Daniels' Orchestral Music

Music Finders
Series Editor: David Daniels

Designed with working musicians, conductors, program directors, and librarians in mind, these practical reference books put the music you need at your fingertips: title, publisher, duration, instrumentation, and appendixes for cross-referencing are all provided in these carefully researched volumes. Using the orchestral repertoire as a starting point, this series will also encompass chamber music, ballet, opera, thematic music, and repertoire of individual instruments.

The Music Finders series is based on the Scarecrow titles *Orchestral Music: A Handbook*, by David Daniels (2005) and *Orchestral "Pops" Music: A Handbook*, by Lucy Manning (2008).

Chamber Orchestra and Ensemble Repertoire: A Catalog of Modern Music , by Dirk Meyer, 2011.

The Canon of Violin Literature: A Performer's Resource, by Jo Nardolillo, 2011.

Arias, Ensembles, and Choruses: An Excerpt Finder for Orchestras, by John Yaffé and David Daniels, 2012.

Orchestral "Pops" Music: A Handbook, 2nd edition, by Lucy Manning, 2013.

The Opera Manual, by Nicholas Ivor Martin, 2014.

Ballet Music: A Handbook, by Matthew Naughtin, 2014.

Daniels' Orchestral Music, Fifth Edition, by David Daniels, 2015.

Daniels' Orchestral Music

Fifth Edition

David Daniels

ROWMAN & LITTLEFIELD
Lanham • Boulder • New York • London

Published by Rowman & Littlefield
A wholly owned subsidiary of The Rowman & Littlefield Publishing Group, Inc.
4501 Forbes Boulevard, Suite 200, Lanham, Maryland 20706
www.rowman.com

Unit A, Whitacre Mews, 26-34 Stannary Street, London SE11 4AB

British Library Cataloguing in Publication Information Available

Library of Congress Cataloging-in-Publication Data
Daniels, David, 1933-
  Daniels' orchestral music / David Daniels. — Fifth edition.
     pages cm. — (Music finders)
  Includes bibliographical references and index.
  ISBN 978-1-4422-4537-2 (cloth : alk. paper) 1. Orchestral music—Bibliography. I.
Title.
  ML128.O5D3 2015
  016.7842—dc23
                              2015004505

♾™ The paper used in this publication meets the minimum requirements of American
National Standard for Information Sciences—Permanence of Paper for Printed Library
Materials, ANSI/NISO Z39.48-1992.

Printed in the United States of America

Dedicated to the memory of

JAMES A. DIXON

conductor, mentor, friend

CONTENTS

PREFACE

This 5th edition of *Orchestral Music* includes some 8500 entries, which is about a 33% increase over the roughly 6400 entries in the 4th edition. Moreover, about one-third of those 6400 holdovers from the 4th edition have been corrected or updated in the interim. Of course none of these additions or corrections will be news to subscribers to the website OrchestralMusic.com, which is updated monthly. By the time this book appears, the website itself will have had a major makeover as well.

Users of previous editions of *Orchestral Music* will find the familiar format relatively unchanged, with just the addition of dates of composition and revision in most cases, as well as a more convenient manner of listing individual movements with their durations.

Instrumentation formula. The formulaic arrangement of wind instruments, familiar to all in the field, is used here: flute, oboe, clarinet, bassoon — horn, trumpet, trombone, tuba. Amplifications, if any, are spelled out in brackets. A dot (.) separates one player from another; a slash (/) indicates doubling. Thus, the following example...

3[1.2.3/pic] 2[1.Eh] 3[1.2.3/Ebcl/bcl] 3[1.2/cbn.cbn]

...should be understood as:

3 flutists,	the 3rd player doubling on piccolo
2 oboists,	the 2nd playing English horn throughout
3 clarinetists,	the 3rd doubling also on E-flat clarinet and bass clarinet
3 bassoonists,	the 2nd doubling on contrabassoon, and the 3rd playing contra throughout

Unfortunately, in the first three editions of Orchestral Music, some 4500 works were listed using a cruder scheme involving the symbols * , + , and = . These showed that certain auxiliary woodwinds were present, but not how many of them, nor in which part. Over the years I have attempted to find the full doubling information for each of these older entries, but almost 400 still are in this inconclusive state. For the latter I have had to resort to such expressions as: "3[incl pic]", meaning that one or more of the three flutists must play, or double on, piccolo.

In the notes to individual works, for "2fl" read "2 flutes." For "fl2," read "flute 2" (i.e. 2nd flute).

Composers. For composers' names and dates, my main source has been Grove Music Online, supplemented as needed. Because Russia did not adopt the Gregorian calendar, standard in the West, until 1918, Grove gives birth and/or death dates in both the Julian and Gregorian calendars for many late 19th- and early 20th-century Russian composers. In such cases it is the Julian date (about 10 days earlier than the Gregorian) that comes first.

You will find "see-references" from divergent spellings of a composer's surname.

For composers whose output is prolific or in some way confusing, thematic index numbers are employed. The most well-established of these, of course, are the K-numbers

for Mozart, familiar to all musicians. In all such cases, the source of these numbers is given at the beginning of that composer's entries.

Titles. For generic titles (Symphony, Concerto, etc.) I have adapted the uniform title system of American libraries. Recognizing that this book is being used all over the world, I have generally rendered distinctive titles (i.e., non-generic) in their original form, if it is in one of the languages with which most musicians have a passing acquaintance (English, Italian, German, French, Spanish, Latin). Titles in other languages are generally given first in English, with the original title following in parentheses, transliterated if necessary; however, this principle is not followed slavishly, if common sense dictates otherwise (e.g., Stravinsky's *Les noces*).

If you have trouble finding a title you think should be here, try the **Title Index** in the back of the book. All distinctive titles, title translations, and nicknames should be listed there, with directions to the composer and whatever form of the title I have chosen for the entry. International users who may not be sure of the common English version of, for example, *Vesna svyashchennaya* or *Sacre du printemps*, may look for either one in the Title Index, which will refer them to Stravinsky's *Rite of Spring*. The Title Index is also useful should you momentarily forget who composed, say, *La bayadère*.

Initial articles in all languages are ignored for purposes of alphabetization.

Introductory recitative titles for concert arias are given in plain font, while the arias proper are in boldface.

Many, but not all, titles are followed by the dates of composition and/or revision in angle-brackets; e.g., <1979; rev 1986>.

Durations. Durations will of course vary from one performance to the next, even under the same conductor. The durations in this book should be considered reasonable approximations only. Quite aside from tempo variances and cuts, some performers may choose not to honor certain repeats as indicated, which will cause further divergence.

Publishers. Sources of scores and parts appear in short form across the bottom of each entry, in a grey bar. Consult the directory of **Publishers & Sources** in the back of the book for further contact information. I give websites for publishers where possible; some of these are excellent sources of information, though perhaps not always paragons of scholarly exactitude.

Instruments and instrumental practices. General information that will be helpful in using this book.

FLUTES and RECORDERS. When a baroque composer used the term *flauto* unmodified, or perhaps *flauto dolce*, he meant recorder. If he wanted a transverse flute, he took pains to call it *traversa* or *flauto traverso* or some such term.

WOODWIND DOUBLING. As late as the time of Mozart, players were likely to alternate on several instruments. This explains why an eighteenth-century work otherwise for 2 oboes, 2 horns and strings, suddenly uses 2 flutes and strings for a middle movement. The oboists simply switched to flute. Nowadays, of course, that is

largely impractical.

CLARINETS. There is a huge plethora of clarinet types, to which this book does not do justice. I repent my previous naiveté (apparent in earlier editions of this book) in assuming that everything found in orchestral works would be played by standard clarinets in B-flat or A, piccolo clarinets in E-flat, or bass clarinets in B-flat. I have gradually realized that instruments in D and C actually exist and are owned by some (but by no means all) professionals; and that even the bass-clarinet in A is not entirely unknown.

Of course the motives of the composer in choosing a particular type of clarinet may not be fully known. Sometimes it may have been mere convenience, but at least on some occasions it was clearly the desire for a particular tone color. In any case, it is important that musicians and librarians know in advance what is called for in the score. Even if the non-standard instrument will be covered by a feat of transposition at sight, still, forewarned is forearmed.

I have gone back through many scores in an attempt to rectify this shortcoming—and received very welcome help on the matter from many active clarinetists, conductors and librarians—but I know I have only scratched the surface; there must be many works in which my entries fail to specify these important details. Hence these warnings for entries that have not yet been updated:

∞   If my entry merely gives a number of clarinetists required, it is possible that some of them actually call for clarinets in C (abbreviation: **C-cl**)

∞   If the entry reads **Ebcl**, it is certainly possible, especially in music from the late nineteenth- and early twentieth-centures, that the composer specified clarinet in D (abbreviation: **D-cl**)

∞   If you find **bcl** you may be facing a part for bass clarinet in A that goes below the standard range available on a bass clarinet in B-flat—though professional bass clarinets nowadays are constructed to go all the way down to C2. When I have been able to verify that the part was originally in A, I have used the abbreviation **bcl(A)**.

Sometimes my findings, if complicated, are given in the notes rather than the instrumentation formula; such oddities as "clarinet in A-flat" (Bartok: Scherzo, op. 2) will be mentioned in the notes also.

BASSOONS. In eighteenth-century practice, a bassoon played the bass line of an orchestral work, whether specified in the score or not. The bassoon may have been optional in works for string orchestra, but if other wind instruments were present, the bassoon was *de rigueur*. In such cases, some editions list the bassoon and some do not. I have merely followed the edition in hand, but in awareness of this practice, conductors may wish to employ the bassoon, perhaps playing from a cello or bass part, whether it is called for or not.

Nineteenth-century French orchestras normally had 4 bassoons doubling two real parts. Occasionally they might split into four parts for a few bars. I have attempted to distinguish between the number of bassoons called for and the number of real parts involved, if different.

SARRUSOPHONE. Originally this was a whole family of double-reed brass instruments, analogous to the single-reed saxophone family. Only the contrabass size made inroads into the orchestra, where it competed with, and was eventually superseded by, the contrabassoon.

TROMBONES. In eighteenth-century choral music, it was customary for trombones to double the altos, tenors, and basses of the chorus, and sometimes for a *cornetto* (also known as *Zink*, a soprano relative of the serpent) to double the sopranos. These *colla parte* instruments (as they were called) were often not mentioned in the score at all. You may add them when they are not indicated, or omit them when they are—since in any case, a modern chorus with large-bore trombones is not going to sound much like an eighteenth-century chorus (using boy sopranos and male altos) with the sackbut-like trombones of the period.

SERPENT, OPHICLEIDE, and CIMBASSO. These cup-mouthpiece keyed instruments were ultimately replaced by the tuba. The ophicleide was the brass bass instrument of choice for such meticulous orchestrators as Berlioz and Mendelssohn.

In 19th-century Italy the term *cimbasso* was used generically for the lowest brass instrument. This could have been either a wooden serpent, a valved ophicleide, or (after 1845) a newly developed instrument: the *pelittone*. Giuseppe Verdi preferred a small-bore instrument for these parts, and caused a *trombone basso Verdi* to be made to his specification. The modern revival of the cimbasso is essentially a bass trombone: a slide-, rather than a keyed-instrument. The confusion of nomenclature may be seen in many late 19th-century and early 20th-century Italian scores which may call for 3 trombones and a cimbasso—or alternatively for 4 trombones. Sometimes the scores call the bass instrument a trombone but the parts label it a tuba or cimbasso; sometimes the labeling in the score changes from movement to movement, but the intention is for the same instrument to be used throughout.

BASS DRUM & CYMBALS. In nineteenth-century bass drum parts, especially Italian opera, cymbals were expected to be played along with the bass drum, even though they were not specifically notated in the part. Probably the cymbals weren't added indiscriminately to every single note, but were applied with a certain amount of taste and discretion—a vague and not terribly helpful recipe.

A related question is whether two players are required in these cases, or whether mounting one cymbal on the bass drum and clashing it with the other is acceptable. Some say that attaching one cymbal spoils its tone; others that having a single musician play both instruments has compensating virtues. Personally, I switched from the former to the latter position after hearing Jeffrey Fischer, a Boston percussionist, play with exquisite delicacy the two instruments at once.

For the purposes of the percussion count in this book, I have indicated two players in all these situations—even in cases where I was pretty sure the composer had in mind one player, and I as a conductor would prefer only one.

TENOR DRUM & FIELD DRUM. In American practice it seems clear that of these two deeper drums, the field drum has snares and the tenor drum does not. Other nations have other traditions, and especially with such terms as *tamburo rullante*, *caisse*

roulante, or *Rührtrommel*, it is not always entirely clear in a particular composition which instrument is intended. Sometimes the composer helps by specifying: *caisse roulante avec cordes* ("… with snares"), for example.

DOUBLE BASS TUNING. When the double bass is used as a solo instrument, a traditional scordatura comes into play. Each string is tuned up a whole step, to F#1–B1–E2–A2, respectively. The music is normally transposed for the convenience of the player, so that the solo part becomes essentially a D-transposition, the player fingering it as it appears. The resulting heightened tension on the strings serves to mitigate the balance problems that might arise between solo double bass and orchestral accompaniment. Parts for works for solo double bass are often available in two keys, depending on whether or not the soloist employs the traditional scordatura.

❄ ❄ ❄

Acknowledgements. It was over a half-century ago that the late **Jim Dixon** (to whose memory this edition is dedicated) lent me his personal notebook of durations of orchestral works. This was before Xerox machines were ubiquitous, so my wife, **Jimmie Sue Daniels** (to whom several earlier editions of this book were dedicated), spent a couple of weeks typing a copy of the Dixon notebook for my own use. It was only gradually that it dawned on me, as a neophyte conductor, that adding the instrumentation and publisher would make it even more useful.

    Knox College, where I was employed in the 1960s, gave me a generous research grant to begin the actual work, and (astonishingly) renewed the grant for a second summer, even after I had resigned my position to move to Michigan. At that point, **Oakland University** (Rochester, Michigan) took over and supported my work with grants and sabbaticals for the better part of three decades.

    All this time, many **friends**, **colleagues**, and **perfect strangers** from around the globe have helped with the project by sending me suggestions, additions, and corrections. I can't possibly name them all, but they all have my unstinting gratitude. You know who you are.

    One who must be named, however, is **Clinton F. Nieweg**, Principal Librarian of the Philadelphia Orchestra (ret.), who has sent suggestions, corrections and encouragement almost from the beginning.

    In 2004, Los Angeles Philharmonic librarian **Kazue McGregor** made the well-timed suggestion that my database be combined with that of OLIS (Orchestra Library Information Service). That suggestion has proved to be a game-changer for the 4th edition and the subsequent history of this book. The owner of OLIS, then the **American Symphony Orchestra League** (now League of American Orchestras) agreed with the plan, as did **Tom Gaitens** of **Fine Arts Software** who helped hugely with the conversion to my system, and who uses the combined version as the repertoire module in the **OPAS** orchestra management software, for which he is the North American representative.

    Now having passed the age of 80, I naturally wonder what will happen to this work when I am gone. Perhaps I will be lucky enough to recruit **David Alexander Rahbee** to carry on. He is Senior Artist in Residence at the University of Washington School of Music in Seattle, where he serves as director of orchestral activities. He has been sending

me additions, corrections, durations and suggestions for many years, and his fierce passion to nail down every last detail is inspiring.

When languages gave me problems I found willing experts to help me out: **Jack Moeller** (German), **Anna Barnes** (Italian and Spanish), **Dolores Burdick** (French), **Paweł Kotla** (Polish), **Irina Tikhonova** (Russian), **Mads Skovbjerg Paldam** (Danish), and for Czech both **David Mascitelli** and his Czech-born wife **Hana Baudys**.

Percussion problems quickly yielded to the vast knowledge and generous advice of **Russ Girsberger**, percussionist, author, and librarian now at the School of Music of the United States Navy and Marine Corps.

Barbara Levine of **MicroServ LLC** was able, in a ten-minute phone call, to fix an issue of formatting that had plagued me forever, and in the process taught me how to handle such things in the future.

The list of Jewish composers in the Appendix was verified by **Helen Rowin**, Music Librarian (ret.), Detroit Public Library. She has performed this daunting task ever since the 2nd edition of the book.

Another group too numerous to list, but too important to pass over: the **rental librarians** and **promotion specialists** of every publishing company, who have sent me perusal scores by the dozen with nary a complaint, even when I fail to return them in a timely fashion. Many self-published **composers** have been equally generous. And a special mention is required for **Luck's Music Library**, which happens to be within 20 minutes' drive of my home; I've imposed on them a lot.

The **Edwin A. Fleisher Collection of Orchestral Music**, unlike Luck's, is hundreds of miles away in Philadelphia—but its assistant curator **Stuart Serio**, like the previous curator **Kile Smith**, has been an unfailing source of information.

And of course I have depended on the university libraries closest to me: **Oakland University**, **Wayne State University**, and the splendid collection at the **University of Michigan** in Ann Arbor.

Every researcher should have a daughter who is a librarian: who can find obscure facts with a few clicks of a mouse, and use her influence to get tricky inter-library loans at the drop of a hat. I have been thus blessed with **Abigail Daniels**, who has performed those feats on demand, as well as supplied more depth to my appendix on Youth Concerts; she had proofed several of the earlier editions of this book, putting her knowledge of German and Russian to good use.

Oh yes, and every single time I had a computer issue in the last two decades—right up to and including the week before my deadline—**Rob Burns** appeared and solved it. He is an IT specialist for Oakland University, an early music junky, and a mean flute player. He also is the only person I know who owns (and plays!) a cimbalom.

ABBREVIATIONS

&

PITCH CHART

ABBREVIATIONS

4t quartet

5t quintet

A alto voice

acl alto clarinet

afl alto flute
flute in G; British usage: bass flute

almglock Almglocken
herdbells

alt alternative
abwechselnd

alto tbn alto trombone

ampd amplified

arr arranged, arrangement
bearbeitet

asx alto saxophone

atp tromba contralta
contralto trumpet pitched in F and used in late 19th-century and early 20th-century Russian scores; parts are playable on a B-flat trumpet.

b sxhn bass saxhorn

Bar baritone voice

bar hn baritone horn
a baritone saxhorn in B-flat, narrower in bore than a euphonium

basset hn basset horn

bcl bass clarinet

bcl(A) bass clarinet in A

bd bass drum

bd/cym bass drum with attached cymbal

bfl bass flute in C
not to be confused with alto flute in G

bgtr bass guitar

bn bassoon

brake dr brake drum

Bs bass voice

Bs-Bar bass-baritone voice

bsx baritone saxophone

btbn bass trombone

btp bass trumpet

C-cl C clarinet

cast castanets

cb sxhn contrabass saxhorn

cb tbn contrabass trombone

cbcl contrabass clarinet

cbn contrabassoon

cel celesta

chimes chimes
tubular bells, cloches, campane

Chinescym Chinese cymbal

chmb chamber
as in "chamber orchestra."

chor chorus

cimb cimbalom
dulcimer of Hungarian origin; not to be confused with cimbasso, *a brass bass instrument.*

cimbasso cimbasso

cl clarinet
B-flat or A clarinet if unmodified; occasionally may refer to C clarinet (see Preface, p. xi)

cnt continuo

crit ed critical edition
an edition based on scholarly evaluation of the sources and taking into account historical performance practice.

crot crotales
antique cymbals

crt cornet

cym cymbals (pair)

D-cl D clarinet

d'am d'amore

db double bass
contrabass

dbl doubling, doubles, doubled
doppio, doppelt

dr drum

dur duration

Ebcl E-flat clarinet
sometimes used in this book generically to indicate the piccolo clarinet, whether in E-flat or D (see Preface, p. xi).

ed edited; edition

Eh English horn
cor anglais

elec electric
as in electric bass, electric guitar, etc.

ens ensemble

euph euphonium

field dr field drum
deep drum with snares (military drum, parade drum, Rührtrommel, tamburo rullante con corde, caisse roulante avec cordes)

fig. rehearsal figure
in this book, rehearsal letters or numbers are enclosed in square brackets: [ ]

fl flute
NB: in baroque usage, flauto *indicates recorder*

flag flageolet
an end-blown flute which served in the 18th century as a predecessor to the orchestral piccolo.

flug flugelhorn, fluegelhorn

glock glockenspiel
orchestra bells, campanelli, carillon

gtr guitar

harm harmonium

heckl heckelphone

herdbells herdbells
Almglocken, sheepbells, etc. (i.e., bells with internal clapper)

hi-hat high-hat cymbal

hn horn

hp harp

hpsd harpsichord

incl including

indef indefinite
as in "indefinite pitch," or unpitched

inst instrument(s);
instrumentation

kybd keyboard

kybd glock keyboard
glockenspiel

mand mandolin

marac maracas

marim marimba

max maximum
massimo

mic microphone

min minimum
minimo, mindestmass

Ms mezzo-soprano voice

mvt movement
Satz; mouvement

ob oboe
hautbois

ob d'am oboe d'amore

ob da cacc oboe da caccia

ondes ondes martenot

oph ophicleide

opt optional

orch; orchd orchestra;
orchestrated

org organ

orig original

pcs pieces
as in "2 pieces of metal"

perc percussion

pf piano
Klavier

pf-cond piano-conductor score

pic piccolo
ottavino, kleine Flöte, petite flûte

pic tp piccolo trumpet
usually in Bb or A

posthn posthorn

pr pair
paire; Paar; paio

pub published, publisher

ratch ratchet
raganella, crécelle, Ratsche

rec recorder
Blockflöte, flûte à bec

red reduced, reduction

rev revised; revision

S soprano voice

sandblks sandpaper blocks

sarr sarrusophone

sd snare drum
*caisse claire, tambour, kleine Trommel,
side drum*

serp serpent

set drum set, trap set

sirenwhstl siren whistle
cyclone whistle

slgh-bells sleighbells
pellet bells, grelots, Schellen, sonagli

ssx soprano saxophone

str strings

str 4t string quartet
2 violins, viola, cello

str 5t string quintet
2 violins, viola, cello, double bass

sus cym suspended cymbal

sx saxophone

synth synthesizer

szl cym sizzle cymbal

T tenor voice

tambn tambourine
tambour de basque, tamburino

tambn prov tambourin provençal;
tambour de provence
*long narrow 2-headed drum without
snares; not to be confused with the
tambourine*

tbn trombone
Posaune

td tenor drum
*deep drum without snares (Rührtrommel
ohne Saiten; Wirbeltrommel, Rolltrommel,
tamburo rullante, caisse roulante, or
tambour roulant sans timbre)*

templeblks temple blocks

ten tenor
*as applied to an instrument: e.g., tenor
banjo*

thunder thundersheet

tmp timpani
*NB: the number of drums is not specified
in these listings; 2tmp means 2 players,
not 2 drums*

tp trumpet

Treb treble voice
boy soprano, child soprano

tri triangle

tsx tenor saxophone

va viola

var variable

vc violoncello
cello

vib vibraphone

vibrslp vibraslap
jawbone

vn violin

vn pic violino piccolo

w/ with
con, avec, mit

w/o without
senza, sans, ohne

Wag tb Wagner tuba

whip whip
slapstick, frusta, Peitsche, fouet

wnd mach wind machine

woodblk woodblock

xyl xylophone

PITCH CHART

Letter names for musical pitches in this book use the system known loosely as scientific pitch notation (or American Standard Pitch Notation). It is often abbreviated "ASA", referring to the Acoustical Society of America. This method, given below, is simple and easy to remember: just think that "middle C" is C4, and the complete octave below it is C3 – B3. On the piano, C8 would be the top note, and C1 would be almost the lowest note. (The next lower octave would be C0 – B0.)

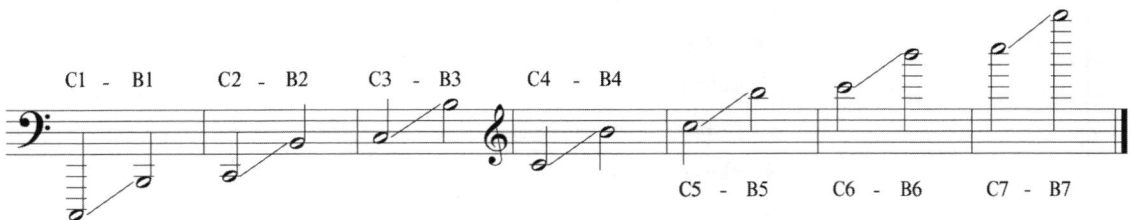

A

Abel, Karl Friedrich   1723-1787

(b Cöthen, 22 Dec 1723; d London, 20 June 1787). German

Symphony, op.1, no.5, F major <1759>   10'

0 2 0 0 — 2 0 0 0 — opt cnt — str
Oboes and horns may be omitted, or may be replaced by flutes and
clarinets respectively.
  Ed. Hilmar Hoeckner.

Vieweg	Luck's

Symphony, op.1, no.6, G major <1759>   10'

0 2 0 0 — 2 0 0 0 — opt cnt — str
Oboes and horns may be omitted, or may be substituted for by flutes and
clarinets respectively.
  Ed. Hilmar Hoeckner.

Vieweg	Luck's

Symphony, op.7, no.6, E-flat major <1767>   13'

0 0 2 1 — 2 0 0 0 — str
Originally scored for 0 2 0 0 — 2 0 0 0 — str, presumably including
bassoon as part of the general bass part. The young Mozart copied it,
changing the oboes to clarinets and making the bassoon part distinct.
Mozart's copy survived, and was later published by Breitkopf as his
Symphony No.3; this work is still listed under Mozart by Kalmus (a
reprint of the original Breitkopf edition).
  I. Molto allegro   4'
  II. Andante   5'
  III. Presto   4'

Breitkopf	Kalmus	Kneusslin	Peters

Symphony, op.14, no.2, E-flat major <1778>   15'

0 2 0 1 — 2 0 0 0 — cnt — str
2fl may substitute for 2ob. Ed. Gwilym Beechey.

Oxford

Abels, Michael   1962-

(b Phoenix AZ, 8 October 1962). American

Affectionate Objects <2004>   10'

3[1.2.pic] 2 3[1.2/Ebcl.3/bcl] 2 — 4 3 3 1 — tmp+3 — hp — str
perc: bd, sus cym, set, tri, glock, marim, chimes, bongos, xyl[opt], cabasa,
4tomtoms, Chinescym or small tamtam

Subito

American Variations on "Swing Low, Sweet Chariot"   9'
<1993>

solo trumpet
3[1.2.pic] 3[1.2.Eh] 3[1.2.bcl] 2 — 4 3 3 1 — ampd db — tmp+3 —
pf — str

Subito

Dance for Martin's Dream <1997>   10'

3[1.2.pic] 2[1.2/Eh] 2[1.2/Ebcl] 2 — 4 3 3 1 — tmp+2 — hp — str
Musicians chant nonsense syllables at end.

Subito

Delights and Dances <2007>   13'

solo string quartet
str

Subito

Frederick's Fables <1993–1994>   37'

narrator
2[1.2/pic] 2[1.2/Eh] 2[1.2/bcl] 2 — 2 2 2 0 — tmp+2 — hp — cel —
str
  Frederick   7'
  The Greentail Mouse   10'
  Theodore & the Talking Mushroom 9'
  Alexander & the Wind-Up Mouse   11'

Subito

Global Warming <1991>   8'

3[1.2.pic] 2[1.2/opt Eh] 2 2 — 4 3 3 1 — tmp+2 — hp — str
perc: timbales, tri, tambn, tamtam, xyl, marim, guiro, congas, bodhran, tablas;
optional additional percussionists playing ethnic instruments

Subito

Outburst <2005>   5'

3[1.2.pic] 2 2[1/Ebcl.2] 2 — 4 3 3 1 — tmp+3 — str
perc: bd, sus cym, Chinescym, sd, tri, glock, whip, bongos, bd/ped

Subito

Accolay, Jean-Baptiste   1833-1900

(b Brussels, 17 April 1833; d Bruges, 19 August 1900)

Concerto, Violin, No.1, A minor   10'

str
Rev. & ed. George Perlman.

Kalmus	Luck's

Actor, Lee   1952-

(b Denver, 29 October 1952). American

Celebration Overture <2007>   11'

3[1.2.pic] 2 2 3[1.2.cbn] — 4 2 3 1 — tmp+3 — str
perc: bd, cym, sus cym, sd, tri, tamtam

Polygames

Circus Symphonicus <2008>   6'

3[1.2.pic] 3[1.2.Eh] 3[1.2.bcl] 3[1.2.cbn] — 4 3 3 1 — tmp+3 — str
perc: bd, cym, sus cym, sd, tri, tambn, woodblk
Original title: *Philharmonic Fun*. The finale of the composer's *Symphony
No.2*.

Polygames

Concerto, Alto Saxophone <2009>   22'

2 2 2 2 — 2 2 0 0 — tmp+1 — str
perc: tri, sus cym, tambn, bd
  I. Andante appassionato   9'
  II. Adagio   6'
  III. Allegro molto   7'

Polygames

Concerto, Guitar <2011>   23'

2 2 2 2 — 2 2 0 0 — tmp+1 — str
perc: bd, sus cym, cym, tri, woodblk, tambn
I. Allegro   10'
II. Remembrance (Adagio)   6'
III. Allegro deciso   7'

> Polygames

Concerto, Horn <2007>   14'

2 2 2 2 — tmp — str
I. Allegro moderato   5'
II. Adagio   5'
III. Allegro vivo   4'

> Polygames

Concerto, Timpani <2005>   11'

3[1.2.pic] 2 2 2 — 4 2 3 1 — 2perc — str
perc: bd, sus cym, sd, tri, glock, woodblk

> Polygames

Concerto, Violin <2005>   31'

2 2 2 2 — 2 2 0 0 — tmp+1 — str
perc: bd, sus cym, sd, tri
1. Proclamation   15'
2. Meditation   8'
3. Exhilaration   8'

> Polygames

Dance Rhapsody <2010>   16'

3[1.2.pic] 2 3[1.2.bcl] 2 — 4 2 3 1 — tmp+2 — str
perc: tri, bd, cym, sus cym, tambn, sd, woodblk, cast
Movements are played without pause.
Waltz   _'
Interlude 1   _'
Slow Tango   _'
Fast Tango   _'
Slow Tango Reprise _'
Interlude 2   _'
Fandango   _'

> Polygames

Divertimento for Small Orchestra <2011>   10'

2 1 2 2 — 2 1 0 0 — tmp — str

> Polygames

Meditation for Violin & Orchestra <2008>   8'

2 2 2 2 — 2 0 0 0 — tmp — str
The 2nd mvt of the composer's *Violin Concerto*.

> Polygames

Opening Remarks <2009>   6'

2 2 2 2 — 2 2 0 0 — tmp — str

> Polygames

Prelude to a Tragedy <2003>   12'

3[1.2.pic] 3[1.2.Eh] 3[1.2.bcl] 2 — 4 2 3 1 — tmp+2 — hp — str
perc: bd, cym, sus cym, sd, tri, tamtam

> Polygames

Premonition <2012>   11'

3[1.2.pic] 2 2 2 — 4 2 3 1 — tmp+2 — str
perc: bd, cym, sus cym, tamtam

> Polygames

Redwood Fanfare <2002>   3'

2 2 2 2 — 4 3 3 1 — tmp+2 — str
perc: bd, cym

> Polygames

Symphony No.1 <2002>   34'

2 2 2 2 — 4 2 3 1 — tmp+2 — hp — str
perc: bd, cym, sus cym, sd, tamtam
Prelude   14'
Lament   10'
Finale   10'

> Polygames

Symphony No.2 <2008>   25'

3[1.2.pic] 3[1.2.Eh] 3[1.2.bcl] 3[1.2.cbn] — 4 3 3 1 — tmp+3 — str
perc: bd, cym, sus cym, sd, tri, tambn, tamtam, glock, woodblk
The last mvt is available separately as "Circus Symphonicus."
I. Andante maestoso   11'
II. Adagio molto   8'
III. Allegro molto vivace 6'

> Polygames

Symphony No.3 <2013>   36'

3[1.2.pic] 2 2 2 — 4 2 3 0 — tmp+2 — str
perc: bd, cym, sus cym, tamtam, sd, tri, woodblk
I. Premonition   11'
II. Scherzo 1   4'
III. Reflections 7'
IV. Scherzo 2   4'
V. Finale   10'

> Polygames

Variations & Fugue <2001>   9'

2 2 2 2 — 4 2 2 1 — tmp — str

> Polygames

Adam, Adolph-Charles   1803-1856

(b Paris, 24 July 1803; d Paris, 3 May 1856). French

Le brasseur de Preston (The Brewer of Preston):   7'
Overture <1838>

2[1.pic] 2 2 2 — 4 2 3 0 — tmp — str
This work is out of print and very rare.

> Richault

Le corsaire <1856>   122'

2[1.2/pic] 2 2 2 — 4 4[2crt, 2tp] 3 1 — tmp+4 — hp — str
perc: bd, cym, sd, tri, tambn, cast
Varied productions over the years have included added music by Léo
Delibes, Riccardo Drigo, Boris Fitingof-Shel, Yuli Gerber, Ludwig
Minkus, Pyotr von Oldenburg, Cesare Pugni, and Albert Zabel; all are
included in the Lars Payne materials.

> Payne

Le corsaire: Pas de deux <1856>

3[1.2.pic] 2 2 2 — 4 3 3 1 — tmp+4 — hp — str
perc: tri, sd, cym, bd

> Payne

Giselle <1841>   126'

2[1.2/pic] 2[1/opt Eh.2/opt Eh] 2 2 — 4 4[2tp, 2crt] 3 1 — tmp+3 — hp — str

perc: bd, cym, tri, sd, bells in G & E

Eh parts are cued in clarinets.

The Lars Payne material includes the interpolations by Burgmüller and Minkus as well as traditional inserts and transpositions.

Two reductions of this ballet are available:

William McDermott (Kalmus):

2[1.2/pic] 2[1.2/Eh] 2 2 — 3 2 3 0 — tmp+perc — hp — str

Humphrey Searle (Faber):

1/pic 1/Eh 1 1 — 1 1 1 0 tmp+1 — pf — str

Act I   63'

Act II   63'

Kalmus	Payne

Si j'étais roi (If I Were King): Overture <1852>   7'

2[1.pic] 2 2 2 — 4 2[2crt] 3 0 — tmp+4 — hp — str

perc: sd, tri, bd, cym, glock

Leduc brass as listed; Kalmus and Luck's brass 2 2 3 1

Kalmus	Leduc	Luck's

Adamo, Mark   1962-

(b Philadelphia 1962). American composer of Italian descent

Alcott Music   16'

1perc — pf/cel — str

perc: tmp, chimes, glock, ratch, sd, sus cym, tamtam, vib

From the opera *Little Women*.

I. Jo   9'

II. Meg   4'

III. Alma and Gideon 3'

Schirmer

Four Angels (Concerto for Harp & Orchestra) <2007>   25'

2[1.2/pic] 2[1.2/Eh] 2[1.2/bcl] 2[1.2/cbn] — 4 2 3 1 — tmp+3 — pf/cel — str

perc: glock, xyl, marim, chimes, crot, brake dr, belltree, tamtam, tri, sd, bd, congas, guiro, templeblks, woodblk, vibrslp, whip, tambn, cast, vib, sandblks, 2gong, 3opera gong, 2sus cym

I. Overture: Metatron   _'

II. Scherzo: Sraosha   _'

III. Aria: Regina coeli   _'

IV. Finale: Mik'hail   _'

Schirmer

Late Victorians <1994; rev 2007>   28'

2 voices: medium-high singing voice & amplified speaking voice

2[1.2/pic] 2[1.Eh] 2 2[1.2/cbn] — 2 2 0 0 — tmp — hp — str

Speaking voice notated mostly as *Sprechstimme*.

I. Nineteen eighty-nine   8'

II. He had been born in South America 7'

III. I stood aloof   6'

IV. Sometimes no family came   7'

Schirmer

Lysistrata: Overture <2005>   4'

2[1/pic.2/pic] 2[1.Eh] 2[1.asx(or cl2)] 2 — 2 2 0 0 — tmp+2 — hp — str

perc: brake dr, glock, marim, sd, sus cym, tamtam, templeblks, tri, vib, whip, xyl, anvil, 5congas

From the opera *Lysistrata, or The Nude Goddess*.

Schirmer

Prepositions and the Names of Fish <©2011>   3'

2[1.2/pic] 2 2 2[1.2/cbn] — 4 2 3 1 — tmp+3 — hp — pf/cel — str

perc: bd, sus cym, sd, brake dr, tri, tambn, gong, glock, xyl, belltree, woodblk, templeblks, whip, guiro, cast, vibrslp, sandblks, 3opera gongs

Schirmer

Adams, John   1947-

(b Worcester, MA, 15 Feb 1947). American

Century Rolls <1997>   29'

solo piano

3[1.2.pic] 3[1.2.Eh] 3[1.2.bcl] 2 — 3 3 2 0 — tmp+2 — hp — cel[opt dbl kybd glock] — str[14.12.8.8.6]

perc: vib, xyl, woodblk, bongos, crot, marim, glock, chimes

Piano must be lightly amplified. Composer suggests recommended string count of 14.12.8.8.6.

I. First Movement   15'

II. Manny's Gym   6'

III. Hail Bop   8'

Boosey

The Chairman Dances; Foxtrot for Orchestra <1986>   12'

2[1/pic.2/pic] 2 2[1.2/bcl] 2 — 4 2 2 1 — tmp+3 — hp — pf — str

perc: pedal bd, cym, sus cym, szl cym, hi-hat, sd, tri, tambn, glock, xyl, vib, crot, belltree, claves, cast, sandblks, 2woodblks

AMP

Chamber Symphony <1992>   22'

1[fl/pic] 1 2[1/Ebcl.2/bcl] 2[1.2/cbn] — 1 1 1 0 — 1perc — synth — str[1.0.1.1.1]

perc: set [includes pedal bd, 3tomtoms, 2timbales, sd, bongos, 4rototoms, conga, claves, cowbell, woodblock, hi-hat, tambn]

Mongrel Airs   7'

Aria with Walking Bass   9'

Roadrunner   6'

Boosey

Christian Zeal and Activity <1973>   10'

1 0 1 1 — hp — str[or str5t]

A pre-recorded tape is to be created by the performers; it does not have to have particular religious content. Alternatively, a pre-recorded DAT tape of a sermon is available from the publisher with the rental materials.

Boosey

City Noir <2009>   35'

4[1.2.3/pic.pic] 4[1.2.3.Eh] 4[1.2.3/bcl.bcl] 3[1.2.cbn] — 6 4 3 1 — asx — tmp+6 — 2hp — pf, cel — str

perc: bd, sd, set, tri, tambn, glock, xyl, marim, vib, chimes, crot, templeblks, cowbell, claves, cast, congas, 5sus cym, 2timbales, 2tamtam, 2bongos[2pairs], 20 tuned gongs[2 octaves]

If absolutely necessary, certain gong pitches may be left tacet.

I. The City and its Double   14'

II. The Song is for You   9'

III. Boulevard Night   12'

Boosey

Common Tones in Simple Time <1979; rev 1986>   20'

3[1.2.3/pic] 2 3 2 — 2 2 0 0 — 2perc — hp — str

perc: glock, 2marim, metronome

AMP

Concerto, Violin <1993>   32'

2[1/pic.2/pic] 2[1.2/Eh] 2[1.2/bcl] 2 — 2 1 0 0 — 2perc — 2synth — str[min 6.6.5.5.2]

perc: bd, sus cym, tomtoms, timbales, roto-toms, tambn, marim, vib w/ bow, chimes, cowbell, bongos, guiro, claves, 2congas, tmp

Synth: Yamaha SY99 & Kurzweil K2000, or 2 Kurzweil K2000.

1. Quarter note = 78   15'

2. Chaconne: Body Through Which the Dream Flows   11'

3. Toccare   7'

Boosey

Doctor Atomic Symphony   25'

3[1.2.pic] 3[1.2.3/Eh] 3[1.2/Ebcl.3/bcl] 3[1.2.3/cbn] — 4 4[1.2.3.4/pic tp] 3 1 — tmp+4 — hp — cel — str

perc: chimes, crot, glock, bd, thunder, 2tamtam, 2sus cym, 8gong[tuned]

Derived and reworked from the composer's opera *Doctor Atomic*.

N.B., the mvt titles given below have been used on some recordings; they are not indicated in the score.

1. The Laboratory	*3'*
2. Panic	*15'*
3. Trinity	*7'*

Boosey

El Dorado <1991>   29'

3[1.2/pic.3/pic] 3[1.2.3/Eh] 3[1.2/Ebcl.3/bcl] 3[1.2.3/cbn] — 4 3[1/flug.2/flug.3] 3 1 — tmp+4 — hp — kybd samplers — str

perc: tambn, claves, marim, cowbell, xyl, sd, vib, bongos, templeblks, crot, hi-hat, td, guiro, marac, woodblk, logdrum, sandblks, cabasa, bd/ped, metalpipe, 4timbales, 5tomtom, 2db bows

Kybd sampler software, specific to the model being used, will be provided with the rental materials.

Part 1. A Dream of Gold	*13'*
Part 2. Soledades	*16'*

Boosey

Eros Piano <1989; rev 1990>   17'

solo piano

2[1/pic.2/pic] 2 2[1.2/bcl] 2 — 2 0 0 0 — 1perc — opt synth — str[min 6.6.4.4.2]

perc: vib (mallets & bow), crot (mallets & bow), marac

Boosey

Fearful Symmetries <1988; rev 1989>   27'

2[1/pic.2/pic] 2[1.2/Eh] 3[1.2.bcl] 1 — 2 3 3 0 — ssx, 2asx, bsx — tmp — pf, synth, sampler — str[min 6.6.4.4.2]

Boosey

Gnarly Buttons <1996>   25'

solo clarinet

0 1[Eh] 0 1 — 0 0 1 0 — gtr/banjo/mandolin — 2kybd samplers[1.2/pf] — str[min: 1.1.1.1.1; max: 6.6.4.4.2]

Kybd sampler software, specific to the model being used, will be provided with the rental materials.

I. The Perilous Shore	*10'*
II. Hoedown (Mad Cow)	*6'*
III. Put Your Loving Arms Around Me	*9'*

Boosey

Grand Pianola Music <1982>   32'

2 solo pianos   3 amplified female voices (mostly non-text)

2[1/pic.2/pic] 2 2[1.2/bcl] 2 — 2 2 2 1 — 3perc — [no str]

perc: glock, crot, marim, sus cym, marac, woodblk, tri, tamtam, xyl, tambn, bd, cym, 2db bows, 2metallophones, bd w/ ped, 5td (more equipment may be necessary, depending on how much can be shared)

The 3 female voices are treated not as soloists. but as members of the orchestra.

Part 1a	*15'*
Part 1b: Slow	*8'*
Part 2: On the Dominant Divide	*9'*

AMP

Harmonielehre <1984–1985>   40'

4[1.2/pic.3/pic.4/pic] 3[1.2.3/Eh] 4[1.2.3/bcl1.4/bcl2] 4[1.2.3.cbn] — 4 4 3 2 — tmp+4 — 2hp — cel, pf — str

perc: chimes, glock, belltree, bd, gong, xyl, crot, tamtam, szl cym, vib, cym, 4sus cym, 2marim, 3tri, 2vc bows

Part 1	*17'*
Part 2: The Anfortas Wound	*12'*
Part 3: Meister Eckhardt and Quackie	*11'*

AMP

Harmonium <1980–1981>   33'

chorus (minimum of 90)

4[1.2/pic.3/pic.4/pic] 3 3[1.2.bcl] 3[1.2.3/cbn] — 4 4 3 1 — tmp+4 — hp — cel, pf/synth — str

perc: bd, cym, sus cym, szl cym, tri, tambn, glock, xyl, vib, chimes, crot, anvil, 4cowbells, 2marim, 2tamtams

N.B. The quality of the rental vocal scores is said to be very poor [8-18-11].

Negative Love	*11'*
Because I Could Not Stop	*10'*
Wild Nights	*12'*

AMP

Lollapalooza <1995>   6'

3[1.2/pic.pic] 3[1.2.Eh] 4[1.2.Ebcl.bcl] 3[1.2.cbn] — 4 3 3 1 — tmp+4 — pf — str

perc: xyl, sus cym, gong, sd, marac, tambn, claves, woodblk, bongos, tomtom, vib, bd, 3rototoms, bd/ped

Boosey

Naive and Sentimental Music <1997–1998>   44'

4[1.2.3/pic.4/pic] 3[1.2.3/Eh] 4[1.2/bcl.3.bcl] 3[1.2.3/cbn] — 4 4 3 2 — gtr (ampd) — tmp+5 — 2hp — pf, cel, kybd sampler — str

perc: bd, szl cym, tamtam, glock, xyl, marim, vib, chimes, crot, slgh-bells, almglocken (2 8ves), 7tri, shaker, anvil, 2sus cym, 5gongs, 2bells, 5temple bowls, 3cello bows

Kybd sampler software, specific to the model being used, will be provided with the rental materials.

I. Naive and Sentimental Music	*18'*
II. Mother of the Man	*15'*
III. Chain to the Rhythm	*11'*

Boosey

El Niño: A Nativity Oratorio <1999–2000>   110'

SMsBar   male ens (3 countertenors), chorus, opt children's chor

2[1/pic.2/pic] 2[1/Eh.2/Eh] 2[1.2/bcl] 2[1.2/cbn] — 3 0 3 0 — 2gtr — 3perc — hp — pf/cel, sampler/cel — str[min 14.6.6.4]

perc: tamtam, glock, chimes, crot, templeblks, cowbell, guiro, marac, claves, 6tri, 3gong, tuned almglocken, 2temple bowls

PART ONE	
1. I sing of a maiden	*6'*
2. Hail, Mary, gracious!	*5'*
3. La anunciación	*10'*
4. For with God no thing shall be impossible	*1'*
5. The babe leaped in her womb	*4'*
6. Magnificat	*3'*
7. Now she was sixteen years old	*3'*
8. Joseph's Dream	*5'*
9. Shake the Heavens	*6'*
10. Se habla de Gabriel	*8'*
11. The Christmas Star	*7'*
PART TWO	
12. Pues me dios ha nacido	*5'*
13. When Herod heard	*2'*
14. Woe unto them that call evil good	*4'*
15. And the star went before them	*2'*
16. The Three Kings	*5'*
17. And when they were departed	*1'*
18. Dawn Air	*4'*
19. And he slew all the children	*2'*
20. Memorial de Tlatelolco	*9'*
21. In the day of the great slaughter	*3'*
22. Pues está tiritando	*4'*
23. Jesus and the Dragons	*3'*
24. A Palm Tree	*8'*

Boosey

On the Transmigration of Souls <2002>   23'

mixed chorus, children's chorus
4[1.2.3/pic.pic] 3 4[1.2.bcl.cbcl] 3[1.2.cbn] — 4 4 3 2 — pre-recorded multichannel soundtrack — tmp+4 — 2hp — pf, cel, quarter-tone pf — str

perc: sus cym, glock, chimes, crot, 5tri, 3brake dr
    Solo tp in balcony behind audience at beginning quotes from Ives' *The Unanswered Question*. Six violins within the orchestra constitute "Quarter-tone Ensemble" (no scordatura required).
    Soundtrack composed in collaboration with sound designer Mark Grey.

> Boosey

Shaker Loops <1978; rev 1982>   26'

str orch
Originally for str septet (3vn, va, 2vc, db); orchestra parts reflect this division.
    I. Shaking and Trembling   9'
    II. Hymning Slews   6'
    III. Loops and Verses   7'
    IV. A Final Shaking   4'

> AMP

Short Ride in a Fast Machine <1986>   4'

4[1.2.pic1.pic2] 3[1.2.Eh] 4[1.2.(3&4 opt)] 4[1.2.3.cbn] — 4 4 3 1 — tmp+3 — opt synth — str
perc: bd, bd/ped, sus cym, szl cym, sd, tri, tambn, tamtam, glock, xyl, crot, 2woodblk

> Boosey

Slonimsky's Earbox <1996>   14'

3[1.2.pic] 3[1.2.Eh] 4[1.2.3/Ebcl.bcl] 3 — 4 4 3 1 — tmp+3 — hp — pf, kybd sampler[or cel + jazz org] — str[16.14.10.8.6]
perc: crot, marim, glock, xyl, woodblk, claves, sd, hi-hat, templeblks, cast, tamtam, tambn, tri, shaker, 2sus cym
Kybd sampler software, specific to the model being used, will be provided with the rental materials.

> Boosey

Son of Chamber Symphony <2007>   24'

1[fl/pic] 1 2[cl.bcl] 1 — 1 1 1 0 — 2perc — pf/cel — str 5t
perc: sus cym, hi-hat, glock, chimes, woodblk, templeblks, cowbell, bongos, claves, cast, congas, kybd sampler, bd/ped, 3tomtom
    I. quarter-note = 116   9'
    II. eighth-note = 92   8'
    III. Presto: half-note = 138   7'

> Boosey

Tromba lontana <1986>   4'

2 solo trumpets
4[1.2.pic1.pic2] 2 2 0 — 4 0 0 0 — 3perc — hp — pf — str
perc: sus cym, glock, vib, crot

> Boosey

The Wound-Dresser <1988–1989>   20'

solo baritone voice
2[1/pic.2] 2 2[1.bcl] 2 — 2 1[pic tp] 0 0 — tmp — synth — str[min 6.6.4.4.2]
Synth: Yamaha Electone HX-1, SY77, SY99, or Korg Wavestation.

> Boosey

Adams, John Luther   1953-

(b Meridian, MS, 23 Jan 1953). American

Become Ocean <2013>   42'

3 3[1.2.3/Eh] 3[1.2.3/bcl] 3[1.2.3/cbn] — 4 3 3 1 — 3 — 2hp — cel, pf — str
Special seating is required:
    Woodwinds, perc 1 & hp1 are up right.
    Brass, perc 2 & hp 2 are up left.
    Remainder far downstage in as wide an arc as possible.
    (Each string section divisi into two parts.)

> Madigan

Adams, Leslie   1932-

(b Cleveland, 20 Dec 1932). American

Ode to Life <1982; rev 1985>   12'

2[1.2/pic] 2 2 2 — 4 3 3 1 — tmp+3 — opt cel — str
perc: bd, cym, sd, tri, tamtam, glock, xyl, chimes, tambn, sus cym

> ACA

Three Dunbar Songs <1981>   20'

solo voice (mezzo-soprano or baritone)
1[1/pic] 1 1 1 — 2 0 0 0 — tmp+2 — hp — str

> ACA

Adaskin, Murray   1906-2002

(b Toronto, 28 March 1906; d Victoria, 6 May 2002). Canadian

Algonquin Symphony <1957–1958>   22'

3[1.2.pic] 3[1.2.Eh] 3[1.2.bcl] 2 — 4 3 3 1 — tmp+4 — hp — str
perc: bd, cym, sus cym, sd, td, tri, tambn, woodblk
    I. Allegretto   9'
    II. Lento sostenuto   6'
    III. Largo; Allegro   7'

> Ricordi

Saskatchewan Legend <1959>   12'

3[1.2/pic.3] 2 2 1 — 2 3 3 1 — tmp+2 — str
perc: bd, sd, cym, glock, tambn, sus cym

> Ricordi

Serenade Concertante <1954>   8'

2[1.2/pic] 2 2 2 — 2 1 0 0 — str

> Ricordi

Addinsell, Richard   1904-1977

(b London, 13 Jan 1904; d Chelsea, London, 14 Nov 1977). English

Warsaw Concerto <1941>   9'

solo piano
2 1[1/Eh] 2 2 — 4 3 3 0 — tmp — str

> Warner

Adès, Thomas   1971-

(b London, 1 March 1971). English

Asyla, op.17 <1997>   25'

3[1.2/pic.2/bfl] 3[1.2/Eh.3/bass ob/opt Eh] 3[1.2/bcl.cbcl] 3[1.2.cbn] — 4 3 3 1 — tmp+6 — hp — 2pf* — str[16.16.14.12.10]

perc: cowbell[tuned], chimes, Chinescym, glock, cym, bd, crot, géophone, washboard, choke cym, sandblks, bd/ped, bag of cutlery[metal knives & forks], 2sd, 11gong[tuned], 2sus cym, 2watergong, 3rototom, 5finger dr[or bongo], 2bell plate, 2hi-hat, 3tin, 2ratchet

*Keyboards:
1st player: grand piano, doubling on upright piano.
2nd player: upright piano[tuned 1/4 tone lower], doubling on celesta and second grand piano

> Faber

Chamber Symphony, op.2 <1990>   13'

1[fl/pic/afl] 1 2[basset cl.bcl] 0 — 1 1[tp/wine bottle] 1 0 — 2perc — prepared pf/accordion — str 5t

perc: tri, cowbell, woodblk, sd, hi-hat, guiro, crot, belltree, marim, flexatone, wood chimes, shell chimes, 2frame drums, 3tamtam

Composer's note: "The accordion part is simple and does not require a trained player."

The three sections/movementsx are played without a break.

> Faber

Living Toys, op.9 <1993>   18'

1[1/pic] 1[1/Eh/sopranino rec] 1[1/Ebcl/bcl] 1[1/cbn] — 1[1/whip] 1[1/pic tp] 1 0 — 1perc — pf — str 5t

perc: sd, field dr, tri, templeblks, guiro, cast, vibrslp, 3gongs, tmp, 2crot, talking drum, 2sus cym, suspended sheet of paper, 2cowbells, bd/pedal, whip

I. Angels	2'
II. Aurochs	2'
BALETT	1'
III. Militiamen	2'
IV. H.A.L.'s Death	3'
BATTLE	2'
V. Playing Funerals	4'
TABLET	2'

> Faber

Adler, Samuel   1928-

(b Mannheim, 4 March 1928). American composer of German birth

Arcos Concerto   15'

soloists: flute, oboe, clarinet, bassoon
str

I. Slowly and very lyrically	_'
II. Fast and fluid	_'
III. Slow and quiet	_'
IV. Fast and vigorous	_'

> Presser

Art Creates Artists; A Celebration for Orchestra <1996>   3'

3[1.2.pic] 3[1.2.Eh] 3[1.2.bcl] 3 — 4 3 3 1 — tmp+3 — str

perc: bd, sus cym, sd, xyl, marim, 3tomtom, 3woodblk

> Presser

Beyond the Pale; Portrait of a Klezmer <2003>   14'

solo clarinet
str

> Presser

Centennial; A Celebration for Symphony Orchestra <1993>   4'

3[1.2.pic] 2 3[1.2.bcl] 3[1.2.cbn] — 4 3 3 1 — tmp+3 — str

perc: bd, cym, sus cym, sd, tri, tamtam, glock, xyl, marim, vib, 3timbales

> Presser

Concerto for Orchestra <1971>   20'

4[1.2.3/pic.4/pic] 3[1.2.Eh] 4[1.2.Ebcl.bcl] 3[1.2.cbn] — 4 3 4 1 — tmp+4 — hp — pf — str

perc: bd, cym, sus cym, sd, toms, tri, tamtam, glock, xyl, marim, vib, crot, templeblks

> Boosey

Concerto, Guitar <1994>   21'

2 2 2 2 — 2 2 0 0 — tmp+1 — str

perc: bd, rototom, tri, tambn, glock, marim, claves, cast, 3tomtom, 4timbales, 3woodblk

I. Very fast and rhythmic	_'
II. Very slowly; Suddenly much faster	_'
III. Fast and rhythmic	_'

> Presser

Concerto, Horn <2000>   20'

3[1.2.pic] 3[1.2.Eh] 3[1.2.bcl] 2 — 4 3 3 1 — tmp+2 — str

perc: bd, cym, sd, rototom, tri, tamtam, xyl, marim, vib, templeblks, whip, 3woodblk

I. Slowly and declamatory	_'
II. Slowly	_'
III. Fast and very rhythmic	_'

> Presser

Drifting on Wind and Currents; A Poem for Orchestra <2010>   9'

3[1.2.pic] 2 2 — 4 3 3 1 — tmp+2 — str

perc: bd, szl cym, sd, glock, marim

> Presser

Elegy for String Orchestra <1962>   8'

str

> Presser

Lux perpetua <1999>   14'

solo organ
3[1.2.pic] 3[1.2.Eh] 3[1.2.bcl] 3[1.2.cbn] — 4 3 3 1 — tmp+3 — str

> Presser

Summer Stock; Overture for Orchestra <1955>   5'

2 2 2 2 — 2 2 3 0 — tmp+2 — str

> AMP   Luck's

Symphony No.5 (We Are the Echoes) <1975>   26'

mezzo-soprano solo
3[1.2.pic] 3[1.2.Eh] 3[1.2.bcl] 3[1.2.cbn] — 4 3 3 1 — tmp+3 — pf — str

perc: bd, cym, sus cym, szl cym, sd, td, tri, tamtam, glock, xyl, vib, crot, bongos

I. We Go	4'
II. Even During War	5'
III. The Future	5'
IV. We Are the Echoes	7'
V. God Follows Me Everywhere	5'

> Boosey

Symphony No.6 <1984–1985>   22'

3[1.2.pic] 3[1.2.Eh] 3[1.2.bcl] 3[1.2.cbn] — 4 3 3 1 — tmp+3 — pf
— str
perc: xyl, marim, sus cym, td, bd, sd, tri, tambn, tamtam, glock, vib, templeblks,
bongos, cast, congas, 3tomtom, 2timbales, 3brake dr, 3woodblk
I. Fast and with much excitement   _'
II. Slowly and very expressively   _'
III. Fast and rhythmic   _'

Presser

Those Were the Days; Four Nostalgic Songs <2000>   9'

solo soprano
2 2 3[1.2.bcl] 2 — 2 2 0 0 — tmp+2 — str
perc: bd, sd, tri, glock, xyl, marim, 4tomtom, 5woodblk
I. Nostalia and Complaint of the Grandparents   _'
II. At the Young Composers' Concert   _'
III. Time and the Weather   _'
IV. Mrs. Snow   _'

C. Fischer

Adolphe, Bruce   1955-

(b New York, 31 May 1955). American

Carnival of the Creatures <2010>   30'

2[1.2/pic] 2 2 2 — 4 2 3 0 — tmp+3 — hp — str
perc: bd, cym, tomtom, tri, gong, marim, vib, chimes, woodblk, templeblks
"A carnival of overlooked creatures." Humorous verses are provided,
presumably to be read prior to each movement. The narrator will need to
approximate a Boston accent to make some of the rhymes work. (A
French translation of the verses is also available.)
    Audience participation in mvt XII (an audience-leader is needed).
Introduction [spoken only; no orchestra]   _'
I. The Pterosaur   _'
II. The Iguana   _'
III. The Owl   _'
IV. The Shrimp   _'
V. The Spider   _'
VI. The Shark   _'
VII. The Mudskipper   _'
VIII. Moratorium: Meditiation on Endangered and Extinct Creatures   _'
IX. The Virus   _'
X. The Conductor   _'
XI. The Teddy Bear   _'
XII. The Audience   _'
XIII. The Unicorn   _'

LKMP

I'm Inclined to New Music <1991>   8'

str
A comic parody on *Eine kleine Nachtmusik.*

MMB

Marita and Her Heart's Desire <1993>   27'

narrator (actress with multiple voices)
1[pic] 1 1 1 — 0 0 1 0 — 1perc — hp — str 5t

MMB

Oceanophony <2003>   35'

narrator (opt)
1 1 1 1 — 2 1 2 0 — 1perc — pf — str
perc: sus cym, tomtom, tri, marim, vib, templeblks
Accompanying optional narration and slide show available from the
publisher.
    Also available for octet: fl, cl, bn, vn, vc, db, pf, perc.
I. Marine Snow   _'
II. Pufferfish   _'
III. Coral Music   _'
IV. Stoplight Parrotfish   _'
V. Parrotfish Lullaby   _'
VI. Octopus   _'
VII. Sea Horse Greeting Dance   _'
VIII. Sarcastic Fringehead Fish   _'

LKMP

The Purple Palace <1998>   34'

narrator
1[fl/pic] 1 1 1 — 2 1 1 0 — 2perc — str
perc: bd, cym, sus cym, marim, vib, chimes, 3tomtom, tmp

LKMP

THREE PIECES for Kids & Chamber Orchestra   3'
1. Ta Woop! <1989>

solo flute & oboe
str
Kids (in the audience) sing.

MMB

2. Rainbow <1989>   4'

2 2 2 2 — 2 2 0 0 — str
Kids (in the audience) sing.

MMB

3. T-D-T (Texture-Dynamics-Timbre) <1989>   5'

1 2 2 2 — 2 0 0 0 — str
Kids (in the audience) clap, "click," and stamp.

MMB

Tyrannosaurus Sue: A Cretaceous Concerto <1999>   28'

narrator
0 1 1 1 — 1 1 1 0 — 1perc — str 5t or str orch
perc: bd, sus cym, tri, gong, 3tomtom, tmp
Duration includes the passages of narration which precede each
movement.
I. Birth of Sue   3'
II. Youth—Sue Explores Her World   4'
III. Competing for Food with the Troodon   3'
IV. Chasing the Parasaurolophus   3'
V. Battle with the Triceratops   4'
VI. Old Age and the Death of Sue   6'
VII. Dawning of a New World (After the Dinosaurs)   5'

LKMP

Aho, Kalevi   1949-

b Forssa, Finland, 9 Mar 1949) Finnish

Concerto, Flute (Huilukonsertto) <2002>   30'

2[1.pic] 2[1.Eh] 2 2 — 3 2 2 1 — baritone horn — 2perc — hp — str
perc: cym, sd, field dr, tomtom, tambn, tamtam, vib, thunder, 2sus cym, 2tri,
2woodblk, tmp, steel castanets, bamboo windchimes, glass windchimes
Flute soloist also plays alto flute.
I. Misterioso, adagio   15'
II. Presto, leggiero   9'
III. Epilogue   6'

Fennica

Kellot; Concerto for Saxophone Quartet & Orchestra   *28'*
(The Bells) <2008>

saxophone quartet (soprano, alto, tenor & baritone saxophones)
2 2 2 2 — 2 2 2 0 — 2perc — str[min 8.7.6.5.4]
perc: bd, sus cym, glock, chimes, templeblks, tmp, 2tri, 2tamtam, 2woodblk, 2cowbell
I. Prologue   _'
II. Chorale   _'
III. Scherzo (Presto)   _'
IV. Epilogue (Andante — Presto)   _'

> Fennica

Minea; Concertante Music for Orchestra <2008>   *18'*

4[1.2.3.pic] 4[1.2.3.Eh] 4[1.2.3.bcl] 4[1.2.3.cbn] — 6 4 3 1 — tmp+3 — hp — pf — str[16.14.12.10.8]
perc: vib, glock, bd, tamtam, chimes, congas, bongos, field dr, 3sus cym, iron chain, 4tomtom, darabucca

> Fennica

Symphony No.1 <1969>   *29'*

2[both/pic] 2 2 2[1.2/cbn] — 2 2 2 0 — 1perc — hp — str
perc: bd, cym, sus cym, tamtam
Trombones in mvts 3 & 4 only.
I. Andante   9'
II. Allegretto   6'
III. Presto   5'
IV. Andante — Allegro non troppo 9'

> Fazer   Fennica

Symphony No.2 <1970; rev 1995>   *24'*

3[1.2.pic] 3[1.2.3/Eh] 4[1.2.Ebcl.bcl] 3[1.2.cbn] — 6 4 3 1 — tmp+2 — str
perc: bd, cym, sd, field dr, tamtam

> Fazer   Fennica

Albéniz, Isaac   1860-1909

(b Camprodon, Gerona, 29 May 1860; d Cambo-les-Bains, 18 May 1909). Spanish

Catalonia (Suite populaire, no.1) <1899>   *7'*

3[1.2.pic] 3[1.2.Eh] 3[1.2.bcl] 3 — 4 4 3 1 — tmp+4 — 2hp — str
perc: bd, cym, sd, tri, tambn
Originally for piano; orchestrated by the composer. Part I of an intended (but never-completed) three-part work.

> Durand   Kalmus   Luck's

Concerto, Piano, No.1, op.78, A minor (Concierto   *24'*
fantástico) <1887?>

2 2 2 2 — 2 2 3 0 — tmp — str

> UME

Iberia (arr. E. F. Arbós) <1906–1907>   *28'*

3[1.2.3/pic] 3[1.2.Eh] 4[1.2.3/Ebcl.4/bcl] 3[1.2.cbn] — 4 4 3 1 — tsx — tmp+6 — 2hp — cel — str
Nos. 1-3 and 6-7 of the suite, originally for piano; orchestrated by Enrique Fernández Arbós.
Evocation   7'
El puerto   7'
Fête Dieu â Seville   5'
Triana   4'
El Albaicín   5'

> Eschig

Iberia (arr. Carlos Surinach) <1906–1908>   *50'*

2[1.2/pic] 2[1.2/Eh] 2 2 — 4 2 3 1 — tmp+2 — hp — str
Nos. 4-5 and 8-12 of the suite, originally for piano.
Rondeña   7'
Almería   7'
El polo   9'
Lavapies   7'
Málaga   5'
Jérez   8'
Eritaña   7'

> AMP

Navarra <1912>   *5'*

3[1.2.3/pic] 3[1.2.3/Eh] 3[1.2.3/bcl] 3 — 4 3 3 1 — tmp+4 — 2hp — str
perc: field dr, tri, tambn, cym, sus cym, bd
An unfinished piano work; completed by D. de Séverac, 1912, and orchestrated by Enrique Fernández Arbós.

> Eschig

Rapsodia española, op.70 <1887>   *18'*

solo piano
3[1.2.pic] 3[1.2.Eh] 2 2 — 4 2 3 1 — tmp+4 — hp — cel — str
perc: xyl, sd, cast, tambn, cym, sus cym, bd
Originally for 2 pianos; orchestrated by Cristóbal Halffter.

> UME

Albert, Adrienne   1937-

(b Los Angeles, 1 Aug 1937). American

Courage <2000>   *5'*

2 2 2 2 — 4 3 3 1 — tmp+2 — str
perc: cym, sus cym, sd, td, tri, glock

> Kenter Canyon

Fanfare   *4'*

0 0 0 0 — 4 4 4 1 — [no str]

> Kenter Canyon

Interiors   *7'*

str

> Kenter Canyon

Western Suite <1999>   *12'*

2 2 2 2 — 4 2 3 1 — tmp+2 — hp — pf — str
An earlier title for this work, *Montana Morning,* has been superseded.
Sunrise   _'
Hoedown   _'

> Kenter Canyon

Albert, Eugen d'   1864-1932

b Glasgow, 10 April 1864; d Riga, 3 March 1932). German

Concerto, Violoncello, op.20, C major <1899>   *22'*

2 2 2 2 — 4 2 0 0 — tmp — str
I. Allegro moderato   9'
II. Andante con moto   7'
III. Allegro vivace   6'

> Forberg   Kalmus

Albert, Stephen   1941 - 1992

(b New York City, 6 Feb 1941; d Truro, MA, 1992). American

Anthem and Processionals <1988>   16'

3[1.2.3/pic] 3[1.2.Eh] 3[1.2.3/bcl] 3[1.2.cbn] — 4 3 3 1 — tmp+5 — hp — pf/cel — str

perc: bd, cym, sus cym, rototom, gong, glock, vib, chimes, crot, 3tomtom, 4woodblk, 2metalplate, tambn[on pf strings]

> Schirmer

Flower of the Mountain <1985>   16'

soprano solo
2[1.2/pic] 2[1.2.Eh] 2 2 — 2 2 0 0 — tmp+2 — hp — str
perc: tri, glock, xyl, vib
Movement 2 of the composer's *Distant Hills*.
    Also available for soprano & chamber orchestra:
1[fl/afl] 1[1/Eh] 1 1 — 1 0 0 0 — pf — str 5t

> Schirmer

Into Eclipse <1982; rev 1986>   30'

tenor
2[1.2/pic/afl] 2[1.2.Eh] 2[1.2/bcl] 2[1.2.cbn] — 4 2 3 1 — mandolin — tmp+4 — hp — cel, pf — str
perc: bd, sd, gong, glock, xyl, marim, vib, chimes, crot, claves, 2rototom
Originally composed for tenor & chamber orchestra (1981):
    1[fl/pic] 0 1[cl/Ebcl] 0 — 1 1 0 0 — 2perc — hp — pf — str 5t
Full orchestra version, 1986.

I. Prologue and Riddle Song	_'
II. Oedipus 1	_'
III. A Quiet Fate	_'
IV. Ghosts	_'
V. Oedipus 2	_'

> Schirmer

RiverRun (Symphony No.1) <1983–1984>   33'

3[1.2/afl.3/pic] 3[1.2.Eh] 4[1.2.Ebcl.bcl] 3[1.2.cbn] — 4 3 3 1 — asx — tmp+3 — 2hp — pf — str
perc: vib, glock, bd, xyl, gong, bell
Subsets of these four movements are authorized for performance independently: *Rain Music* (mvt 1); *Rivers End* (mvt 4); *Rivering Waters* (mvts 1 & 4).

1. Rain Music	8'
2. Leafy Speafing	9'
3. Beside the Rivering Waters	6'
4. Rivers End	10'

> Schirmer

Sun's Heat <1989>   15'

solo tenor
2[1.2/pic] 2[1.2.Eh] 2 2 — 2 2 0 0 — tmp+2 — hp — pf — str
perc: bd, glock, vib, chimes
Tmp+1 if the timpanist plays 7 notes on vib.
Movement 1 from the composer's *Distant Hills*.
Also available for tenor & chamber orchestra:
    1[fl/afl] 1 1 1 — 1 0 0 0 — pf — str 5t

> Schirmer

Symphony No.2 <1992>   31'

3[1.2.3/pic] 3[1.2.3/Eh] 3[1.2.3/bcl] 4[1.2.3.cbn] — 4 3 3 1 — tmp+2 — hp — pf — str
perc: bd, chimes, glock, sd, sus cym, tri, vib, woodblk, xyl
Completed in short score by the composer before his death; orchestration completed by Sebastian Currier, 1994.

I. quarter-note = 58-60	13'
II. dotted quarter-note = 72	5'
III. quarter-note = 54-56	13'

> Schirmer

Wind Canticle <1991>   14'

solo clarinet
2 2[1.2/Eh] 2[1.2/bcl] 2 — 4 2 0 0 — hp — pf — str

> Schirmer

Albinoni, Tomaso   1671 - 1750

(b Venice, 8 June 1671; d Venice, 17 Jan 1750/51). Italian

Adagio, Organ & Strings, G minor <1694–1741>   10'

str orch
Actually composed by Remo Giazotto (1910-1998); an elaboration of a fragment supposedly from one of Albinoni's sonatas.

> Ricordi

Concerto, op.5, no.4, G major <1707>   5'

cnt — str
Ed. Raffaele Cumar.

> Ricordi

Concerto, op.5, no.7, D minor <1707>   10'

cnt — str
Ed. Ettore Bonelli.

> Zanibon   Luck's

Concerto, op.9, no.9, C major <1722>   11'

0 2 0 0 — cnt — str

> Musica Rara   Ricordi

Concerto, Oboe, op.7, no.3, B-flat major <1715>   9'

cnt — str
Ed. Bernhard Paumgartner.

> Boosey   Luck's

Concerto, Oboe, op.9, no.2, D minor <1722>   14'

cnt — str

> Kalmus   Kneusslin   Luck's   Zerboni

Concerto, Oboe, op.9, no.11, B-flat major <1722>   9'

cnt — str
Ed. Franz Giegling.

Allegro	4'
Adagio	2'
Allegro	3'

> Musica Rara

Concerto, Trumpet, A major, op.6, no.11 (St. Marc) <1712>   8'

cnt — str
Originally for violin, viola & harpsichord; "freely transcribed" by Gerald Webster. A version in B-flat major is also available from the publisher.

1. Grave	2'
2. Allegro	2'
3. Andante (Minuet)	1'
4. Allegro	3'

> Hoyt

Concerto, Violin, op.9, no.10, F major <1722>   11'

cnt — str
Ed. Remo Giazotto.

> Ricordi

Albrechtsberger, Johann Georg   1736-1809

(b Klosterneuburg, nr Vienna, 3 Feb 1736; d Vienna, 7 March 1809). Austrian

Concerto, Trombone, B-flat major <1769>   15'

str[no va]
Arr. Paul Angerer.
Allegro moderato   6'
Andante   6'
Allegro moderato   3'

> Reift

Alfvén, Hugo   1872-1960

(b Stockholm, 1 May 1872; d Falun, 8 May 1960). Swedish

Bergakungen, op.37 (The Mountain King): Vallflickans Dans (Herd Maiden's Dance; Shepherd-Girl's Dance) <1916–1923>   4'

3[1.2.pic] 3[1.2.3/Eh] 2 3 — 4 0 0 0 — str
Extract from the ballet. Optional: ob3/Eh, bn3.

> Nordiska

Midsommarvaka, op.19 (Midsummer Vigil; Swedish Rhapsody No.1) <1903>   12'

3[1.2.3/pic] 3[1.2.3/Eh] 3[1.2/Ebcl.bcl] 3 — 4 2 3 1 — tmp+2 — 2hp — str
perc: cym, tri, glock

> Hansen   Kalmus   Luck's

Swedish Rhapsody No.3, op.47 (Dalarapsodien) <1931>   18'

3[1.2/pic.3/pic] 3[1.2.Eh] 3[1/opt ssx.2.bcl] 3[1.2.cbn] — 4 2 3 1 — tmp+2 — hp — str
perc: bd, cym
The soprano saxophone, if used, should preferably be off stage. Optional instruments: fl3, Eh, bcl, cbn.

> Hansen

Alkan, Charles-Valentin   1813-1888

(b Paris, 30 Nov 1813; d Paris, 29 March 1888). French

Andante romantique <1837>   5'

solo piano
str
Slow movement of a lost piano concerto, reconstructed by Mark Starr from a related piece, no.2 of the *Trois andantes romantiques*, op.13.

> Noteworthy

Concerto, Piano <1857>   52'

3[1.2/pic2.3/pic1] 3[1.2.Eh] 3[1.2.bcl] 3[1.2.cbn] — 4 3 3 1 — tmp+3 — str
perc: bd, cym, sus cym, sd, tambn, tamtam, glock, sleighbells, cast, field drum, large bell (C#), tocsin
An orchestration by Mark Starr of Alkan's *Concerto pour piano seul*, op.39, nos.8-10.
   2 small ensembles (drawn from the above complement) are deployed off-stage briefly in the 1st mvt (optional).
Allegro assai   30'
Adagio   12'
Allegretto alla barbaresca   10'

> Noteworthy

Le Festin d'Esope (Aesop's Feast) <1857>   10'

3[1.2.pic] 2 3[1.2.bcl] 3[1.2/cbn.cbn] — 4 3 3 1 — tmp+5 — hp — pf/cel — str
perc: bd, cym, sus cym, sd, tri, glock, xylorimba, templeblk, whip, ratch, lion roar, wind machine, thundersheet, guiro
Orchestrated by Mark Starr from a set of variations for solo piano (op.39, no.12).

> C. Fischer

Ouverture de concert <1857>   9'

3[1.2.pic] 2 2 3[1.2.cbn] — 4 3 3 1 — tmp+2 — str
perc: bd, cym
Orchestrated by Mark Starr from a work for solo piano (op.39, no.11).

> C. Fischer

Symphony, op.39 (Symphonie macabre) <1857>   34'

3[1.2/pic.3/pic] 2 2 4[1.2.3.cbn] — 4 3 3 1 — tmp+2 — hp — str
perc: bd, cym, sus cym, tri, tambn, chimes
Orchestrated by Mark Starr from four etudes for solo piano (op.39, nos.4-7).
Allegro moderato [op.39 no.4]   12'
Marche funèbre: Andantino [op.39 no.5]   9'
Menuet: Tempo di minuetto [op.39 no.6]   7'
Finale: Presto [op.39 no.7]   6'

> C. Fischer

Allen, Brett Lensley   1958-

(b Princeton NJ, 8 December 1958). American

Nativity Scenes <2002>   22'

optional narrator
str[min 4.4.2.3.2]
If narration is used, 28'.
1. O Come, O Come, Emmanuel   4'
2. We Three Kings   3'
3. Handelia   6'
4. Silent Night   5'
5. Good Christian Men Rejoice   4'

> Oxford

Alwyn, William   1905-1985

(b Northampton, 7 Nov 1905; d Southwold, 11 Sept 1985). English

Autumn Legend <1954>   12'

solo English horn
str

> Lengnick

Elizabethan Dances <1957>   16'

2[1.2/pic] 2[1.2/Eh] 2 2 — 4 3 3 0 — tmp+4 — hp — cel — str
perc: bd, cym, sd, td, tri, tambn, glock, xyl, woodblk, cast, marac[opt]
Dances reflective of the time of Elizabeth I, alternating with others reflective of the time of Elizabeth II.
I. Moderato e ritmico   3'
II. Waltz tempo—languidamente   2'
III. Allegro scherzando [ma non troppo allegro]   2'
IV. Moderato   4'
V. Poco allegretto e semplice   2'
VI. Allegro giocoso   3'

> Lengnick

Festival March <1950>   8'

3[incl pic] 3[incl Eh] 3[incl bcl] 3[incl cbn] — 4 3 3 1 — tmp+2 — hp — str
Possible with woodwinds: 3[incl pic] 2 2 2

> Lengnick

Lyra angelica <1954>   30'

solo harp
str
I. "I looke for angels' songs, and heare Him crie"   8'
II. "Ah! who was He such pretious perills found?"   7'
III. "And yet, how can I heare Thee singing goe?"   9'
IV. "How can such joy as this want words to speake?"   6'

> Lengnick

The Moor of Venice; Dramatic Overture <1956>   10'

2[1.2/pic] 2[1.2/Eh] 2 2[1.2/cbn] — 4 2 3 1 — tmp+3 — hp — str
perc: bd, cym, sd, tri, tamtam, chimes
Originally for brass band; orchestrated by Philip Lane, 2000.

> Boosey

Sinfonietta <1970>   26'

str
1. Moderato molto ritmico   8'
2. Adagio e poco rubato   7'
3. Allegro   11'

> Lengnick

Symphony No.1 <1949>   41'

3[1.2.3/pic] 3[1.2.Eh] 2 2 — 4 3 3 1 — tmp+3 — hp — cel — str
1. Adagio; Allegro ritmico   11'
2. Allegro leggiero   9'
3. Adagio   10'
4. Allegro jubilante   11'

> Lengnick

Symphony No.2 <1953>   30'

3[1.2.3/pic] 3[1.2.Eh] 2 2 — 4 3 3 1 — tmp+3 — 2hp[2nd opt] — str
Part 1: Con moto — Molto moderato — Quasi adagio molto calmato   13'
Part 2: Allegro molto — Moderato largamente — Molto tranquillo   17'

> Lengnick

Symphony No.3 <1955–1956>   45'

3[1.2.3/pic] 3[1.2.Eh] 2 2 — 4 3 3 1 — tmp+4 — hp — cel — str
perc: bd, cym, sd, td, tri, tambn, glock, xyl, chimes, cast
1. Allegro molto   11'
2. Poco adagio   10'
3. Allegro con fuoco   14'

> Lengnick

Symphony No.4 <1959>   38'

1[1.2/pic] 2[1.2/Eh] 2 2 — 4 3 3 1 — tmp — str
1. Maestoso ma con moto; Allegro   12'
2. Molto vivace   12'
3. Adagio e molto calmato   14'

> Lengnick

Symphony No.5 (Hydriotaphia) <1972–1973>   17'

3[1.2.3/pic] 3[1.2.Eh] 2 2 — 4 3 3 1 — tmp+4 — hp — str
perc: sd, td, bd, cym, tamtam, xyl, chimes, sus cym
1. Moderato — Allegro ma non troppo   3'
2. Andante sostenuto   5'
3. Allegro con fuoco   3'
4. Tempo di marcia funebre   6'

> Lengnick

Amaya, Efraín   1959-

(b Caracas, 2 Oct 1959). American composer of Venezuelan birth

Angelica <2000>   6'

str

> LaFi

Un Camino (Concerto for Cello & Orchestra) <2013>   19'

3[1.2.pic] 3[1.2.Eh] 3[1.2.bcl] 2 — 4 2 0 0 — tmp+2 — str
perc: tri, sus cym, claves, templeblks, woodblk, tambn, guiro, vib, marim, tamtam, 2gong, cabasa, shaker

> LaFi

Indigo Concerto <2001>   22'

solo flute
1[pic] 2[1.2/Eh] 2[cl.Ebcl] 2 — 2 1 0 0 — 3perc — pf — str[min 6.6.5.4.2]
perc: xyl, marim, vib, glock, sd, bd, cym, sus cym, whip, tri, tamtam, marac, congas, windchimes, wine glass [F#; or bowed vib], 5woodblk
I. Moderato   14'
II. Lento — III. Dance   8'

> LaFi

Maroon Dreams <2004>   12'

solo tenor
1 1 1 2 — 2 1 0 0 — 1perc — str
I. Chestnut Oak Tree   5'
II. For You   3'
III. Dreamplace   4'

> LaFi

Mater Dei (For God is Love) <2009>   4'

solo soprano
hp — str

> LaFi

Pájaros de tres alas (Birds of Three Wings) <1993>   7'

3[1.2.pic] 2 3[1.2.bcl] 2 — 4 3[3crts] 3 1 — tmp+3 — hp — str
perc: xyl, vib, glock, tambn, bd, cym, sus cym, whip, tri, tamtam, guiro, marac, rainstick

> LaFi

Parasol <2002>   4'

3[1.2.pic] 2 2 2 — 4 2 3 1 — tmp+5 — str
perc: claves, guiro, sus cym, bd, shaker

> LaFi

Soledad y el Mar (Maid of Blue)   11'

3[1.2.pic] 3[1.2.Eh] 4[1.2.Ebcl.bcl] 3[1.2.cbn] — 4 3 3 1 — tmp+5 — hp — pf/cel — str
perc: bd, gong, sus cym, cym, glock, tamtam, tri, xyl

> LaFi

Wuaraira Repano <2006>   15'

solo clarinet
1 1[Eh] 1[bcl] 1 — 1 1 1 0 — 2perc — pf — str
perc: vib, marim, glock, bd, cym, sus cym, tri, tamtam, crot, timbales, windchimes, rainstick, shaker

> LaFi

Amram, David   1930-

(b Philadelphia, 17 Nov 1930). American

Autobiography for Strings <1959>   8'

str

> Peters

Shakespearian Concerto <1959>   22'

0 1 0 0 — 2 0 0 0 — str

> Peters

Triple Concerto <1970>   25'

3 solo quintets: woodwind (fl, ob, cl, bn, hn), brass (2tp, hn, tbn, tuba), and jazz (asx, bsx, pf, db, drums)
2[incl pic] 2[incl Eh] 2[incl bcl] 2[incl cbn] — 2 2 2 0 — tmp+5 — cel — str
The 15 soloists are *in addition* to the accompanying orchestral complement.

> Peters

Amrhein, Karen Amanda   1970-

(b Detroit, 21 May 1970). American

Bestiary <2005; rev 2009>   15'

2[1/pic.2] 1 2 2 — 2 0 3 1 — tmp+1 — hp — str[12.9.8.8.6]
perc: bd, sus cym, tri, glock
Originally titled *House of the Sudden Sea*; revised 2009.
1. Phoenix   3'
2. Chimera   1'
3. Idyll (Wind in the Branches)   3'
4.Griffin   3'
5. Sea Serpent   2'
6. Procession   3'

> Happy Lemon

Concerto, Euphonium <2005–2006>   13'

str[8.8.6.6.2]
I. Daydream on a Thanksgiving Chorale   5'
II. A Song from the Seashore   4'
II. Cascades   4'

> Happy Lemon

Concerto, Piano <2005>   18'

1 1 1 1 — 2 1 1 1 — str[8.8.6.6.4]
A Gathering   7'
A Ballad   6'
A Dance   5'

> Happy Lemon

Event Horizon (clarinet concerto) <2002>   15'

solo clarinet
1 1 1 1 — 2 0 0 0 — euph — marimba — pf — str
Prelude   5'
Night   4'
Event Horizon 6'

> Happy Lemon

Event Horizon (alternative version) <2002–2006>   15'

1 1 1 1 — 1 1 0 0 — euph — marimba — pf — str 5t or str orch [8.8.6.6.4]
Prelude   5'
Night   4'
Event Horizon 6'

> Happy Lemon

Hamilton Street Concerto <1998>   12'

solo guitar
1 1 1 1 — 1 0 0 0 — str[8.8.6.6.2]
Allegro   2'
Episode 1 [gtr unaccompanied]   1'
Autumn Woods   3'
Episode 2 [gtr unaccompanied]   1'
Episode 3 (Two, for Moonlight) [fl & gtr]   3'
(after Purcell)   2'

> Happy Lemon

Little Nemo in Slumberland <2002; rev 2006>   12'

2 2 2 2 — 2 2[or 4] 3 1 — tmp+1 — pf[opt] — str
perc: glock
The publisher also offers a chamber orchestra version, scored for
1 1 1 1 — 1 1 2 0 — 1perc — str; and a version for wind ensemble.

> Happy Lemon

Missa humanis <2000>   11'

chorus   solos SATB
1 1 2 1 — 2 2 0 0 — euph — tmp — str[10vn.8va.6vc.2db]
Kyrie   2'
Gloria   1'
Credo   2'
Sanctus   2'
Agnus dei   4'

> Happy Lemon

Serenade <1994>   5'

2 1[ob/Eh] 2 1 — 2 0 0 0 — tmp — hp — str[10.10.8.8.4]

> Happy Lemon

Semi-Suite <1997>   12'

2 1 2 1 — 2 2 3 0 — tmp+1 — pf — str[12.10.8.8.4]
perc: bd, sus cym, sd, crot
Prelude   4'
Passacaglia   3'
Badinerie   1'
Air   2'
Scherzo   2'

> Happy Lemon

Symphony of Seasons <2001>   22'

2 2 3[1.2.bcl] 2 — 2 2 3 1 — tmp — pf — str
Autumn   9'
Winter   5'
Spring   4'
Summer   4'

> Happy Lemon

Variants for Flute, Guitar & Strings (Finegold Variants) <2003>   11'

solo flute, solo guitar
str[6.6.4.4.2]

> Happy Lemon

Amundson, Steven   1955-

(b Brooklyn, NY, 25 Oct 1955). American

Angels' Dance <1995>   5'

3[1.2.pic] 3[1.2.Eh] 2 2 — 4 3 3 1 — tmp+3 — hp — cel — str
perc: tri, tambn, glock, xyl, marim, chimes

> MMB

Joyous Noel <2002>   4'

handbell choir (5-octave)
3[1.2.pic] 3[1.2.Eh] 2 2 — 4 3 3 1 — tmp+3 — hp — str
perc: tri, glock, chimes

> Tempo

Reindeer Rock   4'

jazz vocalist *or* children's choir
3[1.2.pic] 2 2 2 — 4 3 3 1 — 3perc — str
perc: set, glock, sleighbells

> Tempo

Rejoicing <1999>   6'

3[1.2.pic] 3[1.2.Eh] 3[1.2.bcl] 2 — 4 3 3 1 — tmp+3 — hp — str
perc: sd, hi-hat, tri, tambn, glock, xyl, opt marim

> Tempo

Sola gratia <2000>   7'

2 3[1.2.Eh] 2 2 — 4 3 3 1 — tmp+2 — hp — pf — str
perc: sus cym, glock, vib, chimes, windchimes, finger cym

> Tempo

Three's Company <2002>   6'

3 solo bassoons
3 perc or set — str
perc: bd, sus cym, sd

> Tempo

Amy, Gilbert   1936-

(b Paris, 29 Aug 1936). French

D'un espace déployé (From a Space Unfolded)   31'
<1971–1973>

solo soprano & 2 obbligato pianos
4[1.2/pic.3/pic.4.afl] 4[1.2.3.Eh] 5[1.2.3.Ebcl.bcl] 4[1.2.3.4/cbn] — 6 4
4 2 — tmp+5 — elec org, pf — str[14.12.10.8.8]
perc: templeblks, tri, field dr, bd, metal claves, 2woodblk, 2logdrum, 2anvil, 3sus
cym, 5Chinese cym, 3tamtam, 13Chinese gong
Orchestra 1 (above) led by Conductor 1.
Orchestra 2, led by Conductor 2: 3perc[vib, glock, tamtam, marim, xyl,
gong, chimes], elec gtr, 2hp, cel, pf, str[16.0.8.8.4], solo soprano
voice[textless; syllables to be pronounced as in French]
I. Très modéré mais souple   _'
II. Très calme et souple   _'
III. Assez vif   _'

> Universal

Mouvements, for 17 Solo Instruments <1958>   10'

1 1 2[1.bcl] 1 — 1 1 1 0 — 1perc — 2hp — pf — str 5t
perc: templeblks, marac, bongos, gong, 3tomtom, 2tamtam

> Heugel

Refrains <1972>   15'

4[1/pic.2/pic.3/pic.afl/pic] 3[1.2.Eh] 3[1.2.bcl] 3[1.2.cbn] — 4 3 3 1
— elec gtr[or 2nd hp] — tmp+4 — hp — pf, cel — str[14.12.10.8.6]
perc: glock, chimes, marim, vib, 2tamtam
I. eighth-note = 82   _'
Ib. eighth-note = 82   _'
II. Très modéré   _'
IIb. Assez vif   _'
III. Très modéré   _'

> Universal

Anderson, Leroy   1908-1975

(b Cambridge, MA, 29 June 1908; d Woodbury, CT, 18 May 1975). American

The Classical Jukebox <1950>   3'

3[1.2.pic] 3[1.2.Eh] 3[1.2.bcl] 3[1.2.cbn] — 4 4 3 1 — tmp+3 — pf
— str
perc: tri, cym, bd, ratch, cowbell, woodblk, sd, sirenwhistle
Based on *Music, Music, Music*, by B. Baum & S. Weiss.

> Woodbury

Concerto, Piano, C Major <1953>   22'

3[1.2.pic] 2[1.2/Eh] 2 2 — 4 3 3 1 — tmp+1 — str
perc: sus cym, marac, sd, cowbell, claves (covered by tmp)
1. Allegro moderato   9'
2. Andante   6'
3. Allegro vivo   7'

> Woodbury

Goldilocks: Overture <1958>   5'

3[1.2.pic] 2 2 2 — 4 3 2 1 — tmp+2 — hp[opt] — str
perc: set, glock, xyl, sirenwhstl
Ed. Robert Wendel.

> Wendel

Irish Suite   20'

3[incl pic] 2 2 2 — 4 3 3 1 — tmp+3 — hp — str
perc: tri, chimes, tamtam, glock, xyl, sd, cym, sus cym, bd
Complete suite available for purchase from Alfred; individual mvts
available for rental only.
The Irish Washerwoman   3'
The Minstrel Boy   4'
The Rakes of Mallow   3'
The Wearing of the Green 3'
The Last Rose of Summer   4'
The Girl I Left Behind Me 3'

> Alfred

Anderson, T(homas) J(efferson)   1928-

(b Coatesville, PA, 17 Aug 1928). American

Chamber Symphony <1968>   14'

1[incl pic] 1 1 1 — 1 1 1 0 — 2perc — hp — cel — str

> CFE

Andriessen, Louis   1939-

(b Utrecht, 6 June 1939). Dutch

Dances <1991>   25'

solo soprano
1perc — hp — pf — str

> Donemus

Mausoleum <1979; rev 1981>   30'

2 high baritones
0 0 0 0 — 8 3 4 0 — bass gtr, cimbalom — 2perc — 2hp — 2pf —
str[0.0.4.4.2]
Some instruments must be amplified.

> Donemus

De Staat (The Republic) <1972–1976>   35'

4 female voices
0 4[1.2.3/Eh.4/Eh] 0 0 — 4 4 4 0 — 2elec gtr, bass gtr — 2hp — 2pf
— 4va
All instruments should be amplified for a perfect dynamic balance.

> Donemus

Antheil, George

1900 - 1959

(b Trenton, NJ, 8 July 1900; d New York, 12 Feb 1959). American

Ballet mécanique (1953 version) <1923–1925; rev 1953>   18'

tmp+10 — 4pf — [no str]
perc: bd, cym, sd, td, tri, gong, glock, 2xyl, woodblk, 2 elec bells, 2 airplane sounds
Original version (1923-25) is longer (30') and for a much larger ensemble, according to the publisher: 3xyl, elec bells, 3propellers, tamtam, 4sd, siren, 2pf, 16 pianolas[min 4, written in 4 parts]. A realization (MIDI) of the mechanical piano [pianola] parts is available on rental.

> Schirmer

Cabeza de Vaca <1955–1956>   52'

chorus   solo Bar, T, boy soprano
1[fl/pic] 1 3[1.2.bcl] 1 — 2 2 2 0 — tmp+1 — hp — pf — str
perc: bd, cym, sus cym, sd, field dr, tri, tamtam, glock, xyl, vib
Orchestrated posthumously by Ernest Gold.

> Schirmer

Concerto, Piano, No.1 <1922>   22'

3[1.2.pic] 2 2 2 — 2 3 3 1 — tmp+3 — 2hp — cel — str
perc: cym, sd, tamtam, xyl

> Schirmer

Concerto, Violin <1946>   30'

2[1/pic.2/pic] 2 2 2 — 4 3 2 0 — tmp+2 — hp — str
perc: bd, sus cym, sd, tri, tambn, xyl, woodblk, cast
Revised edition, 2011, based on performance materials used at the premiere, plus the archive recording.
   I. Moderato assai   _'
   II. Andante   _'
   III. Presto capriccio   _'

> Schirmer

A Jazz Symphony [original 1925 version] <1925>   12'

solo piano
0 2 2 0 — 0 3 3 1 — 3perc — 2pf[orch] — str
perc: set, glock, xyl, boatwhistle

> Weintraub

A Jazz Symphony [1955 version] <1925; rev 1955>   8'

1[fl/pic] 0 3 0 — 0 3 3 0 — tmp+1 — pf — str[3vn, va, vc, db]
perc: sus cym, xyl, tambn, cast, set
Originally composed 1925; revised in 1955 for this 19-player version.

> Weintraub

Serenade [I] <1948>   16'

str
   Allegro   3'
   Andante molto   8'
   Vivo   5'

> Weintraub

Spectre of the Rose Waltz <1946; rev 1947>   4'

2 2 2 2 — 2 2 2 0 — tmp — hp — cel — str

> Weintraub

Symphony No.3 (American) <1936–1939; rev 1946>   25'

2 2 2 2 — 4 2 3 1 — tmp+3 — str
perc: bd, sus cym, sd, tri, tambn, glock, xyl
Composed 1936-39; revised in 1946.
   I. Allegro   9'
   II. Andante   7'
   III. The Golden Spike   4'
   IV. Back to Baltimore   5'

> Schirmer

Symphony No.4 (1942) <1942>   34'

3[1/pic.2/pic.3/pic] 3[1.2.3/Eh] 3[1.2.bcl] 3[1.2.cbn] — 4 3 3 1 — tmp+4 — hp — pf — str
perc: bc, cym, sd, tri, tambn, gong, xyl, vib, woodblk, cast
   1. Moderato; Allegretto   11'
   2. Allegro   10'
   3. Scherzo: Presto   5'
   4. Allegro non troppo   8'

> Boosey

Symphony [No.5; withdrawn] (Tragic) <1945–1946>   30'

4[[incl pic]] 3[1.2.Eh] 3[1.2.bcl] 3[1.2.cbn] — 4 3 3 1 — tmp+4 — hp — str
This work from 1945-46 was published by Schirmer, but was withdrawn by the composer, and superseded by his *Symphony No.5 (The Joyous)*, 1947-48, *q.v.*

Symphony No.5 (The Joyous) <1947–1948>   23'

3[[incl pic]] 3[[incl Eh]] 3[[incl bcl]] 3[[incl cbn]] — 4 3 3 1 — tmp+5 — pf — str
A prior symphony, composed in 1945-46 and subtitled *Tragic*, was apparently designated No.5, but then withdrawn.
   1. Allegro   8'
   2. Adagio molto   9'
   3. Allegretto maestoso; Allegro giocoso   6'

> MCA

Symphony No.6 (After Delacroix) <1948; rev 1950>   26'

3[1.2.pic] 3[1.2.Eh] 3[1.2.bcl] 3[1.2.cbn] — 4 3 3 1 — tmp+4 — pf — str
   Maestoso; Allegro molto   9'
   Larghetto   9'
   Allegro   8'

> Weintraub

Antunes, Jorge

1942 -

(b Rio de Janeiro, 23 April 1942). Brazilian

Intervertige <1974>   11'

1 1 1 1 — 1 0 0 0 — 2perc — str 4t[ampd]
perc: bd, sus cym, tri, tamtam, glock, xyl, vib, chimes, crot, templeblks, whip, marac, 3tomtom, 3woodblk, anvil
Electronic equipment required: 2 tape recorders, 4 microphones (in addition to the 4 contact mics for the str 4t), 2 mixers, 4 speakers, 2 amplifiers.
   Each string instrument tunes its lowest string down to a designated pitch, the upper strings of each instrument remaining at normal tuning.

> Zerboni

Poetica II <1973>   15'

str
Scordatura is required throughout: each instrument tunes its lowest string down to a designated pitch, the upper strings of each instrument remaining at normal tuning.

> Billaudot

Arensky, Anton

1861 - 1906

(b Novgorod, 30 June/12 July 1861; d nr Terioki, Finland [now Zelenogorsk, Russia], 12/25 Feb 1906). Russian

Concerto, Piano, op.2, F minor <1882>

30'

2 2 2 2 — 4 2 3 0 — tmp+3 — str
perc: bd, cym, tri

I. Allegro maestoso	13'
II. Andante con moto	9'
III. Scherzo-Finale: Allegro molto	8'

C. Fischer	Kalmus	Simrock

Suite No.1, op.7, G minor <1885>

29'

3[1.2.pic] 2 2 2 — 4 2 3 0 — tmp+3 — hp — str
perc: tri, cym, bd
Mvt IV, *Basso ostinato*, is often performed separately; its instrumentation: 2 2 2 2 — 2 0 0 0 — str.

I. Variations sur un thème russe	7'
II. Air de danse	4'
III. Scherzo	8'
IV. Basso ostinato	4'
V. Marche	6'

Jurgenson	Kalmus

Symphony No.1, op.4, B minor <1883>

35'

3[1.2.pic] 2 2[1/Ebcl.2] 2 — 4 2 3 1 — tmp+3 — str
perc: bd, cym, tri, tambn
Ebcl plays only 4 bars, in the 4th mvt; written in the first part, it could easily be taken by either player.

I. Adagio; Allegro patetico	12'
II. Andante pastorale con moto	10'
III. Scherzo: Allegro con spirito	6'
IV. Finale: Allegro giocoso	7'

Jurgenson	Kalmus

Variations on a Theme by Tchaikovsky, op.35a <1894>

16'

str
Arrangement of the slow mvt of the composer's *String Quartet No.2*, based on the song *Legend* by Tchaikovsky (op.54, no.5).

Theme: Moderato	1'
I. Un poco piu mosso	2'
II. Allegro non troppo	1'
III. Andantino tranquillo	2'
IV. Vivace	2'
V. Andante	3'
VI. Allegro con spirito	2'
VII. Andante con moto	1'
Coda: Moderato	2'

Forberg	Kalmus	Luck's

Argento, Dominick

1927 -

(b York, PA, 27 Oct 1927). American

Bravo Mozart!; An Imaginary Biography <1969>

30'

solo oboe, horn & violin
2[1.2/pic] 0 2[1.2/bcl] 0 — 0 2 2 0 — 1perc [incl tmp] — pf, cel[played by perc] — str[min 12vn, 9va, 6vc, 6db]
perc: tmp, cym, sus cym, tamtam, xyl, chimes, windchimes, marac, cel[played by perc]

> String deployment:
> vn I, II, III (at least 4 of each)
> va I, II, III (at least 3 of each)
> vc I, II, III (at least 2 of each)
> db I, II, III (at least 2 of each)

6 Mozart piano works are used (K.1, 3, 355, 574, 399, 236).

Salzburg: January 27, 1756	_'
The Child Prodigy	_'
Aloysia or Constanze?	_'
Lunch in Prague with Da Ponte and Casanova	_'
The Stranger in Grey	_'
Vienna: December 5, 1791	_'

Boosey

Casa Guidi <1983>

20'

mezzo-soprano solo
3[1.2/pic.3/afl] 3[1.2.Eh] 3[1.2.bcl] 2 — 4 3 3 1 — opt mand — tmp+2 — hp — pf — str
perc: bd, cym, sd, tri, glock, vib, chimes, belltree, shell wind chimes
Chamber orchestra version by the composer also available:
  2[1.2/pic] 2[1.2/Eh] 2[1.2/bcl] 2 — 2 1 1 0 — tmp+1 — hp, pf, mand — str

Casa Guidi	4'
The Italian Cook and the English Maid	4'
Robert Browning	6'
The Death of Mr. Barrett	3'
Domesticity	5'

Boosey

Fire Variations; Eight Variations & Finale on a Blacksmith's Worksong <1981–1982>

22'

3[1.2.3/pic] 3[1.2.Eh] 3[1.2.3/bcl] 3 — 4 3 3 1 — tmp+2 — hp — pf/cel — str
perc: bd, cym, sus cym, sd, td, tamtam, glock, vib, 2tri, 2anvils

Boosey

In Praise of Music; Seven Songs for Orchestra <1977>

30'

3[1.2/pic.3/afl] 3[1.2.3/Eh] 3[1.2.3/bcl] 3[1.2.3/cbn] — 4 3 3 1 — tmp+3 — hp — pf/cel — str
perc: bd, cym, 3sus cym, sd, tri, tamtam, glock, xyl, marim, vib, chimes, crot, belltree, temple blks, bongos, brass wind chimes, shell wind chimes, bamboo wind chimes

Boosey

A Ring of Time (Preludes and Pageants for Orchestra and Bells) <1977>

28'

4[1.2.3/pic.4/pic] 4[1.2.3.4/Eh] 4[1.2.Ebcl.Ebcl/bcl] 4[1.2.3.4/cbn] — 4 3 3 1 — tmp+3 — hp — pf/cel — str
perc: bd, cym, sus cym, sd, td, glock, vib, chimes, crot, belltree, 2tri, 2tamtams, brass wind chimes

Spring (Dawn, Parade)	_'
Summer (Noon, Procession)	_'
Fall (Twilight, March)	_'
Winter (Midnight, Cortege, Postlude)	_'

Boosey

Royal Invitation (Homage to the Queen of Tonga) <1964>

23'

1 2 0 2 — 2 0 0 0 — str

Boosey

Armer, Elinor   1939-

(b Oakland, CA, 6 Oct 1939). American

The Great Instrument of the Geggerets <1989>   16'

narrator
2[incl pic] 2 2[incl bcl] 2[incl cbn] — 2 2 1 1 — tmp+1 — pf —
str[10.8.6.6.3]
Part III of the series *Uses of Music in Uttermost Parts.*

MMB

Arne, Thomas   1710-1778

(b London, 12 March 1710; d London, 5 March 1778). English

Symphony No.1, C major <1767>   8'

0 2 0 1 — 2 0 0 0 — cnt — str
Ed. Richard Platt.
1.   3'
2.   2'
3.   3'

Oxford

Symphony No.2, F major <1767>   9'

0 2 0 1 — 2 0 0 0 — cnt — str
Ed. Richard Platt.
1.   3'
2.   3'
3.   3'

Oxford

Symphony No.3, E-flat major <1767>   11'

0 2 0 1 — 2 0 0 0 — tmp — cnt — str
Ed. Richard Platt.
1.   5'
2.   3'
3.   3'

Oxford

Symphony No.4, C minor <1767>   15'

2 2 0 1 — 2 0 0 0 — cnt — str
Ed. Richard Platt. Flute parts reconstructed by the editor.
1.   5'
2.   5'
3.   5'

Oxford

Arnold, Malcolm   1921-2006

(b Northampton, 21 Oct 1921; d Norfolk County, 23 Sept 2006). English

The Bridge on the River Kwai <1957>   24'

3[1/pic.2/pic.3/pic] 3[incl Eh] 3[incl Ebcl,bcl] 3[incl cbn] — 4 3 3 1
— tmp+6 — 1 or 2hp — 1 or 2pf — str
Music from the film of the same title. Arr. Christopher Palmer.
Prelude (the Camp) and Escape   _'
Sunset   _'
The Jungle Trek   _'
Finale—The River Kwai March   _'

Novello

Burlesque <1944>   6'

solo horn
3[1.2.pic] 2 2 2 — 0 0 0 0 — tmp — str
Ed. Philip Lane.

Novello

Concerto, Clarinet, No.2, op.115 <1974>   17'

2[1.2/pic] 2 0 2 — 2 0 0 0 — tmp/perc — str
perc: tmp(mvts 1-2), set(mvt 3: bd, sd, woodblk, cowbell, cym)
1. *Allegro vivace*   6'
2. *Lento*   8'
3. *Allegro non troppo (The Pre-Goodman Rag)*   3'

Faber

Concerto, Flute, op.45 <1954>   13'

str

Paterson

Concerto for 28 Players, op.105 <1970>   15'

1[fl/pic] 2 0 1 — 2 0 0 0 — str[6.6.4.4.2]

Faber

Concerto, Guitar, op.67 <1959>   21'

1 0 1 0 — 1 0 0 0 — str[or str 5t]

Schirmer

Concerto, Harmonica, op.46 <1954>   10'

0 0 0 0 — 4 3 3 1 — tmp+2 — str
perc: sd, tamtam, glock, cast, cym, woodblk, bd, td, tambn

Paterson

Concerto, Oboe, op.39 <1952>   15'

str

Paterson

Concerto, Organ, op.47 <1954>   12'

0 0 0 0 — 0 3[in D, D, Bb] 0 0 — tmp — str

Paterson

Concerto, Trumpet, op.125 <1982>   12'

2 2 2 2 — 4 2 3 1 — tmp+2 — hp — str
perc: cym, sd, glock

Faber

Concerto, 2 Violins & String Orchestra, op.77 <1962> 17'

str
1. *Allegro risoluto*   6'
2. *Andantino*   8'
3. *Vivace*   3'

Faber

Electra, op.79 <1963>   15'

3[1.2.pic] 2 2 3[1.2.cbn] — 4 3 3 1 — tmp+4 — hp — str
perc: bongos, timbales, tomtom, bd, sd, cym, chimes, tamtam

Novello

English Dances: Set One <1950>   8'

3[1.2.pic] 2 2 2 — 4 3 3 1 — tmp+2 — hp — str
perc: tamtam, glock, sd, chimes, cym, bd, woodblk

Lengnick

English Dances: Set Two <1951>   9'

3[1.2.pic] 2 2 2 — 4 3 3 1 — tmp+2 — hp — cel — str
perc: sd, tambn, cym, glock, chimes, bd, tamtam

Lengnick

Four Cornish Dances, op.91 <1966>   8'

3[1.2.3/pic] 2 2 2 — 4 3 3 1 — tmp+2 — hp — str
1. Vivace   2'
2. Andantino   2'
3. Con moto e sempre senza parodia 2'
4. Allegro ma non troppo   2'

    Faber

Four Irish Dances, op.126 <1986>   11'

3[1.2.pic] 2 2 2 — 4 3 3 1 — tmp+2 — hp — str
perc: bd, cym, td

    Faber

Four Scottish Dances, op.59 <1957>   10'

2[1/pic.pic] 2 2 2 — 4 2 3 0 — tmp+1 — hp — str
perc: sd, tamtam, cym, bd, woodblk
1. Pesante   3'
2. Vivace   2'
3. Allegretto 4'
4. Con brio   1'

    Paterson

Four Welsh Dances, op.138 <1988>   10'

3[1.2.3/pic] 2 2 2 — 4 3 3 1 — tmp+2 — hp — str

    Novello

A Grand, Grand Festival Overture, op.57 <1956>   8'

soloists: organ, 3 vacuum cleaners, floor polisher
3[1.2.pic] 2 2 2 — 4 3 3 1 — tmp+3 — hp — str
perc: chimes, tamtam, sd, sus cym, bd, 4rifles[1 by tmp]
Created for one of the legendary Hoffnung concerts.

    Paterson

The Holly and the Ivy (Fantasy on Christmas Carols) <1991>   6'

3[1.2.3/pic] 2 2 2 — 4 3 3 1 — tmp+3 — hp — pf/cel — str
Arr. Christopher Palmer.

    Novello

Homage to the Queen, op.42: Suite, op.42a <1953>   17'

3[1/pic.2/pic.pic] 2 2 2 — 4 3 3 1 — tmp+2 — hp — cel — str
perc: tambn, cym, sus cym, sd, bd, glock, xyl, vib, tamtam
Prelude and Opening Scene _'
Dance of the Insects   _'
Water   _'
Fire Dance   _'
Pas de Deux   _'
Finale   _'

    Novello

The Inn of the Sixth Happiness: Suite <1992>   14'

3[incl pic] 2 3[incl bcl] 2 — 4 3 3 1 — tmp+4 — 2hp — pf/cel — str
Music from the film of the same title. Arr. Christopher Palmer.
London Prelude   _'
Romantic Interlude   _'
Happy Ending (Mountain Crossing—The Children) _'

    Novello

Little Suite [No.1], op.53 <1955>   8'

2 2 2 2 — 4 3 3 1 — tmp+2 — str
Composer authorizes performance with fewer winds and percussion.
Prelude 3'
Dance   2'
March   3'

    Paterson

Little Suite No.2, op.78 <1961>   9'

2 2 2 2 — 4 3 3 1 — tmp+3 — str
Composer authorizes performance with fewer winds and percussion.
Overture 3'
Ballad   4'
Dance   2'

    Paterson

Little Suite No.4, op.80a <1999>   7'

2[1.2/pic] 2[1.2/Eh] 2 2 — 4[hn3&4 opt] 3 3 1 — tmp+2 — str
perc: cym, sus cym, tamtam, tri, marac, sd, glock, xyl
Arr. by Philip Lane of the composer's Little Suite No.1 for Brass Band, op.80 (1963).
I. Prelude   2'
II. Siciliano 3'
III. Rondo   2'

The Padstow Lifeboat, op.94a: March for Orchestra <1967>   5'

2[1.pic] 2 2 2[1.cbn] — 4 3 3 1 — 3perc — str
perc: bd, sd, sus cym, cym
Originally for brass band (1967); orchestrated by Philip Lane (2000).

    Novello

Peterloo; Overture for Orchestra, op.97 <1968>   10'

3[1.2.pic] 2 2 2 — 4 3 3 1 — tmp+4 — hp — str
perc: bd, cym, 2sd, td, tamtam, glock, chimes

    Faber

Roots of Heaven <1958>   4'

2[1/pic.2/pic] 2 2 2[1.cbn] — 4 3 3 1 — tmp+2 — hp — pf/cel — str
perc: cym, tamtam, tomtom, marac, glock, bd

    Novello

Sinfonietta No.1, op.48 <1954>   10'

0 2 0 0 — 2 0 0 0 — str
I. Allegro comodo   3'
II. Allegretto   4'
III. Allegro con brio 3'

    Novello

Sinfonietta No.2, op.65 <1958>   14'

2 0 0 0 — 2 0 0 0 — str
Allegro non troppo 5'
Lento   6'
Allegro con brio   3'

    Paterson

The Sound Barrier, op.38 <1952>   8'

3[1/pic.2/pic.3/pic] 2 2 2 — 4 3 3 1 — tmp+2 — hp — cel — str

    Novello

Symphonic Study, op.30 (Machines) <1984>   6'

0 0 0 0 — 4 3 3 1 — tmp+2 — str
perc: bd, xyl, tamtam, sd, cym

    Faber

Symphony for Strings <1946>   22'

str

    Lengnick

Symphony No.2, op.40 <1953>   27'

3[1.2.pic] 2 2 3[1.2.cbn] — 4 3 3 1 — tmp+2 — hp — str
perc: glock, td, cym, xyl, bd, tamtam, chime (F#)

I. Allegretto	6'
II. Vivace	4'
III. Lento	11'
IV. Allegro con brio	6'

Paterson

Symphony No.3, op.63 <1957>   33'

3[1.2.pic] 2 2 2 — 4 3 3 1 — tmp — str

1. Allegro; Vivace	12'
2. Lento	14'
3. Alelgro con brio; Presto	7'

Paterson

Symphony No.4, op.71 <1960>   42'

3[1.2.pic] 2 2 3[1.2.cbn] — 4 3 3 1 — tmp+3 — hp — cel — str
perc: bd, cym, sd, tamtam, marim, bongos, marac, 2tomtom

I. Allegro	14'
II. Vivace ma non troppo	5'
III. Andantino	13'
IV. Con fuoco	9'

Paterson

Symphony No.5, op.74 <1961>   30'

3[1.2/pic.pic] 2 2 2 — 4 3 3 1 — tmp+2 — hp — cel — str
perc: bd, cym, sus cym, sd, tomtom, tamtam, glock, chimes, bongos

Tempestuoso	9'
Andante con moto	9'
Con fuoco	5'
Risoluto	7'

Novello

Symphony No.6, op.95 <1967>   27'

3[1.2.3/pic] 2 2 2 — 4 3 3 1 — tmp+3 — str
perc: sd, bd, td, tambn, cym, tamtam, sus cym, chimes
1st mvt is a tribute to jazz saxophonist Charlie Parker.

1. Energico	9'
2. Lento	11'
3. Con fuoco	7'

Faber

Symphony No.8, op.124 <1979>   25'

3[incl pic] 2 2 2 — 4 3 3 1 — tmp+2 — hp — str
perc: cym, tamtam, sd, glock, bd, vib

1. Allegro	10'
2. Andantino	9'
3. Vivace	6'

Faber

Symphony No.9, op.128 <1986>   52'

3[1.2.pic] 2 2 2 — 4 3 3 1 — tmp+2 — hp — str
perc: cym, bd, glock, xyl

1. Vivace	9'
2. Allegretto	11'
3. Giubiloso	8'
4. Lento	24'

Novello

Tam O'Shanter Overture, op.51 <1955>   8'

3[1.2/pic.pic] 2 2 2 — 4 3 3 1 — tmp+2 — str
perc: bd, cym, sus cym, sd, td, tamtam, chimes, whip

Paterson

Arriaga, Juan Crisóstomo   1806-1826

(b Bilbao, 27 Jan 1806; d Paris, 12/17 Jan 1826, bur. 17 Jan 1826). Basque

Los esclavos felices: Overture <1820>   8'

2 2 2 2 — 2 0 0 0 — tmp — str

Heugel	Kalmus	Luck's

Symphony in D <1825>   28'

2 2 2 2 — 2 2 0 0 — tmp — str

1. Adagio	11'
2. Andante	8'
3. Minuetto	4'
4. Allegro con moto	5'

Kalmus	Luck's

Arutiunian, Aleksandr Grigori   1920-2012

(b Yerevan, 23 Sept 1920; d Yerevan 28 March 2012). Armenian

Concerto, Trumpet <1950>   17'

2[1.2/pic] 2 2 2 — 4 2 3 1 — tmp+3 — hp — str
perc: bd, cym, sd, tri

International	Russian

Aschaffenburg, Walter   1927-

(b Essen, 20 May 1927). American composer born in Germany

Three Dances for Orchestra, op.15 <1972>   13'

3[incl pic] 3 4[incl Ebcl,bcl] 3[incl cbn] — 4 3 3 1 — tmp+6 — hp — str

1.	3'
2.	4'
3.	6'

Presser

Asia, Daniel   1953-

(b Seattle, 27 June 1953). American

Gateways <1993>   5'

4[1.2.3/afl.pic] 4[1.2.3.Eh] 4[1.2.3/Ebcl.bcl] 3[1.2.cbn] — 4 4 3 1 — tmp+3 — pf — str
perc: bd, 2sus cym, sd, td, timbales, tri, tamtam, xyl, vib, woodblk, claves

Merion

Symphony No.1 <1987>   25'

3[1.2.3/pic] 3[1.2.3/Eh] 3[1.2.3/bcl] 3[1.2.3/cbn] — 4 3 3 1 — tmp+3 — hp — pf/cel — str

Adagio	8'
Scherzo	4'
Allegretto	3'
Scherzo	4'
Adagio	6'

Merion

Symphony No.2 (Khagiga) <1990>   27'

3[1.2.3/pic] 3[1.2.3/Eh] 3[1.2.3/bcl] 3[1.2.3/cbn] — 4 3 3 1 — tmp+4 — hp — pf/cel/synth — str

Ma Toru	5'
Ashrenu	3'
L'Kha Adonai	6'
Hine El Yeshuat	5'
Halleluyah	8'

Merion

What About It <2003>   7'

3[1.2.pic] 3[1.2.3/Eh] 3[1.2.3/bcl] 3[1.2.3/cbn] — 4 3 3 1 — tmp+4
— hp — pf — str
perc: bd, 4 sus cym, sd, toms, 2tri, xyl, marim, vib, woodblk, templeblks, whip,
bongos

> Merion

Atterberg, Kurt   1887 - 1974

(b Göteborg, 12 Dec 1887; d Stockholm, 15 Feb 1974). Swedish

Adagio amoroso <1967>   8'

solo flute or violin
str

> Swedish MIC

Bäckahästen, op.24 (Midsummer Night): Midsummer   15'
Dances <1923–1924>

2[1.2/pic] 2[1.2/Eh] 2 2 — 4 2 2 0 — 2perc — hp — cel[ad lib] — str
perc: bd, cym
  I. At Evening   *5'*
  II. In the Amusement Park   *10'*

> Universal

Ballade & Passacaglia, op.38 <1935>   9'

2[1.2/pic] 2 2 2[1.2/cbn] — 4 2 3 1 — tmp+1 — hp — str
perc: cym, sus cym, sd, tomtom, woodblk, tamtam

> Eulenburg

Concerto, Piano, op.37, B-flat minor <1935>   34'

2[1.2/pic] 2 2 2 — 4 2 3 1 — tmp+2 — str
perc: tri, cym, sus cym, bd
  I. Pesante allegro   *13'*
  II. Andante   *12'*
  III. Furioso   *9'*

> Breitkopf

Concerto, Violin, op.7, E minor <1913>   38'

2 2 2 2 — 2 2 1 0 — tmp — str[8.8.6.4.4]
  I. Moderato—Agitato   *14'*
  II. Adagio cantabile   *9'*
  III. Rondo: Allegro molto *15'*

> Breitkopf

Sinfonia per archi (Symphony for Strings)   29'

str
May also be performed as a string quintet [2vn, va, 2vc].
  I. Con moto   *7'*
  II. Allegro molto   *6'*
  III. Tranquillo   *9'*
  IV. Allegro molto e ritmico *7'*

> Kunzelmann

Suite pastorale in modo antico, op.34 <1931>   19'

3 solo strings: 2 violins & viola (or violoncello or violin)
str[db opt]
  Preludio   *2'*
  Aria   *2'*
  Gavotte I & II   *4'*
  Pastorale   *2'*
  Serenata   *6'*
  Giga   *3'*

> Breitkopf

Symphony No.2, op.6, F major <1911–1913>   41'

3[1.2.3/pic] 2[1.2/Eh] 3[1.2.bcl] 2 — 4 2 3 1 — tmp+2 — pf — str
perc: cym, sus cym
The composer recommends that a 3rd tp double tp1 in certain designated
passages.
  I. Allegro don moto   *13'*
  II. Adagio—Presto—Adagio—Presto—Adagio   *16'*
  III. Allegro con fuoco   *12'*

> Nordiska

Symphony No.3, op.10 (West Coast Pictures;   35'
Västkustbilder) <1914–1916>

4[1.2.3/pic.opt afl] 3[1.2.3/Eh] 3[1.2.bcl] 3[1.2.cbn] — 4 3 3 1 —
tmp+3 — hp — cel — str
perc: bd, cym, tri
  I. Sonnenrauch (Sun-smoke; Soldis)   *7'*
  II. Sturm (Storm)   *12'*
  III. Sommernacht (Summer Night; Sommarnatt) *16'*

> Breitkopf

Symphony No.5, op.20, D minor (Sinfonia funebre)   33'
<1919–1922>

3[1.2.3/pic] 3[1.2.3/heckl or Eh] 3 2 — 4 3 3 1 — tmp+2 — pf — str
perc: cym, sd, tamtam
  1. Pesante Allegro   *9'*
  2. Lento   *9'*
  3. Allegro molto — Tempo di Valse *15'*

> Breitkopf

Symphony No.7, op.45 (Sinfonia Romantica) <1942>   29'

2[1.2/pic] 2[1.2/Eh] 2 2 — 4 3 3 1 — tmp+4 — hp — cel[ad lib] —
str
perc: bd, cym, tri, sd, tambn, cast, 2woodblk
  1. Drammatico   *10'*
  2. Semplice   *12'*
  3. Feroce   *7'*

> Swedish MIC

Symphony No.8, op.48, E minor (On Swedish National   33'
Melodies) <1944>

2[1/pic.2] 2[1.2/Eh] 2 2[1.2] — 2 2 3 0 — tmp — str
Optional instruments: fl2, ob2, bn2, tbn 1&2. Eh is not optional; if only
one oboist, s/he must double on Eh.
  I. Largo—Allegro   *9'*
  II. Adagio   *10'*
  III. Molto vivo   *5'*
  IV. Con moto   *9'*

> Swedish MIC

A Varmlands Rhapsody (Eine Värmlandsrhapsodie; En   9'
Värmlandsrapsodi) <1933>

2 2 2 2 — 2 3[tp3 opt] 2[1.btbn] 0 — 2perc — hp — cel[opt] — str
perc: tri, cym, sus cym, bd

> Universal

Auber, Daniel-François-Esprit   1782 - 1871

(b Caen, 29 Jan 1782; d Paris, 12 May 1871). French

Le cheval de bronze (The Bronze Horseman): Overture   7'
<1835>

2[1.pic] 2 2 2 — 4 2 3 0 — tmp+2 — str
perc: bd, cym, tri

> Mario Bois   Kalmus   Luck's

Concerto, Violin, D major <1808>   14'

1 2 0 2 — 2 0 0 0 — str
  1. Allegro ma non troppo   8'
  2. Andante   2'
  3. Presto   4'

Kalmus	Luck's

Les diamants de la couronne (The Crown Diamonds): Overture <1841>   8'

2[1.pic] 2 2 2 — 4 2 3 0 — tmp+3 — str
Ed. Clark McAlister.

Kalmus	Luck's

Le domino noir (The Black Domino): Overture <1837>   8'

2[1.2/pic] 2 2 2 — 4 2 3 0 — tmp+3 — str
perc: tri, cym, bd

Breitkopf	Kalmus	Ricordi	Luck's

Fra Diavolo: Overture <1830>   8'

2[1.pic] 2 2 2 — 4 2 3 0 — tmp+4 — str
perc: sd, tri, cym, bd

Breitkopf	Kalmus	Luck's	Ricordi

Lestocq: Overture <1834>   8'

2[incl pic] 2 2 2 — 4 2 1 0 — tmp+3 — str

Luck's

Marco Spada (La fille du bandit): Overture <1852>   8'

2[1.pic] 2 2 2 — 4 2 3 0 — tmp+3 — str

Kalmus	Luck's

Masaniello (La muette de Portici): Overture <1828>   8'

3[1.2.pic] 2 2 2 — 4 2 3 1 — tmp+4 — str
perc: bd, cym, field dr, tri

Breitkopf	Kalmus	Luck's

La part du diable (The Devil's Portion; Des Teufels Anteil): Overture <1843>   8'

2[1.pic] 2 2 2 — 4 2 3 0 — tmp+3 — str
perc: bd, cym, tri

Breitkopf	Luck's

Zanetta: Overture <1840>   9'

2[1.pic] 2 2 2 — 4 2 3 0 — tmp+3 — str
perc: bd, cym, tri

Luck's

Auric, Georges   1899-1983

(b Lodeve, 15 Feb 1899; d Paris, 23 July 1983). French

La chambre <1955>   18'

2[1/pic.2/pic] 1 2 1 — 2 2 1 1 — tmp+2 — pf — str
perc: bd, cym, tamtam, tambn, tri, woodblk

Ricordi

Phèdre: Suite symphonique <1949>   20'

3[1/pic.2/pic.pic] 3[1.2.3/Eh] 3[1.2.bcl] 3[1.2.cbn] — 4 4 3 1 —
tmp+4 — 2hp — cel — str
perc: bd, cym, sd, tamtam, tambn, vib, xyl
From the ballet.
Ob3/Eh plays oboe only in the last 7 bars.
  I. Largamente   _'
  II. Large   _'
  III. Très large   _'
  IV. Assez modéré   _'

Salabert

Avshalomov, David   1946-

(b New York NY, 6 May 1946). American

Concertino, Oboe <2002; rev 2009>   17'

hp — str
  Shifting Masks   6'
  Lament (To Grieve)   6'
  Hushabye (Rondo)   5'

Raven

Concerto con timpani (Battaglia) <1992; rev 2005>   14'

solo timpani
hpsd — str
Published under the pseudonym "G.F. Salomon." In baroque style, and
with precise suggestions for baroque string practice. Harpsichord part
(not included in the score) is intended to be improvised in baroque
manner, though it can be played from the written part if necessary.
  Solo part intended to be played on 6 (or 7) hand-tuned drums; if pedal
drums are used, pedals are only for tuning between movements.
  Materials are available either in an edited version for players not
conversant with historically-informed baroque style, or in an "Urtext"
version intended for baroque players.
  I. Intrada   4'
  II. Largo, sostenuto   6'
  III. Presto   4'

Raven

Elegy <1990>   8'

str

Raven

Gems; Suite of Miniatures <2005>   13'

3[1.2.pic] 2 3[1.2.bcl] 3[1.2.cbn] — 4 3 3 1 — tmp+3 — hp — cel[or
glock or pf] — str
perc: bd, cym, sus cym, sd, tri, tambn, tamtam, glock, xyl, vib, windchimes, whip,
ratch, 4tomtom
Optional: bcl, cbn, hn3-4, tp3, hp, xyl, windchimes, whip, ratchet.
Instrumentation varies from movement to movement.
  1. Brilliant   1'
  2. Starry Night   2'
  3. Whirlwind   1'
  4. Galaxy   2'
  5. Forever   3'
  6. March of the Giant Robots, or Wheels of Industry 2'
  7. Sweet Melody   1'
  8. The Sky's Limit   1'

Raven

Pangs of Love; Romantic Variations on a Rachmaninoff Melody <2003>   31'

str

Raven

Siege <1967; rev 1992>   9'

2 2 3[1.2.bcl] 2 — 4 3 3 1 — tmp+3 — pf — str
perc: bd, cym, sus cym, sd, tamtam, glock, xyl, marim, chimes

Raven

Songs of Life & Songs of Death <2003>   24'

solo baritone
3[1.2.pic] 2 3[1.2.bcl] 3[1.2.cbn] — 4 3 3 1 — tmp+4 — hp —
cel/opt pf — str
perc: bd, cym, tri, tambn, glock, xyl, vib, whip, ratch, 3sus cym, 2sd, 3tamtam
Poems by Emily Dickinson.

SONGS OF LIFE
1. A Narrow Fellow in the Grass (The Snake)	2'
2. The Railway Train	3'
3. Wild Nights—Wild Nights!	2'
4. Hope is the Thing with Feathers	2'

SONGS OF DEATH
5. It Was Not Death, for I Stood Up	4'
6. The Heart asks Pleasure first	2'
7. I Felt a Funeral in my Brain	4'
8. Tie the Strings to My Life, My Lord	2'
9. Because I Could Not Stop for Death (Tango/Encore)	3'

> Raven

Trotzky's Train <2007; rev 2009>   40'

pf — str
Originally for piano & str 5t.
1. Romanovs' Last Ball	10'
2. Memento mori	12'
3. Trotzky's Train	18'

> Raven

Avshalomov, Jacob   1919-2013

(b Qingdao, China, 28 March 1919). American

Cues from "The Little Clay Cart" <1941>   12'

2[1.2/pic] 1 2 0 — banjo — 4perc — hp — str
perc: bd, sus cym, sd, tri, tamtam, gong, glock, xyl, chimes, woodblk, templeblk, 3
Chinese toms, finger cym
Pro & Epilogue	_'
Maitreya	_'
Shampooer	_'
Illusion of a Storm	_'
Sharvilaxa	_'

> Fleisher

Evocations; Concerto for Clarinet & Chamber Orchestra <1947>   17'

solo clarinet (or viola)
1[1/pic] 0 0 0 — tmp+3 — pf — str
perc: cym, sus cym, sd, tri, tambn, glock, xyl
Originally for clarinet or viola with piano; orchestrated by the composer.

> CFE   Fleisher

Ayers, Jesse   1951-

(b Knoxville TN, 26 May 1951). American

... and they gathered on Mount Carmel <2006>   25'

6-20 offstage women's voices (opt)
3[1.2.pic] 3[1.2.opt Eh] 4[1.2.bcl.opt cbcl] 3[1.2.opt cbn] — 4 6 6[incl
solo euph] 2 — tmp+5 — pf[or elec kybd] — str
perc: sus cym, glock, xyl, congas, vib, marim, bd, chimes, cym, sd, cowbell,
bongos, tamtam, 8tomtom, 2field dr, 4-8whistling tubes[behind audience]
A "surround sound" work that requires unusual seating of the brass
sections; the chorus and the whistling tubes are to be behind the audience.
An extra 4-8 players are required for the whistling tubes.
   The solo euphonium in the 2nd mvt may be replaced by a solo horn.
   A reduced orchestra version uses standard brass (4 3 3 1) and tmp+3,
along with woodwind and strings as indicated. A version for wind band is
also available.
   The movements may be performed separately.
I. The Incantations of the Prophets of Baal	8'
II. The Prayer of Elijah	8'
III. The Fire of the Living God	9'

> Ayers

Fanfare and Carol for Christmas <1996; rev 2013>   3'

optional chorus (with possible audience participation)
2[1.pic] 2 2 1 — 4 3 3 1 — tmp+3[or 4] — str
perc: bd, cym, 1 or 2sd, glock
Fanfare with embedded carol "Joy to the World." Several performance
options are listed:
   1. Orch alone, no chorus.
   2. Orch + chorus.
   3. Orch + audience sing-along.
   4. Orch + chorus & audience.
   5. Orch alone: fanfare, no carol, taking optional cuts indicated.
A separate version with reduced orch is also available:
   1[pic] 1 1 1 — 2 2 1 1 — opt tmp+3 — org — str
A version for wind band is also available.

> Ayers

Jericho; A Surround-Sound, Audience-Participation Piece for Orchestra & Narrator <2004–2005>   16'

narrator   opt SATB chorus
3[1.2.3/pic] 3[1.2.Eh] 3[1.2.bcl] 3[1.2.cbn] — 4 4[incl 2offstage] 3 1
— 3 or 6perc — hp — pf — str
perc: hi-hat, tri, tambn, glock, xyl, marim, chimes, templeblks, whip, bongos,
claves, vibrslp, guiro, 3bd or lg tomtom, 4sus cym, marktree or windchimes, 3-7
whistling tubes
Originally for band; orchestrated by the composer.
   Audience participates with shouts, simple hand gestures, and singing of
a hymn-phrase.
   There are 2 versions of the percussion parts: one for 6 players and one
for 3 players; neither involves timpani.

> Ayers

The Passion of John Brown <2009>   19'

narrator, baritone voice (optionally offstage)
3[1.2/pic.3] 3[1.2/Eh.3] 3 3[1.2.3/cbn] — 4 4 3 1 — tmp+3 — hp —
pf/elec pf — str
perc: bd, cym, sus cym, sd, tri, tamtam, glock, xyl, chimes, woodblk, whip,
2tomtom
Optional instruments: fl3, ob3, bn3/cbn.
   Trumpets 3&4 positioned behind audience, right & left.

> Ayers

Veni Emmanuel <1997; rev 2014>   *10'*

chorus (optional)   narrator (optional)

2[1.2/pic] 1 2 1 — 4 3 3 1 — tmp+2 — hp — pf, org — str

perc: cym, sus cym, tamtam, glock, chimes

May be done with or without chorus. Optional narration is only a few
sentences.

Within the orchestra, the following instruments are optional: cl 2, bn,
hn3-4, tp3, tbn3, tuba, hp, org. Suitable for procession of multiple choirs,
but may be done purely instrumentally.

A version for wind band & chorus is also available.

> Ayers

B

Babadjanyan, Arno   1921-1983

(b Erevan, 22 Jan 1921; d Erevan, 11 Nov 1983). Armenian [also spelled
Babadzhanian]

Concerto, Violoncello <1962>   *17'*

3[incl pic] 2 3[incl bcl] 2 — 4 1 0 0 — tmp+1 — pf/cel — str

> Russian

Babbitt, Milton   1916-2011

(b Philadelphia, PA, 10 May 1916). American

All Set <1957>   *8'*

0 0 0 0 — 0 1 1 0 — asx, tsx — perc, vib — pf — db

> AMP

Ars combinatoria <1981>   *19'*

2[incl pic] 2[incl Eh] 2[incl bcl] 2[incl cbn] — 2 2 1 1 — 3perc — hp
— cel, pf — str

> Peters

Composition for Twelve Instruments <1948; rev 1954>   *7'*

1 1 1 1 — 1 1 0 0 — hp — cel — vn, va, vc, db

> AMP

Concerto, Piano <1985>   *20'*

2[incl pic] 2[incl Eh] 3[incl Ebcl,bcl] 2[incl cbn] — 3 2 2 1 — 4perc
— hp — cel — str

> Peters

Correspondences <1967>   *10'*

synthesized tape — str

> AMP

Relata I <1965>   *18'*

3[1.2.3/pic] 3[1.2.Eh] 3[1.2.bcl] 3[1.2.3/cbn] — 4 4 3 1 — 6perc —
hp — pf, cel — str

This work may be followed by *Relata II* (1968) *attacca*.

> AMP

Transfigured Notes <1985–1986>   *19'*

str

> Peters

Bacewicz, Grażyna
1909-1969

(b Łódż, 5 Feb 1909; d Warsaw, 17 Jan 1969). Polish

Concerto for String Orchestra <1948>   15'
str
1. *Allegro*   5'
2. *Andante*   5'
3. *Vivo*   5'

PWM

Concerto, Violoncello, No.2 <1963>   21'
3[1.2.3/pic] 2 4[1.2.3/Ebcl.bcl] 2 — 4 2 0 0 — tmp+4 — 2hp — cel, pf — str
perc: sus cym, sd, tamtam xyl, vib, woodblk, whip, bongos

PWM

Contradizione <1966>   16'
1[1/pic] 1 1[1/Ebcl] 1 — 1 1 0 0 — 2perc — hp — cel — str 5t
perc: sus cym, sd, tamtam, vib, bongos, guiro, 2woodblk, timpano basso

Moeck

Music for Strings, Trumpets & Percussion (Muzyka na smyczki, trąbki i perkusję) <1958>   20'
0 0 0 0 — 0 5 0 0 — tmp+2 — cel — str
perc: sd, xyl

PWM

Pensieri notturni <1961>   8'
1 1 3[1/asx.2/scl.3/bcl] 1 — 1 1 1 0 — tmp+3 — hp — cel — str[5.0.3.2.1]
perc: sd, xyl, vib, woodblk, guiro

PWM

Symphony No.3 <1954>   28'
3[1.2.3/pic] 2 2 2 — 4 3 3 1 — tmp+2 — str

PWM

Bach, Carl Philipp Emanuel
1714-1788

(b Weimar, 8 March 1714; d Hamburg, 14 Dec 1788). German

H = E.E. Helm: *Thematic Catalogue of the Works of Carl Philipp Emanuel Bach* (New Haven, CT, 1989)

W = Wotquenne: *Thematisches Verzeichnis der Werke von Carl Philipp Emanuel Bach (1714–1788)* (Leipzig, 1905)

Concerto, Flute, H.425 (W.22), D minor <1747>   26'
cnt — str
Transcription (perhaps not by the composer) of C.P.E. Bach's *Concerto, Harpsichord, H.425 (W.22).*
I. *Allegro*   9'
II. *Un poco andante*   10'
III. *Allegro di molto*   7'

EMB	Leuckart	Möseler

Concerto, Harpsichord, H.427 (W.23), D minor <1748>   23'
cnt — str
The continuo is in addition to the solo harpsichord.
I. *Allegro*   9'
II. *Poco andante*   7'
III. *Allegro assai*   7'

Breitkopf

Concerto, Oboe, H.466 (W.164), B-flat major <1765>   20'
cnt — str
The same work exists as *Concerto, Harpsichord, H.465 (W.39).*

Eulenburg	Forberg	Kalmus	Kunzelmann	Leuckart

Concerto, Oboe, H.468 (W.165), E-flat major <1765>   17'
cnt — str
The same work exists as *Concerto, Harpsichord, H.467 (W.40).*

EMB	Kunzelmann	Sikorski

Concerto, Violoncello, H.436 (W.171), B-flat major <1751>   21'
cnt — str
Ed. Walter Schulz. Solo part also possible for viola da gamba or solo viola.
1. *Allegretto*   8'
2. *Adagio*   7'
3. *Allegro assai*   6'

Breitkopf	Kalmus	Luck's

Concerto, Piano & Harpsichord, H.479 (W.47), E-flat major <1788>   17'
2 0 0 0 — 2 0 0 0 — str

Kalmus

Magnificat, H.772 (W.215) <1749>   43'
chorus   solos SATB
2 2 0 0 — 2 3 0 0 — tmp — cnt — str
I. *Magnificat*   3'
II. *Quia respexit*   6'
III. *Quia fecit*   4'
IV. *Et misericordia ejus*   8'
V. *Fecit potentiam*   4'
VI. *Deposuit potentes*   6'
VII. *Suscepit Israel*   5'
VIII. *Gloria*   2'
IX. *Et misericordia ejus*   5'

Eulenburg	Kalmus	Luck's

Symphony, H.657 (W.182/1), G major <1773>   12'
cnt — str
I. *Allegro di molto*   4'
II. *Poco adagio*   4'
III. *Presto*   4'

Peters	Schott

Symphony, H.658 (W.182/2), B-flat major <1773>   12'
cnt — str
I. *Allegro di molto*   3'
II. *Poco adagio*   4'
III. *Presto*   5'

Bärenreiter	Kalmus	Luck's	Peters

Symphony, H.659 (W.182/3), C major <1773>   11'
cnt — str
I. *Allegro assai*   3'
II. *Adagio*   3'
III. *Allegretto*   5'

Kalmus	Nagel	Luck's	Peters

Symphony, H.660 (W.182/4), A major <1773>   11'
cnt — str
Allegro ma non troppo   4'
Largo ed innocentemente   4'
Allegro assai   3'

Breitkopf	Peters	Schott

Symphony, H.661 (W.182/5), B minor <1773>   10'

cnt — str
I. Allegretto   4'
II. Larghetto   3'
III. Presto   3'

Kalmus	Nagel	Luck's	Peters

Symphony, H.662 (W.182/6), E major <1773>   8'

cnt — str
I. Allegro di molto   2'
II. Poco andante   3'
III. Allegro spiritoso 3'

Peters

Symphony, H.663 (W.183/1), D major <1775–1776>   11'

2 2 0 2[bn2 opt] — 2 2[opt] 0 0 — opt tmp — str
Packard ed. by David Kidger, from the C.P.E. Bach collected edition (in progress); parts for this edition will be provided in PDF form, to be printed out by the user.
I. Allegro di molto   6'
II. Largo   2'
III. Presto   3'

Breitkopf	Kalmus	Luck's	Packard	Peters

Symphony, H.664 (W.183/2), E-flat major <1775–1776>   10'

2 2 0 1 — 2 0 0 0 — cnt — str
Packard ed. by David Kidger, from the C.P.E. Bach collected edition (in progress); parts for this edition will be provided in PDF form, to be printed out by the user.
1. Allegro di molto   _'
2. Larghetto   _'
3. Allegretto   _'

Kalmus	Nagel	Packard

Symphony, H.665 (W.183/3), F major <1775–1776>   9'

2 2 0 1 — 2 0 0 0 — cnt — str
Packard ed. by David Kidger, from the C.P.E. Bach collected edition (in progress); parts for this edition will be provided in PDF form, to be printed out by the user.
1. Allegro di molto   4'
2. Larghetto   3'
3. Presto   2'

Kalmus	Luck's	Packard	Peters

Symphony, H.666 (W.183/4), G major <1775–1776>   10'

2 2 0 1 — 2 0 0 0 — cnt — str
Packard ed. by David Kidger, from the C.P.E. Bach collected edition (in progress); parts for this edition will be provided in PDF form, to be printed out by the user.
1. Allegro assai   3'
2. Poco andante   3'
3. Presto   4'

Packard

Bach, Jan   1937-

(b Forrest, IL, 11 Dec 1937). American

Concerto, Euphonium <1990>   30'

2[1/pic.2] 2 3[1.2.bcl] 2 — 3 3 3 1 — tmp+4 — pf — str[min 8.8.6.4.2]
perc: bd, cym, sus cym, small splash cym, water gong (lg cym), 2tomtoms, 2sd, tri, tambn, glock, xyl, marim, vib, chimes, glass windchimes, 3woodblk, templeblk, whip, ratch, pu ili (or marac)
Composer indicates tmp+3perc, which may be possible; in either case, timpanist is expected to cover several accessory percussion.
   Movements may be played separately.
Legend   12'
Burlesca   7'
Meditation 11'

Tuba-Euph

Concerto, Steelpan <1994>   22'

2[1.2/pic] 1 3[1.2.bcl] 1 — 2 2 2 1 — tmp+2 — hp — str[min 6.6.4.4.2]
Reflections 11'
Toccata   11'

Meadow

The Happy Prince <1978>   38'

narrator
1[1/pic] 1[1/Eh] 1 1 — 2 2 1 0 — 1 or 2perc — hp — pf/cel/hpsd — str[6.5.4.3.2]
perc: bd, sus cym, sd, tomtom, tri, tamtam, glock, xyl, vib, chimes, glass wind chimes, glass harmonica (or bowed vib), 3 woodblk or templeblks, quica (or small string drum)

Highgate

Variations on a Theme of Brahms <1997>   20'

2[1.2/pic] 2 3[1.2.bcl] 3[1.2.cbn] — 4 3 3 1 — tmp+3 — hp — pf — str[min 9.6.6.4.4]
perc: bd, cym, sus cym, sd, td, tomtoms, 2tri, tamtam, glock, chimes, woodblk, cowbell, bongos, cast

Meadow

Bach, Johann Christian   1735-1782

(b Leipzig, 5 Sept 1735; d London, 1 Jan 1782). German

W = E. Warburton: *The Collected Works of Johann Christian Bach 1735–1782 , xlviii/1: Thematic Catalogue* (New York, 1999)

La clemenza di Scipione, W. G10: Overture <1778>   4'

2 2 0 2 — 2 0 0 0 — cnt — str

Doblinger

Concerto, Harpsichord, op.7, no.5, W. C59, E-flat major <1770>   17'

str[no va]
Ed. Christian Doebereiner.

Kalmus	Luck's	Peters

Concerto, Harpsichord, op.13, no.2, W. C63, D major <1777>   14'

2 2 0 0 — 2 0 0 0 — str

Kalmus	Luck's	Peters

Concerto, Harpsichord, op.13, no.4, W. C65, B-flat major <1777>   20'

0 2 0 0 — 2 0 0 0 — str

Kalmus	Peters	Luck's

Concerto, Violoncello, C minor [spurious] <ca.1916>   14'

str
Attributed to J.C. Bach, but in all likelihood forged by Henri Casadesus in about 1916.
   Peters publishes a piano reduction with viola solo as a substitute for cello.
I. Allegro molto ma maestoso   4'
II. Adagio molto espressivo   7'
III. Allegro molto energico   3'

Credo breve, W. E5 <1758>   20'

chorus
0 2 0 0 — 2 0 0 0 — org — str
Ed. Heinz Hofmann.

| Hänssler |

Sinfonia concertante, W. C34, A major <1773>   18'

solo violin and violoncello
0 2 0 0 — 2 0 0 0 — cnt — str
I. Andante di molto   11'
II. Rondeau: Allegro assai   7'

| Eulenburg | Kalmus | Luck's |

Sonatas, Piano, op.5, nos.2-4

see: Mozart, Wolfgang Amadeus, 1756-1791
       Concertos, Piano, K.107 (21b) nos.1-3

Symphony, op.3, no.1, W. C1, D major <1765>   11'

0 2 0 0 — 2 0 0 0 — cnt — str
Allegro con spirito   4'
Andante   4'
Presto   3'

| Doblinger | Eulenburg |

Symphony, op.3, no.2, W. C2, C major <1765>   10'

0 2 0 0 — 2 0 0 0 — cnt — str
Ed. Erik G. S. Smith.
Allegro   3'
Andante   5'
Allegro assai   2'

| Doblinger |

Symphony, op.3, no.4, W. C4, B-flat major <1765>   15'

0 2 0 0 — 2 0 0 0 — cnt — str
Some editions do not include continuo.
I. Allegro con spirito   5'
II. Andante   5'
III. Tempo di menuetto più tosto allegro 5'

| Doblinger | Kalmus | Kneusslin | Luck's |

Symphony, op.6, no.1, W. C7, G major <1770>   9'

0 2 0 0 — 2 0 0 0 — cnt — str
Allegro con brio   4'
Andante   3'
Allegro assai   2'

| Eulenburg |

Symphony, op.6, no.6, W. C12, G minor <1770>   13'

0 2 0 0 — 2 0 0 0 — cnt — str
Ed. Fritz Stein.
I. Allegro   4'
II. Andante più tosto adagio 6'
III. Allegro molto   3'

| Breitkopf | Luck's |

Symphonies, op.9

see his: Symphonies, op.21

Symphony, op.18, no.1, W. C26, E-flat major <1779>   12'

2 2 0 2 — 2 0 0 0 — cnt (opt) — str
For double orchestra. **Orch 1**: obs, bns, hns, str; **Orch 2**: fls, cnt, str.
I. Allegro spiritoso   5'
II. Andante   5'
III. Allegro   2'

| Kalmus | Luck's | Peters |

Symphony, op.18, no.2, W. G9, B-flat major (Lucio Silla) <1779>   11'

2 2 2 2 — 2 0 0 0 — str
Ed. Fritz Stein. Overture to the opera *Lucio Silla*.
I. Allegro assai   3'
II. Andante   5'
III. Presto   3'

| Kalmus | Peters |

Symphony, op.18, no.3, W. G15, D major (Endimione) <1782>   14'

2 2 0 1 — 2 0 0 0 — cnt — str
For double orchestra. **Orch 1**: obs, bns, hns, str; **Orch 2**: fls, cnt, str.
Overture to the opera *Endimione*.
I. Allegro   5'
II. Andante   6'
III. Allegro assai 3'

| Kalmus | Peters |

Symphony, op.18, no.4, W. C27, D major <1779>   12'

2 2 0 1 — 2 2 0 0 — tmp — cnt[opt] — str
Flutes are optional. Ed. Alfred Einstein.
I. Allegro con spirito 4'
II. Andante   5'
III. Rondo: Presto   3'

| Eulenburg | Luck's |

Symphony, op.18, no.5, W. C28, E major <1779>   17'

2 2 0 1 — 2 0 0 0 — cnt — str
For double orchestra. **Orch 1**: obs, bns, hns, str; **Orch 2**: fls, cnt, str.
Ed. Fritz Stein.
I. Allegro moderato   7'
II. Andante   4'
III. Tempo di minuetto 6'

| Breitkopf | Luck's |

Symphony, op.18, no.6, W. XC1, D major <1781>   14'

2 2 0 1 — 2 0 0 0 — cnt — str
Ed. Fritz Stein.
Allegro   4'
Andante   4'
Allegretto   3'
Allegro   3'

| Breitkopf |

Symphony, op.21 [or op.9], no.1, W. C17, B-flat major <1773>   15'

0 2 0 0 — 2 0 0 0 — cnt — str
Ed. Fritz Stein. Op.21 originally published as op.9; both designations
remain in use.
I. Allegro con spirito _'
II. Andante   _'
III. Presto   _'

| Breitkopf |

Symphony, op.21 [or op.9], no.2, W. C18, E-flat major <1773>   12'

0 2 0 0 — 2 0 0 0 — cnt — str
Oboes may be replaced by flutes; horns are optional.
Ed. Fritz Stein.
  J.C. Bach's op.9 was later republished as op.21; both designations
remain in use, and in fact, this Eulenburg edition (and Kalmus reprint) are
listed as op.9.
I. Allegro   5'
II. Andante con sordini   3'
III. Tempo di menuetto   4'

| Eulenburg | Kalmus | Luck's |

Symphony, op.21 [or op.9], no.3, W. C19, B-flat major <1767>   8'

0 2 0 0 — 2 0 0 0 — cnt — str
Flutes may be substituted for oboes. Ed. Adam Carse.
Op.21 originally published as op.9; both designations remain in use.
I. Allegro _'
II. Andante _'
III. Allegro _'

Augener

Symphony, W. G8, D major (Overture to *Temistocle*) <1772>   10'

2 2 3[1.2.bcl] 2 — 2 2 0 0 — tmp — cnt — str
Ed. Fritz Stein. Overture to the opera *Temistocle*. The original called for 3 *clarinette d'amore* in D, which the editor has adapted for 2cl and bcl.
I. Allegro di molto _'
II. Andante _'
III. Presto _'

Breitkopf

Bach, Johann Ludwig   1677-1731

(b Thal, nr Eisenach, 4 Feb 1677; d Meiningen, bur. 1 May 1731). German

Denn du wirst meine Seele

see: Bach, Johann Sebastian, 1685-1750
Cantata no.15

Suite, G major <1715>   12'

0 2 0 1 — cnt — str

Hänssler

Bach, Johann Sebastian   1685-1750

(b Eisenach, 21 March 1685; d Leipzig, 28 July 1750). German

BWV = W. Schmieder: *Thematisch-systematisches Verzeichnis der musikalischen Werke Johann Sebastian Bachs: Bach-Werke-Verzeichnis* (Leipzig, 1950, enlarged 1990, rev. and abridged 1998 by A. Dürr, Y. Kobayashi and K. Beisswenger as *Bach-Werke-Verzeichnis*)

Bist du bei mir (If Thou be Near) <1725>   3'

2 2 0 2 — 2 0 0 0 — str
Arranged by Thomas Frost. Actual composer is Gottfried Heinrich Stölzel.

Tetra

Brandenburg Concerto No.1, BWV 1046, F major <1717>   20'

solos: 3 oboes, 2 horns, violin [originally violino piccolo]
0 0 0 1 — cnt — str
I. [Allegro]   4'
II. Adagio   6'
III. Allegro   5'
IV. Menuet; Trio 1; Menuet; Polonaise; Menuet; Trio 2; Menuet   7'

Bärenreiter	Breitkopf	Kalmus	Luck's	Peters

Brandenburg Concerto No.2, BWV 1047, F major <1717–1718>   13'

solos: recorder, oboe, trumpet, violin
cnt — str
I. [Allegro]   5'
II. Andante   5'
III. Allegro assai   3'

Bärenreiter	Breitkopf	Kalmus	Luck's	Peters

Brandenburg Concerto No.3, BWV 1048, G major <1711–1713>   10'

solos: 3vn, 3va, 3vc
cnt — db
The two movements are separated by a tutti phrygian cadence; the implication is that this cadence marks the end of some sort of improvised cadenza or other middle movement. The Breitkopf edition includes a cadenza by Emil Platen at this point.
[Allegro]   7'
Allegro   3'

Bärenreiter	Breitkopf	Kalmus	Luck's	Peters

Brandenburg Concerto No.4, BWV 1049, G major <1720>   17'

solos: 2 recorders, violin
cnt — str
This work subsequently arranged by the composer as:
Concerto, Harpsichord, No.6, BWV 1057, F major, *q.v.*
I. Allegro   7'
II. Andante   5'
III. Presto   5'

Bärenreiter	Breitkopf	Kalmus	Luck's	Peters

Brandenburg Concerto No.5, BWV 1050, D major <1720–1721>   21'

solos: harpsichord, flute, violin
str[no vn2]
I. Allegro   10'
II. Affettuoso   6'
III. Allegro   5'

Bärenreiter	Breitkopf	Kalmus	Luck's	Peters

Brandenburg Concerto No.6, BWV 1051, B-flat major <1708–1710>   18'

2 solo violas ["viole da braccio"], 2 solo viole da gamba
cnt — vc, db
I. [Allegro]   7'
II. Adagio ma non tanto   5'
III. Allegro   6'

Bärenreiter	Breitkopf	Kalmus	Luck's	Peters

Cantata No.1 (Wie schön leuchtet der Morgenstern) <1725>   26'

chorus   solos STB
0 2[2ob da cacc] 0 0 — 2 0 0 0 — cnt — str
I. Chorale: "Wie schön leuchtet der Morgenstern"   10'
II. Recitative: "Du wahrer Gottes und Marien Sohn"   1'
III. Aria: "Er füllet, ihr himmlischen göttlichen Flammen"   5'
IV. Recitative: "Ein ird'scher Glanz, ein leiblich Licht"   1'
V. Aria: "Unser Mund und Ton der Saiten"   7'
VI. Chorale: "Wie bin ich doch so herzlich froh"   2'

Breitkopf	Carus	Kalmus	Luck's

Cantata No.2 (Ach Gott, vom Himmel sieh darein) <1724>   18'

chorus   solos ATB
0 2 0 0 — 0 0 4 0 — cnt — str
The 4tbn dbl choral parts.
I. Chorus: "Ach Gott, vom Himmel sieh darein"   4'
II. Recitative: "Sie lehren eitel falsche List"   1'
III. Aria: "Tilg, o Gott, die Lehren"   4'
IV. Recitative: "Die Armen sind verstört"   2'
V. Aria: "Durchs Feuer wird das Silber rein"   6'
VI. Chorus: "Das wollst du, Gott bewahren rein"   1'

Breitkopf	Carus

Cantata No.3 (Ach Gott, wie manches Herzeleid [I]) <1725>   *24'*

chorus   solos SATB
0 2[2ob d'amore] 0 0 — 1 0 1 0 — cnt — str
Brass used only to strengthen the cantus firmus.

I. Chorus: "Ach Gott, wie manches Herzeleid"	*5'*
II. Recitative: "Wie schwerlich lässt sich Fleisch und Blut"	*2'*
III. Aria (Duet): "Empfind ich Höllenangst und Pein"	*6'*
IV. Recitative: "Es mag mir Leib und Geist verschmachten"	*1'*
V. Aria: "Wenn Sorgen auf mich dringen"	*9'*
VI. Chorus: "Erhalt mein Herz im Glauben rein"	*1'*

Breitkopf	Carus

Cantata No.4 (Christ lag in Todesbanden) <1708>   *20'*

chorus   (optional solos SATB)
0 0 0 0 — 0 1[cornetto] 3 0 — cnt — str
The cornetto and 3tbn double choral parts.
   A critical edition of the score with historical and analytical essays is
available from Norton.

I. Sinfonia	*1'*
II. Versus 1: "Christ lag in Todesbanden"	*5'*
III. Versus 2: "Den Tod niemand zwingen kunnt"	*3'*
IV. Versus 3: "Jesus Christus, Gottes Sohn"	*2'*
V. Versus 4: "Es war ein wunderliche Krieg"	*3'*
VI. Versus 5: "Hier ist das rechte Osterlamm"	*3'*
VII. Versus 6: "So feieren wir das hohe Fest"	*2'*
VIII. Versus 7: "Wir essen und leben wohl"	*1'*

Bärenreiter	Breitkopf	Carus	Kalmus	Luck's

Cantata No.5 (Wo soll ich fliehen hin) <1724>   *21'*

chorus   solos SATB
0 2 0 0 — 0 1 0 0 — cnt — str

I. Chorus: "Wo soll ich fliehen hin"	*4'*
II. Recitative: "Der Sünden Wust hat mich nicht nur befleckt"	*1'*
III. Aria: "Ergiesse dich reichlich du göttliche Quelle"	*6'*
IV. Recitative: "Mein treuer Heiland tröstet mich"	*2'*
V. Aria: "Verstumme, Höllenheer"	*6'*
VI. Recitative: "Ich bin ja nur das kleinste Teil der Welt"	*1'*
VII. Chorus: "Führ auch mein Herz und Sinn"	*1'*

Breitkopf	Carus

Cantata No.6 (Bleib bei uns, denn es will Abend werden) <1725>   *20'*

chorus   solos SATB
0 3[1.2.ob da cacc] 0 0 — vc piccolo — cnt — str

I. Chorus: "Bleib bei uns, denn es will Abend werden"	*6'*
II. Aria: "Hochgelobter Gottessohn"	*4'*
III. Aria (Choral): "Ach, bleib bei uns, Herr Jesu Christ"	*4'*
IV. Recitative: "Es hat die Dunkelheit an vielen Orten"	*1'*
V. Aria: "Jesu, lass uns auf dich sehen"	*4'*
VI. Chorus: "Beweis dein Macht, Herr Jesu Christ"	*1'*

Bärenreiter	Breitkopf	Carus	Kalmus	Luck's

Cantata No.7 (Christ unser Herr zum Jordan kam) <1724>   *26'*

chorus   solos ATB
0 2[2ob d'amore] 0 0 — cnt — str

I. Chorus: "Christ unser Herr zum Jordan kam"	*8'*
II. Aria: "Merkt und hört, ihr Menschenkinder"	*6'*
III. Recitative: "Dies hat Gott klar mit Worten"	*1'*
IV. Aria: "Des Vaters Stimme liess sich hören"	*5'*
V. Recitative: "Als Jesus dort nach seinen Leiden"	*1'*
VI. Aria: "Menschen, glaubt doch dieser Gnade"	*4'*
VII. Chorus: "Das Aug allein das Wasser sieht"	*1'*

Breitkopf	Carus	Kalmus	Luck's

Cantata No.8 (Liebster Gott, wann werd' ich sterben)   *16'*   <1724>

chorus   solos SATB
1 2[2ob d'amore] 0 0 — 1 0 0 0 — cnt — str
Horn is used only to strengthen the cantus firmus. A later version exists,
which requires a 3rd oboist, playing oboe da caccia.

I. Chorus: "Liebster Gott, wann werd ich sterben?"	*5'*
II. Aria: "Was willst du dich, mein Geist, entsetzen"	*3'*
III. Recitative: "Zwar fühlt mein schwaches Herz"	*1'*
IV. Aria: "Doch weichet, ihr tollen, vergeblichen Sorgen"	*5'*
V. Recitative: "Behalte nur, o Welt, das Meine"	*1'*
VI. Chorus: "Herrscher über Tod und Leben"	*1'*

Breitkopf	Carus	Kalmus	Luck's

Cantata No.9 (Es ist das Heil uns kommen her) <1735>   *23'*

chorus   solos SATB
1 1[ob d'amore] 0 0 — cnt — str

I. Chorus: "Es ist das Heil uns kommen her"	*5'*
II. Recitative: "Gott gab uns ein Gesetz"	*1'*
III. Aria: "Wir waren schon zu tief gesunken"	*7'*
IV. Recitative: "Doch musste das Gesetz erfüllet werden"	*1'*
V. Duet: "Herr, du siehst statt guter Werke"	*7'*
VI. Recitative: "Wenn wir die Sünd aus dem Gesetz erkennen"	*1'*
VII. Chorus: "Oh sich's anliess, als wollt er nicht"	*1'*

Breitkopf	Carus	Kalmus	Luck's

Cantata No.10 (Meine Seel erhebt den Herren) <1724>   *21'*

chorus   solos SATB
0 2 0 0 — 0 1 0 0 — cnt — str
Trumpet used only to strengthen the cantus firmus.

I. Chorus: "Meine Seel erhebt den Herren"	*4'*
II. Aria: "Herr, der du stark und mächtig bist"	*7'*
III. Recitative: "Des Höchsten Güt und Treu'"	*1'*
IV. Aria: "Gewaltige stösst Gott vom Stuhl"	*4'*
V. Duet: "Er denket der Barmherzigkeit"	*2'*
VI. Recitative: "Was Gott den Vätern alter Zeiten"	*2'*
VII. Chorus: "Lob und Preis sei Gott dem Vater"	*1'*

Breitkopf	Carus	Kalmus	Luck's

Cantata No.11 (Lobet Gott in seinen Reichen) <1735>   *28'*

chorus   solos SATB
2 2 0 0 — 0 3 0 0 — tmp — cnt — str
Also known as *Ascension Oratorio* or *Himmelfahrts-Oratorium*.
   Bärenreiter ed. Paul Brainard.

I. Chorus: "Lobet Gott in seinen Reichen"	*5'*
II. Recitative: "Der Herr Jesus hub seine Hände auf"	*1'*
III. Recitative: "Ach, Jesu, ist dein Abschied"	*1'*
IV. Aria: "Ach, bleibe doch, mein liebstes Leben"	*6'*
V. Recitative: "Und ward aufgehoben zusehends"	*1'*
VI. Chorus: "Nun lieget alles unter dir"	*1'*
VII. Recitative (Duet): "Und da sie ihm nachsahen"	*1'*
VIII. Recitative: "Ach ja, so komme bald zurück"	*1'*
IX. Recitative: "Sie aber beteten ihn an"	*1'*
X. Aria: "Jesu, deine Gnadenblicke"	*6'*
XI. Chorus: "Wann soll es doch geschehen"	*4'*

Bärenreiter	Breitkopf	Carus	Kalmus	Luck's

Cantata No.12 (Weinen, Klagen, Sorgen, Zagen) <1714>   *23'*

chorus   solos ATB
0 1 0 1 — 0 1 0 0 — cnt — str

I. Sinfonia	*2'*
II. Chorus: "Weinen, Klagen, Sorgen, Zagen"	*6'*
III. Recitative: "Wir müssen durch viel Trübsal"	*1'*
IV. Aria: "Kreuz und Krone sind verbunden"	*6'*
V. Aria: "Ich folge Christo nach"	*3'*
VI. Aria: "Sei getreu, alle Pein"	*4'*
VII. Chorus: "Was Gott tut, das ist wohlgetan"	*1'*

Bärenreiter	Breitkopf	Carus	Kalmus	Luck's

28

Cantata No.13 (Meine Seufzer, meine Tränen) <1726>   23'

chorus   solos SATB
2[2rec] 1[ob/ob da cacc] 0 0 — cnt — str
I. Aria: "Meine Seufer, meine Tränen"   8'
II. Recitative: "Mein liebster Gott lässt mich"   1'
III. Aria: "Der Gott, der mir hat versprochen"   3'
IV. Recitative: "Mein Kummer nimmet zu"   1'
V. Aria: "Achzen und erbärmlich weinen"   9'
VI. Chorus: "So sei nu, Seele, deine"   1'

| Breitkopf | Carus |

Cantata No.14 (Wär Gott nicht mit uns diese Zeit) <1735>   17'

chorus   solos STB
0 2 0 0 — 1[corno da caccia] 0 0 0 — cnt — str
I. Chorus: "Wär Gott night mit uns diese Zeit"   6'
II. Aria: "Unsre Stärke heisst zu schwach"   4'
III. Recitative: "Ja, hätt es Gott nicht zugegeben"   4'
IV. Aria: "Gott, bei deinem starken Schützen"   5'
V. Chorus: "Gott Lob und Dank, der nicht zugab"   1'

| Breitkopf | Carus |

Cantata No.15 (Denn du wirst meine Seele) <1714>   15'

solos SATB   chorus in final movement only
0 0 0 0 — 0 3 0 0 — tmp — cnt — str
Actually composed by Johann Ludwig Bach.

| Breitkopf | Kalmus | Luck's |

Cantata No.16 (Herr Gott, dich loben wir) <1726>   18'

chorus   solos ATB
0 2[1.2/ob da cacc] 0 0 — 1[corno da caccia] 0 0 0 — cnt — str
Oboe da caccia in one mvt only; may be played on *violetta* (= viol; possible on viola).
I. Chorus: "Herr Gott, dich loben wir"   2'
II. Recitative: "So stimmen wir bei deiser frohen Zeit"   1'
III. Aria with Chorus: "Lasst uns jauchzen, lasst uns freuen"   4'
IV. Recitative: "Ach treuer Hort"   1'
V. Aria: "Geliebter Jesu, du allein"   9'
VI. Chorus: "All solch dein Güt wir preisen"   1'

| Breitkopf | Carus | Kalmus | Luck's |

Cantata No.17 (Wer Dank opfert, der preiset mich) <1726>   18'

chorus   solos SATB
0 2[2ob d'amore] 0 0 — cnt — str
I. Chorus: "Wer Dank opfert, der preiset mich"   5'
II. Recitative: "Es muss die ganze Welt"   1'
III. Aria: "Herr, deine Güte reicht so weit"   4'
IV. Recitative: "Einer aber unter ihnen, da er sahe"   1'
V. Aria: "Welch Übermass der Güte schenkst du mir"   4'
VI. Recitative: "Sieh meinen Willen an"   1'
VII. Chorus: "Wie sich ein Vatr erbarmet"   2'

| Breitkopf | Carus | Kalmus | Luck's |

Cantata No.18 (Gleichwie der Regen und Schnee) <1714>   14'

chorus   solos STB
2[2rec] 0 0 1 — cnt — 4va, vc[db]
An earlier Weimar version (in G minor rather than A minor) uses no recorders.
I. Sinfonia   3'
II. Recitative: "Gleichwie der Regen und Schnee"   1'
III. Recitative: "Mein Gott, hier wird mein Herze sein"   6'
IV. Aria: "Mein Seelenschatz ist Gottes Wort"   3'
V. Chorus: "Ich bitt, o Herr, aus Herzensgrund"   1'

| Bärenreiter | Breitkopf | Carus | Kalmus | Luck's |

Cantata No.19 (Es erhub sich ein Streit) <1726>   21'

chorus   solos STB
0 3[1/d'am.2/d'am.da cacc] 0 0 — 0 3 0 0 — tmp — cnt — str
I. Chorus: "Es erhub sich ein Streit"   5'
II. Recitative: "Gottlob, der Drache liegt"   1'
III. Aria: "Gott schickt uns Mahanaim zu"   4'
IV. Recitative: "Was ist der schnöde Mensch"   1'
V. Aria: "Bleibt, ihr Engel, bleibt bei mir"   7'
VI. Recitative: "Lasst uns das Angesicht der frommen Engel"   1'
VII. Chorus: "Lass dein' Engel mit mir fahren"   2'

| Breitkopf | Carus | Kalmus | Luck's |

Cantata No.20 (O Ewigkeit, du Donnerwort [I]) <1724>   26'

chorus   solos ATB
0 3 0 0 — 0 1 0 0 — cnt — str
I. Chorus: "O Ewigkeit, du Donnerwort"   5'
II. Recitative: "Kein Unglück ist in aller Welt zu finden"   1'
III. Aria: "Ewigkeit, du machst mir bange"   3'
IV. Recitative: "Gesetzt, es dau'rte der Verdammten Qual"   1'
V. Aria: "Gott ist gerecht in seinen Werken"   4'
VI. Aria: "O Mensch, errette deine Seele"   2'
VII. Chorus: "Solang ein Gott im Himmel lebt"   1'
VIII. Aria: "Wacht auf, wacht auf, verlorne Schafe"   3'
IX. Recitative: "Verlass, o Mensch, die Wollust dieser Welt"   1'
X. Duet (Aria): "O Menschenkind, hör auf geschwind"   4'
XI. Chorus: "O Ewigkeit; du Donnerwort"   1'

| Breitkopf | Carus | Kalmus | Luck's |

Cantata No.21 (Ich hatte viel Bekümmernis) <1714>   38'

chorus   solos SATB
0 1 0 1 — 0 3 4 0 — tmp — cnt — str
Trombones only double choral parts. The timpani part was lost and has been reconstructed.
I. Sinfonia   3'
II. Chorus: "Ich hatte viel Bekümmernis"   3'
III. Aria: "Seufzer, Tränen, Kummer, Not"   4'
IV. Recitative: "Wie hast du dich, mein Gott, in meiner Not"   2'
V. Aria: "Bäche von gesalznen Zähren"   5'
VI. Chorus: "Was betrübst du dich, meine Seele"   4'
VII. Recitative: "Ach Jesu, meine Ruh, mein Licht"   1'
VIII. Aria (Duet): "Komm, mein Jesu, und erquicke"   5'
IX. Chorus: "Sei nun wieder zufrieden, meine Seele"   5'
X. Aria: "Erfreue dich, Seele, erfreue dich, Herze"   3'
XI. Chorus: "Das Lamm, das erwürget ist"   3'

| Bärenreiter | Breitkopf | Carus | Kalmus | Luck's |

Cantata No.22 (Jesus nahm zu sich die Zwölfe) <1723>   18'

chorus   solos ATB
0 1 0 0 — cnt — str
I. Chorus: "Jesus nahm zu sich die Zwölfe"   5'
II. Aria: "Mein Jesu, ziehe mich nach dir"   5'
III. Recitative: "Mein Jesu, ziehe mich, so werd ich laufen"   2'
IV. Aria: "Mein alles in allem, mein ewiges Gut"   4'
V. Chorus: "Ertöt uns durch dein Güte"   2'

| Breitkopf | Carus | Kalmus | Luck's |

Cantata No.23 (Du wahrer Gott und Davids Sohn) <1723>   19'

chorus   solos SAT
0 2 0 0 — 0 1[cornetto] 3 0 — cnt — str
The cornetto and 3tbn double choral parts.
I. Duet: "Du wahrer Gott und Davids Sohn"   8'
II. Recitative: "Ach, gehe nicht vorüber"   2'
III. Chorus: "Aller Augen warten, Herr"   4'
IV. Chorus: "Christe, du Lamm Gottes"   5'

| Breitkopf | Carus | Kalmus | Luck's |

Cantata No.24 (Ein ungefärbte Gemüte) <1723>   18'

chorus   solos SATB
0 2[1/d'am.2/d'am] 0 0 — 0 1 0 0 — cnt — str

I. Aria: "Ein ungefärbt Gemüte"	5'
II. Recitative "Die Redlichkeit ist eine von den Gottesgaben"	2'
III. Chorus: "Alles nun, das ihr wollet"	3'
IV. Recitative: "Die Heuchelei ist eine Brut"	2'
V. Aria: "Treu und Wahrheit sei der Grund"	4'
VI. Chorus: "O Gott, du frommer Gott"	2'

Breitkopf	Carus	Kalmus	Luck's

Cantata No.25 (Es ist nichts gesundes an meinem Leibe) <1723>   15'

chorus   solos STB
3[3rec] 2 0 0 — 0 1[cornetto] 3 0 — cnt — str

I. Chorus: "Es ist nichts Gesundes an meinem Leibe"	5'
II. Recitative: "Die ganze Welt ist nur ein Hospital"	1'
III. Aria: "Ach, wo hol ich Armer Rat"	3'
IV. Recitative: "O Jesu, lieber Meister"	1'
V. Aria: "Öffne meinen schlechten Liedern"	4'
VI. Chorus: "Ich will alle meine Tage"	1'

Breitkopf	Carus

Cantata No.26 (Ach wie flüchtig, ach wie nichtig) <1724>   14'

chorus   solos SATB
1 3 0 0 — 1 0 0 0 — cnt — str
Horn used only to strengthen cantus firmus.

I. Chorus: "Ach wie flüchtig, ach wie nichtig"	2'
II. Aria: "So schnell ein rauschend Wasser schiesst"	5'
III. Recitative: "Die Freude wird zur Traurigkeit"	1'
IV. Aria: "An irdische Schätze das Herze zu hängen"	4'
V. Recitative: "Die höchste Herrlichkeit und Pracht"	1'
VI. Chorus: "Ach wie flüchtig, ach wie nichtig"	1'

Breitkopf	Carus	Kalmus	Luck's

Cantata No.27 (Wer weiss, wie nahe mir mein Ende!) <1725>   16'

chorus   solos SATB
0 2[1.2/ob da cacc] 0 0 — 1 0 0 0 — org, cnt — str
Horn used only to strengthen cantus firmus.

I. Chorus: "Wer weiss, wie nahe mir mein Ende!"	5'
II. Recitative: "Mein Leben hat kein ander Ziel"	1'
III. Aria: "Willkommen! will ich sagen"	5'
IV. Recitative: "Ach, wer doch schon im Himmel wär!"	1'
V. Aria: "Gute Nacht, du Weltgetümmel"	3'
VI. Chorus: "Welt, ade! ich bin dein müde"	1'

Breitkopf	Carus	Kalmus	Luck's

Cantata No.28 (Gottlob! nun geht das Jahr zu Ende) <1725>   16'

chorus   solos SATB
0 3[1.2.ob da caccia] 0 0 — 0 1[cornetto] 3 0 — cnt — str
Cornetto and 3tbn doubling choral parts.

I. Aria: "Gottlob! nun geht das Jahr zu Ende"	5'
II. Chorus: "Nun lob, mein Seel, den Herren"	5'
III. Recitative: "So spricht der Herr"	2'
IV. Recitative: "Gott ist ein Quell"	1'
V. Duet: "Gott hat uns in heurigen Jahre"	2'
VI. Chorus: "All solch dein Güt wir preisen"	1'

Breitkopf	Carus	Kalmus	Luck's

Cantata No.29 (Wir danken dir, Gott, wir danken dir) <1731>   22'

chorus   solos SATB
0 2 0 0 — 0 3 0 0 — tmp — org, cnt — str

I. Sinfonia	3'
II. Chorus: "Wir danken dir, Gott, wir danken dir"	3'
III. Aria: "Halleluja, Stärk und Macht"	5'
IV. Recitative: "Gottlob! es geht uns wohl"	1'
V. Aria: "Gedenk an uns mit deiner Liebe"	5'
VI. Recitative: "Vergiss es ferner nicht"	1'
VII. Aria: "Halleluja, Stärk und Macht"	2'
VIII. Chorus: "Sei Lob und Preis mit Ehren"	2'

Breitkopf	Carus	Kalmus	Luck's

Cantata No.30 (Freue dich, erlöste Schar) <1738>   35'

chorus   solos SATB
2 2[1/ob d'amore.2] 0 0 — 0 3 0 0 — tmp — cnt — str

I. Chorus: "Freue dich, erlöste Schar"	4'
II. Recitative: "Wir haben Rast, und des Gesetzes Last"	1'
III. Aria: "Gelobet sei Gott, gelobet sei sein Name"	5'
IV. Recitative: "Der Herold kommt und meldt den König an"	1'
V. Aria: "Kommt, ihr angefochtnen Sünder"	5'
VI. Chorus: "Eine Stimme lässt sich hören"	1'
VII. Recitative: "So bist du denn, mein Heil bedacht"	1'
VIII. Aria: "Ich will nun hassen"	7'
IX. Recitative: "Und ob wohl sonst der Unbestand"	1'
X. Aria: "Eilt, ihr Stunden, kommt herbei"	6'
XI. Recitative: "Geduld, der angenehme Tag"	1'
XII. Chorus: "Freue dich, geheilgte Schar"	5'

Breitkopf	C. Fischer	Kalmus	Luck's

Cantata No.30a (Angenehmes Wiederau, freue dich in deinen Auen!) <1737>   47'

solos SATB   chorus
2 2[1/ob d'amore.2] 0 0 — 0 3 0 0 — tmp — cnt — str
Characters: Zeit (S), Glück (A), Elster (T), Schicksal (B).
The original form of Cantata No.30.

I. Chorus: "Angenehmes Wiederau, freue dich in deinen Auen!"	_'
II. Recit.: "So ziehen wir in diesem Hause hier"	_'
III. Aria: "Willkommen im Heil, willkommen in Freuden"	_'
IV. Recit.: "Da heute dir, gepriesner Hennicke"	_'
V. Aria: "Was die Seele kann ergötzen"	_'
VI. Recit.: "Und wie ich jederzeit bedacht"	_'
VII. Aria: "Ich will dich halten und mit dir walten"	_'
VIII. Recit.: "Und obwohl sonst der Unbestand"	_'
IX. Aria: "Eilt, ihr Stunden, wie ihr wollt"	_'
X. Recit.: "So recht, ihr seid mir werte Gäste"	_'
XI. Aria: "So wie ich die Tropfen zolle"	_'
XII. Recit.: "Drum, angenehmes Wiederau"	_'
XIII. Chorus: "Angenehmes Wiederau, prange nun in deinen Auen"	_'

Breitkopf

Cantata No.31 (Der Himmel Lacht! die Erde jubilieret) <1715>   20'

chorus   solos STB
0 4[1.2.3.ob da caccia] 0 1 — 0 3 0 0 — tmp — cnt — str

I. Sonata	3'
II. Chorus: "Der Himmel lacht! die Erde jubilieret"	4'
III. Recitative: "Erwünschter Tag! sei, Seele, wieder froh"	2'
IV. Aria: "Fürst des Lebens, starker Streiter"	2'
V. Recitative: "So stehe denn, du gottergebne Seele"	1'
VI. Aria: "Adam muss in uns verwesen"	2'
VII. Recitative: "Weil denn das Haupt sein Glied"	1'
VIII. Aria: "Letzte Stunde, brich herein"	4'
IX. Chorus: "So fahr ich hin zu Jesu Christ"	1'

Bärenreiter	Breitkopf	Carus	Kalmus	Luck's

Cantata No.32 (Liebster Jesu, mein Verlangen) <1726>   25'

solos SB   chorus in final chorale only

0 1 0 0 — cnt — str

I. Aria: "Liebster Jesu, mein Verlangen"	6'
II. Recitative: "Was ists, dass du mich gesuchet?"	1'
III. Aria: "Hier, in meines Vaters Stätte"	8'
IV. Recitative: "Ach! heiliger und grosser Gott"	3'
V. Duet: "Nun verschwinden alle Plagen"	6'
VI. Chorus: "Mein Gott, öffne mir die Pforten"	1'

Breitkopf	Carus	Kalmus	Luck's

Cantata No.33 (Allein zu dir, Herr Jesu Christ) <1724>   20'

chorus   solos ATB

0 2 0 0 — cnt — str

I. Chorus: "Allein zu dir, Herr Jesu Christ"	5'
II. Recitative: "Mein Gott und Richter"	1'
III. Aria: "Wie furchtsam wankten meine Schritte"	8'
IV. Recitative: "Mein Gott verwirf mich nicht"	1'
V. Aria (Duet): "Gott, der du die Liebe heisst"	4'
VI. Chorus: "Ehr sei Gott in dem höchsten Thron"	1'

Breitkopf	Carus	Kalmus	Luck's

Cantata No.34 (O ewiges Feuer, o Ursprung der Liebe) <1740>   19'

chorus   solos ATB

2 2 0 0 — 0 3 0 0 — tmp — cnt — str

I. Chorus: "O ewiges Feuer, O Ursprung der Liebe"	8'
II. Recitative: "Herr, unsre Herzen halten dir"	1'
III. Aria: "Wohl euch, ihr auserwählten Seelen"	7'
IV. Recitative: "Erwählt sich Gott die heilgen Hütten"	1'
V. Chorus: "Friede über Israel! Dankt den höchsten Wunderhänden"	2'

Bärenreiter	Breitkopf	Carus	Kalmus	Luck's

Cantata No.35 (Geist und Seele wird verwirret) <1726>   26'

alto solo

0 3[1.2.ob da cacc] 0 0 — org — str

I. Sinfonia	5'
II. Aria: "Geist und Seele wird verwirret"	9'
III. Recitative: "Ich wundre mich, denn alles, was man sieht"	2'
IV. Aria: "Gott hat alles wohl gemacht"	3'
V. Sinfonia	3'
VI. Recitative: "Ach, starker Gott, lass mich doch dieses"	1'
VII. Aria: "Ich wünsche mir, bei Gott zu leben"	3'

Breitkopf	Carus	Kalmus	Luck's

Cantata No.36 (Schwingt freudig euch empor) <1731>   29'

chorus   solos SATB

0 2[2ob d'amore] 0 0 — cnt — str

There is an earlier version of this cantata, without mvts.2, 4 or 6, and with a different final chorale.

I. Chorus: "Schwingt freudig euch empor"	4'
II. Chorus: "Nun komm, der Heiden Heiland"	3'
III. Aria: "Die Liebe zieht mit sanften Schritten"	5'
IV. Chorus: "Zwingt die Saiten in Cythara"	1'
V. Aria: "Willkommen, werter Schatz"	4'
VI. Chorus: "Der du bist dem Vater gleich"	2'
VII. Aria: "Auch mit gedämpften, schwachen Stimmen"	9'
VIII. Chorus: "Lob sei Gott, dem Vater, g'ton"	1'

Bärenreiter	Breitkopf	Carus	Kalmus

Cantata No.37 (Wer da gläubet und getauft wird) <1724>   16'

chorus   solos SATB

0 2[2ob d'amore] 0 0 — cnt — str

I. Chorus: "Wer da gläubet und getauft wird"	3'
II. Aria: "Der Glaube ist das Pfand der Liebe"	5'
III. Duet: "Herr Gott Vater, mein starker Held"	3'
IV. Recitative: "Ihr Sterblichen, verlanget ihr mit mir"	1'
V. Aria: "Der Glaube schafft der Seele Flügel"	3'
VI. Chorus: "Den Glauben mir verleihe"	1'

Breitkopf	Carus	Kalmus	Luck's

Cantata No.38 (Aus tiefer Not schrei ich zu dir) <1724>   18'

chorus   solos SATB

0 2 0 0 — 0 0 4 0 — cnt — str

The trombones only double choral parts.

I. Chorus: "Aus tiefer Not schrei ich zu dir"	4'
II. Recitative: "In Jesu Gnade wird allein"	1'
III. Aria: "Ich höre mitten in dem Leiden"	8'
IV. Recitative: "Ach! dass mein Glaube noch so schwach"	1'
V. Trio: "Wenn meine Trübsal als mit Ketten"	3'
VI. Chorus: "Ob bei uns ist der Sünden viel"	1'

Breitkopf	Carus	Kalmus

Cantata No.39 (Brich dem Hungrigen dein Brot) <1726>   21'

chorus   solos SAB

2[2recorders] 2 0 0 — cnt — str

I. Chorus: "Brich dem Hungrigen dein Brot"	7'
II. Recitative: "Der reiche Gott wirft seinen Überfluss"	1'
III. Aria: "Seinem Schöpfer noch auf Erden"	3'
IV. Aria: "Wohlzutun und mitzuteilen"	3'
V. Aria: "Höchster, was ich habe ist nur deine Gabe"	3'
VI. Recitative: "Wie soll ich dir, o Herr"	2'
VII. Chorus: "Selig sind, die aus Erbarmen"	1'

Breitkopf	Carus	Kalmus	Luck's

Cantata No.40 (Dazu ist erschienen der Sohn Gottes) <1723>   18'

chorus   solos ATB

0 2 0 0 — 2 0 0 0 — cnt — str

I. Chorus: "Dazu ist erschienen der Sohn Gottes"	5'
II. Recitative: "Das Wort ward Fleisch"	2'
III. Chorus: "Die Sünd macht Leid"	1'
IV. Aria: "Höllische Schlange, wird dir nicht bange"	3'
V. Recitative: "Die Schlange, so im Paradies"	1'
VI. Chorus: "Schüttle deinen Kopf und sprich"	1'
VII. Aria: "Christenkinder, freuet euch"	4'
VIII. Chorus: "Jesu, nimm dich deiner Glieder"	1'

Breitkopf	Carus	Kalmus

Cantata No.41 (Jesu, nun sei gepreiset) <1725>   28'

chorus   solos SATB

0 3 0 0 — 0 3 0 0 — vc piccolo — tmp — cnt — str

I. Chorus: "Jesu, nun sei gepreiset"	9'
II. Aria: "Lass uns, o höchster Gott, das Jahr vollbringen"	7'
III. Recitative: "Herr, deine Hand, dein Segen"	1'
IV. Aria: "Woferne du den edlen Frieden"	8'
V. Recitative: "Doch weil der Feind bei Tag und Nacht"	1'
VI. Chorus: "Dein ist allein die Ehre"	2'

Breitkopf	Carus	Kalmus	Luck's

Cantata No.42 (Am Abend aber desselbigen Sabbats) <1725>   28'

solos SATB   chorus in final chorale only

0 2 0 1 — cnt — str

I. Sinfonia	6'
II. Recitative: "Am Abend aber desselbigen Sabbats"	1'
III. Aria: "Wo zwei und drei versammelt sind"	11'
IV. Duet: "Verzage nicht, o Häuflein klein"	3'
V. Recitative: "Man kann hiervon ein schön Exempel"	1'
VI. Aria: "Jesus ist ein Schild der Seinen"	4'
VII. Chorus: "Verleih uns Frieden gnädiglich"	2'

Breitkopf	Carus	Kalmus	Luck's

Cantata No.43 (Gott fähret auf mit Jauchzen) <1726>   22'

chorus   solos SATB
0 2 0 0 — 0 3 0 0 — tmp — cnt — str

I. Chorus: "Gott fähret auf mit Jauchzen"	4'
II. Recitative: "Es will der Höchste sich"	1'
III. Aria: "Ja tausend mal tausend begleiten den Wagen"	2'
IV. Recitative: "Und der Herr, nachdem er mit ihnen"	1'
V. Aria: "Mein Jesu hat nunmehr"	3'
VI. Recitative: "Es kommt der Helden Held"	1'
VII. Aria: "Er ists, der ganz allein"	3'
VIII. Recitative: "Der Vater hat ihm ja"	1'
IX. Aria: "Ich sehe schon im Geist"	3'
X. Recitative: "Er will mir neben sich"	1'
XI. Chorus: "Du Lebensfürst; Herr Jesu Christ"	2'

Breitkopf	Carus	Kalmus	Luck's

Cantata No.44 (Sie werden euch in den Bann tun [I])   18'
<1724>

chorus   solos SATB
0 2 0 1 — cnt — str

I. Duet: "Sie werden euch in den Bann tun"	2'
II. Chorus: "Es kömmt aber die Zeit"	2'
III. Aria: "Christen müssen auf der Erden"	5'
IV. Recitative: "Ach Gott, wie manches Herzeleid"	1'
V. Recitative: "Es sucht der Antichrist"	1'
VI. Aria: "Es ist und bleibt der Christen Trost"	6'
VII. Chorus: "So sei nun, Seele, deine"	1'

Breitkopf	Carus	Kalmus	Luck's

Cantata No.45 (Es ist dir gesagt, Mensch, was gut ist)   21'
<1726>

chorus   solos ATB
2 2 0 0 — cnt — str

I. Chorus: "Es ist dir gesagt, Mensch, was gut ist"	7'
II. Recitative: "Der Höchste lässt mich seinen Willen wissen"	1'
III. Aria: "Weiss ich Gottes Rechte"	4'
IV. Arioso: "Es werden viele zu mir sagen"	3'
V. Aria: "Wer Gott bekennt aus wahrem Herzensgrund"	4'
VI. Recitative: "So wird denn Herz und Mund"	1'
VII. Chorus: "Gib, dass ich tu mit Fleiss"	1'

Bärenreiter	Breitkopf	Carus

Cantata No.46 (Schauet doch und sehet) <1723>   19'

chorus   solos ATB
2[2rec] 2[2ob da caccia] 0 0 — 1[corno da tirarsi] 0 0 0 — cnt — str
Corno da tirarsi part given to trumpet in Breitkopf materials & Kalmus reprint.

I. Chorus: "Schauet doch und sehet"	7'
II. Recitative: "So klage du, zustörte Gottesstadt"	2'
III. Aria: "Dein Wetter zog sich auf von weiten"	3'
IV. Recitative: "Doch bildet euch, o Sünder"	1'
V. Aria: "Doch Jesus will auch bei der Strafe"	4'
VI. Chorus: "O grosser Gott der Treu"	2'

Breitkopf	Carus	Kalmus	Luck's

Cantata No.47 (Wer sich selbst erhöhet) <1726>   23'

chorus   solos SB
0 2 0 0 — org — str
2nd movement calls for obligato organ *or* solo violin.

I. Chorus: "Wer sich selbst erhöhet"	7'
II. Aria: "Wer ein wahrer Christ will heissen"	8'
III. Recitative: "Der Mensch ist Kot, Stank, Asch und Erde"	2'
IV. Aria: "Jesu, beuge doch mein Herze"	5'
V. Chorus: "Der zeitlichen Ehrn will ich gern entbehrn"	1'

Breitkopf	Carus	Kalmus	Luck's

Cantata No.48 (Ich elender Mensch) <1723>   16'

chorus   solos AT
0 2 0 0 — 0 1 0 0 — cnt — str

I. Chorus: "Ich elender Mensch, wer wird mich erlösen"	4'
II. Recitative: "O Schmerz, o Elend, so mich trifft"	2'
III. Chorus: "Solls ja so sein"	1'
IV. Aria: "Ach lege das Sodom der sündlichen Glieder"	3'
V. Recitative: "Hier aber tut des Heilands Hand"	1'
VI. Aria: "Vergibt mir Jesus meine Sünden"	4'
VII. Chorus: "Herr Jesu Christ, einiger Trost"	1'

Breitkopf	Carus	Kalmus	Luck's

Cantata No.49 (Ich geh und suche mit Verlangen)   27'
<1726>

solos SB
0 1[ob d'amore] 0 0 — vc piccolo — org, cnt — str

I. Sinfonia	7'
II. Aria: "Ich geh und suche mit Verlangen"	6'
III. Recitative: "Mein Mahl ist zubereit"	2'
IV. Aria: "Ich bin herrlich, ich bin schön"	5'
V. Recitative: "Mein Glaube hat mich selbst so angezogen"	2'
VI. Duet: "Dich hab ich je und je geliebet"	5'

Breitkopf	Carus	Kalmus	Luck's

Cantata No.50 (Nun ist das Heil und die Kraft) <1727>   5'

double chorus
0 3 0 0 — 0 3 0 0 — tmp — cnt — str
This single movement probably a fragment of a planned or lost cantata for St. Michael.

Breitkopf	Carus	Kalmus	Luck's

Cantata No.51 (Jauchzet Gott in allen Landen!) <1730>   19'

soprano solo   trumpet solo
cnt — str

I. Aria: "Jauchzet Gott in allen Landen!"	5'
II. Recitative: "Wir beten zu dem Tempel an"	3'
III. Aria: "Höchster, mache deine Güte"	5'
IV. Aria: "Sei Lob und Preis mit Ehren"	4'
V. Aria: "Alleluja"	2'

Breitkopf	Carus	Kalmus	Luck's

Cantata No.52 (Falsche Welt, dir trau ich nicht) <1726>   15'

soprano solo   chorus in final chorale only
0 3 0 1 — 2 0 0 0 — cnt — str
The *Sinfonia* is the same as the 1st mvt of the Brandenburg Concerto No.1, though without the violino piccolo.

I. Sinfonia	5'
II. Recitative: "Falsche Welt, dir trau ich nicht"	1'
III. Aria: "Immerhin, immerhin, wenn ich gleich verstossen bin"	3'
IV. Recitative: "Gott ist getreu"	1'
V. Aria: "Ich halt es mit dem lieben Gott"	4'
VI. Chorus: "In dich hab ich gehoffet, Herr"	1'

Breitkopf	Carus	Kalmus	Luck's

Cantata No.53 (Schlage doch, gewünschte Stunde)   10'

alto solo
bells — cnt — str
Wrongly attributed to Bach; actual composer is Georg Melchior Hoffmann.

Breitkopf	Kalmus	Luck's

Cantata No.54 (Widerstehe doch der Sünde) <1714>   12'

alto solo
cnt — str
Fragment of a two-part cantata.

I. Aria: "Widerstehe doch der Sünde"	7'
II. Recitative: "Die Art verruchter Sünden"	2'
III. Aria: "Wer Sünde tut, der ist vom Teufel"	3'

Breitkopf	Carus	Kalmus	Luck's

Cantata No.55 (Ich armer Mensch, ich Sündenknecht)   *14'*
<1726>

tenor solo   chorus in final chorale only
1 1[ob d'amore] 0 0 — cnt — str
Oboe d'amore part playable on oboe.

I. Aria: "Ich armer Mensch, ich Sündenknecht"	*5'*
II. Recitative: "Ich habe wider Gott gehandelt"	*2'*
III. Aria: "Erbarme dich, lass die Tränen dich erweichen"	*4'*
IV. Recitative: "Erbarme dich! jedoch nun"	*2'*
V. Chorus: "Bin ich gleich von dir gewichen"	*1'*

Breitkopf	Carus	Kalmus	Luck's

Cantata No.56 (Ich will den Kreuzstab gerne tragen)   *20'*
<1726>

bass solo   chorus in final chorale only
0 3[1.2.ob da caccia] 0 0 — cnt — str

I. Aria: "Ich will den Kreuzstab gerne tragen"	*8'*
II. Recitative: "Mein Wandel auf der Welt"	*2'*
III. Aria: "Endlich, endlich wird mein Joch"	*6'*
IV. Recitative: "Ich stehe fertig und bereit"	*2'*
V. Chorus: "Komm, o Tod, du Schlafes Bruder"	*2'*

Bärenreiter	Breitkopf	Carus	Kalmus	Luck's

Cantata No.57 (Selig ist der Mann) <1725>   *28'*

solos SB   chorus in final chorale only
0 3[1.2.ob da caccia] 0 0 — cnt — str

I. Aria: "Selig ist der Mann"	*5'*
II. Recitative: "Ach! dieser süsse Trost erquickt"	*2'*
III. Aria: "Ich wünschte mir den Tod"	*7'*
IV. Recitative: "Ich reiche dir die Hand"	*1'*
V. Aria: "Ja, ja, ich kann die Feinde schlagen"	*6'*
VI. Recitative: "In meinem Schoss liegt Ruh und Leben"	*2'*
VII. Aria: "Ich ende behende mein irdisches Leben"	*4'*
VIII. Chorus: "Richte dich, Liebste, nach meinem Gefallen"	*1'*

Breitkopf	Carus	Kalmus	Luck's

Cantata No.58 (Ach Gott, wie manches Herzeleid [II])   *12'*
<1727>

solos SB
0 3[1.2.ob da caccia] 0 0 — cnt — str

I. Duet: "Ach Gott, wie manches Herzeleid"	*4'*
II. Recitative: "Verfolgt dich gleich die arge Welt"	*1'*
III. Aria: "Ich bin vergnügt in meinem Leiden"	*4'*
IV. Recitative: "Kann es die Welt nicht lassen"	*1'*
V. Duet: "Nur getrost, ihr Herzen" — "Ich hab für mir"	*2'*

Breitkopf	Carus

Cantata No.59 (Wer mich liebet [I]) <1724>   *14'*

solos SB   chorus in chorale only
0 0 0 0 — 0 2 0 0 — tmp — cnt — str
The composer may have intended a final chorale to be appended.

I. Duet: "Wer mich liebet, der wird mein Wort halten"	*3'*
II. Recitative: "O, was sind das für Ehren"	*2'*
III. Chorus: "Komm, heiliger Geist, Herre Gott"	*2'*
IV. Aria: "Die Welt mit allen Königreichen"	*3'*

Bärenreiter	Breitkopf	Carus	Kalmus	Luck's

Cantata No.60 (O Ewigkeit, du Donnerwort [II]) <1723>   *16'*

solos ATB   chorus in final chorale only
0 2[2ob d'amore] 0 0 — 1 0 0 0 — cnt — str
Horn is used only to strengthen the cantus firmus.

I. Duet: "O Ewigkeit, du Donnerwort" — "Herr, ich warte"	*5'*
II. Recitative: "O schwerer Gang zum letzten Kampf"	*2'*
III. Duet: "Mein letztes Lager will mich schrecken"	*3'*
IV. Recitative: "Der Tod bleibt"	*5'*
V. Chorus: "Es ist genug, Herr, wenn es dir gefällt"	*1'*

Breitkopf	Carus	Kalmus

Cantata No.61 (Nun komm, der Heiden Heiland [I])   *14'*
<1714>

chorus   solos STB
0 0 0 1 — cnt — str

I. Overture: "Nun komm, der Heiden Heiland"	*3'*
II. Recitative: "Der Heiland ist gekommen"	*1'*
III. Aria: "Komm, Jesu, komm zu deiner kirche"	*4'*
IV. Recitative: "Siehe, ich stehe vor der Tür"	*1'*
V. Aria: "Offne dich, mein ganzes Herze"	*4'*
VI. Chorus: "Amen, komm du schöne Freudenkrone"	*1'*

Bärenreiter	Breitkopf	Carus	Kalmus	Luck's

Cantata No.62 (Nun komm, der Heiden Heiland [II])   *21'*
<1724>

chorus   solos SATB
0 2 0 0 — 1 0 0 0 — cnt — str
Horn used only to strengthen the cantus firmus.

I. Chorus: "Nun komm, der Heiden Heiland"	*5'*
II. Aria: "Bewundert, o Menschen, dies grosse Geheimnis"	*7'*
III. Recitative: "So geht aus Gottes Herrlichkeit"	*1'*
IV. Aria: "Streite, siege, starker Held"	*6'*
V. Recitative: "Wir ehren diese Herrlichkeit"	*1'*
VI. Chorus: "Lob sei Gott, dem Vater, g'ton"	*1'*

Bärenreiter	Breitkopf	Carus	Kalmus	Luck's

Cantata No.63 (Christen, äzet diesen Tag) <1713>   *28'*

chorus   solos SATB
0 3 0 1 — 0 4 0 0 — tmp — cnt, org — str
A later variant of the 3rd mvt calls for obligato organ (replacing solo ob).

I. Chorus: "Christen, ätzet diesen Tag"	*6'*
II. Recitative: "O selger Tag! O ungemeines Heute"	*3'*
III. Aria: "Gott, du hast es wohl gefüget"	*6'*
IV. Recitative: "So kehret sich nun heut"	*1'*
V. Aria: "Ruft und fleht den Himmel an"	*4'*
VI. Recitative: "Verdoppelt euch demnach"	*1'*
VII. Chorus: "Höchster, schau in Gnaden an"	*7'*

Bärenreiter	Breitkopf	Carus	Kalmus	Luck's

Cantata No.64 (Sehet welch eine Liebe) <1723>   *21'*

chorus   solos SAB
0 1[ob d'amore] 0 0 — 0 1[cornetto] 3 0 — cnt — str
Cornetto and 3tbn doubling choral parts.

I. Chorus: "Sehet, welch eine Liebe"	*3'*
II. Chorus: "Das hat er Alles uns getan"	*1'*
III. Recitative: "Geh, Welt! behalte nur das Deine"	*1'*
IV. Chorus: "Was frag ich nach der Welt"	*1'*
V. Aria: "Was die Welt in sich hält"	*6'*
VI. Recitative: "Der Himmel bleibet mir gewiss"	*1'*
VII. Aria: "Von der Welt verlang ich nichts"	*7'*
VIII. Chorus: "Gute Nacht; o Wesen"	*1'*

Breitkopf	Carus	Kalmus	Luck's

Cantata No.65 (Sie werden aus Saba alle kommen)   *17'*
<1724>

chorus   solos TB
2[2rec] 2[2ob da caccia] 0 0 — 2 0 0 0 — cnt — str

I. Chorus: "Sie werden aus Saba alle kommen"	*5'*
II. Chorus: "Die Kön'ge aus Saba kamen dar"	*1'*
III. Recitative: "Was dort Jesaias vorhergesehn"	*2'*
IV. Aria: "Gold aus Ophir ist zu schlecht"	*3'*
V. Recitative: "Verschmähe nicht, du, meiner Seelen Licht"	*1'*
VI. Aria: "Nimm mich dir zu eigen hin"	*4'*
VII. Choral: "Ei nun, mein Gott, so fall ich dir"	*1'*

Breitkopf	Carus	Kalmus	Luck's

Cantata No.66 (Erfreut euch, ihr Herzen) <1724> 33'

chorus   solos ATB
0 2 0 1 — 0 1 0 0 — cnt — str
Trumpet is optional.

I. Chorus: "Erfreut euch, ihr Herzen"	11'
II. Recitative: "Es bricht das Grab und damit unsre Not"	1'
III. Aria: "Lasset dem Höchsten ein Danklied erschallen"	7'
IV. Recitative: "Bei Jesu Leben freudig sein"	5'
V. Duet: "Ich fürchte nicht/zwar des Grabes Finsternissen"	8'
VI. Chorus: "Alleluja! Des solln wir alle froh sein"	1'

Breitkopf	Carus

Cantata No.67 (Halt im Gedächtnis Jesum Christ) <1724> 15'

chorus   solos ATB
1 2[2ob d'amore] 0 0 — 1[corno da tirarsi] 0 0 0 — cnt — str
Corno da tirarsi part given to trumpet in Breitkopf parts (and presumably the Kalmus reprint).

I. Chorus: "Halt im Gedächtnis Jesum Christ"	3'
II. Aria: "Mein Jesus ist erstanden"	3'
III. Recitative: "Mein Jesu, heissest du des Todes Gift"	1'
IV. Chorus: "Erschienen ist der herrlich Tag"	1'
V. Recitative: "Doch scheinet fast, dass mich der Feinde Rest"	1'
VI. Aria: "Friede sei mit euch"	5'
VII. Chorus: "Du Friedefürst, Herr Jesu Christ"	1'

Breitkopf	Carus	Kalmus

Cantata No.68 (Also hat Gott die Welt geliebt) <1725> 19'

chorus   solos SB
0 3[1.2.ob da caccia] 0 0 — 1 1[cornetto] 3 0 — vc piccolo — cnt — str
Horn strengthens cantus firmus; cornetto and 3tbn double choral parts.

I. Chorus: "Also hat Gott die Welt geliebt"	5'
II. Aria: "Mein gläubiges Herze"	4'
III. Recitative: "Ich bin mit Petro nicht vermessen"	1'
IV. Aria: "Du bist geboren mir zugute"	5'
V. Chorus: "Wer an ihn glaubet; der wird nicht gerichtet"	4'

Bärenreiter	Breitkopf	Carus	Kalmus	Luck's

Cantata No.69 (Lobe den Herrn, meine Seele [I]) <1747> 22'

chorus   solos SATB
0 3[1/ob d'am.2.3] 0 1 — 0 3 0 0 — tmp — cnt — str

I. Chorus: "Lobe den Herrn, meine Seele"	6'
II. Recitative: "Wie gross ist Gottes Güte doch"	2'
III. Aria: "Meine Seele, auf! erzähle"	6'
IV. Recitative: "Der Herr hat grosse Ding an ans getan"	2'
V. Aria: "Mein Erlöser und Erhalter"	4'
VI. Chorus: "Es danke, Gott, und lobe dich"	2'

Breitkopf	Carus

Cantata No.70 (Wachet! betet! betet! wachet!) <1723> 24'

chorus   solos SATB
0 1 0 1 — 0 1 0 0 — cnt — str

I. Chorus: "Wachet! betet! betet! wachet!"	4'
II. Recitative: "Erschrecket, ihr verstockten Sünder!"	1'
III. Aria: "Wenn kömmt der Tag"	4'
IV. Recitative: "Auch bei dem himmlischen Verlangen"	1'
V. Aria: "Lasst der Spötter Zungen schmähen"	3'
VI. Recitative: "Jedoch bei dem unartigen Geschlechte"	1'
VII. Chorus: "Freu dich sehr, o meine Seele"	1'
VIII. Aria: "Hebt euer Haupt empor"	3'
IX. Recitative: "Ach, soll nicht dieser grosse Tag"	2'
X. Aria: "Seligster Erquickungstag"	3'
XI. Chorus: "Nicht nach Welt; nach Himmel nicht"	1'

Breitkopf	Carus	Kalmus	Luck's

Cantata No.71 (Gott ist mein König) <1708> 18'

chorus   solos SATB
2[2rec] 2 0 1 — 0 3 0 0 — tmp — org — str
The above instruments constitute a fourfold orchestra:
(1) 3tp+tmp; (2) 2rec+vc solo; (3) 2ob+bn; (4) str+org

I. Chorus: "Gott ist mein König"	2'
II. Aria (Duet): "Ich bin nun achtzig Jahr" — "Soll ich auf dieser Welt"	4'
III. Chorus: "Dein Alter sei wie deine Jugend"	2'
IV. Arioso: "Tag und Nacht ist dein"	3'
V. Aria: "Durch mächtige Kraft"	1'
VI. Chorus: "Du wollest dem Feinde nicht geben"	3'
VII. Chorus: "Das neue Regiment"	3'

Breitkopf	Carus	Kalmus	Luck's

Cantata No.72 (Alles nur nach Gottes Willen) <1726> 17'

chorus   solos SAB
0 2 0 0 — cnt — str

I. Chorus: "Alles nur nach Gottes Willen"	4'
II. Recitative: "O seliger Christ"	2'
III. Aria: "Mit allem, was ich hab und bin"	4'
IV. Recitative: "So glaube nun! Dein Heiland saget"	1'
V. Aria: "Mein Jesus will es tun"	5'
VI. Chorus: "Was mein Gott will, das g'scheh allzeit"	1'

Breitkopf	Carus	Kalmus	Luck's

Cantata No.73 (Herr, wie du willt, so schicks mit mir) <1724> 15'

chorus   solos STB
0 2 0 0 — 1 0 0 0 — cnt — str
Organ may substitute for horn.

I. Chorus: "Herr, wie du willt, so schicks mit mir"	5'
II. Aria: "Ach senke doch den Geist der Freuden"	4'
III. Recitative: "Ach, unser Wille bleibt verkehrt"	1'
IV. Aria: "Herr, so du willt"	4'
V. Chorus: "Das ist des Vaters Wille"	1'

Breitkopf	Carus	Kalmus	Luck's

Cantata No.74 (Wer mich liebet [II]) <1725> 22'

chorus   solos SATB
0 3[1.2.ob da caccia] 0 0 — 0 3 0 0 — tmp — cnt — str

I. Chorus: "Wer mich liebet, der wird mein Wort halten"	3'
II. Aria: "Komm, komm, mein Herze steht dir offen"	3'
III. Recitative: "Die Wohnung ist bereit"	1'
IV. Aria: "Ich gehe hin und komme wieder zu euch"	3'
V. Aria: "Kommt, eilet, stimmet Sait und Lieder"	5'
VI. Recitative: "Es ist nichts Verdammliches an denen"	1'
VII. Aria: "Nichts kann mich erretten"	5'
VIII. Chorus: "Kein Menschenkind hier auf der Erd"	1'

Breitkopf	Carus	Kalmus	Luck's

Cantata No.75 (Die Elenden sollen essen) <1723> 40'

chorus   solos SATB
0 2[1/ob d'amore.2] 0 1 — 0 1 0 0 — cnt — str

I. Chorus: "Die Elenden sollen essen"	5'
II. Recitative: "Was hilft des Purpurs Majestät"	1'
III. Aria: "Mein Jesus soll mein alles sein"	6'
IV. Recitative: "Gott stürzet und erhöhet"	1'
V. Aria: "Ich nehme mein Leiden mit Freuden auf mich"	5'
VI. Recitative: "Indes schenkt Gott ein gut Gewissen"	1'
VII. Chorus: "Was Gott tut, das ist wohlgetan"	2'
VIII. Sinfonia	2'
IX. Recitative: "Nur eines kränkt ein christliches Gemüte"	1'
X. Aria: "Jesus macht mich geistlich reich"	3'
XI. Recitative: "Wer nur in Jesu bleibt"	1'
XII. Aria: "Mein Herze glaubt und liebt"	4'
XIII. Recitative: "O Armut, der kein Reichtum gleicht"	1'
XIV. Chorus: "Was Gott tut; das ist wohl getan"	2'

Breitkopf	Carus

Cantata No.76 (Die Himmel erzählen die Ehre Gottes) <1723>   38'

chorus   solos SATB

0 2[1/ob d'amore.2] 0 0 — 0 1 0 0 — va da gamba — cnt — str

I. Chorus: "Die Himmel erzählen die Ehre Gottes"	5'
II. Recitative: "So lässt sich Gott nicht unbezeuget"	1'
III. Aria: "Hört, ihr Völker, Gottes Stimme"	5'
IV. Recitative: "Wer aber hört, da sich der grösste Haufen"	1'
V. Aria: "Fahr hin abgöttische Zunft"	3'
VI. Recitative: "Du hast uns, Herr, von allen Strassen"	1'
VII. Chorus: "Es woll uns Gott genädig sein"	2'
VIII. Sinfonia	2'
IX. Recitative: "Gott segne noch die treue Schar"	1'
X. Aria: "Hasse nur, hasse mich recht"	3'
XI. Recitative: "Ich fühle schon im Geist"	1'
XII. Aria: "Liebt, ihr Christen, in der Tat"	3'
XIII. Recitative: "So soll die Christenheit"	1'
XIV. Chorus: "Es danke, Gott, und lobe dich"	2'

Breitkopf	Carus	Kalmus	Luck's

Cantata No.77 (Du sollt Gott, deinen Herren, lieben) <1723>   17'

chorus   solos SATB

0 2 0 0 — 0 1 0 0 — cnt — str

I. Chorus: "Du sollt Gott, deinen Herren, lieben"	5'
II. Recitative: "So muss es sein"	1'
III. Aria: "Mein Gott, ich liebe dich von Herzen"	5'
IV. Recitative: "Gib mir dabei, mein Gott, ein Samariterherz"	1'
V. Aria: "Ach, es bleibt in meiner Liebe"	4'
VI. Chorus: "Herr, durch den Glauben wohn in mir"	1'

Breitkopf	Carus

Cantata No.78 (Jesu, der du meine Seele) <1724>   21'

chorus   solos SATB

1 2 0 0 — 1 0 0 0 — cnt — str

Horn used only to strengthen the cantus firmus.

I. Chorus: "Jesu, der du meine Seele"	5'
II. Aria-duet: "Wir eilen mit schwachen doch emsigen Schritten"	5'
III. Recitative: "Ach! ich bin ein Kind der Sünden"	2'
IV. Aria: "Das Blut, so meine Schuld durchstreicht"	3'
V. Recitative: "Die Wunden, Nägel, Kron und Grab"	2'
VI. Aria: "Nun du wirst mein Gewissen stillen"	3'
VII. Chorus: "Herr, ich glaube, hilf mir Schwachen"	1'

Bärenreiter	Breitkopf	Carus	Kalmus	Luck's

Cantata No.79 (Gott der Herr ist Sonn und Schild) <1725>   16'

chorus   solos SAB

2 2 0 0 — 2 0 0 0 — tmp — cnt — str

I. Chorus: "Gott der Herr ist Sonn und Schild"	5'
II. Aria: "Gott ist unser Sonn und Schild"	4'
III. Chorus: "Nun danket alle Gott"	2'
IV. Recitative: "Gottlob, wir wissen den rechten Weg"	1'
V. Aria-duet: "Gott, ach Gott, verlass die Deinen nimmermehr"	3'
VI. Chorus: "Erhalt uns in der Wahrheit"	1'

Breitkopf	Carus	Kalmus	Luck's

Cantata No.80 (Ein feste Burg ist unser Gott) <1724>   25'

chorus   solos SATB

0 3[1/d'am.2/d'am.ob da caccia] 0 0 — 0 3 0 0 — tmp — org — str

An earlier version, Cantata No.80a, *Alles, was von Gott geboren*, consists of mvts 2, 3, 4, 6, 7 plus a final chorale (*Mit unser Macht ist nichts getan*).

The 3tp and tmp in Cantata No.80 were added ca.1744-7 by W.F. Bach.

I. Chorus: "Ein feste Burg ist unser Gott"	6'
II. Aria: "Alles was Gott geboren" — "Mit unsrer Macht ist nichts getan"	4'
III. Recitative: "Erwäge doch, Kind Gottes"	2'
IV. Aria: "Komm in mein Herzenshaus"	3'
V. Chorus: "Und wenn die Welt voll Teufel wär"	4'
VI. Recitative: "So stehe denn bei Christi blutgefärbten Fahne"	1'
VII. Duet: "Wie selig sind doch die, die Gott im Munde tragen"	4'
VIII. Chorus: "Das Wort sie sollen lassen stahn"	1'

Bärenreiter	Breitkopf	Carus	Kalmus	Luck's

Cantata No.81 (Jesus schläft, was soll ich hoffen?) <1724>   16'

solos ATB   chorus in final chorale only

2[2rec] 2[2ob d'amore] 0 0 — cnt — str

I. Aria: "Jesus schläft, was soll ich hoffen?"	4'
II. Recitative: "Herr! warum trittest du so ferne"	1'
III. Aria: "Die schäumenden Wellen von Belials Bächen"	3'
IV. Arioso: "Ihr Kleingläubigen, warum seid Ihr so furchtsam?"	1'
V. Aria: "Schweig, aufgetürmtes Meer!"	5'
VI. Recitative: "Wohl mir, mein Jesus spricht ein Wort"	1'
VII. Chorus: "Unter deinen Schirmen"	1'

Breitkopf	Carus	Kalmus	Luck's

Cantata No.82 (Ich habe genung [genug]) <1727; rev 1735>   24'

solo bass voice

0 1 0 0 — cnt — str

A later version (1735, as yet unpublished?) is for solo bass or mezzo-soprano; instrumentation is similar, but organ is required and an ob da caccia is optional.

For a version for solo soprano, see Cantata No.82a.

I. Aria: "Ich habe genung"	8'
II. Recitative: "Ich habe genung. Mein Trost ist nur allein"	2'
III. Aria: "Schlummert ein, ihr matten Augen"	9'
IV. Recitative: "Mein Gott! wenn kömmt das schöne: Nun!"	1'
V. Aria: "Ich freue mich auf meinen Tod"	4'

Breitkopf	Carus	Kalmus	Luck's

Cantata No.82a (Ich habe genung [genug]) <1714; rev 1730>   24'

solo soprano voice

1 0 0 0 — cnt — str

A 1730 version of Cantata 82, transposed for soprano from C minor to E minor, and calling for flute rather than oboe. Reconstructed by Diethard Hellmann.

I. Aria: "Ich habe genung"	8'
II. Recitative: "Ich habe genung. Mein Trost ist nur allein"	2'
III. Aria: "Schlummert ein, ihr matten Augen"	9'
IV. Recitative: "Mein Gott! wenn kömmt das schöne: Nun!"	1'
V. Aria: "Ich freue mich auf meinen Tod"	4'

Breitkopf	Carus

Cantata No.83 (Erfreute Zeit im neuen Bunde) <1724>   21'

solos ATB   chorus in final chorale only

0 2 0 0 — 2 0 0 0 — cnt — str

I. Aria: "Erfreute Zeit im neuen Bunde"	8'
II. Intonation & Recitative: "Herr, nun lässest du deinen Diener in Friede"	4'
III. Aria: "Eile, Herz, voll Freudigkeit"	7'
IV. Recitative: "Ja, merkt dein Glaube"	1'
V. Chorale: "Er ist das heil und selig Licht"	1'

Breitkopf	Carus

Cantata No.84 (Ich bin vergnügt mit meinem Glücke) <1727>   13'

soprano solo   chorus in final chorale only

0 1 0 0 — cnt — str

I. Aria: "Ich bin vergnügt mit meinem Glücke"	5'
II. Recitative: "Gott ist mir ja nichts schuldig"	1'
III. Aria: "Ich esse mit Freuden mein weniges Brot"	5'
IV. Recitative: "Im Schweisse meines Angesichts"	1'
V. Chorus: "Ich leb indes in dir vergnüget"	1'

Breitkopf	Carus	Kalmus	Luck's

Cantata No.85 (Ich bin ein guter Hirt) <1725>   18'

solos SATB   chorus in final chorale only
0 2 0 0 — vc piccolo — cnt — str
I. Aria: "Ich bin ein guter Hirt"   4'
II. Aria: "Jesus ist ein guter Hirt"   4'
III. Aria: "Der Herr ist mein getreuer Hirt"   5'
IV. Recit.: "Wenn die Mietlinge schlafen"   1'
V. Aria: "Seht, was die Liebe tut"   3'
VI. Chorus: "Ist Gott mein Schutz und treuer Hirt"   1'

| Breitkopf | Carus | Kalmus | Luck's | Ricordi |

Cantata No.86 (Wahrlich, wahrlich, ich sage euch) <1724>   14'

solos SATB   chorus in final chorale only
0 2[2ob d'amore] 0 0 — cnt — str
I. Aria: "Wahrlich, wahrlich, ich sage euch"   2'
II. Aria: "Ich will doch wohl Rosen brechen"   5'
III. Aria: "Und was der ewig gütig Gott"   2'
IV. Recit.: "Gott macht es nicht gleich wie die Welt"   1'
V. Aria: "Gott hilft gewiss"   3'
VI. Chorus: "Die Hoffnung wart' der rechten Zeit"   1'

| Breitkopf | Carus | Kalmus | Luck's |

Cantata No.87 (Bisher habt ihr nichts gebeten) <1725>   19'

solos ATB   chorus in final chorale only
0 3[1.2/da cacc.da cacc.] 0 0 — cnt — str
I. Aria: "Bisher habt ihr nichts gebetenin meinem Namen"   2'
II. Recitative: "O Wort, das Geist und Seel erschreckt"   1'
III. Aria: "Vergib, o Vater, unsre Schuld"   8'
IV. Recit.: "Wenn unsre Schuld bis an den Himmel steigt" 1'
V. Aria: "In der Welt habt ihr Angst"   2'
VI. Aria: "Ich will leiden, ich will schweigen"   4'
VII. Chorus: "Muss ich sein betrübet"   1'

| Breitkopf | Carus |

Cantata No.88 (Siehe, ich will viel Fischer aussenden) <1726>   23'

solos SATB   chorus in final chorale only
0 3[2ob d'amore.ob da cacc] 0 0 — 2 0 0 0 — cnt — str
I. Aria: "Siehe, ich will viel Fischer aussenden"   8'
II. Recitative: "Wie leichtlich könnte doch"   1'
III. Aria: "Nein, Gott ist allezeit geflissen"   4'
IV. Recitative: "Fürchte dich nicht"   3'
V. Duet: "Beruft Gott selbst, so muss der Segen"   3'
VI. Recitative: "Was kann dich denn in deinem Wandel schrecken"   3'
VII. Chorus: "Sing, bet und geh auf Gottes Wegen"   1'

| Breitkopf | Carus | Kalmus | Luck's |

Cantata No.89 (Was soll ich aus dir machen, Ephraim?) <1723>   12'

solos SAB   chorus in final chorale only
0 2 0 0 — 1 0 0 0 — cnt — str
I. Aria: "Was soll ich aus dir machen, Ephraim?"   4'
II. Recitative: "Ja, freilich sollte Gott"   1'
III. Aria: "Ein unbarmherziges Gerichte"   3'
IV. Recitative: "Wohlan! mein Herze legt Zorn"   1'
V. Aria: "Gerechter Gott, ach, rechnest du"   2'
VI. Chorus: "Mir mangelt zwar sehr viel"   1'

| Breitkopf | Carus | Kalmus |

Cantata No.90 (Es reisset euch ein schrecklich Ende) <1723>   13'

solos ATB   chorus in final chorale only
0 0 0 0 — 0 1 0 0 — cnt — str
I. Aria: "Es reisset euch ein schrecklich Ende"   6'
II. Recitative: "Des Höchsten Güte wird von Tag zu Tag neu"   1'
III. Aria: "So löschet im Eifer der rächende Richter"   4'
IV. Recitative: "Doch Gottes Auge sieht auf uns als Auserwählte"   1'
V. Chorus: "Leit uns mit deiner rechten Hand"   1'

| Breitkopf | Carus |

Cantata No.91 (Gelobet seist du, Jesu Christ) <1724>   18'

chorus   solos SATB
0 3 0 1 — 2 0 0 0 — tmp — cnt — str
I. Chorus: "Gelobet seist du, Jesu Christ"   3'
II. Recitative: "Der Glanz der höchsten Herrlichkeit" 2'
III. Aria: "Gott, dem der Erden Kreis zu klein"   3'
IV. Recitative: "O Christenheit! Wohlan"   1'
V. Aria (duet): "Die Armut, so Gott auf sich nimmt"   8'
VI. Chorus: "Das hat er alles uns getan"   1'

| Bärenreiter | Breitkopf | Carus | Kalmus | Luck's |

Cantata No.92 (Ich hab in Gottes Herz und Sinn) <1725>   28'

chorus   solos SATB
0 2[2ob d'amore] 0 0 — cnt — str
I. Chorus: "Ich hab in Gottes Herz und Sinn"   7'
II. Recitative: "Es kann mir fehlen nimmermehr"   3'
III. Aria: "Seht, seht, wie reisst, wie bricht, wie fällt"   3'
IV. Aria: "Zudem ist Weisheit und Verstand"   3'
V. Recitative: "Wir wollen nun nicht länger zagen"   1'
VI. Aria: "Das Brausen von den rauhen Winden"   5'
VII. Chorus: "Ei nun, mein Gott, so fall ich dir"   2'
VIII. Aria: "Meinem Hirten bleib ich treu"   3'
IX. Chorus: "Soll ich denn auch des Todes Weg"   1'

| Breitkopf | Carus |

Cantata No.93 (Wer nur den lieben Gott lässt walten) <1724>   19'

chorus   solos SATB
0 2 0 0 — cnt — str
I. Chorus: "Wer nur den lieben Gott lässt walten"   5'
II. Recitative: "Was helfen uns die schweren Sorgen?" 2'
III. Aria: "Man halte nur ein wenig stille"   3'
IV. Aria (duet): "Er kennt die rechten Freudenstunden" 3'
V. Recitative: "Denk nicht in deiner Drangsalshitze"   2'
VI. Aria: "Ich will auf den Herren schauen"   3'
VII. Chorus: "Sing, bet und geh auf Gottes Wegen"   1'

| Breitkopf | Carus | Kalmus | Luck's |

Cantata No.94 (Was frag ich nach der Welt) <1724>   28'

chorus   solos SATB
1 2[1/d'amore.2/d'amore] 0 0 — cnt — str
I. Chorus: "Was frag ich nach der Welt"   4'
II. Aria: "Die Welt ist wie ein Rauch und Schatten"   2'
III. Aria: "Die Welt sucht Ehr und Ruhm"   4'
IV. Aria: "Betörte Welt, betörte Welt"   5'
V. Recitative: "Die Welt bekümmert sich"   3'
VI. Aria: "Die Welt kann ihre Lust und Freud"   5'
VII. Aria: "Es halt es mit der blinden Welt"   4'
VIII. Chorus: "Was frag ich nach der Welt!"   1'

| Breitkopf | Carus | Kalmus | Luck's |

Cantata No.95 (Christus, der ist mein Leben) <1723>   16'

chorus   solos STB
0 2[1/d'amore.2/d'amore] 0 0 — 1 0 0 0 — cnt — str
I. Chorus: "Christus, der ist mein Leben"   4'
II. Recitative: "Nun, falsche Welt"   1'
III. Aria: "Valet will ich dir geben"   2'
IV. Recitative: "Ach könnte mir doch bald so wohl geschehn"   1'
V. Aria: "Ach, schlage doch bald, selge Stunde"   6'
VI. Recitative: "Denn ich weiss dies"   1'
VII. Chorus: "Weil du vom Tod erstanden bist"   1'

| Breitkopf | Carus | Kalmus | Luck's |

Cantata No.96 (Herr Christ, der einge Gottessohn) <1724>   20'

chorus   solos SATB

1[fl/sopranino rec] 2 0 0 — 1[or tbn] 0 1[or hn] 0 — vn piccolo (opt) — cnt — str

Score calls for *flauto piccolo*, by which a sopranino recorder in F is probably intended (the modern piccolo did not yet exist). In a later performance (probably 1734) Bach replaced this instrument with a violino piccolo (in that case, a transverse flute is still needed for the 3rd mvt).

    Horn used only to strengthen the cantus firmus; in performances around 1744, Bach used a trombone for this purpose.

I. Chorus: "Herr Christ, der einge Gottessohn"	5'	
II. Recit.: "O Wunderkraft der Liebe"	2'	
III. Aria: "Ach, ziehe die Seele mit Seilen der Liebe"	9'	
IV. Recit.: "Ach führe mich, o Gott, zum rechten Wege"	1'	
V. Aria: "Bald zur Rechten, bald zur Linken"	2'	
VI. Chorus: "Ertöt uns durch dein Güte"	1'	

Breitkopf   Carus

Cantata No.97 (In allen meinen Taten) <1734>   28'

chorus   solos SATB

0 2 0 1 — cnt — str

I. Chorus: "In allen meinen Taten"	5'
II. Aria: "Nichts ist es spat und frühe"	4'
III. Recit.: "Es kann mir nichts geschehen"	1'
IV. Aria: "Ich traue seiner Gnaden"	5'
V. Recit.: "Er wolle meiner Sünden"	1'
VI. Aria: "Leg ich mich späte nieder"	5'
VII. Duet: "Hat er es denn beschlossen"	3'
VIII. Aria: "Ihm hab ich mich ergeben"	3'
IX. Chorus: "So sei nun, Seele, deine"	1'

Breitkopf   Carus

Cantata No.98 (Was Gott tut, das ist wohlgetan [I]) <1726>   14'

chorus   solos SATB

0 3[1.2.ob da caccia] 0 0 — cnt — str

2nd ob and ob da caccia only double inner chorus parts.

I. Chorus: "Was Gott tut, das ist wohlgetan"	4'
II. Recit.: "Ach Gott! wann wirst du mich einmal"	1'
III. Aria: "Hört, ihr Augen, auf zu weinen"	4'
IV. Recit.: "Gott hat ein Herz, das des Erbarmens Uberfluss!"	1'
V. Aria: "Meinen Jesum lass ich nicht"	4'

Breitkopf   Carus   Kalmus   Luck's

Cantata No.99 (Was Gott tut, das ist wohlgetan [II]) <1724>   17'

chorus   solos SATB

1 1[ob d'amore] 0 0 — 1 0 0 0 — cnt — str

Horn used only to strengthen the cantus firmus.

I. Chorus: "Was Gott tut, das ist wohlgetan"	5'
II. Recit.: "Sein Wort der Wahrheit stehet fest"	1'
III. Aria: "Erschüttre dich nur nicht, verzagte Seele"	6'
IV. Recit.: "Nun, der von Ewigkeit geschlossne Bund"	1'
V. Aria (duet): "Wenn des Kreuzes Bitterkeiten"	3'
VI. Chorus: "Was Gott tut, das ist wohlgetan"	1'

Breitkopf   Carus

Cantata No.100 (Was Gott tut, das ist wohlgetan [III]) <1735>   23'

chorus   solos SATB

1 1[ob d'amore] 0 0 — 2 0 0 0 — tmp — cnt — str

I. Chorus: "Was Gott tut, das ist wohlgetan, es bleibt gerecht"	5'
II. Duet: "Was Gott tut, das ist wohlgetan, er wird mich nicht betrügen"	4'
III. Aria: "Was Gott tut, das ist wohlgetan, er wird mich wohl bedenken"	4'
IV. Aria: "Was Gott tut, das ist wohlgetan, er ist mein Licht und Leben"	4'
V. Aria: "Was Gott tut, das ist wohlgetan, muss ich den Kelch"	4'
VI. Chorus: "Was Gott tut, das ist wohlgetan, dabei will ich verbleiben"	2'

Breitkopf   Carus

Cantata No.101 (Nimm von uns, Herr, du treuer Gott) <1724>   25'

chorus   solos SATB

1 3[1.2.ob da caccia] 0 0 — 0 1[cornetto] 3 0 — cnt — str

Cornetto and 3tbn doubling choral parts.

I. Chorus: "Nimm von uns, Herr, du treuer Gott"	7'
II. Aria: "Handle nicht nach deinen Rechten"	3'
III. Recit.: "Ach! Herr Gott, durch die Treue dein"	3'
IV. Aria: "Warum willst du so zornig sein"	4'
V. Recit.: "Die Sünd hat uns verderbet sehr"	2'
VI. Aria (duet): "Gedenk an Jesu bittern Tod"	5'
VII. Chorus: "Leit uns mit deiner rechten Hand"	1'

Breitkopf   Carus

Cantata No.102 (Herr, deine Augen sehen) <1726>   23'

chorus   solos ATB

1 2 0 0 — cnt — str

I. Chorus: "Herr, deine Augen sehen nach dem Glauben"	8'
II. Recit.: "Wo ist das Ebenbild, das Gott uns eingepräget"	1'
III. Aria: "Weh der Seele, die den Schaden nicht mehr kennt"	5'
IV. Arioso: "Verachtest du den Reichtum seiner Gnade"	3'
V. Aria: "Erschrecke doch, du allzu sichre Seele"	3'
VI. Recit.: "Beim Warten ist Gefahr"	1'
VII. Chorus: "Heut lebst du, heut bekehre dich"	2'

Breitkopf   Carus   Kalmus   Luck's

Cantata No.103 (Ihr werdet weinen und heulen) <1724>   17'

chorus   solos AT

1[rec or fl] 2[2ob d'amore] 0 0 — 0 1 0 0 — cnt — str

Score calls for *flauto piccolo*, by which a recorder in D is probably intended (the modern piccolo did not yet exist). In a later performance (1731) Bach designated this part for solo violin or transverse flute.

I. Chorus: "Ihr werdet weinen und heulen"	6'
II. Recit.: "Wer sollte nicht in Klagen untergehn"	1'
III. Aria: "Kein Arzt ist ausser dir zu finden"	5'
IV. Recit.: "Du wirst mich nach der Angst"	1'
V. Aria: "Erholet euch, betrübte Sinnen"	3'
VI. Chorus: "Ich hab dich einen Augenblick"	1'

Breitkopf   Carus   Kalmus   Luck's

Cantata No.104 (Du Hirte Israel, höre) <1724>   19'

chorus   solos TB

0 3[1/d'am.2/d'am.da cacc] 0 0 — cnt — str

I. Chorus: "Du Hirte Israel, höre"	4'
II. Recit.: "Der höchste Hirte sorgt für mich"	1'
III. Aria: "Verbirgt mein Hirte sich zu lange"	4'
IV. Recit.: "Ja, dieses Wort ist meiner Seelen Speise"	1'
V. Aria: "Beglückte Herde, Jesu Schafe"	8'
VI. Chorus: "Der Herr ist mein getreuer Hirt"	1'

Breitkopf   Carus   Kalmus   Luck's   Ricordi

Cantata No.105 (Herr, gehe nicht ins Gericht) <1723>   25'

chorus   solos SATB

0 2 0 0 — 1 0 0 0 — cnt — str

I. Chorus: "Herr, gehe nicht ins Gericht"	7'
II. Recit.: "Mein Gott, verwirf mich nicht"	1'
III. Aria: "Wie zittern und wanken"	7'
IV. Recit.: "Wohl aber dem, der seinen Bürgen weiss"	2'
V. Aria: "Kann ich nur Jesum mir zum Freunde machen"	6'
VI. Chorus: "Nun, ich weiss, du wirst mir stillen"	2'

Breitkopf   Carus   Kalmus   Luck's

CANTATA NO.106 <1707>

This cantata was composed in the key of F Lydian (no B-flat). Because the organ in the church for which it was written was at a very high pitch (Chorton), the organ part was prepared in E-flat while the rest of the score was in F. Editors of the 19th-century Bach-Gesellschaft misunderstood the situation and treated E-flat as the concert key and all the other instruments (which were written in the lower Kammerton) as transposing. However, the E-flat version is impractical for the recorders; the version in F is available from Bärenreiter and Carus.

Cantata No.106 — F major version (Gottes Zeit ist die allerbeste Zeit [Actus tragicus]) <1707>   23'

chorus   solos SATB

2[2rec] 0 0 0 — 2va da gamba — cnt — [no other str]

In these editions the intended original key is restored; it is the only key that is practical for the recorders.

I. Sonatina	*3'*
IIa. Chorus: "Gottes Zeit ist die allerbeste Zeit"	*2'*
IIb. Arioso: "Ach Herr, lehre uns bedenken"	*2'*
IIc. Aria: "Bestelle dein Haus! denn du wirst sterben"	*1'*
IId. Chorus: "Es ist der alte Bund"	*3'*
IIIa. Aria: "In deine Hände befehl ich meinen Geist"	*2'*
IIIb. Arioso: "Heute wirst du mit mir im Paradies sein"	*4'*
IV. Chorus: "Glorie, Lob, Ehr und Herrlichkeit"	*2'*

Bärenreiter	Carus		

Cantata No.106 — E-flat Major version (Gottes Zeit ist die allerbeste Zeit [Actus tragicus]) <1707>   19'

chorus   solos SATB

2[2rec] 0 0 0 — 2va da gamba — cnt — [no other str]

This Breitkopf edition (with Kalmus and Luck's reprints) is based on the Bach Gesellschaft, which misinterpreted the intended key. Not playable by the recorders.

I. Sonatina	*3'*
IIa. Chorus: "Gottes Zeit ist die allerbeste Zeit"	*2'*
IIb. Arioso: "Ach Herr, lehre uns bedenken"	*2'*
IIc. Aria: "Bestelle dein Haus! denn du wirst sterben"	*1'*
IId. Chorus: "Es ist der alte Bund"	*3'*
IIIa. Aria: "In deine Hände befehl ich meinen Geist"	*2'*
IIIb. Arioso: "Heute wirst du mit mir im Paradies sein"	*4'*
IV. Chorus: "Glorie, Lob, Ehr und Herrlichkeit"	*2'*

Breitkopf	Kalmus	Luck's

Cantata No.107 (Was willst du dich betrüben) <1724>   19'

chorus   solos STB

2 2[2ob d'amore] 0 0 — 1 0 0 0 — cnt — str

Horn used only to strengthen the cantus firmus.

I. Chorus: "Was willst du dich betrüben"	*4'*
II. Recit.: "Denn Gott verlässet keinen"	*1'*
III. Aria: "Auf ihn magst du es wagen"	*3'*
IV. Aria: "Wenn auch gleich aus der Höllen"	*3'*
V. Aria: "Er richt's zu seinen Ehren"	*3'*
VI. Aria: "Drum ich mich ihm ergebe"	*3'*
VII. Chorus: "Herr, gib, dass ich dein Ehre"	*2'*

Breitkopf	Carus	

Cantata No.108 (Es ist euch gut, dass ich hingehe) <1725>   17'

chorus   solos ATB

0 2[2ob d'amore] 0 0 — cnt — str

I. Aria: "Es ist euch gut, dass ich hingehe"	*4'*
II. Aria: "Mich kann kein Zweifel stören"	*4'*
III. Recit.: "Dein Geist wird mich also regieren"	*1'*
IV. Chorus: "Wenn aber jener, der Geist der Wahrheit"	*3'*
V. Aria: "Was mein Herz von dir begehrt"	*4'*
VI. Chorus: "Dein Geist, den Gott von Himmel gibt"	*1'*

Breitkopf	Carus	Kalmus	Luck's

Cantata No.109 (Ich glaube, lieber Herr) <1723>   26'

chorus   solos AT

0 2 0 0 — 1 0 0 0 — cnt — str

I. Chorus: "Ich glaube, lieber Herr, hilf meinem Unglauben"	*7'*
II. Recit.: "Des Herren Hand ist ja noch nicht vekürzt"	*2'*
III. Aria: "Wie zweifelhaftig ist mein Hoffen"	*6'*
IV. Recit.: "O fasse dich, du zweifelhafter Mut"	*1'*
V. Aria: "Der Heiland kennet ja die Seinen"	*6'*
VI. Chorus: "Wer hofft in Gott und dem vertraut"	*4'*

Breitkopf	Carus	Kalmus

Cantata No.110 (Unser Mund sei voll Lachens) <1725>   27'

chorus   solos SATB

2 3[1/d'am.2.3/da cacc] 0 1 — 0 3 0 0 — tmp — cnt — str

I. Chorus: "Unser Mund sei voll Lachens"	*9'*
II. Aria: "Ihr Gedanken und ihr Sinnen"	*4'*
III. Recit.: "Dir, Herr, ist niemand gleich"	*1'*
IV. Aria: "Ach Herr, was ist ein Menschenkind"	*4'*
V. Duet: "Ehre sei Gott in der Höhe"	*4'*
VI. Aria: "Wacht auf! ihr Adern und ihr Glieder"	*4'*
VII. Chorus: "Alleluia! Gelobt sei Gott!"	*1'*

Breitkopf	Carus	Kalmus	Luck's

Cantata No.111 (Was mein Gott will, das g'scheh allzeit) <1725>   17'

chorus   solos SATB

0 2 0 0 — cnt — str

I. Chorus: "Was mein Gott will, das g'scheh allzeit"	*5'*
II. Aria: "Entsetze dich, mein Herze, nicht"	*3'*
III. Recit.: "O Törichter, der sich von Gott entzieht"	*1'*
IV. Aria: "So geh ich mit beherzten Schritten"	*6'*
V. Recit.: "Drum wenn der Tod zuletzt den Geist"	*1'*
VI. Chorus: "Noch eins, Herr, will ich bitten dich"	*1'*

Breitkopf	Carus	Kalmus	Luck's

Cantata No.112 (Der Herr ist mein getreuer Hirt) <1731>   14'

chorus   solos SATB

0 2[2ob d'amore] 0 0 — 2 0 0 0 — cnt — str

I. Chorus: "Der Herr ist mein getreuer Hirt"	*3'*
II. Aria: "Zum reinen Wasser er mich weist"	*4'*
III. Recit.: "Und ob ich wandert' im finstern Tal"	*2'*
IV. Duet: "Du bereitest vor mir einen Tisch"	*4'*
V. Chorus: "Gutes und die Barmherzigkeit"	*1'*

Breitkopf	Carus	Kalmus

Cantata No.113 (Herr Jesu Christ, du höchstes Gut) <1724>   25'

chorus   solos SATB

1 2[2ob d'amore] 0 0 — cnt — str

I. Chorus: "Herr Jesu Christ, du höchstes Gut"	*4'*
II. Aria: "Erbarm dich mein in solcher Last"	*5'*
III. Aria: "Fürwahr, wenn mir das kömmet ein"	*3'*
IV. Recit.: "Jedoch dein heilsam Wort, das macht"	*2'*
V. Aria: "Jesus nimmt die Sünder an"	*5'*
VI. Recit.: "Der Heiland nimmt die Sünder an"	*2'*
VII. Duet: "Ach Herr, mein Gott, vergib mirs doch"	*3'*
VIII. Chorus: "Stärk mich mit deinem Freudengeist"	*1'*

Breitkopf	Carus	Kalmus	Luck's

Cantata No.114 (Ach, lieben Christen, seid getrost) <1724>   24'

chorus   solos SATB

1 2 0 0 — 1 0 0 0 — cnt — str

Horn used only to strengthen the cantus firmus.

I. Chorus: "Ach, lieben Christen, seid getrost"	*4'*
II. Aria: "Wo wird in diesem Jammertale"	*9'*
III. Recit.: "O Sünder, trage mit Geduld"	*2'*
IV. Aria: "Kein Frucht das Weizenkörnlein bringt"	*2'*
V. Aria: "Du machst, O Tod, mir nun nicht ferner bange"	*5'*
VI. Recit.: "Indes bedenke deine Seele"	*1'*
VII. Chorus: "Wir wachen oder schlafen ein"	*1'*

Breitkopf	Carus

Cantata No.115 (Mache dich, mein Geist, bereit) <1724>   21'

chorus   solos SATB

1 1[ob d'amore] 0 0 — 1 0 0 0 — vc piccolo — cnt — str
Horn used only to strengthen the cantus firmus.

   I. Chorus: "Mache dich, mein Geist, bereit"   4'
   II. Aria: "Ach, schläfrige Seele, wie ruhest du noch?"   9'
   III. Recit.: "Gott, so für deine Seele wacht"   1'
   IV. Aria: "Bete aber auch dabei"   5'
   V. Recit.: "Er sehnet sich nach unserm Schreien"   1'
   VI. Chorus: "Drum so lasst uns immerdar"   1'

Breitkopf	Carus	Kalmus	Luck's

Cantata No.116 (Du Friedefürst, Herr Jesu Christ) <1724>   18'

chorus   solos SATB

0 2[2ob d'amore] 0 0 — 1 0 0 0 — cnt — str
Horn used only to strengthen the cantus firmus.

   I. Chorus: "Du Fredefürst, Herr Jesu Christ"   6'
   II. Aria: "Ach, unaussprechlich ist die Not"   4'
   III. Recit.: "Gedenke doch, o Jesu, dass du noch"   1'
   IV. Aria: "Ach, wir bekennen unsre Schuld"   5'
   V. Recit.: "Ach, lass uns durch die scharfen Ruten"   1'
   VI. Chorus: "Erleucht auch unser Sinn und Herz"   1'

Breitkopf	Carus

Cantata No.117 (Sei Lob und Ehr dem höchsten Gut) <1731>   22'

chorus   solos ATB

2 2[1/d'amore.2/d'amore] 0 0 — cnt — str

   I. Chorus: "Sei Lob und Ehr dem höchsten Gut"   4'
   II. Recit.: "Es danken dir die Himmelsheer"   1'
   III. Aria: "Was unser Gott geschaffen hat"   3'
   IV. Chorus: "Ich rief dem Herrn in meiner Not"   1'
   V. Recit.: "Der Herr ist noch und nimmer nicht"   2'
   VI. Aria: "Wenn Trost und Hülf ermangeln muss"   3'
   VII. Aria: "Ich will dich all mein Leben lang"   3'
   VIII. Recit.: "Ihr, die ihr Christi Namen nennt"   1'
   IX. Chorus: "So kommet vor sein Angesicht"   4'

Breitkopf	Carus	Kalmus	Luck's

Cantata No.118 [1st setting] (O Jesu Christ, meins Lebens Licht) <1737>   5'

chorus

0 0 0 0 — 2 1[cornetto] 3 0 — [no str or cnt]
Although classified in BWV as a cantata, this is actually a motet, and was probably performed out of doors at a burial service.
   The 2 high horn parts are designated *litui* [plural of *lituus*]—archaic Roman brass instruments that no longer existed in Bach's time. Though horns are apparently intended, these parts are given to 2 cornets in the Breitkopf edition.

Breitkopf	Carus

Cantata No.118 [2nd setting] (O Jesu Christ, meins Lebens Licht) <1737>   5'

chorus

0 3[1.2.ob da caccia] 0 1 — 2 0 0 0 — cnt — str
Although classified in BWV as a cantata, this is actually a motet.
   The woodwinds are optional ("*se piace*") to strengthen the vocal lines. The Breitkopf and Carus editions assign the woodwind parts to ob, Eh, & 2bn.
   The 2 high horn parts are designated *litui* [plural of *lituus*]—archaic Roman brass instruments that no longer existed in Bach's time. Though horns are apparently intended, these parts are given to 2 cornets or trumpets in the Breitkopf edition by M. Schneider and the Kalmus and Luck's reprints.

Breitkopf	Carus	Kalmus	Luck's

Cantata No.119 (Preise, Jerusalem, den Herrn) <1723>   25'

chorus   solos SATB

2[2rec] 3[1/da cacc.2/da cacc.3] 0 0 — 0 4 0 0 — tmp — cnt — str

   I. Chorus: "Preise, Jerusalem, den Herrn"   5'
   II. Recit.: "Gesegnet Land, glückselge Stadt"   1'
   III. Aria: "Wohl dir, du Volk der Linden"   4'
   IV. Recit.: "So herrlich stehst du, liebe Stadt"   2'
   V. Aria: "Die Obrigkeit ist Gottes Gabe"   3'
   VI. Recit.: "Nun! wir erkennen es und bringen dir" 1'
   VII. Chorus: "Der Herr hat Guts an uns getan"   7'
   VIII. Recit.: "Zuletzt! da du uns, Herr"   1'
   IX. Chorus: "Hilf deinem Volk, Herr Jesu Christ" 1'

Breitkopf	Carus

Cantata No.120 (Gott, man lobet dich in der Stille) <1729>   21'

chorus   solos SATB

0 2[2ob d'amore] 0 0 — 0 3 0 0 — tmp — cnt — str

   I. Aria: "Gott, man lobet dich in der Stille"   6'
   II. Chorus: "Jauchzet, ihr erfreuten Stimmen"   7'
   III. Recit.: "Auf, du geliebte Lindenstadt"   1'
   IV. Aria: "Heil und Segen soll und muss zu alter Zeit" 5'
   V. Recit.: "Nun, Herr, so weihe selbst das Regiment" 1'
   VI. Chorus: "Nun hilf uns, Herr, den Dienern dein" 1'

Breitkopf

Cantata No.120a (Herr Gott, Beherrscher, aller Dinge) <1729>

chorus   solos SATB

0 2[1/d'amore.2/d'amore] 0 0 — 0 3 0 0 — tmp — org — str
A later version of Cantata 120, incompletely preserved. Reconstruction by F. Hudson, 1955; this work may be out of print.

   I. Chorus: "Herr Gott, Beherrscher aller Dinge"   _'
   II. Recit.: "Wie wunderbar, o Gott, sind deine Werke" _'
   III. Aria: "Leit, o Gott, durch deine Liebe"   _'
   IV. Sinfonia   _'
   V. Recit.: "Herr Zebaoth, Herr unsrer Väter Gott"   _'
   VI. Aria (duet): "Herr, fange an und sprich den Segen" _'
   VII. Recit.: "Der Herr, Herr unser Gott, sei so mit euch" _'
   VIII. Chorale: "Lobe den Herren, der deinen Stand" _'

Curwen

Cantata No.121 (Christum wir sollen loben schon) <1724>   20'

chorus   solos SATB

0 1[ob d'amore] 0 0 — 0 1[cornetto] 3 0 — cnt — str
Cornetto and 3tbn doubling choral parts.

   I. Chorus: "Christum wir sollen loben schon"   4'
   II. Aria: "O du von Gott erhöhte Kreatur"   5'
   III. Recit.: "Der Gnade unermesslich's Wesen"   1'
   IV. Aria: "Johannis freudenvolles Springen"   8'
   V. Recit.: "Doch wie erblickt es dich in deiner Krippe?" 1'
   VI. Chorus: "Lob; Ehr' und Dank sei dir gesagt"   1'

Breitkopf	Carus

Cantata No.122 (Das neugeborne Kindelein) <1724>   17'

chorus   solos SATB

3[3rec] 3[1.2.ob da caccia] 0 0 — cnt — str

   I. Chorus: "Das neugeborne Kindelein"   4'
   II. Aria: "O Menschen, die ihr täglich sündigt"   6'
   III. Recit.: "Die Engel, welche sich zuvor"   2'
   IV. Aria (Trio): "O wohl uns" — "Ist Gott versöhnt" 3'
   V. Recitative: "Dies ist ein Tag, den selbst der Herr gemacht" 1'
   VI. Chorus: "Es bringt das rechte Jubeljahr"   1'

Breitkopf	Carus

Cantata No.123 (Liebster Immanuel, Herzog der Frommen) <1725>

21'

chorus   solos ATB

2 2[2ob d'amore] 0 0 — cnt — str

I. Chorus: "Liebster Immanuel, Herzog der Frommen"	5'
II. Recit.: "Die Himmelssüssigkeit"	1'
III. Aria: "Auch die harte Kreuzesreise"	5'
IV. Recit.: "Kein Höllenfeind kann mich verschlingen"	1'
V. Aria: "Lass, o Welt, mich aus Verachtung"	8'
VI. Chorus: "Drum fahrt nur immer hin"	1'

Breitkopf	Carus	Kalmus	Luck's

Cantata No.124 (Meinen Jesum lass ich nicht) <1725>

15'

chorus   solos SATB

0 1[ob d'amore] 0 0 — 1 0 0 0 — cnt — str

Horn used only to strengthen the cantus firmus.

I. Chorus: "Meinum Jesum lass ich nicht"	4'
II. Recit.: "Solange sich ein Tropfen Blut"	1'
III. Aria: "Und wenn der harte Todesschlag"	3'
IV. Recit.: "Doch ach! welch schweres Ungemach"	4'
V. Aria (Duet): "Entziehe dich eilends, mein Herze, der Welt"	5'
VI. Chorus: "Jesum lass ich nicht von mir"	1'

Breitkopf	Carus	Kalmus	Luck's

Cantata No.125 (Mit Fried und Freud ich fahr dahin) <1725>

25'

chorus   solos ATB

1 1[ob/ob d'amore] 0 0 — 1 0 0 0 — cnt — str

Horn used only to strengthen the cantus firmus.

I. Chorus: "Mit Fried und Freud ich fahr dahin"	5'
II. Aria: "Ich will auch mit gebrochnen Augen"	9'
III. Recit.: "O Wunder, dass ein Herz"	3'
IV. Aria (Duet): "Ein unbegreiflich Licht erfüllt den ganzen Kreis"	6'
V. Recit.: "O unerschöpfter Schatz der Güte"	1'
VI. Chorus: "Er ist das heil und selig Licht"	1'

Breitkopf	Carus

Cantata No.126 (Erhalt uns, Herr, bei deinem Wort) <1725>

15'

chorus   solos ATB

0 2 0 0 — 0 1 0 0 — cnt — str

I. Chorus: "Erhalt uns, Herr, bei deinem Wort"	3'
II. Aria: "Sende deine Macht von oben"	4'
III. Recit.: "Der Menschen Gunst und Macht"	2'
IV. Aria: "Stürze zu Boden schwülstige Stolze"	3'
V. Recit.: "So wird dein Wort und Wahrheit offenbar"	1'
VI. Chorus: "Verleih uns Frieden gnädiglich"	2'

Breitkopf	Carus	Kalmus

Cantata No.127 (Herr Jesu Christ, wahr' Mensch und Gott) <1725>

20'

chorus   solos STB

2[2rec] 2 0 0 — 0 1 0 0 — cnt — str

I. Chorus: "Herr Jesu Christ, wahr' Mensch und Gott"	6'
II. Recit.: "Wenn alles sich zur letzten Zeit"	1'
III. Aria: "Die Seele ruht in Jesu Händen"	8'
IV. Recit. and Aria: "Wenn einstens die Posaunen schallen"	4'
V. Chorus: "Ach Herr, vergib all unsre Schuld"	1'

Breitkopf	Carus	Kalmus

Cantata No.128 (Auf Christi Himmelfahrt allein) <1725>

18'

chorus   solos ATB

0 3[1/d'am.2/d'am.da caccia] 0 0 — 2 1 0 0 — cnt — str

I. Chorus: "Auf Christi Himmelfahrt allein"	5'
II. Recit.: "Ich bin bereit, komm, hole mich!"	1'
III. Aria: "Auf, auf, mit hellem Schall"	4'
IV. Aria (Duet): "Sein Allmacht zu ergründen"	7'
V. Chorus: "Alsdenn so wirst du mich"	1'

Breitkopf	Carus	Kalmus	Luck's

Cantata No.129 (Gelobet sei der Herr, mein Gott) <1727>

19'

chorus   solos SAB

1 2[1/d'amore.2] 0 0 — 0 3 0 0 — tmp — cnt — str

I. Chorus: "Gelobet sei der Herr, mein Gott, mein Licht"	4'
II. Aria: "Gelobet sei der Herr, mein Gott, mein Heil"	4'
III. Aria: "Gelobet sei der Herr, mein Got, mein Trost"	4'
IV. Aria: "Gelobet sei der Herr, mein Gott, der ewig lebet"	5'
V. Chorus: "Dem wir das heilig itzt"	2'

Breitkopf	Carus	Kalmus	Luck's

Cantata No.130 (Herr Gott, dich loben alle wir) <1724>

15'

chorus   solos SATB

1 3 0 0 — 0 3 0 0 — tmp — cnt — str

I. Chorus: "Herr Gott, dich loben alle wir"	3'
II. Recit.: "Ihr heller Glanz und hohe Weisheit zeigt"	1'
III. Aria: "Der alte Drache brennt vor Neid"	4'
IV. Recit.: "Wohl aber uns, dass Tag und Nacht"	1'
V. Aria: "Lass, o Fürst der Cherubinen"	5'
VI. Chorus: "Darum wir billig loben dich"	1'

Bärenreiter	Breitkopf	Carus	Kalmus	Luck's

Cantata No.131 (Aus der Tiefen rufe ich, Herr, zu dir) <1707>

26'

chorus   solos TB

0 1 0 1 — cnt — str[2 va parts; only 1 vn part]

Title often given as *Aus der Tiefe*.

Soprano and alto sing the cantus firmus in the arias for bass and tenor respectively (mvts.2&4); some consider these SA lines to be solos also, rather than choral sections.

In addition to the version in G minor (offered by Breitkopf, Carus & Kalmus), the work may legitimately be performed in A minor; Carus publishes it separately in this key.

I. Chorus: "Aus der Tiefen rufe ich, Herr, zu dir"	5'
II. Duet: "So du willst, Herr, Sünde zurechnen"	5'
III. Chorus: "Ich harre des Herrn"	5'
IV. Duet: "Meine Seele wartet auf den Herrn"	6'
V. Chorus: "Israel, hoffe auf den Herrn"	5'

Breitkopf	Carus	Kalmus	Luck's

Cantata No.132 (Bereitet die Wege, bereitet die Bahn!) <1715>

20'

solos SATB   chorus in final chorale only

0 1 0 1 — cnt — str

Final chorale missing in Bach's score, but evident from Salomo Franck's libretto. Apparently a transposition (B-flat to A) of the final chorale from Cantata No.164 is intended.

I. Aria: "Bereitet die Wege, bereitet die Bahn"	8'
II. Recit.: "Willst du dich Gottes Kind und Christi Bruder nennen"	2'
III. Aria: "Wer bist du? frage dein Gewissen"	3'
IV. Recit.: "Ich will, mein Gott, dir frei heraus bekennen"	2'
V. Aria: "Christi Glieder, ach bedenket"	4'
VI. Chorus: "Ertöt uns durch dein Güte"	1'

Bärenreiter	Breitkopf	Carus	Kalmus	Luck's

Cantata No.133 (Ich freue mich in dir) <1724>

20'

chorus   solos SATB

0 2[2ob d'amore] 0 0 — 0 1[cornetto] 0 0 — cnt — str

Cornetto used only to strengthen the cantus firmus.

I. Chorus: "Ich freue mich in dir"	5'
II. Aria: "Getrost! es fasst ein heilger Leib"	5'
III. Recit.: "Ein Adam mag sich voller Schrecken"	1'
IV. Aria: "Wie lieblich klingt es in den Ohren"	7'
V. Recit.: "Wohlan, des Todes Furcht und Schmerz"	1'
VI. Chorus: "Wohlan, so will ich mich an dich"	1'

Breitkopf	Carus	Kalmus	Luck's

Cantata No.134 (Ein Herz, das seinen Jesum lebend weiss) <1724>   26'

chorus   solos AT

0 2 0 0 — cnt — str

I. Recit.: "Ein Herz, das seinen Jesum lebend weiss"   *1'*
II. Aria: "Auf, Gläubige, singet die lieblichen Lieder"   *4'*
III. Recit.: "Wohl dir, Gott hat an dich gedacht"   *2'*
IV. Aria (Duet): "Wir danken und preisen dein brünstiges Lieben"   *9'*
V. Recit.: "Doch würke selbst den Dank in unserm Munde"   *2'*
VI. Chorus: "Erschallet, ihr Himmel, erfreue dich, Erde"   *8'*

Bärenreiter	Breitkopf	Kalmus

Cantata No.135 (Ach Herr, mich armen Sünder) <1724>   15'

chorus   solos ATB

0 2 0 0 — 0 1[cornetto] 1 0 — cnt — str

Cornetto and trombone used only to strengthen the cantus firmus.

I. Chorus: "Ach Herr, mein armen Sünder"   *6'*
II. Recit.: "Ach heile mich, du Arzt der Seelen"   *1'*
III. Aria: "Tröste mir, Jesu, mein Gemüte"   *3'*
IV. Recit.: "Ich bin von Seufzen müde"   *1'*
V. Aria: "Weicht, all ihr Übeltäter"   *3'*
VI. Chorus: "Ehr sei ins Himmels Throne"   *1'*

Breitkopf	Carus

Cantata No.136 (Erforsche mich, Gott) <1723>   19'

chorus   solos ATB

0 2[1/d'amore.d'amore] 0 0 — 1 0 0 0 — cnt — str

I. Chorus: "Erforsche mich, Gott, und erfahre mein Herz"   *4'*
II. Recit.: "Ach, dass der Fluch, so dort die Erde schlägt"   *4'*
III. Aria: "Es kömmt ein Tag, so das Verborgne richtet"   *5'*
IV. Recit.: "Die Himmel selber sind nicht rein"   *1'*
V. Aria (duet): "Uns treffen zwar der Sünden Flecken"   *4'*
VI. Chorus: "Dein Blut, der edle Saft"   *1'*

Breitkopf

Cantata No.137 (Lobe den Herren) <1725>   15'

chorus   solos SATB

0 2 0 0 — 0 3 0 0 — tmp — cnt — str

I. Chorus: "Lobe den Herren, den mächtigen König der Ehren"   *4'*
II. Aria: "Lobe den Herren, der alles so herrlich regieret"   *6'*
III. Aria: "Lobe den Herren, der künstlich und fein dich bereitet"   *4'*
IV. Aria: "Lobe den Herren, der deinen stand sichtbar gesegnet"   *3'*
V. Chorus: "Lobe den Herren, was in mir ist, lobe den Namen"   *1'*

Breitkopf	Carus	Kalmus	Luck's

Cantata No.138 (Warum betrübst du dich, mein Herz?) <1723>   18'

chorus   solos SATB

0 2[2ob d'amore] 0 0 — cnt — str

I. Chorus: "Warum betrübst du dich, mein Herz?"   *5'*
II. Recit.: "Ich bin veracht', der Herr hat mich zum Leiden"   *1'*
III. Chorus: "Er kann und will dich lassen nicht"   *3'*
IV. Recit.: "Ach süsser Trost, Wenn Gott mich nicht verlassen"   *1'*
V. Aria: "Auf Gott steht meine Zuversicht"   *5'*
VI. Recit.: "Ei nun, so will ich auch recht sanfte ruhn"   *1'*
VII. Chorus: "Weil du mein Gott und Vater bist"   *7'*

Breitkopf

Cantata No.139 (Wohl dem, der sich auf seinen Gott) <1724>   20'

chorus   solos SATB

0 2[2ob d'amore] 0 0 — cnt — str

I. Chorus: "Wohl dem, der sich auf seinen Gott"   *5'*
II. Aria: "Gott ist mein Freund; was hilft das Toben"   *6'*
III. Recit.: "Der Heiland sendet ja die Seinen"   *1'*
IV. Aria: "Das Unglück schlägt auf allen Seiten"   *6'*
V. Recit.: "Ja, trag ich gleich den grössten Feind in mir"   *1'*
VI. Chorus: "Dahero Trotz der Höllen Heer!"   *1'*

Breitkopf

Cantata No.140 (Wachet auf, ruft uns die Stimme) <1731>   29'

chorus   solos STB

0 3[1.2.ob da caccia] 0 1 — 1 0 0 0 — vn piccolo — cnt — str

A critical edition of the score with historical and analytical essays is available from Norton.

I. Chorus: "Wachet auf, ruft uns die Stimme"   *6'*
II. Recit.: "Er kommt, der Bräutgam kommt!"   *1'*
III. Duet: "Wenn kommst du, mein Heil"   *6'*
IV. Aria: "Zion hört die Wächter singen"   *4'*
V. Recit.: "So geh herein zu mir"   *2'*
VI. Duet: "Mein Freund ist mein, und ich bin dein"   *8'*
VII. Chorus: "Gloria sei dir gesungen"   *2'*

Bärenreiter	Boosey	Breitkopf	Carus	Kalmus

Cantata No.141 (Das ist je gewisslich wahr) <1740>   10'

chorus   solos ATB

0 2 0 0 — cnt — str

Wrongly attributed to Bach; actual composer is G. P. Telemann.

I. Chorus: "Das ist je gewisslich wahr"   *_'*
II. Aria: "Jesus ist der Menschen Heil"   *_'*
III. Recit.: "Wir müssen recht im Geiste nach ihm fragen"   *_'*
IV. Aria: "Jesu, Trost der geistlich Armen"   *_'*

Breitkopf

Cantata No.142 (Uns ist ein Kind geboren) <1715>   13'

chorus   solos ATB

2[2recorders] 2 0 0 — cnt — str

Actual composer believed to be Johann Kuhnau, Bach's predecessor at the Thomasschule in Leipzig.

I. Concerto   *2'*
II. Chorus: "Uns ist ein Kind geboren"   *2'*
III. Aria: "Dein Geburtstag ist erschienen"   *2'*
IV. Chorus: "Ich will den Namen Gottes loben"   *1'*
V. Aria: "Jesu, dir sei Dank gesungen"   *2'*
VI. Recit.: "Immanuel! Du wollest dir gefallen lassen"   *1'*
VII. Aria: "Jesu, dir sei Preis gesungen"   *2'*
VIII. Chorus: "Alleluia, gelobet sei Gott"   *1'*

Breitkopf	Galaxy	Kalmus	Luck's

Cantata No.143 (Lobe den Herrn, meine Seele [II]) <1714>   14'

chorus   solos STB

0 0 0 1 — 3 0 0 0 — tmp — cnt — str

Authenticity doubtful.

I. Chorus: "Lobe den Herrn, meine Seele"   *1'*
II. Choral (Aria): "Du Friedefürst, Herr Jesu Christ"   *2'*
III. Recit.: "Wohl dem, des Hülfe der Gott Jakob ist"   *1'*
IV. Aria: "Tausendfaches Unglück, Schrecken"   *4'*
V. Aria: "Der Herr ist König ewiglich"   *2'*
VI. [Aria]: "Jesu, Retter deiner Herde"   *2'*
VII. Chorus: "Gedenk, Herr Jesu, an dein Amt" — "Halleluja"   *2'*

Breitkopf	Carus

Cantata No.144 (Nimm, was dein ist, und gehe hin) <1724>   13'

chorus   solos SAT

0 2[1/ob d'amore.2] 0 0 — cnt — str

I. Chorus: "Nimm, was dein ist, und gehe hin"   *2'*
II. Aria: "Murre nicht, lieber Christ"   *5'*
III. Chorus: "Was Gott tut, das ist wohl getan"   *1'*
IV. Recit.: "Wo die Genügsamkeit regiert"   *1'*
V. Aria: "Genügsamkeit ist ein Schatz in diesem Leben"   *3'*
VI. Chorus: "Was mein Gott will, das g'scheh allzeit"   *1'*

Breitkopf	Carus	Kalmus	Luck's

Cantata No.145 (Ich lebe, mein Herze, zu deinem Ergötzen; Auf, mein Herz, des Herren Tag) <1729>   9'

chorus   solos STB

1 2[2ob d'amore] 0 0 — 0 1 0 0 — cnt — str
Oboe d'amore parts are playable on oboe.

Five mvts are by Bach; 2 initial mvts were added, probably after his death: a chorale by Bach, *Auf, mein Herz, des Herren Tag*, and the chorus *So du mit deinem Munde bekennest Jesum*, from an Easter cantata by G. P. Telemann. The title *Ich lebe, mein Herze, zu deinem Ergötzen*, is actually the 3rd mvt, but it is the first of the movements intended by Bach for this cantata.

I. Aria: "Ich lebe, mein Herze zu deinem Ergötzen"	*3'*
II. Recit.: "Nun fordre, Moses, wie du willt"	*1'*
III. Aria: "Merke, mein Herze, beständig nur dies"	*3'*
IV. Recit.: "Mein Jesus lebt"	*1'*
V. Chorus: "Drum wir auch billig fröhlich sein"	*1'*
— The following order uses the added two mvts —	
I. Chorus: "Auf, mein Herz, des Herren Tag"	
II. Chorus: "So du mit deinem Munde bekennest Jesum"	
III. Aria: "Ich lebe, mein Herze zu deinem Ergötzen"	
IV. Recit.: "Nun fordre, Moses, wie du willt"	
V. Aria: "Merke, mein Herze, beständig nur dies"	
VI. Recit.: "Mein Jesus lebt"	
VII. Chorus: "Drum wir auch billig fröhlich sein"	

Breitkopf

Cantata No.146 (Wir müssen durch viel Trübsal) <1728>   38'

chorus   solos SATB

1 3[1/d'am.2/d'am.da caccia] 0 0 — org — str
The first two mvts of this cantata are from the Harpsichord Concerto No.1 (BWV 1052).

Text of last mvt lost; new text substituted.

I. Sinfonia	*8'*
II. Chorus: "Wir müssen durch viel Trübsal"	*6'*
III. Aria: "Ich will nach dem Himmel zu"	*8'*
IV. Recit.: "Ach! wer doch schon im Himmel wär'!"	*2'*
V. Aria: "Ich säe meine Zähren"	*6'*
VI. Recit.: "Ich bin bereit"	*1'*
VII. Duet: "Wie will ich mich freuen"	*6'*
VIII. Chorus: ["Denn wer selig dahin fähret"]	*1'*

Breitkopf	Carus	Kalmus	Luck's

Cantata No.147 (Herz und Mund und Tat und Leben) <1723>   28'

chorus   solos SATB

0 2[1/d'am/da cacc.2/da cacc] 0 1 — 0 1 0 0 — cnt — str
The well-known *Jesu, Joy of Man's Desiring*, for chorus, oboe, trumpet, strings and continuo, appears twice in this cantata: the sixth movement (*Wohl mir, dass ich Jesum habe*), and the tenth and final movement, with identical music but a different text (*Jesu bleibet meine Freude*).

I. Chorus: "Herz und Mund und Tat und Leben"	*4'*
II. Recit.: "Gebenedeiter Mund"	*2'*
III. Aria: "Schäme dich, o Seele, nicht"	*4'*
IV. Recit.: "Verstockung kann Gewaltige verblenden"	*2'*
V. Aria: "Bereite dir, Jesu, noch jetzo die Bahn"	*4'*
VI. Chorus: "Wohl mir, dass ich Jesum habe"	*2'*
VII. Aria: "Hilf, Jesu, hilf, dass ich auch dich bekenne"	*3'*
VIII. Recit.: "Der höchsten Allmacht Wunderhand"	*2'*
IX. Aria: "Ich will von Jesu Wundern singen"	*3'*
X. Chorus: "Jesus bleibet meine Freude"	*2'*

Bärenreiter	Breitkopf	Carus	Kalmus	Luck's

Cantata No.147a (Herz und Mund und Tat und Leben) <1716>   15'

chorus   solos SATB   solo violin

0 1[ob da caccia] 0 1 — 0 1 0 0 — org — str
Original form of Cantata 147, which can be only partially reconstructed. Carus ed. Diethard Hellmann; Doblinger ed. Redulescu.

I. Chorus: "Herz und Mund und Tat und Leben"	*4'*
II. Aria: "Schäme dich, o Seele, nicht"	*4'*
III. Aria: "Hilf, Jesu, hilf, dass ich auch dich bekenne"	*3'*
IV. Aria: "Bereite dir, Jesu, noch jetzo die Bahn"	*4'*
V. Aria: "Lass mich der Rufer Stimmen hören" [Lost]	*_'*
VI. Chorus: "Dein Wort lass mich bekennen" [Lost]	*_'*

Carus	Doblinger

Cantata No.148 (Bringet dem Herrn Ehre seines Namens) <1723>   19'

chorus   solos AT

0 3 0 0 — 0 1 0 0 — cnt — str
3rd oboe part perhaps intended for ob da caccia.

I. Chorus: "Bringet dem Herrn Ehre seines Namens"	*4'*
II. Aria: "Ich eile, die Lehren des Lebens zu hören"	*5'*
III. Recit.: "So, wie der Hirsch nach frischem Wasser schreit"	*2'*
IV. Aria: "Mund und Herze steht dir offen"	*6'*
V. Recit.: "Bleib auch, mein Gott, in mir"	*1'*
VI. Chorus: "Amen, zu aller Stund"	*1'*

Breitkopf	Carus	Kalmus	Luck's

Cantata No.149 (Man singet mit Freuden) <1728>   18'

chorus   solos SATB

0 3 0 1 — 0 3 0 0 — tmp — cnt — str

I. Chorus: "Man singet mit Freuden vom Sieg"	*4'*
II. Aria: "Kraft und Stärke sei gesungen"	*2'*
III. Recit.: "Ich fürchte mich vor tausend Feinden nicht"	*1'*
IV. Aria: "Gottes Engel weichen nie"	*5'*
V. Recit.: "Ich danke dir, mein lieber Gott, dafür"	*1'*
VI. Duet: "Seid wachsam, ihr heiligen Wächter"	*3'*
VII. Chorus: "Ach Herr, lass dein lieb Engelein"	*2'*

Breitkopf	Carus	Kalmus	Luck's

Cantata No.150 (Nach dir, Herr, verlanget mich) <1709>   15'

chorus   solos SATB

0 0 0 1 — cnt — str[no va]
This work in B minor was probably intended to be heard in D minor, because of the discrepancy between the *Chorton* and *Kammerton* in Bach's time. However, all editions are in B minor.

I. Sinfonia	*1'*
II. Chorus: "Nach dir, Herr, verlanget mich"	*4'*
III. Aria: "Doch bin und bleibe ich vergnügt"	*1'*
IV. Chorus: "Leite mich in deiner Wahrheit"	*2'*
V. Trio: "Zedern müssen von den Winden"	*2'*
VI. Chorus: "Meine Augen sehen stets"	*2'*
VII. Chorus: "Meine Tage in den Leiden"	*3'*

Breitkopf	Carus	Kalmus	Luck's

Cantata No.151 (Süsser Trost, mein Jesus kömmt) <1725>   19'

solos SATB   chorus in final chorale only

1 1[ob d'amore] 0 0 — cnt — str

I. Aria: "Süsser Trost, mein Jesus kömmt"	*10'*
II. Recit.: "Erfreue dich, mein Herz"	*2'*
III. Aria: "In Jesu Demut kann ich Trost"	*5'*
IV. Recit.: "Du teurer Gottessohn"	*1'*
V. Chorus: "Heut schleusst er wieder auf die Tür"	*1'*

Boosey	Breitkopf	Carus	Kalmus	Luck's

Cantata No.152 (Tritt auf die Glaubensbahn) <1714>   20'

solos SB
1[rec] 1 0 0 — va d'amore, va da gamba — cnt — [no other str]
This work in E minor was probably intended to be heard in G minor,
because of the discrepancy between the *Chorton* and *Kammerton* in
Bach's time.

I. Sinfonia	4'
II. Aria: "Tritt auf die Glaubensbahn"	3'
III. Recit.: "Der Heiland ist gesetzt"	2'
IV. Aria: "Stein, der über alle Schätze"	4'
V. Recit.: "Es ärgre sich die kluge Welt"	2'
VI. Duet: "Wie soll ich dich, Liebster der Seelen, umfassen"	5'

Breitkopf	Carus	Kalmus	Luck's

Cantata No.153 (Schau, lieber Gott, wie meine Feind)   17'
<1724>

solos ATB   chorus in three chorales only
cnt — str

I. Chorus: "Schau, lieber Gott, wie meine Feind"	1'
II. Recit.: "Mein liebster Gott, ach lass dichs doch erbarmen"	1'
III. Arioso: "Fürchte dich nicht, ich bin mit dir"	2'
IV. Recit.: "Du sprichst zwar, lieber Gott, zu meiner Seele Ruh"	2'
V. Chorus: "Und ob gleich alle Teufel"	1'
VI. Aria: "Stürmt nur, stürmt, ihr Trübsalswetter"	3'
VII. Recit.: "Getrost! mein Herz"	2'
VIII. Aria: "Soll ich meinen Lebenslauf"	3'
IX. Chorus: "Drum will ich, weil ich lebe noch"	2'

Breitkopf	Carus

Cantata No.154 (Mein liebster Jesus ist verloren) <1724>   17'

solos ATB   chorus in two chorales only
0 2[2ob d'amore] 0 0 — cnt — str

I. Aria: "Mein liebster Jesus ist verloren"	3'
II. Recit.: "Wo treff ich meinen Jesum an"	1'
III. Chorus: "Jesu, mein Hort und Erretter"	1'
IV. Aria: "Jesu, lass dich finden"	4'
V. Arioso: "Wisset ihr nicht, dass ich sein muss"	1'
VI. Recit.: "Dies ist die Stimme meines Freundes"	2'
VII. Duet: "Wohl mir, Jesus ist gefunden"	4'
VIII. Chorus: "Meinen Jesum lass ich nicht"	1'

Breitkopf	Kalmus	Luck's

Cantata No.155 (Mein Gott, wie lang, ach lange) <1716>   14'

solos SATB   chorus in final chorale only
0 0 0 1 — cnt — str

I. Recit.: "Mein Gott, wie lang, ach lange"	2'
II. Duet: "Du musst glauben, du musst hoffen"	6'
III. Recit.: "So sei, o Seele, sei zufrieden"	2'
IV. Aria: "Wirf, mein Herze, wirf dich noch"	3'
V. Chorus: "Ob sichs anliess, als wollt er nicht"	1'

Breitkopf	Carus	Kalmus	Luck's

Cantata No.156 (Ich steh mit einem Fuss im Grabe)   16'
<1729>

solos ATB   chorus only in final chorale and one soprano cantus firmus
0 1 0 0 — cnt — str

I. Sinfonia	3'
II. Duet: "Ich steh mit einem Fuss im Grabe" — "Machs mit mir, Gott"	5'
III. Recit.: "Mein Angst und Not"	1'
IV. Aria: "Herr, was du willt soll mir gefallen"	5'
V. Recit.: "End willst du, dass ich nicht soll kranken"	1'
VI. Chorus: "Herr, wie du willt, so schicks mit mir"	1'

Breitkopf	Kalmus	Luck's

Cantata No.157 (Ich lasse dich nicht) <1727>   20'

solos TB   chorus in final chorale only
1 1[ob d'amore] 0 0 — cnt — str

I. Duet: "Ich lasse dich nicht, du segnest mich denn"	4'
II. Aria: "Ich halte meinen Jesum feste"	7'
III. Recit.: "Mein lieber Jesu du"	2'
IV. Aria: "Ja, ja, ich halte Jesum feste"	6'
V. Chorus: "Meinen Jesum lass' ich nicht"	1'

Breitkopf	Carus

Cantata No.158 (Der Friede sei mit dir) <1728>   12'

bass solo   chorus in final chorale & one soprano cantus firmus
1[or vn] 1 0 0 — cnt — vn[or ob]; vc &/or db
Oboe used only to strengthen the cantus firmus.

I. Recit.: "Der Friede sei mit dir"	2'
II. Duet: "Welt, ade! ich bin dein müde"	7'
III. Recit.: "Nun Herr, regiere meinen Sinn"	2'
IV. Chorus: "Hier ist das rechte Osterlamm"	1'

Bärenreiter	Breitkopf	Carus	Kalmus	Luck's

Cantata No.159 (Sehet, wir gehn hinauf gen Jerusalem)   14'
<1729>

solos ATB   chorus only in final chorale and one soprano cantus firmus
0 1 0 1 — cnt — str

I. Arioso & Recitative: "Sehet, wir gehn hinauf gen Jerusalem"	3'
II. Duet: "Ich folge dir nach" — "Ich will hier bei dir stehen"	4'
III. Recitative: "Nun will ich mich, mein Jesu"	1'
IV. Aria: "Es ist vollbracht"	5'
V. Chorus: "Jesu, deine Passion"	1'

Breitkopf	Carus	Kalmus	Luck's

Cantata No.160 (Ich weiss, dass mein Erlöser lebt)   15'
<1740>

tenor solo
0 0 0 1 — cnt — vn
Wrongly attributed to Bach; actual composer is Telemann.

I. Aria: "Ich weiss, dass mein Erlöser lebt"	_'
II. Recit.: "Erlebt und ist von Todten auferstanden!"	_'
III. Aria: "Gott Lob, dass mein Erlöser lebt"	_'
IV. Recit.: "So biet' ich allen Reufeln Trutz!"	_'
V. Aria: "Nun, ich halte mich bereit"	_'

Breitkopf	Kalmus	Luck's

Cantata No.161 (Komm, du süsse Todesstunde) <1715>   18'

chorus   solos AT
2[2rec] 0 0 0 — org — str
Bach's performance in 1735 replaced the recorders with transverse flutes.

I. Duet: "Komm, du süsse Todesstunde"	5'
II. Recitative: "Welt! deine Lust ist Last!"	2'
III. Aria: "Mein Verlangen ist, den Heiland zu umfangen"	5'
IV. Recitative: "Der Schluss ist schon gemacht;"	2'
V. Chorus: "Wenn es meines Gottes Wille"	3'
VI. Chorus: "Der Leib zwar in der Erden"	1'

Boosey	Breitkopf	Carus	Kalmus	Luck's

Cantata No.162 (Ach, ich sehe, jetzt) <1715>   17'

solos SATB   chorus in final chorale only
0 0 0 1 — 1[corno da tirarsi] 0 0 0 — cnt — str
Corno da tirarsi part given to trumpet in Breitkopf edition.

I. Aria: "Ach! ich sehe, jetzt, da ich zur Hochzeit gehe"	4'
II. Recitative: "O grosses Hochzeitfest"	2'
III. Aria: "Jesu, Brunnquell aller Gnaden"	3'
IV. Recitative: "Mein Jesu, lass mich nicht"	2'
V. Duet: "In meinem Gott bin ich erfreut"	5'
VI. Chorus: "Ach, ich habe schon erblicket"	1'

Breitkopf

Cantata No.163 (Nur jedem das Seine) <1715>   18'

solos SATB   chorus in final chorale only
0 1[ob d'amore] 0 0 — cnt — str
I. Aria: "Nur jedem das Seine"	5'
II. Recitative: "Du bist, mein Gott, der Geber aller Gaben"	2'
III. Aria: "Lass mein Herz die Münze sein"	4'
IV. Arioso [Duet]: "Ich wollte dir, o Gott"	3'
V. Duet: "Nimm mich mir und gib mich dir"	3'
VI. Chorus: "Führ auch mein Herz und Sinn"	1'

Breitkopf	Carus

Cantata No.164 (Ihr, die ihr euch von Christo nennet) <1725>   18'

solos SATB   chorus in final chorale only
2 2 0 0 — cnt — str
I. Aria: "Ihr, die ihr euch von Christo nennet"	4'
II. Recitative: "Wir hören zwar, was selbst die Liebe spricht"	2'
III. Aria: "Nur durch Lieb und durch Erbarmen"	5'
IV. Recitative: "Ach, schmelze doch durch deinen Liebesstrahl"	2'
V. Duet: "Händen, die sich nicht verschliessen	4'
VI. Chorus: "Ertöt uns durch dein Güte"	1'

Breitkopf	Carus	Kalmus	Luck's

Cantata No.165 (O heilges Geist- und Wasserbad) <1715>   12'

solos SATB   chorus in final chorale only
0 0 0 1 — cnt — str
I. Aria: "O heiliges Geist- und Wasserbad"	3'
II. Recitative: "Die sündige Geburt vedammter Adamserben"	1'
III. Aria: "Jesu, der aus grosser Liebe"	2'
IV. Recitative: "Ich habe ja, mein Seelenbräutigam"	2'
V. Aria: "Jesu, meines Todes Tod"	3'
VI. Chorus: "Sein Wort, sein Tauf, sein Nachtmahl"	1'

Breitkopf

Cantata No.166 (Wo gehest du hin?) <1724>   18'

solos ATB   chorus in final chorale and one soprano cantus firmus only
0 1 0 0 — cnt — str
I. Aria: "Wo gehest du hin?"	2'
II. Aria: "Ich will an den Himmel denken"	7'
III. Aria: "Ich bitte dich, Herr Jesu Christ"	3'
IV. Recitative: "Gleichwie die Regenwasser bald verfliessen"	1'
V. Aria: "Man nehme sich in acht"	4'
VI. Chorus: "Wer weiss, wie nahe mir mein Ende"	1'

Bärenreiter	Breitkopf	Carus	Kalmus

Cantata No.167 (Ihr Menschen, rühmet Gottes Liebe) <1723>   17'

solos SATB   chorus in final chorale only
0 1[1/ob da caccia] 0 0 — 0 1 0 0 — cnt — str
Trumpet used only to strengthen the cantus firmus.
I. Aria: "Ihr Menschen, rühmet Gottes Liebe;"	4'
II. Recitative: "Gelobet sei der Herr Gott Israel;"	2'
III. Duet: "Gottes Wort, das trüget nicht"	7'
IV. Recitative: "Des Weibes Samen kam"	1'
V. Chorus: "Sei Lob und Preis mit Ehren"	3'

Breitkopf	Carus

Cantata No.168 (Tue Rechnung! Donnerwort) <1725>   16'

solos SATB   chorus in final chorale only
0 2[2ob d'amore] 0 0 — cnt — str
I. Aria: "Tue Rechnung! Donnerwort"	4'
II. Recitative: "Es ist nur fremdes Gut"	2'
III. Aria: "Kapital und Interessen"	4'
IV. Recitative: "Jedoch, erschrocknes Herz"	2'
V. Duet: "Herz, zerreiss des Mammons Kette"	3'
VI. Chorus: "Stärk mich mit deinem Freudegeist"	1'

Breitkopf	Kalmus	Luck's

Cantata No.169 (Gott soll allein mein Herze haben) <1726>   25'

solo alto   chorus in final chorale only
0 3[2ob d'amore, ob da caccia] 0 0 — cnt, org — str
I. Sinfonia	8'
II. Arioso: "Gott soll allein mein Herze haben; zwar merk ich"	3'
III. Aria: "Gott soll allein mein Herze haben; ich find in ihm"	6'
IV. Recitative: "Was ist die Liebe Gottes"	1'
V. Aria: "Stirb in mir, Welt und alle deine Liebe"	5'
VI. Recitative: "Doch meint es auch dabei"	1'
VII. Chorus: "Du süsse Liebe, schenk uns deine Gunst"	1'

Breitkopf	Kalmus	Luck's

Cantata No.170 (Vergnügte Ruh, beliebte Seelenlust) <1726>   24'

alto solo
1[opt] 1[ob d'amore] 0 0 — org, cnt — str
Ob d'amore only doubles vn1.
I. Aria: "Vergnügte Ruh, beliebte Seelenlust;"	6'
II. Recitative: "Die Weit, das Sündenhaus"	2'
III. Aria: "Wie jammern mich doch die verkehrten Herzen"	7'
IV. Recitative: "Wer sollte sich demnach wohl hier zu leben"	2'
V. Aria: "Mir ekelt mehr zu leben"	7'

Boosey	Breitkopf	Carus	Kalmus	Luck's

Cantata No.171 (Gott, wie dein Name) <1729>   16'

chorus   solos SATB
0 2 0 0 — 0 3 0 0 — tmp — cnt — str
I. Chorus: "Gott, wie dein Name, so ist auch dein Ruhm"	2'
II. Aria: "Herr, so weit die Wolken gehen"	4'
III. Recitative: "Du süsser Jesus-Name du"	1'
IV. Aria: "Jesus soll mein erstes Wort"	5'
V. Recitative: "Und da du, Herr, gesagt"	2'
VI. Chorus: "Lass uns das Jahr vollbringen"	2'

Breitkopf	Carus

Cantata No.172 [1724 version, D major] (Erschallet, ihr Lieder) <1714; rev 1724>   20'

chorus   solos SATB
1 1[ob/ob d'amore] 0 1 — 0 3 0 0 — tmp — cnt — str[divided va]
I. Chorus: "Erschallet, ihr Lieder, erklinget, ihr Saiten!"	4'
II. Recit.: "Wer mich liebet, der wird mein Wort halten"	1'
III. Aria: "Heiligste Dreieinigkeit"	2'
IV. Aria: "O Seelenparadies, das Gottes Geist"	5'
V. Duet: "Komm, lass mich nicht länger warten"	3'
VI. Chorus: "Von Gott kommt mir ein Freudenschein"	1'
VII. Chorus: "Erschallet, ihr Lieder, erklinget, ihr Saiten!"	4'

Carus

Cantata No.172 [1731 version, C major] (Erschallet, ihr Lieder) <1714; rev 1731>   16'

chorus   solos SATB
0 0 0 1 — 0 3 0 0 — tmp — org — str[divided va]
An oboe can substitute for organ in one movement.
I. Chorus: "Erschallet, ihr Lieder, erklinget, ihr Saiten!"	4'
II. Recit.: "Wer mich liebet, der wird mein Wort halten"	1'
III. Aria: "Heiligste Dreieinigkeit"	2'
IV. Aria: "O Seelenparadies, das Gottes Geist"	5'
V. Duet: "Komm, lass mich nicht länger warten"	3'
VI. Chorus: "Von Gott kommt mir ein Freudenschein"	1'

Bärenreiter	Breitkopf	Kalmus	Luck's

Cantata No.173 (Erhöhtes Fleisch und Blut) <1724>   14'

chorus   solos SATB
2 0 0 0 — cnt — str
I. Recit.: "Erhöhtes Fleisch und Blut"	1'
III. Aria: "Ein geheiligtes Gemüte"	4'
III. Aria: "Gott will, o ihr Menschenkinder"	2'
IV. Duet: "So hat Gott ide Welt geliebt"	4'
V. Recit. [Duet]: "Undendlichster, den man doch Vater nennt"	1'
VI. Chorus: "Rühre, Höchster, unsern Geist"	2'

Breitkopf	Carus

Cantata No.174 (Ich liebe den Höchsten) <1729>   21'

solos ATB   chorus in final chorale only

0 3[1.2.ob da caccia] 0 1 — 2 0 0 0 — cnt — str[3vn, 3va, 3vc, db]

The Sinfonia to this cantata is the 1st movement of
Brandenburg Concerto No.3 (with added wind parts).

I. Sinfonia	6'
II. Aria: "Ich liebe den Höchsten von ganzem Gemüte"	8'
III. Recit.: "O Liebe, welcher keine gleicht"	2'
IV. Aria: "Greifet zu! fasst das Heil"	4'
V. Chorus: "Herzlich lieb hab ich dich"	1'

Breitkopf

Cantata No.175 (Er rufet seinen Schafen mit Namen) <1725>   16'

solos ATB   chorus in final chorale only

3[3rec] 0 0 0 — 0 2 0 0 — vc piccolo — cnt — str

I. Recit.: "Er rufet seinen Schafen mit Namen"	1'
II. Aria: "Komm, leite mich"	4'
III. Recit.: "Wo find ich dich?"	1'
IV. Aria: "Es dünket mich, ich seh dich kommen"	3'
V. Recit.: "Sie vernahmen aber nicht"	1'
VI. Aria: "Offnet euch; ihr beiden Ohren"	4'
VII. Chorus: "Nun, werter Geist, ich folge dir"	2'

Bärenreiter   Breitkopf   Carus

Cantata No.176 (Es ist ein trotzig und verzagt Ding) <1725>   14'

chorus   solos SAB

0 3[1.2.ob da caccia] 0 0 — cnt — str

I. Chorus: "Es ist trotzig und verzagt Ding"	3'
II. Recit.: "Ich meine, recht verzagt"	1'
III. Aria: "Dein sonst hell beliebter Schein"	3'
IV. Recit.: "So wundre dich, o Meister, nicht"	2'
V. Aria: "Ermuntert euch, furchtsam und schüchterne Sinne"	3'
VI. Chorus: "Auf dass wir also allzugleich"	2'

Bärenreiter   Breitkopf   Carus   Kalmus

Cantata No.177 (Ich ruf zu dir, Herr Jesu Christ) <1732>   27'

chorus   solos SAT

0 2[1/ob da cacc.2] 0 1 — cnt — str

I. Chorus: "Ich ruf zu dir, Herr Jesu Christ"	7'
II. Aria: "Ich bitt noch mehr, o Herre Gott"	7'
III. Aria: "Verleih, dass ich aus Herzensgrund"	6'
IV. Aria: "Lass mich kein Lust noch Furcht von dir"	5'
V. Chorus: "Ich lieg im Streit und widerstreb"	2'

Breitkopf

Cantata No.178 (Wo Gott, der Herr, nicht bei uns hält) <1724>   23'

chorus   solos ATB

0 2[1/d'am.2/d'am] 0 0 — 1 0 0 0 — cnt — str

Horn used only to strengthen the cantus firmus.

I. Chorus: "Wo Gott, der Herr, nicht bei uns hält"	5'
II. Recit.: "Was Menschen Kraft und Witz anfäht"	3'
III. Aria: "Gleichwie die wilden Meereswellen"	4'
IV. Aria: "Sie stellen uns wie Ketzern nach"	3'
V. Chorus & Recit.: "Aufsperren sie den Rachen weit"	2'
VI. Aria: "Schweig nur, taumelnde Vernunft"	4'
VII. Chorus: "Die Feind sind all in deiner Hand"	2'

Breitkopf   Carus   Kalmus   Luck's

Cantata No.179 (Siehe zu, dass deine Gottesfurcht) <1723>   13'

chorus   solos STB

0 2[1/da cacc.2/da cacc] 0 0 — cnt — str

I. Chorus: "Siehe zu, dass deine Gottesfurcht"	3'
II. Recit.: "Das heutge Christentum"	1'
III. Aria: "Falscher Heuchler Ebenbild"	2'
IV. Recit.: "Wer so von innen wie von aussen ist"	2'
V. Aria: "Liebster Gott, erbarme dich"	4'
VI. Chorus: "Ich armer Mensch, ich armer Sünder"	1'

Breitkopf   Carus

Cantata No.180 (Schmücke dich, o liebe Seele) <1724>   23'

chorus   solos SATB

2[1/rec1.rec2] 2[1.ob da caccia] 0 0 — vc piccolo — cnt — str

I. Chorus: "Schmücke dich, o liebe Seele"	6'
II. Aria: "Ermuntre dich: dein Heiland klopft"	6'
III. Recit.: "Wie teuer sind des heilgen Mahles Gaben?"	3'
IV. Recit.: "Mein Herz fühlt in sich Furcht und Freude"	2'
V. Aria: "Lebens Sonne, Licht der Sinnen"	4'
VI. Recit.: "Herr, lass an mir dein treues Lieben"	1'
VII. Chorus: "Jesu, wahres Brod des Lebens"	1'

Breitkopf   Carus   Kalmus   Luck's

Cantata No.181 (Leichtgesinnte Flattergeister) <1724>   14'

chorus   solos SATB

1 1 0 0 — 0 1 0 0 — cnt — str

I. Aria: "Leichtgesinnte Flattergeister"	3'
II. Recit.: "O unglückselger Stand"	2'
III. Aria: "Der schädlichen Dornen unendliche Zahl"	3'
IV. Recit.: "Von diesen wird die kraft erstickt"	1'
V. Chorus: "Lass, Höchster, uns zu allen Zeiten"	5'

Breitkopf   Carus

Cantata No.182 (Himmelskönig, sei willkommen) <1714>   31'

chorus   solos ATB

1[rec] 0 0 0 — cnt — str

I. Sonata	3'
II. Chorus: "Himmelskönig, sei willkommen"	4'
III. Recit.: "Siehe, siehe, ich komme"	1'
IV. Aria: "Starkes Lieben, das dich, grosser Gottessohn"	3'
V. Aria: "Leget euch dem Heiland unter"	8'
VI. Aria: " Jesu, lass durch Wohl und Weh"	4'
VII. Chorus: "Jesu, deine Passion"	3'
VIII. Chorus: "So lasset uns gehen in Salem der Freuden"	5'

Breitkopf   Carus   Kalmus   Luck's

Cantata No.183 (Sie werden euch in den Bann tun [II]) <1725>   14'

solos SATB   chorus in final chorale only

0 4[2ob d'am, 2ob da cacc] 0 0 — vc piccolo — cnt — str

The oboe d'amore parts are playable on oboe.

I. Recit.: "Sie werden euch in den Bann tun"	1'
II. Aria: "Ich fürchte nicht des Todes Schrecken"	7'
III. Recit.: "Ich bin bereit, mein Blut und armes Leben"	1'
IV. Aria: "Höchster Tröster, heilger Geist"	4'
V. Chorus: "Du bist ein Geist, der lehret"	1'

Breitkopf   Carus   Kalmus   Luck's

Cantata No.184 (Erwünschtes Freudenlicht) <1724>   23'

chorus   solos SAT

2 0 0 0 — cnt — str

I. Recit.: "Erwünschtes Freudenlicht"	3'
II. Duet: "Gesegnete Christen, glückselige Herde"	9'
III. Recit.: "So freuet euch, ihr auserwählten Seelen"	2'
IV. Aria: "Glück und Segen sind bereit"	5'
V. Chorus: "Herr, ich hoff je, du werdest die"	1'
VI. Chorus: "Guter Hirte, Trost der Deinen"	3'

Breitkopf   Carus

Cantata No.185 (Barmherziges Herze der ewigen Liebe) <1715>   16'

solos SATB   chorus in final chorale only
0 1 0 1 — 0 1[opt] 0 0 — cnt — str

I. Duet: "Barmherziges Herze der ewigen Liebe"	4'
II. Recit.: "Ihr Herzen, die ihr euch in Stein und Fels verkehret"	3'
III. Aria: "Sei bemüht in dieser Zeit"	4'
IV. Recit.: "Die Eigenliebe schmeichelt sich"	1'
V. Aria: "Das ist der Christen Kunst"	3'
VI. Chorus: "Ich ruf' zu dir, Herr Jesu Christ"	1'

Breitkopf   Carus   Kalmus   Luck's

Cantata No.186 (Ärgre dich, o Seele, nicht) <1723>   38'

chorus   solos SATB
0 3[1.2.ob da caccia] 0 1 — cnt — str

I. Chorus: "Ärgre dich, o Seele, nicht"	3'
II. Recit.: "Die Knechtsgestalt, die Not, der Mangel"	1'
III. Aria: "Bist du, der mir helfen soll"	3'
IV. Recit.: "Ach, dass ein Christ so sehr"	2'
V. Aria: "Mein Heiland lässt sich merken"	3'
VI. Chorus: "Ob sichs anliess, als wollt er nicht"	2'
VII. Recit.: "Es ist die Welt, die grosse Wüstenei"	2'
VIII. Aria: "Die Armen will der Herr umarmen"	3'
IX. Recit.: "Nun mag die Welt mit ihrer Lust vergehen"	1'
X. Duet: "Lass, Seele, kein Leiden"	5'
XI. Chorus: "Die Hoffnung wart' der rechten Zeit"	2'

Breitkopf   Kalmus   Luck's

Cantata No.186a (Ärgre dich, o Seele, nicht) <1716>   20'

chorus   solos SATB
0 2 0 1 — org — str
The original form of Cantata No.186. Reconstruction by Diethard Hellmann.

I. Chorus: "Ärgre dich, o Seele, nicht"	_'
II. Aria: "Bist du, der mir helfen soll"	_'
III. Aria: "Messias lässt sich merken"	_'
IV. Aria: "Die Armen will der Herr umarmen"	_'
V. Duet: "Lass, Seele, kein Leiden"	_'
VI. Chorus: "Darum ob ich schon dulde"	_'

Carus

Cantata No.187 (Es wartet alles auf dich) <1726>   23'

chorus   solos SAB
0 2 0 0 — cnt — str

I. Chorus: "Es wartet alles auf dich"	7'
II. Recit.: "Was Kreaturen hält"	1'
III. Aria: "Du Herr, du krönst allein das Jahr mit deinem Gut"	4'
IV. Aria: "Darum sollt ihr nicht sorgen"	3'
V. Aria: "Gott versorget alles Leben"	4'
VI. Recit.: "Halt ich nur fest an ihm"	2'
VII. Chorus: "Gott hat die Erde zugericht'"	2'

Breitkopf   Carus   Kalmus   Luck's

Cantata No.188 (Ich habe meine Zuversicht) <1728>   26'

solos SATB   chorus in final chorale only
0 3[1.2.ob da caccia] 0 0 — cnt, org — str
Includes the sinfonia of Cantata no.146, which is believed to belong with this work. (This sinfonia is also the 3rd mvt of the harpsichord concerto BWV 1052.) Ed. W. Breig.

I. Sinfonia [from Cantata no.146]	8'
II. Aria: "Ich habe meine Zuversicht"	8'
III. Recit.: "Gott meint es gut mit jedermann"	2'
IV. Aria: "Unerforschlich ist die Weise"	6'
V. Recit.: "Die Macht der Welt verlieret sich"	1'
VI. Chorus: "Auf meinen lieben Gott"	1'

Breitkopf

Cantata No.189 (Meine Seele rühmt und preist) <1710>   20'

solo tenor
1[rec] 1 0 0 — cnt — solo violin
Wrongly attributed to Bach; the actual composer is Georg Melchior Hoffmann.

I. Aria: "Meine Seele rühmt und preist"	_'
II. Recit.: "Denn seh' ich mich"	_'
III. Aria: "Gott hat sich hoch gesetzet"	_'
IV. Recit.: "O was vor grosse Dinge"	_'
V. Aria: "Deine Güt, dein Erbarmen währet"	_'

Breitkopf   Kalmus   Luck's

Cantata No.190 (Singet dem Herrn ein neues Lied!) <1724>   16'

chorus   solos ATB
0 3[1/d'amore.2.3] 0 1 — 0 3 0 0 — tmp — cnt — str
Portions of the first two movements were lost and have been reconstructed by Diethard Hellmann.

I. Chorus: "Singet dem Herrn ein neues Lied!"	4'
II. Chorus and Recit.: "Herr Gott, dich loben wir!"	2'
III. Aria: "Lobe, Zion, deinen Gott"	3'
IV. Recit.: "Es wünsche sich die Welt"	1'
V. Duet: "Jesus soll mein alles sein"	3'
VI. Recit.: "Nun, Jesus gebe, dass mit dem neuen Jahr"	2'
VII. Chorus: "Lass uns das Jahr vollbringen"	7'

Breitkopf

Cantata No.190a (Singet dem Herrn ein neues Lied!) <1724; rev 1730>   15'

chorus   solos ATB
0 3[1/d'amore.2.3] 0 1 — 0 3 0 0 — tmp — cnt — str
A version of Cantata No.190 prepared for the 200-year celebration of the Augsburg Confession. Mvts 1-3 were taken over exactly. Mvt 5 uses a new text. The recitatives mvts 4 & 6 were new, and the music has not survived. Mvt 7 is a different chorale from that of the source cantata. Breitkopf reconstruction by Diethard Hellmann; Carus reconstruction by Masato & Masaaki Suzuki (listed by Carus as Cantata No.190).

I. Chorus: "Singet dem Herrn ein neues Lied!"	_'
II. Chorus and Recit.: "Herr Gott, dich loben wir!"	_'
III. Aria: "Lobe, Zion, deinen Gott"	_'
IV. Recit.: "Herr, wenn dein Evangelium" [Lost]	_'
V. Duet: "Selig sind wir durch das Wort"	_'
VI. Recit.: "Nun, Gott, dir opfern wir" [Lost]	_'
VII. Chorus: "Es danke Gott und lobe dich"	_'

Breitkopf   Carus

Cantata No.191 (Gloria in excelsis Deo) <1740>   15'

chorus   solos ST
2 2 0 0 — 0 3 0 0 — tmp — cnt — str
Three mvts from Bach's *Mass in B Minor*, slightly altered.

I. Chorus: "Gloria in excelsis Deo"	7'
II. Duet: "Gloria Patri et Filio et Spiritui sancto"	4'
III. Chorus: "Sicut erat in principio"	4'

Breitkopf   Schirmer   Kalmus   Luck's

Cantata No.192 (Nun danket alle Gott) <1730>   12'

chorus   solos SB
2 2 0 0 — cnt — str
The tenor part of the chorus is lost and has been reconstructed.

I. Chorus: "Nun danket alle Gott"	5'
II. Duet: "Der ewig reiche Gott"	4'
III. Chorus: "Lob, Ehr und Preis sei Gott"	3'

Breitkopf   Carus   Kalmus   Luck's

Cantata No.193 (Ihr Tore [Pforten] zu Zion) <1727>   20'

chorus   solos SA

0 2 0 0 — 0 3 0 0 — tmp — cnt — str

Missing parts have been reconstructed.

I. Chorus: "Ihr Tore zu Zion"	4'
II. Recit.: "Der Hüter Israel entschläft"	1'
III. Aria: "Gott, wir danken deiner Güte"	6'
IV. Recit.: "O Leipziger Jerusalem"	1'
V. Aria: "Sende, Herr, den Segen ein"	3'
VI. Recit.: [Lost]	1'
VII. Chorus: "Ihr Tore zu Zion" [repetition of mvt 1]	4'

Carus	Doblinger

Cantata No.194 (Höchsterwünschtes Freudenfest) <1723>   40'

chorus   solos STB

0 3 0 1 — cnt — str

I. Chorus: "Höchsterwünschtes Freudenfest"	5'
II. Recit.: "Unendlich grosser Gott"	1'
III. Aria: "Was des Höchsten Glanz erfüllt"	5'
IV. Recit.: "Wie könnte dir, du höchstes Angesicht"	1'
V. Aria: "Hilf, Gott, dass es uns gelingt"	6'
VI. Chorus: "Heilger Geist ins Himmels Throne"	2'
VII. Recit.: "Ihr Heiligen, erfreuet euch"	1'
VIII. Aria: "Des Höchsten Gegenwart allein"	4'
IX. Recit.: "Kann wohl ein Mensch zu Gott"	2'
X. Duet: "O wie wohl ist uns geschehen"	9'
XI. Recit.: "Wohlan demnoch, du heilige Gemeine"	1'
XII. Chorus: "Sprich Ja zu meinen Taten"	1'

Breitkopf

Cantata No.195 (Dem Gerechten muss das Licht) <1737>   18'

chorus   solos SB

2 2[1/d'amore.2/d'amore] 0 0 — 2 3 0 0 — tmp — cnt — str

SATB solos from chorus used as a concertante.

I. Chorus: "Dem Gerechten muss das Licht"	5'
II. Recit.: "Dem Greudenlicht gerechter Frommen"	1'
III. Aria: "Rühmet Gottes Güt und Treu"	4'
IV. Recit.: "Wohlan; so knüpfet denn ein Band"	1'
V. Chorus: "Wir kommen; deine Heiligkeit"	6'
VI. Chorus: "Nun danket all und bringet Ehr"	1'

Breitkopf	Kalmus	Luck's

Cantata No.196 (Der Herr Denket an uns) <1708>   11'

chorus   solos STB

cnt — str

I. Sinfonia	2'
II. Chorus: "Der Herr denket an uns"	2'
III. Aria: "Er segnet, die den Herrn fürchten"	2'
IV. Duet: "Der Herr segne euch"	2'
V. Chorus: "Ihr seid die Gesegneten das Herrn"	3'

Breitkopf	Kalmus	Luck's

Cantata No.197 (Gott ist unsre Zuversicht) <1742>   31'

chorus   solos SAB

0 2[1/d'amore.2/d'amore] 0 1 — 0 3 0 0 — tmp — cnt — str

I. Chorus: "Gott ist unsre Zuversicht"	6'
II. Recit.: "Gott ist und bleibt der beste Sorger"	1'
III. Aria: "Schläfert allen Sorgenkummer"	7'
IV. Recit.: "Drum folget Gott und seinem Triebe"	1'
V. Chorus: "Du süsse Lieb, schenk uns deine Gunst"	1'
VI. Aria: "O du angenehmes Paar"	6'
VII. Recit.: "So wie es Gott mit dir getreu und väterlich"	2'
VIII. Aria: "Vergnügen und Lust"	5'
IX. Recit.: "Und dieser frohe Lebenslauf"	1'
X. Chorus: "So wandelt froh auf Gottes Wegen"	1'

Breitkopf	Luck's

Cantata No.197a (Ehre sei Gott in der Höhe) <1728>   11'

solos AB   chorus only in final chorale

2 1[ob d'amore] 0 1[or vc] — cnt — str

Mvts 1-3 lost; mvts 4-7 reconstructed by Diethard Hellmann.

I. [Chorus: "Ehre sei Gott in der Höhe"] Lost	_'
II. [Aria: "Erzählet; ihr Himmel; die Ehre Gottes"] Lost	_'
III. [Recit.: "O Liebe, der kein Lieben gleich"] Lost	_'
IV. Aria: "O du angenehmer Schatz"	5'
V. Recit.: "Das Kind ist mein und ich bin sein"	1'
VI. Aria: "Ich lasse dich nicht"	4'
VII. Chorus: "Wohlan! so will ich mich"	1'

Carus

Cantata No.198 (Lass, Fürstin, lass noch einen Strahl) <1727>   31'

chorus   solos SATB

2 2[2ob d'amore] 0 0 — 2lute, 2va da gamba — org, hpsd — str

Mvts 1, 3, 5, 8, & 10 are from the lost *St. Mark Passion*.
Breitkopf edition by Hans Grüss.

I. Chorus: "Lass, Fürstin, lass noch einen Strahl"	5'
II. Recit.: "Dein Sachsen, dein bestürztes Meissen"	1'
III. Aria: "Verstummt, verstummt, ihr holden saiten"	4'
IV. Recit.: "Der glocken bebendes Getön"	1'
V. Aria: "Wie starb die Heldin so vergnügt"	7'
VI. Recit.: "Ihr Leben liess die Kunst zu sterben"	1'
VII. Chorus: "An dir, du Fürbild grosser Frauen"	2'
VIII. Aria: "Der Ewigkeit saphirnes Haus"	4'
IX. Recit.: "Was Wunder ists? Du bist es wert"	2'
X. Chorus: "Doch, Königin, du stirbest nicht"	4'

Breitkopf	Carus	Kalmus	Luck's

Cantata No.199 (Mein Herze schwimmt im Blut) <1714>   25'

soprano solo

0 1 0 1 — cnt — str

I. Recit.: "Mein Herze schwimmt im Blut"	2'
II. Aria: "Stumme Seufzer, stille Klagen"	9'
III. Recit.: "Doch Gott muss mir genädig sein"	1'
IV. Aria: "Tief gebückt und voller Reue"	7'
V. Recit.: "Auf diese Schmerzensreu"	1'
VI. Aria: "Ich, dein betrübtes Kind"	2'
VII. Recit.: "Ich lege mich in diese Wunden"	1'
VIII. Aria: "Wie freudig ist mein Herz"	2'

Breitkopf	Carus	Kalmus	Luck's

Cantata No.200 (Bekennen will ich seinen Namen) <1735>   4'

alto solo

cnt — str

Only one aria surviving from an otherwise lost cantata. Peters listed two versions not as a cantata, but as an aria: catalog no. 4209: *Bekennen will ich seinen Namen* (ed. Landshoff); catalog no. 66032: *With Joyful Heart I Praise My Saviour*. However, these may be out of print.

Peters

Cantata No.201 (Der Streit zwischen Phoebus und Pan) <1729>   *49'*

chorus   solos SATTBB
2 2[1/ob d'amore.2] 0 0 — 0 3 0 0 — tmp — cnt — str
Characters: Momum (S), Mercurius (A), Tmolus (T), Midas (T), Phoebus (B), Pan (B).

I. Chorus: "Geschwinde, ihr wirbelnden Winde"	*5'*
II. Recit.: "Und du bist doch so unverschämt und frei"	*2'*
III. Aria: "Patron, das macht der Wind"	*2'*
IV. Recit.: "Was braucht ihr euch zu zanken?"	*1'*
V. Aria: "Mit verlangen drück ich deine zarten Wangen"	*10'*
VI. Recit.: "Pan, rücke deine Kehle"	*1'*
VII. Aria: "Zu Tanze, zu Sprunge, so wackelt das Herz"	*5'*
VIII. Recit.: "Nunmehro Richter her"	*1'*
IX. Aria: "Phoebus, deine Melodei"	*6'*
X. Recit.: "Komm, Midas, sage du"	*1'*
XI. Aria: "Pan ist Meister, lasst ihn gehn"	*5'*
XII. Recit.: "Wie, Midas, bist du toll"	*1'*
XIII. Aria: "Aufgeblasne Hitze, aber wenig Grütze"	*6'*
XIV. Recit.: "Du guter Midas, geh nun hin"	*1'*
XV. Chorus: "Labt das Herz, ihr holden Saiten"	*2'*

Breitkopf	Kalmus	Luck's

Cantata No.202 (Weichet nur, betrübte Schatten) <1723>   *25'*

soprano solo
0 1 0 0 — cnt — str

I. Aria: "Weichet nur, betrübte Schatten"	*7'*
II. Recit.: "Die Welt wird wieder neu"	*1'*
III. Aria: "Phoebus eilt mit schnellen Pferden"	*4'*
IV. Recit.: "Drum sucht auch Amor"	*1'*
V. Aria: "Wenn die Frühlingslüfte streichen"	*3'*
VI. Recit.: "Und dieses ist das Glücke"	*1'*
VII. Aria: "Sich üben im Lieben"	*5'*
VIII. Recit.: "So sei das Band der keuschen Liebe"	*1'*
IX. Aria (Gavotte): "Sehet in Zufriedenheit"	*2'*

Breitkopf	Kalmus	Luck's	Peters

Cantata No.203 (Amore traditore) <1725>   *15'*

bass solo   hpsd
hpsd — [no str]
Of doubtful authenticity.

I. Aria: "Amore traditore"	*7'*
II. Recit.: "Voglio provar, se posso"	*1'*
III. Aria: "Chi in amore ha nemica la sorte"	*7'*

Breitkopf

Cantata No.204 (Ich bin in mir vergnügt) <1726-27>   *30'*

solo soprano
1 2 0 0 — cnt — str

I. Recit.: "Ich bin in mir vergnügt"	*2'*
II. Aria: "Ruhig und in sich zufrieden"	*7'*
III. Recit.: "Ihr Seelen, die ihr ausser euch"	*2'*
IV. Aria: "Die Schätzbarkeit der weiten Erden"	*4'*
V. Recit.: "Schwer ist es zwar"	*2'*
VI. Aria: "Meine Seele sei vergnügt"	*6'*
VII. Recit.: "Ein edler Mensch ist Perlenmuscheln gleich"	*3'*
VIII. Aria: "Himmlische Vergnügsamkeit"	*4'*

Breitkopf

Cantata No.205 (Zerreisset, zersprenget, zertrümmert die Gruft [Der zufriedengestellte Äolus]) <1726 or 1727>   *41'*

chorus   solos SATB
2 2[1/ob d'amore.2] 0 0 — 2 3 0 0 — va d'amore, va da gamba — tmp — cnt — str
Characters: Pallas (S), Pomona (A), Zephyrus (T), Äolus (B).

I. Chorus: "Zerreisset, zersprenget, zertrümmert die Gruft"	*6'*
II. Recit.: "Ja! ja! die Stunden sind nunmehro nah"	*2'*
III. Aria: "Wie will ich lustig lachen"	*4'*
IV. Recit.: "Gefürcht'ter Aolus"	*1'*
V. Aria: "Frische Schatten, meine Freude"	*5'*
VI. Recit.: "Beinahe wirst du mich bewegen"	*1'*
VII. Aria: "Können nicht die roten Wangen"	*3'*
VIII. Recit.: "So willst du, grimm'ger Aolus"	*1'*
IX. Aria: "Angenehmer Zephyrus"	*4'*
X. Recit.: "Mein Aolus, ach, störe nicht die Fröhlichkeiten"	*2'*
XI. Aria: "Zurücke, geflügelten Winde"	*3'*
XII. Recit.[trio]: "Was Lust! Was Freude! Welch Vergnügen!"	*2'*
XIII. Aria [duet]: "Zweig und Aste zollen dir"	*3'*
XIV. Recit.: "Ja, ja! ich lad euch selbst zu dieser Feier ein"	*1'*
XV. Chorus: "Vivat! August, August vivat"	*3'*

Breitkopf	Kalmus	Luck's

Cantata No.206 (Schleicht, spielende Wellen) <1736>   *43'*

chorus   solos SATB
3 2[1/d'am.2/d'am] 0 0 — 0 3 0 0 — tmp — cnt — str
Characters: Pleisse (S), Donau (A), Elbe (T), Weichsel (B).

I. Chorus: "Schleicht, spielende Wellen"	*7'*
II. Recit.: "O glückliche Veränderung"	*1'*
III. Aria: "Schleuss des Janustempels Türen"	*5'*
IV. Recit.: "So recht, beglückter Weichselstrom"	*2'*
V. Aria: "Jede Woge meiner Wellen"	*8'*
VI. Recit.: "Ich nehm zugleich an deiner Freude teil"	*1'*
VII. Aria: "Reis von Habsburgs hohem Stamme"	*7'*
VIII. Recit.: "Verzeiht, bemooste Häupter starker Ströme"	*2'*
IX. Aria: "Hört doch! der sanften Flöten Chor"	*4'*
X. Recit.: "Ich muss, ich will gehorsam sein"	*2'*
XI. Chorus: "Die himmlische Vorsicht der ewigen Güte"	*4'*

Bärenreiter	Breitkopf	Kalmus	Luck's

Cantata No.207 (Vereinigte Zwietracht der wechselnden Saiten) <1726>   *32'*

chorus   solos SATB
2 3[2ob d'am.ob da cacc] 0 0 — 0 3 0 0 — tmp — cnt — str
Characters: Glück (S), Dankbarkeit (A), Fleiss (T), Ehre (B).
Cantatas 207 and 207a are the same, except for text and recitatives.

I. Chorus: "Vereinigte Zwietracht der wechselnden Saiten"	*_'*
II. Recit.: "Wen treibt ein edler Trieb"	*_'*
III. Aria: "Zieht euren Fuss nur nicht zurücke"	*_'*
IV. Recit.: "Dem nur allein soll meine Wohnung"	*_'*
V. Aria [Duet]: "Den soll mein Lorbeer schützend decken"	*_'*
VI. Recit.: "Es ist kein leeres Wort"	*_'*
VII. Aria: "Atzet dieses Angedenken"	*_'*
VIII. Recit.: "Ihr Schläfrigen; herbei!"	*_'*
IX. Chorus: "Kortte lebe, Kortte blühe"	*_'*
Anhang: Marsch	*_'*

Bärenreiter	Breitkopf	Kalmus	Luck's

Cantata No.207a (Auf, schmetternde Töne) <1735>   *31'*

chorus   solos SATB
2 3[2ob d'am.ob da cacc] 0 0 — 0 3 0 0 — tmp — cnt — str
Cantatas 207 and 207a are the same, except for text and recitatives.

I. Chorus: "Auf, schmetternde Töne der muntern Trompeten"	_'
II. Recit.: "Die stille Pleisse spielt"	_'
III. Aria: "Augustus' Namenstages Schimmer"	_'
IV. Recit.[duet]: "Augustus Wohl ist der treuen Sachsen Wohlergehn"	_'
V. Aria [duet]: "Mich kann die süsse ruhe laben"	_'
VI. Recit.: "Augustus schützt die frohen Felder"	_'
VII. Aria: "Preiset späte Folgezeiten"	_'
VIII. Recit.: "Ihr Fröhlichen, herbei!"	_'
IX. Chorus: "August lebe, lebe König"	_'
Anhang: March	_'

> Breitkopf

Cantata No.208 (Was mir behagt) <1713>   *35'*

chorus   solos SSTB
2[2rec] 3[1.2.ob da caccia] 0 1 — 2 0 0 0 — cnt — str
Characters: Diana (S), Pales (S), Endymion (T), Pan (B).
    The well-known aria *Sheep May Safely Graze* (for soprano, 2rec & cnt) is movement 9 of this cantata.

I. Recit.: "Was mir behagt, ist nur die muntre Jagd!"	1'
II. Aria: "Jagen ist die Lust der Götter"	2'
III. Recit.: "Wie? schönste Göttin, wie?"	1'
IV. Aria: "Willst du dich nicht mehr ergötzen"	5'
V. Recit.[duet]: "Ich liebe dich zwar noch"	2'
VI. Recit.: "Ich, der ich sonst ein Gott"	1'
VII. Aria: "Ein Fürst ist seines Landes Pan"	3'
VIII. Recit.: "Soll denn der Pales Opfer hier das letzte sein"	1'
IX. Aria: "Schafe können sicher weiden"	5'
X. Recit.: "So stimmt mit ein"	1'
XI. Chorus: "Lebe, Sonne dieser Erden"	3'
XII. Duet: "Entzücket uns beide"	2'
XIII. Aria: "Weil die wollenreichen Herden"	2'
XIV. Aria: "Ihr Felder unf Auen"	3'
XV. Chorus: "Ihr lieblichste Blicke, ihr freudige Stunden"	3'

> Bärenreiter   Breitkopf   Kalmus   Luck's

Cantata No.209 (Non sa che sia dolore) <1734>   *25'*

soprano solo
1 0 0 0 — cnt — str

I. Sinfonia	8'
II. Recit.: "Non sa che sia dolore"	1'
III. Aria: "Parti pur, e con dolore"	9'
IV. Recit.: "Tuo saver al tempo"	1'
V. Aria: "Ricetti gramezza e pavento"	6'

> Breitkopf   Kalmus   Luck's

Cantata No.210 (O holder Tag, erwünschte Zeit) <1740>   *32'*

soprano solo
1 1[ob d'amore] 0 0 — cnt — str

I. Recit.: "O holder Tag, erwünschte Zeit"	1'
II. Aria: "Spielet, ihr beseelten Lieder"	7'
III. Recit.: "Doch haltet ein, ihr muntern Saiten"	1'
IV. Aria: "Ruhet hie, matte Töne"	6'
V. Recit.: "So glaubt man denn, dass die Musik verführe"	2'
VI. Aria: "Schweigt, ihr Flöten, schweigt, ihr Töne"	4'
VII. Recit.: "Was Luft, was Grab"	2'
VIII. Aria: "Grosser Gönner, dein Vergnügen"	3'
IX. Recit.: "Hochteurer Mann, so fahre ferner fort"	1'
X. Aria: "Seid beglückt, edle Beide"	5'

> Breitkopf

Cantata No.211 (Coffee Cantata [Schweigt stille]) <1735>   *26'*

solos STB   optional chorus (STB) in last movement
1 0 0 0 — cnt — str
Characters: Lieschen (S), Schlendrian (B), Narrator (T).

I. Recit.: "Schweigt stille, plaudert nicht"	1'
II. Aria: "Hat man nicht mit seinen Kindern"	3'
III. Recit.: "Du böses Kind, du loses Mädchen"	1'
IV. Aria: "Ei, wie schmeckt der Coffee süsse"	4'
V. Recit.: "Wenn du mir nicht den Coffee lässt"	1'
VI. Aria: "Mädchen, die von harten Sinnen"	3'
VII. Recit.: "Nun folge, was dein Vater spricht"	1'
VIII. Aria: "Heute noch, lieber Vater, tut es doch"	1'
IX. Recit.: "Nun geht und sucht der alte Schlendrian"	1'
X. Chorus: "Die Katze lässt das Mausen nicht"	4'

> Breitkopf   Kalmus   Luck's   Ricordi

Cantata No.212 (Peasant Cantata [Mer hahn en neue Oberkeet]) <1742>   *38'*

solos SB
1 0 0 0 — 1 0 0 0 — cnt — str

I. Overture	2'
II. Aria [duet]: "Mer hahn en neue Oberkeet"	1'
III. Recit.[duet]: "Nu, Mieke, gib dein Guschel immer her"	1'
IV. Recit.: "Ach es schmeckt doch gar zu gut"	1'
V. Recit.: "Der Herr ist gut: Allein der Schösser"	1'
VI. Aria: "Ach, Herr Schösser, geht nicht gar zu schlimm"	1'
VII. Recit.: "Es bleibt dabei, dass unser Herr der beste sei"	1'
VIII. Aria: "Unser trefflicher, lieber Kammerherr"	2'
IX. Recit.[duet]: "Er hilft uns allen, alt und jung"	1'
X. Aria: "Das ist galant, es spricht niemand"	1'
XI. Recit.: "Und unsre gnädge Frau"	1'
XII. Aria: "Fünfzig Taler bares Geld"	1'
XIII. Recit.: "Im Ernst ein Wort"	1'
XIV. Aria: "Klein-Zschocher müsse so zart und süsse"	7'
XV. Recit.: "Das ist zu klug vor dich"	1'
XVI. Aria: "Es nehme zehntausend Dukaten"	1'
XVII. Recit.: "Das klingt zu liederlich"	1'
XVIII. Aria: "Gib, Schöne, viel Söhne"	2'
XIX. Recit.: "Du hast wohl recht"	1'
XX. Aria: "Dein Wachstum sei feste"	6'
XXI. Recit.: "Und damit sei es auch genung"	1'
XXII. Recit.: "Und dass ihrs alle wisst"	1'
XXIII. Recit.: "Mein Schatz, erraten!"	1'
XXIV. Duet or Chorus: "Wir gehn nun, wo der Dudelsack"	1'

> Breitkopf   Kalmus   Luck's   Peters

Cantata No.213 (Lasst uns sorgen, lasst uns wachen [Hercules auf dem Scheidewege]) <1733>   *47'*

chorus   solos SATB
0 2[1/ob d'amore.2] 0 0 — 2 0 0 0 — cnt — str
Characters: Wollust (S), Hercules (A), Tugend (T), Mercur (B).

I. Chorus: "Lasst uns sorgen, lasst uns wachen"	7'
II. Recit.: "Und wo? Wo ist die rechte Bahn"	1'
III. Aria: "Schlafe, mein Liebster, und pflege der Ruh"	9'
IV. Recit.: "Auf! folge meiner Bahn"	1'
V. Aria: "Treues Echo dieser Orten"	5'
VI. Recit.: "Mein hoffnungsvoller Held"	1'
VII. Aria: "Auf meinen Flügeln sollst du schweben"	5'
VIII. Recit.: "Die weiche Wollust locket zwar"	1'
IX. Aria: "Ich will dich nicht hören"	4'
X. Recit.[duet]: "Geliebte Tugend; du allein"	1'
XI. Aria [duet]: "Ich bin deine, du bist meine"	8'
XII. Recit.: "Schaut, Götter, dieses ist ein Bild"	1'
XIII. Chorus: "Lust der Völker, Lust der Deinen"	3'

> Breitkopf

Cantata No.214 (Tönet, ihr Pauken! Erschallet, Trompeten!) <1733>   25'

chorus   solos SATB
2 2[1/ob d'amore.2] 0 0 — 0 3 0 0 — tmp — cnt — str
I. Chorus: "Tönet, ihr Pauken! Erschallet, Trompeten!"   8'
II. Recit.: "Heut ist der Tag"   1'
III. Aria: "Blast die wohlgegriffnen Flöten"   3'
IV. Recit.: "Mein knallendes Metall"   1'
V. Aria: "Fromme Musen! meine Glieder!"   4'
VI. Recit.: "Unsre Königin im Lande"   1'
VII. Aria: "Kron und Preis gekrönter Damen"   4'
VIII. Recit.: "So dringe in das weite Erdenrund"   1'
IX. Chorus: "Blühet, ihr Linden in Sachsen, wie Zedern"   2'

| Breitkopf | Kalmus | Luck's |

Cantata No.215 (Preise dein Glücke, gesegnetes Sachsen) <1734>   33'

double chorus   solos STB
2 2 0 1 — 0 3 0 0 — tmp — cnt — str
I. Chorus: "Preise dein Glücke, gesegnetes Sachsen"   7'
II. Recit.: "Wie können wir, grossmächtigster August"   1'
III. Aria: "Freilich trotzt Augustus Name"   7'
IV. Recit.: "Was hat dich sonst, Sarmatien, bewogen"   2'
V. Aria: "Rase nur, verwegner Schwarm"   3'
VI. Recit.: "Ja, ja! Gott ist uns noch mit seiner Hülfe nah"   2'
VII. Aria: "Durch die von Eifer entflammeten Waffen"   4'
VIII. Recit.[trio]: "Lass doch, o teurer Landesvater, zu"   3'
IX. Chorus: "Stifter der Reiche, Beherrscher der Kronen"   4'

| Bärenreiter |

Chaconne, BWV 1004, D minor (arr. Casella) <1720>   18'

3[1.2.3/pic] 3[1.2.Eh] 4[1.2.Ebcl.bcl] 3[1.2.cbn] — 4 3 4 0 — tmp — org — str
Transcribed by Alfredo Casella from the 5th movement of the *Partita No.2* for unaccompanied violin.

| Carisch |

Chaconne, BWV 1004, D minor (arr. Starr) <1720>   15'

cnt — str
Transcribed by Mark Starr from the 5th movement of the *Partita No.2* for unaccompanied violin.

| Noteworthy |

Chorale-Variations [or Canonic Variations] on "Vom Himmel hoch"

see under: Stravinsky, Igor, 1882-1971

Christmas Oratorio

see his: Weihnachtsoratorium

Concerto, Flute (or Violin), BWV 971, G major (Italian Concerto) <1735>   12'

cnt — str
Concerto nach italienischem Gusto, from Part 2 of Bach's *Clavierübung*, originally for harpsichord unaccompanied (in F major). Arrangement by Mark Starr (transposed to G major).
Allegro   4'
Andante   4'
Presto   4'

| Noteworthy |

Concerto, Flute, Violin & Harpsichord, BWV 1044, A minor <1730>   22'

str
I. Allegro   9'
II. Adagio ma non tanto e dolce   6'
III. Alla breve   7'

| Breitkopf | Kalmus | Luck's | Peters |

Concerto, Harpsichord, No.1, BWV 1052, D minor <1729–1736>   24'

str
I. Allegro   8'
II. Adagio   9'
III. Allegro   7'

| Bärenreiter | Breitkopf | Kalmus | Luck's | Peters |

Concerto, Harpsichord, No.2, BWV 1053, E major <1729–1736>   19'

str
I. [Allegro]   8'
II. Siciliano   5'
III. Allegro   6'

| Bärenreiter | Breitkopf | Kalmus | Luck's | Peters |

Concerto, Harpsichord, No.3, BWV 1054, D major <1717–1723>   16'

str
I. [No tempo indicated]   7'
II. Adagio e sempre piano   6'
III. Allegro   3'

| Bärenreiter | Breitkopf | Kalmus | Luck's | Peters |

Concerto, Harpsichord, No.4, BWV 1055, A major <1729–1736>   14'

str
I. Allegro   5'
II. Larghetto   5'
III. Allegro ma non tanto   4'

| Bärenreiter | Breitkopf | Kalmus | Luck's | Peters |

Concerto, Harpsichord, No.5, BWV 1056, F minor <1729–1736>   10'

str
I. [No tempo indicated]   3'
II. Largo   3'
III. Presto   4'

| Bärenreiter | Breitkopf | Kalmus | Luck's | Peters |

Concerto, Harpsichord, No.6, BWV 1057, F major <1720>   17'

2[2rec] 0 0 0 — str
An arrangement by the composer of his *Brandenburg Concerto No.4*.
I. [No tempo indicated]   7'
II. Andante   5'
III. Allegro assai   5'

| Bärenreiter | Breitkopf | Luck's | Peters |

Concerto, Harpsichord, No.7, BWV 1058, G minor <1717–1723>   14'

str
I. [No tempo indicated]   4'
II. Andante   6'
III. Allegro assai   4'

| Bärenreiter | Breitkopf | Kalmus | Luck's | Peters |

Concerto, 2 Harpsichords, No.1, BWV 1060, C minor   *14'*
<1727–1736>

str
  I. Allegro   *5'*
  II. Adagio   *5'*
  III. Allegro   *4'*

Breitkopf	Kalmus	Luck's	Peters

Concerto, 2 Harpsichords, No.2, BWV 1061, C major   *17'*
<1727–1736>

str
  I. [No tempo indicated]   *7'*
  II. Adagio ovvero largo   *4'*
  III. Fuga   *6'*

Breitkopf	Kalmus	Luck's	Peters

Concerto, 2 Harpsichords, No.3, BWV 1062, C minor   *15'*
<1717–1723>

str
  I. [No tempo indicated]   *4'*
  II. Andante   *6'*
  III. Allegro assai   *5'*

Breitkopf	Kalmus	Luck's

Concerto, 3 Harpsichords, No.1, BWV 1063, D minor   *16'*
<1733>

str
  I. [No tempo indicated]   *6'*
  II. Alla siciliana   *5'*
  III. Allegro   *5'*

Breitkopf	Kalmus	Luck's	Peters

Concerto, 3 Harpsichords, No.2, BWV 1064, C major   *18'*
<1733>

str
  I. [Allegro]   *7'*
  II. Adagio   *6'*
  III. Allegro   *5'*

Breitkopf	Kalmus	Luck's	Peters

Concerto, 4 Harpsichords, BWV 1065, A minor   <1733>   *10'*

str
After Vivaldi's *Concerto, 4 Violins & Violoncello, op.3, no.10, RV 580, B minor.*
  I. [No tempo indicated]   *4'*
  II. Largo   *3'*
  III. Allegro   *3'*

Breitkopf	Kalmus	Luck's

Concerto, Violin, No.1, BWV 1041, A minor <1730>   *15'*

cnt — str
  I. [No tempo indicated]   *4'*
  II. Andante   *7'*
  III. Allegro assai   *4'*

Bärenreiter	Breitkopf	Kalmus	Luck's	Peters

Concerto, Violin, No.2, BWV 1042, E major <before   *19'*
1730>

cnt — str
A 2004 Breitkopf edition by Klaus Hofmann includes 3 alternative violin parts: (1) based on the new edition, (2) with markings and notes by baroque violinist Sigiswald Kuijken, (3) a facsimile of the manuscript source.
  I. Allegro   *9'*
  II. Adagio   *7'*
  III. Allegro assai   *3'*

Bärenreiter	Breitkopf	Kalmus	Luck's	Peters

Concerto, 2 Violins, BWV 1043, D minor <1730–1731>   *17'*

cnt — str
  I. Vivace   *4'*
  II. Largo; ma non tanto   *7'*
  III. Allegro   *6'*

Bärenreiter	Breitkopf	Kalmus	Luck's	Peters

Concerto, Violin & Oboe, BWV 1060R <1727–1736>   *17'*

cnt — str
A reconstruction of what is believed to have been the original version of the *Concerto No.1 for 2 Harpsichords* (BWV 1060). The Bärenreiter edition (Wilfried Fischer) is in C minor; the Breitkopf (Max Schneider 1921, reprinted Luck's; Klaus Hofmann 1997) has been transposed to D minor.
  I. Allegro   *5'*
  II. Adagio   *8'*
  III. Allegro   *4'*

Bärenreiter	Breitkopf	Luck's

Concerto, Violin & Viola, G major <1727>   *14'*

cnt — str
Reconstruction by Robert Bridges. Based on 3 arias from *Matthuspassion* (BWV 244): no.13 (*Ich will dir mein Herzen schenken*); no.39 (*Erbarme dich*); no.42 (*Gebt mir meinen Jesum wieder*).
  [Ich will dir mein Herzen schenken]   *4'*
  [Erbarme dich]   *7'*
  [Gebt mir meinen Jesum wieder]   *3'*

RBP

Fantasia & Fugue, BWV 537, C minor <after 1723>   *9'*

3[1.2.pic] 3[1.2.Eh] 3[1.2.bcl] 3[1.2.cbn] — 4 3 3 1 — tmp+4(or 6) — 2hp[1part] — str
perc: glock, sd, cym, bd, opt tri, opt tambn
Originally for organ; arr. by Edward Elgar.

Luck's	Novello

Fugue, BWV 577, G major (Fugue à la gigue)   *3'*
<1705–1706>

2 2 2 2 — 2 2 2 1 — str
Originally for organ; arr. by Gustav Holst.

Novello

Fugue, BWV 578, G minor (The Little) <1717–1723>   *4'*

3[1.2.pic] 3[1.2.Eh] 3[1.2.bcl] 3[1.2.cbn] — 4 3 3 1 — tmp+4 — hp — str
perc: bd, cym, sd, sus cym
Originally for organ; arr. by Lucien Cailliet.

C. Fischer	Luck's

Jesu, Joy of Man's Desiring (arr. from Cantata No.147)   *3'*
<1723>

2 2 2 2 — 4 3 3 1 — str
Arr. Arthur Luck; chorus may substitute for brass.

Luck's

Johannespassion, BWV 245 (St. John Passion) <1723;   *114'*
rev 1725, 1732, 1749>

chorus   solos SATBB
2 2[1/d'am/da cacc.2/da cacc] 0 1 — lute, 2va d'amore, va da gamba — org — str
Over the course of 25 years, Bach produced at least 4 versions of this work: 1724, 1725, 1732(?), an unfinished revision in 1739, and 1749.
    Breitkopf offers the original version in an edition by G. Sievers. Bärenreiter gives the 1725 version, ed. Arthur Mendel. Carus gives the 1749 version, with materials from the earlier versions in an appendix.
  Part I   *42'*
  Part II   *72'*

Bärenreiter	Breitkopf	Carus	Kalmus	Peters

Komm, Gott, Schöpfer, heiliger Geist, BWV 631 <1717>   5'

4[1.2.pic1.pic2] 4[1.2.Eh1.Eh2] 6[1.2.Ebcl1.Ebcl2.bcl1.bcl2]
4[1.2.cbn1.cbn2] — 4 4 4 1 — tmp+2 — 2hp — str
perc: glock, cym, tri
Orchestrated by Arnold Schoenberg from an organ chorale prelude.

Universal

Komm süsser Tod (Come Sweet Death) <1736>   4'

3 3[1.2.Eh] 1[bcl] 2[1.cbn] — 4 3 4 1 — tmp — hp — str
Arr. Leopold Stokowski.

Broude Bros.	Luck's

Magnificat, BWV 243a, E-flat major [original version] <1723>   36'

chorus   solos SSATB
2[2rec] 2 0 1 — 0 3 0 0 — tmp — cnt — str
The original version of this work, interpolating 4 Christmas texts (2 in
German and 2 in Latin) into the traditional *Magnificat*.
Ed. Alfred Dürr.

I. Magnificat anima mea	3'
II. Et exsultavit	3'
Interpolation A: "Vom Himmel hoch"	2'
III. Quia respexit	3'
IV. Omnes generationes	1'
V. Quia fecit	2'
Interpolation B: "Freut euch und jubiliert"	1'
VI. Et misericordia	4'
VII. Fecit potentiam	2'
Interpolation C: "Gloria in excelsis Deo"	1'
VIII. Deposuit	2'
IX. Esurientes	3'
Interpolation D: "Virga Jesse floruit"	3'
X. Suscepit Israel	2'
XI. Sicut locutus	2'
XII. Gloria Patri	2'

Bärenreiter

Magnificat, BWV 243, D major <1732–1735>   29'

chorus   solos SSATB
2 2[1/d'am.2/d'am] 0 1 — 0 3 0 0 — tmp — cnt — str
A later reworking, in a lower but more brilliant key, of BWV 243a,
excising the 4 Christmas additions so as to render the work suitable for
other feast days.
    The Bärenreiter edition includes in an appendix the 4 Christmas
interpolations of BWV 243a, transposed to D major for use with BWV
243 if desired.

I. Magnificat anima mea	3'
II. Et exsultavit	3'
III. Quia respexit	3'
IV. Omnes generationes	1'
V. Quia fecit	2'
VI. Et misericordia	4'
VII. Fecit potentiam	2'
VIII. Deposuit	2'
IX. Esurientes	3'
X. Suscepit Israel	2'
XI. Sicut locutus	2'
XII. Gloria Patri	2'

Bärenreiter	Kalmus	Luck's	Peters

Mass, BWV 232, B minor <1747–1749>   108'

chorus   solos SSATB
2 3[1/d'am.2/d'am.3] 0 2 — 1 3 0 0 — tmp — cnt — str

I. KYRIE	(18')	
1. Kyrie eleison (Chorus)		9'
2. Christe eleison (Soprano & Alto)		5'
3. Kyrie eleison (Chorus)		4'
II. GLORIA	(36')	
4. Gloria in excelsis (Chorus)		2'
5. Et in terra pax (Chorus)		5'
6. Laudamus te (Soprano)		4'
7. Gratias agimus tibi (Chorus)		3'
8. Domine Deus (Soprano & Tenor)		5'
9. Qui tollis (Chorus)		3'
10. Qui sedes (Alto)		5'
11. Quoniam tu solus (Bass)		5'
12. Cum sancto spiritu (Chorus)		4'
III. CREDO	(31')	
13. Credo in unum Deum (Chorus)		2'
14. Patrem omnipotentem (Chorus)		2'
15. Et in unum Dominum (Soprano & Alto)		5'
16. Et incarnatus est (Chorus)		3'
17. Crucifixus (Chorus)		3'
18. Et resurrexit (Chorus)		4'
19. Et in Spiritum sanctum (Bass)		5'
20. Confiteor (Chorus)		4'
21. Et expecto (Chorus)		3'
IV. SANCTUS	(15')	
22. Sanctus (Chorus)		3'
23. Pleni sunt coeli (Chorus)		2'
24. Osanna (Double Chorus)		3'
25. Benedictus (Tenor)		4'
24. [repeated] Osanna (Double Chorus)		3'
V. AGNUS DEI	(8')	
26. Agnus Dei (Alto)		5'
27. Dona nobis pacem (Chorus)		3'

Bärenreiter	Breitkopf	Kalmus	Luck's	Peters

Mass, BWV 233, F major (Lutheran Mass No.1) <1737>   29'

chorus   solos SAB
0 2 0 2[1 part] — 2 0 0 0 — cnt — str

I. Kyrie	5'
II. Gloria	7'
III. Domine Deus	4'
IV. Qui tollis	5'
V. Quoniam	5'
VI. Cum sancto Spiritu	3'

Bärenreiter	Breitkopf	Bärenreiter	Luck's	Peters

Mass, BWV 234, A major (Lutheran Mass No.2) <1737–1738>   37'

chorus   solos SAB
2 0 0 0 — cnt — str

I. Kyrie	9'
II. Gloria	6'
III. Domine Deus	7'
IV. Qui tollis	7'
V. Quoniam	4'
VI. Cum sancto Spiritu	4'

Bärenreiter	Breitkopf	Kalmus	Luck's	Peters

Mass, BWV 235, G minor (Lutheran Mass No.3) <1737>   33'

chorus   solos ATB
0 2 0 0 — cnt — str

I. Kyrie	8'
II. Gloria	4'
III. Gratias agimus tibi	4'
IV. Domine Fili	6'
V. Qui tollis	5'
VI. Cum sancto Spiritu	6'

Bärenreiter	Breitkopf	Kalmus	Luck's	Peters

Mass, BWV 236, G major (Lutheran Mass No.4) <1737–1738>   32'

chorus   solos SATB
0 2 0 0 — cnt — str
I. Kyrie	4'
II. Gloria	5'
III. Gratias agimus tibi	6'
IV. Domine Deus	5'
V. Quoniam	7'
VI. Cum sancto Spiritu	5'

| Bärenreiter | Breitkopf | Kalmus | Luck's | Peters |

Matthäuspassion, BWV 244 (St. Matthew Passion) <1729>   131'

double chorus   solos SATBB   semi-chorus of sopranos (boys)
4[1/rec.2/rec.3.4] 4[all/d'am;1&2/da cacc] 0 0 — va da gamba — org,
hpsd — str
Double chorus & double orchestra.
   Numerous smaller solo parts may be taken by members of the chorus.
   Recorders in one movement only; probably the 2 recorder parts were
originally intended for 6 players or so, perhaps covered by some of the
violinists not otherwise occupied in that particular movement.
   1 viola da gamba will suffice, though score calls for 1 in each
orchestra.
| Part I | 61' |
| Part II | 70' |

| Bärenreiter | Breitkopf | Kalmus | Peters |

Motet No.2, BWV 226 (Der Geist hilft unser Schwachheit auf) <1727>   8'

double chorus
0 3[1.2.ob da caccia] 0 1 — cnt — str

| Bärenreiter | Kalmus | Luck's |

Musikalisches Opfer, BWV 1079 (Landshoff) (Musical Offering) <1727>   47'

1 3[1/d'am.2.ob da cacc.] 0 1 — cnt — str
Ed. Ludwig Landshoff.
I. Ricercar 1	6'
II. Canones 1-5	6'
III. Trio Sonata for Flute, Violin, and Continuo	18'
IV. Canones 6-10	10'
V. Ricercar 2	7'

| Kalmus | Luck's | Peters |

Musikalisches Opfer, BWV 1079 (Pillney) (Musical Offering) <1747>   47'

1 0 0 0 — cnt — str[no vn2]
Orchestrated by Karl H. Pillney.
I. Ricercar 1	6'
II. Canones 1-5	6'
III. Trio Sonata for Flute; Violin and Continuo	18'
IIIa. Largo	
IIIb. Allegro moderato	
IIIc. Andante larghetto	
IIId. Allegro	
IV. Canones 6-10	10'
V. Ricercar 2	7'

| Breitkopf |

Musikalisches Opfer (Musical Offering): Ricercare (arr. Anton Webern) <1747>   8'

1 2[1.Eh] 2[1.bcl] 1 — 1 1 1 0 — tmp — hp — str

| Universal |

Oster-Oratorium, BWV 249 (Easter Oratorio; Kommt, eilet und laufet) <1725>   38'

chorus   solos SATB
2[2rec] 2[1/d'am.2] 0 1 — 0 3 0 0 — tmp — cnt — str
One recorder doubles on optional flute.
   Characters: Maria Jacobi (S), Maria Magdalena (A), Petrus (T),
Johannes (B).
I. Sinfonia	4'
II. Adagio	3'
III. Duet: "Kommt; eilet und laufet"	5'
IV. Recitative: "O kalter Männer Sinn"	1'
V. Aria: "Seele, deine Spezereien"	11'
VI. Recitative: "Hier ist die Gruft"	1'
VII. Aria: "Sanfte soll mein Todeskummer"	6'
VIII. Recitative: "Indessen seufzen wir"	1'
IX. Aria: "Saget, saget mir geschwinde"	6'
X. Recitative: "Wir sind erfreut"	1'
XI. Chorus: "Preis und Dank bleibe, Herr, dein Lobgesang"	2'

| Breitkopf | Kalmus | Schott |

Partita, BWV 1004, Violin Unaccompanied: Chaconne

see his: Chaconne, BWV 1004

Passacaglia, BWV 582, C minor (orch. Respighi) <1716–1717>   13'

4[1.2.3.pic] 4[1.2.3.Eh] 4[1.2.3.bcl] 4[1.2.3.cbn] — 6 4 3 1 — tmp —
org — str
Orchestrated by Ottorino Respighi; originally for organ. This
orchestration does not include the fugue that was part of Bach's original
organ composition.

| Ricordi |

Passacaglia & Fugue, BWV 582, C minor <1716–1717>   13'

4[1.2/afl.3.4/pic] 4[1.2.3.Eh] 4[1.2.3.bcl] 4[1.2.3.cbn] — 8 4 4 2[tuba,
tenor tuba] — tmp — str
Arr. Leopold Stokowski from a work for organ. May be performed with
winds: 3[incl pic] 3[incl Eh] 3[incl bcl] 3[incl cbn] — 4 3 3 1.

| Broude Bros. |

Prelude & Fugue, BWV 552, E-flat major (St. Anne) <1723>   16'

4[1.2.pic1.pic2] 4[1.2.Eh1.Eh2] 6[1.2.bcl1.bcl2.Ebcl1.Ebcl2]
4[1.2.cbn1.cbn2] — 4 4 4 1 — tmp+2 — hp — cel — str
perc: bd, cym, glock, tri, xyl
Orchestrated by Arnold Schoenberg; originally for organ. Publisher offers
also a reduced version by Erwin Stein with woodwinds 4 3 4 3.

| Universal |

Prelude & Fugue, BWV 558, G minor <1708–1717>   4'

2 3[1.2.Eh] 3[1.2.bcl] 3[1.2.cbn] — 4 3 3 1 — tmp — hp — str
Orchestrated by Lucien Cailliet. Originally an organ work, believed by
some to have been composed by Bach's pupil Johann Ludwig Krebs
(1713-1780) and wrongly attributed to Bach; this is not universally
accepted, however.

| C. Fischer |

Saint John Passion

see his: Johannespassion

Saint Matthew Passion

see his: Matthäuspassion

Schmücke dich, o liebe Seele, BWV 654 (Deck Thyself, O My Soul) <1717>   5'

4[1.2.pic1.pic2] 4[1.2.Eh1.Eh2] 6[1.2.Ebcl1.Ebcl2.bcl1.bcl2] 4[1.2.cbn1.cbn2] — 4 4 4 1 — tmp+1 — hp — cel — str
perc: glock, tri
Originally for organ; orchestrated by Arnold Schoenberg.

Universal

Sheep May Safely Graze (from Cantata No.208) <1713>   5'

3[1.2.pic] 3[1.2.opt Eh] 3[1.2.opt bcl] 3[1.2.opt cbn] — 4 3 3 1 — tmp — opt hp — str
Arr. Lucien Cailliet.

Boosey

Suite (Overture) No.1, BWV 1066, C major <1717–1723>   21'

0 2 0 1 — cnt — str

I. Overture	6'
II. Courante	2'
III. Gavotte I & II	3'
IV. Forlane	2'
V. Menuet I & II	3'
VI. Bourrée I & II	3'
VII. Passepied I & II	2'

Bärenreiter	Breitkopf	Kalmus	Luck's	Peters

Suite (Overture) No.2, BWV 1067, B minor <1736–1739>   20'

solo flute
cnt — str

I. Overture	7'
II. Rondeau	2'
III. Sarabande	3'
IV. Bourrée I & II	2'
V. Polonaise & Double	3'
VI. Menuet	1'
VII. Badinerie	2'

Bärenreiter	Breitkopf	Kalmus	Luck's	Peters

Suite (Overture) No.3, BWV 1068, D major <1729–1731>   20'

0 2 0 0 — 0 3 0 0 — tmp — cnt — str

I. Overture	7'
II. Air	5'
III. Gavotte I & II	4'
IV. Bourrée	1'
V. Gigue	3'

Bärenreiter	Breitkopf	Kalmus	Luck's	Peters

Suite (Overture) No.4, BWV 1069, D major <1717–1723>   19'

0 3 0 1 — 0 3 0 0 — tmp — cnt — str

I. Overture	10'
II. Bourrée I & II	3'
III. Gavotte	2'
IV. Minuet	2'
V. Rejouissance	2'

Bärenreiter	Breitkopf	Kalmus	Luck's	Peters

Tilge, Höchster, meine Sünden, BWV 1083 <1736>   43'

solos SA
cnt — str
An arrangement by J.S. Bach of Giovanni Battista Pergolesi's *Stabat Mater*, with German text based on Psalm 51.

Versus 1: "Tilge Höchster, meine Sünden"	4'
Versus 2: "Ist mein Herz"	3'
Versus 3: "Missetaten, die mich drücken"	3'
Versus 4: "Dich erzürnt mein Tun und Lassen"	3'
Versus 5/6: "Wer wird sein Schuld vermeinen"	2'
Versus 7: "Sieh! Ich bin in Sünd empfangen"	1'
Versus 8: "Sieh, du willst die Wahrheit haben:	4'
Versus 9: "Wasche mich doch rein von Sünden"	3'
Versus 10: "Lass mich Freud und Wonne spüren"	2'
Versus 11/15: "Schaue nicht auf meine Sünden"	6'
Versus 16: "Offne Lippen, Mund und Seele"	5'
Versus 17/18: "Denn du willst kein Opfer haben"	4'
Versus 19/20: "Lass dein Zion blühend dauern"	2'
Amen	1'

Bärenreiter

Toccata & Fugue, BWV 565, D minor <1708>   9'

4[1.2.3/pic1.4/pic2] 4[1.2.3.Eh] 4[1.2.3.bcl] 4[1.2.3.cbn] — 6 4 4 1 — tmp — 2hp — cel — str
Originally for organ; orchestrated by Leopold Stokowski. May be performed with winds: 4 3[incl Eh] 3[incl bcl] 3incl cbn] — 4 4 3 1.

Broude Bros.

WEIHNACHTSORATORIUM, BWV 248 (Christmas Oratorio) <1734>   169'

chorus   solos SATB
2 4[1/d'am.2/d'am.da cacc1.da cacc2] 0 1 — 2[2corno da caccia] 3 0 0 — tmp — cnt — str
A series of six cantatas, though available only as a single publication.

Cantata I: On the First Day of the Festival of Christmas	27'
Cantata II: On the Second Day of the Festival of Christmas	32'
Cantata III: On the Third Day of Christmas	26'
Cantata IV: On New Year's Day	26'
Cantata V: On the Sunday after New Year	27'
Cantata VI: On the Feast of the Epiphany	31'

Bärenreiter	Breitkopf	Kalmus	Peters

1. Jauchzet, frohlocket, auf, preiset die Tage <1734>   27'

chorus   solos ATB
2 2[1/d'amore.2/d'amore] 0 1 — 0 3 0 0 — tmp — cnt — str
A cantus firmus for soprano in mvt 7 could be for soloist or choral section.

1. Chorus: "Jauchzet, frohlocket"	8'
2. Recit.: "Es begab sich aber zu der Zeit"	1'
3. Recit.: "Nun wird mein liebster Bräutigam"	1'
4. Aria: "Bereite dich, Zion"	6'
5. Chorale: "Wie soll ich dich empfanger"	1'
6. Recit.: "Und sie gebar ihren ersten Sohn"	1'
7. Chorale & Recit.: "Er ist auf Erden kommen arm"	3'
8.Aria: "Grosser Herr, o starker König"	5'
9. Chorale: "Ach mein herzliebes Jesulein"	1'

2. Und es waren Hirten in derselben Gegend <1734>   32'

chorus   solos ATB
2 4[2ob d'am.2ob da cacc] 0 0 — cnt — str

10. Sinfonia (Pastorale)	5'
11. Recit.: "Und es waren Hirten"	1'
12. Chorale: "Brich an, o schönes Morgenlicht"	1'
13. Recit.: "Und der Engel sprach zu ihnen"	1'
14. Recit.: "Was Gott dem Abraham verheissen"	1'
15. Aria: "Frohe Hirten, eilt, ach eilet"	4'
16. Recit.: "Und das habt zum Zeichen"	1'
17. Chorale: "Schaut hin, dort liegt im finstern Stall"	1'
18. Recit.: "So geht denn hin, ihr Hirten geht"	1'
19. Aria: "Schlafe, mein Liebster"	9'
20. Recit.: "Und alsobald war da"	1'
21. Chorus: "Ehre sei Gott in der Höhe"	4'
22. Recit.: "So recht, ihr Engel"	1'
23. Chorale: "Wir singen dir in deinem Heer"	1'

3. Herrscher des Himmels, erhöre das Lallen <1734>   26'

chorus   solos SATB
2 2[1/d'amore.2/d'amore] 0 0 — 0 3 0 0 — tmp — cnt — str

24. Chorus: "Herrscher des Himmels"	2'
25. Recit.: "Und da die Engel"	1'
26. Chorus: "Lasset uns nun gehen"	1'
27. Recit.: "Er hat sein Volk getröst"	1'
28. Chorale: "Dies hat er alles uns getan"	1'
29. Duet: "Herr, dein Mitleid, dein Erbarmen"	8'
30. Recit.: "Und sie kamen eilend"	1'
31. Aria: "Schliesse, mein Herze"	5'
32. Recit.: "Ja, ja, mein Herz"	1'
33. Chorale: "Ich will dich mit Fleiss bewahren"	1'
34. Recit.: "Und die Hirten kehrten wieder um"	1'
35. Chorale: "Seid froh dieweil"	1'
24. [repeated] Chorus: "Herrscher des Himmels"	2'

4. Fallt mit Danken, fallt mit Loben <1734>   26'

chorus   solos STB
0 2 0 0 — 2[2corno da caccia] 0 0 0 — cnt — str

36. Chorus: "Fallt mit Danken, fallt mit Loben"	7'
37. Recit.: "Und da acht Tage um waren"	1'
38. Recit. & Chorale: "Immanuel, o süsses Wort" — "Jesu, du mein…"	3'
39. Aria: "Flösst mein Heiland"	6'
40. Recit. & Chorale: "Wohlan, dein Name soll allein" — "Jesu, meine…"	2'
41. Aria: "Ich will nur dir zu Ehren leben"	5'
42. Chorale: "Jesus richte mein Beginnen"	2'

5. Ehre sei dir, Gott, gesungen <1734>   27'

chorus   solos SATB
0 2[2ob d'amore] 0 0 — cnt — str

43. Chorus: "Ehre sei dir, Gott, gesungen"	8'
44. Recit.: "Da Jesus geboren war"	1'
45. Chorus & Recit.: "Wo ist der neugeborne König der Juden?"	2'
46. Chorale: "Dein Glanz all Finsternis verzehrt"	1'
47. Aria: "Erleucht auch meine finstre Sinnen"	4'
48. Recit.: "Da das der König Herodes hörte"	1'
49. Recit.: "Warum wollt ihr erschrecken?"	1'
50. Recit.: "Und liess versammlen alle Hohepriester"	1'
51. Aria: "Ach, wenn wird die Zeit erscheinen"	6'
52. Recit.: "Mein Liebster herrschet schon"	1'
53. Chorale: "Zwar ist solche Herzensstube"	1'

6. Herr, wenn die stolzen Feinde schnauben <1734>   31'

chorus   solos SATB
0 2[1/d'am.2/d'am] 0 0 — 0 3 0 0 — tmp — cnt — str

54. Chorus: "Herr, wenn die stolzen Feinde schnauben"	6'
55. Recit.: "Da berief Herodes die Weisen"	1'
56. Recit.: "Du Falscher, suche nur den Herrn"	1'
57. Aria: "Nur ein Wink von seinen Händen"	8'
58. Recit.: "Als sie nun den König gehöret hatten"	1'
59. Chorale: "Ich steh an deiner Krippen hier"	1'
60. Recit.: "Und Gott befahl ihnen im Traum"	1'
61. Recit.: "So geht! genug, mein Schatz"	2'
62. Aria: "Nun mögt ihr stolzen Feinde schrecken"	5'
63. Recit.: "Was will der Höllen Schrecken nun"	1'
64. Chorus: "Nun seid ihr wohl gerochen"	4'

Bach, P.D.Q.   1807-1742?

(ostensibly b 1807; d 1742). An imaginary composer.

An imaginary person, the creation of composer and humorist Peter Schickele, q.v.

Bach, Wilhelm Friedemann   1710-1784

(b Weimar, 22 Nov 1710; d Berlin, 1 July 1784). German

Sinfonia, D minor <1764>   9'

2 0 0 0 — str
Schott ed. Walter Lebermann, under the title *Adagio & Fugue in D minor*.

Kalmus	Luck's	Schott

Sinfonia, F major <1746>   12'

cnt — str

I. Vivace	4'
II. Andante	3'
III. Allegro	3'
IV. Menuetto	2'

Breitkopf	Kalmus	Luck's	Schott

Bacon, Ernst   1898-1990

(b Chicago, 26 May 1898; d Orinda, CA, 16 March 1990). American

Bearwalla <1936>   4'

2[1.2/pic] 2[1.2/Eh] 2 2 — 4 2 2 1 — 1perc — pf — str
perc: tri, woodblk, tmp

Fleisher

By Blue Ontario <1958>   47'

solo alto, baritone; narrator   SATB chorus
2[1.2/pic] 2 2 2 — 4 3 3 1 — tmp+3 — cel — str
perc: bd, sus cym, sd, field dr, tri, gong, glock, xyl, bongos, chimes (opt)
Celesta can be played by a percussionist.

1. Preface: As a Strong Bird	3'
2. Vision: By Blue Ontario's Shore	4'
3. Soul of Love and Tongue of Fire	8'
4. Discourse: Come Muse	4'
5. Long and Long	3'
6. Had I the Choice to Tally Greatest Bards	3'
7. The Commonplace I Sing	2'
8. And Whence and Why Come You?	2'
9. Years Prophetical: What Whispers are These	4'
10. Thou Mother With Thy Equal Brood	11'
11. Chorale: One Thought Ever at the Fore	3'

Fleisher

Concerto, Piano, No.2 <1982>   33'

2[1/pic.2/pic] 2 2 2 — 4 3 3 1 — tmp+3 — cel — str
perc: bd, sus cym, sd, tri, tambn, glock, xyl, woodblk, bongos, wine glass, marim
or vib
Orchestration completed by Paul Schiavo.

Grave; Risoluto	6'
Allegretto	7'
Tranquillo	8'
Vivace	12'

> Fleisher

Concerto Grosso <1957>   19'

str orch [*or* str 5t]

Allegro moderato	_'
Moderato	_'
Grave, quasi andante	_'
Allegro	_'

> Fleisher

Ecclesiastes <1936>   34'

solo soprano, bass   chorus SATB
2[1.2/pic] 2 2[1.2/bcl] 2 — 4 3 3 1 — tmp — cel — str

1. Vanity of Vanities (Bass)	2'
2. The Sun Also Riseth (Soprano)	2'
3. All Things are Filled With Labor (Bass)	1'
4. The Thing That Has Been (Chorus)	2'
5. To Everything There is a Season (Soprano)	2'
6. Sermon and Passacaglia (Bass)	4'
7. Chorale: For What Hath Man (Chorus)	2'
8. And the Whole Earth (Chorus)	1'
9. What Profit Hath He (Bass)	1'
10. There is a Generation (Chorus)	2'
11. There Be Three Things (Soprano & Chorus Sopranos)	2'
12. And Further, By These (Chorus)	4'
13. While the Sun or the Light (Bass, Soprano, Chorus)	5'
14. All the Rivers Run Into the Sea (Chorus	4'

> Elkus   MMB

Elegy for Oboe & Strings: On an Air by Bartolomeo Tromboncino, Venice, 1504 <1957>   9'

solo oboe
str
On an air by Bartolomeo Tromboncino, Venice, 1504. Oboe plays only in
middle section (*Air of Peri*). Mvts played without pause.

Andante	_'
Air of Peri	_'
Fugato	_'

> Fleisher

Enchanted Isle <1943; rev (orchd) 1954>   22'

2[1/pic.2/pic] 2 2 2[1.2/cbn] — 4 3 3 1 — opt accordion — 2tmp+2
— pf/cel — str
perc: bd, sus cym, sd, tambn, gong, glock, xyl, vib, chimes, cowbell, bongos,
guiro, thunder, 2tri, flyswatter
Originally a piano quintet; orchestrated by the composer.

1. Shipwreck	3'
2. Ariel	2'
3. Miranda	2'
4. Caliban	2'
5. Ariel and the Conspirators	2'
6. The Shapes	2'
7. Ariel (again)	1'
8. Dance of Certain Reapers and Nymphs	4'
9. Prospero's Farewell	2'
10. Marriage Blessing	3'

> Schirmer

Erie Waters <1961>   13'

2[1.2/pic] 2[1.2/Eh] 2 2 — 4 2 3 1 — tmp+3 — cel — str
perc: bd, sus cym, sd, xyl, woodblk, 2stones (or woodblk)
Cel may be covered by percussionist.

Andante con moto	_'
Allegretto	_'
Larghetto	_'
Allegro moderato	_'

> Fleisher

Fables (The Secretary-Bird and Associates [Seven Studies in the Ecology of Democracy]) <1953>   30'

narrator
1[fl/pic] 1[ob/Eh] 1 1 — 2[or tbn] 0 0 0 — tmp+3 — pf/cel — str
perc: bd, sus cym, sd, tri, tambn, xyl, woodblk, cowbell, bongos, ratch, guiro,
marac, sandblks
The order of movements seems not to be definitively fixed.

1. Preface	2'
2. The Jay and the Lark	4'
3. The Two Dogs and a Cow	2'
4. The Possum and the Skunk	4'
5. A Question of Diet	3'
6. The Secretary Bird	5'
7. The Praying Mantis	3'
8. The Well	7'

> Fleisher

Ford's Theatre; A Few Glimpses of Easter Week, 1865 <1946>   31'

3[1.2/pic.pic] 3[1.2.Eh] 3[1.2.bcl] 3[1.2.cbn] — 4 3 3 1 — tmp+3 —
hp — cel — str
perc: bd, cym, sus cym, sd, tri, glock, chimes, clock sound
Mvt 4, *Telegraph Fugue*, available as an independent string orch work.

1. Preamble	2'
2. Walt Whitman and the Dying Soldier	2'
3. Passing Troops	3'
4. The Telegraph Fugue	6'
5. Moonlight on the Savannah	2'
6. The Theatre	2'
7. The River Queen	2'
8. Premonition	1'
9. Pennsylvania Avenue, April 9, 1865	5'
10. Good Friday, 1865	3'
11. The Long Rain	1'
12. Conclusion	2'

> AMP

From Emily's Diary <1947>   20'

solo soprano & alto   women's chorus SSAA
1[fl/pic] 1 1 1 — 1 0 0 0 — 1perc — pf — str
perc: tri, glock, cym, tmp

1. Preface	_'
2. Air for Chorus: My River Runs to Thee	_'
3. Air for Soprano: I Dwell in Possibility	_'
4. Song (Sopr & Chor): A Drop Fell on the Apple Tree	_'
5. Choral Duet: The Daisy Follows Soft the Sun	_'
6. Choral Song: What Soft Cherubic Creatures	_'
7. Choral Recitation: Our Share of Night	_'
8. Air for Alto: When Roses Cease to Bloom	_'
9. The Postponeless Creature	_'
10. Duet & Chorus: Unto Me?	_'
11. Chorale: Not What We Did	_'
12. Afterthought	_'

> Schirmer

From These States; Gathered Along Unpaved Roads <1951> 24'

3[1.2/pic.3/pic] 3[1.2.Eh] 3[1.2.bcl] 3[1.2.cbn] — 4 3 3 1 — tmp+3 — cel — str
perc: bd, cym, tri, gong, glock, vib

1. Laying the Rails (A Sledge-Hammer Song)	2'
2. Source of the Tennessee	2'
3. The Sunless Pines	2'
4. The Saluda Barn Dance	2'
5. The Cliff Dwellers (No Ancient Cliffs, These)	2'
6. Wizard Oil	2'
7. Storm Over Huron	2'
8. Lullaby to a Sick Child	3'
9. Polly's Murder	4'
10. Hickory Gap	1'
11. The Timberline Express	2'

AMP

Great River; The Rio Grande <1956> 41'

narrator
2[1/pic.2/pic] 2[1.2/Eh] 2 2 — 4 3 3 1 — tmp+3 — hp — pf, cel — str
perc: bd, cym, sus cym, sd, tri, xyl, vib, bongos, cast

Preface [strings only]	3'
I. A River Created	4'
II. The Peaks—Colorado	2'
III. Pastoral Valleys, N.M.	3'
IV. Desert and Canyon (Texas—Mexico)	5'
V. Mexico Bay (the Gulf)	3'
VI. A Pueblo Dance Prayer	2'
VII. An Indian Death	3'
VIII. Spanish Soldiers before Battle	3'
IX. Mountain Man (Taos 1829-1830)	2'
X. Soldiers by Firelight (Texas 1846)	3'
XI. The Honey-Eaters	4'
XII. American Visions	4'

Fleisher

Hymn to the United Nations 4'

chorus SATB
2 2 2 2 — 3[hn3 opt] 3 3 0 — tmp+2 — str
perc: bd, sd

Fleisher

The Last Invocation; A Requiem <1968–1971> 48'

solos: S, B, opt A   chorus
2[1/pic.2/pic] 2 2 2 — 4 3 3 1 — tmp+2 — pf/cel — str
perc: bd, sus cym, sd, tri, gong, glock, xyl, marim, chimes, bongos, stones

1. Preamble [orchestra]	3'
2. Dark Mother	6'
3. Shadow on the Grass	2'
4. Whispers of Heavenly Death	4'
5. The Postponeless Creature	3'
6. Summer's Papse [orchestra]	2'
7. The Voice of the Rain	5'
8. Eternity	2'
9. She Went	2'
10. Farewell	4'
11. Dies non [orchestra]	2'
12. This Quiet Dust	2'
13. This Day, O Soul	2'
14. This Place (After a Hundred Years)	3'
15. Passenger of Infinity	2'
16. The Unknown Region	4'
17. Lingering Last Drops	3'

Bacon   Fleisher

The Lord Star <1949> 12'

solo baritone   chorus
0 0 0 0 — 2 3 2 1 — org — str

Fleisher

The Muffin Man <1960> 4'

2[1.pic] 2 2 2 — 4 3 3 1 — tmp+3 — cel — str

Schirmer

The Nantucket Fling <1970s> 6'

3[1.2.pic] 2 2 2 — 4 3 3 1 — tmp+5 — cel [can be played by perc] — str
perc: sus cym, sd, tri, tambn, xyl, woodblk, 2stones

Fleisher

Passacaglia & Aria

see his: Symphony No.1, 2nd mvt

Remembering Ansel Adams (A Mountain Threnody) <1985> 13'

0 0 1 0 — tmp/bongos — str

Fleisher

Riolama; Ten Places, for Piano & Orchestra (Concerto, Piano, No.1) <1963> 33'

solo piano
2[1/pic.2/pic] 2[1.2/Eh] 2[1.2.bcl] 2[1.2.cbn] — 4 3 3 1 — tmp+5 — cel — str
perc: bd, sus cym, sd, tri, tambn, gong, glock, xyl, vib, chimes, woodblk, bongos, cast, 2water glasses, 2stones; 1perc plays on the interior of soloist's piano
Strings use banjo plectra in 10th mvt. Cel part can be covered by perc.
    Mvt 10, Pico Perdido, may be played separately.

1. Salem, Massachusetts	3'
2. The Chama River, New Mexico	5'
3. Creede, Colorado	2'
4. Nantahala, North Carolina	3'
5. Ruwenzori, Africa	4'
6. Gnaw-Bone, Indiana	2'
7. Gaspé, Ontario	2'
8. Nicasio Valley, California	3'
9. Riolama, Venezuela	3'
10. Pico Perdido, Spain	3'
Supplement (for encore): 156 W. 55 St., N.Y.	3'

Fleisher

Smoky Mountain Scherzo <1937>

see his: Symphony No.2

Symphony No.1, D minor <1932> 30'

3[1.2.pic] 3[1.2.Eh] 3[1.2.bcl] 3[1.2.cbn] — 4 3 3 1 — 2sx opt[ssx, asx] — tmp+3 — hp — pf, cel — str
perc: bd, cym, sus cym, sd, tri
2nd mvt, Passacaglia and Aria, about 10', is available separately from Schirmer.

Allegro	-'
Passacaglia and Aria: Andante sostenuto	-'
Diversion: Allegretto moderato	-'
Fugue: Finale	-'

AMP

Symphony No.2 (Americana) <1937> 29'

2[1/pic2.2/pic1] 2[1.2/Eh] 2 2[1.2/cbn] — 4 3 3 1 — tmp+2 — hp — cel — str
perc: bd, cym, sd, tri, glock, xyl, woodblk
The 2nd movement may be performed independently, under the title Smoky Mountain Scherzo.

Grave and Agitato	10'
Interlude and Diversion	6'
Air	4'
Fugue	9'

AMP

USania; A Small Oratorio <1977> 25'

2narrators   solo bass, opt soprano   chorus SATB
2[1/pic.2/pic] 2 2 2 — 3 3 2 1 — tmp+3 — hp or pf — pf/cel — str
perc: bd, cym, sd, tri, glock, xyl, woodblk, bongos

1. Preamble (Melville)	2'
2. Freedom (Whittier)	3'
3. The Passing Moment (Emerson)	1'
4. Distribution (B. Franklin)	1'
5. The Commonplace (Whitman)	2'
6. Places (Bacon)	2'
7. The Ancient Redwood (Whitman)	2'
8. Pollutics (American saying)	2'
9. My Land (Bacon)	2'
10. Aspiration (Dickinson)	1'
11. The Reckoning (Whitman)	7'

Fleisher

Bacri, Nicolas 1961-

(b Paris, 23 Nov 1961). French

Une prière, op.52 (A Prayer) <1995–1997> 23'

solo viola (or violoncello, or violin)
2[1.2/pic] 2 2 1 — 2 0 0 0 — tmp — str

I. Canon	8'
II. Passacaglia	3'
III. Scherzo	7'
IV. Ricapitolazione	5'

Durand

Badings, Henk 1907-1987

(b Bandung, Java, 17 Jan 1907; d Maarheeze, 26 June 1987). Dutch

Concerto, Harp <1967> 21'

2 2 2[1.bcl] 2 — 4 2 2 0 — tmp+2 — cel — str

Donemus

Concerto, Piano (1940) <1939> 27'

2[incl pic] 2 3[incl bcl] 2 — 4 3 3 1[opt] — tmp+3 — cel — str

Donemus

Symphonietta 12'

2 0 2 0 — 0 2 0 0 — tmp — str[va & db opt]
The 2nd fl & 2nd cl may be played by other wind instruments; the
trumpets may be given to other brass instruments.

Harmonia

Symphony No.5 30'

3[1.2.3/pic] 3[1.2.Eh] 3[1.2.bcl] 3[1.2.cbn] — 4 3 3 1 — tmp+2 — hp
— cel — str
perc: bd, cym, sus cym, sd, tamtam, xyl, vib

Donemus   Schott

Symphony No.7 (Louisville) <1954> 23'

2[1.2/pic] 2[1.2/Eh] 3[1.2.(bcl opt)] 2 — 4 2 3 1 — tmp+2 — hp —
opt pf/cel — str
perc: bd, cym, sus cym, sd, tambn, tamtam, xyl, chimes, opt vib
Score is ambiguous as to whether the entire pf/cel part is optional, or just
the celesta (3rd mvt only); all pf notes throughout the symphony,
however, are doubled in other instruments, suggesting that the entire
keyboard part is optional.

Lento; Allegro appassionato	8'
Scherzo	3'
Adagio	8'
Allegro vivace	4'

Donemus

Baermann, Heinrich Joseph 1784-1847

(b Potsdam, 14 Feb 1784; d Munich, 11 June 1847). German

Adagio, Clarinet & Strings, D-flat major <1817> 4'

str
2nd mvt from Baermann's *Clarinet Quintet*, op.23. This *Adagio*
previously attributed to Richard Wagner.

Breitkopf

Baird, Tadeusz 1928-1981

(b Grodzisk Mazowiecki, 26 July 1928; d Warsaw, 2 Sept 1981). Polish

Concerto lugubre <1975> 19'

solo viola
3[1.2.3/afl] 3[1.2.3/Eh] 3[1.2.3/bcl] 3 — 4 3 3 0 — tmp+5 — 2hp —
pf, hpsd — str
perc: sd, tambn, marac, templeblks, tri, gong, tamtam, vib, 3bd, 3td, 4tomtom,
3whip, 3sus cym
In one mvt.

PWM

Four Essays for Orchestra <1958> 19'

1 2[1.Eh] 2[1.bcl] 1 — 2 2 2 0 — tmp+5 — 2hp — cel, pf, pf/hpsd —
str[incl vn 1, 2, 3]

PWM

Variations Without a Theme (Wariacje bez tematu) <1962> 10'

4 1 4[1.2.3.4/bcl] 0 — 4 4 4 0 — tmp+5 — 2hp — cel, pf, pf/hpsd —
str

PWM

Baker, David 1931-

(b Indianapolis, 21 Dec 1931). American

Le chat qui pêche <1974> 28'

soloists: textless soprano voice; jazz quartet (alto/tenor saxophone;
acoustic/electric piano; acoustic/electric bass; drums)
3[incl pic] 3[incl Eh] 3[incl bcl] 3[incl cbn] — 4 3 3 1 — tmp+3 —
hp — str

Soleil d'Altamira (The Sunshine of Altamira)	5'
L'odeur du blues (The Smell of the Blues)	6'
Sons voiles (Veiled Sounds)	8'
Guadeloupe calypso	4'
Le miroir noir (The Black Mirror)	5'

AMP

Concerto, Violoncello <1975> 17'

1 1 1 1 — 2 0 0 0 — tmp+1 — str[no vc]

1. Fast	6'
2. Slow	6'
3. Fast	5'

AMP

Kosbro <1973> 13'

3[incl pic] 3[incl Eh] 3[incl bcl] 3[incl cbn] — 4 3 3 1 — tmp+4 — pf
— str

Schirmer

Baksa, Robert   1938-

(b New York, 7 Feb 1938). American

Variations from the Heart   13'

narrator
0 0 1 0 — 0 0 0 1 — str

Theme	_'
Variation I: Being Frightened	_'
Variation II: Getting Angry	_'
Variation III: Feeling Sad	_'
Variation IV: Feeling Happy	_'

Presser

Balada, Leonardo   1933-

(b Barcelona, 22 Sept 1933). American composer of Spanish birth

Concerto, Violoncello & 9 Players <1962>   15'

1[fl/pic] 1[ob/Eh] 1[cl/bcl] 1 — 1 2 1 — tmp/perc — [no other str]
perc: sus cym, sd, tri, glock, xyl

I. Quasi allegretto	_'
II. Lento	_'
III. Allegretto	_'

EMI

Balakirev, Mily   1837-1910

(b Nizhniy Novgorod, 21 Dec 1836/2 Jan 1837; d St Petersburg, 16/29 May 1910).
Russian

Islamey (arr. Alfredo Casella) <1869>   9'

4[1.2.3.4/pic] 3[1.2.Eh] 3[1.2.Ebcl] 4[1.2.3.cbn] — 4 4 3 1 — tmp+6
— 2hp — str
perc: bd, cym, sus cym, sd, tri, tambn, tamtam, glock, chimes
Originally for piano.

Kalmus	MCA	Simrock

Islamey (arr. Sergei Lyapunov) <1869>   9'

4[1.2.pic1.pic2] 2[1.Eh] 3[1.2.Ebcl] 2 — 4 4 3 1 — tmp+5 — 2hp —
str
perc: bd, cym, sd, tri, tambn
Originally for piano.

Kalmus	Luck's	Russian

King Lear (Korol' Lir): Incidental Music <1858–1861;   35'
rev 1902-5>

3[1.2.3/pic] 2[1.Eh] 3 2 — 4 4 3 1 — tmp+4 — hp — str
perc: tri, tamtam, sd, cym, bd
The music that was originally for a separate elaborate stage band is here
incorporated into the main orchestra.

1. Overture	11'
2. Act I: Lear's Train	_'
3. Music for a Festive Procession	5'
4. Prelude to Act II	3'
5. Act II, Scene 1 (Gloucester), Scene 2 (Kent)	_'
6. Prelude to Act III	5'
7. Prelude to Act IV	8'
8. Act IV, Scenes 6 & 7	_'
9. Prelude to Act V	2'
10. Act V, Scenes 1, 2, & 3	_'

Fleisher	Zimmerman

Overture on Three Russian Folk Songs (Uvertyura na   8'
temï tryokh russkikh pesen) <1858; rev 1881>

2 2 2 2 — 2 2 3 0 — tmp — str
perc: ad lib: bd, cym

Russian	Luck's	Simrock

Russia (2nd Overture on Russian Themes; In Russia)   15'
<1863-4; rev 1884>

3 2 2 2 — 4 2 3 1 — tmp+4 — 2hp — str
perc: tri, tambn, tamtam, cym, bd

Kalmus	Luck's

Symphony No.1, C major <1864–1866; rev 1893-1897>   45'

3[1.2.3/pic] 2[1.Eh] 3 2 — 4 2 3 1 — tmp+5 — 2hp[1part] — str
perc: tri, tambn, sd, cym, bd

Largo; Allegro vivo	14'
Scherzo: Vivo	8'
Andante	14'
Finale: Allegro moderato	9'

Kalmus

Symphony No.2, D minor <1900–1908>   37'

3[1.2.3/pic] 2[1.Eh] 3 2 — 4 2 3 1 — tmp+5 — hp — str
perc: tri, tambn, sd, cym, bd

Allegro ma non troppo	10'
Scherzo alla cosacca: Allegro ma non troppo, ma con fuoco e energico	9'
Romanza: Andante	9'
Finale: Polonaise	9'

Kalmus

Tamara <1867–1882>   20'

3[1.2.3/pic] 2[1.Eh] 3 2 — 4 2 3 1 — tmp+6 — 2hp — str
perc: tri, tambn, sd, cym, bd, tamtam
Symphonic poem after Mikhail Lermontov.

Breitkopf	Kalmus

Balassa, Sándor   1935-

(b Budapest, 20 Jan 1935). Hungarian

Cantata Y, op.21 <1970>   10'

solo soprano
3 2 3 2 — 3 2 3 0 — tmp+5 — cel, pf — str[12.12.8.6.4]
perc: bd, cym, 2 sus cym, sd, 5toms, tri, tamtam, 4gong, glock, xyl, vib, chimes,
crot, slgh-bells, woodblk, bongos, marac

EMB

Ballard, Louis   1931-2007

(b Devil's Promenade, OK, 8 July 1931; d Santa Fe, 9 Feb 2007). American

Incident at Wounded Knee <1973>   16'

1[1/pic] 1[1/Eh] 1[1/Ebcl] 2 — 2 0 0 0 — 1perc[opt] — str[4.4.3.3.1]
perc: sus cym, sd, tri, guiro, marac, claves, cabasa, tmp

I. Procession	_'
II. Prayer	_'
III. Blood and War	_'
IV. Ritual	_'

Belwin

Bamert, Matthias
1942-

(b Ersigen, 5 July 1942). Swiss

Circus Parade <1974>
12'

narrator (may be the conductor)
2[1/pic.2/pic] 2 2[1.2/bcl] 2 — 4 2 2 0 — tmp+2 — hp — pf — str
   1. Ringmaster   _'
   2. Horses   _'
   3. Tightrope Walkers   _'
   4. Bears   _'
   5. Jugglers   _'
   6. Lions   _'
   7. Magician   _'
   8. Little Monkeys   _'
   9. Clowns   _'

EAM

Once Upon an Orchestra <1975>
50'

narrator
3[1.2.pic] 3[1.2.Eh] 3[1.2.bcl] 3[1.2.cbn] — 4 3 3 1 — tmp+3 — hp — str

EAM

Snapshots
15'

3[incl pic] 3[incl Eh] 3[incl bcl] 3[incl cbn] — 4 3 3 1 — tmp+3 — hp — pf — str
13 short movements with humorous titles.

EAM

Bantock, Granville
1868-1946

(b London, 7 Aug 1868; d London, 16 Oct 1946). English

Hamabdil; Hebrew Melody <1919>
6'

solo violoncello
tmp — hp[or pf] — str

Kalmus

Hebridean Symphony <1915>
32'

3[1.2.pic] 3[1.2.Eh] 3[1.2.bcl] 3[1.2.cbn] — 4 3 3 1 — tmp+3 — hp — cel — str
perc: bd, cym, sus cym, sd, tri
This work, originally published by Breitkopf, may be out of print; a score may be found at <imslp.org>.
   Although the work is through-composed, and mvts are not indicated in the score, four distinct sections may be discerned:
   1. beginning through fig [29]   *14'*
   2. [29] – [45]   *3'*
   3. [45] – 2 bars before [71]   *7'*
   4. 2 before [71] to end   *8'*

Breitkopf

In the Far West <1900; rev (orchd) 1912>
_'

str
A serenade based on the composer's string quartet of 1900. This serenade, originally published by Breitkopf, may be out of print; a score may be found at <imslp.org>.
   I. Lento; Poco allegro; Animato   _'
   II. Andante, con espressione   _'
   III. Scherzo: Vivo quasi presto   _'
   IV. Finale: Con brio   _'

Fleisher

The Pierrot of the Minute <1908>
12'

3[1.2.pic] 2 2 1 — 3 2 1 0 — tmp+1 — hp — str
perc: tambn, tri, glock
A "comedy overture."

Breitkopf   Kalmus

Barab, Seymour
1921-2014

(b Chicago, 9 Jan 1921; d Manhattan, 28 June 2014). American

G-A-G-E, A Christmas Story
20'

narrator
2 2 2 2 — 2 2 2 0 — tmp+2 — hp — cel, pf — str
perc: bd, cym, sus cym, sd, tambn, glock, chimes, ratch
Major piano part (pf player can cover cel as well). Narrator must sing a verse of "Silent Night."

Schirmer

Barber, Samuel
1910-1981

(b West Chester, PA, 9 March 1910; d New York, 23 Jan 1981). American

Adagio for Strings <1936>
8'

str orch

Schirmer

Andromache's Farewell, op.39 <1962>
12'

soprano solo
3[1.2.pic] 3[1.2.Eh] 3[1.2.bcl] 2 — 4 3 3 1 — tmp+3 — hp — cel — str
perc: bd, cym, sd, td, tambn, tamtam, xyl, crot, woodblk, whip, anvil

Schirmer

Antony and Cleopatra, op.40: Two Scenes <1966>
16'

solo soprano
3[1.2.pic] 3[1.2.Eh] 3[1.2.bcl] 2 — 4 3 3 1 — tmp+4 — 2hp[1part] — pf — str
perc: bd, cym, sus cym, szl cym, sd, td, field dr, military drum, tomtom, 4 small untuned drums, tri, tambn, tamtam, glock, xyl, vib, crot, belltree, woodblk, whip, claves, anvil
   1. Give Me Some Music   *8'*
   2. Death of Cleopatra   *8'*

Schirmer

Canzonetta for Oboe & String Orchestra, op.48 posth. <1977–1978>
8'

solo oboe
str
Orchestrated by Charles Turner.

Schirmer

Capricorn Concerto <1944>
15'

solo flute, oboe, & trumpet
str
   I. Allegro ma non troppo   *7'*
   II. Allegretto   *3'*
   III. Allegro con brio   *5'*

Schirmer   Luck's

Commando March for Orchestra <1943>
4'

3[1.2.pic] 3[1.2.Eh] 4[1.2.Ebcl.bcl] 3[1.2.cbn] — 4 3 3 1 — tmp+2 — str
perc: bd/cym, sd, tri, woodblk, xyl
Originally for band.

Schirmer

Concerto, Piano, op.38 <1962>
26'

3[1.2.3/pic] 3[1.2.Eh] 3[1.2.bcl] 2 — 4 3 3 0 — tmp+2 — hp — str
perc: bd, cym, sd, small sd w/o snares, tomtoms, tri, tamtam, xyl, crot, whip
   I. Allegro appassionato   *13'*
   II. Canzone   *7'*
   III. Allegro molto   *6'*

Schirmer

Concerto, Violin, op.14 <1939–1940; rev 1949>   25'

2[1.2/pic] 2 2 2 — 2 2 0 0 — tmp/sd — pf — str
I. Allegro   12'
II. Andante   9'
III. Presto in moto perpetuo   4'

Schirmer

Concerto, Violoncello, op.22 <1945>   27'

2 2[1.Eh] 2[1.2/bcl] 2 — 2 3 0 0 — tmp+1 — str
perc: sd
I. Allegro moderato   12'
II. Andante sostenuto   7'
III. Molto allegro ed appassionato   8'

Schirmer

Die natali, op.37; Chorale Preludes for Christmas <1960>   16'

3[1.2.3/pic] 3[1.2.Eh] 3[1.2.bcl] 2 — 4 3 3 1 — tmp+4 — hp — cel — str
perc: bd, cym, td, tri, tamtam, glock, xyl, crot

Schirmer   Luck's

Die natali: Silent Night <1960>   3'

1 2[1.Eh] 3[1.2.bcl] 0 — 4 0 3 1 — hp — cel — str
Cued to be playable with winds: 1 1 2 1 — 2 0 1 0

Schirmer

Essay No.1, op.12 <1937>   8'

2 2 2 2 — 4 3 3 1 — tmp — pf — str

Schirmer

Essay No.2, op.17 <1942>   10'

3[1.2.pic] 3[1.2.Eh] 2[1.2/bcl] 2 — 4 3 3 1 — tmp+2 — str
perc: bd, cym, field drum, tamtam

Schirmer   Luck's

Essay No.3, op.47 <1978>   14'

3[1.2.pic] 3[1.2.Eh] 4[1.2.Ebcl.bcl] 3[1.2.cbn] — 4 3 3 1 — opt euph — 2tmp+5 — 2hp — pf — str
perc: bd, cym, 2sd, tamtam, gong, glock, xyl, crot, whip, bongo, metal sheet

Schirmer

Fadograph of a Yestern Scene, op.44 <1971>   7'

3[1.2.pic] 3[1.2.Eh] 3[1.2.bcl] 2 — 4 3 3 1 — tmp+1 — 1 or 2hp — cel, pf — str
perc: sd, tri, vib, bd, tamtam, tambn, sus cym, crot[E5,A5]

Schirmer   Luck's

Four Songs <1936–1943; rev (orchd) 1945>   10'

mezzo-soprano solo
1 2 3[1.2.bcl] 2 — 3 2 2 0 — tmp — hp — str
Composed for voice & piano at various times from 1936 to 1943;
orchestrated by the composer 1945. Instrumentation varies from song to
song, within the aggregate listed above.
I. Nocturne, op.13, no.4, D major   4'
II. Monks and Raisins, op.18, no.2, F major 1'
III. Sure on this Shining Night, op.13, no.3, B-flat major   2'
IV. I Hear an Army, op.10, no.3, C minor   3'

Schirmer

Knoxville: Summer of 1915, op.24 <1947>   16'

high voice
1[1/pic] 1[1/Eh] 1 1 — 2 1 0 0 — 1perc[opt] — hp — str
perc: tri (one note!)

Schirmer   Luck's

The Lovers, op.43 <1971>   31'

solo baritone   chorus
4[1.2.pic.afl] 3[1.2.Eh] 3[1.2.bcl] 2 — 4 3 3 1 — tmp+3 — hp — cel, pf — str
perc: cym, xyl, tamtam, bd, crot, belltree, tri, 2woodblk, 3bongos
I. Body of a woman (baritone)   _'
II. Lithe girl, brown girl (men's chorus, women's voices)   _'
III. In the hot depth of this summer (women's voices)   _'
IV. Close your eyes (chorus)   _'
V. The Fortunate Isles (chorus with incidental soprano solo)   _'
VI. Sometimes (baritone)   _'
VII. We have lost even this twilight (chorus)   _'
VIII. Tonight I can write (baritone)   _'
IX. Cemetery of kisses (chorus)   _'

Schirmer

Medea [original version], op.23 (Cave of the Heart) <1946; rev 1947>   28'

1[fl/pic] 1[ob/Eh] 1 1 — 1 0 0 0 — pf — str
The original 1946 ballet; in 1947 it was reorchestrated for larger
orchestra. For subsequent versions, see next two entries.
I. Parados   3'
II. Chorus   2'
III. Medea Solo   5'
IV. Princess Solo   1'
V. Jason Solo   2'
VI. Chorus   3'
VII. Medea, Chorus, Jason and Princess: Medea's Dance of Vengeance   7'
VIII. Chorus   2'
IX. Exodus   3'

Schirmer

Medea, op.23 (Ballet Suite) <1948>   27'

2[1.2/pic] 2[1.2/Eh] 2 2 — 2 2 2 0 — tmp+3 — hp — pf — str
perc: bd, cym, sus cym, sd, tom, xyl
A suite for orchestra, drawn from the original ballet.
I. Parados   3'
II. Choros. Medea and Jason   5'
III. The Young Princess. Jason   3'
IV. Choros   3'
V. Medea   7'
VI. Kantikos Agonias 3'
VII. Exodos   3'

Schirmer

Medea's Meditation and Dance of Vengeance, op.23a <1953>   13'

3[1.2.3/pic] 3[1.2.Eh] 4[1.2.Ebcl.bcl] 3[1.2.cbn] — 4 3 3 1 — tmp+5 — hp — pf — str
perc: bd, cym, sd, tomtoms, tri, tamtam, xyl, whip
Created 1953, based on the 1946 ballet.

Schirmer

Music for a Scene from Shelley, op.7 <1933>   8'

3 3[1.2.Eh] 3[1.2.bcl] 3 — 4 3 3 1 — tmp+1 — hp — str
perc: sus cym, tamtam, glock

Schirmer

Night Flight, op.19a <1944; rev 1947; 1964>   8'

3[1.2.3/pic] 3[1.2.Eh] 4[1.2.Ebcl.bcl] 2 — 4 3 3 1 — 1perc — pf — str
perc: sus cym
An "electric instrument", imitating a signal or radio beam, may substitute
for the E-flat clarinet. This work is a revised version of a movement from
the composer's *Symphony No.2*.

Schirmer   Luck's

Prayers of Kierkegaard, op.30 <1954>   20'

chorus   solo soprano
3[1.2.pic] 3[1.2.Eh] 3[1.2.bcl] 2 — 4 3 3 1 — tmp+4 — hp — pf —
str
perc: bd, cym, tamtam, xyl, low bell (E)
Incidental alto & tenor solos drawn from chorus.

Schirmer

The School for Scandal: Overture <1931>   8'

3[1.2.pic] 3[1.2.Eh] 3[1.2.bcl] 2 — 4 3 3 1 — tmp+3 — hp — cel[can
be played by perc] — str
perc: bd, cym, tri, glock

Schirmer	Luck's

Serenade, op.1 <1928>   10'

str 4t or str orch
I. Un poco adagio; Allegro con spirito   4'
II. Andante con moto   3'
III. Allegro giocoso   3'

Schirmer

Souvenirs, op.28: Suite <1952>   20'

2[1.2/pic] 2[1.2/Eh] 2 2 — 4 3 3 0 — tmp+3 — hp — cel — str
perc: bd, cym, sd, tri
I. Tempo di walzer   4'
II. Schottische   3'
III. Pas de deux   4'
IV. Two-step   2'
V. Hesitation-Tango   4'
VI. Galop   3'

Schirmer

Symphony No.1 in One Movement, op.9 <1935–1936>   21'

3[1.2.3/pic] 3[1.2.Eh] 3[1.2.bcl] 3[1.2.cbn] — 4 3 3 1 — tmp+1 — hp
— str
perc: bd, cym
Allegro ma non troppo   7'
Allegro molto   4'
Andante tranquillo   5'
Con moto (Passacaille)   5'

Schirmer

Symphony No.2, op.19 <1944; rev 1947>   26'

3[1.2.3/pic] 3[1.2.Eh] 4[1.2.Ebcl.bcl] 3[1.2.cbn] — 4 3 3 1 — tmp+2
— pf — str
perc: bd, sus cym, sd, woodblk
I. Allegro ma non troppo   10'
II. Andante un poco mosso   7'
III. Presto — Allegro risoluto   9'

Schirmer

Toccata festiva, op.36 <1960>   14'

solo organ
3[1.2.pic] 3[1.2.Eh] 3[1.2.bcl] 2 — 4 3 3 1 — tmp+4 — str
perc: bd, cym, sd, tri, tamtam, xyl
Alternate version: organ solo, trumpet, timpani, strings.

Schirmer	Luck's

Vanessa: Intermezzo <1957>   4'

3[1.2.3/pic] 3[1.2.Eh] 3[1.2.bcl] 2 — 4 2 3 1 — tmp+1 — hp — str
perc: bd, sus cym

Schirmer	Luck's

Vanessa: Under the Willow Tree (Country Dance) <1957>   4'

optional mixed chorus
3[1.2.pic] 3[1.2.Eh] 3[1.2.bcl] 2 — 4 2 3 0 — tmp+3 — hp — cel —
str
perc: bd, cym, sd, crot

Schirmer	Luck's

Barlow, Wayne   1912-1996

(b Elyria, OH, 6 Sept 1912; d Rochester, NY, 17 Dec 1996). American

The Winter's Past; Rhapsody for Oboe <1938>   5'

solo oboe
str

C. Fischer	Luck's

Bartholomew, Greg   1957-

(b St. Paul, Minnesota, 29 July 1957). American

Ah, My Children <2008>   8'

1 1 1 1 — 4 1 1 1 — tmp — str
Adaptation of the opera *Razumov*, Act II, sc.1.

Burke&Bagley

Suite for String Orchestra <2006>   12'

Originally for string trio (*String Trio for George Crumb*).
1. Adagio—Animato   4'
2. Grave all'antico—Moderato   4'
3. Presto—Legato dolce   4'

Burke&Bagley

Sunshine Music <2011>   10'

1 2[1.Eh] 1 1 — 1 0 0 0 — str
Mvts played without pause. An alternative orchestration is available for:
2 1 1 1 — 1 0 0 0 — str
1. Sunshine in the Dooryard   _'
2. Sunshine in the City   _'
3. Sunshine in the Mountains   _'

Burke&Bagley

Bartók, Béla   1881-1945

(b Nagyszentmiklós, Hungary [now Sînnicolau Mare, Romania], 25 March 1881; d
New York, 26 Sept 1945). Hungarian

BB = László Somfai: *Béla Bartók: Composition, Concepts, and
Autograph Sources* (Berkeley, Univ. of California Press, 1996)

Cantata profana, BB 100 (A kilenc csodaszarvas; The   18'
Nine Enchanted Stags) <1930>

double chorus   solo tenor & baritone
3[1.2/pic.3/pic] 3 3[1.2/bcl.3/bcl] 3[1.2/cbn.3/cbn] — 4 2 3 1 —
tmp+2 — hp — str
perc: bd, cym, sd, tamtam
I. Molto moderato   7'
II. Andante   8'
III. Moderato   3'

Boosey

Concerto for Orchestra, BB 123 <1942–1943>   *36'*

3[1.2.3/pic] 3[1.2.3/Eh] 3[1.2.3/bcl] 3[1.2.3/cbn] — 4 3 3 1 — tmp+1 — 2hp — str

perc: bd, cym, sus cym, sd, tri, tamtam
A 2nd percussionist is required if alternate ending is used. Cbn used only in final movement (11 bars).
   An edition (score & parts), revised 1993 by Peter Bartok, is available from the publisher.

I. Introduzione: Andante non troppo - Allegro vivace	*10'*
II. Giuoco delle coppie: Allegretto scherzando	*6'*
III. Elegia: Andante non troppo	*7'*
IV. Intermezzo interrotto: Allegretto	*4'*
V. Finale: Pesante - Presto	*9'*

Boosey

Concerto, Piano, No.1, BB 91 <1926>   *25'*

2[1.2/pic] 2[1.2/Eh] 2[1.2/bcl] 2 — 4 2 3 0 — tmp+3 — str

perc: bd, cym, sus cym, sd w/ snare, sd w/o snares, tri, tamtam

I. Allegro moderato	*9'*
II. Andante	*9'*
III. Allegro molto	*7'*

Boosey

Concerto, Piano, No.2, BB 101 <1930–1931>   *28'*

3[1.2.3/pic] 2[1/Eh.2] 2[1.2/bcl] 3[1.2.3/cbn] — 4 3 3 1 — tmp+2 — str

perc: bd, cym, sus cym, small sd, tri, tambn, tamtam

I. Allegro	*10'*
II. Adagio - Presto - Adagio	*12'*
III. Allegro molto	*6'*

Boosey

Concerto, Piano, No.3, BB 127 <1945>   *23'*

2[1.2/pic] 2[1.2/Eh] 2[1.2/bcl] 2 — 4 2 3 1 — tmp+1 — str

perc: bd, cym, sd, tri, tamtam, xyl
Revised edition from Boosey & Hawkes includes minor modifications of Bartok's that were not incorporated into the first published score, as well as modifications to the last 17 bars (which were orchestrated by Tibor Serly after Bartok's death).

I. Allegretto	*7'*
II. Adagio religioso - Poco più mosso - Tempo I	*9'*
III. Allegro vivace	*7'*

Boosey

Concerto, 2 Pianos and Percussion, BB 121 <1940>   *25'*

2[1.2/pic] 2[1.2/Eh] 2 2[1.2/cbn] — 4 2 3 0 — cel — str

perc: Solo I: tmp, 2sd, tri, cym, sus cym, tamtam
Solo II: xyl, bd, 2sd, tri, cym, sus cym, tamtam
This work is the orchestral version of the *Sonata for 2 Pianos and Percussion*, BB 115, *q.v.*

I. Assai lento - Allegro molto	*12'*
II. Lento; ma non troppo	*6'*
III. Allegro non troppo	*7'*

Boosey

Concerto, Viola, op. posth., BB 128 (Serly version) <1945>   *21'*

3[1.2.3/pic] 2 2 2 — 3 3 2 1 — tmp+2 — str

perc: bd, sd, large cyms, small cyms
Trombones & tuba appear to be optional; they are cued into other instruments.
   Completed by Tibor Serly.

I. Moderato	*11'*
II. Lento - Adagio religioso - Allegretto	*6'*
III. Allegro vivace	*4'*

Boosey

Concerto, Viola, op. posth., BB 128 (rev. version) <1945>   *20'*

3[1.2.pic] 2[1.2/Eh] 2 2[1.2/cbn] — 4 3 2 1 — tmp+2 — str

perc: bd, large cyms, sd, tri
Revised version by Nelson Dellamaggiore & Peter Bartok (1995).

I. Allegro moderato	*10'*
II. Lento	*5'*
III. Finale: Allegretto	*5'*

Boosey

Concerto, Viola, op.posth., BB 128 (Erdélyi version) <1945>   *21'*

3[1.2.pic] 2 2[1.2/bcl] 2 — 4 3 2 1 — tmp+2 — str

Reconstructed from Bartók's incomplete sketches by Csaba Erdélyi (2004). Retail sales and performance rights to this reconstruction are as yet available only in New Zealand and Australia.

Promethean

Concerto, Violin, "No.1", op. posth., BB 48a <1907–1908>   *21'*

2[1.2/pic] 3[1.2.Eh] 2[1.2/bcl] 2 — 4 2 2 1 — tmp+1 — 2hp — str

perc: tri, bd (brief; can be covered by tmp)
1st mvt of this work later used as no.1 of the *Two Portraits*, op.5.

I. Andante sostenuto	*9'*
II. Allegro giocoso	*12'*

Boosey

Concerto, Violin, No.2, BB 117 <1937–1938>   *36'*

2[1.2/pic] 2[1.2/Eh] 2[1.2/bcl] 2[1.2/cbn] — 4 2 3 0 — tmp+2 — hp — cel — str

perc: bd, cym, sus cym, sd, tri, tamtam; 1 percussionist doubles on tmp2

I. Allegro non troppo	*16'*
II. Theme and Variations: Andante tranquillo	*9'*
III. Rondo: Allegro molto	*11'*

Boosey

Concerto, Violoncello, op. posth., BB 128 (Serly adaptation) <1945>   *21'*

3[1.2.3/pic] 2 2 2 — 3 3 2 1 — tmp+2 — str

perc: bd, sd, large cyms, small cyms
Trombones & tuba appear to be optional; they are cued into other instruments.
   Tibor Serly, who completed the Viola Concerto after the composer's death, also made a version of the solo part for violoncello. Use the orchestral parts for the Viola Concerto.

I. Moderato	*11'*
II. Lento - Adagio religioso - Allegretto	*6'*
III. Allegro vivace	*4'*

Boosey

Dance Suite, BB 86a (Táncszvit) <1923>   *17'*

2[1/pic.2/pic] 2[1.2/Eh] 2[1.2/bcl] 2[1.2/cbn] — 4 2 2 1 — tmp+3 — hp — pf, cel/pf — str

perc: bd, cym, sd, td, tri, tamtam, glock
Brief passage requires pf 4-hands (covered by cel player).

I. Moderato	*4'*
II. Allegro molto	*2'*
III. Allegro vivace	*3'*
IV. Molto tranquillo	*3'*
V. Comodo	*1'*
VI. Finale: Allegro	*4'*

Boosey

Dances of Transylvania, BB 102b (Erdélyi táncok) <1915; rev (orchd) 1931>   5'

2[1.2/pic] 2 2[1.2/bcl] 2 — 2 2 2 1 — tmp/tri — hp[or pf] — str
perc: tri
Originally for piano (1915); then for violin & piano (1930).
A version for strings only is available from Kalmus.

I. Allegretto	2'
II. Moderato	1'
III. Allegro vivace	2'

Boosey	Luck's

Divertimento, BB 118 <1939>   24'

str[min 6.6.4.4.2]
Corrected edition, 1999.

I. Allegro non troppo	9'
II. Molto adagio	8'
III. Allegro assai	7'

Boosey

Four Orchestral Pieces, op.12, BB 64 <1912; rev (orchd) 1921>   22'

4[1.2.3/pic2.4/pic1] 3[1.2/Eh2.3/Eh1] 4[1.2.3/Ebcl1/bcl1.4/Ebcl2/bcl2] 4[1.2.3.4/cbn] — 4 4 4 1 — tmp+2 — 2hp — pf, cel/pf — str
perc: bd, cym, sd, tri, tamtam, glock
Originally for 2 pianos; orchestrated by the composer.
Cel helps cover pf 4-hands in 2nd mvt. Eh2 not actually necessary.

I. Preludio: Moderato	7'
II. Scherzo: Allegro	6'
III. Intermezzo: Moderato	4'
IV. Marcia funebre: Maestoso	5'

Boosey

Hungarian Peasant Songs, BB 107 (Magyar parasztdalok) <1933>   9'

2[1.2/pic] 2[1.2/Eh] 2[1.2/bcl] 2 — 2 2 2 1 — tmp/bd — hp — str
Taken from a set of 15 piano works (BB 79); orchestrated by the composer.

I. Ballad (Theme with variations)	3'
II. Hungarian Peasant Dances	6'

Boosey

Hungarian Sketches, BB 103 (Magyar képek; Hungarian Pictures) <1931>   11'

2[1.2/pic] 2 2[1.2/bcl] 2[1.2/cbn] — 2 2 2 1 — tmp+2 — hp — str
perc: bd, cym, sus cym, tri, xyl, sd, sd w/o snare
Bcl has only 2 notes (can be covered by bn 2); cbn has only 10 notes (can be covered by tuba and bn 2).

I. An Evening in the Village (Este a székelyeknél)	3'
II. Bear Dance (Medvetánc)	2'
III. Melody (Melódia)	2'
IV. Slightly Tipsy (Kicsit ázottan)	2'
V. Swineherd's Dance (Urögi kanásztánc)	2'

EMB

Kossuth, BB 31 <1903>   21'

4[1/pic.2.3.pic] 4[1.2.3.Eh] 4[1.2.Ebcl.bcl] 4[1.2.3.cbn] — 8 4 3 1 — bass tp, 2 tenor tubas — tmp+4 — 2hp — str[16.16.12.10.8]
perc: bd, cym, sd, tri, tamtam
Ed. D. Dille.

EMB

Mikrokosmos Suite, BB 105 <1926–1939>   17'

3[1.2.3/pic] 2[1.2/Eh] 2[1.2/bcl] 2[1.2/cbn] — 4 3 3 1 — tmp+4 — hp — cel — str
perc: bd, cym, sd, tomtoms, tri, tambn, tamtam, xyl, chimes, slghbells, woodblk, rattle
Arr. Tibor Serly, with the cooperation and approval of Bartók. From the collection of 153 piano pieces.

I. Prelude	_'
II. Scherzando (Jack in the Box)	_'
III. Unisono	_'
IV. Bourrée	_'
V. Moto perpetuo (From the Diary of a Fly)	_'
VI. Contrasts over Pedal (Study in Overtones)	_'
VII. Bulgarian Rhythm No. 4	_'
VIII. Bulgarian Rhythm No. 6	_'

Boosey

The Miraculous Mandarin, op.19, BB 82 (A csodálatos mandarin) <1919>   30'

textless chorus
3[1.2/pic2.3/pic1] 3[1.2.3/Eh] 3[1.2/Ebcl.3/bcl] 3[1.2/cbn2.3/cbn1] — 4[2&4/Wag tb] 3 3 1 — tmp+5 — hp — cel, pf, org — str
perc: bd, cym, sus cym, sd, td, tri, tamtam, xyl
Cl 2 doubles on E-flat cl as well as D-clarinet. Bcl is in B-flat and in A. Bn2 has only 1 note on cbn, after figure 93; apparently this has been eliminated in the revised edition.
Rev. 2000 by Peter Bartók, restoring music previously cut in an unsuccessful attempt to appease the censors in 1931 (this does not affect any of the music in the suite).

Boosey	Universal

The Miraculous Mandarin, op.19, BB 82 (A csodálatos mandarin): Suite <1918–1919>   20'

3[1.2/pic2.3/pic1] 3[1.2.3/Eh] 3[1.2/Ebcl.3/bcl] 3[1.2.3/cbn1] — 4 3 3 1 — tmp+5 — hp — cel, pf, org — str
perc: bd, cym, sus cym, sd, td, tri, tamtam, xyl
2nd cl doubles on E-flat cl as well as D-clarinet. Bcl is in B-flat and in A. Org has only 8 notes (fig [4]): all pedals, and all doubled in tuba and tbn3.

Boosey	Universal

Music for Strings, Percussion and Celesta, BB 114 <1936>   27'

tmp+3 — hp — cel, pf — double str orch
perc: bd, 2pr cym, sd, sd w/o snares, tamtam, xyl
Cel helps cover pf 4-hands in 4th mvt.

I. Andante tranquillo	7'
II. Allegro	7'
III. Adagio	7'
IV. Allegro molto	6'

Boosey

Rhapsody, Piano & Orchestra, op.1, BB 36b <1905>   17'

3[1.2.3/pic] 2 2[1.2/bcl] 2 — 4 2 3 0 — tmp+2 — str
perc: bd, cym, sd, tri, tamtam

Boosey	EMB	Kalmus	Luck's

Rhapsody No.1 for Violin & Orchestra, BB 94b <1928>   10'

2[1.2/pic] 2 2[1.2/bcl] 2 — 2 2 1 1 — cimbalom[or hp & pf] — 1perc — hp — pf — str
perc: tri
Originally for violin & piano (BB 94a).

I. Lassu	5'
II. Friss	5'

Boosey

Rhapsody No.2 for Violin & Orchestra, BB 96b <1928–1929; rev 1935>   11'

2[1.2/pic] 2[1.2/Eh] 2[1.2/bcl] 2 — 2 2 1 1 — tmp+2 — hp — pf/cel — str
perc: bd, cym, sus cym, sd, tri
I. Lassu   5'
II. Friss   6'

Boosey

Romanian Folk Dances, BB 76 (Román népi táncok) <1915; rev (orchd) 1915>   6'

2[1.2/pic] 0 2 2 — 2 0 0 0 — str
Originally for piano (BB 68); orchestrated by the composer.
Also available for string orchestra, *q.v.*
I. Jocul cu bâta (Stick Dance)   1'
II. Brâul (Waistband Dance)   1'
III. Pe loc (Stamping Dance, or On the Spot)   1'
IV. Buciumeana (Hornpipe Dance)   1'
V. Poarga românesca (Romanian Polka)   1'
VI. Maruntel (Quick Dance)   1'

Boosey   Kalmus

Romanian Folk Dances [string orchestra version], BB 76 (Román népi táncok) <1915>   6'

str
Arranged for string orch by an unknown hand.
I. Jocul cu bâta (Stick Dance)   1'
II. Brâul (Waistband Dance)   1'
III. Pe loc (Stamping Dance, or On the Spot)   1'
IV. Buciumeana (Hornpipe Dance)   1'
V. Poarga românesca (Romanian Polka)   1'
VI. Maruntel (Quick Dance)   1'

Boosey

Scherzo, op.2, BB 35 <1904>   29'

solo piano
4[1.2.3/pic2.pic1] 3[1.2.Eh] 4[1.2.3.Ebcl] 4[1.2.3.cbn] — 4 3 3 1 — tmp+5 — 2hp — str
perc: bd, cym, sd, small sd, tri, tamtam, glock
One of the 4 clarinet parts is written for "clarinet in A-flat."
Originally titled *Burlesque.*

Boosey

Sonata, 2 Pianos & Percussion, BB 115 <1937>   25'

4 players: 2pf & 2 perc
perc: Solo I: tmp, 2sd, tri, cym, sus cym, tamtam
Solo II: xyl, bd, 2sd, tri, cym, sus cym, tamtam
See also the verson of this work with orchestral accompaniment:
Concerto for 2 Pianos and Percussion.
I. Assai lento - Allegro molto   12'
II. Lento; ma non troppo   6'
III. Allegro non troppo   7'

Boosey

Suite No.1 for Orchestra, op.3, BB 39 <1905>   35'

4[1.2.3.pic] 3[1.2.Eh] 4[1.2.Ebcl.bcl] 4[1.2.3.cbn] — 4 3 3 1 — tmp+3 — 2hp — str
perc: bd, cym, sd, tri, tambn, glock
I. Allegro vivace   7'
II. Poco adagio   7'
III. Presto   8'
IV. Moderato   6'
V. Molto vivace   7'

Boosey   Kalmus

Suite No.2 for Small Orchestra, op.4, BB 40 <1905–1907; rev 1920, 1943>   34'

2[1/pic.2] 2[1.2/Eh] 2[1/Ebcl.2/bcl] 2[1.2/cbn] — 3 2 0 0 — tmp+2 — 2hp — str
perc: bd, cym, tri, tambn, gong
I. Comodo   9'
II. Allegro scherzando   9'
III. Andante   8'
IV. Comodo   8'

Boosey

Three Village Scenes, BB 87b (Falun [Tri dedinské scény]) <1926>   12'

female voices (2 or 4 mezzo-sopranos & 2 or 4 altos)
1[1/pic] 1[1/Eh] 2[1/Ebcl.2/asx] 1 — 1 1 1 0 — 1perc — hp — pf — str 5t
perc: cym, sus cym, bd, chimes, 2sd
Originally for voice and piano (BB 87a).
I. Wedding   4'
II. Lullaby   5'
III. Lad's Dance   3'

Boosey

Two Pictures, op.10, BB 59 (Két kép; Deux images) <1910>   17'

3[1.2.3/pic] 3[1.2.Eh] 3[1.2.3/bcl] 3[1.2.3/cbn] — 4 4 3 1 — tmp+1 — 2hp — cel — str
perc: bd, cym, chimes
I. Virágzás (In Full Flower)   8'
II. A falu tánca (Village Dance)   9'

Boosey   Kalmus   Luck's

Two Portraits, op.5, BB 48b (Két portré; Deux portraits) <1907–1911>   12'

2[1/pic.2] 2[1.2/Eh] 2[1/Ebcl1.2/bcl/Ebcl2] 2 — 4 2 2 1 — tmp+4 — 2hp — str
perc: bd, cym, sd, tri, tamtam
First movement is for solo violin with orchestra accompaniment.
I. Egy ideális (One Ideal)   10'
II. Egy torz (One Grotesque)   2'

Boosey   EMB   Kalmus   Luck's

Two Romanian Dances, BB 56 (Két román tánc; Deux danses roumaines) <1909–1910>   10'

2[1.2/pic] 2 2 2 — 4 2 3 0 — tmp+3 — hp — str
perc: bd, cym, sus cym, sd, tri, tambn, tamtam
Originally for piano; orchestrated by Leó Weiner.
I. Allegro vivace   5'
II. Poco allegro   5'

EMB

The Wooden Prince, BB 74 (A fából faragott királyfi): Suite <1921–1924; rev 1932>   30'

4[1.2.3/pic.4/pic] 4[1.2.3/Eh.4/Eh] 4[1.2.3/Ebcl.4/bcl] 4[1.2.3/cbn.4/cbn] — 4 6[4tp.2crt] 3 1 — asx, tsx — tmp+5 — 2hp — cel 4-hands — str
perc: bd, cym, sd, tri, tamtam, glock, xyl, cast
There is also a *Little Concert Suite from The Wooden Prince* (also op.13, BB 74), 12' in duration (3 dances from the ballet).

Boosey

Bassett, Leslie   1923-

(b Hanford, CA, 22 Jan 1923). American

Concerto for Orchestra <1991>   28'

3[incl pic] 3[incl Eh] 3[incl bcl] 3[incl cbn] — 4 3 3 1 — tmp+3 — hp — pf/cel — str

Peters

Concerto lirico <1983>   15'

solo trombone
3[1.2.3/pic] 2 3 2 — 4 2 3 1 — tmp+3 — hp — pf/cel — str
perc: bd, sus cym, sd, tomtom, tri, tamtam, glock, vib, chimes, crot, woodblk,
templeblk, whip, bongo, wind chimes (wood, glass & metal)
I. Expressive, energetic   _'
II. Hushed, singing   _'
III. Scurrying   _'

Peters

Echoes from an Invisible World <1974–1975>   17'

3[1.2.3/pic] 3[1.2.Eh] 3[1.2.3/bcl] 3[1.2.cbn] — 4 4 3 1 — tmp+3 —
hp — cel, pf — str
perc: bd, 4sus cym, szl cym, sd, tomtoms, 4 tri, tamtam, glock, xyl, vib, bongos,
bamboo wnd ch, wood wnd ch, 4marac

Peters

From a Source Evolving <1985>   13'

3[incl pic] 3[incl Eh] 3[incl bcl] 3[incl cbn] — 4 3 3 1 — tmp+3 —
hp — pf, cel — str

Peters

Variations for Orchestra <1963>   23'

2[1.pic] 2[1.Eh] 2[1.2/bcl] 2[1.2/cbn] — 4 2 3 1 — tmp+2 — hp —
cel, pf — str
perc: glock, gong, tri, vib, xyl, 2sd, 2sus cym

Peters

Bates, Mason   1977-

(b Philadelphia, PA, 23 Jan 1977). American

Alternative Energy <2011>   27'

3[1/pic.2/pic/afl.3/pic] 3[1.2.3/Eh] 3[1.2/Ebcl.3] 3[1.2.3/cbn] — 4 3 3
1 — electronica — tmp+3 — hp — pf/cel — str
perc: glock, vib, hi-hat, tomtom, marim, sd, tamtam, bd, gong, szl cym, xyl, crot,
chimes, tri, thunder, buttongong[2 8ves of tuned gongs], shaker, djembe, sticks,
Chinese cym, car parts, scrap metal, 2ratch, 3sus cym, 2woodblk,
2windchimes[bamboo & ceramic], logdrum
Electronica: laptop; 6 house speakers, 2 subwoofers, 5-6 onstage
monitors—all speakers controlled by an in-house sound engineer. Laptop
performer need not have computer expertise; software is supplied by the
publisher.
1. Ford's Farm, 1896   8'
2. Chicago, 2012   6'
3. Xianjiang Province, 2112   8'
4. Reykjavik, 2222   5'

Holab

Attack Decay Sustain Release <2013>   5'

3[1/pic.2.3] 2 2[bcl1.bcl2] 3[1.2.cbn] — 4 3 3 1 — tmp+3 — pf/cel
— str
perc: field dr, bd, hi-hat, sus cym, sd, tambn, claves, cast, tri, tamtam, sandblk,
shaker, 4rototom, 4woodblk

Holab

The B-Sides; Five Pieces for Orchestra <2009>   23'

2[1/pic.2] 2[1.2/Eh(opt)] 3[1.2/bcl.3/Ebcl] 3[1.2.cbn] — 4 3 3 1 —
electronica — tmp+3 — hp — pf/cel — str
perc: sus cym, szl cym, bd, cym, hi-hat, sd, tambn, glock, marim, vib, woodblk,
cast, 2sandblks, 2tri, djembe, typewriter, oildrum, large broom
Electronica: 2 stereo speakers, 5-6 onstage monitors, an in-house sound
engineer; an electronic drumpad, supplied by the publisher and playable
by any percussionist, triggers the electronica part.
I. Broom of the System   _'
II. Aerosol Melody (Hanalei)   _'
III. Gemini in the Solar Wind [attacca]   _'
IV. Temescal Noir [attacca]   _'
V. Warehouse Medicine   _'

Holab

Concerto, Violin <2012>   24'

2[1.2/pic] 2[1.2/Eh] 2[1.2/bcl] 2[1.2/cbn] — 4 3 3 1 — tmp+3 — hp
— pf/cel — str
perc: bd, marim, sus cym, szl cym, tamtam, glock, hi-hat, tambn, sd, tri, cym,
23buttongongs, 2woodblks, djembe, logdrum, eggshaker, 3Tibetan prayer
bells[tuned]
I. Archeopteryx [attacca]   _'
II. Lakebed Memories [attacca]   _'
III. The Rise of Birds   _'

Holab

Desert Transport <2010>   14'

3[1/pic.2/pic3.3] 3[1.2.3/Eh] 3[1.2/Ebcl.3] 3[1.2.cbn] — 4 3 3 1 —
tmp+3 — hp — pf/cel — str
perc: sus cym, bd, marim, sd, glock, tri, templeblks, tambn, tomtom, cym, crot,
vib, lionroar, 2rute, sandblks, eggshaker, finger cym, Indian rattle
At the beginning of mvt 4, a field recording of Pima Indians singing
"Mountain by the Sea" is played (initiated by a percussionist) on a CD
player which may be run through the house system.
    Mvts are played without pause.
1. Dengler's Hangar
2. Sky Ranch
3. Sedona
4. Montezuma's Castle

Holab

Icarian Rhapsody <1999>   12'

str

Holab

Liquid Interface <2007>   23'

3[all/pic] 3[1.2.3/Eh] 3[1.2.3/Ebcl/bcl] 3[1.2.3/cbn] — 4 3 3 1 —
electronica — 3perc — hp — pf — str
perc: bd, szl cym, hi-hat, sd, set, tri, tamtam, glock, xyl, marim, vib, chimes, crot,
bongos, cast, wnd mach, 2sus cym, ride cym, splash, 2harmonicas, gtr, 6musical
glasses, washboard
Electronica: laptop (any kind), 2 stereo speakers, a few onstage monitors,
electronic drumpad (supplied by publisher).
1. Glaciers Calving [attacca]   _'
2. Scherzo Liquido   _'
3. Crescent City [attacca]   _'
4. On the Wannsee   _'

Holab

Mothership <2011>   9'

3 3[1.2.Eh] 3[1.2.Ebcl] 2 — 4 3 3 0 — electronica — tmp+3 — hp —
pf — str
perc: bd, cym, hi-hat, sd, set, glock, marim, 2sus cym, 3woodblk, djembe
Electronica: 2 stereo speakers, 5-6 onstage monitors, in-house sound
engineer, laptop

Holab

Music from Underground Spaces <2008>   15'

2[1.2/afl(opt)] 2 2[1/Ebcl.2] 2[1.2/cbn] — 4 3 3 1 — electronica —
tmp+3 — hp — pf/cel — str
perc: vib, marim, bd, glock, crot, szl cym, sd, hi-hat, xyl, cast, Chinese gong,
fingercym, typewriter, logdrum, 2sus cym, 2woodblk, 2tri
Electronica: 2 stereo speakers, a few small onstage monitors, laptop.
    The movements are played without pause.
1. Tunnels
2. Infernos
3. Crystalline Cities
4. Tectonic Plates

Holab

Ode <2001>   *11'*

3[1.2.pic] 2 3[1.2/bcl.Ebcl] 3[1.2.cbn] — 4 3[tp 1-2 dbl slide whistle] 3 1 — tmp+3 — hp — pf — str
perc: crot, marim, bd, xyl, vib, congas, vibrslp, field dr, gong, wnd mach, glock, chimes, cast, sd, whip, cym, logdrum, sandblk & lg sandpaper board, 2tri, bamboo windchimes, police whistle, anvil, pump shotgun, 4tamtam, 8sus cym, splash, siren

Holab

The Rise of Exotic Computing <2013>   *12'*

1[fl/pic] 1 1 1 — 1 1 0 0 — electronica — 1perc — hp — pf — str
perc: marim, glock, sus cym
Electronica: speakers, on-stage monitors, laptop.

Holab

Sea-Blue Circuitry <2010>   *13'*

2[1/pic.2/opt pic] 2[1.2/Eh] 2 2[1.2/cbn] — 4 3 3 1 — 4perc — hp — prep pf — str
perc: hi-hat, sd, bd, vib, glock, tomtom, typewriter, splash, buttongong, 5rototom
  I. *Circuits*   ˌ'
  II. *Marine Snow*   ˌ'
  III. *Gigawatt Greyhound*   ˌ'

Holab

White Lies for Lomax <2009>   *7'*

2[1.2/pic] 2 2[1.bcl] 2 — 4 3 3 1 — 3perc — hp — pf — str
perc: glock, tri, vib, crot, xyl, marim, sus cym, cym, splash
An optional off-stage boombox in the last 27 measures plays an Alan Lomax field recording of old blues musicians.

Holab

Bavicchi, John   1922-

(b Boston, 25 April 1922). American

Fantasia on Korean Folk Tunes, op.53 <1966>   *8'*

2 1 3[incl bcl] 1 — 2 2 3 1 — tmp+3 — str

BKJ

Mont Blanc Overture, op.72 <1976–1977>   *7'*

3[1.2.opt pic] 1[opt] 3[1.2.opt bcl] 1 — 2 3 3 1[opt] — tmp+4 — str

Oxford

Music for Small Orchestra, op.81 <1981>   *8'*

2 2 2 2 — 2 2 0 0 — tmp — str

BKJ

Bax, Arnold   1883-1953

(b Streatham, 8 Nov 1883; d Cork, 3 Oct 1953). English

An excellent website by Graham Parlett may be found at www.arnoldbax.com. It includes instrumentations, durations, and sources for the complete Bax works, along with much other useful information.

Garden of Fand <1913–1916>   *17'*

4[1.2.3.pic] 3[1.2.Eh] 4[1.2.3.bcl] 3[1.2.cbn] — 4 3 3 1 — tmp+3 — 2hp — cel — str
perc: bd, cym, sus cym, tambn, glock
1 less percussionist, if timpanist covers bd.

Chappell	Kalmus	Luck's

The Happy Forest <1914–1921>   *10'*

3[1.2.3/pic] 3[1.2.Eh] 4[1.2.Ebcl.bcl] 3[1.2.cbn] — 4 3 3 1 — tmp+4 — hp — cel — str
perc: cym, glock, bd, xyl, tambn
Originally published by Murdoch, Murdoch & Sons.

Warner

In the Faery Hills <1909; rev 1921>   *15'*

3[1.2.3/pic] 3[1.2.Eh] 4[1.2.Ebcl.bcl] 2 — 4 3 3 1 — tmp+2 — 2hp — cel — str
perc: glock, cym, sus cym, tamtam, tambn, sd, bd
No.2 of the composer's *Éire* trilogy.

Chappell

Mediterranean <1922>   *3'*

2 3[1.2.Eh] 2 2 — 4 0 0 0 — tmp+2 — hp — str
perc: tambn, glock, cast

Chappell	Kalmus	Luck's

November Woods <1917>   *15'*

4[1.2.3.pic] 3[1.2.Eh] 4[1.2.3.bcl] 3[1.2.cbn] — 4 3 3 1 — tmp+2 — 2hp — cel — str
perc: sus cym, bd, glock, cym

Chappell	Kalmus	Luck's

Overture to a Picaresque Comedy <1930>   *10'*

3[1.2.3/pic] 3[1.2.Eh] 4[1.2.3.bcl] 3[1.2.cbn] — 4 3 3 1 — tmp+3 — hp — str
perc: td, sd, xyl, cym, tambn, glock, bd, tamtam, sus cym, rattle

Chappell

Roscatha (Battle Hymn; Rosc-catha) <1910>   *11'*

3[1.2.3/pic] 3[1.2.Eh] 4[1.2.3.bcl] 3[1.2.cbn] — 4 3 3 1 — tmp+4 — str
perc: bd, field dr, sd, glock, cym, sus cym
The original title, "Rosc-catha", is Irish Gaelic for "battle hymn." This work is no.3 of the composer's *Éire* trilogy.

Saga

Summer Music <1917–1920; rev 1932>   *10'*

3[1.2.3/pic] 3[1.2.Eh] 2 2 — 4 1 0 0 — tmp — hp — str

Warner

Symphony No.1, E-flat <1922>   *32'*

4[1.2.3/afl.4/pic] 3[1.2.Eh.heckl or bass ob] 4[1.2.3/Ebcl.4/bcl(A)] 3[1.2.cbn or sarr] — 4 3 3 1 — tmp+4 — 2hp — cel — str
perc: bd, cym, sd, tri, tambn, tamtam, glock, xyl, chimes, td
  I. *Allegro moderato e feroce; Moderato espressivo; Tempo I*   *13'*
  II. *Lento solenne*   *11'*
  III. *Allegro maestoso; Allegro vivace ma non troppo presto*   *8'*

Chappell

Symphony No.3 <1929>   *50'*

3[1.2.3/pic] 3[1.2.Eh] 4[1.2.3/Ebcl.bcl] 3[1.2.cbn] — 4 3 3 1 — tmp+5 — 1 or 2hp — cel — str
perc: sd, td, tri, tambn, xyl, glock, bd, cym, tamtam, anvil
  I. *Lento moderato; Allegro moderato*   *21'*
  II. *Lento*   *13'*
  III. *Moderato*   *16'*

Chappell

Symphony No.4 <1931>   42'

3[1.2.3/pic] 3[1.2.Eh] 4[1.2.3.bcl(A)] 3[1.2.cbn] — 6 3 3 1 — tenor
tuba — tmp+4 — hp — cel/org — str
perc: sd, xyl, glock, tri, tamtam, bd, tambn, sus cym, cym
- I. Allegro moderato   17'
- II. Lento moderato   14'
- III. Allegro; Tempo di marcia trionfale   11'

> Chappell

Symphony No.5 <1932>   43'

3[1.2/pic.3/pic] 3[1.2.Eh] 4[1.2.3/Ebcl.bcl(A)] 3[1.2.cbn] — 4 3 3 1
— tmp+3 — hp — str
perc: glock, tamtam, tambn, td, sd, tri, bd, cym, sus cym
- I. Poco lento; Allegro con fuoco; Moderato   18'
- II. Poco lento   11'
- III. Poco moderato; Allegro; Epilogue   14'

> Chappell

Symphony No.6 <1934>   40'

3[1.2.3/pic] 3[1.2.Eh] 4[1.2.3/Ebcl.bcl(A)] 3[1.2.cbn] — 4 3 3 1 —
tmp+3 — hp — cel — str
perc: sd, tri, tamtam, glock, td, bd, cym, sus cym
- I. Moderato; Allegro con fuoco   10'
- II. Lento, molto espressivo   11'
- III. Introduction; Scherzo & Trio; Epilogue   19'

> Chappell

Symphony No.7 <1938–1939>   47'

3[1.2.3/pic] 3[1.2.Eh] 4[1.2.3.bcl] 3[1.2.cbn] — 4 3 3 1 — tmp+4 —
hp — str
perc: glock, tambn, tamtam, tri, sd, td, cym, sus cym, bd
- I. Allegro   17'
- II. Lento; In legendary mood   16'
- III. Theme and Variations   14'

> Chappell

The Tale the Pine-Trees Knew <1931>   18'

3[1.2.3/pic] 3[1.2.Eh] 4[1.2.3/Ebcl.bcl] 3[1.2.cbn] — 4 3 3 1 —
tmp+4 — 2hp — cel — str
perc: gong, sd, td, xyl, sus cym, glock, bd, tambn

> Warner

Tintagel <1917–1919>   12'

3[1.2.3/pic] 3[1.2.Eh] 3[1.2.bcl] 3[1.2.cbn] — 4 3 3 1 — tmp+2 — hp
— str
perc: bd, cym, sus cym, tri, glock

> Chappell

Beach, Amy Marcy Cheney   1867-1944

(b Henniker, NH, 5 Sept 1867; d New York, 27 Dec 1944). American

Concerto, Piano, op.45, C-sharp minor <1899>   27'

2 2 2 2 — 4 2 3 1 — tmp+2 — str
- Allegro moderato   8'
- Scherzo (Perpetuum mobile)   6'
- Largo   5'
- Allegro con scioltezza   8'

> Fleisher   Hildegard

Grand Mass in E-flat, op.5 <1890>   63'

solos SATB   chorus
2 3[1.2.Eh] 2 2 — 4 3 3 0 — tmp — hp — org — str
Ed. Oliva.
- I. Kyrie eleison   6'
- II. Gloria in excelsis Deo   6'
- III. Laudamus te; Gratias   5'
- IV. Qui tollis peccata mundi   6'
- V. Quoniam tu solus sanctus   3'
- VI. Graduale: Benedicta es tu   5'
- VII. Credo in unum Deum   13'
- VIII. Sanctus; Hosannah   4'
- IX. Benedictus   5'
- X. Agnus Dei   10'

> Kalmus

Symphony No.2, op.32, E minor (Gaelic) <1894>   41'

3[1.2.pic] 3[1.2.Eh] 3[1.2.bcl(A)] 2 — 4 2 3 1 — tmp+1 — str
perc: tri
Although published as *Symphony No.2*, this work appears to have been
the composer's only symphony.
- I. Allegro con fuoco   11'
- II. Alla siciliana; Allegro vivace 8'
- III. Lento con molto espressione   13'
- IV. Allegro di molto   9'

> Kalmus

Beall, John   1942-

(b Belton, TX, 12 June 1942). American

Concerto, Violin & Double Bass (For Bridging the Gap)   24'
<2004–2005>

2 2 2 2 — 2 2 3 0 — tmp+1 — str
perc: cym, sus cym, sd, tri
- I. Driving   7'
- II. Slowly   8'
- III. Presto   9'

> Beall

Beaser, Robert   1954-

(b Boston, 29 May 1954). American

Chorale Variations for Orchestra <1992>   20'

3[incl pic] 3[incl Eh] 4[incl Ebcl,bcl] 3[incl cbn] — 4 4 3 1 — tmp+4
— hp — pf — str

> Helicon

Concerto, Piano <1989–1990>   30'

3[1.2.pic] 3[1.2.Eh] 3[1.2.bcl] 3[1.2.cbn] — 4 3 3 1 — tmp+3 — hp
— cel — str
perc: bd, cym, 4sus cym, hi-hat, med Chinese cym, sd, field drum, 3toms,
timbales, 2tri, tambn, tamtam, gong, glock, xyl, marim, vib, 1chime (E), crot,
templeblk, cowbell, whip, bongos, ratch, guiro, marac, conga, vibraslap,
2woodblk, 2steel pipes, Mexican bean, gourd

> Helicon

Double Chorus for Orchestra <1990>   11'

3[1.2.3/pic] 3[1.2.3/Eh] 3[1.2.3/bcl] 3[1.2.3/cbn] — 4 4 3 1 — tmp+4
— hp — pf — str

> Helicon

Song of the Bells <1987>   13'

solo flute
1[1/pic] 2[1.2/Eh] 2 2 — 3 1 0 0 — tmp+2 — hp — pf — str
perc: bd, 2 sus cym, szl cym, sd, toms, tri, 3tamtams, glock, xyl, marim, vib, chimes, crot, Mexican bean
Timpanist must cover some percussion.

| Helicon |

Beck, Franz Ignaz   1734-1809

(b Mannheim, 20 Feb 1734; d Bordeaux, 31 Dec 1809). German

Sinfonia, Callen 30, D major   14'

0 2 0 0 — 2 0 0 0 — str
Ed. Allan Badley.
I. Allegro   4'
II. Andante   3'
III. Minuetto   4'
IV. Presto   3'

| Artaria |

Sinfonia, op.10, No.2, D major <before 1758>   8'

str
Ed. Allan Badley.
I. Allegro   2'
II. Andante   2'
III. Presto   4'

| Artaria |

Sinfonia, op.13, no.1, E major   10'

0 0 0 0 — 2 0 0 0 — str
Ed. Allan Badley.
I. Allegro   3'
II. Andante   2'
III. Allegro   5'

| Artaria |

Beckel, James A. Jr.   1948-

(b Marion, OH, 16 July 1948). American

Celebrations <1994>   5'

3[1.2.pic] 3[1.2.Eh] 3[1.2.bcl] 2 — 4 3 3 1 — elec bass — tmp+3 — hp[opt] — opt pf — str
perc: cym, sus cym, set, gong, glock, windchimes, marktree, belltree, templeblk, cowbell, conga, vibraslap

| Beckel |

A Christmas Fanfare (brass choir version) <1992>   3'

0 0 0 0 — 4 4 4 1 — baritone hn — tmp+2 — [no str]
perc: sus cym, glock, chimes, crot (C, G), marktree

| Beckel |

A Christmas Fanfare (orchestra version) <1992>   3'

3[1.2.pic] 2 3[1.2.bcl] 2 — 4 3 3 1 — tmp+3 — hp — cel — str
perc: cym, sus cym, chimes, crot, marktree
A special optional ending permits a segue into Leroy Anderson's *A Christmas Festival*.

| Beckel |

Fantasy After Schubert <2004>   11'

3[1.2.pic] 2 3[1.2.bcl] 2 — 4 3 3 1 — tmp+3 — hp — str
perc: bd, cym, sus cym, sd, tri, glock, xyl, crot, marktree
An alternative ending shortens the duration to 9'.

| Beckel |

Gardens of Stone <2006>   11'

narrator
3[1.2.pic] 3[1.2.Eh] 3[1.2.bcl] 2 — 4 4 3 1 — tmp+4 — hp — pf — str
perc: bd, cym, sus cym, sd, field dr, tri, gong, glock, xyl, crot
Optional: Eh, tp4, perc4, hp, pf. Mvts are played without pause.
    Real rifles may optionally be used for *21 Gun Salute*. Final section allows a color guard to march through the audience to the stage.
Sunrise at Arlington Cemetery   _'
Past Battles   _'
21 Gun Salute   _'
Taps   _'
Parade of the Fallen Heroes   _'

| Beckel |

The Glass Bead Game; Concerto for Horn & Orchestra <1997>   19'

2[1.pic] 2[1.Eh] 2 2 — 2 2 0 0 — 2perc — hp — pf — str
perc: bd, sus cym, sd, tri, glock, xyl, marim, vib, chimes, windchimes, marktree, belltree, tmp, Chinese gong
1. The Call & Awakening   8'
2. Father Jacobus   5'
3. Magister Ludi Coronation & Death   6'

| Beckel |

A Gospel Christmas <1996>   10'

opt chorus & alto solo
2[1.2/pic] 2 2 2 — 4 2 3 1 — elec bass — tmp+2 — hp — str
perc: cym, sus cym, set, tri, tambn, glock, marktree, bongos, congas
Playable with brass 2 2 2 0.

| Beckel |

Imagination; A Children's Narrative Work for Chamber Ensemble <2009>   8'

narrator
1 1 1 1 — 1 1 0 0 — 1perc — pf — 1va, 1vc
perc: sus cym, glock, xyl
Children create their own story by filling in the blanks in the template provided. May be performed simply as a musical work without narrator.

| Beckel |

Liberty for All <2000>   12'

narrator
3[1.2.pic] 2 3[1.2.bcl] 2 — 4 3 3 1 — tmp+4 — hp — opt pf/cel — str
perc: bc, cym, sus cym, sd, tri, gong, glock, xyl, chimes
Texts from Patrick Henry, the U.S. Constitution, Washington, Lincoln, Kennedy, and *My Country 'Tis of Thee*.

| Beckel |

Make a Joyful Noise <2001>   4'

2[1.pic] 2 2 2 — 3 2[pic tp.2] 0 0 — tmp+1 — str
perc: sus cym, tri, glock, xyl, marktree

| Beckel |

Musica Mobilis <1999>   4'

3[1.2.pic] 2 3[1.2.bcl] 2 — 4 3 3 1 — tmp+3 — str
perc: bd, cym, tri, tambn, glock, xyl, vib, windchimes, bongos, 4sus cym

| Beckel |

Night Visions: The American Dream <1992>   4'

3[1.2.pic] 2 3[1.2.bcl] 2 — 4 2 3 1 — tmp+3 — hp[opt] — str
perc: bd, sd, tri, Chinese gong, tambn on stand, glock, xyl, marktree, belltree, woodblk

| Beckel |

Overture for a New Age <2000>   6'
3[1.2.pic] 2 3[1.2.bcl] 2 — 4 3 3 1 — tmp+3 — str
perc: bd, cym, sus cym, sd, tri, glock, xyl, windchimes, belltree, woodblk
> Beckel

Toccata for Orchestra <2007>   9'
3[1.2.pic] 2 3[1.2.bcl] 2 — 4 3 3 1 — tmp+3 — hp — pf — str
perc: bd, cym, sus cym, sd, tri, gong, xyl, 3 crot
> Beckel

Waltz of the Animals <1995>   14'
narrator
3[1.2.pic] 2 3[1.2.bcl] 2 — 4 2 3 1 — tmp+3 — hp — str
perc: bd, cym, sus cym, tri, gong, glock, xyl, chimes, windchimes, marktree, belltree, whip, ratch, whistle
Also available in a smaller orchestration:
 2[1.pic] 2 2 2 — 4 2 3 0 — 2perc — hp — str
> Beckel

Becker, John J.   1886-1961
(b Henderson, KY, 22 Jan 1886; d Wilmette, IL, 21 Jan 1961). American

Concerto arabesque <1930>   13'
solo piano
1 1 1 2[1.cbn] — 1 1 0 0 — str
> ACA

Soundpiece No.1b <1935>   12'
pf — str
> ACA

Soundpiece No.2b (Homage to Haydn) <1936>   13'
str orch
> Presser

Symphony No.3 (Symphonia brevis) <1929>   17'
3[1.2.pic] 3[1.2.Eh] 2 4[1.2.3.cbn] — 4 4 3 1 — tmp+6 — pf — str
1. A Scherzo in the Spirit of Mockery _'
2. Must Life Forever Be a Struggle? _'
> Peters

TWO PIECES FOR ORCHESTRA   3'
1. Among the Reeds and Rushes <1912>
1 1 2 1 — 1 1 0 0 — tmp — hp — str
> Fleisher

2. The Mountains <1912>   3'
3[1.2.pic] 2 2 1 — 2 2 2 1 — tmp+3 — str
> Fleisher

When the Willow Nods <1940>   15'
1 1 1 1 — 1 1 0 0 — tmp+1 — pf — str
> Fleisher

Beethoven, Ludwig van   1770-1827
(b Bonn, bap. 17 Dec 1770; d Vienna, 26 March 1827). German

WoO = *Werk ohne Opuszahl* [work without opus number]

Ah, perfido, op.65 <1795–1796>   13'
soprano scene and aria
1 0 2 2 — 2 0 0 0 — str
> Breitkopf   Kalmus   Luck's

Cantata on the Death of Emperor Joseph II, WoO 87 (Kantate auf den Tod Kaiser Josephs II) <1790>   33'
chorus   solos SSATB
2 2 2 2 — 2 0 0 0 — str
> Breitkopf   Kalmus   Luck's   Schirmer

Christus am Ölberg, op.85 (Christ on the Mount of Olives) <1803; rev 1804>   52'
chorus   solos STB
2 2 2 2 — 2 2 3 0 — tmp — str
Roles: Seraph (S), Jesus (T), Petrus (B).
Breitkopf ed. Anja Mühlenweg.
I. Introduction, Recitative & Aria   15'
II. Recitative, Aria & Chorus   9'
III. Recitative & Duet   7'
IV. Recitative & Chorus   4'
V. Recitative & Chorus   4'
VI. Recitative, Trio & Chorus   13'
> Breitkopf   Kalmus

Calm Sea and Prosperous Voyage
see his: Meeresstille und glückliche Fahrt

Concerto, Piano, No.1, op.15, C major <1795>   36'
1 2 2 2 — 2 2 0 0 — tmp — str
Bärenreiter ed. Jonathan Del Mar.
I. Allegro con brio   17'
II. Largo   10'
III. Rondo: Allegro   9'
> Bärenreiter   Breitkopf   Henle   Kalmus   Luck's

Concerto, Piano, No.2, op.19, B-flat major <1793>   28'
1 2 0 2 — 2 0 0 0 — str
Bärenreiter ed. Jonathan Del Mar.
I. Allegro con brio   14'
II. Adagio   8'
III. Rondo: Molto allegro   6'
> Bärenreiter   Breitkopf   Henle   Kalmus   Luck's

Concerto, Piano, No.3, op.37, C minor <1800>   34'
2 2 2 2 — 2 2 0 0 — tmp — str
Bärenreiter ed. Jonathan Del Mar.
I. Allegro con brio   16'
II. Largo   9'
III. Rondo: Allegro   9'
> Bärenreiter   Breitkopf   Henle   Kalmus   Luck's

Concerto, Piano, No.4, op.58, G major <1805–1806>   34'
1 2 2 2 — 2 2 0 0 — tmp — str
Bärenreiter edition by Jonathan Del Mar.
I. Allegro moderato   19'
II. Andante con moto   5'
III. Rondo: Vivace   10'
> Bärenreiter   Breitkopf   Kalmus   Luck's

Concerto, Piano, No.5, op.73, E-flat major (Emperor)   *38'*
<1809>

2 2 2 2 — 2 2 0 0 — tmp — str
Bärenreiter edition by Jonathan Del Mar.
I. Allegro   20'
II. Adagio un poco mosso   8'
III. Rondo: Allegro   10'

Breitkopf	Kalmus	Luck's

Concerto, Piano, No.6, op.61, D major   <1806; rev 1807>   *42'*

1 2 2 2 — 2 2 0 0 — tmp — str
The composer has provided a piano version of the solo part of his violin
concerto, op.61. Use the orchestral parts for the violin concerto. The only
difference for the orchestra is that timpani participate in the first cadenza;
a timpani part for this purpose may be purchased from Breitkopf.
I. Allegro ma non troppo   23'
II. Larghetto   10'
III. Rondo: Allegro   9'

Breitkopf	Henle	Kalmus

Concerto, Violin, op.61, D major   <1806>   *42'*

1 2 2 2 — 2 2 0 0 — tmp — str
I. Allegro ma non troppo   23'
II. Larghetto   10'
III. Rondo: Allegro   9'

Breitkopf	Henle	Kalmus	Luck's

Concerto, Violin, Violoncello & Piano, op.56, C major   *33'*
(Triple Concerto) <1803–1804>

1 2 2 2 — 2 2 0 0 — tmp — str
Bärenreiter ed. Jonathan Del Mar.
I. Allegro   17'
II. Largo   4'
III. Rondo alla polacca   12'

Bärenreiter	Breitkopf	Henle	Kalmus	Luck's

Consecration of the House

see his: Weihe des Hauses

Contradances, WoO 14 (Kontretänze) <1802>   *12'*

1 2 2 2 — 2 0 0 0 — 1perc — str[no va]
perc: tambn[only in no.8]
Twelve dances.

Breitkopf	Kalmus	Schott

Coriolan Overture, op.62 <1807>   *8'*

2 2 2 2 — 2 2 0 0 — tmp — str

Breitkopf	Henle	Kalmus	Luck's

The Creatures of Prometheus

see his: Prometheus, op.43

Deutsche Tänze

see his: German Dances

Egmont (incidental music), op.84 <1809–1810>   *43'*

soprano solo
2[1.2/pic] 2 2 2 — 4 2 0 0 — tmp — str
perc: sd offstage (can be covered by timpanist)
Breitkopf edition has a narration text by H. Enke for concert performance.
Overture   9'
No.1 Die Trommel gerühret (song)   3'
No.2 Entr'acte I   3'
No.3 Entr'acte II   6'
No.4 Freudvoll und leidvoll (song) 2'
No.5 Entr'acte III   4'
No.6 Entr'acte IV   4'
No.7 Clärchen's Death   4'
No.8 Melodrama   5'
No.9 Siegessymphonie   3'

Breitkopf	Kalmus	Luck's

Egmont: Overture <1809–1810>   *9'*

2[1.2/pic] 2 2 2 — 4 2 0 0 — tmp — str

Breitkopf	Kalmus	Luck's

Elegischer Gesang, op.118 <1814>   *4'*

solos SATB
str 4t
Often performed using chorus and string orchestra, rather than soloists
and string quartet.

Breitkopf	Kalmus	Luck's

Fantasia, Piano, Chorus & Orchestra, op.80 (Choral   *19'*
Fantasy) <1808>

chorus   solos SSATTB   solo piano
2 2 2 2 — 2 2 0 0 — tmp — str
I. Adagio [piano unaccompanied]   4'
II. Finale   15'

Breitkopf	Kalmus	Schirmer

Fidelio: Overture, op.72c <1814>   *6'*

2 2 2 2 — 4 2 2 0 — tmp — str

Breitkopf	Kalmus	Luck's

German Dances (Deutsche Tänze) <1795>   *20'*

3[1.2.pic] 2 2 — 2 2 0 0 — posthorn — tmp+3 — str[no va]
perc: bd, tri, tambn
Twelve dances.

Breitkopf	Kalmus

Die Geschöpfe des Prometheus

see his: Prometheus, op.43

Gratulations-Menuet, WoO 3 (Congratulations Minuet)   *5'*
<1822>

2 0 2 2 — 2 2 0 0 — tmp — str

Breitkopf	Henle	Kalmus	Schott

Grosse Fuge, op.133 <1825–1826>   *16'*

str orch
Edited by Felix Weingartner for string orchestra. Originally for string
quartet.

Breitkopf	Kalmus	Luck's

Jena Symphony

see under: Witt, Friedrich, 1770-1837

König Stephan, op.117 (King Stephen): Overture <1811>   8'

2 2 2 3[1.2.cbn] — 4 2 0 0 — tmp — str

Breitkopf	Kalmus	Luck's

Leonore Overture No.1, op.138 <1807>   10'

2 2 2 2 — 4 2 0 0 — tmp — str

Breitkopf	Kalmus	Luck's

Leonore Overture No.2, op.72a <1804–1805>   13'

2 2 2 2 — 4 2 3 0 — tmp — str
Solo offstage for one of the trumpets; an extra player may be required.

Breitkopf	Kalmus	Luck's

Leonore Overture No.3, op.72b <1805–1806>   14'

2 2 2 2 — 4 2 3 0 — tmp — str
Solo offstage for one of the trumpets; an extra player may be required.

Breitkopf	Kalmus	Luck's

Mass, op.86, C major <1807>   43'

chorus   solos SATB
2 2 2 2 — 2 2 0 0 — tmp — org — str

I. Kyrie	6'
II. Gloria	9'
III. Credo	11'
IV. Sanctus	11'
V. Agnus Dei	6'

Breitkopf	Kalmus	Luck's	Peters

Meeresstille und glückliche Fahrt, op.112 (Calm Sea and Prosperous Voyage) <1814–1815>   10'

chorus
2 2 2 2 — 4 2 0 0 — tmp — str
Breitkopf ed. Armin Raab.

Breitkopf	Kalmus

Minuets, WoO 7 (Zwölf Menuetten) <1795>   24'

3[1.2.pic] 2 2 2 — 2 2 0 0 — tmp — str[no va]

1. D Major	2'
2. B-flat Major	2'
3. G Major	2'
4. E-flat Major	2'
5. C Major	2'
6. A Major	2'
7. D Major	2'
8. B-flat Major	2'
9. G Major	2'
10. E-flat Major	2'
11. C Major	2'
12. F Major	2'

Breitkopf	Kalmus

Missa solemnis, op.123, D major <1819–1823>   81'

chorus   solos SATB
2 2 2 3[1.2.cbn] — 4 2 3 0 — tmp — org — str

I. Kyrie	10'
II. Gloria	18'
III. Credo	20'
IV. Sanctus	17'
V. Agnus Dei	16'

Breitkopf	Kalmus	Peters	Schirmer

Musik zu einem Ritterballet <1791>   12'

1[pic] 0 2 0 — 2 2 0 0 — tmp — str

1. March	2'
2. German Song	1'
3. Hunting-Song	2'
4. Love-Song ("Romance")	1'
5. War Dance	1'
6. Drinking-Song	2'
7. German Dance	1'
8. Coda	2'

Breitkopf	Kalmus

Namensfeier Overture, op.115 <1814–1815>   8'

2 2 2 2 — 4 2 0 0 — tmp — str

Breitkopf	Henle	Kalmus	Luck's

Prometheus, op.43 (Die Geschöpfe des Prometheus) <1800–1801>   63'

2 2 2 2 — 2 2 0 0 — basset hn — tmp — hp — str
Basset horn may be played by one of the clarinetists.

Overture	6'
ACT I	
Introduction	2'
No. 1: Poco adagio	3'
No. 2: Adagio	2'
No. 3: Allegro vivace	2'
ACT II	
No. 4: Maestoso; Andante	1'
No. 5: Adagio	6'
No. 6: Un poco adagio; Allegro	1'
No. 7: Grave	4'
No. 8: Allegro con brio	6'
No. 9: Adagio	4'
No. 10: Pastorale	3'
No. 11: Andante	1'
No. 12: Maestoso	3'
No. 13: Allegro	4'
No. 14: Andante	5'
No. 15: Andantino	4'
No. 16: Finale; Allegretto	6'

Breitkopf	Kalmus

Prometheus (Die Geschöpfe des Prometheus): Overture <1800–1801>   5'

2 2 2 2 — 2 2 0 0 — tmp — str
In the complete ballet, the overture leads directly into the first number. The Breitkopf edition of the overture (and its Kalmus reprint) supplies a simple 5-bar concert-ending consisting of reiterated tonic chords.

Breitkopf	Kalmus

Quartet, Strings, op.95, F minor (arr. Mahler) (Serioso) <1810>   22'

str
Arranged 1899 for string orchestra by Gustav Mahler; ed. David Matthews.

1. Allegro con brio	5'
2. Allegretto ma non troppo	7'
3. Allegro assai vivace ma serioso	5'
4. Larghetto espressivo	5'

Weinberger

Quartet, Strings, op.131, C-sharp minor (arr. Davis) <1825–1826>   37'

str
Arr. Colin Davis.

Weinberger

Romance No.1, op.40, G major <1801–1802>   8'

violin solo
1 2 0 2 — 2 0 0 0 — str
Some editions publish Romances Nos.1 & 2 together.

Bärenreiter	Breitkopf	Henle	Kalmus	Luck's

Romance No.2, op.50, F major <1798>   9'

violin solo
1 2 0 2 — 2 0 0 0 — str
Some editions publish Romances Nos.1 & 2 together.

Bärenreiter	Breitkopf	Henle	Kalmus	Luck's

Romance Cantabile (Hess 13) <1786>   5'

solos: flute, bassoon, piano
0 2 0 0 — str
Originally intended as the slow movement of a larger work. Ed. W. Hess.

Breitkopf

Rondo, Piano & Orchestra, WoO 6, B-flat major <1793>   9'

1 2 0 2 — 2 0 0 0 — str
Originally the finale of his *Piano Concerto No.2, op.19.*

Breitkopf	Kalmus	Luck's

Die Ruinen von Athen, op.113 (The Ruins of Athens) <1811>   40'

solo soprano, baritone, bass; narrator   chorus
2[1.2/pic] 2 2 3[1.2.cbn] — 4 2 3 0 — tmp+3 — str
perc: bd, cym, tri (one part can be covered by tmp, in which case tmp+2 is
sufficient)

Overture	5'
1. Chorus: Tochter des mächtigen Zeus	4'
2. Duet: Ohne Verschulden	4'
3. Chorus: Du hast in deines Armels Falten	2'
4. Turkish March	2'
5. Offstage Music [winds only: 2222-2000]	2'
6. March & Chorus: Schmückt die Altäre	9'
7. Chorus: Wir tragen empfängliche Herzen	8'
8. Chorus: Heil unserm König, heil!	4'

Breitkopf	Kalmus

Die Ruinen von Athen, op.113 (The Ruins of Athens): Overture <1811>   6'

2 2 2 2 — 4 2 0 0 — tmp — str

Breitkopf	Kalmus	Luck's

Die Ruinen von Athen, op.113 (The Ruins of Athens): March and Chorus <1811>   6'

chorus
2[1.2/pic] 2 2 2 — 2 2 3 0 — tmp — str
No.6, *Schmückt die Altäre*, from the incidental music.

Breitkopf	Kalmus	Luck's

Die Ruinen von Athen, op.113 (The Ruins of Athens): Turkish March <1811>   4'

1[pic] 2 2 3[1.2.cbn] — 2 2 0 0 — 3perc — str
perc: bd, cym, tri
No.4 from the incidental music.

Breitkopf	Kalmus	Luck's

Septet, op.20, E-flat major <1800>   40'

0 0 1 1 — 1 0 0 0 — vn, va, vc, db

I. Adagio; Allegro con brio	9'
II. Adagio cantabile	9'
III. Tempo di Menuetto	3'
IV. Tema con variazioni	7'
V. Scherzo: Allegro molto e vivace	3'
VI. Andante con moto alla Marcia; Presto	9'

Luck's	Peters

Symphony No.1, op.21, C major <1800>   26'

2 2 2 2 — 2 2 0 0 — tmp — str
Bärenreiter ed. Jonathan Del Mar; Breitkopf ed. Clive Brown.

I. Adagio molto - Allegro con brio	9'
II. Andante cantabile con moto	7'
III. Menuetto: Allegro molto e vivace	4'
IV. Finale: Adagio - Allegro molto e vivace	6'

Bärenreiter	Breitkopf	Henle	Kalmus	Luck's

Symphony No.2, op.36, D major <1801–1802>   32'

2 2 2 2 — 2 2 0 0 — tmp — str
Bärenreiter ed. Jonathan Del Mar; Breitkopf ed. Clive Brown.

I. Adagio Molto - Allegro con brio	10'
II. Larghetto	11'
III. Scherzo: Allegro	4'
IV. Allegro Molto	7'

Bärenreiter	Breitkopf	Kalmus	Luck's

Symphony No.3, op.55, E-flat major (Eroica) <1803>   47'

2 2 2 2 — 3 2 0 0 — tmp — str
Bärenreiter ed. Jonathan Del Mar; Breitkopf ed. Peter Hauschild.

I. Allegro con brio	15'
II. Marcia funebre: Adagio assai	15'
III. Scherzo: Allegro vivace	5'
IV. Finale: Allegro molto	12'

Bärenreiter	Breitkopf	Kalmus	Luck's

Symphony No.4, op.60, B-flat major <1806>   34'

1 2 2 2 — 2 2 0 0 — tmp — str
Bärenreiter ed. Jonathan Del Mar; Breitkopf ed. Peter Hauschild.

I. Adagio - Allegro vivace	13'
II. Adagio	10'
III. Allegro vivace	4'
IV. Allegro ma non troppo	7'

Bärenreiter	Breitkopf	Kalmus	Luck's

Symphony No.5, op.67, C minor <1807–1808>   31'

3[1.2.pic] 2 2 3[1.2.cbn] — 2 2 3 0 — tmp — str
Piccolo, contrabassoon and trombones play in mvt 4 only.
    A critical edition of the score with historical and analytical essays is
available from Norton.
Bärenreiter ed. Jonathan Del Mar; Breitkopf ed. Clive Brown.

I. Allegro con brio	7'
II. Andante con moto	10'
III. Allegro	6'
IV. Allegro	8'

Bärenreiter	Breitkopf	Kalmus	Luck's

Symphony No.6, op.68, F major (Pastorale) <1808>   39'

3[1.2.pic] 2 2 2 — 2 2 2 0 — tmp — str
Pic & tbns in last 2 mvts only.
Bärenreiter ed. Jonathan Del Mar; Breitkopf ed. Peter Hauschild.

1. Erwachen heiterer Empfindungen bei der Ankunft auf dem Lande	9'
2. Szene am Bach	12'
3. Lustiges Zusammensein der Landleute	5'
4. Gewitter, Sturm (Thunderstorm)	4'
5. Hirtengesang, frohe und dankbare Gefühle nach dem Sturm	9'

Bärenreiter	Breitkopf	Kalmus	Luck's

Symphony No.7, op.92, A major <1811–1812>   36'

2 2 2 2 — 2 2 0 0 — tmp — str
Bärenreiter ed. Jonathan Del Mar; Breitkopf ed. Peter Hauschild.
  I. Poco sostenuto - Vivace   12'
  II. Allegretto   9'
  III. Presto   8'
  IV. Allegro con brio   7'

| Bärenreiter | Breitkopf | Kalmus | Luck's |

Symphony No.8, op.93, F major <1812>   26'

2 2 2 2 — 2 2 0 0 — tmp — str
Bärenreiter ed. Jonathan Del Mar; Breitkopf ed. Peter Hauschild.
  I. Allegro vivace con brio   9'
  II. Allegretto scherzando   5'
  III. Tempo di menuetto   5'
  IV. Allegro vivace   7'

| Bärenreiter | Breitkopf | Kalmus | Luck's |

Symphony No.9, op.125, D minor (Choral) <1822–1824>   65'

chorus   solos SATB
3[1.2.pic] 2 2 3[1.2.cbn] — 4 2 3 0 — tmp+3 — str
perc: bd, cym, tri
Voices, pic, cbn & perc only in 4th mvt; tbn in 2nd & 4th mvts. Scherzo (2nd mvt) calls for clarinets in C.
    Bärenreiter ed. Jonathan Del Mar; Breitkopf ed. Peter Hauschild.
  I. Allegro ma non troppo; un poco maestoso   15'
  II. Molto vivace   13'
  III. Adagio molto e cantabile   13'
  IV. Presto - Allegro assai - Allegro assai vivace   24'

| Bärenreiter | Breitkopf | Kalmus | Luck's |

Die Weihe des Hauses, op.124 (Consecration of the House): Overture <1822>   12'

2 2 2 2 — 4 2 3 0 — tmp — str

| Breitkopf | Henle | Kalmus | Luck's |

Wellingtons Sieg, op.91 (Wellington's Victory) <1813>   15'

3[1.2.pic] 2 2 2 — 4 6 3 0 — tmp+3 — str
perc: bd, cym, tri, 2ratch, 4sd, 2cannon
Off-stage instruments and spatial effects. Extra percussion and trumpets may be desirable.
  I. Schlacht (Battle)   8'
  II. Sieges-Symphonie (Victory Symphony) 7'

| Breitkopf | Henle | Kalmus | Luck's |

Zapfenstreich March <1809>   4'

1[pic] 2 2 3[1.2.cbn] — 2 2 0 0 — 4perc — [no str]
perc: bd, field dr, tri, cym

| Kalmus | Luck's |

Bellini, Vincenzo   1801-1835

(b Catania, 3 Nov 1801; d Puteaux, nr Paris, 23 Sept 1835). Italian

Concerto, Oboe, E-flat major <1822>   7'

2 2 2 1 — 2 0 0 0 — str
  Maestoso e deciso   1'
  Larghetto cantabile   2'
  Allegro (alla polonese) 4'

| Kalmus | Leuckart | Thomi-Berg |

Norma: Overture <1831>   6'

2[1.pic] 2 2 2 — 4 2 3 1 — tmp+2 — hp — str
perc: bd, cym

| Breitkopf | Kalmus | Luck's | Ricordi |

Il pirata: Overture <1827>   7'

2[1.pic] 2 2 2 — 4 2 3 1[serpentone] — tmp+3 — str
perc: bd, cym, tri
Kalmus renders the *serpentone* part as a bass trombone (i.e., a 4th trombone).

| Kalmus | Luck's |

Symphony, C minor <1825>   10'

2 2 2 2 — 2 2 3 0 — str
Ed. Maffeo Zanon.

| Ricordi |

Symphony, D major <1825>   8'

2 2 2 2 — 2 2 3 0 — tmp — str
Ed. Maffeo Zanon.

| Ricordi |

Benda, Georg Anton [Jiří Antonín]   1722-1795

(b Staré Benátky, bap. 30 June 1722; d Kostritz, 6 Nov 1795). Bohemian

Concerto, Viola, F major <1775>   22'

0 0 0 0 — 2[opt] 0 0 0 — cnt — str
Ed. Walter Lebermann.

| Schott |

Symphony No.4, F major   9'

0 2 0 0 — 2 0 0 0 — cnt — str
Ed. Jaroslav Pohanka.

| Kalmus | Luck's |

Symphony No.5, G major   12'

2 0 0 0 — 2 0 0 0 — cnt — str
Ed. Jaroslav Pohanka.
  Allegro   6'
  Andante molto   3'
  Tempo di minuetto   3'

| Kalmus | Luck's |

Benda, Johann (Georg) [Jan Jiří]   1713-1752

(b Staré Benátky, bap. 30 Aug 1713; d Berlin, early 1752). Bohemian

Concerto, Violin, G major   20'

str
Ed. Samuel Dushkin. This work may be spurious; some believe it was composed by Dushkin himself.

| Schott |

Bendix, Victor   1851-1926

(b Copenhagen, 17 May 1851; d Copenhagen, 5 Jan 1926). Danish

Symphony No.3, A minor, op.25 <1894>   31'

2[1.2/pic] 2 2 2 — 4 2 3 1 — tmp+2 — hp — str
perc: tri, bd, cym
  I. Fantasie   13'
  II. Scherzo appassionato (Bunte Bilder) 7'
  III. Elegie   11'

| Hansen |

Ben-Haim, Paul
1897-1984

(b Munich, 1 Oct 1897; d Tel Aviv, 14 Jan 1984). Israeli composer of German birth

Concerto for Strings <1947>
18'

str
I. Preambolo _'
II. Capriccio _'
III. Intermezzo lirico _'
IV. Finale _'

Israeli

Symphony No.1 <1940>
30'

3[1.2.3/pic] 3[1.2.Eh] 3[1.2.bcl] 3[1.2.cbn] — 4 3 3 1 — tmp+3 — hp — str
perc: bd, cym, sd, tri, tamtam

Israeli

Benjamin, Arthur
1893-1960

(b Sydney, 18 Sept 1893; d London, 10 April 1960). Australian-English

Concertino, Piano & Orchestra <1927>
15'

2[incl pic] 2 2 2 — 2 2 0 0 — asx — tmp+4 — str

Schott

Two Jamaican Pieces <1938>
5'

1 1 2[cl 2 opt] 1 — 2 1 0 0 — asx[opt] — tmp[opt]+2 — str
perc: glock, xyl, marac
Percussion in 2nd mvt only.
Jamaican Song _'
Jamaican Rhumba _'

Boosey

Benjamin, George
1960-

(b London, 31 Jan 1960). English

A Mind of Winter <1981>
9'

solo soprano
2[1/pic.2/pic] 2[1.2/Eh] 2 2 — 2 2 0 0 — 1perc — str[6.6.4.4.2]
perc: 2 sus cym, sd, szl cym, 2tri

Faber

Bennett, Richard Rodney
1936-2012

(b Broadstairs, 29 March 1936; d New York, 24 Dec 2012). English

Actaeon (Metamorphoses I) <1977>
20'

solo horn
2[1.2/pic] 2[1.2/Eh] 3[1.2.3/bcl] 2 — 3 3 3 1 — tmp+3 — hp — cel/pf — str
perc: 3timbales, xyl, glock, marim, sd, crot, td, bd, vib, 2sus cym, 2tamtams, 3bongos, 3woodblks

Novello

Anniversaries <1982>
17'

3[1.2.pic] 3[1.2.Eh] 3[1.2.bcl] 3[1.2.cbn] — 4 3 3 1 — tmp+3 — hp — pf/cel — str
perc: xyl, glock, vib, crot, claves, sd, td, bongos, marim, chimes, bd, tamtam, 3timbales, ching-ring, 3woodblk, 3sus cym
1. Vivo e declamato _'
2. Episode 1 (Woodwind) _'
3. Con fuoco _'
4. Episode 2 (Tuned Percussion, Piano, Harp) _'
5. Arioso _'
6. Episode 3 (Strings) _'
7. Tranquillo _'
8. Episode 4 (Percussion) _'
9. Brilliante _'
10. Episode 5 (Brass) _'
11. Finale _

Novello

Birthday Music <2011>
2'

3[1.2.pic] 2 2 2 — 4 3 3 1 — tmp+2 — hp — pf — str
perc: bd, sd, sus cym, tambn

Novello

Chelsea Reach <2009>
3'

str

Novello

Concerto for Orchestra <1973>
23'

3[incl pic] 3[incl Eh] 2[incl bcl] 3[incl cbn] — 4 3 3 1 — tmp+3 — hp — pf/cel — str

Novello

Concerto, Guitar & Chamber Ensemble <1971>
20'

1[1/pic] 1[1/Eh] 1[bcl] 0 — 1 1 0 0 — tmp+1 — cel — vn, va, vc
perc: bongos, marac, sd, cast, tri, tamtam, tambn, claves, 2tomtoms, 3sus cym, 2woodblks

Universal

Concerto, Harpsichord <1980>
22'

2[1/pic.2/pic] 2[1.2/Eh] 2[1.2/Ebcl/bcl] 2 — 2 2 2 1 — tmp+3 — hp — pf/cel — str
Harpsichord should be amplified.

Novello

Concerto, Oboe <1969–1970>
16'

str

Universal

Concerto, Violin <1975>
22'

2[1.2/pic] 2[1.2/Eh] 1[1/bcl] 2 — 4 2 3 1 — tmp+3 — hp — pf/cel — str
perc: bd, 3 sus cym, sd, 3 timbales, tamtam, glock, xyl, vib, crot, 3bongos, claves, ching-ring

Novello

Country Dances, Book 1 <2000–2001>
12'

2[1.2/pic] 2 2 2 — 2 2 0 0 — tmp+1 — hp — pf — str
perc: sd, tri, crot, tambn, xyl, 2sus cym
Tunes from "Playford's Dancing Master," a collection of 525 popular tunes published between 1651 and 1728, ed. John Playford (1623-86) and others.
1. Buskin _'
2. A New Dance _'
3. Enfield Common _'
4. Chelsea Reach _'
5. Nobody's Jig _'

Novello

Diversions <1989>   20'

2[1.2/pic] 2 2 2 — 2 2 0 0 — tmp+2 — pf — str
perc: sd, td, tri, xyl, tambn, chimes, bd, 3sus cym
Theme: Vivo (Whistle and I'll come to you, my lad)	_'
Variation I: Grazioso	_'
Variation II: Scherzando	_'
Interlude 1: Allegretto (In yon garden)	_'
Variation III: Poco lento	_'
Variation IV: Con fuoco	_'
Variation V: Tranquillo	_'
Variation VI: Con brio	_'
Interlude 2: Lento (My love's in Germanie)	_'
Finale: Molto allegro — Alla marcia	_'

Novello

Gormenghast: Suite   16'

0 0 0 0 — 4 3 3 1 — tmp+2 — hp — pf/cel — str
perc: cym, sd, tamtam, chimes, xyl, 2sus cym
From the TV series; orchd by John Wilson.
Celebration	1'
Fuchsia and Lord Groan	4'
Irma's Romance	2'
The Red Room	5'
Farewell to Gormenghast	4'

Novello

Lilliburlero Variations <2008; rev (orchd) 2009>   10'

2[1.2/pic] 2 2 2 — 2 2 2 1 — tmp+1 — hp — str
perc: sd, cym, tamtam, 3sus cym, 3bongos
Originally for 2 pianos; arr. for orchestra by the composer.

Novello

Partita <1995>   17'

2[1.2/pic] 2[1.2/Eh] 2 2 — 2 0 0 0 — tmp — hp — str[min 10.8.6.6.4]
1. Intrada	5'
2. Lullaby	7'
3. Finale	5'

Novello

Reflections on a Scottish Folk Song <2004>   27'

solo violoncello
str[min 14.12.10.8.6]
Based on the folk song "Ca the yowes."

Novello

Reflections on a Sixteenth Century Tune <1999>   16'

str[12.12.8.8.4; min 8.6.4.4.2]
Based on the 16th century French popular song, Á l'ombre d'un Buissonet (1536).
Prelude: Lento	2'
Variation I: Allegretto	2'
Variation II: Allegro vivo	3'
Variation III: Andante (Homage to Peter Warlock)	3'
Variation IV: Con brio e ritmico	2'
Finale	4'

Novello

Serenade <1976>   14'

2[1.2/pic] 2 2 1 — 2 2 1 0 — tmp+3 — pf — str
perc: bd, tambn, glock, bongos, sus cym, tri, xyl, woodblk, sd
I. Aubade	_'
II. Siesta	_'
III. Nocturne	_'

Novello

Sonnets to Orpheus <1979>   30'

solo violoncello
2[incl pic] 2[incl Eh] 2[incl Ebcl,bcl] 2[incl cbn] — 2 2 2 1 — tmp+3 — 2hp — pf/cel — str[min 14.12.10.8.6]

Novello

Sinfonietta <1984>   10'

2[1.2/pic] 2 2 2 — 2 2 0 0 — tmp+1 — pf — str
perc: sd, bd, tri, tambn

Novello

Symphony No.3 <1987>   22'

2 2[1.Eh] 2 1 — 2 0 0 0 — tmp+2 — hp — pf — str
perc: sd, tri, tamtam, chimes, 3sus cym
I. Andante; Vivo	8'
II. Allegretto	6'
III. Adagio	8'

Novello

Troubadour Music <2006>   5'

3[1.2.pic] 3[1.2.Eh] 3[1.2.Ebcl] 3[1.2.cbn] — 4 3 3 1 — tmp+3 — hp — pf/cel — str
perc: sd, td, bd, chimes, xyl, ching-ring

Novello

Zodiac <1975–1976>   17'

3[1.2.3/pic] 3[1.2.Eh] 3[1.2.bcl] 3[1.2.cbn] — 4 3 3 1 — tmp+3 — hp — pf/cel — str
perc: xyl, vib, cast, crot, sd, glock, marac, claves, tamtam, td, bd, chimes, 3timbales, 3bongos, 3sus cym, 3tri, ching-ring

Novello

Bennett, Robert Russell   1894-1981

(b Kansas City, MO, 15 June 1894; d New York, 18 Aug 1981). American

The Four Freedoms; A Symphony after Four Paintings by Norman Rockwell <1943>   20'

2[1.2/pic] 2[1.2/Eh] 3[1.2.3/bcl] 2 — 4 3 3 1 — tmp+3 — str
perc: bd, cym, sus cym, sd, field dr, tri, 2tomtoms
I. Freedom of Speech	5'
II. Freedom of Worship	5'
III. Freedom from Want	4'
IV. Freedom from Fear	6'

Schirmer

Suite of Old American Dances <1949; rev 1950>   19'

2[1.2/pic] 2[1.2/Eh] 3[1.2.bcl] 2 — 4 3 3 1 — tmp+3 — hp — str
perc: sd, bd, cym, tri, xyl, glock
Originally for band; orchestrated by the composer.
1. Western One-Step	3'
2. Wallflower Waltz	4'
3. Rag	4'
4. Schottische	3'
5. Cake Walk	5'

Chappell

Bennett, William Sterndale   1816-1875

(b Sheffield, 13 April 1816; d London, 1 Feb 1875). English

Symphony, op.43, G minor <1863–1867>   24'

2 2 2 2 — 2 2 3 0 — tmp — str
I. Allegro moderato	8'
II. Introduzione al Minuetto, Minuetto & Trio	5'
III. Romanza: Larghetto cantabile	6'
IV. Intermezzo: Tempo di Minuetto, Grave, & Rondo Finale: Presto	5'

Kistner&Siegel   mph

Benson, Warren   1924-2005

(b Detroit, MI, 26 Jan 1924; d Rochester, NY, 6 Oct 2005). American

Chants and Graces <1980>   8'

1[incl pic] 0 0 0 — 4perc — hp — str
This work may be out of print.

> C. Fischer

A Delphic Serenade   12'

2[incl pic] 2 2 2 — 4 3 3 1 — tmp+3 — hp — str

> C. Fischer

Five Brief Encounters <1880>   7'

2 0 2 0 — 2 1 1 0 — tmp — str
This work may be out of print.

> C. Fischer

Bentzon, Niels Viggo   1919-2000

(b Copenhagen, 24 Aug 1919; d Frederiksberg, 25 April 2000). Danish

Chamber Concert for 11 Instruments, op.52 <1948>   17'

0 0 1 1 — 0 2 0 0 — tmp+1 — 3pf — db

I. Allegro moderato	*5'*
II. Adagio	*7'*
III. Allegro	*5'*

> Hansen

Symphony No.4, op.55 (Metamorphoses) <1948>   32'

2[1.2/pic] 2[1.2/Eh] 2 2 — 4 3 3 1 — tmp+5 — hp — cel[can be played by perc] — str
perc: bd, sd, tri, xyl, sus cym, tambn, gong
An optional part for clarinet in Eb or D can be supplied (not notated in the score).

I. Vivace	*12'*
II. Tempo di largamente	*9'*
III. Allegro ma non troppo	*11'*

> Hansen

Symphony No.7, op.83 (De tre versioner; The Three Versions) <1952>   27'

3[1.2.pic] 3[1.2.Eh] 3[1.2.bcl] 2 — 4 3 3 1 — tmp+4 — hp — cel — str
perc: bd, cym, sd, tri, gong, xyl

> Hansen

Symphony No.8, op.113 (Sinfonia discrezione)   44'

2[1.2/pic] 2[1.2/Eh] 2 2 — 4 3 3 1 — tmp+3 — hp — str
perc: bd, cym, sus cym, sd, tri

I. Allegro ma non troppo	*17'*
II. Allegro molto	*6'*
III. Andante tranquillo	*10'*
IV. Allegro	*11'*

> Hansen

Symphony No.9, op.126 (Aerøsymfonien) <1960>   33'

3[1.2.3/pic] 3[1.2.Eh] 3[1.2.bcl] 3[1.2.cbn] — 4 3 3 1 — tmp+5 — cel[played by perc] — str
perc: bd, cym, sus cym, sd, tri, xyl, gong, chimes, cel[played by perc]

I. Tempo giusto	*_'*
II. Andante ma non troppo	*_'*
III. Allegro moderato	*_'*

> Hansen

Symphony No.13, op.181 (Military) <1965>   33'

2 2 2 2 — 4 3 3 1 — tmp+3 — str
perc: bd, cym, sus cym, sd, tri

Allegro ma non troppo	*_'*
Scherzo	*_'*
Andante tranquillo	*_'*
Allegro	*_'*

> Hansen

Berezowsky, Nicolai   1900-1953

(b St Petersburg, 4/17 May 1900; d New York, 27 Aug 1953). American composer of Russian birth

Concerto, Harp, op.31 <1945>   22'

3[1.2.pic] 2 3[1.2.bcl] 2 — 4 2 3 1 — tmp+2 — str

> Elkan-Vogel

Berg, Alban   1885-1935

(b Vienna, 9 Feb 1885; d Vienna, 24 Dec 1935). Austrian

Altenberg Lieder, op.4 <1912>   11'

soprano solo
3[1.2.pic] 3[1.2.3/Eh] 4[1.2.3/Ebcl.bcl] 3[1.2.3/cbn] — 4 3 4 1 — tmp+4 — hp — cel, pf, harm — str
perc: bd, sd, tri, tamtam, glock, xyl; sus cym played by timpanist
Chamber ensemble version arr. Diderik Wagenaar (1985) calls for:
  1[fl/pic] 1 1 1 — 1 0 0 0 — pf, harm — str 5t

1. Seele, wie bist du schöner	*3'*
2. Sahst du nach dem Gewitterregen	*1'*
3. Uber die Grenzen des All	*2'*
4. Nichts ist gekommen	*1'*
5. Hier ist Friede	*4'*

> Universal

Chamber Concerto, op.8 <1923–1925>   32'

solo violin   solo piano
2[1.2/pic] 2[1.Eh] 3[1.Ebcl.bcl] 2[1.cbn] — 2 1 1 0 — [no str]
1st or 2nd mvt may be performed separately.

I. Thema scherzoso con variazione [pf & winds]	*8'*
II. Adagio [vn & winds]	*13'*
III. Rondo ritmico con introduzione [tutti]	*11'*

> Universal

Concerto, Violin <1935>   22'

2[1/pic.2/pic] 2[1.2/Eh] 4[1.2.3/asx.bcl] 3[1.2.cbn] — 4 2 2[1.btbn] 1 — tmp+2 — hp — str
perc: bd w/ cym, cym, sus cym, sd, tri, tamtam, gong
Breitkopf ed. Michael Kube.

I. Andante; Allegretto	*9'*
II. Allegro; Adagio	*13'*

> Breitkopf   Universal

Lulu: Suite <1928–1934; rev Suite: 1935>   32'

opt coloratura soprano solo
3[1/pic1.2/pic2.3/pic3] 3[1.2.3/Eh] 4[1.2/Ebcl.3/Ebcl.bcl] 3[1.2.3/cbn] — 4 3 3 1 — asx — tmp+3 — hp — pf — str
perc: bd, cym, sd, tri, tamtam, gong, vib, sus cym

I. Rondo: Andante (Introduzione) Hymne: Sostenuto	*15'*
II. Ostinato: Allegro	*3'*
III. Lied Der Lulu: Comodo	*3'*
IV. Variationen: Moderato—Thema: Subito tempo moderato	*3'*
V. Adagio: Sostenuto - Lento - Grave	*8'*

> Universal

Lyric Suite (Lyrischen Suite) <1925–1926; rev 1927>   26'

str
Originally for string quartet, 1925-26. In 1927 the composer arranged mvts 2, 3 & 4 for string orchestra. The three remaining movements (nos.1, 5, 6) arr. by Theo Verbey in 2006.

I. Allegretto gioviale [arr. Verbey]	3'
II. Andante amoroso [arr. Berg]	6'
III. Allegro misterioso [arr. Berg]	3'
IV. Adagio appassionato [arr. Berg]	5'
V. Presto delirando [arr. Verbey]	4'
VI. Largo desolato [arr. Verbey]	5'

Universal

Sieben frühe Lieder (Seven Early Songs) <1905–1908>   18'

high voice
2[1.2/pic] 2[1.2/Eh] 3[1.2.bcl(A)] 3[1.2.cbn] — 4 1 2 0 — 1perc — hp — opt cel — str
perc: bd, tri, cym, tamtam, sd, sus cym, tmp [3 notes only]
An arrangement by Heinz Stolba for medium voice is also available from Universal.

1. Nacht (Night)	4'
2. Schilflied (Song Amongst the Reeds)	3'
3. Die Nachtigall (The Nightingale)	2'
4. Traumgekrönt (A Crown of Dreams)	3'
5. Im Zimmer (Indoors)	2'
6. Liebesode (Lovers' Ode)	2'
7. Sommertage (Summer Days)	2'

Universal

Three Pieces for Orchestra, op.6 (Drei Orchesterstücke) <1914–1915>   19'

4[all/pic] 4[1.2.3.4/Eh] 5[1.2.3/Ebcl.4.bcl] 4[1.2.3.cbn] — 6 4 4 1 — 2tmp+6 — 2hp — cel — str
perc: bd w/ cym, cym, sd, td, tri, tamtam, gong, glock, xyl, large hammer
Revised 1929.

Praeludium (Prelude)	4'
Reigen (Round Dance)	6'
Marsch (March)	9'

Universal

Der Wein (concert aria) <1929>   15'

soprano solo
2[1/pic1.2/pic2] 2[1.2/Eh] 3[1.2.bcl] 3[1.2.cbn] — 4 2 2 1 — asx — tmp+2 — hp — pf — str
perc: bd, cym, sus cym, sd, tri, tambn, tamtam, gong, glock [playable with tmp+1 if timpanist covers some percussion]

Universal

Wozzeck: Three Excerpts (Drei Bruchstücke) <1924>   20'

soprano solo
4[1.2.3/pic.4/pic] 4[1.2.3.4/Eh] 5[1.2.3/Ebcl.4/Ebcl.bcl] 4[1.2.3.cbn] — 4 4 4 1 — tmp+4 — hp — cel — str
perc: bd w/ cym, sus cym, sd, tri, tamtam, gong, xyl, rute
Playable with reduced winds: 3 3 3 — 4 3 3 1

Act I: sc.3 (Military March & Lullaby)	_'
Act III: sc.1 (Theme & Variations)	_'
Act III: sc.4, scene change, & sc.5	_'

Universal

Bergsma, William   1921-1994

(b Oakland, CA, 1 April 1921; d Seattle, WA, 18 March 1994). American

A Carol on Twelfth Night <1954>   8'

2[1.pic] 2 2 2 — 4 2 3 1 — tmp+2 — hp — str

Galaxy

Chameleon Variations <1960>   13'

3[1.2.3/pic] 2 3[1.2.3/bcl] 2 — 4 3 3 1 — tmp+3 — hp — pf — str
perc: bd, cym, glock, sd, tambn, xyl

Galaxy

Documentary One; Portrait of a City <1963; rev 1968>   18'

2[1.2/pic] 2[1.Eh] 2[1.2/bcl] 2 — 4 2 3 1 — tmp+2 — str
perc: bd, sus cym, sd, td, tri, tambn, glock, xyl
4th movement may be performed separately under the title *Follow the Leader* (4').

1. Designers, Builders	_'
2. Tintypes and Lithographs	_'
3. Lullaby in a Railroad Flat	_'
4. Rainy Street, Follow the Leader, Kids at Play	_'

Galaxy

Music on a Quiet Theme <1943>   8'

2[1.pic] 2[1.Eh] 2 2 — 4 2 3 1 — tmp+1 — str
perc: cym

Boosey

Berio, Luciano   1925 - 2003

(b Oneglia, Imperia, 24 Oct 1925; d Rome, 27 May 2003). Italian

Allelujah [I] <1955>   10'

4[incl pic] 2 4[incl Ebcl,bcl] 3[incl cbn] — 8 5 3 1 — asx, tsx — tmp+7 — 2hp — cel, pf — str

Zerboni

Concertino, Clarinet & Violin <1951>   11'

solo clarinet & violin
hp — cel — str

Universal

Concerto, 2 Pianos <1972–1973>   25'

3[incl pic] 3[incl Eh] 4[incl Ebcl,bcl] 4[incl cbn] — 3 3 3 1 — asx, tsx — 3perc — elec org, orchestral pf — str
perc: marim, 6insts with heads (toms & bongos), 6almglocken

Universal

Encore <1978–1981>   3'

4[1.2.3/pic.4/pic] 3[1.2.Eh] 4[1.2.Ebcl.bcl] 3[1.2.cbn] — 3 3 3 1 — asx, tsx — tmp+2 — hp — cel, pf — str
perc: woodblk, tri, sd, slgh-bells, chimes, bd, cym

Universal

Folk Songs for Seven Instruments <1964>   21'

solo mezzo-soprano
1[fl/pic] 0 1 0 — 2perc — hp — vn, va
perc: sd, crot, tamtam, tambn, woodblk, chimes, coilspring
Arrangements of folk songs; the mvts are to be performed without pause.
    A transcription by the composer for mezzo-soprano and orchestra was created in 1973; see following entry.

1. Black is the Colour of My True Love's Hair (United States)	3'
2. I Wonder as I Wander (United States)	2'
3. Loosin Yelav (The Moon Has Risen—Armenia)	3'
4. Rossignolet du bois (Little Nightingale of the Woods—France)	1'
5. A la femminisca (A Woman's Prayer—Sicily)	2'
6. La donna ideale (The Ideal Woman—Italy)	1'
7. Ballo (Dance—Italy)	1'
8. Motettu de Tristura (Song of Sadness—Sardinia)	2'
9. Malorous qu'o uno fenno (Wretched Is He Who Has a Wife—Auvergne)	1'
10. Lo fiolaire (The Spinner—Auvergne)	3'
11. Azerbaijan love song—Azerbaijan)	2'

Universal

Folk Songs for Voice & Orchestra <1964; rev 1973>   21'

solo mezzo-soprano

2[1.2/pic] 1 3[1.2.bcl] 1 — 1 1 1 0 — 2perc — hp — str

perc: sd, crot, tamtam, tambn, woodblk, chimes, coilspring

Arrangements of folk songs; the mvts are to be performed without pause.
    Originally for voice & 7 instruments (1964—see previous entry);
transcribed by the composer for voice & orchestra, 1973.

1. Black is the Colour of My True Love's Hair (United States)	3'
2. I Wonder as I Wander (United States)	2'
3. Loosin Yelav (The Moon Has Risen—Armenia)	3'
4. Rossignolet du bois (Little Nightingale of the Woods—France)	1'
5. A la femminisca (A Woman's Prayer—Sicily)	2'
6. La donna ideale (The Ideal Woman—Italy)	1'
7. Ballo (Dance—Italy)	1'
8. Motettu de Tristura (Song of Sadness—Sardinia)	2'
9. Malorous qu'o uno fenno (Wretched Is He Who Has a Wife—Auvergne)	1'
10. Lo fiolaire (The Spinner—Auvergne)	3'
11. Azerbaijan love song—Azerbaijan)	2'

Universal

Nones <1954>   10'

3[incl pic] 2 2 3[incl cbn] — 4 4 3 1 — asx — elec gtr — tmp+5 —
hp — cel/glock, pf — str

perc: bd, 2sus cym, 2militry dr, tri, tamtam, gong, xyl, vib, glock [played by cel
player]

Zerboni

Rendering <1988–1989>   25'

2 2 2 2 — 2 2 3 0 — tmp — cel — str

Based on sketches by Franz Schubert for a symphony (D.936a).

Universal

Requies <1983–1984>   13'

2[1.pic] 2[1.Eh] 3[1.Ebcl.bcl] 2 — 2 2 1 0 — marimba — hp — cel
— str[8.8.4.4.3]

Universal

Ritirata notturna di Madrid <1975>   10'

3[1.2.3/pic] 3[1.2.Eh] 3[1.2.bcl] 3[1.2.cbn] — 4 4 3 1 — tmp+3 — hp
— str

perc: 2sd, bd, tri

Quattro versioni originali della Ritirata notturna di Madrid *di L.
Boccherini sovrapposte e trascritte per orchestra* (Four Original Versions
of the *Ritirata notturna di Madrid* of L. Boccherini, superimposed and
transcribed for orchestra)

Universal

Ritorno degli snovidenia (The Return of the Dreams)   20'
<1976–1977>

solo violoncello

3 2 3[1.2.bcl] 2 — 2 2 2 1 — asx — pf — 3vn, 3va, 3vc, 2db

"Snovidenia" is a Russian word meaning "nostalgic dreams."

Universal

Sinfonia <1968–1969>   27'

eight voices (SSAATTBB)

4[1.2.3.pic] 3[1.2.Eh] 4[1.2.3.Ebcl] 3[1.2.cbn] — 4 4 3 1 — asx, tsx
— tmp+2
— hp — pf, elec org, elec hpsd (Baldwin) — str

perc: bd, sus cym, 3sd, 3tri, tambn, 3tamtam, glock, marim, vib, slgh-bells,
3woodblk, whip, bongos, congas, guiro, cast [tmp must cover some perc]

Section I	7'
Section II	5'
Section III	12'
Section IV	3'

Universal

Still <1973>   12'

3 3[1.2.Eh] 4[1.2.3.4/bcl] 3[1.2.cbn] — 4 4 3 1 — asx, tsx — 3perc
— hp — pf, elec org — str

perc: marim, vib, 4bongos, 2tomtoms, 3tamtams

Universal

Tempi concertati <1958–1959>   16'

soloists: flute, violin, 2 pianos (one doubling on celeste)

1[pic] 2[1.Eh] 3[1.2.bcl] 1 — 1 1 1 0 — 4perc — 2hp — 2va, 2vc, db

perc: 2militry dr, 2sus cym, tri, glock, xyl, marim, vib, chimes, templeblks,
bongos, congas, 5cowbells, 4woodblks, 3tomtoms, 2tamtams

Not to be conducted in performance, though a conductor is necessary in
rehearsal.

Universal

Variazioni per orchestra da camera (Variations for   12'
Chamber Orchestra) <1954>

2[incl pic] 1 2 2 — 2 2 1 0 — str[8.8.6.4.3]

Zerboni

Berkeley, Lennox   1903-1989

(b Boars Hill, Oxford, 12 May 1903; d London, 26 Dec 1989). English

Concerto, Guitar, op.88 <1974>   22'

1 1 1 1 — 2 0 0 0 — str

Chester

Sinfonietta, op.34 <1950>   13'

2 2 2 2 — 2 0 0 0 — tmp — str

1. Allegro	4'
2. Lento; Allegro non troppo	9'

Chester

Symphony No.3 in One Movement, op.74 <1969>   14'

3[1.2.3/pic] 3[1.2.Eh] 2 3[1.2.cbn] — 4 3 3 1 — tmp+2 — hp — str

Chester

Windsor Variations, for Chamber Orchestra <1969>   13'

1 2 0 2 — 2 0 0 0 — str

Chester

Berlioz, Hector   1803-1869

(b La Cote-Saint-Andre, Isere, 11 Dec 1803; d Paris, 8 March 1869). French

Béatrice et Bénédict: Overture <1860–1862>   8'

2[1.pic] 2 2 — 4 3[1.2.crt] 3 0 — tmp — str

Bote & Bock	Breitkopf	Kalmus	Luck's

La belle voyageuse; Légende irlandaise, op.2, no.4 (The   4'
Beautiful Traveller) <1829; rev 1845>

solo mezzo-soprano

1 2 2 1 — str

Also performable with a 2-part female chorus in place of the mezzo. The
orchestration unchanged; chorus parts in the Appendix of the *New
Berlioz Edition*, v.13, p.132.

Bärenreiter

Benvenuto Cellini: Overture <1834–1837>   11'

2[1.2/pic] 2 2[1.2/bcl] 4 — 4 6[4tp, 2crt] 3 1[oph] — 3tmp+3 — str

perc: bd, cym, tri

4 real bassoon parts in only 3 bars of the total piece; otherwise 2 real
parts, each doubled.

Breitkopf	Kalmus	Luck's

La captive, op.12 <1832; rev (orchd) 1848>   7'

solo alto or mezzo
2 2 2 2 — 2 0 0 0 — tmp+2 — str; 2nd str orch ad lib
perc: bd, cym
This work may be available in 2 different keys (for alto or mezzo).

Bärenreiter	Breitkopf	Kalmus	Luck's

Le carnaval romain (Roman Carnival) <1844>   8'

2[1.2/pic] 2[1.2/Eh] 2 4 — 4 4[2tp, 2crt] 3 0 — tmp+4 — str
perc: 2tambn, cym, tri
2 real bassoon parts, each doubled. (The Breitkopf edition, as well as the
reprints deriving from it, indicate 2bn only.)

Breitkopf	Kalmus	Luck's

Le chasseur danois, op.19, no.6 (The Danish Huntsman;   3'
Der dänische Jäger) <1844; rev 1845>

solo bass voice
2[1.2/pic] 2 2 4 — 4 0 3 0 — tmp — str

Bärenreiter	Breitkopf

Le cinq mai; Chant sur la mort de l'Empereur Napoléon,   11'
op.6 (The Fifth of May) <1835>

solo bass voice   chorus
2 0 2 4 — 4 2 3 0 — 1perc — str
perc: bd

Bärenreiter

Cléopâtre <1829>   22'

soprano solo
2[1/pic.2/pic] 2 2 2 — 4 2 3 0 — tmp — str
Often listed as *La Mort de Cléopâtre*. Sometimes the two titles are
incorrectly listed as separate works.

1. C'en est donc fait!	3'
2. Ah! qu'ils sont loin	7'
3. Méditation: Grand Pharaons	5'
4. Non! … non, de vos demeures funèbres	3'
5. Dieux du Nil	4'

Bärenreiter	Breitkopf	Kalmus	Luck's

Le corsaire, op.21 <1844; rev before 1852>   8'

2 2 2 4[2 real parts] — 4 4[2tp, 2crt] 3 1[oph] — tmp — str

Bärenreiter	Breitkopf	Kalmus	Luck's

La damnation de Faust, op.24 <1845–1846>   *136'*

solos MsTBarB   chorus, optional children's chorus
3[1/pic.2/pic.3/pic] 2[1/Eh.2/Eh] 3[1.2.bcl] 4 — 4 4[2tp, 2crt] 3
2[tuba.oph(1 part)] — 2tmp+3 — 2hp — str
perc: bd, cym, sd, tri, tamtam, chimes
Incorporating revised versions of the composer's *Huit scènes de Faust.*

PART I: Plaines de Hongrie (The Plains of Hungary)	17'
1. Introduction	
2. Ronde de paysans	
3. Recitatif et Marche hongroise	
PART II: Nord d'Allemagne (In Northern Germany)	51'
4. Faust seul dans son cabinet de travail	
Chant de la Fêtes de Paques	
5. Faust. Méphistophélès	
6. Chœur des Buveurs. Chanson de Brander. Fugue	
Recitatif et Chanson (Méphistophélès)	
7. Air de Méphistophélès	
Chœur de Gnomes et de Sylphes. Ballet de Sylphes	
8. Chœur de Soldats. Chanson d'Etudiants	
PART III: Dans la chambre de Marguerite (In Marguerite's Room)	36'
9. Tambours et Trompettes sonant la retraite. Air de Faust	
10. Faust et Méphistophélès	
11. Marguerite. Le Roi de Thulé	
12. Evocation. Menuet des Follets. Sérénade de Méphistophélès	
13. Duo	
14. Trio et Chœur	
PART IV	32'
15. Romance de Marguerite	
16. Invocation à la nature	
17. Recitatif et Chasse	
18. L Course à l'Abîme	
19. Pandaemonium	
20. Dans le Ciel	

Breitkopf	Kalmus	Schirmer

La damnation de Faust: Dance of the Sylphs (Ballet des   3'
sylphs) <1845–1846>

3[1.2.pic] 0 2 0 — tmp — 2hp — str

Breitkopf	Kalmus	Luck's

La damnation de Faust: Rákóczy March (Marche   5'
hongroise) <1845–1846>

3[1.2.pic] 2 2 4[2 parts] — 4 4[2tp, 2crt] 3 1 — tmp+4 — str
perc: bd, cym, sd, tri

Breitkopf	Kalmus	Luck's

La damnation de Faust: Will-o-the-Wisps (Menuet de   5'
follets) <1845–1846>

3[1.pic1.pic2] 2 3[1.2.bcl] 4 — 4 4[2tp, 2crt] 3 0 — 2tmp+2 — str
perc: cym, tri

Breitkopf	Kalmus	Luck's

L'enfance du Christ, op.25 (Childhood of Christ)   95'
<1850–1854>

solos S, 2T, Bar, 3B   chorus
2[1.2/pic] 2[1.2/Eh] 2 2 — 2 4[2tp, 2crt; probably opt] 3 0 — tmp —
hp — harm — str
Can be done with solos STBarB.
    Concerning the 2tp and 2crt, which play only 15 bars, see the Foreword
by David Lloyd-Jones to vol.11 of the *New Edition of the Complete
Works*, 1998.

PART I. Le songe d'Hérode (Herod's Dream)	
1. "Dans la crèche, en ce temps"	2'
2. Marche nocturne	7'
3. Air d'Hérode: "Toujours ce rêve"; "O misère des rois!"	10'
4. "Les sages de Judée"	10'
5. Duo: "O mon cher fils"	9'
6. Choeur des anges invisibles: "Joseph! Marie! Ecoutez-nous!"	4'
PART II. La fuite en Egypte (The Flight into Egypt)	
7. Ouverture	5'
8. L'adieu des bergers à la Sainte Famille	6'
9. Le repos de la Sainte Famille	5'
PART III. L'arrivée à Saïs (The Arrival at Sais)	
10. "Depuis trois jours"	3'
11. Duo: "Dans cette ville immense"	5'
12. "Entrez, pauvres Hébreux"	7'
13. Trio for 2 flutes & harp	6'
14. "Vous pleurez, jeune mère"	6'
15. "Ce fut ainsi"	10'

Bärenreiter	Breitkopf	Kalmus	Schirmer

Les Franc-Juges, op.3 (Judges of the Secret Court)   13'
<1826>

2[1/pic.2/pic] 2 2 3[1.2.cbn] — 4 3[1.2.crt] 3 2[2oph] — tmp+1 — str
perc: bd, cym

Bärenreiter	Breitkopf	Kalmus	Luck's

Harold in Italy, op.16   <1834>   43'

solo viola
2[1.2/pic] 2[1/Eh.2] 2 4 — 4 4[2tp, 2crt] 3 1 — tmp+3 — hp — str
perc: cym, tri, 2tambn
2 violins & 1 violoncello play offstage at end of 4th mvt.

I. Harold in the Mountains	15'
II. March of the Pilgrims	8'
III. Serenade of an Abruzzi Mountaineer to his Beloved	7'
IV. Orgy of the Brigands	13'

Bärenreiter	Breitkopf	Kalmus

Huit scènes de Faust (Eight Scenes from Faust)   38'
<1828–1829>

solos SSSSATBarB   chorus SSTTBB
2[1/pic.2/pic] 2[1/Eh.2/Eh] 2 4 — 4 2 0 1[oph] — glass harmonica,
gtr — 4tmp — 2hp — str
Each mvt distinct in orchestration and voice deployment; last mvt for
voice and gtr only. Withdrawn by the composer, and later used in *La
damnation de Faust*, q.v.

1. Chants de la Fête de Pâques	5'
2. Paysans sous les tilleuls	3'
3. Concert de sylphes	9'
4. Ecot de joyeux compagnons	2'
5. Chanson de Méphistophélès	2'
6. Le roi de Thulé	4'
7. Romance de Marguerite	11'
8. Sérénade de Méphistophélès	2'

Bärenreiter

Hymne des Marseillais (La Marseillaise) <1830>   9'

chorus   male chorus   children's chorus
0 0 2 2 — 4 6 3 2[oph] — 3tmp+bd — str
National anthem of France. Words and music by Roget de Lisle; arr.
Berlioz 1830. Six verses.

Bärenreiter

Le jeune pâtre breton, op.13, no.4 (The Young Breton Shepherd) <1833>   3'

mezzo-soprano or tenor solo
1 2 2 1 — 2[2nd hn backstage] 0 0 0 — str[no db]
1hn could cover it, first in the orchestra and then offstage.

Bärenreiter

Lélio, ou Le retour â la vie, op.14b (The Return to Life)   35'
<1831–1832>

speaker   invisible chorus & solos TTB
2[1.2/pic] 2[1.2/Eh] 2 2 — 4 4[2tp, 2crt] 3 1 — 2tmp+1 — hp — pf
4-hands — str
perc: bd, cym, tamtam
Part II of *Épisode de la vie d'un artiste* (Episode in the Life of an Artist):
continuation and ending of the *Symphonie fantastique*. Duration with
spoken text, 53'; duration of music only, 35'.
    Bärenreiter ed. Peter Bloom.
    Breitkopf parts (and consequently Kalmus reprint) lack the brief
(16-bar) appearance of the 1st violins in the first movement.

I. Le Pêcheur [The Fisherman]	4'
II. Choeur d'ombres [Chorus of Shades]	5'
III. Chansons de brigands [Brigands' Song]	4'
IV. Chant de bonheur [Song of Happiness]	5'
V. La Harpe éolienne - Souvenirs [The Aeolian Harp — Memories]	3'
VI. Fantaisie sur la tempête de Shakespeare[Fantasy on The Tempest]	14'

Bärenreiter	Breitkopf	Kalmus	Luck's

Messe solennelle   <1824>   51'

solos STB   chorus STTB
2 2 2 2 — 4 2 3 2[serp.buccin(or oph)] — tmp+2 — opt harps — str
perc: cym, tamtam
The composer added a piccolo (i.e., a 3rd flutist) to the *Resurrexit* and
then deleted it, though Bärenreiter includes the part as an option. Berlioz
vacillated among serpent, buccin, and ophicleide for the lowest member
of the brass family: one mvt calls for buccin *and* serp, while another calls
for buccin *or* oph, and yet another for serp alone. In any case it can be
covered by one player on a modern tuba (high tessitura).
    Ed. Hugh Macdonald.

Introduction	1'
1. Kyrie	6'
2. Gloria	5'
3. Gratias	6'
4. Quoniam	2'
5. Credo	3'
6. Incarnatus	3'
7. Crucifixus	2'
8. Resurrexit	8'
Motet pour l'offertoire	3'
9. Sanctus	2'
10. O salutaris	3'
11. Agnus dei	3'
Domine, salvum	4'

Bärenreiter

La mort de Cléopâtre (The Death of Cleopatra)

see his: Cléopâtre

Les nuits d'été, op.7 <1840–1841>   31'

solo voice (Ms or T or Bar, or several different voices alternating)
2 1 2 2 — 3 0 0 0 — hp — str
The list of contents shows the voices as specified by the composer for
each song. Keys of the original set are given first, in italics. All publishers
offer the keys listed for individual songs, except that those in square
brackets are only available from Bärenreiter. The transpositions involve
some orchestration adjustments because of instrument ranges.

Some scholars believe these songs to have been intended not as a cycle,
but as freestanding individual songs.

1. Villanelle (mezzo or tenor—*A*, G, F)   2'
2. Le spectre de la rose (alto—*B*, D [C])   7'
3. Sur les lagunes (mezzo, alto, or baritone—*f*, g [e])   7'
4. Absence (mezzo or tenor—*F#*, Eb, Db)   6'
5. Au cimetière (tenor—*D*, C, B, Bb)   5'
6. L'île inconnue (mezzo or tenor—*F*, E, D)   4'

Bärenreiter	Breitkopf	Kalmus	Luck's

Requiem, op.5 (Grande messe des morts) <1837>   82'

chorus   tenor solo
4 4[1.2.Eh1.Eh2] 4 8 — 12 16[12tp.4crt] 16 6[2tuba.4oph] — 10tmp,
9perc — str
perc: bd, 10cym, 4tamtam
The above includes the 4 small orchestras of brass instruments (trumpets,
cornets, trombones, tubas & ophicleides) placed at the four corners of the
body of chorus and orchestra; only the horns are seated in the main
orchestra.

Number of real parts for winds and percussion, exclusive of doublings:
4 4[incl Eh] 2 4 — 6 8 8 3 — 4tmp, 3perc.

Kalmus timpani parts are redistributed to permit performance by 6
timpanists.

1. *Requiem et Kyrie*   12'
2. *Dies irae*   12'
3. *Quid sum miser*   3'
4. *Rex tremendae*   6'
5. *Quaerens me*   5'
6. *Lacrimosa*   11'
7. *Offertoire; Choeur des âmes du Purgatoire*   8'
8. *Hostias*   3'
9. *Sanctus*   10'
10. *Agnus Dei*   12'

Bärenreiter	Breitkopf	Kalmus	Luck's

Rêverie et Caprice, op.8 <1841>   11'

violin solo
2[1.pic] 2 2 2 — 2 0 0 0 — str

Bärenreiter	Breitkopf	Kalmus

Rob Roy <1831>   12'

2[1.2/pic] 2[1.Eh] 2 2 — 4 3[1.2.crt] 3 0 — tmp — hp — str

Bärenreiter	Breitkopf	Kalmus	Luck's

Le Roi Lear, op.4 (King Lear) <1831>   16'

2[1.2/pic] 2 2 2 — 4 2 3 1[oph] — tmp — str

Breitkopf	Kalmus	Luck's

Roman Carnival

see his: Carnaval romain

Roméo et Juliette, op.17 <1839>   95'

solos ATB   double chorus, smaller ATB chorus, small male chorus
TTBB
3[1.2.pic] 2[1.2/Eh] 2 4 — 4 4[2tp, 2crt] 3 1[oph] — 2tmp+6 — 2hp
[preferably doubled] — str[min 15.15.10.11.9]
perc: bd, cym, sus cym, 2tri, 2tambn, crot

Act I: Introduction   5'
Prologue   14'
Act II: Romeo Alone   14'
Love Scene   18'
Queen Mab Scherzo   8'
Act III. Juliet's Funeral Procession 10'
Romeo in the Tomb of the Capulets   9'
Finale   17'

Bärenreiter	Breitkopf	Kalmus	Schirmer

Roméo et Juliette: Introduction <1839>   5'

2 2 2 4 — 4 4[2tp, 2crt] 3 1[oph] — tmp — str

Roméo et Juliette: Love Scene <1839>   18'

2 2[1.Eh] 2 4 — 4 0 0 0 — str
In the complete *Roméo et Juliette*, after 42 bars of instrumental
introduction, a lengthy passage for 2 off-stage male choruses ensues—a
passage that is normally omitted for concert performance of this excerpt.
Breitkopf omits the passage in question; Kalmus offers both versions,
identifying the one without chorus as "concert version."

Bärenreiter	Breitkopf	Kalmus	Luck's

Roméo et Juliette: Queen Mab Scherzo <1839>   8'

3[1.2.pic] 2[1.Eh] 2 4 — 4 0 0 0 — 2tmp+1 — 2hp — str
perc: bd, sus cym, crot

Bärenreiter	Breitkopf	Kalmus	Luck's

Roméo et Juliette: Romeo Alone; Festivities at Capulet's <1839>   14'

3[1.2.pic] 2 2 4 — 4 4[2tp, 2crt] 3 0 — 2tmp+6 — 2hp — str
perc: bd, cym, tambn, tri

Bärenreiter	Breitkopf	Kalmus	Luck's

Sara la baigneuse, op.11 (Sarah the Bather) <1834>   7'

3 choruses: SA, STBB, TTBB
3[1.2.pic] 1 2 2 — 3 0 0 0 — str

Bärenreiter	Breitkopf	Kalmus	Luck's

Symphonie fantastique, op.14 (Fantastic Symphony) <1830>   49'

2[1.2/pic] 2[1.2/Eh] 2[1/Ebcl.2] 4 — 4 4[2tp, 2crt] 3 2[2oph] —
4tmp+2 — 4hp [doubling 2 real parts] — str
perc: bd, cym, sus cym, sd, 2 low bells;
2 of the 4 timpanists double on percussion
Offstage oboe (ob1) in mvt 2; offstage low bells in final mvt.

A critical edition of the score with historical and analytical essays is
available from Norton.

A special optional solo cornet part for the 2nd mvt (where trumpets and
cornets are otherwise tacet) may have been written for a performance by
the legendary Jean-Baptiste Arban. This part is included in the Kalmus
set; it is also available in Appendix III of the Bärenreiter collected edition
of Berlioz in a format that can be photocopied and used in performance
(v.16, p.197). The Norton score integrates the part into the score of the
2nd mvt.

1. *Rêveries, Passions*   13'
2. *Un bal (A Ball)*   6'
3. *Scène aux champs (Scene in the Country)*   15'
4. *Marche au supplice (March to the Scaffold)*   5'
5. *Songe d'une nuit du sabbat (Dream of a Witches' Sabbath)* 10'

Bärenreiter	Breitkopf	Kalmus	Luck's

Symphonie funèbre et triomphale, op.15 (Funeral and Triumphal Symphony) <1840>   36'

optional chorus SSTTBB (3rd mvt)
9[5fl.4pic] 5 33[5Ebcl.26cl.2bcl] 9[8bn.1opt cbn] — 12 12[8tp.4crt]
11[btbn opt] 6[6 oph] — tmp+12 — optional str[20.20.15.15.10]
perc: bd, 3cym, 8sd, tamtam, Turkish crescent
Scored for military band. Number of real wind & perc parts, exclusive of doublings:
2[1.pic] 1ob 4[1.2.Ebcl.bcl] 3[1.2.opt cbn] — 6 6[4tp.2crt]
5[1.2.3.4.opt btbn] 2[2 oph] — tmp+5.
   Bärenreiter also offers a separate edition prepared for American wind bands by Jonathan Elkus.
   Marche funèbre   18'
   Oraison funèbre   9'
   Apothéose   9'

Bärenreiter	Breitkopf	Kalmus

Te Deum, op.22 <1849>   52'

solo tenor   double chorus, optional children's chorus
4[1.2.3.4/pic] 4[1.2.3.4/Eh] 4[1.2.3.4/bcl] 4 — 4 4[2tp, 2crt] 6
2[tuba.oph] — tmp+6 — org — str
perc: bd, 5 pr cym, 4sd
Number of real parts for winds and percussion, exclusive of doublings:
   2 2[1.2/Eh] 2[1.2/bcl] 4 — 4 4[2tp, 2crt] 3 2 — tmp+3.
Tuba and ophicleide are in unison or octaves; 1 instrument is probably sufficient.
   Berlioz wrote in a letter to Hans von Bülow that the tenor solo could be sung by a soprano.
   Two additional movements, the *Prélude* and the *March,* are intended only for use on quasi-military occasions; see the following two entries. They are both included (the *Prélude* as an appendix) in the Bärenreiter edition score and parts of the complete work.
   1. Te Deum (Hymne)   8'
   2. Tibi omnes (Hymne)   10'
   3. Dignare (Prière)   9'
   4. Christe, rex gloriae (Hymne) 5'
   5. Te ergo quaesumus (Prière)   8'
   6. Judex crederis (Hymne et prière) 12'

Bärenreiter	Breitkopf	Kalmus	Schirmer

Te Deum, op.22: Prelude <1849>   3'

3[1.2.pic] 4 4 4 — 4 4[2tp, 2crt] 3 2[tuba.oph] — tmp+6 — str
perc: 6field dr [playing a single part]
Number of real parts for non-string instruments, exclusive of doublings:
2 2 2 2 — 4 4 3 1 — tmp+1.
   Intended for use in the *Te Deum* only in quasi-military situations; if used, it would come between the *Tibi omnes* and the *Dignare.*

Bärenreiter

Te Deum, op.22: Marche pour la présentation des drapeaux (March for the Presentation of the Colors) <1849>   5'

4 4 4 4 — 4 4[2tp, 2crt] 6 2[tuba, oph] — petit saxhorn — tmp+4 —
12hp[1part] — org — str
perc: 4sd[1part]
Number of real parts for non-string instruments, exclusive of doublings:
4 2 2 2 — 4 4 3 2 — petit saxhorn — tmp+1 — 1hp — org. Tuba and ophicleide are in unison or octaves; 1 instrument is probably sufficient. Similarly, flutes 3-4 are always in unison or octaves with flutes 1-2, and could be omitted.
   Intended for use as a final movement of the *Te Deum* only in quasi-military situations.

Bärenreiter

TRISTIA, op.18 <1831–1848>   20'

chorus
2 2[1.2/Eh] 2 2 — 4 4[2tp, 2crt] 3 1 — tmp+9 — str
perc: bd, cym, 6sd doubling 1 part, tamtam [all perc offstage]
Optional bn3&4 in no.3.
   The individual components are available separately (see below).
   1. Méditation religieuse   5'
   2. La mort d'Ophélie   6'
   3. Marche funèbre d'Hamlet   9'

Kalmus	Luck's

Tristia, op.18: 1. Méditation religieuse <1831>   5'

chorus SSTTBB
2 0 2 2 — 2 0 0 0 — str

Bärenreiter	Breitkopf

Tristia, op.18: 2. La mort d'Ophélia (Death of Ophelia) <1848>   6'

female chorus
2 1[Eh] 2 0 — 3 0 0 0 — str
Originally for high voice and piano; orchestrated by the composer.

Bärenreiter	Breitkopf

Tristia, op.18: 3. Marche funèbre d'Hamlet (Funeral March from Hamlet) <1844>   9'

wordless chorus
2 2 2 2[bn3&4 opt] — 4 4[2tp, 2crt] 3 1 — tmp+9 — str
perc: bd, cym, 6sd doubling 1 part, tamtam [all perc offstage]

Bärenreiter	Breitkopf

Les Troyens: Overture <1856–1858>   6'

2 2 2[1.bcl] 2 — 4 4[2tp, 2crt] 3 0 — tmp — str

Kalmus	Luck's

Les Troyens: Ballet <1856–1858>   12'

3[1.2.pic] 2[1.2/Eh] 2 2 — 4 4[2tp, 2crt] 3 0 — tmp+2 — str
perc: tambourin provençal, crot
   1. Pas des almées   _'
   2. Danse des esclaves   _'
   3. Pas d'esclaves nubiennes   _'

Choudens	Kalmus	Luck's

Les Troyens: Chasse royale et Orage (Royal Hunt and Storm) <1856–1858>   10'

opt chorus
3[1.2.pic] 2 2 2 — 4 4[2tp, 2crt] 3 1 — 2tmp+1 — str
perc: bd
A 3rd timpanist is optional.

Bärenreiter	Choudens	Kalmus	Luck's

Les Troyens: Marche troyenne (concert version) <1856–1858>   5'

2 2 2 2 — 4 4[2tp, 2crt] 3 1 — tmp+2 — 2hp — str
perc: bd, cym

Bärenreiter	Breitkopf	Choudens	Kalmus	Luck's

Vox populi: Deux grand choeurs, op.20 <1844–1848>   11'

TTBB solos (or small chorus)   chorus
2 2 2 2 — 4 4[2tp & 2crt] 3 1[oph or tuba] — 2tmp — str
Ed. David Charlton.
   1. La menace des Francs (Marche et choeur)   3'
   2. Hymne à la France   8'

Bärenreiter

Waverley, op.1 <1839>   9'

2[1.2/pic] 2 2 4 — 4 3 3 1 — tmp — str

| Kalmus | Luck's |

Zaïde; boléro, op.19, no.1 <1845>   4'

solo soprano
1 2 2 2 — 4 0 0 0 — tmp+1 — str
perc: cast

| Bärenreiter | Breitkopf | Kalmus |

Bernstein, Leonard   1918-1990

(b Lawrence, MA, 25 Aug 1918; d New York, 14 Oct 1990). American

The Age of Anxiety <1949>

see his: Symphony No.2

Arias and Barcarolles (version for strings & percussion) <1988>   30'

solo mezzo-soprano & baritone
2perc — str
perc: xyl, chimes, crot, tri, sus cym, glock, vib, bd, tamtam, tambn, 2sd, 2woodblks, police whistle
Accompaniment originally for piano 4-hands; arr. for strings & percussion by Bright Sheng.
  Another version exists, for chamber orchestra, by Bruce Coughlin:
1[fl/pic] 1[ob/Eh] 1[cl/Ebcl/asx] 1 — 2 1 0 0 — tmp+2 — str [or 5t]

Prelude	*1'*
Love Duet	*4'*
Little Smary	*3'*
The Love of My Life	*4'*
Greeting	*3'*
At My Wedding	*5'*
Mr. & Mrs. Webb Say Goodnight	*7'*
Nachspiel	*3'*

| Boosey |

Candide: Overture <1955–1956>   5'

3[1.2.pic] 2 4[1.2.Ebcl.bcl] 3[1.2.cbn] — 4 2 3 1 — tmp+5 — hp — str
perc: bd, cym, sd, td, tri, glock, xyl

| Boosey | Luck's |

Chichester Psalms <1965>   19'

chorus *or* male chorus   solo boy *or* countertenor
0 0 0 0 — 0 3 3 0 — tmp+7 — 2hp — str
perc: bd, cym, sd, tri, tambn, glock, xyl, chimes, woodblks, templeblks, whip, 3bongos, rasp
Publisher offers a reduction of the instrumental forces for harp, organ, and percussion.

I. Psalm 108:2; Psalm 100	*4'*
II. Psalm 23; Psalm 2:1-4	*6'*
III. Psalm 131; Psalm 133:1	*9'*

| Boosey |

Divertimento for Orchestra <1980>   15'

4[1.2.3/pic2.pic1] 3[1.2.Eh] 4[1.2.Ebcl.bcl] 3[1.2.cbn] — 4 3 3 1[1/euph] — tmp+6 — hp — pf — str
perc: bd, cym, sus cym, 4sd, td, set, tri, tambn, tamtam, glock, xyl, marim, vib, chimes, woodblk, templeblk, marac, congas, 2 Cuban cowbells, rasp, 3bongos, sandblks

1. Sennets and Tuckets	*1'*
2. Waltz	*2'*
3. Mazurka	*2'*
4. Samba	*1'*
5. Turkey Trot	*2'*
6. Sphinxes	*1'*
7. Blues	*2'*
8. In memoriam; March: "The BSO Forever"	*4'*

| Boosey |

Facsimile <1946>   21'

2[1.2/pic] 2 2[1.2/Ebcl] 2 — 4 3[1.2.crt] 2 1 — tmp+2 — pf — str
perc: bd, sd, cym, tri, glock, woodblk

| Boosey |

Fancy Free [complete ballet] <1944>   25'

2[1.2/pic] 2 2 2 — 4 3 3 1 — tmp+3 — pf — str
perc: bd, cym, sd, woodblk, sus cym, cowbell (opt), tri (played by tmp)
The Suite from *Fancy Free*, which was only slightly shorter than the complete ballet listed here, has been withdrawn.

1. Enter Three Sailors	*3'*
2. Scene at the Bar	*2'*
3. Enter Two Girls	*2'*
4. Pas de deux	*3'*
5. Competition Scene	*3'*
6. Three Dance Variations (Galop, Waltz, Danzon)	*7'*
7. Finale	*5'*

| Boosey |

Fancy Free: Three Dance Variations <1944>   7'

2[1.2/pic] 2 2 2 — 4 3 3 1 — tmp+3 — pf — str
perc: bd, sus cym, sd, tri

Galop	*1'*
Waltz	*3'*
Danzon	*3'*

| Boosey |

Halil <1981>   16'

solo flute
2[afl.pic] 0 0 0 — tmp+6 — hp — str
perc: bd, cym, 2sus cym, 4sd, 4tomtoms, 2tri, 2gongs, tamtam, glock, xyl, vib, chimes, 4woodblks, whip
Pic & afl seated with perc section, preferably invisible to audience.

| Boosey |

Jeremiah

see his: Symphony No.1

Kaddish

see his: Symphony No.3

Mass: Three Meditations <1971; rev 1977>   17'

solo violoncello
tmp+7 — hp — pf, org — str
perc: bd, tomtom, cym, sus cym, tri, tambn, xyl, glock, marim, vib, 2sd, 3hand dr, gourds

1. Lento assai	*5'*
2. Andante sostenuto	*4'*
3. Presto	*8'*

| Boosey |

On the Town: Three Dance Episodes <1945>   *11'*

1[1/pic] 1[1/Eh] 3[1/Ebcl.2/asx.3/bcl] 0 — 2 3 3 0 — tmp+2 — pf — str

perc: sd, bd, set, sus cym, tri, woodblk, xyl

Revised edition 2007.

   Mvt 1, *The Great Lover*, has violins split 3 ways: A, B, and C. Current material from the publisher treats this as a 3-part *divisi* in both vn1 and vn2.

The Great Lover	2'
Lonely Town (Pas de deux)	4'
Times Square: 1944	5'

> Boosey

On the Waterfront: Symphonic Suite <1955>   *23'*

3[1.2.pic] 2 4[1.2.Ebcl.bcl] 3[1.2.cbn] — 4 3 3 1 — asx — 2tmp+3 — hp — pf — str

perc: xyl, vib, glock, sd, bd, sus cym, cym, tri, woodblk, chimes, 3tuned dr, 2tamtams

> Boosey

Prelude, Fugue and Riffs <1949>   *9'*

solo clarinet

0 0 0 0 — 0 5 4 0 — 2asx[1/cl.2], 2tsx, bsx — 2perc — pf — solo db

perc: xyl, vib, woodblk, set, 4tomtoms, tmp (last 2 notes only)

1st alto saxophone doubles on clarinet (*not* the solo clarinet). Solo clarinet appears only in 3rd mvt; it should be discreetly amplified.

Prelude for the Brass	_'
Fugue for the Saxes	_'
Riffs for Everyone	_'

> Boosey

Serenade (After Plato's "Symposium") <1954>   *31'*

solo violin

tmp+5 — hp — str

perc: tambn, xyl, glock, sus cym, chimes, tri, sd, td, 2 Chinese blocks, 2bd

I. Phaedras—Pausanias: Lento - Allegro	7'
II. Aristophanes: Allegretto	4'
III. Eryximachus: Presto	5'
IV. Agathon: Adagio	8'
V. Socrates—Alcibiades: Molto tenuto - Allegro molto	10'

> Boosey

Slava! (A Political Overture) <1977>   *4'*

3[1.2.pic] 3[1.2.Eh] 4[1.2.Ebcl.bcl] 3[1.2.cbn] — 4 3 3 1 — ssx — elec gtr, prerecorded tape — tmp+5 — pf — str

perc: sd, td, bd, set, cym, sus cym, chimes, tri, woodblk, tambn, ratch, whip, xyl, glock, marim, vib, small sd, steel pipe, slide whistle

> Boosey

Songfest <1977>   *40'*

solo voices: S Ms A T Bar B

3[1.2.3/pic] 3[1.2.Eh] 4[1.2.Ebcl.bcl] 3[1.2.cbn] — 4 3 3 1 — fender bass — tmp+6 — hp — cel/pf/elec pf — str

perc: td, bd, sd, cym, sus cym, chimes, tambn, tri, slgh-bells, tamtam, woodblk, glock, xyl, marim, vib, 2sd, 3tomtoms, 3rock drums, finger cym, anvil, rasp

I. Sextet	3'
II. Three Solos	11'
III. Three Ensembles	9'
IV. Sextet	2'
V. Three Solos	11'
VI. Sextet	4'

> Boosey

Symphony No.1 (Jeremiah) <1943>   *25'*

solo mezzo-soprano

3[1.2.3/pic] 3[1.2.Eh] 3[1.2.Ebcl/bcl] 3[1.2.cbn] — 4 3 3 1 — tmp+4 — pf — str

perc: bd, cym, sd, tri, woodblk, marac (on tmp)

Said to be many textual problems in score and parts.

Prophecy	8'
Profanation	7'
Lamentation	10'

> Boosey

Symphony No.2 (The Age of Anxiety) <1949; rev 1965>   *35'*

solo piano

3[1.2.pic] 3[1.2.Eh] 3[1.2.bcl] 3[1.2.cbn] — 4 3 3 1 — tmp+5 — 2hp — pianino — str

perc: bd, cym, sus cym, sd, td, tri, tamtam, glock, xyl, chimes, templeblks

The Prologue	2'
The Seven Ages	8'
The Seven Stages	6'
The Dirge	6'
The Masque	5'
The Epilogue	8'

> Boosey

Symphony No.3 (Kaddish) <1963; rev 1977>   *41'*

speaker, soprano solo   mixed chorus, boy's chorus

4[1.2.3/afl.4/pic] 3[1.2.Eh] 4[1.2.Ebcl.bcl] 3[1.2.cbn] — 4 4 3 1 — asx — tmp+7 — hp — cel, pf — str

perc: bd, cym, sd, td, field dr, tri, tambn, tamtam, glock, xyl, vib, chimes, crot, woodblk, templeblk, whip, ratch, Israeli hand dr, sandblks, 3bongos, rasp, 2sus cym, fingercym, marac (also marac played on tmp)

Speaker's original text by the composer; substitute text by Samuel Pisar, 1988.

I. Invocation	3'
I. … Kaddish 1	5'
II. Din-Torah	6'
II. … Kaddish 2	8'
III. Scherzo	5'
III. … Kaddish 3	3'
III. … Finale	11'

> Boosey

West Side Story: Overture <1957>   *5'*

2[1.2/pic] 2[1.2/Eh] 2[1.2/Ebcl/bcl] 2 — 4 3 3 1 — elec gtr (opt) — tmp+3 — hp — pf — str

perc: chimes, set (sd, 2sus cym, bd/ped, hi-hat, tomtom, 3cowbells), marac, vib, bongos, xyl, glock, guiro, timbales

Original publisher G.Schirmer. The Broadway show had no overture at all. The present overture was created (by Sid Ramin?) for very small instrumentation, to be used by summer stock companies, and subsequently arranged by Maurice Peress for full orchestra.

> Boosey   Luck's

West Side Story: Selections (Mason) <1957>   *8'*

2[1.2/pic] 2[1.2/Eh] 2 2 — 4 3 3 1 — optional: 2asx, tsx, bsx — tmp+4 — hp — str

perc: bd, bongos, cast, chimes, glock, claves, cym, hi-hat, marac, sd, tambn, tri, vib, xyl

> Leonard

West Side Story: Symphonic Dances <1957>   24'

3[1.2.3/pic] 3[1.2.Eh] 4[1.2.Ebcl.bcl] 3[1.2.cbn] — 4 3 3 1 — asx —
tmp+4 or 5 — hp — pf/cel — str
perc: vib, timbales, congas, bd, tomtom, set, cym, tambn, woodblk, tri, tamtam,
xyl, glock, chimes, td, 4pitched dr, 2sd, finger cym, 2pr marac, 3cowbells, police
whistle, 3bongos, 2sus cym, guiro
Newly engraved score and parts in 1995 rectify some errors.

I. Prologue	*4'*
II. "Somewhere"	*5'*
III. Scherzo	*1'*
IV. Mambo	*2'*
V. Cha Cha	*1'*
VI. Meeting Scene	*1'*
VII. "Cool" Fugue	*4'*
VIII. Rumble	*2'*
IX. Finale	*4'*

> Boosey

Berwald, Franz   1796-1868

(b Stockholm, 23 July 1796; d Stockholm, 3 April 1868). Swedish

Estrella de Soria: Overture <1862>   8'

2 2 2 2 — 4 2 3 0 — tmp — str
Concert-ending by Moses Pergament.
Bärenreiter ed. by N. Castegren.

> Bärenreiter   Gehrmans

Symphony No.1, G minor (Sinfonie sérieuse) <1842>   34'

2 2 2 2 — 4 2 3 0 — tmp — str
Sometimes listed as *Symphony No.2*.
Ed. L.Hedwall.

I. Allegro con energia	*12'*
II. Adagio maestoso	*8'*
III. Stretto	*6'*
IV. Finale: Adagio; Allegro molto	*8'*

> Bärenreiter   Gehrmans

Symphony No.2, D major (Sinfonie capricieuse) <1842>   24'

2 2 2 2 — 4 2 3 0 — tmp — str
Only the short score draft survives; realization by N. Castegren.

1. Allegro	*7'*
2. Andante	*7'*
3. Finale: Allegro assai	*10'*

> Bärenreiter   Gehrmans

Symphony No.3, C major (Sinfonie singulière) <1845>   29'

2 2 2 2 — 4 2 3 0 — tmp — str
Sometimes listed as *Symphony No.5*. Bärenreiter ed. H.Blomstedt.

I. Allegro fuocoso	*11'*
II. Adagio	*10'*
III. Finale: Presto	*8'*

> Bärenreiter   Hansen   Kalmus

Symphony No.4, E-flat major (Sinfonie naïve) <1845>   28'

2 2 2 2 — 4 2 3 0 — tmp — str
Published as *Symphony No.3*; sometimes referred to as *Symphony No.6*.

1. Allegro risoluto	*9'*
2. Adagio	*6'*
3. Scherzo: Allegro molto	*6'*
4. Finale: Allegro vivace	*7'*

> Bärenreiter   Gehrmans   Simrock

Biber, Heinrich von   1644-1704

(b Wartenberg [now Stráz pod Ralskem], Bohemia, bap. 12 Aug 1644; d Salzburg, 3
May 1704). Austrian composer of Bohemian birth

Battalia <1673>   6'

cnt — str
Alliance ed. by Joel Blahnik; Doblinger ed. by Nikolaus Harnoncourt.

> Alliance   Doblinger

Requiem, F minor <after 1692>   31'

solos SSATB   chorus SSATB
0 0 0 1 — 0 0 3 0 — org — str

I. Introitus	*3'*
II. Kyrie	*2'*
III. Dies irae	*9'*
IV. Domine Jesu Christe	*6'*
V. Sanctus	*2'*
VI. Benedictus	*3'*
VII. Agnus Dei	*6'*

> Handlo

Biggs, John   1932-

(b Los Angeles, 18 October 1932). American

The Ballad of William Sycamore, op.93 <1995>   16'

narrator
2 2 2 2 — 4 3 3 1 — tmp+3 — str
perc: bd, cym, sus cym, sd, td, tambn, chimes, woodblk
Trumpets backstage in last movement.

Prologue	*4'*
Remembrance [spoken]	*2'*
Dance	*3'*
Youth [spoken]	*1'*
Declaration	*3'*
Epilogue	*3'*

> Consort   Fleisher

Concerto for Orchestra, op.75 <1988>   21'

2[1.2/pic] 2[1.2/Eh] 2 2 — 4 3 3 1 — tmp+3 — hp — str
perc: bd, cym, sus cym, td, tri, glock, xyl, chimes, sd, pic sd
Movements attacca without breaks.

Allegro energico [tutti]	*5'*
Briskly [winds]	*4'*
Half as Fast [strings]	*6'*
Immediately Faster [tutti]	*6'*

> Consort   Fleisher

Concerto, Oboe & Strings, op.4 <1958>   21'

str

I. Allegro moderato	*_'*
II. Largo	*_'*
III. Allegro energico	*_'*

> Consort

Concerto, Violin & Classical Orchestra, op.72 <1987>   25'

2 2 2 2 — 2 2 0 0 — tmp — str

I. Allegro	*_'*
II. Largo — mestoso	*_'*
III. Allegro energico	*_'*

> Consort

Concerto, Violoncello & Chamber Orchestra, op.96 <1996>   21'

0 2 0 2 — 2 0 0 0 — str

1. Allegro con bravura	*8'*
2. Andante	*8'*
3. Allegro vivo	*5'*

> Consort   Fleisher

**Passacaglia: In memoriam J.F. Kennedy, op.21 <1978;   10'
rev 1997>**

2[1.2/pic] 2 2 2 — 4 2 2 1 — tmp+3 — str
perc: bd, cym, sus cym, sd, tri

| Consort | Fleisher |

Pastiche; An Overture, op.87 <1992>   6'

2[1.2/pic] 2 2 2 — 4 3 3 1 — tmp+2 — str
perc: bd, cym, sus cym, td, tri, tambn, xyl, woodblk, whip, 2sd
27 quotations from well-known classics, cleverly worked together.

| Consort | Fleisher |

Salutation, op.93 <1993>   6'

2[1.2/pic] 2 2 2 — 4 3 3 1 — tmp+3 — str
perc: bd, cym, sus cym, sd, tri, glock, xyl, chimes

| Consort |

Sousaphernalia; An Overture for Orchestra <1999>   7'

2[1.2/pic] 2 2 2 — 4 2 0 0 — tmp — str
Using interwoven themes from well-known marches by John Philip
Sousa.

| Consort |

Variations on a Theme of Shostakovich, op.52 <1977>   21'

solo piano
2[1.2/pic] 2 2[1.2/Ebcl] 2 — 4 2 2 1 — tmp+2 — str
perc: bd, cym, sus cym, sd, piccolo sd, td, tri, tambn, gong, xyl, chimes,
templeblks
Theme is from the Shostakovich String Quartet No.1, op.49.

| Consort |

Bilik, Jerry H.   1933-

(b New Rochelle, NY, 1933). American

American Civil War Fantasy   8'

2[1.2/pic] 2 2 2 — 4 3 3 1 — tmp+3 — str
perc: sd, field dr, cym, sus cym, tri, bd, glock, cannon (opt)

| Peer | Luck's |

Birtwistle, Harrison   1934-

(b Accrington, Lancs., 15 July 1934). English

Carmen arcadiae mechanicae perpetuum <1977–1978>   12'

1[1/pic] 1 1[1/bcl] 1[1/cbn] — 1 1 1 0 — marim — pf — str 5t, or
str[6.6.4.4.2]

| Universal |

Endless Parade <1987>   18'

0 0 0 0 — 0 1 0 0 — vib — str[7.7.4.4.2]

| Universal |

Machaut à ma manière (Machaut in My Manner)   10'
<1988>

2[1/pic.2/pic] 2[incl Eh] 2[incl Ebcl] 2[incl cbn] — 4 3 2 1 — 2perc
— str[min 10.8.6.6.4]
perc: tambn, bd, claves, 2hi-hat, 2sd, 2glock
A recomposition of 3 pieces by Guillaume de Machaut (ca.1300-1377).
O Livoris Feritas   _'
David Hoquetus   _'
Amen   _'

| Universal |

Nomos <1968>   15'

ampflied solo group: flute, clarinet, horn, bassoon
4[1.2/pic.3/pic.4/pic] 3[1.2.3/Eh] 3[1/Ebcl.2/Ebcl.3/bcl] 3[1.2.3/cbn] —
4 4 3 1 — tmp+6 — hp — cel — 10va, 10vc, 8db
perc: crot, glock, marim, templeblks, marac, tambn, bd, 2xyl, sandblks, 2tri,
3woodblks, 2field dr, 5sus cym, 5timbales, 3tamtams, 5bongos, 9brass bells;
timpanist covers some perc

| Universal |

Verses for Ensembles <1969>   28'

1[pic/afl] 1[ob/Eh] 2[1/Ebcl.2/bcl] 1[bn/cbn] — 1 2 2 0 — 3perc —
[no str]
perc: bd, sd, td, 4bongos, congas, 3glock, 3xyl, 5timbales, 4sus cym, templeblks,
4cowbells
Players move from place to place.

| Universal |

Bissell, Keith   1912-1992

(b Meaford, ON, 12 Feb 1912; d Newmarket, ON, 9 May 1992). Canadian

Andante e Scherzo <1972>   7'

2 2 2 2 — 2 0 0 0 — tmp+1 — str
1. Andante   _'
2. Scherzo   _'

| Counterpoint |

Bizet, Georges   1838-1875

(b Paris, 25 Oct 1838; d Bougival, nr Paris, 3 June 1875). French

L'Arlésienne: Suite No.1 <1872>   17'

2 2[1/Eh.2] 2 2 — 4 4[2tp, 2crt] 3 0 — opt asx — tmp+1 — hp[or
pf)] — str
perc: sd
The original incidental music to Alphonse Daudet's play was for:
   2 1[incl Eh] 1 2 — asx — 2hn — tmp/tmb prov — str.
   Suite No.1 for full orchestra was prepared by the composer. The
Eulenburg is a text-critical edition. The Breitkopf edition (and Kalmus
reprint) by Fritz Hoffmann is cued for performance by a minimum of
1 1 2 1 — 2 2 1 0 — str 4t. Bizet's 2tp & 2crt parts are redistributed by
Hoffmann among the 4tp in an unpredictable, though practical, manner.
Prélude   6'
Minuet   3'
Adagietto   3'
Carillon   5'

| Breitkopf | Choudens | Eulenburg | Kalmus | Luck's |

L'Arlésienne: Suite No.2 <1872>   18'

2[1.2/pic] 2 2 2 — 4 4[2tp, 2crt] 3 0 — opt asx — tmp+3 — hp[or pf]
— str
perc: cym, bd, tambourin provençal
The original incidental music to Alphonse Daudet's play was for:
   2 1[incl Eh] 1 2 — asx — 2hn — tmp/tmb prov — str.
   Suite No.2 for full orchestra was prepared by Ernest Guiraud after
Bizet's death. The Eulenburg is a text-critical edition. The Breitkopf
edition (and Kalmus reprint) by Fritz Hoffmann is cued for performance
by a minimum of 1 1 2 1 — 2 2 1 0 — str 4t. Guiraud's 2tp & 2crt parts
are redistributed by Hoffmann among the 4tp in an unpredictable, though
practical, manner. There is an English horn part which, however, consists
of only 4 notes, all of them saxophone cues.
Pastorale   5'
Intermezzo   4'
Menuet [borrowed by Guiraud from Bizet's Le jolie fille de Perth]   4'
Farandole   5'

| Breitkopf | Choudens | Eulenburg | Kalmus | Luck's |

Carmen: Suite No.1 <1873–1874>   12'

2[1.2/pic] 2[1.2/Eh] 2 2 — 4 2 3 0 — tmp+4 — hp — str
perc: tri, sd, cast, tambn, cym, bd
Ed. Fritz Hoffmann.
  I. Prélude & Aragonaise   2'
  II. Intermezzo   4'
  III. Seguedille   2'
  IV. Les Dragons d'Alcala   2'
  V. Les Toréadors   2'

| Breitkopf | Choudens | Kalmus | Luck's |

Carmen: Suite No.2 <1873–1874>   19'

2[1/pic.2/pic] 2[1.2/Eh] 2 2 — 4 2 3 1 — tmp+4 — hp — str
perc: tri, tambn, cym, bd
Ed. Fritz Hoffmann.
  I. Marche des contrebandiers   4'
  II. Habanera   2'
  III. Nocturne   4'
  IV. Chanson de toréador   2'
  V. La garde montante   3'
  VI. Danse bohème   4'

| Breitkopf | Choudens | Kalmus | Luck's |

Carmen Fantasy

see under: Sarasate, Pablo de, 1844-1908
              Proto, Frank

Carmen Symphony in 12 Scenes [José Serebrier] <1875>   25'

2[1/pic.2/pic] 2[1.2/Eh] 2 2 — 4 2 3 0 — asx — tmp+4 — hp — str
perc: bd, cym, sd, tri, tambn
Compiled and arranged by José Serebrier. Many of the best-known
passages from the opera, with minimal reorchestration and recomposition.
  1. Prelude   _'
  2. The Cavalry   _'
  3. Habanera   _'
  4. Seguidilla   _'
  5. Fugato   _'
  6. Interlude 1   _'
  7. Toreador   _'
  8. Interlude 2   _'
  9. Andante cantabile   _'
  10. Interlude 3   _'
  11. The Wedding   _'
  12. Gypsy Dance   _'

| Kalmus |

Le docteur Miracle (Dr. Miracle): Overture <1856>   5'

2 2 2 2 — 2 2 3 0 — tmp+2 — pf[opt] — str
Arr. David Stone. Many instruments optional; may even be played with
as small an orchestra as woodwinds 1 1 1 0 plus strings.

| Oxford |

Jeux d'enfants, op.22: Petite suite <1871>   12'

2[1.2/pic] 2 2 — 4 2 0 0 — tmp+3 — str
perc: sd, tri, cym
Nos. 6, 3, 2, 11, & 12 of a collection of miniatures originally for piano
duet; orchestrated by the composer.
    There is also a Breitkopf edition under the title *Kleine Orchestersuite*
(Kinderspiele), ed. Fritz Hoffmann, with an added trombone
(piano-conductor score only).
  Marche (Trompette et tambour)   2'
  Berceuse (La poupée)   3'
  Impromptu (La toupie)   1'
  Duo (Petit mari, petite femme)   4'
  Galop (Le bal)   2'

| Durand | Kalmus | Ricordi | Luck's |

La jolie fille de Perth: Scènes bohémiennes <1866>   12'

2[1.2/pic] 2[1.2/Eh] 2 2 — 4 2 3 0 — tmp+3 — hp — str
perc: tri, sd, cym
  Prélude   4'
  Sérénade   2'
  Marche   3'
  Danse bohémienne   3'

| Kalmus | Luck's |

Ouverture <1855>   14'

2[1.pic] 2 2 2 — 4 2 3 1[oph] — tmp — str
Ed. Antonio d'Almeida.

| Universal |

Patrie <1873>   13'

2[1.2/pic] 2 2 2 — 4 4[2tp (opt).2crt] 3 1[oph (opt)] — tmp+3 —
2hp[1part] — str
perc: sd, cym, bd, tri
Trumpets 1&2 are cued in cornet parts; ophicleide is cued in bassoon 1.
Wind parts previously sold by Kalmus were in a reduced version by
Francis Casadesus, and did not agree with the score. Since 2005 Kalmus
has offered the original wind parts.

| Choudens | Kalmus | Luck's |

Les pecheurs de perles (Pearlfishers): Overture <1863>   3'

2 2 2 2 — 4 0 0 0 — tmp — str

| Kalmus | Luck's |

Roma <1868; rev 1871>   33'

2[1.2/pic] 2[1.2/Eh] 2 2 — 4 2 3 0 — tmp — hp — str
Roma is a symphony, though it was posthumously published as *3me Suite
de concert.*
    Breitkopf ed. is arr. Fritz Hoffmann, and includes pic & Eh doublings;
Choudens (reprinted Kalmus) is probably the composer's original version.
  [Une chasse dans la forêt d'Ostie]   13'
  Allegretto vivace   5'
  [Une procession]   9'
  Carneval   6'

| Breitkopf | Choudens | Kalmus |

Symphony No.1, C major <1855>   27'

2 2 2 2 — 4 2 0 0 — tmp — str
  I. Allegro vivo   8'
  II. Adagio   9'
  III. Allegro vivace   4'
  IV. Allegro vivace   6'

| Choudens | Kalmus | Luck's | Universal |

Variations chromatiques <1868>   12'

2[1.2/pic] 2[1.2/Eh] 2 2 — 4 2 3 0 — tmp+3 — hp — str
perc: cym, sus cym, sd, tri
Originally for piano; orchestrated by Felix Weingartner.

| Choudens | Kalmus | Luck's |

Blacher, Boris   1903-1975

(b Niu-chang, China, 19 Jan 1903; d Berlin, 30 Jan 1975). German composer of
Baltic descent

Concertante Musik, op.10 <1937>   11'

2[1.2/pic] 2 2 — 4 2 3 1 — tmp — str

| Bote & Bock |

Concerto, Clarinet & Chamber Orchestra <1971>   12'

0 0 0 0 — 1 1 1 0 — hp — str
  I. Allegro   6'
  II. Theme and Variations 6'

| Bote |

Concerto, Piano, No.1, op.28 <1947>   22'
1 1 1 1 — 2 1 1 0 — str

> Bote & Bock

Concerto, Violoncello <1964>   22'
1 1 1 1 — 1 1 1 0 — str

> Bote & Bock

Hamlet; Symphonic Poem <1940>   16'
3[1.2.3/pic] 3[1.2.Eh] 3[1.2.3/bcl] 3[1.2.3/cbn] — 4 3 3 1 — tmp+4 — str
perc: bd, cym, sd, field drum
Percussion only briefly near end, but very important.

> Bote & Bock

Music for Cleveland, op.53 <1957>   10'
3[1.2.3/pic] 3[1.2.Eh] 3[1.2.bcl] 3[1.2.cbn] — 4 4 3 1 — tmp+5 — hp — str
perc: bd, cym, sd, field drum, 3tomtoms, tri, tambn, glock, xyl, vib

> Bote & Bock

Orchesterfantasie, op.51 <1955>   20'
solo string quartet
3[1.2.3/pic] 3[1.2.Eh] 3[1.2.3/bcl] 3[1.2.3/cbn] — 4 3 3 1 — tmp+4 — hp — str

> Bote & Bock

Orchester-Ornament, op.44 <1953>   14'
3[1.2.3/pic] 3[1.2.Eh] 3 3 — 4 3 3 1 — tmp+4 — str

> Bote & Bock

Orchestra-Variations on a Theme of Paganini <1947>   16'
3[1.2.3/pic] 3[1.2.Eh] 3[1.2.3/bcl] 3[1.2.3/cbn] — 4 3 3 1 — tmp — str

> Bote & Bock

Poème <1973–1974>   22'
3[1/pic.2.3/afl] 3[1.2.3/Eh] 3[1.2.3/bcl] 3 — 4 3 3 1 — tmp+3 — hp — str
perc: 3sus cym, sd, 3tomtoms, tri, tambn, gong, glock, xyl

> Bote & Bock

Studie im Pianissimo, op.45 <1953>   12'
2[1.2/pic] 2 2 2 — 4 3 3 1 — str

> Bote & Bock

Symphony, op.12 <1938>   25'
3[1.2.pic] 2 2 2 — 4 2 3 1 — tmp — str
Largo; Allegro   7'
Adagio   9'
Fuge: Piano   9'

> Bote & Bock

Tanzszenen (Dance Scenes; La vie) <1979>   23'
2[1.2/pic] 2 2 2 — 2 2 2 0 — tmp+1 — str
perc: bd, cym, sd, 2tomtoms, tri, tambn, tamtam, vib, wood drum
Intended for a ballet, *La Vie*. Posthumously published as *Tanzszenen*. Various shorter suites have been proposed:
   Dance Suite No.1 (16'): nos. 6, 7 [Tango only], 4, 8, 5
   Dance Suite No.2 (13'): nos. 1, 2, 3, 4, 9a [= Rhumba], 10
   Dance Suite [No.3] (12'): nos.1-5 inclusive
   1. Intrada   -'
   2. Pas de deux   -'
   3. Scherzo   -'
   4. Rag-Caprice   -'
   5. Valse, La vie   -'
   6. Carnival   -'
   7. Episodes & Tango   -'
   8. Intermezzo   -'
   9. Variations   -'
   10. Danzón   -'
   11. Envoi   -'

> Boosey

Two Inventions, op.46 (Zwei Inventionen) <1954>   12'
2 2 2 2 — 4 2 0 0 — tmp+1 — str
perc: sus cym, sd, tri, tambn

> Bote & Bock

Variations on a Theme of Muzio Clementi, op.61 (Variationen über ein Thema von Muzio Clementi) <1931>   18'
solo piano
2 2 2 2 — 4 2 3 1 — tmp+4 — hp — cel — str
perc: sus cym, sd, field drum, tomtoms, tambn, glock, vib

> Bote & Bock

Blackwood, Easley   1933-

(b Indianapolis, IN, 21 April 1933). American

Symphony No.1, op.3 <1958>   31'
4[1.2.3/pic.4/pic] 3[1.2.3/Eh] 4[1.2.3/Ebcl.bcl] 4[1.2.3.cbn] — 6 4 3 1 — tmp+3 — cel — str
Andante maestoso; Non troppo allegro ma con spirito   9'
Andante comodo   6'
Allegretto grotesco   5'
Andante sostenuto   11'

> Elkan-Vogel

Symphony No.2, op.9 <1961>   24'
3[incl pic] 3[incl Eh] 3[incl bcl] 3[incl cbn] — 4 4 3 1 — tmp+3 — hp — str
Source for orchestral material cannot be verified.

>

Symphony No.5, op.34 <1990>   26'
3 3[1.2.Eh] 3[1.2.bcl] 3[1.2.cbn] — 4 3 3 1 — tmp+2 — str
perc: bd, cym, sus cym, sd, tri, tamtam
I. Allegro inquieto   8'
II. Molto adagio   11'
III. Allegro vivo   7'

> Blackwood

Blake, Howard   1938-

(b London, 28 Oct 1938). English

Concerto, Violin (The Leeds) <1992>   35'
2[incl afl,2pic] 2[incl Eh] 2[incl bcl] 3[incl cbn] — 4 4 0 0 — tmp+1 — hp — str

> Faber

Nursery Rhyme Overture <1984>   8'

2[1/pic.2/pic] 1 1 2 — 2 1 1 0 — tmp+1 — hp — str
perc: tri, sd, cym, glock, slgh-bells, bd, sus cym, templeblks, chimes, 2tambn, birdcall

> Faber

Bliss, Arthur   1891-1975

(b London, 2 Aug 1891; d London, 27 March 1975). English composer of American descent

The Beatitudes <1962>   49'

solo ST   chorus
2[1/pic.2/pic] 2 2 2 — 4 2 3 1 — tmp+2 — 2hp — org — str
perc: sus cym, cym, td, bd, chimes, gong, 2sd

Prelude: A Troubled World	3'
1. The Mount of Olives	4'
2. First & Second Beatitudes	3'
3. Easter	6'
4. I got me flowers to strew Thy way	4'
5. Third Beatitude	2'
6. The lofty looks of man	4'
7. Fourth Beatitude	2'
8. The Call	4'
Interlude	1'
9. Fifth, Sixth, Seventh & Eighth Beatitudes	3'
10. And death shall have no dominion	3'
11. Ninth Beatitude	3'
12. Epilogue: O blessed Jesu	7'

> Novello

Checkmate <1937>   52'

2[1.2/pic] 2[1.2/Eh] 2 2 — 4 2 3 0 — tmp+2 — hp — str
perc: bd, cym, sd, tri, glock, chimes, tamtam, xyl, cast, tambn

I. Prologue	5'
II. Dance of the Red Pawns	2'
III. Dance of the Four Knights	4'
IV. Entry of the Black Queen	6'
V. The Red Knight's Mazurka	4'
VI. Ceremony of the Red Bishops	2'
VII. Entry of the Red Castles	2'
VIII. Entry of the King and Queen	2'
IX. The Attack	7'
X. The Duel	8'
XI. The Black Queen Dances	4'
XII. Finale: Checkmate	6'

> Novello

Checkmate: Prologue & Five Dances, op.57 <1937>   27'

2[1.2/pic] 2[1.2/Eh] 2 2 — 4 2 3 0 — tmp+2 — hp — str
perc: bd, cym, sus cym, sd, chimes, tamtam

I. Prologue: The Players	5'
II. Dance of the Four Knights	4'
III. Entry of the Black Queen	6'
IV. The Red Knight's Mazurka	4'
V. Ceremony of the Red Bishops	2'
VI. Finale: Checkmate	6'

> Novello

A Colour Symphony <1921–1922; rev 1932>   31'

3[all/pic] 3[1.2.Eh] 3[1.2.bcl] 3[1.2.cbn] — 4 3 3 1 — 2tmp+1 — 2hp — str
perc: cym

I. Purple	6'
II. Red	7'
III. Blue	10'
IV. Green	8'

> Boosey

Introduction and Allegro <1926; rev 1937>   12'

3[1.2.pic] 3[1.2.Eh] 3[1.2.bcl] 3[1.2.cbn] — 4 3 3 1 — tmp+2 — hp — str
perc: sd, xyl, glock, gong

> Boosey

Things to Come: Concert Suite <1935>   15'

2[1/pic.2/pic] 2[1.2/Eh] 2 2 — 4 3 3 1 — tmp+3 — hp — str
perc: sd, td, bd, cym, tri
Originally a film score (1936); suite prepared by the composer. Other suites using music dropped from the film have been compiled by Christopher Palmer (22', for a larger orchestra, 1960's), and by Philip Lane (32', 1990's).

1.	4'
2.	2'
3.	2'
4.	2'
5.	1'
6.	4'

> Novello

Blitzstein, Marc   1905-1964

(b Philadelphia, 2 March 1905; d Fort-de-France, Martinique, 22 Jan 1964). American

Concerto, Piano <1931>   24'

3[1.2.pic] 2 2 3[1.2.cbn] — 4 2 3 1 — str

I. Moderato molto; Allegro	_'
II. Largo assai	_'
III. Allegro non troppo	_'

> Boosey

Orchestra Variations <1934>   15'

3[1.2.pic] 3[1.2.Eh] 4[1.2.Ebcl.bcl] 3[1.2.cbn] — 4 4[2tp, 2crt] 3 1 — tmp+2 — pf — str

> Boosey

Surf and Seaweed: Suite <1931>   16'

1 1 1 1[1/cbn] — 0 1 0 0 — pf — str 4t
From the music for the 1931 film.

I. Giocoso	_'
II. Moderato	_'
III. Allegro Vivace	_'
IV. Andante	_'
V. Grave	_'

> Boosey

Bloch, Augustyn   1929-

(b Grudziądz, 13 Aug 1929; d Warsaw 6 April 2006). Polish

Enfiando per orchestra <1970>   11'

3 3 3 — 4 3 3 1 — tmp+3 — org or amplified pf — str[14.12.10.8.6]
perc: gong, td, crot, bd, tomtom, 2field dr, 3sus cym, 2tamtam, 3cowbells, 3tri (played by tmp)

> Schott

Bloch, Ernest

1880-1959

(b Geneva, 24 July 1880; d Portland, OR, 15 July 1959). American composer of Swiss origin

America; An Epic Rhapsody in Three Parts <1926> 50'

3[1.2.3/pic] 3[1.2.Eh] 3[1.2.bcl] 3[1.2.cbn] — 4 3 3 1 — tmp+3 — 2hp — cel, opt org — str
perc: sd, tambn, cym, tamtam, tri, glock, bell (D), sus cym, woodblk, 2bd, Indian dr, 2anvils, steel plate, opt auto hn (Db)
Brief unison choral passage at the end of the work, intended by the composer to be sung by the audience.
    Originally published by Birchard.

I. ... 1620:	*20'*
The Soil	
The Indians	
England	
The Mayflower	
The Landing of the Pilgrims	
II. ... 1861-1865:	*16'*
Hours of Joy	
Hours of Sorrow	
III. 1926...:	*14'*
The Present	
The Future	

> Broude Bros.

Avodath Hakodesh (Sacred Service) <1930–1933> 52'

chorus   solo baritone (cantor), optional narrator
3[1.2/pic.3] 3[1.2.Eh] 3[1.2.bcl] 3[1.2.cbn] — 4 3 3 1 — tmp+3 — 2hp — cel — str[min 10.8.6.6.5]
perc: sd, bd, tambn, cym, sus cym, tamtam, tri
Brief solos (SAATB) for members of the chorus.

Act I. Meditation	*12'*
Act II. Kedushah (Sanctification)	*5'*
Act III. Silent Devotion	*9'*
Act IV. Returning the Scroll to the Ark	*8'*
Act V. Adoration	*18'*

> Broude Bros.

Baal Shem (Three Pictures of Chassidic Life) <1923> 15'

solo violin
2[1.2/pic] 2 2 2 — 4 3 0 0 — tmp+1 — hp — cel — str

I. Vidui (Contrition)	*3'*
II. Nigun (Improvisation)	*7'*
III. Simchas Torah (Rejoicing)	*5'*

> C. Fischer

Concertino, Flute, Viola & Strings <1950> 10'

solo flute   solo viola (or clarinet)
3[1.2.pic] 2 2 — 4 3 3 1 — tmp+3 — str
Winds and percussion play only last 14 bars; they may be omitted by using a special ending for strings.

1. Allegro comodo	*4'*
2. Andante	*3'*
3. Allegro	*3'*

> Schirmer

Concerto, Violin <1937–1938> 36'

3[1.2.3/pic] 3[1.2.Eh] 3[1.2.bcl] 3[1.2.cbn] — 4 3 3 1 — tmp+2 — hp — cel — str
perc: cym, tamtam, bd, sd, sus cym

I. Allegro deciso	*18'*
II. Andante	*7'*
III. Deciso	*11'*

> Boosey

Concerto Grosso No.1 <1924–1925> 25'

obbligato piano
str
A 1984 printing includes many corrections, as well as cuts suggested by the composer.

I. Prelude	*4'*
II. Dirge	*7'*
III. Pastorale and Rustic Dances	*8'*
IV. Fugue	*6'*

> Broude Bros.

Concerto Grosso No.2 <1952> 19'

solo string quartet
string orchestra

I. Maestoso; Allegro	*6'*
II. Andante	*3'*
III. Allegro	*4'*
IV. Tranquillo	*6'*

> Schirmer

Evocations <1937> 18'

3[1.2.3/pic] 2[1.2/Eh] 2 2 — 4 2 3 1 — tmp+3 — hp — cel, pf — str
perc: sd, tri, cym, sus cym, tamtam, glock, bd

Contemplation	*7'*
Houang Ti (God of War)	*5'*
Renouveau (Springtime)	*6'*

> Schirmer

Hiver—Printemps (Winter—Spring) <1904–1905> 15'

3[1.2.pic] 3[1.2.Eh] 2 2 — 4 2 3 1 — tmp/tri — hp — str
perc: tri
Parts for additional instruments (fl3, ob3, cl3, bn3, tp3, hp2) are listed as "supplementary"; they merely double the 1st parts in specified passages.

I. Hiver (Winter)	*7'*
II. Printemps (Spring)	*8'*

> Schirmer

In the Night (A Love Poem) <1922> 6'

3[1.2.3/pic] 3[1.2.Eh] 3[1.2.bcl] 3[1.2.cbn] — 4 3 3 1 — tmp+1 — hp — cel — str
perc: glock

> Schirmer

Poems of the Sea <1922> 13'

3[1.2.3/pic] 3[1.2.Eh] 3[1.2.bcl] 3[1.2.cbn] — 4 3 3 1 — tmp+3 — hp — cel — str
perc: bd, cym, tamtam, tri, glock, sus cym
Originally for piano; orchestrated by the composer.

1. Waves	*4'*
2. Chanty	*3'*
3. At Sea	*6'*

> Schirmer

Prelude and Two Psalms (Deux Psaumes, Précédés d'un Prélude Orchestral) <1912–1914> 14'

soprano solo
4[1.2.3/pic.4/pic] 4[1.2.3.Eh] 4[1.2.3.bcl] 4[1.2.3.cbn] — 6 4 3 1 — tmp+ — 2hp — cel — str
perc: bd, sd, tamtam, sus cym

Prélude	*4'*
Psaume 137: Assis aux fleuves de Babel	*6'*
Psaume 114: Arrachés par Iahvé	*4'*

> Schirmer

Proclamation <1955> 6'

solo trumpet
2 2 2 2 — 4 2 0 0 — tmp+1 — str
perc: bd, cym, sd

> Broude Bros.

Sacred Service

see his: Avodath Hakodesh

Schelomo; Hebraic Rhapsody <1915–1916>   20'

solo violoncello
3[1.2.3/pic] 3[1.2.Eh] 3[1.2.bcl] 3[1.2.cbn] — 4 3 3 1 — tmp+3 —
2hp — cel — str
perc: sus cym, cym, tambn, tamtam, bd, sd

Kalmus	Schirmer

Sinfonia breve <1952>   18'

3[1.2.pic] 3[1.2.Eh] 3[1.2.bcl] 3[1.2.cbn] — 4 3 2 1 — tmp+3 — hp
— cel — str
perc: bd, cym, sd, tamtam

Schirmer

Suite hébraïque <1951>   12'

solo viola (or violin)
2 2 2 2 — 4 3 0 0 — tmp+2 — hp — str
perc: sd, cym, tamtam
1. *Rhapsody*   6'
2. *Processional*   2'
3. *Affirmation*   4'

Schirmer

Suite modale <1956>   12'

solo flute
str

Broude Bros.

Symphony for Trombone & Orchestra <1954>   17'

solo trombone
3[1.2.3/pic] 3[1.2.Eh] 3[1.2.bcl] 3[1.2.cbn] — 4 3 3 1 — tmp+2 — hp
— cel — str
perc: sd, tamtam, cym, sus cym, bd
I. Maestoso   3'
II. Agitato   9'
III. Allegro deciso 5'

Broude Bros.

Symphony in E-flat <1954–1955>   25'

3[1.2.3/pic] 3[1.2.Eh] 3[1.2.bcl] 3[1.2.cbn] — 4 3 3 1 — tmp+2 — str
perc: bd, cym, sus cym, sd
I. Tranquillo; Allegro deciso   9'
II. Allegro   5'
III. Andante   5'
IV. Allegro deciso   6'

Schirmer

Trois poèmes juifs (Three Jewish Poems) <1913>   25'

3[1.2.3/pic] 3[1.2.Eh] 2 3[1.2.cbn] — 4 3 3 1 — tmp+4 — hp — cel
— str
perc: sd, tamtam, cym, sus cym, tri, bd, tambn prov, bells[D3,G3]
Danse   8'
Rite   7'
Cortège funèbre 10'

Kalmus	Luck's	Schirmer

Voice in the Wilderness <1936>   25'

solo violoncello obbligato
3[1.2.3/pic] 3[1.2.Eh] 3[1.2.Ebcl] 3[1.2.cbn] — 4 3 3 1 — tmp+2 —
2hp — pf/cel — str
perc: cym, sd, tri, bd, tamtam
1. *Moderato*   3'
2. *Poco lento*   4'
3. *Moderato*   3'
4. *Adagio piacevole*   5'
5. *Poco agitato; Cadenza* 4'
6. *Allegro giocoso*   6'

Schirmer

Blomdahl, Karl-Birger   1916-1968

(b Växjö, 19 Oct 1916; d Kungsängen, nr Stockholm, 14 June 1968). Swedish

Forma ferritonans <1961>   11'

3[1.2.3/pic] 3 4[1.2.bcl/cbcl.cbcl] 4[1.2.3/cbn.4/cbn] — 4 4 5 0 —
tmp+3 — pf — str
perc: bd, cym, xyl

Schott

Game for Eight; Choreographic Suite (Spiel für Acht)   25'
<1962>

1[fl/pic] 1[ob/Eh] 1[cl/bcl/asx] 1[bn/cbn] — 1 1 2 0 — tmp+7 — hp
— cel, pf — 2vn, 2va, 2vc, 2db
perc: xyl, vib, glock, sd, td, cym, tambn, tri, tamtam, templeblks, cowbell, marac,
guiro, claves, whip, 2woodblks
After the Overture, only 5 percussion required.
Ouverture   _'
I. quarter-note = ca.42   _'
II. quarter-note = ca.126   _'
III. quarter-note = ca.63   _'
IV. half-note = ca.84   _'
V. [without mvt title]   _'
VI. quarter-note = ca.63   _'
VII. eighth-note = ca.84   _'

Schott

Sisyphos; Choreographic Suite for Orchestra <1954>   20'

3[1.2.3/pic] 3[1.2.3/Eh] 3[12.3/bcl] 3[1.2.cbn] — 4 4 3 1 — tmp+6 —
hp — pf — str
perc: sd, td, bd, cym, tambn, bongos, tri, tamtam, marac, claves, xyl, vib, marim

Schott

Symphony No.3 (Facets) <1950>   23'

3[1.2.3/pic] 3[1.2.3/Eh] 3[1.2.3/bcl] 3[1.2.3/cbn] — 4 4 3 1 — tmp+2
— str
perc: td, field dr, cym

Schott

Boccherini, Luigi   1743-1805

(b Lucca, 19 Feb 1743; d Madrid, 28 May 1805). Italian

G = Yves Gérard, *Thematic, Bibliographical and Critical Catalogue of
the Works of Luigi Boccherini*, tr. A Mayor. London: Oxford University
Press, 1969

Concerto, Flute, G.489, D major <1760>   20'

str
Wrongly attributed to Boccherini; actual composer is Franz Xaver
Pokorny.

Kalmus	Luck's	Nagel

Concerto, Violin, G.486, D major <1790>   24'

2 2 0 0 − 2 0 0 0 − str
Ed. S. Dushkin. Authenticity very doubtful.

| Schott | |

Concerto, Violoncello, G.474, E-flat major <1790>   18'

0 2 0 0 − 2 0 0 0 − str
Ed. Franco Gallini.

| Zerboni | |

Concerto, Violoncello, G.477, C major <1770>   15'

0 0 0 0 − 2[opt] 0 0 0 − str
Ed. Walter Lebermann.

| Schott | |

Concerto, Violoncello, G.482, B-flat major [original version] <1771>   22'

0 0 0 0 − 2 0 0 0 − str
Ed. Richard Sturzenegger. This is the original version of the work well-known in the inauthentic Grützmacher arrangement.

I. Allegro moderato	9'
II. Adagio non troppo	6'
III. Rondo: Allegro	7'

| Eulenburg | Kalmus | Luck's |

Concerto, Violoncello, G.482, B-flat major (Grützmacher version) <1771>   22'

0 2 0 0 − 2 0 0 0 − str
Formerly accepted as genuine, this work was put together by cellist Friedrich Grützmacher from 3 different Boccherini works (G.565, G.480, G.482), with a greatly altered solo part and tuttis largely by Grützmacher.

I. Allegro moderato	9'
II. Adagio	6'
III. Rondo: Allegro	7'

| Breitkopf | Kalmus | Luck's |

Minuet in A, G.275 <1771>   4'

str
This is the celebrated minuet, originally the 3rd mvt of *String Quintet No.11, G.275, op.11, no.5.*

| Kalmus | Luck's |

Overture, op.43, G.521, D major <1790>   5'

0 2 0 1 − 2 0 0 0 − str
Breitkopf edition (and Kalmus reprint) calls for 2fl rather than 2ob. This work is listed elsewhere as *Symphony No.19* and (in the Almeida edition) as *Symphony No.28.*

| Breitkopf | Kalmus | Luck's | Zanibon |

Ritirata notturna di Madrid

see under: Berio, Luciano, 1925-2003

| | |

Sinfonia concertante, Strings, G.268, C major <1771>   9'

str
Ed. Pina Carmirelli. Originally a string quintet, op.10, no.4. However, the composer himself indicated orchestral performance as possible.

| Zanibon | Luck's |

SYMPHONIES

The numbering system used here is that of the Doblinger edition of the complete Boccherini symphonies, ed. Antonio de Almeida. Divergent numberings are also noted in the individual listings.

Symphony No.1, G.490, D major <?1765>   7'

0 2 0 1 − 2 0 0 0 − cnt − str
Ed. Antonio de Almeida. Editor stipulates that continuo was not used, no[w] is one indicated in score; however, a continuo part is included in the set o[f] parts for this particular symphony. This work was also the overture to *La confederazione dei Sabini con Roma*, a cantata.

1. Allegro	3'
2. Andante	2'
3. Allegro assai	2'

| Doblinger | |

Symphony No.2, G.491, op.7, C major <1769>   21'

2 solo violins, solo violoncello
0 2 0 2 − 2 0 0 0 − str
Ed. Antonio de Almeida.

I. Allegro	9'
II. Adagio	5'
III. Allegro	7'

| Doblinger | |

Symphony No.3, G.503, op.12, no.1, D major <1771>   25'

1 2 0 1 − 2 0 0 0 − str
Doblinger ed. Antonio de Almeida. G. Schirmer edition (ed. Newell Jenkins) is published as op.16, no.2.

Grave; Allegro assai	8'
Andantino	7'
Minué amoroso	6'
Presto assai	4'

| Doblinger | Luck's | Schirmer |

Symphony No.5, G.505, op.12, no.3, C major <1771>   24'

2 0 0 1 − 2 0 0 0 − str
Ed. Antonio de Almeida

Allegro con moto	8'
Andantino amoroso	6'
Tempo di minué	6'
Presto ma non tanto	4'

| Doblinger | |

Symphony No.6, G.506, op.12, no.4, D minor (La casa del diavolo) <1771>   22'

0 2 0 1 − 2 0 0 0 − str
Listed elsewhere as *Symphony No.4.*
Doblinger ed. Antonio de Almeida; Ricordi ed. Pina Carmirelli; Suvini ed. Gallini.

1. Andante sostenuto; Allegro assai	7'
2. Andantino con moto	6'
3. Allegro con molto	9'

| Doblinger | Ricordi | Zerboni |

Symphony No.7, G.507, op.12, no.5, B-flat major <1771> 20'

2 0 0 0 − 2 0 0 0 − str
Ed. Antonio de Almeida.

Allegro con spirito	8'
Adagio non tanto	4'
Minuetto	4'
Prestissimo	4'

| Doblinger | |

Symphony No.8, G.508, op.12, no.6, A major <1771>   26'

2 0 0 0 − 2 0 0 0 − str
Ed. Antonio de Almeida.

1. Allegro assai	8'
2. Larghetto	7'
3. Minuetto con moto	5'
4. Grave	6'

| Doblinger | |

Symphony No.9, G.493, op.21, no.1, B-flat major <1782>   11'

2 0 0 1 — 2 0 0 0 — str
Ed. Antonio de Almeida.

Allegro assai	5'
Andantino con moto	5'
Presto assai	1'

Doblinger	Luck's

Symphony No.10, G.494, op.21, no.2, E-flat major <1775>   17'

2 0 0 0 — 2 0 0 0 — str
Ed. Antonio de Almeida.

Allegro e con spirito	6'
Andantino	5'
Menuetto	6'

Doblinger

Symphony No.11, G.495, op.21, no.3, C major <1775>   23'

0 2 0 0 — 2 0 0 0 — str
Ed. Antonio de Almeida.

Allegro assai	11'
Larghetto sostenuto	6'
Tempo di Minuetto	6'

Doblinger

Symphony No.12, G.496, op.21, no.4, D major <1775>   8'

0 2 0 0 — 2 0 0 0 — str
Ed. Antonio de Almeida.

Doblinger

Symphony No.13, G.497, op.21, no.5, B-flat major <1775>   16'

0 2 0 1 — 2 0 0 0 — str
Ed. Antonio de Almeida.

Allegro spiritoso	8'
Andantino con moto	5'
Allegro vivace assai	3'

Doblinger

Symphony No.14, G.498, op.21, no.6, A major <1775>   13'

0 2 0 0 — 2 0 0 0 — str
Ed. Antonio de Almeida.

Allegro assai	4'
Andantino grazioso	5'
Tempo di Minuetto e con un poco di moto	4'

Doblinger

Symphony No.15, G.509, op.35, no.1, D major <1782>   11'

0 2 0 1 — 2 0 0 0 — str
Ed. Antonio de Almeida.

Allegro	4'
Andantino lento	4'
Prestissimo	3'

Doblinger

Symphony No.16, G.510, op.35, no.2, E-flat major <1782>   13'

0 2 0 1 — 2 0 0 0 — str
Ed. Antonio de Almeida.

Allegro	5'
Andante	5'
Andante giusto	3'

Doblinger

Symphony No.17, G.511, op.35, no.3, A major <1782>   17'

0 2 0 1 — 2 0 0 0 — str
Doblinger ed. Antonio de Almeida. Zanibon edition (ed. Ettore Bonelli) published as op.1, no.3. Listed elsewhere as *Symphony No.9*.

Allegro giusto	6'
Andante	6'
Allegro ma non presto	5'

Doblinger	Kalmus	Zanibon

Symphony No.18, G.512, op.35, no.4, F major <1782>   13'

0 2 0 1 — 2 0 0 0 — str
Doblinger ed. Antonio de Almeida. G. Schirmer version (ed. Newell Jenkins) is published as op.35, no.4. Ricordi version (ed. Guido Guerrini) also calls for one flute, and is published as *Symphony No.4*. This same work is elsewhere identified as *Symphony No.10*.

Allegro	4'
Andantino	5'
Allegro vivace	4'

Doblinger	Ricordi	Schirmer	Luck's

Symphony No.19, G.513, op.35, no.5, E-flat major <1782>   11'

0 2 0 1 — 2 0 0 0 — str
Ed. Antonio de Almeida.

Allegro con moto	4'
Andante	4'
Minuetto	3'

Doblinger

Symphony No.20, G.514, op.35, no.6, B-flat major <1782>   17'

0 2 0 1 — 2 0 0 0 — str
Doblinger ed. Antonio de Almeida. Zanibon edition (ed. Ettore Bonelli) published as op.1, no.6. Listed elsewhere as *Symphony No.12*.

Allegro	5'
Andante	9'
Presto	3'

Doblinger	Kalmus	Luck's	Zanibon

Symphony No.21, G.515, op.37, no.1, C major <1786>   17'

1 2 0 2 — 2 0 0 0 — str
Ed. Antonio de Almeida.

Allegro con moto	5'
Menuetto	5'
Lento	4'
Finale: Allegro vivo assai	3'

Doblinger

Symphony No.22, G.516, op.37, no.2, D major <1786>

This work has been lost; only the incipit of the first movement survives.

Symphony No.23, G.517, op.37, no.3, D minor <1787>   18'

1 2 0 2 — 2 0 0 0 — str
Doblinger edition ed. Antonio de Almeida. Kalmus title: *Sinfonia a più strumenti obbligati op.37 grande*.

Allegro moderato	6'
Minuetto con moto	3'
Andante amoroso	5'
Allegro vivo ma non presto	4'

Doblinger	Kalmus	Luck's

Symphony No.25, G.518, op.37, no.4, A major <1790>   21'

1 2 0 2 — 2 0 0 0 — str
Doblinger ed. Antonio de Almeida; Ricordi ed. by Riccardo Allorto; Universal ed. by Karl Geiringer. Also listed elsewhere as *Symphony No.16*.

Allegro spiritoso	7'	
Minuetto	4'	
Andante	6'	
Allegro ma non presto	4'	

Doblinger	Ricordi	Luck's	Universal

Symphony No.26, G.519, op.41, C minor <1788>   15'

0 2 0 2 — 2 0 0 0 — str[divided va]
Ed. Antonio de Almeida.

Allegro vivo assai	5'
Pastorale lentarello	4'
Minuetto	3'
Finale: Allegro	3'

Doblinger

Symphony No.27, G.520, op.42, D major <1789>   20'

1 2 0 2 — 2 0 0 0 — str
Doblinger ed. Antonio de Almeida; Suvini ed. Pietro Spada.

Allegro	6'
Andante	7'
Minuetto	4'
Finale: Presto	3'

Doblinger	Zerboni

Symphony No.28

see his: Overture, op.43, G.521, D major

Symphony "A", G.500, D major <1767>   9'

0 0 0 0 — 2[opt] 0 0 0 — str
Ed. Walter Lebermann.
Authenticity has been disputed.

Allegro	2'
Andante	3'
Minuetto	3'
Presto	1'

Schott

Boëllmann, Léon   1862-1897

(b Ensisheim, Haut-Rhin, 25 Sept 1862; d Paris, 11 Oct 1897). French

Symphonic Variations, op.23 (Variations symphoniques) <1890>   13'

solo violoncello
2 2 2 2 — 4 2 3 1 — tmp — hp[perhaps doubled] — str

Durand	Kalmus	Luck's

Boelter, Karl   1952-

(b Milwaukee, WI, 14 Mar 1952). American

Concerto, Violin <1999; rev 2000>   22'

2[1.2/pic] 2 2 2 — 2 2 2 1 — tmp+1 — hp — str
perc: bd, sus cym, sd, tomtom, glock, marim, tamtam

Circles	5'
Orbits	4'
Rotations	3'
Progression	10'

Boelter

Dharma <1982; rev 2001>   12

1 1 1 1 — 2 1 0 0 — tmp+1 — pf — str
perc: bd, sus cym, sd, tri, glock, xyl, chimes

Boelter

Images from Goldsmith <2001>   19

solo horn
0 0 2 2 — str

1. *These Rocks by Custom Turn to Beds of Down*	5'
2. *Sprightly Land of Mirth and Social Ease*	4'
3. *I See the Lords of Human Kind Pass By*	4'
4. *Where the Broad Ocean Leans Against the Land*	6'

Boelter

Boieldieu, François   1775-1834

(b Rouen, 16 Dec 1775; d Jarcy, Seine et Oise, 8 Oct 1834). French

Le Calife de Bagdad (The Caliph of Bagdad): Overture <1800>   8

2[1/pic.2/pic] 2 2 — 2 2 0 0 — tmp+3 — str
perc: cym, bd, 2tri
Numerous discrepancies between score and parts; Breitkopf/Kalmus scores do not indicate trumpets, though 2 trumpet parts are provided. A Mario Bois edition has 3 trombones, but apparently no percussion.

Breitkopf	Heugel	Kalmus	Luck's

Concerto, Harp, C major (In tre tempi) <1801>   22

2 2 0 2 — 2 0 0 0 — str
Another version is available: arr. M.A.Dupin and M. Nordmann, for:
1 1 1 1 — 2 2 0 0 — tmp — str (pub Billaudot).

I. *Allegro brillante*	11'
II. *Andante lento*	4'
III. *Rondeau: Allegro agitato*	7'

Ricordi

La dame blanche: Overture <1825>   9

2[1.2/pic] 2 2 — 2 2 1[btbn] 0 — tmp — str

Breitkopf	Kalmus	Luck's

Boismortier, Joseph Bodin de   1689-1755

(b Thionville, 23 Dec 1689; d Roissy-en-Brie, 28 Oct 1755). French

Concerto, Violoncello, D major <1726>   8'

cnt — str

Symphonia

Bolcom, William   1938-

(b Seattle, WA, 26 May 1938). American

Commedia for (Almost) 18th-Century Orchestra <1971>   10'

1[fl/pic] 2 1[cl/Ebcl] 2 — 2 0 0 0 — opt tmp — pf — str[4.4.2.2.1]
2vn and 1vc (last chairs of the 4.4.2.2.1 count) have offstage solo lines; total strings may be increased to 10.10.9.7.4. Doublings of winds permissible.

Marks

Concerto, Violin <1984>   23'

2[incl pic] 2[incl Eh] 2[incl Ebcl,bcl] 2[incl cbn] — 2 2 2 0 — tmp+3
— hp — pf/cel — str
May be done with chamber orchestra or full-sized orchestra; if the latter,
horns should be doubled.

1. Quasi una fantasia: Tempo giusto; Allegro elegiaco	10'
2. Adagio non troppo ma sostenuto	7'
3. Rondo-Finale	6'

> Marks

Concerto-Serenade <1964>   17'

solo violin
str[min 4.3.3.2.1]

> Marks

Fives <1965–1966>   18'

solo violin & piano
3 str orchestras

> Merion

Humoresk <1969>   12'

solo organ
2[1.2/pic] 2[1.2/Eh] 2[1.2/bcl] 2 — 4 2 3 1 — 2perc — pf/cel — str

> Marks

Orphée-sérénade <1984>   19'

solo piano
1[dbl pic] 1 1[dbl Ebcl] 1 — 1 0 0 0 — 2vn, va, vc, db
Chamber-size string sections may be used instead of individual players.

Ouverture	3'
Romance	4'
Pas des Bacchantes	2'
Hurluberlu	3'
Elégie	4'
Energique	3'

> Marks

Ragomania!—A Classic Festival-Overture <1982>   10'

3[incl pic] 3[incl Eh] 3[incl bcl] 3[incl cbn] — 4 3 3 1 — elec gtr —
tmp+3 — opt hp — pf/opt elec pf — str
Guitar may be dispensed with if pianist has an electric piano in addition
to an acoustic piano.

> Marks

Seattle Slew (Dance Suite) (Three Dances in Forequarter   20'
Time) <1986>

3[incl pic] 3[incl Eh] 3[incl bcl] 3 — 4 3[1.2.flug] 3 1 — tmp+3 —
hp — pf — str[min 10.8.6.6.4]

1. Derby Dressage	5'
2. Preakness Promenade	8'
3. Belmont Bourrée	7'

> Marks

Serenata Notturna (Serenade No.3) <2005>   20'

solo oboe
str

I. Gentle; Allegro	_'
II. Grazioso	_'
III. Scherzo di medianotte	_'
IV. Andante; Allegro	_'

> Marks

Songs of Innocence and of Experience <1956–1981>   160'

SSSAATTBar, country singer, rock singer, folk singer, opt boy soprano
chorus, children's chorus, madrigal group
3[incl rec,afl,2pic] 3[incl Eh] 3[incl Ebcl,bcl] 3[incl cbn] — 6 5[3tp,
2flug] 5 3[2tubas, euph] — asx/tsx, asx/tsx/bsx — gtr/elec gtr, elec bass
— tmp+5 — hp — pf/elec pf, harm/cel/org — str[incl 2 elec vn dbl on
mandolin & fiddle]
perc: templeblks, szl cym, crot, marim, guiro, glock, cowbell, windchimes,
slgh-bells, vib, sd, vibrslp, timbales, bd/ped, 5sus cym, 6tomtoms, anvil, 2marac,
2tambn, 2pr cym, 2tri, toy piano, chimes, 2hihats, 3Chinescym, 2whips,
3woodblk, 3tamtam, sandblks, 3Thai gongs[G2,C2,D2], 2bd
Solo parts may be combined so as to require fewer soloists (5-10 singers);
however, maximum diversity of vocal sound and style is desired.

> Marks

A Summer Divertimento <1973>   25'

2 0 1[incl Ebcl] 1 — 0 1 0 0 — 1perc — pf, hpsd — 3vn, 2va, 2vc,
2db

> Marks

Symphony No.1 <1957>   18'

2 1 1 1 — 4 2 1 0 — tmp+2 — pf — str

1. Allegro molto	5'
2. Adagio	5'
3. Tempo di menuetto	2'
4. Allegro	4'

> Marks

Symphony No.3 <1979>   35'

1[fl/pic/afl] 2[incl Eh] 1[cl/Ebcl/bcl] 2 — 2 0 0 0 — pf/cel/elec pf —
str[6.4.4.3.1]
Formerly titled *Chamber Symphony*, or *Symphony for Chamber
Orchestra*.

Alpha	_'
Scherzo vitale	_'
Chiaroscuro	_'
Omega	_'

> Marks

Symphony No.5 <1989>   23'

3[1.2.3/pic] 3[1.2.Eh] 3[1/Ebcl.2.bcl] 3[1.2.cbn] — 4 3 3 1 — tmp+4
— hp — str
perc: bd, 2sus cym, pic dr, sd, td, tamtam, glock, crot, 7button gongs, bass
marimba

Pensive/active	6'
Scherzo mortale	7'
Hymne à l'amour	6'
Machine	4'

> Marks

Bolzoni, Giovanni   1841-1919

(b Parma, 15 May 1841; d Turin, 21 Feb 1919). Italian

Gavotte   4'

str

> Kalmus   Luck's

Minuetto, B major   3'

str

> Kalmus   Luck's

Bond, Victoria   1945-

(b Los Angeles, 6 May 1945). American

Ancient Keys (Piano Concerto No.2) <2002>   17'

solo piano
2[1.2/pic] 2[1.2/Eh] 2[1.2/bcl] 2 — 2 2 1 0 — tmp+2 — cel — str
perc: bd, sus cym, sd, tri, tamtam, glock, chimes

> Presser

Dreams of Flying <1994>   16'

str
I. Resisting Gravity   5'
II. Floating   2'
III. The Caged Bird Dreams of the Jungle   9'

> Subito

The Frog Prince <1984; rev (chamber version) 1990>   15'

narrator
1 1 1 1 — 3 1 1 0 — tmp+2 — str
perc: set, sd, bd, hi-hat, whip, sus cym, woodblk, tambn, cym, templeblks,
3bongos, 2tri, 4rototom
Based on the familiar Grimm fable. Originally a longer version (24') for
full orchestra; chamber orchestra version by the composer. A version for
woodwind quintet also exists.

> Schirmer

A Modest Proposal <1999>   17'

solo tenor
1 1 1 1 — 2 1 0 0 — tmp+1 — cel — str
perc: bd, tamtam, glock, crot, slgh-bells

> Presser

Thinking Like a Mountain <1994>   16'

narrator
2[incl pic,afl] 2[incl Eh] 2 2 — 4 3 3 1 — tmp+3 — hp — str

> Subito

Urban Bird <1993>   24'

solo alto saxophone
2[incl pic] 2[incl Eh] 2[incl bcl] 2 — 4 4 3 1 — tmp+2 — str

> Presser

Variations on a Theme of Brahms <1998>   16'

3[incl pic] 2[incl Eh] 2 3[incl cbn] — 4 3 3 1 — tmp+2 — str

> Subito

What's the Point of Counterpoint? <1985>   25'

narrator
2[incl pic] 2[incl Eh] 2[incl bcl] 2 — 4 3 3 1 — tmp+3 — hp — str
A chamber version is also available.

> Subito

Bonds, Margaret Allison   1913-1972

(b Chicago, 3 March 1913; d Los Angeles, 26 April 1972). American

The Ballad of the Brown King; A Christmas Cantata   20'
<1954>

solos SATBar   chorus SSAATTBB
2[1.2/pic] 2 2 2 — 2 2 2 0 — 1perc — hp — cel — str
perc: sd, tambn, tmp
I. Of the Three Wise Men   '
II. They Brought Fine Gifts   —'
III. Sing Alleluia [a cappella]   —'
IV. Mary Had Little Baby   —'
V. Now When Jesus Was Born   —'
VI. Could He Have Been an Ethiope?   —'
VII. O Sing of the King Who Was Tall and Brown   —'
VIII. That Was a Christmas Long Ago   —'
IX. Alleluia   —'

> Fox

Boone, Charles   1939-

(b Cleveland, 21 June 1939). American

Second Landscape <1973; rev 1979>   14'

1 1 1 1[1/cbn] — 0 2 0 0 — 2perc — pf/maracas — str

> Salabert□□□□

Borodin, Alexander   1833-1887

(b St Petersburg, 31 Oct/12 Nov 1833; d St Petersburg, 15/27 Feb 1887). Russian

Borodiniana Suite   21'

3[1.2.pic] 3[1.2.Eh] 3[1.2.bcl] 3[1.2.cbn] — 4 3 3 0 — tmp+4 — str
perc: bd, cym, sus cym, tri, tambn, marac, claves, cast
Suite assembled and orchestrated by Mark Starr, from various
lesser-known works of Borodin. Movements available individually.
1. Allegro in D minor (from an unfinished string sextet)   5'
2. Hélène Polka (originally for piano 4-hands)   3'
3. Scherzo in A-flat major (originally for piano)   4'
4. Andantino in E minor (from an unfinished string sextet)   2'
5. Serenata alla spagnola on the name of Belaieff (originally for str 4t)   2'
6. Grande tarantella (originally for piano 4-hands)   5'

> Noteworthy

In the Steppes of Central Asia (V sredney Azii) <1880> 9'

2 2[1.Eh] 2 2 — 4 2 3 0 — tmp — str

> Kalmus   Luck's   Russian

La Mer (More; The Sea) <1869–1870>   8'

solo tenor
2 2 2 2 — 4 2 3 1 — tmp — str
Orchestrated by Rimsky-Korsakov from a song for voice & piano.

> Kalmus   Luck's

Nocturne (arr. N. Rimsky-Korsakov) <1881>   9'

solo violin
2 2 2 2 — 2 2 0 0 — tmp — str
From the composer's *String Quartet No.2*.

> Kalmus   Luck's

Nocturne (arr. Malcolm Sargent) <1881>   9'

str
From the composer's *String Quartet No.2*.

> Boosey   Luck's

Nocturne (arr. N. Tcherepnin) <1881>   9'

3 2 3 2 — 4 3 3 1 — tmp — hp — str
From the composer's *String Quartet No.2*.

> Universal

Petite suite <1885>   23'

3[1.2/pic2.pic1] 2 2 2 — 4 2 3 0 — tmp+2 — str
perc: tri, tambn, tamtam, sus cym (played by timpanist)
Arr. Glazunov.

Au convent	5'
Intermezzo	3'
Mazurka	4'
Rêverie	3'
Serenade	2'
Finale	6'

> Breitkopf Kalmus Leduc Luck's

Petite suite: Scherzo & Nocturne <1885>   6'

3[1.2/pic2.pic1] 2 2 2 — 4 2 3 0 — tmp — str
Arr. Glazunov.
Scherzo & Nocturne together constitute the Finale of the suite.

> Luck's

Prince Igor: Overture <1869>   10'

3[1.2.pic] 2 2 2 — 4 2 3 1 — tmp — str
Completed and orchestrated by Glazunov.

> Kalmus Luck's

Prince Igor: Polovtsian Dances <1869–1887>   14'

optional chorus
3[1.2.pic] 2[1.2/Eh] 2 2 — 4 2 3 1 — tmp+5 — hp — str
perc: bd, cym, sd, tri, tambn, glock
Nos. 8 & 17 from the opera.
Kalmus ed. newly corrected & engraved (2011); ed. Nancy M. Bradburd
& Clinton F. Nieweg.

I. Dance of the Polovtsian Maidens	2'
II. Polovtsian Dance with Chorus	12'

> C. Fischer Kalmus Luck's Schirmer

Prince Igor: Polovtsian March <1869–1887>   5'

optional male chorus
3[1.pic1.pic2] 2 2 2 — 4 2 3 1 — tmp+4 — str
perc: tambn, sd, cym, bd
Optional backstage *banda*: brass 4 2 0 1, & snare drum. Orchestrated by
Rimsky-Korsakov. This is the Prelude to Act III of the opera.

> Belaieff Kalmus Luck's

Symphony No.1, E-flat major <1862–1867>   33'

2 2[1/Eh.2] 2 2 — 4 2 3 0 — tmp — str

I. Adagio; Allegro	13'
II. Scherzo: Prestissimo	7'
III. Andante	7'
IV. Allegro molto vivo	6'

> Breitkopf Kalmus Leduc

Symphony No.2, B minor <1869–1875>   33'

4[1.2.3/pic.pic2] 2[1/Eh.2] 2 2 — 4 2 3 1 — tmp+4 — hp — str
perc: tri, tambn, cym, bd
2pic doubling one real part in 1st & 4th mvts. Some editions do not
mention the doubling of the piccolos, and/or give the Eh part to the 2nd
oboe, rather than the 1st.
Kalmus ed. Clinton F. Nieweg and Nancy M. Bradburd.

I. Allegro	12'
II. Scherzo: Prestissimo	5'
III. Andante	8'
IV. Finale: Allegro	8'

> Breitkopf Kalmus Leduc Luck's

Symphony No.3, A minor <1882–1887>   19'

2 2 2 2 — 4 2 3 0 — tmp — str
Completed and orchestrated by Glazunov.

I. Moderato assai	9'
II. Scherzo: Vivo	10'

> Belaieff Kalmus Luck's

Bossi, Marco Enrico   1861-1925

(b Salò, Lake Garda, 25 April 1861; d Atlantic Ocean, 20 Feb 1925). Italian

Intermezzi goldoniani, op.127 <1905>   25'

str
5th mvt: solo for viola d'amore, or viola, or violin.

1. Preludio e minuetto	7'
2. Gagliarda	4'
3. Coprifuoco	4'
4. Minuetto e musetta	3'
5. Serenatina	3'
6. Burlesca	4'

> Peters

Bottesini, Giovanni   1821-1889

(b Crema, 22 Dec 1821; d Parma, 7 July 1889). Italian

Concerto, Double Bass, No.2, B minor   17'

1 2 0 2 — 2 0 0 0 — tmp — str

I. Allegro moderato	7'
II. Andante	5'
III. Allegro	5'

> Doblinger

Concerto, Double Bass, No.2, B or A minor (arr. Ludwin)   17'

2 2 2 1 — 2 2 0 0 — tmp — str
Originally for smaller orchestra; arr. Norman Ludwin. Available in either
key, depending on whether or not the soloist uses traditional solo
scordatura.
    Ludwin also offers a version for string orchestra.

I. Allegro moderato	7'
II. Andante	5'
III. Allegro	5'

> Ludwin

Elegy   2'

solo double bass
str
Arranged by Norman Ludwin. Offered in D major if traditional solo bass
scordatura is used; or in C major if the soloist uses orchestral tuning.
Specify key when ordering.

> Ludwin

Gran duo concertante, Violin & Double Bass <1880>   15'

2 2 2 2 — 4 2 3 1 — tmp — str
Arr. M. Fleschig.

> Billaudot

Gran duo concertante, Violin & Double Bass (arr. Ludwin) <1880>   *15'*

str
Arranged for string orchestra by Norman Ludwin. Original in A major, with the expectation that the double bass will use traditional solo scordatura; therefore the solo bass part is written in G major.

Ludwin also offers the performance material in G major, in case the solo bass prefers orchestral tuning. However, this means the solo violin part must also be in G major; Ludwin has adjusted the violin part where it would otherwise go below the normal range of the violin, but other awkward passages may occur in this transposition.

Specify key when ordering.

> Ludwin

Grande allegro di concerto (alla Mendelssohn)   *13'*

solo double bass
str
Ed. Umberto Ferrari.

> Nuove Cons

Boudreau, Walter   1947-

(b Montréal, 1947). Canadian

Versus <1988>   *18'*

1 1 1 1 — 1 2 1 0 — 3perc — pf — [no str]
A burlesque of a hockey game.
Préambule   _'
Exercises de réchauffement   _'
Prélude   _'
1ere période   _'
1er intermission   _'
2e période   _'
2e intermission   _'
3e période   _'

> CMC

Boughton, Rutland   1878-1960

(b Aylesbury, 23 Jan 1878; d London, 25 Jan 1960). English

Concerto, Oboe, No.1, C minor <1936>   *23'*

str
1.   *8'*
2.   *6'*
3.   *9'*

> Boosey

Boulanger, Lili   1893-1918

(b Paris, 21 Aug 1893; d Mezy, 15 March 1918). French

D'un matin de printemps <1918>   *5'*

3[incl pic] 3[incl Eh] 3[incl bcl] 3[1.2.sarr] — 4 3 3 1 — 2perc — hp — cel — str
Ed. JoAnn Falletta & Terrie Baune.

> Durand

D'un soir triste <1918>   *12'*

2 3[incl Eh] 3[incl bcl] 3[1.2.sarr] — 4 3 3 1 — tmp+2 — hp — cel — str
Ed. JoAnn Falletta & Terrie Baune.

> Durand

Psalm 24 (La Terre appartient à l'Eternel; The Earth is the Lord's) <1916>   *5'*

chorus
0 0 0 0 — 4 3 4 1 — tmp — hp — org — [no str]
Tenor solo drawn from chorus.

> Durand

Psalm 129 (Ils m'ont assez opprimé; Sorely Have They Afflicted Me) <1916>   *8'*

male chorus or solo baritone
3[1.2.pic] 3[1.2.Eh] 3[1.2.bcl] 3[1.2.sarr] — 4 3 3 1 — tmp+2 — 2hp — cel — str
perc: bd, cym, tamtam

> Durand

Psalm 130 (Du fond de l'abîme; Out of the Depths) <1914–1917>   *25'*

solo soprano or alto   chorus
3[1.2.pic] 3[1.2.Eh] 3[1.2.bcl] 3[1.2.sarr] — 4 3 4 1 — tmp — 2hp — cel, org — str
perc: bd, cym, tamtam

> Durand

Boulez, Pierre   1925-

(b Montbrison, Loire, 26 March 1925). French

Over the course of his career, Boulez tended increasingly to see his music as work-in-progress. This is manifested in both (1) the tendency to see individual pieces as parts of a larger whole, and (2) the subjection of many works to revision—often repeatedly, sometimes drastically—over long periods amounting to as much as 30 years. Therefore, it is not always clear what is to be considered the definitive version of a given work, or indeed whether a definitive version is intended for any particular piece.

cummings ist der Dichter <1970; rev 1986>   *14'*

16 solo voices [4S.4A.4T.4B], *or* chamber choir [up to 48 voices]
2 2[1.Eh] 3[1.2.bcl] 2 — 2 2 2 1 — 3hp — str[3vn, 2va, 2vc, db]

> Universal

Éclat <1965>   *8'*

1[afl] 1[Eh] 0 0 — 0 1 1 0 — mand, gtr, cimbalom — 3perc — hp — pf, cel — va, vc
perc: glock, vib, chimes
Related to *Don* and to *Strophes*. *Éclat* has been extended as *Éclat/Multiples*, for 9perc & orchestra, 1970.

> Universal

Le marteau sans maître (The Hammer Without a Master) <1952–1954>   *36'*

solo mezzo-soprano
afl, gtr, xylorimba, vib — 1perc — va
perc: sd, marac, claves, tri, gong, sus cym, 2pr bongos, cloche double, 2tamtams, 4 cymbalettes
1. avant "l'artisanat furieux"   *2'*
2. commentaire I de "bourreaux de solitude"   *4'*
3. "l'artisanat furieux"   *2'*
4. commentaire II de "bourreaux de solitude"   *4'*
5. "bel édifice et les pressentiments;" version première   *4'*
6. "bourreaux de solitude"   *5'*
7. après "l'artisanat furieux"   *1'*
8. commentaire III de "bourreaux de solitude"   *6'*
9. "bel édifice et les pressentiments;" double   *8'*

> Universal

Memoriale (...explosante-fixe...originel) <1985>   7'

solo flute
0 0 0 0 — 2 0 0 0 — 3vn, 2va, vc

Universal

Notations I-IV <1978>   10'

4[incl pic] 4[incl Eh] 5[incl Ebcl,bcl] 4[incl cbn] — 6 4 4 1 — tmp+8 — 3hp — cel, pf — str[18.16.14.12.10]
perc: xyl, vib, chimes, templeblks, tri, glock, claves, tambn, marac, belltree, marim, bd, 4turkishcym, glass windchimes, 2boobams, 3cowbells, 2anvils, 3sd, 2timbales, 2woodblks, 8bongos, 6tomtoms, 2bellplates[B2,C4], 3woodplanks, 2tablas, 2congas, slitdrum, chromatic cowbells [D4–D#5], 3tamtams, 2gongs, 3Chinescym, 3szl cym
The first four of a projected set of 12 pieces, based on the composer's early piano works. The composer suggests performance in the following order: 1, 4, 3, 2.
Universal shows also a 1984 version.

I. Modéré - Fantasque   2'
II. Trés vif - Strident   2'
III. Trés modéré -   4'
IV. Rythmique   2'

Universal

Pli selon pli (Fold upon Fold): No.1. Don (1962 version) <1960–1962>   11'

soprano solo
4[1.2/pic.3/pic.afl] 1[Eh] 3[1.Ebcl.bcl] 1 — 4 2 3[incl cb tbn] 0 — mand, gtr (both ampd) — tmp+6 — 3hp — cel, pf — [no str]
Originally for soprano & piano; arr. by the composer for soprano & orchestra, 1960-62.

Universal

Pli selon pli (Fold upon Fold): No.1 Don (version nouvelle 1989) <1960; rev 1989-1990>   6'

soprano
4[1.2.3.afl] 1 3[1.Ebcl.bcl] 1 — 4 2 3[incl cb tbn] 0 — mand, gtr — 7perc — 3hp — pf, cel — str[4vn.4va.5vc.3db]
perc: Chinescym, sd, glock, chimes, crot, 2vib, 3bongo, 2xyl, 2bellplates, 3pr claves, 2pr marac, 5sus cym, 6herdbells, 3gongs, 2tamtams, 2bd, tmp
Originally for soprano & piano; arr. by the composer for soprano & orchestra, 1960-62. Revised 1989-90 to include strings.

Universal

Pli selon pli (Fold upon Fold): No.2. Improvisation I sur Mallarmé (Le vierge, le vivace et le bel aujourd'hui; 1962 version) <1957; rev (arr for orch) 1962>   6'

soprano solo
2[1/pic.2/pic] 0 2[1.Ebcl] 0 — 4 0 0 0 — 2asx — gtr, mand — 7 or 8 perc — 3hp — cel — 8va, 6db
perc: chimes, xyl, td, bd, 2vib, 2cowbells, 2tamtams, 6bongos, 2sd, tuned herdbells[G3–C5], 3gongs, 3sus cym, 6crotales (indef pitch), glock[opt]
Originally (1957) for soprano & percussion; arranged 1962 for soprano & orchestra by the composer.
    2nd version; valid only for *Pli selon pli* in its complete form. For performances of *Improvisation I* alone, or in conjunction with *Improvisation II*, the piece must be performed in the version for soprano & percussion.

Universal

Pli selon pli (Fold upon Fold): No.3. Improvisation II sur Mallarmé (Une dentelle s'abolit) <1957>   12'

soprano
6perc — hp — pf, cel — [no str]
perc: sus cym, gong, vib, chimes, crot, 4pr marac, 3pr claves, 2tamtams

Universal

Pli selon pli (Fold upon Fold): No.4. Improvisation III sur Mallarmé (À la nue accablante tu) <1959; rev 1983-84>   19'

soprano solo
4[incl 3pic] 0 0 0 — 0 0 1 0 — 7perc — 3hp — cel — 5vc, 3db
perc: claves, congas, glock, chimes, Chinescym, bd, 2xyl[4-hands], bellplate, 6herdbells, 5bongos
Special tuning required for 2 of the harps.

Universal

Pli selon pli (Fold upon Fold): No.5. Tombeau <1959; rev 1960>   17'

2[1/pic.2] 1[Eh] 3[1.Ebcl.bcl] 1 — 1 2 3 0 — gtr — 8perc — 2hp — cel, pf — str[4vn, 4va, 2vc, 2db]
perc: chimes, 2vib, xylorimba, bell plate, 3gongs, 3tamtams, tmp

Universal

Le soleil des eaux (1958 version) (The Sun of the Waters) <1948–1950; rev 1958>   10'

chorus   solos STB
2[1.2/pic] 2[1.Eh] 2[1.bcl] 2 — 3 2 1 1 — tmp+2 — hp — str[12.10.8.8.6]
perc: cym, glock, vib, xyl, 2tamtams
A 1958 revision of the unpublished 1950 original.

I. Complainte du lezard amoureux (Lay of the Lizard in Love)   4'
II. La Sorgue (Chanson pour Yvonne)   6'

Heugel

Le soleil des eaux (1965 version) (The Sun of the Waters) <1948–1950; rev 1958; 1965>   10'

solo soprano   chorus
2[1.2/pic] 2[1.Eh] 2[1.bcl] 2 — 3 2 1 1 — tmp+5 — 2hp — cel[5 octaves] — str[12.10.8.8.6]
perc: glock, xyl, bd, sus cym, szl cym, Chinescym, sd, tambn, tamtam, chimes, crot, templeblks, whip, guiro, claves, Turkish cym, 2gongs, 2marac[hi & lo]

I. Complainte du lézard amoureux (Lay of the Lizard in Love)   4'
II. La sorgue (Chanson pour Yvonne)   6'

Heugel

Bowles, Paul   1910-1999

(b Jamaica, NY, 30 Dec 1910; d Tangier, 18 Nov 1999). American

Concerto, 2 Pianos, Percussion & Winds <1947>   17'

0 1[incl Eh] 1[incl bcl] 0 — 0 1 0 0 — 2perc — [no str]
1. Allegro   5'
2. Presto   2'
3. Andante   6'
4. Galop   4'

AME

Concerto, 2 Pianos (full orchestra version) <1947; rev (orchd) 1949>   17'

2[1.2/pic] 2[1.2/Eh] 2[1.2/bcl] 1 — 2 2 1 0 — tmp+3 — hp — cel — str
Orchestrated by the composer, 1949.
1. Allegro   5'
2. Presto   2'
3. Andante   6'
4. Galop   4'

AME

Boyce, William
1711-1779

(b London, bap. 11 Sept 1711; d London, 7 Feb 1779). English

Concerto grosso, B minor <1770>
7'

solos: 2 violins, violoncello
cnt — str
Hinrichsen edition gives title as *Double Concerto*.

Eulenburg	Hinrichsen

Overture (Ode for His Majesty's Birthday [1769]) <1769>
7'

0 2 0 1 — 2 0 0 0 — cnt — str
Score only available in the collection *Musica Britannica*, v.13, p.1; parts available from Galaxy.

Galaxy

Overture (Ode for the New Year [1758]) <1758>
4'

0 2 0 1 — 0 2 0 0 — tmp — cnt — str
Score only available in the collection *Musica Britannica*, v.13, p.103; parts available from Galaxy.

Galaxy

Overture (Ode for the New Year [1772]) <1772>
4'

0 2 0 1 — cnt — str
Score only available in the collection *Musica Britannica*, v.13, p.55; parts available from Galaxy.

Galaxy

Overture (Peleus and Thetis) <1740>
7'

0 2 0 1 — cnt — str
Score only available in the collection *Musica Britannica*, v.13, p.131; parts available from Galaxy.

Galaxy

Symphony No.1, B-flat major <1760>
8'

2 2 0 1 — cnt — str
Doblinger edition (ed. Max Goberman) is to be preferred.

Allegro	*3'*
Moderato e dolce	*3'*
Allegro	*2'*

Doblinger	Oxford

Symphony No.2, A major <1760>
5'

0 2 0 1 — cnt — str
Doblinger edition (ed. Max Goberman) is to be preferred.

Allegro assai	*2'*
Andante	*1'*
Presto	*2'*

Doblinger	Oxford

Symphony No.3, C major <1760>
6'

0 2 0 1 — cnt — str
Doblinger edition (ed. Max Goberman) is to be preferred.

Allegro	*3'*
Andante	*1'*
Tempo di Menuetto	*2'*

Doblinger	Oxford

Symphony No.4, F major <1760>
7'

0 2 0 2 — 2 0 0 0 — cnt — str
Doblinger edition (ed. Max Goberman) is to be preferred.

Allegro	*3'*
Vivace ma non troppo	*2'*
Gavott: Allegro	*2'*

Doblinger	Oxford

Symphony No.5, D major
8'

0 2 0 1 — 0 2 0 0 — tmp — cnt — str
Doblinger edition (ed. Max Goberman) is to be preferred.

Allegro ma non troppo — Adagio — Allegro assai	*4'*
Tempo di Gavotta	*2'*
Tempo di Menuetto	*2'*

Doblinger	Oxford

Symphony No.6, F major <1760>
8'

0 2 0 1 — cnt — str
Doblinger edition (ed. Max Goberman) is to be preferred.

| *1. Largo; Allegro* | *5'* |
| *2. Larghetto* | *3'* |

Doblinger	Oxford

Symphony No.7, B-flat major <1760>
10'

2 2 0 1 — cnt — str
Doblinger edition (ed. Max Goberman) is to be preferred.

Andante spirituoso	*5'*
Moderato	*3'*
Jigg: Allegro assai	*2'*

Doblinger	Oxford

Symphony No.8, D minor <1760>
11'

2 2 0 1 — cnt — str
Doblinger edition (ed. Max Goberman) is to be preferred.

Pomposo. Allegro	*6'*
Largo. Andante	*2'*
Tempo di Gavotta. Risoluto	*3'*

Doblinger	Oxford

Boyer, Peter
1970-

(b Providence, RI, 10 Feb 1970). American

American Rhapsody <2007>
13'

solo piano
2[1.2/pic] 2 2 2 — 4 3 3 1 — tmp+3 — hp — str
perc: bd, hi-hat, td, glock, xyl, bongos, congas, 2sus cym, 2tri, 2tambn, shakers, 2sd, 4tomtoms

1. Fast, rhythmic, energetic	*4'*
2. Slowly, expressively	*4'*
3. Very fast, rhythmic	*5'*

Propulsive

Celebration Overture <1997; rev 2001>
7'

3[1.2.pic] 2 3[1.2.3/bcl] 2 — 4 4 4[4th opt] 1 — tmp+3 — hp — pf — str
perc: sd, chimes, bd, hi-hat, glock, tamtam, tambn, tri, 2sus cym, 4tomtoms

Propulsive

The Dream Lives On: A Portrait of the Kennedy Brothers <2010>
15'

4narrators   SSAATTBB chorus (opt)
3[1.2.3/pic] 3[1.2.3/Eh] 3[1.2.3/bcl] 3[1.2.3/cbn] — 4 3 3 1 — tmp+4 — hp — pf/cel — str
perc: glock, vib, marim, sd, bd, tamtam, sus cym, tri, belltree
4 narrators preferred (3 males for the three brothers, and 1 female) — but the work may be performed by a single male narrator.
    May be performed without chorus, in which case the passages for *a cappella* chorus are cued in the orchestra parts.
    In the premiere by the Boston Pops Orchestra, a significant video component accompanied the performance.

Propulsive

Dreaming a World <2006>   20'

narrator   chorus, children's chorus
2[1.2/pic] 2 2 2 — 4 3 3 1 — tmp+4 — hp — pf — str
perc: bd, cym, sd, td, set, tambn, tamtam, glock, xyl, vib, crot, marktree, congas,
4tomtoms, NatAmer dr, 4-6 sus cym, 2tri, shakers, rainstick; *in opt 4th mvt only:*
szl cym, shekere, gourd rattle, pow-wow drum, agyegyewa (or small conga),
talking dr (Donno), 3frame drums, apentema (or small conga or djembe), oprenten
(or djembe), petia (or medium conga), atumpan (or medium & low congas),
2agogo

4th mvt is optional; it uses only narrator, the orchestral percussion, and 6
or more additional percussionists playing African instruments. These
additional percussionists begin offstage and proceed to designated places
within the hall.

I. Prelude, Invocation and Dance	5'
II. Voices of Unity	5'
III. I Dream a World	3'
IV The Great Drum [optional movement]	4'
V. Finale	3'

Propulsive

Ellis Island: The Dream of America <2001–2002>   44'

7 actors (4 female, 3 male), or 2 actors (male & female)
3[1.2.3/pic] 3[1.2.3/Eh] 3[1.2/bcl.3/asx] 3[1.2.3/cbn] — 4 3 3 1 —
projections — tmp+4 — hp — pf/cel — str
perc: bd, cym, sus cym, sd, set, tri, tambn, tamtam, glock, xyl, marim, vib, chimes,
whip, anvil, 4tomtoms

1. Prologue	6'
2. Helen Cohen (emigrated from Poland, 1920)	3'
3. Interlude 1	1'
4. James Apanomith (Greece, 1911)	3'
5. Interlude 2	2'
6. Lillian Galletta (Italy, 1908)	4'
7. Interlude 3	2'
8. Lazarus Salamon (Hungary, 1920)	4'
9. Interlude 4	2'
10. Helen Rosenthal (Belgium, 1940)	4'
11. Interlude 5	1'
12. Manny Steen (Ireland, 1925)	5'
13. Interlude 6	2'
14. Katherine Beychok (Russia, 1910)	3'
15. Epilogue: The New Colossus, by Emma Lazarus, 1883	2'

Propulsive

Festivities <2011>   6'

3[1.2.3/pic] 3 3 3[1.2.3/cbn] — 4 3 3 1 — tmp+5[or 4] — hp —
pf/cel — str
perc: glock, vib, chimes, xyl, sd, td, bd, tamtam, sus cym, tri, tambn

Propulsive

Ghosts of Troy <2000>   15'

2[1.2/pic] 2 2[1.2/bcl] 2 — 2 2 0 0 — 2perc [incl tmp] — hp — pf —
str[min 6.5.4.3.1]
perc: vib, xyl, glock, templeblks, sd, td, bd, sus cym, tamtam, tambn, tri, tmp,
4tomtoms, cabasa

1. The Rage of Achilles	4'
2. The Death of Patroclus	1'
3. Hector and Andromache Bid Farewell	3'
4. The Combat of Hector and Achilles	1'
5. The Supplication of King Priam	3'
6. The Ransom and Burial of Hector	3'

Propulsive

New Beginnings <2000>   11'

3[1.2/pic.3/pic] 3[1.2.3/Eh] 3[1.2.3/bcl] 3[1.2.3/cbn] — 4 3 3 1 —
tmp+4 — hp — pf/cel — str
perc: marim, vib, xyl, glock, crot, sus cym, cym, sd, timbales, congas, bd, tambn,
tri, whip, tamtam, 4tomtoms, shaker, anvil

Propulsive

On Music's Wings <2003–2004>   30'

solos S, Bar   chorus   children's chorus
3[1.2.3/pic] 3[1.2.3/Eh] 3[1.2.3/bcl] 3[1.2.3/cbn] — 4 3 3 1 — tmp+4
— hp — pf/cel — str
perc: crot, vib, xyl, chimes, field dr, bd, tamtam, cym, sus cym, szl cym, tri,
tambn, guiro, whip, belltree, 2glock, 2sd, 4tomtoms, egg shakers, sandblks, anvil
Mvt 4 for chamber choir of 16 voices, *a cappella*. Mvt 6 may include
additional massed children's voices and/or audience participation.

1. Silver Fanfare (orchestra)	4'
2. That Music Always Round Me (Whitman)	7'
3. To Music (Rilke)	6'
4. The Aim Was Song (Frost)	3'
5. Music (Aiken)	5'
6. On Music's Wings (Boyer)	5'

Propulsive

On Music's Wings: Silver Fanfare <2003–2004>   4'

3[1.2.pic] 3[1.2.3/Eh] 3[1.2.3/bcl] 3[1.2.3/cbn] — 4 3 3 1 — tmp+4
— hp — pf — str
perc: vib, glock, belltree, chimes, field dr, bd, cym, sus cym, tri, tambn, whip, 2sd,
4tomtoms, anvil

Propulsive

perchance to dream…: Songs of Sleep <1994–1995>   18'

soprano solo
1 1 1[cl/bcl] 1 — 1 1 0 0 — 1perc — pf — str[min 6.5.4.3.1]
perc: bd, sus cym, sd, tamtam, vib, chimes, crot, marktree, tmp (29")

Prelude	2'
I. How Long Wilt Thou Sleep, O Sluggard	2'
II. I Wander All Night in My Vision	6'
III. Colorless Green Ideas	2'
IV. To Die: to Sleep	3'
V. I Lingered Round Them	2'
Postlude	1'

Propulsive

The Phoenix <1998>   8'

3[1.2.3/pic] 3[1.2.3/Eh] 3[1.2.3/bcl] 3 — 5[incl 1 offstage] 4[incl 1
offstage] 3 1 — tmp+4 — hp — pf/cel — str
perc: bd, cym, sd, tri, tamtam, vib, chimes, belltree, crot (E), 2glock, 6rototoms,
2sus cym

Propulsive

Rolling River (Sketches on "Shenandoah") <2014>   5'

3[1.2.pic] 3[1.2.Eh] 3[1.2.bcl] 3[1.2.3/cbn] — 4 3 3 1 — tmp+3 — hp
— cel — str
perc: sus cym, bd, tri, vib, glock

Propulsive

Symphony No.1 <2012–2013>   24'

3[1.2.3/pic] 3[1.2.Eh] 3[1.2.bcl] 3[1.2.3/cbn] — 4 3 3 1 — tmp+5[or
4] — hp — pf/cel — str
perc: glock, vib, xyl, crot, sd, td, bd, tamtam, sus cym, cym, tri, tambn, shaker

I. Prelude	7'
II. Scherzo/Dance	6'
III. Adagio, un poco rubato	11'

Propulsive

Three Olympians <2000>   15'

str[min 6.5.4.3.1]

I. Apollo	5'
II. Aphrodite	6'
III. Ares	4'

Propulsive

Titanic <1995>   13'

3[1.2/pic.3/pic] 3[1.2.Eh] 3[1.2.3/bcl] 3[1.2.cbn] — 4 4[incl 1 offstage]
3 1 — tmp+5 — hp — cel, pf[upright & grand] — str[min 12.10.8.8.6]
perc: chimes, xyl, crot, cym, marktree, vib, templeblks, bd, glock, tambn, sd,
tamtam, brake dr, 4tomtoms, 2sus cym, watergong

Propulsive		

Brahms, Johannes   1833-1897

(b Hamburg, 7 May 1833; d Vienna, 3 April 1897). German

Akademische Festouvertüre, op.80 (Academic Festival   10'
   Overture) <1880>

3[1.2.pic] 2 2 3[1.2.cbn] — 4 3 3 1 — tmp+3 — str
perc: bd, cym, tri

Breitkopf	Kalmus	Luck's

Alto Rhapsody, op.53 <1869>   13'

alto solo   male chorus
2 2 2 2 — 2 0 0 0 — str

Breitkopf	Broude Bros.	Kalmus	Luck's	Peters

Begräbnisgesang, op.13 <1858>   11'

chorus
0 2 2 2 — 2 0 3 1 — tmp — [no str]

Breitkopf	Carus	Hänssler	Hinshaw

Concerto, Piano, No.1, op.15, D minor <1854–1858>   44'

2 2 2 2 — 4 2 0 0 — tmp — str
Corrected Kalmus edition (2010) by Clinton F. Nieweg & Robert
Sutherland.
 I. Maestoso   *21'*
 II. Adagio   *11'*
 III. Rondo: Allegro non troppo   *12'*

Breitkopf	Kalmus	Luck's

Concerto, Piano, No.2, op.83, B-flat major <1878–1881>   46'

2[1/pic.2] 2 2 2 — 4 2 0 0 — tmp — str
 I. Allegro non troppo   *16'*
 II. Allegro appassionato   *9'*
 III. Andante   *12'*
 IV. Allegretto grazioso   *9'*

Breitkopf	Kalmus	Luck's

Concerto, Viola (or Clarinet), op.120, no.1, F minor (arr.   24'
   Adler) <1894>

solo viola or clarinet
2 2 2 2 — 2 2 0 0 — str
Originally a sonata (op.120, no.1) for clarinet or viola with piano.
Orchestrated by Samuel Adler.
 This same Brahms sonata has been orchestrated by Luciano Berio, pub
Universal, calling for a somewhat larger orchestra:
 3 2 2 3[1.2.cbn]] — 3 3 1 0 — str
 I. Allegro appassionato   *9'*
 II. Andante un poco adagio   *5'*
 III. Allegretto grazioso   *5'*
 IV. Vivace   *5'*

Presser		

Concerto, Violin, op.77, D major <1878>   38'

2 2 2 2 — 4 2 0 0 — tmp — str
Bärenreiter critical edition by Clive Brown.
 I. Allegro non troppo   *21'*
 II. Adagio   *9'*
 III. Allegro giocoso; ma non troppo vivace *8'*

Bärenreiter	Breitkopf	Kalmus	Luck's

Concerto, Violin & Violoncello, op.102, A minor (Double   32'
   Concerto) <1887>

2 2 2 2 — 4 2 0 0 — tmp — str
 I. Allegro   *16'*
 II. Andante   *8'*
 III. Vivace non troppo   *8'*

Breitkopf	Kalmus	Luck's

Ein deutsches Requiem, op.45 (A German Requiem)   68'
   <1857–1868>

chorus   soprano and baritone solos
3[1.2.pic] 2 2 3[1.2.opt cbn] — 4 2 3 1 — tmp — 2 or more hp
[1part] — org[opt] — str
A reduction of the orchestral part, arr. Joachim Linckelmann, is available
from Carus. Instrumentation:
 1[fl/pic] 1 1 1 — 1 0 0 0 — tmp — str 5t
 1. Chorus: "Selig sind die da Leid tragen"   *10'*
 2. Chorus: "Denn alles Fleisch es ist wie Gras"   *14'*
 3. Solo & Chorus: "Herr, lehre doch mich"   *11'*
 4. Chorus: "Wie lieblich sind deine Wohnungen"   *6'*
 5. Solo & Chorus: "Ihr habt nun Traurigkeit"   *6'*
 6. Solo & Chorus: "Denn wir haben hie"   *11'*
 7. Chorus: "Selig sind die Toten"   *10'*

Breitkopf	Kalmus	Luck's	Peters

Eleven Chorale Preludes, op.122 <1896>   25'

3[1.2.opt 3/pic] 3[1.2/Eh] 3[1.2.bcl] 3[1.2.opt cbn] — 4 2 3 1 —
tmp+1 — str
perc: chimes
Originally for organ; orchestrated by Virgil Thomson.

Boosey		

Es ist ein Ros' entsprungen (Lo, How a Rose E'er   6'
   Blooming) <1896>

2 0 2 1 — str
Transcribed by Earl Scott from an organ chorale prelude, op.122 no.8.
Winds are optional.

Luck's	Kalmus

Gesang der Parzen, op.89 (Song of the Fates) <1882>   14'

chorus
2[1/pic.2] 2 2 3[1.2.cbn] — 4 2 3 1 — tmp — str

Breitkopf	Kalmus

Haydn Variations

see his: Variations on a Theme of Joseph Haydn

Hungarian Dances Nos.1, 3, 10 (arr. Brahms) <1868>   7'

3[1.2.pic] 2 2 2 — 4 2 0 0 — tmp+2 — str
perc: tri, bd, cym
Originally for piano 4-hands.
 No.1, G minor   *3'*
 No.3, F major   *2'*
 No.10, F major   *2'*

Breitkopf	Kalmus	Luck's

Hungarian Dances Nos.2, 7 (arr. Andreas Hallén)   5'
   <1868>

2 2 2 2 — 4 2 3 0 — tmp+1 — str
perc: sd
Originally for piano 4-hands.
 No.2   *3'*
 No.7   *2'*

Kalmus	Luck's	Simrock

Hungarian Dance No.4, F-sharp minor (arr. Paul Juon) <1852–1869>   4'

2[1/pic.2/pic] 2 2 2 — 4 2 3 0 — tmp — hp[or pf] — str
Originally for piano 4-hands.

Kalmus	Luck's	Simrock

Hungarian Dances Nos.5, 6 (arr. A. Parlow) <1868>   7'

2[1.pic] 2 2 2 — 4 2 3 0 — tmp — str
Originally for piano 4-hands.
No.5   *3'*
No.6   *4'*

Kalmus	Luck's	Simrock

Hungarian Dances Nos.5, 6, 7 (arr. M. Schmeling) <1868>   9'

3[1.2.pic] 2 2 2 — 4 2 3 0 — tmp+3 — str
perc: bd, cym, tri
Originally for piano 4-hands.
No.5, G minor   *3'*
No.6, D major   *4'*
No.7, F major   *2'*

Breitkopf	Kalmus	Luck's

Hungarian Dances Nos.11-16 (arr. A. Parlow) <1880>   12'

3[1.2.pic] 2 2 2 — 4 2 3 0 — tmp — hp — str
perc: bd, sd
Originally for piano 4-hands.
Hp tacet in nos.12, 13, & 15; perc plays in no.13 only.
No.11, D minor   *2'*
No.12, D minor   *2'*
No.13, D major   *2'*
No.14, D minor   *2'*
No.15, B-flat major   *2'*
No.16, F minor   *2'*

Kalmus	Luck's	Simrock

Hungarian Dances Nos.17-21 (arr. Dvořák) <1880>   10'

2[1.2/pic] 2 2 2 — 4 2 3 0 — tmp+3 — opt hp in no.21 — str
perc: bd, cym, tri
Originally for piano 4-hands.
No.17, F-sharp minor   *2'*
No.18, D major   *2'*
No.19, B minor   *2'*
No.20, E minor   *2'*
No.21, E minor   *2'*

Kalmus	Luck's	Simrock

Liebeslieder Waltzes, op.52 <1874>   25'

str
Originally for solos SATB & piano 4-hands; arr. Friedrich Hermann.

Kalmus	Luck's	Simrock

Liebeslieder Waltzes, from op.52 & 65 (Neun Walzer aus op.52 und 65) <1869–1870>   11'

solos SATB (sometimes performed by chorus)
2[incl pic] 2 2 2 — 2 0 0 0 — str
Originally for solos SATB & piano 4-hands; selected and orchestrated by the composer.
  NB: the vocal parts for *Nagen am Herzen* differ from those of the original version (SATB & pf 4-hands).
Op.52 no.1 (Rede Mädchen, allzuliebes)   *1'*
52/2 (Am Gesteine rauscht die Flut)   *1'*
52/4 (Wie des Abends schöne Röte)   *1'*
52/6 (Ein kleiner, hübscher Vogel)   *2'*
52/5 (Die grüne Hopfenranke)   *1'*
op.65/9 (Nagen am Herzen)   *1'*
52/11 (Nein, es ist nicht auszukommen)   *1'*
52/8 (Wenn so lind dein Auge mir)   *1'*
52/9 (Am Donaustrande)   *2'*

Kalmus	Luck's	Peters

Nänie, op.82 <1880–1881>   14'

chorus
2 2 2 2 — 2 0 3 0 — tmp — 2hp[1part] — str

Breitkopf	Kalmus	Luck's	Peters

Piano Quartet, op.25, G minor; arr. Schoenberg <1861>   43'

3[1.2.3/pic] 3[1.2.3/Eh] 3[1.2/bcl.Ebcl] 3[1.2.cbn] — 4 3 3 1 — tmp+5 — str
perc: xyl, tri, glock, sd, cym, bd, tambn
Originally for piano and strings; orchestrated by Arnold Schoenberg, 1937. Available from Belmont in the US; Schirmer elsewhere.
  N.B.: The changeovers from ob3 to Eh are such that a 4th oboist may be required.
I. Allegro   *14'*
II. Intermezzo: Allegro; ma non troppo   *10'*
III. Andante con moto   *11'*
IV. Rondo alla zingarese: Presto   *8'*

Belmont	Schirmer

Rinaldo, op.50 <1863–1868>   38'

tenor solo   male chorus
3 2 2 2 — 2 2 3 0 — tmp — str
Kalmus orchestral parts are a reprint of Breitkopf, and do not match the Kalmus vocal scores, which are a reprint of Simrock.
I. Introduction & Chorus: "Zu dem Strande"   *5'*
II. Solo & Chorus: "Stelle her der gold'nen Tage"   *14'*
III. Chorus: "Zurücke, nur zurücke!"   *2'*
IV. Solo & Chorus: "Zum zweiten Male"   *10'*
V. The Return Voyage: "Auf dem Meere"   *7'*

Lengnick	Kalmus	Luck's	Simrock

Schicksalslied, op.54 (Song of Destiny) <1868–1871>   18'

chorus
2 2 2 2 — 2 2 3 0 — tmp — str

Breitkopf	Kalmus	Luck's	Simrock

Serenade No.1, op.11, D major <1857–1858>   49'

2 2 2 2 — 4 2 0 0 — tmp — str
I. Allegro molto   *14'*
II. Scherzo   *7'*
III. Adagio non troppo   *14'*
IV. Menuetto I & II   *4'*
V. Scherzo   *4'*
VI. Rondo   *6'*

Breitkopf	Kalmus	Luck's

Serenade No.2, op.16, A major <1858–1859>   29'

3[1.2.pic] 2 2 2 — 2 0 0 0 — str[no vn]
Piccolo plays in movement 5 only.
I. Allegro moderato   *8'*
II. Scherzo: Vivace   *2'*
III. Adagio non troppo   *8'*
IV. Quasi menuetto   *5'*
V. Rondo: Allegro   *6'*

Breitkopf	Kalmus	Luck's

Symphony No.1, op.68, C minor <1855–1876>   45'

2 2 2 3[1.2.cbn] — 4 2 3 0 — tmp — str
Trombones play in mvt 4 only.
I. Un poco sostenuto; Allegro   *13'*
II. Andante sostenuto   *10'*
III. Un poco allegretto e grazioso   *5'*
IV. Adagio; Più andante; Allegro non troppo, ma con brio   *17'*

Breitkopf	Henle	Kalmus	Luck's

Symphony No.2, op.73, D major <1877>   43'

2 2 2 2 — 4 2 3 1 — tmp — str

I. Allegro non troppo		18'
II. Adagio non troppo		10'
III. Allegretto grazioso (Quasi andantino)		5'
IV. Allegro con spirito		10'

Breitkopf	Kalmus	Luck's

Symphony No.3, op.90, F major <1883>   33'

2 2 2 3[1.2.cbn] — 4 2 3 0 — tmp — str

I. Allegro con brio	10'
II. Andante	8'
III. Poco allegretto	6'
IV. Allegro	9'

Breitkopf	Kalmus	Luck's

Symphony No.4, op.98, E minor <1884–1885>   39'

2[1.2/pic] 2 2 3[1.2.cbn] — 4 2 3 0 — tmp+1 — str
perc: tri
Pic & tri in mvt 3 only; tbn in mvt 4 only; cbn in mvts 3&4 only. 3rd mvt calls for clarinets in C.

I. Allegro non troppo	12'
II. Andante moderato	11'
III. Allegro giocoso	6'
IV. Allegro energico e passionato	10'

Breitkopf	Kalmus	Luck's

Tragische Ouvertüre, op.81 (Tragic Overture) <1880>   13'

3[1.2.pic] 2 2 2 — 4 2 3 1 — tmp — str

Breitkopf	Kalmus	Luck's

Variations on a Theme of Joseph Haydn, op.56a (Haydn Variations) <1873>   19'

3[1.2.pic] 2 2 3[1.2.cbn] — 4 2 0 0 — tmp+1 — str
perc: tri
A note by the composer in the autograph indicates that, if necessary, a tuba may substitute for contrabassoon in the chorale and the finale only. Presumably, in such a case, the contrabassoon part would simply be omitted in Variations 1, 2 & 6.
   A critical edition of the score with historical and analytical essays is available from Norton.

Chorale St. Antoni: Andante	2'
Variation I: Poco più animato	1'
Variation II: Più vivace	1'
Variation III: Con moto	2'
Variation IV: Andante con moto	3'
Variation V: Vivace	1'
Variation VI: Vivace	1'
Variation VII: Grazioso	3'
Variation VIII: Presto non troppo	1'
Finale: Andante	4'

Breitkopf	Kalmus	Luck's

Brant, Henry   1913-2008

(b Montréal, 15 Sept 1913; d Santa Barbara, CA, 26 Apr, 2008). American composer of Canadian birth

Angels and Devils <1931>   18'

solo flute, accompanied by a flute orchestra
10 fl [3pic.5fl.2afl] 0 0 0 — [no str]

MCA

Desert Forests (Spatial Panoramas) <1983>   15'

3[incl 3pic] 3 4[incl Ebcl,bcl] 3[incl cbn] — 5 3 3 1 — tmp+3 — hp — cel, opt pf — str
2 conductors are required. Groups of instruments are separated spatially, with some players in balconies and/or boxes.

C. Fischer

Galaxy 2 <1954>   5'

1[1/pic] 0 1 0 — 2 1 1 0 — tmp+1 — [no str]

MCA

Verticals Ascending (After the Rodia Towers) <1967>   8'

2[1.pic] 2 3[1.alto cl.bcl] 2 — 2 2 1 1 — opt asx — tmp+1 — pf, opt elec org — [no str]
Alternate version substitutes violins for organ and/or violas and violoncellos for saxophone. Instruments divided into two widely separated groups, each with its own conductor.

MCA

Bremer, Carolyn   1957-

(b Santa Monica, CA, 28 Oct 1957). American

Early Light <1995>   6'

2[1.pic] 2[1.Eh] 2 2 — 4 3 3 1 — tmp+4 — str
perc: glock, xyl, cym, sus cym, tri, templeblks, chimes, whip, bd, sd

C. Fischer

Brian, Havergal   1876-1972

(b Dresden, Staffs., 29 Jan 1876; d Shoreham, Sussex, 28 Nov 1972). English

Symphony No.22 (Symphonia brevis) <1964–1965>   10'

3[incl pic] 3[incl Eh] 3[incl bcl] 3[incl cbn] — 4 3 3 1 — tmp+7 — hp — str[16.14.12.10.8]

Musica Viva	UMP

Bridge, Frank   1879-1941

(b Brighton, 26 Feb 1879; d Friston, Sussex, 10 Jan 1941). English

Enter Spring <1927>   17'

3[1.2.3/pic] 3[1.2.Eh] 3[1.2.bcl] 3[1.2.cbn] — 4 3 3 1 — tmp+4 — 2hp — cel — str
perc: glock, chimes, tamtam, sd, cym, sus cym, tambn, bd, 2tri

Faber

Oration (Concerto elegiaco) <1930>   28'

solo violoncello
2[1/pic.2/pic] 2 2 — 4 2 3 1 — tmp+1 — hp — str
perc: sd, tri
Ed. Paul Hindmarsh.

Faber

Rebus <1940>   9'

3[1.2.pic] 3[1.2.Eh] 3[1.2.bcl] 3[1.2.cbn] — 4 3 3 1 — tmp+3 — hp — str
perc: sd, cym, sus cym, bd, tri

Boosey

The Sea <1910–1911>   25'

3[1.2.3/pic] 3[1.2.Eh] 3[1.2.bcl] 3[1.2.cbn] — 4 3 3 1 — tmp+4 — hp — str
perc: bd, cym, sd, tri

Seascape (Seestück)	7'
Sea-Foam (Meeresschaum)	5'
Moonlight (Mondlicht)	6'
Storm (Sturm)	7'

Kalmus	Luck's	Stainer

Suite for String Orchestra <1908>   20'

str
I. Prelude	7'
II. Intermezzo	3'
III. Nocturne	6'
IV. Finale	4'

| Curwen | Kalmus | Luck's |

Brief, Todd   1953-

(b New York, 12 February 1953). American

Cantares <1978>   16'

solo soprano
4[all/pic] 4[1.2.3.Eh] 5[1.2.3.4.bcl] 4[1.2.3.cbn] — 4 3 4 1 — tmp+5 — 2hp — cel, pf — str
perc: crot, bd, bongos, cast, chimes, claves, glock, gong, guiro, marim, sd, tamtam, tambn, templeblks, tomtom, tri, vib, woodblk, xyl, sus cym, bamboo wind chimes, glass chimes, hand bell, log drum, 3cowbells

| Universal |

Brindle, Reginald Smith   1917 - 2003

see: Smith Brindle, Reginald

Bristow, George Frederick   1825 - 1898

(b Brooklyn, NY, 19 Dec 1825; d New York, 13 Dec 1898). American

---

The Oratorio of Daniel, op.42 <1862–1866>   118'

solos SMzTTBarBBB   chorus
2 2 2 2 — 4 2 3 1 — tmp+2 — opt prg — str
perc: cym, tri
May be done with one less bass soloist (1 bass covers 2 parts).
    Ed. David Griggs-Janower.
Story 1: The Babylonian Captivity	16'
Story 2: Nebuchadnezzar's Dream	33'
Story 3: The Fiery Furnace	23'
Story 4a: Nebuchadnezzar's Second Dream	12'
Story 4b: Nebuchadnezzar is Turned into a Beast	19'
Story 4c: Nebuchadnezzar Regains His Sanity	15'

| Griggs-Janower |

Rip Van Winkle: Overture <1852–1855>   9'

3[1.2.pic] 2 2 2 — 4 2 3 0 — tmp — str

| Fleisher |

Britten, Benjamin   1913 - 1976

(b Lowestoft, 22 Nov 1913; d Aldeburgh, 4 Dec 1976). English

Ballad of Heroes, op.14 <1939>   17'

solo tenor (or soprano)   chorus
3[1.2/pic.(3 opt)] 3[1.2.Eh.(3 opt)] 3[1.2.(Ebcl opt)] 3[1.2.(opt 3/cbn)] — 4 5[1.2.(3-5 opt)] 3 1 — tmp+3 (or 2) — hp — str
perc: cym, td, xyl, bd, whip, 2sd
The 3 optional trumpets and 1 snare drum are offstage.
1. Funeral March	6'
2. Scherzo (Dance of Death)	4'
3. Recitative and Choral — Epilogue (Funeral March)	7'

| Boosey |

The Building of the House, op.79 <1967>   5'

opt chorus
2 2 2 2 — 2 2 0 1 — tmp+1 — opt org — str
perc: cym, sd, xyl, chimes, tri
The chorus can be replaced or added to by an organ, or by extra brass (3tp & 3tbn).

| Faber |

Canadian Carnival, op.19 <1939>   14'

2[1.2/pic] 2[1.2/Eh] 2 2 — 4 3[tp3 opt] 3 1 — tmp+2 — hp — str
perc: sd, bd, xyl, 2sus cym

| Boosey |

Cantata academica, carmen basiliense, op.62 <1959>   21'

chorus   solos SATB
2[1.2/pic] 2 2 2 — 4 2 3 1 — tmp+4 — 1 or 2hp — pf[dbl opt cel] — str
perc: field dr, tambn, tri, chimes, xyl, glock, cym, bd, tamtam, templeblks

| Boosey |

Cantata misericordium, op.69 <1963>   20'

chorus   solos TB
tmp — hp — pf — solo str 4t — str orch

| Boosey |

Children's Crusade, op.82 <1969>   19'

children's chorus
6perc — elec org, 2pf (or pf 4-hands) — [no str]
perc: gong, woodblk, tri, sd, tambn, chimes, td, xyl, tamtam, bd w/ ped, 3sus cym, tabor, 2glock, guiro
Any number of "tutti percussion" in addition to the 6 solo percussionists.

| Faber |

Concerto, Piano, No.1, op.13 <1938; rev 1945>   33'

2[1/pic.2/pic] 2[1.2/Eh] 2 2 — 4 2 3 1 — tmp+2 — hp — str
perc: sd, td, tambn, glock, whip, cym, bd/cym
I. Toccata: Allegro molto e con brio	12'
II. Waltz: Allegretto	5'
III. Impromptu: Andante lento	7'
IV. March: Allegro moderato; sempre alla marcia	9'

| Boosey |

Concerto, Violin, No.1, op.15 <1939>   31'

3[1.2/pic2.3/pic1] 2[1.2/Eh] 2 2 — 4 3 3 1 — tmp+2 — hp — str
perc: sd, cym, glock, bd, td, tambn
I. Moderato con moto	9'
II. Vivace	9'
III. Passacaglia: Andante lento (un poco meno mosso)	13'

| Boosey |

Concerto, Violin & Viola (Double Concerto) <1932>   25'

2[1.2/pic] 2 2 2 — 2 2 0 0 — tmp+1 — str
perc: cym
Ed. Colin Matthews.
Allegro ma non troppo	7'
Rhapsody: Poco lento	7'
Allegro scherzando	8'

| Oxford | Chester |

Death in Venice: Suite, op.88a <1971–1973; rev 1973-4>   27'

2[1/pic.2/pic] 2 2[1.2/bcl] 2 — 2 2 2 1 — tmp+4 — hp — pf —
str[min 6.4.3.3.2]
perc: cym, chimes, vib, xyl, sus cym, marim, tuned dr[C4], 2gong[D#3,G3],
3tomtom, 3Chinesdr [ad lib], 2tamtam, 2glock
Suite from the opera arr. Steuart Bedford, 1985. The movements are
played without pause.

Summons to Venice	_'
Overture to Venice	_'
First Beach Scene	_'
Tadzio	_'
I love you	_'
Pursuit	_'
Second Beach Scene and Death	_'

> Faber

Diversions on a Theme, op.21 <1940>   23'

solo piano (left hand)
2[1.2/pic] 2[1.2/Eh] 2[1.2/Ebcl] 3[1.2.opt cbn] — 4 2 3 1 — asx (opt)
— tmp+3 (or 2) — hp — str
perc: cym, sd, xyl, tri, bd, sus cym, gong, tambn

> Boosey

Fourteen Folk Songs <1941–1959>   36'

solo voice [mostly high voice; some medium voice]
2[1.2/pic] 2[1.2/Eh] 2[1.2/bcl] 2 — 2 2 0 0 — tmp+1 — hp — str
perc: bd/cym, sd, tambn, woodblk
The complete folk songs for voice and orchestra, though not intended as a
cycle. Originally created over a period of years for voice & piano, and
subsequently orchestrated.

The Bonny Earl o'Moray	3'
Come you not from Newcastle?	1'
Little Sir William	3'
O can ye sew cushions?	2'
Oliver Cromwell	1'
O Waly, Waly	3'
The Plough Boy	2'
The Salley Gardens [version for voice & str]	3'
The Salley Gardens [version for bn (or vc), hp, str]	3'
La belle est au jardin d'amour (Beauty in love's garden)	3'
Eho! Eho!	2'
Fileuse	2'
La Noël passée (The Orphan and King Henry)	4'
Quand j'étais chez mon pere (Heigh ho! heigh hi!)	2'
Le roi s'en va-t'en chasse (The King is gone hunting)	2'

> Boosey

Gloriana: Symphonic Suite, op.53a <1953>   26'

3[1.2.pic] 3[1.2.Eh] 3[1.2.bcl] 3[1.2.cbn] — 4 3 3 1 — tmp+4 — hp
— str
perc: bd, cym, sd, td, tri, tambn, gong

The Tournament	4'
The Lute Song	5'
The Courtly Dances	9'
Gloriana moritura	8'

> Boosey

Gloriana: Courtly Dances <1953>   9'

2[1.2/pic] 2 2 — 4 2 3 1 — tmp+4 — str
perc: td, sd, tambn, cym, bd, tri
This popular extract is no longer available separately; for separate
performance, the publisher will provide the entire "Symphonic Suite" but
will charge only for the "Courtly Dances."
  An arrangement by David Stone for school orchestra is available for
purchase; instrumentation: 1 1 2 1 — 2 2 1 0 — tmp+perc — pf — str

1. March	1'
2. Coranto	1'
3. Pavane	2'
4. Morris Dance	1'
5. Lavolta	2'
6. Reprise of the March	2'

> Boosey

Les illuminations, op.18 <1939>   21'

high voice
str

I. Fanfare: Maestoso (poco presto)	2'
II. Villes: Allegro energico	2'
IIIa. Phrase: Lento ed estatico	1'
IIIb. Antique: Allegretto; un poco mosso	2'
IV. Royauté: Allegro maestoso	2'
V. Marine: Allegro con brio	1'
VI. Interlude: Moderato ma comodo	2'
VII. Being Beauteous: Lento ma comodo	4'
VIII. Parade: Alla marcia	3'
IX. Départ: Largo mesto	2'

> Boosey

Johnson over Jordan: Suite <1939>   14'

1[fl/pic] 1 2[1/Ebcl.2/bcl/asx] 1 — 0 2 1 0 — tmp+1 — pf — str
perc: sus cym, hi-hat, tamtam, sd, td, bd/ped
Originally incidental music for a play by J.B. Priestley; suite compiled
1990 by Paul Hindmarsh.
  Alternative clarinet disposition: 3[1/Ebcl.2.3/bcl/asx]; ossias are
provided if only 2cl are used.

1. Overture	4'
2. Incinerators' Ballet	3'
3. The Spider and the Fly	4'
4. End Music	3'

> Faber

Lachrymae, op.48a <1950; rev 1976>   15'

solo viola
str[vn, va, vc, db: each divisi a2]
Originally (1950) for viola & piano; orchestrated by the composer (1976)
Reflections on a song of John Dowland.
  The orchestral violin parts are intended for the 2nd violins (i.e., 1st
violins are tacet).

> Boosey

Matinées musicales, op.24 (after Rossini) <1941>   16'

2[1.2/pic] 2 2 — 2 2 3 0 — tmp+2 — hp[or pf] — cel[or pf] — str
perc: sd, tambn, bd/cym, sus cym, td, tri, woodblk

I. March	3'
II. Nocturne	4'
III. Waltz	2'
IV. Pantomime	4'
V. Moto perpetuo (Solfeggi e gorgheggi)	3'

> Boosey   Luck's

Men of Goodwill; Variations on a Christmas Carol (God Rest Ye Merry, Gentlemen) <1947>   8'

3[1.2.pic] 2 2 — 4 2 3 1 — tmp+2 — hp — str
perc: cym, sus cym, sd, td, bd, xyl

> Faber

Movements for a Clarinet Concerto <1942>   17'

solo clarinet
2[1.2/pic] 2 1[bcl] 2 — 4 2 3 0 — tmp+1 — hp — str
perc: cym, sus cym, sd, glock
Begun 1942 for Benny Goodman but abandoned; "devised and
orchestrated" by Colin Matthews, 2008, using material from Britten's
Mazurka Elegiaca for 2 pianos (1941) and the orchestral fragment the
composer had abandoned in 1942.

I. Molto allegro	_'
II. Mazurka Elegiaca	_'
III. Finale	_'

> Faber

Nocturne, op.60 <1958>   26'

solo tenor
1 1[Eh] 1 1 — 1 0 0 0 — tmp — hp — str
Seven solo instruments (fl, Eh, cl, bn, hn, hp, tmp) join the solo tenor in
particular mvts; the full forces are heard only in the final postlude.
1. Prologue, from Prometheus Unbound *(Shelley)*   3'
2. The Kraken (Tennyson)–Bassoon obbligato   3'
3. from The Wanderings of Cain *(Coleridge)–Harp obbligato*   2'
4. Blurt, Master Constable (Middleton)–Horn obbligato   3'
5. from The Prelude *(1805, Wordsworth)–Timpani obbligato*   3'
6. The Kind Ghosts (Owen)–English horn obbligato   5'
7. Sleep and Poetry (Keats)–Flute & clarinet obbligato 3'
8. Postlude, Sonnet 43 (Shakespeare)   4'

> Boosey

Now Sleeps the Crimson Petal <1943>   5'

solo tenor, solo horn
str
Originally intended to be part of the composer's *Serenade for Tenor,
Horn & Strings, q.v.* Not to be performed in conjunction with the
Serenade.

> Boosey

Our Hunting Fathers, op.8 <1936; rev 1961>   27'

high voice
2[1.2/pic] 2[1.2/Eh] 2[1.Ebcl/bcl] 2 — 4 2 3 1 — asx — tmp+2 — hp
— str
perc: bd, cym, sus cym, sd, td, tri, tambn, xyl
Prologue   2'
[A] Rats Away!   4'
[B] Messalina   7'
[C] Dance of Death (Hawking for the Partridge)   6'
Epilogue and Funeral March   8'

> Boosey

Paul Bunyan: Overture <1941>   5'

2[1.pic] 1 3[1.2.bcl] 1 — 2 2 2 1 — tmp+2 or 3 — opt hp — opt pf —
str
perc: tri, sd, cym, tambn, bd; td[opt]
Orchestrated by Colin Matthews.

> Faber

Peter Grimes: Four Sea Interludes, op.33a <1944–1945>   16'

2[1/pic2.2/pic1] 2 2[1.2/Ebcl] 3[1.2.cbn] — 4 3 3 1 — tmp+2 — hp
— str
perc: chimes, xyl, sd, tambn, cym, gong, bd
I. Dawn: Lento e tranquillo   3'
II. Sunday Morning: Allegro spiritoso   4'
III. Moonlight: Andante comodo e rubato   4'
IV. Storm: Presto con fuoco   5'

> Boosey

Peter Grimes: Passacaglia, op.33b <1944–1945>   7'

2[1.2/pic] 2 2 3[1.2.cbn] — 4 3 3 1 — tmp+3 — hp — cel — str
perc: sd, gong, cym, tamtam, bd, td, tambn

> Boosey

Phaedra, op.93 <1975>   15'

mezzo-soprano solo
tmp+2 — hpsd — str
perc: cym, chimes, tamtam, td, bd

> Faber

Plymouth Town; A Ballet for Small Orchestra <1931>   25'

1[fl/pic] 1 2 1 — 2 1 1 0 — tmp+2 — str
perc: bd, cym, sus cym
Ed. Colin Matthews. A 2nd tp is advisable for an offstage part.

> Faber

Praise We Great Men <1976>   8'

SATB solos   chorus SATB
3[1.2/pic.3/pic] 2[1.2/Eh] 2[1.2/bcl] 2 — 4 2 0 0 — tmp+2 — hp —
pf — str
perc: bd, cym, sus cym, glock, vib
Fragment edited and orchestrated by Colin Matthews.

> Faber

The Prince of the Pagodas: Pas de six <1956>   11'

3[1.2.pic] 3[1.2.Eh] 3[1.2.Ebcl] 3[1.2.cbn] — 4 3 3 1 — tmp+2 — hp
— pf — str
perc: bd, cym, tambn
Cued so that performance is possible with double woodwind.
   From Act III, Sc.2 of the ballet.
1. Entrée   2'
2. Variation I: Pas de deux   3'
3. Variation II: Girl's solo   1'
4. Variation III: Boy's solo   1'
5. Pas de trois   2'
6. Coda   2'

> Boosey

Quatre chansons françaises <1928>   13'

high voice
2 1 3[1.2.bcl] 2 — 4 0 0 0 — 1perc — hp — pf — str
perc: sus cym [1 note in mvt 3]
Ed. Colin Matthews.
1. Nuits de Juin (June Nights; Die Sommernächte)   3'
2. Sagesse (Wisdom; Weisheit)   3'
3. L'Enfance (Childhood; Die Kindheit)   4'
4. Chanson d'Automne (Autumn Song; Herbstlied   3'

> Faber

Saint Nicolas, op.42 <1948>   50'

tenor solo, 4 boy sopranos   chorus, semi-chorus of female voices
tmp[+2opt perc] — pf 4-hands, org — str
perc: sd, td, whip, tri, tambn, gong, cym, bd
I. Introduction   5'
II. The Birth of Nicholas   3'
III. Nicholas Devotes Himself to God   4'
IV. He Journeys to Palestine   8'
V. Nicholas Comes to Myra and is Chosen Bishop   6'
VI. Nicholas from Prison   3'
VII. Nicholas and the Pickled Boys   6'
VIII. His Piety and Marvellous Works   6'
IX. The Death of Nicholas   9'

> Boosey

Scottish Ballad, op.26 <1941>   13'

2 solo pianos
2[1.pic] 2 2 3[1.2.opt cbn] — 4 2 3 1 — tmp+2 — hp — str
perc: sd, tambn, cym, tamtam, bd/cym, whip

> Boosey

Serenade for Tenor, Horn & Strings, op.31 <1943>   25'

solo tenor, solo horn
str
I. Prologue   2'
II. Pastoral   4'
III. Nocturne   3'
IV. Elegy   5'
V. Dirge   3'
VI. Hymn   2'
VII. Sonnet   4'
VIII. Epilogue   2'

> Boosey

Simple Symphony, op.4 <1933–1934>   16'

str
I. Boisterous Bourrée	3'
II. Playful Pizzicato	3'
III. Sentimental Saraband	7'
IV. Frolicsome Finale	3'

Oxford	Chester

Sinfonia da requiem, op.20 <1940>   21'

3[1.2.3/pic/opt afl] 3[1.2.Eh] 3[1.2/Ebcl.3/bcl] 3[1.2.cbn] — 6[hn5-6 opt] 3 3 1 — opt asx — tmp+3 or 4 — 1 or 2hp — pf — str
perc: xyl, sd, whip, tambn, sus cym, cym, bd, tmp2
I. Lacrymosa	9'
II. Dies Irae	5'
III. Requiem aeternam	7'

Boosey

Sinfonietta, op.1 <1932>   15'

1 1 1 1 — 1 0 0 0 — str 5t[or small str orch]
A version using 2 horns was prepared by the composer in 1936, and is also available from Boosey.
I. Poco presto ed agitato	4'
II. Variations: Andante lento	7'
III. Tarantella: Presto vivace	4'

Boosey

Soirées musicales, op.9 (after Rossini) <1936>   10'

2[1/pic.2/pic] 2 2 2 — 4 2 3 0 — tmp+3 — hp[or pf] — str
perc: sd, cast, bd/cym, tri; optional: sus cym, glock, xyl
Playable with the following reduced instrumentation:
  1 1 1 0 — 0 1 1 0 — 2perc — hp[or pf] — str
I. March	1'
II. Canzonetta	3'
III. Tirolese	2'
IV. Bolero	2'
V. Tarantella	2'

Boosey	Luck's

Spring Symphony, op.44 <1949>   46'

chorus, boy chorus   solos SAT
3[1.2.3/afl/pic] 3[1.2.Eh] 3[1.2.bcl] 3[1.2.cbn] — 4 3 3 1 — cow horn — tmp+4 — 2hp — str
perc: bd, sus cym, gong, sd, td, tambn, whip, xyl, chimes, woodblk, cast, vib, cym
Cow horn usually played by horn player; instrument may be rented from publisher.
PART I:	
Introduction (Anon. 16th century)	9'
The Merry Cuckoo (Spenser)	2'
Spring, the Sweet Spring (Nashe)	2'
The Driving Boy (George Peele — John Clare)	2'
The Morning Star (Milton)	4'
PART II:	
Welcome Maids of Honor (Herrick)	3'
Waters Above (Vaughan)	3'
Out on the Lawn I Lie in Bed (Auden)	6'
PART III:	
When Will My May Come (Barnefield)	3'
Fair and Fair (George Peele)	3'
Sound the Flute (Blake)	1'
PART IV:	
Finale: London; to Thee I Do Present (Beaumont & Fletcher)	8'

Boosey

Suite on English Folk Tunes, op.90 (A Time There Was...) <1966–1975>   15'

2[1.2/pic] 2[1.2/Eh] 2 2 — 2 2 0 0 — tmp+2 — hp — str
perc: sd, chimes, bd, tri, sd w/o sn
I. Cakes and Ale: Fast and Rough	2'
II. The Bitter Withy: Allegretto	3'
III. Hawkin' Booby: Heavily	2'
IV. Hunt the Squirrel: Fast and Gay	1'
V. Lord Melbourne: Slow and Languid	7'

Faber

The Sword in the Stone <1939>   10'

1 0 1 1 — 0 1 1 0 — 1perc — hp — [no str]
perc: bd, td, sd, sus cym, hi-hat, tri, woodblk, gong, glock

Faber

Symphony for Cello & Orchestra, op.68 <1963; rev 1964>   35'

2[1.2/pic] 2 2[1.2/bcl] 2[1.cbn] — 2 2 1 1 — tmp+2 — str
perc: bd, cym, tambn, whip, gong, sd, td, vib, tamtam
I. Allegro maestoso	13'
II. Presto inquieto	4'
III. Adagio	10'
IV. Passacaglia: Andante allegro	8'

Boosey

Te Deum <1934>   8'

treble solo   chorus (treble, alto, tenor, bass)
hp — str
Accompaniment originally for organ; orchestrated by the composer (1936).

Chester

Temporal Variations <1936>   14'

solo oboe
str
Original for oboe & piano; arranged for oboe & string orchestra by Colin Matthews in 1993.
I. Theme	2'
II. Oration	2'
III. March	1'
IV. Exercises	1'
V. Commination	1'
VI. Chorale	2'
VII. Waltz	2'
VIII. Polka	1'
IX. Resolution	2'

Faber

Variations on a Theme of Frank Bridge, op.10 <1937>   26'

str
I. Introduction and Theme	2'
II. Adagio	2'
III. March	1'
IV. Romance	2'
V. Aria italiana	1'
VI. Bourée classique	1'
VII. Wiener Waltz	3'
VIII. Moto perpetuo	1'
IX. Funeral March	4'
X. Chant	2'
XI. Fugue and Finale	7'

Boosey

War Requiem, op.66 <1961>   78'

chorus, boy choir   solos STB   main orch & *chamber orch*
4[1.2.3/pic.*chmb1/pic*] 4[1.2.Eh.*chmb1/Eh*] 4[1.2.3/Ebcl/bcl.*chmb1*]
4[1.2.cbn.*chmb1*] — 7[1-6.*chmb1*] 4 3 1 — tmp+5; *chmb1 — chmb hp*
— pf, harm, opt org — str; *chmb str 5t*

perc: bd, vib, whip, gong, sd, td, tambn, glock, chimes, cym, cast, crot, tri, Chinese block; *chmbr: tmp, sd, bd, cym, gong*

Each of the 2 orchestras has its own conductor. Chamber orchestra indicated above by "*chmb*" and italics. To clarify: the chamber orchestra taken alone has the following instrumentation:
   1[fl/pic] 1[ob/Eh] 1 1 — 1 0 0 0 — 1perc — hp — str 5t

I. Requiem aeternum	9'
II. Dies irae	26'
III. Offertorium	10'
IV. Sanctus	9'
V. Agnus Dei	3'
VI. Libera me	21'

> Boosey

Welcome Ode, op.95 <1976>   9'

SAB chorus [with optional tenors]
2 2 2 2 — 4 2 3 1 — tmp+3 — pf — str
perc: bd, cym, sus cym, sd, tri, tambn, xyl[opt]
May be done with: 2 1 2 1 — 2 2 2 0 — tmp+2 — str

1. March	2'
2. Jig	1'
3. Roundel	3'
4. Modulation	1'
5. Canon	2'

> Faber

The World of the Spirit <1938>   42'

solos SATB, 2 speakers   chorus SATB
2 2 2 2 — 4 2 3 1 — tmp+1 — hp — org — str
perc: sus cym, cym, gong, sd, bd, tambn

Originally a radio feature. Concert version, allowing adjustment of the spoken sections interspersed among the musical sections, prepared by Donald Mitchell. Duration of 42' includes all the spoken sections.

PART I — Prologue	
1. Prelude	1'
2. O Thou that movest all	2'
3. The sun, the moon, the stars	1'
4a. This is my commandment	1'
4b. With wide-embracing love	3'
PART II — The fruits of the Spirit	
5. O Life, O Love, now undivided	4'
6a. A voice within our souls	1'
6b. The fruit of the Spirit is love	1'
6c. The fruit of the Spirit is faith	1'
6d. The fruit of the Spirit is goodness	1'
6e. The fruit of the Spirit is longsuffering	1'
6f. The fruit of the Spirit is joy	1'
7. The spirit of the Lord	4'
PART III — Epilogue	
8. O knowing, glorious Spirit!	2'
9. The world is charged	2'
10. Come, O Creator Spirit, come	4'

> Chester

Young Apollo, op.16 <1939>   10'

solo piano, solo string quartet
str

> Faber

Young Person's Guide to the Orchestra, op.34   18'
(Variations and Fugue on a Theme of Purcell) <1946>

optional speaker
3[1.2.pic] 2 2 — 4 2 3 1 — tmp+5 — hp — str
perc: xyl, tri, sd, cym, bd, tambn, gong, whip, cast, Chinese block
5 percussionists can cover all the notes; composer-authorized omissions make performance possible with 4 percussionists. Curiously, the published score specifies "at least 3" percussionists (apparently a temporary or emergency solution involving discretionary omissions).

Theme: Allegro maestoso e largamente	2'
Variation A (flutes and piccolo): Presto	1'
Variation B (oboes): Lento	1'
Variation C (clarinets): Moderato	1'
Variation D (bassoons): Allegro alla marcia	1'
Variation E (violins): Brillante - Alla polacca	1'
Variation F (violas): Meno mosso	1'
Variation G (cellos): [L'istesso tempo]	1'
Variation H (basses): Comminciando lento ma poco a poco accelerando	1'
Variation I (harp): Maestoso	1'
Variation J (horns): L'istesso tempo	1'
Variation K (trumpets): Vivace	1'
Variation L (trombones): Allegro pomposo	1'
Variation M (percussion): Moderato	1'
Fugue: Allegro molto	3'

> Boosey

Brockway, Howard   1870-1951

(b Brooklyn, NY, 22 Nov 1870; d New York, 20 Feb 1951). American

Cavatina, op.13 <1895>   5'

solo violin
0 0 1 0 — 2 0 0 0 — str

> Margun

Brott, Alexander   1915-2005

(b Montreal, 14 March 1915; d Montreal, 1 April 2005). Canadian

Concordia <1946>   21'

3[1.2.pic] 3[1.2.Eh] 3[1.2.bcl] 3[1.2.cbn] — 4 3 3 1 — tmp+2 — str
perc: bd, cym, sd, tambn, gong, xyl, cast, rattle
Bcl notated in bass clef.
   Composer writes for "gong," "large gong," & "tamtam," one right after the other, all using the identical notation; probably all are intended to be the same instrument.

> CMC

Brouwer, Leo   1939-

(b Havana, 1 March 1939). Cuban

Concerto de Toronto (Concerto No.4) <1990>   34'

solo guitar
1[incl pic] 0 2[incl Ebcl] 0 — 1 1 0 0 — 2perc — pf — str

I. Moderato	10'
II. Tema con variaciones	14'
III. Tempo libero	10'

> EDY

Concerto elegiaco (Concerto No.3) <1986>   22'

solo guitar
tmp+1 — str

I. Tranquilo poco allegro	9'
II. Interludio	4'
III. Finale	9'

> Eschig

Retrats catalans (Catalan Portraits) <1983>   18'

solo guitar
2[incl pic] 0 0 0 — tmp+2 — pf — str[4.3.2.2.1]

Eschig

Brown, Earle   1926-2002

(b Lunenburg, MA, 26 Dec 1926; d Rye, NY, 2 July 2002). American

Available Forms 1 <1961>   12'

1 1 3[1.Ebcl.bcl] 1 — 1 1 1 0 — 2perc — hp — pf — str 5t
perc: glock, marim, xyl, vib, tmp
Duration variable, from approximately 8' to 15'.

AMP

Available Forms 2 <1962>   17'

4[1.2.pic.afl] 3[1.2.Eh] 4[1.2.Ebcl.bcl] 3[1.2.cbn] — 6 4[1.2.3.btp]
4[1.2.btbn.cb tbn] 2[Eb.Bb] — ampd gtr — tmp+3 — 2hp — pf/cel —
str[16.14.12.10.8]
perc: glock, marim, xyl, vib, tmp
2 conductors are required. Duration varies between 15' & 20'.

AMP

Cross Sections and Color Fields <1972–1975>   18'

4[1.2.3.afl] 2[1.Eh] 3[1.2.bcl] 3[1.2.cbn] — 4 3 3 2 — ssx — tmp+4
— 2hp — cel, pf — str[8.7.5.4.3]
Duration variable between 17' & 20'.

Universal

Brubeck, Howard   1916-1993

(b Concord, CA, 11 July 1916; d Escondido, CA, 16 Feb 1993). American

Dialogues for Jazz Combo & Orchestra <1956>   23'

2[incl pic] 2[incl Eh] 2 2 — 4 3 3 1 — tmp+2 — str
The jazz combo may be varied in instrumentation. The length of the solo
sections may be varied.

Shawnee

Bruch, Max   1838-1920

(b Cologne, 6 Jan 1838; d Friedenau, Berlin, 2 Oct 1920). German

Adagio appassionato, op.57 <1891>   8'

solo violin
2 2 2 2 — 4 2 3 0 — tmp — str

C. Fischer	Kalmus	Luck's	Simrock

Adagio nach keltischen Melodien, op.56 (Adagio on Keltish Melodies) <1891>   6'

solo violoncello
2 2 2 2 — 2 2 0 0 — str

Kalmus	Luck's

Ave Maria, op.61 <1892>   4'

solo violoncello
2 2 2 2 — 4 2 3 0 — tmp — str

Fleisher	Simrock	Luck's

Concerto, Clarinet & Viola, op.88, E minor <ca.1911>   19'

2 3[1.2.Eh] 2 2 — 4 2 0 0 — tmp — str
Solo clarinet may be replaced by solo violin.
    Peters ed. by Nicolai Pfeffer, 2008.

Andante con moto	7'
Allegro moderato	6'
Allegro molto	6'

Musica Rara	Peters	Simrock

Concerto, 2 Pianos, op.88a, A-flat Minor <1909; rev 1912>   22'

2 3[1.2.Eh] 2 2 — 4 2 3 0 — tmp — str
Originally the 3rd Suite for Orchestra & Organ (1909); revised for 2
pianos & orchestra 1912.

I. *Andante sostenuto*	5'
II. *Andante con moto—Allegro molto vivace*	5'
III. *Adagio ma non troppo*	5'
IV. *Andante—Allegro*	7'

Boosey	Simrock

Concerto, Violin, No.1, op.26, G minor <1865–1867>   24'

2 2 2 2 — 4 2 0 0 — tmp — str
An excellent concert-ending for the first movement, if it is to be
performed separately, is available at <www.orchestralibrary.com> under
Special parts and items for downloading.

I. *Prelude: Allegro moderato*	9'
II. *Adagio*	8'
III. *Finale: Allegro energico*	7'

Broude Bros.	Kalmus	Luck's	Peters

Concerto, Violin, No.2, D minor <1878>   27'

2 2 2 2 — 4 2 3 0 — tmp — str

I. *Adagio ma non troppo*	13'
II. *Recitative: Allegro moderato*	4'
III. *Finale: Allegro molto*	10'

C. Fischer	Kalmus	Luck's

Concerto, Violin, No.3, op.58, D minor <1891>   38'

2 2 2 2 — 4 2 3 0 — tmp — str

I. *Allegro energico*	18'
II. *Adagio*	11'
III. *Finale: Allegro molto*	9'

Kalmus	Luck's

Hebräische Gesänge (Hebrew Songs) <1888>   8'

chorus
2 2 2 2 — 4 2 3 0 — org[opt] — str
Organ part cued in winds.
    Often in performance the movements are sung in the order 2, 3, 1.

1. *Beweinet, die geweint an Babels Strand (O Weep for Those That Wept…*	3'
2. *In ihrer Schönheit wandelt sie (She Walks in Beauty, Like the Night)*	2'
3. *Arabien's Kameele (On Jordan's Banks the Arabs' Camels Stray)*	3'

Breitkopf	Kalmus

Kol Nidrei, op.47 <1880>   10'

solo violoncello
2 2 2 2 — 4 2 3 0 — tmp — hp — str

C. Fischer	Kalmus	Lengnick	Luck's

Die Loreley: Prelude <1863>   7'

2 2 2 2 — 4 2 3 0 — tmp — hp — str
Adapted by George Dasch. There is what appears to be a keyboard
reduction at the bottom of the score, though not identified as such.

Kistner&Siegel	Luck's

Romance, op.85, F major <1911>   9'

solo viola
1 1 2 2 — 3 2 0 0 — tmp — str

Kalmus	Luck's

Scottish Fantasy, op.46 (Schottische Fantasie) <1880> *30'*

solo violin
2 2 2 2 — 4 2 3 1 — tmp+2 — hp — str
perc: bd, cym

Prelude: Grave & I. Adagio cantabile	9'	
II. Allegro	6'	
III. Andante sostenuto	6'	
IV. Finale: Allegro guerriero	9'	

Kalmus	Luck's	Simrock

Seeräuberlied, op.68, no.1 (Song of the Pirates) <1896> *6'*

male chorus (TTBB)
2[1.pic] 2 2 2 — 4 2 3 0 — tmp+2 — str
perc: cym, tri

Kalmus	Luck's	Simrock

Serenade, op.75, A minor <1900> *41'*

solo violin
2 2 2 2 — 4 2 3 0 — tmp — str

Andante con moto	10'	
Allegro moderato	10'	
Notturno: Andante sostenuto	11'	
Allegro energico	10'	

Kalmus	Luck's	Simrock

Swedish Dances, op.63, nos.1-7 (Series 1) <1890> *12'*

2[1.2/pic] 2[1.2/Eh] 2 2 — 4 2 3 0 — tmp+1 — str
perc: tri

Kalmus	Lengnick	Luck's	Simrock

Swedish Dances, op.63, nos.8-15 (Series 2) <1890> *11'*

2 2[1.2/Eh] 2 2 — 4 2 3 1 — tmp+1 — str
perc: tri

Kalmus	Lengnick	Luck's	Simrock

Symphony No.1, op.28, E-flat major <1870> *29'*

2 2 2 2 — 4 2 3 0 — tmp — str

Allegro maestoso	10'
Scherzo	5'
Grave	6'
Finale	8'

Kalmus

Symphony No.2, op.36, F minor <1870> *37'*

2 2 2 2 — 4 2 3 0 — tmp — str

Allegro passionato, ma un poco maestoso	12'
Adagio ma non troppo	13'
Allegro molto tranquillo	12'

Breitkopf	Kalmus	Simrock

Symphony No.3, op.51, E major <1870> *36'*

2 2 2 2 — 4 3 3 1 — tmp — str

Andante sostenuto	12'
Adagio	11'
Scherzo	7'
Finale: Allegro ma non troppo	6'

Breitkopf	Kalmus

Bruckner, Anton

1824-1896

(b Ansfelden, nr Linz, 4 Sept 1824; d Vienna, 11 Oct 1896). Austrian

WAB = R. Grasberger: *Werkverzeichnis Anton Bruckner* (Tutzing, 1977)
As the present book goes to press, a new "scholarly-practical performing edition" of the complete works of Bruckner has been announced, under the general editorship of Benjamin-Gunnar Cohrs, and puiblished by Verlagsgruppe Hermann. A prospectus may be seen at: www.harrassowitz.de/music_services/documents/AntonBrucknerUrtextCompleteEdition.pdf.
As always with Bruckner, nothing is simple. The Cohrs edition will apparently be in competition with a new MWV complete edition, announced only a few years ago.
Some Bruckner autograph manuscripts may be viewed online at www.onb.ac.at. *Search for the desired work by WAB number, and use the* Digitale Ressourcen *tab at the top of the page. The "digital resources" include manuscripts, printed music, correspondence, and recordings.*

Helgoland, WAB 71 <1893> *14'*

male chorus
2 2 2 2 — 4 3 3 1 — tmp+1 — str
perc: cym

Bärenreiter	MWV	Universal

March in D minor. WAB 96 <1862> *4'*

2 2 2 2 — 2 2 3 0 — tmp — str
Published with his *Three Pieces for Orchestra, q.v.* The Eulenburg version uses the collective title *Four Orchestral Pieces*.

Doblinger	Eulenburg

Mass, WAB 25, C major (Windhaag Mass) <1842> *11'*

solo alto   chorus
0 0 0 0 — 2 0 0 0 — org — str

Kalmus

Mass No.1, D minor, WAB 26 <1864; rev 1876, 1881, 1882> *49'*

chorus   solos SATB
2 2 2 2 — 2 2 3 0 — tmp — org — str
Ed. Leopold Novak (1975).

Kyrie	8'
Gloria	7'
Credo	14'
Sanctus	2'
Benedictus	8'
Agnus Dei	10'

Bärenreiter	MWV

Mass No.2, E minor, WAB 27 <1866; rev 1876, 1882> *44'*

chorus
0 2 2 2 — 4 2 3 0 — [no str]
Two versions are available from MWV, both ed. Leopold Novak: original version of 1866, and revised version of 1882.

Kyrie	9'
Gloria	7'
Credo	11'
Sanctus	4'
Benedictus	7'
Agnus Dei	6'

MWV

Mass No.3, F minor, WAB 28 (Great) <1867–1868>   60'

chorus   solos SATB
2 2 2 2 — 2 2 3 0 — tmp — opt org — str
Ed. Leopold Nowak (1960).

Kyrie	*9'*
Gloria	*12'*
Credo	*19'*
Sanctus	*2'*
Benedictus	*7'*
Agnus Dei	*8'*

Bärenreiter	MWV		

Missa solemnis, B-flat minor, WAB 29 <1854>   31'

chorus   solos SATB
0 2 0 2 — 2 2 3 0 — tmp — org — str
Ed. Leopold Nowak (1957).

Kyrie	*3'*
Gloria	*2'*
Qui tollis	*2'*
Tu solus	*3'*
Credo	*2'*
Et incarnatus	*3'*
Et resurrexit	*4'*
Et vitam venturi	*2'*
Sanctus	*2'*
Benedictus	*3'*
Agnus Dei	*3'*
Dona nobis pacem	*2'*

Bärenreiter	MWV		

Overture, G minor, WAB 98 <1862–1863>   12'

2[1.pic] 2 2 2 — 2 2 3 0 — tmp — str
Posthumous.

MWV	Universal	Kalmus	Luck's

Psalm 150, WAB 38 <1892>   9'

solo soprano   chorus
2 2 2 2 — 4 3 3 1 — tmp — str
Edited by Franz Grasberger.

Bärenreiter	MWV		

Requiem, D minor, WAB 39 <1849>   37'

chorus   solos SATB
0 0 0 0 — 1 0 3 0 — org — str
Revised new edition by Rüdiger Bornhöft (1998).

Bärenreiter	MWV		

SYMPHONIES

A description of the numerous versions of Bruckner's two unnumbered and nine numbered symphonies is far beyond the scope of this book. The list here includes the most widely-performed versions, and employs the Cahis numbering system, which helps clarify the chronology of the revisions.

The Anton Bruckner Website, maintained by David Griegel, seems to have disappeared, but a fine site at www.abruckner.com is maintained by John F. Berky. It includes Berky's invaluable Bruckner Symphony Versions Discography and many other features and links.

Most of these compositions are available from MWV in Austria, and from Bärenreiter world-wide. Corrigenda lists may be obtained from MWV; also errors are corrected in subsequent reprints from the publisher.

UNNUMBERED SYMPHONIES   48'

Symphony (Cahis 1, WAB 99) F minor (Studiensymphonie; Study Symphony) <1863>

2 2 2 2 — 4 2 3 0 — tmp — str
Ed. Leopold Nowak, 1973.
   A student work. Occasionally referred to as *Symphony No.00.*

Allegro molto vivace	*18'*
Andante	*13'*
Scherzo: Schnell	*6'*
Finale: Allegro	*11'*

Bärenreiter	MWV	

Symphony (Cahis 3, WAB 100) D minor (Nullte) <1869>   46'

2 2 2 2 — 4 2 3 0 — tmp — str
Ed. Leopold Nowak, 1968.
   This work, composed in 1869, *after* the *Symphony No.1*, was originally designated *Symphony No.2* by the composer, but later changed to unnumbered status. Occasionally referred to as *Symphony No.0.*

Allegro	*15'*
Andante sostenuto	*14'*
Scherzo: Presto	*7'*
Finale: Moderato; Andante	*10'*

Bärenreiter	MWV	

SYMPHONY NO.1, WAB 101   50'

Symphony No.1 (Linz version 1866, Cahis 2) C minor <1866>

3 2 2 2 — 4 2 3 0 — tmp — str
Slightly revised by the composer in 1877. Ed. Robert Haas, 1935; Leopold Nowak, 1953.
   3rd flute in 2nd movement only.

I. Allegro	*13'*
II. Adagio; Andante	*14'*
III. Scherzo: Lebhaft	*9'*
IV. Finale: Bewegt und feurig	*14'*

Bärenreiter	MWV	Kalmus

Symphony No.1 (Vienna version 1891, Cahis 17) C minor <1866; rev 1891>   48'

3 2 2 2 — 4 2 3 0 — tmp — str
Ed. Robert Haas, 1935; Günter Brosche, 1980.
   3rd flute in 2nd movement only.

I. Allegro	*13'*
II. Adagio; Andante	*13'*
III. Scherzo: Lebhaft	*9'*
IV. Finale: Bewegt und feurig	*13'*

Bärenreiter	MWV	Kalmus

SYMPHONY NO.2, WAB 102   68'

Symphony No.2 (1872 version, Cahis 4) C minor <1871–1872>

2 2 2 2 — 4 2 3 0 — tmp — str
Ed. William Carragan.
   The Robert Haas edition of 1938, although labeled "original version," is actually primarily the 1877 version, with elements of 1872 mixed in.

I. Ziemlich schnell	*20'*
II. Adagio: Feierlich; etwas bewegt	*16'*
III. Scherzo: Schnell	*11'*
IV. Finale	*21'*

Bärenreiter	MWV	Kalmus

Symphony No.2 (1877 version, Cahis 8) C minor <1871–1872; rev 1877>   60'

2 2 2 2 — 4 2 3 0 — tmp — str
Ed. Robert Haas, 1938; Leopold Nowak, 1965; William Carragan, 1997.

I. Ziemlich schnell	*18'*
II. Adagio: Feierlich, etwas bewegt	*18'*
III. Scherzo: Schnell	*7'*
IV. Finale	*17'*

Bärenreiter	MWV	

SYMPHONY NO.3, WAB 103   65'
Symphony No.3 (1873 version, Cahis 5) D minor (Wagner-Symphonie) <1872–1873>

2 2 2 2 — 4 3 3 0 — tmp — str
Ed. Leopold Nowak, 1977.

I. Mässig bewegt	*24'*
II. Adagio (etwas bewegt) quasi Andante	*19'*
III. Scherzo: Ziemlich schnell	*6'*
IV. Finale: Allegro	*16'*

Bärenreiter	MWV	

Symphony No.3 (1877 version, Cahis 9) D minor (Wagner-Symphonie) <1872–1873; rev 1877>   61'

2 2 2 2 — 4 3 3 0 — tmp — str
Ed. Fritz Oeser, 1950; Leopold Nowak, 1981.

I. Mässig bewegt	*21'*
II. Adagio (etwas bewegt) quasi Andante	*17'*
III. Scherzo: Ziemlich schnell	*7'*
IV. Finale: Allegro	*16'*

Bärenreiter	MWV	Kalmus

Symphony No.3 (1889 version, Cahis 15) D minor (Wagner-Symphonie) <1872–1873; rev 1889>   57'

2 2 2 2 — 4 3 3 0 — tmp — str
Ed. Leopold Nowak, 1959.

I. Mässig bewegt	*22'*
II. Adagio (etwas bewegt) quasi Andante	*16'*
III. Scherzo: Ziemlich schnell	*7'*
IV. Finale: Allegro	*12'*

Bärenreiter	MWV	

Symphony No.3: Adagio 2 (1876) <1876>   18'

2 2 2 2 — 4 3 3 0 — tmp — str
Ed. Leopold Nowak, 1980.
   An intermediate version of the 2nd movement, later discarded from the 1877 version of Symphony No.3 (Cahis 9).

Bärenreiter	MWV	

SYMPHONY NO.4, WAB 104   70'
Symphony No.4 (1874 version, Cahis 6) E-flat major (Romantic) <1874>

2 2 2 2 — 4 3 3 0 — tmp — str
Ed. Leopold Nowak, 1975.

Bewegt, nicht zu schnell	*20'*
Andante quasi Allegretto	*20'*
Scherzo: Bewegt	*12'*
Finale: Bewegt, doch nicht zu schnell	*18'*

Bärenreiter	MWV	

Symphony No.4 (1878 version, Cahis 10): Finale 1878 (Volksfest) <1874; rev 1878>   17'

2 2 2 2 — 4 3 3 1 — tmp — str
Ed. Leopold Nowak, 1981.
   This finale to the 1878 version of Symphony no.4 (Cahis 10) was later replaced. To perform the complete Cahis 10, use the first three movements of Cahis 11 (next entry) plus this finale.

Bärenreiter	MWV	

Symphony No.4 (1878/80 version, Cahis 11) E-flat major (Romantic) <1874; rev 1880>   70'

2 2 2 2 — 4 3 3 1 — tmp — str
Ed. Leopold Nowak, 1953.
   This edition includes a further revision of the finale, previously thought to be 1886, but which may be as early as 1881. This revision brings back in its final bars the horn motive from the first movement; it is the most frequently performed version of the symphony. (The Robert Haas edition of 1936, reprinted in 1944, does not include this return of the horn call.)

I. Bewegt; nicht zu schnell	*21'*
II. Andante quasi Allegretto	*15'*
III. Scherzo: Bewegt	*11'*
IV. Finale: Bewegt; doch nicht zu schnell	*23'*

Bärenreiter	MWV	Kalmus

Symphony No.4 (1888 version, Cahis Suppl.1/14+) E-flat major <1874; rev 1888>   65'

3[1/pic.2.3] 2 2 2 — 4 3 3 1 — tmp — str
Bruckner is said to have regarded this as his final, definitive version of this symphony. Critical edition by Benjamin Korstvedt, 2005.

1. Bewegt, nicht zu schnell	*17'*
2. Andante quasi allegretto	*18'*
3. Scherzo: Bewegt	*9'*
4. Finale: Bewegt, doch nicht zu schnell	*21'*

MWV

SYMPHONY NO.5, WAB 105   81'
Symphony No.5 (Cahis 7) B-flat major <1875–1876; rev 1877>

2 2 2 2 — 4 3 3 1 — tmp — str
Ed. Robert Haas, 1935; Leopold Nowak, 1951.
   Extra brass is often added at the end of the symphony.

I. Adagio; Allegro; Langsamer	*21'*
II. Adagio - Sehr langsam	*21'*
III. Scherzo: Molto vivace	*14'*
IV. Finale: Adagio; Allegro	*25'*

Bärenreiter	MWV	Kalmus

SYMPHONY NO.6, WAB 106   54'
Symphony No.6 (Cahis 12) A major <1879–1881>

2 2 2 2 — 4 3 3 1 — tmp — str
Ed. Robert Haas, 1935; Leopold Nowak, 1952.

I. Maestoso	*16'*
II. Adagio: Sehr feierlich	*16'*
III. Scherzo: Ruhig bewegt (etwas gemessen)	*9'*
IV. Finale: Bewegt, doch nicht zu schnell	*13'*

Bärenreiter	MWV	Kalmus

SYMPHONY NO.7, WAB 107   64'
Symphony No.7 (Cahis 13) E major <1881–1883>

2 2 2 2 — 4 3 3 1 — 4 Wagner tubas [2tenor, 2bass] — tmp+2 — str
perc: cym, tri
Ed. Robert Haas, 1944; Leopold Nowak, 1954.
   Although 4tp are listed on the first page of the finale, this is an error; there is no 4th tp part. Wagner tubas in mvts 2 & 4 only. The percussion is controversial; it is said to have been added by Joseph Schalk, but it is unclear whether or not the composer approved it.

I. Allegro moderato	*20'*
II. Adagio: Sehr feierlich und sehr langsam	*22'*
III. Scherzo: Sehr schnell	*10'*
IV. Finale: Bewegt, doch nicht schnell	*12'*

Bärenreiter	MWV	Kalmus

Symphony No.7 (Cahis 13) E major (chamber orchestra version) <1881–1883>   64'

0 0 1 0 — 1 0 0 0 — pf[4-hands], harm — str 5t
Arranged by various members of the *Verein für Musikalische Privataufführung*: Hanns Eisler (mvts. 1 & 3), Erwin Stein (mvt. 2), Karl Rankl (mvt. 4). Optional timpani were later added by editor Alan Leighton, but are probably best omitted.

I. Allegro moderato	20'
II. Adagio: Sehr feierlich und sehr langsam	22'
III. Scherzo: Sehr schnell	10'
IV. Finale: Bewegt, doch nicht schnell	12'

> Breitkopf

SYMPHONY NO.8, WAB 108   84'
Symphony No.8 (1887 version, Cahis 14) C minor <1884–1887>

3[1.2.3/pic] 3 3 3[1.2.3/cbn] — 8[5-8/Wag tb] 3 3 1 — tmp+2 — 3hp[1part] — str
perc: cym, tri
Ed. Leopold Nowak, 1972.

I. Allegro moderato	17'
II. Scherzo: Allegro moderato	15'
III. Adagio: Feierlich langsam, doch nicht schleppend	28'
IV. Finale: Feierlich nicht schnell	24'

> Bärenreiter   MWV

Symphony No.8 (1890 version, Cahis 16) C minor <1884–1887; rev 1890>   74'

3 3 3 3[1.2.3/cbn] — 8[5-8/Wag tb] 3 3 1 — tmp+2 — 3hp[1part] — str
perc: cym, tri
There are two editions of Symphony No.8 (1890, Cahis 16) offering differing notions of what revisions to the work the composer truly intended. The Robert Haas edition (1935) is preferred by some conductors and scholars because it includes more music; Haas "restored" certain cuts made by Bruckner on grounds that the composer had been subjected to undue outside influences (principally by Josef Schalk). The Leopold Nowak edition (1955) takes a more pristine view and accepts all Bruckner's cuts as valid.

I. Allegro moderato	15'
II. Scherzo: Allegro moderato	13'
III. Adagio: Feierlich langsam, doch nicht schleppend	24'
IV. Finale: Feierlich nicht schnell	22'

> Bärenreiter   MWV

SYMPHONY NO.9, WAB 109   63'
Symphony No.9 (Cahis 18) D minor <1887–1894>

3 3 3 3 — 8[5-8/Wag tb] 3 3 1 — tmp — str
Ed. Alfred Orel, 1934; Leopold Nowak, 1951; Benjamin-Gunnar Cohrs, 2000.
     See the following entries for the finale, which was left unfinished at the composer's death.
     Also two posthumous trios (1889 & 1893) for the Scherzo, with viola solo, ed. Cohrs, are separately available from Doblinger; the second one, ed. Armin Knab, also available from Bärenreiter.

Feierlich, misterioso	25'
Scherzo: Bewegt, lebhaft	11'
Adagio: Langsam, feierlich	27'

> Bärenreiter   MWV   Kalmus

Symphony No.9: Finale (Documentation of the Fragment) <1887–1896>   36'

speaker
3 3 3 3 — 4 3 3 1 — 4 Wagner tubas — tmp — str
Intended for workshop concerts or pre-concert presentation only. Duration allows 21' for the music and 15' for the interspersed spoken commentary.
Ed. John A. Phillips, 2002.

> Bärenreiter   MWV

Symphony No.9: Finale (Carragan) <1887–1896>   22'

3 3 3 3 — 8[5-8/Wag tb] 3 3 1 — tmp — str
Completion of the finale by William Carragan, based on the composer's sketches.

Symphony No.9: Finale ("SPCM" version) <1887–1896>   25'

3 3 3 3 — 4 3 3 1 — 4Wagner tubas — tmp — str
Completed performing version by Nicola Samale, John A. Phillips, Benjamin-Gunnar Cohrs & Giuseppe Mazzuca (SPCM); new edition by Samale & Cohrs, 2004.

> Artium

Te Deum, WAB 45 <1881–1884>   24'

chorus   solos SATB
2 2 2 2 — 4 3 3 1 — tmp — opt org — str
Ed. Leopold Nowak.

I. Te Deum laudamus	6'
II. Te ergo quaesumus	3'
III. Aeterna fac cum sanctis tuis	2'
IV. Salvum fac populum tuum	7'
V. In te Domine, speravi	6'

> Bärenreiter   MWV   Kalmus

Three Pieces for Orchestra, WAB 97 <1862>   8'

2 2 2 2 — 2 2 1 0 — tmp — str
Published with his *March in D minor, q.v.* The Eulenberg edition gives the collective title *Four Orchestral Pieces*.

> Doblinger   Eulenberg

Brüll, Ignaz   1846-1907

(b Prossnitz [now Prostějov], 7 Nov 1846; d Vienna, 17 Sept 1907). Austrian

Concerto, Piano, No.1, op.10, F major   27'

2 2 2 2 — 4 2 0 0 — tmp — str

1. Allegro moderato	14'
2. Andante: Molto espressive	5'
3. Finale: Presto	8'

> Boosey   Fleisher

Serenade No.2, op.36, E major   15'

3 2 2 2 — 3 2 0 0 — tmp — str

I. Allegro vivace	_'
II. Marcia	
III. Allegro moderato	_'

> Fleisher   Kalmus   Schott

Bryant, Curtis   1949-

(b Atlanta, GA, 1949). American

Dinosaurs; A Primeval Symphony <1991>   17'

narrator
2[1.2/pic] 2[1.2/Eh] 2 2 — 2 2 1 1 — tmp+2 — hp — cel — str
perc: bd, cym, sus cym, tambn, tamtam, glock, xyl

1. Ultimate Tangle	4'
2. Plated March	3'
3. Pterrible Flight	4'
4. Duckbilled Ragtime	3'
5. Tyrannical Tarantelle	3'

> Bryant

Buck, Dudley

1839-1909

(b Hartford, CT, 10 March 1839; d West Orange, NJ, 6 Oct 1909). American

Festival Overture on the American National Air (The Star Spangled Banner) <c.1879>

7'

optional chorus
3[1.2.pic] 2 2 2 — 4 3 3 1 — tmp+3 — str
perc: sd, cym, bd
Ends with the singing of *The Star Spangled Banner* by audience or chorus.

> Fleisher

Buhr, Glenn

1954-

(b Winnipeg, 18 Dec 1954). Canadian

Akasha (Sky) <1989>

4'

2[1.pic] 0 2 0 — 2 1 1 0 — 1perc — str

> Counterpoint

Chant of Water and Sky <2007>

4'

str

> Counterpoint

Chant of Wind and Thunder <2007>

4'

str
perc: Several tamtam notes, played by conductor.

> Counterpoint

Concerto, Bassoon, No.2 <2010>

1 1 0 0 — 2 0 0 0 — gtr — hpsd — str
perc: bd, tri, musical saw, bd/ped[played by bn soloist]
"A Melodrama in 3 Acts for Solo Bassoon and Baroque Orchestra."
Act 1: La Commedia   _'
Act 2: and man will only grieve if he believes the sun stands still   _'
Act 3: Joyful Noise   _'

> Counterpoint

The Cycle of Spring <1988>

25'

solo soprano   chorus
1 2[ob.Eh] 0 1 — 0 1 1[btbn] 0 — 2perc — hp — hpsd/pf/cel — str
NIMESHA (the closing of the eyelids)   _'
ACHARYA (the master)   _'
AVIRAVIRMAYEDHI (O self-revealing one reveal thyself in me) _'
ANANDA (joy)   _'

> Counterpoint

Red Sea (Song of the Earth) <2010>

22'

mezzo-soprano solo
1[fl/pic] 1[ob/Eh] 1[cl/bcl] 1 — 1 0 0 0 — tmp+2 — pf — str
Prologue (Hammer Blows)   _'
1. Eye-dropper   _'
2. White Sea Birds   _'
3. Wilderness of Mirrors   _'
Epilogue   _'

> Counterpoint

… this is the murmur of yearning <2009>

3'

2[fl.pic] 0 0 0 — 1perc — 22 solo str[6.6.4.4.2]
perc: vib, crot

> Counterpoint

winter poems <1994>

25'

3[1.2/pic.3/pic] 3[1.2.3/Eh] 3[1.2.3/Ebcl] 3[1.2.cbn] — 4 3 3 1 —
tmp+3 — hp — pf — str
perc: marim, vib, crot, chimes, xyl, sus cym, glock
Individual movements may be performed separately.
1. Tranquillo   10'
2. Vivo   6'
3. Calmando   9'

> Counterpoint

Burge, John

1961-

(b Dryden, ON, 2 Jan 1961). Canadian

The Canadian Shield <2001>

12'

3[1.2/pic.3] 3[1.2.Eh] 4[1.2.Ebcl.bcl] 3[1.2.cbn] — 4 3 3 1 — tmp+6
— str
perc: glock, chimes, tri, tamtam, sd, bd, cym, 2sus cym, tomtom;
optional: td, 2tomtom, 2pair cym
A number of instruments are optional; may be performed with:
2[1.2/pic] 2 2 2 — 4 2 3 1 — tmp+3 — str

> CMC

Snowdrift <1996>

13'

2 2 2 2 — 4 2 3 1 — tmp+2 — str
perc: tri, tamtam, glock, vib, windchimes[assorted non-wood], 2sus cym

> CMC

Burgess, Anthony

1917-1993

(b Manchester, 25 Feb 1917; d London, 22 Nov 1993). English writer & composer

Concerto, Piano, E-flat <1976>

34'

3[1.2.pic] 3[1.2.Eh] 2 2 — 4 3 3 1 — tmp+3 — str
perc: bd, cym, sus cym, sd, tambn, templeblks, xyl, cast
I. Molto moderato; Allegro giocoso   15'
II. Andantino semplicissimo   6'
III. Presto con fuoco   13'

> Barnard

A Manchester Overture <1989>

12'

3[1.2.3/pic] 3[1.2.Eh] 3[1.2.bcl] 3[1.2.cbn] — 4 3 3 1 — tmp+3 —
2hp — str
perc: bd, cym, sd, glock, xyl

> Barnard

Mr W.S. <1979>

35'

2[1.2/pic] 3[1.2.Eh] 2 2 — 4 3 3 1 — tmp+3 — hp — str
perc: bd, cym, sus cym, sd, tambn, gong, glock, xyl, chimes, whip, cast, tabor
Ob1 doubles optional shawm.
Ballet on the life of William Shakespeare.
I. Prelude nel modo di una toccata   6'
II. Sarabande   2'
III. Galliard   1'
IV. Allegretto   3'
V. Quodlibet   4'
VI. Lento   4'
VII. Allegro spiritoso   5'
VIII. Lento   3'
IX. March: Non sanz droict   7'

> Barnard

116

Symphony No.3 <1974–1975>   35'

solo tenor & baritone (4th mvt)

2[1/pic.2/pic] 2[1.Eh] 2 2 — 4 3[1/opt crt.2.3] 3 1 — mand — tmp+3 — hp — pf/cel — str

perc: bd, cym, sus cym, sd, tambn, xyl, woodblk, tabor

Cel can be covered by perc in 1st mvt and by pianist elsewhere.

I. Andantino; Allegro	11'
II. Allegro molto giocoso	3'
III. Andante lugubre	6'
IV. Allegro con spirito ed un po' di malizia	15'

Barnard

Busoni, Ferruccio   1866-1924

(b Empoli, 1 April 1866; d Berlin, 27 July 1924). Italian composer, active chiefly in Austria and Germany

K = J. Kindermann: *Thematisch-chronologisches Verzeichnis der Werke von Ferruccio Busoni* (Regensburg, 1980)

Berceuse élégiaque, op.42, K.252a (Elegie No.1: Des Mannes Wiegenlied am Sarge seiner Mutter) <1909>   10'

3 1 3[1.2.bcl] 0 — 4 0 0 0 — 1perc — hp — cel — str[3vn, 3va, 3vc, 2db]

perc: gong

Breitkopf	Kalmus	Luck's

Die Brautwahl, K.258: Suite, op.45 <1908–1911; rev 1912>   33'

3[1/pic.2/pic.3/pic] 3[1.2.3/Eh] 3[1.2.3/bcl] 3[1.2.3/cbn] — 4 3 3 1 — tmp+3 — hp — cel — str

perc: tamtam, xyl, glock, sd, tri, tambn, cym, sus cym, bd, kybd glock

I. Spukhaftes Stück (Ghostly Music)	4'
II. Lyrisches Stück (Lyrical Music)	10'
III. Mystisches Stück (Mystic Music)	7'
IV. Hebräisches Stück (Hebrew Music)	8'
V. Heiteres Stück (Joyful Music)	4'

Breitkopf

Concertino, Clarinet & Chamber Orchestra, op.48, K.276 <1919>   11'

0 2 0 2 — 2 0 0 0 — 1perc — str

perc: tri

Breitkopf	Kalmus	Luck's

Concerto, Piano, op.39, K.247 <1903–1904>   64'

4[1.2.3/pic.pic] 3[1.2.3/Eh] 3[1.2.3/bcl(A)] 3 — 4 3 3 1 — tmp+3 — str

perc: glock, tri, tamtam, tambn, bd, sd, cym

Optional unseen male chorus of 48 voices in final movement.

Bcl in A, and notated in bass clef. Cl 1 & 2 are in C in mvt 4.

Prologo e Introito	12'
Pezzo giocoso	8'
Pezzo serioso	23'
All'Italiana	12'
Cantico	9'

Breitkopf	Luck's

Divertimento, Flute & Chamber Orchestra, op.52, K.285 <1920>   8'

0 2 2 2 — 2 2 0 0 — tmp+1 — str

perc: tri

Breitkopf	Kalmus	Luck's

Indianische Fantasie, op.44, K.264 (Indian Fantasy) <1913>   28'

solo piano

2[1.2/pic] 2[1.2/Eh] 2 2 — 3 2 0 0 — tmp+3 — hp — str

perc: tri, tamtam, glock, cym, bd, sd

Breitkopf	Kalmus	Luck's

Lustspiel Overture, op.38, K.245 (Comedy Overture) <1897>   8'

3[1.2.pic] 2 2 2 — 4 2 0 0 — tmp+2 — str

perc: tri, cym

Breitkopf	Kalmus	Luck's

Nocturne symphonique, op.43, K.262 <1913>   9'

3 2[1.Eh] 3[1.2.bcl] 3[1.2.cbn] — 3 0 0 0 — tmp+2 — hp — cel — str[12.10.8.8.6]

perc: bd, cym, tamtam

Breitkopf	Kalmus	Luck's

Rondò arlecchinesco, op.46, K.266 (Harlekins Reigen; Harlequin's Round-Dance) <1915>   12'

tenor voice backstage

2[1/pic.2] 1 2 2 — 3 2 3 0 — tmp+3 — str

perc: tri, tambn, glock, cym, sd

Breitkopf	Kalmus	Luck's

Sarabande & Cortège; 2 Studies for *Doktor Faust*, op.51, K.282 (Elegien Nos.5-6) <1918–1919>   19'

3[1.2.3/pic] 4[1.2.Eh1.Eh2] 3[1.2.bcl] 3[1.2.cbn] — 4 3 3 1 — tmp+3 — str

perc: bd, cym, tri, tamtam

Breitkopf	Kalmus	Luck's

Turandot, op.41, K.248: Suite <1904>   37'

3[1.2/pic.3/pic] 3[1.2.3/Eh] 3[1.2.3/bcl] 3[1.2.3/cbn] — 4 4 3 1 — tmp+4 — 2hp — str

perc: sd, td, tambn, tamtam, glock, tri, cym, bd, 2nd tmp

Optional women's chorus in one movement. 2nd harp used only in mvt 5 where much of the part doubles 1st harp.

1. Die Hinrichtung, Das Stadttor, Der Abschied	4'
2. Truffaldino (Introduzione e marcia grotesca)	3'
3. Altoum, Marsch	4'
4. "Turandot" Marsch	7'
5. Das Frauengemach	2'
6. Tanz und Gesang	5'
7. "Nächtlicher Walzer"	3'
8. "In modo di Marcia funebre" e "Finale alla Turca"	9'

Breitkopf	Kalmus

Turandot, op.41, K.248: Verzweiflung und Ergebung (Despair and Resignation) <1911>   5'

4[1.2.3.pic] 3 3 3[1.2.3/cbn] — 4 4 3 1 — offstage: 4tp, sd, cym — tmp+1 — str

perc: cym, sus cym

An addendum to the *Turandot Suite* (previous entry); if used, this work should be inserted between mvts 7 and 8 of the Suite.

Offstage banda in two brief passages: 4tp [in unison, which may be strengthened ("beliebig verstärkt")], sd, cym.

Breitkopf

Butler, Martin   1960-

(b Romsey, 1 March 1960). English

Fixed Doubles <1989>   8'
3[1.2.pic] 3 3[1.2.3/bcl] 3[1.2.3/cbn] — 4 3 3 1 — tmp+3 — hp — pf/cel — str
perc: bd, 3sus cym, sd, tambn, glock, xyl, woodblk, whip, marac

| Oxford |

Butterworth, George   1885-1916

(b London, 12 July 1885; d Pozieres, 5 Aug 1916). English

The Banks of Green Willow <1913>   7'
2 2 2 2 — 2 1 0 0 — hp — str

| Kalmus | Luck's | Stainer |

A Shropshire Lad; Rhapsody for Orchestra <1912>   11'
2 3[1.2.Eh] 3[1.2.bcl] 2 — 4 2 3 1 — tmp — hp — str

| Eulenburg | Kalmus | Luck's |

Two English Idylls <1911>   10'
3[1.2.pic] 2 2 2 — 4 0 0 0 — tmp+1 — hp — str
perc: tri
"Founded on folk-tunes."
  I. Allegro scherzando   _'
  II. Adagio non troppo   _'

| Kalmus | Luck's | Stainer |

Buxtehude, Dietrich   ca.1637-1707

(b ?Helsingborg, c1637; d Lubeck, 9 May 1707). German

BuxWV = *Thematisch-systematisches Verzeichnis der musikalischen Werke von Dietrich Buxtehude: Buxtehude-Werke-Verzeichnis*, ed. G. Karstädt (Wiesbaden, 1974, 2/1985)

| |

Chaconne, BuxWV 160, E minor   7'
4[2fl, 2pic] 3[1.2.Eh] 4[1.2.3.bcl] 3[1.2.cbn] — 4 4 3 1 — tmp — str
Originally for organ; orchestrated by Carlos Chávez, 1937. Score, but no parts, on sale from Kalmus. Chávez also made a version for smaller orchestra: 2 1 1 2 — 2 2 2 0 — str

| EMI |

Four Chorale Preludes <1690>   20'
2[1.2/pic] 2[1.2/Eh] 2 2 — 3 3 3 1 — str
Arr. Gordon Binkerd.
  Gelobet seist du, Jesu Christ   7'
  Puer natus in Bethlehem   3'
  Nun komm der Heiden Heiland   4'
  Wie schön leuchtet der Morgenstern   6'

| AMP |

Magnificat, BuxWV Anh.1   14'
chorus
cnt — str
Attribution to Buxtehude is doubtful.

| Kalmus | Luck's | Presser |

C

Cadman, Charles Wakefield   1881-1946

(b Johnstown, PA, 24 Dec 1881; d Los Angeles, 30 Dec 1946). American

American Suite <1936>   10'
str
  I. Indian   3'
  II. Negro   4'
  III. Old Fiddler   3'

| Luck's |

Oriental Rhapsody from Omar Khayyam <1921>   9'
3[1.2.pic] 2 2 — 4 2 3 1 — tmp+2 — hp — str

| Fleisher |

Cage, John   1912-1992

(b Los Angeles, 5 Sept 1912; d New York, 12 Aug 1992). American

Atlas eclipticalis <1961>   var
3 3 3 3 — 5 3 3 3 — 3tmp+9 — 3hp — str[12.12.9.9.3]
The instrumentation given is the maximum, but not all instruments need be used. The work may be played in whole or in part by any ensemble, chamber or orchestral. Duration is variable.

| Peters |

Suite for Toy Piano (Orchestra Version by Lou Harrison) <1948>   8'
3[1.2.3/pic] 3[1.2.3/Eh] 3 3[1.2.cbn] — 4 3 4 0 — tmp+3 — hp — str

| Peters |

Caltabiano, Ronald   1959-

(b New York City, 7 Dec 1959). American

Concertini <1991>   20'
1[fl/pic] 1 1[cl/Ebcl] 1 — 2 1 1 0 — 1perc — str[min 10.8.7.5.4]
  I. Allegro molto   1'
  II. Andante piacevole   3'
  III. Allegro molto   1'
  IV. Andante moderato   3'
  V. Andante; Presto   3'
  VI. Andante   3'
  VII. Andante; Presto   2'
  VIII. Allegro molto   1'
  IX. Adagio sustenuto   3'
  X. Allegro   2'

| Merion |

Cannabich, Christian   1731-1798

(b Mannheim, bap. 12 Dec 1731; d Frankfurt, 20 Jan 1798). German

Concerto, Violin, B-flat major

See: Haydn, Franz Joseph
       Concerto, Violin, Hob.VIIa:B2, B-flat major

Canning, Thomas   1911-1989

(b Brookville, PA, 12 Dec 1911; d 4 Oct 1989). American

Fantasy on a Hymn by Justin Morgan   10'

2 solo string quartets
str

Heugel

Canteloube, Joseph   1879-1957

(b Annonay, 21 Oct 1879; d Paris, 4 Nov 1957). French

CHANTS D'AUVERGNE, 1st series   2'

1. La pastoura al camps (La bergère aux champs) <1923>

medium voice
3[1.2.pic] 2 2 2 — 2 0 0 0 — pf — str
Text in Provençal with French translation.

Heugel

2. Baïlèro (Chante de berger de Haute-Auvergne) <1923>   7'

medium voice
3[1.2.pic] 1 2 2 — 2 1 0 0 — tmp — pf — str
Text in Provençal with French translation.

Heugel

3. Trois bourrées <1923>   6'

medium voice
3[1.2.pic] 1 2 2 — 2 1 0 0 — tmp+1 — pf — str
perc: tambn
Text in Provençal with French translation.
     Cadenzas for oboe & clarinet, respectively, link the 3 movements.
     a. L'aïo dé rotso (L'eau de source)   1'
     b. Ound' onorèn gorda? (Où irons-nous garder?)   3'
     c. Obal din lou Limouzi (Là-bas dans le Limousin)   2'

Heugel

CHANTS D'AUVERGNE, 2nd series   5'

1. Pastourelle—E passo dédossaï (Ah! viens près de moi) <1923>

medium voice
2 1[Eh] 2 2 — 2 1 0 0 — tmp — pf — str
Text in Provençal with French translation.

Heugel

2. L'Antouèno (L'Antoine) <1923>   3'

medium voice
4[2fl, 2pic] 3[1.2.Eh] 2 2 — 2 2 0 0 — tmp — pf — str
Text in Provençal with French translation.

Heugel

3. La pastrouletta è lou chibalié (La bergère et le cavalier) <1923>   3'

medium voice
3[1.2.pic] 1 2 2 — 2 0 0 0 — pf — str
Text in Provençal with French translation.

Heugel

4. La délaïssádo (La délaissée) <1923>   5'

medium voice
2 2[1.Eh] 2 2 — 2 1 0 0 — tmp — pf — str
Text in Provençal with French translation.

Heugel

5. Bourées <1923>   5'

medium voice
3[1.2.pic] 3[1.2.Eh] 2 2 — 2 2 0 0 — tmp+1 — pf — str
perc: tambn
Text in Provençal with French translation.
     Clarinet cadenza serves as link between the two movements.
     a. N'aï pas ièu dè mil (Je n'ai pas d'amie)   _'
     b. Lo calhé (La caille)   _'

Heugel

CHANTS D'AUVERGNE, 3rd series   3'

1. Lo fiolairé (La fileuse) <1927>

medium voice
2[1.pic] 0 2 2 — 1 1 0 0 — tmp — pf — str
Text in Provençal with French translation.
     Trumpet has one single note.

Heugel

2. Passo pel prat (Viens par le pré) <1927>   4'

medium voice
2[1.pic] 1 2 2 — 2 1 0 0 — tmp+1 — pf — str
perc: sus cym
Text in Provençal with French translation.

Heugel

3. Lou boussu (Le bossu) <1927>   3'

medium voice
2[1.pic] 1 2 2 — 2 1 0 0 — tmp+2 — pf — str
perc: bd, cym, sus cym
Text in Provençal with French translation.

Heugel

4. Brezairola (Berceuse) <1927>   4'

medium voice
1 1 2 2 — 2 1 0 0 — pf — str
Text in Provençal with French translation.

Heugel

5. Malurous qu'o uno fenno (Malheureux qui à une femme) <1927>   2'

medium voice
2[1.pic] 2 2 — 2 1 0 0 — tmp+3 — pf — str
perc: bd, cym, slgh-bells
Text in Provençal with French translation.

Heugel

CHANTS D'AUVERGNE, 4th series   3'
1. Jou l'pount d'o Mirabel (Au pont de Mirabel) <1930>

medium voice
2 2[1.Eh] 2 2 — 2 2 0 0 — tmp+1 — pf — str
perc: sus cym (can be covered by tmp)
Text in Provençal with French translation.

> Heugel

2. Oï ayaï (Oh! yayaï) <1930>   4'

medium voice
1 1 2 2 — 2 1 0 0 — tmp+1 — pf — str
perc: cym
Text in Provençal with French translation.

> Heugel

3. Pour l'enfant (Soun, soun minou minauno) <1930>   2'

medium voice
1 1 1 1 — 2 2 0 0 — pf — str
Text in Provençal with French translation.

> Heugel

4. Chut, chut <1930>   3'

medium voice
2[1.pic] 1 2 2 — 2 1 0 0 — pf — str
Text in Provençal with French translation.

> Heugel

5. Pastorale (Baïlèro, lero lero) <1930>   2'

medium voice
2[1.pic] 2[1.Eh] 2 2 — 2 1 0 0 — tmp+1 — pf — str
perc: sus cym (can be covered by tmp)
Text in Provençal with French translation.

> Heugel

6. Lou coucut (Le coucou) <1930>   2'

medium voice
3[1.2.pic] 2 2 2 — 2 2 0 0 — tmp+1 — pf — str
perc: bd, sus cym
Text in Provençal with French translation.

> Heugel

CHANTS D'AUVERGNE, 5th series   4'
1. Obal, din lo coumbèlo (Au loin, là-bas dan la vallée) <1954>

medium voice
2 1 1 1 — 1 1 0 0 — tmp+1 — hp — cel — str
perc: sus cym
Text in Provençal with French translation.

> Heugel

2. Quand z'eyro petitoune (Lorsque j'étais petite) <1954>   6'

medium voice
1 1 1 1 — 1 1 0 0 — tmp+1 — hp — str
perc: vib, sus cym
Text in Provençal with French translation.

> Heugel

3. Là-haut, sur le rocher (Chanson de Haute Aubergne) <1954>   3'

medium voice
1 1 1 1 — 1 1 0 0 — tmp — hp — cel — str
French text only.

> Heugel

4. Hé! Beyla-z-y dau fé (Hé! Donnez-lui du foin) <1954>   2'

medium voice
2[1.pic] 1 1 1 — 1 1 0 0 — tmp+1 — hp — str
perc: sus cym, slgh-bells
Text in Provençal with French translation.

> Heugel

5. Pastouro, sé tu m'aymo (Bergère, si tu m'aimes) <1954>   3'

medium voice
1 1 1 1 — 1 1 0 0 — tmp+1 — hp — str
perc: sus cym (can be played by tmp)
Text in Provençal with French translation.

> Heugel

6. Tè l'co, tè! (Va, l'chien, va!) <1954>   1'

medium voice
1 1 1 1 — 1 1 0 0 — tmp+1 — hp — str
perc: sus cym (can be played by tmp)
Text in Provençal with French translation.

> Heugel

7. Uno jionto pastouro (Une jolie bergère) <1954>   2'

medium voice
1 1 1 1 — 1 1 0 0 — 1perc — hp — str
perc: vib
Text in Provençal with French translation.

> Heugel

8. Lou diziou bé (On disait bien) <1954>   1'

medium voice
2[1.pic] 1 1 1 — 1 1 0 0 — tmp+1 — hp — str
perc: sus cym, slgh-bells
Text in Provençal with French translation.

> Heugel

Capuzzi, Giuseppe Antonio   1755-1818

(b Breno, Brescia, 1 Aug 1755; d Bergamo, 28 March 1818). Italian

Concerto, Double Bass & Strings (Ludwin)   12'

str
Original in D major for a 6-stringed violone; transcribed and arranged by
Norman Ludwin. Available in F or G, depending on the tuning used by
the soloist.
Allegro moderato   5'
Andante cantabile   3'
Rondo: Allegro   4'

> Ludwin

Concerto, Double Bass & Orchestra (Schaffner)   12'

2 2 2 1 — 2 2[opt] 0 0 — opt tmp — str
Original in D major for a 6-stringed violone.
  ECS version transcribed and arranged by Steven L. Schaffner in F
major—the key in which many bassists learn this work.
Allegro moderato   5'
Andante cantabile   3'
Rondo: Allegro   4'

> ECS

Carpenter, John Alden   1876-1951

(b Park Ridge, IL, 28 Feb 1876; d Chicago, 26 April 1951). American

Adventures in a Perambulator <1914; rev 1941>   27'

3[1.2.3/pic] 3[1.2.Eh] 3[1.2.bcl] 2 — 4 2 3 1 — tmp+3 — hp — cel, pf — str

perc: bd, cym, sus cym, sd, tri, glock, xyl, chimes, [tambn & opt 2xyl in original version only]

Kalmus and Luck's publish the original version, dated 1917; their listed duration of 14' is an error. Schirmer rents the 1941 version (durations as listed herewith).

1. En voiture!	3'
2. The Policeman	4'
3. The Hurdy-Gurdy	4'
4. The Lake	4'
5. Dogs	4'
6. Dreams	8'

Kalmus	Luck's	Schirmer

Concerto, Violin <1936>   20'

2[1.2/pic] 2[1.2/Eh] 2 2 — 4 3 3 1 — tmp+2 — hp — pf, cel — str

perc: bd, cym, sd, glock, vib, gong, chimes, tomtom, cast, sus cym

Schirmer

Sea Drift <1933; rev 1944>   17'

2 2[1.2/Eh] 2 2 — 4 3 3 1 — tmp+2 — hp — cel, pf — str

perc: bd, cym, glock, gong, vib, chimes

Schirmer

Skyscrapers <1924>   28'

optional chorus (6tenors, 6sopranos)

3[1.2.3/pic] 3[1.2.3/Eh] 3[1.2.3/bcl] 3[1.2.3/cbn] — 4 4 3 1 — 3sx[ssx/asx.asx/tsx.tsx/bsx] — banjo — tmp+5 — pf, pf/cel — str[min 6.6.4.4.4]

perc: xyl, cym, bd, sd, tambn, glock, gong, tamtam, woodblk, thunder, chimes, sus cym, tomtom, 3anvils, fac whstle

2 traffic lights, downstage right & left, for which the exact rhythm and duration are notated in the score; they are intended to be "played" by a keyboard offstage.

Score is poorly engraved and with confusing errors and inconsistencies:
• "Cylinder bells" are apparently chimes, abbreviated "Bells," "Cy.B," and "C-bells.""
• Glockenspiel is variously abbreviated "G.S." or "Gl."
Duration with authorized concert cuts: 15'

Schirmer

Carter, Elliott   1908-2012

(b New York, 11 Dec 1908; d New York, 5 Nov 2012). American

Adagio tenebroso <1995>   20'

3[1.2/pic.3/pic] 3[1.2.Eh] 3[1.2/Ebcl.bcl] 3[1.2.cbn] — 4 3 3 1 — tmp+4 — pf — str

perc: bd, glock, templeblks, cowbell, vib, woodblk, sd, xyl, tamtam, marim, 4bongos, 2sus cym, 2tomtoms, wood dr, 2metal blocks

Boosey

Concerto for Orchestra <1969>   20'

3[1.2/pic.3/pic] 3[1.2.3/Eh] 3[1.2/bcl.3/Ebcl] 3[1.2.3/cbn] — 4 3[1.2.3/pic tp] 3 1 — tmp+7 — hp — pf — str[9.8.6.6.5; min 7.6.5.4.3]

perc: glock, gong, tamtam, cym, cast, marim, xyl, tambn, marac, whip, vib, bd, 2tri, 4sus cym, 3sd, 2cowbells, anvil, 2ratch, 3woodblks, 2td (1 played by tmp)

I. Allegro non troppo	5'
II. Presto volando	4'
III. Maestoso	6'
IV. Allegro agitato	5'

AMP

Concerto, Oboe <1986–1987>   20'

1[1/afl/pic] 0 1[1/bcl] 0 — 1 0 1 0 — 2perc — str

perc: glock, templeblks, marim, xyl, bd, tamtam, guiro, field dr, tmp, 2metalblks, 2woodblks, 2cowbells, 4bongos, 2tomtoms, 3sus cym, 2sd, 2vib

The solo oboe, 1 of the percussionists, and 4 of the violas form a concertino.

Boosey

Concerto, Piano <1964–1965>   26'

concertino: pf, fl, Eh, bcl, vn, va, vc, db

2[1/pic.2/pic] 2 2 3[incl cbn] — 4 3 3 1 — 2tmp — str[min 14.12.10.8.6; max 20.18.14.14.10]

AMP

Concerto, Violin <1990>   26'

3[1.2/pic.pic] 3[1.2.Eh] 3[1.2/Ebcl/bcl.bcl] 3[1.2.cbn] — 4 3 3 1 — 2perc — str[either 16.14.12.10.8 or 14.12.10.8.6]

perc: glock, crot, vib, tamtam, bd, tmp, 2sus cym, 2sd

1. Impulsivo	9'
2. Tranquillo/Angosciato	9'
3. Scherzando	8'

Boosey

Double Concerto, Harpsichord & Piano <1961>   23'

1[1/pic] 1 1[1/Ebcl] 1 — 2 1 1 0 — 4perc — vn, va, vc, db.

perc: crot, gong, claves, guiro, marac, whip, templeblks, 2field dr, 4sd, 5sus cym, 2tambn, 2tomtoms, 2tamtams, 2cowbells, 2bd, anvil, 4bongos, 2tri

Two conductors are recommended.

Introduction	4'
Cadenza for Harpsichord	2'
Allegro scherzando	5'
Adagio	5'
Presto	1'
Cadenzas for Piano	3'
Coda	3'

AMP

Elegy for String Orchestra <1952>   5'

str

Originally for viola & piano.

Peer	Luck's

The Harmony of Morning <1944>   9'

female chorus SSAA

1 1 1 1 — 1 0 0 0 — pf — str

AMP

Holiday Overture <1944>   10'

3[1.2.pic] 3[1.2.Eh] 3[1.2.bcl] 3[1.2.cbn] — 4 3 3 1 — tmp+4 — pf — str

perc: sd, tri, whip, cym, bd, tamtam

AMP

In Sleep, In Thunder <1981>   21'

solo tenor

1[1/pic/afl] 1[1/Eh] 1[1/bcl] 1 — 1 1 1 0 — 1perc — pf — str 5t

perc: vib, marim, woodblk, cowbell, guiro, marac, szl cym, sus cym, sd, td, bd, tamtam, bottle

1. Dolphin	3'
2. Across the Yard	3'
3. La Ignota	4'
4. Dies Irae	3'
5. Careless Night	5'
6. In Genesis	3'

Hendon

The Minotaur: Ballet Suite <1947>   25'

2[1.2/pic] 2[1.2/Eh] 2[1.2/bcl] 2 — 4 2 2[1.btbn] 0 — tmp+3 — pf — str

perc: sd, td, cym, tamtam, bd, tri

1. Overture	_'
2. Pasiphaë	_'
3. Entrance of the Bulls—Bull's Dance with Pasiphaë	_'
4. Ariadne and Theseus	_'
5. The Labyrinth	_'
6. Theseus' Farewell on Entering the Labyrinth	_'
7. Theseus Fights and Kills the Minotaur	_'
8. Ariadne Rewinds Her Thread	_'
9. Theseus and the Greeks Emerge	_'
10. Theseus and the Greeks Prepare to Leave	_'

AMP

A Mirror on Which to Dwell <1975>   16'

solo soprano

1[1/pic/afl] 1[1/Eh] 1[1/Ebcl/bcl] 0 — 1perc — pf — vn, va, vc, db

perc: vib, marim, sd, bd, sus cym, tri, 4 bongos

1. Anaphora	3'
2. Argument	2'
3. Insomnia	3'
4. O Breath	3'
5. Sandpiper	2'
6. View of the Capitol from the Library of Congress	3'

AMP

Partita <1993>   18'

3[1.2/pic.pic] 3[1.2.Eh] 3[1.2/Ebcl.bcl] 3[1.2.cbn] — 4 3 3 1 — tmp+4 — hp — pf — str

perc: templeblks, guiro, sd, bd, glock, vib, xyl, marim, 2metalblks, 2cowbells, 2sus cyms, 2woodblks, wood drum, gavel, 4bongos, 2tomtoms

Boosey

Penthode <1985>   18'

1[1/pic/afl] 1[1/Eh] 2[1/Ebcl.bcl/cbcl] 1 — 1 2 1 1 — 3perc — hp — pf — str 5t

perc: marim, templeblks, vib, crot, tri, guiro, td, gong, tamtam, claves, whip, bd, cowbell, 2woodblks, 2sd, 4sus cym, wood drum, gavel, 4bongos, 3tomtoms

5 groups, each consisting of 4 players: (1) tp, tbn, hp, vn; (2) fl/pic/afl, hn, perc, db; (3) ob/Eh, tuba, vn, vc; (4) cl/Ebclcl, bcl/cbcl, tp, perc; (5) bn, pf, perc, va.

Hendon

Pocahontas: Suite <1939; rev 1960>   20'

3[1.2.3/pic] 2 2 2 — 4 3 3 1 — tmp+4 — hp — pf — str

perc: xyl, cym, gong, whip, sd, slgh-bells, bd, td, gourd rattle, tin rattle, 2 Indian drums, 3tri, 2sus cym

Overture	_'
John Smith and Rolfe Lost in the Virginia Forest	_'
Princess Pocahontas and Her Ladies	_'
Torture of John Smith	_'
Pavane (Farewell of Pocahontas)	_'

AMP

Symphony No.1 <1942; rev 1954>   27'

2[1.2/pic] 2 2[1/Ebcl.2] 2 — 2 2 1 0 — tmp — str

I. Moderately, wistfully	9'
II. Slowly, gravely	11'
III. Vivaciously	7'

AMP

A Symphony of Three Orchestras <1976>   17'

3[1.2.pic] 3[1.2.3/Eh] 3[1.2/bcl.Ebcl] 3[1.2.3/cbn] — 5 3 3 1 — tmp+3 — pf — str[18vn.8va.6vc.5db]

perc: xyl, chimes, marim, vib, tomtom, belltree, tambn, long drum, anvil, 2sus cym, 2sd, 2tamtams

Aggregate divided into 3 groups.

AMP

Syringa <1978>   20'

mezzo-soprano & bass soloists

1[afl] 1[Eh] 1[bcl] 0 — 0 0 1 0 — gtr — 1perc — pf — str 4t[vn.va.vc.db]

perc: marim, vib, bongos, timbales, 2tomtoms

AMP

Three Occasions for Orchestra <1986–1989>   16'

3[1.2/pic2.pic1] 3[1.2.Eh] 3[1.2.bcl] 3[1.2.cbn] — 4 3 3 1 — tmp+2 — pf/cel — str[16.14.12.10.8]

perc: vib, marim, xyl, bd, 3sus cym

1. A Celebration of Some 100 x 150 Notes	3'
2. Remembrance	7'
3. Anniversary	6'

Boosey

Variations for Orchestra <1954–1955>   24'

2[1.2/pic] 2 2 — 4 2 3 1 — tmp+3 — hp — str[min 9.6.6.4.4]

perc: woodblk, tambn, bd, tri, cym, tamtam, 2sus cym, 2sd; tmp plays whip, claves

Introduction: Allegro	_'
Theme: Andante	_'
Variations:	
I. Vivace leggero	_'
II. Pesante	_'
III. Moderato	_'
IV. Ritardando molto	_'
V. Allegro misterioso	_'
VI. Accelerando molto	_'
VII. Andante	_'
VIII. Allegro giocoso	_'
IX. Andante	_'
Finale: Allegro molto	_'

AMP

Casella, Alfredo   1883-1947

(b Turin, 25 July 1883; d Rome, 5 March 1947). Italian

La giara: Symphonic Suite, op.41bis <1924>   22'

opt tenor solo

2[1.2/pic] 2 2[1.bcl] 2 — 4 2 1 0 — str

perc: bd/cym, cast, cym, field dr, slgh-bells, tamtam, tambn, tri, xyl

Prelude	5'
Sicilian Dance	4'
La storia della fanciulla rapita dai pirati	3'
Nela's Dance	1'
Entrance of the Peasants	1'
Toast	1'
General Dance	5'
Finale	2'

Universal

Italia, op.11 <1909>   19'

3[1.2.3/pic] 3[1/Eh.2.3] 4[1.2.Ebcl.bcl] 4[1.2.3.cbn] — 4 4 3 1 — tmp+6 — 2hp — str

perc: bd/cym, cym, sd, tamtam, tambn, tri, bell (G), kybd glock

Kalmus   Universal

Paganiniana, op.65 <1941–1942>   18'

2[1.2/pic] 2[1.Eh] 3[1.2.bcl] 2 — 4 2 1 1 — tmp+2 — str

perc: bd, cym, field dr, tamtam, tambn, xyl

I. Allegro agitato	4'
II. Polaccheta: Allegretto moderato	4'
III. Romanza: Larghetto cantabile; amoroso	5'
IV. Tarantella: Presto molto	5'

Universal

Scarlattiana, op.44 <1926>   26'

solo piano
2 2[1.Eh] 3[1.Ebcl.bcl] 2 — 2 1 1 0 — tmp+1 — str[6.0.4.4.3]
perc: tambn, field dr, cast, tri
After Domenico Scarlatti.
I. Sinfonia	6'
II. Minuetto	6'
III. Capriccio	4'
IV. Pastorale	5'
V. Finale	5'

Universal

Serenata, op.46bis <1927; rev 1930>   22'

2 1 2[1.bcl] 2 — 2 1 1 0 — tmp+1 — str[8.6.4.4.3]
perc: xyl, glock, field dr, tambn, tamtam, bd, cym
Arrangement by the composer of a quintet (orig. cl, bn, tp, vn, vc).
I. Marcia	4'
II. Notturno	6'
III. Gavotta	3'
IV. Cavatina	5'
V. Finale	4'

Universal

Suite à Jean Huré, op.13 <1909–1910>   26'

3 2[1.Eh] 3[1.2.3/Ebcl] 3 — 4 3 0 0 — tmp+5 — hp — cel — str
perc: glock, tri, tambn, sd, bd, cym, tamtam
Middle mvt after the composer's *Sarabande* op.10 for harp (later piano).
1. Overture	8'
2. Sarabande	11'
3. Bourée	7'

Kalmus   Universal

Castelnuovo-Tedesco, Mario   1895-1968

(b Florence, 3 April 1895; d Beverly Hills, CA, 16 March 1968). Italian

Concerto, Guitar [No.1], op.99, D major <1939>   19'

1 1 2 1 — 1 0 0 0 — tmp — str[2.2.2.2.1]
I. Allegretto	6'
II. Andantino alla romanza	7'
III. Ritmico e cavalleresco	6'

Schott

Concerto, Guitar, No.2, op.160, C major (Concerto sereno) <1953>   25'

2[1.2/pic] 1 2 1 — 2 1 0 0 — tmp+3 — str[from 4.4.2.2.1 to 6.6.3.3.2]
perc: sus cym, sd, tri, tambn, chime (B-flat), cast

Schott

Concerto, 2 Guitars, op.201 <1962>   20'

2[1.2/pic] 1 2 1 — 2 1 0 0 — tmp+2 — str
perc: bd, sus cym, sd, tri, marac, cast
I. Un poco moderato e pomposo	7'
II. Andante (ma semplice e quieto)	7'
III. Rondo Mexicano: Molto vivace	6'

Bèrben

Genesis Suite: V. The Flood (Noah's Ark) <1944>   11'

narrator   chorus (SATTBB)
3[1.2.3/pic] 2[1.2/Eh] 3[1.2.3/bcl] 2[1.2/cbn] — 4 3 3 1 — tmp+2 — hp — pf/cel — str
perc: bd, cym, sus cym, sd, tri, tambn, gong, xyl
See the entry for "Nathaniel Shilkret: *Genesis Suite*" for a full description of this collaborative work by 7 composers.
Part I	_'
Part II	_'

Milken

Catán, Daniel   1949-

(b Mexico City, 3 April 1949). Mexican

Caribbean Airs <2007>   20'

solo Latin percussion: marimba, steel drums, & 3 percussion
3[1.2.3/pic] 2 4[1.2.3.4/bcl] 2 — 4 4 3 1 — tmp+1 — hp — pf — str
perc: (orchestral) sus cym, bd, gong, cowbell, shekere
(solo) marimba, steel drums, woodblock, bongos, guiro, maracas, congas, shekere
I. quarter-note = 130-140	_'
II. quarter-note = 110	_'
III. quarter-note = 176	_'

AMP

En un doblez del tiempo (A Fold in Time; Scherzo for Orchestra) <1982>   12'

3[1.2.3pic] 3[1.2.3/Eh] 3[1.2.3/bcl] 3 — 4 3 3 1 — tmp+1 — hp — cel — str
perc: bd, xyl

AMP

Florencia en el Amazonas (Florencia in the Amazon): Suite <1996>   28'

2[1.2/pic] 2 3[1.2.3/bcl] 2 — 3 2 2[1/foghorn.2] 1 — tmp+3 — hp — pf — str
perc: bd, cym, sus cym, sd, tambn, gong, marim, chimes, djembe, steel pan
En el muelle (On the Pier)	4'
Arcadio	4'
La tormenta (The Storm)	4'
Amanecer (Sunrise)	3'
Paula	6'
Aria final de Florencia (Florencia's Farewell)	8'

AMP

Caviani, Ronald Joseph   1931-2004

(b Iron Mountain, MI, 12 Mar 1931; d Iron Mountain, MI, 16 Jan 2004). American

Ondee <1976>   10'

2[1.2/pic] 2 2 2 — 4 3 3 1 — tmp+2 — str

UnivPacific

Chabrier, Emmanuel   1841-1894

(b Ambert, Puy-de-Dome, 18 Jan 1841; d Paris, 13 Sept 1894). French

Bourée fantasque <1891>   5'

3[1.2.pic] 3[1.2.Eh] 2 4 — 4 3 3 1 — tmp+4 — 2hp[1part] — str
perc: sd, tambn, tri, cym, sus cym
Originally for piano; orchd Felix Mottl.
   The composer had started his own orchestration for a smaller instrumentation, but left it incomplete; the fragment has been completed by Robin Holloway, and is available from Boosey:
   2[1.2/pic] 1 2 1 — 2 2 1 0 — tmp+2 — pf — str

Enoch   Kalmus   Luck's

España <1883>   8'

3[1.2.pic] 2 2 4 — 4 4[2tp, 2crt] 3 1 — tmp+4 — 2hp — str
perc: tambn, tri, cym, bd
Kalmus ed. by Clinton F. Nieweg & Nancy M. Bradburd, 2009; this edition supplies cues rendering bn 3-4, crt 2, and hp 2 optional.

Enoch   Kalmus   Luck's

Gwendoline: Overture <1885>   9'

3[1.2.pic] 2[1.Eh] 3[1.2.bcl] 4 — 4 4 3 1 — tmp+3 — 2hp — str
perc: bd, cym, tri

Enoch   Kalmus   Luck's

Gwendoline: Prelude, Act II <1885>   5'

3[1.2.pic] 2[1.Eh] 2[1.bcl] 2 — 4 2 3 1 — 2hp — str

Enoch	Kalmus	Luck's

Habanera <1885>   4'

2 1 2 1 — 2 2 0 0 — tmp+1 — str
perc: tri
Originally for piano.

Enoch	Kalmus	Luck's

Joyeuse marche <1888>   4'

3[1.2.pic] 2 2 4 — 4 4[2tp, 2crt] 3 1 — tmp+4 — hp — str
perc: tri, sd, cym, bd

Enoch	Kalmus	Luck's

Ode à la musique <1890>   11'

solo soprano   female chorus (16 singers: 4 S1, 4 S2, 4 Ms, 4 A)
2 2 2 2 — 4 2 3 0 — tmp+1 — 2hp — str
perc: tri

Kalmus

Le roi malgré lui (The King in Spite of Himself; The Reluctant King): Danse slav <1887>   5'

2[1/pic.2/pic] 2 2 2 — 2 2 3 0 — tmp+3 — str
perc: tri, cym, bd

Enoch	Kalmus	Luck's

Le roi malgré lui (The King in Spite of Himself; The Reluctant King): Fête polonaise <1887>   10'

2[1.pic] 2 2 2 — 2 2[crt1.crt2] 3 0 — tmp+3 — str
perc: tri, sd, cym, bd

Enoch	Kalmus	Luck's

Suite pastorale <1888>   21'

2[1.2/pic] 1 2 2 — 2 2[crt1.crt2] 3 0 — tmp+3 — opt hp — str
perc: tri, cym, bd

Idylle	5'
Danse villageoise (Rustic Dance)	5'
Sous bois (In the Woods)	6'
Scherzo-valse	5'

Enoch	Kalmus	Luck's

Chadwick, George Whitefield   1854-1931

(b Lowell, MA, 13 Nov 1854; d Boston, MA, 4 April 1931). American

Aphrodite; Symphonic Fantasy <1912>   20'

3[1.2.3/pic] 3[1.2.Eh] 3[1.2.bcl] 3[1.2.cbn] — 4 4 3 1 — tmp+4 — hp — cel — str
perc: tri, tamtam, cym, sus cym, bd, opt chimes, 4 field dr off stage
4 offstage field drums may be covered by percussionists leaving the stage (i.e., no extra players needed).

Kalmus	Luck's

Elegy (In memoriam Horatio Parker) <1919>   9'

3[fl3 opt] 3[1.2.opt Eh] 2 2 — 4 2 3 0 — tmp — opt hp — opt org — str

Fleisher

Euterpe; Concert Overture <1902>   9'

3[1.2.pic] 2 2 2 — 4 2 3 1 — tmp — hp — str

Kalmus	Luck's	Schirmer

Melpomene; Dramatic Overture <1886>   12'

3[1.2.pic] 2[1.Eh] 2 2 — 4 2 3 1 — tmp+1 — str
perc: bd, cym, sus cym

Kalmus	Luck's

A Pastoral Prelude <1890>   10'

3[1.2.pic] 3[1.2.Eh] 2 2 — 4 2 0 0 — tmp — str
1st clarinet in C; 2nd clarinet in B-flat.

Fleisher

Rip Van Winkle: Overture <1879>   10'

3[1.2.pic] 2 2 2 — 4 2 3 1 — tmp+1 — str
perc: tri

C. Fischer

Serenade, F major <1895>   27'

str
Ed. Russell Girsberger.

Kalmus	Luck's

Sinfonietta, D major <1904>   19'

3[1.2.3/pic] 2 2 — 4 2 3[opt] 0 — tmp+1 — hp — str
perc: tri, sd

Risolutamente	6'
Canzonetta: Allegretto	6'
Scherzino: Vivacissimo e leggiero	5'
Finale: Assai animato	5'

Kalmus	Luck's	Schirmer

Symphonic Sketches <1895–1904>   30'

3[1.2/pic.pic] 3[1.2.Eh] 3[1.2.bcl] 2 — 4 2 3 0 — tmp+4 — hp — str
perc: tri, xyl, tambn, field dr, cym, sus cym, bd
Alternative availability: Jubilee & Noël are available as a pair; the other movements are available separately.

Jubilee	8'
Noël	8'
Hobgoblin	6'
A Vagrom Ballad	8'

Kalmus	Schirmer

Symphony No.2, B-flat major <1885>   37'

2 2 2 2 — 4 2 3 0 — tmp — str

Andante non troppo; Allegro con brio	13'
Allegretto scherzando	6'
Largo e maestoso; Allegro non troppo	9'
Allegro molto animato; Assai animato; Presto	9'

Kalmus

Tam O'Shanter; Symphonic Ballade <1914–1915>   18'

3[1.2/pic.3/pic] 3[1.2.Eh] 4[1.2.Ebcl.bcl] 2 — 4 3 3 1 — tmp+4 — hp — str
perc: bd, cym, glock, tamtam, xyl, Chinese drum, rattle, sandblks, wood drum

Kalmus	Luck's

Tre pezzi (Three Pieces for Orchestra) <1923>   15'

3[1.2.3/pic] 3[1.2.Eh] 2 2 — 4 3 3 1 — tmp+1 — hp — str
perc: tri, xyl

Overture mignon	_'
Canzone vecchia	_'
Fuga giacosa	_'

Fleisher

Chaikovsky, Peter Ilich
1840-1893

This transliteration of the composer's name is used by the U.S. Library of Congress, the Fleisher Collection, and many libraries.

see: Tchaikovsky, Piotr Ilyich, 1840-1893

Chatschaturjan, Aram
1903-1978

This transliteration of the composer's name is occasionally found in German publications.

see: Khachaturian, Aram, 1903-1978

Chaminade, Cécile
1857-1944

(b Paris, 8 Aug 1857; d Monte Carlo, 13 April 1944). French

Callirhoë Suite, op.37 <1890>
14'

3[1.2.pic] 2 2 4 — 4 4 3 1 — tmp+3 — hp — str
perc: tri, cym, bd
Prelude   _'
Pas de Echarpes   _'
Scherzettino   _'
Pas des Cymbales

Kalmus	Luck's

Concertino, Flute, op.107, D major <1902>
8'

1 2 2 2 — 4 0 3 1 — tmp — hp — str

Enoch	Kalmus	Luck's

Chance, John Barnes
1932-1972

(b Beaumont, TX, 20 Nov 1932; d Lexington, KY, 16 Aug 1972). American

Elegy <1997>
8'

2 3[1.2.Eh] 3[1.2.bcl] 3[1.2.cbn] — 4 3 3 1 — tmp+2 — str
perc: sus cym, gong, vib, chimes
Originally for band; transcribed for orchestra by D. Wilson Ochoa.

Boosey

Charpentier, Gustave
1860-1956

(b Dieuze, Moselle, 25 June 1860; d Paris, 18 Feb 1956). French

Impressions d'Italie <1887–1889>
32'

3[1.2.3/pic] 3[1.2.3/Eh] 3[1.2.3/bcl] 4 — 4 4 3 1 — asx/ssx — tmp+4 — 2hp — str
perc: bd, cym, sd, tri, slgh-bells[pitched: G4,Bb4], sus cym, tambn
A 4th trombone may be added in the last mvt.
I. Sérénade   7'
II. A la fontaine (At the Fountain) 3'
III. A mules (On Mules)   4'
IV. Sur les cîmes (On the Summit)   6'
V. Napoli (Naples)   12'

Heugel	Kalmus

Louise: Prelude to Act III & "Air de Louise" <1889–1896>
10'

2 2[incl Eh] 2 2 — 2 2 3 0 — tmp+2 — 2hp — opt cel — str
perc: bd, tri
Arr. Francis Casadesus. Set has special parts for 2 cornets to be used in lieu of trumpets and horns. Piano-conductor score only.
Prelude to Act III   6'
Air de Louise   4'

Luck's

Charpentier, Marc-Antoine
1643-1704

(b in or nr Paris, 1643; d Paris, 24 Feb 1704). French

H = H.W. Hitchcock: *Les oeuvres de Marc-Antoine Charpentier: catalogue raisonné* (Paris, 1982)

Magnificat, H.73 <early 1670s>
4'

3-part male chorus
cnt — str
Over a ground bass repeated 89 times.
    Ed. Claude Crussard.

Foetisch

Messe de minuit pour Noël, H.9 (Midnight Mass for Christmas) <early 1690s>
20'

solos SSATTB   chorus
2 0 0 0 — org — str
Concordia, ed. H. Wiley Hitchcock; Bärenreiter, ed. Rudolf Walter, calls for soloists SSAATTBB.

Bärenreiter	Concordia	Eulenburg

Noëls pour les instruments, H.531 & 534 <early 1680s & 1690s>
15'

2[rec1.rec2] 0 0 1 — cnt — str
Settings of popular French carols. Ed. H. Wiley Hitchcock.
1. Les bourgeois de Châtre (1)   2'
2. Joseph est bien marié   1'
3. Or nous dites, Marie   2'
4. Laissez paître vos bêtes   1'
5. Vous qui désirez sans fin   3'
6. A la venue de Noël   1'
7. O Créateur   1'
8. Une jeune pucelle   1'
9. Où s'en vont ces gais bergers?   1'
10. Le bourgeois de Châtre (2)   2'

Universal

Te Deum, H.146 <1692>
23'

chorus   solos SSATB
2 3[1.2.Eh] 0 1 — 0 1 0 0 — tmp — cnt — str
Bärenreiter edition, ed. Helga Schauerte-Maubouet, calls for: soloists SSAATTBB; no Eh; 2tp (instead of 1) plus 1 tbn.

Bärenreiter	Eulenburg	Universal

Chausson, Ernest
1855-1899

(b Paris, 20 Jan 1855; d Limay, nr Mantes, Yvelines, 10 June 1899). French

Poème, op.25 <1896>
16'

solo violin
2 2 2 2 — 4 2 3 1 — tmp — hp — str
Kalmus ed. Clinton F. Nieweg (2012).

Breitkopf	Kalmus	Luck's

Poème de l'amour et de la mer, op.19 <1882–1890; rev 1893>
27'

solo voice
2 2 2 2 — 2 2 3 0 — tmp — hp — str
Available in 2 keys: G for high voice, or F for medium voice.
I. La fleur des eaux   11'
II. Interlude   3'
III. La mort de l'amour 13'

Kalmus	Luck's	Rouart

Symphony, op.20, B-flat major <1889–1890>   30'
3[1.2.3/pic] 3[1.2.Eh] 3[1.2.bcl] 3 — 4 4 3 1 — tmp — 2hp — str
I. Lent; Allegro vivo   11'
II. Très lent   7'
III. Animé   12'

Kalmus	Luck's	Salabert□□□□

La tempête, op.18 (The Tempest): 2 Excerpts <1888>   8'
3[1.2.pic] 2 2 2 — 2 2 3 0 — tmp+1 — hp — str
perc: cym, tri
Air de danse   3'
Danse rustique   5'

Kalmus	Luck's

Viviane, Symphonic Poem on a Legend of the Round Table, op.5 <1882; rev 1887>   12'
3[1.2.3/pic] 2 2 3 — 4 2 3 1 — tmp+2 — 2hp — str
perc: cym, bd, crot

Kalmus	Luck's

Chávez, Carlos   1899-1978

(b Mexico City, 13 June 1899; d Mexico City, 2 Aug 1978). Mexican

Baile; cuadro sinfónico (Dance; Symphonic Picture) <1953>   4'
3[1.2.3/pic] 3[1.2.Eh] 2 2 — 4 2 3 1 — tmp+1 — pf — str
perc: sus cym, tomtom

Carlanita

Concerto, 4 Horns <1937–1938; rev 1964>   23'
0 1[incl Eh] 4[incl Ebcl,bcl] 3 — tmp — str
Kalmus publishes score only; no parts.
Allegro   _'
Adagio   _'
Rondo   _'

Belwin	Kalmus

Concerto, Piano <1938–1940; rev 1969>   36'
3[1.2.pic] 3[1.2.Eh] 2 3[1.2.cbn] — 4 2 3 1 — tmp+3 — hp — cel — str
perc: glock, sd, sus cym, woodblk, xyl, tambn, bd, tamtam, td, cym, claves, marac
I. Largo non troppo—Allegro agitato   20'
II. Molto lento   9'
III. Finale: Allegro non troppo   7'

Schirmer

La hija de Colquide (The Daughter of Colchis; Dark Meadow): Symphonic Suite <1943>   24'
3[1.2.pic] 3[1.2.Eh] 4[1.2.Ebcl.bcl] 3 — 4 3 3 1 — tmp+3 — hp — str
perc: field dr, sus cym, bd
The original ballet (42') from which this suite was constructed, was for double quartet (fl, ob, cl, bn & str 4t).
I. Preludio   _'
II. Encantamiento (Enchantment)   _'
III. Zarabanda (Saraband)   _'
IV. Peán (Paean)   _'
V. Postludio   _'

Belwin	Carlanita

Initium <1971>   18'
3[1.2.pic] 3[1.2.Eh] 3[1.2.bcl] 3[1.2.3/cbn] — 4 3 3 1 — tmp+3 — hp — str
perc: vib, marim, cym, sd, gong, claves, glock, xyl, 2sus cym

Belwin

Pasajes mexicanas; Variaciones sinfonicos (Mexican Passages) <1973>   20'
3[1.2.pic] 3[1.2.Eh] 3[1.2.bcl] 3[1.2.3/cbn] — 4 3 3 1 — tmp+3 — str
perc: bd, bd/cym, cym, sus cym, sd, td, tambn, glock, xyl, marim, woodblk, guiro, claves, Indian dr

Carlanita

Prometheus Bound <1956>   25'
solo soprano   chorus
3[1.2.pic] 3[1.2.Eh] 3[1.2.bcl] 3[1.2.3/cbn] — 4 2 3 1 — tmp+3 — 2hp — str
perc: bd, sd, td, gong, vib, marac, whip, bongos, 3sus cym, 2metalplate, metal rttl, soft rttl, chain
Cantata based on Aeschylus (trans. R.C. Trevelyan). Characters: **Power**, **Hephaistos**, **Hermes**, **Caller**, *narrators* (all drawn from the chorus); **Io**, *dramatic soprano*; **Prometheus**, *male chorus*; **Oceanids**, *female chorus*.

Schirmer

Resonancias <1964>   15'
3[1.2.pic] 3[1.2.Eh] 3[1.2.bcl] 3[1.2.3/cbn] — 4 2 3 1 — tmp+3 — str
perc: cym, marac, td, 3 small drums, 3sd, 3pr cym, soft rattles, clay rattles, 2bd, 2guiro

Belwin

Sinfonía para orquesta <1915–1919>   30'

Carlanita

Symphony No.1 (Sinfonía de Antígona) <1933>   11'
3[1.afl.pic] 3[1.Eh.heckl] 4[1.2.Ebcl.bcl] 3 — 8 3 0 1 — tmp+3 — 2hp — str
perc: cym, glock, td, 2sus cym, 2sd, Indian drum

Schirmer

Symphony No.2 (Sinfonia india) <1935–1936>   12'
4[1.2.3/pic2.pic1] 3 4[1.2.Ebcl.bcl] 3 — 4 2 2 0 — tmp+4 — hp — str
perc: marac, sus cym, td, claves, xyl, sd, guiro, bd, Indian drum, metal rattle, soft rattle, rattling string, rasping stick
Score contains instructions for the use of primitive Indian instruments, if available, in place of certain percussion.

Schirmer

Symphony No.3 <1951–1954>   27'
3[1.2.pic] 3[1.2.Eh] 4[1.2.Ebcl.bcl] 3[1.2.3/cbn] — 4 3 3 1 — tmp+3 — hp — str
perc: cym, bd, sd, td, 2tamtams
I. Introduzione: Andante moderato   6'
II. Allegro: Allegro non troppo   8'
III. Scherzo   5'
IV. Finale: Molto lento   8'

Carlanita

Symphony No.4 (Sinfonía romántica) <1953>   22'
3[1.2.3/pic] 3[1.2.Eh] 2 3[1.2.3/cbn] — 4 2 3 1 — tmp+3 — str
perc: glock, chimes, xyl, cym, claves, marac, bd, sd, td
I. Allegro   7'
II. Molto lento   7'
III. Vivo non troppo   8'

Boosey

Symphony No.5 <1954>   21'
str
I. Allegro molto moderato   6'
II. Lento   8'
III. Allegro con brio   7'

Belwin	Carlanita	Kalmus

Chen Gang   1935-

(b Shanghai, 10 March 1935). Chinese

The Butterfly Lovers; Violin Concerto (Liang Shanbo yu Zhu Yingtai)

see under: He Zhanhao

Chen Yi   1953-

(b Guangzhou, 4 April 1953). American composer of Chinese birth

Ba yin (The Eight Sounds) <2001>   17'

solo saxophone quartet (ssx, asx, tsx, bsx)
str
Praying for Rain	8'
Song of the Chu	4'
Shifan Gong-and-Drum	5'

Presser

Chinese Folk Dance Suite (Violin Concerto) <2000>   17'

solo violin
2[1.2/pic] 2 2 2 — 4 2 3 0 — 3perc — str
perc: bd, sus cym, sd, tambn, crot, templeblk, 3congas, low tom, 2 Beijing opera gongs, 2 6" Chinese cym, paddle castanets
Orchestra members sing non-pitched syllables extensively in 2nd mvt.
Lion Dance	4'
YangKo	5'
Muqam	8'

Presser

Chinese Myths Cantata <1996>   34'

12 male voices (countertenors, tenors, baritones, basses)
2[1/pic.2/pic] 2 2[1/Ebcl.2/bcl] 2[1.2/cbn] — 4 2 3 0 — 4 traditional Chinese instruments: erhu (fiddle), yangqin (dulcimer), pipa (lute), zheng (zither) — tmp+3 — str[6.6.4.6.4]
perc: bd, cym, sus cym, small Chinese cyms, toms, tambn, tamtam, glock, small bell, sound tree, clappers, woodblk, bongos, ratch, thunder sheet; played by timpanist: sus cym, bamboo tree, crotales
Pan Gu Creates Heaven and Earth	10'
Nü Wa Creates Human Beings	10'
Weaving Maid and Cowherd	8'
Song of Weaving Maid and Cowherd [voices a cappella]	6'

Presser

Concerto, Percussion <1998>   20'

solo percussionist (recites in Chinese while playing)
3[1.2.3/pic] 3 3[1.2.3/bcl] 3[1.2.cbn] — 4 3 3 1 — 3 orchestral perc — str[min 14.12.10.10.8]
perc: cym, sd, crot, tamtam, templeblks, claves, bd, tmp, 3Peking gongs, sus cym, 2szl cym, Chinese cym, 2fingerbells (Pengling), 2gongs, 5woodblks, 3tomtoms; SOLO: vib, xyl, marim, marktree, bowl chime, Chinese cym, 2Peking gongs, 2gongs, tamtam, Japanese high woodblk, templeblks, 5Chinese tomtoms, dagu (Chinese bd)
The Night Deepens	7'
Prelude to Water Tune	7'
Speedy Wind	6'

Presser

Concerto, Piano <1992; rev 2000>   17'

3[1/pic.2/pic.3/pic] 3[1.2.Eh] 3[1.2.bcl] 3[1.2.cbn] — 4 3 3 1 — tmp+3 — str
perc: bd, cym, 2sus cym, sd, tri, tamtam, 2Beijing gongs, 3buttongongs, xyl, vib, chimes, crot, belltree, templeblk, 3woodblk

Presser

Dunhuang Fantasy <1998>   13'

solo organ
1 1 2[1.bcl] 1[cbn] — 1 1 1 0 — 1perc — [no str]
perc: bd, sys cym, sd, toms, tamtam, marktree, bongo

Presser

Duo ye [No.1] <1985>   8'

1 1 2[1.Ebcl] 1 — 1 0 0 0 — 2perc — str[8.6.4.2.2]
perc: sus cym, sd, toms, gong, vib, woodblk

Presser

Duo ye, No.2 <1987>   8'

3[incl 2pic] 3[incl Eh] 3[incl bcl] 3[incl cbn] — 4 3 3 1 — tmp+3 — str[14.14.10.12.8]
A version for chamber orchestra also exists.

Presser

Eleanor's Gift (Concerto for Cello & Orchestra) <1998>   15'

solo violoncello
2 2 2 2 — 2 2 1 0 — tmp+2 — hp — str
perc: bd, sus cym, sd, tambn, templeblks, tamtam, vib, marktree, Japanese high woodblk; timpanist plays templeblk

Presser

Fiddle Suite <1997>   15'

huqin solo [erhu, zhonghu, & jinghu]
str
The *erhu* family (generically called *huqin*) includes the *zhonghu* and the *jinghu*; all may be played by the same soloist.
     There is also a version of this work for huqin and full orchestra:
3 3 3 3[incl cbn] — 4 4 3 1 — 4perc — str
Singing [solo erhu]	5'
Reciting [solo zhonghu]	6'
Dancing [solo jinghu]	4'

Presser

Ge xu (Antiphony) <1994>   8'

2[1.2/pic] 2 2 2 — 4 2 3 0 — tmp+3 — hp — str
perc: bd, cym, sus cym, toms, tamtam, vib, woodblk, 2congas; timpanist doubles on clappers

Presser

Golden Flute (Concerto for Flute & Orchestra) <1997>   20'

solo flute
2[1/pic.2/pic] 2 2 2 — 4 2 3 0 — tmp+2 — hp — str
perc: bd, sus cym, tri, tamtam, 5 set gongs, glock, vib, crot, small bell, templeblk, Japanese high woodblock; timpanist doubles on tri & sus cym
1.	6'
2.	3'
3.	11'

Presser

KC Capriccio <2000; rev 2001>   4'

chorus
2[1.2/pic] 2 3[1.2.bcl] 2 — 4 3 3 1 — asx.tsx.bsx — baritone horn — tmp+2 — [no str]
perc: bd, sus cym, sd, marktree, woodblk

Presser

The Linear <1994>   15'

2 2 2 2 — 4 3 3 1 — tmp+4 — hp — str
perc: 2pr large cym, sus cym, sd, toms, tri, tamtam, 3gongs, small Beijing gong, clappers, woodblk

Presser

Momentum <1998>   12'

3[1.2.pic] 3[1.2.Eh] 3[1.2.bcl] 3[1.2.cbn] — 4 3 3 1 — tmp+3 — hp — str

perc: bd, 2sus cym, sd, tamtam, bongos, high Japanese woodblk

Presser

Romance and Dance <1998>   9'

2 solo violins
str

Romance of Hsiao and Ch'in	4'
Dance [adapted from the 3rd mvt of the composer's Fiddle Suite*]*	5'

Presser

Romance of Hsiao and Ch'in <1995>   4'

2 solo violins
str

Later used as the 1st mvt of *Romance and Dance.*

Presser

Shuo <1994>   9'

str

Presser

Si Ji (Four Seasons) <2005–2005>   14'

4[1.2.3.pic] 4[1.2.3.Eh] 4[1.2.3.bcl] 4[1.2.3.cbn] — 4 3 3 1 — tmp+4 — hp — str

perc: bd, sd, tri, tamtam, xyl, marim, vib, bongos, 2sus cym, opera gong, bass bow
Based on four ancient Chinese poems.

Presser

Sparkle <1992>   12'

1[fl/pic] 0 1[Ebcl] 0 — 2perc — pf — vn, vc, db

perc: bd, marim, vib, claves

Presser

Sprout <1986>   6'

str

An alternate version exists for saxophone orchestra.

Presser

Symphony No.2 <1993>   18'

3 3[1.2.Eh] 3[1.2.Eh] 3[1.2.cbn] — 4 3 3 1 — tmp+4 — hp — str

Presser

Tang Poems Cantata <1995>   15'

solo tenor   chorus
1 1 1 1 — 1 1 1 0 — tmp+1 — pf — vn, va, vc, db
perc: tri, woodblk, 3congas; timpanist doubles on sus cym, claves, tamtam

Riding on My Skiff	_'
Written on a Rainy Night	_'
Wild Grass	_'
Monologue	_'

Presser

Xian shi (Viola Concerto) <1983>   15'

solo viola
2[1.2/pic] 2 2 2 — 4 3 2 0 — tmp+2 — str
perc: hi-hat, sus cym, tri, tambn, gong, glock, xyl, woodblk, templeblk, range drums, range bells

Presser

Cherubini, Luigi   1760-1842

(b Florence, 8/14 Sept 1760; d Paris, 15 March 1842). Italian composer active in France

Les abencérages: Overture <1813>   9'

2 2 2 2 — 4 2 3 0 — tmp — str

Breitkopf	Kalmus	Luck's

Ali-Baba: Overture <1833>   7'

2[1.pic] 2 2 2 — 4 4 3 1 — tmp+3 — str
perc: bd, cym, tri

Bärenreiter	Breitkopf	Kalmus	Luck's

Anacréon: Overture <1803>   9'

2[1.2/pic] 2 2 2 — 4 2 3 0 — tmp — str

Breitkopf	Kalmus	Luck's

Démophoon: Overture <1788>   10'

2 2 2 2 — 2 2 3 0 — tmp — str
Ed. Pietro Spada.

Zerboni

Les deux journées (Le porteur d'eau; Der Wasserträger; The Water Carrier): Overture <1800>   8'

2 2 2 2 — 4 0 1 0 — tmp — str

Breitkopf	Kalmus

Faniska: Overture <1806>   8'

2 2 2 2 — 2 2 1 0 — tmp — str

Breitkopf	Kalmus	Luck's	Ricordi

L'hôtellerie portugaise (The Portuguese Inn): Overture <1799>   8'

2 2 2 2 — 2 2 1 0 — tmp — str

Breitkopf	Kalmus

Lodoïska: Overture <1791>   9'

2 2 2 2 — 2 2 1 0 — tmp — str

Breitkopf	Kalmus	Luck's

March, F major <1805>   6'

0 2 2 3[1.2.cbn] — 2 0 0 0 — [no str]
Double bass may substitute for contrabassoon.

Zerboni

Mass No.4, C major (Messe solennelle) <1816>

chorus   solos SSSSTTBB
2 2 2 2 — 2 2 0 0 — tmp — str

Kalmus	Luck's

Médée (Medea): Overture <1797>   9'

2 2 2 2 — 4 0 0 0 — tmp — str

Bärenreiter	Breitkopf	Kalmus	Luck's

Requiem, C minor <1816>   47'

chorus
0 2 2 2 — 2 2 3 0 — tmp — str
1. Introit: Requiem aeternam   7'
2. Graduale: Requiem aeternam   2'
3. Dies irae   10'
4. Offertorium: Domine Jesu Christe   16'
5. Sanctus   2'
6. Pie Jesu   3'
7. Agnus Dei   7'

Breitkopf	Kalmus	Luck's	

Requiem, D minor <1833>   52'

male chorus
2[1.pic] 2 2 2 — 4 2 3 0 — tmp — str
1. Introit: Requiem aeternam   10'
2. Graduale: Requiem aeternam   4'
3. Dies irae   14'
4. Offertorium: Domine Jesu Christe   7'
5. Sanctus   4'
6. Pie Jesu   4'
7. Agnus Dei   9'

Breitkopf	Kalmus	Luck's	Peters

Solemn Mass, G major (Messa solenne) <1819>   50'

chorus
2 2 2 2 — 2 2 3 0 — tmp — str
Ed. Giovanni Carli Ballola.

Boccaccini			

Symphony, D major <1815>   28'

1 2 2 2 — 2 2 0 0 — tmp — str
I. Lento; Allegro   10'
II. Larghetto cantabile   8'
III. Scherzo: Allegro assai   5'
IV. Finale: Allegro vivace   5'

Bärenreiter	Breitkopf	Kalmus	Luck's	Zerboni

Chiarappa, Richard   1948-

(b Middletown, CT, 7 Nov 1948). American

The Gettysburg Address <2008>   4'

narrator
3[1.2.pic] 2 2 2 — 4 3 3 1 — tmp+3 — str
perc: bd, cym, sd, tri, chimes

Wendel			

Paean to the Scholar, the Athlete and the Artist <2001>   5'

chorus
3[1.2.pic] 2 2 2 — 4 3 3 1 — tmp+ — str
perc: cym, tri, sus cym, sd

Clear Mud			

Chilcott, Bob   1955-

(b Plymouth, England, 9 April 1955). British

Tandem; for Double Orchestra <2002>   21'

4[1.2; 1.2] 4[1.2; 1.2] 4[1.2; 1.2] 4[1.2; 1.2] — 4[1.2; 1.2] 5[1.2.3; 1.2]
6[1.2.3; 1.2.3] 1[1] — tsx — tmp — pf or elec pf — str; str
The above forces are divided into 2 orchestras: **Orchestra 1**
(professional); **Orchestra 2** (amateur or youth, shown in italics). The two
should be spatially separated, left and right, with piano in the center.
   Tenor saxophone may be covered by one of the flute or clarinet
players, doubling on saxophone.

Oxford			

Chin, Unsuk   1961-

(b Seoul, 14 July 1961). Korean composer active in Germany since 1988

santika Ekatala <1993>   15'

3[1/afl.2.3/pic] 3[1/Eh.2.3] 3[1/Ebcl.2.3/bcl] 3[1.2.cbn] — 6 4 3 1 —
5perc — hp — cel, pf — str
perc: bd, tambn, slgh-bells, xyl, vib, glock, cym, crot, chimes, field dr, tamtam,
gong, 6tomtoms, tmp, 3sd, 3thundersheets, 3tri

Boosey			

Die Troerinnen (The Trojan Women) <1986>   22'

solos: 2 sopranos, mezzo-soprano   female chorus
3[1.2.pic] 3 3 3 — 4 3 3 0 — 2perc — hp — cel, pf — str
perc: vib, cym, crot, glock, marim, tambn, tri, gong, xyl, sd, tomtom, chimes, tmp

Boosey			

Chopin, Fryderyk Franciszek   1810-1849

(b Zelazowa Wola, nr Warsaw, 1 March 1810; d Paris, 17 Oct 1849). Polish

Allegro de concert, op.46 <1832–1841>   20'

solo piano
2 2 2 2 — 4 2 3 0 — tmp — str
Arr. Jean Louis Nicodé, from a work for unaccompanied solo piano.

C. Fischer	Kalmus	Luck's	PWM

Chopiniana (piano works orchestrated by Glazunov)

see under: Glazunov, Alexander, 1865-1936

Concerto, Piano, No.1, op.11, E minor <1830>   43'

2 2 2 2 — 4 2 1 0 — tmp — str
No autograph manuscript of the orchestration for this concerto survives,
and it is said that the much-criticized orchestral accompaniment was not
entirely the work of the 19-year-old Chopin. This version, published by
Breitkopf in 1880, has long held sway, but has been challenged by other
contenders (see the following two entries).
   I. Allegro maestoso   21'
   II. Romanze: Larghetto   11'
   III. Rondo: Vivace   11'

Breitkopf	Kalmus	Luck's	PWM

Concerto, Piano, No.1, op.11, E minor (arr. Balakirev) <1829>   43'

2 2[1.Eh] 2 2 — 4 2 1 0 — tmp — str
Reorchestrated by Mily Balakirev in 1910, for the Chopin centennial,
maintaining the structure and the solo piano part exactly as in the original,
though adding English horn, making use of valved horns and trumpets,
and rescoring much of the accompaniment.
   I. Allegro maestoso   21'
   II. Romanze: Larghetto   11'
   III. Rondo: Vivace   11'

Zimmermann			

Concerto, Piano, No.1, op.11, E minor (arr. Yaffé) <1829>   43'

2 2 2 2 — 4 2 1 0 — tmp — str
Revised orchestration by John Yaffé, based on Mily Balakirev's 1910
version, though restoring the 2 oboe parts and eliminating the English
horn.
   I. Allegro maestoso   21'
   II. Romanze: Larghetto   11'
   III. Rondo: Vivace   11'

Ipsilon			

Concerto, Piano, No.2, op.21, F minor <1829–1830>   32'

2 2 2 2 — 2 2 1[btbn] 0 — tmp — str

I. Maestoso	15'
II. Larghetto	9'
III. Allegro vivace	8'

Breitkopf	Kalmus	Luck's	PWM

Fantasy on Polish Airs, op.13 <1828>   16'

solo piano
2 2 2 2 — 2 2 0 0 — tmp — str

1.	5'
2.	4'
3.	4'
4.	3'

Breitkopf	C. Fischer	Kalmus	Luck's	PWM

Grande polonaise brillante, op.22 <1834>   10'

solo piano
2 2 2 2 — 2 0 1[btbn] 0 — tmp — str
Preceded by an *Andante spianato* (4', also op.22) for unaccompanied piano, for a total duration of 14'.

Breitkopf	Kalmus	Luck's	PWM

Krakowiak, op.14 (Rondo à la krakowiak) <1828>   14'

solo piano
2 2 2 2 — 2 2 0 0 — tmp — str

Breitkopf	Kalmus	Luck's	PWM

Mazurka No.7, op.7, no.3, F-sharp minor <1830>   3'

str
Originally a work for solo piano in F minor; transcribed for string orchestra by Mily Balakirev.

Kalmus	Luck's	Zimmermann

Nocturne, op.32, no.2, A-flat major (orchestrated by Stravinsky) <1837>   8'

2 2 2 2 — 4 0 0 0 — 1perc — hp — cel — str
perc: bd
Orchestrated by Stravinsky for *Les sylphides*. Score (wrongly) identifies this work as op.32, no.1.

Boosey

Polonaise, op.40, no.1, A major (Military) <1838>   4'

3[1.2.pic] 2 2 2 — 4 2 3 0 — tmp+3 — str
perc: cym, sd, tri
Arr. Alexander Glazunov.

Kalmus	Luck's

Romanze <1830>   8'

solo violin
2 0 2 2 — 2 0 0 0 — tmp — str
Paraphrase by August Wilhelmj of the slow movement of Chopin's first piano concerto (transposed from E to D).

Kalmus	Luck's

LES SYLPHIDES

[Not to be confused with the similarly-named ballet *La Sylphide*, composed by Herman Løvenskjold.]

This ballet was created in 1907 by choreographer Michel Fokine as *Chopiniana*, set to Chopin piano music as previously orchestrated by Glazunov in an 1893 suite of that same name (*q.v.*, under Glazunov). It was retitled *Les Sylphides* in 1909 for a production of Serge Diaghilev's Ballet Russes, using new orchestrations by Liadov, Taneyev, Tcherepnin, and Stravinsky. Modern productions usually use one of the following orchestrations (below).

N.B. An old orchestration previously offered by Kalmus, and purporting to preserve the Diaghilev orchestrations, is deficient in many ways and should not be used. It has been withdrawn by Kalmus but may still lurk undetected in various collections.

Les Sylphides (arr. Britten) <1833–1847>   27'

2[1.2/pic] 2 2 2 — 2 2 1 0 — tmp+1 — hp — str
perc: sd, tri
Arr. Benjamin Britten, 1941.

1. Prelude, op.28 no.7	1'
2. Nocturne, op.32 no.2	6'
3. Valse, op.70 no.1	2'
4. Mazurka, op.33 no.2	3'
5. Mazurka, op.67 no.3 (reconstructed by Colin Matthews)	2'
6. Prelude, op.28 no.7 [repeated]	2'
7. Valse, op.64 no.2	5'
8. Grande valse brillante, op.18	6'

Boosey

Les Sylphides (arr. Douglas) <1833–1847>   27'

3[1.2/pic.(opt 3/pic)] 2[1.2/Eh] 2 2 — 4 2 3 0 — tmp+2 — hp — str
perc: cym, tri, bd, sd
Arr. Roy Douglas, 1936.

1. Prelude, op.28 no.7	1'
2. Nocturne, op.32 no.2	6'
3. Waltz, op.70 no.1	2'
4. Mazurka, op.33 no.2	3'
5. Mazurka, op.33 no.3 (op.67 no.3 as alternative)	2'
6. Prelude, op.28 no.7	2'
7. Waltz, op.64 no.2	5'
8. Grande valse brillante, op.18	6'

Boosey

Les Sylphides (arr. Douglas—reduced version) <1833–1847>   27'

1 1 2 1 — 2 2 1 0 — tmp+2 — hp — pf — str
perc: cym, tri, bd, sd, sus cym, glock
Arr. Roy Douglas, 1936.

1. Prelude, op.28 no.7	1'
2. Nocturne, op.32 no.2	6'
3. Waltz, op.70 no.1	2'
4. Mazurka, op.33 no.2	3'
5. Mazurka, op.33 no.3 (op.67 no.3 as alternative)	2'
6. Prelude, op.28 no.7	2'
7. Waltz, op.64 no.2	5'
8. Grande valse brillante, op.18	6'

Boosey

Les Sylphides (arr. Lanchbery)   27'

solo piano
2 1 2 1 — 2 2 2 0 — tmp+perc — hp — str
Arr. John Lanchbery.

1. Prelude, op.28 no.7	1'
2. Nocturne, op.32 no.2	6'
3. Valse, op.70 no.1	2'
4. Mazurka, op.33 no.2	3'
5. Mazurka, op.67 no.3	2'
6. Prelude, op.28 no 7 [repeated]	2'
7. Valse, op.64 no.2	5'
8. Grande valse brillante, op.18	6'

Mario Bois

Les Sylphides (arr. McDermott) <1833–1847>   27'

2 2 2 2 — 3 2 2 0 — tmp+3 — hp — str
perc: bd, cym, tri
Arr. William McDermott, rev.1982 and newly engraved.

1. Prelude, op.28 no.7	1'
2. Nocturne, op.32 no.2	6'
3. Valse, op.70 no.1	2'
4. Mazurka, op.33 no.2	3'
5. Mazurka, op.67 no.3	2'
6. Prelude, op.28 no. 7 [repeated]	2'
7. Valse, op.64 no.2	5'
8. Grande valse brillante, op.18	6'

Kalmus

Variations on *Là ci darem la mano*, op.2 <1827>   18'

solo piano
2 2 2 2 — 2 0 0 0 — tmp — str

Introduzione: Largo	4'
Tema: Allegretto	2'
Variation 1: Brillante	1'
Variation 2: Veloce, ma accuratamente	1'
Variation 3: Sempre sostenuto	2'
Variation 4: Con bravura	1'
Variation 5: Adagio	3'
Alla polacca	4'

Kalmus	Luck's	PWM

Chou Wen-chung   1923-

(b Chefoo, Yantai, 29 July 1923). Chinese composer active in the USA; naturalized US citizen.

All in the Spring Wind <1953>   8'

2[incl pic] 2[incl Eh] 2[incl bcl] 2[incl cbn] — 2 2 2 1 — tmp+3 — hp — cel/pf — str

Peters

And the Fallen Petals <1954>   10'

2[1/pic.2/pic] 2[1.2/Eh] 3[1.2.bcl] 2 — 4 2 3 1 — tmp+2 — hp — cel — str
perc: tri, tamtam, tambn, tomtom, td, sd, field dr, bd, cym, 2sus cym

Peters

Beijing in the Mist <1986>   12'

0 0 0 0 — 0 1 1 0 — asx, bsx — elec gtr, elec bass — 3perc — pf, elec pf — [no str]

1.	4'
2.	9'

Peters

Landscapes <1949>   8'

2[1.2/pic] 2[1.2/Eh] 0 0 — 2 0 2 0 — tmp+1 — hp — str
perc: tamtam, 2sus cym, 2pr cym

Peters

Pien; Chamber Concerto <1966>   14'

solo piano
2[incl afl] 1[1/Eh] 1 1 — 1 2 2 0 — 4perc — [no str]

Peters

Soliloquy of a Bhiksuni <1958>   5'

solo trumpet
0 0 0 0 — 4 0 3 1 — tmp+2 — [no str]

Peters

Yü ko <1965>   5'

1[afl] 1[Eh] 1[bcl] 0 — 0 0 2 0 — 2perc — pf — vn

Peters

Cimarosa, Domenico   1749-1801

(b Aversa, 17 Dec 1749; d Venice, 11 Jan 1801). Italian

Concerto (Concertante), 2 Flutes, G major <1793>   17'

0 2 0 1 — 2 0 0 0 — str

I. Allegro vivo	9'
II. Largo	4'
III. Rondo: Allegro	4'

Bote & Bock	Southern

Concerto, Oboe, C minor <1942>   11'

str
Freely adapted by Arthur Benjamin from piano sonatas of Cimarosa.

I. Introduzione: Allegro	6'
II. Siciliana	3'
III. Allegro giusto	2'

Boosey	Luck's

Il giorno felice: Overture <1775–1777>   4'

0 2 2 1 — 2 2 0 0 — 1perc — str
perc: bd

Carisch	Kalmus

Il maestro di cappella <1785–1793>   22'

solo bass or baritone
1 2 0 2 — 2 0 0 0 — tmp — hpsd or pf — str
Overture & comic monologue, ed. Maffeo Zanon.
    A new English libretto by Mark Starr (mentioning such anachronistic things as Urtexts and union rehearsal rules) is available from Noteworthy Music (orchestra parts must be obtained from Ricordi).

Ricordi	Noteworthy

Il maestro di cappella: Overture <1786–1793>   4'

1 2 0 2 — 2 0 0 0 — tmp — str
Carisch edition apparently has 2 flutes.

Carisch	Ricordi

Il matrimonio segreto: Overture (original) <1792>   6'

0 2 2 2 — 2 2 0 0 — tmp — str
Ed. Nick Rossi (2000); the original Vienna 1792 version.

Artaria

Il matrimonio segreto: Overture <1792>   8'

2 2 2 2 — 2 2 0 0 — tmp — str
Well-established and often-performed versions of this popular overture, which, however, are said to be later adaptations (even corruptions) of the original.

Carisch	Kalmus	Luck's

I nemeci generosi (The Gallant Adversaries): Overture <1796>   4'

2 2 2 2 — 2 2 0 0 — tmp — str
Practical performing edition by Clark McAlister.

Kalmus

Sinfonia, D major   8'

1 2 0 0 — 2 0 0 0 — str
Has also been attributed to the Czech composer Josef Mysliveček.

I. Allegro molto con brio	_'
II. Larghetto con moto	_'
III. Tempo primo	_'

Zanibon	Luck's

I traci amanti: Overture <1793>   7'

0 2 0 1 — 2 0 0 0 — str

| Curci | Kalmus | Luck's | Zanibon |

Clarke, Jeremiah   ca.1674-1707

(b c1674; d London, 1 Dec 1707). English

The Prince of Denmark's March (Trumpet Voluntary)

see his: Suite, D major
see also: Purcell, Henry, ca.1659-1695
              Trumpet Prelude
              Trumpet Voluntary

Suite, D major <1700>   10'

solo trumpet
0 2 0 1 — cnt — str
This suite includes the well-known *Prince of Denmark's March* as its 4th
movement. The latter is often wrongly attributed to Henry Purcell, under
the title *Trumpet Voluntary* or *Trumpet Prelude.*

1. Prelude, The Duke of Gloster's March	*1'*
2. Minuet	*1'*
3. Sybelle	*1'*
4. Rondeau, The Prince of Denmark's March	*1'*
5. Serenade	*1'*
6. Bourée	*1'*
7. Ecossaise	*2'*
8. Hornpipe	*1'*
9. Gigue	*1'*

| Musica Rara |

Clementi, Muzio   1752-1832

(b Rome, 23 Jan 1752; d Evesham, Worcs., 10 March 1832). English composer of
Italian birth

Symphony No.1, C major   26'

2 2 2 2 — 2 2 3 0 — tmp — str
Ed. Pietro Spada.

I. Larghetto—Allegro vivace	*9'*
II. Andante con moto	*6'*
III. Menuetto	*5'*
IV. Finale	*6'*

| Zerboni |

Symphony No.2, D major   24'

2 2 2 2 — 2 2 3 0 — tmp — str
Ed. Pietro Spada.

I. Andante sostenuto—Allegro vivace	*9'*
II. Larghetto cantabile	*6'*
III. Minuetto pastorale	*4'*
IV. Finale: Allegro molto vivace	*5'*

| Zerboni |

Symphony No.3, G major (Great National Symphony)   27'

2 2 2 2 — 2 2 3 0 — tmp — str
Ed. Pietro Spada. Quotes *God Save the King* in the slow movement.

I. Andante sostenuto—Allegro con brio	*9'*
II. Andante un poco mosso	*8'*
III. Minuetto: Allegretto	*5'*
IV. Finale: Vivace	*5'*

| Zerboni |

Symphony No.4, D major   28'

2 2 2 2 — 2 2 3 0 — tmp — str
Ed. Pietro Spada.

I. Introduzione e allegro vivace	*10'*
II. Larghetto cantabile	*7'*
III. Minuetto pastorale	*6'*
IV. Finale	*5'*

| Zerboni |

Coates, Eric   1886-1957

(b Hucknall, 27 Aug 1886; d Chichester, 23 Dec 1957). English

London Suite (London Every Day) <1933>   13'

2[1.2/pic] 3[1.2.Eh] 3[1.2.bcl] 2 — 4 3 3 0 — tmp+4 — hp — str
perc: bd, cym, tri, tambn, gong, glock, bell (G)

I. Covent Garden: Tarantelle	*4'*
II. Westminster: Meditation	*4'*
III. Knightsbridge: March	*5'*

| Chappell | Luck's |

Coleman, Linda Robbins   1954-

(b Des Moines, IA, 1 Jan 1954). American

The Celebration; A Symphonic Jubilee <2000>   17'

2[1.2/pic] 2 2 2 — 4 2 2 1 — tmp+3 — hp — pf — str
perc: cym, sus cym, sd, tomtom, tri, glock, cowbell, ratch, marac, claves, cast,
sandblks

1. The Invitation	*3'*
2. Valse Mémoire (Past Times, Absent Friends)	*5'*
3. The Life of the Party!	*3'*
4. Audrey and Cary (A Fantasy in Tango)	*5'*
5. Jubilation (The Grand Finale)	*1'*

| Coleman |

Elegy for the Greatest Generation <2009>   11'

2[1.2/pic] 2 2 2 — 4 2 3 1 — tmp+2 — hp — str
perc: sd, bd, cym, sus cym, tamtam, tri, whip
Tp1 optionally doubles cornet or bugle.

| Coleman |

For a Beautiful Land <1996>   11'

2[1.2/pic] 2 2 2 — 2 0 0 0 — tmp+1 — hp[opt] — str
perc: 2pr cym, sus cym, sd, gong, tri, glock
Also available: a slightly larger orchestration that includes brass 2 2 2 1,
as well as an extra percussionist.

| Coleman |

Hibernia Suite <1997>   17'

str
Also available in a version for str 4t.

Land of Youth (Tir na nóg)	*6'*
The Lover (Leanna'n)	*5'*
Dancing (Damhsa)	*6'*

| Coleman |

In Good King Charles's Golden Days; Symphonic   7'
Overture <1989; rev 1995>

2[1.2/pic] 2 2 2 — 4 2 3 1 — tmp+3 — hp — hpsd (or electronic
substitute) — str
perc: cym, sus cym, sd, tri, glock, xyl
Originally for 8 instruments; orchestral version by the composer (1995).

| Coleman |

Journeys <1992>   11'

2[1.2/pic] 2 2 2 — 4 3 3 1 — tmp+3 — hp — cel/pf — str
perc: bd, cym, sus cym, finger cym, sd, tambn, tamtam, glock, chimes, cast

> Coleman

Lunatics and Lovers (Shakespeare Suite #1)   16'
<1979–1997; rev 2005>

3[1.2.pic] 2 2 2 — 3 0 1 0 — tmp+2 — hp — hpsd — str
perc: cym, sus cym, glock, tri, slgh-bells, tambn, marktree, woodblk
From incidental music to *Midsummer Night's Dream* and *The Merchant
of Venice*.
   1. Overture   6'
   2. Bacchanalia   10'

> Coleman

Suite Antique <1998–2013>   18'

str
The 3rd or 4th movements may be performed separately.
   1. Nouveau   *1'*
   2. Rétro   *2'*
   3. Memoré   *4'*
   4. Valse Calliope   *6'*
   5. Fin de siècle   *5'*

> Coleman

Coleridge-Taylor, Samuel   1875-1912

(b London, 15 Aug 1875; d Croydon, 1 Sept 1912). English

Ballade, op.33, A minor <1898>   13'

3[1.2.pic] 2 2 2 — 4 2 3 1 — tmp+1 — str
perc: cym
Ed. Nancy M. Bradburd.

> Kalmus   Luck's

The Bamboula, op.75 (Rhapsodic Dance No.1) <1911>   8'

3[1.2.pic] 2 2 2 — 4 2 3 1 — tmp+3 — str
perc: bd, cym, glock, sd, tri

> Boosey   Kalmus   Luck's

Christmas Overture <1900>   5'

2 1 2 2 — 2 2 3 0 — tmp+2 — hp — str

> Boosey   Luck's

Danse nègre, op.35, no.4 <1898>   6'

3[1.2.pic] 2 2 2 — 4 2 3 0 — tmp+3 — str
perc: bd, cym, tri
Originally for pf & str 4t; orchestrated by the composer.

> Kalmus   Luck's

Hiawatha: Suite from the Ballet Music, op.82a <1912>   18'

2[1.2/pic] 2 2 2 — 4 2 3 1 — tmp+4 — hp — str
Arr. and orchestrated by P.E. Fletcher, 1924.
   1. The Wooing   _'
   2. The Marriage Feast _'
   3. Bird Scene   _'
   4. Conjuror's Dance   _'
   5. The Departure   _'
   6. Reunion   _'

> Luck's

Novelette, op.52, no.1, A major <1903>   5'

1perc — str
perc: tambn, tri

> Kalmus

Novelette, op.52, no.2, C major <1903>   7'

1perc — str
perc: tambn, tri

> Kalmus

Novelette, op.52, no.3, A minor (Valse) <1903>   5'

1perc — str
perc: tambn, tri

> Kalmus

Novelette, op.52, no.4, D major <1903>   4'

1perc — str
perc: tambn, tri

> Kalmus

Petite suite de concert, op.77 <1911>   16'

3[1.2.pic] 2 2 2 — 4 2 3 0 — tmp+3 — str
   1. Le caprice de Nannette   4'
   2. Demande et réponse   5'
   3. Un sonnet d'amour   4'
   4. Le tarantelle fretillante   3'

> Boosey   Kalmus   Luck's

THE SONG OF HIAWATHA, op.30   31'
1. Hiawatha's Wedding Feast <1898>

chorus   solo tenor
3[1.2.3/pic] 2 2 2 — 4 2 3 1 — tmp+3 — hp — str
perc: bd, cym, sd, tri

> Kalmus   Luck's   Novello   Schirmer

2. The Death of Minnehaha <1899>   40'

chorus   solos SB
3[1.2.3/pic] 2 2 2 — 4 2 3 1 — tmp+2 — hp — str

> Kalmus   Luck's   Novello

3. Hiawatha's Departure <1900>   40'

chorus   solos STB
3[1.2.3/pic] 2 2 2 — 4 2 3 1 — tmp+2 — hp — opt org — str

> Kalmus   Luck's   Novello

Symphonic Variations on an African Air, op.63 <1906>   20'

3[1.2.pic] 2[1/Eh.2] 2 2 — 4 2 3 1 — tmp+2 — hp — str
perc: bd, bd/cym, cym, sd, tri

> Fleisher

Toussaint L'Ouverture, op.46 <1901>   15'

3[1.2.pic] 2 2 2 — 4 2 3 1 — tmp+2 — str
perc: bd, cym, sus cym, sd
Toussaint L'Ouverture was a colorful historical figure, born in slavery,
who rose to rule Haiti in 1801. His surname, which he normally spelled
"Louverture," has nothing to do with the musical form, although
Coleridge-Taylor's work happens to be a concert overture.
   Novello, the ostensible publisher, is apparently unable to find the parts.

> Novello

Colgrass, Michael   1932-

(b Chicago, 22 April 1932). American

As Quiet As ... <1966>   14'

3[1/pic.2.3/afl] 3[1.2.3/Eh] 3[1.2.3/bcl] 3 — 4 3 3 1 — tmp+3 — 2hp
— pf/cel/hpsd — str[12.10.8.8.4]
perc: glock, tamtam, vib, timbales, td, sus cym, szl cym, bd, 3 lg woodblks, chime
(A), Indian dr, glass windchimes, 3tri, crot (C#); played by tmp: little bells

1. A Leaf Turning Colors	_'
2. An Uninhabited Creek	_'
3. An Ant Walking	_'
4. Children Sleeping	_'
5. Time Passing	_'
6. A Soft Rainfall	_'
7. The First Star Coming Out	_'

MCA

Concertmasters <1975>   20'

3 solo violins
2[1.2/pic] 2 2[1.2/bcl] 2[1.2/cbn] — 4 3 3 1 — tmp+5 — 2hp —
cel/hpsd — str

C. Fischer

Déjà vu <1977>   18'

solo percussion quartet & solo jazz double bass
3[1.2/pic.3/afl] 0 3[1.2/Ebcl.3/bcl] 3[1.2.3/cbn] — 4 3 3 1 — 2hp —
pf/cel — str
perc: SOLO I: glock, 8rototoms, 4woodblks, 3szl cym, cym; SOLO II: vib,
tomtom, sd, timbales, bd, bamboo wind chimes, elephant bells, 8"sus cym,
5cowbells, 3tambn, tamtam; SOLO III: marim, 2td, 2field dr, 10"sus cym, 2szl
cym, woodblk, cowbell; SOLO IV: 5tmp, chimes, 4tri

C. Fischer

Letter from Mozart <1976>   16'

2[incl pic,afl] 2 2 2[incl cbn] — 2 2 2 1 — accordion — 4perc — hp
— cel/pf — str
Calls for 2 conductors; accordion part may be played by the keyboard
player.

C. Fischer

Rhapsodic Fantasy <1965>   9'

solo percussionist
2[1/pic.2/afl] 1 1 1 — 1 1 1 0 — tmp+3 — hp — cel — str

MCA

Theatre of the Universe <1975>   17'

solo S Ms T Bar B   chorus
3[1.2/pic.3/afl] 3[1.2.Eh] 3[1.2/Ebcl.3/bcl] 3[1.2.cbn] — 4 3 3 1 —
tmp+4 — 2hp — pf/cel — str

C. Fischer

Collins, Edward   1886-1951

(b Joliet, IL, 10 Nov 1886; d Chicago, 1 Dec 1951). American

Concerto, Piano, No.1, E-flat major <1924>   30'

3[1.2.pic] 3[1.2.Eh] 3[1.2.bcl] 3[1.2.cbn] — 4 2 3 1 — tmp+2 —
cel[played by perc] — str
perc: bd, cym, sus cym, tri, tambn, xyl, cel[played by perc]

I. Molto moderato, quasi adagio; Allegro non troppo	13'
II. Andante mesto	9'
III. Allegro ritmico	8'

ECFAM

Concerto, Piano, No.2, A minor (Concert Piece) <1931>   21'

2 2 2 3[1.2.cbn] — 2 2 3 0 — tmp+2 — str
perc: bd, cym, sd, glock

Andante molto tranquillo; Allegro	_'
Scherzo diabolico: Presto	_'
Allegro	_'

ECFAM

Concerto, Piano, No.3, B minor <1941>   39'

2[1.2/pic] 2 2 2 — 4 2 3 1 — tmp+2 — str
perc: tri, cym, tambn, sd

I. Moderato e patetico	15'
II. Intermezzo: Pièce eccentrique	3'
III. Nocturne (Andante tranquillo)	10'
IV. Rondo alla Tarantella (Presto)	11'

ECFAM

Cowboy's Breakdown <1938–1944>   2'

3[1.2.pic] 2 2 3[1.2.cbn] — 4 2 3 1 — tmp+2 — pf — str
perc: cym, xyl, bd[attached cym or 3rd player]
Originally for piano; arr. for 2 pianos, and then orchestrated (1944) by the
composer.

ECFAM

The Daffodils <1940>   3'

medium voice
1 0 1 0 — 1 0 0 0 — str
Originally for voice & piano; orchestrated by Verne Reynolds.

ECFAM

Hibernia (Irish Rhapsody [1929]) <1929>   18'

3[1.2.3/pic] 4[1.2.3.Eh] 4[1.2.3.bcl] 4[1.2.3.cbn] — 6 3 3 1 — tmp+3
— 2hp — str
perc: bd, cym, sus cym, sd, tri, glock
Not to be confused with the composer's earlier Irish Rhapsody [1927].

ECFAM

Hymn to the Earth <1929>   37'

solos SATB   chorus
2[1.2/pic] 2 2 2 — 2 2 3 0 — tmp+1 — opt hp — str
perc: cym, tri[ad lib]

1. Chorus: Hail! Mother of us all and beautiful	9'
2. Chorus & Bass: Thou changest thy garment	4'
3. Chorus & Tenor: Then one day	3'
4. Soprano: Hour of youth, Springtime of life	4'
5. Chorus: Summer finds thee garbed in yellow	6'
6. Alto, Quartet & chorus: Comes Autumn	11'

ECFAM

Irish Rhapsody <1927>   12'

3[1.2.pic] 3[1.2.Eh] 3[1.2.bcl] 3[1.2.cbn] — 4 2 3 1 — tmp+4 — hp
— pf — str
perc: bd, cym, sd, tri, glock
Not to be confused with the composer's later work Hibernia, composed in
1929 and subtitled Irish Rhapsody.

ECFAM

Lament and Jig <1941>   2'

3[1.2.pic] 3[1.2.Eh] 3[1.2.bcl] 3[1.2.cbn] — 4 3 3 1 — tmp+1 — str
perc: cym, sd
Part of the multi-composer work Variations on an American Folk-Song,
commissioned by the Chicago Symphony Orchestra.

ECFAM

Lil' David Play on Yo' Harp (Negro Spiritual) <1940>   4'

2[1.2/pic] 2 2 2 — 2 2 2 0 — hp — str

ECFAM

Mardi Gras <1922>   15'

3[1.2.pic] 2 3[1.2.bcl] 3[1.2.cbn] — 4 3 3 1 — tmp+3 — hp — str
perc: bd, cym, sus cym, sd, tri, tambn, glock

ECFAM

The Masque of the Red Death: Ballet Suite <1932>   26'

3[1.2.3/pic] 3[1.2.Eh] 3[1.2.bcl] 3[1.2.cbn] — 4 3 3 1 — tmp+4 — hp
— str
perc: bd, cym, sus cym, tri, tambn, tamtam, glock, xyl, chimes (Bb), cast, goblet
drum
  1. Invocation profane   *1'*
  2. Propos subtil et mysterieux   *7'*
  3. Valse seduisante   *5'*
  4. Chez le sultan   *6'*
  5. Orgie   *7'*

ECFAM

A Piper <1942>   2'

medium voice
1 0 1 1 — 1 0 0 0 — str
Originally for voice & piano; orchestrated by Verne Reynolds.

ECFAM

Prayer for C.H.S.   3'

medium voice
str
Originally for voice & piano; orchestrated by Verne Reynolds.

ECFAM

Set of Four <1924; rev 1933>   18'

3[1.2.3/pic] 3[1.2.Eh] 3[1.2.bcl] 3[1.2.cbn] — 4 3 3 1 — tmp+3 —
2hp — pf, cel[played by perc] — str
perc: bd, cym, sus cym, tri, tambn, glock, cel[played by perc]
  1. Prelude   *3'*
  2. Moonlight and Dance *9'*
  3. To Her   *3'*
  4. Passacaglia   *3'*

ECFAM

Song and Suds <1943>   2'

medium voice
str
Originally for voice & piano; orchestrated by Verne Reynolds.

ECFAM

Symphony, B minor (Nos habebit humus) <1929>   36'

4[1.2.3/pic.4] 4[1.2.3.Eh] 4[1.2.3.bcl] 4[1.2.3.cbn] — 6 4 3 1 —
tmp+3 — 2hp[1part] — str
perc: bd, cym, sd, tri, tambn, tamtam, chimes
Harps play only in 6 measures of mvt 2, doubling a single part.
  1. Allegro molto moderato   *14'*
  2. Allegretto soave   *5'*
  3. Elegy (Andante lugubre)   *7'*
  4. Allegro   *10'*

ECFAM

Tragic Overture <1923>   14'

3[1.2.3/pic] 4[1.2.3.Eh] 4[1.2.3.bcl] 4[1.2.3.cbn] — 4 3 3 1 — tmp+4
— pf — str
perc: bd, cym, sus cym, sd, field dr, tambn, tamtam, chimes
Original title: *1914.*

ECFAM

Valse elegante <1921–1924>   3'

3[1.2.pic] 2 2 3[1.2.cbn] — 4 2 3 1 — tmp/tri — hp — cel/pf — str
Originally no.2 of a set of 6 waltzes for piano; later orchestrated by the
composer.

ECFAM

Variations on an Irish Folksong <1931–1932>   18'

3[1.2.3/pic] 3[1.2.Eh] 3[1.2.bcl] 4[1.2.3.cbn] — 6 3 3 1 — tmp+2 —
2hp — str
perc: bd, cym, sd, tri, tambn, glock

ECFAM

Constant, Marius   1925-2004

(b Bucharest, 7 Feb 1925; d Paris, 15 May 2004). French composer of Romanian
birth

Vingt-quatre préludes (24 Preludes for Orchestra)   14'
<1958>

4[1.2.3/pic.afl] 4[1.2.3.Eh] 4[1.2.Ebcl.bcl] 4[1.2.3.cbn] — 6 4 4 1 —
tmp+5 — 2hp — pf, cel — str[min 16.14.12.12.8]
perc: marim, vib, glock, cym, sus cym, marac, tamtam, chimes, rattle, 3bd,
3bongos, 2sd
Each prelude lasts less than one minute.

Ricordi

Conus, Julius   1869-1942

(b Moscow, 1 Feb 1869; d Malenki, Ivanov, 3 Jan 1942). Russian

Concerto, Violin, E minor <1898>   20'

3 2 2 2 — 4 2 3 0 — str

Kalmus   Luck's

Converse, Frederick Shepherd   1871-1940

(b Newton, MA, 5 Jan 1871; d Westwood, MA, 8 June 1940). American

American Sketches <1928>   32'

3[incl pic] 3[incl Eh] 3[incl bcl] 3[incl cbn] — 4 3 3 1 — tmp+5 —
2hp — cel, org — str
  Manhattan   *11'*
  The Father of Waters   *9'*
  Chicken Reel   *4'*
  Bright Angel Trail   *8'*

Fleisher

California; Festival Scenes for Orchestra <1927>   13'

3[incl pic] 3[incl Eh] 4[incl Ebcl,bcl] 3[incl cbn] — 4 3 3 1 — tmp+5
— 2hp — cel — str
  Victory Dance of the First Inhabitants   _'
  Spanish Padres and Explorers   _'
  The March of Civilization   _'
  Land of Poco tiempo   _'
  Invasion of the Gringos   _'
  Midnight at El Paseo *1927*   _'

Presser

Endymion's Narrative, op.10 <1901>   15'

3[1.2.3/pic] 3[1.2.Eh] 2 3[1.2.cbn] — 4 3 3 1 — tmp+5 — hp — str
perc: sd, tri, bd, cym, tamtam, glock, gong

Novello   Presser

Festival of Pan, op.9 <1899>   18'

3[1.2.3/pic] 3[1.2.Eh] 3[1.2.bcl] 3[1.2.cbn] — 4 3 3 1 — tmp+3 — hp
— str
perc: bd, cym, tri

Fleisher   Presser

Flivver Ten Million; A Joyous Epic for Orchestra   12'
<1926>

3[1.2.3/pic] 3[1.2.Eh] 3[1.2.bcl] 3[1.2.cbn] — 4 3 3 1 — tmp+5 —
2hp — cel — str

perc: bd, cym, xyl, glock, tri, sd, tambn, wnd mach, tamtam, whip, sus cym, bell
(Eb), factory whistle [or organ], anvil, autohorn, rattle

> Presser

The Mystic Trumpeter   <1904>   20'

3[1.2.3/pic] 3[1.2.Eh] 3[1.2.bcl] 3[1.2.cbn] — 4 3 3 1 — tmp+5 — hp
— str

perc: sd, bd, cym, tri, glock

Movements are continuous, each corresponding to a section of the poem
by Walt Whitman.

I. "Hark, some wild trumpeter … "	*4'*
II. "… Love, that is the pulse of all … "	*5'*
III. "Blow again trumpeter—conjure war's wild alarums … "	*3'*
IV. "… Utter defeat upon me weighs … "	*3'*
V. "… Joy in the ecstasy of life! … "	*5'*

> Kalmus   Luck's   Schirmer

Night & Day, op.11, Two Poems for Piano & Orchestra   26'
<1901>

solo piano
2[1.2/pic] 3[1.2.Eh] 3[1.2.bcl] 3[1.2.cbn] — 4 2 3 1 — tmp — str
Original publisher: Boston Music Company.

Night	*13'*
Day	*13'*

> Fleisher

Ormazd, op.30 <1911>   10'

3[incl pic] 3[incl Eh] 3[incl bcl] 3[incl cbn] — 6 3 3 1 — tmp+3 —
hp — cel, pf — str

> AME   Presser

Coolidge, Peggy Stuart   1913-1981

(b Swampscott, MA, 19 July 1913; d Cushing, ME, 7 May 1981). American

Pioneer Dances <1980>   11'

3[incl pic] 2 2 2 — 4 3 3 1 — tmp+4 — hp — str
Also available in versions for string orch. and for chamber orch.:
   1 1 2 1 — 1 2 1 0 — tmp+3 — hp — str

Allegro vivo	*3'*
Andante, quasi rubato	*5'*
Allegro vivo	*3'*

> Peer

Copland, Aaron   1900-1990

(b Brooklyn, NY, 14 Nov 1900; d North Tarrytown, NY, 2 Dec 1990). American

APPALACHIAN SPRING: Chronology

This work exists in 4 versions. The chronology:
   1. Original ballet for 13 instruments (1943-44)
   2. Suite (shortened version of the ballet) for 13 instruments (1944)
   3. Suite (same music as no.2) for full orchestra (1945)
   4. Complete ballet for full orchestra (1954)
These are listed below in chronological order.

Appalachian Spring (complete ballet, 13 instruments)   33'
<1943–1944>

1 0 1 1 — pf — str[2.2.2.2.1]
The work as originally conceived.

> Boosey

Appalachian Spring: Suite (13 instruments)   23'
<1943–1944>

1 0 1 1 — pf — str[2.2.2.2.1]
The music of the Suite, using the original instrumentation.

> Boosey

Appalachian Spring: Suite (full orchestra)   23'
<1943–1944; rev 1945>

2[1.2/pic] 2 2 2 — 2 2 2 0 — tmp+2 — hp — pf — str
perc: bd, sus cym, sd, tabor, tri, glock, xyl, woodblk, claves
Shortened version of the ballet, rescored for full orchestra; this is the most
commonly heard version of this work.

> Boosey

Appalachian Spring (complete ballet, full orch version)   33'
<1943–1944; rev 1954>

2[1.2/pic] 2 2 2 — 2 2 2 0 — tmp+2 — hp — pf — str
perc: bd, sus cym, sd, tabor, tri, glock, xyl, woodblk, claves

> Boosey

Billy the Kid: Suite <1938>   22'

3[1.2/pic.pic] 2 2 2 — 4 3 3 1 — tmp+4 — hp — pf — str
perc: xyl, sd, woodblk, glock, cym, slgh-bells, guiro, whip, sus cym, bd, tri

Introduction: The Open Prairie	*3'*
Street in a Frontier Town	*3'*
Mexican Dance and Finale	*4'*
Prairie Night (Card Game at Night)	*4'*
Gun Battle	*2'*
Celebration (After Billy's Capture)	*3'*
Billy's Death	*1'*
The Open Prairie Again	*2'*

> Boosey

Billy the Kid: Prairie Night & Celebration Dance <1938;   5'
rev 1946>

1[1/pic] 1 2 1 — 1 2 2 0 — tmp+2 — pf — str
Excerpts from the ballet, arranged for chamber orchestra.

> Boosey

Billy the Kid: Waltz (Billy and His Sweetheart) <1938;   4'
rev 1946>

1 1 2 1 — 1 2 1 0 — hp[or pf] — str
Excerpt from the ballet, arranged for chamber orchestra. This movement
is not included in the Suite.

> Boosey   Luck's

Canticle of Freedom <1955; rev 1967>   13'

chorus
3[1.2.pic] 2[1.2/opt Eh] 2 2 — 4 3 3 1 — tmp+4 — hp — str
perc: glock, gong, chimes, vib, xyl, cym, sus cym, tamtam, tri, woodblk, whip, sd,
bd

> Boosey

Ceremonial Fanfare <1969>   3'

0 0 0 0 — 4 3 3 1 — [no str]
Score available in the collection *Ceremonial Music*, which includes the
composer's *Fanfare for the Common Man, Jubilee Variation, Preamble
for a Solemn Occasion, Ceremonial Fanfare,* and *Inaugural Fanfare.*
Parts are available separately.

> Boosey

The City <1939>   22'

1[1/pic] 1[1/Eh] 3[1.2.bcl/asx] 1 — 2 2 1 0 — tmp+1 — pf — str
perc: bd, sus cym, chimes
1. New England Countryside	5'
2. The Steel Mill	2'
3. The Sorrow of the City	3'
4. Fire Engines at Lunch Hour	2'
5. Taxi Ja	2'
6. Sunday Traffic	3'
7. The New City	4'
8. The Children	1'

Boosey

Concerto, Clarinet <1948>   18'

hp — pf — str
Slowly and expressively	10'
Rather fast	8'

Boosey

Concerto, Piano <1926>   16'

3[1.2.pic] 3[1.2.Eh] 4[1.2.Ebcl.bcl] 3[1.2.cbn] — 4 3 3 1 — asx — tmp+5 — cel — str
perc: xyl, tamtam, woodblk, field dr, cym, tri, bd, Chinese drum
I. Andante sostenuto	7'
II. Molto moderato (molto rubato) - Allegro assai	9'

Boosey

Connotations <1962>   20'

4[1.2.3/pic2.pic1] 3[1.2.Eh] 4[1.2.Ebcl.bcl] 3[1.2.3/cbn] — 6 4 4 1 — tmp+5 — pf/cel — str
perc: xyl, glock, congas, tamtam, vib, crot, td, timbales, sd, tri, cym, woodblk, bd, templeblks, claves, metal plate

Boosey

Dance Panels; A Ballet in Seven Sections <1959>   29'

2[1/opt afl.2/pic] 1 2 1 — 2 2 1 0 — 2perc — str
perc: sd, sus cym, xyl, tri, field dr, glock, bd, cym, woodblk, templeblks
I. Introduction: Moderato (Tempo di Valzer)	5'
II. Allegretto con tenerezza	5'
III. Scherzando	3'
IV. Pas de trois: Lento	5'
V. Con brio	4'
VI. Con moto	2'
VII. Molto ritimico	5'

Boosey

Dance Symphony <1922–1925>   19'

3[1.2/pic2.3/pic1] 3[1.2.Eh] 4[1.2.Ebcl.bcl(A)] 3[1.2.cbn] — 4 5[3tp.2crt] 3 1 — tmp+4 — 2hp — pf/cel — str
perc: xyl, field dr, woodblk, whip, tri, tamtam, cym, bd
Music taken from the composer's ballet Grogh.
Introduction: Lento	2'
I. Molto allegro; Adagio molto	6'
II. Andante moderato	6'
III. Allegro vivo	5'

Boosey

Danzón cubano <1942>   7'

3[1.2/pic.pic] 3[1.2.Eh] 3[1.2.bcl] 3[1.2.cbn] — 4 3 3 1 — tmp+4 — pf — str
perc: xyl, woodblk, cowbell, marac, sd, whip, claves, guiro, bd, cym, Chinese blocks

Boosey

Down a Country Lane <1962>   3'

2 1 2 1 — 2 1 1 0 — str

Boosey

Eight Poems of Emily Dickinson <1948–1950; rev 1970>   21'

medium voice
1[1/pic] 1 1[Ebcl] 1 — 1 1 1 0 — hp — str[min 8.6.4.3.2]
I. "Nature, the gentlest mother"	4'
II. "There came a wind like a bugle"	2'
III. "The world feels dusty"	2'
IV. "Heart, we will forget him"	2'
V. "Dear March, come in!"	2'
VI. "Sleep is supposed to be"	3'
VII. "Going to heaven!"	3'
VIII. "The chariot"	3'

Boosey

Emblems <1964>   12'

3[1.2.3/pic] 3[1.2.Eh] 4[1.2.3.4/bcl] 3[1.2.3/cbn] — 4 4 4 1 — tmp+4 — pf/cel — str
perc: bd, bongos, congas, cym, glock, gong, sd, sus cym, td, tri, woodblk, xyl
Originally for band; transcribed for orchestra by D. Wilson Ochoa, 2008.

Boosey

Fanfare for the Common Man <1942>   3'

0 0 0 0 — 4 3 3 1 — tmp+2 — [no str]
perc: bd, tamtam
Score available in the collection Ceremonial Music, which includes the composer's Fanfare for the Common Man, Jubilee Variation, Preamble for a Solemn Occasion, Ceremonial Fanfare, and Inaugural Fanfare. Parts are available separately.

Boosey

Inaugural Fanfare <1969; rev 1975>   4'

3[1.2.3/pic] 2 2 0 — 4 3 3 1 — tmp+4 — [no str]
perc: whip, glock, cym, sd, vib, td, sus cym, bd, tamtam
Score available in the collection Ceremonial Music, which includes the composer's Fanfare for the Common Man, Jubilee Variation, Preamble for a Solemn Occasion, Ceremonial Fanfare, and Inaugural Fanfare. Parts are available separately.

Boosey

Inscape <1967>   13'

3[1.2.pic] 3[1.2.Eh] 3[1.2.bcl] 2 — 4 3 3 1 — tmp+4 — hp — pf/cel — str
perc: sd, tambn, td, claves, glock, tri, xyl, vib, 3sus cym

Boosey

John Henry <1940; rev 1952>   4'

2[1.2/pic] 2 2 2 — 2 2 1 0 — tmp+2 — opt pf — str
perc: sd, tri, bd, anvil, sandpaper blks
Possible with woodwinds 1 1 2 1.

Boosey

Jubilee Variation on a Theme by Eugene Goosens <1945>   2'

3[1.2.pic] 3[1.2.Eh] 3[1.2.bcl] 3[1.2.cbn] — 4 3 3 1 — tmp+4 — pf — str
perc: xyl, sd, tri, cym, bd
Score available in the collection Ceremonial Music, which includes the composer's Fanfare for the Common Man, Jubilee Variation, Preamble for a Solemn Occasion, Ceremonial Fanfare, and Inaugural Fanfare. Parts are available separately.

Boosey

Letter from Home <1944; rev 1962>   6'

2 2[ob2 opt] 3[1.2.opt bcl] 2[bn2 opt] — 2 2 2 0 — tmp+2 — opt hp — opt pf — str
perc: glock, bd, cym, tri

Boosey   Luck's

Lincoln Portrait <1942>   14'

speaker
2[1/pic.2/pic] 3[1.2.opt Eh] 3[1.2.opt bcl] 3[1.2.opt cbn] — 4 3[tp3 opt] 3 1 — tmp+3 — hp — opt cel — str
perc: glock, xyl, cym, slgh-bells, sd, tamtam, bd

Boosey

Music for a Great City <1964>   24'

3[1.2/pic1.3/afl/pic2] 3[1.2.Eh] 3[1.2.bcl] 3[1.2.cbn] — 4 3 3 0 — tmp+7 — hp — pf/cel — str
perc: glock, gong, vib, xyl, congas, timbales, cym, sus cym, tri, claves, templeblks, woodblk, whip, bd, sd, td, rattle, sandblks, 2cowbells; tmp plays marac
The city of the title is London.

Skyline	7'
Night Thoughts	7'
Subway Jam	3'
Toward the Bridge	7'

Boosey

Music for Movies <1942>   16'

1[1/pic] 1 1 1 — 1 2 1 0 — 1perc — pf [or hp] — str
perc: sd, bd, tri, sus cym, glock, xyl, tmp
Written for tmp+2, but it is possible for one player to cover tmp and both perc parts.

Contents—New England Countryside	5'
Barley Wagons	2'
Sunday Traffic	3'
Grovers Corners	3'
Threshing Machines	3'

Boosey

Music for the Theatre <1925>   21'

1[1/pic] 1[1/Eh] 1[1/Ebcl] 1 — 0 2 1 0 — 1perc — pf — str[min 2.2.2.2.1]
perc: xyl, glock, td, woodblk, sus cym, bd w/ ped

I. Prologue	6'
II. Dance	3'
III. Interlude	5'
IV. Burlesque	3'
V. Epilogue	4'

Boosey

Nonet for Strings <1960>   18'

str[3vn.3va.3vc]
Performance by larger ensembles of up to 48 strings authorized by the composer.

Boosey

Old American Songs (First Set) <1950; rev 1954>   14'

medium voice or chorus
1[1/pic] 1 2 1 — 1 1 1 0 — hp — str

1. Boatmen's Dance	4'
2. The Dodger	2'
3. Long Time Ago	3'
4. Simple Gifts	2'
5. I Bought Me a Cat	3'

Boosey

Old American Songs (Second Set) <1952; rev 1957>   13'

medium voice or chorus
1[1/pic] 1 2 1 — 2 1 1 0 — hp — str

1. The Little Horses	3'
2. Zion's Walls	2'
3. Golden Willow Tree	4'
4. At the River	2'
5. Ching-a-Ring Chaw	2'

Boosey

Orchestral Variations <1930; rev orchd 1957>   13'

2[1/pic2.2/pic1] 2[1.Eh] 2[1.2/bcl] 2 — 4 2 3 1 — tmp+3 — hp — str
perc: bd, bongos, crot, chimes, congas, cowbell, cym, glock, sd, tamtam, td, woodblk, xyl, sus cym
Originally for piano; orchestrated by the composer.

Boosey

Our Town <1940>   11'

3[fl3 opt] 3[1.2[opt].Eh] 3[1.2.3/bcl] 2 — 3 3 2 1 — 1perc — str
perc: glock
Music from the film of the Thornton Wilder play.

Boosey

An Outdoor Overture <1938>   10'

3[1.2.pic] 2 2 2 — 4 2 3 0 — tmp+3 — pf, opt cel — str
perc: xyl, sd, cym, tri, bd

Boosey

Prairie Journal (Music for Radio; Saga of the Prairie) <1937>   13'

2[1.2/pic] 2 2 1 — 2 3[tp3 opt] 2 1 — 2asx[1/cl.2/cl], tsx[dbl bcl] — tmp+1 — hp — pf/cel — str
perc: vib, xyl, tri, bd
Original title: Music for Radio, Saga of the Prairie. Retitled 1968.
  Cues permit performance with winds: 2[1.2/pic] 2 2 2 — 4 2 2 1 (i.e., 3rd & 4th hn replace 2asx; 2nd bn replaces tsx).

Boosey

Preamble for a Solemn Occasion <1949>   6'

optional narrator
3[1.2/pic2.3/pic1] 3[1.2.Eh] 3[1.2.bcl] 3[1.2.cbn] — 4 3 3 1 — tmp+2 — hp — str
perc: gong, sus cym, vib, tri, bd, td, cym
Score available in the collection Ceremonial Music, which includes the composer's Fanfare for the Common Man, Jubilee Variation, Preamble for a Solemn Occasion, Ceremonial Fanfare, and Inaugural Fanfare. Parts are available separately.

Boosey

Quiet City <1939>   10'

solo trumpet   solo English horn (or oboe)
str

Boosey

The Red Pony <1948>   25'

2[1/pic.2/pic] 2[1.2/Eh] 4[1.2.3/bcl.opt Ebcl] 2 — 4[hn4 opt] 3 3 1 — tmp+4 — hp — pf/cel — str
perc: glock, xyl, vib, marim, sd, td, cym, tri, slgh-bells, bd

I. Morning on the Ranch	5'
II. The Gift	5'
IIIa. Dream March; IIIb. Circus Music	5'
IV. Walk to the Bunkhouse	3'
V. Grandfather's Story	4'
VI. Happy Ending	3'

Boosey

Rodeo [McPhee reduction] <1942>   25'

2[1.2/pic] 2[1.2/Eh] 2[1.2/bcl] 2 — 4 2 3 1 — tmp/whip+2 — opt hp — pf — str
perc: sd, woodblk, tri, sus cym, cym, bd, xyl, glock, rattle
Reduced orchestration by Jonathan McPhee.

Buckaroo Holiday	7'
Interlude & Corral Nocturne	5'
Rag-Time and Rancher's Daughter	4'
Saturday Night Waltz	4'
Hoe-Down	5'

Boosey

RODEO: FOUR DANCE EPISODES   7'
1. Buckaroo Holiday <1942>
3[1.2/pic1.3/pic2] 3[1.2.opt Eh] 3[1.2.opt bcl] 2 — 4 3 3 1 — tmp+4
— hp — pf/cel — str
perc: xyl, glock, sd, woodblk, tri, cym, whip, bd

Boosey

2. Corral Nocturne <1942>   4'
1 1 2 1 — 2 2 1 0 — hp — cel — str

Boosey

3. Saturday Night Waltz <1942>   4'
1 1 3[1.2.opt bcl] 1 — 2 2 1 0 — hp — str

Boosey

4. Hoe-Down <1942>   3'
3[1.2.pic] 3[1.2.opt Eh] 3[1.2.opt bcl] 2 — 4 3 3 1 — tmp+4 — pf —
str
perc: xyl, bd, sd, woodblk, tri, cym
Playable without Eh or bcl.

Boosey

Rodeo: Hoe-Down (string orchestra) <1942>   3'
str

A piano part is included in the set, though not indicated in the score; this
piano part is, if not essential, at least highly desirable.

Boosey

El Salón México <1933–1936>   11'
3[1.2.pic] 3[1.2.opt Eh] 4[1.2.opt Ebcl.opt bcl] 3[1.2.opt cbn] — 4
3[tp3 opt] 3 1 — tmp+4 — pf — str
perc: sd, woodblk, guiro, bd, xyl, cym, sus cym, templeblks, tambourin provençal

Boosey   Luck's

Statements <1935>   19'
3[1.2.3/pic] 3[1.2.Eh] 3[1.2.bcl] 3[1.2.cbn] — 4 3 3 1 — tmp+3 — str
perc: tamtam, sd, whip, cym, glock, bd
Movements often performed individually or in groups.

Military	*3'*
Cryptic	*3'*
Dogmatic	*2'*
Subjective	*4'*
Jingo	*3'*
Prophetic	*4'*

Boosey

Symphonic Ode <1928–1929; rev 1955>   19'
4[1.2.3/pic.pic] 4[1.2.3.Eh] 4[1.2.Ebcl.bcl] 4[1.2.3.cbn] — 8[hn5-8 opt]
4 3 1 — tmp+4 — 2hp — pf — str
perc: tamtam, field dr, bd, glock, templeblks, cym, td, woodblk, xyl, tri, whip,
chimes

Boosey

Symphony for Organ & Orchestra (1924) (Organ Symphony) <1924>   25'
3[1.2/pic2.pic1] 3[1.2.Eh] 2 3[1.2.cbn] — 4 3 3 1 — tmp+4 — 1 or
2hp — opt cel — str
perc: xyl, woodblk, tambn, sd, cym, bd
A revised version without solo organ was later published as *Symphony
No.1*.

I. Prelude: Andante	*7'*
II. Scherzo: Allegro molto	*7'*
III. Finale: Lento	*11'*

Boosey

Symphony No.1 <1928>   25
3[1.2/pic.pic] 3[1.2.Eh] 3[1.2.bcl] 3[1.2.cbn] — 8 5 3 1 — opt asx —
tmp+5 — 2hp — pf/cel — str
perc: xyl, tambn, woodblk, glock, field dr, cym, tamtam, bd
A revision (without organ solo) of his *Symphony for Organ & Orchestra*

I. Prelude: Andante	*7'*
II. Scherzo: Allegro molto	*7'*
III. Finale: Lento	*11'*

Boosey

Symphony No.1: Prelude (arr. for chamber orchestra) <1924>   5'
1 1 1 1 — 1 1 0 0 — hp[or pf] — str
Arranged by the composer.

Boosey   Luck's

Symphony No.2 (Short Symphony) <1932–1933>   15'
3[1/afl.2.pic] 3[1.2.Eh/opt heckl] 3[1.2.bcl] 3[1.2.cbn] — 4 2 0 0 —
pf — str

I. quarter note = 144 (preciso)	*4'*
II. half note = c. 44	*5'*
III. quarter note = 144 (preciso e ritmico)	*6'*

Boosey

Symphony No.3 <1944–1946>   43'
4[1.2.3/pic2.pic1] 3[1.2.3/Eh] 4[1.2.bcl.Eb] 3[1.2.cbn] — 4 4 3 1 —
tmp+5 — 2hp — cel, pf — str
perc: bd, cym, sus cym, sd, td, tri, tamtam, glock, xyl, chimes, woodblk, whip,
ratch, claves, anvil

I. Molto moderato; with simple expression	*11'*
II. Allegro molto	*8'*
III. Andantino quasi allegretto	*10'*
IV. Molto deliberato - Allegro risoluto	*14'*

Boosey

The Tender Land: Suite <1952–1954>   19'
3[1.2.pic] 2[1.Eh] 2[1.2/bcl] 2 — 4 3 3 1 — tmp+2 — hp — opt
pf/cel — str
perc: glock, tri, sd, woodblk, xyl, cym, ratch, bd, whip

I. Introduction and Love Music	*9'*
II. Party Scene	*5'*
III. Finale: The Promise of Living	*5'*

Boosey

The Tender Land: Suite (chamber ensemble version) <1852–1956>   25'
solo soprano & tenor
1 0 1 1 — pf — str[2.2.2.2.1]
Arr. for 13 instruments by Murry Sidlin.

Boosey

Three Latin-American Sketches <1972>   11'
1[1/pic] 1 1 1 — 0 1 0 0 — 1perc — 1 or 2 pf — str[min 6.4.3.2.1]
perc: claves, woodblk, xyl, ratch, whip, tri, congas, sus cym

I. Estribillo	*3'*
II. Paisaje Mexicano	*4'*
III. Danza de Jalisco	*4'*

Boosey

Two Pieces for String Orchestra <1923–1928>   11'
str[or str 4t]

I. Lento molto	_'
II. Rondino	_'

Boosey

Variations on a Shaker Melody <1943–1944; rev 1967>   4'

2[1.2/pic] 2 2 2 — 2 2 2 0 — opt tmp, 1perc — opt hp — pf — str
perc: glock, tri
Adapted from the composer's *Appalachian Spring*.

Boosey

Corelli, Arcangelo   1653-1713

(b Fusignano, 17 Feb 1653; d Rome, 8 Jan 1713). Italian

Concerti grossi, op.5

see: Geminiani, Francesco, 1687-1762
        Concerto grosso in C major, after Corelli, op.5, no.3
        Concerto grosso no.12, after Corelli, op.5, no.12 (La folia)

Concerto grosso, op.6, no.1, D major <1714>   12'

2 solo violins, solo violoncello
cnt — str
1. Largo; Allegro	5'
2. Largo	3'
3. Allegro	2'
4. Allegro	2'

Eulenburg	Kalmus	Luck's	Peters	Ricordi

Concerto grosso, op.6, no.2, F major <1714>   10'

2 solo violins, solo violoncello
cnt — str
1. Vivace; Allegro	4'
2. Allegro	2'
3. Grave; Andante largo; Allegro	4'

Eulenburg	Kalmus	Luck's	Peters	Ricordi

Concerto grosso, op.6, no.3, C minor <1714>   10'

2 solo violins, solo violoncello
cnt — str
1. Largo; Allegro	4'
2. Grave; Vivace	4'
3. Allegro	2'

Eulenburg	Kalmus	Luck's	Peters	Ricordi

Concerto grosso, op.6, no.4, D major <1714>   9'

2 solo violins, solo violoncello
cnt — str

Eulenburg	Kalmus	Luck's	Peters	Ricordi

Concerto grosso, op.6, no.5, B-flat major <1714>   10'

2 solo violins, solo violoncello
cnt — str

Eulenburg	Kalmus	Luck's	Peters	Ricordi

Concerto grosso, op.6, no.6, F major <1714>   12'

2 solo violins, solo violoncello
cnt — str
Adagio	2'
Allegro	2'
Largo	3'
Vivace	2'
Allegro	3'

Eulenburg	Kalmus	Luck's	Peters	Ricordi

Concerto grosso, op.6, no.7, D major <1714>   8'

2 solo violins, solo violoncello
cnt — str
Vivace; Allegro	2'
Allegro	2'
Andante largo	2'
Allegro	1'
Vivace	1'

Eulenburg	Kalmus	Luck's	Peters	Ricordi

Concerto grosso, op.6, no.8, G minor (Christmas Concerto) <1690>   13'

2 solo violins, solo violoncello
cnt — str
I. Vivace - Grave - Allegro	3'
II. Adagio - Allegro - Adagio	3'
III. Vivace	1'
IV. Allegro	2'
V. Pastorale	4'

Eulenburg	Kalmus	Luck's	Peters	Ricordi

Concerto grosso, op.6, no.9, F major <1714>   10'

2 solo violins, solo violoncello
cnt — str
1. Preludio: Largo	1'
2. Allemanda: Allegro	3'
3. Corrente: Vivace	2'
4. Gavotte: Allegro; Adagio	2'
5. Minuetto: Vivace	2'

Eulenburg	Kalmus	Luck's	Peters	Ricordi

Concerto grosso, op.6, no.10, C major <1714>   12'

2 solo violins, solo violoncello
cnt — str
Preludio	2'
Allemanda	2'
Adagio	1'
Corrente	2'
Allegro	3'
Minuetto	2'

Eulenburg	Kalmus	Luck's	Peters	Ricordi

Concerto grosso, op.6, no.11, B-flat major <1714>   9'

2 solo violins, solo violoncello
cnt — str
1. Preludio	2'
2. Allemanda	2'
3. Adagio	2'
4. Sarabanda	1'
5. Gigue	2'

Eulenburg	Kalmus	Luck's	Peters	Ricordi

Concerto grosso, op.6, no.12, F major <1714>   10'

2 solo violins, solo violoncello
cnt — str
Preludio	2'
Allegro	3'
Adagio	1'
Sarabanda	1'
Giga	3'

Eulenburg	Kalmus	Luck's	Peters	Ricordi

Sarabanda, Giga e Badinerie (Suite for String Orchestra) <1700>   8'

str
A pastiche, assembled and arranged by E. Pinelli from individual movements of the composer's 12 sonatas for violin & continuo, op.5.
Sarabanda [from op.5, no.7]	_'
Giga [from op.5, no.9]	_'
Badinerie [from op.5, no.11]	_'

Luck's	Ricordi

Corigliano, John

1938-

(b New York, 16 Feb 1938). American

Aria <1985>

6'

solo oboe
str orch [or str 5t]
Adapted from his *Oboe Concerto*.

Schirmer

Campane di Ravello <1987>

4'

4[1.2.3.pic] 4[1.2.3.Eh] 4[1.2.3.bcl] 4[1.2.3.cbn] — 4 4 3 1 — tmp+5
— hp — pf — str
perc: chimes, glock, crot, marim, xyl, sus cym, bd, 3tamtams
"A celebration piece for Sir Georg Solti." Based on C.F. Summy's *Happy Birthday to You*.

Schirmer

Concerto, Clarinet <1977>

30'

4[1.2.3.pic] 4[1.2.3.Eh] 3[1.2.bcl] 4[1.2.3.cbn] — 6 4 3 1 — 2tmp+3
— hp — pf — str
perc: xyl, vib, templeblks, woodblk, sd, td, tamtam, cym, tri, bd, 5tomtoms, 3sus cym, 2tambn
Preferred number of strings: 14.14.12.12.6 (less or more may be used).
    Special seating, including some players surrounding the audience.

Schirmer

Concerto, Oboe <1975>

28'

2[1.2/pic] 1 2[1.2/Ebcl] 2 — 2 1 1[btbn] 0 — tmp+3 — hp — pf/opt cel — str
perc: bd, sus cym, xyl, tambn, sd, tamtam, tri, whip, cym, td, 3tomtom, hi bells, kazoo

I. Tuning Game	6'
II. Song	6'
III. Scherzo	4'
IV. Aria	7'
V. Rheita Dance	5'

Schirmer

Concerto, Piano <1968>

38'

3[1.2.pic] 3[1.2.Eh] 3[1.2.3/bcl] 2 — 4 3 3 1 — tmp+3 — hp — str
perc: sd, td, xyl, sus cym, tamtam, chimes, tri, bd, ratch, tambn, choke cymbal, 3tomtom

I. Molto allegro	16'
II. Scherzo	6'
III. Andante appassionata	9'
IV. Allegro	7'

Schirmer

Concerto, Violin (The Red Violin) <2003>

39'

3[1.2/pic.3/pic/afl] 2 2[1.2/bcl] 2[1.2/cbn] — 4 2 3 1 — tmp+4 — hp
— pf/cel — str
1st mvt derived from "The Red Violin Chaconne," itself inspired by the film "The Red Violin" (1998), the music for which was composed by Corigliano.

1 Chaconne	16'
2. Pianissimo scherzo	5'
3. Andante flautando	6'
4. Accelerando finale	9'

Schirmer

Conjurer (Concerto for Percussionist & String Orchestra [with optional Brass]) <2007>

37'

solo percussionist
0 0 0 0 — 4 3 3 1 — str
The brass play only in the final mvt, and are optional.
    The soloist performs at one of three stations, corresponding to the particular movement:
    I. WOOD: 2claves, 4woodblocks, 5templeblocks, castanet, coconut, 2wood drums, 3logdrums, marimba, xylophone
    II. METAL: chimes, vibraphone, glockenspiel, crotales, 2tamtams, suspended cymbal
    III. SKIN: 4timpani, 2bongos, 6tomtoms, bass drum, talking drum, 2kickdrums

I. Wood	10'
II. Metal	15'
III. Skin	12'

Schirmer

Creations; Two Scenes from Genesis <1971; rev 1984>

27'

narrator & dancers (or mimes)
2[1.2/pic] 2[1.2/Eh] 2[1.2/bcl] 2[1.2/cbn] — 2 1 1 0 — tmp+1 — hp
— pf — str
perc: bd, sd, sus cym, tambn, tamtam, glock, xyl, vib, ratch, 3tomtom
Much graphic notation.

I. The Creation of the World	15'
II. The Creation of Adam and Eve	12'

Schirmer

A Dylan Thomas Trilogy <1959–1999>

68'

boy soprano, tenor, baritone   chorus
3[1/pic.2/pic.3/pic] 3 3[1.2.3/bcl] 3[1.2.cbn] — 4 3 3 1 — tmp+3 —
hp — pf, hpsd — str
perc: bd, cym, sus cym, sd, td, tambn, tamtam, glock, xyl, vib, chimes, whip, ratch, guiro, anvil, 3tomtom
A compilation of 3 previously existing works, with the addition of the Author's Prologue, Parts I & II. The movements all elide one to another.
    Discreet amplification and lighting effects stipulated in score. Drawn from the aggregate above, on the forestage are the soloists, a chamber chorus of 24 (chmb chor), and a chamber orchestra (chmb orch: 1110—1000—hp—hpsd—str[4.3.2.2.1]) Behind these are seated the remainder of the orchestra (lg orch) and a chorus of 125 (lg chor).

Author's Prologue, Part I (baritone, lg chor, lg orch)	5'
I. Fern Hill (boy sop, chmb chor, chmb orch)	15'
Author's Prologue, Part II (baritone, lg chor, lg orch)	6'
II. Poem in October (tenor, chmb orch)	15'
III. Poem on His Birthday (baritone, tutti chor, tutti orch)	27'

Schirmer

Elegy for Orchestra <1965>

8'

2[1.2/pic] 2 2 2 — 2 1 1[btbn] 0 — tmp+2 — pf [or hp] — str
perc: sd, sus cym, bd, tri, cym

Schirmer

Fancy on a Bach Air <1996>

6'

str

Schirmer

Fantasia on an Ostinato <1986>

14'

3[1.2/pic1.3/pic2] 3 3 3[1.2.3/cbn] — 4 4 3 1 — tmp+5 — hp — pf
— str
perc: brake dr, bd, sd, td, tambn, rototom, templeblks, tamtam, ratch, sus cym, cym, chimes, whip, crot, glock, xyl, tri, vib, 3vc bows

Schirmer

Fern Hill <1960–1961> 16'

solo mezzo-soprano   chorus
2 2 2 2 — 4 2 2 0 — tmp+2 — hp — pf — str
perc: bd, cym, sus cym, sd, tri, tambn, xyl, vib, opt marim
Brief solo 4t (SATB, drawn from chorus).
   This work exists in two other versions of the instrumental accompaniment:
    (1) strings, piano & optional harp
    (2) chamber orch (1999): 1 1 1 0 — 1 0 0 0 — hp — str [in this chamber orchestra version the mezzo-soprano is replaced by a boy soprano.]
    ["Fern Hill" is also the 2nd movement of "A Dylan Thomas Trilogy."]
Schirmer

Gazebo Dances <1981> 13'

2[1.2/pic] 2 2 2 — 4 3 3 1 — tmp+3 — str
perc: bd, cym, sus cym, sd, td, tri, tambn, xyl, handbell
Overture   *4'*
Waltz   *2'*
Adagio   *5'*
Tarantella   *2'*
Schirmer

Jamestown Hymn <2007> 3'

3 3 3 — 4 3 3 1 — tmp+3 — str
perc: bd, sus cym, td, tamtam, vib
Schirmer

Midsummer Fanfare <2004> 5'

3[1.2.pic] 3 3 3 — 4 3 3 1 — tmp+3 — hp — pf — str
perc: bd, sus cym, sd, td, tambn, glock, xyl, vib, crot, belltree, templeblks, ratch, 2tri
Schirmer

Mr. Tambourine Man; Seven Poems of Bob Dylan <2000; rev (orchd) 2003> 36'

soprano (amplified)
3[1.2/pic.3/pic] 3[1.2.3/Eh] 3[1.2.3/Ebcl/bcl] 3[1.2.3/cbn] — 4 4 3 1 — asx/bsx — tmp+3 — hp — pf — str
perc: 2bd, 2sus cym, sd, td, metal plate, hammer, tri, 2tambn, tamtam, gong, glock, xyl, vib, 3 sets chimes (2 offstage), flexatone, woodblk, templeblks, whip, police whistle, vibrslp
Texts are by Bob Dylan, but the music newly composed by Corigliano without reference to Dylan's original musical settings. Corigliano's settings originally (2000) for voice and piano, and later (2003) orchestrated by the composer. In 2009 a version was created for soprano [ampd], flute/pic/bfl, clarinet/Ebcl/bcl, 1percussion, piano, violin[opt dbl va], violoncello. Also in 2009 a transcription with accompaniment for wind ensemble was made by Verena Meisenbichler and approved by the composer.
Prelude: Mr. Tambourine Man   *4'*
1. Clothes Line   *7'*
2. Blowin' in the Wind   *6'*
3. Masters of War   *4'*
4. All Along the Watchtower   *3'*
5. Chimes of Freedom   *7'*
Postlude: Forever Young   *5'*
Schirmer

One Sweet Morning <2011> 27'

solo mezzo-soprano
3[1.2.3/pic] 3 3[1.2.3/Ebcl/bcl] 3[1.2.3/cbn] — 4 3 3 1 — tmp+4 — hp — pf/cel — str
perc: vib, glock, crot, bd, xyl, belltree, sd, templeblks, sus cym, cym, whip, field dr, td, tambn, tri, 2tamtam, 5tomtom, 3bellplates, dagu[=Chinese bass drum]
I. A Song on the End of the World   *9'*
II. Patroclus   *7'*
III. War South of the Great Wall   *6'*
IV. One Sweet Morning   *5'*
Schirmer

Phantasmagoria on "The Ghosts of Versailles" <1999> 23'

3[1.2/pic.3/pic] 3[1.2.3/Eh] 3[1.2/Ebcl.3/bcl] 3[1.2.3/cbn] — 4 4 3 1 — tmp+4 — hp — pf/synth — str
perc: bd, cast, chimes, crot, glock, sd, sus cym, templeblks, tomtom, tri, vib, 2woodblk, xyl, tambn, low drum[=td?]
Schirmer

Pied Piper Fantasy <1979–1981> 38'

solo flute doubling on tin whistle or piccolo; costume suggested
3[1.2/pic.3opt] 3 3[1.2.3/Ebcl/bcl] 3[1.2.3/cbn] — 4 3 3 1 — tmp+4 — hp — pf/cel — str[min 14.12.10.8.6]
perc: bd, sd, td, tambn, glock, xyl, vib, chimes, crot, templeblks, whip, ratch, 2pr cym, 3sus cym, 5tomtom, 3tri, 2tamtam, sandpaper, bell
Children's group: flutes (piccolos, tin whistles) in any multiple of three (*i.e.,* 3, 6, 9, etc.); 1 low drum, 1 high drum; "acting" children if necessary to augment the production.
   Children's group marches in and out; score includes stage directions, as well as lighting and costuming suggestions.
I. Sunrise and the Piper's Song   *10'*
II. The Rats   *2'*
III. Battle With the Rats   *3'*
IV. War Cadenza   *4'*
V. The Piper's Victory   *5'*
VI. The Burghers' Chorale   *4'*
VII. The Children's March   *10'*
Schirmer

Poem in October <1970> 17'

solo tenor
1 1 1 0 — 1 0 0 0 — hpsd — str
See also the composer's "A Dylan Thomas Trilogy," which includes the present work as its penultimate mvt.
   Schirmer also offers a reduced version for: 1 1 1 0 — hpsd — str 4t.
Schirmer

Poem on His Birthday <1976> 32'

solo baritone   chorus
2[1.2/pic] 2 2[1.2/bcl] 2 — 4 2 2 0 — tmp+3 — hp — pf — str
perc: bd, xyl, sus cym, cym, chimes, sd, td, vib, tamtam, 3tomtom, anvil
See also the composer's "A Dylan Thomas Trilogy," which includes the present work as its last mvt.
Schirmer

Promenade Overture <1981> 8'

2[1.2.pic] 2 2 2 — 6[hn5-6 opt] 4 3 1 — tmp+4 — hp — str
perc: bd, sus cym, finger cym, sd, td, tri, tambn, tamtam, glock, xyl, belltree, templeblk, ratch
Starting with a bare stage, the players gradually enter while playing.
Schirmer

The Red Violin; Chaconne for Violin & Orchestra <1997> 17'

solo violin
3[1.2/pic.3/pic] 2 2 2 — 4 2 3 1 — tmp+3 — hp — pf/cel — str
From the music for the 1997 film. See also the composer's *Concerto, Violin (The Red Violin)*.
Schirmer

The Red Violin: Suite <1997; rev 1999> 24'

solo violin
tmp+2 — hp — str
perc: bd, marim, vib, whip, chimes, sd
From the music for the 1997 film. See also the composer's *Concerto, Violin (The Red Violin)*.
Schirmer

Salute <2006> 1'

0 0 0 0 — 4 3 3 1 — kazoos[min 5] — 2perc — [no str]
perc: bd, sd, 2pol whstle

Schirmer

Snapshot: Circa 1909 <2003; rev (arr) 2011> 7'

2 solo violins
str
Originally for string quartet (2003); arranged by the composer (2011).

Schirmer

Symphony No.1 <1988–1989> 41'

4[1.2/pic.3/pic.4/pic] 4[1.2.3.Eh] 4[1.2.3/Ebcl/opt cbcl.4/bcl]
4[1.2.3.cbn] — 6 5 4[1.2.3[btbn].4[btbn]] 2 — 2tmp+6 — hp — pf —
str
perc: glock, vib, rototom, whip, sus cym, flexatone, xyl, brake dr, tamtam, ratch,
td, marim, crot, sd, tambn, field dr, tri, templeblks, chimes, 3sets chimes, anvil,
finger cym, 5tomtoms, metalplate, 3bd, police whistle, tmp3
1-2 stands of violin II double on mandolin. Clarinet 4 doubles on Ebcl if
the optional contrabass clarinet (in the cl3 part) is used.
1. Apologue: Of Rage and Remembrance   14'
2. Tarantella   9'
3. Chaconne: Giulio's Song [attacca]   14'
4. Epilogue   4'

Schirmer

Symphony No.2 <2000> 38'

str[min 6.5.4.4.2]
I. Prelude   4'
II. Scherzo   7'
III. Nocturne   9'
IV. Fugue   9'
V. Postlude   9'

Schirmer

Three Hallucinations <1981> 13'

3[1.2.3/pic] 3 3[1.2.3/Ebcl/bcl] 3[1.2.3/cbn] — 4 3 3 1 — 2tmp+4 —
hp — 2pf[grand pf/elec org.smaller pf mistuned] — str[min 12.10.8.8.6]
Electric organ backstage; also backstage the smaller piano (upright or
baby grand, tuned 1/4 tone flat).
Winds may be increased to 4 4 4 4 — 6 4 3 1, if the remainder of
the ensemble is "large enough."
Based on music for the film Altered States.

Schirmer

To Music <1994> 5'

2[1.2/pic] 2 2[1.2/bcl] 2 — 4 3 3 1 — tmp+1 — str
perc: bd, sus cym
Some of the brass placed offstage around the audience. A fantasy on
Schubert's song An die Musik, and adapted from Corigliano's Fanfares to
Music for double brass quintet.

Schirmer

Tournaments <1967> 12'

3[1.2.3/pic] 3[1.2.Eh] 3[1.2.bcl] 3[1.2.cbn] — 4 4 3 1 — tmp+3 — hp
— pf — str
perc: xyl, whip, tri, sd, sus cym, bd

Schirmer

Troubadours (Variations for Guitar & Chamber Orchestra) <1993> 23'

solo guitar
2[1.2/pic] 2[1.2/Eh] 2 2 — 2 0 0 0 — 2perc — opt pf — str[6.6.4.4.2]
perc: xyl, vib, glock, crot, tambn, tri, sd, td, field dr, bd, tamtam, 3tomtom, 2sus
cym, bell
Ob2/Eh, bn1&2, and hn1&2 are positioned offstage throughout. Perc2
moves offstage at certain times.

Schirmer

Utah Fanfare <2000> 2'

0 0 0 0 — 4[offstage] 4[2pic tp offstage, 2tp onstage] 3 1 — 2perc —
[no str]
perc: sd, bd, tmp

Schirmer

Vocalise <1999> 20'

solo soprano (textless)   sound engineer
3[1.2.3/pic] 2 3[1.2.3/bcl] 2 — 4 4[all off-stage; tp2/pic tp] 3 1[opt]
— electronics — tmp+4 — hp — pf/cel — str
perc: bd, belltree, cym, crot, glock, sd, sus cym, tambn[opt], tamtam, tri, vib, xyl
4microphones, used at times by solo soprano, fl1, cl1, tp1. Electronics
designed by Mathias Gohl; sound engineer and control panel to be
conspicuously visible to audience.
Trumpets 2 & 3 double on crotales; tp4 doubles on glockenspiel; extra
percussion instruments required for these musicians offstage.

Schirmer

Voyage, for Strings <1971; rev 1976> 7'

str
Originally "L'invitation au voyage," a Baudelaire text set for a cappella
chorus (1971). Arranged by the composer for strings (1976) and again for
solo flute accompanied by strings & harp (1983).

Schirmer

Voyage, for Flute & Strings <1971; rev 1976, 1983> 7'

hp — str
Originally "L'invitation au voyage," a Baudelaire text set for a cappella
chorus (1971). Arranged by the composer for strings (1976) and again for
solo flute accompanied by strings & harp (1983).

Schirmer

Cornelius, Peter   1824-1874

(b Mainz, 24 Dec 1824; d Mainz, 26 Oct 1874). German

Der Barbier von Bagdad: Overture (original, B minor) 8'
<1855–1858>

3[1.2.pic] 2 2 2 — 4 2 3 0 — tmp+3 — str
perc: tri, cym, bd
This is the overture originally written for the opera. It is an entirely
different work from the so-called Mottl arrangement of the same title (see
the following entry).

Breitkopf   Kalmus   Luck's

Der Barbier von Bagdad: Overture (D major; arr. Mottl) 7'
<1855–1858>

3[1.2.pic] 2 2 2 — 4 2 3 1 — tmp+2 — hp — str
perc: cym, tri
This second overture was composed shortly before the composer's death;
it is an entirely different work from original B minor overture.
Although the title page states that it was "arranged after the original
score by Felix Mottl," it is believed that Franz Liszt actually orchestrated
the work (S.352 in the Searle index). Mottl revised, shortened, and
reorchestrated the entire opera in the early 1880s, and that is probably the
arrangement referred to; thus the present work may be considered Mottl's
arrangement of Liszt's orchestration of Cornelius's second overture.

Luck's

143

Corrin, Gary   1955-

(b San Jose, CA, 30 July 1955). American

How the Orchestra Grew   55'

narrator
3[1.2/afl.3/pic] 3[1.2.Eh] 3[1.2/Ebcl.3/bcl] 3[1.2.cbn] — 4 3 3 1 — tmp+3 — hp — str
perc: bd, cym, tri, tamtam, deep church bells
Props: natural horn, snake (Peruvian string instrument), drinking straw cut as a double reed, animal horn, empty bottle, two pieces of wood.
    Traces the development of the orchestra from a small group of strings to the full modern ensemble. Each instrument is introduced individually, then added to the orchestra in music that features that instrument and illustrates a new stage in the development of the orchestra.
    Intended for youth; an 85-minute version for adults is available.

> Corrin

Costa, John Vasconcelos   1955-

(b Taunton, MA, 9 Decmeber 1955). American

Allure <1994>   15'

3[1.2.pic] 3[1.2.Eh] 2 2 — 4 2 2 1 — tmp+2 — str
perc: bd, sd, tri, tamtam, marim, vib, 3sus cym, 3tomtoms

> Costa

Espranza <1991>   13'

2[1.2/pic] 2 2 2 — 4 2 2 1 — tmp+2 — str
perc: bd, cym, sd, templeblks, 3sus cym, 3woodblk, 3tri

> Costa

Providence <2002–2003>   13'

2[1.2/pic] 2 2 2 — 4 3 3 1 — tmp+2 — str
perc: sus cym, cym, glock, bd, vib, xyl, sd, tomtom, marim
1 clarinet leaves stage for backstage cadenza, or a 3rd cl may be used.

> Costa

Vignette <1996>   6'

2 2 2 2 — 4 2 2 1 — tmp+2 — hp — str
perc: bd, sus cym, sd, marim, vib

> Costa

Cotton, Jeffery   1957-2013

(b San Fernando, CA, 4 April 1957). American

CityMusic <1995; rev 2000>   12'

narrator
3[1.2.3/pic] 2[1.2/Eh] 2[1.2/bcl] 2[1.2/cbn] — 4 3 3 1 — tmp+3 — hp — str
perc: bd, cym, sus cym, sd, tri, tamtam, bongos, anvil, police whistle, bullhorn

> Cotton

Concerto, Clarinet <2002>   27'

hp — str
1.   9'
2.   8'
3.   10'

> Cotton

Elegy <2001>   5'

str

> Cotton

La folia <2000>   15'

hp — str

> Cotton

Lyra <1999>   13'

str

> Cotton

Pyramus and Thisbe: Suite <2002>   31'

str
1. *Divertissement I*   5'
2. *Pas de deux I (Thisbe's Dream)*   6'
3. *Solo (Thisbe's Lament)*   4'
4. *Pas de deux II*   10'
5. *Prélude et divertissement II*   6'

> Modern Works

Couperin, François   1668-1733

(b Paris, 10 Nov 1668; d Paris, 11 Sept 1733). French

La Sultane: Overture and Allegro <1695>   7'

3[1.2.pic] 3[1.2.Eh] 3[1.2.bcl] 2 — 3 3 3 1 — tmp+1 — hp — str
Orchestrated by Darius Milhaud.

> Elkan-Vogel   Luck's

Cowell, Henry   1897-1965

(b Menlo Park, CA, 11 March 1897; d Shady, NY, 10 Dec 1965). American

HC = William Lichtenwanger, *The Music of Henry Cowell: A Descriptive Catalog* (New York, 1986)

Air and Scherzo for Alto Saxophone & Small Orchestra, HC 897a <1961; rev (orchd) 1963>   9'

2 1 2 1 — str
Originally for alto saxophone & piano; orchestrated by the composer, 1963.
Air   6'
Scherzo (Gay—Sad—Gay)   3'

> AMP

Ancient Desert Drone, HC 597 <1940>   5'

3 3[1.2.Eh] 3 3 — 4 3 3 1 — tmp+2 — hp — str
perc: bd, cym, tomtom, glock
An alternate version exists for:
1 2[1.Eh] 2 1 — 2 2 1 0 — tmp+2 — str

> AMP

Ballad, HC 705 3/b <1954>   4'

str
Originally for woodwind quintet.

> AMP   Luck's

Carol for Orchestra <1965>   9'

2 2 2 2 — 2 2 0 0 — hp [or pf] — str
The composer's own version for "western orchestra" of his *Koto Concerto*.

> AMP

Chiaroscuro, HC 892 <1961>   11'

3[1.2.3/pic] 3 3[1.2.3/bcl] 3 — 4 3 3 1 — tmp+2 — str
perc: cym, sd, 5tomtom, 5metal sounds, 2gong, marim[or xyl], 4woodblk

> AMP

Fanfare for the Forces of our Latin American Allies, HC 634 <1942>   *1'*

0 0 0 0 — 4 3 3 0 — 3perc — [no str]
perc: cym, sd, bd

| Boosey |

Fiddler's Jig, HC 771 <1952>   *2'*

solo violin
str

| AMP | Luck's |

Four Irish Tales, HC 605 (Tales of Our Countryside) <1940>   *14'*

solo piano
3[1.2/pic.3] 3 3 3 — 4 3[crt or tp] 3 1 — tmp+2 — str
perc: bd, cym, sd, woodblk, templeblks, xyl[opt]
Expansion of four early piano pieces: HC 219/1, 328, 384, 463/1.
1. *Deep Tides (aka Tides of Manaunaun)*   *3'*
2. *Exultation*   *2'*
3. *The Harp of Life*   *6'*
4. *Lilt of the Reel*   *3'*

| AMP |

Hymn and Fuguing Tune No.2, HC 657 <1944>   *7'*

str

| AMP |

Hymn and Fuguing Tune No.3, HC 660 <1944>   *7'*

2[incl pic] 2 2 2 — 4[hn3&4 opt] 2 2 1 — tmp+2 — str
perc: cym, xyl, chimes, bd

| AMP | Luck's |

Hymn and Fuguing Tune No.5, HC 673a <1946>   *7'*

str

| AMP |

Hymn and Fuguing Tune No.10, HC 813 <1955>   *10'*

0 1 0 0 — 0 0 0 0 — str
Hymn   *6'*
Fuguing Tune   *4'*

| AMP |

Hymn and Fuguing Tune No.16, HC 921a <1963>   *6'*

2 2 2 2 — 4[hn3-4 opt] 3 3 1 — str

| Peters |

Old American Country Set, HC 567 <1939>   *13'*

2 2 2 1[or bsx or bcl] — 2 2 1 1 — banjo — 3perc — str
perc: xyl, sd, bd
The banjo may be substituted for by xylophone (much of the xyl part already doubles the banjo), ampd guitar, mandolin, or flute.
1. *Blarneying Lilt*   *2'*
2. *Meeting House*   *2'*
3. *Comallye [come-all-ye]*   *3'*
4. *Charivari [pron. "shivaree"]*   *4'*
5. *Cornhuskin' Hornpipe*   *2'*

| AMP |

Ongaku, HC 846 <1957>   *14'*

2 2[1.2/Eh] 2 2 — 2 2 0 0 — tmp+2 — hp — cel — str
perc: bd, glock, 4sus cym, 2gong, 4woodblk
I. *Gagaku*   *6'*
II. *Sankyoku*   *8'*

| AMP |

Polyphonica for Small Orchestra, HC 458 <1925>   *4'*

1 1 1 1 — 1 1 1 0 — str

| AMP | Luck's |

Sinfonietta, HC 443 <1928>   *14'*

1 1 1 1 — 1 1 1 0 — str[2.2.1.1.1]
Larghetto   *7'*
Scherzo   *3'*
Marked Passages   *4'*

| AMP |

Symphony No.3, HC 636 (Gaelic) <1942>   *23'*

3[1.2.pic] 3[1.2.Eh] 4[1.2.3.bcl] 3[1.2.(3opt)] — 4 3 3[1.2.3.euph] 1 — 4sx[2asx.tsx.bsx] — tmp+3 — str
perc: bd, cym, sus cym, sd, tomtom, gong, glock, xyl, chimes[opt], 2woodblk
Saxophones and Eh are cued in other instruments, and probably considered optional.
I. *Maestoso*   _'
II. *Andante cantabile*   _'
III. *Allegretto con moto*   _'
IV. *Allegro*   _'

| AMP |

Symphony No.5, HC 722 <1948>   *28'*

3[1.2/pic.3] 3[1.2.Eh] 3[1.2.3/bcl] 3 — 4 3 3 1 — tmp+3 — pf — str
perc: xyl, glock, chimes, sd, cym, marac, claves, 2tomtom, 2gong

| AMP |

Symphony No.7, HC 776 <1952>   *25'*

2 1[ob/Eh] 2[1.2/bcl] 1 — 2 1 1 0 — tmp+1 — pf — str
perc: glock, xyl, cym
I. *Maestoso*   *10'*
II. *Andante*   *5'*
III. *Presto*   *4'*
IV. *Maestoso*   *6'*

| AMP |

Symphony No.9, HC 787 <1953>   *22'*

2[1.2/opt pic] 2[1.2/opt Eh] 2 2 — 2 2 2 0 — tmp+2 — hp or pf — str
perc: bd, cym, sd, chimes
I. *Largo*   _'
II. *Allegro*   _'
III. *Allegretto quasi andante*   _'
IV. *Presto*   _'
V. *Allegro*   _'

| AMP |

Symphony No.10, HC 788 <1953>   *23'*

2 2[1.2/Eh] 2[1.2/bcl] 2 — 2 2 0 0 — tmp — str
I. *Largo*   _'
II. *Allegro*   _'
III. *Andante con moto*   _'
IV. *Allegro*   _'
V. *Allegretto quasi andante*   _'
VI. *Maestoso*   _'

| AMP |

Symphony No.15, HC 887 (Thesis) <1960>   *23'*

3[1.2.3/pic] 3 3[1.2.3/bcl] 2 — 4 3 3[1.2.opt 3] 1 — tmp+2 — cel — str
perc: gong, cym, bd, xyl, tamtam, 5 metal pieces, 5tomtom
I. *Largo*   _'
II. *Andante*   _'
III. *Presto*   _'
IV. *Allegretto*   _'
V. *Allegro*   _'
VI. *Moderato*   _'

| AMP |

Symphony No.16, HC 912 (Icelandic) <1962>   24'

2 2 2 2 — 2 2 2 1 — tmp+2 — hp — str
perc: gong, cym, xyl, 6tomtom, 6metal sounds
"For large orchestra, third winds double seconds; horns 3-4 double 1-2."

I. Moderato con moto	4'
II. Allegro	4'
III. Adagio cantabile	5'
IV. Vivace	3'
V. Maestoso	8'

AMP

Symphony No.17, HC 916 (Lancaster) <1963>   22'

2 2 2 2 — 4 2 2 1 — tmp+2 — str
perc: cym, bd, chimes, templeblks, gong, sd, glock, 5tomtom, 5metal sounds

I. Moderato	_'
II. Andante vigoroso	_'
III. Drone and Ground: Maestoso	_'
IV. Presto	_'
V. Allegro	_'

AMP

Symphony No.19, HC 943 <1965>   26'

3[1.2.3/pic] 3[1.2.3/Eh] 3[1.2.3/bcl] 3 — 4 3 3 1 — tmp+3 —
cel[played by perc] — str
perc: bd, sd, glock, xyl, marim, vib, 7tuned drums, 5tomtom, 5metal sounds,
3gongs, 2sus cym, 3tri, 7bowls, 2woodblk, cel[played by perc]

1. Allegro moderato	6'
2. Andante	5'
3. Vivace	6'
4. Andante	2'
5. Allegro	7'

AMP

Synchrony, HC 464 <1930>   15'

3[incl 3pic] 3 3[incl 2Ebcl] 3[incl cbn] — 4 3 3 1 — tmp+4 — str

Peters

Crawford (Seeger), Ruth   1901-1953

(b East Liverpool, OH, 3 July 1901; d Chevy Chase, MD, 18 Nov 1953). American

Andante for Strings <1931>   4'

str

Merion

Music for Small Orchestra <1926>

1 0 1 1 — pf — str[4vn.2vc]

A-R Editions

Rissolty Rossolty <1939>   3'

1 1 2 1 — 2 2 1 0 — tmp — str

Merion

Three Songs <1930–1932>   9'

solo oboe, percussion, piano, contralto voice
0 0 1[cl/bcl] 1[bn/cbn] — 1 1 1 0 — str[min 2.2.2.1.1]
perc: [soloist] bd, sus cym, tri, tambn, tamtam, templeblks
The 4 soloist parts ("concertanti") may be performed with or without the
orchestral accompaniment ("ostinati").

I. Rat Riddles	3'
II. Prayers of Steel	2'
III. In Tall Grass	4'

Mercury

Cresswell, Lyell   1944-

(b Wellington, 13 Oct 1944). New Zealand composer, active in Scotland

Alas! How Swift <2006>   11'

solo trumpet
1 2[1.Eh] 2[1.bcl] 2 — 2 0 0 0 — str

Scottish

Cassandra's Songs <2005>   14'

mezzo-soprano solo
2[1/afl.pic] 2[1.Eh] 2[1.bcl] 2[1.cbn] — 2 2 1 0 — str

1. Cassandra's Lament
2.. Day and Night
3. Teach Me, Gods of Songs
4. Cassandra's Gift
5. Exile

Scottish

Concerto, Piano <2010>   20'

3[1.2.pic] 3[1.2.Eh] 3[1.2.bcl] 3[1.2.cbn] — 4 3 3 1 — tmp+3 — hp
— str
perc: szl cym, sd, tambn, glock, xyl, slgh-bells, templeblks, cowbell, marac,
2woodblk

I. Funeral March	_'
II. Adagio 1	_'
III. Scherzo 1	_'
IV; Addolorato	_'
V. Scherzo 2	_'
VI. Adagio 2	_'
VII. Presto	_'

Scottish

Concerto, String Quartet & Orchestra <1996>   25'

solos: 2vn, va, vc
3[1.2.3/pic] 3[1.2.Eh] 3[1.2.bcl] 3[1.2.cbn] — 4 3 3 1 — tmp+3 — hp
— str
perc: bd, sus cym, sd, tri, tambn, marac, claves, rute

Scottish

Concerto, Violoncello <1984>   27'

3[1.2.pic] 3[1.2.3/Eh] 3[1.2.bcl] 3[1.2.3/cbn] — 4 3 3 1 — tmp+3 —
hp — str
perc: glock, chimes, xyl, templeblks, sd, bd, 2sus cym

I. quarter-note = 72	11'
II. quarter-note = 54	8'
III. quarter-note = 88	8'

Waiteata

Kaea (Trombone Concerto) <1997>   18'

2[1.pic] 2[1.Eh] 2[1.bcl] 2[1.cbn] — 2 2 0 0 — str

Scottish

O! <1982>   16'

3 3 3 3 — 4 3 3 1 — tmp+3 — hp — pf — str
perc: sd, chimes, tri, bd, xyl, tamtam, 2sus cym

Waiteata

Of Smoke and Bickering Flame (Concerto for Chamber Orchestra) <2001–2002> 25'

2 2[1.Eh] 2 2 — 2 2 0 0 — str
  I. Con fuoco   _'
  II. Sospirando   _'
  III. Nostalgia 1 — piacevole   _'
  IV. Gorgogliante   _'
  V. Soave   _'
  VI. Animato   _'
  VII. Nostalgia 2 — sfogato   _'
  VIII. Infocato   _'

Scottish

I paesaggi dell'anima (Landscapes of the Soul) <2008> 15'

str

Scottish

Salm <1977> 20'

3[1.2.pic] 3[1.2.Eh] 3[1.2.bcl] 3[1.2.cbn] — 4 3 3 1 — tmp+3 — hp — str
perc: tamtam, bd, cym, chimes, sd, glock, vib, tri, crot, 2woodblk, 3sus cym
  I. quarter-note = c.60   _'
  II. quarter-note = 88   _'

Waiteata

The Voice Inside (Concerto for Violin, Soprano, & Orchestra) <2001> 25'

solos: soprano & violin
2[1/pic.2/pic] 2 2[1.bcl] 2[1.cbn] — 3 2 1 1 — 1perc — str
perc: templeblks
  I. Invocation   4'
  II. Scherzo I   3'
  III. Vigorous   4'
  IV. Slow Movement   5'
  V. Scherzo II   3'
  VI. Burlesque   2'
  VII. Plea   4'

Scottish

Ylur <1991> 27'

2[1.pic] 2[1.Eh] 2[1.bcl] 2[1.cbn] — 4 3 3 0 — 3perc — str
perc: bongos, ratch, tri, tambn, timbales, 3templeblks[3sets], 2claves[2pairs], 3cast, slitdrum, 3sd, 2cowbell, 5woodblk
  I. Risoluto   _'
  II. Sostenuto   _'
  III. Animato   _'
  IV. Piangente   _'
  V. Energico   _'
  VI. Ruvido   _'
  VII. Lontano   _'
  VIII. Feroce   _'

Waiteata

Creston, Paul

1906-1985

(b New York, 10 Oct 1906; d San Diego, CA, 24 Aug 1985). American

Airborne Suite: Night in Mexico 4'

3[1.2.3/pic] 3 3[1.2.3/bcl] 3[1.2.cbn] — 4 3 3 1 — tmp+4 — str
perc: bd, cym, sus cym, td, toms, tri, tambn, marim, marac, claves, cast
Bns & cbn may be replaced by 2bcl & contrabass clarinet in E-flat.

Templeton

Airborne Suite: Afternoon in Montreal 2'

3[1.2.3/pic] 3[ob3 opt] 3 3[1.2.cbn] — 4 1 0 0 — tmp+2 — str
perc: sd, tri, chimes, sleighbells, templeblk
Bns & cbn may be replaced by 2bcl & contrabass clarinet in E-flat.

Templeton

Concertino for Marimba & Orchestra, op.21 <1940> 17'

2 1 1 1 — 2 0 0 0 — tmp — str
  I. Vigorous   _'
  II. Calm   _'
  III. Lively   _'

Schirmer

Concerto, Alto Saxophone, op.26 <1941> 18'

3[1.2.pic] 2 2 2 — 4 2 3 1 — tmp — str
The accompaniment is also available for concert band.
  I. Energetic   6'
  II. Meditative   7'
  III. Rhythmic   5'

Schirmer

Dance Overture, op.62 <1954> 12'

4[1.2.3.pic] 3[1.2.Eh] 3[1.2.bcl] 3[1.2.cbn] — 4 3 3 1 — tmp+3 — str
perc: cast, bd, cym, sd, tamtam, tambn, xyl, tri

Luck's   Templeton

Fanfare for Paratroopers <1942> 1'

0 0 0 0 — 4 3 3 0 — 2perc — [no str]
perc: sd, cym

Boosey

Fantasy for Trombone, op.42 <1947> 13'

3[1.2.pic] 2 2 2 — 4 2 3 1 — tmp — str

Schirmer

Invocation and Dance, op.58 <1953> 12'

4[1.2.3.pic] 3[1.2.Eh] 3[1.2.bcl] 3[1.2.cbn] — 4 3 3 1 — tmp+3 — pf — str
perc: cym, sd, bd, gong, tri, tambn, tomtom, xyl
Possible with winds and percussion: 2 2 2 2 — 4 2 3 1 — tmp+2.

Schirmer

A Rumor <1941> 5'

1 1 2 1 — 2 2 1 0 — str

Schirmer

Symphony No.1, op.20 <1940> 24'

3[1.2.3/pic] 2 2 2 — 4 2 3 1 — tmp — str
  I. With Majesty   7'
  II. With Humor   6'
  III. With Serenity   7'
  IV. With Gaiety   4'

Schirmer

Symphony No.2, op.35 <1944> 23'

4[1.2.3.pic] 3[1.2.Eh] 3[1.2.bcl] 3[1.2.cbn] — 4 3 3 1 — tmp+4 — pf — str
perc: tambn, tri, xyl, tamtam, sd, cym, sus cym, bd, tomtom
  I. Introduction & Song   12'
  II. Interlude & Dance   11'

Schirmer

Symphony No.3, op.48 (Three Mysteries) <1950> 27'

4[1/pic.2.3.4] 3[1.2.Eh] 3[1.2.bcl] 3[1.2.cbn] — 4 3 3 1 — tmp — hp — str
  Nativity   10'
  Crucifixion   9'
  Resurrection   8'

Shawnee

Symphony No.4, op.52 <1951>   26'

3[1.2.3/pic] 2 2 2 — 4 2 3 1 — tmp — str
I. Maestoso; Allegro   7'
II. Andante pastorale   7'
III. Allegretto giocoso   5'
IV. Vivace saltellante   7'

Schirmer

Two Choric Dances, op.17b <1938>   12'

3[1.2.3/pic] 2 2 2 — 4 2 3 1 — tmp+1 — pf — str
perc: sd, tambn, tomtom, cym, tamtam

Schirmer

Crumb, George   1929-

(b Charleston, WV, 24 Oct 1929). American

Echoes of Time and the River; Four Processionals for   20'
Orchestra <1967>

3[1/pic.2/pic.3/pic] 0 3[1.2.Ebcl] 0 — 3 3 3 0 — mand — 6perc — hp
— pf, pf/cel — str[min 15.15.12.12.9]
perc: crot, bd, chimes, congas, glock, gong, marim, slgh-bells, timbales, vib, xyl,
anvils, bamboo windchimes, Chinese belltree, finger cym, glass chimes, bell, 4sus
cym, tmp, 3tamtams, watergong
A number of the wind and string players also play antique cymbals.
    Players move in procession from place to place, on and off stage, while
playing. Many other special effects.
I. Frozen Time   5'
II. Remembrance of Time   5'
III. Collapse of Time   5'
IV. Last Echoes of Time   5'

Belwin

Star-Child; A Parable <1977>   33'

solo soprano; 2 children's choruses (each SA); male speaking chorus also
playing 20 handbells
4[1/pic.2/pic.3/pic.4/pic] 4[1.2.3.4/Eh] 4[1.2.3.4/Ebcl] 4[1.2.3.4/cbn] —
6 7 3 1 — 8perc — org — str
perc: xyl, bongos, wnd mach, thunder, congas, td, sd, 9tamtam, 5db bows, 8sus
cym, 4slgh-bells, 3sets crot, 3tmp, ruler, 3tambn [1 mounted], 2glock, 2sets
chimes, 5pr claves, 2logdrum, 2iron chains, 16tomtoms, 2vib, 4szl cym,
4flexatone, 2pr marac, 2bd, metalplates, bell, hammer
Male speaking chorus (8-16 voices) should be amplified.
2 primary & 2 secondary conductors are required.

Peters

Variazioni <1959>   23'

3[incl 2pic] 3[incl Eh] 4[incl Ebcl,bcl] 3[incl cbn] — 4 3 3 1 — mand
— tmp+6 — hp — cel — str[min 14.14.12.12.10]
perc: crot, bd, cym, glock, sd, tamtam, td, tri, vib, xyl, tambn
Introduzione e Tema   3'
Pezzo Antifonale (Variation I)   1'
Toccata (Variation II)   1'
Fantasia I: Notturno   4'
Scherzo (Variation III)   1'
Trio Estatico: Canone Inversio (Variation IV)   2'
Da Capo: Burlesca (Variation V)   2'
Fantasia II: Cadenza   3'
Ostinato (Variation VI)   2'
Fantasia III: Elegia e Coda - Tema   4'

Peters

Crusell, Bernhard Henrik   1775-1838

(b Uusikaupunki, Finland, 15 Oct 1775; d Stockholm, 28 July 1838).
Swedish-Finnish

Concerto, Clarinet, No.2, op.5, F minor <1815>   25'

1 2 0 2 — 2 2 0 0 — tmp — str
Ed. Howard K. Wolf.
I. Allegro   _'
II. Andante pastorale   _'
III. Rondo: Allegretto   _'

Kalmus

Cunningham, Arthur   1928-1997

(b Piermont, NY, 11 Nov 1928; d Nyack, NY, 31 March 1997). American

Lullabye for a Jazz Baby <1969>   7'

2[incl pic] 2 3[incl bcl] 1 — 2 2 2 0 — 3perc — hp — str

Presser

Curiale, Joseph   1955-

(b Bridgeport, CT, 1 July 1955). American

Blue Windows   8'

solo trumpet
1 2[1.Eh] 2 1 — 4 2 3 0 — tmp+2 — hp — str
perc: cym, sus cym, sd, glock

Orchard Road

Gates of Gold <1993–1994>   19'

1[fl/pic] 2[1.Eh] 2 1 — 4 3 3 0 — tmp+3 — hp — pf/cel — str
perc: cym, sus cym, sd, woodblk, tambn, vib, glock, chimes, tri
NB: The many concertmaster solos in this piece were originally
conceived for erhu (Chinese stringed instrument).
1. Arrival: A View from Sea   3'
2. River of Tears   7'
3. Call of the Mountain   9'

Orchard Road

Sea of Tranquility/Ocean of Storms <2003>   5'

pf — str[no vn2]

Orchard Road

Wind River (I Am) <2000>   15'

2[1.2/pic] 2[1.Eh] 2 2 — 4 4 3 1 — tmp+3 or 4 — hp — cel[played
by perc] — str

Orchard Road

Cushing, Charles   1905-1982

(b Oakland, CA, 8 Dec 1905; d Berkeley, CA, 14 April 1982). American

Divertimento for String Orchestra <1944; rev 1976>   17'

str
I. Saltarello   6'
II. Serenade   3'
III. Nocturne   4'
IV. Finale   4'

Elkus

Czerny, Carl   1791-1857

(b Vienna, 21 Feb 1791; d Vienna, 15 July 1857). Austrian

Concerto, Piano 4-hands, op.153, C major   30'

solo piano 4-hands
2 2 2 2 — 2 2 0 0 — tmp — str
Allegro con brio   *12'*
Adagio   *6'*
Vivace   *12'*

> Four Hands

D

Dahl, Ingolf   1912-1970

(b Hamburg, 9 June 1912; d Frutigen, nr Berne, 6 Aug 1970). American composer of Swedish descent.

Concerto, Alto Saxophone & Wind Orchestra <1949; rev 1953>   22'

4[1.2.3.4/pic] 3[1.2.Eh] 5[1.2.3.Ebcl.bcl] 3[1.2.cbn] — 4 4 3 2 — tmp+3 — 4db
perc: bd, cym, sus cym, sd, field dr, tri, tambn, tamtam, glock, xyl, templeblks, cowbell, whip, bongos, cast, 2tomtoms, 2woodblks, metal block
May be played with full band, in which case certain passages are marked for single players.
1. Recitative   *6'*
2. Adagio (Passacaglia)   *8'*
3. Rondo alla marcia: Allegro brioso   *8'*

> Schott

Elegy Concerto <1963>   14'

solo violin
0 2 0 0 — 2 0 0 0 — str[min 6.6.4.4.2]
Left unfinished at the composer's death; completed by Donal Michalsky (1971).

> Boonin

Quodlibet on American Folk Tunes and Folk Dances <1965>   5'

3 2 3[1.2.opt bcl] 2 — 4 3 3 1[opt] — tmp+2 — opt pf — str
perc: td, woodblk, tri, xyl, glock, bd, 2sd, 2tomtoms, 2sus cym, 2pr cym

> Peters

Symphony concertante for 2 Clarinets & Orchestra <1952>   27'

2 solo clarinets
3[1.2.3/pic] 2 0 2 — 2 2 2 1 — tmp+1 — hp — str
perc: bd, cym, sus cym, td, field dr, tri, tambn, glock, xyl, 2sd [tmp also covers some cym]
Revised 1975 by Donal Michalsky, based on the composer's working copy.
    Carrie Ann Budelman, in a D.M.A. thesis (Rice University, 2008), discusses the historical aspects of this work, and provides a "critical" edition of the score.
I. Allegro; Adagio; Allegro   *_'*
II. Adagio   *_'*
III. Intoduction & Variations   *_'*

> Boonin

Variations on a Theme by C.P.E. Bach <1967>   12'

str
This work is permanently out of print, though sets are available at the Fleisher Collection and at Luck's Music Library.

> Fleisher   Luck's

Dallapiccola, Luigi

1904-1975

(b Pisino d'Istria [now Pazin, Istra, Croatia], 3 Feb 1904; d Florence, 19 Feb 1975).
Italian

Canti di liberazione <1955>   30'

chorus
3[1.2.3/pic] 3[1.2.Eh] 4[1.2.Ebcl.bcl] 3[1.2.cbn] — 4 3 3 1 — asx, tsx
— tmp+8 — 2hp — cel — str
perc: vib, glock, sd, chimes, field dr, bd, cym, gong, tamtam, 2xyl, 2sus cym, sd
w/o sn

O frater, frater	12'
Dominus quasi vir pugnator	6'
Vocasti et clamasti	12'

Zerboni

Canti di prigionia <1941>   25'

chorus
2tmp+8 — 2hp — pf — [no str]
perc: xyl, vib, chimes, sd, td, sus cym, cym, bd, tri, 3tamtams

Preghiera di Maria Stuarda	10'
Invocazione di Boezio	5'
Congedo di Girolamo Savonarola	10'

Carisch

Divertimento in quattro esercizi <1934>   13'

soprano solo
1[1/pic] 1 1 0 — va, vc

I. Introduzione	_'
II. Arietta	_'
III. Bourrée	_'
IV. Siciliana	_'

Carisch

Due pezzi per orchestra <1947>   11'

2 3[1.2.Eh] 2 2[1.2/cbn] — 4 3 2 1 — tmp+4 — 2hp — cel, pf — str
perc: xyl, field dr, tamtam, sus cym, cym, sd, bd

Sarabanda	6'
Fanfara e fuga	5'

Zerboni

Liriche greche: Cinque frammenti di Saffo (Five Fragments from Sapho) <1942>   8'

solo mezzo-soprano
1[1/pic] 1 2[1/bcl.Ebcl] 1 — 1 1 0 0 — hp — pf/cel — vn, va, vc, db

Vespro, tutto riporti	_'
O mia Gongila, ti prego	_'
Muore il tenero Adone, o Citerea	_'
Piena splendeva la luna	_'
Io lungamente	_'

Zerboni

Piccola musica notturna <1954>   7'

2 2 2 2 — 2 2 0 0 — tmp+3 — hp — cel — str
perc: bd, cym, sus cym, field dr, tamtam, gong, xyl, chimes

Schott

Piccola musica notturna (chamber version) <1954; rev 1961>   7'

1 1 1 0 — hp — cel — vn, va, vc

Schott

Tartiniana <1951>   16'

solo violin
3[1.2.pic] 1 4[1.2.Ebcl.bcl] 3[1.2.cbn] — 2 1 0 0 — 1perc — hp —
6va, 3vc, 2db
perc: xyl

Zerboni

Variazioni per orchestra <1954>   15'

2[1/pic.2/pic] 2[1.2/Eh] 2 2 — 4 2 3 1 — tmp+4 — hp — cel — str
perc: xyl, vib, sus cym, cym, tambn, sd, field dr, bd, tamtam, whip, sd w/o sn

Zerboni

Danielpour, Richard

1956-

(b New York, 28 Jan 1956). American

An American Requiem <2001>   63'

mezzo-soprano, tenor, baritone solos   chorus
3[1.2/afl.3/pic] 3[1.2.3/Eh] 3[1.2.3/bcl] 3[1.2.3/cbn] — 4[all dbl Wag
tb] 3 3 1 — tmp+5 — hp — pf/cel — str
perc: cym, sus cym, hi-hat, td, field dr, brake dr, tri, glock, xyl, vib, ratch, guiro,
rute, watergong, 2bd, 2tomtom, 2tamtam, 2chimes, 2crot
Additional offstage instruments: 6tbn.

PART I	
1. Introit: Requiem	_'
2. Dies Irae	_'
3. Vigil II—Lacrimosa—Pie Jesu	_'
PART II	
4. Sanctus—Benedictus	_'
5. Lay this Body Down—Agnus Dei	_'
6. Libera Me—Not in Our Time	_'
7. Lux Aeterna	_'

AMP

Apparitions, for Strings, Percussion & Celesta <2001; rev (orchd) 2002>   27'

tmp+3 — cel/pf — str[min 14.12.10.8.6]
perc: glock, crot, claves, cast, tri, sus cym, guiro, whip, marim, bd, rute, 3vibrslp[1
played by tmp], sandblks, 2xyl, 2chimes, 1 or 2vib
An orchestration by the composer of his String Quartet No.4.

I. Rudolfo's Dream	6'
II. Family Reunion	4'
III. Swan Song [str only]	7'
IV. Last Tango at Teatro Colon	4'
V. Johnnie Brown	6'

AMP

The Awakened Heart <1990>   24'

3[1.2.3/pic] 2[1.2/Eh] 3[1.2.3/bcl] 3[1.2.3/cbn] — 4 3 3 1 — tmp+4
— hp — pf/cel — str
perc: Chinescym, timbales, brake dr, tri, tambn, glock, xyl, marim, vib, chimes,
crot, cowbell, ratch, guiro, cast, 3sus cym, 3gong, 2sd, 4rototom, 2tomtom, 2bd

I. Into the World's Night	9'
II. Epiphany	8'
III. Hy Hero Bares His Nerves	7'

AMP

Concerto for Orchestra (Zoroastrian Riddles) <1996>   29'

3[1.2/pic.3/Eh] 3[1.2.Eh] 3[1.2.3/bcl] 3[1.2.3/cbn] — 4 3 3 1 —
tmp+4 — hp — pf/cel — str
perc: field dr, glock, marim, vib, chimes, 3sd, 7tomtom, 2tamtam, 4cowbell,
5bongos, 2rototom, 2bd, 3sus cym, 3brake dr, 2crot, 2xyl, 2woodblk, 4vibrslp,
3ratchet, 3cast, 4guiro, 3tambn, 2whip, 2rute, 2watergong, anvil, metalplate
N.B. percussion: A reassignment of the percussion parts could reduce the
number of duplicate instruments from that shown above.

I. Quarter-note = 108-112	6'
II. Playfully (scherzando)	5'
III. Adagio non troppo	11'
IV. Con moto leggiero, ben misurato	7'

AMP

Concerto, Piano, No.1

see his: Metamorphosis

Concerto, Piano, No.2 <1993>   31'

2[1.2/pic] 2[1.2/Eh] 3[1.2.bcl] 2[1.2/cbn] — 4 3 3 0 — tmp+3 — hp
— str[min 12.10.8.8.6]
perc: xyl, marim, vib, glock, guiro, cast, tri, tambn, brake dr, sus cym, gong,
tamtam, sd, bd, cowbell, whip, ratch, 2tomtom, 4rototom, chimes[2 sets]
I. Prophecy   _'
II. Lamentation   _'
III. Dénouement: A Cosmic Riddle   _'
AMP

Concerto, Violoncello <1994>   31'

3[1.2.3/pic] 3[1.2.Eh] 3[1.2.3/bcl] 3[1.2.3/cbn] — 4 3 3 1 — tmp+4
— hp — pf/cel — str[min 14.12.10.8.6]
AMP

Concerto, Violoncello, No.2

see his: Through the Ancient Valley

First Light (original version) <1988>   13'

1 1[incl Eh] 1 1 — 2 1 1 0 — tmp+2 — hp — pf [ampd] — str
Subsequently revised for expanded orchestra (see next entry).
AMP

First Light (expanded version); Concerto for Orchestra   13'
in One Movement <1989>

2 2[1.2/Eh] 2 2 — 4 2 2 0 — tmp+3 — hp — pf [ampd] —
str[10.10.8.6.4]
perc: sd, td, chimes, glock, xyl, vib, gong, 2sus cym
Originally for chamber orchestra (see previous entry).
AMP

Lacrimae beati (Tears of the Blessed One) <2008>   11'

str
Based on the first 8 bars of the "Lacrimosa" from Mozart's
Requiem—believed to be the last music that Mozart wrote.
AMP

Metamorphosis (Piano Concerto No.1) <1990>   28'

solo piano
2[1.2/pic] 2[1.2/Eh] 2[1.2/bcl] 2 — 2 2 2 0 — tmp+3 — hp —
str[10.10.8.7.5]
perc: cym, gong, tomtom, sd, tambn, glock, xyl, vib, tri, whip
I. Deciso   _'
II. Atonement   _'
III. Apotheosis   _'
AMP

Song of Remembrance <1991>   17'

3[1.2.3/pic] 2[1.2/Eh] 3[1.2.3/bcl] 3[1.2.3/cbn] — 4 4[tp4 offstage] 3
1 — tmp+4 — hp — pf/cel[ampd] — str
perc: xyl, glock, vib, sus cym, Chinescym, guiro, cast, tomtom, 2bd, 2sd, 2chimes,
3sus cym, 2gong, floortom
AMP

Symphony No.2 (Visions) <1986>   26'

solo tenor & soprano
2 2[1.2/Eh] 3[1.2.bcl] 2 — 4 2 3 1 — tmp+ — hp — pf — str
perc: bd, sus cym, tamtam, gong, glock, xyl, chimes
I. Who are you (tenor)   _'
II. I must lie still (tenor)   _'
III. When the wren bone (soprano)   _'
IV. There crouched bare (tenor & soprano) _'
V. Epilogue: I turn the corner of prayer _'
AMP

Symphony No.3 (Journey Without Distance) <1990>   29'

solo soprano   mixed chorus or male chorus
3[1.2.3/pic] 2[1.2/Eh] 3[1.2.3/bcl] 2[1.2/cbn] — 4 3 3 1 — tmp+3 —
hp — ampd pf (2 players opt)/cel — str
Part 1   16'
Part 2   13'
AMP

Through the Ancient Valley (Violoncello Concerto No.2)   28"
<2000>

violoncello solo
3[1.2/pic/afl.3/pic] 3[1.2.3/Eh] 3[1.2.3/bcl] 3[1.2.3/cbn] — 4 3 3 1 —
tmp+4 — hp — pf/cel — str[16.14.12.10.8]
perc: glock, xyl, chimes, congas, bongos, tambn, sus cym, tamtam, gong, 2vib,
2tomtom, 2bd, dumbek
Offstage instruments:
    fl (may be 1st fl from orch, onstage if necessary)
    ob (= 3rd ob)
    1 or 2 santours (Greek dulcimer)
    kemancheh (spike fiddle) or viola
    string 4t
AMP

Toward the Splendid City <1992>   10'

3[1.2.3/pic] 3[1.2.Eh] 3[1.2.3/bcl] 3[1.2.3/cbn] — 4 3 3 1 — tmp+4
— hp — pf/cel — str
perc: vib, xyl, marim, glock, chimes, sus cym, guiro, tomtom, sd, rototom, cast,
brake dr, timbales, tri, bd, cowbell, whip
AMP

Voices of Remembrance: A Concerto for String Quartet   24'
& Orchestra <1998>

solo string quartet
3[1.2.3/pic] 3[1.2.Eh] 3[1.2.3/bcl] 3[1.2.3/cbn] — 4 3 3 1 — tmp+6
— hp — pf/cel — str[min 16.14.12.10.8]
perc: sus cym, field dr, brake dr, tamtam, glock, vib, crot, cowbell, ratch,
metalplate, 2bd, 2td, 2tomtom, 2marim, 2whip, 2vibrslp
Solo string quartet should be on a raised platform.
    Additional offstage insts (last mvt only):
    Brass: 2hn, 1 or 2tbn (side balconies)
    Str 4t (wings)
    Perc: (3 of the 6 orchestral players at back of hall)
I. Adagio cantabile [attacca]   _'
II. Molto agitato [attacca]   _'
III. Misterioso   _'
AMP

Washington Speaks <2005>   8'

narrator
2 2 2 3[1.2.cbn] — 4 2 3 0 — tmp+2 — str[min 7.6.5.4.3]
perc: glock, crot, chimes, vib, sus cym, tri, bd, tamtam
AMP

A Woman's Life <2007>   22'

solo soprano
3[1.2.3/pic] 2[1.2/Eh] 3[1.2.bcl] 3 — 4 3 3 1 — tmp+3 — hp —
pf/cel — str
perc: bd, sus cym, hi-hat, sd, tomtom, tambn, tamtam, xyl, vib, chimes, woodblk,
cowbell, guiro, 4congas[2pairs], metalplate, sandblks
The solo voice should be amplified discreetly.
I. Little Girl Speakings   3'
II. Life Doesn't Frighten Me   3'
III. They Went Home   3'
IV. Come. And Be My Baby   3'
V. Let's Majeste   4'
VI. My Life Has Turned to Blue   3'
VII. Many and More   3'
AMP

Daugherty, Michael   1954-

(b Cedar Rapids, IA, 28 April 1954). American

Asclepius <2007>   6'

0 0 0 0 — 4 3 3 1 — tmp+2 — [no str]
perc: cym, sus cym, brake dr, glock, chimes

> Boosey

Bay of Pigs <2007>   16'

solo guitar
str 4t or str orch
  I. havana dreams   _'
  II. water fall   _'
  III. anthem   _'

> Boosey

Blue Like an Orange <1987>   10'

1 1 2[1.bcl] 0 — 1 1 1[btbn] 0 — 3perc — synth — str or str 5t
perc: marac, cast, glock, 2tambn, 2gong, 2chimes, 2whip, tmp, 3herdbells[G3,G#3,A#3]
Originally paired with the composer's *Snap!*, a 7-minute piece published by Peer for the same size ensemble (with differing percussion instruments).

> Boosey

Dead Elvis <1993>   10'

solo bassoon
0 0 1 0 — 0 1 1 0 — 1perc — vn, db
Elvis Presley costuming for solo bassoon is optional. Instrumentation is identical to that of Stravinsky's *L'Histoire du soldat*.

> Peer

Flamingo <1991>   9'

2 tambourine soloists
2[1.pic] 1 1 1 — 1 1 1[btbn] 0 — keyboard — str [small sections or str 5t]

> Boosey

Hell's Angels <1998–1999>   15'

solo bassoon quartet (3 bassoons & contrabassoon)
3[1.2.pic] 0 0 0 — 4 4 3 1 — tmp+4 — hp — cel — str
perc: windchimes, thunder, tri, marac, bd, bongos, vibrslp, sd, whip, chimes, crot, wnd mach, xyl, glock, claves, shaker

> Boosey

METROPOLIS SYMPHONY <1988–1993>   42'

3[1/pic.2/pic.3/pic] 3[1.2.3/Eh] 3[1.2/Ebcl.3/bcl] 3[1.2.cbn] — 4 4 3 1 — tmp+4 — synth/pf — str
Movements may be performed separately, as listed below.
  1. Lex   *10'*
  2. Krypton   *7'*
  3. Mxyzptlk (pronounced "Mix-yes-pittle-ick")   *7'*
  4. Oh, Lois!   *5'*
  5. Red Cape Tango   *13'*

> Peer

Metropolis Symphony: 1. Lex <1991>   10'

solo violin (may be concertmaster)
3[1.2.pic] 3[incl Eh] 3[1.Ebcl.bcl] 3[1.2.cbn] — 4 4 3 1 — tmp+4 — synth (or pf) — str
A chamber version exists of this movement alone, calling for amplified or electric violin, 4 percussion, timpani, 1 or 2 synthesizers, and electric bass (no other strings); the chamber version is published by Boosey.

> Peer

Metropolis Symphony: 2. Krypton <1993>   7'

3[1.2.pic] 3 3[1.Ebcl.bcl] 3[1.2.cbn] — 4 4 3 1 — 4perc — synth (or pf) — str
perc: td, tambn, siren, 2lg ship bells, 2cowbells

> Peer

Metropolis Symphony: 3. MXYZPTLK <1988>   7'

2 solo flutes (2nd doubles on piccolo)
0 2 2 2 — 2 1 1 0 — 2perc — synth — str
perc: sus cym, 3woodblks, whip, 2gongs, 3tri
Pronounced "Mix-yes-pittle-ick."

> Peer

Metropolis Symphony: 4. Oh Lois! <1989>   5'

2[1/pic.2] 2 2 2 — 4 3 3 0 — tmp+2 — synth (or keyboard) — str
perc: gong, tamtam, 2tri, 2flexatones, 2whips, 2bd
The 2perc are divided antiphonally.

> Peer

Metropolis Symphony: 5. Red Cape Tango <1993>   13'

3[1.2.pic] 3[1.2.Eh] 3[1.2.bcl] 3[1.2.cbn] — 4 4 3 1 — tmp+4 — pf — str
perc: chimes, sd, brake dr, cast, marac, tamtam, tambn, finger cym, 2pr cym

> Peer

Motorcity Triptych <2000>   30'

3[1.2.pic] 3[1.2.Eh] 3[1.Ebcl.bcl] 3[1.2.cbn] — 4 4 3 1 — tmp+4 — hp — str
perc: glock, xyl, bd, vibrslp, tambn, tamtam, whip, templeblks, ratch, vib, chimes, gong, 2woodblk, tomtom, finger cym, siren, pod rattles, 2djembe, 2tri, 3claves, 2brake dr, 3sus cym
  Motown Mondays   *9'*
  Pedal to the Metal   *10'*
  Rosa Parks Boulevard   *11'*

> Boosey

Route 66 <1998>   7'

3[1.2.pic] 3[1.2.Eh] 3[1.Ebcl.bcl] 3[1.2.cbn] — 4 4 3 1 — tmp+4 — hp — pf — str
perc: glock, xyl, vib, marim, bongos, timbales, brake dr, 2cowbells, 3sus cym, 3tri, 3woodblks

> Boosey

Le tombeau de Liberace <1996>   17'

solo piano
1[fl/pic] 1 1 1 — 2 1 1 1 — 2perc — str
perc: bd, szl cym, sd, tambn, glock, xyl, chimes, windchimes, whip, ratch, 3sus cym, 4tri, cast[2pr], marac[plastic], 2finger cym
Optional: 2fl[1.pic]
  I. Rhinestone Kickstep   *3'*
  II. How Do I Love Thee?   *6'*
  III. Sequin Music [piano only]   *3'*
  IV. Candelabra Rhumba   *5'*

> Boosey

UFO <1999>   35'

solo percussion
3[1.2.3/pic] 3[1.2.Eh] 3[1.Ebcl.bcl] 3[1.2.cbn] — 4 4 3 1 — str
perc: (solo) waterphone, siren, xyl, 3 "resonant metals", 4 "non-resonant metals", vib, marktree, ride cym, 2splash cym, bd with pedal, 5tomtoms, 8octobans, 2bongos, 3 cowbells, 3woodblks, 4sus cym
Solo percussionist moves from one "station" to another. Composer provides optional lighting cues if desired to enhance the theatrical effect.
  Traveling Music   *2'*
  Unidentified   *4'*
  Flying   *15'*
  ???   *4'*
  Objects   *10'*

> Boosey

David, Ferdinand   1810-1873

(b Hamburg, 19 June 1810; d Klosters, Switzerland, 18 July 1873). German

Concertino, Bassoon, op.12, E-flat major   15'

1 2 2 1 — 2 2 0 0 — tmp — str
The composer is said to have provided a version of this work for solo viola & orchestra.

| Kalmus | Luck's |

Concertino, Trombone, op.4, E-flat major   13'

2 2 2 2 — 4 2 3 0 — tmp — str
The composer is said to have provided a version of this work for solo violin & orchestra.

| Kalmus | Luck's |

Davidovsky, Mario   1934-

(b Buenos Aires, 4 March 1934). American composer of Argentine birth

Inflexions <1965>   7'

2[incl pic,afl] 0 1[cl/bcl/asx] 0 — 0 1 1 0 — 4perc — pf/cel — vn, va, vc, db

| Marks |

Davidson, Randall   1953-

(b Pueblo, CO, 31 July 1953). American

Black & Blues <1984>   21'

1 2 1 2 — 2 0 0 0 — 1perc — str
Crane Dancing	8'
Willy	5'
Judgement of the Birds	8'

| Boys Art |

Mexico-Bolivar Tango   5'

1 1 1 1 — str

| Boys Art |

The Young Lutheran's Guide to the Orchestra   24'

narrator
2[incl pic] 2[incl Eh] 2 2 — 4 3 3 1 — 2perc — hp — str

| Boys Art |

Davies, Peter Maxwell   1934-

see: Maxwell Davies, Peter

Davies, Victor   1939-

(b Winnipeg, Manitoba, 1 May 1939). Canadian

Dream Variations <1995>   21'

3[1.2.pic] 3[1.2.Eh] 3[1.2.bcl] 2 — 4[2 parts, each doubled] 3 3 1 — tmp+5 — hp — pf, synth, cel — str
perc: sd, bd, set, cym, sus cym, glock, vib, xyl, chimes, tambn, templeblks, woodblk, tri, ratch, crot, tamtam, belltree, whip, cowbell, brake dr, flexatone, wnd mach, siren whistle, cuckoo, birdcall, duckcall, bike hn, slide whistle, sound effects[cow, dog, "boing"]
Written for a combination of youth orchestras: senior & intermediate orchestras and (optional) junior orchestra. The junior orchestra, if used, has 3 violin parts and no double basses.
   A Lullaby and 15 "Dreams."

| Counterpoint |

Mennonite Piano Concerto <1975>   32'

2[1.2/pic] 2 2 2 — 4 3 3 0 — tmp+2 — str
perc: bd, cym, hi-hat, sd, set, tri, tambn, gong, glock, chimes, woodblk, cowbell, 3sus cym, 2tomtom
Based on Mennonite hymns.
1. Sonata	11'
2. Theme & Variations on "In the Rifted Rock I'm Resting"	14'
3. Rondo (Scherzo)	7'

| Counterpoint |

A Short Symphony <1974>   22'

2[1.2/pic] 2 2 2 — 4 3 3 1 — tmp+2 — str
perc: set, cowbell, hi-hat, bd, sus cym, sd, gong, whip, glock, tomtom, szl cym, marac, belltree, 2tomtom, fingercym
An oboe solo at the beginning and end of the 2nd mvt requires amplification with a reverb unit.
1. Glory, Glory	_'
2. The Comet	_'
3. Romance	_'
4. Jubilee	_'

| Counterpoint |

Davis, Anthony   1951-

(b Paterson, NJ, 20 Feb 1951). American

Esu Variations <1995>   11'

4[1.2/pic.3.4] 4 4 4[1.2.3.4/cbn] — 4 4 3 1 — tmp+3 — str
perc: vib, glock, chimes, marim, set
The title refers to the trickster god of Yoruban mythology.

| Schirmer |

Jacob's Ladder <1997>   8'

2 3[1.2.Eh] 3[1.2.bcl] 2 — 4 3 3 1 — tmp+3 — hp — str
perc: sus cym, set, marim, vib, bongos, congas

| Schirmer |

Litany of Sins <1992>   30'

1 1 1 1 — 1 0 0 0 — hp — str 5t

| Schirmer |

Notes from the Underground <1988>   9'

2[incl pic] 2 2 2 — 2 2 2 1 — tmp+4 — pf — str

| Schirmer |

Tales (Tails) of the Signifying Monkey <1998>   15'

3[1.2.pic] 3[1.2.Eh] 3[1.2.bcl] 3[1.2.cbn] — 4 3 3 1 — tmp+3 — hp — str
perc: bd, set, marim, vib

| Schirmer |

Wayang No.5 <1984>   25'

solo piano (must improvise)
2[incl pic] 1 2[incl bcl] 1 — 2 1 2 0 — tmp+4 — str
N.B. The 2nd clarinet doubles on contrabass clarinet in E-flat (sometimes called "contra-alto clarinet"); however the range of the part does not exceed that of the normal bass clarinet, so, with proper transposition, the part may be played on the latter instrument.

Schirmer

Davison, John   1930-1999

(b Istanbul, 31 May, 1930; d Haverford, PA, 5 March 1999). American

Arthur's Return <1983>   9'

bagpipe in B-flat
str

Fleisher

Dawson, William   1899-1990

(b Anniston, AL, 26 Sept 1899; d Montgomery, AL, 2 May 1990). American

Negro Folk Symphony <1934; rev 1952>   36'

3[1.2.pic] 3[1.2.Eh] 4[1.2.Ebcl.bcl] 3[1.2.cbn] — 4 3 3 1 — tmp+4 — hp — str
perc: gong, chimes, tri, td, sd, xyl, cym, bd, steel plate
The Bond of Africa: Adagio—Allegro con brio   14'
Hope in the Night: Andante—Allegretto (alla scherzando) 13'
O Le' Me Shine, Shine Like a Morning Star: Allegro con brio 9'

Shawnee

Dean, Brett   1961-

(b Brisbane, 23 Oct 1961). Australian

The Lost Art of Letter Writing, for Violin & Orchestra   34'
<2006; rev 2007>

3[1/pic1.2/afl.3/pic2] 2[1/Eh.2/Eh] 3[1.2/bcl2.bcl1/cbcl] 2[1.2/cbn] — 4 2 2 1 — tmp+4 — hp — pf[grand].cel/pf[upright] — str[14.12.10.8.6]
perc: bd, szl cym, hi-hat, sd, td, tambn, glock, vib, chimes, crot, slgh-bells[+ assorted keys, toy bells, etc.], whip, 4sus cym, 2Chinescym, 3tomtom, 2tamtam, 2marim, bass bow, 6tuned gong, rainstick, 2watergong, 2steelpan[7 pitches]
I. Hamburg, 1854 (Johannes Brahms)   12'
II. The Hague, 1882 (Vincent Van Gogh) 10'
III. Vienna, 1886 (Hugo Wolf)   4'
IV. Jerilderie, 1879 (Ned Kelly)   8'

Bote

Debussy, Claude   1862-1918

(b St Germain-en-Laye, 22 Aug 1862; d Paris, 25 March 1918). French

Berceuse héroïque <1914>   4'

2 3[1.2.Eh] 3 3 — 4 2 3 1 — tmp — 2hp — str
Originally for piano solo; orchestrated by the composer.

Durand	Kalmus	Luck's

La boîte à joujoux (The Toybox) <1913>   35'

2[1.2/pic] 3[1.2.Eh] 2 2 — 2 2 0 0 — tmp+4 — hp — cel, pf — str
perc: sd, tri, ratch, cym, bd
The beginning orchestrated by Debussy, the rest by André Caplet from Debussy sketches.
Peters "Urtext" ed. R.Zimmermann.
1. Prélude: Le sommeil de la boîte (The Toybox Asleep)   3'
2. Le magasin de jouets (The Toy Store)   11'
3. Le champ de bataille (The Battlefield)   10'
4. La bergerie a vendre (The Sheepfold for Sale)   7'
5. Après fortune faite (After Making a Fortune)   2'
6. Epilogue   2'

Durand	Kalmus	Luck's	Peters

Children's Corner (Le coin des enfants; arr. Caplet)   17'
<1906–1908>

2[1.2/pic] 2 2 2 — 4 2 0 0 — 2perc — hp — str
perc: tri, cym, bd, sd
Originally for piano; orchestrated by André Caplet, 1910.
Doctor Gradus ad Parnassum   3'
Jumbo's Lullaby (Berceuse des éléphants)   3'
Serenade for the Doll (Sérénade à la poupée) 3'
The Snow is Dancing (La neige danse)   3'
The Little Shepherd (Le petit berger)   2'
Golliwogg's Cake-Walk   3'

Durand	Kalmus	Luck's

Children's Corner (Le coin des enfants; arr.   17'
Abrahamsen) <1906–1908>

2[1.2/pic] 2[1.2/Eh] 2[1.2/bcl] 2 — 2 2 2 1 — tmp+3 — 2hp — cel/pf — str
perc: glock, chimes, xyl, crot, cym, bd, tambn, tamtam, tri, cast, slgh-bells
Originally for piano; orchestrated by Hans Abrahamsen, 2012.
Doctor Gradus ad Parnassum   3'
Jimbo's Lullaby (Berceuse des éléphants)   3'
Serenade of the Doll (Sérénade à la poupée) 3'
The Snow is Dancing (La neige danse)   3'
The Little Shepherd (Le petit berger)   2'
Golliwogg's Cake-Walk   3'

Hansen

Clair de lune (arr. Caplet) <1905>   5'

2 2 2 2 — 2 0 0 0 — hp — str
Originally for piano; from *Suite bergamasque*. Arr. André Caplet.
Many other arrangements of this work include those of Lucien Cailliet (Elkan-Vogel), Carmen Dragon (pub. Dragon); Wm. Gleichmann (Elkan-Vogel), Arthur Luck (Luck's), Alfred Reed (Kalmus), and Leopold Stokowski (Stokowski Collection).

Jobert

Clair de lune (arr. Luck) <1905>   5'

2 2 2 2 — 4 0 0 0 — hp — cel — str
Originally for piano; from *Suite bergamasque*. Arr. Arthur Luck.
Many other arrangements of this work include those of Lucien Cailliet (Elkan-Vogel), André Caplet (Jobert), Carmen Dragon (pub. Dragon); Wm. Gleichmann (Elkan-Vogel), Alfred Reed (Kalmus), and Leopold Stokowski (Stokowski Collection).

Luck's

La damoiselle élue (The Blessed Damozel) <1887–1888;   20'
rev (reorchd) 1902>

mezzo-soprano solo (or 2 Ms)   female chorus SSAA
3 3[1.2.Eh] 3[1.2.3/bcl] 3 — 4 3 3 0 — 2hp — str

Durand	Kalmus	Luck's

Danse <1890; rev 1903>   6'

2 2 2 2 — 2 2 0 0 — tmp+3 — hp — str
perc: sd, tri, bd, cym, crot
Orchestrated by Maurice Ravel, from Debussy's *Tarentelle styrienne* for
solo piano.

Jobert			

Danses sacrée et profane (Sacred and Profane Dances) <1904>   9'

solo harp
str
  I. Danse sacrée: Très modéré   5'
  II. Danse profane: Modéré   4'

Durand	Kalmus	Luck's	Peters

L'enfant prodigue (The Prodigal Son) <1884; rev 1907-08>   36'

solos STBar   optional chorus
3[1.2.3/pic] 3[1.2.Eh] 2 2 — 4 2 3 1 — tmp+2 — 2hp — str
perc: tambn, cym
  I. Prélude   2'
  II. Recit et Air (Lia): "L'année en vain chasse l'année"   5'
  III. Recit (Simeon): "Eh bien, encore des pleurs?"   1'
  IV. Cortège et Air de danse   4'
  V. Recit et Air (Azaël): "Ces airs joyeux"   6'
  VI. Recit (Lia): "Je m'enfuis"   3'
  VII. Duo (Lia; Azaël): "Rouvre les yeux"   5'
  VIII. Recit et Air (Simeon): "Mon fils est revenu!"   4'
  IX. Trio (Lia; Azaël; Simeon): "Mon coeur renaît à l'espérance"   6'

Durand	C. Fischer	Kalmus	Luck's

L'enfant prodigue: Cortège et Air de danse <1884; rev 1907-08>   7'

3[1.2.pic] 3[1.2.Eh] 2 2 — 4 2 0 0 — tmp+2 — hp — str
perc: sus cym, tambn

Durand	Kalmus	Luck's

Fantaisie, Piano & Orchestra <1889–1896>   25'

3 3[1.2.Eh] 3[1.2.bcl] 3 — 4 3 3 0 — tmp+1 — 2hp — str
perc: cym
Peters ed. M. Pommer.
  I. Andante; Allegro   9'
  II. Lento e molto espressivo   8'
  III. Allegro molto   8'

Jobert	Peters

Fantaisie, Piano & Orchestra (2nd version) <1889–1890; rev 1916-1917>   25'

3[1.2.3/pic] 3[1.2.Eh] 3[1.2.bcl] 3 — 4 3 3 0 — tmp+1 — hp — str
perc: cym
2nd version, with orchestration lightened by the composer (1916-1917),
ed. Jean-Pierre Marty, with Denis Herlin & Edmond Lemaître, first pub'd
in the Complete Works, 2007.
  I. Andante ma non troppo; Allegro giusto   9'
  II. Lent (très expressif)   8'
  III. Allegro molto   8'

Durand		

Five Etudes <1915>   18'

2[1.2/pic] 2[1.2/Eh] 2[1.2/bcl] 2[1.2/cbn] — 2 2 0 0 — 2perc — hp
— pf/cel — str
perc: marim, cym, bd, xyl, tri, glock, crot, tambn, sus cym, tamtam, tmp, 2sd
Originally for piano (1915); orchestrated by Aaron Jay Kernis (1996).
  1. Pour les "cinq doigts"—d'après Monsieur Czerny   3'
  2. Pour les sistes   3'
  3. Pour les notes repétées   3'
  4. Pour les sonorités opposées   5'
  5. Pour les octaves   3'

AMP		

IMAGES   7'
1. Gigues <1909–1912>

4[1.2.pic1.pic2] 4[1.2.Eh.ob d'amore] 4[1.2.3.bcl] 4[1.2.3.cbn] — 4 4
3 0 — tmp+2 — 2hp — cel — str
perc: xyl, sd, cym

Durand	Kalmus	Luck's	Peters

2. Ibéria <1905–1908>   20'

4[1.2.3/pic.pic] 3[1.2.Eh] 3 4[1.2.3.cbn] — 4 3 3 1 — tmp+4 — 2hp
— cel [dbl on chimes] — str
perc: cast, xyl, tambn, sd, cym, chimes[played by cel]
Kalmus ed. Clinton F. Nieweg & Kenneth Bonebrake.
  Par les rues et par les chemins (In the Streets and Byways)   7'
  Les parfums de la nuit (The Fragrances of the Night)   8'
  Le matin d'un jour de fête (The Morning of a Festival Day)   5'

Durand	Kalmus	Peters

3. Rondes de printemps <1905–1909>   9'

3[1.2.3/pic] 3[1.2.Eh] 3 4[1.2.3.cbn] — 4 0 0 0 — tmp+3 — 2hp —
cel — str
perc: tri, cym, tambourin provençal

Durand	Kalmus	Luck's	Peters

L'isle joyeuse <1903–1904>   7'

3[1.2.3/pic] 3[1.2.Eh] 4[1.2.3.bcl] 3[1.2.3/cbn] — 4 4 3 1 — tmp+4
— 2hp — cel — str
perc: cym, tambn, tri, xyl
Orchestrated by Bernardino Molinari following Debussy's indications;
originally for piano solo.

Durand		

Jeux; poème dansé <1912–1913>   17'

4[1.2.pic1.pic2] 4[1.2.3.Eh] 4[1.2.3.bcl] 4[1.2.3.sarr] — 4 4 3 1 —
tmp+3 — 2hp — cel — str
perc: xyl, tri, tambn, cym, sus cym
Kalmus edition by Clinton F. Nieweg. Durand critical edition (from the
Debussy *Oeuvres complètes*) by Pierre Boulez & Myriam Chimènes,
1999; Peters ed. M. Pommer.

Durand	Kalmus	Peters

Marche écossaise sur un thème populaire (Scottish March on a Popular Theme) <1890; rev (orchd) 1908>   7'

3[1.2.pic] 3[1.2.Eh] 2 2 — 4 2 3 0 — tmp+2 — hp — str
perc: sd, cym
Orchestrated by the composer from a work for piano 4-hands.

Jobert	Kalmus	Luck's

Le martyre de Saint Sébastien (The Martyrdom of Saint Sebastian) <1910–1911>   72'

chorus   solos SAA
4[1.2.3/pic1.4/pic2] 3[1.2.Eh] 4[1.2.3.bcl] 4[1.2.3.cbn] — 6 4 3 1 —
tmp+1 — 3hp — cel, harm — str
perc: cym, bd, tamtam
Incidental music to a play by Gabriele d'Annunzio; orchestrated in part by
André Caplet. Most often performed in a format devised by D.E.
Inghelbrecht, with the approval of Debussy and d'Annunzio, using a
narrator. The music alone, without narration, lasts about an hour.
  I. La cour de lys (The Court of Lilies)   19'
  II. La chambre magique (The Magic Chamber)   13'
  III. Le concile des faux dieux (The Council of the False Gods)   19'
  IV. Le laurier blessé (The Broken Laurel)   15'
  V. Le paradis (Paradise)   6'

Durand		

Le martyre de Saint Sébastien: Fragments symphoniques <1910–1911>   22'

4[1.2.3/pic1.4/pic2] 3[1.2.Eh] 4[1.2.3.bcl] 4[1.2.3.cbn] — 6 4 3 1 — tmp+1 — 3hp — cel — str
perc: bd, tamtam
3rd harp mostly doubles the other two; only 3 independent bars, which could be covered by hp1.

La cour des lys (Prelude)	4'
Danse extatique et Final du premier acte	7'
La passion (Act III, Scene 4)	6'
Le Bon Pasteur (Prelude to Act IV)	5'

Durand	Kalmus	Luck's	Peters

Le martyre de Saint Sébastien: La chambre magique (The Magic Chamber) <1910–1911>   2'

4[1.2.pic1.pic2] 2[1.Eh] 4[1.2.3.bcl] 4[1.2.3.cbn] — 6 2 3 1 — tmp+1 — 3hp — cel — str
perc: sus cym, tamtam

Durand

Le martyre de Saint Sébastien: Two Fanfares <1910–1911>   3'

0 0 0 0 — 6 4 3 1 — tmp — [no str]

Elkan-Vogel	Luck's

La mer <1903–1905>   23'

3[1.2.pic] 3[1.2.Eh] 2 4[1.2.3.cbn] — 4 5[1.2.3.crt1.crt2] 3 1 — tmp+3 — 2hp — str
perc: glock[or cel in mvt 2], tamtam, cym, tri, bd
Kalmus edition by Clinton F. Nieweg & Nancy M. Bradburd, 1991; Durand critical edition (from the Debussy *Oeuvres complètes*) by Marie Rolf, 1997; Breitkopf edition ed. P. Jost. Peters edition [not recommended] ed. M. Pommer.
    The controversial brass figures in the last movement before figure 60 do not appear in the Nieweg/Bradburd, Rolf, or Jost editions. The composer was apparently ambivalent about these figures; they appeared in the autograph MS (as an afterthought) and in the 1905 first edition. They were stricken in the 1909 edition at the composer's direction.

I. De l'aube à midi sur la mer [From Dawn to Noon on the Sea]	8'
II. Jeux des vagues [Play of the Waves]	7'
III. Dialogue du vent et de la mer [Dialogue of Wind and Sea]	8'

Breitkopf	Durand	Kalmus	Luck's	Peters

Nocturnes (original version) <1897–1899>   25'

16 women's voices (positioned in the orchestra) in last mvt
3[1.2.3/pic] 3[1.2.Eh] 2 3 — 4 3 3 1 — tmp+2 — 2hp — str
perc: field dr, cym
Kalmus ed. 2005 by Clinton F. Nieweg.
    Percussion in 2nd mvt only.
    A choral score, with piano reduction for rehearsal, is available from Kalmus (W7492).

Nuages (Clouds)	8'
Fêtes (Festivals)	6'
Sirènes (Sirens)	11'

Kalmus

Nocturnes (revised version) <1897–1899>   25'

16 women's voices (positioned in the orchestra) in last mvt
3[1.2.3/pic] 3[1.2.Eh] 2 3 — 4 3 3 1 — tmp+2 — 2hp — str
perc: field dr, cym
Both the *Édition definitive*, 1930, based on changes the composer had entered into his personal score, and the *Nouvelle édition après corrections*, 1964, are published by Jobert; both, however, are said to be riddled with errors and discrepancies between score and parts.
    Recommended: Durand critical edition (from the Debussy *Oeuvres complètes*) by Denis Herlin, 1999.
Percussion in 2nd mvt only.

Nuages (Clouds)	8'
Fêtes (Festivals)	6'
Sirènes (Sirens)	11'

Durand	Jobert	Peters

Pelléas et Mélisande symphonie (Marius Constant) <1893–1902>   24'

3 3[1.2.Eh] 2 3 — 4 3 3 1 — tmp+1 — 2hp — str
perc: chime[G4]
Orchestral passages from Debussy's opera—largely transitions between scenes, and beginnings and ends of acts—compiled by Marius Constant in 1983.

Durand

Petite suite <1886–1889>   13'

2[1.2/pic] 2[1.2/Eh] 2 2 — 2 2 0 0 — tmp+3 — hp — str
perc: tri, cym, tambn
Orchestrated by Henri Büsser, 1907, from a work originally for piano 4-hands.

En bateau (In the Boat)	3'
Cortège	4'
Menuet	3'
Ballet	3'

Durand	Kalmus	Luck's

La plus que lente <1910>   4'

1 0 1 0 — cimbalom — pf — str
Originally for piano solo; orchestrated by the composer.

Durand	Kalmus	Luck's

Prélude à "L'après-midi d'un faune" (Afternoon of a Faun) <1891–1894>   10'

3 3[1.2.Eh] 2 2 — 4 0 0 0 — 1perc — 2hp — str
perc: crot
A critical edition of the score with historical and analytical essays, and including the composer's own metronome marks, is published by Norton.
    Bärenreiter ed. Douglas Woodfull-Harris; Breitkopf edition by Fr. Reinisch; Kalmus edition by Clinton F. Nieweg; Peters ed. M. Pommer.

Bärenreiter	Breitkopf	Jobert	Kalmus	Peters

Prélude à "L'après-midi d'un faune" (arr.) (Afternoon of a Faun) <1891–1894>   10'

1 1 1 0 — 1perc — pf, harm — 2vn, va, vc, db
perc: crot
Arr. "under the supervision of Arnold Schoenberg" for chamber ensemble.

Belmont

Printemps <1887>   15'

2[1.2/pic] 2[1.2/Eh] 2 2 — 4 2 3 0 — tmp+2 — hp — pf 4-hands — str
perc: cym, sd, tri
The original version, a symphonic suite with female chorus, was lost; it was reorchestrated 1912 by Henri Büsser under Debussy's supervision from a 1904 arrangement for piano 4-hands. Kalmus edition by Clinton F. Nieweg.

I. Très modéré	9'
II. Modéré	6'

Durand	Kalmus

Rhapsody, Alto Saxophone & Orchestra <1901–1908>   10'

3[1.2.3/pic] 3[1.2.Eh] 2 2 — 4 2 3 1 — tmp+2 — hp — str
perc: cym, tambn, tri
Previously believed to have been completed and orchestrated by Jean Roger-Ducasse in 1919. However, recent scholarship suggests that the work was structurally complete and supplied with orchestration indications in Debussy's hand in 1903, and that Roger-Ducasse merely prepared the work for publication, perhaps with the assistance of André Caplet.
    Kalmus ed. Clinton F. Nieweg.

Durand	Kalmus	Luck's

Rhapsody, Clarinet & Orchestra (Première rapsodie) <1909–1910>   8'

3 3[1.2.Eh] 2 3 — 4 2 0 0 — 2perc — 2hp — str
perc: cym, tri
Originally for clarinet & piano; orchestrated 1911 by the composer.
   Kalmus ed. Clinton F. Nieweg & Gregory Vaught; Peters ed.
   R.Zimmermann.

Durand	C. Fischer	Kalmus	Luck's	Peters

Le roi Lear; Incidental Music (King Lear) <1904–1905>   5'

2 2 2 2 — 4 3 2 1 — tmp+1 — 2hp — str
perc: sd
   I. Fanfare   2'
   II. Le sommeil de Lear (Lear Asleep)   3'

Jobert

Sarabande <1894–1901>   6'

2 2[1.Eh] 2 2 — 2 1 0 0 — 1perc — hp — str
perc: tamtam, cym
Orchestrated by Maurice Ravel, 1923, from a movement of the suite
Pour le piano.

Jobert	Luck's

Six épigraphes antiques <1914>   16'

3[incl pic] 3[incl Eh/opt ob d'am] 3[incl bcl] 3[incl cbn] — 4 3 3 0 —
tmp+2 — 2hp — cel — str
perc: cym, tamtam, tri, bd, glock, crot, xyl
Orchestrated by Ernest Ansermet, from a work for piano 4-hands.
   1. Pour invoquer Pan, dieu du vent d'été   3'
   2. Pour un tombeau sans nom   3'
   3. Pour que la nuit soit propice   2'
   4. Pour la danseuse aux crotales   2'
   5. Pour l'égyptienne   3'
   6. Pour remercier la pluie au matin   3'

Durand	Luck's

Symphony, B minor (orch. Finno) <1880–1881>   12'

2[incl pic] 2[incl Eh] 2 2 — 4 2 2 0 — tmp+2 — hp — str
Orchestrated by Tony Finno, from the composer's arrangement for piano
4-hands.

Fleisher

Le triomphe de Bacchus <1882>   4'

3[1.2.pic] 3[1.2.Eh] 2 3 — 4 3 3 1 — tmp+2 — 2hp — str
perc: bd, sus cym
Orchestrated by Marius François Gaillard, 1928, from a work for piano
4-hands.

Choudens	Kalmus	Luck's

Trois ballades de François Villon <1910>   11'

solo voice (medium)
3 3[1.2.Eh] 2 3 — 4 2 0 0 — hp — str
Ballade de Villon à s'amye   5'
Ballade que Villon fait à la requeste de sa mère 4'
Ballade des femmes de Paris   2'

Durand	Kalmus	Luck's

Delden, Lex van   1919-1988

(b Amsterdam, 10 Sept 1919; d Amsterdam, 1 July 1988). Dutch

Concerto per due orchestre d'archi, op.71 <1961>   20'

double string orchestra

Donemus

In memoriam, op.38 <1953>   10'

2[1/pic.2] 2 3[1.2.bcl] 2 — 4 3 3 1 — tmp+2 — hp — str
perc: field dr, cym, bd, tamtam, sus cym

Donemus

Musica sinfonica, op.93 <1967>   20'

2[1.2/pic] 3[1.2.Eh] 3[1.2.bcl] 3[1.2.cbn] — 4 3 3 1 — tmp+2 — hp
— pf — str
perc: bd, td, sd, tambn, sus cym
Could be played by tmp+1, if timpanist covers some suspended cymbal.

Donemus

Piccolo concerto, op.67 (Little Concerto) <1960>   10'

2[1/pic.2/pic] 2 2[1.2/Ebcl] 2 — 2 2 0 0 — tmp+1 — pf — [no str]
perc: td, bd, sus cym, woodblk, xyl
Woodwinds are divided into 2 stereophonically opposing quartets.

Donemus

Symphony No.3, op.45 (Facetten; Facets) <1955>   14'

2[1.2/pic] 2 3[1.2.bcl] 3[1.2.cbn] — 4 3 3 1 — tmp+2 — hp — str
perc: cym, bd, field dr, tamtam, xyl

Donemus

Delibes, Léo   1836-1891

(b St Germain du Val, 21 Feb 1836; d Paris, 16 Jan 1891). French

Coppélia <1870>   92'

2[1.2/pic] 2 2 4 — 4 4[2tp, 2crt] 3 1 — tmp+4 — hp — str
perc: bd, cym, tri, sd
Kalmus ed Wm. McDermott; also an orchestral reduction by McDermott
is available from Kalmus:
   2[incl pic] 2[incl Eh] 2 2 — 2 2 1 0 — tmp, perc — hp — str
   ACT I   37'
   1a. Prélude - Mazurka
   b. Valse lente
   2. Scène (Swanhilda and Frantz)
   3. Mazurka
   4. Scène (Préparatifs de fête)
   5. Ballade de l'épi
   6. Thème slave varié
   7. Czardas
   ACT II   55'
   Scène 1
   8. Entr'acte - Valse
   9. Scène (L'atelier de Coppélius)
   10. Scène
   11. Musique des automates
   12. Scène
   13. Chansons à boire - Scène
   14. Scène - Valse de la poupée
   15. Scène
   16. Boléro
   17. Gigue
   18. Finale
   Scène 2
   19. Marche de la cloche
   20. Fête de la cloche (Divertissement):
   a. Valse des heures
   b. L'aurore
   c. La prière
   d. Le travail (La fileuse)
   e. L'hymen (Noce villageoise)
   f. La discorde et la guerre
   g. La paix
   h. Dance de fête
   i. Galop final

Heugel	Kalmus	Payne

Coppélia: Suite No.1 <1870>   25'

2[1.2/pic] 2 2 2 — 4 2 3 0 — tmp+3 — hp — str
perc: tri, cym, sd, bd

1. Thème slave varié (Slav Folk-Tune)	6'
2. Danse de fête et Valse des heures (Festive Dance & Waltz of the Hours)	6'
3. Notturno (Nocturne)	3'
4. Scène des automates et Valse (Music of the Automatons & Waltz)	6'
5. Czardas	4'

Kalmus

COPPÉLIA: 4 PETITES SUITES <1870>   24'

The following are sometimes grouped together as Ballet Suite No.2. They are published separately. Some of the movements also appear in Suite No.1, q.v.

1. Entr'acte & Waltz <1870>   4'

2[1.2/pic] 2 2 2 — 2 2 3 1 — tmp — hp — str
Kalmus ed. Clark McAlister.

Heugel	Kalmus	Luck's

2. Prelude & Mazurka <1870>   6'

2[1.2/pic] 2 2 2 — 4 4[2tp, 2crt] 3 1 — tmp+4 — hp — str
perc: bd, cym, sd, tri
Kalmus ed. Clark McAlister.

Heugel	Kalmus	Luck's

3. Ballade & Thème slave varié <1870>   9'

2[1.2/pic] 2[1.2/Eh] 2 4 — 4 4[2tp, 2crt] 3 1 — tmp+3 — hp — str
perc: bd, cym, tri
Kalmus ed. Clark McAlister.

Heugel	Kalmus	Luck's

4. Valse de la poupée & Czardas <1870>   5'

2[1.pic] 2 2 2 — 4 4[2tp, 2crt] 3 1 — tmp+3 — str
perc: bd, tri, tambn
Kalmus ed. Clark McAlister.

Heugel	Kalmus	Luck's

Lakmé: Airs de danse <1883>   8'

2[1.2/pic] 2 2 2 — 4 2 3 1 — tmp+3 — hp — str
perc: bd, crot, cym, timbales, tambn, tri

Introduction	_'
I. Teràna	_'
II. Rektah	_'
III. Persian	_'
IV. Coda	_'

Kalmus	Luck's

Le roi l'a dit (The King Hath Said): Overture <1873>   6'

2[1.2/pic] 2 2 2 — 4 2 3 0 — tmp+2 — str
perc: bd, cym, tri

Heugel	Luck's

Le roi s'amuse: Six airs de danse dans le style ancien <1882> 13'

2 2 2 2 — 2 2 0 0 — tmp — str
Incidental music for the Victor Hugo play; it originally included at the end a *chanson* for voice, mandolin and ensemble, which is not included in orchestral performances.

Gailliarde	3'
Pavane	1'
Scène du bouquet	2'
Lesquercade	2'
Madrigal	2'
Passepied	2'
Final	1'

Heugel	Kalmus	Luck's

Sylvia, ou La nymphe de Diane <1876>   100'

2[1.2/pic] 2[1.2/Eh] 2[1.2/asx] 4 — 4 4[2crt, 2tp] 3[oph] 1 — tmp+3 — 2hp[1part] — str
perc: bd, cym, field dr, tomtom, tri, tambn, tamtam, crot
Solo horn backstage may be covered by a player from the main orchestra. Possible with only 2bn and minor adjustments in the few passages where they split into more than two parts.

ACT I: Prelude	5'
Faunes et Dryades (Scherzo)	7'
Le Berger (Pstorale)	3'
Les Chasseresses (Fanfare)	3'
Intermezzo	1'
Valse lente	5'
Scène	5'
Cortège rustique	3'
Scène	5'
Entrée du Sorcier et Final	5'
ACT II: Entr'acte	3'
La grotte d'Orion	6'
Pas de Ethiopiens	2'
Chant bachique	3'
Scène et Danse de la Bacchante	5'
Scène finale	5'
ACT III: Marche et Cortège de Bacchus	7'
Scène	1'
Barcarolle	3'
Divertissement: (a) Pizzicati	3'
(b) Solo de Violin	7'
(c) Pas des Exclaves	2'
(d) Variation de Sylvia—Valse	1'
(e) Strette—Galop	4'
Scène finale	4'
Apotheosis	3'

Payne

Sylvia: Suite <1876; rev Suite: 1880>   17'

2[1.2/pic] 2 2 2 — 4 4[2tp, 2crt] 3 1 — tmp+3 — hp — str
perc: sd, tri, cym, bd

Prélude	3'
Intermezzo et Valse lente	6'
Pizzicato	2'
Cortège de Bacchus	6'

Heugel	Kalmus	Luck's

Delius, Frederick   1862-1934

(b Bradford, 29 Jan 1862; d Grez-sur-Loing, 10 June 1934). English

Air and Dance <1915>   5'

str
Boosey also offers a version by Eric Fenby for flute & strings.

Boosey	Luck's

Appalachia; Variations on an Old Slave Song with Final Chorus <1986> 34'

baritone solo   chorus
3[all/pic] 4[1.2.3.Eh] 4[1.2.Ebcl.bcl] 4[1.2.3.cbn] — 6 3 3 1 — tmp+3 — 2hp — str
perc: tri, tamtam, bd, sd, cym
Ed. Thomas Beecham.
Boosey also offers a reduced orchestration by Eric Fenby:
2[incl pic] 2[incl Eh] 2 2 — 4 2 3 1 — tmp, perc — hp — str

Boosey	Kalmus	Luck's

Brigg Fair; An English Rhapsody <1907>   16'

3 3[1.2.Eh] 4[1.2.3.bcl] 4[1.2.3.cbn] — 6 3 3 1 — tmp+3 — hp[1 or more] — str
perc: bd, chimes, tri
Universal ed. Thomas Beecham.

Boosey	Kalmus	Luck's	Universal

Concerto, Piano, C minor <1897; rev 1904-06>   22'

3[1.2.3/pic] 3[1.2.Eh] 2 3 — 4 2 3 1 — tmp+2 — str
perc: bd, cym
Two versions: (1) 3-mvt original version, 1897; (2) rev 1-mvt version,
1906. Both are available on rental from Boosey or for sale from Kalmus.
  1. Allegro ma non troppo   _'
  2. Largo   _'
  3. [revised version] Tempo primo   _'

Boosey	Kalmus	Luck's

Concerto, Violin <1916>   24'

2 2[1.Eh] 2 2 — 4 2 3 1 — tmp — hp — str
Ed. Thomas Beecham.

Augener	Kalmus	Luck's	Schott

Concerto, Violin & Violoncello (Double Concerto)   20'
<1916>

2 2[1.Eh] 2 2 — 4 2 3 1 — tmp — hp — str
A version for violin & viola, arr. Lionel Tertis, is available from Augener.
  1. Quietly   6'
  2. Slowly and quietly   7'
  3. Accel... Tempo I   7'

Augener	Kalmus	Luck's

Concerto, Violoncello <1921>   22'

2 2[1.Eh] 2 2 — 4 2 3 1 — tmp — hp — str
Slow   7'
Becoming slower   5'
Very quietly   1'
Con moto tranquillo   2'
With animation (Allegramente)   7'

Boosey	Kalmus

Dance Rhapsody No.1 <1908>   12'

3[1.2.3/pic] 3[1.Eh.bass ob] 4[1.2.3.bcl] 4[1.2.3.sarr or cbn] — 6 3 3
1 — tmp+2 — 2hp — str
perc: tambn, tri, cym
Universal ed. Thomas Beecham.

Kalmus	Luck's	Universal

Dance Rhapsody No.2 <1916>   8'

3[1.2.pic] 3[1.2.Eh] 2 2 — 4 2 3 1 — tmp+3 — hp — cel — str
perc: bd, cym, sd, tambn, tri, glock

Stainer	Luck's

Eventyr (Once Upon a Time) <1917>   16'

20 male voices [offstage]
3[1.2.3/pic] 3[1.2.Eh] 4[1.2.3.bcl] 4[1.2.3.sarr] — 4 3 3 1 — tmp+4
— 2hp — cel — str
perc: cym, sus cym, tri, glock, chimes, sd, xyl, bd, gong, tamtam, tambn
Off-stage voices have only 2 notes ("wild shouts") to sing; these could
well be uttered by orchestra members.

Augener

Florida—Suite <1887; rev 1889>   34'

3[1.2.3/pic] 3[1.2.Eh] 3[1.2.bcl] 2 — 4 2 3 1 — tmp+3 — hp — str
perc: tambn, tri, cym, bd
Rev. & ed. Thomas Beecham.
  I. Daybreak   10'
  II. By the River 7'
  III. Sunset   8'
  IV. At Night   9'

Boosey

Hassan: Intermezzo & Serenade <1920–1923>   4

1 2[1.Eh] 1 1 — 2 1 0 0 — tmp — hp — str
Movements may be performed independently (*Serenade* is for solo vn, h
& str only). Arr. Thomas Beecham.

Boosey	Luck's

In a Summer Garden <1908; rev 1912>   13

3 3[1.2.Eh] 3[1.2.bcl] 3 — 4 2 3 1 — tmp+1 — hp[1 or more] — str
perc: glock, tri
Ed. Thomas Beecham.

Boosey	Kalmus	Universal

Irmelin: Prelude <1890–1892>   4

2 2[1.Eh] 3[1.2.opt bcl] 2 — 2 0 0 0 — hp — str
Boosey also offers a reduced orchestration by Robert Threlfall:
  1 1 1 0 — str[min 3.3.3.2.1]

Boosey	Luck's

Marche caprice <1889–1890>   4

2[incl pic] 2 2 — 4 2 3 1 — tmp+4 — str
perc: sd, tri, cym, bd
Ed. & arr. Thomas Beecham.

Kalmus	Stainer

A Mass of Life <1904–1905>   100

solos SATBar   double chorus
3[1/pic.2.3] 4[1.2.3.Eh/bass ob] 4[1.2.3.bcl] 4[1.2.3.cbn] — 6 4 3 1
— tmp+4 — 2hp — str
perc: bd, cym, sd, tri, tamtam, cast, glock, chimes (F#, G#)
Boosey offers a reduced orchestration by Eric Fenby:
  2[1/pic.2/pic] 3[1.2.bass ob/Eh] 4[1.2.3.bcl] 3[1.2.cbn] — 4 3 3 1
— tmp+4 — hp — str

Boosey

Prelude and Idyll (Once I Passed through a Populous   16'
City) <1930–1932>

soprano & baritone solos
2 3[1.2.Eh] 2 2 — 4 2 3 1 — tmp — hp — str

Boosey

Sea Drift <1903–1904>   30'

chorus   baritone solo
3 4[1.2.3.Eh] 4[1.2.3.bcl] 4[1.2.3.cbn] — 6 3 3 1 — tmp+1 — 2hp —
str
perc: bd
Ed. Thomas Beecham.

Boosey	Kalmus	Luck's

Sleigh Ride <1890>   5'

3[1.2.3/pic] 2 2 — 4 4[2tp, 2crt] 3 1 — tmp+2 — str
perc: cym, slgh-bells

Boosey	Luck's

A Song of the High Hills <1911>   35'

chorus[min 32 voices]
3[1.2.3/pic] 3[1.2.Eh] 4[1.2.3.bcl] 4[1.2.3.sarr or cbn] — 6 3 3 1 —
3tmp+1 — 2hp[1part] — cel — str
perc: bd, glock, cym
Brief passages for solo soprano & solo tenor, marked "in the chorus."
Ed. Thomas Beecham.

Kalmus	Universal

Summer Evening <1890>   6'

3[incl pic] 2 2 — 4 2 3 1 — tmp — str
Ed. & arr. Thomas Beecham.

Kalmus	Stainer

TWO PIECES for Small Orchestra   7'
1. On Hearing the First Cuckoo in Spring <1912>
1 1 2 2 — 2 0 0 0 — str

| Kalmus | Luck's | Oxford |

2. Summer Night on the River <1911>   5'
2 1 2 2 — 2 0 0 0 — str

| Kalmus | Luck's | Oxford |

The Walk to the Paradise Garden <1900–1901>   8'
2 2[1.Eh] 2 2 — 4 2 3 0 — tmp — hp — str
From *A Village Romeo and Juliet*.
   Two differing versions are available from the publisher: one arr. by
Thomas Beecham; the other by Keith Douglas. The present listing is
Beecham's; Douglas differs in that the Eh doubles on ob2, and the hp may
be replaced by pf.

| Boosey |

Dello Joio, Norman   1913-2008

(b New York, 24 Jan 1913; d East Hampton, NY, 24 Jul 2008). American

Air <1967>   4'
str

| Marks |

Arietta <1978>   4'
str

| Marks |

Five Images for Orchestra <1957>   8'
3[1.2.pic] 2 3[1.2.bcl] 2 — 4 2 3 1 — tmp+3 — str
perc: chimes, glock, xyl, sd, bd, cym
Originally piano 4-hand sketches for young players; orchestrated by the
composer.

Cortège	*2'*
Promenade	*1'*
Day Dreams	*1'*
The Ballerina	*2'*
The Dancing Sergeant	*2'*

| Marks |

Lyric Fantasies <1972>   17'
solo viola
str orch or str 5t

| AMP | Luck's |

Meditations on Ecclesiastes <1955–1956>   31'
str

I. Introduction: Largo (To everything there is a season…)	*4'*
II. Theme: Adagio con sentimento (…a time to be born…)	*3'*
III. Solenne (…and a time to die…)	*3'*
IV. Soave e leggerio (…a time to plant, and a time to pluck up…)	*1'*
V. Grave con ruvidezza (…a time to kill…)	*2'*
VI. Larghetto con legerezza (…and a time to heal…)	*3'*
VII. Animato (…a time to break down. and a time to build up…)	*1'*
VIII. Adagio con intensità (…a time to weep and to mourn…)	*3'*
IX. Spumante (…and a time to dance and to laugh…)	*2'*
X. Adagio libermante (…a time to embrace…)	*4'*
XI. Con brio; Semplice (…a time of hate…a time to love…)	*5'*

| C. Fischer |

New York Profiles <1949>   18'
2[1.2/pic] 2[1.2/Eh] 2 2 — 2 2 0 0 — tmp+1 — str
perc: cym, sus cym, sd, xyl

1. Prelude, *The Cloisters*	4'
2. Caprice, *The Park*	4'
3. Chorale Fantasy, *The Tomb*	6'
4. Festal Dance, *Little Italy*	4'

| C. Fischer |

The Triumph of Saint Joan <1951>   29'
2[1.2/pic] 2[1.2/Eh] 2 2 — 4 2 3 1 — tmp+1 — str
perc: glock, cym, bd, sd

The Maid	11'
The Warrior	8'
The Saint	10'

| C. Fischer |

Variations, Chaconne & Finale <1947>   24'
3[1.2.pic] 3[1.2.Eh] 3[1.2.bcl] 3[1.2.cbn] — 4 3 3 1 — tmp+3 — str
perc: bd, chimes, cym, glock, sd, sus cym, tambn, xyl

I. Theme and 7 variations	*11'*
II. Chaconne: Adagio serioso	*9'*
III. Finale: Allegro vivo, giocoso e ritmico	*4'*

| C. Fischer |

Del Tredici, David   1937-

(b Cloverdale, CA, 16 March 1937). American

Acrostic Song <1987>   8'
soprano solo
1[fl/pic] 0 1 0 — 1 1 0 0 — 1perc — pf — str 5t
perc: chimes
"Whisper chorus" (members of the ensemble).
   Arrangement by the composer of the ending of his *Final Alice* with an
additional *Postlude*.

| Boosey |

AN ALICE SYMPHONY <1969>   35'
solo soprano (amplified and with bullhorn)
2[1/pic.2/pic] 2[1.2/Eh] 2[1/Ebcl.2/bcl] 2[1.2/cbn] — 4 2 2 1 —
ssx/asx, ssx/asx/tsx — accordion, mand, tenor banjo — tmp+5 — str
perc: whip, xyl, cym, siren, marim, wnd mach, bd, glock, ratch, sd,
chimes, tri, templeblks, tambn, vib, field dr, hi-hat, 4cowbells, 2anvils, 3slgh-bells,
several glass windchimes, theremin, 2sus cym
This work may be excerpted in various ways. See subsequent entries.

1. Speak Roughly/Speak Gently	7'
2. The Lobster Quadrille	12'
3. 'Tis the Voice of the Sluggard	6'
4. Who Stole the Tarts; Dream Conclusion	10'

| Boosey |

An Alice Symphony: Illustrated Alice <1969; rev   17'
1976>
solo soprano (amplified and with bullhorn)
2[1/pic.2/pic] 2 2 2[1.2/cbn] — 4 2 2 1 — ssx/asx, ssx/asx/tsx —
tmp+5 — str
perc: whip, xyl, cym, siren, marim, wnd mach, sus cym, tamtam, gong, bd, glock,
ratch, sd, chimes, 4cowbells, 2anvils, 3slgh-bells, several glass windchimes

Speak Roughly/Speak Gently	_'
Who Stole the Tarts	_'
Dream Conclusion	_'

| Boosey |

An Alice Symphony: In Wonderland <1969>   24'

solo soprano (amplified)
2[1/pic.2/pic] 2[1.2/Eh] 2[1/Ebcl.2/bcl] 2[1.cbn] — 4 2 2 1 — 2ssx —
accordion, mand, tenor banjo — tmp+4 — str
perc: tri, templeblks, chimes, xyl, cym, tambn, vib, marim, field dr, tamtam, gong,
hi-hat, bd, sd, glock, theremin, 2sus cym
The Lobster Quadrille   _'
'Tis the Voice of the Sluggard   _'
Dream Conclusion   _'

Boosey

An Alice Symphony: The Lobster Quadrille <1969;   13'
rev 1974>

optional soprano or tenor solo (amplified)
2[pic.pic/fl] 2[1.2/Eh] 2[1/Ebcl.2/bcl] 2[1.cbn] — 4 2 2 1 — 2ssx —
accordion, mand, tenor banjo — 4perc — str
perc: chimes, tri, templeblks, vib, cym, tambn, field dr, glock, bd, sd, tmp,
theremin, 2sus cym, 2tamtam
"Folk group," a subset from the above instrumentation: 2 soprano
saxophonists, accordion, mandolin, tenor banjo.

Boosey

All in the Golden Afternoon <1981>   32'

soprano solo (amplified)
3[1.2/pic.3/pic] 3[1.2.3/Eh] 4[1.2.3/Ebcl.bcl] 3[1.2.3/cbn] — 4 4 3 1
— tmp+5 — 2hp — cel — str
perc: chimes, crot, tamtam, gong, tri, woodblk, cowbell, wnd mach, slgh-bells,
tambn, xyl, marim, glock, vib, cym, ratch, whip, cast, bongos, templeblks, sd, field
dr, td, bd, 2sus cym, 2birdcalls, glass windchimes
Spoken chorus (members of the orchestra).
From *Child Alice*, Part II, *q.v.*

Boosey

Child Alice <1977–1981>   141'

soprano solo (amplified)
3[1.2/pic.3/pic] 3[1.2.3/Eh] 4[1.2.3/Ebcl.bcl] 3[1.2.3/cbn] — 4 4 3 1
— tmp+5 — 2hp — cel — str
perc: chimes, crot, gong, tamtam, tri, woodblk, cowbell, wnd mach, slgh-bells,
tambn, xyl, marim, glock, vib, cym, ratch, whip, cast, bongos, templeblks, sd, field
dr, td, bd, siren, hi-hat, guiro, 2sus cym, 2birdcalls, glass windchimes, anvil
The components of this full-evening entertainment based on Lewis
Carroll's *Alice in Wonderland* may be excerpted individually and in
various combinations. The composer has supplied concert-beginnings and
concert-endings for this purpose. See listings for individual movements.
Part I: In Memory of a Summer Day   63'
Part II: Quaint Events   25'
  Happy Voices   21'
  All in the Golden Afternoon   32'

Boosey

Final Alice <1976>   70'

solo soprano (amplified and with bullhorn)
4[1.2/pic.3/pic.4/pic] 4[1.2.3.4/Eh] 4[1.2.3/bcl.4/Ebcl] 4[1.2.3.4/cbn] —
6 4 4 1 — 2ssx — accordion, mand, tenor banjo — tmp+7 — 2hp —
cel — str
perc: glock, crot, chimes, vib, marim, xyl, bongos, cowbell, cym, hi-hat, tamtam,
tri, ratch, templeblks, whip, bd, sd, tambn, siren, 4tomtoms, anvil, 2sus cym, 2td,
theremin, glass windchimes, wood windchimes
The composer indicates a possible cut which reduces the duration to 60',
and lessens the complexity of the folk group amplification.

Boosey

Haddock's Eyes <1985>   20'

soprano-narrator
1[fl/pic] 0 1 0 — 1 1 0 0 — pf — str 5t
Amplification needed for selected passages.

Boosey

Happy Voices; Fuga for Orchestra <1980>   21'

3[1.2/pic.3/pic] 3[1.2.3/Eh] 4[1.2.Ebcl.bcl] 3[1.2.3/cbn] — 4 4 3 1 —
tmp+5 — 2hp — cel — str
perc: whip, tambn, sd, td, bd, woodblk, cowbell, templeblks, tamtam, cym, marim,
xyl, tri, ratch, cast, glock, chimes, vib, wnd mach, crot, slgh-bells, 2sus cym, anvi
glass windchimes
From *Child Alice*, part II, *q.v.*

Boosey

In Memory of a Summer Day <1980>   63'

solo soprano (amplified)
3[1.2/pic.3/pic] 3[1.2.3/Eh] 4[1.2.3/Ebcl.bcl] 3[1.2.3/cbn] — 4 4 3 1
— tmp+5 — 2hp — cel — str
perc: tri, cowbell, cym, tambn, tamtam, gong, glock, woodblk, crot, bd, vib, xyl,
whip, sd, td, wnd mach, marim, chimes, ratch, siren, 2sus cym, anvil
String players form an antiphonal whisper-chorus.
From *Child Alice*, part I, *q.v.*
1. Introduction (Dawn)   _'
2. Song ("Simple Alice")   _'
3. A Tale is Told: <Marcia> ("Triumphant Alice")   _'
4. Interlude   _'
5. Aria ("Ecstatic Alice")   _'
6. Postlude   _'
7. Concert Ending   _'

Boosey

Pop-Pourri <1968; rev 1973>   28'

solo soprano (amplified)   chorus   opt counter-tenor or
mezzo-soprano
2[1/pic.2/pic] 2[1.2/Eh] 2[1.2/bcl] 2[1.2/cbn] — 0 2 2 0 — ssx,
ssx/tsx — elec gtr, elec bass gtr — 3perc — str
perc: chimes, tamtam, bd, wnd mach, anvil
One technician required. Chorus may be omitted by cutting one
movement.

Boosey

Quaint Events <1981>   25'

soprano solo (amplified)
3[1.2/pic.3/pic] 3[1.2.3/Eh] 4[1.2.Ebcl.bcl] 3[1.2.3/cbn] — 4 4 3 1 —
tmp+5 — 2hp — cel — str
perc: marim, vib, glock, chimes, crot, cym, tamtam, gong, hi-hat, tri, tambn,
cowbell, ratch, whip, cast, guiro, slgh-bells, wnd mach, bd, sd, td, field dr, siren,
2sus cym, glass windchimes, anvil
Spoken chorus (members of the orchestra).
From *Child Alice*, part II, *q.v.*

Boosey

Syzygy <1966>   24'

solo group: soprano (amplified), horn, tubular bells with extended range
(2 players)
2[1/pic2.pic/afl] 2[1.2/Eh] 2[1.2/bcl] 2[1.2/cbn] — 0 2 0 0 — 2perc
— 2vn, 2va, vc, db
perc: chimes w/ extended range (2 players)

Boosey

Vintage Alice; Fantascene on a Mad Tea-Party <1972>   28'

solo soprano (amplified)
1[1/pic] 1 1[Ebcl] 1 — 2 1 1 0 — 2ssx — accordion, mand, tenor
banjo — tmp+1 — str or str 5t
perc: cym, whip
If a large string complement is used, winds may be doubled.

Boosey

Demersseman, Jules 1833-1866

(b Hondschoote, Belgium, 9 Jan 1833; d Paris, 1 Dec 1866). Belgian

Concerto italien, op.82 (Grand solo de concert no.6) 13'

solo flute
2[1.2/pic] 2 2 2 — 4 2 0 0 — tmp+3 — str
perc: bd, cym, sd, tri, tambn
Orchestrated by Mark Starr from a work for flute and piano.

> Noteworthy

Denisov, Edison 1929-1996

(b Tomsk, 6 April 1929; d Paris, 24 Nov 1996). Russian

Bells in the Mist (Glocken im Nebel) <1987> 15'

4 1 4 0 — 6 4 4 0 — 5perc — hp — cel — str
perc: glock, crot, vib, chimes, 4tri, 3sus cym

> Breitkopf   Sikorski

Chamber Symphony No.2 <1994> 17'

1 1 1 1 — 1 1 1 0 — 1perc — hp — pf — str 5t
perc: woodblk, sd, tamtam, 5bongos, 2sus cym
In one movement.

> Chant

Concerto, Bassoon & Violoncello <1982> 32'

1 1 1 0 — 2 1 1 0 — 1perc — str[min 5.4.3.2.1; max 15.12.10.8.4]
In one movement.

> Russian

Concerto, Clarinet <1989> 26'

4 4 4[1.2.3.4/bcl] 0 — 6 4 3 0 — tmp+3 — hp — cel — str
perc: vib, sus cym, glock, tamtam
  I. Agitato   14'
  II. Lento   12'

> Sikorski

Concerto, Flute & Harp <1994–1995> 25'

0 2 0 0 — 2 0 0 0 — str
  I. Poco agitato   14'
  II. Lento   5'
  III. Agitato   6'

> Billaudot

Crescendo e diminuendo <1965> 6'

hpsd — str[6vn, 3va, 2vc, db]

> Universal

Little Suite, op.13 (Malen'kaya suita; Kleine Suite) <1958> 7'

2[1.2/pic] 1 2[1.2/bcl] 2 — 2 1 0 0 — asx — tmp+2 — hp — pf/cel — str
perc: sus cym, glock, tamtam, bd
  I. Melodie   _'
  II. Divertissement _'
  III. Landschaft   _'
  IV. Zwischenspiel   _'
  V. Spiel   _'

> Russian

Postludio in memoriam Witold Lutoslawski <1994> 12'

0 0 0 0 — 0 3 2 0 — 1perc — hp — pf — str[8.6.6.4.2]
perc: vib, chimes

> Breitkopf

Deussen, Nancy Bloomer 1931-

(b New York City, 1 Feb 1931). American

American Hymn <2005> 5'

3[1.2.pic] 2 2 2 — 4 3 3 1 — tmp+3 — hp — str
perc: bd, cym, sus cym, td, tri, glock, chimes, 2woodblk

> Wendel

Ascent to Victory <1997> 8'

1 1 2 1 — 2 1 0 0 — 1perc — str

> Wendel

Carmel by-the-Sea <1987> 8'

2 2 2 2 — 2 1 0 0 — 1perc — str
perc: tmp, glock

> Wendel

Concerto, Clarinet <1995> 24'

tmp+1 — hp — str

> Accessibility

A Field in Pennsylvania <2006> 7'

3[1.2.pic] 3[1.2.Eh] 3[1.2.bcl] 2 — 4 3 2 1 — tmp+3 — str
perc: bd, cym, sus cym, sd, tri, tamtam, glock, chimes

> Wendel

Peninsula Suite <1994> 10'

solo string quartet
str
A version for string orchestra alone (no solo quartet) was created in 2008.

> Accessibility

Reflections on the Hudson <1994> 11'

2[1.2/pic] 2[1.2/Eh] 2 2 — 4 3 3 1 — tmp+1 — hp — cel — str

> Wendel

A Silver Shining Strand <2001> 24'

2[1.2/pic] 2[1.2.Eh] 2 2 — 4 3 3 1 — tmp+4 — hp — str
perc: sd, tri, woodblk, sus cym, glock
The 2nd mvt (Regalos) is available separately; it is 6' in duration.
  Watchers of Stone   _'
  Regalos   _'
  A Silver Shining Strand _'
  The Beacon   _'

> Wendel

Tico <2004> 9'

2 2 2 2 — 2 2 0 0 — 2perc — str
perc: tmp, cym, bongos, marac, claves, congas, afuche

> Accessibility

The Transit of Venus <2013> 10'

2 2 2 2 — 2 2 0 0 — tmp+3 — hp[or synth] — str
perc: chimes, glock, sus cym, tri, td, cym

> Accessibility

Trinity Alps <1999–2008> 10'

2[1.2/pic] 2 2 — 2 2 1 0 — tmp+1 — str

> Accessibility

Devienne, François   1759-1803

(b Joinville, Haute-Marne, 31 Jan 1759; d Paris, 5 Sept 1803). French

Concerto, Bassoon, B-flat major

see: Mozart, Wolfgang Amadeus, 1756-1791
Concerto, Bassoon, No.2, K.Anh.C14.03, B-flat major

Concerto, Flute, No.7, F major   10'

0 2 0 0 — 2 0 0 0 — str
Arr. Fernand Oubradous, whose contribution may have been extensive, since there is no indication that Devienne ever wrote a flute concerto in F major, and his Concerto No.7 is in E minor!

> EMT

Devore, Derek   1973-

(b Clinton, IL, 18 April 1973). American

Heartland <1995>   7'

3[1.2.pic] 3[1.2.Eh] 3[1.2.bcl] 3[1.2.cbn] — 4 2 3 1 — tmp+3 — str
perc: bd, sus cym, tri

> Devore

In Common Ragtime   6'

3[1.2.pic] 3[1.2.Eh] 3[1.2.bcl] 3[1.2.cbn] — 4 3 3 1 — tmp+3 — hp
— pf — str
perc: bd, cym, sus cym, tri, tambn, tamtam

> Devore

Diamond, David   1915-2005

(b Rochester, NY, 9 July 1915; d Brighton, NY, 13 June 2005). American

Concerto, Violin, No.3 <1967–1968>   23'

4[incl pic,afl] 3[incl Eh] 4[incl Ebcl,bcl] 3[incl cbn] — 4 3 3 1 —
tmp+3 — hp — pf — str

> Peer

Elegy in Memory of Ravel <1938; rev (arr) 1938-39>   7'

tmp+1 — str
perc: td, tamtam, glock
Originally for brass 4331, perc, 2hp; arr. by the composer.

> Southern   Luck's

Kaddish, for Violoncello & Orchestra <1987–1989>   13'

3[1.2.pic] 3[1.2.Eh] 3[1.2.bcl] 3[1.2.cbn] — 4 3 3 1 — tmp+2 — hp
— str
perc: td, tri, cym, gong

> Schirmer

Music for Shakespeare's Romeo and Juliet <1947>   18'

2[1.2/pic] 2[1.2/Eh] 2[1.2/bcl] 2 — 2 2 1 0 — tmp+1 — hp — str
perc: sd, glock, xyl, tri, chimes
I. Overture   3'
II. Romeo and Juliet: Balcony Scene   4'
III. Romeo and Friar Laurence   3'
IV. Juliet and Her Nurse   2'
V. The Death of Romeo and Juliet   6'

> Boosey

Rounds for String Orchestra <1944>   13'

str
I. Allegro; molto vivace   4'
II. Adagio   3'
III. Allegro vigoroso   6'

> Elkan-Vogel

Symphony No.1 <1940–1941>   22'

3[1.2.3/pic] 3[1.2.Eh] 3[1.2.bcl] 3[1.2.cbn] — 4 3 3 1 — tmp+2 — str
perc: bd, cym, chimes
I. Allegro moderato con energia   7'
II. Andante mestoso   9'
III. Maestoso - Adagio - Allegro vivo   6'

> Southern

Symphony No.2 <1942–1943>   42'

3[1.2.3/pic] 3[1.2.Eh] 3[1.2.bcl] 3[1.2.cbn] — 4 3 3 1 — tmp+4 — str
perc: xyl, glock, sd, tri, cym, tamtam, bd
Adagio funèbre   14'
Allegro vivo   6'
Andante espressivo, quasi adagio   14'
Allegro vigoroso   8'

> Peer

Symphony No.3 <1945>   31'

3[1.2.3/pic] 3[1.2.Eh] 3[1.2.bcl] 3[1.2.cbn] — 4 4 3 1 — tmp+3 — hp
— pf — str
perc: bd, cym, sd, td, tri, xyl
I. Allegro deciso   9'
II. Andante   9'
III. Allegro vivo   6'
IV. Adagio assai   7'

> Southern

Symphony No.4 <1945>   16'

4[1.2.3/pic.4/pic] 4[1.2.3.Eh] 4[1.2.3.bcl] 4 — 6 4 3 1 — tmp+2 —
2hp — pf — str
perc: bd, cym, sd, td, tri, gong, xyl
A version with reduced winds is also available, calling for:
3[1.2.3/pic] 3[1.2.Eh] 3[1.2.bcl] 3 — 4 4 3 1
1. Allegretto   5'
2. Adagio - Andante   5'
3. Allegro   6'

> Schirmer

Symphony No.5 <1951–1964>   21'

3[1.2.pic] 3[1.2.Eh] 4[1.2.Ebcl.bcl] 3[1.2.cbn] — 4 4 3 1 — 2tmp+3
— pf, org — str
perc: xyl, td, sd, glock, cym

> Peer

Symphony No.6 <1951–1954>   25'

3[1.2.pic] 3[1.2.Eh] 4[1.2.Ebcl.bcl] 3[1.2.cbn] — 4 4 3 1 — tmp+3 —
pf — str
perc: bd, chimes, cym, glock, tamtam, sus cym, td, xyl, gavel, snap
I. Introduzione: Adagio; Allegro fortemente mosso   _'
II. Adagio   _'
III. Deciso: Poco allegro; Fuga   _'

> Fleisher   Luck's   Warner

Symphony No.7 <1959>   16'

3[1.2.pic] 3[1.2.Eh] 4[1.2.Ebcl.bcl] 3[1.2.cbn] — 4 4 3 1 — tmp+3 —
hp — pf — str
perc: bd, cym, sus cym, sd, td, gong, xyl
I. Andante; Allegro, ma non troppo   _'
II. Andante   _'
III. Allegro moderato   _'

> Southern

Symphony No.8 <1960>   31'

3[1.2.pic] 3[1.2.Eh] 4[1.2.Ebcl.bcl] 3[1.2.cbn] — 4 4 3 1 — tmp+2 —
hp — pf — str

perc: bd, cym, sd, td, tri, gong, glock, xyl, vib

I. Moderato; Allegro vivo   13'
II. Theme & Variations   17'

> Southern

The World of Paul Klee <1957>   12'

3[1.2.pic] 3[1.2.Eh] 3[1.2.bcl] 2 — 4 3 3 0 — tmp+3 — hp — pf/cel
— str

perc: glock, xyl, cym, sus cym, tri, tamtam, tomtom, tambn, woodblk, guiro, td,
paper thunder sheet

1 *Frame*   _'
2 *The Dance of the Grieving Child*   _'
3 *Frame*   _'
4 *The Black Prince*   _'
5 *Frame*   _'
6 *Pastorale*   _'
7 *Frame*   _'
8 *The Twittering Machine*   _'

> Southern

Diemer, Emma Lou   1927-

(b Kansas City, Missouri, 24 Nov 1927). American

Concerto, Piano (Concerto in One Movement) <1991>   25'

3[1.2.pic] 2 3[1.2.bcl] 3[1.2.cbn] — 4 3 3 1 — tmp+2 — cel — str

perc: bd, sd, tomtom, timbales, tambn, tamtam, xyl, woodblk, 3sus cym, 2tri,
2gongs, finger cym, metal windchimes

> Fleisher

Homage to Tchaikovsky <2000>   7'

3[1.2.pic] 2 2 2 — 4 2 3 1 — tmp — str

> MMB

Dimas, Blas Galindo   1910-1993

see: Galindo, Blas

Di Vittorio, Salvatore   1967-

(b Palermo, 22 October 1967). Italian

Overtura Palermo <2013>   7'

3[1.2.pic] 2[1.2/Eh] 2 3[1.2.cbn] — 4 3 3 1 — tmp+3 — hp — cel —
str

perc: crot, bd, cym, chimes, sd, tambn, tri, tamtam, cast

> Panastudio

Overtura Respighiana (Respighiana Overture)   6'

2[1.pic] 2[1.Eh] 2 2 — 2 2 3 1 — tmp+3 — hp — cel — str
perc: bd, cym, sd, tri, tambn, tamtam, glock, crot
Based on music of Respighi, as well as Rossini (as transcribed by
Respighi in *Rossiniana* and *La boutique fantasque*).

> Panastudio

San Michele Arcangelo <2005>   8'

solo baritone   chorus SATB
2[1.2/pic] 1 1 1 — 2 1 1 0 — tmp+1 — hp — str
perc: bd, cym, tamtam, chimes
Also serves as prolog to the composer's opera *Fausto*.

> Panastudio

Stabat Mater speciosa <2012>   9'

chorus SATBB
1 1[ob/Eh] 0 1 — 0 0 0 0 — 1perc — org[opt] — str
perc: tri, crot
NB: The text is a joyful Christmas counterpart to the *Stabat Mater
dolorosa*, likewise attributed to the 13th-century poet Jacopone da Todi.

> Panastudio

Symphony No.1 (Isolation) <1994; rev 1999>   19'

str
I. Preludio   6'
II. Fantasia   7'
III. Fuga   3'
IV. Finale   3'

> Panastudio

Symphony No.2 (Lost Innocence) <1997; rev 2000>   16'

2[1.2/pic] 2 2 — 4 2 3 1 — tmp+2 — hp — cel/pf — str
perc: bd, cym, sd, tamtam, glock, xyl, crot, chimes, finger cym
I. Requiem for a Child — March, on Lost Innocence   4'
II. Dance of Tears   3'
III. Childheart, Song of Truth — Revelation: The Abandoned Cradle 4'
IV. Elegy   5'

> Panastudio

Symphony No.3 (Templi di Sicilia; Temples of Sicily) <2011>   14'

3[1.2.pic] 3[1.2/Eh] 2 3[1.2.cbn] — 4 3 3 1 — tmp+3 — hp — cel —
str
perc: bd, cym, sd, tri, tambn, tamtam, chimes, crot
Sections played without pause.
Naxos: Tempio di Venere   _'
Siracusa: Tempio di Apollo   _'
Himera: Tempio della Vittoria   _'
Segesta: Tempio di Diana   _'
Akragas: Tempio della Concordia _'

> Panastudio

Il tallone di Achille, per piccola orchestra (Achilles' Heel) <2010–2013>   7'

1 2[ob.Eh] 0 1 — 1 1 0 0 — 1perc — hp — str
perc: crot, bd

> Panastudio

Dittersdorf, Karl Ditters von   1739-1799

(b Vienna, 2 Nov 1739; d Neuhof [now Novy Dvur], nr Sobeslav, Bohemia, 24 Oct
1799). Austrian

G = M. Grave: thematic index in *Carl Ditters von Dittersdorf: Six
Symphonies*, ed. E. Badura-Skoda, The Symphony 1720–1840, ser. B, i
(New York, 1985)

Concerto, Double Bass, E major   11'

2 0 0 0 — 2 0 0 0 — cnt — str
Ed. Franz Tischer-Zeitz.

> Schott

Concerto, Double Bass, E-flat major   17'

2 2 0 0 — 2 0 0 0 — str
Ed. Franz Ortner. Wind parts may be omitted.

> Schott

Concerto, Harp, A major   22'

0 2 0 0 — 2 0 0 0 — str
Arr. K.H. Pillney.

> Peters

Concerto, Harpsichord, B-flat major <by 1773> 14'

2 0 0 0 — 2 0 0 0 — str[no va]
Winds used only in slow movement.

Kalmus	Luck's	Peters

Sinfonia, A minor [G.a2] (Il delirio delli compositori, ossia Il gusto d'oggidi) <by 1779> 23'

0 2 0 0 — 2 0 0 0 — str
Ed. Allan Badley

I. Allegro assai	10'
II. Andantino	4'
III. Minuetto	4'
IV. Presto [non troppo]	5'

Artaria

Sinfonia, A major [G.A10] (Nazionale nel gusto di cinque nazioni) <by 1766> 20'

0 2 0 0 — 2 0 0 0 — str
Ed. Allan Badley. 4 movements in the styles of Germany, Italy, England, and France; 5th mvt is a rondo in which *Tedesco* (Germany) is the recurring ritornello, and the interspersed episodes represent respectively Italy, England, France, and Turkey(!).

I. Tedesco: Andantino	5'
II. Italiano: Allegro	2'
III. Inglese: Allegretto	2'
IV. Francesco: Minuetto	6'
V. [Rondo]: Allegro	5'

Artaria

Sinfonia, C major (Die vier Weltalter; The Four Ages; Les quatre âges du monde) 12'

1 2 0 2 — 2 2 0 0 — tmp — str
From the collection *3 simphonies, exprimant 3 Métamorphoses d'Ovide* (Vienna, 1791).

Allegro molto	3'
Larghetto	3'
Menuetto 1: Vivace — Menuetto 2: Tranquillo	3'
Finale: Prestissimo	3'

Doblinger	Luck's

Sinfonia, D major [G.D16] (Il combattimento delle passioni umani; The Contest of Human Passions) <c.1771> 27'

0 2 0 0 — 2 0 0 0 — str
Ed. Allan Badley.

I. Il Superbo (Pride): Andante con maesta	4'
II. Il Humile (Humility): Andante	1'
II. Il Matto [minuet], Il Amante [trio] (Madness & Love): Minuetto	3'
IV. Il Contento (Contentment): Andante	3'
V. Il Constante (Constancy): Minuetto	5'
VI. Il Malinconico (Melancholy): Adagio	2'
VII. Il Vivace (Liveliness): Allegro assai	9'

Artaria

Sinfonia, D minor [G.d1] <btn 1773-79> 23'

0 2 0 0 — 2 0 0 0 — str
Ed. Allan Badley.

I. Adagio	4'
II. Allegro vivace	10'
III. Minuetto — Allegretto	5'
IV. Presto non troppo	4'

Artaria

Sinfonia, F major [G.F7] <c.1763> 14

0 2 0 0 — 2 0 0 0 — str
Ed. Allan Badley.

I. Allegro	6'
II. Andante	2'
III. Minuetto	4'
IV. Presto	2'

Artaria

Sinfonia, G minor [G.g1] <by 1768> 31'

1 2 0 0 — 2 0 0 0 — str
Ed. Allan Badley.

I. Allegro	10'
II. Andante sempre piano	5'
III. Minuetto	5'
IV. Presto con garbo	11'

Artaria

Sinfonia concertante, Double Bass & Viola 16'

0 2 0 0 — 2 0 0 0 — str
Ed. Wilhelm Altmann.

Hofmeister	Luck's

Dohnányi, Ernö [Ernst von] 1877 - 1960

(b Pozsony [now Bratislava], 27 July 1877; d New York, 9 Feb 1960). Hungarian

American Rhapsody, op.47 <1953> 14'

3[1.2.3/pic] 2[1.2/Eh] 2 2[1.2/cbn] — 4 3 3 1 — tmp+2 — str
perc: cym, sd

AMP

Concerto, Piano, No.1, op.5, E minor <1898> 45'

3[1.2.pic] 2 2 3[1.2.cbn] — 4 2 3 0 — tmp — str[min 12.12.8.8.6]

1. Adagio maestoso; Allegro; Adagio	18'
2. Andante	10'
3. Vivace; Cadenza con orchestra; Vivace	17'

Doblinger	Kalmus	Luck's

Concerto, Violin, No.1, op.27, D minor <1914–1915> 41'

2 2[1.2/Eh] 2 3[1.2.cbn] — 4 2 3 0 — tmp/tri — str
perc: tri (6 notes)

I. Molto moderato, maestoso e rubato	13'
II. Andante	8'
III. Molto vivace	6'
IV. Tempo del primo pezzo, rubato; Allegro non troppo	14'

EMB	Kalmus	Luck's

Ruralia hungarica, op.32b <1924> 25'

3[1.2.3/pic] 3[1.2.Eh] 3[1.2.3/Eh/bcl] 3[1.2.cbn] — 4 3 3 1 — tmp+4 — hp — cel — str
perc: sd, tri, bd, cym, tamtam, xyl

EMB

DER SCHLEIER DER PIERRETTE (The Veil of Pierrette), op.18 5'
1. Pierrot's Complaint of Love <1908–1909>

1 2 2 2 — 4 0 0 0 — tmp — str

Kalmus	Luck's

2. Walzer-Reigen (Waltz-Round Dance) <1908–1909> 2'

2 2[1.Eh] 2 2 — 2 0 0 0 — str

Kalmus	Luck's

3. Lustiger Trauermarsch (Jolly Funeral March) <1908–1909>   3'

1 1 2 3[1.2.cbn] — 4 2 3 0 — tmp — str

Kalmus	Luck's

4. Hochzeitswalzer (Wedding Waltz) <1908–1909>   6'

2 2 2 2 — 4 2 3 0 — tmp+2 — str
perc: cym, sd, tri
Sometimes incorrectly listed as "Wedding March."

Doblinger	Kalmus	Luck's

5. Menuett <1908–1909>   2'

1 1 2 2 — 2 0 0 0 — str

Kalmus	Luck's

6. Pierrettens Wahnsinnstanz (Pierrette's Dance of Madness) <1908–1909>   7'

2 2 3[1.2.Ebcl] 3[1.2.cbn] — 4 2 3 1 — tmp+1 — hp — str
perc: tamtam

Kalmus	Luck's

Symphonic Minutes, op.36 (Szimfónikus percek) <1933>   15'

2[1.2/pic] 2[1.2/Eh] 2[1.2/bcl] 2 — 4 2 3 0 — tmp+2 — hp — cel — str
perc: tri, sd, cym, glock, bd

I. Capriccio	3'
II. Rapsodia	4'
III. Scherzo	2'
IV. Tema con variazioni	4'
V. Rondo	2'

EMB	Eulenburg

Variations on a Nursery Song, op.25 <1914>   22'

solo piano
3[1.2.pic] 2 2 3[1.2.cbn] — 4 3 3 1 — 2tmp+2 — hp — cel[can be played by perc] — str
perc: chimes, glock, xyl, bd, tri, sus cym, cym

Kalmus	Luck's	Simrock

Donizetti, Gaetano   1797-1848

(b Bergamo, Nov 1797; d Bergamo, 8 April 1848). Italian

Allegro in C major   6'

str

Peters

Ave Maria <1842>   4'

chorus   soprano solo
str

Luck's	Peters

Concertino, Clarinet, B-flat major <1817>   8'

0 2 0 0 — 2 0 0 0 — str
Reconstructed by R.Meylan; original manuscript was untitled.

Eulenburg	Peters

Concertino, English Horn, G major <1817>   11'

1 2 0 1 — 2 0 0 0 — str
Ed. R.Meylan.

Peters

Concertino, Flute, C major <1819>   7'

0 2 0 1 — 2 0 0 0 — str
Orchestrated by Wolfgang Hofmann after the composer's Sonata for Flute and Piano.

Peters

Concertino, Oboe, F major <1817>   7'

2 0 0 1 — 2 0 0 0 — str
Orchestrated by Wolfgang Hofmann after the composer's Sonata for Oboe and Piano.

Peters

Don Pasquale: Overture <1843>   6'

2[1.pic] 2 2 2 — 4 2 3 0 — tmp+2 — str
perc: cym, bd

Kalmus	Luck's	Ricordi

La fille du régiment (Daughter of the Regiment): Overture <1840>   7'

2[1.2/pic] 2 2 2 — 4 2 3 0 — tmp+3 — str
perc: sd, cym, bd

Breitkopf	Kalmus	Luck's	Ricordi

Linda di Chamounix: Prelude <1842>   7'

3[1.2.pic] 2 2 2 — 4 2 3 1[oph] — tmp+1 — str
perc: bd (perhaps with cymbals)

Kalmus	Luck's

Roberto Devereux: Overture <1837>   8'

3[1.2.pic] 2 2 2 — 4 2 3 0 — tmp+2 — str
perc: bd, tri

Ricordi

Sinfonia for Winds, G minor <1817>   5'

1 2 2 2 — 2 0 0 0 — [no str]
Kunzelmann ed. Päuler; Tetra ed. Douglas Townsend.

Kunzelmann	Tetra

Doppler, Franz   1821-1883

(b Lemberg [now L'viv], 16 Oct 1821; d Baden, nr Vienna, 27 July 1883). Polish, active in Hungary

Concerto, 2 Flutes, D minor   18'

2 2 2 2 — 4 2 3 0 — tmp — hp[opt] — str
Reconstructed and adapted by András Adorján.

1. Allegro maestoso	8'
2. Andante	3'
3. Allegro	7'

Billaudot

Fantasie pastorale, op.26   12'

solo flute
1 1 2 1 — 2 2 3[ad lib] 1[ad lib] — tmp — str
Originally for flute & piano; arranged by A. Klautzsch. Novello also offers an edition by James Galway for solo flute, with:
1 1 1 1 — 2 1 1 0 — tmp — str.

Kalmus	Luck's

Dorati, Antal   1906-1988

(b Budapest, 9 April 1906; d Gerzensee, nr Berne, 13 Nov 1988). American
conductor and composer of Hungarian birth.

Concerto, Piano <1977>   32'

3[1.2/pic.3/pic] 3[1.2.Eh] 3[1.2.3/bcl] 3[1.2.cbn] — 4 3 3 1 — tmp+3
— str

> Zerboni

Dorff, Daniel   1956-

(b New Rochelle, NY, 7 March 1956). American

Billy and the Carnival; A Children's Guide to the   14'
Instruments <1985; rev 1988>

narrator
2[1.2/pic] 2 2 2 — 2 2 1 0 — tmp+2 — str[min 6.6.4.3.2]
perc: glock, chimes(opt), tri, tambn, sd, hi-hat, whip, sus cym, cym, bd, slide
whistle, bike hn

> Presser

Blast Off! <1999>   10'

narrator
2[1.pic] 2[1.Eh] 2 2[1.cbn] — 4 3 3 1 — tmp+3 — hp — str
perc: glock, tamtam, chimes, sd, cowbell, xyl, szl cym, bd, 4tomtom, 3tri

> Presser

Concerto, Contrabassoon <1991>   11'

0 0 1 0 — 1 0 0 0 — str

> MMB

Concerto, Percussion <1991–1992>   20'

solo percussionist
2[1.pic] 2 2 2[1.2/opt cbn] — 4 3 3 1 — opt euph — tmp+3 — hp —
str
perc: field dr, tamtam, glock, cym, chimes, bd, slgh-bells, crot, sus cym, 3tri,
2tambn, 2sd
solo: templeblocks, 2woodblk, 2sus cym, bd, 4tomtom, bongos, sd, tambn, marim,
szl cym, 2tri, 3windchimes, marktree, belltree, glock, vib, xyl
  I. Moderato, intense   _'
  II. Mysterious, fleempo   _'
  III. Allegro volante   _'

> Presser

Concerto, Percussion: Allegro volante <1991–1992>   5'

solo xylophone
2[1.pic] 2 2 2 — 4 3 3 1 — tmp+3 — hp — str
Third mvt of the composer's *Concerto, Percussion* (see previous entry).

> Presser

Fanfare Overture <1983>   3'

2 2 2 2 — 4 3 3 1 — 3perc — str

> MMB

Fast Walk <1989–1990>   3'

2 2 3[incl bcl] 2 — 4 3 3 0 — tmp+1 — str

> MMB

Goldilocks and the Three Bears <2000>   8'

narrator
1 1 1 1 — 1 1 1 0 — 2perc — hp — str

> Presser

It Takes Four to Tango <1990; rev 1998>   3'

str orch, str 4t or 5t

> Presser

The Kiss <2001>   14'

3[1.2/afl.pic] 3[1.2.Eh] 2 2 — 4 3 3 1 — tsx — tmp+3 — hp — cel
— str
perc: bd, cym, sus cym, sd, 4tomtoms, 2tri, glock, xyl, vib, cowbell, shaker

> Presser

Lamentations <1977>   5'

str

> Presser

Pachelbel's Christmas; A Merry Melange for Orchestra   5'
<1886; rev (orchd) 2005>

2[1.pic] 2 2 2 — 2[3-4 opt] 2 2 1 — tmp+2 — str
44 carols in canon and quodlibet over the Pachelbel canon. Originally for
brass 5t; orchestrated by the composer.

> Presser

Philly Rhapsody <1997>   12'

3[1.2.pic] 2 3[1.2.bcl] 2 — 4[hn3-4 opt] 3[tp1/opt flugelhorn] 3 1 —
4perc — hp [or synth] — pf — str
perc: glock, vib, marim, tambn, szl cym, sd, sus cym, tri, tamtam, bd, guiro, marac
belltree, cym, shaker, police whistle, 4tomtom
Options: 1st ob may be taken by ssx or fl; ob2, bn2, hn3-4 may be
omitted; hp may be covered by a synth.
  Playable by school orchestras; a set of preparatory exercises are
provided to familiarize young players with certain syncopated rhythms.

> Presser

Summer Solstice <1993>   18'

solo clarinet
str

> MMB

Sunburst <1998>   3'

solo violin
str

> Presser

Three Fun Fables <1996; rev 1999>   11'

narrator
1 1 1 2[incl cbn] — 1 1 1 0 — 1 or 2perc — hp — str
The Fox and the Crow (tp & db)   4'
The Dog and His Reflection (tbn & vn/hp/perc)   2'
The Tortoise and the Hare (cbn & cl)   5'

> MMB

Three Fun Fables: The Tortoise and the Hare <1996>   6'

narrator
1 1 1 2[incl cbn] — 1 1 1 0 — 1 or 2perc — hp — str

> MMB

Dorman, Avner   1975-

(b Tel Aviv, 14 April, 1975). Israeli

Astrolatry <2011>   10'

2[fl.pic] 2 2[1.2/Ebcl] 2 — 4 2 2 1 — tmp+4 — hp[ampd] — pf — str
perc: crot, glock, vib, marim, sus cym, brake dr, sd, bd, 4tomtom, claves, 2shakers,
sticks
  I. Celestial Revelations   _'
  II. The Worship of the Stars   _'

> Schirmer

Azerbaijani Dance <2005; rev (orchd) 2010>   7'

3[1.2/pic.pic] 2 3[1.2.bcl] 2 — 4 3 3 1 — tmp+3 — hp — pf — str
perc: bd, cym, tri, tamtam, glock, xyl, vib, ratch, djembe, windchimes[Arabic], slgh-bells[Arabic], 2sus cym, 2tomtom, 4tambn
Originally for piano; orchestrated by the composer.

> Schirmer

Chorale for String Orchestra <1999>   5'

str[min 2.2.2.2.1]

> Schirmer

Concerto, Piccolo <2001>   15'

pf — str
I. Allegro — groovy serious, and dramatic	6'
II. Adagio cantabile	5'
III. Presto	4'

> Schirmer

Concerto, Soprano Saxophone <2003>   14'

1 1 1 2 — 2 0 0 0 — 1perc — str
perc: drum set
Certain passages provide for optional improvisation on the part of the soloist.

> Schirmer

Concerto, Violin <2006>   23'

2[1/pic.2/pic] 1 2[1.2/bcl] 1 — 2 2 1 1 — tmp+3 — hp — pf, hpsd — str
perc: sus cym, hi-hat, glock, marim, vib, chimes, flexatone, cowbell, guiro, marac, vibrslp, 3tomtom, 5woodblk
Pf & hpsd may be covered by a single player.
I. Fast; rhythmic and frantic	_'
II. In baroque style	_'
III. Presto	_'

> Schirmer

Ellef Symphony <2000>   19'

3[1.2.3/pic] 3[1.2.Eh] 3[1.2.bcl] 3[1.2.3/cbn] — 4 3 3 1 — tsx — tmp+5 — hp — pf/cel — str
perc: tamtam, windchimes, chimes, sd, sus cym, bd, xyl, marim, vib, glock, tambn, tri, vibrslp, shaker, 4tomtom, 2woodblk
Mvts are played without pause.
I. Fear	_'
II. Slaughter	_'
III. Elegy	_'
IV. …(silence)	_'

> Schirmer

Lost Souls <2009>   23'

solo piano
2[1.2/pic] 2[1.Eh] 3[1.2/Ebcl.3/bcl] 2[1.2/cbn] — 4 3[tp2 dbl pic tp] 3 1 — tmp+3 — hp — pf[upright]/cel — str
perc: bd, cym, sus cym, hi-hat, sd, rototom, gong, glock, xyl, marim, vib, crot, flexatone, woodblk, whip, bongos, batá, djembe, 2shakers, 2tomtom, 2tamtam, 3cowbell
The soloist of course performs on a concert grand; the upright piano is in the orchestra. Movements are played without pause.
I. Séance	
II. Twilight	
III. Exorcism	

> Schirmer

Prayer for the Innocents <2009>   8'

double str 4t

> Schirmer

Reflections <2011>   6'

2 2 2 2 — 2 2 0 0 — 2perc — hp — pf — str[min 6.6.6.6.4]

> Schirmer

Variations Without a Theme <2001–2003>   15'

4[1.2/afl.3.4/pic] 3[1.2.3/Eh] 3[1.2/Ebcl.3/bcl] 3[1.2.3/cbn] — 4 4 3 1 — tmp+3 — hp — pf/cel — str
perc: bd, cym, hi-hat, sd, tri, tambn, vib, chimes, crot, flexatone, slgh-bells, windchimes, belltree, woodblk, vibrslp, 2glock

> Schirmer

Uzu and Muzu from Kakaruzu <2012>   40'

narrator   2 solo percussion
2[1.2/pic] 2 2[1.2/bcl] 2 — 3 2 2 1 — tmp — str
perc: [soloists] vib, belltree, glock, sd, tambn, guiro, brake dr, gong, sus cym, bd, set, rototom, cym, 2marim, 2vibrastick, 8tomtoms, shaker, 2hi-hat, caxixi

> Schirmer

Draeseke, Felix   1835-1913

(b Coburg, 7 Oct 1835; d Dresden, 26 Feb 1913). German

Symphony No.1, op.12, G major <1868–1872>   35'

2 2 2 2 — 4 3 0 0 — tmp — str
I. Introduzione ed Allegro	10'
II. Scherzo: Presto leggiero	6'
III. Adagio	12'
IV. Finale: Allegro con brio e vivace	7'

> Kahnt   mph

Dragonetti, Domenico   1763-1846

(b Venice, 7 April 1763; d London, 16 April 1846). Italian

Concerto, Double Bass, A or G major   16'

str
Specify key when ordering: A major if soloist uses traditional solo scordatura; G major if soloist used orchestral tuning.
    An arrangement for string orchestra is also available in either key from Ludwin.
Allegro moderato	5'
Andante	6'
Allegro vivo	5'

> Ludwin

Pezzo di concerto   9'

solo double bass
1 2 0 1 — 2 0 0 0 — str
Ed. Rudolf Malaric.

> Doblinger

Drattell, Deborah   1956-

(b Brooklyn, NY, 27 Dec 1956). American

Be Still My Spirit <1994>   12'

solo alto saxophone
1 1 1 1 — 1 1 1 0 — tmp+2 — str
perc: glock, xyl, marim, vib, 3sus cym, 4tomtoms

> Subito

Fire Dances (Concerto for Clarinet & Orchestra) <1988>   13'

soloist employs both Bb & Eb clarinets
3[1.2.3/pic] 3[1.2.3/Eh] 3[1.2.bcl] 3[1.2.3/cbn] — 3 3 2 1 — tmp+4 — pf/cel — str
perc: bd, tri, tambn, glock, xyl, marim, vib, chimes, crot, woodblk, templeblks, marac, 2sus cym, finger cym, 5tomtoms

> Subito

The Fire Within <1989>   14'

solo flute

2[1/pic.2] 2 2[1.2/Ebcl] 2 — 2 2 1 0 — tmp+2 — pf/cel — str

perc: bd, tambn, xyl, marim, vib, chimes, woodblk, marac, cast, congas, 3sus cym, 2tomtom, finger cym

Subito

Lilith <1988>   13'

3[1.2/afl.3/pic] 3[1.2.3/Eh] 3[1.2/Ebcl.3/bcl] 3[1.2.3/cbn] — 5 4 3 1 — tmp+4 — pf/cel — str

perc: bd, cym, tri, tambn, glock, xyl, marim, vib, chimes, crot, marac, cast, lionroar, 2sus cym, fingercym, 2timbales, metalsheet, 3tamtams, 3tomtoms

This 1988 orchestral work is not to be confused with the composer's opera of the same title, premiered 2001.

I. Stato ipnotico   10'
II. Infiammare di passione   3'

Subito

Sorrow Is Not Melancholy <1993>   11'

str 4t or str orch

Subito

Syzygy <1987>   10'

3[1.2.3/pic] 3[1.2.3/Eh] 3[1.2.3/bcl] 3[1.2.cbn] — 3 3 3 1 — tmp+4 — pf/cel — str

perc: bd, sus cym, tamtam, glock, xyl, marim, vib, chimes, crot, 4tomtom, metal sheet

Subito

Drigo, Riccardo   1846-1930

(b Padua, 30 June 1846; d Padua, 1 Oct 1930). Italian

Diane et Actéon Pas de deux <1903>   8'

3[1.2.pic] 3[1.2.Eh] 3[1.2.bcl] 3[1.2.cbn] — 4 4[2crt, 2tp] 3 1 — tmp+4 — hp — str

perc: tri, sd, tambn, cym, bd, glock

Attributed to Drigo, though the music, at least in part, may have been composed originally by Cesare Pugni (1802-1870). Much later (1935) this excerpt was inserted in the Pugni ballet *La Esmeralda*, and its association with the latter work has stuck.

The Lars Payne edition is the original; there is also an arrangement by William McDermott for reduced orchestra, available from Kalmus:

2 2 2 2 — 4 2 3 0 — tmp+1 — hp — str

Introduction   _'
Adagio   _'
Variation I (Acteon)   _'
Variation II (Diana)   _'
Coda   _'

Payne

Druckman, Jacob   1928-1996

(b Philadelphia, 26 June 1928; d New Haven, CT, 24 May 1996). American

Aureole <1979>   12'

3[1.2.afl] 3[1.2.Eh] 3[1.2.bcl] 2 — 4 3 3 1 — tmp+3 — hp — pf — str

perc: bongos, bd, chimes, congas, flexatone, glock, gong, szl cym, templeblks, timbales, vib, vibrslp, woodblk, 2sus cym, 3tamtams, 2tomtoms, tmpl bell

Boosey

Brangle <1989>   22'

3[1.2/pic.3/afl] 3[1.2.Eh] 3[1.2.bcl] 2 — 4 3 3 1 — tmp+3 — hp — pf — str

perc: vib, marim, glock, chimes, szl cym, congas, bd, tambn, tri, cowbell, slgh-bells, marac, vibrslp, 2sus cym, 2tamtams, 2timbales, 5tomtoms

Boosey

Dark Upon the Harp <1962>   22'

mezzo-soprano solo

0 0 0 0 — 1 2 1 1 — 2perc — [no str]

Psalm XXII	2'
Psalm LVII	5'
Psalm XVIII	4'
Psalm XXX	3'
Psalm CXXXIII	4'
Psalm XVI	4'

Presser

Lamia <1974; rev 1975>   24'

soprano solo

3[1.2.3/pic] 2 3[1.2.bcl] 2 — 4 3 3 1 — 3perc — hp — pf, elec org — str

perc: vib, templeblks, chimes, timbales, szl cym, tri, sd, glock, marim, 4sus cym, 4cowbells, 2woodblk, 2congas, 2bongos, 2tamtams, 2gongs, 2bd, Japanese templeblk on tmp, coil spring w/ sizzles

Orchestra is divided into 2 groups, each with its own conductor.

Alternative version for soprano & small orchestra (1 conductor):

1 1 2[1.bcl] 1 — 1 1 1 0 — 2perc — synth — str

Boosey

Mirage <1975>   24'

3[1.2.3/pic] 3[1.2.Eh] 3[1.2.bcl] 2 — 4 3 3 1 — tmp+4 — hp — pf, elec org, elec pf — str

perc: vib, congas, tambn, glock, marim, claves, bongos, timbales, tomtom, belltree, szl cym, marac, bd, sd, cym, bd/cym, 5sus cym, 2woodblk, 3tri, 2tamtams, 2gongs, 2sets templeblks, brass windchimes, glass windchimes

Boosey

Nor Spell Nor Charm <1990>   15'

1[1/afl] 2 2[1.2/bcl] 2 — 2 0 0 0 — pf/synth — str

Boosey

Prism <1980>   22'

3[1.2/pic.afl] 3[1.2.Eh] 3[1.2.bcl] 2 — 4 3 3 1 — tmp+3 — hp — pf/elec hpsd or synth — str

perc: vib, tri, templeblks, marim, crot, glock, chimes, bongos, bd, szl cym, timbales, 4sus cym, 3tamtams, 2tomtoms

One-third of the strings in a separate section toward the rear of the stage.

Treats the Medea & Jason story in three movements.

1. after Marc-Antoine Charpentier   _'
2. after Francesco Cavalli   _'
3. after Luigi Cherubini   _'

Boosey

Windows <1972>   21'

3[1.2.3/pic] 3[1.2.Eh] 3[1.2.bcl] 3[1.2.cbn] — 4 3 3 1 — 3perc — hp — pf, elec org — str

perc: glock, vib, marim, chimes, congas, sd, timbales, templeblks, szl cym, steeldrum, 2bd, 2bongos, 2woodblks, 2tamtams, 2gongs, 4sus cym, coilspring, saw

Both pf & elec org should be amplified and with reverberation.

Boosey

Dubois, Pierre Max   1930-1995

(b Graulhet, 1 March 1930; d Rocquencourt, 29 August 1995). French

Concerto, Alto Saxophone   17'

str

1. Lento espressivo; Allegro   7'
2. Sarabande lento nostalgico   6'
3. Rondo: Allegretto   4'

Leduc

Dubois, Théodore
1837-1924

(b Rosnay, Marne, 24 Aug 1837; d Paris, 11 June 1924). French

Les sept paroles du Christ (The Seven Last Words of Christ) <1867>   46'
chorus   solos STB
2[incl pic] 2 2 2 — 4 2 3 0 — tmp+1 — hp — org (opt) — str

Kalmus	Luck's

Duffy, John
1926-

(b Manhattan, NY, 23 Jun 1926). American

American Fantasy Overture <1990>   4'
2[1.2/pic] 2 2 2 — 4 2 3 1 — tmp+2 — hp — pf — str
perc: cym, sus cym, sd, tambn, glock, xyl, woodblk

Schott

American Fantasy Overture (chamber orchestra version) <1994>   4'
2[1.2/pic] 2 2 2 — 2 2 0 0 — 1perc — pf — str
perc: tmp, cym, sd, xyl, woodblk

Schott

Freedom Overture <1990>   4'
3[1.2.pic] 2 2 2 — 4 3 3 1 — tmp+3 — str
perc: bd, cym, sd, tamtam, chimes

Schott

Heritage: Symphonic Suite with Narration   53'
narrator
2[1.2/pic] 2[1.2/Eh] 2[1.2/Ebcl] 2 — 4 2 3 1 — tmp+4 — hp — pf/cel — str
perc: bd, cym, sus cym, szl cym, 2 sets finger cym, sd, td, roto-toms, tri, tambn, tamtam, gong, 3 bronze bell plates (or synth), glock, xyl, marim, vib, chimes, crot, animal bells (2 strings) or sleighbells, 4 Japanese temple bells (or chimes), windchimes, marktree, belltree, log drum (slit drum or 2 lg templeblks), hand drum,woodblk, 2cowbells, 2congas, marac, claves, cabasa, windmachine
4th hn doubles on shofar; timpanist also covers animal bells.

Part I: In the beginning	*26'*
Part II: The living legacy	*27'*

Schott

Heritage: Suite   25'
2[1.2/pic] 2[1.2/Eh] 2[1.2/Ebcl] 2 — 4 2 3 1 — tmp+3 — hp — pf — str
perc: bd, cym, sus cym, szl cym, sd, 4tomtoms, timbales, hand drum, tri, tambn, tamtam, glock, xyl, chimes, sleighbells, 2woodblk, 2cowbells, bongos, marac, claves, 3congas, cabasa, finger cym

Overture; David and Bathsheba	*11'*
Dance of the Golden Calf	*2'*
Destruction of the Temple	*2'*
Diaspora	*6'*
Finale: Prophecy	*4'*

Schott

Heritage Dances   16'
2[1.2/pic] 2[1.2/Eh] 2 2 — 4 2 3 1 — tmp+3 — hp — pf/cel — str
perc: bd, cym, sus cym, sd, 4tomtoms, timbales, rototoms, tambn, tamtam, glock, xyl, chimes, sleighbells, woodblk, bongos, marac, cast

David's Dance	*3'*
The Rabbi's Dance	*2'*
Renaissance Dance	*2'*
Spanish Dance	*2'*
America	*4'*
Waltz	*3'*

Schott

Heritage Fanfare and Chorale   3'
0 0 0 0 — 4 2 3 1 — tmp+3 — [no str]
perc: bd, cym, sd, gong
Ed. Richard Williams.

Schott

Symphony No.1 (Utah) <1989>   25'
2[1.2/pic] 2 2 — 4 2 3 1 — tmp+3 — hp — str
perc: bd, cym, sus cym, sd, tambn, tamtam, glock, xyl, chimes, whip, bongos, marac, claves

God's Wildness	*–'*
Requiem	*–'*
Puwa ["Puwa" means "Life Force" in Ute]	*–'*

Schott

Three Jewish Portraits <1996>   10'
2[1.2/pic] 2 2[1.2/Ebcl] 2 — 4 2 3 1 — tmp+2 — hp — pf/cel — str
perc: bd, cym, sys cym, sd, 3tomtoms, tambn, glock, xyl, woodblk, cast

The Golden Age of Spanish Jewry	*2'*
The Shtetl	*6'*
The Rabbi's Dance	*2'*

Schott

Three Jewish Portraits (chamber version) <1995>   10'
2[1.2/pic] 2 2[1.2/Ebcl] 2 — 2 2 1 0 — tmp+2 — hp — pf/cel — str
perc: bd, cym, sus cym, sd, 3tomtoms, tambn, glock, xyl, woodblk, cast

The Golden Age of Spanish Jewry	*2'*
The Shtetl	*6'*
The Rabbi's Dance	*2'*

Schott

A Time for Remembrance; A Peace Cantata <1991; rev 1993>   24'
narrator; solo soprano (or mezzo)
2[1.2/pic] 2 2[1.2/bcl] 2 — 4 3 3 1 — tmp+4 — hp — str
perc: bd, 2pr cym, sus cym, szl cym, sd, td, fielddrum, tamtam, glock, xyl, vib chimes, woodblk, metal pipe or plate, opt cannon

1. The Dead	*7'*
2. Letters Home	*3'*
3. I Want to Die Easy	*6'*
4. An End to War	*5'*
5. Epilogue: Blow Out, You Bugles, Over the Rich Dead	*3'*

Schott

Dukas, Paul
1865-1935

(b Paris, 1 Oct 1865; d Paris, 17 May 1935). French

L'apprenti sorcier (The Sorcerer's Apprentice) <1897>   12'
3[1.2.pic] 2 3[1.2.bcl] 4[1.2.3.cbn (or sarr)] — 4 4[2tp, 2crt] 3 0 — tmp+4 — hp — str
perc: glock, sus cym, tri, cym, bd
Kalmus edition by Clinton F. Nieweg.
    Glock part probably intended for keyboard glockenspiel, but usually played on a mallet instrument.
    A narration, cued to the music and suitable for youth and family concerts, has been prepared by Neal Gittleman; it may be found online at https://db.tt/kuDuihtD.

Durand	Kalmus	Luck's

La Péri; Poème dansé <1911>   19'
3[1.2.3/pic] 3[1.2.Eh] 3[1.2.bcl] 3 — 4 3 3 1 — tmp+6 — 2hp — cel — str
perc: xyl, sd, tri, tambn, cym, bd

Durand	Kalmus

La Péri: Fanfare <1912>   3'
0 0 0 0 — 4 3 3 1 — [no str]

Durand

Polyeucte: Overture <1891>   15'
2 3[1.2.Eh] 3[1.2.bcl] 3 — 4 2 3 1 — tmp — hp — str

| Durand | Kalmus | Luck's |

Symphony, C major <1895–1896>   40'
3[1.2.3/pic] 2[1/Eh.2] 2 2[bn3-4 opt] — 4 3 3 1 — tmp — str
I. Allegro non troppo vivace, ma con fuoco   *15'*
II. Andante espressivo e sostenuto   *14'*
III. Allegro spiritoso   *11'*

| Kalmus | Rouart |

Villanelle (orchd Miller) <1906>   6'
solo horn
2[1.2/pic] 2 2 2 — 2 2 0 0 — tmp+2 — str
perc: tri, glock
Originally for horn & piano, with orchestration only sketched by the
composer; subsequently orchestrated by Donald Garfield Miller. Ed. &
revised 2009 by Clinton F. Nieweg & Nancy M. Bradburd.
  Other versions:
  Donemus (arr. Hans Henkemans): 3333—4331—tmp, perc, 2hp, cel—str
  Elkan-Vogel (arr. Norman Pickering): 2222—str

| Donemus | Elkan-Vogel | Kalmus |

Dun, Tan   1957-

see under: Tan Dun ["Tan" is surname]

Duparc, Henri   1848-1933

(b Paris, 21 Jan 1848; d Mont-de-Marsan, 12 Feb 1933). French

Chanson triste, op.2, no.4 <1868; rev 1902, orchd 1912>   4'
solo soprano
2 0 0 0 — 4 0 0 0 — hp — str
Originally for voice and piano; orchestrated by the composer. E-flat or C.

| Kalmus | Rouart |

L'invitation au voyage <1870; rev (orchd) ?1892-5>   5'
solo soprano
2[1.2/pic] 2 2 2 — 4 0 0 0 — 1perc — hp — typophone or cel[opt] —
str
perc: bd
Originally for voice and piano; orchestrated by the composer. C minor.

| Kalmus | Rouart |

Lénore <1874–1875>   13'
3[1.2.3/pic] 2 2 4[bn4 ad lib] — 4 2 3 1 — tmp+3 — str
perc: bd, cym, 2tamtam
Symphonic poem after a ballad by Gottfried August Bürger.

| Kalmus | Leuckart |

Le manoir de Rosemonde <1879; rev (orchd) by 1912>   3'
solo soprano
2 2[1.Eh] 2 2 — 4 2 0 0 — tmp — str
Originally for voice and piano; orchestrated by the composer. D minor

| Kalmus | Rouart |

La vie antérieure <1884; rev (orchd) 1911-13>   5'
solo soprano
2 2[1.Eh] 2 2 — 4 2 3 0 — tmp+1 — hp — str
Originally for voice and piano; orchestrated by the composer. E-flat
major.

| Kalmus | Rouart |

Dupré, Marcel   1886-1971

(b Rouen, 3 May 1886; d Meudon, 30 May 1971). French

Symphony, op.25, G minor <1928>   28
solo organ
3[1.2.3/pic] 3[1.2.Eh] 3[1.2.bcl] 3[1.2.cbn] — 4 3 3 1 — tmp+2 — h|
— cel — str
perc: bd, cym, tri, tambn, glock
1. Modérément lent; Allegro   *8'*
2. Vivace   *6'*
3. Lent   *7'*
4. Animé   *7'*

| Salabert□□□□ |

Durand, Joël-François   1954-

(b Orléans, 17 Sept 1954). French composer, active in USA

Athanor <2001>   19'
3[1.2.3/pic] 3[1.2.Eh] 3[1.2.bcl] 3[1.2.3/cbn] — 4 3 3 1 — tmp+4 —
str[14.14.10.10.8]
perc: tamtam, chimes, sus cym, bd, glock, tambn, 2Japanese templebells,
3metalplates; each percussionist also has 1 timpano.

| Durand |

Concerto, Piano <1993>   21'
2[1.2/pic] 2[1.2.Eh] 2 2 — 2 2 1 1 — tmp+2 — hp — cel —
str[6.4.4.3.2]
perc: cowbell, tambn, bd, glock, woodblk, bongos, sd, td, 2tri, 3tomtom, 3brake dr,
2tamtam, 3sus cym
In one mvt. Timpanist and harpist each asked to double on small triangle.

| Durand |

Lichtung <1987>   15'
1[1/afl] 1 1 0 — 1 0 0 0 — 1perc — pf — str 5t

| Durand |

Durante, Francesco   1684-1755

(b Frattamaggiore, Aversa, 31 March 1684; d Naples, 30 Sept 1755). Italian

Concerto No.1, F minor <1738–1742>   14'
str[no va]
I. Un poco andante - Allegro   *4'*
II. Andante   *6'*
III. Amoroso   *2'*
IV. Allegro assai   *2'*

| Carisch | Schott |

Concerto No.5, A major <1738–1742>   8'
str
I. Presto   *3'*
II. Largo   *4'*
III. Allegro molto *1'*

| Carisch |

Vespro breve   21'
soli or chorus: SATB
org — str[no va]
I. Dixit Dominus   *3'*
II. Confitebor   *5'*
III Beatus vir à 3   *5'*
IV. Laudate pueri   *3'*
V. Magnificat   *5'*

| Tropp |

Duruflé, Maurice

1902-1986

(b Louviers, 11 Jan 1902; d Paris, 16 June 1986). French

Requiem, op.9 <1947>   45'

chorus   solos Ms, Bar
3[1.2/pic.3/pic] 3[1.2/Eh.Eh] 3[1.2.bcl] 2 — 4 3 3 1 — tmp+3 — hp — cel, opt organ — str
perc: cym, bd, tamtam, sus cym

I. Introit	4'
II. Kyrie	5'
III. Domine Jesu Christe	9'
IV. Sanctus	4'
V. Pie Jesu	4'
VI. Agnus Dei	5'
VII. Lux Aeterna	4'
VIII. Libera Me	6'
IX. In Paradisum	4'

Durand

Requiem, op.9 (reduced version) <1947>   41'

chorus   solos Ms, Bar
0 0 0 0 — 0 3[opt] 0 0 — opt tmp — opt hp — org — str
Reduction by the composer.

I. Introit	8'
II. Kyrie	8'
III. Domine Jesu Christe	3'
IV. Sanctus	3'
V. Pie Jesu	3'
VI. Agnus Dei	4'
VII. Lux Aeterna	4'
VIII. Libera Me	5'
IX. In Paradisum	3'

Durand   Leonard   Luck's

Dutilleux, Henri

1916-2013

(b Angers, 22 Jan 1916; d Paris, 22 May 2013). French

Métaboles <1959–1964>   17'

4[1.2.3.pic] 4[1.2.3.Eh] 4[1.2.Ebcl.bcl] 4[1.2.3.cbn] — 4 4 3 1 — tmp+6 — hp — cel — str
perc: templeblks, sd, bd, cym, sus cym, Chinescym, tri, cowbell, xyl, glock, 3tomtom, 2tamtam

1. Incantatoire	3'
2. Linéaire	4'
3. Obsessonel	3'
4. Torpide	3'
5. Flamboyant	4'

Heugel

Mystère de l'instant, for 24 Strings, Cymbalum and Percussion <1985–1989>   18'

tmp+2 — cimb — str[8.6.4.4.2]
perc: gong, tamtam, 2sus cym

I. Appels	2'
II. Échos	2'
II. Prismes	2'
IV. Espaces lointains	2'
V. Litanies	2'
VI. Choral	1'
VII. Rumeurs	1'
VIII. Soliloques	1'
IX. Métamorphoses (sur la nom SACHER)	3'
X. Embrasement	2'

Leduc

Symphony No.2 (Le double) <1958–1959>   30'

3[1/pic2.2.3/pic1] 3[1.2/Eh.3] 3[1.2/bcl.3] 3[1.2/cbn.3] — 2 3 3 1 — tmp+3 — hp — cel, hpsd — str
perc: xyl, vib, tri, bd, glock, cym, tamtam, 2sd
Divided into 2 orchestras, one large and the other for 12 players, included in the aggregate above: ob, cl, bn, tp, tbn, tmp, cel, hpsd, str 4t.

I. Animato, ma misterioso	8'
II. Andantino sostenuto	10'
III. Allegro fuocoso - Calmato	12'

Heugel

Timbres, espace, mouvement (La nuit étoilée; Starry Night) <1976–1978; rev 1990>   15'

4[1.2/afl.3/pic.4/pic] 4[1.2.3.ob'am] 4[1.2.3.bcl] 4[1.2.3.cbn] — 4 3 3 1 — tmp+4 — hp — cel — 12vc, 10db
perc: crot, sd, bd, marim, kybd glock, 2sus cym, 3tamtam, 3bongos, 3tomtom
The subtitle is a reference to the well-known Van Gogh painting.

I. quarter-note = ca. 72	8'
II. eighth-note = ca. 56	7'

Heugel

Tout un monde lointain… ; Concerto for Violoncello & Orchestra (A Whole Remote World) <1967–1970>   30'

3[1.2.pic] 2 3[1.2.bcl] 3[1.2.cbn] — 3 2 2 1 — tmp+5 — hp — cel — str
perc: sd, bd, cym, crot, tri, xyl, marim, glock, 3bongos, 3tomtom, 2gong, 2tamtam

I. Enigme (Enigma)	7'
II. Regard (Gaze)	7'
III. Houles (Surges)	5'
IV. Miroirs (Mirrors)	6'
V. Hymne (Hymn)	5'

Heugel

Dvořák, Antonín

1841-1904

(b Nelahozeves, nr Kralupy, Bohemia, 8 Sept 1841; d Prague, 1 May 1904). Czech

B = J. Burghauser: Antonín Dvořák: Thematický katalog, bibliografie přehled života a díla [Thematic Catalogue, Bibliography, Survey of Life and Work] (Prague, 1960, enlarged 1996, additional bibliography with J. Clapham)

The American Flag, op.102, B.177 <1892–1893>   21'

solos ATB   chorus SATB
3[1.2.pic] 3[1.2.Eh] 3[1.2.bcl] 2 — 4 3 3 1 — tmp+4 — hp — str
perc: bd, cym, sd, tri
Ed. Jan Kachlík. Alto soloist may be replaced by a small choir of 4 voices. This work has also been listed as op.94 and op.99.

I. The Colors of the Flag	5'
II. First Apostrophe to the Eagle	2'
Second Apostrophe to the Eagle	2'
III. Interlude—March	2'
First Apostrophe to the Flag (The Foot-Soldier)	2'
Second Apostrophe to the Flag (The Cavalryman)	2'
Third Apostrophe to the Flag (The Sailor)	3'
IV. Finale (Prophetic)	3'

EBP

Amid Nature, op.91

see his: In Nature's Realm, op.91, B.168

Biblical Songs, op.99, B.185 (Biblické písně; Biblische Lieder, Chants bibliques) <1894>   26'

solo alto (or baritone)
2 0 2 0 — 2 2 0 0 — tmp+1 — hp — str
perc: tri
Originally for voice & piano. Nos.1-5 orchestrated by the composer; nos.6-10 by V. Zemánek. Available in keys for high or low voice.

1. Clouds and Darkness (Oblak a mrákota jest vůkol Něho)	2'
2. Thou Art My Hiding-Place (Skrýše má a paveza má Ty jsí)	2'
3. Give Ear to My Prayer (Slyš, ó Bože, slyš modlitbu mou)	3'
4. The Lord is My Shepherd (Hospodin jest můj pastýř)	3'
5. I Will Sing a New Song (Bože! Bože! Píseň novou)	3'
6. Hear My Cry (Slyš, ó Bože, volání mé)	3'
7. By the Rivers of Babylon (Při řekách babylonských)	3'
8. Turn Thee unto Me (Popatřiž na mne a smiluj se nade mnou)	3'
9. I Will Lift Up Mine Eyes (Pozdvihuji očí svých k horám)	2'
10. O Sing unto the Lord (Zpívejte Hospodinu píseň novou)	2'

| Kalmus | Luck's | Simrock | Supraphon |

Carnival Overture, op.92, B.169 (Karneval) <1891>   10'

3[1.2.pic] 3[1.2.Eh] 2 2 — 4 2 3 1 — tmp+3 — hp — str
perc: tambn, tri, cym

| Bärenreiter | Kalmus | Luck's | Supraphon |

Concerto, Piano, op.33, B.63, G minor <1876>   34'

2 2 2 2 — 2 2 0 0 — tmp — str

I. Allegro agitato	15'
II. Andante sostenuto	10'
III. Finale: Allegro con fuoco	9'

| Bärenreiter | Kalmus | Luck's | Peters | Supraphon |

Concerto, Violin, op.53, B.96, A minor <1879–1880>   32'

2 2 2 2 — 4 2 0 0 — tmp — str

I. Allegro; ma non troppo	10'
II. Adagio; ma non troppo	11'
III. Finale: Allegro giocoso; ma non troppo	11'

| Bärenreiter | Breitkopf | Kalmus | Luck's | Supraphon |

Concerto, Violoncello, op.104, B.191, B minor <1894–1895>   40'

2[1.2/pic] 2 2 2 — 3 2 3 1 — tmp+1 — str
perc: tri
Bärenreiter edition by Jonathan Del Mar; Breitkopf edition by Klaus Döge.

I. Allegro	16'
II. Adagio ma non troppo	11'
III. Finale: Allegro moderato	13'

| Bärenreiter | Kalmus | Luck's | Supraphon |

Concerto, Violoncello (No.2) op.posth., B.10, A major <1865>   30'

2 2 2 2 — 2 2 0 0 — tmp — str
A youthful work, originally for violoncello & piano. Bärenreiter edition orchestrated by Jarmil Burghauser. Breitkopf edition (which calls for 4hn rather than 2) orchestrated by Günter Raphael.

| Bärenreiter | Breitkopf |

Czech Suite, op.39, B.93, D major (Česká suita) <1879>   23'

2 3[1.2.Eh] 2 2 — 2 2 0 0 — tmp — str
English horn plays only in 4th mvt; composer indicates that a basset horn played by a clarinetist may substitute for Eh (clarinets are tacet in the 4th mvt).

I. Praeludium (Pastorale): Allegro moderato	4'
II. Polka: Allegretto grazioso	5'
III. Menuetto (Sousedská): Allegro giusto	4'
IV. Romanze: Andante con moto	4'
V. Finale (Furiant): Presto	6'

| Bärenreiter | Kalmus | Luck's | Supraphon |

Festival March, op.54a, B.88 (Slavnostní pochod; Fest-Marsch) <1879>   5'

2 2 2 2 — 4 2 3 1 — tmp+1 — hp[opt] — str
perc: tri

| Bärenreiter | Bote & Bock | Kalmus | Luck's | Supraphon |

Golden Spinning Wheel, op.109, B.197 (Zlatý kolovrat) <1896>   27'

2[1.2/pic] 3[1.2.Eh] 2 3[1.2.cbn] — 4 2 3 1 — tmp+3 — hp — str
perc: tri, cym, bd

| Bärenreiter | Kalmus | Luck's | Supraphon |

A Hero's Song, op.111, B.199 (Píseň bohatýrská; Heldenlied) <1897>   23'

2 2 2 2 — 4 2 3 1 — tmp+3 — str
perc: tri, cym, bd

| Bärenreiter | Kalmus | Luck's | Supraphon |

Humoresque, op.101, no.7, B.187 (Humoresky; Humoreske) <1894>   5'

2 2 2 2 — 2 2 1 0 — tmp — hp[opt] — str
Arr. Adolf Schmid, from a piano work.

| Kalmus | Lengnick | Luck's |

Hussite Overture, op.67, B.132 (Husitská) <1883>   14'

3[1.2.pic] 2[1/Eh.2] 2 2 — 4 2 3 1 — tmp+2 — hp[opt] — str
perc: bd, tri, cym

| Bärenreiter | Kalmus | Luck's | Supraphon |

In Nature's Realm, op.91, B.168 (V přírodě) <1891>   12'

2 3[1.2.Eh] 3[1.2.bcl] 2 — 4 2 3 1 — tmp+1 — str
perc: cym, tri

| Bärenreiter | Kalmus | Luck's | Supraphon |

Legends, op.59, B.122 (Legendy): Nos.1-5 <1881>   25'

2 2 2 2 — 4 2 0 0 — tmp — hp — str
perc: tri [played by timpanist]
Originally for pf duet; arr. by the composer.

1. Allegretto [2222—4000—tmp—str]	5'
2. Molto Moderato [1222—4000—str]	4'
3. Allegro giusto - Andante giusto [2222—4000—1perc—str]	4'
4. Molto maestoso [2222—4200—tmp/tri—str]	7'
5. Allegro giusto [2222—hp—str]	5'

| Bärenreiter | Kalmus | Luck's | Simrock |

Legends, op.59, B.122 (Legendy): Nos.6-10 <1881>   21'

2 2 2 2 — 4 0 0 0 — tmp — hp — str
Originally for pf duet; arr. by the composer.

6. Allegro con moto - Moderato [2222—2000—hp—str]	5'
7. Allegretto grazioso - pocu più mosso [2222—2000—tmp—str]	4'
8. Un poco allegretto e grazioso [2222—4000—str]	5'
9. Andante con moto [2222—2000—tmp—str]	3'
10. Andante [2222—4000—str]	4'

| Bärenreiter | Kalmus | Luck's | Simrock |

Mass, op.86, B.153, D major <1887>   43'

chorus   opt soloists SATB
0 2 0 2 — 3 2 3 0 — tmp — org — str

1. Kyrie	7'
2. Gloria	9'
3. Credo	13'
4. Sanctus	2'
5. Benedictus	7'
6. Agnus Dei	5'

| Bärenreiter | Kalmus | Supraphon |

Midday Witch, op.108, B.196 (Polednice; Noon Witch)   *14'*
   <1896>

3[1.2.pic] 2 3[1.2.bcl] 2 — 4 2 3 1 — tmp+3 — str
perc: tri, chime[A4], cym, bd
Bcl largely in A, though early passages in B-flat; all of the bcl part is in
treble clef.

Bärenreiter	Luck's	Supraphon

My Homeland, op.62, B.125a (Domov můj; Mein Heim)   *10'*
   <1881>

2 2 2 2 — 4 2 3 0 — tmp+1 — str
perc: tri

Kalmus	Lengnick	Luck's	Simrock	Supraphon

Nocturne, op.40, B.47, B major <1875; rev 1882 or   *7'*
1883>

str

Originally part of the composer's *String Quartet No.4*, from which it was
later adapted as (a) *Nocturne* for violin & piano, (b) a movement
temporarily in the composer's *String Quintet op.77* but subsequently
withdrawn, and (c) the present independent work for string orchestra.

Bote & Bock	Kalmus	Luck's

Othello Overture, op.93, B.174 <1891–1892>   *15'*

2[1.2/pic] 3[1.2.Eh] 2 2 — 4 2 3 1 — tmp+2 — hp — str
perc: cym, bd

Bärenreiter	Luck's	Supraphon

The Peasant a Rogue, B.67 (Šelma sedlák; The Cunning   *11'*
Peasant): Overture <1877>

2[1.2/pic] 2 2 2 — 4 2 3 0 — tmp+1 — str
perc: tri

Kalmus	Lengnick	Luck's	Simrock

Prague Waltzes, B.99 (Pražské valčiky) <1879>   *9'*

2 2 2 2 — 4 2 3 0 — tmp — str

Czech

Requiem, op.89, B.165 <1890>   *90'*

chorus   solos SATB
3[1.2.pic] 3[1.2.Eh] 3[1.2.bcl] 3[1.2.cbn] — 4 4 3 1 — tmp+1 — hp
— org — str
perc: tamtam, chimes
Bärenreiter offers also an arrangement by Joachim Linckelmann that
reduces the orchestra to:
   1 1[ob/Eh] 1[cl/bcl] 1 — 1 0 0 0 — tmp — str.
   Eh & bcl are optional.

I. Requiem aeternam	*10'*
II. Requiem aeternam	*5'*
III. Dies Irae	*2'*
IV. Tuba mirum	*8'*
V. Quid sum miser	*6'*
VI. Recordare; Jesu pie	*7'*
VII. Confutatis maledictis	*5'*
VIII. Lacrymosa	*6'*
IX. Offertorium	*11'*
X. Hostias	*10'*
XI. Sanctus	*5'*
XII. Pie Jesu	*5'*
XIII. Agnus Dei	*10'*

Bärenreiter	Kalmus	Supraphon

Rhapsody, op.14, B.44, A minor (Symfonická básen;   *19'*
Symphonic Poem) <1874>

3[1.2.pic] 3[1.2.Eh] 2 2 — 4 2 3 1 — tmp+3 — hp — str
perc: tri, cym, bd

Bärenreiter	Kalmus	Supraphon

Romance, Violin & Orchestra, op.11, B.39, F minor   *12'*
   <1873–1877>

2 2 2 2 — 2 0 0 0 — str
Originally the slow movement of the String Quartet in F minor, op.9.

Bärenreiter	Kalmus	Luck's	Supraphon

Rondo, Violoncello & Orchestra, op.94, B.181, G minor   *7'*
   <1891; rev 1893>

0 2 0 2 — tmp — str
Originally for violoncello & piano; orchestrated by the composer.

Kalmus	Lengnick	Luck's	Simrock	Supraphon

Scherzo capriccioso, op.66, B.131 <1883>   *12'*

3[1.2.pic] 3[1.2.Eh] 3[1.2.bcl(A)] 2 — 4 2 3 1 — tmp+3 — hp — str
perc: tri, cym, bd

Bärenreiter	Bote & Bock	Kalmus	Luck's	Supraphon

Serenade, op.22, B.52, E major <1875>   *27'*

str

I. Moderato	*4'*
II. Tempo di valse	*6'*
III. Scherzo: Vivace	*6'*
IV. Larghetto	*5'*
V. Finale: Allegro vivace	*6'*

Bärenreiter	Bote & Bock	Kalmus	Luck's	Supraphon

Serenade, op.44, B.77, D minor <1878>   *24'*

0 2 2 3[1.2.opt cbn] — 3 0 0 0 — vc, db

I. Moderato quasi marcia	*4'*
II. Menuetto - Trio: Presto	*6'*
III. Andante con moto	*7'*
IV. Finale: Allegro molto	*7'*

Bärenreiter	Kalmus	Luck's	Simrock	Supraphon

Silent Woods, B.182 (Klid; Waldesruhe) <1893>   *5'*

solo violoncello
1 0 2 2 — 1 0 0 0 — str
Originally a work for 2 pianos, op.68 no.5; arranged by the composer.

Kalmus	Lengnick	Simrock	Supraphon

Slavonic Dances, op.46, B.83, nos.1-4 (Slovanské tance;   *19'*
   Slawische Tänze; Danses slaves) <1878>

3[1.2/pic.3] 2 2 2 — 4 2 3 0 — tmp+3 — str
perc: bd, cym, tri
3rd flute appears in 3rd dance only.
   Originally for piano 4-hands; orchestrated by the composer.
   Breitkopf edition by Klaus Döge.

No. 1 in C major: Presto	*4'*
No. 2 in E minor: Allegretto scherzando	*5'*
No. 3 in A-flat major: Poco allegro	*4'*
No. 4 in F major: Tempo di menuetto	*6'*

Bärenreiter	Breitkopf	Kalmus	Luck's	Simrock

Slavonic Dances, op.46, B.83, nos.5-8 (Slovanské tance;   *16'*
   Slawische Tänze; Danses slaves) <1878>

2[1.2/pic] 2 2 — 4 2 3 0 — tmp+3 — str
perc: bd, cym, tri
2nd flute part is entirely piccolo, except in dance no.5.
   Originally for piano 4-hands; orchestrated by the composer.
   Breitkopf edition by Klaus Döge.

No. 5 in A major: Allegro vivace	*3'*
No. 6 in D major: Allegretto scherzando	*6'*
No. 7 in C minor: Allegro assai	*4'*
No. 8 in G minor: Presto	*3'*

Bärenreiter	Breitkopf	Kalmus	Luck's	Simrock

Slavonic Dances, op.72, B.147, nos.1-4 (9-12) (Slovanské tance; Slawische Tänze; Danses slaves) <1886–1887>   *18'*

2 2 2 2 — 4 2 3 0 — tmp+3 — str
perc: tri, cym, bd
Originally for piano 4-hands; orchestrated by the composer.
No. 1 in B major: Molto vivace   4'
No. 2 in E minor: Allegretto grazioso   6'
No. 3 in F major: Allegro   3'
No. 4 in D-flat major: Allegretto grazioso 5'

Bärenreiter	Kalmus	Luck's	Simrock

Slavonic Dances, op.72, B.147, nos.5-8 (13-16) (Slovanské tance; Slawische Tänze; Danses slaves) <1886–1887>   *17'*

2[1.2/pic] 2 2 2 — 4 2 3 0 — tmp+3 — str
perc: bd, cym, tri, handbell[G#3]
Tbn & perc tacet no.6; tbn tacet no.8.
Originally for piano 4-hands; orchestrated by the composer.
No. 5 in B-flat minor: Poco adagio - Vivace   3'
No. 6 in B-flat major: Moderato; quasi menuetto 4'
No. 7 in C major: Allegro vivace   3'
No. 8 in A-flat major: Grazioso e lento   7'

Bärenreiter	Kalmus	Luck's	Simrock

Slavonic Rhapsody, op.45, B.86, no.1, D major <1878>   *10'*

3[1.2.pic] 2 2 2 — 4 2 3 0 — tmp+3 — str
perc: bd, cym, tri

Bärenreiter	Kalmus	Luck's	Simrock

Slavonic Rhapsody, op.45, B.86, no.2, G minor <1878>   *13'*

2 2 2 2 — 4 2 3 0 — tmp+3 — hp — str
perc: tri, cym, bd

Bärenreiter	Kalmus	Luck's	Simrock

Slavonic Rhapsody, op.45, B.86, no.3, A-flat major <1878>   *14'*

2[1.2/pic] 2 2 2 — 4 2 3 0 — tmp+3 — hp[doubled if possible] — str
perc: bd, cym, tri

Bärenreiter	Kalmus	Luck's	Simrock

The Spectre's Bride, op.69, B.135 (Svatební košile; Die Geisterbraut; Les chemises des noces) <1884>   *80'*

solos STB   chorus
2[1.2/pic] 3[1.2.Eh] 2[1.2/bcl] 2 — 4 2 3 1 — tmp+2 — hp — str
perc: tri, tamtam,
handbells[E4,A4,E5,G#5]
Score and parts not in agreement about the distribution of the clarinet parts; parts are clearer in this respect.

Kalmus	Supraphon

Stabat Mater, op.58, B.71 <1876–1877>   *81'*

chorus   solos SATB
2 2[1/Eh.2] 2 2 — 4 2 3 1 — tmp — org or harm [in 1 mvt] — str
Breitkopf edition by Klaus Döge.
Tuba in 3rd mvt only (12 bars).
I. Stabat Mater dolorosa   17'
II. Quis est homo   10'
III. Eia Mater, fons amoris   7'
IV. Fac ut ardeat cor meum   9'
V. Tui nati vulnerati   6'
VI. Fac me vere tecum flere   7'
VII. Virgo virginum praeclara   6'
VIII. Fac ut portem Christi mortem 6'
IX. Inflammatus et accensus   6'
X. Quando corpus morietur   7'

Bärenreiter	Kalmus	Schirmer	Supraphon

Suite, op.98b, B.190, A major (American) <1895>   *19'*

3[1.2.pic] 2 2 3[1.2.cbn] — 4 2 3 1 — tmp+3 — str
perc: bd, cym, tri
Originally for piano; orchestrated by the composer.
1. Andante con moto   5'
2. Allegretto   3'
3. Moderato (Alla Polacca) 4'
4. Andante   4'
5. Allegro   3'

Bärenreiter	Luck's	Simrock	Supraphon

Symphonic Variations, op.78, B.70 <1877>   *21'*

2[1.2/pic] 2 2 — 4 2 3 0 — tmp+1 — str
perc: tri

Bärenreiter	Kalmus	Luck's	Supraphon

Symphony No.1, op.3, B.9, C minor (Bells of Zlonice; Zlonické zvony) <1865>   *40'*

3[1.2.pic] 3[1.2.Eh] 2 2 — 4 2 3 0 — tmp — str
Eh in 1st mvt only: just a few notes.
I. Allegro   11'
II. Adagio molto   13'
III. Allegretto   6'
IV. Finale: Allegretto   10'

Bärenreiter	Kalmus	Supraphon

Symphony No.2, op.4, B.12, B-flat major <1865>   *48'*

3[1.2.pic] 2 2 — 4 2 3 0 — tmp — str
I. Allegro con moto   12'
II. Poco adagio   13'
III. Scherzo: Allegro con brio 13'
IV. Finale: Allegro con fuoco   10'

Bärenreiter	Kalmus	Supraphon

Symphony No.3, op.10, B.34, E-flat major <1873>   *33'*

3[1.2.pic] 3[1.2.Eh] 2 2 — 4 2 3 1 — tmp+1 — hp — str
perc: tri
I. Allegro moderato   10'
II. Adagio molto; Tempo di marcia 14'
III. Finale: Allegro vivace   9'

Bärenreiter	Kalmus	Simrock	Supraphon

Symphony No.4, op.13, B.41, D minor <1874>   *38'*

2[1/pic.2/pic] 2 2 — 4 2 3 0 — tmp+3 — hp — str
perc: tri, cym, bd
I. Allegro   10'
II. Andante sostenuto e molto cantabile 12'
III. Scherzo: Allegro feroce   6'
IV. Allegro con brio   10'

Bärenreiter	Kalmus	Simrock	Supraphon

Symphony No.5, op.76, B. 54, F major <1875>   *36'*

2 2 2[1/bcl.2] 2 — 4 2 3 0 — tmp+1 — str
perc: tri
Bcl in 4th mvt only: brief solo.
Formerly known as *Symphony No.3*.
I. Allegro ma non troppo   9'
II. Andante con moto   8'
III. Scherzo: Allegro scherzando 7'
IV. Finale: Allegro molto   12'

Bärenreiter	Kalmus	Supraphon

Symphony No.6, op.60, B.112, D major <1880>   *41'*

2[1.2/pic] 2 2 — 4 2 3 1 — tmp — str
Formerly known as *Symphony No.1*.
I. Allegro non tanto   13'
II. Adagio   11'
III. Scherzo (Furiant): Presto 7'
IV. Finale: Allegro con spirito 10'

Bärenreiter	Kalmus	Luck's	Supraphon

Symphony No.7, op.70, B.141, D minor <1884–1885>   *35'*

2[1.2/pic] 2 2 2 — 4 2 3 0 — tmp — str
Formerly known as *Symphony No.2.*
　　Bärenreiter ed. by Jonathan Del Mar is said to include 2 versions of the 2nd mvt.
　I. Allegro maestoso　　*11'*
　II. Poco adagio　　　*9'*
　III. Scherzo: Vivace　*7'*
　IV. Finale: Allegro　*8'*

Bärenreiter	Kalmus	Luck's	Supraphon

Symphony No.8, op.88, B.163, G major <1889>   *34'*

2[1.2/pic] 2[1.2/Eh] 2 2 — 4 2 3 1 — tmp — str
Just a few notes for piccolo and English horn.
　　Breitkopf edition by Klaus Döge.
　　Formerly known as *Symphony No.4.*
　I. Allegro con brio　　*9'*
　II. Adagio　　　　*10'*
　III. Allegretto grazioso　*6'*
　IV. Allegro ma non troppo　*9'*

Bärenreiter	Breitkopf	Kalmus	Luck's	Supraphon

Symphony No.9, op.95, B.178, E minor (From the New World; Z nového světa; Aus der Neuen Welt; Le nouveau monde) <1893>   *40'*

2[1.2/pic] 3[1.2.Eh] 2 2 — 4 2 3 1 — tmp+1 — str
perc: tri, cym
Playable with 2 oboists, the 2nd doubling English horn.
　　Breitkopf critical ed. by Christian Rudolf Riedel.
　　Formerly known as *Symphony No.5.*
　I. Adagio - Allegro molto　*8'*
　II. Largo　　　　*12'*
　III. Molto vivace　　*8'*
　IV. Allegro con fuoco　*12'*

Bärenreiter	Breitkopf	Kalmus	Luck's	Supraphon

Te Deum, op.103, B.176 <1892>   *21'*

chorus　　solos SB
2 3[1.2.Eh] 2 2 — 4 2 3 1 — tmp+3 — str
perc: tri, cym, bd
　I. Te deum laudamus: Allegro moderato maestoso　*7'*
　II. Tu Rex gloriae: Lento maestoso　*5'*
　III. Aeterna fac cum Sanctis: Vivace　*3'*
　IV. Dignare Domine: Lento　*6'*

Bärenreiter	Kalmus	Luck's	Simrock	Supraphon

Water Goblin, op.107, B.195 (Vodnik; Watersprite; Der Wassermann; L'ondin) <1896>   *19'*

3[1.2.pic] 3[1.2.Eh] 2[1.2/bcl(A)] 2 — 4 2 3 2[tuba2 opt] — tmp+4 — str
perc: tri, cym, bd, tamtam, handbell[A#4]
Bcl plays only 21 bars near the end (bars 760-780); could be covered either by cl 1 or cl 2.

Bärenreiter	Kalmus	Luck's	Supraphon

The Wood Dove, op.110, B.198 (The Wild Dove; The Forest Dove; Holoubek) <1896>   *19'*

2[1/pic.2] 3[1.2.Eh] 3[1.2.bcl] 2 — 4 3 3 1 — tmp+3 — hp — str
perc: tri, cym, bd, tambn, sus cym
Tp1&2 backstage for one passage; tp3 entirely backstage.

Bärenreiter	Simrock	Luck's	Supraphon

E

Earnest, John David   1940-

(b Lubbock TX, 11 August 1940). American

Chasing the Sun <1987>   *6'*

3[1.2.pic] 2 2 2 — 4 3 3 1 — tmp+3 — hp — str
perc: bd, sus cym, sd, tamtam, glock, xyl, vib, 3tomtom

ECS

Southern Exposure <2002; rev 2010>   *10'*

3[1.2.3/pic] 3[1.2.3/Eh] 3 3 — 4 3 3 1 — tmp+4 — hp — pf — str
perc: bd, sus cym, sd, tambn, tamtam, glock, xyl, vib, templeblks, cast, 4tomtom

ECS

Eccles, Henry   ca.1680-ca.1740

(b ?1675-85; d ?1735-45). English

Sonata in A minor   *9'*

double bass
str
Originally from the composer's violin sonatas, Book 1, no.11; widely known in arrangements for viola and for cello, with piano accompaniment. Arranged for double bass and string orchestra by Norman Ludwin.
　　The solo part, like the violin original, is written in G minor. If traditional solo double bass scordatura is used, it will sound in A minor. Ludwin offers score and parts in either A minor or G minor; specify key when ordering.
　I. Largo　　　　*3'*
　II. Allegro con spirito　*2'*
　III. Adagio　　　*2'*
　IV. Vivace　　　*2'*

Ludwin

Eck, Friedrich Johann   1767-1838

(b Schwetzingen, 24 May 1767; d ? France, 22 Feb 1838). Bohemian

Concerto, Violin, E-flat major

　　see: Mozart, Wolfgang Amadeus
　　　　Concerto, Violin, No.6, K.268 (Ang.C14.04), E-flat major

Effinger, Cecil   1914-1990

(b Colorado Springs, CO, 22 July 1914; d Boulder, CO, 22 Dec 1990). American

Little Symphony No.1, op.31 <1945>   *15'*

2[1.2/pic] 1 2 1 — 2 1 0 0 — str
　Moderato　　　*5'*
　Presto　　　　*2'*
　Adagio　　　　*5'*
　Allegro vivace　　*3'*

C. Fischer

Egk, Werner   1901-1983

(name orig. Werner Mayer; b Auchsesheim, nr Donauwörth, 17 May 1901; d Inning, nr Munich, 10 July 1983). German

French Suite <1949>   20'
3[1.2.pic] 3 3 3[1.2.cbn] — 4 3 3 1 — tmp+4 — hp — str
perc: cym, glock, sd, tri, gong, bd, tamtam, 2sus cym
After Rameau.
1. *Le rappel des oiseaux*   _'
2. *Gigue en rondeau*   _'
3. *Les tendres plaintes*   _'
4. *La vénetienne*   _'
5. *Les tourbillons*   _'
```
Schott
```

La tentation de Saint Antoine (The Temptation of St.   23'
Anthony) <1947; rev 1952>

alto solo
str 4t & str orch
Originally for alto & string quartet; revised 1952 for alto, string quartet & string orchestra; revised 1978 for chorus & orchestra.
   After 18th-century airs and verse; the contents list gives the text incipit.
1. *Ciel! l'Univers va-t-il donc se dissoudre?*   2'
2. *C'étoit ainsi, c'étoit ainsi*   1'
3. *On vit sortir d'une grotte profonde*   2'
4. *On vit des Démons de tous les cantons*   1'
5. *Quelques-uns prirent le cochon*   2'
6. *Sur un sopha*   3'
7. *Ronflant comme un cochon*   1'
8. *Courez vite, prenez le patron*   1'
9. *Le saint, craignant de pécher*   2'
10. *Piqué dans ce bachanal*   2'
11. *Tel qu'un voleur, sitôt qu'il voit main forte* 3'
12. *Ah! mon Dieu! que je l'échappe belle!*   1'
13. *Le Démon, quoiqu'il passe pour fin*   2'
```
Schott
```

Variations on a Caribbean Theme (Variationen über ein   30'
karibisches Thema) <1959>

2 2 2 2 — 4 3 3 0 — tmp+3 — hp — pf — str
perc: sd, cym, tri, vib, chimes, congas, 3bongos, 3tomtoms
1. *Thema (Choucoune)*   _'
2. *Perpetuum mobile*   _'
3. *Chaconne*   _'
4. *Ostinato*   _'
5. *Concertino*   _'
6. *Evokation*   _'
7. *Finale*   _'
```
Schott
```

Einem, Gottfried von   1918-1996

(b Berne, 24 Jan 1918; d Oberdurnbach, Lower Austria, 12 July 1996). Austrian

Ballade, op.23 <1957>   14'
3[1.2.3/pic] 2 2 2 — 4 3 3 1 — tmp — str
```
Schirmer
```

Bruckner Dialog, op.39 <1971>   15'
3[1.2.pic] 2 2 2 — 4 3 3 1 — tmp — str
Based largely on the chorale theme from the unfinished 4th mvt of Bruckner's *Symphony No.9*.
```
Boosey
```

Capriccio, op.2 <1943>   8'
3[1.2.3/pic] 2 2 2 — 4 3 3 1 — tmp — str
```
Bote & Bock
```

Meditations, op.18 <1954>   21'
2[1.2/pic] 2 2 2 — 4 2 2 0 — tmp — str
```
Universal
```

Philadelphia Symphony, op.28 <1960–1961>   16'
3[1.2.pic] 2 2 2 — 4 3 3 1 — tmp — str
1. *Allegro giusto*   3'
2. *Andante*   6'
3. *Allegro vivace*   7'
```
Boosey
```

Wiener Symphonie, op.49 (Vienna Symphony) <1976>   32'
3[1.2.pic] 2 2 2 — 4 3 3 1 — tmp — str
Allegro ma non troppo   9'
Im Tempo eines Geschwindmarsches   6'
Adagio   8'
Allegro   9'
```
Bote & Bock
```

Einhorn, Richard   1952-

(b 1952). American

The Fourth Manner of Loving <1996>
chorus (SSAATTBB)
2 2 0 0 — str
Medieval Dutch text; pronunciation guide available from composer.
```
Einhorn
```

My Many Colored Days By Dr. Seuss <1997>   25'
narrator
2[1.2/pic] 2 2 2 — 4 2 3 1 — tmp+2 — 2hp — cel — str
perc: bd, sd, 2marim
I. *Some Days*   _'
II. *Bright Red Days*   _'
III. *Bright Blue Days*   _'
IV. *Sort of Brown Days*   _'
V. *A Yellow Day*   _'
VI. *Gray Day*   _'
VII. *My Orange Days*   _'
VIII. *Green Days*   _'
IX. *On Purple Days*   _'
X. *Happy Pink Days*   _'
XI. *My Black Days*   _'
XII. *Mixed Up Days / Finale*   _'
```
Einhorn
```

Voices of Light <1993>   70'
solos SATB   chorus
2 2 0 0 — 3gambas — sampler — str[min 30]
Oratorio intended to accompany the Carl Dreyer silent film *The Passion of Joan of Arc*.
I. *Prelude*   3'
II. *First Interrogation Part 1* 5'
III. *Interrogation 1 Part 2*   7'
IV. *The Jailers 1*   3'
V. *Interrogation 2*   9'
VI. *The Jailers 2*   5'
VII. *Torture*   4'
VIII. *Illness*   5'
IX. *Sacrament*   8'
X. *Abjuration*   4'
XI. *Haircut*   2'
XII. *Massien and Joan*   5'
XIII. *The Final Walk*   3'
XIV. *The Burning*   3'
XV. *Protest*   4'
```
Einhorn
```

Elfman, Danny   1953-

(b Los Angeles, 29 May 1953). American

Serenada Schizophrana <2005>   39'

solo soprano and female chorus (mvts 5-6)
3[1/pic.2/afl.3/pic/afl] 3[1.2/Eh.3/Eh] 3[1/Ebcl.2/bcl.3/bcl/asx]
3[1.2.3/cbn] — 6 3 4[1.2.3/btbn.btbn/cb tbn] 1[tuba/cimbasso] —
tmp+5 — hp — synth, 2pf[1.2/synth2] — str[14.10.8.8.6]
perc: tomtom, glock, xyl, vib, chimes, claves, cast, cym, sd, tambn, tamtam, bd,
Wuhan cymbal, 4woodblks, 3templeblks, 2marim, 4sus cym, Chinese tamtam,
Peking gong, metal shaker, wooden shaker, rattlesnake shaker, songbells, MIDI
pad, Octapad
Mvt 4 orchestrated by Edgardo Simone; remainder by Steve Bartek.

I. Pianos	7'
II. Blue Strings	10'
III. A Brass Thing	5'
IV. Quadruped Patrol	3'
V. I Forget	6'
VI. Bells and Whistles	7'
End Tag	1'

AMP

Elgar, Edward   1857-1934

(b Broadheath, nr Worcester, 2 June 1857; d Worcester, 23 Feb 1934). English

The Apostles, op.49 <1902–1903>   130'

solos SATBBB   chorus, semi-chorus (24 voices) of boys or women
3[1.2.pic] 3[1.2.Eh] 3[1.2.bcl] 3[1.2.cbn] — 4 4 3 1 — tmp+4 — 1 or
2hp — org — str
perc: sd, tambn, tri, gong, tamtam, cym, crot, bd, kybd glock
The 4th trumpet represents the shofar. The 2 oboes and English horn play
offstage in one passage.

Part I	75'
Part II	55'

Novello

Chanson de matin, op.15, no.2 <1901>   3'

1 1 2 1 — 2 0 0 0 — hp[or pf] — str

Kalmus	Luck's	Novello

Chanson de nuit, op.15, no.1 <1901>   4'

1 1 2 1 — 2 0 0 0 — hp[or pf] — str

Kalmus	Luck's	Novello

Cockaigne, op.40 (In London Town) <1900–1901>   13'

2[1.2/pic] 2 2 3[1.2.cbn] — 4 4[2tp, 2crt] 3[tbn4-5 opt] 1 — tmp+5
— opt org — str
perc: sd, tri, slgh-bells, tambn, cym, bd

Boosey	Kalmus	Luck's

Concerto, Violin, op.61, B minor <1909–1910>   48'

2 2 2 3[1.2.opt cbn] — 4 2 3 1[opt] — tmp — str

I. Allegro	18'
II. Andante	11'
III. Allegro molto	19'

Kalmus	Luck's	Novello

Concerto, Violoncello, op.85, E minor <1919>   30'

2 2 2 2 — 4 2 3 1[opt] — tmp — str
Optional piccolo part for 10 bars in the last movement. Bärenreiter
edition by Jonathan Del Mar; Kalmus ed. Nancy Bradburd.
   An arrangement of the solo part for viola has been made by Lionel
Tertis; it is available from Novello. In this case, the orchestral parts for
the Cello Concerto are used, but Novello will supply a different full score
showing the solo viola part.

I. Adagio; Moderato	7'
II. Lento; Allegro molto	6'
III. Adagio	6'
IV. Allegro; Moderato; Allegro, ma non troppo	11'

Bärenreiter	Kalmus	Luck's	Novello

The Crown of India: Suite <1912>   17'

3[1.2.pic] 2 3[1.2.opt bcl] 3[1.2.opt cbn] — 4 4[3&4 opt] 3 1 —
tmp+5 — hp — str
perc: bd, cym, sus cym, sd, tomtom, tri, tambn, tamtam, gong, glock, slgh-bells

1. (a) Introduction (b) Dance of the Nautch Girls	5'
2. Menuetto	2'
3. Warrior's Dance	2'
4. Intermezzo	4'
5. March of the Mogul Emperors	4'

Boosey	Kalmus

The Crown of India: March of the Mogul Emperors   4'
<1912>

3[1.2.pic] 2 3[1.2.bcl] 3[1.2.cbn] — 4 3 3 1 — tmp+5 — str
perc: bd, cym, sd, tambn, tamtam, gong, slgh-bells

Boosey	Kalmus

Dream Children, op.43 (Enfants d'un rêve) <1902>   6'

2 2 2 2 — 4 0 0 0 — tmp — hp — str

1. Andantino	3'
2. Allegretto piacevole	3'

Kalmus	Luck's	Novello

The Dream of Gerontius, op.38 <1899–1900>   100'

large chorus, semi-chorus (18 voices)   solos Ms TB
3[1.2.pic] 3[1.2.Eh] 3[1.2.bcl] 3[1.2.cbn] — 4 3 3 1 — tmp+4 — 1 or
2hp — org — str
perc: sd, slgh-bells, tri, cym, glock, bd, tamtam
8 bars of the work call for 3 extra trumpets ad lib.

Kalmus	Luck's	Novello

Elegy, op.58 <1909>   5'

str

Kalmus	Luck's	Novello

Enigma Variations, op.36 (Variations on an Original 31'
Theme) <1898–1899>

2[1.2/pic] 2 2 3[1.2.cbn] — 4 3 3 1 — tmp+3 — opt org — str
perc: sd, tri, cym, bd
Organ only in the finale; percussion only in variations 7, 11, & finale.
   Bärenreiter ed. by Christopher Hogwood.

Enigma: Andante	1'
Var.I. "C.A.E." L'istesso tempo	2'
II. "H.D.S.- P." Allegro	1'
III. "R.B.T." Allegretto	1'
IV. "W.M.B." Allegro di molto	1'
V. "R.P.A." Moderato	2'
VI. "Ysobel" Andantino	1'
VII. "Troyte" Presto	1'
VIII. "W.N." Allegretto	2'
IX. "Nimrod" Moderato	4'
X. "Dorabella - Intermezzo" Allegretto	3'
XI. "G.R.S." Allegro di molto	1'
XII. "B.G.N." Andante	3'
XIII. " *** - Romanza" Moderato	3'
XIV. "E.D.U." - Finale	5'

Bärenreiter	Kalmus	Luck's	Novello

Falstaff, op.68 <1913>   *30'*

3[1.2.pic] 3[1.2.Eh] 3[1.2.bcl] 3[1.2.cbn] — 4 3 3 1 — tmp+3 (or 4)
— 2hp — str
perc: sd, tambn, tri, cym, bd, tabor

Kalmus	Novello

Froissart, op.19 <1890; rev 1901>   *12'*

2[1.2/pic] 2 2 3[1.2.opt cbn] — 4 2 3 0 — tmp+1 opt — str
perc: opt cym

Kalmus	Luck's	Novello

In the South, op.50 (Alassio) <1903–1904>   *20'*

3[1.2.3/pic] 3[1.2.Eh] 3[1.2.bcl] 3[1.2.cbn] — 4 3 3 1 — tmp+3 — hp
— str
perc: tri, sd, glock, cym, bd

Kalmus	Luck's	Novello

Introduction and Allegro, op.47 <1904–1905>   *14'*

solo string quartet
str

Kalmus	Luck's	Novello

The Kingdom, op.51 <1901–1906>   *104'*

solos SATB   chorus
3[1.2.3/pic] 3[1.2.Eh] 3[1.2.bcl] 3[1.2.cbn] — 4 3 3 1 — tmp+3 —
2hp — org — str
perc: sd, cym, bd

Kalmus	Novello

The Music Makers, op.69 <1912>   *39'*

contralto solo   chorus
3[1.2.pic] 3[1.2.Eh] 3[1.2.bcl] 3[1.2.cbn] — 4 3 3 1 — tmp+3 — 2hp
— org — str
perc: bd, cym, sd, tri

Novello

POMP AND CIRCUMSTANCE, military marches, op.39   *5'*
No.1, D major <1901>

4[1.2.pic1.opt pic2] 2 2 3[1.2.bcl(A)] 3[1.2.cbn] — 4 4[2tp, 2crt] 3 1 —
tmp+5 — 2hp — org — str
perc: sd, tri, tambn, slgh-bells, cym, bd, opt glock

Boosey	Kalmus	Luck's

No.2, A minor <1901>   *3'*

3[1.2.pic] 2 3[1.2.bcl(A)] 3[1.2.cbn] — 4 4[2tp, 2crt] 3 1 — tmp+5 —
str
perc: tri, glock, slgh-bells, cym, bd, 2sd

Boosey	Kalmus	Luck's

No.3, C minor <1904>   *5'*

3[1.2.pic] 3[1.2.Eh] 3[1.2.bcl] 4[1.2.3.cbn] — 4 4[2tp, 2crt] 3 1 —
tmp+5 — str
perc: sd, tri, td, cym, bd
Perhaps possible with 4perc.

Boosey	Kalmus	Luck's

No.4, G major <1907>   *4'*

3[1.2.3/pic] 3[1.2.Eh] 3[1.2.bcl] 3[1.2.cbn] — 4 3 3 1 — tmp+3 —
2hp — str
perc: sd, cym, bd

Boosey	Kalmus	Luck's

No.5, C major <1929–1930>   *5'*

3[1.2.pic] 3[1.2.Eh] 3[1.2.bcl] 3[1.2.cbn] — 4 3 3 1 — tmp+4 — str
perc: sd, tri, cym, bd

Boosey

Salut d'amour, op.12 (Love's Greeting) <1888>   *4'*

1 2 2 2 — 2 0 0 0 — str
Originally for violin & piano; arr. by the composer.

Kalmus	Luck's

Sea Pictures, op.37 <1897–1899>   *23'*

alto solo
2 2 2 3[1.2.cbn] — 4 2 3 1 — tmp+2 — hp — opt org — str
perc: gong, sus cym, bd
Cbn in no.5 only. Occasionally sung by baritones.

I. Sea Slumber Song (Roden Noel)	5'
II. In Haven (Capri) (C. Alice Elgar)	2'
III. Sabbath Morning at Sea (Elizabeth Barrett Browning)	6'
IV. Where Corals Lie (Dr. Richard Garnett)	4'
V. The Swimmer (Adam Lindsay Gordon)	6'

Boosey	Kalmus	Luck's

Serenade, op.20, E minor <1892>   *12'*

str

I. Allegro piacevole	3'
II. Larghetto	6'
III. Allegretto	3'

Breitkopf	Kalmus	Luck's

Severn Suite <1930>   *19'*

3[1.2.pic] 3[1.2.Eh] 3[1.2.bcl] 3[1.2.cbn] — 4 3 3 1 — tmp+3 — str
perc: bd, cym, sd
Originally for brass band; orchestrated by the composer. Mvts are all
attacca.

1. Introduction (Worcester Castle)	2'
2. Toccata (Tournament)	5'
3. Fugue (The Cathedral)	4'
4. Minuet (Commandery)	6'
5. Coda	2'

Goodmusic

Sospiri, op.70 <1913–1914>   *6'*

hp[or pf] — opt org or harm — str

Breitkopf	Kalmus	Luck's

Spanish Serenade, op.23 (Stars of the Summer Night)   *4'*
<1892>

chorus
2 2 2 2 — 2 0 0 0 — tmp+1 — str
perc: tri, tambn

Kalmus	Luck's

Sursum corda, op.11 (Lift Your Hearts; Elévation)   *8'*
<1894>

0 0 0 0 — 4 2 3 1 — tmp — org — str
An arrangement by Adolf Schmid that includes woodwinds, is available
from Schott, and reprinted by Luck's. The instrumentation is:
  2 2 2 2 — 4 2 3 1 — tmp — hp — str

Luck's

Symphony No.1, op.55, A-flat major <1907–1908>   50'

3[1.2.3/pic] 3[1.2.Eh] 3[1.2.bcl] 3[1.2.cbn] — 4 3 3 1 — tmp+3 —
2hp — str
perc: sd, cym, bd
Perc tacet in mvts. 1 & 3.
   This work has string solo passages throughout, including solos for the
last stand of every string section.

I. Andante; nobilmente e semplice - Allegro	19'
II. Allegro molto	7'
III. Adagio	12'
IV. Lento - Allegro	12'

Kalmus	Novello

Symphony No.2, op.63, E-flat major <1909–1911>   53'

3[1.2.3/pic] 3[1.2.Eh] 4[1.2.Ebcl.bcl] 3[1.2.cbn] — 4 3 3 1 — tmp+4
— 2hp — str
perc: sd, tambn, cym, bd

I. Allegro vivace e nobilmente	17'
II. Larghetto	14'
III. Rondo	8'
IV. Moderato e maestoso	14'

Kalmus	Novello

Symphony No.3 <1932–1933>   58'

3[incl pic] 3[incl Eh] 3[incl bcl] 3[incl cbn] — 4 3 3 1 — tmp+3 —
2hp — str
perc: bd, cym, sd, tamtam, tambn
Elgar's sketches for a third symphony, elaborated by Anthony Payne.

Boosey

Three Bavarian Dances <1895; rev 1896>   12'

2[1.2/pic] 2 2 2 — 4 2 3 1 — tmp+4 or 5 — str
perc: sd, tri, bd, cym, glock ad lib.
Possible with perc: tmp+3. Nos. 1, 3 & 6 of the choral suite *From the
Bavarian Highlands*, op.27.

The Dance (Sonnenbichl)	4'
Lullaby (In Hammersbach)	3'
The Marksmen (Bei Murnau)	5'

Kalmus	Luck's	Stainer

Variations on an Original Theme, op.36

   see his: Enigma Variations

Ellington, Edw. Kennedy "Duke"   1899-1974

(b Washington, DC, 29 April 1899; d New York, 24 May 1974). American

   *Ellington's music is in dire need of a savior. Publisher G. Schirmer is
to be commended for keeping these works alive and available. However,
the condition of many of the scores and parts leaves much to be desired,
and the catalog descriptions frequently conflict with the scores
themselves. The situation is reminiscent of Haydn and Rossini
publications of the mid-20th century.*
   *Many works exist in multiple versions, some of which may be viewed
and compared at www.MusicSalesClassical.com/OnDemand. Still, it is
wise for users to obtain the materials well in advance, in order to absorb
any surprises and make adjustments.*

Black, Brown and Beige: Suite <1943>   18'

3[1.2.pic/afl] 2 3[1.2.bcl/bsx] 3[1.2.cbn] — 4 4 3 1 — asx — jazz
bass — tmp+3 — hp — str
Symphonic orchestration by Maurice Peress.

Black (A Work Song)	8'
Brown (Come Sunday)	5'
Beige (Light)	5'

Schirmer

Grand Slam Jam   12'

jazz soloists, as many as possible   optional dance band
2 3[1.2.Eh] 4[1.2.3.bcl] 3[1.2.cbn] — 4 4 3 1 — tmp+2 — hp — str
perc: set
Arr. Luther Henderson, Jr.; ed. Maurice Peress.
   Piece may be extended *ad lib.*

Schirmer

Harlem <1950>   18'

3[1.2.3/pic] 3[1.2.Eh] 3[1.2.bcl] 2 — 4 4 3 1 — 2asx, 2tsx, bsx —
tmp+3 — hp — str
perc: bd, cym, sd, set, tamtam, cowbell, 2gourds, shaker, 2sus cym, 3tomtom
Arr. Luther Henderson & Maurice Peress.

Schirmer

New World A-Comin' <1945>   10'

solo piano (must ad lib)   optional dance band
2[1.2/pic] 2 3[1.2.bcl] 2 — 4 4 3 1 — tmp+3 — hp — str
perc: set, bd, cym, sus cym, tambn, glock, xyl
Arr. & ed. Maurice Peress.

Schirmer

Night Creature   17'

2 1 2 1 — 2 4 3 1 — 2asx, 2tsx, bsx — jazz bass — tmp+2 — hp —
pf — str

Schirmer

Nutcracker Suite (After Tchaikovsky) <1960>   19'

2 2[incl Eh] 3[incl bcl] 2 — 4 3 3 1 — asx/tsx — jazz bass — 1perc
— str
perc: set
Composed & arr. by Ellington & Billy Strayhorn; orchd Jeff Tyzik.

Overture	4'
Toot Toot Tootie Toot (Dance of the Reed Pipes)	3'
Dance of the Floreadors (Waltz of the Flowers)	4'
Sugar Rum Cherry (Dance of the Sugar Plum Fairy)	3'
Peanut Brittle Brigade (March)	5'

Schirmer

The River <1970>   30'

2[incl pic] 2[1.2/Eh] 2[incl bcl] 2 — 4 3 3 1 — tmp+2 — hp — pf —
str
arr. Ron Collier.

Spring	—'
Meander	—'
Giggling Rapids	—'
Lake	—'
Vortex	—'
Falls	—'
Riba	—'
Two Cities	—'

Schirmer

Les trois rois noirs (The Three Black Kings)   15'

3[1.2.pic] 3[1.2.Eh] 3[1.2.bcl] 3[1.2.cbn] — 4 4[all/flug (tp4 opt)]
4[tbn4 opt] 1 — opt elec gtr — tmp+2 — hp — pf — str
Trumpets double on flugelhorn.
   According to the publisher's catalog, there is also a version for jazz
soloist (Eb, Bb or C instrument) and orchestra (ed. Maurice Peress);
however, Mr. Peress reports that this is the same as the original version.

King of the Magi	—'
King Solomon	—'
Martin Luther King	—'

Schirmer

Emerson, Keith

1944-

(b Todmorden, 1 Nov 1944). English

Concerto, Piano, No.1 <1977>

18'

3[1.2.3/pic] 2 2 3[1.2.cbn] — 4 3 3 1 — tmp+2 — str
perc: bd, sd, field dr, tri, tambn, tamtam, glock, chimes, crot, belltree, whip
I. quarter-note = 104 9'
II. Andante con moto 2'
III. quarter-note = c.150 7'

Presser

Enesco, Georges

1881-1955

(b Liveni Vîrnav [now George Enescu], nr Dorohoi, 19 Aug 1881; d Paris, 3/4 May 1955). Rumanian

Romanian Rhapsody, op.11, no.1, A major <1901>

11'

3[1.2.3/pic] 3[1.2.Eh] 2 2 — 4 4[2tp, 2crt] 3 1 — tmp+3 — 2hp — str
perc: cym, sd, tri
For this work only, the US representative of Enoch is Peermusic Classical.

Enoch	Kalmus	Luck's	Peer

Romanian Rhapsody, op.11, no.2, D major <1901>

11'

3 3[1.2.Eh] 2 2 — 4 2 3 0 — tmp+1 — 2hp — str
perc: cym

Kalmus	Luck's

Suite No.1, op.9, C major <1903>

26'

3[1.2.pic] 2[1.2/Eh] 2 2 — 4 2 3 0 — tmp+1 — hp — str[20.18.14.12.12]
perc: cym, sus cym
Prélude a l'unisson 7'
Menuet lent 9'
Intermède 4'
Final 6'

Enoch	Kalmus	Luck's

Symphonie concertante, op.8, B minor <1901>

23'

solo violoncello
2 2[1.2/Eh] 2 2 — 4 2 3 0 — tmp — str
Assez lent 15'
Majestueux 8'

Enoch	Kalmus

Symphony No.1, op.13, E-flat major <1905>

36'

3[1.2.pic] 3[1.2.Eh] 3[1.2.Ebcl/bcl] 4[1.2.3.cbn] — 4 4[2tp, 2crt] 3 1 — tmp+3 — 2hp — str[20.18.14.12.12]
perc: bd, cym, sus cym, tri, tambn
I. Assez vif et rythmé 13'
II. Lent 13'
III. Vif et vigoureux 10'

Boosey	Enoch	Kalmus

Eötvös, Peter

1944-

(b Székelyudvarhely [now Odorheiv Secviesc], Transylvania, 2 Jan 1944). Hungarian

CAP-KO (dedicated to Béla Bartók) <2005>

20

solo piano
2[1/pic.2/pic/afl] 2[1.2/Eh] 3[1.2/Ebcl.bcl/cbcl] 2[1.2/cbn] — 2 2 2 2 — ssx/asx/bsx — 3perc — cel — str[10.8.6.6.4]
perc: bd, tamtam, chimes, tambn, crot, surf fx, 3sd, 3sus cym, 5Chinescym, 6bellplates, 3tri, 3pod rattles, 2tomtom, 3bongos, 2slgh-bells, 2gong
2 grand pianos are required:
  1. Normal acoustic grand with pedal locked with a rubber wedge.
  2. Roland KR 17 or similar midi piano.
Celesta player also covers the "keyboard control," which modifies the sound of the Roland by adding parallel voices at various intervals (somewhat like an organ mixture stop).
I. quarter-note = 69 4'
II. half-note = 69 4'
III. eighth-note = 69 4'
IV. eighth-note = 84 5'
V. quarter-note = 120 3'

Schott

Chinese Opera <1986>

26

2[1/pic.afl.2/pic/afl] 2[1/Eh.2/Eh] 3[1/Ebcl1.2/Ebcl2.3/bcl] 2 — 2 2[1/pic tp.2/pic tp] 2 1 — tmp+2 — hp — synth DX7 — str[2.0.2.2.1]
perc: cym, crot, templeblks, 2bd, 2Chinese bd, 2gongs, 2Chinese opera gongs, 2tamtam, 2Chinescym, 3ratchets, 2pelletbells, 2tanggu
All flutes & piccolos to be tuned 1/4 tone lower. Tuba, harp & double bass to be amplified.
Erste Szene in E und Gis (First Scene in E and G-sharp) 11'
Zweite Szene in F und G (Second Scene in F and G) 8'
Dritte Szene in Fis und C (Third Scene in F-sharp and C) 7'

Salabert

DoReMi (Violin Concerto No.2) <2011–2012; rev 2013>

24

3[1.2/pic.3/afl] 2[1.2/Eh] 3[1.2/Ebcl.3/bcl] 2[1.2/cbn] — 2 2 1[alto tbn] 0 — 3perc — hp — cel — str[12.10.8.8.6]
perc: glock, bongos, xyl, crot, chimes, guiro, tamtam, tambn, 3tri, 3woodblk, 3Chinescym, 2gong, caxixi, 2sus cym, 2szl cym, 2marac, cowbells[chromatic], 2metalpipe
FIRST PART: quarter-note = 116 _'
SECOND PART: quarter-note = 120 _'
THIRD PART: quarter-note = 50 _'

Schott

Hommage à Domenico Scarlatti <2013>

9

solo horn
str[5.4.3.3.1]
Originally an opera aria; arr. by the composer.

Schott

Seven (Memorial for the Columbia Astronauts) <2006; rev 2007>

24

solo violin
3[1/afl.2/pic.3/pic] 3 4[1.2.3.bcl] 3 — 2 2 2 1 — bsx — 4perc — hp[ampd] — kybd[sampler] — 6vn.5va.5vc.4db
perc: 4chimes, 6sus cym, 2szl cym, 2Chinescym, 13gong, 4anvil, 4dome cym, 4coilspr, 2sistrum, 4tri, 3tamtam, 3glock, 2vib, 2crot
The visual aspect of this piece is specified in great detail (e.g., including the precise placement of each instrument, and the height at which each gong is mounted). 4 suspended loudspeakers are required. 6vn are in various positions in the balcony.
PART I: Cadenza with Accompaniment
  first cadenza (for Husband and McCool) 2'
  second cadenza (for Anderson) 1'
  third cadenza (for Clark and Brown) 3'
  fourth cadenza (for Chawla and Ramon) 6'
PART II 12'

Schott

Shadows <1996>   15'

solo flute & clarinet
1[pic] 1 2[bcl.cbcl] 1 — 2 1 1 0 — bsx — tmp+1 — cel —
str[8.0.6.4.2]
perc: szl cym, hi-hat, sd
Solo fl, solo cl, perc & cel all amplified.
   For smaller ensemble version, strings may be reduced to [4.0.2.2.2]
First movement   3'
Second movement   4'
Third movement   8'

Ricordi

zeroPoints <1999>   14'

4[1.2.pic1.pic2] 3[1.2.Eh] 4[1.2.Ebcl.bcl] 3[1.2.cbn] — 4 3[1.2.pic tp]
3 1 — ssx, tsx — 5perc[incl tmp] — 2hp — pf/cel — str[14.12.10.10.8]
perc: bd, cym, glock, xyl, marim, chimes, crot, lionroar, windchimes, 3tamtam,
4steeldrums, 3tri, 2slgh-bells, 5tmp[3 players], 2vib, 4sus cym

Schott

Erb, Donald   1927-2008

(b Youngstown, OH, 17 Jan 1927; d Cleveland Heights, OH, 12 Aug 2008).
American

Concerto, Brass <1987>   19'

3[1.2.3/pic/afl] 3[1.2.Eh] 3[1.2.bcl] 3[1.2.cbn] — 4 3 3 1 — tmp+3 —
hp — 2[or1]pf/synth/cel — str
perc: rototom, glock, xyl, marim, crot, 3bd, 3sus cym, 2sd, 5tomtom, 3tamtam,
2vib, 2chimes, 2db bows, nipplegong (C), 4harmonicas (Bb, B, C, D), 5wine
glasses
I. dotted quarter-note = 72-84   5'
II. quarter-note = 48-56   7'
III. eighth-note = c.132   6'

Merion

Concerto for Orchestra <1985>   26'

3[1.2.3/pic/afl] 3[1.2.Eh] 3[1.2/Ebcl.bcl] 3[1.2.cbn] — 4 3 3 1 —
tmp+3 — hp — pf/elec pf/cel — str
perc: sd, timbales, rototom, glock, xyl, marim, vib, crot, bongos, congas, 3bd, 3sus
cym, 6tomtom, 3tamtam, metal windchimes, nipplegong (C), cello bow,
5harmonicas (C, D, G, G. Ab), 4water goblets, 2gallon jug, tape
I. quarter-note = c.84   6'
II. [untitled]   8'
III. Scherzo   6'
IV. quarter-note = 60   6'

Presser

Concerto for Solo Percussionist & Orchestra <1966>   10'

3[1.2.3/pic] 2 3[1.2.bcl] 3[1.2.cbn] — 4 3 3 1 — tmp — hp — pf/cel
— str
perc: soloist: sd, marim, templeblks, vib, xyl, glock, chimes, bongos, timbales,
4woodblks, pf, 4sus cym; opt set for 3rd mvt improvised cadenza
I. quarter-note = 60   _'
II. quarter-note = 40-44   _'
III. eighth-note = 144   _'

Concerto, Trombone <1976>   17'

3[1.2.3/pic] 2 3[1.2.bcl] 3[1.2.cbn] — 4 3 3 1 — tmp+3 — hp —
pf/cel — str
perc: szl cym, sd, timbales, tri, glock, xyl, marim, vib, templeblks, bongos, 3bd,
4sus cym, 4tomtom, 3tamtam, fingercym, slide whistle, harmonica (D), jug
I. quarter-note = 112   4'
II. quarter-note = 36   5'
III. eighth-note = 132   4'
IV. dotted quarter-note = 120 4'

Merion

Cummings Cycle <1963>   8'

chorus
3[1/pic.2/pic.3] 2[1.2/Eh] 2 2 — 4 3 3 1 — tmp+2 — pf/cel — str
perc: bd, sus cym, sd, tri, woodblk, templeblks, cast
Score is not absolutely clear on whether 2nd fl doubles on pic.
I. your birthday comes to tell me this   _'
II. first robin the: _'
III. silence   _'
IV. off a pane (the   _'
V. ADHUCSUBJUDICE LIS   _'
VI. this   _'

Merion

Evensong (Laus amicorum) <1993>   23'

3[1.2.3/pic/afl] 3[1.2.Eh] 3[1.2.bcl] 3[1.2.cbn] — 4 3 3 1 — tmp+3 —
hp — pf/synth — str
perc: sd, timbales, xyl, marim, vib, chimes, bongos, 3bd, 3sus cym, 4tomtom,
6rototom, 3tamtam, 3glock, 3harmonica (C), 3slide whistle, gong (C), buttongong,
bass bow, fingercym
I. Laus amicorum   7'
II. Elegy for Marcel Dick 8'
III. Old Badman   8'

Merion

New England's Prospect <1974>   30'

narrator   triple chorus, opt children's chorus
3[1.2.3/pic] 2 3[1.2.bcl] 3[1.2.cbn] — 4 3 3 1 — asx — tmp+2 — hp
— pf/cel — str
perc: bd, cym, sd, timbales, tri, tambn, glock, xyl, vib, bongos, marac, claves, cast,
2sus cym, 2tomtom, 2tamtam, 2sl whistle, finger cym, glass wind chimes
Includes 16 Marine Band harmonicas [4 each in C, Db, D, Eb], played by
chorus members. Alto saxophone (mvt VI) must improvise and use
multiphonics.
I. A Prophecy for North America   _'
II. Mediations Divine & Morall   _'
III. Liberty for All   _'
IV. The Volunteer   _'
V. Ode for the American Dead in Asia   _'
VI. I Too Hear America Singing   _'
VII. Thomas Jefferson's Letter to Thomas Jefferson Smith _'
VIII. Illegitimate Things   _'

Presser

Ritual Observances <1991>   30'

3[1.2.3/pic] 3[1.2.Eh] 4[1.2.3/Ebcl.bcl] 3[1.2.cbn] — 4 3 3 1 —
tmp+3 — hp — pf/synth — str
perc: sd, glock, xyl, marim, vib, chimes, crot, marktree, bongos, 3bd, 3sus cym,
4tomtom, 2timbales, 3rototom, 3tamtam, 2buttongong (D4, G4), 3slide whistles,
gong[C4], metal windchimes, bass bow, 3harmonicas[C], 2harmonica[F#,G],
chromatic harmonica
Bns & cbn each play 4 telephone bells.
I. Lacrymosa   12'
II. Genesis' Thunder   5'
III. My Father's Ghost Is Climbing in the Rain   8'
IV. Light Breaks Where No Sun Shines   5'

Merion

The Seventh Trumpet <1969>   16'

3[1.2.3/pic] 3[1.2.Eh] 3[1.2.bcl] 3[1.2.cbn] — 4 3 3 1 — tmp+3 — hp
— pf/cel — str
perc: bd, cym, sd, timbales, tri, tambn, glock, xyl, vib, templeblks, bongos, ratch,
marac, lionroar, sus cym, tamtam, 2tomtom, 4woodblk, 3police whistles, 2jug,
3bottles, pf[played inside]

Merion

Symphony of Overtures <1964>   16'

3[1.2.3/pic] 2 3[1.2.bcl] 3[1.2.cbn] — 4 3 3 1 — tmp+3 — hp — pf — str

perc: bongos, chimes, claves, cym, marac, sd, sus cym, tambn, templeblks, td, vib, xyl, bd, finger cym, slide whistle, 4tomtoms, 2woodblks

The Blacks	5'
Endgame	4'
The Maids	3'
Rhinoceros	4'

Galaxy

Etler, Alvin   1913-1973

(b Battle Creek, IA, 19 Feb 1913; d Northampton, MA, 13 June 1973). American

Elegy for Small Orchestra <1959>   5'

1 1 2 2 — 2 0 0 0 — str

AMP

Ewazen, Eric   1954-

(b Cleveland, OH, 1954). American

Ballade   12'

solo clarinet
hp — str

SMC

F

Falla, Manuel de   1876-1946

(b Cadiz, 23 Nov 1876; d Alta Gracia, Argentina, 14 Nov 1946). Spanish

El amor brujo: Ballet Suite <1914–1915; rev 1915-16>   24'

mezzo-soprano solo
2[1.2/pic] 1[1/opt Eh] 2 1 — 2 2 0 0 — tmp+1 — pf — str
perc: chimes[A3,D4,E4]

1. Introduction & Scene/At the Gypsies/Song of Love's Sorrow	4'
2. The Ghost/Dance of Terror	2'
3. The Magic Circle (The Fisherman's Story)	2'
4. Midnight (The Magic Spell)/Ritual Fire Dance	4'
5. Scene/Song of the Will-o'-the-Wisp	3'
6. Pantomime/Dance of the Game of Love/Finale	9'

Chester

El amor brujo: Suite (arr. Ryden) <1914–1915>   12'

3[1.2.pic] 2 2 2 — 4 2 3 0 — tmp+1 — str
perc: bd, sus cym, tamtam, xyl (opt)
Arranged by William Ryden.

Allegro furioso, ma non troppo vivo	_'
Chez les gitanes	_'
Cancion del amor dolido	_'
El circulo magico	_'
A medio noche	_'
Danza ritual del fuego	_'

Kalmus

El amor brujo: Ritual Fire Dance <1914–1915>   5'

2[1.2/pic] 1 2 1 — 2 2 0 0 — tmp — pf — str

Chester

Concerto, Harpsichord [or Piano], D major <1923–1926>   15'

1 1 1 0 — vn, vc

1. Allegro	4'
2. Lento	6'
3. Vivace	5'

Eschig

Homenajes <1926–1941>   17'

3[1.2.pic] 3[1.2.Eh] 3[1.2.bcl] 3[1.2.cbn] — 4 3 3 1 — tmp+2 — hp — cel — str
perc: tambn, field dr, sd, tri, tamtam, bd, sus cym

A 1939 compilation, orchestration, and in some cases extension of earlier works for various media.

1. Fanfare (Sobre el nombre de Enrique Fernández Arbós)	1'
2. Á Claude Debussy (Elegía de la guitarra)	3'
3. Rappel de la Fanfare	1'
4. Á Paul Dukas (Spes vitae)	4'
5. Pedrelliana	8'

Ricordi

FALLA, MANUEL DE

Noches en los jardines de España (Nights in the Gardens of Spain) <1909–1915>   *23'*

solo piano
3[1.2.3/pic] 3[1.2.Eh] 2 2 — 4 2 3 1 — tmp+2 — hp — cel — str
perc: cym, tri
A 1926 chamber orchestra version of the accompaniment calls for:
2[1.2/pic] 3[1.2.Eh] 2 2 — 2 2 0 0 — tmp+2 — hp — cel — str
This work is published by Eschig, but listed by both Chester and Eschig. To rent orchestra materials of either version, consult the regional representatives for the following publishers:
Chester - for USA, Canada, Latin America, Japan, Australia
Falla (Manuel de Falla Ediciones) - for Spain
Eschig - for the rest of the world
En el Generalife (In the Gardens of the Generalife)   *10'*
Danza lejana (A Dance Is Heard in the Distance)   *5'*
En los jardines de la Sierra de Córdoba (In the Gardens of...)   *8'*

Chester	Eschig	Falla

Siete canciones populares españolas (Seven Popular Spanish Songs) <1914>   *12'*

medium voice
2 2[1.Eh] 3[1.2/bcl] 2 — 2 0 0 0 — tmp+1 — hp — str
Originally for voice & piano; orchestrated by Ernesto Halffter, 1938-1945. Also orchestrated by Luciano Berio (Universal) in 1978 for:
2 2[1.Eh] 3 3 — 2 2 2 1 — tmp+2 — str

Chester

El sombrero de tres picos (Three-Cornered Hat) <1916–1917; rev 1919>   *34'*

solo mezzo-soprano
3[1/pic2.2.3/pic1] 3[1.2.Eh] 2 2 — 4 3 3 1 — tmp+5 — hp — pf/cel — str
perc: bd, cym, sus cym, sd, tri, tamtam, glock, xyl, cast
Dancers (on stage) clap and shout briefly; for concert presentation, this may be done by the orchestra.
Originally a pantomime entitled *El corregidor y la molinera*.
Chester critical edition by Yvan Nommick, 1999.
Introduction   *1'*
PART I:
Afternoon   *5'*
Dance of the Miller's Wife (Fandango)   *3'*
The Grapes   *4'*
PART II:
Dance of the Neighbors (Seguidillas)   *3'*
The Miller's Dance   *6'*
The Corregidor's Dance   *6'*
The Final Dance   *6'*

Chester	Kalmus

El sombrero de tres picos (Three-Cornered Hat): Suite No.1 <1919>   *12'*

2[1.2/pic] 2[1.2/Eh] 2 2 — 2 2 0 0 — tmp+1 — hp — pf — str
perc: xyl, sus cym, glock
Kalmus ed. Clinton F. Nieweg & Julie McAlister, 2011; Chester critical ed. by Yvan Nommick, 2001.
Introduction - Afternoon   *4'*
Dance of the Miller's Wife (Fandango)   *3'*
The Corregidor   *1'*
The Grapes   *4'*

Chester	Kalmus	Luck's

El sombrero de tres picos (Three-Cornered Hat): Suite No.2 (Three Dances) <1916–1921>   *12'*

3[1.2/pic.pic] 3[1.2.Eh] 2 2 — 4 3 3 1 — tmp+5 — hp — pf/cel — str
perc: bd, cym, sus cym, sd, tri, tamtam, xyl, cast
Kalmus ed. Nancy M. Bradburd; Chester critical ed. by Yvan Nommick, 2001.
The Neighbors   *3'*
Miller's Dance (Farruca)   *3'*
Final Dance   *6'*

Chester	Kalmus

La vida breve: Interlude & Dance <c.1904–1913>   *8'*

3[1.2.pic] 3[1.2.Eh] 3[1.2.bcl] 2 — 4 2 3 1 — tmp+5 — 2hp — cel — str
perc: glock, tri, cast, cym, bd
If celesta player covers a few bars of glockenspiel, only 4 percussionists are required.

Eschig

La vida breve: Spanish Dance No.1 <1905>   *4'*

3[1.2.pic] 2 2 2 — 4 2 3 0 — tmp+4 — str

Eschig	Luck's

La vida breve: Spanish Dance No.1 (Chapelier) <1905>   *4'*

2[1.pic] 1 2 1 — 2 2 3 0 — tmp+2 — pf — str
Arr. S. Chapelier; condensed score only.

Eschig	Luck's

FARKAS, Ferenc   1905-2000

(b Nagykanizsa, 15 Dec 1905; d Budapest, 10 Oct 2000). Hungarian

Prelude & Fugue <1944–1947>   *9'*

3[1.2.pic] 3[1.2.3/Eh] 3[1.2.3/bcl] 3[1.2.cbn] — 4 2 3 0 — tmp+1 — str
perc: cym (one note)

Belwin	EMB

FASCH, Johann Friedrich   1688-1758

(b Buttelstadt, nr Weimar, 15 April 1688; d Zerbst, 5 Dec 1758). German

Concerto, Trumpet, D major <1743>   *6'*

0 2 0 0 — cnt — str
Ed. Winschermann.
1. Allegro   *2'*
2. Largo   *1'*
3. Allegro   *3'*

Sikorski

FAURÉ, Gabriel   1845-1924

(b Pamiers, Ariege, 12 May 1845; d Paris, 4 Nov 1924). French

Ballade, op.19 <1881; rev 1901>   *15'*

solo piano
2 2 2 2 — 2 0 0 0 — str

Hamelle	Kalmus	Luck's

Caligula, op.52 <1888>   *20'*

female chorus
3[1.2.pic] 2 2 2 — 4 3 3 0 — tmp+2 — 2hp — str
perc: crot, tri, sd, tambn
Incidental music to the play by Alexandre Dumas *père*.
I. Prologue: Fanfares, Marche, et Chœurs   *7'*
II. Chœur: Allegretto   *3'*
III. Air de danse: Allegro   *2'*
IV. Mélodrame et chœur: Allegro moderato   *4'*
V. Mélodrame et chœur: Andante molto moderato   *4'*

Leduc	mph

Cantique de Jean Racine, op.11 <1865>   *6'*

SATB chorus
2 2 2 2 — 2 0 0 0 — hp or pf — str
Originally for chorus & organ; revised 1866 for chorus, harmonium & str 5t; orchestrated by the composer, 1906.

Leduc

Dolly, op.56 <1894–1897>   18'

2[1.2/pic] 2 2 2 — 4 2 3 0 — tmp+3 — hp — str
perc: tri, tambn, cym, bd
Originally for pf 4-hands; orchestrated by Henri Rabaud, 1906.

I. Berceuse	3'
II. Mi-a-ou	2'
III. Le jardin de Dolly	3'
IV. Kitty-Valse	3'
V. Tendresse	4'
VI. Le pas espagnol	3'

Kalmus	Luck's

Elegy, op.24 <1896>   8'

solo violoncello
2 2 2 2 — 4 0 0 0 — str

C. Fischer	Kalmus	Luck's

Fantasy, op.79, Flute & Chamber Orchestra <1918>   6'

0 2 2[opt] 2 — 2 0 0 0 — str
Originally for flute & piano; orchestrated by Louis Aubert, 1957.

Hamelle

Fantasy, Piano & Orchestra, op.111 <1918>   18'

2 2 2 2 — 4 1 0 0 — tmp — hp — str

Durand	Kalmus	Luck's

Four Pieces <1893–1910>   13'

2[1.2/pic] 2 2 2 — 2 2 1 0 — tmp+1 — hp — str
perc: bd, cym, sus cym, sd, tri, tambn, glock, cel[or glock]
Originally for piano; orchestrated by Stanley Hollingsworth.

1. Nocturne, op.84, no.8	2'
2. Prelude, op.103, no.7	2'
3. Prelude, op.103, no.4	2'
4. Valse-caprice No.4, op.62	7'

Fleisher

Masques et bergamasques, op.112 <1919>   14'

2 2 2 2 — 2 2 0 0 — tmp — hp — str

1 Ouverture	4'
2 Menuet	3'
3 Gavotte	3'
4 Pastorale	4'

Durand	Kalmus	Luck's

Pavane, op.50 <1887>   7'

optional chorus
2 2 2 2 — 2 0 0 0 — str
Bärenreiter ed. Robin Tait.

Bärenreiter	Hamelle	Kalmus	Luck's

Pelléas et Mélisande, op.80: Suite <1898>   18'

2 2 2 2 — 4 2 0 0 — tmp — hp — str
Score lists "harpes" (plural), though there is only a single part.

1. Prélude	7'
2. Entr'acte: Fileuse (The Spinner)	2'
3. Sicilienne	4'
4. La mort de Mélisande (The Death of Melisande)	5'

Hamelle	Kalmus	Luck's

Pelléas et Mélisande: Melisande's Song <1900>   2

mezzo-soprano
2 2 2[ob d'am.Eh] 2 1 — 2 0 0 0 — 1perc [opt] — str
perc: bd [opt]
Orchestrated by Charles Koechlin.
    Oboe may substitute for the oboe d'amour; 2nd horn may be covered
by a 2nd bassoon or a bass clarinet.
    Text is in English (Fauré's incidental music was commissioned for an
English production of the Maeterlinck play).

Hamelle

Pénélope: Prelude <1913>   7'

2 3[1.2.Eh] 3[1.2.bcl] 2 — 4 2 3 1 — tmp — str

Heugel	Kalmus	Luck's

REQUIEM, op.48 <1887; rev 1900>

This work, assembled over a period of years, offers a convoluted history.
The earliest version of **1887-1888** included only five movements: 1.
Introit et Kyrie; 2. *Sanctus;* 3. *Pie Jesu;* 4. *Agnus Dei;* 5. *In paradisum.*
    The **1893** version added two more movements and various instruments;
it may be considered the definitive expression of the composer's wishes.
    In **1899-1900** a version using a larger, more standard orchestra was
prepared at the behest of the publisher Hamelle. While this version is the
most commonly performed, there is little or no evidence that Fauré had a
hand in preparing it.
    The choral parts of the 1893 version were not changed in the
subsequent orchestrations.

Requiem, op.48 (1888 & 1893 versions; ed. Legge)   23'
<1887; rev 1893>

chorus SATTBB   solo soprano (& baritone for 1893 version)
0 0 0 2[opt] — 4[3&4 opt] 2[opt] 3[opt] 0 — tmp[opt] — hp[opt] —
org — str[solo vn, va I&II, vc I&II, db]
Ed. Philip Legge. Either the 1888 (23') or 1893 (36') version may be
performed using this material.

Introit and Kyrie	7'
Offertorium [not in 1888 version]	8'
Sanctus	3'
Pie Jesu	3'
Agnus Dei	6'
Libera me [not in 1888 version]	5'
In paradisum	4'

IMSLP

Requiem, op.48 (1893 version; ed. Nectoux & DeLage)   36'
<1887–1893>

children's chor (SA) & male chor (TTBB)   solo treble & baritone
0 0 0 0 — 2 2 3 0 — tmp — hp — org — str[solo vn, va I&II, vc
I&II, db]
Reconstruction of the 1893 version by Jean-Michel Nectoux & Roger
DeLage (1994).

I. Introit and Kyrie	7'
II. Offertorium	8'
III. Sanctus	3'
IV. Pie Jesu	3'
V. Agnus Dei	6'
VI. Libera me	5'
VII. In paradisum	4'

Hamelle

Requiem, op.48 (1893 version; ed. Rutter) <1877; rev 1887-93>   36'

chorus SATTBB   solo soprano & baritone
0 0 0 2[opt] — 4[3-4 opt] 2[opt] 0 0 — tmp[opt] — hp — org —
str[solo vn; min 0.0.5.4.1]
Reconstruction of the 1893 version. Ed. John Rutter (1984).

I. Introit and Kyrie	7'
II. Offertorium	8'
III. Sanctus	3'
IV. Pie Jesu	3'
V. Agnus Dei	6'
VI. Libera me	5'
VII. In paradisum	4'

Hinshaw	Luck's

Requiem, op.48 (full orchestra version, 1900) <1877; rev 1887-93>   36'

chorus SATTBB   solo soprano & baritone
2 0 2 2 — 4 2 3 0 — tmp — hp — org — str
Score lists "harpes," though there is only a single part.
    The orchestration of this work may have been carried out by another hand, possibly that of Jean Roger-Ducasse.
    This is the version published by Dover (score only; no parts).
Bärenreiter ed. Christina Stahl & Michael Stegemann; Hamelle edition by Jean-Michel Nectoux; Peters ed. credited to Nectoux & Zimmermann.
    There are said to be many errors in the orchestral parts.

I. Introit and Kyrie	7'
II. Offertorium	8'
III. Sanctus	3'
IV. Pie Jesu	3'
V. Agnus Dei	6'
VI. Libera me	5'
VII. In paradisum	4'

Bärenreiter	Carus	Hamelle	Kalmus	Peters

Shylock, op.57: Suite <1889>   19'

solo tenor
2 2 2 2 — 4 2 0 0 — tmp+1 — hp — str
perc: tri

I. Chanson	3'
II. Entr'acte	3'
III. Madrigal	3'
IV. Epithalame	3'
V. Nocturne	3'
VI. Final	4'

Kalmus	Leduc	Luck's

Shylock, op.57: Nocturne <1890>   3'

str

Kalmus	Luck's

Felciano, Richard   1930-

(b Santa Rosa, CA, 7 Dec 1930). American

Galactic Rounds <1972>   10'

4[1.2.3.4/pic] 4 4 4 — 4 4 4 1 — tmp+4 — hp — pf — str

ECS

Orchestra <1980>   20'

4[1.2.3/pic.pic] 3[1.2.3/Eh] 3[1.2.3/bcl] 3[1.2.3/cbn] — 4 3 3 1 —
tmp+4 — hp — pf, pf/cel — str

ECS

Feldman, Morton   1926-1987

(b New York, 12 Jan 1926; d Buffalo, NY, 3 Sept 1987). American

Atlantis <1959>   8'

3[incl pic] 0 2[incl bcl] 2[incl cbn] — 1 1 1 1 — 2perc — hp — pf —
vc, db
Graph notation. Alternate version:
    1 0 1[incl bcl] 0 — 1 1 1 0 — 2perc — hp, pf — vc

Peters

Intersection No.1 for Orchestra <1951>   13'

Woodwind, brass, strings (the precise number of players being indeterminate). Graph notation.

Peters

Marginal Intersection <1951>   6'

"Large orchestra," unspecified except that it includes piano, xylophone, vibraphone, amplified guitar, 2 oscillators, recording of riveting, and 6 percussionists, together with the usual woodwinds, brass, and strings. Graph notation.

Peters

...Out of "Last Pieces" <1961>   9'

2 3[incl Eh] 3[incl bcl] 2 — 4 3[1.2.btp] 3 0 — elec gtr — 8perc —
hp — cel/pf — str[no vn or va]
Graph notation.

Peters

Structures for Orchestra <1962>   10'

3[incl afl] 3[incl Eh] 3[incl bcl] 2 — 4 3 3 1 — 2perc — hp — cel —
str
perc: chimes, crot
Conventional notation.

Peters

Violin and Orchestra <1979>   51'

solo violin
4[1.2.3.pic] 4[1.2.3.Eh] 4[1/Ebcl.2.3.bcl] 4[1.2.3.cbn] — 3 3 4 1 —
4perc — 2hp — 2pf — str
perc: marim, glock, claves, templeblks, sd, sus cym, woodblk, tmp, 4gong, 2tamtam

Universal

Ferneyhough, Brian   1943-

(b Coventry, 16 Jan 1943). English

Carceri d'invenzione III <1986>   11'

2[1/pic.2/pic/afl] 2[1.2/Eh] 3[1.2/Ebcl.bcl] 1[bn/cbn] — 2 2 2 1 —
3perc — [no str]
perc: szl cym, whip, slgh-bells, td, bd, 2wood drum, 10tomtom, 2timbales, 3congas, 4gong, 5bongos, 5woodblk, 3tambn, 3sus cym, 3tamtam
Microtones and unusual meter-signatures are called for.

Peters

Plötzlichkeit (Suddenness) <2006>   23'

3 female voices
3[1.2/pic.pic] 3[1.2.Eh] 3[1.2.bcl] 3[1.2.cbn] — 6 4[1.2.3.btp] 5[2sop tbn; 3ten tbn] 1[cimbasso] — 3perc — 2hp — pf — str

perc: bd, tri, tambn, glock, xyl, marim, vib, chimes, templeblks, whip, ratch, guiro, claves, cast, vibrslp, thunder, 3sus cym, 2sd, 2td, 3tomtom, 3rototom, 3brake dr, 2gong, 2crot, 3slgh-bells, 5woodblk, 3bongos, 2marac[2 sets], 4buttongong, 2logdrum, sandblks, 3anvils, rute, 2tindrum

Tuning: a quarter-tone low: hp2
one-sixth tone low: hn2, hn5, tp2
one-third tone low: hn3, hn6, tp3
(A simple method for tuning of the brass is described in the score.)

> Peters

Fine, Irving   1914-1962

(b Boston, 3 Dec 1914; d Boston, 23 Aug 1962). American

Blue Towers <1959>   3'

3[1.2.pic] 2 2 2 — 4 3 3 1 — opt saxes: 2asx, tsx — tmp+3 — opt pf — str

perc: cym, sus cym, sd, tri, tambn, glock, xyl

> Boosey

Diversions for Orchestra <1959–1960>   8'

2 2[1.2/opt Eh] 2 2 — 4 3 3 1 — opt saxes: 2asx, tsx, bsx — tmp+2 — pf or cel — str

perc: tambn, sd, tri, glock, sus cym, cym

Little Toccata	1'
Flamingo Polka	2'
Koko's Lullaby	3'
The Red Queen's Gavotte	2'

> Broude Bros.

Music for Orchestra <1947>   16'

3[1.2.pic] 2 2 2 — 4 2 3 1 — tmp+2 — str

perc: td, bd, whip, tri, woodblk, cym, bongos, tambn, xyl, vib, glock, templeblks, sd

Orchestrated by Joel Spiegelman (1974) from the composer's *Music for Piano* (1947).

Prelude	1'
Waltz-Gavotte	3'
Variations	9'
Interlude-Finale	3'

> Boosey

Notturno <1950–1951>   13'

hp — str[min 6.4.3.3.1]

I. Lento	6'
II. Animato	2'
III. Adagio	5'

> Boosey

Serious Song; a Lament for String Orchestra <1955>   10'

str

> Broude Bros.

Symphony (1962) <1962>   23'

3[1.2.pic] 3[1.2.Eh] 3[1.2.bcl] 3[1.2.cbn] — 4 3 3 1 — tmp+4 — hp — pf/cel — str

perc: sd, bd, tambn, cym, sus cym, woodblk, tri, tamtam, xyl, glock, crot, chimes, timpano piccolo

I. Intrada	7'
II. Capriccio	6'
III. Ode	10'

> Belwin

Toccata concertante <1947>   10

3[1.2.pic] 3[1.2.Eh] 3[1.2.bcl] 3[1.2.cbn] — 4 2 3 1 — tmp+3 — pf — str

perc: bd, cym, sd

> Boosey

Fine, Marshall   1956-

(b Cleveland, OH, 14 Dec 1956). American

Missouriana, op.44 <1985>   5

2[1.2/pic] 2 2 2 — 2 2 0 0 — tmp/tri — pf — str

> C. Fischer

Fine, Vivian   1913-2000

(b Chicago, 28 Sept 1913; d Bennington, VT, 20 March 2000). American

Drama for Orchestra <1982>

4[1.2.3/pic.4/pic] 4[1.2.3.4/Eh] 4[1.2.3.4/bcl] 4[1.2.3.4/cbn] — 6 4 3 1 — tmp+4 — hp — pf/cel — str

perc: glock, vib, xyl, whip, tri, templeblks, woodblk, sus cym, gong

After paintings by Edvard Munch.

1. Mid-Summer Night	_'
2. The Embrace	_'
3. Jealousy	_'
4. The Scream	_'
5. Two Figures by the Shore	_'

Finko, David   1936-

(b Leningrad [now St Petersburg], 15 May 1936). Russian composer, active in the USA

Concerto, Harp <1979>   19

1[incl pic] 1[incl Eh] 1[incl bcl] 0 — 2 0 0 0 — 2perc — str

> Dako   Fleisher

Concerto, Viola <1971>   16

1 0 1[incl bcl] 0 — 2 0 0 0 — tmp+2 — str

> Dako   Fleisher

Concerto, Viola & Double Bass <1977>   22

3[incl pic] 0 2 1[cbn] — 2 1 1 0 — 2perc — vn I & II; vc I & II

> Dako

Concerto, Viola D'Amore & Harpsichord (or Guitar) <1977>   21'

2 1[incl Eh] 1[incl bcl] 0 — 2perc — 5vn, 2vc, db

Guitar part written as an *ossia* (i.e., not identical to hpsd part).

> Dako   Fleisher

Concerto, Violin <1992>   24'

2[incl pic] 0 2 0 — 2 1 1 0 — 2perc — str

> Dako   Fleisher

The Holocaust; An Uprising in the Ghetto (Der Holocaust; der Aufstand im Ghetto) <1985>   10'

2[incl pic] 1 2[incl Ebcl] 1 — 2 2 2 0 — tmp+2 — str

> Dako   Fleisher

Russia (Russland) <1974; rev 1989>   15'

4[incl 2pic] 2 2 2 — 4 2 3 1 — tmp+3 — str

> Dako   Fleisher

Symphony No.1 <1969>   *23'*

3[incl pic] 2[incl Eh] 3[incl Ebcl] 2 — 4 2 3 1 — tmp+3 — str

    Elkin   Fleisher

Symphony No.2 <1972>   *25'*

3[incl pic] 2 2 2 — 4 2 3 1 — tmp+2 — str

    Elkin   Fleisher

The Wailing Wall (Die Klagemauer) <1983>   *12'*

2 2 3[incl bcl] 1 — 2 2 2 0 — 3perc — str

    Dako   Fleisher

Finney, Ross Lee   1906-1997

(b Wells, MN, 23 Dec 1906; d Carmel, CA, 4 Feb 1997). American

Hymn, Fuguing Tune & Holiday <1943>   *10'*

3[1.2.pic] 3[1.2.Eh] 3[1.2.bcl] 3[1.2.cbn] — 4 3 3 1 — tmp+3 — 1 or 2hp — cel — str

    C. Fischer

Landscapes Remembered <1971>   *14'*

1[1/pic/afl] 0 1 0 — 0 1 1 0 — 1perc — hp — pf — str[5t or max 4.4.4.2.2]

    Peters

Finzi, Gerald   1901-1956

(b London, 14 July 1901; d Oxford, 27 Sept 1956). English

Concerto, Clarinet, op.31 <1948–1949>   *30'*

str

1. Allegro vigoroso	8'
2. Adagio, ma senza rigore	13'
3. Rondo: Allegro giocoso	9'

    Boosey

Dies natalis, op.8 <1925–1939>   *25'*

solo soprano (or tenor)

str

Intrada (strings only)	5'
Rhapsody (recitativo stromentato)	7'
The Rapture (Danza)	4'
Wonder (Arioso)	4'
The Salutation (Aria)	5'

    Boosey

The Fall of the Leaf, (Elegy) op.20 <1929; rev 1939-41>   *9'*

3[1.2.pic] 3[1.2.Eh] 2 3[1.2.cbn] — 4 2 3 1 — tmp+2 — hp — str
perc: gong, cym, bd
Orchestration completed posthumously by Howard Ferguson.

    Boosey

In terra pax; Christmas Scene (original version) <1954>   *15'*

small chorus   solo soprano & baritone

1perc — hp[or pf] — str
perc: cym

    Boosey

In terra pax; Christmas Scene (large chorus version) <1954; rev 1956>   *15'*

chorus   solo soprano & baritone

2 2 2 2 — 4 2 3 0 — tmp+1 — 2hp[1part] — cel — str
perc: cym, tri

    Boosey

In terra pax; Christmas Scene (large chorus; reduced orchestra) <1954; rev 1956>   *15'*

chorus   solo soprano & baritone

2 2 2 2 — 0 2 2 0 — tmp+1 — hp — cel — str
perc: cym, tri

    Boosey

Introit, op.6 <1925; rev 1942>   *8'*

solo violin

1 2[1.Eh] 2 1 — 2 0 0 0 — str[max 10.8.6.6.4]
Originally the 2nd mvt of a violin concerto, of which the outer mvts were later withdrawn.

    Boosey   Kalmus   Luck's

New Year Music, op.7 (Nocturne) <1926; rev 1945-6>   *9'*

2[1.2/pic] 3[1.opt 2.Eh] 3[1.2.opt bcl] 3[1.2.opt cbn] — 4 3 3 1 — tmp+1 — hp — str
perc: cym

    Boosey

Prelude, op.25 <1920's>   *4'*

str

    Boosey

Romance, op.11 <1928>   *6'*

str

    Boosey

A Severn Rhapsody, op.3 <1923>   *6'*

1 1[1/Eh] 1[1/bcl or bn] 0 — 1 0 0 0 — str

    Boosey   Kalmus   Luck's

Fišer, Luboš   1935-1999

(b Prague, 30 Sept 1935; d Prague, 22 June 1999). Czech

Fifteen Prints after Dürer's Apocalypse (Patnáct listů podle Dürerovy Apokalypsy) <1965>   *9'*

3 2 3 2 — 2 2 2 0 — tmp+1 — hpsd — str
perc: claves, field dr

    Harth

Flagello, Nicolas   1928-1994

(b New York, 15 March 1928; d New Rochelle, NY, 16 March 1994). American

Aria sinfonica, op.9 <1951>   *5'*

4[1.2.3.pic] 3[1.2.Eh] 3[1.2.bcl] 3[1.2.cbn] — 4 3 3 1 — tmp+1 — hp — str
perc: cym, tamtam

    Schirmer

Concerto, Piano, No.2, op.19 <1956>   *26'*

2 2 2 2 — 4 2 3 0 — tmp+2 — str

    Schirmer

A Goldoni Overture, op.54 <1966>   *5'*

2[1.pic] 2 2 — 4 2 2 1 — tmp+3 — hp — cel — str
perc: bd, cym, sus cym, sd, tri, glock, xyl, chimes
Composed as an overture to Vittorio Giannini's opera *The Servant of Two Masters*.

    Schirmer

Lautrec; Suite for Orchestra, op.47 <1965>   17'

3[1.2.3/pic] 2[1.2/Eh] 2 2 — 4 2 3 1 — tmp+2 — hp — cel — str
perc: bd, cym, sus cym, sd, tri, tambn, tamtam, glock, chimes, belltree, ratch

1. Le plaisir à Paris [aka Paris—La belle époque]	4'
2. Les histoires naturelles	3'
3. Elles	5'
4. Moulin Rouge	5'

Schirmer

Serenata per orchestra, op.58 <1968>   18'

1 1 1 1 — 2 0 0 0 — hp — str

1. Psalmus	5'
2. Passe-pied	3'
3. Siciliana	6'
4. Giga	4'

Schirmer

Symphony No.1, op.57 <1964–1968>   37'

3[1.2.pic] 3[1.2.Eh] 3[1.2.bcl] 3[1.2.cbn] — 4 3 3 1 — tmp+3 — hp
— pf/cel — str

1. Allegro molto	9'
2. Andante lento	10'
3. Allegretto brusco	6'
4. Ciaccona: Maestoso andante	12'

Schirmer

Theme, Variations & Fugue, op.20 <1956>   29'

3[1.2.pic] 3[1.2.Eh] 3[1.2.bcl] 3[1.2.cbn] — 4 3 3 1 — tmp+5 — hp
— pf/cel, opt org — str
perc: bd, cym, sus cym, sd, tri, tamtam, xyl, tambn, kybd glock

Tema: Andante comodo	2'
Variazione I: Andante con moto	2'
Variazione II: Andantino misurato	2'
Variazione III: Allegro con brio	1'
Variazione IV: Andante calmo	4'
Variazione V: Andantino	2'
Variazione VI: Allegro marziale	1'
Variazione VII: Allegro comodo	2'
Variazione VIII: Andante con moto	3'
Variazione IX: Allegro marcato	3'
Fuga: Allegro giusto	7'

Schirmer

Flotow, Friedrich von   1812-1883

(b Toitendorf [Teutendorf] estate, nr Neu-Sanitz, Mecklenburg-Schwerin, 27 April 1812; d Darmstadt, 24 Jan 1883). German

Alessandro Stradella: Overture <1844>   7'

2[1.2/pic] 2 2 2 — 4 2 3 0 — tmp+1 — str
perc: bd

Luck's

Martha: Overture <1847>   9'

2[1.pic] 2 2 2 — 4 2 3 1 — tmp+3 — str
perc: sd, bd, tri

Breitkopf   Kalmus   Luck's

Floyd, Carlisle   1926-

(b Latta, SC, 11 June 1926). American

In Celebration <1971>   10'

2 2[1.2/Eh] 2 2 — 4 2 2 1 — tmp+2 — hp — cel — str

Belwin

Foerster, Josef Bohuslav   1859-1951

(*b* Prague, 30 Dec 1859; *d* Vestec, nr Stará Boleslav, Bohemia, 29 May 1951). Czech

From Shakespeare, op.76 (Ze Shakespeara) <1908–1909>   26'

3[1.2.3/pic] 3[1.2.Eh] 3[1.2.bcl] 3[1.2.cbn] — 4 3 3 1 — tmp+3 — h
— str
perc: tri, tambn, cym, tamtam

Introduction	1'
I. Perdita	7'
II. Viola	5'
III. Lady Macbeth	6'
IV. Katherine, Petruchio and Eros	7'

Supraphon

Symphony No.4, op.54, C minor (Easter Eve; Veliká noc) <1904–1905>   50'

3[1.2.pic] 3[1.2.Eh] 3[1.2.bcl] 3[1.2.cbn] — 6 3 3 1 — tmp+2 — org
— str
perc: sus cym, tri
Cues in the woodwinds are to be played only in the absence of an organ.

I. Molto sostenuto—Allegro	16'
II. Allegro—Allegro moderato	9'
III. Andante sostenuto	9'
IV. Lento lububre—Animato—Allegro moderato	16'

mph   Universal

Foote, Arthur   1853-1937

(b Salem, MA, 5 March 1853; d Boston, 8 April 1937). American

Air and Gavotte   7'

2 0 0 0 — str

Kalmus   Luck's

Four Character Pieces after the *Rubáiyát* of Omar Khayyám <1912>   20'

2 2 2 2 — 4 2 3 1 — tmp+2 — hp — str
perc: bd, cym, tambn

I. Andante comodo (Iram indeed is gone)	'
II. Allegro deciso; Più moderato (They say the lion and the lizard)	'
III. Comodo (A book of verses)	'
IV. Andantino ben marcato; Molto allegro (Yon rising moon)	'

Kalmus   Luck's

Francesca da Rimini; Symphonic Prologue, op.24 <1890>   18'

2 2 2 2 — 4 2 3 1 — tmp — str
Breitkopf parts newly engraved in 2000; they match the score published by Dover, except for rehearsal figures. Kalmus edition is believed to be a reprint of Jurgenson, and has a number of errors.

Breitkopf   Kalmus   Luck's

Irish Folk Song   4'

str

Kalmus   Luck's

A Night Piece <1918; rev 1922>   9'

solo flute
str
Originally for flute and str 4t.

Luck's

Serenade, op.25 <1894–1895>   17'

str
Originally published by Arthur P. Schmidt, Leipzig, 1892.

1. Praeludium: Allegro comodo	2'
2. Air: Adagio, ma non troppo	5'
3. Intermezzo: Allegretto grazioso	3'
4. Romanze: Andante con moto	4'
5. Gavotte: Allegro deciso	3'

Luck's

Suite, op.63, E major <1907; rev 1908>   15'

str

I. Praeludium	4'
II. Pizzicato	7'
III. Fuge	4'

Kalmus	Luck's

Fortner, Wolfgang   **1907 - 1987**

(b Leipzig, 12 Oct 1907; d Heidelberg, 5 Sept 1987). German

The Creation (Die Schöpfung) <1954>   25'

solo voice (medium)
2 2[1.Eh] 2[1.bcl] 1[cbn] — 0 2 2 0 — tmp+5 — hp — hpsd — str
perc: sd, field dr, bd, sus cym, gong, vib

Schott

Foss, Lukas   **1922 - 2009**

(b Berlin, 15 Aug 1922; d Manhattan, 1 Feb 2009). American

American Fanfare <1990>   4'

2 2 2 2 — 4 3 3 1 — tmp+3 — 1 or 2hp — pf, opt elec org — str
perc: vib, chimes, cym, sus cym, tomtom, sd, bd, musical saw
Woodwinds may be doubled.

C. Fischer

Baroque Variations <1967>   25'

3[1.2/pic.3/pic/opt rec] 2[1.2/Eh] 3[1.2.3/ssx or Ebcl] 1 — 3 3 1 1 —
elec gtr — tmp+3 — elec pf/cel, elec org/hpsd — str
perc: bd, chimes, claves, cym, gong, templeblks, tri, vib, whip, xyl, anvil, bottle,
church bell, elephant bells, hammer, wood windchimes
The optional recorder, which occurs in the 2nd mvt, could if preferred be
covered by one of the other instruments that are tacet in that mvt: clarinet,
bassoon, or a brass player.

1. On a Handel Larghetto	8'
2. On a Scarlatti Sonata	7'
3. On a Bach Prelude (Phorion)	10'

C. Fischer

Cello Concert <1966>   23'

solo violoncello
0 0 0 0 — 2 1 2 0 — 4perc — hp — pf, org (or harm or accordion) —
str
perc: crot, glock, cowbell, chimes, woodblk, whip, vib, fingercym, anvil

C. Fischer	Schott

Concerto, Percussion <1974>   30'

1[incl pic] 1 1[1/ssx] 1 — 1 2 2 1 — elec gtr — 3perc — pf, elec org
— str[min 3.2.2.2.1]
May be extended to 45' duration.

Salabert

Elegy for Anne Frank <1989>   7'

solo piano   optional narrator
0 0 2[opt] 2[opt] — 1[and/or tp] 1[and/or hn] 1[and/or tuba] 1[and/or
tbn] — 1perc — str
perc: td, field dr, sd
Later revised to become the 2nd mvt of his *Symphony No.3*.
Brass clarification: tp or hn (or both); tbn or tuba (or both).

Pembroke

Exeunt <1982>   18'

2[incl pic] 2 2 2 — 4 2 3 1 — elec gtr — tmp+3 — hp — pf —
str[min 8.6.6.6.4]
perc: vib, sd, chimes, gong, bd, xyl, anvil, 2sus cym, bass bow

Pembroke

Folksong for Orchestra <1975>   15'

3[incl 2pic] 3 3 — 5 3 3 1 — tmp+3 — hp — pf — str

Salabert

Night Music for John Lennon <1979–1980>   15'

solos: 2tp, hn, tbn, tuba (or 2nd tbn)
1 1 1 1 — 1 1 1 0 — elec gtr — 1perc — pf — str[min 5.4.4.3.1]
perc: gong, sus cym, sd, td, vib, musical saw, anvil

Pembroke

Ode for Orchestra <1945; rev 1958>   10'

3[1.2.pic] 3[1.2.Eh] 3[1.2.bcl] 3[1.2.cbn] — 4 3 3 1 — tmp+3 — 1 or
2hp — pf — str
perc: chimes, xyl, cym, cowbell, sus cym, sd, td, tri, bd, gong

C. Fischer

Quintets for Orchestra <1979>   15'

2 3[1.2.Eh] 3[1.2.bcl] 2 — 3 3 3 1 — tmp — elec org — str
perc: chimes[played by tmp]
Originally for brass quintet.

Pembroke

Renaissance Concerto <1985>   21'

solo flute
1[incl pic] 1 1 1 — 1 2 1 0 — tmp+2 — hp — opt hpsd — str

Intrada	5'
Baroque Interlude (after Rameau)	4'
Recitative (after Monteverdi)	5'
Jouissance	7'

C. Fischer

Salomon Rossi Suite <1975>   10'

1[incl pic] 2[incl Eh] 0 2 — 0 2 2 0 — tmp — hp — str

Salabert

Song of Anguish <1945>   19'

solo baritone (or bass)
3[1.2.pic] 2 3[1.2.bcl] 3[1.2.cbn] — 4 3 3 1 — tmp+3 — hp — pf/cel
— str
perc: vib, bd, sus cym, tri, tamtam, sd, tomtom, chimes, xyl

C. Fischer

Song of Songs <1946>   33'

soprano (or mezzo-soprano) solo
3[1.2.pic] 3[1.2.Eh] 3[1.2.bcl] 3[1.2.cbn] — 4[3-4 opt] 3 2 0 —
tmp+2 — hp — str
perc: cym, glock, sd, tomtom, tri

I. Awake; O North Wind	6'
II. Come; My Beloved	7'
III. By Night on My Bed	13'
IV. Set me as a Seal	7'

C. Fischer

Symphony No.1 <1944>   32'
3[1.2.pic] 3[1.2.opt Eh] 3[1.2.bcl] 3[1.2.cbn] — 4 3 3 0 — tmp+3 — hp — pf — str
perc: cym, sus cym, sd, bd, tri, xyl, glock[opt], tamtam[opt]
I. Andantino; Allegretto _'
II. Adagio _'
III. Scherzo: Vivace _'
IV. Andantino; Allegro _'

    Schirmer

Symphony No.3 (Symphony of Sorrows) <1991>   28'
3[1.2.pic] 3[1.2.Eh] 3[1.2.bcl] 3[1.2.cbn] — 4 3 3 1 — tmp+3 — hp — org/pf/cel — str
1. Fugue: Of Strife and Struggle _'
2. Elegy for Anne Frank _'
3. Wasteland _'
4. Prayer _'

    Pembroke

Time Cycle <1959–1960>   21'
solo soprano
2[1.2/pic] 0 2[1.2/bcl] 0 — 2 2 1 0 — tmp+2 — hp — cel/pf — str
perc: vib, xyl, glock, chimes, crot, templeblks, gong, tambn, sd, bd, tri, 2woodblks, 2sus cym
Chamber version by the composer:
    soprano — cl — 1perc — pf/cel — vc
We're Late (W. H. Auden)   4'
When the Bells Justle (A. E. Housman)   5'
Sechzehnter Januar (Franz Kafka)   6'
O Mensch, gib Acht (Friedrich Nietzsche)   3'

    C. Fischer

Frackenpohl, Arthur   1924-
(b Irvington, NJ, 23 April 1924). American

Short Overture   4'
1 1 2 2 — 2 2 2 1 — tmp+3 — str

    Boosey   Luck's

Françaix, Jean   1912-1997
(b Le Mans, 23 May 1912; d Paris, 25 Sept 1997). French

Concertino, Piano <1932>   9'
2 2 2 2 — 2 2 2 0 — str
1. Presto leggiero   2'
2. Lent   3'
3. Allegretto   2'
4. Rondeau: Allegretto vivo 2'

    Schott

Sei preludi (Six Preludes) <1963>   15'
str[3.3.2.2.1]
1. Apertura _'
2. Elegia _'
3. Scherzo _'
4. Intermezzo alla tedesca _'
5. Sogno _'
6. Finale _'

    Schott

Serenade for Small Orchestra <1934>   10'
1 1 1 1 — 1 1 1 0 — str

    Schott

La ville mystérieuse <1973>   15'
3[1.2.pic] 3[1.2.Eh] 3[1.2.bcl] 3[1.2.cbn] — 4 3 3 1 — tmp+5 — 2hp — cel — str
perc: tri, crot, tamtam, sd, field dr, bd, xyl, glock, cym, 2sus cym, 3tomtom, police whistle, slide whistle
Fantaisie pour grand orchestre d'après une nouvelle de Jules Verne.

    Schott

Francesconi, Luca   1956-
(b Milan, 17 March 1956). Italian

Da capo <1985–1986>   14'
1[fl/pic] 0 1 1 — 1perc — hp — pf — 1vn, 1va, 1vc
perc: vib, marim, glock

    Ricordi

Inquieta limina; Un omaggio a Berio <1996>   8'
1[fl/pic] 1[ob/Eh] 1 1 — 1 1 1 0 — accordion — 1perc — pf — str[1.1.1.1.1]
perc: vib, marim, glock

    Ricordi

Islands; Concerto per pianoforte e 12 strumente <1992>   15'
solo piano
1[fl/pic] 1 1[cl/bcl] 1 — 1 0 0 0 — 2perc — str[1.1.1.1.1]
perc: xyl, tri, hi-hat, congas, marim, glock, bd/ped, 5sus cym, 4tomtom, 2pr bongos, 2hi-hat, 2gong, 2woodblk

    Ricordi

Plot in Fiction <1986>   10'
solo oboe doubling English horn
1[fl/pic] 0 1[cl/bcl] 1 — 1 0 0 0 — 1perc — pf — str[1.1.1.1.1]
perc: vib, marim, glock

    Ricordi

Franck, César   1822-1890
(b Liège, 10 Dec 1822; d Paris, 8 Nov 1890). French composer of Belgian birth

Le chasseur maudit (The Accursed Huntsman) <1882>   14'
3[1.2.pic] 2 2 4 — 4 4[2tp, 2crt] 3 1 — tmp+3 — str
perc: chimes, cym, bd, tri
Newly engraved & corrected Kalmus edition (2010) by Clinton F. Nieweg & Nancy M. Bradburd.

    Kalmus   Luck's   Presser   Ricordi

Les djinns (The Spirits) <1884>   13'
solo piano
2 2 2 4 — 4 2 3 1 — tmp — str

    Enoch   Kalmus   Luck's

Eight Short Pieces (Huit pièces brèves): Nos.1-4 <1863>   10'
1 1 1 1 — 1 1 0 0 — tmp — str
Originally for organ; orchestrated by Henri Busser.
1. Trés lent _'
2. Andantino poco allegretto _'
3. Poco lento _'
4. Molto moderato _'

    Enoch   Kalmus   Luck's

Eight Short Pieces (Huit pièces brèves): Nos.5-8   9'

1[1/pic] 1[1/Eh] 1 1 — 1 1 0 0 — tmp — str
Originally for organ; orchestrated by Henri Busser.
> 5. *Quasi lento*   _'
> 6. *Andante*   _'
> 7. *Andantino*   _'
> 8. *Allegretto (quasi allegro)*   _'

Enoch	Kalmus	Luck's

Les Éolides   <1875–1876>   11'

2 2 2 2 — 4 2 0 0 — tmp+1 — hp — str
perc: sus cym

Enoch	Kalmus	Luck's

Psalm 150   <1883>   5'

chorus
2 2 2 2 — 4 2 3 0 — tmp+1 — hp — org — str
perc: cym

Breitkopf	Kalmus	Luck's	Peters	Ricordi

PSYCHÉ   8'

1. Le sommeil de Psyché (Psyché Asleep)   <1887–1888>

2 3[1.2.Eh] 3[1.2.bcl] 4 — 4 4[2tp, 2crt] 3 1 — tmp — str

Kalmus	Luck's

2. Psyché enlevée par les Zéphirs (Psyché Carried Away by the Zephyrs)   <1887–1888>   3'

2 3[1.2.Eh] 3[1.2.bcl] 4 — 4 4[2tp, 2crt] 0 0 — tmp — 2hp — str

Kalmus	Luck's

3. Les jardins d'Eros (The Gardens of Eros) <1887–1888>   4'

3[1.2.pic] 3[1.2.Eh] 3[1.2.bcl] 4 — 4 4[2tp, 2crt] 3 1 — tmp — str

Kalmus	Luck's

4. Psyché et Eros   <1887–1888>   6'

2 3[1.2.Eh] 3[1.2.bcl] 4 — 4 4[2tp, 2crt] 3 1 — tmp — str

Kalmus	Luck's

Rédemption   <1871–1872; rev 1874>   73'

chorus   solo soprano
2 2 2 2 — 4 2 3 1[oph] — tmp+1 — str
perc: cym
> PART I
> *Introduction*   4'
> *1. Choeur terrestre*   7'
> *2. Récit et Choeur des anges*   5'
> *3. Choeur; Récit et Air de L'archange* 10'
> *4. Choeur général*   4'
> PART II:
> *5. Morceau symphonique*   14'
> *6. Choeur d'hommes*   6'
> *7. Choeur des anges*   8'
> *8. Air de l'archange*   8'
> *9. Choeur général*   7'

Heugel	Kalmus

Rédemption: Morceau symphonique (Symphonic Interlude)   <1874>   14'

2 2 2 2 — 4 2 3 1[oph] — tmp — str
No.5, from the 1874 final version of *Rédemption*.

Heugel	Kalmus	Luck's	Ricordi

Symphonic Variations   <1885>   15'

solo piano
2 2 2 2 — 4 2 0 0 — tmp — str

Breitkopf	Enoch	Kalmus	Luck's

Symphony, D minor   <1886–1888>   37'

2 3[1.2.Eh] 3[1.2.bcl] 2 — 4 4[2tp, 2crt] 3 1 — tmp — hp — str
Breitkopf ed. by Peter Jost; Kalmus ed. by Clinton F. Nieweg & Jennifer A. Johnson (2012, updated 2014).
> *I. Lento - Allegro non troppo*   17'
> *II. Allegretto*   10'
> *III. Allegro non troppo*   10'

Breitkopf	Hamelle	Kalmus	Luck's

Frank, Gabriela Lena   1972-

(b Berkeley, CA, Sep 1972). American composer of mixed descent (Peruvian, Chinese & Lithuanian).

Compadrazgo; Double Concerto for Cello, Piano & Chamber Orchestra   <2007>   26'

2[1/pic2.2/pic1] 2 2 2 — 2perc — hp — str[no db]
perc: bd, sus cym, woodblk, templeblks, cowbell, whip, thunder, 2tri, tmp

Schirmer

Concertino Cusqueño   <2012>   10'

2[1.2/pic] 2 2[1.2.bcl] 2 — 2 2 0 0 — tmp+3 — hp — cel — str
perc: sd, 2sus cym, 2tri, 2marim
The four string principals are used as a solo concertino. Other prominent solos for piccolo, bass clarinet, & timpani.

Schirmer

Elegía Andina (Andean Elegy)   <2000>   11'

2[1.2/pic] 2 2 2 — 2 2 0 0 — tmp+1 — str[8.8.6.4.2]
perc: glock, whip, sus cym, templeblks, woodblk, 2tri

Schirmer

Escaramuza   <2010>   8'

tmp+4 — hp — pf — str
perc: bd, cym, sd, rototom, tambn, whip, claves, cast, 2sus cym, 4tri, buttongong, 3marim

Schirmer

Havana Jila (Hava Nagila)   <2003>   5'

solo violin
2perc — str[no db]
perc: sus cym, tomtom, tri, marim, templeblks

Schirmer

Illapa   <2004>   14'

solo flute
2[1.2/pic] 2 2 — 4 2 2 0 — tmp+4 — hp — pf — str
perc: bd, tamtam, claves, congas, xyl, chimes, cym, marim, sus cym, thunder, whip, sd, rainstick
This work also exists in a purely symphonic version as the middle movement of *Three Latin American Dances*.
> *I. Introducción: Soliloquio Serrano (Introduction: Mountain Soliloquy)*   _'
> *II. Harawi*   _'

Schirmer

Leyendas: An Andean Walkabout   <2001; rev 2008>   21'

str
Originally for string 4t; arr. for string orch by the composer.
> *I. Toyos*   2'
> *II. Tarqueada*   3'
> *III. Himno de Zampoñas*   3'
> *IV. Chasqui*   3'
> *V. Canto de Velorio*   7'
> *VI. Coqueteos*   3'

Schirmer

La Llorona; Tone Poem for Viola & Orchestra (The Crying Woman) <2007>   20'

2[1.2/pic] 2[1.2/Eh] 2[1.2/bcl] 2 — 2 2 2 0 — tmp+3 — hp — pf/cel — str

perc: cym, sus cym, tri, tamtam, xyl, woodblk, whip, 2marim
The mvts are played without pause.
   I. Slumber   _'
   II. Awakening   _'
   III. Flight   _'
   IV. Danza de las Chullpas   _'
   V. Canto de la Luna   _'
   VI. Flight   _'
   VII. Coda   _'

   Schirmer

Manchay tiempo (Time of Fear) <2005>   13'

tmp+4 — hp — pf — str

perc: cym, sus cym, tri, tambn, tamtam, xyl, templeblks, cowbell, whip, thunder, 2bd, 2marim, 2woodblk

   Schirmer

Peregrinos (Pilgrims) <2008>   22'

2[1.2/pic] 2 2 2 — 2 2 0 0 — tmp+3 — hp — pf/cel — str

perc: bd, cym, sus cym, tri, tamtam, chimes, 2marim, buttongong
   Testimonio I: Arbol de Sueños (Dream Tree)
   Testimonio II: Hero Brothers
   Testimonio III: Fireflies
   Testimonia IV: Devotional for Sarita Colonia
   Testimonial V: Arbol de Sueños (Dream Tree)

   Schirmer

Raíces (Roots; Concerto Suite for Orchestra) <2012>   15'

2[1.2/pic] 2[1.2/Eh] 2 2 — 2 2 0 0 — tmp+2 — hp — str
perc: bd, sus cym, sd, tri, templeblks, whip, 2marim, 2woodblk
   I. Allegro Nazca   _'
   II. Sombras (Shadows)   _'
   III. Muñequitos de Madera (Little Wooden Dolls)   _'
   IV. Danza Selvática (Jungle Dance)   _'
   V. Adios al Altiplano (Goodbye to the Highland)   _'
   VI. Allegro Costeño   _'

   Schirmer

Requiem for a Magical America (El dia de los muertos) <2006; rev 2012>   23'

2[1/pic.2/pic] 2[1.2/Eh] 2[1.2/bcl] 2[1.2/cbn] — 4 2 3 0 — tmp+3 — pf — str
perc: bd, cym, rototom, tamtam, xyl, chimes, templeblks, bongos, cast, sd, 3sus cym, 2tri, 2tambn, 2marim, 2woodblk, 2cowbell, shekere, 2pail
Originally for band; arranged for orchestra by the composer, 2012.
   Musicians not otherwise occupied hum in the brief last mvt.
   I. Preludio: Canto Religioso (Prelude: Religious Song)   _'
   II. Sacando a los Espíritus Malos (Driving Away the Evil Spirits)   _'
   III. Danza del Pueblo (Village Dance)   _'
   IV. Calaveras (Skeletons/Satiric Verses)   _'
   V. El Cementerio (The Cemetery)   _'
   VI. La Llegada de los Muertos (The Arrival of the Dead)   _'
   VII. Almas Perdidas (Lost Souls)   _'
   VIII. Danza sel Guerrero Precolombino (Dance of the … Warrior)   _'
   IX. Epílogo: Canto Religioso (Epilogue: Religious Song)   _'

   Schirmer

Three Latin American Dances <2003>   20'

3[1.2.3/pic] 3[1.2.Eh] 3[1.2.bcl] 3 — 4 3 3 0 — tmp+4 — hp — pf — str
perc: bd, cym, sd, tambn, tamtam, xyl, chimes, woodblk, templeblks, whip, bongos, congas, thunder, cast, claves, shekere, 2tri, 2sus cym, 2marim, rainstick
The middle movement also exists in a version for solo flute and orchestra: *Illapa,* q.v.
   I. Introduction: Jungle Jaunt   8'
   II. Highland Harawi   9'
   III. The Mestizo Waltz   3'

   Schirmer

Two American Portraits <2008>   15'

3[1.2.pic] 2 2 2 — 2 2 2 0 — tmp+3 — hp — str
perc: cym, sus cym, tambn, xyl, tri, cast, templeblks, marim, 2woodblk
First mvt is for 2 solo clarinets, unaccompanied except for a brief timpani roll; movements are played without pause.
   I. Frank's Alborada   _'
   II. Old Modesto   _'

   Schirmer

Frazelle, Kenneth   1955-

(b Jacksonville, NC, 1955). American

From the Air <2000>   10'

3[1.2.pic] 2 2 2 — 4 3 3 1 — tmp+3 — hp — str
perc: cym, sus cym, sd, field dr, tri, glock, xyl, claves, crot[G#4]

   Notevole

Shivaree   11'

3[1.2.pic] 2 2 2 — 4 3 3 1 — tmp+3 — hp — cel — str

   Notevole

The Swans at Pungo Lake <2006>   6'

3[1.2.pic] 3[1.2.Eh] 3[1.2.bcl] 3[1.2.cbn] — 4 3 3 1 — tmp+3 — hp — str
perc: bd, sus cym, sd, tri, marim, templeblks, marac, 2woodblk, 2flexible tmp covers

   Notevole

Frederick II ("The Great")   1712-1786

(b Berlin, 24 Jan 1712; d Potsdam, 17 Aug 1786). German

Concerto, Flute, No.3, C major   14'

cnt — str
Ed. Gustav Lenzewski.
   1. Allegro   5'
   2. Grave   5'
   3. Allegro assai   4'

   Luck's   Vieweg

Concerto, Flute, No.4, D major   15'

cnt — str
Ed. Gustav Lenzewski.

   Luck's   Vieweg

Symphony No.1, G major   8'

cnt — str
Ed. Gustav Lenzewski.

   Luck's   Vieweg

Symphony No.2, G major   8'

cnt — str
Ed. Gustav Lenzewski.

   Luck's   Vieweg

Frescobaldi, Girolamo Alessandro 1583-1643

(b Ferrara, bap. mid-Sept 1583; d Rome, 1 March 1643). Italian

Toccata 6'

3[1.2.pic] 2 3[1.2.bcl] 2 — 4 3 3 1 — tmp+1 — str

Almost certainly not by Frescobaldi. The work is believed to be a forgery by the cellist Gaspar Cassadó (1897-1966), who passed it off as a "transcription" of a keyboard work by Frescobaldi. It was then (presumably innocently) orchestrated by conductor Hans Kindler in 1942.

| Belwin | Luck's | Warner |

Fry, William Henry 1813-1864

(b Philadelphia, 19 Aug 1813; d Santa Cruz, Virgin Islands, 21 Dec 1864). American

The Dying Soldier 8'

2[1.pic] 2 2 2 — 4 4[2tp, 2crt] 3 1 — tsx — 3tmp+1 — str
perc: bd, cym, sd

The 3 timpanists briefly double on other percussion.

| Fleisher |

Evangeline: Overture <1860> 9'

1 1 2 1 — 2 2[crt1.crt2] 1 0 — tmp/perc — str
perc: sd, tri (1 player covers tmp & perc)

| Fleisher |

Niagara Symphony <by 1854> 14'

2[1.pic] 2 2 3[1.2.cbn] — 4 4[2tp, 2crt] 3 2[see note] — 5tmp — str

2 real parts for the multiple brass bass instruments, designated as "tubas, ophicleides, bombardones," and in a very high register.

| Fleisher |

Macbeth: Overture <1862> 11'

2 2 2 2 — 4 2 3 1 — tmp+2 — str

| Fleisher |

Santa Claus (Christmas Symphony) <1853> 25'

3[incl pic] 2 2 2 — 4 6[4tp, 2crt] 3 1 — opt: ssx & flageolet — tmp+3 — str

Optional: unspecified toy instruments, in addition to the flageolet and sopr sax. Could readily be performed with 2tp rather than 6. Fleisher Collection has an elaborate synopsis of the programmatic events in the score, which could be adapted as a narration.

| Fleisher |

Fuchs, Robert 1847-1927

(b Frauental, nr Deutschlandsberg, Styria, 15 Feb 1847; d Vienna, 19 Feb 1927). Austrian

Serenade, No.3, op.21, E minor <1878> 22'

str

1. Romanze: Andante sostenuto	4'
2. Menuetto	6'
3. Allegretto grazioso	7'
4. Finale alla Zingarese: Allegro con fuoco	5'

| Kistner&Siegel |

Fučik, Julius 1872-1916

(b Prague, 18 July 1872; d Berlin, 25 Sept 1916). Czech

Der alte Brummbär, op.210 (The Old Grumbling Bear; The Old Sore-Head) 5'

solo bassoon (or saxophone)
2[1.2/pic] 2 2 0 — 3 2 3 0 — 2perc — str

| Apollo | Luck's |

Fuleihan, Anis 1900-1970

(b Kyrenia, Cyprus, 2 April 1900; d Stanford, CA, 11 Oct 1970). American

Fanfare for the Medical Corps <1943> 2'

0 0 0 0 — 4 3 3 1 — [no str]

| Boosey |

Fux, Johann Joseph 1660-1741

(b Hirtenfeld, nr St Marein, Styria, 1660; d Vienna, 13 Feb 1741). Austrian

Overture, C major <1717> 12'

cnt — str
Ed. Paul Angerer.

| Doblinger |

G

Gabrieli, Giovanni   1554/7 - 1612

(b ?Venice, c1554-7; d Venice, Aug 1612). Italian

Canzon XVI (arr. Jeff Tyzik)   3'

2 2 2 2 — 4 3 3 1 — tmp — str
Brass, listed above, are deployed antiphonally as follows:
    Choir 1, stage left: 2tp, hn, tbn
    Choir 2, stage right: tp, hn, 2tbn
    Remainder (2hn, tuba) in the main orchestra, center stage.

Schirmer

Canzona   6'

double string orchestra
Ed. Franco Michele Napolitano.

Kalmus	Luck's	Zanibon

Canzona noni toni, a 12, for Three Brass Choirs <1597>   6'

0 0 0 0 — 0 6 6 3[opt] — [no str]
3hn may substitute for 3 of the trombones.
Ed. Robert Austin Boudreau.

Peters

Sonata pian' e forte <1597>   7'

0 0 0 0 — 1 2 4 1 — baritone horn — [no str]
Possible with brass 4 1 3 0, or a variety of other combinations. One of the
parts originally intended for viola.

King

Sonata pian' e forte (ed. Fritz Stein) <1597>   7'

0 0 0 0 — 2 2 4 1[opt] — [no str]

Peters

Gade, Niels   1817 - 1890

(b Copenhagen, 22 Feb 1817; d Copenhagen, 21 Dec 1890). Danish

Concerto, Violin, op.56, D minor <1880>   25'

2 2 2 2 — 2 2 0 0 — tmp — str

Breitkopf	Kalmus

Echoes of Ossian, op.1 (Efterklange af Ossian; Nachklänge von Ossian) <1840>   14'

2[1.2/pic] 2 2 — 4 2 2 1[or cbn] — tmp — hp — str

Breitkopf	Kalmus	Luck's

Hamlet, op.37 <1861>   12'

3[1.2.3/pic] 2 2 — 4 2 3 1 — tmp — str

Breitkopf

In the Highlands, op.7 (I højlandene; Scottish Overture) <1844>   7'

2[1.2/pic] 2 2 2 — 4 2 2 1[or oph] — tmp — str

Kalmus	Luck's

Michelangelo, op.39 <1861>   9'

3[1.2.3/pic] 2 2 2 — 4 2 3 1 — tmp — str

Kalmus	Kistner & Siegel

Novelette [No.1] op.53, F major <1874>

str

Breitkopf	Kalmus	Luck's

Novelette No.2, op.58, E major <1883; rev 1886>   20'

str

Breitkopf	Kalmus	Luck's

Symphony No.1, op.5, C minor (Paa Sjølunds fagre sletter; On Sjoland's Fair Plains) <1842>   32'

3[1.2.pic] 2 2 — 4 2 3 1[or cbn] — tmp — str
Moderato con moto; Allegro energico   9'
Scherzo   7'
Andantino grazioso   9'
Finale   7'

Kalmus

Symphony No.2, op.10, E major <1843>   29'

2 2 2 2 — 4 2 3 0 — tmp — str
Andantino quasi allegretto   8'
Andante con moto   8'
Scherzo   4'
Allegretto   9'

Breitkopf	Kalmus

Symphony No.3, op.15, A minor <1847>   26'

2 2 2 2 — 4 2 1[btbn] 0 — tmp — str
Presto   7'
Andante sostenuto   6'
Allegretto, assai moderato   6'
Finale: Allegro molto e con fuoco   7'

Breitkopf	Kalmus

Symphony No.4, op.20, B-flat major <1849–1850>   21'

2 2 2 2 — 4 2 0 0 — tmp — str
Andantino; Allegro vivace e grazioso   7'
Andante con moto   6'
Scherzo: Allegro, ma non troppo e tranzuillamente   3'
Finale: Allegro molto vivace   5'

Kalmus	Kistner&Siegel	Luck's

Symphony No.5, op.25, D minor <1852>   28'

3[1.2.pic] 2 2 — 4 2 3 0 — tmp — pf — str
N.B.: The piano part, while not rising to the level of a concerto, is very
elaborate and prominent.
1. Allegro con fuoco   9'
2. Andante sostenuto   7'
3. Scherzo: Allegro molto vivace   4'
4. Finale: Andante con moto; Allegro vivace   8'

Breitkopf	Kalmus

Symphony No.6, op.32, G minor <1857>   25'

3 2 2 2 — 4 2 1 0 — tmp — str
1. Andantino; Allegro molto vivace   6'
2. Andante sostenuto   7'
3. Allegro moderato e energico   4'
4. Finale: Andante quasi allegretto; Allegro vivace e animato   8'

Kalmus	Kistner & Siegel

Symphony No.7, op.45, F major <1864>   *33'*

2 2 2 2 — 4 2 3 0 — tmp — str
  1. Allegro risoluto   10'
  2. Andante   10'
  3. Scherzo: Allegro vivace   9'
  4. Finale: Allegro vivace   4'

| Breitkopf | Kalmus |

Symphony No.8, op.47, B minor <1869–1871>   *27'*

3[1.2.pic] 2 2 2 — 4 2 3 0 — tmp — str
  1. Allegro molto e con fuoco   9'
  2. Allegro moderato   5'
  3. Andantino   7'
  4. Finale: Allegro non troppo e marcato   6'

| Kalmus |

Zion, op.49 <1874>   *29'*

solo baritone   chorus
2 2 2 2 — 2 2 3 1 — tmp — str
  Einleitung   _'
  Wanderung aus Aegypten   _'
  Gefangenschaft in Babylon   _'
  Heimkehr   _'

| Kistner&Siegel | Luck's |

Gál, Hans   1890-1987

(b Brunn, nr Vienna, 5 Aug 1890; d Edinburgh, 3 Oct 1987). Austrian

Musik für Streichorchester, op.73 <1937>   *21'*

str
  1. Toccata   _'
  2. Tema con variazioni   _'
  3. Rondo giocoso   _'

| Breitkopf |

Symphony No.4, op.105 (Sinfonia concertante) <1973>   *36'*

soloists: flute, clarinet, violin, violoncello
0 2 0 2 — 2 0 0 0 — tmp — str
  I. Improvvisazione   11'
  II. Scherzo leggiero   8'
  III. Duetto   9'
  IV. Buffoneria   8'

| Simrock |

Galbraith, Nancy   1951-

(b Pittsburgh, PA, 17 Jan 1951). American

De profundis ad lucem <2002>   *20'*

3[1.2.pic] 2 2 2 — 4 3 3 1 — tmp+3 — hp — pf — str
perc: bd, sus cym, timbales, tamtam, glock, vib, woodblk, templeblks, bongos, claves, 4tomtoms

| Subito |

Fantasy for Orchestra <1993>   *10'*

3[1.2.3/pic] 2 2 2 — 4 3 3 1 — tmp+4 — pf — str
perc: bd, sus cym, timbales, rototom[played by tmp], tri, glock, xyl, marim, vib, templeblks, bongos, claves, congas, 4tomtoms, 2cowbells, logdrum[2pitches], tuned gongs[B2,F#3,A3,E4]

| Subito |

A Festive Violet Pulse <1997>   *3'*

2[1.2/pic] 2 2 2 — 4 2 3 0 — tmp+2 — str
perc: bd, sus cym, timbales, tri, tamtam, xyl, marim, vib, crot, templeblks, bongos, marac, sandblks, 2tomtoms

| Subito |

Missa mysteriorum (Mass of the Mysteries) <1999>   *43'*

chorus SSAATTBB   solos SSATB
3[1.2.pic] 2 4[1.2.3.bcl] 2 — 4 3 3 1 — 3perc — hp — pf, org[or synth] — 1vc, 1db
perc: bd, sd, td, tri, tambn, glock, xyl, marim, vib, chimes, crot, templeblks, bongos, marac, claves, cast, tmp, 2woodblk, 4sus cym, 4tomtom, logdrums [or templeblks], sandblks
  Kyrie   10'
  Gloria   5'
  Credo   13'
  Sanctus   7'
  Agnus Dei   8'

| Subito |

Requiem <2004>   *58'*

chorus SSAATTBB
3[1.2.pic] 2 2 2 — 2 2 2 1 — tmp+3 — str
perc: sus cym, bd, hi-hat, sd, timbales, tri, tamtam, glock, xyl, vib, chimes, crot, templeblks, cowbell, ratch, marac, 2woodblk, 5tuned gongs, 3gongs [indefinite pitch], 4tomtom, whistle, 3cowbells, Japanese singing bowls [or crot or marim]
  I. Requiem aeternam   _'
  II. Dies irae   _'
  1. Dies irae   _'
  2. Tuba mirum   _'
  3. Quid sum miser   _'
  4. Rex tremendae   _'
  5. Ingemisco   _'
  6. Confutatis   _'
  7. Lacrimosa   _'
  III. Offertorium   _'
  IV. Sanctus   _'
  V. Agnus Dei   _'
  VI. Lux aeterna   _'
  VII. Libera me   _'

| Subito |

Tormenta del sur <1994>   *9'*

3[1.2.3/pic] 2 3 3[1.2.cbn] — 4 2 3 1 — tmp+3 — hp — pf — str
perc: bd, sus cym, tamtam, glock, xyl, marim, vib, windchimes [glass or metal], whip, bongos, sandblk, 2tomtom, 2woodblk

| Subito |

Galindo, Blas   1910-1993

(b San Gabriel [now Venustiano Carranza], 3 Feb 1910; d Mexico City, 19 April 1993). Mexican composer of Huichol Indian descent

Sones de mariachi <1953>   *8'*

3[1.2.pic] 3[1.2.Eh] 4[1.2.Ebcl.bcl] 3 — 4 3 3 1 — tmp+3 — hp — str
perc: cym, sd, td, marac, xyl, bd, guiro

| EMM |

Galuppi, Baldassare   1706-1785

(b Burano, nr Venice, 18 Oct 1706; d Venice, 3 Jan 1785). Italian

Concerto, Flute, D major   *13'*

cnt — str
Ed. Felix Schroeder.

| Breitkopf |

Concerto, 2 Flutes, E minor   *21'*

cnt — str
Ed. Felix Schroeder.

| Kalmus | Luck's | Peters |

Concerto, Harpsichord, F major   14'
str
Ed. Edoardo Farina.

Luck's	Zanibon

Concerto a quattro, No.1, G minor   9'
cnt — str
Ed. Horst Heussner.

Doblinger

Concerto a quattro, No.2, G major   4'
cnt — str
Ed. Horst Heussner.

Doblinger

Domine ad adjuvandum me <1753>   3'
SA soli   chorus SATB
0 2 0 0 — 2 0 0 0 — org — str
Ed. Thomas J. Tropp. Can be performed with only strings & continuo.

Tropp

Laudate pueri   27'
SA(T) soli   chorus SATB
0 2 0 0 — 2 2 0 0 — org — str
Ed. Thomas J. Tropp. Wind parts could be omitted. Solo tenor part is only 7 bars; could be performed by a chorus member.
   I. Coro: Laudate pueri Dominum   7'
   II. Due (Canto e Alto): A solis ortu   5'
   III. Coro: Quis sicut Dominus   3'
   IV. Coro: Suscitans a terra inopem   2'
   V. Canto: Qui habitare   4'
   VI. Alto: Gloria Patri   3'
   VII. Coro: Sicut erat in principio   3'

Tropp

Sinfonia, D major   7'
0 0 0 0 — 2 0 0 0 — str
Ed. Ettore Bonelli.

Luck's	Zanibon

Sinfonia, F major (Della serenata)   7'
0 0 0 0 — 2 0 0 0 — str
Ed. Ettore Bonelli.

Luck's	Zanibon

Gang, Chen   1935-
see: Chen Gang

Garcia, José Mauricio Nunés   1767-1830
see: Nunés-Garcia, José Mauricio, 1767-1830

Garcia, José Pablo Moncayo   1912-1958
see: Moncayo (Garcia), José Pablo

Gedike, Alexander   1877-1957
see: Goedicke, Alexander, 1877-1957

Gellis, Herbert Sidney   1948-
(b New York City, 10 Apr 1948). American

Allegro sauvage <1997–1998>   5'
solo timpani
3[1.2.pic] 2 2 1 — 2 2 2 1 — 3perc — str
perc: bd, sd, cym, tambn

Harmonic

Corduroy; Concertino for Baritone Saxophone &   11'
Orchestra <2002–2003>
3[1.2.pic] 2 2 2 — 2 2 2 1 — tmp+2 — str
perc: set, xyl, glock, tri, cym, woodblk, tambn, gong
   1. Medium Wale   3'
   2. Fine Wale   4'
   3. Wide Wale   4'

Harmonic

Duplex <2000; rev 2002>   10'
2[1.pic] 2[1.2/opt Eh] 3[1.2.bcl] 2 — 2 2 2 1 — tmp+3 — str
perc: chimes, xyl, sd, cym, gong, woodblk, tambn, sus cym, tri

Harmonic

Hymn for Strings <2000–2002>   7'
str

Harmonic

Short Symphony on Eastern Modes <2005>   19'
3[1.2.pic] 2[1.2/Eh(opt)] 2 2 — 4 3 3 1 — tmp+2 — str
perc: sd, sus cym, tambn, bd, claves, tri
Mvts played without pause.
   I. Allegro moderato   4'
   II. Grave   5'
   III. Scherzo   3'
   IV. Tempo giusto   7'

Harmonic

Geminiani, Francesco   1687-1762
(b Lucca, bap. 5 Dec 1687; d Dublin, 17 Sept 1762). Italian

Concerto grosso, C major, after Corelli, op.5, no.3   11'
<1727>
solo concertino: 2vn, vc
cnt — str
Ed. Hugo Ruf.

Luck's	Nagel

Concerto grosso no.5, G minor, after Corelli op.5, no.5   9'
solos: 2vn, va, vc
cnt — str
Ed. Michelangelo Abbado.
   I. Adagio   3'
   II. Vivace   2'
   III. Adagio   2'
   IV. Allegro   2'

Ricordi

Concerto grosso no.12, D minor, after Corelli, op.5, no.12   12'
(*La folia* [also spelled *La follia*]) <1727>

solo concertino: 2vn, va, vc
cnt — str[no va]
Ricordi ed. Fasano; Schott ed. Walter Kolneder.

Ricordi	Schott

Concerto grosso, op.2, no.2, C minor <1732>   9'

str

Galaxy	Luck's

Concerto grosso, op.2, no.3, D minor   7'

cnt — str
Ed. Walter Upmeyer.
Presto   3'
Adagio   2'
Allegro   2'

Luck's	Vieweg

Concerto grosso, op.3, no.1, D major   14'

solo concertino: 2vn, va, vc
cnt — str[no va]

Kalmus	Luck's	Peters

Concerto grosso, op.3, no.2, G minor   16'

solo concertino: 2vn, va, vc
cnt — str[no va]

Kalmus	Luck's	Peters	Schirmer

Concerto grosso, op.3, no.3, E minor   9'

solo concertino: 2vn, va, vc
cnt — str[no va]
1. Grave   1'
2. Allegro moderato 2'
3. Andante   2'
4. Allegro   4'

Kalmus	Luck's	Peters

Concerto grosso, op.3, no.4, D minor   13'

solo concertino: 2vn, va, vc
cnt — str[no va]

Kalmus	Luck's	Peters

Concerto grosso, op.3, no.5, B-flat major   9'

solo concertino: 2vn, va, vc
cnt — str[no va]

Kalmus	Luck's	Peters

Concerto grosso, op.3, no.6, E minor   10'

solo concertino: 2vn, va, vc
cnt — str[no va]

Kalmus	Luck's	Peters

Concerto grosso, op.7, no.1, D major   9'

solo concertino: 2vn, va, vc
cnt — str

Bärenreiter	Luck's	Nagel

Gerhard, Roberto   1896-1970

(b Valls, 25 Sept 1896; d Cambridge, 5 Jan 1970). Catalan composer, active in England; a naturalized British citizen

Albada, interludi i dansa <1936>   10'

2[1.2/pic] 2[1.2/Eh] 2 2 — 2 2 2 1 — tmp+2 — str[10.10.8.6.6]
perc: cym, bd, tambn

Boosey

Alegrías: Suite <1942>   13'

2[1.pic] 2[1.Eh] 2[1.bcl] 1 — 2 1 1 0 — tmp+1 — hp — pf — str
perc: cym, sd, tambn, tamtam, cast, tomtom, xyl

Boosey

Cancionero de Pedrell <1941>   19'

high voice
1[1/pic] 1[1.Eh] 2 0 — 2perc — hp — pf — str[min 2.2.1.1.1]
perc: tambn, sd, cym, tmp
Arrangements of Spanish folksongs collected by Felipe Pedrell. In Catalan and English. Originally for high voice & piano; arr. for high voice & 13 instruments by the composer.
1. Sa ximbomba   2'
2. La mal maridada 2'
3. Laieta   1'
4. Soledad   3'
5. Muera yo…   2'
6. Farruquiño   3'
7. Alalá   3'
8. Corrandes   3'

Boosey

Concerto for Orchestra <1964–1965>   21'

3[1/pic.2/pic.3/pic] 3[1.2.3/Eh] 3[1.2.3/bcl] 3[1.2.cbn] — 4 4 3 1 — 2tmp+3[or 4] — hp — str[16.14.12.10.8]
perc: glock, timbales, templeblks, vib, xyl, cast, sd, marim, crot, 3woodblk, 7sus cym, 3Chinese tomtoms, 2tamtam, 3bd, 2pr claves

Oxford

Concerto, Piano <1951>   22'

str
I. Tiento   6'
II. Diferencias 10'
III. Folia   6'

Boosey

Don Quixote: Dances <1958>   16'

2[1.2/pic] 2 2[1.2/bcl] 2 — 2 2 2 0 — tmp+2 — pf — str
perc: xyl, sus cym, cym, bd, sd, tambn, cast, tamtam, tri, 3Chinese tomtoms
Introduction   _'
Dance of the Muleteers   _'
The Golden Age   _'
In the Cave of Montesinos _'
Epilogue   _'

Boosey

Epithalamion <1965–1966; rev 1968>   17'

4[1.2.3/pic.4/pic] 4[1.2.3.4/Eh] 4[1.2.3.bcl] 4[1.2.3.cbn] — 4 4 3 1 — 2tmp+6 — hp — pf — str[16.14.12.10.8]

Oxford

Metamorphoses <1967–1968>   33'

4[1.2.pic1.pic2] 4[1.2.3.Eh] 4[1.2.3.4/bcl] 4[1.2.3.cbn] — 4 4 4 1 —
accordion — tmp+7 — hp — pf — str
perc: marim, xyl, vib, glock, crot, tambn, claves, cast, bd, sd, tamtam, templeblks,
timbales, 3sus cym, 3Chinese tomtoms, 7woodblks, wooden scraper w/ jingles
A recomposition of the composer's Symphony No.2 (1957-59). Last
movement not completed; performing version of this movement by Alan
Boustead. Score includes a facsimile of the composer's manuscript of that
final section.

Belwin

Pedrelliana (en memoria) <1941>   12'

3[1.2.pic] 2[1.2/Eh] 2 2 — 4 2 2 1 — tmp+3 — hp — str
perc: glock, xyl, sus cym, cym, sd, bd, tamtam, tambn, cast, 2Chinese tomtom
3rd movement of the composer's symphony *Homenaje de Pedrell*.

Boosey

Symphony No.1 <1952–1953>   39'

2[1.2/pic] 2[1.Eh] 2 2 — 4 2 2 1 — tmp+2 — hp — pf — str
perc: xyl, sd, tambn, bd, tamtam, 3Chinese tomtoms, 2sus cym, 2tri
  I. Allegro animato   *11'*
  II. Adagio   *11'*
  III. Allegro spiritoso   *17'*

Boosey

Symphony No.4 (New York) <1967; rev 1968>   26'

4[1.2.3/pic.4/pic] 4 4 4[1.2.3.cbn] — 6 4 4 1 — tmp+4 — 2hp — cel
— str
perc: glock, crot, timbales, tri, xyl, claves, chimes, marim, tamtam, bd, templeblks,
8sus cym, 6Chinese blks, 6tambn, 2sd, 4Chinese toms
In one mvt.

Oxford

German, Edward   1862-1936

(b Whitchurch, Shropshire, 17 Feb 1862; d London, 11 Nov 1936). English

Henry VIII: Three Dances <1892>   8'

2 2 2 2 — 2 2 3 0 — tmp+2 — str
  Morris Dance   2'
  Shepherd's Dance   4'
  Torch Dance   2'

Kalmus	Luck's	Novello

Nell Gwyn: Three Dances <1900>   8'

2[1.2/pic] 1 2 2 — 2 2[2crts] 3 0 — tmp+3 — hp — str
perc: bd, cym, tambn, tri, sd
Incidental music to *Nell Gwyn*, originally titled *English Nell*.
  I. Country Dance   3'
  II. Pastoral Dance   3'
  III. Merrymakers' Dance 2'

Chappell	Kalmus	Luck's

Gernsheim, Friedrich   1839-1916

(b Worms, 17 July 1839; d Berlin, 11 Sept 1916). German

Symphony No.4, op.62, B-flat major   31'

2 3[1.2.Eh] 3[1.2.bcl] 2 — 4 2 3 0 — tmp — str
  I. Allegro   *11'*
  II. Andante sostenuto   *8'*
  III. Vivace scherzando e con grazia *4'*
  IV. Allegro con spirito e giocoso   *8'*

Simrock

Gershwin, George   1898-1937

(b Brooklyn, NY, 26 Sept 1898; d Hollywood, CA, 11 July 1937). American

> *Under the editorship of Mark Clague, a "George and Ira Gershwin
> Critical Edition," has been initiated in 2013 by the University of
> Michigan in collaboration with the estates of the two brothers. It will be
> published by European American Music and Schott International.*
> The Gershwin Initiative, *at* www.music.umich.edu/ami/gershwin.

An American in Paris <1928>   16'

3[1.2.3/pic] 3[1.2.Eh] 3[1.2.bcl] 2 — 4 3 3 1 — asx, tsx, bsx —
tmp+4 — cel — str
perc: sd, woodblk, cym, bd, tri, 2tomtoms, 4autohorns, xyl, glock (xyl/glock
player can also cover cel)
Rev. F. Campbell-Watson.
  A facsimile of the composer's autograph score, which differs from the
Campbell-Watson edition, is available from Warner; one such deviation
is said to be that the sax parts are more prominent from [63] to the end:
the players all switch to soprano saxes in harmony at [63], and all three
switch to alto sax before [74].

Warner	Luck's	Schott

Catfish Row: Symphonic Suite from "Porgy and Bess"   23'
<1935–1936>

2[1.2/pic] 2[1.2/Eh] 4[1.2.3.4/bcl] 1 — 3 3 2 1 — banjo — tmp+1 —
pf — str
Gershwin's own suite from "Porgy and Bess," 1935-36.
  Another arrangement available from Warner, ed. Steven D. Bowen,
same instrumentation.
  1. Catfish Row   6'
  2. Porgy Sings   5'
  3. Fugue   2'
  4. Hurricane   3'
  5. Good Mornin', Sistuh 7'

Warner	Schott

Concerto, Piano, F major <1925>   31'

3[1.2.pic] 3[1.2.Eh] 3[1.2.bcl] 2 — 4 3 3 1 — tmp+3 — str
perc: cym, glock, xyl, sd, woodblk, whip, bd, tri, gong
Ed. F. Campbell-Watson.
  A separate jazz band orchestration of this work was prepared for Paul
Whiteman by Ferde Grofe, with the composer's permission. See the
following entry.
  I. Allegro   *13'*
  II. Adagio - Andante con moto *11'*
  III. Allegro agitato   *7'*

Warner	Luck's	Schott

Concerto, Piano, F major (arr. for jazz band) <1925> 31'

solo piano
2[1/pic2.2/pic1] 2[1.2/Eh/bass oboe] 4[1.2.3/bcl.Ebcl] 3 — 0 4 4 1 —
6sx[ssx1.ssx2/asx4.asx1/ssx3.asx2/ssx4.tsx1/asx3.tsx2/bsx], tenor banjo
— tmp+3 — pf/cel — vns (divisi) [no va, no vc] db
perc: xyl, vib, glock, bd/cym, sus cym, sd, tri, gong, whip, set
Arranged 1928 for the Paul Whiteman Orchestra by Ferde Grofé. Ed. Ella
M. Fredrickson for symphony orchestra, maintaining the Grofé
instrumentation, but rendering the woodwind and saxophone doublings
more practical for symphony orchestras.
  I. Allegro   *13'*
  II. Adagio - Andante con moto *11'*
  III. Allegro agitato   *7'*

Gershwin Music

Cuban Overture <1932>   10'

3[1.2.3/pic] 3[1.2.Eh] 3[1.2.bcl] 3[1.2.cbn] — 4 3 3 1 — tmp+6 — str
perc: xyl, glock, sd, bongos, guiro, marac, cym, woodblk, bd, claves
Original title, *Rhumba*.

Warner	Luck's	Schott

Girl Crazy: Overture (arr. McBride) <1930>   7'

3[1.2.pic] 3[1.2.Eh] 3[1.2.bcl] 2 — 4 3 3 1 — tmp+3 — hp — pf — str

Arr. by Robert McBride. There are also arrangements available from Warner by Don Rose (similar size orchestra) and Robert Russell Bennett (1 1 0 0 — 0 3 2 0 — 2asx, tsx — perc — pf — str).

Warner	Schott

"I Got Rhythm" Variations (arr. Schoenfeld) <1930>   9'

solo piano
2[1.2/pic] 2[1.2/Eh] 4[1.2.3.bcl] 2 — 4 3 3 1 — opt 2asx, tsx, bsx — tmp+4 — str

perc: glock, xyl, sd, ratch, sus cym, tamtam, woodblk, bd, muffled drum

Arr. William C. Schoenfeld.

Percussion may be covered by 3 players if a drum set is used.

Warner	Luck's	Schott

Let 'Em Eat Cake: Overture <1924>   8'

3[1.2.3/pic] 3[1.2.Eh] 3[1.2.bcl] 3[1.2.cbn] — 4 3 3 1 — tmp+4 — hp — pf — str

Arr. Don Rose.

Warner	Schott

Lullaby <1924>   8'

str
Originally for str 4t; double bass part added, but otherwise unchanged.

Warner	Schott

Of Thee I Sing: Overture <1931>   5'

3 3[1.2.Eh] 3[1.2.bcl] 3[1.2.cbn] — 4 3 3 1 — tmp+4 — hp — pf — str

Arr. Don Rose. Other arrangements available from Warner: Robert Russell Bennett, Robert McBride (both similar-size orchestra); as well as the original: 1 1 0 0 — 1 3 1 0 — 2asx/2cl, tsx — perc — pf — str

Luck's	Warner	Schott

Porgy and Bess: Symphonic Picture <1935>   24'

3[1.2.pic] 3[1.2.Eh] 3[1.2.bcl] 2 — 4 3 3 1 — 2asx, tsx — banjo — tmp+3 — 2hp — str

perc: glock, xyl, woodblk, cym, tri, sd, sus cym, bd

Symphonic version by Robert Russell Bennett. Bennett has also arranged a shorter and simpler *Selections from Porgy and Bess* (11'), which is available on rental from Luck's.

Saxes & banjo are cued in other instruments.

Warner	Schott

Promenade (Walking the Dog; The Real McCoy) <1937>   3'

2[1.2/pic] 2 3[1.2.bcl] 2 — 4 3 2 1 — tmp+2 — hp — opt cel — str

perc: sus cym, tri, glock, xyl, vib, woodblk

Originally an interlude in the 1937 film *Shall We Dance*. Arr. Sol Berkowitz. Often adapted as a novelty solo for clarinet or other instrument.

Originally published by Gershwin Music.

Warner	Schott

Rhapsody in Blue (original jazz band version) <1924>   16'

solo piano
0 1 2[1.2/bcl] 0 — 2 2 2 1[tuba/string bass] — 3sx[asx1/ssx, asx2/bsx, tsx/Ebcl] — banjo — tmp+1 — pf[orchestral],cel — 8vn

perc: set, glock, tri, gong, bd, cym, sus cym, sd, Turkish cym

Instrumentation by Ferde Grofé. New set of engraved parts and MS score (2009) is a vast improvement over what was previously available.

The above instrumentation shows how the parts are laid out; for practicality, however, certain adaptations could be made:

E-flat clarinet (in tsx part) could readily be covered by cl1.
String bass (in tuba part) may be given to a separate player.
Tmp & perc might be covered by one nimble player (but tmp+1 is better).
Celesta plays only 19 bars — all of it doubled in glockenspiel.
Oboe plays only 9 bars. In the score it is shown as a double for cl1, but in the set it is provided with its own part.

EAM

Rhapsody in Blue (1926 orchestration) <1924>   16'

solo piano
1 1 2 1 — 2 2 1 0 — 3sx[asx.tsx.asx] — banjo — tmp+2 — str

perc: bd, cym, sus cym, sd, tri, gong, glock

Rescored by Ferde Grofé for standard concert orchestra, 1926. Published by Harms, Inc., but believed to be out of print. Parts are engraved; Fleisher Collection created a manuscript full score.

Percussion could be handled by 2 players (tmp+1) if drumset used; the part may have been intended for one agile player covering tmp and all perc.

EAM	Fleisher

Rhapsody in Blue (full orchestra, 1942) <1924>   16'

solo piano
2 2 3[1.2.bcl] 2 — 3 3 3 1 — 3 opt saxes[2asx, tsx] — opt banjo — tmp+3 — str

perc: sd, sus cym, cym, glock, tri, bd, tamtam

Ferde Grofé's 1926 orchestration further fleshed out in 1942, incidentally making the saxophones and banjo "almost optional" according to the preface by editor Frank Campbell Watson.

This is the most commonly performed version.

Warner	Luck's	Schott

Second Rhapsody for Piano & Orchestra <1931>   15'

3[1.2.pic] 3[1.2.Eh] 3[1.2.bcl] 2 — 4 3 3 1 — tmp+3 — hp — str

perc: glock, xyl, cym; set: bd, sd, woodblk

Originally composed as *Manhattan Rhapsody for Delicious*.

Warner has two versions of this work: (1) Gershwin's original orchestration in very poor manuscript copies; (2) Robert McBride's orchestration, as engraved for New World Music. Luck's has the McBride orchestration only. The solo piano part is identical in both.

Schott has both versions in what appear to be newly engraved editions.

Warner	Luck's	Schott

Tip-Toes: Overture <1925>

2[1.2/pic] 2[1.2/Eh] 2[1.2/Ebcl] 2 — 4 3 3 1 — 4sax[2asx, tsx, bsx] — tmp+1 — hp — pf — str

perc: sus cym

Arr. Don Rose

Warner	Schott

Ghedike, Alexander   1877 - 1957

see: Goedicke, Alexander, 1877-1957

Giannini, Vittorio   1903-1966

(b Philadelphia, 19 Oct 1903; d New York, 28 Nov 1966). American

Symphony No.2 <1956>   22'

3[1.2.pic] 2 2 2 — 4 3 3 1 — tmp+1 — str

Chappell	Luck's	

Giazotto, Remo   1910-1998

(b Rome, 4 Sept 1910; d Pisa, 26 Aug 1998). Italian musicologist and critic

Adagio, Organ & Strings, G minor

see under: Albinoni, Tomaso (1671-1750)
       Adagio, Organ & Strings, G minor

Gilbert, Henry F.   1868-1928

(b Somerville, MA, 26 Sept 1868; d Cambridge, MA, 19 May 1928). American

Dance in the Place Congo <1908>   20'

3[1.2.3/pic] 2 3[1.2.bcl] 3[1.2.cbn] — 4 3 3 1 — tmp+4 — hp — str
perc: tri, tambn, sd, bd, cym, glock, xyl, chime[Eb3]

Belwin	Fleisher	Gray

Gilbert, Jan   1946-

(b New York, 6 Aug 1946). American

Dream Carver; A Story from Oaxaca <2009>   22'

narrator
2[1/pic.2] 1 2 1 — 1 1 1 0 — 1perc — str
perc: sus cym, sd, tri, tambn, slgh-bells, woodblk, cowbell, whip, ratch, guiro, marac, claves, vibrslp, cabasa, rainstick
The inserted *El Toro Relajo* can use, as options, a tenor soloist, and extra Latin percussion.

A. *Village Fiesta Music I / Zapotec Ruins*   '
B. *Carving Music I*   '
C. *Parade of the Dream Animals I*   '
D. *Freely/Mateo and his Father*   '
E. *Mateo's longing*   '
F. *Dream Music I*   '
G. *Carving Music II*   '
H. *Carving Music III*   '
J. *Parade of the Dream Animals II*   '
K. *Andante / Mateo's love for his father / Dream Music II*   '
FIESTA-INSERT El Toro Relajo (The Disturbed Bull)   '
L. *Village Fiesta Music II*   '

ACA		

In the Beginning <2007>   20

narrator
2 2 2[1.Eh] 2 2 — 4 2 3 1 — 2perc — hp — str
perc: bd, cym, sus cym, sd, tri, gong, xyl, windchimes, belltree, templeblks, cowbell, whip, guiro, marac, claves, congas, hoof rattle, ocean drum, rainstick
A Native American legend from the Tlingit tribe of the Northwest Coast. Mvts may be performed as excerpts.

A. *The Soft Darkness*   '
B. *Raven Arrives*   '
C. *The Ghosts*   '
D. *The Fish*   '
E. *Calypso I*   '
F. *The Magic Spring*   '
G. *Raven's Waltz*   '
H. *Storytelling by the Fire*   '
I. *Bossa Nova*   '
J. *Storytelling*   '
K. *Calypso II*   '
L. *Raven's Escape*   '
M. *The Wobbly Flight*   '
N. *The Creation of the Crooked Rivers*   '
O. *The Endless Night*   '

ACA		

Khoj; The Search for Light   23'

narrator
2[1/.2pic] 2[1.Eh] 2 2 — 4 2 0 1 — 3perc — hp — str
perc: belltree, cast, chimes, claves, congas, cym, glock, guiro, marac, marim, slgh-bells, sd, tambn, templeblks, tri, whip, windchimes, woodblk, xyl, oceandrum, rainstick, 2sus cym
A contemporary North Indian folktale by Gita Kar.
    Movements may be performed separately.

A. *The Earth is Dark*   2'
B. *The Koel Bird*   2'
C. *The Flight of the Flamingos*   1'
D. *The Camels*   1'
E. *March of the Elephants*   3'
F. *The Wonder of the Child Elephants*   1'
G. *The River*   1'
H. *The Sea Turtles*   1'
I. *The Cheetal Deer*   2'
J. *The Western Wind*   1'
K. *The Search for Light*   2'
L. *Dance of the Peacocks*   3'
M. *The Enchanted Night*   3'

ACA		

Nine-in-One Grr! Grr! <2003>   17'

narrator
2[1/pic.2] 2[1.Eh] 2 2 — 4 2 0 1 — qeej[opt] — 2perc — str
perc: sus cym, sd, tri, tambn, gong, glock, xyl, chimes, belltree, woodblk, templeblks, guiro, marac, logdrum, rainstick
A Hmong folktale.
    The *qeej* is a Hmong free-reed mouth organ, also known as *geeng*. The optional *qeej* part is entirely improvised; if a *qeej* is not used, a cut of about 2' should be observed.
    An optional children's dance with improvised *qeej* accompaniment (3-4' extra duration) may be inserted.

ACA		

Suite for South Indian Veena & Orchestra <2007>   20'

solo veena [a.k.a. vina]
2[both/pic] 2[1.Eh] 2 2 — 4 2 0 1 — 2perc — str
perc: cym, sus cym, sd, tri, tambn, gong, glock, vib, chimes, woodblk, templeblks, marac, claves, congas, bamboo windchimes, metal windchimes, finger cym, bowlgong, rainstick, shaker
Sunada veena, an electric veena, may be used; much of the veena part is improvised, especially in the *Alap*. Optional accompaniment by a *mridangam* drum, in which case a mridangam improvised solo passage may be inserted in mvt 5.

I. Alap (raga-mayamalavagaula)	_'
II. Thillana (raga-mayamalavagaula)	_'
III. Alap (raga-risabhapriya)	_'
IV Thillana (raga-janaranjani)	_'
V. Jati	_'
VI. Alap (raga-rasikapriya)	_'

ACA

Gilbertson, Michael   1987-

(b Dubuque, IA, 31 May 1987). American

Reflections on Rushmore <2006>   10'

2[1.2/pic] 2 2 2 — 4 3 3 1 — tmp+3 — str
perc: bd, cym, sus cym, sd, tamtam, glock, chimes, whip

I. Fanfare for the Founding Father	_'
II. Monticello Song	_'
III. Riders in the Rough	_'
IV. Hymn to Lincoln	_'

Wendel

Gillis, Don   1912-1978

(b Cameron, MO, 17 June 1912; d Columbia, SC, 10 Jan 1978). American

Short Overture to an Unwritten Opera <1944>   4'

2 2 3[1.2.bcl] 2 — 3 3 3 1 — tmp+2 — hp — str

Boosey   Luck's

Ginastera, Alberto   1916-1983

(b Buenos Aires, 11 April 1916; d Geneva, 25 June 1983). Argentine

Concerto for Strings (Concerto per corde), op.33 <1965>   24'

str

Variazioni per i solisti	9'
Scherzo fantastica	4'
Adagio angoscioso	6'
Finale furioso	5'

Boosey

Concerto, Harp, op.25 <1956>   23'

2[1.2/pic] 2 2 2 — 2 2 0 0 — tmp+4 — cel — str[8.8.6.6.4]
perc: tambn, tamtam, crot, claves, woodblk, sd, bd, guiro, td, whip, marac, xyl, glock, field dr, 2tri, 4tomtoms, 4cowbells, 3sus cym, 3bongos

I. Allegro giusto	8'
II. Molto moderato	6'
III. Cadenza: Liberamente capriccioso - Vivace	9'

Boosey

Concerto, Piano, No.1, op.28 <1961>   27'

3[1.2.3/pic] 3[1.2.Eh] 4[1.2.Ebcl.bcl] 3[1.2.cbn] — 4 3 3 1 — tmp+5 — hp — cel — str
perc: sd, cym, cast, tamtam, bd, tri, crot, glock, tambn, xyl, 3tomtoms, 2sus cym; 1perc covers tmp2

I. Cadenza e varianti	9'
II. Scherzo allucinante	6'
III. Adagissimo	7'
IV. Toccata concertata	5'

Barry

Concerto, Violin, op.30 <1963>   27'

3[1.2.pic] 3[1.2.Eh] 4[1.2.Ebcl.bcl] 3[1.2.cbn] — 4 3 3 1 — tmp+8 — hp — cel — str[16.16.12.12.6]
perc: windchimes, crot, guiro, woodblk, sus cym, cym, bd, marac, tambn, claves, td, reco-reco, 4tri, 6templeblks, 3bongos, 2sd, 2glock, 3tamtam, 3tomtom

I. Cadenza e Studi	11'
II. Adagio per 22 soloisti	9'
III. Scherzo pianissimo e Perpetuum mobile	7'

Boosey

Estancia: Four Dances, op.8a <1941>   13'

2[1/pic2.pic1] 2 2 2 — 4 2 0 0 — tmp+6 — pf — str
perc: tambn, cym, field dr, tri, td, cast, tamtam, sus cym, bd, xyl

1. Los trabajadores agrícolas (The Land Workers)	3'
2. Danza del trigo (Wheat Dance)	4'
3. Los peones de hacienda (The Cattlemen)	2'
4. Danza final (Malambo—Final Dance)	4'

Barry

Glosses sobre temes de Pau Casals, (full orchestra version) op.48 (Glosses on Themes of Pablo Casals) <1976–1977>   18'

3[1.2.pic] 3[1.2.3/Eh] 3[1.2.3/Ebcl/bcl] 3[1.2.3/cbn] — 4 3 3 1 — tmp+4 — hp — pf/cel/harm — str
perc: bd, cym, 2 sus cym, sd, field dr, tri, tambn, 2tamtam, glock, xyl, crot, flexatone, sleighbells, woodblk, templeblk, guiro, marac, claves, 4cowbells, sandblk, slide flute, sistro
[Pablo Casals' given name was "Pau."]

Introducció	7'
Romanç	3'
Sardanes	3'
Cant	3'
Conslusió delirant	2'

Boosey

Iubilum; Symphonic Celebration, op.51 <1979–1980>   11'

3[1.2.3/pic] 3[1.2.3/Eh] 3[1.2.3/bcl] 3[1.2.3/cbn] — 4 4 4 1 — tmp+4 — hp — cel — str
perc: tri, glock, sd, cym, vib, chimes, field dr, sus cym, bd, 2sd, 3tamtams

Boosey

Oberatura para el "Fausto" Criollo, op.9 (Overture to the Creole "Faust") <1943>   9'

2[incl pic] 2 2 2 — 4 3 3 1 — tmp+5 — hp — pf — str
perc: tambn, sd, cym, bd, xyl

Barry

Ollantay, op.17 <1947>   14'

3[1.2.pic] 3[1.2.Eh] 3[1.2.bcl] 2 — 4 3 3 1 — tmp+7 — hp — pf/cel — str
perc: xyl, tambn, cym, tamtam, tri, bd, td, sd, marac, 3Indian drums

1. Paisaje de Ollantaytambo (Landscape of Ollantaytambo)	5'
2. Los guerreros (The Warriors)	3'
3. La muerte de Ollantay (The Death of Ollantay)	6'

Barry

Pampeana No.3, op.24 <1954>   18'

3[1.2.3/pic] 2[1.2/Eh] 2 2 — 4 3 3 1 — tmp+2 — hp — pf/cel — str
perc: xyl, tambn, sd, td, cym, bd, tamtam

1. Adagio contemplativo	6'
2. Impetuosamente	6'
3. Largo con poetica esaltazione	6'

Barry

Panambí: Suite, op.1a <1934–1936>   13'

4[1.2.3/pic.4/pic] 4[1.2.3.Eh] 4[1.2.3.4/Ebcl/bcl] 4[1.2.3.4/cbn] — 4 4 3 1 — tmp+7 — 2hp — cel, pf — str
perc: bd, sd, claves, tri, tambn, cym, tamtam, xyl, 3cajas

1. Claro de luna sobra el Paranà (Moonlight on the Parana)	6'
2. Invocación a los espìritus poderosos (Invocation of the Powerful	1'
3. Lamento de las concellas (Lament of the Maidens)	3'
4. Fiesta indìgena—Danza de los guerreros (Dance of Warriors)	3'

> Barry

Popol vuh, op.44 (The Creation of the Maya World) <1975–1983>   23'

3[1.2/pic.3/pic] 3[1.2.3/Eh] 3[1.2/Ebcl.3/bcl] 3[1.2.3/cbn] — 4 4 4 1 — tmp+4 — 2hp — pf/cel — str
perc: marim, vibrslp, claves, tamtam, templeblks, marac, guiro, xyl, gong, glock, bd, sd, flexatone, 5tomtoms, 5cowbells, sistro, 5bongos, 5congas, 5woodblks, chocalho, reco-reco, cuica, 2sus cym
1 percussionist doubles on 2nd tmp.

> Boosey

Variaciones concertantes, op.23 <1953>   25'

2[1.2/pic] 1 2 1 — 2 1 1 0 — tmp — hp — str
Solos for fl, ob, cl, bn, hn, tp, tbn, hp, vn, va, vc, db.

I. Tema per Violoncello ed Arpa	2'
II. Interludio per Corde	2'
III. Variazione giocosa per Flauto	1'
IV. Variazione in modo di Scherzo per Clarinetto	2'
V. Variazione drammatica per Viola	4'
VI. Variazione canonica per Oboe e Fagotto	3'
VII. Variazione ritmica per Trombe e Trombone	1'
VIII. Variazione in modo di Moto perpetuo per Violino	1'
IX. Variazione pastorale per Corno	2'
X. Interludio per Fiati	1'
XI. Represa dal Tema per Contrabasso	2'
XII. Variazione finale in modo di Rondo per Orchestra	4'

> Boosey

Giuliani, Mauro   1781 - 1829

(b Bisceglie, nr Bari, 27 July 1781; d Naples, 8 May 1829). Italian

Concerto, Guitar, op.36, A major <1808>   24'

str

> Kalmus   Luck's   Zerboni

Glanville-Hicks, Peggy   1912 - 1990

(b Melbourne, 29 Dec 1912; d Sydney, 25 June 1990). Australian

Gymnopédie No.1 <1934>   4'

0 1 0 0 — hp — str

> AMP   Luck's

Sinfonia da Pacifica <1953>   12'

1 1 1 1 — 1 1 1 0 — tmp+4 — str

> AMP

Glass, Philip   1937 -

(b Baltimore, 31 Jan 1937). American

Arioso No.2 <1967>   6'

str

> Elkan-Vogel

The Canyon <1988>   18'

3[1.2.pic] 2 2 2 — 4 3 3 1 — tmp+7 — pf — str
perc: chimes, glock, marac, woodblk, tri, tambn, ratch, bd, sd, td

> Chester   Dunvagen

Company <1983>   10'

str orch (or str 4t)
From the composer's String Quartet No.2.

I. quarter-note = 96	3'
II. dotted quarter = 120	2'
III. quarter = 90	2'
IV. quarter = 160	3'

> Dunvagen

Concerto, Piano, No.2 (After Lewis and Clark) <2004>   35'

1[fl/pic] 1 1 1 — 2 1 0 0 — 2perc — str
perc: sd, tambn, cym, bd, td, cast, hi-hat, glock, sus cym, tri, anvil
An optional Native American flute is called for in the 2nd mvt; the part may be played on a standard flute an 8ve higher.

I. The Vision	11'
II. Sacagawea	11'
III. The Land	13'

> Chester   Dunvagen

Concerto, Violin, No.2 (American Four Seasons) <2009>   40'

synth — str

Prologue	2'
Movement 1	6'
Song No.1	4'
Movement 2	10'
Song No.2	2'
Movement 3	6'
Song No.3	3'
Movement 4	7'

> Dunvagen

Concerto Grosso <1992>   19'

1 1 1 1 — 2 1 1 1 — str

> Dunvagen

Days and Nights in Rocinha: Dance for Orchestra <1997>   20'

3[1.2.pic] 2 4[1.2.Ebcl.bcl/cbcl] 2 — 4 3 3 1 — tmp+5 — hp — pf — str
perc: sd, td, bd, tri, marim, woodblk, tambn, cym, xyl, cast, tamtam

> Dunvagen

Dracula: Suite <1999>   31'

pf — str
Arr. by Michael Riesman from the composer's film score for the 1931 classic silent film Dracula.

Dracula	1'
Journey to the Inn	1'
The Inn	3'
Carriage Without a Driver	2'
Dr. van Helsing and Dracula	2'
In the Theater	6'
Seward Sanatorium	3'
Mina on the Terrace	4'
Mina's Bedroom/The Abbey	4'
The End of Dracula	4'
Epilogue	1'

> Dunvagen

Music in Similar Motion <1969; rev 1981>   12'

3[1.2.pic] 3[1.2.Eh] 4[1.2.Ebcl.bcl] 2 — 4 2 2 1 — elec org or pf — str
May be performed by any group of instruments.

> Dunvagen

The Passion of Ramakrishna <2006>   45'

solo S, Ms, T, Bs-Bar, B   Chorus
3[1.2.pic] 2[1.2/Eh] 3[1.2/Ebcl./] 2 — 4 3 3 1 — tmp+4 — hp — pf
— str
Prologue   3'
Part 1—The Master's Visions   11'
Part 2—Sarada Devi   10'
Part 3—The Master's Illness   10'
Part 4—The Mahasamadhi of the Master   7'
Epilogue   4'

> Dunvagen

Phaedra <1986>   13'

gtr — tmp+7 — 1 or 2hp — str
perc: chimes, glock, sd, bd, cym, tri, woodblk, windchimes, set, opt vib, opt crot
Ballet score based on music for the film *Mishima*.

> Dunvagen

The Secret Agent: Three Pieces   11'

1 1[Eh] 0 0 — 0 0 0 0 — 1perc — hp — cel — str
perc: tamtam
From the film sound track.
1. Secret Agent   5'
2. The First Meridian   3'
3. Secret Agent Ending   3'

> Dunvagen

Symphony No.2 <1994>   44'

3[1.2.pic] 2[1.2/Eh] 4[1.2.Ebcl.bcl/cbcl] 2 — 4 3 3 1 — 5perc —
2hp[1part] — elec pf, cel[played by perc] — str
perc: glock, sd, td, bd, tri, chimes, hi-hat, tambn, cym, tamtam, cel[played by perc]
Movement I   18'
Movement II   14'
Movement III   12'

> Dunvagen

Symphony No.3 <1995; rev 1996>   24'

str[6.4.4.3.2]
Movement I: quarter-note = 112   5'
Movement II: quarter-note = 144   6'
Movement III: quarter-note = 112   10'
Movement IV: quarter-note = 144   3'

> Dunvagen

Symphony No.7 (A Toltec Symphony) <2005>   34'

chorus SSATB
3[1.2.pic] 3[1.2.Eh] 3[1.2/Ebcl.bcl] 2 — 4 3 3 1 — 5perc — hp —
cel, pf, org — str
perc: woodblk, bd, tamtam, glock, sus cym, tambn, td, sd, cast, tri, xyl, tomtom,
marim, rattle, anvil, shaker, finger cym, tmp
I. The Corn   11'
II. The Sacred Root   10'
III. The Blue Deer   13'

> Chester   Dunvagen

Symphony No.8 <2005>   38'

3[1.2.3/pic] 2[1.2/Eh] 3[1.2/Ebcl.bcl] 2 — 4 3[1.2/Ebtp.3] 3 1 —
tmp+4 — hp — pf/cel — str
perc: xyl, vib, glock, chimes, sd, td, bd, sus cym, hi-hat, cowbell, tri, marac, cast,
woodblk, tambn, whip
I. quarter-note = 144   19'
II. quarter-note = 96   12'
III. quarter-note = 96   7'

> Chester   Dunvagen

Glazunov, Alexander   1865-1936

(b St Petersburg, 29 July/10 Aug 1865; d Paris, 21 March 1936). Russian

Carnaval Overture, op.45 <1892>   9'

3[1.2.3/pic] 2 3 2 — 4 3 3 1 — tmp+4 — opt org — str
perc: tri, tambn, cym, bd

> Belaieff   Kalmus   Luck's

Chant du ménestrel, op.71 <1900>   3'

solo violoncello
3[1.2.pic] 2 2 2 — 2 0 0 0 — str

> Belaieff   Kalmus   Luck's

Chopiniana, op.46 <1893>   14'

3[1.2.pic] 2 2 2 — 4 2 3 0 — tmp+4 — str
perc: tri, tambn, sd, cym, bd
Chopin piano works orchestrated by Glazunov.
Polonaise, op.40, no.1   4'
Nocturne, op.15, no.1   3'
Mazurka, op.50, no.3   3'
Tarentelle, op.43   4'

> Belaieff   Kalmus   Luck's

Concerto, Alto Saxophone, op.109, E-flat major <1934> 13'

str
Bärenreiter 2010 critical edition ed. Regina Back & Douglas
Woodfull-Harris.

> Bärenreiter   Kalmus   Leduc   Luck's

Concerto, Violin, op.82, A minor <1904>   21'

3[1.2.pic] 2 2 2 — 4 2 3 0 — tmp+3 — hp — str
perc: glock, tri, cym
1. Moderato   5'
2. Andante sostenuto   10'
3. Allegro   6'

> Belaieff   Kalmus   Luck's

Cortège solennel [No.1], op.50, D major <1894>   6'

3[1.2.pic] 2 3 2 — 4 3 3 1 — tmp+4 — hp — str
perc: tri, tambn, cym, bd

> Belaieff   Kalmus   Luck's

Cortège solennel No.2, op.91, B-flat major <1910>   4'

3[1.2.pic] 2 3 2 — 4 3 3 1 — tmp+4 — str
perc: tri, sd, cym, bd

> Belaieff   Fleisher

Elegy in Memory of Belaieff, op.105 (Élegiya pamyati   7'
M.P. Belyayeva)

str
Originally for string quartet; db part added by an unknown hand.

> Belaieff

Finnish Fantasy, op.88 (Fantasie finnoise) <1909>   16'

3[1.2.pic] 3[1.2.Eh] 3[1.2.3/bcl] 3[1.2.cbn] — 4 3 3 2 — tmp+4 — hp
— str

> Belaieff

The Kremlin, op.30 (Kreml') <1890>   27'

3[1.2.3/pic] 3[1.2.Eh] 3[1.2.bcl] 3[1.2.cbn] — 4 3 3 1 — tmp+5 — hp — str

perc: bd, cym, sd, tri, tambn, tamtam, glock

Optional banda of "at least" 6 cornetti, 4 corni alti, 4 corni tenori, 6 tubas; however, this banda could be covered by 3 cornets, 2 tubas, and 6 medium-range instruments (horns and/or trombones). Essential banda parts are cued into the orchestral brass.

1. Popular Festival	*8'*
2. In the Monastery	*10'*
3. The Meeting and Entrance of the Prince	*9'*

Belaieff	Fleisher

March des noces, op.21 (Svadebnoye shestviye; Wedding Procession) <1889>   6'

3[1.2.pic] 2 2 2 — 4 2 3 1 — tmp+3 — hp — str

perc: bd, cym, tri

Belaieff	Kalmus	Luck's

Overture No.1 on Three Greek Themes, op.3 <1882>   15'

3[1.2.pic] 2 2 2 — 4 2 3 1 — tmp+4 — opt hp — str

perc: bd, cym, td, tri

Belaieff	Kalmus	Luck's

Overture solennelle, op.73 <1900>   11'

3[1.2.pic] 2 2 2 — 4 2 3 1 — tmp+3 — str

perc: bd, cym, tri

Belaieff	Kalmus	Luck's

Raymonda: Act III [McPhee reduction]   31'

2[1.2/pic] 2[1.2/Eh] 2 2 — 4 2 3 1 — tmp+3 — hp — pf[pianino] — str

perc: bd, cym, sd, tambn, tri, glock

Reduced orchestration by Jonathan McPhee. This is apparently intended for a ballet production of the so-called 1964 Nureyev version of *Raymonda*.

Entre-acte (Allegro moderato)	*3'*
Grand pas hongroise (Moderato maestoso)	*4'*
Entrée (Allegretto)	*2'*
Pas classique hongrois (Adagio)	*4'*
Variation I (Prestissimo)	*1'*
Danse des enfants (Allegro moderato)	*1'*
Variation IV (Raymonda, Allegretto)	*1'*
Variation II (Moderato)	*2'*
Variation III (Allegretto)	*1'*
Variation III (pour un danseur, Allegro)	*1'*
Variation IV (Raymonda; Adagio)	*3'*
Coda (Allegro)	*3'*
Galop (Allegro assai)	*4'*
Apothéose (Le tournoi, Andante)	*1'*

Boosey

Raymonda: Suite, op.57a <1898>   40'

3[1.2.3/pic] 2[1.2/Eh] 3 2 — 4 3 3 1 — tmp+3 — hp — cel — str

perc: bd, cym, tri, tambn, glock, field dr

I. Introduction: In the Castle	_'
II. Dance of Pages and Young Girls	_'
III. Arrival of the Stranger	_'
IV. Entrance of Raymonda	_'
V. Moonlight	_'
VI. Prelude and La Romanesca	_'
VII. Variations	_'
VIII. Raymonda's Dream	_'
IX. Spanish Dance	_'
X. Valse fantasque	_'
XI. Grand Adagio	_'
XII. Raymonda's Variation	_'
XIII. Arab Boy's Dance	_'
XIV. Entrance of the Saracens	_'
XV. Love Triumphant	_'
XVI. Wedding Feast	_'

Belaieff	Kalmus	Luck's

Rêverie, op.24 <1890>   3'

solo horn

2 1 2 2 — tmp — hp[or pf] — str

Originally for horn and piano; arr. by the composer.

Belaieff	Kalmus	Luck's

Scènes de ballet, op.52 <1894>   27'

3[1.2.pic] 2[1.2/Eh] 3 2 — 4 3 3 1 — tmp+4 — hp — str

perc: tri, tambn, sd, glock, cym, bd

I. Préambule	*3'*
II. Marionnettes	*2'*
III. Mazurka	*4'*
IV. Scherzino	*1'*
V. Pas d'action	*5'*
VI. Danse orientale	*3'*
VII. Valse	*4'*
VIII. Polonaise	*5'*

Belaieff	Kalmus

THE SEASONS, op.67   9
The Seasons (Vremena goda): 1. Winter <1899>

3[1.2.pic] 2 2 — 4 2 3 1 — tmp+1 — hp — cel — str

perc: sus cym, sd, tri, glock

Introduction	*3'*
Le givre [Frost]	*1'*
La glace [Ice]	*1'*
La grêle [Hail]	*1'*
La neige [Snow]	*3'*

Belaieff	C. Fischer	Kalmus	Luck's

The Seasons (Vremena goda): 2. Spring <1899>   5

3[1.2.pic] 2 2 — 4 2 3 0 — tmp+1 — hp — str

perc: tri

Kalmus	Luck's

The Seasons (Vremena goda): 3. Summer <1899>   11

3[1.2.pic] 2 2 — 4 2 3 1 — tmp+4 — hp — pf — str

perc: bc, cym, sus cym, tri, glock

L'Eté	*2'*
Valse des Bluets et des Pavots	*2'*
Barcarolle	*2'*
Variation	*1'*
Coda	*4'*

Belaieff	C. Fischer	Kalmus	Luck's

The Seasons (Vremena goda): 4. Autumn <1899>   11

3[1.2.pic] 2[1.2/Eh] 2 2 — 4 2 3 1 — tmp+5 — hp — cel — str

perc: bd, cym, sd, tri, tambn, glock

Bacchanal	*4'*
Petit adagio	*4'*
Variation (Le satyre)	*3'*

Belaieff	Kalmus	Luck's

The Seasons (Vremena goda): Three Movements <1899>   4

2[1.2/pic] 2 2 — 2 2 3 0 — tmp+5 — hp — cel — str

perc: bd, cym, tri, tambn, glock

Arr. Norman Richardson.

Barcarolle	*2'*
La Glace	*1'*
Bacchanal	*1'*

Boosey

Serenade No.1, op.7, A major <1883>   5'

2 2[1.Eh] 2 2 — 4 2 0 0 — tmp+2 — str

perc: tri, tambn

Kalmus	mph

Serenade No.2, op.11, F major <1884>   4'

2 1 2 2 — 2 0 0 0 — str

Kalmus		mph	

Stenka Razin, op.13 <1885>   16'

3[1.2.3/pic] 2 2 2 — 4 2 3 1 — tmp+3 — hp — str
perc: cym, bd, tamtam

Belaieff	Kalmus	Luck's

Symphony No.4, op.48, E-flat major <1893>   31'

3[1.2/pic.3/pic] 2[1.2/Eh] 3 2 — 4 2 3 1 — tmp — str
1. Andante; Allegro moderato	*13'*
2. Allegro vivace	*5'*
3. Andante; Allegro	*13'*

Belaieff	Kalmus

Symphony No.5, op.55, B-flat major <1895>   34'

3[1.2.3/pic] 2 3[1.2.3/bcl] 2 — 4 3 3 1 — tmp+4 — hp — str
perc: tri, cym, glock, bd
1. Moderato maestoso; Allegro	*11'*
2. Scherzo: Moderato	*5'*
3. Andante	*10'*
4. Allegro maestoso	*8'*

Belaieff	Kalmus

Symphony No.6, op.58, C minor <1896>   35'

3[1.2.3/pic] 2 3 2 — 4 3 3 1 — tmp+2 — str
perc: bd, cym, sd, tri, glock
1. Adagio; Allegro passionato	*11'*
2. Theme and Variations	*10'*
3. Intermezzo: Allegretto	*4'*
4. Finale: Andante maestoso	*10'*

Belaieff	Kalmus	Luck's

Symphony No.7, op.77, F major (Pastoral; Pastoral'naya) <1902>   37'

3[1.2.3/pic] 2 2 2 — 4 2 3 1 — tmp+3 — hp — str
perc: tri, bd, cym
I. Allegro moderato	*9'*
II. Andante	*11'*
III. Scherzo: Allegro giocoso	*6'*
IV. Finale: Allegro maestoso (molto pesante)	*11'*

Belaieff	Kalmus

Symphony No.8, op.83, E-flat major <1906>   44'

3[1.2/afl.3/pic] 3[1.2.Eh] 3[1.2.bcl] 3[1.2.cbn] — 4 3 3 1 — tmp+3 — str
perc: tri, cym, bd
I. Allegro moderato	*11'*
II. Mesto	*13'*
II. Allegro	*7'*
IV. Finale: Moderato sostenuto—Allegro moderato	*13'*

Belaieff	Kalmus

Symphony No.9, D minor <1910>   7'

3[1.2.pic] 3[1.2.Eh] 3 3[1.2.cbn] — 4 3 3 1 — tmp+2 — str
perc: cym, sus cym, bd
One mvt (Adagio), left in piano score, 1910; orchd by Gavril
Yakovlevich Yudin, 1948, rev.1986

Belaieff

Valse de concert, No.1, op.47, D major (Concert Waltz No.1) <1893>   11'

3[1.2.3/pic] 2[1.Eh] 3 2 — 4 2 3 0 — tmp+5 — hp — str
perc: sd, bd, cym, tri, glock

Belaieff	Kalmus	Luck's

Valse de concert, No.2, op.51, F major (Concert Waltz No.2) <1894>   10'

3[1.2.pic] 2 2 2 — 4 2 3 0 — tmp+3 — hp — str

Belaieff	Kalmus	Luck's

Glière, Reinhold   1875-1956

(b Kiev, 30 Dec 1874/11 Jan 1875; d Moscow, 23 June 1956). Russian

Concerto, Coloratura Soprano & Orchestra, op.82 <1943>   14'

2 2 2 2 — 3 0 0 0 — tmp+1 — hp — str
perc: tri, glock
| *I. Andante* | *9'* |
| *II. Allegro* | *5'* |

Russian

Concerto, Harp, op.74, E-flat major <1938>   27'

2 2 2 2 — 3 0 0 0 — tmp+1 — str
I. Allegro moderato	*11'*
II. Tema con variazioni	*11'*
III. Allegro giocoso	*5'*

Russian

Concerto, Horn, op.91, B-flat major <1950>   26'

3 2 2 2 — 3 2 3 1 — tmp+4 — hp — str
perc: tri, sd, cym, bd

Russian

The Red Poppy (Roter mohn): Suite <1927>   27'

3[1.2/pic.3/pic] 3[1.2.Eh] 3[1.2.3/Ebcl/bcl] 3[1.2.3/cbn] — 4 3 3 1 — tmp+7 — 2hp — cel — str
perc: xyl, glock, tamtam, tri, tambn, sd, cym, bd, 2small pitched gongs
Victorious Dance of the Coolies	*4'*
Scene and Dance with the Golden Fingers	*9'*
Coolie Dance	*2'*
The Phoenix	*6'*
Waltz	*2'*
Russian Sailors' Dance	*4'*

Russian

The Red Poppy (Roter mohn): Russian Sailors' Dance (Yablochko) <1926–1927> 4'

3[1.2.pic] 3[1.2.Eh] 3[1.2.bcl] 3[1.2.cbn] — 4 3 3 1 — tmp+5 — str
perc: tri, tambn, sd, cym, bd

Kalmus	Russian

Symphony No.1, op.8, E-flat major <1899–1900>   36'

3[1.2.3/pic] 2 2 2 — 4 2 3 1 — tmp+2 — str
perc: cym, bd
1. Andante; Allegro moderato; Andante	*14'*
2. Allegro molto vivace	*7'*
3. Andante	*8'*
4. Finale: Allegro	*7'*

Belaieff	Kalmus	Russian

Symphony No.2, op.25, C minor <1907–1908>   45'

3[1.2.3/pic] 3[1.2.Eh] 3[1.2.3/bcl] 3 — 4 3 3 1 — tmp+4 — hp — str
perc: tri, field dr, tambn, xyl, bd, cym, sus cym, glock
I. Allegro pesante	*14'*
II. Allegro giocoso	*7'*
III. Andante con variazioni	*13'*
IV. Allegro vivace	*11'*

Belaieff	Kalmus	Russian

Symphony No.3, op.42 (Il'ya Muromets) <1911>   76'

4[1.2.3/pic.pic] 4[1.2.3.Eh] 4[1.2.3.bcl] 4[1.2.3.cbn] — 8 4 4 1 —
tmp+4 — 2hp — cel — str
perc: tri, field dr, tamtam, glock, cym, bd; 1 player covers tmp2
The 4 movements are sold separately.
    This work has been subjected in performance to radical cuts of as much
as one-third of its original length; 76' is believed to be the uncut duration.

1. *Wandering Pilgrims: Il'ya Murometz and Svyatogor*		22'
2. *Il'ya Murometz and Solovei the Brigand*		22'
3. *At the Court of Vladimir the Mighty Sun*		7'
4. *The Heroic Deeds and Petrification of Il'ya Murometz*		25'

Kalmus	Luck's	Russian

Les Syrènes, op.33 <1908>   17'

4[1.2.3.pic] 3[1.2.Eh] 4[1.2.3.bcl] 3[1.2.cbn] — 6 3 3 1 — tmp+2 —
2hp — cel — str
perc: cym, sus cym, glock, tamtam

Kalmus

The Zaporozhy Cossacks, op.64 (Dnieper Cossacks) <1921>   18'

3[1.2.pic] 3[1.2.Eh] 3[1.2.bcl] 3[1.2.cbn] — 4 3 3 1 — tmp+5 — str
perc: bd, cym, tri, tambn, field dr

Introduction	3'
The Cossacks Write the Letter Then Read It	1'
They Laugh	2'
They Dance and Rejoice	9'
Finale	3'

Luck's	Russian

Glinka, Mikhail   1804-1857

(b Novospasskoye [now Glinka], nr Yelnya, Smolensk district, 20 May/1 June 1804;
d Berlin, 3/15 Feb 1857). Russian

Capriccio brillante on the "Jota aragonesa" (Spanish Overture No.1) <1845>   9'

2 2 2 2 — 4 2 3 1 — tmp+3 — hp — str
perc: cym, cast, bd
Because there are never more than 2hn playing at once, it would be
possible to adapt this work for performance with only 2 horns.

Kalmus	Luck's	Universal

Kamarinskaya; Fantasy for Orchestra on Two Russian Folksongs <1848>   7'

2 2 2 2 — 2 2 1 0 — tmp — str

Belaieff	Kalmus	Luck's

A Life for the Tsar (Zhizn' za tsarya): Overture <1834–1836>   10'

2 2 2 2 — 4 2 3 0 — tmp — str

Breitkopf	Kalmus	Luck's	Simrock

A Life for the Tsar (Zhizn' za tsarya): Krakoviak <1834–1836>   5'

2 2 2 2 — 4 2 3 0 — tmp — str

Kalmus	Luck's	Russian

Ruslan and Lyudmila (Ruslan i Lyudmila): Overture <1837–1842>   5'

2 2 2 3[1.2.cbn] — 4 2 3 0 — tmp — str

Belaieff	Kalmus	Luck's	Schott	Universal

Summer Night in Madrid (Spanish Overture No.2) <1851>   10

2 2 2 2 — 4 2 1 0 — tmp+5 — str
perc: tri, field dr, cym, bd, cast
Original title: *Recuerdos de Castilla*.

Belaieff	Kalmus	Luck's	Russian

Valse fantaisie <1839; rev 1856>   6'

2 2 2 2 — 2 2 1 0 — tmp+1 — str
perc: tri [can be played by timpanist]
Originally for pf, 1839; orchestrated 1845 but lost; reorchestrated 1856.

Kalmus	Luck's	Schirmer	Universal

Gluck, Christoph Willibald   1714-1787

(b Erasbach, Upper Palatinate, 2 July 1714; d Vienna, 15 Nov 1787). Bohemian

Airs de ballet, Suite No.2 <1744–1787>   22'

2 2 2 2 — 2 2 0 0 — tmp+1 — str
perc: tambn
Arr. F. A. Gevaert, from various Gluck operas.
    Tuba, tps & fl2 in mvt 5 only; tambourine in 3 only; clarinets & oboes
in 2 & 5 only.

I. *Air (Iphigénie en Aulide)*	_'
II. *Dance of the Slaves (Iphigénie en Aulide)*	_'
III. *Tambourin (Iphigénie en Aulide)*	_'
IV. *Gavotte (Armide)*	_'
V. *Grande chaconne (Iphigénie en Aulide & Orfeo ed Euridice)*	_'

Kalmus	Luck's

Alceste: Overture <1767>   10'

2 2 2 3[1.2.opt cbn] — 2 0 3 0 — str
Concert-ending by Felix Weingartner.

Breitkopf	Kalmus	Luck's

Alceste (Paris version of 1776): Overture <1776>   8'

2 2 0 2 — 2 0 3 0 — str
Ed. Rudolf Gerber. includes a concert-ending.

Bärenreiter

Ballet Suite No.1 (arr. Mottl)   16'

3[1.2.pic] 2[1/Eh.2] 2 2 — 4 2 0 0 — tmp+2 — str
perc: tri, tamb prov
Arr. Felix Mottl. Freely adapted from ballet music of various Gluck
operas.
    Pic in mvt 1 only; Eh in mvt 2 only (playable by either oboist).

1. *Introduction (Don Juan), Air gai (Iphigenie en Aulide), Lento*	4'
2. *Dance of the Blessed Spirits (Orpheus)*	6'
3. *Musette [Gavotte] (Armide)*	2'
4. *Air gai (Iphigenie en Aulide), Sicilienne (Armide)*	4'

Kalmus	Luck's	Peters

Ballet Suite No.2 (arr. Mottl)   15'

2[1.2/pic] 2 2 — 2 2 3 0 — tmp+2 — str
perc: tri, tamb prov
Arr. Felix Mottl. Freely adapted from ballet music of various Gluck
operas.

1. *March (Alceste), Menuet (Iphigenie en Aulide)*	_'
2. *Grazioso (Paride e Elena)*	_'
3. *Slave Dance (Iphigenie en Aulide)*	_'

Kalmus	Luck's	Peters

Concerto, Flute, G major   15'

0 0 0 0 — 2 0 0 0 — str

Kalmus	Luck's	Peters

Don Juan: Four Movements <1761>   28'

2 2 0 2 — 2 0 1 0 — str
Arr. by Hermann Kretzschmar.
I. Overture and Andante grazioso   _'
II. Brilliante; Allegretto risoluto; Tranquillo _'
III. Allegro molto; Grazioso   _'
IV. Larghetto e Allegro non troppo   _'

| Breitkopf | Kalmus | Luck's |

Iphigénie en Aulide (Iphigenie in Aulis): Overture   4'
<1774>

2 2 0 2 — 2 2 0 0 — tmp — str
Ed. Marius Flothuis. Concert-ending included.

| Bärenreiter |

Iphigénie en Aulide (Iphigenie in Aulis): Overture   10'
(Wagner ending) <1774>

2 2 2 3 — 4 3 0 0 — tmp — str
Concert-ending by Richard Wagner.

| Breitkopf | Kalmus | Luck's |

Orfeo ed Euridice: Overture <1762>   5'

0 2 0 1 — 2 2 0 0 — tmp — str

| Kalmus | Luck's |

Orfeo ed Euridice: Dance of the Blessed Spirits <1762>   6'

2 1[Eh] 0 0 — 2 0 0 0 — str
Arr. Felix Mottl.

| Kalmus | Luck's |

Orfeo ed Euridice: Dance of the Furies <1762>   5'

0 2 0 1 — 2 0 0 0 — str

| Kalmus | Luck's |

Overture, D major   5'

cnt — str
Ed. Gerber.

| Kalmus | Luck's |

Sinfonia, D major   5'

0 0 0 0 — 4 0 0 0 — str

| Supraphon |

Sinfonia, F major   13'

0 0 0 0 — 2 0 0 0 — str
Ed. Gerber.

| Kalmus | Luck's |

Sinfonia, G major   8'

cnt — str
Ed. Hoffmann.

| Kalmus | Luck's |

Goedicke, Alexander   1877-1957

(b Moscow, 20 Feb/4 March 1877; d Moscow, 9 July 1957). Russian composer of German extraction

Concert Etude, Trumpet & Orchestra, op.49   6'

1 1[or fl2] 1 1 — 1 0 0 0 — tmp — opt hp — str
Orchestrated by Gene Mullins.
   A version for solo trumpet with larger orchestra is available from Sikorski; a version for trumpet & strings is available from Kalmus (composer's name spelled "Gedike" in Kalmus catalog—probably more correctly).

| Brass Press |

Goehr, Alexander   1932-

(b Berlin, 10 August 1932). English omposer of German birth

Symphony in One Movement, op.29 <1969; rev 1981>   29'

3[1.2/pic.3/Eh] 3[1.2.Eh] 3[1.2/Ebcl.bcl] 3[1.2.cbn] — 4 3 3 1 — tmp+3 — hp — cel — str
perc: gong, xyl, cym, bd, field dr, tri, tamtam, chimes, crot, woodblk, whip, guiro, anvil, 3sus cym, 2tomtom

| Schott |

When Adam Fell (Durch Adams Fall) <2010–2011>   15'

3[1.2.3/afl/pic] 2[1.2/Eh] 3[1.2/bcl.3/Ebcl] 2[1.2/cbn] — 3 2 3 0 — 2perc — hp — str
perc: guiro, belltree, lionroar, crot, logdrum, 2tri, 2tambn

| Schott |

Goetz, Hermann   1840-1876

(b Königsberg [now Kaliningrad], 7 Dec 1840; d Hottingen, nr Zürich, 3 Dec 1876). German

Concerto, Piano, No.2, op.18, B-flat Major <1867>   37'

2 2 2 2 — 2 2 0 0 — tmp — str
I. Mässig bewegt   15'
II. Mässig langsam   11'
III. Langsam—Belebter—Lebhaft 11'

| Kistner&Siegel |

Concerto, Violin, G major, op.22   18'

2 2 2 2 — 2 0 0 0 — tmp+1 — str
perc: tri
In one mvt.

| Kistner&Siegel |

Frühlings-Ouvertüre, op.15 <1864>   13'

2 2 2 2 — 4 2 0 0 — tmp — str

| Kistner&Siegel |

Nenie, op.10 <1874>   12'

chorus
2 2 2 2 — 4 0 0 0 — tmp — str

| Kistner&Siegel |

Symphony, op.9, F major <1873>   33'

2 2 2 2 — 4 2 3 0 — tmp — str
I. Allegro moderato   9'
II. Intermezzo: Allegretto, un poco meno moto 7'
III. Adagio ma non troppo lento   10'
IV. Finale: Allegro con fuoco   7'

| Kistner&Siegel | Fleisher |

Gołąbek, Jakub   1739-1789

(b Silesia, c1739; d Kraków, 30 March 1789). Polish

Symphony, C major   14'

2 2 0 0 — 2 0 0 0 — str
Probably originally calling for 2tp rather than 2hn; manuscript indicates *"clarini."*

PWM

Symphony, D major (I)   14'

0 2 0 1 — 2 0 0 0 — str

PWM

Symphony, D major (II)   18'

0 2 0 0 — 2 0 0 0 — str

PWM

Goldmark, Karl   1830-1915

(b Keszthely, 18 May 1830; d Vienna, 2 Jan 1915). Austro-Hungarian

Concerto, Violin, op.28, A minor <1877>   33'

2 2 2 2 — 4 2 3 0 — tmp — str
I. Allegro moderato   14'
II. Air: Andante   7'
III. Moderato   12'

Kalmus	Luck's

Im Frühling, op.36 (Springtime) <1889>   10'

3[1.2.3/pic] 2 2 2 — 4 3 3 1 — tmp — str
Apparent discrepancy about the number of flutes:
    Current Schott catalog: 2[1.2/pic]
    Current Kalmus catalog: 3fl+1pic
    Current Breitkopf catalog: 3fl

Breitkopf	Kalmus	Schott

Die Königin von Saba, op.27 (The Queen of Sheba): Einzugsmarsch <1875>   9'

chorus SSATTBB
3[1.2.pic] 3[1.2.Eh] 3[1.2.bcl] 2 — 4 3 4 0 — tmp+4 — 2hp — str
perc: tri, bd, cym, 2sd, anvil
Chorus often omitted when played as an orchestral piece.

Kalmus	Luck's

Die Königin von Saba, op.27 (The Queen of Sheba): Ballet Music <1875>   14'

female chorus
3[1.2.pic] 3[1.2.Eh] 3[1.2.bcl] 2 — 4 3 4 1 — tmp+4 — hp — str
perc: tri, sd, cym, bd, glock
Chorus often omitted when played as an orchestral piece.

Kalmus	Luck's

Ländliche Hochzeit, op.26 (Rustic Wedding Symphony) <1877>   43'

2 2 2 2 — 4 2 3 0 — tmp+3 — str
perc: bd[mvt 1 only], cym[mvts 1&5 only], tri[mvts 1, 2 & 5]
1. Hochzeitsmarsch (Wedding March), Variationen   15'
2. Brautlied (Bridal Song), Intermezzo   4'
3. Serenade, Scherzo   5'
4. Im Garten (In the Garden), Andante   10'
5. Tanz (Dance), Finale   9'

Kalmus	Schott

Penthesilea Overture, op.31 <1879>   18'

2[1.2/pic] 2 2 2 — 4 2 3 1 — tmp — str
Piccolo called for only in a single chord, apparently in order to provide a high C#.
    Subtitle: *Penthesilea und Achilles—das Rosenfest—Kampf und Tod*

Kalmus

Sakuntala (Overture), op.13: Overture <1965>   19'

2 3[1.2.Eh] 2 2 — 4 2 3 1 — tmp — hp — str

Kalmus	Luck's

Scherzo, A major, op.45 <1894>   11'

2 2 2 2 — 4 2 3 0 — tmp — str

Kalmus	Luck's	Peters

Symphony No.2, op.35, E-flat major <1887>   34'

2 2 2 2 — 4 2 3 1 — tmp/tri — str
Original publisher: Schott.
1. Allegro   11'
2. Andante   9'
3. Allegro quasi presto   6'
4. Andante assai: Allegro alla breve   8'

Kalmus	Luck's

Goldschmidt, Berthold   1903-1996

(b Hamburg, 18 Jan 1903; d London, 17 Oct 1996). British composer of German origin

Ciaccona sinfonica <1934–1936>   11'

2[1.pic] 2[1.2/Eh] 2[1.2/bcl] 2[1.2/opt cbn] — 2 2 2 0 — tmp+4 — hp — str
perc: sd, glock, xyl, tri, tamtam, cym, tambn, bd

Boosey

Concerto, Violin <1952–1955>   24'

2[1.2/pic] 2[1.2/Eh] 2 2 — 2 2 0 0 — tmp+1 — str
perc: gong, xyl, glock, tri, sus cym

Boosey

Concerto, Violoncello <1953>   23'

2[1.2/pic] 2[1.2/Eh] 2 2 — 2 2 3 0 — tmp+2 — hp — str
perc: chimes, xyl, cym, tamtam, tri, bd, sd

Boosey

Golijov, Osvaldo   1960-

(b La Plata, Argentina, 5 Dec 1960). Argentinian-born American composer.

Azul <2006; rev 2007>   27'

solo violoncello
3[all/pic] 1[Eh] 2[1.basset hn] 1 — 4 3 3 0 — 4perc — hp — str[each section divided]
perc: tri, tamtam, marim, vib, slgh-bells, templeblks, congas, gong[D], cajon, bottle shaker, caxixi, cricket, djembe[w/ broom], dumbek, finger cym, frame drum, 2goat's nail, 2gourds, khanjeri, pandeiro, seedrattles, shaker, pellet bells, static whip [aka theatre lightning], surdo, talking drum, waterphone, wind whistle, tmp, bass bow, spring
Hyperaccordion & 2 ethnic percusssion from the above list form an "obbligato group." Score includes helpful photos of unusual percussion instruments employed.

Ytalianna

The Dreams and Prayers of Isaac the Blind <1993–1994; rev 2000>
34'

soloist: klezmer clarinet, playing in turn: cl in A, cl in Bb, bcl, cl in C (opt Bb) & bcl (or bassett horn)
string orchestra
Originally for klezmer clarinet and string quartet; orchestrated by the composer.

Prelude: Calmo, sospeso	*3'*
I. Agitato, minaccioso	*9'*
II. Graceful, densely slow	*11'*
III. K'vakarat	*8'*
Postlude: Rubato sempre; lento, liberamente	*3'*

Ytalianna

Last Round <1996>
13'

str
3 methods of performance:
    1. 9 players [4vn, 2va, 2vc, db]
    2. small string orchestra
    3. large string orchestra [ideally 12.16.12.8.6]
Violin & viola "soloists" [i.e., 4vn, 2va] stand as in the traditional tango orchestras.

I. Movido, urgente	*7'*
II. Muertes del angel (Deaths of the Angel)	*6'*

Ytalianna

Mariel <2007>
13'

solo violoncello
3[1.2.3/afl] 2[1.Eh] 2[1.2/bcl] 2 — 4 2 3 1 — tmp+4 — hp — cel — str
perc: marim, vib, chimes, crot, 2 or 3tri, 2tamtams

Ytalianna

Oceana <1996>
28'

vocalist (Brazilian jazz style), boy soprano (or small boys chorus), double chorus
3[1.2.3/pic/afl] 0 0 0 — 2gtr — 3 or 4 perc — hp — str[6.5.4.3.2 or larger]
perc: talking drums (or clay drums), shekere, opt marac, dumbek (or bongos), 2rainsticks
Ampd: vocalist, boy soprano, alto flute, solo db, 2gtr.

1. Call	*4'*
2. First Wave: "Oceana nupcial, cadera de las islas"—Rain Tree Interlude	*2'*
3. Second Wave: "Quiero oir lo invisible"	*3'*
4. Second Call	*2'*
5. Third Wave: "Oceana, reclina tu noche en el castillo"	*2'*
6. Aria: "Tengo hambre de no ser sino piedra marina"	*6'*
7. Coral del arrecife (Chorale of the Reef): "Oceana, dame las conchas"	*9'*

Ytalianna

La pasión según San Marcos (St. Mark Passion) <2000>
88'

chorus[min 54]   principal soloists [SABar, 2dancers]
soloists from chorus [5A, 6T, Bar]
0 0 0 0 — 0 2[1/pic tp.2] 2 0 — gtr/tres, accordion, berimbau — 3perc — pf — str[6vn, 6vc, 1db]
perc: timbales, windchimes, bongos, guiro, marac, claves, 2bd, 3sd, 3cowbell, 3congas, 3batá drums, 2shekere, 3quitiplas, 2shell windchimes, 4metal tomtom, caxixi, coil spring, agogo, udu pot, whistle, shaker, cuica, ganza, gua-gua, cajon
Elaborate amplification & sound effects. A sound designer and/or engineer is required.
    Some of the numerous ethnic percussion instruments are to be played by chorus members and instrumentalists other than percussionists.

1. Visión: Bautismo en la Cruz (Baptism on the Cross)	*1'*
2. Danza del Pescador Pescado (Dance of the Ensnared Fisherman)	*1'*
3. Primer Anuncio (First Announcement)	*4'*
4. Segundo Anuncio (Second Announcement)	*2'*
5. Tercer Anuncio: En Fiesta No (Not During the Feast)	*1'*
6. Dos Días (Two Days)	*2'*
7. Unción en Betania (Anointment in Bethany)	*2'*
8. ¿Por Qué? (Why?)	*4'*
9. Oración Lucumí (Aria con Grillos) (Aria with Crickets)	*2'*
10. El Primer Día (The First Day)	*2'*
11/12. Judas y El Cordero Pascual (The Pascal Lamb)	*4'*
13. Quisiera Yo Renegar (Aria de Judas) (I Forswear This World)	*3'*
14. Eucaristía (Eucharist)	*3'*
15. Demos Gracias al Señor (We Give Thanks)	*5'*
16. Al Monte (To the Mount)	*1'*
17. Cara a Cara (Face to Face)	*1'*
18. En Getsemaní (In Gethsemane)	*1'*
19. Agonía (Aria de Jesús) (Agony; Aria of Jesus)	*8'*
20. Arresto (Arrest)	*3'*
21. Danza Sábana Blanca (Dance of the White Sheet)	*2'*
22. Ante Caifás (Before Caiphas)	*2'*
23. Soy Yo (Confesión) (Yes, I Am; Confession)	*2'*
24. Escarnio y Negación (Scorn and Denial)	*2'*
25. Desgarro de la Túnica (The Rending of the Robe)	*1'*
26. Lúa Descolorida (Aria de las Lágrimas de Pedro) (Colorless Moon)	*6'*
27. Amanecer: Ante Pilato (Dawn: Before Pilate)	*4'*
28. Silencio (Silence)	*2'*
29. Sentencia (Sentence)	*2'*
30. Comparsa al Gólgota (Parade: To Golgotha)	*3'*
31. Danza de la Sábana Púrpura-Manto Sagrado (Dance of the Holy	*2'*
32. Crucifixión (Crucifixion)	*2'*
33. Muerte (Death)	*1'*
34. Kaddish	*7'*

Ytalianna

She Was Here <2008>

soprano solo
2[1.2/pic/afl] 2[1.Eh] 2[1.2/basset hn/bcl] 2 — 2 2 1[bass tbn] 0 — 1perc — hp — cel — str
perc: tamtam, crot, windchimes, 2tri, tuned glass
Four songs by Franz Schubert, orchestrated and with an Introduction by Osvaldo Golijov.

Introduction	*–'*
I. Wandrers Nachtlied	*–'*
II. Lied der Mignon: Nur weg die Sehnsucht Kennt	*–'*
Interlude	*–'*
III. Dass sie hier gewese	*–'*
IV. Nacht und Träume	*–'*

Ytalianna

Three Songs
22'

soprano
2[1.2/pic/afl] 2[1.Eh] 2[1/basset hn.2/bcl] 2[1.2/cbn] — 2 0 0 0 — 2perc — hp — cel — str
perc: tamtam, marim, vib, chimes, bass bow
    Alternative versions: **No.1** also available in instrumental version [no voice]; **No.2** originally for voice & piano, or voice & str 4t; **No.3** also available for voice & str 4t.

1. Night of the Flying Horses (Lullaby, Doina, Gallop)	*8'*
2. Lúa descolorida	*6'*
3. How Slow the Wind	*8'*

Ytalianna

ZZ's Dream <2008>   4'

1 1 1 1 — 1 1 1 0 — vib — hp — cel — str

> Ytalianna

Gomes, Antônio Carlos   1836-1896

(b Campinas, 11 July 1836; d Belém, 16 Sept 1896). Brazilian

Il Guarany: Overture <1871>   7'

3[1.2.pic] 2 2 2 — 4 4[2tp,2crt] 3 1 — tmp+3 — hp — str
perc: cym, bd, tri
Arr. Ross Jungnickel.

> Kalmus   Luck's   Ricordi

Goossens, Eugene   1893-1962

(b London, 26 May 1893; d Hillingdon, Middlesex, 13 June 1962). English composer of Belgian descent

Concerto in One Movement for Oboe & Orchestra, op.45 <1927>   11'

2[1.2/pic] 0 2[1.2/bcl] 1 — 2 1 0 0 — 2perc — hp — cel — str
perc: bd, cym, tamtam, glock, xyl

> Leduc

Fanfare for the Merchant Marine <1943>   2'

0 0 0 0 — 4 4[one off-stage] 3 1 — tmp+5 — [no str]
perc: bd, sd, sus cym, thundersheet, td, gong, cym, leatherpad

> Boosey

Tam O'Shanter; Scherzo after Burns, op.17a <1919>   4'

3[1.2.3/pic] 3[1.2.Eh] 3 3[1.2.cbn] — 4 3 3 1 — hp — pf — str
perc: chimes, cym, gong, drum

> Chester   Luck's

Gordeli, Otar   1928-1994

(b Tbilisi, Georgia, 18 Nov 1928; d 1994). Georgian

Concertino, Flute, op.8 <1958>   12'

2[1.pic] 2 2 2 — 4 3 3 1 — tmp+2 — hp — str
perc: bd, cym, sus cym, xyl

> Schirmer

Gordon, Michael   1956-

(b Miami, 20 July 1956). American

Beijing Harmony <2013>   12'

3 3 3 3[1.2.3/cbn] — 4 3 3 1 — tmp+2 — pf — str
perc: bd, szl cym, tamtam, chimes
Violins divided into 4 sections. Special seating is recommended for most of the orchestra, in order to take advantage of spatial elements.

> Red Poppy

Dystopia <2007>   29'

4[1/pic.2/pic.pic1.pic2] 3[1.2.Eh] 3[1.2.bcl] 1[cbn] — 4 3 3 1 — asx — 5perc — hp — pf, org, elec bass — str
perc: hi-hat, slgh-bells, chimes, sus cym, 3szl cym, 2sus cym, 3woodblk, 3tambn, 4thunder, 3gong, 4sd, 2tomtom, 3bd, almglocken (pitched), 2glock

> Red Poppy

ReWriting Beethoven's Seventh Symphony <2006>   22'

3 2 3 3[1.2.cbn] — 4 3 3 1 — elec bass — tmp+4 — str
perc: bd, sus cym, szl cym, sd, tri, tamtam, glock, thunder, 2tambn, 2flexatone, 3cowbell, 2marac

> Red Poppy

Romeo <1992>   9'

2 2 2 2 — 2 2 2 0 — tmp+2 — str
perc: glock, cym, bd, 2tamtam

> Red Poppy

Sunshine of Your Love <1999>   10'

4[all/pic] 4 4 4[1.2.cbn1.cbn2] — 4 4 4 2 — 4asx, 2elec gtr, 2bgtr — 2tmp+4 — 4kybd — str
Tuning requirements: half the instruments tune normally; the others are split into 3 groups, which tune, respectively, 1/8 tone lower, 1/8 tone higher, and 1/4 tone higher. The 4kybds are "tunable" and "splitable" synthesizers; they do not appear in the score, but double the (divided) violins, saxes, and trumpets for the purpose of tuning as well as sound reinforcement.

> Red Poppy

Górecki, Henryk Mikołaj   1933-2010

(b Czernica, nr Rybnik, 6 Dec 1933; d Katowice, 12 Nov 2010). Polish

Ad matrem, op.29 (Do matki) <1971>   11'

soprano solo   chorus
4[1.2.3/pic.4/pic] 4 4 4[1.2.3/cbn.4/cbn] — 4 4 4 0 — 2tmp+2 — hp — pf — str
perc: bd, sd

> Boosey   PWM

Beatus vir, op.38 <1979>   35'

solo baritone   chorus
4 4 4 4[1.2.3/cbn.4/cbn] — 4 4 4 4[or 2tbn & 2 tubas] — 2perc — 2hp — pf 4-hands — str
perc: glock, chimes

> Boosey   Chester   PWM

Concerto for Five Instruments and String Quartet, op.11 <1957>   12'

solo flute, clarinet, trumpet, xylophone, mandolin
str 4t
   1. Sostenuto   4'
   2. Dolce   3'
   3. Non troppo   2'
   4. Marcato, ritmico   3'

> Boosey   PWM

Concerto, Harpsichord (or Piano), op.40 <1980>   9'

str
Harpsichord must be amplified electronically; strings 6.6.4.4.2 should be used for hpsd version. Piano version calls for strings 16.14.12.10.8.

> Boosey   Chester   PWM

Genesis III: Monodramma, op.19 no.3 <1963>   10'

soprano
13perc — 6db[or 12 db]
perc: chimes, 12 blocks, 8sus cyms, 4gongs, 12tri, 8cyms, 4tamtams

> Boosey   Eulenburg   PWM

Muzyczka 3, op.25 (La Musiquette 3-me) <1967>   14'

any number of violas divided equally among 3 parts

> Boosey   PWM

Old Polish Music, op.24 (Muzyka staropolska) <1969>   27'

0 0 0 0 — 5 4 4 0 — str[min 8.8.8.8.8]

Boosey

Refrain for Orchestra, op.21 (Refren na orkiestrę) <1965>   17'

0 4 4 4 — 4 4 4 0 — 3tmp+1 — str[24vn, 8va, 8vc, 8db]
perc: tamtam

Boosey   PWM

Scontri, op.17 (Collisions) <1960>   18'

4[2fl, 2pic] 0 4[1.2.Ebcl.bcl] 4[2bn, 2cbn] — 4 4 3 1 — 8perc — 2hp
— pf — str[30vn, 12va, 10vc, 8db]
perc: bongos, glock, templeblks, vib, marim, timbales, 2tamtams, 6sus cym,
4tomtoms, 4cowbells, 3horseshoes, 4sd, 2bd, 3woodblks, 2gongs
Graphic notation.

Boosey   PWM

Symphony No.1 "1959", op.14 <1959>   18'

tmp+7 — hp — pf, hpsd — str[16.16.14.12.10]
perc: td, xyl, marim, vib, 4sd, 3sus cym
Inwokacja   5'
Antyfona   6'
Choral   3'
Lauda   4'

Boosey

Symphony No.3, op.36 (Symphony of Sorrowful Songs; Symfonia pieśni żałosnych) <1976>   56'

solo soprano
4[1.2.3/pic.4/pic] 0 4 4[2bn, 2cbn] — 4 0 4 0 — hp — pf —
str[16.14.12.10.8]
Lento — sostenuto tranzuillo ma cantabile   27'
Lento e largo — tranquillissimo — cantabillissimo — dolcissimo   10'
Lento — cantabile semplice   19'

Boosey

Three Dances for Orchestra, op.34 (Trzy tańce na orkiestrę) <1973>   12'

2[1.2/pic] 2 2 2 — 4 3 3 1 — 2tmp — str
No.1   3'
No.2   4'
No.3   5'

Chester   PWM

Three Pieces in Old Style (Trzy utwory w dawnym stylu) <1963>   10'

str
No.1   3'
No.2   2'
No.3   5'

Boosey   Chester   PWM

Gossec, François Joseph   1734-1829

(b Vergnies, 17 Jan 1734; d Passy, Paris, 16 Feb 1829). South Netherlands composer, active in France

Christmas Suite (Première suite de noëls)   10'

optional chorus in last movement only
0 2 0 0 — 2 0 0 0 — cnt — str
Horns are said to be optional; however there are some solo passages for
horns. Flutes may substitute for oboes. Ed. Karlheinz Schultz-Hauser.

Vieweg

Sinfonia, op.12, no.2, G major   15'

0 2 0 0 — 2 0 0 0 — str
Ed. Allan Badley.
I. Allegro molto   4'
II. Andante moderato   5'
III. Presto   6'

Artaria

Sinfonia, op.12, no.4, B-flat major   12'

0 2 0 0 — 2 0 0 0 — str
Ed. Allan Badley.
I. Allegro molto   4'
II. Largo   6'
III. Allegro   2'

Artaria

Symphony op.6, no.6, B-flat major <1762>   21'

str
Ed. Fritz Zobeley.
1. Allegro molto   7'
2. Larghetto poco lento   4'
3. Largo con sordini   1'
4. Fuga   3'
Menuetto 1, 2   6'

Breitkopf

Gottschalk, Louis Moreau   1829-1869

(b New Orleans, 8 May 1829; d Tijuca, Brazil, 18 Dec 1869). American

D = J.G. Doyle: *Louis Moreau Gottschalk 1829–1869: a
Bibliographical Study and Catalog of Works* (Detroit, 1983)

Cakewalk

see under: Kay, Hershy, 1919-1981

Grande Tarantelle, Piano & Orchestra, D.66, op.67 (arr. Kay) <1868>   9'

2 2 2 2 — 2 2 0 0 — tmp+2 — str
perc: cym, tri, bd, sd, tambn
Originally conceived for violin & piano, this piece gradually evolved into
a concerto-like work. The composer's own orchestration is not published.
Reconstructed and orchestrated by Hershy Kay.

Boosey

Grande Tarantelle, Piano & Orchestra, D.66, op.67 (arr. McDermott) <1868>   9'

2 2 2 2 — 4 2 2 0 — tmp+2 — str
perc: cym, tambn, glock
Originally conceived for violin & piano, this piece gradually evolved into
a concerto-like work. The composer's own orchestration is not published.
Orchestrated by William McDermott.

Kalmus

Souvenir de Porto Rico <1857>   4'

3[1.2.pic] 3[1.2.Eh] 3[1.2.bcl] 3[1.2.cbn] — 4 3 3 1 — tmp+3 — str
perc: bd, cym, sd, marac, congas
Originally for piano solo; arranged by Phillip James for band (published
Presser); band version adapted for orchestra by Thor Johnson.

Fleisher

Symphony No.1, D.104 (La nuit des tropiques; Night in the Tropics) <1852; rev 1858>   19'

3[1.2.pic] 2 5[4cl, Ebcl] 2 — 4 3 2 1 — baritone horn — bsx — tmp+6 — str
perc: guiro, marac, claves, cym, bd, congas
Reconstructed by Gaylen Hatton.
I. Andante   13'
II. Allegro moderato   6'

> Boosey

Symphony No.2, D.99 (Romantique; Montevideo) <1868>   16'

3[incl pic] 2 2 2 — 2 2 2 1[oph] — tmp — str

> Belwin

Gould, Morton   1913-1996

(b New York, 10 Dec 1913; d Orlando, FL, 21 Feb 1996). American

AMERICAN BALLADS <1976>   33'

A series of American tunes in orchestral settings.

1. Star-Spangled Overture (on "The Star-Spangled Banner") <1976>   5'

3[1.2.pic] 2 3[1.2.Ebcl] 2[1.2/cbn] — 4 3 3 1 — tmp+4 — hp — str
perc: bd, cym, sus cym, sd, tri, tambn, chimes, ratch

> Schirmer

2. Amber Waves (on "America the Beautiful") <1976>   7'

3[1.2.pic] 2[1.Eh] 3[1.2.bcl] 2[1.2/cbn] — 4 3 3 1 — 2perc — hp — str
perc: sus cym, gong

> Schirmer

3. Jubilo (on "Year of Jubilo") <1976>   3'

3[1/pic.2.pic] 2[1.2/Eh] 3[1.2.bcl] 2[1.2/cbn] — 4 3 3 1 — tmp+3 — hp — str
perc: bd, sus cym, td, tri, tambn, glock

> Schirmer

4. Memorials (on "Taps") <1976>   7'

3[1.2.pic] 2[1.2/Eh] 3[1.2.3/bcl] 2[1.cbn] — 4 3[tp1 offstage] 3 1 — tmp+3 — hp — str
perc: bd, sd, td, field dr

> Schirmer

5. Saratoga Quickstep (on "The Girl I Left Behind Me") <1976>   4'

3[1.2.pic] 2[1.2/Eh] 3[1.2.bcl] 2[1.2/cbn] — 4 3 3 1 — tmp+3 — hp — str
perc: sd, td, field dr, tri, glock

> Schirmer

6. Hymnal (on "We Shall Overcome") <1776>   7'

3[1.2.pic] 2[1.2/Eh] 3[1.2.bcl] 2[1.2/cbn] — 4 3 3 1 — tmp+3 — hp — str
perc: sd, sus cym, bd, cym, tambn, gong, bd/cym

> Schirmer

American Salute <1943>   5'

3[1.2.3/pic] 2[1.2/Eh] 3[1.2.3/bcl] 2 — 4 3 3 1 — gtr — tmp+3 — hp — pf — str
perc: sd, cym, glock, bd, chimes

> Belwin

Cheers! A Celebration March <1979>   5'

3[all/pic] 3[1.2.3/Eh] 3 3[1.2.3/cbn] — 4 4 3 1 — tmp+5 — hp — org[opt] — str
perc: chimes, glock, xyl, vib, cym, sus cym, sd, td, bd, cast, tri, tomtom, 3bongos
The parts are cross-cued for smaller instrumentation.

> Schirmer

Classical Variations (on Colonial Themes) <1984–1985>   14'

2[1/pic.2/pic] 2 2 2 — 4 2 2 0 — tmp+3 — hp — str
perc: sd, tambn, cym, chimes, bd

> Schirmer

Concerto, Flute <1983–1984>   34'

2[pic1.pic2] 3 3 3[1.2.3/cbn] — 4 3 3 1 — tmp+3 — hp — cel — str
perc: bd, sd, xyl, cym, td, tri, chimes, finger cym, 4bongos

> Schirmer

Fall River Legend: Ballet Suite (1961 version) <1947; rev 1961>   21'

2[1.2/pic] 2 2 2 — 4 2 3 0 — tmp+3 — pf — str
perc: tamtam, tri, tambn, glock, xyl, cym, sd, bd, finger cym
Ballet composed 1947; there is also a different 1948 version of the Suite.
I. Prologue and Waltz   3'
II. Elegy   3'
III. Church Social   4'
IV. Hymnal Variations 5'
V. Cotillion   4'
VI. Epilogue   2'

> Chappell

Interplay <1945>   13'

solo piano
2 2 2 2 — 4 3 3 1 — tmp+2 — str
perc: bd, sus cym, sd, xyl, glock, woodblk
I. [untitled]   4'
II. Gavotte   2'
III. Blues   3'
IV. Concertette   4'

> Belwin

The Jogger and the Dinosaur; For Rapper (Narrator) & Orchestra in 7 Scenes <1992>   22'

2 narrators/actors (2nd is optional)
2[1.2/pic] 1 2 1 — 2 2 2 1 — tmp+2 — str
perc: xyl, glock, set, sd, td, bd, thundersheet, guiro, cym, tri, templeblks, tambn, cowbell, marac, 4tomtoms, 4bongos, sneakers, kitchenware
Score claims tuba is optional, and shows it cued in bn and db; however, these cues are not present in the parts supplied by the publisher.
   The work is intended for performance with mimes or dancers.
Alternate versions are possible without narrator: *Suite* (16'); *Dinosauria Dances* (11').

> Schirmer

Latin-American Symphonette (Symphonette No.4) <1941>   17'

3[1/pic.2.3] 2 4[1.2.3.bcl] 2 — 4 3 3 1 — 4opt sx [2asx, tsx, bsx] — opt gtr — tmp+4 — hp — opt pf — str
perc: bd, claves, cowbell, cym, guiro, marim, sd, tambn, templeblks, tomtom, xyl, shakers
All saxophones double on clarinet; saxophones, guitar, and piano are optional, as are other (unspecified) instruments.
Rhumba   5'
Tango   4'
Guaracha 3'
Conga   5'

> Mills

Notes of Remembrance <1989>   10'

2[1.pic] 1 2 1 — 2 2 2 0 — tmp+1 — str
perc: tri, guiro, sd

Schirmer

Soundings <1969>   16'

3[1/pic.2/pic.3/pic] 3[1.2.3/Eh] 3[1.2/Ebcl.3/bcl] 3[1.2.3/cbn] — 4 3 3
1 — tmp+4 — hp — str
perc: tamtam, tomtom, cym, field dr, bd, 2sd, 3sus cym, finger cym, 2cowbells,
2tri, hammer, thunder drum
Threnodies   10'
Paeans   6'

Chappell

Spirituals <1941>   20'

3[1.2.opt pic] 2 3[1.2.bcl] 2 — 4 3 3 1 — tmp+3 — hp — opt pf —
str
perc: sd, bd, vib, xyl, cym, glock, chimes, sandblks, anvil[or cym]
Proclamation   5'
Sermon   4'
A Little Bit of Sin 5'
Protest   3'
Jubilee   3'

Belwin	Luck's

Stringmusic <1993>   29'

str
Prelude   6'
Tango   4'
Dirge   10'
Ballad   4'
Strum (perpetual motion) 5'

Schirmer

Symphonette No.2 (Second American Symphonette)   9'
<1935>

2 2 2 2 — 4 3 3 0 — tmp+1 — hp — str
perc: set (sd, sus cym, bd)
(The well-known *Pavane* is the 2nd movement.)
   There seems to be another instrumentation of this work, in which the
woodwinds are reduced to 1 each and the horns reduced to 2, while 4
saxophones, piano & guitar are added.
I. Moderately fast   3'
II. Pavane: Allegretto 3'
III. Very fast - racy 3'

Belwin	Kalmus

Symphony of Spirituals <1976>   27'

3[1.2.pic] 3[1.2.Eh] 3[1.2/Ebcl.3/bcl] 3[1.2.cbn] — 4 3 3 1 — tmp+3
— hp — pf — str
perc: bd, cast, chimes, claves, cym, field dr, guiro, bongos, templeblks, marac,
whip, sd, tamtam, tambn, td, tri, woodblk, 2sus cym, sandblks, 3tomtoms
Hallelujah   8'
Blues   8'
Rag   4'
Shout   7'

Schirmer

Tap Dance Concerto <1952>   16'

solo tap dancer
2[1/pic.2] 2 2 — 4 2 2 0 — tmp — str
Toccata   5'
Pantomime   3'
Minuet   4'
Rondo   4'

Chappell

Goulet, Maxime   1980-

(b Montreal, 7 June, 1980). Canadian

Chocolats symphoniques; Suite orchestrale en quatre   11'
saveurs (Symphonic Chocolates; Orchestral Suite in
Four Flavors) <2012>

2 2 2 2 — 2 2 0 0 — str
I. Chocolat au caramel (Caramel Chocolate)   2'
II. Chocolat noir (Dark Chocolate)   3'
III. Chocolat à la menthe (Mint Chocolate)   3'
IV. Chocolat au Café (Coffee-infused Chocolate) 3'

CMC

Citius, altius, fortius! (Faster, Higher, Stronger) <2008>   3'

2 2 2 2 — 4 3 3 1 — tmp+2 — str
perc: bd, cym, sus cym, tamtam, vib, sd, 3tomtom

CMC

Gounod, Charles   1818-1893

(b Paris, 17 June 1818; d Saint-Cloud, 18 Oct 1893). French

La Colombe: Entr'acte <1860>   4'

2 1 2 2 — 4 0 0 0 — 1perc — hp — str
perc: tri

Choudens	Luck's

Concertino, Flute   4'

0 2 2 2 — 2 0 0 0 — str
Ed. Dominik Sackmann.

Amadeus

Faust: Ballet Music <1852–1859>   15'

2[1.2/pic] 2 2[1.2/bcl] 2 — 4 4[2tp, 2crt] 3 1 — tmp+3 — hp — str
perc: bd, cym, tri, tambn
An error in the score makes it appear that a 3rd clarinetist is required. Not
so: the 2nd player covers bcl.
I. Dance of the Nubian Slaves   2'
II. Cleopatra and the Golden Cup   4'
III. Antique Dance   2'
IV. Dance of Cleopatra and Her Slaves 1'
V. Dance of the Trojan Maidens   2'
VI. Mirror Dance   2'
VII. Dance of the Phryne   2'

Chappell	Choudens	Kalmus	Luck's

Marche funèbre d'une marionette (Funeral March of a   6'
Marionette) <1879>

2[1.pic] 2 2 2 — 2 2[2crt] 3 1[oph] — tmp+3 — str
perc: tri, cym, bd

Bote & Bock	Kalmus	Luck's

Messe solennelle (St. Cecilia) <1883>   47'

chorus   solos STB
3[1.2.pic] 2 2 4 — 4 4[2tp, 2crt] 3 0 — tmp+2 — 6hp[1part] — org
— str
perc: cym, bd
Composer calls for *octobasse* (an obsolete form of giant double bass) in
one movement.
I. Kyrie   5'
II. Gloria   9'
III. Credo   12'
IV. Invocation—Offertoire 4'
V. Sanctus   6'
VI. Benedictus   3'
VII. Agnus Dei   4'
VIII. Dominum salvum   4'

Kalmus	Leduc	Luck's

Mors et vita: Judex <1855>   5'

2 2 2 2 — 4 3 3 0 — tmp+1 — hp — org[opt] — str
perc: bd/cym
Piano-conductor score.

Kalmus	Luck's

Petite symphonie (Little Symphony for Wind Instruments) <1885>   21'

1 2 2 2 — 2 0 0 0 — [no str]
I. Adagio et Allegretto	6'
II. Andante cantabile	6'
III. Scherzo	4'
IV. Finale	5'

Costallat	Kalmus	Luck's

Symphony No.1, D major <1855>   27'

2 2 2 2 — 2 2 0 0 — tmp — str
Ed. Bradburd/Wolf.
I. Allegro molto	7'
II. Allegretto moderato	5'
III. Scherzo: Non troppo presto	6'
IV. Finale: Adagio - Allegro vivace	9'

Kalmus	Luck's

Grainger, Percy   1882-1961

(b Brighton, Victoria, 8 July 1882; d White Plains, NY, 20 Feb 1961).
Australian-American

Children's March (Over the Hills and Far Away) <1918>   4'

2[1.pic] 2[1.Eh] 2 2 — 4 3 3 1 — tmp+7(6) — hp — opt pf — str
perc: cym, bd, sus cym, sd, tambn, tamtam, xyl, chimes, woodblk, cast, 2glock[2nd opt]
Originally for 2 pianos; orchestrated by Adolf Schmid (piano-conductor score only). Instrumentation flexible.

Schirmer

The Immovable Do (The Cyphering C) <1939>   4'

4[incl pic] 3[incl Eh] 3[incl bcl] 3[incl cbn] — 4 3 3 1 — tmp+4 — str
May be performed with: 3[incl pic] 2 2 2 — 4 3 3 1 — tmp+4 — str; or by winds without strings; or by string orchestra; or by 9 solo strings.

Schirmer

In a Nutshell <1916>   15'

3[incl pic] 3[incl ob] 3[incl opt bcl] 3[incl opt cbn] — 4 3 3 1 — tmp+8 to 12perc — hp — cel, pf — str
perc: bd, cym, sus cym, sd, woodblk, glock, tamtam, marim[2players], vib[2players], xyl, kybd glock
Arrival Platform Humlet	2'
Gay but Wistful	2'
Pastoral	8'
The Gum-Suckers March	3'

Kalmus	Luck's

Irish Tune from County Derry (Londonderry Air) <1911>   3'

0 0 0 0 — 2[opt] 0 0 0 — str
Schott also offers 2 other orchestrations of this work, by Stokowski and Adolf Schmid, respectively.

Kalmus	Luck's	Schott

Lincolnshire Posy <1937>   18'

3[1.2.pic] 3[1.2.Eh] 3[1/Ebcl.2.bcl] 2 — 4 3[1/flug.2.3] 3 1 — tmp+ — str
perc: bd, cym, sd, glock, xyl, chimes
Originally for military band; transcribed for orchestra by Joseph Kreines
   Optional: E-flat clarinet, soprano saxophone (replaces English horn), baritone horn & euphonium, handbells (briefly). May be performed with 3perc.
1. Lisbon	2'
2. Horkstow Grange	3'
3. Rufford Park Poachers (Version A)	4'
4. The Brisk Young Sailor	2'
5. Lord Melbourne	4'
6. The Lost Lady Found	3'

Aeolus

Molly on the Shore <1907>   3'

3[1.2.pic] 2 2 2 — 4 2 3 1 — tmp+4 — cel — str
perc: glock, marim, xyl
"To any or all of the original 4 string parts (2 violins, viola & cello) can be added any or all of the [winds & percussion listed]."

Kalmus	Luck's	Schott

Shepherd's Hey <1909>   3'

3[1.2.pic] 2 2 2 — 4 3 3 1 — tmp+6 — 2hp — pf — str
perc: sd, bd, cym, tri, glock, xyl
May be performed with: 2[incl pic] 2 2 2 — 4 2 3 1 — tmp+3 — hp — str. Another available version calls for: fl, cl, opt hn, concertina, 3vn 2va, 2vc, db.

Kalmus	Luck's	Schott

Granados, Enrique   1867-1916

(b Lérida, 27 July 1867; d at sea, English Channel, 24 March 1916). Spanish (Catalan) composer

Dante, op.21 <1908>   15'

alto solo
3[1.2.3/pic] 3[1.2.Eh] 3[1.2.bcl] 3[1.2.cbn] — 4 3 4 1 — 4Wagner tubas — tmp+1 — 2hp — str
Harps preferably doubled.

Schirmer

Goyescas: Intermezzo <1916>   4'

3 2[1.2/Eh] 2 3 — 4 1 3 0 — tmp+2 — 2hp — str
perc: tri, tambn, cast
From the opera Goyescas, rather than the piano work of the same name.
   There are numerous versions of this piece, all differing somewhat in instrumentation. The instrumentation given is that of the Schirmer "revised version." Two different versions from Tritó appear to be for reduced orchestra.

Luck's	Schirmer	Tritó	Ximart

Tres danzas españolas <1900>   13'

3[1.2.pic] 3[1.2.Eh] 3[1.2.bcl] 2 — 4 2 3 1 — tmp+3 — hp — str
Orchestrated by J. Lamote de Grignon.
   UME offers a reduced version, also by Grignon:
   2[1.pic] 2[1.Eh] 2[1.bcl] 1 — 2 0 2 1 — tmp+3 — hp — str
Orienta	_'
Andaluza	_'
Rondalla aragonesa	_'

Luck's	UME

Grandjany, Marcel
1891-1975

(b Paris, 3 Sept 1891; d New York, 24 Feb 1975). American composer of French birth

Aria in Classic Style <1950>
4'

solo harp
str

> AMP

Graun, Johann Gottlieb
1703-1771

(b Wahrenbruck, 1702-3; d Berlin, 27 Oct 1771). German

Concerto, Violin & Viola, C minor
23'

cnt — str

> Breitkopf   Kalmus   Luck's

Sinfonia, F major, M.95
8'

2 0 0 0 — 2 0 0 0 — str
Ed. H.T. David.

> Kalmus   Luck's

Graupner, Christoph
1683-1760

(b Kirchberg, Saxony, 13 Jan 1683; d Darmstadt, 10 May 1760). German

Concerto, Bassoon, G major
8'

cnt — str

> Kalmus   Luck's

Concerto, Oboe, F major
8'

cnt — str

> Kalmus   Luck's

Greenberg, Jay
1991-

(b New Haven, CT, 13 Dec 1991). American

Concerto, Piano Trio & Orchestra <2008>
20'

3[1.2.pic] 2[1.2/Eh] 2[1.2/bcl] 3[1.2.3/cbn] — 4 2 3 0 — tmp+2 — hp — str
perc: bd, cym, sus cym, sd, tri, tambn, tamtam, xyl, crot

> Schirmer

Concerto, Violin <2007>
25'

2[1.2/pic] 2[1.2/Eh] 2[1.2/bcl] 2[1.2/cbn] — 4 2 3 1 — tmp+3 — pf — str
perc: bd, cym, sus cym, sd, tri, tamtam, glock, xyl
One continuous movement; an alternate ending is included.

> Schirmer

Intelligent Life <2006>
32'

4[1.2.3.pic] 4[1.2.3.Eh] 4[1.2.3.bcl] 4[1.2.3.cbn] — 4 3 3 1 — tmp+2 — 2hp — pf, cel — str
perc: bd, cym, sus cym, tamtam, xyl, marim, vib, chimes
| I. The March of the Dead | _' |
| II. The Gate of the Dead | _' |

> Schirmer

Neon Refracted <2010>
25'

1[fl/pic] 1 2[1.2/bcl] 2 — 2 2 1 0 — tmp+2 — pf — str
perc: bd, cym, sus cym, hi-hat, sd, td, tri, tambn, tamtam, xyl
I. Intrata	_'
II. Aria	_'
III. Burlesca	_'
IV. Passacaglia	_'
V. Finale	_'

> Schirmer

Skyline Dances: A Terpsichorean Couplet <2008>
15'

3[1.2.3/pic] 3[1.2.3/Eh] 3 3 — 4 3 3 1 — tmp+3 — hp — str
perc: bd, cym, sus cym, sd, tri, tambn, tamtam, glock
| I. Andante maestoso | _' |
| II. Allegro vivo | _' |

> Schirmer

Symphony No.5 <2005>
34'

3[1.2.pic] 2 3[1.2.bcl] 3[1.2.cbn] — 4 3 3 1 — tmp+3 — hp — str
perc: bd, cym, sus cym, sd, tamtam, xyl, chimes
I. Allegro molto	10'
II. Scherzo: Vivace assai	6'
III. Fantasia: Lento, quasi fantasia	11'
IV. Finale: Allegro con brio e deciso	7'

> Schirmer

Grétry, André
1741-1813

(b Liège, 8 Feb 1741; d Montmorency, Seine-et-Oise, 24 Sept 1813). Liégeois, later French, composer of Walloon descent

Concerto, Flute, C major <c.1766>
14'

0 0 0 0 — 2 0 0 0 — str
Ed. Dieter Sonntag.

> Kalmus   Luck's   Peters

Zémire et Azor: Ballet Suite <1771>
14'

2[1.2/pic] 2 2 2 — 2 0 0 0 — 2perc — str
perc: tri, glock
Ed. and arr. by Thomas Beecham.

> Boosey

Grieg, Edvard
1843-1907

(b Bergen, 15 June 1843; d Bergen, 4 Sept 1907). Norwegian

At the Cloistergate, op.20 (Foran sydens kloster; Vor der Klosterpforte; Before a Southern Convent) <1871>
9'

solo soprano, alto   female choir (SSAA)
2 2 2 2 — 4 2 0 0 — tmp — hp — org — str
The score has a piano, but it looks like a reduction rather than an orchestral part.

> Luck's   Peters

Bell Ringing, op.54, no.6 (Klokkeklang) <1891; rev (orchd) 1904>
3'

2 2 2 2 — 4 2 3 1 — tmp+1 — hp — str
perc: tamtam [perhaps could be covered by tmp]
Originally for piano; orchestrated by the composer.

> Norwegian MIC

Bergliot; A Declamation with Orchestra, op.42 <1871; rev (orchd) 1885>
18'

reciter
3[1.2.pic] 2 2 2 — 4 2 3 1 — tmp+4 — str
perc: bd, cym, sus cym, sd, tri, tamtam

> Kalmus   Luck's   Peters

Concerto, Piano, op.16, A minor <1868>   30'

2[1.2/pic] 2 2 2 — 4 2 3 0 — tmp — str
Originally calling for 2 horns rather than 4. Horns 3&4 were not added
until a fourth reprinting of the concerto (Peters, 1917), based on Grieg's
revisions of 1907. The additions are largely doublings of horns 1&2, and
are sometimes omitted in modern performances.
   Piccolo plays only 11 bars near the end of the 3rd mvt.
   I. Allegro molto moderato   13'
   II. Adagio   7'
   III. Allegro moderato molto e marcato 10'

Kalmus	Luck's	Peters

Erotik, op.43, no.5 <1886>   3'

opt hp — str
Arr. Max Spicker, from a work for piano solo.

Kalmus	Luck's

Holberg Suite, op.40 (From Holberg's Time; Fra   21'
   Holbergs tid; Aus Holbergs Zeit) <1884>

str
   I. Prelude   4'
   II. Sarabande   4'
   III. Gavotte and Musette   4'
   IV. Air   5'
   V. Rigaudon   4'

Kalmus	Luck's	Peters

From Monte Pincio, op.39, no.1 (Fra Monte Pincio; Vom   5'
   Monte Pincio) <1869–1884>

solo voice (medium)
2 0 2 2 — 2 0 0 0 — 1perc — hp — str
perc: tri
Originally for voice & pf.

Luck's	Peters

In Autumn, op.11 (I høst) <1866; rev & orchd 1887>   10'

3[1.2.pic] 2 2 2 — 4 2 3 1 — tmp+3 — str
perc: tri, cym, bd

Kalmus	Peters

Landsighting, op.31 (Landkjenning) <1872>   7'

male chorus   solo baritone
2 2 2 2 — 4 2 3 1 — tmp — opt org — str

Luck's	Peters

Lyric Pieces, op.68, nos.4 & 5 (To lyriske stykker)   9'
   <1898>

0 1 0 0 — 1 0 0 0 — str
Piano works arranged by the composer.
   1. Evening in the Mountains (Aften på høfjeldet)   5'
   2. At the Cradle (Bådnlåt) [strings only]   4'

Luck's	Peters

Lyric Suite, op.54 (Lyrisk suite) <1891>   17'

3[1.2.pic] 2 2 2 — 4 2 3 1 — tmp+2 — hp — str
perc: cym, tamtam, bd
Originally for piano; orchestrated by the composer.
   Shepherd's Boy (Gjetergutt)   5'
   Gangar   4'
   Notturno   4'
   March of the Dwarfs (Trolltog) 4'

Kalmus	Luck's	Peters

Norwegian Dances, op.35 <1881>   17'

3[1.2.pic] 2 2 2 — 4 2 3 1 — tmp+2 — hp — str
perc: cym, tri
Orchestrated by Hans Sitt; originally for piano 4-hands.
   I. Allegro marcato   6'
   II. Allegretto tranquillo grazioso 2'
   III. Allegro moderato alla marcia 4'
   IV. Allegro molto   5'

Kalmus	Luck's	Peters

Old Norwegian Melody with Variations, op.51   22'
   (Gammelnorsk romanse med variasjoner) <1890; rev
   (orchd) 1900-05>

3[1.2.3/pic] 2 2 2 — 4 2 3 1 — tmp+4 — hp — str
perc: tri, sd, cym, bd
Originally for 2 pianos; orchestrated by the composer.

Kalmus	Luck's	Peters

Peer Gynt, op.23 <1874–1875; rev 1885; 1891-2>   82

solos SSSBarB   chorus
3[1/pic.2/pic.3/pic] 2 2 2 — 4 2 3 1 — tmp+4 — hp[or 2hp] — org,
   opt pf — str
perc: bd, cym, sd, tri, tambn, tamtam, xyl, chimes
26 mvts; mvt 2 orchestrated by Johan Halvorsen.
   ACT 1
   1 Bryllupsgården [At the Wedding, Prelude to Act 1]   5
   2 Halling [orchestrated by Johan Halvorsen]   1
   3 Springar [Norwegian Dances]   2
   ACT 2
   4 Bruderovet. Ingrids klage [The Abduction of the Bride. Ingrid's Lament] 4
   5 Peer Gynt og seterjentene [Peer Gynt and the Herd Girls]   4
   6 Peer Gynt og Den grønnkledte [Peer Gynt and the Woman in Green]   2
   7 Peer Gynt: 'På ridestellet skal storfolk kjendes!'   1'
   8 I Dovregubbens hall [In the Hall of the Mountain King]   3
   9 Dans av Dovregubbens datter [Dance of the Mountain King's Daughter] 2
   10 Peer Gynt jages av troll [Peer Gynt Hunted by the Trolls]   3
   11 Peer Gynt og Bøygen [Peer Gynt and The Bøyg]   5
   ACT 3
   12 Åses død [The Death of Åse, Prelude to Act 3]   4
   ACT 4
   13 Morgenstemning [Morning Mood]   4
   14 Tyven og heleren [The Thief and the Receiver]   1
   15 Arabisk dans [Arabian Dance]   5
   16 Anitras dans [Anitra's Dance]   3
   17 Peer Gynts serenade [Peer Gynt's Serenade]   3
   18 Peer Gynt og Anitra [Peer Gynt and Anitra]   3
   19 Solveigs sang [Solveig's Song]   5
   20 Peer Gynt ved Memnonstøtten [Peer Gynt at the Statue of Memnon]   2
   ACT 5
   21 Peer Gynts hjemfart. Stormfull aften ved havet [Homecoming. Stormy] 3
   22 Skipsforliset [The Shipwreck]   1
   23 Solveig synger i hytten [Solveig Sings in the Hut]   2
   24 Nattscene [Night Scene]   8
   25 Pinsesalme: Velsignede morgen [Whitsun Hymn: Oh Blessed Morning]   1
   26 Solveigs vuggevise [Solveig's Cradle Song]   6

Kalmus

Peer Gynt: Prelude (I bryllupsgarden; Im Hochzeitshof)   10
   <1874–1875; rev 1885, 1891-2, 1902>

3[1.2.pic] 2 2 2 — 4 2 3 0 — tmp — hp — str
Includes backstage viola solo.

Kalmus	Luck's

Peer Gynt: Suite No.1, op.46 <1874–1875; rev 1885>   15'

3[1.2.pic] 2 2 2 — 4 2 3 1 — tmp+2 — str
perc: tri, cym, bd
From the incidental music, nos. 13, 12, 16, 8.
The 2nd mvt (*Ase's Death*) is for strings only. The 3rd mvt (*Anitra's Dance*) is for strings and triangle only, and may be performed by 9 solo strings [2.2.2.2.1].

Morning (Morgenstemning)		*4'*
Ase's Death (Ases død)		*4'*
Anitra's Dance (Anitras dans)		*4'*
In the Hall of the Mountain King (I dovregubbens hall)		*3'*

Kalmus	Luck's	Peters

Peer Gynt: Suite No.2, op.55 <1874–1875; rev 1885; 1890-92>   15'

3[1/pic.2.pic] 2 2 2 — 4 2 3 1 — tmp+4 — hp — str
perc: tri, sd, cym, bd; tambn [played by timpanist]
From the incidental music, nos. 4, 15, 21, 19.

Abduction of the Bride & Ingrid's Lament (Bruderovet, & Ingrids klage)	*3'*
Arabian Dance (Arabisk dans)	*4'*
Peer Gynt's Homeward Journey (Peer Gynts hjemfart)	*4'*
Solveig's Song (Solveigs sang)	*4'*

Kalmus	Luck's	Peters

Sigurd Jorsalfar, op.56: Three Orchestral Pieces <1872; rev 1892>   18'

2[1/pic.2/pic] 2 2 2 — 4 3 3 1 — tmp+3 — hp — str
perc: sd, cym, bd, tri

1. Prelude (In the King's Hall; Ved mannjevningen)	*4'*
2. Intermezzo (Borghild's Dream; Borghilds drøm)	*5'*
3. Triumphal March (Hyldningsmarsj; Huldigungsmarsch)	*9'*

Kalmus	Luck's	Peters

Symphonic Dances (Symfoniske danser), op.64 <1896–1897>   30'

3[1.2.pic] 2 2 2 — 4 2 3 1 — tmp/tri — hp — str
perc: tri (can be covered by timpanist)

I. Allegro moderato e marcato	*7'*
II. Allegretto grazioso	*7'*
III. Allegro giocoso	*5'*
IV. Andante - Allegro molto e risoluto	*11'*

C. Fischer	Kalmus	Luck's

Symphony, C minor <1863–1864>   32'

2 2 2 2 — 2 2 3 0 — tmp — str
Composed 1863-1864; withdrawn 1867. The Musikproduktion Höflich (mph) score and parts (2014) are edited by Klaus Henning Oelmann and Marius Hristescu.

1. Allegro molto	*12'*
2. Adagio expressivo	*7'*
3. Intermezzo: Allegro energico	*5'*
4. Finale: Allegro molto vivace	*8'*

mph	Peters

Two Elegiac Melodies, op.34 (To elegiske melodier) <1881>   9'

str

Heartwounds (Hjertesår)	*4'*
Last Spring (Våren)	*5'*

Kalmus	Luck's	Peters

Two Melodies, op.53 (To melodier) <1891>   8'

str
Originally for voice & piano.

Norwegian (Norsk)	*4'*
The First Meeting (Det første møte)	*4'*

Kalmus	Luck's	Peters

Two Norwegian Airs, op.63 (Nordiske melodier) <1869>   11'

str
Originally for piano; orchestrated by the composer.

Popular Song (I folketonestil) [melody by Fredrik Due]	*6'*
Cow Keeper's Tune and Country Dance (Kulokk og Stabbelåtten).	*5'*

Kalmus	Luck's

Wedding Day at Troldhaugen, op.65, no.6 (Bryllupsdag på Troldhaugen) <1896>   6'

2 2 2 2 — 4 2 3 1 — 2perc — str
This popular work, originally for piano, exists in several arrangements with various instrumentations. The above version is that of **Luck's**, arr. Theo. M. Tobani. Other versions:
  Schirmer (arr. Morton Gould): 2222-4331-tmp+perc-cel, hp-str.
  Peters (arr. Breuer): 2222-4230-tmp+perc-hp-str.
  Kalmus (arr. Huppertz): 1121-3210-perc-str (reprint of a different Peters arrangement; piano-conductor score only).

Luck's	Schirmer	Peters	Kalmus

Griffes, Charles Tomlinson   1884-1920

(b Elmira, NY, 17 Sept 1884; d New York, 8 April 1920). American

Bacchanale <1919>   5'

3[1.2.pic] 3[1.2.Eh] 3[1.2.bcl] 4[1.2.3.cbn] — 4 3 3 1 — tmp+2 — 2hp — cel — str
perc: cym, tambn, sus cym, tamtam, bd
A version of the *Scherzo* for piano (1913); orchestrated by the composer in 1919.
G. Schirmer score and parts are in the original key of E-flat minor. Fleisher Collection parts (but not the score) have been transposed to the key of E minor (more practical for the musicians).

Fleisher	Schirmer

Clouds <1916; rev 1919>   5'

3[1.2.3/pic] 3[1.2.3/Eh] 3[1.2.bcl] 3[1.2.cbn] — 4 0 0 0 — 1perc — 2hp — cel — str
perc: tamtam
Originally a piano piece: No.4 of the *Roman Sketches*, op.7; orchestrated by the composer.

Schirmer

The Pleasure Dome of Kubla Khan, op.8 <1912–1915; rev 1917>   13'

3[1.2.3/pic] 3[1.2.Eh] 3[1.2.bcl] 3 — 4 3 3 1 — tmp+2 — 2hp — cel, pf — str
perc: bd, cym, gong, tambn
Originally for piano; orchestrated by the composer, 1917.
  Kalmus edition (ed. Gregory Vaught, 1996) is the composer's original orchestration.
  The G. Schirmer edition is a reworking of the score by the conductor Frederick Stock, originally published in 1929, with changes in dynamics, phrasing, and orchestration. First printings (with plate no. 46121) make no mention of Stock's participation, though later reprints (no plate no.) do, and they also provide helpful prefatory material by Donna K. Anderson, Griffes' biographer. Although described as "combining Griffes' original version with Frederick Stock's 1920 revisions," this is misleading to say the least; it is Stock's version with a few footnotes thrown in, and of course the preface to provide context.
  The Luck's edition appears to be a reprint of Schirmer.

Kalmus	Luck's	Schirmer

Poem for Flute and Orchestra <1918>   9'

0 0 0 0 — 2 0 0 0 — 2perc — hp — str
perc: sd, bd, gong, tambn

Luck's	Schirmer

The White Peacock <1915; rev 1919>   6'

2[1.2/pic] 2 2 2 — 2 3 2 0 — tmp+1 — 2hp — cel — str
perc: cym, tamtam
Originallly a piano piece: No.1 of the *Roman Sketches*, op.7, orchestrated by the composer.

| Luck's | Schirmer |

Grimm, Julius Otto   1827-1903

(b 6 Mar, Pernau, Livonia [now Pärnu, Estonia]; d 7 Dec 1903, Münster, Ger). German

Suite in Canonform, op.10 <c.1865>   23'

str
Out of print; original publisher J. Rieter-Biedermann, 1866.
1. Allegro con brio	*6'*
2. Andante lento	*5'*
3. Tempo di minuetto, ben moderato	*7'*
4. Allegro risoluto	*5'*

| Fleisher |

Symphony, D minor, op.19   30'

2 2 2 2 — 4 2 3 0 — tmp — str
Out of print. Original publisher J. Rieter-Biedermann, 1875. Score available at IMSLP.org.
1. Sostenuto; Allegro	_'
2. Trauermarsch: Andante	_'
3. Scherzo: Presto	_'
4. Finale: Allegro vivace	_'

Grofé, Ferde   1892-1972

(b New York, 27 March 1892; d Santa Monica, CA, 3 April 1972). American

Grand Canyon Suite <1931>   33'

3[1.2.3/pic] 3[1.2.Eh] 3[1.2.bcl] 3[1.2.cbn] — 4 3 3 1 — tmp+3 — hp — pf/cel — str
perc: glock, tri, chimes, bd, sd, wnd mach, vib, horse hooves, 2sus cym, "lightning machine" [one bar]
Sunrise	5'
Painted Desert	6'
On the Trail	8'
Sunset	5'
Cloudburst	9'

| Luck's | Robbins |

Kentucky Derby; A Tone Poem <1938>   7'

3 3[1.2.Eh] 3[1.2.bcl] 3[1.2.cbn] — 4 3 3 1 — tmp+3 — hp — cel — str
perc: set, xyl, chimes, sandblks, popgun, elecbell, horse hooves
Ed. Lucas Richman.

| LeDor |

Mississippi Suite <1925>   11'

3[1.2.pic] 3[1.2.3/Eh] 3[1.2.bcl] 3[1.2.cbn] — 4 3 3 1 — tmp+3 — hp — str
perc: bd, chimes, cym, glock, sd, sus cym, 2tomtoms, tri, woodblk, whistle, sandblks
A number of arrangements, adaptations and reductions of this work exist; e.g., a version for smaller orchestra, calling for winds:
1 1/Eh 2 1 — 2 3 2 0 — 4sx
I. Father of Waters	3'
II. Huckleberry Finn	2'
III. Old Creole Days	2'
IV. Mardi Gras	4'

| Luck's | Robbins | Schirmer |

Gross, Murray   1955-

(b Buffalo, NY, 8 Nov 1955). American

Reaching <1990>   12'

solo clarinet
1 1 0 1 — 2 2 1 0 — str

| Gross |

Watchman, Tell Us of the Night <1992>   7'

0 0 0 0 — 4 3 3 0 — [no str]
2tp are stereophonically separated, perhaps backstage, at the beginning; then move into the group.

| Gross |

You Must Remember This... <2004>   14'

3[1.2.pic] 3[1.2.Eh] 3[1.2.bcl] 3[1.2.cbn] — 4 3 3 1 — tmp+3 — hp — str
perc: crot, marim, xyl, vib, tri, tamtam, glock, woodblk, bd, 3sus cym, bass bow, 4tomtoms

| Gross |

Gruber, H[einz] K[arl]   1943-

(b Vienna, 3 Jan 1943). Austrian

Concerto, Violoncello <1989>   22'

1[incl pic] 1 1 1 — 1 1 1 0 — 1perc — pf — str[min 1.1.1.1.1]
perc: marim, vib, glock, tri, sd, bd, hi-hat, xylorimba

| Boosey |

Frankenstein!! A Pan-Demonium for Chansonnier & Ensemble <1976-77>   28'

baritone chansonnier
1[1/pic] 1 1 1 — 3 1 1 1 — tmp+2 — hp — cel — str
perc: xyl, vib, flexatone, set, sd, hi-hat, bongos, sus cym, tri, cowbell, woodblk, guiro, tambn, bd/ped, 4tomtoms, 2 tuned gongs, slide whistle
Baritone and all players (except strings) double on an array of toy instruments, which are available with the rental material.
    An alternate version for baritone & 12 instruments is available:
    1[incl pic] 0 1 1 — 1 1 0 0 — 1perc — pf — str[1.1.1.1.1]

| Boosey |

Nebelsteinmusik (Violin Concerto No.2) <1988>   17'

solo violin
str[min 2.2.2.1]
Requires a five-string double bass.
1. This Is My Home	4'
2. Im Herzschlag (In time with the heartbeat)	6'
3. Cadenza	4'
4. Concertino	3'

| Boosey |

Gruenberg, Louis   1884-1964

(b nr Brest-Litovsk [now Brest], 22 July/3 Aug 1884; d Beverly Hills, CA, 10 June 1964). American composer of Russian origin

Concerto, Violin, op.47 <1944>   37'

3[1.2.3/pic] 3[1.2.Eh] 3[1.2.bcl] 3[1.2.cbn] — 4 3 3 1 — harmonica — tmp+3 — hp — cel/pf — str

| Fleisher |

The Creation; A Negro Sermon for Voice and Eight Instruments, op.23 <1925>   22'

medium voice
1 0 1 1[or vc] — 1 0 0 0 — tmp+1 — pf — va

    Gunmar

Gubaydulina, Sofiya Asgatovna   1931-

(b Chistopol', 24 Oct 1931). Russian composer resident in Germany

Feast During a Plague <2006>   25'

4[1.2.3/pic.4/pic] 4 4[1.2.3/Ebcl.bcl] 4[1.2.3.4/cbn] — 6 4 3 1 — audio CD — tmp+3 — 2hp — pf/cel — str
perc: cym, tri, tamtam, glock, marim, vib, chimes, marktree, 4bd, 3sus cym, 2sd, bellplates

    Russian

The Light of the End (Svyet kontsa) <2003>   24'

4[1.2.afl.4/pic] 3[1.Eh.heckl] 3[1.2.bcl] 3[1.2.cbn] — 4 3 3[1.2.cb tbn] 1 — tmp+5 — hp — str[min 16.14.12.10.8]
perc: bd, cym, tamtam, glock, marim, vib, crot, marktree, 5sus cym, 2chimes, 2antique cym[C5,Db5], 2bellplates[G#2,A2]

    Russian

Offertorium; Concerto for Violin & Orchestra <1980–1986>   40'

solo violin
3[1.2.pic] 2 3[incl Ebcl] 2 — 3 3 3 1 — tmp+4 — 2hp — pf/cel — str[16.14.12.10.8]
perc: tri, templeblks, tamtam, glock, bd, xyl, marim, whip, vib, crot, chimes, sd, 3sus cym, 3woodblks, 5bongos, 5tomtoms
Graphic notation.

    Sikorski

Two Paths (A Dedication to Mary and Martha)   24'

2 solo violas
3[1.2/bfl.pic] 2 4[1.2.Ebcl.bcl] 3[1.2.cbn] — 4 3 3[tbn, btbn, cb tbn] 1 — tmp+5 — cel, pf — str
perc: glock, vib, marim, crot, chimes, tamtam, sd, marktree, bellplates, 4gong
A concerto for two violas & orchestra.

    Russian

Guilmant, Alexandre   1837-1911

(b Boulogne-sur-Mer, 12 March 1837; d Meudon, 29 March 1911). French

Symphony No.1, Organ & Orchestra, op.42 <1879>   23'

2 2 2 2 — 4 2 3 1 — tmp+2 — str
perc: bd, cym
    I. Introduction & Allegro   9'
    II. Pastorale   7'
    III. Final   7'

    Kalmus   Luck's   Schott

Gutche, Gene   1907-2000

(b Berlin, 3 July 1907; d 2000). American composer born in Germany

Epimetheus USA, op.46 <1969>   8'

3[1.2.3/pic] 3[1.2.3/Eh] 3[1.2.Ebcl] 3[1.2.cbn] — 4 4 3 1 — asx — tmp+3 — str

    Galaxy

Holofernes Overture, op.27, no.1 <1958>   9'

3[1.2/opt afl.pic] 3[1.2.3/Eh] 3[1.2.3/bcl] 3[1.2.cbn] — 4 4[tp 3-4 opt] 3 1 — opt asx — tmp+8 — str
May be performed with 3 percussionists.

    Highgate

Perseus and Andromeda XX, op.50 <1976>   17'

3 3[1.2.3/Eh] 3[1.2.Ebcl] 3[1.2.cbn] — 4 4 3 1 — asx — tmp+5 — str
Originally published by Regus, the composer's own imprint.

    Fleisher

Symphony No.5, op.34 <1962>   17'

str
    I. = 96   6'
    II. Burletta   3'
    III. Mesto   4'
    IV. Lesto (agile, nimble, quick)   4'

    Highgate

Symphony No.6 <1971>   27'

3[1.2.3/pic] 3[1.2.3/Eh] 3[1.2/bcl.Ebcl] 3[1.2.cbn] — 4 4 3 1 — tmp+4 — hp — str

    Highgate

Guy-Ropartz, Joseph   1864-1955

see: Ropartz, Joseph Guy, 1864-1955

Guzzo, Anne   1968-

(b Laramie, WY, 1 July 1968). American

Fanfare for Mountains and Peace <2007>   6'

3[1.2.pic] 3 3 3 — 3 3 3 1 — tmp+4 — hp — str
perc: bd, cym, sus cym, tri, chimes, crot, slgh-bells, windchimes [alt for South American instrument], 2tomtoms, fingercym

    Guzzo

H

Hadley, Henry   1871-1937

(b Somerville, MA, 20 Dec 1871; d New York, 6 Sept 1937). American

Salome, op.55 <1905–1906>   24'
3[1.2.3/pic] 3[1.2.Eh] 3[1.2.bcl] 3[1.2.cbn] — 4 4 3 1 — tmp+2 — 2hp — str
perc: bd, cym, tambn, tri, tamtam, glock, sus cym

Fleisher	Ries

San Francisco, op.121 <1931>   12'
3[1.2.3/pic] 3[1/ob d'am.2.Eh] 3[1.2.bcl] 2 — 4 3 3 1 — tmp+3 — hp — str

The Harbor	_'
Chinese Quarter	_'
Mardi Gras	_'

Birchard	Fleisher

Symphony No.2, op.30, F minor (The Four Seasons; Die vier Jahreszeiten) <1901>   36'
3[1.2.pic] 2[1.2/Eh] 2 2 — 4 2 3 1 — tmp+2 — str
perc: bd, cym, glock, tri

Winter	11'
Spring	7'
Summer	10'
Autumn	8'

Fleisher	Schmidt

Hagen, Daron Aric   1961-

(b Milwaukee, 4 Nov 1961). American

Gesture Drawings <2005>   18'
3 3 3 3 — 4 3 3 1 — tmp+3 — pf/cel — str
perc: cym, sd, tri, tamtam, chimes

1. Tones in Black and White (Chaconne)	6'
2. Koine (Passacaglia)	3'
3. To Wash Our Souls (Melodia & Chorale)	5'
4. Day Lily in Pastel (Theme & Variations)	4'

C. Fischer

Hahn, Reynaldo   1875-1947

(b Caracas, 9 Aug 1875; d Paris, 28 Jan 1947). French composer of Venezuelan birth

Le Bal de Beatrice d'Este: Suite <1905>   18
2[1/pic.2] 1 2 2 — 2 1 0 0 — tmp+1 — 2hp — pf — [no str]
perc: cym, sus cym, tri
The 2hp mostly double a single part.
   Original score and parts are riddled with errors. A critical edition and dissertation by Jared Chase for the University of Cincinnati College-Conservatory of Music may be found at:
   http://rave.ohiolink.edu/etdc/view?acc_num=ucin1298394760
   A score and set of parts for this edition may be acquired by contacting Mr. Chase directly at chase.jared@gmail.com or through his website, www.jaredgchase.com.

Entrée pour Ludovic le More	2'
Lesquercade	4'
Romanesque	3'
Ibérienne	2'
Léda et l'Oiseau	2'
Courante	4'
Salut final au Duc de Milan	1'

Heugel	Kalmus	Luck's

Concerto, Piano, E major <1931>   27
2[incl pic] 2[incl Eh] 2 2 — 4 2 3 0 — tmp+2 — hp — str

Modéré	13'
Danse	3'
Réverie, Toccata et Finale	11'

Heugel

Concerto, Violoncello (Inachevé; Unfinished)   22
2 2 2 2 — 2 2 0 0 — str[5.4.3.2.2]
Revision & cadenza by Fernand Pollain under the direction of the composer; orchestration by M.F. Gaillard.

Salabert

Mozart: Overture <1925>   5
2 1 1 1 — 2 1 0 0 — pf — str

Heugel

Hailstork, Adolphus   1941-

(b Rochester, NY, 17 April 1941). American

An American Port of Call <1984>   10
3[1.2.3/pic] 2 2 3[1.2.3/cbn] — 4 3 3 1 — tmp+3 — pf — str
perc: bd, cym, sus cym, sd, td, tri, tamtam, glock, xyl, woodblk, whip, 2gong

Presser

Celebration <1974>   3
3[1.2.pic] 3 3 2 — 4 3 3 1 — tmp+5 — str
perc: cym, sus cym, sd, td, tri, tamtam, gong, glock, xyl, chimes, whip, cast, 4tomtoms, opt rototom
This work may be out of print.

Wimbledon

Earthrise <2005>   28
two choruses
2[1.2/pic] 2 2 2[1.2/cbn] — 4 3 3 1 — tmp+2 — hp — pf — str
perc: bd, sus cym, tamtam, xyl, marim, bongos, afuche, 3tomtom
One of the choruses should be African-American. Brief soprano solo (member of the African-American chorus).

Presser

HAILSTORK, ADOLPHUS 1941-

Fanfare on "Amazing Grace" <2003> 3'

2 2 3 2 — 2 3 3 1 — tmp+1 — str
perc: cym
Another version exists for brass quintet, timpani & organ.

> Presser

Symphony No.3 <2002> 41'

3[1.2.3/pic] 2[1.2/Eh] 2 2 — 4 3 3 1 — tmp+3 — str
perc: timbales, marac, xyl, glock, sus cym, cym, marim, vib, tri, tabla, 2cowbell
1. Vivace 12'
2. Moderato 12'
3. Scherzo 5'
4. Finale 12'

> Presser

Halévy, Fromental 1799-1862

b Paris, 27 May 1799; d Nice, 17 March 1862). French

La Juive: Overture <1835> 13'

3[1.2.pic] 2 2 2 — 4 4 3 1[oph] — tmp+3 — str

> Bärenreiter   Kalmus   Luck's

Halffter, Ernesto 1905-1989

b Madrid, 16 Jan 1905; d Madrid, 5 July 1989). Spanish

La muerte de Carmen (The Death of Carmen): Habanera <1931> 9'

3[incl pic] 3[incl Eh] 3[incl bcl] 3 — 4 3 3 1 — tmp+6 — 2hp — str

> Eschig

Halvorsen, Johan 1864-1935

b Drammen, 15 March 1864; d Oslo, 4 Dec 1935). Norwegian

Entry of the Boyars (Bojarernes intogsmarsch; Einzugsmarsch der Bojaren) <1893> 5'

2[1.pic] 2 2 — 4 2 3 1 — 3perc — str
perc: bd, cym, sd, tri

> Kalmus   Luck's

Hamilton, Iain 1922-2000

b Glasgow, 6 June 1922; d London, 21 July 2000). Scottish

Circus <1969> 17'

2 solo trumpets
2 2 2 2 — 4 0 3 1 — ampd gtr — tmp+1 — hp — pf — str

> Presser

Voyage, for Horn & Chamber Orchestra <1970> 18'

1[incl pic] 1 1[incl Ebcl] 0 — 0 2 1 0 — 1perc — pf — str[single str or sections]
perc: chimes, glock, crot, td, tamtam, bd, windchimes, 3sus cym

> Presser

Handel, George Frideric 1685-1759

b Halle, 23 Feb 1685; d London, 14 April 1759). German; naturalized English from 1726

HWV = *Händel Werke Verzeichnis*, referring to the numeration of works in the *Händel-Handbuch*, i–iv (Leipzig, 1978–85)

Acis and Galatea, HWV 49a: Overture <1718; rev 1732-1736> 4'

0 2 0 0 — cnt — str

> Bärenreiter

Acis and Galatea, HWV 49a: Overture (arr. Mozart) <1732> 4'

0 2 2 2 — 2 0 0 0 — str
Clarinets, bassoons & horns added by Mozart (K.566). Ed. Berthold Tours.

> Fleisher   Novello

Agrippina, HWV 6: Overture <1708> 7'

0 1 0 0 — cnt — str

> Breitkopf   Kalmus   Luck's

Alceste, HWV 45: Instrumental Pieces <1749–1750> 10'

0 2 0 1 — 0 1 0 0 — cnt — str
Ed. H.T. David.
Overture _'
Symphony _'
Grand Entrée _'

> Kalmus   Luck's

Alcina, HWV 34: Overture <1735> 5'

0 2[opt] 0 0 — cnt — str
Published as *Festival Music (Overture and Dances from* Alcina*) for String Orchestra.*

> Hofmeister   Kalmus   Luck's

Alessandro, HWV 21: Overture <1726> 6'

0 2 0 0 — cnt — str

> Bärenreiter

Alexander's Feast, HWV 75 <1736> 85'

chorus solos STB
2[rec1.rec2] 2 0 3 — 2 2 0 0 — tmp — cnt — str
Parte Prima 56'
Parte Seconda 29'

> Bärenreiter   Kalmus

Alexander's Feast, HWV 75: Overture <1736> 5'

0 2 0 0 — cnt — str

> Bärenreiter   Kalmus   Luck's

L'Allegro, il penseroso ed il moderato, HWV 55 <1740> 98'

chorus solos SATB
2[rec1.rec2] 2 0 2 — 2 2 0 0 — tmp — cnt — str
perc: carillon
Part I 51'
Part II 47'

> Bärenreiter   Kalmus

Belshazzar, HWV 61 <1744> 147'

chorus solos SAATTBB
0 2 0 0 — 0 2 0 0 — tmp — cnt — str
Act I 78'
Act II 36'
Act III 33'

> Bärenreiter   Peters

Belshazzar, HWV 61: Overture <1744> 6'

0 2 0 1 — cnt — str

> Bärenreiter   Kalmus

Brockes' Passion, HWV 48

see his: Passion nach Barthold Heinrich Brockes

The Choice of Hercules, HWV 69 <1751>   55'

chorus   solos SSAT

2 2 0 1 — 2 2 0 0 — cnt — str

Bärenreiter	Novello			

Concerto, Harp, op.4, no.6, HWV 294, B-flat major <1736>   12'

2[rec1.rec2] 0 0 1 — cnt — str

Solo part is for harp or organ.

   I. Andante allegro   *4'*
   II. Larghetto   *6'*
   III. Allegro moderato   *2'*

Bärenreiter	Breitkopf	Luck's	Peters	Schott

Concerto, Oboe, No.1, HWV 301, B-flat major <1703–1706>   8'

cnt — str

Also known as *Concerto Grosso No.8.*

   I. Adagio   *2'*
   II. Allegro   *2'*
   III. Siciliana: Largo   *2'*
   IV. Vivace   *2'*

Breitkopf	Kalmus	Luck's

Concerto, Oboe, No.2, HWV 302, B-flat major <1703–1706>   9'

cnt — str[no va]

Also known as *Concerto Grosso No.9.*

   I. Vivace   *2'*
   II. Allegro   *2'*
   III. Andante   *3'*
   IV. Allegro   *2'*

Breitkopf	Kalmus	Luck's

Concerto, Oboe, No.3, HWV 303, G minor <1703–1709>   8'

cnt — str

Also known as *Concerto Grosso No.10.*

   I. Grave   *_'*
   II. Allegro   *_'*
   III. Sarabande   *_'*
   IV. Allegro   *_'*

Breitkopf	Kalmus	Luck's

Concerto, Oboe, E-flat major <1740>   10'

cnt — str

Ed. Fritz Stein, with added embellishments. The work is probably spurious.

   I. Largo   *_'*
   II. Allegro   *_'*
   III. Largo   *_'*
   IV. Vivace   *_'*

Peters

Concerto, Organ, op.4, no.1, HWV 289, G minor <1736>   16'

0 2 0 1 — cnt — str

Breitkopf ed. Ton Koopman; Breitkopf numbering: *No.1.*

   I. Larghetto e staccato   *5'*
   II. Allegro   *6'*
   III. Adagio   *1'*
   IV. Andante   *4'*

Bärenreiter	Breitkopf	Kalmus	Luck's	Schott

Concerto, Organ, op.4, no.2, HWV 290, B-flat major <1735>   10

0 2 0 1 — cnt — str

Breitkopf ed. Ton Koopman; Breitkopf numbering: *No.2.*

   I. A tempo ordinario e staccato   *1'*
   II. Allegro   *5'*
   III. Adagio e staccato & IV. Allegro, ma non presto   *4'*

Bärenreiter	Breitkopf	Kalmus	Luck's	Schott

Concerto, Organ, op.4, no.3, HWV 291, G minor <1735>   12

solo vn & solo vc, in addition to solo organ

0 2 0 1 — cnt — str

Breitkopf ed. Ton Koopman; Breitkopf numbering: *No.3.*

   I. Adagio   *4'*
   II. Allegro   *4'*
   III. Adagio   *1'*
   IV. Allegro   *3'*

Bärenreiter	Breitkopf	Kalmus	Luck's	Schott

Concerto, Organ, op.4, no.4, HWV 292, F major <1735>   16

0 2 0 1 — cnt — str

Breitkopf ed. Ton Koopman; Breitkopf numbering: *No.4.*

   I. Allegro   *4'*
   II. Andante   *7'*
   III. Adagio   *2'*
   IV. Allegro   *3'*

Bärenreiter	Breitkopf	Kalmus	Luck's	Schott

Concerto, Organ, op.4, no.5, HWV 293, F major <1735>   7

0 2 0 1 — cnt — str

Breitkopf ed. Ton Koopman; Breitkopf numbering: *No.5.*

   I. Larghetto   *2'*
   II. Allegro   *2'*
   III. Alla siciliana   *1'*
   IV. Presto   *2'*

Bärenreiter	Breitkopf	Kalmus	Luck's	Schott

Concerto, Organ, op.4, no.6, HWV 294, B-flat major <1736>   12

2[rec1.rec2] 0 0 1 — cnt — str

Solo part for organ or harp.

Breitkopf ed. Ton Koopman; Breitkopf numbering: *No.6.*

   I. Andante allegro   *4'*
   II. Larghetto   *6'*
   III. Allegro moderato   *2'*

Bärenreiter	Breitkopf	Kalmus	Peters	Schott

Concerto, Organ, op.7, no.1, HWV 306, B-flat major <1740>   11

0 2 0 1 — cnt — str

Breitkopf ed. Ton Koopman; Breitkopf numbering: *No.7.*

   I. Andante   *4'*
   II. Andante   *3'*
   III. Largo e piano   *2'*
   IV. Bourrée: Allegro   *2'*

Bärenreiter	Breitkopf	Kalmus	Schott

Concerto, Organ, op.7, no.2, HWV 307, A major <1743>   16

0 2 0 1 — cnt — str

Breitkopf ed. Ton Koopman; Breitkopf numbering: *No.8.*

   I. Ouverture: Grave   *7'*
   II. A tempo ordinario: Allegro (1 & 2)   *3'*
   III. Organo ad libitum: Adagio & IV. Allegro   *6'*

Breitkopf	Kalmus	Luck's	Schott

Concerto, Organ, op.7, no.3, HWV 308, B-flat major <1751>   16'

0 2 0 1 — cnt — str
Breitkopf ed. Ton Koopman; Breitkopf numbering: *No.9*.

I. Allegro	5'		
II. Spirituoso	3'		
III. Menuet	4'		
IV. Menuet	4'		

Breitkopf	Kalmus	Luck's	Schott

Concerto, Organ, op.7, no.4, HWV 309, D minor <1740–1750>   16'

0 2 0 2 — cnt — str
Breitkopf ed. Ton Koopman; Breitkopf numbering: *No.10*.

Adagio	6'
Allegro	4'
Organo ad libitum	3'
Allegro	3'

Breitkopf	Kalmus	Luck's	Schott

Concerto, Organ, op.7, no.5, HWV 310, G minor <1750>   13'

0 2 0 1 — cnt — str
Breitkopf ed. Ton Koopman; Breitkopf numbering: *No.11*.

I. Allegro ma non troppo; e staccato	4'
II. Andante larghetto; e staccato - Adagio	5'
III. Menuett	2'
IV. Gavotte	2'

Breitkopf	Kalmus	Luck's	Schott

Concerto, Organ, op.7, no.6, HWV 311, B-flat major <1749>   10'

0 2 0 1 — cnt — str
Breitkopf ed. Ton Koopman; Breitkopf numbering: *No.12*.

I. Pomposo	3'
II. Adagio; quasi una fantasia	3'
III. A tempo ordinario	4'

Breitkopf	Luck's	Schott

Concerto, Organ, HWV 295, F major (The Cuckoo and the Nightingale) <1739>   14'

0 2 0 1 — cnt — str
Breitkopf ed. Ton Koopman; Breitkopf numbering: *No.13*.

I. Larghetto	2'
II. Allegro ("The Cuckoo and the Nightingale")	3'
III. Organo ad libitum	?'
IV. Larghetto	3'
V. Allegro	3'

Bärenreiter	Breitkopf	Kalmus	Luck's

Concerto, Organ, HWV 296a, A major <1739>   18'

0 2 0 1 — cnt — str
Breitkopf ed. Ton Koopman; Breitkopf numbering: *No.14*.

I. Largo e staccato	5'
II. Organo ad libitum	1'
III. Andante	4'
IV. Grave	1'
V. Allegro	7'

Breitkopf

Concerto, Organ, HWV 304, D minor <1739>   12'

cnt — str
Breitkopf ed. Ton Koopman; Breitkopf numbering: *No.15*.

I. Andante	_'
II. Organo ad libitum	_'
III. Allegro	_'

Breitkopf	Kalmus	Luck's

Concerto, Organ, HWV 305a, F major <1746>   18'

0 2 0 1 — cnt — str
Breitkopf ed. Ton Koopman; Breitkopf numbering: *No.16*.

I. Ouverture	2'
II. Allegro	3'
III. Allegro ma non troppo	4'
IV. Adagio	1'
V. Andante	4'
VI. Allegro	2'
VII. Marche: Allegro	2'

Breitkopf	Kalmus

Concerto, Viola, B minor <1925>   12'

2 0 0 2 — str
Perhaps a pastiche of movements from various works of Handel, compiled and arranged as a viola concerto by Henri Casadesus. Alternatively, this may be a complete forgery by Casdesus.

I. Allegro moderato	5'
II. Andante ma non troppo	4'
III. Allegro molto	3'

Eschig	Luck's

Concerto a due cori, No.1, HWV 332, B-flat major <1747>   14'

0 4 0 2 — cnt — str
Breitkopf title is *Concerto grosso No.27*, ed. Max Seiffert. Kalmus and Luck's sets are from manuscripts of unknown provenance.

Two separated orchestras are intended, but the parts are confusingly laid out in the Breitkopf edition; two sets of parts may be needed. 2nd mvt of this work is an instrumental version of *And the glory of the Lord*, from Handel's *Messiah*, though in B-flat major rather than A major.

I. Ouverture	1'
II. Allegro ma non troppo	3'
III. Allegro	2'
IV. Lento	1'
V. Allegro	2'
VI. Alla breve [Moderato]	2'
VII. Menuets	3'

Bärenreiter	Breitkopf	Kalmus	Luck's

Concerto a due cori, No.2, HWV 333, F major <1747>   16'

0 4 0 2 — 4 0 0 0 — cnt — str
Some authorities believe this and the *Concerto a due cori No.3* are actually a single work. Breitkopf title for *No.2* is *Concerto grosso No.28*, ed. Max Seiffert. Kalmus and Luck's sets are heavily edited copies — editing attributed to "Kogel" — and differ substantially from the original text.

3rd mvt of this work is an instrumental version of *Lift up your heads* from Handel's *Messiah*.

Pomposo	2'
Allegro	2'
A tempo giusto	3'
Largo	2'
Allegro non troppo	4'
A tempo ordinario	3'

Bärenreiter	Breitkopf	Kalmus	Luck's

Concerto a due cori, No.3, HWV 334, F major <1747>   13'

0 4 0 2 — 4 0 0 0 — cnt — str
Some authorities believe this and the *Concerto a due cori No.2* are actually a single work. Breitkopf title for *No.3* is *Concerto grosso No.29*, ed. Max Seiffert. Kalmus and Luck's sets are of unknown provenance.

1. Overture	1'
2. Allegro	3'
3. Allegro ma non troppo	3'
4. Adagio	1'
5. Andante larghetto	3'
6. Allegro	2'

Bärenreiter	Breitkopf	Kalmus	Luck's

Concerto grosso, op.3, no.1, HWV 312, B-flat major <1734>   *10'*

2[rec1.rec2] 2 0 2 — 2cnt — str
Breitkopf numbering: *Concerto grosso No.1.*

  I. Allegro moderato   *3'*
  II. Largo   *5'*
  III. Allegro   *2'*

Bärenreiter	Breitkopf	Kalmus	Luck's	Peters

Concerto grosso, op.3, no.2, HWV 313, B-flat major <1734>   *12'*

solo concertino: 2 violins, violoncello
0 2 0 1 — 2cnt — str
Breitkopf numbering: *Concerto grosso No.2.*

  1. Vivace   *2'*
  2. Largo   *3'*
  3. Allegro   *2'*
  4. [Menuet]   *2'*
  5. [Gavotte]   *3'*

Bärenreiter	Breitkopf	Kalmus	Luck's	Peters

Concerto grosso, op.3, no.3, HWV 314, G major   *8'*

solo concertino: violin, flute (or oboe)
2cnt — str
Breitkopf numbering: *Concerto grosso No.3.*

  I. Largo e staccato - Allegro   *3'*
  II. Adagio   *1'*
  III. Allegro   *4'*

Bärenreiter	Breitkopf	Kalmus	Luck's	Peters

Concerto grosso, op.3, no.4, HWV 315, F major <1734>   *11'*

0 2 0 1 — cnt — str
Breitkopf numbering: *Concerto grosso No.4.*

  1. Andante; Allegro; Lentement   *4'*
  2. Andante   *2'*
  3. Allegro   *2'*
  4. Minuetto alternativo   *3'*

Bärenreiter	Breitkopf	Eulenburg	Kalmus	Peters

Concerto grosso, op.3, no.5, HWV 316, D minor <1734>   *10'*

0 2 0 0 — cnt — str
Breitkopf numbering: *Concerto grosso No.5.*
  See also Handel's *Prelude & Fugue,* HWV 316, D minor (a free
transcription by Hans Kindler of movements from this concerto grosso).

  1. [untitled]   *2'*
  2. Allegro   *2'*
  3. Adagio   *1'*
  4. Allegro ma non troppo   *2'*
  5. Allegro   *3'*

Bärenreiter	Breitkopf	Kalmus	Luck's	Peters

Concerto grosso, op.3, no.6, HWV 317, D major <1734>   *7'*

0 2 0 1 — org — str
Breitkopf numbering: *Concerto grosso No.6.*

  I. Allegro moderato   *3'*
  II. Allegro   *4'*

Bärenreiter	Breitkopf	Kalmus	Luck's	Peters

Concerto grosso, No.7, HWV 318, C major (Alexanderfest) <1736>   *13'*

solo concertino: 2 violins, violoncello
0 2 0 0 — 2cnt — str

Bärenreiter	Breitkopf	Kalmus	Peters

Concerto grosso, Nos.8-10, HWV 301-303

  see his: Concerto, Oboe, Nos.1-3, HWV 301-303

Concerto grosso, op.6, no.1, HWV 319, G major <1739>   *12*

solo concertino: 2 violins, violoncello
2cnt — str
Bärenreiter edition includes 2ob & 1bn.
  Breitkopf numbering: *Concerto grosso No.12.*

  I. A tempo giusto   *2'*
  II. Allegro   *2'*
  III. Adagio   *2'*
  IV. Allegro   *3'*
  V. Allegro   *3'*

Bärenreiter	Breitkopf	Kalmus	Luck's	Peters

Concerto grosso, op.6, no.2, HWV 230, F major <1739>   *11*

solo concertino: 2 violins, violoncello
2cnt — str
Bärenreiter edition includes 2ob & 1bn (the 2ob were apparently later additions).
  Breitkopf numbering: *Concerto grosso No.13.*

  I. Andante larghetto   *4'*
  II. Allegro - Menuetto: Moderato, non troppo   *2'*
  III. Largo   *3'*
  IV. Allegro, ma non troppo   *2'*

Bärenreiter	Breitkopf	Kalmus	Luck's	Peters

Concerto grosso, op.6, no.3, HWV 321, E minor <1739>   *12*

solo concertino: 2 violins, violoncello
2cnt — str
Breitkopf numbering: *Concerto grosso No.14.*

  I. Larghetto   *1'*
  II. Andante   *2'*
  III. Allegro   *3'*
  IV. Polonaise: Andante   *5'*
  V. Allegro; ma non troppo   *1'*

Bärenreiter	Breitkopf	Kalmus	Luck's	Peters

Concerto grosso, op.6, no.4, HWV 322, A minor <1739>   *11*

solo concertino: 2 violins, violoncello
2cnt — str
Breitkopf numbering: *Concerto grosso No.15.*

  I. Larghetto affettuoso - Allegro   *3'*
  II. Allegro   *3'*
  III. Largo e piano   *2'*
  IV. Allegro   *3'*

Bärenreiter	Breitkopf	Kalmus	Luck's	Peters

Concerto grosso, op.6, no.5, HWV 323, D major <1739>   *16*

solo concertino: 2 violins, violoncello
2cnt — str
Bärenreiter edition includes 2ob & 1bn.
  Breitkopf numbering: *Concerto grosso No.16.*

  I. [Maestoso]   *2'*
  II. Allegro   *2'*
  III. Presto   *3'*
  IV. Largo   *2'*
  V. Menuet: Un poco larghetto   *3'*
  VI. Finale: Allegro   *4'*

Bärenreiter	Breitkopf	Kalmus	Luck's	Peters

Concerto grosso, op.6, no.6, HWV 324, G minor <1739>   *17'*

solo concertino: 2 violins, violoncello
2cnt — str
Bärenreiter edition includes 2ob & 1bn.
  Breitkopf numbering: *Concerto grosso No.17.*

  I. Larghetto affettuoso   *4'*
  II. Allegro ma non troppo   *2'*
  III. Musette: Allegretto   *6'*
  IV. Allegro molto vivace   *3'*
  V. Finale: Allegro con fuoco   *2'*

Bärenreiter	Breitkopf	Kalmus	Luck's	Peters

Concerto grosso, op.6, no.7, HWV 325, B-flat major <1739>   14'

solo concertino: 2 violins, violoncello
2cnt — str
Concertino merely doubles ripieno in this work.
    Breitkopf numbering: *Concerto grosso No.18.*
Largo   *1'*
Allegro   *2'*
Largo e piano   *3'*
Andante   *5'*
Hornpipe: Spiritoso *3'*

Bärenreiter	Breitkopf	Kalmus	Luck's	Peters

Concerto grosso, op.6, no.8, HWV 326, C minor <1739>   14'

solo concertino: 2 violins, violoncello
2cnt — str
Breitkopf numbering: *Concerto grosso No.19.*
Allemande: Andante *4'*
Grave   *2'*
Andante allegro   *2'*
Adagio   *1'*
Siciliana: Andante *4'*
Allegro   *1'*

Bärenreiter	Breitkopf	Kalmus	Luck's	Peters

Concerto grosso, op.6, no.9, HWV 327, F major <1739>   15'

solo concertino: 2 violins, violoncello
2cnt — str
Breitkopf numbering: *Concerto grosso No.20.*
Largo   *1'*
Allegro   *4'*
Larghetto   *4'*
Allegro   *2'*
Menuet: Andante   *2'*
Gigue: Allegro   *2'*

Bärenreiter	Breitkopf	Kalmus	Luck's	Peters

Concerto grosso, op.6, no.10, HWV 328, D minor <1739>   14'

solo concertino: 2 violins, violoncello
2cnt — str
Breitkopf numbering: *Concerto grosso No.21.*
I. Ouverture: [Maestoso]   *4'*
II. Allegro   *3'*
III. Air: Lento   *2'*
IV. Allegro moderato   *3'*
V. Finale: Allegro [con fuoco] *2'*

Bärenreiter	Breitkopf	Kalmus	Luck's	Peters

Concerto grosso, op.6, no.11, HWV 329, A major <1739>   18'

solo concertino: 2 violins, violoncello
2cnt — str
Breitkopf numbering: *Concerto grosso No.22.*
Andante larghetto e staccato *5'*
Allegro   *2'*
Largo e staccato   *1'*
Andante   *4'*
Allegro   *6'*

Bärenreiter	Breitkopf	Kalmus	Luck's	Peters

Concerto grosso, op.6, no.12, HWV 330, B minor <1739>   12'

solo concertino: 2 violins, violoncello
2cnt — str
Breitkopf numbering: *Concerto grosso No.23.*
Largo   *2'*
Allegro   *3'*
Aria: Larghetto   *4'*
Largo   *1'*
Allegro   *2'*

Bärenreiter	Breitkopf	Kalmus	Luck's	Peters

Dettingen Te Deum, HWV 283 <1743>   35'

chorus   solo bass voice
0 2 0 1 — 0 3 0 0 — tmp — org, hpsd — str
The Kalmus edition (believed to be a reprint of an old Breitkopf edition) is full of added dynamics and other spurious interpretive markings.

Bärenreiter	Kalmus	Luck's	Peters

Dixit Dominus, HWV 232 (Psalm 109) <1707>   33'

chorus   solos SSATB
cnt — str
1. Chorus: Dixit Dominus, Domino meo   *6'*
2. Air: Virgam virtutis tuae   *3'*
3. Air: Tecum principium   *3'*
4. Chorus: Juravit Dominus   *2'*
5. Chorus: Secundum ordinem Melchisedech *2'*
6. Chorus: Dominus a dextris tuis   *7'*
7. Chorus: De torrente in via bibet   *4'*
8. Chorus: Gloria Patri et Filio   *6'*

Bärenreiter	Kalmus

Esther, HWV 50a [1st version] <1718–1732>   90'

solos SSATTTTB   chorus SATTBB
0 1 0 2 — 2 1 0 0 — hp — cnt — str
Ed. Howard Serwer.

Bärenreiter	Kalmus	Novello

Israel in Egypt, HWV 54 <1738>   123'

double chorus   solos SSATBB
0 2 0 2 — 0 2 3 0 — tmp — org, hpsd — str
Bärenreiter edition includes 2fl.
Part 1   41'
Part 2   31'
Part 3   51'

Bärenreiter	Kalmus	Luck's	Peters

Joshua, HWV 64 <1748>   126'

chorus   solos SSATB
2 2 0 1 — 2 3 0 0 — tmp — cnt — str
Act I   53'
Act II   73'

Kalmus	Luck's	Peters

Jubilate for the Peace of Utrecht, HWV 279 <1713>   19'

chorus   solos AAB
0 2 0 1 — 0 2 0 0 — cnt — str
I. O be joyful in the Lord   *2'*
II. Serve the Lord with gladness   *2'*
III. Be ye sure that the Lord He is God *3'*
IV. O go your way into his gates   *3'*
V. For the Lord is gracious   *3'*
VI. Glory be to the Father   *6'*

Kalmus

Judas Maccabaeus, HWV 63 <1746>   132'

chorus   solos SSATBB
2 2 0 2 — 2 3 0 0 — tmp — org, hpsd — str
Overture   6'
Act I   42'
Act II   49'
Act III   35'

Kalmus	Luck's	Peters

Judas Maccabaeus, HWV 63: Overture <1746>   7'

0 2 0 1 — cnt — str

Kalmus	Luck's

Largo <1738>

see his: Xerxes, HWV 40: Largo

Let Thy Hand be Strengthened (Coronation Anthem   7'
No.4) HWV 259 <1727>

chorus

0 2 0 0 — cnt — str

Kalmus	Luck's	Schirmer

Messiah, HWV 56 <1741>   159'

chorus   solos SATB

0 2 0 2 — 0 2 0 0 — tmp — cnt, org — str

Novello edition (ed. Watkins Shaw) offers the most extensive number of
variant movements. See also *Messiah: The Solo Variants*, ed. Chester
Alwes (the various options for arias and recitatives in piano-vocal score
format).

Part I	60'
Part II	64'
Part III	35'

    [For full contents, see Appendix J]

Bärenreiter	Novello	Peters

Messiah, HWV 56 (orchestrated by W. A. Mozart)   120'
<1741>

chorus   solos SATB

2[1/pic.2] 2 2 2 — 2 2 3 0 — tmp — org — str

Bärenreiter	Peters

Messiah, HWV 56 (orchestrated by Ebenezer Prout)   120'
<1741>

chorus   solos SATB

2 2 2 2 — 2 2 3 0 — tmp — org, pf — str

Schirmer

Occasional Oratorio, HWV 62 (Festoratorium) <1746>   148'

double chorus   solos SSATB

0 2 0 2 — 2 3 0 0 — tmp — cnt — str

Several of the movements were borrowed from the composer's *Israel in
Egypt*. Some of these borrowed movements used 3 trombones in the
earlier setting, and parts for trombones are included by the editor of the
Breitkopf edition with the *Occasional Oratorio* materials, though
apparently they were not intended by Handel; nor are they found in the
Bärenreiter materials.

Overture	10'
Act I	48'
Act II	45'
Act III	45'

Bärenreiter	Breitkopf

Occasional Oratorio, HWV 62: Overture <1746>   10'

0 2 0 0 — 0 3 0 0 — tmp — cnt — str

Kalmus	Luck's

Ode for St. Cecilia's Day, HWV 76 <1739>   41'

chorus   solos ST

1 2 0 1 — 0 2 0 0 — lute — tmp — cnt — str

I. Recit (Tenor) & Chorus: From Harmony, From Heavenly Harmony	6'
II. Air (Soprano): What passion cannot Music raise and quell!	7'
III. Air (Tenor) & Chorus: The Trumpet's loud clangor	3'
IV. March	2'
V. Air (Soprano): The soft complaining Flute	5'
VI. Air (Tenor): Sharp Violins proclaim	4'
VII. Air (Soprano): But oh! What art can teach	4'
VIII. Air (Soprano): Orpheus could lead the savage race	2'
IX. Recit (Soprano): But bright Cecilia rais'd the wonder high'r	1'
X. Chorus: As from the pow'r of sacred lays	7'

Carus	Kalmus

Orlando, HWV 31: Overture <1733>   6'

0 2 0 0 — cnt — str

Bärenreiter	Kalmus

Overture, HWV 337, D major <1722–1723>   5'

2 3 2 3[1.2.cbn] — 4 3 0 0 — tmp — str

Arr. Franz Wüllner.

    Kalmus title: *Overture in D arr. from Royal Fireworks Music.*

I. [No tempo indicated]	1'
II. Adagio	2'
III. Allegro	2'

Kalmus	Luck's

Passion nach Barthold Heinrich Brockes, HWV 48   150'
(Brockes Passion) <1716>

chorus   solos: 6S, 4A, 3T, 5B

0 2 0 2 — cnt — str

Original title: *Der für die Sünde der Welt gemartete und sterbende Jesus*
    Possible, by combining roles, with solos SATTBB.

Bärenreiter

Il pastor fido, HWV 8 (The Faithful Shepherd): Suite   25'
<1712>

2 2 2 2 — 4 2 0 0 — tmp+1 — str

perc: tri, sd

Arr. Thomas Beecham.

I. Introduction and Fugue	5'
II. Adagio	6'
III. Gavotte	2'
IV. Bourrée	2'
V. Minuet	3'
VI. Pastorale	4'
VII. Finale	3'

Boosey

Prelude & Fugue, HWV 316, D minor <1735>   6'

3[incl pic] 3[incl Eh] 3[incl bcl] 2 — 4 3 3 1 — tmp — pf — str

Freely transcribed by Hans Kindler from the *Concerto Grosso, op.3,
no.5.*

Belwin	Luck's

Psalm 89, HWV 252 (My Song Shall Be Alway) <1720>   30'

chorus   solos STB

0 1 0 1 — cnt — str[no va]

Luck's	Peters

Psalm 96, HWV 249 (O Sing unto the Lord) <1714>   20'

chorus   solos ST

0 1 0 1 — cnt — str[no va]

Luck's	Peters

Rinaldo, HWV 7: Overture <1711; rev 1731>   5'

1[rec] 2 0 1 — cnt — str

There are 2 versions of this opera: 1711 and 1731. The overture is the
same in both, except for the absence of the recorder in the 1731 version.

Kalmus	Peters

Rodrigo, HWV 5: Overture <1707>   19'

0 2 0 1 — cnt — str
A French overture, followed, as is traditional, by a series of dances.

Overture	5'
Gigue	1'
Sarabande	2'
Matelot	1'
Menuet	1'
Bouree I & II	3'
Menuet	1'
Passacaille	5'

Kalmus	Peters

Royal Fireworks Music, HWV 351 <1749>   19'

0 3 0 3[1.2.cbn] — 3 3 0 0 — tmp — cnt — str[opt]
Handel's original performance used 24ob, 12bn, unknown numbers of
contrabassoons and serpents, 3hn, 3tp, and 3 sets of timpani. The strings
were added later by the composer and may be considered optional.
The Kalmus edition (ed. Max Seiffert) uses no cbn. Another separate
Peters edition (ed. Robert A. Boudreau) uses no strings and calls for one
or more snare drums in addition to timpani.

Overture	9'
Bourrée	2'
La Paix	3'
La Réjouissance	2'
Menuet I & II	3'

Bärenreiter	Breitkopf	Kalmus	Luck's	Peters

Royal Fireworks Music, HWV 351 (ed. Baines &   19'
Mackerras) <1749>

2[1/pic.2/pic] 3 3 3[1.2.cbn] — 3 5 3 0 — tmp+3 — str
perc: bd, cym, sd
Arr. Anthony Baines & Charles Mackerras. Playable by a variety of
instrumentations from a maximum (above) to a minimum of:
    0 3 0 2 — 2 2 0 0 — tmp+1 — [no str].

1. Ouverture	9'
2. Bourée	2'
3. La Paix	3'
4. La Réjouissance	2'
5. Minuet/Trio	3'

Oxford

Royal Fireworks Music, HWV 351 (arr. Hamilton Harty)   15'
<1749>

0 2 0 2 — 4 3 0 0 — tmp+1 — str
perc: sd

Overture	6'
Alla siciliana	5'
Bourrée	1'
Menuetto.	3'

Chappell	Luck's

Samson, HWV 57 <1741>   167'

chorus   solos SATBB
2 2 0 2 — 2 2 0 0 — tmp — cnt — str
Additional minor solos (SSTT) drawn from the chorus.

Act I	78'
Act II	83'
Act III	53'

Bärenreiter	Kalmus	Peters

Samson, HWV 57: Overture <1741>   7'

0 2 0 1 — 2 0 0 0 — cnt — str

Bärenreiter	Kalmus	Luck's

Saul, HWV 53 <1739>   151'

chorus   solos: 2S, A , 5T, 4B
2[rec1.rec2] 2 0 2 — 0 2 3 0 — tmp+1 — hp — cnt, org — str
perc: chimes

Overture	14'
Act I	70'
Act II	48'
Act III	48'

Bärenreiter

Saul, HWV 53: Overture <1738>   14'

0 2 0 1 — cnt, org — str

Bärenreiter	Kalmus

Saul, HWV 53: Overture (arr. Prout) <1738>   15'

2 2 2 2 — 2 0 0 0 — str
Arr by Ebenezzer Prout.

Kalmus	Luck's

Solomon, HWV 67 <1749>   142'

chorus   solos SSSSATB
2 2 0 2 — 2 2 0 0 — tmp — cnt — str

Overture	4'
Act I	57'
Act II	52'
Act III	38'

Bärenreiter	Breitkopf

Solomon, HWV 67: Overture <1749>   4'

0 2 0 0 — cnt — str

Kalmus	Luck's

Solomon, HWV 67: Entrance of the Queen of Sheba   4'
<1748>

0 2 0 0 — cnt — str
Neither publisher supplies the continuo part that is *de rigueur* for such
works. The harpsichordist will have to extemporize from the bass line or
from full score, unless a part is prepared for the purpose.

Kalmus	Luck's

Te Deum

see his: Dettingen Te Deum, HWV 283
         Utrecht Te Deum, HWV 278

Theodora, HWV 68: Overture <1749>   12'

0 2 0 0 — cnt — str

Kalmus	Luck's

Utrecht Te Deum, HWV 278 <1713>   25'

solos SSAATB   chorus SSAATTB
1 2 0 1 — 0 2 0 0 — org — str
Bärenreiter ed. Gerald Hendrie; Novello ed. Shaw.

Bärenreiter	Kalmus	Luck's	Novello	Schirmer

Water Music, HWV 348-350 (Wassermusik) <1717>   50'

1[1/flag or sopranino rec] 2 0 1 — 2 2 0 0 — cnt — str
Breitkopf previously identified this version as *Concerto grosso No.25*; it
is based on the old collected edition of Handel's works. More recent
scholarship suggests that the division into three separate suites (as in
subsequent entries) is preferable.

Breitkopf	Luck's	Peters

Water Music: Suite No.1, HWV 348, F major <1717>   32'

0 2 0 1 — 2 0 0 0 — cnt — str
1. Overture	4'
2. Adagio e staccato	2'
3. [Allegro]	8'
4. Andante	4'
5. [Presto]	3'
6. Air	3'
7. Minuet	2'
8. Bourrée	2'
9. Hornpipe	4'
10. Allegro moderato [a transition to Suite No.2]	

Bärenreiter   Eulenburg

Water Music: Suite No.2, HWV 349, D major <1717>   12'

0 2 0 1 — 2 2 0 0 — cnt — str
11. Allegro	3'
12. Alla Hornpipe	4'
13. Minuet	1'
14. Lentement	3'
15. Bourée	1'

Bärenreiter   Eulenburg

Water Music: Suite No.3, HWV 350, G major <1717>   11'

1[flag or sopranino rec] 2 0 1 — cnt — str
Flute doubles on flageolet or sopranino recorder.
16. [Sarabande]	-'
17. Rigaudon	-'
18. [Allegro]	-'
19. Menuets I & II	-'
20. ["flauto piccolo" & str]	-'
21. ["flauto piccolo" & str]	-'
22. [bn & str]	-'

Bärenreiter   Eulenburg

Water Music Suite (arr. Hamilton Harty) <1717>   16'

2[1.2/pic] 2 2 2 — 4 2 0 0 — tmp — str
Arr. Hamilton Harty.
I. Allegro	2'
II. Air	5'
III. Bourrée	1'
IV. Horn-Pipe	1'
V. Andante espressivo	4'
VI. Allegro deciso	3'

Chappell   Luck's

Xerxes, HWV 40 (Serse): Overture <1738>   6'

0 2 0 1 — cnt — str

Bärenreiter   Kalmus   Luck's

Xerxes, HWV 40 (Serse): Largo (arr.) <1738>   5'

2 2 2 2 — 4 3 3 1 — hp — str
The well-known aria *Ombra mai fu*, arr. Arthur Luck for full orchestra.

Luck's

Zadok the Priest (Coronation Anthem No.1), HWV 258 <1727>   6'

chorus   solos SSAATBB
0 2 0 2 — 0 3 0 0 — tmp — cnt — str

Kalmus   Luck's   Schirmer

Hanson, Howard   1896-1981

(b Wahoo, NE, 28 Oct 1896; d Rochester, NY, 26 February 1981). American
composer of Swedish ancestry

Before the Dawn <1919>   4'

3[1.2.pic] 2 2 2 — 4 2 3 1 — tmp — str

C. Fischer

Cherubic Hymn <1949>   12'

chorus
3[1.2.pic] 2 2 2 — 4 3 3 1 — tmp+1 — pf — str

C. Fischer

Concerto, Organ & Harp, op.22, no.3 <1921>   15'

str

C. Fischer

Elegy in Memory of Serge Koussevitsky, op.44 <1956>   14'

2[incl pic] 2[incl Eh] 2 2 — 4 3 3 1 — tmp — hp — str

C. Fischer

Fanfare for the Signal Corps <1943>   1'

0 0 0 0 — 4 3 3 1 — tmp+2 — [no str]
perc: sd, td

Boosey

Lament for Beowulf, op.25 <1925>   19'

chorus
3[1.2.str] 2 2 3[incl cbn] — 4 3 3 1 — 2tmp+2 — hp — str

C. Fischer

Lux aeterna, op.24 <1923>   15'

solo viola
3[1.2.pic] 2 2 3[1.2.cbn] — 4 3 3 1 — tmp+2 — 2hp — cel, pf — str

C. Fischer

Merry Mount: Suite <1933>   15'

3[1.2.3/pic] 3[1.2.Eh] 3[1.2.bcl] 3[1.2.cbn] — 4 3 3 1 — tmp+6 —
2hp — str
perc: Chinese cym, chimes, cym, gong, marim, sd, sus cym, tambn, templeblks,
tri, woodblk, xyl
I. Overture	3'
II. Children's Dance	2'
III. Love Duet	4'
IV. Prelude to Act II and Maypole Dances	6'

Luck's   Warner

Serenade, op.35 <1945>   6'

solo flute
hp — str

C. Fischer   Luck's

Song of Democracy, op.44 <1957>   12'

SATB chorus
3[1.2.pic] 3[1.2.Eh] 2 2 — 4 3 3 1 — tmp+3 — hp[or pf] — cel — str
perc: tri, sd, gong, sus cym, cym, xyl

C. Fischer

Symphony No.1, op.21, E minor (Nordic) <1922>   27'

3[1.2.pic] 2 2 3[1.2.cbn] — 4 3 3 1 — tmp+2 — hp — str
perc: bd, cym, sus cym
1. Andante solenne — Allegro con forza	12'
2. Andante tenerament, con semplicita	6'
3. Allegro con fuoco	9'

C. Fischer   Luck's

Symphony No.2, op.30 (Romantic) <1930>   28'

3[1.2.pic] 3[1.2.Eh] 2 3[1.2.3/cbn] — 4 3 3 1 — tmp+2 — hp — str
perc: sd, bd, cym, sus cym
Fischer critical edition by Clinton F. Nieweg; score for sale but parts that
agree with the Nieweg score are rental only.

Adagio; Allegro moderato	14'
Andante con tenerezza	7'
Allegro con brio	7'

| C. Fischer | Luck's |

Symphony No.3, op.33 <1937–1938>   33'

3[1.2.3/pic] 3[1.2.Eh] 3[1.2.3/bcl] 3[1.2.cbn] — 4 3 3 1 — tmp — str

I. Andante lamentando	10'
II. Andante tranquillo	8'
III. Tempo scherzando	6'
IV. Largamente e pesante	9'

| C. Fischer | Luck's |

Symphony No.4, op.34 (Requiem) <1943>   27'

3[1.2.pic] 2 2[1.2/bcl] 2[1.2/cbn] — 4 3 3 1 — tmp+2 — str
perc: sd, xyl

1. Kyrie	10'
2. Requiescat	6'
3. Dies irae	3'
4. Lux aeterna	8'

| C. Fischer | Luck's |

Symphony No.5, op.43 (Sinfonia sacra) <1955>   13'

3[1.2.3/pic] 2 2 — 4 3 3 1 — tmp+2 — hp — str
perc: cym, gong, sd, sus cym, xyl

| C. Fischer | Luck's |

Symphony No.6 <1968>   21'

3[1.2.pic] 3[1.2.Eh] 3[1.2.bcl] 3[1.2.cbn] — 4 3 3 1 — tmp+3 — str
perc: bd, sus cym, tri, xyl, 2sd
Movements are played without pause.

I. Andante	4'
II. Allegro scherzando	5'
III. Adagio	5'
IV. Allegro assai	2'
V. Adagio	3'
VI. Allegro	2'

| C. Fischer |

Harbison, John   1938-

(b Orange, NJ, 20 Dec 1938). American

Closer to My Own Life <2011>   19'

solo mezzo-soprano
2[1.2/pic] 2[1.2/Eh] 2[1.2/bcl] 2[1.2/cbn] — 2 2 0 0 — tmp+1 — hp
— cel — str
perc: bd, sus cym, tri, tambn, glock, vib, 2tamtam

I. Home	_'
II. Lying under the apple tree	_'
III. What do you want to know for	_'
IV. Messenger	_'

| Presser |

Concerto, Bass Viol <2005>   20'

2[1.2/pic/afl] 2[1.2/Eh] 2[1.2/bcl] 2[1.2/cbn] — 2 2 0 0 — tmp+1 —
pf — str[max 12.12.8.8.6]
perc: vib, marim, sd, sus cym, tri, templeblks, flexatone, glass ch
In C if soloist uses orchestral tuning; in D if traditional solo scordatura is
used. Specify which version is desired when ordering.

I. Lamento	_'
II. Cavatina	_'
III. Rondo	_'

| AMP |

Concerto, Flute <1994>   19'

2[1.2/pic] 2 2 2[1.2/cbn] — 2 2 0 0 — tmp+2 — hp — cel — str

| AMP |

Concerto, Oboe <1991>   21'

2[1.2/pic] 0 3[1.2.asx/bcl] 3[1.2.3/cbn] — 2 2 2 1 — tmp+3 — hp —
str
perc: chimes, xyl, tamtam, sus cym, cym, gong, glock, vib, sd, tri, templeblks,
marim, 3woodblk
Movements played without pause.

I. Aria	_'
II. Passacaglia	_'
III. Fantasia	_'

| AMP |

Concerto, Oboe, Clarinet & Strings <1985>   14'

str orch [or str 5t]

I. Declamando	5'
II. Larghetto	6'
III. Furioso	3'

| AMP |

Concerto, Viola <1989>   23'

2[1.2/pic] 2[1.2/Eh] 2[1.bcl] 2[1.2/cbn] — 2 2 0 0 — tmp+1 — hp —
cel — str[min 6vn, 5va, 4vc, 2db]
perc: vib, cym, gong

I. Con moto, rubato	9'
II. Allegro brillante	2'
III. Andante	6'
IV. Molto allegro, gioioso	6'

| AMP |

Crane Sightings: Eclogue for Solo Violin with String   15'
Accompaniment <2004>

str

I. Encounter	_'
II. Flight	_'
III. The Sadness of Marshes	_'
IV. Dance–Variations	_'

| AMP |

Double Concerto, Violin & Violoncello <2009>   25'

2[1.2/pic] 2 2[1.2/bcl] 2[1.2/cbn] — 4 2 0 0 — tmp+1 — hp — cel —
str
perc: bd, sus cym, sd, tri, marim, vib, metalplate, 5cowbell[or kalimba]

I. Affetuoso, poco inquieto	_'
II. Notturno; Adagio	_'
III. Tempo giusto	_'

| AMP |

The Flight into Egypt: Sacred Ricercar <1986>   14'

solo soprano, baritone   chorus
0 3[1.2.Eh] 0 1 — 0 0 3 0 — org — str[min 4.4.2.2.1]

| AMP |

The Great Gatsby: Suite <1999; rev 2007>   30'

3[1.2.3/pic] 3[1.2.Eh] 4[1.2/Ebcl.3/ssx.bcl] 3[1.2.cbn] — 4 3 3 1 —
ten banjo — tmp+3 — hp — pf — str
perc: bd, cym, set, tomtom, tri, tamtam, glock, xyl, marim, vib, chimes, crot,
cowbell, marac, cast, 3sus cym, 4brake dr
Suite prepared 2007 by the composer, from the 1999 opera.

| AMP |

Merchant of Venice: Incidental Music <1971>   12'

str[or str 4t]

| AMP |

Milosz Songs <2006>   34'

solo soprano
3[1.2/pic.3/afl] 2[1.2/Eh] 2[1.2/bcl] 2[1.2/cbn] — 2 2 2 0 — tmp+3
— hp — cel — str[max 10.10.8.6.4]
perc: vib, marim, templeblks, crot, chimes, tamtam, cym, sus cym, sd, bd, tambn,
3tri, 2gong[Bb3,B3]
Concertino of instruments from the orchestra positioned forward: 3 flutes,
cel, hp, perc1.

Prologue from Lauda	_'
1. A Task	_'
2. Encounter	_'
3. You Who Wronged	_'
4. When the Moon	_'
5. O!	_'
6. What Once Was Great	_'
7. So Little	_'
8. On Old Women	_'
Epilogue: from Winter	_'
Post-Epilogue: Rays of Dazzling Light	_'

AMP

The Most Often Used Chords (Gli accordi più usati) <1993>   18'

2 2 2 2 — 2 2 0 0 — tmp+1 — hp — cel/pf — str
perc: vib, glock, marim, tri, sd, td, crot[D5,E5]

AMP

Mottetti di Montale: Il saliscendi bianco <1999>   11'

solo mezzo-soprano
1[fl/pic] 1 1[cl/bcl] 0 — 1 0 0 0 — org — vn, va, vc, db
Book 1 of the *Mottetti di Montale* is for voice and piano.

LIBRO 2 (BOOK 2)	
VII. Il saliscendi bianco e nero (The black and white span)	2'
VIII. Ecco il segno (Behold the sign)	1'
IX. Il ramarro (The green lizard)	2'
X. Perché tardi? (Why are you late?)	2'
XI. L'anima che dispensa (The soul which scatters)	2'
XII. Ti libero la fronte (I free your forehead)	2'

AMP

Music for 18 Winds <1986>   11'

2[1.2/pic] 2 2 2[1.2/cbn] — 4 2 2 1 — asx — [no str]

AMP

Partita (for Orchestra) <2000>   18'

2[1.2/pic] 2[1.2/Eh] 2[1.2/bcl] 2[1.2/cbn] — 4 2 2 0 — tmp+3 — str
perc: bd, cym, sd, tamtam, glock, xyl, marim, vib, templeblks, whip, bongos, ratch,
claves, congas, wood drum, 3sus cym, 3tomtom, 3tri, 2woodblk, 3cowbell

I. Praeludium–Fantasia	_'
II. Rondo–Capriccio	_'
III. Aria–Sarabande	_'
IV. Courante–Gigue	_'

AMP

Remembering Gatsby; Foxtrot for Orchestra <1985; rev 1990>   7'

3[1.2.3/pic] 3[1.2.3/Eh] 3[1.2.3/bcl/ssx] 3[1.2.cbn] — 4 3 3 1 —
tmp+5 — pf — str
perc: xyl, sd, bd, cym, tri, claves, glock, flexatone, 5sus cym, set (sd, bd, hi-hat,
2cowbells, woodblk, cym)
Reduced version by John Moody:
2[1.2/pic] 2[1.2/Eh] 2[1.2/ssx] 2 — 2 2 2 1 — tmp+perc — pf — str

AMP

Requiem <2002>   58

solos SATBs-bar   chorus
2[1.2/pic] 2 2 2[1.2/cbn] — 2 2 3 0 — tmp+3 — hp — pf/cel — str
perc: cym, szl cym, sd, glock, vib, marim, chimes, crot, flexatone, woodblk,
templeblks, guiro, churchbell, 2bd, 3wood drum, 4 cowbell, 4tri, 4tamtam,
5tomtom, 2tuned gongs

Introit	_'
SEQUENCE I: Dies irae	_'
Tuba mirum	_'
Liber scriptum	_'
Quid sum miser	_'
Recordare	_'
Confutatis—Lacrymosa	_'
PART II. Offertorium	_'
Sanctus	_'
Agnus Dei	_'
Lux aeterna	_'
Libera me	_'
In paradisum	_'

AMP

Symphony No.1 <1981>   24'

3[1.2.3/afl/pic] 3[1.2.3/Eh] 3[1.2.3/bcl] 3[1.2.3/cbn] — 4 2 3 1 —
tmp+5 — hp — str
perc: bd, chimes, claves, marac, marim, sd, tambn, templeblks, rototom, vib,
2tamtams, 2metalblks, 4sus cym, 3tomtoms, 2woodblks, wooddrum, 2tri

I. Drammatico	9'
II. Allegro sfumato	2'
III. Paesaggio (Landscape): Andante	7'
IV. Tempo giusto	6'

AMP

Symphony No.2 <1987>   23'

3[1.2.3/pic] 3[1.2.Eh] 4[1.2.Ebcl.bcl] 3[1.2.cbn] — 4 4 3 1 — tmp+3
— hp — pf/cel — str
perc: glock, sd, tri, templeblks, gong, thunder, vib, tamtam, cast, lionroar, crot, bd,
cym, szl cym, 4sus cym, 4tomtoms

Dawn	5'
Daylight	4'
Dusk	6'
Dark	8'

AMP

Symphony No.3 <1990>   21'

3[1.2.3/pic] 3[1.2.3/Eh] 3[1.2.3/bcl] 3[1.2.3/cbn] — 4 3 3 1 — tmp+4
— pf — str
perc: bd, sd, td, tri, tambn, tamtam, glock, xyl, marim, vib, chimes, crot, woodblk,
templeblks, cowbell, lujon[or wood drums], 4sus cym, 4tomtom, 4timbales,
4brake dr

AMP

Symphony No.4 <2004>   25'

3[1.2.3/pic] 3[1.2.3/Eh] 3[1.2.3/bcl] 3[1.2.3/cbn] — 4 2 2 1 — tmp+3
— hp — pf — str
perc: bd, sus cym, sd, td, tri, tambn, glock, marim, vib, chimes, templeblks,
3tomtom, 2tamtam

I. Fanfare	_'
II. Intermezzo	_'
III. Scherzo	_'
IV. Threnody	_'
V. Finale	_'

AMP

Symphony No.5   35'

solo baritone, mezzo-soprano
3[1.2.3/pic] 3[1.2.3/Eh] 3[1.2/Ebcl.3/bcl] 3[1.2.cbn] — 4 2 2 1 —
elec gtr — tmp+3 — hp — pf — str
perc: glock, vib, sus cym, guiro, whip, marim, tri, td, marac, cowbell, sd, bd, ratch,
tamtam, 2metalblks, 2bell, 2claves, 2gong, 2sandblks
Movements played without pause.
I. The death of Orpheus	–'
At the entrance to Hades	–'
He remembered her words	–'
In a labyrinth	–'
He sang the brightness …	–'
II. He sang	–'
But there are conditions	–'
It happened as he expected	–'
III. Where would I be without my sorrow	–'
IV. Be ahead of all parting	–'

AMP

Symphony No.6   25'

solo mezzo-soprano
3[1.2.3/pic] 3[1.2.3/Eh] 3[1.2.3/bcl] 3[1.2.3/cbn] — 4 3 3 1 —
tmp+2[or 3] — hp — cimb[or prepared piano] — str
perc: cym, sd, tamtam, glock, marim, vib, chimes, flexatone, bongos, congas,
2gong
I. Con moto	–'
II. Con anima	–'
III. Vivo, ruvido	–'
IV. Moderato cantabile e semplice	–'

AMP

Umbrian Landscape With Saint   23'

optional chorus
1 1[Eh] 1 1 — 1 2 1 1 — pf — str 5t
Chorus only in III (Cantico delle creature, to a text by St. Francis of
Assisi).
I. Semplice	–'
II. Panels from Giotto's St. Francis Cycle in Assisi	–'
1. Francis Offers His Cloak	–'
2. Francis Drives the Demons out of Arezzo	–'
3. Dream of the Flaming Chariot	–'
4. Vision of the Heavenly Thrones	–'
5. Trial by Fire	–'
6. St. Francis in Ecstasy	–'
7. The Miracle of the Stream	–'
8. Francis Preaches to the Birds	–'
9. Francis Receives the Stigmata	–'
10. The Death of St. Francis	–'
III. Cantico delle creature	–'

AMP

Harmon, John   1935-

(b Oshkosh, WI, 25 Oct 1935). American

Earth Day Portrait <2001>   21'

1-4 narrators
3[1.2.pic] 3[1.2.Eh] 3[1.2.bcl] 2 — 4 3 3 1 — tmp+4 — hp — str
perc: bd, cym, sus cym, sd, tri, glock, xyl, chimes, windchimes
Texts by John Muir, Aldo Leopold, Gaylord Nelson; concept and
connecting texts by Jon Becker.
1. Fanfare for Our Common Earth	3'
2. Invocation	1'
3. Music for the Earth	4'
4. Words for the Earth	10'
5. Pledge for Our Common Earth	3'

Alliance

Fanfare for Our Common Earth <2001>   3'

3[1.2.pic] 3[1.2.Eh] 3[1.2.bcl] 2 — 4 3 3 1 — tmp+4 — hp — str
perc: cym, sus cym, tri, glock, bd
The first movement of the composer's Earth Day Portrait. 2 versions:
D-flat major (original) & D major.

Alliance

Prelude & Fugue for String Orchestra   3'

str

Alliance

A Suite of Migrations: Flight of the Monarch <2002>   7'

3[1.2.pic] 3[1.2.Eh] 3[1.2.bcl] 2 — 4 3 3 1 — tmp+3 — hp — str
perc: cym, sus cym, tri, glock, belltree, cast

Alliance

A Suite of Migrations: Geese—Majestic Travelers <2002>   6'

3[1.2.pic] 3[1.2.Eh] 3[1.2.bcl] 2 — 4 3 3 1 — tmp+4 — hp — str
perc: cym, sus cym, tri, glock, aluminum windchimes, opt recording of geese
sounds (played by tmp)
Recording of geese sounds (opt), provided by publisher.

Alliance

Harris, Ross   1945-

(b Amberley, 1 Aug 1945). New Zealander

Concerto, Violin, No.1 <2010>   23'

2[1.pic] 2[1.Eh] 2[1.bcl] 2[1.cbn] — 2 2 2 1 — tmp+3 — hp — str
perc: bd, sd, tambn, tamtam, xyl, chimes

SOUNZ

Concerto, Violoncello <2012>   24'

2 3[1.2.Eh] 3[1.2.bcl] 3[1.2.cbn] — 4 2 3 0 — tmp+1 — hp — str
perc: bd

SOUNZ

The Floating Bride, the Crimson Village <2008>   20'

solo soprano
1 2[1.Eh] 1 1 — 2 1 1[btbn] 0 — tmp+2 — hp — cel — str
perc: bd, sus cym, sd, tambn, tamtam, glock
1. A rooster is walking the bluest night	–'
2. Tu es ma belle	–'
3. The dancer	–'
4. The ladder to the moon	–'
5. The rabbi	–'
6. Give me a green horse	–'
7. As the night	–'
8. You can talk	–'
9. I know the road	–'
10. Like a scarlet lake	–'
11. Mon Dieu	–'

SOUNZ

Music for Jonny <2000>   6'

str

SOUNZ

Symphony No.2 <2006>   29'

solo soprano
3[1.2.pic] 3[1.2.Eh] 2 3[1.2.cbn] — 4 3 3 1 — tmp+3 — hp — str
perc: bd, cym, sd, rototom, tamtam, chimes
I. The blaring of the brass _'
II. She stands with the other women _'
III. There is knocking at the door _'
IV. I shall never be there _'

SOUNZ

Symphony No.3 <2009>   44'

3[1.2.pic] 3[1.2.Eh] 3[1.2.Ebcl] 3[1.2.cbn] — 4 3 3 1 — tmp+3 — hp — pf, cel, accordion — str
perc: bd, cym, sd, glock, xyl, chimes, 3tomtom

SOUNZ

Symphony No.4 (To the Memory of Mahinarangi Tocker)   25'

2[1.2/pic] 3[1.2.Eh] 3[1.2.bcl] 3[1.2.cbn] — 4 3 3 1 — tmp+4 — hp — cel — str
perc: bd, cym, tri, tambn, glock, xyl, vib, chimes, crot, 4sd
1. "the sea mimics a thousand applauding kanuka" _'
2. I'm happy, dressed for laughter…" _'
3. The window fogs to track my finger…" _'
4. I'm the only one turning…" _'
5. "no sky in her day…" _'

SOUNZ

Harris, Roy   1898-1979

(b nr Chandler, OK, 12 Feb 1898; d Santa Monica, CA, 1 Oct 1979). American

Chorale, op.3 <1944>   6'

str[no db]
Violas & cellos are each divided.

Shawnee

Elegy for Orchestra <1958>   6'

3[1.2.pic] 3[1.2.Eh] 2 3[1.2.cbn] — 4 3 3 1 — tmp+2 — hp — cel — str
perc: vib, bd, glock, chimes

AMP   Luck's

Epilogue to Profiles in Courage—J.F.K. <1964; rev 1964>   10'

3[1.2.pic] 3[1.2.Eh] 3[1.2.bcl] 3 — 6 3 3 1 — tmp+3 — str
perc: bd, sd, field dr, marim, vib, chimes

AMP

Horn of Plenty <1964>   10'

3[1.2.3/pic] 3[1.2.Eh] 3[1.2.bcl] 3 — 4 4 3 1 — baritone horn — tmp+3 — str
perc: sd, cym, sus cym, bd, vib

AMP

Ode to Consonance <1957>   10'

2[incl pic] 2[incl Eh] 3[incl bcl] 2 — 2 3 2 1 — baritone horn — tmp+1 — hp — str
perc: vib, sd

AMP

Symphony No.3, in One Movement <1938>   18'

3[1.2.3/pic] 3[1.2.Eh] 3[1.2.bcl] 2 — 4 3 3 2 — tmp+2 — str
perc: xyl, vib, sus cym, bd

AMP

Symphony No.5 <1942>   25

3[1.2.3/pic] 3[1.2/Eh2.Eh1] 4[1.2.bcl.Ebcl(opt)] 3 — 4[opt doubled] 3 3 1 — opt tsx — opt baritone tuba — tmp+6 — hp — pf — str
perc: vib, marim, chimes, sd, cym, sus cym, bd, 2field dr
I. Dotted quarter note = 66   5'
II. Quarter note = 46   11'
III. Dotted half note = 72: Appassionato   9'

Mills

Symphony No.7 <1952; rev 1955>   19'

4[1.2.3/pic2.pic1] 4[1.2.3/Eh2.Eh1] 4[1.2.3.bcl] 4[1.2.3.cbn] — 6[hn5&6 opt] 4[tp4 opt] 3 1 — baritone horn — tmp+3 — hp — pf — str
perc: xyl, chimes, bd, vib, 2field dr, 2sus cym, 2sd
1.   7'
2.   3'
3.   5'
4.   4'

AMP

Symphony No.9 <1962>   27'

4[1.2.3.pic] 4[1.2.Eh1.Eh2] 4[1.2.3.bcl] 4[1.2.3.4/cbn] — 6 4 4 1 — baritone horn — tmp+3 — hp — pf — str
perc: vib, field dr, cym, sus cym, tambn, bd, chimes, 2sd
I. "We, the people …"   5'
II. "…to form a more perfect union"   11'
III. "…to promote the general welfare"   11'

AMP

Symphony No.11 <1967>   22'

4[1.2.3.pic] 4[1.2.3.Eh] 4[1.2.3.bcl] 4[1.2.3.4/cbn] — 6 4 5[1.2.3.4.ba.hn] 1 — 2tmp+5 — hp — cel, pf — str
perc: bd, cym, chimes, field dr, gong, 3sd, 2vib

AMP

When Johnny Comes Marching Home <1935>   8'

3[1.2.pic] 3[1.2.Eh] 3[1.2.Ebcl.bcl] 3 — 4 3 3 1 — euphonium — 2tmp+2 — str
perc: field dr, cym, bd, sus cym

AMP

Harrison, Lou   1917-2003

(b Portland, OR, 14 May 1917; d Lafayette, IN, 2 Feb 2003). American

Suite, Violin, Piano & Chamber Orchestra <1951>   16'

2[1.2/pic] 1 0 0 — 1perc — hp — cel, tack pf — 2vc, db
perc: tamtam

Peters

Harsányi, Tibor   1898-1954

(b Magyarkanisza, 27 June 1898; d Paris, 19 Sept 1954). French composer of Hungarian birth

L'histoire du petite tailleur (The Story of the Little Tailor) <1939>   30'

narrator (optional)
1[incl pic] 0 1 1 — 0 1 0 0 — 1perc — pf — vn, vc
25' without narration. Composed for marionettes, after a tale of Grimm.

Eschig

Hartke, Stephen
1952-

(b Orange, NJ, 6 July 1952). American

Symphony No.3 <2002–2003>
28'

soloists: countertenor, 2 tenors, baritone
3[1.2.3/pic] 3[1.2.Eh] 3[1.2.bcl] 3[1.2.3/cbn] — 4 4 4 1 — tmp+3 — hp — pf/cel — str
perc: bd, marim, vib, cym[2pr], Chinese opera cymbal, 4noah bells[Ab, Eb, E, Db]
Voices may be amplified if necessary.

LKMP

Hartmann, Karl Amadeus
1905-1963

(b Munich, 2 Aug 1905; d Munich, 5 Dec 1963). German

Concerto funèbre <1939>
20'

solo violin
str
I. Introduktion (Largo)   2'
II. Adagio   6'
III. Allegro di molto   8'
IV. Choral (Langsamer Marsch) 4'

Schott

Gesangsszene <1963>
24'

solo baritone
3[1.2/pic.3/afl] 3[1.2.3/Eh] 3[1.2.3/bcl] 3[1.2.3/cbn] — 3 4[incl pic tp] 3 1 — 2tmp+7 — hp — cel, pf — str
perc: sd, bd, field dr, tambn, sus cym, tri, gong, glock, xyl, marim, vib, chimes, 2tomtom, 3timbales, 3tamtam
The composer's manuscript ends after 756 measures. Because of a fatal illness he could not complete the work. It was his wish that the final sentences of the text, which he was not able to set to music, be spoken by the soloist.
In passages for pf 4-hands, the cel player plays pf.

Schott

Miserae <1933–1934>
14'

2[1.2/pic] 2[1.2/Eh] 2 2 — 4 3 3 1 — tmp+6 — cel — str
perc: tambn, sd, bd, tri, sus cym, ratch, wood drum, splash cym, 2gong, rute

Schott

Symphony No.1 (Versuch eines Requiems; Essay for a Requiem) <1935–1936; rev 1954-55>
28'

alto solo
3[all/pic] 4[1.2.3/Eh.Eh] 3[1.2.3/bcl] 4[1.2.3.cbn] — 4 4 3 1 — tmp+5 — hp — pf, cel — str
perc: bd, cym, sd, td, tomtom, tri, tamtam, glock, xyl, vib, gong (G), low bell
I. Introduktion: Elend (Introduction: Misery)   3'
II. Frühling (Spring)   5'
III. Thema mit vier Variationen (Theme with Four Variations) 8'
IV. Tränen (Tears)   8'
V. Epilog: Bitte (Epilogue: Request)   4'

Schott

Symphony No.2 (Adagio) <1945–1946>
17'

3[1/pic.2/pic.3/pic] 3[1.2.3/Eh] 3[1.2.3/bsx] 3[1.2.3/cbn] — 4 3 3 1 — tmp+5 — hp — cel, pf — str
perc: vib, cym, sd, xyl, bd, 2gong, glock, tambn, tri, deep bells [F3,G3,A3,B3]

Schott

Symphony No.4 for Strings <1946–1947>
34'

str
1. Lento assai, con passione 16'
2. Allegro di molto, risoluto 10'
3. Adagio appassionato   8'

Schott

Symphony No.6 <1951–1953>
26'

3[1/pic.2/pic.3/pic] 3[1.2/Eh.3] 3[1.2/bcl.3] 3[1.2.cbn] — 4 4 3 1 — mand — tmp+8 — hp — cel, pf 4-hands — str
perc: bd, sd, td, field dr, tambn, tamtam, tri, cym, sus cym, wood drum, 2tomtoms, 2xyl, 2glock, tmp2, splash cym
I. Adagio   12'
II. Toccata variata 14'

Schott

Symphony No.7 <1957–1958>
32'

3[1.2.3/pic] 3 3 3[1.2.3/cbn] — 4 3 3 1 — 2tmp+7 — hp[dbl if possible] — cel, pf 4-hands — str
perc: bd, field dr, xyl, marim, vib, sd, tri, gong, templeblks, chimes, td, sus cym, cym, tamtam, splash cym, 3tomtom, 3timbales, 2glock
I. Teil (Part I)
  Introduction und Ricercare   11'
II. Teil (Part II)
  Adagio mesto   12'
  Finale: Scherzo virtuoso   7'

Schott

Hartway, James
1944-

(b Detroit, 24 Apr 1944). American

Cityscapes <1981>
22'

jazz quartet: asx, pf, db, drums
3[1.2.pic] 2 3[1.2.bcl] 3[1.2.opt cbn] — 6 4 4 1 — tmp+3 — str
perc: glock, vibrslp, tri, sus cym, chimes, sd, cym, bd, vib, 3tomtoms. Tmp in 1st mvt only; otherwise tmp covers various percussion
Duration varies between 20' & 25', depending on the extent of the jazz solos.
Sunday Morning   _'
Weekdays   _'
Saturday Night   _'

Hard Wall

Country Suite <1985>
17'

jazz quartet: fl, pf, db, drums
str
Duration varies between 15' & 20', depending on the extent of the jazz solos.
1. Hoe Down   _'
2. The Lass and the Lad _'
3. Barn Dance   _'

Hard Wall

Freedom Festival <1990>
10'

optional speaking chorus
3[1.2.pic] 3[1.2.Eh] 3[1.2.bcl] 3[1.2.cbn] — 4 3 3 1 — tmp+4 — hp — pf — str[12.10.8.8.6 preferred]
perc: chimes, vib, tamtam, cym, bd, 5sus cym, 4tomtoms, 2sd
Players (or chorus members) whisper, speak, and shout cries for freedom in 7 different languages at various points. Fragments of 12 different national anthems occur.

Hard Wall

Island Dances <2000>
23'

2 solo harps
3[1.afl.pic] 3[1.2.Eh] 3[1.2.bcl] 3[1.2.cbn] — 4 3 3 0 — tmp+3 — str
perc: cym, sus cym, sd, timbales, tamtam, bongos, guiro, claves, congas, vibrslp, djembe* (or congas), Wuhan cym*, 2cowbells, steel drum (opt) [* available from publisher]
1. Calypso   _'
2. Dream Tango _'
3. Mambo   _'

Hard Wall

Star Dancer <1997>   11'

4[1.2.pic.afl] 2 3[1.2.bcl] 3[1.2.cbn] — 4 4 4 1 — tmp+5 — hp — pf
— str
perc: rototom, tamtam, brake dr, vib, flexatone, cym, vibrslp, sd, bd/cym,
4tomtoms, 4sus cym, 2cowbells, 2tri, log drum, Wuhan cym*, Japanese bell*,
djembe* (or conga) [* available from publisher]

Hard Wall

Urban Pictures   19'

solo jazz quintet: 2tenor sax [1 dbl soprano sax], piano, bass, drums
4[1.2.pic.afl] 2 3[1.2.bcl] 3[1.2.cbn] — 4 4 4 1 — tmp+3 — str
perc: sus cym, sd, brake dr, vib, whip, claves, police whistle
1. Mean Streets   11'
2. Renaissance Cities   8'

Hard Wall

Harty, Hamilton   1879-1941

(b Hillsborough, Co. Down, 4 Dec 1879; d Brighton, 19 Feb 1941). Irish

A John Field Suite <1939>   18'

1[1/pic] 1 1 1 — 1 1 0 0 — tmp+1 — hp — str
perc: glock, chimes, tri, bd, sd, tambn
Transcription by Harty of John Field piano works.
I.   Polka   5'
II. Nocturne   5'
III. Slow Waltz (Remembrance)   4'
IV. Rondo (Midi)   5'

Boosey

Haydn, Franz Joseph   1732-1809

(b Rohrau, Lower Austria, 31 March 1732; d Vienna, 31 May 1809). Austrian

Hob = A. van Hoboken: *Joseph Haydn: Thematisch-bibliographisches
Werkverzeichnis, i: Instrumentalwerke; ii: Vokalwerke; iii: Register,
Addenda und Corrigenda* (Mainz, 1957–78)

Armida, Hob. XXVIII:12: Overture <1784>   7'

1 2 0 2 — 2 0 0 0 — str

Bärenreiter	Breitkopf	Luck's

Concertino, Harpsichord, Hob.XIV:11, C major <1760>   10'

str
Ed. H.C. Robbins Landon.
1. Moderato   3'
2. Adagio   5'
3. Allegro   2'

Doblinger	Henle

Concerto, Flute, Hob.VIIf:D1, D major <1771>   20'

cnt — str
Ed. Alexander Kowatscheff. Authenticity doubtful.

Leuckart	Luck's

Concerto, 2 Flutes, Hob.VIIh:1, C major <1786–1787>   13'

0 0 0 0 — 2 0 0 0 — str
Ed. H.C. Robbins Landon. Originally for 2 solo *lire organizzate*, rather
than 2 flutes.
I.   Allegro con spirito   4'
II. Andante   4'
III. Finale: Allegro con brio   5'

Doblinger

Concerto, Flute & Oboe, Hob.VIIh:2, G major   12'
<1786–1787>

0 0 0 0 — 2 0 0 0 — str
Ed. H.C. Robbins Landon. Originally for 2 solo *lire organizzate*, rather
than flute & oboe.
I.   Vivace assai   5'
II. Adagio ma non troppo   3'
III. Rondo: Presto   4'

Doblinger

Concerto, Flute & Oboe, Hob.VIIh:3, G major   13'
<1786–1787>

0 0 0 0 — 2 0 0 0 — str
Ed. H.C. Robbins Landon. Originally for 2 solo *lire organizzate*, rather
than flute & oboe.
I.   Allegro con spirito   5'
II. Romance: Allegretto   4'
III. Finale: Allegro   4'

Doblinger

Concerto, Flute & Oboe, Hob.VIIh:4, F major <1786>   14'

0 0 0 0 — 2 0 0 0 — str
Ed. H.C. Robbins Landon. Originally for 2 solo *lire organizzate*, rather
than flute & oboe.
I.   Allegro   5'
II. Andante   5'
III. Finale: Presto   4'

Doblinger

Concerto, Flute & Oboe, Hob.VIIh:5, F major   12'
<1786–1787>

0 0 0 0 — 2 0 0 0 — str
Ed. H.C. Robbins Landon. Originally for 2 solo *lire organizzate*, rather
than flute & oboe.
I.   Allegro   5'
II. Andante   4'
III. Finale: Vivace   3'

Doblinger

Concerto, Harpsichord, Hob.XVIII:4, G major <1781>   21'

0 2[opt] 0 0 — 2[opt] 0 0 0 — str
For harpsichord or piano.
1. Allegro moderato   9'
2. Adagio   8'
3. Rondo: Presto   4'

Henle	Kalmus	Luck's	Nagel	Peters

Concerto, Harpsichord, Hob.XVIII:5, C major <1765>   13'

str[no va]
Perhaps intended for piano rather than harpsichord. Ed. Horst Heussner.
This work has also been attributed to Wagenseil, though it is probably
by Haydn.

Luck's	Nagel

Concerto, Harpsichord, Hob.XVIII:7, F major   12'

str[va opt]
Ed. Klaas Weelink. Authenticity questioned by some authorities;
attributed to Wagenseil in one manuscript.

KaWe	Luck's

Concerto, Harpsichord, Hob.XVIII:11, D major <1784>   18'

0 2 0 0 — 2 0 0 0 — str
I.   Vivace   7'
II. Un poco adagio   7'
III. Rondo all'ungherese: Allegro assai 4'

Breitkopf	Luck's	Peters

Concerto, Harpsichord, Hob.XVIII:F1, F major <1780>   *12'*

2 0 0 0 — str
Ed. Gustav Lenzewski. Actual composer is Georg Joseph Vogler.

Kalmus	Luck's	Vieweg

Concerto, Horn, No.1, Hob.VIId:3, D major <1762>   *17'*

0 2 0 0 — cnt — str
Boosey ed. HH Steves; Kalmus ed. Clark McAlister.

I. Allegro vivace	6'
II. Adagio	7'
III. Allegro vivace	4'

Boosey	Bote & Bock	Kalmus	Luck's

Concerto, Horn, No.2, Hob.VIId:4, D major <1781>   *18'*

str
Authenticity doubtful. Boosey ed. HH Steves; Kalmus ed. Clark McAlister.

I. Allegro moderato	7'
II. Adagio	6'
III. Allegro	5'

Boosey	Breitkopf	Kalmus	Luck's

Concerto, 2 Horns, E-flat major   *20'*

0 2 0 0 — 2 0 0 0 — str
Attribution to Haydn is acknowledged to be incorrect; actual composer remains unknown.
   Practical performing edition by Clark McAlister.

1. Allegro maestoso	_'
2. Romance: Adagio	_'
3. Rondeau: Allegretto	_'

Kalmus

Concerto, Oboe, Hob.VIIg:C1, C major   <1800>   *23'*

0 2 0 0 — 2 2 0 0 — tmp — str
Authenticity doubtful. Breitkopf ed. Alexander Wunderer; Oxford ed. Evelyn Rothwell; Peters ed. Rolf Julius Koch.

I. Allegro spiritoso	11'
II. Andante	6'
III. Rondo: Allegretto	6'

Breitkopf	Oxford	Peters

Concerto, Organ, Hob.XVIII:1, C major <1756>   *20'*

0 2 0 0 — str
Ed. Michael Schneider.

1. Allegro moderato	8'
2. Largo	7'
3. Allegro molto	5'

Breitkopf

Concerto, Organ, No.2, Hob.XVIII:8, C major <1766>   *11'*

0 0 0 0 — 0 2[opt] 0 0 — opt tmp — str
Ed. H.C. Robbins Landon.

I. Moderato	5'
II. Adagio	3'
III. Finale: Allegro	3'

Doblinger

Concerto, Organ, Hob.XVIII:7, F major   *14'*

0 0 0 0 — 2 0 0 0 — str
Ed. Belsky and Sramek. First published in 1962, and not listed in Hoboken. Attribution to Haydn is doubtful.

I. Moderato	6'
II. Adagio	5'
III. Allegro	3'

Breitkopf	Luck's

Concerto, Piano

see his: Concerto, Harpsichord

Concerto, Trumpet, Hob.VIIe:1, E-flat major <1796>   *13'*

2 2 0 2 — 2 2 0 0 — tmp — str
Universal edition (1982) is by Edward Tarr & H.C. Robbins Landon. New Kalmus "Practical Performing Edition" (A7278, 2009) ed. Clark McAlister.

I. Allegro	6'
II. Andante	3'
III. Finale: Allegro	4'

Boosey	Breitkopf	C. Fischer	Kalmus	Universal

Concerto, Violin, Hob.VIIa:1, C major <1769>   *19'*

cnt — str
Bärenreiter ed. H. Lohmann & G. Thomas.

I. Allegro moderato	10'
II. Adagio	5'
III. Finale: Presto	4'

Bärenreiter	Breitkopf	Eulenburg	Kalmus	Luck's

Concerto, Violin, Hob.VIIa:4, G major <1769>   *21'*

cnt — str

I. Allegro moderato	9'
II. Adagio	8'
III. Finale: Allegro	4'

Breitkopf	Doblinger	Kalmus	Luck's

Concerto, Violin, Hob.VIIa:B2, B-flat major <1767>   *27'*

str
Actual composer: Christian Cannabich.

I. Allegro con giusto	_'
II. Adagio	_'
III. Tempo di menuetto	_'

Breitkopf

Concerto, Violin & Piano (or Harpsichord), Hob.XVIII:6, F major <1766>   *18'*

str
Ed. Paul Bormann.

1. Allegro moderato	7'
2. Largo	7'
3. Allegro	4'

Boosey	Breitkopf	Luck's

Concerto, Violoncello, Hob.VIIb:1, C major <c1761–1765>   *24'*

0 2 0 0 — 2 0 0 0 — str
2 Bärenreiter editions: (1) ed. Oldrich Pulkert, 1962, when the concerto was rediscovered (reprinted Kalmus); (2) ed. Sonja Gerlach (for the Haydn collected edition). Supraphon edition has cadenzas by Benjamin Britten.

I. Moderato	10'
II. Adagio	8'
III. Allegro molto	6'

Bärenreiter	Kalmus	Supraphon

Concerto, Violoncello, Hob.VIIb:2, D major <1783>   *25'*

0 2 0 1 — 2 0 0 0 — str
Bärenreiter ed. Sonja Gerlach; Peters (& Kalmus reprint) ed. Kurt Soldan; Schott ed. Maurice Gendron.
   Lengnick edition (ed. H.C. Robbins Landon, based on the rediscovered autograph) incorporates baroque bowings in solo & orchestral parts.

I. Allegro moderato	13'
II. Adagio	6'
III. Allegro	6'

Bärenreiter	Kalmus	Lengnick	Peters	Schott

Concerto, Violoncello, Hob.VIIb:2, D major (arr. Gevaert) <1783>   25'

Arr. François-Auguste Gevaert.
2 2 2 2 — 2 0 0 0 — str
Arr. François-Auguste Gevaert, with added woodwinds and various romanticizations. The added cadenzas are believed to have been written not by Gevaert, but by Adrien-François Servais (1806-1866), a great cello virtuoso of his day.

I. Allegro moderato	13'
II. Adagio	6'
III. Allegro	6'

Breitkopf	Kalmus	Luck's

Concerto, Violoncello, Hob.VIIb:5, C major <1769>   17'

2 2 2 2 — 2 0 0 0 — str
Completed by David Popper after a sketch by Haydn.

I. Allegro moderato	_'
II. Andante	_'
III. Allegretto vivace	_'

Kalmus

The Creation

see his: Schöpfung

Divertimento, Hob.II:46, B-flat major (St. Antony Chorale) <1784>   10'

0 2 0 4[1.2.3.cbn (orig serp)] — 2 0 0 0 — [no str]
Authenticity doubtful.

I. Allegro con spirito	4'
II. Chorale St. Antoni: Andante quasi allegretto	2'
III. Menuetto	2'
IV. Rondo: Allegretto	2'

Peters

L'isola disabitata (The Desert Island; Die wüste Insel): Overture <1779>   8'

1 2 0 1 — 2 2 0 0 — tmp — str

Bärenreiter

Die Jahreszeiten (The Seasons) <1799–1801>   134'

chorus   solos STB
2[1.2/pic] 2 2 3[1.2.cbn] — 4 3 3 0 — tmp+2 — pf — str
perc: tri, tambn
Trumpet 3 and horns 3-4 have very little to play. Percussion play only in part 3, *Autumn*. (Originally the percussion parts were intended to be improvised; written-out parts have been created editorially.)
   Bärenreiter edition includes a harpsichord part.

I. Spring	31'
II. Summer	37'
III. Autumn	34'
IV. Winter	32'

Bärenreiter	Breitkopf	Kalmus	Peters

Kindersymphonie, Hob.II:47, C major (*Toy Symphony; Sinfonia Berchtolsgadensis*) <1786>   10'

5-7 players of toy insts — str[no va]
Toy instruments: trumpet, drum, cuckoo, nightingale, rattle, triangle, quail.
   Published variously under the names of Joseph Haydn and Leopold Mozart (Breitkopf & Doblinger editions are under Leopold Mozart's name; Kalmus & Luck's [reprints of earlier editions] are under that of Franz Joseph Haydn).
   This work has also been attributed to Michael Haydn and to Edmund Angerer (also Augener, Angener). Some early sources are titled *Berchtolds Gaden Musick*, and some use viola instead of 2nd violin as th middle of the 3 string voices.
   A corruption of this work was later incorporated into a *Cassation* that has been attributed, probably incorrectly, to Leopold Mozart.

I. Allegro	5'
II. Menuetto	3'
III. Finale: Allegro	2'

Breitkopf	Doblinger	Kalmus	Luck's	Peters

March for the Royal Society of Musicians, Hob.VIII:3bis <1792–1795>   4

2 0 2 2 — 2 2 0 0 — tmp — str
Ed. H.C. Robbins Landon. The second (orchestral) version of the *March for the Prince of Wales*.

Doblinger

Mass, Hob.XXII:1, F major (Missa brevis; Jugendmesse) <1749>   12

chorus   2 solo sopranos
org — str[no va]
Bärenreiter and Faber editions include the additional instrumental parts which were supplied later, supposedly at Haydn's suggestion:
1 0 2 2 — 0 2 0 0 — tmp

I. Kyrie	1'
II. Gloria	2'
III. Credo	3'
IV. Sanctus	1'
V. Benedictus	3'
VI. Agnus Dei	2'

Bärenreiter	Doblinger	Faber

[Mass, Hob.XXII:2]

This work is for chorus *a cappella*—thus outside the scope of this book.

Mass, Hob.XXII:3, G major (Rorate coeli desuper; Missa brevis alla capella)   10'

chorus
org — str[no va]
Ed. H.C. Robbins Landon.

Universal

Mass, Hob.XXII:4, E-flat major (Grosse Orgelsolo Messe; Missa in honorem beatissimae virginis Mariae) <1774>   37'

chorus   solos SATB
0 2[Eh1.Eh2] 0 1 — 2 0 0 0 — org — str[no va]
Ed. Alois Strassl. Doblinger edition includes parts for 2tp & tmp believed to be by Haydn.

I. Kyrie	5'
II. Gloria	9'
III. Credo	10'
IV. Sanctus	2'
V. Benedictus	5'
VI. Agnus Dei	6'

Bärenreiter	Doblinger

Mass, Hob.XXII:5, C major (St. Cecilia Mass; Missa   70'
cellensis) <1766>

chorus   solos SATB
0 2 0 2 — 0 2 0 0 — tmp — org — str
In the *Benedictus* the composer may have added 2hn later.
Both this work and Hob.XXII:8 are known as *Missa cellensis*.

I. Kyrie	9'
II. Gloria	31'
III. Credo	17'
IV. Sanctus	2'
V. Benedictus	6'
VI. Agnus Dei	5'

Bärenreiter	Universal

Mass, Hob.XXII:6, G major (Missa Sancti Nicolai; Missa   27'
St. Josephi) <1772>

chorus   solos SATB
0 2 0 1 — 2 0 0 0 — org — str
Faber ed. by H.C. Robbins Landon.

1. Kyrie	3'
2. Gloria	5'
3. Credo	6'
4. Sanctus	2'
5. Benedictus	5'
6. Agnus Dei	6'

Bärenreiter	Faber	Kalmus	Luck's

Mass, Hob.XXII:7, B-flat major (Kleine Orgelmesse;   20'
Missa brevis sancti Johannis de deo) <1778>

chorus   solo soprano
org — str[no va]
Ed. H.C. Robbins Landon.
   Bärenreiter offers an arrangement for female chorus (SMsAA) by
Herbert Breuer.

1. Kyrie	2'
2. Gloria	1'
3. Credo	5'
4. Sanctus	1'
5. Benedictus	5'
6. Agnus Dei	6'

Bärenreiter	Carus

Mass, Hob.XXII:8, C major (Mariazeller Messe; Missa   36'
cellensis) <1782>

chorus   solos SATB
0 2 0 1 — 0 2 0 0 — tmp — org — str
Both this work and Hob.XXII:5 are known as *Missa cellensis*.

I. Kyrie	5'
II. Gloria	8'
III. Credo	8'
IV. Sanctus	3'
V. Benedictus	7'
VI. Agnus Dei	5'

Bärenreiter	Kalmus	Luck's

Mass, Hob.XXII:9, C major (Missa in tempore belli;   40'
Mass in Time of War; Paukenmesse) <1795>

chorus   solos SATB
1 2 2 2 — 2 2 0 0 — tmp — org — str
Composer provided various versions and distributions of the wind parts,
affecting fl, cl, hn.

I. Kyrie	5'
II. Gloria	10'
III. Credo	10'
IV. Sanctus	3'
V. Benedictus	6'
VI. Agnus Dei	6'

Bärenreiter	Kalmus	Luck's	Schirmer

Mass, Hob.XXII:10, B-flat major (Heiligmesse; Missa   42'
Sancti Bernardi von Offida) <1796>

chorus   solos SATB (or SSATBB)
0 2 2 2 — 0 2 0 0 — tmp — org — str
Clarinets are used only in the *Incarnatus* and *Et vitam*. Peters edition
treats them as an alternative to the oboes (i.e., 2ob *or* 2cl).

I. Kyrie	5'
II. Gloria	11'
III. Credo	11'
IV. Sanctus	2'
V. Benedictus	6'
VI. Agnus Dei	7'

Bärenreiter	Luck's	Peters

Mass, Hob.XXII:11, D minor [original instrumentation]   42'
(Lord Nelson Mass; Missa in angustiis; Nelsonmesse;
L'Impérial; Coronation Mass) <1798>

chorus   solos SATB
0 0 0 0 — 0 3 0 0 — tmp — org — str
Solo 2nd soprano required for 4 bars only. 3rd tp has no independent part;
doubles 2nd tp in certain passages.
   Includes a *konzertierenden* organ part, because at the time the
Esterhazy winds were gone. Haydn later suggested putting the concerted
part of the organ back in the winds, resulting in two subsequent editions
of this mass [2nd instrumentation & 3rd instrumentation]. It is possible to
play any of the three instrumentations from the Bärenreiter set of parts.

Kyrie	5'
Gloria	11'
Credo	10'
Sanctus & Benedictus	9'
Agnus Dei	7'

Bärenreiter	Schott

Mass, Hob.XXII:11, D minor [2nd instrumentation]   42'
(Lord Nelson Mass; Missa in angustiis; Nelsonmesse;
L'Impérial; Coronation Mass) <1798>

chorus   solos SATB
1 2 0 2 — 0 3 0 0 — tmp — org — str
Solo 2nd soprano required for 4 bars only. 3rd tp has no independent part;
doubles 2nd tp in certain passages.
   Woodwinds added supposedly at Haydn's suggestion. It is possible to
play any of the three instrumentations from the Bärenreiter set of parts.

Kyrie	5'
Gloria	11'
Credo	10'
Sanctus & Benedictus	9'
Agnus Dei	7'

Bärenreiter	Breitkopf	Luck's	Peters

Mass, Hob.XXII:11, D minor [3rd instrumentation]   42'
(Lord Nelson Mass; Missa in angustiis; Nelsonmesse;
L'Impérial; Coronation Mass) <1798>

chorus   solos SATB
1 2 2 1 — 2 3 0 0 — tmp — org — str
Solo 2nd soprano required for 4 bars only. 3rd tp has no independent part;
doubles 2nd tp in certain passages.
   Optional clarinets and horns added supposedly at Haydn's suggestion.
It is possible to play any of the three instrumentations from the
Bärenreiter set of parts.

Kyrie	5'
Gloria	11'
Credo	10'
Sanctus & Benedictus	9'
Agnus Dei	7'

Bärenreiter	

Mass, Hob.XXII:12, B-flat major (Theresienmesse) <1799>   43'

chorus   solos SATB

0 0 2 1 — 0 2 0 0 — tmp — org — str

An authentic copy has additional parts for 2ob and 2hn, though these are not as yet available in any modern edition.

I. Kyrie	5'
II. Gloria	12'
III. Credo	11'
IV. Sanctus	2'
V. Benedictus	6'
VI. Agnus Dei	7'

Bärenreiter

Mass, Hob.XXII:13, B-flat major (Schöpfungsmesse; Creation Mass) <1801>   41'

chorus   solos SATB (or SSATTB)

0 2 2 2 — 2 2 0 0 — tmp — org — str

I. Kyrie	7'
II. Gloria	11'
III. Credo	9'
IV. Sanctus	3'
V. Benedictus	5'
VI. Agnus Dei	6'

Bärenreiter   Kalmus

Mass, Hob.XXII:14, B-flat major (Harmoniemesse) <1802>   48'

chorus   solos SATB (or SSATTB)

1 2 2 2 — 2 2 0 0 — tmp — org — str

I. Kyrie	9'
II. Gloria	13'
III. Credo	12'
IV. Sanctus	3'
V. Benedictus	4'
VI. Agnus Dei	7'

Bärenreiter   Kalmus   Peters   Schirmer

Notturno No.1, Hob.II:25, C major <1774–1775>   15'

1 1 0 0 — 2 0 0 0 — str

Ed. H.C. Robbins Landon.

   Originally for strings, 2 horns, and 2 *lire organizzate*.

I. Marcia	2'
II. Allegro	4'
III. Adagio	5'
IV. Finale: Presto	4'

Doblinger   Luck's

Il ritorno di Tobia, Hob.XXI:1: Overture <1786>   6'

0 2 0 2 — 2 2 0 0 — tmp — str

Bärenreiter

Salve regina, Hob.XXIIIb:2, G minor <1771>   20'

solos SATB

org — str

Doblinger ed. by H.C. Robbins Landon.

   Originally intended for 4 solo voices, though sometimes performed chorally.

Doblinger   Luck's   Peters

Scherzando, Hob.II:33, F major <1765>   8'

1 2 0 0 — 2 0 0 0 — str[no va]

Flute only in the Trio.

Allegro	1'
Menuet & Trio	3'
Adagio	3'
Finale: Presto	1'

Henle

Scherzando, Hob.II:34, C major <1765>   9

1 2 0 0 — 2 0 0 0 — str[no va]

Flute only in the Trio.

Allegro	2'
Menuet & Trio	3'
Adagio	3'
Finale: Presto	1'

Henle

Scherzando, Hob.II:35, D major <1765>   9'

1 2 0 0 — 2 0 0 0 — str[no va]

Flute only in the Trio.

Allegro	1'
Menuet & Trio	4'
Andante	3'
Finale: Presto	1'

Henle

Scherzando, Hob.II:36, G major <1765>   10'

1 2 0 0 — 2 0 0 0 — str[no va]

Flute only in the Trio.

Allegro	2'
Menuet & Trio	4'
Adagio	3'
Finale: Presto	1'

Henle

Scherzando, Hob.II:37, E major <1765>   9'

1 2 0 0 — 2 0 0 0 — str[no va]

Flute only in the Trio.

Allegro	3'
Menuet & Trio	3'
Andante	2'
Finale: Presto	1'

Henle

Scherzando, Hob.II:38, A major <1765>   11'

1 2 0 0 — 2 0 0 0 — str[no va]

Allegro	3'
Menuet & Trio	3'
Adagio	4'
Finale: Presto	1'

Henle

Die Schöpfung (The Creation) <1798>   109'

chorus   solos SSTBB (or STB)

3 2 2 3[1.2.cbn] — 2 2 3 0 — tmp — hpsd — str

Fl 3 plays only in the first 32 bars of Part III. Probably in the 18th century one of the oboists (both of whom are tacet in this passage) switched to flute to cover the 3rd part.

   Carus ed. Wolfgang Gersthofer; Bärenreiter ed. Annette Oppermann; Novello ed. Michael Pilkington; Peters ed. Nicholas Temperley.

Part I	40'
Part II	40'
Part III	29'

Bärenreiter   Breitkopf   Carus   Novello   Peters

Die Schöpfung (ed. A. Peter Brown) (The Creation) <1798>   109'

chorus   solos STB (or SSTBB)

3 2 2 3[1.2.cbn] — 2 2 3 0 — tmp — fortepiano[or hpsd] — str

Includes markings that permit reconstruction of Haydn's own practice, including, for performances with the very largest forces, the use of up to 3 "wind bands" and 2 brass groups. The aggregate largest ensemble would be: 9 6 6 7[incl cbn] — 6 4 5 0 — 2tmp — fortepiano or hpsd — "with a string body comparable to modern dimensions."

Part I	40'
Part II	40'
Part III	29'

Oxford

The Seasons
see his: Jahreszeiten

Die sieben letzten Worte [choral version, Hob.XX/2]   56'
(Seven Last Words of Christ) <1795–1796>

chorus   solos SATB
2 2 2 3[1.2.cbn] — 2 2 2 0 — tmp — str

Introduction	5'
1. Vater, vergib ihnen	7'
2. Fürwahr, ich sag es dir: Heute wirst du bei mir	6'
3. Frau, hier siehe deinen Sohn	7'
4. Mein Gott, mein Gott, warum hast du mich verlassen?	7'
Introduction	5'
5. Jesus rufet: Ach, mich dürstet	4'
6. Es ist vollbracht	5'
7. Vater, in deine Hände empfehle ich meinen Geist	8'
Il terremoto (The Earthquake): Er ist nicht mehr (He is no more)	2'

Bärenreiter	Breitkopf	Kalmus	Luck's	Peters

Die sieben letzten Worte [orchestral version,   67'
Hob.XX/1A] (Seven Last Words of Christ) <1787>

2 2 0 2 — 4 2 0 0 — tmp — str
Horns 3&4 only in 2 mvts; flute 2 only in 2 movements; trumpets & tmp only in last mvt.

I. Introduzione	5'
II. Sonata 1: "Pater, dimitte illis"	7'
III. Sonata 2: "Hodie mecum eris in Paradiso"	9'
IV. Sonata 3: "Mulier, ecce filius tuus"	10'
V. Sonata 4: "Deus meus, Deus meus, utquid dereliquisti me?"	8'
VI. Sonata 5: "Sitio"	9'
VII. Sonata 6: "Consummatum est"	7'
VIII. Sonata 7: "In manus tuas, Domine, commendo spiritum meum"	10'
IX. Il terremoto	2'

Bärenreiter

Sinfonia Berchtolsgadensis
see his: Kindersymphonie

Sinfonia concertante, op.84, Hob.I:105, B-flat major   22'
<1792>

solos: oboe, bassoon, violin, violoncello
1 2 0 2 — 2 2 0 0 — tmp — str

I. Allegro	9'
II. Andante	6'
III. Allegro con spirito	7'

Breitkopf	Luck's

Stabat Mater, Hob.XXbis <1767>   80'

chorus   solos SATB
0 2[Eh1.Eh2] 0 1 — org — str
Faber ed. by H.C. Robbins Landon.
   Bärenreiter edition includes the original scoring (as above) as well as a version with enlarged winds, prepared probably in 1803 by Sigismund Neukomm under Haydn's guidance:
   1 2 2 2 — 2 2 3 0 — tmp — org — str

Bärenreiter	Breitkopf	Faber	Kalmus

SYMPHONIES

Although there are many editions of the various Haydn symphonies, many 19th- and 20th-century editions failed to meet modern standards of scholarship. The editions cited here (those of the Haydn-Mozart Presse, edited by H.C. Robbins Landon) are by far the best. Publishers are Doblinger (Symphonies A, B, and 1-49) and Universal (Symphonies 50-104).
   Henle editions, from the Haydn Complete Works, are also cited, as are the excellent Bärenreiter editions where available.

Symphony A, Hob.I:107, B-flat major <1762>   15'

0 2 0 1 — 2 0 0 0 — cnt — str

I. Allegro	6'
II. Andante	4'
III. Allegro molto	5'

Doblinger

Symphony B, Hob.I:108, B-flat major <1765>   15'

0 2 0 1 — 2 0 0 0 — cnt — str

I. Allegro molto	3'
II. Menuet	4'
III. Andante	5'
IV. Presto	3'

Doblinger

Symphony No.1, D major <1759>   11'

0 2 0 1 — 2 0 0 0 — cnt — str

I. Presto	5'
II. Andante	4'
III. Presto	2'

Doblinger

Symphony No.2, C major <1764>   9'

0 2 0 1 — 2 0 0 0 — cnt — str

I. Allegro	3'
II. Andante	3'
III. Presto	3'

Doblinger

Symphony No.3, G major <1762>   16'

0 2 0 1 — 2 0 0 0 — cnt — str

I. Allegro	5'
II. Andante moderato	6'
III. Menuet	3'
IV. [Allegro]	2'

Doblinger

Symphony No.4, D major <1762>   13'

0 2 0 1 — 2 0 0 0 — cnt — str

I. Presto	4'
II. Andante	4'
III. Tempo di menuetto	5'

Doblinger

Symphony No.5, A major <1762>   17'

0 2 0 1 — 2 0 0 0 — cnt — str

I. Adagio ma non troppo	5'
II. Allegro	6'
III. Menuet	4'
IV. Presto	2'

Doblinger

Symphony No.6, D major (Le matin) <1761>   24'

1 2 0 1 — 2 0 0 0 — cnt — str

I. Adagio - Allegro	6'
II. Adagio - Andante - Adagio	8'
III. Menuet	5'
IV. Allegro	5'

Bärenreiter	Doblinger	Henle

Symphony No.7, C major (Le midi) <1761>   21'

2 2 0 1 — 2 0 0 0 — cnt — str

I. Adagio - Allegro	5'
II. Recitativo: Adagio - Allegro - Adagio	7'
III. Adagio	4'
IV. Menuet	2'
V. Allegro	3'

Bärenreiter	Doblinger	Henle

Symphony No.8, G major (Le soir) <1761>   23'

1 2 0 1 — 2 0 0 0 — cnt — str
I. Allegro molto   5'
II. Andante   8'
III. Menuet   5'
IV. La tempesta: Presto   5'

Bärenreiter   Doblinger   Henle

Symphony No.9, C major <1762>   12'

2 2 0 1 — 2 0 0 0 — cnt — str
Flutes in 2nd mvt only, where the oboes are tacet (probably in the 18th century the oboists doubled on flute).
I. Allegro molto   4'
II. Andante   5'
III. Menuet: Allegretto   3'

Doblinger

Symphony No.10, D major <1766>   13'

0 2 0 1 — 2 0 0 0 — cnt — str
I. Allegro   5'
II. Andante   5'
III. Presto   3'

Doblinger

Symphony No.11, E-flat major <1769>   18'

0 2 0 1 — 2 0 0 0 — cnt — str
I. Adagio cantabile   8'
II. Allegro   3'
III. Menuet   4'
IV. Presto   3'

Doblinger

Symphony No.12, E major <1763>   16'

0 2 0 1 — 2 0 0 0 — cnt — str
I. Allegro   3'
II. Adagio   9'
III. Presto   4'

Doblinger

Symphony No.13, D major <1763>   21'

1 2 0 1 — 4 0 0 0 — tmp — cnt — str
I. Allegro molto   5'
II. Adagio cantabile   6'
III. Menuet   5'
IV. Allegro molto   5'

Doblinger

Symphony No.14, A major <1764>   15'

0 2 0 1 — 2 0 0 0 — cnt — str
I. Allegro molto   4'
II. Andante   4'
III. Menuet: Allegretto   4'
IV. Allegro   3'

Doblinger

Symphony No.15, D major <1764>   18'

0 2 0 1 — 2 0 0 0 — cnt — str
I. Adagio   6'
II. Menuet   5'
III. Andante   5'
IV. Presto   2'

Doblinger

Symphony No.16, B-flat major <1766>   12'

0 2 0 1 — 2 0 0 0 — cnt — str
I. Allegro   4'
II. Andante   5'
III. Allegro   3'

Doblinger

Symphony No.17, F major <1766>   14

0 2 0 1 — 2 0 0 0 — cnt — str
I. Allegro   5'
II. Andante ma non troppo 6'
III. Allegro molto   3'

Doblinger

Symphony No.18, G major <1766>   16

0 2 0 1 — 2 0 0 0 — cnt — str
I. Andante moderato   7'
II. Allegro molto   5'
III. Tempo di menuet   4'

Doblinger

Symphony No.19, D major <1766>   12

0 2 0 1 — 2 0 0 0 — cnt — str
I. Allegro molto   5'
II. Andante   4'
III. Presto   3'

Doblinger

Symphony No.20, C major <1766>   15

0 2 0 1 — 2 2 0 0 — tmp — cnt — str
I. Allegro molto   3'
II. Andante (cantabile) 5'
III. Menuet   4'
IV. Presto   3'

Doblinger

Symphony No.21, A major <1764>   15

0 2 0 1 — 2 0 0 0 — cnt — str
I. Adagio   5'
II. Presto   4'
III. Menuet   3'
IV. Allegro molto 3'

Doblinger

Symphony No.22, E-flat major (The Philosopher) <1764>   16

0 2[Eh1.Eh2] 0 1 — 2 0 0 0 — cnt — str
I. Adagio   7'
II. Presto   3'
III. Menuet   4'
IV. Presto   2'

Doblinger

Symphony No.23, G major <1764>   16

0 2 0 1 — 2 0 0 0 — cnt — str
I. Allegro   5'
II. Andante   6'
III. Menuetto   3'
IV. Presto assai 2'

Doblinger

Symphony No.24, D major <1764>   15

1 2 0 1 — 2 0 0 0 — cnt — str
I. Allegro   4'
II. Adagio   4'
III. Menuetto   4'
IV. Allegro   3'

Doblinger

Symphony No.25, C major <1766>   12

0 2 0 1 — 2 0 0 0 — cnt — str
I. Adagio - Allegro molto   6'
II. Menuet   3'
III. Presto   3'

Doblinger

**Symphony No.26, D minor (Lamentatione;   17'
   Weihnachtssymphonie) <1770>**

0 2 0 1 — 2 0 0 0 — cnt — str
The title *Lamentatione* may be authentic; the title *Weihnachtssymphonie* is probably not.
   Bärenreiter ed. Andreas Friesenhagen & Christin Heitmann.
I. Allegro assai con spirito   6'
II. Adagio   6'
III. Menuet   5'
   Bärenreiter   Doblinger

Symphony No.27, G major (Hermannstadt) <1766>   11'

0 2 0 1 — 2 0 0 0 — cnt — str
I. Allegro molto   4'
II. Andante (Siciliano) 4'
III. Presto   3'
   Doblinger

Symphony No.28, A major <1765>   17'

0 2 0 1 — 2 0 0 0 — cnt — str
I. Allegro di molto   6'
II. Poco adagio   6'
III. Menuet: Allegro molto 2'
IV. Presto assai   3'
   Doblinger

Symphony No.29, E major <1765>   17'

0 2 0 1 — 2 0 0 0 — cnt — str
I. Allegro di molto   4'
II. Andante   5'
III. Menuet: Allegro   4'
IV. Presto   4'
   Doblinger

Symphony No.30, C major (Alleluja) <1765>   12'

1 2 0 1 — 2 0 0 0 — cnt — str
I. Allegro   4'
II. Andante   4'
III. Tempo de menuetto più tosto allegretto 4'
   Doblinger

Symphony No.31, D major (Horn Signal) <1765>   25'

1 2 0 1 — 4 0 0 0 — cnt — str
I. Allegro   4'
II. Adagio   6'
III. Menuet   5'
IV. Moderato molto - Presto 10'
   Doblinger

Symphony No.32, C major <1766>   17'

0 2 0 1 — 2 2 0 0 — tmp — cnt — str
I. Allegro molto   4'
II. Menuet   4'
III. Adagio ma non troppo 6'
IV. Presto   3'
   Doblinger

Symphony No.33, C major <1767>   18'

0 2 0 1 — 2 2 0 0 — tmp — cnt — str
I. Vivace   5'
II. Andante   7'
III. Menuet   3'
IV. Allegro   3'
   Doblinger

Symphony No.34, D minor <1767>   15'

0 2 0 1 — 2 0 0 0 — cnt — str
I. Adagio   6'
II. Allegro   4'
III. Menuet   3'
IV. Presto assai 2'
   Doblinger

Symphony No.35, B-flat major <1767>   20'

0 2 0 1 — 2 0 0 0 — cnt — str
I. Allegro di molto   5'
II. Andante   7'
III. Menutto: un poco allegretto 4'
IV. Presto   4'
   Doblinger

Symphony No.36, E-flat major <1769>   17'

0 2 0 1 — 2 0 0 0 — cnt — str
I. Vivace   5'
II. Adagio   4'
III. Menuet   4'
IV. Presto   4'
   Doblinger

Symphony No.37, C major <1769>   13'

0 2 0 1 — 2 0 0 0 — cnt — str
An alternative version substitutes 2 trumpets and timpani for the horns.
I. Presto   3'
II. Menuet   3'
III. Andante   4'
IV. Presto   3'
   Doblinger

Symphony No.38, C major <1769>   13'

0 2 0 1 — 2 2 0 0 — tmp — cnt — str
I. Allegro molto   4'
II. Andante molto   3'
III. Menuetto   3'
IV. Allegro di molto   3'
   Doblinger

Symphony No.39, G minor <1770>   16'

0 2 0 1 — 4 0 0 0 — cnt — str
I. Allegro assai   5'
II. Andante   4'
III. Menuet   3'
IV. Allegro molto   4'
   Doblinger

Symphony No.40, F major <1763>   18'

0 2 0 1 — 2 0 0 0 — cnt — str
I. Allegro   5'
II. Andante più tosto allegretto 5'
III. Menuet   5'
IV. Allegro   3'
   Doblinger

Symphony No.41, C major <1770>   19'

1 2 0 1 — 2 2 0 0 — tmp — str
I. Allegro con spirito 6'
II. Un poco andante   6'
III. Menuetto   4'
IV. Presto   3'
   Doblinger

Symphony No.42, D major <1771>   29'

0 2 0 2 — 2 0 0 0 — str
- *I. Moderato e maestoso*   10'
- *II. Andantino e cantabile*   10'
- *III. Menuet: Allegretto*   5'
- *IV. Scherzando e presto*   4'

Doblinger

Symphony No.43, E-flat major (Merkur; Mercury)   25'
<1772>

0 2 0 1 — 2 0 0 0 — str
- *I. Allegro*   7'
- *II. Adagio*   9'
- *III. Menuet*   4'
- *IV. Allegro*   5'

Doblinger

Symphony No.44, E minor (Trauer-Symphonie) <1772>   22'

0 2 0 1 — 2 0 0 0 — str
- *I. Allegro con brio*   7'
- *II. Menuet: Allegretto; canon in diapason*   6'
- *III. Adagio*   6'
- *IV. Presto*   3'

Doblinger

Symphony No.45, F-sharp minor (Abschieds-Symphonie;   25'
Farewell Symphony) <1772>

0 2 0 1 — 2 0 0 0 — str
Musicians gradually leave the stage during finale.
- *I. Allegro assai*   6'
- *II. Adagio*   7'
- *III. Menuet: Allegretto*   4'
- *IV. Presto - Adagio*   8'

Bärenreiter   Doblinger

Symphony No.46, B major <1772>   19'

0 2 0 1 — 2 0 0 0 — str
- *I. Vivace*   6'
- *II. Poco adagio*   5'
- *III. Menuet: Allegretto*   4'
- *IV. Presto e scherzando*   4'

Bärenreiter   Doblinger

Symphony No.47, G major <1772>   22'

0 2 0 1 — 2 0 0 0 — str
- *I. [Allegro]*   6'
- *II. Un poco adagio; cantabile*   8'
- *III. Menuet al roverso - Trio al roverso*   3'
- *IV. Presto assai*   5'

Doblinger

Symphony No.48, C major (Maria Theresia) <1772>   27'

0 2 0 1 — 2 2 0 0 — tmp — str
Trumpet & timpani parts by another hand, though probably similar to
Haydn's original parts which were lost.
- *I. Allegro*   8'
- *II. Adagio*   10'
- *III. Menuet: Allegretto*   6'
- *IV. Allegro*   3'

Bärenreiter   Doblinger

Symphony No.49, F minor (La passione) <1768>   24'

0 2 0 1 — 2 0 0 0 — cnt — str
- *I. Adagio*   10'
- *II. Allegro di molto*   5'
- *III. Menuet*   6'
- *IV. Presto*   3'

Bärenreiter   Doblinger

Symphony No.50, C major <1773>   18'

0 2 0 1 — 2 2 0 0 — tmp — str
- *I. Adagio e maestoso - Allegro di molto*   4'
- *II. Andante moderato*   4'
- *III. Menuet*   6'
- *IV. Presto*   4'

Universal

Symphony No.51, B-flat major <1774>   23'

0 2 0 1 — 2 0 0 0 — str
- *I. Vivace*   7'
- *II. Adagio*   8'
- *III. Menuetto*   4'
- *IV. Allegro*   4'

Universal

Symphony No.52, C minor <1774>   23'

0 2 0 1 — 2 0 0 0 — str
- *I. Allegro assai con brio*   7'
- *II. Andante*   7'
- *III. Menuetto: Allegretto*   5'
- *IV. Presto*   4'

Universal

Symphony No.53, D major (L'imperiale) <1778>   26'

1 2 0 1[or 2bn] — 2 0 0 0 — tmp — str
The Philharmonia edition of the score offers three alternate finales:
  A. Finale: Capriccio (6') — this is found in the Esterhazy set of parts.
  B. Presto (5') — this was found in most 18th-century manuscripts and
prints.
  C. Presto (4') — believed to be spurious.
- *I. Largo maestoso - Vivace*   8'
- *II. Andante*   7'
- *III. Menuetto*   5'
- *IV. Capriccio: Moderato*   6'

Universal

Symphony No.54, G major <1774>   28'

2 2 0 2 — 2 2 0 0 — tmp — str
- *I. Adagio maestoso - Presto*   6'
- *II. Adagio assai*   11'
- *III. Menuet: Allegretto*   5'
- *IV. Presto*   6'

Universal

Symphony No.55, E-flat major (Der Schulmeister)   22'
<1774>

0 2 0 2 — 2 0 0 0 — str
- *I. Allegro di molto*   5'
- *II. Adagio; ma semplicemente*   8'
- *III. Menuetto*   5'
- *IV. Presto*   4'

Universal

Symphony No.56, C major <1774>   25'

0 2 0 1 — 2 2 0 0 — tmp — str
- *I. Allegro di molto*   6'
- *II. Adagio*   8'
- *III. Menuet*   7'
- *IV. Prestissimo*   4'

Universal

Symphony No.57, D major <1774>   23'

0 2 0 1 — 2 0 0 0 — tmp — str
- *I. Adagio - Allegro*   8'
- *II. Adagio*   6'
- *III. Menuet: Allegretto*   5'
- *IV. Prestissimo*   4'

Universal

Symphony No.58, F major <1775>   18'
0 2 0 1 — 2 0 0 0 — cnt — str
I. Allegro	5'
II. Andante	6'
III. Menuet alla zoppa: Un poco allegretto	3'
IV. Presto	4'

Universal

Symphony No.59, A major (Feuersymphonie; Fire Symphony) <1769>   17'
0 2 0 1 — 2 0 0 0 — cnt — str
I. Presto	5'
II. Andante o più tosto allegretto	5'
III. Menuet	4'
IV. Allegro assai	3'

Universal

Symphony No.60, C major (Il distratto) <1774>   24'
0 2 0 1 — 2 2 0 0 — tmp — str
I. Adagio - Allegro di molto	6'
II. Andante	4'
III. Menuet	5'
IV. Presto	3'
V. Adagio	4'
VI. Prestissimo	2'

Universal

Symphony No.61, D major <1776>   22'
1 2 0 2 — 2 0 0 0 — tmp — str
I. Vivace	7'
II. Adagio	7'
III. Menuet: Allegretto	5'
IV. Prestissimo	3'

Universal

Symphony No.62, D major <1781>   20'
1 2 0 2 — 2 0 0 0 — str
I. Allegro	5'
II. Allegretto	5'
III. Menuet: Allegretto	3'
IV. Allegro	7'

Universal

Symphony No.63, C major [1st version] (La Roxelane) <1777>   20'
1 2 0 2 — 2 2 0 0 — tmp — str
Reconstructed by H.C. Robbins Landon.
The Universal edition includes *both* versions of this symphony in a single publication. Both versions are pastiches, the 1st mvt being the overture to Haydn's opera *Il mondo della luna.*
I. Allegro	6'
II. "La Roxelane": Allegretto (o più tosto allegro)	6'
III. Menuet: Allegretto	4'
IV. Finale: Prestissimo	4'

Universal

Symphony No.63, C major [2nd version] (La Roxelane) <1777–1780>   20'
1 2 0 1 — 2 0 0 0 — str
The Universal edition includes *both* versions of this symphony in a single publication. Both versions are pastiches, the 1st mvt being the overture to Haydn's opera *Il mondo della luna.*
An appendix in the score (but not the parts) includes several versions of added trumpet and timpani parts to the 2nd version, which are, however, of very doubtful authorship.
I. Allegro	6'
II. "La Roxelane": Allegretto (o più tosto allegro)	6'
III. Menuet	4'
IV. Finale: Presto	4'

Universal

Symphony No.64, A major (Tempora mutantur) <1778>   21'
0 2 0 1 — 2 0 0 0 — str
I. Allegro con spirito	6'
II. Largo	9'
III. Menuet: Allegretto	3'
IV. Presto	3'

Universal

Symphony No.65, A major <1778>   17'
0 2 0 1 — 2 0 0 0 — str
I. Vivace e con spirito	5'
II. Andante	5'
III. Menuet	3'
IV. Presto	4'

Universal

Symphony No.66, B-flat major <1779>   23'
0 2 0 2 — 2 0 0 0 — str
I. Allegro con brio	9'
II. Adagio	6'
III. Menuet	4'
IV. Scherzando e presto	4'

Universal

Symphony No.67, F major <1779>   18'
0 2 0 2 — 2 0 0 0 — str
I. Presto	4'
II. Adagio	6'
III. Menuet	3'
IV. Allegro di molto - Adagio cantabile - Primo tempo	5'

Universal

Symphony No.68, B-flat major <1779>   21'
0 2 0 2 — 2 0 0 0 — str
I. Vivace	4'
II. Menuetto: Allegretto	4'
III. Adagio	8'
IV. Presto	5'

Universal

Symphony No.69, C major (Laudon) <1779>   16'
0 2 0 2 — 2 2 0 0 — tmp — str
I. Vivace	4'
II. Un poco adagio; più tosto andante	5'
III. Menuet	3'
IV. Presto	4'

Universal

Symphony No.70, D major <1779>   18'
1 2 0 1 — 2 2 0 0 — tmp — str
I. Vivace con brio	8'
II. Andante: Specie d'un canone in contrapunto doppio	4'
III. Menuet: Allegretto	3'
IV. Allegro con brio	3'

Universal

Symphony No.71, B-flat major <1780>   23'
1 2 0 1 — 2 0 0 0 — str
I. Adagio - Allegro con brio	7'
II. Adagio	6'
III. Menuetto	4'
IV. Vivace	6'

Universal

Symphony No.72, D major <1781>   23'

1 2 0 1 — 4 0 0 0 — tmp — cnt — str
Timpani part may not be authentic.
   I. Allegro   5'
   II. Andante   5'
   III. Menuet   4'
   IV. Andante - Presto   9'
   Universal

Symphony No.73, D major (La chasse) <1782>   25'

1 2 0 2 — 2 2 0 0 — tmp — str
   I. Adagio   10'
   II. Andante   5'
   III. Menuet: Allegretto   5'
   IV. La chasse   5'
   Universal

Symphony No.74, E-flat major <1781>   23'

1 2 0 2 — 2 0 0 0 — str
   I. Vivace assai   7'
   II. Adagio cantabile   7'
   III. Menuetto: Allegro   4'
   IV. Allegro assai   5'
   Universal

Symphony No.75, D major <1781>   20'

1 2 0 1 — 2 2 0 0 — tmp — str
   I. Grave - Presto   6'
   II. Poco adagio   8'
   III. Menuetto: Allegretto   3'
   IV. Vivace   3'
   Universal

Symphony No.76, E-flat major <?1782>   24'

1 2 0 2 — 2 0 0 0 — str
   I. Allegro   6'
   II. Adagio cantabile, ma non troppo 8'
   III. Menuet: Allegretto   3'
   IV. Allegro, ma non troppo 7'
   Universal

Symphony No.77, B-flat major <1783>   18'

1 2 0 2 — 2 0 0 0 — str
   I. Vivace   6'
   II. Andante sostenuto   5'
   III. Menuetto: Allegro   3'
   IV. Allegro   4'
   Universal

Symphony No.78, C minor <1783>   20'

1 2 0 2 — 2 0 0 0 — str
   I. Vivace   6'
   II. Adagio   6'
   III. Menuetto: Allegretto   4'
   IV. Presto   4'
   Universal

Symphony No.79, F major <1784>   21'

1 2 0 2 — 2 0 0 0 — str
   I. Allegro con spirito   6'
   II. Adagio cantabile - un poco allegro 6'
   III. Menuetto: Allegretto   4'
   IV. Vivace   5'
   Universal

Symphony No.80, D minor <1784>   21'

1 2 0 2 — 2 0 0 0 — str
   I. Allegro spiritoso   5'
   II. Adagio   7'
   III. Menuetto   4'
   IV. Presto   5'
   Universal

Symphony No.81, G major <1784>   26'

1 2 0 2 — 2 0 0 0 — str
   I. Vivace   7'
   II. Andante   8'
   III. Menuetto: Allegretto   6'
   IV. Allegro; ma non troppo 5'
   Universal

Symphony No.82, C major (L'ours; The Bear) <1786>   27'

1 2 0 2 — 2 0 0 0 — tmp — str
Trumpets may replace horns in C alto in mvts 1, 3, & 4; horns in F are
required in mvt 2 (trumpets tacet).
   I. Vivace assai   8'
   II. Allegretto   8'
   III. Menuetto   5'
   IV. Vivace   6'
   Bärenreiter   Universal

Symphony No.83, G minor (La poule) <1785>   24'

1 2 0 2 — 2 0 0 0 — str
   I. Allegro spiritoso   8'
   II. Andante   6'
   III. Menuet: Allegretto   5'
   IV. Vivace   5'
   Bärenreiter   Universal

Symphony No.84, E-flat major <1786>   24'

1 2 0 2 — 2 0 0 0 — str
   I. Largo - Allegro   7'
   II. Andante   7'
   III. Menuet: Allegretto 4'
   IV. Vivace   6'
   Bärenreiter   Universal

Symphony No.85, B-flat major (La reine; The Queen of France) <1785–1786>   20'

1 2 0 2 — 2 0 0 0 — str
   I. Adagio - Vivace   8'
   II. Romanze: Allegretto 5'
   III. Menuetto: Allegretto 4'
   IV. Presto   3'
   Bärenreiter   Universal

Symphony No.86, D major <1786>   26'

1 2 0 2 — 2 2 0 0 — tmp — str
   I. Adagio - Allegro spiritoso 7'
   II. Capriccio: Largo   7'
   III. Menuet: Allegretto   6'
   IV. Allegro con spirito 6'
   Bärenreiter   Universal

Symphony No.87, A major <1785>   23'

1 2 0 2 — 2 0 0 0 — str
   I. Vivace   7'
   II. Adagio   7'
   III. Menuet   5'
   IV. Vivace   4'
   Bärenreiter   Universal

Symphony No.88, G major <?1787>   23'
1 2 0 2 — 2 2 0 0 — tmp — str
I. Adagio - Allegro	7'
II. Largo	8'
III. Menuetto: Allegretto	4'
IV. Allegro con spirito	4'

Universal

Symphony No.89, F major <1787>   22'
1 2 0 2 — 2 0 0 0 — str
I. Vivace	7'
II. Andante con moto	6'
III. Menuet: Allegretto	4'
IV. Vivace assai	5'

Universal

Symphony No.90, C major <1788>   24'
1 2 0 2 — 2 2 0 0 — tmp — str
I. Adagio - Allegro assai	7'
II. Andante	7'
III. Menuet	5'
IV. Allegro assai	5'

Universal

Symphony No.91, E-flat major <1788>   25'
1 2 0 2 — 2 0 0 0 — str
I. Largo - Allegro assai	9'
II. Andante	7'
III. Menuet: Un poco allegretto	4'
IV. Vivace	5'

Universal

Symphony No.92, G major (Oxford) <1789>   28'
1 2 0 2 — 2 2 0 0 — tmp — str
I. Adagio - Allegro spiritoso	8'
II. Adagio cantabile	8'
III. Menuetto: Allegretto	6'
IV. Presto	6'

Universal

Symphony No.93, D major <1791>   21'
2 2 0 2 — 2 2 0 0 — tmp — str
I. Adagio - Allegro assai	6'
II. Largo cantabile	6'
III. Menuetto: Allegro	4'
IV. Presto ma non troppo	5'

Bärenreiter   Universal

Symphony No.94, G major (Surprise; Mit dem Paukenschlag) <1791>   23'
2 2 0 2 — 2 2 0 0 — tmp — str
I. Adagio; Vivace assai	7'
II. Andante	7'
III. Menuetto: Allegro molto	5'
IV. Allegro di molto	4'

Bärenreiter   Henle   Universal

Symphony No.95, C minor <1791>   21'
1 2 0 2 — 2 2 0 0 — tmp — str
I. Allegro moderato	7'
II. Andante	6'
III. Menuet	5'
IV. Vivace	3'

Bärenreiter   Universal

Symphony No.96, D major (The Miracle; Das Wunder) <1791>   20'
2 2 0 2 — 2 2 0 0 — tmp — str
I. Adagio - Allegro	5'
II. Andante	6'
III. Menuet: Allegretto	6'
IV. Vivace	3'

Bärenreiter   Universal

Symphony No.97, C major <1792>   25'
2 2 0 2 — 2 2 0 0 — tmp — str
I. Adagio - Vivace	8'
II. Adagio ma non troppo	5'
III. Menuetto: Allegretto	5'
IV. Spiritoso	7'

Bärenreiter   Universal

Symphony No.98, B-flat major <1792>   28'
1 2 0 2 — 2 2 0 0 — tmp — hpsd — str
I. Adagio - Allegro	8'
II. Adagio	5'
III. Menuet: Allegro	6'
IV. Presto	9'

Bärenreiter   Universal

Symphony No.99, E-flat major <1793>   25'
2 2 2 2 — 2 2 0 0 — tmp — str
I. Adagio - Vivace assai	9'
II. Adagio	8'
III. Menuetto: Allegretto	4'
IV. Vivace	4'

Bärenreiter   Henle   Universal

Symphony No.100, G major (Military) <1793>   24'
2 2 2 2 — 2 2 0 0 — tmp+3 — str
perc: bd, cym, tri
Although 2 flutes are clearly indicated, the 2nd flute either doubles the 1st or is tacet throughout.
I. Adagio - Allegro	7'
II. Allegretto	5'
III. Menuet: Moderato	6'
IV. Presto	6'

Bärenreiter   Universal

Symphony No.101, D major (The Clock; Die Uhr) <1793>   29'
2 2 2 2 — 2 2 0 0 — tmp — str
I. Adagio - Presto	9'
II. Andante	8'
III. Menuet: Allegretto	7'
IV. Vivace	5'

Bärenreiter   Henle   Universal

Symphony No.102, B-flat major <1794>   24'
2 2 0 2 — 2 2 0 0 — tmp — str
I. Largo - Vivace	7'
II. Adagio	6'
III. Menuet: Allegro	6'
IV. Presto	5'

Bärenreiter   Henle   Universal

Symphony No.103, E-flat major (Paukenwirbel; Drum Roll) <1795>   27'
2 2 2 2 — 2 2 0 0 — tmp — str
A critical edition of the score with historical and analytical essays is available from Norton.
I. Adagio - Allegro con spirito	8'
II. Andante più tosto allegretto	9'
III. Menuet	4'
IV. Allegro con spirito	6'

Bärenreiter   Henle   Universal

Symphony No.104, D major (London; Salomon) <1795>   29'

2 2 2 2 — 2 2 0 0 — tmp — str

I. Adagio - Allegro	8'
II. Andante	9'
III. Menuet: Allegro	5'
IV. Spiritoso	7'

| Bärenreiter | Henle | Universal |

Te Deum for the Empress Maria Therese, Hob.XXIIIc:2 <1800>   12'

chorus

1 2 0 2 — 2 3 3 0 — tmp — org — str

Ed. H.C. Robbins Landon.

   Trombones provide a simplified doubling of choral passages; trombones not in original score, but reconstructed by Robbins Landon from authentic parts.

| Doblinger |

Toy Symphony

see his: Kindersymphonie

Haydn, Michael   1737 - 1806

(b Rohrau, Lower Austria, bap. 14 Sept 1737; d Salzburg, 10 Aug 1806). Austrian

MH = C.H. Sherman and T.D. Thomas: *Johann Michael Haydn (1737–1806): a Chronological Thematic Catalogue of his Works* (Stuyvesant, NY, 1993)

P = Michael Haydn: *Instrumentalwerke*, ed. L. Perger, *Denkmäler der Tonkunst in Österreich*, xxix, Jg.xiv/2 (1907)

Andromeda ed Perseo, MH 438 (P.25): Overture <1787>   5'

0 2 0 2 — 2 2 0 0 — tmp — str

| Bärenreiter | Doblinger |

Concertino, Horn, MH 134 (P.134), D major <1776>   12'

0 2 0 1 — 2 0 0 0 — cnt — str

Ed. Charles H. Sherman.

| Universal |

Concertino, Trumpet, P.52*bis*, D major   9'

str

Ed. T. Donley Thomas. Minuet movement omitted in this edition.

| I. Adagio | 6' |
| II. Allegro | 3' |

| Medici |

Concerto, Trumpet, No.2, MH 60 (P.34), C major   13'

2 0 0 0 — cnt — str

Ed. Edward H. Tarr.

| 1. Adagio | 5' |
| 2. Allegro molto | 8' |

| Musica Rara |

Concerto, Violin, MH 207, A major <1776>   25'

0 2 0 1 — 2 0 0 0 — str

Ed. Charles H. Sherman.

| 10' |
| 10' |
| 5' |

| Doblinger |

Concerto, Violoncello, B-flat major   31'

0 2 0 2 — 2 0 0 0 — cnt — str

Reconstructed & edited by Mark Starr. Recent research by Starr, yet to be published, now suggests that this cello concerto may actually be the work of Franz Joseph Haydn.

1. Moderato	17'
2. Romance	7'
3. Rondeau	7'

| Noteworthy |

Mass, MH 17 (Missa Sancti Gabrielis) <1754–1757; rev 1768>

chorus   solos SATB

0 0 0 0 — 0 2[opt] 0 0 — opt tmp — str[no va]

Includes both long and short settings for the Gloria and Credo.

   Ed. Otto Biba.

| Carus | Coppenrath |

Mass, MH 182 (Missa Sancti Joannis Nepomuceni) <1772>   20'

chorus

0 2 0 1 — 0 4[2 clarini, 2 trombe] 3[tbn3 opt] 0 — tmp — org — str

Ed. Charles H. Sherman.

| Carus |

Mass, MH 254 (Missa Sancti Hieronymi) <1777>   45'

chorus

0 4 0 2 — 0 0 3 0 — org — double basses

Ed. Charles H. Sherman.

| Universal |

Mass, MH 796 [or 797] (Missa sub titulo Sanctae Theresiae; Theresienmesse) <1801>   40'

solos SATB   chorus

0 2 0 1 — 0 2 0 0 — tmp — org — str

Ed. Charles H. Sherman. Title page says MH 797; Sherman thematic index says MH 796.

| Carus |

Mass, MH 826 (Missa sub titulo Sancte Francisci Seraphici) <1803>   45'

solos SATB   chorus

0 2 0 1 — 0 2 0 0 — tmp — org — str

Ed. Charles H. Sherman.

| Carus |

Pastorello, MH 83 (P.91) (Christmas Music, Salzburg, 1766) <1766>   10'

0 0 0 0 — 0 4 0 0 — tmp — cnt — str

3rd & 4th trumpet parts are low, and may be played on trombones.

| Luck's | Peters |

Requiem, MH 155 [or 154], C minor (Missa pro defuncto Archiepiscopo Sigismundo) <1771>   45'

chorus   solos SATB

0 0 0 1 — 0 4[2 clarini, 2 trombe] 3[tbn3 opt] 0 — tmp — cnt — str[no va]

Carus & Universal editions by Charles Sherman. Title page says MH 154; thematic index says MH 155.

| Carus | Hänssler | Universal |

Salve Regina, MH 634, A major <1796>   4'

chorus

0 0 0 1 — 2 0 0 0 — cnt — str[no va]

Ed. Thomas C. Pamberger.

| Carus |

Symphony, MH 181 (P.8), G major   5'
  str
  Ed. Charles H. Sherman.

  Doblinger

Symphony, MH 272 (P.42), D major <1778>   16'
  0 2 0 1 — 2 0 0 0 — str
  Ed. H.C. Robbins Landon.
  I. Introduction: Adagio; Allegro molto   7'
  II. Andante   5'
  III. Finale: Presto   4'

  Doblinger

Symphony, MH 334 (P.16), G major <1783>   19'
  1 2 0 2 — 2 0 0 0 — hpsd — str
  Doblinger ed. Charles Sherman.
    Previously known as Symphony no.37 by Mozart, whose contribution
  was only an adagio introduction.
  1. Allegro con spirito   7'
  2. Andante sostenuto   5'
  3. Finale: Allegro molto   7'

  Breitkopf   Doblinger

Symphony, MH 399 (P.21), D major <1785>   19'
  1 2 0 2 — 2 0 0 0 — str
  Ed. Pál Gombás.

  Doblinger

Symphony, MH 473 (P.26), E-flat major <1788>   9'
  0 2 0 2 — 2 0 0 0 — str
  Ed. Antal Várhelyi.
  1. Allegro con brio   3'
  2. Adagietto   3'
  3. Finale — Fugato: Allegro 3'

  Doblinger

Symphony, MH 476 (P.29), D major <1788>   8'
  1 2 0 2 — 2 0 0 0 — str
  Ed. Lászlo Kalmár.

  Doblinger

Symphony, MH 508 (P.33), A major <1789>   15'
  0 2 0 2 — 2 0 0 0 — str
  Ed. Charles H. Sherman.

  Doblinger

Veni Sancte Spiritus, MH 39 <1761>   5'
  0 2 0 0 — 2 0 3[opt] 0 — org — str[no va]

  Carus   Hug

He Zhanhao   1933-

(b Hejiashan village, Zhuji, Zhejiang province, 29 Aug 1933). Chinese

**The Butterfly Lovers; Violin Concerto (Liang Shanbo yu   27'
Zhu Yingtai; Liang Zhu Xiao Ti Qin Xie Zou Qu)
<1959>**
  (composed with Chen Gang)
  2 2 2 2 — 4 2 3 0 — tmp+3 — hp — pf — str
  perc: cym, tamtam, clappers [gu ban; or woodblks]
  The publisher also offers a reduction for solo violin, string quintet,
  woodwind quintet & piano.

  HNH

Heath, Dave   1956-

(b Manchester, 1956). British

Out of the Cool <1989>   6'
  solo saxophone (or flute or violin)
  2[1.2/pic] 2 2[1.2/bcl] 2 — 4 0 0 0 — str

  Chester

Heggie, Jake   1961-

(b West Palm Beach, FL, 31 Mar 1961). American

**Cut Time; Variations for Piano & Chamber Orchestra   12'
<2001>**
  1 1 2[1.bcl] 1 — 2 1 1 0 — 1perc — hp — str
  perc: sus cym, sd, tri, tamtam, xyl

  Bent Pen

**Dead Man Walking: Orchestral Excerpts <2000; rev   20'
2002>**
  3[1.2.3/pic/afl] 3[1.2.Eh] 3[1.2.bcl] 3[1.2.3/cbn] — 4 3 3 0 — tmp+2
  — hp — str
  perc: bd, cym, sus cym, sd, tri, tamtam, glock, xyl, vib, templeblks, 4tomtom
  Part 1   _'
  Part 2   _'
  Part 3   _'

  Bent Pen

Heinrich, Anthony Philip   1781-1861

(b Schönbüchel [now Krásny Buk], Bohemia, 11 March 1781; d New York, 3 May
1861). American composer of German-Bohemian birth

The Columbiad; Petite fantasie <1837>   11'
  1[pic/fl] 0 2 1 — 2 1 0 0 — 2vn, 2va, vc, db
  Ed. Andrew Stiller.

  Kallisti

The Tower of Babel (Language Confounded) <1837> 15'
  1 0 2 1 — 2 1 0 0 — st[1.1.2.1.1]
  Ed. Joe Brumbeloe.
    This is one of several versions of this work; other versions are in
  preparation by Kallisti.

  Kallisti

Heitzeg, Steve   1959-

(b Albert Lea, MN, 15 Oct 1959). American

Aqua (Homage à Jacques-Yves Cousteau) <1999>   7'
  2[1.2/pic] 2 2 2 — 4 3 3 1 — tmp+3 — hp — str
  perc: bd, chimes, claves, crot, glock, tamtam, templeblks, button gong (C), 4brake
  drums, 4cowbells, rainstick, 4steel pipes; other perc supplied with parts
  Unconventional percussion supplied with the parts include coral,
  driftwood, fogbell, ocean drum, plastic rings, seashells, seashell
  windchime, river stones. Further optional extra percussion around and
  behind audience playing various assorted bells.

  Stone Circle

Blessed are the Peacemakers <1997> 17'

solo alto   chorus

2[1.2/pic] 2 2 2 — 4 3 3 1 — tmp+4 — hp — str

perc: bd, belltree, crot, glock, guiro, marac, cym, sd, tambn, td, thunder, timbales, tri, chimes, 3bongos, 2cowbells, logdrum, 2metal pipes, 4stones, 4tomtoms, herdbells

1perc placed in balcony. Movements may be performed separately.

1. Injustice Anywhere is a Threat to Justice Everywhere	7'
2. I Am the One Whose Praise Echoes on High	3'
3. Lord, Make Me an Instrument of Your Peace	3'
4. Vägen, du skall följa den (I Hope the Peace So Longed For)	4'

Stone Circle

Blue Liberty <2002> 5'

3[1.2.pic] 3[1.2.Eh] 3[1.2.bcl] 3[1.2.cbn] — 4 3 3 1 — tmp+4 — hp — str

perc: bd, cym, sus cym, sd, td, tamtam, glock, xyl, chimes, marac, 2stones

Stone Circle

Flower of the Earth (Homage to Georgia O'Keefe) <1987> 15'

1 2 0 1 — 2 0 0 0 — str

Slides of the paintings available from the publisher. Movements may be performed separately.

1. White Calico Flower	5'
2. Black Cross, New Mexico	4'
3. Sky Above Clouds II	2'
4. Evening Star III	4'

Stone Circle

Litanies for the Living <1992> 15'

chorus

2[1.2/pic] 2[1.2/Eh] 2 2 — 4 3 3 1 — tmp+3 — hp — str

perc: chimes, glock, vib, tamtam, cym, sus cym, bd, sd, templeblks, tomtom, xyl, 3rainsticks

Gatha for All Threatened Beings	7'
Song (4)	8'

Stone Circle

Mahkato Wakpa (Blue Earth River) <1992> 17'

2[1.2/pic] 2 2 — 4 3 3 1 — tmp+3 — hp — str

perc: bd, chimes, glock, cym, tamtam, td, windchimes (bamboo/wood), xyl, 4tomtoms

Stone Circle

Mustang <1995> 6'

2[1.2/pic] 2 2 — 4 3 3 1 — tmp+3 — hp — str

perc: bd, cast, chimes, cym, slgh-bells, tambn, tamtam, templeblks, td, whip, xyl, 4tomtoms; provided with parts: 2horseshoes, hubcap

Stone Circle

Nine Surrealist Studies (After Salvador Dali) <1985> 19'

3[1.2.3/pic] 3[1.2.Eh] 3 3 — 4 3 3 1 — tmp+3 — hp — pf — str

perc: glock, chimes, tamtam, sd, tomtom, bd, templeblks, xyl, 2sus cym

Accompanying slides available from publisher.

Illumined Pleasures	2'
Three Young Surrealist Women	2'
The Persistence of Memory	2'
Hand (Remorse of Conscience)	2'
The First Days of Spring	1'
Evocation of the Apparition of Lenin	4'
Honey is Sweeter Than Blood	2'
Daddy Long Legs of the Evening… Hope!	1'
Skull with Its Lyric Appendage Resting on a Night Table	3'

Stone Circle

Nobel Symphony; A Symphony for Peace and Justice <2001> 73'

solo Ms, Bar   chorus   children's chorus

3[1.2.3/pic] 3[1.2.Eh] 3[1.2.bcl] 3[1.2.cbn] — 4 3 3[tbn1&2/Tibetan hns] 1 — tmp+4 — pf — str

perc: bd, bongos, brake dr, chimes, claves, congas, glock, guiro, cym, marac, marim, ratch, sd, tamtam, templeblks, td, timbales, vib, vibrslp, whip, woodblk, xyl, agogo, 2cowbells, djembe, gourd rattle, kalimba, logdrum, talking dr, 4tomtoms, 2tri, plus extensive additional instruments

An extensive array of unconventional instruments (including Tibetan horns, but mostly percussion) provided with the parts.

Texts from various Nobel laureates. Optional narrations before certain movements (these add about 5' to the total duration).

Preamble For Known and Unknown Worlds	2'
I. Literature: War is Wide…	11'
II. Chemistry: Anthem and Elements	9'
Proclamation for Economic Justice	1'
III. Economics: To Have and Have Not	9'
IV. Physics: Universal Scherzo	6'
Proclamation for the Sick and Suffering	3'
V. Physiology or Medicine: Chaconne for Healing	4'
VI. Peace: Circles of Compassion	24'
Postlude For the Rights of All	4'

Stone Circle

On the Day You Were Born <1995> 18'

narrator

2[1.2/pic] 2 2 2 — 4 3 3 1 — tmp+3 — hp — str

perc: bd, belltree, chimes, glock, cym, marim, tambn, tamtam, templeblks, vib, xyl, 4tomtoms, wood windchimes; provided with the parts: llama hooves rattle, shell windchimes, 2stones

Also available in a version for chamber orchestra & narrator:

1 2 1 2 — 2 1 0 0 — tmp+1 — pf — str

Stone Circle

Sacred Stones (Symphony in Stone) <1993> 23'

3[1.2.3/pic] 3[1.2.Eh] 3[1.2.bcl] 3[1.2.cbn] — 4 3 3 1 — tmp+3 — h — str

perc: bd, tamtam, chimes, glock, vib, marim, cym, xyl, sus cym, 4tomtoms; provided with the parts: obsidian wind gong, ankle bells, stone windchimes, various stones

String players also strike pairs of stones together; conductor shakes 4 obsidian arrowheads briefly. Stones and arrowheads provided with the parts. Movements may be performed separately.

Agate (Stone of Truth)	5'
Turquoise (Stone of Life)	3'
Jade (Stone of Wisdom and Justice) and Amethyst (The Healing Stone)	6'
Black Obsidian "Apache Tear" (The Protective Stone)	9'

Stone Circle

Symphony in Sculpture <2012> 29'

3[1.2.pic] 3[1.2.Eh] 3[1.2.bcl] 3[1.2.cbn] — 4 3 3 1 — tmp+4 — hp — pf, cel — str

perc: bd, chimes, glock, cym, ratch, slgh-bells, tambn, tamtam, thunder, tri, whip, xyl, agogo, bamboo windchimes, car parts, finger cym, pod rattle, singing bowl, shruti box, 3dumbek, small bells, clappers, 2Coke bottles, 5noah bells, 2sus cym

1. Moonrise, east. january, 2005; Moonrise, east. august, 2006	4'
2. Spider	2'
3. Back of a Snowman (White); Back of a Snowman (Black)	2'
4. Ancient Forest	5'
5. Post-Balzac	4'
6. T8	1'
7. White Ghost	4'
8. Thinker on a Rock	1'
9. Namade	6'

Stone Circle

Symphony to the Prairie Farm <2002>   25'

2[1.2/pic] 2 2 2 — 4 3 3 1 — gtr — tmp+3 — str
perc: bd, cym, sus cym, bass bow, tamtam, xyl, woodblk, gourd rattle, CD of crop circle sounds; additional unconventional percussion instruments (including farm equipment items) and CD supplied with parts
Movements may be performed separately.
Ghosts of the Grasslands   10'
Rows of Green on Black (Farms, Not Arms)   5'
Night Pasture (All Cows Are Sacred)   5'
Field Dances and Harvest Waltz   5'

Stone Circle

The Tin Forest   10'

narrator
3[1.2.pic] 3[1.2.Eh] 3[1.2.bcl] 3[1.2.cbn] — 4 3 3 1 — gtr — tmp+4 — hp — pf — str
perc: bd, bongos, brake dr, chimes, claves, flexatone, glock, guiro, cym, marac, marim, tamtam, tri, xyl, gourd, cuica, rainstick, samba whistle, springdrum, cricket, 2stones, 3sus cym, 3cowbell.
props & special effects: 3plastic bags, 6-7 aluminum pop cans, plastic water bottles, 3glass bottles, plastic 5-gallon pail, 2metal pipes, tin-can bell tree, tin-can temple blocks, tin soup can, junk cymbal.

Stone Circle

Together (Divided We Are Nothing) <2006>   6'

chorus
2[1.2/pic] 2 2 2 — 4 3 3 1 — tmp+4 — str
perc: bd, chimes, claves, congas, glock, cym, marac, marim, sus cym, tambn, tamtam, buttongong[E3], cuica, cabasa, Tibetan prayer chimes, 2stones.
props & special effects: 2plowshares, 2 small fallen tree branches.

Stone Circle

Voice of the Everglades (Epitaph for Marjory Stoneman Douglas) <2000>   17'

narrator
2[1.2/pic] 2 2 2 — 4 3 3 1 — tmp+3 — hp — cel[also manatee CD] — str
perc: bd, chimes, claves, crot, glock, cym, sd, tamtam, td, thundersheet, tri, woodblk, cuica, bellplate, 2brake dr, rainstick, sandblks, 4steel pipes; provided with parts: 2 manatee bones, 2 sawgrass bundles, 2 seaglass shards, 12-15 seashells, manatee sounds (CD)

Stone Circle

Wounded Fields (Dedicated to Victims of War and Genocide) <2003>   4'

str

Stone Circle

Hensel, Fanny Mendelssohn   1805 - 1847

(b Hamburg, 14 Nov 1805; d Berlin, 14 May 1847). German

Hiob (Job) <1831>   8'

chorus   solos SATB
2 2 2 2 — 2 2 0 0 — tmp — str
Ed. Conrad Misch.
1.   3'
2.   2'
3.   3'

Furore

Lobgesang <1831>   12'

chorus   SA solos
2 2 2 2 — 2 2 0 0 — str
Ed. Conrad Misch.
1.   2'
2.   3'
3.   1'
4.   3'
5.   3'

Furore

Overture, C major <c1830>   11'

2 2 2 2 — 4 2 0 0 — tmp — str
Ed. JoAnn Falletta.

C. Fischer   Furore

Henze, Hans Werner   1926 - 2011

(b Gutersloh, 1 July 1926; d Dresden, 27 October 2012). German

Antifone <1960>   17'

4 0 0 0 — 0 2 2 0 — 4sx[ssx.asx.tsx.bsx] — tmp+6 — cel, pf — str[3.3.2.2.1]
perc: marim, vib, crot, cowbell, field dr, bd, 4tri, 4sus cym, 2tambn, 4tomtoms, 4tamtams, 4Glockenstab[C6,G5#,B4,A4#]
The saxophones may be replaced by 4 B-flat clarinets.

Schott

Aria de la Folía española <1977>   20'

1[1/pic] 2[1.2/ob d'am/Eh] 1[1/Ebcl/bcl] 2 — 2 0 0 0 — mand — 1perc — cel/pf — str
perc: crot, gong, cast, templeblks, marac, tmp, 3bongos, 3tomtoms, 3sus cym

Schott

Barcarola <1979>   20'

3[1/pic.2/pic.3/pic/afl] 3[1.2/Eh.3/Eh/heckl] 3[1/Ebcl.2/Ebcl/bcl.3/Ebcl/cbcl] 3[1.2.3/cbn] — 6 4 4 1 — ssx, bsx — tmp+2 — 2hp — cel, pf — str
perc: bongos, glock, vib, field dr, marim, bd, cym, crot, chimes, 3tamtams, tamtam on tmp head, 6tomtoms, metalplate, 3sus cym, 3bell plates[A#2,C#3,C#4]; tmp covers some percussion

Schott

Los caprichos; Fantasia per orchestra <1963>   20'

3[1.2.pic] 3[1.2.Eh] 3[1.2.bcl] 3[1.2.cbn] — 4 3 3 1 — tmp+3 — hp — cel, pf — str
perc: sus cym, tamtam, tri, cym, xyl, field dr, glock, vib, bd/cym, 3bongos, 3tomtoms played by timpanist

Schott

Compases para preguntas ensimismadas (Music for Viola and 22 Players) <1969–1970>   26'

solo viola
2[1/afl/pic.rec] 1[1/Eh] 1[1/bcl] 1 — 1 0 0 0 — 2perc — hp — cel/pf — ampd hpsd — str[6.0.0.4.1]
perc: vib, glock, windchimes, marim, boobam[F4->F5], logdrums[G3->C4], 4almglock, tmp, bamboo tubes

Schott

Concerto, Piano, No.2 <1967>   45'

3[1.2/pic.3/pic] 3[1.2.Eh] 3[1.2/Ebcl.bcl] 3[1.2.cbn] — 4 2 2 1 — tmp+7 — hp — str
perc: xyl, vib, chimes, field dr, tamtam, cym, bd, 3cowbells, 3bongos, 2tri, 3sus cym, marac (played by tmp)

Schott

Concerto, Violin, No.2 <1971>   29'

solo violin & solo bass-baritone
3[1/pic.2/pic.3/pic] 2[1.Eh] 3[1.2.bcl] 2 — 2 2 1 0 — gtr, mand —
tape (vns & voices) — 4perc — hp — pf, prepared pf — 4va, 3vc, 2db
perc: vib, woodblk, guiro, chimes, thunder, marac, flexatone, marimbula,
3almglock, 3tomtoms, logdrums, bamboo windchimes, 8boobams[F4–>F5], bd w/
ped, 3sus cym, 3tamtams, tmpl bell
Gtr, mand, & 1st clarinet with contact microphones. Soloist occasionally
plays a violin with contact microphone. In one passage soloist may speak
some text ad lib. Voice parts on tape may all be sung live.

> Schott

Double Concerto, Oboe, Harp & Strings <1966>   30'

str[soloistic: 8.0.4.4.2]

> Schott

L'heure bleue (Twilight; Die blaue Stunde) <2001>   10'

2[fl.afl] 2[ob d'am.Eh] 2[cl.bcl] 1 — 1 0 0 0 — Wag tb[or euph] —
1perc — hp — pf — str[vn.va.vc.db]
perc: vib, bd/cym, tamtam, sistrum, tmp, 11Thai gongs, 3tuned tomtoms, log drum

> Chester

Ode an den Westwind <1953>   22'

violoncello solo
2[1.2/pic] 2[1.Eh] 2[1.bcl] 2[1.cbn] — 2 2 1 1 — tmp+8 — hp — cel,
pf — str[20.0.12.0.8]
perc: xyl, marim, vib, chimes, tri, sd, marac, claves, cym, bd, tamtam, 4tomtoms,
2sus cym

> Schott

Quattro poemi (Four Poems) <1955>   10'

3[1.2.pic] 3[1.2.Eh] 3[1.2.bcl] 3[1.2.cbn] — 4 2 2 1 — str

Elogio	*3'*
Egloga	*2'*
Elegia	*2'*
Ditirambo	*3'*

> Schott

Requiem; Neun geistliche Konzerte (Nine Sacred   78'
Concerto) <1990–1992>

solo piano   trumpet concertante
2[1/pic.2/pic/afl] 2[1.Eh] 2[1/Ebcl.2/bcl/cbcl] 1[1/cbn] — 2 2[1.2/btp]
2[1.2/cb tbn] 0 — ssx/asx/bsx — tmp+3 — hp — cel — 4vn, 3va, 3vc,
db
perc: vib, whip, marim, flexatone, cast, bd, tambn, marac, woodblk, sd, crot, glock,
guiro, thunder, wnd mach, chimes, bd/cym, templeblks, ratch, handbells,
3tomtoms, 3sus cym, 3tamtams, rod, steeldrum, rattle, stringdrum, metraca
Many of the movements available separately.

Introitus	*5'*
Dies irae	*8'*
Ave verum corpus	*8'*
Lux aeterna	*12'*
Rex tremendae	*11'*
Agnus Dei	*7'*
Tuba mirum	*10'*
Lacrimosa	*7'*
Sanctus	*10'*

> Schott

Scorribanda sinfonica, sopra la tomba di una Maratona   15'
(Symphonic Raid on the Grave of a Marathon)
<2001>

4[1.2/pic.3/pic.4/pic/afl] 4[1.2.ob d'am.Eh] 4[1.2.3/bcl.4/bcl]
4[1.2.3.4/cbn] — 4 3 3 1 — tmp+5 — hp — cel, pf — str
perc: bd/cym, szl cym, sd, tambn, glock, marim, vib, crot, templeblks, marac,
claves, cast, 4sus cym, tomtoms[pitched], 3tamtam, 6bongos, 3ratch, 2guiro,
Chinese gongs, 2sistrum
Maratona (Marathon) is a dance drama composed in 1956, "revisited,
raided and ravished by its composer" for this 2001 work.

> Chester

Symphony No.1 <1947; rev 1963, 1991>   18

2[1/pic.afl/pic] 2[1.Eh] 2[1.bcl] 0 — 2 2 0 0 — tmp — hp — cel, pf
— str

Allegretto, con grazia	*6'*
Notturno: Lento	*6'*
Allegro con motot	*6'*

> Schott

Symphony No.2 <1949>   21

3[1.2.3/pic] 3[1.2.Eh] 3[1.2.bcl] 3[1.2.cbn] — 4 4 3 1 — tmp+4 — h
— pf — str
perc: vib, cym, glock, xyl, sd, tri, bd, tamtam

Lento	*8'*
Allegro molto vivace	*4'*
Adagio	*9'*

> Schott

Symphony No.3 <1949–1950>   24

3[1.2.pic] 3[1.2.Eh] 3[1.2.bcl] 3[1.2.cbn] — 4 4 3 1 — tsx — tmp+4
— hp — cel, pf — str
perc: sd, tri, glock, td, xyl, tamtam, vib, bd/cym, cym (2pr)

Anrufung Apolls (Invocation of Apollo)	*8'*
Dithyrambe	*11'*
Beschwörungstanz (Conjuring Dance)	*5'*

> Schott

Symphony No.4 <1955>   28

3[1.2.pic] 3[1.2.Eh] 3[1.2.bcl] 3[1.2.cbn] — 4 3 2 1 — tmp+3 — hp
— cel, pf — str
perc: glock, vib, tri, cym

> Schott

Symphony No.5 <1962>   20

4[1.2.3/pic.afl] 4[1.2.Eh1.Eh2] 0 0 — 4 4 4 0 — tmp — 2hp — 2pf
— str

Movimentato	*8'*
Adagio	*6'*
Moto perpetuo	*6'*

> Schott

Symphony No.6, for 2 Chamber Orchestras <1969; rev   37
1994>

3[1.2/pic.afl] 3[1.2.Eh] 3[1.2/Ebcl.bcl] 2[1.2/cbn] — 4 3[1.2.3/pic tp]
3[1.2.3/ten tuba] 0 — tsx — gtr/banjo — tmp+4 — hp — pf, elec org —
str[8.8.8.8.6]
perc: vib, glock, marim, marac, bd, sd, guiro, 3bongos, bamboo windchimes,
chains (on tmp & cym), 2steel plates, 3almglock, 3sus cym, 2tamtams, 6tomtoms
1vn, gtr & banjo have contact microphones; charango (with contact
microphone) may substitute for banjo.
Divided into two orchestras.

Part 1	*13'*
Part 2	*15'*
Part 3	*9'*

> Schott

Symphony No.8 <1992–1993>   27

2[1/pic.2/pic/afl] 2[1.2/Eh] 2[1.2/bcl] 2[1.2/cbn] — 4 2 2 1 — tmp+5
— hp — cel, pf — str
perc: vib, marim, crot, glock, whip, tambn, bd/cym, field dr, templeblks, 3sus cym
3tomtoms, 2tamtams, 3 tuned Chinese gongs[D4,E4,F#4]
Based on scenes from Shakespeare's "Midsummer Night's Dream."

Allegro moderato	*8'*
Ballabile	*10'*
Adagio	*9'*

> Schott

L'usignolo dell'imperatore (Des Kaisers Nachtigall) 17'
<1959>

1[fl/pic] 0 1[bcl] 0 — 0 0 0 0 — 5perc — cel, pf — va, vc
perc: marim, cowbell, 3sus cym, 3tomtom, 2tri, 3tamtam
Ballet-pantomime by Giulio di Majo, freely adapted from Hans Christian
Andersen.
Nine mvts, played without pause.

    Schott

Il Vitalino raddoppiata (Vitali Redoubled) <1977> 35'

solo violin
1[1/pic] 1[1/Eh] 1[bcl] 1 — 1 0 0 0 — hp — str[1.1.1.1.1]
Based on a chaconne by Tomaso Vitali.

    Schott

Herbert, Victor
1859-1924

(b Dublin, 1 Feb 1859; d New York, 26 May 1924). American composer of Irish birth

Concerto, Violoncello, No.1, op.8, D major <1884> 30'

2 2 2 2 — 4 2 3 0 — tmp — hp — str

    Kalmus   Luck's

Concerto, Violoncello, No.2, op.30, E minor <1894> 24'

2 2 2 2 — 4 2 3 0 — tmp+1 — str
perc: tri, cym
Allegro impetuoso 10'
Andante tranquillo 7'
Allegro 7'

    Kalmus   Luck's

Hero and Leander, op.33 <1901> 29'

3[1.2.pic] 2[1/Eh.2] 3[1.2.bcl] 2 — 4 3 3 1 — tmp+2 — hp — str
perc: bd, tri, cym, sus cym, tamtam

    Fleisher

Serenade, op.12 <1889> 27'

str
1. Aufzug (Procession) 5'
2. Polonaise 5'
3. Liebes-Scene (Love Scene) 7'
4. Canzonetta 2'
5. Finale 8'

    Kalmus   Luck's

Suite romantique, op.31 <1901> 18'

3[1.2.pic] 2[1/Eh.2] 3[1.2.bcl] 2 — 4 3 3 1 — tmp+3 — hp — str
perc: bd, cym, tri, tambn, glock
Visions _'
Aubade _'
Triomphe d'amour _'
Fête nuptiale _'

    Kalmus   Luck's   Simrock

Yesterthoughts <1900> 4'

solo violoncello
str
Transcribed by Sam Dennison; ed. Lynn Harrell.

    Kalmus

Herman, Jerry
1933-

(b New York, 10 July 1933). American

La cage aux folles: Overture <1983> 5'

3[1.2.pic] 2 2 2 — 4 3 3 1 — tmp+4 — hp — str
perc: bd, cym, set, glock, xyl
Arr. Don Pippin & Robert Wendel; orchestrated by G. Harrell & Robert
Wendel.

    Wendel

Hello Dolly!: Overture <1996> 5'

3[1.2.pic] 2 2 2 — 4 3 3 1 — tmp+3 — hp[opt] — str
perc: bd/cym, set, glock, xyl, woodblk, bell[indef pitch]
The original musical had no overture; this 1996 version was put together
by Don Pippin using material from the show, orchestrated by Larry
Blank, and edited for symphony orchestra by Robert Wendel.

    Wendel

Mack & Mabel: Overture <1974> 5'

3[1.2.pic] 2 3[1.2.bcl] 2 — 4 3 2 1 — opt banjo — tmp+3 — hp — pf
— str
perc: bd, cym, sus cym, set, glock, xyl, ratch
Arr. Donald Pippin; orchestrated Philip J. Lang; ed. Robert Wendel.

    Wendel

Mame: Overture <1966> 4'

3[1.2.pic] 2 2 — 4 3 3 1 — opt banjo/gtr — tmp+3 — opt hp — str
perc: bd, cym, set, glock, xyl, chimes
Arr. Donald Pippin; orchestrated Philip J. Lang; ed. Robert Wendel.

    Wendel

Milk and Honey: Overture <1961> 4'

3[1.2.pic] 2 2 2 — 4 3 3 1 — tmp+3 — hp — str
perc: bd, cym, set, timbales, tambn, tamtam, glock, woodblk
Arr. & orchestrated by Hershy Kay; ed. Robert Wendel.

    Wendel

Hérold, Louis Joseph F.
1791-1833

(b Paris, 28 Jan 1791; d Paris, 19 Jan 1833). French

Zampa: Overture <1831> 8'

2[1.pic] 2 2 — 4 2 3 1[oph] — tmp+3 — str
perc: tri, cym, bd

    Kalmus   Luck's   Ricordi

Hertel, Johann Wilhelm
1727-1789

(b Eisenach, 9 Oct 1727; d Schwerin, 14 June 1789). German

Double Concerto (Doppelkonzert), E-flat major <1754> 14'

solo trumpet & oboe
cnt — str
Ed. Edward H. Tarr.
I. Allegro 5'
II. Arioso 5'
III. Allegro 4'

    Schott

Hervig, Richard   1917-2010

(b Story City, IA, 24 Nov 1917; d 6 Sept 2010). American

In Summer Season   12'

pf — str

> SMC

Heseltine, Philip   1894-1930

see: Warlock, Peter, 1894-1930

Higdon, Jennifer   1962-

(b Brooklyn, NY, 31 Dec 1962). American

All Things Majestic <2011>   23'

2 2 2 2 — 4 3 3 1 — tmp+3 — hp — cel — str
perc: vib, glock, crot, Chinescym, tamtam, sd, tomtom, bd, templeblks, 2sus cym
1. Teton Range   _'
2. String Lake [strings]   _'
3. Snake River   _'
4. Cathedrals   _'

> Lawdon

blue cathedral <1999>   11'

2[1.2/pic] 2[1.Eh] 2 2 — 4 3 3 1 — tmp+3 — hp — pf/cel — str
perc: crot, marim, tamtam, vib, glock, belltree, szl cym, sus cym, chimes, bd, tomtom, 2tri

8 crystal glasses (played by hns, tbns & tuba); 60-70 Chinese bells (played by most orchestra players; available from publisher). Piano must be prepared (2 screws) for last 7 bars.

> Lawdon

Celebration Fanfare <2003>   3'

str

> Lawdon

City Scape <2002>   29'

3[1.2.pic] 3[1.2.Eh] 3[1.2.bcl] 3[1.2.cbn] — 4 3 3 1 — tmp+3 — hp — str
perc: bd, cym, 2sus cym, szl cym, Chinescym, sd, floor tom, 2tri, brakedrum, tambn, tamtam, glock, xyl, marim, vib, crot, woodblk, templeblk, bongo, guiro, watergong

Movements may be performed separately; see separate entries for individual instrumentation requirements.
SkyLine   7'
river sings a song to trees   16'
Peachtree Street   6'

> Lawdon

Concerto for Orchestra <2002>   32'

3[1.2.3/pic] 3 3[1.2.bcl] 3[1.2.cbn] — 4 3 3 1 — tmp+3 — hp — pf/cel — str
perc: bd, 2sus cym, szl cym, Chinescym, sd, toms, floortom, 2tri, tamtam, glock, marim, vib, chimes, crot, flexatone, 3woodblk, sandblk, 2 sets templeblk, whip, bongos, guiro, marac, cast, vibraslap

2nd mvt (which is for strings only) may be performed as a separate piece, entitled *String*, q.v.
  Timpanist doubles on 4th percussion.
I   8'
II   4'
III   9'
IV   5'
V   6'

> Lawdon

Concerto, Oboe <2005>   18'

2[1.2/pic] 1[ob/Eh] 2 2 — 2 2 0 0 — 1perc — str
perc: sus cym, szl cym, sd, brake dr, tri, tambn, vib, woodblk, templeblks, bongos, cast
This work was later arranged by the composer as a Concerto for Soprano Saxophone.

> Lawdon

Concerto, Piano <2009>   30'

2[1.2/pic] 2 2 2 — 4 3 3 1 — tmp+2 — hp — str
perc: bd, Chinescym, brake dr, tambn, tamtam, marim, vib, templeblks, cowbell, cast, 2sus cym, 2woodblk, bowlgong (C, E, or F) or Peking opera gong
1. quarter-note = 60; quarter-note = 152-160   _'
2. quarter-note = 52   _'
3. quarter-note = 142-152   _'

> Lawdon

Concerto, Soprano Saxophone <2005>   18'

2[1.2/pic] 1[ob/Eh] 2 2 — 2 2 0 0 — 1perc — str
perc: sus cym, szl cym, sd, brake dr, tri, tambn, vib, woodblk, templeblks, bongos, cast
Arranged by the composer from her Oboe Concerto.

> Lawdon

Concerto, Violin <2009>   32'

2[1.2/pic] 2[1.2/Eh] 2 2 — 4 3 3 1 — tmp+4 — hp — str
perc: bd, szl cym, Chinescym, glock, marim, chimes, crot, 2sus cym, rute
N.B. The title of the first movement refers to the street address of the Curtis Institute of Music, one of the four institutions that commissioned this concerto.
1. 1726   14'
2. Chaconni   13'
3. Fly Forward   5'

> Lawdon

Concerto 4-3 <2008>   20'

soloists: 2 violins & double bass
2 2 2 2 — 4 3 3 1 — tmp+2 — str
perc: bd, sus cym, Chinescym, tambn, tamtam, glock, marim, vib, woodblk, guiro, sandblks, cabasa, shaker
Optional cadenzas (improvised) between mvts 1 & 2, and mvts 2 & 3. For a shorter version, perform mvts 2 & 3 only. Durations without cadenzas:
  complete work, 17'-20'
  mvts 2 & 3 only, 13'-15'
1. The Shallows   5-6'
2. Little River   7-9'
3. Roaring Smokies   5'

> Lawdon

Fanfare ritmico <1999>   6'

3[1.2.3/pic] 3 3[1.2.bcl] 3[1.2.cbn] — 4 3 3 1 — tmp+4 — hp — pf — str

> Lawdon

Loco <2004>   10'

3[1.2.pic] 3 3 — 4 3 3 1 — tmp+3 — pf — str
perc: bd, cym, sd, tambn, marim, vib, cowbell, bongos, guiro, cast, 2sus cym, 2tomtom, sandblks, 2woodblk

> Lawdon

Machine <2002>   3'

2[1.pic] 2 2 2 — 4 2 3 1 — tmp — str

> Lawdon

On a Wire <2010>   25'

soloists: flute/piccolo/alto flute; clarinet/bass clarinet; violin/viola;
violoncello; marimba; piano
2 2 2 2[1.cbn] — 4 3 2 1 — 2perc — str
perc: bd, sd, szl cym, Chinescym, glock, xyl, vib, chimes, templeblks, guiro,
sandblks, rute
All soloists participate in playing on the interior of the piano (plucking,
scraping, bowing with rosined fishing line). Composed for the ensemble
"eighth blackbird."

> Lawdon

On the Death of the Righteous <2009>   12'

SATB chorus
3[1.2.3/pic] 2 2 4 — 4 8[5tp, 3pic tp] 3 1 — tmp+1 — str
perc: bd, sus cym, szl cym, Chinescym, tamtam, chimes, crot; tmp uses 2 low crot
or sus cym placed on head

> Lawdon

Peachtree Street <2002>   7'

2 2 2 2 — 4 2 2 1 — tmp+2 — str
perc: bd, cym, sus cym, Chinescym, sd, floortom, brakedrum, glock, xyl
3rd movement of *City Scape*.

> Lawdon

river sings a song to trees <2002>   16'

3[1.2.pic] 3[1.2.Eh] 3[1.2.bcl] 3[1.2.cbn] — 4 3 3 1 — tmp+3 — hp
— str
perc: bd, 2 sus cym, szl cym, Chinescym, 2 tri, floortom, tamtam, marim, vib, crot,
watergong
2nd movement of *City Scape*.

> Lawdon

Shine <1995>   10'

3[1.2.3/pic] 3[1.2.Eh] 3[1.2.3/bcl] 3[1.2.3/cbn] — 4 3 3 1 — tmp+3
— hp — pf/cel — str

> Lawdon

The Singing Rooms <2006>   38'

solo violin   SATB chorus
2 2[1.2/Eh] 2 2 — 4 3[1/pic tp.2.3] 3 1 — tmp+2 — hp — str
perc: bd, sus cym, szl cym, Chinescym, sd, brake dr, tambn, tamtam, marim, vib,
chimes, crot, slgh-bells, marktree, templeblks, cowbell, bongos, claves, 2tri,
2woodblk, rute
Movements are continuous.
  1. Three Windows: Two Versions of the Day   5'
  2. Things Aren't Always   3'
  3. The Interpretation of Dreams   6'
  4. Confession   7'
  5. History Lesson   3'
  6. A Word with God   9'
  7.Three Windows: Two Versions of the Day   5'

> Lawdon

SkyLine <2002>   7'

3[1.2.pic] 3[1.2.Eh] 3[1.2.bcl] 3[1.2.cbn] — 4 3 3 1 — tmp+3 — str
perc: bd, 2 sus cym, szl cym, Chinescym, sd, high tri, tambn, tamtam, vib,
woodblk, templeblk, bongos, guiro
1st movement of *City Scape*.

> Lawdon

Soliloquy <1989>   7'

solo English horn (or cello, or clarinet, or flute)
str 4t or str orch
Available in 6 scorings:
  A. solo Eh, str orch
  B. solo vc, str orch
  C. solo cl, str 4t
  D. solo cl, str orch
  E. solo Eh, str 4t
  F. solo fl, str 4t

> Lawdon

Spirit <2006>   5'

0 0 0 0 — 4 3 3 1 — tmp+3 — [no str]
perc: bd, sus cym, Chinescym, tomtom, brake dr, tamtam, glock, chimes, crot

> Lawdon

String <2002>   4'

str
2nd mvt of *Concerto for Orchestra*.

> Lawdon

To the Point <2003>   4'

str
Derived from the 2nd mvt of the composer's String Quartet No.4,
Impressions.

> Lawdon

Wind Shear <2000>   3'

3 3 3[1.2.bcl] 3[1.2.cbn] — 4 0 0 0 — [no str]

> Lawdon

Hindemith, Paul   1895-1963

(b Hanau, nr Frankfurt, 16 Nov 1895; d Frankfurt, 28 Dec 1963). German; US
citizenship 1945

Amor und Psyche

see his: Cupid and Psyche

Chamber Music

see his: Kammermusik

Concert Music

see his: Konzertmusik

Concerto for Orchestra, op.38 <1925; rev 1958>   13'

2[1.2/pic] 2 3[1.Ebcl.bcl] 3[1.2.cbn] — 3 2 2 1 — tmp+5 — str
perc: tambn, sd, tri, whip, cym, 2bd (med & lg), wood drum
Composed 1925; last mvt reorchestrated 1958.
  I. Mit Kraft; mässig schnelle   3'
  II. Sehr schnelle Halbe   3'
  III. Marsch für Holzbläser   4'
  IV. Basso ostinato   3'

> Schott

Concerto, Clarinet <1947>   21'

3[1.2.pic] 2 0 2 — 2 2 2 0 — tmp+3 — str
perc: sd, bd, cym, tri, tambn, glock

> Schott

Concerto, Horn <1949>   15'

1[1/pic] 2 2 2 — tmp — str
I. Moderately fast   3'
II. Very fast   2'
III. Very slow   10'

Schott

Concerto, Organ (1962) <1962>   25'

2[1.pic] 2 2 3[1.2.cbn] — 2 2 3 1 — tmp+2 — cel — str
perc: sd, glock, bd, cym

Schott

Concerto, Trumpet & Bassoon <1949–1952>   16'

str
I. Allegro spiritoso   6'
II. Molto adagio   8'
III. Vivace   2'

Schott

Concerto, Violin <1939>   29'

2[1.2/pic] 2 3[1.2.bcl] 2 — 4 2 3 1 — tmp+3 — str
perc: sd, tambn, tri, cym, bd, tamtam
Mässig bewegte Halbe   9'
Langsam   10'
Lebhaft   10'

Schott

Concerto, Violoncello <1940>   25'

2[1.2/pic] 2 3[1.2.bcl] 2 — 4 2 3 1 — tmp+4 — cel — str
perc: bd, cym, sus cym, sd, field dr, tri, tambn, glock
I. Mässig schnell   8'
II. Ruhig bewegt; Sehr lebhaft 8'
III. Marsch: Lebhaft   9'

Schott

Concerto for Woodwinds, Harp & Orchestra <1949>   16'

solos: flute, oboe, clarinet, bassoon, harp
0 0 0 0 — 2 2 1 0 — str
I. Moderately fast   8'
II. Grazioso   3'
III. Rondo: Rather fast   5'

Schott

Concertpiece (Konzertstück), Trautonium & Strings <1931>   9'

trautonium
str
A clarinet may substitute for trautonium as soloist.
I. Leicht bewegt   3'
II. Lied, ruhig, bewegt   3'
III. Im ersten Zeitmass   3'

Schott

Cupid and Psyche (Amor und Psyche): Overture <1943>   6'

2[1.pic] 2 2 2 — 2 2 2 0 — tmp+1 — str
perc: tri, sus cym, glock

Schott

Drei Gesänge, op.9 (Three Songs) <1917>   18'

solo soprano
3[all/pic] 3[1.2.Eh] 3[1.2.Ebcl] 3[1.2.3/cbn] — 8 4 3 1 — tmp+5 —
2hp — str
perc: bd/cym, cym, sus cym, sd, field dr, tri, gong
Harps in 3rd song only.
1. Meine Nächte sind heiser zerschrien…   4'
2. Weltende   7'
3. Aufbruch der Jugend   7'

Schott

Five Pieces for String Orchestra, op.44, no.4 <1927>   14'

str
I. Langsam   3'
II. Langsam   2'
III. Lebhaft   2'
IV. Sehr langsam   3'
V. Lebhaft   4'

Schott

The Four Temperaments

see his: Theme and Variations

Die Harmonie der Welt (Symphony) <1951>   35'

2[1.2/pic] 2 3[1.2.bcl] 3[1.2.cbn] — 4 2 3 1 — tmp+6 — str
perc: glock, tambn, sd, td, tri, gong, cym, bd, chimes[E,A,B]
Musica Instrumentalis   11'
Musica Humana   10'
Musica Mundana   14'

Schott

Kammermusik No.1 mit Finale 1921, op.24, no.1 <1921–1922>   16'

1[1/pic] 0 1 1 — 0 1 0 0 — accordion [or harm] — 1perc — pf — str
5t
perc: xyl, sd, sus cym, tambn, tri, siren, glock, wood drum, metal shaker (sand)
Sehr schnell und wild   1'
Mässig schnell Halbe; Sehr streng im Rhythmus   4'
Quartett: sehr langsam und mit Ausdruck   5'
Finale 1921: Ausserst lebhaft   6'

Luck's   Schott

Kammermusik No.2 for Piano & 12 Solo Instruments, op.36, no.1 <1924>   20'

1[1/pic] 2 2[1.bcl] 1 — 1 1 1 0 — 1vn, 1va, 1vc, 1db

Schott

Kammermusik No.3 for Violoncello & 10 Solo Instruments, op.36, no.2 <1925>   16'

1[1/pic] 1 1[1/Ebcl] 1 — 1 1 1 0 — vn, vc, db

Schott

Kammermusik No.4 for Violin & Large Chamber Orchestra, op.36, no.3 <1925; rev 1951>   23'

2[2pic] 0 3[1.Ebcl.bcl] 3[1.2.cbn] — 0 1[crt] 1 1 — 1perc — 4va,
4vc, 4db
perc: 4 frame drums
Composed 1925; 1st mvt rev. 1951.

Schott

Kammermusik No.5 for Viola & Large Chamber Orchestra, op.36, no.4 <1927; rev 1930>   17'

1[1/pic] 1 3[1.Ebcl.bcl] 3[1.2.cbn] — 1 2 2 1 — 4vc, 4db

Schott

Kammermusik No.6 for Viola d'amore & Chamber Orchestra, op.46, no.1 <1927>   16'

1 1 2[1.bcl] 1 — 1 1 1 0 — 3vc, 2db

Schott

Kammermusik No.7 for Organ & Chamber Orchestra, op.46, no.2 <1927>   16'

2[1.pic] 1 2[1.bcl] 3[1.2.cbn] — 1 1 1 0 — str[no vn or va]
Could be performed using minimum strings of just 2vc and 1db, though the score clearly indicates sections (*Violoncelli* and *Kontrabässe*, respectively).

I. Nicht zu schnell	*3'*
II. Sehr langsam und ganz ruhig	*7'*
III. [Eighth-note] bis 184	*6'*

Schott

Konzertmusik (Concert Music) for Strings and Brass, op.50 <1930>   17'

0 0 0 0 — 4 4 3 1 — str

Part I: Massig schnell; mit Kraft - Sehr breit; stets fleissend	*9'*
Part II: Lebhaft - Langsam - Im ersten Zeitmass (Lebhaft)	*8'*

Schott

Konzertmusik (Concert Music) for Viola & Large Chamber Orchestra, op.48 (original version) <1929–1930>   23'

2[1.pic] 2[1.Eh] 2[1.bcl] 3[1.2.cbn] — 3 1 1 0 — 4vc, 4db

ERSTER TEIL (PART ONE)	
1. Lebhaft; Bewegte Halbe	_'
2. Ruhig gehend	_'
3. Lebhaft	_'
ZWEITER TEIL (PART TWO)	
4. Langsam; Schreitende Achtel	_'
5. Leicht bewegt	_'
6. Lebhaft und munter	_'

Schott

Konzertmusik (Concert Music) for Viola & Large Chamber Orchestra, op.48 (definitive version) <1929–1930; rev 1930>   20'

2[1.pic] 2[1.Eh] 2[1.bcl] 3[1.2.cbn] — 3 2 1 1 — 4vc, 4db

1. Lebhaft; Bewegte Halbe	*5'*
2. Ruhig gehend	*7'*
3. Lebhaft	*2'*
4. Leicht bewegt	*4'*
5. Sehr lebhaft	*2'*

Schott

Lustige Sinfonietta, op.4 <1916>   30'

2[1/pic.2/pic] 3[1.2.Eh] 2 3[1.2.cbn] — 2 2 0 0 — tmp+2 — str[8.6.6.6.4]
perc: sd, bd/cym, 2sus cym

Die Galgenbrüder	*11'*
Intermezzo (Zoologische Merkwürdikeiten)	*4'*
Palmström	*15'*

Schott

Das Marienleben: Sechs Lieder (Six Songs) <1922–1942; rev 1959>   26'

soprano solo
2[1.2/pic] 3[1.2.Eh] 3[1.2.bcl] 2 — 2 2 2 0 — tmp+2 — str
perc: bd, sus cym, tri, glock, 2pr cym
Originally 15 songs for voice & piano, 1922-23; new version 1936-42. 4 songs orchestrated 1939; 2 more 1959.

1. Geburt Mariä (Birth of Mary)	*4'*
2. Argwohn Josephs (Joseph's Suspicions)	*2'*
3. Geburt Christi (Birth of Christ)	*5'*
4. Rast auf der Flucht nach Agypten (Rest on the Flight to Egypt)	*4'*
5. Vor der Passion (The Passion)	*8'*
6. Vor dem Tode Mariä III (The Death of Mary)	*3'*

Schott

Marsch über den alten *Schweizerton* <1960>   4'

2[1.2/pic] 2 2 2 — 4 2 3 1 — tmp+3 — str
perc: field dr, 2sd

Schott

Mathis der Maler (Symphony) <1933–1934>   25'

2[1.2/pic] 2 2 2 — 4 2 3 1 — tmp+3 — str
perc: glock, bd, cast, sd, tri, cym

Engelskonzert (Angelic Concert)	*8'*
Die Grablegung (Entombment)	*4'*
Versuchung des heiligen Antonius (Temptation of St. Anthony)	*13'*

Schott

Neues vom Tage (News of the Day): Concert Overture <1929>   8'

2[1.2/pic] 2[1.Eh] 3[1.2/Ebcl.bcl] 3[1.2.cbn] — 1 2 2 1 — asx — 3perc — str
perc: tri, sd, tomtom, cym, bd, small cym
With concert-ending.

Schott

Nobilissima visione: Suite <1938>   21'

2[1.2/pic] 2 2 — 4 2 3 1 — tmp+4 — str
perc: tri, td, sd, glock, cym, bd

Introduction & Rondo	*7'*
March & Pastorale	*9'*
Passacaglia	*5'*

Schott

Philharmonic Concerto <1932>   20'

3[1.2.3/pic] 3[1.2.Eh] 3[1.2.bcl] 3[1.2.cbn] — 4 3 3 1 — tmp+3 — str
perc: sd, cym, bd, tri, *Rührtrommel* (probably field drum in this case)

Thema: Ruhig schreitend	*3'*
Variation I: Massig schnell	*2'*
Variation II: Sehr ruhig	*2'*
Variation III: Massig lebhafte	*3'*
Variation IV: Ruhig bewegt	*4'*
Variation V: Leicht bewegt	*6'*
Variation VI: Im Marschzeitmass	*3'*

Schott

Pittsburgh Symphony <1958>   21'

2[1.2/pic] 3[1.2.Eh] 3[1.2.bcl] 3[1.2.cbn] — 4 2 3 1 — tmp+4 — str
perc: glock, tri, woodblk, cast, tomtom, cym, bd, gong, 2sd

I. Molto energico	*6'*
II. Slow March	*11'*
III. Ostinato	*4'*

Schott

Rag Time (wohltemperierte) <1921>   4'

3[1.pic1.pic2] 2 3[1.2.Ebcl] 2 — 4 2 3 1 — tmp+3 — str
Uses a fugue subject from J.S. Bach's *Das wohltemperierte Klavier (The Well-Tempered Clavier)*.

Schott

Der Schwanendreher <1935; rev 1936>   27'

solo viola
2[1.2/pic] 1 2 2 — 3 1 1 0 — tmp — hp — str[no vn or va]
Based on old folksongs.

1. Zwischen Berg und tiefem Tal	*8'*
2. Nun laube, Lindlein laube… Der Gutzgauch auf dem Zaune sass	*9'*
3. Seid ihr nicht der Schwanendreher (Variations)	*10'*

Schott

Sinfonietta in E <1949>   19'

2[1.pic] 2 2 2 — 3 1 2 1 — tmp+1 — cel — str
perc: glock, cym

I. Schnell	5'
II. Adagio und Fugato	7'
III. Intermezzo ostinato	2'
IV. Rezitativ and Rondo	5'

Schott

Spielmusik, op.43, no.1 <1927>   7'

2 2 0 0 — str

Mässig bewegte Halbe	_'
Langsam schreitende Viertel	_'
Schnell Halbe	_'

Schott

Suite of French Dances (Suite französicher Tänze) <1958>   15'

2[1.pic] 2[1.Eh] 0 1 — 0 1 0 0 — lute — str[3va, 2vc; *or* 2vn, va, 2vc; *or* string orchestra]
Winds are optional.
     After 16th-century dances by Claude Gervaise & Estienne du Tertre, as published by Pierre d'Attaignant.

I. Pavane und Gaillarde	2'
II. Tourdion	1'
III. Bransle simple	1'
IV. Bransle de Bourgongne	1'
V. Bransle simple	2'
VI. Bransle d'Escosse	2'
VII. Pavane	6'

Schott

Symphonia serena <1946>   29'

3[1.2.pic] 3[1.2.Eh] 3[1.2.bcl] 3[1.2.cbn] — 4 2 2 1 — tmp+4 — cel — str
perc: tri, tambn, glock, sd, cym, bd, 2woodblks
2nd mvt (a paraphrase of Beethoven's *Geschwindmarsch*) is for winds, cel, perc [no str]. 3rd mvt for strings only, divided into 2 groups. 1st & 4th mvts are tutti.

I. Moderately Fast	8'
II. Geschwindmarsch by Beethoven; Paraphrase for Winds	4'
III. Colloquy for 2 String Orchestras	9'
IV. Finale: Gay	8'

Schott

Symphonic Dances (Symphonische Tänze) <1937>   28'

2[1.2/pic] 2 2 2 — 4 2 3 1 — tmp+3 — str
perc: sd, tri, tambn, cym, bd, small sus cym, kybd glock

Langsam; lebhaft	14'
Sehr langsam	6'
Mässig bewegt, mit Kraft	8'

Schott

Symphonic Metamorphosis of Themes by Carl Maria von Weber <1943>   21'

3[1.2.pic] 3[1.2.Eh] 3[1.2.bcl] 3[1.2.cbn] — 4 2 3 1 — tmp+4 — str
perc: tri, tambn, glock, tomtom, sd, td, chimes, cym, woodblk, bd, gong
Original Schott score (1943) has some errors, which were corrected in a 1973 edition.

I. Allegro	4'
II. Turandot: Scherzo	8'
III. Andantino	4'
IV. March	5'

Schott

Symphony in E-flat <1940>   31'

3[1.2.pic] 3[1.2.Eh] 3[1.2.bcl] 3[1.2.cbn] — 4 3 3 1 — tmp+4 — str
perc: sd, glock, tambn, cym, tri, bd, rute

Sehr lebhaft	5'
Sehr langsam	9'
Lebhaft	7'
Mässig schnelle Halbe	10'

Schott

Theme and Variations (The Four Temperaments; Die vier Temperamente) <1940>   29'

solo piano
str

Theme		7'
Variation I:	*Melancholic*	7'
Variation II:	*Sanguine*	6'
Variation III:	*Phlegmatic*	4'
Variation IV:	*Choleric*	5'

Schott

Trauermusik (Music of Mourning) <1936>   6'

solo viola (or violin or violoncello)
str

Schott

Tuttifäntchen: Suite <1922>   19'

1[fl/pic] 1 1 1 — 1 1 0 0 — tmp+1 — str
perc: sd, bd/cym, tambn, glock
The work from which the suite is drawn is a Christmas fairy tale in three scenes.

1. Vorspiel	1'
2. Lied	1'
3. Intermezzo	1'
4. Lied	2'
5. Marsch	1'
6. Musik zum Kaspertheater	1'
7. Tanz der Holzpuppen	4'
8. Lied	3'
9. Melodram	3'
10. Wiegenlied	1'
11. Schlusslied	1'

Schott

Das Unaufhörliche <1931>   85'

STBarB solos   boy choir   chorus
3[1.2.pic] 2 2 3[1.2.opt cbn] — 3 2 2 1 — tmp+1 — opt org — str
perc: sd, td, cym
Baritone solo may be covered by the bass soloist.

Schott

When Lilacs Last in the Door-Yard Bloom'd (Als Flieder jüngst mir im Garten blüht) <1946>   66'

mezzo-soprano, baritone solos   chorus
2[1.pic] 2[1.Eh] 2[1.bcl] 2[1.cbn] — 3 3[1.2.bugle backstage] 2 1 — tmp+3 — org — str
perc: cym, glock, chimes, gong, tri, sd, bd, field dr

Prelude	5'
1. "When Lilacs"	5'
2. Arioso—"In the Swamp"	3'
3. March—"Over the Breast of the Spring"	7'
4. "O Western Orb" (O Westgestirn)	2'
5. Arioso—"Sing On, There in the Swamp"	2'
6. Song—"O How Shall I Warble"	4'
7. Introduction & Fugue—"Lo! Body and Soul!"	5'
8. "Sing On! You Gray-brown Bird"	10'
9. Death Carol—"Come Lovely and Soothing Death"	8'
10. "To the Tally of My Soul"	7'
11. Finale—"Passing the Visions" (Schwinden die Bilder)	8'

Schott

When Lilacs Last in the Door-Yard Bloom'd: Prelude <1946>   5'

2[1.pic] 2[1.Eh] 2[1.bcl] 2[1.cbn] — 3 2 2 1 — tmp+1 — org — str
perc: bd

> Schott

Ioag, Charles Kelso   1931-

(b 1931). American

An After-Intermission Overture for Youth Orchestra <1972>   3'

2 2 2 2 — 4 3 3 1 — tmp+1 — pf — str
perc: tri, sd, tambn

> Schirmer

Hoddinott, Alun   1929-2008

(b Bargoed, Glam., 11 Aug 1929; d Gower, Swansea, 12 March 2008). Welsh

Concerto, Horn, op.65 <1969>   14'

2[1.2/pic] 2 2 — 3 2 3 0 — tmp+2 — hp — str

> Oxford

Fioriture, op.60 <1968>   19'

3[1.2.3/pic] 3[1.2.Eh] 3[1.2.bcl] 3[1.2.cbn] — 4 3 3 1 — tmp+3 — hp — str
perc: vib, xyl, crot, sd, woodblk, sus cym, marim, bd, cym, glock, claves, tamtam, templeblks, tri, whip, 2gong, bamboo windchimes, 3tomtom, 3bongos

> Oxford

Sinfonietta No.3, op.71 <1970>   12'

3[incl pic] 2 2 3[incl cbn] — 4 2 3 0 — tmp+2 — hp — str

> Oxford

Symphony No.3, op.61 <1968>   22'

3[1.2.3/pic] 3[1.2.Eh] 3[1.2.bcl] 3[1.2.cbn] — 4 3 3 1 — tmp+3 — hp — pf/cel — str
perc: gong, sd, xyl, vib, tambn, bd, marim, sus cym, tomtom, chimes, tamtam, claves, cym, field dr, glock, marac, bongos, marktree, 2tri

| I. Adagio; Presto | 12' |
| II. Allegro; Adagio | 10' |

> Oxford

Symphony No.5, op.81 <1973>   25'

3[incl pic] 3[incl Eh] 3[incl bcl] 3[incl cbn] — 4 3 3 1 — tmp+4 — hp — str

| Allegro | 11' |
| Adagio; Allegro; Andante; Allegro; Adagio; Presto | 14' |

> Oxford

Hofer, Andreas   1629-1684

(b Reichenhall [now Bad Reichenhall], 1629; d Salzburg, 25 Feb 1684). Austrian

Te Deum   9'

double chorus
0 2[alt for cornetti] 2[alt for cornetti] 3[1.2opt.cbn opt] — 0 5[2clarini, 2tp, btp(or bn)] 3 0 — org — str
Forces are divided into 3 orchestras and 2 choruses.
Ed. Charles H. Sherman.

> Universal

Hoffmann, Georg Melchior   ca.1679-1715

(b Barenstein, nr Dresden, c1679; d Leipzig, 6 Oct 1715). German

Meine Seele rühmt und preist

see: Bach, Johann Sebastian, 1685-1750
      Cantata no.189

Schlage doch, gewünschte Stunde

see: Bach, Johann Sebastian, 1685-1750
      Cantata no.53

Hofmann, Leopold   1738-1793

(b Vienna, 14 Aug 1738; d Vienna, 17 March 1793). Austrian

B = A. Badley *Leopold Hofmann; Thematic Catalogue* [in preparation]

Concerto, Violin, B.A2, A major <by 1766>   20'

str
Ed. Allan Badley.

I. Allegro moderato	10'
II. Adagio	5'
III. Allegro molto	5'

> Artaria

Concerto, Violin, B.Bb1, B-flat major <late 1760s>   17'

str
Ed. Allan Badley.

I. Tempo giusto	8'
II. Adagio	3'
III. Vivace	6'

> Artaria

Concerto, Violin & Violoncello, B.G1, G major (Double Concerto) <1782?>   23'

str
Ed. Allan Badley.

I. [Tempo giusto]	9'
II. Andante un poco tarde	7'
III. [Allegro]	7'

> Artaria

Concerto, Violoncello, B.C1, C major   13'

0 0 0 0 — 2 0 0 0 — str
Ed. Allan Badley.

I. Tempo giusto	8'
II. Adagio ma non molto	5'
III. Allegro molto	5'

> Artaria

Concerto, Violoncello, B.C3, C major   13'

str[no va]
Ed. Allan Badley.

I. [Tempo giusto]	5'
II. Adagio	3'
III. Vivace	5'

> Artaria

HOFMANN, LEOPOLD   1738-1793

Concerto, Violoncello, B.D3, D major   27'

0 0 0 0 — 2 0 0 0 — str
Ed. Allan Badley.
I. Allegro moderato   10'
II. Adagio un poco andante   6'
III. Allegro molto   11'

> Artaria

Sinfonia, B-flat major <before 1764>   11'

0 2 0 0 — 0 0 0 0 — str
Ed. Allan Badley.
I. Allegro ma non molto   4'
II. Andante   4'
III. Vivace   3'

> Artaria

Sinfonia, C major   19'

0 2 0 0 — 2 0 0 0 — str
Ed. Allan Badley.
I. Vivace   6'
II. Andante   3'
III. Menuet   3'
IV. Presto   7'

> Artaria

Sinfonia, D major <by 1762>   13'

0 2 0 0 — 2 0 0 0 — str
Ed. Allan Badley.
I. Adagio; Allegro   4'
II. Andante   3'
III. Menuet   3'
IV. Presto   3'

> Artaria

Sinfonia, B.F1, F major <before 1767>   17'

str
Ed. Allan Badley.
I. Allegro molto   3'
II. Andantino   6'
III. Menuet   3'
IV. Allegro assai   5'

> Artaria

Sinfonia, B.F2, F major <ca 1760>   12'

0 2 0 0 — 0 0 0 0 — str
Ed. Allan Badley.
I. Allegro molto; Andante   5'
II. Menuet   3'
III. Presto   4'

> Artaria

Hoiby, Lee   1926- 2011

(b Madison, WI, 17 Feb 1926; d New York City, 28 Mar, 2011). American

Concerto, Piano, No.2, op.33 <1980>   29'

2[1.2/pic] 2[1.2/Eh] 2[1.2/bcl] 2 — 2 2 1 0 — 1perc — str
perc: bd, cym, sus cym, sd, tri, tmp

> Fleisher

Höller, York   1944-

(b Leverkusen, 11 Jan 1944). German

Aura <1991–1992>   20'

4[1.2.3/pic.4/pic] 3[1.2.3/Eh] 3[1.2.3/bcl] 3[1.2.3/cbn] — 4 3 3 1 —
tmp+5 — hp — cel/pf/synth (2 players) — str[14.12.10.8.6]
perc: vib, woodblk, chimes, tomtom, marim, td, slgh-bells, glock, xyl, crot, bd,
tambn, marac (hi, med, lo), 5sus cym, 4gongs, 3tamtams

> Boosey

Pensées (Piano Concerto No.2) <1990–1992>   25'

solo piano (MIDI grand)
3[1.2.3/pic] 3[1.2.Eh] 3[1.2.bcl] 3[1.2.cbn] — 4 3 3 1 — tmp+5 — hp
— synth, computer — str[14.12.10.8.6]
perc: xyl, marim, vib, crot, glock, bd, chimes, tomtom, woodblk, marac, td,
belltree, gongs, 6sus cym, 3tamtams, 2sd

> Boosey

Holliger, Heinz   1939-

(b Langenthal, canton of Berne, 21 May 1939). Swiss

Ardeur noire <2008>   7'

chorus (backstage)
3[1.2.3/pic/afl] 3[1.2/Eh.Eh] 4[1.2.3/bcl.cbcl] 3[1.2.3/cbn] — 4 3 3 1
— tmp+3 — 2hp — cel — str[14.12.10.8.7]
perc: crot, gong, szl cym, bd, bell plate, 2sus cym, 3tamtam
After the 1917 piano work of Claude Debussy, *Les soirs illuminés par
l'ardeur du charbon*.
    Backstage chorus may be doubled by 2 or 4 horns.

> Schott

Janus (Double Concerto for Violin, Viola & Small   21'
Orchestra) <2011–2012>

solo violin & viola
2[1/afl.2/pic/afl] 2[1.Eh] 2[1.bcl] 2 — 2 0 0 0 — 2-3perc — hp — cel
— str[6.4.3.3.3]
perc: glock, marim, cym, bd, crot, guiro, flexatone, tomtom, tmp, sandblks, glass
windchimes, 3tamtam

> Schott

Meta arca <2012>   12'

solo violin
str[4.4.3.2.1]
All the string parts are written for individuals; only vc2 and db may be
doubled if necessary. The soloist acts also as the 1st of the 4 vn1 players.

> Schott

Hollingsworth, Stanley   1924-2003

(b Berkeley, CA, 27 Aug 1924; d Rocklin, CA, 29 Oct 2003). American

Concerto, Piano <1980>   14'

2[1.2/pic] 2 2 2 — 2 1 0 0 — tmp+2 — str
perc: sd, xyl, sus cym
1. Allegro con brio   4'
2. Romanza: Andante   6'
3. Allegro molto   4'

> Belwin

Concerto, Violin (Lirico) <1991>   14'

2 2[1.2/Eh] 2 2 — 2 1 0 0 — str
Allegretto grazioso   5'
Andante   4'
Allegro moderato   5'

> Fleisher

Death Be Not Proud (Holy Sonnet X) <1978>   3'

chorus
2 1 2 2 — 2 2 2 0 — tmp+2 — hp — str
perc: sus cym, xyl

> Fleisher

Divertimento <1982>   14'

2[1.2/pic] 2[1.2/Eh] 2 2 — 4 2 2 1 — tmp+2 — hp — cel, pf — str
perc: sus cym, sd, tri, tambn, xyl, sleighbells, woodblk

Entrance	*1'*
Pas de deux	*4'*
Merci Monsieur J.I.	*3'*
Soliloquy	*3'*
Introduction & Finale	*3'*

> Belwin

A Dubious Piety <1985>   2'

solo clarinet
1 1 1 1 — 0 1 0 0 — tmp+1 — hp — str
perc: sus cym, sd, tri
A movement from his *Reflections and Diversions* for clarinet & piano,
orchestrated by the composer.

> Fleisher

Dumbarton Oaks Mass <1950 or 1953?>   19'

chorus
str

Kyrie	*4'*
Gloria	*3'*
Credo	*4'*
Sanctus	*3'*
Agnus Dei	*5'*

> Fleisher

A Song of David <?1963>   8'

solo tenor   chorus
2 2 2 2 — 4 2 2 1 — tmp/sus cym — hp — pf — str
perc: sus cym

> Fleisher

Stabat Mater <1957>   12'

chorus SATB
2 2 2 2 — 2 2 1 0 — tmp — hp — pf — str

Stabat Mater dolorosa	*3'*
Quis est homo qui no flerit	*2'*
Eja Mater fons amoris	*4'*
Virgo virginum praeclara	*3'*

> Schirmer

Three Ladies Beside the Sea <1984>   12'

narrator
2[1.2/pic] 1 1 1 — 0 1 0 0 — tmp+1 — hp — cel, pf — str
perc: tri, tambn, sus cym, xyl, timbales, sd (tmp covers some perc)

> Belwin

Holloway, Robin   1943-

(b Leamington Spa, 19 Oct 1943). English

Concerto, Viola, op.56 <1983–1984>   24'

2 2[1.Eh] 1 1 — 2 1 1 0 — cel — str

> Boosey

Romanza, op.31 <1976>   16'

solo violin
2[1/pic.2/pic] 1 2 1 — 2 0 0 0 — hp — str

> Boosey

Scenes from Schumann, op.13 <1970; rev 1986>   22'

3[1/pic.2/pic.3/pic/afl] 2[1.2/Eh] 2[1.2/bcl] 2[1.2/cbn] — 2 2 1 0 —
1perc — hp — pf — str[min 8.6.4.4.2; max 12.12.10.8.6]
perc: tri, sus cym, tamtam

> Boosey

Second Concerto for Orchestra, op.40 <1978–1979>   35'

3[1/pic.2/pic.3/pic/afl] 3[1.2.3/Eh] 3[1/Ebcl.2.3/bcl] 3[1.2.3/cbn] — 4
3 3 1 — asx — tmp+4 — hp — pf/cel — str[min 16.14.12.10.8]
perc: glock, gong, chimes, vib, xyl, belltree, cym, tamtam, claves, marac, ratch,
templeblks, woodblk, whip, bd, sd, tambn, td, 9anvils, 2sus cym, 3tri

> Boosey

Holmboe, Vagn   1909-1996

(b Horsens, 20 Dec 1909; d Ramløse, 1 Sept 1996). Danish

Concerto for Orchestra <1929>   14'

3[1.2.pic] 2 2 2 — 4 3 3 2 — 2perc ad lib — str
perc: bd, cym
In one mvt.

> Hansen

Concerto, Flute, op.126 <1975–1976>   22'

1[fl/pic] 2[1.2/Eh] 2 2 — 4 2 0 0 — tmp+4 — cel[played by perc] —
str
perc: xyl, vib, sus cym, tri, 2sd, cel[played by perc]

I. Allegro con spirito	*6'*
II. Andante tranquillo	*7'*
III. Poco lento—Allegro	*9'*

> Hansen

Concerto, String Quartet & String Orchestra, op.195 <1995–1996>   15'

str

I. Allegro	*_'*
II. Allegretto	*_'*
III. Andante con moto	*_'*
IV. Allegro con brio	*_'*

> Hansen

Concerto, Tuba, op.127 <1976>   17'

2 2 2 2 — 4 2 0 0 — tmp+4 — str
perc: td, sd, vib, xyl
In one mvt.

> Hansen

Concerto, Violoncello, op.120 <1994; rev 1979>   25'

3[1.2.3/pic] 3[1.2.Eh] 3[1.2.bcl] 3[1.2.cbn] — 4 3 0 0 — tmp+4 —
cel[played by perc] — str
In one mvt.

> Hansen

Symphony No.1, op.4 <1935>   15'

1 1 1 1 — 1 1 1 0 — tmp+3 — str
perc: bd, cym, sus cym, sd, tri, gong, whip

| *I. Allegro* | *7'* |
| *II. Andante—Allegro energico* | *8'* |

> Hansen

Symphony No.2, op.15 <1938–1939>   28'

3[1.2.3/pic] 3[1.2.Eh] 3[1.2.bcl] 3[1.2.cbn] — 4 3 3 1 — tmp+4 — str
perc: bd, cym, sus cym, sd, td, gong, xyl

I. Impressioni	*12'*
II. Lamentazione	*10'*
III. Espressione	*6'*

> Hansen

Symphony No.3, op.25 (Sinfonia rustica) <1941>   27'

3[1.2.pic] 2 2 2 — 4 3 3 1 — tmp+3 — cel — str
perc: sus cym, cym, sd, td
Movement titles refer to ancient Danish ballads.
  1. Brujdans (Bridal Dance)   5'
  2. Skammelsen-Variationer (Skammelsen Variations)   16'
  3. Bryde Kloster (Break Down the Convent Wall)   6'
> Hansen

Symphony No.4, op.29 (Sinfonia sacra) <1941; rev 1945>   27'

chorus SATB
3[1.2.pic] 3[1.2.Eh] 3[1.2.bcl] 3[1.2.cbn] — 4 3 3 1 — tmp+3 — pf
— str
  I. Timor serpit per hominum vitas   7'
  II. Terra jacet deserta   7'
  III. Ego volue   2'
  IV. Pacem desideramus   4'
  V. Gloria in excelsis Deo   3'
  VI. Laudate Dominum   4'
> Hansen

Symphony No.6, op.43 <1947>   32'

3[1.2.pic] 3[1.2.Eh] 3[1.2.bcl] 3[1.2.cbn] — 4 3 3 1 — tmp+2 — cel
— str
perc: sd, field dr, bd, xyl, sus cym
  1. Adagio—Allegro—Adagio   18'
  2. Allegro molto e con vuoco   14'
> Hansen

Symphony No.7, op.50 <1950>   24'

3[1.2.3/pic] 2[1.2/Eh] 2 2 — 4 3 3 1 — tmp+4 — cel[played by perc]
— str
perc: xyl, bd, cym, sus cym, tri, 3sd, cel[played by perc]
  1. Allegro con fuoco   4'
  2. Intermedio I   1'
  3. Adagio   6'
  4. Intermedio II   1'
  5. Presto   7'
  6. Intermedio III   1'
  7. Coda   4'
> Hansen

Symphony No.8, op.56 (Sinfonia boreale) <1951–1952>   34'

3[1.2.3/pic] 3[1.2.3/Eh] 3[1.2.3/bcl] 3[1.2.cbn] — 4 3 3 1 — tmp+3
— cel[played by perc] — str
perc: bd, cym, sus cym, xyl, 2sd, cel[played by perc]
  1. Allegro molto intensivo   7'
  2. Tempo giusto   7'
  3. Andante con moto   10'
  4. Allegro passionato   10'
> Hansen

Symphony No.9, op.95 <1967–1968>   31'

3[1.2.3/pic] 3[1.2.Eh] 3[1.2.bcl] 3[1.2.cbn] — 4 3 3 1 — tmp+5 —
cel[played by perc] — str
perc: xyl, vib, tri, bd, gong, 3sd, 2sus cym, cel[played by perc]
  I. Allegro fluente   9'
  II. Intermezzo I   4'
  III. Allegro con fuoco   7'
  IV. Intermezzo II   4'
  V. Andante austero   7'
> Hansen

Symphony No.10, op.105 <1970–1971>   26'

3[1.2.pic] 3[1.2.Eh] 3[1.2.bcl] 3[1.2.cbn] — 4 3 3 1 — tmp+5 —
cel[played by perc] — str
perc: cym, sd, field dr, bd, tamtam, xyl, vib, cel[played by perc]
  I. Poco sostenuto—Allegro espansivo   9'
  II. Andante affettuoso   9'
  III. Allegro con forza   8'
> Hansen

Symphony No.11, op.144 <1980–1981>   21

3[1.2.pic] 3[1.2.Eh] 3[1.2.bcl] 3[1.2.cbn] — 4 3 3 1 — tmp+3 — cel
— str
perc: tri, cym, sd, field dr, bd, xyl, vib, gong
  I. Allegro non troppo   8'
  II. Tempo giusto   6'
  III. Andante   7'
> Hansen

Symphony No.12, op.175 <1988>   24

3[1.2.3/pic] 3[1.2.Eh] 3[1.2.bcl] 3[1.2.cbn] — 4 3 3 1 — tmp+2 — h
— str
perc: cym, tri, field dr, xyl, vib, 2tomtom
  I. Allegro con forza   9'
  II. Andante sereno   6'
  III. Adagio—Allegro con brio 9'
> Hansen

Symphony No.13, op.192 <1993–1994>   20

3[1.2.3/pic] 3[1.2.Eh] 3[1.2.bcl] 3[1.2.cbn] — 4 3 3 1 — tmp+2 —
cel[played by perc] — str
perc: bd, cym, sd, xyl, vib, 3tomtom, cel[played by perc]
  1. Allegro assai   6'
  2. Allegro moderato   5'
  3. Allegro con brio   9'
> Hansen

Holst, Gustav   1874 - 1934

(b Cheltenham, 21 Sept 1874; d London, 25 May 1934). English

Beni Mora; Oriental Suite for Orchestra, op.29, no.1   15"
<1909–1910>

3[1.2.3/pic] 3[1.2.Eh] 2 2 — 4 3 3 1 — tmp+3 — 1 or 2hp — str
perc: tambn, tri, cym, bd, gong
  I. First Dance (Oriental Dance)   6'
  II. Second Dance   4'
  III. Third Dance: In the Street of the Ouled Näils   7'

| Curwen | Kalmus | Luck's |

Brook Green Suite <1933>   8"

1[opt] 1[opt] 1[opt] 1[opt] — str
  1. Prelude   2'
  2. Air   3'
  3. Dance   3'
> Curwen

Capriccio <1932>   6'

1[1/pic] 2[1.2/Eh] 2[1.2/bcl] 2 — 2 3 2 1 — 2perc — hp — cel, pf
str
perc: marim or vib (ad lib.), chimes (ad lib.), sd, tri, glock, bd, sus cym, tmp
Original title: *Jazz-Band Piece*. Ed. Imogen Holst.
> Faber

A Choral Fantasia, op.51 <1930>   17"

soprano solo   chorus
0 0 0 0 — 0 3 3 1 — tmp+1 — org — str
perc: cym, bd, tamtam
> Curwen

Christmas Day <1910>   7'

chorus   solos SATB
2[1.2/opt pic] 2 2 2 — 2 2 2[opt] 0 — tmp+1[opt] — str
perc: glock
A keyboard part (pf or org) in the full score is intended only for choral
rehearsal.

| Kalmus | Luck's | Novello |

Concerto, 2 Violins, op.49 (Double Concerto) <1929>   16'

2[fl2 opt] 2[ob2 opt] 2 2 — 2[hn2 opt] 2[tp2 opt] 0 0 — tmp — str
Rev. Imogen Holst.

1. Scherzo: Allegro	5'
2. Lament: Andante	5'
3. Variations on a Ground: Allegro	6'

Kalmus	Luck's

Egdon Heath, op.47 <1927>   15'

2 3[1.2opt.Eh] 2 3[1.2.opt cbn] — 4[hn3-4 opt] 3[tp3 opt] 3 1[opt] — str

Novello

First Choral Symphony, op.41 <1923–1924>   48'

chorus   solo soprano
3[1.2.3/pic] 3[1.2.Eh] 3[1.2.bcl] 3[1.2.cbn] — 4 3 3 1 — tmp+2 — hp — cel, org — str
perc: cym, chimes, slgh-bells, tambn, bd, glock, xyl, gong
Minimum instrumentation (should be used if the chorus is small):
   2[incl pic] 2[incl Eh] 2 2 — 2 2 3 0 — tmp — hp — str

Prelude: Invocation to Pan	2'
Song and Bacchanal	6'
"Whence came ye, merry Damsels, whence came ye?"	1'
"Within his car, aloft, young Bacchus stood"	1'
"Whence came ye, jolly Satyrs, whence came ye?"	1'
"Onward the tiger"	1'
"Bacchus, young Bacchus!"	1'
Ode on a Grecian Urn	11'
"Ever let the Fancy roam"	3'
Folly's Song	3'
"Spirit here that reignest!"	1'
"God of the golden bow"	2'
"Then, though thy Temple wide, melodious swells"	1'
"'Tis awful silence then again"	4'
"Next thy Tasso's ardent numbers"	1'
"But when Thou joinest with the Nine"	7'
"Spirit here that reignest!"	2'

Novello

A Fugal Concerto, op.40, no.2 <1923>   8'

solo fl (or vn1); solo oboe (or vn2)
str

I. Moderato	2'
II. Adagio	3'
III. Allegro	3'

Luck's	Novello

Hammersmith, op.52 <1930; rev 1931>   15'

3[1.2.pic] 3[1.2.Eh] 3[1.2.bcl] 3[1.2.cbn] — 4 3 3 1 — tmp+2 — str
perc: gong, tri, cym, xyl, bd
Originally for military band; orchestrated by the composer.
May be played with: 2[1.pic] 2[1.Eh] 2 1 — 2 2 3 1 — tmp — str

Prelude	5'
Scherzo	10'

Boosey

The Hymn of Jesus <1917>   20'

2 choruses & female semi-chorus [SA]
3[1.2/pic.3] 3[1.2.Eh] 2 2 — 4 2 3 0 — tmp+1 — cel, pf, org — str
perc: bd, cym, sd, tambn
Some instruments optional; may be performed with:
   2[1.2/pic] 2[1.Eh] 2 1 — 2 2 0 0 — pf — str
   Also possible to perform using the choruses, the piano accompaniment from the piano-vocal score, and special string parts (not the same as the orchestral string parts).

Kalmus	Stainer

In the Bleak Midwinter <1904–1905>   5'

2 2 4[1.2.3.bcl] 2 — 2 3 3 1 — tmp+4 — str
perc: bd, cym, sus cym, tri, gong, glock, chimes, windchimes
Originally for SATB & org; arr. Robert W. Smith.

Warner

Invocation, op.19, no.2 <1911>   10'

solo violoncello
2 2 2 2 — 2 1 0 0 — 2perc — hp — str
perc: tri, sus cym

Faber

The Lure <1921>   9'

3[1.2.pic] 3[1.2.Eh] 3[1.2.bcl] 3[1.2.cbn] — 4 3 3 1 — tmp+3 — hp — cel — str
perc: sus cym, xyl, bd, tri, glock, tambn, gong, cym

Faber

Lyric Movement for Viola & Small Orchestra <1933>   10'

solo viola
1 1 1 1 — str
Ed. Colin Matthews.

Luck's	Oxford

The Perfect Fool: Ballet Music <1918–1922>   12'

3[1.2.pic] 3[1.2.Eh] 3[1.2.bcl] 3[1.2.cbn] — 4 4 3 1 — tmp+3 — hp — cel — str
perc: xyl, slgh-bells, cym, sus cym, tamtam, bd, tambn
Playable with: 3[incl pic] 2[incl Eh] 2 2 — 4 2 3 1 — tmp+3 — hp — str

Dance of the Spirits of Earth	5'
Dance of the Spirits of Water	3'
Dance of the Spirits of Fire	4'

Novello

The Planets <1914–1916>   51'

hidden female chorus in last movement
4[1.2.3/pic1.4/afl/pic2] 4[1.2.3/bass ob.Eh] 4[1.2.3.bcl] 4[1.2.3.cbn] — 6 4 3 1 — tenor tuba — 2tmp+4 — 2hp — cel, org — str
perc: glock, xyl, tamtam, chimes, sd, tambn, bd, tri, cym

   Schirmer edition prepared by Imogen Holst & Colin Matthews; Kalmus critical edition by Clinton F. Nieweg & Gregory Vaught.
   The parts are cued to make performance possible with the following minimum instrumentation: 3[incl pic] 3[incl Eh] 3[incl bcl] 2 — 4 3 3 1 — 2tmp+3 — 2hp, cel — str. Not all the cues are to be found in the scores, but a list prepared by Hitomi Tsuchiya Sipher that covers them all may be found at mola-inc.org. Some performances have successfully replaced the wordless female chorus with a synthesizer. The "bass flute" called for in the score is a misnomer; the part, reflecting British nomenclature of the period, is for alto flute in G.
   A separate composition by Colin Matthews, *Pluto, the Renewer, q.v.*, is intended for use with Holst's *The Planets*, thus completing the roster. (The planet Pluto was not discovered until 14 years after Holst's composition; in 2006, however, Pluto was demoted to the status of a dwarf planet.)

1. Mars, the Bringer of War	6'
2. Venus, the Bringer of Peace	10'
3. Mercury, the Winged Messenger	4'
4. Jupiter, the Bringer of Jollity	7'
5. Saturn, the Bringer of Old Age	11'
6. Uranus, the Magician	6'
7. Neptune, the Mystic	7'

Kalmus	Luck's	Schirmer

St. Paul's Suite, op.29, no.2 <1912–1913>   12'

str
The composer also prepared additional parts for woodwinds, brass and
percussion, available from Chester. This instrumentation is:
   2 2 2 1 — 1 1 0 0 — tmp+2[tri, tambn] — str.
I. Jig	3'
II. Ostinato	2'
III. Intermezzo	4'
IV. Finale (The Dargason)	3'

| Curwen | Kalmus |

A Somerset Rhapsody, op.21, no.2 <1906–1907>   10'

2[1.2/pic] 2[1.2/opt ob d'amore] 2 2 — 4 2 3 1 — tmp+3 — str
perc: sd, cym, bd

| Boosey | Luck's |

Suite No.1, op.28, no.1, E-flat major (First Suite for Band) <1909>   11'

3[1.2.pic] 2 2 2 — 4 3 3 1 — tmp+3 — str
perc: bd, cym, sus cym, sd, tri, tambn
Transcribed for orchestra by Chris Hazell.
1. Chaconne	5'
2. Intermezzo	3'
3. March	3'

| LudwigMasters |

Suite No.2, op.28, no.2, In F major (Second Suite for Band) <1911>   12'

3[1.2.pic] 2 2 2 — 4 2 3 1 — tmp+3 — str
perc: bd, cym, sus cym, sd, tri, tambn
Transcribed for orchestra by Adam Kent.
1. March	5'
2. Song Without Words	2'
3. Song of the Blacksmith	2'
4. Fantasia on the Dargason	3'

| LudwigMasters |

Suite for Orchestra [McPhee] <1909–1911>   13'

2[1.2/pic] 2 2 2 — 4 2 3 1 — tmp+3 — str
perc: bd, cym, sd, tambn, tri
Arranged for orchestra by Jonathan McPhee, using movements from both
the Holst suites for military band.
1. March [from Suite No.1]	3'
2. Song Without Words [from Suite No.2]	2'
3. Intermezzo [from Suite No.1]	3'
4. March [from Suite No.2]	5'

| Boosey |

Honegger, Arthur   1892-1955

(b Le Havre, 10 March 1892; d Paris, 27 Nov 1955). Swiss-French

Une cantate de Noël (A Christmas Cantata; Eine Weihnachtskantata) <1952–1953>   27'

solo baritone   chorus (SSAATTBB), children's chorus
2[1.2/pic] 2 2 2 — 4 3 3 0 — hp — org — str
A brief passage (10 notes) for solo treble voice from the children's
chorus. A number of Christmas tunes are quoted.

| Salabert |

Chant de joie <1922–1923>   7'

3[1.2.pic] 3[1.2.Eh] 3[1.2.bcl] 3[1.2.cbn] — 4 3 3 1 — 2perc — hp —
cel — str
perc: sus cym, bd

| Salabert |

Le chant de Nigamon <1917>   11'

3[1.2.pic] 2[1.Eh] 2 3[1.2.cbn] — 4 2 3 1 — tmp+3 — str
perc: sus cym, bd, tri

| Salabert |

Concertino, Piano & Orchestra <1924>   10'

2[incl pic] 2[incl Eh] 2[incl bcl] 2 — 2 2 1 0 — str

| Salabert |

Concerto da camera <1948>   18'

solo flute & English horn
str
1. Allegretto amabile	6'
2. Andante	8'
3. Vivace	4'

| Salabert |

Le dit des jeux du monde <1918>   50'

1[1/pic] 0 0 0 — 0 1 0 0 — tmp+3 — str[2.2.2.2.2]
perc: sd, sus cym, bd, bouteillophone [4-5 bottles unpitched; alt. tri]

| Salabert |

Horace victorieux; Symphonie mimée <1920–1921>   23'

3[1.2.3/pic] 3[1.2.Eh] 3[1.2.bcl] 3[1.2.cbn] — 4 3 3 1 — tmp+3 — hp
— str
perc: bd, cym, sd, tamtam, ratch [tmp+2 are sufficient if tmp plays tamtam &
ratchet]
1. Introduction	1'
2. Camille et Curiace	7'
3. Entrée des Horaces (Entrance of the Horatii)	2'
4. Entrée de la foule précédant les hérauts (Entrance of the Crowd)	2'
5. Annonce et préparatifs du combat (Fanfares Announcing the Combat)	4'
6. Le combat	3'
7. Triomphe d'Horace	1'
8. Lamentations et imprécations de Camille	2'
9. Meutre (Murder of Camille)	1'

| Salabert |

L'Impératrice aux rochers (Un miracle de Nôtre-Dame): Suite <1925; rev suite: 1926>   18'

3[1.2.pic] 3[1.2.Eh] 3[1.2.bcl] 3[1.2.cbn] — 4 3 3 1 — 3perc — hp —
cel — str
perc: sus cym, tamtam, bd, tambn
Suite from the incidental music to the play by S.-G. de Bouhélier.
I. La chasse de l'Empereur	3'
II. La neige sur Rome	3'
III. Orage	4'
IV. Le jardin	4'
V. Orgie	4'

| Salabert |

Jeanne d'Arc au bûcher (Joan of Arc at the Stake) <1935; rev 1944>   77'

chorus, children's chorus   solos SSSATB
4 spoken roles (1 female, 3 male)
2[1.2/pic] 2 3[1.Ebcl.bcl] 4[1.2.3.cbn] — 0 4 4 0 — 3asx — tmp+2
— 2pf, cel, ondes martenot — str
perc: bd, cym, sd, td, field dr, tri, tamtam, woodblk, ratch
4th trombone may be replaced by tuba.

Prologue	*8'*
Scene I, The Voices from Heaven	*3'*
Scene II, The Book	*3'*
Scene III, The Voices of the Earth	*4'*
Scene IV, Joan Given up to the Beasts	*9'*
Scene V, Joan at the Stake	*3'*
Scene VI, The Kings, or the Invention of the Game of Cards	*5'*
Scene VII, Catherine and Margaret	*3'*
Scene VIII, The King Who is Going to Rheims	*11'*
Scene IX, Joan's Sword	*15'*
Scene X, Trimazo	*1'*
Scene XI, Joan of Arc in the Flames	*12'*

Salabert

Mouvement symphonique no.3 <1933>   10'

3[1.2.pic] 3[1.2.Eh] 2 3[1.2.cbn] — 4 3 3 1 — asx — 2perc — str
perc: sus cym, tamtam, bd

Salabert

Nocturne <1936>   9'

3[1.2.pic] 3[1.2.Eh] 3[1.2.bcl] 3 — 4 3 0 1 — asx — 3perc — hp —
str
perc: tri, cym, ratch, woodblk, sd, tambn

Boosey

Pacific 231 (Mouvement symphonique no.1) <1923>   7'

3[1.2.pic] 3[1.2.Eh] 3[1.2.bcl] 3[1.2.cbn] — 4 3 3 1 — 4perc — str
perc: td, cym, bd, tamtam

Salabert

Pastorale d'été <1920>   7'

1 1 1 1 — 1 0 0 0 — str

Kalmus   Luck's   Salabert

Prelude, Fugue, Postlude <1929; rev extracts: 1948>   13'

3[1.2.3/pic] 3[1.2.Eh] 3[1.2.3/bcl] 3[1.2.cbn] — 4 3 3 1 — asx (opt)
— 3perc — hp — cel — str
perc: sus cym, bd, tamtam, tri
Three extracts from the ballet *Amphion*.

Prelude	*5'*
Fugue	*5'*
Postlude	*3'*

Salabert

Prélude pour "La Tempête" de Shakespeare <1923>   8'

2[1.pic] 2[1.Eh] 2[1.bcl] 2[1.cbn] — 4 2 3 1 — 4perc — str
perc: tri, tamtam, sus cym, bd

Salabert

Le roi David [original, 1921] (King David) <1921>   74'

chorus   solos SAT   speaker
2[1.2/pic] 1[1/Eh] 2[1.2/bcl] 1 — 1 2 1 0 — tmp+3 — pf, cel, harm
— db, opt vc
perc: cym, sd, bd, gong, tambn, tambn prov
Many errors and discrepancies in score and parts.

Part I	*32'*
Part II	*14'*
Part III	*28'*
[For full contents, see Appendix J]	

Foetisch

Le roi David [large orchestra version, 1923] (King David) <1921; rev (reorchestrated) 1923>   74'

chorus   solos SAT   speaker
2[1.2/pic] 2[1.2/Eh] 2[1.2/bcl] 2[1.2/cbn] — 4 2 3 1 — tmp+3 — hp
— cel, org — str
perc: cym, sd, bd, gong, tambn, tambn prov
Originally for small orchestra; rescored by the composer.

Part 1	*32'*
Part 2	*14'*
Part 3	*28'*
[For full contents, see Appendix J]	

Foetisch

Rugby (Mouvement symphonique no.2) <1928>   8'

3[1.2.pic] 3[1.2.Eh] 3[1.2.bcl] 3[1.2.cbn] — 4 3 3 1 — str

Salabert

Suite archaïque <1950–1951>   16'

2 2 2 2 — 0 2 2 0 — str

I. Ouverture	*5'*
II. Pantomime	*2'*
III. Ritournelle et Sérénade	*5'*
IV. Processional	*4'*

Salabert

Symphony No.1 <1930>   21'

3[1.2.3/pic] 3[1.2.Eh] 3[1.2.bcl] 3[1.2.cbn] — 4 3 3 1 — 1perc — str
perc: bd, tamtam

I. Allegro marcato	*6'*
II. Adagio	*8'*
III. Presto	*7'*

Salabert

Symphony No.2 <1941>   25'

0 0 0 0 — 0 1[opt] 0 0 — str
Tp plays end of mvt 3 only.

I. Molto moderato - Allegro	*11'*
II. Adagio mesto	*9'*
III. Vivace; non troppo	*5'*

Salabert

Symphony No.3 (Symphonie liturgique) <1946>   30'

3[1.2.3/pic] 3[1.2.Eh] 3[1.2.bcl] 3[1.2.cbn] — 4 3 3 1 — tmp+4 — pf
— str
perc: td, sus cym, bd, tri, tamtam

I. Dies irae	*6'*
II. De profundis clamavi	*12'*
III. Dona nobis pacem	*12'*

Salabert

Symphony No.4 (Deliciae basiliensis) <1946>   28'

2[1.2/pic] 1 2 1 — 2 1 0 0 — 2perc — pf — str
perc: sus cym, tri, tamtam, glock, tambour bâlois or caisse roulante [in this case
probably with snares]
Spelling on the score itself: *Deliciae basilienses*.

I. Lento e misterioso	*12'*
II. Larghetto	*8'*
III. Allegro	*8'*

Salabert

Symphony No.5 (Di tre re) <1951>   23'

3[1.2.3/pic] 3[1.2.Eh] 3[1.2.bcl] 3 — 4 3 3 1 — opt tmp — str

I. Grave	*8'*
II. Allegretto	*9'*
III. Allegro marcato	*6'*

Salabert

Hoover, Katherine   1937 -

(b Elkins, WV, 2 Dec 1937). American

Concerto, Clarinet, op.38 <1987>   22'

2[1.2/pic] 2 1 2 — 2 3 3 0 — asx — 1 or 2perc — str
Written for jazz clarinetist Eddie Daniels; some improvisation by soloist
required.

Presser

Concerto, 2 Violins, op.40 (Double Concerto) <1989>   17'

str
No.1   6'
No.2   6'
No.3   5'

Papagena

Eleni; A Greek Tragedy, op.36 <1986>   15'

3[1.2.3/pic] 3[1.2.Eh] 3[1.2.bcl] 3[1.2.cbn] — 4 3 3 1 — gtr, alto
voice (seated in orchestra) — tmp+2 — str

Presser

J. M. W. Turner: Impressions <2006>   23'

3[all/pic] 3[1.2.3/Eh] 3[1.2.bcl] 3[1.2.cbn] — 4 3 3 1 — tmp+3 — hp
— pf/hpsd — str
Each movement describes a painting by J.M.W. Turner.
I. The Grand Canal   7'
II. Steamboat in a Snowstorm   4'
III. The Music Room   6'
IV. The First Rater   6'

Papagena

Medieval Suite   20'

solo flute
1[fl/pic] 1 2 1 — 2 0 2 0 — 2perc — hp — str
perc: sus cym, td, glock, xyl, vib, woodblk, tmp[briefly in last mvt]
I. Virelai   5'
II. The Black Knight   5'
III. The Drunken Friar   2'
IV. On the Betrothal of Princess Isabelle of France, Aged Six Years 4'
V. Demon's Dance   4'

Presser

Night Skies, op.46 <1992>   25'

4[1.2/shakuhachi.3/pic.4/pic] 3 3[1/Ebcl.2.3/bcl] 3 — 6 4 4 0 —
tmp+5 — hp — str
Brass divided into 2 sections seated left & right across from each other.

Papagena

Stitch-te Naku, op.47 <1994>   18'

solo violoncello
2[incl pic] 2 2 2[incl cbn] — 4 2 1 0 — tmp+3 — pf/cel — str
One percussionist covers 2nd tmp in 2 brief passages.

Papagena

Summer Night, op.34 <1985>   8'

solo flute & horn
str

Presser

Two Sketches, op.42 <1989>   11'

2[1.2/pic] 2[1.2/Eh] 2[1.2/bcl] 3[1.2(opt).3/cbn] — 2 2 1 0 — tmp+3
— hp — cel, pf — str
Winter Sands   5'
Turnabout   6'

Presser

Horne, David   1970 -

(b Tillicoultry, 12 Dec 1970). Scottish

Concerto, Piano <1992>   21'

2[1/afl.2/pic] 2 2[1.2/bcl] 2[1.cbn] — 2 2 2 1 — 2perc — hp — cel -
str
perc: chimes, marim, vib, xyl, crot, glock, tamtam, 3sus cym, tmp

Boosey

Horwood, Michael   1947 -

(b Buffalo, NY, 24 May 1947). American-Canadian.

Amusement Park Suite <1986>   17'

3[1.2.pic] 2 2 2 — 4 2 3 1 — tmp+3 — str
perc: bd, cym, sus cym, hi-hat, sd, toms, tri, tambn, tamtam, glock, ratch
3rd tbn *or* tuba *or* both may be used.
The Sky Ride   4'
The Log Flume   4'
The Carousel   3'
The Dark Ride   3'
The Roller-Coaster 3'

CMC

Concerto, Double Bass <1967; rev 2003>   15'

str
Largo   _'
Allegro molto _'

CMC

Do You Live for Weekends? <1996>   6'

1 1 1 1 — 1 1 1 0 — 1 or 2 perc — str[5.4.3.3.1]
perc: tmp, bd, sus cym, Chinese cym, hi-hat, sd, glock, chimes, glass chimes, whip

CMC

Intravariations <1997>   19'

solo piano
3[1.2.pic] 2 2 2 — 4 2 3 1 — tmp+3 — str
perc: bd, cym, sus cym, sd, td, tri, tambn, tamtam, glock, woodblk, cowbell, guiro,
marac, wooden plank

CMC

National Park Suite <1991>   22'

3[1.2.pic] 2[1.2/Eh] 2 2 — 4 2 3 1 — tmp+2 — hp — str
perc: bd, cym, sus cym, szl cym, swish cym, sd, tri, tambn, headless tambn,
tamtam, glock, xyl, woodblk, marac, vibraslap, chains or beads, box of marbles,
cardboard scraper, cedar windchimes
Forillon National Park (Québec)   6'
Bryce Canyon National Park (Utah)   3'
Fathom Five Marine Park (Ontario)   5'
Yellowstone National Park (Wyoming) 2'
Jasper National Park (Alberta)   6'

CMC

Symphony No.1 <1984>   19'

2[1.2/pic] 2[1.2/Eh] 2[1.2/bcl] 2 — 2 2 0 0 — tmp+2 — str
perc: bd, sus cym, sd, tri, tambn, tamtam, glock, xyl, chimes, finger cym
Allegro frammenti   8'
Passacaglia funebre   6'
Vivace in moto perpetuo 5'

CMC

Symphony No.2 (Visions of a Wounded Earth) <1995> 50'

chorus
3[1.2.pic] 2 2 2 — 4 2 3 1 — tmp+2 — str
perc: bd, cym, 2sus cym, sd, tri, tambn, tamtam, xyl, woodblk, bongos
English text by 8 different Canadian poets.

I. Out of the Past	13'
II. Northern Images	11'
III. Change	2'
IV. Specifically	11'
V. Toward Healing	13'

> CMC

Symphony No.3 <1996> 26'

solo tenor saxophone
3[1.2.pic] 3[1.2.Eh] 4[1.2.Ebcl.bcl] 3[1.2.cbn] — 4 4 3 1 — tmp+4 — pf — str
perc: bd, cym, sus cym, szl cym, hi-hat, sd, td, set, toms, floortom, brakedrum, tri, tambn, tamtam, glock, xyl, vib, chimes, woodblk, guiro, claves, gourd rattle

> CMC

Three Interludes <1995> 10'

2[1.2/pic] 2 2 2 — 4 2 0 0 — tmp+2 — str
perc: sd, tri, tambn, sus cym
Drawn from the composer's Symphony No.2.

> CMC

Women of Trachis <1966> 17'

1[fl/pic] 1 1 0 — 1 1 0 0 — opt mand — 2perc — 2vn, va, vc, db
perc: bd, sus cym, sd, timbales, brakedrum, tri, tambn, tamtam, xyl, vib, woodblk, templeblk, ratch, cast
Incidental music for the drama by Sophocles. Horn & double bass double on percussion in one movement.

> CMC

Hovhaness, Alan 1911-2000

(b Somerville, MA, 8 March 1911; d Seattle, 21 June 2000). American composer of Armenian and Scottish descent

Alleluia and Fugue, op.40b <1941> 9'

str

> Rongwen

And God Created Great Whales, op.229, no.1 <1970> 12'

3[1.2.3/pic] 2 2 2 — 4 3 3 1 — tape of whale sounds — tmp+4 — 2hp — str
perc: tamtam, glock, vib, chimes, bd, gong, 1perc controls tape

> Peters

Armenian Rhapsody No.2, op.51 <1944> 7'

str

> Rongwen

Artik, op.78 <1949> 15'

solo horn
str

> Peters

Celestial Fantasy, op.44 <1944> 7'

str

> Rongwen

Floating World, op.209 (Ukiyo) <1964> 12'

3 3[1.2.Eh] 2 2 — 4 3 3 1 — tmp+7 — 1 or 2hp — cel — str
perc: tamtam, xyl, bd, 2glock (1 opt), 2vib (1 opt), 2sets chimes (1 opt)
4 of the percussionists are optional.

> Peters

Fra Angelico, op.220 <1967> 17'

3 3[1.2.Eh] 3[1.2.bcl] 3[1.2.cbn] — 4 3 3 1 — tmp+6 (or 4) — 2hp — cel — str[16.16.12.12.10(or 8)]

> Peters

Magnificat, op.157 <1958> 33'

chorus   solos STB
0 2 0 0 — 2 2 1 0 — 2perc — hp — str
perc: tamtam, chime[C5]

> Peters

Meditation on Orpheus, op.155 <1957> 13'

3 3[1.2.Eh] 3[1.2.bcl] 3[1.2.cbn] — 4 3 3 1 — tmp+1 — hp — cel — str
perc: tamtam

> Peters

Overture, op.76, no.1 <1948> 5'

solo trombone
str

> Peters

Prelude and Quadruple Fugue, op.128 <1936; rev 1954> 6'

2 2 2 2 — 4 2 3 0 — tmp — str

> AMP   Luck's

Psalm and Fugue, op.40a <1941> 11'

str

> Peters

Symphony No.1, op.17 (Exile) <1937> 20'

2 2 2 2 — 4 3 3 1 — tmp — hp — str

Andante espressivo; Allegro	7'
Grazioso	4'
Finale: Andante; Presto	9'

> Peters

Symphony No.2, op.132 (Mysterious Mountain) <1955> 15'

3 3[1.2.Eh] 3[1.2.bcl] 3[1.2.cbn] — 5 3 3 1 — tmp — hp — cel — str

I. Andante con moto	5'
II. Double Fugue: Moderato maestoso - Allegro vivo	5'
III. Andante espressivo: Con moto	5'

> AMP

Symphony No.10, op.184 (Vahaken) <1944; rev 1965> 19'

2 2 2 2 — 2 2 3 0 — tmp+2 — hp — str
perc: xyl, chimes, bd (opt)
Playable with 1 1 1 1 — 1 1 1 0 — tmp+1 — hp — str

1. Andante; Allegro	6'
2. Intermezzo (Allegretto)	3'
3. Andante; Allegro	10'

> Peters

Symphony No.15, op.199 (Silver Pilgrimage) <1962>   25'

2 2[1.2/Eh] 2 2 — 4 3 3 1 — tmp+2 — hp — str
perc: bd, tamtam, chimes

Mount Ravana	5'
Marava Princess	3'
River of Meditation	11'
Heroic Gates of Peace	6'

Peters

Symphony No.22, op.236 (City of Light) <1971>   30'

3[1.2.3/pic] 2 3[1.2.bcl] 3[1.2.cbn] — 4 3 3 1 — tmp+3 — hp — str
perc: vib, glock, tamtam, chime[D5]

1. Allegro moderato	10'
2. Angel of Light (Largo)	4'
3. Allegretto grazioso	3'
4. Finale (Largo maestoso)	13'

Peters

Symphony No.24, op.273 (Majnun) <1973>   25'

tenor solo   chorus
0 0 0 0 — 0 1 0 0 — str

AMP

Symphony No.29, op.289 <1976>   25'

solo baritone horn
3 2 2 2 — 4 3 3 1 — tmp+3 — hp — str

Fujihara

Talin, op.93 (Concerto for Viola & String Orchestra) <1952>   14'

str
AMP is said to offer a version for solo clarinet and strings.

I.Chant	_'
II. Estampie	_'
III. Canzona	_'

AMP

Variations and Fugue, op.18 <1964>   13'

3 3[incl Eh] 2 2 — 4 3 3 1 — tmp+1 — hp — str

Peters

Howells, Herbert   1892-1983

(b Lydney, Glos., 17 Oct 1892; d London, 23 Feb 1983). English

Elegy for Viola, String Quartet & String Orchestra, op.15 <1917>   10'

solo viola; solo string quartet
opt org pedals — str

Boosey

An English Mass <1955>   34'

1 1 0 0 — 0 0 0 0 — tmp — hp — org — str

I. Kyrie eleison	6'
II. Credo	8'
III. Sursum corda	1'
IV. Sanctus	3'
V. Benedictus	4'
VI. Agnus Dei	3'
VII. Gloria	9'

Novello

Hymnus Paradisi <1938; rev 1950>   45'

solo soprano, tenor   double chorus
2[1.2/opt pic] 3[1.2.opt Eh] 3[1.2.opt bcl] 3[1.2.opt cbn] — 4 3 3 1 — tmp+1 — hp — opt org, opt cel — str
perc: bd, cym, sd

I. Preludio	4'
II. Requiem aeternam	9'
III. The Lord is My Shepherd	7'
IV. Sanctus—I Will Lift Up Mine Eyes	10'
V. I Heard a Voice from Heaven	5'
VI. Holy is the True Light	10'

Novello

Penguinski <1933>   5'

2[1/pic.2] 2[1.2/Eh] 2 2 — 4 2 3 1 — tmp+3 — hp — pf — str
perc: bd, cym, sd, tri, tambn, xyl
An affectionate tribute to Stravinsky.

Novello

Sir Patrick Spens, op.23 <1917>   20'

baritone solo   chorus
2[1.2/pic] 2[1.2/Eh] 2[1.2/bcl] 2 — 4 2 3 1 — tmp+3 — hp — org — str
perc: sd, bd, tri, cym
Brief tenor solo for a member of the chorus.

Novello

Stabat Mater <1963–1965>   52'

solo tenor   chorus
2[1.2/pic] 3[1.2.Eh] 3[1.2.bcl] 3[1.2.cbn] — 4 3 3 1 — tmp+2 — hp — pf/cel, org — str

1. Stabat Mater dolorosa	8'
2. Cujus animam gementem	10'
3. Quis est homo qui non fleret	5'
4. Eia, Mater, fons amoris	5'
5. Sancta Mater, istud agas	6'
6. Fac, ut portem Christi mortem	8'
7. Christe com sit hinc exire	10'

Novello

Hoyt, George   1947-2014

(b Bremerton, WA, 7 February 1947; d Bremerton, WA, 7 November 2014). American

Symphony No.1 <1985–1988>   43'

3[1.2.pic] 2 3[1.2.bcl] 2 — 4 3 3 1 — tmp+3 — str
perc: bd, cym, sd, field dr, tri, tamtam, glock

I. Allegro non troppo, ma con brio	11'
II. Allegro, quasi scherzo	9'
III. Adagio	9'
IV. Allegro moderato con bravura	14'

Fleisher   Hoyt

Hummel, Johann Nepomuk   1778-1837

(b Pressburg [now Bratislava], 14 Nov 1778; d Weimar, 17 Oct 1837). Austrian

Concerto, Piano, op.113, A-flat major <1827>   35'

2 0 2 2 — 2 2 0 0 — tmp — str

I. Allegro moderato	17'
II. Romanza: Larghetto con moto	6'
III. Rondo alla spagniola: Allegro moderato	11'

A-R Editions   Kalmus   Luck's

Concerto, Trumpet, E major [original key] <1803>   19'

1 2 2 2 — 2 0 0 0 — tmp — str
Breitkopf ed. Michael Kube; Universal ed. Edward Tarr. For the same
work in a transposed version, see subsequent entry.

I. Allegro con spirito	10'
II. Andante	5'
III. Rondo	4'

Breitkopf	Universal

Concerto, Trumpet, E-flat major [transposed version] <1803>   21'

1 2 2 2 — 2 0 0 0 — tmp — str
Breitkopf ed. Michael Kube; Kalmus "practical edition" in E-flat major,
ed. by Clark McAlister. (The original work is in E major.)
    A version without clarinets is published by Billaudot; a version without
clarinets or timpani is published by EMT.

I. Allegro con spirito	12'
II. Andante	5'
III. Rondo	4'

Breitkopf	Kalmus

Fantaisie, Viola & Orchestra   9'

0 0 2 0 — str
Arr. Fernand Oubradous.

EMT

Humperdinck, Engelbert   1854-1921

(b Siegburg, 1 Sept 1854; d Neustrelitz, 27 Sept 1921). German

Dornröschen (Sleeping Beauty): Suite <1902>   19'

2 2 2 2 — 4 2 3 1 — tmp+1 — hp — str

Prelude	8'
Ballade	4'
Irrfahrten (Wanderings)	3'
Das Dornenschloss (The Castle of Thorns)	2'
Festklänge (Festive Sounds)	2'

Fleisher

Hänsel und Gretel: Prelude <1890–1893>   8'

3[1.2.pic] 2 2 2 — 4 2 3 1 — tmp+2 — str
perc: tri, tambn, cym

Kalmus	Luck's	Schott

Hänsel und Gretel: Hexenritt (Witch's Ride) <1890–1893>   4'

3[1.2.pic] 2 2 2 — 4 2 3 1 — tmp+4 — str
perc: bd, cym, sus cym, tri, tambn, cast

Kalmus	Luck's

Hänsel und Gretel: Knusperwalzer (Crackle-Waltz) <1890–1893>   5'

2[1.pic] 2 2 2 — 4[hn3&4 opt] 2 3[opt] 0 — tmp+2 — str
perc: glock, tri
Arr. Hans Steiner.

Kalmus	Luck's

Hänsel und Gretel: Suite <1890>   32'

3[1.2.pic] 2[1.2/Eh] 3[1.2.bcl] 2 — 4 2 3 1 — tmp+3 — hp — str
perc: glock, tri, cym, tamtam, tambn, bd, cast, thunder sheet
Suite compiled by Omar Abad. Score lists 2perc, but 3 are needed.

1. Vorspiel (Prelude)   —'
2. "Rallalala"   —'
3. Hexenritt (The Witch's Ride)   —'
4. Im Walde (In the Forest)   —'
5. Abendsegen (Evening Prayer)   —'
6. Das Knusperhäuschen (The Gingerbread House at the Ilsenstein)   —'
7. Knusperwalzer und Pantomime (The Witch's Waltz and Pantomime)   —'

Schott

Hänsel und Gretel: Three Excerpts <1890–1893>   13'

3[1.2.pic] 2[1.2/Eh] 2 2 — 4 2 3 1 — tmp+1 — hp — str
perc: tri, cym

Lied des Sandmännchens (Sandman's Song)	3'
Abendsegen (Evening Prayer)	3'
Traumpantomime (Dream Pantomime)	7'

Kalmus	Luck's	Schott

Königskinder: Prelude <1897>   8'

3[1.2.pic] 2 3[1.2.bcl] 3[1.2.cbn] — 4 3 3 1 — tmp+1 — str
perc: cym, tri

Fleisher	Luck's

Königskinder: Introduction to Act II <1897>   4'

3[1.2.pic] 2 2 3[1.2.cbn] — 4 2 3 1 — tmp+2 — str
perc: cym, tri, rattle

| Hellafest | —' |
| Kinder-Reigen | —' |

Kalmus	Luck's

Königskinder: Introduction to Act III <1897>   9'

3[1.2.3/pic] 2[1.Eh] 3[1.2.bcl] 3[1.2.cbn] — 4 3 3 1 — tmp — hp —
str

Kalmus	Luck's

Maurische Rhapsodie (Moorish Rhapsody) <1887; rev 1890; 1898>   41'

3[1.2.pic] 2[1.Eh] 3[1.2.bcl] 3[1.2.cbn] — 4 2 3 1 — tmp+2 — str
perc: tri, glock, cym, tambn
Originally Maurische Suite, 1887; revised as Maurische Symphonie,
1890; revised to its present form (and title), 1898.

I. Tarifa: Elegie bei Sonnenuntergang	15'
II. Tanger: Eine Nacht in Mohrencafé	11'
III. Tetuan: Ritt in der Wüste	15'

Kalmus	Luck's

Eine Trauung in der Bastille <1905>   10'

2[1.2/pic] 2[1.2/Eh] 2 2 — 4 3 3 1 — tmp+2 — hp — opt org or harm
— str
perc: sd, cym, glock, tamtam
Introduction and interlude from the opera Die Heirat wider Willen.
    Backstage: 1tp, org, sd & tamtam.

Fleisher

Hurwit, Albert
1931-

(b Hartford, CT, 20 May 1931). American

Symphony No.1 (Remembrance)
59'

3[1.2.pic] 3[1.2.Eh] 3[1.2/Ebcl.3/bcl] 2 — 4 3 3 1 — klezmer band[cl, accordion, balalaika (or mand), db] — tmp+2 — 1 or 2 hp — str

perc: bd, cym, sus cym, sd, tri, tambn, tamtam, glock, woodblk, whip, cast
Klezmer group in 2nd mvt only; solo klezmer db is from the orchestra. The group (except the db) enters from the wings and must move to their places while playing.

1. Origins — Andante piacevole	*17'*
2. Separation (Variations) — Tempestuoso	*11'*
3. Remembrance — Adagio	*16'*
4. Arrival — Maestoso	*15'*

Fleisher

Husa, Karel
1921-

(b Prague, 7 Aug 1921). American composer of Czech birth

Apotheosis of This Earth <1972>
26'

chorus
4[1.2.3.4/pic] 4[1.2.3.Eh] 4[1.2.3.bcl] 3[1.2.cbn] — 4 4 4 1 — tmp+4 — str

Originally for band and optional chorus, 1971; adapted by the composer, 1972.

I. Apotheosis	*13'*
II. Tragedy of Destruction	*7'*
III. Postscript	*6'*

AMP

Celebration Fanfare <1996>
2'

3[1.2.pic] 3[1.2.Eh] 3[1.2.bcl] 3[1.2.cbn] — 4 3 3 1 — tmp+3 — str
perc: gong, cym, sus cym, chimes, vib

AMP

Concerto for Orchestra <1986>
38'

3[1/afl.2/pic.3/pic] 3[1.2.Eh] 3[1.2.bcl] 3[1.2.3/cbn] — 5 4 3 1 — tmp+4 — 2hp — pf — str
5th horn in last movement only.

AMP

Concerto, Trumpet & Wind Orchestra <1973>
14'

3[1.2.pic] 3[1.2.Eh] 2 3[1.2.cbn] — 4 3 3 1 — asx — tmp+4 — 3 or 4db

AMP

Concerto, Violin <1991>
28'

3[1.2.3/pic] 3[1.2.Eh] 3[1.2.bcl] 3[1.2.cbn] — 4 3 3 1 — tmp+3 — 2hp — str
perc: marim, vib, xyl, glock, chimes, crot, sus cym, gong, templeblks, gamelan gong, 5tomtom, 5woodblk

I. Moderato, ma deciso	_'
II. Adagio	_'
III. Allegro giocoso	_'

AMP

Fantasies for Orchestra <1956–1957>
20'

2[1.pic] 1 1 0 — 0 3 0 0 — 2perc — pf — str["symphonic or chamber"]
perc: sd, bd, cym, gong, tri, glock, xyl

Schott

Festive Ode <1955>
5'

mixed chorus or male chorus
3[incl pic] 3[incl Eh] 3[incl bcl] 3[incl cbn] — 4 3 3 1 — tmp+3 — str

Instruments such as English horn, bass clarinet, contrabassoon, 2nd & 4th horns and others may be omitted. Where orchestra is not available, either band or brass ensemble with percussion may be used.

Highgate

Music for Prague 1968 [orchestral version] <1968>
24'

3[1.2.3/pic] 3[1.2.Eh] 3[1.2.bcl] 3[1.2.cbn] — 4 4 3 1 — tmp+4 — hp — pf — str

perc: crot, bd, chimes, cym, marim, vib, xyl, 3sus cym, 3tomtoms, 4tri, 2tamtams, 2sd
Originally for concert band; orhestrated by the composer.

I. Introduction and Fanfare	*7'*
II. Aria	*6'*
III. Interlude	*4'*
IV. Toccata and Chorale	*7'*

AMP

Overture (Youth) <1991>
5'

3[1.2.3/pic] 3[1.2.Eh] 3[1.2.bcl] 3[1.2.3/cbn] — 4 3 3 1 — tmp+4 — 2hp — pf — str
perc: marim, vib, xyl, sd, chimes, templeblks, cym, 2sus cym, 2gong, 5tomtom

AMP

Pastoral <1979>
7'

str

AMP

The Steadfast Tin Soldier <1974>
27'

narrator
2[1/pic.2/pic] 2 1 2[1.2/cbn] — 2 2 1[btbn] 0 — asx — tmp+3 — hp — str
perc: vib, glock, chimes, xyl, sd, bd, gong, whip, cym, szl cym, ratch, 3tomtom, 2sus cym

Introduction and March	_'
Games of the Toys	_'
The Rain	_'
The Rat and the Fish	_'
The Tin Soldier and the Little Dancer	_'
The Flames	_'

AMP

Symphonic Suite for Orchestra <1984>
19'

3[1.2.3/pic] 3 3[1.2.3/bcl] 3[1.2.3/cbn] — 4 3 3 1 — tmp+3 — hp — pf — str

perc: vib, xyl, marim, chimes, sus cym, cym, sd, bd, templeblks, tri, 2gong, 5tomtom, 3woodblk, sandblks
Note in the score: "The 1st & 3rd mvts allow the optional use of antiphonally place[d] brass choirs." However, no further instructions are to be found; apparently these additional brass choirs are to double the orchestral brass at the discretion of the conductor.

Celebration	_'
Meditation	_'
Vision	_'

AMP

Symphony No.1 <1953>
28'

3[1.2.pic] 3[1.2.Eh] 3[1.2.bcl] 3[1.2.cbn] — 4 3 3 1 — tmp+3 — 1 or 2hp — pf — str
perc: sd, bd/cym, cym, xyl, 2tamtams

1. Adagio misterioso; Allegro assai
2. Grave attacca
3. Poco più viva; Con moto; Maestoso

Schott

Symphony No.2 (Reflections) <1982–1983>   25'

2[1/afl.2/pic] 2[1.2/Eh] 2[1.2/bcl] 2[1.2/cbn] — 2 2 0 0 — tmp+2 —
hp[opt dbl] — str
perc: vib, xyl, templeblks, bd, sd, sus cym, gong, 5tomtom
   I. Moderate   _'
   II. Very fast   _'
   III. Slow   _'

AMP

Two Sonnets from Michelangelo <1971>   16'

3[1.2.pic] 3[1.2.Eh] 2 2 — 4 3 3 1 — asx — tmp+2 — hp — str
perc: marim, vib, sd, gong, sus cym, cym, crot[E5,A5], tmp2

AMP

Hutter, Gregory   1971-

(b Michigan City, IN, 10 Jan 1971). American

Deploration <2005>   11'

str
Movements played without pause.
   I. Prelude   _'
   II. Fugue   _'
   III. Chorale   _'

ECS

Electric Traction <2002>   7'

3[1.2.pic] 3[1.2.Eh] 3[1.2.bcl] 3[1.2.cbn] — 4 3 3 1 — tmp+3 — hp
— pf — str
perc: sus cym, hi-hat, sd, field dr, tambn, tamtam, glock, xyl, marim, vib, whip

ECS

Sinfonietta concertante <2006>   10'

1 1 1 1 — 1 1 0 0 — 1perc — pf — str
perc: glock, xyl, tmp

ECS

Skyscrapers <2001>   9'

3[1.2.pic] 3[1.2.Eh] 3[1.2.bcl] 3[1.2.cbn] — 4 3 3 1 — tmp+3 — hp
— pf/cel — str
   I. Mies (Homage, Ludwig Mies van der Rohe)   5'
   II. Steel and Glass   4'

ECS

Still Life <2004>   11'

solo oboe
str

ECS

Urban Collision <2003>   7'

3[1.2.pic] 3[1.2.Eh] 3[1.2.bcl] 3[1.2.cbn] — 4 3 3 1 — tmp+3 — hp
— pf — str

ECS

I

Iannaccone, Anthony   1943-

(b Brooklyn, NY, 14 Oct 1943). American

Concertante, Clarinet <1994>   15'

3[1.2.pic] 2 2[1.bcl] 2 — 4 2 3 0 — tmp+3 — hp — cel, pf — str
perc: bd, sd, timbales, tamtam, glock, xyl, marim, vib, crot, 2sus cym, 2tomtom

Presser

Divertimento <1983>   11'

3[1.2.3/pic] 2 3[1.2.bcl] 2 — 4 3 3 1 — 3perc — hp — pf/cel — str
perc: bd, sus cym, sd, tomtom, tamtam, glock, tambn, xyl, marim, vib, bongos,
tmp
   1. Night Music (Nocturne)   6'
   2. Morning Music (Aubade)   5'

Presser

From Time to Time: Fantasias on Appalachian   13'
Folksongs <2000>

3[1.2.pic] 2 2 2 — 4 2 2 0 — tmp+2 — pf/cel — str
perc: bd, sd, glock, xyl, marim, vib, bongos, 2sus cym, 3tomtom, 2tambn
   I. Once Upon a Time: Crosscurrents Remembered   _'
   II. Moving Time: A Millennium Ride   _'

Presser

Lysistrata <1968>   8'

3[1.2.pic] 3[1.2.Eh] 3[1.2.bcl] 3[1.2.cbn] — 4 3 3 1 — tmp+2 — hp
— pf/cel — str
perc: cym, sus cym, sd, tri, glock, xyl, woodblk, templeblks

Subito

Symphony No.3 (Night Rivers) <1991>   19'

3[1.2.3/pic] 2 3[1.2.bcl] 2 — 4 3 3 1 — tmp+3 — hp — pf, cel — str
perc: bd, sd, timbales, tri, tamtam, glock, xyl, marim, vib, crot, 2sus cym, 2tomtom

Presser

Waiting for the Sunrise on the Sound   11'

3[1.2.pic] 2 3[1.2.bcl] 2 — 4 3 3 1 — tmp+3 — hp — pf — str
perc: bd, sd, glock, xyl, marim, vib, bongos, 3sus cym, 3tomtom

Presser

West End Express <1997>   7'

3[1.2.pic] 2 3[1.2.bcl] 2 — 4 3 3 1 — tmp+3 — hp — pf — str
perc: bd, sd, tri, tambn, glock, xyl, marim, vib, crot, whip, bongos, 3sus cym,
3tomtom

Presser

Ibert, Jacques
1890 - 1962

(b Paris, 15 Aug 1890; d Paris, 5 Feb 1962). French

Bacchanale <1956>
10'

3[incl pic] 3[1.2.Eh] 3[1.2.bcl] 4[1.2.3.cbn] — 4 3 3 1 — tmp+6 — hp — str
perc: xyl, sd, tambn, field dr, bd, tomtom, cym

Leduc

La ballade de la geôle de Reading (The Ballad of Reading Gaol) <1921>
26'

3[1.2.3/pic] 3[1.2.Eh] 3[1.2.bcl] 3[1.2.sarr] — 4 3 3 1 — tmp+5 — 2hp — cel — str
perc: bd, cym, tri, sd, tamtam, xyl, sus cym
1. Il n'avait plus sa tunique écarlate — 13'
2. Cette nuit là, les corridors vides furent pleins de formes effrayents — 7'
3. Le vent frais du matin commença à gémir — 6'

Leduc

Bostoniana <1955>
8'

3[incl pic] 3[1.2.Eh] 3[1.2.bcl] 3[1.2.cbn] — 4 4 3 1 — tmp+2 — 2hp — str
perc: tri, cym, xyl, sd, sus cym

Leduc

Le chevalier errant: Symphonic Suite <1935>
27'

3[1.2.3/pic] 3[1.2.Eh] 3[1.2.bcl] 4[1.2.cbn] — 6 4 3 1 — asx — gtr — tmp+5 — 2hp — cel — str
perc: glock, xyl, tri, tamtam, sd, cym, bd, tambn, chimes[B4,E5,F#5], tambourin provençal (or tomtom)
Les moulins — _'
Danse des galériens — _'
L'age d'or — _'
Les comédiens et Finale — _'

Leduc

Concertino da camera, Alto Saxophone & Orchestra <1935>
13'

1 1 1 1 — 1 1 0 0 — str 5t or small str complement
I. Allegro con moto — 5'
II. Larghetto - Animato — 8'

Leduc

Concerto, Flute <1932–1933>
18'

2 2 2 2 — 2 1 0 0 — tmp — str
I. Allegro — 5'
II. Andante — 6'
III. Allegro scherzando — 7'

Leduc

Diane de Poitiers: Suite No.1 <1934>
17'

3[incl pic] 3[incl Eh] 3[incl bcl] 4[incl cbn] — 4 4 3 1 — opt ob d'amour, opt basset horn — tmp+5 — 2hp — str
perc: glock, vib, tri, sd, tambn, tomtom, cym, bd, tamtam
Several movements are based on 16th-century French tunes.
Introduction — 2'
Entrée des pages — 4'
Diane — 2'
Danse des boyards — 2'
Le Marchand d'Orviétans — 3'
Danse de l'arc — 2'
Finale — 2'

Leduc

Diane de Poitiers: Suite No.2 <1934>
27'

3[incl pic] 3[incl Eh] 3[incl bcl] 4[incl cbn] — 4 4 3 1 — tmp+6 — 2hp — str
perc: glock, sd, tri, tambn, tamtam, tomtom, cym, bd, cast, vib (or cel), chimes[D#4,F4,A#4], tambourin provençal
Based on 16th-century French tunes.
Introduction et allegro — 7'
Intermezzo et Adage — 8'
Marche et Finale — 12'

Leduc

Divertissement <1929–1930>
15'

1[1/pic] 0 1 1[1/cbn] — 1 1 1 0 — 1perc — pf/cel — 3vn, 2va, 2vc, db
perc: timbales, tri, woodblk, sd, tambn, sus cym, bd, cast, tamtam, police whistle
From Ibert's incidental music to the farce by E. Labiche, *Un chapeau de paille d'Italie*, 1929.
I. Introduction — 1'
II. Cortège — 5'
III. Nocturne — 2'
IV. Valse — 3'
V. Parade — 2'
VI. Finale — 2'

Durand

Escales (Ports of Call) <1922>
14'

3[1.2/pic2.pic1] 3[1.2.Eh] 2 3 — 4 3 3 1 — tmp+7 — 2hp — cel[played by perc] — str
perc: xyl, field dr, tri, tambn, cast, tamtam, cym, bd, cel[played by perc]
I. Rome—Palermo — 6'
II. Tunis—Nefta — 3'
III. Valencia — 5'

Leduc

Féerique <1924>
9'

3[1.2.pic] 3[1.2.Eh] 3[1.2.bcl] 3 — 4 3 3 1 — tmp+6 — 2hp — str
perc: sd, tri, tambn, tamtam, cym, bd

Leduc

Histoires: Suite No.1 <1926>
21'

2 2 2 1 — 2 2[crt1.crt2] 1 0 — tmp — str
Originally for piano solo and piano 4-hands; orchestrated by Hubert Henri F. Mouton.
Piano-conductor score only.
1. Le petit âne blanc (The Little White Donkey) — _'
2. A Giddy Girl — _'
3. Le palais abondonné (The Abandoned Palace) — _'
4. La cage du crystal (The Crystal Cage) — _'

Leduc

Hommage à Mozart <1956>
5'

2 2 2 2 — 2 2 0 0 — tmp — str

Leduc

Louisville Concerto <1953>
12'

2[1.2/pic] 2 2 2 — 4 2 3 1 — tmp+3 — hp — str
perc: sd, tri, field dr, tambn, tamtam, glock, cym, bd/cym

Leduc

Les rencontres: 3 pièces de ballet <1924–1925>
9'

3[1.2.3/pic] 3[1.2.Eh] 3[1,2,BC] 3 — 4 3 3 1 — tmp+6 — 2hp — cel[or glock] — str
perc: sd, tri, tambn, tamtam, cast, cym, bd
The 3tp are offstage for the *Introduction*.
Introduction — _'
I. Les bouquetières (The Flower Girls) — _'
II. Les créoles (The Creoles) — _'
III. Les bavardes (The Chatterers) — _'

Leduc

Suite symphonique (Paris) <1930>   14'

1 1 1[cl/asx] 0 — 0 1 1 0 — tmp+4 — pf/cel/harm/kybd glock — str[min 3.0.2.2.1; max 5.0.4.3.2]

perc: bd, cym, sus cym, sd, tri, tambn, tamtam, xyl, woodblk, ratch, chimes[A#4,D#5], darabucca, police whistle

I. Le Métro (The Metro)	2'
II. Faubourgs (The Suburbs)	3'
III. Le Mosquée de Paris (The Mosque of Paris)	2'
IV. Restaurant au Bois de Boulogne (Restaurant in the Bois de Boulogne)	3'
V. Le paquebot Ile-de-France (The Steamship Ile-de-France)	2'
VI. Parade foraine (Parade at the Fair)	2'

Peters

Symphonie marine <1931>   14'

0 0 1 1 — 1 1 1 0 — asx — 2perc — hp — pf/cel — str[max 6.4.4.4.2]

perc: bd, cym, sd, tri, tamtam, tambn

Leduc

Tropismes pour des amours imaginaires <1957>   25'

2 2 2 2 — 2 2 2 0 — tmp+4 — cel, pf — str

perc: xyl, tamtam, bd, cym, sd, tomtom, tambn, templeblks

Billaudot

Imbrie, Andrew   1921-2007

(b New York, 6 April 1921; d Berkeley, CA, 5 Dec 2007). American

Chamber Symphony <1968>   17'

1 1 1 1 — 1 1 1 0 — 3perc — hp — pf; cel[played by perc] — str[min 4.4.3.3.2]

perc: bd, sd, td, tri, tambn, tamtam, gong, glock, xyl, vib, chimes, bongos, 3timbales, 3sus cym, 3woodblk, tmp, cel[played by perc]

I. Fantasy	_'
II. Variations	_'

Shawnee

Concerto, Piano, No.2 <1974>   27'

3[1.2.pic] 3[1.2.Eh] 3[1.2.bcl] 3[1.2.cbn] — 4 3 3 1 — tmp+ — hp — cel — str

perc: td, bd, tri, tambn, tamtam, gong, glock, xyl, marim, 5tomtom, 3sus cym, 2woodblk

I. Andante misterioso	_'
II. Andantino, dolce ma ben misurato	_'
III. Allegro molto	_'

Shawnee

Concerto, Piano, No.3 <1992>   39'

2[1.2/pic] 2 2 2 — 2 2 0 0 — tmp+2 — str

perc: bd, cym, sus cym, tri, tamtam, glock, xyl, marim, vib, 7tomtom

I. Allegro	16'
II. Lento	9'
III. Presto	14'

Malcolm

Concerto, Violin <1954>   37'

3[1.2.pic] 3[1.2.Eh] 3[1.2.bcl] 3[1.2.cbn] — 4 3 3 1 — tmp+3 — hp — cel — str

Malcolm

Concerto, Violoncello <1972–1973>   30'

3[1.2.3/pic] 3[1.2.Eh] 3[1.2/Ebcl.bcl] 3[1.2.cbn] — 4 3 3 1 — tmp+ — hp — cel — str

perc: tambn, td, tri, gong, tamtam, chimes, 5tomtom, 2bd, 3sus cym, 2woodblk

I. Allegro	_'
II. Vivace	_'

Shawnee

Legend <1959>   14'

3[1.2.pic] 3[1.2.Eh] 3[1.2.bcl] 3[1.2.cbn] — 4 3 3 1 — tmp+3 — hp — cel — str

Malcolm

Little Concerto for Piano Four-Hands and Orchestra   11'
<1955–1956>

2[1.2/pic] 2 2 2 — 2 2 2[ten.btbn] 1 — tmp+3 — str

perc: sus cym, tamtam, sd, bd, cym[2pr]

In 1 mvt.

Shawnee

Symphony No.1 <1965>   32'

3[1.2.pic] 3[1.2.Eh] 3[1.2/Ebcl.bcl] 3[1.2.cbn] — 4 3 3 1 — tmp+4 — 2hp — cel — str

perc: bongos, tomtom, sd, bd, tri, tamtam, tambn, whip, cast, xyl, glock, chimes, 2timbales, 3sus cym, 2cym

1.	12'
2.	8'
3.	4'
4.	8'

Malcolm

Symphony No.3 <1970>   19'

3[1.2.pic] 3[1.2.Eh] 3[1.2.bcl] 3[1.2.cbn] — 4 3 3 1 — tmp+1 — 2hp — cel — str

I. Prologue; Maestoso	3'
II. Allegro	7'
III. Andantino	4'
IV. Vivace	5'

Shawnee

Ince, Kamran   1960-

(b Glendive, MT, 6 May 1960). American composer of Turkish descent

Academica; Rhapsodic Overture <1998>   14'

3[1.2.pic] 2 3[1.2.bcl] 3[1.2.cbn] — 4 3 3 1 — tmp+3 — hp — pf — str

perc: bd, sd, td, toms, glock, xyl, vib, chimes

EAM

Arches <1994>   13'

1 0 1 0 — 0 1 0 0 — synth — vn, vc

EAM

Before Infrared <1986>   9'

3[1.2.pic] 2 3[1.2/Ebcl.bcl] 3[1.2.cbn] — 4 3 3 1 — tmp+3 — hp — str

perc: bd, sus cym, szl cym, Chinese cym, sd, td, timbales, 8toms (2 sets), 4logdrum, tambn, tamtam, glock, xyl, vib, 2woodblk, ratch, marac, claves, cast

May be played alone, or before the composer's Infrared Only.

EAM

Concerto, Piano <1984>   19'

3[1.2.pic] 2 2[1/Ebcl.2] 3[1.2.cbn] — 4 2 3 1 — tmp+3 — str

perc: bd, 2sus cym, Chinese cym, sd, toms, tamtam, glock, xyl, vib, crot

EAM

Deep Flight <1986>   11'

1 1 1 1 — 2 2 3 1 — tmp+1 (or 2) — pf — str[min 6.5.4.3.2]

perc: bd, 2sus cym, szl cym, td, toms, glock, xyl, vib, bongos

Although one percussionist is probably intended, a second player would alleviate some rapid changes of instrument.

EAM

Domes <1993>   12'

1 0 2[1.Ebcl/bcl] 1 — 2 1 1 0 — hp — pf — str

EAM

Ebullient Shadows <1987>   12'

4[1.2.3.pic] 3 4[1.2.Eb.bcl] 4[1.2.3.cbn] — 4 3 3 1 — tmp+3 — hp —
pf — str
perc: bd, 4sus cym, szl cym, Chinese cym, sd, td, toms, timbales, tamtam, glock,
xyl, marim, vib, chimes, crot, 4bongos

EAM

F E S T, for New Music Ensemble & Orchestra <1998>   26'

solo ensemble: asx/siren, tsx/cl, perc, synth, elec gtr, elec bgtr, vn
(amplified), vc (amplified)
2[1.2/pic] 2 2[1/Ebcl.2/bcl] 2 — 4 2 2 0 — str
perc: (solo) tmp, bd, sus cym, tamtam, glock, marim, crot
Prologue   _'
Dance I   _'
Dance II   _'
Reflections   _'
Dance III   _'
Epilogue   _'

EAM

Hot, Red, Cold, Vibrant <1992>   10'

2[1.2/pic] 3[1.Eh1.Eh2] 3[Ebcl1.Ebcl2.bcl] 2 — 4 3 3 0 — 3perc —
hp — pf — str
perc: bd, Chinese cym, td, toms, 4timbales, tri, glock, xyl, marim, vib, 4bongos

EAM

In White <1999>   18'

solo violin (amplified)
1[ampd] 0 0 0 — asx, tsx — elec bass gtr — female voice & male voice
[both voices ampd & with straight sound] — synth/pf — vc[ampd]

EAM

Symphony No.2 (Fall of Constantinople) <1994>   24'

2[1/pic.2] 2 3[Ebcl.2.3/bcl] 3[1.2.cbn] — 4 3[1.2.3/pic] 2[1.btbn] 1 —
elec gtr, bgtr — tmp+2 — hp — pf, synth — str
perc: bd, Chinese cym, sd, td, toms, tri, tamtam, glock, xyl, marim, vib, chimes,
crot, 2logdrum
I. City and the Walls   10'
II. Hagia Sophia   3'
III. Speeches of Emperor Constantine and Mehmet the Conqueror 3'
IV. Ships on Rails: The Marine Battle   4'
V. Fall of Constantinople   4'

EAM

Symphony No.3 (Siege of Vienna) <1995>   25'

3[1.2/pic.3/pic] 3[1.2.Eh] 4[1/Ebcl/tsx.2/Ebcl.3.bcl] 3[1.2.3/cbn] —
4[all/Wag tb] 3[1.2.3/pic] 3 1 — tmp+2 — pf, synth — str
perc: 2bd, sd, toms, 2tri, susp metal plate, glock, xyl, marim, vib, bongos; covered
by timpanist: 2brakedrum, td, bd.
Only 10 bars of tsx (in the cl 1 part).
Long March   5'
City Under Siege   3'
War of the Worlds   3'
Forgotten Souls   5'
Calls   1'
Final Assault   3'
Victorious City   1'
The Great Retreat   4'

EAM

Indy, Vincent d'   1851-1931
(b Paris, 27 Mar 1851; d Paris, 2 Dec 1931). French

Chanson et danses, op.50 <1898>   14

1 1 2 2 — 1 0 0 0 — [no str]

Kalmus   Luck's

Fervaal: Introduction to Act I <1889–1893>   7

2 2 2 2 — 4 1 3 0 — str

Durand   Kalmus   Luck's

Istar; Variations symphoniques, op.42 <1896>   13

3[1.2.pic] 3[1.2.Eh] 3[1.2.bcl] 3 — 4 3 3 1 — tmp+2 — 2hp — str
perc: cym, tri
Très lent   3'
Un peu plus animé   3'
Très animé   4'
Le double plus vite   3'

Durand   Kalmus   Luck's

Jour d'été à la montagne, op.61 (Summer Day in the   31
Mountains) <1905>

3[1.2.3/pic] 3[1.2.Eh] 3[1.2.bcl] 3 — 4 3 4 0 — tmp+1 — 2hp — pf
— str
perc: bd, cym, sus cym, sd
Aurore   8'
Jour (Après-midi sous les pins)   12'
Soir   11'

Durand   Kalmus

Lied, op.19 <1884>   7

solo violoncello
2 0 2 2 — 2 0 0 0 — tmp — str

Hamelle   Kalmus   Luck's

Symphonie sur un chant montagnard français, op.25   24
(Symphony on a French Mountain Air; Symphonie
cévenole) <1886>

solo piano
3[1.2.3/pic] 2[1/Eh.2] 3[1.2.bcl] 3 — 4 4[2tp, 2crt] 3 1 — tmp+3 —
hp — str
perc: bd, cym, tri
I. Assez lent - Modérément animé   11'
II. Assez modéré; mais sans lenteur   6'
III. Animé   7'

Hamelle   Kalmus   Luck's

Symphony No.2, op.57, B-flat major <1902–1903>   42

3[1.2.3/pic] 3[1.2.Eh] 3[1.2.bcl] 3 — 4 3 4[1.2.3.cb tbn] 0 — tmp+2
— 2hp — str
perc: tri, bd, cym, sus cym
I. Extrêmement lent - Tres vif   12'
II. Modérément lent   11'
III. Modéré   5'
IV. Lent   13'

Durand   Kalmus

Symphony No.3, op.70 (Sinfonia brevis de bello gallico) 33
<1916–1918>

3[1.2.3/pic] 3[1.2.Eh] 4[1.2.Ebcl.bcl] 3 — 4 4 4[1.2.3.cb tbn] 0 —
tmp+5 — 2hp — pf — str
perc: bd, cym, field dr, xyl, 2sd
I. Lent et calm - Animé   10'
II. Assez vite   5'
III. Lent   9'
IV. Très animé   9'

Salabert

ngelbrecht, Désiré-Émile
1880 - 1965

(b Paris, 17 Sept 1880; d Paris, 14 Feb 1965). French

Rapsodie de printemps <1910>
10'

3[incl pic] 3[incl Eh] 4[incl bcl] 2 — 4 3 3 1 — tmp+2 — 2hp — pf, harm — str
backstage: 10 children's voices, harm, solo va, triangle.

> Salabert

ppolitov-Ivanov, Mikhail
1859 - 1935

(b Gatchina, nr St Petersburg, 7/19 Nov 1859; d Moscow, 28 Jan 1935). Russian

Armenian Rhapsody, op.48 (Armyanskaya rapsodiya) <1895>
12'

2 2 2 2 — 3 2 0 0 — tmp+4 — str
perc: bd, cym, tri, tambn

> Kalmus   Luck's

Caucasian Sketches, op.10 (Kavkazskiye eskizï; Suite No.1) <1894>
21'

3[1.2.pic] 3[1.2.Eh] 2 2 — 4 4[2tp, 2 opt crt] 3 0 — tmp+5 — hp — str
perc: tri, tambn, cym, bd, field dr, 2timpani piccoli orientali
Cornets appear only in last mvt, and are optional.

In the Mountain Pass	8'
In the Village	4'
In the Mosque	4'
Procession of the Sardar	5'

> Kalmus   Luck's   Russian

Turkish Fragments, op.62 (Tyurkskiye fragmentï; Suite No.3) <?1928>
13'

3[1.2.3/pic] 3[1.2.Eh] 2 2 — 3 2 3 1 — tmp+5 — hp — str
Kalmus edition is permanently out of print.

The Caravan	3'
During a Rest	5'
In the Night	2'
At the Festival	3'

> Kalmus   Russian

Ireland, John
1879 - 1962

(b Bowdon, Cheshire, 13 Aug 1879; d Rock Mill, Washington, Sussex, 12 June 1962). English

Concertino pastorale <1939>
20'

str

I. Eclogue	9'
II. Threnody	7'
III. Toccata	4'

> Boosey

The Forgotten Rite <1913>
8'

3[1.2.3/pic] 3[1.2.Eh] 3[1.2.bcl] 2 — 4 2 3 0 — tmp — hp — cel — str

> Augener

A London Overture <1936>
12'

2[1.2/pic] 2 2 2 — 4 3 3 1 — tmp+2 — str
perc: tri, tambn, glock, sd, bd, cym, sus cym, xyl, gong, slgh-bells

> Boosey

These Things Shall Be <1937>
20'

solo baritone (or tenor)   chorus
3[incl 2pic] 3[incl Eh] 3[incl Ebcl] 3[incl cbn] — 4 3 3 1 — tmp+4 — cel, org — str
perc: xyl, glock, chimes, sd, tri, cym, sus cym, bd, tamtam

> Boosey

Ishii, Maki
1936 - 2003

(b Tokyo, 28 May 1936; d Tokyo, 8 April 2003). Japanese

Kyō-Sō <1969>
22'

3[1/pic.2/pic.3/pic] 3 3[1.2.3/bcl] 3[1.2.cbn] — 6 4 3 1 — tmp+5 — hp — cel — str[min 16.14.10.8.6]
perc: templeblks, crot, cast, field dr, glock, marim, bd, xyl, vib, 4sus cym, 2sd, sistro, 6pr maracas, opt high bells, 4tri, 3bongos, 3congas, 2pr claves, 2tamtams

> Moeck

Mono-Prism <1976>
24'

3[1.2.3/pic] 3 3[1.2.3/bcl] 3[1.2.cbn] — 6 4 3 1 — tmp+5 — 2hp — pf/cel — str
Tibetan trumpet (ad lib).

> Moeck

Sho-ko, op.39 (Faint Dawn) <1980>
16'

3[1/pic.2/pic.3/pic] 3 3 3[1.2.cbn] — 6 3 3 1 — 5perc — 2hp — cel, pf — str
perc: bd, cast, congas, cym, sd, field dr, glock, tamtam, gong, marim, slgh-bells, tambn, vib, woodblk, xyl, 2sus cym, tmp

> Moeck

Itkin, David
1957 -

(b Portland, OR, 2 May 1957). American

Jonah
18'

narrator
3[1.2.3/pic] 2[1.2/Eh] 3[1.2.3/bcl] 2 — 4 3 3 1 — tmp+2 — hp — cel — str

> DCI Music

Ivanovici, Iosif
1845 - 1902

(b?1845; d Bucharest, 28 Sept 1902). Romanian

Donauwellen (Waves of the Danube; Valurile Dunarii) <1880>
7'

2[1.pic] 2 2 2 — 4 2 3 1 — tmp+3 — str
Originally for military band; orchestrated by Emil Waldteufel. There are numerous other arrangements of this popular piece, differing somewhat in instrumentation.

> Kalmus   Luck's   Schott

Ives, Charles

1874-1954

(b Danbury, CT, 20 Oct 1874; d New York, 19 May 1954). American

The Charles Ives Society since 1973 has been supporting the preparation of performing editions of Ives' music along scholarly-critical lines. These are brought out by various publishers, and should be sought out as they become available, since the previous editions have many errors. Executive editor of the Charles Ives Society is scholar and conductor James B. Sinclair. Website: charlesives.org.

S = James B. Sinclair, *A Descriptive Catalogue of the Music of Charles Ives*. New Haven [Conn.]: Yale University Press, c1999

Central Park in the Dark, S.34 <1906–1909; rev 1936>   9'

2[1.pic] 1 1[1/Ebcl] 1 — 0 1 1 0 — 2perc — 2 or 3pf — str
perc: sd, bd/cym

Boelke

Charlie Rutlage, S.226 <1920–1921>   3'

optional medium voice
1[pic] 1[Eh] 1[Ebcl] 1 — 0 1 1 1 — 3perc — pf — str
perc: sd, bd, 2tomtoms (1 opt)
Realized by Kenneth Singleton, based on the original piano-vocal score with the composer's directions for instrumentation (Ives Society).
  Can be done with 2perc.

AMP	Luck's

Chromâtimelôdtune, S.35 <1923>   6'

0 1 1 1 — 1 1 1 1 — 2perc — pf — 3vn, va, vc, db
perc: sd, chimes[B3,D4]
Reconstructed and completed by Gunther Schuller, 1963. Alternative realizations exist by Kenneth Singleton and by Gerard Schwarz.

MJQ

The Circus Band, S.33 [version 2] <1894>   3'

optional chorus SSATTBB
2[1.pic] 0 2 0 — 1 1 3 1 — 1-2perc — str[no va, vc opt]
perc: set; or bd/cym & sd
Original for voice & piano; orchestrated by George F. Roberts under Ives' supervision.

Peer

A Concord Symphony <1920s–1940s>   51'

3[1/pic.2/pic.3/pic] 3[1.2.3/Eh] 3[1.2.3/bcl] 3[1.2.3/cbn] — 4 3 3 1 — tmp+3 — hp — pf/cel — str
perc: xyl, glock, chimes, vib, cym, bd, set, sus cym, sd, woodblk, templeblks, cowbell, 2tomtom, cel[covered by perc when pianist is otherwise occupied]
Originally the composer's Piano Sonata No.1 ("Concord, Mass., 1840-1860"); orchestral transcription by Henry Brant (1995).

I. Emerson	18'
II. Hawthorne	15'
III. The Alcotts	6'
IV. Thoreau	12'

AMP

"Country Band" March, S.36 <1910–1911; rev 1914>   4'

1[1/pic] 0 1 0 — 0 1[crt] 2 0 — asx — 3perc — pf — str[no va]
perc: set; or bd/cym & sd
Ed. James Sinclair (Ives Society).

Luck's	Merion

Emerson Overture (Concerto) for Piano & Orchestra, S.22   22

3[1.2.pic] 0 2 3[1.2.cbn] — 2 2 3 1 — tmp — glock/cel — str[12.12.8.8.6]
Realization by David Porter, from Ives' developed but not quite complete sketches (the music eventually was used in the *Emerson* movement of Ives' *Concord Sonata*). Timpani part added by James B. Sinclair.

AMP

Evening, S.15, no.4 <1974>   2

1 1[or medium voice] 0 0 — pf, cel[or glock] — 3vn
Ives Society critical edition. From *Set No.6: From the Side Hill*.

AMP

Fugue in Four Keys on "The Shining Shore", S.69 <1903>   3

1 0 0 0 — 0 1[crt] 0 0 — str
Critical ed. 1975 by John Kirkpatrick (Ives Society).

Merion

General William Booth Enters into Heaven, S.255 <1914; rev c1933>   5

medium voice (or chorus)
1 1 1 1 — 1 1 1 0 — 1perc — pf — str
perc: bd [or low timpano]
Originally for voice & piano; orchestrated by John J. Becker in collaboration with the composer.

Merion

The Gong on the Hook and Ladder, S.38 (Firemen's Parade on Main Street) <1934>   3

1 0 1 1 — 0 2 1 0 — tmp+2 — pf — str
perc: gong[opt], sd, tri
Critical ed. 1979 by James Sinclair (Ives Society).

Peer

Hymn (Largo cantabile), S.84 no.1 <1907–1908>   3

str 5t or str orch
Used as the first mvt of *A Set of Three Short Pieces*, S.84.

Peer

Johnny Poe, S.183 <1927–1929>   4

male chorus
3[1.2/pic.pic] 2 3[1.2.bcl] 3[1.2.cbn] — 4 3 3 1 — tmp+3 — pf — str
perc: sd, bd, cym, chimes
Incomplete; realized & ed. John Kirkpatrick (Ives Society critical edition).

Peer

Lincoln the Great Commoner, S.184 <1922–1923>   4

chorus
2[incl opt pic] 2 2 2 — 0 2 2 1 — tmp+1 — pf — str
perc: low bell
There is as yet no Ives Society critical score, and the composer's intentions with respect to instrumentation remain ambiguous. One of the flutists may optionally double on piccolo. Additional brass (2tp, 2tbn) double the chorus in places. (Octaves indicated in the tuba part are probably intended as performance options, rather than a requirement for a 2nd tuba.)

Kalmus	Luck's	Presser

NEW ENGLAND HOLIDAYS
9'

1. Washington's Birthday, S.5 no.1 <1915–1917>

1[1/pic] 0 0 1[opt; or tbn] — 1 0 1[opt; or bn] 0 — Jew's harp
[1player; 3 insts in A, Ab & F] (or 2cl) — bells (or pf) — str
Critical edition by James B. Sinclair, 1987 (Ives Society).

> AMP

2. Decoration Day, S.5 no.2 <1915–1920; rev 1923-24>
10'

3[1.2.opt pic] 3[1.2.Eh] 3[1.2.opt Ebcl] 2 — 4 2[tp3 opt] 3 1 —
tmp+5 — str
perc: sd, bd, cym, chimes[low bells], glock[or cel]
An *ossia* is provided for the E-flat clarinet.
Critical edition by James B. Sinclair, 1987 (Ives Society).

> Peer

3. The Fourth of July, S.5 no.3 <1914–1918; rev 1931>
7'

3[1.2.pic] 2 2 3[1.2.cbn] — 4 4[1.2.3.crt] 3 1 — tmp+6 — pf — str
perc: xyl, sd, cym, bd, bells (hi, mid, lo)
Critical edition by Wayne D. Shirley (Ives Society).

> AMP

4. Thanksgiving and Forefathers' Day, S.5 no.4 <1911–1916; rev 1933>
15'

optional chorus
3[1.2.opt pic] 2 2 3[1.2.opt cbn] — 4 3 3 1 — tmp+1 to 5 — cel, pf
— str
perc: chimes, bells (hi, mid, lo), churchbells
In several isolated passages, Ives suggests various additional instruments:
fl, cl, bn, cbn, hn, tp. An optional offstage band can be covered by
instrumentalists who leave the stage.
  Critical edition by Jonathan Elkus, 1991 (Ives Society).

> Peer

Orchestral Set No.2, S.8 <1910–1914; rev 1920-21>
16'

optional unison chorus
2[1.2/pic] 0 3 2 — 3[hn3 opt] 5[tp5 opt] 4[tbn4 opt] 1 — zither, opt
theremin, accordion — tmp+4 — hp — 2pf, cel/glock, org — str
perc: sd, bd, cym, tamtam, gong, tri, chimes
Critical edition by James B. Sinclair (Ives Society).
  1. *An Elegy to our Forefathers*   4'
  2. *The Rockstrewn Hills Join in the People's Outdoor Meeting* 5'
  3. *From Hanover Square North, at the End of a Tragic Day*   7'

> Peer

Over the Pavements; Scherzo, S.82 <1906–1913>
5'

1[pic] 0 1 1[or bsx] — 0 1 3 0 — 1perc — pf — [no str]
perc: bd/cym

> Peer

Overture and March "1776" for Theater Orchestra, S.24 <1909–1910>
3'

2[1/pic.2/pic] 1 1 0 — 0 2[crt1.crt2] 1 0 — 2-3perc — pf — str
perc: bd/cym, sd, opt glock
Ed. James B. Sinclair (Ives Society).

> Merion

Postlude in F <1895>
5'

2 2 2 2 — 4 2 3 1 — tmp+1 — str
perc: bd/cym
Critical ed. 1991 by Kenneth Singleton (Ives Society).
  Originally for organ; orchestrated by the composer.

> AMP

Ragtime Dances, S.43 <1915–1921>
11'

1[1.pic] 1 1 1 — 1 1 1 1 — asx/bsx — 2perc — pf — str[max
6.6.4.4.2]
perc: chimes, set
Ed. James B. Sinclair (Ives Society).
  1. *Allegro moderato*   3'
  2. *Allegro moderato*   2'
  3. *Allegro*   3'
  4. *Allegro*   3'

> Peer

Robert Browning Overture, S.27 <1912–1914; rev 1936-42>
17'

3[1.2.pic] 3[1.2.Eh] 2 3[1.2.cbn] — 4 3 4 1 — tmp+3 — str
perc: sd, chimes, cym, bd, 3bellplates[G#2,A2,C#3], Indian drum
Omissions in bell part; check with score.
Ives Society critical ed. by Jonathan Elkus in preparation.

> Peer

A Set of Pieces for Theatre or Chamber Orchestra, S.20 <1907–1930>
7'

1 2[1.Eh] 2 1 — 1 0 0 0 — opt bsx — tmp+2 — hp[or hps] — pf
4-hands (or 2pf), opt org — str
perc: bells or chimes (2 players & timpanist)
The composer's instructions for instrumentation are extremely permissive,
and list numerous options, in the spirit of the theatre orchestra of the early
20th-century United States. A minimum instrumentation might be: 1 1 1
1 — 1perc — pf 4-hands — str.
  Ives Society critical edition in preparation.
  In the Cage   1'
  In the Inn   4'
  In the Night   2'

> Kalmus   Luck's   Presser

Set No.1 for Chamber Orchestra, S.10 <1915–1916>
10'

1[1/pic] 1[1/Eh] 2 2 — 0 2 1 0 — bsx — tmp+3 — 2pf — str
perc: sd, td, bd, cym, tambn, chimes
The composer's instructions for instrumentation are extremely permissive,
and list numerous options, in the spirit of the theatre orchestra of the early
20th-century United States. The Gunther Schuller arrangement is given
here; the Ives Society instrumentation differs somewhat.
  Movements are published separately, some by companies other than
Merion, as shown in the contents below in square brackets; however, the
work as a whole may be had from Merion.
  1. *The Seer [pub. AMP]*   1'
  2. *A Lecture (Tolerance)*   1'
  3. *The Ruined River (The New River) [pub. Peer]*   1'
  4. *Like a Sick Eagle*   2'
  5. *Calcium Light Night (arr. Cowell)*   3'
  6. *Allegretto sombreoso (Incantation) [pub. Peer]*   2'

> Merion

Symphony No.1, S.1, D minor <1898–1908>
32'

2 3[1.2.Eh] 2 3[1.2.opt cbn] — 4 2 3 1 — tmp[+2 opt] — str
perc: sd, bd/cym
Percussion parts occur in last movement only, and are optional; they are
not indicated in the score.
  Ed. James Sinclair, for the Ives Society.
  I. Allegro   10'
  II. Adagio molto   6'
  III. Scherzo   4'
  IV. Allegro molto   12'

> Peer

Symphony No.2, S.2 <1907–1909>   37'

3[1.2.pic] 2 2 3[1.2.cbn] — 4 2 3 1 — tmp+2 — str
perc: sd, bd, tri
Ives Society critical edition by Jonathan Elkus, 2007.

I. Andante moderato	6'
II. Allegro	11'
III. Adagio cantabile	8'
IV. Lento maestoso	2'
V. Allegro molto vivace	10'

> Southern

Symphony No.3, S.3 (The Camp Meeting) <1908–1911>   19'

1 1 1 1 — 2 0 1 0 — "distant bells" & opt tmp [1 player] — str
Critical edition by Kenneth Singleton, 1989 (Ives Society). The optional timpani part appears on p.42 of the score.

Old Folks Gatherin'	7'
Children's Day	8'
Communion	4'

> AMP

Symphony No.4, S.4

Publication history of this complex work, composed from 1910 to 1925, but not published complete for 40 more years; the publisher's nomenclature is followed:

Facsimile edition: "Facsimile" only in the sense that the movements are for the most part not engraved, but are reproductions of manuscript produced by the editors: Romulus Franceschini (mvts 1 & 2), Nicholas Falcone (mvt 3) and Theodore A. Seder (mvt 4). Preface by John Kirkpatrick, AMP, 1965.

Critical edition: A Charles Ives Society edition: James B. Sinclair, executive editor; William Brooks (mvt 1), James B. Sinclair (mvt 2), Kenneth Singleton (mvt 3), Wayne D. Shirley (mvt 4). An accompanying CD includes manuscript facsimiles, some from Ives, most from his copyist, a Mr. Reis, as well as a color-coded "Quotation Analysis." AMP, 2011.

Performance edition: Prepared by Thomas M. Brodhead on the basis of the "critical edition." This is the only practical edition for performance; see the following entry. AMP, 2012.

Symphony No.4, S.4 (Performance Edition)   29'
<ca.1910–1925>

chorus   solo piano
4[1.2.3.pic] 2 3 2 — 4 6[tp5/crt] 4 1 — tsx/bsx — tmp+9 — hp — pf 4-hands, cel, org, opt quarter-tone pf — str[min12.12.12.10.8]
perc: sd, tri, bd/cym, bells[hi, lo], 2tamtam, xyl (opt), Indian dr, piccolo tmp
A "Distant Choir Ensemble" [hp, 5vn] is drawn from main body (mvts 1, 4); the harp is never on stage. Also called for: an optional "ether organ," for which an ondes martenot (or failing that, a synthesizer or a theremin) might be a suitable replacement.

"Performance Edition" (score and parts) for this extraordinarily complex work newly prepared (2012) by Thomas M. Brodhead. The score includes a dozen very helpful essays by the editor, such as a "Survival Guide," "Where Additional Conductors Might Be Employed," and "Checklist for Orchestra Librarians."
    The score and essays may be viewed at:
issuu.com/scoresondemand/docs/symphony_no_4_perf_ed_47475
    Certain of the essays may be downloaded in PDF format at:
http://www.musicsalesclassical.com/composer/work/764/47475
    Although this Performance Edition is based on the 2011 Ives Society "Critical Edition," ed. James B. Sinclair, the latter is not intended for performance. The Brodhead Performance Edition is the only recommended orchestral material.

I. Prelude: Maestoso	3'
II. Comedy: Allegretto	11'
III. Fugue: Andante moderato con moto	8'
IV. Very slowly (Largo maestoso)	7'

> AMP

Symphony No.4: Fugue (From Greenland's Icy Mountains) <1912–1924>   8'

1 0 1 0 — 1[or tbn] 0 1[or hn] 0 — tmp — opt org — str
3rd mvt of the Symphony No.4, ed. Leopold Stokowski.

> AMP

They Are There!, S.188 (A War Song March) <1918–1921; rev 1942>   3'

unison chorus
4[1.2.3/pic.4/pic] 2 2 2 — 4 2 2 1 — 3perc — pf — str
perc: glock, xyl, sd, cym, bd
Ives Society edition in preparation.
    This is "version 2" of the work. "Version 1" calls for unison chorus, fl/fife, 2pf, vn; it is also available from Peer.

> Peer

Three Harvest Home Chorales <1912–1915>   8'

chorus
0 0 0 0 — 0 4 3 1 — org — db
Ives Society critical edition in preparation.

1. The Harvest Dawn Is Near	_'
2. Lord of the Harvest, Thee We Hail	_'
3. Come Ye Thankful People, Come	_'

> Mercury

THREE PLACES IN NEW ENGLAND, S.7

This work exists in 4 versions:
    Version 1: original, for full orchestra, completed 1914
    Version 2: rescored for chamber orchestra, together with compositional changes, 1929
    Version 3: 1929 version with enhanced instrumentation for publication, 1935
    Version 4: restoration of the original full orchestration, but retaining compositional changes from 1929

Three Places in New England, S.7, version 1   19'
<1911–1914>

2[1.2/pic] 2[1.2/Eh] 2 3[1.2.cbn] — 4 2 3 1 — tmp+3 — str
perc: sd, gong, bd/cym
Ed. & reconstruction of mvt 2 by James B. Sinclair (Ives Sociey).

1. An Impression of the "St. Gaudens" on Boston Common	9'
2. Putnam's Camp	6'
3. The Housatonic at Stockbridge	4'

> Mercury

Three Places in New England, S.7, version 2 <1914; rev 1929>   19'

2[1.opt pic] 2[1.Eh] 1 1 — 2[hn2 opt] 2[tp2 opt] 1 0 — tmp+1 — pf 4-hands[2nd player opt] — str[4.4.2.2.1]
perc: sd, bd/cym [tmp plays perc in 2nd mvt]
Ed. James B. Sinclair (Ives Society).

1. The "St. Gaudens" on Boston Common	9'
2. Putnam's Camp	6'
3. The Housatonic at Stockbridge	4'

> Mercury

Three Places in New England, S.7, version 3 <1914; rev 1934>   19'

2[1.opt pic] 2[1.Eh] 1 1 — 4[2-4 opt] 4[tp3-4 opt] 2 1 — tmp+1 — p 4-hands[2nd player opt], opt cel, opt org — str
perc: sd, bd/cym [tmp plays perc in 2nd mvt]
This version is a bit of a hodge-podge, hastily prepared for publication. There is little reason to perform it now; version 2 is better for chamber orchestra, and version 4 for full orchestra.

1. The "St. Gaudens" on Boston Common	9'
2. Putnam's Camp	6'
3. The Housatonic at Stockbridge	4'

> Mercury

Three Places in New England, S.7, version 4 <1914; rev 1929>   19'

3[1.2.3/pic] 2[1.2/Eh] 2 3[1.2.cbn] — 4 2 3 1 — tmp+3 — 1 or 2hp — cel/pf, org — str
perc: bd/cym, sd, gong
Full orchestration restored and edited by James B. Sinclair (Ives Society), but retaining compositional changes from version 2 (1929).

1. The "St. Gaudens" on Boston Common	9'
2. Putnam's Camp	6'
3. The Housatonic at Stockbridge	4'

> Mercury

Tone Roads No.1, S.49, version 2 <1911>   3'

1 0 1 1 — str
Ives Society critical edition in preparation. (Version 1 of this work is a quartet for fl, cl, bn, pf.)

> Peer

Tone Roads No.3, S.49 <1915>   3'

1 0 1 0 — 0 1 1 0 — 1perc — pf — str
perc: chimes[G3–>A4]
Ives Society critical edition in preparation.
[Tone Roads No.2 is lost.]

> Peer

The Unanswered Question, S.50 <1906>   6'

4 0 0 0 — 0 1 0 0 — backstage str 4t or str orch
Flute 3 may be taken by oboe; flute 4 by clarinet. Possible substitutions for tp: Eh, ob, or cl.
> Composer's comments: "The trumpet should use a mute unless playing in a very large room, or with a larger string orchestra... If a large string orchestra is playing, the full treble woodwind choir may be used at the discretion of the conductor..."
> Critical ed. by Paul Echols & Noel Zahler, 1985 (Ives Society).

> Luck's   Peer

UNIVERSE SYMPHONY, S.6 <1915–1928>

This massive work survives mainly in sketches. There are 3 modern realizations of the piece:
> **David Porter**: An Ives Society edition of only the mvts completed by Ives (1, 4, & Coda of 6)
> **Larry Austin**: complete work
> **Johnny Reinhard**: complete work
See subsequent listings.

Universe Symphony, S.6 (Porter realization) <1915–1928>   62'

1[incl pic] 4 2 3[1.2.cbn] — 4 4 5 2 — tmp+21 — cel, opt pf — str
Ed. David Porter; Ives Society critical edition of only those mvts completed by Ives (1, 4, & Coda of 6).
Earth group: vns, vc, db; *Heavens* group: vns, 3fl, cl.

Prelude No.1 [repeated an indefinite number of times]	_'
Section A	_'
Coda of Section C	_'

> Peer

Universe Symphony, S.6 (Austin realization) <1915–1928>   37'

4[1.2.pic1.afl/pic2] 3[1.2.Eh] 4[1.2.3.bcl] 3[1.2.cbn] — 4 4 4 1 — 16-track tape & 25 headphones — 24perc — hp — 2pf[1 dbl cel], opt org — str
Requires principal conductor plus 4 assistant conductors. Forces divided into 7 separate orchestras. Extra bn may substitute for tuba; extra tuba may substitute for 4th tbn.
> A fantasia based on Ives' sketches and descriptions, realized & completed by Larry Austin.

Past	_'
Present	_'
Future	_'

> Peer

Universe Symphony, S.6 (Reinhard realization) <1915–1928>   66'

9 2 3[1.2.3/bcl] 5[1.2.3.4/cbn1.5/cbn2] — 4 5 4 2 — 12perc — pf/cel, org, overtone machine — str
A somewhat controversial reordering of Ives' original material, realized by Johnny Reinhard.

Fragment. Earth Alone	3'
Prelude 1. Pulse of the Cosmos	4'
Section A. Wide Valleys and Clouds	1'
Prelude 2. Birth of the Oceans	5'
Section B. Earth and the Firmament	11'
Preludes 3. And Lo, Now it is Night	30'
Section C. Earth is of the Heavens	12'

> Peer

Variations on "America" <1891>   8'

3[1.2/pic.3/pic] 2 2 2 — 4 3 3 1 — tmp+3 — str
perc: xyl, glock, cast, bd, sd, tri, cym, tambn
Originally for organ; orchestrated by William Schuman.

> Merion

Yale-Princeton Football Game, S.51 (Sinclair version) <1898–1899; rev ca 1910-11>   2'

2[1.2/pic] 2 2 3[1.2.cbn] — 4 3 3 1 — tmp+2 — str
perc: sd, bd/cym
Realized by James B. Sinclair from Ives' pencil score-sketch.

> AMP

Yale-Princeton Football Game, S.51 (Schuller version) <1898–1899; rev ca 1910-11>   3'

4[1.2.3/pic.pic] 4[1.2.3.4/Eh] 3 4 — 4 4 3 1 — bsx — tmp+3 — pf — str
perc: sd, bd/cym, glock
Realized, with expanded instrumentation, by Gunther Schuller.

> AMP

J

Jacob, Gordon   1895-1984

(b London, 5 July 1895; d Saffron Walden, 8 June 1984). English

The Barber of Seville Goes to the Devil; Comedy Overture   4'

2[1.pic] 1 2 1 — 2 2 2 0 — tmp+3 — hp[or pf] — str
perc: woodblk, cast, cym, bd, sd, tri

> Oxford

Concerto, Horn <1951>   22'

str
I. Allegro moderato	9'
II. Adagio	7'
III. Allegro con spirito, quasi presto	6'

> Galaxy

Concerto, Trombone <1952>   18'

2[1.2/pic] 2 2 2 — 2 2 0 0 — tmp+1 — str
perc: xyl, glock, sd, tambn, tri, cym

> Stainer

Fantasia on the Alleluia Hymn <1949>   8'

2 2 2 2 — 4[hn3-4 opt] 2 3 1 — tmp+2 — str

> Galaxy   Luck's

Janáček, Leoš   1854-1928

(b Hukvaldy, Moravia, 3 July 1854; d Moravská Ostrava [now Ostrava], 12 Aug 1928). Czech

Adagio <1891>   6'

2[1.2/pic] 2[1.Eh] 2 2 — 2 2 2 0 — tmp — str

> Bärenreiter   Universal

Amarus <1896–1897; rev 1901 & 1906>   27'

solo tenor, baritone   chorus SATB
3[1.2.pic] 3[1.2.Eh] 3[1.2.bcl] 3[1.2.cbn] — 4 2 3 1 — tmp+2 — hp — str
perc: tri, tamtam, chimes
Baritone solo brief (20 bars) but important; brief soprano solo (could be in chorus).
   Cbn plays only 5 bars, all doubled in the db.
I. Always he'd lived in the monastery	_'
II. A tall man, and pale-faced	_'
III. Days and years were passing	_'
IV. Today Amarus did not fill the lamp	_'
V. Epilog: Amarus they named him	_'

> Kalmus

Capriccio for Piano (Left Hand) & Winds (Vzdor; Defiance) <1926>   17'

1[1/pic] 0 0 0 — 0 2 3 0 — tenor tuba — [no str]
Ed. Jarmil Burghauser.

> Kalmus   Supraphon

Concertino <1925>   16

solo piano
0 0 1 1 — 1 0 0 0 — 2vn, va

> Bärenreiter   Kalmus   Supraphon

The Cunning Little Vixen (Příhody Lišky Bystroušky): Suite (Talich/Smetáček) <1922–1923; rev 1924>   16

4[1.2.3/pic.4/pic] 3[1.2.3/Eh] 3[1.2.bcl] 3[1.2.cbn] — 4 3 3 1 — tmp+4 — hp — cel — str
perc: bd, cym, glock, xyl, sus cym, sd, tri, tambn, tamtam
Arr. Vaclav Talich; rev. Vaclav Smetácek, 1964.
In 2 mvts.

> Universal

The Cunning Little Vixen (Příhody Lišky Bystroušky): Suite (Jílek) <1922–1923; rev 1924>   15

4[1.2.3.4/pic] 3[1.2.Eh] 3[1.2.bcl] 3[1.2.3/cbn] — 4 3 3 1 — tmp+2 — hp — cel — str
perc: bd, cym, glock, xyl, chimes
Arr. František Jílek, 1990.

> Universal

The Fiddler's Child (Šumařovo dítě; Dorfgeigers Kind) <1913>   12

2 2 3[1.2.bcl] 2 — 3 2 3 1 — tmp+1 — hp — str
perc: cym, tri, glock

> EBP   Kalmus   Supraphon

From the House of the Dead (A mrtvého domu): Overture <1927–1928>   6'

4[1.2.3/pic.4/pic] 3[1.2.Eh] 3[1.2.3/bcl] 3[1.2.3/cbn] — 4 3 3 1 — tenor tuba/btp — tmp+2 — hp — cel — str
perc: tri, glock, xyl
This overture is a revision of what was originally a sketch for a never-completed violin concerto (1926).

> Universal

From the House of the Dead (A mrtvého domu): Suite (arr. Jílek)   20'

4[1.2.3/pic.4/pic] 3[1.2.Eh] 3[1.2/Ebcl.3/bcl] 3[1.2.3/cbn] — 4 3 3 1 — tenor tuba/btp — tmp+3 — hp — cel — str
perc: bd, cym, sus cym, sd, field dr, tri, tamtam, glock, xyl, ratch, whip, chains, stroke of an ax
Arr. by František Jílek from the opera.

> Universal

Glagolitic Mass (1927 original version) (Mša glagolskaja; Missa solemnis) <1926–1927>   42'

SATB solos   chorus SSAATTBB
4[1.2/pic.3/pic.4/pic] 3[1.2.Eh] 3[1.2.3/bcl] 3[1.2.3/cbn] — 4 4 3 1 — 3cl offstage [or recording] — tmp+3 — 2hp[2nd opt] — org, cel[can be played by org or perc] — str
perc: sus cym, sd, tri, glock, chimes, tamtam
Ed. Paul Wingfield, 1995.
   2 of the 3 percussionists dbl on tmp in mvt V. The sung text is in Old Church Slavonic.
   This edition seeks to present the composer's original conception of the work, before the alterations that were made for the 1928 première.
I. Intrada	2'
II. Uvod (Introduction)	3'
III. Gospodi pomiluj (Kyrie)	3'
IV. Slava (Gloria)	6'
V. Věruju (Credo)	12'
VI. Svet (Sanctus)	6'
VII. Agneče Božij (Agnus dei)	5'
VIII. Varhany solo (Organ solo)	3'
IX. Intrada da capo	2'

> Universal

Glagolitic Mass (1928 revision; Fassung letzter Hand) (Mša glagolskaja; Missa solemnis) <1926–1927; rev 1928>   40'

SATB solos   chorus SSAATTBB
4[1.2/pic.3/pic.4/pic] 3[1.2.Eh] 3[1.2.3/bcl] 3[1.2.3/cbn] — 4 4 3 1 — 3cl offstage [or recording] — tmp+1 — 2hp[2nd opt] — org, cel[can be played by org or perc] — str
perc: sus cym, sd, tri, glock, chimes, tamtam
Bärenreiter ed. Jiří Zahrádka & Leoš Faltus; Universal ed. Paul Wingfield, 2010. The sung text is in Old Church Slavonic.
   This edition is the version revised by the composer for the 1928 première, but not published until after his death. It is the most frequently performed version, for the nonce. For an edition that seeks to present the composer's original conception, see the preceding entry.

I. Uvod (Introduction)	3'
II. Gospodi pomiluj (Kyrie)	3'
III. Slava (Gloria)	6'
IV. Věruju (Credo)	12'
V. Svet (Sanctus)	6'
VI. Agneče Božij (Agnus dei)	5'
VII. Varhany solo (Organ solo)	3'
VIII. Intrada	2'

> Bärenreiter   Universal

Idylla <1878>   30'

str
1. Andante; Meno mosso; Da capo	4'
2. Allegro; Moderato; [Allegro]	3'
3. Moderato; Con moto; [Moderato]	4'
4. Allegro	4'
5. Adagio; Presto; Adagio	7'
6. Scherzo	4'
7. Moderato	4'

> Bärenreiter   Kalmus   Supraphon

Jealousy (Žárlivost) <1895>   6'

2[1.2/pic] 3[1.2.Eh] 3[1.2.bcl] 2 — 4 2 3 1 — tmp+1 — hp — str
perc: glock
Originally the prelude to the composer's opera *Jenůfa*.

> Bärenreiter   Universal

Jenůfa-Rhapsodie <1896–1903; rev 1903-1908>   25'

2[1.2/pic] 2[1.2/Eh] 2 2[bn2 ad lib] — 4[hn3 ad lib] 2 3 1[ad lib] — tmp+2 — hp — str
perc: bd, cym, sus cym, sd, tri, tambn, glock
Arr. by Max Schönherr, 1940, from the opera.

> Universal

Lachian Dances (Lašské tance) <1924>   19'

2[1.2/pic] 3[1.2.opt Eh] 3[1.2.opt bcl] 2 — 4 2 3 0 — tmp+1 — hp — opt org — str
perc: chimes, glock
1. Old Fashioned (Starodávny)	6'
2. Blessed (Pocehnany)	2'
3. Town Piper (Dymák)	2'
4. Old Fashioned(Starodávny) [II]	4'
5. Country Bumpkin's Dance (Celadensky)	2'
6. Handsaw Dance (Pilky)	3'

> Bärenreiter   Kalmus   Supraphon

Moravian Dances (Moravské tance; Mährische Volkstänze) <1957>   8'

2 2 2 2 — 3 2 2 0 — tmp+1 — hp — str
perc: glock
1. Kožich	3'
2. Kalamajka	1'
3. Trojky	2'
4. Silnice	1'
5. Rožek	1'

> Universal

Sinfonietta <1926>   24'

4[1.2.3.4/pic] 2[1.2/Eh] 3[1.2/Ebcl.bcl] 2 — 4 12 4 1 — 2 bass tp, 2 tenor tubas — tmp+1 — hp — str
perc: cym, chimes, glock, sus cym
Two reduced versions are available from the publisher: by Erwin Stein and Joseph Keilberth, respectively.
I. Allegretto	3'
II. Andante - Allegretto	6'
III. Moderato	5'
IV. Allegretto	3'
V. Andante con moto	7'

> Universal

Sokol Fanfare <1926>   3'

0 0 0 0 — 0 9 0 0 — 2 bass tp [or tbn], 2 tenor tubas [or bar hns, or tbn] — tmp — [no str]
Composed as theme music for a sporting event in Czechoslovakia, and later used as the 1st movement of the composer's *Sinfonietta*.
   An arrangement by James Olcott (Triplo Press, *www.triplo.com*) is said to add the final seven measures of the *Sinfonietta* "… for a more fulfilling and exuberant finish."

> Universal

Taras Bulba <1915–1918>   23'

3[1.2.3/pic] 3[1.2.Eh] 2 3[1.2.3/cbn] — 4 3 3 1 — tmp+2 — hp — org — str
perc: chimes, tri, sd, sus cym
I. Death of Andril (Smrt Andrijova)	9'
II. Death of Ostap (Smrt Ostapova)	5'
III. Death and Prophesy of Taras Bulba (Proroctví a smrt Bulby)	9'

> Bärenreiter   Supraphon

Janello, David A.   1960-

(b Bridgeport, CT, 16 May 1960). American

At the Sea of Clouds <1990>   7'

2 2 2 2 — 2 2 2 1 — elec gtr — 3perc — hp — pf/cel — str[min 5.5.4.3.2]
Bassoonists also play on crystal glasses.

> Argon

Janiewicz, Feliks   1762-1848

(b Vilnius, 1762; d Edinburgh, 21 May 1848). Polish; lived in Britain after 1815

Divertimento

see under: Panufnik, Andrzej, 1914-1991

Janssen, Werner   1899-1990

(b New York, 1 June 1899; d Stony Brook, NY, 19 Sept 1990). American

New Year's Eve in New York <1929>   20'

4[1.2.3.pic] 3[1.2.3/Eh] 4[1.2.3.bcl] 3[1.2.3/cbn] — 4 5 3 1 — 3sx[asx, asx/ssx, tsx/ssx] — tenor banjo — tmp+4 — 2hp — pf — str
Original publisher: Birchard
Reflections on the Passing Year	_'
The Dying Year	_'
Midnight and the Stroke of Twelve	_'
Happy New Year!	_'
Celebration of the New Year	_'

> Fleisher

Järnefelt, Armas   1869-1958

(b Viipuri [now Vyborg, Russia], 14 Aug 1869; d Stockholm, 23 June 1958). Swedish composer of Finnish birth

Berceuse <1904>   4'

0 0 2 1 — 2 0 0 0 — str

Breitkopf	Kalmus	Luck's

Praeludium   3'

1 1 2 1 — 2 2 0 0 — tmp+2 — str

Breitkopf	Kalmus	Luck's

Jenkins, Karl   1944-

(b Penclawdd, Wales, nr Swansea, 17 Feb 1944). Welsh

Gloria <2010>   36'

solo voice   chorus
2[1.2/pic] 2[opt] 2[1.2/bcl] 2[1.2/cbn] — 4 3[tp3 opt] 3 1[opt] — tmp+3 — hp — org [opt] — str
perc: bd, cym, sus cym, sd, tri, tambn, glock, xyl, congas, surdo, finger cym, cabasa, hand dr
The solo voice (mvt IV) may be "any suitable voice," male or female; the music is in D major, but orchestra parts for this mvt include a transposition in E-flat major if preferred.

I. The Proclamation: Gloria in excelsis Deo	5'
Reading from the Hindu Bhagavadgītā	1'
II. The Prayer: Laudamus te	7'
Reading from the Buddhist Diamond Sūtra	1'
III. The Psalm: Tehillim—Psalm 150	4'
Reading from the Taoist Tao Te Ching	1'
IV. The Song: I'll make music	6'
Reading from the Qur'an	1'
V. The Exaltation: Domine Deus	10'

Boosey

Palladio   15'

str

1. Allegretto	4'
2. Largo	5'
3. Vivace	6'

Boosey

Joachim, Joseph   1831-1907

(b Kitsee, nr Pressburg [now Bratislava], 28 June 1831; d Berlin, 15 Aug 1907). Austro-Hungarian

Concerto, Violin, op.11, D minor (Hungarian) <1861>   35'

2 2 2 2 — 4 2 0 0 — tmp — str

1. Allegro	19'
2. Romanze	9'
3. Finale alla zingara	7'

Breitkopf	Kalmus	Luck's

Hamlet, op.4 <c1855>   17'

2 2 2 2 — 4 2 3 0 — tmp — str

Breitkopf

Jolivet, André   1905-1974

(b Paris, 8 Aug 1905; d Paris, 20 Dec 1974). French

Les amants magnifiques (The Magnificent Lovers) <1961>   12

2[1.2/pic] 2 0 2 — 2 2 0 0 — tmp+4 — hp — hpsd[or pf] / cel — str
perc: cym, sus cym, field dr, tri, xyl, sd, bd, slgh-bells, tambn, cast
Variations on a theme of Lully from a comédie-ballet of Molière.
    Use of an electronic keyboard with harpsichord and celesta stops would facilitate some rapid instrument changes.

Boosey

Concertino, Trumpet <1948>   9

pf — str

Durand

Concerto, Harp <1952>   18

1[fl/pic] 1[ob/Eh] 1 1 — 2 1 0 0 — str

I. Allegro volubile	6'
II. Andante cantabile	7'
III. Allegramente	5'

Billaudot

Concerto, Ondes Martenot <1947>   23

2[1.2/pic] 2[1.2/Eh] 2 2 — 2 3 2 1 — asx — tmp+5 — hp — cel — str[min 12.10.8.8.6]
perc: tambn, sd, bd, templeblks, sus cym, Chinescym, tamtam, tri, marac, whip, cym, vib, xyl, kybd glock

I. Allegro moderato	10'
II. Allegro vivace	6'
III. Largo cantabile	7'

Heugel

Concerto, Percussion <1958>   21

2[1.2/pic] 2[1.Eh] 2[1.Ebcl] 2 — 2 2 2 1 — asx — pf — str
perc: (solo) 4tmp, sd, field dr, woodblk, vib, sus cym, Chinescym, xyl, ratch, whi, templeblks, chimes, hi-hat, cym, bd, 3cowbell, 3tomtom

I. Robuste	6'
II. Dolent	5'
III. Rapidement	4'
IV. Allègrement	6'

Salabert

Concerto, Piano <1949–1950>   27

3[all dbl pic] 2[1.Eh] 2[1.Ebcl] 2 — 2 3 2 1 — tmp+3 — hp — cel — str
perc: marac, sd, field dr, bd, woodblk, vib, xyl, glock, hi-hat, tambn, tri, ratch, whip, crot, cym, sus cym, gong, Chinescym, tamtam, slgh-bells, 5Chinesblks, goblet, 2tambn prov

I. Allegro deciso	9'
II. Senza rigore	9'
III. Allegro frenetico	9'

Heugel

Symphonie de danses <1940>   17

2[1.2/pic] 2[1.2/Eh] 2 2 — 2 2 2 1[or cbn] — 4perc — hp — pf — st
perc: sus cym, tambn, field dr, templeblks, tri, bd, gong, tamtam, sd, marac, darabucca

Billaudot

Symphonie pour cordes (Symphony for Strings) <1961>   22

str [max 16.14.12.10.8; min 5.4.4.3.2]

I. Farouche	8'
II. Flottant	7'
III. Trépidant	7'

Boosey

Symphony No.1 <1953>   25'

3[1.2/pic.3/pic] 3[1.2.Eh] 3[1.2.3/bcl] 3 — 4 4 3 1 — tmp — hp —
str[14.12.10.10.8]

    I. Allegro strepitoso   _'
    II. Adagio   _'
    III. Allegro veloce   _'
    IV. Allegro corruscante   _'

Heugel

Symphony No.3 <1964>   25'

3[1.2/pic.3/pic] 3[1.2.Eh] 3[1.2.Ebcl] 3[1.2.cbn] — 4 3 3 1 — asx,
tsx[or bn] — 3perc — str

perc: templeblks, cast, guiro, chimes, hi-hat, sd, field dr, bd, woodblk, whip,
tambn, Chinescym, tamtam, tri, marac, sleighbells, anvil, tambn prov, police
whistle, bd/ped, 2cowbell, 3tomtom, 2sus cym

    I. Obstiné (Obstinately)   12'
    II. Fulgural (Lightning-like)   7'
    III. Lyrique (Lyrical)—Véhément (Vehement) 6'

Boosey

Jones, Samuel   1935-

(b Inverness, Mississippi, 2 June 1935). American

Aurum aurorae; Fanfare-Overture <2001>   6'

0 0 0 0 — 4 3 3 1 — tmp — org — [no str]

Campanile

Benediction <1999>   9'

1 1 1 1 — 1 2 1 1 — str

"Chorale Prelude on the Celebrated Benediction and Sevenfold Amen by
Peter Lutkin."
    An orchestration by the composer of his 1999 work for chorus &
strings, Reunion benediction, q.v.

Campanile

Chorale-Overture for Organ and Orchestra

see his: Mount Rainier Overture

A Christmas Memory: Suite <1965>   17'

2[1.2/pic] 2[1.2/Eh] 2[1.2/bcl] 2 — 2 2 1 1 — tmp+1 — hp — str

perc: chimes, glock, tambn, bd, tri, tamtam, sd, sus cym, xyl

    I. Prelude   4'
    II. It's Christmas Weather   3'
    III. Pecan Gatherers' Little March   4'
    IV. Best Friends in the Whole Wide World 6'

Campanile

Concerto, Horn <2007–2008>   25'

3[1.2.pic] 3[1.2.Eh] 3[1.2.bcl] 3[1.2.cbn] — 5[2opt] 3 3 1 — tmp+3
— hp — str

perc: bd, cym, sus cym, sd, tri, gong, glock, crot[C#4], Indian bell[G4]
3 horns in orchestra; 2 additional optional echo horns off stage.

    I. Andante serioso   11'
    II. Lento   6'
    III. Lento; Allegro vivace   8'

Campanile

Concerto, Trombone (Vita Accademica) <2009>   25'

3[1.2.3/pic] 3[1.2.3/Eh] 3[1.2.3/bcl] 3[1.2.cbn] — 4 3 3 1 — tmp+3
— hp — str

perc: bd, cym, sus cym, sd, tri, tambn, gong, chimes

    I. Andante vigoroso   11'
    II. Romanza: Andante amabile   4'
    III. Allegro moderato; Allegro   10'

Campanile

Concerto, Tuba <2005>   24'

3[1.2/afl.3/pic] 3[1.2.Eh] 3[1.2/Ebcl.3/bcl] 3[1.2.cbn] — 4 3 3 0 —
tmp+3 — hp — str

perc: sd, field dr, tri, tambn, gong, glock, xyl, chimes, crot, 2sus cym, anvil (or
iron pipe)

    1. Andante con moto   9'
    2. Andante mosso; Poco adagietto   6'
    3. Largo; Allegro molto   9'

Campanile

Concerto, Violin <2013>   24'

2[1.2/pic] 2[1.Eh] 2[1.2/bcl] 2 — 2 2 0 1 — tmp+1 — str

perc: sus cym, chimes, sd

    I. Andante moderato   11'
    II. Larghetto con moto—Largo cantabile   7'
    III. Allegro inquieto ed appassionato   7'

Campanile

Concerto, Violoncello <2010>   21'

2[1.2/pic] 2[1.Eh] 2[1.2/bcl] 2 — 2 2 0 0 — tmp+1 — str

perc: sus cym, sd, xyl, crot

    I. Con brio; Andante mosso   10'
    II. Largo   5'
    III. Allegro   6'

Campanile

Elegy <1963>   5'

str

C. Fischer

Eudora's Fable: The Shoe Bird <2002>   51'

narrator   children's chorus
2[1/pic.2/afl] 2[1.2/Eh] 3[1/Ebcl.2/bcl.3/asx] 2[1.2/cbn] — 2 3 1 0 —
tmp+1 — hp — str

perc: bd, sus cym, sd, field dr, toms, gong, glock, xyl, cowbell, small mouth siren,
slidewhistle, duckcall
Timpanist covers 2 gong notes.
    An alternative text, slightly shorter, reduces the duration to 48'.

Campanile

Fanfare and Celebration <1980>   5'

4[1.2.3.pic] 4[1.2.3.Eh] 4[1.2.3.bcl] 4[1.2.3.cbn] — 4 3 3 1 — tmp+5
— 2hp — str

perc: bd, cym, sus cym, sd, tri, glock, xyl
A second version ("Version B" as opposed to the present "Version A")
calls for 4 less woodwinds, thus: 3[1.2.3/pic] 3[1.2.3/Eh] 3[1.2.bcl]
3[1.2.cbn]. Brass, percussion, harps and strings remain the same.
    Yet a third version is a transcription by the composer and Carl Simpson
for symphonic band.

C. Fischer

Festival Fanfare <1964>   2'

0 0 0 0 — 5 3 3 1 — [no str]

C. Fischer

Hear the Music <2011>   2'

children's voices (chorus and/or audience) and clapping
3[1.2.pic] 3[1.2.Eh] 3[1.2.bcl] 3[1.2.cbn] — 4 3 3 1 — tmp+2 — hp
— str

perc: sd, bd, whip, tri, tamtam, sus cym
Adapted from the composer's Reflections: Songs of Fathers and
Daughters (q.v.). Commissioned by the Seattle Symphony for use as a
signature song for their youth concerts. May be customized to serve the
same purpose for your own orchestra.
    Also available in a small orchestra version:
    2[1.2/pic] 2 2 — 2 2 1 1 — tmp+2 — hp — str

Campanile

Hymn to the Earth (Roundings: Suite No.1) <2000> 12'

3[1.2.3/pic] 3[1.2.Eh] 3[1.2.bcl] 3[1.2.cbn] — 4 3 3 1 — tmp+5 — hp — str

perc: bd, cym, sus cym, sd, field dr, gong, glock, chimes, farm bell, tractor sound (CD)

Movements 1, 6 & 7 from the composer's *Roundings*. CD supplied by publisher (tractor sound in *Plow* only).

Hymn to the Earth	1'
Plow	7'
To Every Thing There Is a Season	4'

Campanile

Janus <1998> 17'

2[1.2/pic] 2[1.2.Eh] 2 2 — 2 2 1 0 — tmp+1 — hp — str

perc: sus cym, gong, glock, xyl, chimes

Movements may be performed separately.

| *In retrospect* | *8'* |
| *In prospect* | *9'* |

Campanile

Let Us Now Praise Famous Men <1972> 16'

3[1.2/pic.pic] 3[1.2.Eh] 3[1.2.bcl] 3[1.2.cbn] — 4 3 3 1 — tmp+3 — hp — str

perc: bd, cym, sys cym, sd, tri, gong, glock, churchbell (or chime)

Offstage fl choir: 3fl & afl, preferably doubled or tripled at the conductor's discretion.

May be performed without the offstage flute choir by using 4 flutes, including alto flute, in the orchestra.

C. Fischer

Listen Now, My Children; Overture on Texas Frontier Children's Songs <1985> 11'

3[1.2.pic] 3[1.2.Eh] 2 2 — 4 3 3 1 — tmp+4 — hp — str

perc: bd, cym, sus cym, sd, glock, xyl

C. Fischer

Machines (Roundings: Suite No.2) <2000> 14'

3[1.2.3/pic] 3[1.2.3/Eh] 3[1.2.3/bcl] 3[1.2.3/cbn] — 4 3 3 1 — tmp+5 — hp — str

perc: bd, cym, sus cym, 3sd, field dr, gong, glock, xyl, chimes, sandblks, ironpipe, chain, 2 LP shakers, eggshaker, cabasa, locomotive bell, metallic screech

Movements 3 & 4 from the composer's *Roundings*.

| Oil Well | 6' |
| Locomotive | 8' |

Campanile

Mount Rainier Overture: Chorale-Overture for Organ and Orchestra <2003> 7'

3[1.2.3/pic] 3[1.2.Eh] 3[1.2.3/bcl] 3[1.2.3/cbn] — 4 3 3 1 — tmp+3 — str

perc: sd, bd, chimes, tambn, glock, xyl, sus cym, gong

Original title: Chorale-Overture for Organ and Orchestra.

Campanile

The Open Range (Roundings: Suite No.3) <2000> 15'

3[1.2.3/pic] 3[1.2.3/bcl] 3[1.2.cbn] — 4 3 3 1 — tmp+5 — hp — str

perc: bd, cym, 3 sus cym, sd, 3tri, gong, glock, xyl, crot, windchimes, woodblk, templeblk, vibraslap

Movements 2 & 5 from the composer's *Roundings*.

| Windmill | 8' |
| Lariat | 7' |

Campanile

Organ Benediction <1999; rev 2010> 9'

org — str

"Chorale Prelude on the Celebrated *Benediction and Sevenfold Amen* by Peter Lutkin."

An arrangement by the composer of his *Reunion Benediction*.

Campanile

Overture for a City <1964> 8'

3[1.2.3/pic] 3[1.2.Eh] 3[1.2.3/bcl] 3[1.2.cbn] — 4 3 3 1 — tmp+2 [or 3] — hp — str

perc: bd, cym, sus cym, sd, gong, glock, xyl

C. Fischer

A Parliament of Owls; Fanfare & Processional March <1977; rev 1991> 5

0 0 0 0 — 4 3 3 1 — tmp — [no str]

Campanile

Reflections (Songs of Fathers and Daughters) <2011> 18

3[1.2.3/pic] 3[1.2.Eh] 3[1.2.3/bcl] 3[1.2.cbn] — 4 3 3 1 — tmp+3 — hp — str

perc: cym, sus cym, sd, tri, gong, glock, xyl, chimes, crot, Indian bell [B# approx]

Tone poem/Suite for orchestra.

Campanile

Reunion Benediction <1999> 9'

chorus SSAATTBB

str

"Chorale Prelude on the Celebrated *Benediction and Sevenfold Amen* by Peter Lutkin."

A later fully instrumental version is entitled simply *Benediction*; a version for organ and strings, *Organ Benediction*; see above.

Campanile

Roundings; Musings and Meditations on Texas New Deal Murals <2000> 41'

3[1.2.3/pic] 3[1.2.3/Eh] 3[1.2.3/bcl] 3[1.2.3/cbn] — 4 3 3 1 — tmp+5 — hp — str

perc: bd, cym, 3 sus cym, 3sd, field dr, 3tri, gong, glock, xyl, chimes, crot, windchimes, woodblk, templeblk, vibraslap, cabasa, sandblks, farm bell, locomotive bell, tractor sound (CD), iron pipe, chain, metalic screech, 2 LP shakers, egg shaker

CD supplied by publisher (tractor sound, in 6th mvt only). Individual movements may be performed separately, or sub-suites may be used; *see*:

Hymn to the Earth [mvts. 1, 6, 7], *12'*
Machines [mvts. 3, 4], *14'*
The Open Range [mvts 2, 5], *15'*

1. Prologue: Hymn to the Earth	*1'*
2. Windmill	*8'*
3. Oil Well	*3'*
4. Locomotive	*8'*
5. Lariat	*7'*
6. Plow	*7'*
7. Epilogue: To Every Thing There Is a Season	*4'*

Campanile

The Seas of God; Fanfare-Overture <1992> 8'

chorus (SSAATTBB)

3[1.2.3/pic] 3[1.2.Eh] 3[1.2.bcl] 3[1.2.cbn] — 4 3 3 1 — tmp+4 — str

perc: bd, cym, sus cym, sd, tri, tambn, gong, glock, xyl, chimes

Text by Walt Whitman. Composed for the 500th anniversary of the voyages of Columbus.

Campanile

The Shoe Bird

see under: Eudora's Fable: The Shoe Bird

A Symphonic Requiem (Variations on a Theme of Howard Hanson) <1983; rev 2002> 25'

3[1.2.3/pic] 3[1.2.Eh] 3[1.2.3/bcl] 3[1.2.cbn] — 4 3 3 1 — tmp+3 — hp — str

perc: bd, cym, sus cym, sd, field dr, toms, glock, xyl, chimes

Campanile

Symphony No.1 <1959–1960>   28'

3[1.2.3/pic] 3[1.2.Eh] 3[1.2.3/bcl] 3[1.2.cbn] — 4 3 3 1 — tmp+3 — hp — pf/cel — str
perc: bd, cym, sus cym, sd, field dr, tri, gong, glock, xyl, woodblk, templeblk
Mvts 2 & 3 may be performed separately as "Chaconne and Burlesque," 12'.

Andante	11'
Chaconne	6'
Burlesque	5'
Finale	6'

C. Fischer

Symphony No.2 (Canticles of Time) <1990>   27'

chorus (double chorus in one movement)
3[1.2.3/pic] 2[1.2/Eh] 2[1.2/bcl] 3[1.2.cbn] — 4 3 3 1 — tmp+5 — hp — cel[played by perc] — str
perc: bd, cym, sus cym, sd, field dr, tri, tambn, tamtam, gong, glock, xyl, vib, chimes, Indian bell, cel[played by perc]
Text by John Stone.

Prologue	3'
Scio (I Know)	4'
Credo (I Believe)	9'
Gaudeo (I Rejoice)	11'

Campanile

Symphony No.3 (Palo Duro Canyon) <1992>   23'

3[1.2.3/pic] 3[1.2.3/Eh] 3[1.2.3/bcl] 3[1.2.cbn] — 4 3 3 1 — tmp+5 — hp — cel (played by percussionist) — str
perc: bd, cym, sus cym, 2sd, toms, tri, tambn, tamtam, gong, glock, xyl, chimes, claves, bundle of sticks, tape of wind sounds
A special percussion instrument, "bundle of sticks," is supplied with the rental material, as is a recording of wind sounds. Celesta may be played by one of the percussionists.

Campanile

The Temptation of Jesus <1995>   73'

mixed chorus, small chorus, children's chorus   solo bass
2[1.2/pic] 2[1.2/Eh] 2[1.2/bcl] 2 — 2 2 3 0 — tmp+1 — hp — cel[played by perc] — str
perc: bd, cym, sus cym, sd, tri, tambn, gong, glock, xyl, windchimes, whip, ratch, rute, tambour provençal, Indian bell, chime, cel[played by perc]
Timpanist doubles on some percussion; otherwise tmp+2 is required.
   Text from the Bible and writings of Thomas Merton.

Campanile

The Trumpet of the Swan <1985>   19'

chorus
3[1.2.pic] 2[1.2/Eh] 2[1.2/bcl] 2[1.2/cbn] — 4 3 3 1 — tmp+3 — hp — str
perc: tri, glock, xyl, sd, bd, cym, tamtam, tambn, 2sus cym, 3tomtom, 3sd (graduated in size), field dr
The text is excerpted from Eudora Welty's story "The Wanderers," from her short story cycle *The Golden Apples*. (Not be confused with E.B.White's well-known children's book *The Trumpet of the Swan*.)

Campanile

Jongen, Joseph   1873-1953

(b Liège, 14 Dec 1873; d Sart, 12 July 1953). Belgian

Symphonie concertante, Organ & Orchestra, op.81   40'
<1926–1927>

3[1.2.3/pic] 3[1.2.Eh] 3[1.2.bcl] 3[1.2.opt cbn] — 4 3 3 1 — tmp+2 — hp — str
perc: tri, cym
Exercise caution: a 1965 printing of the solo organ part differs from the orchestral score and parts printed in 1967.

Allegro, molto moderato	10'
Divertimento, molto vivo	10'
Molto lento, misterioso	14'
Toccata (Moto perpetuo, allegro moderato	6'

Schott

Joplin, Scott   1868-1917

(b northeast TX, between July 1867 and mid-Jan 1868; d New York, 1 April 1917). American

see also: Turok, Paul

The Entertainer <1902>   5'

1[incl pic] 0 1 0 — 0 1 1 1 — 1perc — pf — opt str[2vn, va, vc]
perc: set
Arr. D.S. Delisle; ed. Gunther Schuller.

Belwin   Luck's

Maple Leaf Rag <1899>   3'

1[incl pic] 0 1 0 — 0 1 1 1 — 1perc — pf — str[2vn, va, vc, opt db]
perc: set
Arranger unknown; ed. Gunther Schuller.

Belwin   Luck's

Ragtime Dance <1906>   4'

1 0 1 0 — 0 1 1 1 — 1perc — pf — str[2vn, va, vc, db]
perc: set
Ed. Gunther Schuller.

Belwin   Luck's

K

Kabalevsky, Dmitri   1904-1987

(b St Petersburg, 17/30 Dec 1904; d Moscow, 14 Feb 1987). Russian

Colas Breugnon, op.24 (Kola Bryun'yon): Overture   5'
<1936–1938; rev 1953 & 1968>

3[1.2.3/pic] 3 3 3[1.2.3/cbn] — 4 3 3 1 — tmp+5 — hp — str

perc: xyl, tri, field dr, cym, bd

Russian	Sikorski

Colas Breugnon (Kola Bryun'yon): Suite, op.24a   20'
<1936–1938; rev 1953 & 1968>

3[1.2.3/pic] 3[1.2.3/Eh] 3 3[1.2.3/cbn] — 4 3 3 1 — tmp+5 — hp — str

perc: xyl, tamtam, sd, cym, sus cym, bd, tri, tambn

Overture	4'
Fête populaire	6'
Fléau publique	6'
Insurrection	4'

Russian	Sikorski

The Comedians, op.26; Suite for Small Orchestra   13'
(Komedianti) <1940>

1[1/pic] 1[1/Eh] 2 1 — 2 2 1 1 — tmp+4 — pf — str

perc: xyl, tambn, field dr, cym, sus cym, bd, tri

1. Prologue	1'
2. Galop	1'
3. March	1'
4. Waltz	1'
5. Pantomime	2'
6. Intermezzo	1'
7. Little Lyrical Scene	1'
8. Gavotte	1'
9. Scherzo	2'
10. Epilogue	2'

Russian	Sikorski

The Comedians, op.26 (Komedianti): Galop <1940>   2'

1 1 2 1 — 2 2 1 1 — tmp+3 — pf — str

perc: bd, cym, sd, xyl

Russian

Concerto, Piano, No.3, op.50, D major (Youth) <1952>   18'

2 2 2 2 — 2 2 2 0 — tmp+3 — str

perc: bd, xyl, sd, tri, cym, sus cym

Russian	Sikorski

Concerto, Violin, op.48 <1948>   16'

1 1 2 1 — 2 1 1 0 — tmp+4 — str

perc: xyl, tri, sd, tambn, cym, bd

Russian	Sikorski

Concerto, Violoncello, No.2, op.77, C major <1964>   29

2 2 2 3[1.2.cbn] — 4 2 2 0 — asx — tmp+2 — hp — str

perc: bd, sus cym, sd, tambn, tamtam

The asx plays only in the second movement.

I. Molto sostenuto; Allegro molto e energico	10'
Cadenza I	2'
II. Presto marcato	6'
Cadenza II	3'
III. Andante con moto; Allegro	8'

Russian

Overture pathétique, op.64 <1960>   4

3[incl pic] 3[incl Eh] 3[incl bcl] 3[incl cbn] — 4 3 3 1 — tmp+3 — hp — pf — str

Kalmus

Symphony No.1, op.18, C-sharp minor <1932>   21

3[1.2.pic] 3[1.2.Eh] 3[1.2.bcl] 3[1.2.cbn] — 4 3 3 1 — tmp+4 — str

perc: field dr, tri, cym, sus cym, bd

I. Andante molto sostenuto	10'
II. Allegro molto agitato e con spirito	11'

Russian

Symphony No.2, op.19, C minor <1934>   29

3[1.2.3/pic] 3[1.2.Eh] 3[1.2.bcl] 3[1.2.cbn] — 4 3 3 1 — tmp+4 — st

perc: field dr, tri, cym, sus cym, bd

I. Allegro quasi presto	9'
II. Andante non troppo	12'
III. Prestissimo scherzando	8'

Kalmus	Russian	Sikorski

Symphony No.3, op.22, B-flat minor (Requiem) <1933>   19

chorus

3[1.2.3/pic] 3[1.2.Eh] 3[1.2.bcl] 3[1.2.cbn] — 4 3 3 1 — tmp+4 — pf — str

perc: field dr, cym, sus cym, bd, tamtam

I. Allegro impetuoso	7'
II. Andante marciale, lugubre	12'

Russian

Kagel, Mauricio   1931-2008

(b Buenos Aires, 24 Dec 1931; d Cologne, 18 Sept 2008). German composer of Argentine birth

Broken Chords <2000–2001>   21'

4[1.2.3/pic/afl.4/pic/afl] 4 5[1.2.3.4.bcl] 4 — 4 4 4 1 — str

Peters

Das Konzert (The Concert) <2001–2002>   27'

soloists: flute [dbl pic, afl], harp, percussion

str[8.7.6.5.4]

perc: (soloist) congas, templeblks, vib, marim, Chinescym, 4tri, 3gong

In one mvt. The percussion solo, though intended for 1 performer, may be divided among 2 players if desired: one playing the mallets and the other the remainder.

Peters

Konzertstück, Timpani & Orchestra <1990–1992>   19'

4[1/pic.2/pic.3/pic/afl.4/pic/afl] 4[1.2.3.4/Eh] 4[1.2.3.bcl] 3[1.2.3/cbn] — 4 3 3 1 — 3perc — str

perc: (soloist) 5timpani, 1timpano or bass drum w/ paper membrane (orch) xyl, vib, crot, hi-hat, marim, chimes, bd, angklung, 2guiro, 6tomtom, 4sandblks, 3cast, 2tamtam, 6cowbell, 3tri, 6woodblk, 3sus cym

Peters

Variationen ohne Fuge (Variations without Fugue) <1971–1972>   25'

optional: 2 actors representing Brahms (speaking) and Handel (silent)
3[1.2/pic.3/pic] 3[1.2.Eh] 4[1.2.Ebcl.bcl] 3[1.2.bcl] — 4 3 4 1 —
tmp+1 — 2hp — pf/hpsd, cel — str[12.12.10.10.8]
perc: glock, bd
Based on the Brahms piano work *Variations and Fugue on a Theme by Handel*, op.24.
    Actors, if present, are in costume, makeup, and mask to represent the two elderly composers; an exact impersonation is important. If actors are not used, the duration is about 21'.
    A "ripieno ensemble," drawn from the above, may be either (Ripieno A): vn, va, vc, db, or (Ripieno B): fl, ob, cl, bn, tp, vn, va, vc, db.

Universal	

Kalinnikov, Vassili   1866-1901

(b Voina, Oryol district, 1/13 Jan 1866; d Yalta, 29 Dec/11 Jan 1901). Russian
[not to be confused with Victor Kalinnikov (1870-1927)]

Chanson triste <1893>   2'

str
Originally a piano piece, *Grustnaya pesenka*, arranged by Moritz Kohler.

Kalmus	Luck's

Serenade for Strings <1891>   10'

str

Muzyka	Russian

Suite, D Major <1892>   40'

2[1.2/pic] 2 2 — 4 2 3 0 — tmp+3 — hp — str
perc: bd, cym, tri

I. Andante	11'
II. Allegro scherzando	4'
III. Adagio	19'
IV. Allegro moderato	6'

Jurgenson	Kalmus

Symphony No.1, G minor <1895>   35'

3[1.2.pic] 3[1.2.Eh] 2 2 — 4 2 3 1 — tmp+1 — hp — str
perc: tri

1. Allegro moderato	11'
2. Andante commodamente	6'
3. Scherzo: Allegro non troppo	7'
4. Finale: Allegro moderato	11'

Kalmus	Luck's	Russian

Symphony No.2, A major <1897>   37'

3[1.2.pic] 2[1.2/Eh] 2 2 — 4 2 3 1 — tmp — hp — str

1. Moderato; Allegro non troppo	10'
2. Andante cantabile	8'
3. Allegro scherzando	8'
4. Andante cantabile; Allegro vivo	11'

Kalmus	

Kallman, Daniel   1956-

(b Heidelberg, 11 Aug 1956). American composer born in Germany

A Holiday Hoedown <1992>   5'

2[1.2/pic] 2 2 2 — 4 3 3 1 — tmp+3 — opt hp — opt pf — str[incl separate parts for 3 solo violins]
Christmas carols in country-western style.
    A separate chamber orchestra version is available with brass reduced to 2.2.1.0 (no hp or pf).

MMB	

Trinity Canticles <1989>   19'

3[1.2.pic] 3[1.2.Eh] 3[1.2.bcl] 2 — 4 3 3 1 — tmp+3 — hp — str
Messiah, Prince of Peace (7') may be performed separately.

Prelude	_'
Yahweh, God of the Covenant	_'
Messiah, Prince of Peace	_'
Paraclete, Holy Advocate	_'

MMB	

Kancheli, Giya   1935-

(b Tbilisi, 10 Aug 1935). Georgian

And Farewell Goes Out Sighing… <1999>   20'

soloists: countertenor & violin
4[1.2.3/pic.4/afl/pic] 3[1.2.3/Eh] 2 3[1.2.cbn] — 4 4 3 1 — elec bgtr — tmp+5 — hp — pf — str
perc: bd, cym, sus cym, sd, tri, tambn, tamtam, glock, xyl, marim, chimes, marktree, templeblks, claves

Russian	

Don't Grieve <2001>   38'

solo baritone
4[1.2.3/pic./afl/pic] 3[1.2.3/Eh] 3[1.2.3/bcl] 3[1.2.cbn] — 4 4 4 1 — elec bgtr — tmp+6 — hp — pf, accordion — str
perc: tri, templeblks, tambn, td, bd, sus cym, cym, claves, tamtam, glock, chimes, 3cowbell, 3bongos
Texts, alternating Russian and English, are a melange of fragments from many authors.

Russian	

Symphony No.7 (Epilogue) <1986>   31'

4[1.2/pic.3/pic.afl/pic] 3 3[1.2.3/bcl] 3[1.2/cbn.3/cbn] — 6 6 4 1 — bass gtr — tmp+5 — hp — pf, spinet (=hpsd) — str
It is conceivable, though difficult, that 1 keyboard player could cover pf & spinet.

Russian	Sikorski

V & V <1994; rev 1996>   10'

solo violin
taped voice — str

Russian	

Karidoyanes, Steven   1957-

(b Boston, 5 Nov 1957). Dual American & Greek citizenship

Café Neon; Fantasy on Greek Songs and Dances <2000>   9'

2 2 2 2 — 2 2 0 0 — tmp/perc — str
perc: [played by tmp] tri, 2sus cym

Pegasus	

Yerakína; Dionysian Dance for Orchestra <2006>   3'

2 2 2 2 — 4 2 3 1 — tmp+2 — str
perc: sd, tri, 2sus cym, 2tri

Pegasus	

Karłowicz, Mieczysław

1876-1909

(b Wiszniew, Święcany district, Lithuania, 11 Dec 1876; d nr Zakopane, Tatra Mountains, 8 Feb 1909). Polish

Concerto, Violin, op.8, A major <1902>

27'

2 2 2 2 — 4 2 3 1 — tmp — str

  1. Allegro moderato   *12'*
  2. Andante   *8'*
  3. Finale: Vivace assai   *7'*

> PWM

Eternal Songs, op.10 (Odwieczne pieśni) <1904–1906>

24'

3[1.2.3/pic] 3[1.2.Eh] 3[1.2.bcl] 3[1.2.cbn] — 4 3 3 1 — tmp+2 — str
perc: cym, tri, tamtam

  1. Song of Erernal Longing (Pieśń o wiekuistej tęsknocie)   *9'*
  2. Song of Love and Death (Pieśń o miłości i o śmierci)   *10'*
  3. Song of Eternity (Pieśń o wszechbycie)   *5'*

> PWM

Lithuanian Rhapsody, op.11 (Rapsodia litewska) <1906>

19'

3[1.2.3/pic] 3[1.2.Eh] 3[1.2.bcl] 2 — 4 2 3 0 — tmp+2 — str
perc: cym, tri

> PWM

Serenade, op.2, C major <1897>

22'

str

  1. March   *6'*
  2. Romance *7'*
  3. Waltz   *5'*
  4. Finale   *4'*

> PWM

Stanisław and Anna Oświęcimowie, op.12 (Stanisław i Anna Oświęcimowie) <1907>

22'

4[1.2.3.4/pic] 4[1.2.3.Eh] 4[1.2.Ebcl.bcl] 4[1.2.3.cbn] — 6 3 3 1 — tmp+3 — 2hp — str
perc: bd, cym, tri, tamtam, sus cym

> PWM

Kats-Chernin, Elena

1957-

(b Tashkent, 4 Nov 1957). Australian composer of Uzbek origin

Mythic <2004>

12'

2[1/pic.2] 2 2 2 — 4 2 3 1 — tmp+1 — hp — hp
perc: bd, sus cym, hi-hat, vib, claves, 4tomtoms, corrugated iron

> Boosey

Zoom and Zip <1997>

13'

str

> Boosey

Kay, Hershy

1919-1981

(b Philadelphia, 17 Nov 1919; d Danbury, CT, 2 Dec 1981). American

Cakewalk: Concert Suite <1951>

24

2[1.2/pic] 2 2[1.2/bcl] 2 — 4 2[1/crt.2/crt] 3 1 — tmp+3 — hp — pf/cel — str
perc: bd, sd, cym, sus cym, templeblks, woodblk, tri, xyl, glock, chimes, marac, tambn, tomtoms
After piano melodies of Louis Moreau Gottschalk and early minstrel tunes.

  1. Great Walkaround   *3'*
  2. Three Variations: Wallflower Waltz   *6'*
    Sleight of Feet
    Perpendicular Points
  3. Freebee   *4'*
  4. Magic Act: Introduction of the Magicians   *7'*
    Venus and the Three Graces
    The Wild Pony
    Pas de deux
  5. Finale: Gala Cakewalk   *4'*

> Boosey

Kay, Ulysses

1917-1995

(b Tucson, AZ, 7 Jan 1917; d Englewood, NJ, 20 May 1995). American

Chariots <1978>

15

3[incl pic] 3[incl Eh] 3[incl bcl] 3[incl cbn] — 4 3 3 1 — tmp+3 — hp — str

> C. Fischer

Fantasy Variations <1963>

15

2[incl pic] 2 2 2 — 4 3 3 1 — tmp+4 — str

> MCA

Markings <1966>

18

3[incl pic] 3[incl Eh] 3[incl bcl] 3[incl cbn] — 4 3 3 1 — tmp+4 — str

> MCA

Of New Horizons <1944>

8

3[1.2.pic] 3[1.2.Eh] 3[1.2.bcl] 3[1.2.cbn] — 4 3 3 1 — tmp+4 — hp — pf/cel — str

> Peters

Scherzi musicali, For Chamber Orchestra <1968>

17

1 1 1 1 — 1 0 0 0 — str

> MCA

Serenade for Orchestra <1954>

18

2[1.2/pic] 2 2 2 — 4 2 3 1 — tmp — str

> AMP

Six Dances for String Orchestra <1954?>

19

str

> MCA

Southern Harmony <1975>   20'

3[1.2/pic2.pic1] 3[1.2.opt Eh] 3[1.2.bcl] 3[1.2.opt cbn] — 4 3 3 1 —
tmp+2 — str
perc: crot, tambn, bd/cym, td, 2sd, 3sus cym, 2tomtoms, 3tri, 2woodblks
Quotes tunes from the shape-note collection *Southern Harmony*.

1. Prelude: Land of Beginnings   _'
2. Fifes and Drums   _'
3. Variants   _'
4. Elysium   _'

    C. Fischer

Suite for Orchestra <1945>   17'

3[incl pic] 3[incl Eh] 3[incl bcl] 3[incl cbn] — 4 3 3 1 — tmp+5 — pf
— str
perc: xyl, tri, woodblk, sd, cym, sus cym, bd, tambn

    Schirmer

Suite for Strings <1947>   14'

str

    Peters

Theater Set for Orchestra <1968>   15'

3[incl pic] 3[incl Eh] 3[incl bcl] 2 — 4 3 3 1 — tmp+3 — hp — str

    MCA

Umbrian Scene <1963>   15'

2 2 2 2 — 4 3 3 1 — tmp+3 — hp — str
perc: vib, sus cym, sd, glock, tamtam, tri, bd, tambn

    MCA

Kechley, David   1947-

(b Seattle, WA, 16 Mar 1947). American

Alexander and the Wind-Up Mouse <1981>   17'

narrator
2[incl pic] 2 2[incl bcl] 2 — 2 2 1 0 — 2perc — hp — pf/cel — str
Based on a children's book by Leo Lionni.

    Pine Valley

Clocks and More Clocks <1981>   13'

narrator
3[incl pic] 3 3[incl bcl] 3 — 4 3 3 1 — tmp+3 — hp — pf — str
Based on a book by Pat Hutchins.

    Pine Valley

The Funky Chicken <1976>   3'

str

    Pine Valley

Karasuma; A Fast Funk for Orchestra <1993> 7'

3[incl pic] 3[incl Eh] 3[incl bcl] 3[incl cbn] — 4 3 3 1 — tmp+4 —
opt hp — pf — str

    Pine Valley

The Skylark Sings <1995>   29'

solo soprano   chorus (last mvt only)
2[incl pic] 2[incl Eh] 2 2 — 4 3 3 1 — tmp+3 — hp — pf — str

Skylarks   6'
Fireflies   3'
Starlight Night   3'
Magic Mushrooms   4'
Scarecrows   4'
The Giant Tortoise   5'
Quiet Birds   4'

    Pine Valley

Transformations; An Orchestral Triptych <1998>   18'

3[incl pic] 3[incl Eh] 3[incl bcl] 3[incl cbn] — 4 3 3 1 — ssx, asx —
tmp+3 — hp — pf/cel — str

Still on the Edge   5'
Funeral Music with Dance   9'
Past Refrains   4'

    Pine Valley

Tuahku; A Dark Samba for Orchestra <1997>   9'

3[incl pic] 3[incl Eh] 3[incl bcl] 3[incl cbn] — 4 3 3 1 — tmp+3 —
hp — pf — str

    Pine Valley

Kelley, Edgar Stillman   1857-1944

(b Sparta, WI, 14 April 1857; d New York, 12 Nov 1944). American

The Pit and the Pendulum <1930>   16'

3[1.2.3/pic] 3[1.2.Eh] 3[1.2.bcl] 3 — 4 3 3 1 — tmp+3 — hp — str

    Fleisher   Schirmer

Kelterborn, Rudolf   1931-

(b Basle, 3 Sept 1931). Swiss

Changements <1972–1973>   12'

4[1.2.3/pic.4/pic] 2[1.Eh] 4[1.2.3/bcl.Ebcl] 2[1.cbn] — 4 4 4[1.2.3.cb
tbn] 0 — tmp+4 — 2hp — str

    Bärenreiter

Kennan, Kent   1913-2003

(b Milwaukee, WI, 18 April 1913; d Austin, TX, 1 November 2003). American

Night Soliloquy <1936>   4'

solo flute
pf — str

    C. Fischer   Luck's

Kernis, Aaron Jay   1960-

(b Philadelphia, 15 Jan 1960). American

Air, for Violoncello and Orchestra <1996; rev 2000>   11'

2[1.2/pic] 1 2 1 — 2 2 0 0 — tmp+1 — hp — pf — str[min 6.6.4.4.3;
max 12.12.8.8.6]
perc: crot
Originally (1996) for violin & orchestra; arr. by the composer for cello &
orchestra, 2000.

    AMP

Colored Field; Concerto for English Horn & Orchestra   41'
<1994>

3[1.2/pic.3/pic] 2 3[1.2/bcl.3/Ebcl] 2[1.2/cbn] — 4 3 3 1 — tmp+3 —
hp — pf/cel — str[2 str orchs]
perc: bd, bd/cym, cast, chimes, glock, guiro, marim, ratch, whip, sd, tambn, td,
bongos, vib, xyl, rute, sandblks, woodrattle, 4almglock, 5bell plate, 4brake dr,
4buttongong, 4steel pipe, 4sus cym, 4tamtam, 2timbales, 2tomtom, 3tri, 2woodblk
Originally (1994) for English horn & orchestra; also arr by the composer
for violoncello & orchestra, 2000, *q.v.*

I. Colored Field   12'
II. Pandora Dance   6'
III. Hymns and Tablets 23'

    AMP

Colored Field; Concerto for Violoncello & Orchestra <1994; rev 2000>   41'

3[1.2/pic.3/pic] 2 3[1.2/bcl.3/Ebcl] 2[1.2/cbn] — 4 3 3 1 — tmp+3 — hp — pf/cel — str[2 str orchs]
perc: bd, bd/cym, cast, chimes, glock, guiro, marim, ratch, whip, sd, tambn, td, bongos, vib, xyl, rute, sandblks, woodrattle, 4almglock, 5bell plate, 4brake dr, 4buttongong, 4steel pipe, 4sus cym, 4tamtam, 2timbales, 2tomtom, 3tri, 2woodblk
Originally (1994) for English horn & orchestra, *q.v.*; arr by the composer for violoncello & orchestra, 2000.

I. Colored Field	12'
II. Pandora Dance	6'
III. Hymns and Tablets	23'

AMP

Concerto With Echoes <2009>   17'

0 2[1.2/pic] 0 2 — 2 1 0 0 — tmp+2 — str[4va, 4vc, 2db]
perc: vib, chimes, gong, sus cym
Winds only in mvts 2-3; perc only in mvt 2. Strings may be in multiples (i.e., doubled or tripled).

I. Lontano—Toccata: Molto allegro	_'
II. Slowly	_'
III. Aria: dolente, grazioso	_'

AMP

Concierto de "Dance Hits" <1993; rev 1995, 1998>   12'

solo guitar (amplified)
str
Originally for guitar & string quartet; the composer arranged the 3rd mvt in 1995 and added mvts 1 & 2 in 1998.

I. Double Echo	_'
II. Slow Dance Ballad	_'
III. Salsa Pasada	_'

AMP

Garden of Light <1999>   50'

soloists: SMTBar, boy soprano   chorus   children's chorus
4[1.2.3/pic2.4/pic1] 4[1.2.3.4/Eh] 4[1.2/bcl2.3/Ebcl/bcl2.4/bcl1] 4[1.2.3.cbn] — 6 4 4 1 — ssx, asx, tsx, bsx — elec gtr, elec bass — tmp+6 — hp — cel, pf, synth — str
perc: vib, chimes, marim, xyl, crot, 3szl cym, glock, marac, whip, sd, ratch, 7tri, 4metalshaker, 8bell, 2bellplates[F#5,G5], 6herdbells, 15sus cym, anvil, 2wooden clappers, 2timbales, 2tomtom, 2lionroar, 3tambn, 3Chinese gong[E2,G#3#,C5]], 2deskbell, 6tamtam, woodenshaker, cym[3pr], 2bd, 2woodblk, 3bongos
The 1st bcl is always in the 4th cl part, but the 2nd bcl is sometimes in the 3rd cl part and other times in 2nd cl; it would be simple and logical to combine all bcl2 into one or the other part, since never do more than 2 bcl play at any one time.

Morning of the World	12'
Tapestry of Home	38'

AMP

Lament and Prayer <1995>   25'

solo violin
0 1[offstage] 0 0 — 4-6perc — 1-2hp — str[min 12.12.8.8.6]
perc: chimes[balcony or offstage]; array of small metal perc on stage: triangles, jingles, metal shakers, sizzle cymbals, small Asian bells, and the like.
Solo oboe, harps and percussion appear only near the end of the work.

AMP

Musica celestis <1990>   11'

str
Originally the 2nd movement of the composer's String Quartet (1990); arr. for string orchestra by the composer.

AMP

New Era Dance <1992>   6'

3[1.2.pic] 2 2[1/Ebcl.2/bcl] 2 — 4 3 3 1 — tmp+4 — pf, synth — str
DAT tape (operated by synth player) supplied with orchestral materials.
Police whistles (optional) for several players.

AMP

Newly Drawn Sky <2005>   16'

3[1.2.3/pic] 3[1.2.3/Eh] 3[1.2/Ebcl.3/bcl] 3[1.2.3/cbn] — 4 3 3 1 — tmp+4 — hp — pf — str
perc: bd, timbales, glock, xyl, vib, chimes, crot, bongos, ratch, cast, 5sus cym, 6woodblk, 3cowbell, 3tri, 2tamtam, 2cym

AMP

Symphony of Meditations (Symphony No.3) <2009>   65'

solos: soprano & baritone; tenor[in chorus]   chorus SATB
3[1.2.3/pic] 3[1.2.3/Eh] 3[1.2/Ebcl.3/bcl] 3[1.2.3/cbn] — 4 3 3 1 — elec bgtr — tmp+4 — hp — pf — str
perc: sd, rototom, glock, xyl, marim, vib, crot, thunder, 2bd, 5tomtom, 6tri, 3tambn, 4tamtam, 5woodblk, 3pr bongos, 12almglock[tuned], 2steel plate, 4cym[4pr], 7sus cym, 5gong[tuned], 3tomtom[pitched]

I. Invocation	_'
II. Meditation on Oneness	_'
III. Supplication	_'

AMP

Symphony in Waves <1989>   38'

1[1/pic] 2[1.2/Eh] 1[1/Ebcl/bcl] 2[1.2/cbn] — 3 1[pic tp] 0 0 — 1perc — pf/cel — str[min 6.6.4.4.2]

Continuous Wave	10'
Scherzo	4'
Still Movement	15'
Intermezzo	2'
Finale	7'

AMP

Symphony No.2 <1991>   26'

3[1.2.3/pic] 3[1.2.Eh] 3[1.2.bcl] 3[1.2.3/cbn] — 4 4 4 1 — tmp+4 — hp — pf — str
perc: td, bongos, congas, crot, vib, xyl, glock, marim, chimes, tamtam, 2sd, 2bd, logdrum, reco-reco, 2metalpipe, cabasa, 2tri, 4sus cym, 2cym[2pr], 4tomtom, 4brake dr, 3woodblk, 3cowbell, 2thunder sheets, 4mounted handbells

Alarm	6'
Air/Ground	12'
Barricade	8'

AMP

Too Hot Toccata <1996; rev 2007>   6'

2[1.2/pic] 2 2[1/Ebcl.bcl] 2 — 2 2 0 0 — tmp+2 — pf — str
perc: tri, 3cowbells, 2woodblks, opt vib, set (2sus cym, hi-hat, 2tomtoms, sd, td, pedal bd)

AMP

Ketting, Otto   1935-

(b Amsterdam, 3 Sept 1935). Dutch

Symphony No.1 <1959>   18'

3 3[1.2.Eh] 3[1.2.bcl] 3[1.2.3/cbn] — 4 4 3 1 — asx — 2hp — cel — str

Donemus

Keuris, Tristan   1946-1996

(b Amersfoort, 3 Oct 1946; d Amsterdam,15 Dec 1996). Dutch

Sinfonia <1974>   12'

4[1.2.3/pic.4/pic] 4[1.2.Eh1.Eh2] 3[1.2.bcl] 4[1.2.3.cbn] — 8 4 3 2 — 2asx — 4perc — pf — str
perc: cym, sd, tri, bd, td, 2tamtams

Donemus

Khachaturian, Aram   1903-1978
(b Tbilisi, 24 May/6 June 1903; d Moscow, 1 May 1978). Armenian

Concerto, Piano <1936>   33'
2[1/pic.2] 2 3[1.2.bcl] 2 — 4 2 3 1 — tmp+3 — str
perc: sd, sus cym, bd, flexatone [or vib]
Only 12 bars of pic; could be covered by either flutist.
   According to James Holland (*Practical Percussion*, 2005), in the 1970s
the composer insisted that a musical saw replace the flexatone.

I. Allegro ma non troppo e maestoso	*14'*
II. Andante con anima	*11'*
III. Allegro brillante	*8'*

Russian

Concerto, Flute (Rampal version) <1940>   35'
3[1.2.pic] 3[1.2.Eh] 2 2 — 4 3 3 1 — tmp+3 — hp — str
perc: tambn, sd, sus cym, bd
The composer's violin concerto, with solo part adapted by Jean-Pierre
Rampal for flute. Use the orchestral parts for the violin concerto.

I. Allegro con fermezza	*14'*
II. Andante sostenuto	*12'*
III. Allegro vivace	*9'*

Russian

Concerto, Violin <1940>   35'
3[1.2.pic] 3[1.2.Eh] 2 2 — 4 3 3 1 — tmp+3 — hp — str
perc: tambn[?], sd, sus cym, bd
N.B. Many percussionists and conductors believe that the indication of
"tambourine" may have been a copyist's error, and that the intended
instrument is actually snare drum throughout; this is based mainly on
stylistic and idiomatic grounds, and some experts strongly dispute this
suggestion.

I. Allegro con fermezza	*14'*
II. Andante sostenuto	*12'*
III. Allegro vivace	*9'*

Russian

Concerto-Rhapsody, Violin & Orchestra <1962>   23'
3[1.2.3/pic] 2 2 2 — 4 2 0 0 — tmp+3 — hp — str
perc: sd, sus cym, tamtam, bd

Russian

Concerto-Rhapsody, Violoncello & Orchestra <1963>   23'
2 2 2 2 — 4 2 0 0 — tmp+4 — hp — str
perc: xyl, tamtam, field dr, cym, sus cym, bd

Russian

Gayane: Suite No.1 <1943>   36'
3[1.2.pic] 3[1.2.Eh] 3[1.2.bcl] 2 — 4 3 3 1 — asx [covered by one of
the clarinetists] — tmp+4 — hp — cel — str
perc: bd, cym, glock, gong, sd, tambn, tri, xyl, tubaphone

Introduction	_'
Dance of the Young Maidens	_'
Ayshe's Awakening and Dance	_'
Mountaineers' Dance	_'
Lullaby	_'
Gayane and Guiko	_'
Gayane's Adagio	_'
Lesginka	_'

Russian

Gayane: Suite No.2 <1943>   30'
3[1.2.pic] 3[1.2.Eh] 3[1.2.bcl] 2 — 4 3 3 1 — tmp+4 — hp — pf —
str
perc: bd, cym, glock, sd, tamtam, tambn, tri, vib, woodblk, xyl, frame drum

Dance of Welcome	_'
Lyric Duet	_'
Russian Dance	_'
Noune's Variation	_'
Dance of an Old Man and Carpet Weavers	_'
Armen's Variation	_'
Fire	_'

Russian

Gayane: Suite No.3 <1943>   23'
3[1.2.pic] 3[1.2.Eh] 3[1.2.bcl] 2 — 4 3 3 1 — asx — tmp+4 — hp —
pf — str
perc: bd, cym, glock, sd, tambn, tri, xyl, frame drum

Cotton Picking	*5'*
Dance of the Young Kurds	*2'*
Introduction and Dance of the Old Men	*2'*
The Carpet Weavers	*5'*
Sabre Dance	*5'*
Hopak	*4'*

Russian

Gayane: Dance of the Rose Maidens <1943>   2'
3[1.2.pic] 3[1.2.Eh] 2 2 — 4 3[1(crt).tp2.tp3] 3 0 — tmp+2 — hp —
str
perc: sus cym, tubaphone

Russian

Gayane: Lullaby <1943>   5'
3[1.2.pic] 3[1.2.Eh] 2 2 — 4 0 0 0 — tmp+2 — hp — cel[played by
perc] — str
perc: glock, cym, cel[played by perc]

Russian

Gayane: Sabre Dance <1943>   2'
3[1.2.pic] 3[1.2.Eh] 3[1.2.bcl] 2 — 4 3 3 1 — asx — tmp+3 — hp —
cel[played by perc] — str
perc: xyl, sus cym, woodblk, sd, tambn, cel[played by perc]
Celesta plays last 3 bars only.

Russian

Gayane: Three Pieces <1943>   9'
3[1.2.pic] 3[1.2.Eh] 3[1.2.bcl] 2 — 4 3[1/crt.2.3] 3 1 — asx — tmp+3
— hp — cel[played by perc] — str
perc: cym, glock, sd, tambn, sus cym, woodblk, xyl, tubaphone, cel[played by
perc]
Originally published (wrongly) by Leeds as *Suite No.1* from *Gayane*.

Dance of the Rose Maidens	2'
Lullaby	5'
Sabre Dance	2'

Russian

Masquerade: Suite <1941>   18'
2[1.2/pic] 2 2 2 — 4 2 3 1 — tmp+3 — str
perc: bd, cym, glock, sd, xyl

Waltz	*4'*
Nocturne	*5'*
Mazurka	*3'*
Romance	*3'*
Galop	*3'*

Russian

Spartacus: Suite No.1 <1955>   26'

3[1.2.3/pic] 3[1.2.Eh] 3[1.2.3/bcl] 2 — 4 4 3 1 — tmp+5 — hp — cel, pf — str

perc: tri, tambn, sd, cym, bd, tamtam, glock, xyl, tubaphone

1. Introduction and Dance of Nymphs	5'
2. Introduction, Adagio of Aegina and Harmodius	8'
3. Variation of Aegina and Bacchanalia	4'
4. Scene and Dance with Crotalums	4'
5. Dance of Gaditanae and Victory of Spartacus	6'

Russian

Spartacus: Suite No.2 <1955>   21'

3[1.2.3/pic] 3[1.2.Eh] 3[1.2.3/bcl] 2 — 4 3 3 1 — tmp+4 — hp — pf — str

perc: bd, cym, sus cym, sd, tri, tambn

1. Adagio of Spartacus and Phrygia	9'
2. Entrance of Merchants, Dance of a Roman Courtesan, General Dance	6'
3. Entrance of Spartacus, Quarrel, Treachery of Harmodius	5'
4. The Dance of the Pirates	1'

Russian

Spartacus: Suite No.3 <1955>   16'

3[1.2.pic] 3[1.2.Eh] 3[1.2.bcl] 2 — 4 3 3 1 — tmp+6 — hp — pf — str

perc: xyl, glock, tambn, sd, cym, sus cym, bd, tri, woodblk, tubaphone

1. Market	3'
2. Dance of a Greek Slave	2'
3. Dance of an Egyptian Girl	3'
4. Dance of Phrygia and the Parting Scene	5'
5. Sword Dance of Young Thracians	3'

Russian

Symphony No.2 (Symphony with a Bell; Simfoniya s kolokolom) <1943; rev 1944>   43'

3[1.2.3/pic] 3[1.2.Eh] 4[1.2.Ebcl.bcl] 2 — 4 3 3 1 — tmp+4 — hp — pf — str

perc: tamtam, xyl, glock, sd, chimes, woodblk, sus cym, cym, bd

Andante maestoso	13'
Allegro risoluto	9'
Andante sostenuto	11'
Andante mosso; Allegro sostenuto	10'

Russian

Symphony No.3 (Symphony-Poem) <1947>   24'

for full orchestra, organ and 15 trumpets
3[1.2.pic] 3[1.2.Eh] 2 2 — 4 3 3 1 — tmp+4 — hp — str
perc: sd, cym, bd, tamtam

Russian

The Valencian Widow: Suite <1940>   19'

2[1/pic.2/pic] 2 2 2 — 4 3 3 1 — tmp+3 — hp — cel — str
perc: sd, cym, xyl, glock, woodblk, bd, tri, cast

Suite from the incidental music for the play, *La viuda valenciana*, by Lope de Vega (1562-1635).

I. Introduction	3'
II. Serenade	4'
III. Song	2'
IV. Song (Dance) of Joke	3'
V. Intermezzo	2'
VI. Dance	5'

Sikorski	Zen-On

Khrennikov, Tikhon   1913-2007

(b Yelets, 28 May/10 June 1913; d Moscow, 14 Aug 2007). Russian

Concerto, Violin, op.14 <1958–1959>   20

3[1.2.pic] 2 3[1.2.bcl] 3[1.2.cbn] — 4 3 0 0 — tmp+4 — hp — pf/cel — str

1. Allegro non troppo; Allegro con brio	9'
2. Andante espressivo	6'
3. Allegro agitato	5'

Russian

Symphony No.1, op.4 <1933–1935>   18

3[1.2.pic] 2 2 2 — 4 2 3 1 — tmp+4 — cel — str
perc: bd, cym, glock, sd, tri

I. Allegro non troppo	6'
II. Adagio; molto expressivo	5'
III. Allegro molto	7'

Russian

Kilar, Wojciech   1932-2013

(b Lwów [now L'viv, Ukraine], 17 July 1932; d Katowice, 29 Dec 2013). Polish

Angelus (Ave Maria) <1984>   23

solo soprano   chorus
4[all/pic] 4 4 4[1.2.3.4/cbn] — 4 4 4 1 — 6perc — 2hp — cel, pf — str
perc: bd, sd, glock, chimes, cym, 2tri, 2gong, tmp
Text is a Polish translation of the antiphon *Ave Maria*.

PWM

Exodus <1979–1981>   23

chorus
4[1/pic.2/pic.3/pic.4/afl/pic] 4[1.2.3.4/Eh] 4[1.2.3.4/Ebcl/bcl] 4[1.2.3.4/cbn] — 6 6 6 1 — tmp+5 — 2hp[doubled if possible] — 2pf[1.2/cel] — str[18.16.14.12.10]
perc: bd, cym, tambn, chimes, guiro, thunder, 4sus cym, 2sd, 4tomtom, 6gong, 4woodblk

Chorus doesn't enter until about the last 100 bars of this 673-bar work.
    Score not totally clear about which woodwind parts have which auxiliaries; some adjustment may be needed for maximum convenience.

PWM

Krzesany <1974>   17

4[1.2.3/pic.4/pic] 4 4[1.2.3/Ebcl.4/Ebcl] 4[1.2.3/cbn.4/cbn] — 4 4 4 — 6perc — org[ad lib] — str[12.12.10.10.8]
perc: bd, cym, sd, 8tmp, 4tomtom, 4gong, 2cowbell; also as many as possible slgh-bells, herdbells, tri, crot, cowbells, etc.

PWM

Orawa <1986>   9

str[5.4.3.2.1]

PWM

Pan Tadeusz: Polonaise <1998>   5

3 3 3 2 — 4 3 3 0 — tmp+2 — str[16.12.12.8.8]
perc: cym, sd
Extract from the film score.

PWM

Kirchner, Leon

(b Brooklyn, NY, 24 Jan 1919; d Manhattan NY, 17 Sept 2009). American-born composer of Russian extraction

Concerto, Piano, No.1 <1953>
25'

3[1.2.pic] 3[1.2.Eh] 3[1.2.Ebcl] 3[1.2.cbn] — 4 3 3 1 — tmp+4 — cel — str

AMP

Concerto, Piano, No.2 <1963>
19'

3[1.2.pic] 3[1.2.Eh] 3[1.2.bcl] 3[1.2.cbn] — 4 3 3 1 — tmp+5 — cel — str

perc: glock, xyl, sd, td, tomtom, bd, crot, sus cym, tri, tamtam, templeblks, marac, chimes, metal blk, 4woodblk, 3bongos

AMP

Concerto, Violin, Violoncello, 10 Winds & Percussion <1960>
19'

1[1/pic] 1 1 2[1.cbn] — 1 2 2 0 — tmp+2 — cel — [no other str]

AMP

The Forbidden
12'

2 3[1.2.Eh] 2 2 — 4 3 3 1 — 4perc — pf/cel — str

perc: bd, sus cym, sd, tri, tamtam, xyl, vib, chimes, templeblks, 3tomtom, 3woodblk

Based on the composer's Piano Sonata (2003).

AMP

Music for Cello and Orchestra <1992>
18'

3[1.2.3/pic] 3[1.2.Eh] 3[1.2.bcl] 3[1.2.cbn] — 4 3 3 1 — tmp+4 — pf/cel — str

perc: bd, sd, td, tambn, tamtam, glock, xyl, chimes, crot, templeblks, claves, 3woodblk

AMP

Music for Flute and Orchestra <1978>
13'

3[1.2.3/pic] 3[1.2.Eh] 3[1.2.bcl] 3[1.2.cbn] — 4 3 3 1 — tmp+4 — hp — pf/cel/elec pf — str

AMP

Music for Orchestra <1969>
13'

3[1.2.3/pic] 3[1.2.Eh] 3[1.2.3/bcl] 3[1.2.cbn] — 4 3 3 1 — tmp+5 — pf/cel — str

AMP

Of Things Exactly as They Are <1997>
30'

solo soprano & baritone   chorus
3[1.2.3/pic] 3[1.2.Eh] 3[1.2.bcl] 3[1.2.cbn] — 4 3 3 1 — tmp+3 — hp — pf/cel — str

perc: bd, td, tri, tamtam, xyl, vib, chimes, crot, templeblks, bongos, claves, 2sus cym, 2sd, 2woodblk

AMP

Orchestra Piece (Music for Orchestra II) <1989>
10'

3[1.2.3/pic] 3[1.2.Eh] 3[1.2.bcl] 3[1.2.cbn] — 4 3 3 1 — tmp+4 — pf/cel — str

perc: bd, sus cym, sd, td, tri, tamtam, glock, chimes, crot, templeblks, bongos, claves, 2gong, 3woodblk

Original title: *Kaleidoscope.*

AMP

Toccata <1955>
14'

0 1 1 1 — 1 1 1 0 — 4perc — cel — str

perc: bd, sd, tamtam, tambn, td, woodblk, xyl

AMP

Kirk, Theron

(b Alamo, TX, 28 Sept 1919; d San Antonio, TX, 1 Oct 1999). American

An Orchestra Primer <1959>
13'

narrator
2[1/pic.2] 2 2 2 — 4 3 3 1 — tmp+2 — str
perc: sd, bd, tri, cym, glock, sus cym
Possible with reduced winds: 1/pic 1 2 1 — 3 2 1 0

Oxford

Klein, Gideon

(b Přerov, Moravia, 6 Dec 1919; d ?Fürstengrube, nr Katowice, Poland, end of Jan 1945). Moravian

Partita <1944>
17'

str
Originally (1944) for string trio; arranged for string orchestra (1990) by Vojtěch Saudek.
I. Allegro	4'
II. Variations on a Moravian Folk Song: Lento	10'
III. Molto vivace	3'

Bote

Kleinsinger, George

(b San Bernardino, CA, 13 Feb 1914; d New York, 28 July 1982). American

Tubby the Tuba <1942>
13'

solo tuba   narrator
2[1.2/pic] 1 2[1.2/opt bcl] 1 — 2 2 1 0 — tmp+1 — pf/cel — str
perc: sus cym, sd, woodblk, templeblks, xyl
Bcl part may be played on bn.

Music Theatre

Klengel, Julius

(b Leipzig, 24 Sept 1859; d Leipzig, 27 Oct 1933). German

Serenade, op.24, F major
26'

str

Breitkopf   Luck's

Knecht, Justin Heinrich

(b Biberach an der Riss, 30 Sept 1752; d Biberach an der Riss, 1 Dec 1817). German

Le portrait musical de la nature, ou Grande sinfonie (Pastoralsymphonie) <1784–1785>
28'

2 2 0 2 — 2 2 0 0 — tmp[opt] — str
The elaborate program of this symphony anticipates that of Beethoven's 6th, and it is said [*Oxford Dictionary of Music*, 2nd ed, 1994] that Beethoven would have known of it, since the program was printed in an advertisement on the cover of Beethoven's earliest published piano sonatas (1783).
I. Allegretto	10'
II. Tempo medemo	3'
III. Allegro molto	6'
IV. Tempo medemo	2'
V. L'inno con variazioni: Andantino	7'

Fleisher   Garland

Knehans, Douglas
1957-

(b St. Louis, MO, 3 Apr 1957). American/Australian

glow (double concerto for violin & clarinet)
31'

solo violin, solo clarinet
2[1.2/pic] 2 2 2 — 4 2 2 1 — tmp+2 — hp — str
perc: bd, sd, tri, tamtam, glock

I. Lyrical, floating	*12'*
II. Adagio lamentoso	*6'*
Cadenza	*6'*
III. (in a broken 4: 3+2+2+3 quavers)	*7'*

Armadillo

lamentation <2005>
10'

str[min 12.10.8.6.4]

Armadillo

… mist, memory, shadow…
8'

solo violin
str

Armadillo

ripple <2002>
13'

3[1.2.pic] 3[1.2.Eh] 3[cl.Ebcl.bcl] 3[1.2.cbn] — 4 2 2 1 — tmp+4 — pf — str
perc: bd, sd, tri, tambn, marim, vib, anvil

Armadillo

shoah requiem
120'

S,Ms,T,Bs-Bar soloists   chorus SATB
2[1/pic.2/pic] 2[1.2/Eh] 2 2 — 4 2 3 1 — tmp+2 — hp — str[min 12.10.8.6.4]
perc: bd, cym, sus cym, sd, tomtom, tri, tamtam, xyl, vib

1. introit/fear	*14'*
2. kyrie/the bear	*14'*
3. dies irae/blue	*8'*
4. liber scriptus	*3'*
5. quid sum miser/the pond	*7'*
6. rex tremendae	*7'*
7. recordare	*3'*
8. ingemisco	*3'*
9. the garden	*3'*
10. confutatis	*6'*
11. lacrymosa	*7'*
12. offertorium	*7'*
13. agnus dei/the legacy	*5'*
14. sanctus/benedictus	*5'*
15. lux aeterna	*4'*
16. libra me	*4'*
17. break down	*7'*

Armadillo

soar (concerto for cello & orchestra) <2006>
15'

solo violoncello
2[1.2/pic] 2 2 — 2 1 1 1 — tmp+1 — hp — str
perc: sd, glock, xyl

Armadillo

winter steps
11'

3[1.2.pic] 3[1.2.Eh] 3[1.2.bcl] 3[1.2.cbn] — 4 3 3 1 — tmp+3 — pf/cel — str[14.12.10.8.6]
perc: bd, cym, xyl, marim, whip

Armadillo

Knussen, Oliver
1952-

(b Glasgow, 12 June 1952). English

Choral, op.8 <1970–1972>
10

4[1.2.3.4/pic] 4[1.2.3.Eh] 5[1.2/Ebcl.3.4.cb cl] 4[1.2.3.cbn] — 4 3 4 2 — 2asx, tsx, bsx — 3perc — 1-4db
perc: sus cym, chimes, bongos, bd, glock, templeblks, td, crot, 2tamtams, Burmese gong, 2tomtoms, 2tri
4 extra horns may be substituted for saxophones. If possible, one additional Eh should be used to double the written Eh part in selected passages.

Gunmar

Fanfares for Tanglewood <1986>
2'

0 0 0 0 — 6 3 3 1 — 3perc — [no str]
perc: sus cym, 2tamtams, 2sets chimes
Hns 5&6 may be doubled, or may be replaced by Wagner tubas, euphoniums, etc. Percussion may be omitted completely (but not partially). Multiple conductors may be desirable.
    Instruments are divided into 3 groups, spatially separated. A juxtaposition of 3 independent fanfares (*Fanfare for the 80th Birthday of Sir Michael Tippett*; *Serenak Chorale*; Fanfare for the final scene of the opera *Higglety Pigglety Pop*).

Faber

Flourish with Fireworks, op.22 <1988; rev 1993>
4'

4[1.2.3.4/pic] 3[1.2.Eh] 4 3[1.2.cbn] — 4 3 3 1 — tmp+4 — hp — cel (dbl kybd glockenspiel ad lib) — str
perc: glock, tamtam, bd, tri, td, vib, whip, sd, 2sus cym, 3woodblks, coil spring

Faber

Symphony No.2, op.7 <1970–1971>
16'

high soprano solo
2 2 2 2 — 2 0 0 0 — 4perc (opt) — str[min 6.6.4.4.2]
perc: 4 bowed crotales [these parts may also be prerecorded or omitted]

1. [untitled]	*5'*
2. The Rats (Die Ratten)	*3'*
3. Edge	*4'*
4. To the Sister (An die Schwester)	*4'*

Faber

Where the Wild Things Are: Songs and a Sea-Interlude, op.20a <1979–1981>
17'

solo soprano
3[1.2.3/pic] 2[1.Eh] 3[1.2.3/Ebcl] 2[1.cbn] — 4 0 3 0 — 4perc — hp — pf 4-hands — str[min 6.6.4.4.4]
perc: vib, chimes, tri, templeblks, td, xyl, szl cym, marac, whip, glock, tamtam, tambn, claves, wnd mach, 4cowbells, 3sus cym, clogs (2 pr), anvil, 2bd, coil spring

Schirmer

Koch, Anton Peter
1972-

(b 1972). Australian

The Adventures of Sinbad: Overture <2006>
5'

3[1.2.pic] 2[1.Eh] 2 2[1.cbn] — 4 3 3 1 — tmp+5 — hp — str
perc: bd, cym, sus cym, szl cym, sd, tri, tambn, tamtam, glock, chimes, marktree, belltree, whip, bongos, congas, anvil

Wendel

Kodály, Zoltán

1882 - 1967

(b Kecskemet, 16 Dec 1882; d Budapest, 6 March 1967). Hungarian

Concerto for Orchestra <1939–1940>   21'

3[1.2.3/pic] 2 2 2 — 4 3 3 1 — tmp+1 — hp — str
perc: tri
1. Allegro risoluto	4'
2. Largo	8'
3. Tempo primo	5'
4. Largo	3'
5. Tempo primo	1'

Boosey

Dances of Galánta (Galántai táncok) <1933>   16'

2[1.2/pic] 2 2 2 — 4 2 0 0 — tmp+2 — str
perc: glock, sd, tri
I. Lento	5'
II. Allegretto moderato	3'
III. Allegro con moto, grazioso	1'
IV. Allegro	3'
V. Allegro vivace	4'

Universal

Dances of Marosszek (Marosszéki táncok) <1923–1927;   13'
rev (orchd) 1929>

2[1.2/pic] 2 2 2[1.cbn] — 4 2 0 0 — tmp+3 — str
perc: sd, cym, bd
Originally for piano; orchestrated for ballet 1929.
1.	2'
2.	1'
3.	2'
4.	3'
5.	1'
6.	1'
7.	1'
8.	2'

Universal

Háry János: Suite <1926–1927>   25'

3[1/pic.2/pic.3/pic] 2 2[1/Ebcl.2/asx] 2 — 4 6[3tp, 3crt] 3 1 —
cimbalom [or hpsd, or pf] — tmp+6 — cel, pf — str
perc: xyl, tambn, chimes, glock, sd, tri, cym, bd, tamtam
3 cornets in last mvt only.
I. Prelude; The Fairy Tale Begins	4'
II. The Viennese Musical Clock	2'
III. Song	6'
IV. The Battle and Defeat of Napoleon	4'
V. Intermezzo	5'
VI. Entrance of the Emperor and his Court	4'

Universal

Háry János: Intermezzo <1926–1927>   5'

3[fl3 opt] 2 2 2 — 4 3[tp3 opt] 0 0 — cimbalom [or hpsd, or pf] —
tmp+4 — str
perc: bd, sd, tri, cym

Luck's   Universal

Háry János: Song <1926–1927>   6'

1 1 1 0 — 2 0 0 0 — cimbalom [or hpsd, or pf] — str

Universal

Kállai kettös (Kálló Double Dance) <1937; rev 1950>   9'

chorus SATB
0 0 3[1.2.Ebcl] 0 — cimb — str
Originally a song for low voice & piano; arr. 1950 by the composer.

EMB

Missa brevis <1948>   31'

solos SATB   chorus
3[1.2.3/pic] 2 2 — 4 3 3 1 — tmp — opt org — str
Introitus	2'
Kyrie	3'
Gloria	5'
Credo	6'
Sanctus	2'
Benedictus	4'
Agnus Dei	6'
Ite, missa est	3'

Boosey

Psalmus hungaricus, op.13 <1923>   22'

solo tenor   chorus   opt boy choir
3 2 2 2 — 4 3 3 0 — tmp+1 — hp — opt org — str
perc: cym
1. Mikoron Dávid nagy búsultában	8'
2. Keserüségem annyi nem volna	6'
3. Te azért lelkem, gondolatodat	8'

Universal

Summer Evening (Nyári este) <1906; rev 1929-30>   16'

1 2[1.Eh] 2 2 — 2 0 0 0 — str

Universal

Symphony in C <1930s–1961>   29'

3[1.2.3/pic] 2 2 — 4 3 3 1 — tmp+1 — str
perc: cym, tri
Allegro	12'
Andante moderato	9'
Vivo	8'

Boosey

Te Deum (Budavári Te Deum) <1936>   21'

chorus   solos SATB
2 2 2 2 — 4 3 3 1 — tmp — opt org — str

Universal

Theater Overture (Szinházi nyitány) <1927; rev   12'
1929-32>

3[1.2.3/pic] 2 2 2 — 4 3 3 1 — tmp+4 — pf — str
perc: tri, sd, cym, bd
Also known as the *Overture for Háry János*.

Universal

Variations on a Hungarian Folksong (The Peacock;   25'
Felszállott a páva; Der Pfau flog) <1937–1939>

3[1.2.3/pic] 2[1.2/Eh] 2 2 — 4 3 3 0 — tmp+1 — hp — str
perc: glock, tri, cym
I. Con brio	_'
II. [No tempo indicated]	_'
III. Più mosso	_'
IV. Poco calmato	_'
V. Appassionato	_'
VI. Tempo (calmato)	_'
VII. Vivo	_'
VIII. Più vivo	_'
IX. [No tempo indicated]	_'
X. Molto vivo	_'
XI. Andante expressivo	_'
XII. Adagio	_'
XIII. Tempo di marcia funebre	_'
XIV. Andante; tempo rubato	_'
XV. Allegro giocoso	_'
XVI. Maestoso	_'
Finale	_'

Boosey

Koechlin, Charles
1867-1950

(b Paris, 27 Nov 1867; d Le Canadel, Var, 31 Dec 1950). French

Les Bandar-Log, op.176 (Scherzo des singes) <1939–1940>
15'

4[1.2.3/pic.pic] 3[1.2.Eh] 4[1.2.Ebcl.bcl] 3[1.2.cbn] — 4 4 4 1 — ssx, tsx — bugle in B-flat — tmp+9 — 2hp — cel, pf — str
perc: bd, cym, sus cym, sd, tamtam, tambn, tri, woodblk, gong, xyl, kybd glock
Symphonic poem after Kipling's *The Jungle Book*.

> Eschig

La course de printemps, op.95 <1908–1927>
28'

4[all/pic] 3[incl Eh,ob d'am] 3[incl bcl] 3[incl cbn] — 4 4 4 2 — 2tmp+3 — 2hp — cel, pf, org — str[min 14.12.10.8.8]
Symphonic poem after Kipling's *Second Jungle Book*.

> Eschig

Partita, op.205 <1945–1946>
16'

2[incl pic] 2[incl Eh] 2 2 — 1 1 0 0 — tmp — opt ondes martenot — str
  1.   2'
  2.   2'
  3.   4'
  4.   4'
  5.   4'

> Salabert

Kolb, Barbara
1939-

(b Hartford, CT, 10 Feb 1939). American

Chromatic Fantasy <1979>
13'

narrator (amplified)
1[afl (ampd)] 1 0 0 — 0 1 0 0 — ssx — elec gtr [or elec hpsd or elec pf] — vib (ampd) — [no str]
Text by Howard Stern.

> Boosey

Grisaille <1978–1979>
15'

4[1.2.3.pic] 3[1.2.Eh] 4[1.2.Ebcl.bcl] 3[1.2.cbn] — 4 3 3 1 — 5perc — str[12.12.8.8.6]
perc: chimes[D#], tamtam, 5sd

> Boosey

Soundings <1971–1972; rev 1975, 1978>
16'

3 3 3 3 — 3 0 0 0 — 2perc — 2hp — str[3.3.3.3.0]
perc: chimes
Divided into 2 orchestras, requiring 2 conductors. Also possible in a chamber version for pre-recorded tape and 11 players (1 conductor):
  1 1 1 1 — 1 0 0 0 — 1perc[chimes] — hp — str 4t

> Boosey

Voyants <1991>
21'

solo piano
2[1/pic.2] 1 1 1 — 1 1 1 0 — 1perc — str[or str 5t]
perc: vib, sus cym, timbales, sd, chimes

> Boosey

Korngold, Erich Wolfgang
1897-1957

(b Brno, 29 May 1897; d Hollywood, CA, 29 Nov 1957). Austrian

Baby-Serenade, op.24 <1928–1929>
20'

2[1.2/pic] 1 2[1/Ebcl.2/bcl] 1 — 1 3 1 0 — 2asx, tsx — bamjo (opt) — tmp+3 — hp — pf — str
perc: cym, sus cym, sd, tri, tambn, tamtam, glock, xyl, woodblk
Saxophone parts are cued in other instruments. Banjo plays in 1st mvt only.
  I. Ouvertüre: Baby tritt in die Welt
  II. Lied: Es ist ein braves Baby
  III. Scherzino: Es hat auch die schönsten Spielsachen
  IV. Jazz: Baby erzählt eine Geschichte
  V. Epilog: Und nun singt es in den Schlaf

> Schott

Captain Blood: Overture <1935>
3'

2 2 3[1.2.bcl] 2 — 4 4 3 1 — tmp — hp — str

> Warner

Concerto, Violin, op.35, D major <1937; rev 1945>
24'

2[1.2/pic] 2[1.2/Eh] 3[1.2.bcl] 2[1.2/cbn(2 notes only)] — 4 2 1 0 — tmp+2 — hp — cel — str
perc: glock, xyl, vib, cym, bd
  Moderato nobile   9'
  Romance: Andante   8'
  Finale: Allegro assai vivace   7'

> Schott

Märchenbilder, op.3 <1910>
22'

3[1.2.3/pic] 2 2 — 4 2 3 0 — tmp+2 — hp — str
perc: bd, cym, sus cym, sd, tri, tambn, tamtam, glock, xyl
Originally for piano; orchestrated by the composer.
  I. Die verzauberte Prinzessin (The Enchanted Princess)   3'
  II. Rübezahl (Ruler of the Spirits)   3'
  III. Wichtelmännlein (Goblins)   3'
  IV. Ball beim Märchenkönig (The Fairy King's Ball)   4'
  V. Das tapfere Schneiderlein (The Brave Little Tailor)   5'
  VI. Das Märchen spricht den Epilog (The Fairy Tale's Epilogue) 4'

> Schott

Military March, B-flat major (Militär-Marsch) <1917>
8'

2 2 2 2 — 4 2 3 0 — tmp+2 — hp — str
perc: bd/cym, cym, sus cym, sd, tri, glock

> Schott

Much Ado About Nothing, op.11 (Viel Lärmen um Nichts): Suite <1918–1919>
14'

1[1/pic] 1 1 1 — 2 1 1 0 — tmp+3 — hp — pf, harm — str 4t [may be doubled]
perc: bd, cym, sd, tri, tambn, tamtam, glock, chimes, ratch, rute
  1. Overture   5'
  2. Mädchen in Brautgemach [The Maiden in the Bridal Chamber] 3'
  3. Holzapfel und Schlehwein [Dogberry and Verges]   2'
  4. Intermezzo (Gartenszene) [Garden Scene]   2'
  5. Hornpipe [Masquerade]   2'

> Kalmus   Luck's   Schott

Schauspiel-Ouvertüre, op.4 (Dramatic Overture) <1911>
16'

3[1.2.pic] 2 3[1.2.bcl] 3[1.2.cbn] — 4 3 3 1 — tmp+3 — hp — str
perc: cym, tri, xyl

> Kalmus   Luck's   Schott

Der Schneemann (The Snowman): Overture <1908>   5'

2[1.2/pic] 2 2 2 — 4 2 3 0 — tmp+2 — hp — str
perc: tri, sd, glock, cym

The pantomime *Der Schneemann* by the 11-year-old Korngold was orchestrated by his teacher, Alexander Zemlinsky.

Kalmus	Luck's	Universal

Sinfonietta, op.5 <1912>   43'

3[1.2.3/pic] 2[1.2/Eh] 3[1.2.bcl] 3[1.2.cbn] — 4 3 3 1 — tmp+2 — 2hp — cel, pianino — str[16.16.12.12.8]
perc: sd, cym, glock, tri, chimes

1. Fliessend, mit heiterem Schwunge	11'
2. Scherzo: Molto agitato, rasch und feuerig	9'
3. Molto andante	8'
4. Finale: Patetico; Allegro giocoso	15'

Kalmus	Schott

Straussiana <1953>   6'

3[1.2.pic] 1[opt] 2 1[opt] — 2[opt] 2 2 0 — tmp+2 — opt hp — pf — str
perc: cym, sd, tri, glock

Kalmus	Schott

Symphonic Overture, op.13 (Sursum corda) <1919>   18'

3[1.2.3/pic] 3[1.2.Eh] 4[1.2.3.bcl] 3[1.2.cbn] — 4 4[1.2.3.btp] 3 1 — tmp+5 — 2hp — pf — str
perc: bd, cym, sus cym, sd, tri, tambn, tamtam, glock
String disposition:
    Violin I (14)
    Violin II (8)
    Violin III (8)
    Viola I (6)
    Viola II (6)
    Violoncello I (6)
    Violoncello II (6)
    Double Bass (8) — with C string

Kalmus	Schott

Symphonic Serenade in B-flat major, op.39 <1947>   35'

str[16.16.12.12.8]

1. Allegro moderato, semplice	10'
2. Intermezzo: Allegro molto	4'
3. Lento religioso	14'
4. Finale: Allegro con fuoco	7'

Schott

Symphony, op.40, F-sharp <1947–1952>   50'

3[1.2.3/pic] 2 3[1.2.bcl] 3[1.2.cbn] — 4 3 4 1 — tmp+2 — hp — pf/cel — str[12.14.10.10.8]
perc: bd, cym, sus cym, gong, glock, xyl, marim
Tmp must cover occasional perc notes.

I. Moderato ma energico	15'
II. Scherzo: Allegro molto	10'
III. Adagio	15'
IV. Finale: Allegro	10'

Schott

Theme and Variations, op.42 <1953>   7'

2 1[opt] 2 1[opt] — 2[opt] 2 2 0 — tmp+2 — opt hp — pf — str
perc: cym, sd, glock

Schott

Koussevitzky, Serge   1874-1951

(b Vïshniy Volochek, 26 July 1874; d Boston, 4 June 1951). American composer of Russian birth

Andante, op.1   3'

solo double bass
str

Accompaniment arr. for string orchestra by Norman Ludwin. Solo part written in G major; orchestration offered in A major or G major, depending on the tuning used by the soloist (solo scordatura or orchestral tuning). Specify key when ordering.

Ludwin

Chanson triste, op.2   3'

solo double bass
str

Accompaniment arr. for string orchestra by Norman Ludwin. Solo part written in D minor; orchestration offered in E minor or D minor depending on the tuning used by the soloist (solo scordatura or orchestral tuning). Specify key when ordering.

Ludwin

Concerto, Double Bass, op.3, F-sharp minor <1905>   17'

2 2 2 2 — 4 0 0 0 — tmp — hp — str
The solo double bass part is written in E minor, which sounds F# minor using the traditional solo scordatura.

I. Allegro	6'
II. Andante	6'
III. Allegro	5'

Boosey

Concerto, Double Bass, op.3, F-sharp minor (arr. Ludwin)   17'

2 2 2 2 — 4[hns3&4 opt] 2 0 0 — tmp — str
Orchestrated by Norman Ludwin, and offered either in F# minor (if the soloist is using solo tuning) or E minor (if orchestral tuning is used). In either case, the solo double bass part is written in E minor. Specify key when ordering.

I. Allegro	6'
II. Andante	6'
III. Allegro	5'

Ludwin

Concerto, Double Bass, op.3, F-sharp minor (arr. Meyer-Tormin) <1905>   17'

2 2 3[1.2.bcl] 2 — 3 2 0 0 — tmp — str
Orchestrated by Wolfgang Meyer-Tormin.
The solo double bass part is written in E minor, which sounds F# minor using the traditional solo scordatura.

I. Allegro	6'
II. Andante	6'
III. Allegro	5'

Forberg

Humoresque, op.4   3'

solo double bass
str

Accompaniment arr. for string orchestra by Norman Ludwin. Solo part written in G major; orchestration offered in A major or G major, depending on the tuning used by the soloist (solo tuning or orchestral tuning). Specify key when ordering.

Ludwin

Valse miniature, op.1, no.2   3'

solo double bass
str
Accompaniment arr. for string orchestra by Norman Ludwin. Solo part
written in G major; orchestration offered in A major or G major,
depending on the tuning used by the soloist (solo tuning or orchestral
tuning). Specify key when ordering.

> Ludwin

Kozeluch, Johann Antonin   1738-1814

(b Velvary, 14 Dec 1738; d Prague, 3 Feb 1814). Bohemian

Concerto, Bassoon, C major   18'

0 2 0 0 — 2 2 0 0 — tmp — str
I. Allegro   7'
II. Larghetto - Adagio   8'
III. Vivace   4'

> Elkan-Vogel   Musica Rara

Kraft, William   1923-

(b Chicago, 6 Sept 1923). American

Configurations; Concerto for 4 Percussionists & Jazz   16'
Orchestra <1968>

4 percussion soloists
2[1/pic.2/afl] 0 3[1.2.bcl] 0 — 2 3 3 1 — asx, tsx, bsx — elec gtr —
pf — 1db
perc: **1**: 4tmp, marim, xyl, tamtam, crot; **2**: glock, chimes, bd, 3woodblks,
templeblks; **3**: bd, vib, 6 graduated membranic drums; **4**: drum set
Above is a possible deployment of woodwinds and saxes suitable for a
symphony orchestra. The piece actually calls for 3 woodwind players
with extensive doublings: 1. pic/fl/cl/asx; 2. fl/afl/cl/tsx; 3. cl/bcl/bsx)
   This work is not to be confused with the composer's *Concerto for 4
Percussionists & Orchestra.*

> MCA

Contextures: Riots — Decade '60 <1967>   17'

offstage jazz quartet: ssx, tp, bass, drums
4[1.2.3.4/pic] 4[1.2.3.Eh] 4[1.2.3/Ebcl.4/bcl/asx] 4[1.2.3.4/cbn] — 4 4
4 1 — tmp+5 — hp — pf/cel — str[16.14.12.12.10]
perc: vib, chimes, td, xyl, marim, szl cym, tri, timbales, lionroar, templeblks, crot,
2bd, 4sd, 2pr bongos, 2anvils, 2bellplates[low chimes C3,D3], 4windchimes
(glass, bamboo, metal tubes, metal leaves), 6nipplegongs, 4tamtams, 3pr cym,
2sus cym, 2field dr, 6rototoms, 2woodblks, 2glock, 5 muted cowbells
Timpanist also covers many percussion instruments; one of the
percussionists can also play drumset in the offstage jazz quartet.
1. Adagio   2'
2. Prestissimo   4'
3. Con calore   3'
4. Presto   3'
5. Molto adagio   5'

> MCA

A Simple Introduction to the Orchestra <1958>   4'

narrator
4[1.2.3.pic] 4[1.2.3.opt Eh] 4[1.2.3.opt bcl] 4[1.2.opt 3.opt cbn] — 4 3
3 1 — tmp+3 — opt hp — opt pf — str
perc: bd, chimes, cym, field dr, glock, tri, xyl, whip
Fl 1-3 are also optional.

> Belwin

Three Miniatures for Percussion & Orchestra <1958>   14'

4 percussionist soloists
3[incl pic] 2 3[incl bcl] 3[incl cbn] — 4 3 3 1 — tmp+2 — str

> Belwin

Kraus, Joseph Martin   1756-1792

(b Miltenberg am Main, 20 June 1756; d Stockholm, 15 Dec 1792). German-Swedish
composer

Symphony, C minor (1783) <1783>   23'

0 2 0 2 — 4 0 0 0 — str
Ed. Richard Engländer.
1. Larghetto; Allegro   10'
2. Andante   6'
3. Allegro assai   7'

> Kalmus   Luck's   Nordiska

Der Tod Jesu (The Death of Jesus) <1776>   46'

solos SAB   chorus
0 0 0 0 — 2 2 0 0 — tmp — cnt — str
Ed. Bertil van Boer, Jr.
Introduzione	2'
Recitativo "Kommt! Geliebte, zur Schedelstädte"	2'
Aria, "Er starb!"	5'
Recitativo, "O weinet mit mir, Ihr Sterblichen!"	1'
Duetto, "Weine Sünder"	3'
Coral, "Jesus ruft dir"	2'
Recitativo, "Ja, man schleppte ihn vor der Richter"	3'
Intermezzo	6'
Coro, "Der Rächer kömmt"	4'
Recitativo, "An jenem Tage"	2'
Aria, "Sey ewig mir gesegnet"	8'
Recitativo, "Komm, gottseeliger Pilgrim!"	1'
Coral, "O Traurigkeit"	1'
Recitativo, "Sind wir frei von seinem Tode?"	1'
Aria, "Wenn einst die Ungewitter"	2'
[Alternate aria, "Wenn mich mein Heyland schützet"]	1'
Coro ultimo, "Erbarme dich unser"	2'

> A-R Editions

Kreisler, Fritz   1875-1962

(b Vienna, 2 Feb 1875; d New York, 29 Jan 1962). American violinist and composer
of Austrian birth

Liebesfreud   4'

0 0 2 2 — 2 0 0 0 — str
Originally for solo violin & piano; arranged by Clark McAlister for
orchestra alone. No.1 of *Three Old Viennese Dances*.

> Kalmus

Krenek, Ernst   1900-1991

(b Vienna, 23 Aug 1900; d Palm Springs, CA, 22 [or 23?] Dec 1991). American
composer of Austrian birth

Concerto, Organ, op.230 <1979>   10'

str

> Universal

Concerto, Piano, No.1, op.18, F-sharp major <1923>   30'

2 2 2 2 — 2 1 0 0 — str

> Universal

Concerto, Piano, No.2, op.81 <1937>   23'

2[1/pic.2/pic] 2 2[1.2/bcl] 2[1/cbn.2/cbn] — 4 2 2 1 — tmp+2 — str
perc: bd, cym, sus cym, sd, tri, tamtam, gong, glock, cast
Only 1 cbn plays at a time.

> Universal

Eleven Transparencies for Orchestra, op.142 (Elf Transparente) <1954>   20'

2[1.2/pic] 2 2 2 — 4 2 2 1 — tmp+2 — hp — str
perc: cym, glock, tri, woodblk, gong, xyl, sd, bd
Jointly published by Schott and Universal.

| Schott | Universal |

Kleine Symphonie, op.58 <1928>   15'

2 0 3[1/Ebcl.2/Ebcl/bcl.3] 2[1.2/cbn] — 0 3 2 1 — tmp+2 — hp — 2mand, gtr, 2banjo — str[no va, no vc; min 2vn, 2db]
perc: bd, cym, sus cym, sd, field dr, tri, cast
    I. Andante sostenuto; Allegro energico ma non troppo
    II. Andantino (poco lento)
    III. Allegretto, poco grave

| Universal |

Sinfonietta (The Brazilian; La Brasileira) <1952>   15'

str

| Universal |

Symphonic Elegy, op.105 <1946>   12'

str

| Elkan-Vogel | Luck's |

Symphony, op.137 (Pallas Athena) <1954>   21'

2[1.2/pic] 2 2[1.2/bcl] 2[1.2/cbn] — 4 2 2 0 — tmp+3 — hp — cel/pf — str
perc: sd, bd, field dr, cym, sus cym, tambn, tri, woodblk, ratch, xyl, wood drum, 2gongs
Jointly published by Schott and Universal.

| Schott | Universal |

Kubik, Gail   1914-1984

(b South Coffeyville, OK, 5 Sept 1914; d West Covina, CA, 20 July 1984). American

Divertimento I for Thirteen Players <1958>   16'

1[1/pic] 1[1/Eh] 1[1/bcl] 1 — 1 1 1 0 — tmp — pf/hpsd — vn, va, vc, db

| MCA |

Gerald McBoing Boing <1950>   9'

solo percussion   narrator
1 1 1 1 — 1 1 0 0 — pf — va, vc
perc: 2tmp, sd, td, bd, tomtom, sus cym, cym, tamtam, thundersheet, templeblks, cowbell, tri, cast, tambn, ratch, whip, xyl, glock, vib, 2woodblks [substitutions possible for many of the perc insts]
Narrator plays a few notes.

| Presser | Luck's | Southern |

Symphony concertante <1951; rev 1953>   25'

solos: trumpet, viola, piano
2[1.2/pic] 2 2[1.2/bcl] 2[1.2/cbn] — 2 1 1 0 — 1perc — str

| Peer |

Kuhlau, Friedrich   1786-1832

(b Uelzen, nr Hanover, 11 Sept 1786; d Copenhagen, 12 March 1832). Danish composer of German birth

Concertino, 2 Horns & Orchestra, op.45, F minor <1821>   23'

2 2 2 2 — 2 2 1 0 — tmp — str

| Fleisher | Hofmeister | Musica Rara |

Concerto, Piano, op.7, C major <1812>   30'

1 2 2 2 — 2 2 0 0 — tmp — str

| Samfundet |

William Shakespeare, op.74: Overture <1826>   11'

2[1.2/pic] 2 2 2 — 4 2 1 0 — tmp+2 — str
perc: bd, cym, tri

| Samfundet |

Kuhnau, Johann   1660-1722

(b Geising, Erzgebirge, 6 April 1660; d Leipzig, 5 June 1722). German

Uns ist ein Kind geboren
    see: Bach, Johann Sebastian, 1685-1750
        Cantata no.142

Kurka, Robert   1921-1957

(b Cicero, IL, 22 Dec 1921; d New York, 12 Dec 1957). American composer of Czech descent

The Good Soldier Schweik: Suite <1956>   19'

2[1.pic] 2[1.Eh] 2[1.bcl] 2[1.cbn (or db)] — 3 2 1 0 — tmp+1 — [no str]
Double bass may substitute for contrabassoon.
    1. Overture   3'
    2. Lament   4'
    3. March   3'
    4. War Dance   2'
    5. Pastoral   4'
    6. Finale   3'

| Weintraub |

Kurtág, György   1926-

(b Lugoj, Romania, 19 Feb 1926). Hungarian

Concerto, Viola <1953–1954>   19'

2 2 2 2 — 3 2 0 0 — tmp — str
The first movement may be performed independently under the title "Movement for Viola and Orchestra."
    1. Allegro molto moderato e poco rubato   12'
    2. Allegro molto   7'

| EMB |

Movement for Viola and Orchestra <1953–1954>   12'

2 2 2 2 — 3 2 0 0 — tmp — str
The first movement of the composer's Viola Concerto, when performed as an independent work.

| EMB |

Kuster, Kristin   1973-

(b 1973). American

Iron Diamond <2005>   6'

3[1.2.pic] 2 2 2 — 4 3 3 1 — tmp+3 — str
perc: bd, sd, td, brake dr, tri, tambn, xyl, vib, chimes, 3sus cym, sandblocks, 4tomtom

| Kuster |

L

Lachenmann, Helmut   1935-

(b Stuttgart, 27 Nov 1935). German

"… zwei Gefühle… ", Musik mit Leonardo ("… Two   23'
Feelings… ", Music with Leonardo) <1992>

2 narrators [slightly ampd; possible with 1, but not preferred]
2[afl/fl/pic.bfl] 1[Eh] 2[bcl.cbcl] 1[cbn] — 0 2 1 1 — gtr[slightly
ampd] — 2tmp/perc — hp — pf[plus 1 "lid lifter"] — str[2.0.2.2.1]
perc: Played by 2 timpanists: 2tamtams, large tomtom[or bd]

> Breitkopf

Laderman, Ezra   1924- 2015

(b Brooklyn, NY, 29 June 1924; d 28 Feb 2015). American

Concerto for Orchestra <1968>   22'

3[1.2.3/pic] 3[1.2.3/Eh] 3[1.2.3/bcl] 3[1.2.cbn] — 4 3 3 1 — tmp+5
— hp — cel — str
perc: bd, chimes, cym, glock, tambn, tamtam, tomtom, tri, vib, woodblk, xyl

I. Sections	11'
II. Variations	4'
III. Combinations	7'

> Presser

Concerto, Clarinet <1994>   28'

str

I. Andante	11'
II. Allegro	3'
III. Andante	9'
IV. Allegro assai	5'

> Schirmer

Concerto, Flute <1985>   29'

3[1.2.3/pic] 3[1.2.Eh] 3[1.2.bcl] 3[1.2.cbn] — 4 2 3 0 — tmp+3 — hp
— str
perc: bd, cym, sus cym, sd, tambn, tamtam, glock, xyl, marim, vib, woodblk,
templeblks

I. Moderato	_'
II. Andante	_'
III. Allegro	_'

> Schirmer

Magic Prison <1967>   25'

2 narrators (one female, one male)
2[1.2/pic] 2 3[1.2.bcl] 2 — 4 3 3 0 — tmp+2 — hp — cel, org — str
perc: tri, sus cym, glock, sd, field dr, cym, tambn
Text selected by Archibald MacLeish from the poems and letters of
Emily Dickinson and the recollections of T.W. Higginson.

> Presser

Symphony No.7 <1984>   40'

3[1.2.3/pic/afl] 3[1.2.3/Eh] 3[1.2.3/bcl] 3[1.2.cbn] — 4 3 3 1 —
tmp+3 — str
perc: vib, marim, sd, woodblk, templeblks, bd, cym, tambn, whip, wind machine,
tomtom, 2tamtam, 2xyl, 2glock

I. Moderato con mysterioso	_'
II. Allegro con brio e leggiero	_'
III. Andante grazioso	_'
IV. Allegro ma non troppo	_'

> Schirmer

Lajtha, László   1892-1963

(b Budapest, 30 June 1892; d Budapest, 16 Feb 1963). Hungarian

Suite No.3, op.56 <1952>   30'

2[1.2/pic] 2 2 2 — 4 2 0 0 — tmp+5 — 2hp — cel — str
perc: cym, sd, field dr, bd, templeblks, chimes, glock, tri

> Leduc

Lalande, Michel-Richard de   1657-1726

(b Paris, 15 Dec 1657; d Versailles, 18 June 1726). French

Symphonie de Noël (Christmas Symphony;   10'
Weihnachtssinfonie)

2[or 2ob] 0 0 1 — cnt — str
Ed. F. Schroeder.

> Luck's   Vieweg

Lalo, Édouard   1823-1892

(b Lille, 27 Jan 1823; d Paris, 22 April 1892). French

Concerto, Piano, F minor <1889>   23'

2 2 2 2 — 4 4 3 0 — tmp — str

> Heugel   Kalmus   Luck's

Concerto, Violin, op.20, F major <1873>   27'

3[1.2.pic] 2 2 — 2 2 3 0 — tmp+1 — str
perc: tri
Pic & tri in Finale only.

Part I: Andante - Allegro non troppo	15'
Part II: Romance	6'
Final - Allegro con fuoco	6'

> Durand   Kalmus   Luck's

Concerto, Violoncello, D minor <1877>   26'

2 2 2 2 — 4 2 3 0 — tmp — str
Bärenreiter ed. by Hugh Macdonald.

I. Prélude: Lento - Allegro maestoso	13'
II. Intermezzo: Andantino con moto - Allegro presto	6'
III. Introduction: Andante - Allegro vivace	7'

> Bärenreiter   Bote & Bock   Kalmus   Luck's

Namouna: Ballet Suite No.1 <1882>   25'

2 2 2 4 — 4 4 3 1 — tmp+3 — 2hp — str
perc: tri, sd, cym, bd

1. Prélude	7'
2. Sérénade	3'
3. Thème varié	6'
4. Parade de foire	5'
5. Fête foraine	4'

> Hamelle   Kalmus   Luck's

Namouna: Ballet Suite No.2 <1882>   15'

2[1.2/Eh] 2[1/Eh.2/Eh] 2 4 — 4 4 3 1[oph] — tmp+3 — 2hp — str
perc: tri, cast, sus cym, sd, bd, tambn prov

1. Danse marocaine	3'
2. Mazurka	3'
3. Dolce far niente (La sieste)	4'
4. Pas des cymbales	3'
5. Danse des esclaves	2'

Hamelle	Kalmus	Luck's

Rapsodie norvégienne (Norwegian Rhapsody) <1879>   10'

3[1.2.pic] 2 2 2 — 4 4 3 1[oph] — tmp+2 — hp — str
perc: bd, tambn, tri
Also known as *Rapsodie pour orchestre.*

Bote & Bock	Kalmus	Luck's

Le roi d'Ys: Overture <1875–1888>   11'

2 2 2 4[2 real parts] — 4 4[2tp, 2crt] 3 1 — tmp+2 — str
perc: sd, bd
Newly engraved Kalmus edition (ed. Clinton F. Nieweg & Nancy M. Bradburd, 2010) cues bn 3-4 into bn 1-2, so that the 3rd & 4th player are optional.

Heugel	Kalmus	Luck's

Symphonie espagnole, op.21 <1874>   33'

solo violin
3[1.2.pic] 2 2 2 — 4 2 3 0 — tmp+2 — hp — str
perc: sd, bd
A 2006 Breitkopf "Urtext" edition by Christian Rudolf Riedel makes use of new sources to resolve previous discrepancies & problems.

I. Allegro non troppo	8'
II. Scherzando: Allegro molto	4'
III. Intermezzo: Allegretto non troppo	6'
IV. Andante	7'
V. Rondo	8'

Breitkopf	Durand	Kalmus	Luck's

Lambert, Constant   1905-1951

(b London, 23 Aug 1905; d London, 21 Aug 1951). English

Les Patineurs

see: Meyerbeer, Giacomo (1791-1864)
      Patineurs

Rio Grande   15'

solo piano   chorus   solo alto
0 0 0 0 — 0 4 3 1 — tmp+4 — str
perc: bd, cym, sus cym, sd, td, tamtam, cast, tri, tambn, woodblk, cowbell, xyl

Oxford

La Montaine, John   1920-2013

(b Chicago, 17 March 1920; d Hollywood, CA, 29 April 2013). American

Birds of Paradise, op.34 <1964>   13'

solo piano
3[1.2.pic] 3[1.2.Eh] 2 2 — 4 3 3 1 — tmp+3 — hp — str

C. Fischer

Concerto, Piano, op.9 <1958>   25'

3[1.2.pic] 3[1.2.Eh] 3[1.2.bcl] 3[1.2.cbn] — 4 3 3 0 — tmp+2 — str

Galaxy

Songs of the Rose of Sharon, op.6 <1956>   15'

solo soprano
2 2 2 3[1.2.cbn] — 4 2 3 1[opt] — tmp[opt] — hp — str
Tuba and timpani are optional.

Broude Bros.

A Summer's Day; Sonnet for Orchestra, op.32 <1964>   5'

1 1 1 0 — 1 1 0 0 — tmp — hp — str

Luck's	Schirmer

Lang, David   1957-

(b Los Angeles, 8 Jan 1957). American

Grind to a Halt <1996>   11'

3[1.2.pic] 3 3[1.2.bcl] 3[1.2.cbn] — 4 3 3 1 — tmp+4 — hp — pf — str
perc: vib, chimes, marim, brake dr, xyl, glock, 2bd

Red Poppy

how to pray <2002>   8'

3 2 3[1.2.bcl] 3 — 4 3 3 1 — tmp+3 — pf — str
perc: vib, marim, bd

Red Poppy

International Business Machine; An Overture for Tanglewood <1990>   5'

3[1.2.pic] 3 3 3 — 4 3 3 1 — 4perc — hp — cel — str
perc: glock, tri, chimes, bd, thunder, tamtam, 4metal pipe, 4brake dr, 2sus cym

Red Poppy

loud love songs <©2004>   15'

solo percussionist
1 2 2 2 — 2 1 1 1 — tmp+3 — pf — str
perc: bd, glock, vib, tamtam, tri, 3brake dr, 5 "nasty metals"
soloist: 7 graduated tambourines, 1 bell (D-flat5), "woodthing" (3 tiny woodblocks)

Red Poppy

statement to the court <2010>   10'

chorus
bd — str
The parts marked "solo women" or "solo men" are each to be performed by a different singer of the chorus. The bass drum may be played by a percussionist or by a member of the bass section of the chorus.

Red Poppy

Langgaard, Rued Immanuel   1893-1952

(b Copenhagen, 28 July 1893; d Ribe, 10 July 1952). Danish

Music of the Spheres (Sfaerernes Musik; Sphärenmusik; L'harmonie des sphères) <1916–1918>   36'

solos SAA   Chorus SSAATTTBB
4[1.2.3.4/pic] 3[1.2.3/Eh] 3 3 — 8 3 3 1 — 4tmp+2 — org, pf — str
perc: cym, tamtam, chimes [pealing of bells]
Distant orchestra, in addition to the above:
    2 1 2 0 — 1 0 0 0 — tmp — hp — str
    Solo soprano is also with the distant orchestra. Piano (main orchestra) is termed a "glissando-piano."

Hansen

Sphinx (Sfinx) <1909–1910; rev 1913>   9'

3 3[1.2.Eh] 3[1.2.bcl] 3 — 4 3 4 1 — tmp — str

Hansen

Symphony No.7 <1925–1926; rev 1930-32>   18'

3[1.2.pic] 3 3 3 — 4 3 3 1 — tmp+2 — hp — str
perc: tri, tamtam, cym

I. Maestoso fiero	4'
II. Allegro moderato maestoso	7'
III. Scherzoso grazioso	3'
IV. Fastoso allegro	4'

> Hansen

Lankester, Michael   1944-

(b London, 1944). English

Make Your Own Orchestra; A Piece for Home-Made Instruments & Orchestra <1984>   15'

2 2 2 2 — 3 2 0 1 — 3perc — hp — str
Orchestra members also play instruments made from junk: hosepipe in F (1st hn); bamboo flute (1st fl); tuned bottles (2perc); drinking straws (1st ob); washtub/broomstick bass (principal db).

> MMB

A Pocket-Sized Guide to the Orchestra (The Time-Machine, Part 1) <1989>   8'

narrator (rap style)
1[1/pic] 1 1 1 — 2 1 1 0 — 1perc — str
perc: sd, woodblk, templeblks, bongos, cowbell, tri, set, 3tomtoms, autohorn
Instruments are introduced and enter the stage one by one.

> MMB

Lanner, Joseph   1801-1843

(b St Ulrich, Vienna, 11 April 1801; d Oberdöbling, nr Vienna, 14 April 1843). Austrian

Die Schönbrunner Walzer, op.200 <1842>   7'

2[1.pic] 1 2 1 — 2 2 1 1 — tmp+2 — str

> Kalmus   Luck's

Die Werber Walzer, op.103 <1835>   7'

2[1.pic] 1 2 1 — 2 2 1 0 — tmp+1 — str

> Luck's

Laparra, Raoul   1876-1943

(b Bordeaux, 13 May 1876; d Suresnes, 4 April 1943). French

Un dimanche basque (A Basque Sunday) <1922>   15'

solo piano
3[1.2.pic] 2[1.2/Eh] 2 2 — 4 4 3 1 — tmp+2 — 2hp — opt org — str

Vers l'église (Toward the Church)	6'
Au jeu de pelote (At the Game of Pelote)	4'
Devant une maison blanche (In Front of a White House)	3'
A la fête (At the Feast).	2'

> Choudens   Fleisher

La habanera: Prélude <1908>   5'

3[1/pic.2/pic.3/pic] 3[1.2.3/Eh] 3[1.2.bcl] 3[1.2.cbn] — 4 4 3 1 — tmp+3 — hp — str

> Enoch   Fleisher

La habanera: Three Entr'actes <1908>   7'

2 3[1.2.Eh] 3[1.2.bcl] 3[1.2.cbn] — 4 2 3 1 — tmp+2 — hp — str
perc: bd, cym
One hp part, though the score uses the plural ("*harpes*"). Trumpets play only 3 bars (mvt 2) and are otherwise tacet.

1. Doloroso e appassionato	2'
2. Tempo di havanera	2'
3. A Bad Night: Andantino	3'

> Enoch   Fleisher

Rythmes espagnols <1914; rev (orchd) 1932>   10'

2[1.2/pic] 2[1.2/Eh] 2 2 — 4 4 3 1 — tmp+2 — 2hp — str
perc: bd, cym, sd, tri, cast
Originally for harp; later orchestrated by the composer.

Paseo	2'
Petenera	1'
Tientos	2'
Rueda	3'
Calesera	2'

> Enoch   Fleisher

Suite italienne <1929>   9'

solo trumpet
3[1.2.pic] 2[1.2/Eh] 2 2 — 2 0 0 0 — tmp+1 — 2hp — str

Préambule	_'
Le Lac tranquille (Nemi)	_'
Burla du fol	_'

> Ricordi

Larsen, Libby   1950-

(b Wilmington, DE, 24 Dec 1950). American

The Atmosphere As a Fluid System <1992>   14'

solo flute
3perc — str

> Oxford

Mary Cassatt; Seven Songs   29'

solo mezzo-soprano   solo trombone
3[1.2.3/pic] 2 2 2 — 4 2 0 1 — tmp+2 — hp — str
2 slide projectors with a dissolve unit to project 15 slides of Mary Cassatt's paintings; exact slides and fades are shown in score.

1. To Be a Painter	_'
2. Travels	_'
3. Franco-Prussian War	_'
4. Early Work	_'
5. Degas	_'
6. Maturity	_'

> Oxford

Northern Star Fanfare   1'

0 0 0 0 — 4 3 3 1 — [no str]

> ECS

Overture for the End of a Century <1994>   6'

3[1.2.pic] 2 2 2 — 4 3 3 1 — tmp+3 — pf — str
perc: tambn, sd, sus cym, woodblk, xyl, tri, glock, bongos, marim, 2tomtoms

> Oxford

Solo Symphony (Symphony No.5) <1999>   30'

3[1.2.pic] 2 3[1.2.bcl] 2 — 4 3 3 1 — elec bass — tmp+3 — pf — str

1. Solo-Solos	9'
2. One Dancer, Many Dancers	10'
3. Once Around	3'
4. The Cocktail Party Effect	6'

> Oxford

String Symphony (Symphony No.4) <1999>   23'

str
Elegance	*6'*
Beauty Alone	*10'*
Ferocious Rhythm	*7'*

> Oxford

Larsson, Lars-Erik   1908-1986

(b Åkarp, Skåne, 15 May 1908; d Helsingborg, 26 Dec 1986). Swedish

Concertino, Horn, op.45, no.5 <1955>   13'

str
I. Allegro moderato	*4'*
II. Lento cantabile	*4'*
III. Allegro vivace	*5'*

> Gehrmans

Concertino, Trumpet, op.45, no.6 <1953>   7'

str
I. Allegro moderato	*2'*
II. Ritornell: Andante semplice	*3'*
III. Allegro risoluto	*2'*

> Gehrmans

Concertino, Trombone, op.45, no.7 <1955>   12'

str
1. Prelude	*5'*
2. Aria	*3'*
3. Finale	*4'*

> Gehrmans

Lauridsen, Morten   1943-

(b Colfax WA, 1943). American

O magnum mysterium <1994>   6'

str
Originally for chorus *a cappella*; transcribed for string orchestra by
Sandra Dackow.

> Peer

Lavista, Mario   1943-

(b Mexico City, 3 April 1943). Mexican

Clepsidra <1990>   10'

3[1.2.pic] 3[1.2.Eh] 3[1.2.bcl] 2 — 4 2 2 0 — 1perc — hp — cel —
str
perc: tamtam

> Peer

Lazarof, Henri   1932-

(b Sofia, Bulgaria, 12 April 1932; d Los Angeles, 29 Dec 2013). American composer
of Bulgarian origin

Chamber Symphony <1976>   18'

1[fl/afl] 2[1/Eh.2] 0 2 — 2 0 0 0 — str[8.6.4.4.2]
I. quarter-note = 50	
II. quarter-note = 60	
III. dotted quarter-note = 88	

> Merion

Concerto for Orchestra <1977>   21'

4[incl 2pic] 4[incl 2Eh] 4[incl bcl] 4[incl cbn] — 6 4 4 1 — tmp+3 —
2hp — cel, pf — str

> Merion

Poema <1985>   14'

3 3[1.2.3/Eh] 3[1.2.3/bcl] 3 — 4 3 3 1 — tmp+3 — hp — pf/cel — str
perc: glock, chimes, tamtam, 3vib
Timpanist covers glock, chimes, tamtam.

> Merion

Symphony No.7 <2000>   16'

3 3 3 3 — 4 3 3 1 — tmp+3 — hp — pf — str
perc: bd, sd, tomtom, tamtam, glock, xyl, marim, vib, chimes, bongos, claves, 2sus
cym, 2woodblks

> Merion

Tableaux <1989>   27'

solo piano
4[1.2.3.4/pic/afl] 4[1.2.3.4/Eh] 4[1.2.3.4/bcl] 4[1.2.3.4/cbn] — 6 4 6 1
— tmp+4 — hp — pf, cel/harm — str[16.14.12.10.10]
perc: sd, bd, sus cym, chimes, td, templeblks, tambn, tamtam, marim, 8bongos,
3woodblk, 5tomtom, 3tri, 2vib, 2glock
After Kandinsky.

> Merion

Leclair, Jean-Marie [l'aîné]   1697-1764

(b Lyons, 10 May 1697; d Paris, 22 Oct 1764). French

Concerto, Violin, op.7, no.4, F major   14'

cnt — str
Ed. Claude Crussard.
I. Allegro moderato	*5'*
II. Adagio	*5'*
III. Allegro	*4'*

> Foetisch

Concerto, Violin, op.7, no.5, A minor   15'

cnt — str
Ed. Hugo Ruf.
1. Vivace	*6'*
2. Largo; Adagio	*4'*
3. Allegro	*5'*

> Luck's   Nagel

Sonata, D major (arr.)   10'

str
Transcribed for string orchestra by Held.

> Kalmus

Lee, James III   1975-

(b St. Joseph, MI, 26 Nov 1975). American

Beyond Rivers of Vision <2005>   13'

2 3[1.2.Eh] 2 3[1.2.cbn] — 4 3 3 1 — tmp+3 — hp — cel/pf — str
perc: bd, cym, sus cym, tomtom, tambn, glock, xyl, marim, vib, chimes, 3tri, glass
windchimes, 2tamtams, 4woodblks
I. Hiddekel	*3'*
II. The 24th Day of Abib	*5'*
III. ...and on either side of the river	*5'*

> Subito

A Different Soldier's Tale <2008>   23'

3[1.2.pic] 3[1.2.Eh] 3[1.2.bcl] 3[1.2.cbn] — 4 3 3 1 — tmp+3 — hp — cel/pf — str

perc: glock, tambn, tamtam, marim, sd, xyl, woodblk, vib, bd, templeblks, tri, cym, sus cym, glass windchimes, 3tomtom

I. Vigilant Patrol   _'
II. I Must Survive   _'
III. Capture! Funeral?   _'
IV. Celebration on Broad Street   _'

Subito

Lees, Benjamin   1924-2010

(b Harbin, China, 8 Jan 1924; d Glen Cove, NY, 31 May 2010). American composer of Russian parentage

Concerto, Brass Choir & Orchestra <1983>   20'

soloists: 4 horns, 3 trumpets, 3 trombones, tuba
3[1.2/pic.3/pic] 0 0 0 — tmp+4 — cel — str

Boosey

Concerto for Chamber Orchestra <1966>   17'

2[1/pic.2/pic] 2[1.2/Eh] 2[1.2/bcl] 2[1.2/cbn] — 2 2 0 0 — 1perc [incl tmp] — str

perc: cym, tri, bd, sd, tmp

Boosey

Concerto for Orchestra <1959>   22'

3[1.2.3/pic] 3[1.2.3/Eh] 3[1.2.3/bcl] 3[1.2.3/cbn] — 4 3 3 1 — tmp+4 — pf/cel — str

perc: xyl, cym, woodblk, bd, sd

Boosey

Concerto, Horn <1992>   25'

3[1.2/pic.3/pic] 3 3[1.2.3/bcl] 3[1.2.3/cbn] — 4 3 3 1 — tmp+2 — cel — str

perc: glock, tamtam, chimes, bd, sd

Boosey

Concerto, Oboe <1963>   17'

2[1.2/pic] 0 2 2 — 2 0 0 0 — tmp+1 — str

perc: cym, sus cym, tri, woodblk, tambn

Boosey

Concerto, Piano, No.2 <1966>   22'

3[1.2.3/pic] 3 3[1.2.3/bcl] 3[1.2.3/cbn] — 4 3 3 1 — tmp+3 — str

perc: glock, xyl, cym, sus cym, tamtam, tri, bd, sd, anvil, 2woodblks

Boosey

Concerto, String Quartet & Orchestra <1964>   22'

solos: 2vn, va, vc
2[1.2/pic] 2[1.2/Eh] 2 2 — 4 3 3 1 — tmp+3 — str

perc: glock, xyl, cym, tri, bd, sd

Allegro con brio   8'
Andante cantando   8'
Allegro energico   6'

Boosey

Concerto, Violin <1958>   24'

3[1.2.3/pic] 3[1.2.3/Eh] 3[1.2.3/bcl] 3[1.2.cbn] — 4 3 3 1 — tmp+2 — str

perc: xyl, cym, sus cym, tamtam, tri, woodblk, bd, sd, tambn

I. Andante con brio   11'
II. Adagio   8'
III. Allegro giusto   5'

Boosey

Passacaglia <1975>   12'

3[1.2.pic] 2 2 3[1.2.3/cbn] — 4 3 3 1 — tmp+3 — pf — str

perc: sd, bd, cym, sus cym, tamtam, templeblks, woodblk, glock, xyl, chimes

Boosey

Scarlatti Portfolio <1979>   25'

2 2 2 2 — 2 2 1 0 — tmp+1 — str

perc: sd, bd, cast, tambn, tri, glock

"Transformation" of seven keyboard sonatas by Domenico Scarlatti: Longo nos. 58, 465, 382, 104, 64, 282, 499 (= Kirkpatrick nos. 64, 96, 69, 159, 148, 133, 30, respectively).

Boosey

Spectrum <1964>   10'

2[1/pic.2/pic] 2 2 2 — 2 2 1 0 — tmp+1 — pf — str

perc: glock, cym, sus cym, tri

Boosey

Symphony No.2 <1958>   26'

2[1.2/pic] 2[1.2/Eh] 2 2 — 4 3 3 1 — tmp+3 — hp — str

perc: xyl, cym, bd, sd

I. Andante mesto - Vivo   11'
II. Scherzo   8'
III. Adagio   7'

Boosey

Symphony No.3 <1969>   29'

3[1.2.3/pic] 3[1.2.3/Eh] 3[1.2.3/bcl] 3[1.2.3/cbn] — 5 4 3 1 — tsx — tmp+3 — cel — str

perc: glock, sus cym, tamtam, templeblks, woodblk, bd, sd

1. Interlude   2'
2. Andante; Allegro, molto risoluto   9'
3. Interlude   2'
4. Andante; Allegro molto, affonosamente   3'
5. Interlude   2'
6. Andante; Molto calmo   11'

Boosey

Symphony No.5 (Kalmar Nyckel) <1986>   26'

3[1.2/pic.3/pic] 3 3[1.2.3/bcl] 3[1.2.3/cbn] — 4 3 3 1 — tmp+4 — hp — cel — str

perc: xyl, glock, chimes, bd, sd, cym, woodblk, field dr, tri, cast, tambn

Boosey

The Trumpet of the Swan <1972>   17'

narrator
2[1.2/pic] 2[1.2/Eh] 2 2 — 4 3 3 1 — tmp+4 — str

perc: xyl, cym, sus cym, tamtam, tri, bd, sd, tambn, pane of glass, pistol

Boosey

Leeuw, Reinbert de   1938-

(b Amsterdam, 8 Sept 1938). Dutch

Abschied; Symphonic Poem <1973>   19'

4[1.2.3/pic.4/pic] 4 5[1.2.3/bcl.Ebcl.bcl] 5[1.2.3.4.cbn] — 8 5 4 2 — asx, tsx — tmp+6 — 2hp — pf — str

Donemus

Leeuw, Ton de   1926-1996

(b Rotterdam, 16 Nov 1926; d Paris, 31 May 1996). Dutch

Mouvements retrograde <1957>   13'

3[1.2.pic] 3[1.2.3/Eh] 3[1.2.3/bcl] 3[1.2.cbn] — 4 3 3 1 — tmp+3 — hp — pf/cel — str

Donemus

Lehár, Franz   **1870-1948**

(b Komáron, Hungary, 30 April 1870; d Bad Ischl, 24 Oct 1948). Austro-Hungarian

Gold und Silber Walzer, op.79 (Gold and Silver Waltz)   8'
<1902>

2[1/pic.2/pic] 2 2 2 — 4 2[crt1.crt2] 3 1[opt] — opt asx, opt tsx —
tmp+3 — hp — str

perc: bd, cym, sd, tri, gong, glock

Kalmus provides parts for tuba and saxes, but they are not shown in the
score; they are believed to be a late addition (1930) by Lehar.

| Kalmus | Luck's |

Die lustige Witwe (The Merry Widow): Overture   9'
<1905>

3[1.2/pic.3/pic] 3[1.2.Eh] 3[1.2.bcl] 3[1.2.cbn] — 4 2 3 1 — tmp+4
— hp — cel — str

perc: bd, cym, glock, sd, tamtam, tri

Not the overture to the 1905 operetta itself, but rather a symphonic
concoction — longer and for larger orchestra — written in 1940 for a
celebration of the composer's 70th birthday.

| Glocken | Luck's |

Lentini, James   **1958-**

(b Detroit, MI, 7 February 1958). American

Dreamscape   <1994>   8'

1 1 1 1 — 1 1 1 0 — 1perc — str
perc: bd, sus cym, sd, tri, glock, vib, chimes

| MMB |

Sinfonia di festa   <1996>   9'

3[1.2.pic] 3[1.2.Eh] 3[1.2.bcl] 3[1.2.cbn] — 4 3 3 1 — tmp+3 — hp
— str

perc: bd, cym, sus cym, sd, tri, tambn, tamtam, glock, xyl, marim, vib, chimes,
windchimes, woodblk, bongos

| MMB |

Leo, Leonardo   **1694-1744**

(b San Vito degli Schiavoni [now San Vito dei Normanni], 5 Aug 1694; d Naples, 31
Oct 1744). Italian

Concerto, Violoncello, D major   14'

cnt — str[no va]
Ed. Felix Schroeder.

| Eulenburg | Luck's |

Santa Elena al Calvario: Sinfonia   <1732>   5'

0 2 0 0 — 2 0 0 0 — cnt — str
From the oratorio. Ed. Richard Engländer.

| Eulenburg | Luck's |

León, Tania   **1943-**

(b Havana, 14 May 1943). Cuban-American composer of mixed descent (French,
Spanish, African, Chinese)

Ácana, for Chamber Orchestra   <2008>   13'

2[1/pic.2/pic] 2 2[1.2/bcl] 2 — 2 2 1 0 — 2perc — pf — str

perc: bd, congas, bongos, cast, templeblks, hi-hat, szl cym, marac, tamtam, claves,
guiro, windchimes, logdrum, dumbek, frame drum, caxixi, bamboo windchimes,
2sus cym, 2marim, 2djembe

| Peer |

Batá   <1985; rev 1988>   7'

2[1.2/pic] 2[1.2/Eh] 2[1.2/bcl] 2 — 2 2 2 1 — tmp+2 — hp — pf/cel
— str

| Peer |

"Desde..."   <©2001>   18'

3[1.2/pic.3/pic] 2 3[1.2.bcl] 3[1.2.cbn] — 4 3 3 1 — tmp+3 — hp —
pf/cel — str

perc: rototom, bongos, tomtom, congas, vib, szl cym, marac, tambn, sd, glock,
timbales, cast, cowbell, tamtam, logdrum, 2bd, 2sus cym

Each of the 3 percussionists requires an array of about 6 drums (bd,
rototoms, congas, bongos, timbales, etc.).

| Peer |

Horizons   <1999>   10'

2[1.2/pic] 2[1.2/Eh] 3[1.2.bcl] 2[1.2/cbn] — 4 3 2[1.btbn] 1 — tmp+2
— hp — pf — str

perc: vib, bd, sus cym, rototom, tomtom, sd, bongos, marim, tamtam

The 2 percussionists require a considerable array of drums, tomtoms,
rototoms, and the like.

| Peer |

Para viola y orquesta (For Viola & Orchestra)   <1994>   18'

solo viola
2[incl pic,afl] 2 2[incl bcl] 2[incl cbn] — 2 2 1 0 — 2perc — cel/hpsd
— str

1.	3'
2.	3'
3.	8'

| Southern |

Leoncavallo, Ruggero   **1857-1919**

(b Naples, 8 March 1857; d Montecatini, 9 Aug 1919). Italian

Mattinata   <1904>   3'

solo tenor
1 1 2 0 — 1 0 0 0 — hp — str
Score in E major only, but Luck's offers parts in D-flat or C. A large
orchestration (Chiaramello) is available in E or D.

| Kalmus | Luck's |

I pagliacci: Intermezzo   <1892>   4'

3[1.2.pic] 2[1.Eh] 3[1.2.bcl] 3 — 4 2 3 1 — tmp — 2hp[1part] — str

| Kalmus | Luck's |

Levy, Marvin David   **1935-**

(b Passaic, NJ, 2 Aug 1932). American

Canto de los marranos   <1977>   28'

solo soprano
2 2 2 2 — 2 1 1 0 — hp — pf/cel/elec pf — str
perc: crot, chimes, marim, xyl, cym, sus cym, cast, whip, bd, sd, td, windchimes,
Burmese gongs, Chinese belltree, 3tamtams, 3tri, 3woodblks

| Boosey |

Lewis, John   **1920-2001**

(b La Grange, IL, 3 May 1920; d New York, 29 March 2001). American

The Golden Striker   5'

solo piano, bass, drums
0 0 0 0 — 4 4 2 1 — [no str]

| MJQ |

Jazz Ostinato   6'

solo jazz quartet: vibraphone, piano, bass, drums
3[incl pic] 3[incl Eh] 3[incl bcl] 3[incl cbn] — 4 4 3 1 — tmp+2 —
hp — cel — str

MJQ

Lewis, Robert Hall   1926-1996

(b Portland, OR, 22 April 1926; d Baltimore, MD, 22 March 1996). American

Three Movements on Scenes of Hieronymous Bosch   23'
<1989>

4[incl afl,2pic] 3[incl Eh] 3[incl Ebcl,bcl] 3[incl cbn] — 4 3 3 1 —
cimbalom, mand — tmp+4 — hp — cel, pf — str
2nd conductor may be needed briefly in one passage.

Garden of Earthly Delights	_'
The Last Judgement	_'
Visions of the Hereafter	_'

Presser

Liadov, Anatol   1855-1914

(b St Petersburg, 29 April/11 May 1855; d Polïnovka, Novgorod district, 16/28 Aug 1914). Russian

Baba-Yaga, op.56 <1891–1904>   4'

3[1.2.pic] 3[1.2.Eh] 3[1.2.bcl] 3[1.2.cbn] — 4 2 3 1 — tmp+3 — str
perc: xyl, cym, bd

Belaieff	Kalmus	Luck's

Eight Russian Folk Songs, op.58 <1906>   13'

3[1.2.pic] 3[1.2.Eh] 2 2 — 4 2 0 0 — tmp+2 — str
perc: tri, tambn

1. Religious Chant	2'
2. Christmas Carol	1'
3. Plainte	2'
4. Humorous Song	1'
5. Legend of the Birds	2'
6. Cradle Song	2'
7. Round Dance	1'
8. Village Dance Song	2'

Belaieff	Kalmus	Luck's

The Enchanted Lake, op.62 (Volshebnoye ozero) <1909>   6'

3 2 3 2 — 4 0 0 0 — tmp+1 — hp — cel — str
perc: bd

Belaieff	Kalmus	Luck's

From the Apocalypse, op.66 (Iz Apokalipsisa)   10'
<1910–1912>

3[1.2.3/pic] 3[1.2.Eh] 3 3[1.2.cbn] — 4 3 3 2 — 2tmp+4 — hp — cel
— str
perc: bd, cym, sus cym, tri, tamtam, gong

Belaieff	Kalmus	Luck's

Kikimora, op.63 <1909>   7'

3[1.2.pic] 3[1.2.Eh] 3[1.2.bcl] 2 — 4 2 0 0 — tmp+1 — cel — str
perc: xyl

Belaieff	Kalmus	Luck's

Liebermann, Lowell   1961-

(b New York, 22 Feb 1961). American

Concerto, Piccolo, op.50 <1996>   25'

2 2 2 2 — 2 2 0 0 — tmp+1 — hp — pf — str
perc: bd, cym, sd, tri, xyl, vib

I. Andante comodo	10'
II. Adagio	10'
III. Presto	5'

Presser

The Domain of Arnheim, op.33 <1990>   16'

2 2 2 2 — 2 2 1 0 — tmp+1 — hp — cel, pf — str

Presser

Liebermann, Rolf   1910-1999

(b Zürich, 14 Sept 1910; d Paris, 2 Jan 1999). Swiss

Concerto for Jazz Band & Symphony Orchestra <1954>   17'

Jazz band: 5sx[2asx, 2tsx, bsx], 4tp, 4tbn, pf, db, drums.
3[all/pic] 3 3[1.2.bcl] 3 — 4 3 3 1 — tmp+4 — hp — pf — str
perc: bd, sus cym, sd, set, tri, tamtam, gong, xyl, woodblk, cowbell, tumba, shaker ("Rohr")
Another version of this work was created in 1998 for jazz band alone and published by Universal under the title *Symphony for Jazz Ensemble* (9').
Its 4 mvts correspond to (1) *Jump*; (2) *Blues*; (3) *Boogie-Woogie*; (4) the last 50 bars of *Interludium* plus the complete *Mambo*.

Introduction	3'
Jump	2'
Scherzo I	2'
Blues	2'
Scherzo II	2'
Boogie-Woogie	1'
Interludium	2'
Mambo	3'

Universal

Furioso <1947>   9'

2[both/pic] 2[1/Eh.2] 2 2 — 4 3 3 1 — 2tmp+1 — pf — str
perc: bd, cym, sus cym, sd, field dr

Universal

Geigy Festival Concerto (Eine Fantasie über Basler   12'
Themen) <1958>

solo Basle drum [field drum]
3[1.2.3/pic] 3 3[1.2/bcl.3] 3 — 4 3 3 1 — tmp+1 — pf — str
perc: bd, cym, sus cym, tamtam, handbell (Bb)
Soloist has one brief passage on sd ("tamburo [piccolo] militare").

Introduzione (Adagio; Allegro)	_'
Maestoso (Andante)	_'
Scherzo e Trio (Allegro)	_'
Finale (Vivace)	_'

Universal

Suite über sechs schweizerische Volkslieder (Suite on Six   12'
Swiss Folksongs) <1947>

2 2[1.2/Eh] 2 2 — 2 0 0 0 — hp — str

1. Es isch kei sölige Stamme	2'
2. Im Aargäu sind zwei Liebi	2'
3. Schönster Abestärn	2'
4. Durs Oberland uf und durs Oberland ab	2'
5. S'isch äben e Mönsch uf Arde	2'
6. Üsen Atti	2'

Universal

Symphony for Jazz Ensemble

see his: Concerto for Jazz Band & Symphony Orchestra

Lieberson, Peter   1946-2011

(b New York, 25 Oct 1946; d Tel Aviv, 23 April 2011). American

Ashoka's Dream: Suite <2008>   30'

3[1.2.3/pic] 2[1.2/Eh] 3[1.2.bcl] 2[1.2/cbn] — 4 3 3 1 — asx — tmp+2 — hp — pf/cel — str

perc: bd, cym, tomtom, tamtam, glock, marim, vib, crot, 3sus cym, gong[G#2]

AMP

Drala <1986>   18'

3[1/pic.2/afl/pic.3/pic] 2 3[1.2.3/Ebcl] 3[1.2.cbn] — 4 3 3 1 — tmp+6 — 1 or 2hp — pf — str

perc: vib, crot, slgh-bells, sd, chimes, tambn, whip, bd, xyl, templeblks, cuica, 3tomtom, 3cym, 3sus cym, 2woodblk, 3rototom, 2tri, 2glock

Invocation	*3'*
I. Gathering	*3'*
II. Offerings and Praises	*8'*
III. Raising Windhorse	*4'*

AMP

Remembering JFK (An American Elegy) <2011>   15'

narrator

2[1.2/pic] 2[1.2/Eh] 3[1.2.3/bcl] 2[1.2/cbn] — 4 2 0 0 — tmp+1 — hp — pf — str

perc: sus cym, chimes, crot

Excerpts from speeches of President John Fitzgerald Kennedy.

AMP

Ligeti, György   1923-2006

(b Dicsöszentmárton [Diciosânmartin, now Tîrnăveni], Transylvania, 28 May 1923; d Vienna, 12 June 2006). Hungarian-born; later took Austrian citizenship.

Apparitions <1958–1959>   9'

3[1.2.3/pic] 0 3[1.2.3/Ebcl] 3[1.2.cbn] — 6 4 3 1 — 4perc — hp — cel, pf, hpsd — str[12.12.8.8.6]

perc: xyl, bd, glock, cast, templeblks, marac, tamtam, sd, whip, woodblk, guiro, tambn, claves, crot, tmp, dishes

Universal

Atmosphères <1961>   9'

4[1/pic.2/pic.3/pic.4/pic] 4 4[1.2.3.4/Ebcl] 4[1.2.3.cbn] — 6 4 4 1 — 2perc — str[14.14.10.10.8]

perc: pf[played by 2perc]

Universal

Concerto, Piano <1985–1988>   24'

1[fl/pic] 1 1[cl/alto ocarina in G] 1 — 1 1 1 0 — 2-3 perc — str[8.6.6.4.3]

perc: bd, sd, tri, tambn, glock, xyl, crot, flexatone, templeblks, whip, guiro, cast, 2handbell, 4woodblk, 3bongos, 4tomtom, siren whistle, whistle, sl whistle, Chronomica in C (Hohner 270)

I. Vivace molto ritmico e preciso	*4'*
II. Lento e deserto	*7'*
III. Vivace cantabile	*4'*
IV. Allegro risoluto, molto ritmico	*5'*
V. Presto luminoso	*4'*

Schott

Concerto, Violoncello <1966>   15'

1[1/pic] 1[1/Eh] 2[1,2/bcl] 1 — 1 1 1 0 — hp — str[8.7.6.5.4; or str 5t]

I. quarter note = 40	*7'*
II. quarter note = 40	*8'*

Donemus   Peters

Hamburgisches Konzert (Hamburg Concerto) <1998–2002>   15'

solo horn

2[1.2/pic] 1 2[1/basset hn1.basset hn2/Ebcl] 1 — 4[natural horns] 1 1 0 — tmp+2 — str

perc: chimes, marim, vib, crot, sd, tambn, bd, xyl, sus cym, glock, 4bongos, temple bowl

I. Praeludium	*3'*
II. Signale—Tanz—Choral	*2'*
III. Aria—Aksak—Hoketus	*1'*
IV. Solo—Intermezzo—Mixtur—Kanon	*4'*
V. Spectra	*3'*
VI. Capriccio	*1'*
VII. Hymnus	*1'*

Schott

Lontano <1967>   11'

4[1.2/pic.3/pic.4/afl] 4[1.2.3.4/Eh] 4[1.2.3/bcl.4/opt cbcl] 4[1.2.3.cbn] — 4 3 3 1 — str

Schott

Macabre Collage <1974–1977; rev 1996>   17'

3[1.2/pic1.3/pic2] 3[1.2/ob d'am.3/Eh] 3[1.2/Ebcl/asx.3/bcl] 3[1.2.3/cbn] — 4 6[1.2.3.4.flug.btp] 3 1 — tmp+3 — hp — cel/hpsd, pf/elec pf, elec org — str[3.0.2.6.4]

perc: tambn, cym, claves, xyl, tamtam, cast, tomtom, templeblks, woodblk, td, chimes, glock, flexatone, congas, field dr, gong, bd, sd, 12autohorn, 2vib, slide whistle, 3bongos, bass xyl, 2siren, gunshot, logdrum

Arr. by Elgar Howarth from the opera *Le Grand Macabre*.

Schott

Melodien (Melodies) <1971>   13'

1[1/pic] 1[1/ob d'amore] 1 1 — 2 1 1 1 — 1perc — pf/cel — str[8.7.6.5.4; or str 5t]

perc: xyl, vib, glock, crot, tmp

Schott

Mysteries of the Macabre <1974–1977; rev 1992>   9'

coloratura soprano *or* solo trumpet

2[1.pic] 3[1.2.3/Eh] 2[1.2/bcl] 2[1.2/cbn] — 4 2 1[cb tbn] 1 — mand — tmp+3 — hp — cel/hpsd, pf/elec org — str[3.0.2.6.4]

perc: glock, crot, xyl, tri, cast, marac, guiro, sus cym, woodblk, templeblks, sd, tambn, congas, tomtom, tamtam, field dr, bd, police whistle, slide whistle, signal pipe, 2cym, rattle, 3bongos, sandpaper, large sheet of paper which can be crumpled loudly

3 arias from the opera *Le Grand Macabre*.

A reduced version of the orchestra (by Elgar Howarth) is available:
1[fl/pic] 1 1[cl/bcl] 1[bn/cbn] — 1 1 1 0 — tmp+perc — mand — pf/cel — str 5t

Schott

Ramifications <1968–1969>   9'

str orch; or 12 solo str[7.0.2.2.1]

Two groups, tuned a quarter-tone apart.

Schott

Requiem <1963–1965>   27'

2 mixed choruses   solos S, Ms

3[1.2/pic.3/pic] 3[1.2.3/Eh] 3[1/Ebcl.2/bcl.3/cbcl] 3[1.2.cbn] — 4 4[1.2.3.btp] 3[1.2.cb tbn] 1 — 3perc — hp — hpsd, cel — str[12.12.10.8.6]

perc: sd, bd, tamtam, tambn, whip, sus cym, xyl, glock

Peters

San Francisco Polyphony <1973–1974>   12'

3[1/afl.2/pic.3/pic] 3[1.2/ob d'am.3/Eh] 3[1.2/Ebcl.3/bcl] 3[1.2.cbn] —
2 2 2 1 — 2perc — hp — pf/cel — str[12.12.10.8.6]
perc: bd, whip, tamtam, glock, vib, xyl

Schott

Lindberg, Magnus   1958-

(b Helsinki, 27 June 1958). Finnish

Arena <1994–1995>   15'

2[1.2/pic] 3 3 2[1.2/cbn] — 2 3 3 0 — 2perc — hp — pf/cel — str
perc: bd, tri, tamtam, glock, marim, vib, marktree, bongos, 2sus cym, 4tomtom,
2woodblk
The composer later (1996) revised this work for 16 instruments; materials
available from Chester:
   1[fl/pic] 1 1 1[bn/cbn] — 2 1 1 0 — 1perc — hp — pf/cel — str
5t[or str sections]

Chester

Aura (In memoriam Witold Lutosławski) <1994>   37'

3[1.2.pic] 3[1.2.Eh] 4[1.2.3/bcl.bcl] 3[1.2.cbn] — 4 3[1.2.3/btp] 3 1
— tmp+3 — hp — pf/cel — str[rec: 16.14.12.10.8]
perc: vib, marktree, claves, bd, marim, sd, crot, glock, tri, Chinescym, 2opera
gong, 3temple bells, 2sus cym, 4tomtom, 4bongos, 2tamtam, 2woodblock
I. quarter-note = 72   *13'*
II. quarter-note = 54   *13'*
III. quarter-note = 84   *6'*
IV. quarter-note = 144   *5'*

Chester

Concerto, Piano, [No.1] <1990; rev 1994>   29'

2[1.2/pic] 3[1.2.Eh] 3[1.2.bcl] 2[1.2/cbn] — 2 1 1 1 — 2perc — hp
— str[8.8.6.4.4]
perc: glock, vib, tamtam, crot, marktree, bongos, bd, 3temple bells, 2sus cym
The three mvts are played without pause.
I. quarter-note = 54   *10'*
II. quarter-note = 108   *11'*
III. quarter-note = 126   *8'*

Hansen

Corrente II <1992>   18'

0 3[1.2.Eh] 3[1.2/Ebcl.bcl] 3[1.2.cbn] — 4 2 3 0 — tmp+1 — hp —
pf — str
perc: tamtam, vib, bd, glock
Expanded and adapted from an earlier work for 16 instruments, *Corrente*
(also 1992).

Chester

Era <2012>   18'

3[1.2.3/pic] 3[1.2.Eh] 4[1.2.3.bcl] 3[1.2.cbn] — 4 3 3 1 — tmp+2 —
hp — str
perc: chimes, tri, bd, crot, td, tamtam, 2sus cym, 2Chinescym

Boosey

Joy <1989–1990>   27'

2[1.2/pic] 1 3[1.2/Ebcl.bcl] 1[1/cbn] — 2 1 1 1 — 2perc — pf/cel,
kybd[AKAI S1000; Yamaha KX88, SY77, DX7, DMP7 or DMP11;
stereo amplification] — str[2vn.2va.2vc.1db]
perc: vib, belltree, bongos, tamtam, crot, marktree, chimes, bd, metalplate[Bb3],
3templebells, almglocken, anvil, tmp

Hansen

Marea (Tides) <1990>   11'

2[1.2/pic] 2[1.Eh] 2[1.bcl] 2[1.cbn] — 2 1 1 1 — tmp+ — pf — str
perc: crot, tamtam, bd, tri, sus cym, chimes, marktree

Hansen

Ritratto, For 18 Players <1979–1983>   14'

2[1.2/pic/crot] 1 2[1.2/Ebcl] 1 — 2 0 0 0 — 1perc — pf — str[3vn,
2va, 2vc, db]
perc: bd, sus cym, tri, tambn, tamtam, glock, marim, crot, slgh-bells, templeblks,
bongos, claves, 3herdbells, 5tomtom, 3woodblk

Fennica

Sculpture <2005>   23'

4[1.2.3/pic.afl] 4[1.2.3.Eh] 4[1.2.3/bcl.bcl] 4[1.2.3/cbn.cbn] —
6[hn5&6/Wag tb] 4 4 2 — tmp+4 — 2hp — 2pf[1.2/org] — str[no
violins]
perc: bd, td, tri, marim, vib, crot, marktree, belltree, templeblks, bongos,
2Chinescym, 4sus cym, 4tomtom, 2tamtam, 2buttongong[Db2,Eb2]

Boosey

Tribute <2004>   3'

3[1.2.pic/afl] 3[1.2.Eh] 4[1.2.3.bcl] 3[1.2.cbn] — 4 3 3 1 — tmp+3 —
hp — pf/cel — str
perc: bd, tamtam, marim, vib, crot, templeblks, buttongong[Db2]

Boosey

Zona <1983; rev 1990>   20'

solo violoncello
1[afl] 0 1[bcl] 0 — 1perc — hp — pf — 1vn, 1db
perc: bd, Chinescym, hi-hat, sd, tomtom, tamtam, glock, marim, crot, woodblk,
templeblks, bongos, cowbell, 3sus cym, 3tri, wood windchimes, herdbells, bow

Fennica

Liszt, Franz   1811-1886

(b Raiding (Doborján), 22 Oct 1811; d Bayreuth, 31 July 1886). Hungarian

S = numbering system by Humphrey Searle, in the works list for the
article "Liszt, Franz," *The New Grove Dictionary of Music & Musicians*
(ed. Stanley Sadie, 1980).
    The Searle numbers are also used in the Kalmus catalog (though alas as
"G" numbers—presumably for "Grove"). Searle numbers may also be
found in *Oxford Music Online*, www.oxfordmusiconline.com, where they
are the *secondary* numbering system for Liszt—the *primary* system being
from R. Charnin Mueller & M. Eckhardt: *Thematisches Verzeichnis der
Werke Franz Liszts* [Munich, in prep.]. Confusion is compounded
because Mueller & Eckhardt assign letters to the various categories of
works; "G" (entirely different from the Kalmus G numbers) is the letter
designating orchestral works.

A la Chapelle Sixtine, S.360 (At the Sistine Chapel)   18'
<1862>

2 2 2 2 — 4 2 3 1 — tmp+2 — str
perc: bd, tamtam
Based on the celebrated *Miserere* of Gregorio Allegri (1582-1652) and
the *Ave verum corpus* of Mozart. Originally for piano; orchestral version
by the composer.

EMB

Angelus! Prière aux anges gardiens, S.378 (Prayer to the   6'
Guardian Angels) <1880–1882>

str 5t or str orch
Originally for piano (*Années de pèlerinage, troisième année, no.1*).
   Arranged by Liszt for str 4t; db part added by Walter Bache.

Kalmus   Luck's

Battle of the Huns

see his: Hunnenschlacht, S.105

Ce qu'on entend sur la montagne, S.95 (Bergsymphonie; Symphonic Poem No.1) <1847–1856>

38'

3[1.2.pic] 2 3[1.2.bcl] 2 — 4 3 3 1 — tmp+3 — hp — str
perc: bd, cym, tamtam, sus cym

Breitkopf	Kalmus

Christus, S.3 <1866–1872>

162'

chorus   solos SATB
3[1.2.pic] 3[1.2.Eh] 2 2 — 4 3 3 1 — tmp+2 — hp — org, opt harm — str
perc: cym, bd, chimes
Harmonium offstage (may be replaced by cued woodwinds).
 I. ORATORIUM IN NATIVITATE DOMINI (CHRISTMAS ORATORIO)

1.Rorate coeli (Einleitung)	*14'*
2 Angelus Domini (Pastorale und Verkündigung des Engels)	*7'*
3 Stabat Mater speciosa (Hymnus)	*11'*
4 Hirtenspiel an der Krippe (Pastorale)	*13'*
5 Et ecce stella (Die heiligen drei Könige Marsch)	*15'*

 II. POST EPIPHANIAM (AFTER EPIPHANY)

6 Beati pauperes spiritu (Die Seligkeiten)	*11'*
7 Pater Noster (Gebet)	*8'*
8 Tu es Petrus (Die Gründung der Kirche)	*6'*
9 Et ecce motus magnus (Das Wunder)	*9'*
10 Hosanna, benedictus qui venit (Der Einzug in Jerusalem)	*14'*

 III. PASSIO ET RESURRECTIO

11 Tristis est anima mea	*14'*
12 Stabat Mater dolorosa (Jacopone da Todi)	*33'*
13 O filii et filiae (Hymnus Paschalis)	*2'*
14 Resurrexit!	*5'*

Kalmus	Peters

Christus: Die heiligen drei Könige (March of the Three Kings) <1866–1872>

12'

3[1.2.pic] 2 2 2 — 4 3 3 1 — tmp — hp — str

Kalmus	Luck's

Christus: Hirtengesang an der Krippe (Shepherd's Song at the Manger) <1866–1872>

18'

2 3[1.2.Eh] 2 2 — 4 2 0 0 — tmp — hp — str

Kalmus	Luck's

Concerto, Piano, No.1, S.124, E-flat major <1835–1856>

19'

3[1.2.pic] 2 2 — 2 2 3 0 — tmp+2 — str
perc: tri, cym

I. Allegro maestoso	6'
II. Quasi adagio - Allegretto vivace	7'
III. Allegro marziale animato	6'

Breitkopf	Kalmus	Luck's

Concerto, Piano, No.2, S.125, A major <1839–1861>

21'

3[1.2.3/pic] 2 2 — 2 2 3 1 — tmp+1 — str
perc: cym

1. Adagio sostenuto assai - Allegro agitato assai	7'
2. Allegro moderato	8'
3. Allegro deciso - Marziale un poco meno allegro	7'
4. Allegro animato	2'

Breitkopf	Kalmus	Luck's

Concerto, Piano, S.125a, op. posth., E-flat major (1839) <1839>

15'

3[incl pic] 2 2 — 2 3 3 0 — tmp+1 — str
Ed. Jay Rosenblatt
Sometimes referred to as *Concerto No.3*.

EMB

Concerto pathétique, S.258 <1856; rev 1885>

14'

solo piano
3[1.2.pic] 2 2 — 2 2 3 0 — tmp+2 — hp — str
perc: tri, cym
Originally for 2 pianos; arr for solo piano with orchestral accompaniment by Eduard Reuss; rev. Liszt, 1885 & pubd posthumously.

Breitkopf	Kalmus

Dante Symphony, S.109 (Eine Symphonie zu Dantes Divina Commedia) <1855–1856>

52'

chorus of women's or boys' voices
3[1.2.3/pic] 3[1.2.Eh] 3[1.2.bcl(A)] 2 — 4 2 3 1 — 2tmp+3 — 2hp — harm — str
perc: cym, bd, tamtam
Brief solo for soprano.

Inferno	23'
Purgatorio	29'

Breitkopf	Kalmus

Episodes from Lenau's "Faust", S.110

see separate entries:
 1. Nächtliche Zug (Nocturnal Procession)
 2. Mephisto Waltz No.1

Fantasie über ungarische Volksmelodien, S.123 (Hungarian Fantasy) <1849–1852>

15'

solo piano
3[1.2.pic] 2 2 2 — 2 2 3 0 — tmp+3 — str
perc: bd, cym, sd

Kalmus	Luck's	Peters

Fantasy on Motives from Beethoven's "Ruins of Athens", S.122 <1848–1852>

11'

solo piano
3[1.2.pic] 2 2 2 — 2 2 3 0 — tmp+3 — str
perc: bd, cym, tri

Kalmus	Luck's

A Faust Symphony, S.108 <1854–1857; rev 1861>

65'

male chorus   tenor solo
3[1.2.3/pic] 2 2 — 4 3 3 1 — tmp+2 — hp — org — str
perc: cym, tri
Voices enter only in the 3rd movement. An alternative ending without organ or voices is 5-7' shorter.

Faust	23'
Gretchen	19'
Mephistopheles	23'

Breitkopf	Kalmus

Festklänge, S.101 (Symphonic Poem No.7) <1853–1861>

18'

2 2 2 2 — 4 3 3 1 — tmp+2 — str
perc: bd, cym

Breitkopf	Kalmus	Luck's

From the Cradle to the Grave

see his: Von der Wiege bis zum Grabe, S.107

The Funeral Triumph of Tasso

see his: Triomphe funèbre du Tasse, S.112, no.3

Hamlet, S.104 (Symphonic Poem No.10) <1858>   10'

3[1.2.pic] 2 2 2 — 4 2 3 1 — tmp — str

| Breitkopf | Kalmus | Luck's |

Héroïde funèbre, S.102 (Heroic Elegy; Heldenklage; Symphonic Poem No.8) <1849–1850; rev 1854-6>   26'

3[1.2.pic] 3[1.2.Eh] 2 2 — 4 2 3 1 — tmp+5 — str
perc: field dr, tamtam, cym, bd, chimes

| Breitkopf | Kalmus | Luck's |

Huldigungs-Marsch, S.357 <1853; rev (orchd) 1857>   6'

3[1.2.pic] 2 2 2 — 4 2 3 1 — tmp+1 — str
perc: cym
Originally for solo piano; orchestrated by the composer.

| Bote & Bock | Kalmus | Luck's |

Hungaria, S.103 (Symphonic Poem No.9) <1854>   22'

3[1.2.pic] 3[1.2.Eh] 2 2 — 4 3 3 1 — tmp+5 — str
perc: field dr, tri, tamtam, cym, bd

| Breitkopf | Kalmus | Luck's |

Hungarian Attack March

see his: Ungarischer Sturmmarsch, S.119

HUNGARIAN RHAPSODIES, S.359 (Ungarische Rhapsodien)

Of the nineteen Hungarian Rhapsodies for solo piano (S.244), six were orchestrated by the composer in collaboration with Franz Doppler, and were renumbered in the process. Some of these orchestral versions were also transposed up or down a half-step from the piano originals. Later orchestrators did not always follow Liszt's numbering or choice of keys (as in the case of the well-known Müller-Berghaus version of No.2).

Hungarian Rhapsody No.1 [S.359 no.1], F minor <1853; rev 1857-60>   11'

3[1.2.pic] 2 2 3 — 4 3 3 1[oph] — tmp+2 — 2hp[1part] — str
perc: cym, tri
Piano version No.14; orchestrated by the composer and Franz Doppler.

| Kalmus | Luck's |

Hungarian Rhapsody No.2 [S.359 no.4], D minor <1851>   11'

3[1.2.pic] 2 3[1.2.D-cl] 2 — 4 2 3 1 — tmp+2 — str
perc: cym, tri
Piano version No.2; original in C-sharp minor. Orchestrated by the composer and Franz Doppler in D minor, and published as No.4 of the orchestral series (i.e., S.359 no.4); renumbered by Kalmus & Luck's in the reprinting, apparently to coincide with the popular piano original, as well as the oft-played Müller-Berghaus arrangement. (Kalmus and Luck's list the work incorrectly as 359/2 rather than 359/4.)

| Kalmus | Luck's |

Hungarian Rhapsody No.2 [S.359 no.4], C minor (arr. Müller-Berghaus) <1851>   11'

2[1/pic.2/pic] 2 2 2 — 4 2 3 0 — tmp+4 — hp — str
perc: sd, tri, bd, cym
Piano version No.2; original in C-sharp minor. Transcribed for orchestra from the piano original, S.244 no.2, by Karl Müller-Berghaus. Listed by Kalmus incorrectly as S.359/2 rather than 359/4.
   Piccolo could readily be consolidated into the 2nd flute part if desired (i.e., never do the 2 flutes play pic simultaneously).

| Kalmus | Luck's | Simrock |

Hungarian Rhapsody No.3 [S.359 no.3], D major <1853>   7'

3[1.2.pic] 2 2 2 — 4 2 3 1[oph] — cimbalom — tmp+3 — hp — str
perc: bd, cym, tri
Piano version No.6; original in D-flat major. Orchestrated by the composer and Franz Doppler.

| Kalmus | Luck's |

Hungarian Rhapsody No.4 [S.359 no.2], D minor <1853>   11'

3[1.2.pic] 2 2 2 — 4 2 3 1 — tmp+3 — hp — str
perc: tri, cym, bd
Piano version No.12; original in C-sharp minor. Orchestrated by the composer and Franz Doppler. Originally published as No.2 (i.e., S.359 no.2) of the orchestral series; renumbered in the reprinting, and incorrectly listed by Kalmus as S.359/4 rather than 359/2.

| Kalmus | Luck's |

Hungarian Rhapsody No.5 [S.359 no.5], E minor (Héroïde-élégiaque) <1853>   8'

2 2 2 2 — 4 0 3 0 — tmp — hp — str
Piano version No.5. Orchestrated by the composer and Franz Doppler.

| Kalmus | Luck's |

Hungarian Rhapsody No.6 [S.359 no.6], D major (Pesther Carneval) <1848; rev 1853>   10'

3[1.2.pic] 2 2 2 — 4 2 3 1[oph] — tmp+3 — hp — str
perc: tri, cym, bd
Piano version No.9; originally in E-flat major. Orchestrated by the composer and Franz Doppler.

| Kalmus | Luck's |

Hungarian Rhapsody, S.244, no.1, C minor <1851>   10'

3[1.2.pic] 2 2 2 — 4 2 3 1 — tmp+5 — hp — str
Piano version No.1; original in C-sharp minor. Transcribed for orchestra from the piano original, S.244 no.1, by Karl Müller-Berghaus.
   This work is not to be confused with the *Hungarian Rhapsody No.1 in F minor*, which is an arrangement of piano original S.244 no.14.

| Fleisher | Simrock |

Hunnenschlacht, S.105 (Battle of the Huns; Symphonic Poem No.11) <1857>   16'

3[1.2.pic] 2 2 2 — 4 3 3 1 — tmp+1 — opt org — str
perc: cym, sus cym
The organ part is cued in the winds.

| Breitkopf | Kalmus | Luck's |

Die Ideale, S.106 (Symphonic Poem No.12) <1856–1857>   30'

2 2 2 2 — 4 2 3 1 — tmp+1 — str
perc: cym

| Breitkopf | Kalmus | Luck's |

Die Legende von der heiligen Elisabeth, S.2 (The Legend of St. Elizabeth) <1857–1862>   *146'*

solo soprano, mezzo, bass; 4 smaller roles (A/Bar, 2Bar, Bass)
chorus, opt children's chorus
3[1.2.3/pic] 3[1.2.Eh] 2 2 — 4 3 3 1 — tmp+2 — 2hp — harm, org — str
perc: sd, cym, bd, chime[E3]
The score indicates that the four smaller roles may all be sung by one baritone.

PART I	
Introduction	*10'*
1. Ankunft der Elisabeth auf Wartburg (Arrival of Elizabeth ...)	*15'*
2. Landgraf Ludwig (Count Ludwig)	*22'*
3. Die Kreuzritter (The Crusaders)	*25'*
PART II	
4. Landgräfin Sophie (Counstess Sophia)	*20'*
5. Elisabeth (Elizabeth)	*33'*
6. Feierliche Bestattung der Elisabeth (Solemn Burial of Elizabeth)	*21'*

> EMB

Légendes, S.354 <1863>   *18'*

3[1.2.3/pic] 3[1.2.opt Eh] 2 2 — 4 2 3 1 — tmp+1 — hp — str
perc: cym, sus cym
Previously unknown rediscovered score, ed. Friedrich Schnapp, 1983.
Probably an orchestration of piano pieces (S.175) by the composer,
though it is claimed by Schnapp that the orchestra version came first, and
the piano pieces are later transcriptions.

San Francesco d'Assisi	*9'*
San Francesco di Paola	*9'*

> EMB

Légendes: Die Vogelpredigt des heiligen Franz von Assisi (The Sermon to the Birds of St. Francis of Assisi) <1863>   *9'*

2 2 2 2 — 4 2 3 1 — tmp — 2hp — str
Orchestrated from the piano work (S.175/1) by Felix Mottl, presumably
unaware that Liszt had orchestrated it himself.
   Kalmus lists this work as S.354/1, which strictly should be reserved for
the Liszt orchestration; Mottl's transcription should be S.175/1.

> Kalmus

Malédiction, S.121 <1833–1840>   *13'*

solo piano
str

> Breitkopf   Kalmus   Luck's

Mazeppa, S.100 (Symphonic Poem No.6) <1851–1854>   *17'*

3[1.2.pic] 3[1.2.Eh] 3[1(in D or A).2.bcl] 3 — 4 3 3 1 — tmp+3 — str
perc: tri, cym, bd
Score shows 1st Clarinet in D (sopranino), but the published part
(Breitkopf and reprints) is in A, mostly lying extremely high. The bass
clarinet part is in bass clef and in C. Kalmus, as of 2012, offers alternative
parts for cl 1 in Eb, cl 2 in A, and bcl in Bb treble clef.
   The final portion of this work (about 4') can be performed
independently, beginning at the *Allegro*, 41 bars before figure [L].

> Breitkopf   Kalmus   Luck's

Mephisto Waltz No.1, S.110/2 (Der Tanz in der Dorfschenke) <1857–1861>   *11'*

3[1.2.3/pic] 2 2 2 — 4 2 3 1 — tmp+2 — hp — str
perc: tri, cym, sus cym
No.2 of two *Episodes from Lenau's Faust.*

> Breitkopf   Kalmus   Luck's

Mephisto Waltz No.2, S.111 <1880–1881>   *11'*

3[1.2.pic] 2 2 2 — 4 2 3 1 — tmp+2 — hp — str
perc: cym, tri

> Kalmus   Luck's

Der nächtliche Zug, S.110/1 (Nocturnal Procession) <1857–1861>   *15'*

3[1.2.3/pic] 3[1.2.opt Eh] 2 2 — 4 2 3 1 — tmp+1 — hp — str
perc: bell (C#) or tamtam
No.1 of two *Episodes from Lenau's Faust.*

> Kalmus

Orpheus, S.98 (Symphonic Poem No.4) <1853–1854>   *13'*

3[1.2.pic] 3[1.2.Eh] 2 2 — 4 2 3 1 — tmp — 2hp — str

> Breitkopf   Kalmus   Luck's

Polonaise No.2, S.223/2, E major <1851>   *10'*

3[1.2.pic] 2 2 2 — 4 2 3 1 — tmp+5 — hp — str
perc: glock, sd, tri, cym, bd
Originally for solo piano; orchestrated by Karl Müller-Berghaus.

> Kalmus   Simrock

Les Préludes, S.97 (Symphonic Poem No.3) <1848>   *16'*

3[1.2.3/pic] 2 2 2 — 4 2 3 1 — tmp+3 — hp — str
perc: field dr, cym, bd

> Breitkopf   Kalmus   Luck's

Prometheus, S.99 (Symphonic Poem No.5) <1849–1855>   *12'*

3[1.2.pic] 3[1.2.Eh] 2 2 — 4 2 3 1 — tmp — str

> Breitkopf   Kalmus   Luck's

Rákóczi-Marsch, S.117 (Hungarian March) <1863–1867>   *6'*

3[1.2.pic] 2 2 2 — 4 2 3 1 — tmp+3 — str
perc: bd, cym, tri
Originally for solo piano; arranged for orchestra by the composer.

> Breitkopf   Kalmus   Luck's

Rhapsodie espagnole, S.254 <1858>   *15'*

solo piano
3[1.2.3/pic] 2 2 — 4 2 3 1 — tmp+2 — str
perc: cym, tri, tambn, cast
Originally for solo piano; arranged as a concert piece for piano and
orchestra by Ferruccio Busoni.

Introduction	*1'*
I. Folies d'Espagne: Andante moderato	*4'*
II. Jota aragonesa: Allegro	*3'*
III. Un poco meno allegro - Allegretto piacevole	*7'*

> Kalmus   Luck's

Ruins of Athens: Fantasy

see: Liszt, Franz, 1811-1886
      Fantasy on Motives from Beethoven's "Ruins of Athens"

Tasso; lamento e trionfo, S.96 (Tasso; Lament and Triumph; Symphonic Poem No.2) <1847–1854>   *19'*

3[1.2.pic] 2 3[1.2.bcl] 2 — 4 4 3 1 — tmp+4 — hp — str
perc: tri, field dr, cym, bd

> Breitkopf   Kalmus   Luck's

Totentanz, S.126 <1847–?1862>   *16'*

solo piano
3[1.2.pic] 2 2 2 — 2 2 3 1 — tmp+3 — str
perc: tri, cym, tamtam

> Breitkopf   Kalmus   Luck's

Totentanz, S.126; Fantasy for Piano & Orchestra (1st version) <1847?>   17'

3[1.2.3/pic] 2 2 2 — 2 2 3 1 — tmp+3 — str
perc: bd, cym, tri, tamtam
Ed. Ferruccio Busoni.

Kalmus		

Le triomphe funèbre du Tasse, S.112, no.3 (Funeral Triumph of Tasso; Symphonic Poem No.2a) <1866>   11'

3[1.2.pic] 2 2 2 — 4 2 3 1 — tmp+1 — str
perc: deep bell [F] or tamtam
Epilogue to the composer's *Tasso; lamento e trionfo*, S.96, *q.v.*

Breitkopf	Kalmus	Luck's

Ungarischer Sturmmarsch, S.119 (Hungarian Attack March; Magyar induló; Marche militaire hongroise) <1844; rev (orchd) 1875>   4'

3[1.2.pic] 2 2 2 — 4 2 3 1 — tmp+2 — optional cimbalom — str
perc: cym, tri
Based on his *Seconde marche hongroise* (1844) for solo piano; rev. & orchestrated by the composer, 1875. The instrument identified in the score as "Cymbal" is actually an optional cimbalom, which plays for some 42 bars in the middle of the work. (The "cym" in the percussion section is labeled "Becken.")

Kalmus	Luck's

Die Vogelpredigt des heiligen Franz von Assisi

see under his: Légendes, S.354

Von der Wiege bis zum Grabe, S.107 (From the Cradle to the Grave; Du berceau jusqu'a la tombe; Symphonic Poem No.13) <1881–1882>   14'

3[1.2.pic] 2[1.2/Eh] 2 2 — 4 2 3 1 — tmp+1 — opt hp — str
perc: cym

Bote & Bock	Kalmus	Luck's	Schirmer

Wanderer Fantasy

see under: Schubert, Franz, 1797-1828

Litolff, Henry Charles   1818-1891

(b London, 7 Aug 1818; d Bois-Colombes, 5 Aug 1891). French

Concerto symphonique, No.4, op.102, D minor <ca 1852>   38'

solo piano
2[1.2/pic] 2 2 2 — 4 2 3 0 — tmp+1 — str
I. Allegro con fuoco   13'
II. Scherzo: Presto   7'
III. Adagio religiosos; Cantabile   7'
IV. Allegro impetuoso   11'

Kalmus	Leuckart	Luck's

Maximilian Robespierre, op.55 <1856>   10'

2[1.2/pic] 2 2 2 — 4 2 3 0 — tmp+3 — str

Kalmus	Peters

Lloyd, Jonathan   1948-

(b London, 30 September 1948). English

Symphony No.2 <1983–1984>   25'

3[1/pic.2/pic.3/afl] 3[1.2.3/Eh] 3[1.2.3/bcl] 3[1.2.3/cbn] — 4 3 3 1 — opt 4rec[descant, 2 trebles, bass] off-stage — opt asx[doubled by clarinetist] — tmp+2 — hp — cel — str[16.14.12.10.8]
perc: sus cym, hi-hat, sd, szl cym, tamtam, lionroar, wnd mach, siren, chimes, anvil, 9 tuned gongs

Boosey		

Locatelli, Pietro   1695-1764

(b Bergamo, 3 Sept 1695; d Amsterdam, 30 March 1764). Italian

Concerto grosso, op.1, no.6, C minor <1721>   12'

cnt — str
Ed. Arthur Egidi.

Eulenburg	Kalmus	Luck's	Vieweg

Concerto grosso, op.1, no.8, F minor <1721>   20'

solos: 2 violins, 2 violas, violoncello
cnt — str
Ed. Arnold Schering.

Eulenburg	Kahnt	Luck's

Concerto grosso, op.1, no.9, D major <1721>   12'

solos: 2 violins, violoncello
str
Ed. Ettore Bonelli.

Eulenburg	Kalmus	Luck's	Zanibon

Concerto grosso, op.7, no.6, E-flat major (Il pianto d'Arianna) <1741>   14'

solos: 2 violins, viola, violoncello
str
Ed. Remo Giazotto.
Adagio   1'
Andante   1'
Allegro   1'
Largo   2'
Largo andante   3'
Grave   2'
Allegro   1'
Largo   3'

Luck's	Ricordi

Concerto grosso, op.7, no.12, F major <1741>   12'

4 solo violins
cnt — str
Ed. Newell Jenkins.

Peters	

Trauer-Symphonie (Funeral Symphony)   15'

cnt — str
Authenticity has been questionsd.

Kahnt	Kalmus	Luck's

Locklair, Dan   1949-

(b Charlotte, NC, 7 Aug 1949). American

Concerto, Harp <2004>   19'

2 2 2 2 — 2 2 0 0 — tmp+2 — str
perc: sus cym, tri, tamtam, glock, xyl, marim, vib, chimes, crot, belltree, bass bow, 4tomtoms
> I. Dialogues (Heralding and Joyous)   6'
> II. Variants (Still and Gently Moving)   9'
> III. Contrasts (Very Quick and Vibrant)   4'

Subito

Concerto, Harpsichord, Strings & Percussion   21'
<1990–1992>

1perc — str[3 or 4.3 or 4.3.2.2]
perc: sus cym, tri, glock, xyl, vib, chimes, bass bow, 4tomtoms
> I. Majestic and never hurried; Driving   7'
> II. Gently, with rubato   7'
> III. Fast and exuberant   7'

Subito

"Ere Long We Shall See... "; Concerto brevis for Organ   10'
& Orchestra <1995>

2[1.2/pic] 2[1.2/Eh] 2 2 — 4 2 3 1 — tmp+2 — str
perc: cym, sus cym, tamtam, glock, xyl, vib, chimes, crot, belltree, bass bow, 4tomtoms, 5woodblks

Subito

Hues; Three Brief Tone Poems <1992–1993>   12'

2[1.2/pic] 2[1.2/Eh] 2 2 — 4 2 3 1 — tmp+3 — pf — str
perc: bd, cym, sus cym, sd, tri, tamtam, glock, xyl, marim, vib, chimes, crot, belltree, bass bow, 3tomtoms
> I. Cloudburst   3'
> II. Moonshine   6'
> III. Sunburst   3'

Subito

In Memory — H.H.L. <2005>   4'

str
In memory of the composer's mother, Hester Helms Locklair, 1918-2005.

Subito

Phoenix <1985; rev (orchd) 2006-07>   10'

3[1.2.pic] 2 2 2 — 4 4 4 1 — tmp+2 — hp — org[opt] — str
perc: bd, cym, sus cym, tamtam, glock, xyl, chimes, vib, crot
Of the above, 2tp & 2tbn form an off-stage antiphonal group.
    Originally a work for brass, percussion & organ; orchestrated by the composer.

Subito

Phoenix and Again; An Overture for Orchestra <1983>   5'

2 2 2 2 — 4 2 3 1 — tmp+2 — str
perc: bd, cym, sus cym, glock, vib, chimes

Subito

Since Dawn <1995>   20'

narrator   chorus
2[1.2/pic] 2[1.2/Eh] 2 2 — 4 2 3 1 — tmp+3 — pf — str
perc: bd, cym, sus cym, tamtam, glock, xyl, marim, vib, chimes, crot, belltree, templeblks, 3tomtoms, cello bow
Chorus must whistle on pitch.

Subito

Symphony No.1 (Symphony of Seasons) <2000–2002>   31'

3[1.2.pic] 3[1.2.Eh] 3[1.2.bcl] 2 — 4 3 3 1 — tmp+3 — hp — pf — str
perc: bd, sus cym, cym, tri, tambn, tamtam, glock, xyl, vib, chimes, crot, belltree, opt wnd mach
> 1. Autumn   7'
> 2. Winter   9'
> 3. Spring   7'
> 4. Summer   8'

Subito

When Morning Stars Begin to Fall <1986; rev 1999>   13'

3[1.2.pic] 3[1.2.Eh] 3[1.2.bcl] 3[1.2.cbn] — 4 3 3 1 — tmp+3 — hp — pf — str
perc: bd, cym, sus cym, sd, tri, tambn, tamtam, glock, xyl, vib, chimes, crot, belltree, 3tomtoms, bass bow

Subito

Lockwood, Normand   1906-2002

(b New York, 19 March 1906; d Denver, CO, 9 March 2002). American

Carol Fantasy <1952>   15'

chorus
0 2 0 0 — 0 2 0 0 — tmp — str

AMP

Loeffler, Charles Martin   1861-1935

(b Schöneberg bei Berlin, 30 Jan 1861; d Medfield, MA, 19 May 1935). German-born American composer

Canticum fratris solis <1925>   18'

solo voice
3 1[Eh] 0 0 — 2 0 0 0 — 2hp — pf, cel — str
This work also arranged for female chorus and orchestra.

Fleisher

Divertissement espagnole pour orchestre et saxophone   11'

solo alto saxophone
2[1.2/pic] 2 2 2 — 2 2 3 0 — tmp+1 — hp — str
perc: tambn

Fleisher

Evocation <1930>   15'

female chorus   male speaker
3[1/afl.2.3/pic] 3[1.2.Eh] 3[1.2.bcl] 3[1.2.cbn] — 4 4 3 1 — asx, 2tsx — tmp+4 — 2hp — cel, pf — str
perc: tambn, xyl, bd, tamtam, sus cym, crot, tri, vib (or 2nd pf)

AME

Five Irish Fantasies <1920>   28'

solo voice (high)
4[incl 2pic] 3[incl Eh] 3[incl bcl] 3[incl cbn] — 4 4 3 1 — tmp+4 — 2hp — cel — str
4 real trumpet parts only in the last 2 bars.
> The Hosting of the Sidhe (Ceol-shee)   2'
> The Host of the Air (Suantraige)   6'
> The Fiddler of Dooney (Geantraige)   3'
> Ballad of the Foxhunter (Goltraige)   10'
> Caitilin Ni Uallachain (The Blind)   7'

Schirmer

Memories of My Childhood (Life in a Russian Village)   *14'*
   <1924>

3[1.2.3/pic] 3[1.2.Eh] 3[1.2.bcl] 3[1.2.cbn] — 4 3 3 1 —
4harmonicas[in F] — tmp+2 — 2hp — cel, pf — str
perc: chimes, xyl, tamtam, bd, cym, tambn

   Schirmer

La Mort de Tintagiles, op.6 <1897; rev 1900>   *25'*

solo viola d'amore
3[1.2.3/pic] 3[1.2.Eh] 4[1.2.Ebcl.bcl] 2 — 4 4[2tp, 2crt] 3 1 —
2tmp+3 — hp — str
perc: sd, tamtam, bd, cym
Originally for 2 solo va d'amore & orch; rev.1900 for a single soloist.

   Kalmus   Luck's   Schirmer

A Pagan Poem, op.14 <1902; rev 1906>   *22'*

3[1.2.3/pic] 3[1.2.Eh] 3[1.2.bcl] 2 — 4 6[3 are offstage] 3 1 — tmp+1
— hp — pf — str
perc: tamtam, glock
Originally *Poème païen* (1902, for 13 insts); revised and orchestrated by
the composer.

   Kalmus   Luck's   Schirmer

La villanelle du diable, op.9 <1901>   *10'*

3[1.2.3/pic] 3[1.2.Eh] 3[1.2.bcl] 3 — 4 4[2tp, 2crt] 3 1 — tmp+3 —
hp — org — str
perc: bd, cym, chimes, sd

   Kalmus   Luck's   Schirmer

Lofstrom, Doug   1949-

(b Chicago, 4 March 1949). American

Concertino, Oboe <2007>   *9'*

2[1.2/pic] 1[Eh] 2 2 — 2 2 0 0 — tmp+1 — str
perc: cym, sus cym, sd, tri, glock

   Little Miracles

Irish Suite #1 (Celtic Morning) <2007>   *8'*

2[1.2/pic] 2 2 2 — 2 2 0 0 — ssx — tmp+1 or 2 — hp[or pf] — str
perc: cym, sd, tambn, bodhrán
   1. Celtic Morning, by Amy Shoemaker   _'
   2. Apples in Winter, & Micho's Jig, by John Williams   _'
   Little Miracles

Two Soldiers: Prelude & Wedding Scene   *10'*

1[1/pic] 1[1/Eh] 1[1/bcl] 2 — 4 2 3 0 — tmp/perc — pf — str
perc: sus cym, sd, tri, glock, tmp
Opt: fl2, ob2, cl 2
   1. Prelude   _'
   2. Wedding Scene   _'
   Little Miracles

The Woodcarver's Daughter: Suite [No.1] <1994>   *33'*

2[1.2/pic] 2 2[1.2/bcl] 2 — 4 3 3 1 — tmp+2 — hp — pf — str
perc: bd, cym, sd, tambn, tamtam, glock, xyl

   Little Miracles

Lombardo, Mario   1931-

(b Elizabeth, NJ, 30 May 1931). American

Drakestail; A Symphonic Fairy Tale for Children   *18'*
   <1976>

narrator
3[1.2.3/pic] 3[1.2.Eh] 3[1.2.bcl] 2 — 4 3 3 1 — tmp+3 — hp — cel
— str
perc: sd, tri, bd, glock, cym, duck horn

   Chappell

London, Edwin   1929-

(b Philadelphia, 16 March 1929). American

A Hero of our Time <1992>   *17'*

4[incl pic] 3[incl Eh] 4[incl Ebcl,bcl] 3[incl cbn] — 4 4 3 1 — tmp+4
— hp — pf — str

   Peters

The Imaginary Invalid: Overture   *4'*

1 0 2[incl bcl] 1 — 0 1 0 0 — str
This work may be out of print.

   EAM

In Heinrich's Shoes   *30'*

1[1/pic/afl] 1[1/Eh] 2[1.bcl/ssx] 0 — 2 1 2 0 — tmp+2 — str
An orchestral fantasy based on the *St. John's Passion* by Heinrich Schütz.

   Peters

Peter Quince at the Clavier <1987>   *30'*

solo tenor
3[incl pic] 2 3[incl bcl] 2 — 4 3 3 1 — tmp+2 — hp — cel/pf —
str[min 10.8.6.5.3]

   Peters

Long, Zhou   -

see under: Zhou Long ["Zhou" is surname]

Lorenz, Ricardo   1961-

(b Maracaibo, 24 May 1961). Venezuelan

En tren vá changó (Destination Macondo) <2001>   *8'*

3[1.2/pic.pic] 3[1.2.Eh] 3[1.2/bcl.Ebcl] 3[1.2.cbn] — 4 4[tp2/flug or
crt] 3 1 — tmp+3 — hp — pf — str[prefer 16.14.12.10.8]

   MMB

Lortzing, (Gustav) Albert   1801-1851

(b Berlin, 23 Oct 1801; d Berlin, 21 Jan 1851). German

Zar und Zimmermann: Overture   *7'*

2[1.2/pic] 2 2 2 — 4 2 3 0 — tmp+2 — str
perc: tri, bd
Playable with winds: 1 0 2 0 — 2 2 1 0.

   Breitkopf   Kalmus   Luck's

Løvenskjold, Herman   1815-1870

(b Holmestrand, Norway, 30 July 1815; d Copenhagen, 5 Dec 1870). Danish composer of Norwegian descent

La Sylphide (Sylfiden) <1836>   70'

2[1.2/pic] 2 2 2 — 4 2 3 0 — tmp+2 — hp — str
perc: bd, cym, tri, sd
Not to be confused with the similarly-named ballet *Les Sylphides*, on music by Chopin.
   Original orchestration (1836). Piano reduction available from Payne.
   Arrangement for larger orchestra by John Lanchbery (Oxford):
3[1.2.3/pic] 2[1.2/Eh] 2 2 — 4 3 3 1 — tmp+3 — hp — str.
   Yet another arrangement by Bonynge is offered by Mario Bois; instrumentation not available.

Overture	7'
Act 1	28'
Act 2	35'

Payne

Luening, Otto   1900-1996

(b Milwaukee, 15 June 1900; d New York, 2 Sept 1996). American

Prelude to a Hymn Tune by William Billings <1937>   10'

1 1 1 1 — 1 0 0 0 — pf — str

Luck's   Peters

Rhapsodic Variations <1954>   17'

(composed with Vladimir Ussachevsky)
2[1.2/pic] 2 2 2 — 4 2 3 0 — electronic tape — tmp+1 — str

Peters

Synthesis <1962>   9'

2[1.pic] 2 2 2 — 2 2 3 0 — electronic tape — 3perc — pf — str

Peters

Luigini, Alexandre   1850-1906

(b Lyons, 9 March 1850; d Paris, 29 July 1906). French composer of Italian descent

Ballet égyptien <1875>   20'

3[1.2/pic.3/pic] 2 2 2 — 4 2 3 1 — tmp+4 — 2hp — str

Kalmus   Luck's

Lully, Jean-Baptiste   1632-1687

(b Florence, 29 Nov 1632; d Paris, 22 March 1687). French composer of Italian birth

Ballet Suite   16'

2 2 2 2 — 4 2 0 0 — tmp — str
Arr. Felix Mottl from ballet music of five Lully operas.

1. Introduction (Le temple de la paix)	_'
2. Nocturno (Le triomphe de l'amour)	_'
3. Menuetto (Le temple de la paix)	_'
4. Prelude (Alceste), Les Vents (Alceste), Marche (Thésée)	_'

Kalmus   Luck's   Peters

Roland: Suite <1685>   9'

1 2 0 1 — 2 2 0 0 — tmp — str
Arr. William Lynen.

Overture	_'
Marsch	_'
Air	_'
Menuet	_'
Gavotte	_'
Gigue	_'

Kalmus   Luck's

Le triomphe de l'amour: Ballet Suite <1681>   20'

str
Ed. Paul Angerer.

Doblinger

Lutosławski, Witold   1913-1994

(b Warsaw, 25 Jan 1913; d Warsaw, 9 Feb 1994). Polish

Chain 1 (Łańcuch 1) <1983>   9'

1[1/pic/afl] 1[1/Eh] 1 1 — 1 1 1 0 — 1perc — hpsd — str 5t
perc: marim, xyl, gong, tamtam, 2sus cym

Chester   PWM

Chain 2: Dialog for Violin & Orchestra (Łańcuch 2) <1984–1985>   18'

2[1/pic.2/pic] 2[1.2/Eh] 2[1.2/bcl] 2 — 0 2 2 0 — 2perc — pf/cel — str[min 6.6.4.4.2]
perc: chimes, marim, xyl, vib, glock, bongos, sd, 5tomtom, tmp

1. Ad libitum	4'
2. A battuta	5'
3. Ad libitum	5'
4. A battuta	4'

PWM

Chantefleurs et chantefables <1989–1990>   22'

solo soprano
1 1 1[cl/bcl/Ebcl] 1[bn/cbn] — 1 1 1 0 — tmp+1 — hp — pf/cel — str[min 8.6.4.4.2]

1. La Belle-de-Nuit (The Marvel of Peru)	3'
2. La Sauterelle (The Grasshopper)	2'
3. La Véronique (The Speedwell)	2'
4. L'Eglantine, l'aubépine et la glycine (Wild Rose, Hawthorn, Wisteria)	2'
5. La Tortue (The Tortoise)	2'
6. La Rose (The Rose)	3'
7. L'Alligator (The Alligator)	3'
8. L'Angélique (The Ravishing Angelica Flower)	3'
9. Le Papillon (The Butterfly)	2'

Chester

Concerto for Orchestra <1950–1954>   28'

3[1.2/pic.3/pic] 3[1.2.3/Eh] 3[1.2.3/bcl] 3[1.2.3/cbn] — 4 4 4 1 — tmp+5 — 2hp — cel, pf — str
perc: cym, sus cym, tambn, glock, tamtam, td, sd, bd, field dr, xyl, 3tomtoms

I. Intrada	7'
II. Capriccio notturno e arioso	6'
III. Passacaglia, toccata e corale	15'

Chester   PWM

Concerto, Oboe, Harp & Chamber Orchestra (Double Concerto) <1979–1980>   19'

2perc — str[7vn, 2va, 2vc, db]
perc: vib, xyl, bongos, bd, marim, glock, gong, tamtam, td, sd, tri, templeblks, 5tomtoms, tmp, 3sus cym

I. Rapsodico; Appassionato	5'
II. Dolente	7'
III. Marciale e grotesco	7'

Chester   PWM

Concerto, Piano <1987–1988>   26'

3[1.2/pic.3/pic] 3 3[1.2/Ebcl.3/bcl] 3[1.2.3/cbn] — 4 2 3 1 — tmp+2 — hp — cel — str
perc: bd, xyl, bongos, 3tamtam, 4tomtom
Movements are played without pause.

1. dotted quarter-note = 110	6'
2. quarter-note = 160	5'
3. eighth-note = 85	7'
4. quarter-note = 84	8'

Chester

Concerto, Violoncello <1969–1970>   24'

3[1.2/pic.3/pic] 3 3[1.2.3/bcl] 3[1.2.3/cbn] — 4 3 3 1 — tmp+2 — hp — cel, pf — str

perc: xyl, tamtam, whip, vib, sus cym, sd, td, bd/cym, 5tomtoms, 3woodblk, bellplate

Chester	PWM

Dance Preludes (Preludia taneczne) <1954; rev (orchd) 1955>   7'

solo clarinet

tmp+1 — hp — pf — str[8.8.6.6.4]

perc: sd; timpanist covers bd, sus cym, sd w/o snares

Originally for clarinet & piano; orchestrated by the composer.
   In 1959 arr. for 9 instruments: woodwind 5t, vn, va, vc, db.

PWM

Little Suite [rev.1951] (Mała suita) <1950; rev 1951>   11'

2[1.pic] 2 2 2 — 4 3 3 1 — tmp+1 — str

perc: sd

Originally for chamber orchestra; revised for full orchestra.

1. Fife	3'
2. Hurra pulka	2'
3. Song	3'
4. Dance	3'

Chester	PWM

Livre pour orchestre (Książka na orkiestrę) <1968>   20'

3[1.2/pic.3/pic] 3 3 3[1.2.3/cbn] — 4 3 3 1 — 3perc — hp — cel, pf — str

perc: bongos, sd, vib, field dr, gong, tamtam, chimes, glock, bd, td, tmp, 2xyl, 2tomtoms, 2sus cym

Chester	PWM

Mi-parti <1976>   15'

3[1/pic.2/pic.3/pic] 3 3[1.2.3/bcl] 3 — 4 3 3 1 — tmp+3 — hp — cel, pf — str

perc: glock, marim, xyl, vib, chimes, tamtam, 2sus cym

Chester	PWM

Musique funèbre (Muzyka żałobna) <1958>   14'

str

In memory of Béla Bártòk.

Chester	PWM

Novelette <1978–1979>   18'

3[1.2/pic.3/pic] 3[1.2.3/Eh] 3[1.2/Ebcl.3/bcl] 3[1.2.3/cbn] — 4 3 3 1 — tmp+4 — 2hp — pf, cel — str

perc: bd, sd, td, glock, xyl, marim, vib, chimes, 2sus cym, 5tomtom

I. Announcement	2'
II. First Event	3'
III. Second Event	4'
IV. Third Event	2'
V. Conclusion	7'

Chester

Overture for Strings <1949>   5'

str

Chester	PWM

Polish Dances (10 tańców polskich) <1951>   12'

1[fl/pic] 1 2 1 — 1 1 0 0 — 2perc — str

perc: tri, tambn, sd, td, sus cym, bd

1. Koziorajka (Silesian Folk Dance)	'
2. Nie chcę cię znać (I Don't Want to Know You)	'
3. Gołąbek (A Little Pigeon)	'
4. Grozik (Kaszuby Folk Dance)	'
5. Kaczok (Duckling)	'
6. Kowal (Blacksmith)	'
7. I ty i ja [Laura] (And You and Me [Laura])	'
8. Maryszunka (Kaszuby Folk Dance)	'
9. Dobra tabaczka (Good Little Snuff)	'
10. Szejper (Skipper)	'

PWM

Postludium <1958–1963>   4'

3[1.2.pic] 3 3[1.2.bcl] 3[1.2.cbn] — 4 3 3 1 — tmp+2 — hp — cel, pf — str

perc: xyl, bd, sd, tambn

No.1 of the *Three Postludes*.

Chester	PWM

Prelude for GSMD (Worldes Blis Ne Last No Throwe) <1989>   2'

2 2 2 2 — 2 2 2 1 — 2perc — hp — str

perc: sd, glock, vib, chimes, tmp

GSMD = Guildhall School of Music and Drama.

Chester	Hansen

Preludes & Fugue for 13 Solo Strings <1970–1972>   34'

7vn, 3va, 2vc, 1db

Any of the preludes in any order can be played with or without the fugue, which can itself be shortened four possible ways. Duration given is the longest possible.

Chester	Hansen	PWM

Symphony No.1 <1941–1947>   26'

3[1.2/pic.pic] 3[1.2.Eh] 3[1.2/Ebcl.3/bcl] 3[1.2.cbn] — 4 3 3 1 — tmp+3 — hp — pf, cel — str

perc: bd, cym, sus cym, sd, tambn, tamtam, glock, xyl, woodblk

I. Allegro giusto	6'
II. Poco adagio	10'
III. Allegretto misterioso	5'
IV. Allegro vivace	5'

Chester

Symphony No.2 <1965–1967>   28'

3[1/pic.2/pic.3/pic] 3[1.2.3/Eh] 3[1.2.3/bcl] 3 — 4 3 3 1 — tmp+2 — hp — pf, cel[played by perc] — str[16.14.12.9.6]

perc: bd, td, sd, field dr, tambn, chimes, xyl, vib, 2sus cym, cel[played by perc], bamboo windchimes; timpanist covers 5tomtoms, glock

| 1. Hésitant | 14' |
| 2. Direct | 14' |

Chester	Hansen	PWM

Symphony No.3 <1981–1983>   28'

3[1.2/pic.3/pic] 3[1.2.3/Eh] 3[1.2/Ebcl.3/bcl] 3[1.2.3/cbn] — 4 4 4 1 — tmp+4 — 2hp — cel, pf 4-hands — str

perc: xyl, sd, tambn, bongos, glock, tamtam, bd, chimes, vib, marim, td, gong, 3sus cym, 5tomtoms

Chester

Symphony No.4 <1988–1992>   22'

3[1.2.3/pic] 3[1.2.3/Eh] 3[1.2/Ebcl.3/bcl] 3[1.2.3/cbn] — 4 3 3 1 — tmp+3 — 2hp — cel, pf — str

perc: bd, sd, td, tambn, tamtam, glock, xyl, marim, vib, chimes, bongos, 3sus cym, 4tomtom

Chester

Three Postludes (Trzy postludia) <1958`1963`>   18'

3[1.2/pic.pic] 3 3[1.2.3/bcl] 3[1.2.3/cbn] — 4 3 3 1 — tmp+3 — 2hp
— pf, cel[played by perc] — str[16.14.12.12.8]
perc: sd, field dr, xyl, bd, tamtam, vib, td, cel[played by perc], 2sus cym; timpanist
covers tambn, tri, glock
  I. Pour le centenaire de la Croix-Rouge   4'
  II. quarter-note = 160   5'
  III. quarter-note = 150   9'

Chester	PWM

Venetian Games (Jeux vénitiens) <1960–1961>   13'

2[1.2/pic] 1 3[1.2.3/bcl] 1 — 1 1 1 0 — tmp+3 — hp — pf 4-hands
doubling cel — str[4vn.3va.3vc.2db]
perc: td, xyl, cym, tamtam, vib, claves, 3sd, 5tomtoms, 3sus cym

Moeck	PWM

Lysenko, Mykola   1842-1912

(b Hrynky, nr Kremenchug, Poltava district, 10/22 March 1842; d Kiev, 24 Oct/6
Nov 1912). Ukrainian

Taras Bulba: Overture <1880–1891>   5'

3[1.2.pic] 3[1.2.Eh] 3[1.2.bcl] 3[1.2.cbn] — 4 3 3 1 — tmp+4 — hp
— str
perc: tri, bd, cym, sus cym, sd, tambn
Revised by L. Revutsky.

Russian	Schirmer

M

MacDowell, Edward   1860-1908

(b New York, 18 Dec 1860; d New York, 23 Jan 1908). American

Concerto, Piano, No.1, op.15, A minor <1882>   25'

2 2 2 2 — 4 2 0 0 — tmp — str
  Maestoso; Allegro con fuoco   10'
  Andante tranquillo   7'
  Presto   8'

Breitkopf	Kalmus	Luck's

Concerto, Piano, No.2, op.23, D minor <1884–1886>   26'

2 2 2 2 — 4 2 3 0 — tmp — str
  I. Larghetto calmato   13'
  II. Presto giocoso   5'
  III. Largo - Molto allegro   8'

Breitkopf	Kalmus	Luck's

Hamlet & Ophelia, op.22 <1884–1885>   17'

3[1.2.pic] 2 2 2 — 4 2 3 0 — tmp+1 — str
perc: cym, sus cym, bd
Sometimes construed as 2 separate symphonic poems.
  1. Hamlet (above instrumentation)   10'
  2. Ophelia (2 2 2 2 — 4 2 0 0 — tmp — str).   7'

Kalmus	Luck's

Lamia, op.29 (Symphonic Poem No.3) <1887>   18'

3[1.2.pic] 2 2 2 — 4 2 3 1 — tmp+1 — str
perc: cym, tamtam
Original publisher: Arthur P. Schmidt.

Kalmus

Lancelot and Elaine, op.25 (Symphonic Poem No.2) <1886>   20'

3[1.2.pic] 2 2 2 — 4 2 3 1 — tmp+2 — str
perc: cym, sus cym, bd

Kalmus	Schirmer

The Saracens; Two Fragments after the "Song of   10'
Roland," op.30 (Die Sarazenen) <1886–1890>

3[1.2.pic] 2 2 2 — 4 2 3 1 — tmp+2 — str
perc: cym, bd
  The Saracens (Die Sarazenen)   3'
  Lovely Aldâ (Die schöne Aldâ)   7'

Breitkopf	Kalmus

Suite No.1, A minor, op.42 <1888–1891; rev (3rd mvt   20'
added) 1893>

3[1.2.pic] 2 2 2 — 4 2 3 1 — tmp+2 — str
perc: cym, sus cym, bd
  1. In einem verwünschten Walde (In a Haunted Forest)   6'
  2. Sommer-Idylle (Summer Idyll)   2'
  3. Im Oktober (In October)   3'
  4. Gesang der Hirtin (The Shepherdess's Song)   4'
  5. Waldgeister (Forest Spirits)   5'

Kalmus	Luck's

Suite No.2, E minor, op.48 (Indian) <1891–1895>   30'

3[1.2.pic] 2 2 2 — 4 2 3 1 — tmp+2 — str
perc: bd, cym

1. Legend	7'
2. Love Song	6'
3. In War-Time	5'
4. Dirge	6'
5. Village Festival	6'

Breitkopf	Kalmus	Luck's

Mackey, Steven   1956-

(b Frankfurt, 14 Feb 1956). American

Beautiful Passing <2008>   20'

solo violin
3[1.2/pic1.pic2] 2[1.2/Eh] 3[1.2/Ebcl.bcl] 2[1.2/cbn] — 4 2 2 1 — tmp+2 — hp — pf — str
perc: bd, set, brake dr, gong, glock, xyl, marim, vib, crot[E-flat, dipped in water], flexatone, woodblk, 2sus cym, 3tomtom, peking gng, bow, 2tennisball

Boosey

Deal <1995>   20'

solo electric guitar; solo drum set (optional)
1[1/pic/afl] 1[1/Eh] 1[1/bcl] 1 — 1 1 1 0 — pre-recorded tape — 1perc — hp — pf — str 5t
perc: marim, vib, glock, chimes, szl cym, tamtam, bd, woodblk, cowbell, ratch, tmp, 2sus cym, tuned gong, herdbells
Amplification required.
   A later version (1996) of this work for full orchestra exists.

Boosey

Eating Greens <1993>   23'

3[1.2/pic.3/pic] 3[1.2.3/Eh] 3[1.2.bcl/cbcl] 3[1.2.cbn] — 4 3 3 1 — tsx/bsx — pre-recorded tape — tmp+4 — hp — pf/cel/harm — str
perc: marim, sd, bongos, windchimes, vib, xyl, cym, szl cym, cowbell, glock, templeblks, cast, ratch, belltree, chimes, bd, hi-hat, lionroar, marac, claves, flexatone, woodblk, guiro, 3tamtams, 3sus cym, 3tri, party horn, harmonica, sandblks, 2buttongongs, 3logdrums, 3tambn, 3glass jars, prayer stones, whistle, 3tomtoms, 3glass bottles
Pizza is delivered to principal double bass.

Boosey

Square Holes, Round Pegs <1987>   15'

2[1/afl.2/pic] 2[1.2/Eh] 2[1.2/bcl] 2[1.cbn] — 2 2 0 0 — tmp+1 — hp — pf — str
perc: bd, sus cym, szl cym, tambn, tamtam, chimes, windchimes[wood or bamboo], woodblk, claves, lionroar, 8buttongong[tuned], 3tri

Margun

TILT <1992>   13'

3[1.2/pic.3/pic] 3[1.2.3/Eh] 3[1.2/asx.bcl/cbcl] 3[1.2.3/cbn] — 4 3 3 1 — tmp+4 — hp — pf — str
perc: xyl, tamtam, glock, lionroar, guiro, ratch, claves, marim, templeblks, chimes, vib, bd, hi-hat, szl cym, steelpan, 3sus cym, whistle, 4cowbells, herdbells, 3tri, 2woodblks, 2buttongongs, metalpipe, anvil, bike bell, bike hn, 2tambn, glass windchimes, autohorn

Boosey

MacMillan, James   1959-

(b Kilwinning, 16 July 1959). Scottish

Britannia <1994>   12'

3[1.2.3/pic] 3[1.2.Eh] 3[1.2.3/bcl] 3[1.2.cbn] — 4 3 3 1 — tmp+3 — hp — str
perc: bd, cym, sd, tri, tamtam, vib, flexatone, whip, autohorn, bodhran, cocoshells, duckcall, klaxon, whistle, 2cowbells, 5tomtoms, 2woodblks

Boosey

The Confession of Isobel Gowdie <1990>   20'

2[1.2/pic] 2[1.2/Eh] 2[1.2/bcl] 2[1.2/cbn] — 4 3 3 1 — tmp+2 — str
perc: congas, xyl, chimes, sd, vib, bd, tamtam, 3tamtams, anvil

Boosey

Epiclesis <1993>   25'

solo trumpet
3[1.2.3/pic] 3[1.2.3/Eh] 3[1.2.3/bcl] 3[1.2.cbn] — 6 3 3 1 — tmp+4 — str[min 14.12.10.8.8]
perc: marim, thundersheet, vib, crot, bongos, glock, cym, chimes, bd, belltree, tri, sd, bowlgong, 2tamtams, 4gamelan gongs, sanctus bell, 4cowbells, 6tomtoms, anvil, cencerros (chromatic cowbells), 4woodblks

Boosey

Seven Last Words From the Cross <1993>   47'

chorus SATB
str

I. Father, forgive them, for they know not what they do	6'
II. Woman, behold thy Son! …Behold thy Mother!	5'
III. Verily, I say unto you, today thou shalt be with me in Paradise	8'
IV. Eli, Eli, lama sabachthani	7'
V. I thirst	6'
VI. It is finished	7'
VII. Father, into Thy hands I commend my Spirit	8'

Boosey

Veni, veni, Emmanuel <1992>   26'

solo percussion
2[1.2/pic] 2[1.2/Eh] 2[1.2/bcl] 2[1.2/cbn] — 2 2 2[tbn.btbn] 0 — tmp — str[min 8.6.4.4.2]
perc: (solo) congas, timbales, marim, marktree, sus cym, szl cym, chimes, 2tamtams, 2sd, 6tomtoms, bd/ped, 6chinese gongs, 6templeblks, logdrum, 2woodblks, 2cowbells

Boosey

Maderna, Bruno   1920-1973

(b Venice, 21 April 1920; d Darmstadt, 13 Nov 1973). Italian

Aura <1972>   20'

4[all/pic] 4[incl Eh] 5[incl Ebcl,2bcl] 3[incl cbn] — 4 5 4 0 — tmp+13 — 2hp — cel — str[12.12.12.10.8]
perc: vib, glock, whip, claves, congas, bd, 2xyl, 2marim, 4sus cym, 2sets slgh-bells, 4tri, 6templeblks, 4gongs[A#3,G#3,D3,E3]; (tmp covers 1slgh-bells & 1sus cym)

Ricordi

Concerto, Oboe, No.3 <1973>   15'

4[1.2.3.4/pic] 4[1.2.3.Eh] 4[1.2.Ebcl.bcl] 3[1.2.3/cbn] — 4 5 4 0 — tmp+3 — 2hp — cel — str
perc: glock, vib, marim, xyl (covered by tmp)

Salabert

Serenata No.2 <1954>   16'

1[1/pic] 0 2[incl bcl] 0 — 1 1 0 0 — 1perc — hp — pf/glock — vn, va, db
perc: xyl, vib; glock (covered by pianist)

Zerboni

Venetian Journal <1972>   20'

solo tenor
1[1/pic] 1[1/Eh] 1[1/bcl] 1 — 1 1 1 0 — pre-recorded tape — 2perc — hp — cel — str
perc: xyl, tri, bd/cym, marim, templeblks

Ricordi

Magnard, Albéric
1865-1914

(b Paris, 9 June 1865; d Baron, Oise, 3 Sept 1914). French

Chant funèbre, op.9 <1895>
15'

2 2 2 2 — 4 1 3 0 — tmp — hp — str

Kalmus	Luck's	Salabert

Hymne à la justice, op.14
14'

3 2 3 2 — 4 3[tp4 ad lib] 3 0 — tmp — hp — str

An optional part for a 4th tp is included in the material though not in the score; it doubles tp1 in the tutti from fig. [23] to [24] at the discretion of the conductor.
  The material is said to be riddled with errors.

Kalmus	Luck's	Salabert

Symphony No.3, op.11, B-flat minor <1896>
38'

2 2[1.2/Eh] 2 2 — 4 2 3 0 — tmp — str

I. Introduction et Ouverture	12'
II. Danses	7'
III. Pastorale	10'
IV Final	9'

Kalmus	Luck's	Salabert

Mahler, Gustav
1860-1911

(b Kalischt, nr Iglau [now Kaliste, Jihlava], Bohemia, 7 July 1860; d Vienna, 18 May 1911). Austrian

Mahler frequently revised his works. Though much of his music is available through reprint houses, these are often not the final versions.
  The International Gustav Mahler Society maintains an excellent website at www.gustav-mahler.org.
  Mahler's scores include elaborate and meticulous instructions for conductor and players; German-English glossaries of these indications are available from the Conductors Guild (conductorsguild.com). These are typically 2-4 pages per work, and are intended to be reproduced and handed out to orchestral players. Available glossaries: Symphonies 1-8, Kindertotenlieder, Lieder eines fahrenden Gesellen, *and* Das Lied von der Erde.

Des Antonius von Padua Fischpredigt <1893>
4'

solo voice
2 2 2 3 — 4 0 0 0 — tmp+2 — str
perc: cym, tri, bd, tamtam, rute
From *Des Knaben Wunderhorn*. Available in C minor (original key) and D minor. Also available in B minor from Luck's.

Kalmus	Universal

Blicke mir nicht in die Lieder! <1901>
2'

solo voice
1 1 1 1 — 1 0 0 0 — hp — str[no db]
From *Rückert Lieder*. Available in F major (original key), and A-flat major or E-flat major.

Kalmus	Luck's	Universal

Blumine
see his: Symphony No.1: *Blumine*

Ich atmet' einen Linden Duft <1901>
2'

solo voice
1 1 1 2 — 3 0 0 0 — hp — cel — vn, va
From *Rückert Lieder*. Available in F major, D major (original key), and C major.

Kalmus	Luck's	Universal

Ich bin der Welt abhanden gekommen <1901>
5'

solo voice
0 2[1.Eh] 2 2 — 2 0 0 0 — hp — str
From *Rückert Lieder*. Available in F major (original key), and E-flat major, or D-flat major.

Kalmus	Luck's	Universal

Das irdische Leben <1892–1893>
3'

solo voice
2 3[1.2.Eh] 2 2 — 3 1 0 0 — 1perc — str
perc: cym
From *Des Knaben Wunderhorn*. Available in E-flat minor (original key), and D minor.

Kalmus	Luck's	Universal

Kindertotenlieder <1901–1904>
26'

solo voice (medium)
3[1.2.pic] 3[1.2.Eh] 3[1.2.bcl] 3[1.2.cbn] — 4 0 0 0 — tmp+1 — hp — cel — str
perc: glock, tamtam
Peters (Kahnt) ed. Zoltan Roman, 1979.
  Bcl is partly in A and partly in B-flat, but always in treble clef ("French notation").
  A reduced orchestration by de Leeuw is published by Donemus.

1. Nun will die Sonn' so hell aufgeh'n	6'
2. Nun seh' ich wohl	5'
3. Wenn dein Mütterlein	5'
4. Oft denk' ich, sie sind nur ausgegangen	3'
5. In diesem Wetter	7'

Kalmus	Luck's	Peters	Universal

Das klagende Lied (original version in 3 mvts) <1878–1880>
65'

solos SATBar, 2boys[S&A]   chorus
6[1.2/pic.3/pic; *1.2.pic*] 3[1.2.Eh] 7[1.2.bcl; *1.2.Ebcl1.Ebcl2*] 6[1.2.3; *1.2.3*] — 4[all dbl hand horns] 10[1/crt1.2/crt2.3.4; *1/flg1.2/flg2.3/flg3.flg4.crt1.crt2*] 3 2 — tmp+3; *tmp+2* — 6hp[2real parts] — str
perc: tri, cym, tamtam, bd; *tri, cym*
In addition to the main orchestra, a *Fernorchester* ("distant orchestra") of winds and percussion. Specifications for the *Fernorchester* are included above in italics.
  Ed. Reinhold Kubik, 1997.

1. Waldmärchen (Forest Legend)	28'
2. Der Spielmann (The Minstrel)	18'
3. Hochzeitsstück (Wedding Piece)	19'

Universal

Das klagende Lied (2nd version in 2 mvts) <1878–1880; rev 1892-3, 1898-9>
37'

chorus   solos SAT, opt boy alto
6[1.2.3/pic; *1.2.pic*] 5[1.2.3/Eh; *1.2*] 7[1.2.3/bcl; *1.2.Ebcl1.Ebcl2*] 3[1.2.3/cbn] — 8[1-4; *1-4*] 6[1-4; 2tp or flg] 3 1 — tmp+3; *<tmp+2>* — 2hp — str
perc: tri, cym, tamtam, bd; *tri, cym*
In addition to the main orchestra, a *Fernorchester* ("distant orchestra") of winds and percussion. Specifications for the *Fernorchester* are included above in italics.
  Universal ed. Rudolf Stephan, 1978.

1. Der Spielmann (The Minstrel)	18'
2. Hochzeitsstück (Wedding Piece)	19'

Kalmus	Luck's	Universal

Liebst du um Schönheit? <1902>
3'

solo voice
0 3[1.2.Eh] 2 2 — 4 0 0 0 — hp — str
From *Rückert Lieder*. Available in E-flat major, C major (original key), and B-flat major.
  This particular song was orchestrated not by Mahler himself, but by Max Puttmann.

Kalmus	Luck's	Universal

Lied des Verfolgten im Turm <1898>   5'

solo voice
2 2 2 2 — 4 2 0 0 — tmp — str
From *Des Knaben Wunderhorn*. Available in C minor (original key), and
D minor.

Kalmus	Luck's	Universal

Das Lied von der Erde <1908–1909>   63'

alto (or baritone) & tenor solos
4[1.2.3.pic] 3[1.2.3/Eh] 4[1.2.3/Ebcl.bcl/3] 3[1.2.3/cbn] — 4 3 3 1 —
mand — tmp+3 — 2hp — cel — str
perc: bd, cym, sus cym, tri, tambn, tamtam, glock
The composer apparently had 5 clarinetists (including E-flat clarinet and
bass clarinet) in mind, but the parts can be readily covered by four
players; the 3rd clarinet part must be taken by the E-flat clarinetist and
bass clarinetist alternately (a single bcl note has to be omitted in mvt 1,
bar 37). The bcl is mostly in B-flat, though there are about 40 bars for bcl
in A in the 6th mvt.
    Universal edition by Karl Heinz Füssl, 1990.
    The early piano-vocal score prepared by Mahler does not entirely agree
with the orchestral version; use instead the piano-reduction by Erwin
Stein (Boosey & Universal).

   1. Das Trinklied von Jammer der Erde (tenor)   9'
   2. Der Einsame im Herbst (alto)   10'
   3. Von der Jugend (tenor)   3'
   4. Von der Schönheit (alto)   7'
   5. Der Trunkene im Frühling (tenor)   4'
   6. Der Abschied (alto)   30'

Kalmus	Universal

Lieder aus "Des Knaben Wunderhorn" (Youth's Magic Horn) <1892–1898>   42'

solo voice
3[1.2.pic] 3[1.2.Eh] 3[1.2.Ebcl] 3 — 4 2 1 1 — tmp+4 — hp — str
perc: cym, bd/cym, tamtam, sus cym, sd, field dr, tri, rute
Songs are available individually, each with a choice of high or low key
(the original keys are indicated by italics in the contents list below).
Instrumentation varies from song to song within the aggregate given
above.
    Other songs from *Des Knaben Wunderhorn*: two appear in *Sieben
Lieder aus letzter Zeit*; others appear as mvts of Symphonies nos. 2, 3,
and 4, and are also available separately, though only in the original keys.
    Of those below, nos. 2, 4, 7, 9, & 10 are available from Presser in
arrangements by Philip West for voice and chamber orchestra (20').

   1. Der Schildwache Nachtlied (C major, *B-flat major*)   6'
   2. Verlorne Müh' (*A major*, G major)   4'
   3. Trost im Unglück (*A major*, G major)   4'
   4. Wer hat dies Liedlein erdacht? (*F major*, E-flat major)   2'
   5. Das irdische Leben (*E-flat minor*, D minor)   3'
   6. Des Antonius von Padua Fischpredigt (D minor, *C minor*)   4'
   7. Rheinlegendchen (*A major*, G major)   3'
   8. Lied des verfolgten im Turm (*D minor*, C minor)   5'
   9. Wo die schönen Trompeten blasen (*D minor*, C minor)   7'
   10. Lob des hohen Verstandes (*D major*, C major)   4'

Kalmus	Luck's	Universal

Lieder eines fahrenden Gesellen (Songs of a Wayfarer) <1883–1885; rev ?1891-6>   16'

solo voice (medium)
3[1.2.3/pic] 2[1.2/Eh] 3[1.2.3/bcl] 2 — 4 2 3 0 — tmp+2 — hp — str
perc: bd, cym, tri, tamtam, glock
Weinberger ed. Zoltan Roman, 1982.
   1. Wenn mein Schatz Hochzeit macht   4'
   2. Ging heut Morgen über's Feld   4'
   3. Ich hab' ein glühend Messer   3'
   4. Die zwei blauen Augen   5'

Kalmus	Luck's	Weinberger

Lob des hohen Verstandes <1896>   4

solo voice
2 2 3[1.2.Ebcl] 2 — 4 1 1 1 — tmp+1 — str
perc: tri
From *Des Knaben Wunderhorn*. Available in D major (original key), and
C major.

Kalmus	Luck's	Universal

Revelge <1899>   7'

solo voice
2[1.2/pic] 2 2 3[1.2.cbn] — 4 3 0 0 — tmp+3 — str
perc: tri, sus cym, sd, tamtam, bd/cym
From *Sieben Lieder aus letzten Zeit*. Available in D minor (original key),
C minor, B-flat minor.

Kalmus	Luck's	Universal

Rheinlegendchen <1893>   3'

solo voice
1 1 1 1 — 1 0 0 0 — str
From *Des Knaben Wunderhorn*. Available in A major (original key), and
G major.

Kalmus	Luck's	Universal

Rückert Lieder <1901–1902>   18'

solo voice
2 3[1/ob d'am.2.Eh] 2 3[1.2.cbn] — 4 2 3 1 — tmp — hp[dbl in no.4]
— cel/pf — str
Nos.3-7 of his *Sieben Lieder aus letzten Zeit* (i.e., "seven recent songs," a
collection cobbled together by the publisher). Often sung as a cycle, the
order being at the discretion of the performer.
    Songs are available individually, each with a choice of high, medium,
or low key (the original keys are indicated by italics in the contents list
below). Instrumentation varies from song to song, within the aggregate
given above.
   1. Blicke mir nicht in die Lieder (A-flat major, *F major*, E-flat major)   2'
   2. Ich atmet' einen Linden Duft (F major, *D major*, C major)   2'
   3. Ich bin der Welt abhanden gekommen (*F major*, Eb major, Db major)   5'
   4. Um Mitternacht (B-minor, *A minor*, G minor)   6'
   5. Liebst du um Schönheit? (E-flat major, *C major*, B-flat major)   5'

Kalmus	Luck's	Universal

Der Schildwache Nachtlied <1892>   6'

solo voice
3[1.2.pic] 3[1.2.Eh] 2 2 — 4 2 0 0 — tmp+4 — hp — str
perc: tri, field dr, cym, bd/cym
From *Des Knaben Wunderhorn*. Available in B-flat major (original key),
and C major.

Kalmus	Universal

Sieben Lieder aus letzten Zeit <1899–1902>   30'

solo voice
2[1.2/pic] 3[1/ob d'am.2/Eh.3/Eh] 3[1.2.bcl] 3[1.2.cbn] — 4 3 3 1 —
tmp+3 — hp[dbl in no.6] — pf/cel — str
perc: tri, sus cym, sd, tamtam, bd/cym, cym
Songs are available individually, each with a choice of high, medium, or
low key (the original keys are indicated by italics in the contents list
below). Instrumentation varies from song to song, within the aggregate
given above. Not intended as a cycle, but merely "seven recent songs"
published together.
    Nos.3-7 are known as *Rückert Lieder*, after the poet of the texts
(nos.1-2 use texts from *Des Knaben Wunderhorn*).
    Nos.4, 3, 7 & 5 are available from Presser with orchestration arranged
by Philip West for woodwind quintet, harp, and string quartet (12').
   1. Revelge (*D minor*, C minor, B-flat minor)   7'
   2. Der Tamboursg'sell (E minor, *D minor*, C minor)   5'
   3. Blicke mir nicht in die Lieder (A-flat major, *F major*, E-flat major)   2'
   4. Ich atmet' einen Linden Duft (F major, *D major*, C major)   2'
   5. Ich bin der Welt abhanden gekommen (*F major*, Eb major, Db major)   5'
   6. Um Mitternacht (B-minor, *A minor*, G minor)   6'
   7. Liebst du um Schönheit? (E-flat major, *C major*, B-flat major)   3'

Kalmus	Luck's	Universal

Symphonic Prelude (Sinfonisches Präludium) <1876>   10'

2[1.2/pic] 2 2 2[1.2/cbn] — 4 2 3 1 — tmp+1 — hp — str
perc: sus cym[one note]
The attribution of this 1876 work to Mahler is not universally accepted; some scholars believe it to be by Bruckner. The original manuscript is lost. What survives is a preliminary sketch for the score, prepared by another hand (perhaps a fellow-student of Mahler's) with some notations about orchestration. From this, Albrecht Gürsching created a "reconstruction" of the score.

Sikorski

Symphony No.1, D major (Titan) <1884–1888; rev 1893-6; 2nd rev. ca 1906>   53'

4[1.2/pic2.3/pic1.4/pic3] 4[1.2.3/Eh.4] 4[1.2.3/bcl/Ebcl2.4/Ebcl1] 3[1.2.3/cbn] — 7 4 3 1 — 2tmp+3 — hp — str
perc: bd, bd/cym, cym, sus cym, tri, tamtam
A 5th trumpet and 4th trombone may be used in the last movement to strengthen the horns if necessary. Also in the last movement, the 4th clarinet (playing Ebcl) should be "at least" doubled; thus a 5th or even 6th player.
    Universal ed. Sander Wilkens ("corrected new printing"), 1995.
    A reduced version by Erwin Stein is available from Universal, supposedly calling for:
    2 2 3 2 — 4 3[4 opt] 3[4 opt] 1 — 2tmp+3 — hp — str

I. Langsam schleppend	15'
II. Kräftig bewegt	8'
III. Feierlich und gemessen	12'
IV. Stürmisch bewegt	18'

Kalmus	Luck's	Universal

Symphony No.1: Blumine <1884–1888>   8'

2 2 2 2 — 4 1 0 0 — tmp — hp — str
In its original form, the symphony included this piece as the second of five movements. The five-movement version was performed under Mahler's direction in 1889 and 1894, but this movement was deleted in the published version of 1899.

Presser

Symphony No.2, C minor (Resurrection; Auferstehungssymphonie) <1888–1894; rev 1903>   80'

chorus   solos SA
4[1/pic.2/pic.3/pic.4/pic] 4[1.2.3/Eh.4/Eh] 5[1.2.3/bcl.4/Ebcl2.Ebcl1] 4[1.2.3.4/cbn] — 10 8 4 1 — 2tmp+6 — 2hp[preferably dbl] — org — str
perc: bd, cym, glock, sus cym, 3tri, 3sd, 2tamtams, 3bells (indefinite pitch), rute, tmp (additional in 5th mvt)
Cl 1-3 play C-clarinets in parts of the 2nd & 3rd mvts (81 bars totale) Cbn is sometimes in the 3rd bn part and sometimes in the 4th; however, only 1 cbn is required. Possible with 6tp. Important offstage passages for players (drawn from the above aggregate): 4hn, 4tp, 3perc.
    Universal ed. Gilbert Kaplan & Renate Stark-Voit, 2010.
    Universal offers a reduced version by Erwin Stein with winds:
3[incl pic] 3[incl Eh] 3[incl bcl] 3[incl cbn] — 4 3 3 1 — [no org]
    An improved choral score by Tom Cunningham (Goodmusic Publishing) is available at tomcunningham.org.uk/editions/mahler-2.

I. Allegro maestoso	22'
II. Andante moderato	11'
III. In ruhig fliessender Bewegung	11'
IV. Urlicht (Primeval Light)	4'
V. Im Tempo des Scherzo	32'

Kalmus	Luck's	Universal

Symphony No.3, D minor <1893–1896; rev 1906>   99'

alto solo   women's chorus, boys' chorus
4[all/pic] 4[1.2.3.4/Eh] 5[1.2.3/bcl.4/Ebcl2.Ebcl1] 4[1.2.3.4/cbn] — 8 4[1/posthn offstage] 4 1 — 2tmp+5 — 2hp — str
perc: glock, tambn[or possibly *tambourin provençal?*], tri, sd, chimes[Bb3(opt),C4,D4,F4,G4,A4], bd/cym, tamtam, rute, 3pr cym, 2sus cym, several sd offstage
Ebcl1 doubled if possible. Voices and chimes "on high" (*in der Höhe*).
    Universal ed. Erwin Ratz & Karl Heinz Füssl, 1974.
    Improved choral scores at tomcunningham.org.uk/editions/mahler-3.
    Universal offers a reduced instrumentation with triple woodwinds and brass 4 3 3 1.
    ☛*See also* the composer's "What the Wild Flowers Tell Me": a 1941 arrangement for reduced orchestra by Benjamin Britten of the 2nd mvt of this symphony.

I. Kräftig; Entschieden	33'
II. Tempo di menuetto: Sehr mässig	10'
III. Comodo; scherzando; ohne Hast	18'
IV. Sehr langsam; misterioso	9'
V. Lustig im Tempo und keck im Ausdruck	4'
VI. Langsam; ruhevoll; empfunden	25'

Kalmus	Universal

Symphony No.4, G major <1892–1900; rev 1901-10>   54'

soprano solo
4[1.2.3/pic1.4/pic2] 3[1.2.3/Eh] 3[1.2/Ebcl.3/bcl] 3[1.2.3/cbn] — 4 3 0 0 — tmp+4 — hp — str
perc: slgh-bells, glock, tri, cym, tamtam, bd
Scordatura solo violin in mvt 2. 1st cl plays C-clarinet for 10 bars in 1st mvt, and 3rd cl plays C-clarinet for 8 bars. Bcl mostlly in B-flat, though scattered passages for bcl in A (9 bars in 1st mvt & 29 bars in 3rd mvt).
    Universal ed. Erwin Ratz & Karl Heinz Füssl, 1995 ("corrected edition").
    A chamber orchestra version by Klaus Simon (2007) is available from Universal; the instrumentation is:
    1 1 1 1 — 1 0 0 0 — 2perc — harm, pf — str[1.1.1.1.1 to max 6.6.5.4.2]

I. Bedächtig; nicht eilen	17'
II. In gemächlicher Bewegung; ohne Hast	10'
III. Ruhevoll	18'
IV. Sehr behaglich	9'

Kalmus	Luck's	Universal

Symphony No.5, C-sharp minor <1901–1902; rev repeatedly>   68'

4[all/pic] 3[1.2.3/Eh] 3[1.2.3/D-cl/bcl] 3[1.2.3/cbn] — 6 4 3 1 — tmp+4 — hp — str
perc: sd, tri, tamtam, glock, whip, cym, bd/cym, bd
All 3 clarinets are in C in mvt 2 for 30 bars. Bcl is in A for 13 bars near the end of the 1st mvt; elsewhere bcl is in B-flat.
    Various critical editions, all published by Peters: Reinhold Kubik 2001; Erwin Ratz & Karl Heinz Füssl, 1989; Erwin Ratz, 1964, 1975.
    Movement durations given are those of a performance led by Mahler on March 12, 1905. Records also show on that occasion a 2' interval between mvts 1 and 2, 3' between 2 and 3, and 3' between 3 and 4 (mvts 4 & 5 are *attacca*).

PART I	
1. Trauermarsch	12'
2. Stürmisch bewegt	15'
PART II	
3. Scherzo: Kräftig, nicht zu schnell	17'
PART III	
4. Adagietto	9'
5. Rondo-Finale	15'

Kalmus	Peters

Symphony No.5: Adagietto <1901–1902>   9'

hp — str

Kalmus	Luck's	Peters

Symphony No.6, A minor (Tragic) <1903–1904; rev 1906; scoring repeatedly revised>   79'

5[1.2.3/pic.4/pic.pic] 5[1.2.3/Eh.4/Eh.Eh] 5[1.2.3.Ebcl.bcl]
5[1.2.3.4.cbn] — 8 6 4 1 — 2tmp+3 — 2hp — cel — str
perc: glock, xyl, sd, tamtam, bd, herdbells, hammer, 3tri, 2sd, tmp 2, 3pr cym, rute, deep bellsounds offstage

Ed. Erwin Ratz / Karl Heinz Füssl / Reinhold Kubik; new engraving, 1998. New edition by Kubik, 2010.

    The score suggests in places that the 2 harp parts be doubled. The composer also calls for 2 or more celestas if possible. Oboe parts may need some adjustment: Eh is a separate part in the 4th mvt (the only mvt requiring 5 players); mvts 2 & 3 each call briefly for 2Eh (in the ob3 & ob4 parts). Net result: never are more than 2Eh called for simultaneously. In 4th mvt, 4th cl plays D-cl, and bcl is in A (in the earlier mvts in B-flat). Tmp2 should cover perc in the *Scherzo*; otherwise an extra percussionist is required.

    There is some controversy over the order of the inner movements; *Andante* second and *Scherzo* third has the most adherents at the moment. Rehearsal numbers for these two mvts vary; score and parts must therefore be collated to ensure agreement.

    Also somewhat controversial: whether there are 2 or 3 great hammerstrokes in mvt 4.

I. Allegro energico, ma non troppo	22'
II. Andante moderato	14'
III. Scherzo	11'
IV. Finale	32'

Kahnt	Kalmus

Symphony No.7, E minor <1904–1905; rev scoring repeatedly revised>   77'

5[1.2.3.4/pic2.pic1] 4[1.2.3.Eh] 5[1.2.3.Ebcl.bcl(A & Bb)] 4[1.2.3.cbn]
— 4 3 3 1 — tenorhorn — gtr, mand — tmp+5 — 2hp — str
perc: glock, tamtam, sd, tri, cym, bd, bd/cym, tambn, deep bellsounds, rute, 2sets herdbells (1 offstage)

Tenorhorn in mvt 1 only; gtr & mand in mvt 4 only.

    Bote & Bock ed. Reinhold Kubik, 2010.

I. Langsam - Allegro	22'
II. Nachtmusik I	15'
III. Scherzo: Schattenhaft	9'
IV. Nachtmusik II	15'
V. Rondo-Finale	16'

Bote & Bock	Kalmus

Symphony No.8, E-flat major (Symphony of a Thousand) <1906–1907>   79'

double chorus, boys' chorus   solos SSSAATBB
6[1.2.3.4.5/pic.pic] 5[1.2.3.4.Eh] 6[1.2.3.Ebcl1.Ebcl2.bcl]
5[1.2.3.4.cbn] — 8 8 7 1 — mand [preferably dbl] — tmp+4 —
2hp[preferably dbl] — cel, pf, harm, org — str
perc: cym, glock, tamtam, tri, bd, 2deep bells[G#,A]

Universal ed. Karl Heinz Füssl, 1977.

    Bcl mostly in B-flat, but some passages in 1st mvt for bcl in A.

    A reduced version is available from the publisher.

Hymnus: Veni, Creator Spiritus	24'
Final Scene from Goethe's Faust	56'

Kalmus	Universal

Symphony No.9, D major <1908–1909>   81'

5[1.2.3.4.pic] 4[1.2.3.4/Eh] 5[1.2.3.Ebcl.bcl] 4[1.2.3.4/cbn] — 4 3 3 1
— tmp+4 — 1 or 2hp — str
perc: glock, tamtam, sd, cym, bd, 3deep bells[F#,A,B], tmp2

2nd hp, if used, merely doubles certain passages.

    Ed. Erwin Ratz, 1969; corrected in 1998 and again 2004.

I. Andante comodo	29'
II. Im Tempo eines gemächlichen Ländlers	18'
III. Rondo - Burleske	13'
IV. Adagio	21'

Kalmus	Universal

SYMPHONY NO.10 <1910>

This work was left incomplete at the composer's death. In Mahler's manuscript, the first two movements are complete, or almost complete, in score sketch; the third movement has 30 measures of score sketch, and the whole movement in short score; the fourth and fifth movements are in 4-stave short score, with sparse indications of instrumentation.

    The following entries show various attempts to complete the work, listed in chronological order. The Cooke, Wheeler, Carpenter and Mazzetti versions are discussed in Theodore Bloomfield's article "In Search of Mahler's Tenth," Musical Quarterly, vol.74 no.2, 1990.

Symphony No.10 (Krenek): Movements I and III only <1910>   24'

3[1.2.3/pic] 3 3 3 — 4 4 3 1 — tmp+1 — hp — str
perc: cym, gong

Performing version by Ernst Krenek, 1924 (ed. Otto A. Jokl).

    The publisher identifies these incorrectly as mvts 1 & 2; the second of this pair is the *Purgatorio* movement, which was intended to be the 3rd movement.

Mvt I. Andante - Adagio	20'
Mvt III. Allegretto moderato - Allegro non troppo	4'

AMP

Symphony No.10 (Ratz): 1st movement (Adagio) only <1910>   22'

3[1.2.3/pic] 3 3 3 — 4 4 3 1 — hp — str
Ed. Erwin Ratz, 1969.

Universal

Symphony No.10 (Cooke) <1910>   72'

4[1.2.3.4/pic] 4[1.2.3.4/Eh] 5[1.2.3.4.Ebcl.bcl] 4[1.2.3/cbn.4/cbn] — 4
4 4 1 — 2tmp+3 — hp — str
perc: glock, xyl, cym, bd/cym, rute, large double-sided military drum; 2nd timpanist covers tri, sd, tamtam

Performing version by Deryck Cooke (in collaboration with Berthold Goldschmidt, Colin Matthews & David Matthews), 1964; 2nd version 1972, rev.1976.

    Score is published by Faber; parts are available from AMP.

PART I	
1. Adagio	23'
2. Scherzo I	12'
PART II	
3. Purgatorio	5'
4. Scherzo II	12'
5. Finale	20'

AMP	Faber	Luck's

Symphony No.10 (Wheeler) <1910>   74'

4[incl 2pic] 4[incl 2Eh] 5[incl bcl,2Ebcl] 4[incl 2cbn] — 4 4 4 1 —
tmp+3 — 2 or more hp — str
Cuing permits performance with 3bn (one doubling on cbn), 3tbn, and 1hp.

    Performing version by Joseph Wheeler, 1965.

I. Adagio	23'
II. Scherzo I	12'
III. Purgatorio oder Inferno	5'
IV. Scherzo II	12'
V. Finale	22'

AMP

Symphony No.10 (Carpenter) <1910>   66'

5[incl pic] 4[incl Eh] 5[incl Ebcl,bcl] 4[incl 2cbn] — 4 4 3 1 —
tmp+4 — 2hp — str
perc: glock, tamtam, tri, bd/cym, cym, bd

Completion by Clinton A. Carpenter, 1966, rev. 1988.

1. Adagio: Andante — Adagio	19'
2. Scherzo I: In gemächlicher Bewegung. Ohne Hast	12'
3. Purgatorio: Un heimlich bewegt	4'
4. Scherzo II: Kräftig, nicht zu schnell	12'
5. Finale: Langsam — Allegro moderato — Andante comodo, aber nicht	19'

AMP

Symphony No.10 (Mazzetti) <1910>   75'

5[incl pic] 4[incl Eh] 5[incl Ebcl,bcl] 4[incl 2cbn] — 4 4 4 1 —
2tmp+4 — 2hp — str
perc: glock, field dr, sd, tri, tamtam, cym, bd/cym, tmp2
Completion by Remo Mazzetti Jr., 1985, rev. 1986, and again 1997.

1. Adagio	24'
2. Scherzo I	12'
3. Purgatorio oder Inferno	4'
4. Scherzo II	11'
5. Finale	24'

> AMP

Symphony No.10 (Gamzou) <1910>   78'

4[1.2.3.4/pic] 4[1.2.3/Eh.4] 4[1.2.3/Ebcl.4/bcl] 4[1.2.3/cbn.4/cbn] — 4
4 4 1 — tmp+3 — hp — str[max 14.12.10.8.6]
perc: bd, cym, sus cym, sd, tri, tamtam, glock, extra bd, extra tmp
Realization and further development of the uncompleted sketches;
concert setting by Yoel H. Gamzou (2003-2010).

PART I	
1. Adagio	–'
2. Scherzo	–'
3. Purgatorio	–'
PART II	
4. Wild. Der Teufel tanzt es mit mir	–'
5. Finale	–'

> Schott

Der Tamboursg'sell <1901>   5'

solo voice
0 2[1/Eh.2/Eh] 3[1.2.bcl] 3[1.2.cbn] — 4 0 0 1 — tmp+3 — str[no vn
or va]
perc: sd, cym, bd, tamtam
From *Sieben Lieder aus letzten Zeit*. Available in E minor, D minor
(original key), and C minor.

> Kalmus   Luck's   Universal

Totenfeier <1888; rev 1894>   20'

3[incl pic] 3[incl Eh] 3[incl bcl] 3 — 4 3 3 1 — tmp+3 — hp — str
perc: tri, tamtam, cym, bd
Ed. Rudolf Stephan, 1988.
   An early version (1888) of the 1st movement of the composer's
Symphony No.2.

> Universal

Trost im Unglück <1892>   4'

solo voice
3[1.2.pic] 2 2 2 — 4 2 0 0 — tmp+2 — str
perc: sd, tri
From *Des Knaben Wunderhorn*. Available in A major (original key), and
G major.

> Kalmus   Luck's   Universal

Um Mitternacht <1901>   6'

solo voice
2 1[ob d'amore] 2 3[1.2.cbn] — 4 2 3 1 — tmp — hp — pf — [no str]
From *Rückert Lieder*. Available in B minor (original key), as well as A
minor and G minor.

> Kalmus   Luck's   Universal

Verlorne Müh' <1892>   3'

solo voice
2[1/pic.2/pic] 2 2 — 2 0 0 0 — 1perc — str
perc: tri
From *Des Knaben Wunderhorn*. Available commercially in A major
(original key) and G major. Also a Bb major version is (or was) available
at www.mola-inc.org/page/Resource%20Sharing.

> Kalmus   Luck's   Universal

Waldmärchen (A Forest Legend) <1878–1880>   28'

solo SATBar   chorus
3[1.2.pic] 3[1.2.Eh] 3[1.2.bcl] 3 — 4 4 3 1 — tmp+2 — 2-6hp — str
perc: tri, bd, cym
2 real harp parts; composer asks that each be tripled in certain passages.
   Originally composed as Part I of *Das klagende Lied* and subsequently
withdrawn.
   Kalmus publishes the score, but no parts.

> Kalmus

Wer hat dies Liedlein erdacht? <1982>   2'

solo voice
2 2 2 2 — 2 0 0 0 — 1perc — str
perc: tri
From *Des Knaben Wunderhorn*. Available in F major (original key), and
E-flat major.

> Kalmus   Luck's   Universal

What the Wild Flowers Tell Me <1893–1896; rev 1906>   10'

2[1.2/pic] 2 2 — 4 3 0 0 — 2perc — hp — str
perc: tri, sus cym, glock, tambn, rute
The 2nd mvt of the composer's Symphony No.3, in a 1941 arrangement
for reduced orchestra by Benjamin Britten.

> Universal

Wo die schönen Trompeten blasen <1898>   7'

solo voice
2 2 2 0 — 4 2 0 0 — str
From *Des Knaben Wunderhorn*. Available in D minor (original key), and
C minor.

> Kalmus   Luck's   Universal

Malipiero, Gian Francesco   1882 - 1973

(b Venice, 18 March 1882; d Treviso, 1 Aug 1973). Italian

Armenia: canti armeni tradotti sinfonicamente <1917>   12'

3[1.2.pic] 3[1.2.Eh] 3[1.2.bcl] 2 — 4 2 0 0 — tmp+2 — hp — cel —
str
perc: cym, tri, tambn

> Kalmus

Concerto, Violoncello <1937>   14'

3[incl pic] 2 2 2 — 4 0 0 0 — 2perc — str

> Zerboni

Dialogo no.1 con Manuel de Falla, in memoria   11'
<1955–1956>

1 1 1 2 — 2 0 0 0 — 2perc — pf — str[4.4.4.3.2]
perc: bd, field dr, tambn

> Ricordi

Impressioni dal vero (Impressions of Life): Part I   13'
<1910–1911>

3[1.2.3/pic] 3[1.2.Eh] 3[1.2.bcl] 2 — 4 2 0 0 — tmp+2 — hp — str
perc: tri, cast, bd, glock

Il capinero (The Garden-Warbler)	5'
Il picchio (The Woodpecker)	3'
Il chiù (The Owl)	5'

> Kalmus   Salabert

Impressioni dal vero (Impressions of Life): Part II <1914–1915> 19'

4[incl 2pic] 3[incl Eh] 3[incl bcl] 3[incl cbn] — 4 3 3 1 — tmp+4 — hp — cel — str

Colloquio di campane (Colloquy of Bells)	9'
I cipressi e il vento (The Cypresses and the Wind)	6'
Baldoria campestre (Bonfire in the Countryside)	4'

> Chester   Kalmus

Impressioni dal vero (Impressions of Life): Part III <1921–1922> 10'

3[1.2.3/pic] 3[1.2.Eh] 3[1.2.bcl] 3[1.2.cbn] — 4 3 3 1 — tmp+6 — hp — cel — str

perc: bd, cym, sus cym, field dr, tri, tambn, glock, xyl

Festa in val d'inferno (Festival in the Valley of Hell)	4'
I galli (The Cocks)	4'
La tarantella a Capri (The Tarantella in Capri)	2'

> Universal

Oriente immaginario; Tre studi per piccola orchestra <1920> 15'

1[1/pic] 1 0 1 — 4perc — hp — cel, pf — str[4.4.4.4.2]

> Chester

Pause del silenzio I <1917> 13'

3[incl pic] 3[incl Eh] 3[incl bcl] 3[incl cbn] — 4 3 3 1 — tmp+2 — hp — cel — str

> Chester   Universal

Per una favola cavalleresca; Illustrazioni sinfoniche per orchestra (For a Tale of Chivalry) <1921> 25'

3[incl pic] 3[incl Eh] 3[incl bcl] 3[incl cbn] — 4 3 3 1 — tmp+2 — hp — cel — str

> Ricordi

Sette invenzioni (Seven Inventions) <1933> 19'

3[incl pic] 2 2 3[incl cbn] — 4 2 3 1 — tmp+3 — cel — str

Adapted from film score Acciaio.

> Carisch

Sinfonia per Antigenida <1962> 17'

3[1.2.pic] 3[1.2.Eh] 2 2 — 4 2 3 1 — 3perc — hp — cel — str

1. Ritenuto	4'
2. Lento	6'
3. Allegro	3'
4. Lento	4'

> Ricordi

Symphony No.1 (Sinfonia in quattro tempi, come le quattro stagioni; The Four Seasons) <1933> 23'

3[incl pic] 3[incl Eh] 2 2 — 4 2 2 1 — tmp+3 — hp — cel — str

1. Quasi andante; Sereno	6'
2. Allegro	6'
3. Lento, ma non troppo	5'
4. Allegro quasi allegretto	6'

> Ricordi

Symphony No.2 (Elegiaca) <1936> 22'

3[incl pic] 2 2 2 — 4 2 3 1 — tmp+2 — hp — str

1. Allegro non troppo	5'
2. Lento non troppo	6'
3. Mosso	3'
4. Lento	8'

> Ricordi

Symphony No.3 (Delle campane) <1944–1945> 18'

2[1.2/pic] 3[1.2.Eh] 3[1.2.bcl] 2 — 4 2 3 1 — tmp+2 — hp — cel, pf — str

> Zerboni

Symphony No.6 <1947> 20'

str[6.6.4.4.2]`

> Ricordi

Symphony No.8 (Symphonia brevis) <1964> 20'

3[incl pic] 3[incl Eh] 2 2 — 4 2 0 0 — 5perc — hp — cel, pf — str

> Ricordi

Symphony No.9 (Dell' ahimè) <1966> 16'

3[incl pic] 3[incl Eh] 2 2 — 4 2 0 0 — 4perc — hp — cel, pf — str

1. Allegro	7'
2. Lento, ma non troppo	4'
3. Allegro	5'

> Ricordi

Symphony No.10 (Atropo) <1967> 13'

2[incl pic] 2[incl Eh] 2 2 — 4 2 0 0 — 2perc — hp — cel, pf — str

Lento; Andante	4'
Tranquillo	2'
Mosso	3'
Mosso, molto vivace	4'

> Ricordi

Symphony No.11 (Della cornamuse) <1969> 11'

2[incl pic] 2[incl Eh] 1 2 — 4 2 0 0 — 4perc — hp — cel, pf — str

> Ricordi

Maltz, Richard 1958-

(b Everett, MA, 7 June 1958). American

Aesop's Fables 22'

narrator

1[fl/pic] 1 1 1 — 1 1 0 0 — tmp+1 — str or str 5t

perc: bd, cym, 2sus cym, sd, tambn, xyl, metal wind chimes; timpanist plays tri & finger cym

Overture	3'
The Hare and the Tortoise	3'
The Fox and the Grapes	3'
The Ants and the Grasshopper	3'
The Oak and the Reeds	3'
The Milkmaid and Her Pail	3'
Finale	4'

> Maltz

Mamlok, Ursula 1928-

(b Berlin, 1 Feb 1928). American composer of German birth

Grasshoppers; Six Humoresques for Orchestra <1957> 6'

3[1.2.pic] 2 2 3[1.2.opt cbn] — 2 2 3 1 — tmp+2 — str

perc: sus cym, sd, tambn, marac, guiro, tri, claves, xyl, bd, templeblks, woodblk, 3bongos, bamboo windchimes

Originally for piano; arranged by the composer.

1. Sunday Walk	1'
2. Night Serenade	1'
3. In the Rain	1'
4. Minuet	1'
5. In the Army	1'
6. Hurrying Home	1'

> ACA

Manevich, Alexander 1908-1976

(b Starodube, Russia, 1908; d 1976). Russian

Concerto, Clarinet <1955> 13'

2[1.2/pic] 2[1.2/Eh] 0 2 — 3 1 1 0 — tmp+2 — hp — str

> Russian

Manfredini, Francesco 1684-1762

(b Pistoia, 22 June 1684; d Pistoia, 6 Oct 1762). Italian

Concerto grosso, op.3, no.9, D major <1718> 11'

solo concertino: 2 violins, violoncello
str
Ed. Ettore Bonelli.

> Kalmus   Luck's   Zanibon

Concerto grosso, op.3, no.10, G minor <1718> 12'

solo concertino: 2 violins
cnt — str
Ed. Bernhard Paumgartner.

> Luck's   Peters

Concerto grosso, op.3, no.12, C major (Christmas Concerto) <1718> 10'

solo concertino: 2 violins
cnt — str

Pastorale: Largo	5'
Largo	2'
Allegro	3'

> Eulenburg   Kahnt   Luck's   Schott

Sinfonia da chiesa, op.2, no.12, D major (Sinfonia pastorale per il santissimo natale; Christmas Symphony) <1709> 6'

org — str
De Santis ed. Riccardo Nielsen; Vieweg ed. Felix Schroeder.

Largo	2'
Adagio	1'
Largo e puntato	3'

> Vieweg

Marcello, Alessandro 1669-1747

(b Venice, 24 Aug 1669; d Venice, 19 June 1747). Italian

Concerto, Oboe, C minor <1717> 12'

cnt — str
Ed. R. Lauschmann. Score not published, though the Philadelphia Orchestra Library caused one to be computer-engraved and has it on file.
   Previously attributed to Benedetto Marcello (1686-1739), and published under his name by Zanibon (reprinted by Kalmus).

> Forberg

Marcello, Benedetto 1686-1739

(b Venice, 24 June or 24 July 1686; d Brescia, 24 July 1739). Italian

Concerto, Oboe, C minor <1717> 12'

str
Ed. Ettore Bonelli. Actually by Alessandro Marcello; published under Alessandro Marcello's name by Forberg.

I. Allegro moderato	3'
II. Adagio	5'
III. Allegro	4'

> Kalmus   Zanibon

Concerto grosso, op.1, no.1, D major <1708> 10'

solo concertino: 2 violins, violoncello
cnt — str
Ed. Ettore Bonelli.

> Luck's   Zanibon

Concerto grosso, op.1, no.2, E minor <1708> 12'

solo concertino: 2 violins, viola, violoncello
cnt — str
Ed. Ettore Bonelli.

> Luck's   Zanibon

Concerto grosso, op.1, no.3, E major <1708> 10'

solo concertino: 2 violins, viola, violoncello
cnt — str
Ed. Ettore Bonelli.

> Luck's   Zanibon

Concerto grosso, op.1, no.4, F major <1708> 15'

solo concertino: 2 violins, viola, violoncello
cnt — str
Ed. Ettore Bonelli.

> Luck's   Zanibon

Concerto grosso, op.1, no.5, B minor <1708> 13'

solo concertino: 2 violins, viola, violoncello
cnt — str
Ed. Ettore Bonelli.

> Luck's   Zanibon

Concerto grosso, op.1, no.6, B-flat major <1708> 10'

solo concertino: 2 violins, violoncello
cnt — str
Ed. Ettore Bonelli.

> Luck's   Zanibon

Concerto grosso, op.1, no.7, F minor 10'

solo concertino: 2 violins, violoncello
cnt — str
Ed. Ettore Bonelli.

> Luck's   Zanibon

Concerto grosso, op.1, no.8, F major <1708> 9'

solo concertino: 2 violins, violoncello
cnt — str
Ed. Ettore Bonelli.

> Luck's   Zanibon

MARCELLO, BENEDETTO   1686-1739

Concerto grosso, op.1, no.9, A major <1708>   10'
solo concertino: 2 violins, violoncello
cnt — str
Ed. Ettore Bonelli.
> Luck's   Zanibon

Concerto grosso, op.1, no.10, C major <1708>   12'
solo concertino: 2 violins, violoncello
cnt — str
Ed. Ettore Bonelli.
> Luck's   Zanibon

Introduction, Aria & Presto, A minor   9'
str
Ed. Ettore Bonelli.
> Luck's   Zanibon

Markevitch, Igor   1912-1983
(b Kiev, 27 July 1912; d Antibes, 7 March 1983). French composer of Ukrainian birth

Rebus <1931>   24'
2[1.2/pic] 2 2[1.Ebcl] 2 — 4 2 3 1 — tmp+3 — str
perc: tri, tambn, sd, field dr, bd, cym
> Breitkopf

Márquez, Arturo   1950-
(b Alamos, Sonora, Mexico, 20 Dec 1950). Mexican

Danzón No.2 <1994>   10'
2[1.2/pic] 2 2 2 — 4 2 3 1 — tmp+3 — pf — str
perc: bd, sus cym, sd, guiro, claves, 3tomtoms
> Peer

Danzón No.3 (version for flute, guitar & small orchestra) <1994>   13'
solo flute & guitar
0 0 2 0 — 2 0 0 0 — 2perc — str[4-8. 4-8. 3-6, 3-6, 2-4]
perc: sus cym, timbales, tamtam, guiro, claves
> Peer

Danzón No.3 (version for guitar & chamber orchestra) <1994>   13'
0 1 2[Ebcl.Bbcl] 1 — 1 0 0 0 — 2perc — hp — pf — str[no va]
perc: sus cym, tamtam, guiro, claves, tmp
> Peer

Danzón No.4 (full orchestra) <1996>   11'
2[1.2/pic] 2 2 2 — 4 2 3 1 — tmp+3 — pf — str
perc: bd, sus cym, timbales, tamtam, guiro, marac (2 prs), claves (2 prs)
> Peer

Danzón No.4 (chamber orchestra) <1996>   11'
1 1 1 1 — 1 1 1 0 — ssx — 2perc — str[single or small]
perc: sus cym, timbales, guiro, marac, claves
> Peer

Paisajes bajo el signo de cosmos (Landscapes Under the Sign of the Cosmos) <1993>   10'
2 2 2 2 — 4 2 3 1 — tmp+4 — hp — str
perc: bd, cym, sus cym, sd, tambn, glock, xyl, guiro, marac, claves
> Peer

Marschner, Heinrich   1795-1861
(b Zittau, 16 Aug 1795; d Hanover, 14 Dec 1861). German

Hans Heiling, op.80: Overture <1833>   9'
2 2 2 2 — 4 2 3 0 — tmp — str
> Breitkopf   Peters

Marshall, Ingram   1942-
(b Mount Vernon, NY, 10 May 1942). American

Fog Tropes <1982>   10'
0 0 0 0 — 2 2 2 0 — pre-recorded tape — [no str]
> Ibu Music

Martin, Frank   1890-1974
(b Geneva, 15 Sept 1890; d Naarden, 21 Nov 1974). Swiss

Ballade, Flute & Orchestra <1939; rev 1941>   8'
pf — str
Originally for flute & piano; orchestrated by the composer.
> Universal

Ballade, Flute & Orchestra (arr. Ansermet) <1939; rev 1941>   8'
0 2[1.2/Eh] 2[1/asx.2/bcl] 1 — 2 0 0 0 — tmp — hp — cel — str
Arranged by Ernest Ansermet.
> Universal

Ballade, Saxophone & Orchestra <1938>   13'
solo alto saxophone
tmp+1 — pf — str
perc: sd, bd, cym
> Universal

Concerto, Piano, No.2 <1968–1969>   25'
2[1.pic] 2[1.Eh] 2[1.Ebcl] 2[1.cbn] — 2 2 1 0 — asx — tmp+3 — hp — str
perc: sd, tri, xyl, cym, bd, sus cym
> Universal

Concerto, 7 Winds <1949>   20'
solos: fl, ob, cl, bn, hn, tp, tbn
tmp+3 — str
perc: sd, cym, bd
  I. Allegro   6'
  II. Adagietto - Misterioso ed elegante   7'
  III. Allegro vivace   7'
> Universal

Etudes for String Orchestra <1955–1956>   20'
str
  Ouverture   4'
  1st Etude: Pour l'enchaînement des traits   2'
  2nd Etude: Pour le pizzicato   3'
  3rd Etude: Pour l'expression et le sostenuto   4'
  4th Etude: Pour le style fugué, ou "Chacun et chaque chose à sa place"   7'
> Universal

Maria-Triptychon <1967–1968>   21'

solo soprano & solo violin
2 2[1.2/Eh] 2 2[1.2/cbn] — 2 2 1 0 — tmp — hp — pf — str
I. Ave Maria: Gegrüsset seist du   *4'*
II. Magnificat: Meine Selle erhebt den Herren   *10'*
III. Stabat Mater   *7'*

Universal

Ouverture en hommage à Mozart (Overture in Homage   6'
to Mozart) <1956>

3[1.2.pic] 2 2 2 — 2 2 0 0 — tmp — str[max 12.12.8.8.6]

Universal

Passacaille (String Orchestra version) <1944; rev 1952>   11'

str
Originally for organ (1944); orchestrated for strings, 1952; for full orchestra, 1962.

Universal

Passacaille pour grand orchestre <1944; rev (orchd)   12'
1962>

3[1.2.3/pic] 3[1.ob d'am.Eh] 3[1.2.basset hn] 3[1.2.cbn] — 4 2 3 1 — tmp — str
Originally for organ (1944); orchestrated for strings, 1952; for full orchestra, 1962.

Universal

Petite symphonie concertante <1944–1945>   23'

hp — pf, hpsd — 2 string orchestras [each 4-6, 3-5, 2-4, 2-3, 1-2]
I. Adagio - Allegro con moto   *14'*
II. Adagio   *5'*
III. Allegretto con marcia   *4'*

Universal

Polyptyque (Six images de la Passion du Christ) <1973>   26'

solo violin
str[2 small str orchs]
I. Image des Rameaux (Image of the Palms)   *4'*
II. Image de la chambre haute (Image of the Upper Room)   *7'*
III. Image de Judas (Image of Judas)   *2'*
IV. Image de Géthsémané (Image of Gethsemane)   *4'*
V. Image du Jugement (Image of the Judgement)   *4'*
VI. Image de la Glorification (Image of the Glorification)   *5'*

mph   Universal

Les quatre éléments (The Four Elements) <1963–1964>   20'

3[1.2/pic.pic] 3[1.2.Eh] 3[1.2/Ebcl.bcl] 3[1.2.cbn] — 4 3 3 1 — asx — tmp+4 — 2hp — cel, pf — str
perc: vib, xyl, sd, glock, cym, tamtam, bd, tri, chimes[A3,B3,C#4]
1. La terre (Earth)   *5'*
2. L'eau (Water)   *5'*
3. L'air (Air)   *4'*
4. Le Feu (Fire)   *6'*

Universal

Three Dances (Trois danses) <1970; rev 1972>   19'

solo oboe, harp, string quintet
str[max 7.6.5.4.3]
I. Seguiriya   *8'*
II. Soledad   *7'*
III. Rumba   *4'*

Universal

Le vin herbé <1938–1941>   93'

12 solo voices: 3S, 3A, 3T, 3B
pf — 2vn, 2va, 2vc, db
Act I   *32'*
Act II   *21'*
Act III *40'*

Universal

Martineau, Jason   1969-

(b Ithaca, NY, 24 October 1969). American

Concertino, Piano & Orchestra <1995>   17'

3[1.2.pic] 3[1.2.Eh] 3[1.2.bcl] 3[1.2.cbn] — 4 2 3 1 — tmp+1 — hp — str
perc: bd, cym, sus cym, sd, tri, tamtam

Hoyt

Martino, Donald   1931-2005

(b Plainfield, NJ, 16 May 1931; d at sea in the Caribbean, 8 Dec 2005). American

Concerto, Alto Saxophone <1987>   24'

1[incl pic] 2[incl Eh] 1 2[incl cbn] — 2 1[1/opt flug] 2 0 — 2perc — pf — str[min 6.4.3.3.2]

Dantalian

Concerto, Piano <1965>   27'

3[1.2/pic.3/pic] 2[1.2/Eh] 3[1.2.bcl/cbcl] 3[1.2.cbn] — 4 2 3 1[1/euph] — tmp+4 — hp — cel/pf[orchestral] — str[min 14.12.10.10.8]
perc: bd, bongos, claves, cym, glock, guiro, tomtom, marim, field dr, templeblks, xyl, vib, 2sd, 2woodblks, 2gongs, rattle, 2sus cym, 2tambn
I. Moderato; tempo rubato   *_'*
II. Presto   *_'*
III. Adagio molto   *_'*

Ione

Concerto, Violoncello <1996>   28'

3[1.2/pic.3/pic] 3[incl Eh] 3[1.2.bcl/cbcl] 3[incl cbn] — 4 4 3 1 — tmp+4 — hp — pf/cel — str[min 12.10.8.6.4; preferred 16.14.12.10.8]

Dantalian

Divertisements for Youth Orchestra <1981>   7'

2 2 2 2 — 2 2 2 0 — 2-3perc — pf — str
Oboes, bassoons, horns & trombones are optional.
1. The Kick-Off Quadrille   *_'*
2. Songs of Solitaire   *_'*
3. Miss Phoebe's Waltz   *_'*
4. Little Joe's Lament   *_'*

Dantalian

Mosaic for Grand Orchestra <1967>   16'

4[incl afl,2pic] 4[incl Eh] 4[1.2.3.bcl/cbcl] 4[incl cbn] — 4 4 4 1 — elec gtr — tmp+5 — 2hp — cel/elec org — str[16.14.10.10.9]

Dantalian

Paradiso Choruses <1974>   29'

chorus (incl opt children's voices)   solos 3S, 4Mz, 3T, 2Bar
3[1.2/pic.3/pic] 3[incl Eh] 3[incl bcl] 4[incl cbn] — 4 4 4 1 — pre-recorded tape — tmp+4 — hp — org, pf[preferably elec] — str

Dantalian

Ritorno <1976>   15'

2 3[incl Eh] 3[incl bcl] 2 — 4 3 3 1 — tmp+3 — hp — cel/pf — str

Dantalian

The White Island <1985>   22'

chorus
1[1/pic] 1[1/Eh] 2[1.bcl/cbcl] 1 — 1 1[1/flg] 2 0 — 2perc — cel, pf
— str[min 6.4.3.3.2] *or* solo str 5t
Cbn doubling bn2 may substitute for bcl/cbcl.

> Dantalian

Martinů, Bohuslav   1890-1959

(b Polička, Bohemia, 8 Dec 1890; d Liestal, Switzerland, 28 Aug 1959). Czech

H = H. Halbreich: Martinu: Werkverzeichnis, Dokumentation und
Biographie (Zürich, 1968)

Comedy on the Bridge, H.251 (Veselohra na moste):   6'
Little Suite <1935>

1[1/pic] 1 1 1 — 2 1 1 0 — 3perc — pf — str
perc: field dr, cym, bd
  I. Introduction and Poco Allegro   _'
  II. Andantino poco moderato   _'
  III. Marcia   _'

> Boosey

Concertino, Piano Trio & String Orchestra, H.232   17'
<1933>

solo violin, violoncello & piano
str

> Kalmus   Luck's   Supraphon

Concerto, Flute & Violin, H.252 <1936>   20'

1 2 2 2 — 2 1 0 0 — pf — str

> Bärenreiter   Kalmus   Luck's

Concerto, Oboe, H.353 <1955>   15'

2 0 2 1 — 2 1 0 0 — pf — str
  1. Moderato   5'
  2. Poco andante   6'
  3. Poco allegro   4'

> Eschig

Concerto, Violin, No.2, H.293 <1943>   28'

2 2 2 2 — 4 3 3 1 — tmp+2 — str
perc: cym, tri, bd, sd
  1. Andante; Poco allegro   12'
  2. Andante moderato   8'
  3. Poco allegro   8'

> Bärenreiter   Boosey   Kalmus   Luck's

Double Concerto, 2 String Orchestras, Piano & Timpani,   20'
H.271 <1938>

tmp — pf — str
  I. Poco allegro   6'
  II. Largo   8'
  III. Allegro   6'

> Boosey

Estampes, H.369 <1958>   19'

2[1.2/pic] 2[1.2/Eh] 2 2 — 4 2 3 0 — tmp+2 — hp — pf — str
  1. Andante   6'
  2. Adagio; Allegretto; Tempo primo   7'
  3. Poco allegro   6'

> Peer

Fantasia concertante, Piano & Orchestra, H.366   23'
(Concerto, Piano, No.5) <1958>

3[1.2.pic] 2 2 2 — 4 2 3 0 — tmp+3 — str
perc: sd, field dr, woodblk, cym, xyl, bd, tri
  I. Poco allegro; risoluto   7'
  II. Poco andante   10'
  III. Poco allegro   6'

> Universal

The Frescos of Piero della Francesca, H.352 (Les   18'
Fresques de Piero della Francesca) <1953–1955>

4[1.2.3.pic] 3[1.2.3/Eh] 3 3 — 4 3 3 1 — tmp+3 — hp — str
perc: xyl, sd, td, tri, cym, bd, tamtam
  1. Andante poco moderato   7'
  2. Adagio   6'
  3. Poco allegro   5'

> Universal

Inventions, H.234 (Invence) <1934>   12'

2 2 2 2 — 4 2 2 0 — tmp+3 — pf — str
perc: bd, cym, sus cym, sd, toms, tri, xyl, woodblk

> Bärenreiter   Kalmus   Luck's   Supraphon

Memorial to Lidice, H.296 (Památník Lidicím) <1943>   8'

3 3[1.2.Eh] 3 2 — 4 2 3 1 — tmp+2 — hp — pf — str
perc: cym, tamtam, bd

> Bärenreiter   Kalmus   Luck's   Supraphon

Overture, H.345 <1953>   8'

2 2 2 2 — 4 2 0 0 — tmp — str

> Eschig

Rhapsody-Concerto, H.337 <1952>   22'

solo viola
2 2 2 2 — 4 2 0 0 — tmp/sd — str
perc: sd[played by timpanist]
  1. Moderato   10'
  2. Molto adagio   12'

> Bärenreiter   Kalmus   Luck's

Sextet for String Orchestra, H.224a <1932; rev (arr. for 16'
str orch) 1958>

str
Originally for six strings (2vn, 2va, 2vc).
  I. Lento; Allegro poco moderato   7'
  II. Andantino   5'
  III. Allegretto poco moderato   4'

> AMP

Sinfonia concertante, for 2 orchestras, H.219 <1932>   19'

2[1.2/pic] 3 2 2 — 4 2 3 1 — tmp+2 — str
perc: tri, cym, sd, bd
Division of instruments:
  1st orch: 0 3 0 1 — 2 0 0 0 — str
  2nd orch: 2[1.2/pic] 0 2 1 — 2 2 3 1 — tmp+2 — str
  1. Allegro non troppo   6'
  2. Vivace   3'
  3. Andante   5'
  4. Allegretto   5'

> Schott

Symphony No.1, H.289 <1942>   36'

3[1.2.pic] 3[1.2.Eh] 3 3[1.2.cbn] — 4 3 3 1 — tmp+3 — hp — pf — str

perc: sd, tri, tambn, cym, tamtam, bd

I. Moderato	10'
II. Allegro	8'
III. Largo	8'
IV. Allegro non troppo	10'

Boosey

Symphony No.2, H.295 <1943>   24'

3[1.2.pic] 3 3 2 — 4 3 3 1 — tmp+3 — hp — pf — str

perc: sd, tri, tamtam, cym, bd

1. Allegro moderato	6'
2. Andante moderato	8'
3. Poco allegro	5'
4. Allegro	5'

Boosey

Symphony No.3, H.299 <1944>   26'

3[1.2.pic] 3[1.2.Eh] 3 2 — 4 3 3 1 — tmp+4 — hp — pf — str

perc: sd, tri, tamtam, cym, bd

1. Alletro poco moderato	9'
2. Largo	7'
3. Allegro; Andante	10'

Boosey

Symphony No.4, H.305 <1945>   33'

4[1.2.3.pic] 4[1.2.3.Eh] 3 2 — 4 3 3 1 — tmp+3 — pf — str

perc: sd, tri, tambn, cym, woodblk, tamtam, bd

I. Poco moderato	7'
II. Allegro vivo	9'
III. Largo	9'
IV. Poco allegro	8'

Boosey

Symphony No.5, H.310 <1946>   31'

3[1.2.pic] 3 3 3 — 4 3 3 1 — tmp+3 — pf — str

perc: sd, tri, cym, tamtam, bd

1. Adagio; Allegro	9'
2. Larghetto	10'
3. Lento; Allegro	12'

Boosey

Symphony No.6, H.343 (Fantaisies symphoniques) <1953>   28'

4[1.2.3.pic] 3 3 3 — 4 3 3 1 — tmp+4 — str

perc: sd, tamtam, tambn, tri, cym, bd

1. Lento; Allegro	9'
2. Poco allegro	8'
3. Lento	11'

Boosey

Toccata e due canzoni, H.311 <1946>   25'

1[pic] 2 1 1 — 0 1 0 0 — tmp+1[opt] — pf — str

perc: cym, sd, tri (all can be covered by timpanist)

Toccata: Allegro moderato	9'
Canzone No.1: Andante moderato	7'
Canzone No.2: Allegro (poco); Adagio	9'

Boosey

Martirano, Salvatore   1927-1995

(b Yonkers, NY, 12 Jan 1927; d Urbana, IL, 17 Nov 1995). American

Contrasto <1954>   9'

3[1.2.pic] 3[1.2.Eh] 3[1.2.bcl] 3[1.2.cbn] — 4 3 3 1 — tmp+3 — hp — cel — str

perc: bd, cym, xyl, field dr, td, 2sus cym, 2tamtams

Schott

Martucci, Giuseppe   1856-1909

(b Capua, 6 Jan 1856; d Naples, 1 June 1909). Italian

Tarantella, op.44, no.6 <1880; rev (orchd) 1908>   9'

3[1.2.pic] 3[1.2.Eh] 3[1.2.bcl] 3 — 4 2 3 0 — tmp+4 — hp — str

perc: tambn, cast, tri, cym

Originally for piano, 1880; orchestrated by the composer 1908.

Ricordi

Mascagni, Pietro   1863-1945

(b Livorno, 7 Dec 1863; d Rome, 2 Aug 1945). Italian

Amica: Intermezzo <1905>

3[1.2.pic] 3[1.2.Eh] 3[1.2.bcl] 3[1.2.cbn] — 4 3 3 1 — tmp+4 — hp — str

perc: bd, cym, sd, tambn, tamtam, chimes

Luck's

L'amico Fritz: Intermezzo <1891>   4'

3[1.2.pic] 2 2 2 — 4 2 3 1 — tmp+1 — hp — str

perc: cym

Luck's

Cavalleria rusticana: Intermezzo <1888>   3'

2[incl pic] 2 2 2 — 2 0 0 0 — hp — opt org — str

There appear to be 4 or 5 different instrumentations of this excerpt, differing in mostly insignificant ways. Any of the versions may be covered by the above instrumentation, in some cases with slight adaptations.

Kalmus   Luck's

Cavalleria rusticana: Prelude & Siciliana <1888>   6'

3[1.2.pic] 2 2 2 — 4 2 3 1 — tmp+2 — hp[opt] — str

perc: cym, bd

Kalmus   Luck's

Mascari, Edward Paul   1949-

(b Patterson, NJ, 20 December 1949). American

Meet the Orchestra <1995; rev 1997>   17'

narrator

3[1.2.3/pic] 2 2 2 — 4 3 3 1 — tmp+2 — str

perc: cym, sus cym, sd, tri, tambn, marim, cowbell, cast

MMB

Maslanka, David   1943-

(b New Bedford, MA, 30 Aug 1943). American

11:11 (A Dance at the Edge of the World) <2001>   17'

3[1.2.pic] 2 3[1.2/ssx.bcl] 2 — 4 2 2 1 — tmp+2 — hp — pf — str

perc: cym, sus cym, sd, toms, glock, xyl, vib, ratch, anvil

C. Fischer

Music for String Orchestra <1992>   17'

str

I. Aria	4'
II. Elegy	7'
III. Dance	6'

C. Fischer

Symphony No.6 (Living Earth) <2004> 34'

3[1.2.3/pic] 3 4[1.2.3/Ebcl.bcl] 3[1.2.3/cbn] — 4 3[1/flug.2.3] 3 1 — tmp+3 — hp — pf/cel — str
perc: bd, szl cym, sd, tambn, tamtam, glock, xyl, marim, vib, chimes, crot, slgh-bells, belltree, 2sus cym, cello bow, eggshaker, rainstick, 4gongs, cabasa

1. Living Earth 1	*10'*
2. Rain	*8'*
3. November—Geese on the Wing	*3'*
4. Dreamer	*7'*
5. Living Earth 2	*6'*

C. Fischer

Mason, Daniel Gregory
1873-1953

(b Brookline, MA, 20 Nov 1873; d Greenwich, CT, 4 Dec 1953). American

Chanticleer; Festival Overture, op.27 <1926> 15'

3[1.2.3/pic] 3[1.2.Eh] 3[1.2.bcl] 3[1.2.cbn] — 4 3 3 1 — tmp+2 — hp — str

Presser

Massenet, Jules
1842-1912

(b Montaud, St Etienne, 12 May 1842; d Paris, 13 Aug 1912). French

Le Cid: Ballet Music <1884–1885> 17'

2[1.2/pic] 2[1/Eh.2] 2 2 — 4 4[2tp, 2crt] 3 1 — tmp+3 — 2hp — str
perc: bd, cym, sd, td, tri, tambn, cast

1. Castillane	*3'*
2. Andalouse	*2'*
3. Aragonaise	*2'*
4. Aubade	*1'*
5. Catalane	*3'*
6. Madrilene	*3'*
7. Navarraise	*3'*

Heugel   Kalmus   Luck's

La cigal: Suite <1904> 15'

3[1.2.pic] 3[1.2.Eh] 2 2 — 4 3 3 1 — tmp+3 — 2hp[1part] — cel — str
perc: bd, cym, tri, tamtam, tambn prov

1. Valse tourbillon des autans (Waltz-Whirlwind of the Winter Winds)	_'
2. Cantabile	_'
3. Variations	_'
4. Vieux Noël	_'
[5.] La ronde des cigales	_'

Kalmus

Concerto, Piano, E-flat major <1903> 30'

3[1.2.pic] 2 2 2 — 4 2 3 0 — tmp+3 — cel — str

1. Andante moderato	*14'*
2. Largo	*9'*
3. Airs slovaques: Allegro	*7'*

Heugel

Hérodiade: Prelude to Act III <1881> 2'

0 1 2 2 — 4 0 0 1 — tmp — hp — str

Heugel   Luck's

Manon: Minuet & Gavotte <1884> 5'

1 2 2 2 — 2 2 1 0 — tmp+1 — str
perc: tri
Arr. Theo. M. Tobani; piano-conductor score only.

Minuet	*3'*
Gavotte	*2'*

Kalmus   Luck's

Phèdre: Overture <1900> 9'

3[1.2.pic] 2 2 2 — 4 4[2tp, 2crt] 3 1 — tmp — str

Heugel   Kalmus   Luck's

Scènes alsaciennes (Suite No.7) <1882> 21'

2[1.pic] 2 2 2 — 4 4 3 1 — tmp+4 — str
perc: sd, tri, cym, bd

1. Sunday Morning	*7'*
2. In the Tavern	*5'*
3. Under the Linden Trees	*5'*
4. Sunday Evening	*4'*

Heugel   Kalmus   Luck's

Scènes hongroises (Suite No.2) <ca 1870> 18'

3[1.2.pic] 2 2 2[or 4] — 4 4[2tp, 2crt] 3 1["saxtuba"] — tmp+4 — hp — str
perc: bd, cym, fielddrum, tri

1. Entrèe en forme de danse	_'
2. Intermède	_'
3. Adieux à la fiancée	_'
4. Cortège	_'
5. Bénédiction nuptiale	_'
6. Sortie de l'eglise	_'

Fleisher   Leduc

Scènes pittoresques (Suite No.4) <?1872> 18'

2[1.2/pic] 2 2 2 — 4 4 3 0 — tmp+4 — str
perc: sd, tri, cym, bd

1. Marche	*4'*
2. Air de ballet	*3'*
3. Angelus	*6'*
4. Fête bohême	*5'*

Heugel   Kalmus   Luck's

Suite No.1, op.13 <1865> 23'

3[1.2.pic] 2 2 2 — 4 4 3 1["saxtuba"] — tmp+3 — 2hp — str
perc: bd, cym, field dr

1. Pastorale et Fugue	*6'*
2. Variations	*5'*
3. Nocturne	*6'*
4. Marche et Strette	*6'*

Durand   Kalmus

Thaïs: Méditation <1894> 5'

solo violin
2 2[1.Eh] 3[1.2.bcl] 3[1.2.cbn] — 4 0 0 0 — tmp — hp[1part marked "Harpes soli"] — str
Playable with: 0 0 2 2 — 1 0 0 0 — hp — str
   Instructions *au théâtre*: backstage ob, Eh & wordless chorus.
   Instructions *au concert*: 4 or 8 solo voices seated in orchestra. (The voices sing only for 15 bars and are often omitted; Kalmus version gives these notes to 2tp & 2tbn.)

Kalmus   Luck's

Matthews, Colin
1946-

(b London, 13 Feb 1946). English

Landscape, op.17 (Sonata No.5) <1978–1980> 30'

3[1.2/pic.3/pic] 3[1.2.Eh] 4[1.2.3/bcl.cbcl (or cbn)] 3 — 4 3 3 1 — tmp+4 — 2hp — str[min 12.12.8.8.6]
perc: bongos, field dr, cym, hi-hat, cast, claves, templeblks, marac, cowbell, crot, vib, marim, 8tomtoms, 2td, 2bd, 4sus cym, 2tri, 1 or 2 gongs, 2tamtams, 2whips, 2glock
Cbn may substitute for contrabass cl; an alternative part is provided.

Faber

Pluto, the Renewer <1999–2000>   6'

7-part female chorus offstage
4[1.2.pic.afl] 4[1.2.Eh.bass ob] 4[1.2.3.bcl] 4[1.2.3.cbn] — 6 4 3 1 —
tenor tuba — 2tmp+4 — 2hp — cel, org — str
perc: bd, cym, sus cym, td, tri, tamtam, glock, chimes, crot
Intended for use with Gustav Holst's *The Planets*, thus completing the
roster. Then in 2006, Pluto was reclassified as a "dwarf planet."

> Faber

Matthews, David   1943-

(b Walthamstow, London, 9 March 1943). English

Symphony No.3, op.37 <1983–1985>   20'

3[1/pic.2/pic.3/pic] 3[1.2.3/Eh] 3[1.2/Ebcl.bcl] 3[1.2.3/cbn] — 4 4 3 1
— tmp+2 — hp — str[16.14.12.10.8]
perc: bd, sus cym, Chinescym, tamtam, gong, glock, vib, crot

> Faber

Mauldin, Michael   1947-

(b Port Arthur, TX, 14 June 1947). American

The American West <1986>   21'

narrator
3[1.2.pic] 2 2 2 — 4 3 3 1 — tmp+2 — hp — str
perc: bd, sus cym, sd, tri, glock, vib, chimes

> Mauldin

Dawn at San Juan Mesa <1995>   5'

2 2 2 2 — 4[2 real parts each dbl] 3 3 1 — tmp+2 — hp — str
perc: sus cym, glock

> Harmonic

Desert Light; Four Episodes for Chamber Orchestra <1988>   13'

2 2 2 2 — 2 2 1 1 — tmp — hp — str
1.   4'
2.   2'
3.   3'
4.   4'

> Mauldin

Dreams of the Child of Light <2004>   12'

solo Native American flute
str
1. *Friendly Traveler*   4'
2. *Sorrows of My People*   3'
3. *Return to Lhasa*   5'

> Mauldin

Earthsongs <2010>   24'

soloists SATB & boy sopr   children's chorus   SATB chorus
3[1.2.pic] 2 2 2 — 4 3 3 1 — tmp+2 — hp — str
perc: bd, sus cym, vib, 4tomtom, vn bow
I. *My Words Are Tied in One*   6'
II. *The Dance of the Sun*   2'
III. *Our Mother the Earth*   4'
IV. *She Languishes*   3'
V. *Exodus from Chaco*   3'
VI. *May All Creation Dance for You*   6'

> Mauldin

Enchanted Land <1989>   18'

narrator
2 2 2 2 — 2 2 1 1 — tmp+2 — str
perc: sus cym, sd, vib
Narration from *The House at Otowi Bridge*, by Peggy Pond Church.
1. *Prologue*   2'
2. *Where the River Makes a Noise*   4'
3. *Dance to Life*   5'
4. *If Our Hearts Are Right…*   4'
5. *The Rain Will Come*   3'

> Mauldin

Entrada <1994>   3'

2 2 2 2 — 2 2 0 0 — tmp — [no str]

> Mauldin

Fajada Butte; An Epiphany <1982>   14'

3[1.2.pic] 2 2 2 — 4 3 3 1 — tmp+2 — cel — str
perc: bd, sus cym, sd, tri, vib, chimes

> Mauldin

High Places <1981>   8'

3[1.2.pic] 2 2 2 — 3 2 2 1 — tmp+2 — pf — str
perc: sus cym, sd, tri, glock, chimes

> Kjos

Kokopelli: His Flutesong <1999; rev 2009>   7'

3[1.2.pic] 2 3[1.2.bcl] 2 — 4 3 3 1 — tmp+1 — hp — str
perc: sus cym, sd, tri, glock
Re-arranged for orchestra, from a work for organ.

> Mauldin

The Last Musician of Ur <2009>   7'

3[1.2.pic] 2 2 2 — 4 3 3 1 — tmp+2 — hp — str
perc: glock, tri, bd, sus cym

> Mauldin

Mountain Light; Four Landscapes for Orchestra <1987>   21'

3[1.2.pic] 2 3[1.2.bcl] 2 — 4 3 3 1 — tmp+2 — hp — str
perc: bd, sus cym, sd, tri, glock, vib, chimes
I. *Summer Afternoon*   8'
II. *Autumn Morning*   5'
III. *Winter Evening*   3'
IV. *Spring Midday*   5'

> Mauldin

Music for the Mountain Air <1988>   9'

2 2 2 2 — 2 2 0 0 — tmp — pf — str

> Mauldin

Petroglyph <1978>   11'

str

> Mauldin

Prayer of Mesas <1988>   7'

chorus
3[1.2.pic] 2 3[1.2.bcl] 3 — 4 3 3 1 — 4sx opt[2asx, tsx, bsx] —
tmp+2 — hp — str
perc: bd, sus cym, sd, tri, glock, vib, chimes

> Mauldin

Prayers of the Children <1993>   11'
chorus   opt children's chorus
3[1.2.pic] 2 3[1.2.bcl] 2 — 4 3 3 1 — tmp+2 — str
perc: sus cym, sd, tri, glock
Please Don't Let Them Die   7'
God Bless the Winds and the Waters of the World 4'
> Mauldin

Promontory Night <1977>   8'
2 1 2 2 — 2 1 0 0 — 1perc — str
perc: glock
> Harmonic

Santa Fe Magic <2003>   11'
narrator
3[1.2.pic] 2 3[1.2.bcl] 2 — 4 3 3 1 — tmp+2 — hp — str
perc: sus cym, sd, glock, vib
I. October Sundown   3'
II. The Children   3'
III. Ecstasy   5'
> Mauldin

Three Dances from Chaco Canyon; Concertpiece for Chamber Orchestra <1980>   10'
1 2 1 2 — 2 0 0 0 — tmp — pf — str
> Mauldin

Three Jemez Landscapes; Fantasy on a Huron Carol <1973>   9'
2 2 2 2 — 4 3 3 1 — tmp+2 — opt pf — str
perc: sus cym, sd, glock[or cel]
Celesta may substitute for glockenspiel.
1. Calavaras Dawn/Moonset (an old carol)   2'
2. Rio de las Vacas (some old jokes)   3'
3. Paliza Sun-Cliffs (some old echoes)   4'
> Harmonic

The Valley at Annacarla <2006>   5'
2 2 3[1.2.bcl] 2 — 4 3 3 1 — tmp+3 — hp — str
perc: bd, sus cym, sd, tri, glock
> Harmonic

Maurice, Paule   1910-1967
(b Paris, 29 Sept 1910; d Paris, 18 Aug 1967). French

Tableaux de Provence <1954–1959>   12'
solo alto saxophone
2[incl pic] 2[incl opt Eh] 2 1 — 2 1 0 0 — tmp+1 — hp — cel — str
1. Farandoulo di chatouno (Farandoles des jeunes filles)   2'
2. Cansoun per ma Mio (Chanson pour ma mie)   1'
3. La Boumiano (La Bohémienne)   1'
4. Dis Alyscamps, l'amo souspire (Des Alyscamps, l'ame soupire) 4'
5. Lou Cabridan (Le Cabridan)   4'
> Lemoine

Maw, Nicholas   1935-2009
(b Grantham, 5 Nov 1935; d Washington, DC, 19 May 2009). English

Odyssey <1972–1987>   95'
3[1.2/afl.3/pic] 3[1.2.3/Eh] 3[1.2/Ebcl.3/Ebcl/bcl] 3[1.2.3/cbn] — 8 4 3 1 — 2tmp+3 — hp — cel — str[min 16.14.12.10.8; max 20.18.14.12.10]
perc: bd, cym, sd, td, tri, tambn, gong, vib, chimes, whip, marac, claves, 3sus cym 3tomtom, 3tamtam, 2glock, 3bongos
The Eb clarinet part is sometimes in the 2nd part and other times in the 3rd; however, only one Ebcl at a time is required.
    The 4 trumpet parts are high and difficult [use of piccolo trumpets is recommended by the composer].
> Faber

Maxwell Davies, Peter   1934-
(b Salford, Greater Manchester, 8 Sept 1934). English

The J-numbers previously used for this composer's works (from Judy Arnold & Colin Bayliss, *Integrated List of Published and Unpublished Works*) were removed from the composer's official website www.maxopus.com in 2007 and have been replaced by opus numbers. For convenience, the J-numbers are included in brackets in the listings below.

Black Pentecost, op.82 [J.218] <1979>   54'
solo mezzo-soprano & baritone
3[1.2.afl] 3[1.2.Eh] 3[1.2.bcl] 3[1.2.cbn] — 4 3 2 0 — tmp+5 — cel — str
perc: marim, bd, glock, crot, Chinescym, marac, whip, claves, rototom, jptmplbell 2flexatones, tamtam (with plastic soap dish)
1. Adagio   18'
2. Lentissimo   10'
3. Lentissimo—Allegro   8'
4. Andante   18'
> Chester

Caroline Mathilde: Suite from Act I, op.144b [J.297] <1990>   29'
2[1.2/pic/afl] 2[1.2/Eh] 2[1.2/bcl] 2[1.2/cbn] — 2 2 2 0 — tmp+2 — hp — str
perc: cym, glock, flexatone, bd, tamtam, crot, 2sus cym, anvil
1. A Public Square   _'
2. Inside the Castle   _'
3. The Queen's Chamber   _'
4. The Royal Chambers   _'
> Chester

Caroline Mathilde: Suite from Act II, op.144c [J.298] <1990>   32'
female voices (a small chorus SA, or 2 soloists)
2[1.2/pic/afl] 2[1.2/Eh] 2[1.2/bcl] 2[1.2/cbn] — 2 2 2 0 — tmp+2 — hp — str
perc: cym, glock, flexatone, bd, tamtam, crot, 2sus cym, anvil
1. A Public Square   3'
2. The Conspiracy   4'
3. Court Dance   5'
4. Pas-de-deux   6'
5. The Arrest   5'
6. The Execution   7'
7. Exile of Caroline Mathilde 2'
> Chester

Carolísima Serenade, op.168 [J.334] <1994>   19'

1[1/pic] 1 2[1.bcl] 1[1/cbn] — 1 1 1 0 — 1perc — str 5t
perc: field dr, sd, bd, crot, belltree, 2sus cym
1. *Introduction*   _'
2. *Allegro*   _'
3. *Adagio*   _'
4. *Allegro*   _'
5. *Epilogue*   _'

> Schott

Chat Moss, op.164 [J.329] <1993>   6'

2 1 1 1 — 0 2 0 0 — tmp+2 — str
perc: cym, sus cym, bd
Intended for school orchestra.

> Chester

Concerto, Trumpet, op.132 [J.281] <1988>   31'

3[1.2.afl] 3[1.2.Eh] 3[1.2.bcl] 3[1.2.cbn] — 4 3 3 1 — tmp+4 — str
perc: glock, marim, crot, tambn, belltree, bd; Japanese templegong (played by tmp)
1. *Adagio; Allegro*   14'
2. *Adagio*   10'
3. *Presto*   7'

> Boosey

Concerto, Violin, [No.1], op.123 [J.267] <1985>   30'

2 2 2 2 — 2 2 0 0 — tmp — str
1. *Allegro moderato*   _'
2. *Adagio*   _'
3. *Allegro non troppo*   _'

> Chester

Concerto, Violin, No.2 (Fiddler on the Shore) <2009>   25'

3[1.2.pic] 2 3[1.2.bcl] 3[1.2.cbn] — 4 3 3 0 — tmp+3 — str
perc: glock, marim, crot, tambn, bd, sd
In one mvt.

> Chester

Cross Lane Fair, op.167 [J.332] <1994>   16'

solo: Northumbrian pipes & bodhran
2[1.2/pic] 2 2 2[1.cbn] — 2 2 2 1 — tmp+2 — str
perc: tambn, flexatone, lionroar, vib, templeblks, belltree, bd/ped, tamtam (rubbed with plastic soapbox), choke cym, 4woodblks, 2sus cym
1. *Introduction*   2'
2. *The Fairground*   1'
3. *Ghost Train*   2'
4. *Transition (The Fairground)*   1'
5. *The Bearded Lady and the Five-Legged Sheep*   2'
6. *Transition (The Fairground)*   1'
7. *The Juggler*   3'
8. *Transition (The Fairground)*   1'
9. *Carousel*   3'

> Chester

Eight Songs for a Mad King, op.39 [J.129] <1969>   33'

solo male voice
1[1/pic] 0 1 0 — 1perc — pf/hpsd/dulcimer — vn, vc
perc: sd, hi-hat, bd, ratch, tomtom, tamtam, tambn, rototom, templeblks, windchimes, crot, slgh-bells, glock, railwhstle, 2sus cym, 2woodblks, chain, 2birdcalls, steelbars, didjeridoo
1. *The Sentry (King Prussia's Minuet)*   _'
2. *The Country Walk (La Promenade)*   _'
3. *The Lady-in-Waiting (Miss Musgrave's Fancy)*   _'
4. *To be Sung on the Water (The Waterman)*   _'
5. *The Phantom Queen (He's Ay A-Kissing Me)*   _'
6. *The Counterfeit (Le Contrefaite)*   _'
7. *Country Dance (Scotch Bonnett)*   _'
8. *The Review (A Spanish March)*   _'

> Boosey

First Fantasia on an "In nomine" of John Taverner, op.19 [J.97] <1962>   11'

2 2 2 2 — 2 2 2 1 — 1perc — str
perc: handbells

> Schott

Five Klee Pictures, op.12 [J.58] <1960; rev 1976>   10'

2 2 2 2 — 4 2 2 0 — 5perc — pf — str
perc: sd, bd, cym, cast, woodblk, templeblks, tamtam, tambn, tri, xyl, nightingale
Intended for school orchestra.
1. *A Crusader*   1'
2. *Oriental Garden*   2'
3. *The Twittering Machine*   2'
4. *Stained Glass Saint*   2'
5. *Ad Parnassum*   3'

> Boosey   Luck's

Into the Labyrinth, op.111 [J.254] <1983>   32'

solo tenor
2 2 2 2 — 2 2 0 0 — str
1. *Lento*   _'
2. *Allegro*   _'
3. *Lento*   _'
4. *Adagio (moving between Lento and Allegro)*   _'
5. *Lento recitando - Largo*   _'

> Chester

Jimmack the Postie, op.124 [J.269] <1986>   9'

2[1/pic.2/afl] 2 2[1.2/bcl] 2 — 2 2 2 0 — tmp — str

> Chester

Mavis in Las Vegas <1996>   15'

3[1.2.afl] 3 3[1.2.bcl/tsx] 3[1.2.cbn] — 4 3 3 1 — banjo — tmp+5 — hp — cel/pf/elec kybd — str
perc: glock, marim, crot, sd, templeblks, flexatone, belltree, Chinescym, tambn, guiro, bd, cym, slide whistle, 3sus cym, 4woodblk

> Chester

A Mirror of Whitening Light, op.75 [J.149] (Speculum luminis dealbensis) <1976–1977>   22'

1[fl/pic] 1[ob/Eh] 1 1 — 1 1 1 0 — 1perc — cel — str 5t
perc: glock, crot, marim

> Boosey

Ojai Festival Overture, op.147 [J.305] <1991>   6'

2[1.2/pic] 2[1.2/Eh] 2 2 — 2 2 0 0 — tmp — str

> Boosey

An Orkney Wedding, With Sunrise, op.120a [J.264] <1984; rev chamber orch version 1986>   13'

solo bagpiper
2 2 2[1.2/bcl] 2 — 4 2 2 1 — tmp+4 — str
perc: marim, crot, glock, tambn, sd, sus cym, cym, whip, 4woodblks, bd/ped, slide whistle
Piper marches through hall in traditional costume.
   A chamber orchestra version (op.120b) dispenses with 3 of the percussionists, 2 horns, & tuba.

> Boosey

Prolation, op.8 [J.53] <1958>   20'

3[1.2.pic] 3[1.2.Eh] 3 2[1.2/cbn] — 4 3 4 1 — tmp+3 — hp — cel — str
perc: glock, xyl, 5sus cym, 2bd (1 muffled)

> Schott

St. Thomas Wake; Foxtrot for Orchestra on a Pavan by John Bull, op.37 [J.127] <1969> 21'

4[1.2.pic; *fl/pic*] 2 4[1.2.bcl; *cl*] 3[1.2.cbn] — 4 4[1.2.3; *tp*] 4[1.2.3; *tbn*] 1 — tmp+3; *perc* — hp — *pf [out-of-tune]* — str
perc: sd, td, tamtam, claves, whip, 2whstles, 4sus cym, metal sheet, 3hammers, upright pf w/ action removed, 4woodblks, 3rattles, 4metal pipes, 2bd, tindrum; *set*
Musicians are divided into 2 ensembles: the main orchestra and a quasi-1930s dance band, distinguished above by italics.
   Hp sometimes ampd.

Boosey

Second Fantasia on John Taverner's "In nomine," op.23 [J.103] <1964> 40'

2[1.2/pic/afl] 2[1.2/Eh] 2[1.2/bcl] 2[1.2/cbn] — 4 4 2 2 — tmp+4 — hp — str
perc: sd, sus cym, glock, xyl, chimes, tamtam, 2bd, handbells

Boosey

The Shepherds' Calendar, op.30 [J.112] <1965> 21'

chorus   treble soloist
1 1 5 1 — 0 1 1 0 — 6rec — 9perc — str 4t
perc: marac, woodblk, templeblks, tamtam, td, claves, crot, xyl, glock, 3sd, 3sus cym, washboard, Japanese jingles, anvil, rattle, 2bd, 2stone discs, metal claves, handbells
Treble soloist may be replaced by a soprano, or group of trebles and/or sopranos, doubled by a flute if necessary.
   Suitable for church choirs, amateur, school or professional choruses.
   1. Letabund rediit _'
   2. Vestiunt silve tenera memorem _'
   3. De ramis cadunt folia _'
   4. Veniet Dominus, et non tardabit _'

Boosey

Sinfonia concertante, op.106 [J.247] <1982> 37'

solo woodwind 5t (fl, ob, cl, bn, hn)
tmp — str
   1. Adagio molto - Allegro molto   16'
   2. Andante   11'
   3. Flessibile - Allegro   10'

Chester

Sinfonia for Chamber Orchestra, op.20 [J.98] <1962> 23'

1 1 1 1 — 1 0 0 0 — str
   1. Lento recitando   _'
   2. Allegro molto moderato   _'
   3. Allegro   _'
   4. Lento   _'

Schott

Sinfonietta accademica, op.112 [J.255] <1983> 32'

2[1.2/pic] 2 2 2 — 2 2 0 0 — str
   1. Allegro moderato   _'
   2. Largo   _'
   3. Andante - Allegro - Lento   _'

Chester

Sir Charles His Pavan, op.157 [J.320] <1992> 4'

3[1.2.afl] 2 3[1.2.bcl] 3[1.2.cbn] — 4 2 3 1 — tmp+1 — hp — str
perc: bd

Schott

A Spell for Green Corn, op.161 [J.325] (The MacDonald Dances) <1993> 20'

solo violin
2[1.2/pic] 2 2[1.bcl] 2[1.2/cbn] — 2 2 2[opt] 0 — tmp+1[opt] — str
perc: tambn, glock, crot, bd, belltree

Chester

Stone Litany; Runes from a House of the Dead, op.57 [J.168] <1973> 20'

solo mezzo-soprano
2[1.pic] 0 2[1.bcl/Ebcl] 2[1.cbn] — 2 2 2 1 — tmp+5 — hp — cel —
perc: glock, marim, flexatone, crot, belltree, templeblks, marac, rototom, bd, chimes, Chinescym, sus cym, tamtam, 2wine glasses, 2woodblks, tabor, 3buttongongs[G#,E,C], bass bow, anvil
The text is in Old Norse.
   1.   4'
   2.   1'
   3.   3'
   4.   2'
   5.   3'
   6.   7'

Boosey

Strathclyde Concerto No.1, op.128 [J.277] <1986> 27'

solo oboe
2[1.2/pic] 0 2[1.2/bcl] 0 — 2 0 0 0 — tmp — str
   Adagio molto - Allegro moderato   _'
   Adagio   _'
   Allegro   _'

Boosey

Strathclyde Concerto No.2, op.131 [J.280] <1987> 35'

solo violoncello
2[1.2/pic] 2 2[1.bcl] 2 — 2 2 0 0 — tmp — str
   Moderato   12'
   Lento   12'
   Allegro moderato - Lento - Lentissimo   11'

Chester

Strathclyde Concerto No.3, op.139 [J.290] <1989> 29'

solo horn & trumpet
2[1.2/afl] 2[1.2/Eh] 2[1.2/bcl] 2[1.2/cbn] — tmp — str
   Adagio (Introduction)   9'
   Allegro moderato   6'
   Cadenza   3'
   Andante   6'
   Allegro   5'

Boosey

Strathclyde Concerto No.4, op.143 [J.295] <1990> 30'

clarinet solo
2[1.2/pic] 2 1[bcl] 2[1.2/cbn] — 2 0 0 0 — 1perc — str
perc: tmp, marim, crot, Japanese temple gong
   Lento (Introduction)   2'
   Allegro moderato   9'
   Adagio   12'
   Cadenza   4'
   Adagio   3'

Chester

Strathclyde Concerto No.5, op.151 [J.310] <1991> 34'

solo violin & viola
str
   Adagio - Allegro moderato   15'
   Allegro moderato - Adagio   10'
   Allegro - Più lento   9'

Boosey

Strathclyde Concerto No.6, op.152 [J.312] <1991> 25'

solo flute
0 0 2[1.2/bcl] 1 — 2 2 0 0 — tmp+1 — str[no vn]
perc: glock, claves, tambn
   Andante - Allegro moderato   11'
   Adagio   7'
   Allegro - Andante   7'

Chester

Strathclyde Concerto No.7, op.156 [J.319] <1992>   21'

solo double bass
2[1.2/afl] 2[1.2/Eh] 2[1.bcl] 2[1.2/cbn] — 2 0 0 0 — str
Moderato　　　　*11'*
Lento - Allegro　　*10'*

Boosey

Strathclyde Concerto No.8, op.159 [J.323] <1993>   25'

solo bassoon
2[1/pic.afl] 0 2[1.bcl] 1[cbn] — 2 0 0 0 — tmp — str
Presto - Allegro moderato　*12'*
Andante　　　　　　*6'*
Recit, Allegro　　　　*7'*

Chester

Strathclyde Concerto No.9, op.170 [J.337] <1994>   25'

solos: pic, afl, Eh, Ebcl, bcl, cbn
str
Moderato　　　*_'*
Allegro　　　　*_'*
Lentissimo　　*_'*

Chester

Strathclyde Concerto No.10; Concerto for Orchestra,   30'
op.179 [J.348] <1996>

2[1.2/pic/afl] 2[1.2/Eh] 2[1.2/bcl] 2[1.2/cbn] — 2 2 0 0 — tmp — str
Allegro non troppo　*13'*
Lento　　　　　*9'*
Moderato　　　*9'*

Boosey

Symphony No.1, op.71 [J.198] <1976>   55'

3[1.2/pic2.pic1/afl] 3[1.2.Eh] 3[1.2.bcl] 3[1.2.cbn] — 4 3 3 0 —
tmp+4 — hp — cel — str
perc: marim, chimes, flexatone, glock, crot
1. Presto　　　　　　　　　*17'*
2. Lento (accelerating to Presto)　*10'*
3. Adagio　　　　　　　　　*15'*
4. Presto　　　　　　　　　*13'*

Boosey

Symphony No.2, op.91 [J.231] <1980>   55'

3[1.2.pic/afl] 2 3[1.2.bcl] 3[1.2.cbn] — 4 3 2 0 — tmp+3 — hp — str
perc: glock, marim, crot
I. Allegro molto　　　　　　　　*17'*
II. Adagio　　　　　　　　　　*16'*
III. Allegro molto; leggiero　　　*9'*
IV. Adagio, flessibile - Moderato - Allegro　*13'*

Boosey

Symphony No.3, op.119 [J.263] <1984>   58'

3[1.2/afl.3/pic] 3[1.2.Eh] 3[1.2.bcl] 3[1.2.cbn] — 4 3 3 1 — tmp —
str
1. Lento - Allegro alla breve　*19'*
2. Scherzo I: Allegro　　　*9'*
3. Scherzo II: Allegro vivace　*8'*
4. Lento/Adagio flessibile　*22'*

Boosey

Symphony No.4, op.136 [J.287] <1989>   43'

2[1.2/pic/afl] 2[1.2/Eh] 2[1.2/bcl] 2[1.2/cbn] — 2 2 0 0 — tmp — str
Moderato　　　　*14'*
Allegro　　　　　*7'*
Adagio　　　　　*11'*
Andante - Allegro　*11'*

Boosey

Symphony No.5, op.166 [J.331] <1994>   26'

3[1.2/afl.pic] 3[1.2.Eh] 3[1.2.bcl] 3[1.2.cbn] — 4 3 3 1 — tmp+4 —
hp — cel — str
perc: marim, glock, crot, flexatone, cym, sus cym, tambn, 2bd

Boosey

Symphony No.6, op.176 [J.280] <1996>   49'

3[1.2/afl.pic] 3[1.2.Eh] 3[1.2.bcl] 3[1.2.cbn] — 4 3 3 1 — tmp+5 —
hp — cel — str
perc: cym, sd, tambn, glock, marim, crot, 2bd, 2sus cym, 2woodblk, rainsticks
I. Adagio; Allegro　　　　　　*20'*
II. Adagio non troppo; Allegro　*9'*
III. Adagio; Più animato　　　　*20'*

Boosey

Symphony No.7, op.211 <1999–2000>   45'

3[1.2/afl.pic] 3[1.2.Eh] 3[1.2.bcl] 3[1.2.cbn] — 4 3 3 1 — tmp+5 —
hp — cel — str
perc: cym, Chinescym, sd, tambn, tamtam, glock, marim, chimes, crot, 2bd, 2sus
cym, 2woodblk, pelletbell, antique cymbals (indefinite pitch)
1. Exposition　　　*_'*
2. Minuet and Trio　*_'*
3. Slow Movement　*_'*
4. Development　　*_'*

Boosey

Symphony No.8, op.215 [J.320] (Antarctic Symphony)   40'
<2000>

3[1.2.pic] 3[1.2.Eh] 3[1.2.bcl] 3[1.2.cbn] — 4 3 3 1 — tmp+4 — hp
— cel — str
perc: cym, Chinescym, sd, tambn, tamtam, glock, xyl, marim, chimes, crot,
belltree, woodblk, 2bd, 6sus cym, buttongong, Japanese temple gong, 5tuned
brandy glasses, 2pebbles, cog rattle, 3metalpipe, plastic soap dish, biscuit tin filled
with broken glass
In one mvt.

Boosey

Symphony No.9   25'

3[1.2.pic] 3[1.2.Eh] 3[1.2.bcl] 3[1.2.cbn] — 4 3 3 1 — tmp+3 — str
perc: td, marim, glock, crot, chimes, 2bd, 2sd, 3sus cym, 2woodblk
Additional brass sextet, positioned away from the orchestra: 3tp, 2tbn,
tuba.
　In one mvt.

Chester

Threnody on a Plainsong for Michael Vyner, op.141   3'
[J.292] <1989>

0 2 0 2 — 2 2 0 0 — tmp — str

Chester

Veni sancte spiritus, op.22 [J.102] <1963>   20'

solos SAB　　chorus
1 1 0 2 — 2 2 2 0 — str
1. Dum complementur dies pentecosts　*_'*
2. Veni, sancte spiritus　　　　　　*_'*
3. O lux, beatissima　　　　　　　*_'*
4. Da virtutis meritum　　　　　　*_'*

Boosey

A Welcome to Orkney, op.90 [J.229] <1980>   3'

1 1 1 1 — 1 0 0 0 — 2 str quartets & db [or small str ensemble]

Boosey

Worldes Blis; Motet for Orchestra, op.38 [J.128] <1969>   *37'*

3[1.2.pic] 2 3[1.2.bcl] 3[1.2.cbn] — 4 3 3 1 — 2tmp+5 — 2hp — org (or chamber org) — str
perc: glock, xyl, claves, td, chimes, 3sus cym, 5cym, 2whips, 5woodblks, 2sd, anvil, handbells or crot, hammer, 2tamtams, upright pf (action removed), 2bd, 2templeblks

Boosey

Mayuzumi, Toshirō   1929-1997

(b Yokohama, 20 Feb 1929; d Kawasaki, 10 April 1997). Japanese

Concertino, Xylophone <1965>   *13'*

2 2 2 2 — 2 2 2 1 — asx — tmp+1 — hp — str

Peters

McBride, Robert   1911-

(b Tucson, AZ, 20 Feb 1911). American

Pumpkin-Eater's Little Fugue <1955>   *4'*

2[1.pic] 2[ob2 opt] 2 2[bn2 opt] — 4 2 3[tbn3 opt] 1 — tmp+2 — str

AMP   Luck's

McCabe, John   1939-2015

(b Huyton, 21 April 1939; d 13 Feb 2015). English

Arthur: Three Portraits <1998–2000; rev 2010>   *21'*

3[1.2.pic(opt)] 3[1.2(opt).3/Eh] 3[1.2.bcl] 3[1.2.cbn(opt)] — 4 3[tp3 opt] 3 1 — asx — tmp+3 — hp — cel[or pf] — str
perc: cym, sd, bd, tamtam, xyl, glock, chimes, rototom[or marim or pf]
Taken from the ballet diptych *Arthur, Part I: Arthur Pendragon* and *Arthur, Part II: Le Mort d'Arthur*, with some recomposition.
  Lancelot Alone (Passacaglia)   _'
  Guinevere (Courtly Dance and Pas de deux)   _'
  Arthur (The Last Battle, and Transformation)   _'

Novello

Arthur Pendragon: Suite No.1 <1998–2000>   *28'*

2[1.2/pic] 2 2 2 — 4 2 3 1 — asx — tmp+3 — hp — pf — str
perc: bd, sd, tambn, cym, sus cym, tamtam, flexatone, whip, glock, xyl, crot, chimes, rainstick, waterphone, 2agogo bells, 2cowbell, 3rototom
Suite from the ballet.
  1. Uther and the Tribes   7'
  2. Igraine and Uther   7'
  3. The Tourney   6'
  4. The Lovers   8'

Novello

Concerto, Horn <2005–2006>   *24'*

2[1.2/pic] 2 2[1.bcl] 2 — 2 2 2 1 — tmp+3 — hp — str
perc: claves, marac, sus cym, bd, tamtam, marim

Novello

Concerto, Trumpet (La primavera) <2012>   *19'*

1 1 1 1 — 1 1 1 0 — 1perc — str
perc: td, sus cym, bd, tamtam, woodblk, tambn, 4bongos
Solo trumpet doubles on flugelhorn. Percussion is prominent, and considered an obbligato.

Novello

Concerto, Violoncello (Songline) <2007>   *23'*

2 2 2 2 — 4 2 3 1 — tmp+2 — hp — str
perc: marac, sus cym, bd, tamtam, whip, woodblk, xyl, vib
In one mvt.

Novello

Concerto funèbre, for Viola & Chamber Orchestra <1962; rev 2006>   *13'*

0 2 0 0 — 2 0 0 0 — str
  1. Prefazione   _'
  2. Elegia I   _'
  3. Notturno   _'
  4. Elegia II   _'
  5. Cadenza   _'
  6. Elegia III   _'

Novello

The Lion, the Witch and the Wardrobe: Suite <1968>   *15'*

1 1 2 1 — 1 2 1 0 — tmp+2 — pf — str

Novello

Symphony "Edward II" <1994–1995; rev 1997>   *38'*

3[1.2.3/pic] 3[1.2.3/Eh] 3[1.2/Ebcl.bcl] 3[1.2.cbn] — 4 3 3 1 — elec gtr — tmp+3 — hp — pf, cel — str
perc: sus cym, cym, sd, td, bd, woodblk, whip, tamtam, xyl, glock, vib, marim, chimes, 3tomtom, anvil
Movements from the ballet, made into a symphony by the composer.
  I. Adagio; Allegro, poco pesante   _'
  II. Romanza   _'
  III. The Barons   _'
  IV. Finale   _'

Novello

Symphony No.4 (Of Time and the River) <1993–1994>   *30'*

3[1.2.3/pic] 3[1.2.3/Eh] 3[1.2.3/bcl] 3[1.2.cbn] — 4 3 3 1 — asx — tmp+3 — hp — pf/cel — str
perc: bd, sd, td, sus cym, whip, glock, xyl, vib, crot, chimes, 3tomtom
  Part One   _'
  Part Two   _'

Novello

Symphony No.7 (Labyrinth) <2007>   *20'*

3[1.2.3/pic] 3[1.2.Eh] 3[1.2.bcl] 3 — 4 3 3 1 — asx — tmp+3 — str
perc: sus cym, cym, td, bd, tamtam, xyl, glock, chimes
In one mvt.

Novello

Symphony on a Pavane <2006>   *21'*

2[1.2/pic] 2[1.bass ob] 2 2 — 4 2 2 1 — 3perc — cel — str
perc: sus cym, cym, bd, chimes, rototom, windchimes
Mvts played without pause.
  Allegro vivace   _'
  Dissolve I   _'
  Scherzando   _'
  Dissolve II   _'
  Largo   _'
  Dissolve III   _'
  L'istesso tempo   _'

Novello

McCarter, Kevin   1956-

American

Landscape Scenes for Clarinet & Strings   *6'*

solo clarinet
str

McCarter

Opening Ideas <2004>   *6'*

str

McCarter

Prelude and Excursion   4'

0 0 0 0 — 4 3 3 1 — [no str]

> McCarter

McCarthy, Daniel   1955-

(b Onekoma, MI, 1955). American

American Dance Music   10'

solos: 2tp, hn, tbn, tuba, perc
2[incl pic] 2 3[incl bcl] 2 — 3 2 2 0 — tmp+2 — str

1. The Unsquare Dance	2'
2. Latina	1'
3. Serenade	2'
4. Jazz	3'
5. Rokit!	2'

> MMB

McCartney, Paul   1942-

(b Liverpool, 18 June 1942). English

Spiral <1997>   10'

2[1.2/pic] 2[1.Eh] 2 2 — 2 0 0 0 — tmp — hp — str
Horns may be doubled in one passage.
Orchestrated by Richard Rodney Bennett.

> Faber

McClure, Glenn   1964-

(b Warsaw, NY, 27 Dec 1964). American

Caribbean Christmas Mass <2005>   54'

chorus   4 steelpans (lead, double 2nd, cello, bass)   narrator
2[1.2/pic] 1 1 1 — 2 2 2 1 — tmp+2 — str
perc: sus cym, set, cowbell, marac, congas, agogo
Brief alto solo (16 bars); optional audience sing-along.
Intended originally for youth chorus. Movements may be performed separately.

1. O magnum mysterium	4'
2. Veni, veni Emmanuel (samba)	5'
3. Hodie Christus natus est	3'
4. Kyrie (waltz; includes interpolated text by St. Francis of Assisi)	4'
Reading, from Bonaventure's Major Life of St. Francis of Assisi	3'
5. Gloria (calypso)	4'
6. His Love Endures forever (Psalm 118)	4'
7. Credo (salsa)	4'
Reading, from St. Francis' Nativity Psalm	1'
8. Sanctus (calypso)	4'
9. Agnus Dei	5'
10. Silent Night (jazz waltz)	6'
Reading, from St. Francis' Nativity Psalm	1'
11. Puer natus est (salsa—Joy to the World)	4'
12. His Love Endures Forever (reprise)	2'

> McClure

McGlaughlin, William   1946-

(b Philadelphia, PA, 3 October 1943). American

Bela's Bounce <1998>   9'

3[1.2.3/pic] 3[1.2.Eh] 3[1.2.bcl] 3[1.2.cbn] — 4 3 3 1 — tmp+2 — hp — str
perc: bd, sus cym, hi-hat, sd, tambn, vib, claves

> Subito

Solstice; An Orchestral Fantasy on Old English Carols <1997>   12'

3[1.2/afl.pic] 3[1.2.Eh] 3[1.2.bcl] 2 — 4 3 3 1 — tmp+2 — hp — str
perc: bd, cym, sus cym, sd, tambn, glock, xyl, crot, 2tomtoms, shaker

I. In dulci jubilo	_'
II. Rorate	_'
III. Coventry Carol	_'

> Subito

McKay, George Frederick   1899-1970

(b Harrington, WA, 11 June 1899; d Stateline, NV, 4 Oct 1970). American

Symphonette in D

2 2 2 2 — 4 3 3 1 — tmp — pf — str

> Galaxy

McLoskey, Lansing   1964-

American

Chanson pour cordes <1999>   8'

str[min 4.4.3.4.1]

> Odhecaton

Moraine <1995>   13'

2[1.2/pic] 2 2 2 — 2 2 2 0 — 1perc — pf — str
perc: bd, Chinescym, tamtam, glock, chimes, 2sd, 3congas

> Odhecaton

post- <2010>   8'

2[1.2/pic] 2 2 2 — 2 2 2 1 — tmp+1 — hp — str
perc: bd, sd, tambn, xyl, cowbell, whip, bongos, ratch, vibrslp, 2sus cym, 3tomtom, police whistle
Timpanist covers some percussion.

> Odhecaton

Prex penitentialis (The Prayer of Petrarch) <1997–1998>   23'

soprano solo
2[1.2/pic] 2[1.2/Eh] 2 2 — 2 0 0 0 — 1perc — str[min 4.3.3.3.1]
perc: sus cym, sd, tri, tamtam, glock, marim, 3tomtom, timpani

I. The Air is the Work of Your Fingers	11'
II. The Hiss and Roar of Gehenna; I Dwelt in Dreams	12'

> Odhecaton

Requiem, ver.2.001x <2001; rev (orchd) 2009>   15'

2[1/afl.2/pic] 2[1.2Eh] 2[1.2/bcl] 2 — 2 2 3 0 — 2perc — pf — str[min 5.4.4.3.1]
perc: bd, szl cym, Chinescym, tri, tamtam, marim, vib, 2sus cym, 3sd, 3buttongong, 3bongos, crot[A#5]
Originally a chamber work; rev. 2009 for orchestra.

I. Introit	_'
II. R.I.P.	_'
Trope [virus]	_'
III. Eulogy	_'
IV. Epitaph	_'
Obit.	_'

> Odhecaton

Symphoniae sacrae <1991>   18'

2[1.2/pic] 2[1.2/Eh] 2 3[1.2.cbn] — 4 2 0 1 — tmp+2 — str
perc: bd, sd, tri, tambn, windchimes, whip, 2sus cym, 6tomtom

I. Magnificat	6'
II. Gaudeamus	3'
III. Orbis factor	4'
IV. Sanctus, sanctus, sanctus	3'
V. Alleluia	2'

> Odhecaton

McPhee, Colin   1900-1964

(b Montréal, 15 March 1900; d Los Angeles, 7 Jan 1964). American composer of Canadian birth

Symphony No.2 (Pastorale) <1957>   17'

2[1.2/pic] 2 2 2 — 4 2 3 1 — tmp+3 — hp — pf — str
perc: bd, sd, tri, tambn, glock, xyl, marim, finger cym
   I. Moderato misterioso; Più animato   7'
   II. Elegy   5'
   III. Molto energico   5'

> AMP

Tabuh-Tabuhan; Toccata for Orchestra and 2 Pianos <1936>   19'

4[1.2.pic1.pic2] 3[1.2.Eh] 3[1.2.bcl] 3[1.2.cbn] — 4 3 3 1 — 6perc — hp — cel, 2pf — str
perc: cym, tri, bd, tamtam, xyl, marim, glock, chimes, sus cym, Balinese cym [or tambn], sandblks, 2Balinese gongs[A2,F#3 (opt)]
   1. Ostinatos   7'
   2. Nocturne   6'
   3. Finale   6'

> AMP

Transitions <1954>   15'

3[1.2.pic] 3[1.2.Eh] 2 2 — 4 3 3 1 — tmp+2 — pf — str
perc: bd, sus cym, sd, tri, tamtam, glock, xyl, chimes

> AMP

McTee, Cindy   1953-

(b Tacoma, WA, 20 Feb 1953). American

Adagio for String Orchestra <2002>   12'

str
2nd mvt of the composer's *Symphony No.1: Ballet for Orchestra*, for which it was adapted from an earlier organ work, *Agnus Dei*.

> Rondure

Circuits <1990; rev 1992>   6'

3 3 3 3 — 4 3 3 1 — 3perc — opt pf — str
perc: bd, sd, tambn, glock, vib, templeblks, cowbell, 2sus cym, 2woodblk, 4almglocken, metal plate
May also be played in a chamber orchestra version with the following instrumentation:
   2 2 2 2 — 2 2 1 0 — 3perc — opt pf — str
   The optional piano part is not to be found in the score of either version, but a part is provided.

> LKMP

Double Play <2009–2010>   17'

3[1.2.pic] 3 3[1.2.Ebcl] 3 — 4 3 3 1 — tmp+3 — hp — str
perc: bd, szl cym, hi-hat, tambn, tamtam, vib, marktree, templeblks, bongos, guiro, cast, congas, vibrslp, 5sus cym, 2sd, 4tomtom, 2tri, 6woodblk, shaker, rainstick, 4cowbell
Movements may be performed separately; see individual entries.
   I. The Unquestioned Answer   8'
   II. Tempus fugit   9'

> Rondure

Einstein's Dream <2004>   14'

pre-recorded sounds (CD) — 3perc — str
perc: bd, tamtam, glock, chimes, marktree, belltree, ratch, marac, cast, 4sus cym, 2tri, 2flexatone, opt gong, 2vc bows
   1. Warps and Curves in the Fabric of Space and Time   2'
   2. Music of the Spheres   1'
   3. Chasing after Quanta   1'
   4. Pondering the Behavior of Light   3'
   5. The Frantic Dance of Subatomic Particles   2'
   6. Celestial Bells   3'
   7. Wondering at the Secrets   2'

> Rondure

Finish Line <2005>   7'

3[1.2.pic] 3[1.2.Eh] 3 3 — 4 3 3 0 — tmp+3 — str
perc: bd, sus cym, Chinescym, tri, tambn, tamtam, glock, vib, woodblk, ratch, guiro, cast, vibrslp, 4brake dr or metal plates, shaker
Instrumentation may be reduced from full orchestra to chamber orchestra by eliminating the following: Eh, cl 3, bn3, hn2, hn4, tp3, tbn3, thus leaving: 3[1.2.pic] 2 2 2 — 2 2 2 0 — tmp+3 — str

> Rondure

Solstice, for Trombone & Orchestra <2007>   19'

0 0 0 0 — 4 3 3 1 — tmp+3 — str
perc: bd, cym, tambn, tamtam, marktree, cowbell, claves, cast, vibrslp, 4brake dr, 2tri, 4sus cym
   I. Allegro [attacca]   _'
   II. Adagio   _'
   III. Allegro   _'

> Rondure

Symphony No.1 (Ballet for Orchestra) <2002>   31'

3[1.2.pic] 3 3[1.2/bcl.Ebcl] 3[1.2.cbn] — 4 3 3 1 — tmp+3 — hp — pf — str
perc: bd, hi-hat, sd, flexatone, cowbell, bongos, ratch, vibrslp, 4sus cym, 4tomtom, 2tri, 2tambn, cabasa, cuica, cello bow
   I. Introduction: On with the Dance   8'
   II. Adagio: Till a Silence Fell   12'
   III. Waltz: Light Fantastic   4'
   IV. Finale: Where Time Plays the Fiddle   7'

> Rondure

Tempus fugit <2010>   9'

3[1.2.pic] 3 3[1.2.Ebcl] 3 — 4 3 3 1 — tmp+3 — str
perc: bd, szl cym, hi-hat, tambn, templeblks, bongos, ratch, guiro, cast, congas, vibrslp, 5sus cym, 4tomtom, 2tri, 6woodblk, 2sd, 4cowbell
2nd movement of the composer's *Double Play*, q.v.

> Rondure

Timepiece <2000>   8'

3[1.2.pic] 3[1.2.Eh] 3[1.2.Ebcl] 3[1.2.cbn] — 4 3 3 1 — tmp+3 — pf — str
perc: hi-hat, tri, tambn, xyl, ratch, claves, cast, vibrslp, 5sus cym, 4tomtom, 2cowbell, 4bongos, metalshakr, washboard

> LKMP

The Twittering Machine <1993>   13'

1[fl/pic] 1 1 1 — 1 1 1 0 — 1perc — hp — pf — str
perc: bd, hi-hat, sd, tomtom, vib, templeblks, 2sus cym
May be performed with single strings on each part.

> LKMP

The Unquestioned Answer <2009; rev 2010>   7'

3[1.2.pic] 3 3[1.2.Ebcl] 3 — 4 3 3 1 — tmp+3 — hp — str
perc: bd, szl cym, sd, tamtam, vib, marktree, 4sus cym, rainstick
1st movement of the composer's *Double Play*, q.v.

> Rondure

Mechem, Kirke   1925-

(b Wichita, KS, 16 Aug 1925). American composer

The Jayhawk; Magic Bird Overture, op.43 <1974>   8'

3[incl pic] 2 3[incl bcl] 2 — 4 3 3 1 — tmp+2 — opt pf — str

> Schirmer

Songs of the Slave, op.51b <1993>   34'

solos: bass-baritone, soprano   chorus
3[1.2.3/pic] 3[1.2.Eh] 3[1.2.3/bcl] 3[1.2.cbn] — 4 3 3 1 — tmp+4 — hp — str
perc: tri, tambn, sd, field dr, bd, whip, xyl, glock, chimes, tamtam, cym, sus cym
From the composer's opera *John Brown*. A reduced orchestration is available:
   2[1.2/pic] 2 2[1.2/bcl] 2 — 4 2 2 0 — tmp+2 — hp — str

1. Blow Ye the Trumpet (chorus)	_'
2. The Songs of the Slave (solo bs-bar)	_'
3. Dan-u-el (solo baritone & chorus)	_'
4. Dear Husband (solo soprano)	_'
5. A Speech by Frederick Douglass (solo bs-bar)	_'
6. Declaration (solo bs-bar & chorus)	_'

> Schirmer

Méhul, Etienne-Nicolas   1763-1817

(b Givet, 22 June 1763; d Paris, 18 Oct 1817). French

La chasse du jeune Henri <1797>   11'

2 2 2 2 — 4 0 0 0 — tmp — str
Originally the overture to Méhul's opera *Le jeune Henri*, though much-performed as an independent excerpt.

> Heugel   Luck's

Joseph: Overture <1807>   6'

2 2 2 2 — 2 2 0 0 — tmp — str

> Breitkopf   Kalmus   Luck's

Symphony No.2, D Major <1809>   28'

2 2 2 2 — 2 0 0 0 — tmp — str
Kalmus ed. Clinton B. Fairlamb.

1. Adagio; Allegro	9'
2. Andante	7'
3. Menuett	4'
4. Finale: Allegro vivace	8'

> Breitkopf   Kalmus

Melartin, Erkki   1875-1937

(b Käkisalmi, Finland [now Priozersk, Russia], 7 Feb 1875; d Pukinmäki, Helsinki, 14 Feb 1937). Finnish

Serenade, op.31, no.4 <1904>   17'

str

I. Alla Marcia	_'
II. Idyll	_'
III. Menuetto	_'
IV. Canzone	_'
V. Gavotte-Rondo	_'

> FIMIC

Symphony No.3, op.40, F major <1906–1907>   35'

2[1/pic.2/pic] 2[1.2/Eh] 2 2 — 4 3 3 1 — tmp+2 — hp — str
perc: glock, tri, tambn, sd, cym, bd, tamtam, sus cym

I. Allegro moderato	9'
II. Andante (poco recitando)	9'
III. Scherzo: Vivacissimo	10'
IV. Largo	7'

> Fennica

Symphony No.4, op.80, E major (Summer Symphony)   40'

solo voices: S, Ms, A
3[1.2.pic] 2[1.2/Eh] 2 3[1.2.cbn] — 4 3 3 1 — tmp+2 — 2hp — cel — str
perc: tri, cym, bd, tamtam, xyl, sd, sus cym, low bell [E]
Cues in ob and 2cl in case solo voices not used.

I. Allegro moderato	11'
II. Scherzo: Vivace	5'
III. Andante	14'
IV. Rondo-Finale: Allegro	10'

> Melartin

Symphony No.5, op.90, A minor (Sinfonia brevis) <1914–1915>   32'

3[1.2.pic] 2[1.2/Eh] 2 3[1.2.cbn] — 4 3 3 1 — tmp+2 — hp — cel — str
perc: tri, cym, bd, sus cym, tamtam

1. Moderato; Allegro	12'
2. Andante	7'
3. Intermezzo: Allegro	6'
4. Finale: Largo; Allegro moderato	7'

> Melartin

Symphony No.6, op.100 (Symphony of the Elements) <1918–1924>   35'

3[1.2.3/pic] 2[1.2/Eh] 3[1.2.bcl] 3[1.2.cbn] — 4 3 3 1 — tmp+2 — hp — cel (opt) — str
perc: glock, sd, tambn, tri, xyl, bd, cym, sus cym, cast
The composer disavowed the subtitle "… because the matter is not of 'Program-Music'."

I. Andante	8'
II. Andante—Moderato—Andante	11'
III. Allegro	6'
IV. Finale: Allegro con fuoco	10'

> Hansen

Melby, John   1941-

(b Whithall, WI, 1941). American

Symphony No.1 <1993>   41'

3[incl pic,afl] 3[incl Eh] 4[incl Ebcl,bcl,cbcl] 3[incl cbn] — 4[4hn/4Wag tub] 3[1.2.3/flg] 3 1 — tmp+3 — 2hp — str

> Merion

Mendelssohn, Fanny   1805-1847

see: Hensel, Fanny Mendelssohn, 1805-1847

Mendelssohn, Felix   1809-1847

(b Hamburg, 3 Feb 1809; d Leipzig, 4 Nov 1847). German

Athalie, op.74: Overture <1845>   10'

2 2 2 2 — 2 2 3 0 — tmp — hp — str

> Breitkopf   Kalmus   Luck's

Athalie: Kriegsmarsch der Priester (War March of the Priests) <1845>   5'

2 2 2 2 — 2 2 3 1[oph] — tmp — str

> Kalmus   Luck's

Beautiful Melusina

see his: Märchen von der schönen Melusine

Calm Sea and Prosperous Voyage

see his: Meeresstille und glückliche Fahrt

Capriccio brillant, op.22, B minor <1825>   12'

solo piano
2 2 2 2 — 2 2 0 0 — tmp — str

Breitkopf	Kalmus	Luck's

Christus, op.97 <1847>   21'

chorus   solos STBB
2 2 2 2 — 2 2 3 0 — tmp — str
Fragments of an unfinished oratorio. An organ part, though not indicated
in the score, may be included in the set of parts.
Carus ed. Larry R. Todd.
   DIE GEBURT CHRISTI (THE BIRTH OF CHRIST)   8'
  1. Recitative: "Da Jesus geboren ward"
  2. Trio: "Wo ist der neugeborne König"
  3. Chorus: "Es wird ein Stern aus Jakob"
   DAS LEIDEN CHRISTI (THE PASSION OF CHRIST)   13'
  1. Recitative: "Und der ganze Haufe stand auf"
  2. Chorus: "Diesen finden wir, dass er das Volk abwendet"
  3. Recitative: "Pilatus sprach"
  4. Chorus: "Er hat das Volk erregt"
  5. Recitative: "Pilatus aber sprach"
  6. Chorus: "Hinweg mit diesem"
  7. Recitative: "Da rief Pilatus abermals"
  8. Chorus: "Kreuzige ihn"
  9. Recitative: "Pilatus spricht zu ihnen"
  10. Chorus: "Wir haben ein Gesetz"
  11. Recitative: "Da überantwortete er ihn"
  12. Chorus: "Ihr Töchter Zions"
  13. Chorale: "Er nimmt auf seinen Rücken"

Breitkopf	Carus	Luck's

Concerto, Piano & Strings, A minor <1822>   36'

str
Ed. Chr. Hellmundt.

Breitkopf

Concerto, Piano, No.1, op.25, G minor <1831>   21'

2 2 2 2 — 2 2 0 0 — tmp — str
  I. Molto allegro con fuoco   8'
  II. Andante   7'
  III. Presto - Molto allegro e vivace   6'

Breitkopf	Kalmus	Luck's

Concerto, Piano, No.2, op.40, D minor <1837>   25'

2 2 2 2 — 2 2 0 0 — tmp — str
Breitkopf ed. Christoph Hellmundt.
  I. Allegro appasionato   11'
  II. Adagio - Molto sostenuto   6'
  III. Finale - Presto scherzando   8'

Breitkopf	Kalmus	Luck's

Concerto, 2 Pianos, A-flat major <1828>   30'

2 2 2 2 — 2 2 0 0 — tmp — str
Ed. Karl-Heinz Köhler.
  I. Allegro vivace   13'
  II. Andante   8'
  III. Allegro vivace   9'

Breitkopf	Kalmus

Concerto, 2 Pianos, E major <1823>   28'

1 2 2 2 — 2 2 0 0 — tmp — str
Ed. Karl-Heinz Köhler.
  I. Allegro vivace   12'
  II. Adagio non troppo - Più mosso   8'
  III. Allegro   8'

Breitkopf	Kalmus

Concerto, Violin, op.64, E minor <1844; rev 1845>   26'

2 2 2 2 — 2 2 0 0 — tmp — str
Bärenreiter edition (by R. Larry Todd) includes the original version of th
concerto as well as the later 1845 version commonly used.
  I. Allegro molto appassionato   12'
  II. Andante   8'
  III. Allegretto non troppo - Allegro molto vivace   6'

Bärenreiter	Breitkopf	Kalmus	Luck's	Peters

Concerto, Violin (posth.), D minor (1822) <1822>   22'

str
Discovered and edited by Yehudi Menuhin for Peters; Breitkopf edition
ed. R. Unger.
  I. Allegro   9'
  II. Andante   9'
  III. Allegro   4'

Breitkopf	Peters

Concerto, Violin & Piano, D minor (original str orch   37' version) <1823>

str
  I. Allegro   18'
  II. Adagio   10'
  III. Allegro molto   9'

Breitkopf	Kalmus

Concerto, Violin & Piano, D minor (full orchestral   37' version) <1823; rev 1823>

2 2 2 2 — 2 2 0 0 — tmp — str
  I. Allegro   18'
  II. Adagio   10'
  III. Allegro molto   9'

Breitkopf

Elijah, op.70 (Elias) <1846; rev 1847>   133'

chorus   solos SSATB (or more)
2 2 2 2 — 4 2 3 1 — tmp — org — str
Breitkopf ed. Christian Martin Schmidt.
  PART I   66'
  PART II   67'
  [For full contents, see Appendix J]

Breitkopf	Kalmus	Luck's	Peters	Schirmer

Die erste Walpurgisnacht, op.60 <1832; rev 1842>   34'

chorus   solos ATBB
3[1.2.pic] 2 2 2 — 2 2 3 0 — tmp+2 — str
perc: bd, cym
  1. Overture   9'
  2. Es lacht der Mai!   4'
  3. Könnt ihr so verwegen handeln?   2'
  4. Wer opfer heit' zu bringen scheut   2'
  5. Verteilt euch hier   2'
  6. Dies dumpfen Pfaffenchristen   7'
  7. So weit gebracht   8'

Breitkopf	Kalmus	Peters	Schirmer

Fair Melusina

see his: Märchen von der schönen Melusine

Hear My Prayer (Hör mein Bitten) <1844>   10'

solo soprano   chorus
0 2 2 2 — 2 0 0 0 — tmp — str
Ed. R. Larry Todd.

Carus	Kalmus	Luck's

The Hebrides, op.26 (Fingal's Cave) <1830>   10'

2 2 2 2 — 2 2 0 0 — tmp — str
Bärenreiter ed. Christopher Hogwood; Breitkopf ed. Christian Martin Schmidt.

Bärenreiter	Breitkopf	Kalmus	Luck's

Heimkehr aus der Fremde, op.89 (Son and Stranger):   7'
Overture <1829>

2 2 2 2 — 2 2 0 0 — str

Breitkopf	Kalmus

Die Hochzeit des Camacho, op.10 (Camacho's Wedding):   6'
Overture <1825>

2 2 2 2 — 4 2 3 0 — tmp — str

Breitkopf	Kalmus

Hymne, op.96 (Lass', o Herr, mich Hülfe finden) <1843>   10'

mezzo-soprano or alto solo   chorus
2 2 2 2 — 2 2 0 0 — tmp — str

Breitkopf	Kalmus	Luck's

Jesu, meine Freude <1828>   9'

chorus
0 1[opt] 0 1[opt] — opt org — str 5t or str orch
Ed. Günter Graulich.

Carus

Konzertstück No.1, op.113, F minor <1832; rev (orchd)   8'
1833>

solo clarinet & basset horn (or 2 clarinets)
2 2 0 2 — 2 2 0 0 — tmp — str
Ed. Trio di Clarone (Sabine Meyer, Wolfgang Meyer, Reiner Wehle).
  Originally for clarinet, basset horn & piano (1832). Accompaniment orchestrated by the composer (1833).
  2nd clarinet part provided as alternative to basset horn.

Breitkopf

Kyrie, D minor <1825>   10'

chorus SSATB
2 2 2 2 — 2 2 3 0 — str
Ed. R. Larry Todd.

Carus

Lauda Sion, op.73 <1846>   28'

chorus   solos SATB
2 2 2 2 — 2 2 3 0 — tmp — str
1. Chorus: Lauda Sion salvatorem   _'
2. Chorus: Laudis thema specialis   _'
3. Soprano solo & Chorus: Sit laus plena   _'
4. Solo quartet: In hac mensa novis regis   _'
5. Chorus: Docti sacris institutis   _'
6. Soprano solo: Caro cibus, sanguis potus   _'
7. Solo quartet & Chorus: Sumit umus, sument mille   _'

Breitkopf	Belwin

Lobgesang, op.52 (Hymn of Praise) <1840>   71'

chorus   solos SST
2 2 2 2 — 4 2 3 0 — tmp — org — str
A "symphony-cantata." The opening instrumental sections are separately published as *Symphony No.2*; however, Breitkopf's publication, entitled *Symphony No.2*, includes the entire work (symphony plus cantata).
  I. SYMPHONIE
Maestoso con moto - Allegro   13'
Allegretto un poco agitato   6'
Adagio religioso   8'
  II. KANTATE
Chorus: Alles was Odem hat   5'
Solo & chorus: Lobe den Herrn, meine Seele   3'
Recit. & Aria: Saget es, die ihr erlöst seid   3'
Chorus: Sagt es, die ihr erlöst seid   2'
Duet & Chorus: Ich harrete des Herrn   5'
Tenor solo: Stricke des Todes   4'
Chorus: Die Nacht ist vergangen   5'
Chorale: Nun danket alle Gott   4'
Duet: Drum sing ich mit meinem Liede   4'
Chorus: Ihr Völker, bringet her den Herrn   6'

Breitkopf	Kalmus	Schirmer

Märchen von der schönen Melusine, op.32 (Fair   10'
Melusina) <1833>

2 2 2 2 — 2 2 0 0 — tmp — str
Bärenreiter ed. Christopher Hogwood; Breitkopf ed. Christian Martin Schmidt.

Bärenreiter	Breitkopf	Kalmus	Luck's

Meeresstille und glückliche Fahrt, op.27 (Calm Sea and   12'
Prosperous Voyage) <1828; rev 1834>

3[1.2.pic] 2 2 3[1.2.cbn] — 2 3 0 1[serp] — tmp — str
Composed 1828 and revised in 1834. Bärenreiter (ed. Christopher Hogwood) includes both versions in a single volume; all other publications are the revised 1834 version only.
  The composer's indication "contrafagotto e serpente" suggests the doubling of the cbn part with a tuba. However, no separate tuba part is provided in published materials.

Bärenreiter	Breitkopf	Kalmus	Luck's

A Midsummer Night's Dream, op.21 & 61 (Ein   61'
Sommernachtstraum) <1827–1843>

women's chorus   2 solo sopranos
2 2 2 2 — 2 3 3 1[oph] — tmp+2 — str
perc: tri, cym
Overture   13'
1. *Scherzo (after Act I)*   5'
2. *Act II, Sc I: "Over hill, over dale"; Entry of Oberon & Titania*   2'
3. *Act II, Sc.2: "You Spotted Snakes, With Double Tongue"*   4'
4. *Act II, Sc 2: "What thou seest, when thou dost wake"*   1'
5. *Intermezzo, after Act II*   4'
6. *Act III, Sc 1: "What hempen homespuns have we swaggering here"*   5'
7. *Nocturne (end of Act III)*   7'
8. *Act IV, Sc 1: "But first I will release the Fairy Queen"*   2'
9. *Wedding March (after Act IV)*   5'
10. *Act V, Sc 1: Dialogue and Funeral March*   2'
11. *A Dance of Clowns*   2'
12. *Reprise of Wedding March (exit of lovers)*   1'
Finale. Dialogue & Song: "Through this house give glimmering light"   5'

C. Fischer	Kalmus	Luck's

A Midsummer Night's Dream: Overture, op.21 <1827>   12'

2 2 2 2 — 2 2 0 1[oph] — tmp — str
Bärenreiter ed. Christopher Hogwood; Breitkopf ed. Christian Martin Schmidt.

Bärenreiter	Breitkopf	Kalmus	Luck's

A Midsummer Night's Dream, op.61: Intermezzo <1843>   4'

2 2 2 2 — 2 0 0 0 — str

Breitkopf	Kalmus	Luck's

A Midsummer Night's Dream, op.61: Nocturne <1843>   6'

2 2 2 2 — 2 0 0 0 — str

Breitkopf	Kalmus	Luck's

A Midsummer Night's Dream, op.61: Scherzo <1843>   5'

2 2 2 2 — 2 2 0 0 — tmp — str

Breitkopf	Kalmus	Luck's

A Midsummer Night's Dream, op.61: Wedding March <1843>   5'

2 2 2 2 — 2 3 3 1[oph] — tmp+1 — str
perc: cym

Breitkopf	Kalmus	Luck's

Nocturno <1824–1826>   10'

1 2 2 2 — 2 1 0 1[opt serp] — [no str]
The "corno di basso" (i.e.. serpent) was probably considered optional by
the composer, who referred to this piece as being for 10 winds.
This work was later revised for full wind band as *Overture for Winds*,
op.24, C major, *q.v.*
    Ed. Christopher Hogwood.

Bärenreiter

O Haupt voll Blut und Wunden (O Sacred Head Now Wounded) <1830>   14'

solo bass   chorus
2 2 2 2 — 2 0 0 0 — str
Ed. Oswald Bill.
1. Chorus: O Haupt voll Blut und Wunden	*7'*
2. Aria: Du desen Todeswunden	*5'*
3. Chorale: Ich will hier bei dir stehen	*2'*

Carus

Octet, Strings, op.20, E-flat major <1825>   33'

4vn, 2va, 2vc
I. Allegro moderato ma con fuoco	*13'*
II. Andante	*10'*
III. Scherzo - Allegro legierissimo	*4'*
IV. Presto	*6'*

Kalmus	Luck's

Octet, Strings, op.20, E-flat major: Scherzo; arr. <1825>   4'

2 2 2 2 — 2 2 0 0 — tmp — str
Orchestrated by Mendelssohn for use with his *Symphony No.1*, in place of
that work's *Menuetto.*

Kalmus	Luck's	Novello

Overture for Winds, op.24, C major <1824; rev 1838>   10'

2[1.pic] 2 4[2cl, 2Ebcl] 3[1.2.cbn] — 4 2 3 1[oph] — 2 basset horns
— 4perc — [no str]
perc: sd, bd, cym
Original version for 10 winds entitled *Nocturno, q.v.*
    2 of the clarinets are in F, the other 2 in C. As for a bass brass
instrument, the score indicates "corno basso," while the parts say
"ophicleide."
    Carus ed. Christopher Hogwood.
    An arrangement by Felix Greissle for contemporary band is published
by G. Schirmer.

Bärenreiter	Breitkopf	Carus	Kalmus	Luck's

Psalm 42, op.42 (Wie der Hirsch schreit; As Pants the Hart) <1837>   26'

chorus   solo soprano   solo male quartet (TTBB)
2 2 2 4[2 real parts] — 4 2 3 0 — tmp — str
Chorus: Wie der Hirsch schreit	*6'*
Aria: Meine Seele dürstet nach Gott	*3'*
Recit. & Aria: Meine Tränen/Denn ich wollte gern hingehen	*3'*
Chorus: Was betrübst du dich, meine Seele	*2'*
Recitative: Mein Gott, betrübt ist meine Seele	*2'*
Quintet: Der Herr hat des Tages verheissen seine Güte	*5'*
Chorus: Was betrübst du dich, meine Seele	*5'*

Kalmus	Luck's	Schirmer

Psalm 95, op.46 (Kommt, lasst uns anbeten; O Come Let Us Sing) <1838>   27'

chorus   solos SST
2 2 2 2 — 2 2 3 0 — tmp — str

Breitkopf	Kalmus	Luck's

Psalm 98, op.91 (Singet dem Herrn ein neues Lied; Sing unto the Lord) <1843>   8'

double chorus
2 2 2 2 — 2 2 3 0 — tmp — hp — org — str

Breitkopf	Kalmus	Luck's

Psalm 114, op.51 (Da Israel aus Ägypten zog; When Israel out of Egypt Came) <1839>   15'

chorus
2 2 2 2 — 4 2 3 0 — tmp — str

Breitkopf	Kalmus	Luck's

Psalm 115, op.31 (Nicht unserm Namen, Herr; Not unto us, O Lord; Non nobis, Domine) <1830>   12'

chorus   solos STBar
2 2 2 2 — 2 0 0 0 — str

Breitkopf	Kalmus	Luck's

Rondo brillant, op.29 <1834>   10'

solo piano
2 2 2 2 — 2 2 0 0 — tmp — str

Breitkopf	C. Fischer	Kalmus	Luck's

Ruy Blas, op.95: Overture <1839>   7'

2 2 2 2 — 4 2 3 0 — tmp — str
Bärenreiter ed. Christopher Hogwood;

Bärenreiter	Breitkopf	Kalmus	Luck's

St. Paul, op.36 (Paulus) <1836>   125'

chorus   solos SATBB
2 2 2 3[1.2.cbn] — 4 2 3 1[serp] — tmp — org — str
The composer's indication "contrafagotto e serpente" suggests the
doubling of the cbn part with a tuba. However, no separate tuba part is
provided in published materials.
    Bärenreiter ed. Michael Cooper; Breitkopf edition by Michael Märker,
1997.
Overture	*7'*
PART I	*62'*
PART II	*56'*
[For full contents, see Appendix J]	

Bärenreiter	Breitkopf	Kalmus	Luck's	Peters

St. Paul: Overture <1836>   7'

2 2 2 2 — 2 2 3 1[serp] — tmp — org — str
The serpent part usually given to contrabassoon.

Breitkopf	Kalmus	Luck's

Die schöne Melusine
see his: Märchen von der schönen Melusine

Sinfonia No.1, C major <1821> — 10'
str
Allegro	*3'*			
Andante	*4'*			
Allegro	*3'*			

Breitkopf	Eulenburg	Kalmus	Luck's

Sinfonia No.2, D major <1821> — 9'
str
Allegro	*3'*			
Andante	*4'*			
Allegro vivace	*2'*			

Breitkopf	Eulenburg	Kalmus	Luck's

Sinfonia No.3, E minor <1821> — 7'
str
Allegro di molto	*2'*			
Andante	*3'*			
Allegro	*2'*			

Breitkopf	Eulenburg	Kalmus	Luck's

Sinfonia No.4, C minor <1821> — 8'
str
Grave; Allegro	*3'*			
Andante	*3'*			
Allegro vivace	*2'*			

Breitkopf	Eulenburg	Kalmus	Luck's

Sinfonia No.5, B-flat major <1821> — 7'
str
Allegro vivace	*2'*			
Andante	*2'*			
Presto	*3'*			

Breitkopf	Eulenburg	Kalmus	Luck's

Sinfonia No.6, E-flat major <1821> — 11'
str
Allegro	*3'*			
Menuetto	*4'*			
Prestissimo	*4'*			

Breitkopf	Eulenburg	Kalmus	Luck's

Sinfonia No.7, D minor <1821–1822> — 21'
str
Allegro	*5'*			
Andante amorevole	*5'*			
Menuetto	*5'*			
Allegro molto	*6'*			

Breitkopf	Eulenburg	Kalmus	Luck's

Sinfonia No.8, D major (string version) <1822> — 31'
str
Adagio e grave; Allegro	*10'*			
Adagio	*6'*			
Menuetto	*5'*			
Allegro molto	*10'*			

Deutscher	Kalmus	Luck's

Sinfonia No.8, D major (version with winds) <1822> — 31'
2 2 2 2 — 2 2 0 0 — tmp — str
Arranged by the composer.
Adagio e grave; Allegro	*10'*			
Adagio	*6'*			
Menuetto	*5'*			
Allegro molto	*10'*			

Breitkopf	Kalmus

Sinfonia No.9, C major (Swiss) <1823> — 32'
str
Sometimes listed as C minor, though only the introduction to the first movement is in minor.
Grave; Allegro	*11'*			
Andante	*8'*			
Scherzo (La Suisse)	*3'*			
Allegro vivace	*10'*			

Deutscher	Kalmus	Luck's

Sinfonia No.10, B minor <1823> — 11'
str
Adagio	*2'*			
Allegro	*9'*			

Breitkopf	Kalmus	Luck's

Sinfonia No.11, F major <1823> — 40'
tmp+2 — str
perc: tri, cym
Tmp & perc in one brief passage in the 3rd mvt only.
Adagio; Allegro molto	*12'*			
Scherzo: commodo (Schweizer Lied)	*4'*			
Adagio	*8'*			
Menuetto: Allegro moderato	*6'*			
Allegro molto	*10'*			

Deutscher	Kalmus	Luck's

Sinfonia No.12, G minor <1823> — 20'
str
Grave; Allegro	*5'*			
Andante	*7'*			
Allegro molto	*8'*			

Breitkopf	Kalmus	Luck's

Sinfonia [No.13], C minor
see his: Symphony Movement, C minor

Ein Sommernachtstraum
see his: Midsummer Night's Dream

Son and Stranger
see his: Heimkehr aus der Fremde, op.89

Symphony Movement, C minor (Sinfoniesatz) <1823> — 6'
str
Also known as *Sinfonia No.13*. Similar to the juvenile series of string sinfonias, though in one movement only.

Kalmus

Symphony No.1, op.11, C minor <1824> — 32'
2 2 2 2 — 2 2 0 0 — tmp — str
I. Allegro di molto	*10'*	
II. Andante	*7'*	
III. Menuetto: Allegro molto	*7'*	
IV. Allegro con fuoco	*8'*	

Breitkopf	Kalmus	Luck's	Peters

Symphony No.2, op.52a (from "Lobgesang") <1840>   27'

2 2 2 2 — 4 2 3 0 — tmp — str

This symphony consists of the opening instrumental sections of the symphony-cantata *Lobgesang*. Breitkopf previously offered also an edition of this symphony "with final chorus in the version shortened by Mendelssohn"; this requires chorus and solos SST in addition to the above instrumentation, but it may now be out of print. Total duration of that version: 37'.

I. Allegro	12'
II. Allegretto un poco agitato	6'
III. Adagio religioso	9'

Kalmus	Luck's

Symphony No.3, op.56, A minor (Scottish) <1829–1842; rev 1843>   40'

2 2 2 2 — 4 2 0 0 — tmp — str

Breitkopf ed. Thomas Schmidt-Beste. The Bärenreiter edition (ed. Christopher Hogwood) includes performance material both for the standard version of 1843, and an earlier "London" version of 1842.

I. Andante con moto - Allegro un poco agitato	14'
II. Vivace non troppo	5'
III. Adagio	11'
IV. Allegro vivacissimo - Allegro maestoso assai	10'

Bärenreiter	Breitkopf	Kalmus	Luck's

Symphony No.4, op.90, A major (Italian) <1833>   27'

2 2 2 2 — 2 2 0 0 — tmp — str

Breitkopf ed. of the standard 1833 version by Thomas Schmidt-Beste.

Mendelssohn, never satisfied, revised mvts 2, 3 & 4 of this work in 1834 but did not complete planned revisions to the 1st mvt. This partially-revised version was published for the first time in 1999. Score and parts, ed. John Michael Cooper, are available from Reichert.

The Bärenreiter ed., by Christopher Hogwood, includes all the performance material for the standard 1833 version, as well as the revised 1834 version of mvts 2, 3 & 4.

I. Allegro vivace	8'
II. Andante con moto	7'
III. Con moto moderato	6'
IV. Saltarello: Presto	6'

Bärenreiter	Breitkopf	Kalmus	Luck's	Reichert

Symphony No.5, op.107, D major (Reformation) <1830; rev 1832 (alternative ending)>   27'

2 2 2 3[1.2.cbn] — 2 2 3 1[serp] — tmp — str

Score calls for "contrafagotto e serpente," (4th mvt only) playing in unison. This suggests the doubling of the cbn part with a modern tuba. However, no separate tuba part is provided in published materials; the part is normally played on contrabassoon.

The Bärenreiter ed. by Christopher Hogwood includes a 30-bar transition between the 3rd & 4th mvts—a transition that was later deleted by the composer.

I. Andante - Allegro con fuoco	10'
II. Allegro vivace	5'
III. Andante	4'
IV. Chorale: Andante con moto - Allegro vivace	8'

Bärenreiter	Breitkopf	Kalmus	Luck's

Trumpet Overture, op.101 (Trompeten-Ouvertüre) <ca.1825; rev 1833>   8'

2 2 2 2 — 2 2 3 0 — tmp — str

Bärenreiter ed. Christopher Hogwood.

Bärenreiter	Breitkopf	Kalmus	Luck's

Tu es Petrus, op.111 <1827>   10'

chorus

2 2 0 0 — 2 2 3 0 — tmp — str

Carus ed. John Michael Cooper.

Carus	Harmonia

Verleih' uns Frieden (Dona nobis pacem) <1831>   6'

chorus

2 0 2 2 — str

Breitkopf

Mennin, Peter   1923-1983

(b Erie, PA, 17 May 1923; d New York, 17 June 1983). American

Canto <1963>   8'

3[1.2.pic] 3[1.2.Eh] 3[1.2.bcl] 2 — 4 3 3 1 — tmp+3 — str

C. Fischer

The Christmas Story <1949>   24'

chorus   solos ST

0 0 0 0 — 0 2 2 0 — tmp — str

C. Fischer

Concertato for Orchestra (Moby Dick) <1961>   11'

3[1.2.pic] 3[1.2.Eh] 3[1.2.bcl] 2 — 4 3 3 1 — tmp+3 — str
perc: bd, cym, sd, sus cym

C. Fischer

Symphony No.6 <1953>   28'

3[1.2.pic] 3[1.2.Eh] 3[1.2.bcl] 2 — 4 2 3 1 — tmp+3 — str
perc: bd, cym, sus cym, sd

I. Maestoso - Allegro	8'
II. Grave	10'
III. Allegro vivace	10'

C. Fischer

Symphony No.7 (Variation-Symphony) <1964>   27'

3[1.2.pic] 3[1.2.Eh] 3[1.2.bcl] 3[1.2.cbn] — 4 3 3 1 — tmp+3 — str

1. Adagio	7'
2. Allegro	5'
3. Andante	8'
4. Moderato	4'
5. Allegro vivace	3'

C. Fischer

Menotti, Gian Carlo   1911-2007

(b Cadegliano, 7 July 1911; d Monaco, 1 Feb 2007). American composer of Italian birth

Apocalypse (Apocalisse) <1951>   24'

3[1.2.pic] 3[1.2.Eh] 3[1.2.bcl] 3[1.2.cbn] — 6 4 3 1 — tmp+4 — hp — pf, cel — str
perc: glock, chimes, xyl, cym, sd, bd, tamtam, tri, gong

| I. Improperia |
| II. La Città Celeste |
| III. Gli Angelic Militanti |

Schirmer

Concerto, Piano, F major <1945>   33'

3[1.2.pic] 2 2[1.2/Ebcl] 2 — 4 3 3 1 — tmp+4 — str

1. Allegro	14'
2. Lento	9'
3. Allegro	10'

Ricordi

Concerto, Double Bass <1983>   23'

3[1.2.pic] 2 3[1.2.bcl] 2[4] — 2 3 1 — tmp+3 — hp — str
perc: bd, cym, sus cym, sd, tri, tambn, glock, xyl, woodblk, 3tomtom

I. [Allegro]	_'
II. Adagio	_'
III. Allegro	_'

Schirmer

Concerto, Violin, A minor <1952>   31'

3[1.2.pic] 2 2 2 — 2 2 0 0 — tmp+3 — hp — str
perc: bd, cym, tambn, tri
I. Allegro moderato   *14'*
II. Adagio ma non troppo   *10'*
III. Vivace   *7'*

> Schirmer

Fantasia, Violoncello & Orchestra <1975>   30'

3[1.2.pic] 3[1.2.Eh] 3[1.2.bcl] 2 — 4 2 3 1 — tmp+2 — hp — str
perc: bd, sus cym, sd, tambn, tri, xyl
In one mvt.

> Schirmer

Lewisohn Stadium Fanfare <1965>   5'

0 0 0 0 — 4 3 3 1 — tmp+4 — str
perc: bd, cym, sus cym, sd, tri, xyl

> Schirmer

My Christmas <1987>   15'

male chorus
1 1 1 0 — 1 0 0 0 — bell[B3] — hp — db
The brief bell part (22 bars, 1 repeated note) could be covered by a chorus
member. Brief solos (5 bars) for a tenor and bass from the chorus.

> Schirmer

Nocturne <1982>   6'

solo soprano
hp — str 4t or str orch

> Schirmer

Pastorale (Pensiero e danza) <1933>   8'

pf — str
1. Pensiero   _'
2. Danza   _'

> Schirmer

Sebastian: Suite <1945>   24'

1[1/pic] 1[1/Eh] 2[1.2/bcl] 1 — 2 2 2 0 — tmp+2 — hp — pf — str
From the ballet.
1. Introduction   *2'*
2. Barcarolle   *4'*
3. Baruffa (Street Fight)   *2'*
4. Cortège   *5'*
5. Sebastian's Dance   *3'*
6. Dance of the Wounded Courtesan   *4'*
7. Pavane   *4'*

> Ricordi

Suite, 2 Violoncellos & Strings   20'

2 solo violoncellos
str
Arr. Hans Kunstovny.
I. Introduction   _'
II. Scherzo   _'
III. Arioso   _'
IV. Finale   _'

> Ricordi

Symphony No.1, A minor (The Halcyon) <1976>   30'

3[1.2.pic] 3[1.2.Eh] 3[1.2.bcl] 2 — 4 3 3 1 — tmp+2 — hp — pf —
str
perc: bd, cym, sus cym, sd, tri, tambn
I. Allegro vivace   _'
II. Adagio, ma non troppo   _'
III. Andante mosso; Allegro con brio _'

> Schirmer

Triplo Concerto a Tre <1970>   22'

9 soloists in 3 groups: (1) piano, harp, percussion;
(2) oboe, clarinet, bassoon; (3) violin, viola, violoncello.
2[1.2/pic] 1 1 1 — 2 2 2 1[or btbn] — tmp+1 — str
perc: (orch) bd; (soloist) cym, tri, tambn, xyl, 3sd, cel, bd

> Schirmer

Mercadante, Saverio   1795-1870

(b Altamura, bap. 17 Sept 1795; d Naples, 17 Dec 1870). Italian

Concerto, Flute, E minor <1813?>   19'

str
Ed. Agostino Girard.
Allegro maestoso   *8'*
Largo   *4'*
Rondò russo: Allegro vivace scherzando   *7'*

> Zerboni

Mercurio, Steven   1956-

(b Bardonia, NY, 11 May 1956). American

Mercurial Overture <1999>   6'

3[1.2.3/pic] 3[1.2.Eh] 3[1.2.bcl] 2 — 4 3 3 1 — tmp+2 — hp — str
perc: tamtam, cym

> Subito

Messiaen, Olivier   1908-1992

(b Avignon, 10 Dec 1908; d Paris, 28 April 1992). French

L'Ascension; 4 méditations symphoniques <1932–1933>   27'

3 3[1.2.Eh] 3[1.2.bcl] 3 — 4 3 3 1 — tmp+3 — str[16.16.14.12.10]
perc: bd, cym, tambn, tri
1. Majesté du Christ demandant sa gloire à son Père   *6'*
2. Alléluias sereins d'un âme que désire le ciel   *6'*
3. Alléluia sur la trompette, alléluia sur la cymbale   *5'*
4. Prière du Christ montant vers son Père   *10'*

> Leduc

Concert à quatre <1990–1992>   26'

solo flute, oboe, violoncello, piano
5[1.2.3.pic1.pic2] 4[1.2.3.Eh] 5[1.2.3.Ebcl.bcl] 4[1.2.3.cbn] — 4
4[1.2.3.pic tp] 3 1 — 7perc — cel — str
perc: chimes, whip, templeblks, sus cym, crot, bd, xyl, marim, glock, wnd mach,
reco-reco, 3tri, 3tamtam
I. Entrée   *7'*
II. Vocalise   *4'*
III. Cadenza   *5'*
IV. Rondeau   *10'*

> Leduc

Chronochromie <1959–1960>   25'

4[1.2.3.pic] 3[1.2.Eh] 4[1.2.Ebcl.bcl] 3 — 4 4 3 1 — 5perc — kybd
glock — str
perc: xyl, marim, chimes, sus cym, Chinescym, tamtam, 3gongs
1. Introduction   *4'*
2. Strophe I   *2'*
3. Antistrophe I   *3'*
4. Strophe II   *2'*
5. Antistrophe II   *6'*
6. Epôde   *5'*
7. Coda   *3'*

> Leduc

Couleurs de la cité céleste (Colours of the Celestial City) <1963> *18'*

solo piano
0 0 3 0 — 2 4 4 0 — 6perc — [no str]
perc: xyl, marim, chimes, xylorimba, tuned herdbells[C5–>D6], 4gongs, 2tamtams

> Leduc

Des canyons aux étoiles (From the Canyons to the Stars) <1971–1974> *92'*

soloists: piano, horn, xylorimba, glockenspiel
4[incl pic,afl] 3[incl Eh] 4[incl Ebcl,bcl] 3[incl cbn] — 2 3 3 0 —
5perc — 6vn, 3va, 3vc, db
perc: chimes, crot, tri, slgh-bells, marac, guiro, whip, claves, woodblk, congas, bd,
thunder, wnd mach, bamboo windchimes, glass windchimes, shell windchimes,
6templeblks, 3sus cym, 4gongs, 2tamtams, geophone

PART ONE	
1. Le désert	4'
2. Les orioles	6'
3. Ce qui est écrit sur les étoiles	6'
4. Le cossyphe d'Heuglin	4'
5. Cedar Breaks et le don de crainte	7'
PART TWO	
6. Appel interstellaire	8'
7. Bryce Canyon et les rochers rouge-orange	13'
PART THREE	
8. Les ressuscités et le chant de l'étoile Aldébaran	10'
9. Le moqueur polyglotte	10'
10. La grive des bois	5'
11. Omao, Leiothrix, Elepaio, Shama	9'
12. Zion Park et la Cité Céleste	10'

> Leduc

Hymne <1947> *12'*

3 3[1.2.Eh] 3[1.2.bcl] 3 — 4 3 3 0 — tmp+2 — str
perc: sus cym, bd, tri
A reconstruction by the composer of his 1932 work *Hymne au Saint-Sacrement*.

> Broude Bros.

Les offrandes oubliées (The Forgotten Offerings) <1930> *11'*

3 3[1.2.Eh] 3[1.2.bcl] 3 — 4 3 3 1 — tmp+3 — str
perc: tri, cym, bd

> Durand

Oiseaux exotiques (Exotic Birds) <1955–1956> *14'*

solo piano
2[1.pic] 1 4[1.2.Ebcl.bcl] 1 — 2 1 0 0 — 7perc — [no str]
perc: xyl, templeblks, woodblk, sd, tamtam, kybd glock (possible on mallet glock),
3gongs

> Universal

Sept haïkaï; Esquisses Japonaises (Seven Haiku) <1962> *23'*

solo piano
2[incl pic] 3[incl Eh] 4[incl Ebcl,bcl] 2 — 0 1 1 0 — 6perc — 8vn
perc: xyl, marim, crot, tri, chimes, Chinescym, tuned herdbells, 2turkish cym,
2gongs, 2tamtams

1. Introduction	2'
2. Le parc de Nara et les lanternes de pierre	2'
3. Yamanaka: cadenza	4'
4. Gagaku	4'
5. Miyajima et le torii dans la mer	2'
6. Les oiseaux de Karuizawa	7'
7. Coda	2'

> Leduc

Un Sourire (A Smile) <1989> *10'*

4[incl pic] 4[incl Eh] 3 3 — 4 1 0 0 — 4perc — str[16.16.14.12.no db]
perc: xyl, chimes, sus cym, xylorimba

> Leduc

La Transfiguration de Notre-Seigneur Jésus-Christ <1965–1969> *110*

chorus   soloists: fl, cl, xylorimba, vib, marimba, vc, pf
5[incl 2pic] 4[incl Eh] 5[incl Ebcl,bcl] 4[incl cbn] — 6 4 4 2 — 6perc
— str[16.16.14.12.10]
perc: tri, slgh-bells, guiro, sus cym, cym, crot, claves, woodblk, marac, chimes, bd,
3turkish cym, 6templeblks, luminophone, 7gongs, 3tamtams, 3tomtoms

> Leduc

Trois petites liturgies de la Présence Divine <1943–1944> *37*

solo piano, solo ondes martenot   women's chorus
4perc — cel — str
perc: vib, marac, tamtam, Chinescym (or small tamtam)
If 18 voices, str 4.4.3.3.2; if 36 voices, str 8.8.6.6.4.

1. Antienne de la conversation intérieure	10'
2. Séquence du Verbe, cantique divin	7'
3. Psalmodie de l'ubiquité par Amour	20'

> Durand

Turangalîla-symphonie <1946–1948; rev 1990> *74*

solo piano, solo ondes martenot
3[1.2.pic] 3[1.2.Eh] 3[1.2.bcl] 3 — 4 5[1.2.3.crt.pic tp] 3 1 — 11perc
— cel — str[16.16.14.12.10]
perc: vib, chimes, bd, sd, templeblks, marac, tri, tambn, woodblk, cym, sus cym,
Chinescym, tamtam, kybd glock (or 2mallet glocks), tambn prov, small Turkish
cym
Bcl is said to be in A.

1. Introduction	7'
2. Chant d'amour I	7'
3. Turangalîla I	5'
4. Chant d'amour II	12'
5. Joie du sange des étoiles	5'
6. Jardin du sommeil d'amour	11'
7. Turangalîla II	4'
8. Développement de l'amour	11'
9. Turangalîla III	5'
10. Final	7'

> Durand

Un vitrail et des oiseaux (Stained Glass Window and Birds) <1986> *15*

solo piano
4[1.2.3.afl] 4[1.2.3.Eh] 5[1.2.3.Ebcl.bcl] 3 — 0 1 0 0 — 8perc — [no str]
perc: xyl, marim, chimes, tri, woodblk, xylorimba, 6templeblks, 2sus cym,
2tamtams

> Leduc

Meyerbeer, Giacomo **1791-1864**

(b Vogelsdorf, nr Berlin, 5 Sept 1791; d Paris, 2 May 1864). German

Fackeltanz No.1 (Torch Dance No.1) <1842> *6*

2[1.pic] 2 2 2 — 4 2 3 1 — tmp+3 — str
Originally for military band; arranged for orchestra, perhaps by the composer.

> Bote & Bock   Kalmus   Luck's

Les Huguenots: Overture <1836> *7*

3[1.2.pic] 3[1.2.Eh] 2 2 — 4 4 3 1[oph] — tmp+2 — str
perc: cym, bd

> C. Fischer   Kalmus   Luck's

Les Patineurs <1937>   20'

2[1.2/pic] 2 2 2 — 4 2 3 1 — tmp+2 — hp — str
perc: bd, cym, tri, slgh-bells, cast
Ballet by Constant Lambert, 1937, after excerpts from Meyerbeer's *Le prophète* and *L'étoile du nord*.
    Kalmus publication edited by William McDermott.

I. Entrée	*3'*
II. Pas seul	*1'*
III. Pas de deux	*3'*
IV. Pas de trois	*2'*
V. Duet	*2'*
VI. Pas de patineurs	*3'*
VII. Finale	*4'*

Boosey	Kalmus

Le prophète: Ballet Music <1849>   16'

3[1.2.pic] 2 2 4 — 4 4 3 1 — tmp+3 — str
perc: tri, cym, bd

Waltz	_'
Air de ballet	_'
Quadrille	_'
Galop	_'

Kalmus

Le prophète: Coronation March <1849>   4'

3[1.2.pic] 2 2 4 — 4 4 3 1[oph] — tmp+3 — str
perc: bd, cym, sd

Breitkopf	Kalmus	Luck's

Miari, Giangiacomo   1929-

(b 1929). Italian

Concerto, Double Bass   12'

str

Luck's	Zanibon

Miaskovsky, Nikolai   1881-1950

(b the fortress of Novo-Georgiyevsk [now Modlin], Poland, 8/20 April 1881; d Moscow, 8 Aug 1950). Russian

Sinfonietta, op.32, no.2, B minor <1928–1929>   24'

str

1. Allegro pesante e serioso	*7'*
2. Theme and Variations	*11'*
3. Presto	*6'*

Russian

Symphony No.6, op.23, E-flat minor <1922–1923>   65'

optional double chorus (4th mvt only)
3[1.2.3/pic] 3[1.2.Eh] 3[1.2.3/bcl] 3[1.2.cbn] — 6 3 3 1 — tmp+2 — hp — cel — str
perc: bd, cym, field dr, sus cym, tamtam

1. Poco largamente; Precipitato; Allegro feroce	*23'*
2. Presto tenebroso; Andante moderato; Tempo I	*9'*
3. Andante appassionato	*15'*
4. Allegro vivace (quasi Presto)	*18'*

Universal

Symphony No.21, op.51, F-sharp minor <1940>   16'

3[1.2.pic] 3[1.2.Eh] 3[1.2.bcl] 3[1.2.cbn] — 4 3 3 1 — tmp — str
In one movement.

Russian

Symphony No.22, op.54, B minor (Symphonic Ballad) <1941>   35'

3[1.2.pic] 3[1.2.Eh] 3[1.2.bcl] 3[1.2.cbn] — 4 3 3 1 — tmp+3 — str

Russian

Milhaud, Darius   1892-1974

(b Marseilles, 4 Sept 1892; d Geneva, 22 June 1974). French

Aubade, op.387 <1960>   18'

2[1.2/pic] 2 2 2 — 2 2 2 0 — tmp+3 — hp — cel — str
perc: sd, td, cym, tri, whip, cast, bd, tamtam, tambn, xyl, tambn prov

I. Vif	_'
II. Nonchalant	_'
III. Vif	_'

Heugel

Le boeuf sur le toit, op.58 <1919>   15'

2[1/pic.2] 1 2 1 — 2 2 1 0 — 2perc — str
perc: guiro, tambn, bd, tambn prov
There exists also a version for solo violin and orchestra, op.58b, with the same instrumentation.

Eschig

Le carnaval d'Aix; Fantasy for Piano & Orchestra, op.83b <1920>   19'

2[1.2/pic] 1 2 1 — 2 2 1 1 — tmp+3 — str
perc: sd, td, cast, cym, tamtam, bd, tambn, tambn prov

Heugel

Le carnaval de Londres, op.172 <1937>   30'

1[1/pic] 1 1 1 — 0 1 1 0 — asx — 1perc — hp — str
perc: sd, td, cym, woodblk, tri, tambn, bd

Salabert

Chamber Symphonies

see his: Symphonies de chambre

Les Choéphores, op.24 <1915–1916>   35'

chorus   solos SSA
3[incl pic] 3[incl Eh] 3[incl bcl] 4 — 4 3 3 1 — tmp+14 — hp — cel — str
perc: cym, slgh-bells, ratch, tri, cast, whip, tambn, td, sd, tamtam, wnd mach, metal cast, tambn prov, muffled dr, 2bd, woodplank, hammer
Part two of Milhaud's Orestian trilogy.
    Certain of the movements are scored for speaking chorus and percussion only.

Vocifération funèbre (Funeral Clamor)	*6'*
Libation [chorus alone]	*3'*
Incantation	*14'*
Présages (Omens) [chorus & percussion only]	*3'*
Exhortation	*3'*
La justice et la lumière (Justice and Light)	*5'*
Conclusion [chorus & percussion only]	*1'*

Heugel

Concertino de printemps, Violin & Orchestra, op.135 <1934>   9'

1 1 1 1 — 1 1 0 0 — tmp+1 — str
perc: sd, td, bd, tri

Salabert

Concertino d'hiver, Trombone & Strings, op.327 <1953>   18'

str

AMP	Luck's

Concerto, Marimba & Vibraphone, op.278 <1947>   19'

1 solo percussionist, alternating on marimba & vibraphone
2 2 2 2 — 2 2 2 1 — tmp+3 — hp — cel — str
perc: sd, td, tambn, cast, xyl, cym, bd, tamtam, tri, woodblk, tambn prov
May be performed with a piano soloist, rather than marimba and
vibraphone, under the title *Suite concertante, Piano & Orch., op.278*, q.v.

Animé	5'
Lent	9'
Vif	5'

> Enoch

Concerto, Percussion & Small Orchestra, op.109   7'
<1929–1930>

1 percussion soloist, using a large number of solo instruments
2[1/pic.2/pic] 0 2 0 — 0 1 1 0 — str[2.2.2.2.1]
perc: (solo) timbales, sd, td, tri, sus cym, woodblk, cym, cast, whip, ratch, tambn,
tamtam, bd/ped w/ detachable cym, tambn prov, cowbell

> Universal

Concerto, Piano, No.1, op.127 <1933>   12'

2[incl pic] 2 3[incl Ebcl,bcl] 2 — 2 3 2 1 — tmp+2 — hp — str
perc: cast, sd, td, tri, xyl, bd, cym, tambn prov

1. Très vif	4'
2. Barcarolle	4'
3. Final: Animé	4'

> Salabert

Concerto, Piano, No.3, op.270 <1946>   19'

2[incl pic] 2 2 2 — 2 2 2 1 — tmp+2 — str

> AMP

Concerto, Violin, No.2, op.263 <1946>   22'

2[incl pic] 3[incl Eh] 3[incl bcl] 2 — 2 2 2 1 — tmp+1 — str
perc: sd, td, bd, cym, tamtam, tri

> AMP

Concerto, Violoncello, No.1, op.136 <1934>   14'

2[incl pic] 2[incl Eh] 2 2 — 2 2 2 1 — tmp+1 — hp — str
perc: sd, td, tambn, tri, bd, cym, cast, tambn prov

1. Nonchalant	5'
2. Grave	6'
3. Joyeux	3'

> Salabert

Concerto, Violoncello, No.2, op.255 <1945>   20'

2[1.2/pic] 2 2 2 — 2 2 2 1 — tmp+2 — hp — str
perc: sd, td, tambn, bd, cym, tamtam, tri

> AMP

Cortège funèbre, op.202 <1939>   14'

2[1.pic] 1 2[or 2asx] 1 — 0 2 2 1 — 2perc — hp — str
perc: sd, td, cym, tamtam, bd/ped

> AMP

La création du monde, op.81 (The Creation of the   16'
World) <1923>

2[1/pic.2] 1 2 1 — 1 2 1 0 — asx — tmp+1 — pf — 2vn, vc, db
perc: tambn, cowbell, woodblk, cym, sd, td, tambn prov, bd/ped; for timpanist: 2
extra tmp (high)
Two reduced versions exist: (1) for str 4t & pf, presumably by the
composer; (2) an arrangement by Jean-Marie Londeix for asx, perc, pf &
str[1.1.0.1.1]

Overture	4'
1er tableau: The Chaos Before Creation	1'
2e tableau: The Slowly Lifting Darkness	3'
3e tableau: Man and Woman Created	2'
4e tableau: The Desire of Man and Woman	4'
5e tableau: Coda—The Man and Woman Kiss	2'

> Eschig

A Frenchman in New York, op.399 (Un français à New   20'
York) <1962>

3[1.2.3/pic] 3[1.2.Eh] 3[1.2.bcl] 3[1.2.cbn] — 4 3 3 1 — tmp+5 — hp
— cel[played by perc] — str
perc: bd, cym, sus cym, sd, td, tri, tambn, tamtam, glock, xyl, woodblk, cast,
tambn prov, cel[played by perc]

I. New York with Fog on the Hudson River	3'
II. The Cloisters	4'
III. Horse and Carriage in Central Park	3'
IV. Times Square	3'
V. Gardens on the Roofs	4'
VI. Baseball in Yankee Stadium	3'

> Salabert

Les funérailles de Phocion (Hommage á Poussin), op.385   8'
<1960>

3[1.2.pic] 2 3[1.2.bcl] 3[1.2.cbn] — 4 3 3 1 — tmp+3 — str
perc: sd, td, tamtam, bd, cym, tambn prov

> Heugel

Genesis Suite: IV. Cain and Abel, op.241 <1944>   5'

narrator
2 2 2 2 — 2 2 2 0 — tmp+1 — hp — str
perc: cym, sd, tri, tambn
See the entry for "Nathaniel Shilkret: *Genesis Suite*" for a full description
of this collaborative work by 7 composers.
    Reconstructed by Patrick Russ.

> Milken

Kentuckiana, op.287; Divertissement on 20 Kentucky   9'
Airs <1948>

2[1.pic] 2 2 2 — 4 2 2 0 — tmp+1 — str

> Elkan-Vogel

Murder of a Great Chief of State, op.405 (Meurtre d'un   4'
grand chef d'etat) <1963>

2 2 2 2 — 4 3 3 1 — tmp — str

> Eschig

Ouverture méditerranéene, op.330 <1953>   5'

2 2 2 2 — 4 2 2 0 — tmp+3 — str
perc: td, sd, cym, tambn, bd, tambn prov

> Heugel

Ouverture philharmonique, op.397 <1962>   9'

2[1.2/pic] 2[1.2/Eh] 3[1.2.bcl] 3[1.2.cbn] — 4 3 3 1 — tmp+3 — hp
— str
perc: sd, td, bd, tri, cym, sus cym, glock, whip, tambn, tamtam, xyl, woodblk,
tambn prov

> EMT

Saudades do Brazil; Suite of Dances, op.67 <1920–1921>   25'

2[1.2/pic] 2[1.2/Eh] 2 2 — 2 2 2 0 — tmp — str

Overture	1'
I. Sorocaba	2'
II. Botofago	2'
III. Leme	3'
IV. Copacabana	3'
V. Ipanema	2'
VI. Gavea	2'
VII. Corcovado	2'
VIII. Tijaca	2'
IX. Sumaré	2'
X. Paineras	1'
XI. Larenjeiras	1'
XII. Paysandú	2'

> Eschig

Scaramouche, op.165c <1937; rev 1939>   9'

solo alto saxophone or clarinet
2[incl pic] 2 2 2 — 2 2 2 0 — 1perc — str
perc: sd, td, cast, tri, cym, bd, tambn, woodblk, tambn prov
From the incidental music to Moliere's *Le médecin volant* (op.165); also
used in Milhaud's *Scaramouche* for 2pf (op.165b) as well as various other
incarnations.

I. Vif	*3'*
II. Modèrè	*3'*
III. Brazileira	*3'*

Salabert

Suite concertante, Piano & Orchestra, op.278 <1952>   19'

2 2 2 2 — 2 2 2 1 — tmp+3 — hp — cel — str
perc: sd, td, tambn, cast, xyl, cym, bd, tamtam, tri, woodblk, tambn prov
May be performed using a marimba/vibraphone soloist instead of piano,
under the title *Concerto, Marimba & Vibraphone*, q.v.

Animé	*5'*
Lent	*9'*
Vif	*5'*

Enoch

Suite française, op.248 <1945>   15'

2[1.2/pic] 2 2 2 — 2 2 2 0 — tmp+2 — str
perc: sd, td, cym, bd, tambn prov
Orchestrated by the composer from a work for concert band.

I. Normandie	*2'*
II. Bretagne	*3'*
III. Ile de France	*2'*
IV. Alsace-Lorraine	*5'*
V. Provence	*3'*

MCA

Suite provençale, op.152b <1936>   16'

2[1/pic.2] 3[1.2.Eh] 2[1.Ebcl] 2 — 4 3 3 1 — tmp+3 — str
perc: sd, td, cym, bd, tambn, tamtam, tambn prov

I. Animé	*2'*
II. Très Modéré	*2'*
III. Modéré	*2'*
IV. Vif	*1'*
V. Modéré	*2'*
VI. Vif	*1'*
VII. Lent	*2'*
VIII. Vif	*4'*

Salabert

Suite symphonique no.2, op.57 (Protée) <1919>   22'

3[1.2.3/pic] 3[1.2.Eh] 3[1.2.bcl] 4 — 4 3 3 1 — tmp+1 — hp — cel
— str
perc: whip, cym, tri, bd, tambn prov
Drawn from incidental music to Paul Claudel's *Protée*.

Durand

SYMPHONIES DE CHAMBRE (Chamber Symphonies)   3'
1. Le Printemps, op.43 <1917>

2[1.pic] 1 1 0 — hp — str 4t

Allant	*1'*
Chantant	*1'*
Et Vif!	*1'*

Luck's	Universal

2. Pastorale, op.49 <1918>   5'

1 1[Eh] 0 1 — vn, va, vc, db

Joyeux	*1'*
Calme	*3'*
Joyeux	*1'*

Luck's	Universal

3. Sérénade, op.71 <1921>   3'

1 0 1 1 — vn, va, vc, db

Vivement	*1'*
Calme	*1'*
Rondement	*1'*

Luck's	Universal

4. Dixtuor à cordes, op.74 <1921>   7'

4vn, 2va, 2vc, 2db

1.	*2'*
2.	*3'*
3.	*2'*

Luck's	Universal

5. Dixtuor d'instruments à vent, op.75 <1922>   5'

2[1.2/pic] 2[1.Eh] 2[1.bcl] 2 — 2 0 0 0 — [no str]

Rude	*1'*
Lent	*3'*
Violent	*1'*

Luck's	Universal

6. Sinfonie, op.79 <1923>   8'

chorus *or* soloists SATB
0 1 0 0 — vc

1.	*3'*
2.	*2'*
3.	*3'*

Universal

Symphony No.1, op.210 <1939>   29'

3[1.2.3/pic] 3[1.2.Eh] 3[1.2.bcl] 3[1.2.cbn] — 4 3 3 1 — tmp+3 — hp
— str
perc: sd, td, tamtam, cym, tri, bd, tambn, tambn prov

I. Pastoral: Modérément animé	*8'*
II. Très vif	*5'*
III. Très modéré	*9'*
IV. Final: Animé	*7'*

Heugel

Symphony No.2, op.247 <1944>   27'

3[1.2.pic] 3[1.2.Eh] 3[1/asx.2.bcl] 3[1.2.cbn] — 4 3 3 1 — tmp+3 —
hp — cel — str
perc: sd, td, cast, tamtam, cym, bd, tambn, xyl, tambn prov

I. Paisible	*6'*
II. Mysterieux	*5'*
III. Douloureux	*8'*
IV. Avec sérénité	*3'*
V. Allelouia	*5'*

Heugel

Symphony No.3, op.271 (Te Deum) <1946>   32'

chorus
3[1.2.pic] 3[1.2.Eh] 4[1.2.Ebcl.bcl] 3[1.2.cbn] — 4 3 3 1 — tmp+4 —
hp — str
perc: sd, td, cast, tamtam, cym, bd, tambn, xyl, tambn prov

1. Fièrement	*5'*
2. Très recueilli	*11'*
3. Pastorale	*4'*
4. Te Deum (Hymnis Ambrosianus)	*12'*

Heugel

Symphony No.10, op.382 <1960>   23'

3[1.2.pic] 3[1.2.Eh] 3[1.2.bcl] 3[1.2.cbn] — 4 3 3 1 — tmp+3 — hp
— str
perc: sd, td, tamtam, cym, tambn, tri, bd, cast, xyl, whip, woodblk, tambn prov

Décidé	*4'*
Expressif	*9'*
Fantasque	*5'*
Emporté	*5'*

Heugel

Symphony No.11, op.384 (Romantique) <1960>   18'

3[1.2.pic] 3[1.2.Eh] 3[1.2.bcl] 3[1.2.cbn] — 4 3 3 1 — tmp+2 — hp — str

perc: sd, td, cast, cym, whip, tamtam, tri, bd, xyl, woodblk, tambn, tambn prov

1.	4'
2.	9'
3.	5'

Heugel

Symphony No.12, op.390 (Rurale) <1962>   17'

2[1.2/pic] 2 3[1.2.bcl] 2 — 2 2 3 1 — tmp+5 — hp — str

perc: sd, td, cym, tri, bd, tambn, xyl, tambn prov

Heugel

Miller, Scott Aaron   1962-

(b Minneapolis, 1962). American

Scenes Unseen: Views from Ivory Towers   12'

str

Into the Ether	2'
Schiaparelli's Dream	3'
Through a Wormhole	3'
Event Horizon	4'

EMF

Minkus, Ludwig   1826-1917

(b Vienna, 23 March 1826; d Vienna, 7 Dec 1917). Czech composer of Austrian birth, active in Russia

La bayadère <1877>   125'

3[1.2.pic] 2 2 2 — 4 4[2crt, 2tp] 3 1 — tmp+4 — hp — str

perc: bd, cym, field dr, tri, glock

Payne provides the original orchestration of this work, newly computer-engraved. A piano reduction is in preparation.

Act I	50'
Act II	40'
Act III	35'

Payne

La bayadère: Act II <1877>   22'

2 2 2 2 — 4 2 2 0 — tmp+2 — hp — str

perc: cym, sd, tri, glock

Orchestrated by William McDermott.

Kalmus

La bayadère: Pas de deux <1877>   12'

2[1.2/pic] 2 2 — 4 2 3 0 — tmp+3 — hp — str

perc: cym, sd, tri, glock

Orchestrated by William McDermott.

Kalmus

Don Quixote <1869>   137'

3[1.2.3/pic] 2 2 — 4 4[2tp, 2crt] 3 1 — tmp+4 — hp — pf/cel — str

perc: bd, cym, tri, tambn, sd, glock, xyl, cast

The uncut Bolshoi material, which includes traditional added music by Vasily Solov'yev-Sedoy, Reinhold Glière, Anton Simon, Valery Zhelobinsky, Riccardo Drigo, Yuly Gerber, Cesare Pugni, & Eduard Napravnik. Original orchestration, newly computer-engraved.
    Piano, celesta, harp 2, and xylophone only required for certain of these added movements.

Introduction & PROLOGUE	13'
ACTE I	41'
ACTE II	55'
ACTE III	27'
[For full contents, see Appendix J]	

Payne

Don Quixote [arr. McPhee]   125'

2[1.2/pic] 2[1.2/Eh] 2 2 — 4 2 3 1 — tmp+2 — hp — str

perc: bd, cym, sd, tambn, tri, glock, wnd mach

Arranged from the piano score by Jonathan McPhee.

Boosey

Don Quixote: Pas de deux (original) <1869>   9'

3[1.2.pic] 2 2 2 — 4 4[2tp, 2crt] 3 1 — tmp+4 — hp — str

perc: tri, field dr, cym, bd

Original orchestration, newly computer-engraved.

Introduction	_'
I. Valse entrée	_'
II. Adagio	_'
III. Basilio's variation	_'
IV. Kitri's Variation	_'
Coda	_'

Payne

Don Quixote: Pas de deux (arr. McDermott) <1869>   9'

2[1.2/pic] 2 2 — 4 2 3 0 — tmp+3 — hp — str

perc: cym, sd, tri, glock

Orchestrated by William McDermott.

Kalmus   Luck's

Paquita   40'

3[1.2.pic] 2 2 — 4 4[2crt, 2tp] 3 1 — tmp+4 — 2hp — cel — str

perc: tri, tambn, sd, cym, bd, glock

As was customary in the classic ballet tradition, movements by other composers (Adolphe Adam, Anton Simon, Riccardo Drigo, Cesare Pugni, Nikolay Tcherepnin, Albert Zabel, and Yuli Gerber) have been interpolated over the course of various productions.
    2nd harp plays in two movements only.

1. Polonaise	_'
1a. Mazurka	_'
2. Allegro	_'
3. Maestoso	_'
4. Allegro non troppo	_'
5. Allegro	_'
5a. Allegretto	_'
6. Moderato	_'
7. Moderato	_'
8. Moderato (Adolphe Adam)	_'
9. Allegro moderato	_'
9a. Souvenir du bal (Anton Simon; orchd R. Drigo)	_'
10. Tempo di Valse (Riccardo Drigo)	_'
11. Tempo di Valse (Cesare Pugni)	_'
12. Moderato; Tempo di Valse (Riccardo Drigo)	_'
13. Allegro	_'
14. Allegro ma non troppo (Nikolay Tcherepnin)	_'
15. Andante (Alfred Zabel)	_'
16. Allegro (Yuly Gerber)	_'
17. Allegro	_'
18. Allegro moderato	_'
19. Allegro con fuoco	_'

Payne

Paquita [McPhee reduction] <1846>   40*

2[1.2/pic] 2 2 — 4 2 3 1 — tmp+3 — hp — cel — str

perc: bd, cym, sd, tri, glock

Reduced orchestration by Jonathan McPhee.

Boosey

Paquita: Suite <1846>   25*

2[1.2/pic] 2 2 — 2 2 2 0 — tmp+1 — hp — cel — str

Orchestrated by William McDermott.

Kalmus

Miyoshi, Akira   1933-

b Tokyo, 10 Jan 1933). Japanese

Concerto for Orchestra <1964>   11'

3 3[1.2.3/Eh] 3[1/Ebcl.2.3] 3 — 6 4 3 1 — tmp+5 — hp — pf, cel — str

Ongaku

Mjaskowsky, Nikolai   1881-1950

The German transliteration of the composer's name, used by Universal Edition.

see: Miaskovsky, Nikolai, 1881-1950

Moeran, E. J.   1894-1950

b Heston, 31 Dec 1894; d nr Kenmare, Ireland, 1 Dec 1950). English composer of Anglo-Irish descent

Overture to a Masque <1944>   10'

2[1.2/pic] 2 3[1.2.bcl(ad lib)] 2 — 4 3 3 0 — tmp+3 — str
perc: cym, sd, glock, bd, tri
Bass clarinet cued in bn2.

Stainer

Molter, Johann Melchior   1696-1765

(b Tiefenort, nr Eisenach, 10 Feb 1696; d Karlsruhe, 12 Jan 1765). German

Concerto, Clarinet, No.1, A major   13'

cnt — str
Ed. Heinz Becker. Written for Clarinet in D; material includes a transposed part for Clarinet in A.
  1. Moderato   4'
  2. Largo   5'
  3. Allegro   4'

Breitkopf

Moncayo (García), José Pablo   1912-1958

(b Guadalajara, 29 June 1912; d Mexico City, 16 June 1958). Mexican

Amatzinac <1935>   8'

solo flute
str

Peer

Homenaje a Cervantes (Homage to Cervantes) <1947>   8'

0 2 0 0 — 0 0 0 0 — str

Peer

Huapango <1941>   7'

3[1.2.pic] 2 3[1.2.Ebcl] 2 — 4 3 3 1 — tmp+4 — hp — str
perc: xyl, claves, guiro, bd, metal rttl, American Indian drum
There is also a chamber orchestra version, calling for:
  1 1 2 1 — 2 2 1 0 — 4perc — pf[or hp] — str

EMM

Sinfonietta <1945>   9'

3[1.2.pic] 2 3[1.2.Ebcl] 2 — 4 2 1 1 — tmp+3 — str
perc: bd, cym, sus cym, sd

EMM

Tierra de temporal (Land of Tempests)   11'

3[1.2.pic] 3[1.2.Eh] 2 2 — 4 3 3 1 — tmp+3 — hp — str
perc: bd, sus cym, sd, marac

Peer

Moniuszko, Stanisław   1819-1872

(b Ubiel, nr Minsk, 5 May 1819; d Warsaw, 4 June 1872). Polish

Fairy Tale; Fantastic Overture (Bajka; Conte d'hiver) <1848>   13'

2[1.pic] 2 2 2 — 4 2 3 1 — tmp — str

PWM

Halka: Mazur <1846–1847>   4'

2[1.pic] 2 2 2 — 4 2 3 1 — tmp+4 — str

PWM

Halka: Overture <1846–1847; rev 1857>   9'

2[1.pic] 2 2 2 — 4 2 3 1 — tmp+3 — str
perc: bd, cym, tri
Ed. Grzegorz Fitelberg.

PWM

Hrabina (The Countess): Overture <1859>   8'

2[1.2/pic] 2 2 2 — 4 2 3 1 — tmp+4 — str

PWM

Monroe, Ervin   1942-

(b Springfield, LA, 25 Nov 1942). American

The Amazing Symphony Orchestra <1976>   24'

narrator
3[1.2.3/pic] 2[1.2/Eh] 2 2 — 4 2 3 1 — tmp+3 — str
perc: bd, cym, sus cym, sd, tri, tambn, xyl
  I. Moods   9'
  II. Pictures   8'
  III. Dances   7'

Little Piper

Monteverdi, Claudio   1567-1643

(b Cremona, 15 May 1567; d Venice, 29 Nov 1643). Italian

SV = *Claudio Monteverdi: Verzeichnis der erhaltenen Werke: kleine Ausgabe*, ed. M.H. Stattkus (Bergkamen, 1985)

Arianna: Lamento d'Arianna (Ariadne's Lament) <1608>   8'

solo mezzo-soprano
3 3 0 2 — 0 3 3 1 — hp — str
Orchestrated by Ottorino Respighi, P.88 (1908). Ed. Salvatore Di Vittorio.

Panastudio

Combattimento di Tancredi e Clorinda, SV 153 <1624>   22'

solos SAT
cnt — str
Chester edition (& Luck's reprint) by G.F. Malipiero; Oxford ed. Denis
Stevens; Suvini ed. G.F. Ghedini.

Sinfonia	2'		
Tancredi, che Clorinda un uomo stima	2'		
Sinfonia	3'		
Non schivar, non parar	2'		
E stanco e anelante	3'		
Così tacendo e rimirando	2'		
Torna ira nei cori, e li trasporta	1'		
Ma ecco omai l'ora fatal	2'		
Amica, hai vinto	2'		
In queste voci languide	3'		

Chester	Luck's	Oxford	Zerboni

Laudate dominum (Psalm 117), SV 272 <1641>   4'

chorus   solos SSTTB
0 0 0 0 — 0 0 4[opt] 0 — cnt — str[no va]
Originally for 5 solo voices, optional chorus, 4va da braccio, 4 opt tbn,
continuo. Ed. Denis Arnold.

Eulenburg

Orfeo, SV 318: Overture <1607>   5'

2[incl pic] 2 0 0 — 0 2 3 0 — 2hp[or lute & chittarone] — org — str
Arranger not identified.

Kalmus	Luck's

Orfeo, SV 318: Sinfonie e ritornelli <1607>   9'

str
Arr. G.F. Malipiero.

Kalmus	Luck's	Ricordi

Orfeo, SV 318: Toccata & ritornelli <1607>   4'

3[1.pic.pic] 2 3[1.2.bcl] 2 — 4 3 4[tbn4 opt] 0 — 1perc — hp — str
Arr. Maurice Peress.

Luck's

VESPRO DELLA BEATA VERGINE, SV 206 <1610>

*Ch.1 of Jeffrey Kurtzman's book "The Monteverdi Vespers of 1610:
Music, Context, Performance" (Oxford University Press, 1999) has a
critical study of the various editions and recordings of this vast and
complex work. Two of the best editions are given below.*

Vespro della Beata Vergine, SV 206 (Kurtzman) <1610>   80'

solos: 2S, 3T, 2B   double chorus: SATTB - SATTB
4[2fl, 2rec] 0 0 0 — 0 3[3cornetti or 3tp] 3 0 — org — str[2 or 3vn,
or 3va, 2vc, db]
Ed. Jeffrey Kurtzman.
Mvts. 10, 13, & 14 have alternate versions (10b, 13b, 14b) transposed
down a 4th reflecting the 17th-century practice of "chiavette."
Antiphons for feasts of the B.V.M. are given for possible use in a
liturgical setting.

1. Domine ad adjuvandum	_'
2. Dixit Dominus	_'
3. Nigra sum	_'
4. Laudate pueri	_'
5. Pulchra es	_'
6. Laetatus sum	_'
7. Duo Seraphim	_'
8. Nisi Dominus	_'
9. Audi coelum	_'
10a & b. Lauda Jerusalem	_'
11. Sonata sopra Sancta Maria	_'
12. Ave maris stella	_'
13a & b. Magnificat à 7	_'
14a & b. Magnificat à 6	_'

Oxford

Vespro della Beata Vergine, SV 206 (Jürgens) <1610; rev 1615>   93'

double chorus   solos SSATTBB
2[1/rec.2/rec] 3[alt for cornetti or tp] 0 2 — 0 3[3cornetti or 3tp] 4 0
— chitarrone/lute — hp — org, hpsd — str
A "practical Urtext" edition, ed. Jürgen Jürgens, 1977.

I. Versicle & Response: Deus in adjutorium / Domine ad adjuvandum	2'
II. Psalm 109: Dixit Dominus	8'
III. Motet: Nigra sum	4'
IV. Psalm 112: Laudate pueri	6'
V. Motet: Pulchra es	4'
VI. Psalm 121: Laetatus sum	7'
VII. Motet: Duo Seraphim	7'
VIII. Psalm 126: Nisi Dominus	5'
IX. Motet: Audi coelum	10'
X. Psalm 147: Lauda Jerusalem	4'
XI. Sonata sopra "Sancta Maria; ora pro nobis"	7'
XII. Hymn: Ave maris stella	8'
XIII. Magnificat	21'

Universal

Montsalvatge, Xavier   1912-2002

b Gerona, 11 March 1912; d Barcelona, 7 May 2002). Spanish (Catalan)

Cuatro variaciones sobre un tema de *La flauta mágica* (Variations on a theme from "Magic Flute") <1991>   8'

2 2 2 2 — 2 2 0 0 — str
Based on Sarastro's aria "In diesen heil'gen Hallen."

Trító

Manfred (Ballet for Orchestra) <1945>   20'

2[1.2/pic] 1[ob/Eh] 2 1 — 2 2 3 1 — tmp+3 — hp — str
perc: cym, sus cym, sd, tri, tamtam, bd

Trító

Simfonia de Rèquiem <1985>   24'

3[1.2.pic] 3[1.2.Eh] 3[1.2.bcl] 2 — 4 3 3 0 — soprano voice — tmp+3 — pf — str

perc: vib, glock, cym, sus cym, tamtam, sd, bd, tomtom, cast, tri, whip, 3finger cym

The soprano sings only the last 23 bars; the composer specifies that she is not intended as a soloist, but as another instrument. If possible the audience should not even see her on stage.

I. Introitus	3'
II. Kyrie	4'
III. Dies irae	4'
IV. Agnus Dei	4'
V. Lux aeterna	5'
VI. Libera me, Domine	4'

Tritó

Tres reflejos sobre una pastoral de invierno (Three Reflections on a Winter Pastoral) <2002>   13'

str

Orchestration completed by Albert Guinovart.

I. Andantino violeta (Violet Andantino)	_'
II. Adagietto blanc (White Adagietto)	_'
III. Spiritoso carmesí (Crimson Spiritoso)	_'

Tritó

Moore, Carman   1936-

(b Lorain, OH, 8 Oct 1936). American

Gospel Fuse <1975>   23'

gospel quartet: S solo with accompanying trio SAA
3[incl pic] 3[incl Eh] 4[incl bcl] 3[incl cbn] — 4 3 3 1 — ssx — elec bass — tmp+2 — hp — pf, elec org — str

Pianist & organist do some improvisation.

The Call	_'
The Dream	_'
Love Sermons	_'

Peer

Moore, Douglas   1893-1969

(b Cutchogue, NY, 10 Aug 1893; d Greenport, NY, 25 July 1969). American

Overture on an American Tune <1931>   6'

3[1.2.pic] 2 2 — 4 3 3 1 — tmp+3 — hp — str

C. Fischer

Pageant of P.T. Barnum <1924>   18'

3[1.2.pic] 3[1.2.Eh] 3[1.2.bcl] 3[1.2.cbn] — 4 3 3 1 — tmp+6 — hp — cel — str

1. Boyhood at Bethel	3'
2. Joice Heth, 161 Year Old Negress	4'
3. General and Mrs. Tom Thumb	2'
4. Jenny Lind	5'
5. Circus Parade	4'

C. Fischer   Luck's

Moore, Undine Smith   1904-1989

(b Jarratt, VA, 25 Aug 1904; d Petersburg, VA, 6 Feb 1989). American

Scenes from the Life of a Martyr <1978>   43'

solos SATB   chorus   narrator
3[1.2.pic] 3[1.2.Eh] 3[1.2.bcl] 3[1.2.cbn] — 4 3 3 1 — tmp+3 — hp — str

perc: bd, cym, sus cym, sd, field drum, tri, xyl

Orchestrated by Donald Rauscher.

Prologue 1: What is Precious is Never to Forget	_'
Prologue 2: O Stay in the Field, Children	_'
Prologue 3: Lay Dis Body Down	_'
1. Whenever a People Is Oppressed They Wait in Hope	_'
2. His mother Rocked Him Gently with Love and Freedom on Her Mind	_'
3. Songs at the Cradle, No.1	_'
4. Songs at the Cradle, No.2	_'
5. Songs at the Cradle, No.3	_'
6. Ring Game	_'
7. The Voice of My Beloved	_'
8. Arise My Love, My Fair One	_'
9. Set Me As a Seal on Thy Heart	_'
10. He Hath Anointed Me to Preach the Gospel	_'
11. I Never Felt Such Love in My Soul Before	_'
12. Martin's Song (Lord, Thou Knowest)	_'
13. Martin's Lament	_'
14. Oh God, How Many Are Them That Hate Me!	_'
15. They Tell Me Martin Is Dead	_'
16. Tell All My Father's People Don't You Grieve for Me (Alleluia)	_'

C. Fischer

Moravec, Paul   1957-

(b Buffalo, NY, 2 Nov 1957). American

The Blizzard Voices <2008>   70'

solo soprano, mezzo-soprano, tenor, baritone, bass   chorus SATB
2[1.2/7] 2 2 2 — 4 2 2 0 — tmp+1 — str

perc: cym, sus cym, tri, glock, xyl, chimes, crot, windchimes

1. Prologue: The Plains	_'
2. There was a Day	_'
3. The Blizzard Bore Down	_'
4. Billy	_'
5. I never see a sunflower…	_'
6. All Night the Wind Moaned	_'
7. Lois Mae Royce	_'
8. Fare Thee Well, Mother	_'
9. Telegraph	_'
10. Minnie Freeman	_'
11. My Sister Was Born	_'
12. In the Morning	_'
13. Light the Fire	_'
14. The Searching Parties	_'
15. In Remembrance	_'
16. Epilogue	_'

Subito

Concerto, Oboe & Strings <2006>   21'

str

I. Lively	_'
II. Expressive, melancholy	_'
III. Quarter-note = 56	_'

Subito

Concerto, Piano & Orchestra <1992>   30'

2[1.2/pic] 2 2 2 — 2 2 2 0 — tmp+1 — str

perc: sus cym, tri, tamtam, glock, marim, 4tomtoms

Subito

Montserrat; Concerto for Violoncello & Orchestra <1999>   18'

3[1.2.pic] 2 3[1.2.bcl] 2 — 2 2 1 0 — 2perc — str
perc: sus cym, glock, chimes, windchimes

> Subito

Sempre diritto! (Straight Ahead!) <1991>   14'

0 2 0 0 — 2 0 0 0 — str

> Subito

Songs of Love and War <1998>   25'

baritone solo   solo trumpet   chorus
str
1. *Don't Ask (Vietnam War)*   2'
2. *Dearest Rowland (World War II)*   6'
3. *Here Hard by That Lonely Grave (World War I)* 7'
4. *Always, Always (Civil War)*   10'

> Subito

Morawetz, Oskar   1917-2007

(b Světlá nad Sázavou, 17 Jan 1917; d Toronto, 13 June 2007). Canadian composer of Czech birth

From The Diary of Anne Frank <1970>   19'

solo soprano or mezzosoprano
2[1.2/pic] 2 2 2 — 4 2[brief tp3 opt] 3 1 — tmp+3 — hp — pf/cel — str
perc: sd, bd, tri, cym, tamtam, chimes, vib, glock, xyl

> CMC

Mosolov, Aleksandr Vasil'yevich   1900-1973

(b Kiev, 29 July/11 Aug 1900; d Moscow, 12 July 1973). Russian

Iron Foundry, op.19 (Zavod) <1926–1928>   3'

3[1.2.pic] 3[1.2.Eh] 3[1.2.bcl] 3[1.2.cbn] — 4 3 3 1 — tmp+5 — str
perc: field dr, sus cym, bd, tamtam, thunder sheet
An orchestral episode from the ballet *Stal.*

> Kalmus   Russian

Moussorgsky, Modeste   1839-1881

see: Mussorgsky, Modest, 1839-1881

Mozart, Leopold   1719-1787

(b Augsburg, 14 Nov 1719; d Salzburg, 28 May 1787). German-Austrian

Cassatio ex G (mit der *Kindersinfonie*) (Toy Symphony)   15'

0 0 0 0 — 2 0 0 0 — 5-7 players of toy insts — str[vn I, vn II & "basso"]
Toy instruments: drum, ratchet, *Pfeife* in G, cuckoo, trumpet, quail, windmill, organ. The notation of the toys is largely inexact and suggestive, and the distribution of parts is not clear.
    The preface to the score suggests the presence of a harpsichord continuo, but no such part is included; presumably in the 18th century the continuo player would improvise from the all-purpose *basso* part, along with cello, double bass, and perhaps a bassoon.
    Ed. H.C. Robbins Landon.
    Some scholars (though apparently not Robbins Landon) question the attribution to L. Mozart.
    Three of the movements of this work are from the widely-known *Berchtolds Gaden Musick* of unknown authorship. For further information, see Leopold Mozart, *Kindersymphonie.*
1. *Marche*   _'
2. *Menuetto*   _'
3. *Allegro*   _'
4. *Menuetto*   _'
5. *Allegretto*   _'
6. *Menuetto*   _'
7. *Presto*   _'

> Doblinger

Concerto, Trumpet, D major <1762>   9'

0 0 0 0 — 2 0 0 0 — cnt — str

> Kalmus   Kneusslin   Luck's   Schott

Kindersymphonie, C major (*Toy Symphony; Sinfonia Berchtolsgadensis*) <1786>   10'

5-7 players of toy insts — str[no va]
Toy instruments: trumpet, drum, cuckoo, nightingale, rattle, triangle, quail.
    Published variously under the names of Joseph Haydn and Leopold Mozart (Breitkopf & Doblinger editions are under Leopold Mozart's name; Kalmus & Luck's [reprints of earlier editions] are under that of Franz Joseph Haydn).
    This work has also been attributed to Michael Haydn and to Edmund Angerer (also Augener, Angener). Some early sources are titled *Berchtolds Gaden Musick*, and some use viola instead of 2nd violin as the middle of the 3 string voices.
    A corruption of this work was later incorporated into a *Cassation* that has been attributed, perhaps incorrectly, to Leopold Mozart.
I. *Allegro*   5'
II. *Menuetto*   3'
III. *Finale: Allegro* 2'

> Breitkopf   Doblinger   Kalmus   Luck's   Peters

Musikalische Schlittenfahrt (Musical Sleigh-Ride) <1755>   25'

0 2 0 2 — 2 4 0 0 — tmp+3 — str
perc: tuned slgh-bells [5pitches; 3players]
Ed. Raimund Rüegge.

> Kunzelmann

Symphonies, B-flat major

see: Mozart, Wolfgang Amadeus, 1756-1791
        Symphony, No.2, K.17 (Anh.C 11.02), B-flat major
        Symphony, K.Anh.216 (Anh.C11.03; K.74g), B-flat major

Toy Symphony

see his: Kindersymphonie

Mozart, Wolfgang Amadeus   1756-1791

(b Salzburg, 27 Jan 1756; d Vienna, 5 Dec 1791). Austrian

K [or **KV**] = Ludwig von Köchel, *Chronologisch-thematisches Verzeichnis sämtlicher Tonwerke Wolfgang Amade Mozarts* (Leipzig, 1862; 6th ed. 1964 by F. Giegling, A. Weinmann and G. Sievers)

In the works of this composer, the original K-number (from the first edition of the Köchel Verzeichnis) is primary; K-numbers with letters appended indicate the additions or renumberings of the 3rd and 6th editions (the 2nd, 4th, and 5th editions may be disregarded for scholarly purposes). In this book, the original K-number is generally given first; the K-number from the 6th edition, if different, is second. If a third K-number is found, it is from the 3rd edition, and is included because some published editions (such as those of Bärenreiter) follow that numbering.

The complete works of Mozart may be examined online in the edition of the Neue Mozart-Ausgabe *at:*
dme.mozarteum.at/DME/nma/nmapub_srch.php?l=2

A questo seno / Or che il cielo, K.374 <1781>   9'

soprano recitative and rondo
0 2 0 0 — 2 0 0 0 — str

Bärenreiter	Breitkopf	Luck's

Abduction from the Seraglio

see his: Entführung aus dem Serail

Adagio, Violin & Orchestra, K.261, E major <1776>   5'

2 0 0 0 — 2 0 0 0 — str
Written for the *Concerto, Violin, No.5, K.219.*

Breitkopf	Kalmus	Luck's

Adagio & Fugue, K.546, C minor <1788>   9'

str
Fugue originally for 2 pianos; orchestrated by the composer.

Bärenreiter	Breitkopf	Eulenburg	Kalmus	Luck's

Ah, lo previdi / Ah, t'invola / Deh, non varcar, K.272 <1777>   12'

soprano recitative, aria, and cavatina
0 2 0 0 — 2 0 0 0 — str

Bärenreiter	Breitkopf	Luck's

Ah se in ciel, benigne stelle, K.538 <1788>   7'

soprano aria
0 2 0 2 — 2 0 0 0 — str

Bärenreiter	Breitkopf	Kalmus	Luck's

Al desio di chi t'adora, K.577 <1789>   7'

solo soprano
0 0 0 2 — 2 0 0 0 — 2 basset hn — str
Intended as a substitute for the aria *Deh vieni non tardar,* in the composer's *Nozze di Figaro.*

Breitkopf

Alcandro, lo confesso / Non so d'onde viene, K.294 <1778>   8'

soprano recitative and aria
2 0 2 2 — 2 0 0 0 — str
Not to be confused with the composer's later version for bass voice of this same text, K.512.

Bärenreiter	Breitkopf	Kalmus	Luck's

Alcandro, lo confesso / Non so d'onde viene, K.512 <1787>   9'

bass recitative and aria
1 2 0 2 — 2 0 0 0 — str
Not to be confused with the composer's earlier version for soprano of this same text, K.294.

Bärenreiter	Breitkopf	Luck's

Alma dei creatoris, K.277 (272a) <1777>   5'

chorus   solos SAT
0 0 0 1 — 0 0 3 0 — org — str

Kalmus	Peters	Luck's

Alma grande e nobil core, K.578 <1789>   4'

soprano aria
0 2 0 2 — 2 0 0 0 — str
The old Breitkopf edition, as well as its Kalmus and Luck's reprints, calls for a pair of trumpets rather than horns. Horns are likely correct.

Bärenreiter	Breitkopf	Kalmus	Luck's

Andante, Flute & Orchestra, K.315 (285e), C major <1779–1780>   6'

0 2 0 0 — 2 0 0 0 — str

Bärenreiter	Breitkopf	Kalmus	Luck's

Apollo et Hyacinthus, K.38: Prelude <1767>   3'

0 2 0 0 — 2 0 0 0 — str

Bärenreiter	Kalmus	Luck's

Ascanio in Alba: Overture

see his: Symphony, K.111

Ave verum corpus, K.618 <1791>   4'

chorus
org — str

Bärenreiter	Breitkopf	Kalmus	Luck's

Un bacio di mano, K.541 <1788>   2'

bass arietta
1 2 0 2 — 2 0 0 0 — str

Bärenreiter	Breitkopf	Kalmus	Luck's

Basta, vincesti / Ah non lasciarmi (K.295a; 486a) <1778>   7'

soprano recitative and aria
2 0 0 2 — 2 0 0 0 — str
This work was not given a K-number in the 1862 edition of the *Köchel Verzeichnis.* K.295a is from the 6th edition; K.486a from the 3rd edition.

Bärenreiter	Breitkopf

Bastien und Bastienne, K.50 (46b): Overture <1768>   2'

0 2 0 0 — 2 0 0 0 — str

Breitkopf	Kalmus	Luck's

Bella mia fiamma / Resta, oh cara, K.528 <1787>   10'

soprano recitative and aria
1 2 0 2 — 2 0 0 0 — str

Bärenreiter	Breitkopf	Kalmus	Luck's

Benedictus sit deus, K.117 (66a) <1768>   9'

chorus   soprano solo
2 0 0 0 — 2 2 0 0 — tmp — org — str

Kalmus	Luck's

Betulia liberata, K.118 (74c) <1771>   *145'*

    solos SSSATB   chorus
    2 2 0 2 — 4 2 0 0 — str

Bärenreiter			

Betulia liberata, K.118 (74c): Overture <1771>   *5'*

    0 2 0 2 — 4 2 0 0 — str

Breitkopf	Kalmus	Luck's

Cassation No.1, K.63, G major <1769>   *22'*

    0 2 0 0 — 2 0 0 0 — str
    I. [March]   2'
    II. Allegro   3'
    III. Andante   3'
    IV. Menuet   3'
    V. Adagio   6'
    VI. Menuet   3'
    VII. Finale   2'

Breitkopf	Kalmus	Luck's

Cassation No.2, K.99 (63a), B-flat major <1769>   *20'*

    0 2 0 0 — 2 0 0 0 — str
    I. [March]   3'
    II. Allegro molto   2'
    III. Andante   3'
    IV. Menuet   3'
    V. Andante   3'
    VI. Menuet   2'
    VII. Allegro   4'

Breitkopf	Kalmus	Luck's

Ch'io mi scordi di te / Non temer, amato bene, K.505 <1786>   *7'*

    soprano scene and rondo, with obligato piano
    0 0 2 2 — 2 0 0 0 — str

Bärenreiter	Breitkopf	Grande	Kalmus	Luck's

Chi sà, chi sà, qual sia, K.582 <1789>   *3'*

    soprano aria
    0 0 2 2 — 2 0 0 0 — str

Bärenreiter	Breitkopf	Kalmus	Luck's

Church Sonatas

    see his: Sonatas, Organ & Strings
                 Sonatas, Organ & Orchestra

Clarice cara mia sposa, K.256 <1776>   *2'*

    tenor aria
    0 2 0 0 — 2 0 0 0 — str

Bärenreiter	Kalmus	Luck's

La clemenza di Tito, K.621: Overture <1791>   *5'*

    2 2 2 2 — 2 2 0 0 — tmp — str

Bärenreiter	Breitkopf	Kalmus	Luck's

La clemenza di Tito, K.621: March <1791>   *2'*

    2 2 2 2 — 2 2 0 0 — tmp — str
    This excerpt may be out of print.

Breitkopf			

Con ossequio, con rispetto, K.210 <1775>   *3'*

    tenor aria
    0 2 0 0 — 2 0 0 0 — str

Bärenreiter	Breitkopf

Concerto, Bassoon, K.191 (186e), B-flat major <1774>   *20'*

    0 2 0 0 — 2 0 0 0 — str
    I. Allegro   8'
    II. Andante ma adagio   6'
    III. Rondo: Tempo di menuetto   6'

Bärenreiter	Breitkopf	Kalmus	Luck's

Concerto, Bassoon, No.2, K.Anh.C14.03, B-flat major   *19'*

    0 2 0 0 — 2 2 0 0 — tmp — str
    Ed. Max Seiffert. Probably spurious; perhaps composed by François
    Devienne (1759-1803).
    I. Allegro moderato   7'
    II Andante   7'
    III. Rondo: Allegro moderato   5'

Peters			

Concerto, Clarinet, K.622, A major <1791>   *25'*

    2 0 0 2 — 2 0 0 0 — str
    The Bärenreiter score shows also what is believed to be the original
    version for basset-clarinet.
    I. Allegro   12'
    II. Adagio   7'
    III. Rondo: Allegro   6'

Bärenreiter	Breitkopf	Kalmus	Luck's

Concerto, Flute, No.1, K.313 (285c), G major <1778>   *25'*

    2 2 0 0 — 2 0 0 0 — str
    The 2 orchestral flutes are used in the second movement only, where the
    oboes are tacet. (Probably in Mozart's time the oboists doubled on flute.)
    I. Allegro maestoso   10'
    II. Adagio non troppo   9'
    III. Rondo: Tempo di menuetto   6'

Bärenreiter	Breitkopf	Kalmus	Luck's

Concerto, Flute, No.2, K.314 (285d), D major <1778>   *21'*

    0 2 0 0 — 2 0 0 0 — str
    A reworking, possibly by the composer, of the oboe concerto in C major,
    K.314 (285d).
    I. Allegro aperto   8'
    II. Andante ma non troppo   7'
    III. Allegro   6'

Bärenreiter	Breitkopf	Kalmus	Luck's

Concerto, Flute & Harp, K.299 (297c), C major <1778>   *30'*

    0 2 0 0 — 2 0 0 0 — str
    I. Allegro   11'
    II. Andantino   9'
    III. Rondo: Allegro   10'

Bärenreiter	Breitkopf	Kalmus	Luck's

Concerto, Horn, No.1, K.412 & K.514 (= 386b), D major <1791–1792>   *9'*

    0 2 0 2 — str
    1st mvt is K.412; 2nd mvt, completed by Franz Xaver Süssmayer after
    Mozart's death, is K.514. The whole (in the numeration of the Köchel 6th
    ed.) is K.386b.
        Breitkopf offers separately a new version of the 2nd mvt (K.514) ed.
    K. Marguerre.
    I. Allegro   5'
    II. Allegro   4'

Bärenreiter	Breitkopf	Kalmus	Luck's

Concerto, Horn, No.2, K.417, E-flat major <1783>   *16'*

    0 2 0 0 — 2 0 0 0 — str
    I. Allegro maestoso   8'
    II. Andante   4'
    III. Rondo   4'

Bärenreiter	Breitkopf	Kalmus	Luck's

Concerto, Horn, No.3, K.447, E-flat major <1784–1787>   16'

0 0 2 2 — str
I. *Allegro*	7'
II. *Romanza: Larghetto*	5'
III. *Allegro*	4'

| Bärenreiter | Breitkopf | Kalmus | Luck's |

Concerto, Horn, No.4, K.495, E-flat major <1786>   16'

0 2 0 0 — 2 0 0 0 — str
I. *Allegro moderato*	9'
II. *Romanza: Andante*	4'
III. *Rondo: Allegro vivace*	3'

| Bärenreiter | Breitkopf | Kalmus | Luck's |

Concerto, Oboe, K.314 (285d), C major <1778>   21'

0 2 0 0 — 2 0 0 0 — str
The original version of the D major flute concerto, K.314 (285d).
Bärenreiter ed. Franz Giegling; Boosey ed. Bernhard Paumgartner.
I. *Allegro aperto*	8'
II. *Adagio non troppo*	7'
III. *Rondo: Allegretto*	6'

| Bärenreiter | Boosey | Luck's |

Concerto, Piano, No.1, K.37, F major <1767>   15'

0 2 0 0 — 2 0 0 0 — str
Based on sonata movements by Hermann Friedrich Raupach & Leontzi
Honauer.
I. *Allegro*	5'
II. *Andante*	5'
III. *[Allegro]*	5'

| Bärenreiter | Breitkopf |

Concerto, Piano, No.2, K.39, B-flat major <1767>   15'

0 2 0 0 — 2 0 0 0 — str
Based on sonata movements by Hermann Friedrich Raupach & Johann
Schobert.
I. *Allegro spiritoso*	5'
II. *Andante*	6'
III. *Molto allegro*	4'

| Bärenreiter | Breitkopf |

Concerto, Piano, No.3, K.40, D major <1767>   13'

0 2 0 0 — 2 2 0 0 — str
Based on sonata movements by Leontzi Honauer, Johann Gottfried
Eckard, & C.P.E. Bach.
I. *Allegro maestoso*	5'
II. *Andante*	5'
III. *Presto*	3'

| Bärenreiter | Breitkopf | Kalmus | Luck's |

Concerto, Piano, No.4, K.41, G major <1767>   14'

2 0 0 0 — 2 0 0 0 — str
Based on sonata movements by Leontzi Honauer & Hermann Friedrich
Raupach.
I. *Allegro*	5'
II. *Andante*	5'
III. *Molto allegro*	4'

| Bärenreiter | Breitkopf |

Concerto, Piano, K.107 (21b) no.1, D major <1772>   13'

str[no va]
After Johann Christian Bach's piano sonata, op.5, no.2; not considered
one of the 27 piano concertos in the Mozart canon.

| Möseler | Schott |

Concerto, Piano, K.107 (21b) no.2, G major <1772>   10'

str[no va]
After Johann Christian Bach's piano sonata, op.5, no.3; not considered
one of the 27 piano concertos in the Mozart canon.

| AMP | Schott |

Concerto, Piano, K.107 (21b) no.3, E-flat major <1772>   9'

str[no va]
After Johann Christian Bach's piano sonata, op.5, no.4; not considered
one of the 27 piano concertos in the Mozart canon.

| Möseler | Schott |

Concerto, Piano, No.5, K.175, D major <1773>   21'

0 2 0 0 — 2 2 0 0 — tmp — str
See also his *Concert-Rondo, K.382, D major*, which was composed as a
new finale for this concerto.
I. *Allegro*	7'
II. *Andante ma un poco adagio*	9'
III. *Allegro*	8'

| Breitkopf | Kalmus | Luck's |

Concerto, Piano, No.6, K.238, B-flat major <1776>   20'

2 2 0 0 — 2 0 0 0 — str
The 2 flutes are used in the second movement only, where the oboes are
tacet. (Probably in Mozart's time the oboists doubled on flute.)
I. *[Allegro aperto]*	6'
II. *Andante un poco adagio*	3'
III. *Rondeau: Allegro*	3'

| Bärenreiter | Breitkopf | Kalmus | Luck's |

Concerto, 3 Pianos, No.7, K.242, F major (Lodron) <1776>   20'

0 2 0 0 — 2 0 0 0 — str
A version by the composer for 2 solo pianos is also available; use the
same orchestral materials.
   Bärenreiter publishes the score of the 3-piano version, and a piano
reduction of the 2-piano version.
I. *Allegro*	8'
II. *Adagio*	7'
III. *Rondo: Tempo di menuetto*	5'

| Bärenreiter | Breitkopf | Kalmus | Luck's |

Concerto, Piano, No.8, K.246, C major (Lützow) <1776>   20'

0 2 0 0 — 2 0 0 0 — str
I. *Allegro aperto*	7'
II. *Andante*	7'
III. *Tempo di menuetto*	6'

| Bärenreiter | Breitkopf | Kalmus | Luck's |

Concerto, Piano, No.9, K.271, E-flat major (Jeunehomme) <1777>   32'

0 2 0 0 — 2 0 0 0 — str
I. *Allegro*	11'
II. *Andantino*	12'
III. *Rondo: Presto*	9'

| Bärenreiter | Breitkopf | Kalmus | Luck's |

Concerto, 2 Pianos, No.10, K.365 (316a), E-flat major <1779>   24'

0 2 2[opt] 2 — 2 2[opt] 0 0 — opt tmp — str
The parts for 2cl, 2tp, and tmp were added later, and may be considered
optional.
I. *Allegro*	11'
II. *Andante*	7'
III. *Rondo: Allegro*	6'

| Bärenreiter | Breitkopf | Kalmus | Luck's |

Concerto, Piano, No.11, K.413 (387a), F major <1782>   23'

0 2 0 2 — 2 0 0 0 — str
Peters edition lists the wind parts as optional.
I. Allegro   10'
II. Larghetto   8'
III. Tempo di menuetto   5'

Bärenreiter	Breitkopf	Kalmus	Luck's	Peters

Concerto, Piano, No.12, K.414 (385p), A major <1782>   25'

0 2 0 0 — 2 0 0 0 — str
Peters edition lists the wind parts as optional.
I. Allegro   10'
II. Andante   9'
III. Allegretto 6'

Bärenreiter	Breitkopf	Kalmus	Luck's	Peters

Concerto, Piano, No.13, K.415 (387b), C major <1782>   26'

0 2 0 2 — 2 2 0 0 — tmp — str
Peters edition lists the wind and timpani parts as optional.
I. Allegro   10'
II. Andante   8'
III. Allegro 8'

Bärenreiter	Breitkopf	Kalmus	Luck's	Peters

Concerto, Piano, No.14, K.449, E-flat major <1784>   21'

0 2 0 0 — 2 0 0 0 — str
Peters edition lists the wind parts as optional.
I. Allegro vivace   8'
II. Andantino   7'
III. Allegro ma non troppo 6'

Bärenreiter	Breitkopf	Kalmus	Luck's	Peters

Concerto, Piano, No.15, K.450, B-flat major <1784>   25'

1 2 0 2 — 2 0 0 0 — str
I. Allegro   11'
II. Andante 6'
III. Allegro 8'

Bärenreiter	Breitkopf	Kalmus	Luck's

Concerto, Piano, No.16, K.451, D major <1784>   25'

1 2 0 2 — 2 2 0 0 — tmp — str
I. Allegro assai   10'
II. Andante   8'
III. Allegro di molto 7'

Bärenreiter	Breitkopf	Kalmus	Luck's

Concerto, Piano, No.17, K.453, G major <1784>   30'

1 2 0 2 — 2 0 0 0 — str
I. Allegro   12'
II. Andante   10'
III. Allegretto 8'

Bärenreiter	Breitkopf	Kalmus	Luck's

Concerto, Piano, No.18, K.456, B-flat major (Paradis) <1784>   30'

1 2 0 2 — 2 0 0 0 — str
I. Allegro vivace   12'
II. Andante un poco sostenuto 11'
III. Allegro vivace   7'

Bärenreiter	Breitkopf	Kalmus	Luck's

Concerto, Piano, No.19, K.459, F major <1784>   28'

1 2 0 2 — 2 0 0 0 — str
I. Allegro   13'
II. Allegretto   8'
III. Allegro assai 7'

Bärenreiter	Breitkopf	Kalmus	Luck's

Concerto, Piano, No.20, K.466, D minor <1785>   30'

1 2 0 2 — 2 2 0 0 — tmp — str
I. Allegro   13'
II. Romanza   9'
III. Rondo: Allegro assai 8'

Bärenreiter	Breitkopf	Kalmus	Luck's

Concerto, Piano, No.21, K.467, C major <1785>   29'

1 2 0 2 — 2 2 0 0 — tmp — str
I. [Allegro maestoso]   13'
II. Andante   9'
III. Allegro vivace assai 7'

Bärenreiter	Breitkopf	Kalmus	Luck's

Concerto, Piano, No.22, K.482, E-flat major <1785>   34'

1 0 2 2 — 2 2 0 0 — tmp — str
Bärenreiter edition has 2 extra measures (bars 282-283 of the 1st mvt)
which do not appear in the Breitkopf or Kalmus score or parts. These two
measures are identical to bars 19-20.
I. Allegro   14'
II. Andante   8'
III. Rondo: Allegro 12'

Bärenreiter	Breitkopf	Kalmus	Luck's

Concerto, Piano, No.23, K.488, A major <1786>   26'

1 0 2 2 — 2 0 0 0 — str
I. Allegro   11'
II. Adagio   7'
III. Allegro assai 8'

Bärenreiter	Breitkopf	Kalmus	Luck's

Concerto, Piano, No.24, K.491, C minor <1786>   31'

1 2 2 2 — 2 2 0 0 — tmp — str
I. Allegro   14'
II. Larghetto   8'
III. Allegretto 9'

Bärenreiter	Breitkopf	Kalmus	Luck's

Concerto, Piano, No.25, K.503, C major <1786>   30'

1 2 0 2 — 2 2 0 0 — tmp — str
A reprint of the Bärenreiter score, together with historical and analytical
essays, is published by Norton (ed. Joseph Kerman).
I. Allegro maestoso 15'
II. Andante   7'
III. Allegretto   8'

Bärenreiter	Breitkopf	Kalmus	Luck's

Concerto, Piano, No.26, K.537, D major (Coronation) <1788>   28'

1 2 0 2 — 2 2 0 0 — tmp — str
I. Allegro   13'
II. Larghetto   6'
III. Allegretto 9'

Bärenreiter	Breitkopf	Kalmus	Luck's

Concerto, Piano, No.27, K.595, B-flat major <1788–1791>   32'

1 2 0 2 — 2 0 0 0 — str
Bärenreiter edition has 7 extra measures (bars 47-53 of the 1st mvt)
which do not appear in the Breitkopf or Kalmus score or parts.
I. Allegro   15'
II. Larghetto 8'
III. Allegro   9'

Bärenreiter	Breitkopf	Kalmus	Luck's

Concerto, Piano, No.28, K.382, D major

see his: Concert-Rondo, K.382, D major

Concerto, 2 Pianos, K.242, F major

See note to No.7 in the series of piano concertos.

Concerto, 2 Pianos, K.365 (316a), E-flat major

Listed as No.10 in the series of piano concertos.

Concerto, 3 Pianos, K.242, F major

Listed as No.7 in the series of piano concertos.

Concerto, Violin, No.1, K.207, B-flat major <1775>   21'

0 2 0 0 — 2 0 0 0 — str

I. Allegro moderato	7'		
II. Adagio	8'		
III. Presto	6'		

Bärenreiter	Breitkopf	Kalmus	Luck's

Concerto, Violin, No.2, K.211, D major <1775>   21'

0 2 0 0 — 2 0 0 0 — str

I. Allegro moderato	8'		
II. Andante	9'		
III. Rondo: Allegro	4'		

Bärenreiter	Breitkopf	Kalmus	Luck's

Concerto, Violin, No.3, K.216, G major (Strassburg) <1775>   24'

2 2 0 0 — 2 0 0 0 — str

The 2 flutes are used in the second movement only, where the oboes are tacet. (Probably in Mozart's time the oboists doubled on flute.)

I. Allegro	9'			
II. Adagio	9'			
III. Rondo: Allegro	6'			

Bärenreiter	Breitkopf	Kalmus	Luck's	Schott

Concerto, Violin, No.4, K.218, D major <1775>   26'

0 2 0 0 — 2 0 0 0 — str

I. Allegro	10'		
II. Andante cantabile	9'		
III. Rondeau: Andante grazioso - Allegro ma non troppo	7'		

Bärenreiter	Breitkopf	Kalmus	Luck's

Concerto, Violin, No.5, K.219, A major (Turkish) <1775>   31'

0 2 0 0 — 2 0 0 0 — str

For an alternative slow movement, see his *Adagio, Violin & Orchestra, K.261.*

I. Allegro aperto	10'		
II. Adagio	12'		
III. Rondo: Tempo di menuetto	9'		

Bärenreiter	Breitkopf	Kalmus	Luck's

Concerto, Violin, No.6, K.268 (Anh.C 14.04), E-flat major <1780>   24'

1 2 0 2 — 2 0 0 0 — str

Authenticity doubtful; actual composer believed to be Friedrich Johann Eck.

I. [Allegro moderato]	12'		
II. Un poco adagio	7'		
III. Rondo: Allegretto	5'		

Breitkopf	Kalmus	Luck's

Concerto, Violin, No.7, K.271a (271i), D major <1777>   29'

0 2 0 0 — 2 0 0 0 — str

Substantially by Mozart, though the earliest extant source (the autograph is lost) shows signs of alterations made in the early 19th century.

I. Allegro maestoso	10'	
II. Andante	10'	
III. Allegro	9'	

Breitkopf	Kalmus	Luck's

Concertone, 2 Violins, K.190 (186e), C major <1774>   28'

0 2 0 0 — 2 2 0 0 — str

I. Allegro spiritoso	8'		
II. Andantino grazioso	11'		
III. Tempo di menuetto	9'		

Bärenreiter	Breitkopf	Kalmus	Luck's

Concert-Rondo, K.371, E-flat major <1781>   5'

solo horn or violoncello

0 2 0 0 — 2 0 0 0 — str

Breitkopf edition (& Kalmus reprint) for horn solo completed by Waldemar Spiess. Universal edition arr. Bernhard Paumgartner for horn or violoncello & orchestra.

Breitkopf	Luck's	Universal

Concert-Rondo, K.382, D major <1782>   8'

solo piano

1 2 0 0 — 2 2 0 0 — tmp — str

Composed as a new finale for Mozart's *Concerto, Piano, No.5, K.175.* Sometimes listed as *Piano Concerto No.28.*

Breitkopf	Kalmus	Luck's

Concert-Rondo, K.386, A major <1782>   9'

solo piano

0 2 0 1[opt] — 2 0 0 0 — str

Completed by Alan Tyson, Paul Badura-Skoda & Charles Mackerras. Perhaps originally intended as a finale for the piano concerto no.12.

Schott

Contradances, K.267 (271c) <1777>   6'

1 2 0 1 — 2 0 0 0 — str[no va]

No. 1 in G major	1'	
No. 2 in E-flat major	2'	
No. 3 in A major	1'	
No. 4 in D major	2'	

Breitkopf	Kalmus	Luck's

Contradances, K.462 (448b) <1784>   10'

0 2 0 0 — 2 0 0 0 — str[no va]

1. C major	2'	
2. E-flat major	2'	
3. B-flat major	1'	
4. D major	2'	
5. B-flat major	1'	
6. F major	2'	

Breitkopf	Kalmus	Luck's

Contradance, K.535 (La battaille; The Siege of Belgrade) <1788>   2'

1[pic] 0 2[or 2ob] 1 — 0 1 0 0 — 1perc — str[no va]
perc: sd

Escobar edition includes 3 contradances: K.535, K.587, & K.610.

Breitkopf	Escobar

Contradance, K.587 (Der Sieg vom Helden Koburg) <1789>   2'

1 1 0 1 — 0 2 0 0 — str[no va]

Escobar edition includes 3 contradances: K.535, K.587, & K.610.

Breitkopf	Escobar

Contradances, K.603 <1791>   4'

1[pic] 2 0 2 — 2 2 0 0 — tmp — str[no va]
2 dances.
D major   2'
B-flat major   2'

> Bärenreiter

Contradances, K.609 <1791>   7'

1 0 0 0 — 1perc — str[no va]
perc: sd
Snare drum in nos.3-4 only.
No. 1 in C major   1'
No. 2 in E-flat major   1'
No. 3 in D major   1'
No. 4 in C major   3'
Alternativo I (in C major)   _'
Alternativo II (in F major)   _'
Alternative III (in A minor)   _'
No. 5 in G major   1'

> Breitkopf   Kalmus   Luck's   Vieweg

Contradance, K.610, G major (Les filles malicieuses)   2'
<1791>

2 0 0 0 — 2 0 0 0 — str[no va]
Escobar edition includes 3 contradances: K.535, K.587, & K.610.

> Escobar

Così dunque / Aspri rimorsi atroci, K.432 (421a)   5'
<c1982–1783>

bass recitative and aria
2 2 0 2 — 2 0 0 0 — str

> Bärenreiter   Breitkopf   Kalmus   Luck's

Così fan tutte, K.588: Overture <1790>   5'

2 2 2 2 — 2 2 0 0 — tmp — str

> Bärenreiter   Breitkopf   Kalmus   Luck's

Davidde penitente, K.469 <1785>   47'

chorus   solos SST
1 2 1 2 — 2 2 3 0 — tmp — str
Most of the music adapted from the Mass, K.427 (417a).
    The Breitkopf edition, and its Kalmus and Luck's reprints, has a 4th
(soprano) trombone part in the 1st mvt—a part that is probably spurious.

> Bärenreiter   Breitkopf   Kalmus   Luck's

Deutsche Tänze

see his: German Dances

Dite almeno in che mancai, K.479 <1785>   5'

solo quartet: soprano, tenor, 2 basses
0 2 2 2 — 2 0 0 0 — str

> Bärenreiter   Breitkopf

Divertimento [No.1] K.113, E-flat major <1771; rev   14'
1773>

0 4[1.2.Eh1.Eh2] 2 2 — 2 0 0 0 — str
Alternative version: 0 0 2 0 — 2 0 0 0 — str
I. Allegro   4'
II. Andante   5'
III. Menuetto   2'
IV. Allegro   3'

> Breitkopf   Kalmus   Luck's

Divertimento [No.2] K.131, D major <1772>   31'

1 1 0 1 — 4 0 0 0 — str
I. [Allegro]   5'
II. Adagio   6'
III. Menuetto   6'
IV. Allegretto   3'
V. Menuetto   4'
VI. Adagio — Allegro molto   7'

> Breitkopf   Kalmus   Luck's

Divertimenti, K.136, 137, 138 (125a, 125b, 125c) <1772>   38'

str
    K.136 (125a), D major
I. Allegro   6'
II. Andante   6'
III. Presto   3'
    K.137 (125b), B-flat major
I. Andante   5'
II. Allegro di molto   4'
III. Allegro assai   3'
    K.138 (125c), F major
I. Allegro   5'
II. Andante   4'
III. Presto   2'

> Bärenreiter   Kalmus   Luck's   Peters

Divertimento, K.166 (159d), E-flat major <1773>   13'

0 4[1.2.Eh1.Eh2] 2 2 — 2 0 0 0 — [no str]

> Breitkopf   Luck's

Divertimento, K.186 (159b), B-flat major <1773>   12'

0 4[1.2.Eh1.Eh2] 2 2 — 2 0 0 0 — [no str]

> Breitkopf

Divertimento, K.188 (240b), C major <1773>   10'

2 0 0 0 — 0 5 0 0 — tmp — [no str]

> Breitkopf

Divertimento [No.7] K.205 (167a), D major <?1773>   21'

0 0 0 1 — 2 0 0 0 — str[no vn2]
Solo strings may have been intended. The March K.290, *q.v.*, was
intended to accompany this Divertimento.
I. Largo - Allegro   5'
II. Menuetto   3'
III. Adagio   6'
IV. Menuetto   3'
V. Finale: Presto   4'

> Breitkopf   Kalmus   Luck's

Divertimento [No.10] K.247, F major (First Lodron)   31'
<1776>

0 0 0 0 — 2 0 0 0 — str
I. Allegro   8'
II. Andante grazioso   4'
III. Menuetto   4'
IV. Adagio   6'
V. Menuetto   3'
VI. Andante; Allegro assai   6'

> Breitkopf   Kalmus   Luck's

Divertimento [No.11] K.251, D major <1776>   26'

0 1 0 0 — 2 0 0 0 — str
I. Allegro molto   5'
II. Menuetto   4'
III. Andantino - Adagio - Allegretto   4'
IV. Menuetto: Tema con variazione   5'
V. Rondo: Allegro assai   6'
VI. Marcia alla francese   2'

> Breitkopf   Kalmus   Luck's

Divertimento [No.15] K.287 (271h), B-flat major (Second Lodron) <1777>   37'

0 0 0 0 — 2 0 0 0 — str

I. Allegro	7'
II. Thema mit Variationen: Andante grazioso	8'
III. Menuetto	3'
IV. Adagio	8'
V. Menuetto	4'
VI. Andante - Allegro molto	7'

Breitkopf	Kalmus	Luck's

Divertimento [No.17] K.334 (320b), D major (Robinig von Rottenfeld) <1779>   43'

0 0 0 0 — 2 0 0 0 — str

The March, K.445, *q.v.*, is intended to close this Divertimento.

I. Allegro	7'
II. Thema mit Variationen: Andante	8'
III. Menuetto	5'
IV. Adagio	6'
V. Menuetto	8'
VI. Rondo: Allegro	9'

Breitkopf	Kalmus	Luck's

Dixit et Magnificat, K.193 (186g) <1774>   17'

chorus   solos STB

0 0 0 1 — 0 2 3 0 — tmp — org — str

Schirmer

Don Giovanni, K.527: Overture <1787>   7'

2 2 2 2 — 2 2 0 0 — tmp — str

In the opera, the overture leads directly into the first number, thus necessitating a special ending for concert performance. There are three concert-endings:

(1) a 13-bar ending by Mozart himself, though it is unclear whether this ending should be inserted at bar 282 or 286 of the original overture; either option is feasible. A new Breitkopf (ed. Bastiaan Blomhert) allows either possibility; Bärenreiter inserts the special ending at bar 286; Kalmus A6417 (reprint of Peters) starts the insert at bar 282.

(2) a 9-bar ending beginning at bar 275 of the original, attributed to Johann Anton André, though that attribution has been questioned. The "André" ending is found in an earlier Breitkopf edition (reprinted Kalmus A1735).

(3) a more elaborate ending by Ferruccio Busoni, substantially longer, and requiring 3tbn; see subsequent entry.

Bärenreiter	Breitkopf	Kalmus	Luck's

Don Giovanni, K.527: Overture (arr. Busoni) <1787>   9'

2 2 2 2 — 2 2 3 0 — tmp — str

Concert-ending by Ferruccio Busoni, using material from Act I and from the closing scene of the opera.

Kalmus	Luck's

Die Entführung aus dem Serail, K.384 (The Abduction from the Seraglio): Overture (Mozart ending) <1781–1782>   6'

1[1/pic] 2 2 2 — 2 2 0 0 — tmp+3 — str
perc: tri, cym, bd

In the opera the overture elides with the first number, necessitating a concert ending for performance of the overture independently. This edition, ed. Bastiaan Blomhert, employs an ending alleged to have been composed by Mozart himself for the wind-band version of his *Entführung*. Blomhert reorchestrated the wind-band ending to close the original overture.

Breitkopf

Die Entführung aus dem Serail, K.384 (The Abduction from the Seraglio): Overture (André ending) <1781–1782>   6'

1[1/pic] 2 2 2 — 2 2 0 0 — tmp+3 — str
perc: tri, cym, bd

In the opera the overture elides with the first number, necessitating a concert ending for performance of the overture independently. This commonly-used ending was provided by Johann Anton André (1775-1842): composer, music publisher, and generally acknowledged father of Mozart research.

Bärenreiter edition includes the original elided version of the overture (ending inconclusively on the dominant) as well as the André ending.

The Kalmus edition uses the title *Abduction*; Luck's uses *Seraglio*.

Bärenreiter	Breitkopf	Kalmus	Luck's

Die Entführung aus dem Serail, K.384 (The Abduction from the Seraglio): Overture (Busoni ending) <1781–1782>   6'

1[1/pic] 2 2 2 — 2 2 0 0 — tmp+3 — str
perc: tri, cym, bd

In the opera the overture elides with the first number, necessitating a concert ending for performance of the overture independently. This ending is by Feruccio Busoni; both Kalmus and Luck's editions are reprints of an earlier Breitkopf edition.

The Kalmus edition uses the title *Abduction*; Luck's uses *Seraglio*.

Kalmus	Luck's

Die Entführung aus dem Serail: Marsch der Janitscharen (Janissary March) <1781>   2'

2 0 2 2 — 2 2 0 0 — 2perc — [no str]
perc: bd ("Turkish drum"), field dr ("German drum")

Bärenreiter

Ergo interest / Quaere superna, K.143 (73a) <1772–1773>   6'

soprano recitative and aria

org — str

Breitkopf

Exsultate jubilate, K.165 (158a) <1771>   17'

soprano solo

0 2 0 0 — 2 0 0 0 — org — str

I. Exsultate, jubilate	5'
II. Recitative: Fulget amica dies	1'
III. Tu virginum corona	8'
IV. Alleluja!	3'

Bärenreiter	Breitkopf	Kalmus	Luck's	Oxford

Fantasia, K.608, F minor (arr. Harbison) <1791>   10'

1 2 2 2 — 2 0 0 0 — str

Originally for mechanical organ, 1791; arr. 1991 by John Harbison.

AMP

La finta giardiniera, K.196: Overture <1774–1775>   5'

0 2 0 0 — 2 0 0 0 — str

See also his: Symphony, K.196/121, D major.

| I. Allegro molto | 3' |
| II. Andantino grazioso | 2' |

Bärenreiter	Breitkopf	Kalmus	Luck's

La finta semplice, K.51 (46a): Overture <1768>   6'

2 2 0 2 — 2 0 0 0 — str

Drawn from the composer's Symphony No.7, K.45, D major.

I. [Allegro[	3'
II. Andante	2'
III. [Molto allegro]	1'

Bärenreiter	Breitkopf

German Dances, K.509 (Deutsche Tänze) <1787>   17'

3[1.2.flautino] 2 2 2 — 2 2 0 0 — tmp — str[no va]
The *flautino* is not the same instrument as the modern transverse piccolo.

1. D major	_'
2. G major	_'
3. E-flat major	_'
4. F major	_'
5. A major	_'
6. C major	_'

Breitkopf	Kalmus	Luck's

German Dances, K.536 (Deutsche Tänze) <1788>   12'

3[1.2.flautino] 2 0 2 — 2 2 0 0 — tmp — str[no va]
The *flautino* is not the same instrument as the modern transverse piccolo.

1. C major	2'
2. G major	2'
3. B-flat major	2'
4. D major	2'
5. F major	2'
6. F major	2'

Breitkopf

German Dances, K.567 (Deutsche Tänze) <1789>   10'

3[1.2.flautino] 2 2 2 — 2 2 0 0 — tmp/sd — str[no va]
perc: sd (played by tmp)
The *flautino* is not the same instrument as the modern transverse piccolo.

1. B-flat major	1'
2. E-flat major	1'
3. G major	2'
4. D major	2'
5. A major	2'
6. C major	2'

Breitkopf	Kalmus	Luck's

German Dances, K.571 (Deutsche Tänze) <1789>   10'

2[1.2/flautino] 2 2 2 — 2 2 0 0 — tmp+2 — str[no va]
perc: (in no.6 only) cym, sd
6 dances. The *flautino* is not the same instrument as the modern
transverse piccolo.

1. D major	2'
2. A major	1'
3. C major	1'
4. G major	2'
5. B-flat major	2'
6. D major	2'

Breitkopf	Kalmus	Luck's

German Dances, K.586 (Deutsche Tänze) <1789>   23'

3[1.2.flautino] 2 2 2 — 2 2 0 0 — tmp — str[no va]
12 dances. The *flautino* is not the same instrument as the modern
transverse piccolo.

1. C major	2'
2. G major	2'
3. B-flat major	2'
4. F major	2'
5. A major	2'
6. D major	1'
7. G major	2'
8. E-flat major	2'
9. B-flat major	2'
10. F major	2'
11. A major	2'
12. C major	2'

Breitkopf	Kalmus	Luck's

German Dances, K.600 (Deutsche Tänze) <1791>   12'

3[1.2.flautino] 2 2 2 — 2 2 0 0 — tmp — str[no va]
The *flautino* is not the same instrument as the modern transverse piccolo.

1. C major	2'
2. F major	2'
3. B-flat major	2'
4. E-flat major	2'
5. G major (*Der Kanarienvogel*)	2'
6. D major	2'

Breitkopf	Kalmus	Luck's

German Dances, K.602 (Deutsche Tänze) <1791>   8'

3[1.2.flautino] 2 2 2 — 2 2 0 0 — lira — tmp — str[no va]
The *flautino* is not the same instrument as the modern transverse piccolo.

1. B-flat major	2'
2. F major	2'
3. C major (*Der Leiermann*)	2'
4. A major	2'

Breitkopf	Kalmus	Luck's

German Dances, K.605 (Deutsche Tänze) <1791>   7'

2[1.2/flautino] 2 0 2 — 2 4[2tp, 2posthn] 0 0 — tmp/perc — str[no
va]
perc: tuned sleighbells[C5,E5,F5,G5,A5]
The *flautino* is not the same instrument as the modern transverse piccolo.
Posthorns probably played by horn players. Conductor Michael Griffith
suggests the following solution for the tuned sleighbells: use 2 players,
one playing normal untuned sleighbells, while the other plays the
specified sleighbell pitches on glockenspiel, using brass mallets.

1. D major	2'
2. G major	2'
3. C major (*Die Schlittenfahrt*)	3'

Breitkopf	Kalmus	Luck's

Gloria from the Twelfth Mass, K.Anh.C 1.04   4'

chorus
0 2 0 2 — 2 2 0 0 — tmp — str
Spurious; is probably by Wenzel Müller (1759-1835).

Kalmus	Luck's	Schirmer

Ich möchte wohl der Kaiser sein, K.539 <1788>   3'

bass solo
1[pic] 2 0 2 — 2 0 0 0 — 3perc — str

Bärenreiter

Idomeneo, K.366: Overture (original version) <1780–1781>   5'

2 2 2 2 — 2 2 0 0 — tmp — cnt — str
No continuo in Breitkopf or Kalmus edition.

Bärenreiter	Breitkopf	Kalmus	Luck's

Idomeneo, K.366: Overture (with concert-ending) <1780–1781>   5'

2 2 2 2 — 2 2 0 0 — tmp — cnt — str
Concert-ending by Carl Reinecke.

Breitkopf	Kalmus	Luck's

Idomeneo: Ballet Music, K.367 <1780–1781>   23'

2 2 2 2 — 2 2 0 0 — tmp — str
Clarinets in mvt 5 only.
The original opera, K.366, was composed in 1781; ballet music, K.367,
was added for a production in 1786.

Chaconne	10'
Pas seul	4'
Passe-pied	3'
Gavotte	3'
Passacaille	3'

Breitkopf	Kalmus	Luck's

Idomeneo: March, D major [No.8] <1780–1781>   3'
2 2 0 2 — 2 2 0 0 — tmp — str

Breitkopf

Idomeneo: March, C major [No.14] <1780–1781>   3'
2 2 2 2 — 2 2 0 0 — tmp — str

Breitkopf

Idomeneo: March, F major [No.25] <1780–1781>   2'
0 2 0 0 — 0 0 0 0 — str

Breitkopf

The Impresario, K.486
see his: Schauspieldirektor

Inter natos mulierum, K.72 (74f) <1771>   6'
chorus
org — str[no va]

Bärenreiter	Breitkopf	Luck's

Io ti lascio, K.621a <1791>   4'
bass aria
str

Bärenreiter	Kalmus	Luck's

Kirchensonaten
see his: Sonatas, Organ & Strings
Sonatas, Organ & Orchestra

Eine kleine Nachtmusik (Serenade, K.525) <1787>   16'
str
I. Allegro	5'
II. Romance: Andante	5'
III. Menuetto: Allegretto	2'
IV. Rondo: Allegro	4'

Bärenreiter	Breitkopf	Kalmus	Luck's	Peters

Kommet her, ihr frechen Sünder, K.146 (317b) <1770s>   5'
solo soprano
org — str
Sacred aria on the Passion; 3 verses.

Breitkopf

Kyrie, K.341 (368a) <1780–1781>   6'
chorus
2 2 2 2 — 4 2 0 0 — tmp — org — str

Bärenreiter	Breitkopf	Kalmus	Luck's

Laut verkünde unsre Freude, K.623 <1791>   15'
male chorus   solos TTB
1 2 0 0 — 2 0 0 0 — str
I. Chorus: Laut verkünde unsre Freude	4'
II. Recitative	1'
III. Aria: Dieser Gottheit Allnacht ruher	4'
IV. Recitative	1'
V. Duet: Lange sollen dies Mauern	3'
VI. Chorus: Laut verkünde unsre Freude	2'

Bärenreiter	Breitkopf	Kalmus

Litaniae de venerabili altaris sacramento, K.125, B-flat major <1772>   31'
chorus   solos SATB
2 2 0 0 — 2 2 0 0 — org — str
I. Kyrie	4'
II. Panis vivus	5'
III. Verbum caro factum	1'
IV. Hostia sancta	3'
V. Tremendum	1'
VI. Panis omnipotentia	5'
VII. Viaticum	1'
VIII. Pignus	4'
IX. Agnus Dei	7'

Bärenreiter	Kalmus	Luck's

Litaniae de venerabili altaris sacramento, K.243, E-flat major <1776>   33'
chorus   solos SATB
2 2 0 2 — 2 0 3 0 — org — str
I. Kyrie	4'
II. Panis vivus	5'
III. Verbum caro factum	1'
IV. Hostia sancta	4'
V. Tremendum	2'
VI. Dulcissimum convivium	4'
VII. Viaticum	2'
VIII. Pignus	5'
IX. Agnus dei	6'

Breitkopf	Kalmus	Luck's

Litaniae lauretanae, K.109 (74e), B-flat major (Litaniae de Beata Virgine) <1771>   10'
chorus   solos SATB
org — str[no va]

Breitkopf	Kalmus	Luck's

Litaniae lauretanae, K.195 (186d), D major (Litaniae de Beata Virgine) <1774>   27'
chorus   solos SATB
0 2 0 0 — 2 0 0 0 — org — str
Kyrie	6'
Sancta Maria	7'
Salus infirmorum	3'
Regina angelorum	5'
Agnus Dei	6'

Breitkopf	Kalmus	Luck's

Lucio Silla, K.135: Overture <1772>   9'
0 2 0 0 — 2 2 0 0 — tmp — str

Bärenreiter	Breitkopf	Kalmus	Luck's

Ma che vi fece / Sperai vicino il lido, K.368 <1779>   9'
soprano recitative and aria
2 0 0 2 — 2 0 0 0 — str

Bärenreiter	Breitkopf	Luck's

The Magic Flute, K.620
see his: Zauberflöte

Mandina amabile, K.480 <1785>   5'
trio for soprano, tenor, & bass
2 2 2 2 — 2 0 0 0 — str

Bärenreiter	Breitkopf	Kalmus	Luck's

March, K.62, D major <1769>   4'

0 2 0 0 — 2 2 0 0 — tmp — str
Believed to have been intended as an introduction to the Serenade, K.100 (62a).

Deutscher

March, K.189 (167b), D major <1773>   5'

2 0 0 0 — 2 2 0 0 — str[no va]
Used as introduction to the Serenade, K.185 (167a). The Bärenreiter edition of the serenade includes the march.

Deutscher	Kalmus	Luck's

March, K.214, C major <1775>   4'

0 2 0 0 — 2 2 0 0 — str

Deutscher	Kalmus	Luck's

March, K.215 (213b), D major <1775>   4'

0 2 0 0 — 2 2 0 0 — str
Used as introduction to the Serenade, K.204 (213a).

Deutscher

March, K.237 (189c), D major <1774>   4'

0 2 0 2 — 2 2 0 0 — str[no va]
Used as introduction to the Serenade, K.203 (189b). The Bärenreiter edition of the serenade includes the march.

Deutscher

March, K.248, F major <1776>   5'

0 0 0 0 — 2 0 0 0 — str

Deutscher

March, K.249, D major <1776>   4'

0 2 0 2 — 2 2 0 0 — str
Used as introduction to the Serenade, K.250 (248b), "Haffner." The Bärenreiter edition of the serenade includes the march.

Deutscher	Kalmus	Luck's

March, K.290 (167AB), D major <1772>   4'

0 0 0 0 — 2 0 0 0 — str[no vn2]
Intended to accompany the Divertimento, K.205 (167A).

Deutscher

Marches, K.335 (320a), D major <1779>   8'

2 2 0 0 — 2 2 0 0 — str
Oboes appear in the 1st march only; flutes only in the 2nd march.
   These two marches are used as the introduction and conclusion, respectively, of Serenade no.9, K.320. The Bärenreiter edition of the serenade includes the two marches.
No.1   4'
No.2   4'

Deutscher

Marches, K.408 (383e, 385a, 383F) <1782>   12'

2 2 0 2 — 2 2 0 0 — tmp — str
No.2, K.385a, was originally intended as the introduction to the abortive serenade which became Symphony No.35 (Haffner).
No.1, K.383e, C major   5'
No.2, K.385a, D major   3'
No.3, K.383F, C major   4'

Deutscher	Kalmus

March, K.445 (320c), D major <1780>   4'

0 0 0 0 — 2 0 0 0 — str
Intended to close the Divertimento, K.334 (320b).

Deutscher

March, K.544, D major <1788>   4'

1 0 0 0 — 1 0 0 0 — str[no vn2]

Deutscher

The Marriage of Figaro, K.492

see his: Nozze di Figaro

Masonic Funeral Music

see his: Maurische Trauermusik

Mass

see also: Missa brevis

Mass, K.66, C major (Dominicus) <1769>   41'

chorus   solos SATB
2 2 0 0 — 2 4 0 0 — tmp — org — str
Probably in Mozart's time 2 woodwind players alternated on flute and oboe in this work. Bärenreiter and Breitkopf editions include 3 *colla parte* trombones.

Bärenreiter	Breitkopf	Kalmus	Luck's

Mass, K.139 (47a), C minor (Waisenhaus; Orphanage) <1768>   45'

chorus   solos SATB
0 2 0 0 — 0 4 3 0 — tmp — org — str

Bärenreiter	Breitkopf

Mass, K.167, C major (Trinity) <1773>   30'

chorus
0 2 0 0 — 0 2 2 0 — tmp — org — str[no va]
Trombone parts were originally for trumpet in C basso. The Bärenreiter edition calls for 4 trumpets and 3 *colla parte* trombones.
I. Kyrie   3'
II. Gloria   4'
III. Credo   13'
IV. Sanctus   1'
V. Benedictus   4'
VI. Agnus Dei   5'

Bärenreiter	Breitkopf	Kalmus	Luck's

Mass, K.257, C major (Credo-Messe) <1776>   26'

chorus   solos SATB
0 2 0 0 — 0 2 3 0 — tmp — org — str[no va]
I. Kyrie   2'
II. Gloria   3'
III. Credo   8'
IV. Sanctus   2'
V. Benedictus   5'
VI. Agnus Dei   6'

Bärenreiter	Breitkopf

Mass, K.258, C major (Spaur-Messe; Piccolomini)   *17'*
<?1775 >

chorus   solos SATB

0 2 0 0 — 0 2 3 0 — tmp — org — str[no va]

The autograph score of this mass does not include the oboes or *colla parte* trombones. However, 2 oboe parts in Mozart's hand are in existence. Different editions call for different winds:

    Bärenreiter: as above
    Breitkopf: 0 0 0 0 — 0 2 3 0
    Kalmus & Luck's: 0 0 0 0 — 0 2 0 0

I. Kyrie	*2'*
II. Gloria	*3'*
III. Credo	*6'*
IV. Sanctus	*1'*
V. Benedictus	*2'*
VI. Agnus Dei	*3'*

Bärenreiter	Breitkopf	Kalmus	Luck's

Mass, K.262 (246a), C major (Longa) <1775; rev c1777>   *30'*

chorus   solos SATB

0 2 0 0 — 2 2 3 0 — tmp — org — str[no va]

I. Kyrie	*3'*
II. Gloria	*6'*
III. Credo	*13'*
IV. Sanctus	*1'*
V. Benedictus	*3'*
VI. Agnus Dei	*4'*

Bärenreiter	Breitkopf

Mass, K.317, C major (Coronation) <1779>   *24'*

chorus   solos SATB

0 2 0 1 — 2 2 3 0 — tmp — org — str[no va]

I. Kyrie	*3'*
II. Gloria	*4'*
III. Credo	*6'*
IV. Sanctus	*2'*
V. Benedictus	*3'*
VI. Agnus Dei	*6'*

Bärenreiter	Breitkopf	Kalmus	Luck's

Mass, K.337, C major (Missa solemnis; Aulica) <1780>   *22'*

chorus   solos SATB

0 2 0 2 — 0 2 3 0 — tmp — org — str[no va]

Kyrie	*3'*
Gloria	*3'*
Credo	*5'*
Sanctus	*2'*
Benedictus	*3'*
Agnus Dei	*6'*

Bärenreiter	Breitkopf	Kalmus	Luck's

MASS, K.427 (417a), C MINOR (THE GREAT) <1782–1783>

This work was unfinished at its first performance in 1783. Various attempts to complete it are listed below in chronological order. The very earliest attempted completion, by Johann Anton André (1840) is not in print.

Mass, K.427 (417a), C minor (Schmitt) <1782–1783>   *75'*

chorus   solos S Ms T B

2 2 2 2 — 2 2 4 0 — tmp — org — str

Ed. Alois Schmitt, 1901.

    Mozart's unfinished score does not constitute a liturgically complete mass; Schmitt attempted to complete it by substituting movements from other works of Mozart: K.139, 262, 322, 333, 337, and K.Anh.21 (= K.Anh.A2 = K.93c; this movement, wrongly attributed to Mozart, is actually by Ernst Eberlin). Schmitt also adapted the opening *Kyrie* to form a final *Agnus Dei*.

Breitkopf	Kalmus

Mass, K.427 (417a), C minor (Robbins Landon)   *56'*
<1782–1783>

chorus   solos SSTB

1 2 0 2 — 2 2 3 0 — tmp — org — str

Ed. H.C. Robbins Landon, 1956.

    Individual movements have been reconstructed by the editor, but no movements have been added.

    Parts for this version do not always agree in all details with the score.

Kyrie	*6'*
Gloria in excelsis	*3'*
Laudamus te	*5'*
Gratias	*1'*
Domine	*3'*
Qui tollis	*6'*
Quoniam	*5'*
Jesu Christe - Cum sancto spiritu	*5'*
Credo in unum Deum	*3'*
Et incarnatus	*8'*
Sanctus	*4'*
Benedictus	*7'*

Peters

Mass, K.427 (417a), C minor (Holl & Köhler)   *56'*
<1782–1783>

chorus   solos SSATB

1 2 0 2 — 2 2 3 0 — tmp — org — str

Ed. Monika Holl in collaboration with Karl-Heinz Köhler, 1987. *Credo in unum deum, Et incarnatus est, Sanctus,* and *Hosanna* reconstructed and completed by Helmut Eder.

Kyrie	*6'*
Gloria in excelsis	*3'*
Laudamus te	*5'*
Gratias	*1'*
Domine	*3'*
Qui tollis	*6'*
Quoniam	*5'*
Jesu Christe - Cum sancto spiritu	*5'*
Credo in unum Deum	*3'*
Et incarnatus	*8'*
Sanctus	*4'*
Benedictus	*7'*

Bärenreiter

Mass, K.427 (417a), C minor (Beyer) <1782–1783>   *62'*

chorus   solos SSATB

1 2 0 2 — 2 2 3 0 — tmp — org — str

Ed. Franz Beyer, 1989. A piano-vocal score of this edition is available from Peters.

    Beyer's completion is relatively conservative; it is mainly distinguished by the repetition of the *Kyrie* music at the end of the mass, retexted as an *Agnus Dei.*

Kyrie	*6'*
Gloria	*3'*
Laudamus te	*5'*
Gratias	*1'*
Domine Deus	*3'*
Qui tollis	*6'*
Quoniam	*5'*
Jesu Christe - Cum sancto spiritu	*5'*
Credo	*3'*
Et incarnatus	*8'*
Sanctus	*4'*
Benedictus	*7'*
Agnus Dei	*6'*

Amadeus

Mass, K.427 (417a), C minor (Maunder) <1782–1783>   *55'*

Solos SSTB   double chorus

1 2 0 2 — 2 2 3 0 — tmp — org — str

Ed. & reconstructed by Richard Maunder, 1990. The introduction to this edition has a particularly good history of the work and its various completions.

Oxford	Carus

Mass, K.427 (417a), C minor (Levin) <1782–1783>   75'

Solos SSTB   double chorus
1 2 0 2 — 2 2 3 0 — tmp — org — str
Completed and edited by Robert D. Levin, 2005, using hitherto unused
sketch material from 1783, as well as music adapted from the cantata
Davidde penitente, K.469, for which Mozart had already adapted music
from the Kyrie and Gloria of K.427.
    KYRIE
1. *Kyrie (Solo Soprano, Chorus)*   7'
    GLORIA
2. *Gloria (Chorus)*   2'
3. *Laudamus te (Solo Soprano)*   5'
4. *Gratias (Chorus)*   1'
5. *Domine (Duet)*   3'
6. *Qui tollis (Double Chorus)*   4'
7. *Quoniam (Trio)*   4'
8. *Jesu Christe (Chorus & Trio)*   5'
    CREDO
9. *Credo (Chorus)*   3'
10. *Et incarnatus est (Solo Soprano)*   9'
11. *Crucifixus (Chorus)*   4'
12. *Et resurrexit (Chorus)*   3'
13. *Et in Spiritum Sanctum (Solo Tenor)*   4'
14. *Et unam sanctam (Chorus)*   2'
15. *Et vitam venturi (Chorus)*   3'
    SANCTUS
16. *Sanctus (Double Chorus)*   3'
    BENEDICTUS
17. *Benedictus (Quartet, Double Chorus)*   5'
    AGNUS DEI
18. *Agnus Dei (Solo Soprano, Chorus)*   4'
19. *Dona nobis pacem (Solo Quartet, Chorus)*   4'

| Carus | | | |

Mass, K.427 (417a), C minor : Agnus Dei (Rodriguez)   9'

Composed in 2006 for use as the final missing movement of K.427,
though not in the style of Mozart.

see: Rodriguez, Robert Xavier
    Agnus Dei

| | | | |

Die Maurerfreude, K.471 (Sehen, wie dem starren   7'
Forscherauge die Natur) <1785>

tenor solo   male chorus
0 2 1 0 — 2 0 0 0 — str

| Breitkopf | Kalmus | Luck's |

Maurerische Trauermusik, K.477 (479a) (Masonic   6'
Funeral Music) <1785>

0 2 1 0 — 2 0 0 0 — basset hn — str
Original version given above. The composer later provided 2 additional
basset horn parts in lieu of the horns, and added a part for *Gran Fagotto*,
which may or may not have been intended for contrabassoon, thus
arriving at:
    0 2 1 1[cbn?] — 3 basset hn — str

| Bärenreiter | Breitkopf | Kalmus | Luck's |

Mentre ti lascio, o figlia, K.513 <1787>   8'

bass aria
1 0 2 2 — 2 0 0 0 — str

| Bärenreiter | Breitkopf | Kalmus | Luck's |

Mia speranza / Ah, non sai, K.416 <1783>   10'

soprano scene and rondo
0 2 0 2 — 2 0 0 0 — str

| Bärenreiter | Breitkopf | Kalmus | Luck's |

Minuet, K.409 (338f), C major <1782>   5'

2 2 0 2 — 2 2 0 0 — tmp — str
This minuet is believed by some to belong to Symphony No.34, which,
however, does not have flutes in the orchestration.

| Breitkopf | Kalmus | Luck's |

Misera, dove son / Ah, non son io che parlo, K.369   7'
<1781>

soprano recitative and aria
2 0 0 0 — 2 0 0 0 — str

| Bärenreiter | Breitkopf | Kalmus | Luck's |

Misericordias domini, K.222 (205a) <1775>   6'

chorus
org — str

| Bärenreiter | Kalmus | Luck's |

Misero, o sogno / Aura, che intorno spiri, K.431 (425b)   10'
<1783>

tenor recitative and aria
2 0 0 2 — 2 0 0 0 — str

| Bärenreiter | Breitkopf | Kalmus | Luck's |

Missa brevis, K.49 (47d), G major <1768>   18'

chorus   solos SATB
org — str
Bärenreiter, Breitkopf & Kalmus editions include 3 *colla parte*
trombones.

| Bärenreiter | Breitkopf | Kalmus | Luck's |

Missa brevis, K.65 (61a), D minor <1769>   15'

chorus   solos SATB
0 0 0 0 — 0 0 3 0 — org — str[no va]
Kalmus edition does not include the 3 *colla parte* trombones.

| Bärenreiter | Breitkopf | Kalmus | Luck's |

Missa brevis, K.140 (Anh.C1.12), G major <?>   15'

chorus   solos SATB
org — str[no va]
Bärenreiter, Breitkopf and Luck's editions include 3 *colla parte*
trombones.
    The authenticity of this work is doubtful.

| Bärenreiter | Breitkopf | Luck's |

Missa brevis, K.192 (186f), F major <1774>   25'

chorus   solos SATB
0 0 0 0 — 0 2[added later] 0 0 — org — str[no va]
The Bärenreiter edition shows also 3 trombones, in keeping with
18th-century *colla parte* practice for choral music.

| Bärenreiter | Breitkopf | Kalmus | Luck's | Schirmer |

Missa brevis, K.194 (186h), D major <1774>   22'

chorus   solos SATB
org — str[no va]
Bärenreiter and Breitkopf editions include 3 *colla parte* trombones.

| Bärenreiter | Breitkopf | Kalmus | Luck's |

Missa brevis, K.220 (196b), C major (Spatzenmesse;   20'
Sparrow Mass) <1775–1777>

chorus   solos SATB
0 0 0 0 — 0 2 0 0 — tmp — org — str[no va]
Bärenreiter and Breitkopf editions include 3 *colla parte* trombones.

| Bärenreiter | Breitkopf | Kalmus | Luck's |

Missa brevis, K.259, C major (Orgelsolo) <1776>   *14'*

chorus   solos SATB
0 0 0 0 — 0 2 0 0 — tmp — org — str[no va]
Bärenreiter and Breitkopf editions include 3 *colla parte* trombones.

Bärenreiter	Breitkopf	Kalmus	Luck's	Peters

Missa brevis, K.275 (272b), B-flat major <1777>   *20'*

chorus   solos SATB
org — str[no va]
Bärenreiter edition includes 3 *colla parte* trombones.

Kyrie	2'
Gloria	3'
Credo	5'
Sanctus	1'
Benedictus	3'
Agnus Dei	6'

Bärenreiter	Breitkopf	Kalmus	Peters

Mitridate, K.87 (74a): Overture <1770>   *6'*

2 2 0 0 — 2 0 0 0 — str

Allegro	2'
Andante grazioso	2'
Presto	2'

Breitkopf	Luck's

Un moto di gioia, K.579 <1789>   *2'*

solo soprano
1 1 0 1 — 2 0 0 0 — str
Intended as a substitute for the aria *Veniti inginocchiatevi*, in the
composer's *Nozze di Figaro*.

Breitkopf	Kalmus	Luck's

Ein musikalischer Spass, K.522 (A Musical Joke) <1787>   *18'*

0 0 0 0 — 2 0 0 0 — str 5t

I. Allegro	3'
II. Menuetto maestoso	5'
III. Adagio cantabile	6'
IV. Presto	4'

Breitkopf	Kalmus	Luck's	Peters

Nehmt meinen Dank, K.383 <1782>   *4'*

soprano solo
1 1 0 1 — str

Bärenreiter	Breitkopf	Kalmus	Luck's

No, no, che non sei capace, K.419 <1783>   *4'*

soprano aria
0 2 0 0 — 2 2 0 0 — tmp — str

Bärenreiter	Breitkopf	Kalmus	Luck's

Notturno, K.286 (269a)

see his: Serenade No.8, K.286 (269a), D major

Le nozze di Figaro, K.492: Overture <1785–1786>   *4'*

2 2 2 2 — 2 2 0 0 — tmp — str

Bärenreiter	Breitkopf	Kalmus	Luck's

Nun liebes Weibchen, ziehst mit mir, K.625 (592a) <1790>   *2'*

duet for soprano and bass
1 2 0 2 — 2 0 0 0 — str
Arrangement by Mozart of a duet with keyboard accompaniment; the
original possibly by Mozart, but more likely not.

Kalmus	Luck's

Ombra felice / Io ti lascio, K.255 <1776>   *8'*

alto recitative and aria
0 2 0 0 — 2 0 0 0 — str

Bärenreiter	Breitkopf	Kalmus	Kneusslin	Luck's

Overture, K.311a (Anh.C11.05), B-flat major (Paris)   *10'*

2 2 2 2 — 2 2 0 0 — tmp — str
Authenticity doubtful.

Luck's	Peters

Per pietà, non ricercate, K.420 <1783>   *6'*

tenor aria
0 0 2 2 — 2 0 0 0 — str

Bärenreiter	Breitkopf	Kalmus	Luck's

Per questa bella mano, K.612 <1791>   *8'*

bass aria with obligato double bass
1 2 0 2 — 2 0 0 0 — str

Bärenreiter	Breitkopf	Doblinger	Kalmus	Luck's

Les Petits Riens, K.Anh.10 (299b) <1778>   *22'*

2 2 2 2 — 2 2 0 0 — tmp — str
21 brief movements for a pantomime, not all of them by Mozart. Using
the numbering of the Neue Mozart-Ausgabe, the categories are:
    Authentic Mozart: Overture, Nos.9, 10, 11, 12, 15, 16, 18
    Possibly by Mozart: Nos.4, 5, 7, 8, 13, 14, 17
    Not by Mozart: Nos.1, 2, 3, 6, 19, 20

Bärenreiter	Breitkopf	Kalmus	Luck's

Popoli di Tessaglia / Io non chiedo, eterni dei, K.316 (300b) <1778–1779>   *11'*

soprano recitative and aria
0 1 0 1 — 2 0 0 0 — str

Bärenreiter	Breitkopf	Luck's

Il ré pastore, K.208: Overture <1775>   *4'*

0 2 0 0 — 2 2 0 0 — str

Breitkopf	Kalmus	Luck's

Regina coeli, K.108 (74d), C major <1771>   *15'*

chorus   solo soprano
2 2 0 0 — 2 2 0 0 — tmp — org — str

Breitkopf	Carus

Regina coeli, K.127, B-flat major <1772>   *15'*

chorus   solo soprano
2 2 0 0 — 2 0 0 0 — org — str

Breitkopf

Regina coeli, K.276 (321b), C major <late 1770s>   *7'*

chorus   solos SATB
0 2 0 0 — 0 2 0 0 — tmp — org — str[no va]

Breitkopf	Kalmus	Luck's

REQUIEM, K.626 <1791>

This work was left incomplete upon the composer's death. The completion of the work by Mozart's pupil, Franz Xaver Süssmayr, was accepted for nearly two centuries as the standard version. More recently, attempts have been made to improve upon Süssmayr, and/or return to Mozart's original intention.

In addition to the versions listed herewith, others are in preparation and will doubtless become available in time.

Requiem, K.626 (Süssmayr) <late 1791>   48'

chorus   solos SATB
0 0 0 2 — 0 2 3 0 — 2basset hns — tmp — org — str
Basset horns may be replaced by clarinets.
    Completed by Mozart's pupil Franz Xaver Süssmayr.

I. Introitus - Requiem	6'
II. Kyrie	3'
III. Sequenz	
Dies irae	2'
Tuba mirum	4'
Rex tremendae	2'
Recordare	5'
Confutatis	2'
Lacrimosa	5'
IV. Offertorium	
Domine Jesu	4'
Hostias	4'
V. Sanctus	2'
VI. Benedictus	6'
VII. Agnus Dei	3'
VIII. Communio	3'

Bärenreiter	Breitkopf	Kalmus	Luck's	Peters

Requiem, K.626 (Robbins Landon) <late 1791>   50'

chorus   solos SATB
0 0 0 2 — 0 2 3 0 — 2basset hns — tmp — org — str
Mozart's fragment supplemented by Joseph Eybler and Franz Xaver Süssmayr; completed and edited by H.C. Robbins Landon, 1991.

I. Introitus - Requiem	6'
II. Kyrie	3'
III. Sequenz	
Dies irae	2'
Tuba mirum	4'
Rex tremendae	2'
Recordare	5'
Confutatis	2'
Lacrimosa	5'
IV. Offertorium	
Domine Jesu	4'
Hostias	4'
V. Sanctus	2'
VI. Benedictus	6'
VII. Agnus Dei	3'
VIII. Communio	3'

Breitkopf

Requiem, K.626 (Beyer) <late 1791>   48'

chorus   solos SATB
0 0 0 2 — 0 2 3 0 — 2basset hns — tmp — org — str
Described as a reorchestration, but actually much more than that. Franz Beyer left the voice parts unchanged from the traditional Süssmayr version, but attempted to improve the rest of the texture and voice-leading. Though both Eulenburg (1971) and Kunzelmann (1979) editions are by Beyer, and are very similar, there are a few differences in detail. Kunzelmann edition offers clarinet parts as alternatives to basset horns.

I. Introitus - Requiem	6'
II. Kyrie	3'
III. Sequenz	
Dies irae	2'
Tuba mirum	4'
Rex tremendae	2'
Recordare	5'
Confutatis	2'
Lacrimosa	5'
IV. Offertorium	
Domine Jesu	4'
Hostias	4'
V. Sanctus	2'
VI. Benedictus	6'
VII. Agnus Dei	3'
VIII. Communio	3'

Eulenburg	Kunzelmann

Requiem, K.626 (Maunder) <late 1791>   44'

chorus   solos SATB
0 0 0 2 — 0 2 3 0 — 2basset hns — tmp — org — str
    Richard Maunder (1988) starts from Mozart's autograph, using none of Süssmayr's contributions. Orchestration reworked throughout. *Lacrymosa* has new continuation which leads to a completion of Mozart's sketch for an *Amen* fugue. (Süssmayr's *Sanctus* and *Benedictus* are included as appendices.)
    Maunder's related book, *Mozart's Requiem: On Preparing a New Edition* (Oxford, 1988), appeared simultaneously with the edition.
    Carus materials for sale; Oxford for rental only.

Carus	Oxford

Requiem, K.626 (Levin) <late 1791>   46'

chorus   solos SATB
0 0 2[2cl/2basset hns] 2 — 0 2 3 0 — tmp — org — str
Robert Levin (1994) provides an *Amen* fugue, and makes many changes in orchestration and structure.
    Clarinets play only in the *Sanctus* and the two iterations of the *Hosanna*; the bulk of the Requiem is for basset horn. Alternative clarinet parts are provided to be used in the absence of basset horns.

Requiem	5'
Kyrie	2'
Dies irae	2'
Tuba mirum	3'
Rex tremendae	2'
Recordare	5'
Confutatis	2'
Lacrimosa	4'
Domine Jesu	3'
Hostias	3'
Sanctus	2'
Benedictus	5'
Agnus Dei	3'
Lux aeterna	3'
Cum sanctis	2'

Hänssler

Requiem, K.626 (Druce) <1791>   50'

chorus   solos SATB
0 0 0 2 — 0 2 3 0 — 2basset hns — tmp — org — str
Duncan Druce edition commissioned 1984, but not published until 1993. Includes more changes and newly composed music than any other recent version. Clarinet parts are available as alternatives to basset horns.

Novello

Rivolgete a lui lo sguardo, K.584 <1789>   5'

bass aria
0 2 0 2 — 0 2 0 0 — tmp — str

Breitkopf

Rondo, Flute & Orchestra, K.373 (Anh.184), D major <1781>   5'

solo flute
0 2 0 0 — 2 0 0 0 — str
Arrangement (and transposition), by an unknown hand, of Mozart's
Rondo, Violin & Orchestra, K.373, C major.

Heinrichshofen	Luck's

Rondo, Horn & Orchestra, K.371, E-flat major

see his: Concert-Rondo, Horn & Orchestra, K.371, E-flat major

Rondo, Piano & Orchestra, K.382, D major <1782>

see his: Concert-Rondo, Piano & Orchestra, K.382, D major

Rondo, Violin & Orchestra, K.269 (261a), B-flat major <1776>   8'

0 2 0 0 — 2 0 0 0 — str

Breitkopf	Kalmus	Luck's

Rondo, Violin & Orchestra, K.373, C major <1781>   4'

0 2 0 0 — 2 0 0 0 — str

Breitkopf	Kalmus	Luck's

Sancta Maria, K.273 <1777>   4'

chorus
org — str

Bärenreiter	Breitkopf	Kalmus	Luck's

Scande coeli limina, K.34 (Offertorium in festo St. Benedicti) <early 1767>   5'

chorus   solo soprano
0 0 0 0 — 0 2 0 0 — tmp — org — str[no va]
Authenticity doubtful.

Breitkopf

Der Schauspieldirektor, K.486 (The Impresario): Overture <1786>   5'

2 2 2 2 — 2 2 0 0 — tmp — str

Breitkopf	Kalmus	Luck's

Se al labbro mio non credi, K.295 <1778>   9'

tenor aria
2 2 0 2 — 2 0 0 0 — str

Bärenreiter	Breitkopf	Luck's

Serenade No.1, K.100 (62a), D major <1769>   27'

2 2 0 0 — 2 2 0 0 — str
The 2 flutes are used in a single movement only, where the oboes are
tacet. (Probably in Mozart's time the oboists doubled on flute.)
    The March, K.62, is believed to have been intended as an introduction
to this serenade.
  I. Allegro   4'
  II. Andante   6'
  III. Menuetto   2'
  IV. Allegro   3'
  V. Menuetto   3'
  VI. Andante   4'
  VII. Menuetto   2'
  VIII. Allegro   3'

Breitkopf	Kalmus	Luck's

Serenade No.2, K.101 (250a), F major <1776>   6'

1 2 0 1 — 2 0 0 0 — str[no va]
Four contradances.
  I. [Contredanse]   1'
  II. Andantino   2'
  III. Presto   2'
  IV. Gavotte   1'

Breitkopf	Kalmus	Luck's

Serenade No.3, K.185 (167a), D major (Andretter) <1773>   37'

2 2 0 0 — 2 2 0 0 — str
The March, K189 (167b), is used as an introduction to this serenade; the
Bärenreiter edition includes the march (an extra 5').
  I. Allegro assai   6'
  II. Andante   8'
  III. Allegro   3'
  IV. Menuetto   3'
  V. Andante grazioso   6'
  VI. Menuetto   5'
  VII. Adagio - Allegro assai   6'

Bärenreiter	Breitkopf	Kalmus	Luck's

Serenade No.4, K.203 (189b), D major <1774>   41'

solo violin
2 2 0 1 — 2 2 0 0 — str
Solo violin printed in ripieno part. The March, K.237 (189c), is used as
an introduction to this serenade; the Bärenreiter edition includes the
march (an extra 4').
  I. Andante maestoso - Allegro assai   7'
  II. Andante   6'
  III. Menuetto   3'
  IV. Allegro   6'
  V. Menuetto   4'
  VI. Andante   5'
  VII. Menuetto   5'
  VIII. Prestissimo   5'

Bärenreiter	Breitkopf	Kalmus	Luck's

Serenade No.5, K.204 (213a), D major <1775>   39'

2 2 0 1 — 2 2 0 0 — str
The March, K.215 (213b), is used as an introduction to this serenade.
Movements 1, 5, 6, & 7 are used as the Symphony, K.204 (231a).
  I. Allegro assai   6'
  II. Andante moderato   8'
  III. Allegro   6'
  IV. Menuetto   3'
  V. Andantino   6'
  VI. Menuetto   4'
  VII. Andantino grazioso - Allegro   6'

Breitkopf	Kalmus	Luck's

Serenade No.6, K.239, D major (Serenata notturna) <1776>   13'

solos: 2vn, va, db

tmp — str 4t [2vn, va, vc; no db], *or* str orch

Commonly available editions of this work show 2 solo violins with accompaniment for timpani and string orchestra. This is a misrepresentation of the basic double-string-group structure. These editions also may indicate a solo cello doubling the solo double bass; this doubling is spurious.

     If performed with single players on each part, the combined string count, including soloists, would be 2.2.2.1.1.

I. Marcia maestoso	4'
II. Menuetto	4'
III. Rondo: Allegretto - Adagio - Allegro	5'

Bärenreiter	Breitkopf	Kalmus	Luck's

Serenade No.7, K.250 (248b), D major (Haffner) <1776>   54'

2 2 0 2 — 2 2 0 0 — str

The March, K.249, is used as an introduction to this serenade; the Bärenreiter edition includes the march (an extra 4').

     Three of the 8 movements (2. *Andante*, 3. *Menuetto*, 4. *Rondeau*) constitute a mini-concerto, complete with cadenza and *Eingänge*, for the concertmaster.

     The remaining movements (nos. 1, 5, 6, 7 & 8) are used (with timpani part added by Leopold Mozart) as the Symphony, K.250 (248b). The latter is *not*, however, the "Haffner" Symphony (K.385).

I. Allegro maestoso - Allegro molto	7'
II. Andante	12'
III. Menuetto	4'
IV. Rondo: Allegro	8'
V. Menuetto galante	6'
VI. Andante	8'
VII. Menuetto	6'
VIII. Adagio - Allegro assai	7'

Bärenreiter	Breitkopf	Kalmus	Luck's

Serenade No.8, K.286 (269a), D major (Notturno) <1776–1777>   19'

0 0 0 0 — 8 0 0 0 — str

4 orchestras, each consisting of 2hn & str.

I. Andante	9'
II. Allegretto grazioso	3'
III. Menuetto	7'

Breitkopf	Kalmus	Luck's

Serenade No.9, K.320, D major (Posthorn) <1779>   40'

2[1.2/pic] 2 0 2 — 2 2 0 0 — posthorn — tmp — str

Posthorn may be covered by one of the other brass players.

     The two marches, K.335 (320a) *q.v.*, are used as introduction and conclusion, respectively, to this serenade; the Bärenreiter edition includes the two marches (an extra 4' each).

     Movements 1, 5 & 7 are used as Symphony, K.320.

I. Adagio maestoso - Allegro con spirito	8'
II. Menuetto: Allegretto	4'
III. Concertante: Andante grazioso	8'
IV. Rondo: Allegro ma non troppo	6'
V. Andantino	5'
VI. Menuetto	5'
VII. Finale: Presto	4'

Bärenreiter	Breitkopf	Kalmus	Luck's

Serenade No.10, K.361 (370a), B-flat major (Gran partita) <1783–1784>   43'

0 2 2 3[1.2.cbn] — 4 0 0 0 — 2basset horns — [no str]

Double bass may substitute for contrabassoon. 3rd & 4th clarinet parts are provided as alternatives to basset horns.

     Bärenreiter edition by Daniel N. Leeson & Neal Zaslaw; Henle ed. Henrik Wiese.

I. Largo - Allegro Molto	7'
II. Menuetto	9'
III. Adagio	5'
IV. Menuetto: Allegretto	5'
V. Romanze: Adagio - Allegretto - Adagio	5'
VI. Thema mit Variationen	9'
VII. Rondo: Allegro molto	3'

Bärenreiter	Breitkopf	Henle	Kalmus	Luck's

Serenade No.11, K.375, E-flat major <1781>   24'

0 2 2 2 — 2 0 0 0 — [no str]

An earlier version without oboes also exists.

I. Allegro maestoso	8'
II. Menuetto I	4'
III. Adagio	6'
IV. Menuetto II	6'
V. Allegro	3'

Breitkopf	Kalmus	Luck's

Serenade No.12, K.388 (384a), C minor (Nachtmusik) <1782–1783>   21'

0 2 2 2 — 2 0 0 0 — [no str]

I. Allegro	6'
II. Andante	4'
III. Menuetto in canone	4'
IV. Allegro	7'

Breitkopf	Kalmus	Luck's

Serenade K.525, G major

see his: Kleine Nachtmusik

Si mostra la sorte, K.209 <1775>   3'

tenor aria

2 0 0 0 — 2 0 0 0 — str

Bärenreiter	Breitkopf

Sinfonia concertante, K.297b (Anh. C14.01), E-flat major <1778>   32'

soloists: oboe, clarinet, horn, bassoon

0 2 0 0 — 2 0 0 0 — str

The authenticity of this well-known work is in question; it is believed to be an arrangement by another hand of a lost Mozart composition for flute, oboe, horn, and bassoon.

I. Allegro	14'
II. Adagio	9'
III. Andantino con variationi	9'

Breitkopf	Kalmus	Luck's

Sinfonia concertante, K.297b (Anh. I/9), E-flat major (Levin reconstruction) <1778>   30'

solos: flute, oboe, horn, bassoon

0 2 0 0 — 2 0 0 0 — str

A reconstruction by Robert D. Levin of the hypothetical original. The music of the solo quartet has been adapted to the changed instrumentation, and the orchestral tuttis and accompaniments have been recomposed. The score includes the solo quartet parts of the "standard version" (K.Anh. C14.01) for comparison.

Allegro	10'
Adagio	7'
Andantino con variazioni	13'

Bärenreiter

Sinfonia concertante, K.364 (320d), E-flat major <1779>   30'

solo violin, solo viola
0 2 0 0 — 2 0 0 0 — str
Solo viola part originally notated in D major, with the intention that the instrument be tuned a half-step higher than normal, the extra string tension compensating for the lesser brilliance of the viola *vis-à-vis* the violin. Bärenreiter includes parts for the solo viola either in D major (using scordatura), or in E-flat major (using normal tuning).

I. Allegro maestoso	*13'*
II. Andante	*11'*
III. Presto	*6'*

Bärenreiter	Breitkopf	Kalmus	Luck's

Il sogno di Scipione, K.126

see his: Symphony, K.141a, D major

SONATAS, ORGAN & ORCHESTRA (Church Sonatas; Kirchensonaten)

Certain of the sonatas, from Kalmus (*Church Sonatas*) and Bärenreiter (*Kirchensonaten*) can only be purchased in collections (*e.g.,* Nos.1-8 published together).

Sonata, Organ & Strings, No.1, K.67 (41h), E-flat major <late 1771–1772>   3'

str[no va]

Bärenreiter	Kalmus	Mercury

Sonata, Organ & Strings, No.2, K.68 (41i), B-flat major <late 1771–1772>   2'

str[no va]

Bärenreiter	Kalmus	Mercury

Sonata, Organ & Strings, No.3, K.69 (41k), D major <late 1771–1772>   2'

str[no va]

Bärenreiter	Kalmus	Mercury

Sonata, Organ & Strings, No.4, K.144 (124a), D major <early 1774>   2'

str[no va]

Bärenreiter	Kalmus	Mercury

Sonata, Organ & Strings, No.5, K.145 (124b), F major <early 1774>   2'

str[no va]

Bärenreiter	Kalmus	Mercury

Sonata, Organ & Strings, No.6, K.212, B-flat major <1775>   2'

str[no va]

Bärenreiter	Kalmus	Mercury

Sonata, Organ & Strings, No.7, K.224 (241a), F major <1779–1780>   3'

str[no va]

Bärenreiter	Kalmus	Mercury

Sonata, Organ & Strings, No.8, K.225 (241b), A major <1779–1780>   3'

str[no va]

Bärenreiter	Kalmus	Mercury

Sonata, Organ & Strings, No.9, K.244, F major <1776>   6'

str[no va]

Bärenreiter	Kalmus	Luck's	Mercury

Sonata, Organ & Strings, No.10, K.245, D major <1776>   3'

str[no va]

Bärenreiter	Kalmus	Luck's	Mercury

Sonata, Organ & Strings, No.11, K.274 (271d), G major <1777>   3'

str[no va]

Bärenreiter	Kalmus	Mercury

Sonata, Organ & Orchestra, No.12, K.278 (271e), C major <1777>   4'

0 2 0 0 — 0 2 0 0 — tmp — str[no va]

Bärenreiter	Breitkopf	Kalmus	Luck's	Mercury

Sonata, Organ & Strings, No.13, K.328 (317c), C major <1779>   5'

str[no va]

Bärenreiter	Kalmus	Luck's	Mercury

Sonata, Organ & Orchestra, No.14, K.329 (317a), C major <1779>   4'

0 2 0 0 — 2 2 0 0 — tmp — str[no va]
Believed to have some connection with the Mass, K.317 (*Coronation*).

Bärenreiter	Breitkopf	Kalmus	Mercury

Sonata, Organ & Strings, No.15, K.336 (336d), C major <1780>   5'

str[no va]

Bärenreiter	Kalmus	Luck's	Mercury

Sonata, Organ & Strings, No.16, K.241, G major <1776>   2'

str[no va]

Bärenreiter	Mercury

Sonata, Organ & Orchestra, No.17, K.263, C major <1776>   3'

0 0 0 0 — 0 2 0 0 — str[no va]

Bärenreiter	Mercury

SYMPHONIES

The published symphonies that are not a part of the established canon (Nos.1-41) are inserted below in the order of their K-numbers in the 1st or 3rd ed. of Köchel. Symphonies relegated to the Anhang *come first.*

Symphony, K.Anh.214 (45b), B-flat major   14'

0 2 0 0 — 2 0 0 0 — str
Ed. E.H. Müller von Asow; Peters ed. Alfred Einstein.
   Breitkopf numbering: *Symphony no.55.*
   Attribution uncertain.

1. Allegro	*2'*
2. Andante	*5'*
3. Minuetto	*3'*
4. Allegro	*4'*

Breitkopf	Peters

Symphony, K.Anh.216 (Anh.C11.03; K.74g), B-flat major <?>   15'

0 2 0 1 — 2 0 0 0 — str
Breitkopf numbering: *Symphony no.54.*
   Some authorities believe this work to have been composed by Leopold Mozart.

Allegro	4'
Andante	4'
Menuet	3'
Allegro molto	4'

Breitkopf	Kalmus

Symphony, K.Anh.220 (16a), A minor (Odense)   12'

0 2 0 2 — 2 0 0 0 — str
Very doubtful authenticity.

Allegro moderato	4'
Andantino	5'
Rondo: Allegro moderato	3'

Bärenreiter

Symphony, K.Anh.221 (45a), G major (Lambacher Sinfonie; Old Lambach) <1766; rev 1767>   15'

0 2 0 0 — 2 0 0 0 — str
Bärenreiter ed. Gerhard Allroggen; Bote ed. Heinrich Wollheim; Schott ed. Georg Röthke.

Allegro maestoso	6'
Andante	7'
Presto	2'

Bärenreiter	Bote & Bock	Ricordi	Schott

Symphony, K.Anh.223 (19a), F major <1766>   11'

0 2 0 1 — 2 0 0 0 — cnt — str

Allegro assai	5'
Andante	4'
Presto	2'

Bärenreiter

Symphony No.1, K.16, E-flat major <1764–1765>   13'

0 2 0 0 — 2 0 0 0 — str

I. Molto allegro	6'
II. Andante	5'
III. Presto	2'

Breitkopf	Kalmus	Luck's

Symphony No.2, K.17 (Anh.C 11.02), B-flat major   12'

0 2 0 0 — 2 0 0 0 — str
Believed to be by Leopold Mozart.

I. Allegro	_'
II. [Andante]	_'
III. Menuetto	_'
IV. Presto	_'

Breitkopf	Kalmus	Luck's

Symphony No.3, K.18 (Anh.A 51), E-flat major <1767>   12'

0 0 2 1 — 2 0 0 0 — str
Though published under Mozart's name, this is actually *Symphony op.7, no.6,* by Karl Friedrich Abel, somewhat reorchestrated by Mozart. For details, see the entry under Abel.

Molto allegro	_'
Andante	_'
Presto	_'

Kalmus	Luck's

Symphony No.4, K.19, D major <1765>   7'

0 2 0 0 — 2 0 0 0 — str

I. Allegro	2'
II. Andante	3'
III. Presto	2'

Breitkopf	Kalmus	Luck's

Symphony No.5, K.22, B-flat major <1765>   7'

0 2 0 0 — 2 0 0 0 — str

I. Allegro	3'
II. Andante	3'
III. Allegro molto	1'

Breitkopf	Kalmus	Luck's

Symphony No.6, K.43, F major <1767>   17'

0 2 0 0 — 2 0 0 0 — str

I. Allegro	5'
II. Andante	6'
III. Menuetto	2'
IV. Allegro	4'

Breitkopf	Kalmus	Luck's

Symphony No.7, K.45, D major <1767>   12'

0 2 0 0 — 2 2 0 0 — tmp — str
This symphony was later revised for use as the overture to the opera *La finta semplice*, K.51 (46a), *q.v.*

I. Allegro	3'
II. Andante	2'
III. Menuetto	4'
IV. Finale	3'

Bärenreiter	Kalmus	Luck's

Symphony No.8, K.48, D major <1768>   15'

0 2 0 0 — 2 2 0 0 — tmp — str

I. [Allegro]	4'
II. Andante	4'
III. Menuetto	4'
IV. [Allegro]	3'

Kalmus	Luck's

Symphony No.9, K.73, C major <1772>   12'

2 2 0 0 — 2 2 0 0 — tmp — str
The 2 flutes are used in the 2nd movement only, where the oboes are tacet. (Probably in Mozart's time the oboists doubled on flute.)

I. Allegro	3'
II. Andante	4'
III. Menuetto	3'
IV. Allegro molto	2'

Bärenreiter	Breitkopf	Kalmus	Luck's

Symphony No.10, K.74, G major <1770>   8'

0 2 0 0 — 2 0 0 0 — str

I. [Allegro]	3'
II. [Andante]	3'
III. [Allegro]	2'

Bärenreiter	Breitkopf	Kalmus	Luck's

Symphony, K.75, F major <1771>   14'

0 2 0 0 — 2 0 0 0 — str
Bärenreiter ed. Gerhard Allroggen.
   Breitkopf numbering: *Symphony no.42.*
   Attribution uncertain.

Allegro	3'
Menuetto	4'
Andantino	5'
Allegro	2'

Bärenreiter	Breitkopf

Symphony, K.76 (42a), F major   15'

0 2 0 2 — 2 0 0 0 — str
Bärenreiter ed. Gerhard Allroggen.
   Breitkopf numbering: *Symphony no.43.*
   Attribution uncertain.

Allegro maestoso	4'
Andante	4'
Menuetto	4'
Allegro	3'

Bärenreiter	Breitkopf	Kalmus

Symphony, K.81 (73-l), D major <before 1775>   10'

0 2 0 0 − 2 0 0 0 − str
Bärenreiter ed. Gerhard Allroggen.
   Breitkopf numbering: *Symphony no.44.*
   Attribution uncertain; possibly by Leopold Mozart.
Allegro   3'
Andante   5'
Allegro molto 2'

Bärenreiter	Breitkopf	Kalmus	

Symphony No.11, K.84 (73q), D major <1770>   10'

0 2 0 0 − 2 0 0 0 − str
Attribution uncertain.
I. Allegro   4'
II. Andante 2'
III. Allegro 4'

Bärenreiter	Breitkopf	Kalmus	Luck's

Symphony, K.95 (73n), D major <1770>   11'

2 2 0 1[opt] − 0 2 0 0 − str
Flutes in 2nd mvt only, while oboes are tacet.
   Bärenreiter ed. Gerhard Allroggen.
   Breitkopf numbering: *Symphony no.45.*
   Attribution uncertain.
Allegro   2'
Andante 3'
Menuetto 3'
Allegro   3'

Bärenreiter	Breitkopf	Kalmus	

Symphony, K.96 (111b), C major <1771>   14'

0 2 0 0 − 2 2 0 0 − tmp − str
Bärenreiter ed. Gerhard Allroggen.
   Breitkopf numbering: *Symphony no.46.*
   Attribution uncertain.
Allegro   2'
Andante 5'
Menuetto 4'
Molto allegro 3'

Bärenreiter	Breitkopf	Kalmus	

Symphony, K.97 (73m), D major <1770>   11'

0 2 0 0 − 2 2 0 0 − tmp − str
Bärenreiter ed. Gerhard Allroggen.
   Breitkopf numbering: *Symphony no.47.*
   Attribution uncertain.
Allegro   3'
Andante 3'
Menuetto 3'
Presto   2'

Bärenreiter	Breitkopf	Kalmus	

Symphony No.12, K.110 (75b), G major <1771>   17'

0 2 0 0 − 2 0 0 0 − str
I. Allegro   7'
II. [Andante] 4'
III. Menuetto 4'
IV. Allegro   2'

Bärenreiter	Breitkopf	Kalmus	Luck's

Symphony, K.111/120 (111a), D major <1771>   7'

2 2 0 0 − 2 2 0 0 − tmp − str
Overture and No.1 from *Ascanio in Alba* (K.111) with a new finale
(K.120).
Allegro assai 4'
Andante   2'
Presto   1'

Bärenreiter			

Symphony No.13, K.112, F major <1771>   14'

0 2 0 0 − 2 0 0 0 − str
I. Allegro   5'
II. Andante 5'
III. Menuetto 2'
IV. Molto allegro 2'

Bärenreiter	Breitkopf	Kalmus	Luck's

Symphony No.14, K.114, A major <1771>   19'

2 2 0 0 − 2 0 0 0 − str
The 2 oboes are used in the second movement only, where the flutes are
tacet. (Probably in Mozart's time the flutists doubled on oboe.)
I. Allegro moderato 7'
II. Andante 5'
III. Menuetto 3'
IV. Molto allegro 4'

Bärenreiter	Breitkopf	Kalmus	Luck's

Symphony No.15, K.124, G major <1772>   16'

0 2 0 0 − 2 0 0 0 − str
I. Allegro   5'
II. Andante 5'
III. Menuetto 3'
IV. Presto   3'

Bärenreiter	Breitkopf	Kalmus	Luck's

Symphony No.16, K.128, C major <1772>   13'

0 2 0 0 − 2 0 0 0 − str
I. Allegro maestoso 4'
II. Andantino grazioso 5'
III. Allegro 4'

Bärenreiter	Breitkopf	Kalmus	Luck's

Symphony No.17, K.129, G major <1772>   16'

0 2 0 0 − 2 0 0 0 − str
I. Allegro   6'
II. Andante 6'
III. Allegro 4'

Bärenreiter	Breitkopf	Kalmus	Luck's

Symphony No.18, K.130, F major <1772>   18'

2 0 0 0 − 4 0 0 0 − str
I. Allegro   5'
II. Andantino grazioso 4'
III. Menuetto 2'
IV. Molto allegro 7'

Bärenreiter	Breitkopf	Kalmus	Luck's

Symphony No.19, K.132, E-flat major <1772>   17'

0 2 0 0 − 4 0 0 0 − str
An alternative slow movement exists for this symphony.
I. Allegro   5'
II. Andante 3'
III. Menuetto 5'
IV. Allegro 4'

Bärenreiter	Breitkopf	Kalmus	Luck's

Symphony No.20, K.133, D major <1772>   19'

1 2 0 0 − 2 2 0 0 − str
Flute plays only in the second movement, during which the other winds
are tacet. In Mozart's time one of the oboists would have doubled on
flute.
   This work probably originally called for timpani.
I. Allegro   7'
II. Andante 4'
III. Menuetto 3'
IV. [Allegro] 5'

Bärenreiter	Breitkopf	Kalmus	Luck's

Symphony No.21, K.134, A major <1772>   20'

2 0 0 0 — 2 0 0 0 — str

I. Allegro	6'
II. Andante	5'
III. Menuetto	4'
IV. Allegro	5'

Bärenreiter	Breitkopf	Kalmus	Luck's

Symphony, K.141a, D major (Il sogno di Scipione) <1773–1774>   8'

2 2 0 0 — 2 2 0 0 — tmp — str

The first two movements are the overture to the composer's *Il sogno di Scipione*, K.126. The finale, K.161/163, was added later.

I. Allegro moderato	3'
II. Andante	3'
III. Presto	2'

Bärenreiter	Kalmus

Symphony No.22, K.162, C major <1773>   10'

0 2 0 0 — 2 2 0 0 — str

This work probably originally called for timpani.

I. Allegro assai	4'
II. Andantino grazioso	4'
III. Presto assai	2'

Bärenreiter	Breitkopf	Kalmus	Luck's

Symphony No.23, K.181 (162b), D major <1773>   9'

0 2 0 0 — 2 2 0 0 — str

This work probably originally called for timpani.

I. Allegro spiritoso	5'
II. Andantino grazioso	2'
III. Presto assai	2'

Bärenreiter	Breitkopf	Kalmus	Luck's

Symphony No.24, K.182 (173dA; 166c), B-flat major <1773>   9'

2 2 0 0 — 2 0 0 0 — str

Flutes play only in the second movement, during which the oboes are tacet. (In Mozart's time the oboists would have doubled on flute.)

I. Allegro spiritoso	4'
II. Andantino grazioso	2'
III. Allegro	3'

Bärenreiter	Breitkopf	Kalmus	Luck's

Symphony No.25, K.183 (173dB), G minor <1773>   24'

0 2 0 2 — 4 0 0 0 — str

I. Allegro con brio	10'
II. Andante	5'
III. Menuetto	2'
IV. Allegro	7'

Bärenreiter	Breitkopf	Kalmus	Luck's

Symphony No.26, K.184 (161a; 166a), E-flat major <1773>   8'

2 2 0 2 — 2 2 0 0 — str

This work probably originally called for timpani.

I. Molto presto	3'
II. Andante	3'
III. Allegro	2'

Bärenreiter	Breitkopf	Kalmus	Luck's

Symphony, K.196/121, D major (La finta giardiniera) <1774–1775>   8'

0 2 0 0 — 2 0 0 0 — str

The first two movements are the overture to the composer's *La finta giardiniera*, K.196. The finale, K.121 (207a) was added to the overture to form this symphony.

I. Allegro molto	3'
II. Andantino grazioso	2'
III. Allegro	3'

Bärenreiter	Kalmus

Symphony No.27, K.199 (161b; 162a), G major <1773>   18'

2 0 0 0 — 2 0 0 0 — str

I. Allegro	6'
II. Andantino grazioso	6'
III. Presto	6'

Bärenreiter	Breitkopf	Kalmus	Luck's

Symphony No.28, K.200 (189k; 173e), C major <1774>   23'

0 2 0 0 — 2 2 0 0 — str

This work originally called for timpani; an autograph copy of the timpani part once existed, but has been lost.

I. Allegro spiritoso	7'
II. Andante	6'
III. Allegretto	4'
IV. Presto	6'

Bärenreiter	Breitkopf	Kalmus	Luck's

Symphony No.29, K.201 (186a), A major <1774>   28'

0 2 0 0 — 2 0 0 0 — str

I. Allegro moderato	10'
II. Andante	7'
III. Menuetto	4'
IV. Allegro con spirito	7'

Bärenreiter	Breitkopf	Kalmus	Luck's	Peters

Symphony No.30, K.202 (186b), D major <1774>   16'

0 2 0 0 — 2 2 0 0 — str

This work probably originally called for timpani.

I. Molto allegro	5'
II. Andantino con moto	3'
III. Menuetto	4'
IV. Presto	4'

Bärenreiter	Breitkopf	Kalmus	Luck's

Symphony, K.204 (213a), D major <1775>   22'

2 2 0 1 — 2 2 0 0 — str

Movements 1, 5, 6, & 7 of the Serenade K.204 (213a).

I. Allegro assai	6'
II. Andantino	6'
III. Menuetto	4'
IV. Andantino grazioso - Allegro	6'

Bärenreiter

Symphony, K.250 (248b), D major <1776>   34'

2 2 0 2 — 2 2 0 0 — tmp — str

Movements 1, 5, 6, 7 & 8 of the Serenade, K.250 (248b) (*Haffner*)—with a new tmp part (added by Leopold Mozart) and other revisions.

I. Allegro maestoso - Allegro molto	7'
II. Menuetto galante	6'
III. Andante	8'
IV. Menuetto	6'
V. Adagio - Allegro assai	7'

Bärenreiter

Symphony No.31, K.297 (300a), D major (Paris) <1778>   *17'*

2 2 2 2 — 2 2 0 0 — tmp — str

Mozart supplied two slow movements for this symphony:
Andante [or *Andantino*], G major, 6/8, ca.6'
Andante, G major, 3/4, ca.5'
    It is not entirely clear which came first. Most editions give the 6/8 version; Bärenreiter includes both, with the 3/4 mvt as an alternative. The Bärenreiter score (but not the parts) also includes the original version of the 1st movement, the differences of which are interesting, but not particularly striking.

I. Allegro assai	7'		
II. Andantino	6'		
III. Allegro	4'		

Bärenreiter	Breitkopf	Kalmus	Luck's

Symphony No.32, K.318, G major <1779>   *9'*

2 2 0 2 — 4 2 0 0 — tmp — str

I. Allegro spiritoso	3'
II. Andante	4'
III. Tempo primo	2'

Bärenreiter	Breitkopf	Kalmus	Luck's

Symphony No.33, K.319, B-flat major <1779>   *20'*

0 2 0 2 — 2 0 0 0 — str

I. Allegro assai	7'
II. Andante moderato	5'
III. Menuetto	3'
IV. Allegro assai	5'

Bärenreiter	Breitkopf	Kalmus	Luck's

Symphony, K.320, D major <1779>   *17'*

0 2 0 2 — 2 2 0 0 — tmp — str

Movements 1, 5 & 7 of the Serenade K.320 (*Posthorn*), with added timpani.

I. Adagio maestoso - Allegro con spirito	8'
II. Andantino	5'
III. Presto	4'

Bärenreiter

Symphony No.34, K.338, C major <1780>   *21'*

0 2 0 2 — 2 2 0 0 — tmp — str

This symphony lacks a minuet. Sometimes the Minuet K.409 (338f) is inserted, in which case 2 flutes are needed.

I. Allegro vivace	7'
II. Andante di molto	6'
III. Allegro vivace	8'

Bärenreiter	Breitkopf	Kalmus	Luck's

Symphony No.35, K.385, D major (Haffner) <1782>   *18'*

2 2 2 2 — 2 2 0 0 — tmp — str

Originally intended as a serenade, with the March, K.408/2 (385a) and another minuet, which has been lost. Not related to the "Haffner" Serenade, K.250 (248b).

I. Allegro con spirito	5'
II. Andante	6'
III. Menuetto	3'
IV. Presto	4'

Bärenreiter	Breitkopf	Kalmus	Luck's

Symphony No.36, K.425, C major (Linz) <1783>   *26'*

0 2 0 2 — 2 2 0 0 — tmp — str

I. Adagio - Allegro spiritoso	9'
II. Poco adagio	7'
III. Menuetto	4'
IV. Presto	6'

Bärenreiter	Breitkopf	Kalmus	Luck's

Symphony No.37, K.444 (425a), G major <1783 or 84>   *14'*

1 2 0 0 — 2 0 0 0 — str

Only the adagio introduction is by Mozart; the remainder of this symphony is by Michael Haydn (MH 334; P.16). Breitkopf and Doblinger publish this work under Michael Haydn's name.

I. Adagio maestoso - Allegro con spirito	5'
II. Andante sostenuto	5'
III. Allegro molto	4'

Breitkopf	Kalmus	Luck's

Symphony No.38, K.504, D major (Prague) <1786>   *26'*

2 2 0 2 — 2 2 0 0 — tmp — str

I. Adagio - Allegro	11'
II. Andante	9'
III. Presto	6'

Bärenreiter	Breitkopf	Kalmus	Luck's	Peters

Symphony No.39, K.543, E-flat major <1788>   *29'*

1 0 2 2 — 2 2 0 0 — tmp — str

I. Adagio - Allegro	10'
II. Andante con moto	10'
III. Menuetto: Allegretto	4'
IV. Allegro	5'

Bärenreiter	Breitkopf	Kalmus	Luck's	Peters

Symphony No.40, K.550, G minor <1788>   *35'*

1 2 2 2 — 2 0 0 0 — str

A critical edition of the score with historical and analytical essays is available from Norton.
    An earlier version of the work did not use clarinets; the Bärenreiter set has alternative parts permitting performance of the early version, though a separate score must be purchased.

I. Molto allegro	7'
II. Andante	14'
III. Menuetto: Allegretto	5'
IV. Allegro assai	9'

Bärenreiter	Breitkopf	Kalmus	Luck's	Peters

Symphony No.41, K.551, C major (Jupiter) <1788>   *31'*

1 2 0 2 — 2 2 0 0 — tmp — str

I. Allegro vivace	11'
II. Andante cantabile	9'
III. Allegretto	4'
IV. Molto allegro	7'

Bärenreiter	Breitkopf	Kalmus	Luck's	Peters

Tantum ergo, K.142 (Anh.C3.04; 186d), B-flat major   *5'*

chorus   solo soprano

0 0 0 0 — 0 2 0 0 — org — str

Believed to be by Jan Zach (1699-1773), arranged by Mozart, and with a newly composed *Amen*.

Bärenreiter	Kalmus	Luck's

Tantum ergo, K.197 (Anh.186e), D major   *4'*

chorus

0 0 0 0 — 0 2 0 0 — tmp — org — str

Authenticity doubtful.

Bärenreiter	Kalmus	Luck's

Te Deum laudamus, K.141 (66b) <1769>   11'

chorus

0 0 0 1 — 0 4 0 0 — tmp — org — str[no va]

Ed. Hellmut Federhofer. The Bärenreiter score, following the original performance material with Leopold Mozart's handwritten annotations, calls for 2 *clarini* (typical Mozart trumpet parts) and 2 *trombe* (somewhat lower than the *clarini*, though still in a trumpet range). The lost timpani part has been reconstructed by the editor.

Parts for the Kalmus edition—a reprint of an Anton Böhm edition, clearly spurious—distribute the *clarini* and *trombe* music among pairs of oboes, bassoons and trumpets, although the score shows only the strings. Breitkopf catalog lists only chorus, organ and strings.

Bärenreiter	Breitkopf

Thamos, König in Ägypten, K.345 (336a): Zwischenaktmusiken (Entr'actes) <?1776–1779>   19'

0 2 0 2 — 2 2 0 0 — tmp — str

1. Maestoso - Allegro	7'
2. Andante	5'
3. Allegro - Allegretto	3'
4. Allegro vivace assai	4'

Bärenreiter	Kalmus

Titus

see his: Clemenza di Tito

Turkish March, from Piano Sonata in A major, K.331 (300i) <1784>   4'

3[1.2.pic] 2 2 2 — 2 2 0 0 — 3perc — str

perc: bd, cym, tri

Arr. Prosper Pascal.

Luck's

Vado, ma dove, o dei, K.583 <1789>   4'

soprano aria

0 0 2 2 — 2 0 0 0 — str

Bärenreiter	Breitkopf	Grande	Kalmus	Luck's

Veni sancte spiritus, K.47 <before 1770>   4'

chorus   solos SATB

0 2 0 0 — 2 2 0 0 — tmp — org — str

Kalmus	Luck's

Venite populi, K.260 (248a) (Offertorium de venerabili sacramento) <1776>   5'

double chorus

0 0 0 1 — 0 0 3 0 — org — str[no va]

Bärenreiter	Breitkopf	Luck's

Vesperae de dominica, K.321 <1779>   35'

chorus   solos SATB

0 0 0 1 — 0 2 3 0 — tmp — org — str[no va]

1. Dixit Dominus	5'
2. Confitebor	8'
3. Beatus vir	5'
4. Laudate pueri	5'
5. Laudate Dominum	6'
6. Magnificat	6'

Bärenreiter	Breitkopf	Kalmus	Luck's

Vesperae solennes de confessore, K.339 <1780>   26'

chorus   solos SATB

0 0 0 1 — 0 2 3 0 — tmp — org — str[no va]

I. Dixit	4'
II. Confitebor	4'
III. Beatus vir	4'
IV. Laudate pueri	4'
V. Laudate Dominum	5'
VI. Magnificat	5'

Bärenreiter	Breitkopf	Kalmus	Luck's

Voi avete un cor fedele, K.217 <1775>   6'

soprano aria

0 2 0 0 — 2 0 0 0 — str

Bärenreiter	Breitkopf	Luck's

Vorrei spiegarvi, oh Dio, K.418 <1783>   6'

soprano aria

0 2 0 2 — 2 0 0 0 — str

Bärenreiter	Breitkopf	Kalmus	Luck's

Die Zauberflöte, K.620 (The Magic Flute): Overture <1791>   7'

2 2 2 2 — 2 2 3 0 — tmp — str

Bärenreiter	Breitkopf	Kalmus	Luck's	Ricordi

Mozetich, Marjan   1948-

(b Gorizia, Italy, 1948). Canadian composer of Italian birth

Postcards from the Sky <1996>   13'

str

1. Unfolding Sky	5'
2. Weeping Clouds	4'
3. A Messenger	4'

CMC

Procession of Duos <2011>   21'

2 2 3[1.2.bcl] 3[1.2.cbn] — 4 2 3 1 — tmp+2 — hp — str

perc: bd, sus cym, sd, tambn, glock, marim, vib, 3tomtom, 2tamtam

CMC

Steps to Ecstasy <2001; rev 2002>   12'

2 2 0 2 — hpsd[or pf] — str

CMC

Muczynski, Robert   1929-2010

(b Chicago, 19 March 1929; d Tucson, AZ, 25 May 2010). American

Concerto, Piano, No.1, op.7 <1954>   15'

2 2 2 2 — 4 2 3 1 — tmp+3 — hp — str

perc: bd, cym, sus cym, field dr, tri, glock

Harp in mvts 2 & 3 only.

I. Maestoso; Allegro con brio	7'
II. Andante pastorale	4'
III. Vivace	4'

Schirmer

Dovetail Overture, op.12 <1960>   5'

3[1.2.pic] 2 2 2 — 4 3 3 1 — tmp+5 — str

perc: tri, woodblk, cym, tambn, sd, bd, glock, xyl

Luck's	Schirmer

Müller, Wenzel   1759-1835

(b Tyrnau [now Trnava], 26 Sept 1759; d Baden, nr Vienna, 3 Aug 1835). Austrian

Gloria from the Twelfth Mass

see: Mozart, Wolfgang Amadeus, 1756-1791
    Gloria from the Twelfth Mass, K.Anh.C 1.04

Murail, Tristan   1947-

(b Le Havre, 11 March 1947). French

Pour adoucer le cours de temps… <2005>   17'

2 1 3[1.2.3/bcl] 1 — 2 1 1 0 — pf, clavier/MIDI — str[3vn, va, vc, db]
Graphic notation.

Lemoine

Musgrave, Thea   1928-

(b Barnton, Midlothian, 27 May 1928). Scottish composer, now resident in the USA

Chamber Concerto No.1 <1962>   10'

0 1 1 1 — 1 1 1 0 — vn, va, vc

Chester

Concerto for Orchestra <1967>   20'

3[1.2.3/pic] 3[1.2.Eh] 3[1.2.bcl] 3[1.2.cbn] — 4 3 3 1 — tmp+3 — hp — str

Chester

Concerto, Viola <1973>   24'

1 2[1.Eh] 2[1.bcl] 1 — 3 2 1 0 — 1perc — hp — str
perc: chimes, sus cym, tamtam

Novello

Festival Overture <1965>   11'

2[1.2/pic] 2 2 2 — 4 2 3 0 — tmp+1 — str
perc: sd, sus cym, bd, vib, bongos, woodblk, templeblks, tamtam

Chester

Largo, In Homage to B.A.C.H. <2013>   6'

str[5.4.3.2.1]

Novello

Night Music, for Chamber Orchestra <1969>   18'

1[1/pic] 2 0 1 — 2 0 0 0 — str[min 6.4.3.2.1; max 10.8.6.4.3]

Chester

Peripeteia <1981>   15'

2[incl pic] 2 2 2 — 4 2 3 1 — tmp+2 — hp — str

Novello

Rainbow <1990>   12'

2[1.2/pic] 2 2 2 — 4 3 3 1 — tmp+3 — hp — synth — str
perc: vib, sd, 2tomtom, td, bd, marim, sus cym, glock, tamtam

Novello

Scottish Dance Suite <1959>   8'

2[1.2/pic] 2 2 2 — 4 2 3 1 — tmp+2 — hp — str
perc: xyl, bd, sus cym, 3woodblk
  I. Andante   _'
  II. Andante con moto   _'
  III Tempo di rumba   _'
  IV. Reel tempo   _'

Chester

Turbulent Landscapes <2004>   25'

3[1.2.3/pic] 3[1.2.Eh] 3[1.2.bcl] 3[1.2.cbn] — 4 3 3 1 — tmp+3 — hp — str
perc: bd, tamtam, chimes, xyl, td, vib, bongos, marim, 3sus cym, 2sd, 4tomtom
Depictions of various paintings by Turner.

I. Sunrise with Sea Monsters	3'
II. The Shipwreck	6'
III. Snowstorm: Hannibal and his army crossing the Alps	4'
IV. War: the Exile and the Rock Limpet	3'
V. 16th October, 1834: The Burning of the Houses of Parliament	5'
VI. Sunrise, with a boat between Headlands	4'

Novello

Two's Company; A Concerto for Oboe, Percussion and Orchestra <2005>   21'

2 2[1.Eh] 2 2 — 3 2 2 1 — hp — str
perc: (solo) tamtam, chimes, marktree, vib, bd, sd, templeblks, marim, Chinese belltree, 3sus cym, 5congas, 5tomtom, 5bongos, 2woodblk
Soloists are stationed at particular locations and move from place to place according to elaborate stage directions (e.g., "Turn toward English horn and play in response"). Sections (i.e., mvts) are played without pause.

I. Desolate, lonely	7'
II. Frivolous, playful	4'
III. Dramatic: furioso/espressivo	5'
IV. Warm; Passionate; Exultant	5'

Novello

Mussorgsky, Modest   1839-1881

(b Karevo, Pskov district, 9/21 March 1839; d St Petersburg, 16/28 March 1881). Russian

Boris Godunov: Polonaise <1871–1872>   6'

3[1.2.3-pic] 3[1.2.Eh] 3 3 — 4 4[2tp, 2crt] 3 1 — tmp+4 — hp — str
perc: sd, tri, cym, bd
Arr. Rimsky-Korsakov.

Breitkopf	Kalmus

The Fair at Sorochinski (Sorochinskaya yarmarka): Introduction <1874–1880>   5'

3[1.2.3/pic] 3[1.2.Eh] 2 2 — 4 2 3 1 — tmp+2 — str
perc: tri, tambn
Orchestrated by Anatol Liadov.

Breitkopf	Kalmus	Luck's

The Fair at Sorochinski (Sorochinskaya yarmarka): Gopak <1874–1880>   3'

3[1.2.pic] 2 2 2 — 4 2 3 1 — tmp+2 — str
perc: tri, tambn
Orchestrated by Anatol Liadov.

Breitkopf	Kalmus	Luck's

Intermezzo in the Classic Style (Intermezzo in modo classico) <1867>   7'

2 2 2 2 — 4 2 3 1 — tmp+1 — str
perc: bd
Arr. & ed. Rimsky-Korsakov, 1883; Universal edition arr. Paul Lamm.

Kalmus	Russian	Luck's	Universal

Khovantchina: Introduction (Dawn on the Moskva River) (Rimsky-Korsakov) <1872–1880>   5'

2 2 2 2 — 4 0 0 0 — tmp+1 — hp — str
perc: tamtam
The opera was completed and orchestrated by Rimsky-Korsakov, 1883; however, Mussorgsky wrote all of the introduction.

Breitkopf	Kalmus	Luck's

Khovantchina: Introduction (Dawn on the Moskva River) (Shostakovich) <1872–1880>   5'

3 3[1.2.Eh] 3 3[1.2.cbn] — 4 0 0 0 — tmp+2 — 2hp — pf/cel — str
perc: chimes, tamtam
Orchestrated by Shostakovich.

Schirmer	Sikorski

Khovantchina: Dance of the Persian Maidens (Persian Dances) <1872–1880>   6'

3[1.2.pic] 2[1/Eh.2] 2 2 — 4 2 3 1 — tmp+3 — hp — str
perc: field dr, tambn, tri, cym
Completed and orchestrated by Rimsky-Korsakov, 1883.

Breitkopf	Kalmus	Luck's	Russian

Khovantchina: Prince Galitzin's Journey into Exile; Entr'acte   <1872–1880>   4'

3 2 2 2 — 4 2 3 1 — tmp — str
Entr'acte to Act 4, Scene 2
   Completed and orchestrated by Rimsky-Korsakov, 1883.

Kalmus	Luck's

Night on Bald Mountain (original version) (Ivanova noch' na Lïsoy gore; St John's Night on Bald Mountain) <1866–1867; rev 1872; 1880>   12'

3[1.2.pic] 2 2 2 — 4 4[2tp, 2crt] 3 1 — tmp+4 — str
perc: tri, tambn, sd, cym, bd, tamtam
Ed. Georgi Kirkor; rev. Clark McAlister.

Kalmus	Russian	Scores Ref

Night on Bald Mountain (arr. Rimsky-Korsakov) <1866–1867; rev 1872; 1880>   12'

3[1.2.pic] 2 2 2 — 4 2 3 1 — tmp+3 — hp — str
perc: cym, bd, tamtam, chimes[D4]
Arr. Rimsky-Korsakov, 1886. Kalmus edition by Clinton F. Nieweg.

Kalmus	Luck's	Russian	Universal

PICTURES AT AN EXHIBITION (Kartinki s vïstavki)

This piano work has been orchestrated many times. A list prepared by Clinton F. Nieweg of all available orchestrations of this work may be found at www.mola-inc.org/resources.html or www.orchestrallibrary.com under Special Interest>The Nieweg Charts. The Ravel orchestration is the most commonly performed.

Pictures at an Exhibition (arr. Funtek) (Kartinki s vïstavki) <1874>   40

4[1.2.3/pic.pic] 3[1.2.3/Eh] 4[1.2.3/bcl.Ebcl] 3[1.2.cbn] — 6 4 4 1 — tmp+4 — 2hp — pf, cel — str
perc: sd, cym, sus cym, glock, xyl, tri, tamtam, bd, tambn
Originally for piano; orchestrated by Leo Funtek, 1922.

Promenade I	2'
Gnomus	3'
Promenade II	1'
Das alte Schloss (Il vecchio castello)	5'
Promenade III	1'
Tuileries (Spielende Kinder im Streit)	1'
Bydlo	4'
Promenade IV	1'
Ballet der Küchlein in ihren Eierschalen	1'
Samuel Goldenberg und Schmuyle	3'
Promenade V	2'
Der Marktplatz in Limoges	2'
Catacombae	2'
Con mortuis in lingua mortua	2'
Die Hütte der Baba Yaba	3'
Das grosse Tor von Kiew	7'

Fazer

Pictures at an Exhibition (arr. Goehr) (Kartinki s vïstavki) <1874>   25

2[1.2/pic] 2[1.2/Eh] 2[1.2/bcl/asx] 2 — 4 2 3 0 — tmp+3 — hp — org, pf — str
perc: glock, sd, tomtom, woodblk, templeblks, xyl, vib, gong, cym, tri, bd, chimes[D#4]
Originally for piano; orchestrated by Walter Goehr, 1942. Cross-cued for smaller combinations. *Gnomus* omitted.

Boosey

Pictures at an Exhibition (arr. Gorchakov) (Kartinki s vïstavki) <1874>   31

3[1.2.3/pic] 3[1.2.3/Eh] 4[1.2.3/ssx.bcl] 3[1.2.cbn] — 4 3 3 2 — tmp+5 — hp — cel — str
perc: bd, chimes, cym, glock, sd, tamtam, tri, woodblk, xyl
Originally for piano; orchestrated by Sergei Gorchakov, 1954.

Introduction - Promenade	_'
I. Gnomus	_'
II. Il vecchio castello	_'
III. Tulleries	_'
IV. Bydlo	_'
V. Ballet of Little Chicks in their Shells	_'
VI. Two Polish Jews	_'
VII. Limoges	_'
VIII. Catacombae - Cum mortius in lingua mortua	_'
IX. Baba-Yaga - The Hut on Hen's Legs	_'
X. The Great Gate of Kiev	_'

Russian

Pictures at an Exhibition (arr. Ravel) (Kartinki s vïstavki) <1874>   *35'*

3[1.2/pic.3/pic] 3[1.2.3/Eh] 3[1.2.bcl] 3[1.2.cbn] — 4 3 3 1 — asx — tmp+5 — 2hp — cel [can be covered by perc] — str
perc: xyl, sd, tamtam, tri, whip, ratch, cym, bd, glock, sus cym, chimes[D#4]
Originally for piano; orchestrated by Maurice Ravel, 1922. This is the most frequently played of the various orchestrations of this work.

Bcl entirely treble clef; about evenly divided between bcl in B-flat and bcl in A.

Promenade	2'
1. Gnomus	3'
Promenade	1'
2. The Old Castle	4'
Promenade	1'
3. Tuileries	1'
4. Bydlo	3'
Promenade	1'
5. Ballet of the Chicks in Their Shells	1'
6. Samuel Goldenberg and Schmuyle	3'
7. Limoges	2'
8. Catacombs	2'
Cum mortuis in lingua mortua	2'
9. The Hut on Fowl's Legs	4'
10. The Great Gate of Kiev	5'

Boosey	Ed. Russe

Pictures at an Exhibition (arr. Stokowski) (Kartinki s vïstavki) <1874>   *27'*

4[1.2/afl.3/pic.4/pic] 4[1.2.3.Eh] 4[1.2.3/Ebcl.bcl/asx] 4[1.2.3.cbn] — 8 4 4 1[1/opt euph] — tmp+4 — 2hp[1part] — cel, opt org — str
perc: sd, tambn, tri, cym, bd, tamtam, chimes, marim[or xyl], vib[or glock]
Originally for piano; orchestrated by Leopold Stokowski. Brass parts could be covered with 5.3.3.1.

1. Promenade	2'
2. Gnomus	2'
3. Promenade	1'
4. Il vecchio castello	4'
5. Bydlo	3'
6. Promenade	1'
7. Ballet de poussins dan leur coques	1'
8. Samuel Goldenberg and Schmuyle	2'
9. Catacombae: Sepulcrum romanum, Con mortuis in lingua mortua	2'
10. La cabane sur les pattes de poule (Baba Yaga)	3'
11. La grande porte de Kiev	6'

Peters

Pictures at an Exhibition (arr. Tushmalov) (Kartinki s vïstavki) <1874>   *20'*

3[1.2.pic] 3[1.2.Eh] 3[1.2.bcl] 2 — 4 2 3 1 — tmp+5 — hp — pf — str
perc: glock, tri, cym, sus cym, bd, tamtam, chime[Eb: 8ve unspecified]
Originally for piano; instrumentation by Mikhail Tushmalov (ca.1891) with collaboration by Rimsky-Korsakov. Three "pictures" and 4 "promenades" are omitted from the original piano version.

Promenade	_'
The Old Castle	_'
Ballet of the Chicks	_'
Two Jews	_'
Limoges	_'
Catacombs	_'
Con mortuis	_'
Baba Yaga	_'
Great Gate of Kiev	_'

Kalmus	Luck's

Pictures at an Exhibition (arr. Yu) (Kartinki s vïstavki) <1874>   *32'*

1[fl/pic/afl] 1[ob/Eh] 1[cl/bcl] 1[bn/cbn] — 1 1 1 0 — 1-3perc — hp — pf/cel — str 5t or str orch
perc: bd, sus cym, tamtam, glock, xyl, marim, vib, chimes, tmp, 4woodblks
Originally for piano; orchestrated by Julian Yu for 16 players or chamber orchestra, 2002. Contains a number of liberties and changes from Mussorgsky's original piano work.

Promenade	_'
Gnomus	_'
Promenade	_'
Il vecchio castello	_'
Promenade	_'
Les Tuileries (Dispute d'enfants après jeux)	_'
Bydlo	_'
Promenade	_'
Ballet of the Unhatched Chickens	_'
Samuel Goldenberg und Schmuÿle	_'
Promenade	_'
Limoges. Le marché (La grand nouvelle)	_'
Catacombae (Sepulcrum romanum)	_'
Cum mortuis in lingua mortua	_'
The Hut on Chucken's [sic] Legs (Baba-Yaga)	_'
The Heroic Gate (in the Imperial City of Kiev)	_'

Zen-On

Scherzo, B-flat major <1858>   *5'*

2 2 2 2 — 2 2 3 0 — tmp — str
Originally for piano; arr. Rimsky-Korsakov, 1883.

Kalmus	Luck's	Russian	Universal

Solemn March in A-flat (Vzyatiye Karsa; The Capture of Kars) <1880>   *6'*

3[1.2.pic] 2 2 2 — 4 4[2tp, 2crt] 3 1 — tmp+4 — str
perc: sd, tri, cym, bd, tambn [played by tmp]
Arr. Rimsky-Korsakov.

Originally from the unfinished opera *Mlada*, with a new middle section. Alternative titles: *Feierlicher Marsch, Festive March, March with Trio alla turca, Triumphal March, Turkish March, Marche solennelle.*

Kalmus	Luck's	Russian	Universal

Songs and Dances of Death (Pesni i plyaski smerti) <1875–1877>   *19'*

solo voice (medium)
2[1.2/pic] 2 2[1.2/bcl] 2[1.2/cbn] — 4 2 3 1 — tmp+2 — hp — str
perc: sd, tamtam, cym
Orchestrated by Shostakovich.

1. Kolabelnaya (Lullaby)	5'
2. Serenada (Serenade)	4'
3. Trepak	5'
4. Polkavodets (Commander in Chief)	5'

Kalmus	Luck's	Russian

Myaskovsky, Nikolay Yakovlevich   **1881-1950**

The composer's name as transliterated by *Grove Music Online.*

see: Miaskovsky, Nikolai, 1881-1950

N

Nelhybel, Vaclav
1919-1996

(b Polanka nad Odrou, Czechoslovakia, 24 Sept 1919; d Scranton, PA, 22 March 1996). American composer of Czech birth

Music for Orchestra   8'

4[incl pic] 2 3[incl bcl] 2 — 4 3 3 1 — tmp+4 — str

Belwin			

Nelson, Marie Barker
1926-

(b 1926). American

Ode to Antigone <1997>   11'

3[1.2.pic] 3[1.2.Eh] 3[1.2.bcl] 3[1.2.cbn] — 4 3 3 1 — tmp+3 — hp — str
perc: bd, sus cym, tri, tamtam, gong, glock, xyl, vib, chimes, crot, cowbell

Nelson, Ron
1929-

(b Joliet, IL, 14 Dec 1929). American

Five Pieces for Orchestra after Paintings by Andrew Wyeth <1975>   25'

solo baritone (wordless)
3[1.2.pic] 3[1.2.Eh] 2[1.2.bcl] 3[1.2.cbn] — 4 3 3 1 — tmp+4 — hp — pf, cel[played by perc] — str
perc: glock, marim, vib, xyl, cel[played by perc]
I. Winter 1946   _'
II. Young America   _'
III. Christina's World _'
IV. The Drifter   _'
V. The Patriot   _'

Boosey			

Sarabande for Katharine in April <1954>   5'

2 2[1.2/Eh] 2 2 — 2 2 0 0 — 1perc — hp — cel — str

Boosey			

Savannah River Holiday <1957 or 1952(?)>   9'

2[1.2.pic] 2 2 2 — 4 3 3 1 — tmp+3 — hp — pf/cel — str
perc: bd, cym, glock, gong, sd, sus cym, tambn, td, tri, xyl

C. Fischer			

This Is the Orchestra <1960 or 63>   22'

narrator
2[1.2.pic] 2 2 2 — 4 3 3 1 — tmp+5 — hp — str
perc: bd, chimes, cast, glock, gong, sd, sus cym, templeblks, tambn, tri, woodblk, xyl, sandblks, slidewhistle

Boosey			

Nicolai, Otto
1810-1849

(b Königsberg [now Kaliningrad], 9 June 1810; d Berlin, 11 May 1849). German

Die lustigen Weiber von Windsor (The Merry Wives of Windsor): Overture <1849>   8'

2[1.2/pic] 2 2 2 — 4 2 3 0 — tmp+2 — str
perc: bd, cym

Bote & Bock	Breitkopf	Kalmus	Luck's

Nielsen, Carl
1865-1931

(b Sortelung, nr Nørre Lyndelse, Funen, 9 June 1865; d Copenhagen, 3 Oct 1931). Danish

Aladdin, op.34: 7 Pieces <1918–1919>   23'

optional chorus (wordless)
3[1.2/pic.pic] 2[1.2/Eh] 2 2 — 4 2 3 1 — tmp+4 — cel[played by perc] — str
perc: field dr, tambn, tri, tamtam, sd, cym, xyl, bd, cast, cel[played by perc]
The new critical edition of the complete works of Nielsen (Series 1, v.8, 2002) includes the composer's instructions for the 4th mvt, "Market Place in Ispahan," in which the orchestra is divided into 4 separate ensembles playing independently of one another, each in its own tempo.
    This work can be done with only 2 flutes, both doubling piccolo, via a very slight adjustment.
1. Oriental Festive March   3'
2. Aladdin's Dream and Dance of the Morning Mist   3'
3. Hindu Dance   3'
4. Chinese Dance   3'
5. Marketplace in Ispahan   3'
6. Prisoners' Dance   4'
7. Negro Dance   4'

Hansen	Kalmus	Luck's	

Bohemian-Danish Folk Tune; Paraphrase for String Orchestra (Bøhmisk-dansk folkeone) <1928>   8'

str

Hansen	Kalmus	Luck's	

Concerto, Clarinet, op.57 <1928>   24'

0 0 0 2 — 2 0 0 0 — 1perc — str
perc: sd

Kalmus	Luck's	Samfundet	

Concerto, Flute (1926) <1926>   19'

0 2 2 2 — 2 0 1 0 — tmp — str
I. Allegro moderato   12'
II. Allegretto   7'

Luck's	Samfundet		

Concerto, Violin, op.33 <1911>   34'

2[1.2/pic] 2 2 2 — 4 2 3 0 — tmp — str
1. Prelude: Largo   6'
2. Allegro cavalleresco   12'
3. Poco adagio   6'
4. Rondo: Allegro scherzando   10'

Hansen	Kalmus	Luck's	

A Fantasy Journey to the Faroes (En fantasirejse til Faerøene; Rhapsodic Overture) <1927>   10'

3[1.2.3/pic] 2 2 2 — 4 2 3 0 — tmp+3 — str
perc: tri, sus cym, sd, bd

Hansen	Kalmus	Luck's	

Helios Overture, op.17 <1903>   12'

3[1.2.3/pic] 2 2 2 — 4 3 3 1 — tmp — str

Hansen	Kalmus	Luck's	

Little Suite, op.1 <1888>   16'

str
I. Präludium	4'
II. Intermezzo	5'
III. Finale	7'

Hansen	Kalmus	Luck's

Maskarade: Overture <1904–1906>   5'

3[1.2.3/pic] 2 2 2 — 4 3 3 1 — tmp+2 — str
perc: cym, bd

Hansen	Kalmus	Luck's

Maskarade: Hanedans (Dance of the Cocks) <1906>   5'

3[1.2.pic] 2 2 2 — 4 3 3 1 — tmp — str

Hansen	Kalmus	Luck's

Pan and Syrinx, op.49 (Pan og Syrinx) <1917–1918>   9'

2[1.2/pic] 2[1.2/Eh] 2 2 — 4 2 0 0 — tmp+4 — str
perc: cym, tambn, tri, sd, ratch, glock, xyl
The original edition of this work incorrectly called for crotales; the 2004 critical edition (ed. Niels Bo Foltmann & Peter Hauge) corrects this to ratchet (raganella). Likewise, the original edition called for fl1 to double on piccolo; the piccolo has been put in the fl2 part in the 2004 edition.

Hansen

Saga Dream, op.39 (Saga-drøm) <1907–1908>   7'

3 2 2 2 — 4 3 3 1 — tmp+1 — str
perc: sus cym, glock

Hansen	Kalmus	Luck's

Saul and David (Saul og David): Prelude to Act II   6'
<1901>

3 2 2 2 — 4 3 3 1 — tmp — str

Hansen

Sleep, op.18 (Søvnen) <1903–1904>   20'

SATB chorus
3[1/pic.2/pic.3] 2 2 2 — 4 3 3 1 — tmp+1 — str
perc: glock, tamtam

Hansen

Symphonic Rhapsody (Symfonisk rhapsodi) <1888>   9'

2 2 2 2 — 4 2 3 0 — tmp — str

Hansen

Symphony No.1, op.7 <1890–1892>   27'

3[1/pic.2.3] 2 2 2 — 4 2 3 0 — tmp — str
I. Allegro orgoglioso	8'
II. Andante	6'
III. Allegro comodo	6'
IV. Finale: Allegro con fuoco	7'

Hansen	Kalmus

Symphony No.2, op.16 (The Four Temperaments; De fire   32'
temperamenter) <1901–1902>

3[1/pic.2.3/pic] 2[1.2/Eh] 2 2 — 4 3 3 1 — tmp — str
Layout of flute parts is confusing: In the 1st mvt, piccolo is in the 1st flute part, and the 2nd flute has all the solos. Elsewhere piccolo is in the 3rd flute part. It is believed that this problem has been alleviated in the new collected edition of Nielsen's works (Hansen, beginning in 1998). Brief Eh part (4 measures) in 2nd mvt.
I. Allegro collerico	8'
II. Allegro comodo e flemmatico	4'
III. Andante malincolico	12'
IV. Allegro sanguineo	8'

Hansen	Kalmus

Symphony No.3, op.27 (Sinfonia espansiva)   39'
<1910–1911>

soprano and baritone voices (textless)
3[1.2.3/pic] 3[1.2.3/Eh] 3 3[1.2.3/cbn] — 4 3 3 1 — tmp — str
A clarinet and trombone are cued to substitute for the voices.
I. Allegro espansivo	12'
II. Andante pastorale	10'
III. Allegretto un poco	7'
IV. Finale: Allegro	10'

Hansen	Kahnt	Kalmus

Symphony No.4, op.29 (The Inextinguishable; Det   36'
uudslukkelige) <1914–1916>

3[1.2.3/pic] 3 3 3[1.2.3/cbn] — 4 3 3 1 — 2tmp — str
1. Allegro	12'
2. Poco allegretto	5'
3. Poco adagio quasi andante	10'
4. Allegro	9'

Hansen	Kalmus	Luck's

Symphony No.5, op.50 <1921–1922>   34'

3[1.2.3/pic] 2 2 3[1.2.cbn (opt?)] — 4 3 3 1 — tmp+3 — cel[played by perc] — str
perc: tambn, tri, sus cym, cel[played by perc], 2sd[1 offstage]
A revised version by Erik Tuxen (pub. 1950) was not specifically authorized by the composer. The Hansen edition is apparently the original 1923 publication; Kalmus offers both the original and the Tuxen revision, each with a useful preface by Clark McAlister.
    The Tuxen material has a contrabassoon part which, however, never appears in the score. The part appears to be a doubling of the 2nd bn in certain passages; perhaps it is intended to be optional.
| I. Tempo giusto - Adagio | 19' |
| II. Allegro - Andante | 15' |

Hansen	Kalmus

Symphony No.6 (Sinfonia semplice) <1924–1925>   31'

2[1.2/pic] 2 2 2 — 4 2 3 1 — tmp+3 — str
perc: glock, xyl, tri, sd, bd, sus cym; tmp plays tri in Variation IX.
Although the score lists 2 flutes plus piccolo, the composer apparently intended 2 players, one doubling on piccolo.
    2nd mvt is for 9 players: 1[pic] 0 2 2 — 0 0 1 0 — 3perc — [no str]
    Kalmus offers "original version"; apparently a revised version exists.
I. Tempo giusto - Allegro passionato	12'
II. Humoreske [no str]	4'
III. Proposta seria	5'
IV. Tema con variazioni	10'

Hansen	Kalmus	Luck's	Samfundet

Nielsen, Ludolf   1876-1939

(b Nørre Tvede, nr Naestved, 29 Jan 1876; d Copenhagen, 16 Oct 1939). Danish

Symphony No.3, op.32, C major: 1st movement   12'
<1911–1913>

3[1.2/pic.3/pic] 3[1.2.Eh] 3[1.2.bcl] 3[1.2.cbn] — 6 3 3 1 — tmp+3 — hp — str
perc: glock, tri, bd, sus cym, cym, sd

Harmonic

Nono, Luigi   1924-1990

(b Venice, 29 Jan 1924; d Venice, 8 May 1990). Italian

Canti di vita e d'amore; Sul ponte di Hiroshima <1962>   18'

soprano and tenor solos
3 3 3 3 — 4 4 4 0 — 4-6perc — str[8.8.8.6.6]
perc: 4perc (min), each with an array that includes tmp and 3 chime pitches, as well as various snare drums, cymbals, tamtams & bass drums. Total complement: 8tmp, chimes (1set), 8sus cym, 8sd, 4tamtams, 4bd.

Schott

Il canto sospeso <1955–1956>   28'

chorus   solos SAT
4[1.2.3.4/pic] 2 3[1.2.bcl] 2 — 6 5 4 0 — 3tmp+2 — 2hp —
cel[played by perc] — str
perc: chimes, glock, xyl, vib, marim, 6sus cym, 4sd, cel[played by perc]
Letters of Resistance fighters.

Schott

La victoire de Guernica <1954>   13'

SATB chorus
3 3 4[1.2.3.bcl] 3 — 4 4 3 1 — tmp+6 — 2hp — cel — str
perc: bd, marim, xyl, vib, 4sd, 4field dr, 4sus cym

Ars Viva	Schott

Nørgård [Norgard], Per   1932-

(b Gentofte, 1932). Danish

Symphony No.3 <1972–1975>   48'

2 choruses (large chorus & chamber chorus)
3[1/pic/afl.2/pic.3/pic] 3[1.2.Eh] 2[1/Ebcl.2/Ebcl] 3[1.2.cbn] — 4
3[1.2.3/btp] 3 1 — tmp+5 — 1 or 2hp[ampd] — pf[ampd], org,
cel[played by perc] — str[14.10.8.8.6]
perc: bd, glock, xyl, marim, vib, chimes, crot, flexatone, slgh-bells, whip,
2tamtam, 3td, 4tomtom, 3tri, 2pr cym, cel[played by perc], recorder[played by
perc or chorus member]
Brief mezzo solo, ampd if necessary. Choristers whistle. Descant recorder
played either by a member of the chorus, or of the percussion section.
  I. Moderato   20'
  II. Allegretto   28'

Hansen

Symphony No.8 <2010–2011>   35'

4[1.2/afl.3/afl.4/pic] 4[1.2.3.Eh] 4[1.2.3/Ebcl.bcl] 4[1.2.3.cbn] — 4
4[1/pic tp] 4[1.2.3.btbn] 1 — tmp+4 — hp — pf, cel[played by perc] —
str
perc: glock, vib, xyl, marim, crot, chimes, gong, tamtam, cowbell, marac,
woodblk, templeblks, field dr, bd, marktree, 8buttongong, steeldrum, 3sus cym,
2tambn, 4bongos, 4tomtom, watergong, 2metalstave
  I. Tempo giusto   _'
  II. Adagio molto   _'
  III. quarter-note = 96   _'

Hansen

Tributes; Album for Strings <1994–1995>   18'

str
Movements may be programmed individually (the Bartok movement,
"Observations from an Infinite Rapport," is in 4 sections).
  I. Observations d'un rapport infini (Homage to Bela Bartok)   5'
  II. Out of this World (Homage to Lutoslawski)   6'
  III. Voyage into the Broken Screen (Homage to Sibelius)   7'

Hansen

Twilight <1976–1977; rev 1979>   17'

optional dancer
3[1/pic.2/pic.3/pic] 3[1.2.Eh] 3[1.2/Ebcl.bcl] 3[1.2.cbn] — 4 3 3 1 —
tmp+4 — hp[ampd] — pf[ampd], cel[played by perc] — str
perc: sus cym, sd, tomtom, tamtam, glock, marim, vib, chimes, templeblks, marac,
3congas, 4logdrum, 2gong, xylorimba, cel[played by perc]
N.B.: The conga part is prominent and difficult; the composer directs that
the player be recognized in the program as a soloist.

Hansen

Voyage into the Golden Screen (Rejse ind i den gyldne   18'
skærm) <1968–1969; rev 2010>

2[1/afl.2] 1 1 1 — 2 2 1 0 — 1perc — hp — pf — str[4.4.3.2.1]
perc: tamtam, vib, chimes
Scordatura applied to half the strings.
  I. Lento molto   12'
  II. Lento, poco rubato   6'

Hansen

Noskowski, Zygmunt   1846-1909

(b Warsaw, 2 May 1846; d Warsaw, 23 July 1909). Polish

The Steppe (Step) <1896>   18'

3[1.2.pic] 2 2 2 — 4 2 3 1 — tmp+1 — hp — str
perc: tambn, cym

Fleisher	PWM

Nunés-Garcia, José Mauricio   1767-1830

(b Rio de Janeiro, 22 Sept 1767; d Rio de Janeiro, 18 April 1830). Brazilian

Requiem   40'

chorus
2 2 2 2 — 2 0 0 0 — tmp — str
Ed. Dominique-René de Lerma.

Schirmer

Sinfonia funebre, E-flat major <1790>   6'

2 2 0 2 — 2 2 0 0 — str
Ed. Cleofe Person de Mattos.
  Score published in *The Symphony in the New World* (New York:
Garland Pub., 1984); parts may not be available.

Zemira Overture <1803>   7'

2 0 0 2 — 2 0 2 0 — str
Ed. Cleofe Person de Mattos.
  Score published in *The Symphony in the New World* (New York:
Garland Pub., 1984); parts may not be available.

O'Boyle, Sean

1963-

b Hexham, UK, 20 Nov 1963). Australian composer of English birth & Irish descent

An Australian in New York <2012>   16'

3[1.2.pic] 3[1.2.Eh] 3[1.2.bcl] 3[1.2.cbn] — 4 3 3 1 — tmp+ — hp — str

perc: siren, cym, bd, sd, cast, tri, tamtam, tambn, woodblk, glock, vib, xyl, 2sus cym, chimes (6 chimes placed in orchestra for various orchestra members to play)

Leonard

Ballycroy (Baile Cruiach)   6'

3[1.2.pic] 3[1.2.Eh] 3[1.2.bcl] 3[1.2.cbn] — 4 5 3 1 — tmp+2 — hp — str

perc: bd, cym, sus cym, sd, td, tri, tambn, tamtam, glock, xyl, chimes, windmachine, ship's bell, rainstick
2 of the trumpets are offstage throughout.

Leonard   Queensland

Celtic Suite   14'

solo violin
3[1.2.pic] 3[1.2.Eh] 3[1.2.bcl] 3[1.2.cbn] — 4 3 3 1 — tmp+3 — hp — str
Movements may be performed separately.

She Moved Through the Fair	*3'*
Molly	*3'*
Beauty in Tears [after Irish harper O'Carolan]	*3'*
Celtic Dance.	*5'*

Leonard   Queensland

Concerto, Didgerido   20'

3[1.2.pic] 3[1.2.Eh] 3[1.2.bcl] 3[1.2.cbn] — 4 3 3 1 — tmp+3 — hp — str

perc: 2bd, sus cym, sd, toms, tamtam, xyl, marim, vib, chimes, windchimes, clap sticks, bull roarer, box of marbles, watergong, temple bells
Composed in collaboration with didgerido performer William Barton. The solo part is basically improvised, folllowing stipulated rhythmic patterns. Some amplification may be needed for didgerido.

Earth	*6'*
Wind	*3'*
Water	*5'*
Fire	*6'*

Leonard   Queensland

Concerto, Percussion <2013>   15'

soloists: 1 timpanist, 3 percussionists playing a large array of instruments
2 2 2 2 — 4 3 3 1 — hp — cel — str
solo percussion insts: 4tmp, bd, cym, 3sus cym, sd, 5tomtom, timbales (2 sets), 3tri, tambn, tamtam, glock, chimes, crot (2 sets), flexatone, sleighbells, windchimes (2 sets), marktree, woodblk, templeblks, 4cowbell, whip, bongos, ratch, guiro, cast, vibraslap, siren, lionroar, wind machine, thunder sheet, 2police whistle, train whistle, belltree, waterphone (or springdrum), washboard, 20 tuned beer bottles, 4birdcalls (duck, cuckoo, dove, nightingale), 3energy chimes, 2cellophane balls, chain, sandblocks, go-go bells, metal frypan, fingercymbals, tinkly bells, LagerPhone

Leonard

Conflict, Sadness, Victory, and Resolution <2013>   19'

solo soprano
2[1.2/pic] 2 2 2 — 2 2 0 0 — tmp — str

1. *Conflict: "The Dead"*	4'
2. *Sadness: "Sonnet 30"*	5'
3. *Victory: "Victory"*	6'
4. *Resolution: "Sunrise on the Coast"*	4'

Leonard

Country Kazoo Overture   2'

2[1.2/pic] 2 2 2 — 4 2 3 1 — tmp+3 — hp — str
perc: sus cym, sd, glock, xyl, chimes, woodblk
Orchestra members play kazoos and make animal sounds in middle section. A version for single woodwinds, single brass, 3perc & str is available under the title *Kazzoo* [sic] *Overture.*

Leonard   Queensland

Music That Goes with "The Tale of Peter Rabbit"   7'

narrator
2[1.2/pic] 2 2[1.bcl] 2 — 4 3 3 1 — tmp+1 — str
perc: tri

Queensland

Olympia Australis   2'

2[1/pic.2/pic]] 2 3[1.2.bcl] 2 — 4 6 6 1 — 3perc — hp — str
perc: bd, cym, sd, tri
Piccolo doublings are optional.

Leonard   Queensland

Ragtime Overture <2001>   2'

3[1.2.pic] 3[1.2.Eh] 2 3 — 4 3 3 1 — tmp+4 — hp — str
perc: set, 2xyl, ratch, mouth whistle

Leonard   Queensland

River Symphony: Suite <2004>   10'

3[1.2.3/pic] 3[1.2.Eh] 3[1.2.bcl] 3[1.2.cbn] — 4 3 3 1 — tmp+3 — hp — str
perc: bd, cym, sus cym, sd, tomtom, tri, tamtam, glock, xyl, chimes, windchimes

Leonard   Queensland

River Symphony: Fanfare <2004>   4'

3[1.2.3/pic] 3[1.2.Eh] 3[1.2.bcl] 3[1.2.cbn] — 4 3 3 1 — tmp+3 — hp — str
perc: bd, cym, sus cym, sd, tri, xyl, chimes

Leonard   Queensland

Scottish Piano Rhapsody <2009>   6'

1 1 0 0 — 2 2 0 0 — 2perc — str
perc: tri, bd, sd, sus cym, cym

Leonard

She Moved Through the Fair (string orchestra version)   3'

str

Leonard   Queensland

Silent Movie Music   2'

2[1.pic] 2 2[1.2/bcl] 2 — 4 3 3 1 — 3perc — hp — str
perc: bd, cym, sd, 2xyl, train whistle, cap gun

Leonard   Queensland

SNAPSHOT CONCERTOS

A series of 1-minute character pieces featuring specific instruments (listed here in score order). Many of them are available alternatively in a large or a small orchestration.

Mini Dance   1'

solo piccolo
hp — str

Leonard

Flipperdiperus   1'

solo flute
2[1.(2opt).pic] 3[1.2.Eh] 3[1.2.bcl] 3[1.2.cbn] — 4 3 3 1 — tmp+2 — hp — str
perc: tambn, xyl, woodblk, templeblk, whip

Leonard   Queensland

A Quiet Place   1'

solo oboe
hp — str

Leonard   Queensland

The Pretty Girl Milking Her Cow   1'

solo English horn
2 1 2[1.bcl] 2 — hp — str

Leonard   Queensland

Liquorice Noodles   1'

solo clarinet
3[1.2.pic] 3[1.2.Eh] 2[1.bcl] 3[1.2.cbn] — 4 3 3 1 — tmp+3 — hp — str
perc: bd, sd, tri, tambn, glock, xyl, vib

Leonard   Queensland

Liquorice Noodles (small orchestra)   1'

solo clarinet
1 1 0 1 — 1 1 1 0 — tmp+2 — str
perc: bd, sd, tri, tambn, glock, xyl, vib

Queensland

Bassett Hound   1'

solo bass clarinet
2 2 0 0 — 4 3 3 0 — 2perc — hp — str
perc: sus cym, vib

Leonard

A Bundle of Sticks   1'

solo bassoon
2 1 2 0 — 1 1 0 0 — 1perc — str
perc: tri

Leonard   Queensland

The Big Broomstick   1'

solo contrabassoon
2 2[1.Eh] 2 2 — 4 3 3 0 — tmp+2 — hp — str
perc: sus cym, tambn, tamtam, vib

Leonard   Queensland

Curly Bits   1'

horn section soli
3[1.2.pic] 3[1.2.Eh] 3[1.2.bcl] 3[1.2.cbn] — 0 3 3 1 — tmp+3 — hp — str
perc: bd, sd, tri, tamtam, xyl, vib, ratch

Leonard   Queensland

Lonesome Prairie   1'

solo trumpet
3 2 3[1.2.bcl] 2 — 4 0 3 0 — 3perc — hp — str
perc: sus cym, tri, glock, xyl, templeblk

Leonard   Queensland

Lonesome Prairie (small orchestra) <1997>   1'

solo trumpet
1 1 1 1 — 1 0 1 0 — 3perc — str
perc: sus cym, tri, glock, xyl, templeblks

Queensland

Buy, Swap or Sell!   1'

solo trombone
2[1.pic] 2 2 — 4 3 0 1 — tmp+1 — hp — str
perc: xyl

Leonard   Queensland

Tuba Toothpaste   1'

solo tuba
3[1.2.pic] 3[1.2.Eh] 3[1.2.bcl] 3[1.2.cbn] — 4 3 3 0 — tmp+2 — hp — str
perc: bd, sd, tri, glock, xyl

Leonard   Queensland

Galloping Goanna   1'

solo xylophone
3[1.2.pic] 3[1.2.Eh] 3[1.2.bcl] 3[1.2.cbn] — 4 3 3 1 — tmp+1 — str
perc: sd

Leonard   Queensland

The Big Bang   1'

percussion section soli (tmp+2)
3[1.2.pic] 3[1.2.opt Eh] 3[1.2.opt bcl] 3[1.2.opt cbn] — 4 3 3 1 — hp — str
perc: [soloists] tmp, cym, sd, tri, tambn, woodblk, templeblks, bongos, ratch, guiro, cast, vibrslp, siren, 4tomtom, duckcall, agogo, whistle
Harp plays only 2 bars.

Leonard

Pale Moonlight   1'

solo harp
2 2[1.Eh] 2[1.bcl] 0 — 2perc — str
perc: sus cym, vib

Leonard   Queensland

Dueling Fiddles   1'

2 solo violins
1 1 3[1.2.bcl] 1 — 4 2 2 1 — 2perc — str
perc: set, xyl

Leonard   Queensland

Dueling Fiddles (small orchestra)   1'

2 solo violins
1 1 1 1 — 1 1 1 0 — 2perc — str[no vn]
perc: set, xyl

Queensland

Tumbleweeds at Ten Paces   1'

solo violin
3[1.2.pic] 3[1.2.Eh] 3[1.2.bcl] 3[1.2.cbn] — 4 3 3 1 — tmp+2 — hp — str
perc: bd, tri, tambn

| Leonard | Queensland |

The Songbird   1'

solo viola
2 2 0 0 — 1perc — str
perc: sus cym

| Leonard | Queensland |

Changing Seasons   1'

solo violoncello
2 2 2 2 — 4 3 3 1 — tmp+2 — hp — str
perc: tri, glock

| Leonard | Queensland |

Quando, quando, basso   1'

solo double bass
2[1.pic] 2 2 2 — 4 3 3 1 — tmp+1 — hp — str
perc: sd, tri, xyl, tambn

| Leonard | Queensland |

The Song Bird: Scissor Dance   2'

2[1.pic] 2 2[1.bcl] 2 — 4 3 3 1 — tmp+1 — hp — str
perc: xyl

| Leonard | Queensland |

O'Connor, Mark   1961-

(b Seattle, 5 Aug 1961). American

The Fiddle Concerto <1992–1993>   37'

solo violin
3[1.2.pic] 2 2 3[1.2.cbn] — 4 2 2 1 — tmp+5 — hp — str
perc: tri, sd, bd, xyl, sus cym, tambn, cym
I. Quite fast (Lightly energetic)   18'
II. Moderately slow   13'
III. Moderately fast   6'

| O'Connor |

Three Pieces for Violin and Orchestra <1994–1995>   56'

3[1.2.pic] 3[1.2.Eh] 3[1.2.bcl] 3[1.2.cbn] — 4 3 3 1 — tmp+2 — hp — pf/cel — str
perc: bd, cym, sus cym, sd, tri, tambn, gong, glock, xyl, chimes
1. Call of the Mockingbird   20'
2. Trail of Tears   16'
3. Fanfare for the Volunteer   20'

| O'Connor |

Offenbach, Jacques   1819-1880

(b Cologne, 20 June 1819; d Paris, 5 Oct 1880). French

La belle Hélène: Overture <1864>   8'

2[1.pic] 2 2 2 — 4 2 3 0 — tmp+4 — hp — str
perc: sd, tri, tambn, cym, bd
Not actually the overture to the 1864 operetta, but a pastiche of various
instrumental passages from it.

| Kalmus | Luck's |

Concerto militaire, Violoncello & Orchestra <1847>   21'

2 2 2 2 — 4 2 3 0 — tmp — str

| Belwin |

Les contes d'Hoffmann (Tales of Hoffmann): Intermezzo   6'
& Barcarolle <1877–1881>

2 2 2 2 — 4 2 3 0 — tmp+3 — hp — str
perc: bd, cym, tri
1. Prelude & Entr'acte to Act II   2'
2. Intermezzo from end of Act IV (incl orch reprise of the Barcarolle).   4'

| Bote & Bock | Kalmus | Luck's |

L'île de Tulipatan: Overture <1868>   5'

2[1.pic] 2 2 2 — 4 2 3 0 — tmp+1 — str
perc: bd

| Boosey | Bote & Bock |

Kakadu: Ballet Suite <1869>   19'

2[1.2/pic] 2 2 2 — 4 2 3 0 — tmp+2 — hp — str
Arr. by Wolfgang Ebert, from the opera *Vert-vert*
I. Allegro molto   _'
II. Valse lento   _'
III. Allegro vivo   _'
IV. Andantino   _'
V. Allegro molto   _'

| Weinberger |

Orphée aux enfers (Orpheus in the Underworld):   10'
Overture <1858>

2[1.pic] 2 2 2 — 4 2 3 1 — tmp+3 — hp — str
perc: bd, cym, sd, tri
Ed. Clark McAlister. Not the actual overture to the operetta, but
composed by Carl Binder on tunes from the operetta.
    Percussion parts do not appear in the score.

| Kalmus | Luck's |

La Périchole: Overture <1868>   3'

2[1.pic] 1 2 2 — 4 2 3 0 — tmp+2 — str
perc: bd, sd

| Bote & Bock | Kalmus |

Le '66': Overture <1856>   5'

2[1.2/pic] 2 2 2 — 4 3 3 0 — tmp — str

| Bote & Bock | Luck's |

La vie parisienne: Overture <1866>   5'

2[1.2/pic] 2 2 2 — 4 2 2 0 — 2asx, tsx — tmp+3 — str
perc: bd, cym, tri
Arr. Antal Dorati on themes of Offenbach.

| Kalmus | Luck's |

Ohana, Maurice   1913-1992

(b Casablanca, 12 June 1913; d Paris, 13 Nov 1992). French composer of Spanish
descent, with British citizenship

Anneau du Tamarit <1976>   22'

solo violoncello
2[both/pic] 2 2 2 — 2 2 1 0 — 3perc — pf — str
perc: Chinescym, vib, bongos, gong, 4sus cym, 2cym[laid on felt], 2woodblk,
templeblks, 4tomtom, 2tambn, 2sd, 3tamtam

| Jobert |

Livre des prodiges (Book of Marvels) <1978–79>   31'

4[1/pic1.2/pic2.3.afl] 4[1.2.3.Eh] 4[1.2.Ebcl.bcl] 4[1.2.3.cbn] — 6 4 4 1 — tmp+4 — 2hp — pf — str

perc: cym, sd, tambn, marac, vib, Chinescym, bongos, crot, bd, congas, szl cym, xylorimba, 6tomtom, 3tamtam, 2gong, 6woodblk, 3cym [laid on felt]

PART ONE
1. Clair de terre (Earthlight)   2'
2. Cortège des taureaux ailés (Procession of Winged Bulls)   4'
3. Immémorial   4'
4. Hydra   2'
5. Clè des songes (Key of Dreams)   2'
6. Clair de terre (Earthlight)   2'
7. Soleil renversé (Inverted Sun)   2'
PART TWO
1. Conjuration des sorts (Conjuring of Spells)   3'
2. Alecto (Alekto)   1'
3. Son noir (Black Sound)   2'
4. Jeu des masques (Play of Masks)   2'
5. Clair de terre (Earthlight)   2'
6. Korô-Ngô   3'

| Jobert |

Suite pour un mimodrame, pour 10 musiciens <1914>   15'

1 1 1 0 — 0 1 0 0 — 4perc — pf — vn, va, vc, db

perc: sd, bd, tamtam, sus cym, tomtom, tambn, tri, woodblk

Music for a scene by Georges Schehadé.
1. [untitled]   _'
2. Concertino   _'
3. Interlude   _'
4. Mouvement perpétuel (Danse de mort)   _'
5. Finale   _'

| Billaudot |

Tombeau de Claude Debussy <1962>   28'

soloists: soprano, piano, one-third-tone zither

1[fl/pic] 1 1 1 — 1 1 0 0 — 6perc — cel — str[min 4.4.3.2.1; max 6.6.4.4.2]

perc: xyl, marim, glock, vib, tambn, bd, tamtam, marac, tri, crot, templeblks, 8tomtom, 3sd, rasp, 2sus cym, conga

The solo "one-third-tone zither" is an instrument invented by the composer and used in several of his works.
Hommage   _'
Soleils   _'
Ballade de la grande guerre   _'
Autres Soleils   _'
Miroir endormi   _'
Rose des vents et de la pluie   _'
Envoi   _'

| Amphion | Durand |

Oliverio, James   1956-

(b Cleveland, OH, 11 April 1956). American

Concerto, Timpani, No.1 (The Olympian) <1990>   23'

3[1.2.pic] 3[1.2.Eh] 3[1.2.bcl] 3[1.2.cbn] — 4 3 3 1 — 3perc — hp — str

perc: xyl, woodblk, sd, glock, vib, sus cym, marim, cowbell, cym, bd, chimes, 4templebowl, leadpipe, watertub
I. Volitivo con precisione   7'
II. Lento introspettivo   8'
III. Feroce con brio   8'

| OMI Music |

Dynasty; Double Timpani Concerto <2011>   26'

soloists: 2 timpanists

3[1.2/afl.pic] 3[1.2.Eh] 4[1.2.Ebcl.bcl] 3[1.2.cbn] — 4 4 3 1 — 3perc — 2hp — str

perc: marim, xyl, cym, 2sus cym, 2bd
I. Impetuous   4'
II. Naiveté   5'
III. Interlude [for unaccompanied timpani]   2'
IV. Ancestors Within   6'
V. Destiny   9'

| OMI Music |

Generations <2000>   25'

soloists: 2 females, 2 males   youth chorus

3[1.2.3/pic] 3[1.2.Eh] 3[1.2.bcl] 3 — 4 3 3 1 — tmp+4 — hp — pf — str

perc: bd, bd/cym, cym, sus cym, hi-hat, tri, tambn, xyl, marim, chimes, cabasa, sandblks, anvil, shakere, 2tomtom, 2woodblk
I. Overture   3'
II. Parents   2'
III. Sibs !!!   1'
IV. Grandparents   3'
V. Mating Dance   3'
VI. The Bond   2'
VII. The Challenge   3'
VIII. Childhood Memory   2'
IX. Progeny   3'
X. Every Generation   3'

| OMI Music |

Go Gently My Friend <1984; rev 1994>   6'

1 2[1.Eh] 1 1 — 4 0 0 0 — str

| OMI Music |

The Messenger; Concerto for Percussion & Orchestra <2001>   17'

3[1.2/pic.pic] 3[1.2.Eh] 3[1.2.bcl] 3[1.2.3/cbn] — 4 3 3 1 — 1perc — str

perc: (orch) sus cym, bd, cym, sandblks
(soloist) tmp, chimes, Tibetan prayer bowls, xyl, scraper, rainstick, shakers, ethnic xyl, 5hand drums, 3tri, vib, crot, glock, tamtam
I. Legend   5'
II. Spark   4'
III. Code   8'

| OMI Music |

The Story of Snow White; A Child's Introduction to the Symphony Orchestra <1976; rev 1991>   17'

narrator

2[1.2/pic] 2[1.Eh] 2[1.bcl] 2 — 4 3 3 1 — tmp+1 — hp — str

perc: bd, cym, sus cym, sd, tri, gong, glock, chimes, templeblks, ratch

Some of the narrator's speech is rhythmically notated.

| OMI Music |

UnStoppable <1999>   6'

3[1.2.3/pic] 2 2 2 — 4 3 3 1 — tmp+3 — str

perc: bd, sus cym, marim, tambn, cym, whip, sd, hi-hat, tomtom, sandblks, shaker

| OMI Music |

Voyage Through the Musical Universe; A Child's Introduction to the Symphony Orchestra <1988>   17'

narrator

2[1.2/pic] 2[1.2/Eh] 2[1.2/bcl] 2[1.cbn] — 2 2 2 1 — tape — tmp+2 — hp — str

perc: sd, bd, marim, chimes, xyl, tomtom, cym, cowbell

| OMI Music |

Orbón, Julián
1925-1991

(b Avilés, 7 Aug 1925; d Miami Beach, 20 May 1991). Cuban composer of Spanish birth

Tres versiones sinfónicas <1989>
23'

4[1.2.3.pic] 2 4[1.2.3.bcl] 4[1.2.3.cbn] — 4 4 3 1 — tmp+6 — hp — cel, pf — str

Luis Milan	10'
Perotin	10'
Congo	3'

> Peer

Orff, Carl
1895-1982

(b Munich, 10 July 1895; d Munich, 29 March 1982). German

Carmina burana (Songs of Beuren) <1936>
65'

large chorus, small chorus, children's chorus   solos STBar, short solos TTTBB

3[1.2/pic.3/pic] 3[1.2.3/Eh] 3[1.2/bcl.3/Ebcl] 3[1.2.cbn] — 4 3 3 1 — tmp+6 — cel, 2pf — str

perc: xyl, cast, ratch, slgh-bells, tri, crot["piatti piccoli"], cym, tamtam, chimes, tambn, bd, 3glock, 2sus cym, 2sd, 2nd tmp

With minor adjustments, one of the pianists can cover the celesta part.

A small version by Wilhelm Killmayer is scored for 2 pianos, 5 percussion, & the above voices; this version is intended for school and amateur performances. Schott also publishes a version by Juan Vicente Mas Quiles, for wind band plus the above voices.

This work is part 1 of **Trionfi**, a "trittico teatrale" that also includes *Catulli Carmina* and *Trionfo de Afrodite*.

FORTUNA IMPERATRIX MUNDI (Fortune, Empress of the World)	
1. O Fortuna	3'
2. Fortune plango vulnera	3'
I. PRIMO VERE (In Springtime)	
3. Veris leta facies	4'
4. Omnia Sol temperat	3'
5. Ecce gratum	3'
UF DEM ANGER (On the Green)	
6. Tanz	2'
7. Floret silva	3'
8. Chramer, gip die varwe mir	4'
9. Reie	4'
10. Were diu werlt alle min	1'
II. IN TABERNA (In the Tavern)	
11. Estuans interius	3'
12. Cignus ustus cantat	4'
13. Ego sum abbas	2'
14. In taberna quando sumus	3'
III. COUR D'AMOURS (The Court of Love)	
15. Amor volat undique	3'
16. Dies, nox et omnia	3'
17. Stetit puella	2'
18. Circa mea pectora	2'
19. Si puer com puellula	1'
20. Veni, veni, venias	1'
21. In trutina	2'
22. Tempus est iocundum	3'
23. Dulcissime	3'
BLANZIFLOR ET HELENA (Blanziflor and Helena)	
24. Ave formosissima	2'
FORTUNA IMPERATRIX MUNDI (Fortune, Empress of the World)	
25. O Fortuna	3'

> Schott

Trionfo di Afrodite <1949–1951>
41'

chorus   solos SSTTB

3[1/pic3.2/pic1.3/pic2] 3[1.2/Eh1.3/Eh2] 3[1.2.3/Ebcl] 3[1.2.3/cbn] — 6 3 3 2 — gtr — tmp+9 — 2hp — 3pf — str[12 to 14.12 to 14.12.12.8]

perc: tri, tamtam, chimes, tambn, cast, xyl, woodblk, 3pr cym, 2sd, 2bd, trough xyl, 2marim, 3glock, 4marac[played by tmp]

This work is part 3 of **Trionfi**, a "trittico teatrale" that also includes (1) *Carmina burana*, and (2) *Catulli Carmina*.

I. Canto amebeo di vergini e giovani a Vespero	7'
II. Corteo nuziale ed arrive della sposa e dello sposo	2'
III. Sposa e sposo	8'
IV. Invocazione dell' Imeneo	3'
Inno all' Imenzo	3'
V. Ludi e canti nuziale davanti al talamo; La sposa viene accolta	4'
La sposa viene condotte alla camera nuziale	3'
Epitilamo	6'
VI. Canto di novello sposi dal talamo	2'
VII. Apparizione di Afrodite	2'

> Schott

Ott, David
1947-

(b Crystal Falls, Michigan, 5 July 1947). American

The Angel's Harp
7'

solo harp

3[incl pic] 2 2 2 — 4 2 3 1 — tmp+2 — str

> Park Press

First Trip to the Symphony <2002>
23'

narrator

3[1.2.bcl] 2 2 2 — 4 3 3 1 — tmp+2 — hp — str

perc: bd, cym, sus cym, sd, tri, glock, xyl, chimes, whip

> Park Press

The Water Garden <1985>
9'

3[1.2.3/pic] 3[1.2.Eh] 3 3[1.2.cbn] — 4 3 3 1 — tmp+3 — hp — pf/cel — str

perc: bd, cym, sus cym, szl cym, sd, tamtam, glock, xyl, vib, chimes, crot, woodblk, 4tomtom

There is also a chamber orchestra version, calling for:
1 1 1 1 — 1 1 1 0 — hp — tmp+1 — str

> MMB

Overton, Hall
1920-1972

(b Bangor, MI, 23 Feb 1920; d New York, 24 Nov 1972). American

Symphony for Strings <1955>
21'

str

> Peters

Symphony No.2 <1962>
14'

3[incl pic] 2 2 2 — 4 3 3 1 — tmp+4 — hp — str

> Peters

P

Pachelbel, Johann   1653-1706

(b Nuremberg, bap. 1 Sept 1653; d Nuremberg, bur. 9 March 1706). German

Canon <late 17th c.>   5'

opt cnt — str
Arr. Helmut May. Originally for 3 solo violins and continuo.

| Schott | | |

Canon

see also: Dorff, Daniel
           Pachelbel's Christmas; A Merry Melange

| | | |

Pachulski, Henryk   1859-1921

(b Łazy, nr Siedlce, 4 Oct 1859; d Moscow, Dec 1921). Polish

Suite, op.13 <1897>   18'

2 2 2 2 — 2 0 0 0 — tmp — str
1. Prélude   5'
2. Scherzo   3'
3. Momento lirico   5'
4. Scène de ballet   5'

| Fleisher | Jurgenson | |

Paderewski, Ignacy Jan   1860-1941

(b Kuryłówka, Podolia, 6/18 Nov 1860; d New York, 29 June 1941). Polish

Concerto, Piano, op.17, A minor <1882–1888>   33'

3[1.2.pic] 2[1/Eh.2] 2 2 — 4 2 3 0 — tmp — str
I. Allegro   16'
II. Romanza   8'
III. Allegro molto vivace   9'

| Bote & Bock | Kalmus | Luck's |

Fantaisie polonaise sur des thèmes originaux, op.19 (Polish Fantasy on Original Themes) <1893>   24'

solo piano
3[1.2.pic] 3[1.2.Eh] 2 2 — 4 2 3 1 — tmp+2 — hp — str
perc: tri, tambn, cym, glock

| Bote | Luck's | Schirmer |

Symphony, op.24, B minor (Polonia) <1903–1908>   59'

3[1.2.3/pic] 3[1.2.Eh] 3[1.2.bcl] 3[1.2.cbn] — 4 4 3 1 — 3 contrabass sarrusophones — tmp+2 — hp — org — str
perc: bd, cym, sus cym, field dr, tri, tambn, tamtam, glock, thunder sheet ("tonitruone")
The contrabass sarrusophones are written in E-flat, in treble clef.
I. Adagio maestoso   22'
II. Andante con moto   14'
III. Vivace   23'

| Heugel | | |

Paganini, Nicolò   1782-1840

(b Genoa, 27 Oct 1782; d Nice, 27 May 1840). Italian

Concerto, Violin, No.1, op.6, D major <1816>   35'

2 2 2 2[1.cbn] — 2 2 3 0 — tmp+2 — str
perc: bd, cym, sus cym
Originally in E-flat, with the soloist tuned a half-step sharp; now normally performed in D.
I. Allegro maestoso   20'
II. Adagio   5'
III. Rondo: Allegro spiritoso   10'

| Breitkopf | Kalmus | Luck's |

Concerto, Violin, No.1, op.6, D major (arr. Wilhelmj) <1816>   20'

2 2 2 2 — 4 2 1 0 — tmp — str
A free transcription of the first movement of the concerto by August Wilhelmj.

| Kalmus | Luck's | Simrock |

Concerto, Violin, No.2, op.7, B minor (La clochette; La campanella) <1826>   31'

2[1.opt 2] 2 2 2 — 2 2 3 1[opt serp or euph] — opt tmp+1 or 2 — str
perc: glock, opt bd
Kalmus ed. Gregory Vaught.
I. Allegro maestoso   15'
II. Adagio   7'
III. Rondo   9'

| C. Fischer | Kalmus | Lemoine | Luck's |

Concerto, Violin, No.3, E major <1826>   34'

2 2 2 2 — 2 2 3 1 — tmp+2 — str
I. Introduzione - Allegro marziale   _'
II. Adagio cantabile spianato   _'
III. Polacca: Andantino vivace   _'

| Boccaccini | | |

MOTO PERPETUO, op.11 <1831–1832>

The following are only a few of the many versions and arrangements of this popular work, some with violin solo and some without. The work was originally composed for solo violin and orchestra.

Moto perpetuo, op.11 <1831–1832>   4'

solo violin
2 2 2 2 — 2 0 3 1 — str

| Luck's | | |

Moto perpetuo, op.11 (arr. Jerger) <1831–1832>   4'

solo violin
2[incl pic] 2 2 2 — 2 0 0 0 — 1perc — str
Arr. Wilhelm Jerger.

| Universal | | |

Moto perpetuo, op.11 (arr. Molinari) <1831–1832>   4'

2 2 2 2 — 2 0 3 1 — str
Arr. by Bernardino Molinari, 1934; first violins play original solo part in unison. Trombones & tuba enter only at the end.

| Ricordi | | |

Paine, John Knowles   1839-1906

(b Portland, ME, 9 Jan 1839; d Cambridge, MA, 25 April 1906). American

As You Like It: Overture, op.28 <c1876>   8'
3[1.2.pic] 2 2 2 — 4 2 3 0 — tmp — str

| Kalmus | Luck's |

Azara: Orchestral Scene & 3 Moorish Dances   17'
<1883–1898>
3 3[1.2.Eh] 3[1.2.bcl] 3 — 4 3 3 1 — tmp+4 — hp — str
perc: bd, cym, tri, tambn
Additional 4hn backstage (cued in orchestral parts).
Orchestral Scene (Act II, sc.1b)   7'
Three Moorish Dances (Act III, sc.3)   10'

| Fleisher |

Mass, op.10, D major <1865>   102'
solos SATB   chorus
2 2 2 2 — 2 2 3 0 — tmp — org — str

| AMP |

Oedipus tyrannus: Prelude <1880–1881; rev 1895>   8'
2 2 2 2 — 4 2 3 0 — tmp — str

| Kalmus | Luck's |

Poseidon and Amphitrite; An Ocean Fantasy <c1888>   10'
3[1.2.pic] [1.2.Eh] 2 2 — 4 2 3 1 — tmp — hp — str
Original title: *An Island Fantasy.*

| Kalmus |

Symphony No.1, op.23, C minor <1875>   38'
2 2 2 2 — 4 2 3 0 — tmp — str
1. Allegro con brio   11'
2. Allegro vivace   8'
3. Adagio   10'
4. Allegro vivace   9'

| AMP | Kalmus |

Symphony No.2, op.34, A major (In the Spring; Im   51'
Frühling) <1879>
2 2 2 2 — 4 2 3 0 — tmp — str
The original publisher was Arthur Schmidt of Boston.
1. Introduction   16'
2. Scherzo   10'
3. Adagio   14'
4. Allegro giojoso   11'

| Fleisher |

The Tempest, op.31 <c1876>   25'
3[1.2.pic] 2 2 2 — 4 2 3 1 — tmp — hp — str
Symphonic poem after Shakespeare.
1. Allegro furioso: The Storm   _'
2. Adagio tranquillo: Calm and Happy Scene before Prospero's Cell _'
3. Allegro moderato e maestoso: Prospero's Tale   _'
4. Allegro non troppo: _'
The Happy Love of Ferdinand and Miranda
Episode with Caliban
Triumph of Prospero's "Potent Art"

| Breitkopf | Kalmus | Luck's |

Paisiello, Giovanni   1740-1816

(b Roccaforzata, nr Taranto, 9 May 1740; d Naples, 5 June 1816). Italian

Nina (La pazza per amore): Overture <1789>   5'
0 2 2 2 — 2 0 0 0 — str
Ed. Giuseppe Piccioli.

| Carisch | Kalmus |

La scuffiara: Overture <1787>   6'
2 2 0 2 — 2 2 0 0 — str
Ed. Giuseppe Piccioli. Alternative titles: *La modista raggiratrice; La scuffiara raggiratrice; La scuffiara amante; La cuffiara.*

| Carisch | Kalmus | Luck's |

Sinfonia, D major   7'
0 2 0 0 — 2 0 0 0 — str
Ed. Bernhard Päuler. Authenticity doubtful.

| Peters |

Sinfonia funebre <1797>   10'
2 2 2 2 — 2 2 0 0 — tmp — str
Ed. Giuseppe Piccioli.

| Carisch |

Sinfonia in tre tempi, D major   6'
0 2 0 0 — 2 0 0 0 — str
Ed. Giuseppe Piccioli.

| Carisch | Kalmus | Luck's |

Pann, Carter   1972-

(b La Grange, IL, 21 Feb 1972). American

Mercury Concerto <2008–2009>   23'
solo flute
1 2 2 1 — 2 1 0 0 — tmp+2 — hp — str
perc: bd, cym, sd, tri, glock, xyl, vib, marktree, templeblks, whip, bongos, ratch, sandblks, 2logdrum, 3sus cym
I. Moderato, liberamente   _'
II. Contemplative   _'
III. Allegro molto, winged   _'

| Presser |

Rags to Richard; Two Symphonic Dances <1998>   12'
solo clarinet
2[1.2/pic] 2 2[1.2/bcl] 2 — 4 2 3 1 — tmp+3 — hp — pf/cel — str
I. Terrifying yet Marvelous   7'
II. Fresh, Innocent   5'

| Presser |

Slalom <1999>   10'
3[1.2/pic.3/pic] 3 3[1.2.3/bcl] 3[1.2.3/cbn] — 4 3 3 1 — tmp+3 — hp — pf/cel — str
perc: bd, cym, 2sus cym, 2hi-hat, 4tomtom, 2tri, tambn, tamtam, glock, xyl, marim, crot, woodblk, templeblk, 3whip, 3sandblks, rute, thundersheet, siren whistle

| Presser |

Triple Trombone Concerto <2001>   17'

2 solo tenor trombones, 1 solo bass trombone
2perc — str[6.6.4.4.2, or 8.8.6.4.3, or 12.10.8.8.4]
perc: hi-hat, sd, tomtom, tambn, glock, xyl, woodblk, templeblks, cowbell, whip, bongos, 3sus cym, 3tmp, 2tri, bd/ped
  I. Rutherford's Rag   _'
  II. Angela's Waltz   _'
  III. Gall   _'

Presser

Panufnik, Andrzej   1914-1991

(b Warsaw, 24 Sept 1914; d London, 27 Oct 1991). Polish; settled in England from 1954

Autumn Music <1962; rev 1965>   16'

3 0 3 0 — 2perc — hp — cel, pf — str[0.0.6.6.4 or 0.0.3.3.2]
perc: glock, tri, bd, sd, td

Boosey

Concertino for Timpani, Percussion & Strings   16'
<1979–1980>

solo timpani, solo percussionist
str
perc: **Solo 1:** tmp; **Solo 2:** glock, xyl, vib, chimes, congas, 3tri, 3sus cym, 2tomtoms
  1. Entrada   3'
  2. Canto I   4'
  3. Intermezzo   2'
  4. Canto II   4'
  5. Fine   3'

Boosey

Concerto in modo antico <1951; rev 1955>   15'

solo trumpet
tmp — 1 or 2hp — opt hpsd — str[max 8.8.12.8.6; min 3.3.4.3.2]

Boosey

Concerto, Bassoon <1985>   20'

1 0 2 0 — str[min 6.5.4.3.2]
  1.   2'
  2.   4'
  3.   2'
  4.   10'
  5.   2'

Boosey

Concerto, Piano <1961–1962; rev 1972, 1982>   24'

3[1.2.3/pic] 3[1.2.Eh] 3[1.2.bcl] 3[1.2.cbn] — 4 3 3 1 — 2perc — str
perc: xyl, sus cym, tamtam, tri, bd, sd, td
Originally in 3 mvts, 1961-62. Recomposed 1972 with only 2 mvts (*Molto tranquillo, Molto agitato*). In 1982, *Entrata* added as a first mvt.
  1. Entrata   4'
  2. Larghetto molto tranquillo 13'
  3. Presto molto agitato   7'

Boosey

Divertimento <1947; rev 1955>   15'

str
After string trios by Feliks Janiewicz (1762-1848).

Boosey

Harmony; A Poem for Chamber Orchestra <1989>   17'

2 2 2 2 — str[min 6.4.4.3.0; max 12.10.8.6.0]

Boosey

Heroic Overture (Uwertura bohaterska) <1950–1952;   6'
rev 1969>

3[1.2.pic] 2 3[1.2.bcl] 3[1.2.cbn] — 4[or 6] 3 3 1 — 4perc — str
perc: glock, sd, td, bd, tamtam, cym
Composer prefers extra horns & percussion.

Boosey

Jagiellonian Triptych <1966>   7'

str[min 6.6.4.3.2]
Based on 16th & 17th century Polish fragments.
  Preambulum   _'
  Cantio   _'
  Chorea polonica   _'

Boosey

Lullaby (Kołysanka) <1947; rev 1955>   8'

2hp — str[6.6.6.6.5]

Boosey

Nocturne <1947; rev 1955>   16'

3[1.2.3/pic] 2 3[1.2.bcl] 3[1.2.cbn] — 4 3 3 1 — tmp+4 — pf — str
perc: sd, td, cym, tri, bd, tamtam

Boosey

Old Polish Suite (Suita staropolska) <1950; rev 1955>   12'

str
  Cenar   _'
  Interlude   _'
  Wyrwany   _'
  Chorale   _'
  Hayduk   _'

Boosey

Symphony No.8 (Sinfonia votiva) <1981; rev 1984>   22'

3[1.2.pic] 3[1.2.Eh] 3[1.2.bcl] 3[1.2.cbn] — 4 3 3 1 — 5perc — 1 or 2hp — str[min 14.12.10.8.6]
perc: glock, vib, chimes, 3tri, 3sus cym, 3tamtam
  I. Con devozione: Andante rubato   14'
  II. Con passione: Allegro assai   8'

Boosey

Symphony No.10 <1988; rev 1990>   21'

3 2 3[1.2.3/bcl] 3[1.2.cbn] — 6 3 3 1 — 2perc — hp — pf[ampd if possible] — str
perc: sd, td, bd, gong, tamtam, 2sus cym

Boosey

Tragic Overture (Uwertura tragiczna) <1942; rev   7'
reconstructed 1945; rev. 1955>

3[1.2.3/pic] 0 3[1.2.bcl] 3[1.2.cbn] — 4 3 3 1 — 3perc — str
perc: bd, cym, field dr, tamtam

Boosey

Parker, Horatio   1863-1919

(b Auburndale, MA, 15 Sept 1863; d Cedarhurst, NY, 18 Dec 1919). American

Hora novissima <1893>   62'

chorus   solos SATB
2 2 2 2 — 4 2 3 1 — tmp+2 — hp — org — str
perc: bd, cym
PART I

1. Introduction & Chorus: Hora novissima	7'
2. Quartet: Hic breve vivitur	6'
3. Aria (bass): Spe modo vivitur	5'
4. Chorus: Pars mea, Rex meus	5'
5. Aria (soprano): O bona patria	5'
6. Quartet & Chorus: Tu sine littore	5'
PART II	
7. Solo (tenor): Urbs Syon aurea	5'
8. Double Chorus: Stant Syon atria	4'
9. Solo (alto): Gens duce splendida	5'
10. Chorus a cappella: Urbs Syon unica	4'
11. Quartet & chorus: Urbs Syon inclyta	11'

Kalmus   Luck's

A Northern Ballad, op.46 <1899>   12'

3[incl 2pic] 2[incl Eh] 2 2 — 4 2 3 1 — tmp+1 — hp — str

Fleisher

Parry, Hubert   1848-1918

(b Bournemouth, 27 Feb 1848; d Rustington, Sussex, 7 Oct 1918). English

An English Suite <1890–1918>   21'

str

1. Prelude	4'
2. In Minuet Style	3'
3. Sarabande	4'
4. Caprice	3'
5. Pastoral	2'
6. Air	2'
7. Frolic	3'

Kalmus   Luck's

Ode on St. Cecilia's Day <1889>   45'

chorus   solos SBar
2 2 3[1.2.bcl] 3[1.2.cbn] — 4 2 3 1 — tmp — hp — org — str

Kalmus

Suite in F (Lady Radnor's Suite) <1894>   15'

str

1. Prelude	3'
2. Allemande	2'
3. Sarabande	3'
4. Bourée	3'
5. Slow minuet	2'
6. Gigue	2'

Kalmus   Luck's   Novello

Symphony No.3 in C (The English) <1887–1889; rev 1902>   34'

2 2 2 2 — 4 2 3[opt] 0 — tmp — str

1. Allegro energico	8'
2. Andante sostenuto	10'
3. Allegro molto scherzoso	5'
4. Moderato	11'

Kalmus   Novello

Symphony No.5 (Symphonic Fantasia '1912') <1912>   27'

2 3[1.2.Eh] 3[1.2.bcl] 3[1.2.cbn] — 4 2 3 1 — tmp — 2hp — str

Stress	7'
Love	6'
Play	5'
Now	9'

Curwen

Pärt, Arvo   1935-

(b Paide, 11 Sept 1935). Estonian

Cantus in Memory of Benjamin Britten <1977>   6'

1perc — str
perc: chime[A3]

Universal

Credo <1968>   12'

chorus   solo piano
4[2fl, 2pic] 2 4[2cl, 2bcl] 4[2bn, 2cbn] — 4 4 3 1 — tmp+10 — str
perc: vib, xyl, bd, tamtam, cym, sus cym, sd, tri, glock

Universal

Festina lente <1988; rev 1990>   6'

opt hp — str

Universal

Fratres <1977; rev 1991>   12'

1perc — str
perc: claves, bd
Originally a chamber work for 12 instruments (1977). Arranged by the composer for various combinations, including this one (1991); also a version for violin, strings & perc (1992), and one for trombone, strings & perc (1993).

Universal

Nekrolog, op.5 <1960>   12'

3[1.2.pic] 3[1.2.Eh] 4[1.2.Ebcl.bcl] 3[1.2.cbn] — 4 4 3 1 — tmp+3 — pf — str
perc: sd, cym, xyl

Belaieff

Silouans Song (My Soul Yearns after the Lord…) <1991>   5'

str

Universal

Wenn Bach Bienen gezüchtet hätte … (If Bach Had Raised Bees …) <1976; rev 1984>   10'

1[1/pic] 1 1 1 — 1 0 0 0 — 1perc[woodblk] — pf — str[4.4.4.4.2 (or 8.8.8.8.4)]

Universal

Partos, Ödön   1907-1977

(b Budapest, 1 Oct 1907; d Tel Aviv 6 July 1977). Israeli

Yiskor (In memoriam) <1947>   9'

solo viola
str

Israeli

Pasatieri, Thomas
1945-

(b New York, 20 Oct 1945). American

Alleluia <1991>
3'

medium voice (baritone or mezzo-soprano)
2 2 2 2 — 3 2 0 0 — tmp/perc — hp — str
perc: cym, sus cym, finger cym

Presser

Concerto, Piano
27'

2[1/pic.2] 2 2[1.2/bcl] 2[1.2/cbn] — 2 2 2 0 — tmp+2 — hp — str
perc: xyl, vib, tri, woodblk, szl cym, sus cym, cym, sd, tomtom, bd, whip, finger cym
   I. Allegro   _'
   II. Lento   _'
   III. Allegro   _'

Subito

Concerto, 2 Pianos & Strings <1994>
32'

str
   I. Andante serioso   _'
   II. Lento cantabile   _'
   III. Allegro serioso   _'

Subito

In the Light of Angels
27'

solo soprano & mezzo-soprano   children's chorus
2 2[1.ob da cacc] 0 1 — 0 0 0 0 — str
   1. Overture
   2. The Angel of the Lord
   3. At the break of day
   4. Interlude
   5. And in that region
   6. Mary stayed outside the tomb
   7. When the Lamb opened the seventh seal

Presser

Sieben Lehmannlieder <1988>
26'

solo soprano
2[incl pic] 2 2[incl bcl] 2[incl cbn] — 4 2 2 1 — tmp+1 — hp — cel — str
Poems by Lotte Lehmann.
   1. Ich bin allein auf Bergesgipfeln   _'
   2. Wie lieb' ich diese klare Stunde   _'
   3. So hört' ich wieder deiner Stimme Ton   _'
   4. In Flammen starb dein Bild   _'
   5. Wie schön ist dieser tiefe Schlummer   _'
   6. Narzissus (Auf ein Bild): Nicht eines Rehes flücht'ge Spur   _'
   7. Die Welt scheint ganz aus Glut gesponnen   _'

Presser

Symphony <2009>
22'

3 3 3 2 — 4 3 3 0 — tmp+3 — hp — str
perc: bd, cym, sus cym, sd, tri, tamtam, glock, xyl, belltree, marac, finger cym, glass windchimes, 2tomtom, 2woodblk
In one mvt.

Presser

Paulus, Stephen
1949-2014

(b Summit, NJ, 24 Aug 1949). American

Concertante <1989>
11'

3[1.2.pic] 3 3 3 — 4 3 3 1 — tmp+3 — pf — str

EAM

Concerto for Orchestra <1983>
27'

3[1.2.pic] 3[1.2.Eh] 3 3[1.2.cbn] — 4 4 3 1 — tmp+3 — hp — pf/cel — str
   I. Bold and Impetuous   _'
   II. With Abandon   _'
   III. Tenderly and Somewhat Mournful   _'
   IV. Lively and with Buoyancy   _'
   V. Austere; Explosive   _'

EAM

Voices from the Gallery <1991>
33'

narrator
1 1 1 1 — 1 1 0 0 — tmp/perc — str[min 3.3.2.2.1]
perc: vib, glock, sus cym, sd, ratch, brake dr, woodblk, whip, flexatone, claves, belltree, hi-hat, tambn, bd, cym, chimes, sandblks, 4tomtom
Each mvt based on a famous work of art; the narrator (a virtuoso part) speaks the thoughts of the subjects.
   I. The Winged Victory of Samothrace   5'
   II. American Gothic   2'
   III. The Garden of Earthly Delights   2'
   IV. Infanta Margarita   3'
   V. Picasso's Goat   2'
   VI. Nude Descending a Staircase   3'
   VII. The Birth of Venus   3'
   VIII. Mona Lisa   4'
   IX. The Beggars   2'
   X. Christina's World   4'
   XI. Dance at Bougival   3'

EAM

Peck, Russell
1945-2009

(b Detroit, 25 Jan 1945; d Greensboro, NC, 1 Mar 2009). American

Don't Tread on Me <1995>
4'

str
This work is also used as the 1st mvt of *Signs of Life II*.

Pecktackular

Flying on Instruments; Concerto for Orchestra <1997>
20'

3[1.2.3/pic] 3[1.2.Eh] 3[1.2.Eb] 3[1.2.cbn] — 4 3 3 1 — tmp+3 — str
perc: bd, cym, 3 sus cym, szl cym, hi-hat, sd, 3tomtom, tri, tambn, tamtam, glock, xyl, chimes, belltree, 2woodblk, claves, cast, vibraslap
   Mysterious Fire   6'
   Out of the Blue   9'
   Flying on Instruments   5'

Pecktackular

Freedom Fanfare <1995>
3'

3[1.2.pic] 2 3[1.2.opt bcl] 2 — 4 3 3 1 — tmp+2 — str
perc: bd, small bd, 3sus cym, hi-hat, sd, 3tomtom, tambn, mounted tambn, xyl, chimes, crot [set may be used if absolutely necessary]

Pecktackular

The Glory and the Grandeur; Concerto for Percussion Trio <1988>
12'

3 solo percussion
3[1.2.3/pic] 2 3[1.2.bcl] 3[1.2.cbn] — 4 3 3 1 — tmp+1 — hp — str

Pecktackular

Harmonic Rhythm; Concerto for Timpani <2000>
22'

timpani solo
3[1.2.3/pic] 3[1.2.Eh] 3[1.2.bcl] 3[1.2.cbn] — 4 3 3 1 — 2(or 3)perc — pf — str
perc: bd, cym, 3 sus cym, Chinesecym, sd, 3toms, 3roto-toms, brakedrum, tri, tambn, tamtam, glock, xyl, marim, vib, chimes, crot, woodblk, templeblk, marac

Pecktackular

Jack and Jill at Bunker Hill <1976; rev 1997> 9'

narrator
3[1.2.3/pic] 3[1.2.Eh] 3[1.2.bcl] 3[1.2.cbn] — 4 3 3 1 — tmp+2 — hp — str
perc: xyl, glock, chimes, tamtam, templeblks, bd, thunder, whip, ratch, set, 2balloons & pin
Cued to be playable with:
   2[1.pic] 2 2 2 — 4 2 3 1 — tmp+2[incl set] — str
A separate smaller version is also available for:
   2[1.pic] 2 2 2 — 2 2 1 0 — tmp+1[incl set] — str (plus opt tuba & hp)

Pecktackular

Mozart Escapes the Museum; Concerto for Orchestra <1997> 23'

3[1.2.pic] 2 2 3[1.2.cbn] — 4 3 3 1 — tmp+3 — str
perc: bd, sd, tamtam, glock, xyl, marim(4th mvt only), chimes, crot, marktree, templeblks, 3sus cym, 2tri, 3tomtoms
Based on Mozart keyboard sonata movements; each movement highlights a section of the orchestra.
   1. Revolutionary Brass (K.310, 1st mvt)   5'
   2. Amadeus Meets Stradivarious (K.310, 2nd mvt)   7'
   3. Woodwinds à la Wolfgang (K.333, final mvt)   5'
   4. Mallets and Mozart (K.332, final mvt)   6'

Pecktackular

Peace Overture <1988> 11'

3[1.2.3/pic] 3[1.2.Eh] 3[1.2.bcl] 3[1.2.cbn] — 4 3 3 1 — tmp+4 — pf — str
perc: xyl, glock, chimes, bd, szl cym, cym, hi-hat, tamtam, ratch, 3tomtom, 3sus cym, 2tri
Cued to be playable with:
   2[1.2/pic] 2 2 2 — 4 3 3 1 — tmp+2 — pf — str

Pecktackular

Playing With Style <1991; rev 1999> 10'

narrator (may be conductor)
2 2 2 2 — 4 2 3 1 — tmp+2 — str
perc: xyl, glock, sd, bd, hi-hat, sus cym, cym, tri, woodblk, tambn, vibrslp, belltree, ratch, 3tomtom, sandblks, sirenwhstl, pol whstle, klaxon
Also available for: 2 2 2 2 — 2 2 1 1 — tmp/perc — str.

Pecktackular

Signs of Life <1983> 12'

str[min 3.3.2.2.1]
   I. Arioso   6'
   II. Scherzo   6'

Pecktackular

Signs of Life II <1986> 16'

str[min 3.3.2.2.1]
This work is the combination of the composer's *Don't Tread on Me* with the 2 mvts of *Signs of Life*.
   I. Allegro [Don't Tread on Me]   4'
   II. Arioso   6'
   III. Scherzo   6'

Pecktackular

The Thrill of the Orchestra <1985> 13'

narrator
3[1.2.3/pic] 3[1.2.Eh] 3[1.2.bcl] 3[1.2.cbn] — 4 3 3 1 — tmp+3 — str
perc: tambn, glock, bd, szl cym, tamtam, sd, templeblks, belltree, xyl, chimes, cym, marac, metal windchimes, 3sus cym, 3tomtoms, 2tri, opt vib
Cued to be playable with: 2 2 2 2 — 4 2 3 1 — tmp+2 — str.
A separate smaller version is also available for:
   2 2 2 2 — 2 2 0 0 — tmp/perc — str (plus opt tbn, tuba & perc)

Pecktackular

The Upward Stream; Concerto for Tenor Saxophone <1985> 20'

solo tenor saxophone
3[1.2.3/pic] 2 2 2 — 4 3 3 1 — tmp+2 — str
perc: bd, sd, tri, tambn, tamtam, glock, xyl, chimes, marktree, belltree, templeblks, guiro, vibrslp, woodblk, cym, 3tomtoms, 2sus cym
   Adagietto   5'
   Allegro; Adagietto   8'
   Allegro molto   7'

Pecktackular

Voice of the Wood; Concerto for Cello Quartet <1999> 21'

4 solo violoncelli
3[1.2.3/pic] 3[1.2.Eh] 3[1.2.bcl] 3[1.2.cbn] — 4 3 3 1 — tmp+3 — hp — pf — str[no vc]
perc: bd, small bd, cym, 3 sus cym, sd, 3tomtom, tambn, tamtam, glock, xyl, chimes, crot, 2woodblk, claves, cast, vibraslap, lion roar
   Prelude   5'
   Fantasia   16'

Pecktackular

Where's Red Robin? (Song of the Little Robin) <1973; rev 1995> 17'

narrator
3[1.2.3/pic] 3 3[1.2.3/Ebcl] 3[1.2.cbn] — 4 3 3 1 — tmp+2 — hp — pf — str
perc: xyl, vib, chimes, bd, sd, hi-hat, tamtam, cym, tambn, ratch, woodblk, tri, lionroar, siren, templeblks, glock, crot, marim[opt], 3tomtoms, 3sus cym, glass windchimes, 2crickets, slide whistle, whistle, 2cowbells, clown's horn
Cued to be playable with:
   2[1.pic] 2 2[1.2/Ebcl] 2 — 4 2 3 1 — tmp+2 — hp — pf — str
Score includes options for reduced duration.

Pecktackular

Penderecki, Krzysztof 1933-

(b Dębica, 23 Nov 1933). Polish

Adagio

see his: Symphony No.4

Anaklasis <1959–1960> 9'

tmp+5 — hp — cel, pf — str[20.0.8.8.6]
perc: bongos, chimes, congas, gong, glock, tamtam, tri, vib, woodblk, 6pr cym, 6tomtom, xylorimba

Moeck   PWM

The Awakening of Jacob (Przebudzenie Jakuba; Als Jakob erwachte) <1974> 8'

3[1/pic.2/pic.3] 3[1.2.3/Eh] 3 3[1.2.3/cbn] — 5 3 3 1 — tmp+1 — str[24.0.10.10.8]
perc: bd, tamtam
All woodwind players double on ocarinas.

Schott

Capriccio, Violin & Orchestra <1967> 10'

4 4 5[1.2.3.cbcl.Ebcl] 4[1.2.3.cbn] — 6 4 4 1 — 4sx[ssx, 2asx, bsx] — gtr, elec bass — tmp+5 — hp — harm, pf — str
perc: vib, bongos, ratch, bd, guiro, whip, tri, cym, sus cym, 2sets chimes, 5woodblks, 4cowbells, 2tamtams, 2Javanese gongs; covered by tmp: claves, saw

Schott

Concerto, Viola <1983>   18'

2[1.2/pic] 2 2 2[1.2/cbn] — 2 2 2 0 — tmp+3 — cel — str

perc: sus cym, crot, tamtam, chimes, field dr, tambn, glock, xyl, tomtom, bongos, 4tri

Also transcribed for violoncello & orchestra by Boris Pergamenschikow. A version also exists with accompaniment for strings, perc & cel.

Schott

Concerto, Violin <1976–1977; rev 1988>   39'

3[1.2.3/pic] 3[1.2.3/Eh] 5[1.2.3/Ebcl.bcl.cbcl] 3[1.2.cbn] — 4 3 3 1 — 2tmp+3 — hp — cel — str

perc: sd, gong, tamtam, tambn, chimes, cym, bd, 3sus cym, tri[played by tmp2]

Schott

De natura sonoris No.1 <1966>   8'

4[1.2.3/pic.4/pic] 4[1.2.3.Eh] 3[1.2.bcl] 4[1.2.3.cbn] — 6 4 3 1 — asx — tmp+5 — pf, harm — str[24.0.8.8.6]

perc: vib, glock, bongos, sd, bd, whip, claves, woodblk, cym, gong, tamtam, flexatone, 6tomtom

Moeck	PWM

De natura sonoris No.2 <1970–1971>   10'

0 0 0 0 — 4 0 4 1 — tmp+4 — pf, harm — str[24.0.8.8.6]

perc: flexatone, chimes, crot, slide whistle, 4sus cym, iron rail, 2tamtams, 2gongs, metalblks, bell; played by tmp: cowbell, saw, woodblk

PWM	Schott

Emanations (Emanacje) <1958>   8'

2 str orchs tuned a half-step apart [24.0.10.8.8]

Moeck	PWM

Flourescences (Fluorescencje) <1961–1962>   14'

4[1.2.3.4/pic] 4 4 4 — 6 4 3 2 — tmp+5 — pf — str[24.0.8.8.6]

perc: tri, bongos, gong, vib, guiro, chimes, flexatone, tamtam, claves, ratch, siren, 2sus cym, metalblks, 4woodblks, 6whistles, Javanese gong, 4tomtoms, 2cowbells, 2field dr, elecbell, saw, typewriter; pieces of iron, glass & wood

Moeck	PWM

Passio et mors domini nostri Iesu Christi secundum Lucam (St. Luke Passion) <1963–1966>   80'

3 mixed choruses, boy choir   solos SBarB, reciter
4[1.2.3/pic.4/pic/afl] 0 1[bcl] 4[1.2.3.cbn] — 6 4 4 1 — 2asx — tmp+6 — hp — pf, harm, org — str[24.0.10.10.8]

perc: bd, bongos, field dr, whip, guiro, claves, glock, vib, 6tomtoms, 4woodblks, 4sus cym, 2tamtams, 2gongs

Moeck	PWM

Polymorphia <1961>   10'

str[24.0.8.8.8]

Moeck

Sonata, Violoncello & Orchestra <1964>   10'

0 0 0 4[1.2.3.cbn] — 6 0 3 1 — 4perc — pf — str

perc: sd, bongos, whip, claves, guiro, tamtam, 3woodblks

Belwin	PWM

Symphony No.1 <1972–1973>   31'

3[1/pic.2/pic.3] 3[1.2.3/Eh] 4[1.2.3/Ebcl.bcl] 3[1.2.3/cbn] — 5 3 4 1 — 2tmp+4 — hp — cel, pf, harm — str[24.0.8.8.6]

perc: glock, templeblks, congas, whip, vibrslp, bd, guiro, vib, marim, bongos, ratch, gong, claves, chimes, crot, 4sus cym, 2tamtams, 5cowbells, 6tomtoms, clappers, 5woodblks, 2tri, iron, 5wood drums

| *1. Arche I; Dynamics I* | *20'* |
| *2. Dynamics II; Arche II* | *11'* |

Schott

Symphony No.2 (Christmas Symphony; Wigilijna; Weihnachtssinfonie) <1979–1980>   35'

3[1.2.pic] 3[1.2.Eh] 3[1.2.3/Ebcl/bcl] 3[1.2.cbn] — 5 3 3 1 — 2tmp+ — cel — str

perc: bd, field dr, cym, tri, 2tamtams, gong, glock, chimes, xyl

In one movement.

Moderato	*8'*
Allegretto	*4'*
Lento	*10'*
Tempo I	*4'*
Allegretto	*9'*

Schott

Symphony No.4 (Adagio) <1989>   31'

3[1.2.pic] 3[1.2.Eh] 4[1.2.Ebcl.bcl] 3[1.2.cbn] — 5 6[3tp are offstage] 4 1 — tmp+3 — str

perc: tri, sus cym, tamtam, field dr, tambn, rototom, belltree, chimes, xyl, triangle-tree, crotales-tree

Adagio is not an excerpt, but is in fact the title of Penderecki's *Symphony No.4*.

Adagio	*5'*
Più animato	*3'*
Tempo I	*13'*
Allegro	*6'*
Tempo II	*4'*

Schott

To the Victims of Hiroshima (Threnody; Tren ofiarom Hiroszimy; Threnos den Opfern von Hiroshima) <1960>   9'

str[24.0.10.10.8]

EMI	Schott

Pentland, Barbara   1912-2000

(b Winnipeg, 2 Jan 1912; d Vancouver, 5 Feb 2000). Canadian

Symphony No.3 (Symphony for Ten Parts) <1957>   10'

1 1 0 0 — 1 1 0 0 — tmp+1 — vn, va, vc, db

Berandol

Perera, Ronald   1941-

(b Boston, 25 Dec 1941). American

Chamber Concerto, Brass Quintet, Winds & Percussion <1983>   19'

2[1.2/pic] 1 2[1.2/bcl] 1 — 1 1 1[btbn] 0 — 2perc — pf — [no str]

perc: crot, chimes, cym, glock, marim, sd, sus cym, tamtam, templeblks, vib, woodblk, xyl, tmp, 5tomtoms

Brass quintet = 2tp, hn, tbn, tuba.

Introduction	_'
Seven Variations:	_'
L'istesso tempo	_'
Driving; Jazzy	_'
Volatile	_'
Broad and Sustained	_'
Very Fast and Bright	_'
Elegant	_'
Dark	_'

ECS

THE SAINTS; Three Pieces for Orchestra with Audience Participation
1. Choirs <1990>   3'

audience sings
2 2 2 2 — 2 2 2 0 — tmp — str

Music Assoc

2. Joyful Noise <1990>   3'

audience provides sound effects
2 2 2 2 — 2 2 0 0 — prerecorded tape — tmp — str

Music Assoc

3. Marching In <1990>   3'

audience sings
1[1/pic] 2 1 2 — 2 2 2 0 — ssx (or asx), asx, tsx — opt banjo —
tmp+1 — pf — str
2cl & bcl may substitute for 3 saxophones.

Music Assoc

Pergolesi, Giovanni Battista   1710-1736

(b Iesi, Marche, 4 Jan 1710; d Pozzuoli, nr Naples, 16 March 1736). Italian

P = Marvin E. Paymer, *Giovanni Battista Pergolesi: A Thematic
Catalogue of the Opera Omnia.* New York: Pendragon Press, 1977.

*Many works attributed to Pergolesi are spurious or doubtful. The
collected edition begun in 1986 (ed. B.S. Brook, Marvin Paymer, and
others) will be helpful in sorting these out, when completed.*

Concertino, E-flat major   7'

str
Ed. Renato Fasano. Authenticity doubtful.

Ricordi

Concerto, Flute, P.33, G major   13'

cnt — str[no va]
Authenticity doubtful.

Boosey	Luck's	Sikorski

Concerto, Violin, B-flat major   18'

0 2 0 1 — 2 0 0 0 — str
Ed. Adriano Lualdi. Authenticity doubtful.

Carisch

Magnificat, P.59   11'

chorus   solos SATB
cnt — str
Ed. Clayton Westermann. Authenticity doubtful; believed to be by
Francesco Durante.

I. Magnificat anima mea	2'
II. Et misericordia	2'
III. Deposuit potentes	2'
IV. Suscepit Israel	2'
V. Sicut locutus	1'
VI. Sicut erat in principio	2'

Kalmus

Stabat Mater, P.77   39'

soprano and alto solos
cnt — str
Although sometimes performed with treble chorus, the work
is intended for soloists, not chorus.
   Kunzelmann score does not match the orchestral parts, which are more
heavily edited.

I. Stabat Mater	4'
II. Cujus animam	3'
III. O quam tristis	2'
IV. Quae moerebat	3'
V. Quis ost homo	3'
VI. Vidit suum	3'
VII. Eia Mater	3'
VIII. Fac ut ardeat	2'
IX. Sancta Mater	6'
X. Fac ut portem	4'
XI. Inflammatus	2'
XII. Quando corpus - Amen	4'

Bärenreiter	Kalmus	Kunzelmann	Ricordi	Schott

Stabat Mater

see also: Bach, Johann Sebastian
          Tilge, Höchster, meine Sünden

Perkinson, Coleridge Taylor   1932-2004

(b Winston-Salem, NC, 14 June, 1932; d Chicago, 9 March 2004). American

Grass; Poem for Piano, Strings & Percussion <1973>   16'

tmp+1 — pf — str
perc: bd, sus cym, sd, tamtam

MMB

Sinfonietta No.1 <1976>   15'

str
I. Sonata Allegro	4'
II. Song Form	5'
III. Rondo	6'

MMB

Sinfonietta No.2 (Generations) <1996>   18'

str
I. Misterioso	6'
II. Alla sarabande	5'
III. Alla burletta	2'
IV. Allegro vivace	5'

MMB

Perle, George   1915-2009

(b Bayonne, NJ, 6 May 1915; d New York City, 23 January 2009). American

Adagio for Orchestra <1993>   8'

4[1.2.pic1.pic2] 4[1.2.3.Eh] 4[1.2.3.bcl] 4[1.2.3.cbn] — 4 4 4 1 —
tmp — hp — cel — str

Galaxy

Concerto, Piano, No.1 <1990>   25'

4[1.2.3.4/pic] 4[1.2.3.Eh] 4[1.2.3.bcl] 4[1.2.3.cbn] — 4 4 3 1 —
tmp+3 — hp — cel[played by perc] — str
perc: cym, sus cym, sd, tamtam, xyl, marim, 2tri
Errata sheet for score available from publisher.
I. Allegro	11'
II. Scherzo	3'
III. Adagio	5'
IV. Allegro	6'

ECS

Concerto, Piano, No.2 <1992>   19'

2[1.2/pic] 2 2 2 — 4 2 0 0 — tmp+2 — str
perc: sd, glock, vib, whip
   I. Allegro molto   8'
   II. Adagio   6'
   III. Allegro   5'

> ECS

New Fanfares <1987>   2'

0 0 0 0 — 4 3 3 0 — [no str]

> Galaxy

Serenade No.2 for Eleven Players <1968>   15'

1 1 1 1 — 0 1 0 0 — tsx — 1perc (incl tmp) — pf — vn, va, vc

> Presser

Six Bagatelles <1965>   6'

3[incl pic] 3[incl Eh] 3[incl bcl] 3[incl cbn] — 4 3 3 1 — tmp+2 — hp — cel — str

> Presser

Three Movements for Orchestra <1960>   18'

4[1.2.3.pic] 3 3[1.2.bcl] 2 — 4 3 3 1 — tmp+3 — hp — cel, pf — str
perc: sd, cym, woodblk, vib, xyl, glock
  Prelude   5'
  Contrasts   9'
  Ostinato   4'

> Merion

Transcendental Modulations <1993>   21'

4[1.2.3/pic1.4/pic2/afl] 4[1.2.3.Eh] 4[1.2.3/Ebcl.bcl] 4[1.2.3.4/cbn] — 4 4 4[2ten, 2bass] 1 — tmp+3 — hp — pf, cel — str
perc: bd, sus cym, tamtam, glock, xyl, vib, chimes, templeblks

> Galaxy

Perosi, Lorenzo   1872-1956

(b Tortona, 20 Dec 1872; d Rome, 12 Dec 1956). Italian

La risurrezione di Lazzaro <1898>   84'

chorus   solos SSTBarB
2 2 2 2 — 4 3 4 0 — tmp — hp — str
  PART 1
  Preludio   7'
  La malattia di Lazzaro   6'
  La dilezione — La consolazione   30'
  PART 2
  Preludio — Pianto de Cristo   31'
  Inno — Finale   10'

> Ricordi

Perry, Julia   1924-1979

(b Lexington, KY, 25 March 1924; d Akron, OH, 24 April 1979). American

Concerto, Violin <1963–1965; rev 1968>   17'

2[1.2/pic] 2 2 — 3 2 2 0 — tmp+3 — hp — pf — str
perc: xyl, cym, sd
Score (photoprinted from manuscript) very difficult to read. Tenor sax written in score in bass clef (a minor 7th below sounding pitch!); check the part.

> C. Fischer

Persichetti, Vincent   1915-1987

(b Philadelphia, 6 June 1915; d Philadelphia, 14 Aug 1987). American

Concerto, English Horn, op.137 <1977>   24'

str
  I. Con fantasia   9'
  II. Amabile   6'
  III. Spiritoso   9'

> Elkan-Vogel

Dance Overture, op.20 <1942>   8'

3[1.2.pic] 3[1.2.Eh] 3[1.2.bcl] 3[1.2.cbn] — 4 4 3 1 — tmp+3 — pf — str
perc: sd, cym, bd, sus cym

> Elkan-Vogel

The Hollow Men <1944>   8'

solo trumpet
str

> Elkan-Vogel

Night Dances, op.114 <1970>   22'

3[1.2.pic] 3[1.2.Eh] 3[1.2.bcl] 2 — 4 3 3 1 — tmp+3 — str
perc: woodblk, timbales, sd, tambn, tamtam, td, bd, xyl, glock, 2sus cym
  I. Shadow Dancers Alive in Your Blood Now (Carl Sandburg)   3'
  II. Their Radiant Spirals Crease Our Outer Night (Daniel Hoffman)   2'
  III. Sleep to Dreamier Sleep Be Wed (James Joyce)   4'
  IV. The Incendiary Eve of Deaths and Entrances (Dylan Thomas)   3'
  V. The Loneliness Includes Me Unawares (Robert Frost)   3'
  VI. Through the Black Amnesias of Heaven (Sylvia Plath)   4'
  VII. Where at Midnight Motion Stays (Robert Fitzgerald)   3'

> Elkan-Vogel

Serenade No.1, op.1 <1929>   8'

1 1 1 1 — 2 2 1 1 — [no str]

> Elkan-Vogel

Symphony No.4, op.51 <1951>   24'

3[1.2.pic] 3[1.2.Eh] 3[1.2.bcl] 2 — 4 2 3 1 — tmp — str
  I. Adagio; Allegro   8'
  II. Andante   6'
  III. Allegretto   4'
  IV. Presto   6'

> Elkan-Vogel

Symphony No.5, op.61 (Symphony for Strings) <1953>   19'

str
  1. Sostenuto   4'
  2. Allegro   3'
  3. Adagio   4'
  4. Andante   4'
  5. Allegro   4'

> Elkan-Vogel

Symphony No.9, op.113 (Sinfonia janiculum) <1970>   23'

4[1.2.pic1.pic2] 3[1.2.Eh] 4[1.2.Ebcl.bcl] 3[1.2.cbn] — 4 3 3 1 — tmp+3 — hp — str
perc: sd, sus cym, tamtam, td, bd, glock, xyl, chimes, 2timbales
In one mvt.

> Elkan-Vogel

Petering, Mark   1973-

(b Milwaukee, 13 Aug 1973). American

Concerto, Clarinet (Three Psalms) <2008>   16'

str
Also available for solo violin, solo flute, solo alto saxophone, or as a double concerto for clarinet & violin.
I. Psalm Prelude   _'
II. Quilters' Psalm   _'
III. "…like rain on the fields…"   _'

| Petering |

Concerto, Tuba <2009>   15'

2[1/pic.2/pic] 2 2 2 — 2 2 2 0 — 3perc — str
perc: tmp, bd, sus cym, hi-hat, tamtam, glock, marim, vib, chimes, woodblk

| Petering |

Fanfare and Reflection after Ravel <2003>   6'

2[1.2/pic] 2 2 2[1/cbn.2] — 2 2 0 0 — tmp/perc — pf — str
perc: sus cym, marim

| Petering |

Lake Summit after Stravinsky; Prelude for Chamber Orchestra <2001>   12'

1[1/pic] 1 1 1 — 1 0 0 0 — tmp — pf — str
perc: sus cym (played by tmp)
Abridged version (200-bar cut): 7'

| Petering |

Lamentations <2004–2007>   9'

3[1.2/pic.3/pic] 3 3[1.2.3/bcl] 3[1.2.cbn] — 4 3 3 1 — 3perc — pf — str
perc: vib, 2bd

| Petering |

The Swimming Pool <2003>   10'

2 2 2 2 — 2 2 2 1 — asx, tsx — 4perc — [no str]
perc: bd, cym, sus cym, szl cym, tamtam, glock, marim, vib, crot, tmp

| Petering |

Symphony No.2 <2008>   23'

tape [opt] — str
Also playable by string quartet with optional tape, as *String Quartet No.1*.
I. Train & Tower   7'
II. Quilters' Psalm   8'
III. Open Road   8'

| Petering |

Train & Tower after Sibelius <2003>   7'

2 2 2 2 — 2 2 2 0 — tmp/perc+1 — str
perc: cym, sd, tri, szl cym, 2sus cym
Optional recording (CD of train sounds).

| Petering |

Peterson, Wayne   1927-

(b Albert Lea, MN, 8 March 1927). American

The Face of the Night, the Heart of the Dark <1991>   19'

3[incl pic,afl] 3[incl Eh] 3[incl bcl] 3[incl cbn] — 4 3 3 1 — tmp+3 — hp — pf/cel — str

| Peters |

Petrassi, Goffredo   1904-2003

(b Zagarolo, nr Palestrina, 16 July 1904; d Rome, 2 Mar 2003). Italian

Concerto for Orchestra No.1 <1933–1934>   22'

3[1.2.3/pic] 3[1.2.Eh] 3[1.2.bcl] 3[1.2.cbn] — 4 3 3 1 — asx — pf — str
I. Allegro   7'
II. Adagio   10'
III. Tempo di marcia 5'

| Ricordi |

Pettersson, Allan   1911-1980

(b Västra Ryd, Uppland, 19 Sept 1911; d Stockholm, 20 June 1980). Swedish

Symphony No.4 <1958–1959>   39'

3[1.2.pic] 3[1.2.Eh] 3[1.2.bcl] 3[1.2.cbn] — 4 3 3 1 — tmp+7 — cel — str
perc: tri, tambn, sd, field dr, cym, sus cym, bd, tamtam, gong, xyl
In one mvt.

| Nordiska |

Pfitzner, Hans   1869-1949

(b Moscow, 5 May 1869; d Salzburg, 22 May 1949). German

Das Christ-Elflein, op.20 (The Christmas Elf): Overture <1906; rev 1917>   10'

2[1.2/pic] 2 2 2 — 2 0 0 0 — tmp+1 — hp — str
perc: tri

| Boosey | Kalmus | Luck's | Schott |

Concerto, Piano, op.31, E-flat Major <1922>   41'

3[1.2.3/pic] 3 3 3[1.2.3/cbn] — 4 3 3 1 — tmp+1 — hp — str
perc: cym, tri
I. Pomphaft, mit Kraft und Schwung   16'
II. Heiterer Satz: Ziemlich schnell, in einheitlich atemlosen Zeitmass 6'
III. Ausserst ruhig, versonnen, schwärmisch   9'
IV. Rasch ungeschlacht, launig   10'

| Boosey | Fürstner |

Das Kätchen von Heilbronn, op.17a: Overture <1905>   13'

3[1.2.pic] 2 2 2 — 4 3 3 1 — tmp+2 — hp — str
perc: cym, sus cym, tri

| Eulenburg | Kalmus | Ries |

Kleine Sinfonie, op.44, G major <1939>   16'

2 2 2 2 — 0 1 0 0 — 1perc — hp — str
perc: cym
This work may be out of print. The original publisher was Brockhaus.
1. Gemächlich   6'
2. Im Tempo (Allegro) 2'
3. Adagio   5'
4. Heiter bewegt   3'

| Fleisher |

Palestrina: Prelude, Act I <1911–1915>   6'

4 3[1.2.Eh] 4[1.2.3.bcl] 4[1.2.3.cbn] — 4 2 4 1 — tmp — hp — str
Schott also offers also a reduced version by Hans Zanotelli.

| Kalmus | Schott |

Palestrina: Prelude, Act II <1911–1915>   7'

4[1.2.3/pic.4/pic] 3[1.2.Eh] 4[1.2.3/Ebcl.bcl] 4[1.2.3.cbn] — 6 4 4 1
— tmp+2 — str
perc: chimes, cym, sus cym, tamtam, field dr
Schott offers also a reduced version by Hans Zanotelli.

Kalmus	Schott

Palestrina: Prelude, Act III <1911–1915>   8'

2 3[1.2.Eh] 3[1.2.bcl] 3 — 4 0 4 1 — tmp+2 — hp — str
perc: chimes, cym, sus cym, tamtam, field dr
Schott also offers also a reduced version by Hans Zanotelli.

Kalmus	Schott

Scherzo, C minor <1888>   11'

3[1.2.pic] 2 2 — 2 2 0 0 — tmp — str

Kalmus

Phillips, Burrill   1907-1988

(b Omaha, NE, 9 Nov 1907; d Berkeley, CA, 22 June 1988). American

Selections from McGuffey's Reader <1934>   17'

3[1.2.pic] 2 2 2 — 4 3 3 1 — tmp+3 — hp — cel — str

C. Fischer

Phillips, Paul Schuyler   1956-

(b Newark, NJ, 28 April 1956). American

Brownian Motion <1995>   9'

3[1.2/afl.3/pic] 3[1.2.3/Eh] 3[1.2.3/bcl] 3 — 4 3 3 1 — tmp+4 — hp
— pf — str
perc: bd, cym, tri, glock, xyl, marim, vib, chimes, crot, woodblk, marac, 4tomtoms

Barnard

Celestial Harmonies <1996–1997>   25'

str[min 4.3.3.3.1]
I. Adagio misterioso	8'
II. Allegro spiritoso	5'
III. Lento, mesto	4'
IV. Allegro molto ed energico	4'
VI. Adagio mol	4'

Barnard

Piazzolla, Astor   1921-1992

(b Mar del Plata, 11 March 1921; d Buenos Aires, 5 July 1992). Argentine

Two useful websites for Piazzolla's music:
  www.yonezawa.com/piazzolla/scores.htm
  www.piazzolla.org
*Beware: abbreviations are not always what one might expect. For
example,* bn *stands for* bandoneon *(not bassoon).*

Aconcagua; Concerto for Bandoneon   20'

tmp+1 — hp — pf — str[10.8.6.5.4]
perc: bd, tri, guiro
Allegro marcato	7'
Moderato	7'
Presto	6'

Curci

Oblivion   3'

1 1 1 1 — 0 1 0 0 — tmp+1 — str
perc: sus cym
Originally for oboe (or bandoneon) & strings; arr. Eduardo Marturet.

Pagani

Piccinni, Niccolò   1728-1800

(b Bari, 16 Jan 1728; d Passy, nr Paris, 7 May 1800). Italian

Iphigenie en Tauride: Overture <1781>   8'

2 2 0 2 — 0 2 0 0 — tmp — str

Doblinger

Picker, Tobias   1954-

(b New York, 18 July 1954). American

Keys to the City (Piano Concerto No.2) <1983>   18'

solo piano
2[1.2/pic] 2 2[1/ssx.2/asx/bcl] 2[1.2/cbn] — 4 2 3 1 — tmp+1 — str
Reduced version of the accompaniment available, scored for:
ob, cl, bn, str 5t.

Helicon

Old and Lost Rivers <1986>   6'

3[1.2.pic] 2 3[1.2.bcl] 3 — 6 2 0 1 — tmp+2 — hp — pf — str
Originally for piano; orchestrated by the composer.
  2 trombones may substitute for horns 5 & 6.

Helicon

Symphony No.1, in 2 Movements <1982>   27'

3[1.2.3/pic] 3[1.2.Eh] 3[1.2.bcl] 3 — 4 2 3 1 — tmp+1 — 2hp — pf
— str
perc: bd, sus cym, hi-hat, chimes, glock

Picker

Pierné, Gabriel   1863-1937

(b Metz, 16 Aug 1863; d Ploujean, Finistere, 17 July 1937). French

Cydalise et le chèvre-pied: Suite No.1 <1923>   28'

6[all/pic] 4[1.2.3.Eh] 5[1.2.3.Ebcl.bcl] 4[1.2.3.cbn] — 4 3 3 1 —
tmp+3 — 2hp — cel/hpsd/pf — str
perc: tri, sd, tambn, xyl, bd, cym, glock, sus cym, "claquoir" (clapper)
Optional: fl5, fl6, ob3, cl3.
A. L'Ecole des Ægipans	2'
B. La leçon de flûte de Pan	3'
C. Marche des élèves nymphes	2'
D. La leçon de danse (sur le mode Hypolydien)	9'
Ballet de "la Sultane des Indes"	
A. Entrée	1'
B. Pantomime	1'
C. Pas des apothicaires	3'
D. Danse des esclaves	1'
E. Variation de Cydalise	2'
F. Finale du ballet de "La Sultane des Indes"	1'
Danse de Styrax (Final du 2e. Tableau)	3'

Heugel	Kalmus

Cydalise et le chèvre-pied: Suite No.2 <1923>   14'

6[1.2.3/pic.4/pic.5/pic.6/pic] 4[1.2.3.Eh] 5[1.2.3.Ebcl.bcl] 4[1.2.3.cbn] — 4 3 3 1 — tmp+3 — 2hp — cel/opt pf — str

perc: xyl, cym, bd, sd, tri, sus cym

The Suite No.2 is the entire 3rd Tableau of the ballet. A wordless chorus, intended for the full ballet, is replaced by cues in the orchestra parts in Suite No.2

A. Entrée de Cydalise	1'
B. Entree des suivantes et du Négrillon	2'
C. Pas des billets doux	3'
D. Entrée de Styrax et Danse	4'
E. Final du 3e Tableau	4'

| Heugel | Kalmus | Luck's |

Cydalise et le chèvre-pied: Entrance of the Little Fauns <1923>   2'

2[pic1.pic2] 1 2 1 — 2 2 3[opt] 0 — 2-3perc — str

perc: bd, sd, tambn

Kalmus and Luck's versions available only with the entire Suite No.1 from the ballet.

| Heugel | Kalmus | Luck's |

Marche des petits soldats de plomb, op.14, no.6 (March of the Little Lead Soldiers) <1887>   4'

1 0 1 0 — 0 1 0 0 — 1perc — pf — str

perc: sd

Originally for piano; orchestrated by the composer.

| Kalmus | Leduc | Luck's |

Serenade, op.7   3'

str

Double bass is optional.

| Kalmus | Leduc | Luck's |

Pijper, Willem   1894-1947

(b Zeist, 8 Sept 1894; d Leidschendam, 18 March 1947). Dutch

Six Symphonic Epigrams (Zes Symphonische Epigrammen) <1927–1928>   9'

4[1.2.3.4/pic] 4[1.2.3.Eh] 4[1.2.3.bcl] 4[1.2.3.cbn] — 4 4 4 1 — tmp+3 — cel — str

1. Grave	1'
2. Grazioso	1'
3. Molto tranquillo	2'
4. Allegro assai	1'
5. Adagio molto	2'
6. Pesante, maestoso	2'

| Donemus |

Pinkham, Daniel   1923-2006

(b Lynn, MA, 5 June 1923; d Boston, 18 Dec 2006). American

Catacoustical Measures <1962>   5'

4[incl pic] 3[incl Eh] 4[incl bcl] 4[incl cbn] — 4 4 4 1 — tmp+3 — hp — cel, pf — str

| Peters |

Signs of the Zodiac <1964>   21'

optional speaker

3[incl pic] 3[incl Eh] 3[incl bcl] 2 — 4 3 3 1 — tmp+2 — hp — pf/cel — str

| Peters |

Symphony No.1 <1961>   17'

3[incl pic] 3[incl Eh] 3[incl bcl] 3[incl cbn] — 4 3 3 1 — tmp+2 — hp — pf/cel — str

| Peters |

Symphony No.2 <1962>   16'

3[incl pic] 3[incl Eh] 3[incl bcl] 2 — 4 3 3 1 — tmp+5 — hp — pf — str

| Peters |

Piston, Walter   1894-1976

(b Rockland, ME, 20 Jan 1894; d Belmont, MA, 12 Nov 1976). American

Bicentennial Fanfare <1975>   2'

3[1.2.pic] 3[1.2.Eh] 3[1.2.bcl] 3[1.2.cbn] — 4 3 3 1 — tmp+4 — str

perc: bd, cym, sd, tamtam, tambn, tri, woodblk

| AMP |

Capriccio <1963>   8'

solo harp

str

| AMP |

Concertino, Piano & Chamber Orchestra <1937>   14'

2[1.pic] 2 2 2 — 2 0 0 0 — str

| AMP |

Concerto for Orchestra <1933>   13'

3 3[1.2.Eh] 3[1.2.bcl] 3[1.2.cbn] — 4 3 3 1 — tmp+5 — pf — str

perc: bd, cym, glock, sd, tambn, tri, woodblk, sus cym

I. Allegro moderato ma energico	3'
II. Allegro vivace	4'
III. Adagio - Allegro moderato	6'

| AMP |

Concerto for String Quartet, Wind Instruments & Percussion <1976>   12'

solo string quartet

3[1.2.pic] 3[1.2.Eh] 3[1.2.bcl] 2 — 2 2 2 0 — tmp+3 — [no other str]

perc: cym, sus cym, sd, tambn, tamtam, glock, woodblk, templeblks, 2tri

In one mvt.

| AMP |

Concerto, Flute <1971; rev 1973>   19'

2 3[1.2.Eh] 3[1.2.bcl] 2 — 4 2 0 0 — tmp+2 — hp — str

perc: tambn, tri, sus cym, woodblk

| AMP |

Concerto, 2 Pianos <1959>   19'

3[1.2.pic] 3[1.2.Eh] 3[1.2.bcl] 3[1.2.cbn] — 4 2 3 1 — tmp+3 — str

perc: bd, tri, sus cym, woodblk, tambn, sd

I. Allegro non troppo	7'
II. Adagio	8'
III. Con spirito	4'

| AMP |

Concerto, Viola <1957>   23'

3[1.2.pic] 3[1.2.Eh] 3[1.2.bcl] 3[1.2.cbn] — 4 2 3 1 — tmp+4 — hp — str

perc: bd, sd, cym, tri

1. Con moto moderato e flessíble	8'
2. Adagio con fantasia	9'
3. Allegro vivo	6'

| AMP |

Divertimento for Nine Instruments <1946>   *13'*

1 1 1 1 — str 5t

AMP	Luck's

Fanfare for the Fighting French <1942>   *1'*

0 0 0 0 — 4 3 3 1 — tmp+4 — [no str]
perc: bd, cym, field dr, sd

Boosey

Fantasy for English Horn, Harp & Strings <1953>   *10'*

str

AMP

The Incredible Flutist <1938>   *35'*

3[1.2.pic] 3[1.2.Eh] 3[1.2.bcl] 3[1.2.cbn] — 4 3 3 1 — tmp+4 — pf — str

perc: bd, bd/cym, cym, sus cym, sd, tri, tambn, glock, cast

AMP

The Incredible Flutist: Suite <1938>   *18'*

3[1.2.pic] 3[1.2.Eh] 3[1.2.bcl] 3[1.2.cbn] — 4 3 3 1 — tmp+4 — pf — str

perc: cast, cym, bd, glock, sd, tambn, tri

Introduction - Siesta in the Market Place	*1'*
Entrance of the Vendors	*2'*
Entrance of the Customers	*1'*
Tango of the Merchant's Daughters	*3'*
Arrival of the Circus	*1'*
Circus March	*1'*
The Flutist	*2'*
Minuet	*1'*
Spanish Waltz	*1'*
Eight O'Clock Strikes	*1'*
Siciliana	*2'*
Polka Finale	*2'*

AMP

Lincoln Center Festival Overture <1962>   *12'*

3[1.2.pic] 3[1.2.Eh] 3[1.2.bcl] 3[1.2.cbn] — 4 3 3 1 — tmp+4 — 2hp — str
perc: bd, cym, gong, sd, tambn, tri

AMP

Pine Tree Fantasy <1965>   *10'*

3[1.2.pic] 3[1.2.Eh] 3[1.2.bcl] 3[1.2.cbn] — 4 2 3 1 — tmp+3 — str
perc: sd, tri, cym, sus cym, tamtam, bd, tambn

AMP

Prelude & Allegro for Organ & Strings <1943>   *9'*

str

Prelude: Andantino	*4'*
Allegro	*5'*

AMP

Serenata <1956>   *12'*

2 2 2 2 — 4 2 0 0 — tmp — hp — str

I. Con allegrezza	*3'*
II. Con sentimento	*6'*
III. Con spirito	*3'*

AMP

Sinfonietta <1941>   *15'*

2 2 2 2 — 2 0 0 0 — str

I. Allegro grazioso	*6'*
II. Adagio	*5'*
III. Allegro vivo	*4'*

Boosey

Symphonic Prelude <1961>   *10'*

3[1.2.pic] 3[1.2.Eh] 3[1.2.bcl] 3[1.2.cbn] — 4 3 3 1 — tmp — hp — str

AMP

Symphony No.1 <1937>   *28'*

3[1.2.pic] 3[1.2.Eh] 3[1.2.bcl] 3[1.2.cbn] — 4 3 3 1 — tmp — str

I. Andantino quasi adagio; Allegro	*10'*
II. Adagio	*12'*
III. Allegro con fuoco	*6'*

Schirmer

Symphony No.2 <1943>   *25'*

3[1.2.pic] 3[1.2.Eh] 3[1.2.bcl] 3[1.2.cbn] — 4 3 3 1 — tmp+4 — str
perc: bd, cym, sd, tambn, tri

I. Moderato	*10'*
II. Adagio	*11'*
III. Allegro	*4'*

AMP

Symphony No.3 <1947>   *34'*

3[1.2.pic] 3[1.2.Eh] 3[1.2.bcl] 3[1.2.cbn] — 4 3 3 1 — tmp+4 — 2hp — str
perc: glock, xyl, cym, bd, sd, tri

I. Andantino	*10'*
II. Allegro	*5'*
III. Adagio	*13'*
IV. Allegro	*6'*

Boosey

Symphony No.4 <1950>   *23'*

3[1.2.pic] 3[1.2.Eh] 3[1.2.bcl] 3[1.2.cbn] — 4 3 3 1 — tmp+5 — 2hp — str
perc: bd, cym, sd, tri, woodblk

I. Piacevole	*6'*
II. Ballando	*5'*
III. Contemplativo	*8'*
IV. Energico	*4'*

AMP

Symphony No.5 <1954>   *22'*

3[1.2.pic] 3[1.2.Eh] 3[1.2.bcl] 3[1.2.cbn] — 4 3 3 1 — tmp+3 — 2hp — str
perc: sd, cym, bd

I. Lento - Allegro con spirito	*9'*
II. Adagio	*8'*
III. Allegro lieto	*5'*

AMP

Symphony No.6 <1955>   *28'*

3[1.2.pic] 3[1.2.Eh] 3[1.2.bcl] 3[1.2.cbn] — 4 3 3 1 — tmp+4 — 2hp — str
perc: bd, cym, field dr, sd, sus cym, tamtam, tambn, tri

I. Fluendo espressivo	*8'*
II. Leggerissimo vivace	*3'*
III. Adagio sereno	*13'*
IV. Allegro energico	*4'*

AMP

Symphony No.7 <1960>   *19'*

3[1.2.pic] 3[1.2.Eh] 3[1.2.bcl] 3[1.2.cbn] — 4 3 3 1 — tmp+5 — 2hp — str
perc: sd, tamtam, tambn, tri, woodblk, cym, sus cym, bd

I. Con moto	*6'*
II. Adagio pestorale	*9'*
III. Allegro festevole	*4'*

AMP

Symphony No.8 <1965>   24'

3[1.2.pic] 3[1.2.Eh] 3[1.2.bcl] 3[1.2.cbn] — 4 3 3 1 — tmp+4 — 2hp
— str
perc: bd, cym, sd, tamtam, tambn, tri
I. Moderato mosso   10'
II. Lento assai   10'
III. Allegro marcato   4'

> AMP

Three New England Sketches <1959>   17'

3[1.2.pic] 3[1.2.Eh] 3[1.2.bcl] 3[1.2.cbn] — 4 3 3 1 — tmp+4 — 2hp
— str
perc: tambn, tamtam, tri, glock, sd, woodblk, cym, sus cym, bd
I. Seaside   8'
II. Summer Evening   3'
III. Mountains   6'

> AMP

Toccata <1948>   9'

3[1.2.pic] 3[1.2.Eh] 3[1.2.bcl] 3[1.2.cbn] — 4 3 3 1 — tmp+5 — str
perc: bd, cym, sd, tambn, tri

> Boosey

Plain, Gerald   1940-

(b 1940). American

Clawhammer   12'

2[1.2/pic] 2 2 2 — 2 1 1 0 — 2perc — hp — elec kybd —
str[6.5.4.3.2]

> Oxford

Pleyel, Ignaz   1757-1831

(b Ruppersthal, 18 June 1757; d Paris, 14 Nov 1831). Austro-French

Symphony, op.3, no.1, D major   16'

0 2 0 0 — 2 0 0 0 — str
Ed. Helmut Riessberger.
Allegro   6'
Andante   3'
Minuetto: Allegretto   2'
Finale, Rondo: Allegro   5'

> Doblinger

Pokorny, Franz Xaver   1729-1794

(b Mies [now Stříbro, Czech Republic], 20 Dec 1729; d Regensburg, 2 July 1794).
Bohemian

Concerto, Flute, D major

see: Boccherini, Luigi, 1743-1805
       Concerto, flute, G.489, D major

Ponce, Manuel   1882-1948

(b Fresnillo, Zacatecas, 8 Dec 1882; d Mexico City, 24 April 1948). Mexican

Chapultepec; Tres bocetos sinfonicos <1934>   15'

3[1.2.pic] 2 3[1.2.bcl] 2 — 4 3 3 1 — tmp+3 — cel[can be played by
perc] — str
I. Primavera   5'
II. Nocturno   6'
III. Canto y Danza 4'

> Southern

Concierto del sur <1941>   25'

solo guitar
1 1 1 1 — tmp — str
1. Allegro moderato   13'
2. Andante   6'
3. Allegro moderato e festivo 6'

> Peer

Ponchielli, Amilcare   1834-1886

(b Paderno Fasolaro [now Paderno Ponchielli], 31 Aug 1834; d Milan, 17 Jan 1886).
Italian

Elegia   12'

2 3[incl Eh] 4[incl 2bcl] 2 — 4 2 4 0 — tmp/bd — hp — str
Ed. Pietro Spada.

> Zerboni

La Gioconda: Dance of the Hours (Danza delle ore)   9'
<1876; rev 1879>

3[1.2.pic] 2 2 2 — 4 4 3 1[bombardone] — tmp+3 — 2hp — str
perc: glock, tri, bd [bd/cym may have been intended]
Although the score calls for *campanelli a tastiera* (keyboard
glockenspiel), the part is normally played on the hammered glock.

> Kalmus   Luck's   Ricordi

Gran quartetto concertante   15'

solo quartet: flute, oboe, E-flat clarinet, clarinet [original] *or* 3 flutes &
alto flute
2[1.2/pic] 2 2 2 — 4 3 3 0 — tmp+3 — str
perc: bd, cym, tri, tambn, whip, cast, thundersheet
Orchestrated, arranged & edited by Mark Starr.

> Noteworthy

Popper, David   1843-1913

(b Prague, 18 June 1843; d Baden, Vienna, 7 Aug 1913). Austrian

Hungarian Rhapsody, op.68 (Ungarischer Rhapsodie)   8'
<1894>

solo violoncello
2 2 2 2 — 4 2 3 0 — tmp+1 — str
perc: glock, tri [these parts are not reflected in the score]
Orchestrated by Max Schlegel, from a work for violoncello & piano.

> Hofmeister   Kalmus   Luck's

Tarantelle, op.33   5'

solo violoncello
2 2 2 2 — 2 0 0 0 — tmp[opt]+2 — str
Orchestrated by Paul Gilson from a work for violoncello & piano.

> Kalmus   Luck's

Porter, Quincy   1897-1966

(b New Haven, CT, 7 Feb 1897; d Bethany, CT, 12 Nov 1966). American

Symphony No.2 <1962>   27'

3[incl pic] 2[incl Eh] 2 2 — 4 2 3 1 — tmp+1 — str
Lento   8'
Scherzando   3'
Adagio, molto espressivo   6'
Allegro   10'

> Peters

Poulenc, Francis   1899-1963

(b Paris, 7 Jan 1899; d Paris, 30 Jan 1963). French

Les animaux modèles, op.111 (Model Animals): Suite   21'
<1940–1942; rev 1942>

3[1.2.pic] 3[1.2.Eh] 4[1.2..Ebcl.bcl] 4[1.2.3.cbn] — 4 3[1.2.3/crt] 3 1 — tmp+3 — 2hp — cel, pf — str

perc: bd, cym, sus cym, sd, tri, tambn, tamtam, glock, crot, chimes[Bb4,F5]

1. Le petit jour (Dawn)	*4'*
2. Le lion amoureux (The Lion in Love)	*2'*
3. L'homme entre deux âges et ses deux maîtresses (The Middle-Aged	*2'*
4. La mort et la bûcheron (Death and the Woodcutter)	*6'*
5. Les deux cocqs (The Two Roosters)	*4'*
6. Le repas de midi (The Midday Meal)	*3'*

Eschig

Aubade; Concerto chorégraphique <1929>   22'

solo piano

2 2 2[1.2/Eh] 2 2 — 2 1 0 0 — tmp — 2va, 2vc, 2db

I. Toccata	*3'*
II. Récitatif: Les compagnes de Diane	*2'*
III. Rondeau: Diane et compagnes	*3'*
IV. Presto: Toilette de Diane	*2'*
V. Récitatif: Introduction à la variation de Diane	*2'*
VI. Andante: Variaton de Diane	*3'*
VII. Allegro feroce: Désespoir de Diane	*1'*
VIII. Conclusion: Adieux et départ de Diane	*6'*

Rouart

Le bal masqué (The Masked Ball) <1932>   19'

solo baritone or mezzo

0 1 1 1 — 0 1 0 0 — 1perc — pf — vn, vc

1. Préambule et air de bravoure	*4'*
2. Intermède	*3'*
3. Malvina	*2'*
4. Bagatelle	*2'*
5. La dame aveugle	*3'*
6. Finale	*5'*

Salabert

Les biches (The Does): Suite <1923; rev 1939-40>   16'

3[1.2.pic] 3[1.2.Eh] 3[1.2.bcl] 3[1.2.cbn] — 4 3 3 1 — tmp+2 — hp — cel — str

perc: sd, td, tri, sus cym, glock, tambn, field dr, bd

Rondeau	*3'*
Adagietto	*3'*
Rag-mazurka	*4'*
Andantino	*3'*
Final	*3'*

Heugel

Concerto, Organ, G minor <1938>   24'

tmp — str

Andante	*3'*
Allegro giocoso	*2'*
Subito andante moderato	*8'*
Tempo allegro; Molto agitato	*3'*
Très calme; Lent	*3'*
Tempo de l'allegro initial	*2'*
Tempo introduction; Largo	*3'*

Salabert

Concerto, Piano <1949>   20'

2[1.2/pic] 2[1.2/Eh] 2 2 — 4 2 3 1 — tmp — str

I. Allegro	*10'*
II. Andante con moto	*6'*
III. Rondo à la française	*4'*

Salabert

Concerto, 2 Pianos, D minor <1932>   20'

2[1.pic] 2[1.2/Eh] 2 2 — 2 2 2 1 — 1perc — str[8.8.4.4.4]

perc: sd, td, field dr, tri, cast, sus cym, bd

I. Allegro ma non troppo	*8'*
II. Larghetto	*5'*
III. Finale: Allegro molto	*7'*

Salabert

Concerto champêtre, Harpsichord (or Piano)   25'
<1927–1928>

2[1/pic.2/pic] 2[1.2/Eh] 2 2 — 4 2 1 1 — tmp+2 — str[8.8.4.4.4]

perc: bd, cym, sd, td, tambn, tri, xyl

I. Allegro molto	*11'*
II. Andante	*6'*
III. Finale: Presto	*8'*

Salabert

Deux marches et un intermède (Two Marches and an   6'
Interlude) <1937>

1 1 1 1 — 0 1 0 0 — str

Marche (1889)	*2'*
Intermède champêtre	*2'*
Marche (1937)	*2'*

Salabert

Gloria <1959–1960>   28'

chorus   solo soprano

3[1.2/pic.pic] 3[1.2.Eh] 3[1.2.bcl] 3[1.2.cbn] — 4 3 3 1 — tmp — hp — str

Orchestral parts are said to have many errors [2013]; see various articles by Lee Barrow: lbarrow@northgeorgia.edu.

I. Gloria	*3'*
II. Laudamus Te	*3'*
III. Domine Deus	*5'*
IV. Domine Fili unigenite	*1'*
V. Domine Deus Agnus Dei	*8'*
VI. Qui sedes ad dexteram Patris	*8'*

Salabert

L'histoire de Babar, le petit éléphant (The Story of   22'
Babar, the Little Elephant) <1940–1945>

narrator (text in French or English)

2[1/pic.2/pic] 2[1.2/Eh] 2[1.2/bcl] 2[1.2/cbn] — 2 2[1/crt.2] 1 1 — tmp+1 — hp — str

perc: tri, sd, bd, tambn, cym, tamtam, whistle, autohorn

Originally for narrator & pf; orchestrated by Jean Françaix, 1962. Other orchestrations, both from Chester: Bastiaan Blomhert (similar inst except for brass 2 1 0 1); David Matthews (1/pic 1/Eh 1/Ebcl/bcl 1 — 1 0 0 0 — perc — pf — str 5t)

Chester

Sécheresses (Droughts) <1937>   17'

chorus

2[1.2/pic] 2[1.2/Eh] 2 2 — 4 2 3 1 — tmp+1 — hp — cel — str

perc: field dr, bd, tambn, sus cym, tamtam

1. Les sauterelles (The Grasshoppers)	*6'*
2. Le village abandonné (The Abandoned Village)	*4'*
3. Le faux avenir (The False Prospects)	*2'*
4. Le squelette de la mer (The Skeleton of the Sea)	*5'*

Durand

Sinfonietta <1947–1948>   29'

2 2 2 2 — 2 2 0 0 — tmp — hp — str

I. Allegro con fuoco	*8'*
II. Molto vivace	*6'*
III. Andante cantabile	*8'*
IV. Finale: Prestissimo et tres gai	*7'*

Chester

Stabat Mater <1950–1951>   31'
chorus   solo soprano
3[1.2.pic] 3[1.2.Eh] 3[1.2.bcl] 3 — 4 3 3 1 — tmp — 2hp — str
I. Stabat Mater dolorosa	4'
II. Cujus animam gementem	1'
III. O quam tristis	3'
IV. Quae moerebat	1'
V. Quis est homo	1'
VI. Vidit suum	4'
VII. Eja Mater	1'
VIII. Fac et Ardeat	2'
IX. Sancta Mater	3'
X. Fac ut portem	4'
XI. Inflammatus et accensus	2'
XII. Quando corpus	5'

Salabert

The Story of Babar, the Little Elephant
see his: Histoire de Babar, le petit éléphant

Suite française <1935>   13'
0 2 0 2 — 0 2 3 0 — 1perc — hpsd — [no str]
perc: sd, bd/cym
After Claude Gervaise (16th century).
Bransle de Bourgogne	2'
Pavane	3'
Petite marche militaire	1'
Complainte	1'
Bransle de Champagne	2'
Sicilienne	2'
Carillon	2'

Durand

Powell, Mel   1923-1998
(b New York, 12 Feb 1923; d Van Nuys, CA, 24 April 1998). American

Duplicates (A Concerto for Two Pianos and Orchestra)   30'
<1987–1990>
3[1/afl.2.pic] 3[1.2.Eh] 4[1.2.Ebcl.bcl] 3[1.2.cbn] — 4 3 3 1 — 3perc — 2hp — str[14.12.10.10.8]
perc: glock, xyl, vib, marim, crot, chimes, tri, szl cym, Chinescym, bongos, timbales, sd, field dr, td, guiro, vibrslp, cast, claves, templeblks, belltree, finger cymbals, 2sus cym, 2tamtam, elephant bells, bell plate, 6almglocken, 4brake dr, 2tomtom, 2bd, chocalho
I. ONTA	15'
II. Three Interludes	6'
Interlude 1: Madrigal	
Interlude 2: Immobile	
Interlude 3: Mobile	
III. ONTA Variants	9'

Schirmer

Modules; An Intermezzo for Chamber Orchestra   14'
<1985>
1 1 1 1 — 2 1 1 0 — 2perc — hp — cel — vn, va, vc, db
perc: glock, tri, belltree, td, vib, xyl, bongos, bd, templeblks, marac, tambn, tmpl bell, 2sus cym, 2tamtams, 2sd, 3tomtoms, 3woodblks

Schirmer

Prelleur, Peter   1705-1741
(b ?London, ? Dec 1705; d 25 June 1741). English

Concerto, 2 Trumpets, D major <ca.1740>   7'
cnt — str
Ed. Gerald Webster.
1. Allegro	2'
2. Largo	2'
3. Allegro	3'

Hoyt

Previn, André   1929-
(b Berlin, 6 April 1929). American composer of German birth

Concerto, Harp <2007>   15'
3[1.2.3/pic] 2[1.2/Eh] 3[1.2.bcl] 3[1.2.cbn] — 4 2 3 1 — tmp+2 — cel — str
perc: glock, xyl, sd, bd, tamtam, sus cym, tri, claves, choke cym
I. Andante	_'
II. Slowly and rubato	_'
III. Quasi cadenza; Suddenly fast	_'

Schirmer

Concerto, Violin (Anne-Sophie) <2001>   40'
3[1.2.3/pic] 3[1.2.Eh] 3[1.2.bcl] 3[1.2.cbn] — 4 3 3 0 — tmp+2 — hp — cel — str
perc: bd, cym, sus cym, sd, tamtam, xyl, vib, woodblk, bongos, 4rototom, bell plate
I. Moderato	10'
II. Cadenza	13'
III. Andante ("from a train in Germany")	17'

Schirmer

Concerto, Violin, No.2, for Violin and String Orchestra   24'
(with two Harpsichord interludes) <2012>
hpsd — str
Unaccompanied harpsichord solo between mvts I and II, and between mvts II and III.
I. Molto rubato; Allegro	_'
II. Slow	_'
III. Fast	_'

Schirmer

Concerto, Violin & Double Bass (Double Concerto)   28'
<2007>
3[1.2.3/pic] 3[1.2.Eh] 4[1.2.Ebcl.bcl] 3[1.2.cbn] — 4 2 3 1 — tmp+2 — hp — cel — str
perc: glock, xyl, tamtam, cym, sd, whip, woodblk, bd, claves, tambn, 2sus cym, 3tri
I. Allegro	9'
Interlude	4'
II. Slowly	8'
III. Allegro	7'

Schirmer

Concerto, Violin & Viola <2009>   20'
3[1.2.pic] 3[1.2.Eh] 3[1.2.bcl] 2 — 4 3 3 1 — tmp+2 — hp — str
perc: bd, sus cym, sd, xyl, claves
I. Andante	_'
II. Adagio; Suddenly fast	_'

Schirmer

Concerto, Violoncello <1960>   26'

3[1.2.3/pic] 3[1.2.Eh] 3[1.2.bcl] 2 — 4 3 3 1 — tmp+2 — hp — str
perc: xyl, tamtam, woodblk, sd, bd, sus cym
  I. Moderato   _'
  II. quarter-note = 72 _'
  III. Allegro, with energy _'

   Schirmer

Diversions <1999>   24'

2[1.2/pic] 2 2[1.2/Ebcl/bcl] 2[1.2/cbn] — 2 1 0 0 — tmp+2 — hp —
cel — str[12.10.8.6.4]
perc: bd, sd, xyl, vib, tamtam
  I. Prologue   5'
  II. Passacaglia   6'
  III. Fast   5'
  IV. Slowly   8'

   Schirmer

The Magic Number <1997>   17'

solo soprano
2 2[1.2/Eh] 2[1.2/bcl] 2[1.2/bcl] — 4 2 0 0 — 1perc — hp — cel —
str
perc: bd, sus cym, sd

   Schirmer

Night Thoughts <2006>   20'

3[1.2.3/pic] 3[1.2.Eh] 4[1.2.Ebcl.bcl] 2 — 4 3 3 1 — tmp+2 — hp —
cel — str
perc: cym, sus cym, sd, xyl, marim, vib

   Schirmer

Overture to a Comedy <1967>   9'

3[incl pic] 2 3[incl bcl] 2 — 4 3 3 1 — tmp+3 — hp — str
perc: tamtam, tambn, cym, xyl, sd, tri, bd, glock

   MCA

Owls <2008>   15'

2[1.2/pic] 2[1.2/Eh] 3[1.2.bcl] 2 — 4 2 0 0 — tmp/perc — hp — cel
— str
perc: bd, sus cym

   Schirmer

Triple Concerto for Horn, Trumpet, & Tuba   18'

3[1.2.3/pic] 3[1.2.Eh] 3[1.2.bcl] 2 — 0 0 3 0 — tmp+1 — hp — str
perc: bd, sd, sus cym, tamtam, cast
  I. quarter-note = 138 _'
  II. Very slow   _'
  III. quarter-note = 120 _'

   Schirmer

Vocalise <1996>   4'

solo soprano, solo cello
1 1 0 0 — 1 0 0 0 — hp — str

   Chester

Price, Florence   1887-1953

(b Little Rock, AR, 9 April 1887; d Chicago, 3 June 1953). American

Dances in the Canebrakes <1953>   9'

2[1.2/pic] 2 2[1.2/bcl] 2 — 3 3 2 0 — asx — tmp+1 — hp — str
perc: glock, sus cym, sd, vib, cast, tri, claves [tmp covers some perc]
From a collection of piano pieces; orchestrated by Wm. Grant Still; ed.
Michael Kibbe.
  1. Nimble Feet   2'
  2. Tropical Noon   4'
  3. Silk Hat and Walking Cane 3'

   WGS

Symphony No.3, C minor <1940>   30'

4[1.2.3.pic] 3[1.2.Eh] 3[1.2.bcl] 2 — 4 3 3 1 — tmp+5 — hp — cel
— str
perc: bd, cym, sus cym, sd, tri, tambn, tamtam, glock, xyl, chimes, woodblk, cast,
sandblks, opt whip
  I. Andante; Allegro   11'
  II. Andante ma non troppo 9'
  III. Juba: Allegro   5'
  IV. Scherzo. Finale   5'

   Fleisher

Prokofiev, Serge   1891-1953

(b Sontsovka [now Krasnoye, Selidovsky district, Donetsk region, Ukraine], 15/27
April 1891; d Moscow, 5 March 1953). Russian

Ala and Lolly

see his: Scythian Suite

Alexander Nevsky, op.78 (Aleksandr Nevskiy) <1939>   36'

chorus   solo mezzo-soprano
3[1.2.pic] 3[1.2.Eh] 3[1.2.bcl] 3[1.2.cbn] — 4 3 3 1 — tsx — tmp+7
— hp[dbl if possible] — str
perc: bd, chimes (A#), cym, woodblk, marac, glock, sd, tamtam, tambn, tri, xyl,
sus cym
  I. Russia under the Mongolian Yoke 3'
  II. Song about Alexander Nevsky 3'
  III. The Crusaders in Pskov 6'
  IV. Arise, Ye Russian People 2'
  V. The Battle on the Ice 12'
  VI. The Field of the Dead 6'
  VII. Alexander's Entry into Pskov 4'

   Russian

Andante, op.50bis <1930>   9'

str
Arr. from *String Quartet No.1*, op.50, 3rd movement.

   Boosey

Chout, op.21 (Skazka pro shuta; The Tale of the   55'
Buffoon) <1920>

3[1.2.pic] 3[1.2.Eh] 3[1.2.3/bcl] 3 — 4 3[1.2.atp] 3 1 — tmp+6 —
2hp — pf — str
perc: glock, xyl, tri, tambn, field dr, cym, bd

   Boosey

Chout, op.21bis (Skazka pro shuta; The Tale of the   35'
Buffoon): Symphonic Suite <1920>

3[1.2.pic] 3[1.2.Eh] 3[1.2.3/bcl] 3 — 4 3[1.2.atp] 3 1 — tmp+6 —
2hp — pf — str
perc: glock, xyl, tri, tambn, field dr, cym, bd
  1. The Buffoon and His Wife 4'
  2. Dance of the Wives 3'
  3. The Buffoons Kill Their Wives 3'
  4. The Buffoon as a Young Woman 4'
  5. Third Entr'acte 2'
  6. Dance of the Buffoons' Daughters 3'
  7. Entry of the Merchant and His Welcome 4'
  8. In the Merchant's Bedroom 2'
  9. The Young Woman Becomes a Goat 3'
  10. Fifth Entr'acte and The Goat's Burial 3'
  11. The Buffoon and the Merchant Quarrel 2'
  12. Final Dance 4'

   Boosey

Cinderella (Zolushka): Suite No.1, op.107 <1940–1944;   29'
rev 1946>

3[1.2.pic] 3[1.2.Eh] 3[1.2.bcl] 3[1.2.cbn] — 4 3 3 1 — tmp+6 — hp
— pf — str
perc: glock, xyl, tri, tambn, field dr, cym, bd, chimes[C4], tamtam, woodblk, cast

1. Introduction	3'
2. Pas de chat (Cat's Dance)	4'
3. Quarrel	3'
4. Fairy Godmother & Fairy Winter	5'
5. Mazurka	6'
6. Cinderella Goes to the Ball	3'
7. Cinderella's Waltz	3'
8. Midnight	2'

Russian

Cinderella (Zolushka): Suite No.2, op.108 <1940–1944;   29'
rev 1946>

3[1.2.pic] 3[1.2.Eh] 3[1.2.bcl] 3[1.2.cbn] — 4 3 3 1 — tmp+4 — hp
— pf/cel — str
perc: xyl, tri, tambn, field dr, cym, marac, glock, bd, woodblk, cast

1. Cinderella's Dream	4'
2. Dancing Lesson and Gavotte	6'
3. Fairy of Spring & Fairy of Summer	4'
4. Bourrée	2'
5. Cinderella in the Castle	8'
6. Galop	5'

Russian

Cinderella (Zolushka): Suite No.3, op.109 <1940–1944;   26'
rev 1946>

3[1.2.pic] 3[1.2.Eh] 3[1.2.bcl] 3[1.2.cbn] — 4 3 3 1 — tmp+4 — hp
— pf/cel — str
perc: glock, xyl, field dr, cast, cym, tambn, bd, tri
Celesta appears only in the last 4 bars of the suite on the glockenspiel part
(campanelli); it could easily be covered by the percussionist.

1. Pavana	4'
2. Cinderella and the Prince	5'
3. The Three Oranges	1'
4. Southern Borders (Temptation)	4'
5. Orientalia	2'
6. The Prince Has Found Cinderella	2'
7. Waltz Melody	4'
8. Amoroso	4'

Russian

Classical Symphony, op.25 (Symphony No.1)   14'
<1916–1917>

2 2 2 2 — 2 2 0 0 — tmp — str
Kalmus edition by Clinton F. Nieweg.

I. Allegro con brio	5'
II. Larghetto	4'
III. Gavotte: Non troppo allegro	2'
IV. Finale: Molto vivace	4'

Kalmus   Russian

Concerto, Piano, No.1, op.10, D-flat major <1911–1912>   16'

3[1.2.pic] 2 2 3[1.2.cbn] — 4 2 3 1 — tmp+1 — str
perc: glock[3-octave range, C5–>B7, requires kybd glock]

I. Allegro brioso	7'
II. Andante assai	5'
III. Allegro scherzando	4'

Forberg   Kalmus   Luck's

Concerto, Piano, No.2, op.16, G minor <1912–1913; rev   31'
1923>

2 2 2 2 — 4 2 3 1 — tmp+2 — str
perc: bd, cym, tambn, sd

I. Andantino	11'
II. Scherzo: Vivace	3'
III. Moderato	7'
IV. Finale: Allegro tempestoso	10'

Boosey

Concerto, Piano, No.3, op.26, C major <1917–1921>   27'

2[1.2/pic] 2 2 2 — 4 2 3 0 — tmp+1 — str
perc: bd, cym, cast, tambn

I. Andante - Allegro	9'
II. Andantino	9'
III. Allegro ma non troppo	9'

Boosey

Concerto, Piano (Left Hand), No.4, op.53, B-flat <1931>   25'

2 2 2 2 — 2 1 1 0 — 1perc — str
perc: bd

I. Vivace	4'
II. Andante	11'
III. Moderato	8'
IV. Vivace	2'

Russian

Concerto, Piano, No.5, op.55, G major <1931–1932>   23'

2[1.2/pic] 2 2 — 2 2 2[1.btbn] 1 — tmp+2 — str
perc: sd, bd

I. Allegro con brio	5'
II. Moderato ben accentuato	4'
III. Toccata: Allegro con fuoco	2'
IV. Larghetto	7'
V. Vivo	5'

Boosey

Concerto, Violin, No.1, op.19, D major <1916–1917>   22'

2[1.2/pic] 2 2 — 4 2 0 1 — tmp+2 — hp — str
perc: tambn, sd

I. Andantino	10'
II. Scherzo: Vivacissimo	4'
III. Moderato	8'

Boosey

Concerto, Violin, No.2, op.63, G minor <1935>   26'

2 2 2 2 — 2 2 0 0 — 1perc — str
perc: cym, tri, cast, bd, sd

I. Allegro moderato	10'
II. Andante assai	9'
III. Allegro; ben marcato	7'

Boosey

Ivan the Terrible, op.116 (Ivan Grozniy) <1942–1945>   74'

narrator   solos ABar   chorus   optional children's chorus
3[1.2/pic.pic] 3[1.2.Eh] 5[1.2.3.Ebcl.bcl] 4[1.2.3.cbn] — 4 5 3 2 —
asx, tsx — 2opt dulcimers or psalteries [cued in hp] — tmp+6 — 2hp —
pf — str
perc: xyl, tambn, chimes, glock, tri, field dr, woodblk, whip, cym, bd, tamtam
Film music arranged in the form of an oratorio by Abram Stasevich,
1961.

    There are also orchestral suites from this music arr. by Christopher
Palmer (Boosey, 25') and by P. Haletzki (Russian, 20').

Russian

Lieutenant Kijé, op.60 (Poruchnik Kizhe): Suite <1934>   20'

opt baritone voice
3[1.2/pic] 2 2 — 4 3[1.2.opt crt] 3 1 — tsx (opt if voice is used) —
3perc — hp — pf/cel — str
perc: sd, slgh-bells, cym, tambn, bd, tri

The Birth of Kijé	4'
Romance	5'
Kijé's Wedding	3'
Troika	2'
The Burial of Kijé	6'

Boosey

The Love for Three Oranges, op.33bis (Lyubov' k tryom apel'sinam): Symphonic Suite <1919; rev 1924>   15'

3[1.2.pic] 3[1.2.Eh] 3[1.2.bcl] 3[1.2.3/cbn] — 4 3 3 1 — tmp+6 — 2hp — str
perc: glock, xyl, tri, tamtam, field dr, cym, bd, tambn
Kalmus edition by Clinton F. Nieweg & Nancy M. Bradburd.

1. *The Ridiculous People*	3'
2. *Scene from Hades (Fata Morgana Playing Cards)*	3'
3. *March*	2'
4. *Scherzo*	2'
5. *The Prince and the Princess*	3'
6. *Flight*	2'

> Boosey   Luck's

The Love for Three Oranges, op.33bis (Lyubov' k tryom apel'sinam): March & Scherzo <1919>   4'

3[1.2.pic] 3[1.2.Eh] 3[1.2.bcl] 3[1.2.cbn] — 4 3 3 1 — tmp+6 — 2hp — str
perc: glock, xyl, tri, field dr, cym, bd

March	2'
Scherzo	2'

> Boosey

March, op.99, B-flat major <1943–1944>   3'

3[1.2.pic] 2 2 2 — 4 3 3 1 — tmp+3 — str
perc: bd, cym, sd, tambn
Originally for military band; transcribed for orchestra by D. Wilson Ochoa.

> Schirmer

Overture, op.42 (American) <1926>   8'

1 1 2 1 — 0 2 1 0 — tmp — 2hp — cel, 2pf — 1vc, 2db
A version of this work exists for full orchestra:
    3 3 3 3 — 4 2 3 1 — tmp+2 — 2hp — cel, pf — str

> Boosey

Peter and the Wolf, op.67 (Petya i volk) <1936>   25'

narrator
1 1 1 1 — 3 1 1 0 — tmp+1 — str
perc: bd, sd, cast; tmp covers cym, sus cym, tri, tambn
Text by the composer in Russian; English version by Thomas Dunhill; Spanish text by Juan Serrallonga. For a Norwegian text, contact Helen Farr at the Stavanger Symphony, Norway. A French translation is said to be in the Kalmus score, and doubtless narrations in many other languages exist.

> Russian

Romeo and Juliet, op.64 (Romeo i Dzhuletta) <1935–1936>   130'

3[1.2.pic] 3[1.2.Eh] 3[1.2/Ebcl.bcl] 3[1.2.cbn] — 6 4[1.2.3.crt] 3 1 — tsx — 2mand, va d'amore[or va] — tmp+5 — 2hp — pf/cel/org — str
perc: field dr, xyl, tri, woodblk, marac, glock, tambn, chimes[A5], cym, bd
Complete ballet in 4 acts, after Shakespeare.
    An onstage *banda* (6hn, 6tp, 2tubas + perc) may be cued into the pit parts.
    Reduction by Wm. McDermott (pub. Russian; no score):
    2 2 2 2 — 2 2 1 1 — tmp+2 — hp — pf — str

> Russian

Romeo and Juliet (Romeo i Dzhuletta): Suite No.1, op.64bis <1935–1936>   27'

3[1.2.pic] 3[1.2.Eh] 3[1.2.bcl] 3[1.2.cbn] — 4 3[1.2.crt] 3 1 — tsx — tmp+4[opt 5] — hp — pf — str
perc: glock, xyl, tambn, field dr, tri, cym, bd, sd
Presenters frequently cobble together a version of *Romeo and Juliet* by mixing movements from the three suites; durations and instrumentations of individual movements for this purpose may be found at orchestralibrary.com, under Special Interest>Nieweg Charts.

1. *Folk Dance*	4'
2. *Scene*	2'
3. *Madrigal*	4'
4. *Minuet*	3'
5. *Masks*	2'
6. *Romeo and Juliet*	8'
7. *The Death of Tybalt*	4'

> Russian

Romeo and Juliet (Romeo i Dzhuletta): Suite No.2, op.64ter <1935–1936>   30'

3[1.2.pic] 3[1.2.Eh] 3[1.2.bcl] 3[1.2.cbn] — 4 3[1.2.crt] 3 1 — tsx — opt va d'amore — tmp+2 — hp — pf/cel — str
perc: glock, tambn, cym, sd, bd, marac, tri
Presenters frequently cobble together a version of *Romeo and Juliet* by mixing movements from the three suites; durations and instrumentations of individual movements for this purpose may be found at orchestralibrary.com, under Special Interest>Nieweg Charts.

1. *The Montagues and the Capulets*	5'
2. *Juliet—The Young Girl*	4'
3. *Friar Laurence*	3'
4. *Dance*	2'
5. *Romeo and Juliet before Parting*	8'
6. *Dance of the Maids from the Antilles*	2'
7. *Romeo at Juliet's Grave*	6'

> Russian

Romeo and Juliet (Romeo i Dzhuletta): Suite No.3, op.101 <1935–1936; rev 1946>   18'

3[1.2.pic] 3[1.2.Eh] 3[1.2.bcl] 3[1.2.cbn] — 4 3 3 1 — tmp+2 — hp — cel, pf — str
perc: woodblk, glock, bd, cym, sus cym, tambn, tri, sd
Presenters frequently cobble together a version of *Romeo and Juliet* by mixing movements from the three suites; durations and instrumentations of individual movements for this purpose may be found at orchestralibrary.com, under Special Interest>Nieweg Charts.

1. *Romeo at the Fountain*	2'
2. *Morning Dance*	2'
3. *Juliet*	5'
4. *Nurse*	2'
5. *Morning Serenade (Aubade)*	2'
6. *The Death of Juliet*	5'

> Russian

Russian Overture, op.72 (Ouverture russe) <1936; rev 1937>   14'

3[1.2.pic] 3[1.2.Eh] 3[1.2.bcl] 3[1.2.cbn] — 4 3 3 1 — tmp+4 — 2hp — pf — str
perc: tri, bd, tamtam, tambn, sd, cym, cast, xyl, glock
The original 1936 version employed quadruple woodwinds.

> Boosey

Scythian Suite, op.20 (Skifskaya syuita) <1914–1915>   20'

4[1.2.3/afl.pic] 4[1.2.3.Eh] 4[1.2.3/Ebcl.bcl] 4[1.2.3.cbn] — 8 5[1.2.3/pic tp.atp.5 opt] 4 1 — tmp+9 — 2hp — cel, pf — str
perc: glock, xyl, tri, tambn, sd, bd, tamtam, 2pr cym
From the withdrawn ballet, *Ala and Lolly (Ala i Lolli)*.

1. *Adoration of Vélèss and Ala*	7'
2. *The Hostile God & Dance of the Dark Spirits*	3'
3. *Night*	5'
4. *Glorious Departure of Lolli & Cortège of the Sun*	5'

> Boosey

Sinfonia concertante, op.125 <1950–1951; rev 1952> 37'
solo violoncello
2[1.2/pic] 2 2 2 — 4 3[tp3 opt] 3 1 — tmp+2 — cel[can be covered by perc] — str
perc: tambn, sd, sus cym, bd, tri
A reworking of the composer's *Concerto, Violoncello*, op.58.

I. Andante	11'
II. Allegro giusto	16'
III. Andante con moto - Allegretto - Allegro marcato	10'

Boosey

Sinfonietta, op.5/48 <1909; rev 1914-15; rev 1929 as op.48> 20'
2 2 2 2 — 4 2 0 0 — str
Composed 1909 as op.5; rev. 1914-15; rev. again 1929 as op.48.

1. Allegro giocoso	5'
2. Andante	4'
3. Intermezzo: Vivace	3'
4. Scherzo: Allegro risoluto	4'
5. Allegro giocoso	4'

Boosey

The Steel Step, op.41 (Stal'noy skok; Le Pas d'acier) <1925–1926> 35'
3[1.2.pic] 3[1.2.Eh] 4[1.2.Ebcl.bcl] 3[1.2.cbn] — 4 4 3 1 — tmp+4 — pf — str
perc: xyl, glock, sd, tri, cym, cast, bd, tambn

Boosey

The Steel Step (Stal'noy skok; Le Pas d'acier): Suite, op.41bis <1926> 13'
3[1.2.pic] 3[1.2.Eh] 3[1.2.bcl] 3[1.2.cbn] — 4 4 3 1 — tmp+4 — pf — str
perc: xyl, glock, sd, tri, cym, cast, bd, tambn

1. Entry of the People	2'
2. The Officials	5'
3. The Sailor and the Factory Worker	3'
4. The Factory	3'

Boosey

Summer Day, op.65bis; Children's Suite for Small Orchestra (Letniy den') <1935; rev (orchd) 1941> 13'
2 2 2 2 — 2 2 0 0 — tmp+2 — str
perc: tri, cym, bd, tambn, sd, cast
From piano pieces, op.65; 7 of the 12 piano pieces were orchestrated by the composer, 1941.

1. Morning	2'
2. Tip and Run	1'
3. Waltz	2'
4. Repentance	3'
5. March	1'
6. Evening	2'
7. The Moon is Over the Meadows	2'

Russian

Symphony No.1, D major
see his: Classical Symphony, op.25

Symphony No.2, op.40, D minor <1924–1925> 36'
3[1.2.pic] 3[1.2.Eh] 3[1.2.bcl] 3[1.2.cbn] — 4 3 3 1 — tmp+2 — pf — str
perc: cym, tri, sd, bd, tambn, cast

| I. Allegro ben articolato | 12' |
| II. Andante | 24' |

Boosey

Symphony No.3, op.44, C minor <1928> 34'
3[1.2.pic] 3[1.2.Eh] 3[1.2.bcl] 3[1.2.cbn] — 4 3 3 1 — tmp+2 — 2hp — str
perc: sd, tamtam, cym, cast, bd, tambn, bell
Material taken from his opera, *The Fiery Angel (Ognenniy angel)*.

I. Moderato	14'
II. Andante	7'
III. Allegro agitato	7'
IV. Andante mosso - Allegro moderato	6'

Boosey

Symphony No.4 (first version), op.47, C major <1929–1930> 29'
3[1.2.pic] 3[1.2.Eh] 3[1.2.bcl] 3[1.2.cbn] — 4 2 3 1 — tmp+3 — str
perc: bd, cym, sd, tambn
Material taken from his ballet, *The Prodigal Son (Bludniy sin)*

1. Andante assai; Allegro eroico	8'
2. Andante tranquillo	7'
3. Moderato, quasi allegretto	6'
4. Allegro risoluto	8'

Boosey

Symphony No.4 (revised version), op.112, C major <1947> 34'
3[1.2.pic] 3[1.2.Eh] 4[1.2.Ebcl.bcl] 3[1.2.cbn] — 4 3 3 1 — tmp+3 — hp — pf — str
perc: sd, woodblk, cym, tambn, tri, bd
Revision of the composer's *Symphony No.4*, op.47.

I. Andante; Allegro eroico	12'
II. Andante tranquillo	7'
III. Moderato; quasi allegretto	6'
IV. Allegro risoluto	9'

Boosey

Symphony No.5, op.100, B-flat major <1944> 46'
3[1.2.pic] 3[1.2.Eh] 4[1.2.Ebcl.bcl] 3[1.2.cbn] — 4 3 3 1 — tmp+5 — hp — pf — str
perc: sd, tambn, tri, cym, bd, tamtam, woodblk

I. Andante	14'
II. Allegro moderato	9'
III. Adagio	13'
IV. Allegro giocoso	10'

Russian

Symphony No.6, op.111, E-flat minor <1945–1947> 43'
3[1.2.pic] 3[1.2.Eh] 4[1.2.Ebcl.bcl] 3[1.2.cbn] — 4 3 3 1 — tmp+4 — hp — cel, pf — str
perc: sd, tambn, tamtam, woodblk, cym, bd, tri

I. Allegro moderato	15'
II. Largo	16'
III. Vivace	12'

Russian

Symphony No.7, op.131, C-sharp minor <1951–1952> 31'
3[1.2.pic] 3[1.2.Eh] 3[1.2.bcl] 2 — 4 3 3 1 — tmp+4 — hp — pf — str
perc: sd, tambn, glock, woodblk, xyl, cym, tri, bd

I. Moderato	9'
II. Allegretto	8'
III. Andante espressivo	5'
IV. Vivace	9'

Russian

The Ugly Duckling, op.18 (Gadkiy utyonok) <1914> 12'
solo mezzo-soprano
2[1.2/pic] 2 3[1.2.bcl] 2 — 2 2 2 0 — 1perc — hp — str
perc: bd, cym, sd, glock
Originally for voice & piano; orchestrated by the composer.

Boosey

Visions fugitives, op.22 (Mimoletnosti) <1915-1917>   17'

str

Originally 20 pieces for piano; 15 of these arranged for string orchestra by Rudolf Barshai.

Lentamente	*1'*
Andante	*2'*
Allegretto	*1'*
Animato	*1'*
Molto giocoso	*1'*
Con eleganza	*1'*
Comodo	*1'*
Allegretto tranquillo	*1'*
Ridiculosamente	*1'*
Con vivacita	*1'*
Assai moderato	*1'*
Allegretto	*1'*
Feroce	*1'*
Inquieto	*1'*
Dolente	*2'*

Breitkopf	Kalmus

Proto, Frank   1941-

(b Brooklyn, NY, 18 July 1941). American

A Carmen Fantasy, For Double Bass & Orchestra   25'

2[1.2/pic] 2[1.Eh] 2[1.bcl] 0 — 2perc — hp — pf/cel — str[min 8.8.6.4.2]

perc: sus cym, sd, tri, tambn, glock, xyl, vib, cast, tmp

Solo double bass should be amplified.

The composer also has a *Carmen Fantasy* for Trumpet & Orchestra.

1. Prelude	*2'*
2. Aragonaise	*6'*
3. Nocturne: Michaela's Aria	*4'*
4. Toreador Song	*8'*
5. Bohemian Dance	*5'*

Liben

Casey at the Bat <1973>   13'

narrator

3[incl pic] 3[incl Eh] 3[incl bcl] 3[incl cbn] — 4 3 3 1 — tape (crowd noises, etc.) — elec bass — tmp+4 — hp — pf — str

Jazz trumpeter (tp2) must improvise on the blues; pf, elec bass & drums also must swing.

Liben

Doodles; An Introduction to the Orchestra <1975>   var

2[1.2/pic] 2 3[1.2.bcl] 2 — 4 2 3 1 — elec bass — tmp+2 — hp — pf — str

It is not intended that all movements be played; the work can be as short as 8' or as long as 30'.

   Playable with: 2 2 2 2 — 2 2 0 0 — 1perc — pf — elec bass — str

Pf, elec bass & drummer must be capable jazz players.

Liben

Fantasy on the Saints <1975>   8'

3[incl pic] 3[incl Eh] 3[incl bcl] 3[incl cbn] — 4 3 3 1 — opt elec bass — tmp+4 — hp — pf/cel — str

Optional jazz section that can be stretched out into a Dixieland jam session, increasing the duration to about 12'.

Liben

Psathas, John   1966-

(b Wellington, 3 July 1966). New Zealand composer of Greek parentage

---

Djinn <2010>   20'

solo marimba

3perc — hp — str

perc: bd, tomtom, tri, tamtam, glock, chimes, crot, windchimes, marktree, whip, 2sus cym, finger cym, djembe, waterphone, frame drum, 4 Japanese singing bowls, springdrum

1. Pandora	_'
2. Labyrinth	_'
3. Outdreaming the Genie	_'

Promethean

Omnifenix (Concerto for Tenor Saxophone & Orchestra)   16'
<2000>

soloists: tenor saxophone, drumset

2[1/pic.2/pic] 2 2 2[1/Ebcl(opt).2] 2 — 4 3 3 1 — tmp+3 — str

perc: tamtam, chimes, cowbell, 2bd, 2sus cym, 2sd, tomtom, 2tri, vib, 2windchimes

The 2 concertante parts (tsx & set) consist largely of instructions for directed improvisation.

Promethean

Orpheus in Rarohenga <2002>   45'

solos STBar   chorus SATB

3[1.2.3/pic] 3[1.2.3/Eh] 3[1.2.3/bcl] 3[1.2.cbn] — 4 3 3 1 — tmp+5 — hp — pf/cel, org — str

perc: bd, szl cym, Chinescym, rototom, tri, tambn, tamtam, glock, marim, vib, chimes, crot, slgh-bells, windchimes, marktree, claves, 4cym, 5sus cym, 2sd, 9tomtom, 4woodblk, finger cym

Part 1: The Transit of Venus	_'
Part 2: The Death of Cook	_'
Part 3: Captain Cook in Rarohenga	_'

Promethean

Planet Damnation <2007>   7'

solo timpani

2[1.2/pic] 2 2 2[1.cbn] — 4 3 3 1 — 3 or 4 perc — str

perc: bd, cym, sus cym, rototom, tri, tambn, tamtam, marim, vib, chimes, windchimes, 2sd, thundersheet, finger cym

Promethean

Pounamu <2011>   40'

soloist: vocals/gtr/bgtr

2[1.2/pic] 2 2 2[1.cbn] — 4 3 3 1 — tmp+3 — hp — str

perc: bd, cym, sus cym, rototom, tri, tamtam, glock, marim, vib, chimes, marktree, templeblks, whip, bongos, congas, waterphone, automobile sample

Written for "roots musician" Warren Maxwell (guitar, bass guitar, vocals). Solo part mostly improvised.

1. Complexities	_'
2. Nemesis	_'
3. Grandma's Tears	_'
4. Shadows	_'
5. Treasures	_'

Promethean

Seikilos <1998>   12'

2[1/pic.2/pic] 2 2 2 — 4 3 3 1 — tmp+2 — str

perc: bd, cym, sd, rototom, tri, vib, 6tomtom, china crash cym

Promethean

Tarantismo <2010>   7'

2 2 2 2[1.2/cbn] — 4 3 3 1 — tmp+3 — hp — str

perc: bd, cym, sus cym, tri, tamtam, xyl, vib, chimes, finger cym

Promethean

Three Psalms (Concerto for Solo Piano, Percussion, Harp & String Orchestra) <2003>   23'

solo piano
hp — str
perc: bd, tambn, tamtam, marim, vib, chimes, slgh-bells, windchimes, marktree, bongos, 2tri, finger cym, china crash cym, tmp
I. Aria   _'
II. Inferno   _'
III. Sergei Bk.3 Ch.1   _'

> Promethean

View from Olympus (Double Concerto for Percussion, Piano & Orchestra) <2001>   21'

solo percussion & piano
3[1.2/pic.pic] 2 2[1/Ebcl.2] 2 — 4 3 3 1 — tmp+2(or 4) — hp — str
perc: bd, cym, sus cym, Chinescym, sd, tri, tambn, tamtam, glock, marim, vib, chimes, marktree, cowbell, 3tomtom, finger cym.
solo perc: vib, marim, simtak, dulcimer, bass steel drums, windchimes (2-3 sets), belltree, marktree, tri, finger cym, 4octobans, 4tomtom, hi-hat, multiple cymbals.
Piano is amplified in mvts I & III.
   Includes "Fragment," a duet for vib & pf which may be performed as an encore; included in the soloist parts (no orchestral accompaniment).
I. The Furies   _'
II. To Yelastro Paithi (The Smiling Child)   _'
III. Dance of the Maenads   _'

> Promethean

Zahara (Concerto No.2 for Saxophone & Orchestra) <2005>   23'

solo saxophone (soprano/tenor)
3[1.2.3/pic] 3[1.2.3/Eh] 3 3[1.2.3/cbn] — 4 3 2 1 — tmp+3 — str
perc: bd, cym, tri, marim, vib, crot, slgh-bells, whip, finger cym, spring drum, waterphone
Timpanist also plays windchimes (2 sets) & finger cymbals.
Mirologio   _'
Movement II   _'
Interlude   _'
Movement III   _'

> Promethean

Ptaszyńska, Marta   1943-

(b Warsaw, 29 July 1943). Polish; resident in US since 1972

Holocaust Memorial Cantata <1992>   40'

solos STBar   chorus
2 2 2 2 — 2 2 2 1 — 2perc — str

> Presser

Puccini, Giacomo   1858-1924

(b Lucca, 22 Dec 1858; d Brussels, 29 Nov 1924). Italian

Capriccio sinfonico <1883>   16'

3[1.2.pic] 2 2 2 — 4 2 3 1 — tmp+2 — hp — str
perc: cym, tri
Boccaccini & Elkan-Vogel ed. Pietro Spada; Carus ed. Dieter Schickling.

| Boccaccini | Carus | Elkan-Vogel |

I crisantemi (The Chrysanthemums) <1890>   6'

str
Originally for string quartet. Kalmus (ed. Lucas Drew) adds a bass part, as does Fischer (ed. Y. Talmi); other editions consist of the original 4 string parts.

| Boccaccini | C. Fischer | Kalmus | Luck's | Ricordi |

Edgar: Preludio <1890; rev 1905>   8'

3[1.2.3/pic] 3[1.2.Eh] 3[1.2.bcl] 2 — 4 4 3 1 — tmp+2 — hp — str
Ed. Pietro Spada.

| Elkan-Vogel |

Manon Lescaut: Prelude, Act II <1891–1893>   3'

2 3[1.2.Eh] 2 3 — 4 0 0 0 — tmp — hp — str

| Boccaccini |

Manon Lescaut: Intermezzo from Act III <1891–1893>   5'

3[1.2.3/pic] 3[1.2.Eh] 3[1.2.bcl] 2 — 4 3 3 1 — tmp+1 — hp — str
perc: bd

| Kalmus | Luck's | Ricordi |

Preludio sinfonico <1876>   12'

3[1.2.pic] 2[1.2/Eh] 2 2 — 4 2 3 1 — tmp+2 — hp — str
perc: bd, cym
Elkan-Vogel ed. Pietro Spada; Kalmus ed. Michael Kaye (title: *Symphonic Prelude*); Peters ed. Wojciechowski.

| Elkan-Vogel | Kalmus | Peters |

Suor Angelica: Intermezzo <1918>   4'

3[1.2.pic] 3[1.2.Eh] 3[1.2.bcl] 2 — 4 2 0 0 — tmp+1 — hp — cel — str
perc: bd, tri

| Ricordi |

Pugni, Cesare   1802-1870

(b Genoa, 31 May 1802; d St Petersburg, 14/26 Jan 1870). Italian

La Esmeralda

see under: Drigo, Riccardo
            Diane et Actéon Pas de deux

Purcell, Henry   1659-1695

(b ?Westminster, London, ?10 Sept 1659; d Westminster, London, 21 Nov 1695). English

> **Z** = F.B. Zimmerman: *Henry Purcell, 1659–1695: An Analytical Catalogue of his Music* (London, 1963)

Abdelazer, Z.570: Suite <1695>   13'

cnt — str
Ed. Edvard Fendler.
   Includes a *Rondeau* (mvt 2) which became the theme used in Britten's *Young Person's Guide to the Orchestra*.
1. Overture   4'
2. Rondeau   1'
3. Air   1'
4. Air   2'
5. Minuet   1'
6. Air   1'
7. Jig   1'
8. Hornpipe   1'
9. Air   1'

> Mercury

Canon on a Ground Bass, Z.731 <before 1680>   4'

str
Originally for 3 violins or 3 recorders, with harpsichord; arr. Wallingford Riegger.

| AMP | Luck's |

Chacony in G minor, Z.730 <1680>   7'

opt hpsd — str
Ed. Benjamin Britten.

Boosey	Luck's

Come, Ye Sons of Art, Z.323 <1694>   25'

solo soprano, 2 countertenors, bass   chorus SATB
2[2recorders] 2 0 1 — 0 2 0 0 — tmp — cnt — str

Symphony	*4'*
Come, ye sons of art, away	*2'*
Sound the trumpet	*3'*
Come ye sons of art	*1'*
Strike the viol	*4'*
The day that such a blessing gave	*3'*
Bid the Virtues	*3'*
These are the sacred charms	*2'*
See, Nature, rejoicing	*3'*

Schirmer	Schott

Dido and Aeneas, Z.626: Suite <1689>   10'

cnt — str
Ed. E.J. Dent. Perhaps out of print.

1. Overture	*2'*
2. The Triumphing Dance	*2'*
3. Echo Dance of Furies	*1'*
4. Second Act Tune	*1'*
5. Third Act Tune	*1'*
6. Sailors' Dance	*1'*
7. Dance of Witches and Sailors	*2'*

Oxford	Fleisher

The Double Dealer, Z.592: Suite <1693>   8'

cnt — str
Ed. Paul Stassevitch.

Mercury

The Fairy Queen, Z.629: Suite No.1 <1692>   18'

cnt [opt] — str 4t or str orch
Hortus Musicus No.50; publisher's title: *Spielmusik zum
"Sommernachtstraum" I.* (Reprinted by Kalmus, under the title
Midsummer Night's Dream Music Vol.1.)
   Ed. Hilmar Höckner.
   Vn3 may replace va; winds (fl, ob, bn) may be added.

1. Prelude	*_'*
2. Hornpipe	*_'*
3. Overture	*_'*
4. Air	*_'*
5. Rondeau	*_'*
6. Prelude	*_'*
7. Entry Dance	*_'*
8. Hornpipe	*_'*
9. Dance for the Fairies	*_'*
10. Chaconne	*_'*

Bärenreiter

The Fairy Queen, Z.629: Suite No.2 <1692>   15'

cnt [opt] — str 4t or str orch
Hortus Musicus No.58; publisher's title: *Spielmusik zum
"Sommernachtstraum" II.* (Reprinted by Kalmus, under the title
Midsummer Night's Dream Music Vol.2.)
   Ed. Hilmar Höckner.
   Vn3 may replace va; winds (fl, ob, bn) may be added.

1. Air (Second Music)	*_'*
2. Jig (First Act Tune)	*_'*
3. Prelude	*_'*
4. Dance for the Followers of Night	*_'*
5. Air (Fourth Act Tune)	*_'*
6. Dance for the Green Men	*_'*
7. Monkey's Dance	*_'*
8. Air (Second Act Tune)	*_'*
9. Air	*_'*

Bärenreiter

The Fairy Queen, Z.629: Two Suites <1692>   15'

str
Two suites published together; ed. William Reed.

SUITE NO.1	*6'*
1. Prelude	*_'*
2. Rondeau	*_'*
3. Jig	*_'*
4. Hornpipe	*_'*
5. Dance of the Fairies	*_'*
SUITE NO.2	*9'*
1. Air	*_'*
2. Monkey Dance	*_'*
3. Dance for the Followers of the Night	*_'*
4. Chaconne	*_'*

Eulenburg	Kalmus	Kunzelmann	Luck's

Fantasias, Strings, Z.732-743, 745 <1679–1680>   38'

str[no db]
Transcribed by Peter Warlock; ed. André Mangeot. Published under the
title *Three-, Four-, and Five-Part Fantasias for Strings.*

FANTASIAS a 3	
Z.732, D minor	*3'*
Z.733, F major	*3'*
Z.734, G minor	*2'*
FANTASIAS a 4	
Z.735, G minor	*3'*
Z.736, B-flat major	*3'*
Z.737, F major	*3'*
Z.738, C minor	*4'*
Z.739, D minor	*3'*
Z.740, A minor	*3'*
Z.741, E minor	*3'*
Z.742, G major	*3'*
Z.743, D minor	*3'*
Fantasia upon One Note, a 5, Z.745, F major	*2'*

Curwen	Kalmus	Luck's

Funeral Music for Queen Mary, Z.58c & 860   10'

3[1.2.3/pic] 3[1.2.Eh] 3 3[1.2.cbn] — 4 2 3 1 — tmp+2 — hp — pf
— [no str]
perc: bd, tamtam, glock, vib, chimes
Originally choral movements (Z.58c) alternating with instrumental
movements (Z.860). Transcribed and elaborated by Steven Stucky, 1992;
choral passages from the original are rendered by instruments in this
arrangement.

March	*_'*
Anthem	*_'*
Canzona	*_'*
March	*_'*

Merion

Funeral Music for Queen Mary: March & Canzona,   4'
Z.860 <1692>

0 0 0 0 — 0 2 2 0 — tmp — [no str]
Originally for 4 trumpets. Timpani optional. Ed. Thurston Dart.

1. March	*2'*
2. Canzona	*2'*

Oxford

The Gordian Knot Untied, Z.597: Suite No.1 <1691>   11'

2 2 2 1 — 2 2 0 0 — tmp — str
Winds and timpani, added by Gustav Holst, are optional.

1. Overture	*_'*
2. Air	*_'*
3. Rondeau Minuet	*_'*
4. Air	*_'*
5. Jig	*_'*

Luck's	Novello

The Gordian Knot Untied, Z.597: Suite No.2 <1691>   7'

2 2 2 1 — 2 2 0 0 — tmp — str
Winds and timpani, added by Gustav Holst, are optional.
1. Chaconne _'
2. Air _'
3. Minuet _'

Luck's	Novello

Indian Queen, Z.630: Trumpet Overture <1695>   3'

0 0 0 0 — 0 1 0 0 — tmp — str
Arr. Lionel Salter.

Luck's	Oxford

The Married Beau, Z.603: Suite <1694>   12'

2 2 2 1 — 2 2 0 0 — tmp — str
Arr. Gustav Holst.

Novello

Midsummer Night's Dream Music

see his: Fairy Queen, Z.629

Ode for St. Cecilia's Day, Z.328 (ed. Dennison) (Hail, Bright Cecilia) <1692>   40'

chorus   solos SAATBB
2[2rec] 2 0 0 — 0 2 0 0 — bass rec — tmp — cnt — str
Ed. Peter Dennison.

Novello

Ode for St. Cecilia's Day, Z.328 (ed. Tippett & Bergmann) (Hail, Bright Cecilia) <1692>   56'

chorus   solos SAATBB
2 2 0 0 — 0 2 0 0 — tmp — cnt — str
Ed. Tippett and Bergmann.

I. Symphony	*11'*
II. Hail! Bright Cecilia	*5'*
III. Hark; Each Tree	*5'*
IV. 'Tis Nature's Voice	*4'*
V. Soul of the World	*3'*
VI. Thou Tun'st This World	*4'*
VII. With that Sublime Celestial…	*3'*
VIII. Wondrous Machine	*3'*
IX. The Airy Violin	*2'*
X. In Vain the Am'rous Flute	*5'*
XI. The Fife; and All the Harmony of War	*3'*
XII. Let These Among Us Contest	*3'*
XIII. Hail! Bright Cecilia	*5'*

Schott

Ode for St. Cecilia's Day, Z.329 (Laudate Ceciliam) <1683>   11'

solos ATB
cnt — str[no va]
Ed. Bruce Wood.

Symphony / Laudate Ceciliam, in voce et organo	2'
Modelemini psalmum novum	3'
Symphony	2'
Dicite Virgini, canite Martyri	4'

Novello

Ode for St. Cecilia's Day, Z.334 (Raise, Raise the Voice) <ca.1685>   12'

chorus (STB)   solos SB
cnt — str[no va]
Ed. Bruce Wood.

Symphony	3'
Raise, Raise the Voice, All Instruments Obey	3'
The God Himself Says He'll Be Present Here	2'
Mark How Readily Each Pliant String	4'

Novello

Ode for St. Cecilia's Day, Z.339 (Welcome to All the Pleasures) <1683>   15'

chorus   solos SSATB
cnt — str
Ed. Walter Bergmann.

Symphony	2'
Welcome to All the Pleasures	2'
Here the Deities Approve	5'
Then Lift Up Your Voices	2'
Beauty, Thou Scene of Love	3'
In a Consort of Voices	1'

Luck's	Schott

The Rival Sisters, Z.609: Overture   7'

cnt — str
Ed. Paul Stassevitch.

Luck's	Mercury

Sonata for Trumpet & Strings, Z.850 <1964>   6'

str
Ed. Alan Lumsden.

Musica Rara

Spielmusik zum Sommernachtstraum

see his: Fairy Queen, Z.629

Te Deum and Jubilate, Z.232 <1694>   19'

chorus SSATB   solos SSAATB
0 0 0 0 — 0 2 0 0 — cnt — str
Ed. Denis Arnold

Eulenburg	Luck's

Trumpet Prelude (Trumpet Voluntary) <1700>   3'

3[1.2.pic] 2 2 2 — 4 3 3 1 — tmp+1 — hp — str
perc: sd
Orchestrated by Arthur Luck. Neither the title of this work nor its attribution to Purcell is correct. Actually it is *The Prince of Denmark's March*, by Jeremiah Clarke, found as the 4th movement of his *Suite, D major, q.v.*

Luck's

Trumpet Voluntary (arr. Westermann) <1700>   4'

3[1.2.pic] 2 2 2 — 4 2 3 1 — tmp+3 — str
Arr. Clayton Westermann. Wrongly attributed to Purcell, this work is actually the 4th movement of Jeremiah Clarke's *Suite, D major, q.v.*

Kalmus

The Virtuous Wife, Z.611: Suite <1694>   10'
2 2 2 1 — 2 2 0 0 — tmp — str
Arr. Gustav Holst.
I. *Overture*   _'
II. *Slow Air*   _'
III. *Hornpipe*   _'
IV. *Minuet I*   _'
V. *Minuet II*   _'
VI. *Allegro*   _'

Novello

Puts, Kevin   1972-
(b St. Louis, MO, 3 January 1972). American

Concerto, Marimba <1997>   22'
2[1.pic] 2 2 2[1.cbn] — 2 1 0 0 — 1perc — str
perc: xyl
I. "*…terrific sun on the brink*"   _'
II. "*…into the quick of losses*"   _'
III. "*…logarithms, exponents, the damnedest of metaphors*"   _'

Aperto

Exalted Virelai <1997>   14'
3[1.2.pic] 3[1.2.3/Eh] 3[1/Ebcl.2.3] 3[1.2.cbn] — 4 3 3 1 — tmp+3 — pf — str
perc: bd, cym, tri, glock, xyl, marim, vib, crot, claves, 2brakedrums, 2woodblks, 3tamtams
After Guillaume de Machaut, c1300-1377.

Aperto

Falling Dream <2001>   16'
3 3 3 3[1.2.cbn] — 4 3 3 1 — tmp+4 — hp — pf — str
perc: bd, sus cym, szl cym, tri, glock, vib, chimes, crot, 5gongs, 3tamtams

Aperto

Hymn to the Sun <2008>   7'
3[1.2.pic] 3[1.2.Eh] 3[1.2.Ebcl] 3[1.2.cbn] — 4 3 3 1 — tmp+4 — hp — pf — str
perc: bd, cym, sus cym, szl cym, Chinescym, tri, tamtam, glock, xyl, marim, vib, chimes, crot

Aperto

Inspiring Beethoven <2001>   15'
3[1.2.pic] 2 2 3[1.2.cbn] — 4 3 3 1 — tmp+3 — pf — str
perc: bd, sus cym, szl cym, tomtom, tamtam, glock, xyl, vib, chimes
References to Beethoven *Symphony No.7*.

Aperto

John Brown's Body <2001>   14'
narrator
3[1.2.pic] 3[1.2.Eh] 3[1.2.bcl] 3[1.2.cbn] — 4 3 3 1 — tmp+3 — hp — pf — str
perc: bd, cym, sus cym, sd, tri, tambn, tamtam, glock, vib, chimes, marktree, woodblk, vibrslp

Aperto

Millennium Canons <2001>   7'
3[1.2.3/pic] 3 3 3[1.2.cbn] — 4 4 3 1 — tmp+4 — hp — pf — str
perc: bd, cym, sus cym, tri, 3tamtams, glock, vib, chimes, crot, 2woodblk, templeblk

Aperto

Network <1997>   7'
3[1.2.pic] 2 2 3[1.2.cbn] — 4 4 3 1 — 3perc — pf — str
perc: bd, kick bd, sus cym, sd, brakedrum, tri, glock, xyl, marim, vib, crot, woodblk, metal plates, 3tamtams, 2 bass bows

Aperto

Symphony No.1 <1998–1999>   24'
3[1.2.pic] 3[1.2.Eh] 2 2 — 4 3 3 1 — tmp+3 — hp — str
perc: bd, cym, sus cym, sd, tri, glock, xyl, marim, vib, chimes, crot, woodblk, templeblk, cowbell, 2tamtams, 2brakedrums, 4tomtom

Aperto

Symphony No.2 (Island of Innocence) <2001>   12'
3[1.2.3/pic] 3[1.2.Eh] 3 3[1.2.cbn] — 4 3 3 1 — tmp+3 — hp — pf — str
perc: bd, cym, sus cym, tamtam, glock, xyl, vib, chimes, crot

Aperto

Symphony No.3 (Vespertine) <2003; rev 2005>   21'
3[1.2.3/pic] 3[1.2.Eh] 3[1.2.3/Ebcl] 3[1.2.cbn] — 4 3 3 1 — tmp+3 — hp — cel — str
perc: bd, cym, szl cym, Chinescym, tri, glock, vib, chimes, claves, 2sus cym, 2tamtam, 3woodblk, 3cowbell
3rd mvt may be performed separately as *Vespertine Elegy*.
I. "*…through the warmthest cord*"   6'
II. "*…I have a recurrent dream*"   4'
III. "*…it's not meant to be a strife*" 11'

Aperto

Symphony No.4 <2007; rev 2007>   28'
3[1.2/pic2.3/pic1] 3[1.2.Eh] 3 2 — 4 3 3 1 — tmp+3 — hp — str
perc: bd, cym, sus cym, szl cym, Chinescym, tri, tamtam, glock, xyl, vib, chimes, crot, opt marim
I. *PRELUDE: Mission San Jua Bautista, ca.1800*   6'
II. *ARRIQUETPON (the diary of Francisco Arroyo de la Cuesta, 1818)*   8'
III. *INTERLUDE*   6'
IV. *HEALING SONG*   8'

Aperto

"… this noble company" <2003>   6'
3[1.2.pic] 3[1.2.Eh] 3[1.2.3/bcl] 3[1.2.cbn] — 4 3 3 1 — tmp — hp — str
May be performed with *Millennium Canons* under the title *Two Orchestral Fanfares (I. "…this noble company"; II. Millennium Canons)*.

Aperto

Two Mountain Scenes <2007>   14'
3[1.2.pic] 3[1.2.Eh] 3 3[1.2.cbn] — 4 4 3 1 — tmp+3 — hp — pf — str
perc: bd, cym, sus cym, szl cym, tri, tamtam, glock, xyl, vib, chimes, crot, 4woodblk
I. *Maestoso*   _'
II. *Furioso*   _'

Aperto

Q

R

Quantz, Johann Joachim   1697-1773

(b Oberscheden, Hanover, 30 Jan 1697; d Potsdam, 12 July 1773). German

Concerto, Flute, C major   14'

cnt — str
Ed. Hanns-Dieter Sonntag.

Kalmus	Luck's	Peters

Concerto, Flute, C minor   16'

cnt — str
Ed. Hanns-Dieter Sonntag.

Peters

Concerto, Flute, D major   15'

cnt — str
Ed. Hanns-Dieter Sonntag.

Kalmus	Luck's	Möseler

Concerto, Flute, D major (Pour Potsdam)   16'

cnt — str
Ed. Walter Upmeyer.

Bärenreiter	Kalmus	Luck's

Concerto, Flute, G major   16'

cnt — str
Ed. Felix Schroeder.

I. Allegro	5'
II. Mesto	6'
III. Allegro vivace	5'

Eulenburg	Luck's

Rabaud, Henri   1873-1949

(b Paris, 10 Nov 1873; d Paris, 11 Sept 1949). French

Divertissement sur des chansons russes, op.2   13'
(Divertissement on Russian Songs) <1899>

2 2 2 2 — 4 2 3 0 — tmp+1 — hp — str
perc: cym

Enoch

La procession nocturne, op.6 <1910>   16'

3 2 2 2 — 4 2 3 1 — tmp+1 — hp — str
perc: bd (could be covered by timpanist)

Durand	Kalmus	Luck's

Rachmaninoff, Sergei   1873-1943

(b Oneg, 20 March/1 April1873; d Beverly Hills, CA, 28 March 1943). Russian

The Bells, op.35 (Kolokola; Die Glocken; Les cloches)   35'
<1913; rev 1936 and later>

chorus   solos STB
4[1.2.3.pic] 4[1.2.3.Eh] 4[1.2.3.bcl] 4[1.2.3.cbn] — 6 3 3 1 — tmp+5
— hp — cel, pianino, opt org — str
perc: bd, cym, sd, tri, tambn, tamtam, glock, chimes
Revisions of the vocal parts from 1936 and later (intended principally for
performances in English) may be found in the appendix of the Boosey
choral score of 1971, corrected 1973. These revisions are not to be found
in any published full score.

1. The Silver Sleigh Bells	6'
2. The Mellow Wedding Bells	10'
3. The Loud Alarum Bells	8'
4. The Mournful Iron Bells	11'

Boosey	Kalmus	Luck's

Caprice bohémien, op.12 (Kaprichchio na tsïganskiye   20'
temï; Capriccio on Gypsy Themes) <1892–1894>

3[1.2.pic] 2 2 2 — 4 2 3 1 — tmp+5 — hp — str
perc: tri, tambn, sd, cym, bd

Boosey	Kalmus	Luck's

Cinq Études-tableaux <1911–1917>   25'

3[1.2.3/pic] 3[1.2.Eh] 3[1.2.bcl] 3[1.2.cbn] — 4 3 3 1 — tmp+4 — hp
— str
perc: tri, glock, tambn, field dr, chimes, cym, bd, tamtam
Selected and orchestrated by Ottorino Respighi, from Rachmaninoff's
Etudes-tableaux for piano, op.33 no.7 & op.39 nos.2, 6, 7, 9.

1. La mer et les mouettes (The Sea and the Seagulls)	8'
2. La foire (The Fair)	2'
3. Marche funèbre (Funeral March)	8'
4. Le Chaperon rouge et le Loup (Little Red Riding Hood and the Wolf)	3'
5. Marche (March)	4'

Boosey

CONCERTO, PIANO, No.1, op.1, F# MINOR (history) <1890–1891; rev 1917, 1919>

There are three extant versions of this concerto:

Original version, 1891. Published originally by Gutheil; republished by Muzyka, 1971, ed. Irina Jordan & Georgi Kirkor; score and parts are available from Boosey & Hawkes, though this is not clear from the Boosey website. May be seen on the IMSLP website, imslp.org.

Intermediate version, 1917. The composer's revisions of the solo piano part, but *not* of all of the orchestration. Published by Muzyka, 1965, and reprinted by Kalmus, 1973 (A2418—since withdrawn), as well as Dover. Sets of parts for this version may exist, undetected, in many orchestra libraries. This too may be seen on the IMSP website, imslp.org, where a free downloadable audio file of this version may also be found.

Definitive final version, 1919. As the composer's last word on the matter, this should be the choice of performers, absent some special historical intent. Published by Gutheil, 1919; reprinted by Boosey & Hawkes (1947 miniature score) and Kalmus (A8062). Also published in a Boosey & Hawkes Masterworks score (including concertos 1 *and* 2) in which it is wrongly identified as the 1917 version.

Concerto, Piano, No.1, op.1, F-sharp minor (definitive final version, 1919) <1890–1891; rev 1917; 1919>   27'

2 2 2 2 — 4 2 3 0 — tmp+2 — str
perc: cym, tri
See previous entry for the history of this work.

I. Vivace	13'	
II. Andante	6'	
III. Allegro vivace	8'	

Boosey	Kalmus	Luck's

Concerto, Piano, No.2, op.18, C minor <1900–1901>   33'

2 2 2 2 — 4 2 3 1 — tmp+2 — str
perc: bd, cym
Luck's provides Eh part (in lieu of ob1) for 3rd mvt, 16 bars before [31].

I. Moderato	11'	
II. Adagio sostenuto	11'	
III. Allegro scherzando	11'	

Boosey	Kalmus	Luck's

Concerto, Piano, No.3, op.30, D minor <1909>   39'

2 2 2 2 — 4 2 3 1 — tmp+2 — str
perc: bd, cym, sus cym, sd

I. Allegro ma non tanto	15'	
II. Intermezzo	10'	
III. Finale	14'	

Boosey	Kalmus	Luck's

CONCERTO, PIANO, NO.4   31'

Concerto, Piano, No.4, op.40, G minor (1926 version) <1926>

3[1.2.pic] 3[1.2.Eh] 2 2 — 4 2 3 1 — tmp+5 — str
perc: tri, tambn, sd, cym, bd
This original version was never published during the composer's lifetime. Boosey offers the score for sale and the parts for rent. This version has been recorded.

Boosey

Concerto, Piano, No.4, op.40, G minor (1927 version) <1926; rev 1927>   29'

3[1.2.pic] 3[1.2.Eh] 2 2 — 4 2 3 1 — tmp+5 — str
perc: tri, tambn, sd, cym, bd
The composer revised this concerto for its publication, making cuts and other changes. Kalmus had offered it under the slightly misleading heading "original version"; since the 2005-06 Kalmus catalog, it is listed as "1927 version." This version has been recorded.

Kalmus

Concerto, Piano, No.4, op.40, G minor (1941 version) <1926; rev 1941>   24'

3[1.2.pic] 3[1.2.Eh] 2 2 — 4 2 3 1 — tmp+5 — str
perc: tri, tambn, sd, cym, bd
The composer revised the work a second time in 1941; this version was published in 1944, and became the standard for concert performances and recordings. It is the shortest, and technically the least demanding on the soloist.

I. Allegro vivace	9'	
II. Largo	6'	
III. Allegro vivace	9'	

Boosey	Kalmus

The Isle of the Dead, op.29 (Ostrov myortvïkh; Die Toteninsel) <1909>   20'

3[1.2.3/pic] 3[1.2.Eh] 3[1.2.bcl] 3[1.2.cbn] — 6 3 3 1 — tmp+2 — hp — str
perc: bd, cym

Boosey	Kalmus	Luck's

Prelude, op.3, no.2 <1892>   4'

2 2 2 2 — 4 2 3 0 — tmp+1 — hp — str
The celebrated *Prelude in C-sharp minor*, originally for piano; transposed to C minor and orchestrated by Adolf Schmid. Piano-conductor score only.

Boosey	Kalmus	Luck's

Rhapsody on a Theme of Paganini, op.43 <1934>   22'

solo piano
3[1.2.pic] 3[1.2.Eh] 2 2 — 4 2 3 1 — tmp+4 — hp — str
perc: glock, sus cym, sd, tri, cym, bd

Boosey

The Rock; Fantasy, op.7 (Utyos) <1893>   18'

3[1.2.pic] 2 2 — 4 2 3 1 — tmp+2 — hp — str
perc: tri, tambn, cym, bd, tamtam

Forberg	Kalmus	Luck's	Russian

Symphonic Dances, op.45 <1940>   35'

3[1.2.pic] 3[1.2.Eh] 3[1.2.bcl] 3[1.2.cbn] — 4 3 3 1 — asx — tmp+5 — hp — pf — str
perc: bd, cym, sd, tri, tambn, tamtam, glock, xyl, chimes
Saxophone briefly in 1st mvt only; could be covered by contrabassoonist or bass clarinetist. Piano in mvts 1 & 2 only. Bcl in bass clef throughout; mostly in B-flat but some passages for bcl in A.

Kalmus offers a score for sale, but parts are rental only.

It is said that the title originally was to be "Fantastic Dances," with movement titles "Noon," "Twilight," and "Midnight."

I. Non allegro - Lento - Tempo I [original title "Noon"]	11'	
II. Andante con moto (Tempo di valse) [original title "Twlight"]	10'	
III. Lento assai - Allegro vivace [original title "Midnight"]	14'	

Boosey

Symphony, D minor (1891) (Youth Symphony) <1891>   13'

2 2 2 2 — 4 2 3 1 — tmp — str
Only first mvt was completed. Ed. Paul Lamm.

Kalmus	Luck's	Sikorski

Symphony No.1, op.13, D minor <1895>   42'

3[1.2.3/pic] 2 2 — 4 3 3 1 — tmp+5 — str
perc: bd, cym, sus cym, sd, tri, tambn, tamtam

I. Grave - Allegro ma non troppo	13'	
II. Allegro animato	9'	
III. Larghetto	8'	
IV. Allegro con fuoco	12'	

Fleisher	Kalmus	Russian	Sikorski

Symphony No.2, op.27, E minor <1906–1907>   60'

3[1.2.3/pic] 3[1.2.3/Eh] 3[1.2.bcl(A)] 2 — 4 3 3 1 — tmp+3 — str
perc: bd, cym, sd, glock
Many 20th-century conductors made cuts in this work, allegedly with the
composer's approval. Fleisher Collection has one set of parts of this sort.
However, more and more conductors perform the work as written.
  Kalmus ed. Clinton F. Nieweg & Christopher R. Morgan, 2011.

I. Largo - Allegro moderato	20'
II. Allegro molto	11'
III. Adagio	14'
IV. Allegro vivace	15'

| Boosey | Kalmus | Luck's |

Symphony No.3, op.44, A minor <1935–1936; rev 1938>   39'

3[1.2.pic] 3[1.2.Eh] 3[1.2.bcl(A)] 3[1.2.cbn] — 4 3[1.2.atp] 3 1 —
tmp+5 — hp — cel — str
perc: bd, cym, sd, tri, tamtam, xyl
Score, but not parts, available from Kalmus.

Lento; Allegro moderato	13'
Adagio ma non troppo	12'
Allegro	14'

| Boosey | Luck's |

Three Russian Songs, op.41 (Trois chansons russes)   12'
<1926>

chorus of altos and basses
3[1.2.3/pic] 3[1.2.Eh] 3[1.2.bcl] 3[1.2.cbn] — 4 3[1.2.atp] 3 1 —
tmp+4 — hp — pf — str
perc: tri, tamtam, glock, sd, cym, bd, rute

Across the River (Cherez rechku)	3'
Oh, Ivan (Akh tï, Van'ka)	5'
Whiten My Rouged Cheeks (Belelitsï, rumyanitsï vï moy)	4'

| EMI |

Die Toteninsel

see his: Isle of the Dead, op.29

VOCALISE   6'
Vocalise (voice & orchestra) <1912; rev 1915>

soprano or tenor solo
2 3[1.2.Eh] 2 2 — 2 0 0 0 — str
Originally for voice & piano (op.34, no.14); arr. by the composer for
voice & orchestra.

| Luck's |

Vocalise (orchestra) <1912; rev 1915>   6'

2 3[1.2.Eh] 2 2 — 2 0 0 0 — str
16-20 violins playing solo line, accompanied by the remainder of the
orchestra. Originally for voice & piano (op.34, no.14); arr. by the
composer for orchestra. Kalmus ed. Clinton F. Nieweg.

| Boosey | Kalmus | Luck's |

Vocalise (arr. Daniel Braden) <1912; rev 1915>   6'

solo soprano
str

| Kalmus |

Raff, Joachim   1822 - 1882

(b Lachen, nr Zurich, 27 May 1822; d Frankfurt, 24/5 June 1882). German

Ein feste Burg ist unser Gott, op.127 <1854; rev 1865>   19'

3[1.2.pic] 2 2 2 — 4 2 3 0 — tmp — str
Originally the overture to incidental music for *Bernhard von Weimar*, by
W. Genast.

| Fleisher | Hofmeister |

Ode au printemps, op.76 <1857>   13'

solo piano
3[1.2.pic] 2 2 2 — 4 2 0 0 — tmp — str

| Luck's | Schott |

Sinfonietta, op.188, F major <1873>   21'

2 2 2 2 — 2 0 0 0 — [no str]

I. Allegro	7'
II. Scherzo: Allegro molto	4'
III. Larghetto	6'
IV. Finale: Vivace	4'

| Luck's |

Symphony No.1, op.96, D major (An das Vaterland; To   69'
the Fatherland) <1859–1861>

2 2 2 2 — 4 2 3 0 — tmp — str

1. Allegro	18'
2. Scherzo: Allegro molto vivace	10'
3. Larghetto	13'
4. Allegro dramatico	6'
5. Larghetto sostenuto; Un poco meno lento … ; Allegro deciso, trionfante	22'

| Kalmus |

Symphony No.3, op.153, F major (Im Walde; In the   31'
Forest) <1869>

3[1.2.pic] 2 2 2 — 4 2 3 0 — tmp+1 — str
perc: tri

I. AM TAGE	11'
Eindrücke und Empfindungen	
II. IN DER DAMMERUNG	9'
Träumerei	
Tanz der Dryaden	
III. NACHTS	11'
Stilles Wehen der Nacht im Walde	
Einzug und Auszug der Wilden Jagd mit Frau Holle und Wotan	
Anbruch des Tages	

| Kalmus | Kistner&Siegel |

Symphony No.5, op.177, E major (Lenore) <1872>   34'

3[1.2.pic] 2 2 2 — 4 2 3 0 — tmp+2 — str
perc: sd, tri

Liebesglück	17'
Trennung	7'
Wiedervereinigung im Tode	10'

| Kalmus |

Symphony No.6, op.189, D minor <1873>   29'

2 2 2 2 — 4 2 3 0 — tmp — str

1. Allegro non troppo	9'
2. Vivace	5'
3. Larghetto, quasi marcia funebre	7'
4. Allegro con spirito	8'

| Kalmus |

Symphony No.8, op.204, A major (Frühlingsklänge;   41'
Sounds of Spring) <1876>

2 2 2 2 — 4 2 3 0 — tmp — str
Part 1 of the symphonic cycle *Die Jahreszeiten*.

Frühlings Ruckkehr	14'
In der Walpurgisnacht	8'
Mit dem ersten Blumenstrauss	7'
Wanderlust	12'

| Kalmus | Kistner&Siegel |

Symphony No.9, op.208, E minor (Im Sommer; In Summer) <1878>   39'

3[1.2.3/pic] 2 2 2 — 4 2 3 0 — tmp — str
Part 2 of the symphonic cycle *Die Jahreszeiten*.

Ein heisser Tag	12'
Die Jagd der Elfen	11'
Ekloge	7'
Zum Erntekrantz	9'

Kalmus	Kistner&Siegel

Raksin, David   1912-2004

(b Philadelphia, 4 Aug 1912; d Los Angeles, 9 Aug 2004). American

Toy Concertino   6'

concertino (8 musicians)
2[1.2/pic] 1 2 1 — 2 2 0 0 — tmp+1 — str
perc: bd/cym
Instrumentation of concertino: (1) tin fife; (2) piccolo trumpet or normal trumpet muted; (3) ocarina in G; (4) ocarina in C; (5) toy glockenspiel; (6) bird warble alternating ratchets & duck squawk; (7) toy snare drum alternating triangle and pop-gun; (8) cuckoo call alternating toy accordion or toy concertina or harmonica.

Broude Bros.

Rameau, Jean-Philippe   1683-1764

(b Dijon, bap. 25 Sept 1683; d Paris, 12 Sept 1764). French

Ballet Suite <1739 & 1749>   12'

2[1.2/pic] 2[1.2/Eh] 2 2 — 2 2 0 0 — tmp+2 — str
perc: tambn, tri
Arr. Felix Mottl from various Rameau stage works.

1. Menuett (from Platée*)*	_'
2. Musette (from Fêtes d'Hébé*)*	_'
3. Tambourin (from Fêtes d'Hébé*)*	_'

Kalmus	Peters

Dardanus: Suite <c1739>   11'

2 2 0 2 — str
Ed. Paul Henry Lang.

Mercury

Les fêtes d'Hébé: Divertissement <c1739>   20'

2[incl pic] 2 0 1 — 2 1 0 0 — tmp — str
Arr. Fernand Oubradous.

EMT

Les Paladins: Suite No.2 <1760>   20'

2[incl pic] 2 0 2 — 2 0 0 0 — cnt — str
Ed. Roger Desormière. (This work may be out of print.)

Oiseau Lyre

Platée: Suite des danses <1749>   8'

2[incl pic] 2 0 1 — str
Arr. Fernand Oubradous.

EMT

Suite for String Orchestra   15'

str
Arranged by R. Temple-Savage from six harpsichord pieces.

Boosey	Luck's

Zaïs: Overture <1748>   5'

2[2pic] 2 0 2 — 1perc — cnt — str
perc: "tambour"
Arr. Vincent d'Indy.

Durand	Kalmus

Ran, Shulamit   1949-

(b Tel Aviv, 21 Oct 1949). American composer of Israeli birth

Chicago Skyline <1991>   5'

0 0 0 0 — 6 4 3 2 — tmp+3 — [no str]

Presser

Concerto for Orchestra <1986>   26'

2[1/pic.2/afl] 2[1.2/Eh] 3[1/Ebcl.2.3/bcl] 3[1.2.3/cbn] — 4 3 3[1/euph.2.3] 1 — tmp+3 — pf — str
perc: bd, cym, szl cym, sd, tri, tambn, tamtam, gong, xyl, chimes, crot, woodblk, templeblks, 4sus cym, 6tomtom

I. quarter-note = 52	9'
II. quarter-note = 72	5'
III. quarter-note = 88	8'
IV. quarter-note = 58	4'

Presser

Concert Piece (1970) <1970>   13'

solo piano (amplified; also doubling celesta)
4[1.2.3/pic.4/pic] 2 4[1.2.3.bcl] 3[1.2.cbn] — 5 4 3 1 — 2tmp+4 — str
perc: bd, sus cym, sd, 6tomtom, tambn, gong, glock, marim, vib, chimes, 3woodblk

Presser

Concerto, Violin <2002–2003>   20'

2[1.2/pic] 2 2[1/Ebcl.2/bcl] 2[1.2/cbn] — 2 2 2 0 — tmp+2 — cel — str
perc: 4 sus cym, tomtom, tamtam, glock, xyl, vib, chimes, bongos, vibraslap, bass bow
If timpanist covers percussion also, only 2 players required (tmp+1).

Presser

Double Vision, for 2 Quintets & Piano <1976>   18'

1[fl/pic] 1 2[1/Ebcl.2/bcl] 1 — 1 2 2 0 — pf — [no str]

Presser

Ensembles for 17 <1975>   18'

solo soprano
2[1/pic.2/afl] 0 2[1/Ebcl.2/bcl] 1 — 1 1 2 0 — 2perc — pf — str 4t
perc: bd, sus cym, 4tomtom, 3timbales, gong, marim, vib, chimes, 2woodblk, templeblk

Presser

Legends <1992–1993; rev 2001>   20'

3[1.2/afl.3/pic] 2[1.2/Eh] 3[1.2/Ebcl/bcl.3/bcl] 3[1.2.3/cbn] — 4 3 3 2 — tmp+5 — hp — cel, pf — str[min 12.10.8.8.6]
perc: bd, cym, 3sus cym, szl cym, sd, 4tomtoms with bd flat, 3tri, 3tambn, 2tamtam, nipplegong, 2glock, xyl, marim, vib, chimes, crot, marktree, glass windchimes, 3woodblk, templeblk, whip, marac, rute, 2 bass bows

1.	10'
2.	10'

Presser

Symphony <1991>   34'

2[incl pic] 2[incl Eh] 3[incl Ebcl,bcl] 3[incl cbn] — 6 4 3 1 — tmp+4 — str

Presser

Three Fantasy Movements <1971; rev (orchd) 1993; rev 1996>   20'

solo violoncello
2 2 2 2 — 2 2 2 0 — tmp+2 — str
perc: bd, cym, 2 sus cym, szl cym, tomtoms, 6roto-toms, tambn, 2glock, xyl, marim, 2vib, chimes, crot, windchimes, marktree, ratchet, guiro, suspended key chimes
Originally *Three Fantasy Pieces* for violoncello & piano; arr. for orchestra by Cliff Colnot.
   Timpanist must cover several percussion instruments.

Presser

Vessels of Courage and Hope <1998>   13'

3[1.2.3/pic] 3[1.2.Eh] 3[1.2/Ebcl.3/bcl] 3[1.2.cbn] — 4 3 3 1 — tmp+5 — pf — str
perc: bd, cym, 3 sus cym, sd, tomtoms, tri, tamtam, nipplegong, xyl, vib, 2 sets chimes, crot, woodblk, templeblk, whip, ratch, vibraslap, sandblks

Presser

Voices <2000>   16'

flute soloist (doubles also on amplified alto flute & piccolo)
2[1.2/pic] 2 2[1.2/bcl] 2 — 2 2 2 1 — 3perc — str
perc: bd, cym, 5 sus cym, szl cym, 7tomtoms, 3tri, 2tambn, tamtam, glock, xyl, vib, chimes, crot, marktree, woodblk, templeblk, bongos, vibraslap
Quasi Passacaglia (flute)   7'
Voice of the Wood (amplified alto flute)   4'
Big Bands, Little Bands (flute/piccolo)   5'

Presser

Rands, Bernard   1934-

(b Sheffield, 2 March 1934). American composer of English birth

Agenda, For Young Players <1969–1970>   13'

2 2 2 2 — 2 2 2 0 — 2perc — str[6.6.4.4.2]
2-6 percussion players who need have no knowledge of conventional music notation may be added. Wind and string forces may be increased. Graphic notation.

Helicon

Canti del sole (small ensemble version) <1983–1984>   28'

solo tenor
1[1/pic/afl] 0 1[1/Ebcl/bcl] 0 — 0 1 1 0 — 2perc — pf — vn, va, vc, db
Originally for large orchestra with tenor solo; reduction by the composer, 1984

Helicon

Canti lunatici <1980; rev 1981>   29'

solo soprano
2[incl pic,afl] 2 2[incl Ebcl,bcl] 2 — 2 2 2 0 — 2perc — 2hp — cel, pf — str[min 8.8.6.4.2]
Originally for soprano & small ensemble; arr. for soprano & orchestra, 1981.

Helicon

Fanfare for a Festival <1986>   2'

2 2 2 2 — 2 2 2 0 — tmp — str

Helicon

Hiraeth <1987>   30'

solo violoncello
3[incl pic,2afl] 3[1.2.Eh] 4[incl bcl] 3[incl cbn] — 4 3 3 1 — tmp+4 — 2hp — cel, pf, elec org — str

Helicon

Madrigali (after Monteverdi/Berio) <1977>   20'

1 1 0 0 — 1 1 0 0 — 2perc — str[6.6.4.2.1]
perc: sd, tamtam, vib, bongos, 2tomtoms
"... based upon the musical characteristics found in Monteverdi's Eighth Book of Madrigals. ... refers constantly to Luciano Berio's transcription of *Il Combattimento*."
   1. Lento tranquillo   4'
   2. Un poco misterioso   5'
   3. Allegro con forza   3'
   4. from Scherzi   3'
   5. Legatissimo sempre, senza accenti   5'

Helicon   Schott

Ránki, György   1907-1992

(b Budapest, 30 Oct 1907; d Budapest, 22 May 1992). Hungarian

Symphony No.1 <1977>   19'

2[1.2/pic] 2[1.2/Eh] 2[1.2/bcl] 2[1.2/cbn] — 4 2 3 1 — tmp+3 — hp — pf/cel — str
perc: sd, tambn, bd, vib, xyl, glock, chimes, gong, 2sus cym, 2tomtoms, 4woodblks, 3bongos
   I. Con moto appassionato   _'
   II. Andante cantabile   _'
   III. Alla danza macabra   _'

EMB

Rathaus, Karol   1895-1954

(b Tarnopol, 16 Sept 1895; d New York, 21 Nov 1954). American composer of Polish origin

Praeludium and Gigue   7'

2 2 2 2 — 4 2 3 1 — tmp — str

Boosey

Rautavaara, Einojuhani   1928-

(b Helsinki, 9 Oct 1928). Finnish

Cantus arcticus; Concerto for Birds & Orchestra <1972>   18'

2 2 2 2 — 2 2 1 0 — audio CD — tmp[opt]+1 — hp — cel — str
perc: cym, tamtam
CD operator must be able to read a score.
   1. The Bog   7'
   2. Melancholy   4'
   3. Swans Migrating   7'

Fennica

Concerto, Piano, No.3 (Gift of Dreams) <1998>   28'

2 2 2 2 — 4 2 2 0 — tmp+2 — str
perc: bd, sd, tamtam, gong, vib, chimes, 4tomtom
   I. Tranquillo   10'
   II. Adagio assai   12'
   III. Energico   6'

Fennica

Fiddlers, op.1 (Pelimannit) <1952; rev (orchd) 1972>   8'

str
Originally for piano; orchestrated by the composer.
   1. The Närbö Villagers in Fine Fettle (Närböläisten braa speli)   2'
   2. Mr. Jonas Kopsi (Kopsin Jonas)   2'
   3. Bellringer Samuel Dikström (Klockar Samuel Dikström)   1'
   4. Devil's Schottische (Pirun polska)   2'
   5. Jumps (Hypyt)   1'

Fazer

Lintukoto (Isle of Bliss) <1995>   11'

2 2 2 2 — 2 1 1 0 — tmp+1 — hp — str
perc: tamtam, vib, woodblk

Fennica

A Requiem in Our Time <1953>   11'

0 0 0 0 — 4 4 3 1 — bar hn — tmp+2 — [no str]
perc: cym, sus cym, sd, glock, xyl, bell[E4]

Hymnus	*3'*
Credo et dubito	*2'*
Dies irae	*3'*
Lacrymosa	*3'*

King

Suite for Strings (Sarja jousille) <1952>   13'

str
Originally String Quartet No.1, with bass part added by the composer.

I. Presto	*3'*
II. Andante assai	*7'*
III. Vivace assai (Alla giga)	*3'*

Fennica

Symphony No.1 (1988 revision) <1955–1956; rev 1988,   17'
2003>

2[1.2/pic] 2 2 2 — 4 3 2 1 — tmp+2 — str
perc: bd, cym, sus cym, sd, tomtom, xyl, guiro, cuica

I. Andante	*13'*
II. Allegro	*4'*

Fennica

Symphony No.2 (Sinfonia intima) <1957; rev 1984>   22'

2[1.pic] 2[1.Eh] 3[Ebcl.cl.bcl] 2[1.cbn] — 2 1 1 0 — tmp+2 — str
perc: bd, cym, sus cym, sd, tamtam, glock, xyl, marim, vib, whip, guiro, 3tomtoms

I. Quasi grave	*10'*
II. Vivace	*3'*
III. Largo	*6'*
IV. Presto	*3'*

Fennica

Symphony No.3 <1959–1960>   33'

2 2 2 2 — 2 2 3 1 — 4Wag tb[2ten.2b] — tmp — str

1. Langsam, breit, ruhig; Bewegt	*12'*
2. Langsam, doch nicht schleppend	*7'*
3. Sehr schnell	*7'*
4. Bewegt	*7'*

Fennica

Symphony No.4 (Arabescata) <1963>   18'

3[1.2/afl.3/pic] 2[1.Eh] 3[Ebcl.cl.bcl] 2[1.cbn] — 3[1.2.Wag tb
tenor/bass] 3[pic tp. tp1.tp2] 4[2tenor, 2 bass] 1 — asx — tmp+8 — hp
— cel, pf — str
perc: bd, cym, sus cym, td, field dr, tri, tambn, tamtam, gong, glock, xyl, vib,
chimes, marac, cast, 2sd, 2tomtoms, 2woodblks
The work originally titled *Symphony No.4* (1965, rev.1968) was
withdrawn in 1986, and the preexisting *Arabescata* (1963) was given the
designation *Symphony No.4*.
   Rigorously serialized in many aspects; nevertheless ambiguities exist
in the score.

Arabescata I	*4'*
Arabescata II (Quadratus — Zigzag — Figurae — Dedicatio — Rotatus)	*6'*
Arabescata III	*3'*
Arabescata IV	*5'*

Fennica

Symphony No.5 <1985>   31'

3[1.2.3/pic] 3[1.2.Eh] 3[1.2.bcl] 3[1.2.cbn] — 4 4 4 1 — tmp+4 — str
perc: bd, sus cym, marim, vib, chimes, 6tomtom, 3tamtam, glass windchimes,
bamboo windchimes
In one movement.

Fennica

Symphony No.6 (Vincentiana) <1992>   38'

2 2 3[1.2.bcl] 3[1.2.cbn] — 4 4 3 1 — tmp+3 — hp — synth (DX7)
— str
perc: bd, glock, xyl, marim, vib, chimes, crot, flexatone, woodblk, guiro, 3sus
cym, 4tomtom, 3tamtam
4th mvt revised in 1996 for performance as an independent work entitled
Apotheosis; in that revision the synthesizer is replaced by harp.

I. Starry Night (Tähiyö)	*16'*
II. The Crows (Varikset)	*6'*
III. Saint-Rémy	*9'*
IV. Apotheosis	*7'*

Fazer

Symphony No.7 (Angel of Light) <1994>   35'

2 2 2 2 — 4 3 3 1 — tmp+2 — hp — str
perc: sus cym, sd, glock, xyl, marim, vib, 4tomtoms, 3tamtams

I. Tranquillo	*12'*
II. Molto allegro	*6'*
III. Come un sogno	*9'*
IV. Pesante	*8'*

Fennica

Symphony No.8 (The Journey; Matka) <1999>   30'

3[1.2.pic] 3[1.2.Eh] 3[1.2.bcl] 3[1.2.cbn] — 4 4 3 1 — tmp+2 — 2hp
— str
perc: sus cym, gong, glock, xyl, vib, chimes, 4tomtoms, 3tamtams

I. Adagio assai	*11'*
II. Feroce	*3'*
III. Tranquillo	*6'*
IV. Con grandezza; Sciolto; Tempo primo	*10'*

Fennica

Ravel, Maurice   1875-1937

(b Ciboure, Basses-Pyrenees, 7 March 1875; d Paris, 28 Dec 1937). French composer
of Swiss-Basque parentage

Alborada del gracioso <1904–1905; rev (orchd) 1918>   8'

3[1.2.3/pic] 3[1.2.Eh] 2 3[1.2.cbn] — 4 2 3 1 — tmp+6 — 2hp — str
perc: bd, cym, sd, tri, tambn, xyl, crot, cast
Originally for piano (*Miroirs*, mvt 4); orchestrated by the composer.
   Kalmus ed. Clinton F. Nieweg, 2005; corrected transposed parts for the
Nieweg edition available from Luck's.

Eschig	Kalmus	Schott

Une barque sur l'ocean <1904–1905; rev (orchd) 1906>   7'

3[1.2/pic2.3/pic1] 3[1.2.Eh] 3[1.2.bcl] 2 — 4 2 3 1 — tmp+3 — 2hp
— cel — str
perc: bd, cym, tri, gong, glock
Originally for piano (*Miroirs*, 3rd mvt); orchestrated by the composer.
   If cel player covers the gong, one less percussionist is needed.
   Kalmus edition by Clinton F. Nieweg & Nancy M. Bradburd.

Eschig	Kalmus	Schott

Bolero <1928>   13'

3[1.2/pic2.pic1] 3[1.2/ob d'am.Eh] 3[1.2/Ebcl.bcl] 3[1.2.cbn] — 4
4[pic tp.1.2.3] 3 1 — ssx, tsx — tmp+4 — hp — cel[played by perc] —
str
perc: bd, cym, 2sd, tamtam, cel[played by perc]
Score actually calls for a 3rd saxophone, a sopranino, but the passage in
question is normally covered by the soprano saxophonist.
Breitkopf ed. Jean-François Monnard.
   Schott ed. by Arbie Orenstein; parts in this edition are on rental from
Schott in many countries, though not in the USA.

Breitkopf	Durand	Schott

Cinq mélodies populaires grecques (Five Greek Folk Songs) <1904–1906>   8'

solo voice
2[1/pic.2/ opt pic] 2[1.2/Eh] 2 2 — 2 1 0 0 — tmp+4 — hp — cel — str
Originally for voice & piano; nos.1 & 5 orchestrated by the composer; nos.2-4 orchestrated by Manuel Rosenthal, 1913.
     Kalmus ed. by Clinton R. Nieweg.

1. Chanson de la mariée (Awakening of the Bride)	1'
2. Là bas, vers l'église (Over by the Church)	2'
3. Quel galant m'est comparable (What Dandy Can Compare with Me)	1'
4. Chanson des cueilleuses de lentisques (Song of the Lentisk Pickers)	3'
5. Tout gai! (Very Merrily!)	1'

Durand	Kalmus

Concerto, Piano, G major <1929–1931>   23'

2[1.pic] 2[1.Eh] 2[1.Ebcl] 2 — 2 1 1 0 — tmp+3 — hp — str
perc: bd, sus cym, sd, tri, tamtam, woodblk, whip

I. Allegramente	9'
II. Adagio assai	9'
III. Presto	5'

Durand

Concerto, Piano (Left Hand), D major <1929–1930>   19'

3[1.2.3/pic] 3[1.2.Eh] 4[1.2.Ebcl.bcl] 3[1.2.cbn] — 4 3 3 1 — tmp+4 — hp — str
perc: bd, cym, sd, tri, tamtam, woodblk
Bcl in A and in B-flat (all treble clef).

Durand

Daphnis et Chloé <1909–1912>   50'

wordless chorus
4[1.2/pic2.3/pic1.afl] 3[1.2.Eh] 4[1.2.Ebcl.bcl] 4[1.2.3.sarr] — 4 4 3 1 — tmp+8 — 2hp — cel — str
perc: bd, cym, sd, military drum, tri, tambn, tamtam, xyl, crot, cast, windmachine, jeu de timbres à clavier
The chorus may be dispensed with by playing the cues in the orchestral parts; these cues are not indicated in the score.
     Kalmus edition by Clinton F. Nieweg; a compatible choral score (vocal lines only; no piano accompaniment) is available from Kalmus. Durand publishes a piano reduction (with chorus lines) which may be used for choral or ballet rehearsal.

Durand	Kalmus

Daphnis et Chloé: Suite No.1 <1909–1912>   12'

optional wordless chorus
4[1.2/pic2.3/pic1.afl] 3[1.2.Eh] 4[1.2.Ebcl.bcl] 4[1.2.3.sarr] — 4 4 3 1 — tmp+6 — 2hp — cel — str
perc: bd, cym, sd, tri, tambn, tamtam, glock, crot, windmachine
Kalmus edition by Clark McAlister.

Nocturne	5'
Interlude	3'
Danse guerrière	4'

Durand	Kalmus

Daphnis et Chloé: Suite No.2 <1909–1912>   18'

optional wordless chorus
4[1.2/pic2.pic1.afl] 3[1.2.Eh] 4[1.2.Ebcl.bcl] 4[1.2.3.sarr] — 4 4 3 1 — tmp+8 — 2hp — cel — str
perc: bd, cym, sd, military drum, tri, tambn, cast, jeu de timbres à clavier
Kalmus edition by Clinton F. Nieweg. **N.B.:** In all publications all wind parts of Daphnis Suite II must be marked that the Suite starts at fig.[155], instead of fig.[153].
     Kalmus publishes a score-format version of the percussion parts, which may allow percussion sections to use less than the 8 players for which Ravel originally scored, by having one player handle several instruments. The precise number of players should be determined by the principal percussionist.

Lever du jour	6'
Pantomime	7'
Danse générale	5'

Durand	Kalmus

Don Quichotte à Dulcinée (Don Quixote to Dulcinea) <1932–1933>   7'

solo baritone
2 2[incl Eh] 2 2 — 2 1 0 0 — 1perc — hp — str
perc: vib, cast

Chanson romanesque	2'
Chanson épique	3'
Chanson à boire	2'

Durand

Gaspard de la nuit <1908>   22'

3[incl pic,afl] 3[incl Eh] 4[incl Ebcl,bcl] 3[incl cbn] — 4 3[1/flug] 3 1 — tmp+6 — 2hp — cel — str
perc: bd, cym, 2sus cym, szl cym, sd, military drum, tri, tamtam, gong, glock, xyl, chimes, crot, woodblk, whip, ratch, cast, windmachine, thundersheet, géophone
Originally for piano; orchestrated by Marius Constant.

Ondine	7'
Le gibet	6'
Scarbo	9'

Durand

Introduction & Allegro <1905>   11'

solo harp
1 0 1 0 — str 4t
A double bass part of uncertain provenance (but definitely not from Ravel) exists, presumably intended for performances using string sections rather than a quartet.

Kalmus	Luck's

Le jardin magique (The Magic Garden)   12'

2[1.2/pic] 2[1.Eh] 2 2 — 2 2 2 0 — 3perc — hp — cel — str
perc: bd, sus cym, field dr, tri, tambn, tamtam, glock, xyl, chimes, tmp
A suite of little pieces by Ravel, orchestrated by Bo Holten, 1991-1996. (Nos.1 & 8 are arrangements of Ravel's own orchestrations.) The mvts are played without pause.

1. Fanfare (L'Eventail de Jeanne)	_'
2. Sainte	_'
3. Menuet sur le nom de Haydn	_'
4. Prelude	_'
5. Berceuse sur le nom de Fauré	_'
6. Prelude	_'
7. Menuet	_'
8. Noël des Jouets	_'

Hansen

Ma Mère l'Oye (Mother Goose) <1908–1910; rev (orchd) 1911>   29'

2[1.2/pic] 2[1.2/Eh] 2 2[1.2/cbn] — 2 0 0 0 — tmp+4 — hp — cel — str

perc: bd, cym, sd, tri, tamtam, xyl, jeu de timbres à clavier, sus cym
Complete ballet; originally a 5-movement suite for piano 4-hands; orchestrated by the composer, with the addition of 2 movements and connecting material. Kalmus edition by Nancy M. Bradburd & Clinton F. Nieweg.
   The *Prélude & Danse rouet* with the *5 Pièces enfantines* from *Ma Mère l'Oye* (next 2 entries) contain between them nearly all the music of the complete ballet; some connecting transitions are missing, and the order of movements is changed slightly.

1. Prélude	*3'*
2. Danse du rouet et scène	*4'*
3. Pavane de la belle au bois dormant	*2'*
4. Les entretriens de la belle et de la bête	*5'*
5. Petit poucet	*4'*
6. Laideronnette, impératrice des pagodes	*5'*
7. Le jardin féerique	*6'*

Durand	Kalmus	Luck's

Ma Mère l'Oye (Mother Goose): Prélude & Danse du rouet <1911>   7'

2[1.2/pic] 2[1.2/Eh] 2 2 — 2 0 0 0 — tmp+3 — hp — cel — str
perc: cym, sus cym, sd, tri, tamtam, jeu de timbres à clavier, xyl
Kalmus ed. by Clinton F. Nieweg.
   The end of this excerpt leads directly into the *Pavane de la Belle au bois dormant*. There is no concert ending provided.

1. Prélude	*3'*
2. Danse du rouet et scène (Dance of the Spinning Wheel & Scene)	*4'*

Durand	Kalmus	Luck's

Ma Mère l'Oye (Mother Goose): 5 pièces enfantines (Suite) <1908–1910>   16'

2[1.2/pic] 2[1.2/Eh] 2 2[1.2/cbn] — 2 0 0 0 — tmp+3 — hp — cel — str

perc: bd, cym, tri, tamtam, xyl, jeu de timbres à clavier, sus cym
Originally for piano 4-hands; orchestrated 1911 by the composer.
   Kalmus edition by Clinton F. Nieweg & Nancy M. Bradburd.

1. Pavane de la Belle au bois dormant	*2'*
2. Petit Poucet	*3'*
3. Laideronnette, Impératrice des pagodes	*3'*
4. Les Entretiens de la Belle et de la Bête	*4'*
5. Le Jardin féerique	*4'*

Durand	Kalmus	Luck's

Menuet antique <1895; rev (orchd) 1929>   7'

3[1.2.pic] 3[1.2.Eh] 3[1.2.bcl] 3[1.2.cbn] — 4 3 3 1 — tmp — hp — str
Originally for piano; orchestrated by the composer.

Enoch

Pavane pour une infante défunte (Pavane for a Dead Princess) <1899; rev (orchd) 1910>   6'

2 1 2 2 — 2 0 0 0 — hp — str
Originally for piano; orchestrated by the composer. A reduced version for piano and string orchestra is availble from Schott.

Eschig	Kalmus	Luck's	Schott

Rapsodie espagnole <1907–1908>   16'

4[1.2.pic1.pic2] 3[1.2.Eh] 3[1.2.bcl] 4[1.2.3.sarr] — 4 3 3 1 — tmp+6 — 2hp — cel — str
perc: bd, cym, sd, tri, tambn, tamtam, xyl, cast
3rd mvt calls for bass clarinet in A (other mvts all bcl in B-flat).
Kalmus edition by Nancy M. Bradburd & Clinton F. Nieweg.

I. Prélude a la nuit	*4'*
II. Malagueña	*2'*
III. Habanera	*3'*
IV. Feria	*7'*

Durand	C. Fischer	Kalmus	Luck's

Shéhérazade [voice & orchestra] <1903>   17'

soprano solo
3[1.2.pic] 3[1.2.Eh] 2 2 — 4 2 3 1 — tmp+3 — 2hp — cel — str
perc: bd, cym, sd, tri, tambn, tamtam, glock
Kalmus edition by Clinton F. Nieweg.

Asie (Asia)	*10'*
La flûte enchantée (The Enchanted Flute)	*3'*
L'indifférent (The Indifferent One)	*4'*

Durand	C. Fischer	Kalmus

Shéhérazade; ouverture de féerie <1898>   14'

3[incl pic] 3[incl Eh] 2 4[1.2.3.sarr] — 4 4 3 1 — tmp+5 — 2hp — cel — str
perc: bd, cym, sd, tri, tambn, gong

Salabert

Le Tombeau de Couperin <1914–1917; rev (orchd) 1919>   17'

2[1.2/pic] 2[1.2/Eh] 2 2 — 2 1 0 0 — hp — str
Originally six mvts for piano; four of them later orchestrated by the composer to create the present work.
   Kalmus ed. Clinton F. Nieweg & Nancy M. Bradburd.

I. Prélude	*3'*
II. Forlane	*6'*
III. Menuet	*5'*
IV. Rigaudon	*3'*

Durand	Kalmus	Luck's

Trois poèmes de Stéphane Mallarmé <1913>   11'

solo voice (mezzo-soprano or baritone)
2[1.2/pic] 0 2[1.2/bcl] 0 — pf — str 4t

Soupir	*4'*
Placet futile	*4'*
Surgi de la croupe et du bond	*3'*

Durand	Kalmus

Tzigane, rapsodie de concert, for Violin & Orchestra <1924>   10'

2[1.2/pic] 2 2 2 — 2 1 0 0 — 1perc — hp — cel — str
perc: sus cym, tri, glock
Originally for violin & piano-with-*luthéal* (a device that causes a piano to sound somewhat like a cimbalom); orchestrated by the composer.
   Bärenreiter ed. Douglas Woodfull-Harris, 2012.

Durand	C. Fischer

La valse, poème chorégraphique <1919–1920>   12'

3[1.2.3/pic] 3[1.2.3/Eh] 3[1.2.bcl] 3[1.2.cbn] — 4 3 3 1 — tmp+6 — 2hp — str
perc: bd, cym, sd, tri, tambn, tamtam, glock, crot, cast
Breitkopf ed. Jean-François Monnard; Kalmus ed. Clinton F. Nieweg & Nancy M. Bradburd.
   Bcl largely in A, though with passages for bcl in B-flat (all treble clef).

Breitkopf	Durand	Kalmus	Luck's

Valses nobles et sentimentales <1911; rev (orchd) 1912>   16'

2 3[1.2.Eh] 2 2 — 4 2 3 1 — tmp+6 — 2hp — cel — str
perc: bd, cym, sd, tri, tambn, glock
Originally for piano; orchestrated by the composer.
   Kalmus edition by Clinton F. Nieweg.

I. Modéré	*1'*
II. Assez lent	*2'*
III. Modéré	*2'*
IV. Assez animé	*2'*
V. Presque lent	*1'*
VI. Assez vif	*1'*
VII. Moins vif	*4'*
VIII. Epilogue	*3'*

Durand	Kalmus	Luck's

Read, Gardner   1913-2005

(b Evanston, IL, 2 Jan 1913; d Manchester-by-the-Sea, MA, 10 Nov 2005). American

First Overture, op.58 <1943>   8'

3[incl pic] 3[incl opt Eh] 3[incl opt bcl] 3[incl opt cbn] — 4 3 3 1 —
tmp+3 — opt hp — opt pf — str
Original publisher was Composers Press. This work may be out of print.

> Fleisher

Night Flight, op.44 <1942>   7'

4[incl pic] 3[incl Eh] 3[incl bcl] 3[incl cbn] — 4 3 3 1 — tmp+3 —
hp — str

> Peters

Pennsylvania Suite, op.67 <1947>   16'

4[incl pic] 3[incl Eh] 3[incl bcl] 3[incl cbn] — 4 3 3 1 — tmp+2 —
hp — pf — str
Based on folk songs of western Pennsylvania.
    May be performed with:
    3[incl pic] 2[incl Eh] 2 2 — 4 3 3 1 — tmp+2 — str
Dunlap's Creek   _'
I'm a Beggar   _'
John Riley   _'

> Belwin

Prelude & Toccata for Small Orchestra, op.43 <1937>   7'

2[1.pic] 2 2 2 — 2 2 2 0 — tmp — str

> Colombo

Symphony No.3, op.75 <1948>   25'

3[incl pic] 3[incl Eh] 3[incl bcl] 3[incl cbn] — 4 3 3 1 — tmp+3 — pf
— str

> Belwin

Reed, H. Owen   1910-2014

(b Odessa, MO, 17 June 1910; d Athens, GA, 6 Jan 2014). American

La fiesta mexicana <1964>   23'

3[1.2.pic] 3[1.2.opt Eh] 3[1.2.bcl] 3[1.2.opt cbn] — 4 3 3 1 — tmp+4
— hp — str
perc: templeblks, marim, xyl, chimes, cast, sd, tambn, sus cym, bd, gong, finger
cym, 2rototom
Off-stage band (mvt I, bars 158-196): cl, 2crt, hn, tbn, tuba, sd, bd/cym;
off-stage parts are cued in the on-stage instruments.
    Movements may be performed separately.
Prelude & Aztec Dance   9'
Mass   7'
Carnival   7'

> Belwin   Luck's

Reger, Max   1873-1916

(b Brand, nr Bayreuth, 19 March 1873; d Leipzig, 11 May 1916). German

Serenade, B-flat major   8'

2 2 2 2 — 4 0 0 0 — [no str]
Completed by Martien van Woerkum & Kees Verheijen. This work may
be out of print.

> Compusic

Symphonischer Prolog zu einer Tragödie (Symphonic Prolog to a Tragedy), op.108 <1908>   35'

3[1.2.3/pic] 3[1.2.Eh] 3[1.2.bcl] 3[1.2.cbn] — 6 3 3 1 — tmp+2 — str
perc: cym, bd
A note in one of the Peters scores describes a cut (bars 290 through 412),
to be employed at the conductor's discretion; this would reduce the
overall duration to 26'.

> Peters

Variations and Fugue on a Merry Theme of Joh. Adam Hiller, op.100 <1907>   39'

2 2 2 3[1.2.cbn] — 4 2 3 1 — tmp — hp — str

> Bote & Bock   Kalmus

Variations and Fugue on a Theme of Mozart, op.132 <1914>   35'

3 2 2 2 — 4 2 0 0 — tmp — hp — str
Breitkopf critical ed. by Bruno Weil.

> Breitkopf   Kalmus   Luck's   Peters

Vier Tondichtungen nach Arnold Böcklin, op.128 (Four Tone-Poems after Arnold Böcklin) <1913>   24'

3[1.2.3/pic] 2[1.2/Eh] 2 3[1.2.cbn] — 4 3 3 1 — tmp+3 — hp — str
perc: tri, tamtam, cym, bd
1. Der geigende Eremit (The Hermit Fiddler)   8'
2. Im Spiel der Wellen (Play of the Waves)   4'
3. Die Toteninsel (Isle of the Dead)   8'
4. Bacchanal (Bacchanale)   4'

> Kalmus   Luck's

Weihnachten, op.145, no.3 (Christmas) <1915–1916>   7'

str
Originally no.3 of a set of seven organ pieces; arr. Otto Meyer for strings.
    Quotes several German Christmas tunes.

> Luck's

Reich, Steve   1936-

(b New York, 3 Oct 1936). American

The Desert Music <1982–1984>   46'

amplified chorus of 27 voices
4[1.2/pic.3/pic.4/pic] 4[1.2/Eh.3/Eh.4/Eh] 4[1.2/bcl.3/bcl.4/bcl]
4[1.2.3.4/cbn] — 4 4[1/opt pic tp] 3 1 — 2tmp+7 — 2pf (4
players[1/synth.2.3/synth.4/synth]) — str[12.12.9.9.6]
perc: marac, 2marim, 2vib, 2xyl, 2glock, sticks, 2bd
Woodwinds are amplified, and 2va use contact microphones.
    An alternative version is for 10 singers (amplified) and reduced
orchestra.

> Boosey

The Four Sections <1987>   25'

4[1.2.3.4/pic] 4 4[1.2.3.4/bcl] 4[1.2.3.4/cbn] — 4 4 4 1 — tmp+4 —
2pf[dbl 2 synth] — str[18.16.12.8.6]
perc: 2vib, 2marim, 2bd
I. Strings (with Winds and Brass)   11'
II. Percussion   2'
III. Winds and Brass (with Strings)   6'
IV. Full Orchestra   6'

> Boosey

Music for Mallet Instruments, Voices & Organ <1973>   18'

3 female voices
7perc — elec org — [no str]
perc: vib, 4marim, 2glock
8 mics with amplifiers & speakers.

> Boosey

Tehillim [small ensemble version] <1981>   30'

solo voices SSSA
2[1.pic] 2[1.Eh] 2 1 — 6perc — 2elec orgs (or 2 players on 4 synths) — str 5t
perc: marac, marim, vib, crot, clapping, 4 tuned tambn w/o jingles
Amplification required for voices, woodwinds (except piccolo), and strings.

> Boosey

Tehillim [orchestral version] <1981>   30'

solo voices SSSA
4[1.2.3.pic] 3[1.2.Eh] 2 1 — 6perc — 2elec orgs (or 2 players on 4 synths) — str[6.6.4.2.1]
perc: marac, marim, vib, crot, clapping, 4 tuned tambn w/o jingles
Amplification required for voices, woodwinds (except piccolo), and db.

> Boosey

Three Movements <1986>   15'

4[1.2.pic1.pic2] 3[1.2.3/Eh] 3 4[1.2.3/cbn.cbn] — 4 3 3 1 — 5perc — pf[8-hands] — str[14.14.8.8.8]
perc: bd, 2marim, 2vib
Strings divided into 2 equal groups, right and left.
I. quarter note = 176   7'
II. quarter note = 88   4'
III. quarter note = 176   4'

> Boosey

Variations, for Winds, Strings & Keyboards <1979; rev 1980>   21'

3 3 0 0 — 0 3 3 1 — 2pf, 3elec org [synth] — str
For performance in "ensemble form," strings may play parts singly [min 2.2.2.2.1].

> Boosey

Reinagle, Alexander   1756-1809

(b Portsmouth, bap. 23 April 1756; d Baltimore, 21 Sept 1809). American composer of English birth.

Madison's March & Mrs. Madison's Minuet <1809 & 1796 resp.>   3'

str
Arr. Sam Denison from piano works.
Madison's March   2'
Mrs. Madison's Minuet   1'

> Fleisher

Reinecke, Carl   1824-1910

(b Altona, 23 June 1824; d Leipzig, 10 March 1910). German

Concerto, Flute, op.283, D major <ca.1908>   22'

2 2 2 2 — 4 2 0 0 — tmp+1[opt] — str
perc: optional tri
Ed. Henrik Wiese.
Allegro molto moderato   8'
Lento e mesto   8'
Moderato   6'

> Breitkopf

Concerto, Harp, op.182, E minor <1885>   24'

2 2 2 2 — 4 2 0 0 — tmp+1 — str
perc: tri
I. Allegro moderato   11'
II. Adagio   6'
III. Scherzo-Finale: Allegro vivace   7'

> Kalmus   Simrock

Kinder-Symphonie, op.239 (Toy-Symphony) <1897>   14'

7 players of toy instruments — pf — str[no va, no db]
Toy instruments: nightingale, cuckoo, 2 trumpets [G, D], drum, rattle (or perhaps ratchet?), crescent, *Theebrett* (tea-tray?), glass bell in B. Only the cuckoo, the glass bell, and the trumpets (which should be played by 1 player—1 toy trumpet in each hand) are given definite pitches to play. The precise nature and method of playing the tea-tray may be left to the ingenuity of the percussionist.
   The 2nd mvt is a quodlibet, combining several melodies from other composers, including Mozart, Beethoven, Weber, and Wenzel Müller.
I. Allegro un poco maestoso   4'
II. Andantino   6'
III. Moderato   2'
IV. "Steeple chase": Molto vivace   2'

> Kalmus

Serenade, op.242, G minor   25'

str
I. Marcia: Molto moderato   3'
II. Arioso: Andante sostenuto   4'
III. Scherzo: Allegretto   3'
IV. Cavatine: Adagio   6'
V. Fughetta gioiosa: Vivace   4'
VI. Finale: Allegretto   5'

> Kalmus   Zimmermann

Symphony No.1, op.79, A major   <?1870>   28'

2 2 2 2 — 4 2 3 0 — tmp — str
1. Lento; Allegro con brio   8'
2. Andante   8'
3. Scherzo: Molto vivace   6'
4. Finale: Allegro ma non troppo   6'

> Kalmus

Symphony No.2, op.134, C minor (Hakon Jarl) <1875>   35'

2 2 2 2 — 4 2 3 0 — tmp — str
Hakon Jarl   11'
Thora   7'
In Odin's Hain   5'
Oluf's Sieg   12'

> Kalmus

Symphony No.3, op.227, G minor <c1895>   33'

2 2 2 2 — 4 2 3 0 — tmp — str
1. Allegro   9'
2. Andante sostenuto   9'
3. Scherzo: Allegro vivace   7'
4. Finale: Maestoso; Allegro con fuoco; Molto più animato; Presto   8'

> Kalmus   Luck's

Respighi, Ottorino   1879-1936

(b Bologna, 9 July 1879; d Rome, 18 April 1936). Italian

P = P. Pedarra: "Catalogo delle composizioni di Ottorino Respighi," in *Ottorino Respighi*, ed. G. Rostivolta (Turin, 1985), pp. 327-404.

Adagio con variazioni, P.133, Violoncello & Orchestra <1921>   8'

3[1.2.pic] 3[1.2.Eh] 2 2 — 2 0 0 0 — hp — str
1921 revision of the 2nd mvt of an otherwise lost Violoncello Concerto from 1902.

> Bongiovani   Fleisher

Antiche danze ed arie (Ancient Airs and Dances): Suite I, P.109 <1917>   16'

2 3[1.2.Eh] 0 2 — 2 1 0 0 — hp — hpsd — str
Based on lute music of the 16th century. Later arr. for 2pf.
   1. Simone Molinaro (1599): Balletto detto "Il Conte Orlando"   3'
   2. Vincenzo Galilei (155…): Gagliarda   4'
   3. Anon. (late 16th Century): Villanella   5'
   4. Anon. (late 16th Century): Passo mezzo e Mascherada   4'

| Eulenburg | Kalmus | Luck's | Ricordi |

Antiche danze ed arie (Ancient Airs and Dances): Suite II, P.138 <1923>   19'

3[1.2.3/pic] 3[1.2.Eh] 2 2 — 3 2 3 0 — tmp — hp — hpsd 4-hands [1player/cel] — str
Based on lute music of the 16th & 17th centuries. Later arr. for 2pf.
   1. Fabritio Caroso (1581): Laura soave   4'
   2. Giovanni Battista Besardo (1617): Danza rustica   4'
   3. Marin Mersenne (17th Century): Campanae parisienses - Aria   5'
   4. Bernardo Gianoncelli (1650): Bergamasca   6'

| Eulenburg | Ricordi |

Antiche danze ed arie (Ancient Airs and Dances): Suite III, P.172 <1931>   19'

str
Based on lute music of the 16th & 17th centuries. Respighi arranged the pieces first for piano, then str 4t, then string orchestra.
   1. Anon. (late 16th century): Italiana   4'
   2. Giovanni Battista Besardo (17th century): Arie di Corte   8'
   3. Anon. (late 17th century): Siciliana   3'
   4. Lodovico Roncalli (1692): Passacaglia   4'

| Eulenburg | Ricordi |

Aria, P.32 <1901>   6'

str or str 5t
Originally for strings & organ; ed. & transcribed for string orchestra or string quintet by Salvatore Di Vittorio.

| Panastudio |

Ballata delle gnomidi, P.124 (Ballad of the Gnomes) <1919>   18'

4[1.2.pic1.pic2] 3[1.2.Eh] 4[1.2.Ebcl.bcl] 4[1.2.cbn] — 4 4[1.2.3.pic tp] 3 1 — tmp+6 — 2hp — str
perc: xyl, glock, tri, sd, cym, bd

| Kalmus | Luck's | Ricordi |

Belkis, regina di Saba (Belkis, Queen of Sheba): Suite, P.177 <1931–1932; rev 1934>   22'

3[1.2.pic] 3[1.2.Eh] 4[1.2.Ebcl.bcl] 3[1.2.cbn] — 4 4 4 0 — tmp+5 — 2hp — cel, pf — str
perc: tambn, field dr, xyl, glock, tri, cym, bd, tamtam, sd, darabucca
Offstage: 3tp, voce interna [tenor voice; trumpet may substitute].
   Perhaps the 4th trombone is intended to be a tuba part; the score of the complete ballet is said to call for 3tbn and 1 tuba (see Preface, p. xii, *supra*).
   I. Il sogno di Salomone (The Dream of Solomon)   8'
   II. La danza di Belkis all'aurora (The Dance of Belkis at Dawn)   6'
   III. Danza guerresca (War Dance)   3'
   IV. Danza orgiastica (Orgiastic Dance)   5'

| Ricordi |

La boutique fantasque, P.120 [after Rossini] (The Fantastic Toy Shop) <1918>   40'

3[1.2.pic] 3[1.2.Eh] 2 2 — 4 3 3 1 — tmp+5 — hp — cel — str
perc: bd, sus cym, sd, glock, xyl, tri, tambn, cym, cast
Ballet based on music of Rossini. Kalmus ed. Nancy M. Bradburd.
   N.B. Although the US Library of Congress and Grove Music OnLine both catalog this work under **Respighi**, other sources, including Chester and Luck's, list it under **Rossini**. Kalmus puts it after the end of the Rossini list, under the heading **Rossini-Respighi**.

| Chester | Kalmus |

La boutique fantasque [after Rossini] (The Fantastic Toy Shop): Suite, P.120a <1918>   21'

3[1.2.pic] 3[1.2.Eh] 2 2 — 4 3 3 1 — tmp+5 — hp — cel — str
perc: glock, tambn, tri, xyl, sd, cym, bd, cast
From the ballet based on music of Rossini. Kalmus ed. Nancy M. Bradburd.
   N.B. Although the US Library of Congress and Grove Music OnLine both catalog this work under **Respighi**, other sources, including Chester and Luck's, list it under **Rossini**. Kalmus puts it after the end of the Rossini list, under the heading **Rossini-Respighi**.
   1. Overture   2'
   2. Tarantella   2'
   3. Mazurka   3'
   4. Danse cosaque   2'
   5. Can-can   2'
   6. Valse lente   4'
   7. Nocturne   4'
   8. Galop   2'

| Chester | Kalmus |

Cinq Études-tableaux, P.160

see under: Rachmaninoff, Sergei, 1873-1943

Concerto a cinque, P.174 (Concerto for Five) <1933>   25'

soloists: oboe, trumpet, violin, double bass, piano
str
   Moderato   7'
   Adagio   12'
   Allegro vivo   6'

| Ricordi |

Concerto, Violin, P.49, A major <1903>   21'

2 2 2 2 — 4 2 0 0 — tmp — str
Mvts. 1 & 2 completed by Respighi (orchestration has been "enhanced" by Salvatore Di Vittorio); 3rd mvt completed in 2009 by Di Vittorio, based on Respighi's early sketches.
   I. Allegro energico   7'
   II. Molto lento; Agitato; Tranquillo   9'
   III. Allegro (Rondo)   5'

| Panastudio |

Fantasia slava, P.50 <1903>   13'

solo piano
3[1.2.pic] 2[1.2/Eh] 2 2 — 4 2 0 0 — tmp+1 — str
perc: tambn, cym

| Ricordi |

Feste romane, P.157 (Roman Festivals) <1928>   24'

3[1.2.3/pic] 3[1.2.Eh] 4[1.2.D-cl.bcl] 3[1.2.cbn] — 4 4 3 1 — 3 buccine or extra trumpets — mand — tmp+9 — pf 4-hands, org — str
perc: glock, xyl, tambn, sd, slgh-bells, field dr, tri, ratch, tamtam, cym, bd, chimes[A#3,A#4], 2tavolette
Bcl in A and B-flat.
   I. Circenses (Circus Games)   5'
   II. Il giubileo (The Jubilee)   7'
   III. L'ottobrata (Harvest Festivals in October)   7'
   IV. La Befana (Epiphany)   5'

| Ricordi |

Fontane di Roma, P.106 (Fountains of Rome) 15'
<1915–1916>

3[1.2.pic] 3[1.2.Eh] 3[1.2.bcl] 2 — 4 3 3 1 — tmp+3 — 2hp — cel,
pf, opt org — str
perc: tri, cym, chimes[D4], kybdglock
Kalmus ed. Clinton F. Nieweg & Nancy M. Bradburd.
   Bcl said to be in A, at least in part.
   I. La fontana di Valle Giulia all'alba   *4'*
   II. La Fontana del Tritone al mattino   *3'*
   III. La Fontana de Trevi al meriggio   *3'*
   IV. La fontana di Villa Medici al tramonto *5'*

Kalmus	Luck's	Ricordi

Impressioni brasiliane, P.153 (Brazilian Impressions) 20'
<1928>

3[1.2.3/pic] 3[1.2.Eh] 3[1.2.bcl] 2 — 4 3 2 1 — tmp+3 — hp — cel,
pf — str
perc: tri, tambn, bd, sus cym, sd, chimes[A4]
   Notte tropicale (Tropical Night)   *10'*
   Butantan (In a Snake-Garden Near São Paulo) *5'*
   Canzone e danza (Song and Dance)   *5'*

Ricordi

Lamento d'Arianna, P.88

   see: Monteverdi, Claudio (1567-1643)
         Arianna: Lamento d'Arianna

Lauda per la natività del Signore, P.166 <1928–1930> 26'

chorus   solos SSA (or SAT)
2[1.2/pic] 2[1.Eh] 0 2 — 1perc — pf 4-hands — [no str]
perc: tri
   1. Pastor, voie che vegghiate   *6'*
   2. Segnor, tu sei desceso   *5'*
   3. O car dolce mio figlio   *5'*
   4. Segnor puoie ch'hai degnato   *3'*
   5. Voglio ve consolare   *7'*

Ricordi

Pini di Roma, P.141 (Pines of Rome) <1923–1924> 23'

3[1.2.3/pic] 3[1.2.Eh] 3[1.2.bcl] 3[1.2.cbn] — 4 3 4 0 — 6 buccine
[2sopr, 2ten, 2bass] — tmp+5 — hp — cel, pf, org — str
perc: glock, tamtam, tri, cym, tambn, bd, 2small cym, nightingale recording
[supplied with parts], ratch [played by tmp]
Bcl (otherwise in B-flat) is in A in the 3rd mvt.
   Buccina was a metal signaling instrument of ancient Rome; Respighi
calls for the parts to be played by "flicorni" (= flugelhorns). Actually the
soprano and tenor buccine work fine on flugelhorns, while the 2 bass
instruments are best played on euphoniums or baritone horns. They
appear only in the last mvt, and are often stationed in three groups out in
the hall, on the sides and rear of the audience. Buccine may be substituted
for by cues present in the orchestral brass plus an additional 5th & 6th hn
and a 4th tp; of course this practice sacrifices much of the drama.
   There is also a brief but prominent solo for "tromba interna" (offstage
trumpet, as distant as possible); this could be played by one of the
flugelhorn players, though of course on trumpet (not flugelhorn).
   In the main orchestra, the score shows a 4th tbn, but the relevant *part* is
labeled "Tuba bassa," and is often played on tuba. Nightingale recording
supplied with rental materials.
   Mvts played without pause.
   1. I pini di Villa Borghese (The Pines of the Villa Borghese) *3'*
   2. Pini presso una catacomba (Pines Near a Catacomb) *7'*
   3. I pini del Gianicolo (The Pines of the Janiculum) *7'*
   4. I pini della Via Appia (The Pines of the Appian Way) *6'*

Ricordi

Rossiniana, P.148 <1925> 24'

3[1.2.3/pic] 3[1.2.Eh] 2 2 — 4 3 3 1 — tmp+5 — hp — cel — str
perc: xyl, glock, tri, tambn, cast, tamtam, bd, cym, chimes[C4]
Freely transcribed from Rossini's *Les Riens*.
   1. Capri e Taormina (Barcarola e Siciliana) *7'*
   2. Lamento   *7'*
   3. Intermezzo   *2'*
   4. Tarantella Puro sangue   *8'*

Simrock

Serenata per piccola orchestra, P.54 (Serenade for Small Orchestra) <1904> 4'

1 1 1 0 — 0 0 0 0 — str
Ed. Salvatore Di Vittorio.

Panastudio

Sinfonia drammatica, P.102 <1914> 60'

3[1.2.pic] 3[1.2.Eh] 4[1.2.Ebcl.bcl] 3[1.2.cbn] — 6 3 3 1 — tmp+4 —
hp — org — str
perc: glock, tamtam, sd, cym, sus cym, bd
   I. Allegro energico   *25'*
   II. Andante sostenuto *17'*
   III. Allegro impetuoso *18'*

Universal

Suite for Strings, P.41 <1902> 25'

str
Ed. Salvatore Di Vittorio.
   I. Ciacona   *7'*
   II. Siciliana   *5'*
   III. Giga   *3'*
   IV. Sarbanda *3'*
   V. Burlesca   *3'*
   VI. Rigaudon   *4'*

Panastudio

Suite, G major, P.58 <1901–1905> 23'

solo organ
str
Ed. Salvatore Di Vittorio.
   Preludio   *5'*
   Aria   *6'*
   Pastorale *5'*
   Cantico   *7'*

Panastudio

Toccata, P.156 <1928> 18'

solo piano
3 3 0 2[1.cbn] — 3 0 0 0 — str

Ricordi

Il tramonto, P.101 (The Sunset) <1914> 16'

mezzo-soprano or baritone solo
str 4t or str orch
A double bass part, independent of the cello, is provided, though not
reflected in the score.

Ricordi

Tre liriche, P.99a <1906–1912; rev (orchd) 1913> 10'

solo mezzo-soprano (or baritone)
3[1.2.3/pic] 3[1.2.Eh] 2 2 — 2 0 3 1 — 2perc — hp — cel — str
perc: sus cym, tri, tamtam
Originally for mezzo-soprano & piano; orchestrated by the composer, but
partially lost after the composer's death. Orchestration completed and ed.
by Salvatore Di Vittorio.
   1. Notte (Night)   *4'*
   2. Nebbie (Fog)   *3'*
   3. Pioggia (Rain)   *3'*

Panastudio

Respighi, Ottorino   1879-1936

Trittico Botticelliano, P.151 <1927>   18'

1 1 1 1 — 1 1 0 0 — 1perc — hp — cel, pf — str
perc: glock, tri

La primavera (Spring)	6'
L'adorazione dei Magi (Adoration of the Magi)	7'
La nascita di Venere (The Birth of Venus)	5'

Ricordi

Gli uccelli, P.154 (The Birds) <1927>   19'

2[1.2/pic] 1 2 2 — 2 2 0 0 — hp — cel — str
The movements are based on works of 17th- and 18th-century composers.

1. *Preludio (Prelude, after Bernardo Pasquini)*	3'
2. *La colomba (The Dove, after Jacques de Gallot)*	5'
3. *La gallina (The Hen, after Jean-Phillipe Rameau)*	3'
4. *L'usignolo (The Nightingale—unknown 17th-century English composer)*	4'
5. *Il cuccù (The Cuckoo, after Bernardo Pasquini)*	4'

Ricordi

Vetrate di chiesa, P.150 (Church Windows) <1925–1926>   27'

3[1.2.3/pic] 3[1.2.Eh] 3[1.2.bcl] 3[1.2.cbn] — 4 3 3 1 — tmp+4 — hp — cel, pf, org — str
perc: cym, bd, chimes[C#4], 3tamtams

Mvts 1-3 based on the composer's *3 preludi sopra melodie gregoriane*, P.131, for piano.

La fuga in Egitto (Flight into Egypt)	6'
San Michele arcangelo (St. Michael, Archangel)	6'
Il mattutino di Santa Chiara (The Matins of Santa Chiara)	5'
San Gregorio Magno (St. Gregory the Great)	10'

Ricordi

Reuter, Paul   1945-

(b 1945). American

We Have a Dream <1993>   7'

children's chorus
1 1 1 1 — 2 1 0 0 — 2perc — str
perc: sus cym, sd, td, tambn
Based on children's poetry; may be performed with projections.
A larger orchestration is available:
2[fl.pic] 2 2 2 — 4 2 3 1 — 3perc — str

MMB

Revueltas, Silvestre   1899-1940

(b Santiago Papasquiaro, Durango, 31 Dec 1899; d Mexico City, 5 Oct 1940). Mexican

Alcancías <1932>   8'

1[pic] 1 2[1.Ebcl] 0 — 1 2 1 0 — tmp+6 — str
perc: xyl, marac, sd, cym, bd, guiro

Southern

Homenaje a Federico Garcia Lorca (Homage to Lorca) <1935>   10'

1[pic] 0 1[Ebcl] 0 — 0 2 1 1 — 1perc — pf — 2vn, db [or small str sections]
perc: xyl, 2tamtams

1. *Baile (Dance)*	3'
2. *Duelo (Sorrow)*	4'
3. *Son*	3'

Southern

Janitzio <1933>   7'

3[1.2.pic] 2 2[1.Ebcl] 2 — 4 2 2 1 — 3perc — str
perc: sd, bd, tamtam, sus cym

Peer

La noche de los Mayas (The Night of the Maya): Limantour four-movement suite <1939>   31'

2[1/pic.2/pic] 2 3[1/Ebcl.2/Ebcl.bcl] 2 — 4 3 2 1 — tmp+13 — pf — str
perc: bd, td, field dr, tomtom, tamtam, xyl, bongos, guiro, congas, metal rattle, Indian drum, logdrum, conch shell (or tenor tuba)
Originally a film score; suite compiled by José Yves Limantour, 1959.
An improvised cadenza for the expanded percussion in the 4th movement was later added by Enrique Diemecke.
Conch shell (caracol) may be replaced by tenor tuba playing high E.

I. *Noche de los Mayas (Night of the Maya)*	7'
II. *Noche de jaranas (Night of Revelry)*	6'
III. *Noche de Yucatán (Yucatan Night)*	8'
IV. *Noche de encantamiento (Night of Enchantment); Tema y variaciones*	10'

Peer

La noche de los Mayas (The Night of the Maya): Hindemith two-movement suite <1939>   13'

2[1/pic.2/pic] 1 2 1 — 4 1 1 1 — 4perc — str
perc: bd, cym, tamtam, xyl, guiro, marac, 2 Indian drums, tmp
Originally a film score; suite compiled by Paul Hindemith.

I. *Lento; Andantino; Allegretto; Andante*	6'
II. *Lento; Moderato; Lento; Allegro*	7'

Peer

Ocho por radio [8 x radio] (Eight on the Radio) <1933>   6'

0 0 1 1 — 0 1 0 0 — 1perc — 2vn, vc, db
perc: cym, marac, Indian drum
May also be performed as chamber orchestra (i.e., with string sections).

Southern

Sensemayá [chamber version] <1937>   7'

1[pic] 0 3[1.Ebcl.bcl] 1 — 0 2 1 0 — 4perc — pf — str[1.1.0.0.1]
perc: sus cym, xyl, guiro, marac, claves, 2tomtom
Based on a poem by the Afro-Cuban revolutionary Nicolás Guillén.
Revueltas composed two versions: (1) for chamber ensemble and (2) for full orchestra.

Schirmer

Sensemayá [full orchestra version] <1938>   7'

4[1.2.pic1.pic2] 3[1.2.Eh] 4[1.2.Ebcl.bcl] 4[1.2.3.cbn] — 4 4 3 1 — tmp+5 — pf, cel[played by perc] — str
perc: xyl, claves, cym, glock, bd, 2gongs, 2tomtoms, small Indian drum, raspador, gourd, cel[played by perc]
Based on a poem by the Afro-Cuban revolutionary Nicolás Guillén.
Revueltas composed two versions: (1) for chamber ensemble and (2) for full orchestra.

Schirmer

Reynolds, Roger   1934-

(b Detroit, 18 July 1934). American composer

Fiery Wind <1977>   15'

3[1.2/pic.pic] 2[1.Eh] 2[1.Ebcl] 2[1.cbn] — 3 3 3 1 — 4perc — pf — str
perc: glock, xyl, vib, sus cym, gong, tamtam, sd, claves, crot, chimes, 2tri, 3bd, 2db bow

Peters

Graffiti <1964>   9'

3[incl pic] 3[incl Eh] 3[incl bcl] 3[incl cbn] — 4 3 3 1 — tmp+7 — 2hp — pf — str
perc: xyl, vib, glock, chimes, sd, tri, tambn, templeblks, bd, tamtam, woodblk, 3tomtom, 3sus cym, bass bow

Peters   Barnhouse

Quick Are the Mouths of Earth <1964–1965>   18'

3 1 0 0 — 0 1 2 0 — 2perc — pf — 3vc

> Peters

Wedge <1961>   8'

2[1.2/pic] 0 0 0 — 0 2 2 1 — 3perc — pf/cel — db

> Peters

Rezniček, Emil Nikolaus von   1860-1945

(b Vienna, 4 May 1860; d Berlin, 2 Aug 1945). Austrian

Donna Diana: Overture <1894; rev 1908 (?)>   5'

3[1.2.3/pic] 2 2 2 — 4 2 0 0 — tmp+1 — opt hp — str
perc: tri

> Kalmus   Luck's   Universal

Eine Lustspiel-Ouverture (A Comedy Overture) <1895>   12'

3[1.2.pic] 2 2 2 — 4 2 0 0 — tmp — str

> Kalmus

Der Sieger (Symphonisches-satyrisches Zeitbild) <1913>   48'

solo alto   chorus
4[1.2.3.pic] 4[1.2.3.Eh] 5[1.2.3.Ebcl.bcl] 4[1.2.3.cbn] — 8 6 6 1 —
tmp+5 — 3hp — cel — str[24.20.16.12.10]
perc: bd, cym, sus cym, sd, tri, tambn, whip, ratch, cast, tamtam, chimes
Solo alto and chorus enter only at the end of the 3rd mvt. Optional: hn5-8,
tp4-6, hp3. The indicated string count is only an ideal setting.

I. Der Aufstieg und die Gefährtin (The Ascent and the Companion)	17'
II. Der Tanz um das goldene Kalb (The Dance Around the Golden Calf)	12'
III. Der Tod (Death)	19'

> Bote

Symphonic Suite No.1, E minor <1893>   25'

3[1.2.3/pic] 2 2 2 — 4 2 3 1 — tmp+1 — str
perc: cym, tri

I. Ouverture	_'
II. Adagio	_'
III. Scherzo finale	_'

> Kalmus

Symphony No.2, B-flat major (Ironische; Ironic) <1904>   26'

3[1.2.pic] 2 2 2 — 2 2 0 0 — tmp — str[10.8.6.6.4]

I. Lustig, aber nicht sehr schnell	7'
II. Rasch und leicht	5'
III. Mit abgeklärter Ruhe	9'
IV. Sehr lustig, aber nicht zu schnell	5'

> Boosey   Kalmus

Symphony No.5 (Tanz-Symphonie; Vier Sinfonische   39'
Tänze; Dance Symphony) <1924>

3[1.2.3/pic] 3[1.2.Eh] 3[1.2.bcl] 3[1.2.cbn] — 4 3 3 1 — tmp+4 —
hp[dbl if possible] — cel — str
perc: sd, tri, bd/cym, tamtam, cast, tambn, bd, cym, spurs
Full instrumentation only in last mvt.

1. Polonaise	11'
2. Csárdás	11'
3. Ländler	5'
4. Tarantella	12'

> Kalmus

Rheinberger, Joseph   1839-1901

(b Vaduz, Liechtenstein, 17 March 1839; d Munich, 25 Nov 1901). German

Concerto, Organ, No.1, op.137, F major (The Romantic)   24'
<1890–1901>

0 0 0 0 — 3 0 0 0 — str

I. Maestoso	8'
II. Andante	8'
III. Finale: Con moto	8'

> Forberg   Kalmus   Luck's

Concerto, Organ, No.2, op.177, G minor <1890>   25'

0 0 0 0 — 2 2 0 0 — tmp — str

1. Grave	10'
2. Andante	8'
3. Con moto	7'

> Forberg   Luck's

Der Stern von Bethlehem, op.164 (The Star of   47'
Bethlehem)

solos STBarB   chorus SSAATTBB
2 2 2 2 — 2 2 3 0 — tmp — hp — org — str
Carus ed. Harold Wanger.

1. Erwartung (Expectation)	8'
2. Die Hirten (The Shepherds)	7'
3. Erscheinung des Engels (The Appearance of the Angel)	3'
4. Bethlehem	3'
5. Die Hirten an die Krippe (The Shepherds at the Manger)	5'
6. Der Stern (The Star)	6'
7. Anbetung der Weisen (Adoration of the Wise Men)	5'
8. Maria an der Krippe (Mary at the Manger)	5'
9. Erfüllung (Fulfillment)	5'

> Carus   Forberg   Kalmus

Richman, Lucas   1964-

(b Los Angeles, CA, 31 Jan 1964). American

American Fanfare <1984>   3'

2 2 2 2 — 2 3 2 1 — tmp+2 — str
perc: bd, cym, sd, glock, xyl

> LeDor

Be a Composer <1990>   8'

narrator (may be the conductor)
3[incl pic] 2 2 2 — 4 3 3 1 — tmp+2 — hp — str

> LeDor

Be a Conductor   3'

see his: Western Fanfare

Behold the Bold Umbrellaphant <2009>   29'

narrator
3[1.2.3/pic] 3[1.2.Eh] 3[1.2.bcl] 3[1.2.cbn] — 4 3 3 1 — tmp+2 — hp — pf — str
perc: bd, bd/cym, cym, sus cym, sd, tri, tambn, tamtam, glock, xyl, chimes, woodblk, congas, 2metalplate, sandpaper, chain, deskbell, tabla, washboard, popgun

Behold the Bold Umbrellaphant	2'
The Bizarre Alarmadillos	1'
The Ballpoint Penguins	2'
The Lynx of Chain	1'
The Pop-up Toadsters	2'
Shoehornets	1'
Here Comes a Panthermometer	2'
The Circular Sawtoise	2'
The Limber Bulboa	2'
The Clocktopus	1'
The Eggbeaturkey	2'
Hatchickens	1'
The Trumpetoos and Tubaboons	2'
The Tweasels of the Forest	1'
The Tearful Zipperpotamuses	2'
The Ocelock	2'
The Solitary Spatuloon	2'
Finale	1'

LeDor

The Brentwood Rag <1987>   4'

2[1.pic] 2 2 2 — 2 2 1 0 — 1-2perc — pf — str
perc: bd, sd (or set)

LeDor

A Christmas Wish: Reindeer Variations <2001>   8'

2 2 2[1/asx.2] 2 — 2 2 2 1 — tmp+2 — hp — pf — str
perc: bd, cym, sus cym, szl cym, hi-hat, sd, set, glock, xyl, marim, sleighbells, belltree
Separate variation for each reindeer.

LeDor

Colonial Liberty Overture <1998>   6'

3[1.2.pic] 2 2 2 — 4 3 3 1 — tmp+3 — hp — str
perc: bd, cym, sus cym, sd, tri, tamtam, glock, chimes (G)

LeDor

Dachau Lied (Arbeit macht frei) <1998>   9'

narrator   male chorus
2[1.2/pic] 2 2 2 — 4 3 3 1 — tmp+3 — hp — str
perc: bd, sus cym, sd, tri, tamtam, glock, xyl
Original song by Herbert Zipper & Jura Soyfer; adapted and orchestrated by Lucas Richman.
   Narrator's text in English; chorus sings in German and English.

LeDor

Hanukkah Festival Overture <1994>   6'

3[incl pic] 2 2 2 — 4 3 3 1 — tmp+2 — hp — str

LeDor

Homework Blues <2002>   3'

voice
2 2 2 2 — 4 3 3 1 — tmp+1 — pf — str
perc: set

LeDor

I Remember a Lullaby <2001>   12'

soloists: soprano, violin, ballet dancer, 2 actors   children's chorus (SA)
2 3[1.2.Eh] 2 2 — 2 2 2 0 — tmp+1 — hp — pf/cel — str
perc: sus cym, sd, glock, windchimes, marktree, cricket
The soprano, violinist and dancer also have spoken lines.

LeDor

Jalopy and Blues (Salutation No.2) <2005>   4'

2[1.pic] 1 2 1 — 2 2 0 0 — tmp — hp — pf — str

LeDor

Kol Nidre <1996>   4'

str

LeDor

Music Can Make Your Life Complete <2001>   5'

mezzo-soprano solo
3[1.2.3/pic] 2 2 2 — 4 3 3 1 — tmp+3 — hp — str
perc: sus cym, hi-hat, sd, glock, xyl, vib, sandblks

LeDor

An Overture to Blanche <1984>   9'

2 2 2 2 — 2 2 2 1 — tsx — tmp+2 — pf — str
perc: cym, sus cym, hi-hat, sd, set, tri, glock, xyl

LeDor

Playground Escapades <1999>   3'

3[1.2.pic] 3[1.2.Eh] 3[1.2.bcl] 3[1.2.cbn] — 4 3 3 1 — tmp+3 — hp — str
perc: cym, sus cym, sd, toms, tri, glock, xyl, chimes, electric school bell

LeDor

Prayer and Freylach <1999>   11'

solo violoncello
2 2 2 2 — 2 2 0 0 — tmp+1 — hp — str
perc: bd, tambn

LeDor

Sheva B'rachot (The Seven Blessings)   7'

tenor (or soprano)   solo clarinet
hp — str

LeDor

The United Symphony <2003>   8'

3[1.2.pic] 3[1.2.Eh] 3[1.2.bcl] 3[1.2.cbn] — 4 3 3 1 — tmp+4 — str
perc: bd, cym, sus cym, hi-hat, sd, 4tomtoms, tri, gong, xyl, vib, chimes, comga

Toccata for Percussion	2'
Hornpipe for Brass	2'
Arabesque for Winds	2'
Scherzo for Strings	1'
The United Symphony	1'

LeDor

Wake Me a Song <1999>   9'

chorus
3[1.2.3/pic] 3[1.2.Eh] 3[1.2.bcl] 3[1.2.cbn] — 4 3 3 1 — tmp+3 — hp — pf — str
perc: bd, cym, sus cym, sd, tomtoms, 2tri, gong, glock, xyl, crot, chime[F#]

LeDor

A Western Fanfare (Be a Conductor) <1997>   3'

2 2 2 2 — 2 2 1 0 — tmp+1 — hp — str
perc: sd, tri

LeDor

Riegger, Wallingford   1885-1961

(b Albany, GA, 29 April 1885; d New York, 2 April 1961). American

Dance Rhythms, op.58 <1955>   8'

2[1.2/pic] 2 2 2 — 2 2 2 0 — tmp+4 — hp — str

AMP   Luck's

The Dying of the Light, op.59a <1954; rev (orchd) 1955>   4'
solo voice [range C4-G5]
3[1.2.pic] 3[1.2.Eh] 2 2 — 4 2 0 0 — tmp — str
Originally for voice and piano (1954); orchestrated by the composer.
> AMP

Music for Orchestra, op.50 <1951>   7'
3[1.2.3/pic] 3[1.2.Eh] 2 3[1.2.cbn] — 4 3 3 1 — tmp+3 — str
perc: sd, cym, bd
> AMP   Luck's

New Dance, op.18b <1935>   5'
3[1.2.pic] 3[1.2.3/Eh] 3[1.2.3/bcl/asx] 3[1.2.3/cbn] — 4 3 3 1 — tmp+3 — hp — str
perc: xyl, marim, sd, tambn, cym, bd, sus cym
Originally part three of a choreographic trilogy.
> AMP

Study in Sonority, op.7 <1926-1927>   9'
10vn, or any multiple thereof
> AMP

Rietz, Julius   1812-1877
(b Berlin, 28 Dec 1812; d Dresden, 12 Sept 1877). German

Concert Overture, op.7   11'
2 2 2 2 — 4 2 3 0 — tmp — str

Riisager, Knudåge   1897-1974
(b Port Kunda, Estonia, 6 March 1897; d Copenhagen, 26 Dec 1974). Danish

Fools' Paradise (Slaraffenland): Suite No.1 <1942>   16'
3[1.2.pic] 2 2 3[1.2.cbn] — 4 3[1/crt.2.3] 3 1 — tmp+ — cel[played by perc] — str
perc: sd, cym, bd, tri, vib, tambn, xyl, glock, cel[played by perc]
1. Prelude (Forspil)   2'
2. Departure (Rejsen derhen)   1'
3. Princess Sweets (Prinsesse Sukkergodt)   3'
4. The Lazy Dogs' Polka (Dovendidrikernes Polka)   2'
5. Fountains of Liqueurs (Likørfontænerne)   2'
6. The Royal Guardsmen (Vagtparaden)   1'
7. Procession of Gluttons (Ædedolkenes Procession)   4'
8. Punctum Finale (Punktum Finale)   1'
> Hansen

Fools' Paradise (Slaraffenland): Suite No.2 <1942>   13'
3[1.2.pic] 2 2 2 — 4 3 3 1 — tmp+4 — hp — cel/pf — str
perc: bd, cym, sus cym, sd, tri, gong, xyl, chimes
1. Lullaby (Berceuse)   2'
2. The Rocking-Chair (Gyngestolen)   1'
3. The Three Musketeers (De tre Musketerer)   1'
4. Spry Dance (Springedans)   1'
5. Pas de deux   4'
6. The Dance of the Dishes (Retternes Dans)   4'
> Hansen

Little Overture (Lille Ouverture) <1934>   5'
str
> Hansen

Mardi Gras, op.20 (Fastelavn; Carnival) <1929-1930>   9'
3[1.2.pic] 2 3[1.2.bcl] 2 — 4 3 3 1 — tmp+4 — cel[played by perc] — str
perc: bd, cym, sus cym, sd, tri, xyl, chimes, flexatone, slgh-bells, woodblk, whip, cast, Chinese drum, cel[played by perc]
Bcl part written in A in score.
> Hansen

Qarrtsiluni, op.36 <1938>   9'
3[1.2.pic] 2 2[1/Ebcl.2] 2 — 4 3 3 1 — tmp+4 — hp — str
perc: bd, cym, sus cym, tri, tamtam, xyl, vib, 2sd, 2tomtom
Originally a ballet. "Qarrtsiluni" is said to be a word in the Inupiaq language, the tongue of Native Americans in the Alaska region. It means "sitting together in darkness" or "waiting for something to burst forth"; it is believed that songs are born in that silence.
> Hansen

Twelve by the Mail, op.37 (Tolv med posten): Six Dances <1942>   11'
3[1.2.pic] 2 2 2 — 4 3 3 1 — tmp+5 — hp — cel/pf — str
perc: bd, cym, sus cym, tri, xyl, chimes
From the ballet based on a tale of Hans Christian Andersen.
The cel/pf part could perhaps be covered by a percussionist.
1. January   3'
2. April   1'
3. May   2'
4. July   2'
5. August   2'
6. Intermezzo; October   1'
> Hansen

Riley, Terry   1935-
(b Colfax, CA, 24 June 1935). American

At the Royal Majestic (Concerto for Organ & Orchestra)   33'
solo organ
6[3pic, 2fl, 1afl] 0 2[2bcl] 6[5bn, 1cbn] — 2 5[4tp, 1flug] 2 2 — asx — tmp+5 — str
perc: cym, hi-hat, sd, set, tambn, glock, xyl, vib, chimes, slgh-bells, windchimes, belltree, templeblks, buttongong, waterdrum, 5sus cym, 3tomtom, 5rototom, 2tamtam, 4woodblk, 2Chinese gong
I. Negro Hall   14'
II. Lizard Tower Gang   5'
III. Circling Kailash   14'
> AMP

Half-Wolf Dances Mad in Moonlight   9'
str
> AMP

The Palmian Chord Ryddle <2012>   35'
solo electric violin
3[1.2.pic] 2[1.Eh] 1[bcl] 2[1.cbn] — 0 3[1.2.flug] 2 1 — asx — tmp+4 — hp — pf, USB kybd — str
perc: bd, cym, hi-hat, sd, set, tri, tambn, xyl, slgh-bells, windchimes, belltree, templeblks, cowbell, ratch, claves, metal pipe, clay pot, buttongong, 2chinese gong, 3sus cym, 3tomtom, 2rototom, 2tamtam
I. Starting From Here   -'
II. Iberia   -'
III. Slow Drag   -'
IV. Towrds the Clouds   -'
V. For Maresa   -'
VI. Ghandi-Ji's Danda   -'
VII. Wedding Music for Gyan and Nicole   -'
VIII. The Afterglow   -'
> AMP

The Sands <1991>   31'
solo string quartet
2[1.afl] 2[1.Eh] 2[1.bcl] 2 — 2 2 0 0 — tmp+1 — pf — str
perc: set, bd, cym, sus cym, hi-hat, sd, tri, tambn, gong, templeblks

AMP

SolTierraLuna <2007>   41'
soloists: violin, 2 guitars
1 1 0 1 — 0 1 0 0 — 1perc — str[6.6.5.4.3]
perc: vib, bd, sus cym, hi-hat, sd, set, bongos, fingercym, 2tomtom
The soloists should be lightly amplified to balance with the sound of the
orchestra.
1. *Sol (The Royal 88)*   13'
2. *Moonwaves*   5'
3. *Tierra*   10'
4. *Sarabande for Iraq* 13'

AMP

Zephir <2009>   19'
solo violin
4[2fl.2afl] 0 0 0 — 0 2 2 1 — gtr[nylon-string] — 3perc — hp — cel
— str[6.6.5.4.3]
perc: bd, tambn, glock, xyl, templeblks, bongos, cast, tmp, frog-scraper, 2gong,
2Chinescym, 3tomtom
If needed the solo vn, gtr & hp should be amplified.

AMP

Rimelis, David   1954-
(b Irvington, NJ, 28 Aug 1954). American

The Cool Ghoul   3'
optional narrator
2[1.2/pic] 2 2 2 — 4 3 3 1 — tmp+3 — str

MMB

Phonefare (Friendly Cell Phone Reminder) <2004>   1'
announcer (backstage)
3[1.2.pic] 2 2 2 — 4 3 3 1 — xyl — str
To be played after oboe tuning note has ended; orchestra simulates a
number of common ringtones (including *Für Elise* and *1812 Overture*).

MMB

Please Turn Your Cell Phones On! <2003>   9'
2 2 2 2 — 4 3 3 1 — tmp+2 — str
perc: set, tambn, hand dr, shaker, cabasa, 2tomtoms, splash cym
Humorous piece involving cell phones, both on stage and via audience
participation.

MMB

Rimsky-Korsakov, Nikolai   1844-1908
(b Tikhvin, 6/18 Mar 1844; d Lyubensk, nr Luga [now Pskov district], 8/21 June
1908). Russian

Antar, Symphonic Suite
see his: Symphony No.2

Capriccio espagnol, op.34 (Kaprichchio na ispanskiye   15'
temï) <1887>
3[1.2.pic] 2[1/Eh.2] 2 2 — 4 2 3 1 — tmp+5 — hp — str
perc: bd, cym, sd, tri, tambn, cast
Kalmus ed. Clinton F. Nieweg & Stuart S. Serio.
    The original Belaieff edition puts the Eh doubling in the ob1 part as
was customary at the time. The Nieweg/Serio edition puts it in ob2.
Neither ob is playing during the Eh passage, so it may be covered by
either player.
1. *Alborada*   1'
2. *Variazioni*   5'
3. *Alborada*   1'
4. *Scena e canto gitano* 5'
5. *Fandango asturiano*   3'

Belaieff	Kalmus	Luck's

Christmas Eve (Noch' pered rozhdestvom): Suite   23'
<1894–1895>
optional chorus
3[1.2.3/pic] 2 3[1.2.3/D-cl] 2 — 4 3[1.2.atp] 3 1 — tmp+4 — hp —
str
perc: bd, cym, sd, tri, glock, tambn, xyl, tamtam, chimes[C]
I.   *Introduction*   _'
II. *Tableaux 6 and 7*   _'
III. *Polonaise*   _'
IV. *Tableau 8*   _'

Belaieff	Boosey	Kalmus	Luck's

Christmas Eve (Noch' pered rozhdestvom): Polonaise   6'
<1894–1895>
optional chorus
3[1.2.pic] 2 3[1.2.D-cl] 2 — 4 3[1.2.atp] 3 1 — tmp+4 — hp — str
perc: bd, cym, sd, tri

Belaieff	Kalmus	Luck's

Concerto, Clarinet & Military Band, E-flat major   9'
<1878>
3[1.2.pic] 2 6[1.2.3.Ebcl.acl.bcl] 2 — 4 4[2tp, 2crt] 3 2 — euph —
3perc — [no str]
perc: sd, cym, bd
Ed. Clark McAlister. The numbers given are the number of separate parts;
normally in band music the Bb clarinets, and perhaps other winds, would
be doubled or tripled.
Allegro moderato   _'
Adagio   _'
Allegro moderato   _'

Kalmus

Concerto, Piano, op.30, C-sharp minor <1882–1883>   14'
2 2 2 2 — 2 2 3 0 — tmp — str
In one movement.

Belaieff	Kalmus	Luck's

Concerto, Trombone & Military Band, B-flat major <1877>   11'

3[1.2.pic] 2 6[1.2.3.Ebcl.acl.bcl] 2 — 4 6[4tp, 2crt] 3 2 — euph — 3perc — [no str]
perc: sd, cym, bd

Kalmus edition, faithful to the composer's original, by Clark McAlister. The numbers given are the number of separate parts; normally in band music the Bb clarinets, and perhaps other winds, would be doubled or tripled.

MCA version, adapted for American band by Walter Nallin, includes 4 saxophones (2asx, tsx, bsx) and reduces the number of trumpets. Orchestral arrangements:
Obrasso version, arr. Howard Lorriman:
2 2 2 2 — 4 4 3 1 — tmp+3 — str
Southern Music version, arr. Richard Thurston:
3[1.2.pic] 2 2 2 — 4 2 3 0 — tmp, perc — str

1. Allegro vivace	3'		
2. Andante cantabile	3'		
3. Allegro	5'		

Kalmus	MCA	Obrasso	SMC

Conte féerique, op.29

see his: Skazka, op.29 (Russian Fairy Tale)

Le coq d'or (Zolotoy petushok; The Golden Cockerel): Suite <1906–1907>   25'

3[1.2/pic2.pic1] 3[1.2.Eh] 3[1.2.bcl] 3[1.2.cbn] — 4 3[1.2.atp] 3 1 — tmp+4 — 2hp — cel — str
perc: cym, sd, tri, tambn, glock, tamtam, bd

Said to have been extracted in 1913 by Glazunov and Steinberg, following the composer's intentions.

King Dodon at His Palace	9'
King Dodon on the Battlefield	4'
King Dodon with the Queen of Chamakka	6'
Nuptials and the Deplorable End of Dodon	6'

Kalmus	Luck's	Russian

Le Coq d'or (Zolotoy petushok; The Golden Cockerel): Introduction & Wedding March <1906–1907>   9'

3[1.2.pic] 3[1.2.Eh] 3[1.2.bcl] 3[1.2.cbn] — 4 3[1.2.atp] 3 1 — tmp+4 — 2hp — cel — str
perc: bd, cym, sd, tri, chimes

Sometimes referred to as a suite; extracted by the composer for concert performance in 1907.

Introduction (Le Tsar Dodon dans son palais)	5'
Wedding March (Cortège de noces)	4'

Forberg	Kalmus	Luck's

Dubinushka [2nd version], op.62 (The Little Oak Stick) <1905–1906>   4'

optional chorus
3[1.2.pic] 2 3 2 — 4 3[tp3 opt] 3 1 — tmp+4 — str
perc: bd, cym, sd, tri

Belaieff	Kalmus	Luck's	Russian

Fantasia on Two Russian Themes, op.33 (Fantaisie de concert sur les thèmes russes) <1886–1887>   12'

solo violin
2 2 2 2 — 2 2 0 0 — tmp+1 — str
perc: tri

Belaieff	Kalmus	Luck's

Fantasia on Serbian Themes, op.6 <1867; rev 2nd version, 1886-1887>   7'

3[1.2.pic] 2 2 2 — 4 2 3 0 — tmp+4 — str
perc: bd, cym, tri, tambn

2 versions of this work exist: 1867, and 1886-7; both may be seen in the Rimsky-Korsakov collected edition, v.19b. Forces required are identical.

Belaieff	Kalmus	Luck's

The Legend of the Invisible City of Kitezh (Skazaniye o nevidimom grade Kitezhe i deve Fevronii): Massacre at Kerzhentz (Battle of Kerzhenets) <1903–1904>   5'

3[1.2.pic] 3[1.2.Eh] 3[1.2.bcl] 3[1.2.cbn] — 4 3 3 1 — tmp+4 — str
perc: bd, cym, sd, tri, tamtam, glock, chimes, slgh-bells
Entr'acte between Act 3, sc i and sc ii.

Kalmus	Luck's

The Legend of the Invisible City of Kitezh (Skazaniye o nevidimom grade Kitezhe i deve Fevronii): Suite <1907>   24'

3[1.2.3/pic] 3[1.2.Eh] 3[1.2.3/bcl] 3[1.2.cbn] — 4 3 3 1 — dombras & balalaikas[ad lib] — tmp+5 — 1 or 2 hp — cel[can be played by perc] — str
perc: bd, cym, sd, tri, tamtam, glock, chimes[written C3–C4], slgh-bells
Suite from the opera, arr. Maximilian Steinberg.

Eh, bcl, cbn cued in other parts; 2nd hp opt; glock & cel may be played on pf; campane are pitched C3-C4 (i.e., in the 8ve below the normal range of tubular chimes).

I. Prelude — Adoration of Solitude	5'
II. Wedding Procession — Invasion of the Tartars	3'
III. Massacre at Kerzhentz	5'
IV. The Death of the Maiden Fevroniya — Pilgrimage to the Invisible City	11'

Belaieff	Fleisher

The Maid of Pskov (Pskovityanka): Overture <1868–1877; rev 1892>   8'

3[1.2.3/pic] 3[1.2.Eh] 3[1.2.bcl] 3[1.2.cbn] — 4 3[1.2.atp] 3 1 — tmp — str

This is the overture to the opera proper (3rd version), and *not* the same work as the overture listed together with the entr'actes (see next entry).

Breitkopf	Kalmus	Luck's

The Maid of Pskov (Pskovityanka): Overture & Entr'actes <1876–1877>   23'

3[1.2.pic] 2 2 — 4 2 3 1 — tmp+2 — str
perc: cym, tri, tambn

Although published under this title, the overture is actually that of *Boyarina Vera Sheloga*, op.54, which was a prologue to the second version of *The Maid of Pskov*. This is a different overture from the one listed as *Overture to The Maid of Pskov* (see previous entry).

1. Overture (before the Prolog)	6'
2. Entr'acte before Act I: Olga	4'
3. Entr'acte before Act II: The Assembly	5'
4. Entr'acte before Act III: Street Scene	2'
5. Entr'acte before Act IV: Pyechorsky Monastery	6'

Breitkopf	Kalmus

May Night (Mayskaya noch): Overture <1878–1879>   8'

2 2 2 2 — 4 2 3 0 — tmp — str

Belaieff	Kalmus	Luck's

Mlada: Suite <1889–1890>   15'

optional chorus
4[1.2.pic(3).4/afl] 3[1.2.Eh] 4[1.2.3/D-cl.bcl] 3[1.2.cbn] — 6 3[1.2.atp] 3 1 — tmp+5 — 3hp[1part] — str
perc: bd, cym, sd, tri, tambn

Harps play only in Cortège, and only for 18 bars total; they could be omitted.

Bcl in A and treble clef in mvt 4; in B-flat in mvt 5 (a mix of bass and treble clef).

I. Introduction	2'
II. Rédowa	4'
III. Danse lithuanienne	2'
IV. Danse indienne	2'
V. Cortège (Procession of the Nobles)	5'

Belaieff	Kalmus	Luck's

Mlada: Procession of the Nobles (Cortège) <1889–1890>   5'

optional chorus
4[1.2.3.pic] 3[1.2.Eh] 4[1.2.3.bcl] 3[1.2.cbn] — 6 3[1.2.atp] 3 1 —
tmp+5 — 3hp[1part] — str
perc: bd, cym, sd, tri, tambn
Harps play only for 18 bars total; they could be omitted.
Reduced versions:
  Kalmus (Concertmaster Series) arr. Kennedy:
  3[1.2.pic] 2 2 2 — 4 3 3 1 — tmp+perc — str
  Obrasso, arr. Howard Lorriman:
  2 2 2 2 — 4 3 3 1 — tmp+3 — str

| Belaieff | Kalmus | Luck's | Obrasso |

Overture on Russian Themes, op.28 (1880 version) <1866; rev 1979-80>   12'

2[1.2/pic] 2 2 2 — 4 2 3 0 — tmp+1 — opt hp — str
perc: tambn
First version of 1866 required 3fl[1.2.pic], an extra percussionist, and the
harp was obligatory.

| Belaieff | Kalmus | Luck's |

Russian Easter Overture, op.36 (Svetlïy prazdnik; Grand Paque russe) <1888>   14'

3[1.2.3/pic] 2 2[C-cl] 2 — 4 2 3 1 — tmp+5 — hp — str
perc: bd, cym, sus cym, tri, tamtam, glock
Kalmus ed. Clinton F. Nieweg & Nancy Bradburd.

| Belaieff | Kalmus | Luck's |

SADKO, op.5: Chronology

This work exists in 3 versions:
  1st version: 1867 (not published until 1951, in the collected edition).
  Entitled *Épizod iz bïlïnï o Sadko (Episode from the Legend of Sadko)*.
  2nd version: 1869 (published 1870). Entitled *Muzïkal'naya
  kartina—Sadko (Musical Picture—Sadko)*.
  3rd version: 1891-92 (published 1892). Also entitled *Muzïkal'naya
  kartina—Sadko (Musical Picture—Sadko)*.
  N.B.: These orchestral works are not to be confused with the
  "opera-bïlina" *Sadko* (1895-96), though some of their music was
  incorporated into the opera.

Sadko, op.5 (1869 version) <1867; rev 1869-1870>   12'

3[1.2.pic] 2 2 — 4 2 3 0 — tmp+3 — hp — str
perc: bd, cym, sus cym, tamtam
Listed by Kalmus as the 1st version, though actually it is the 2nd.

| Kalmus |

Sadko, op.5 (1892 version) <1867; rev 1869-70 and 1891-92>   12'

3[1.2.pic] 2 2 — 4 2 3 1 — tmp+3 — hp[doubled or tripled] — str
perc: bd, cym, sus cym, tamtam
Listed by Kalmus as the 2nd version, though actually it is the 3rd.

| Kalmus |

Sheherazade, op.35 <1888>   42'

3[1.2/pic.pic] 2[1.2/Eh] 2 2 — 4 2 3 1 — tmp+5 — hp — str
perc: bd, cym, sus cym, sd, tri, tambn, tamtam
Kalmus ed. Clinton F. Nieweg & Andrew S. Holmes.
  The German transliteration of the title, spelled "Scheherazade," is
frequently encountered in English and other languages as well.
  A short story by Alton Thompson, "1,001 Nights: A Tale Retold", is
intended for a reading on stage by a storyteller just prior to a performance
of this work; it takes about 5-7 minutes. The text is available at US $0.99
from www.smashwords.com/books/view/444501, and other sources.
  1. The Sea and Sinbad's Ship   10'
  2. The Tale of Prince Kalendar   11'
  3. The Young Prince and the Princess   10'
  4. The Festival at Bagdad; The Sea; The Ship Goes to Pieces on a Rock   11'

| Belaieff | Kalmus | Luck's |

Sinfonietta on Russian Themes, op.31 <1879–1884>   24'

2 2 2 2 — 4 2 3 0 — tmp — str
Based on the first three mvts of his *String Quartet on Russian Themes*.
  1. In the Field (V pole)   8'
  2. At the Wedding-Eve Party (Na devichnike)   10'
  3. At the Khorovod (V khorovode)   6'

| Belaieff | Kalmus | Luck's |

Skazka, op.29 (Russian Fairy Tale) <1879–1880>   13'

3[1.2.pic] 2 2 — 4 2 3 1 — tmp+3 — hp — str
perc: bd, cym, sus cym, tri
Sometimes referred to as *Conte féerique*; original title: *Baba-Yaga*.

| Belaieff | Kalmus | Luck's |

The Snow Maiden (Snegurochka): Suite <1880–1881; rev c1895>   13'

3[1.2.pic] 2[1.2/Eh] 2 2 — 4 2 3 1 — tmp+4 — str
perc: bd, cym, tambn, tamtam, tri
  1. Introduction   4'
  2. Dance of the Birds   3'
  3. Cortège   2'
  4. Dance of the Skomorokhi [i.e., Buffoons, Tumblers, Clowns]   4'

| Breitkopf | Kalmus | Luck's | Universal |

The Snow Maiden (Snegurochka): Dance of the Skomorokhi [Buffoons, Tumblers, Clowns] <1880–1881>   4'

3[1.2.pic] 2 2 2 — 4 2 3 1 — tmp+4 — str
perc: bd, cym, tri, tambn [or possibly sd]

| Kalmus |

Symphony No.1, op.1, E minor (1884 version) <1861–1865; rev 1884>   27'

2 2 2 2 — 4 2 3 0 — tmp — opt hp — str
Original version (1865) was in E-flat minor; in 1884, the composer recast
the work in E minor.
  Hp in 2nd mvt only (and opt).
  The Harmonic Services Group edition has been corrected by Herb
Gellis.
  I. Largo assai - Allegro   8'
  II. Andante tranquillo   8'
  III. Scherzo: Vivace   5'
  IV. Allegro assai   6'

| Breitkopf | Harmonic | Kalmus | Luck's |

Symphony No.2, op.9, F-sharp minor (Antar, Symphonic Suite) <1868–1897>   32'

3[1.2.3/pic] 2[1/Eh.2] 2 2 — 4 2 3 1 — tmp+4 — hp — str
perc: tri, tambn, cym, tamtam, bd
Brief history of this work:
  1st version, 1868, published in score form (1970) in the
Rimsky-Korsakov collected edition, vol. 17A.
  2nd version, 1875, available from Kalmus (no. A1925, a reprint of the
original 1880 Bessel publication).
  3rd version, 1897, definitive final version, though not published by
Bessel until 1913. Renamed by the composer in this version as a
Symphonic Suite, rather than a Symphony. Distinguishable from the other
versions by the fact that the 2nd mvt is in D minor, rather than C# minor.
Available from Kalmus (A8179, reprint of Bessel)) and Breitkopf
(Breitkopf lists the work under *Antar*).
  "4th version," 1903. Spurious and unauthorized, this seems to have
been an opportunistic undertaking by Bessel using the plates from the 2nd
version, and incorporating only such revisions from the 3rd version as
could be fitted to the old plates. Published only in score form in the
Rimsky-Korsakov collected edition, vol.17B.
  1. Largo; Allegro giocoso   12'
  2. Allegro   5'
  3. Allegro risoluto alla marcia   6'
  4. Allegretto; Adagio   9'

| Breitkopf | Kalmus |

Symphony No.3, op.32, C major <1866–1873; rev 1886>   35'
3[1.2.pic] 2 2 2 — 4 2 3 1 — tmp — str
1st version, 1873; 2nd version 1886. Kalmus edition is a reprint of
Belaieff, presumably the 2nd version.
I. Moderato assai - Allegro   14'
II. Scherzo   6'
III. Andante   9'
IV. Allegro con spirito   6'

Belaieff	Kalmus

Tale of the Tsar Saltan (Skazka o Tsare Saltane): Suite, op.57 <c1901>   17'
3[1.2.pic] 3[1.2.Eh] 3[1.2.3/bcl] 3[1.2.opt cbn] — 4 3 3 1 — tmp+4
— hp — cel — str
perc: bd, cym, sd, tri, glock, xyl
The popular *Flight of the Bumblebee* (see next two entries) is sometimes
inserted in performance between mvts 2 and 3.
1. The Tsar's Farewell and Departure (Introduction to Act I)   4'
2. The Tsarina in a Barrel at Sea (Introduction to Act II)   6'
3. The Three Wonders (Introduction to Act IV, Sc.2)   7'

Breitkopf	Kalmus

Tale of the Tsar Saltan (Skazka o Tsare Saltane): Flight of the Bumblebee <c1901>   2'
2 2 2 2 — 2 0 0 0 — str
Parts include a trumpet covering a vocal line that would otherwise be
absent; it may be omitted for this excerpt. The very first chord is scored
for full orchestra, including full brass, tmp & cym; this single note may
simply be played by the above complement.
  Often used as a showpiece for solo flute, by simply omitting most
chromatic passages in violins and orchestral flutes; retain clarinet
chromatic passages which generally occur when the melody dips below
the range of the flute.
  Numerous arrangements of this popular piece exist (see, for example,
the subsequent entry).

Breitkopf	Kalmus	Luck's	Russian

Tale of the Tsar Saltan (Skazka o Tsare Saltane): Flight of the Bumblebee ("Scherzo" arr. J. Strimer) <c1901>   4'
3[1.2.pic] 2 2 2 — 4 2 3 1 — tmp+1 — str
perc: cym [1 note only]
A concert-version of this popular extract arr. by J. Strimer. It is extended
to more than twice the length of the original by means of the insertion of
a lengthy episode in G minor; the beginning and end are unchanged.

Breitkopf

The Tsar's Bride (Tsarskaya nevesta): Overture <1898>   7'
3[1.2.pic] 2 2 2 — 4 2 3 1 — tmp — hp — str

Belaieff	Kalmus	Luck's

Ritchie, Anthony   1960-
(b Christchurch, 18 Sept 1960). New Zealander

A Bugle Will Do, op.67 <1995>   9'
3[1.2.pic] 2 3[1.2.Ebcl] 3[1.2.cbn] — 4 3 3 1 — tmp+3 — str
perc: bd, sus cym, sd, tri, tamtam, xyl, 3tomtom, logdrum

Concerto, Flute, op.56 <1993>   18'
2 2 2[1.bcl] 1 — 1 2 1 0 — tmp/tri — str
I. Allegretto   6'
II. Slow, freely — Lento, with serenity   6'
III. Allegro   6'

Ritchie

Concerto, Viola, op.64 <1995>   25'
2[1.2/pic] 2 2 — 1 2 2 0 — tmp+1 — str[min 6.6.3.2.1]
perc: bd, sus cym, hi-hat, tri, tamtam, glock, xyl, marim, woodblk, marac,
2tomtom
Tmp covers sus cym.
I. Allegro tempestuoso   7'
II. Adagio   8'
III. Cadenza   3'
IV. Vivace   7'

Bellbird

French Overture, op.138 <2008>   11'
1 2 2 2 — 2 2 0 0 — tmp — str

Ritchie

The Hanging Bulb, op.36 <1989>   15'
2[1.2/pic] 2 2 — 2 2 0 0 — 2perc — pf — str[approx 6.6.4.5.2]
perc: bd, xyl

Ritchie

Symphony No.1, op.59 (Boum) <1993>   32'
3[1.2.3/pic] 2 3[1.2.bcl] 2 — 4 3 3 1 — asx — tmp+1 — str[min
8.8.6.6.4]
perc: bd, cym, sus cym, tri, tambn, tamtam, glock, xyl, chimes, logdrum, 2tomtom
Timpanist also covers tomtoms.
I. Largo con molto rubato — Allegro   11'
II. Allegro energico   5'
III. Adagio, mesto   7'
IV. Allegro   9'

Ritchie

Symphony No.2, op.95 (The Widening Gyre) <2000>   31'
2[1.2/pic] 2 3[1.2.Ebcl] 2 — 4 2 3 1 — tmp+2 — hp — pf/elec pf —
str
perc: bd, cym, tamtam, glock, xyl, marim, 2sus cym, 5tomtom, logdrum, anvil,
poi, rubberball
I. Strategem of Trumpets   14'
II. Mi-1st   8'
III. Double Helix   9'

Ritchie

Symphony No.3, op.150 (Janus) <2008–2010>   30'
3[1.2.pic] 3[1.2.Eh] 3[1.2.bcl] 2 — 4 3 3 1 — tmp+3 — hp — elec
kybd [can be played by perc] — str
perc: bd, cym, sus cym, tamtam, glock, xyl, 4tomtom
I. UP   13'
II. DOWN   17'

Promethean

Ritchie, John   1921-
(b Wellington, 29 Sept 1921). New Zealander

Aquarius: Suite No.2 for String Orchestra <1982>   13'
str
I. Allegro vivace   _'
II. Andante pastorale   _'
III. Allegro moderato   _'

Promethean

Concertino, Clarinet <1957>   14'
str
I. Allegro moderato   _'
II. Andante piacevole   _'
III. Allegro scherzando   _'

Massey

Pisces: Partita Concertante (revised version) <1984; rev 1995>

20'

solo violin
2 0 2 0 — 2 0 0 0 — tmp — str
I. Ritornello _'
II. Arioso _'
III. Alla Giga _'

Massey

Suite No.1 for String Orchestra <1956>

13'

str
I. Triptych _'
II. Air _'
III. Intrada & Fugue _'

Promethean

Rival, Robert Carl

1975-

(b Calgary, 29 Sept 1975). Canadian

Achilles & Scamander <2012>

8'

2[1.2/pic] 2 2 2 — 4 2 3 1 — tmp+2 — hp — str
perc: tri, sus cym, cym, tamtam, woodblk, tambn, sd, td[or tambn prov], bd

Rival

Delights & Dischords <2014>

17'

chorus
2 2 2 2 — 4 2 3 1 — tmp+2 — hp — pf, org[opt] — [no str]
perc: sd, bd, tambn, tri, sus cym, cym, glock, crot, tamtam, set, slgh-bells, ratch, whip, tambn prov[or td], button gong[or chime]
1. Rose-Cheek'd Laura Come (Thomas Campion) 2'
2. On My First Son (Ben Jonson) 3'
3. Now Winter Nights Enlarge (Campion) 2'
4. The Glories of Our Blood and State (James Shirley) 3'
5. Delight in Disorder (Robert Herrick) 2'
6. The Sun Is Set (Robert Sidney) 5'

Rival

Elegy <2007; rev (orchd) 2009>

4'

str
Originally for piano; orchestrated by the composer for strings.

Rival

Lullaby <2011>

5'

2 2 2 2 — 4 2 0 0 — 1perc — hp — cel — str
perc: sus cym, claves, bd, vib, 3buttongong

Rival

Northwest Passage Variations <2014>

12'

2[1.2/pic] 2 2 2 — 4 2 3 1 — tmp+1 — str
perc: sd, tri, cym, crot, tambn prov[or td], 3sus cym

Rival

Scherzo <2010>

7'

1 1 1 1 — 1 0 0 0 — str
Originally a nonet; orchestral version by the composer.

Rival

Spring <2012>

8'

str

Rival

Symphony No.2 (Water) <2013>

24'

2[1.2/pic] 2 2 2 — 4 2 3 1 — tmp+2 — hp — str
perc: bd, sd, cast
2nd mvt for strings alone (solo octet & tutti); may be performed independently.
I. Moderate. Expansive 10'
II. Very slowly. Tranquil 9'
III. Fast. Exuberant 5'

Rival

Whirlwind <2012>

8'

2[1.2/pic] 2 2 2 — 4 2 3 1 — tmp+2 — hp — str
perc: tri, sus cym, cym, glock, xyl, marim, chimes, tambn, sd, timbales, bd, crot, 2woodblk

Rival

Rochberg, George

1918-2005

(b Paterson, NJ, 5 July 1918; d Bryn Mawr, PA, 29 May 2005). American

Black Sounds <1965>

12'

2[1/pic.2/pic] 1 2[1/Ebcl.2/bcl] 0 — 2 2 2 1 — tmp+3 — pf/cel — [no str]

Presser

Cheltenham Concerto <1958>

15'

1 1 1 1 — 1 1 1 0 — str

Presser

Concerto, Oboe <1983>

18'

2[1.2/pic] 0 2 2 — 4 2 3 1 — tmp+2 — hp — cel — str
perc: xyl, tambn, chimes, bd, gong, sus cym

Presser

Concerto, Violin & Orchestra <1974>

36'

3[1.2.3/pic] 3[1.2.3/Eh] 3[1.2.3/bcl] 3[1.2.cbn] — 4 3 3 1 — tmp — 2hp — cel — str

Presser

EDEN: Out of Time and Out of Space <1997>

20'

solo guitar
1 0 1 0 — 1 0 0 0 — vn, va, vc
Chamber concerto for guitar and ensemble.

Presser

Imago mundi <1973>

22'

3[1.2.3/pic] 3[1.2.Eh] 3[1.2.3/bcl] 3[1.2.cbn] — 4 3 3 1 — tmp+3 — hp — cel — str
perc: glock, crot, tamtam, tambn, sus cym, bd, logdrum, 2guiro

Presser

Music for the Magic Theater <1965>

27'

1[fl/pic] 1 1[cl/Ebcl] 1 — 2 1 1 1 — pf — str 5t
Much of the work consists of open un-metered passages in proportional (or visual) notation. There are many quotations from other composers; the bulk of Act II is a transcription of the *Adagio* from Mozart's K.287 Divertimento. The composer provides a lengthy Preface explaining the surreal aspect of the work, and giving specific suggestions for performance.
    This work may also be performed by a small orchestra, using string sections and 4 horns rather than 2.
Act I: in which the present and the past are all mixed up… 9'
Act II: in which the past haunts us with its nostalgic beauty… 8'
Act III: in which we realize that only the present is really real… 10'

Presser

Night Music <1948>   12'

3[1.2.3/pic] 3[1.2.3/Eh] 3[1.2.3/bcl] 3[1.2.3/cbn] — 4 3 3 1 — tmp+1 — hp — str

perc: bd, cym

Night Music is the 2nd mvt of the composer's *Symphony No.1*.

Presser

Symphony No.1 <1948–1957; rev 1971-77>   65'

3[1.2.3/pic] 3[1.2.3/Eh] 3[1/Ebcl.2.3/bcl] 3[1.2.cbn] — 4 3 3 1 — tmp+4 — hp — pf — str

perc: bd, cym, sus cym, sd, tomtom, tri, tambn, chimes, bongos, 2gong

I. Allegro molto ma un poco pesante: exultant!	*11'*
II. Night Music: Poco adagio, like a slow march	*14'*
III. Capriccio: Fast and impetuous, like a curtain-raiser	*14'*
IV. Variations: Moldo adagio, very slow and stately	*18'*
V. Finale: Adagio, parlando e molto rubato; Allegro gioioso	*8'*

Presser

Symphony No.2 <1955–1956>   32'

3[1.2.pic] 3[1.2.Eh] 3[1.2.bcl] 3[1.2.cbn] — 4 3 3 1 — tmp+5 — str

perc: xyl, sd, td, bd, cym, gong, tri, tambn, sus cym

Declamando	*9'*
Allegro scherzoso	*5'*
Adagio	*10'*
Quasi tempo primo, ma capriccioso	*5'*
Adagio sostenuto e calmo	*3'*

Presser

Symphony No.4 <1976>   45'

3[1.2.3/pic] 3[1.2.3/Eh] 3[1.2.bcl] 3[1.2.cbn] — 4 3 3 1 — tmp+3 — hp — cel — str

perc: glock, tambn, tri, sd, bd, cym, 2sus cym

I. Adagio; Andante con moto	_'
II. Serenade; Scherzo	_'
III. Introduction and Finale	_'

Presser

Symphony No.5 <1984; rev 1985-86>   25'

3[1.2.3/pic] 3[1.2.Eh] 3[1.2.bcl] 3[1.2.cbn] — 4 4 3 1 — tmp+4 — hp — pf, cel — str

perc: vib, xyl, chimes, sd, td, bd, sus cym, cym, 4rototom

In 7 sections, which follow each other without pause.

Presser

Symphony No.6 <1986–1987>   35'

4[1.2.3.pic] 4[1.2.3.Eh] 5[1.2.3.Ebcl.bcl] 4[1.2.3.cbn] — 4 4 3 1 — 2tmp+5 — 2hp — cel — str

perc: xyl, vib, chimes, tri, cym, tamtam, whip, guiro, sd, td, bd, 2sus cym

I. Fantasia	_'
II. Marcia	_'

Presser

Time-Span II <1960; rev 1964>   10'

3 3[1.2.Eh] 3[1.2.bcl] 2 — 4 3 3 1 — 2perc — cel, pf — str

perc: vib, tamtam, chimes

A 1964 revision of the original *Time-Span* (1960), which was withdrawn.

MCA

Rodgers, Richard   1902-1979

(b Hammels Station, Long Island, NY, 28 June 1902; d New York, 30 Dec 1979). American

Carousel: The Carousel Waltz <1945>   8'

3[1/pic.2/pic.3/pic] 3[1.2.Eh] 3[1.2.bcl] 3[1.2.cbn] — 4 3 3 1 — tmp+4 — hp — str

perc: bd, cym, glock, sd, sus cym, tri

Orchestrated by Don Walter. Said to be playable with:
    2 1 2 1 — 3 2 3 1 — tmp, perc — hp — str

R&H

Slaughter on Tenth Avenue <1936>   10'

2[1.2/pic] 2[1.Eh] 3[1.2.bcl] 2 — 4 3 3 1 — tmp+3 — hp — pf/cel — str

perc: bd, cym, glock, sd, vib, woodblk, xyl, pol whstle, gunshot

Arr. Robert Russell Bennett. From the 1936 musical *On Your Toes*. R&H also has alternate arrangements of this work, mostly for pit orchestra with extensive woodwind/sax doublings.

Chappell	R&H

The Sound of Music; A Symphonic Picture <1959>   10'

3[1.2.pic] 2 3[1.2.bcl] 2 — 4 3 3 1 — tmp+5 — hp — opt org — str

perc: bd, cym, glock, sd, xyl

Arr. Robert Russell Bennett.

Chappell

Rodrigo, Joaquín   1901-1999

(b Sagunto, 22 Nov 1901; d Madrid, 6 July 1999). Spanish

A la busca del más allá (In Search of the Beyond) <1977>   17'

3[1.2.pic] 3[1.2.Eh] 2 2 — 4 3 3 1 — tmp+1 — hp — cel — str

perc: cym, tri, tamtam, xyl

Schott

Concierto andaluz <1967>   24'

4 solo guitars

2[1.2/pic] 2 2 — 4 2 0 0 — str

1. Tempo di bolero	*8'*
2. Adagio	*10'*
3. Allegretto	*6'*

EJR	Schott

Concierto de Aranjuez <1939>   21'

solo guitar

2[1.2/pic] 2[1.2/Eh] 2 2 — 2 2 0 0 — str

Available from EJR for Spain; Schott elsewhere.

At the request of Nicanor Zabaleta, the composer in 1974 made a version of this concerto for solo harp with orchestra, published by Schott; Zabaleta supplied the fingering for the solo harp part. That version uses the same score and parts of the guitar concerto.

I. Allegro con spirito	*6'*
II. Adagio	*10'*
III. Allegro gentile	*5'*

EJR	Schott

Concierto de estío <1943>   21'

solo violin

2[1.2/pic] 2 2 — 2 2 0 0 — str

1. Prélude	*8'*
2. Siciliano	*8'*
3. Rondino	*5'*

EJR

Concierto madrigal <1969>   30'

2 solo guitars
2[1.pic] 1 1 1 — 1 1 0 0 — str
1. Fanfare	2'
2. Madrigal	3'
3. Entrada	2'
4. "Pastorcico, tú que vienes, Pastorcico tú que vas"	2'
5. Girardilla	1'
6. Pastoral	2'
7. Fandango	2'
8. Arietta	6'
9. Zapateado	5'
10. Caccia a la española	5'

Schott

Concierto serenata <1952>   24'

solo harp
2[1.2/pic] 2 2 2 — 2 2 0 0 — str
1. Estudiantina	8'
2. Intermezzo con aria	10'
3. Sarao	6'

EJR   UME

Cuatro madrigales amatorios (Four Madrigals of Love) 9'
<1947>

solo soprano or mezzo-soprano
2[1.2/pic] 2 1 0 — 1 1 0 0 — 1perc — str
perc: tri
Arrangements of four 16th-century songs, originally for voice & piano.
Available for **high voice** (F minor, A minor, F major, A major) or
medium voice (D minor, F-sharp minor, D major, G major).
1. ¿Con qué la lavaré? (With What Shall I Wash?)	3'
2. Vos me matásteis (You Have Destroyed Me)	3'
3. ¿De dónde venis, amore? (Whence Do You Come, Beloved?)	1'
4. De los álamos vengo, madre (I Have Come from the Poplars, Mother)	2'

Chester

Fantasía para un gentilhombre (Fantasia for a 21'
Nobleman) <1954>

solo guitar
2[1.2/pic] 1 0 1 — 0 1 0 0 — str
Based on several short pieces by the 17th-century Spanish guitar virtuoso
Gaspar Sanz.
1. Villano y Ricercare	5'
2. Españoleta y Fanfare de la caballería de Nápoles	9'
3. Danza de las hachas	2'
4. Canario	5'

Schott

Fantasía para un gentilhombre [flute version] (Fantasia 22'
for a Nobleman) <1954; rev 1978>

solo flute
0 1 1 1 — 0 1 0 0 — str
Originally for guitar & orchestra; transcribed 1978 for James Galway.
1. Villano y Ricercare	5'
2. Españoleta	5'
3. Fanfare de la caballería de Nápoles	5'
4. Danza de las hachas	2'
5. Canario	5'

Schott

Zarabanda lejana y Villancico (Distant Sarabande and 9'
Villancico) <1930>

str
| 1. Zarabanda lejana | 4' |
| 2. Villancico | 5' |

EJR

Rodríguez, Robert Xavier   1946-

(b San Antonio, TX, 28 June 1946). American

Agnus Dei, for Mozart's Mass in C minor, K.427 <2006>   9'

solos SSTB   double chorus   opt handbell choir [10 players]
1 2 0 2 — 2 2 3 0 — tmp+1[opt] — org — str
perc: chimes
Composed in 2006 for use as the final missing movement of the
incomplete Mozart Mass, K.427, though not in the style of Mozart.

Schirmer

A Colorful Symphony <1987>   20'

narrator
3[1.2.3/pic] 2 2 2 — 4 2 3 1 — tmp+3 — hp — pf — str

Schirmer

De rerum natura (On the Nature of Things) <2013>   27'

2[1.2/pic] 2[1.Eh] 2 2 — 4 2 3 0 — tmp+2 — hp — pf — str
perc: vib, chimes, sus cym, td, tambn, templeblks, brass windchimes, cym, szl
cym, crot, tamtam, bd, congas, sd, marac, whip, tri, 2shaker, 2cowbell
Mvts are performed *attacca*. Major solos for violin and violoncello.
I. Invocation of Venus ("…the place of fierce desire")	4'
II. Ricercare ("…where the mind soars at liberty")	4'
III. Variations: Skolion of Seikilos ("…loosening our bonds")	5'
IV. Scherzo ("…atoms that touch the senses with pleasure")	3'
V. Fanfare & Cadenza ("…the swerve")	3'
VI. Finale ("…heralds of godlike beauty")	8'

Schirmer

Estampie <1981>   18'

2[1.2/pic] 2[1.2/Eh] 2[1.2/asx] 2 — 2 2 2 0 — tmp+3 — hp — pf —
str
Based on a medieval tune, which should be performed before the present
work whenever possible.
1. Istanpitta Ghaetta	1'
2. The Reversible Rag	2'
3. The Intermezzo	4'
4. Scherzo	2'
5. The Slow Sleazy Rag	4'
6. The Couple Action Rag	1'
7. Rimbonbo	2'
8. The Reversible Rag Reversed	2'

Schirmer

Favola boccaccesca (Fable of Boccaccio) <1979>   21'

3[1.2.3/pic] 3[1.2.3/Eh] 4[1.2.3.4/bcl] 3[1.2.3/cbn] — 4 3 3 1 —
tmp+3 — hp — cel — str

Schirmer

Forbidden Fire <1998>   22'

solo bass-baritone   double chorus
3[1.2.pic] 2 2 2 — 4 3 3 1 — tmp+3 — hp — pf — str
perc: vib, windchimes, bd, chimes, gong, crot, tri, sus cym, glock, marim, cym
All 3perc need a selection of drums for an improvisation section in mvt 2.
Conceived as a companion piece to Beethoven's *Symphony No.9*.

Schirmer

A Gathering of Angels; Bolero for Orchestra <1989>   8'

opt. handbell choir (5 octaves, 12 players)
3[all/pic] 3[1.2.3/Eh] 3[1.2.3/Ebcl] 2 — 4 3 3 1 — tmp+3 — hp — pf
— str

Schirmer

Hot Buttered Rhumba <1996>   6'

3[1.2.pic] 2 2 2 — 4 3 3 1 — asx — tmp+3 — hp — pf — str

Schirmer

Jargon; The Story of the American Constitution <1987>   15'

narrator   optional chorus
2[1/pic.2/pic] 2 2 2 — 4 2 3 1 — tmp+3 — str
Narrative centers on Benjamin Franklin.

> Schirmer

Oktoechos; Concerto Grosso for 2 Groups of Soloists <1983>   22'

soloists: vn, cl, tp, perc, vc, bn, tbn, pf
3[1.2.3/pic] 3[1.2.Eh] 3[1.2.bcl] 2[1.2.cbn] — 4 2 2 1 — tmp+2 — hp — str

perc: crot, tambn, glock, cym, sd, td, marac, woodblk, claves, bd, gong, glass windchimes, fingercym, logdrum

> Schirmer

Piñata <1991>   6'

3[1.2.pic] 2 2 2 — 4 3 3 1 — asx — tmp+3 — hp — pf — str

> Schirmer

The Salutation Rag <1978>   5'

3[1.2.3/pic] 2 2 2 — 4 3 3 1 — tmp+3 — str
Happy Birthday in the manner of Scott Joplin.

> Schirmer

Scrooge <1994>   20'

solo bass-baritone   chorus
2[1.2/str] 2[1.2/Eh] 2[1.2/Ebcl/bcl] 2[1.2/cbn] — 2[or 4] 2 2 0 — tmp+3 — hp — pf/cel/hpsd — str

perc: chimes, sus cym, tri, vibrslp, guiro, slgh-bells, td, vib, whip, thunder, marac, ratch, cym, woodblk, crot, bd, belltree, sl whistle, cashregister, 2gong, 2tambn, coins, chain, br windchimes, bamboo windchimes
Concert scenes from Dickens' *A Christmas Carol*.
   Cel & hpsd may be synthesized.

> Schirmer

Sinfonía à la mariachi <1997>   20'

3[1.2.pic] 3[incl Eh] 2[incl Ebcl] 2 — 4 4 3 0 — ampd gtr(s), accordion — tmp+3 — hp — pf/synth — str

perc: cym, vibrslp, marim, guiro, marac, vib, sus cym, tri, tambn, gong, chimes, ratch, claves, templeblks, 2woodblk, metalshakr, glass windchimes, brass windchimes
From the above forces, a separate mariachi orchestra is drawn, which consists of 2tp, 1perc, accordion, hp, gtr(s) & strings.
   Optional costumed mariachi band in 4th mvt (in addition to the above instrumentation): 2tp, violins, gtrs, bass gtr.
   One percussionist doubles on a 2nd pair of timpani.

1. Mariage	_'
2. Calaveras	_'
3. Las barricadas misteriosas	_'
4. Plaza de los mariachis	_'

> Schirmer

Trunks; A Circus Story for Narrator & Orchestra <1983>   18'

narrator
2[1.pic] 2 2 2[1.cbn] — 4 2 3 1 — tmp+3 — hp — pf/cel — str
perc: bd, cym, sus cym, sd, td, tri, tambn, gong, glock, xyl, whip, bongos, marac, claves, congas, chain, 2typewriters, sirens, effects[broken dishes, glass, etc.], police whistle

> Schirmer

Rogers, Bernard   1893-1968

(b New York, 4 Feb 1893; d Rochester, NY, 24 May 1968). American

Five Fairy Tales (Once Upon a Time) <1936>   13'

2[1/pic.2/pic] 2 2 2 — 2 2 1[btbn] 0 — tmp+3 — hp — "clavi-cembalo (adapted piano)" — str

1. The Tinder-Box Soldier	2'
2. The Song of Rapunzel	3'
3. The Story of a Darning Needle	1'
4. Dance of the Twelve Princesses	4'
5. The Ride of Koschei the Deathless	3'

> Kalmus

The Musicians of Bremen <1958>   22'

narrator
1[1/pic] 1 1 1 — 1 1 0 0 — tmp+1 — pf — 2vn, vc, db; or small sections[no va]

> Presser

Soliloquy No.1, for Flute & Strings <1922>   6'

str

> C. Fischer   Luck's

Three Japanese Dances <1933>   12'

optional mezzo-soprano
3[incl pic; afl & bfl opt] 3[incl Eh] 3[incl bcl] 3[incl cbn] — 4 2 3 1 — tmp+4 — hp — cel, pf — str

> Presser

Rollin, Catherine   1952-

(b Detroit, MI, 2 April 1952). American

Concerto romantique <1999>   12'

2 2 2 2 — 2 2 0 0 — tmp — str
Intended for the intermediate piano student; composed in the style of Robert Schumann, and orchd by David Daniels also in that style.

I. Allegro	5'
II. Romance: Andante molto cantabile e espressivo	3'
III. Tarantella: Allegro molto e scherzando	4'

> Alfred

Ropartz, Joseph Guy   1864-1955

(b Guingamp, Côtes du Nord [now Côtes d'Armor], 15 June 1864; d Lanloup, Côtes du Nord, 22 Nov 1955). French

Serenade <ca.1892>   3'

str 4t or str orch
Db opt.

> Kalmus

Sérénade champêtre <1932>   9'

1 1 2 1 — 2 1 0 0 — tmp+1 — str
perc: cym, sus cym, tri

> Durand

Symphony No.5, G major <1944>   30'

2 2 2 2 — 4 2 3 0 — tmp+2 — hp — str
perc: cym, sus cym, tri, xyl, sd

I. Allegro assai	9'
II. Presto	4'
III. Largo	11'
IV. Allegro moderato	6'

> Durand

Rorem, Ned   1923-

(b Richmond, IN, 23 Oct 1923). American

Air Music; Ten Variations for Orchestra <1974>   34'

3[all/pic] 3[1.2.Eh] 3[1.2.3/Ebcl] 3[1.2.3/cbn] — 4 3 3 1 — 4perc — hp — cel, pf — str

perc: sd, td, bd, cym, sus cym, gong, tamtam, tri, cowbell, glock, xyl, chimes, vib, anvil, metalplate

> Boosey

Concerto, Organ <1985>   25'

0 0 0 0 — 2 1 1 0 — tmp — str

> Boosey

Concerto, Piano, No.3, in 6 Movements <1969>   23'

3[1.2.3/pic] 3[1.2.3/Eh] 3[1.2.3/Ebcl/asx] 3[1.2.cbn] — 4 3 3 1 — tmp+7 — hp — cel — str

perc: glock, chimes, vib, xyl, bongos, congas, cym, sus cym, tamtam, tri, templeblks, whip, bd, sd, td, anvil

> Boosey

Concerto, Piano, No.4 (Left Hand) <1991>   25'

2[1.2/pic] 2 2 2 — 2 2 2 0 — tmp+3 — hp — cel — str

perc: bd, sd, td, tomtom, bongos, tri, gong, glock, marim, cym, chimes, whip, vib, anvil, metalplate

> Boosey

Concerto, Violin <1985>   22'

1[1/pic] 1 2 1 — 0 1 0 0 — tmp — str

> Boosey

Design <1953>   18'

2[1.2/pic] 2 2 2 — 4 2 2 0 — tmp+5 — hp — cel, pf — str

perc: gong, xyl, cym, bd, tri, sd

> Boosey

Eagles <1958>   8'

3[1.2.pic] 3[1.2.Eh] 4[1.2.Ebcl.bcl] 3[1.2.cbn] — 4 3 3 1 — tmp+7 — hp — cel/pf — str

perc: tamtam, xyl, cym, tri, cast, whip, bd, sd, tambn, td, ratch, 2woodblks

Celesta and Piano are said to be "interchangeable." It appears that one player doubles the two, except that they both play simultaneously in 3 of the last dozen bars.

> Boosey

Eleven Studies for Eleven Players <1959–1960>   28'

1[1/pic] 1[1/Eh] 1 0 — 0 1 0 0 — 2perc — hp — pf — vn, va, vc

perc: xyl, gong, tri, cym, bd, sd, cast, glock, td, tomtom, bongos, tambn, whip, 2woodblks

1. Prelude (eleven: trumpet solo)	2'
2. Allegretto (nine)	2'
3. Bird Call (four: flute solo)	2'
4. The Diary (six)	2'
5. Contest (five)	1'
6. Invention for Battery (two)	2'
7. In Memory of My Feelings (ten: cello solo)	5'
8. Fugato (eleven)	3'
9. Elegy (eleven: English horn solo)	4'
10. Presto (five)	1'
11. Epilogue (eleven: clarinet solo)	4'

> Boosey

Ideas for Easy Orchestra <1961>   12'

1 1 1 1 — 2 1 1 0 — tmp+2 — hp — pf — str

perc: cym, tri, gong, sd, tambn

Eight movements, any of which may be performed separately, and each of which uses a different combination of instruments.

> Boosey

Lions (A Dream) <1963>   14'

combo: asx, drum set, pf, db

3[1.2.3/pic] 3[1.2.Eh] 3[1.2.Ebcl] 2 — 4 3 3 1 — tmp+6 — hp — cel — str

perc: tri, tambn, cast, tamtam, sd, xyl, vib, glock, cym, td, woodblk, templeblks, bongos, chimes[C#,G]

> Boosey

Pilgrims <1958>   6'

str

> Boosey

A Quaker Reader <1975; rev (orchd) 1988>   20'

2[1.2/pic] 2[1.2/Eh] 2 2 — 2 1 1 0 — str

Originally a group of 11 pieces for organ; 8 of these selected and orchestrated by the composer, 1988.

> Boosey

Sinfonia <1957>   9'

3[1.2.pic] 3[1.2.Eh] 4[1.2.Ebcl.bcl] 3[1.2.cbn] — 2 0 0 0 — (opt tmp+5) — (opt pf/cel) — [no str]

Tmp, perc, & pf/cel are all optional.

> Peters

String Symphony <1985>   23'

str

1. Waltz	5'
2. Berceuse	2'
3. Scherzo	2'
4. Nocturne	8'
5. Rondo	6'

> Boosey

Symphony No.1 <1950>   23'

2[incl pic] 2 2 2 — 4 2 2 0 — tmp+5 — hp — str

Maestoso	5'
Andantino	4'
Largo	7'
Allegro	7'

> Southern

Symphony No.2 <1956>   22'

2[1.2/pic] 2[1.2/Eh] 2 2 — 2 1 1 0 — tmp+2 — hp — pf — str

perc: sd, tri, cym, tamtam, xyl, tambn

Broad; Moderate	15'
Tranquillo	4'
Allegro	3'

> Boosey

Symphony No.3 <1958>   24'

3[1.2.pic] 3[1.2.Eh] 3[1.2.bcl] 3[1.2.cbn] — 4 3 3 1 — tmp+6 — hp — cel, pf — str

perc: gong, chimes, xyl, tomtom, cym, tri, cast, woodblk, whip, bd, sd, tambn, td

1. Passacaglia	6'
2. Allegro molto vivace	3'
3. Largo	2'
4. Andante	4'
5. Allegro molto	7'

> Boosey

Water Music <1966>   17'

solo clarinet & violin

1[1/pic] 1[1/Eh] 0 1 — 1 0 0 0 — 2perc — hp — pf/cel — str

perc: glock, gong, vib, bongos, cym, tri, bd, sd, td

Boosey

Rosenberg, Hilding   1892-1985

(b Bosjökloster, Ringsjön, Skåne, 21 June 1892; d Stockholm, 19 May 1985).
Swedish

Bergslagsbilder, op.72 (Scenes from the Bergslag) <1937>   16'

2 1 2 1 — 2 2 1 0 — tmp+2 — str

perc: tri, sus cym, bd, sd, tambn, woodblk

Suite from the film score.

I. Folket (The People)   _'
II. Bygden (The Countryside)   _'
III. Forsen (The Mill-Race)   _'
IV. Den Ljusa Sommernatten (Light Summer Nights)   _'
V. Det gamla bruket (The Old Manor)   _'
VI. Bergslagsindustri (Bergslag Industry)   _'

Nordiska

Concerto No.1 for String Orchestra <1946>   23'

str

I. Allegro con fuoco	10'
II. Andantino ma tranquillo	8'
III. Allegro assai	5'

Kalmus	Nordiska

Concerto No.2 (Concerto for Orchestra) <1949>   27'

3[1.2.pic] 2[1.2/Eh] 2[1.2/bcl] 2 — 4 3 3 1 — tmp+4 — hp — str

perc: bd, sd, cym, tri, woodblk

Gehrmans

Concerto No.3 (Louisville Concerto) <1954; rev 1968>   25'

soloists: violin, viola, violoncello

2[1.2/pic] 2[1.2/Eh] 2 2 — 4 2 3 1 — tmp+2 — hp — cel — str

perc: sd, bd, cym, tomtom, tri, tambn

I. Andante quieto—Allegro vivace	10'
II. Poco adagio	9'
III. Allegro energico	6'

Suecia

Concerto, Viola <1942>   30'

2 2 2[1.2/bcl] 2 — 3 2 0 0 — tmp+3 — hp — str

perc: bd, cym, sd, tambn

I. Moderato—Allegro assai	13'
II. Andante	10'
III. Allegro energico	7'

Kalmus	Nordiska

Orpheus in Town (Orfeus i sta'n): Dance Suite <1938>   13'

2[1/pic1.2/pic2] 2[1.2/Eh] 2 2 — 4 3 3 1 — tmp+4 — pf, cel — str

perc: sd, bd, cym, glock, templeblks, tri, xyl, tambn, sus cym, brushes, 3tomtom

Suite from the ballet.

1. Rhythm of the Times	2'
2. Bartender's Dance	2'
3. Girl's Dance	1'
4. Dance of the Negress	3'
5. Trio Dance	1'
6. Tango	2'
7. Finale	2'

Nordiska

Overtura bianca-nera <1946>   9'

str

Kalmus	Nordiska

Reflessioni no.2 <1960>   17'

str

Nordiska

Sinfonie concertante <1935>   22'

solo violin, viola, oboe, bassoon

0 0 0 0 — 2 2 0 0 — str

I. Allegro vivace	_'
II. Andante molto alla ballata	_'
III. Molto moderato	_'
IV. Allegro vivace ma non troppo	_'

Fleisher

Suite on Swedish Folktunes <1927>   21'

str

I. Allegro assai	6'
II. Moderato	8'
III. Poco allegro	2'
IV. Andante mesto	3'
V. Devil's Polka: Allegro energico	2'

Nordiska

Suite, Violin & Orchestra <1922>   17'

2[1/pic.2/pic] 1 2 1 — 0 0 0 0 — str

I. Introduction	_'
II. Tempo di Valse	_'
III. Melodi	_'
IV. Pastorale	_'
V. Humoresk	_'

Nordiska

Symphonic Metamorphosis No.3 (Metamorfosi sinfoniche no.3) <1964>   18'

1[fl/pic] 1 1 0 — 0 0 0 0 — pf — str

Suecia

Symphony No.2 (Sinfonia grave) <1928–1935>   33'

2[1.2/pic] 2 2 2 — 4 2 3 1 — tmp+4 — str

perc: xyl, glock, tri, field dr, tambn, cym, bd, 3tomtom

I. Allegro energico	11'
II. Poco adagio—Allegro assai	11'
III. Allegro risoluto	11'

Gehrmans

Symphony No.3, op.80 (The Four Ages of Man; De fyra tidsåldrarna) <1939; rev 1952>   37'

2[1.2/pic] 2[1.2/Eh] 2 2 — 4 2 3 1 — tmp+3 — hp — str

perc: sd, field dr, tri, xyl, chimes

Clarinet solo in mvt 2 requires amplification ("Must be played with a megaphone!!" [= bullhorn?]).

1. Moderato	13'
2. Andante sostenuto	10'
3. Allegro con fuoco, molto marcato	8'
4. Andante semplice	6'

Nordiska

Symphony No.4 (The Revelation of St. John; Johannes uppenbarelse) <1940>   75'

solo baritone   double chorus
2[1.2/pic] 2[1.2/Eh] 2 2 — 4 4 3 1 — 2tmp+3 — hp — cel, pf — str
perc: bd, cym, sd, xyl, chimes
I. This is now the revelation of Jesus Christ   _'
Recitative: I, John who also am your brother   _'
II. Holy, Almighty   _'
Choral a cappella: The flames rise from an isle   _'
III. And there appeared a great wonder   _'
Choral a cappella: We earthly women   _'
Recitative: And I saw a wild beast   _'
IV. If any give captivity   _'
Choral a cappella: Here is wisdom fulfilled   _'
V. And these things saidth he   _'
Choral a cappella: I know thee, know what fails thee   _'
Recitative: And I looked   _'
VI. Fear the Lord!   _'
Choral a cappella: That hour is worth all glory   _'
Recitative: And I saw Heaven   _'
VII. O vision of white horses   _'
Recitative: And I saw a new heaven   _'
Choral and finale: And he upon the throne made proclamation   _'

> Nordiska

Symphony No.5 (Hortulanus, The Keeper of the Garden; Hortulanus, Örtagårdsmästaren) <1944>   46'

contralto solo   chorus
2[both/pic] 2 2 2 — 4 2 3 1 — tmp+3 — pf — str
perc: bd, cym, tri, tambn, glock, chimes
1.   14'
2.   8'
3.   9'
4.   8'
5.   7'

> Gehrmans

Symphony No.6 (Sinfonia semplice) <1951>   23'

2[1.2/pic] 2[1.2/Eh] 2 2 — 3 2 3 0 — tmp+2 — str
perc: bd, cym, sd, xyl, glock
I. Poco adagio   9'
II. Alla marcia   6'
III. Recitativo   3'
IV. Inno   7'

> Nordiska

Symphony No.8 (In candidum) <1974; rev 1980>   18'

3[1.2.pic] 3[1.2.Eh] 2 2 — 4 3 3 1 — tmp+2 — hp — cel — str
perc: sd, tri, tambn, cym, sus cym, bd, glock
In one mvt.

> Nordiska

Rossini, Gioachino   1792-1868

(b Pesaro, 29 Feb 1792; d Passy, 13 Nov 1868). Italian

> *Rossini editions in general have been poor and untrustworthy. There are many competing versions, and the scores frequently conflict with the parts.*
>   *Critical editions of the Fondazione Rossini Pesaro, published by Ricordi, are a great improvement as they become available.*

L'assedio di Corinto

see his: Siège de Corinthe

Il barbiere di Siviglia (The Barber of Seville): Overture (critical edition) <1816>   8'

2 2 2 2 — 2 2 0 0 — tmp+1 — str
perc: bd[probably with attached cym]
This overture originally written for his *Aureliano in Palmira* (1813).
   Ricordi critical edition by Alberto Zedda, 1969; Kalmus "Practical Performing Edition" ed. McAlister. Luck's also offers what it terms the "original Italian edition," the instrumentation of which resembles the above, but with the addition of a trombone; this is a reprint of an earlier Ricordi edition.

> Ricordi   Kalmus

Il barbiere di Siviglia (The Barber of Seville): Overture ("German edition") <1816>   8'

2[1.pic] 2 2 — 2 2 3 0 — tmp+1 — str
perc: bd, cym
This overture originally written for his *Aureliano in Palmira* (1813).
   Luck's identifies this version with 3tbn and pic as the "German edition;" it is a reprint of Breitkopf.

> Breitkopf   Luck's

La boutique fantasque

see under: Respighi, Ottorino, 1879-1936

La Cenerentola (Cinderella): Overture <1817>   8'

2[1/pic.2] 2 2 — 2 2 1 0 — tmp+1 — str
perc: bd
Kalmus identifies this as the "original Italian edition." Breitkopf offers a version with the following instrumentation:
   2 2 2 1 — 2 2 1 0 — tmp+perc — str

> Kalmus   Ricordi

Elisabetta, regina d'Inghilterra: Overture <1815>   7'

2[1.pic] 2 2 — 2 2 3 0 — tmp+1 — str
This work may be out of print.

> Breitkopf

La gazza ladra (The Thieving Magpie): Overture <1817>   10'

2[1.pic] 2 2 — 4 2 1 0 — tmp+4 — str
perc: bd, tri, 2sd
Ricordi critical edition by Alberto Zedda, 1979; Kalmus ed. Clark McAlister.

> Kalmus   Luck's   Ricordi

La gazza ladra (The Thieving Magpie): Overture (arr. Kogel) <1817>   10'

2[1.pic] 2 2 — 4 2 3 1 — tmp+3 — str
perc: bd, sd, tri
Ed. & arr. Gustav Kogel. This arrangement, which is not recommended, is sometimes referred to as "the German edition." It calls for extra brass not found in the original, and contains an extra 120 bars of music as well.

> Breitkopf   Kalmus   Luck's

Guillaume Tell (William Tell): Overture <1829>   12'

2[1.pic] 2[1.2/Eh] 2 2 — 4 2 3 0 — tmp+3 — str
perc: tri, cym, bd

> Breitkopf   Kalmus   Luck's   Ricordi

Guillaume Tell (William Tell): Pas de six <1828–1829>   6'

2[1.pic] 2 2 2 — 2 2 0 0 — str

> Kalmus   Luck's

Introduction, Theme & Variations <ca.1822>   14'

solo clarinet
1 2 0 1 — 2 0 0 0 — str
Introduction in E-flat major, followed by (in B-flat) a theme, 3 variations,
a "minore" variation, and a "maggiore" coda-finale.
   Sikorski ed. Jost Michaels; Art of Sound ed. arr. Craig Levesque, who
has added parts for fl2 and bn2.
   The authenticity of this work is uncertain, although it is
well-established in the clarinet repertoire. It is not to be confused with
Rossini's *Variations for Clarinet & Orchestra* in C major, or his
Variazioni a più strumenti, q.v.

Art of Sound	Sikorski	SMC

L'Italiana in Algeri: Overture (original version) <1813>   9'

1[pic] 2 2 1 — 2 2 0 0 — 2perc — str
perc: bd, Turkish crescent
Ricordi critical ed. by Azio Corghi, 1981; Kalmus ed. Clark McAlister.

Ricordi	Kalmus

L'Italiana in Algeri: Overture <1813>   9'

1 2 2 2 — 2 2 0 0 — tmp — str
Luck's (reprint of Breitkopf) identifies this as the "German concert
edition." Various other corrupt editions may still be had, some with a
trombone part.

Breitkopf	Luck's

The Journey to Rheims

see his: Viaggio a Reims

Matinées musicales

see under: Britten, Benjamin, 1913-1976

Petite messe solennelle <1863; rev (orchd) 1869>   86'

solos SATB   chorus SATB
3[1.2.pic] 2 2 3 — 4 4[1.2.3/crt.4/crt] 4 0 — tmp — 2hp — harm[or
pf] — str
Originally (1863) composed for voices, 2pf, & harmonium. Orchestrated
by the composer in 1869.
   1. Kyrie   7'
   2. Gloria   3'
   3. Gratias   5'
   4. Domine Deus   6'
   5. Qui tollis   7'
   6. Quoniam   8'
   7. Cum Sancto Spiritu 6'
   8. Credo   4'
   9. Crucifixus   3'
   10. Et resurrexit   12'
   11. Preludio religioso 8'
   12. Sanctus   3'
   13. O Salutaris   6'
   14. Agnus Dei   8'

Kalmus	Luck's	Ricordi

Prelude, Theme, and Variations   10'

solo horn
1 2 2 2 — 0 0 0 0 — str
From the composer's *Péchés de vieillesse* (*Sins of Old Age*), vol ix, no.8.
Originally for horn and piano; orchestrated by Clark McAlister.

Kalmus

Les riens

see: Respighi, Ottorino, 1879-1936
      Rossiniana

Robert Bruce: Overture <?1819>   7'

2[1.2/pic] 2 2 2 — 4 4[2tp, 2crt] 3 1[oph] — tmp+3 — str
Adapted by Abraham-Louis Niedermeyer (1846) for his opera pastiche on
this subject. The music came from various Rossini operas, especially *La
donna del lago* (1819).

Kalmus	Luck's

Rossiniana

see under: Respighi, Ottorino, 1879-1936

La scala di seta (The Silken Staircase): Overture <1812>   7'

1[1/pic] 2 2 1 — 2 0 0 0 — str

Breitkopf	Kalmus	Luck's	Ricordi

Semiramide: Overture <1823>   12'

2[1.pic] 2 2 2 — 4 2 3 0 — tmp+1 — str
perc: cym, bd

Breitkopf	Kalmus	Luck's	Ricordi

Serenata per piccolo complesso (Serenade for Small   8'
Ensemble) <1823>

1 2[1.Eh] 0 0 — str 4t

Kalmus	Luck's

Le siège de Corinthe (The Siege of Corinth; L'assedio di   10'
Corinto): Overture <1822–1826>

3[1.2.pic] 2 2 2 — 4 2 4 0 — tmp+2 — str
perc: bd, cym, td or field dr
A revision for Paris of the composer's Italian opera *Maometto II*.
   4th tbn part often played on tuba; Breitkopf edition (and Kalmus
reprint) calls for 3tbn plus serpent.

Breitkopf	Carisch	Heugel	Kalmus	Ricordi

Il signor Bruschino: Overture <1812>   5'

1 2 2 1 — 2 0 0 0 — str
Carisch ed. E. De Guarnieri; Ricordi critical ed. by Arrigo Gazzaniga,
1986.

Carisch	Kalmus	Luck's	Ricordi

Sinfonia di Bologna <1808–1809>   5'

1 2 2 1 — 2 2 0 0 — tmp — str

Kalmus	Luck's

Sinfonia di Odense <1808–1809>   5'

2 2 2 2 — 4 2 2 0 — tmp+1 — str
perc: bd

Kalmus	Luck's

Soirées musicales

see under: Britten, Benjamin, 1913-1976

Sonata No.1, G major <1804>   13'

2vn, vc, db
Frequently performed by string orchestra.
   I. Moderato   7'
   II. Andante   4'
   III. Allegro   2'

Kalmus	Luck's

Sonata No.2, A major <1804> 12'

2vn, vc, db
Frequently performed by string orchestra.

I. Allegro	7'
II. Andante	3'
III. Allegro	2'

Kalmus	Luck's

Sonata No.3, C major <1804> 12'

2vn, vc, db
Frequently performed by string orchestra.

I. Allegro	5'
II. Andante	4'
III. Moderato	3'

Kalmus	Luck's

Sonata No.4, B-flat major <1804> 14'

2vn, vc, db
Frequently performed by string orchestra.

I. Allegro vivace	7'
II. Andante	4'
III. Allegretto	3'

Kalmus	Luck's

Sonata No.5, E-flat major <1804> 20'

2vn, vc, db
Frequently performed by string orchestra.

I. Allegro vivace	12'
II. Andante	4'
III. Allegretto	4'

Kalmus	Luck's

Sonata No.6, D major <1804> 17'

2vn, vc, db
Frequently performed by string orchestra.

I. Allegro spiritoso	8'
II. Andante assai	3'
III. Tempesta: Allegro	6'

Kalmus	Luck's

Stabat Mater <1832–1841> 61'

chorus   solos SSTB
2 2 2 2 — 4 2 3 0 — tmp — str

I. Sabat Mater dolorosa	7'
II. Cujus animam	6'
III. Quis est homo	7'
IV. Pro peccatis	6'
V. Eja Mater	5'
VI. Sancta Mater	10'
VII. Fac ut portem	5'
VIII. Inflammatus	5'
IX. Quando corpus morietur	5'
X. In sempiterna saecula, Amen.	5'

EAM	Kalmus	Ricordi	Schirmer	Schott

Tancredi: Overture <1813> 6'

2 2 2 2 — 2 2 0 0 — tmp+1 — str
perc: Turkish crescent
This overture originally written for his *La pietra del paragone*. Ricordi critical ed. by Philip Gossett, 1984. Kalmus edition includes tmp but no perc.

Kalmus	Luck's	Ricordi

The Thieving Magpie

see his: Gazza ladra

Il Turco in Italia: Overture <1814> 9'

2 2 2 2 — 2 2 1[btbn] 0 — tmp+2 — str
perc: bd, cym
Ricordi critical ed. by Margaret Bent, 1988; Kalmus ed. Clark McAlister.

Breitkopf	Kalmus	Luck's	Ricordi

Variations, Clarinet & Orchestra, C major (original) <1809–1810> 9'

1 0 2 1 — 2 0 0 0 — str
Originally for solo clarinet in C; for a set of parts transposed for solo B-flat clarinet, see subsequent entry.
    Consists of an introductory *Andante*, followed by the theme, 4 variations (the third of which is "minore"), and a coda. Amadeus ed. Siegfried Beyer; Eufonia ed. Sergio Bosi & Michele Mangani; Kalmus & Luck's editions are reprints of a Quaderni Rossiniani edition, ed. A Cerasa.
    Not to be confused with the better-known *Introduction, Theme and Variations* attributed to Rossini, or his *Variazioni a più strumenti*, q.v.

Amadeus	Eufonia	Kalmus	Luck's

Variations, Clarinet & Orchestra (transposed) <1809–1810> 9'

1 0 2 1 — 2 0 0 0 — str
Originally for solo clarinet in C; this set of parts is to be used if the soloist is playing a B-flat clarinet. For the original, see previous entry.
    Consists of an introductory *Andante*, followed by the theme, 4 variations (the third of which is "minore"), and a coda.
    Not to be confused with the better-known *Introduction, Theme and Variations* attributed to Rossini, or his *Variazioni a più strumenti*, q.v.

Ipsilon

Variazioni a più strumenti obbligati, F major (Variations for Several Solo Instruments) <c1809> 6'

solo clarinet; solo string quartet
1 0 2 1 — 2 0 0 0 — str
Not to be confused with the other two sets of variations with solo clarinet attributed to Rossini: *Introduction, Theme and Variations* and *Variations for Clarinet & Orchestra*, q.v.

Kalmus

Il viaggio a Reims (The Journey to Rheims): Overture <1825> 8'

2[1.pic] 2 2 2 — 2 2 3 0 — tmp+2 — str
perc: bd, tri
This opera has no overture. The present work was cobbled together in 1936—a pastiche by an unknown person, using a set of *airs de danse* in Rossini's *Le siège de Corinth* (1826).
    Ricordi edition calls for an extra flute and an extra trombone.

Carisch	Kalmus	Luck's	Ricordi

William Tell

see his: Guillaume Tell

Rota, Nino 1911-1979

(b Milan, 3 Dec 1911; d Rome, 10 April 1979). Italian

Concerto for String Orchestra <1964–1965; rev 1977> 17'

str

1. Preludio	4'
2. Scherzo	5'
3. Aria	5'
4. Finale	3'

Ricordi

Roter, Bruce Craig   1962-

(b Brooklyn, 2 June 1962). American

Camp David Overture; Prayer for Peace <1988; rev   12'
1995>

3[1.2.3/pic] 3[1.2.3/Eh] 3[1.2.Ebcl/bcl] 3[1.2.cbn] — 4 3 3 1 —
tmp+3 — hp — pf — str

> MMB

TR: A "Bully" Portrait <2000>   16'

narrator
3[incl pic,afl] 3[incl Eh] 3[incl bcl] 3[incl cbn] — 4 3 3 1 — tmp+2
— hp — str
Text from Theodore Roosevelt.

> Coho

With Courage and Compassion; A Salute to First   15'
Responders <2003>

3[1.2.pic] 2 2 — 4 3 3 1 — tmp+2 — hp — str[16.14.10.10.6]
perc: bd, cym, sus cym, sd, td, tomtoms, tri, tambn, tamtam, glock, xyl, crot

> Coho

Rott, Hans   1858-1884

(b Vienna, 1 Aug 1858; d Vienna, 25 June 1884). Austrian

Symphony No.1, E major <1878–1880>   57'

2 2 2 3[1.2.cbn] — 4 3 3 0 — tmp+1 — str
perc: tri

I. Alla breve	9'
II. Sehr langsam	12'
III. Frisch und lebhaft	13'
IV. Sehr langsam	23'

> Ries

Rouse, Christopher   1949-

(b Baltimore, 15 Feb 1949). American

Bump <1985>   8'

3 3 4[1.2.Ebcl.bcl/bsx] 3[incl cbn] — 4 3 3 1 — 5perc — hp — pf/cel
— str
perc: claves, Chinescym, thundersheet, marim, guiro, bongos, tambn, xyl, bd,
congas, crot, woodblk, timbales, field dr, chimes, sus cym, szl cym, marac, td, sd,
vib, 4tomtoms, 2cowbells, hammer
This is the 3rd movement of the composer's *Phantasmata, q.v.*

> Boosey   Helicon

Concerto, Flute <1993>   28'

3 2 2 2[1.2/cbn] — 4 2 3 1 — tmp+3 — hp — str
perc: glock, xyl, sus cym, cym, tamtam, chimes, sd, td, tambn, vib, bd, sandblks,
rute

> Boosey

Concerto, Oboe <2004>   20'

3[1.2.pic/afl] 0 2 2 — 2 2 3 0 — 3perc — hp — cel — str
perc: bd, sus cym, Chinescym, sd, tambn, tamtam, glock, xyl, woodblk,
templeblks, guiro, claves, 4tomtom

> Boosey

Concerto, Trombone <1991>   30'

0 0 0 3[1.2.cbn] — 4 3 3 1 — tmp+4 — hp — str
perc: xyl, sd, cym, glock, td, marim, bd, chimes, bongos, 2sus cym, 5tomtoms,
2tamtams, hammer

I. Adagio; doloroso - Cadenza - attacca	11'
II. quarter-note = 144 - Cadenza - attacca	7'
III. Elegiaco, lugubre	12'

> Boosey

Concerto, Violin <1991>   22'

2[1.2/pic] 2[1.2/Eh] 2[1.2/bcl] 2[1.2/cbn] — 4 2 3 1 — tmp+3 — hp
— cel — str
perc: chimes, sd, Chinescym, bd, bongos, tambn, woodblk, tri, glock, td, field dr,
tamtam, 2sus cym

> Boosey

Concerto, Violoncello <1992–1993>   27'

2[1.2/pic] 2[1.2/Eh] 2[1.2/bcl] 2 — 4 3 3 1 — tmp+4 — hp — str
perc: cast, bongos, sus cym, guiro, vibrslp, sd, tambn, glock, chimes, ratch, tri, td,
xyl, marac, claves, whip, td, Chinescym, tamtam, 4woodblks, sandblks, hammer,
metalplate, rute, 2water gongs

> Boosey

The Infernal Machine <1981>   5'

3[all/pic] 3 4[1.2.Ebcl.bcl] 3[1.2.cbn] — 4 3 3 1 — 5perc — hp — cel
— str
perc: glock, claves, Chinescym, xyl, tambn, bongos, crot, bd, congas, tamtam,
ratch, whip, tri, field dr, marac, vibrslp, td, sd, cast, sus cym, szl cym, 4tomtoms,
2metal plates, rute, sandblks, 2timbales, friction drum, hammer
Flutes & oboes all play crystal goblets (optional). This work later
incorporated as 2nd movement of *Phantasmata, q.v.*

> Helicon

Iscariot <1989>   12'

1[1/pic] 2[1.Eh] 1 2 — 3 1 0 0 — 2perc — cel — str
perc: field dr, bongos, bd, Chinescym, tamtam, whip, sd, td, timbales, sus cym,
4tomtoms, hammer

> Boosey

Karolju <1990>   23'

chorus
2[1.2/pic] 2 2 2 — 4 3 3 1 — tmp+4 — hp — str
perc: glock, sd, tri, bd, chimes, slgh-bells, marac, guiro, 2tambn, 2pr cym, rute, sm
cym
Original carols in Latin, Swedish, French, Spanish, Russian, Czech,
German, & Italian.

> Boosey

The Nevill Feast <2003>   8'

3[1.2.pic] 3 3[1.2.bcl] 3[1.2.3/cbn] — 4 3 3 1 — elec bass — tmp+3
— hp — str
perc: bd, Chinescym, hi-hat, sd, set, tomtom, timbales, glock, xyl, marim, bongos,
guiro, marac, claves, 2cowbells, police whistle

> Boosey

Phantasmata <1981–1985>   18'

3[all/pic/opt crystal goblets] 3[all/opt crystal goblets] 4[1.2.Ebcl.bcl/bsx]
3[1.2.3/cbn] — 4 3 3 1 — 5perc — hp — pf/cel — str
perc: glock, claves, Chinescym, thundersheet, crot, xyl, tambn, bongos, guiro, bd,
congas, tamtam, chimes, ratch, timbales, whip, tri, field dr, vib, vibrslp, sd, td,
cast, sus cym, szl cym, 4tomtoms, 2metalplates, rute, sandblks, cuica, hammer, 2pr
marac, 3woodblks, 2cowbells
Two of the movements (*Bump* and *The Infernal Machine*) may be
performed independently.

1. The Evestrum of Juan de la Cruz in the Sagrada Familia, 3 A.M.	5'
2. The Infernal Machine	5'
3. Bump	8'

> Boosey

Rapture <2000>   13'

3 3 3 3 — 4 4 4 1 — 2tmp+3 — hp — str
perc: bd, crot, chimes, tamtam, glock, Chinescym, sus cym, 5tri

> Boosey

Symphony No.1 <1986>   24'

2[1.2/pic] 2[1.2.ob d'am/Eh] 2[1.2/bcl] 2[1.2/cbn] — 4[all/Wag tb or euph] 3 3 1 — tmp+3 — str
perc: Chinescym, sd, bongos, td, bd, xyl, tambn, metalplate, hammer

> Boosey

Symphony No.2 <1994>   27'

3[1.2.pic] 3[1.2.Eh] 3[1.2.bcl] 3 — 4 3 3 1 — 2tmp+3 — hp — str
perc: cym, sus cym, Chinescym, bongos, bd, sd, glock, td, field dr, tambn, tamtam, xyl
1. Allegro   7'
2. Adagio (In memoriam Stephen Albert)   13'
3. Allegro   7'

> Boosey

Symphony No.3 <2011>   25'

3[1.2.pic] 3[1.2.Eh] 3[1.2.bcl] 3[1.2.cbn] — 4 4 4 1 — tmp+3 — 2hp — str
perc: bd, cym, Chinescym, sd, timbales, tri, tambn, tamtam, glock, xyl, chimes, 2sus cym, 2td, 3tomtom, 4woodblk, 2opera gong
I. quarter note = 176   _'
II. Tema [Theme & Variations]   _'

> Boosey

Roussel, Albert   1869-1937

(b Tourcoing, 5 April 1869; d Royan, 23 Aug 1937). French

Aeneas, op.54 <1935>   37'

Chorus SATB
3[1.2.3/pic] 3[1.2.Eh] 3[1.2.bcl] 3[1.2.cbn] — 4 3 3 1 — tmp+3 — pf — str
perc: bd, cym, sus cym, tri, tamtam
Ballet in one act.
Prélude   _'
Introduction   _'
Danse des ombres   _'
Danse d'Enée (La Solitude)   _'
Apparition de la Sybille   _'
Les joies funestes   _'
Interlude   _'
Danse de Didon (Les amours tragiques)   _'

> Durand

Bacchus et Ariane, op.43: Suite No.1 <1930>   16'

3[1.2.pic] 3[1.2.Eh] 3[1.2.bcl] 3[1.2.cbn] — 4 4 3 1 — tmp+4 — 2hp — cel — str
perc: sd, tri, cym, bd, tamtam, tambn
Act I of the ballet.
Prélude   2'
Jeux des éphèbes et des vierges   3'
Bacchus apparait déguise   3'
Les nuages   2'
Danse de Bacchus   2'
Ariane, toujours endormie, prend part à la danse avec Bacchus   4'

> Durand

Bacchus et Ariane, op.43: Suite No.2 <1930>   21'

3[1.2/pic2.pic1] 3[1.2.Eh] 3[1.2.bcl] 3[1.2.cbn] — 4 4 3 1 — tmp+4 — 2hp — cel — str
perc: sd, tambn, tri, cym, bd, tamtam
Act II of the ballet.
Prélude: Le sommeil d'Ariane (Ariadne's sleep)   3'
Reveil d'Ariane (Ariadne's awakening)   3'
Bacchus danse seul (Bacchus dances alone)   2'
Le baiser (The kiss)   3'
Danse d'Ariane (Dance of Ariadne)   4'
Danse d'Ariane et Bacchus (Dance of Ariadne and Bacchus)   1'
Bacchanale   4'
Le couronnement d'Ariane (The coronation of Ariadne)   1'

> Durand

Concerto for Small Orchestra, op.34 (Concert pour petit orchestre) <1926–1927>   12'

2[1.2/pic] 2 2 — 2 1 0 0 — tmp — str
I. Allegro   3'
II. Andante   6'
III. Presto   3'

> Durand

Concerto, Piano, op.36, G major <1927>   18'

2[1.2/pic] 2[1.Eh] 2 2 — 2 2 0 0 — tmp+3 — str
perc: sd, tri, cym, bd
I. Allegro   4'
II. Adagio   9'
III. Finale: Allegro con spirito   5'

> Durand

Évocations, op.15, no.1: Les dieux dans l'ombre des cavernes <1910–1911>   15'

3[1.2.3/pic] 3[1.2.Eh] 3[1.2.bcl] 3[1.2.cbn] — 4 3 3 1 — tmp+4 — 2hp — str
perc: sd, tri, tamtam, cym, bd, td

> Durand   Kalmus   Luck's

Évocations, op.15, no.2: La ville rose <1910–1911>   13'

3[1.2.3/pic] 3[1.2.Eh] 3[1.2.bcl] 3[1.2.cbn] — 4 3 3 1 — tmp+3 — 2hp — str
perc: bd, cym, sus cym, tri, glock

> Durand   Kalmus

Évocations, op.15, no.3: Aux bords du fleuve sacré <1910–1911>   18'

solos ATBar   chorus
3[1.2.3/pic] 3[1.2.Eh] 3[1.2.bcl] 3[1.2.cbn] — 4 3 3 1 — tmp+2 — 2hp — cel[played by perc] — str
perc: tri, cym, sd, sus cym, bd, tamtam, cel[played by perc]

> Durand   Kalmus   Luck's

Fanfare pour un sacre païen (Fanfare for a Pagan Rite) <1921>   2'

0 0 0 0 — 4 4 3 0 — tmp — [no str]

> Durand

Le festin de l'araignée, op.17 (The Spider's Feast): Symphonic Fragments <1912–1913>   16'

2[1.2/pic] 2[1.2/Eh] 2 2 — 2 2 0 0 — tmp+1 — hp — cel — str
perc: sd, cym, bd; tri[played by tmp or cel]

> Durand   Kalmus   Luck's

Le marchand de sable qui passe (The Sand Vendor Passing By) <1908>   19'

1 0 1 0 — 1 0 0 0 — hp — str
Prelude   *4'*
Scene   *4'*
Interlude and Scene   *4'*
Scene finale   *7'*

Eschig	Kalmus	Luck's

Padmâvatî, op.18: Suite No.1 <1913–1918>   17'

solo tenor & baritone
4[1.2/pic2.3/pic1.afl] 4[1.2.3.Eh] 4[1.2.Ebcl.bcl] 4[1.2.3.cbn] — 4 4 3
1 — tmp+4 — 2hp — cel — str
perc: bd, sd, tambn, tri, tamtam, cym
Parts cued for performance without afl, ob3, Ebcl.

Durand

Padmâvatî, op.18: Suite No.2 <1913–1918>   14'

4[1.2/pic2.3/pic1.afl] 4[1.2.3.Eh] 4[1.2.Ebcl.bcl] 4[1.2.3.cbn] — 4 4 3
1 — tmp+4 — 2hp — cel — str
perc: bd, sd, tambn, tri, tamtam, cym
Parts cued for performance without afl, ob3, Ebcl.

Durand

Petite suite, op.39 <1929>   13'

2[1.2/pic] 2 2 2 — 2 2 0 0 — tmp+3 — str
perc: sd, tri, cym, bd, tambn, cast
I.   Aubade   *3'*
II. Pastorale   *7'*
III. Mascarade   *3'*

Durand

Pour un fête de printemps, op.22 <1920>   12'

3[1.2.pic] 3[1.2.Eh] 2 3 — 4 2 3 1 — tmp+2 — hp — str
perc: tri, tambn, cym, bd

Durand	Kalmus

Rapsodie flamande, op.56 <1936>   9'

3[1.2.pic] 3[1.2.Eh] 3[1.2.bcl] 3[1.2.cbn] — 4 3 3 1 — tmp+3 — hp
— str
perc: tri, sd, tamtam, field dr, tambn, cym, bd

Durand

Sinfonietta, op.52 <1934>   8'

str
I.   Allegro molto   *3'*
II. Andante   *2'*
III. Allegro   *3'*

Durand

Suite in F, op.33 <1926>   15'

3[1.2/pic.pic] 3[1.2.Eh] 3[1.2.bcl] 3 — 4 4 3 1 — tmp+3 — hp —
cel[played by perc] — str
perc: sd, xyl, tri, tamtam, tambn, cym, bd, cel[played by perc]
I.   Prélude   *4'*
II. Sarabande   *6'*
III. Gigue   *5'*

Durand

Symphony No.2, op.23, B-flat <1919–1921>   38'

3[1.2.3/pic] 3[1.2.Eh] 3[1.2.bcl] 4[1.2.3.cbn] — 4 4 3 1 — tmp+3 —
2hp — cel — str
perc: tri, tamtam, cym, bd, tambn
I.   Lent - Modérément animé   *15'*
II. Modéré   *8'*
III. Très lent - Modéré   *15'*

Durand

Symphony No.3, op.42, G minor <1929–1930>   23'

3[1.2/pic2.3/pic1] 3[1.2.Eh] 3[1.2.bcl] 3[1.2.cbn] — 4 4 3 1 — tmp+(
— 2hp — cel[played by perc] — str
perc: tri, tambn, sd, tamtam, cym, bd, cel[played by perc]
I.   Allegro vivo   *6'*
II. Adagio   *8'*
III. Vivace   *3'*
IV. Allegro con spirito   *6'*

Durand

Symphony No.4, op.53, A major <1934>   20'

3[1.2.pic] 3[1.2.Eh] 3[1.2.bcl] 3[1.2.cbn] — 4 4 3 1 — tmp+3 — hp
— str
perc: sd, tri, tamtam, cym, bd
I.   Lento - Allego con brio   *6'*
II. Lento molto   *7'*
III. Allegro scherzando   *3'*
IV. Allegro molto   *4'*

Durand

Rózsa, Miklós   1907 - 1995

(b Budapest, 18 April 1907; d Los Angeles, 27 July 1995). American composer of
Hungarian birth

Concerto, Violoncello, op.32 <1968>   30'

2[incl pic] 2[incl Eh] 2[incl Ebcl] 2 — 4 3 3 1 — tmp+3 — hp — cel
— str

Breitkopf

The Jungle Book <1942>   30'

narrator, solo contralto
2[1/pic.2/pic] 2[1/Eh.2opt] 2[1.2/asx] 2[1/cbn.2opt] — 4[3, 4 opt] 2 2
1[opt] — tmp+3 — hp — pf/cel — str
perc: chimes, glock, vib, tri, cym, tomtom, sd, bd, gong, Indian cym
From the film score for *The Jungle Book*, based on the book by Rudyard
Kipling.

Broude Bros.

Theme, Variations & Finale, op.13 <1933; rev 1943, 1966>   19'

2[1.2/pic] 2 2 2[1.2/cbn] — 4 2 3 1[ad lib] — tmp+2 — hp — cel ad
lib — str
perc: sd, bd, cym, tri, tamtam, xyl
The above information represents the original 1933 version. The 1966
revision is available from Peters.

Eulenburg

Three Hungarian Sketches, op.14a <1938; rev 1958>   20'

2[1.2/pic] 2 2 2 — 4 2 3 0 — tmp+3 — hp — cel — str
perc: sd, bd, cym, tri, glock
Originally published as *Capriccio, pastorale e danza*, op.14, 1938.
I.   Capriccio   *5'*
II. Pastorale   *7'*
III. Danza   *8'*

Eulenburg

Rubbra, Edmund   1901 - 1986

(b Northampton, 23 May 1901; d Gerrards Cross, 14 Feb 1986). English

Concerto, Viola, op.75, A major <1952>   25'

2 2 2 2 — 4 2 3 1 — tmp+1 — hp — str
perc: sd, tri
I.   Introduzione quasi una fantasia   *10'*
II. Molto vivace   *5'*
III. Collana Musicale: Andante moderato   *10'*

Lengnick

Festival Overture, op.62 <1947>   8'

2 2 2 2 — 4 2 3 1 — tmp+1 — str

> Lengnick

Improvisation for Violin & Orchestra, op.89 <1956>   12'

2 2[1.2/Eh] 2 2 — 2 2 0 0 — tmp+1 — hp — cel — str

> Lengnick

Rubinstein, Anton   1829-1894

(b Vïkhvatintsï on the Dnestr, nr Balta, Ukraine [Podoliya], 16/28 Nov 1829; d Peterhof [now Petrodvorets], nr St Petersburg, 8/20 Nov 1894). Russian

Concerto, Piano, No.3, op.45, G major <1858>   31'

2 2 2 2 — 2 2 0 0 — tmp — str
I. Moderato assai   *11'*
II. Moderato   *7'*
III. Allegro non troppo   *13'*

> C. Fischer   Kalmus

Concerto, Piano, No.4, op.70, D minor <1864; rev 1872>   29'

3[1.2.pic] 2 2 2 — 2 2 0 0 — tmp — str
I. Moderato   *11'*
II. Andante   *9'*
III. Allegro   *9'*

> Kalmus   Simrock

Concerto, Violoncello, No.2, op.96, D minor <1874>   18'

2 2 2 2 — 2 2 0 0 — tmp — str

> Kalmus

Melody in F, op.3, no.1 <1852>   5'

solo violoncello
2 2 2 2 — 2 0 0 0 — tmp — str
Originally for piano; arr. Vincent d'Indy.

> Kalmus

Symphony No.1, op.40, F major <1850>   37'

3[1.2.pic] 2 2 2 — 4 2 3 0 — tmp — str
Allegro con fuoco   *10'*
Allegro   *7'*
Moderato con moto   *11'*
Allegro   *9'*

> Kahnt

SYMPHONY NO.2, OP.42, C MAJOR (Océan)

This symphony, composed in 1851, was revised twice, each time by adding movements and, confusingly, changing certain of the tempo headings and even the meter signatures, not to mention the order of movements!

Two movements were added in 1863, and yet another in 1880. A chart with color graphics may be found online at www.groups.yahoo.com/group/OrchLibInfo/files/David%20Daniels%20updates.

Symphony No.2, op.42, C major [1851 version]   39'
(Océan) <1851>

3[1.2.pic] 2 2 2 — 4 2 3 1 — tmp — str
This version of the symphony is available online at IMSLP.org.
I. Allegro maestoso (3/2, C major)   *12'*
II. Adagio non tanto (4/4, E minor)   *9'*
III. Allegro (2/4, G major)   *5'*
IV. Adagio (4/4, C minor), Allegro con fuoco (2/2, C major)   *13'*

Symphony No.2, op.42, C major [1863 version]   54'
(Océan) <1851; rev 1863>

3[1.2.pic] 2 2 2 — 4 2 3 1 — tmp — hp — str
Harp only in mvt 2.
I. Allegro maestoso (3/2, C major)   *12'*
II. Adagio (3/4, D major, added 1863)   *9'*
III. Allegro (2/4, G major)   *5'*
IV. Adagio (8/8, E minor, originally mvt 2)   *9'*
V. Scherzo: Presto (3/4, F major, added 1863)   *6'*
VI. Adagio (8/8, C min), Allegro con fuoco (2/2, C maj) (orig. mvt 4)   *13'*

> mph

Symphony No.2, op.42, C major [1880 version]   73'
(Océan) <1851; rev 1863, 1880>

3[1.2.pic] 2 2 2 — 4 2 3 1 — tmp+1 — hp — str
perc: bd
Bass drum only in mvt 2; harp only in mvt 3.
I. Moderato assai (3/2, C major)   *12'*
II. Lento assai (4/4, A min), Con moto moderato (2/2, A min, added 1880)   *19'*
III. Andante (3/4, D major, added 1863)   *9'*
IV. Allegro (2/4, G major, originally mvt 3)   *5'*
V. Andante (8/8, E minor, originally mvt 2)   *9'*
VI. Scherzo: Allegro (3/4, F major, added 1863)   *6'*
VII. Andante (8/8, C min), Allegro con fuoco (2/2, C maj) orig mvt 4   *13'*

> Kalmus

Symphony No.3, op.56, A major <1854–1855>   38'

2 2 2 2 — 4 2 0 0 — tmp — str
1. Allegro risoluto   *11'*
2. Adagio: Moderato   *8'*
3. Scherzo: Allegro vivace assai *7'*
4. Finale: Allegro maestoso   *12'*

> Fleisher

Symphony No.4, op.95, D Minor (Symphonie   65'
dramatique) <1874>

3[1.2.pic] 2 2 2 — 2 2 3 0 — tmp — str
1. Lento; Allegro moderato   *22'*
2. Presto   *15'*
3. Adagio   *15'*
4. Largo; Allegro con fuoco *13'*

> Fleisher

Symphony No.5, op.107, G minor <1880>   38'

2 2 2 2 — 4 2 0 0 — tmp — str
I. Moderato assaid   *11'*
II. Allegro non troppo *7'*
III. Andante   *9'*
IV. Allegro vivace   *11'*

Rudow, Vivian Adelberg   1936-

(b Baltimore, MD, 1 Apr 1936). American

> *Many of the works of this composer exist in several different versions. The best source for a detailed grasp of her diverse output is the website: www.vivianadelbergrudow.com.*

Dark Waters <1984>   8'

solo treble instrument (trumpet or any other)
2[1/afl/pic.2] 2[1/crot.Eh] 2[1/crot.2/bcl] 1[1/tri] — 1[1/slide whistle] 0 0 0 — 2perc — pf — 1vn, 1vc, 1db [*or* sections of vn & vc; no va]
perc: sd, tamtam, gong, glock, vib, chimes, crot, belltree, 3sus cym, 2bd, 5tomtoms, 4vc bows, slide whistle[played by hn]
Crotales are all bowed; conductor also plays a crotale with vc bow.
Optional visuals: performers sway; colored lights.
See also the composer's *Journey of Waters*.

> Hollins

Dark Waters of Elba <2005>   8'

solo trumpet
2 2 2 2 — 2 1 0 0 — tmp+1 — pf — str
perc: sus cym, tamtam, tri, cym
Optional visuals include directions for musicians to sway in certain
designated passages, and colored lights (color and location within the
music specified).
    May be performed with voices (solo or choral) replacing the trumpet
melody, under the title *Journey of Waters II*.

> Hollins

Dark Waters of the Chesapeake <2010>   9'

solo trumpet
2 2 2 2 — 2 1 0 0 — 2perc — pf — str
perc: vib, chimes, glock, sd, crot, 3szl cym, 2bd, 2tamtam, 5tomtom
May be performed separately or, together with *Go Green*, under the title
Earth Day Suite.
    Optional visuals include directions for musicians to sway in certain
designated passages, and colored lights (color and location within the
music specified).

> Hollins

Fanfare for My Hero in the Pinstriped Suit <1993>   4'

3[1.2.pic] 3 3 3[1.2.cbn] — 4 4 3 1 — tmp+3 — pf, kybd, or org —
str
perc: bd, cym, set, tri, tambn, chimes; tmp plays: vib, glock
2 versions: (1) Professional orchestra (as above) (2) Community orchestra
(only 3tp, in a somewhat lower tessitura).

> Hollins

Force III <1979>   13'

3[1.2.3/afl/pic] 3[1.2.3/Eh] 3[1.2.3/asx/opt tsx] 3[1.2.3/cbn] — 4 3 3
1 — tmp+4 — str
perc: bd, cym, rototom, tamtam, xyl, vib, chimes, crot, whip, marac, claves, cast,
templeblks, 6sus cym, 3small gongs, 5woodblks, anvil, 2sd, 2vc bows, 2glock,
8tomtoms

> Hollins

Go Green! (The Ocean Sings) <2010>   5'

solo flute
1 2 2 2 — 2 2 0 0 — 2perc — pf[opt] — str
perc: vib, bd, set, 2szl cym

> Hollins

Journey of Waters <1984>   8'

medium voice also playing crotales (bowed) & belltree
Identical to the composer's *Dark Waters*, *q.v.*, except that solo is sung
rather than played by a treble instrument. Singer also replaces one
percussionist (crotales & belltree).

> Hollins

Spirit of America <1999; rev 2006>   10'

chorus of children or adults
2[1/pic.2] 2 2 2 — 4 3 3 1 — tmp+2 — hp — str
perc: cym, 2szl cym, set, 3tomtom, tri, vib, chimes, marktree, congas, 5 metal
surfaces (pots, pipes, etc.); timpanist plays claves, chimes & breaking glass
Interactive options for audience & musicians: shout, applaud, whistle,
make noise, stamp feet, movement.
    2 versions: one without chorus.
    Original title *Urbo Turbo* (for "urban turbulence")

> Rudow

Weeping Rocker III <1993>   6'

chorus SATB
2 2 2 2 — 2 2 2 1 — 2perc — str
perc: sd, tambn, tamtam, glock, xyl, vib, chimes, crot, templeblks, ratch, guiro,
3sus cym, bd/ped, cello bow; played by members of the chorus: sus cym, tri,
windchimes, marac

> Hollins

Ruggles, Carl   1876-1971

(b East Marion, MA, 11 March 1876; d Bennington, VT, 24 Oct 1971). American

Angels <1920–1921; rev 1938>   3'

0 0 0 0 — 0 4 3 0 — [no str]
Although scored for muted brass, it was originally suggested that this
composition could be played by any seven instruments of equal timbre;
however this possibility was withdrawn in the 3rd published version
(1960).

> AME

Evocations <1941; rev (orchd) 1942>   12'

4[1.2.3.4/pic] 4[1.2.3.Eh] 4[1/Ebcl.2.3.bcl] 4[1.2.3.cbn] — 4 3 3 1 —
tmp+1 — pf — str
Originally *Evocations No.2*, the second of four piano pieces by this title;
orchestrated by the composer.

> AME

Men and Mountains (original 1924 version) <1924>   10'

2[1.pic] 2[1.Eh] 1 1 — 2 2 1 0 — 1perc — pf — 2vn, 2va, 2vc, db
I. Men   3'
II. Lilacs   3'
III. Marching Mountains 4'

> AME

Men and Mountains (1936 version for large orchestra)   10'
<1924; rev 1936; 1941>

3[1.2.3/pic] 3[1.2.Eh] 3[1.2.bcl] 3[1.2.cbn] — 4 3 3 1 — tmp+2 — pf
— str
perc: cym, td, bd, sus cym
I. Men, A Rhapsodic Proclamation 3'
II. Lilacs   3'
III. Marching Mountains   4'

> AME

Organum <1944–1947>   8'

3[1.2.pic] 3[1.2.Eh] 4[1.2.Ebcl.bcl] 3[1.2.cbn] — 4 3 3 1 — tmp+1 —
pf — str
perc: cym

> AME

Portals <1925; rev 1929, 1941, 1952-53>   6'

str
Originally for 13 solo strings; then repeatedly revised for string orchestra

> AME

Sun-Treader <1926–1931>   15'

5[1.2.3.4/pic.5/pic] 5[3ob, 2Eh] 5[1.2.3.Ebcl.bcl] 4[1.2.3.cbn] — 6 5 5
1 — tenor tuba — tmp+1 — 2hp[1part] — str
perc: cym, 2sus cym

> AME

Rush, Loren   1935-

(b Los Angeles, 23 Aug 1935). American

The Cloud Messenger <1966–1970>   18'

opt group of 16 sopranos
4[1.2.3/pic.4/pic/afl] 4[1.2.3.Eh] 4[1.2.Ebcl.bcl] 4[1.2.3.cbn] — 4
4[1.2.3.flug] 4 1 — gtr[ampd], elec bass — 6perc — 2hp —
hpsd[ampd], cel, pf — str

> Jobert

Song and Dance <1975>   22'

5[1.2.afl1.afl2.pic] 4[1.2.Eh1.Eh2] 4[1.2.Ebcl1.Ebcl2] 2 — 6 4 2 1 —
quadraphonic tape — 5perc — hp — pf, cel — str

> Presser

Rush, Tracey Ryan   1955-

(b Milwaukee, WI, 10 May 1955). American

Angels in the Snow <1998>   4'

solos SATB   chorus SATB, 2-part treble choir
2 2 2 2 — 4 3 3 1 — tmp+3 — hp — str

> Wendel

Spirit of Freedom <1997>   4'

2 2 2 2 — 4 3 3 1 — tmp+5 — str

> Fountain Park

Russo, William   1928-2003

(b Chicago, 25 June 1928; d Chicago, 11 Jan 2003). American

Street Music; A Blues Concerto <1975>   31'

solo harmonica & piano (may be played by one performer)
3[1.2.pic] 3 3 3 — 4 4 3 1 — tmp+3 — str
perc: sd, bd, cym, xyl, sus cym, marim, finger cym, 3tambn
Harmonica and piano soloist(s) have improvised solos as well as
written-out passages. 9 members of the main orchestra constitute a "small
ensemble" (ob, cl, bn, tp, tbn, 1perc, vn, vc, db).
> *I. Slow*   8'
> *II. quarter-note = 108*   5'
> *III. Very slow*   9'
> *IV. quarter-note = 108*   9'

> Southern

Symphony No.2, op.32 (Titans) <1958>   20'

4[1.2.3.4/pic] 4[1.2.3.Eh] 4[1.2.3.bcl] 4[1.2.3.cbn] — 4 5 4 1 —
tmp+2 — hp — pf — str
One of the trumpets (marked "solo trumpet") very high and jazzy.

> Southern

Rutter, John   1945-

(b London, 1945). English

Gloria (original version) <1974>   17'

chorus SATB
0 0 0 0 — 0 4 3 1 — tmp+2 — org — [no str]
perc: cym, sus cym, sd, glock, xyl
This work was arranged for full orchestra in 1988; see next entry.
> Brief soli for SSA.
> *I. Gloria in excelsis Deo*   5'
> *II. Domine Deus*   7'
> *III. Quoniam tu solus sanctus*   5'

> Oxford

Gloria (full orchestra version) <1974; rev 1988>   17'

chorus SATB
2 2 2 2 — 4 3 3 1 — tmp+2 — hp — str
perc: cym, sus cym, sd, tambn, glock, xyl
Accompaniment originally for organ, brass & percussion; orchestrated by
the composer. See previous entry.
> Brief soli for SSA.
> *I. Gloria in excelsis Deo*   5'
> *II. Domine Deus*   7'
> *III. Quoniam tu solus sanctus*   5'

> Oxford

Magnificat <1990>   37'

soprano or mezzo-soprano   chorus
2 2 2 2 — 4 3 3 1 — tmp+2 — hp — str
perc: glock, sd, cym, sus cym, tambn, bongos
A version using chamber orchestra is also available:
    1 1 1 1 — 1 0 0 0 — tmp+1 or 2 — hp — str [min 2.2.2.1.1]
> *1. Magnificat anima mea*   7'
> *2. Of a Rose, a Lovely Rose*   5'
> *3. Quia fecit mihi magna*   5'
> *4. Et misericordia*   5'
> *5. Fecit potentiam*   4'
> *6. Esurientes*   6'
> *7. Gloria Patri*   5'

> Oxford

Shepherd's Pipe Carol   3'

chorus
1[fl/pic] 0 1 1 — 2 0 0 0 — str

> Oxford

Suite antique <1979>   17'

solo flute
hpsd — str
> *1. Prelude*   3'
> *2. Ostinato*   2'
> *3. Aria*   3'
> *4. Waltz*   3'
> *5. Chanson*   3'
> *6. Rondeau*   3'

> Oxford

Suite for Strings   12'

str
> *1. A-Roving*   3'
> *2. I Have a Bonnet Trimmed With Blue* 3'
> *3. O Waly Waly*   4'
> *4. Dashing Away*   3'

> Goodmusic

S

Saariaho, Kaija
1952-

(b Helsinki, 14 Oct 1952). Finnish

Aile du songe; Concerto for Flute & Orchestra (Wing of the Dream) <2001>
18'

solo flute
tmp+3 — hp — cel — str[14.12.10.8.8]
perc: crot, marac, gong, glock, tamtam, tambn, Chinescym, claves, bd, xyl, chimes, vib, 3windchimes[glass, metal & shell], marim, sandblks, framedrum, 3sus cym, 2tri, 2guiro

A cadenza may be inserted, improvised or not (a written-out cadenza is supplied). The performer is encouraged to extend flute sounds with the voice; instructions are given for these extended techniques.

I. Aérienne	
Prélude	3'
Jardin des oiseaux	4'
D'autres rives	4'
II. Terrestre	
L'oiseau dansant	6'
Oiseau, un satelite infime de notre orbite planétaire	5'

Chester

Asteroid 4179: Toutatis <2005>
4'

3[1.2.3/pic] 3 3 2[1.2/cbn] — 6 4 3 1 — 2tmp+3 — hp — cel — str
perc: crot, glock, tamtam, sus cym, vib

Chester

D'om le vrai sens <2010>
30'

solo clarinet
2[1/pic.2/afl] 2[1.2/Eh] 3[1.2/Ebcl.bcl] 1[bn/cbn] — 4 1 0 0 — tmp+4 — hp — cel — str
perc: crot, glock, vib, marim, bd, chimes, marktree, xyl, tamtam, guiro, td, frame drum, 3windchimes[glass, wood, shell], 3tomtom, 4sus cym, 2tri

The soloist plays from different positions within the hall and on the stage. In the last mvt, members of the violin sections, in addition to the soloist, walk slowly among the audience while playing.

The enigmatic title of this work is an anagram of the title of the last mvt. The various mvt titles refer to a celebrated series of six medieval tapestries, known as *La Dame à la Licorne* (*The Lady and the Unicorn*).

I. L'Ouïe (Hearing)	7'
II. La Vue (Sight)	3'
III. L'Odorat (Smell)	7'
IV. Le Toucher (Touch)	3'
V. Le Goût (Taste)	4'
VI. A mon seul Désir (According to My Desire Alone)	6'

Chester

Forty Heartbeats for Orchestra <1998>
var

1[fl/pic] 1 1 1 — 2 1 1 1 — tmp+2 — hp — pf — str
perc: crot, vib, xyl, tri, templeblks, tamtam, bd, 2sus cym, metalplate

12 fragments of 1 page each, which may be played in any order; one or more pages can appear several times, but all pages must be played at leas once.

Composed to mark the 40th birthdays of fellow Finnish composers Esa-Pekka [Salonen] and Magnus [Lindberg].

Five beats for surrounding cities
First beat for being born
Two beats for two daughters
Three beats for three composers
Five beats for surrounding nature
Five beats for life force
Four beats for two times two sisters
Four beats for three friends
One beat for a good night's sleep with one beat in slow motion
One beat for life in us
Three beats for two instruments
Five beats for life surrounding us

Chester

Laterna Magica <2009>
20

3[1.2.3/pic/afl] 3 3 2[1.2/cbn] — 6 4 3 1 — 2tmp+3 — hp — cel, pf — str
perc: crot, xyl, glock, chimes, Chinescym, marktree, td, vib, marim, 2glass windchimes, bamboo windchimes, shell windchimes, 5sus cym, 2tomtom, 2tri, 2crot, 3tamtam, 2bd

Chester

Lumière et Pesanteur <2009>
6

3[1.2.3/pic] 2 2 2[1.2/cbn] — 4 2 2 1 — tmp+3 — hp — cel — str
perc: tamtam, crot, vib, bd, marim, glass windchimes, 3gong[G#,A,B]

Chester

Nymphea Reflection <2001>
22

str[min 7.6.6.4.2]

In mvt 6 the musicians are asked to whisper a poem by Arseniy Tarkovsky in English, French or German. Individual players may choose different languages if they wish.

I. Sostenuto	4'
II. Feroce	4'
III. Dolcissimo	4'
IV. Lento espressivo	3'
V. Furioso	4'
VI. Misterioso	3'

Chester

Oltra mar (Across the Sea) <1998–1999>
22

chorus
4[1.2.3/afl.4/pic] 4 4 4 — 4 4 4 1 — tmp+3 — hp — pf — str[16.14.12.14.8]

"Seven Preludes for the New Millennium." French texts in mvts 2, 4, 6; chorus sings abstract vowels and consonants in mvts 1, 3, 5, 7.

I. Départ	5'
II. Amour	3'
III. Vagues	2'
IV. Temps	4'
V. Souvenir de vagues	1'
VI. Mort	4'
VII. Arrivée	3'

Chester

Orion <2002>
25

4[1.2.3/afl/pic.4/pic] 4[1.2.3.4/Eh] 4 4[1.2.3.4/cbn] — 6 4 3 1 — 2tmp+4 — 2hp — pf, org — str
perc: bd, tri, tamtam, glock, xyl, marim, vib, chimes, crot, belltree, bullroarer, 2Chinescym, 2bowlgong, 4tomtom, 3sus cym, 2windchimes[glass, shell]

I. Memento mori	7'
II. Winter Sky	9'
III. Hunter	6'

Chester

Quatre instants (Four Moments) <2003>   22'

solo soprano
2[1.2/pic/afl] 2 2 2[1.2/cbn] — 2 0 0 0 — 2perc — hp — cel — str
perc: crot, marim, tamtam, vib, tri, glass windchimes, 2sus cym
Originally for soprano & piano; arranged by the composer for soprano & orchestra (2003).

I. Attente (Longing)	5'
II. Douleur (Torment)	6'
III. Parfum de l'instant (Perfume of the Instant)	4'
IV. Résonances (Echoes)	7'

Chester

Song for Betty <2001>   4'

4[1.2.3/pic.afl] 3[1.2/ob d'am.3/Eh] 3 3 — 4 2 3 1 — tmp+4 — hp — pf — str[14.12.10.8.6]
perc: crot, vib, marim, glock, tri, tamtam, bd, 2sus cym
Arrangement of the last mvt from the composer's opera L'amour de loin.

Chester

Saint-Georges, Joseph Boulogne   1745-1799

(b Baillif, Guadeloupe, 25 Dec 1745; d Paris, 9 June 1799). French

Concerto, Violin, No.1, G major <1773>   16'

0 2 0 0 — 2 0 0 0 — str
Ed. Dominique-René de Lerma. This work was also published as "op.10."

Peer

Symphonie concertante, op.6, no.1, C major <1775>   12'

solos: 2 violins; or 1 violin & 1 violoncello
0 2 0 0 — 2 0 0 0 — str
Score in Barry S. Brook, ed., The Symphony 1720-1840, Series D—Volume IV—Score 7. Artaria edition in progress.

Artaria

Symphonie concertante, op.10, no.2, A major <1779>   10'

solos: 2 violins & viola
0 2 0 0 — 2 0 0 0 — str

Artaria

Symphonie concertante, op.13, G major <1782>

2 solo violins
str
Originally published as op.12, no.2.
   Ed. J. F. Paillard.

Costallat

Symphony No.1, op.11, no.1, G major <1779>   13'

0 2 0 0 — 2 0 0 0 — str
Ed. Dominique-René de Lerma.
   This work believed to be spurious.

1. Allegro	5'
2. Andante	5'
3. Allegro assai	3'

Peer

Saint-Saëns, Camille   1835-1921

(b Paris, 9 Oct 1835; d Algiers, 16 Dec 1921). French

Africa, op.89 <1891>   11'

solo piano
2 2 2 2 — 2 2 3 0 — tmp+1 — str
perc: tri, cym

| Durand | Kalmus | Luck's |

Allegro appassionato, Piano & Orchestra, op.70 <1884>   7'

2 2 2 2 — 2 2 0 0 — str

| Durand | C. Fischer | Kalmus | Luck's |

Allegro appassionato, Violoncello & Orchestra, op.43 <1873>   4'

2 2 2 2 — 2 0 0 0 — str

| Durand | Kalmus | Luck's |

Le carnaval des animaux (Carnival of the Animals) <1886; rev Le cygne added 1887>   21'

2 solo pianos
1[1/pic] 0 1 0 — 1perc — glass harmonica[glock or cel] — str 5t
perc: xyl
Breitkopf ed. Peter Jost; Kalmus ed. Clinton F. Nieweg & Nancy M. Bradburd.

   Often performed with full string sections. The part labeled "harmonica" was originally intended for glass harmonica; it is generally played on glockenspiel, or occasionally celesta.

   Narrations are often used; humorous verses for that purpose have been supplied by various writers, including Ogden Nash (available from Brown), Peter Schickele (Presser), Loriot (in German, French, & English; Breitkopf), Charles & Denise Kirkland (Charles.Kirkland@valpo.edu), Bruce Adolphe (bruce.adolphe@gmail.com), and Jack Prelutsky (Random House). Other individuals and ensembles have their own proprietary verses (e.g., Martin Bookspan, or The Mum Puppet Theatre) which may be used only by those performers. Still others have been published as children's books (e.g., John Lithgow's scenario with verses for the New York City Ballet).

   Although the music is in the public domain, none of the verses are; permissions must be negotiated in each case with the copyright holder.

1. Intro et Marche royale du lion (Intro & Royal March of the Lion)	2'
2. Poules et coqs (Hens and Roosters)	1'
3. Hémiones—Animaux véloces (Wild Donkeys—Fleet Animals)	1'
4. Tortues (Tortoises)	2'
5. L'éléphant	1'
6. Kangourous (Kangaroos)	1'
7. Aquarium	2'
8. Personnages à longues oreilles (People with Long Ears)	1'
9. Le coucou au fond des bois (Cuckoo in the Depths of the Woods)	2'
10. Volière (Aviary)	1'
11. Pianistes (Pianists)	1'
12. Fossiles (Fossils)	1'
13. Le cygne (The Swan)	3'
14. Final (Finale)	2'

| Breitkopf | Durand | Kalmus | Luck's |

Le carnaval des animaux (Carnival of the Animals): Le cygne (The Swan) <1887>   5'

solo violoncello
0 0 0 0 — 2 0 0 0 — pf or hp — str
Orchestrated by Paul Vidal (1863-1931) for use as a ballet presentation, in which case it is usually taken much more slowly than in the original context.
   The 2hn are not strictly essential, all their notes being doubled in the strings.

Payne

Christmas Oratorio

see his: Oratorio de Noël, op.12

Concerto, Piano, No.1, op.17, D major <1858>   27'

2 2 2 2 — 4 2 0 0 — tmp — str

I. Andante - Allegro assai	12'
II. Andante sostenuto quasi adagio	8'
III. Allegro con fuoco	7'

| Durand | C. Fischer |

Concerto, Piano, No.2, op.22, G minor <1868>   24'

2 2 2 2 — 2 2 0 0 — tmp+1[opt] — str
perc: cym[opt]
The extra percussionist would be required if 3 optional cymbal notes in
last movement are to be played.
 Kalmus ed. Clinton F. Nieweg & Nancy M. Bradburd.

I. Andante sostenuto	11'
II. Allegro scherzando	6'
III. Presto	7'

| Durand | Kalmus | Luck's |

Concerto, Piano, No.3, op.29, E-flat major <1869>   30'

2 2 2 2 — 2 2 3 0 — tmp — str

I. Moderato assai	14'
II. Andante	8'
III. Allegro non troppo	8'

| Durand | Kalmus |

Concerto, Piano, No.4, op.44, C minor <1875>   27'

2 2 2 2 — 2 2 3 0 — tmp — str
Kalmus ed. Nancy M. Bradburd.

| I. Allegro moderato - Andante | 13' |
| II. Allegro vivace - Andante - Allegro | 14' |

| Durand | Kalmus |

Concerto, Piano, No.5, op.103, F major (Egyptian) <1896>   29'

3[1.2.pic] 2 2 2 — 4 2 3 0 — tmp — str
perc: tamtam[played by tmp]

I. Allegro animato	11'
II. Andante	12'
III. Molto allegro	6'

| Durand | Kalmus |

Concerto, Violin, No.1, op.20, A major (Konzertstück; Concert Piece) <1859>   11'

2 2 2 2 — 2 2 0 0 — tmp — str

I. Allegro	4'
II. Andante espressivo	2'
III. Tempo I	5'

| Kalmus | Luck's |

Concerto, Violin, No.2, op.58, C major <1858>   28'

2 2 2 2 — 2 2 3 0 — tmp — hp — str

I. Allegro moderato e maestoso	13'
II. Andante espressivo	8'
III. Allegro scherzando quasi allegretto	7'

| Durand | Kalmus |

Concerto, Violin, No.3, op.61, B minor <1880>   29'

2[1.2/pic] 2 2 — 2 2 3 0 — tmp — str
Kalmus ed. Clinton F. Nieweg & Nancy M. Bradburd.

I. Allegro non troppo	9'
II. Andantino quasi allegretto	9'
III. Molto moderato e maestoso; Allegro non troppo	11'

| Durand | Kalmus | Luck's |

Concerto, Violoncello, No.1, op.33, A minor <1872>   19'

2 2 2 2 — 2 2 0 0 — tmp — str
Kalmus ed. Clinton F. Nieweg & Nancy M. Bradburd.

I. Allegro non troppo	5'
II. Allegretto con moto	5'
III. Allegro non troppo	9'

| Durand | Kalmus | Luck's |

Concerto, Violoncello, No.2, op.119, D minor <1902>   17'

2 2 2 2 — 4 2 0 0 — tmp — str

| I. Allegro moderato e maestoso; Andante sostenuto | 11' |
| II. Allegro non troppo | 6' |

| Durand | Kalmus | Luck's |

Coronation March

see his: Marche du couronnement, op.117

Danse macabre, op.40 <1874>   8'

3[1.2.pic] 2 2 2 — 4 2 3 1 — tmp+3 — opt hp — str
perc: xyl, bd, tri, cym
Concertmaster solo with scordatura throughout.
 Kalmus ed. Clinton F. Nieweg.

| Durand | Kalmus | Luck's |

Le déluge, op.45 (The Flood) <1875>   49'

chorus   solos SATB
3[1.2.pic] 2 2 2 — 4 4 5 3 — 2tmp+3 — 2hp — str
perc: cym, tamtam, bd
Included in the above count is the *banda* from Part 2, consisting of 2tp, 2
valve tbn, 2 tubas in Eb, tuba in Bb.

Prélude; Timo de Leo	8'
Part 1: Corruption de l'homme; Colère de Dieu; Alliance avec Noé	14'
Part 2: L'Arche; Le Déluge	9'
Part 3: La Colombe; Sortie de l'Arche; Bénédiction de Dieu	18'

| Durand | Kalmus |

Le déluge, op.45 (The Flood): Prélude <1875>   7'

str

| Kalmus |

La foi, op.130 (The Faith): Trois tableaux symphoniques <1908>   28'

3[1.2.pic] 2[1.2/Eh] 2 2 — 4 3 3 0 — tmp+3 — 2hp[1part] — harm — str
perc: crot, tamtam, tri, cym, sistres

1. Poco allegro	11'
2. Andantino	7'
3. Allegro moderato e maestoso	10'

| Durand |

Havanaise, op.83 <1887>   11'

solo violin
2 2 2 2 — 2 2 0 0 — tmp — str
Kalmus ed. Clinton F. Nieweg & Nancy M. Bradburd.

| Kalmus | Luck's |

Introduction & Rondo capriccioso, op.28 <1963>   10'

solo violin
2 2 2 2 — 2 2 0 0 — tmp — str
Kalmus ed. Clinton F. Nieweg & Nancy M. Bradburd.

| Kalmus | Luck's |

La jeunesse d'Hercule, op.50 <1877>   16'

3[1.2.pic] 2 2 2 — 4 5[2crt, 2tp, petite bugle] 3 1 — tmp+3 — 2hp[1part] — str
perc: tri, tambn, bd, cym
The 5th trumpet ("petite bugle in B-flat") sounds a minor 7th higher than
written; the part is playable on a Bb cornet.

| Durand | Kalmus | Luck's |

Marche du couronnement, op.117 (Coronation March) <1902>   8'

3[1.2.pic] 2 2 3[1.2.cbn] — 4 4 3 1 — tmp+3 — hp — str
perc: cym, bd, chimes

| Kalmus | Luck's |

Marche héroïque, op.34 <1870>   7'

3[1.2.pic] 2 2 2 — 4 2 3 1 — tmp+3 — hp — str
perc: field dr, cym, bd

C. Fischer	Kalmus	Luck's

Morceau de concert, Harp & Orchestra, op.154 <1918>   16'

2 2 2 2 — 2 2 0 0 — tmp — str

Durand	Kalmus	Luck's

Morceau de concert, Horn & Orchestra, op.94 <1887>   9'

2 2 2 2 — 0 0 3 0 — tmp — str

Durand	Kalmus	Luck's

La nuit, op.114 <1900>   10'

female chorus   solo soprano
2 2 2 2 — 4 0 0 0 — hp — str

Durand	Luck's

Odelette, op.162 <1920>   14'

solo flute
0 2 0 2 — str

Durand	Kalmus	Luck's

Oratorio de Noël, op.12 (Christmas Oratorio) <1858>   38'

chorus   solos SMzATBar
hp — org — str

1. Prelude (in the style of Seb. Bach)	3'
2. Recitative & Chorus: Et pastores errant	6'
3. Air: Expectans	4'
4. Air & Chorus: Domine, ego credidi	4'
5. Duo: Benedictus	4'
6. Chorus: Quare fremuerunt gentes?	4'
7. Trio: Tecum principium	4'
8. Quartet: Alleluia	2'
9. Quintet & Chorus: Consurge, Filia Sion	5'
10. Chorus: Tollite hostias	2'

Durand	Kalmus	Luck's	Schirmer

Orient et Occident, op.25 <1869>   6'

3[1.2.pic] 3[1.2.Eh] 3[1.2.bcl] 3[1.2.cbn] — 4 3 3 1 — tmp+4 — str
perc: tri, tambn, cym, tamtam, bd
Originally for military band; arranged for orchestra by the composer.

Durand	Kalmus	Luck's

Phaéton, op.39 <1873>   9'

3[1/pic2.2/pic3.pic1] 2 2 3[1.2.opt cbn] — 4 2 3 1 — 3tmp+3 — 2hp
— str
perc: cym, bd, tamtam [bd & tamtam could be covered by the same player]

Durand	Kalmus	Luck's

La princesse jaune, op.30: Overture <1872>   6'

2[1.2/pic] 2[1/Eh.2] 2 2 — 4 2 3 0 — tmp+1 — hp — str
perc: tri, gong[G4]

Durand	Kalmus	Luck's

Requiem, op.54 <1878>   40'

chorus   solos SATB
4 4[1.2.Eh1.Eh2] 0 4 — 4 0 4 0 — 4hp[2parts] — org — str

Requiem aeternam; Kyrie	5'
Absolve Domine	3'
Dies irae	6'
Rex tremendae	4'
Oro supplex	4'
Domine Jesu Christe	3'
Hostias et preces	2'
Sanctus	2'
Benedictus	2'
Agnus Dei	9'

Durand	Kalmus	Luck's

Rhapsodie d'Auvergne, op.73 <1884>   10'

solo piano
3[1.2.pic] 2 2 — 4 2 3 0 — tmp+1 — str
perc: tri, cym

Durand	Kalmus	Luck's

Rigaudon, op.93, no.2 <1884>   4'

2 2 2 2 — 2 2 2 0 — tmp — str
Often paired with the composer's Sarabande, op.93, no.1.

Durand	Kalmus

Romance, op.36 <1874>   5'

solo horn (or violoncello)
2 1 2 1 — str

Durand	Kalmus	Luck's

Romance, op.37 <1871>   6'

solo flute (or violin)
0 2 2 2 — 4 2 0 0 — tmp — str

Durand	Kalmus	Luck's

Romance, op.48 <1874>   7'

solo violin
1 1 1 1 — 2 0 0 0 — str

Durand	Luck's

Le rouet d'Omphale, op.31 (Omphale's Spinning Wheel)   9'
<1871>

3[1.2.pic] 2 2 3[1.2.cbn] — 4 2 3 0 — tmp+2 — hp — str
perc: sus cym, tri, bd
Cbn only doubles bn1&2 from [J] to 3 after [K]; otherwise tacet.

Durand	Kalmus	Luck's

Samson et Dalila: Bacchanale <1859–1877>   8'

3[1.2.pic] 3[1.2.Eh] 3[1.2.bcl] 3[1.2.cbn] — 4 4[2tp, 2crt] 3 1 —
tmp+4 — 2hp[1part] — str
perc: tri, cym, bd, finger cym, cast [from figure C to E only; covered by tmp]
Kalmus ed. Clinton F. Nieweg & Nancy M. Bradburd.

Durand	Kalmus	Luck's

Sarabande, op.93, no.1 <1892>   6'

str
Often paired with the composer's Rigaudon, op.93, no.2.

Durand	Kalmus

Septet, op.65 <1880>   15'

0 0 0 0 — 0 1 0 0 — pf — str 5t

Durand	Luck's

Saint-Saëns, Camille

Suite algérienne, op.60 <1880>   19'
3[1.2.pic] 2 2 2 — 4 4[2tp, 2crt] 3 1 — tmp+3 — str
perc: tambn, field dr, tri, cym, bd
   1. Prélude (En Vue d'Alger)   4'
   2. Rhapsodie mauresque   6'
   3. Rêverie du soir   5'
   4. Marche militaire française   4'

| Durand | Kalmus | Luck's |

Suite algérienne, op.60: Marche militaire française <1880>   4'
3[1.2.pic] 2 2 2 — 4 4[2tp, 2crt] 3 1 — tmp+3 — str
perc: bd, cym, field dr

| Kalmus | Luck's |

Symphony, A major <c.1850>   25'
2 2 2 2 — 2 2 0 0 — tmp — str
An early work, rediscovered and first published in 1974.
   1. Poco adagio; Allegro vivace   7'
   2. Andantino   9'
   3. Scherzo: Vivace   3'
   4. Finale: Allegro molto; Presto   6'

| EFdM |

Symphony No.1, op.2, E-flat major <1853>   29'
3[1.2.pic] 2[1/Eh.2] 3[1.2.bcl] 2 — 4 4 3 2[b sxhn, cb sxhn] — 2tmp+1 — 4hp[1part] — str
perc: cym
   I. Adagio - Allegro   9'
   II. Marche: Scherzo   4'
   III. Adagio   10'
   IV. Allegro maestoso   6'

| Durand | Kalmus |

Symphony No.2, op.55, A minor <1859>   23'
3[1.2.pic] 2[1.2/Eh] 2 2 — 2 2 0 0 — tmp — str
   I. Allegro marcato   7'
   II. Adagio   4'
   III. Scherzo presto   5'
   IV. Prestissimo   7'

| Durand | Kalmus | Luck's |

Symphony No.3, op.78, C minor (Organ Symphony) <1886>   36'
3[1.2.3/pic] 3[1.2.Eh] 3[1.2.bcl] 3[1.2.cbn] — 4 3 3 1 — tmp+2 — org, pf 4-hands — str
perc: cym, tri, bd
Kalmus edition by Nancy M. Bradburd.
   PART I
   Adagio - Allegro moderato   11'
   Poco adagio   10'
   PART II
   Allegro moderato - Presto   7'
   Maestoso - Allegro   8'

| Durand | Kalmus | Luck's |

Tarantelle, op.6 <1857>   7'
solo flute   solo clarinet
1[pic] 2 0 2 — 2 2 2 0 — tmp — str

| Durand | Kalmus | Luck's |

Wedding Cake, op.76 <1885>   6'
solo piano
str

| Durand | Kalmus | Luck's |

Salieri, Antonio   1750-1825
(b Legnago, 18 Aug 1750; d Vienna, 7 May 1825). Italian composer, mainly resident in Vienna

La grotta di Trofonio (Trofonio's Cave): Overture <1785>   7'
2 2 2 2 — 0 2 0 0 — tmp — str
Practical performing edition by Clark McAlister.

| Kalmus |

Mass, D major <1788>
chorus
0 2 0 2 — 0 4 2 0 — tmp — org — str
Ed. Jane Schatkin Hettrick.
An alternative Dona nobis pacem for chorus, 2ob & str, ends quietly.
   I. Kyrie   _'
   II. Gloria   _'
   III. Credo   _'
   IV. Sanctus   _'
   V. Benedictus   _'
   VI. Agnus Dei   _'

| A-R Editions |

Mass, D minor <1805>
solos SATB   chorus
0 2 0 2 — 0 4 2 0 — tmp — org — str
Ed. Jane Schatkin Hettrick.
   I. Kyrie   _'
   II. Gloria   _'
   III. Credo   _'
   IV. Sanctus   _'
   V. Benedictus   _'
   VI. Agnus Dei   _'

| A-R Editions |

Sinfonia, D major (Il giorno onomastico) <1775>   20'
2 2 0 2 — 2 2 0 0 — tmp — str
2nd bn is optional. Boccaccini ed. by Pietro Spada; Ricordi ed. by Renzo Sabatini.
   1. Allegro, quasi presto   5'
   2. Larghetto   5'
   3. Minuetto   3'
   4. Allegretto   7'

| Boccaccini | Ricordi |

Sinfonia, D major (Veneziana) <1778–1779>   10'
0 2 0 0 — 2 0 0 0 — str
Boccaccini ed. by Pietro Spada; Kalmus ed. by Clark McAlister; Ricordi ed. by Renzo Sabatini.
   This work is also the overture to the composer's opera buffa La scuola de' gelosi, 1779.
   1. Allegro assai   4'
   2. Andantino grazioso   3'
   3. Presto   3'

| Boccaccini | Kalmus | Ricordi |

Sallinen, Aulis   1935-
(b Salmi, 9 April 1935). Finnish

Chamber Music I, op.38 <1975>   13'
str[min 5.3.2.2.1]

| Novello |

Chamber Music II <1975–1976>   14'
solo alto flute
str

| Novello |

Chamber Music III (The Nocturnal Dances of Don Juanquixote [Don Juan-Quijotten yölliset tanssit]) <1985–1986>   20'

solo violoncello
str[min 4.3.2.2.1]

Novello

Concerto for Chamber Orchestra <1959–1960>   22'

1[incl pic] 1 2[incl bcl] 1 — 1 0 0 0 — str

Novello

Shadows; Prelude for Orchestra, op.52 <1982>   11'

3[1.2.3/pic] 3 3[1.2.3/bcl] 3[1.2.3/cbn] — 4 3 3 0 — tmp+4 — hp — pf — str
perc: sd, td, bd, tamtam, cym, sus cym, chimes, vib, glock, tri
Uses material from the composer's opera, *The King Goes Forth to France.*

Novello

Symphony No.1, op.24 <1971>   16'

3[1.2.3/pic] 3 3[1.2.3/bcl] 3[1.2.cbn] — 4 3 3 0 — tmp+4 — hp — str
perc: glock, marim, chimes, woodblk, tamtam, vib, bd, cym, sd

Novello

Symphony No.3 <1975>   23'

4[incl 2pic] 3 4[incl bcl] 3[incl cbn] — 4 3 3 1 — tmp+3 — hp — cel, pf — str

Tempo energico ed sostenuto	7'
Chaconne	7'
Vivace giocoso — Finale	9'

Novello

Symphony No.5, op.57 (Washington Mosaics) <1985>   39'

4[1.2/pic.3/pic.4] 4 4[1.2/Ebcl.3.4/bcl] 4[1.2.3.4/cbn] — 6 4 4 1 — tmp+4 — hp — cel, pf — str
perc: bd, field dr, sd, td, cast, tamtam, cym, sus cym, tri, cowbell, glock, xyl, vib, marim, chimes, 3tomtom, 3bongos, 3woodblk

Washington Mosaics 1	14'
Intermezzo 1	5'
Intermezzo 2	5'
Intermezzo 3	7'
Washington Mosaics 2	8'

Novello

Variations for Orchestra (14 juventas variaatiota), op.8 <1963>   12'

2[incl pic] 2 2 2 — 2 2 2 0 — 1perc — str
perc: marim

Novello

Salonen, Esa-Pekka   1958-

(b Helsinki, 30 June 1958). Finnish

Concerto, Violin <2008–2009>   29'

3[1.2/afl.3/pic] 3[1.2.Eh] 3[1.2.bcl] 3[1.2.cbn] — 2 2 2 0 — tmp+3 — hp — cel — str[12.12.10.8.8]
perc: vib, bd, glock, marim, tamtam, set, logdrum, 4tomtom, 13 tuned gongs
Drum set (perc3) plays in 3rd mvt only.

I. Mirage	8'
II. Pulse I	4'
III. Pulse II	5'
IV. Adieu	12'

Chester

Giro <1982; rev 1997>   10'

2[1.2/afl] 2[1.2/Eh] 2[1.2/bcl] 2[1.2/cbn] — 2 2 2 0 — 1perc — hp — pf — str
perc: vib, marim, chimes, 2tamtam

Chester

Insomnia <2002>   20'

3[1.2/afl.3/pic] 3[1.2.3/Eh] 3[1.2/Ebcl/bcl.bcl] 3[1.2.cbn] — 8[4hn, 4Wag tb] 3 3 1 — tmp+4 — hp — pf/cel — str
perc: vib, chimes, congas, marim, rototom, crot, tri, bd, marktree, sus cym, sd, 2glock, 4tomtom, 4tamtam, 4logdrum, 15 tuned gongs, Chinese gong [F#]

Chester

L.A. Variations <1996>   19'

3[1.2/afl.pic] 3[1.2.Eh] 4[1.2/Ebcl.bcl.cbcl] 3[1.2.cbn] — 4 3 3 1 — sampler — tmp+3 — hp — cel — str[min 16.14.12.10.8]
perc: vib, marim, chimes, crot, szl cym, congas, glock, rototom, marktree, 4 tuned gongs, 4logdrum, 2 pairs bongos, 4tomtom, 3tamtam
For details on the sampler, see www.chesternovello.com.

Chester

NYX <2011>   17'

4[1.2.3/pic.pic] 4[1.2.3.Eh] 4[1.2.3/Ebcl.bcl] 4[1.2.3.cbn] — 4 3 3 1 — tmp+3 — hp — cel/pf — str
perc: vib, glock, tamtam, tomtom, bd, bongos, woodblk, chimes, szl cym, 5 tuned gongs

Chester

Wing on Wing <2003–2004>   26'

2 solo sopranos (textless)
4[1.2/pic/bfl.3/pic.4/afl] 4[1.2.3.Eh] 4[1.2.Ebcl/bcl.cbcl] 4[1.2.3.cbn] — 4 4 3 1 — sampler[played from computer] — tmp+4 — 2hp — cel — str
perc: szl cym, vib, chimes, crot, wnd mach, belltree, 3glock, 5sus cym, 4bongos, almglocken, 8bellplates, 4tomtom, 19 tuned gongs, sandblks, 3tamtam, 4tri, 2congas, 4logdrum

Chester

Sammartini, Giovanni Battista   1701-1775

(b 1700/01; d Milan, 15 Jan 1775). Italian

J-C = N. Jenkins and B. Churgin: *Thematic Catalogue of the Works of Giovanni Battista Sammartini: Orchestral and Vocal Music* (Cambridge, MA, 1976)

Concertino, G major   8'

cnt — str
Ed. Newell Jenkins.

Peters   Kalmus   Luck's

Concerto, E-flat   7'

solo string quartet
str orch
Arr. and ed. Adam Carse.

Augener

Concerto, Violin (or Violoncello Piccolo), J-C 69, C major   12'

cnt — str
Ed. Newell Jenkins.

Eulenburg

Magnificat, J-C 111   20'

chorus   solos SATB
0 2 0 0 — 0 2 0 0 — cnt — str

Eulenburg	Schirmer

Sinfonia, J-C 2, C major   15'

0 2 0 1 — 2 0 0 0 — tmp — str
Ed. Fausto Torrefranca.

Carisch	Kalmus

Sinfonia, J-C 4, C major   7'

0 0 0 0 — 2 0 0 0 — str
Ed. Ettore Bonelli.

Zanibon	Kalmus

Sinfonia, J-C 32, F major   12'

cnt — str
Ed. Newell Jenkins.

Kalmus	Luck's	Peters

Sinfonia, J-C 39, G major   7'

cnt — str
Ed. Newell Jenkins.

Luck's	Peters

Sinfonia, J-C 47, G major   9'

2[opt] 2[opt] 0 0 — 2 0 0 0 — cnt — str
Ed. Fausto Torrefranca.

Carisch	Luck's

Sammartini, Giuseppe   1695-1750

(b Milan, 6 Jan 1695; d London, ?17-23 Nov 1750). Italian

Concerto, Recorder, F major   12'

str

Amadeus	Schott

Concerto grosso, op.5, no.6 (Christmas Concerto)   15'

2 solo violins
cnt — str
Ed. Karlheinz Schultz-Hauser.

Vieweg

Samuel, Gerhard   1924-2008

(b Bonn, 20 April 1924). American composer of German birth

Looking at Orpheus Looking <1971>   16'

4 4 4 4 — 4 4 3 1 — 4perc — hp — elec hpsd, elec org — str
perc: bd, sus cym, sd, tri, tamtam, glock, xyl, vib, crot, windchimes, whip[or bak], 2gongs, bell[E3]

MMB

Requiem for Survivors; And Suddenly it's Evening <1974>   18'

4[all/pic] 4 4[1.2.3/bcl.4/tsx] 4[1.2.3.4/cbn] — 0 4 3 1 — tmp+4 — hp — str
perc: vib, marim, glock, chimes, crot, bd, td, sd, tomtom, sus cym, templeblks, woodblk, claves, marac, guiro, tri, flexatone, whip, 3tamtams, washboard, thermos
Based on the last music Mozart wrote: the first 9 bars of the *Lacrimosa* of his Requiem.

MMB

Sapieyevsky, Jerzy   1945-

(b Łódż, Poland, 1945). American composer of Polish birth.

Summer Overture <1977>   10'

3[1.2.pic] 3 3[1.2.bcl] 3 — 5 3 3 1 — tmp+2 — hp — str
perc: marim, templeblks, sus cym, bd, tamtam

Mercury

Surtsey   15'

str

Mercury

Sarasate, Pablo de   1844-1908

(b Pamplona, 10 March 1844; d Biarritz, 20 Sept 1908). Spanish

Fantasy on Bizet's "Carmen," op.25 <?1883>   12'

solo violin
2[1.2/pic] 2 2 2 — 4 2[crt1.crt2] 3 0 — tmp+1 — hp — str
perc: tambn

Kalmus	Luck's

Introduction and Tarantella, op.43 <1899>   7'

solo violin
2 2 2 2 — 2 2 0 0 — tmp+1 — str
perc: tambn, sd
  I. Moderato   _'
  II. Tarantella: Allegro vivace   _'

C. Fischer	Kalmus	Luck's

Navarra, op.33 <1889>   8'

2 solo violins
2 2 2 2 — 2 2 3 0 — tmp+2 — str
perc: tambn, tri, bd, field dr

Kalmus

Zigeunerweisen, op.20 (Gypsy Airs) <1878>   10'

solo violin
2 2 2 2 — 2 2 0 0 — tmp[+1opt] — str
perc: tri[opt]

C. Fischer	Kalmus	Luck's

Sartor, David P.   1956-

(b Nashville, TN, 25 May 1956). American

Black Ball Counts Double <2001; rev 2003>   4'

str
Originally for string quartet.

Metamorphic

Dies irae <2007>   3'

0 0 0 0 — 4 4 3 1 — euph — tmp — [no str]

Metamorphic

Metamorphic Fanfare <2000>   3'

3[1.2.pic] 2 2 2 — 4 3 3 1 — tmp+3 — str
perc: bd, cym, sus cym, sd, tamtam, glock, chimes

Metamorphic

Portent and Apotheosis <2003>   12'

3[1.2.3/pic] 3[1.2.Eh] 3[1.2.bcl] 3[1.2.cbn] — 4 3 3 1 — tmp+4 — pf
— str
perc: bd, cym, sus cym, sd, tri, tambn, tamtam, glock, xyl, vib, chimes, woodblk
Formerly titled *Concerto for Orchestra*.

    Metamorphic

Reveries <2007>   6'

str

    Metamorphic

Satie, Erik   1866-1925

(b Honfleur, 17 May 1866; d Paris, 1 July 1925). French

Les aventures de Mercure <1924>   14'

2[1.pic] 1 2 1 — 2 2 1 1 — 3perc — str
An arrangement for smaller orchestra by Harrison Birtwistle (1980) is
also published by Universal, under the title *Mercure; Poses plastiques*; it
calls for:
    1[1/pic/afl] 1[1/Eh] 1[1/bcl] 1[1/cbn] — 1 1 1 0 — perc — pf — str 5t
    1. *Overture*   1'
    2. *La nuit*   1'
    3. *Danse de tendresse*   2'
    4. *Signes du zodiaque*   1'
    5. *Entré et danse de Mercure* 1'
    6. *Danse des Graces*   1'
    7. *Bain des Graces*   1'
    8. *Fuite de Mercure*   1'
    9. *Colére de Cerbére*   1'
    10. *Polka des lettres*   1'
    11. *Nouvelle danse*   1'
    12. *Le Chaos*   1'
    13. *Final*   1'

    Universal

Cinq grimaces pour "Un songe d'une nuit d'été" <1915>   3'

3[1/pic.2.3] 3[1.2.Eh] 2 3[1.2.cbn] — 2 3 3 1 — tmp+3 — str
perc: cym, bd, tarole
From incidental music for Jean Cocteau's adaptation of Shakespeare's
Midsummer Night's Dream.

    Universal

Deux Préludes posthumes et une Gnossienne   9'

2 2[1.Eh] 2 2 — 2 2 2 0 — hp — str
Orchestrated by Francis Poulenc.
    1. *Fête donnée par les chevaliers normands en l'honneur d'une jeune*   –'
    2. *1er Prélude du Nazaréen*   –'
    3. *3e Gnossienne*   –'

    Salabert

Gymnopédies <1888>   7'

2 1 0 0 — 4 0 0 0 — 1perc — 2hp — str
perc: sus cym
Orchestrated by Claude Debussy. Labeled nos.1 & 2, though actually nos.
3 & 1, respectively, of the original *Gymnopédies* for piano.
    1. *Lent et grave*   4'
    2. *Lent et douloureux* 3'

    Kalmus   Luck's   Salabert□□□□

Gymnopédie No.2 <1895>   4'

2 1 1 0 — 4 1 0 0 — 2perc — 2hp — cel — str
perc: sus cym, tambn
Celesta part can be covered by one of the percussionists.
    Orchestrated by Roland Manuel. No.2 of the original *Gymnopédies* for
piano.

    Salabert

Jack in the Box <1899>   7'

2[1.2/pic] 2 2 2 — 2 2 2 0 — tmp+3 — str
perc: cym, bd, tarole
Originally piano pieces for a pantomime, 1899; orchestrated by Darius
Milhaud, 1926.
    1. *Prelude*   3'
    2. *Entr'acte* 2'
    3. *Final*   2'

    Universal

Parade; Ballet realiste sur un thème de Jean Cocteau   17'
<1916–1917; rev 1919>

3[1.2.pic] 3[1.2.Eh] 3[1.2.Ebcl] 2 — 2 3[1.2.crt] 3 1 — tmp+4 — hp
— str
perc: bd, cym, sus cym, tarole, tri, lottery wheel, tambn, tamtam, xyl, siren, fog
horn, water splashes, *claquers* (players clap hands), typewriter, pistol,
bouteillophone (sometimes played on xyl), organ pedals
Opening Choral & Final added 1919.
    1. *Choral*   1'
    2. *Prélude du rideau rouge*   1'
    3. *Prestidigitateur chinois*   4'
    4. *Petite fille americaine*   4'
    5. *Acrobates*   4'
    6. *Final*   2'
    7. *Suite au "Prélude du Rideau rouge"* 1'

    Kalmus   Salabert□□□□

Trois petites pièces montées <1919>   5'

1 1 1 1 — 1 2 1 0 — 2perc — str
perc: cym, bd/cym, tarole
    1. *De l'enfance de Pantagruel (Rèverie)* 2'
    2. *Marche de Cocagne (Démarche)*   1'
    3. *Jeux de Gargantua (Coin de polka)*   2'

    Eschig   Kalmus   Luck's

Sauer, Emil   1862-1942

(b Hamburg, 8 Oct 1862; d Vienna, 27 April 1942). German

Concerto, Piano, No.1, E minor   31'

2[1.2/pic] 2 2 2 — 3 2 3 0 — tmp — str
    I. *Allegro patetico*   11'
    II. *Scherzo: Molto vivace*   7'
    III. *Cavatina: Larghetto amoroso* 8'
    IV. *Rondo: Tempo giusto*   5'

    Fleisher   Schott

Scarlatti, Alessandro   1660-1725

(b Palermo, 2 May 1660; d Naples, 22 Oct 1725). Italian

Christmas Cantata (Cantata pastorale per la natività di   15'
Nostro Signore Gesu Cristo)

solo soprano
cnt — str
Ed. Edward Dent.

    Oxford

Concerto grosso No.1, F minor <c1740>   9'

cnt — str
Ed. Walter Upmeyer.

    Kalmus   Luck's   Vieweg

Concerto grosso No.2, C minor <c1740>   7'

cnt — str
Ed. Walter Upmeyer.

    Kalmus   Vieweg

Concerto grosso No.3, F major <c1740>   8'

2 solo violins, solo violoncello
cnt — str

| Kalmus | Luck's | Vieweg | Zanibon |

Concerto grosso No.6, E major <c1740>   9'

2 solo violins, solo violoncello
cnt — str
Ed. Renato Fasano.

| Ricordi |

Piccola Suite   10'

str
A pastiche, assembled by Franco Michele Napolitano from various works
of Scarlatti.

| Kalmus | Luck's | Zanibon |

Sinfonia No.1, F major <1715>   6'

2[2rec] 0 0 0 — cnt — str
Ed. Raymond Meylan.

| Bärenreiter | Kalmus | Luck's |

Sinfonia No.2, D major <1715>   7'

1 0 0 0 — 0 1 0 0 — cnt — str
Ed. Raymond Meylan.

| Bärenreiter | Kalmus | Luck's |

Sinfonia No.4, E minor <1715>   9'

1 1 0 0 — cnt — str
Ed. Raymond Meylan.

| Bärenreiter | Kalmus | Luck's |

Sinfonia No.5, D minor <1715>   9'

2 0 0 0 — cnt — str
Ed. Raymond Meylan.

| Bärenreiter | Kalmus | Luck's |

Sinfonia No.6, A minor <1715>   12'

1[rec] 0 0 0 — cnt — str
Ed. Rolf-Julius Koch.

| Peters |

Sinfonia No.8, G major <1715>   12'

1[rec] 0 0 0 — cnt — str
Ed. Rolf-Julius Koch.

| Peters |

Sinfonia No.10, A minor <1715>   12'

1[rec] 0 0 0 — cnt — str
Ed. Rolf-Julius Koch.

| Peters |

Su le sponde del Tebro   15'

solo soprano, trumpet
cnt — str[no va]
Cantata for soprano, trumpet & strings. Ed. Bernhard Paumgartner.

Sinfonia	*1'*
Recitativo: Su le sponde del Tebro	*1'*
Sinfonia	*1'*
Aria: Contentatevi, o fidi pensieri	*2'*
Recitativo: Mesto, stanco e spirante	*1'*
Largo: Infelici miei lumi	*3'*
Aria: Dite almeno	*3'*
Ritornello	*1'*
Recitativo: All'aura, al cielo	*1'*
Aria: Tralascia pur di piangere	*1'*

| Kalmus |

Scarlatti, Domenico   1685 - 1757

(b Naples, 26 Oct 1685; d Madrid, 23 July 1757). Italian composer active in Portugal

Contesa delle stagioni (Contest of the Seasons)   50'

chorus   solos SMzTB
1 0 0 0 — 2 2 0 0 — cnt — str
Ed. Renato Fasano.

| Ricordi |

Five Sonatas in Form of a Suite   13'

str
"Freely elaborated" by Ettore Bonelli, from harpsichord sonatas of
Scarlatti.

| Kalmus | Luck's | Zanibon |

The Good-Humored Ladies: Suite   14'

2 2 2 2 — 4 2 0 0 — tmp+1 — hpsd[or pf] — str
Five harpsichord sonatas arr. by Vincenzo Tommasini.

| Chester | Kalmus | Luck's |

Scelsi, Giacinto   1905 - 1988

(b La Spezia, 8 Jan 1905; d Rome, 9 Aug 1988). Italian

Chukrum <1963>   18'

str

I. quarter-note = 88	*6'*
II. quarter-note = 72	*4'*
III. quarter-note = 76	*3'*
IV. quarter-note = 88	*5'*

| Salabert |

Uaxuctum <1966>   21'

vocal soloists SSTB (ampd)   chorus SATB
0 0 2[Ebcl.bcl] 0 — 4 3 2 2 — tmp+8 — ondes martenot — 6db
perc: vib, bongos, td, gong, chimes, sistrum, thumbo, 2tamtam, 3bd, calotta,
2thunder sheets, bidone. Certain instruments may be obtained from the composer,
together with the orchestral material: tamburo basso[low drum with snares],
calotta[aluminum hemisphere], 2 lamine[small thunder sheets], bidone[200-liter
can], low chime in E-flat; the thumbo remains mysterious.
"La Légende de la cité Maya, détruite par eux-mêmes pour des raisons
religieuses. (The legend of the Mayan city which they themselves
destroyed for religious reasons.)"
   Chorus and vocal soloists are textless and are treated like instruments
of the orchestra; score includes elaborate instructions for producing and
amplifyng the vocal sounds.

Part One	*7'*
Part Two	*4'*
Part Three	*3'*
Part Four	*3'*
Part Five	*4'*

| Salabert |

Schafer, R. Murray   1933-

(b Sarnia, ON, 18 July 1933). Canadian

Adieu Robert Schumann <1976>   19'

mezzo-soprano solo
2 2 2 2 — 2 2 2 0 — pre-recorded piano — 2perc — pf — str
perc: bd, guiro, sus cym, xyl, tri, belltree, glock, szl cym, bongos, sd, woodblk,
tamtam, tambn, 2tomtoms, tiny high-pitched bell, tmp

> Universal

The Garden of the Heart <1981>   24'

medium voice
3[incl pic] 2 2[incl bcl] 2 — 4 2 1 1 — 2perc — str
Bcl part may be taken by bn.

> Arcana

Schaffner, Steven   1952-

(b Butler, PA, 21 Sept 1952). American

A Whirlwind Tour of the Orchestra <2010>   6'

narrator
3[1.2.pic] 3[1.2.Eh] 3[1.2.bcl] 2 — 4 3 3 1 — tmp+4 — str
perc: bd, cym, sus cym, sd, glock, xyl

> Schaffner

Scharwenka, Xaver   1850-1924

(b Samter [now Szamotuły], 6 Jan 1850; d Berlin, 8 Dec 1924). Polish-German

Concerto, Piano, No.1, op.32, B-flat minor <1876>   28'

2[1/pic.2] 2 2 2 — 2 2 3 0 — tmp — str
I. Allegro patetico - Adagio   10'
II. Scherzo: Allegro assai   7'
III. Allegro non tanto   11'

> C. Fischer   Fleisher

Schein, Johann Hermann   1586-1630

(b Grünhain, nr Annaberg [now Annaberg-Bucholz], 20 Jan 1586; d Leipzig, 19 Nov 1630). German

Banchetto musicale: Suite No.1 <1617>   9'

str
Ed. Arnold Schering.

> Kahnt   Luck's

Scherchen, Tona   1938-

(b Neuchâtel, 12 March 1938). French composer of Eurasian origin

Hsun <1968>   8'

0 1 0 0 — 0 1 1 0 — tmp+2 — 2vc

> Universal

Schickele, Peter   1935-

(b Ames, IA, 17 July 1935). American

Celebration with Bells <1960>   7'

2 2 3[incl bcl] 2 — 4 3 3 1 — opt asx, opt tsx — tmp+3 — str
Possible with winds: 2 1 3[incl bcl] 1 — 2 3 2 1

> Elkan-Vogel

The Chenoo Who Stayed to Dinner <1977>   22'

narrator
2[incl pic] 2 2 — 3 2 2 1 — 2perc — str[min 6.5.3.3.2]

> Elkan-Vogel

Concerto, Bassoon <1998>   23'

2[incl pic] 2 2 1 — 2 2 0 0 — 1perc — pf — str
1. Blues   6'
2. Intermezzo   4'
3. Scherzo   6'
4. Song   5'
5. Romp   2'

> Elkan-Vogel

Elegy <1992>   7'

str

> Elkan-Vogel

Fanfare for the Common Cold, S.98.7   2'

0 0 0 0 — 2 2 1 0 — [no str]
Attributed to P.D.Q. Bach, 1807-1742 ?

> Presser

Symphony No.2 (The Sweet Season) <2003>   18'

2[incl pic] 2 2[incl bcl] 2 — 2 2 0 0 — tmp+2 — hp — pf — str[min 6.6.4.4.2]
perc: bd, tri, vib, bongos, metal windchimes, finger cym, birdcall, duckcall,
3tomtoms, 2sus cym, 2tambn, 2woodblks
1. Piper at the Gates of Dawn   4'
2. Renaissance   3'
3. Vernal Jukebox   4'
4. A Birthday   3'
5. Maypole Dance   3'

> Elkan-Vogel

A Zoo Called Earth <1970>   15'

taped narration (the composer's voice, altered to sound like that of an
extraterrestrial visitor)
2[incl pic] 2 2 — 4 3 3 1 — tmp+3 — cel — str
An insert correcting some omissions in the percussion parts is available
from the publisher.

> Presser

Schiff, David   1945-

(b Bronx, NY, 30 Aug 1945). American

Canti di Davide <2001>   30'

solo clarinet
3[1.2.pic] 2 2 2 — 4 3 3 0 — tmp+2 — hp — str
perc: crot, tri, sus cym, claves, marac, bongos, sd, bd, glock, chimes, xyl, marim,
vib, 2tomtoms, hammer
Mvt 3, Consolation, may be performed alone.
1. Lament   _'
2. Big Al   _'
3. Consolation   _'
4. Corso Magenta   _'
5. Isola San Michaele   _'

> MMB

Schmidt, Franz   1874-1939

(b Pressburg [now Bratislava], 22 Dec 1874; d Perchtoldsdorf, nr Vienna, 11 Feb 1939). Austrian

Das Buch mit sieben Siegeln (The Book with Seven Seals)   110'
<1935–1937>

solos SATB & Heldentenor   chorus

3[1.2.pic] 3[1.2.Eh] 3[1.2.Dcl/bcl] 3[1.2.cbn] — 4 3 3 1 — tmp+3 — org — str

perc: cym, sus cym, sd, bd, tamtam, tri, xyl; optional: 2 additional tamtams
2 of the percussionists must cover tmp briefly.

   The composer gives elaborate instructions for the doubling of woodwind instruments: passages to be doubled are indicated "*a 2*" in the score; players of auxiliary woodwinds cover part of the doubling, so that only 1 extra player of each woodwind group is required—i.e., 4 4 4 4. If the doubling cannot be accomplished according to the composer's specifications, then he stipulates there should be no doubling at all.

   Universal

Notre Dame: Entr'acte & Carnival Music (Zwischenspiel   16'
   und Karnevalsmusik) <1902–1904>

3[1.2.3/pic] 2 2 3[1.2.cbn] — 4 3 3 0 — tmp+2 — 2hp — str
perc: cym, tamtam
Kalmus ed. Clinton F. Nieweg.

   Kalmus

Symphony No.2, E-flat major <1911–1913>   47'

4[1.2.3.pic] 3[1.2.Eh] 5[incl Ebcl,bcl] 3[1.2.cbn] — 8 4 3 1 — tmp+4 — str

perc: sd, tri, tambn, sus cym, cym, bd, tamtam

I. Lebhaft	*15'*
II. Allegretto con variazioni	*16'*
III. Finale	*13'*

   Kalmus   Universal

Symphony No.4, C major <1932–1933>   42'

2[incl pic] 3[incl Eh] 3[incl Ebcl] 3[incl cbn] — 4 3 3 1 — tmp+3 — 2hp — str

perc: sd, tamtam, cym, bd

Allegro molto moderato	*13'*
Adagio	*12'*
Molto vivace	*8'*
Allegro molto moderato	*9'*

   Universal

Schmitt, Florent   1870-1958

(b Blâmont, Meurthe-et-Moselle, 28 Sept 1870; d Neuilly-sur-Seine, Paris, 17 Aug 1958). French

Feuillets de voyage, op.26 <1903–1913>   14'

3[1.2.pic] 2[1.2/Eh] 2 3[1.2.cbn] — 4 2 3 1 — tmp+3 — hp — str
perc: field dr, tri, tambn, cym, sus cym, bd
Originally for piano 4-hands; orchestrated by the composer (5 of the original 10 piano pieces).

1. Sérénade	*4'*
2. Le retour à l'endroit familier	*2'*
3. Danse brittanique	*2'*
4. Berceuse	*4'*
5. Marche burlesque	*2'*

   Kalmus

Janiana, op.101   17'

str
This work may be out of print.

I. Assez animé	*4'*
II. Musette	*3'*
III. Choral	*6'*
Avec entrain, sans précipitation	*4'*

   Durand

Légende, op.66 <1918>   10'

viola (or alto saxophone or violin)
3[1.2.pic] 3[1.2.Eh] 3[1.2.bcl] 3[1.2.cbn] — 4 3 3 1 — tmp+2 — hp — cel — str
perc: sus cym, cym, tri

   Durand

Mirages, op.70: Tristesse de Pan <1920–1921>   9'

3[1.2.pic] 3[1.2.Eh] 3[1.2.bcl] 3[1.2.cbn] — 4 3 3 1 — tmp+4 — hp[doubled ad lib] — cel — str
perc: tambn, tamtam, tri, bd, cym
Originally for piano; orchestrated by the composer.

   Durand

Musiques de plein air, op.44 (Outdoor Music)   19'
<1897–1900>

3[1.2/pic.3opt] 3[1.2opt.Eh] 2 3[1.2.opt sarr] — 4 2 3 1 — tmp+2 — 1 or 2hp — str
perc: cym, tri, sus cym

1. La Procession dans la montagne	*_'*
2. Danse désuète	*_'*
3. Accalmie	*_'*

   Durand   Kalmus

Le palais hanté; Symphonic Étude, op.49 (The Haunted   15'
   Palace) <1900–1904>

3[1.2.pic] 3[1.2.Eh] 3[1.2.bcl] 3[1.2.opt sarr] — 4 2 3 1 — tmp+2 — hp — str

   Durand   Kalmus

Psalm 47, op.38 <1904>   26'

chorus   solo soprano
3[1.2.3/pic] 3[1.2.3/Eh] 3[1.2.3/bcl] 4[1.2.3.cbn(or sarr)] — 4 3 3 1 — tmp+5 — 2hp — cel, org — str
perc: glock [kybd glock], tamtam, field dr, tambn, tri, cym, sus cym, bd
Horns may be doubled.

   Salabert

Rapsodie viennoise, op.53, no.3 <1903–1904>   8'

3[1.2.pic] 2 2 3[1.2.sarr] — 4 2 3 1 — tmp+3 — hp — str
Orchestrated by the composer from a group of 3 rhapsodies, op.53, originally for 2 pianos.

   Kalmus

Reflets d'Allemagne <1905>   10'

3[1.2.pic] 2 2 — 4 2 3 1 — tmp+2 — hp — str
perc: tri, cym, bd
Originally for piano 4-hands (op.28); orchestrated by the composer as a ballet *Reflets* (1932).
   A number of the instruments are called for only in the 4th mvt.

1. Nuremberg	*3'*
2. Dresde (Dresden)	*1'*
3. Werder	*2'*
4. Munich	*4'*

   Kalmus

Ronde burlesque, op.78 <1927>   7'

3[incl pic] 2 2 3[incl cbn] — 4 2 3 1 — tmp+6 — 1 or 2hp — cel — str

   Heugel

Salammbô, op.76: Suite No.2 <1925>   15'

3[1.2.pic] 3[1.2.Eh] 3[1.2.bcl] 3[1.2.cbn] — 4 3 3 1 — tmp+5 — hp[doubled ad lib] — cel — str
perc: sd, tambn, tamtam, tri, bd, cym, glock, xyl
From the film score.

   Durand

La tragédie de Salomé, op.50: Suite <1907; rev 1910>   24'

3-6 female voices backstage (optional)
3[1.2.pic] 3[1.2.Eh] 3[1.2.bcl] 3[1.2.sarr] — 4 3 3 1 — tmp+5 — 2hp
— str
perc: tamtam, glock [kybd glock], sd, tri, cym, sus cym, bd
Suite from the ballet.

1. Prélude	*8'*
2. Danse des perles (Dance of the Pearls)	*3'*
3. Les enchantements sur la mer (The Apparitions on the Sea)	*8'*
4. Danse les éclairs (Dance amid the Lightning Flashes)	*3'*
5. Danse de l'effroi (Dance of Terror)	*2'*

Kalmus

Schnittke, Alfred   1934-1998

(b Engels, 24 Nov 1934; d Hamburg, 3 Aug 1998). Russian composer of German descent

Concerto, Oboe, Harp & String Orchestra <1971>   13'

str

Universal

Concerto, Piano & Strings   26'

str[12.12.8.8.4]

Russian   Sikorski

Concerto, Violin, No.4 <1982>   33'

3[incl afl] 3[1.2.Eh] 3[1.2.bcl] 3[1.2.cbn] — 4 4 4 1 — asx — tmp+6
— hp — cel, prepared pf — str

I. Andante	*5'*
II. Vivo (Cadenza visuale)	*7'*
III. Adagio	*9'*
IV. Lento (Cadenza visuale)	*12'*

Sikorski   Universal

Concerto grosso No.3   22'

2 solo violins
1perc — hpsd/pf/cel — str[4.4.3.2.1]
perc: chimes

I. Allegro	*3'*
II. Risoluto	*4'*
III. Pesante	*6'*
IV.	*6'*
V. Moderato	*3'*

Sikorski

Fragment-Suite <2001>   22'

str
Compiled by Gidon Kremer.

I. Alban Berg: Kanon "An das Frankfurter Opernhaus" arr Schnittke	*2'*
II. Schnittke: Fragment from the 1st mvt of an unfinished cantata	*4'*
III. Schnittke: Piano 4t arr for str orch by Alexander Asteriades	*8'*
IV. Schnittke: Fragment from "Five Fragments after Hieronymus Bosch"	*8'*

Sikorski

In memoriam ... <1976; rev (orchd) 1978>   27'

3[incl pic,afl] 3[incl Eh] 3[incl bcl] 3[incl cbn] — 4 4 4 1 — elec gtr
— tmp+4 — hp — cel, 2pf, hpsd, org — str[min 7.6.5.4.3]
perc: vib, glock, chimes, marim, 2tamtams
Originally for piano quintet; orchestrated by the composer.

1. Moderato	*6'*
2. Tempo di valse	*5'*
3. Andante	*7'*
4. Lento	*5'*
5. Moderato pastorale	*4'*

Peters

Moz-Art à la Haydn <1977>   12'

2 solo violins
str[3.3.2.2.1]
A humorous "deconstruction" involving dueling violinists, lighting effects, and an ending reminiscent of the Haydn *Farewell Symphony*.

Russian   Sikorski

Quasi una sonata <1968; rev (orchd) 1987>   20'

solo violin
2[incl pic] 2 2 2 — 2 0 0 0 — pf/hpsd — str[5.4.3.3.1]
Orchestration of the composer's 1968 *Sonata No.2 for Violin & Piano*.

Universal

Requiem <1974–1975>   35'

solos SSSAT   chorus
0 0 0 0 — 0 1 1 0 — elec gtr, bass gtr — tmp+3 — org, pf, cel — [no str]
Originally intended to be part of the incidental music to Schiller's *Don Carlos*, but ultimately a separate concert work.

1. Requiem	*4'*
2. Kyrie	*2'*
3. Dies irae	*1'*
4. Tuba mirum	*3'*
5. Rex tremendae	*1'*
6. Recordare	*3'*
7. Lacrimosa	*3'*
8. Domine Jesu	*1'*
9. Lacrimosa	*1'*
10. Sanctus	*4'*
11. Benedictus	*2'*
12. Agnus Dei	*2'*
13. Credo	*4'*
14. Requiem	*4'*

Peters

Symphony No.4 <1983>   42'

chorus or vocal quartet
1[incl afl] 1 1 1 — 1 1 1 0 — 4perc — cel, pf, hpsd — str[or str 5t]
perc: vib, glock, tamtam, 7gongs[tuned], 3sets chimes

1. Andante poco pesante	*9'*
2. "Cadenza"	*5'*
3. Moderato	*5'*
4. Molto pesante—Moderato	*12'*
5. Vivo	*1'*
6. Moderato—Andante poco pesante	*5'*
7. "Coro"	*5'*

Chant   Russian

Schoeck, Othmar   1886-1957

(b Brunnen, 1 Sept 1886; d Zürich, 8 March 1957). Swiss

Sommernacht, op.58, Pastoral Intermezzo <1945>   16'

str

Hug

Schoenberg, Arnold
1874-1951

(b Vienna, 13 Sept 1874; d Los Angeles, 13 July 1951). Austro-Hungarian composer

*Many of the works of Schoenberg are handled by **Belmont** for the United States, Canada and Mexico, and by **Universal** for the rest of the world. The Belmont website, www.schoenbergmusic.com, is a goldmine of information.*

Begleitungsmusik zu einer Lichtspielscene, op.34 (Accompaniment to a Cinematographic Scene) <1929–1930>
8'

1[1/pic] 1 2 1 — 2 2 1 0 — tmp+4 — pf — str
perc: xyl, glock, sd, tambn, cym, tri, tamtam, bd, sus cym

Peters		

Chamber Symphony No.1, op.9 (Kammersymphonie) <1906>
21'

1 2[1.Eh] 3[1.Ebcl.bcl] 2[1.cbn] — 2 0 0 0 — str 5t

In the score and original parts, the sopranino clarinet is mostly in D, but changes to E-flat from figure [39] to [64]. Likewise, the bcl in A changes to B-flat from [39] to [77]; the bcl part is in bass clef throughout.

However, parts transposed for Ebcl, and for bcl in B-flat/treble clef, are available both from Kalmus, and at imslp.org.

Continuous texture, though some commentators discern a 4- or 5-movement underlying basis related to sonata-allegro form.

Langsam	6'
Sehr rasch	2'
Viel langsamer, aber doch fliessend	3'
Viel langsamer	4'
Etwas bewegter	6'

Belmont	Kalmus	Universal

Chamber Symphony No.1, op.9b (orchestral version) (Kammersymphonie) <1905; rev 1922, 1935>
21'

3[1.2.3/pic] 3[1.2.3/Eh] 3[1.Ebcl.bcl] 3[1.2.cbn] — 4 2 3 0 — str
Orchestrated by the composer, 1922; rev. 1935.

Langsam	6'
Sehr rasch	2'
Viel langsamer, aber doch fliessend	3'
Viel langsamer	4'
Etwas bewegter	6'

Schirmer	Universal

Chamber Symphony No.2, op.38 (Kammersymphonie) <1906–1916; rev 1938>
22'

2[1.2/pic] 2[1.2/Eh] 2 2 — 2 2 0 0 — str

1. *Adagio*	9'
2. *Con fuoco*	13'

Schirmer	

Concerto, Piano, op.42 <1942>
21'

2[1.2/pic] 2 2 2 — 4 2 3 1 — tmp+3 — str
perc: glock, xyl, cym, sd, gong, bd
One continuous movement, though in four sections.

1. *Andante*	5'
2. *[bar 176] Molto allegro*	3'
3. *[bar 264] Adagio*	7'
4. *[bar 329] Giocoso*	6'

Belmont	Schirmer

Concerto, Violin, op.36 <1935–1936>
32'

3[1.2.3/pic] 3 3[1.Ebcl.bcl] 3 — 4 3 3 1 — tmp+5 — str
perc: xyl, field dr, tambn, glock, tri, cym, tamtam, bd

I. *Poco Allegro*	12'
II. *Andante grazioso*	8'
III. *Allegro*	12'

Schirmer	

Concerto, Violoncello <1932–1933>
16'

2[1/pic.2/pic] 2 2 2 — 2 2 1[btbn] 0 — tmp+3 — hp — cel — str
perc: glock, tri, xyl, sd, cym, tambn, bd, tamtam
After a harpsichord concerto by G. M. Monn (1746).

I. *Allegro moderato*	6'
II. *Adagio (Alla marcia)*	5'
III. *Tempo di menuetto*	5'

Schirmer	

Five Pieces for Orchestra, op.16 (original version) <1909>
16'

4[1.2.3/pic2.pic1] 4[1.2.3.Eh] 5[1.2.3/cbcl.D-cl.bcl] 4[1.2.3.cbn] — 6 ?
4 1 — tmp+3 — hp — cel — str
perc: xyl, sus cym, tamtam, tri, bd, cym, cello bow
Contrabass clarinet is in A.

1. *Vorgefühle (Premonitions)*	2'
2. *Vergangenes (Yesteryears)*	5'
3. *Farben (Colors)*	3'
4. *Peripetie (Peripetia)*	2'
5. *Das obligate Rezitativ (The Obligatory Recitative)*	4'

Kalmus	Peters

Five Pieces for Orchestra, op.16 (revised version) <1909; rev 1949>
16'

4[1.2.3/pic.pic] 3[1.2.Eh] 4[1.2.Ebcl.bcl] 3[1.2.cbn] — 4 3 3 1 —
tmp+3 — hp — cel — str
perc: xyl, sus cym, tamtam, tri, bd, cym, cello bow
A 1973 edition by Richard Hoffmann makes many corrections in this 1949 version.

1. *Vorgefühle (Premonitions)*	2'
2. *Vergangenes (Yesteryears)*	5'
3. *Farben (Colors)*	3'
4. *Peripetie (Peripetia)*	2'
5. *Das obligate Rezitativ (The Obligatory Recitative)*	4'

Peters	

Five Pieces for Orchestra, op.16 (chamber orchestra version) <1909>
16'

1[1/pic] 1 1 1 — 1 0 0 0 — pf, harm — str 5t
Arr. Felix Greissle, 1920.

1. *Vorgefühle (Premonitions)*	2'
2. *Vergangenes (Yesteryears)*	5'
3. *Farben (Colors)*	3'
4. *Peripetie (Peripetia)*	2'
5. *Das obligate Rezitativ (The Obligatory Recitative)*	4'

Peters	

Friede auf Erden, op.13 (Peace on Earth) <1907; rev (orchd) 1911>
8'

chorus
2 2 2 2 — 2 0 0 0 — str
Composed 1907 for *a cappella* performance; in 1911, the composer provided optional parts for small orchestra, if necessary to support the voices.

Belmont	Schott

Genesis Suite: I. Prelude [Schoenberg] <1945>   6'

wordless chorus

3[1.2.pic] 3[1.2.3/Eh] 3[1.2/Ebcl.3/bcl] 3[1.2.cbn] — 4 3 3 1 —
tmp+3 — hp — str

perc: xyl, glock, tamtam, cym, bd, tambn, tri

See the entry for "Nathaniel Shilkret: *Genesis Suite*" for a full description
of this collaborative work by 7 composers.

Belmont		

Gurre-Lieder <1900–1911>   99'

chorus, male chorus   solos SATTB   Sprechstimme

8[4fl, 2fl/pic, 2pic] 5[3ob, 2Eh] 7[3cl, 2Ebcl, 2bcl] 5[3bn, 2cbn] —
10[7-10/Wag tb] 6[6tp, btp] 7[alto tbn, 4tbn, btbn, cb tbn] 1 — 2tmp+8
— 4hp — cel — str[20.20.16.16.14]

perc: glock, ratch, xyl, tri, sd, td, cym, bd, tamtam, several iron chains

The difficult sustained *pp* high B in piccolos (in *Des Sommerwindes
wilde Jagd*, Part III, after fig. [74]) can be covered by a tiny tuned pipe,
or, alternatively, a bowed crotale.

	PART I	
1.	Prelude	7'
2.	Nun dämpft die Dämmerung	4'
3.	O wenn des Mondes Strahlen	3'
4.	Ross! Mein Ross!	3'
5.	Sterne jubeln	2'
6.	So tanzen die Engel vor Gottes Thron nicht	2'
7.	Nun sag ich dir zum ersten Mal	4'
8.	Es ist Mitternachtszeit	5'
9.	Du sendest mir einen Liebestlick	5'
10.	Du wunderliche Tove!	4'
11.	Orchestral interlude	5'
12.	Tauben von Gurre!	11'
	PART II	
1.	Herrgott, weisst du, was du tatest	4'
	PART III	
1.	Erwacht, König Waldemars Mannen wert!	2'
2.	Deckel des Sanges klappert	3'
3.	Gegrüsst, o König	4'
4.	Mit Toves Stimme flüstert der Wald	5'
5.	Ein seltsamer Vogel	6'
6.	Du strenger Richter droben	2'
7.	Der Hahn erhebt den Kopf zur Kraht	5'
8.	Des Sommerwindes wilde Jagd	3'
9.	Herr Gänsefuss, Frau Gänsekraut	5'
10.	Seht die Sonne	5'

Belmont	Kalmus	Universal

Gurre-Lieder [reduced orchestra] <1900–1911>   99'

chorus, male chorus   solos SATTB   Sprechstimme

3[all/pic (opt fl4)] 3[1.2/Eh.3/Eh] 4[1.2.3/bcl.4/Ebcl] 3[1.2.3/cbn] — 6
4 4 1 — 2tmp+8 — 2hp — cel, pf, harm — str

perc: glock, ratch, xyl, tri, sd, td, cym, bd, tamtam, several iron chains

Orchestra reduction by Erwin Stein.

The difficult sustained *pp* high B in piccolos (in *Des Sommerwindes
wilde Jagd*, Part III, after fig. [74]) can be covered by a tiny tuned pipe,
or, alternatively, a bowed crotale.

For contents and durations, see the original version (preceding entry).

Universal		

Gurre-Lieder: Lied der Waldtaube (chamber version)   13'
<1900–1911>

solo soprano

1[1/pic] 2[1.Eh] 3[1.2/Ebcl.bcl] 2[1.2/cbn] — 2 0 0 0 — pf, harm —
str 5t

This excerpt arr. for chamber orchestra by the composer, 1922. Versions
for the huge *Gurre-Lieder* orchestra, and for a normally large orchestra
are also available.

Belmont	Universal	

Kammersymphonie

see his: Chamber Symphony

Kol nidre, op.39 <1938>   18'

chorus   speaker

2[1.2/pic] 1 3[1.Ebcl.bcl] 1 — 2 2 2 1 — tmp+3 — str

perc: tamtam, bd, cym, field dr, xyl, bell, flexatone[played by tmp]

Belmont edition has been corrected.

Belmont	Boelke	

Moderne Psalm, op.50c (O du mein Gott) <1950>   7'

speaker   chorus

2[1.2/str] 2[1.2/Eh] 3[1.Ebcl.bcl] 2 — 2 2 1 0 — 1perc —
str[4.4.4.4.4]

perc: glock, bd, tamtam

Belmont	Schott	

Ode to Napoleon Bonaparte, op.41 <1942>   16'

reciter

pf — str 4t or str orch

Belmont edition has been corrected.

Belmont	Schirmer	

Pelléas und Mélisande, op.5 <1902–1903>   41'

4[1.2.3/pic.pic] 4[1.2.3.Eh] 5[1.2.3/bcl.bcl.Ebcl] 4[1.2.3.cbn] — 8 4 5
1 — tmp+4 — 2hp — str

perc: glock, td, tri, tamtam, cym, bd, sus cym

Revised 1920. Score calls for 2 timpanists, but may be covered by 1
player. Bcl is said to be (at least in part) in A.
Belmont edition has been corrected.
Version by Erwin Stein for reduced orchestra is also available.

Belmont	Kalmus	Universal

Pierrot lunaire, op.21 <1912>   34'

Sprechstimme

1[1/pic] 0 1[1/bcl] 0 — pf — vn/va, vc

Belmont edition has been corrected.

Part I	12'
Part II	11'
Part III	11'

Belmont	Kalmus	Luck's	Universal

Serenade, op.24 <1920–1923>   34'

bass-baritone voice [4th mvt only]

0 0 2[1.bcl] 0 — gtr, mand — vn, va, vc

1.	Marsch	4'
2.	Menuett	8'
3.	Variationen	5'
4.	Sonnet 217 [recte 256] von Petrarca: O könnt ich je der Rach' …	3'
5.	Tanzscene	7'
6.	Lied [ohne Worte]	2'
7.	Finale	5'

Hansen		

Six Songs, op.8 (Sechs Orchester-Lieder) <1903–1904>   23'

soprano solo

3[1.2.3/pic] 3[1.2.Eh] 3[1.2.3/bcl] 3[1.2.3/cbn] — 4 3 3 1 — tmp+3
— hp — str

perc: cym, td, tri

Arrangements are available from Universal of 3 of the songs for voice &
chamber ensemble: by Hanns Eisler (no.1) and Erwin Stein (nos.2 & 5);
instrumentation: fl, ob, cl — pf, harm — str 5t

1.	Natur (Nature)	4'
2.	Das Wappenschild (The Coat-of-Arms)	3'
3.	Sehnsucht (Longing)	2'
4.	Nie ward ich, Herrin müd' (Ne'er, mistress, did I weary)	4'
5.	Voll jener Süsse (Filled with that sweetness)	5'
6.	Wenn Vöglein klagen (When little birds complain)	5'

Belmont	Universal	

Suite for String Orchestra <1934>   28'

str
1. Ouverture	5'
2. Adagio	5'
3. Menuet & Trio	5'
4. Gavotte	6'
5. Gigue	7'

> Schirmer

A Survivor from Warsaw, op.46 <1947>   9'

male narrator   unison male chorus
2[1/pic.2/pic] 2 2 2 — 4 3 3 1 — tmp+5 — hp — str[10.10.6.6.6]
perc: xyl, cast, glock, field dr, tri, tamtam, cym, bd; tambn[played by tmp]
Revised score by Jacques-Louis Monod (1979) makes textual changes
based on rigorous observance of serial principles; a questionable
procedure. The score that comes with the rental parts is identical with that
of the Schoenberg collected edition (ed. Josef Rufer & Christian Martin
Schmidt); it is recommended.

> Belmont   Boelke

Theme and Variations, op.43b <1943>   12'

3[1.2.pic] 3[1.2.Eh] 3[1.2.bcl] 3[1.2.cbn] — 4 3 3 1 — tmp+5 — str
perc: glock, xyl, sd, tambn, gong, cym, bd
Originally for concert band; orchestrated by the composer, 1943.
Theme: Poco allegro	_'
I. A tempo	_'
II. Allegro molto	_'
III. Poco adagio	_'
IV. Tempo di valse	_'
V. Molto moderato	_'
VI. Allegro	_'
VII. Moderato	_'
Finale: Moderato	_'

> Belmont   Schirmer

Variations for Orchestra, op.31 <1926–1928>   22'

4[1.2.3/pic2.4/pic1] 4[1.2.3.4/Eh] 5[1.2.3.4/Ebcl.bcl] 4[1.2.3.4/cbn] —
4 3 4 1 — mand — tmp+5 — hp — cel — str
perc: xyl, tri, glock, sd, flexatone, tambn, cym, tamtam, bd
Composer's note: The part for the small clarinet may be played on E-flat
or D clarinet; the middle parts on A, B-flat, or C instruments; and the bass
clarinet on A or B-flat.
Introduction: Mässig; ruhig	2'
Theme: Molto moderato	1'
I. Moderato	1'
II. Langsam	2'
III. Mässig	1'
IV. Waltz-tempo	1'
V. Bewegt	2'
VI. Andante	2'
VII. Langsam	2'
VIII. Sehr rasch	1'
IX. L'istesso tempo; aber etwas langsamer	1'
Finale	6'

> Belmont   Universal

Verklärte Nacht, op.4 (1917 version) (Transfigured Night) <1899; rev (orchd) 1917>   30'

str
Originally for string sextet. Arr. by the composer for string orchestra.
  Kalmus ed. Clinton F. Nieweg & Mark Laycock.

> Kalmus   Luck's

Verklärte Nacht, op.4 (1943 version) (Transfigured Night) <1899; rev (orchd) 1917, 1943>   30'

str
Originally for string sextet. The 1917 arrangement for string orchestra
substantially revised by the composer, 1943.

> Belmont   Luck's   Universal

Waltzes for String Orchestra <early works>   15'

str
I. Kräftig	1'
II. Nicht zu rasch	1'
III. Etwas langsam	1'
IV. Etwas rasch	2'
V. Rasch	2'
VI. [no tempo indication]	2'
VII. Kräftig	1'
VIII. Getragen	1'
IX. Lebhaft	1'
X. Nicht rasch	2'

> Belmont

Schoenfeld, Paul   1947-

(b Detroit, 24 Jan 1947). American
[Surname spelled "Schoenfield" in some sources; the composer prefers "Schoenfeld"

Four Parables <1982–1983>   28'

solo piano
3[1.2.pic] 3[1.2.Eh] 3[1.2.3/Ebcl/bcl] 3[1.2.cbn] — 4 3 3 1 — elec
bass — 4perc — synth — str
perc: tmp, whip, belltree, thunder, set, bd, timbales, cym, szl cym, hi-hat, field dr,
rototom, crot, xyl, vibrslp, bongos, marktree, ratch, congas, sd, windchimes, vib,
glass windchimes, wood windchimes, sirenwhstl, tumba, 2tomtom, 2tri, 2tambn,
2tamtam, 2bd
I. Rambling Till the Butcher Cuts Us Down	6'
II. Senility's Ride	8'
III. Elegy	7'
IV. Dog Heaven	7'

> Schirmer

Schostakowitsch, Dmitri   1906-1975

The German spelling of this composer's name, used by the publishers Sikorski,
Universal and others.

> *see:* Shostakovich, Dmitri, 1906-1975

Schreiner, Adolf   1841-1894

(b Plauen, 10 May 1841; d Neustrelitz 19 Feb 1894). German

Immer kleiner (Always Smaller)   6'

solo clarinet
2[1.2/pic] 1 3 2 — 4 2 3 1 — opt asx, opt tsx — tmp+3 — str
perc: bd, cym, sd
Originally for clarinet & piano; transcribed for clarinet & band by George
S. Howard; string adaptation by Albert O. Davis.
  A humorous novelty in which the soloist gradually disassembles the
instrument while continuing to play.

> LudwigMasters

The Worried Drummer (Der Pauker in Ängsten)   8'

solo percussionist
2[1.2/pic] 2 2 2 — 2 2 3 0 — str
Ed. Saul Goodman. Luck's version (not Goodman) has only 1 tbn.

> Kalmus   Luck's   LudwigMasters

Schreker, Franz

1878-1934

(b Monaco, 23 March 1878; d Berlin, 21 March 1934). Austrian

Ekkehard, op.12

14'

2 3[1.2.Eh] 3[1.2.bcl] 3[1.2.cbn] — 4 3 3 1 — tmp+2 — hp — org [opt] — str

perc: bd, cym, sus cym, tri, tamtam, low bells [C#3,G#2,E2]

Organ part is cued in the winds.

| Kalmus | Luck's | Universal |

Der Geburtstag der Infantin (The Birthday of the Infanta): Suite <1908; rev Suite: 1923>

20'

3[1.2.3/pic] 3[1.2.Eh] 3[1.2.bcl] 3[1.2.cbn] — 4 3 3 1 — gtr, 4mand — tmp+7 — 2hp — cel — str

perc: tri, glock, xyl, tambn, bd, sd, field dr, cym, cast

1. Reigen (Round Dance)	*2'*
2. Aufzug und Kampfspiel (Pageant & Combat)	*2'*
3. Die Marionetten (The Marionettes)	*3'*
4. Menuett der Tänzerknaben (Minuet of the Dancing Boys)	*2'*
5. Die Tänze des Zwerges (The Dances of the Dwarf)	*1'*
6. Mit dem Wind im Frühling (With the Wind in Springtime)	*2'*
7. In blauen Sandalen über das Korn (In Blue Sandals Over the Rye)	*2'*
8. Im Roten Gewand im Herbst (In a Red Gown in Autumn)	*1'*
9. Die Rose der Infantin (The Rose of the Infanta)	*4'*
10. Nachklang (Reminiscence)	*1'*

| Universal |

Intermezzo, op.8 <1900>

5'

str

Later included in the composer's *Romantische Suite*, op.14 (1903).

| Kalmus | Luck's | Universal |

Kammersymphonie <1916>

25'

1 1 1 1 — 1 1 1 0 — tmp+1 — hp — cel, pf, harm — str[2.2.2.3.2]

perc: tri, cym, tamtam, xyl, glock

Strings may be augmented to 6.6.4.6.3.

| Kalmus | Luck's | Universal |

Ein Tanzspiel; Vier Stücke im alten Stil <1908>

13'

2 2 2 2 — 4 2 3 1[opt] — tmp+3 — hp — str

perc: cym, sus cym, sd, tri, tambn, glock

I. Sarabande	*3'*
II. Menuett	*3'*
III. Madrigal	*4'*
IV. Gavotte	*3'*

| Kalmus | Luck's | Universal |

Vorspiel zu einem Drama (Prelude to a Drama: Die Gezeichneten) <1913–1915>

22'

4[1.2.3.pic] 4[1.2.3.Eh] 5[1.2.3.4/Ebcl.bcl] 3[1.2.cbn] — 6 4 3 1 — 2tmp+5 — 2hp — cel, pf — str[20.20.16.12.10]

perc: bd, bd/cym, cym, sus cym, sd, tri, tambn, tamtam, glock, xyl, cast, low bells [E2,F2,F#2,G#2,A2,A#2,B2,C#3,D#3,E3]

Cel & hps should be doubled if possible.

A shortened version of this work (9') became the actual prelude to the opera *Die Gezeichneten*.

| Kalmus | Luck's | Universal |

Schtschedrin, Rodion

1932-

The German transliteration of this composer's name, used by the publishers Sikorski, Universal and others.

see: Shchedrin, Rodion

Schubert, Franz

1797-1828

(b Vienna, 31 Jan 1797; d Vienna, 19 Nov 1828). Austrian

D = W. Dürr, A. Feil, C. Landon and others: *Franz Schubert: Thematisches Verzeichnis seiner Werke in chronologischer Folge von Otto Erich Deutsch*, Neue Ausgabe sämtlicher Werke, viii/4 (Kassel, 1978)

Alfonso und Estrella, D.732: Overture <1821–1822>

7'

2 2 2 2 — 2 2 3 0 — tmp — str

Later borrowed to be used as the overture to the *Rosamunde* incidental music, and published that way in the old Breitkopf collected edition. There are certain differences in orchestration detail between that version and that of the new Bärenreiter collected edition.

N.B.: This overture in D major is *not* the same work as the well-known *Rosamunde* overture in C major, D.644, *q.v.* The latter was originally composed for the melodrama *Die Zauberharfe*.

| Bärenreiter | Breitkopf | Kalmus | Luck's |

An die Musik, D.547

3'

solo voice

1 1 1 1 — 2 0 0 0 — tmp — str

Originally for voice and piano; arranged by an unknown hand (possibly Max Reger). Available in D major (original key) or B-flat major (score in B-flat only).

| Kalmus | Luck's |

Claudine von Villa Bella, D.239: Overture <c1815>

8'

2 2 2 2 — 2 2 0 0 — tmp — str

| Breitkopf |

Deutsche Messe, D.872, 2nd version (Gesänge zur Feier des heiligen Opfers der Messe) <1827>

22'

chorus

0 2 2 2 — 2 2 3 0 — tmp — org — "basso ad lib."

Original version was for chorus & organ; orchestrated by the composer.

| Doblinger | Schirmer |

Deutsche Tänze, D.820 <1824>

9'

2 2 2 2 — 2 0 0 0 — str

Originally for piano solo; orchestrated by Anton Webern.

| Universal |

Fantasy, D.940, op.103, F minor <1828>

19'

1 2 1 2 — 2 0 0 0 — 1perc — pf — vc, db

Arr. Randall Davidson; originally for piano 4-hands.

| Boys Art |

Fierrabras, D.796: Overture <1823>

9'

2 2 2 2 — 4 2 3 0 — tmp — str

| Breitkopf | Kalmus | Luck's |

Die Freunde von Salamanka, D.326: Overture <1815>

7'

2 2 2 2 — 2 2 0 0 — tmp — str

| Breitkopf |

Gesang der Geister über den Wassern, D.714, op.167 <1821>

11'

male chorus TTTTBBBB

str[va, vc, db]

| Breitkopf |

Grand duo, op.140

see his: Symphony, D.812, op.140, C major (Grand duo)

Grande marche héroïque <1824> 4'

3[1.2.pic] 2 2 2 — 4 2 3 1 — tmp+2 — str
perc: cym, bd
Orchestrated by Franz Liszt from a work for piano 4-hands, D.819 (= op.40) no.3.

Kalmus	Luck's

Der häusliche Krieg, D.787: Overture <1822–1823> 7'

2 2 2 2 — 2 2 0 0 — tmp — str
Completed by Fritz Racek.

Doblinger

Konzertstück, D.345, D major <1816> 8'

solo violin
0 2 0 0 — 0 2 0 0 — tmp — str

Breitkopf	Kalmus	Luck's

Lebensstürme, D.947, op.posth.144 (Allegro caratteristico) <1828> 18'

2 2 2 2 — 4 2 3 0 — tmp — str
Originally for piano 4-hands; orchestrated by Mark Starr.

Noteworthy

Magnificat, D.486 <1815> 13'

chorus   solos SATB
0 2 0 2 — 0 2 0 0 — tmp — org — str
Faber edition by Brian Newbould; Schirmer edition by Robert S. Hines.

Faber	Kalmus	Luck's	Schirmer

Marche hongroise, D.818 (Hungarian March) <1824> 5'

2 2 2 2 — 4 2 3 1 — tmp+4 — str
perc: bd, cym, sd, tri
Adapted by Franz Liszt from Schubert's Divertimento à l'hongroise, op.54, for piano 4-hands.

Fürstner	Kalmus

Marche militaire, D.733 (op.51), no.1 <1818> 5'

3[incl pic] 2 2 2 — 4 3 3 1 — tmp+5 — str
perc: glock, sd, tri, cym, bd
Arr. Leopold Damrosch, from the popular work for piano 4-hands.

Luck's	Schirmer

Mass No.1, D.105, F major <1814> 43'

chorus   solos SSATTB
0 2 2 2 — 2 2 3 0 — tmp — org — str
I. Kyrie	5'
II. Gloria	14'
III. Credo	8'
IV. Sanctus	3'
V. Benedictus	5'
VI. Agnus Dei	8'

Bärenreiter	Breitkopf	Schirmer

Mass No.2, D.167, G major <1815> 22'

chorus   solos STB
0 2[or 2cl] 0 2 — 0 2 0 0 — tmp — org — str
Wind and timpani parts were added later, so it would be plausible to omit them if desired. However, Brian Newbould, in his Faber edition, has established that these parts were added by the composer himself—not, as had been previously thought, by his brother Ferdinand Schubert.
I. Kyrie	3'
II. Gloria	3'
III. Credo	5'
IV. Sanctus	2'
V. Benedictus	4'
VI. Agnus Dei	5'

Breitkopf	Faber	Kalmus	Luck's

Mass No.3, D.324, op.141, B-flat major <1815> 35'

chorus   solos SATB
0 2 0 2 — 0 2 0 0 — tmp — org — str
I. Kyrie	5'
II. Gloria	9'
III. Credo	6'
IV. Sanctus	3'
V. Benedictus	6'
VI. Agnus Dei	6'

Bärenreiter	Breitkopf	Kalmus	Luck's

Mass No.4, D.452, op.48, C major <1816> 26'

chorus   solos SATB
0 2[opt, or 2cl] 0 0 — 0 2[opt] 0 0 — opt tmp — org — str[no va]
Clarinets may substitute for oboes, or all winds & timpani may be omitted.

In 1828, Schubert composed an alternative Benedictus for this mass (D.961, A minor); it is included in the Bärenreiter and Breitkopf editions (and Kalmus reprint) as an appendix.
I. Kyrie	3'
II. Gloria	4'
III. Credo	6'
IV. Sanctus	2'
V. Benedictus	7'
VI. Agnus Dei	4'

Bärenreiter	Breitkopf	Kalmus	Luck's	Schirmer

Mass No.5, D.678, A-flat major <1819–1822> 45'

chorus   solos SATB
1 2 2 2 — 2 2 3 0 — tmp — org — str
A little-known early (first) version of this mass may be found in the Schubert collected edition.

The Bärenreiter score and parts of the present (second) version include an alternative Cum Sancto Spiritu fugue from the first version, as well as an alternate Osanna.
I. Kyrie	5'
II. Gloria	13'
III. Credo	10'
IV. Sanctus	3'
V. Benedictus	8'
VI. Agnus Dei	6'

Bärenreiter	Breitkopf	Kalmus

Mass No.6, D.950, E-flat major <1828> 58'

chorus   solos SATTB
0 2 2 2 — 2 2 3 0 — tmp — str
Breitkopf ed. Peter Jost.
I. Kyrie	7'
II. Gloria	14'
III. Credo	17'
IV. Sanctus	4'
V. Benedictus	6'
VI. Agnus Dei	10'

Breitkopf	Kalmus	Luck's	Peters

Mirjams Siegesgesang, D.942, op.136 (Miriam's Song of Triumph) <1828>   16'

soprano solo   chorus
2[1.2/pic] 2 2 3[1.2.cbn] — 4 3 3 1 — tmp+2 — hp — str
Originally with piano accompaniment; orchestrated by Felix Mottl. An earlier orchestration by Franz Lachner (for 2 2 2 2 — 2 2 3 0 — tmp — str) may be found on IMSLP.

Breitkopf	Kalmus	Luck's

Octet, D.803, F major <1824>   63'

0 0 1 1 — 1 0 0 0 — str 5t
1. *Adagio - Allegro*   15'
2. *Andante un poco mosso*   13'
3. *Allegro vivace*   6'
4. *Andante & Variations*   11'
5. *Menuetto & Trio*   7'
6. *Andante molto - Allegro*   11'

Luck's	Peters

Offertorium, D.963 (Intende voci) <1828>   15'

tenor solo   chorus
0 1 2 2 — 2 0 3 0 — str

Breitkopf

Overture, D.8, C minor (arr. Hess) <1811>   6'

str
Ed. Ernst Hess. Originally for string quintet (2vn, 2va, vc); later arranged by Schubert for string quartet (identified as D.8A). This latter version (D.8A) has been arranged by Hess for string orchestra.

Peters

Overture, D.8, C minor (arr. Hofmann) <1811>   6'

1 0 2 1 — 2 0 0 0 — str
Originally for string quintet (2vn, 2va, vc); later arranged by Schubert for string quartet (identified as D.8A). Orchestrated by Wolfgang Hofmann.

Peters

Overture, D.12, D major <1811 or 1812>   9'

2 2 2 2 — 2 2 3 0 — tmp — str

Breitkopf	Kalmus	Luck's

Overture, D.26, D major <1812>   9'

2 2 2 2 — 2 2 3 0 — tmp — str

Breitkopf	Kalmus	Luck's

Overture, D.470, B-flat major <1816>   7'

0 2 0 2 — 2 2 0 0 — tmp — str
Possibly intended for the cantata, D.472.

Breitkopf

Overture, D.556, D major <1817>   7'

2 2 2 2 — 2 0 0 0 — tmp — str

Breitkopf

Overture, D.590, D major (In the Italian Style) <1817>   8'

2 2 2 2 — 2 2 0 0 — tmp — str

Breitkopf	Kalmus	Luck's

Overture, D.591, op.170, C major (In the Italian Style) <1817>   7'

2 2 2[C-cl] 2 — 2 2 0 0 — tmp — str

Breitkopf	Kalmus

Overture, D.648, E minor <1819>   8'

2 2 2 2 — 4 2 3 0 — tmp — str
Possibly intended for the composer's unfinished opera, *Adrast*, D.137.

Breitkopf

Quartet, Strings, D.810, D minor (Der Tod und das Mädchen; Death and the Maiden) <1824>   40'

str
Arr. for string orchestra by Gustav Mahler.
Ed. David Matthews & Donald Mitchell.

Weinberger

Rondo, Violin & Strings, D.438, A major <1816>   14'

str

Breitkopf	Kalmus	Luck's

Rosamunde, D.797 <1823>   55'

alto solo   chorus
2 2 2 2 — 4 2 3 0 — tmp — str
1. *Entr'acte I*   11'
2. *Ballet Music I*   9'
3a. *Entr'acte II*   4'
3b. *Romance [alto aria]*   4'
4. *Spirits' Chorus [male chorus]*   4'
5. *Entr'acte III*   8'
6. *Pastoral Music [no strings]*   2'
7. *Shepherds' Chorus [mixed chorus]*   4'
8. *Huntsmen's Chorus [mixed chorus]*   2'
9. *Ballet Music II*   7'

Breitkopf

Rosamunde: Overture, D.644   10'

2 2 2 2 — 4 2 3 0 — tmp — str
Actually the overture to *Die Zauberharfe*, and published by Breitkopf under that title, though commonly known as *Rosamunde*.

Bärenreiter	Breitkopf	Kalmus	Luck's

Rosamunde, D.797: Ballet Music <1823>   16'

2 2 2 2 — 2 2 3 0 — tmp — str
Nos.2 and 9 of the incidental music.
Balletmusik I [No.2]: Allegro moderato - Andante un poco assai   9'
Balletmusik II [No.9]: Andantino   7'

Breitkopf	Kalmus	Luck's

Rosamunde, D.797: Entr'actes <1823>   23'

2 2 2 2 — 2 2 3 0 — tmp — str
Nos.1, 3a, and 5 of the incidental music.
Entr'acte after Act I [No.1]: Allegro molto moderato   11'
Entr'acte after Act II [No.3a]: Andante   4'
Entr'acte after Act III [No.5]: Andantino   8'

Breitkopf	Kalmus	Luck's

Salve Regina, D.106, B-flat major <1814`>   8'

tenor solo
0 2 0 2 — 2 0 0 0 — org — str

Breitkopf

Salve Regina, D.223, op.47, F major <1815>   6'

soprano solo
0 0 2 2 — 2 0 0 0 — org — str
Two versions exist.

Kalmus

Salve Regina, D.676, op.153, A major <1819>   13'

soprano solo
str

Breitkopf	Kalmus	Luck's

She Was Here
see under: Golijov, Osvaldo

Der Spiegelritter, D.11: Overture <1811–1813>   10'
2 2 2 2 — 2 2 0 0 — tmp — str

Breitkopf

Stabat Mater, D.175, G minor (The Little) <1815>   6'
chorus
0 2 2 2 — 0 0 3 0 — org — str
Faber edition by Brian Newbould.

Faber	Kalmus	Luck's

Stabat Mater, D.383, F minor <1816>   37'
chorus   solos STB
2 2 0 3[1.2.cbn] — 2 0 3 0 — str
Oratorio, with text by Friedrich Gottlieb Klopstock.

Breitkopf	Kalmus	Luck's

SYMPHONIES
The numbering of the first 6 complete Schubert symphonies appears to be well-established, but thereafter various competing numbering systems come into play. In the following list, the symphonies are organized by D-number.

Symphony, D.2b, D major [fragment] <?1811>   1'
2 2 2 2 — 2 2 3 0 — tmp — str
Fragment in full score, edited by Brian Newbould. 30 bars of a slow introduction and part of an Allegro, believed to have been composed around 1811.

Newbould

Symphony No.1, D.82, D major <1813>   29'
1 2 2 2 — 2 2 0 0 — tmp — str
Bärenreiter ed. A.Feil & Chr.Landon.
I. Adagio; Allegro vivace	*11'*
II. Andante	*7'*
III. Allegro	*5'*
IV. Allegro vivace	*6'*

Bärenreiter	Breitkopf	Kalmus	Luck's

Symphony No.2, D.125, B-flat major <1814–1815>   29'
2 2 2 2 — 2 2 0 0 — tmp — str
Bärenreiter ed. A.Feil & Chr.Landon.
I. Largo; Allegro vivace	*10'*
II. Andante	*9'*
III. Menuetto	*4'*
IV. Presto vivace	*6'*

Bärenreiter	Breitkopf	Kalmus	Luck's

Symphony No.3, D.200, D major <1815>   26'
2 2 2 2 — 2 2 0 0 — tmp — str
Bärenreiter ed. A.Feil & Chr.Landon.
I. Adagio maestoso; Allegro con brio	*10'*
II. Allegretto	*5'*
III. Menuetto	*4'*
IV. Presto vivace	*7'*

Bärenreiter	Breitkopf	Kalmus	Luck's

Symphony No.4, D.417, C minor (Tragic) <1816>   31'
2 2 2 2 — 4 2 0 0 — tmp — str
Bärenreiter ed. A.Feil & D.Woodfull-Harris.
I. Adagio molto; Allegro vivace	*7'*
II. Andante	*10'*
III. Menuetto: Allegro vivace	*6'*
IV. Allegro	*8'*

Bärenreiter	Breitkopf	Kalmus	Luck's

Symphony No.5, D.485, B-flat major <1816>   27'
1 2 0 2 — 2 0 0 0 — str
Bärenreiter ed. A.Feil & D.Woodfull-Harris; Breitkopf ed. Hauschild.
I. Allegro	*5'*
II. Andante con moto	*11'*
III. Menuetto: Allegro molto	*5'*
IV. Allegro vivace	*6'*

Bärenreiter	Breitkopf	Kalmus	Luck's

Symphony No.6, D.589, C major (Little C major) <1817–1818>   27'
2 2 2 2 — 2 2 0 0 — tmp — str
Bärenreiter ed. A.Feil & D.Woodfull-Harris.
I. Adagio; Allegro	*7'*
II. Andante	*5'*
III. Scherzo: Presto - Più lento	*6'*
IV. Allegro moderato	*9'*

Bärenreiter	Breitkopf	Kalmus	Luck's

Symphony, D.615, D major [fragments] <1818>   7'
2 2 2 2 — 2 2 0 0 — tmp — str
From an uncompleted symphony of 1818, Schubert's fragments (piano score) of the first mvt and finale, as orchestrated by Brian Newbould. Materials are available only to professional organizations, only from BBC, and only with Newbould's express permission.
| *Fragment of 1st mvt* | *4'* |
| *Fragment of Finale* | *3'* |

BBC

Symphony, D.708a, D major: Scherzo <after 1820>   17'
2 2 2 2 — 2 2 0 0 — tmp — str
Schubert left fragments in piano score of four movements of a symphony from after 1820. These have been orchestrated by Brian Newbould.
    The Scherzo (8') was almost complete, and has been finished by Newbould, who can supply performance material.
    Movements 1, 2 & 4 remain fragments. Newbould's orchestrations of these are available only to professional organizations, only from BBC, and only with Newbould's express permission.
First movement fragment	*3'*
Slow movement fragment	*3'*
Completion of Scherzo	*8'*
Fragment of Finale	*3'*

BBC	Newbould

Symphony, D.729, E major (Weingartner) <1821>   36'
2 2 2 2 — 4 2 3 0 — tmp — str
Completed from Schubert's sketches by Felix Weingartner, and published as *Symphony No.7*.
1. Adagio; Allegro	*12'*
2. Andante	*8'*
3. Scherzo	*7'*
4. Allegro vivace	*9'*

Luck's	Universal

Symphony, D.729, E major (Newbould) <1821>   39'

2 2 2 2 — 4 2 3 0 — tmp — str
Realization by Brian Newbould from Schubert's sketches. Originally published by the University of Hull Press (1992) as *Symphony No.7*.

1. Adagio; Allegro	*12'*
2. Andante	*8'*
3. Scherzo	*6'*
4. Allegro vivace	*13'*

Newbould

Symphony, D.759, B minor (Unfinished) <1822>   25'

2 2 2 2 — 2 2 3 0 — tmp — str
Traditionally known as *Symphony No.8*; more recently published by Bärenreiter and Breitkopf as *No.7*.
   A critical edition of the score with historical and analytical essays is available from Norton.
   Bärenreiter ed. W. Aderhold; Breitkopf ed. P. Gülke; Peters ed. K. Schubert.

I. Allegro moderato	*12'*
II. Andante con moto	*13'*

Bärenreiter	Breitkopf	Kalmus	Luck's	Peters

Symphony, D.759, B minor (Unfinished): Scherzo (completed Newbould) <1822>   7'

2 2 2 2 — 2 2 3 0 — tmp — str
3rd mvt completed by Brian Newbould, based on Schubert's sketch. A complete 4-movement symphony may be performed by using the traditional mvts 1 & 2, the present Scherzo, and (as recommended by Newbould) the B minor Entr'acte No.1 from the composer's *Rosamunde*, D.797, as a 4th movement. Thus the movements would be, respectively, 12', 13', 7', 11' = 43' total.

Newbould

Symphony, D.812, C major (Grand duo) <1824>   42'

3[1.2.pic] 2 2 2 — 4 2 3 0 — tmp — str
Schubert's *Grand duo*, op.140, originally for piano 4-hands. Orchestrated by Joseph Joachim, acting on a suggestion by Brahms. Other orchestrations exist by Fritz Oeser (Alkor), Raymond Leppard (Faber), and René Leibowitz (Boelke-Bomart).

1. Allegro moderato	*13'*
2. Andante	*11'*
3. Scherzo & Trio: Allegro vivace	*5'*
4. Allegro vivace	*13'*

Kalmus

Symphony, D.936a, D major (Newbould) <1828>   28'

2 2 2 2 — 2 2 3 0 — tmp — str
Realization by Brian Newbould in 1980-81. Published as *Symphony No.10*, it is a 3-movement work, the functions of scherzo and finale being combined in the third movement. Despite the earlier D-number, this work was composed after the "Great" C major symphony, D.944.

I. Allegro maestoso	*9'*
II. Andante	*11'*
III. Scherzo: Allegro moderato	*8'*

Faber

Symphony, D.936a

see also under: Berio, Luciano, 1925-2003
            Rendering

Symphony, D.944, C major (The Great C major) <1825–1828>   48'

2 2 2 2 — 2 2 3 0 — tmp — str
Bärenreiter ed. W. Aderhold; Breitkopf ed. Peter Hauschild.
   Traditionally listed as *Symphony No.7*, or *Symphony No.9*; more recently published by Bärenreiter and Breitkopf as *No.8*.

I. Andante; Allegro ma non troppo	*14'*
II. Andante con moto	*12'*
III. Scherzo: Allegro vivace	*10'*
IV. Allegro vivace	*12'*

Bärenreiter	Breitkopf	Kalmus	Luck's

Tantum ergo, D.962 <1828>   6'

chorus   solos SATB
0 2 2 2 — 2 2 3 0 — tmp — str

Luck's	Peters	Schirmer

Der Teufel als Hydraulicus, D.4: Overture <?1812>   5'

2 0 2 2 — 2 0 0 0 — str

Breitkopf	Carisch	Luck's

Des Teufels Lustschloss, D.84: Overture <c1813>   9'

2 2 2 2 — 2 2 3 0 — tmp — str

Breitkopf	Kalmus	Luck's

Der vierjährige Posten, D.190: Overture <1815>   8'

2 2 2 2 — 2 2 0 0 — tmp — str

Breitkopf	Heugel

Wanderer Fantasy, D.760, op.15 (Wandererfantasie) <1822>   21'

solo piano
2 2 2 2 — 2 2 3 0 — tmp — str
Arr. by Franz Liszt, from a work for piano.

I. Allegro con fuoco	*6'*
II. Adagio	*6'*
III. Presto	*5'*
IV. Allegro	*4'*

Kalmus

Die Zauberharfe: Overture

see his: Rosamunde: Overture, D.644

Die Zwillingsbrüder, D.647: Overture <1818–1819>   5'

2 2 2 2 — 2 2 0 0 — tmp — str

Breitkopf	Kalmus	Luck's

Schuetz, Heinrich   1585-1672

see: Schütz, Heinrich, 1585-1672

Schulhoff, Erwin   1894-1942

(b Prague, 8 June 1894; d Wülzburg,18 Aug 1942). Czech composer of German descent

Hot-Sonate (Jazz Sonate) <1930>   16'

solo alto saxophone
1 1 1 1 — 1 1 0 0 — str 5t[or str orch]
Originally for alto saxophone & piano; arranged (2000) by Harry-Kinross White for alto saxophone & orchestra. There is also a 1994 arrangement for alto saxophone and large orchestra by Detlef Bensmann.

I. quarter-note = 66	4'
II. half-note = 112	2'
III. quarter-note = 80	5'
IV. half-note = 132	5'

Schott

Schuller, Gunther   1925-

(b New York, 22 Nov 1925). American

American Triptych; A Study in Textures <1964–1965>   14'

3[1.2.3/pic] 3[1.2.3/Eh] 3[1.2.3/bcl] 3[1.2.3/cbn] — 4 3 3 1 — tmp+3 — hp — str
perc: glock, vib, tri, tamtam, hi-hat, woodblk, bd, szl cym, sd, 5sus cym, 2gongs

AMP

Capriccio stravagante <1972>   19'

3[1/pic.2/pic.3/pic] 3[1.2.Eh] 4[1.2.Ebcl.bcl] 3[1.2.3/cbn] — tmp+5 — hp — cel, hpsd, pf — str

AMP

Concertino, Jazz Quartet & Orchestra   19'

solo jazz quartet: vibraphone, piano, percussion, string bass
2[1.2/pic] 2 2 2 — 2 3 2 0 — 1perc — str
perc: sus cym, tri

I. Slow	7'
II. Passacaglia	7'
III. quarter note = 88	6'

MJQ

Concerto for Orchestra, No.2 <1976>   22'

4[1/pic.2/pic.3/afl.pic] 4[1.2.3/ob d'am.Eh]
5[1/Ebcl.2.3/bcl.4/asx.bcl/cbcl] 4[1.2.3.4/cbn] — 4 4 4 1 — tmp+5 — hp — cel, pf, opt org — str

AMP

Contours, for Chamber Orchestra <1955–1958>   23'

1[1/pic] 1 2[1/Ebcl.bcl] 1 — 1 1 1 0 — 3perc — hp — str
perc: tambn, tri, glock, xyl, 6sus cym, 2field dr, 2tomtoms, 2gongs

AMP   Schott

Dramatic Overture <1951>   10'

3[1.2/pic3.3/pic] 3[1.2.Eh] 4[1.2.Ebcl.bcl] 3[1.2.cbn] — 4 3 3 1 — tmp+4 — 2hp — pf/cel — str
perc: glock, tri, cym, tambn, bd, td, xyl, 2tamtams

AMP

Five Bagatelles <1964>   15'

3[1.2.pic] 3[1.2.Eh] 2[1.2/bcl] 3[1.2.cbn] — 4 3 3 1 — tmp+2 — hp — pf — str
perc: bd, cym, glock, sd, sus cym, tamtam, tambn, tomtom, tri

AMP

Five Etudes for Orchestra <1966>   14'

3[1.2.3/pic] 3 2 2 — 4 3 3 1 — tmp+3 — hp — pf — str

AMP

Journey into Jazz <1962>   16'

jazz ensemble: asx, tsx, tp, db, drums   narrator
1 1 1 1 — 1 1 0 0 — 1perc — hp — str
perc: hi-hat, szl cym, sd, sus cym

AMP

Of Reminiscences and Reflections <1993>   15'

4[1/pic.2/pic.3/afl.4/afl] 4[1.2.3/Eh.4/Eh] 4[1.2.3/bcl.4/bcl] 4[1.2.3.4/cbn] — 6 4 4 1 — tmp+5 — hp — pf/cel — str

Schirmer

Seven Studies on Themes of Paul Klee <1959>   21'

3[1.2/pic2.3/pic1] 3[1.2.Eh] 3[1.2.bcl] 3[1.2.cbn] — 4 3 3 1 — tmp+5 — hp — pf — str
perc: vib, glock, sd, bd, woodblk, guiro, claves, tri, hi-hat, 2sus cym

1. Antike Harmonien (Antique Harmonies)	2'
2. Abstraktes Trio (Abstract Trio)	2'
3. Kleiner blauer Teufel (Little Blue Devil)	3'
4. Die Zwitschermaschine (The Twittering-Machine)	2'
5. Arabische Stadt (Arab Village)	7'
6. Ein unheimlicher Moment (An Eerie Moment)	2'
7. Pastorale	3'

Universal

Spectra <1958>   23'

4[1.2.pic.afl] 4[1.2.3/Eh.Eh] 4[1.2.Ebcl.bcl] 4[1.2.3.cbn] — 4 4 3 1 — tmp+4 — hp — str
perc: sd, bd, cym, tamtam, tambn, tri, glock, gong, bongos, 3tomtoms

AMP   Schott

Schuman, William   1910-1992

(b New York, 4 Aug 1910; d New York, 15 Feb 1992). American

Amaryllis: Variants for Strings on an Old English Song <1976>   8'

str

Merion

American Festival Overture <1939>   9'

3[1.2.3/pic] 3[1.2.Eh] 3[1.2.bcl] 3[1.2.opt cbn] — 4 3 3 1 — tmp+3 — str
perc: xyl, sus cym, sd, bd

Schirmer

Casey at the Bat <1953; rev 1976> 40'

soloists: baritone, soprano   chorus
3[1.2.pic] 3[1.2.Eh] 3[1.2.bcl] 2 — 4 3 3 1 — tmp+3 (or 4) — pf — str

perc: bd, bd/cym, cym, sus cym, sd, td, tamtam, glock, xyl, chimes, whip, wnd mach, whistle

A baseball cantata adapted from the composer's 1953 opera *The Mighty Casey*. The solo baritone takes many roles; there is an optional role for a boy soprano.

BEFORE THE GAME
1. *Noon of the Big Day* _'
2. *The Championship of the State* _'
3. *The Mighty Casey* _'
4. *Autograph* _'
5. *You look so sweet today* _'
6. *Kiss me not goodbye* _'
THE GAME
7. *Last half of the ninth* _'
8. *Two out* _'
9. *If only Casey* _'
10. *A prayer* _'
11. *Surprise* _'
12. *This gladdened multitude* _'
13. *It looked extremely rocky* _'
14. *You're doin' fine kid* _'
15. *That ain't my style* _'
16. *Rhubarb* _'
17. *With a smile of Christian charity* _'
18. *Hist'ry hangs on a slender thread* _'
19. *The sneer has gone from Casey's lips* _'
AFTER THE GAME
20. *Oh, somewhere (Requiem)* _'

> AMP

Circus Overture (Side Show for Orchestra) <1944> 7'

3[1.2/pic1.3/pic2] 3[1.2.Eh] 4[1.2.Ebcl.bcl] 3[1.2.cbn] — 4 3 3 1 — tmp+4 — pf — str

perc: sd, bd, cym, tamtam, tomtom (opt)

Also available in reduced orchestration:
  2 2 3 0 — 2 3 3 1 — tmp+perc — pf — str

> Schirmer

Concerto, Piano <1938–1942> 24'

  1 1 1 0 — 2 2 1 0 — str
  I. With energy and precision 8'
  II. Deliberately 8'
  III. half-note = ca.144 8'

> Schirmer

Concerto, Violin <1947; rev 1954 & 1958-59> 31'

3[1.2.3/pic] 3[1.opt2.Eh] 4[1.2.opt3.bcl] 3[1.opt2.cbn] — 4 3 3 0 — tmp+3 — str

perc: sd, sus cym, bd, chimes

  I. Allegro risoluto; Molto tranquillo; Tempo I; Cadenza; Agitato, fervente 15'
  II. Introduzione: Adagio; Quasi cadenza; Presto leggiero; Allegretto 16'

> Merion

Credendum; An Article of Faith <1955> 17'

4[1.2/pic1.3/pic2.4] 4[1.2.3.Eh] 5[1.2.3.Ebcl.bcl] 4[1.2.3.cbn] — 6 4 3 2[1.ten tuba] — tmp+4 — pf — str

perc: bd, chimes, cym, sd, sus cym, tamtam, td, xyl, steel plate

  1. *Declaration [no str]* 3'
  2. *Chorale* 6'
  3. *Finale* 8'

> Merion

Judith; Choreographic Poem <1949> 24'

3[1.2.pic] 3[1.2.Eh] 3[1.2.bcl] 3[1.2.cbn] — 4 2 3 1 — tmp+3 — pf — str

perc: xyl, bd, sd, cym, sus cym

May be performed with woodwinds: 2[incl pic] 2[incl Eh] 2 2.

> Schirmer

New England Triptych <1956> 16'

3[1.2.3/pic] 3[1.2.Eh] 4[1.2.Ebcl.bcl] 2 — 4 3 3 1 — tmp+3 — str

perc: bd, cym, sd, td; 2 or 3 opt additional sd or field dr at end

"Three Pieces for Orchestra after William Billings."
  1. *Be Glad Then America* 6'
  2. *When Jesus Wept* 7'
  3. *Chester* 3'

> Merion

Newsreel (In Five Shots) <1941> 8'

3[1.2.3/pic] 3[1.2.Eh] 5[1.2.3.Ebcl.bcl] 4[1.2.3.cbn] — 4 3 3 1 — 2asx, tsx — tmp+4 — pf — str

perc: glock, xyl, sd, cym, sus cym, bd, tri, tamtam

Possible with reduced instrumentation:
  2[hpstr] 1 2 1 — 2 3 3 1 — tmp+4 — str
  If piano/conductor is used, possible with:
  0 0 2 0 — 0 1 1 0 — 1perc — 4vn, 2va
  1. *Horse Race* 2'
  2. *Fashion Show* 2'
  3. *Tribal Dance* 1'
  4. *Monkeys at the Zoo* 2'
  5. *Parade* 1'

> Luck's   Schirmer

On Freedom's Ground; An American Cantata <1985> 40'

baritone solo   chorus
3[1/pic.2/pic.3/pic] 3[1.2.3/Eh] 3[1.2.3/bcl] 2 — 4 3 3 1 — tmp+4 — pf/cel — str

  1. *Back Then* _'
  2. *Our Risen States* _'
  3. *Like a Great Statue* _'
  4. *Come Dance* _'
  5. *Immigrants Still* _'

> Merion

The Orchestra Song <1963> 4'

2[1.pic] 1 2[1.opt bcl] 1 — 4 3 3 1 — tmp+5 (or 8) — str

perc: glock, sd, tambn, sus cym, bd, opt xyl, opt vib, opt tri

> Merion

A Song of Orpheus; Fantasy for Violoncello & Orchestra <1961> 20'

violoncello solo
3[1.2.3/pic] 3[1.2.Eh] 3[1.2.bcl] 2 — 4 0 0 0 — hp — str

> Merion

Symphonies Nos. 1 & 2

These two early symphonies (1935 & 1937, respectively) were withdrawn by the composer.

Symphony No.3 <1941> 33'

4[1.2.(opt3/pic2).pic] 4[1.2.(opt3).Eh] 5[1.2.(opt3).Ebcl.bcl] 4[1.2.(opt3).(opt cbn)] — 8[hn5-8 opt] 4 4 1 — tmp+3 — opt pf — str

perc: bd, cym, sd, xyl

Optional instruments termed "very desirable." All the optional woodwinds and the piano are carefully notated in the score; however, the horns 5-8 are not notated at all, nor does the publisher have parts for them. It would seem unlikely that so careful an orchestrator as Wm.Schuman would want *all* the horns doubled *all* the time. Possibly the request for 4 additional horns was an afterthought, or perhaps the composer intends the conductor to specify where the horns are doubled.

  PART I
  Passacaglia 7'
  Fugue 7'
  PART II
  Chorale 11'
  Toccata 8'

> Schirmer

Symphony No.4 <1941>   26'

3[1.2.3/pic] 4[1.2.3.Eh] 5[1.2.3.Ebcl.bcl] 4[1.2.3.cbn] — 4 3 3 1 —
tmp+3 — str
perc: sd, cym, bd, glock, xyl

I. quarter-note = circa 72   9'
II. Tenderly, simply   9'
III. quarter-note = 144   8'

> Schirmer

Symphony No.5 (Symphony for Strings) <1943>   17'

str
1. Molto agitato ed energico   4'
2. Larghissimo   8'
3. Presto   5'

> Schirmer

Symphony No.6 <1948>   30'

3[1.2.3/pic] 3[1.2.Eh] 3[1.2.bcl] 3[1.2.cbn] — 4 3 3 1 — tmp+2 — str
perc: sd, glock, cym, sus cym, bd
In one movement.

> Schirmer

Symphony No.7 <1960>   29'

3[incl pic] 3[incl Eh] 3[incl bcl] 3[incl cbn] — 4 3 3 1 — tmp+3 — pf
— str

perc: bd, chimes, glock, sd, sus cym, woodblk, xyl
Opt additional insts increase the size of the wind sections to:
    4[incl pic] 4[incl Eh] 5[incl Ebcl,bcl] 4[incl cbn] — 6 4 3 2
I. Largo assai   11'
II. Vigoroso   3'
III. Cantabile intensamente   9'
IV. Scherzando brioso   6'

> Merion

Symphony No.8 <1962>   31'

4[1.2.3/pic1.4/pic2] 4[1.2.(3opt).Eh] 4[1.2.(3opt).bcl] 4[1.2.(3opt).cbn]
— 6 4 4 1 — tmp+5 — 2hp — pf — str
perc: sd, bd, cym, tamtam, woodblk, chimes, glock, vib, xyl, 2sus cym, tmp2
I. Lento sostenuto - Pressante vigoroso - Lento   10'
II. Largo - Tempo più mosso   13'
III. Presto - Prestissimo   8'

> Merion

Symphony No.9 (Le fosse ardeatine) <1968>   28'

3[incl pic] 3[incl Eh] 3[incl bcl] 3[incl cbn] — 4 4 3 1 — tmp+5 — pf
— str

perc: chimes, xyl, sus cym, sd, td, tamtam, bd, 3pr cym
Anteludium   8'
Offertorium   10'
Postludium   10'

> Merion

Symphony No.10 (American Muse) <1975>   31'

4[1.2/pic1.3/pic2.(4opt)] 4[1.2.(3opt).Eh] 5[1.2.(3opt).Ebcl.bcl]
4[1.2.(3opt).cbn] — 6 4 4 1 — tmp+4 — hp — cel, pf — str
perc: xyl, glock, sd, cym, bd, tamtam, chimes, sus cym, vib, crot
I. Con fuoco   6'
II. Larghissimo   13'
III. Presto; Andantino; Leggero; Pesante; Presto possibile   12'

> Merion

Three Colloquies <1979>   23'

solo horn
3[incl pic] 2 3[incl bcl] 2 — 0 3 0 0 — tmp+4 — hp — pf/cel — str
1. Rumination   5'
2. Renewal   10'
3. Remembrance   8'

> Merion

Undertow: Choreographic Episodes from the Ballet <1945>   25'

3[1.2/pic.3/pic] 3[1.2.Eh] 3 3 — 4 2 3 1 — tmp+2 — pf — str
perc: tambn, cym, tamtam, glock, sd, bd, sus cym, rattle

> Schirmer

Schumann, Clara Wieck   1819-1896

(b Leipzig, 13 Sept 1819; d Frankfurt, 20 May 1896). German

Concerto, Piano, op.7, A minor <1833–1836>   21'

2 2 2 2 — 2 2 1 0 — tmp — str
Breitkopf ed. Janina Klassen; Hildegard ed. Kile Smith.
    In mvt 2 the only instruments that play are the solo piano, solo cello
and timpani.
I. Allegro maestoso   6'
II. Romanze: Andante non troppo, con grazia   5'
III. Finale: Allegro non troppo   10'

> Breitkopf   Hildegard

Schumann, Georg   1866-1952

(b Königstein, Saxony, 25 Oct 1866; d Berlin, 23 May 1952). German

Liebesfrühling; Ouvertüre, op.28 <1901>   15'

3[1.2.pic] 2 2 3[1.2.cbn] — 4 3[1.2.crt] 3 1 — tmp+2 — str
perc: tri, cym

> Breitkopf   Fleisher

Schumann, Robert   1810-1856

(b Zwickau, Saxony, 8 June 1810; d Endenich, nr Bonn, 29 July 1856). German

Adagio and Allegro, op.70 <1849>   12'

solo horn (or violoncello)
2 1 2 2 — 2 0 0 0 — tmp — str
Originally for horn (or violin or violoncello) & piano. Orchestrated by
Blair Fairchild.

> Schott

Adventlied, op.71 <1848>   18'

solo soprano   chorus SSAATTB
2 2 2 2 — 4 2 3 0 — tmp — str
1. Dein König kommt in niedern Hüllen   _'
2. O mächt'ger Herrscher ohne Heere   _'
3. Und wo du commest hergezogen   _'
4. O Herr von grosser Huld und Treue   _'
5. Noth ist es, dass du selbst hienieden   _'
6. Dagegen sich die Welt empört   _'_'
7. Und lösch' der Zwietracht Glimmern aus   _'

> Breitkopf   Kalmus

Bilder aus Osten, op.66 (Scenes from the East) <1848>   21'

3[1.2.pic] 2 2 2 — 2 2 0 0 — tmp+2 — str
Originally 6 impromptus for piano 4-hands. Orchestrated by Karl
Reinecke.
I. Vivace ma non troppo   4'
II. Andante con moto   3'
III. Un poco maestoso   2'
IV. Andantino   3'
V. Vivace   3'
VI. Molto moderato   6'

> Kalmus   Kistner&Siegel

Braut von Messina, op.100: Overture <1850–1851>   9'

3[1.2.pic] 2 2 2 — 2 2 3 0 — tmp — str

> Breitkopf   Kalmus

Carnaval, op.9 (orchestrated) <1834–1835>   31'

3[1.2.3/pic] 2 2 2 — 4 2 3 1 — tmp+3 — hp — str
perc: bd, cym, sd, tri, glock
Originally for piano; orchestrated ca.1902 by a group of Russian
composers, as indicated in parentheses in the Contents note below.
    Ed. Howard K. Wolf & Nancy M. Bradburd.

1. Preambule (Glazunov)	2'
2. Pierrot (Glazunov)	2'
3. Arlequin (Nikolai Klenovsky)	1'
4. Valse noble (A. Petrov)	2'
5. Eusebius (Glazunov)	2'
6. Florestan (Rimsky-Korsakov)	1'
7. Coquette (Vasily Kalafati)	2'
8. Réplique (Kalafati)	1'
9. Papillons (Tcherepnin)	1'
10. Lettres dansantes (Liadov)	1'
11. Chiarina (Kalafati)	2'
12. Chopin (Glazunov)	1'
13. Estrella (Alexander Winkler)	1'
14. Reconnaissance (Joseph Wihtol)	2'
15. Pantalon et Colombine (Arensky)	1'
16. Valse allemande (Liadov)	1'
17. Paganini (Liadov)	1'
18. "Aveu" (Nikolai Sokolov)	1'
19. Promenade (Klenovsky)	2'
20. Pause (Glazunov & Kalafati)	1'
21. Marche des "Davidsbündler" (Glazunov & Kalafati)	3'

Kalmus

Carnaval, op.9: 3 excerpts <1834–1835>   11'

2[1.2/pic] 2 2 2 — 2 2 0 0 — tmp+2 — str
perc: sus cym, sd
Originally for piano; orchestrated 1914 by Maurice Ravel.
    I. Préambule
    II. Valse allemande
    III. Paganini — Marche des Davidsbündler contre les Philistins

Salabert

Concert-Allegro with Introduction, op.134   13'

solo piano
2 2 2 2 — 2 2 1 0 — tmp — str

Breitkopf	Kalmus	Luck's

Concerto, Piano, op.54, A minor <1841–1845>   31'

2 2 2 2 — 2 2 0 0 — tmp — str
Breitkopf ed. Peter Jost.

I. Allegro affettuoso	15'
II. Intermezzo: Andantino grazioso	5'
III. Allegro vivace	11'

Breitkopf	Kalmus	Luck's

Concerto, Violin, op.129, A minor <1850; rev 1854>   25'

2 2 2 2 — 2 2 0 0 — tmp — str
Ed. Joachim Draheim. Around 1854, the composer produced a violin
version of his violoncello concerto, apparently for the use of Joseph
Joachim. The manuscript solo violin part had lain amongst the material in
Joachim's estate for many years, but was unrecognized until ca.1987.
    Use the orchestral score and parts for the cello concerto, with only
minor changes in the last 2 bars (755-756), as specified in the Preface to
the violin version. The latter is published only as a solo violin part with
piano accompaniment.

I. Nicht zu schnell	12'
II. Langsam	5'
III. Sehr lebhaft	8'

Breitkopf

Concerto, Violin, D minor <1853>   33'

2 2 2 2 — 2 2 0 0 — tmp — str
Completed 1853, but neither performed nor published until 1937. The
Breitkopf edition (by Christian Riedel) is recommended over Schott (ed.
Reinhard Kapp).

1. In kräftigem, nicht zu schnellem Tempo	16'
2. Langsam [attacca]	5'
3. Lebhaft, doch nicht zu schnell	12'

Breitkopf	Schott

Concerto, Violoncello, op.129, A minor <1850>   25'

2 2 2 2 — 2 2 0 0 — tmp — str

I. Nicht zu schnell	12'
II. Langsam	5'
III. Sehr lebhaft	8'

Breitkopf	Kalmus	Luck's

Concertstück, 4 Horns, op.86, F major <1849>   21'

4 solo horns
3[1.2.pic] 2 2 2 — 2[opt] 2 3 0 — tmp — str

I. Lebhaft	8'
II. Romanze: Ziemlich langsam	5'
III. Sehr lebhaft	6'

Breitkopf	Kalmus	KaWe	Luck's

Fantasia, op.131, C major <1853>   14'

solo violin
2 2 2 2 — 2 2 0 0 — tmp — str

Breitkopf	Kalmus	Luck's

Faust

see his: Scenen aus Goethes "Faust"

Fest-Ouvertüre, op.123 (Rheinweinlied) <1853>   8'

solos SATB   chorus
2 2 2 2 — 4 2 3 0 — tmp — str
Voices enter only near the end.

Breitkopf	Kalmus	Luck's

Genoveva, op.81: Overture <1847–1848>   10'

2 2 2 2 — 4 2 3 0 — tmp — str

Breitkopf	Kalmus	Luck's

Das Glück von Edenhall, op.143 <1853>   15'

solos TB   male chorus
2 2 2 2 — 4 3 3 1 — tmp+1 — str
perc: tri

Breitkopf

Hermann und Dorothea, op.136: Overture <1851>   8'

3[1.2.pic] 2 2 2 — 2 2 0 0 — 1perc — str
perc: sd

Breitkopf	Kalmus	Luck's

Introduction & Allegro appassionato, op.92   15'
(Konzertstück) <1849>

solo piano
2 2 2 2 — 2 2 0 0 — tmp — str

1. Introduction	3'
2. Allegro appassionato	12'

Breitkopf	Kalmus	Luck's

Julius Caesar, op.128: Overture <1851>   9'

2[1.pic] 2 2 2 — 4 2 3 1 — tmp — str

Breitkopf	Kalmus	Luck's

Der Königssohn, op.116 (The King's Son) <1851>   24'

solos ATBarB   chorus SATTBB
3[1.2.pic] 2 2 2 — 4 4[2tp, 2crt] 3 1 — tmp — str

1. Der alte graue König;	3'
2. Der Jüngling steht auf dem Verdeck	5'
3. Was spähest du nach der Angel	3'
4. Im Walde läuft ein wildes Pferd	2'
5. Es steht ein hoher schroffer Fels	6'
6. Der König und die Königin	5'

Breitkopf	Kalmus

Manfred, op.115 <1848–1849>   45'

chorus   solos SATBBBB; various speaking parts
3[1.2.3/pic] 2[1.2/Eh] 2 2 — 4 3 3 1 — tmp+2 — hp — org — str
perc: cym, bd

Overture	12'
1. Gesang der Geister (Song of the Spirits)	3'
2. Erscheinung eines Zauberbildes (Apparition)	1'
3. Geisterbannfluch (Incantation)	4'
4. Alpenkuhreigen (Swiss Alpine Melody)	2'
5. Zwischenaktmusik (Entr'acte)	2'
6. Rufung der Alpenfee (Invocation of the Witch of the Alps)	2'
7. Hymnus der Geister Arimans (Hymn of the Spirits of Arimanes)	3'
8 & 9. [brief snippets, often omitted in concert]	1'
10. Beschwörung der Astarte (Conjuring of Astarte)	1'
11. Manfred's Ansprache an Astarte (Manfred Addresses Astarte)	5'
12. Melodrama	2'
13. Abschied von der Sonne (Manfred's Farewell to the Sun)	2'
14. Melodrama	2'
15. Klostergesang (Final Scene)	3'

Breitkopf	C. Fischer	Kalmus	Luck's

Manfred, op.115: Overture <1848–1849>   12'

2 2 2 2 — 4 3 3 0 — tmp — str

Breitkopf	Kalmus	Luck's

Manfred, op.115: Suite <1848–1849>   6'

2 2[1.2/Eh] 2 2 — 2 1 0 0 — hp — str

1. Entr'acte	2'
2. Ranz des vaches [unaccompanied Eh solo]	2'
3. Apparition de la fée des Alpes	2'

Durand	Fleisher

Mass, op.147, C minor <1852–1853>   42'

chorus   solos STB
2 2 2 2 — 2 2 3 0 — tmp — opt org — str

I. Kyrie	5'
II. Gloria	9'
III. Credo	6'
IV. Offertorium	3'
V. Sanctus	12'
VI. Agnus Dei	7'

Breitkopf	Kalmus	Luck's

Neujahrslied, op.144 (New Year's Song) <1849–1850>   20'

chorus SATB   solos (from chorus) SAB
2 2 2 2 — 2 2 4 0 — tmp — str

1. Mit eherner Zunge da gibt es, gebt acht!	_'
2. Du herrschtest noch eben	_'
3. Heil! Heil! Neuer Gebieter der harrenden Welt	_'
4. Hebt, Brüder, die Blicke	_'
5. Lernt Sicheln zu schleifen	_'
6. Fürst, auf dem Throne	_'
7. Schliesst, Brüder, die Runde	_'

Breitkopf	Kalmus

Overture, Scherzo, & Finale, op.52 <1841; rev 1845>   17'

2 2 2 2 — 2 2 3[opt] 0 — tmp — str
Optional trombones are in Finale only.

I. Overture	7'
II. Scherzo	4'
III. Finale	6'

Breitkopf	Kalmus	Luck's

Das Paradies und die Peri, op.50 <1843>   99'

solos SSMsATTBarB   chorus SSAATTBB
3[1.2.pic] 2 2 2 — 4 2 3 1[oph] — tmp+2 — hp — str
perc: bd, cym, tri
Hp only in no.9; perc only in nos.11 & 18. 2 mvts call for pic: no.6
(*kleine flöte in Es*—actually notated in the score as if in Db) and no.12
(normal pic in C). A new Breitkopf engraving of this work shows a
normal pic in C in both these movements.
    The number of soloists could be reduced somewhat by combining
roles.

PART I	
1. Vor Edens Thor im Morgenprangen	4'
2. Wie glücklich sie wandeln	2'
3. Der hehre Engel, der die Pforte	2'
4. Wo find' ich sie?	2'
5. So sann sie nach	1'
6. Doch seine Ströme sind jetzt roth	3'
7. Und einsam steht ein Jüngling	2'
8. Weh', weh', er fehlte das Ziel	2'
9. Die Peri sah das Mal der Wunde	7'
PART II	
10. Die Peri tritt mit schüchterner Geberde	3'
11. Ihr erstes Himmelshoffen schwand	4'
12. Fort streift von hier das Kind der Lüfte	4'
13. Die Peri weint	3'
14. Im Waldesgrün am stillen See	3'
15. Verlassener Jüngling	4'
16. O lass mich von der Luft durchdringen	5'
17. Schlaf' nun und ruhe in Träumen voll Duft	4'
PART III	
18. Schmücket die Stufen zu Allahs Thron	3'
19. Dem Sang von ferne lauschend	3'
20. Verstossen! Verschlossen auf's neu'	5'
21. Jetzt sank des Abends gold'ner Schein	4'
22. Und wie sie niederwärts	4'
23. Hinab zu jenem Sonnentempel	6'
24. O heil'ge Thränen inn'ger Reue	4'
25. Es fällt ein Tropfen	8'
26. Freud', ew'ge Freude, mein Werk is gethan	7'

Breitkopf

Requiem, op.148, D-flat major <1852>   39'

chorus   solos SATB
2 2 2 2 — 2 2 3 0 — tmp — str

Requiem	4'
Te decet	5'
Dies irae	3'
Liber scriptus	6'
Qui Mariam absolvisti	5'
Domine Jesu Christe	3'
Hostias et preces tibi	2'
Sanctus	4'
Benedictus	7'

Breitkopf	Kalmus	Luck's

Requiem für Mignon, op.98b <1849>   15'

chorus   solos SSAAB
2 2 2 2 — 2 2 3 0 — tmp — opt hp — str

Breitkopf	Kalmus	Luck's

Des Sängers Fluch, op.139 <1852>   39'

solos: SSATBarBarBs   chorus
2 2 2 2 — 4 2 3 1 — tmp — str
Movements performed without pause.
1. Es stand in alten Zeiten	3'
2. Die Stunde ist gekommen	4'
3. Schon steh'n die beiden Sänger	4'
4. Provençalisches Lied	2'
5. Wie schlägt der Greis die Saiten	1'
6. Genug des Frühlings und der Lust	1'
7. Ballade	3'
8. Nicht diese wilden blut'gen Lieder	2'
9. Den Frühling kundet der Orkane Sausen	5'
10. Kamt ihr hier her mit euren Liedern	2'
11. Fangt an! Lausche, Jungfrau, aus der Höhe	4'
12. Und wie vom Sturm zerstoben	2'
13. Weh euch, ihr stolzen Hallen!	3'
14. Der Alte hat's gerufen	3'

| Breitkopf |

Scenen aus Goethes "Faust" (Scenes from Goethe's "Faust") <1844–1853>   115'

solos STBBB   chorus, boy choir
3[1.2.pic] 2 2 2 — 4 2 3 1 — tmp — hp — str
Lesser SATB solos drawn from chorus; boy choir includes SSAA soli.
Overture	8'
PART I	
Scene in the Garden	5'
Gretchen before the Picture of the Mater Dolorosa	4'
Scene in the Cathedral	8'
PART II	
Sunrise	17'
Midnight	13'
Faust's Death	14'
PART III	
Faust's Transfiguration	46'

| Breitkopf | Kalmus |

Scenen aus Goethes "Faust": Overture <1844–1853>   6'

2 2 2 2 — 4 2 3 0 — tmp — str

| Breitkopf |

Der Rose Pilgerfahrt, op.112 <1851>   63'

solos SSAATTBB   chorus
2 2 2 2 — 4 2 3 0 — tmp — str

| Peters |

Symphony, WoO 29, G minor (Zwickau) <1832–1833>   18'

2 2 2 2 — 2 2 3 0 — tmp — str
Ed. Marc Andreae. 2 movements of an unfinished early symphony.
| I. Moderato alletro | 10' |
| II. Andantino quasi allegretto; Intermezzo quasi scherzo; Andantino | 8' |

| Peters |

Symphony No.1, op.38, B-flat major (Spring) <1841>   30'

2 2 2 2 — 4 2 3 0 — tmp+1 — str
perc: tri
Triangle in 1st mvt only.
I. Andante un poco maestoso; Allegro molto vivace	12'
II. Larghetto	6'
III. Scherzo: Molto vivace	5'
IV. Allegro animato e grazioso	7'

| Breitkopf | Kalmus | Luck's |

Symphony No.2, op.61, C major <1845–1846>   38'

2 2 2 2 — 2 2 3 0 — tmp — str
I. Sostenuto assai; Allegro ma non troppo	13'
II. Scherzo: Allegro vivace	8'
III. Adagio expressivo	9'
IV. Allegro molto vivace	8'

| Breitkopf | Kalmus |

Symphony No.3, op.97, E-flat major (Rhenish) <1850>   32'

2 2 2 2 — 4 2 3 0 — tmp — str
I. Lebhaft	9'
II. Scherzo: Sehr mässig	7'
III. Nicht schnell	4'
IV. Feierlich	6'
V. Lebhaft	6'

| Breitkopf | Kalmus | Luck's |

Symphony No.4, op.120, D minor (original version 1841) <1841>   29'

2 2 2 2 — 4 2 3 0 — tmp — str
Breitkopf ed. J. Finson.
   Originally titled Symphonic Fantasy, and first performed as Symphony No.2. Later replaced by a major revision in 1851, as Symphony No.4.

| Breitkopf | Kalmus | Luck's |

Symphony No.4, op.120, D minor (1851 revision) <1841; rev 1851>   28'

2 2 2 2 — 4 2 3 0 — tmp — str
Breitkopf ed. J. Draheim.
   The definitive version of this work, considerably revised from the 1841 original.
I. Ziemlich langsam - Lebhaft	10'
II. Romanze: Siemlich langsam	3'
III. Scherzo: Lebhaft	5'
IV. Langsam - Lebhaft	10'

| Breitkopf | Kalmus | Luck's |

Träumerei <1838>   3'

str
Originally for piano, from Kinderscenen, op.15, no.7. Arr. Arthur Luck.

| Luck's |

Verzweifle nicht im Schmerzenstal, op.93 <1849; rev (orchd) 1852>   17'

double male chorus (TTBB/TTBB)
2 2 2 2 — 4 2 3 0 — tmp — org (ad lib) — str
Originally for male chorus a capella; orchestrated by the composer. Text by Rückert.
1. Verzweifle nicht im Schmerzensthal	5'
2. Viel Winter sind dir über's Haupt gegangen	3'
3. Harr' aus im Leid	3'
4. Und hoffe Gut's vom Hauch des Herrn	1'
5. Freuden ohne Zahl lässt blüh'n	5'

| Breitkopf |

Schurmann, Gerard   1924-

(b Kertosono, Dutch East Indies [now Indonesia], 19 Jan 1924). British-Dutch composer, resident in the USA

Concerto, Piano <1972–1973>   29'

2[incl pic] 2[incl Eh] 2 2 — 4 2 3 1 — tmp+3 — str

| Novello |

Six Studies of Francis Bacon <1968>   30'

3[1/pic.2/pic.3/pic] 3[1.2.3/Eh] 3[1.2.3/Ebcl/bcl] 3[1.2.cbn] — 4 4 3 1 — tmp+4 — hp — pf/cel — str
perc: glock, xyl, vib, chimes, sd, td, claves, tambn, 6pr crot, 2bd, 2tamtams, 2gongs, 2pr cym, 2sus cym, 2woodblks, rattle
Introduction	_'
1. Figures in a Landscape	_'
2. Popes	_'
3. Isabel	_'
4. Crucifixion	_'
5. George and the Bicycle	_'
6. Self-Portrait	_'

| Novello |

Variants, For Small Orchestra <1968–1970>   18'

1[1/pic] 2[1.2/Eh] 0 2 — 2 0 0 0 — str

> Novello

Schütz, Heinrich   1585-1672

(b Köstritz [now Bad Köstritz], nr Gera, bap. 9 Oct 1585; d Dresden, 6 Nov 1672).
German

SWV = *Schütz-Werke-Verzeichnis: kleine Ausgabe*, ed., W. Bittinger
(Kassel, 1960)

Historia der Auferstehung Jesu Christi, SWV 50 (Easter   35'
Oratorio) <1623>

chorus   solos SSAATTBB

hpsd, org — str

Bärenreiter ed. Walter Simon Huber.

> Bärenreiter   Kalmus

Historia der Geburt Jesu Christi, SWV 435 (Christmas   38'
Oratorio) <1664>

chorus   solos STB

2[2rec] 0 0 1 — 0 2 2 0 — 2 violettas (= treble viols) — cnt — str
This listing follows the Bärenreiter version, ed. Friedrich Schöneich,
which is based on the Schütz collected edition. Other editions from
Breitkopf, Kalmus, and G. Schirmer differ somewhat in instrumentation.

Introduction	*1'*
Es begab sich aber zu derselbigen Zeit	*3'*
Fürchtet euch nicht	*3'*
Und alsbald war da bei dem Engel	*1'*
Ehre sei Gott in der Höhe	*2'*
Und da die Engel	*1'*
Lasset uns nun gehen gen Bethlehem	*1'*
Und sie kamen eilend	*3'*
Wo ist der neugeborne König	*2'*
Da das der König Herodes hörete	*1'*
Zu Bethlehem im jüdischen Lande	*3'*
Da berief Herods die Weisen heimlich	*1'*
Ziehet hin, und forschet fleissig	*2'*
Als sie nun den König ge höret hatten	*2'*
Stehe auf, Joseph	*2'*
Und er stund auf und nahm das Kindlein	*4'*
Stehe auf Joseph	*2'*
Und er stund auf und nahm das Kindlein	*2'*
Dank sagen wir alle Gott	*2'*

> Bärenreiter

Schwantner, Joseph   1943-

(b Chicago, 22 March 1943). American

Aftertones of Infinity <1978>   14'

2[1/pic.2] 2[1.Eh] 2 2 — 4 2 3 1 — tmp+2 — hp — pf/cel — str
perc: belltree, chimes, glock, crot, marim, timbales, vib, 2sus cym, 2tri, 2bd,
2tamtams, 2gongs, 3temple bells, 3tomtoms
Oboists each play 2 crystal glasses. Orchestral players sing.

> Peters

Angelfire; Fantasy for Amplified Violin & Orchestra   18'
<2001>

solo violin (amplified)
2 2[1.Eh] 2[1.2/bcl] 2 — 4 2 2 0 — tmp+3 — hp — pf — str
perc: bd, tri, glock, xyl, marim, vib, chimes, crot, belltree, congas, 2tamtams, 2db
bows, 2sus cym, 4brake dr

> Helicon

Chasing Light … <2008>   20'

2[1.2/pic] 2 2 2 — 2 2 1 0 — tmp+1 — pf[ampd] — str
perc: vib, xyl, crot, tamtam, tri, bd, 3tomtom

I. Sunrise Ignites Daybreak's Veil	*5'*
II. Calliope's Rainbowed Song	*5'*
III. A Kaleidoscope Blooms	*5'*
IV. Morning's Embrace Confronts the Dawn	*5'*

> Schott

Concerto, Percussion [No.1] <1994>   28'

3[1.2.pic] 3[1.2.Eh] 3[1.2.bcl] 3[1.2.cbn] — 4 3 3 1 — tmp+3 — hp
— pf[ampd] — str
perc: [orch] bd, tamtam, xyl, chimes, vib, windchimes, marktree, belltree, marim,
4woodblk, timbales, claves, glock, 2sus cym, 4tomtom, 2brake dr, 6tri, anvil
[solo] bd, 2tomtom, timbales, bongos, water gong, vib, marin, xyl, crot, 2sus cym,
2tri, td, 9almglocken, shekere

1. Con forza	*6'*
2. Misterioso	*11'*
3. Ritmico con brio	*11'*

> Schott

Concerto, Percussion, No.2 <2011>   30'

soloists: 1 timpanist, 3 percussionists playing a large array of instruments
3[1.2.pic] 3[1.2.Eh] 3[1.2.bcl] 3[1.2.cbn] — 4 2 3 1 — hp —
pf[ampd] — str
perc: (solo insts, some ampd): tmp, xyl, marim, vib, chimes, crot, bongos, 3bd,
3sus cym, 2tomtom, 2timbales, 3brake dr, 2tri, 3tamtam[with bows],
2windchimes, 2belltree, 3cowbell, 3claves, 3rainstick, 3bucket dr, waterphone,
2mixing bowls, 2Tibetan singing bowls, 2water triangle

I. Feroce	_'
II. Misterioso e buio	_'
III. Con fervore	_'

> Schott

Concerto, Piano <1988>   29'

2[1.2/pic] 2[1.2/Eh] 2[1.2/bcl] 2 — 2 2 2 1 — 2perc — cel — str
perc: vib, marim, chimes, bd, glock, xyl, timbales, bongos, tamtam, sus cym,
belltree, crot, 3tomtoms, watergong, 2tri, tmp
"The piano should be discreetly amplified to slightly enhance its
presence."

> Helicon

Distant Runes and Incantations <1984>   15'

solo piano
2[1.2/pic] 2[1.2/Eh] 2[1.2/bcl] 2 — 2 2 0 0 — tmp+1 — cel — str
The piano should be discreetly amplified.
   A chamber version exists, for fl, cl, pf, perc & str 4t.

> Helicon

Freeflight; Fanfares & Fantasy for Orchestra <1989>   6'

3[1.2.3/pic] 3 3[1.2.3/bcl] 3[1.2.3/cbn] — 4 3 3 1 — tmp+3 — hp —
pf — str
perc: vib, crot, xyl, chimes, marim, bd, glock, tamtam, 2sus cym, 4tomtoms, 2tri

> Helicon

From a Dark Millennium <1981>   12'

3[1.2/pic.3/pic] 3[1.2.Eh] 3[1/Ebcl.2/bcl.3/bcl] 3 — 4 3 4 1 — tmp+4
— amplified pf, amplified cel — 2db
Players must sing and whistle in specified passages.

> Helicon

From Afar; Fantasy for Guitar & Orchestra <1987>   16'

3[1.2.3/pic] 3[1.2.3/Eh] 3[1.2.bcl] 3[1.2.3/cbn] — 4 3 3 1 — tmp+3
— hp — pf/cel — str
Guitar must be amplified.

> Helicon

New Morning for the World (Daybreak of Freedom) <1982>   27'

narrator
4[1.2.3/pic.4/pic] 3[1.2.Eh] 3[1.2.3/bcl] 3 — 4 3 4 1 — tmp+4 — hp
— cel[ampd], pf[ampd] — str
perc: vib, glock, marim, crot, xyl, chimes, 3tomtoms, buttongong, 2pr timbales,
2sus cym, 3tomtoms, 2tri, 2tamtams, 2bd
Words of Martin Luther King Jr.
   Orchestra members sing pitches at end.
   A chamber orchestra version is also available, calling for:
   2[incl pic] 2[incl Eh] 2[incl bcl] 2 — 2 2 0 0 — 1perc — pf — str

Helicon

A Sudden Rainbow <1986>   15'

3[1.2.3/pic] 3[1.2.3/Eh] 3[1.2.3/bcl] 3[1.2.3/cbn] — 4 3 3 1 — tmp+3
— hp — pf/cel[both ampd] — str

Helicon

Toward Light <1987>   22'

3[incl pic] 3[incl Eh] 3[incl bcl] 3[incl cbn] — 4 3 3 1 — tmp+3 —
hp — 2pf[1pf dbl cel] — str
perc: timbales, vib, xyl, claves, marim, chimes, crot, glock, 3tamtams, 2sus cym,
2bd, 3tomtoms, 2tri
1. Someday Memories   _'
2. Toward Light   _'
3. Shadowed Images   _'

Helicon

Schwartz, Elliott   1936-

(b Brooklyn, NY, 19 Jan 1936). American

Island <1970>   12'

3[1.2.pic] 2 3[1.2.bcl] 2[1.2/cbn] — 4 2 3 1 — tmp+2 — pf — str
perc: templeblks, glock, vib, xyl, sus cym, tamtam, bd, chimes, ratch, 4tomtoms,
slide whistle, toy gun, party noisemaker, 2balloons

C. Fischer

Texture <1966>   8'

1 1 1 1 — 1 1 1 0 — str[or str 5t]
Graphic notation and aleatoric procedures; all instruments play from
score.

Tetra

Schwertsik, Kurt   1935-

(b Vienna, 25 June 1935). Austrian

Concerto, Violin, op.31 <1977>   20'

2[1.pic] 1 2[1.Ebcl/bcl] 2 — 2 1 0 1 — tmp+1 — hp — str
perc: chimes, marim, bd
Subtitle: Romanzen in Schwartztinten-Ton und der geblümten
Paradies-Weis (Romances in Black Ink and Flourescent Paradise-White).
1. Phantasie I   _'
2. Albumblatt   _'
3. Vogellied   _'
4. Aubade   _'
5. Phantasie II   _'

Boosey

Draculas Haus- und Hofmusik; Eine transsylvanische   12'
Symphony für Streicher, op.18 (Dracula's House- and
Court Music; A Transylvanian Symphony for Strings)

str
1. Taglied   3'
2. Nachtstück   3'
3. Morgengrauen   3'
4. Abendrot   3'

Doblinger

Fünf Naturstücke (Five Nature Pieces), op.45 (Der   16'
irdischen Klänge 2) <1984>

3[1.2.3/pic] 2 3[1.2.bcl] 3[1.2.cbn] — 3 3 3 1 — tmp+5 — hp — str
perc: vib, thunder, marim, tamtam, chimes, windmachine, rainmachine,
watermachine, bottles (blown)
1. Wind   _'
2. Donner (Thunder) _'
3. Regen (Rain)   _'
4. Wasser (Water)   _'
5. Vogel (Bird)   _'

Boosey

Scriabin, Alexander   1872-1915

(b Moscow, 25 Dec 1871/6 Jan 1872; d Moscow, 14/27 April 1915). Russian

Concerto, Piano, op.20, F-sharp minor <1896>   28'

3[1.2.pic] 2 2 2 — 4 2 3 0 — tmp — str
I. Allegro   8'
II. Theme & Variations   9'
III. Allegro moderato   11'

Belaieff	Kalmus	Luck's	Russian

The Divine Poem; Symphony No.3, op.43   50'
(Bozhestvennaya poema; Le poème divin)
<1902–1904>

4[1.2.3.pic] 4[1.2.3.Eh] 4[1.2.3.bcl] 4[1.2.3.cbn] — 8 5 3 1 — tmp+2
— 2hp — str[16.16.12.12.8]
perc: sus cym, tamtam, glock, tri, bd
I. Luttes (Struggles)   25'
II. Voluptés (Pleasures)   15'
III. Jeu divin (Divine Game) 10'

Belaieff	Kalmus

The Poem of Ecstasy; Symphony No.4, op.54 (Poema   22'
èkstaza; Le Poème de l'extase) <1905–1908>

4[1.2.3.pic] 4[1.2.3.Eh] 4[1.2.3.bcl] 4[1.2.3.cbn] — 8 5 3 1 — tmp+5
— 2hp — cel, org[or harm] — str
perc: tri, cym, bd, tamtam, kybd glock, bell[C]
Keyboard glockenspiel player (perc) can also cover celesta.

Belaieff	Kalmus	Luck's

Prometheus, Poem of Fire; Symphony No.5, op.60   24'
(Prometey, poema ognya; Prométhée, le poème du feu)
<1908–1910>

solo piano   color organ [opt]   opt chorus
4[1.2.3.pic] 4[1.2.3.Eh] 4[1.2.3.bcl] 4[1.2.3.cbn] — 8 5 3 1 — tmp+6
— 2hp — cel, org — str
perc: tri, chimes, cym, bd, tamtam, glock[2 players, or vib for lower part]
Various attempts have been made to realize the composer's wishes with
respect to the color organ (clavier à lumières, or tastiera per luce), using
projections, flashing lights, and lasers.

Boosey	Ed. Russe	Kalmus	Luck's	Russian

Symphony No.1, op.26, E major <1899–1900>   51'

chorus   solo tenor & mezzo-soprano
3[1.2.3/pic] 2 3 2 — 4 3 3 1 — tmp/glock — hp — str
I. Lento   8'
II. Allegro dramatico   9'
III. Lento   10'
IV. Vivace   3'
V. Allegro   8'
VI. "O du des Lebens höchste Zier"   13'

Belaieff	Kalmus	Luck's

Symphony No.2, op.29, C minor <1901>   41'

3[1.2.3/pic] 2 3 2 — 4 3 3 1 — tmp+2 — str
perc: tamtam, sus cym
Russian State Publishers ed. Sergei Pavchinskii, 1972.
   The suspended cymbal part in the Pavchinskii edition is not found in
the original 1903 Belaieff score or Kalmus reprint. It is supposedly based
on an authentic performance tradition established during Scriabin's
lifetime. If the cymbal is not used, tmp+1 is sufficient.

   I. Andante; Allegro giocoso   6'
   II. Allegro   9'
   III. Andante; Piu vivo, poco agitato 12'
   IV. Tempestoso   6'
   V. Maestoso   8'

Belaieff	Kalmus	Russian

Sculthorpe, Peter   1929-2014

(b Launceston, Tasmania, 29 April 1929; d Sydney, 8 August 2014). Australian

Kakadu <1988>   15'

2 3[1.2.Eh] 2 3[1.2.cbn] — 4 4 3 1 — tmp+3 — str
perc: tamtam, sus cym, cym, bd, bongos, congas, Beijing gong, 3tomtoms
A cut from figure [13] to [28] is said to have been approved by the
composer for use in youth concerts.

Faber

Mangrove <1979>   13'

0 0 0 0 — 4 2 3 1 — 3perc — str
perc: tamtam, sus cym, Chinescym, bd, bongos, congas, crot, vib

Faber

Seeger, Ruth Crawford   1901-1953

See: Crawford (Seeger), Ruth, 1901-1953

Seither, Charlotte   1965-

(b Landau/Pfalz, 31 Aug 1965). German

Kammersinfonie (objet diaphane) <1993>   9'

1[fl/afl] 1[ob/Eh] 1 1[bn/cbn] — 1 1 1 0 — 1perc — str[1.1.1.1.1]
perc: vib, marim, tamtam, bd, chimes, tmp

Bärenreiter

Seitz, Friedrich   1848-1918

(b Günthersleben nr.Gotha, 12 Jun 1848; d 22 May 1918). German

Concerto, Violin, op.13, no.2, G Major (Student   9'
Concerto No.2) <1893>

1 2 2 2 — 2 2 0 0 — tmp — str
Originally for violin & piano; orchestrated by Bruce Adolphe, 2000.

Allegro non troppo   4'
Adagio   2'
Allegretto moderato   3'

MMB

Serly, Tibor   1901-1978

(b Losonc, 25 Nov 1901; d London, England, 8 Oct 1978). American composer of
Hungarian birth

Concertino 3 x 3 <1965>   28'

solo piano
2[incl pic] 1[incl Eh] 2 1 — 1 1 1 0 — tmp+1 — str
Each of 3 mvts played first by piano only, then orchestra only, then pf &
orch; thus a total of 9 mvts.

Fleisher

Serocki, Kazimierz   1922-1981

(b Toruń, 3 March 1922; d Warsaw, 9 Jan 1981). Polish

Segmenti <1961>   7'

1[1/pic] 1 2[Ebcl.bcl] 1 — 1 2[1.pic crt or tp] 2[1.tenor saxhorn or
tbn] 1 — asx — elec gtr, elec mand — tmp+3 — hp — pf, hpsd/cel —
[no str]
perc: xyl, glock, marim, vib, tamtam, guiro, ratch, templeblks, bongos, sd, tambn,
bd, 4tri, 6marac, 6herdbells, 5sus cym, 3hi-hats, 2gong, 4bottles (susp),
5woodblks, 3timbales, 3td
Graphic notation.

Moeck

Sessions, Roger   1896-1985

(b Brooklyn, NY, 28 Dec 1896; d Princeton, NJ, 16 March 1985). American

The Black Maskers: Suite <1923; rev suite: 1928>   22'

3[1/pic1.2/pic2.3/afl/pic3] 3[1.2.3/Eh] 4[1.2.Ebcl.bcl] 3[1.2.cbn] — 4 4
3 1 — tmp+4 — pf, opt org — str
perc: cym, field dr, sd, tamtam, tri, xyl, tambn, Chinese tambn

   I. Dance: Stridente sarcastico   4'
   II. Scene: Agitato molto   8'
   III. Dirge: Larghissimo   4'
   IV. Finale: Andante moderato un poco agitato 6'

Marks

Concertino for Chamber Orchestra <1971–1972>   17'

1[1/afl/pic] 1[1/Eh] 1[1/Ebcl/bcl] 1[1/cbn] — 2 1 1 0 — 2perc — pf
— str[2.2.2.2.1]
perc: xyl, marim, tambn, cym, sus cym, sd, timbales, marac, woodblk, whip,
claves, bd, tmp, tambn prov, Chinese drum

Marks

Concerto for Orchestra <1981>   15'

3[1.2/pic.pic] 3[1.2.Eh] 4[1.2.bcl.bcl] 3[1.2.cbn] — 4 3 3 1 — tmp+4
— hp — str
perc: cym, glock, field dr, sd, tamtam, td, tri, vib, whip, woodblk, xyl, tambn,
Chinese drum

Merion

Concerto, Violin <1927–1935>   29'

3[1.2/pic.3/afl] 3[1.2/Eh2.Eh1] 4[1.Ebcl.basset hn(or alto cl).bcl]
3[1.2.cbn] — 4 2 2 0 — tmp+1 — str[no vn]
perc: tri, sd, tambn, cym

   I. Large e tranquillo   9'
   II. Scherzo   6'
   III. Romanza   4'
   IV. Molto vivace   10'

Marks

Concerto, Violin & Violoncello <1970–1971> *20'*

3[incl pic] 2[incl Eh] 3[incl bcl] 2[incl cbn] — 3 1 2 0 — tmp+5 — pf — str

perc: xyl, marac, marim, glock, vib, cym, tamtam, claves, sd, tri, woodblk, bd, whip, 3tambn prov, Chinese drum, 2tambn, 3pr marac, 2sus cym

> Merion

Idyll of Theocritus <1954> *42'*

soprano solo

2[1.2/pic] 2[1.Eh] 2[1.bcl] 2 — 4 2 3 1 — tmp+2 — hp — cel — str[max 8.8.6.5.4]

perc: cym, tamtam, sd, xyl

> Marks

Montezuma: Suite <1935–1963> *15'*

3[1.2.pic] 3[1.2.Eh] 4[1.2.Ebcl.bcl] 3[1.2.cbn] — 4 4 3 1 — tmp+8 — hp — pf, cel — str

perc: bd, cym, sus cym, sd, td, field dr, timbales, tri, tambn, marim, vib, whip, bongos, guiro, marac, claves, tambour de provence, 2xyl, Chinese drum, 3tamtams, rattle, logdrum[or 2 lg woodblks]

> Marks

Symphony No.1, E minor <1926–1927> *19'*

3[1.2.3/pic] 3[1.2.3/Eh] 4[1.2.Ebcl.bcl] 3[1.2.cbn] — 4 4 3 1 — tmp+5 — pf — str

perc: xyl, chimes, cym, sus cym, bd, tri, tambn, 2Chinese drums, 2sd

I. Giusto	6'
II. Largo	7'
III. Allegro vivace	6'

> Marks

Symphony No.2 <1944–1946> *28'*

3[1.2.pic] 3[1.2.Eh] 3[1.2.bcl] 2 — 4 3 3 1 — tmp+3 — pf — str

perc: xyl, tamtam, tri, tambn, sd, bd, td, cym, sus cym

I. Molto agitato; Tranquillo e misterioso	10'
II. Allegretto capriccioso	2'
III. Adagio, tranquillo ed espressivo	9'
IV. Allegramente	7'

> Schirmer

Symphony No.3 <1957> *30'*

3[1.2/pic.pic] 3[1.2.Eh] 4[1.2.Ebcl.bcl] 3[1.2.cbn] — 4 2 3 1 — tmp+4 — hp — cel — str

perc: xyl, tamtam, tambn, sd, field dr, cym, sus cym, bd, templeblks, tri, vib, woodblk, tambn prov, Chinese drum

I. Allegro grazioso	6'
II. Allegro, un poco ruvido	6'
III. Andante sostenuto	11'
IV. Allegro con fuoco	7'

> Marks

Symphony No.4 <1958> *24'*

3[1.2.pic] 3[1.2.Eh] 4[1.2.alto cl.bcl] 3[1.2.cbn] — 4 3 3 1 — tmp+4 — hp — pf/cel — str

perc: xyl, vib, woodblk, tambn, bd, ratch, cym, sus cym, tambn prov, Chinese drum

I. Burlesque: Allegro giocoso	6'
II. Elegy: Adagio	9'
III. Pastorale: Andante tranquillo e grazioso un poco idolente	9'

> Marks

Symphony No.5 <1964> *16'*

3[1.2/afl.3/pic] 3[1.2.Eh] 4[1.2.Ebcl.bcl] 3[1.2.cbn] — 4 2 3 1 — tmp+4 — hp — pf, cel — str

perc: xyl, marim, vib, sus cym, tri, cym, tambn, td, sd, woodblk, whip, marac, tamtam, bd, tambn prov, Chinese drum

Mvts played without pause.

I. Tranquillo	_'
II. Lento	_'
III. Allegro deciso	_'

> Marks

Symphony No.6 <1966> *20'*

3[1.2.pic] 3[1.2.Eh] 4[1.2.Ebcl.bcl] 3[1.2.cbn] — 4 2 3 1 — tmp+7 — hp — pf — str

perc: xyl, marim, glock, vib, sd, field dr, td, tambn, claves, tri, cym, sus cym, bd, marac, guiro, whip, Chinese drum, tambn prov, 2tamtams

Allegro	7'
Adagio e tranquillo	6'
Allegro moderato	7'

> Merion

Symphony No.7 <1966–1967> *23'*

3[1.2.pic] 3[1.2.Eh] 4[1.2.Ebcl.bcl] 3[1.2.cbn] — 4 3 3 1 — tmp+5 — hp — pf — str

perc: xyl, marim, glock, vib, whip, tambn, sd, woodblk, field dr, marac, cym, sus cym, bd, tamtam, Chinese drum, tambn prov

Allegro con fuoco	9'
Lento e dolce	7'
Allegro misurato	7'

> Merion

Symphony No.8 <1968> *14'*

3[1.2/afl.pic] 3[1.2.Eh] 4[1.2.Ebcl.bcl] 4[1.2.3.cbn] — 4 3 4 1 — tmp+5 — hp — pf — str

Adagio e mesto	6'
Allegro con brio	8'

> Marks

Symphony No.9 <1975–1978> *28'*

3[1.2.pic] 3[1.2.Eh] 4[1.2.Ebcl.bcl] 3[1.2.cbn] — 4 4 3 1 — tmp+6 — hp — pf — str

perc: sd, guiro, tambn, xyl, marac, whip, field dr, cym, sus cym, marim, vib, chimes, tri, woodblk, td, bd, glock, Chinese drum, rattle, 3tamtams, tambn prov

I. Allegro	11'
II. Con movimento adagio	5'
III. Allegro vivace	12'

> Merion

When Lilacs Last in the Dooryard Bloom'd <1964–1970> *42'*

solo soprano, contralto & baritone   chorus

3[1.pic.afl] 3[1.2.Eh] 4[1.2.Ebcl.bcl] 3[1.2.cbn] — 4 2 3 1 — tmp+9 — hp — pf, cel — str

perc: bd, cym, sus cym, sd, td, field dr, tri, tambn, glock, xyl, marim, vib, woodblk, whip, ratch, marac, claves, chime[G#3], tambn prov, Chinese drum, 2tamtams

I. When Lilacs Last in the Dooryard Bloom'd	6'
II. Over the Breast of the Spring	16'
III. Now, While I Sat in the Day	20'

> Merion

Shapey, Ralph *1921-2002*

(b Philadelphia, 12 March 1921; d Chicago, 13 June 2002). American

Concerto fantastique <1991> *54'*

3[1/pic.2/pic.3/pic] 3[incl Eh] 3[incl bcl,2Ebcl] 3[incl cbn] — 4 4 5 1 — 2tmp+11 — str

> Presser

Rituals <1959> *12'*

3[incl pic] 3[incl Eh] 3[incl bcl] 3[incl cbn] — 3 2 2 1 — asx, tsx, bsx — tmp+8 — pf — str

I.	9'
II.	3'

> Presser

Symphonie concertante <1985>   29'

11 soloists: fl/pic — ob/Eh — cl/Ebcl/bcl — bn/cbn — hn — tp — tbn
— vn — va — vc —db
3[1/pic.2/pic.pic] 3[1.2.3/Eh] 3[1/Ebcl.2/Ebcl.3/bcl] 3[1.2.cbn] — 3 3
4 1 — 2tmp+8 — cel, pf — str
perc: templeblks, bd, tamtam, xyl, glock, crot, chimes, 3woodblk, 3tomtom, 3sus
cym, 3ironpipe

I. Maestoso, brillante	*11'*
II. Scherzo	*5'*
III. Song	*13'*

Presser

Shchedrin, Rodion   1932-

(b Moscow, 16 Dec 1932). Russian

Anna Karenina: Romantic Music <1971; rev suite,   27'
1972>

optional female narrator
4[incl pic,afl] 3[incl Eh] 3[incl Ebcl] 3[incl cbn] — 4 3 3 1 — tmp+4
— 2hp — cel/pf — str[16.14.12.10.8]
Suite from the ballet.

Bad Omen	3'
Anna's Love	7'
Anna's Lie	4'
Anna's Rebellion	4'
Anna's Nightmares	5'
Anna's Death	4'

Russian   Sikorski

Carmen Suite (Karmen-syuita) <1967>   44'

tmp+4 — str[18.16.14.12.10]
perc: bd, hi-hat, td, tamtam, glock, xyl, marim, vib, chimes, crot, templeblks, whip,
marac, claves, cast, field dr, 3cowbells, 4bongos, 3sd, 3guiros, 2woodblks, shaker,
2tri, 2tambn, 5tomtoms
After Georges Bizet; a recomposition of movements from his *Carmen*
and other works.

1. Introduction	*1'*
2. Dance	*2'*
3. First Intermezzo	*1'*
4. Changing of the Guard	*2'*
5. Carmen's Entrance and Habanera	*4'*
6. Scene	*7'*
7. Second Intermezzo	*2'*
8. Bolero [the Farandole, from L'Arlésienne]	*1'*
9. Torero	*3'*
10. Torero and Carmen [Danse bohémienne from La jolie fille de Perth]	*4'*
11. Adagio	*6'*
12. Fortune-Telling	*5'*
13. Finale	*6'*

Russian

Concerto for Orchestra No.1 (Naughty Limericks;   8'
Ozornïye chastushki) <1963>

3[1.2.pic] 3[1.2.Eh] 3[1.2.3/bcl] 3[1.2.cbn] — 4 4 4 0 — tmp+5 — hp
— pf — str
perc: crot, whip, sd, cym, bd, tamtam, sus cym, wooden spoons
The composer provides a built-in optional encore that may add a minute
or two to the duration. The explanation for this sometimes-misunderstood
feature has been translated into English, together with the numerous other
notes and interpretive comments (e.g., paper under the piano dampers to
simulate a balalaika); these translations may be found via the **Conductors
Guild**, **Orchestra Library Information** or **MOLA** websites.

Russian

Concerto for Orchestra No.2 (The Chimes; Zvoni)   10'
<1968>

4[1.2.pic1.pic2] 2 4[1.2.bcl1.bcl2] 2 — 4 4 4 0 — tmp+4 — pf/cel —
str[16.14.12.10.8]

Russian   Sikorski

The Geometry of Sound (Geometriya zvuka) <1987>   15'

1 1 1 1 — 1 1 1 0 — 2perc — hp — cel, hpsd, synth — str 5t
Ensemble divided into 2 groups: one on stage (*Sul podio*) and one
backstage or in a balcony (*Dietro il podio, oppore ai balconi*).

Universal

The Little Humpbacked Horse (Konyok-gorbunok):   25'
Suite No.1 <1955–1956>

3[incl pic] 3[incl Eh] 3[incl bcl] 3[incl cbn] — 4 3 3 1 — tmp+4 —
2hp — pf/cel — str

1. Introduction	_'
2. Grief	_'
3. Elder Brothers and Ivan	_'
4. The Little Humpbacked Horse	_'
5. Revival of the Tzar Maiden	_'
6. Tzar—the Pea	_'
7. Silver Mountain	_'
8. Gypsy Dance	_'
9. Adagio and Finale	_'

Sikorski   Russian

Music for Strings, Oboes, Horns & Celesta   22'

0 2 0 0 — 2 0 0 0 — cel — str

Sikorski

The Seagull (Chayka): Suite <1979>   20'

3[1.2/afl.3/pic] 3[1.2.Eh] 3[1.2.3/bcl] 2 — 4 3 3 1 — tmp+3 — hp —
cel, hpsd — str
perc: bongos, crot, flexatone, xyl, vib, slgh-bells, chimes, bd, glock

Schirmer

Self-Portrait (Avtoportret) <1984>   19'

3[incl pic,afl] 3[incl Eh] 3 3[incl cbn] — 4 3 3 1 — tmp+4 — hp —
pf/cel — str[16.14.12.10.8]

Russian   Sikorski   Universal

Stikhira for the Millennium of Russian Christianity 23'
<1988>

4[incl pic,2afl] 3[incl 2Eh] 3[incl Ebcl] 3[incl cbn] — 4 3 3 1 —
tmp+4 — hp — cel/pf — str[16.14.12.10.8]
perc: marim, chimes, bd, crot, tamtam, gong, 5Russian bells, chocalho, glass
windchimes, bell plate

Russian   Sikorski

Symphonic Fanfares (Festive Overture) <1967>   5'

3[incl pic] 2 2 2 — 4 3 3 1 — tmp+4 — str
perc: cym, sus cym, bd, 2sd

Sikorski   Russian

Shelley, Harry Rowe   1858-1947

(b New Haven, CT, 2 June 1858; d Short Beach, CT, 12 Sept 1947). American

Santa Claus Overture   6'

2 2 2 2 — 4 2 3 1 — tmp+4 — str

Kalmus

Sheng, Bright   1955-

(b Shanghai, 6 Dec 1955). Chinese-American

Black Swan <2006>   7'

2 2 2 3[1.2.cbn] — 4 2 3 0 — hp — str
An arrangement of Johannes Brahms' *Intermezzo* [piano], op.18, no.2.

Schirmer

China Dreams <1992–1995>   25'

3[1.2/pic.3/pic] 3[1.2.3/Eh] 3[1.2/Ebcl.3/bcl] 3[1.2.cbn] — 4 3[1/pic tp.2.3] 3 1 — tmp+4 — hp — pf/cel — str

perc: tri, tambn, glock, xyl, chimes, crot, belltree, woodblk, whip, bongos, 2sus cym, 2tamtams, 2bd, small Peking opera gong

Prelude	5'
Fanfare	4'
The Stream Flows [strings only]	7'
The Three Gorges of the Long River	9'

Schirmer

China Dreams: Fanfare   4'

3[1.2/pic.3/pic] 3[1.2.Eh] 3[1.2/Ebcl.3/bcl] 3[1.2.cbn] — 4 3[1/pic tp.2.3] 3 1 — tmp+4 — hp — pf/cel — str

perc: bongos, tambn, bd, belltree, tri, glock, xyl, tamtam, crot, 2woodblks, Peking opera gong, 2sus cym

Original title *Arrows to the Page.*

Schirmer

Flute Moon <1999>   18'

solo piccolo (1st mvt), flute (2nd mvt)

2tmp+3 — hp — pf — str

perc: bd, cym, brake dr, tamtam, glock, xyl, marim, whip, ratch, chimes (2sets), 2cowbells, windgong

2nd mvt based on an art song *Evanescent Fragrances* by Jiang Kui (dated 1155-1221).

I. Chi Lin's Dance	6'
II. Flute Moon	12'

Schirmer

H'un (Lacerations): In memoriam 1966-1976 <1988>   22'

2[1/pic.2/pic/afl] 2[1.2/Eh] 2[1/bcl.2/bcl] 2[1.2/cbn] — 3 2 2 0 — 2perc — hp — pf — str

perc: marim, sus cym, tamtam, templeblks, whip, guiro, 4Chinese tomtom, 2Peking gng, tmp, Chinese bd, japwoodblk, 2tambn

Schirmer

Nanking! Nanking! <1999>   26'

solo pipa (ampd)

3[1.2/pic2.3/pic1] 3[1.2.3/Eh] 3[1.2/Ebcl.3/bcl] 3[1.2.3/cbn] — 4 3 3 1 — tmp+4 — hp — pf — str

perc: ratch, whip, lionroar, bd, templeblks, tamtam, woodblk, guiro, brake dr, xyl, rute, Chinese opera gong, Chinese opera cymbal, windgong, 4cowbell, 4bongos

Schirmer

The Phoenix <2004>   23'

solo soprano

3[1.2/afl/pic.3/pic] 3[1.2.Eh] 3[1.2/Ebcl.3/bcl] 3[1.2.cbn] — 4 3 3 1 — tmp+4 — hp — str

perc: crot, glock, belltree, cym, sus cym, tamtam, tri, bd, guiro, ratch, wind gong, 2tambn, 2flexatone

Schirmer

Postcards <1997>   17'

1[fl/pic] 2[1.2/Eh] 1[cl/Ebcl/bcl] 2 — 2 1 0 0 — 2perc — pf/cel — str

perc: bd, sus cym, brake dr, tambn, tamtam, glock, marim, chimes, crot, bongos, guiro, tmp, windgong

I. From the Mountains	5'
II. From the River Valley	3'
III. From the Savage Land	4'
IV. Wish You Were Here	5'

Schirmer

Red Silk Dance <1998>   20'

solo piano

2[1/pic.2/pic] 2 2[1.2/Ebcl] 2 — 4 2 3 0 — tmp+3 — str

perc: bd, sus cym, tri, tambn, tamtam, glock, xyl, vib, chimes, templeblks, whip, ratch, congas, windgong, rute, 4bongos

Schirmer

Shanghai Overture <2007>   9'

3[fl.pic1.pic2] 3[1.2.Eh] 3[1.2.Ebcl] 3[1.2.cbn] — 4 3 3 1 — tmp+4 — hp — str

perc: bd, tri, tamtam, glock, crot, templeblks, ratch, 2Chinese opera cymbal, 2Chinese opera gong, Chinese tomtom, windgong

Schirmer

Two Chinese Folk Tunes   4'

children's choir   treble solo

str

I. Mountain Echo	_'
II. A Happy Sunny Day	_'

Schirmer

Shilkret, Nathaniel   1889-1982

(b Queens, NY, 25 Dec 1889; d Long Island, NY, 18 Feb 1982). American

GENESIS SUITE   58'

narrator   chorus

3[1.2.3/pic] 3[1.2.3/Eh] 3[1.2/Ebcl.3/bcl] 3[1.2.cbn] — 4 3 3 1 — tmp+3 — hp — pf/cel — str

perc: bd, cym, sus cym, sd, tri, tambn, gong, xyl, glock, tamtam, vib, chimes, marktree

This suite, based on the biblical book of Genesis, was commissioned by Shilkret as a collaborative effort of seven composers: one movement each, composed by Schoenberg, Shilkret himself, Tansman, Milhaud, Castelnuovo-Tedesco, Toch, and Stravinsky.

The Schoenberg and Stravinsky movements were published; the Milhaud and Castelnuovo-Tedesco were preserved in manuscript; the Shilkret, Toch and Tansman movements were destroyed in a fire, but reconstructed in 2000 by Patrick Russ, based on surviving condensed scores and a 1945 recording of the originals.

Sources for scores and parts vary from movement to movement, as do the forces required. Therefore each movement is listed individually below, as well as under each individual composer.

I. Prelude [Schoenberg]	6'
II. Creation [Shilkret]	11'
III. Adam and Eve [Tansman]	12'
IV. Cain and Abel [Milhaud]	5'
V. The Flood (Noah's Ark) [Castelnuovo-Tedesco]	11'
VI. The Covenant (The Rainbow) [Toch]	6'
VII. Babel [Stravinsky]	7'

Genesis Suite: I. Prelude [Schoenberg] <1945>   6'

wordless chorus

3[1.2.pic] 3[1.2.3/Eh] 3[1.2/Ebcl.3/bcl] 3[1.2.cbn] — 4 3 3 1 — tmp+3 — hp — str

perc: xyl, glock, tamtam, cym, bd, tambn, tri

Belmont

Genesis Suite: II. Creation [Shilkret] <1945>   11'

narrator   female chorus (SSA)

3[1.2.3/pic] 3[1.2.Eh] 3[1.2.bcl] 3[1.2.cbn] — 4 3 3 1 — tmp+2 — hp — pf/cel — str

perc: bd, cym, sus cym, tamtam, glock, vib, chimes

Reconstructed by Patrick Russ.

Milken

Genesis Suite: III. Adam and Eve [Tansman] <1944>   12'

narrator

3[1.2.3/pic] 3[1.2.Eh] 3[1.2.3/bcl] 3[1.2.cbn] — 4 3 3 1 — tmp+3 — hp — pf/cel — str

perc: sus cym, tamtam, glock, xyl, vib, marktree

Reconstructed by Patrick Russ.

Milken

Genesis Suite: IV. Cain and Abel [Milhaud] <1944>   5'

narrator

2 2 2 2 — 2 2 2 0 — tmp+1 — hp — str

perc: cym, sd, tri, tambn

> Milken

Genesis Suite: V. The Flood (Noah's Ark)   11'
[Castelnuovo-Tedesco] <1944>

narrator   chorus (SATTBB)

3[1.2.3/pic] 2[1.2/Eh] 3[1.2.3/bcl] 2[1.2/cbn] — 4 3 3 1 — tmp+2 — hp — pf/cel — str

perc: bd, cym, sus cym, sd, tri, tambn, gong, xyl

> *Part I*   _'
> *Part II*   _'

> Milken

Genesis Suite: VI. The Covenant (The Rainbow)   6'
[Toch] <1945?>

narrator

3[1.2.3/pic] 3[1.2.Eh] 3 3[1.2.cbn] — 4 3 3 1 — tmp+1 — hp — pf — str

perc: sus cym, vib

Reconstructed by Patrick Russ.

> Milken

Genesis Suite: VII. Babel [Stravinsky] <1944>   7'

narrator   male chorus (TB)

3[1.2.3/pic] 2 3[1.2.bcl] 3[1.2.cbn] — 4 3 3 0 — tmp — hp — str

> Schott

Shostakovich, Dmitry   1906-1975

(b St Petersburg, 12/25 Sept 1906; d Moscow, 9 Aug 1975). Russian

The Age of Gold, op.22a (Zolotoy vek): Suite   16'
<1929–1930>

2[1.pic] 2[1.Eh] 3[1.Ebcl.bcl] 2[1.cbn] — 4 3 3 1 — ssx — baritone horn — tmp+4 — harm — str

perc: bd, cym, sd, tamtam, tri, woodblk, xyl

> *I. Introduction*   3'
> *II. Adagio*   9'
> *III. Polka*   2'
> *IV. Danse*   2'

> Russian   Universal

The Age of Gold, op.22a (Zolotoy vek): Polka   2'
<1927–1930>

2[1.pic] 2[1.Eh] 3[1.Ebcl.bcl] 2[1.cbn] — 4 3 3 1 — ssx — tmp+2 — str

perc: sd, tambn, tri, woodblk, xyl

> Russian

Ballet Suite No.1   14'

2[1.2/pic] 1 2 1 — 3 2 2 1 — tmp+3 — pf/cel — str

Arr. Lev Atovmian, 1949.

> *1. Valse lyrique*   2'
> *2. Dance*   2'
> *3. Romance*   3'
> *4. Polka*   2'
> *5. Valse badinage*   3'
> *6. Galop*   2'

> Russian   Sikorski

Chamber Symphony, op.110a (Kammersinfonie) <1960>   22

str

Originally String Quartet No.8 in C minor (1960); arranged for string orchestra by Rudolf Barshai in 1978.

> *I. Largo*   5'
> *II. Allegro molto*   4'
> *III. Allegretto*   4'
> *IV. Largo*   5'
> *V. Larto*   4'

> Peters   Russian   Sikorski

Concerto, Piano, No.1, op.35, C minor <1933>   21'

solo trumpet as well as solo piano

str

> *I. Allegro moderato*   6'
> *II. Lento*   8'
> *III. Moderato*   1'
> *IV. Allegro brio*   6'

> Russian   Sikorski

Concerto, Piano, No.2, op.102, F major <1957>   20'

3[1.2.pic] 2 2 2 — 4 0 0 0 — tmp/sd — str

perc: sd

> *I. Allegro*   7'
> *II. Andante*   7'
> *III. Allegro*   6'

> Russian   Sikorski

Concerto, Violin, No.1, op.77 (99), A minor <1947–1948;   39'
rev 1955>

3[1.2.3/pic] 3[1.2.3/Eh] 3[1.2.3/bcl] 3[1.2.3/cbn] — 4 0 0 1 — tmp+2 — 2hp[1part] — cel — str

perc: xyl, tambn, tamtam

Published in some editions as op.99, but designated by the composer as op.77.

> *I. Nocturne*   12'
> *II. Scherzo*   6'
> *III. Passacaglia* 16'
> *IV. Burlesca*   5'

> Russian   Sikorski

Concerto, Violoncello, No.1, op.107, E-flat major <1959>   30'

2[1.2/pic] 2 2 2[1.2/cbn] — 1 0 0 0 — tmp — cel — str

> *I. Allegretto*   6'
> *II. Moderato*   12'
> *III. Cadenza*   7'
> *IV. Allegro con moto*   5'

> Russian   Sikorski

Concerto, Violoncello, No.2, op.126, G major <1966>   33'

2[1.pic] 2 2 3[1.2.3/cbn] — 2 0 0 0 — tmp+3 — 2hp[1part] — str

perc: xyl, bd, sd, tomtom, woodblk, whip, tambn

> *I. Largo*   14'
> *II. Allegretto*   4'
> *III. Allegretto*   15'

> Russian   Sikorski

Festive Overture, op.96 <1954>   7'

3[1.2.pic] 3 3 3[1.2.cbn] — 4 3 3 1 — opt *banda*[brass 4 3 3 0] — tmp+4 — str

perc: tri, sd, cym, bd

> Russian   Sikorski

The Gadfly (Ovod): Suite, op.97a <1956>   45'

3[1.2.pic] 3 3[1/asx.2/asx.3/asx] 3[1.2.cbn] — 4 3 3 1 — tmp+5 — hp
— cel/pf — str
perc: glock, xyl, tri, sd, tambn, tamtam, cym, bd
Arranged by Lev Atovmian, from the film score.

1. Overture	3'
2. Counter Dance	3'
3. Fair	3'
4. Interlude	3'
5. Barrel Organ Waltz	2'
6. Galop	2'
7. Introduction	6'
8. Romance	6'
9. Intermezzo	7'
10. Nocturne	4'
11. Scene	2'
12. Final	4'

Russian	Sikorski

The Golden Age

see his: Age of Gold

Hamlet (Gamlet): Incidental Music (1932), op.32   22'
   <1931–1932>

1 1 1 1 — 2 2 1 1 — tmp+3 — str
perc: sd, tri, cym, tamtam, bd, tambn
This work is not to be confused with the composer's film music for
Hamlet (op.116, 1964).

1. Introduction and Night Watch	3'
2. Funeral March	2'
3. Flourish and Dancing Music	2'
4. Desire	2'
5. Actors' Pantomime	2'
6. Procession	1'
7. Musical Pantomime	1'
8. The Banquet	1'
9. Ophelia's Song	2'
10. Cradle Song	2'
11. Requiem	1'
12. Tournament	1'
13. March of Fortinbras	2'

Russian

Hamlet (Gamlet): Film Suite (1964), op.116a   34'
   <1963–1964>

3[1.2.pic] 2 2 2 — 4 3 3 1 — tmp+5 — hp — pf/hpsd — str
Arranged by Lev Atovmian, from the film score. This work is not to be
confused with the composer's incidental music for *Hamlet* (op.32, 1932).

1. Introduction	3'
2. Ball at the Palace	3'
3. The Ghost	5'
4. In the Garden	2'
5. Scene of the Poisoning	8'
6. The Arrival and Scene of the Players	2'
7. Ophelia	4'
8. The Duel and Death of Hamlet	7'

Russian	Sikorski

Song of the Forests, op.81 (Pesn' o lesakh) <1949>   37'

chorus, boys' chorus   tenor & bass solos
3[1.2.3/pic] 3[1.2.Eh] 3 2 — 4 3 3 1 — brass choir[6tp, 6tbn] —
tmp+4 — 2hp — str
perc: glock, tri, sd, cym
Brass choir in last mvt only.

1. When the War Was Over	6'
2. Clothe the Homeland in Forests	3'
3. Recollection of the Past	6'
4. Pioneers Plant the Forests	2'
5. Young Communists Forge Onwards	4'
6. A Walk into the Future	7'
7. Glory	9'

Russian

Suite for Jazz Orchestra, No.1 <1934>   8'

0 0 0 0 — 0 2 1 0 — 3sx[ssx/asx, asx, tsx] — banjo, Hawaiian gtr —
1perc — pf — 1vn, 1db
perc: sus cym, sd, glock, xyl, woodblk
1 player could double on Hawaian guitar & banjo.

1. Waltz	2'
2. Polka	2'
3. Foxtrot (Blues)	4'

Russian

Suite for Jazz Orchestra, No.2 <1938>   7'

0 0 0 0 — 0 4 2 1 — 5sx[2asx, 2tsx, bsx] — guitars/banjos — 2perc
— pf — str[3.3.0.0.2]
perc: set, tri, glock, xyl, woodblk, cast, slide whistle
Guitars & banjos: all playing most of the time from a single part; number
unspecified but clearly more than one of each.
   The music of this work was lost, but has been reconstructed &
orchestrated by Gerard McBurney (2000) from the original piano sketch.

I. Scherzo	3'
II. Lullaby	2'
III. Serenade	2'

Russian

Suite for Variety Orchestra, No.1   25'

2[1.2/pic] 1 2 1 — 3 3 3 1 — 4sx[2asx, 2tsx] — gtr, accordion —
tmp+2 — hp — pf, cel/pf — str
perc: bd, cym, sus cym, sd, tri, tambn, glock, xyl, vib
Often performed and even recorded under the erroneous title *Suite for
Jazz Orchestra No.2, q.v.* Actually this work is a compilation—by
unknown colleagues of Shostakovich—of arrangements from his film and
stage music.

1. March	3'
2. Dance I	3'
3. Dance II	4'
4. Little Polka	3'
5. Lyrical Waltz	3'
6. Waltz I	3'
7. Waltz II	4'
8. Finale	2'

Russian

Suite for Variety Orchestra, No.2   11'

2[1.pic] 1 2 1 — 3 3 3 1 — 4sx[2asx, 2tsx] — gtr, accordion —
tmp+3 — hp — cel/pf — str
perc: bd, cym, sus cym, field dr, tri, tambn, glock, xyl, vib

1. Introduction	3'
2. Waltz	2'
3. Intermezzo	3'
4. Finale	3'

Russian

Symphony No.1, op.10, F minor <1924–1925>   28'

3[1.2/pic2.3/pic1] 2 2 2 — 4 3[1.2.atp] 3 1 — tmp+4 — pf — str
perc: sd, tri, tamtam, glock, cym, bd

I. Allegretto; Allegro non troppo	8'
II. Allegro	4'
III. Lento	8'
IV. Allegro molto; Lento	8'

Russian	Sikorski

Symphony No.2, op.14, B major (To October;   21'
   Oktyabryu) <1927>

chorus
3[1.2.pic] 2 2 2 — 4 3 3 1 — tmp+4 — str
perc: tri, glock, sd, cym, bd, factory whistle [F#3(or tbns)]
The chorus enters in last 7' of this one-mvt symphony.

Largo; Allegro molto	13'
"My shli, my prosili raboty i khleba"	8'

Russian	Sikorski

Symphony No.3, op.20, E-flat major (The First of May; Pervomayskaya) <1929>   27'

chorus
3[1.2.pic] 2 2 2 — 4 2 3 1 — tmp+3 — str
perc: sd, xyl, glock, tri, tamtam, cym, bd
The work has sometimes been performed without chorus; this works because all the musical material given to the chorus is also doubled in the orchestra, largely in the brass.
Movements played without pause.

1. Allegretto	4'
2. Più mosso; Allegro	5'
3. Andante	4'
4. Allegro; Allegro molto	6'
5. Andante; Largo	3'
6. "The First of May"	5'

Russian	Sikorski

Symphony No.4, op.43, C minor <1935–1936>   60'

6[1.2.3.4.pic1.pic2] 4[1.2.3.4/Eh] 6[1.2.3.4.Ebcl.bcl] 4[1.2.3.cbn] — 8 4 3 2 — 2tmp+7 — 2hp — cel[can be played by perc] — str
perc: xyl, glock, sd, woodblk, tri, sus cym, cast, cym, bd, tamtam
A reduced version by Jesse Taynton (1963) was made for the Philadelphia Orchestra and published by MCA; it has since disappeared. instrumentation of the Taynton reduction:
4 4 4 4 — 7 4 3 2 [or 6 4 4 1] — tmp, perc — 2hp, cel — str

I. Allegretto poco moderato; Presto	25'
II. Moderato con moto	9'
III. Largo; Allegro	26'

Russian	Sikorski

Symphony No.5, op.47, D minor <1937>   44'

3[1.2.pic] 2 3[1.2.Ebcl] 3[1.2.cbn] — 4 3 3 1 — tmp+4 — 2hp[1part] — pf/cel — str
perc: xyl, glock, tri, sd, cym, tamtam, bd

I. Moderato	15'
II. Allegretto	5'
III. Largo	14'
IV. Allegro non troppo	10'

Russian	Sikorski

Symphony No.6, op.54, B minor <1939>   30'

3[1.2.pic] 3[1.2.Eh] 4[1.2.3/Ebcl.bcl] 3[1.2.3/cbn] — 4 3 3 1 — tmp+5 — hp — cel[can be played by perc] — str
perc: tamtam, xyl, sd, tri, tambn, cym, bd

I. Largo	15'
II. Allegro	7'
III. Presto	8'

Russian	Sikorski

Symphony No.7, op.60, C major (Leningrad) <1941>   69'

3[1.2/afl.3/pic] 3[1.2.Eh] 4[1.2.3/Ebcl.bcl] 3[1.2.cbn] — 8 6 6 1 — tmp+5[7] — 2hp — pf — str
perc: xyl, sd, tri, tambn, tamtam, cym, bd, 2opt sd[2extra players]

I. Allegretto	26'
II. Moderato; Poco allegretto	11'
III. Adagio	17'
IV. Allegro non troppo	15'

Russian	Sikorski

Symphony No.8, op.65, C minor <1943>   61'

4[1.2.3/pic2.4/pic1] 3[1.2.Eh] 4[1.2.Ebcl.bcl] 3[1.2.3/cbn] — 4 3 3 1 — tmp+5 — str
perc: xyl, tambn, sd, sus cym, cym, bd, tamtam, tri

I. Adagio; Allegro non troppo	23'
II. Allegretto	6'
III. Allegro non troppo	7'
IV. Largo	10'
V. Allegretto	15'

Russian	Sikorski

Symphony No.9, op.70, E-flat major <1945>   27'

3[1.2.pic] 2 2 2 — 4 2 3 1 — tmp+2 — str
perc: sd, tri, cym, bd, tambn

I. Allegro	5'
II. Moderato	8'
III. Presto	3'
IV. Largo	5'
V. Allegretto	6'

Russian	Sikorski

Symphony No.10, op.93, E minor <1953>   57'

3[1.2/pic2.pic1] 3[1.2.3/Eh] 3[1.2.3/Ebcl] 3[1.2.3/cbn] — 4 3 3 1 — tmp+4 — str
perc: sd, tamtam, tri, tambn, xyl, cym, bd

I. Moderato	25'
II. Allegro	5'
III. Allegretto	12'
IV. Andante; Allegro	15'

Russian	Sikorski

Symphony No.11, op.103, G minor (The Year 1905; 1905 god) <1956–1957>   55'

3[1.2.3/pic] 3[1.2.3/Eh] 3[1.2.3/bcl] 3[1.2.3/cbn] — 4 3 3 1 — tmp+5 — 2-4hp[1part] — cel — str
perc: xyl, sd, cym, bd, tri, tamtam, chimes[C4,G4,A#4,B4]

1. The Palace Square	14'
2. The 9th of January	17'
3. In Memoriam	10'
4. The Tocsin	14'

Russian	Sikorski

Symphony No.12, op.112, D minor (The Year 1917; 1917 god) <1959–1961>   38'

3[1.2.3/pic] 3 3 3[1.2.3/cbn] — 4 3 3 1 — tmp+5 — str
perc: tri, sd, cym, bd, tamtam

1. Revolutionary Petrograd	12'
2. The Rising	11'
3. Aurora	5'
4. Dawn of Humanity	10'

Russian	Sikorski

Symphony No.13, op.113, B-flat minor (Babi Yar) <1962>   59'

bass solo   male chorus
3[1.2.pic] 3[1.2.3/Eh] 3[1.2.3/Ebcl.bcl] 3[1.2.3/cbn] — 4 3 3 1 — tmp+4 — 2-4hp[1part] — cel, pf — str
perc: cym, whip, sd, tambn, cast, woodblk, tri, tamtam, xyl, bd, chimes[G3,G#3,A#3,C#4,F4], kybdglock

1. Babi Yar	16'
2. Humor	8'
3. In the Store	11'
4. Fears	12'
5. A Career	12'

Russian	Sikorski

Symphony No.14, op.135 <1969>   52'

soprano & bass solos
2perc — cel — str[5.5.4.3.2]
perc: xyl, vib, whip, cast, woodblk, 3tomtoms, chimes[G3,G#3,A#3,C#4,F4]

1. De Profundis (García Lorca)	5'
2. Malagueña (García Lorca)	3'
3. Loreley (Apollinaire, after Clemens Brentano)	9'
4. The Suicide (Apollinaire)	8'
5. On Watch (Apollinaire)	3'
6. Madam, Look! (Apollinaire)	2'
7. In the Santé Prison (Apollinaire)	9'
8. The Zaporozhean Cossack's Answer (Apollinaire)	2'
9. O Delvig! Delvig! (Küchelbecker)	4'
10. The Poet's Death (Rilke)	6'
11. Conclusion (Rilke)	1'

Russian	Sikorski

Symphony No.15, op.141, A major <1971>   42'

3[1.2.pic] 2 2 2 — 4 2 3 1 — tmp+5 — cel — str[min 16.14.12.12.10]
perc: xyl, tri, glock, vib, sd, cast, woodblk, tomtom, cym, whip, bd, tamtam

I. Allegretto	8'
II. Adagio	16'
III. Allegretto	4'
IV. Adagio; Allegretto	14'

| Russian | Sikorski |

TAHITI TROT, op.16 (Taiti Trot; Tea for Two) <1927>

The history of the two versions of this arrangement of Victor Youmans'
popular tune *Tea for Two* is not entirely clear.

The small instrumentation is believed to have been written in 1927 in
response to a challenge by Nicolai Malko; it was later added to the ballet
The Age of Gold (1930) as an entr'acte before Act III.

The larger instrumentation, perhaps by Veniamin Basner and/or Yuri
Simonov, was likely created for use in the radically changed 1982
(posthumous) production of *The Age of Gold*, not as an entr'acte, but as
one of the dances.

Tahiti Trot, op.16 [small instrumentation] (Taiti Trot;   4'
Tea for Two) <1928>

2[1.pic] 2 1 1 — 4 2 1 0 — tmp+3 — hp — cel — str
perc: cym, sus cym, sd, tri, glock, xyl
Arrangement of Vincent Youmans' *Tea for Two*.

| Russian |

Tahiti Trot, op.16 [large instrumentation] (Taiti Trot;   4'
Tea for Two) <1928>

2[1.pic] 2[1.Eh] 3[1.Ebcl.bcl] 2[1.cbn] — 4 3 3 1 — 2sx "in B-flat" [
= 2ssx?] — tmp+3 — hp — cel — str
perc: cym, sus cym, sd, tri, glock, xyl
Arrangement of Vincent Youmans' *Tea for Two*.

The saxophones are identified only as "in B-flat," and are usually listed
in catalogs as being tenor saxophones. However, soprano saxophones are
almost certainly intended.

| Schirmer |

Shulman, Alan   1915-2002

(b Baltimore, 4 June 1915; d Hudson, NY, 10 July 2002). American

Ben Franklin Suite   7'

str
Uses themes from a string quartet attributed to the American patriot
Benjamin Franklin. Expansion of Shulman's music for a television show
on Franklin.

I. Overture	2'
II. Minuet I	1'
III. Caprice	2'
IV. Minuet II	1'
V. Finale	1'

| Leonard | Marks |

The Bop Gavotte <1954>   3'

str

| Fox |

Concerto, Violoncello <1948>   28'

2 1 2 1 — 2 2 2 0 — tmp — hp — str

| Chappell | Warner |

An Elizabethan Legend <1954>   3'

str
Violins divided A, B, & C; Violas A & B.

| Fox |

Four Moods <1942>   5'

str
Originally for string quartet; arr. for string orchestra by the composer.

| Shulman |

Homage to Erik Satie <1938; rev 1969>   2'

solo violoncello or viola
str

| Shulman |

Hup-Two-Three-Four; Jazz March for Symphony   3'
<1953>

2 2 2 2 — 4 3 3 1 — tmp+3 — hp — str

| Shawnee |

In Memoriam—Sophie (1916-1982) <1983>   4'

2 2 2 2 — str

| EAM |

Interstate 90   3'

2[incl pic] 2 2 2 — 4 3 3 1 — tmp+2 — hp — str
Originally for band; orchestrated by the composer.

| Shulman |

Kol nidre <1970>   10'

solo violoncello
2[incl pic] 2 2 2 — 3 0 0 0 — str

| EAM |

A Laurentian Overture <1951>   9'

3[incl pic] 3[incl Eh] 3[incl bcl] 2 — 4 3 3 1 — tmp+3 — hp — str

| Chappell | Warner |

Minuet   4'

str

| Shulman |

Minuet for Moderns <1954>   4'

str

| Fox |

A New England Tarantella <1978>   4'

str

| Shulman |

A Nocturne for Strings <1938>   4'

str

| Fox |

Pastorale and Dance <1944>   11'

solo violin
1 1 2 1 — 2 2 2 0 — tmp+1 — hp — str

| Pastorale | 7' |
| Dance | 4' |

| EAM |

Poem for Violin & Orchestra <1941; rev orchd 1942>   11'

3[incl pic] 3[incl Eh] 3[incl bcl] 3 — 4 0 0 0 — hp — cel — str
This work, commissioned for Heifetz but rejected by him, has not yet
been performed (2015).

| Shulman |

Popocatepetl <1952>   5'
3[incl pic] 2 2 2 — 4 3 3 1 — tmp+3 — hp — str
> Shawnee

Portrait of Lisa   3'
str
> Fox

Prelude <1952>   6'
2[incl pic] 2 2[incl bcl] 2 — 4 2 2 0 — tmp+1 — hp — cel — str
> Chappell   Warner

Quilt <1985>   14'
2[incl pic] 3[incl Eh] 3[incl bcl] 2[incl cbn] — 4 2 3 1 — tmp+2 —
hp — str
> EAM

Rendezvous <1946>   4'
solo clarinet
str
> Warner

Ricky-Tick Serenade <1953>   3'
gtr — 1perc — hp — pf — str
> Shawnee

Ripe for Plucking <1987>   6'
str
> Presser

Suite for String Orchestra <1963>   8'
str
Based on thematic material from the string quartet of Benjamin Franklin.
> Shulman

Suite Miniature <1956>   9'
8vc
> *Bourée d'Auvergne*   _'
> *Berceuse bretonne*   _'
> *Le Gayant de Douai*   _'
> Shulman

Suite parisienne (after Bréval) <1972>   12'
solo violoncello
str
> Shulman

Theme & Variations, Viola & Orchestra <1940; rev   14'
1954>
2 2 2 2 — 4 2 3 1 — tmp+1 — hp — str
Also available in a version for solo viola, harp & strings (1954).
> Chappell   Warner

Theme & Variations, Violoncello & Orchestra <1966>   19'
2 2 2 2 — 2 1 0 0 — hp — db
> EAM

Threnody <1950>   6'
str
> Luck's   Tetra

Top Brass <1958>   6
0 0 0 0 — 4 4 3 1 — [no str]
> *1.*   2'
> *2.*   2'
> *3.*   2'
> Shulman

Variations 1984 <1984; rev 1985>   14'
solo viola
hp — str
> Gems

Viennese Lace <1954>   4'
str
> Fox

Waltzes for Orchestra <1949>   9'
2 2 2 2 — 4 3 3 1 — tmp+2 — hp — cel/pf — str
> Chappell   Warner

Woodstock Waltzes <1986>   13'
2 2 2 2 — 2 1 0 0 — tmp — str
> EAM

Sibelius, Jean   1865-1957
(b Hämeenlinna, 8 Dec 1865; d Järvenpää, 20 Sept 1957). Finnish

Andante festivo <1922; rev 1938>   5'
opt tmp — str
perc: opt tmp
Originally for string quartet; arr. by the composer for string orch with ad
lib timpani (last 4 bars).
> Fennica   Kalmus   Peer   Presser

Arioso, op.3 <1911>   4'
solo soprano
str
> Breitkopf

Autrefois (Scène pastorale), op.98b <1919>   6'
solo soprano & alto
2 0 2[in lieu of voices] 2 — 2 0 0 0 — tmp — str
2 clarinet parts provided so that the work may be performed without the
solo voices.
> Breitkopf

The Bard, op.64 (Barden) <1913>   6'
2 2 3[1.2.bcl] 2 — 4 2 3 0 — tmp+1 — hp — str
perc: bd, tamtam
> Breitkopf   Luck's

Belshazzar's Feast, op.51 (Belsazars gästabud): Suite   14'
<1906; rev 1907>
2[1.2/pic] 1 2 0 — 2 0 0 0 — 4perc — str
perc: bd, cym, tri, tambn
Suite from the incidental music to the play by H. Procopé.
> *1. Oriental Procession*   2'
> *2. Solitude*   3'
> *3. Night Music*   5'
> *4. Khadra's Dance*   4'
> Kalmus   Lienau   Luck's

Canzonetta, op.62a <1911>   *4'*

str

Breitkopf	Kalmus

Canzonetta, op.62a (arr. Stravinsky) <1911>   *4'*

0 0 2[1.bcl] 0 — 4 0 0 0 — hp — db
Orchestrated by Stravinsky, 1963

Breitkopf	Luck's

The Captive Queen, op.48 (Vapautettu kuningatar) <1906>   *15'*

2[1.2/pic] 2 2[1.bcl] 1 — 4 2 3 0 — tmp+3 — str
perc: tri, cym, bd

Hansen	Lienau

Cassazione, op.6 <1904–1905>   *10'*

2 2 0 0 — 2 1 1 0 — tmp — str

Fazer

Concerto, Violin, op.47, D minor <1903–1904; rev 1905>   *31'*

2 2 2 2 — 4 2 3 0 — tmp — str
I. Allegro moderato   16'
II. Adagio di molto   8'
III. Allegro, ma non tanto 7'

Kalmus	Lienau	Luck's

The Dryad, op.45, no.1 (Dryaden) <1910>   *6'*

3[1.2.pic] 2 3[1.2.bcl] 2 — 4 3 3 1 — 2perc — str
perc: bd, tambn, sd, cast

Breitkopf	Kalmus	Luck's

En saga

see his: Saga, op.9

Finlandia, op.26 <1900>   *8'*

2 2 2 2 — 4 3 3 1 — tmp+1 — str
perc: cym, bd, tri

Breitkopf	Kalmus	Luck's

Humoresque I, op.87, no.1, D minor <1917>   *4'*

solo violin
2 2 2 2 — 2 0 0 0 — tmp — str

Hansen

Humoresque II, op.87, no.2, D major <1917>   *3'*

solo violin
0 0 0 0 — 2 0 0 0 — tmp — str

Hansen

Karelia Overture, op.10 <1893>   *9'*

3[1.2.pic] 2 2 2 — 4 3 3 1 — tmp+3 — str
perc: tambn, tri, bd

Breitkopf	Kalmus	Luck's

Karelia Suite, op.11   *14'*

3[1.2.pic] 3[1.2.opt Eh] 2 2 — 4 3 3 1 — tmp+3 — str
perc: tambn, bd, cym, tri
1. Intermezzo   4'
2. Ballade   6'
3. March   4'

Breitkopf	Kalmus	Luck's

King Kristian II, op.27: Suite <1898>   *22'*

2[1.pic1.2/pic2] 2 2 — 4 2 3 0 — tmp+1 — str
perc: tambn, tri, bd, cym
I. Nocturne   3'
II. Elegy and Musette   7'
III. Serenade   4'
IV. Ballade   5'

Breitkopf	Kalmus

Kullervo, op.7 <1891–1892>   *72'*

solo baritone & soprano   male chorus TTBB
3[1.2.pic] 3[1.2.Eh] 2[1.2/bcl] 2 — 4 3 3 1 — tmp+2 — str
perc: cym, sus cym, tri
Ed. Glenda Dawn Goss.

Problems have been known to occur in getting a piano-vocal score that is compatible with this new Breitkopf edition. Compatible piano-vocal scores do exist, but must be rented; allow plenty of time. (The problem is that the piano-vocal score from the new Breitkopf collected edition of Sibelius is *not* the definitive version of the work, but rather an earlier iteration, intended more for scholars than for practical use.)

A 4th tp is indicated in 2 brief passages, but is a doubling, and probably the result of a hasty oversight.
I. Introduction   13'
II. Kullervo's Youth   14'
III. Kullervo and His Sister 24'
IV. Kullervo Goes to War   11'
V. Kullervo's Death   10'

Breitkopf

Kuolema (Death): Valse triste, op.44, no.1 <1903; rev 1904>   *6'*

1 0 1 0 — 2 0 0 0 — tmp — str

Breitkopf	Kalmus	Luck's

Kuolema (Death): Scene with Cranes (Kurkikohtaus), op.44, no.2 <1903; rev 1906>   *5'*

0 0 2 0 — tmp — str

Fazer

LEMMINKÄINEN SUITE (Lemminkäis-sarja), op.22 (Legends) <1896>

1. Lemminkäinen and the Maidens of the Island (Lemminkäinen ja saaren neidot) <1895; rev 1897, 1939>   *16'*

2[1/pic.2/pic] 2 2 2 — 4 3 3 0 — tmp+2 — str
perc: bd, tri, cym

Breitkopf

2. The Swan of Tuonela (Tuonelan joutsen) <1895; rev 1897, 1900>   *10'*

solo English horn
0 1 1[bcl] 2 — 4 0 3 0 — tmp+1 — hp — str
perc: bd
Originally No.3; later switched with No.2.

Breitkopf	Kalmus	Luck's

3. Lemminkäinen in Tuonela (Lemminkäinen Tuonelassa) <1893; rev 1897, 1939>   *15'*

2 2[1.Eh] 2[1.bcl] 2 — 4 3 3 0 — 2perc — str
perc: bd, cym, sd, tri
Originally No.2; later switched with No.3.

Breitkopf

4. Lemminkäinen's Return (Lemminkäinen palaa kotitienoille) <1895; rev 1897, 1900> *7'*

2[pic1.pic2] 2 2 2 — 4 3 3 1 — tmp+2 — str
perc: bd, tri, tambn, cym, glock[covered by tmp]

Breitkopf	Kalmus	Luck's

Luonnotar, op.70 (Kalevala) <1913> *10'*

soprano solo
2 2 3[1.2.bcl] 2 — 4 2 3 0 — 2tmp — 2hp — str

Breitkopf

Night Ride and Sunrise, op.55 (Öinen ratsastus ja auringonnousu) <1908> *16'*

3[1.2.pic] 2 3[1.2.bcl] 3[1.2.cbn] — 4 2 3 1 — tmp+3 — str
perc: sd, tri, tambn, bd, sus cym
At figure [41], the composer asks that the horns be doubled if possible.

Kalmus	Lienau	Luck's

The Oceanides, op.73 (Aallottaret) <1914> *11'*

3[1.2.pic] 3[1.2.Eh] 3[1.2.bcl] 3[1.2.cbn] — 4 3 3 0 — 2tmp/perc — 2hp — str
perc: [all covered by tmp2] tri, glock

Breitkopf	Kalmus	Luck's

Overture, A minor <1902> *9'*

2 2 2 2 — 4 4 2 1 — tmp — str

Fazer

Overture, E major <1890–1891> *11'*

2 2 2 2 — 4 2 2 1 — tmp+2 — str
perc: cym, tri

Fazer

Pan and Echo; Dance Intermezzo No.3, op.53a <1906> *5'*

2[1.2/pic] 2 2 — 4 2 3 0 — tmp+2 — str
perc: cym, bd, tri

Kalmus	Lienau	Luck's

Pelléas and Mélisande, op.46 <1904–1905> *29'*

1[1/pic] 1[1/Eh] 2 2 — 2 0 0 0 — tmp/perc — str
perc: [covered by tmp] tri, bd

1. At the Castle-Gate (Vid slottsporten)	*4'*
2. Mélisande	*4'*
2a. At the Seashore (På stranden vid hafvet)	*2'*
3. A Spring in the Park (Vid en källa i parken)	*3'*
4. The Three Blind Sisters (De trenne blinda systrar)	*3'*
5. Pastorale	*2'*
6. Mélisande at the Spinning Wheel (Mélisande vid spinnrocken)	*2'*
7. Entr'acte	*3'*
8. The Death of Mélisande (Mélisandes död)	*6'*

Kalmus	Lienau	Luck's

Pohjola's Daughter, op.49 (Pohjulan tytär) <1905–1906> *17'*

3[1.2.pic] 3[1.2.Eh] 3[1.2.bcl] 3[1.2.cbn] — 4 4[2tp, 2crt] 3 1 — tmp — hp — str

Kalmus	Lienau	Luck's

Rakastava, op.14 (The Lover) <1894; rev 1911-1912> *11'*

tmp/triangle — str
Originally for unaccompanied male chorus, 1894; recomposed 1911-12.

1. The Lover	*4'*
2. The Lovers' Path	*2'*
3. Good Night—Farewell!	*5'*

Breitkopf	Kalmus	Luck's

The Rapid-Rider's Brides, op.33 (Koskenlaskijan morsiamet; Des Fährmanns Bräute) <1897> *9'*

solo baritone or mezzo-soprano
2 2 2 2 — 4 2 3 0 — tmp+2 — str
perc: bd, cym, tri

Breitkopf

Romance, op.42, C major <1904> *5'*

str

Breitkopf	Kalmus

A Saga, op.9 (En saga) <1892> *20'*

2[1.2/pic] 2 2 — 4 3 3 1 — 2perc — str
perc: cym, tri, bd
Breitkopf ed. Tuija Wicklund.

Breitkopf	Kalmus	Luck's

Scène de ballet <1891> *8'*

2[incl pic] 2[incl Eh] 2[incl bcl] 2 — 4 2 2 1 — 3perc — str
perc: tri, cast, sus cym

Fazer

Scènes historiques, Suite No.1, op.25: All' overtura <1911> *5'*

2 2 2 2 — 4 3 3 0 — tmp — str

Breitkopf	Kalmus

Scènes historiques, Suite No.1, op.25: Scena <1911> *6'*

2[1/pic.2/pic] 2 2 — 4 3 3 0 — tmp+3 — str
perc: tri, sd, bd, cym

Breitkopf	Kalmus

Scènes historiques, Suite No.2, op.66: Minnelied (Love Song) <1912> *5'*

2 2 2 2 — 4 0 0 0 — tmp — hp — str

Breitkopf	Kalmus

Scènes historiques, Suite No.2, op.66: An der Zugbrücke (At the Drawbridge) <1912> *7'*

3[1.2.pic] 2 2 — 4 0 0 0 — tmp+1 — hp — str
perc: tri, tamtam

Breitkopf	Kalmus

Serenade (Serenad) <1895> *6'*

baritone solo
0 2 2 2 — 4 0 0 0 — str

Breitkopf

Spring Song, op.16 (Vårsång) <1894> *12'*

2[1/pic1.2/pic2] 2 2 2 — 4 3 3 1 — tmp+1 — str
perc: chimes[C#4,D#4,F#4]

Breitkopf	Kalmus	Luck's

Swanwhite, op.54 (Svanevit): Suite <1908; rev suite: 1909> *26'*

2 2 2 2 — 4 0 0 0 — tmp+1 — hp — str
perc: tri, cast, bells

1. The Peacock	*3'*
2. The Harp	*4'*
3. The Maiden with the Roses	*3'*
4. Listen, the Robin Sings	*5'*
5. The Prince Alone	*4'*
6. Swanwhite and the Prince	*4'*
7. Song of Praise	*3'*

Kalmus	Lienau	Luck's

The Swan of Tuonela

see his: Lemminkäinen Suite, op.22, no.2

Symphony No.1, op.39, E minor <1899; rev 1900>   38'

2[1/pic.2/pic] 2 2 2 — 4 3 3 1 — tmp+2 — hp — str
perc: cym, bd, tri
Breitkopf ed. Timo Virtann.

I. Andante, ma non troppo - Allegro energico	11'
II. Andante, ma non troppo lento	9'
III. Scherzo: Allegro	5'
IV. Finale (quasi una fantasia)	13'

Breitkopf	Kalmus	Luck's

Symphony No.2, op.43, D major <1901–1902>   43'

2 2 2 2 — 4 3 3 1 — tmp — str

I. Allegretto	10'
II. Andante; ma rubato	14'
III. Vivacissimo	7'
IV. Finale: Allegro moderato	12'

Breitkopf	Kalmus	Luck's

Symphony No.3, op.52, C major <1907>   29'

2 2 2 2 — 4 2 3 0 — tmp — str
Breitkopf score ed. Timo Virtanen; Breitkopf does not publish parts for this work.

I. Allegro moderato	10'
II. Andantino con moto; quasi allegretto	8'
III. Moderato - Allegro; ma non tanto	11'

Kalmus	Lienau	Luck's

Symphony No.4, op.63, A minor <1910–1911>   36'

2 2 2 2 — 4 2 3 0 — tmp+1 — str
perc: chimes

I. Tempo molto moderato, quasi adagio	10'
II. Allegro molto vivace	5'
III. Il tempo largo	11'
IV. Allegro	10'

Breitkopf	Kalmus

Symphony No.5, op.82, E-flat major <1915; rev 1916; 1919>   30'

2 2 2 2 — 4 3 3 0 — tmp — str
Hansen offers an edition revised in 1974 by Berglund.

I. Tempo molto moderato; Allegro moderato - Presto	13'
II. Andante mosso, quasi allegretto	9'
III. Allegro molto; Misterioso	8'

Hansen	Kalmus	Luck's

Symphony No.6, op.104, D minor <1923>   28'

2 2 3[1.2.bcl] 2 — 4 3 3 0 — tmp — hp — str
Revised ed. 1981.

I. Allegro molto moderato	8'
II. Allegretto moderato	6'
III. Poco vivace	4'
IV. Allegro molto	10'

Hansen	Kalmus

Symphony No.7, op.105, C major <1924>   21'

2[1/pic.2/pic] 2 2 2 — 4 3 3 0 — tmp — str
In one movement. Rev. ed.1980.

Adagio	8'
Un pochetto meno adagio; Vivacissimo; Adagio	4'
Allegro molto moderato	4'
Vivace; Presto; Adagio; Largamente molto; Affetuoso	5'

Hansen

Tapiola, op.112 <1926>   18'

3[1.2.3/pic] 3[1.2.Eh] 3[1.2.bcl] 3[1.2.cbn] — 4 3 3 0 — tmp — str

Breitkopf

The Tempest (Stormen): Prelude (op.109 no.1) <1925>   5'

3[1.2.pic] 2 3[1.Ebcl.bcl] 2 — 4 3 3 1 — tmp+3 — str
perc: field dr, bd, cym

Hansen

The Tempest (Stormen): Suite No.1 (op.109 no.2) <1925; rev suites: 1927>   23'

3[1.2.3/pic] 2 3[1.2/Ebcl.bcl] 2 — 4 3 3 1 — tmp+4 — hp — str
perc: xyl, tri, field dr, cym, bd

1. The Oak Tree	3'
2. Humoresque	1'
3. Caliban's Song	1'
4. The Harvesters	2'
5. Canon	2'
6. Scena	2'
7. Intrada and Berceuse	4'
8. Entr'acte	2'
9. Ariel's Song	2'
10. The Storm	4'

Hansen

The Tempest (Stormen): Suite No.2 (op.109 no.3) <1925; rev suites: 1927>   17'

2[1.2/pic] 2 2[1.2/bcl] 2 — 4 0 0 0 — tmp+1 — hp — str
perc: tri, bd
2nd flute switches to pic in last mvt (Dance Episode), bars 64-65, then back to flute; a correction in the revised score of 2006.

1. Chorus of the Winds	3'
2. Intermezzo	2'
3. Dance of the Nymphs	2'
4. Prospero	2'
5. Song 1	1'
6. Song 2	1'
7. Miranda	2'
8. The Naiads	2'
9. Dance Episode	2'

Hansen

Valse chevaleresque, op.96c <1921>   4'

2 2 2 2 — 4 2 3 0 — tmp+1 — str
perc: sd
Originally for piano; orchestrated by the composer.

Hansen

Valse lyrique, op.96a <1919; rev (orchd) 1920>   5'

2 2 2 2 — 4 2 3 0 — tmp+1 — str
perc: tri
Originally for piano; orchestrated by the composer.

Hansen

Valse triste

see his: Kuolema: Valse triste

Wedding March <1911>   4'

2 1 3[incl bcl] 0 — 0 2 2 0 — tmp+3 — str
For a play by A. Paul, Die Sprache der Vögel.

Fazer

Siegmeister, Elie   1909-1991

(b New York, 15 Jan 1909; d Manhasset, NY, 10 March 1991). American

American Holiday <1933>   7'

2[1.2/pic] 3[1.2.Eh] 2 2 — 3 3 3 1 — tmp+3 — pf — str
perc: tri, sus cym, cym, bd, sd, tambn, woodblk

    C. Fischer

Five Fantasies of the Theater <1967>   12'

2[incl pic] 2[incl Eh] 3[incl Ebcl, bcl] 3[incl cbn] — 4 3 3 1 — tmp+4
— hp — pf — str
1. Beckett   _'
2. Ionesco   _'
3. Brecht   _'
4. Pirandello   _'
5. O'Casey   _'

    C. Fischer

Lonesome Hollow <1946>   7'

2[1.2/pic] 2[1.2/Eh] 2[1.2/Ebcl] 2 — 4 2 2 0 — tmp+1 — hp [or pf]
— str
perc: sd, bd, tri, tambn, sus cym, glock

    C. Fischer

Sunday in Brooklyn <1946>   16'

3[incl 2pic] 2[incl Eh] 3[incl Ebcl, bcl] 2 — 4 3 3 1 — asx — tmp+4
— hp — cel, pf — str
1. Prospect Park   4'
2. Sunday Driver   3'
3. Family at Home   4'
4. Children's Story 1'
5. Coney Island   4'

    C. Fischer

Theater Set <1960>   15'

2[incl pic] 2[incl Eh] 3[incl bcl] 2[incl opt cbn] — 4 3 3 1 — tmp+3
— hp — pf — str
1. Intrada   3'
2. Blues and Pursuit 4'
3. Revelation   5'
4. Triple Attack   3'

    C. Fischer

Western Suite <1945>   20'

2[incl pic] 2[incl Eh] 3[incl Ebcl, bcl] 2 — 4 3 3 1 — tmp+4 — str
1. Prairie Morning 6'
2. Round-Up   3'
3. Night-Herding   4'
4. Buckaroo   3'
5. Riding Home   4'

    C. Fischer

Sierra, Roberto   1953-

(b Vega Baja, Puerto Rico, 9 Oct 1953). Puerto Rican

Alegría <1996>   10'

3[1.2.pic] 2 2 2 — 4 3 3 1 — tmp+3 — str
perc: bd, sus cym, sd, tamtam, gong, xyl, marim, vib, chimes, cowbell, bongos,
guiro, marac, claves, congas, cabasa, 4tomtoms

    Subito

The Bacchae <2006>   12'

3[1.2.pic] 3[1.2.Eh] 3[1.2/Ebcl.bcl] 3[1.2.cbn] — 4 3 3 1 — tmp+3 —
hp — pf — str
perc: bd, cym, sus cym, sd, tri, tambn, tamtam, gong, xyl, marim, vib, bongos,
ratch, guiro, marac, cast, congas, 5cowbells, 2cencerros (salsa type)

    Subito

Beyond the Silence of Sorrow <2002>   22'

solo soprano
3[1.2.pic] 3[1.2.Eh] 3[1.2.bcl] 3[1.2.cbn] — 4 3 3 1 — tmp+2 — hp
— cel — str
perc: bd, cym, sd, tri, gong, marim, vib, woodblk, 3sus cym
1. Prayer to the Land   _'
2. About Me Like a Robe   _'
3. To Tell You of My Love   _'
4. A Cradle for This Child   _'
5. Little Newborn, Sleep   _'
6. The Woman Who Walked Here _'

    Subito

Borikén <2005>   12'

3[1.2.pic] 3[1.2.Eh] 3[1.2.bcl] 3[1.2.cbn] — 4 3 3 1 — tmp+4 — hp
— pf — str
perc: bd, cym, szl cym, sd, tri, tambn, gong, xyl, marim, vib, whip, bongos, guiro,
marac, congas, vibrslp, cabasa, 2sus cym

    Subito

Carnaval <2008>   21'

2[1.2/pic] 2[1.2/Eh] 2[1.2/bcl] 2 — 4 2 3 1 — tmp+3 — hp — cel —
str
perc: bd, cym, tamtam, vib, hi-hat, sd, timbales, tri, gong, glock, xyl, marim,
chimes, cowbell, bongos, guiro, marac, claves, cast, congas, 2sus cym, cabasa
I. Gargoyles   4'
II. Sphynxes   4'
III. Unicorns   6'
IV. Dragons   3'
V. The Phoenix 4'

    Subito

Concerto for Orchestra <2000>   18'

3[1.2.pic] 3[1.2.Eh] 3[1.2.bcl] 3[1.2.cbn] — 4 3 3 1 — tmp+4 — hp
— pf/cel — str
perc: bd, cym, szl cym, sd, tri, tambn, tamtam, gong, glock, xyl, marim, vib,
chimes, crot, marktree, woodblk, templeblks, cowbell, whip, bongos, ratch, guiro,
marac, claves, congas, 6tomtoms, herdbells, cabasa, 3sus cym
I. Dibujos   _'
Cadenza luminosa   _'
II. Atardecer   _'
III. Danzas imaginarias _'

    Subito

Concerto, Saxophone <2002>   20'

soloist alternates tenor & soprano saxophone
3[1.2.pic] 2 3[1.2.bcl] 2 — 4 3 3 0 — tmp+4 — hp — pf/cel — str
perc: bd, set, tri, tambn, tamtam, gong, marim, vib, woodblk, bongos, claves,
cabasa, 4sus cym
I. Rhythmic   5'
II. Tender   7'
III. Playful   4'
IV. Fast (with swing) 4'

    Subito

Concerto, Viola <2006>   16'

tmp+3 — str
perc: tamtam, gong, xyl, marim, vib, cowbell, whip, claves, 3sus cym
I. Lento expresivo _'
II. Expresivo   _'
III. Veloz   _'
IV. Ritmico   _'

    Subito

Concerto, Violin & Viola (Doble concierto para violín y viola) <2002> 20'

3[1.2.pic] 3[1.2.Eh] 3[1.2.bcl] 3[1.2.cbn] — 4 3 3 1 — tmp+3 — hp — pf/cel — str

perc: bd, cym, hi-hat, sd, tri, tamtam, gong, xyl, marim, vib, bongos, guiro, claves, cabasa, 4tomtoms, 3sus cym

1. Con intensidad y emoción	_'
2. Con precisión rítmica	_'
3. Lento, con profunda emoción	_'
4. Rápido	_'

Subito

Cuatro Versos (Cello Concerto) <1999> 20'

2 2 2 2 — 2 1 1 0 — 2perc — pf/cel — str

perc: tri, tambn, gong, glock, marim, vib, cabasa, 4sus cym, 2woodblks

I. Intenso	5'
II. Emotivo	6'
Cadenza	2'
III. Vivo y ligero	3'
IV. Rítmico	4'

Subito

Fandangos <2000> 13'

3[1.2.pic] 3[1.2.Eh] 3[1.2.bcl] 3[1.2.cbn] — 4 3 3 1 — tmp+3 — hp — pf/cel — str

perc: bd, cym, sus cym, sd, toms, tri, tambn, tamtam, xyl, marim, vib, cast, cencerros

Subito

Folias for Guitar & Orchestra <2002> 12'

solo guitar

2 2 2 2 — 2 2 0 0 — 1perc — str

perc: bd, sus cym, tri, tambn, gong, cast

Subito

Güell concert <2006> 11'

1 1 1 1 — 1 1 1 0 — tmp+2 — pf — str

perc: bd, hi-hat, tamtam, gong, glock, xyl, marim, vib, bongos, guiro, congas, 4cowbells, 3sus cym

1. Cantiga: Porque trobar é cousa en que jaz	_'
2. Primera diferencia	_'
3. Cantiga	_'
4. Segunda diferencia	_'
5. Cantiga	_'
6. Tercera diferencia	_'
7. Cantiga	_'
8. Cuarta diferencia	_'
9. Cantiga	_'
10. Quinta diferencia	_'

Subito

A Joyous Overture <1991> 5'

3[1.2.pic] 2 2 2 — 4 3[tp3 opt] 2 1[or btbn] — tmp+2 — str

perc: bd, cym, sus cym, tri, tambn, xyl, woodblk

Schirmer

Missa latina (pro pax) <2003–2005> 68'

solo soprano & baritone   chorus

3[1.2.pic] 3[1.2.Eh] 3[1.2.bcl] 3[1.2.cbn] — 4 3 3 1 — tmp+4 — hp — pf — str

perc: bd, cym, hi-hat, sd, timbales, tri, tamtam, gong, glock, xyl, marim, vib, guiro, marac, claves, congas, vibrslp, cabasa, 4tomtoms, 2cowbells, 4bongos, 3sus cym

1. Introitus	6'
2. Kyrie	6'
3. Gloria	15'
4. Credo	21'
5. Offertorium	7'
6. Sanctus	5'
7. Agnus Dei	8'

Subito

Saludo <1995> 4'

3[1.2.pic] 3[1.2.Eh] 3[1.2.bcl] 3[1.2.cbn] — 4 3 3 1 — tmp+4 — str

perc: bd, sus cym, sd, tri, tamtam, xyl, marim, vib, chimes, templeblks, bongos, congas, 2cowbells, 2gongs

Subito

Serenata for Chamber Orchestra <2003> 16'

2[1.2/pic] 2 2[1.2/bcl] 2 — 2 2 0 0 — tmp+2 — pf — str

perc: cym, hi-hat, sd, tamtam, gong, glock, xyl, marim, vib, woodblk, bongos, guiro, 3sus cym

Entrada	1'
Mazurka criolla	4'
Interludio	1'
Nocturno (Felices días)	7'
Guaracha	3'

Subito

Sinfonía No.1 <2002> 16'

2[1.2/pic] 2 2 2 — 2 2 0 0 — tmp+1 — pf — str

perc: cym, hi-hat, sd, xyl, marim, vib, cowbell, bongos, bd/ped, 2sus cym

I. Lento; Rítmico y preciso	5'
II. Con intensidad y gran expresión	4'
III. Juguetón y rítmico	3'
IV. No muy lento; Movido	4'

Subito

Sinfonía No.2 (Gran passacaglia) <2004–2005> 15'

3[1.2.pic] 3[1.2.Eh] 3[1.2.bcl] 3[1.2.cbn] — 4 3 3 1 — tmp+4 — hp — pf/cel — str

perc: bd, cym, sd, tri, tamtam, gong, xyl, marim, vib, bongos, congas, 3sus cym, 4tomtoms

Subito

Sinfonía No.3 (La Salsa) <2005> 28'

3[1.2.pic] 3[1.2.Eh] 3[1.2.bcl] 2 — 4 3 3 0 — tmp+4 — pf — str

perc: marim, xyl, vib, sus cym, claves, sd, bd, tamtam, guiro, 3cowbells, 3bongos, 3congas

Movements may be performed separately.

I. Tumbao	7'
II. Habanero	7'
III. Danzas	5'
IV. Jolgorio	9'

Subito

Tropicalia: Celebration <1991> 7'

3[1.2.pic] 3[1.2.Eh] 3[1.2.bcl] 3[1.2.cbn] — 4 3 3 1 — tmp+4 — hp — pf/cel — str

perc: crot, glock, vib, xyl, marim, claves, marac, guiro, bongos, congas, tri, sus cym, cym, sd, bd, tamtam, tambn

Schirmer

Silvestrov, Valentin 1937-

(b Kiev, 30 Sept 1937). Ukrainian

Symphony No.2 <1965> 12'

1 0 0 0 — 0 0 0 0 — tmp+2 — pf — str[4.4.3.2.1]

perc: bd, tamtam, vib, glock, 3sus cym

In one movement.

Belaieff   Sikorski

Sinding, Christian   1856-1941

(b Kongsberg, 11 Jan 1856; d Oslo, 3 Dec 1941). Norwegian

Concerto, Piano, op.6, D-flat major <1889>   32'

2 2 2 2 — 4 2 3 1 — tmp — str
I. Allegro non troppo   13'
II. Andante   9'
III. Allegro non assai   10'

Hansen	Kalmus	Luck's

Symphony No.1, op.21, D minor <1880–1890>   40'

3[1.2.pic] 2 2 2 — 4 3 3 1 — tmp — str
Allegro moderato   12'
Andante   10'
Vivace   8'
Allegro   10'

Kalmus	Peters	Luck's

Singleton, Alvin   1940-

(b Brooklyn, NY, 28 Dec 1940). American

After Fallen Crumbs <1987>   7'

3 3[1.2.Eh] 3 3[1.2.cbn] — 4 3 3 1 — tmp — str

EAM

Blueskonzert <1995>   17'

solo piano
2 2 2 2 — 2 2 2 0 — str

Schott

Shadows <1987>   20'

3[1.2.pic/afl] 3[1.2.3/Eh] 3[1.2/Ebcl.3/bcl] 3[1.2.3/cbn] — 4 3 3 1 — 2tmp+2 — hp — str
perc: xyl, marim

EAM

When Given a Choice <2004>   16'

3[1.2.pic] 3[1.2.Eh] 3[1.2/Ebcl.3/bcl] 2 — 4 3 3 1 — tmp+3 — str
perc: marim, xyl, vib

Schott

A Yellow Rose Petal <1982>   20'

2[1/pic.2/pic] 2[1.2/Eh] 2[1.2/bcl] 2[1.2/cbn] — 2 2 1 0 — 2perc — cel — str[min 10.8.6.5.3]
perc: glock, marim, xyl, vib

Schott

Sinigaglia, Leone   1868-1944

(b Turin, 14 Aug 1868; d Turin, 16 May 1944). Italian

Adagio tragico, op.21   7'

str

Bärenreiter	Carisch

Le baruffe chiozzotte, op.32 <1907–1908>   8'

3[1.2.pic] 2 2 2 — 4 2 3 0 — tmp+3 — str
perc: glock, sd, tri, cym

Breitkopf	Carisch	Kalmus	Luck's

Concerto, Violin, op.20, A major <1900>   40'

2 2 2 2 — 4 2 0 0 — tmp — str
I. Allegro risoluto   _'
II. Adagio   _'
III. Allegro vivo e con grazia   _'

Breitkopf

Danze piemontesi sopra temi popolare, No.1, A major <1903>   8'

3[1.2.pic] 2 2 2 — 4 2 0 0 — tmp — hp — str

Breitkopf	Kalmus

Danze piemontesi sopra temi popolare, No.2, D major <1903>   7'

3[1.2.pic] 2 2 2 — 4 2 3 0 — tmp=2 — str
perc: cym, tri, glock

Breitkopf	Kalmus

Rapsodia piemontese, op.26 <1900>   4'

solo violin
2 2 2 2 — 4 2 0 0 — tmp — str

Breitkopf

Skalkottas, Nikos   1904-1949

(b Halkis, Evia, 21 March 1904; d Athens, 20 Sept 1949). Greek

Concertino, Oboe & Chamber Orchestra <1939>   12'

2 1[ob/Eh] 2[cl.bcl] 1 — 2 1 1 1 — hp — str
Arr. Gunther Schuller.
I. Allegro giocoso   5'
II. Andante tranquillo   5'
III. Rondo: Allegro vivo   2'

Margun

Concerto, Piano, No.3 <1938–1939>   66'

1 2[ob.Eh] 1 2[bn.cbn] — 1 1 1 1 — tmp+4 — [no str]
perc: bd, cym, sd, tomtom, tri, tambn, xyl, whip
I. Moderato   21'
II. Andante sostenuto   26'
III. Allegro giocoso   19'

Margun

Five Greek Dances (Ellenike chori) <1931–1936; rev (reorchd) 1948-1949>   9'

str
Selected & ed. Walter Goehr, from the composer's *36 Greek Dances*.
1. Epirotikos   2'
2. Kretikos   1'
3. Tsamikos   2'
4. Arkadikos   2'
5. Kleftikos   2'

Universal

The Return of Ulysses (E epistrophe tou Odysseus) <1943–1944>   30'

3[1/pic.2/pic.3/pic] 4[1.2.3.Eh] 4[1.2.Ebcl.bcl] 3[1.2.cbn] — 6 4[1.2.3.crt] 4 1 — tmp+5 — 2hp — cel — str
perc: bd, cym, glock, sd, vib, xyl
Overture to an unwritten opera, published by Margun under the title *Symphony in One Movement*.

Margun

Ten Sketches for Strings <1940>   19'

str, or str 4t

Universal

Skoryk, Myroslav   1938-

(b Lwów [now Lviv, Ukraine], 13 July 1938). Ukrainian

Hutsul Triptych (Hutsuls'ky tryptykh) <1965>   15'

3[1.2.pic] 3[1.2.Eh] 3[1.2.bcl] 3[1.2.cbn] — 4 3 3 1 — tmp+2 — hp
— pf — str
perc: tri, cym, xyl
1. Childhood	4'
2. Ivan and Maritsa	5'
3. Death of Ivan	6'

Schirmer	Sikorski

Melody   4'

str

Duma

Skrowaczewski, Stanisław   1923-

(b Lwów [now L'viv, Ukraine], 3 Oct 1923). American composer of Polish birth

Ricercari notturni   27'

solo saxophone, doubling on soprano, alto and baritone
3[incl pic] 0 0 2 — 2 2 3 1 — tmp+3 — ampd hpsd — str[8.8.6.6.4]
Alternative soloist: B-flat clarinet doubling on bass clarinet.

EAM

Skryabin, Alexander   1872-1915

see: Scriabin, Alexander, 1872-1915

Sleeper, Thomas   1956-

(b. Wagoner, OK, 16 Feb 1956). American

Concerto, Violin (Hypnagogia) <2011>   18'

3[1.2.pic] 2 2 2 — 4 2 3 1 — tmp+5 — hp — str
perc: xyl, vib, bd, sd, tamtam, cym, sus cym, marac, 5tomtom, rainstick
I. Agitato; Adagio; Andante; Allegro; Veloce	5'
II. eighth-note = 80	5'
III. Un poco adagio; Lento espressivo; Allegro furioso	8'

Uroboros

Concerto, Violoncello <2008>   21'

3[1.2.pic] 2 2 2 — 4 2 3 1 — tmp+4 — hp — str
perc: bd, cym, sd, tamtam, claves, 2sus cym, 4tomtom, rainstick
I. Andante; Allegro	6'
II. sacre	6'
III. Vivace	9'

Uroboros

Symphony No.1 <2007>   26'

3[1.2.pic] 2 2 2 — 4 2 3 1 — tmp+2 — hp — str
perc: xyl, tri, sd, bd, cym, szl cym, rute, 2sus cym
I. Andante mosso	5'
II. Adagio	14'
III. Misterioso	3'
IV. Allegro energico	4'

Uroboros

Symphony No.2 (Little Leylie) <2012>   12'

3[1.2.pic] 2 2 2 — 4 2 3 1 — tmp+4 — hp — str
perc: glock, tri, sus cym, tamtam, sd, bd, cym(2pr)
I. Poco andante; Allegro	5'
II. Andante	4'
III. Leylie's Great Escape	3'

Uroboros

Symphony No.4 <2014>   22'

2[1/pic.2] 2[1.2/Eh] 2 2 — 4 2 3 1 — tmp+4 — hp — str
perc: bd, cym, tamtam, crot, chimes, vib, 3tomtom, 2sus
I. Adagio misterioso; Allegro giocoso	7'
II. "good friday ... "	5'
III. Allegro giocoso	5'
IV. Adagio estatico	5'

Uroboros

Translucence <2009>   18'

solo trombone
2 2 2 2 — 2 2 3 1 — tmp+3 — hp — pf/cel — str
perc: chimes, tamtam, cym, tri, sd, bd, 2sus cym
I. nocturne	5'
II. ... stellar effusion ...	6'
III. dance	7'

Uroboros

Slonimsky, Nicolas   1894-1995

(b St Petersburg, 15/27 April 1894; d Los Angeles, 25 Dec 1995). American composer of Russian birth

My Toy Balloon; Variations on a Brazilian Tune <1942>   6'

3[1.2.pic] 2 2 2 — 2 2 3 1 — tmp+6 — opt hp — pf/opt cel — str
"Toy balloons may, for decorative purposes, be attached to the desks, and
the players supplied with hatpins to explode the balloons." The rhythmic
location for popping balloons is specified in the score and perc part.

Shawnee

Smetana, Bedřich   1824-1884

(b Litomyšl, 2 March 1824; d Prague, 12 May 1884). Czech

The Bartered Bride (Prodaná nevěsta): Overture   7'
<1863–1866; rev 4th (definitive) version: 1870>

3[1.2.pic] 2 2 2 — 4 2 3 0 — tmp — str

Breitkopf	Kalmus	Luck's

The Bartered Bride (Prodaná nevěsta): Three Dances   11'
<1863–1866; rev 4th (definitive) version: 1870>

3[1.2.pic] 2 2 2 — 4 2 3 0 — tmp+3 — str
perc: bd, cym, td, tri
The Kalmus arrangement by Hugo Riesenfeld has many errors; the
version by Clark McAlister (also from Kalmus) is recommended.
Polka	4'
Furiant	2'
Dance of the Comedians	5'

Kalmus	Luck's

Hakon Jarl, op.16 <1860–1861>   10'

3[1.2.pic] 2 3[1.2.bcl] 2 — 4 2 3 1 — tmp+3 — hp — str
perc: tri, cym, bd
Also spelled *Haakon Jarl*.
   Bcl apparently optional; a solo cello cue is provided at one point, "in
the absence of a bass clarinet."

Kalmus	Lengnick	Simrock	Supraphon

MÁ VLAST (My Fatherland)   72'

A cycle of six symphonic poems on nationalist themes. Composed between 1872 and 1879.

1. Vysehrad (The High Castle) <1872–1874>   12'

3[1.2.pic] 2 2 2 — 4 2 3 1 — tmp+2 — 2hp — str
perc: cym, tri

Breitkopf	Kalmus	Luck's	Supraphon

2. Vltava (The Moldau) <1874>   12'

3[1.2.pic] 2 2 2 — 4 2 3 1 — tmp+3 — hp — str
perc: tri, bd, cym
Bärenreiter ed. Hugh Macdonald.

Bärenreiter	Breitkopf	Kalmus	Luck's	Supraphon

3. Sárka <1875>   9'

3[1.2.pic] 2 2 2 — 4 2 3 1 — tmp+2 — str
perc: tri, cym

Kalmus	Luck's	Supraphon

4. From Bohemia's Forests and Meadows (Z ceskych luhuv a hájuv) <1875>   12'

3[1.2.pic] 2 2 2 — 4 2 3 1 — tmp+2 — str
perc: tri, cym

Breitkopf	Kalmus	Luck's	Supraphon

5. Tábor <1878>   13'

3[1.2.pic] 2 2 2 — 4 2 3 1 — tmp+1 — str
perc: cym

Kalmus	Luck's	Supraphon

6. Blaník <1879>   14'

3[1.2.pic] 2 2 2 — 4 2 3 1 — tmp+2 — str
perc: tri, cym

Kalmus	Luck's	Supraphon

Richard III, op.11 <1857–1858>   11'

3[1.2.pic] 2 2 2 — 4 2 3 1 — tmp+3 — hp — str
perc: tri, bd, cym

Kalmus	Lengnick	Supraphon

Wallenstein's Camp (Valdstynuv tabor) <1858–1859>   14'

3[1.2.pic] 2 2 2 — 4 4 3 1 — tmp+4 — str
perc: tri, field dr, bd, cym

Kalmus	Luck's	Simrock	Supraphon

Smith, Gregory   1957-

(b Salem, OR, 30 Dec 1957). American

A MAJOR-minor Mystery <1997>   22'

narrator (low voice; must sing pitches and speak rhythms accurately)
3[1.2.3/pic] 2[1.2/Eh] 2 2 — 4 3 3 1 — tmp+2 — hp — str
perc: bd, sd, brake dr, tri, tamtam, glock, xyl, vib, marktree, templeblks, whip, vibrslp, duckcall, crowcall, finger cym, sirenwhstl, bulbhorn, 2sus cym, sl whistle

Geocoso

The Melodic Life <2006>   23'

narrator (sings a bit; baritone range)
3[1.2.3/pic] 2[1.2/Eh] 2 2 — 4 3 3 1 — tmp+2 or 3 — hp — str
perc: bd/cym, sus cym, sd, set, brake dr, tri, tambn, glock, xyl, vib, chimes, marktree, whip, bongos, guiro, cast, sirenwhstl, shaker, pol whstle, basketball, 2baseball bats, tap shoe simulator

Geocoso

Mr. Smith's Bowl of Notes <2003>   30'

actor
3[1.2.3/pic] 2[1.2/Eh] 2 2 — 4 3[1/pic tp.2.3] 3 1 — tmp+2 — hp — str
perc: bd, cym, sus cym, sd, tomtom, tri, tamtam, glock, xyl, marim, vib, chimes, windchimes, marktree, woodblk, whip, ratch, vibrslp, finger cym, sirenwhstl, bulbhorn, bamboo windchimes, CD [provided], popgun, sl whistl

Geocoso

Mr. Smith's Composition <1990>   19'

narrator
3[incl pic] 3[incl opt Eh] 3[incl opt bcl] 3[incl opt cbn] — 4 3 3 1 — tmp+2 — hp — str

Geocoso

The Orchestra Games <1995>   27'

narrator
3[incl pic] 2 2 2 — 4 3 3 1 — tmp+3 — hp — str

Geocoso

Zoo Song <1998>   17'

narrator
3[1.2.3/pic] 2[1.2/Eh] 2 2 — 4 3 3 1 — tmp+2 — hp — str
perc: bd, sus cym, sd, glock, marim, marktree, belltree, woodblk, templeblks, cowbell, whip, bongos, ratch, guiro, congas, 2tamtams, shaker, bamboo windchimes

Geocoso

Smith, Hale   1925-2009

(b Cleveland, 29 June 1925). American

Contours <1961>   9'

2[incl pic] 2 2[incl bcl] 2 — 4 4 3 1 — tmp+5 — hp — pf/cel — str

Peters

Ritual and Incantations <1974>   16'

2[incl pic] 2[incl Eh] 2[incl bcl] 2 — 4 3 3 1 — tmp+3 — hp — pf — str

Peters

Smith, Julia   1911-1989

(b Denton, TX, 25 Jan 1911; d New York, 27 April 1989). American

Folkways Symphony <1948>   13'

2[incl pic] 2 2 2[opt] — 2 2 1 0 — opt asx — tmp+2 — opt hp — pf 4-hands — str
Harp, bassoons, & saxophone are optional.
  1. Day's A-Breakin'   _'
  2.Night Herding Song   _'
  3.Cowboy's Waltz   _'
  4. Stomping Leather   _'

C. Fischer

Smith, Kile   1956-

(b Camden, NJ, 24 Aug 1956). American

Alabanza <2003>   6'

mezzo-soprano   Latin ensemble: vn, pf, bass gtr, 3perc
2 2 2 2 — 4 3 3 1 — tmp+2 — str
perc: (*Latin ensemble*) marac, tambn, congas;
(*orch*) sus cym, sd, belltree, woodblk, templeblks, bongos
Some improvisation may be expected in the performance of this piece.
This work is a companion piece to *Song of Sonia Sanchez*, *q.v.*, and may
be performed immediately following it.

> Fleisher

Concerto, Trombone   28'

2[1.2/pic] 2[1.2/Eh] 2[1.2/bcl] 0 — 4 2 3 1 — tmp+2 — pf — str
I. Kyrie	4'
II. Credo	6'
III. Gloria	6'
IV. Sanctus	7'
V. Nunc dimittis	5'

> Fleisher

Exsultet   18'

solo horn
str
1. In the darkness, fire is kindled	5'
2. Procession	7'
3. Exsultet	6'

> Fleisher

Four French Carols   11'

3[1.2.pic] 3[1.2.Eh] 2 2 — 4 3 3 1 — tmp+2 — str
perc: bd, cym, sus cym, sd, tri, glock
The composer also made a string orchestra version of this work, as well
as a version for brass quintet.
1. A Cry Went Up at Midnight	4'
2. Bring a Torch, Jeanette, Isabella	2'
3. Saw You Never	3'
4. O Come, Divine Messiah	2'

> Fleisher

Hymn and Fugue No.1 <1990>   10'

str
| Hymn | 4' |
| Fugue | 6' |

> Fleisher

Poems of Gerard Manley Hopkins   10'

high voice
2 2 2 2 — 2 2 0 0 — str
1. Spring and Fall	2'
2. As Kingfishers Catch Fire	3'
3. Henry Purcell	5'

> Fleisher

Psalm 46 <2003–2004>   15'

solo baritone   SATB chorus
2[1.pic] 2 2 — 2 2 3 1 — tmp+1 — str
perc: bd, cym, sus cym, tamtam, glock, bongos, marac

> Fleisher

A Song of Sonia Sanchez <2000>   7'

mezzo-soprano   Latin ensemble: vn, pf, bass gtr, 3perc
2 2 2 2 — 4 3 3 1 — tmp+2 — str
perc: (*Latin ensemble*) marac, cast, claves, tambn, congas, vibrslp;
(*orch*) sus cym, guiro, bongos, tambn, slitdrum (or 2templeblks)
Some improvisation may be expected in the performance of this piece.
In performance, this work may be followed by *Alabanza*, *q.v.*, which is a
companion piece.

> Fleisher

Symphony: Lumen ad revelationem   20'

2 2 2 2 — 2 2 0 0 — tmp/perc — str
perc: bd, 3tomtom, tri, tamtam
1. Lumen ad revelationem	9'
2. Passer invenit sibi domum	3'
3. The Lord God is a Sun and Shield	8'

> Fleisher

Three Dances <1995>   12'

2[incl pic] 2 2 2 — 2 2 0 0 — 1perc — str
perc: tomtom, rute
A version for string orchestra and 1 percussionist also exists.
Introduction	1'
1. Country Dance	4'
2. Waltz	4'
3. Fuguing Tune	3'

> Fleisher

The Three Graces   11'

solo oboe, horn, violoncello
str

> Fleisher

Variations on a Theme of Schubert   17'

solo piano
2 2 2 2 — 2 1 0 0 — tmp+1 — str

> Fleisher

The Voice of One Who Spoke <2002–2003>   20'

3[1.2.pic] 2 2 2[1.cbn] — 4 2 3 1 — tmp+3 — str
perc: bd, timbales, tambn, xyl, chimes, templeblks, bongos, guiro, congas,
2woodblk, 3pr marac, 3pr sandblk, cabasa, shekere [played by tmp]

> Fleisher

Smith Brindle, Reginald   1917-2003

(b Bamber Bridge, 5 Jan 1917; d 9 Sept 2003). English

Concerto, Guitar <1976>   15'

1 1 1 1 — 3perc — pf, elec org — str[5.4.3.2.1]

> Schott

Sousa, John Philip   1854-1932

(b Washington, DC, 6 Nov 1854; d Reading, PA, 6 March 1932). American

The Glass-Blowers (The American Maid): Overture <1909> 7'

2 1 2 2 — 2 2[2crt] 3 0 — 3perc — hp — str
perc: bd, cym, sd, glock, xyl, rattle, pipelophone [=vib?]

> Fleisher

Humoresque on George Gershwin's "Swanee" <1920>   4'

3[1.2.pic] 2 4[1.2.3.bcl] 2 — 4 4 2 1 — tmp+3 — hp — str

> Willow Blossom

Tales of a Traveler <1911>   16'

3[1.2.3/pic] 2 3[1.2.3/bcl] 3[1.2.cbn] — 4 4[2tp, 2crt] 3 1 — tmp+4 — hp — str
perc: bd, cym, sus cym, sd, tri, tambn, glock, xyl, chimes
Ed. R. Mark Rogers.
1. The Kaffir on the Karroo   4'
2. In the Land of the Golden Fleece 6'
3. Coronation March   6'

Southern

Sowerby, Leo   1895-1968

(b Grand Rapids, MI, 1 May 1895; d Port Clinton, OH, 7 July 1968). American

Comes Autumn Time   5'

3[incl pic] 2 3[incl bcl] 2 — 4 3 3 1 — tmp+3 — hp — cel — str
perc: glock, chimes, cym, sus cym
Original publisher: Boston Music Co.

Kalmus	Luck's

From the Northland; Impressions of the Lake Superior Country <1923>   19'

3[incl pic] 3[incl Eh] 4[incl Ebcl, bcl] 3[incl cbn] — 4 3 3 1 — tmp+3 — hp — cel, pf — str
1. Forest Voices   5'
2. Cascades   3'
3. Rock Pool   4'
4. The Lonely Fiddle-Maker 2'
5. The Shining Big-Sea Water 5'

Schirmer

Medieval Poem <1926>   16'

solo organ   off-stage voice (woman or boy)
1 1[1/Eh] 2[incl bcl] 1 — 2 1 0 0 — tmp+1 — str

C. Fischer	Fleisher

Prairie; A Poem for Orchestra <1929>   17'

3[incl pic] 3[incl Eh] 3[incl bcl] 3[incl cbn] — 4 3 3 1 — tmp+4 — cel — str

C. Fischer

Spohr, Ludwig (Louis)   1784-1859

(b Brunswick, 5 April 1784; d Kassel, 22 Oct 1859). German

Concerto, Clarinet, No.1, op.26, C minor <1808>   22'

2 2 0 2 — 2 2 0 0 — tmp — str
1. Adagio - Allegro   12'
II. Adagio   4'
III. Rondo: Vivace   6'

Bärenreiter	Kalmus	Luck's	Musica Rara	Peters

Concerto, String Quartet, op.131, A minor <1845>   25'

2 2 2 2 — 2 2 3 0 — tmp — str
I. Allegro moderato   10'
II. Adagio   8'
III. Rondo: Allegretto 7'

Breitkopf	Luck's

Concerto, Violin, No.8, op.47, A minor (Gesangsszene; In modo de scena cantante) <1816>   19'

1 0 2 1 — 2 0 0 0 — tmp — str
Movements are played without pause.
1. Allegro molto (Recitative)   4'
2. Adagio; Andante   7'
3. Allegro moderato   8'

Breitkopf	Kalmus	Luck's	Peters

Concerto, Violin, No.9, op.55, D minor <1820>   27'

2 2 2 2 — 2 2 3 0 — tmp — str
I. Allegro   10'
II. Adagio   8'
III. Rondo: Allegretto 9'

Breitkopf	Kalmus

Nonet, op.31, F major <1813>   32'

1 1 1 1 — 1 0 0 0 — vn, va, vc, db
1. Allegro   11'
2. Scherzo: Allegro 6'
3. Adagio   7'
4. Finale: Vivace   8'

Peters

Octet, op.32, E major <1814>   29'

0 0 1 0 — 2 0 0 0 — vn, 2va, vc, db
1. Adagio; Allegro   9'
2. Menuetto: Allegro   6'
3. Andante con variazioni   8'
4. Finale: Allegretto   6'

Bärenreiter

Symphony No.3, op.78, C minor <1828>   29'

2 2 2 2 — 4 2 3 0 — tmp — str
Ed. Horst Heussner.
Andante grave; Allegro   8'
Larghetto   6'
Scherzo   6'
Finale: Allegro   9'

Bärenreiter

Symphony No.4, op.86, F major (Die Weihe der Töne; The Consecration of Sound) <1832>   40'

2[1.2/pic/flauto terzo] 2 2 2 — 4 2 3 0 — tmp+4 — str
"Flauto terzo" is apparently an E-flat flute, analogous to Ebcl.
Ed. Joshua Berrett.
Largo; Allegro   11'
Andantino   7'
Tempo di marcia; Andante maestoso (Ambrosian Ode) 14'
Larghetto; Allegretto   8'

Garland	Luck's

Symphony No.6, op.116, G major (Historische Symphonie; Historic Symphony) <1839>   30'

2[incl pic] 2 2 — 4 2 3 0 — tmp+4 — str
"Historische Symphonie im Styl und Geschmack vier verschiedener Zeitabschnitte" (Historical Symphony in the Style and Taste of Four Differemt Time-Periods).
Ed. Joshua Berrett.
1. Bach-Händel'sche Periode 1720   8'
2. Haydn-Mozart'sche Periode 1780   9'
3. Beethoven'sche Periode 1810   6'
4. Allerneueste Periode 1840 [Latest Period] 7'

Garland

Symphony No.7, op.121, C major (Irdisches und Göttliches im Menschenleben; The Earthly and Divine in Human Life) <1841>   34'

3 2 3 2 — 4 2 3 0 — tmp — str
Ed. Joshua Berrett. Double orchestra:
orch I: 1 1 1 1 — 2 0 0 0 — str
orch II: 2 1 2 1 — 2 2 3 0 — tmp — str
1. Kinderwelt (The World of Childhood)   12'
2. Zeit der Leidenschaften (The Age of Passion)   12'
3. Endlicher Sieg des Göttlichen (Final Triumph of the Heavenly) 10'

Garland	Schuberth

Stamitz, Anton   1750 - ca.1809

(b Německý Brod [now Havlíčkův Brod], 27 Nov 1750; d Paris or Versailles, between 1796 and 1809). Bohemian

Concerto, Viola, No.4, D major <1784–1786>   25'

str
Ed. W. Lebermann.

Breitkopf

Stamitz, Carl   1745 - 1801

(b Mannheim, bap. 8 May 1745; d Jena, 9 Nov 1801). Bohemian

Concerto, Bassoon, F major   15'

0 2 0 0 — 2 0 0 0 — str
Ed. Johannes Wojciechowski.

Sikorski

Concerto, Clarinet, E-flat major   17'

2 0 0 0 — 2 0 0 0 — str
1. Allegro   8'
2. Aria   5'
3. Rondo alla scherzo   4'

Hofmeister	Luck's	Sikorski

Concerto, Clarinet, F major   17'

0 2 0 0 — 2 0 0 0 — str
1. Allegro   8'
2. Andante moderato   4'
3. Rondeau   5'

EMB	Eulenburg

Concerto, Clarinet, No.3, B-flat major <c1777>   14'

0 2 0 0 — 2 0 0 0 — str
Ed. Johannes Wojciechowski.
1. Allegro   8'
2. Romanze   3'
3. Rondo: Presto   3'

Luck's	Peters

Concerto, Clarinet & Bassoon, B-flat major   20'

0 0 0 0 — 2 0 0 0 — str
Ed. Johannes Wojciechowski.

Sikorski

Concerto, Clarinet & Violin (or 2 Clarinets)   18'

0 2 0 0 — 2 0 0 0 — str
Oboes & horns are optional. Published under the title *Concerto no.4.*
1. Allegro   8'
2. Andante moderato   6'
3. Tempo di minuetto   4'

Boosey	EMB	Luck's

Concerto, Flute, G major   18'

str
Ed. Ingo Gronefeld.
1. Allegro   8'
2. Andante non troppo moderato 5'
3. Rondo: Allegro   5'

Leuckart

Concerto, Viola, op.1, D major   19'

0 0 2 0 — 2 0 0 0 — str
Ed. Kurt Soldan.
1. Allegro   9'
2. Andante moderato   6'
3. Rondo   4'

Kalmus	Luck's	Peters

Concerto, Violoncello, No.1, G major   20'

2 0 0 0 — 2 0 0 0 — str
Ed. Walter Upmeyer.
1. Allegro con spirito   10'
2. Romanze: Andantino   4'
3. Rondo: Allegro; Moderato; Allegro   6'

Bärenreiter	Kalmus	Luck's

Concerto, Violoncello, No.2, A major   19'

2 0 0 0 — 2 0 0 0 — str
Ed. Walter Upmeyer.
1. Allegro con spirito   9'
2. Romance: Andantino   5'
3. Rondo: Allegretto   5'

Bärenreiter	Kalmus	Luck's

Concerto, Violoncello, No.3, C major   18'

0 2 0 0 — 2 0 0 0 — str
Ed. Walter Upmeyer.
Allegro con spirito   9'
Andante poco moderato   5'
Rondo: Allegro   4'

Bärenreiter	Kalmus	Luck's

Orchestral Quartet, op.1, no.1, C major <1770>   12'

str
Ed. Allan Badley.
I. Allegro vivace   5'
II. Andante moderato   3'
III. Allegro vivace   4'

Artaria

Orchestral Quartet, op.1, no.2, G major <1770>   14'

str
Ed. Allan Badley.
I. Allegro vivace   5'
II. Andante moderato   4'
III. Allegro presto   5'

Artaria

Orchestral Quartet, op.1, no.3, E-flat major <1770>   10'

str
Ed. Allan Badley.
I. Allegro vivace   4'
II. Andantino   3'
III. Minuetto   3'

Artaria

Orchestral Quartet, op.1, no.4, B-flat major <1770>   12'

str
Ed. Allan Badley.
I. Allegro assai   6'
II. Andante   2'
III. Presto   4'

Artaria

Orchestral Quartet, op.1, no.5, F major <1770>   11'

str
Ed. Allan Badley.
I. Allegro molto   5'
II. Andante   3'
III. Minuetto   3'

> Artaria

Orchestral Quartet, op.1, no.6, D major <1770>   11'

str
Ed. Allan Badley.
I. Allegro assai   4'
II. Andante moderato   3'
III. Allegro assai   4'

> Artaria

Orchestral Quartet, op.14, no.1, C major <1776>   19'

str
Ed. Allan Badley.
I. Allegro assai   10'
II. Andante di molto   5'
III. Poco presto   4'

> Artaria

Orchestral Quartet, op.14, no.4, F major <1776>   19'

str
Ed. Allan Badley.
I. Allegro assai   9'
II. Andante ma allegretto   5'
III. Presto assai   5'

> Artaria

Sinfonia concertante, D major   20'

solo violin & viola
0 0 0 0 — 2 0 0 0 — str

> Kalmus   Kneusslin   Luck's

Stamitz, Johann Wenzel Anton   1717-1757

(b Německý Brod [now Havlíčkův Brod], bap. 19 June 1717; d Mannheim, ?27 March, bur. 30 March 1757). Bohemian

Concerto, Flute, C major   25'

cnt — str
Ed. Herbert Koelbel.

> Peters

Concerto, Flute, D major   15'

str[no va]

> Eulenburg   Kalmus   Luck's

Concerto, Oboe, C major   14'

cnt — str
Ed. H. Töttcher & H.F. Hartig.

> Sikorski

Concerto, Viola, G major   15'

cnt — str
Ed. Rudolf Laugg.

> Luck's   Peters

Orchestral Trio, op.1, no.1, Wolf C1, C major <1754–1755>   19'

str[no va]
Ed. Allan Badley.
I. Allegro   5'
II. Andante ma non adagio   6'
III. Menuet   3'
IV. Prestissimo   5'

> Artaria

Orchestral Trio, op.1, no.2, Wolf A1, A major <1754–1755>   17'

str[no va]
Ed. Allan Badley.
I. Allegro assai   5'
II. Andante poco adagio   5'
III. Menuet   3'
IV. Prestissimo   4'

> Artaria

Orchestral Trio, op.1, no.3, Wolf F1, F major <1754–1755>   18'

str[no va]
Ed. Allan Badley.
I. Allegro molto   5'
II. Larghetto   4'
III. Menuet   5'
IV. Giga: Prestissimo   4'

> Artaria

Orchestral Trio, op.4, no.3, Wolf Cm1, C minor <1758>   17'

str[no va]
Ed. Allan Badley.
I. Allegro   5'
II. Andante   4'
III. Menuet I & II   4'
IV. Prestissimo   4'

> Artaria

Orchestral Trio, op.5, no.3, Wolf E1, E major <1759>   16'

str[no va]
Ed. Allan Badley.
I. Allegro   5'
II. Adagio   5'
III. Menuet   3'
IV. Presto   3'

> Artaria

Sinfonia, op.4, no.1, F major   18'

0 2 0 0 — 2 0 0 0 — str
Ed. Allan Badley.
I. Allegro molto   4'
II. Andante   5'
III. Minuetto   3'
IV. Presto assai   6'

> Artaria

Sinfonia pastorale, op.4, no.2, D major   14'

0 2 0 0 — 2 0 0 0 — cnt — str
Artaria ed. Allan Badley.
I. Presto   3'
II. Larghetto   5'
III. Minuetto   3'
IV. Presto   3'

> Artaria   Vieweg

Stamitz, Johann Wenzel Anton 1717-1757

Sinfonia, op.4, no.4, E-flat Major   16'
0 2 0 0 — 2 0 0 0 — str
Ed. Allan Badley.
I. Allegro   *3'*
II. Andante   *4'*
III. Minuetto I & II   *5'*
IV. Presto   *4'*

Artaria

Sinfonia, op.4, no.6, E-flat Major   17'
0 2 0 0 — 2 0 0 0 — str
Ed. Allan Badley.
I. Allegro maestoso   *5'*
II. Adagio   *6'*
III. Minuetto   *3'*
IV. Prestissimo   *3'*

Artaria

Symphony, op.3, no.3, G major   12'
0 0 0 0 — 2[opt] 0 0 0 — str
Ed. Adam Carse.

Augener	Luck's

Three Mannheim Symphonies   37'
str
Ed. Adolf Hoffmann.
No.1, G major   *11'*
No.2, A major   *15'*
No.3, B-flat major   *11'*

Kalmus	Luck's	Möseler

Stamitz, Karl   1745-1801
see: Stamitz, Carl, 1745-1801

Stanford, Charles Villiers   1852-1924
(b Dublin, 30 Sept 1852; d London, 29 March 1924). British

Irish Rhapsody No.1, op.78 <1902>   12'
2[1.2/pic] 2[1.2/Eh] 3[1.2.opt bcl] 3[1.2.cbn] — 4 3 3 1 — tmp+3 — hp — str
perc: sd, cym, bd

Kalmus	Luck's

Phaudrig Crohoore, op.62 <1896>
chorus
2 2 2 2 — 4 2 3 0 — tmp — str

Luck's

Symphony No.3, op.28, F minor (The Irish) <1887>   36'
2 2 2 2 — 4 3 3 0 — tmp — hp — str
I. Allegro appassionato   *11'*
II. Lento espressivo   *10'*
III. Scherzo: Allegro con fuoco   *4'*
IV. Adagio; Allegro moderato; Allegro molto ma non presto *11'*

Kalmus

Symphony No.4, op.31, F major <1889>   44'
2 2 2 3[1.2.cbn] — 4 2 3 0 — tmp — hp — str
I. Allegro vivace e gioioso   *12'*
II. Intermezzo   *9'*
III. Andante molto moderato   *14'*
IV. Finale: Allegro non troppo; Maestoso   *9'*

Kalmus

Symphony No.7, op.124, D minor <1911>   29'
2 2 2 2 — 4 2 3 0 — tmp — str
I. Allegro   *7'*
II. Tempo di minuetto (Allegro molto moderato) *6'*
III. Variations: Andante   *8'*
IV. Finale: Allegro giusto   *8'*

Chiltern	Kalmus

Starer, Robert   1924-2001
(b Vienna, 8 Jan 1924; d Kingston, NY, 22 April 2001). American composer of Austrian birth

Elegy for Strings <1966>   3'
str

MCA

Samson agonistes <1963>   13'
3[1.2.pic] 3[1.2.Eh] 3[1.2.bcl] 3[1.2.cbn] — 4 3 3 1 — tmp+4 — pf/cel — str
perc: td, bd, tamtam, tri, woodblk, xyl, 2sd, 2sus cym, 2cym
"Symphonic portrait" (1963) based on the ballet composed in 1961 for Martha Graham.

MCA

Symphony No.3 <1969>   21'
3[1/pic.2/pic.3/pic] 3[incl Eh] 4[incl Ebcl, bcl] 3[incl cbn] — 4 3 3 1 — tmp+4 — hp — pf — str

MCA

Stenhammar, Wilhelm   1871-1927
(b Stockholm, 7 Feb 1871; d Stockholm, 20 Nov 1927). Swedish

Sången, op.44: Mellanspel (Interlude) <1921>   5'
3 3 4[1.2.3.bcl] 4[1.2.3.cbn] — 4 3 3 1 — tmp — str

Gehrmans	Nordiska

Serenade, op.31, F major <1911–1913; rev 1919>   36'
2 2[1.2/Eh] 2 2 — 4 2 3 0 — tmp+2 — str
perc: sd, bd, cym, tri, glock
Overtura   *7'*
Canzonetta   *5'*
Scherzo   *7'*
Notturno   *8'*
Finale   *9'*

Suecia

Stephan, Rudi   1887-1915
(b Worms, 29 July 1887; d 29 September 1915). German

Musik für Geige und Orchester, in einem Satz <1912>   19'
violin solo
3[1.2.3/pic] 3[1.2.3/Eh] 3[1.2.3/bcl] 3[1.2.cbn] — 4 3 2 1 — tmp+1 — hp — str
perc: sd, glock, tamtam, tri, sus cym

Schott

Musik für Orchester, in einem Satz <1912>   19'

3[1.2/pic.3/pic] 3[1.2.Eh] 3[1.2.3/bcl] 3[1.2.cbn] — 4 3 3 1 — tmp+2
— hp — str

perc: bd, sd, tri, tamtam, glock, sus cym, cym

This 1912 work (published in 1913) was the second work by Stephan
with the title "Musik für Orchester in einem Satz." The original 1910
work of that same name was *later* retitled "Symphonischer Satz für
Orchestra," in a (perhaps futile) attempt to avoid confusion.

Schott

Symphonischer Satz für Orchester <1910>   23'

3[1.2/pic.3/pic] 3[1.ob d'am.Eh] 4[1.2.3.bcl] 4[1.2.3.cbn] — 6 4 3 1
— tmp+2 — hp — org, cel — str

perc: bd, sus cym, sd, tri, tamtam, glock

The composer had an aversion to what he called "poetic titles," and often
called his works "Musik für..." The present work originally bore the title
"Music für Orchester in einem Satz." It was later retitled (either by the
composer or the publisher) to avoid confusion with the 1912 "Musik für
Orchester in einem Satz," which had since been published.

Schott

Stephenson, James   1969-

(b Joliet, IL, 4 Feb 1969). American

American Fanfare <1999>   2'

3[1.2.pic] 3[1.2.Eh] 3[1.2.bcl] 2 — 4 3 3 1 — tmp+3 — org — str
perc: cym, bd, tri, glock, sd, sus cym, tamtam

Stephenson

Celebration Overture <1999>   10'

2[1.2/pic(opt)] 2 2 2 — 2 2 1 0 — tmp — hp(opt) — pf — str
Cued to be playable, if necessary, with:
   1 2 1 2 — 2 1 0 0 — tmp — pf — str

Stephenson

Celestial Suite <2011; rev (orchd) 2013>   20'

3[1.2/afl.3/pic] 3[1.2/bass ob.Eh] 3[1.2.bcl] 2 — 4 3 3 1 — tmp+3 —
hp — str

perc: bd, hi-hat, sd, set, tri, tambn, glock, xyl, chimes, woodblk, 3sus
Originally for brass quintet; orchestrated by the composer.
   Alto flute and bass oboe appear only in last mvt, and could be covered
by any member of their respective sections. In the absence of these
instruments, afl is cued in Eh, and bass ob is cued in bassoon.

   I. Copernicus   4'
   II. Galileo   3'
   III. Newton   4'
   IV. Hubble   4'
   V Hawking   5'

Stephenson

Chamber Concerto <2009>   11'

1 1 1 1 — 1 1 1 0 — tmp+1 — str
perc: bd, sus cym, sd, tri, tambn

Stephenson

Compose Yourself! <2002>   45'

narrator

1 1 1 1 — 1 1[tp/pic tp] 0 1[or tbn] — 1perc — hp[opt] — str 5t
perc: cym, sus cym, sd, tri, tambn, marktree, woodblk, templeblks, cowbell,
bongos, ratch, guiro, marac, claves, sandblks, police whistle, finger cym, shaker,
cabasa

Brass players double on lengths of garden hose.

   For youth concerts. Students learn about the instruments of the
orchestra and even get to participate in composing a piece using three
elements of music—melody, harmony, and rhythm. Light-hearted and
humorous. A charismatic narrator is required.

   A full-orchestra version is also available; instrumentation as follows:
2[1.2/pic] 2[1.2/Eh] 2 2 — 3 2 3 1 — tmp+2 — hp[opt] — str

Stephenson

Concertino and Fanfare <2007>   10'

3[1.2.pic] 3[1.2.Eh] 3[1.2.bcl] 3[1.2.cbn] — 4 3 3 1 — tmp+5 —
cel/pf — str

perc: bd, cym, sus cym, sd, tri, tambn, tamtam, glock, xyl, vib, chimes, whip,
bongos, ratch, guiro, claves, 3tomtom

Stephenson

Concerto, Trombone (Braziliano)   17'

2 2 2 2 — 2 7 0 0 — tmp+1 — str
perc: sd, cym, sus cym, guiro, vibrslp, bd, tri, bongos, claves, shaker

Stephenson

Concerto, Trumpet, No.1 <2003>   23'

1 2 2 2 — 2 1 0 0 — tmp — str
   I. Adagio; Allegro giocoso ma con fiero   15'
   II. Allegro con brio   8'

Stephenson

Concerto, Trumpet, No.2 (Rextreme) <2010>   21'

3[1.2.pic] 3[1.2.Eh] 3[1.2.bcl] 2 — 4 2 3 1 — tmp+4 — hp — pf —
str

perc: sus cym, xyl, td, bd, vib, whip, sd, woodblk, tri, tambn, tamtam, bongos,
cym, cabasa
Soloist doubles on C trumpet, B-flat flugelhorn (2nd mvt), and
(optionally, 3rd mvt) piccolo trumpet.
   I. Vivo, explosive   7'
   II. Adagio   6'
   III. Vivo, presto   8'

Stephenson

The Devil's Tale <2013>   45'

narrator
0 0 1 1 — 0 1 1 0 — 1perc — vn, db
perc: bd, sd, tri, tambn, woodblk, claves, 2sus cym, 3tomtom, police whistle
A sequel to Stravinsky's *L'histoire du soldat (The Soldier's Tale)*. Music alone without narration: 35'
    Options available for dancers, actors, staging.
    Movements marked * are for complete productions only; they may be omitted if desired when only the music is performed.
     PART I
   Intro [percussion solo reprises ending of Stravinsky L'histoire du soldat*]*

I. Never Odd or Even	3'
II. Live, O Devil, revel ever! Live! Do evil	1'
III. Seven Eves	1'
IV. Too Hot to Hoot	2'
V. Three Dances: Cigar, Toss It in a Can, It Is So Tragic	6'
VI. Now, I Won	2'
*VII. Part I Finale	3'

     PART II

VIII. Devil Never Even Lived	4'
*IX. Seven Eves	1'
*X. Never Odd or Even	3'
XI. Evil, a Sin, Is Alive	2'
XII. Name No One Man	2'
XIIa. No, It Is Opposition	3'
*XIII. Never Odd or Even	1'
XIV. Now I Won	1'

Stephenson

A Dialogue of Self and Soul <2013>   24'

solo bassoon
2[1.pic] 2[1.Eh] 3[1.2/Ebcl.bcl] 1 — 2 1 2[1.btbn] 1 — tmp+4 — hp — pf — db
perc: tamtam, tri, bd, sd, td, cym, woodblk, set, glock, xyl, marim, vib, 3sus cym, 2tambn, chimes[opt]
A concerto for bassoon and winds. Optional (but preferred) solo voice appears in the last 71 bars: male voice if bassoonist is male; female voice if bassoonist is female. If no voice used, the part is cued for flugelhorn (tp1).

I. Allegretto moderato assai	10'
II. Allegro – spirited	14'

Stephenson

Duels and Dances <2011>   13'

solo oboe
2[1.2/pic] 0 2 2 — 2 2 2 0 — 1perc — str
perc: sd, bd/cym, cym, sus cym, td, tri, tambn, claves, tmp
Originally for solo oboe and band; revised version for chamber orchestra and solo oboe by the composer.
    Soloist switches among 5 different oboes: bass oboe, oboe d'amore, English horn, oboe, and musette. (Musette sounds a 4th higher than written, *i.e.*, same transposition as trumpet in F).
    Alternatives: 1) soloist may play entire work on oboe; 2) soloist may play only English horn and oboe; 3) 2 soloists may be used—one on oboe and the other on English horn.

Stephenson

La grande vitesse; A Triple Brass Concerto <2009>   19'

soloists: trumpet, horn, trombone
3[1.2.pic] 3[1.2.Eh] 3[1.2.bcl] 2 — 3 2 2 1 — tmp+ — hp — pf —
perc: bd, cym, sus cym, sd, tri, tambn, glock, marim, vib, crot, woodblk, guiro, cabasa, 3tomtom

I. Moderato, spirito	7'
II. Adagio	6'
III. Run with it	6'

Stephenson

Ode to Peace <2012>   10'

solo mezzo-soprano
3[1.2/afl.pic] 2 2 3[1.2.cbn] — 4 2 3 1 — tmp+2 — str
perc: [Native American instruments if possible] tambn, tomtom, bd
Cbn part cued in tuba in case no cbn available.

Stephenson

Pandora's Waltz; A Concerto for Flute <2010>   17'

1 2[1.Eh] 1 1 — 1 1 1 1 — tmp+3 — hp — pf/cel — str
perc: bd, sus cym, hi-hat, sd, tri, tambn, xyl, marim, vib, crot, ratch, guiro, claves, sandblks, 2woodblk
In one mvt.

Stephenson

Printemps <2004>   5'

str

Stephenson

Sounds Awakened; A Concerto for French Horn <2012>   20'

solo horn
2[1.2/pic] 3[1.2.Eh] 2 2 — 3 2 3 1 — tmp+3 — hp — str
perc: hi-hat, sd, tri, tamtam, glock, marim, vib, chimes, crot, woodblk, whip, ratch, claves, bd, 2sus cym, 4tomtom

I. Bold, maestoso	7'
II. Adagio rubato	5'
III. Allegro passionato; Adagio; Allegretto assai	8'

Stephenson

Stars and Stripes Fanfare <2007>   4'

3[1.2.pic] 3[1.2.Eh] 3[1.2.bcl] 2 — 4 3 3 1 — tmp+4 — hp — str
perc: cym, sd, glock, bd, tamtam, sus cym, tri

Stephenson

Tributes (Violin Concerto in Three Movements) <2009>   28'

3[1.2.pic] 3[1.2.Eh] 4[1.2.Ebcl.bcl] 3[1.2.cbn] — 4 3 3 1 — tmp+5 — hp — pf/cel — str
perc: xyl, marim, chimes, glock, sus cym, bd, tri, woodblk, crot, whip, tamtam, bongos, tambn, 2sd, cabasa, 4tomtom, 2stones
A reduced orchestration is in preparation.

I. Allegro deciso	7'
II. Andante	8'
III. Allegro agitato	13'

Stephenson

Violin Fantasie Concerto <2011>   18'

solo violin
3[1.2.pic] 2[1.Eh] 3[1.2.bcl] 2 — 2 2 2 1 — tmp+3 — hp — str
perc: marim, crot, tri, sd, bd, tambn, hi-hat, sus cym, td

Stephenson

Stevens, Halsey   1908-1989

(b Scott, NY, 3 Dec 1908; d Inglewood, CA, 20 Jan 1989). American

Sinfonia breve <1957>   15'

2[1/pic.2/pic] 2 2 2 — 4 2 3 1 — tmp+1 — hp — pf/cel — str

1. Allegro moderato	5'
2. Adagio	6'
3. Allegro ma non troppo	4'

CFE

Symphonic Dances <1958>   15'

3[1.2/afl.3/pic] 3[1.2.3/Eh] 3[1.2.3/bcl] 3[1.2.3/cbn] — 4 3 3 1 — tmp+3 — 2hp — pf/cel — str
perc: xyl, tri, cym, tamtam, sd, glock, sus cym, td, bd, tambn, whip

Peters

Stewart, David Nisbet
1941-

(b 30 Dec 1941). American

Cindy, O Cindy; Variations on an Appalachian Civil War Folksong <2003>
18'

youth chorus
3[1.2.pic] 2 2 2 — 4 3 3 1 — tmp+6 — hp — str
perc: bd, cym, sus cym, sd, td, tri, tamtam, glock, whip

DNS   Fleisher

Concerto, Piano <2008>
23'

3[1.2.pic] 3[1.2.Eh] 3[1.2.bcl] 3[1.2.cbn] — 4 3 3 1 — tmp+3 — str
perc: glock, xyl, sus cym, cym, tri, tambn, sd, bd, tamtam
The plainchant *Victimae paschali laudes* ("Praises to the Paschal Victim"; the Easter Sequence Hymn) is the *cantus firmus* for the first movement.

I. *Vivace; Meno mosso; Vivace ("Victimae paschali laudes")*	11'
II. *Largo*	4'
III. *Allegro*	8'

DNS

Overture in F <2001>
8'

3[1.2.pic] 2 2 2 — 4 2 2 1 — tmp+4 — str
perc: bd, cym, sus cym, tri, glock

DNS   Fleisher

Still, William Grant
1895-1978

(b Woodville, MS, 11 May 1895; d Los Angeles, 3 Dec 1978). American

THE AMERICAN SCENE
8'

The East (Suite 1) <1957>

3[1.2.3/pic] 3[1.2.Eh] 3[1.2.bcl] 2 — 4 3 3 1 — tmp+3 — hp — cel — str
perc: cym, sus cym, sd, glock, xyl

On the Village Green	2'
Berkshire Night	3'
Manhattan Skyline	3'

WGS

The South (Suite 2) <1957>
12'

3[1.2.3/pic] 3[1.2.Eh] 3[1.2.bcl] 2 — 4 3 3 1 — tmp+3 — hp — cel — str
perc: cym, sus cym, tri, tambn, glock, chimes

Florida Night	5'
Levee Land	4'
A New Orleans Street	3'

WGS

The Old West (Suite 3) <1957>
8'

3[1.2.3/pic] 3[1.2.Eh] 3[1.2.bcl] 2 — 4 3 3 1 — tmp+3 — hp — cel — str
perc: cym, 2tomtoms, tri, glock

Song of the Plainsmen	3'
Sioux Love Song	3'
Tribal Dance	2'

WGS

The Far West (Suite 4) <1957>
8'

3[1.2.3/pic] 3[1.2.Eh] 3[1.2.bcl] 2 — 4 3 3 1 — tmp+4 — hp — str
perc: cym, tomtom, tri, gong, glock, xyl, marac, claves, cast, rattle

The Plaza	2'
Sundown Land	4'
Navaho Country	2'

WGS

A Mountain, a Memorial, and a Song (Suite 5) <1957>
15'

3[1.2.3/pic] 3[1.2.Eh] 3[1.2.bcl] 2[1.2/cbn] — 4 3 3 1 — tmp+3 — hp — cel — str
perc: cym, sus cym, sd, glock

Grant Teton	4'
Tomb of the Unknown Soldier	5'
Song of the Rivermen	6'

WGS

Bells <1944>
7'

3[1.2.3/pic] 3[1.2.Eh] 3[1.2.3/bcl] 2[1.2/cbn] — 4 3 3 1 — tmp+1 — hp — cel, pf — str
perc: cym, glock, vib, chimes, 2resonator bells

Phantom Chapel	4'
Fairy Knoll	3'

MCA

Black Bottom <1922>
10'

3[incl pic] 1 3[incl Ebcl,bcl] 2 — 2 3 2 1 — tmp+2 — str
perc: cym, set, glock, whip, guiro

WGS

The Black Man Dances <1935>
11'

solo piano
1 1[incl Eh] 4[incl Ebcl,bcl] 0 — 1 3 3 0 — 2asx, C melody sx, tsx — gtr, ten banjo — 1perc — pf — str
perc: glock, set

1.	4'
2.	2'
3.	3'
4.	2'

WGS

Darker America <1924>
13'

2 2[1.Eh] 2 2 — 1 1 1 0 — 1perc — pf — str
perc: bd

C. Fischer

A Deserted Plantation <1933>
19'

2[1.pic] 2[1.Eh] 4[1.2.3.bcl] 1 — 1 3 3 1 — 4sx[2asx.tsx1.tsx2/bsx] — gtr/banjo — tmp+3 — hp — pf — str
perc: bd, cym, sd, tambn, glock, vib, whip
Ed. Dane Teter.

1. *Prologue*	1'
2. *Yistiddy—An' Today*	4'
3. *Interlude I*	1'
4. *Spiritual*	3'
5. *Interlude II*	1'
6. *Young Missy*	5'
7. *Interlude III*	1'
8. *[optional improvised cadenza for piano]*	
9. *Dance*	3'

WGS

Dismal Swamp <1936>
15'

solo piano
3 3[incl Eh] 4[incl bcl] 3[incl cbn] — 4 3 3 1 — tmp+3 — str
perc: cym, set, tri, vib

Presser

Fanfare for American War Heroes <1944>
1'

3[1.2.pic] 3[1.2.Eh] 3[1.2.bcl] 2 — 4 3 3 1 — tmp+2 — hp — str
perc: cym, sus cym, sd

WGS

Festive Overture <1944>   10'

3[1.2.3/pic] 3[1.2.Eh] 3[1.2.bcl] 2 — 4 3 3 1 — tmp+4 — hp — cel
— str
perc: cym, sd, military dr, tri, tambn, glock, xyl, marim, chimes, resonator bells,
greeko cym

> WGS

Here's One; A Still Medley   13'

mezzo-soprano or baritone
2 2[1.Eh] 2 2 — 2 2 2 1[opt] — tmp+1 — hp[or pf] — str
perc: sus cym, sd
Originally several works for voice and/or violin with piano; arranged as a
medley by Sheldon Bair.

> WGS

In memoriam: The Colored Soldiers Who Died for   6'
Democracy <1943>

3[1.2.3/pic] 3[1.2.Eh] 3[1.2.3/bcl] 2 — 4 3 3 1 — tmp+3 — hp — str
perc: sd, cym, bd, chime[A#3]

> MCA

Lenox Avenue (Choreographic Street Scenes) <1937>   23'

2[1.2/pic] 2[1.2/Eh] 2 2 — 3 3 2 0 — tmp+2 — pf — str
perc: bd, 2sus cym, cym, set, tri, tambn, gong, vib, chimes, whip, cast, sandblk

> WGS

Lenox Avenue: Blues <1937>   3'

1 1 2 1 — 2 2 1 0 — pf — str

> WGS

Old California <1941>   10'

3[1.2.3/pic] 3[1.2.Eh] 3[1.2.bcl] 2 — 4 3 3 1 — tmp+1 — hp — str
perc: bd, sus cym, sd, toms, tambn, gong, vib, chimes, costume bells, marac,
claves, cast, resonator bell

> WGS

Out of the Silence <1939>   4'

pf — str
Originally movement No.4 from the composer's *Seven Traceries* for solo
piano. Orchestrated by the composer.

> WGS

Poem <1944>   14'

3[1.2/pic.3/pic] 3[1.2.Eh] 3[1.2.3/bcl] 2[1.2/cbn] — 4 3 3 1 — tmp+3
— hp — cel — str
perc: sd, cym, bd, tamtam, sus cym, glock

> MCA

Serenade <1957>   9'

pf — str
A larger orchestration is available from C.Fischer:
   21incl pic] 2 2 2 — 3 2 2 1 — tmp+perc — hp — str

> WGS

Suite, Violin & Orchestra <1943>   15'

2 1[1/Eh] 3[1.2.3/bcl] 2[1.cbn] — 4 3 3 1 — tmp+1 — hp — cel —
str
perc: tomtom, chimes
   1. Suggested by Richmond Barthe's African Dancer   6'
   2. Suggested by Sargent Johnson's Mother and Child   6'
   3. Suggested by Augusta Savage's Gamin.   3'

> C. Fischer

Symphony No.1 (Afro-American Symphony) <1930; rev   23'
1969>

3[1.2.3/pic] 3[1.2.Eh] 4[1.2.3.bcl] 2 — 4 3 3 1 — tenor banjo —
tmp+3 — hp — cel — str
perc: cym, set, tri, vib
The 1969 revision requires one less clarinet (i.e., [1.2.bcl]), but parts for
that version may not be available.
   However, there are still many textual problems between score and
parts. A critical edition is definitely needed.
   I. Longing: Moderato assai   7'
   II. Sorrow: Adagio   5'
   III. Humor: Animato   4'
   IV. Aspiration: lento; con risoluzione 7'

> Novello

Symphony No.2, G minor (Song of a New Race) <1937>   29'

3[1.2.3/pic] 3[1.2.Eh] 4[1.2.3.bcl] 2 — 4 3 3 1 — tmp+2 — hp — cel
— str
perc: 2sus cym, cym, set, glock, vib
Revised version.
   1. Slowly   10'
   2. Slowly and deeply expressive   8'
   3. Moderately fast   4'
   4. Moderately slow   7'

> C. Fischer

Symphony No.3 (The Sunday Symphony) <1958>   21'

3[1.2.3/pic] 3[1.2.Eh] 3[1.2.bcl] 2 — 4 3 3 1 — tmp+3 — hp — str
perc: cym, 2sus cym, sd, 3tomtoms, tri, tambn, glock
   Moderately: The Awakening   4'
   Very slowly: Prayer   8'
   Gaily: Relaxation   3'
   Resolutely: Day's End and a New Beginning   6'

> C. Fischer

Symphony No.4 (Autochthonous) <1947>   27'

3[1.2.3/pic] 3[1.2.Eh] 3[1.2.bcl] 2[1.2/cbn] — 4 3 3 1 — tmp+3 — hp
— cel — str
perc: military dr, set, tri, gong, glock, resonator bell

> C. Fischer

Symphony No.5 (The Western Hemisphere) <1945>   20'

3[1.2.3/pic] 3[1.2.Eh] 3[1.2.bcl] 2 — 4 3 3 1 — tmp+3 — hp — cel
— str
perc: cym, 2sus cym, sd, set, glock, marim, chimes
Originally Symphony No.3; later renumbered.
   Briskly   3'
   Slowly, and with utmost grace   7'
   Energetically   3'
   Moderately   7'

> WGS

Wood Notes <1947>   18'

2[1/pic.opt 2/pic] 2[1.opt 2/Eh] 2 2[1.opt 2] — 2[opt] 3 2 0 — tmp+2
— hp[or pf] — cel — str
perc: sus cym, set, tri, glock, vib, sd
Full score also includes piano-conductor.
   1. Singing River   7'
   2. Autumn Night   3'
   3. Moon Dusk   5'
   4. Whippoorwill's Shoes   3'

> Southern

Stillman-Kelley, Edgar   1857-1944

see: Kelley, Edgar Stillman, 1857-1944

Stock, David   1939-

(b Pittsburgh, 3 June 1939). American

Capriccio for Small Orchestra <1963>   7'

1 1 1 1 — 1 1 0 0 — str

> ACA

Inner Space <1973>   13'

3[1.2.pic] 2 2 2 — 4 3 3 1 — tmp+3 — str

> Margun

Stockhausen, Karlheinz   1928-2007

(b Burg Modrath, nr Cologne, 22 Aug 1928; d Kuerten-Kettenberg, Germany, 5 Dec 2007). German

> *Stockhausen did not use opus numbers, but rather a numbering system of his own devising: Nr.1, Nr.2, etc., as well as fractions such as Nr.$^1/_6$, or Nr. 16 $^1/_2$. The numbers are more or less chronological, but not rigorously so.*

Gruppen, for Three Orchestras [Nr.6] <1955–1957>   25'

5[1/pic.2.3/pic.4/pic.afl] 5[3ob, 2Eh] 4[1.2.Ebcl.bcl] 3 — 8 6 7[incl cb tbn(or tuba)] 1 — 2sx[asx/cl, bsx] — elec gtr — 13perc — 2hp — cel, pf — str[26vn.10va.8vc.6db]
perc: marim, glock, vib, chimes[incl A#3 & B3 below middle C], ratch, xylorimba, 13herdbells, 3tamtams, 9sus cym, 12pitched drums[tomtoms and/or congas & bongos], 3sd, 6log drums, 3tambn, 2tri, kybdglock[or cel]
109 players and 3 conductors.

> Universal

Kontra-Punkte [Nr.1] <1952; rev 1953>   12'

1 0 2[1.bcl] 1 — 0 1 1 0 — hp — pf — vn, vc
A "farewell symphony" in which various instruments fade out until just the piano is left.

> Universal

Punkte [Nr.$^1/_2$] <1952; rev 1962, 1964, 1966>   21'

3[1/pic.2/pic.3/afl/pic] 3[1/ob d'am.2.3/Eh] 3[1.Ebcl.bcl] 3[1.2.3/cbn] — 3 3 2 1 — tmp+2 — 2hp — 2pf[2nd/cel] — str[8.8.8.6.4; all soloistic]
perc: vib, marim; played by tmp: chimes, glock
Composed 1952, and revised in 1962, 1964, & 1966.

> Universal

Stojowski, Zygmunt   1869-1946

(b Strzelce, 14 May 1869; d New York, 5 Nov 1946). Polish

Concerto, Piano, No.1, op.3, F-sharp Minor <1893>   35'

2[1.2/pic] 2[1.2/Eh] 2 2 — 4 2 3 0 — tmp+1 — str
perc: tri, cym
  I. Andante poco mosso; Allegro un poco maestoso   15'
  II. Romanza   10'
  III. Allegro con fuoco   10'

> Augener   Fleisher

Symphony, op.21, D minor <1899>   36'

3[1.2.3/pic] 3[1.2.Eh] 3[1.2.bcl] 2 — 4 2 3 1 — tmp — hp — str
perc: glock, tri
  I. Andante mesto; Allegro Moderato   _'
  II. Andante   _'
  III. Scherzo: Molto vivace   _'
  IV. Finale: Allegro con fuoco, ma non vivace   _'

> Peters

Stokowski, Leopold   1882-1977

(b London, 18 April 1882; d Nether Wallop, England, 13 Sept 1977). American

Traditional Slavic Christmas Music   3'

0 0 0 0 — 4 3 3 1 — str

> Tetra

Stölzel, Gottfried Heinrich   1690-1749

(b Grünstädtel, nr Schwarzenberg, Erzgebirge,13 Jan 1690; d Gotha, 27 Nov 1749). German

Bist du bei mir

see under: Bach, Johann Sebastian, 1685-1750

Stookey, Nathaniel   1970-

(b San Francisco, 1970). American

Big Bang <2000>   8'

3[1.2.pic] 2 2 2 — 4 3 3 1 — tmp+4 — str
perc: bd, hi-hat, sd, field dr, rototom, tri, tamtam, glock, xyl, marim, chimes, templeblks, congas, 2sus cym, 4tomtom, 3gong[F#,D,G], 2pr claves

> AMP

The Composer is Dead <2006>   30'

narrator
2[1.2/pic] 2[1.2/Eh] 2[1.2/bcl] 2[1.2/cbn] — 4 2 3 1 — tmp+3 — hp — str
perc: bd, cym, hi-hat, sd, tambn, glock, xyl, marim, vib, chimes, marac, 3tomtom, 3woodblk
The work includes a *Marche funèbre*, which quotes brief passages from celebrated orchestral works of the past. In some concert performances, the work as a whole has been preceded by slightly longer "supplementary excerpts" from these same works, and even a preliminary performance of the *Marche funèbre* itself. The composer endorses this practice, though it is by no means necessary.
  The "supplementary excerpts":
  1. Beethoven: Marcia funebre from Sym. No.3, bars 1–16.
  2. Mahler: Sym. No.5, bars 1–33.
  3. Schubert: Sym. No.8, bars 42–104.
  4. Tchaikovsky: Sym. No.6, 4th mvt, bars 1–18.
  5. Berlioz: Symphonie fantastique, 5th mvt, bars 146–206.

> AMP

Double; Concerto for 2 Violins & String Orchestra <2007>   20'

2 solo violins
str
  I. Imagining   7'
  II. Remembering   13'

> AMP

Into the Bright Lights <2009>   12'

solo mezzo-soprano
1 1 1 1 — 2 0 0 0 — hp — str
  I. S'io   _'
  II. The Golden Thread   _'
  III. Into the Bright Lights   _'

> AMP

Mahl/er/werk <2011>   20'

3[1.2.3/pic] 3[1.2.3/Eh] 3[1.2/Ebcl.3/bcl] 3[1.2.3/cbn] — 4 3 3 1 —
tmp+3 — hp — str

perc: bd, cym, sus cym, sd, tri, 2tamtam, low bell [A-flat], rute
   I. Etwas zurückhalten   _'
   II. Immer quarter = 120   _'
   III. Langsamer, aber nicht schleppen   _'
   IV. Schnell   _'

AMP		

Out of the Everywhere <2003>   22'

3[1.2/afl.3/pic] 3 3[1.2/Ebcl.3/bcl] 3[1.2.3/cbn] — 4 3 3 1 — tmp+3
— hp — pf — str

perc: bd, hi-hat, brake dr, tri, tamtam, glock, xyl, marim, crot, slgh-bells, cast, 2sus
cym, 8tomtoms (2 sets), finger cym
   I. Quickening   _'
   II. Pulse   _'
   III. Tides   _'

AMP		

Strauss, Eduard   1835-1916

(b Vienna, 15 March 1835; d Vienna, 28 Dec 1916). Austrian composer of Hungarian
descent

Bahn frei; Polka, op.45 (Fast Track) <1869>   3'

2[1.pic] 2 2 2 — 4 4 3 1 — 2perc — str
perc: sd, cym, bd, tri, horse hooves

Kalmus	Luck's	Strauss Ed.

Strauss, Franz   1822-1905

(b Parkstein, Upper Palatinate, 26 Feb 1822; d Munich, 31 May 1905). German

Concerto, Horn, op.8, C minor   14'

1 2 2 2 — 2 2 1 0 — tmp — str
New Fleisher edition by Clinton Nieweg, 2007.

Fleisher	Universal

Strauss, Johann, Jr.   1825-1899

(b Vienna, 25 Oct 1825; d Vienna, 3 June 1899). Austrian composer of Hungarian
descent

*Information on the new Strauss critical editions (Johann Jr., Johann
Sr., Josef, Eduard) may be found at www.strauss.at.*

Accelerationen, op.234 (Accelerations) <1860>   8'

2[1.2/pic] 2 2 2 — 2 2 3 0 — tmp+3 — hp — str
perc: sd, tri, bd/cym
Kalmus ed. Clark McAlister.

Doblinger	Kalmus	Luck's	Strauss Ed.

An der schönen blauen Donau, op.314 (On the Beautiful   9'
Blue Danube) <1867>

optional male chorus
2[1.2/pic] 2 2 2 — 4 2 1 1 — tmp+2 — hp — str
perc: tri, sd, bd

Breitkopf	Doblinger	Kalmus	Luck's	Strauss Ed.

Egyptischer Marsch, op.335 (Egyptian March) <1869>   4'

2[1.pic] 2 2 2 — 4 2 3 1 — 5perc — str
perc: chimes, cym, bd, sd, tambn, tri

Doblinger	Kalmus	Luck's	Strauss Ed.

Emperor Waltzes

see his: Kaiser-Walzer

Figaro-Polka, op.320 <1867>   5'

2[1.2/pic] 2 2 2 — 4 4[2tp, 2crt] 3 0 — tmp+4 — str
perc: sd, tri, bd/cym
Ed. Fritz Racek.

Doblinger		

Fledermaus: Overture <1874>   9'

2[1.2/pic] 2 2 2 — 4 2 3 0 — tmp+2 — str
perc: sd, cym, bd, tri, chime (E)

Breitkopf	Doblinger	Kalmus	Luck's

Fledermaus: Du und du, op.367 <1874>   5'

2[1.2/pic] 2 2 2 — 4 2 3 0 — tmp+2 — str
perc: sd, tri, bd/cym

Breitkopf	Kalmus	Luck's

Frühlingsstimmen, op.410 (Voices of Spring) <1883>   6'

2[1.pic] 2 2 2 — 4 2 3 0 — tmp+1 — hp — str
perc: bd, sd

Breitkopf	Doblinger	Kalmus	Luck's	Strauss Ed.

Geschichten aus dem Wienerwald, op.325 (Tales from   11'
the Vienna Woods) <1868>

2[1.2/pic] 2 2[1/Ebcl.2] 2 — 4 3 3 1 — opt zither — tmp+2 — hp —
str
perc: bd, sd, tri

Breitkopf	Doblinger	Kalmus	Luck's	Strauss Ed.

Graduation Ball (arr. Dorati)   48'

2 2 2 2 — 4 2 3 0 — tmp+4 — hp — str
perc: tamtam, sd, bd, cym, tri, glock, bell[G1]
Arranged for David Lichine's ballet (1939) by Antal Dorati, from various
works by Johann Strauss Jr.

EMI		

Gypsy Baron

see his: Zigeunerbaron

Kaiser-Walzer, op.437 (Emperor Waltzes) <1889>   10'

2 2 2 2 — 4 2 3 0 — tmp+1 — hp — str
perc: sd, bd[covered by tmp]

Breitkopf	Doblinger	Kalmus	Luck's	Strauss Ed.

Künstlerleben, op.316 (Artist's Life) <1867>   10'

2[1.pic] 2 2 2 — 4 2 3 1 — tmp+2 — str
perc: bd, sd, tri

Doblinger	Kalmus	Luck's	Strauss Ed.

Künstler Quadrille nach Motiven berühmter Meister,   6'
op.201 <1858>

2[1.pic] 2 2 2 — 4 2 1[btbn] 1 — tmp+1 — str

Doblinger	Kalmus	Luck's	Strauss Ed.

Leichtes Blut, op.319 <1867>   3'

2[1.pic] 2 2 2 — 4 2 1 0 — tmp+3 — str
perc: sd, bd/cym
Polka schnell.

Doblinger	Kalmus	Luck's	Strauss Ed.

Märchen aus dem Orient, op.444 (Fairytales from the Orient) <1892>   8'

2[1.2/pic] 2 2 — 4 2 3 0 — tmp+3 — hp — str

Kalmus

Morgenblätter, op.279 (Morning Papers) <1864>   10'

2[1.2/pic] 2 2 — 4 2 1 1 — tmp+2 — str
perc: sd, tri, bd/cym
The Kalmus and Luck's reprints of this waltz call for 3 trombones.

Doblinger	Kalmus	Luck's	Strauss Ed.

Neu-Wien, op.342 (New Vienna) <1870>   8'

2[1.2/pic] 2 2[Ebcl.2] 2 — 4 2 3 1 — tmp+2 — str
perc: bd, sd, tri
The cl 1 part is for Ebcl.
    Kalmus offers a T.M. Tobani arrangement of this work, for:
    1 1 2 1 — 2 2 1 0 — tmp, perc — str [pf-cond score]

Strauss Ed.

On the Beautiful Blue Danube

see his: An der schönen blauen Donau

Perpetuum mobile; Musikalischer Scherz, op.257 (Musical Joke) <1861>   3'

2[1.2/pic] 2 2[Ebcl.2] 2 — 4 2 1 0 — tmp+1 — hp — str
perc: glock, tamtam
The cl 1 part is for Ebcl.

Doblinger	C. Fischer	Kalmus	Luck's	Strauss Ed.

Pizzicato Polka (composed with Josef Strauss)   3'

2[1.pic] 2 2 2 — 4 3 3 1 — tmp+2 — str
perc: sd, tambn, bd/cym, tri, glock
Frequently performed with just strings and 2perc.

Doblinger	Luck's	Strauss Ed.

Rosen aus dem Süden, op.388 (Roses from the South) <1880>   7'

2[1.pic] 2 2 — 4 2 3 0 — tmp+3 — hp — str
perc: bd, cym, sd, tri
On themes from the comic opera *Das Spitzentuch der Königin.*

Breitkopf	Doblinger	Kalmus	Luck's	Strauss Ed.

Seid umschlungen, Millionen, op.443 <1892>   10'

2[1.2/pic] 2 2 — 4 2 3 0 — tmp+2 — hp — str
perc: bd, sd, tri

Doblinger	Kalmus	Luck's

Tales from the Vienna Woods

see his: Geschichten aus dem Wienerwald

Tausend und eine Nacht, op.346 (One Thousand and One Nights) <1871>   7'

2[1.2/pic] 2 2 — 4 2 3 0 — tmp+2 — str

Kalmus	Luck's	Strauss Ed.

Thunder and Lightning Polka

see his: Unter Donner und Blitz

Tritsch-Tratsch-Polka, op.214 (traditional version) <1858>   3'

1 2 2 2 — 2 2 3 0 — tmp+1 — harm — str
perc: bd, cym, tri
Score includes a "violin obligato," which appears to be a simplification of the vn1 part.

Kalmus

Tritsch-Tratsch-Polka, op.214 (critical edition) <1858>   3'

2[1.pic] 2 2[Ebcl.2] 2 — 4 2 1 1 — tmp+3 — str
perc: bd, cym, sd, tri
Ed. Norbert Rubey.

Doblinger

Unter Donner und Blitz, op.324 (Thunder and Lightning Polka) <1868>   3'

2[1.pic] 2 2 2 — 4 3 3 1 — tmp+3 — str
perc: bd, cym, sd

Doblinger	Kalmus	Luck's	Strauss Ed.

Vergnügungszug, op.281 (Pleasure Train Polka) <1864>   3'

2[1.pic] 2 2 2 — 4 2 1 0 — tmp+4 — str
perc: glock, tri, sd, cym, bd, train whistle, train conductor's horn
Doblinger critical ed. Norbert Rubey (Diletto Musicale). Clarinet 1 in that score is in E (not Eb), though in the part it is in A.
    Kalmus and Luck's publications (believed to be reprints of Spina) have parts for E-flat clarinet (cl 1) and B-flat clarinet (cl 2).

Doblinger	Strauss Ed.	Kalmus	Luck's

Voices of Spring

see his: Frühlingsstimmen

Wein, Weib, und Gesang, op.333 (Wine, Women and Song) <1869>   7'

2[1.2/pic] 2 2[1/Ebcl.2] 2 — 4 2 3 0 — tmp+2 — hp — str
perc: bd, sd, tri

Breitkopf	Doblinger	Kalmus	Luck's	Strauss Ed.

Wiener Blut, op.354 (Vienna Blood) <1873>   7'

2[1.2/pic] 2 2 — 4 2 3 0 — tmp+2 — str
perc: bd, sd, tri

Breitkopf	Kalmus	Luck's	Strauss Ed.

Wo die Citronen blüh'n, op.364 (Where the Citrons Bloom) <1874>   7'

2[1.2/pic] 2 2[incl D-cl] 2 — 4 2 3 0 — tmp+1 — hp — str
perc: sd, tri, glock

Kalmus	Luck's	Strauss Ed.

Zigeunerbaron (Gypsy Baron): Overture <1885>   8'

2[1.2/pic] 2 2 — 4 2 3 0 — tmp+3 — hp — str
perc: sd, bd/cym, glock, spurs
Piccolo has a single note; remainder of the part is 2nd flute.

Doblinger	Kalmus	Luck's

Zigeunerbaron (Gypsy Baron): Einzugsmarsch (Entrance March) <1885>   3'

2 2 2 2 — 4 2 3 0 — 3perc — str
Doblinger ed. Norbert Linke. Kalmus also has an arrangement for similar insrumentation by Max Schoenherr.

Doblinger

Strauss, Johann, Jr. (continued)

Zigeunerbaron (Gypsy Baron): Schatz-Walzer (Treasure Waltz) <1885>   6'

2[1.2/pic] 2 2 2 — 4 2 3 0 — tmp+2 — hp — str
Op.481

Kalmus	Luck's

Strauss, Johann, Sr.   1804-1849

(b Vienna, 14 March 1804; d Vienna, 25 Sept 1849). Austrian composer of Hungarian descent

Radetzky March, op.228 <1848>   3'

3[1.2.pic] 2 2 2 — 4 2 3 1 — 3perc — str
perc: bd, cym, sd, tri
There appear to be various orchestrations for this work, ranging from the largest (above) to as small as:
2[1.pic] 1 2 1 — 2 2 1 0 — 2perc — str

Doblinger	Kalmus	Luck's	Strauss Ed.

Strauss, Josef   1827-1870

(b Vienna, 20 Aug 1827; d Vienna, 22 July 1870). Austrian composer of Hungarian descent

Delirien, op.212 <1867>   7'

2[1.pic] 2 2 2 — 4 2 1 0 — tmp+2 — hp — str
perc: bd, sd, cym

Kalmus	Luck's	Strauss Ed.

Dorfschwalben aus Österreich, op.164 (Village Swallows) <1864>   8'

2[1.2/pic] 2 2 2 — 4 2 1 0 — tmp+3 — hp — str
perc: tri, sd, bd, birdcall

Kalmus	Luck's	Strauss Ed.

Frauenherz, op.166 (Woman's Heart) <1864>   3'

2[1.pic] 2 2[incl Ebcl] 2 — 4 2 1 0 — 3perc — hp — str
perc: sd, tri, bd, cym

Kalmus	Luck's	Strauss Ed.

Mein Lebenslauf ist Lieb' und Lust, op.263 <1869>   7'

2[1.pic] 2 2 2 — 4 4 3 1 — tmp+1 — hp — str
perc: bd, sd

Kalmus	Luck's	Strauss Ed.

Pizzicato Polka

see under: Strauss, Johann, Jr.

Sphärenklänge, op.235 (Music of the Spheres) <1868>   9'

2[1.2/pic] 2 2[incl Ebcl] 2 — 4 4 3 1 — tmp+3 — hp — str
perc: bd, sd, cym, tri

Kalmus	Luck's	Strauss Ed.

Strauss, Richard   1864-1949

(b Munich, 11 June 1864; d Garmisch-Partenkirchen, 8 Sept 1949). German

TrV = Franz Trenner: *Richard Strauss: Werkverzeichnis* (Munich, 1993)

The above is the thematic index cited in this book. There is also an interesting website with much information:
RSQV — Richard-Strauss-Quellenverzeichnis, www.rsi-rsqv.de

Eine Alpensinfonie, TrV 233, op.64 (Alpine Symphony) <1911–1915>   47'

4[1.2.3/pic2.4/pic1] 4[1.2.3/Eh.heckl] 4[1.2.3/bcl.Ebcl] 4[1.2.3.4/cbn] — 20[hn5-8/Wag tb] 6 6 2 — 2tmp+3 — 2hp — cel, org — str[18.16.12.10.8]
perc: glock, tri, sd, wnd mach, cym, thunder, bd, tamtam, sus cym, herdbells
The above instrumentation includes an offstage *banda*:
brass 12 2 2 0
Banda parts are cued in the onstage brass. If these cues are played onstage, only brass 8 4 4 2 is required. If onstage players leave the stage to play the *banda* parts, and all doublings are eliminated, then brass 8 4 5 2 is necessary.
3rd cl also plays C-cl as well as bcl.

1. Nacht (Night)	3'
2. Sonnenaufgang (Sunrise)	1'
3. Der Anstieg (The Ascent)	2'
4. Eintritt in den Wald (Entering the Forest)	5'
5. Wanderung neben dem Bache (Wandering near the Stream)	1'
6. Am Wasserfall (At the Waterfall)	1'
7. Erscheinung (Apparition)	1'
8. Auf blumige Wiesen (On Blooming Meadows)	1'
9. Auf der Alm (On the Alpine Pasture)	2'
10. Durch Dickicht und Gestrüpp auf Irrwegen (Going Astray)	2'
11. Auf dem Gletscher (On the Glacier)	1'
12. Gefahrvolle Augenblicke (Dangerous Moments)	2'
13. Auf dem Gipfel (At the Summit)	5'
14. Vision (View)	4'
15. Nebel steigen auf (Fog Arises)	1'
16. Die Sonne verdüstert sich allmählich (The Sun Gradually Darkens)	1'
17. Elegie (Elegy)	2'
18. Stille vor dem Sturm (Calm Before the Storm)	2'
19. Gewitter und Sturm (Thunder and Storm)	4'
20. Sonnenuntergang (Sunset)	3'
21. Ausklang (Vanishing Sound)	7'
22. Nacht (Night)	2'

Kalmus	Leuckart

Also sprach Zarathustra, TrV 176, op.30 (Thus Spake Zarathustra) <1896>   33'

4[1.2.3/pic2.pic1] 4[1.2.3.Eh] 4[1.2.Ebcl.bcl] 4[1.2.3.cbn] — 6 4 3 2 — tmp+3 — 2hp — org — str[16.16.12.12.8]
perc: glock, tri, cym, bd, sus cym, chimes (E)
2014 Kalmus edition by Clinton F. Nieweg and Stuart S. Serio.

1. Einleitung (Introduction)	2'
2. Von den Hinterweltlern (Of the Backworldsmen)	4'
3. Von der großen Sehnsucht (Of the Great Longing)	2'
4. Von den Freuden und Leidenschaften (Of Joys and Passions)	2'
5. Das Grablied (The Song of the Grave)	2'
6. Von der Wissenschaft (Of Science and Learning)	4'
7. Der Genesende (The Convalescent)	5'
8. Das Tanzlied (The Dance-Song)	8'
9. Nachtwandlerlied (Song of the Night Wanderer)	4'

Kalmus	Luck's	Peters

Aus Italien, TrV 147, op.16 <1886>   47'

3[1.2.pic] 2[1.2/Eh] 2 3[1.2.cbn] — 4 2 3 0 — tmp+4 — hp — str
perc: sd, tri, tambn, cym

1. Auf der Campagna (In the Country)	13'
2. In Roms Ruinen (Amid the Ruins of Rome)	11'
3. Am Strande von Sorrent (On the Beach at Sorrento)	15'
4. Neapolitanisches Volksleben (Neapolitan Life)	8'

Kalmus	Peters

Le Bourgeois Gentilhomme, TrV 228c, op.60 (Der Bürger als Edelmann): Suite <1912; rev Suite: 1920>   *36'*

2[1/pic.2/pic] 2[1.2/Eh] 2 2[1.2/cbn] — 2 1 1 0 — tmp+5 — hp — pf — str[6.0.4.4.2]
perc: sd, tambn, tri, bd/cym, cym, glock

I. Ouvertüre zum 1. Aufzug (Overture to Act I)		4'
II. Menuett (Minuet)		2'
III. Der Fechtmeister (The Fencing-Master)		2'
IV. Auftritt und Tanz der Schneider (The Entrance and Dance of the		5'
V. Das Menuett des Lully (The Minuet of Lully)		2'
VI. Courante		3'
VII. Auftritt des Cleonte, nach Lully (Entrance of Cléonte, after Lully)		5'
VIII. Vorspiel zum 2. Aufzug (Prelude to Act II)		3'
IX. Das Diner: Tafelmusik und Tanz des Küchenjungen (The Dinner)		10'

Fürstner	Kalmus	Leuckart	Luck's

Brentano Lieder

see his: Sechs Lieder, TrV 235, op.68

Burleske, TrV 145 <1885–1886>   *17'*

solo piano
3[1.2.pic] 2 2 2 — 4 2 0 0 — tmp — str

Kalmus	Luck's	Schott

Cäcilie, op.27 (TrV 170), no.2 <1894; rev (orchd) 1897>   *2'*

high voice
2 2 2 2 — 4 2 3 1 — tmp — hp — str[10.10.6.6.4]
Originally for voice & piano; orchestrated by the composer.

Kalmus	Luck's	Universal

Concerto, Horn, No.1, TrV 117, op.11, E-flat major <1882–1883>   *15'*

2 2 2 2 — 2 2 0 0 — tmp — str

I. Allegro	5'
II. Andante	5'
III. Allegro	5'

Kalmus	Luck's	Universal

Concerto, Horn, No.2, TrV 283, E-flat major <1942>   *18'*

2 2 2 2 — 2 2 0 0 — tmp — str

I. Allegro	8'
II. Andante con moto	5'
III. Rondo: Allegro molto	5'

Boosey

Concerto, Oboe, TrV 292 (AV 144), D major <1945; rev 1948>   *28'*

2 1[Eh] 2 2 — 2 0 0 0 — str

I. Allegro moderato	9'
II. Andante	10'
III. Vivace	9'

Boosey

Concerto, Violin, TrV 110, op.8, D minor <1880–1882>   *31'*

2 2 2 2 — 4 2 0 0 — tmp — str

I. Allegro	16'
II. Lento	7'
III. Presto	8'

Kalmus	Universal

Couperin-Tanzsuite

see his: Tanzsuite nach Klavierstücken von François Couperin

Dance of the Seven Veils

see his: Salome, op.54: Salome's Dance

Dance Suite after Couperin

see his: Tanzsuite nach Klavierstücken von François Couperin

Death and Transfiguration

see his: Tod und Verklärung

Don Juan, TrV 156, op.20 <1888–1889>   *17'*

3[1.2.3/pic] 3[1.2.Eh] 2 3[1.2.cbn] — 4 3 3 1 — tmp+3 — hp — str
perc: tri, glock, cym, sus cym
Kalmus critical edition by Clinton F. Nieweg & Nancy M. Bradburd.

Kalmus	Luck's	Peters

Don Quixote; Fantastische Variationen über ein Thema ritterlichen Charakters, TrV 184, op.35 <1897>   *38'*

solo violoncello
3[1.2.pic] 3[1.2.Eh] 3[1.2/Ebcl.bcl] 4[1.2.3.cbn] — 6 3 3 1 — tenor tuba — tmp+2 — hp — str
perc: cym, tri, sd, tambn, bd, glock, wnd mach
Kalmus ed. Gregory Vaught.

In addition to the solo violoncello, major solos for viola, violin & tenor tuba. NB: The tenor tuba part is written in bass clef, but perversely as a B-flat transposition—contrary to customary usage. However, the Kalmus ed. is said to include a C-transposition of the tenor tuba.

Kalmus	Peters

Duet-concertino, TrV 293 <1947>   *18'*

solo clarinet & bassoon
hp — str

I. Allegro moderato	6'
II. Andante	3'
III. Rondo	9'

Boosey

Feierlicher Einzug der Ritter des Johanniter-Ordens, TrV 224 [original version] (Solemn Entrance of the Knights of the Johanniter-Ordens) <1909>   *7'*

0 0 0 0 — 4 15 4 2 — tmp — [no str]

Kalmus	Lienau

Feierlicher Einzug der Ritter des Johanniter-Ordens, TrV 224 [full orchestra] (Solemn Entrance of the Knights of the Johanniter-Ordens) <1909>   *7'*

3[1.2.pic] 2 2 3[1.2.cbn] — 4 3 3 1 — tmp+ — opt org — str
Originally for brass & timpani; arr. for full orchestra by Paul Juon.

Kalmus	Lienau

Festmarsch, TrV 43, op.1 <1876>   *9'*

3[1.2.pic] 2 2 2 — 4 2 3 1 — tmp — str

Breitkopf	Kalmus	Luck's

Four Last Songs

see his: Vier letzte Lieder

Die Frau ohne Schatten: Symphonic Fantasy, TrV 234a   *15'*
<1914–1917; rev 1946>

4[1.2.3/pic.4/pic] 3[1.2.Eh] 5[1.2.C-cl.basset hn.bcl] 4[1.2.3.cbn] — 4
4 3 1 — tmp+3 — 2hp — cel, org[offstage] — str
perc: bd, cym, tri, tambn, glock, xyl, cast

A symphonic fantasy prepared 1946 by the composer, based on his opera
composed 1914-17. The size of the instrumentation is reduced somewhat
from that required in the opera; see the 2009 arrangement by Peter Ruzick
(subsequent entry).
   1 percussionist doubles briefly on timpani.

Boosey	Fürstner	Schott

Die Frau ohne Schatten: Symphonic Fantasy, TrV 234a   *20'*
(arr. Ruzick) <1914–1917; rev 1946>

4[1.2.3/pic.4/pic] 3[1.2.3/Eh] 5[1.2.C-cl1.C-cl2/bcl.basset hn]
4[1.2.3.4/cbn] — 8[hn5-8/Wag tb] 6 4 1 — tmp+4 — 2hp — 2cel,
org[offstage], glass harmonica — str
perc: bd, cym, tri, tambn, glock, xyl, cast

A symphonic fantasy prepared 1946 by the composer, based on his opera
composed 1914-17. The composer had reduced the instrumentation from
that of the opera; in 2009, Peter Ruzick sought to restore this to match the
rather extravagant orchestration of the opera. In the process Ruzick
extended the length of the fantasy somewhat.
   1 percussionist doubles briefly on timpani. The following instruments
appear only briefly near the end of the work: tp5&6, cel2, glass
harmonica, org (a few long pedal notes only).

Fürstner	Schott

Guntram, TrV 168, op.25: Prelude to Act I   *10'*
<1892–1893; rev 1934-1939>

3[1.2.3/pic] 3[1.2.Eh] 3[1.2.bcl] 4[1.2.3.cbn] — 4 3 3 1 — 2tmp+2 —
2hp — str
perc: bd, cym, sm cym, tri

Boosey	Fürstner

Guntram, TrV 168, op.25: Prelude to Act II   *6'*
<1892–1893; rev 1934-1939>

3[1.2.pic] 3 3 4[1.2.3.cbn] — 4 4[1.2.3.btp] 3 1 — 2tmp+5 — str
perc: bd, cym, td, tambn, tri

Boosey	Fürstner

Ein Heldenleben, TrV 190, op.40 (A Hero's Life; A   *40'*
Heroic Life) <1897–1898>

4[1.2.3.pic] 4[1.2.3.4/Eh] 4[1.2.Ebcl.bcl] 4[1.2.3.cbn] — 8 5 3 1 —
tenor tuba — tmp+4 — 2hp — str
perc: sd, cym, tri, tamtam, bd, td, sus cym

Kalmus edition by Clinton F. Nieweg & Stuart S. Serio.
   NB: The tenor tuba part is written in bass clef, but perversely as a
B-flat transposition—contrary to customary usage. However, a
C-transposition of the tenor tuba is included in the Kalmus set.
   It is said that the original ending of the work was soft, and that the
composer changed it. Supposedly the original ending may be heard on a
recording conducted by Fabio Luisi with the Staatskapelle Dresden.

Kalmus	Leuckart

Intermezzo, TrV 246, op.72: Entr'acte after Act I   *7'*
<1918–1923>

2 2[1.Eh] 2 2 — 3 2 2[1.btbn] 0 — tmp — hp — str

Boosey	Fürstner

Intermezzo, TrV 246, op.72: Waltz Scene   *8'*
<1918–1923>

2 2 2 2 — 3 2 2[1.btbn] 0 — tmp+1 — pf — str
perc: sd

Boosey	Fürstner

Josephslegende, TrV 231, op.63 <1912–1914>   *60'*

5[1.2.3/pic.4.pic] 4[1.2.3/Eh.heckl] 4[1.2.Dcl.bcl] 4[1.2.3.cbn] — 6 4
4 2[tenortuba.basstuba] — tmp+6 — 4hp — pf.cel.org[offstage] —
str[vn I,II,III.va I,II.vc I,II.db]
perc: bd, cym, sus cym, sd, tri, tambn, tamtam, glock, xyl, wnd mach, sm
cym[pair], 4pr cast

N.B.: Bass clarinet is in A, bass clef; tenor tuba is in Bb and treble clef; a
contrabass clarinet is called for (4 bars only), to be covered by the 2nd
clarinetist or the D clarinetist [cued in cbn if necessary].
   A 1947 "Symphonic Fragment" from this ballet is available from
Boosey; it was prepared by the composer, and is 20' in duration. The
instrumentation is somewhat smaller.

Boosey	Fürstner

Josephslegende, TrV 231a, op.63 (Legend of Joseph):   *20'*
Symphonic Fragment <1912–1914; rev 1947>

3[1.2.3/pic] 3[1.2.Eh] 3[1.2.bcl] 3[1.2.cbn] — 4 3 3 1 — tmp+4 —
2hp — cel, pf, opt org — str[vn I,II,III.va I,II.vc I,II.db]
perc: glock, cym, tamtam, tri, bd, sd, tambn

Extracted from the ballet of 1914, this late "Symphonic Fragment" (1947)
was arranged for reduced orchestra; a number of passages were also
revised or recomposed. Bass clarinet written in A in bass clef.

Boosey	Kalmus	Luck's

Königsmarsch, TrV 217 <1905>   *5'*

4[2fl, 2pic] 2 4[2cl, 2Ebcl] 3[1.2.cbn] — 8 12 4 1 — tmp+15 — 2hp
— str
perc: bd, cym, sd, tmp[2nd pair]

Originally for piano, but a short score in the composer's hand gives
indications for orchestration. Arranged for large orchestra (presumably
following these autograph indications) by Otto Singer. (Singer also
arranged the work for salon orchestra.)
   Offstage *banda* (incl in aggregate above): 8tp, 12perc.
   Woodwinds may be doubled.

Boosey	Kalmus	Luck's

Macbeth, TrV 163, op.23 <1888>   *18'*

3[1.2.3/pic] 3[1.2.Eh] 3[1.2.bcl] 3[1.2.cbn] — 4 4[1.2.3.btp] 3 1 —
tmp+2 — str
perc: cym, bd, tamtam, sd

Kalmus	Luck's	Peters

Metamorphosen, TrV 290 <1945>   *26'*

23 solo strings[10vn, 5va, 5vc, 3db]

Boosey

Morgen, TrV 170, op.27, no.4 <1894; rev (orchd) 1897>   *2'*

medium or high voice   solo violin
0 0 0 0 — 3 0 0 0 — hp — str

Originally for voice & piano; orchestrated by the composer.
   Available in E for medium voice, or G for high voice.

Kalmus	Luck's	Universal

Parergon zur Sinfonia Domestica, TrV 209a, op.73   *22'*
<1925>

solo piano (left hand)
2 3[1.2.Eh] 3[1.2.bcl] 3[1.2.cbn] — 4 2 3 1 — tmp — hp — str

Boosey

Romanze, TrV 80, E-flat major <1879>   *4'*

solo clarinet
0 2 0 2 — 2 0 0 0 — str

Eulenburg	Schott

Romanze, TrV 118, F major <1883>   *12'*

violoncello solo
2 2 2 2 — 2 0 0 0 — str

> Schott

Der Rosenkavalier, TrV 227d, op.59: Suite [1945]   *22'*
<1909–1910>

3[1.2.3/pic] 3[1.2.3/Eh] 4[1.2.3/Ebcl.bcl] 3[1.2.3/cbn] — 4 3 3 1 — tmp+5 — 1 or 2hp — cel — str
perc: bd, cym, sd, tri, tambn, glock, ratch

2nd harp is noted as optional in the score, but its absence would eliminate important lines; it is not possible to combine the two harp parts into one.

The publisher may supply on request a version of the clarinet parts using only 3 players, and with transpositions more suitable for modern use (i.e., no clarinets in C or D).

The provenance of this 1945 suite is not entirely clear. It is said that Strauss marked up a full opera score with cuts and inserts for Eugene Ormandy, and that this copy was used by the Philadelphia Orchestra for performances of the suite for many years. Possibly he did the same for Artur Rodzinski of the New York Philharmonic, who first conducted it on 5 October 1944. The composer then consented to its publication as a suite in 1945. No editor or arranger is credited in the publication.

> Boosey

Der Rosenkavalier, TrV 227, op.59: Concert Suite [arr.   *20'*
Mandell]

3[1.2.3/pic] 3[1.2.3/Eh] 3[1.2.Ebcl] 3[1.2.3/cbn] — 4 3 3 1 — basset hn — tmp+6 — 2hp — cel — str
perc: bd, cym, sus cym, sd, tambn, glock, ratch

Arr. Robert Mandell.

The score consists of photoprints of pages from the complete opera; these sometimes show the voice parts from the operatic original, but it is not intended that these be sung.

It is said that Kalmus commissioned the creation of this arrangement because the 1945 suite (see previous entry) was under copyright protection and could not be reprinted by Kalmus.

> Kalmus

Der Rosenkavalier, TrV 227, op.59: Waltzes, First   *13'*
Sequence <1909–1910; rev 1944>

3 3 4[1.2.Ebcl.basset hn] 3 — 4 3 3 1 — tmp+5 — 2hp[1part] — str
perc: glock, sd, tri, cym, bd

> Boosey

Der Rosenkavalier, TrV 227, op.59: Waltzes (arr.   *8'*
Doebber) <1909–1910>

2[1.2/pic] 2 2 — 4 2 3 0 — tmp+4 — hp — str
Orch. by Johannes Doebber.

> Fürstner   Kalmus

Salome, TrV 215, op.54: Salome's Dance (Tanz der   *9'*
sieben Schleier; Dance of the Seven Veils)
<1903–1905>

4[1.2.3.pic] 4[1.2.Eh.heckl] 6[1.2.3.4.Ebcl.bcl] 4[1.2.3.cbn] — 6 4 4 1 — 2tmp+6 — 2hp — cel — str
perc: glock, xyl, tamtam, tri, cast, tambn, sd, cym, sus cym, bd

Last page of Boosey score (and Kalmus reprint) has a measure missing; the Schott score is correct in this respect and matches the Boosey parts.

> Boosey   Kalmus   Luck's   Schott

Salome, TrV 215, op.54: Salome's Dance (Boosey red.)   *9'*
<1903–1905>

3[1.2.3/pic] 3[1.2.Eh] 3[1.2.3/bcl] 3[1.2.cbn] — 4 3 3 1 — 2tmp+6 — hp — cel — str
perc: glock, xyl, tamtam, tri, cast, tambn, sd, cym, sus cym, bd

Boosey and Kalmus reductions of this extract are neither identical nor interchangeable.

> Boosey

Salome, TrV 215, op.54: Salome's Dance (Kalmus red.)   *9'*
<1903–1905>

3[1.2.3/pic] 3[1.2.Eh] 4[1.2.bcl.Ebcl(opt)] 3[1.2.cbn] — 4 3 3 1 — 2tmp+6 — hp — cel — str
perc: glock, xyl, tamtam, tri, cast, tambn, sd, cym, sus cym, bd

Boosey and Kalmus reductions of this extract are neither identical nor interchangeable. Kalmus is a reprint of Schott (originally Fürstner).

> Kalmus   Schott

SECHS LIEDER (Brentano Lieder), TrV 235, op.68   *24'*
<1918; rev (orchd) 1933, 1940>

high voice
3[1.2.pic] 3[1.2.Eh] 3[1.2.bcl] 3[1.2.cbn] — 4 3 3 1 — tmp+2 — 2hp — str
perc: bd, tamtam

On poems by Clemens von Brentano, originally for voice & pf (1918); orchestrated by the composer (nos.1-5, 1940; no.6, 1933).

For the instrumentations of the individual songs, see subsequent entries.

1. An die Nacht (To Night)   *3'*
2. Ich wollt ein Sträusslein binden (I Want to Tie a Little Bouquet)   *4'*
3. Säusle, liebe Myrte (Rustle, Dear Myrtle)   *4'*
4. Als mir dein Lied erklang (As I Heard Your Song)   *3'*
5. Amor (Cupid)   *3'*
6. Lied der Frauen (Song of the Women)   *7'*

> Boosey   Fürstner

1. An die Nacht (To Night) <1918; rev (orchd) 1940>   *3'*

high voice
2 3[1.2.Eh] 3[1.2.bcl] 2 — 4 3 3 0 — tmp — hp — str

>

2. Ich wollt ein Sträusslein binden (I Want to Tie a   *4'*
Little Bouquet) <1918; rev (orchd) 1940>

high voice
2 2 2 2 — 2 0 0 0 — hp — str

>

3. Säusle, liebe Myrte (Rustle, Dear Myrtle) <1918;   *4'*
rev (orchd) 1940>

high voice
2 2 2 2 — 2 0 0 0 — str

>

4. Als mir dein Lied erklang (As I Heard Your Song)   *3'*
<1918; rev (orchd) 1940>

high voice
2 2 3[1.2.bcl] 2 — 2 2 0 0 — tmp — str

>

5. Amor (Cupid) <1918; rev (orchd) 1940>   *3'*

high voice
1 1 2[1.bcl] 1 — str

>

6. Lied der Frauen (Song of the Women) <1918; rev   *7'*
(orchd) 1933>

high voice
3[1.2.pic] 3[1.2.Eh] 3[1.2.bcl] 3[1.2.cbn] — 4 2 3 1 — tmp+2 — 2hp — str
perc: bd, tamtam

>

Serenade, TrV 106, op.7, E-flat major <1881>   *10'*

2 2 2 3[1.2.cbn(or tuba or db)] — 4 0 0 0 — [no str]

> Kalmus   Luck's   Universal

Suite, TrV 132, op.4, B-flat major <1884>   24'

2 2 2 3[1.2.cbn(or tuba)] — 4 0 0 0 — [no str]

I. Praeludium	7'
II. Romance	6'
III. Gavotte	4'
IV. Introduction and Fugue	7'

| Kalmus | Leuckart |

Symphonia domestica, TrV 209, op.53 <1902–1903>   44'

4[1.2.3.pic] 4[1.2.Eh.ob d'amore] 5[1.2.3.D-cl.bcl] 5[1.2.3.4.cbn] — 8
4 3 1 — 4opt sx[ssx.asx.bsx.bass sx] — tmp+2 — 2hp — str
perc: cym, tambn, bd, tri, chimes[D4]
Clarinet 3 is most soloistic, and is usually played by the principal clarinet.

1. Introduction (Themes of the Husband, the Wife, the Child)	5'
2. Scherzo (Happiness of the Parents, Childish Games)	7'
3. Wiegenlied (Cradle Song)	6'
4. Adagio	12'
5. Finale	14'

| Bote & Bock | Kalmus |

Symphony, TrV 126, op.12, F minor <1884>   45'

2 2 2 2 — 4 2 3 1 — tmp — str

I. Allegro ma non troppo; un poco maestoso	16'
II. Scherzo: Presto	7'
III. Andante cantabile	10'
IV. Finale: Allegro assai; molto appassionato	12'

| Kalmus | Universal |

Symphony for Winds, TrV 291, op.posth., E-flat major   37'
(Fröhliche Werkstatt; Happy Workshop) <1944–1945>

2 2 5[1.2.3.bcl.basset hn] 3[1.2.cbn] — 4 0 0 0 — [no str]
Also known as *Sonatina No.2 for 16 Wind Instruments.*

1. Allegro con brio	12'
2. Andantino	5'
3. Minuet	4'
4. Introduction and Allegro	16'

| Boosey |

Tanzsuite nach Klavierstücken von François Couperin,   29'
TrV 245 (Dance Suite after Couperin;
Couperin-Tanzsuite) <1923>

2 2[1.2/Eh] 2 2 — 2 1 1 0 — 1perc — hp — cel, hpsd —
str[4.3.2.2.2]
perc: glock, tambn
Rights for staged performances from Boosey.

I. Entrance and Festive Round (Pavane) [Einzug und Feierlicher Reigen]	4'
II. Courante	5'
III. Carillon	2'
IV. Sarabande	4'
V. Gavotte	4'
VI. Whirling Dance (Wirbeltanz, Tourbillon)	3'
VII. Allemande	6'
VIII. March	1'

| Leuckart |

Three Hymns, TrV 240, op.71 (Drei Hymnen) <1921>   29'

high voice
3[1.2.3/pic] 3[1.2.Eh] 4[1.2.3.bcl] 3[1.2.3/cbn] — 4 3 3 1 — tmp —
2hp — cel — str[14.12.8.8.6]

1. Hymne an die Liebe	10'
2. Rückkehr in die Heimat	10'
3. Die Liebe	9'

| Boosey |

Thus Spake Zarathustra

see his: Also sprach Zarathustra

Till Eulenspiegels lustige Streiche, TrV 171, op.28   15'
<1894–1895>

4[1.2.3.pic] 4[1.2.3.Eh] 4[1.2.D-cl.bcl] 4[1.2.3.cbn] — 4[hn5-8 opt]
3[tp4-6 opt] 3 1 — tmp+2 — str
perc: bd, cym, ratch, sd, tri
Kalmus critical ed. Clinton F. Nieweg.

| Kalmus | Luck's | Peters |

Tod und Verklärung, TrV 158, op.24 (Death and   23'
Transfiguration) <1888–1889>

3 3[1.2.Eh] 3[1.2.bcl] 3[1.2.cbn] — 4 3 3 1 — tmp+1 — 2hp — str
perc: tamtam
Kalmus critical edition by Clinton F. Nieweg & Stuart S. Serio.

| Kalmus | Luck's | Peters |

VIER LETZTE LIEDER (Four Last Songs), TrV 296   24'
<1948>

solo soprano
4[1.2.3/pic2.pic1] 3[1.2.Eh] 3[1.2.bcl] 3[1.2.3/cbn] — 4 3 3 1 — tmp
— hp — cel — str
For the instrumentations of the individual songs, see subsequent entries.

1. Frühling (Spring)	5'
2. September	5'
3. Beim Schlafengehen (At Bedtime)	6'
4. Im Abendroth (At Sunset)	8'

| Boosey |

1. Frühling (Spring) <1948>   4'

2 3[1.2.Eh] 3[1.2.bcl] 3 — 4 0 0 0 — hp — str

| Boosey |

2. September <1948>   5'

3 3[1.2.Eh] 3[1.2.bcl] 2 — 4 2 0 0 — hp — str

| Boosey |

3. Beim Schlafengehen (At Bedtime) <1948>   5'

4[2fl, 2pic] 3[1.2.Eh] 3[1.2.bcl] 2 — 4 2 3 1 — cel — str

| Boosey |

4. Im Abendrot (At Sunset) <1948>   8'

2[1/pic1.2/pic2] 3[1.2.Eh] 3[1.2.bcl] 3[1.2.cbn] — 4 3 3 1 — tmp —
str

| Boosey |

Wanderers Sturmlied, TrV 131, op.14 <1884>   16'

chorus
3[1.2.pic] 2 2 3[1.2.cbn] — 4 2 3 0 — tmp — str

| Kalmus | Luck's | Universal |

Wiener Philharmoniker Fanfare, TrV 248 <1924>   3'

0 0 0 0 — 8 6 6 2 — 2tmp — [no str]

| Boosey |

Zueignung, TrV 141, op.10 no.1 (Devotion) <1885; rev   2'
(orchd) 1929>

solo voice
2 2 3[1.2.bcl] 2 — 4 2 1 0 — tmp — hp — str
Originally for voice and piano; orchestrated for high voice by the
composer; for high or medium voice by Robert Heger.
Available in C or A.
   2 other (different) orchestrations, published by Kalmus and Luck's,
respectively; each is available in C or in A.

| Luck's | Universal |

Stravinsky, Igor

1882-1971

(b Oranienbaum, nr St Petersburg, 5/17 June 1882; d New York, 6 April 1971).
Russian composer, later of French (1934) and American (1945) nationality

Abraham and Isaac <1962–1963>   12'

baritone solo
3[1.2.afl] 2[1.Eh] 2[1.bcl] 2 — 1 2 2[1.btbn] 1 — str
Hebrew text with transliteration; English translation of text not intended
for performance.

> Boosey

Agon <1953–1957>   20'

3[1.2.3/pic] 3[1.2.Eh] 3[1.2.bcl] 3[1.2.cbn] — 4 4 3 0 — mand —
tmp/perc — hp — pf — str
perc: (all played by tmp) xyl, cast, tomtom[or hi tmp]

1. Pas de quatre	2'
2. Double Pas de quatre	2'
3. Triple Pas de quatre	1'
4. Prelude	1'
5. First Pas de trois	4'
6. Interlude	1'
7. Second Pas de trois	3'
8. Interlude	1'
9. Pas de deux	4'
10. Four Duos	1'
11. Four Trios	2'

> Boosey

Apollon Musagète [original version] (Apollo) <1927–1928>   30'

str
Kalmus ed. Nancy M. Bradburd. All editions permanently out of print.

TABLEAU 1
1. Naissance d'Apollon	5'

TABLEAU 2
2. Variations d'Apollon (Apollon et les Muses)	3'
3. Pas d'action (Apollon et Calliope, Polymnie et Terpsichore)	4'
4. Variation de Calliope (L'Alexandrin)	1'
5. Variation de Polymnie	1'
6. Variation de Terpsichore	2'
7. Variations d'Apollon	2'
8. Pas de deux (Apollon et Terpsichore)	4'
9. Coda (Apollon et les Muses)	4'
10. Apothéose	4'

> Ed. Russe   Fleisher   Kalmus

Apollon Musagète [1947 version] (Apollo) <1927–1928; rev 1947>   30'

str
The composer suggests 34 strings: 8.8.6.8.4 (cellos are divided).
 Norman Del Mar (*Orchestral Variations*, pp.215-218) lists important
emendations evident in the composer's recording, which Del Mar
describes as "amounting to a further revised version."

TABLEAU 1
1. Naissance d'Apollon	5'

TABLEAU 2
2. Variations d'Apollon (Apollon et les Muses)	3'
3. Pas d'action (Apollon et Calliope, Polymnie et Terpsichore)	4'
4. Variation de Calliope (L'Alexandrin)	1'
5. Variation de Polymnie	1'
6. Variation de Terpsichore	2'
7. Variations d'Apollon	2'
8. Pas de deux (Apollon et Terpsichore)	4'
9. Coda (Apollon et les Muses)	4'
10. Apothéose	4'

> Boosey

LE BAISER DE LA FÉE: Chronology

1928: Ballet, commissioned by Ida Rubinstein
1934: *Divertimento* created from the music of the ballet
1949: *Divertimento* revised
1950: Ballet score revised

Le baiser de la fée (The Fairy's Kiss) <1928; rev 1950>   44'

3[1.2.3/pic] 3[1.2.Eh] 3[1.2.3/bcl] 2 — 4 3 3 1 — tmp+1 — hp — str
perc: bd

1. Prologue: Berceuse de la tempête (Lullaby in the Storm)	8'
2. Une fête au village (A Village Fête)	11'
3. Au moulin (At the Mill); Pas de deux	21'
4. Berceuse des demeures eternelles (Lullaby in the Land of Eternity)	4'

> Boosey

Le baiser de la fée (The Fairy's Kiss): Divertimento <1928; rev 1934, 1949>   22'

3[1.2.pic] 3[1.2.Eh] 3[1.2.3/bcl] 2 — 4 3 3 1 — tmp+1 — hp — str
perc: bd
An orchestra work created from music of the ballet.

1. Sinfonia	5'
2. Danses suisses	6'
3. Scherzo	4'
4. Pas de deux	7'

> Boosey

Canon on a Russian Popular Tune <1965>   1'

3[1.2.pic] 3[1.2.Eh] 3[1.2.bcl] 3[1.2.cbn] — 4 3 3 1 — tmp+1 — hp
— pf — str
perc: bd
"For concert introduction or encore;" same tune as used in the 7/4 passage
from the final stages of *L'oiseau de feu*.

> Boosey

Canticum sacrum ad honorem Sancti Marci nominis <1955>   17'

solo tenor & baritone   chorus
1 3[1.2.Eh] 0 3[1.2.cbn] — 0 4[1.2.3.btp] 4[1.2.btbn.cb tbn] 0 — hp
— org — str[no vn or vc]

1. Dedicatio	1'
2. Euntes in mundum	2'
3. Surge, aquilo	2'
4. Ad tres virtutes hortationes: Caritas, Spes, Fides	7'
5. Brevis motus cantilenae	3'
6. Illi autem profecti	2'

> Boosey

Capriccio for Piano & Orchestra <1928–1929; rev 1949>   17'

concertino: solo vn, va, vc, db
3[1.2.3/pic] 3[1.2.Eh] 3[1.2/Ebcl.3/bcl] 2 — 4 2 3 1 — tmp — str
The original 1929 version is permanently out of print, but available at
Fleisher. Boosey offers only the 1949 revision.

1. Presto	6'
2. Andante rapsodico	6'
3. Allegro capriccioso ma tempo giusto	5'

> Boosey   Ed. Russe   Fleisher

Le chant du rossignol

see his: Song of the Nightingale

Chorale-Variations on "Vom Himmel hoch da komm' ich her" <1955–1956>   18'

chorus
2 3[1.2.Eh] 0 3[1.2.cbn] — 0 3 3 0 — hp — str[no vn or vc]
A "recomposition" of J.S.Bach's *Canonic Variations on "Vom Himmel hoch,"* BWV 769, originally for organ.

> Boosey

Circus Polka; Composed for a Young Elephant <1942; rev (orchd) 1944>   *4'*

2[1.pic] 2 2 2 — 4 2 3 1 — tmp+3 — str
perc: sd, cym, bd
Originally (1942) for piano, and arranged for a wind group with organ the same year; orchestrated by the composer in 1944.

> Schott

Concertino for 12 Instruments <1952>   *6'*

1 2[1.Eh] 1 2 — 0 2 2 0 — vn, vc
An arrangement by the composer of his *Concertino for String Quartet* (1920).

> Boosey

Concerto for Piano & Wind Instruments <1923–1924; rev 1950>   *19'*

3[1.2.pic] 3[1.2.Eh] 2 2[1.2/cbn] — 4 4 3 1 — tmp — db[section]
I. Largo - Allegro	*7'*
II. Largo [original 1924 title, Larghissimo]	*7'*
III. Allegro	*5'*

> Boosey

Concerto, Violin, D major <1931; rev 1961>   *22'*

3[1.2.pic] 3[1.2.Eh] 3[1.2.Ebcl] 3[1.2.3/cbn] — 4 3 3 1 — tmp/bd — str
perc: [1player] bd, tmp
(1) Toccata	*6'*
(2) Aria I	*5'*
(3) Aria II	*5'*
(4) Capriccio	*6'*

> Schott

Concerto in D (Basel Concerto) <1946; rev ca 1950>   *12'*

str
1. Vivace	*6'*
2. Arioso: Andantino	*3'*
3. Rondo: Allegro	*3'*

> Boosey

Concerto in E-flat (Dumbarton Oaks) <1937–1938>   *15'*

1 0 1 1 — 2 0 0 0 — 3vn, 3va, 2vc, 2db
Available from G. Schirmer in the US.
I. Tempo giusto	*5'*
II. Allegretto	*5'*
III. Con moto	*5'*

> Schott

Danses concertantes <1940–1942>   *19'*

1 1 1 1 — 2 1 1 0 — tmp — str[6vn, 4va, 3vc, 2db]
I. Marche-introduction	*2'*
II. Pas d'action	*3'*
III. Thème varié	*8'*
IV. Pas de deux	*5'*
V. Marche-conclusion	*1'*

> Schott

Divertimento

see under: Stravinsky, Igor
Le Baiser de la fée (The Fairy's Kiss)

Ebony Concerto <1945>   *10'*

solo clarinet with jazz orchestra
0 0 0 0 — 1 5 3 0 — 5sx[asx1/cl.asx2/cl.tsx1.tsx2/cl/bcl.bsx] — gtr — 1perc — hp — pf — db
perc: sd, bd, sus cym, 3tomtoms
I. Allegro moderato	*3'*
II. Andante	*3'*
III. Moderato - Con moto	*4'*

> Boosey

Eight Instrumental Miniatures <1921; rev (arr) 1962>   *8'*

2 2 2 2 — 1 0 0 0 — 2vn, 2va, 2vc
An arrangement by the composer of his piano work *Les cinq doigts*, 1921.
I. Andantino	*1'*
II. Vivace	*1'*
III. Lento	*1'*
IV. Allegretto	*1'*
V. Moderato: Alla breve	*1'*
VI. Tempo di marcia	*1'*
VII. Larghetto	*1'*
VIII. Tempo di tango	*1'*

> Chester

The Fairy's Kiss

see his: Baiser de la fée

Fanfare for a New Theatre <1964>   *1'*

2 solo trumpets

> Boosey

The Faun and the Shepherdess, op.2 (Favn' i pastushka; Le Faune et la Bergère) <1906>   *10'*

mezzo-soprano solo
3[1.2.pic] 2 2 2 — 4 2 3 1 — tmp+2 — str
perc: cym, bd
1. Pastushka (The Shepherdess)	*3'*
2. Favn' (The Faun)	*3'*
3. Reka (The River)	*4'*

> Belaieff   Kalmus   Peters

Feu d'artifice, op.4 (Fireworks; Feyerverk) <1908; rev 1909>   *5'*

3[1.2.pic] 2[1.2/] 3[1.2.3/bcl] 2 — 6 3 3 1 — tmp+4 — 2hp — cel — str
perc: glock, tri, cym, bd
Schott critical edition by Ulrich Mosch.

> Kalmus   Schott

The Firebird (Zhar'-ptitsa; L'oiseau de feu) <1909–1910>   *45'*

4[1.2.3/pic2.pic1] 4[1.2.3.Eh] 4[1.2.3/Ebcl.bcl] 4[1.2.3/cbn2.cbn1] — 4 3 3 1 — backstage: 3tp, 4Wag tubas[2ten, 2bass] — tmp+4 — 3hp — cel, pf — str
perc: xyl, tamtam, tambn, tri, glock, cym, bd, sus cym, chimes [backstage: D#,G]
Schott critical edition by Herbert Schneider.
Cl 3 is said to double on D-clarinet (perhaps in addition to Ebcl).
1. Introduction	*3'*
2. Kastchei's Enchanted Garden	*2'*
3. The Firebird Enters, Pursued by Ivan Tsarevich	*2'*
4. The Firebird's Dance	*1'*
5. Ivan Tsarevich Captures the Firebird	*1'*
6. The Firebird Begs to be Released	*5'*
7. Entrance of the Thirteen Enchanted Princesses	*2'*
8. The Princesses Play with the Golden Apples (Scherzo)	*3'*
9. Ivan Tsarevich Appears	*1'*
10. The Princesses' Khorovod (Round Dance)	*5'*
11. Daybreak	*1'*
12. Ivan Tsarevich Enters Kastchei's Palace	*2'*
13. Entrance of Kastchei the Immortal	*1'*
14. Dialogue between Kastchei and Ivan Tsarevich	*1'*
15. The Princesses Plead for Mercy	*1'*
16. The Firebird Enters	*1'*
17. Dance of Kastchei's Retinue under the Firebird's Magic Spell	*1'*
18. Infernal Dance of Kastchei and His Subjects	*5'*
19. The Firebird's Lullaby	*2'*
20. Kastchei Awakens	*1'*
21. Kastchei's Death	*1'*
22. Kastchei's Spell Is Broken	*3'*

> Kalmus   Schott

The Firebird [McPhee reduction] (Zhar'-ptitsa; L'oiseau de feu) <1909> 45'

2[1.2/pic] 2[1.2/Eh] 2 2 — 4 2 3 1 — tmp+3 — hp — pf/cel — str
perc: tri, tambn, bd, cym, tamtam, glock, xyl, vib
Reduced orchestration by Jonathan McPhee, following "the principles Stravinsky himself used when reducing the original orchestration for selections included in his 1919 suite." Passages not present in the 1919 suite have been reduced by McPhee.
  For contents and durations, see main entry for this work.

| Boosey |

The Firebird (Zhar'-ptitsa; L'oiseau de feu): Suite (1911 version) <1909–1910> 23'

4[1.2.3/pic2.pic1] 4[1.2.3.Eh] 4[1.2.3/Ebcl.bcl] 4[1.2.3/cbn2.cbn1] — 4 3 3 1 — tmp+4 — 3hp — cel, pf — str
perc: xyl, tamtam, tambn, tri, glock, cym, bd, sus cym
Originally published by Jurgenson in 1912; sometimes identified as *First Suite from Firebird*.
  Cl 3 is said to double on D-clarinet (perhaps in addition to Ebcl).
1. *Introduction and Kastcheï's Enchanted Garden*   6'
2. *Supplications of the Firebird*   5'
3. *The Princesses Play with the Golden Apples*   3'
4. *Round Dance of the Princesses*   5'
5. *Infernal Dance of All the Subjects of Kastcheï*   4'

| Kalmus | Luck's | Schott |

The Firebird (Zhar'-ptitsa; L'oiseau de feu): Suite (1919 version) <1909–1910> 23'

2[1.2/pic] 2[1.2/Eh] 2 2 — 4 2 3 1 — tmp+3 — hp — pf/opt cel — str
perc: xyl, tambn, tri, cym, bd
Only one bar of Eh; remainder is for 2ob.
  Reorchestrated by the composer in 1919; sometimes identified as *Second Suite from Firebird*. Kalmus ed. Clark McAlister.
1. *Introduction*   3'
2. *L'Oiseau de feu et sa danse & Variation de l'oiseau de feu*   2'
3. *Ronde des princesses*   6'
4. *Danse infernale du roi Kastcheï*   5'
5. *Berceuse*   4'
6. *Final*   3'

| Chester | Kalmus | Schott |

The Firebird (Zhar'-ptitsa; L'oiseau de feu): Suite (1945 version) <1909–1910> 31'

2[1.2/pic] 2 2 — 4 2 3 1 — tmp+3 — hp — pf — str
perc: bd, cym, sd, tambn, tri, xyl
A reorchestration of the 1919 suite, with the insertion of five additional sections from the ballet (*mvts 3-7*). Sometimes identified as *Third Suite from Firebird*.
1. *Introduction*   3'
2. *Prelude, Dance of the Firebird, & Variations*   2'
3. *Pantomime I*   1'
4. *Pas de deux*   3'
5. *Pantomime II*   1'
6. *Scherzo (Dance of the Princesses)*   3'
7. *Pantomime III*   1'
8. *Rondo*   5'
9. *Infernal Dance*   5'
10. *Lullaby (Berceuse)*   4'
11. *Final Hymn*   3'

| Chester | Schott |

The Firebird (Zhar'-ptitsa; L'oiseau de feu): Berceuse & Finale <1909–1910> 6'

2[1.2/pic] 2 2 — 4 2 3 1 — tmp+3 — hp — cel — str
perc: tri, bd, cym
From the 1919 Suite; Kalmus ed. Clark McAlister. Celesta has only 8 notes.
1. *Berceuse*   3'
2. *Finale*   3'

| Kalmus | Luck's |

The Flood; A Musical Play <1961–1962> 24'

narrator, 4 actors, solo TBB   SAT chorus
4[1.2.3/pic.afl] 3[1.2.Eh] 4[1.2.cbn.cbcl] 3[1.2.cbn] — 4 3 3 1 — tmp+2 — hp — cel/pf — str
perc: sus cym, bd, xylorimba, 3tuned tomtoms[played by tmp]
Prelude   6'
Melodrama   5'
The Building of the Ark   3'
The Catalogue of the Animals   2'
The Comedy   2'
The Flood   3'
The Covenant of the Rainbow   3'

| Boosey |

Four Etudes for Orchestra (Quatre études) <1928–1929> 10'

3[1.2.3/pic] 3[1.2.3/Eh] 3[1.2.bcl/Ebcl] 2 — 4 4 3 1 — tmp — hp — pf — str
An arrangement by the composer of his *Three Pieces for String Quartet* (1914), and *Study for Pianola* (1917),
  Available scores are replete with error, to the point that it is difficult to be certain about what instruments are required. 4 notes for a 4th trombone are probably intended for the tuba.
1. *Danse*   1'
2. *Excentrique*   2'
3. *Cantique*   4'
4. *Madrid*   3'

| Boosey |

Four Norwegian Moods <1942> 8'

2[1.2/pic] 2[1.2/Eh] 2 2 — 4 2 2 1 — tmp — str
1. *Intrada*   2'
2. *Song*   3'
3. *Wedding Dance*   1'
4. *Cortège*   2'

| Schott |

Genesis Suite: VII. Babel <1944> 7'

narrator   male chorus (TB)
3[1.2.3/pic] 2 3[1.2.bcl] 3[1.2.cbn] — 4 3 3 0 — tmp — hp — str
See the entry for "Nathaniel Shilkret: *Genesis Suite*" for a full description of this collaborative work by 7 composers.

| Schott |

Greeting Prelude <1955> 1'

3[1.2.pic] 2 2 3[1.2.cbn] — 4 2 3 1 — tmp+1 — pf — str
perc: bd
After C.F. Summy's *Happy Birthday to You*.

| Boosey |

Histoire du soldat (The Soldier's Tale) <1918> 65'

3 spoken parts [Narrator, Soldier, Devil], 1 female dancer
0 0 1 1 — 0 1[crt] 1 0 — 1perc — vn, db
perc: bd, sus cym, tambn, tri, field dr, 2sd
Critical ed. by John Carewe, 1987; percussion part ed. James Blades.
  Other versions of the percussion part exist, by William Kraft and Frank Epstein, respectively.

| Chester |

Histoire du soldat (The Soldier's Tale): Suite <1918>   26'

0 0 1 1 — 0 1[crt] 1 0 — 1perc — vn, db

perc: bd, sus cym, tambn, tri, field dr, 2sd

Critical ed. by John Carewe, 1987; percussion part ed. James Blades.

   Other versions of the percussion part exist, by William Kraft and Frank Epstein, respectively.

   The same materials may be used for the suite as for the complete work.

1. Marche du soldat (The Soldier's March)	2'
2. Petits airs au bord du ruisseau (Airs by a Stream)	3'
3. Pastorale	3'
4. Marche royale (The Royal March)	3'
5. Petit concert (The Little Concert)	3'
6. Trois danses (Three Dances): Tango, Valse, Ragtime	6'
7. Danse du Diable (The Devil's Dance)	1'
8. Grand choral (Great Chorale)	3'
9. Marche triomphale du Diable (Triumphal March of the Devil)	2'

Chester

In memoriam Dylan Thomas <1954>   9'

tenor solo

0 0 0 0 — 0 0 4 0 — str 4t

Dirge-Canons (Prelude)	2'
Song (Do Not Go Gentle …)	5'
Dirge-Canons (Postlude)	2'

Boosey

Introitus (T.S. Eliot in memoriam) <1965>   4'

2tmp+2 — hp — pf — 1va, 1db

perc: 2 tamtams

Boosey

Jeu de cartes (Game of Cards) <1936>   23'

2[1.2/pic] 2[1.2/Eh] 2 2 — 4 2 3 1 — tmp+1 — str

perc: bd

Available from G. Schirmer in the US.

I. First Deal	5'
II. Second Deal	10'
III. Third Deal	8'

Schott

Mass <1944–1948>   18'

chorus   solos SATTB

0 3[1.2.Eh] 0 2 — 0 2 3 0 — [no str]

Children's voices preferred for S and A parts, both solo and chorus.

I. Kyrie	3'
II. Gloria	4'
III. Credo	4'
IV. Sanctus	4'
V. Agnus Dei	3'

Boosey

Monumentum pro Gesualdo di Venosa ad CD annum <1960>   7'

0 2 0 2 — 4 2 3 0 — str[no db]

"Recompositions" of three madrigals by Carlo Gesualdo (ca. 1561-1613).

I. "A sciugate i begli occhi"	2'
II. "Ma tu, cagion di quella"	2'
III. "Beltà poi chet'assenti"	3'

Boosey

Movements for Piano and Orchestra <1958–1959>   10'

2[1.2/pic] 2[1.Eh] 2[1.bcl] 1 — 0 2 3 0 — hp — cel — str

I. eighth-note = 110; Meno mosso, eighth-note = 72	3'
II. quarter-note = 52	2'
III. eighth-note = 72	1'
IV. eighth-note = 80	2'
V. eighth-note = 104	2'

Boosey

Les Noces [definitive version] (Svadebka; The Wedding) <1914–1917; rev 1921-1923>   24'

solos: S Ms T B   chorus SSAATTBB

tmp+6 — 4pf — [no str]

perc: xyl, tri, tambn, sus cym, cym, td, field dr, bd, 2sd, chime (B4), crot[C#5,B5]

Originally (1917) for voices and large instrumental ensemble. This 2005 Chester critical edition (Ed. Margarita Mazo & Millan Sachania) is the edition of choice. *Earlier Chester editions, and reprints thereof by Kalmus and Luck's, should not be considered.*

   The text in this edition is in Russian (Cyrillic alphabet), Russian transliteration (Latin alphabet), and French translation. A separate printing of this Chester edition has text in German and English. Scores may be seen at: http://www.musicsalesclassical.com/OnDemand

PART I	
At the Bride's House	5'
At the Bridegroom's House	6'
The Bride's Departure	3'
PART II	
The Wedding Feast	10'

Chester

Les Noces [1919 draft] (Svadebka; The Wedding) <1914–1917>   24'

solos S Ms T B   chorus SSAATTBB

2perc — harmonium, 2 cimbaloms, pianola — [no str]

perc: bd, tambn, cym, crot, chimes, 3sd, 2sus cym, 2tri

Ed. Millan Sachania; missing passages in Tableaux I & II filled in by Colin Matthews; orchestration and realization of Tableaux III & IV by Theo Verbey. This is a completion of an early version of this seminal work. For the composer's definitive version, see the previous entry.

   Text in Russian (Cyrillic alphabet), Russian transliteration (to the Latin alphabet), and French translation.

Première Partie	
Premier tableau (Chez la mariée)	5'
Deuxième tableau (Chez la mariè)	6'
Troisième tableau (Le départ de la mariée)	3'
Deuxième Partie	
Quatrième tableau (Le repas de noces)	10'

Chester

Les Noces [orchd Steven Stucky] (Svadebka; The Wedding) <1914–1917; rev 1921-1923>   24'

solos S Ms T B   chorus SSAATTBB

3[1.2.pic] 3[1.2.Eh] 4[1.2.Ebcl.bcl] 3[1.2.cbn] — 4 3[1/pic tp.2.3] 3 1 — tmp+6 — 2hp — str

perc: xyl, tri, tambn, sus cym, cym, bd, chimes, crot, 4sd

Instrumental parts arranged for full orchestra by Steven Stucky, 2005.

   Text in Russian (Cyrillic alphabet) with transliteration to the Latin alphabet.

PART I	
Scene 1: At the Bride's House	5'
Scene 2: At the Bridegroom's House	6'
Scene 3: The Bride's Departure	3'
PART II	
Scene 4: The Wedding Feast	10'

Chester

Octet <1922–1923; rev 1952>   14'

1 0 1 2 — 0 2 2 0 — [no str]

I. Sinfonia	4'
II. Tema con variazioni	7'
III. Finale	3'

Boosey

Ode (Triptychon for Orchestra) <1943>   11'

3[incl pic] 2 2 2 — 4 2 0 0 — tmp — str

1. Eulogy	4'
2. Eclogue	3'
3. Epitaph	4'

Schott

Oedipus rex <1926–1927; rev 1948>   51'

male chorus   solos ATTBB   speaker
3[1.2.3/pic] 3[1.2.Eh] 3[1.2.3/Ebcl] 3[1.2.cbn] — 4 4 3 1 — tmp+2
— hp — pf — str
perc: bd, cym, field dr, tambn
The narration is to be given in the vernacular of the audience; the sung
text is to be enunciated in classical Latin (not church Latin).
Act I   24'
Act II   27'

Boosey	Ed. Russe	

L'oiseau de feu

see his: Firebird

Orpheus <1947>   30'

3[1.2.pic] 2[1.2/Eh] 2 2 — 4 2 2 0 — tmp — hp — str
1. Orpheus   3'
2. Air de danse   3'
3. Dance of the Angel of Death   2'
4. Interlude   2'
5. Pas des Furies   3'
6. Air de danse—Interlude—Air de danse   4'
7. Pas d'action   2'
8. Pas de deux   5'
9. Interlude   1'
10. Pas d'action   2'
11. Orpheus' Apotheosis   3'

Boosey	

Pas de deux, from Tchaikovsky's "Sleeping Beauty"   6'

1 1 2 1 — 1 2 2 0 — tmp — pf — str[min 5vn, 4va, 3vc, 2db]
Bluebird Pas-de-deux from Tchaikovsky's *Sleeping Beauty* (Act 3,
nos.10-13), arr. by Stravinsky for small orchestra, 1941. Unaccountably
published under the name of the arranger, rather than that of the
composer.

Schott	

Pastorale <1907; rev 1923>   3'

solo violin
0 2[ob.Eh] 1 1 — 0 0 0 0 — str
Originally for textless soprano & piano; arr. and lengthened by the
composer (1923 & 1933) for solo violin, oboe, English horn, clarinet &
bassoon. Strings added by Leopold Stokowski.

Presser	

Perséphone <1933–1934; rev 1948>   51'

chorus, children's chorus   solo tenor   female narrator
3[1.2.3/pic] 3[1.2.3/Eh] 3[1.2.3/bcl] 3[1.2.3/cbn] — 4 3 3 1 — tmp+1
— 2hp — pf — str
perc: xyl, bd, sd
1. Persephone Abducted   10'
2. Persephone in the Underworld   25'
3. Persephone Restored   16'

Boosey	

Petrushka (original version, 1911) <1910–1911>   34'

4[1.2.3/pic.4/pic] 4[1.2.3.4/Eh] 4[1.2.3.4/bcl] 4[1.2.3.4/cbn] — 4 4[2tp,
2crt] 3 1 — tmp+4 — 2hp — pf, cel 4-hands — str
perc: glock, field dr, tambn, xyl, tamtam, cym, bd, tri, tambn prov
Alternative concert-ending reduces duration by about 3 minutes.
   A critical edition of this version with historical and analytical essays is
available from Norton (score published; no parts).
1. The Shrove-Tide Fair   10'
2. Petrouchka's Cell   4'
3. The Moor's Cell   7'
4. The Shrove-Tide Fair (Towards Evening)   13'

Boosey	Ed. Russe	Kalmus

Petrushka (1947 version) <1910–1911; rev 1946-47>   34'

3[1.2.3/pic] 3[1.2.Eh] 3[1.2.3/bcl] 3[1.2.cbn] — 4 3 3 1 — tmp+3 —
hp — cel, pf — str
perc: tri, xyl, cym, tamtam, tambn, bd/cym, sus cym, 3sd
Alternative concert-ending reduces duration by about 3 minutes.
1. The Shrove-Tide Fair   10'
2. Petrouchka's Cell   4'
3. The Moor's Cell   7'
4. The Shrove-Tide Fair (Towards Evening)   13'

Boosey	

Pribaoutki (Chansons plaisantes; Nonsense Rhymes)   6'
<1914>

male voice (medium)
1 1[1/Eh] 1 1 — vn, va, vc, db
1. Kornilo (L'Oncle Armand)   1'
2. Natáshka (Little Natalie)   1'
3. Polkóvnik (The Colonel)   1'
4. Stárets i zayats (The Old Man and the Hare; Le vieux et le lièvre)   3'

Chester	Kalmus	Luck's

Pulcinella <1919–1920; rev 1948>   40'

solo soprano, tenor, bass   solo str 5t [2vn, va, vc, db]
2[1.2/pic] 2 0 2 — 2 1 1 0 — str[4.4.4.3.3]
A ballet with song.
1. Ouverture: Allegro moderato (Gallo: Trio Sonata I, 1st mvt)   2'
2. Serenata: Larghetto (Pergolesi: Il Flaminio. Act I. Polidoro)   3'
3. Scherzino (Gallo: Trio Sonata II, 1st mvt)   2'
4. Allegro (Gallo: Trio Sonata II, 3rd mvt)   1'
5. Andantino (Gallo: Trio Sonata VIII, 1st mvt)   2'
6. Allegro (Pergolesi: Lo frate 'nnamorato. Act I. Vanella)   2'
7. Ancora poco meno (Pergolesi: Cantata: Luce degli occhi miei)   2'
8. Allegro assai (Gallo: Trio Sonata III, 3rd mvt)   2'
9. Allegro (Pergolesi: Il Flaminio. Act I. Bastiano)   2'
10. Allegro (Pergolesi: Lo frate 'nnamorato. Act III. Ascanio, Vanella)   3'
11. Allegro (Pergolesi: Lo frate 'nnamorato. Act II. Soprano)   1'
12. Presto (Pergolesi: Lo frate 'nnamorato. Act II.)   1'
13. Largo (Pergolesi: Lo frate 'nnamorato. Act II)   1'
14. Allegro alla breve (Gallo: Trio Sonata VII, 3rd mvt)   1'
15. Tarantella: Allegro moderato (Wassenaer / Chelleri)   1'
16. Andantino (Parisotti: Canzona)   3'
17. Allegro (Monza: Harpsichord Suite No. 1)   1'
18. Gavotta: Allegro moderato (Monza: Harpsichord Suite No. 3)   4'
19. Vivo (Pergolesi: Sinfonia for cello and basso)   2'
20. Tempo di minué (Pergolesi: Lo frate 'nnamorato. Act I. Don Pietro)   2'
21. Allegro assai (Gallo: Trio Sonata XII, 3rd mvt)   2'

Boosey	

Pulcinella: Suite <1919–1920; rev 1949>   24'

solo string 5t [2vn, va, vc, db]
2[1.2/pic] 2 0 2 — 2 1 1 0 — str[4.4.4.3.3]
1. Sinfonia   2'
2. Serenata   3'
3. Scherzino   5'
4. Tarantella   2'
5. Toccata   1'
6. Gavotta con due variazioni   5'
7. Vivo   2'
8. Minuetto   2'
9. Finale   2'

Boosey	

Ragtime <1917–1918>   4'

1 0 1 0 — 1 1[crt] 1 0 — cimbalom — 1perc — 2vn, va, db
perc: bd, sus cym, 2sd, 3tomtoms

Chester	Kalmus	Luck's

Renard <1915–1916>   *17'*

solos: 2 tenors, 2 basses
1[1/pic] 1[1/Eh] 1[1/Ebcl] 1 — 2 1 0 0 — cimbalom — tmp+3 — str
5t
perc: tri, sd, cym, bd/cym, tambn, tambn w/o jingles
Full title: *Fable of the Fox, the Cock, the Tomcat and the Ram / Reynard (Bayka pro lisu, petukha, kota da barana / Renard).*

> For staging: clowns, dancers and acrobats, who mime the action; the singers sit in the small orchestra.

> A part for piano (as substitute for the cimbalom) is available with the Chester rental parts; it is of uncertain provenance. It replaces the cimbalom, but the music is retouched to be more pianistic.

Chester	Kalmus

Requiem canticles <1965–1966>   *14'*

chorus   alto & bass solos
4[1.2.3/pic.afl] 0 0 2 — 4 2 3 0 — 2tmp/perc — hp — cel, pf — str
perc: xyl, vib, chimes [all played by the 2 timpanists]
Cel in last mvt only.

I. Prelude	*1'*
II. Exaudi	*2'*
III. Dies Irae	*1'*
IV. Tuba mirum	*1'*
V. Interlude	*3'*
VI. Rex tremendae	*1'*
VII. Lacrimosa	*2'*
VIII. Libera me	*1'*
IX. Postlude	*2'*

Boosey

THE RITE OF SPRING (Vesna svyashchennaya; Le sacre du printemps): Chronology

> An attempt to clarify the confused publication history of this work:
> 1913: first performance
> 1921: first published edition (Éd. Russe de Musique)
> 1929: corrected edition (Éd. Russe de Musique)
> 1943: revision of the *Sacrificial Dance* (Boosey; see entry)
> 1947: "revised version" (Boosey; actually just corrections)
> 1965: more corrections (Boosey)
> 1967: re-engraved (Boosey)
> 2000: Corrected edition (Kalmus; ed. Clinton F. Nieweg)

N.B.: The Dover full score dated 1989 is a reprint of a Muzyka engraving of 1965; it has many errors, and no set of parts fully agrees with it.

The Rite of Spring (Vesna svyashchennaya; Le sacre du printemps) <1911–1913>   *33'*

5[1.2.3/pic2.pic1.afl] 5[1.2.3.4/Eh2.Eh1] 5[1.2.3/bcl2.Ebcl.bcl1]
5[1.2.3.4/cbn2.cbn1] — 8[7-8/Wag tb] 5[pic tp.1.2.3.4/btp] 3 2 —
2tmp+4 — str
perc: bd, tamtam, tri, tambn, guiro, cym, crot[G#7,A#7]
In the Clinton F. Nieweg edition (Kalmus) there is an alternative part for the bass trumpet (tenor clef, concert pitch), in the event it is to be covered by an extra trombonist, as is often the case.

> The proper transposition of the tenor tuba parts has caused confusion; they should almost certainly be transposed like horns in B-flat alto, sounding a major 2nd below written pitch.

> The piccolo clarinet part is in D and E-flat.

PART I: Adoration of the Earth	
Introduction	*3'*
The Augurs of Spring—Dances of the Young Girls	*4'*
Ritual of Abduction	*1'*
Spring Rounds	*4'*
Ritual of the Rival Tribes	*2'*
Procession of the Sage	*1'*
The Sage	*1'*
Dance of the Earth	*1'*
PART II: The Sacrifice	
Introduction	*4'*
Mystic Circle of the Young Girls	*3'*
Glorification of the Chosen One	*1'*
Evocation of the Ancestors	*1'*
Ritual Action of the Ancestors	*3'*
Sacrificial Dance (The Chosen One)	*4'*

Boosey	Kalmus

The Rite of Spring [McPhee reduction] (Vesna svyashchennaya; Le sacre du printemps) <1911–1913>   *33'*

3[1.2/afl.3/pic] 3[1.2.Eh] 3[1/Ebcl.2.3/bcl] 3[1.2.3/cbn] — 4 3[1.2.3]
3[1/btp.2.3] 1 — tmp+3 — str[min 10.8.6.6.4]
perc: bd, cym, tri, tambn, tamtam, guiro, crot[G#7,A#7], 1perc dbl tmp2
Reduced orchestration by Jonathan McPhee. Originally only for staged performances where there is limited space in the pit; as of 2010 the publisher now allows concert performances of this reduced version, but in the USA only.

> In 2010, Mr. McPhee newly computer-engraved this reduction, even creating a score that matches the pagination of the Boosey original version (1967 engraving); this new material should be available from Boosey.

> For contents and durations, see the original version (preceding entry).

Boosey

The Rite of Spring (Rudolf reduction) (Vesna svyashchennaya; Le sacre du printemps) <1911–1913>   *33'*

3[1.2/afl.3/pic] 3[1.2.Eh] 3[1.2.3/bcl] 3[1.2.3/cbn] — 4 3 3 1 —
tmp+2 — str
perc: bd, tamtam, tri, tambn, guiro, cym, sus cym, crot[or glock]
Orchestra reduction by Robert Rudolf (available in the US only), allegedly with the sanction of the composer. However, certain changes in metrical notation are introduced, intended to simplify performance, but with the possible effect of distorting the composer's intentions.

> For contents and durations, see the original version (above).

EMI

The Rite of Spring (Vesna svyashchennaya; Le sacre du printemps): Sacrificial Dance (Danse sacrale) <1911–1913; rev 1943>   9'

5[1.2.3/pic.pic.afl] 5[1.2.3.4.Eh] 5[1.2.3.Ebcl.bcl] 5[1.2.3.4.cbn] — 8 5[1.2.3.4.btp] 3 2 — tmp+1 — str
perc: bd, tamtam
This 1943 revision of the final portion of the ballet, originally published by *AMP*, was intended to be more readily playable than the original because of rescoring, rebarring, enharmonic spelling, and larger metric units. However, in his 1947 and 1965 revisions, the composer did not make use of the 1943 version. It may be assumed that this publication, interesting as it is, is *not* Stravinsky's final word on the subject.

Boosey		

Le roi des étoiles (King of the Stars; Zvezdolikiy) <1911–1912>   6'

male chorus
4[1.2.3/pic2.pic1] 4[1.2.3/Eh.4] 4[1.2.3.Ebcl] 4[1.2.3.cbn] — 8 3 3 1 — tmp+2 — 2hp — cel — str
perc: bd, tamtam
Kalmus ed. Robert Malcolm.

Forberg	Kalmus

Scènes de ballet <1944>   18'

2[1.2/pic] 2 2 1 — 2 3 3 1 — tmp — pf — str
I. Introduction	1'
II. Danses	4'
III. Variation	1'
IV. Pantomime	2'
V. Pas de deux	3'
VI. Pantomime	1'
VII. Variation	1'
VIII. Variation	1'
IX. Pantomime	1'
X. Danses	1'
XI. Apothéose	2'

AMP

Scherzo à la russe (symphonic version) <1943–1944; rev Symphonic version: 1945>   5'

3[1.2.pic] 2 2 2 — 4 3 3 1 — tmp+4 — hp — pf — str
perc: xyl, tambn, tri, sus cym, bd, 2sd
Originally for jazz band; arr. by the composer.

Boosey	Schott

Scherzo fantastique, op.3 (Fantasticheskoye skertso) <1907–1908>   12'

4[1.2/afl.3/pic2.pic1] 3[1.2.Eh] 4[1.2.3/Ebcl.bcl] 3[1.2.cbn] — 4 3[1.2.atp] 0 0 — 1perc — 3hp[or2] — cel — str
perc: sus cym
It is said that the composer reduced the 3 hp parts to 2 in 1930 for the republication of this work by Schott; however, the reduction apparently was applied to the parts only, and not to the 1931 Schott score.

Kalmus	Luck's	Schott

Septet <1952–1953>   11'

0 0 1 1 — 1 0 0 0 — pf — vn, va, vc
I. [untitled]	3'
II. Passacaglia	5'
III. Gigue	3'

Boosey

A Sermon, a Narrative, and a Prayer <1960–1961>   17'

chorus   alto & tenor solos   speaker
2[1.afl] 2 2[1.bcl] 2 — 4 3 3 1 — 2perc — hp — pf — str
perc: 3tamtams

Boosey

Song of the Nightingale (Pesnya solov'ya; Le chant du rossignol) <1917>   21'

2[1.2/pic] 2[1.2/Eh] 2[1.Ebcl] 2 — 4 3 3 1 — tmp+4 — 2hp — cel, pf — str
perc: cym, tamtam, tri, sd, tambn, field dr, bd/cym
A "symphonic poem/ballet" arr. by the composer from Acts 2-3 of his 1914 opera *The Nightingale (Solovey; Le rossignol)*.
1. Presto	2'
2. Chinese March	3'
3. Song of the Nightingale	4'
4. The Mechanical Nightingale (Jeu du rossignol mécanique)	12'

Boosey	Ed. Russe	Kalmus	Luck's

Song of the Volga Boatmen <1917>   1'

2[1.pic] 2 2 3 — 4 3 3 1 — tmp+2 — [no str]
perc: bd, tamtam
Composed on a folktune, just after the Russian revolution, when Diaghilev needed a substitute for the Russian National Anthem.

Chester	Kalmus	Luck's

The Star Spangled Banner <1941>   1'

chorus
3 3[1.2.Eh] 3 3[1.2.opt cbn] — 4 3 3 1 — tmp — str
Stravinsky's harmonization and orchestration of the US national anthem (music attr. John Stafford Smith)—controversial in 1941, but seeming rather innocuous now.
    Available from G.Schirmer in the US.

Mercury

Suite No.1 for Small Orchestra <1917; rev (orchd) 1925>   6'

2[1.2/pic] 1 2 2 — 1 1 1 1 — 1perc — str
perc: bd
Originally for piano 4-hands; arr. by the composer.
1. Andante	2'
2. Napolitana	2'
3. Española	1'
4. Balalaika	1'

Chester	Kalmus

Suite No.2 for Small Orchestra <1914–1917; rev (orchd) 1921>   7'

2[1.2/pic] 1 2 2 — 1 2 1 1 — 3perc — pf — str
perc: sd, cym, bd
Originally for piano 4-hands; arr. by the composer.
1. Marche	1'
2. Valse	2'
3. Polka	2'
4. Galop	2'

Chester	Kalmus

Symphonies of Wind Instruments [1920 version] (Symphonies d'instruments à vent) <1920>   12'

4[1.2.3.afl] 3[1.2.Eh] 3[1.2.alto cl in F] 3[1.2.3/cbn] — 4 3 3 1 — [no str]
Boosey edition corrected and revised by Robert Craft, 2001.

Boosey	Luck's

Symphonies of Wind Instruments [1947 revision] (Symphonies d'instruments à vent) <1920; rev 1947>   12'

3 3[1.2.Eh] 3 3[1.2.3/cbn] — 4 3 3 1 — [no str]

Boosey

Symphony No.1, op.1 E-flat major <1905–1907>   34'

3[1.2.3/pic] 2 3 2 — 4 3 3 1 — tmp+3 — str
perc: tri, cym, bd
I. Allegro moderato   *10'*
II. Scherzo   *6'*
III. Largo   *10'*
IV. Finale   *8'*

Forberg	Kalmus

Symphony in C <1938–1940>   28'

3[1.2.pic] 2 2 2 — 4 2 3 1 — tmp — str
I. Moderato alla breve   *10'*
II. Larghetto concertante   *6'*
III. Allegretto   *5'*
IV. Largo - Tempo giusto   *7'*

Schott

Symphony in Three Movements <1942–1945>   22'

3[1.2.pic] 2 3[1.2.3/bcl] 3[1.2.cbn] — 4 3 3 1 — tmp+1 — hp — pf
— str
perc: bd
I. Allegro   *10'*
II. Andante - Interlude   *6'*
III. Con moto   *6'*

Schott

Symphony of Psalms (Symphonie de psaumes) <1930; rev 1948>   21'

chorus
5[1.2.3.4.5/pic] 5[1.2.3.4.Eh] 0 4[1.2.3.cbn] — 4 5 3 1 — tmp+1 —
hp — 2pf — str[no vn or va]
perc: bd
Chorus should contain children's voices; female voices (soprano & alto)
may be substituted if necessary.
I. Psalm 38: 13-14 [King James Ps.39: 12-13]   *3'*
II. Psalm 39: 2-4 [King James Ps.40:1-3]   *6'*
III. Psalm 150 [King James Ps.150]   *12'*

Boosey	Ed. Russe

Tango (1941 version for large orchestra) <1940>   3'

3 2 3[incl bcl] 2 — 2 3 3 1 — 3sx[2asx, tsx] — gtr — 1perc — pf —
str
perc: cym, sd, bell
Originally for piano (1940); orchestrated by Felix Guenther (1941).
Available from G.Schirmer in the US; Schott handles the work for
Germany, Austria and Britain.

Mercury	Schott

Tango (1953 version for small orchestra) <1940; rev (orchd) 1953>   3'

0 0 5[1.2.3.4.bcl] 0 — 0 4 3 0 — gtr — str[3.0.1.1.1]
Originally for piano (1940); orchestrated 1953 by the composer.
Available from G.Schirmer in the US; Schott handles the work for
Germany, Austria and Britain.

Mercury	Schott

Threni: id est Lamentationes Jeremiae Prophetae <1957–1958; rev 1962>   35'

chorus   solos SATTBB
2 3[1.2.Eh] 3[1.2/acl.bcl] 1[sarr] — 4 1[contralto bugle (= flug)] 3 1
— tmp — hp — cel, pf — str
Introduction   *1'*
I. De elegia prima   *7'*
II. De elegia tertia   *16'*
III. De elegia quinta   *3'*

Boosey

Two Songs by Paul Verlaine, op.9 (Deux poèmes de Paul Verlaine) <1910; rev (orchd) 1951-1952>   6'

solo baritone
2 0 2 0 — 2 0 0 0 — str
Originally for baritone & piano; arr. by the composer.
Un grand sommeil noir   *2'*
La lune blanche   *4'*

Boosey

Variations (Aldous Huxley in memoriam) <1963–1964>   6'

3[1.2.afl] 3[1.2.Eh] 3[1.2.bcl] 2 — 4 3 3 0 — hp — pf — str[12vn,
10va, 8vc, 6db]

Boosey

Strong, George Templeton   1856-1948

(b New York, 26 May 1856; d Geneva, 27 June 1948). American

Chorale on a Theme of Leo Hassler (Wenn ich einmal scheiden soll) <1929>   7'

str
Original publisher: Edition Henn.

Fleisher

Stuart-Coolidge, Peggy   1913-1982

see: Coolidge, Peggy Stuart, 1913-1982

Stucky, Steven   1949-

(b Hutchinson, KS, 7 Nov 1949). American

August 4, 1964 <2007–2008>   72'

solo soprano, mezzo-soprano, tenor, baritone   chorus
3[1.2/afl.3/pic] 3[1.2.Eh] 3[1.2.bcl] 3[1.2.cbn] — 4 3 3 1 — tmp+4 —
hp — str
perc: chimes, marim, xyl, vib, bongos, tamtam, sd, woodblk, cym, sus cym,
templeblks, bd, sandblks, 2brake dr, 5tomtom, 2whip
I. The Saddest Moment   *10'*
II. Historians   *7'*
III. Oval Office 1   *3'*
IV. I Wish to Be a Part of that Fight   *5'*
V. The Secret Heart of America   *8'*
VI. Oval Office 2   *3'*
VII. Elegy   *8'*
VIII. Letter from Mississippi   *5'*
IX. Oval Office 3   *5'*
X. August Fourth   *8'*
XI. Had We Known   *3'*
XII. What is Precious is Never to Forget   *7'*

Merion

Colburn Variations   12'

str

Merion

Concerto for Orchestra <1986–1987>   28'

3[incl afl & 2pic] 3[incl Eh] 3[incl bcl] 3[incl cbn] — 4 4 3 1 —
tmp+3 — hp — pf/cel — str
perc: vib, bd, marim, xyl, claves, templeblks, crot, chimes, glock, bongos, whip,
tamtam, 3woodblks, 4tomtoms, logdrum, 3rototoms, 3sus cym, 3gongs, coilspring

Merion

516

Concerto Mediterraneo, for Guitar & Orchestra <1997–1998>   21'

2 2 2 2 — 2 1 1 0 — tmp+2 — hp — str
perc: vib, marim, xyl, chimes, glock, sus cym, tamtam, bongos, sd, bd, 2coil springs
I. Serenata _'
II. Interludio _'
III. Ciaccona _'
IV. Finale _'

    Merion

Concerto, Percussion & Wind Orchestra <2001>   19'

3[1.2.3/pic] 3[1.2.Eh] 5[1.2.3.Ebcl.bcl] 3[1.2.cbn(or cbcl)] — 4 4 3 1 — pf/cel — [no str]
perc: bd, vib, chimes, tamtam, claves, whip
soloist: 5woodblks, 5templeblks, bongos, 6tomtom, 2congas, 2timbales, bd, tenor steeldrum, marim, xyl, glock, tri, 5templebells, 5almglocken, 5gongs, 2agogo, 3cowbells, 2brake dr, anvil, springcoil
I. Energico _'
II. Moderato delicato, quasi senza tempt _'
III. Vivace _'
IV. Grave _'
V. Gioioso _'

    Merion

Dreamwaltzes <1986>   15'

3[incl 2pic] 3[incl Eh] 3[incl bcl] 3[incl cbn] — 4 4 3 1 — tmp+3 — hp — pf/cel — str
perc: vib, tamtam, templeblks, Chinescym, marim, glock, xyl, tambn, chimes, crot, tri, bd, 3woodblks, 3sus cym, 4tomtoms

    Merion

Funeral Music for Queen Mary <1992>   10'

3[1.2.pic] 3[1.2.Eh] 3 3[1.2.cbn] — 4 2 3 1 — tmp+3 — hp — pf — [no str]
perc: bd, tamtam, chimes, glock, vib
Based on *Music for the Funeral of Queen Mary*, by Henry Purcell.
March _'
Anthem _'
Canzona _'
March _'

    Merion

Impromptus <1991>   18'

3[incl pic] 3[incl Eh] 4[incl bcl] 3[incl cbn] — 4 4 3 1 — tmp+3 — hp — pf — str
perc: marim, vib, tamtam, chimes, glock, Chinescym, bd, 3sus cym, 4tomtoms, gong[G#3], crot[C#5]

    Merion

Jeu de timbres <2003>   4'

3[1.2.pic] 3 3 3[1.2.cbn] — 4 3 3 1 — 2perc — 2hp — pf — str
perc: bd, cym, tambn, tamtam, glock, xyl, chimes, 3sus cym, 3tomtoms

    Merion

Pinturas de Tamayo (Paintings of Tamayo) <1995>   20'

3[1.2/pic2.3/pic2] 3[1.2.3/Eh] 3[1.2/Ebcl.3/bcl] 3[1.2.3/cbn] — 4 3[1/pic tp.2.3] 3 1 — 3perc — hp — pf/cel — str
perc: bd, Chinescym, tamtam, glock, xyl, marim, chimes, vib, marac, claves, tambn, 2tri, 2sus cym, 2woodblks
1. Amigas de los pájaros (Friends of the Birds) 3'
2. Anochecer (Sunset) 4'
3. Mujeres alcanzando la luna (Women Reaching for the Moon) 3'
4. Músicas dormidas (Sleeping Musicians) 5'
5. La gran galaxia (The Great Galaxy) 5'

    Merion

Second Concerto for Orchestra <2003>   29'

3[1.2/afl.3/pic] 3[1.2.3/Eh] 3[1.2.3/bcl] 3[1.2.3/cbn] — 4 4 3 1 — tmp+4 — hp — pf, cel — str
perc: bd, sd, tri, tambn, tamtam, glock, xyl, marim, vib, chimes, whip, bongos, 2sus cym, 3tomtoms, anvil, 2cowbells, 3woodblks
1. Overture (With Friends) 5'
2. Variations 17'
3. Finale 7'

    Merion

Spirit Voices; Concerto for Percussion <2002–2003>   24'

solo percussion
3[1.2/pic.3/pic/afl] 3[1.2.3/Eh] 3[1.2.3/bcl] 3[1.2.cbn] — 4 3[1/pic tp.2.3] 3 1 — hp — str
perc: [solo] tamtam, glock, marim, vib, chimes, crot, bongos, 5sus cym, bass bow, 3gong, 3woodblk, 4log drum, 5 Peking opera gongs, 3tomtoms, 2agogo bells, 2brake dr, 3cowbells, coilspring
Solo percussionist also does some vocalization.
1. Jiu huang ye (Southeast Asia) 3'
2. Bean nighe (Scotland) 4'
3. Ellyllon (Wales) 2'
4. Te Mangoroa (Maori) 4'
5. Coyote (Navaho & other Native American 3'
6. Tengu (Japan) 2'
7. Wah' Kon-Tah (Native American) 6'

    Merion

Styne, Jule   1905-1994

(b London, 31 Dec 1905; d New York, 20 Sept 1994). American composer of British birth

Gypsy: Overture <1959>   5'

3[1.2.pic] 2 3[1.2.bcl] 2 — 4 3 3 1[opt] — tmp+3 — hp — str
perc: bd, cym, sus cym, glock, xyl, vib, wind whistle
Optional reed books:
Reed 1: asx/cl (replaces cl 1)
Reed 2: tsx/cl (replaces cl 2)
Reed 3: bsx/bcl (replaces bcl)
Ed. Robert Wendel.

    Wendel

Subotnick, Morton   1933-

(b Los Angeles, 14 April 1933). American

Lamination <1965>   12'

3[1.2.pic] 3[1.2.Eh] 3[1.Ebcl.bcl] 2 — 4 2 2 1 — mand — tape — tmp+2 — str

    MCA

Play No.2 <1964>   12'

2 2 3[1.2.bcl] 2 — 3 2 2 0 — tape — tmp+1 — str
Graph notation.

    MCA

Suk, Josef   1874-1935

(b Křečovice, 4 Jan 1874; d Benešov, nr Prague, 29 May 1935). Czech

Meditation on the Old Bohemian Chorale "Saint Wenceslas," op.35 (Meditace na starocesky chorál "Svaty Václave") <1914>   7'

str[or str 4t]
Originally published by Fr. A. Urbánek, Prague, 1914.

    Kalmus   Luck's

Fairy Tale, op.16 (Pohádka; Ein Märchen) <1897–1898;   29'
rev suite: 1899-1900>

3[1.2.pic] 3[1.2.Eh] 3[1.2.bcl] 2 — 4 2 3 1 — tmp+3 — hp — str
perc: tri, tamtam, cym, sus cym, bd
Suite from incidental music to *Radúz and Mahulena*.
     The 3rd woodwind players (pic, Eh, bcl) are used only in the last
movement.
1. Liebe und Leid der Königskinder   10'
2. Intermezzo, Volkstanz   4'
3. Intermezzo, Trauermusik   7'
4. Königin Runas Fluch, Sieg der Liebe   8'

Kalmus	Simrock

Scherzo fantastique, op.25 (Fantastické scherzo) <1903>   14'

3[1.2.pic] 3[1.2.Eh] 3[1.2.bcl] 2 — 4 2 3 1 — tmp+3 — hp — str
perc: cym, tri, tambn

Breitkopf	Luck's

Serenade, op.6, E-flat major <1892>   30'

str
I. Andante con moto   6'
II. Allegro ma non troppo e grazioso   6'
III. Adagio   10'
IV. Allegro giocoso, ma non troppo presto 8'

Kalmus	Luck's	Simrock

Symphony No.1, op.14, E major <1897–1899>   48'

2[1.2/pic] 2 2 2 — 4 2 3 1 — tmp — str
I. Allegro ma non troppo   14'
II. Adagio   12'
III. Allegro vivace   7'
IV. Allegro   15'

Kalmus	Luck's	Simrock

Symphony No.2, op.27, C minor (Asrael) <1905–1906>   58'

3[1.2.pic] 3[1.2.Eh] 3[1.2.bcl] 3[1.2.cbn] — 4 3 3 1 — tmp+2 — hp
— str
perc: bd, cym, sus cym, tri
I. Andante sostenuto   15'
II. Andante   7'
III. Vivace   12'
IV. Adagio   10'
V. Adagio maestoso   14'

Breitkopf	Kalmus

Toward a New Life, op.35c (V novy zivot)   6'

chorus SATB
3[1.2.3/pic] 2 3 2 — 4 3 3 1 — tmp+4 — str
perc: bd, cym, tri, sd
Possible without chorus.

Kalmus

Sullivan, Arthur   1842-1900

(b Lambeth, London, 13 May 1842; d London, 22 Nov 1900). English

Concerto, Violoncello, D major <1866>   17'

2 2 2 2 — 2 2 0 0 — tmp — str
Composed 1866. In 1964, score and parts destroyed in a fire.
Reconstructed in 1986 from surviving solo parts by David Mackie &
Charles Mackerras.
I. Allegro moderato   3'
II. Andante expressivo 7'
III. Molto vivace   7'

Weinberger

The Gondoliers: Overture <1889>   7'

2 1 2 2 — 2 2 3 0 — 1 or2perc — str
perc: tri; in opt ending only: tambn, cast

Kalmus	Luck's

The Grand Duke: Overture <1896>   6'

3[incl pic] 2 2 2 — 4 3 3 1 — tmp+4 — str
Arr. Eugene Minor.

Kalmus	Luck's

H.M.S. Pinafore: Overture <1878>   4'

2[1.2/pic] 1 2 1 — 2 2 2 0 — 2perc — str
perc: cym, bd, tri, tmp
Ed. John Bauser.

Kalmus	Luck's

Iolanthe: Overture <1882>   7'

2[1.2/pic] 1 2 1 — 2 2 2 0 — tmp — str

Kalmus	Luck's

The Merchant of Venice: Masquerade Suite <1871>   23'

solo tenor (opt)
2[incl pic] 2 2 2 — 4 2 3 0 — tmp+4 — str
perc: sd, tri, cym, bd
Introduction   2'
Barcarole (Sérenade)   4'
Introduction et Bourée   4'
Danse grotesque   2'
A la Valse   5'
Melodrama   2'
Finale   4'

Kalmus	Luck's

The Mikado: Overture <1885>   8'

2[1.2/pic] 1 2 1 — 2 2 2 0 — tmp+1 — str
perc: bd, cym, tri

Kalmus	Luck's

Overture di ballo <1870>   11'

2[1.2/pic] 2 2 3[1.2.opt serp or tuba2] — 4 2 3 1[opt tuba2 or serp] —
tmp+4 — str
perc: bd, cym, sd, tri
Clyde and Novello editions by Roger Harris. Clyde offers both the
original full-length version, and the later abbreviated version of this work.

Clyde	Kalmus	Luck's	Novello

Overture in C (In memoriam) <1866>   13'

2 2 2 2 — 4 2 3 1[oph] — tmp+2 — org — str

Kalmus	Luck's	Novello

Patience: Overture <1881>   6'

2 1 2 1 — 2 2 2 0 — tmp — str

Kalmus	Luck's

Pineapple Poll: Suite <1860–1900>   18'

2[1/pic.2/pic] 2[1.2/Eh] 2 2[bn2 opt] — 4 2 3 1[opt] — tmp+4 — hp
— str
perc: bd, cast, cym, glock, sd, tamtam, tambn, tri, xyl
Ballet. Music arranged by Charles Mackerras, using excerpts from Gilbert
and Sullivan operettas.

I. Opening Number	4'
II. Poll's Dance	1'
III. Captain Belaye's Dance	2'
IV. Pas de trois	2'
V. Jasper's Dance	2'
VI. Belaye's Hornpipe	2'
VII. Reconciliation of Poll and Jasper	2'
VIII. Finale	3'

Chappell		

The Pirates of Penzance: Overture <1879>   8'

2[1.2/pic] 1 2 1 — 2 2 2 0 — tmp+2 — str
perc: bd, cym, sd, tri

Kalmus	Luck's

The Tempest: Three Dances <1861; rev 1862>   11'

2 2 2 2 — 2 2 3 0 — tmp+2 — str

Masque	2'
Banquet Dance	2'
Dance of Nymphs and Reapers	7'

Kalmus	Novello

The Yeomen of the Guard: Overture <1888>   5'

2 1 2 1 — 2 2 3 0 — tmp — str

Kalmus	Luck's

Suolahti, Heikki   1920-1936

(b Helsinki, 2 Feb 1920; d Helsinki, 27 Dec 1936). Finnish

Sinfonia piccola <1935>   25'

2[1.2/pic] 2[1.2/Eh] 2 2 — 4 3 3 1 — tmp+2 — hp — str
perc: cym, bd, sd
Ed. Thor Johnson.

I. Andante ma non troppo; Allegro moderato	_'
II. Andante	_'
III. Scherzo	_'
IV. Finale: Andante	_'

Boosey	

Suppé, Franz von   1819-1895

(b Spalato, Dalmatia [now Split, Croatia] 18 April 1819; d Vienna, 21 May 1895).
Austrian composer of Belgian descent

Banditenstreiche (Jolly Robbers): Overture <1867>   8'

2[1.pic] 2 2 2 — 4 2 3 0 — gtr — tmp+2 — str
perc: bd, sd, tri
Kalmus ed. Clark McAlister.

Alkor	Kalmus	Luck's

Beautiful Galathea

see his: Schöne Galathée

Boccaccio: Overture <1879>   7'

2[1.pic] 2 2 2 — 4 2 3 0 — tmp+3 — str
perc: sd, cym, bd

Bärenreiter	Kalmus	Luck's

Dichter und Bauer (Poet and Peasant): Overture <1846>   10'

2[1.2/pic] 2 2 2 — 4 2 3 1[oph] — tmp+3 — hp — str
perc: sd, tri, cym, bd
Luck's includes a snare drum part not reflected in the score. Kalmus ed.
Clark McAlister.

Kalmus	Luck's

Fatinitza: Overture <1876>   7'

2[1.2/pic] 2 2 2 — 4 2 3 0 — tmp+2 — str
perc: bd, cym, tri, tambn

Kalmus	Luck's

Jolly Robbers

see his: Banditenstreiche

Leichte Kavallerie (Light Cavalry): Overture <1866>   8'

2[1.pic] 2 2 2 — 4 2 3 0 — 3perc — str
perc: sd, bd, cym
Version available from Luck's includes a timpani part added by an
unknown arranger.

Kalmus	Luck's

Ein Morgen, Mittag und Abend in Wien (Morning, Noon   8'
and Night in Vienna): Overture

2[1.2/pic] 2 2 2 — 4 2 3 0 — tmp+2 — str
perc: bd, sd, cym
Kalmus ed. Clark McAlister.

Kalmus	Luck's

Pique Dame (Die Kartenschlägerin; Queen of Spades):   8'
Overture <1862>

2[1.2/pic] 2 2 2 — 4 2 3 1 — tmp+4 — str
perc: bd, sd, tri, tamtam

Kalmus	Luck's

Poet and Peasant

see his: Dichter und Bauer

Die schöne Galathée (The Beautiful Galathea): Overture   7'
<1865>

2[1.pic] 2 2 — 4 2 3 0 — tmp+2 — str
perc: bd, sd, tri, cym
Kalmus ed. Clark McAlister.

Bärenreiter	Kalmus	Luck's	Simrock

Tantalusqualen: Overture <1868>   6'

2[1.pic] 2 2 — 4 2 3 0 — tmp+3 — str
perc: bd, sd, tri

Kalmus	Luck's

Surinach, Carlos   1915-1997

(b Barcelona, 4 March 1915; d New Haven, CT, 12 Nov 1997). American composer
of Catalan origin

Apasionada <1960>   35'

1[fl/pic] 1[ob/Eh] 1[cl/bcl] 1 — 1 1 1 0 — 2perc — pf — db
perc: sd, tri, td, bd, xyl, glock, sus cym, 2cym[2 pairs], 4tmp

AMP	

Concertino for Piano, Strings & Cymbals <1956>   18'

1perc — str
perc: crot, 4sus cym
I. Chacona   6'
II. Andante   6'
III. Vivace   6'

AMP

Concerto for String Orchestra <1978>   27'

str
A transcription by the composer of his String Quartet.
1. Allegro   8'
2. Larghetto   9'
3. Allegro frenetico 10'

AMP

Drama jondo <1965>   8'

3[1/pic.2.3] 3[1.2.3/Eh] 3[1.2.3/bcl] 2 — 4 3 3 1 — tmp+3 — hp —
str

AMP

Embattled Garden <1957>   21'

1[fl/pic] 1[ob/Eh] 1 1 — 1 1 1 0 — tmp/perc — hp — str
perc: bd, cym, xyl

AMP

Fandango <1954>   8'

3[1.2/pic.3/pic] 3[1.2/Eh.Eh] 3[1.2.bcl] 2 — 4 3 3 1 — tmp+2 — hp
— str

AMP

Feria magica <1956>   6'

2[1/pic.2/pic] 2 2 2 — 4 2 3 1 — tmp+2 — hp — str

AMP

Ritmo jondo; Flamenco for Orchestra <1953>   17'

1[fl/pic] 1[ob/Eh] 1 1 — 1 1 1 0 — 3 hand clappers — 2perc —
str[min 2.2.2.2.1; max 5.4.4.3.2]
perc: tmp, xyl, bd, tamtam, sd, ratch
This ballet is an extended version of the original set of 3 mvts (*Bulerias,
Saeta, Garrotín*) written in 1952 for cl, tp, xyl, td, tmp, & 3 hand
clappers.
I. Tres jaleos   2'
II. Danza chica   3'
III. Bulerias   2'
IV. Rituales   2'
V. Saeta   3'
VI. Danza grande   3'
VII. Garrotín   2'

AMP

Sinfonia chica (Small Symphony) <1957>   14'

2[1/pic.2/pic] 2 2 2 — 2 1 0 0 — tmp/perc — str
perc: cym, tri, xyl, cast
I. Allegro   4'
II. Adagio   6'
III. Frenetico 4'

AMP

Svendsen, Johan   1840-1911

(b Christiania [now Oslo], 30 Sept 1840; d Copenhagen, 14 June 1911). Norwegian

Andante funèbre <1894>   9'

2 2 2 2 — 4 2 3 1 — tmp — str

Hansen	Kalmus

Norwegian Rhapsody No.3, op.21 (Rapsodie   9'
norvégienne) <1876>

2 2 2 2 — 4 2 3 0 — tmp — str

Hansen	Luck's

Romance, op.26 <1881>   8'

solo violin
1 1 2 2 — 2 0 0 0 — tmp — str

Hansen	Kalmus	Peters

Romeo and Juliet, op.18 (Romeo og Julie) <1876>   14'

2 2 2 2 — 4 2 3 1 — tmp — str

Breitkopf	Kalmus

Two Icelandic Melodies, op.30 <1874>   7'

str
I. Maestoso   3'
II. Moderato   4'

Kalmus	Luck's

Two Swedish Folk Melodies, op.27   7'

str
I. Allt under Himmelens Fäste   4'
II. Du gamla, du friska, du fjellhöga Nord   3'

Hansen	Kalmus	Luck's

Svoboda, Tomás   1939-

(b Paris, 6 Dec 1939). American composer of Czech descent

Child's Dream, op.66   11'

children's choir
3[incl pic] 2 2 2 — 4 3 3 0 — tmp+3 — cel, pf — str

Stangland

Concerto for Chamber Orchestra, op.125 <1986>   23'

1 1 1 1 — solo soprano (textless) — 1perc — hp — str
Soprano voice in 3rd mvt only, treated more like another instrument than
a solo voice.

Stangland

Concerto, Marimba, op.148 <1994>   26'

3[incl pic] 2 3[incl bcl] 2 — 4 3 3 1 — tmp+1 — hp — cel, pf — str
1. Con moto   9'
2. Adagio   8'
3. Vivace   9'

Stangland

Concerto, Piano, No.1, op.71 <1974>   18'

1 1 1 1 — 1 1 0 0 — tmp — str

Stangland

Concerto, Piano, No.2, op.134 <1989>   45'

3[incl pic] 2 3[incl bcl] 2 — 4 3 3 1 — tmp+4 — str

Stangland

Concerto, Violin, op.77 <1975>   19'

2 2 2 2 — 2 2 3 0 — tmp — str

Stangland

Dance Suite, op.128 <1987>   23'

3[incl pic] 2 2 2 — 4 2 3 1 — tmp+2 — str

Stangland

Ex libris, op.113 <1983>   8'

3[1.2.pic] 2 3[1.2.bcl] 3[1.2.cbn] — 4 3 4 1 — tmp+4 — str
perc: sus cym, bd, td, cym, tamtam, chimes

Stangland

Festive Overture, op.103 <1982>   9'

3[incl pic] 2 3[incl bcl] 2 — 4 4 4 1 — tmp+5 — str

Stangland

Journey, op.127 <1987>   24'

solo mezzo-soprano & baritone   chorus
2 2 2 2 — 4 3 3 1 — 2asx — tmp+6 — str

Stangland

Meditation, op.143 <1993>   6'

solo oboe
str[or str 5t]

Stangland

Nocturne, op.100 (Cosmic Sunset) <1981>   20'

2 2 2 2 — 2[hn3-4 opt] 2 3[opt] 0 — opt gtr — tmp+2 — hp — pf —
str
Trombones and guitar are optional. Horns may be doubled.

Stangland

Overture of the Season, op.89 <1978>   8'

3[1.2.pic] 2 2 2 — 4 3 3 1 — tmp+2 — str
perc: chimes, 2sus cym

Stangland

Serenade, op.115 <1984>   7'

3[incl pic] 2 2 2 — 4 3 3 1 — tmp+1 — str

Stangland

Sinfoniette (à la renaissance), op.60 <1972>   20'

3[incl pic] 2 2 2 — 4 3 3 1 — tmp+3 — str

Stangland

Swing Dance, op.135a <1992>   6'

3[1.2.pic] 2 2 2 — 4 3 3 1 — asx — tmp+2 — str
perc: cym, bd

Stangland

Symphony No.1, op.20 (Of Nature) <1956; rev 1985>   35'

3[incl pic] 2 3[incl bcl] 2 — 4 3 4 1 — tmp+3 — pf — str

Moderato	10'
Presto	8'
Andante	7'
Allegro; Moderato	10'

Stangland

Symphony No.2, op.41 <1964>   28'

3[incl pic, afl] 2 3[incl bcl] 2 — 4 3 4 1 — tmp+3 — pf — str

Stangland

Symphony No.3, op.43, for Organ & Orchestra <1965>   28'

solo organ; solo string quintet: 2vn, 2va, vc
3[incl pic] 2 5[incl Ebcl, bcl, cbcl] 2 — 4 3 4 1 — asx — tmp+7 — pf
— str[18.16.14.12.8]

Stangland

Symphony No.4, op.69 (Apocalyptic) <1975>   27'

3[incl pic] 2 4[incl bcl, cbcl] 2 — 4 3 4 1 — asx — tmp+7 — hp —
cel — str

Stangland

Symphony No.5, op.92 (In Unison) <1978>   33'

4[incl pic, afl] 3[incl Eh] 4[incl Ebcl, bcl] 2 — 4 3 3 1 — tmp+5 —
hp — pf — str

Stangland

Symphony No.6, op.137, for Clarinet & Orchestra   38'
<1991>

solo clarinet
3[1.2.pic] 2 1 2 — 4 3 3 1 — tmp+2 — str
1. *Lento moderato; Più allegro*
2. *Poco allegro; Allegro comodo; Vivace; Vivacissimo; Presto*
3. *Con moto*

Stangland

Three Cadenzas for Piano & Orchestra, op.135 <1990>   31'

3[incl pic] 2 2 2 — 4 2 3 0 — asx — tmp+3 — str

Stangland

Three Pieces for Orchestra, op.45 <1966>   10'

3[incl pic] 2 2 2 — 4 2 3 1 — tmp+3 — str

Stangland

Swanson, Howard   1907 - 1978

(b Atlanta, GA, 18 Aug 1907; d New York, 12 Nov 1978). American

Concerto for Orchestra <1954>   20'

2 2 2 2 — 2 2 3 1 — tmp+2 — str

Weintraub

Fantasy Piece   19'

solo soprano saxophone or clarinet
str

Weintraub

Music for Strings <1952>   10'

str

Weintraub

Night Music <1950>   9'

1 1 1 1 — 1 0 0 0 — str
Perhaps intended for individual string players rather than sections.

Weintraub

Short Symphony <1948>   12'

2 2 2 2 — 2 2 1 0 — tmp — str

Weintraub

Symphony No.1 <1945>   25'

2[incl pic] 2 2 2 — 4 2 3 1 — tmp+2 — str

Schirmer

Symphony No.3 <1970>   25'

3[incl pic] 3[incl Eh] 3[incl bcl] 2[incl cbn] — 4 3 3 1 — tmp+4 —
cel — str
1.   12'
2.   6'
3.   7'

Schirmer

Szell, George   1897-1970

(b Budapest, 7 June 1897; d Cleveland, 30 July 1970). American composer of Hungarian birth

Variations on an Original Theme, op.4 <1913>   14'

3[1.2.pic] 2[1.2/Eh] 2[1.2/bcl] 2 — 4 3 3 1 — tmp+2 — hp — str
perc: cym, sus cym, tri, cast, tambn, sd, glock

Universal

Szöllősy, András   1921-2007

(b Szászváros [now Orăştie], Transylvania, 27 Feb 1921; d Budapest, 6 Dec 2007). Hungarian

Sonorità <1974>   13'

4 0 4[1.2.3.bcl] 0 — 4 0 0 0 — str
String distribution:
    vn I 8 (10), vn II 8 (10), vn III 8 (10), va 8 (10), vc 6 (8), db 4 (6)

EMB

Szpilman, Władysław   1911-2000

(b Sosnowiec, Poland, 5 Dec 1911; d Warsaw, 6 July 2000). Polish

Concertino, Piano & Orchestra <1940>   11'

1 1 2 1 — 4 3 3 1 — tmp+2 — str
perc: bd, sus cym, sd, tri

Bote & Bock

Szymanowski, Karol   1882-1937

(b Tymoszówka, nr Kiev, 3 Oct 1882; d Lausanne, 29 March 1937). Polish

Concerto, Violin, No.1, op.35 <1916>   26'

3[1.2.3/pic] 3[1.2.3/Eh] 4[1.2.3/Ebcl.bcl] 3[1.2.3/cbn] — 4 3 3 1 —
tmp+4 — 2hp — cel, pf — str
perc: tri, glock, sd, cym, bd, tambn

PWM   Universal

Concerto, Violin, No.2, op.61 <1933>   20'

2[1.2/pic] 2[1.2/Eh] 2[1.2/Ebcl] 3[1.2.cbn] — 4 2 3 1 — tmp+3 — pf
— str
perc: tri, sd, cym, bd

Eschig   PWM

Concert Overture, op.12, E major (Konzert-Ouverture;   16'
Uwertura koncertowa) <1904–1905; rev (reorchd) 1912-1913>

3[1.2.3/pic] 3[1.2.3/Eh] 4[1.2.3/Ebcl.bcl] 3[1.2.3/cbn] — 6 3 3 1 —
tmp+3 — hp — str
perc: tri, sd, cym, bd

Universal

Stabat Mater, op.53 <1925–1926>   20'

solos SABar   chorus
2 2[incl Eh] 2 2[incl cbn] — 4 2 0 0 — tmp+4 — hp — opt org —
str[8.8.6.6.4]
perc: tri, glock, sus cym, bd, tamtam

PWM

Symphony No.2, op.19, B-flat major <1909–1910>   34'

3[1.2.3/pic] 3[1.2.3/Eh] 3[1.2.3/Ebcl/bcl] 3[1.2.3/cbn] — 4 3 3 1 —
tmp+3 — hp — str
perc: bd, cym, tri
Allegro moderato; Grazioso   13'
Lento   12'
Fuga   9'

PWM

Symphony No.3, op.27, B-flat major (Song of the Night;   25'
Pieśń o nocy) <1914–1916>

solo tenor   chorus (wordless)
4[1.2.3./pic] 4[1.2.3./Eh] 5[1.2.3.Ebcl/bcl] 4[1.2.3.cbn] — 6 4
4[1.2.3.cb tbn] 1 — tmp+5 — 2hp — cel, pf, org — str[16.14.12.10.8]
perc: glock, tri, cym, bd, tambn, tamtam, sd
1. *Moderato assai*   8'
2. *Vivace scherzando*   8'
3. *Largo*   9'

Universal

Symphony No.4 for Piano & Orchestra (Symphonie   25'
concertante; Symfonia-Koncertująca) <1932>

solo piano
2[1.2/pic] 2[1.2./Eh] 2[1.2/Ebcl] 2[1.2/cbn] — 4 3 3 1 — tmp+4 —
hp — str
perc: tri, sd, bd, cym, tamtam
1. *Moderato*   10'
2. *Andante molto sostenuto*   8'
3. *Allegro non troppo, ma agitato ed ansioso*   7'

Eschig   PWM

T

Tailleferre, Germaine
1892-1983

(b Parc-St-Maur, nr Paris, 19 April 1892; d Paris, 7 Nov 1983). French

Choral et variations <1979>

1[fl/pic] 1 1 1 — 2 1 0 0 — tmp+2 — hp — cel, pf — str
perc: tri, woodblk, bd, 2tambn
Originally [?] for 2 pianos.

I. Prologue	_'
II. Variation 1: Sarabande	_'
III. Variation 2: La Crouilli	_'
IV. Variation 3: Scarlatino	_'
V. Variation 4: Pastourelle	_'
VI. Variation 5: Ariette	_'
VII. Variation 6: Menuet	_'
VIII. Variation 7: Rigodon	_'
IX. Epilogue	_'

MusikFabrik

Concerto, 2 Guitars <1964>
15'

2 0 1 1 — 1 0 0 0 — tmp — hp — cel — str

I. Allegro moderato	4'
II. [Alla breve]	3'
III. Lento—Tranquillo	5'
IV. Allegro	3'

MusikFabrik

Takemitsu, Toru
1930-1996

(b Tokyo, 8 Oct 1930; d Tokyo, 20 Feb 1996). Japanese

Dream/Window (Yume mado) <1985>
15'

3[incl 2pic & afl] 3[incl Eh] 3[incl bcl] 3[incl cbn] — 4 3 3 0 — ampd gtr — 4perc — 2hp — cel — str[13.13.13.9.8]
perc: crot, glock, vib, chimes, cym, bd, 3tamtams, 3gongs, 3tri, 3sus cym, low tmp
Special seating plan splits the main string body into two separated groups.

Schott

Far Calls, Coming, Far! (Toi yobigoe no kantata e!) <1980>
15'

solo violin
3[1/pic.2.3/afl] 3[1.2.3/Eh] 4[1.2.3/Ebcl.4/bcl] 3[1.2.cbn] — 4 3 2 1 — tmp+4 — 2hp — cel — str[16.14.12.10.8]
perc: chimes, vib, glock, tamtam, crot, gong, 3tamtams, 3sus cym

Schott

A Flock Descends into the Pentagonal Garden (Tori wa hoshigata no niwa ni oriru) <1977>
13'

3[1/pic.2/pic.3/pic/afl] 3[1.2.3/Eh] 3[1/Ebcl.2.3/bcl] 3[1.2.cbn] — 4 2 3 0 — 3perc — 2hp — cel — str[12.10.8.6.6]
perc: bd, chimes, marim, vib, 3sus cym, 2tamtams, 2gongs, 2cowbells

Salabert

Green (November Steps No.2) <1967>
6'

3[1/pic.2/pic3/pic/afl] 3[1.2.3/Eh] 3[1.2.3/Ebcl/bcl] 3[1.2.3/cbn] — 3 3 3 1 — 5perc — hp — pf/cel — str
perc: crot, tri, glock, chimes, Chinescym, 2xylorimbas, fingercym, 3gongs, 3tamtams

Peters

Music of Tree <1961>
17'

3[incl pic & afl] 3[incl Eh] 4[incl Ebcl & bcl] 3[incl cbn] — 4 4 3 1 — ssx — gtr — 3perc — hp — cel, pf — str[16.14.12.10.8]
perc: glock, tri, xyl, vib, sd, bamboo windchimes, 2tamtams, 3sus cym

Peters

Orion and Pleiades (Orion to Pureadesu) <1984>
26'

solo violoncello
3[incl pic & afl] 3[incl ob d'am & Eh] 3[incl Ebcl & bcl] 3[incl cbn] — 4 3 3 1 — 4perc — 2hp — cel — str[14.12.10.8.6]
perc: glock, crot, vib, marim, chimes, 3tamtams

Schott

Quatrain <1975>
17'

solo clarinet, violin, violoncello & piano
3[1.2.3/pic/afl] 2[1.2/Eh] 4[1.2/Ebcl.3/bcl.cbcl] 3[1.2.cbn] — 4 3 3 1 — gtr — 5perc — 2hp — cel — str[12.12.10.8.6]
perc: sus cym, Chinescym, chimes, marim, vib, 2tamtams, 3gongs, 3cowbells, tmpl bells
Not to be confused with *Quatrain II*, a 1977 chamber work for clarinet, violin, violoncello & piano, but without orchestra.

Salabert

Rain Coming (Ame zo furu) <1982>
9'

1[incl afl] 1 1 1 — 1 1 1 0 — 1perc — pf/cel — str 5t
perc: crot, vib, 3tamtams

Schott

Requiem <1957>
10'

str

Salabert

Riverrun <1984>
14'

solo piano
3[incl pic & afl] 3[incl Eh] 4[incl Ebcl & cbcl] 3[incl cbn] — 4 3 3 0 — 4perc — 2hp — cel — str[14.12.10.8.6]
perc: glock, vib, marim, chimes, xyl, tmp, 3tamtams

Schott

A String Around Autumn <1989>
17'

solo viola
3[incl pic & afl] 3[incl ob d'am & Eh] 4[incl Ebcl, bcl & cbcl] 3[incl cbn] — 4 3 3 0 — 4perc — 2hp — pf/cel — str[14.12.10.8.6]
perc: vib, glock, chimes, 3sus cym, 3gongs, 3tamtams, 2cym on tmp

Schott

To the Edge of Dream (Yume no heri e) <1982–1983>
13'

solo guitar
3[1.2/pic.3/pic/afl] 3[1.2.3/Eh] 3[1.2.3/bcl] 3[1.2.3/cbn] — 4 2 3 0 — 4perc — 2hp — cel — str[14.12.10.8.6]
perc: glock, tri, chimes, crot, vib, 2gongs, 3sus cym, 3tamtams

Schott

Tree Line <1988>
14'

1[incl afl] 1 2[incl bcl] 1[incl cbn] — 2 1 1 0 — 2perc — hp — pf/cel — str 5t
perc: vib, crot, chimes, glock, 2cym on tmp

Schott

Twill by Twilight <1988>   12'

4[1.2/pic.3/afl.4/afl] 3[1.2.3/Eh] 4[1.2/Ebcl.3.4/bcl] 3[1.2.3/cbn] — 4 4[incl pic tp] 3 1 — 5perc — 2hp — cel, pf — str[16.14.12.10.8]
perc: vib, glock, crot, chimes, bd, 3sus cym, 3tamtams, cym on tmp
In memory of Morton Feldman.

> Schott

Visions <1990>   13'

4[1.2/pic.3/pic/afl.4/bfl] 3[1.2/ob d'am.3/Eh] 4[incl Ebcl, bcl, & cbcl] 3[incl cbn] — 4 4[1.2.3.btp] 3 0 — 4perc — 2hp — cel, pf — str[16.14.12.10.8]
perc: vib, crot, glock, chimes, 3sus cym, 2Chinescym, 3tamtams, 2cym on tmp
  1. *Mystère*   6'
  2. *Les Yeux clos*   7'

> Schott

Talma, Louise   1906-1996

(b Arcachon, France, 31 Oct 1906; d Saratoga Springs, NY, 13 Aug 1996). American

Full Circle <1985>   11'

2 0 1 0 — tmp+1 — pf — str

> C. Fischer

Toccata <1944>   12'

3[1.2.3/pic] 3[1.2.Eh] 3[1.2.Ebcl] 3[1.2.cbn] — 4 3 3 1 — tmp+2 — pf — str
perc: cym, sus cym, xyl

> C. Fischer

Tan Dun   1957-

(b Simao, Hunan Province, 18 Aug 1957). American composer of Chinese birth

Atonal Rock 'N Roll: Of Youth <2009>   5'

3[1.2.pic] 3[1.2.Eh] 3[1.2.bcl] 2 — 4 3 3 1 — tmp+4 — str
perc: marim, xyl, set, bd, Chinese gong, 2cowbell, 2brake dr
An arrangement of the 1st mvt of the composer's 2009 Violin Concerto "The Love."

> Schirmer

Concerto for Orchestra <1995; rev 2012>   35'

3[1.2.pic] 3[1.2.Eh] 3[1.2.bcl] 3[1.2.cbn] — 4 3 3 1 — tmp+4 — hp — str[14.12.10.10.8]
perc: bd, sus cym, sd, tambn, tamtam, marim, congas, waterphone, Chinese gong, 5rototom, 2woodblk, 3cowbell, 2whip, 4singing bowls(with bows), 4metalcans
From the composer's opera *Marco Polo*.
  1. *Book of Timespace*   9'
  2. *Scent of Bazaar*   5'
  3. *Raga of Desert*   14'
  4. *Forbidden City*   7'

> Schirmer

Concerto for String Orchestra and Pipa or Zheng <1999>   21'

solo pipa (or zheng)
str[max 16.14.12.10.8; min 3.3.3.2.1]
Alternative part for solo zheng is separately notated in the score. Soloist, whether pipa or zheng, must be amplified.
  I. *Andante molto*   4'
  II. *Allegretto*   7'
  III. *Adagio*   5'
  IV. *Moderato*   5'

> Schirmer

Concerto, Guitar (Yi²) <1996>   28'

2[1/pic.2/pic] 2 2[1.bcl] 2[1.cbn] — 2 2 2 0 — 4perc — hp — pf — str[max 12.10.8.8.5; min 6.6.4.4.2]
perc: bd, sus cym, Chinescym, sd, marim, chimes, whip, watergong, 5tmp, 4Chinese bells (2 pairs), 2Chinese gongs, 5rototom, 2tamtam, 2flexatone, 2woodblk, 4cowbell
  1. *Rubato*   8'
  2. *Adagio*   4'
  3. *Andante agitato* 9'
  4. *Cadenza*   5'
  5. *Ending*   3'

> Schirmer

Crouching Tiger Concerto   30'

solo violoncello (or solo erhu)
1[afl/pic] 0 0 0 — 0 0 0 0 — 5perc — hp — str
perc: bongos, tambn, tamtam, bd, 5tmp[1 for each player], 5tar[1 required; 4 opt], 4rototom, 5sus cym w/ bow to play it on the head of tmp
Music from the original sound track of Ang Lee's film *Crouching Tiger, Hidden Dragon*.
  A talking drum may substitute for the "tar." The tar itself is some sort of frame drum, which may or may not have jingles, like a tambourine.
  1. *Crouching Tiger, Hidden Dragon*   _'
  2. *Through the Bamboo Forest*   _'
  3. *Silk Road: Encounters*   _'
  4. *Eternal Vow*   _'
  5. *To the South*   _'
  6. *Farewell*   _'

> Schirmer

Death and Fire (Dialogue with Paul Klee) <1992>   27'

3[1/pic.2/pic.pic/afl] 2 2 3[1.2.cbn] — 4 3 3 1 — 4perc — hp — str
perc: marim, slgh-bells, chimes, xyl, marac, bd, guiro, whip, 4tmp, 5rototom, 3sus cym(bowed on tmp), 2Chinescym, 8stone, 4woodblk, 4whistle
All orchestra members vocalize. Ob2 and cl 2 each need an extra head joint.
  1. *Portrait*   3'
     Insert 1: Animals at Full Moon   3'
     Instert 2: Senicio   2'
     Insert 3: Ad Parnassum   3'
  2. *Self Portrait*   7'
     Insert 4: Twittering Machine   1'
     Insert 5: Earth Witches   1'
     Insert 6: Intoxication   3'
     Insert 7: J.S. Bach   2'
  3. *Death and Fire*   2'

> Schirmer

The Intercourse of Fire and Water (Yi¹) <1993>   25'

solo violoncello
2[1/pic.2/pic] 2 2[1.bcl] 2[1.cbn] — 2 2 2 0 — tmp+3 — hp — pf — str[min 6.6.4.4.2; max 12.10.8.8.5]
perc: bd, sus cym, Chinescym, sd, marim, chimes, whip, watergong, 5rototom, 2tamtam, 2Chinese gong, 2flexatone, 2woodblk, 4cowbell, 4small Chinese bells(4 pair), 5tmp

> Schirmer

On Taoism <1985>   15'

solos: voice, bass clarinet, contrabassoon
3[1.2.3/pic] 1 1 1 — 2 1 2 0 — 6perc — hp — pf — str[14.12.10.8.6]
perc: vib, bd, small bells[6pair], 5woodblk, 5rototom, 2tamtam, 3gong
Voice may be of any kind: soprano, mezzo, tenor, bass, or actor/actress.
  6 pairs of small Chinese bells distributed among the non-percussion players.

> Schirmer

Orchestral Theatre I: Xun <1990> 20'

solo xun (optional)
3[1.2.pic] 2 3[1.2.bcl] 3[1.2.cbn] — 4 3 3 1 — 4perc — hp — str
All players also vocalize. 10 of the woodwind players double on *xuns* (the *xun* is an ancient Chinese ceramic wind instrument, resembling an ocarina). The work may be played in an orchestra-only version, omitting solo and orchestral *xuns* entirely.

Schirmer

Orchestral Theatre II: Re <1992> 22'

bass voice
3[3pic] 3[1.2.Eh] 3[1.2.bcl] 2 — 4 3 3 1 — tmp+3 — hp — pf — str
perc: bd, cym, sus cym, tri, tamtam, chimes, whip, bongos, watergong, watertriangle, bottle (for making bubbling sounds), 2flexatone, 2cowbell, 4stones
2 conductors. Orchestra is divided; woodwinds surround audience. All orchestra members (including conductors) vocalize at certain points, as does the audience. Wind players stand to play (may require neck strap).
    The first 2 pages of the score are laid out non-traditionally, but according to the physical location of the performers: puzzling at first, but logical. A large container of water is required for the watergong, watertriangle, and bottle (bubbling sounds).

Schirmer

Symphonic Poem of 3 Notes <2012> 12'

3[1.2.pic] 3[1.2.bclbcl] 3[1.2.bcl] 3[1.2.cbn] — 4 3 3 1 — tmp+5 — hp — str
perc: chimes, tamtam, marim, vib, bd, 3car wheels, 5rototom, 6stone(3 pairs), 3brake dr, 5tomtom
Musicians vocalize and stamp feet.

Schirmer

Symphony for Strings <1986–2009> 16'

str
I. Adagio misterioso	_'
II. Allegretto scherzo	_'
III. Largo sensibile	_'
IV. Allegretto	_'
V. Moderato festivo	_'
VI. Allegro vivace	_'

Schirmer

Taneyev, Sergey Ivanovich 1856-1915

(b Vladimir-na-Klyaz'me, 13/25 Nov 1856; d Dyud'kovo, nr Moscow, 6/19 June 1915). Russian

Various transliterations of this name are found. The U.S. Library of Congress, as well as many American libraries, use the spelling **Taneev**. Other spellings: **Tanéiew, Tanéiev, Tanejev,** and **Tan'eva.**

Symphony No.1, E minor <1873–1874> 34'

2 2 2 2 — 4 2 3 0 — tmp — str
Not to be confused with the composer's Symphony No.4, op.12, *q.v.*, which was published by Belaeieff as Symphony No.1.
Score published; orchestra parts may be difficult or impossible to find, though the BBC Music Library is said to have a set in the 1948 edition ed. Pavel Lamm.
I. Allegro	*11'*
II. Andantino, quasi Allegretto	*6'*
III. Scherzo: Vivace assai	*6'*
IV. Finale: Allegro molto	*11'*

RepEx

Symphony No.4, op.12, C minor 42'

3[1.2.3/pic] 2 3 3[1.2.cbn] — 4 3 3 1 — tmp+2 — str
perc: cym, sd, tri
Originally published as Symphony No.1.
I. Allegro molto	*12'*
II. Adagio	*14'*
III. Scherzo: Vivace	*6'*
IV. Finale: Allegro energico; Molto maestoso	*10'*

Belaieff	Fleisher

Tann, Hilary 1947-

(b Llwynypia, Glam., 2 Nov 1947). Welsh composer active in the USA

Adirondack Light <1992> 19'

narrator
2[1.2/pic] 2 2 2 — 2 2 0 0 — tmp+1 — str

Oxford

The Grey Tide and the Green <2001> 12'

3[1.2.pic] 2 2 2 — 4 3 3 1 — 3perc — hp — str

Oxford

The Open Field; In memoriam Tiananmen Square (June 1989) <1989> 11'

3[1.2.pic] 2 2 2 — 4 3 3 1 — tmp+3 — str
Special seating for the trumpets.

Oxford

Through the Echoing Timber <1991> 4'

3[1.2.pic] 2 2 2 — 4 3 3 1 — tmp+2 — str

Oxford

Water's Edge <1993> 9'

str
Originally for piano duet; arranged by the composer.
1. Dawn Light	3'
2. From the Riverbed	3'
3. Toward Dusk	3'

Oxford

Water's Edge: Toward Dusk <2001> 3'

2[fl.pic] 0 0 0 — str
Originally for piano duet; arranged by the composer.

Oxford

With the Heather and Small Birds <1994> 10'

2[1/pic.2/pic] 2 2 2 — 2 2 0 0 — tmp+1 — str

Oxford

Tansman, Alexandre 1897-1986

(b Łódż, 12 June 1897; d Paris, 15 Nov 1986). French composer of Polish birth

Concertino, Piano <1931> 15'

3[1.2.pic] 2[1.2/Eh] 2[1.2/bcl] 2 — 4 3 0 0 — tmp+4 — cel — str
perc: tri, sus cym, tambn, bd
I. Toccata	5'
II. Intermezzo Chopiniano	3'
III. Finale	7'

Eschig

Genesis Suite: III. Adam and Eve <1944>   *12'*

narrator
3[1.2.3/pic] 3[1.2.Eh] 3[1.2.3/bcl] 3[1.2.cbn] — 4 3 3 1 — tmp+3 — hp — pf/cel — str
perc: sus cym, tamtam, glock, xyl, vib, marktree
See the entry for "Nathaniel Shilkret: *Genesis Suite*" for a full description of this collaborative work by 7 composers.
   Reconstructed by Patrick Russ.

Milken

Sinfonietta <1924>   *18'*

1 1 1 1 — 1 1 2 0 — tmp+2 — pf/cel — str
perc: cym, tri

I. Allegro assai	*4'*
II. Mazurka	*4'*
III. Notturno	*7'*
IV. Fuga e toccata	*3'*

Universal

Sonatine transatlantique <1930>   *9'*

3[1.2.pic] 2[1.2/Eh] 3[1.2.bcl] 2 — 3 2 3 1 — asx — tmp+3 — cel/xyl, pf — str
perc: tri, cym, tambn, bd, xyl[played by cel]

1. Fox-Trot	*3'*
2. Spiritual and Blues	*4'*
3. Charleston	*2'*

Leduc

Toccata <1926>   *8'*

3[1.2.pic] 3[1.2.Eh] 3[1.2.bcl] 3[1.2.cbn] — 4 4 3 1 — tmp+5 — hp — cel, pf — str
perc: tri, cym, tambn, bd, glock, xyl

Eschig

Tombeau de Chopin <1949>   *10'*

str [or str 5t]

I. Nocturne	*3'*
II. Mazurka	*4'*
III. Postlude	*3'*

Leeds Canada

Triptych <1930>   *16'*

str

I. Allegro risoluto	*3'*
II. Andante	*5'*
III. Finale	*8'*

Eschig

Variations on a Theme by Girolamo Frescobaldi <1937>   *14'*

str

Eschig	Luck's

Tartini, Giuseppe   1692-1770

(b Pirano, Istria [now Piran, Istra, Slovenia], 8 April 1692; d Padua, 26 Feb 1770). Italian

Concerto No.58, F major   *12'*

0 2 0 0 — 2 0 0 0 — str
Ed. Ettore Bonelli.

Kalmus	Luck's	Zanibon

Concerto, Trumpet, D major   *8'*

0 0 0 0 — 2 0 0 0 — cnt — str
Ed. J. Thilde.

I. Allegro	*4'*
II. Andante	*2'*
III. Allegro grazioso	*2'*

Billaudot

Concerto, Violin, No.57, D major   *20'*

0 0 0 0 — 2 2 0 0 — tmp — str
Ed. Ettore Bonelli.

Kalmus	Luck's	Zanibon

Concerto, Violoncello, A major   *12'*

opt org — str
Originally for viola da gamba. Ed. Oreste Ravanello.

Kalmus	Luck's	Zanibon

Sinfonia, D major   *13'*

str
Ed. Hans Erdmann. No.78 in A. Capri's thematic index (*Giuseppe Tartini; con 22 illustrazioni e un catalogo tematico*, Milan, 1945).

Schott

Sinfonia pastorale, D major   *11'*

solo violin
cnt — str

Kahnt

Tavener, John   1944-2013

(b London, 28 Jan 1944; d Child Okeford, Dorset, 12 Nov 2013). English

Akhmatova: Requiem <1979–1980>   *50'*

solos soprano & bass (baritone)
0 0 0 0 — 3 3 3 0 — tmp+5 — cel — str
perc: sus cym, woodblk, chimes, field dr, xyl, bd, tamtam, handbells (mounted), 5tomtom, 4gongs

Chester

Eternal Memory <1991>   *12'*

solo violoncello
str

Chester

Kaleidoscopes; A Tribute to Mozart <2005>   *40'*

solo oboe
1perc — 4 str quartets, 2db
perc: tamtam, 4Tibetan temple bowls
Placement: solo oboist centered, the 4 string quartets as far apart as possible on all 4 sides (north, south, east, west), the 2db with quartet no.1.

Chester

Lalishri <2006>   *35'*

solo violin
str[16.14.12.10.8]
A separate str 4t, "sounding from on high," is taken from the orchestra.

Introduction	*2'*
Cycle 1	*6'*
Cycle 2	*6'*
Cycle 3	*10'*
Cycle 4	*11'*

Chester

Little Ceremonial <2010>   *11'*

2 2 2 2 — 4 2 3 0 — tmp — str

Chester

Mystagogía <1998>   50'

2[1/pic.2/pic/afl] 2 0 0 — 0 2 2 0 — 2tmp+2 — hp — synth — str
perc: Tibetan bowl, handbells (mounted)
The above aggregate is divided into 3 separate orchestras, representing the 3 persons of the Trinity.

> Chester

The Protecting Veil <1987>   46'

solo violoncello
str[min 8.8.6.6.3]

1. The Protecting Veil	9'
2. The Birth of the Mother of God	6'
3. The Annunciation	3'
4. The Incarnation	4'
5. The Lament of the Mother of God at the Cross	10'
6. Christ is Risen!	3'
7. The Dormition of the Mother of God	8'
8. The Protecting Veil	3'

> Chester

Theophany <1993>   30'

2[1/pic.pic/afl] 2 2[1.bcl] 2[1.cbn] — 3 3 2 1 — tape [supplied on a DVD] — tmp+1 — str
perc: bandir drum[= frame drum]

> Chester

The Repentant Thief <1990>   20'

solo clarinet
tmp+1 — str[min 8.6.5.5.5]
perc: tamtam, handbells (mounted)

> Chester

Three Hymns of George Herbert <2013>   15'

SATB choir, and Echo choir
2perc — str[min 5.5.4.3.1]
perc: chimes, 3gong, 2tamtam
The 2 percussionists are in a gallery; in the distance are the Echo Choir (SATB which may be drawn from the main choir) and string quartet (may be drawn from the orchestra). On stage: main choir and main string body (minimum 4.4.3.2.1, not including the distant string quartet).

1. Heaven	_'
2. Love	_'
3. Life	_'

> Chester

Total Eclipse <1999>   40'

solo treble, countertenor, & tenor voices; chorus SATB; solo sopr sax
0 1[baroque ob] 0 0 — 0 1[baroque tp/modern tp] 1[baroque tbn] 0 — 2tmp+baroque tmp+2perc — baroque str
perc: tamtam, Tibetan temple bowl, handbells (mounted)
Chorus always sings in Greek; soloists always in English.
   Spatial separation of the various elements, along lines specified in the score, is important.

1. Stavroménos	_'
2. Metánoia	_'
3. Agápi	_'
4. Parousía	_'

> Chester

The Whale; A Biblical Fantasy <1965–1966>   35'

chamber choir[min 20]   solo mezzo & baritone   speaker
2[1.2/afl/pic] 2 2[1/bcl.2/bcl] 2[1/cbn.2/cbn] — 4 3 3 1 — pre-recorded tape — tmp+8 — hp — pf[ampd], org, Hammond org, cel[played by perc] — str[no vn]
perc: bd, sd, marac, whip, sus cym, cym, chimes, glock, xyl, marim, td, 3bongos, 3tomtoms, 4gongs, handbells (mounted), 2metronomes[ampd], sheet of glass [ampd], 5sanctus bells, fooball rattle[cog rattle], cel[played by perc]
6 male performers with loud hailers [i.e., bullhorns].

> Chester

Taverner, John   ca.1490-1545

(b South Lincs., c1490; d Boston, Lincs., 18 Oct 1545). English

In nomine

see: Maxwell Davies, Peter
    First Fantasia on an "In nomine" of John Taverner
    Second Fantasia on John Taverner's "In nomine"

Taylor, Deems   1885-1966

(b New York, 22 Dec 1885; d New York, 3 July 1966). American

Fanfare for Russia <1942>   2'

0 0 0 0 — 4 3 3 1 — tmp+3 — [no str]
perc: sd, td, cym, bd, tri, sus cym
Arr. Godfrey Turner.

> Boosey

Through the Looking Glass, op.12 <1917–1919; rev 1921-1922>   32'

3[1.2.3/pic] 3[1.2.Eh] 3[1.2.bcl] 3[1.2.cbn] — 4 3 3 1 — tmp+3 — pf — str
perc: cym, tri, sd, glock, xyl, tambn
Originally for chamber orchestra; later arranged for full orchestra.

> Colombo

Tchaikovsky, Piotr Ilyich   1840-1893

(b nr Votkinsk, north-eastern Russia, 25 April/7 May 1840; d St Petersburg, 25 Oct/6 Nov 1893). Russian

TH = *The Tchaikovsky Handbook: A Guide to the Man and His Music*, v.1, compiled by Alexander Poznansky & Brett Langston. Bloomington: Indiana University Press, 2002.
   See also the authors' website at tchaikovsky-research.net.

Andante & Finale, op.79, TH 241 <1892>   19'

piano solo
3[1.2.pic] 2 2 2 — 4 2 3 1 — tmp+1 — str
perc: cym, sd
Completed and orchestrated in 1897 by Sergey Taneyev, to make up the middle and last movements of the *Piano Concerto No.3*. Originally intended for a symphony in E-flat, from which Tchaikovsky had already drawn one movement for use as the first movement of the *Piano Concerto No.3*.

> Belaieff   Fleisher

Andante cantabile [violoncello & strings], TH 63 <1871; rev 1888>   7'

solo violoncello
str
The composer's own transcription of this popular movement from his *String Quartet No.1, op.11*, TH 111; transposed up a half-step to B major.

> Kalmus   Kunzelmann   Wollenweber

Capriccio italien, op.45, TH 47 <1880>   15'

3[1.2.3/pic] 3[1.2.Eh] 2 2 — 4 4[2crt, 2tp] 3 1 — tmp+4 — hp — str
perc: glock, tambn, tri, cym, bd

> Breitkopf   Kalmus   Luck's   Russian

Casse-noisette

see his: Nutcracker

Concerto, Piano, No.1, op.23, TH 55, B-flat minor <1874–1875>   32'

2 2 2 2 — 4 2 3 0 — tmp — str

It is said that the version of this work heard almost universally today incorporates various alterations by Dannreuther, Siloti, and other virtuoso pianists of the period. Pianist Malcolm Frager has recorded for Myrios Classics what purports to be the composer's original version.

I. Allegro non troppo e molto maestoso	17'
II. Andantino semplice	8'
III. Allegro con fuoco	7'

Breitkopf	Kalmus	Luck's	Russian

Concerto, Piano, No.2, op.44, TH 60, G major <1879–1880>   37'

2 2 2 2 — 4 2 0 0 — tmp — str

I. Allegro brillante e molto vivace	21'
II. Andante non troppo	8'
III. Allegro con fuoco	8'

Alkor

Concerto, Piano, No.2, op.44, TH 60, G major (Siloti version) <1879–1880>   30'

2 2 2 2 — 4 2 0 0 — tmp — str

Revised and abridged by Alexander Siloti, though the composer appears to have rejected repeatedly Siloti's proposed changes, which were only published four years after Tchaikovsky's death.

I. Allegro brillante e molto vivace	16'
II. Andante non troppo	7'
III. Allegro con fuoco	7'

Kalmus	Simrock

Concerto, Piano, No.3, op.75, TH 65, E-flat major <1893>   16'

3[1.2.pic] 2 2 2 — 4 2 3 1 — tmp — str

Originally intended to be one movement of a symphony, but recast by the composer as the first movement of a piano concerto. Two other mvts were completed and orchestrated for piano & orchestra by Sergey Taneyev, and published as *Andante & Finale*, op.79, (q.v. under Tchaikovsky's name).

Kalmus	Luck's	Russian	Simrock

Concerto, Violin, op.35, TH 59, D major <1878>   33'

2 2 2 2 — 4 2 0 0 — tmp — str

A trombone part is given in small notes in the Breitkopf score and its Kalmus reprint. This is merely a collection of cues intended for orchestras whose instrumentation is incomplete (lacking 3rd & 4th horns, or 2nd bassoon).

Many soloists make cuts in the last movement, but unfortunately there does not seem to be a single standard set of cuts. Consultation is essential, most efficiently in the form of the soloist providing a copy of the solo part with the cuts marked.

I. Allegro moderato	19'
II. Canzonetta: Andante	7'
III. Finale: Allegro vivacissimo	7'

Breitkopf	Kalmus	Luck's	Russian

Eugene Onegin, TH 5 (Yevgeny Onegin): Polonaise <1877–1878>   4'

2 2 2 2 — 4 2 3 0 — tmp — str

Kalmus	Luck's	Russian	Simrock

Eugene Onegin, TH 5 (Yevgeny Onegin): Waltz <1877–1878>   7'

3[1.2.pic] 2 2 2 — 4 2 3 0 — tmp — str

Breitkopf	Kalmus	Luck's

Fantasie de concert, op.56, TH 61, G major (Concert Fantasy) <1884>   28'

solo piano
3 2 2 2 — 4 2 3 0 — tmp+1 — str
perc: glock, tambn

The composer provides a special ending in case the first movement is to be performed separately.

I. Quasi Rondo	15'
II. Contrastes	13'

Kalmus	Universal

Fatum, op.77, TH 41 <1868>   10'

3[1.2.pic] 3[1.2.Eh] 2 2 — 4 3 3 1 — tmp+4 — hp — str
perc: tri, cym, bd, tamtam

Destroyed by Tchaikovsky, reconstructed by R.R. Shoring, 1896.

Belaieff	EMI	Kalmus	Luck's	Peters

Festival Coronation March, TH 50 (Coronation March for Alexander III; Marche solennelle du couronnement) <1883>   5'

3[1.2.pic] 3[1.2.Eh] 2 2 — 4 4[2tp, 2crt] 3 1 — tmp+3 — str
perc: sd, cym, bd, tri

Original publisher: Jurgenson. Not to be confused with the composer's *Marche solennelle*, TH 52, op.posth.

Kalmus	Luck's

Francesca da Rimini, op.32, TH 46 <1876>   22'

3[1.2.3/pic] 3[1.2.Eh] 2 2 — 4 4[2tp, 2crt] 3 1 — tmp+3 — hp — str
perc: cym, bd, tamtam

Kalmus	Luck's

Hamlet; Fantasy Overture after Shakespeare, op.67, TH 53 <1888>   18'

3[1.2.3/pic] 3[1.2.Eh] 2 2 — 4 4[2tp, 2crt] 3 1 — tmp+3 — str
perc: field dr, cym, bd, tamtam

Not to be comfused with the incidental music to *Hamlet*, op.67a.

Alkor	Kalmus	Luck's	Russian	Universal

Manfred, op.58, TH 28 <1885>   57'

3[1.2.3/pic] 3[1.2.Eh] 3[1.2.bcl] 3 — 4 4[2tp, 2crt] 3 1 — tmp+5 — 2hp — harm — str
perc: tri, tambn, cym, bd, tamtam, chime[A5]

I. Lento lugubre	16'
II. Vivace con spirito	10'
III. Pastorale: Andante con moto	12'
IV. Allegro con fuoco	19'

Kalmus	Russian	Simrock

Marche slave, op.31, TH 45 (Slavonic March; Slavyansky marsh) <1876>   10'

4[2fl, 2pic] 2 2 — 4 4[2crt, 2tp] 3 1 — tmp+4 — str
perc: bd, cym, sd, tamtam

At one point, the Russian state publishers replaced the prominent Czarist hymn in this work and in the composer's *1812 Overture* with a hymn more "correct" politically; these mutilated versions found their way into certain Dover publications. Exercise caution.

Kalmus	Luck's	Simrock

Marche solennelle, TH 52, op.posth. (Coronation March; Jurisprudence March; Pravovedskii marsh) <1885>   5'

3[1.2.pic] 3[1.2.Eh] 2 2 — 4 2 3 1 — tmp+4 — 2hp[1part] — str
perc: sd, cym, bd, tri

Original publisher: Rahter. Not to be confused with the composer's *Festival Coronation March* of 1883, TH 50.

Kalmus	Luck's

Mazeppa, TH 7: Danse cosaque (Cossack Dance)   5'
<1881–1883>

3[1.2.pic] 3[1.2.Eh] 2 2 — 4 4[2tp, 2crt] 3 1 — tmp+3 — str
perc: tambn, tri, cym, bd
Excerpt from the opera.

Kalmus	Luck's

Mozartiana

see his: Suite No.4, op.61, G major

NUTCRACKER, op.71, TH 14 (Shchelkunchik; Casse-noisette)

There are numerous editions of this favorite ballet in its original form as well as for reduced orchestra; only a few of the latter are given here. A chart prepared by Clinton F. Nieweg giving details of many editions may be found at www.mola-inc.org; search for The Nieweg Charts.

Nutcracker, op.71, TH 14 (Shchelkunchik; Casse-noisette) <1891–1892>   86'

backstage children's chorus
3[1.2/pic.3/pic] 3[1.2.Eh] 3[1.2.bcl] 2 — 4 2 3 1 — tmp+2 — 2hp — cel — str
perc: glock, tambn, tamtam, ratch, cast, cym, tri, bd, sd, chimes, whip, sus cym, toydrum, gunshot
Children's chorus passages are doubled in the orchestra.
    Jurgenson critical ed. by Sergei Chebotaryov.
    A harp part combining the 1st and 2nd harp into a single part may be ordered from Kalmus (A8898) or Payne. 5 of the 25 mvts call for bcl in A; otherwise bcl in B-flat.
    Payne sets may be ordered that employ rehearsal letters, rehearsal numbers, and/or bar numbers, as desired. Payne also offers a piano-vocal score for use in rehearsing the children's chorus (mvt no.9).
    Orchestral reductions by Wm. McDermott offered by Kalmus:
    Medium orch: 2[incl pic] 2 2 2—2 2 2 0—tmp+2—hp, cel—str; engraved score that matches the parts now available.
    Small orch: 1 1 2 1 — 2 2 1 0 — tmp, perc — hp, cel — str; score not available.

Overture	4'
ACT I	
1. The Decoration of the Christmas Tree	7'
2. March	2'
3. Children's Galop & Entrance of the Parents	2'
4. Arrival of Drosselmeyer	4'
5. Grossvater Dance	6'
6. Scena	6'
7. Scena (Battle)	4'
8. Scena (Clara's pas de deux)	3'
9. Waltz of the Snowflakes	7'
ACT II	
10. Scena-Confiturembourg	4'
11. Scena	5'
12. Divertissement	
a. Chocolate (Spanish)	1'
b. Coffee (Arab Dance)	3'
c. Tea (Chinese Dance)	1'
d. Trepak (Russian Dance)	1'
e. Mirlitons	3'
f. Mother Ginger	3'
13. Waltz of the Flowers	7'
14. Pas de deux	4'
Variation I (Tarantella)	1'
Variation II (Sugar Plum Fairy)	2'
Coda	1'
15. Waltz	4'
Apotheosis	1'

Jurgenson	Kalmus	Luck's	Payne	Russian

Nutcracker, op.71 (Ceo reduction) (Shchelkunchik; Casse-noisette) <1891–1892>   86'

backstage children's chorus
2[1.2/pic] 2[1.2/Eh] 2[1.2/bcl] 1 — 2 2 1 0 — tmp+2 — hp — cel — str
perc: bd, cym, sus cym, sd, tri, tambn, tamtam, glock, chimes, ratch, cast
Reduced orchestration by Joseph Ceo.
    Children's chorus passages are doubled in the orchestra.
    For contents list and durations, consult the main entry for this work.

Luck's

Nutcracker, op.71 (Golan reduction) (Shchelkunchik; Casse-noisette) <1891–1892>   86'

backstage children's chorus
2[1.2/pic] 2[1.2/Eh] 2[1.2/bcl] 2 — 3 2 3 1 — tmp+1 — hp — cel/glock — str
perc: bd, cym, sus cym, sd, tri, tambn, ratch, cast, chime, tamtam [covered by tmp], glock [covered by cel, along with some tri]
Reduced orchestration by Lawrence Golan.
    Children's chorus passages are doubled in the orchestra.
    For contents list and durations, consult the main entry for this work.

Spurwink

Nutcracker, op.71 (Itkin reduction) (Shchelkunchik; Casse-noisette) <1891–1892>   86'

backstage children's chorus
1[1/pic] 1[1/Eh] 2[1/Ebcl.2/bcl] 1 — 2 2 1 0 — tmp+1 — hp — cel — str
Reduced orchestration by David Itkin.
    Children's chorus passages are doubled in the orchestra.
    For contents list and durations, consult the main entry for this work.

DCI Music

Nutcracker (Shchelkunchik; Casse-noisette): Suite No.1, op.71A, TH 35 <1891–1892>   24'

3[1.2.3/pic] 3[1.2.Eh] 3[1.2.bcl] 2 — 4 2 3 1 — tmp+1 — hp — cel (or pf) — str
perc: glock, tambn, tri, cym

I. Overture miniature	4'
II. Danses caractéristiques: (a) Marche	3'
(b) Danse de la fée-dragée	2'
(c) Danse russe trepak	1'
(d) Danse arabe	2'
(e) Danse chinoise	1'
(f) Danse des mirlitons	4'
III. Valse des fleurs.	7'

Breitkopf	Kalmus	Luck's	Russian

Nutcracker (Shchelkunchik; Casse-noisette): Suite No.2, op.71b <1891–1892>   33'

3[1.2.3/pic] 3[1.2.Eh] 3[1.2.bcl] 2 — 4 2 3 1 — tmp+1 — 2hp — cel[or pf] — str
perc: bd, cast, cym, glock, ratch, tambn, tri

ACT I	
No.10, Scene	4'
No.11; Scene	5'
No.12a, Chocolate	1'
No.14 Pas de deux & Variations	8'
ACT II	
No.1, Decorating and Lighting of the Christmas Tree	7'
No.3, Little Galop of the Children and Entrance of the Parents	2'
No.5, Scene and "Tempo di Gross-Vater"	6'

Kalmus	Luck's

The Nutcracker and the Mouse King <1891–1892; rev (adaptation) 1994>   17'

narrator
2[1.2/pic] 2[1.2/Eh] 2 2 — 4 2 3 1 — tmp+ — hp — cel — str
perc: cym, bd, sd, tambn, tri, sus cym, glock, chimes
Music of Tchaikovsky, adapted and arranged by Jonathan McPhee; story by McPhee, freely adapted from a story by E.T.A. Hoffman. The original tale is greatly shortened, as are most of the movements.

Boosey

Overture 1812, op.49, TH 49 (Ouverture solennelle) <1880>   16'

3[1.2.pic] 3[1.2.Eh] 2 2 — 4 4[2crt+2tp] 3 1 — tmp+5 — str
perc: bd, cym, sd, tri, tambn, bells or chimes ("Glocken"), cannon
Extra brass ("banda") ad libitum: 4 2 2 2 — perc. A useful audio sample cannon shot may be downloaded free from the Robert Wendel Music site wendelmusic.com under "Useful Audio Samples."
    At one point, the Russian state publishers replaced the prominent Czarist hymn in this work and in the composer's *Marche slav* with a hymn more "correct" politically; these mutilated versions found their way into certain Dover publications. Exercise caution.
    Various choral parts have been created for use with this work. Faber publishes one by Carl Davis with English text by Keith Boyd; Schirmer published one by Igor Buketoff with Russian and English texts.

Breitkopf	Kalmus	Luck's

Pezzo capriccioso, op.62, TH 62 <1887>   7'

violoncello solo
2 2 2 2 — 4 0 0 0 — tmp — str

Kalmus	Schott	Sikorski	Simrock	Universal

Romeo and Juliet [original version 1869], TH 42a (Romeo i Dzul'etta) <1869>   23'

3[1.2.pic] 3[incl Eh] 2 2 — 4 2 3 1 — tmp+2 — hp — str

Kalmus	Luck's

Romeo and Juliet overture-fantasy [final version 1880], TH 42c (Romeo i Dzul'etta) <1869; rev 1880>   19'

3[1.2.pic] 3[1.2.Eh] 2 2 — 4 2 3 1 — tmp+2 — hp — str
perc: cym, bd

Bote & Bock	Kalmus	Luck's	Salabert□□□□

Romeo and Juliet (duet), op.posth., TH 215 <?1878>   12'

solo soprano and tenor
2 3[1.2.Eh] 2 2 — 4 2 0 0 — tmp — hp — str
Completed & orchestrated by Sergei Taneyev from the composer's sketches.

Billaudot	Universal

Serenade, op.48, C major, TH 48 <1880>   28'

str
I. Pezzo in forma di Sonatina	9'
II. Walzer	4'
III. Elégie	8'
IV. Finale (Tema Russo)	7'

Breitkopf	Kalmus	Luck's	Peters	Russian

Sérénade mélancolique, op.26, TH 56 <1875>   7'

solo violin
2 1 2 2 — 4 0 0 0 — str

C. Fischer	Kalmus	Luck's	Simrock

Sleeping Beauty, TH 13 (Spyashchaya krasavitsa; Belle au bois dormant) <1888>   157'

3[1.2.pic] 3[1.2.Eh] 2 2 — 4 4[2tp, 2crt] 3 1 — tmp+4 — hp — pf — str
perc: tri, tambn, glock, sd, tamtam, cym, bd
Piano only in 2 movements; could be played by harp.
Introduction	3'
PROLOG: *Le baptême (The Christening)*	
1. *March*	5'
2. *Scène dansante*	5'
3. *Pas de six*	14'
4. *Final*	9'
ACT I: *Le sortilège (The Sorcery)*	
5. *Scène*	8'
6. *Waltz*	5'
7. *Scène*	2'
8. *Pas d'action*	17'
9. *Finale*	8'
ACT II: *La vision et le réveil d'Aurore (Vision and Awakening)*	
10. *Entr'acte et Scène*	3'
11. *Colin-Maillard*	2'
12. *Scène (Danses de duchesses, baronesses, comtesses, marquises)*	5'
13. *Farandole (Scène et Danse)*	2'
14. *Scène*	6'
15. *Pas d'action (Désiré et Aurore)*	10'
16. *Scène*	1'
17. *Panorama*	4'
18. *Entr'acte*	7'
19. *Entr'acte symphonique*	8'
20. *Final*	2'
ACT III: *Les noces (The Wedding)*	
21. *Marche*	4'
22. *Polacca*	4'
23. *Pas de quatre (Or, Argent, Saphir, Diamant)*	7'
24. *Pas de caractère (Le chat botte et la chatte blanche)*	2'
25. *Pas de quatre*	6'
26. *Pas de caractère (Cendrillon et le Prince Fortuné)*	3'
27. *Pas Berrichon*	2'
28. *Pas de deux (Aurore et Désiré)*	11'
29. *Sarabande*	3'
30. *Finale et Apothéose*	9'

Kalmus	Payne	Russian

Sleeping Beauty (Spyashchaya krasavitsa; Belle au bois dormant): Suite, op.66a, TH 234 <1888>   23'

3[1.2.pic] 3[1.2.Eh] 2 2 — 4 4[2tp, 2crt] 3 1 — tmp+3 — hp — str
perc: sd, tamtam, glock, cym, bd
I. *Introduction: La Fée des lilas*	5'
II. *Adagio: Pas d'action*	6'
III. *Pas de caractère: Le chat botté et la chatte blanche*	2'
IV. *Panorama*	4'
V. *Valse*	6'

Kalmus	Luck's	Russian

Sleeping Beauty (Spyashchaya krasavitsa; Belle au bois dormant): Pas de deux (arr. Stravinsky)

see under: Stravinsky, Igor, 1882-1971
                Pas de deux

Souvenir de Florence, op.70, TH 118 (Vospominanie o Florentsii) <1887–1890; rev 1891-92>   34'

str
Originally for string sextet (2vn, 2va, 2vc). Double bass part added by Lucas Drew, for performance as a string orchestra work.
I. *Allegro con spirito*	10'
II. *Adagio cantabile e con moto*	11'
III. *Allegro moderato*	6'
IV. *Allegro vivace*	7'

Kalmus

SOUVENIR D'UN LIEU CHER, op.42 (Vospominanie o dorogom meste) <1878>   18'

Originally for violin & piano (TH 116); arr. by Glazunov for solo violin & orchestra.

1. Méditation <1878>   10'

solo violin
2 2 2 2 — 2 0 0 0 — hp — str
Originally planned as the slow movement for the composer's violin concerto.

C. Fischer	Kalmus	Luck's	Universal

2. Scherzo <1878>   4'

solo violin
2 2 2 2 — 2 0 0 0 — hp — str

C. Fischer	Kalmus	Luck's	Universal

3. Mélodie <1878>   4'

solo violin
2 2 2 2 — 2 0 0 0 — str

C. Fischer	Kalmus	Luck's	Universal

The Storm, op.76, TH 36 (Groza; L'orage; Das Gewitter): Overture <1864>   12'

3[1.2.pic] 3[1.2.Eh] 2 2 — 4 2 3 1 — tmp+3 — hp — str
perc: bd, cym, sd, tamtam

Belaieff	Kalmus	Luck's

Suite No.1, op.43, TH 31, D minor <1878–1879>   41'

3[1.2.3/pic] 2 2 2 — 4 2 0 0 — tmp+2 — str
perc: (in mvt 4 only) glock, tri

1. Introduzione e fuga	11'
2. Divertimento	6'
3. Intermezzo	9'
4. Marche miniature	2'
5. Scherzo	8'
6. Gavotte	5'

Kalmus	Simrock

Suite No.1, op.43, TH 31: Marche miniature <1878–1879>   2'

3[1.2.pic] 2 2 0 — 2perc — vn I & II, each divisi
perc: tri, glock

Kalmus	Luck's

Suite No.2, op.53, TH 32, C major (Caractéristique) <1883>   35'

3[1.2.3/pic] 3[1.2.Eh] 2 2 — 4 2 3 1 — 4 accordions (opt) — tmp+3 — hp — str
perc: tri, tambn, cym, bd
Optional accordions play in mvt 3 only; hp in mvt 4 only.

1. Playing with Sounds	11'
2. Waltz	6'
3. Burlesque Scherzo	5'
4. Dreams of Childhood	9'
5. Baroque Dance	4'

Kalmus	Russian	Simrock

Suite No.3, op.55, TH 33, G major <1884>   41'

3[1.2.3/pic] 3[1.2.Eh] 2 2 — 4 2 3 1 — tmp+3 — hp — str
perc: sd, tambn, tri, cym, bd
Hp in mvt 1 only.

1. Elegy	11'
2. Melancholic Waltz	6'
3. Scherzo	5'
4. Theme and Variations	19'

Kalmus	Simrock

Suite No.4, op.61, TH 34, G major (Mozartiana) <1887>   25'

2 2 2 2 — 4 2 0 0 — tmp+1 — hp — str
perc: glock, cym, sus cym
Arrangements of works by Mozart. Hp in mvt 3 only.

1. Gigue [K.574]	2'
2. Minuet [K.355]	3'
3. Prayer, after a transcription by Liszt [Ave verum corpus, K.618]	5'
4. Theme and Variations [Variations on a theme of Gluck, K.455]	15'

Kalmus	Luck's	Universal

Swan Lake, op.20, TH 12 (Lebedinoye ozero; Le lac des cygnes) <1875–1876>   139'

3[1.2.pic] 2 2 — 4 4[2tp, 2crt] 3 1 — tmp+4 — hp — str
perc: tri, glock, tamtam, cast, field dr, tambn, cym, bd
After the composer's death, this ballet score was edited by Riccardo Drigo, with many excisions and additions (orchestrations of Tchaikovsky piano pieces, op.72). The Lars Payne orchestra material is said to be the most comprehensive, including as it does the Drigo orchestrations, and various transitions and transpositions made necessary by the commonly used reordering.

Introduction	4'
Act I	49'
Act II	31'
Act III	72'

Kalmus	Payne	Russian

Swan Lake, TH 12 (Lebedinoye ozero; Le Lac des cygnes): Suite, op.20a <1875–1876>   31'

3[1.2.pic] 2 2 — 4 4[2tp, 2crt] 3 1 — tmp+3 — hp — str
perc: tri, bd, cym, tambn, cast
There are two suites from *Swan Lake*:

(1) A 6-movement suite, found in the popular Eulenburg miniature score and its reprint by Dover. This was assembled posthumously (1900) by Jürgenson, the original publisher of the ballet.

(2) An 8-movement suite created by Muzgiz, the successor to Jürgenson, using the first 5 movements of the Jürgenson publication, but omitting the 6th movement (*Scène*), and replacing it with three characteristic national dances from Act III (Spanish, Neapolitan, and Polish).

Newly engraved materials from Kalmus (A2185) include all the movements used in either suite, thus permitting performance of either version. The Luck's parts and the contents listed below are for the 8-movement suite.

1. Scène	3'
2. Valse	7'
3. Danse des cygnes	2'
4. Scène	6'
5. Danse hongroise (Czardas)	3'
6. Danse éspagnole	3'
7. Danse napolitaine	2'
8. Mazurka	5'

Kalmus	Luck's

Symphony No.1, op.13, TH 24, G minor (Winter Daydreams; Zimnie grëzy; Rêverie d'hiver) <1866; rev 1874>   44'

3[1.2.pic] 2 2 — 4 2 3 1 — tmp+2 — str
perc: bd, cym
Pic, tbn, tuba & perc in mvt 4 only.

I. Daydreams on a Winter Journey: Allegro tranquillo	11'
II. Land of Gloom, Land of Mist: Adagio cantabile ma non tanto	12'
III. Scherzo: Allegro scherzando giocoso	8'
IV. Finale: Andante lugubre; Allegro moderato; Allegro maestoso	13'

Billaudot	Kalmus	Luck's	Russian	Simrock

Symphony No.2, op.17, TH 25b, C minor (Little Russian; Ukrainian) <1872; rev 1879-1880>   32'

3[1.2.pic] 2 2 2 — 4 2 3 1 — tmp+2 — str
perc: bd, cym, tamtam
Second version, 1879-80 (the original longer version of 1872 may be found at imslp.org).
    The clarinets in the last movement are in C.
    Known as *Little Russian* because of its use of Ukrainian folksongs. In Czarist times, Ukraine was referred to as "Little Russia." The term began to gain a derogatory sense only after Tchaikovsky's death, and now might be considered offensive to Ukrainians.

I. Andante sostenuto - Allegro vivo		11'
II. Andantino marziale, quasi moderato		6'
III. Scherzo: Allegro molto vivace		5'
IV. Finale: Moderato assai - Allegro vivo		10'

Bärenreiter	Breitkopf	Kalmus	Russian	Simrock

Symphony No.3, op.29, TH 26, D major (Polish) <1875>   45'

3[1.2.pic] 2 2 2 — 4 2 3 1 — tmp — str

I. Introduzione e Allegro	14'
II. Alla tedesca: Allegro moderato e semplice	6'
III. Andante elegiaco	10'
IV. Scherzo: Allegro vivo	6'
V. Finale: Allegro con fuoco (tempo di Polacca)	9'

Bärenreiter	Breitkopf	Kalmus	Russian

Symphony No.4, op.36, TH 27, F minor <1877–1878>   44'

3[1.2.pic] 2 2 2 — 4 2 3 1 — tmp+3 — str
perc: tri, bd, cym
Kalmus offers both a "German edition" (reprint of Breitkopf) and a "Russian edition" (reprint of D. Rahter).

I. Andante sostenuto	18'
II. Andantino in modo di canzona	10'
III. Scherzo: Pizzicato ostinato	6'
IV. Finale: Allegro con fuoco	10'

Breitkopf	Kalmus	Luck's	Russian

Symphony No.5, op.64, TH 29, E minor <1888>   44'

3[1.2.3/pic] 2 2 2 — 4 2 3 1 — tmp — str
Kalmus offers both a "German edition" (reprint of Breitkopf) and a "Russian edition" (reprint of D. Rahter).

I. Andante - Allegro con anima	14'
II. Andante cantabile con alcuna licenza	12'
III. Valse: Allegro moderato	6'
IV. Finale: Andante maestoso - Allegro vivace	12'

Breitkopf	Kalmus	Luck's	Russian

Symphony No.6, op.74, TH 30, B minor (Pathétique; Pateticheskaia) <1893>   46'

3[1.2.3/pic] 2 2 2 — 4 2 3 1 — tmp+2 — str
perc: bd, cym, tamtam
In the 1st mvt, 4 bassoon notes at the end of the exposition are sometimes transferred to bass clarinet, covered by the 2nd clarinetist.

I. Adagio - Allegro non troppo	18'
II. Allegro con grazia	8'
III. Allegro molto vivace	9'
IV. Finale: Adagio lamentoso	11'

Breitkopf	Kalmus	Luck's	Russian	Simrock

Symphony No.7, E-flat major, TH 238 <1892>   40'

3[1.2.3/pic] 2 2 — 4 2 3 1 — tmp+3 — hp — str
Reconstructed from Tchaikovsky's sketches by Semyon Semyonovich Bogatïryov. (The composer had already drawn from these sketches for the 1st mvt of his unfinished *Piano Concerto No.3*. Sergey Taneyev fashioned two other concerto movements from the same source, published as Tchaikovsky's *Andante & Finale*, op.79, *q.v.*)

Allegro brillante	13'
Andante	11'
Vivace assai	7'
Allegro maestoso	9'

Kalmus	Russian

The Tempest; Fantasy-Overture, op.18, TH 44 (Burya) <1873>   18'

3[1.2.pic] 2 2 2 — 4 2 3 1 — tmp+2 — str
perc: bd, cym
Symphonic fantasia after Shakespeare's play. This work is not to be confused with the composer's *L'Orage (The Tempest)*, op.76, TH 36, which was inspired by a play of Ostrovsky.

Kalmus	Luck's

Valse-scherzo, op.34, TH 58 <1877>   10'

solo violin
2 2 2 2 — 2 0 0 0 — str
Most soloists favor a cut version that is about 6' in duration. This shortened version is believed to have been established by the Russian virtuoso Vasily Bezekirsky (1835-1919), and published by Jurgenson and various successor firms (Muzyka, Kompozitor); the well-known edition of this work by Josef Gingold (published by International) is identical in this respect.
    That Bezekirsky shortened version requires not only a number of cuts in the orchestral parts, but also the addition of 5 extra bars of music inserted just before the cadenza. New orchestra materials from LarkFrost (ed. Jo Nardolillo) are correct for this shortened version, plus they also permit as an alternative the performance of the complete original. (Other editions, such as Jurgenson, Kalmus, or Luck's, give the complete original text only, and would require significant editing to be usable with the shortened version.)
    Another well-known edition by Theodore Spiering, while including embellishment of the solo part, fits perfectly with the complete original orchestration.

Jurgenson	Kalmus	LarkFrost	Luck's

Variations on a Rococo Theme, op.33, TH 57 (original version) <1877>   18'

solo violoncello
2 2 2 2 — 2 0 0 0 — str
Kalmus ed. Paul Tobias & A. Stogorski; Benjamin ed. Natalia Gutman. A score of this version is also published by Dover. No rehearsal numbers or letters in the score or parts.
    This work is best-known and most frequently performed not in this original version, but in an arrangement by Wilhelm Fitzhagen, the dedicatee—a version, incidentally, that the composer disliked. To distinguish the versions, check the length of the statement of the theme: **Original**—24 bars; **Fitzhagen**—40 bars (8 bars repeated, 8 more bars repeated, 8 bar bridge to the next variation).

Benjamin	Kalmus

Variations on a Rococo Theme, op.33, TH 57 (Fitzenhagen version) <1876>   18'

solo violoncello
2 2 2 2 — 2 0 0 0 — str
Wilhelm Fitzenhagen (1848-1890), the celebrated cellist to whom the work is dedicated, reordered most of the variations and recomposed a few passages. This is the version most commonly known and performed. No rehearsal numbers or letters in the score or parts.
    To distinguish the versions, check the length of the statement of the theme: **Original** — 24 bars; **Fitzhagen** — 40 bars (8 bars repeated, 8 more bars repeated, 8 bar bridge to the next variation).

Kalmus	Luck's	Simrock

Voyevoda, op.3, TH 1 (The Provincial Governor): Overture <1867–1868>   7'

3[1.2.pic] 3[1.2.Eh] 2 2 — 4 2 3 1 — tmp+3 — str
perc: tri, bd, cym
Overture to the opera composed 1867-68. Not to be confused with the symphonic ballad of the same title, op.78, TH 54.

Kalmus	Luck's

Voyevoda, op.78, TH 54; Symphonic Ballad after   10'
Mickiewicz (The Provincial Governor) <1890–1891>

3 3[1.2.Eh] 3[1.2.bcl] 2 — 4 2 3 1 — tmp+1 — hp — cel[or pf] — str
perc: sd
Composed in 1890-91 after Pushkin's translation of Mickiewicz's ballad.
Not to be confused with the opera overture of the same title, op.3, TH 1.

| Belaieff | Kalmus | Luck's | Peters |

Tcherepnin, Alexander   1899-1977

(b St Petersburg, 9/21 Jan 1899; d Paris, 29 Sept 1977). American composer of
Russian origin

Bagatelles, op.5 <1913–1918>   14'

solo piano
2[1.2/pic] 2 2 2 — 2 2 0 0 — tmp+4 — str
perc: field dr, bd, woodblk, cym, tamtam, tri
Originally for piano; orchestral accompaniment added later by the
composer.
I. Allegro marciale	1'
II. Con vivacita—Molto meno mosso, lento	2'
III. Vivo	1'
IV. Lento con tristezza	2'
V. Dolce	2'
VI. Allegro con spirito	1'
VII. Prestissimo	1'
VIII. Allegro marciale	1'
IX. Allegretto	1'
X. Presto	1'
Coda	1'

| Heugel |

Georgiana, op.92 <1959>   17'

2 2 2 2 — 4 2 3 1 — tmp+5 — str
Suite from the composer's ballet *Chota Roustaveli*, 1946.
1. Ceremonial	_'
2. Veils and Daggers	_'
3. Chota and Thamar	_'
4. Kartsuli	_'
5. Apotheosis	_'

| Eulenburg |

Serenade, op.97 <1965>   16'

str

| Eulenburg |

Symphony No.2, op.77, E-flat major <1947–1951>   26'

3[1.2.3/pic] 3[1.2.Eh] 3[1.2.bcl] 3[1.2.cbn] — 4 3 3 1 — tmp+6 — hp
— cel, pf — str
I. Sostenuto; Allegro	10'
II. Lento	5'
III. Allegro	4'
IV. Poco sostenuto; Allegretto	7'

| AMP |

Tcherepnin, Nikolay   1873-1945

(b St Petersburg, 3/15 May 1873; d Issy-les-Moulineaux, nr Paris, 26 June 1945).
Russian composer

The Enchanted Kingdom, op.39 (Zacharovannoye   14'
tsarstvo; Le royaume enchante) <1910>

4[1.2.3.4/pic] 3[1.2.Eh] 3 2 — 4 3 3 1 — tmp+3 — 2hp — cel, pf —
str[14.14.10.8.8]
perc: sus cym, bd, glock, xyl

| Russian |

Teason, Deborah Fischer   1951-

(b Ossining, NY, 27 Aug 1951). American

Trinity; Concerto for Steelband & Orchestra <2002>   18'

5 solo steel pans [tenor, double second, guitar, cello, bass]
2 2 2 2 — 4 2 3 1 — tmp+3 — pf — str
perc: bd, cym, sus cym, hi-hat, set, timbales, brakedrum, tri, tambn, windchimes,
3woodblk, cowbell, bongos, guiro, maraca, claves, conga, cabasa
1. CC's prayer	5'
2. Sisters of Mercy	7'
3. Jump Up and Shout	6'

| Teason |

Telemann, Georg Philipp   1681-1767

(b Magdeburg, 14 March 1681; d Hamburg, 25 June 1767). German

TWV = M. Ruhnke: *Georg Philipp Telemann; thematisch-systematisches
Verzeichnis seiner Werke*. Kassel, 1984-99 [instrumental music only]

TVWV = W. Menke: *Thematisches Verzeichnis der Vokalwerke von
Georg Philipp Telemann*. Frankfurt, 1982-83

Concert Suite, TWV 55:Es2, F major   21'

solo recorder
cnt — str
Ed. Adolf Hoffmann.
    Originally an *Overture* in E-flat major, calling for *flute pastorelle*,
which is a recorder in E-flat, no longer readily available. The editor
transposed the work to F major to suit the modern recorder (pitched in F).
1. Ouverture: Pastorelle	8'
2. Menuet I & II	3'
3. Sarabande	2'
4. Bourrée I en Echo alternat., & Bourrée II	3'
5. Passepied	2'
6. Gavotte	1'
7. Gigue	2'

| Kalmus | Nagel |

Concerto, Flute, TWV 51:D2, D major   17'

cnt — str
Ed. Felix Schroeder.
1. Moderato	4'
2. Allegro	4'
3. Largo	5'
4. Vivace	4'

| Eulenburg |

Concerto, Flute, E minor   12'

cnt — str

| Kalmus | Luck's |

Concerto, 2 Flutes, TWV 52:a2, A minor   8'

cnt — str
Ed. Fritz Stein.
1. Gravement	2'
2. Vistement	2'
3. Largement	2'
4. Vivement	2'

| Kalmus | Nagel |

Concerto, Flute & Violin, TWV 53:A2, A major <1733>   *21'*

cnt — str
Ed. Johann Philipp Hinnenthal.
  From the composer's *Musique de table (Tafelmusik)*, 1733.
  I. *Largo*   4'
  II. *Allegro*   6'
  III. *Gratioso*   4'
  IV. *Allegro*   7'

> Bärenreiter

Concerto, Horn, TWV 51:D8, D major   *9'*

0 1 0 0 — cnt — str
  1. *Vivace*   2'
  2. *Largo*   3'
  3. *Allegro*   4'

> Peters

Concerto, 2 Horns & 2 Violins, TWV 54:Es1, E-flat major <1733>   *16'*

cnt — str
Ed. Max Seiffert, W. Bergmann. From *Tafelmusik* III, no.3.
  Horn parts described as *trombe selvatiche* (= "forest trumpets").

> Breitkopf

Concerto, Oboe, TWV 51:d1, D minor   *8'*

cnt — str
Ed. Hermann Töttcher.
  1. *Adagio*   2'
  2. *[Allegro]*   3'
  3. *Adagio*   1'
  4. *[Allegro]*   2'

> Sikorski

Concerto, Oboe, TWV 51:e1, E minor   *12'*

cnt — str
Ed. Hermann Töttcher.
  1. *Andante*   3'
  2. *Allegro molto* 3'
  3. *Largo*   4'
  4. *Allegro*   2'

> Sikorski

Concerto, Oboe, TWV 51:f1, F minor   *8'*

cnt — str
Ed. Felix Schroeder.
  1. *Allegro*   3'
  2. *Largo e piano*   3'
  3. *Vivace*   2'

> Eulenburg

Concerto, Oboe d'amore, TWV 51:A2, A major <1740>   *14'*

cnt — str
Ed. Felix Schroeder.
  1. *Siciliano*   3'
  2. *Allegro*   3'
  3. *Largo*   3'
  4. *Vivace*   5'

> Eulenburg

Concerto, Recorder, TWV 51:F1, F major   *13'*

cnt — str
Ed. Manfred Ruetz.
  1. *Affettuoso*   3'
  2. *Allegro*   4'
  3. *Adagio*   3'
  4. *Menuet I & II* 3'

> Bärenreiter

Concerto, Recorder & Flute TWV 52:e1, E minor   *13'*

cnt — str
Ed. Herbert Kölbel.
  1. *Largo*   3'
  2. *Allegro*   4'
  3. *Largo*   3'
  4. *Presto*   3'

> Bärenreiter   Kalmus

Concerto, Trumpet & 2 Oboes, TWV 53:D2, D major   *15'*

cnt — str
  1. *Allegro*   3'
  2. *Adagio*   2'
  3. *Aria*   4'
  4. *Vivace*   5'

> Sikorski   Simrock

Concerto, Viola, TWV 51:G9, G major   *12'*

cnt — str
Ed. Hellmuth Christian Wolff.
  1. *Largo*   4'
  2. *Allegro*   3'
  3. *Andante*   3'
  4. *Presto*   2'

> Bärenreiter

Concerto, Violin, TWV 51:a2, A minor   *10'*

cnt — str
Ed. Hellmuth Christian Wolff.
  This work is said to be also the overture to *Emma und Eginhard*.
  1. *Allegro*   4'
  2. *Andante*   2'
  3. *Presto*   3'

> Bärenreiter

Concerto, 2 Violins, TWV 52:C2, C major   *11'*

cnt — str
Ed. Adolf Hoffmann.
  1. *Allegro*   _'
  2. *Adagio*   _'
  3. *Allabreve*   _'

> Kalmus   Möseler

Das ist je gewisslich wahr, TVWV 1:181

see: Bach, Johann Sebastian, 1685-1750
        Cantata no.141

Don Quichotte, TWV 55:G10 (Ouverture burlesque de Quichotte)   *17'*

cnt — str
Ed. Gustav Lenzewski.
  1. *Overture*   5'
  2. *Don Quichottes Erwachen (The Awakening of Don Quixote)*   2'
  3. *Seine Angriff auf die Windmühlen (His Attack on the Windmills)*   2'
  4. *Die Liebesseufzer nach der Prinzessin Aline (Sighs of Love for Aline)* 3'
  5. *Der geprellte Sancho Pansa (Sancho Pansa Swindled)*   2'
  6. *Der Galopp der Rosinante (Rosinante Galloping)*   2'
  7. *Don Quichottes Ruhe (Don Quixote at Rest)*   1'

> Kalmus   Luck's   Vieweg

Ich weiss, dass mein Erlöser lebt, TVWV 1:873

see: Bach, Johann Sebastian, 1685-1750
        Cantata no.160

Laudate Jehovam, omnes gentes, TVWV 7:25 <1758>   7'

chorus
cnt — str[no va]
Psalm 117.

> Concordia

Ouverture des nations anciens et modernes, TWV 55:G4   18'
<1721>

cnt — str
1. *Ouverture*   3'
2. *Menuet I & II*   3'
3. *Les Allemands anciens & Les Allemands modernes*   4'
4. *Les Suédois*   3'
5. *Les Danois*   2'
6. *Les vielles femmes*   2'

> Kalmus   Luck's   Vieweg

Overture, TWV 55:C1, C major   13'

str[no cnt]
Ed. Helmut Mönkemeyer.
1. *Ouverture*   _'
2. *La complaisance*   _'
3. *L'indignation*   _'
4. *Menuet I & II*   _'
5. *Loure*   _'
6. *Très vite*   _'

> Peters

Overture, TWV 55:C3, C major (Wassermusik; Water   26'
Music) <1723>

2[1/rec.2/rec] 2 0 1 — cnt — str
Ed. Friedrich Noack.
1. *Ouverture*   8'
2. *Sarabande: Die schlafende Thetis*   3'
3. *Bourée: Die erwachende Thetis*   2'
4. *Loure: Der verliebte Neptunus*   2'
5. *Gavotte: Die spielenden Najaden*   1'
6. *Harlequinade: Die schertzenden Tritons*   2'
7. *Der stürmende Aeolus*   2'
8. *Menuet: Der angenehme Zephir*   3'
9. *Gig: Ebbe und Fluth*   1'
10. *Canarie: Die lustigen Bots-Leut*   2'

> Bärenreiter

Overture, TWV 55:D21, D major (Pour M. le Landgrave   21'
Louis VIII d'Hessen-Darmstadt) <1765>

0 2 0 1 — 2 0 0 0 — cnt — str
Ed. Friedrich Noack.
1. *Ouverture*   6'
2. *Plainte*   6'
3. *Réjouissance*   1'
4. *Carillon*   2'
5. *Tintamare*   1'
6. *Loure*   2'
7. *Menuet I & II*   3'

> Bärenreiter   Kalmus

Overture, TWV 55:Es2

see his: Concert Suite, TWV 55:Es2, F major

Overture, TWV 55:fis1, F-sharp minor <1701–1767>   20'

cnt — str
Ed. Friedrich Noack.
1. *Ouverture*   7'
2. *Les plaisirs*   2'
3. *Angloise*   1'
4. *La badinerie italienne*   1'
5. *Loure*   2'
6. *Menuet I & II*   3'
7. *Courante*   2'
8. *Le batelage*   1'

> Bärenreiter

Overture, TWV 55:g4, G minor <?1721>   14'

0 3 0 1 — cnt — str
Ed. Friedrich Noack.
1. *Ouverture*   _'
2. *Rondeau*   _'
3. *Les irrésoluts*   _'
4. *Les capricieux*   _'
5. *Loure*   _'
6. *Gasconnade*   _'
7. *Menuet I & II*   _'

> Bärenreiter

Overture, TWV Anh.55:G1, G major (La putain)   10'
<1701–1767>

cnt — str
Ed. Friedrich Noack. Some scholars doubt Telemann's authorship.
1. *Alla breve*   _'
2. *Masquerade: Die Schneckenpost*   _'
3. *Loure: Die Bauren Kirchweyh*   _'
4. *Menuet*   _'
5. *Rondeau: Der Hexen-Tanz*   _'
6. *Sarabande*   _'
7. *Marche*   _'
8. *Gasconnade: In der Laussherberg*   _'
9. *Menuet & Trio*   _'
10. *Bourée: Die Baass Lisabeth*   _'
11. *Hornpipe: Der Vetter Michel Ziehbart* _'

> Bärenreiter   Luck's

So du mit deinem Munde, TVWV 1:1350

Published as the second movement of Cantata no.145 by Johann
Sebastian Bach.

Suite, TWV 44:7, F major   17'

0 0 0 0 — 2 0 0 0 — cnt — str[no va]
Ed. Horst Buettner.
    Probably a chamber work intended for 2hn, 2vn & cnt.
1. *Ouverture*   _'
2. *Sarabande*   _'
3. *Menuet*   _'
4. *Bourée*   _'

> Eulenburg   Kalmus

Suite, TWV 55:a2, A minor <1725>   30'

solo recorder
cnt — str
Ed. Horst Büttner.
1. *Ouverture*   10'
2. *Les plaisirs*   3'
3. *Air à l'italien*   6'
4. *Minuet I & I*   4'
5. *Réjouissance*   2'
6. *Passepied I & II*   2'
7. *Polonoise*   3'

> Eulenburg   Kalmus

Die Tageszeiten, TWV 20:39 <1701–1767>   54'

solos SATB   chorus
2 2 0 1 — cnt — str
Ed. Anton Heilmann. A cycle of cantatas.
    1. Der Morgen (Morning) [nos.1-5]   *16'*
    2. Der Mittag (Noon) [nos.6-9]   *12'*
    3. Der Abend (Evening) [nos.10-13]   *13'*
    4. Die Nacht (Night) [nos.14-17]   *13'*

| Bärenreiter | Kalmus |

Wider die falschen Propheten, TVWV 1:908 (Beware of False Prophets)

chorus or solos SAB
cnt — str
Violas optional. Telemann suggests doubling the upper voices with oboes and/or transverse flutes.
    Ed. Walter Bergmann.

| Eulenburg |

Territo, James   1978-

(b Pontiac, MI, 9 Dec 1978). American

John Henry vs. the Machine <2004>   12'

narrator
1 0 0 1 — 1 0 0 1 — ssx[or oboe or clarinet] — tmp+2 — str or str 4t
perc: sus cym, sd, tamtam, vib, 2marim, chimes[G4,A5]
Virtuoso tuba part, personifying folk hero John Henry. The familiar folk tune "John Henry" does not appear.

| Territo |

Theofanidis, Christopher   1967-

(b 18 Dec 1967). American composer of Greek descent.

Rainbow Body <2000>   13'

3[1.2.3/pic] 3 3[1.2/Ebcl.3/bcl] 3[1.2.3/cbn] — 4 3 3 1 — tmp+3 — hp — pf — str
perc: bd, sus cym, cym, Chinescym, tri, gong, glock, vib, chimes, claves, congas
At a point near the end of the score, there is an option for the string players to erupt in cheering—a tradition originating with the London Symphony Orchestra in 2003. The composer found the practice to be "wonderful and joyous" and has approved it.

| Opus 125 |

Rex tremendae majestatis <2008>   8'

solo organ
0 0 0 0 — 4 4 3 1 — tmp+2 — [no str]
perc: bd, cym, sus cym, szl cym, Chinescym, tamtam, chimes

| Opus 125 |

Thiriet, Maurice   1906-1972

(b Meulan, 2 May 1906; d Puys, 28 Sept 1972). French

Danseries françaises   14'

str
    I. Cadenza et Bransle   _'
    II. Menuet-Carillon   _'
    III. Sarabande et Forlane   _'
    IV. Tourdion   _'
    V. Plainte et Tambourin   _'

| Billaudot |

Thomas, Ambroise   1811-1896

(b Metz, 5 Aug 1811; d Paris, 12 Feb 1896). French

Mignon: Overture <1866>   8'

2[1.pic] 2 2 2 — 4 2 3 0 — tmp+4 — hp — str
perc: bd, cym, tri, tambn, sd
Kalmus ed. (2010) by Clinton F. Nieweg & Nancy M. Bradburd.

| Breitkopf | Heugel | Kalmus | Luck's |

Raymond: Overture <1851>   7'

2[1.2/pic] 2 2 2 — 4 2 3 0 — tmp+4 — str
perc: bd, cym, sd, tri

| Heugel | Kalmus | Luck's |

Thomas, Augusta Read   1964-

(b Glen Cove, NY, 24 April 1964). American

Aureole <2013>   9'

3[1.2.pic] 2 2 3[1.2.cbn] — 4 3 2 1 — 4perc — str
perc: glock, crot, bongos, vib, claves, congas, chimes, td, bd, taiko, 5tri, 2woodblk, 4tomtom, 3fingercym, 2sus cym
Designed to precede a performance of the Beethoven Symphony No.9.
    An optional cut reduces the duration by 1 minute and eliminates the taiko and tenor drum.

| Schirmer |

Ceremonial <1999>   8'

4[1.2.3.pic] 3 4[1.2.3.bcl] 2 — 4 3[1.2.pic tp] 3 1 — 2ssx[opt] — 4perc — hp — str
perc: marim, crot, glock, congas, chimes, woodblk, claves, bongos, bd, 2sus cym, 2vib

| Schirmer |

Helios Choros I (Sun God Dancers) <2006>   9'

3[1.2.pic] 3[1.2.Eh] 3[1.2.3/bcl] 2 — 4 4 3 1 — 4perc — 2hp — pf/cel — str[16.14.12.10.8]
perc: marim, glock, bongos, vib, congas, chimes, sd, bd, claves, xyl, szl cym, 2crot, 4woodblk, 3sus cym, 3tri, 4tomtom
Part I of a 40-minute triptych; may be performed independently.

| Schirmer |

Helios Choros II (Sun God Dancers) <2007>   18'

3[1.2/afl.pic] 3[1.2.Eh] 3[1.2.3/bcl] 2 — 4 4 3 1 — 4perc — 2hp — pf/cel — str[16.14.12.10.8]
perc: glock, marim, bongos, vib, chimes, sd, bd, xyl, szl cym, sus cym, crot, 4woodblk, 5tri, 4tomtom, 3finger cym, 2pr claves, 2tamtam
Part II of a 40-minute triptych; may be performed independently.

| Schirmer |

Helios Choros III (Sun God Dancers) <2007>   11'

3[1.2.pic] 3[1.2.Eh] 3[1.2.3/bcl] 2 — 4 4 3 1 — 4perc — 2hp — pf/cel — str[16.14.12.10.8]
perc: glock, marim, bongos, vib, chimes, sd, bd, xyl, szl cym, sus cym, congas, 4woodblk, 5tri, 4tomtom, 3finger cym, 2pr claves, 2tamtam, 2crot
Part III of a 40-minute triptych; may be performed independently.

| Schirmer |

Hemke Concerto (Prisms of Light) <2014>   19'

solo alto saxophone
3[1.2.pic] 2 2 1 — 2 2 2 1 — 4perc — hp — pf, cel — str[8.7.6.5.4]
Mvts played without pause.
    I. Illuminations   _'
    II. Sunrise Ballad   _'
    III. Chasing Radiance   _'
    IV. Solar Rings   _'

| Schirmer |

Jubilee <2010>   19'

3[1.2.pic] 3[1.2.Eh] 3[1.2.bcl] 2[1.2/cbn] — 4 4 3 1 — 6perc — 2hp
— pf, cel — str[16.14.12.10.8]
perc: bd, sd, glock, xyl, marim, chimes, crot, bongos, claves, congas, 4sus cym,
5tomtom, 5tri, 2tamtam, 2vib (2bows), 3finger cym
4th mvt direction: "Like a be-bop jazz big band meets Varèse."
  I. fanfare: awaking rituals   _'
  II. caprice: effervescent arabesques   _'
  III. reverie: prayer for a departed friend _'
  IV. gambol: whimsical virtuosic romp   _'

Schirmer

Of Paradise and Light <2010>   5'

str[no db]

Schirmer

Orbital Beacons; Concerto for Orchestra <1998>   27'

4[1.2.3.pic] 4 4[1.2/cb cl.3.bcl] 3[1.2.cbn] — 5 4[1.2(pic tp).3.4] 3 1
— 4perc — 2hp — str[14.12.10.10.8]
perc: bd, szl cym, timbales, xyl, vib, crot, bongos, 2sus cym, 5tomtom, 3tri,
2tamtam, 2glock, 2marim, 2chimes, 2woodblk, 2pr claves, 6buttongong, 6tuned
cowbells
Special seating is required: players are divided into 8 "concertinos" of 3-4
musicians each, and 2 "ensembles" (the remainder).
  I. Aquila   4'
  II. Lyra   4'
  III. Eridanus   3'
  IV. Cygnus   4'
  V. Coma Berenices   6'
  VI Andromeda   6'

Schirmer

Tangle <2003>   20'

4[1.2.3.pic] 4[1.2.3.Eh] 4[1.2.3.bcl] 3[1.2.cbn] — 4 4[[2pic tp, 2tp]] 3
1 — tmp+4 — str
perc: bd, sus cym, Chinescym, glock, xyl, marim, vib, chimes, crot, bongos,
congas, 5tomtom, 2tri, 2tamtam, bell[G3], cowbell[G4]
  I. Leaning Against the Sun   _'
  II. Certain Twilights   _'
  III. Cracks in the Glass Horizon _'

Schirmer

Terpsichore's Dream   17'

2[1.2/pic] 1 2[1.2/bcl] 1 — 2 2 1 0 — 4perc — 2hp — pf/cel —
str[9.8.7.6.3]
perc: glock, marim, bongos, claves, sus cym, vib, congas, chimes, sd, bd, xyl, szl
cym, 4woodblk, 5tri, 3finger cym, 2pr claves, 2crot, 4tomtom, 2tamtam

Schirmer

Words of the Sea <1996>   17'

4[1.2.3.pic] 3[1.2.Eh] 4[1.2/cbcl.3.bcl] 3[1.2.cbn] — 4 3 3 1 —
tmp+4 — hp[preferably doubled] — pf — str
perc: szl cym, glock, xyl, marim, vib, chimes, crot, bongos, claves, 2bd, 2tri, 2sus
cym, 2tamtams, 3congas, 5tomtoms, 5rototoms, 4buttongongs[C#,D,G#,A]
2 additional assistant percussionists may be desirable.

Schirmer

Thompson, Randall   1899-1984

(b New York, 21 April 1899; d Cambridge, MA, 9 July 1984). American

Symphony No.1 <1924–1929>   31'

3[1.2.3/pic] 3[1.2.Eh] 3[1.2.bcl] 3[1.2.cbn] — 4 2 3 1 — tmp+3 — hp
— org — str
  1. Allegro brioso   11'
  2. Poco adagio   7'
  3. Allegro   13'

C. Fischer

Symphony No.2 <1931>   28'

3[1.2.3/pic] 3[1.2.3/Eh] 3 3 — 4 3 3 1 — tmp+1 — str
perc: cym
  I. Allegro   8'
  II. Largo   4'
  III. Vivace   6'
  IV. Andante moderato - Allegro con spirito 10'

C. Fischer

Thomson, Virgil   1896-1989

(b Kansas City, MO, 25 Nov 1896; d New York, 30 Sept 1989). American

Bugles and Birds; A Portrait of Pablo Picasso <1940; rev   2'
(orchd) 1944>

2 2 2 2 — 4 2 3 0 — str
Piano work (1940); orchestrated by the composer in 1944.

Schirmer

Dance in Praise (Gaudeamus igitur; Let Us Live, Then,   9'
and Be Glad) <1962>

chorus
2 2[1.2/Eh] 2 2 — 2 2 0 0 — 4perc — pf — str
perc: tri, tambn, sd, field dr, sus cym, cast, glock, xyl
Text, in Latin or English, of *Gaudeamus igitur*, but the familiar tune is
not used.

Boosey

Fanfare for France <1943>   3'

0 0 0 0 — 4 3 3 0 — 2perc — [no str]
perc: sd, field dr

Boosey

Four Saints in Three Acts [oratorio version]   45'
<1927–1928>

solo SSMs ATBarBs   double chorus
1[fl/pic] 1[ob/Eh] 1 1 — 2 1 1 0 — 2perc — harm, accordion — str
Based on the composer's opera of the same title.

Schirmer

Fugue and Chorale on "Yankee Doodle" <1945>   5'

1 1 3[incl bcl] 1 — 2 3 2 0 — tmp+1 — str
perc: cym
From the film score *Tuesday in November*.

Luck's   Schirmer

Louisiana Story: Acadian Songs and Dances (Suite No.2)   15'
<1948>

2[1.2/pic] 2[1.2/Eh] 2 2 — 2 2 2 0 — accordion[or pf] — 2perc —
hp[or pf] — str
perc: sd, field dr, bd, cym, xyl, sus cym
From film score.
  1. Sadness   2'
  2. Papa's Tune   1'
  3. A Narrative   2'
  4. The Alligator and the 'Coon 2'
  5. Super-Sadness   2'
  6. Walking Song   2'
  7. The Squeeze Box   4'

Luck's   Schirmer

Louisiana Story: Boy Fights Alligator (Fugue) <1948>   4'

2 2 2 2 — 4 2 3 1 — tmp+3 — str

Luck's   Schirmer

Louisiana Story: Suite [No.1] <1948>   19'

2[1.2/pic] 2[1.2/Eh] 2[1.2/bcl] 2[1.2/cbn] — 4 2 3 1 — tmp+3 — hp
— str
perc: glock, xyl, cym, sd, field dr, sus cym, bd, tamtam
  1. *Pastoral (The Bayou and the Marsh Buggy)*   5'
  2. *Chorale (The Derrick Arrives)*   3'
  3. *Passacaglia (Robbing the Alligator's Nest)*   7'
  4. *Fugue (Boy Fights Alligator)*   4'

    Schirmer

Parson Weems and the Cherry Tree <1975>   22'

1[fl/pic] 0 1[cl/bcl] 0 — 0 1[tp/flug] 1 0 — 1perc — vn, db
perc: sd, xyl, glock, tmp, 2tomtoms
  1. *The Parson Writes His Book*   1'
  2. *The Parson Instructs George and Martha in the Gentle Art of the Dance* 2'
  3. *The Hatchet*   1'
  4. *The Pitcher and the Bucket*   1'
  5. *Rum is a Demon*   2'
  6. *Martha's Secret Love*   1'
  7. *Molly Whips the Army into Shape*   1'
  8. *Crossing the Delaware*   3'
  9. *Hard Times at Valley Forge*   4'
  10. *On to Glory*   2'
  11. *Cavalry Maneuvers*   1'
  12. *Chopping the Tree and Winging to Heaven*   3'

    Boosey

Pilgrims and Pioneers <1964>   10'

1 1[1/Eh] 2[1.2/bcl] 1 — 4 2 0 0 — 2perc — str
From film score *Journey to America*.

    Luck's   Schirmer

The Plow That Broke the Plains: Suite <1936>   14'

1 1[1/opt Eh] 3[1.2/opt asx.opt bcl/opt tsx] 1[1.2alt to bcl/tsx] — 2 2 2
0 — banjo/gtr [or pf or hp] — tmp+2 — str
perc: bd, sd, tri, cym, sus cym, tambn, tomtom, woodblk, cowbell, horse hooves
If bcl & tsx are both lacking, a 2nd bn must be added.
  1. *Prelude*   1'
  2. *Pastorale (Grass)* 1'
  3. *Cattle*   3'
  4. *Blues (Speculation)* 3'
  5. *Drought*   1'
  6. *Devastation*   5'

    Luck's   Schirmer

The River: Suite <1937>   23'

1[1/pic] 2[1.2/Eh] 2[1.2/bcl] 1 — 2 2 2 0 — banjo — tmp+2 — str
perc: sd, bd, cym, tri, tamtam, glock, iron ratchet, 2iron bars
From the film score.
  1. *The Old South*   9'
  2. *Industrial Expansion in the Mississippi Valley* 4'
  3. *Soil Erosion and Floods*   6'
  4. *Finale*   4'

    Southern

Sea Piece with Birds <1952>   5'

3[1.2.3/pic] 3 3 3 — 4 3 3 0 — 2perc — hp[opt] — str
perc: cym, sus cym, tamtam
May be combined with two other works to form a triptych: *Three
Pictures for Orchestra (1. The Seine at Night; 2. Wheat Field at Noon;
3. Sea Piece with Birds)*

    Schirmer

The Seine at Night <1947>   8'

3[1.2.3/pic] 3[1.2.3/Eh] 3[1.2.3/bcl] 3[1.2.3/cbn] — 4 3 3 1 — 1perc
— 2hp — cel — str
perc: cym, sus cym, tamtam, 2tri
May be combined with two other works to form a triptych: *Three
Pictures for Orchestra (1. The Seine at Night; 2. Wheat Field at Noon;
3. Sea Piece with Birds)*

    Schirmer

A Solemn Music and a Joyful Fugue <1949; rev (orchd)   12'
1962>

3[1.2.3/pic] 3[1.2.3/Eh] 3[1.2.3/bcl] 3 — 4 3 3 1 — tmp+4 — str
perc: sd, field dr, bd, tri, cym, tamtam
A Solemn Music originally for band; orchestrated by the composer.
  1. *A Solemn Music*   7'
  2. *A Joyful Fugue*   5'

    Schirmer

Symphony on a Hymn Tune <1928>   20'

2[1.2/pic] 2 2 3[1.2.cbn] — 4 2 3 1 — tmp+4[or 6] — str
perc: bd, cym, tambn, sd, sus cym, tamtam, tri, glock, rattle
Cbn has only 22 notes, all doubled by 3rd tbn, tuba and double basses.
  1. *Introduction and Allegro*   8'
  2. *Andante cantabile*   4'
  3. *Allegretto*   3'
  4. *Allegro*   5'

    Southern

Symphony No.2 <1931; rev 1941>   16'

3[1.2.3/pic] 3[1.2.Eh] 3[1.2.3/bcl] 3[1.2.3/cbn] — 4 2 3 1 — 3perc —
str
perc: sd, td, cym, sus cym, bd, tamtam
Arr. of *Piano Sonata No.1* (1929).
  1.   4'
  2.   6'
  3.   6'

    MCA

Wheat Field at Noon <1948>   6'

3[1.2.3/pic] 3[1.2.3/Eh] 3[1.2.3/bcl] 3[1.2.3/cbn] — 4 3 3 0 — 3perc
— hp — str
May be combined with two other works to form a triptych: *Three
Pictures for Orchestra (1. The Seine at Night; 2. Wheat Field at Noon;
3. Sea Piece with Birds)*

    Schirmer

Thorne, Francis   1922-

(b Bay Shore, NY, 23 June 1922). American

Elegy for Orchestra <1962–1963>   14'

2[1.2/pic] 2[1.2/Eh] 2[1.2/bcl] 2 — 4 2 3 1 — tmp+2 — hp — str
perc: bd, cym, sus cym, sd, tri, gong

    Merion

Ticheli, Frank   1958-

(b Monroe, LA, 1958). American

Radiant Voices <1993>   20'

3[1.2.pic] 3[1.2.Eh] 2 2 — 4 3 3 1 — tmp+3 — hp — str
perc: bd, cym, sd, timbales, tambn, tamtam, glock, xyl, vib, crot, flexatone,
templeblks, whip, bongos, ratch, vibrslp, 3sus cym, 2tri, 4tomtoms, 2woodblk,
cabasa, 2 police whistles

    Helicon

Tippett, Michael   1905-1998

(b London, 2 Jan 1905; d London, 8 Jan 1998). English

Byzantium <1989–1990>   25'

solo soprano
3[all/pic] 3[incl Eh] 3[incl Ebcl,bcl] 3[incl cbn] — 4 2 3 1 — 7perc
— 2hp — cel, synth — str
perc: glock, chimes, xyl, bd, vib, cym, claves, sd, td, tri, cast, crot, 2sus cym,
2woodblk, tmp, 16rototoms, 4anvils, 5tuned gongs [G2,E3,F#3,D#4,A#4]

    Schott

A Child of Our Time <1939–1941>   72'

chorus   solos SATB
2 3[1.2.Eh] 2 3[1.2.cbn] — 4 3 3 0 — tmp/cym — str
    PART I

1. The World Turns on its Dark Side	5'
2. Man Has Measured the Heavens	3'
3. Is Evil Then Good?	3'
4. Now in Each Nation	1'
5. When Shall the Usurer's City Cease?	2'
6. I Have No Money for My Bread	3'
7. How Can I Cherish My Man in Such Days	4'
8. Steal Away	3'

    PART II

9. A Star Rises in Mid-Winter	4'
10. And a Time Came	1'
11. Away With Them!	1'
12. Where They Could, They Fled	1'
13. We Cannot Have Them in Our Empire	1'
14. And the Boy's Mother Wrote a Letter	1'
15. O My Son!	1'
16. Nobody Knows the Trouble I See, Lord	1'
17. The Boy Becomes Desperate in His Agony	1'
18. They Took a Terrible Vengeance	1'
19. Burn Down Their Houses!	1'
20. Men Were Ashamed of What Was Done	1'
21. Go Down, Moses	3'
22. My Dreams Are All Shattered	4'
23. What Have I Done to You, My Son?	2'
24. The Dark Forces Rise Like a Flood	1'
25. O, By and By	1'

    PART III

26. The Cold Deepens	6'
27. The Soul of a Man	2'
28. The Words of Wisdom Are These	7'
29. I Would Know My Shadow and My Light	6'
30. Deep River	4'

Schott

Concerto for Double String Orchestra <1938–1939>   23'

str

1. Allegro con brio	6'
2. Adagio cantabile	9'
3. Allegro molto	8'

Schott

Concerto for Orchestra <1962–1963>   32'

2 2[1.Eh] 2[1.bcl] 2[1.cbn] — 3 2 2 1 — tmp+3 — hp — pf — str
perc: cym, tri, woodblk, xyl, field dr, tamtam, td, bd
Optimum strings: 6-8vn, 4va, 5vc, 4db (no strings in first mvt).

1. Allegro	10'
2. Lento	12'
3. Allegro molto	10'

Schott

Concerto, Piano <1953–1955>   32'

2 2 2 2 — 4 2 3 0 — tmp — cel — str

Schott

Concerto, Violin, Viola & Violoncello (Triple Concerto)   24'
<1978–1979>

1[1/afl/pic] 2[1.Eh/bass ob] 4[1.2.bcl1.(opt bcl2)] 2[1.cbn] — 4 2 2 0
— tmp+5 — hp — cel — str[min 8.8.6.4.4]
perc: bd, chimes, cast, glock, vib, marim, tri, claves, sus cym, td, sd, field dr, cym,
2woodblks, 5tuned gongs [G#2,A#2,C3,D3,E3]

I. Medium fast	13'
Interlude: Medium slow	3'
II. Very slow - Calmer still	10'
Interlude: Medium fast	2'
III. Medium fast	7'

Schott

Divertimento on "Sellinger's Round" <1953–1954>   20'

1 1 1 1 — 1 1 0 0 — str

1. Allegro	3'
2. Lament (Andante espressivo)	7'
3. Presto	2'
4. Adagio	4'
5. Allegro assai	4'

Schott

Fantasia concertante on a Theme of Corelli (Omaggio a   19'
Italia) <1953>

concertino: 2 violins, violoncello
str
2 string orchestras, one of which (the concerto terzo) acts as continuo.

Schott

Fantasia on a Theme of Handel <1939–1941>   16'

solo piano
2[1/pic.2/pic] 2 2 2 — 4 2 3 0 — tmp+1 — str
perc: cym, tri, sd

Schott

Little Music <1946>   10'

str

1. Prelude	1'
2. Fugue	3'
3. Air	4'
4. Finale	2'

Schott

The Mask of Time <1981–1982>   95'

3[all/pic] 3[1.2.Eh] 3[1.2.bcl] 3[1.2.cbn] — 6 3 3 1 — ssx, asx —
tmp+6 — hp — pf, elec org — str
perc: field dr, td, bd, cym, sus cym, xyl, marim, vib, glock, chimes, woodblk,
claves, cast, marac, tambn, tri, thunder, tamtam, 3tomtoms, boobam, bamboo
windchimes, 2anvils, 2gongs, 4tuned gongs

PART I	
I. Presence	_'
II. Creation of the World by Music	_'
III. Jungle	_'
IV. The Ice-Cap Moves South-North	_'
V. Dream of the Paradise Garden	_'
PART II	
VI. The Triumph of Life	_'
VII. Mirror of Whitening Light	_'
VIII. Hiroshima, mon amour	_'
IX. Three Songs	_'
The Severed Head	
The Beleaguered Friends	
The Young Actor Steps Out	
X. The Singing Will Never Be Done	_'

Schott

The Midsummer Marriage: Ritual Dances <1946–1952>   24'

optional chorus; optional solo voices SMsTB
2[1/pic.2/pic] 2 2 2 — 4 2 3 0 — tmp+1 — hp — cel — str
perc: cym, gong, bd, sus cym, tri

1. Prelude	2'
2. Transformation and Preparation for the First Dance	2'
3. The First Dance: "Earth in Autumn"	2'
4. Transformation and Preparation for the Second Dance	2'
5. The Second Dance: "The Waters in Winter"	3'
6. Transformation and Preparation for the Third Dance	2'
7. The Third Dance: "The Air in Spring"	4'
8. Preparation and the Fourth Dance: "Fire in Summer"	7'

Schott

New Year: Suite <1989>   29'

3[all/pic] 3[1.2.Eh] 3[1.2.bcl] 3[1.2.cbn] — 4 2 3 1 — asx, tsx,
bsx/ssx — elec gtr, bass gtr — taped effects — 5perc — hp — str[min
4.4.4.4.2]

perc: tamtam, glock, brake dr, td, bd, xyl, claves, cym, vib, whip, sus cym, tambn,
cast, tri, chimes, set, woodblk, gong, rattle, 2tomtoms, slit drum

1. The Space Ship Lands	1'
2. Prelude	1'
3. The Shaman Dance	1'
4. The Hunt for the Scapegoat	1'
5. Donny's Skarade	4'
6. Donny's Dream	4'
7. Dream Interlude	1'
8. Jo Ann's Dreamsong	5'
9. Love Scene for Jo Ann and Pelegrin	6'
10. Paradise Dance	2'
11. The Beating-Out of the Scapegoat	1'
12. Ringing in the New Year	1'
13. The Space Ship Takes Off Again	1'

Schott

Songs for Dov <1969–1970>   25'

solo tenor

2[1/pic.2/pic] 2[incl Eh] 2[incl bcl] 2[incl cbn] — 3 1 1 0 — elec
gtr[or elec hpsd] — tmp+4 — hp — pf — str[2.2.2.3.2; may be increased
to 6.6.4.6.4]

perc: vib, xyl, slgh-bells, set, chimes, tri, tamtam, cast, claves, cym, bd, tambn,
templeblks, whip

Schott

Suite for the Birthday of Prince Charles (Suite in D)   16'
<1948>

2[1.2/pic] 2 2 2 — 4 2 3 1 — tmp+1 — hp — str
perc: sd, chimes, cym

I. Intrada	3'
II. Berceuse	3'
III. Procession and Dance	3'
IV. Carol	3'
V. Finale	4'

Schott

Symphony No.1 <1944–1945>   37'

3[all/pic] 2 2 3[incl cbn] — 4 3 3 1 — tmp+1 — str
perc: bd, cym

I. Allegro vigoroso: quasi alla breve	11'
II. Adagio	12'
III. Presto	6'
IV. Allegro moderato ma con brio e più tarde con delicatezza	8'

Schott

Symphony No.2 <1956–1957>   37'

2[incl pic] 2 2 2 — 4 2 3 1 — tmp+1 — hp — pf, opt cel — str
perc: bd, sd, cym

Allegro vigoroso	10'
Adagio molto e tranquillo	12'
Presto veloce	6'
Allegro moderato	9'

Schott

Symphony No.3 <1970–1972>   57'

solo soprano

3[incl 2pic] 3[incl Eh] 3[incl Ebcl,bcl] 3[incl cbn] — 4 2[incl flug] 3
1 — tmp+7 — hp — cel, pf — str
perc: bd, td, field dr, cym, sus cym, tamtam, chimes, claves, marac, templeblks,
woodblk, crot, glock, cast, vib

PART 1	
1. Allegro non troppo e pesante	12'
2. Lento	16'
PART 2	
3. Allegro molto	6'
4. Slow blues (As I Drew Nurture from My Mother's Breast)	4'
5. Fast blues ((O, I'll Go Walking)	2'
6. Slow blues (I Found the Man Grown to a Dwarf)	5'
7. They Sang That When She Waved Her Wings	12'

Schott

Symphony No.4 <1976–1977>   33'

2[1/pic.2/pic] 3[incl Eh] 3[incl bcl] 3[incl cbn] — 6 3 3 2 — tmp+6
— hp — str
perc: glock, marac, cym, xyl, vib, wnd mach, marim, sd, td, sus cym, woodblk,
tomtom, bd, claves, wood windchimes, bells

Introduction and Exposition	4'
Development 1	4'
Slow Movement	8'
Development 2	3'
Scherzo and Trios	4'
Development 3	5'
Recapitulation	5'

Schott

The Vision of Saint Augustine <1963–1965>   35'

solo baritone   chorus

2[1/pic.2/pic] 2[incl Eh] 2[incl bcl] 2[incl cbn] — 4 2 3 1 — tmp+5
— hp — cel, pf — str
perc: xyl, marim, whip, chimes, glock, sus cym, tamtam, field dr, td, tambn,
templeblks, bd, cym, foil rattle, 2woodblks

Part 1: Allegro non troppo	16'
Part 2: Molto adagio	14'
Part 3: Allegro assai	9'

Schott

Toch, Ernst   1887-1964

(b Vienna, 7 Dec 1887; d Santa Monica, CA, 1 Oct 1964). Austrian composer,
naturalized American citizen from 1940

Big Ben: Variation-Fantasy on the Westminster Chimes,   20'
op.62 <1934>

3[1.2.pic] 3[1.2.Eh] 3[1.2.Ebcl] 2 — 4 4 3 1 — tmp+4 — hp — cel
— str
perc: sd, bd, tomtom, tri, cym, sus cym, gong, cast, templeblks, chimes, glock, xyl

AMP

Circus Overture <1953>   6'

3[1.2.3/pic] 2 2 2 — 3 3 3 1 — 4perc — pf — str
perc: bd, cym, sd, tri, woodblk, cast, whip, glock, xyl

Kalmus	Mills

Concerto, Violoncello, op.35 <1925>   29'

1[1/pic] 1 1 1 — 1 0 0 0 — tmp+1 — str 5t
perc: cym, tri, tamtam

1. Allegro assai moderato	11'
2. Agitato	4'
3. Adagio	9'
4. Allegro vivace	5'

Schott

Die chinesische Flöte, op.29 (The Chinese Flute) <1922; rev 1949>   27'

solo soprano
2[1.2/pic] 0 2[1/Ebcl.bcl] 0 — 0 0 0 0 — tmp+2 — cel — str 5t
perc: sus cym, bd/cym, sd, gong, xyl, woodblk, tri, tambn, cym
Prologue	7'
Li Tae Pe	3'
Wayfaring	4'
Sao Han	1'
Procession of Monks	4'
Confucius	8'

AMP

Genesis Suite: VI. The Covenant (The Rainbow) <1945>   6'

narrator
3[1.2.3/pic] 3[1.2.Eh] 3 3[1.2.cbn] — 4 3 3 1 — tmp+1 — hp — pf — str

perc: sus cym, vib
See the entry for "Nathaniel Shilkret: *Genesis Suite*" for a full description of this collaborative work by 7 composers.
Reconstructed by Patrick Russ.

Milken

Pinocchio; A Merry Overture <1936>   6'

3[1.2.pic] 2 2 2 — 2 2 3 0 — tmp+2 — str
perc: cym, sd, tri, xyl

AMP

Symphony No.3, op.75 <1954–1955>   28'

3[1.2.pic] 3[1.2.Eh] 3[1.2.Ebcl] 3[1.2.cbn] — 4 4 3 1 — tmp+5 — org[pipe org or Hammond org] — str
perc: bd, cym, sd, templeblks, xyl, vib, glock, tri, tamtam, sus cym, small cym, tmp2, opt glass harmonica, opt tuned glass balls
Percussion includes glass harmonica and glass balls (struck with mallets); these may be replaced by vibraphone 4-hands.
1. Molto adagio	13'
2. Andante tranquillo - Allegro	6'
3. Allegro impetuoso	9'

Belwin

Symphony No.6, op.93 <1963>   23'

2[incl pic] 2 2 2 — 3 3 3 0 — tmp+4 — str
perc: xyl, woodblk, vib, templeblks, glock, tri, cym, sd, anvil
1. Allegro commodo	10'
2. Molto grazioso e leggiero throughout	4'
3. Allegro energico	9'

Belwin

Tomasi, Henri Frédien   1901-1971

(b Marseilles, 17 Aug 1901; d Paris, 13 Jan 1971). French

Concerto, Clarinet <1956>   19'

hp — str
1. Allegro giocoso	8'
2. Nocturne; tempo di Scherzo	5'
3. Scherzo-final: Vif—scherzando	6'

Leduc

Concerto, Trombone <1956>   17'

2[1.2/pic] 2 2 2 — 2 2 0 0 — tmp+2 — hp — cel[or glock] — str
perc: bd, cym, sus cym, sd, tri, xyl, cel or glock

Leduc

Concerto, Trumpet <1948>   16'

3[incl pic] 3[incl Eh] 2 2 — 4 0 3 1 — tmp+3 — hp — cel — str
1. Allegro & cadenza	7'
2. Nocturne	5'
3. Finale	4'

Leduc

Fanfares liturgiques <1950>   16'

0 0 0 0 — 4 3 3 1[or btbn] — tmp+3 — [no str]
perc: sd, sus cym, tamtam, cym, 2field dr
1. Annonciation	2'
2. Evangile	3'
3. Apocalypse (Scherzo)	3'
4. Procession du Vendredi-saint	8'

Leduc

Tommasini, Matthew   1978-

(b Brussels, 17 Sept 1978). American/Italian

A Letter Home <2004>   9'

2[1.2/pic] 2[1.2/Eh] 2[1.2/bcl] 2[1.2/cbn] — 2 2 1[btbn] 0 — 2perc — hp — str
perc: tamtam, vib, belltree, bd, brake dr, xyl, crot, glock, windchimes, sus cym, td marim

Matalex

Sonic Dreams Made Real <2007; rev 2012>   10'

2[1.2/pic] 2 2 2 — 4 3 3 1 — tmp+3 — pf — str
perc: glock, sd, ratch, whip, tambn, vib, bd, chimes, tri, tamtam, sus cym, windchimes, marim, fingercym, 4tomtom, 2brake dr
Movements played without pause.
| 1. Sonic Dreams | 5' |
| 2. Dreams Made Real | 5' |

Matalex

Tell Me … <2012>   13'

str[min 6.6.4.4.2]
Originally for str 4t; adapted for string orch by the composer.

Matalex

Torn Threads Rewoven <2002>   8'

3[1.2.3/pic] 3 3 — 4 3 3 1 — tmp+3 — hp — str
perc: bd, windchimes, marim, belltree, crot, chimes, xyl, sus cym, vib, whip, tamtam, brake dr, glock, ratch, td, tambn, flexatone, sd, 3tomtom

Matalex

Toovey, Andrew   1962-

(b London, 21 Feb 1962). English

Black Light <1989>   10'

1[1/pic] 1[1/Eh] 1[1/bcl] 1[cbn] — 1 1 1 0 — 2perc — hp — pf — str[min 1.1.1.1.1; max 4.4.3.3.2]
perc: glock, xyl, crot, marim, td, 6sus cym, 3tomtoms, 4gongs, bd/ped, 3woodblks

Boosey

Torelli, Giuseppe   1658-1709

(b Verona, 22 April 1658; d Bologna, 8 Feb 1709). Italian

Concerto, op.6, no.1, G major <1698>   7'

cnt — str
Ed. Walter Kolneder.

Schott

Concerto, Trumpet, D major (Tarr) *6'*

cnt — str
Ed. Edward Tarr. A different work from the concerto edited by Zickler.

Musica Rara

Concerto, Trumpet, D major (Zickler) *10'*

cnt — str
Ed. Heinz Zickler. A different work from the concerto edited by Tarr.

Schott

Concerto, Violin, op.8, no.8, C minor *6'*

cnt — str
Ed. Ernst Praetorius.

Eulenburg Luck's

Concerto, Violin, op.8, no.9, E minor *14'*

cnt — str

Luck's Peters Ricordi Zerboni

Concerto, 2 Violins, op.6, no.10, D minor *5'*

cnt — str
Ed. Hans Engel.

Kalmus Nagel

Concerto, 2 Violins, op.8, no.1, C major *11'*

cnt — str

Ricordi Zerboni

Concerto, 2 Violins, op.8, no.3, E major *7'*

cnt — str
Ed. Piero Santi.

Zerboni

Concerto, 2 Violins, op.8, no.7, D minor *9'*

cnt — str
Ed. Piero Santi.

Zerboni

Concerto grosso, 2 Violins, op.8, no.2, A minor *8'*

cnt — str
Ed. Bernhard Paumgartner.

Schott

Concerto grosso, 2 Violins, op.8, no.5, G major *10'*

cnt — str
Ed. Alfredo Casella.

Ricordi

Concerto grosso, 2 Violins, op.8, no.6, G minor (Christmas Concerto) *6'*

cnt — str
Grave; Vivace 2'
Largo 2'
Vivace 2'

Luck's Peters Vieweg

Sinfonia, op.6, no.6, E minor *7'*

cnt — str
Ed. Arnold Schering.

Kahnt

Sinfonia con tromba, D major *5'*

solo trumpet
cnt — str

King

Torke, Michael 1961 -

(b Milwaukee, 22 Sept 1961). American

Adjustable Wrench <1987> *11'*

0 1 2 1 — 1 2 1 0 — marimba — pf, synth — vn, va, vc, db

Boosey

Ash <1988> *15'*

1 2 1 2 — 3 1 0 0 — tmp — synth — str

Boosey

Concerto, Soprano Saxophone <1993> *20'*

1 2[1.Eh] 2 0 — 4 0 1 0 — hp — str
perc: 2vib, 2marim
I. quarter note = 96-108 7'
II. Slowly; quarter note = 76 7'
III. quarter note = 100 6'

Adjustable

December <1995> *12'*

str[8.8.6.6.4]

Adjustable

Ecstatic Orange <1985> *12'*

3[1.2.pic] 2 2 2 — 4 3 3 1 — tmp+3 — pf — str
perc: xyl, tamtam, claves, tri, sd, vib, glock, sus cym, whip, chimes, marim, tambn, woodblk, bongos

Boosey

Jasper <1998> *12'*

3[1.2.3/pic] 3[1.2.Eh] 3 2 — 4 3 3 1 — tmp+3 — hp — str
perc: sd, bd, bongos, tambn, tri, sus cym, chimes, glock, vib

Adjustable

Javelin <1994> *9'*

3[1.2.3/pic] 3[1.2.Eh] 4[1.2.Ebcl.bcl] 2 — 4 3 3 1 — tmp+3 — hp — str
perc: glock, vib, tambn, tri, claves, woodblk, sus cym, sd, bd

Adjustable

Lucent Variations <1998> *12'*

2 2 2 2 — 2 2 0 0 — tmp — pf — str

Adjustable

Tower, Joan 1938 -

(b New Rochelle, NY, 6 Sept 1938). American

Chamber Dance <2006> *15'*

2[1.2/pic] 2 2 2 — 2 2 0 0 — tmp/perc — str
perc: sus cym, tambn, crot, slgh-bells, woodblk, 2marac(2 sizes)

AMP

Concerto for Orchestra <1991> *29'*

3[1.2.3/pic] 3[1.2.Eh] 3[1.2/Ebcl.3/bcl] 3[1.2.3/cbn] — 4 3 3 1 — tmp+3 — hp — pf — str
Part One 16'
Part Two 13'

AMP

Concerto, Clarinet <1988>   19'

2[1.2/pic] 2 2 2 — 4 2 2 1 — tmp+2 — hp — pf/cel — str
perc: vib, glock, tri, bd, tamtam, marim, templeblks, 3sus cym
In one mvt.

AMP

Concerto, Flute <1989>   15'

1[1/pic] 1 1[1/bcl] 1 — 1   1[btbn] — 2perc — str
perc: bd, td, tomtom, tri, tamtam, glock, xyl, vib, templeblks, 4sus cym
In one mvt.

AMP

Duets <1994>   19'

2 2 2 2 — 2 2 0 0 — tmp+1 — str
perc: vib, glock, templeblks, tambn, marac, tomtom, 3sus cym, rattle

AMP

Fanfare for the Uncommon Woman <1986>   3'

0 0 0 0 — 4 3 3 1 — tmp+2 — [no str]
perc: sd, tamtam, tomtom, templeblks, tri, 2bd, 5sus cym, 2gongs

AMP

For the Uncommon Woman (For Orchestra) <1992>   5'

2[1.2/pic] 2 2 2 — 4 3 3 1 — tmp+3 — str
perc: glock, woodblk, templeblks, marac, xyl, sd, td, slgh-bells, chimes, cast, vib,
tambn, marim, small bell, 4sus cym
Not musically related to the *Fanfare for the Uncommon Woman*;
sometimes referred to as *Fanfare for the Uncommon Woman No.4*.

AMP

Second Fanfare for the Uncommon Woman <1989>   5'

0 0 0 0 — 4 3 3 1 — tmp+3 — [no str]
perc: glock, sd, cast, templeblks, woodblk, tamtam, timbales, td, tomtom, tambn,
tri, marim, chimes, belltree, 5sus cym, 2bd

AMP

Third Fanfare for the Uncommon Woman <1991>   4'

0 0 0 0 — 2 4 2 2 — [no str]
2 brass quintets, each with 2tp, hn, tbn, tuba.

AMP

In Memory <2002>   12'

str

AMP

Made in America <2004>   13'

2[1/pic1.2/pic2] 2 2 2 — 2 2[1/opt pic tp] 1 0 — tmp+3 — str
perc: xyl, glock, vib, sus cym, cym, woodblk, marac, tambn, bd, slgh-bells, egg
maraca

AMP

Purple Rhapsody (Concerto for Viola & Orchestra)   18'
<2005>

2[1.2/pic] 0 2[1.2/bcl] 2 — 0 2 1[btbn] 0 — tmp/perc — str
perc: glock, vib, tamtam, templeblks, marac, tambn, bd, 2sus cym, 2woodblk
In one mvt.

AMP

Sequoia <1981>   16'

2[1/pic.2/pic] 2 2 2 — 4 2 3 1 — tmp+4 — hp — pf/cel — str
perc: tri, crot, sd, td, marim, 8tomtoms, 2bd, templeblks[2 sets], 2cowbells, 5sus
cym

AMP

Silver Ladders <1986>   23"

3[1.2.pic] 3[1.2.Eh] 3[1.2.bcl] 3[1.2.cbn] — 4 3 3 1 — tmp+4 — hp
— pf/cel — str
perc: tri, crot, glock, xyl, td, sd, templeblks, vib, chimes, marim, 2tamtams, 8sus
cym, 4tomtoms, 2bd, 2woodblks

AMP

Stroke <2011>   21'

3[1.2.3/pic] 2 3 2 — 4 3 3 1 — tmp+3 — pf — str
perc: xyl, glock, vib, tamtam, tri, slgh-bells, templeblks, marac, td, tambn, ratch,
2woodblk, 2timbales, 2sd, 2bd, 3sus cym

AMP

Tambor <1998>   15'

2[1.2/pic] 2 2[1.2/bcl] 2 — 4 3 3 1 — tmp+3 — str
perc: hi-hat, sd, td, glock, marim, vib, chimes, slgh-bells, belltree, woodblk,
templeblks, ratch, marac, cast, congas, 2bd, 5sus cym, 4timbales, 2tri, 2tambn

AMP

Tredici, David Del   1937-

see: Del Tredici, David

Trigos, Juan   1965-

(b Mexico City, 26 Feb 1965). American composer of Mexican birth

Concerto, Clarinet <2014>   19'

0 0 0 0 — 2 0 0 0 — tmp+2 — pf — str
perc: marac, guiro, marktree, tri, brake dr, Chinescym, glock, vib, marim, chimes,
2woodblk, buttongong

PromoMusica

Concerto, Guitar, No.1 (Ricercare de Cámara VI)   14'
<1999>

1[fl/pic] 1[ob/Eh] 1[cl/bcl] 0 — 1 1 1[btbn] 0 — 3perc — pf —
str[max 6.6.4.4.2]
perc: bongos, sd, chimes, tamtam, marktree, glock, tri, vib, bd, tomtom, 3sus cym,
2logdrum, Indian dr, palmas (clapping)
Solo guitar should be amplified. The work may be performed with single
strings on a part.

PromoMusica

Concerto, Guitar, No.2 (Hispano) <2006>   34'

2[1.pic] 2[1.Eh] 2[1.bcl] 1 — 2 1 1[btbn] 0 — tmp+3 — hp[ampd ad
lib] — hpsd[ampd], pf — str[min 6.6.4.4.2]
perc: marac, Chinescym, sus cym, sd, tomtom, glock, bongos, vib, templeblks,
gong, bd, chimes, slitdrum, cabasa
Solo guitar may be amplified. Harp, harpsichord and piano are marked
"obbligato."
  I. quarter-note = 92   _'
  II. quarter-note = 126-132   _'

PromoMusica

Magnificat Guadalupano (Cantata concertante No.1) <55'>
<1990; rev 2001>

soloists: soprano, tenor, baritone, guitar[ampd]   double chorus
3[1/pic.2.pic] 2 2 2 — 4 2 2 0 — tmp+2 — pf 4-hands — str
perc: marac, cym, crot, logdrum, bd/ped, 2sus cym, 3tomtom, 2tri, 2sd
Guitar and piano 4-hands marked "soloist"; flute 1 marked "obbligato."
    Text mingles the liturgical *Magnificat* with commentaries in Spanish and Nahuatl; "deconstruction" of the text is used extensively.
*   1. Prologo   '*
*   2. Magnificat anima mea dominum   _'*
*   3. Comentario I   _'*
*   4. Et exsultávit—Quia respéxit   _'*
*   5. Comentario II (Et exultávit - 1º Libro Samuel /2/1)   _'*
*   6. Quia fecit   _'*
*   7. Et misericordia   _'*
*   8. Comentario III (Sólo venimos a dormir)   _'*
*   9. Fecit potentiam   _'*
*   10. Esuriéntes—   _'*
*   11. Comentario IV (Suscépit Isrrael)—¿No estoy yo aqui?   _'*
*   12. Sicut locutus—epilogo   _'*

PromoMusica

Sinfonia breve <2014>   13'

3[1.2.pic] 3[1.2.Eh] 3[1.2.bcl] 3[1.2.cbn] — 4 3 3 1 — tmp+4 — hp — pf — str
perc: sd, whip, glock, guiro, cym, claves, xyl, marim, tamtam, bd, cowbell, vib, 2tri, almglocken
*   I. Allegretto Bartok   _'*
*   II. Scherzo Donatoni   _'*
*   III. Poulenc alla Breve   _'*

PromoMusica

Symphony No.1 <2007>   25'

3[1.2.pic] 3[1.2.Eh] 3[1.2.bcl] 3[1.2.cbn] — 4 4 3 1 — tmp+4 — hp — pf — str
perc: brake dr, templeblks, glock, sus cym, sd, xyl, marac, bongos, chimes, cym, bd, tri, Indian dr [or td], 4cowbell, 4tomtom, 2tamtam
*   I. quarter-note = 96-104   _'*
*   II. quarter-note = 48-52   _'*
*   III. quarter-note = 120-132   _'*

PromoMusica

Symphony No.2 <2010>   21'

1[fl/pic] 1[ob/Eh] 2[1.2/bcl] 1 — 1 1 1 0 — gtr[ampd] — 3perc — hpsd[ampd], pf — str[max 6.6.4.4.2]
perc: tamtam, glock, cowbell, guiro, marac, templeblks, brake dr, marim, sd, bongos, congas, bd, vib, metal rattle, anvil, Indian dr [or td], 2tri, 2sus cym, 2gongs, 5almglock[tuned], 2woodblk, pod rattle
May be performed with single strings on each part. A version of this work for larger orchestra is in preparation.
    In one movement.

PromoMusica

Symphony No.3 (Ofrenda a los muertos; Offering to the Dead) <2013>   40'

3[1.2.pic] 3[1.2.Eh] 4[1.2.Ebcl.bcl] 3[1.2.cbn] — 4 4 3 1 — tmp+4 — hp — prep pf — str
perc: brake dr, glock, marac, sd, guiro, bd, xyl, Chinescym, vib, chimes, marim, tamtam, td, anvil, tenabari, rattling string, slitdrum, 2db bow, 2Indian dr, 2cowbells, 2tri, 4tomtom
*   Introduction   _'*
*   I. quarter-note = 88   _'*
*   II. half-note = 40   _'*
*   III. quarter-note = 100   _'*
*   IV. Pasacalle   _'*

PromoMusica

Trimble, Lester   1923-1986

(b Bangor, WI, 29 Aug 1923; d New York, 31 Dec 1986). American

Duo concertante <1968>   18'

2 solo violins
2[incl pic] 2[incl Eh] 2[incl bcl] 2 — 4 2 3 0 — tmp+4 — hp — cel[played by perc] — str

Peters

Tschaikowsky, Peter Iljitsch   1840-1893

The German transliteration of the composer's name; used in catalogs of Bärenreiter, Breitkopf, Luck's, Schott, and others.

see: Tchaikovsky, Piotr Ilyich, 1840-1893

Tscherepnin, Alexander   1899-1977

The German transliteration of the composer's name, used by Breitkopf, and perhaps other publishers.

see: Tcherepnin, Alexander, 1899-1977

Tsontakis, George   1951-

(b Astoria, NY, 24 Oct 1951). American

Concerto, Violin, No.2 <2003>   18'

1[fl/pic] 1 1[cl/bcl] 1 — 1 1 1 0 — 1perc — hp — pf/cel — str[str 5t or sections]
perc: brake dr, tri, tamtam, vib, crot, sandpaper
If string sections are used, the 5 soli strings still play 60% of the passages, whereas the tutti string sections play only the remaining 40%. Unfortunately it is not clear from the score which passages are intended to be soli and which tutti.
*   I. Surges (among stars)   4'*
*   II. Giocco (Games)   4'*
*   III. Cantilena (Heart)   7'*
*   IV. Just Go!   3'*

Merion

FOUR SYMPHONIC QUARTETS   12'
1. Other Echoes <1997>

3[1.2.3/pic] 3[1.2.Eh] 3[1.2.bcl] 3[1.2.cbn] — 4 3 3 1 — tmp+3 — hp — pf, cel[played by perc] — str
perc: bd, sd, tamtam, glock, marim, vib, chimes, 2sus cym, cel[played by perc]

Merion

2. Perpetual Angelus <1992>   15'

2[incl pic] 2 2 2 — 4 2 1 0 — tmp+2 — hp — str

Merion

3. The Dove Descending <1995>   13'

3[1.2.3/pic] 3[1.2.Eh] 3[1.2.bcl] 3[1.2.cbn] — 4 3 3 1 — tmp+3 — hp — pf — str
perc: bd, tamtam, marim, vib, sandpaper, bass bow

Merion

4. Winter Lightning <1993>   15'

3[incl pic] 3[incl Eh] 3[incl bcl] 3[incl cbn] — 4 3 3 1 — tmp+3 — hp — pf — str

Merion

Mirologhia <2001>   28'

solo percussion
3[1.2/afl.3/pic] 3[1.2.Eh] 3[1.2/Ebcl.bcl] 3[1.2.cbn] — 4 3 3 1 — hp
— pf — str
perc: (soloist) sd, timbales, brake dr, tambn, vib, crot, woodblk, 2bd, 2sus cym,
2cowbell, 8drums, tuned gong, crowbar[8 pitches], incense bells, logdrum, 2egg
shakers, herdbells, cabasa, steelpans, pieces of metal
Orchestra members vocalize (fragments of chant or rhythmic speech) in
certain passages.

I. Introit	5'
II. Crotales Angelorum	1'
III. Soson Kyrie	5'
IV. Labyrinth	9'
V. Eonia Imnimi	8'

> Merion

Tubin, Eduard   1905-1982

(b Alatskivi, nr Kallaste, 18 June 1905; d Stockholm, 17 Nov 1982). Estonian
composer, active in Sweden

ETW = Vardo Rumessen: *The Works of Eduard Tubin;
Thematic-Bibliographical Catalogue of Works* (Tallinn - Stockholm,
2003)

Concerto, Balalaika, ETW 23 <1963–1964>   21'

2[1.2/pic] 2 2 2 — 4 3 3 0 — tmp/perc — str
perc: sd, tomtom[or high tmp]

1. Andante ma rubato; Poco allegretto; Allegro non troppo	7'
2. Andante sostenuto e serioso	6'
3. Allegro giocoso	8'

> Suecia

Concerto, Double Bass, ETW 22 <1948>   19'

2[1.2/pic] 2[1.2/Eh] 2[1.2/bcl] 2[1.2/cbn] — 4 3 3 1 — tmp+1 — hp
— str
perc: sd

1. Allegro con moto	_'
2. Andante sostenuto	_'
3. (attacca) Allegro non troppo, poco marciale	_'

> Gehrmans

Concerto, Violin, No.2, ETW 21, G minor <1945>   26'

2 2 2 2 — 4 2 0 0 — tmp — hp — str

I. Andante	7'
II. Allegro marciale vivace	6'
III. Adagio, quasi recitativo; Allegro non troppo, ma energico	13'

> Gehrmans

Estonian Dance Suite, ETW 15 (Suite on Estonian   13'
Dances; Süit Eesti Tantsudest) <1938>

1[1/pic] 2[1.Eh] 2 1 — 2 2 1 0 — tmp — hp — str
Not to be confused with other similar titles:
ETW 11: Sinfonietta on Estonian Motifs (Sümfonietta eeste motiividel)
ETW 12: Estonian Folk Dances (Eesti rahvatantsud)
ETW 13: Suite on Estonian Motifs (Süit eeste motividel)
ETW 53A: Suite on Estonian Dance Tunes (Süit eesti tantsuviisidest [for
violin & orchestra])

1. Crossed Sticks Dance (Ristpulkade Tants)	4'
2. A Long Anglaise (Pikk Ingliska)	5'
3. Setu Dance (Setu Tants)	4'

> Gehrmans

Music for Strings, ETW 18 (Muusika keelpillidele)   16'
<1962–1963>

str

I. Moderato	5'
II. Allegro	4'
III. Adagio	7'

> Gehrmans   Hansen   Nordiska

Prélude solennel, ETW 16 (Pidulik prelüüd) <1940>   8'

2 2 2 2 — 4 2 3 0 — tmp+2 — hp[opt] — str
perc: cym, sd

> Gehrmans

Symphony No.2, ETW 2, B minor (The Legendary;   32'
Legendaarne) <1937>

3[1.2.3/pic] 3[1.2.Eh] 2 2 — 4 3 3 1 — tmp+1[or 2] — hp — pf — str
perc: cym, sus cym, tamtam, sd

I. Legendaire; Molto allegro e agitato	10'
II. Sostenuto assai, grave e funebre	8'
III. Tempestoso, ma non troppo allegro (quasi toccata); Lento	14'

> Gehrmans   Hansen   Nordiska

Symphony No.4, ETW 4, A major (Sinfonia lirico;   36'
Lüüriline) <1942–1943; rev 1978>

3[1.2.3/pic] 3[1.2.Eh] 3[1.2.3/bcl] 2 — 4 3 3 0 — tmp — hp — str

I. Molto moderato	11'
II. Allegro con anima	7'
III. Andante un poco maestoso	8'
IV. Allegro	10'

> Gehrmans   Hansen   Nordiska

Symphony No.5, ETW 5, B minor <1945–1946>   31'

3[1.2.3/pic] 3[1.2.Eh] 3[1.2.bcl] 3[1.2.cbn] — 4 3 3 1 — 2tmp+1 —
str
perc: cym, sd

I. Allegro energico	11'
II. Andante	9'
III. Allegro assai	11'

> Gehrmans

Symphony No.6, ETW 6 <1952–1954; rev 1956>   33'

3[1.2.3/pic] 3[1.2.3/Eh] 3[1.2/Ebcl.3/bcl] 3[1.2.cbn] — 4 3 3 1 — tsx
— tmp+5 — pf — str
perc: bd, cym, sus cym, sd, td, field dr, tri, tambn, tamtam, woodblk, tambn prov

I. Andante sostenuto, ma ritmico	9'
II. Molto allegro	10'
III. Festoso	14'

> Gehrmans   Hansen   Nordiska

Symphony No.8, ETW 8 <1965–1966>   30'

3[1.2.3/pic] 3[1.2.Eh] 3[1.2.bcl] 3[1.2.cbn] — 4 3 3 1 — tmp+2 —
cel[can be played by perc] — str
perc: sd, tamtam

I. Andante quasi adagio	8'
II. Allegro moderato	8'
III. Allegro vivace	6'
IV. Lento, tenuto e maestoso	8'

> Gehrmans   Nordiska

Toccata, ETW 14 (version I) (Tokaata) <1937; rev 1939>   6'

1[1/pic] 1[1/Eh] 2 1 — 2 2 1 0 — tmp+1 — hp — pf — str
perc: sus cym
Version II calls for:
   2[1.2/pic] 2[1.2/Eh] 2 2 — 4 2 2 0 — tmp+1 — hp — pf — str

> Gehrmans

Tull, Fisher   1934-1994

(b Waco, TX, 24 Sept 1934; d Huntsville, TX, 23 August 1994). American

Capriccio for Small Orchestra, op.23 <1966>   9'

2 1 2 1 — 2 1 1 0 — tmp+1 — pf — str
perc: bd, cym, sd, td, tri, woodblk, templeblks, whip; tmp plays sus cym

> Boosey

Concertino, Oboe & Strings <1970>   9'

str

> Boosey

Concerto No.1, Trumpet <1964>   23'

2[1.2/pic] 2 3[1.2.bcl] 2 — 4 2 3 1 — tmp+2 — pf — str
perc: cym, sus cym, sd, bd/cym, tri, tambn, tamtam, glock, xyl, woodblk
Allegro moderato   9'
Lento   7'
Allegro ritmato   7'

> Boosey

The Final Covenant <1979–1994>   9'

3[1.2.pic] 3[1.2.Eh] 3[1.2.bcl] 2 — 4 3 3 1 — tmp+3 — hp — str
perc: sus cym, tri, tambn, glock, chimes, crot
Originally for band; orchestrated by the composer.

> Boosey

Overture for a Legacy <1981>   11'

2[1/afl.2/pic] 1 2[1.2/bcl] 1 — 2 1[offstage] 0 0 — 2perc — str[min 6.4.4.2.2]
perc: sus cym, rototom, tambn, xyl, vib, woodblk, templeblks, marac, metal windchimes, wood windchimes

> Boosey

Rhapsody for Trumpet & Orchestra <1987>   12'

2[1.2/pic] 2 3[1.2.bcl] 2 — 4 3 3 1 — tmp+4 — hp — str
perc: bd, cym, sus cym, sd, timbales, tri, tambn, glock, xyl, woodblk, templeblks, whip, 4tomtoms, opt field dr

> Boosey

Symphonic Treatise <1986>   14'

3[1.2.pic] 3[1.2.Eh] 3[1.2.bcl] 2 — 4 3 3 1 — tmp+3 — pf — str
perc: bd, sus cym, field dr, tambn, tamtam, glock, xyl, vib, chimes, woodblk, templeblks, whip, bongos, 2tomtoms; timpanist covers belltree, chocalho

> Boosey

Turina, Joaquín   1882 - 1949

(b Seville, 9 Dec 1882; d Madrid, 14 Jan 1949). Spanish

Canto a Sevilla, op.37 <1927>   39'

solo soprano
3[incl pic] 2 2 2 — 4 3 3 1 — tmp+2 — hp — cel — str
1. Preludio   6'
2. Semana Santa   9'
3. Las fuentecitas des Parque 4'
4. Noche de feria   7'
5. El fantasma   4'
6. La Giralda   3'
7. Ofrenda   6'

> UME

Danzas fantásticas, op.22 <1920>   17'

3[1.2.3/pic] 3[1.2.Eh] 3[1.2.bcl] 3[1.2.cbn] — 4 3 3 1 — tmp+3 — hp — str
perc: glock, chimes, tri, tambn, cym, sus cym, bd
1. Exaltación (Exaltation)   5'
2. Ensueño (Fantasy)   7'
3. Orgía (Orgy)   5'

> Luck's   UME

La procesion del rocio, op.9 <1913>   8'

3[1.2.pic] 3[1.2.Eh] 3[1.2.bcl] 3[1.2.cbn] — 4 3 3 1 — tmp+4 — hp — str
perc: bd, cym, sd, tri, tambn, glock
1. Triana en fiesta   3'
2. La procesión   5'

> Kalmus   Luck's

Rapsodia sinfónica, op.66 <1931>   9'

solo piano
str

> UME

Sinfonia sevillana, op.23 <1920>   22'

3[1.2.3/pic] 3[1.2.Eh] 3[1.2.bcl] 3[1.2.cbn] — 4 3 3 1 — tmp+2 — hp — cel — str
1. Panorama   8'
2. Por el Rio Guadalquivir   7'
3. Fiesta de San Juan de Aznalfarache   7'

> UME

Turnage, Mark-Anthony   1960 -

(*b* Grays, Essex, 10 June 1960). English

Snapshots <2002>   3'

2 2[ob.Eh] 2[cl.bcl] 1[cbn] — 2 1 1 0 — 2perc — hp — pf, cel — str 5t
perc: woodblk, tambn, guiro, djembe

> Schott

Three Screaming Popes <1988–1989>   15'

3[all dbl pic & afl] 3[all dbl Eh] 3[1/Ebcl/bcl.2/bcl.3/bcl] 3[1.2.3/cbn] — 6 3 3 1 — euph — 4perc — hp — cel, pf/elec kybd — str[12.12.10.10.8]
perc: templeblks, glock, sus cym, xyl, bd, crot, vib, timbales, 3ratch, bodhran, pol whstle, 2whip, 14handbell, logdrum, 2gong, bd/ped, 2hi-hat

> Schott

Turok, Paul   1929 -

(b New York City, 3 Dec 1929). American

A Joplin Overture <1973>   7'

3[1.2.pic] 3[1.2.Eh] 3[1.2.bcl] 2 — 4 3 3 1 — tmp+3 — hp — str
Appears to be the beginning and ending of Turok's *Great Scott! — Orchestral Suite after Scott Joplin*, spliced together. Joplin's famous rag *The Entertainer* is prominent.

> Schirmer

Tüür, Erkki-Sven   1959 -

(b Kärdla, Hiiumaa Island, 16 Oct 1959). Estonian

Action — Passion — Illusion <1994>   15'

str
I. Action   5'
II. Passion   6'
III. Illusion 4'

> Fennica

Zeitraum <1992>   14'

2 2 2 2 — 4 2 2 1 — tmp+3 — str[14.12.10.10.6-8]
perc: bd, cym, sus cym, sd, tamtam, xyl, marim, chimes, 3tomtom

> Fennica

Tyzik, Jeff
1952-

(b Hyde Park, NY, 1952). American

The Twelve Gifts of Christmas <2000>
10'

high voice
2 2 3[1.2.bcl] 2 — 4 3 3 1 — tmp+2 — hp — pf/cel — str
perc: bd, cym, sd, tri, glock, chimes, slgh-bells, sus cym, 3tomtoms
Clever quotations from standard orchestral repertoire woven into the
familiar Christmas song.

Schirmer

Ussachevsky, Vladimir
1911-1990

(b Hailar, 3 Nov/21 Oct 1911; d New York, 4 Jan 1990). American

Rhapsodic Variations
see under: Luening, Otto, 1900-1996

Ustvolskaya, Galina
1919-2006

(b Petrograd, 17 June 1919; d St. Petersburg, 22 December, 2006). Russian

Concerto, Piano <1946>
20'

tmp — str
In one mvt.

Russian

Valen, Fartein 1887 - 1952

(b Stavanger, 25 Aug 1887; d Haugesund, 14 Dec 1952). Norwegian

Le cimetière marin, op.20 (The Churchyard by the Sea; Kirkegården ved havet) <1933–1934> 10'

2 2 2 2 — 2 2 3 0 — tmp — str

> Lyche

Concerto, Violin, op.37 <1940> 12'

1 1 2 2 — 2 1 0 0 — tmp — str[6.6.4.3.2]
In one mvt.

> Lyche

La isla de las calmas, op.21 (The Island of Silence) <1934> 6'

2 2 2 2 — 2 0 0 0 — str

> Lyche

Symphony No.2, op.40 <1941–1944> 24'

2 2 2 2 — 2 1 1 0 — tmp — str
I. Allegro con brio   7'
II. Adagio   10'
III. Allegretto   2'
IV. Finale: Allegro molto 5'

> Lyche

Symphony No.3, op.41 <1944–1946> 20'

2 2 2 2 — 3 1 1 0 — tmp — str
I. Allegro moderato   7'
II. Larghetto   7'
III. Intermezzo: Allegro 2'
IV. Finale: Allegro   4'

> Lyche

Van Delden, Lex 1919 - 1988

see: Delden, Lex van, 1919-1988

Van de Vate, Nancy 1930 -

(b Plainfield, NJ, 30 Dec 1930). American composer, active in Austria

Adagio for Orchestra <1958> 7'

2 2 2 2 — 2 2 2 1 — tmp — str

> Fleisher   MusicaNeo

Chernobyl <1987> 13'

3[1.2.3/pic] 3[1.2.3/Eh] 3[1.2.3/bcl] 3[1.2.3/cbn] — 4 3 3 1 — tmp+3 — hp — cel, pf — str
perc: bd, rototom, tamtam, glock, xyl, vib, chimes, flexatone, woodblk, templeblks, claves, bell plate, siren (or siren whistle), 3sus cym, 3sd

> Fleisher   MusicaNeo

Concerto, Harp <1996> 15'

str
I. Allegro   6'
II. Slowly   5'
III. Fast   4'

> Fleisher   MusicaNeo

Concerto, Viola <1990> 16'

3[1.2.3/pic] 3[1.2.3/Eh] 3[1.2.3/bcl] 3[1.2.3/cbn] — 4 3 3 1 — tmp+3 — hp — cel, pf — str
perc: glock, xyl, bd, tamtam, marim, chimes, templeblks, whip, cym, vib, td, tambn, 4sus cym, 3sd, 5tomtom

> Fleisher   MusicaNeo

Concerto, Violin, No.1 <1986> 25'

2 2 2 2 — 4 2 2 1 — tmp+2 — hp — pf — str
perc: bd, td, sd, sus cym, whip, xyl, marim, chimes, templeblks, tri, vib, tamtam, tambn, afuche[or cabasa], 4woodblk, 5tomtom
I. quarter-note = 100   9'
II. Slowly   8'
III. quarter-note = 92-100 8'

> Fleisher   MusicaNeo

Concerto, Violin, No.2 <1996> 16'

3[1.2.3/pic] 3[1.2.3/Eh] 3[1.2.3/bcl] 3[1.2.3/cbn] — 4 3 3 1 — tmp+3 — hp — pf, cel — str
perc: glock, xyl, bd, tamtam, marim, chimes, templeblks, whip, cym, vib, td, tambn, 4sus cym, 3sd, 5tomtom

> Fleisher   MusicaNeo

Concertpiece, Violoncello <1979> 9'

5perc — cel, pf — str[8vn, 4va, 4vc, 2db]
perc: vib, sus cym, bd, sd, tri, tambn, glock, xyl, woodblk, whip, 2tambn
A second version of the work, calling for only 3perc but otherwise identical, is also available.

> Fleisher   MusicaNeo

Dark Nebulae <1981> 11'

3[1.2.pic] 2 2 2 — 4 2 2 0 — tmp+2 — hp — cel, pf — str[12.10.8.6.6.]
perc: tamtam, chimes, xyl, bd, sd, tri, glock, vib, 2sus cym

> Fleisher   MusicaNeo

Distant Worlds <1985> 16'

solo violin
3[1.2.pic] 2 2 2 — 4 3 3 1 — tmp+3 — hp — cel, pf — str
perc: vib, marim, xyl, chimes, glock, tamtam, bd, sd, td, templeblks, cast, marac, 2sus cym, 5tomtom, 3woodblk

> Fleisher   MusicaNeo

Four Somber Songs <1970; rev 1991> 13'

solo mezzo-soprano
2[1.2/pic] 2[1.2/Eh] 2 2[1.cbn] — 2 0 1 1 — 1perc — hp — str
perc: glock, xyl, vib, tamtam, sd, sus cym, cym, afuche
I. Eastern Front (Georg Trakl)   4'
II. Alone (Edgar Allan Poe)   3'
III. Mad Song (William Blake)   3'
IV. A Great Dark Sleep (Paul Verlaine) 3'

> MusicaNeo

Gema Jawa (Echoes of Java) <1984>   9'

str

Fleisher	MusicaNeo

Journeys <1981–1984>   15'

3[1.2.pic] 2 2 2 — 4 3 3 1 — tmp+2 — hp — cel, pf — str
perc: chimes, xyl, glock, templeblks, bd, tamtam, tambn, afuche[or marac],
3woodblk, 3sus cym, 3tri, 6tomtom, 2sd

Fleisher	MusicaNeo

Katyn <1989>   15'

chorus SATB
3[1.2.3/pic] 3[1.2.3/Eh] 3[1.2.3/bcl] 3[1.2.3/cbn] — 4 3 3 1 — tmp+3
— hp — pf — str

Fleisher	MusicaNeo

Krakow Concerto <1988>   24'

solo percussion section: tmp+5
3[1.2.3/pic] 2 2 2 — 4 3 3 1 — hp — pf/cel — str
perc: (soloists) xyl, sd, bd, glock, vib, crot, chimes, guiro, td, bongos, marac,
flexatone, tmp, 5tomtom, 4woodblk, 4brake dr, 3cowbell, 3tri, 2tambn, 2sus cym
2nd & 4th mvts (out of 5) for percussion only.

I. quarter-note = 100	5'
II. Slowly	4'
III. Slowly	6'
IV. quarter-note = 80 or faster	2'
V. Slowly	7'

Fleisher	MusicaNeo

Nemo: Suite <1996>   17'

3[1.2.pic] 3[1.2.3/Eh] 3[1.2.3/bcl] 3[1.2.3/cbn] — 4 4 3 1 — tmp+3
— hp — cel, pf — str
perc: bd, cym, sus cym, sd, td, tri, tambn, glock, xyl, marim, vib, chimes,
flexatone, templeblks, whip, marac, cabasa, bell, 5tomtom, 2tamtam
Suite from the opera Nemo: Jenseits von Vulkania.

I. Langsam	3'
II. Heiser, rauh, schreiend	1'
III. Ruhig	3'
IV. Langsam	3'
V. Langsam	4'
VI. Lebhaft, fröhlich	3'

Fleisher	MusicaNeo

A Peacock Southeast Flew (Concerto for Pipa & Orchestra) <1997>   22'

2[1.2/pic] 2[1.2/Eh] 2[1.2/bcl] 2[1.2/cbn] — 2 1 1 0 — 3perc — str
perc: bd, cym, sus cym, szl cym, sd, tambn, tamtam, glock, xyl, marim, vib,
chimes, windchimes, woodblk, tmp, 2tomtom

I. Andante	7'
Interlude I	2'
II. Adagio espressivo	5'
Interlude II	2'
III. Allegro	6'

MusicaNeo

Pura Besakih (Besakih Temple) <1987>   14'

3[1.2.3/pic] 3[1.2.3/Eh] 3 3[1.2.3/cbn] — 4 3 3 1 — tmp+2 — hp —
pf/cel — str
perc: tambn, td, bd, belltree, cym, tamtam, whip, templeblks, glock, vib, chimes,
xyl, marim, 2sd, 2sus cym, 5tomtom, 2tri, 2brake dr

Fleisher	MusicaNeo

Variations for Chamber Orchestra <1958–1959>   9'

1 1 1 1 — str

Theme	1'
Variation 1	1'
Variation 2	2'
Variation 3	1'
Variation 4	1'
Variation 5	3'

Fleisher	MusicaNeo

Voices of Women <1979; rev 1993>   20'

solo soprano, contralto   SSAA chorus
2[fl.pic] 0 1 0 — 2perc — hp — cel — str
perc: vib, tomtom, templeblks, chimes, bd, tmp, 2afuche, 2sus cym, 3tri, 2tambn,
2sd, 2tamtam
Originally a chamber piece, Cantata for Women's Voices; orchestrated by
the composer.

1. Voices	4'
2. Nightlong, Daylong, As the Sweet (soprano solo)	3'
3. Faces	2'
4. The Little Old Women (contralto solo)	3'
5. Tears	8'

MusicaNeo

Western Front <1997>   13'

3[1.2.3/pic] 3[1.2.3/Eh] 3[1.2.3/bcl] 3[1.2.3/cbn] — 4 3 3 1 — tmp+3
— hp — pf/cel — str
perc: bd, sus cym, td, tomtom, tamtam, glock, xyl, chimes, 2sd

MusicaNeo

Vanhal, Johann Baptist (Jan Krt.)   1739-1813

(b Nechanicz [now Nechanice], nr Hradec Králové, Bohemia, 12 May 1739; d
Vienna, 20 Aug 1813). Bohemian composer, active in Austria

also spelled: Wanhal, Johann Baptist

Concerto, Double Bass   18'

0 2 0 0 — 2 0 0 0 — str
Because of the various scordatura tunings used by bass soloists, orchestral
parts must be selected that will match the performamce key of the soloist.
Specify the key when ordering.
Parts in C: Ludwin
... in D: Doblinger, Ludwin, McTier
... in E-flat: Doblinger
... in E: Bärenreiter, Hofmeister, Ludwin

Bärenreiter	Doblinger	Hofmeister	Ludwin	McTier

Sinfonia, G minor   14'

0 2 0 1 — 4 0 0 0 — str
Peters edition calls for 2hn rather than 4, and uses the German spelling of
the composer's name (Wanhal).

Doblinger	Peters

Varèse, Edgard

1883-1965

(b Paris, 22 Dec 1883; d New York, 6 Nov 1965). American composer of French birth

Amériques (1922 version) <1918–1922>

26'

8[4fl, 3pic, afl] 6[4ob, Eh, heckl] 7[4cl, Ebcl, bcl, cbcl] 6[4bn, 2cbn] — 8 10 8 3 — 2tmp+13 — 2hp — cel[played by perc] — str[16.16.14.10.10 w/ low C]

perc: bd, cym, sd, tri, tambn, tamtam, glock, xyl, slgh-bells, whip, cast, siren, lionroar, sirenwhistle, boatwhistle, crowcall, rattle, 2sus cym, rute, cel[played by perc]

4 of the tp & 3 of the tbn are backstage (*fanfare de l'intérieur*).

   Performance edition prepared from the original manuscript by Chou Wen-chung (1997).

Ricordi

Amériques (1929 version) <1918–1922; rev 1927>

23'

5[1.2.pic1.pic2.pic3/afl] 5[1.2.3.Eh.heckl] 5[1.2.3.Ebcl.bcl] 5[1.2.3.cbn1.cbn2] — 8 6 5[1.2.3.btbn.cb tbn] 2 — 2tmp+9 — 2hp — cel[played by perc] — str

perc: xyl, siren, sd, slgh-bells, cym, sus cym, tri, cast, tambn, whip, gong, chimes, glock, lionroar, Chinescym, bd/cym, bd, rattle, cel[played by perc]
Revised and edited by Chou Wen-chung, 1973.

Ricordi

Arcana <1925–1927; rev 1960>

16'

5[1.2.pic1.pic2.pic3] 5[1.2.3.Eh.heckl] 5[1.2.Ebcl1.Ebcl2.bcl] 5[1.2.3.cbn1.cbn2] — 8 5 4[1.2.btbn.cb tbn] 2 — tmp+6 — str

perc: gong, Chinescym, sd, tri, guiro, td, tambn, cym, lionroar, sus cym, xyl, ratch, glock, templeblks, 2tamtams, 2bd, tmp2, chimes, horse

Ricordi

Déserts <1950–1954; rev 1960-61>

24'

2[1/pic.2/pic] 0 2[1.2/bcl/Ebcl] 0 — 2 3 3 2 — tape — tmp+4 — pf — [no str]

perc: vib, sd, claves, glock, cowbell, tambn, templeblks, field dr, guiro, chimes, xyl, marac, 4sus cym, 2timbales, 2bd/cym, 3gongs, 3wood drums, 2lathes[beaten on various surfaces]
2-channel magnetic tapes interpolated between instrumental sections. May be performed without electronic interpolations, in which case the duration is 14'.

Ricordi

Ecuatorial <1932–1934; rev 1961>

11'

several bass voices or male chorus
0 0 0 0 — 0 4 4 0 — 2ondes — tmp+5 — pf, org — [no str]

perc: gong, templeblks, cym, tambn, sus cym, 2sd, 2td, 3bd, 3tamtams, tmp2
Originally for bass voices; revised in 1961 for male chorus. Theremin may be substituted for one or both of the ondes martinots.

Ricordi

Hyperprism <1922–1923>

5'

1[1/pic] 0 1[Ebcl] 0 — 3 2 2 0 — 9perc — [no str]

perc: templeblks, bd, cym, siren, sus cym, lionroar, tamtam, sd, slgh-bells, whip, tambn, tri, Indian dr, 2rattles, anvil
Ed. R. Sacks, 1986.

Ricordi

Intégrales <1924–1925>

12'

2[pic1.pic2] 1 2[1.Ebcl] 0 — 1 2 3[1.btbn.cb tbn] 0 — 4perc — [no str]

perc: sus cym, sd, td, field dr, cast, cym, templeblks, slgh-bells, tambn, gong, tamtam, tri, Chinescym, bd, whip, chain, verges
Rev. ed. by Chou Wen-chung, 1980.

Ricordi

Ionisation <1929–1931>

8'

12perc — pf[also covers some percussion] — [no str]

perc: Chinescym, cowbell, gong, bongos, td, field dr, whip, guiro, templeblks, claves, tri, marac, sus cym, cym, slgh-bells, chimes, tambn, 3bd, 3tamtams, 2sirens, 2sd, tarole, kybd glock, 2anvils

Ricordi

Nocturnal <1961–incomplete>

7'

solo soprano   chorus of bass voices
2[1/pic2.pic1] 1 2[1.Ebcl] 1 — 1 2 3[1.btbn.cb tbn] 0 — tmp+5 — pf — str

perc: sd, field dr, td, marac, guiro, slgh-bells, flexatone, bongos, claves, cym, sandblks, metal sheet, 2woodblks, bambootubes (or templeblks), 2cowbells, 2ratchets, 3gongs, 2bd, rute, 2sus cym
Posthumous work, completed and edited by Chou Wen-chung, 1969.

Ricordi

Octandre <1923>

7'

1[1/pic] 1 1[1/Ebcl] 1 — 1 1 1 0 — db
Rev. ed. by Chou Wen-chung, 1980.

Ricordi

Offrandes <1921>

8'

solo soprano
2[1.2/pic] 1 1 1 — 1 1 1 0 — 8perc — hp — 2vn, va, vc, db

perc: sd, tri, tambn, cast, ratch, cym, bd, 2tamtams
Reinforcement of the string parts authorized to the extent of 6.4.4.2.2 total strings.
   1. Chanson de là-haut   4'
   2. La croix du sud   4'

Ricordi

Tuning Up <1947; rev (reconstructed) 1998>

5'

4[1.2.3/pic2.pic1] 4[1.2.3.Eh] 4[1.2.3.bcl] 4[1.2.3.cbn] — 4 4 3 1 — tmp+6 — 2hp — str

perc: tambn, sd, td, xyl, glock, templeblks, slgh-bells, gong, 3sus cym, 2tamtams, 2anvils, 4tambn, 2tri, 2sirens, 2cym, 2marac
Realized by Chou Wen-chung in 1998, from two drafts by Varese intended for a 1947 movie, but rejected.

Ricordi

Vasks, Pēteris

1946-

(b Aizpute, 16 Apr 1946). Latvian

Symphony No.2 <1998>

35'

3[1/afl.2.3/pic] 3[1.2.3/Eh] 3[1.2.3/bcl] 3[1.2.3/cbn] — 4 3 3 1 — tmp+4 — hp — pf/cel — str

perc: bd, cym, sus cym, field dr, tri, tamtam, glock, xyl, marim, vib, chimes, flexatone, slgh-bells, templeblks, whip, ratch, claves, 2woodblks, 4bongos, 4tomtoms, handbell

Schott

Vaughan Williams, Ralph

1872-1958

(b Down Ampney, Gloucestershire, 12 Oct 1872; d London, 26 Aug 1958). English

Coastal Command: Suite <1942>   15'

2[1.2/pic] 2[1.2/Eh] 2 2 — 4 2 3 1 — tmp+3 — 1 or 2hp — str
perc: bd, cym, sus cym, sd, td, tri, gong, glock
Ed. Christopher Palmer. 3rd mvt may be omitted.

1. Prelude	_'
2. The Hebrides	_'
3. "U-Boat" Alert	_'
4. Taking Off at Night	_'
5. The Hudsons Take Off from Iceland	_'
6. Dawn Patrol (Quiet Determination)	_'
7. The Battle of the Beauforts	_'
8. Finale	_'

Oxford

Concerto, Oboe & Strings, A minor <1944>   19'

str

1. Rondo pastorale	7'
2. Minuet and Musette	3'
3. Finale (Scherzo)	9'

Oxford

Concerto, 1 Piano or 2 Pianos, C major <1926–1931; rev version for 2pf, 1946>   26'

2[incl pic] 2 2 2 — 4 2 3 1 — tmp+2 — opt org — str
perc: cym, tri, tamtam, bd, sd
Originally for 1 solo piano. Version for 2 pianos & orchestra by Joseph Cooper in collaboration with the composer.

1. Toccata: Allegro moderato	6'
2. Romanza: Lento	9'
3. Fuga chromatica con finale alla tedesca: Allegro	11'

Oxford

Concerto, Tuba, F minor <1954>   12'

2[1.2/pic] 1 2 1 — 2 2 2 0 — tmp+2 — str
perc: sd, tri, cym, bd

I. Allegro moderato	4'
II. Romanza: Andante sostenuto	5'
III. Finale; Rondo alla tedesca: Allegro	3'

Oxford

Concerto, Violin, D minor (Concerto accademico) <1924–1925>   16'

str

I. Allegro pesante	_'
II. Adagio	_'
III. Presto	_'

Oxford

Concerto grosso for String Orchestra <1950>   16'

str
Three groups:
(1) Concertino: skilled players approx. 6.6.4.4.2
(2) Tutti: any number of players able to play in 3rd position and simple double stops.
(3) Ad lib parts for less experienced players, including special parts for those using only open strings.
A piano reduction, for rehearsal only, is available.

1. Intrada	2'
2. Burlesca ostinata	6'
3. Sarabande	2'
4. Scherzo	2'
5. March and Reprise of Intrada	4'

Oxford

Death of Tintagiles <1913>   15'

0 1 1 0 — 1 0 0 0 — str
Incidental music to the play by Maeterlinck.
    Ed. & corrected by Roy Douglas.

Prelude: Largo; Andantino; Adagio	6'
Lento	1'
Allegro	1'
Lento; Andante tranquillo; Lento	3'
Moderato	1'
Allegro	1'
Lento	2'

Oxford

The England of Elizabeth: Three Portraits <1955>   17'

2[1.2/pic] 2[1.Eh] 2 1 — 2 2 3 0 — tmp+4 [or 2] — hp — opt cel — str
perc: bd, cym, sus cym, sd, tri, glock, chimes[C,D,E], tuned gong [E (opt)], opt vib
Adapted by Muir Mathieson from the cinema score.

1. Explorer (Sir Francis Drake)	5'
2. Poet (Shakespeare)	7'
3. Queen (Elizabeth I)	5'

Oxford

English Folk Song Suite <1923>   10'

2[1.2/pic] 1 2 1 — 2 2 2 0 — tmp+3 — str
perc: cym, bd, sd, tri
Originally for band; arr. for orchestra by Gordon Jacob (1924).

1. March in F minor (Seventeen Come Sunday)	3'
2. Intermezzo in F minor (My Bonny Boy)	4'
3. March in B-flat major (Folk Songs from Somerset)	3'

Boosey

Fantasia on a Theme by Thomas Tallis <1911–1913; rev 1918, 1933>   15'

solo string quartet
double str orch

Curwen	Kalmus	Luck's

Fantasia on Christmas Carols <1912>   11'

solo baritone   chorus SATB
2 2 2 2 — 4 2 3 1 — tmp+1 — org — str
perc: tri
glock
Wind and percussion parts are optional.

This is the truth sent from above	_'
Come all you worthy gentlemen	_'
On Christmas night all Christians sing	_'
God bless the ruler of this house	_'

Kalmus	Luck's	Presser	Stainer

Fantasia on "Greensleeves" <1934>   4'

1 (or 2) 0 0 0 — hp[or pf] — str
Arr. by Ralph Greaves from the score of the opera *Sir John in Love*.
    Flutes may be covered by 2 solo violins, or 1 flute and 1 violin may be used.

Oxford

Fantasia on Sussex Folk Tunes (Sussex Rhapsody) <1929>   15'

2[1.2/pic] 1 2 2 — 2 1 0 0 — tmp — str

Oxford

Five Mystical Songs <1911>   20'

baritone solo   optional chorus
2 2 2 2 — 4[or 2] 2 3[or 0] 1[or 0] — tmp — hp — str
Two versions of mvt 5 are given: one with chorus & orchestra; the other
with baritone & orchestra.
   May be performed with reduced brass (2 2 0 0) "in case of *absolute
necessity*."
   A separate version of this work with accompaniment for piano &
strings is available from Stainer.

1. Easter	6'
2. I Got Me Flowers	3'
3. Love Bade Me Welcome	6'
4. The Call	2'
5. Antiphon	3'

Kalmus	Luck's	Stainer

Five Variants of "Dives and Lazarus" <1939>   11'

hp[preferably doubled] — str

Oxford

Flos campi (Flower of the Field)   20'

solo viola   textless chorus
1[1/pic] 1 1 1 — 1 1 0 0 — 2perc — hp — cel — str[max 6.6.4.4.2]
perc: cym, bd, tri, tabor

1. As the Lily Among Thorns	2'
2. For Lo, the Winter is Past	3'
3. I Sought Him Whom My Soul Loveth	3'
4. Behold His Bed, Which Is Solomon's	2'
5. Return, Return O Shulamite	3'
6. Set Me As a Seal Upon Thine Heart	7'

Oxford

Hodie (This Day) <1953–1954>   61'

chorus   solos STB
3[1.2.3/pic] 3[1.2.Eh] 2 3[1.2.opt cbn] — 4 3 3 1 — tmp+4 — hp —
cel, pf, opt org — str
perc: sd, td, bd, cym, sus cym, tri, glock, chimes[B3,D4,E4]
Various instruments are optional; possible with:
2[1.3/pic] 2[1.3/Eh] 2 2 — 2 2 3 1 — tmp+4 — cel, pf — str

1. Prologue: Nowell! Nowell!	4'
2. Narration: Now the Birth of Jesus Christ	5'
3. Song: It Was the Winter Wild	5'
4. Narration: And It Came to Pass in Those Days	2'
5. Chorale: The Blessed Son of God	3'
6. Narration: And There Were in the Same Country	7'
7. Song: The Oxen (Christmas Eve and Twelve of the Clock)	3'
8. Narration: And the Shepherds Returned	1'
9. Pastoral: The Shepherds Sing	3'
10. Narration: But Mary Kept All These Things	1'
11. Lullaby: Sweet Was the Song the Virgin Sang	3'
12. Hymn: Bright Portals of the Sky	4'
13. Narration: Now When Jesus Was Born	3'
14. The March of the Three Kings: From Kingdoms of Wisdom	8'
15. Chorale: No Sad Thought His Soul Affright	3'
16. Epilogue: In the Beginning Was the Word	6'

Oxford

In the Fen Country <1904; rev 1935>   14'

3 3[1.2.Eh] 3[1.2.bcl] 2 — 4 2 3 1 — tmp — str
Rev. 1935.

Oxford

Job; A Masque for Dancing <1927–1930>   43'

3[1.2.3/pic/afl] 3[1.2.Eh] 3[1.2.3/bcl] 3[1.2.opt cbn] — 4 3 3 1 — opt
asx — tmp+3 — 2hp — opt org — str
perc: sd, tri, cym, bd, xyl, glock, tamtam
Various instruments are optional; possible with:
2[incl pic] 2[incl Eh] 2 2 — 2 2 3 1 — tmp+4 — str

Oxford

The Lark Ascending <1914; rev 1920>   13'

solo violin
2 1 2 2 — 2 0 0 0 — 1perc — str
perc: tri
Also possible with only one of each wind instrument.

Oxford

Magnificat <1932>   12'

contralto solo   female chorus
2 0 0 0 — hp — opt cel — str
A version with accompaniment for full orchestra is also available:
  2 2[incl Eh] 2 2 — 4 2 0 0 — tmp+2 — hp, opt cel, opt org — str

Oxford

Norfolk Rhapsody No.1, E minor <1905–1906>   10'

2[1.2/pic] 3[1.2.Eh] 3[1.2.opt Ebcl] 2 — 4 2 3 1 — tmp+1 — hp —
str
perc: sd

Oxford

On Wenlock Edge <1908–1909; rev c. 1923>   23'

solo tenor
2[1.2/pic] 2[1.Eh] 2[1.2/bcl] 2 — 4 2 3 0 — tmp+3 — hp — cel — str
perc: sus cym, sd, gong, glock
Originally for tenor, piano and string quartet; orchestrated by the
composer. Tbn in mvt 5 only.

1. On Wenlock Edge	4'
2. From Far, From Even and Morning	2'
3. Is My Team Ploughing?	4'
4. Oh, when I Was in Love with You	1'
5. Bredon Hill	8'
6. Clun	4'

Boosey

An Oxford Elegy <1947–1949>   25'

speaker   chorus
1 2[1.Eh] 2 1 — 2 0 0 0 — str

Oxford

Partita for Double String Orchestra <1946–1948>   20'

str[total min 4.4.4.4.2]
Originally a *Double Trio* for string sextet; arranged by the composer.

I. Prelude	6'
II. Scherzo ostinato	4'
III. Intermezzo (Homage to Henry Hall)	4'
IV. Fantasia	6'

Oxford

The Poisoned Kiss: Overture <1927–1929; rev 1956-57>   7'

2[1.2/pic] 1[1/Eh] 2 1 — 2 2 1 0 — tmp+2 — hp [or pf] — str
perc: bd, cym, sd, tri
Special piano part if used to replace harp.

Oxford

Prelude & Fugue in C minor <1921; rev (orchd) 1930>   10'

3[1.2.3/pic] 2 2 3[1.2.cbn] — 4 3 3 1 — tmp+3 — org — str
Originally for organ; arr. by composer.

Oxford

Prelude "49th Parallel" <1940–1941>   2'

2 2[1.2/Eh] 2 2 — 4 2 3 1 — tmp+1 — hp — str
perc: cym
From the film score. Cued so that it may be played by strings plus any
other available parts.

Luck's	Oxford

Prelude on an Old Carol Tune <1953>   8'

2 1 2 1 — 2 2 2 0 — tmp — str
Based on incidental music for the television serial *The Mayor of Casterbridge*.

> Oxford

Romance <1951>   7'

solo harmonica
str

> Oxford

The Running Set <1933>   5'

2[1.pic] 2[ob2 opt] 2 2 — 2[hn2 opt] 2[tp2 opt] 0 0 — opt pf [or hp] — str
Founded on traditional dance tunes.

> Oxford

Serenade to Music [original version] <1938>   14'

16 solo voices (4S, 4A, 4T, 4B)   solo violin
2[1.2/pic] 2[1.Eh] 2 2 — 4 2 3 1 — tmp+1 — hp — str
perc: tri, bd
May be performed by chorus instead of 16 solo voices, or by some combination of chorus and 4 or more solo voices.

> Oxford

Serenade to Music [reduced version] <1938>   14'

16 solo voices (4S, 4A, 4T, 4B)   solo violin
2[1.2/pic] 2[1.Eh] 2 2 — 2 2 0 0 — tmp/perc — hp — str
perc: tri, bd
May be performed by chorus instead of 16 solo voices, or by some combination of chorus and 4 or more solo voices.
    Reduced orchestration by Roy Douglas.

> Oxford

Serenade to Music [strings & piano] <1938>   14'

16 solo voices (4S, 4A, 4T, 4B)   solo violin
pf — str
May be performed by chorus instead of 16 solo voices, or by some combination of chorus and 4 or more solo voices.
    Arranged for strings & piano by Denis Williams.

> Oxford

Serenade to Music [orchestral version] <1938; rev 1939>   11'

solo violin
2[1.2/pic] 2[1.Eh] 2 2 — 4 2 3 1 — tmp+1 — hp — str
perc: tri
Reworked from the vocal-orchestral version, and shortened by about 3'.

> Oxford

The Story of a Flemish Farm <1943>   24'

2[1.2/pic] 2 2 3[1.2.opt cbn] — 4 2 3 1 — tmp+3 — hp — str
perc: bd, cym, sus cym, sd, tri, gong, glock
Suite from the film.

1. The Flag Flutters in the Wind	*3'*
2. Night by the Sea, Farewell to the Flag	*2'*
3. Dawn in the Old Barn, The Parting of the Lovers	*6'*
4. In the Café	*2'*
5. The Major Goes to Face His Fate	*3'*
6. The Dead Man's Kit	*4'*
7. The Wanderings of the Flag	*4'*

> Oxford

Suite, Viola & Small Orchestra <1934>   25'

2[1.2/pic] 1 2 2 — 2 2 0 0 — tmp+1 — hp — cel[can be played by perc] — str[max 10.8.6.6.4]
perc: sd, tri

GROUP 1	
1. Prelude	*3'*
2. Carol	*2'*
3. Christmas Dance	*2'*
GROUP 2	
1. Ballad	*6'*
2. Moto perpetuo	*4'*
GROUP 3	
1. Musette	*4'*
2. Polka melancolique	*3'*
3. Galop	*2'*

> Oxford

Symphony No.1 (A Sea Symphony) <1903–1909; rev 1923>   63'

soprano & baritone solos   chorus
3[1.2.3/pic] 3[1.2.Eh] 4[1.2.Ebcl.bcl] 3[1.2.cbn] — 4 3 3 1 — tmp+4 — 2hp — org — str
perc: sd, tri, cym, bd
By means of cues and special parts for 2nd fl, Eh, and 2nd bn, playable with the following:
    2[1.2/pic] 2[1.Eh] 2 2 — 4 3 3 1 — tmp+4 — hp — str

1. A Song for All Seas, All Ships	*18'*
2. On the Beach at Night Alone	*10'*
3. Scherzo: The Waves	*7'*
4. The Explorers	*28'*

> Kalmus   Stainer

Symphony No.2, G major (A London Symphony) <1911–1913; rev 1918, 1933>   44'

3[1.2.pic.3/pic] 3[1.2.Eh] 3[1.2.bcl] 3[1.2.cbn] — 4 4[2tp, 2crt] 3 1 — tmp+4 — hp[preferably dbl] — str
perc: glock, tamtam, sd, tri, slgh-bells, cym, bd, sus cym
Playable with winds: 2[1.2/pic] 2[1.2/Eh] 2 2 — 4 2 3 1
    Main revision 1918 (pub. **1920**), available from Kalmus.
    Last revision 1933 (pub. **1934**), available from Stainer. The Stainer score of the 1934 publication is perversely dated 1920; this is also the score reprinted by Dover.

I. Lento - Allegro risoluto	*13'*
II. Lento	*10'*
III. Scherzo (Nocturne)	*7'*
IV. Andante con moto; Maestoso alla marcia	*14'*

> Kalmus   Luck's   Stainer

Symphony No.3 (Pastoral Symphony) <1921>   34'

solo soprano (or tenor)
3[1.2.3/pic] 3[1.2.Eh] 3[1.2.3/bcl] 2 — 4 3 3 1 — tmp+2 — hp — cel[can be played by perc] — str
perc: bd, tri, cym
Possible without the voice, and with the following:
    2[1.2/pic] 2[1.3/Eh] 2 2 — 4 2 3 1 — tmp+2 — hp — str

I. Molto moderato	*10'*
II. Lento moderato	*8'*
III. Moderato pesante	*6'*
IV. Lento; Moderato maestoso	*10'*

> Curwen

Symphony No.4, F minor <1931–1934>   30'

3[1.2.pic.3] 3[1.2/Eh.3] 3[1.2.bcl] 3[1.2.cbn] — 4 2 3 1 — tmp+2 — str
perc: tri, sd, bd, cym, sus cym
Optional: fl3, ob3, bcl, cbn.

I. Allegro	*8'*
II. Andante moderato	*9'*
III. Scherzo	*5'*
IV. Finale con epilogo fugato	*8'*

> Oxford

Symphony No.5, D major <1938–1943; rev 1951>   39'

2[1.2/pic] 2[1.Eh] 2 2 — 2 2 3 0 — tmp — str
Reingraved and corrected 1969.

1. Preludio	12'
2. Scherzo	5'
3. Romanza	12'
4. Passacaglia	10'

Oxford

Symphony No.6, E minor <1944–1947; rev 1950>   31'

3[1.2.3/pic] 3[1.2.Eh] 3[1.2.bcl/tsx] 3[1.2.cbn] — 4 3 3 1 — tmp+3
— hp[doubled ad lib] — str
perc: sd, cym, xyl, bd, tri, sus cym

I. Allegro	7'
II. Moderato	8'
III. Scherzo: Allegro vivace	5'
IV. Epilogue: Moderato	11'

Oxford

Symphony No.7 (Sinfonia antartica) <1949–1952>   41'

brief female chorus & solo soprano
3[1.2.3/pic] 3[1.2.Eh] 3[1.2.bcl] 3[1.2.cbn] — 4 3 3 1 — tmp+4 — hp
— cel, pf, org — str
perc: xyl, vib, sd, td, glock, wnd mach, cym, gong, bd, tri, sus cym, bells[A#2,D3]
Epigraphs at the beginnings of each mvt (Shelley, Psalm 104, Coleridge, Donne, Capt. Scott's journal) are sometimes read in performance by a narrator.
N.B. The composer uses the Italian spelling for *Sinfonia antartica*.

1. Prelude	9'
2. Scherzo	6'
3. Landscape	10'
4. Intermezzo	3'
5. Epilogue	10'

Oxford

Symphony No.8, D minor <1953–1956>   27'

2[1.2/pic] 2 2 3[bn3 opt] — 2 2 3 0 — tmp+5[perc5 opt] — 2hp[hp2 opt] — cel — str
perc: glock, xyl, vib, cym, bd, sd, chimes, tri, 3tuned gongs [D,E,A]
2nd movement is for winds only, and is available separately; 3rd mvt is for strings.

1. Fantasia (Variazioni senza tema)	10'
2. Scherzo alla marcia	4'
3. Cavatina	8'
4. Toccata	5'

Oxford

Symphony No.9, E minor <1956–1958>   33'

3[1.2.3/pic] 3[1.2.Eh] 3[1.2.bcl] 3[1.2.cbn] — 4 3[1.2.flug] 3 1 —
2asx, tsx — tmp+3 — 2hp[1part] — cel — str
perc: very large gong, td, sd, tamtam, tri, cym, xyl, bd, glock, sus cym, bells[E,F#,A#]
2 of the saxophones are optional; 3rd tp may substitute for flugelhorn.

I. Moderato maestoso	8'
II. Andante sostenuto	8'
III. Scherzo: Allegro pesante	5'
IV. Andante tranquillo	12'

Oxford

Three Preludes on Welsh Hymn Tunes <1941>   15'

2[1.2/pic] 1 2 2 — 2 2 0 0 — tmp+1 — str
Originally intended as "household music" for str 4t or other instruments.

1. Crug-y-bar (Fantasia)	_'
2. St. Denio (Scherzo)	_'
3. Aberystwyth (Variations)	_'

Oxford

Toward the Unknown Region <1904–1906>   14'

chorus
3 3[1.2.Eh] 3[1.2.bcl] 2 — 4 3 3 1 — tmp — 2hp — org — str
Cued to permit performance with:
2 1 2 2 — 2 2 0 0 — tmp — hp (or pf) — str

| Kalmus | Luck's | Stainer |

Two Hymn-Tune Preludes <1936>   8'

1 1 1 1 — 1 0 0 0 — str

| *Eventide* | 5' |
| *Dominus regit me* | 3' |

| Luck's | Oxford |

Variations for Orchestra <1957>   12'

2[1.2/pic] 2 2 2 — 4 2 3 1 — tmp+3 — cel[played by perc] — str
perc: bd, cym, sus cym, sd, tri, glock, cel[played by perc]
Originally for brass band; orchestrated by Gordon Jacob.

Oxford

The Wasps: Aristophanic Suite <1909>   25'

2[1.2/pic] 2 2 2 — 4 2 3 0 — tmp+4 — hp — str
perc: tri, tambn, sd, cym, bd, sus cym
Possible with winds: 2[1.2/pic] 1 2 1 — 2 1 0 0

1. Overture	9'
2. Entr'acte	3'
3. March Past of the Kitchen Utensils	3'
4. Entr'acte	4'
5. Ballet and Final Tableau	6'

| Curwen | Kalmus |

The Wasps: Overture <1909>   9'

2[1.2/pic] 2 2 2 — 4 2 0 0 — tmp+3 — hp — str
perc: tri, cym, bd, sus cym
Possible with winds: 2[1.2/pic] 1 2 1 — 2 1 0 0

| Curwen | Kalmus | Luck's |

The Wasps: March Past of the Kitchen Utensils <1909>   4'

2[1.pic] 2 2 2 — 2 1 0 0 — tmp+2 — str
perc: cym, bd, tri
Possible with winds: 2[1.pic] 1 2 1 — 2 1 0 0

| Curwen | Luck's |

Veerhoff, Carlos   1926-

(b Buenos Aires, 3 June 1926). German composer of Argentine origin

Sinfonia panta-rhei <1953–1954>   20'

3[1.2.3/pic] 3[1.2.Eh] 4[1.2.3.bcl] 4[1.2.3.cbn] — 4 4 3 1 — tmp+5
— hp — kybd — str

Schott

Veracini, Francesco Maria   1690-1768

(b Florence, 1 Feb 1690; d Florence, 31 Oct 1768). Italian

Aria schiavona   4'

cnt — str

| Kalmus | Luck's | Zanibon |

Concerto, Violin, D major   6'

cnt — str
Ed. Bernhard Paumgartner.

Bärenreiter

Concerto grande da chiesa; or della incoronazione   12'
solo violin
0 2 0 0 — 0 2 0 0 — tmp — cnt — str

Kalmus	Luck's	Zanibon

Menuet et Gavotte   4'
solo violoncello
str

Kalmus	Luck's	Salabert☐☐☐☐

Quatro pezzi (from Sonate accademiche)   16'
str
Originally for violin and continuo; "elaborated and freely interpreted" by
Ettore Bonelli.
1. Largo   _'
2. Allegro assai _'
3. Giga   _'
4. Aria rustica   _'

Kalmus	Luck's	Zanibon

Verdi, Giuseppe   1813-1901
(b Roncole, nr Busseto, 9 or 10 Oct 1813; d Milan, 27 Jan 1901). Italian

Aïda: Prelude <1871>   6'
3[1.2.pic] 2 2 2 — 4 2 3 1 — tmp — str

Kalmus	Leduc	Luck's	Ricordi

Aïda: Triumphal March & Ballet <1871>   11'
3[1.2.pic] 2 2 2 — 4 4 3 1[cimbasso] — tmp+3 — str
perc: bd, cym, tri
Kalmus also offers an "original version" which includes 13 *banda* parts.
Triumphal March   7'
Ballet   4'

Kalmus	Luck's

Aroldo: Overture <1850>   9'
2[1.pic] 2 2 2 — 4 2 3 1[cimbasso] — tmp+2 — str
perc: sd, bd
The music from an earlier opera, *Stiffelio*.

Kalmus	Ricordi

Un ballo in maschera (A Masked Ball): Preludio <1859>   4'
2[1.pic] 2 2 2 — 4 2 3 1[cimbasso] — tmp — str

Kalmus	Luck's	Ricordi

Birthday Variations [arr. J.McPhee] <1847>   20'
2[1.pic] 2 2 2 — 4 3 3 1 — tmp+2 — hp — str
perc: sd, bd
Arranged and adapted by Jonathan McPhee, largely from the ballet music
for the composer's opera *Jérusalem* (itself a revision of his *I Lombardi*),
and with original material added by McPhee.

Boosey

La forza del destino: Overture <1861>   8'
2[1.pic] 2 2 2 — 4 2 3 1[cimbasso] — tmp+1 — 2hp — str
perc: bd/cym
The bass drum part makes no mention of cymbals, but presumably they
were employed together with the bd in the traditional manner. Some
performers may prefer 2 players for this purpose.

Kalmus	Luck's	Ricordi

Giovanna d'Arco (Joan of Arc): Overture <1845>   8'
2[1.pic] 2 2 2 — 4 2 3 1[cimbasso] — tmp+2 — str
perc: sd, bd [+cym?]
Cym perhaps assumed with bd.

Kalmus	Luck's	Ricordi

Inno delle nazioni (Hymn of the Nations) <1862>   18'
solo tenor   chorus
3[1.2.pic] 2 2 2 — 4 2 3 1[cimbasso] — tmp+1 — 2hp — str
perc: bd
Quotes the national anthems of various nations, tied together by the solo
tenor (*Bardo*).

Kalmus	Ricordi

Luisa Miller: Overture <1849>   6'
3[1.2.pic] 2 2 2 — 4 2 4[1.2.3.btbn] 0 — tmp+1 — str
perc: bd

Kalmus	Ricordi

Messa da requiem (Manzoni requiem) <1874; rev 1875>   84'
chorus   solos SATB
3[1.2.3/pic] 2 2 4 — 4 8[4tp offstage] 3 1[oph] — tmp+1 — str
perc: bd
Bärenreiter critical ed. Marco Uvietta; Carus ed. Norbert Bolin; Ricordi
[collected edition] ed. David Rosen.
I. Requiem and Kyrie   9'
II. Sequence (Dies Irae)   37'
III. Offertorio (Domine Jesu) 10'
IV. Sanctus   3'
V. Agnus Dei   5'
VI. Lux aeterna   6'
VII. Libera me   14'

Bärenreiter	Carus	Peters	Ricordi	Schirmer

Nabucco: Overture <1842>   8'
2[1.2/pic] 2 2 2 — 4 2 3 1 — tmp+3 — str
perc: sd, cym, bd
Kalmus ed. (2010) by Clinton F. Nieweg & Nancy M. Bradburd. Luck's
edition (2012) by Clark Suttle.

Kalmus	Luck's	Ricordi

Requiem
see his: Messa da requiem

Romanze <1835–1847>   25'
solo tenor
2[1.2/pic] 2 2 2 — 2 2 2 1 — tmp+1 — hp — str
8 romanze per tenore e orchestra; orchestral adaptation, including
introductions and endings, by Luciano Berio, 1991. (Verdi's original
musical setting given underneath.)
1. In solitaria stanza   _'
2. Il poveretto   _'
3. Il mistero   _'
4. L'esule   _'
5. Deh, pietoso, oh addolorata _'
6. Il tramonto   _'
7. Ad una stella   _'
8. Brindisi   _'

Universal

Stabat Mater <1896–1897>   12'
chorus
3 2 2 4 — 4 3 4 0 — tmp+1 — hp — str
perc: bd
No.2 of *Quattro pezzi sacri*.

Kalmus	Luck's	Peters	Ricordi

Symphony for Strings, E minor <1873>   23'

str
Originally for string quartet; arr. for string orchestra by Lucas Drew.
   I. Allegro   8'
   II. Andantino   8'
   III. Prestissimo 3'
   IV. Scherzo fuga 4'

Kalmus			

Te Deum <1895–1896>   15'

double chorus   soprano solo
3 3[1.2.Eh] 3[1.2.bcl] 4 — 4 3 4 0 — tmp+1 — str
perc: bd
No.4 of *Quattro pezzi sacri*.

Kalmus	Luck's	Peters	Ricordi

La traviata: Prelude to Act I <1853>   4'

1 1 1 2 — 4 0 0 0 — str

Bärenreiter	Kalmus	Luck's	Ricordi

La traviata: Prelude to Act III <1853>   4'

1 1 2 2 — 1 0 0 0 — str

Kalmus	Luck's	Ricordi	

I vespri siciliani (The Sicilian Vespers): Overture <1854>   9'

2[1.pic] 2 2 2 — 4 4[2tp, 2crt] 3 1 — tmp+3 — str
perc: sd, bd, cym

Kalmus	Luck's	Ricordi	

Veress, Sándor   1907-1992

(b Kolozsvár [now Cluj-Napoca], 1 Feb 1907; d Berne, 4 March 1992). Swiss composer of Hungarian origin

Tromboniade (Double Trombone Concerto) <1989–1990>   14'

2 solo tenor trombones
2[1.2/pic] 1 2[1.2/bcl] 2[1.cbn] — 2 2 0 0 — tmp+5 — hp — cel — str
perc: templeblks, sd, field dr, tamtam, bd, crot, tri, vib, xyl, 2sus cym
In one mvt.

Suvini			

Vieuxtemps, Henri   1820-1881

(b Verviers, 17 Feb 1820; d Mustapha, Algeria, 6 June 1881). Belgian

Concerto, Violin, No.4, op.31, D minor <c1850>   23'

2 2 2 2 — 4 2 3 0 — tmp — hp — str
   1. Andante; Moderato; Cadenza 7'
   2. Adagio religioso   6'
   3. Scherzo & Trio   4'
   4. Finale   6'

C. Fischer	Kalmus		

Concerto, Violin, No.5, op.37, A minor (Grétry) <1861>   18'

1 2 2 2 — 2 2 0 0 — tmp — str
   1. Allegro non troppo 11'
   2. Cadenza   3'
   3. Adagio   3'
   4. Allegro con fuoco   1'

Bote & Bock	C. Fischer	Kalmus	Luck's

Yankee Doodle, op.17; Caprice burlesque (Souvenir d'Amerique) <c1845>   5'

solo violin
2 2 2 2 — 2 2 0 0 — tmp — str
Originally for violin & piano; orchestrated by Clark McAlister.

Kalmus			

Villa-Lobos, Heitor   1887-1959

(b Rio de Janeiro, 5 March 1887; d Rio de Janeiro, 17 Nov 1959). Brazilian

A = David P. Appleby, *Heitor Villa-Lobos; A Bio-Bibliography* (Westport, CT, 1988)

Bachianas brasileiras no.1, A246 <1930>   20'

at least 8 vc
   1. Introdução (Embolada) 7'
   2. Prelúdio (Modinha)   9'
   3. Fuga (Conversa)   4'

AMP			

Bachianas brasileiras no.2, A247 (O trenzinho do Caipira; The Little Train of the Caipira) <1930>   21'

1[1/pic] 1 1 1 — 2 0 1 0 — tsx/bsx — tmp+5 — cel, pf — str
perc: slgh-bells, ratch, guiro, tambn, sd, tri, cym, tamtam, bd, metalshaker, high drum
Although a contrabassoon is called for in the instrumentation list and the first score page, this is almost certainly an error.
   1. Prelúdio: O canto do capadocio (The Song of the Countryman) 7'
   2. Aria: O canto da nossa terra (The Song of our Country) 5'
   3. Dança: Lembrança do sertão (Memory of the Desert) 5'
   4. Toccata: O trenzinho do caipira (The Little Train of the Caipira) 4'

Ricordi			

Bachianas brasileiras no.3, A388 <1938>   27'

solo piano
3[1.2.pic] 3[1.2.Eh] 3[1.2.bcl] 3[1.2.cbn] — 4 2 4 1 — tmp+2 — str
perc: xyl, tamtam, bd
   1. Prelúdio (Ponteio)   7'
   2. Fantasia (Devaneio) 7'
   3. Aria (Modinha)   7'
   4. Tocata (Picapau)   6'

Colombo			

Bachianas brasileiras no.4, A424   22'

3[1.2.pic] 3[1.2.Eh] 3[1.2.bcl] 3[1.2.cbn] — 4 3 2 1 — tmp+3 — cel — str
perc: xyl, bd, tamtam
Originally for piano solo; orchestrated by the composer.
   The parts for this work leave a lot to be desired. Rental sets include a 3rd tbn, but never are there more than 2 trombones playing at the same time.
   1. Prélude (Introdução) 8'
   2. Choral (Canto do Sertão) 4'
   3. Aria (Cantiga)   6'
   4. Danse (Miudinho) 4'

Colombo			

Bachianas brasileiras no.5, for Soprano & Orchestra of Violoncelli, A389 <1938–1945>   10'

soprano solo
at least 8vc
   1. Aria (Cantilena) 6'
   2. Dança (Martelo) 4'

AMP			

Bachianas brasileiras no.5, A389: Ária (full orchestra)   6'

2[1.2/pic] 2[1.Eh] 2[1.2/bcl] 2 — 2 2 2 0 — opt gtr — tmp+7 — opt hp — cel — str

Originally for soprano & 8 violoncellos; arranged for full orchestra by John Krance.

AMP

Bachianas brasileiras no.5, A389: Ária (strings)   7'

opt gtr — str

Originally for soprano & 8 violoncellos; arranged by John Krance.

AMP

Bachianas brasileiras no.6

This work is a duo for flute and bassoon, and thus outside the scope of this book.

Bachianas brasileiras no.7, A432 <1942>   26'

3[1.2.pic] 3[1.2.Eh] 3[1.2.bcl] 3[1.2.cbn] — 4 3 4 1 — tmp+2 — hp — cel — str

perc: bd, tamtam, xyl, woodblk

1. *Prelúdio (Ponteio)*   7'
2. *Giga (Quadrilha caipira)* 4'
3. *Tocata (Desafio)*   8'
4. *Fuga (Conversa)*   7'

Eschig

Bachianas brasileiras no.8, A444 <1944>   27'

3[1.2.pic] 3[1.2.Eh] 3[1.2.bcl] 3[1.2.cbn] — 4 4 4 1 — tmp+3 — str

perc: bd, sd, tamtam, templeblks, xyl

1. *Prelúdio*   7'
2. *Aria (Modinha)*   8'
3. *Tocata (Catira batida)*   6'
4. *Fuga*   6'

Eschig

Bachianas brasileiras no.9, A449 <1945>   10'

str

"Para orquestra de vozes ou de cordas" (For orchestra of human voices [*a cappella*] or of strings).

1. *Prelúdio: Vagaroso e místico*   3'
2. *Fuga: Poco apressado*   7'

Eschig

Chôros no.8, A208 <1925>   20'

2 solo pianos

3[1.2.pic] 3[1.2.Eh] 5[1.2.3.4.5/bcl] 3[1.2.cbn] — 4 2 4 1 — asx — tmp+4 — 2hp — cel — str

perc: tamtam, tri, cym, sd, ratch, bd, xyl, tambn, chocalho, reco-reco, 2guiro, friction drum, caixa de pão, xucalho de pão

Eschig

Chôros no.10, A209 (Rasga o coração) <1926>   12'

chorus

2[incl pic] 2 2 3[1.2.cbn] — 3 2 2 0 — asx — tmp+3 — hp — pf — str

perc: tamtam, gong, sd, tomtom, td, field dr, wood drum, 2frictiondr, 2bd, 2reco-reco, 2chocalho

Eschig

Ciranda das sete notas, A325 <1933>   10'

solo bassoon

str

Southern

Concerto, Guitar & Small Orchestra, A501 <1951>   22'

1 1 1 1 — 1 0 1 0 — str

1. *Allegro preciso*   6'
2. *Andantino e andante*   11'
3. *Allegretto non troppo*   5'

Eschig

Danses africaines, A107 (Danses des indiens métis du Brésil) <1916>   19'

3[1.2.pic] 3[1.2.Eh] 3[1.2.bcl] 3[1.2.cbn] — 4 4 3 1 — tmp+5 — 2hp — cel, pf — str

perc: tamtam, tri, cym, tomtom, guiro, bd, xyl, wood drum, 3tambn, 2bells

1. *Farrapós (Dança dos moços)*   6'
2. *Kankukus (Dança dos velhos)*   7'
3. *Kankikis (Dança dos meninos)*   6'

Eschig

Fantasia para saxophone, A490 <1948>   11'

solo B-flat saxophone (soprano or tenor)

0 0 0 0 — 3 0 0 0 — str

1. *Animé*   5'
2. *Lent*   3'
3. *Très animé*   3'

Southern

Mômoprecóce; fantaisie pour piano et orchestre, A240 (Carnival of the Brazilian Children) <1929>   28'

solo piano

1[1/pic] 2[1.Eh] 1 2[1.2/cbn] — 3 1 1 0 — asx — tmp+2 — cel[played by perc] — str

perc: bd, sd, field dr, slgh-bells, tambn, guiro, toy drum, metal shaker, cel[played by perc]

An elaboration for piano and orchestra of an earlier series of short piano pieces, *Carnaval das Crianças*.

1. *Pierrot's Hobby Horse*   —'
2. *Little Devil's Whip*   —'
3. *The Whining Pierrette*   —'
4. *Domino's Costume Bells*   —'
5. *The Impish Kid in Patches*   —'
6. *The Roguery of the Masked Bandit*   —'
7. *The Precocious Harmonica Player*   —'
8. *Carnival Apotheosis (Breakup of the Snake Dance)*   —'

Eschig

Sinfonietta No.1, B-flat major, A115 (A memória de Mozart) <1916>   22'

2 2 2 2 — 2 2 2 0 — tmp — str

Allegro justo   5'
Andante non troppo   12'
Andantino   5'

Southern

Sinfonietta No.2, C major, A483 <1947>   17'

1[1/pic] 1[1/Eh] 1[1/bcl] 1 — 3 2 2 1 — asx — tmp+1 — hp — cel — str

perc: tamtam, bd, xyl, dinner plates

Southern

Suite for Strings, A54 <1912>   17'

double str 5t or str orch

1. *Timida (Timid Music)*   6'
2. *Misteriosa (Mysterious Music)* 6'
3. *Inquieta (Restless Music)*   5'

Eschig

Uirapurú, A133 (The Magic Bird) <1917>   18'

3[1.2.pic] 3[1.2.Eh] 3[1.2.3/bcl] 3[1.2.cbn] — 4 3 3 1 — ssx — violinophone — tmp+2 — 2hp — cel, pf — str

perc: tamtam, glock, guiro, bd, tambn, cym, xyl, horse hooves

AMP

Villanueva, Felipe
1862-1893

(b Tecámec, Estado de México, 5 Feb 1862; d México, 28 May 1893). Mexican

Vals poético
3'

2 2 3[1.2.bcl] 2 — 4 0 0 0 — tmp+1 — hp — str
perc: tri
Transcribed for orchestra by Gustavo E. Campa.

> Fleisher

Viotti, Giovanni Battista
1755-1824

(b Fontanetto da Po, 12 May 1755; d London, 3 March 1824). Italian

Concerto, Piano, G minor <1792–1794>
41'

2 2 2 2 — 2 2 0 0 — tmp — str
Ed. R. Giazotto.

> Ricordi

Concerto, Violin, No.19, G minor <1791>
31'

2 2 2 0 — 2 0 0 0 — str
1. *Allegro maestoso*   15'
2. *Adagio non troppo*   6'
3. *Presto*   10'

> Ricordi

Concerto, Violin, No.22, A minor <c1793–1797>
27'

1 2 2 2 — 2 2 0 0 — tmp — str
I. *Moderato*   11'
II. *Adagio*   8'
III. *Agitato assai*   8'

> Breitkopf   Kalmus   Luck's

Vitali, Tomaso Antonio
1663-1745

(b Bologna, 7 March 1663; d Modena, 9 May 1745). Italian

Ciaccona [Chaconne], Violin & Strings
14'

solo violin
opt cnt — str
Sometimes attributed to Giovanni Battista Vitali (1632-1692), father of
Tomaso. Probably it is by neither of the Vitalis, but rather by an unknown
composer of the period—or it may even be an anachronistic composition
or pastiche assembled in 1867 by Ferdinand David (1810-1873).
See also the subsequent entry for the Respighi orchestration. There are
numerous other elaborated arrangements of this work:
Solo violin & enlarged orchestra:
Léopold Charlier (Breitkopf)
Alphons Diepenbrock (Donemus)
An orchestra piece (no solo violin):
Alfred Akon (Belwin)
Guido Farina (Carisch)

> Kalmus   Lengnick   Luck's   Zanibon

Ciaccona [Chaconne], Violin & Strings (arr. Respighi)
14'

solo violin
org — str
Sometimes attributed to Giovanni Battista Vitali (1632-1692), father of
Tomaso. Probably it is by neither of the Vitalis, but rather by an unknown
composer of the period—or it may even be an anachronistic composition
or pastiche assembled in 1867 by Ferdinand David (1810-1873).
This edition orchestrated by Ottorino Respighi.

> Kalmus   Luck's

Vittorio, Salvatore Di
1967-

see: Di Vittorio, Salvatore

Vivaldi, Antonio
1678-1741

(b Venice, 4 March 1678; d Vienna, 27/8 July 1741). Italian

RV = Peter Ryom, *Répertoire des oeuvres d'Antonio Vivaldi: Les
compositions instrumentales* (Copenhagen, 1986).
Peter Ryom, *Antonio Vivaldi: Table de concordances des oeuvres*
(Copenhagen, 1973).
A useful concordance of the various numbering systems (by Ryom,
Fanna, Pincherle, Ricordi, and by opus number) may be found at
icking-music-archive.org/lists/vivaldi/intro.html. So far this includes
instrumental works only.

Beatus vir, RV 598, B-flat major
10'

solos SSA   chorus
cnt — str
Ed. Karl Heinz Füssl.
RV 598 is one of several settings of this text by Vivaldi, the others are
RV 597, RV 795, and RV 803. A fifth setting (RV 599) is lost.

> Universal

La cetra <1727>

*The collective title under which the concertos of op.9 (11 for one violin
and 1 for two violins) were published in Amsterdam, 1727. Each
concerto is listed separately in its place.*
*Also the collective title of a separate manuscript collection of
concertos (10 for one violin and 2 for two violins).*
*The contents of the two collections are entirely different; thus there are
24 different concertos with claim to the title* La cetra.

Il cimento dell'armonia e dell'inventione, op.8 <c1725>

*The collective title under which the violin concertos of op.8 were
published in Amsterdam, ca.1725. Each concerto is listed separately in
its place. Two of these concertos, RV 449 and 454, also exist as oboe
concertos. The first four concertos of the collection constitute the
celebrated* Quattro staggioni *(The Four Seasons), q.v.*

Concerto, op.3, no.11, RV 565, D minor (arr. A. Siloti)
8'

2 2 2 3[1.2.cbn] — org — str
Orchestrated by Aleksandr Siloti, from Vivaldi's *Concerto, 2 Violins &
Violoncello, op.3, no.11*, RV 565.
1. *Allegro; Adagio spiccato*   2'
2. *Allegro*   2'
3. *Largo e spiccato*   2'
4. *Allegro*   2'

> Broude Bros.   Kalmus   Luck's

Concerto, Bassoon, RV 477, C major
11'

cnt — str
Ed. Gian Francesco Malipiero.
1. *Allegro*   4'
2. *Largo*   4'
3. *Allegro*   3'

> Ricordi

Concerto, Bassoon, RV 484, E minor   *11'*

cnt — str
   I. Allegro poco   *5'*
   II. Andante   *3'*
   III. Allegro   *3'*
    Ricordi

Concerto, Bassoon, RV 485, F major   *10'*

cnt — str
Ed. Walter Kolneder.
   1. Allegro non molto   *4'*
   2. Andante   *3'*
   3. Allegro molto   *3'*
    Peters

Concerto, Bassoon, RV 498, A minor   *11'*

cnt — str
   I. Allegro ma molto moderato   *4'*
   II. Larghetto   *4'*
   III. Allegro   *3'*
    Ricordi

Concerto, Bassoon, RV 501, B-flat major (La notte)   *10'*

cnt — str
   I. Largo - Andante molto - I fantasmi: Presto   *4'*
   II. Il sonno: Andante molto   *3'*
   III. Sorge l'aurora: Allegro   *3'*
    Eulenburg   Kalmus   Luck's

Concerto, Flute, op.10, no.2, RV 439, G minor (La notte)   *9'*

0 0 0 1 — cnt — str
A reworking of RV 104, which is a chamber concerto for small ensemble (fl, 2vn, bn & cnt).
   I. Largo   *2'*
   II. Fantasmi: Presto   *1'*
   III. Largo   *1'*
   IV. Presto   *1'*
   V. Il sonno: Largo   *2'*
   VI. Allegro   *2'*
    AMP   Luck's   Ricordi

Concerto, Flute, op.10, no.3, RV 428, D major (Il cardellino)   *10'*

cnt — vn
Also variously known as *Del gardellino*, *The Goldfinch*, and *The Bullfinch*. This work is also related musically to the chamber concerto RV 90.
   1. Allegro   *4'*
   2. [Largo]   *3'*
   3. Allegro   *3'*
    Eulenburg   Kalmus   Luck's   Ricordi   Schott

Concerto, Flute, RV 438, G major   *9'*

cnt — str
   I. Allegro molto   *3'*
   II. Largo   *3'*
   III. Allegro   *3'*
    Ricordi

Concerto, Flute, Oboe & Bassoon, op.44, no.16, RV 570, F major (La tempesta di mare)   *7'*

cnt — str
Ed. Felix Schroeder. Flute part possibly intended for recorder.
   I. Allegro   *3'*
   II. Largo   *2'*
   III. Presto   *2'*
    Eulenburg

Concerto, 2 Flutes, RV 533, C major   *7'*

cnt — str
   I. Allegro molto   *3'*
   II. Largo   *2'*
   III. Allegro   *2'*
    Kalmus   Luck's   Ricordi

Concerto, Guitar, RV 93, D major   *9'*

cnt — str
Originally for lute; arr. for guitar.
   I. Allegro giusto   *3'*
   II. Largo   *4'*
   III. Allegro   *2'*
    Doblinger   Kalmus   Peters

Concerto, 2 Horns, RV 538, F major   *7'*

cnt — str
   I. Allegro   *4'*
   II. Larghetto   *3'*
   III. Allegro   *3'*
    Ricordi

Concerto, 2 Horns, RV 539, F major   *10'*

cnt — str
   I. Allegro   *4'*
   II. Largo   *3'*
   III. Allegro non molto   *3'*
    Luck's   Ricordi

Concerto, Mandolin, RV 425, C major   *7'*

cnt — str
Ed. Gian Francesco Malipiero.
   I. Allegro   *3'*
   II. Largo   *2'*
   III. Allegro   *2'*
    Ricordi

Concerto, Oboe, RV 447, C major   *15'*

cnt — str
   1. Allegro non molto   *5'*
   2. Larghetto   *4'*
   3. Minuet   *6'*
    EMB   Eulenburg   Ricordi

Concerto, Oboe, op.8, no.9, RV 454, D minor   *7'*

cnt — str
The same work exists as RV 236, *Concerto for Violin, op.8, no.9.*
   I. Allegro moderato   *3'*
   II. Largo   *2'*
   III. Allegro   *2'*
    Ricordi

Concerto, Oboe, RV 455, F major   *9'*

cnt — str
   I. [Allegro]   *4'*
   II. Grave   *2'*
   III. Allegro   *3'*
    Ricordi

Concerto, Oboe, RV 456, F major <1711–1741>   *9'*

cnt — str
   I. Largo   *4'*
   II. Allegro   *3'*
   III. Presto   *2'*
    Ricordi

Concerto, Oboe & Bassoon, op.42, no.3, RV 545, G major   10'

cnt — str
Ed. Felix Schroeder.
I. Andante molto   4'
II. Largo   3'
III. Allegro molto   3'

| Eulenburg |

Concerto, Oboe & Violin, RV 543, F major   8'

cnt — str
I. Allegro   2'
II. Allegro alla francese 2'
III. Allegro   2'
IV. Minuetto   2'

| Ricordi |

Concerto, Oboe & Violin, RV 548, B-flat major   8'

cnt — str
I. Allegro non molto   3'
II. Largo   3'
III. Allegro   2'

| Ricordi |

Concerto, 2 Oboes, RV 535, D minor   8'

cnt — str
I. Largo - Allegro   3'
II. Largo   2'
III. Allegro molto   3'

| Luck's | Musica Rara | Ricordi |

Concerto, 2 Oboes, Bassoon, 2 Horns, Violin, RV 569, F major   12'

cnt — str
There is also a solo violoncello in the finale.
I. Allegro   5'
II. Grave   2'
III. Allegro   5'

| Ricordi |

Concerto, 2 Oboes, Bassoon, 2 Horns, Violin, RV 574, F major   11'

cnt — str
There is also a solo violoncello in the finale.
I. Allegro   4'
II. Grave   3'
III. Allegro   4'

| Ricordi |

Concerto, 2 Oboes & 2 Clarinets, RV 559, C major   11'

cnt — str
I. Larghetto - Allegro   3'
II. Largo   4'
III. Allegro   4'

| Ricordi |

Concerto, 2 Oboes & 2 Clarinets, RV 560, C major <1711–1741>   9'

cnt — str
I. Larghetto - Allegro   4'
II. Largo   2'
III. (Allegro molto)   3'

| Ricordi |

Concerto for Orchestra, RV 151, G major (Alla rustica)   5'

cnt — str
I. Presto   1'
II. Adagio   2'
III. Allegro   2'

| Kalmus | Peters | Ricordi |

Concerto for Orchestra, RV 152, G minor   6'

cnt — str
Ed. Gian Francesco Mailpiero.
1. Allegro molto   2'
2. Andante molto e sempre pianissimo tutti 2'
3. Allegro molto   2'

| Ricordi |

Concerto for Orchestra, RV 155, G minor   10'

cnt — str
I. Adagio   2'
II. Allegro   2'
III. Largo   3'
IV. Allegro   3'

| Ricordi |

Concerto for Orchestra, RV 158, A major   7'

cnt — str
I. Allegro molto   2'
II. Andante molto   2'
III. Allegro   3'

| Ricordi |

CONCERTOS, PICCOLO

It is not known what instrument Vivaldi had in mind for these concertos. The term he used was flautino, *which could have been sopranino recorder or flageolet. The modern transverse piccolo flute did not yet exist.*

Concerto, Piccolo, RV 443, C major   12'

cnt — str
I. Allegro   4'
II. Largo   5'
III. Allegro   3'

| Eulenburg | Kalmus | Ricordi |

Concerto, Piccolo, RV 445, A minor   10'

cnt — str
Ed. Gian Francesco Malipiero.
I. Allegro   5'
II. Larghetto   4'
III. Allegro   4'

| Ricordi |

Concerto, Recorder, op.44, no.19, RV 441, C minor   13'

cnt — str
Eulenburg ed. Felix Schroeder.
I. Allegro non molto
II. Largo
III. [Allegro]

| Eulenburg | Musica Rara |

Concerto, 2 Trumpets, RV 537, C major   7'

cnt — str
I. Allegro   3'
II. Largo   1'
III. Allegro   3'

| Bärenreiter | Kalmus | Ricordi |

Concerto, Viola d'Amore, RV 392, D major   12'

cnt — str
Kalmus offers an arrangement of this work by H. Newton, transposed to G major for standard viola.
I. [Allegro]   5'
II. Largo   4'
III. Allegro   3'

| Ricordi |

Concerto, Viola d'Amore, RV 394, D minor   *10'*

cnt — str
  I. Allegro   4'
  II. Largo   2'
  III. Allegro   4'

Ricordi		

Concerto, Viola d'Amore & Lute, RV 540, D minor   *12'*
<1711–1741>

cnt — str
  I. Allegro   6'
  II. Largo   3'
  III. Allegro   3'

Luck's	Ricordi	

CONCERTOS FOR SOLO VIOLIN

Concerto, Violin, op.3, no.3, RV 310, G major   *6'*

cnt — str
Bärenreiter edition by W. Upmeyer. This is one of a number of Vivaldi works transcribed by J.S. Bach for various instruments, in this case unaccompanied harpsichord (BWV 978).
  1. Allegro   2'
  2. Largo   2'
  3. Allegro   2'

Bärenreiter	Eulenburg	Kalmus	Luck's	Ricordi

Concerto, Violin, op.3, no.6, RV 356, A minor   *8'*

cnt — str
  1. Allegro   3'
  2. Largo   3'
  3. Presto   2'

Eulenburg	Kalmus	Luck's	Ricordi

Concerto, Violin, op.3, no.9, RV 230, D major   *8'*

cnt — str
Sometimes numbered as op.3, no.7.
  Bärenreiter edition by W. Upmeyer.
  1. Allegro   2'
  2. Larghetto   4'
  3. Allegro   2'

Bärenreiter	Eulenburg	Kalmus	Luck's	Ricordi

Concerto, Violin, op.3, no.12, RV 265, E major   *9'*

cnt — str
  1. Allegro   3'
  2. Largo   3'
  3. Allegro   3'

Eulenburg	Luck's	Ricordi

Concerto, Violin, op.4, no.1, RV 383a, B-flat major *8'*

cnt — str
Bärenreiter edition by W. Upmeyer.
  1. Allegro   3'
  2. Largo   3'
  3. Allegro   2'

Bärenreiter	Kalmus	Luck's	Ricordi

Concerto, Violin, op.4, no.2, RV 279, E minor   *9'*

cnt — str
Bärenreiter edition by W. Upmeyer.
  1. Allegro   4'
  2. Largo   2'
  3. Allegro   3'

Bärenreiter	Kalmus	Luck's	Ricordi

Concerto, Violin, op.4, no.3, RV 301, G major   *7'*

cnt — str
Bärenreiter edition by W. Upmeyer.
  1. Allegro   3'
  2. Largo   2'
  3. Allegro assai 2'

Bärenreiter	Kalmus	Luck's	Ricordi

Concerto, Violin, op.4, no.4, RV 357, A minor   *8'*

cnt — str
  1. Allegro   3'
  2. Grave   2'
  3. Allegro   3'

Ricordi		

Concerto, Violin, op.4, no.5, RV 347, A major   *9'*

cnt — str
  1. Allegro   4'
  2. Largo   2'
  3. Allegro   3'

Ricordi		

Concerto, Violin, op.4, no.6, RV 291, F major   *11'*

cnt — str
  1. Allegro   4'
  2. Larghetto   3'
  3. Allegro   4'

Luck's	Ricordi	

Concerto, Violin, op.4, no.8, RV 249, D minor   *9'*

cnt — str
  1. Allegro   2'
  2. Adagio; Presto   1'
  3. Adagio   2'
  4. Allegro   4'

Ricordi		

Concerto, Violin, op.4, no.9, RV 284, F major   *8'*

cnt — str
  1. Allegro   3'
  2. Largo   3'
  3. Allegro   2'

Ricordi		

Concerto, Violin, op.4, no.10, RV 196, C minor   *9'*

cnt — str
  1. Spiritoso   3'
  2. Adagio   3'
  3. Allegro   3'

Ricordi		

Concerto, Violin, op.4, no.11, RV 204, D major   *8'*

cnt — str
  1. Allegro   3'
  2. Largo   3'
  3. Allegro assai   2'

Ricordi		

Concerto, Violin, op.4, no.12, RV 298, G major   *11'*

cnt — str
  1. Spiritoso e non presto   3'
  2. Largo   4'
  3. Allegro   4'

Luck's	Ricordi	

Concertos, Violin, op.8, no.1-4

see his: Quattro staggioni (The Four Seasons)

Concerto, Violin, op.8, no.5, RV 253, E-flat major (La tempesta di mare)   *10'*

cnt — str
I. Presto   *3'*
II. Largo   *3'*
III. Presto   *4'*

   Ricordi

Concerto, Violin, op.8, no.6, RV 180, C major (Il piacere)   *9'*

cnt — str
I. Allegro   *3'*
II. Largo   *3'*
III. Allegro   *3'*

   Ricordi

Concerto, Violin, op.8, no.7, RV 242, D minor   *8'*

cnt — str
I. Allegro   *3'*
II. Largo   *2'*
III. Allegro   *3'*

   Ricordi

Concerto, Violin, op.8, no.8, RV 332, G minor   *10'*

cnt — str
I. Allegro   *3'*
II. Largo   *3'*
III. Allegro   *4'*

   Luck's   Ricordi

Concerto, Violin, op.8, no.10, RV 362, B-flat major (La caccia)   *7'*

cnt — str
I. Allegro   *3'*
II. Adagio (Grave)   *2'*
III. Allegro   *2'*

   Ricordi

Concerto, Violin, op.8, no.11, RV 210, D major   *13'*

cnt — str
I. Allegro   *5'*
II. Largo   *3'*
III. Allegro   *5'*

   Ricordi

Concerto, Violin, op.8, no.12, RV 178, C major   *8'*

cnt — str
I. Allegro   *3'*
II. Largo   *2'*
III. Allegro   *3'*

   Ricordi

Concerto, Violin, op.9, no.1, RV 181a, C major   *9'*

cnt — str
1. Allegro   *3'*
2. Largo   *3'*
3. Allegro   *3'*

   Ricordi

Concerto, Violin, op.9, no.2, RV 345, A major   *9'*

cnt — str
1. Allegro   *4'*
2. Largo   *2'*
3. Allegro   *3'*

   Ricordi

Concerto, Violin, op.9, no.3, RV 334, G minor   *11'*

cnt — str
1. Allegro non molto   *4'*
2. Largo cantabile   *4'*
3. Allegro non molto   *3'*

   Carisch   Ricordi

Concerto, Violin, op.9, no.4, RV 263a, E major   *12'*

cnt — str
1. Allegro non molto   *5'*
2. Largo   *4'*
3. Allegro non molto   *3'*

   Ricordi

Concerto, Violin, op.9, no.5, RV 358, A minor   *8'*

cnt — str
1. Adagio; Presto   *3'*
2. Largo   *2'*
3. Allegro   *3'*

   Ricordi

Concerto, Violin, op.9, no.6, RV 348, A major   *14'*

cnt — str
1. Allegro   *4'*
2. Largo   *4'*
3. Allegro non molto   *6'*

   Ricordi

Concerto, Violin, op.9, no.7, RV 359, B-flat major   *8'*

cnt — str
1. Allegro   *3'*
2. Largo   *2'*
3. Allegro   *3'*

   Ricordi

Concerto, Violin, op.9, no.8, RV 238, D minor   *10'*

cnt — str
1. Allegro   *4'*
2. Largo   *3'*
3. Allegro   *3'*

   Ricordi

Concerto, Violin, op.9, no.10, RV 300, G major   *10'*

cnt — str
1. Allegro molto   *4'*
2. Largo cantabile   *3'*
3. Allegro   *3'*

   Eulenburg   Kalmus   Luck's   Ricordi

Concerto, Violin, op.9, no.11, RV 198a, C minor   *10'*

cnt — str
1. Allegro   *4'*
2. Adagio   *3'*
3. [Allegro]   *3'*

   Eulenburg   Kalmus   Luck's   Ricordi   Universal

Concerto, Violin, op.9, no.12, RV 391, B minor   *13'*

cnt — str
1. Allegro non molto   *5'*
2. Largo   *4'*
3. Allegro   *4'*

   Kalmus   Luck's   Ricordi   Zanibon

Concerto, Violin, RV 179, C major <1728>   15'

cnt — str

Not published in a modern performing edition.

- *I. Andante*   6'
- *II. Largo*   3'
- *III. Allegro*   6'

Concerto, Violin, RV 270, E major (Il riposo; Natale)   7'

cnt — str

Concerto per il Santissimo Natale.

- *I. Allegro - Molto moderato*   4'
- *II. Adagio*   1'
- *III. Allegro*   2'

Ricordi

Concerto, Violin, RV 271, E major (L'amoroso)   11'

cnt — str

Published by Ricordi as op,35, no.6. From the manuscript collection *La cetra, q.v.*

- *I. Allegro*   4'
- *II. Cantabile*   3'
- *III. Allegro*   4'

Ricordi

Concerto, Violin & Double Orchestra, RV 582, D major <1711–1741>   13'

2cnt — str

- *I. Allegro*   5'
- *II. Grave*   3'
- *III. Allegro*   5'

Kalmus   Ricordi

Concerto, Violin & Double String Orchestra, RV 583, B-flat major <1711–1741>   14'

2cnt — double str orch

- *I. Largo e spiccato - Allegro non molto*   5'
- *II. Andante*   4'
- *III. Allegro*   5'

Ricordi

Concerto, Violin & Woodwinds, RV 577, G minor (Per l'orchestra de Dresda)   10'

solos: violin, 2recorders, 2oboes, bassoon

cnt — str

Kalmus ed. Clark McAlister; Ricordi ed. Angelo Ephrikian.

   Both editions specify solo flutes; however, recorders were intended by the composer. Both editions call for 2 bassoons, but only bn1 is soloistic; the bn2 merely doubles the continuo line.

   2nd mvt scored only for solo ob (or violin) and solo bn (no accompanimental strings).

- *Allegro*   4'
- *Largo non molto*   2'
- *Allegro*   4'

Kalmus   Ricordi

CONCERTOS FOR 2 OR MORE VIOLINS

Concerto, 2 Violins, op.21, no.7, RV 512, D major <1711–1741>   10'

cnt — str

- *I. Allegro molto*   3'
- *II. Largo*   4'
- *III. Allegro*   3'

Ricordi

Concerto, 2 Violins, RV 514, D minor <1735>   11'

cnt — str

- *I. Allegro non molto*   4'
- *II. Adagio*   4'
- *III. Allegro molto*   3'

Ricordi

Concerto, 2 Violins, op.3, no.5, RV 519, A major   8'

cnt — str

Bärenreiter edition by W. Upmeyer.

- *I. Allegro*   3'
- *II. Largo*   2'
- *III. Allegro* 3'

Bärenreiter	Eulenburg	Kalmus	Luck's	Ricordi

Concerto, 2 Violins, op.3, no.8, RV 522, A minor   12'

cnt — str

- *I. Allegro moderato*   4'
- *II. Adagio*   5'
- *III. Allegro*   3'

Eulenburg	Kalmus	Luck's	Peters	Ricordi

Concerto, 2 Violins, op.9, no.9, RV 530, B-flat major   8'

cnt — str

- *1. Allegro*   3'
- *2. Largo e spiccato*   2'
- *3. Allegro*   3'

Ricordi

Concerto, 3 Violins, RV 551, F major <1711–1741>   11'

cnt — str

- *I. Allegro*   5'
- *II. Andante*   2'
- *III. Allegro*   4'

Ricordi

Concerto, 4 Violins, op.3, no.4, RV 550, E minor   8'

cnt — str

- *1. Andante*   3'
- *2. Allegro assai* 2'
- *3. Adagio*   1'
- *4. Allegro*   2'

Eulenburg	Kalmus	Luck's	Ricordi

CONCERTOS FOR 1 OR MORE VIOLINS & VIOLONCELLO

Concerto, Violin & Violoncello, RV 547, B-flat major   9'

cnt — str

- *I. Allegro*   4'
- *II. Andante*   2'
- *III. Allegro molto* 3'

Ricordi

Concerto, 2 Violins & Violoncello, op.3, no.2, RV 578, G minor   10'

cnt — str

- *1. Adagio e spiccato* 2'
- *2. Allegro*   2'
- *3. Larghetto*   3'
- *4. Allegro*   2'

Eulenburg	Kalmus	Luck's	Ricordi

Concerto, 2 Violins & Violoncello, op.3, no.11, RV 565, D minor   *11'*

cnt — str
This work became the basis for J.S. Bach's *Concerto No.5* for solo organ, BWV 596.
   See also Vivaldi's *Concerto, op.3, no.11*, RV 565, D minor (orchestrated Siloti).
   1. Allegro - Adagio - Allegro   *5'*
   2. Largo e spiccato   *3'*
   3. Allegro   *3'*

Eulenburg	Kalmus	Luck's	Ricordi

Concerto, 2 Violins & Violoncello, op.4, no.7, RV 185, C major   *8'*

cnt — str
   1. Largo   *2'*
   2. Allegro   *2'*
   3. Largo   *2'*
   4. Allegro   *2'*

Luck's	Ricordi

Concerto, 4 Violins & Violoncello, op.3, no.1, RV 549, D major   *8'*

cnt — str
Solo violoncello appears in first movement only.
   Bärenreiter edition by W. Upmeyer.
   1. Allegro   *3'*
   2. Largo e spiccato   *3'*
   3. Allegro   *2'*

Bärenreiter	Eulenburg	Kalmus	Luck's	Ricordi

Concerto, 4 Violins & Violoncello, op.3, no.7, RV 567, F major   *10'*

cnt — str
Sometimes numbered as op.3, no.9.
   Bärenreiter edition by W. Upmeyer.
   1. Andante   *3'*
   2. Adagio   *1'*
   3. Allegro   *2'*
   4. Adagio   *2'*
   5. Allegro   *2'*

Bärenreiter	Eulenburg	Kalmus	Luck's	Ricordi

Concerto, 4 Violins & Violoncello, op.3, no.10, RV 580, B minor   *9'*

cnt — str
Probably intended for continuo & 8 strings: 4vn, 2va, vc, db.
   Bärenreiter edition by W. Upmeyer.
   This work became the basis for J.S. Bach's *Concerto, 4 Harpsichords*, BWV 1065, A minor.
   I. Allegro   *4'*
   II. Largo   *2'*
   III. Allegro   *3'*

Bärenreiter	Kalmus	Luck's	Peters	Ricordi

Concerto, 4 Violins, 4 Recorders & Double String Orchestra, RV 585, A major   *9'*

cnt — str[no va]
   I. Allegro   *3'*
   II. Adagio   *3'*
   III. Allegro   *3'*

Ricordi

CONCERTOS FOR 1 OR MORE VIOLONCELLOS

Concerto, Violoncello, RV 401, C minor   *12'*

cnt — str
   I. Allegro non molto   *5'*
   II. Adagio   *3'*
   III. Allegro non molto   *4'*

Ricordi

Concerto, Violoncello, RV.404, D major   *7'*

cnt — str
   I. Allegro   *3'*
   II. Adagio affettuoso   *1'*
   III. Allegro   *3'*

Ricordi

Concerto, Violoncello, RV 406, op.26, no.9, D minor   *9'*

cnt — str
Eulenburg ed. Felix Schroeder.
   I. Allegro non molto   *3'*
   II. Andante   *2'*
   III. Minuet   *4'*

Eulenburg	Ricordi

Concerto, Violoncello, RV 418, op.26, no.17, A minor   *9'*

cnt — str
Peters ed. Walter Kolneder.
   I. Allegro   *3'*
   II. [Largo]   *3'*
   III. Allegro   *3'*

Peters	Ricordi

Concerto, Violoncello, RV 422, A minor   *11'*

cnt — str
   I. Allegro   *4'*
   II. Largo   *4'*
   III. Allegro   *3'*

Kalmus	Luck's	Ricordi

Concerto, 2 Violoncellos, RV 531, G minor   *10'*

cnt — str
   I. Allegro   *4'*
   II. Largo   *3'*
   III. Allegro   *3'*

Eulenburg	Ricordi

Credo, RV 591, E minor   *12'*

chorus
cnt — str
Kalmus ed. Clayton Westermann; Universal ed. Renato Fasano.

Kalmus	Universal	Walton

L'estro armonico, op.3

   The collective title under which the concertos of op.3 for diverse string instruments were published in Amsterdam, ca.1712. The collection was later published in London with a slightly different numbering system, which accounts for the conflicting numbers for certain of these concertos in modern publications. Each concerto is listed separately in its place.

The Four Seasons

   see his: Quattro stagioni

Gloria, RV 589   30'

chorus   solos SSA

0 1 0 0 — 0 1 0 0 — cnt — str

Bärenreiter edition by Malcolm Bruno & Caroline Ritchie; Kalmus edition by Clayton Westermann; Oxford edition by Paul Everett; Ricordi edition by Gian Francesco Malipiero. Also available: Walton edition by Mason Martens.

I. Gloria in excelsis	2'
II. Et in terra pax	5'
III. Laudamus te	2'
IV. Gratias agimus tibi	2'
V. Propter magnam gloriam	2'
VI. Domine Deus	4'
VII. Domine Fili unigenite	2'
VIII. Domine Deus; Agnus Dei	4'
IX. Qui tollis	1'
X. Qui sedes ad dexteram	2'
XI. Quoniam tu solus sanctus	1'
XII. Cum Sancto Spiritu	3'

Bärenreiter	Carus	Kalmus	Oxford	Ricordi

Gloria, RV 589 (arr. Alfredo Casella)   30'

chorus   solos SSA

0 2 0 0 — 0 2 0 0 — org — str

Altered and romanticized. Vocal and orchestral parts for this version are not compatible with those of other editions.

I. Gloria in excelsis	2'
II. Et in terra pax	5'
III. Laudamus te	2'
IV. Gratias agimus tibi	2'
V. Propter magnam gloriam	2'
VI. Domine Deus	4'
VII. Domine Fili unigenite	2'
VIII. Domine Deus; Agnus Dei	4'
IX. Qui tollis	1'
X. Qui sedes ad dexteram	2'
XI. Quoniam tu solus sanctus	1'
XII. Cum Sancto Spiritu	3'

Ricordi

Introduction & Gloria, RV 639 & 588   35'

chorus   solos SSAT

0 2 0 0 — 0 1 0 0 — cnt — str

Ed. Clayton Westermann.

Kalmus

Kyrie, RV 587   12'

double chorus   opt SSAA solos

2cnt — double str orch

Bärenreiter ed. Malcolm Bruno & Caroline Ritchie; Carus ed. Walter Kolneder; Eulenburg ed. Jürgen Braun; Kalmus ed. Clayton Westermann; Universal ed. Karl Heinz Füssl.

Middle section, with SA duets in each choir, could be construed either as soloists or chorus.

Bärenreiter	Carus	Eulenburg	Kalmus	Universal

Lauda Jerusalem (Psalm 147), RV 609   10'

4 solo sopranos   double chorus

2cnt — double str orch

Eulenburg ed. Jürgen Braun; Ricordi ed. Francesco Degrada.

The 2 solo sopranos of chorus 1 sing in unison, as do the 2 solo sopranos of chorus 2.

Eulenburg	Ricordi

MAGNIFICAT

Two versions of this work are readily available. **RV 610** *(about 15' in duration) is the original version.* **RV 611** *(about 23' long) is identical, except that 5 new virtuoso arias (written for particular singers) are substituted for 3 of the movements of RV 610. Several editions include all these alternatives, so as to permit performance of either of the two versions. Details vary from one edition to another.*

The composer also prepared two other versions:

RV 610a *(some movements adapted for double chorus)*

RV 610b *(single-chorus version, but without oboes, and with 2 trumpets added in several movements).*

Magnificat, RV 610 (ed. H.C. Robbins Landon)   15'

chorus   solos SSATB

0 2 0 2 — 0 1[cornetto] 3 0 — cnt — str

Winds are optional.

Universal

Magnificat, RV 610 or 611 (ed. Günter Graulich)   23'

chorus   solos SSAT

0 2 0 0 — cnt — str

RV 610 = 15'; RV 611 = 23'.

I. Magnificat	1'
II. Et exultavit	2'
III. Quia respexit	3'
IV. Quia fecit	2'
V. Et misericordia	4'
VI. Fecit potentiam	1'
VII. Deposuit potentes	1'
VIII. Esurientes	2'
IX. Suscepit Israel	1'
X. Sicut locutus	3'
XI. Gloria	3'

Carus

Magnificat, RV 610 or 611 (ed. G. F. Malipiero)   23'

chorus   solos SSAT

0 2 0 0 — cnt — str

If the RV 611 version is performed, the 2 oboes are not required.

RV 610 = 15'; RV 611 = 23'.

I. Magnificat	1'
II. Et exultavit	2'
III. Quia respexit	3'
IV. Quia fecit	2'
V. Et misericordia	4'
VI. Fecit potentiam	1'
VII. Deposuit potentes	1'
VIII. Esurientes	2'
IX. Suscepit Israel	1'
X. Sicut locutus	3'
XI. Gloria	3'

Ricordi

Magnificat, RV 610 or 611 (ed. Clayton Westermann)   23'

chorus   solos SSATB

0 2 0 0 — cnt — str

RV 610 = 15'; RV 611 = 23'.

I. Magnificat	1'
II. Et exultavit	2'
III. Quia respexit	3'
IV. Quia fecit	2'
V. Et misericordia	4'
VI. Fecit potentiam	1'
VII. Deposuit potentes	1'
VIII. Esurientes	2'
IX. Suscepit Israel	1'
X. Sicut locutus	3'
XI. Gloria	3'

Kalmus

LE QUATTRO STAGIONI, op.8, nos.1-4 (The Four Seasons)   37'

solo violin
str
Four violin concertos published as a collection, ed. Christopher Hogwood.

1. La primavera (Spring), RV 269	*11'*
2. L'estate (Summer), RV 315	*10'*
3. L'autunno (Autumn), RV 293	*9'*
4. L'inverno (Winter), RV 297	*7'*

Bärenreiter

1. La primavera, RV 269, E major (Spring)   11'

solo violin
cnt — str

1. Giunt'e la primavera	*3'*
2. Mormorio di fronde e piante, il capraro che dorme, il cane che grida	*3'*
3. Danza pastorale	*5'*

Carisch	Eulenburg	Kalmus	Luck's	Ricordi

2. L'estate, RV 315, G minor (Summer)   10'

solo violin
cnt — str

1. Languidezza per il caldo	*5'*
2. Toglie alle membra lasse il suo riposo	*2'*
3. Tempo impetuoso d'estate	*3'*

Carisch	Eulenburg	Kalmus	Luck's	Ricordi

3. L'autunno, RV 293, F major (Autumn)   9'

solo violin
cnt — str

1. Ballo e canto di villanelli	*4'*
2. Dormienti ubriachi	*2'*
3. La caccia	*3'*

Carisch	Eulenburg	Kalmus	Luck's	Ricordi

4. L'inverno, RV 297, F minor (Winter)   7'

solo violin
cnt — str

1. Aggiaciatto tremar tra nevi algenti	*3'*
2. Passar al foco i di quieti	*2'*
3. Camminar sopra il giaccio	*2'*

Carisch	Eulenburg	Kalmus	Luck's	Ricordi

Sinfonia Nos. 1 & 2, RV 719 & 146   12'

cnt — str
Ed. Ludwig Landshoff.
  RV 719 is the Sinfonia to the opera *L'incoronazione di Dario*.

Sinfonia No.1, RV 719, C major	*6'*
Sinfonia No.2, RV 146, G major	*6'*

Kalmus	Luck's	Peters

Sinfonia No.3, RV 149, G major   6'

cnt — str
Ed. Ludwig Landshoff.

I. Allegro molto	*2'*
II. Andante	*2'*
III. Allegro	*2'*

Kalmus	Luck's	Peters

Sinfonia, RV 169, B minor (Al santo sepolcro)   7'

str[no cnt]

I. Adagio molto	*3'*
II. Allegro; ma poco	*4'*

Ricordi

Stabat Mater, RV 621 <1727>   20'

contralto solo
org or hpsd — str
Ricordi ed. G.F. Malipiero; Universal ed. Renato Fasano. There is also a Carisch ed. Alfredo Casella, which, however, may be altered and romanticized as with his edition of the *Magnificat*.

1. Stabat Mater	*3'*
2. Cujus animam	*2'*
3. O quam tristis	*2'*
4. Quis est homo	*3'*
5. Quis non posset	*2'*
6. Pro peccatis	*2'*
7. Eja Mater	*3'*
8. Fac, ut ardeat	*2'*
9. Amen	*1'*

Ricordi	Universal

La stravaganza, op.4

The collective title under which the violin concertos of op.4 were published in Amsterdam, ca.1712-13. Each concerto is listed separately in its place.

Vivier, Claude   1948-1983

(b Montreal, 14 April 1948; d Paris, 12 March 1983). Canadian

Orion <1979>   13'

3[1.2.pic] 3[1.2.Eh] 3[1.2.Ebcl] 3 — 4 2 2 1 — 3perc — hp — str[min 12.10.10.8.6]
perc: chimes, crot, gong, woodblk, 2vib, 2marim, 2bd, 5buttongong, 3tamtam, 2metalplate, 4Japanese temple bells ("Rin")
A tenor voice part (2-note figure occuring twice) with the text "Hé-o" appears in the percussion staff; it should be shouted into a tamtam each time.

Boosey

Vladigerov, Pancho   1899-1978

(b Zurich, 13 March 1899; d Sofia, 8 Sep 1978). Bulgarian

Improvisation and Toccata, op.36 <1941>   9'

3[1.2.pic] 3[1.2.Eh] 2 2 — 4 3 3 1 — tmp+4 — hp — cel, pf — str
perc: glock, tri, cym, bd, tamtam, sd

I. Improvisation	*5'*
II. Toccata	*4'*

Fleisher

Vogler, Georg Joseph   1749-1814

(b Würzburg, 15 June 1749; d Darmstadt, 6 May 1814). German

Concerto, Harpsichord, No.6, F major

see under: Haydn, Franz Joseph (1732-1809)
    Concerto, Harpsichord, Hob.XVIII:F1, F major

Voříšek, Jan Václav   1791-1825

(b Vamberk, north-east Bohemia, 11 May 1791; d Vienna, 19 Nov 1825). Bohemian

Symphony, D major <1823>   27'

2 2 2 2 — 2 2 0 0 — str

I. Allegro con brio	*8'*
II. Andante	*8'*
III. Scherzo: Allegro ma non troppo	*6'*
IV. Allegro con brio	*5'*

Czech

W

Wachsman, Dianne
1960-

(b Champaign-Urbana, IL, 26 August 1960). American

Fanfares for String Orchestra <1992>
6'

str
1. *Blues [vn only]* — 1'
2. *Viola Fanfare [va only]* — 1'
3. *Cello Fanfare [vc only]* — 1'
4. *Double Bass Tango, orig version [db only]* — 1'
5. *Double Bass Tango, expanded version [db only]* — 2'
6. *All-Strings Fanfare [str orch]* — 2'

MMB

Wagenaar, Bernard
1894-1971

(b Arnhem, 18 July 1894; d York, ME, 19 May 1971). American composer of Dutch origin

Fanfare for Airmen <1942>
1'

0 0 0 0 — 4 3 3 1 — tmp+1 — [no str]
perc: sd

Boosey

Wagenseil, Georg Christoph
1715-1777

(b Vienna, 29 Jan 1715; d Vienna, 1 March 1777). Austrian

Concerto, Harpsichord, D major
16'

str[no va]

Breitkopf   Luck's

Concerto, Trombone, E-flat major
13'

2 0 0 1 — 2 0 0 0 — cnt — str
Ed. Paul R. Bryan. Editor suggests use of an alto trombone, though the solo part is readily playable on a tenor trombone.

Universal

Concerto, Violoncello, A major <1752>
10'

cnt — str
Ed. Enrico Mainardi & Fritz Racek.

Doblinger

Concerto, Violoncello, C major <1763>
22'

0 2 0 0 — 2 2[opt] 0 0 — opt cnt — str
Ed. Fritz Racek.

Doblinger

Sinfonia, G minor
15'

0 2 0 1 — cnt — str
Ed. Alison Copland.

Universal

Wagner, Melinda
1957-

(b Philadelphia, 25 Feb 1957). American

Concerto, Flute <1998>
24'

tmp+3 — hp — pf/cel — str

Presser

Concerto, Trombone <2006>
24'

3[1.2.3/pic] 3[1.2.Eh] 3[1.2.bcl] 3[1.2.cbn] — 4 3[1&2 opt flug] 3 1 — tmp+4 — hp — pf/cel — str
perc: bd, szl cym, tambn, glock, xyl, marim, vib, chimes, crot, belltree, woodblk, bongos, ratch, claves, 3sus cym, 4tomtom, 3tri, 2tamtam, waterphone, bass bow, bell plate, eggshaker, pelletbells, watergong, cricket
I. Satyr — 10'
II. Elemental Things — 7'
Litany (Interlude) — 1'
III. Catch — 6'

Presser

Falling Angels; Poem for Orchestra <1992>
14'

3[1.2.pic] 3[1.2.Eh] 3[1.2.bcl] 3[1.2.cbn] — 4 3 3 1 — tmp+5 — hp — pf, cel — str
perc: bd, cym, szl cym, sd, tri, tambn, tamtam, glock, xyl, marim, vib, chimes, crot, belltree, woodblk, templeblks, whip, bongos, vibrslp, bamboo windchimes, slide whistle, 3sus cym, 4tomtom

Presser

Little Moonhead <2008>
17'

solo violin
2 0 0 0 — 0 0 0 0 — hpsd — str[4.4.4.3.1]
I. Little Prelude (with Rills) — _'
II. Moon Ache — _'
III. Fiddlehead — _'

Presser

Wagner, Richard
1813-1883

(b Leipzig, 22 May 1813; d Venice, 13 Feb 1883). German

WWV = John Deathridge, Martin Geck & Egon Voss, eds.: *Wagner Werk-Verzeichnis; Verzeichnis der musikalischen Werke Richard Wagners und ihrer Quellen* (Mainz, 1986)

Adagio, clarinet & strings, D-flat major

see under: Heinrich Joseph Baermann, 1784-1847

Christoph Columbus, WWV 37A: Overture <1834–1835>
8'

3[1.2.pic] 2 2 2 — 4 6 3 1 — tmp — str
Breitkopf (and Kalmus & Luck's reprints) ed. Felix Mottl; Schott ed. Egon Voss. Overture to a drama by Theodor Apel.

Breitkopf   Kalmus   Luck's   Schott

Concert Overture No.1, WWV 20, D minor <1831>
7'

2 2 2 2 — 4 2 0 0 — tmp — str
Ed. Egon Voss.

Schott

Concert Overture No.2, WWV 27, C major <1832>
10'

2 2 2 2 — 4 2 3 0 — tmp — str
Ed. Egon Voss.

Schott

Eine Faust-Ouvertüre, WWV 59 (A Faust Overture) <1839–1840; rev 1855>   *12'*

3[1.2.pic] 2 2 3 — 4 2 3 1 — tmp — str
Rev. 1855.

Breitkopf	Kalmus	Luck's

Der fliegende Holländer, WWV 63 (The Flying Dutchman): Overture <1841; rev 1860>   *11'*

3[1.2.pic] 2[1.2/Eh] 2 2 — 4 2 3 1 — tmp — hp — str
Two versions available from Kalmus: original (reprint of Fürstner) and Hoffmann (reprint of Breitkopf). The Fritz Hoffmann version includes numerous cues, permitting performance with reduced forces. The current Breitkopf edition is probably not the Hoffmann version, though this is uncertain.
   The last 90 bars or so of the overture are written for clarinets in C.

Breitkopf	Kalmus	Luck's	Schott

Götterdämmerung, WWV 86d: Gesang der Rheintöchter (Song of the Rhinemaidens) <1872>   *10'*

2 2 2 2 — 4 2 3 0 — tmp+2 — hp — str
perc: tri, cym
Concert version, arr. Herman Zumpe.

Kalmus	Schott	Luck's

Götterdämmerung: Brünnhilde's Immolation <1872–1874>   *18'*

soprano solo
4[1.2.3.pic] 4[1.2.3.Eh] 4[1.2.3.bcl] 3 — 8[hn5-7/Wag tb] 4[1.2.3.btp]
4[incl cb tbn] 1 — 2tmp+3 — 6hp[2parts] — str
perc: cym, sus cym, tri, tamtam

Kalmus	Luck's	Schott

Götterdämmerung: Siegfried's Funeral Music (Trauermarsch; Siegfrieds Tod) <1872–1874>   *8'*

4[1.2.3.pic] 4[1.2.3.Eh] 4[1.2.3.bcl] 3 — 8[4hn, 4Wag tb] 4[1.2.3.btp]
4 1 — 2tmp+3 — 6hp[2parts] — str
perc: td, cym, tri

Breitkopf	Kalmus	Luck's	Schott

Götterdämmerung: Siegfried's Death & Funeral Music (Stasny)   *12'*

2[1.2/pic] 2 2 — 4 2 3 1 — tmp+3 — hp — str
perc: td, cym, tri
Reduced orchestration arr. L.Stasny. This excerpt begins earlier in the opera than other versions: just after Siegfried has received the fatal blow. The remainder of his dying lines are given to the trumpet—an awkward solution that might best be deleted.

Kalmus	Luck's	Schott

Götterdämmerung: Siegfried's Rhine Journey (Rheinfahrt)   *10'*

3[1.2opt.pic] 2 2 — 4 3[tp3 opt] 3 1 — tmp+2 — hp — str
perc: tri, cym, glock[opt]
Arr. Englebert Humperdinck. An insert available from Luck's restores 45 bars omitted by Humperdinck; it includes additional parts (not essential) for Eh, bcl, and 3rd bn. Duration with insert: 13'.

Kalmus	Luck's	Schott

Grosser Festmarsch, WWV 110 (American Centennial March) <1876>   *12'*

4[1.2.3.pic] 3 3 4[1.2.3.cbn] — 4 4[1.2.3.btp] 3 1 — tmp+4 — str
perc: sd, tri, cym, bd, tamtam
Schott ed. Peter Jost.

Kalmus	Luck's	Schott

Huldigungsmarsch, WWV 97 <1864; rev (orchd) 1871>   *7'*

3[1.2.pic] 2 3[1.2.bcl] 2 — 4 3 3 1 — tmp+4 — str
perc: sd, tri, cym, bd
Originally for military band, 1864; orchestrated by the composer, 1871.
   Snare drum part may be tripled, requiring 2 extra players.

Kalmus	Luck's	Schott

Kaisermarsch, WWV 104   *10'*

3[1.2.pic] 3 3 — 4 3 3 1 — tmp+4 — str
perc: tri, field dr, cym, bd
Apparently intended to include an optional unison male chorus ("people's chorus") singing "Heil! Heil! dem Kaiser." This chorus is not shown in the most published scores, but may be found in the *Sämtliche Werke*, v.18 no.3, p.158; the same volume contains an SATB version of the vocal part (p.269).

Breitkopf	Kalmus	Luck's

König Enzio: Overture, WWV 24 <1831–1832>   *7'*

2 2 2 2 — 4 2 0 0 — tmp — str
Breitkopf ed. Felix Mottl; Schott ed. Egon Voss. Overture for a drama by Ernst Raupach.

Breitkopf	Schott

Lohengrin, WWV 75: Prelude, Act I <1846–1847>   *8'*

3 3[1.2.Eh] 3[1.2.bcl(A)] 3 — 4 3 3 1 — tmp+1 — str
perc: cym

Breitkopf	Kalmus	Luck's

Lohengrin: Prelude, Act III <1846–1847>   *3'*

3 3 3 — 4 3 3 1 — tmp+3 — str
perc: cym, tri, tambn
In the opera, the prelude segues into the quiet *Wedding Chorus* of Act III (sometimes referred to as the "Hoffmann ending").
   Kalmus also offers a version with the "Toscanini ending," which ends climactically after stating the *Warning* motive from Act I (sung first by Lohengrin to the words "Nie sollst du mich befragen"). Musicians sometimes refer to this as the "Swan Lake" ending, because the *Warning* motive resembles a prominent theme in Tchaikovsky's ballet.
   Perhaps the simplest procedure for ending this work is merely to make a fermata at the climactic G major chord (at rehearsal letter [E]), holding it until the pent-up energy has dissipated.

Breitkopf	Kalmus	Luck's

Lohengrin: Elsa's Procession to the Cathedral (Feierlicher Zug zum Münster) <1846–1847>   *4'*

opt double male chorus & chorus of women & boys
3 3[1.2.Eh] 3[1.2.bcl] 3 — 4 3 3 1 — tmp — str

Breitkopf	Kalmus	Luck's

Die Meistersinger, WWV 96: Prelude <1861–1862>   *9'*

3[1.2.pic] 2 2 — 4 3 3 1 — tmp+2 — hp — str
perc: tri, cym
The concert ending, penciled into the composer's autograph and reproduced in all modern editions, is sometimes adapted to resemble the end of the opera.

Breitkopf	Kalmus	Luck's	Schott

Die Meistersinger: An Orchestral Tribute <1861–1862>   47'
3[1.2.3/pic] 2 2 2 — 4 3 3 1 — tmp+4 — hp — str
perc: bd, cym, tri, glock, 2field dr
"Symphonic compilation" arr. Henk de Vlieger, 2005. Optional offstage
insts: 1 or 2hn; 1 or 2tp. Movements are played continuously.
1. Vorspiel (Prelude)	*9'*
2. Versammlung der Meistersinger (Assembly of the Meistersinger)	*5'*
3. Gesang der Lehrbuben (Song of the Apprentices)	*2'*
4. Sachsens Monolog (Sachs' Monologue)	*3'*
5. Vorspiel III (Prelude to Act III)	*5'*
6. Taufspruch (Baptismal Verse—Quintet)	*3'*
7. Züge der Zünfte (Procession of the Guilds)	*5'*
8. Tanz der Lehrbuben (Dance of the Apprentices)	*3'*
9. Aufzug der Meistersinger (Entrance of the Meistersingers)	*3'*
10. Walther's Preislied (Walther's Prize Song)	*6'*
11. Schlussgesang (Finale Ode)	*3'*

Schott		

Die Meistersinger: Three Excerpts from Act III   13'
3[1.2.pic] 2 2 2 — 4 3 3 1 — tmp+2 — hp — str
perc: tri, glock, cym
Arr. Wouter Hutschenruyter. Kalmus reprint is listed as "*Suite*."
   Schott has a longer version that includes at the end the *Gruss an Hans
Sachs (Homage to Sachs)* [reprinted Kalmus as "*Suite (Urtext)*"].
1. Einleitung zum 3. Akt (Introduction to Act III)	*5'*
2. Tanz der Lehrbuben (Dance of the Apprentices)	*4'*
3. Aufzug der Meistersinger (Procession of the Meistersingers)	*4'*

Breitkopf	Kalmus	Luck's

Parsifal, WWV 111: Prelude <1877–1881>   13'
3 4[1.2.3.Eh] 3 4[1.2.3.cbn] — 4 3 3 1 — tmp — str
Breitkopf	Kalmus	Luck's	Schott

Parsifal: Good Friday Spell (Charfreitagszauber) <1877–1881>   11'
3 4[1.2.3.Eh] 4[1.2.3.bcl] 4[1.2.3.cbn] — 4 3 3 1 — tmp — str
Ed. W. Hutschenruyter; playable with:
   3 3[1.2.Eh] 2 2 — 4 2 3 1 — tmp —str
Breitkopf	Kalmus	Luck's	Schott

Polonia, WWV 39 <1832–1836>   11'
4[1.2.pic1.pic2] 2 2 2 — 4 4 3 1[oph] — tmp+5 — str
perc: bd, cym, td, field dr, tri
Ed. Felix Mottl.
Breitkopf	Kalmus	Luck's

Das Rheingold, WWV 86a: Entry of the Gods into Valhalla (Einzug der Götter) <1853–1854>   9'
2 2 2 2 — 4 3 3 1 — tmp+1 — hp — str
perc: cym
Arr. Herman Zumpe.
Kalmus	Luck's	Schott

Rienzi, WWV 49: Overture <1840>   12'
3[1.2.pic] 2 2 3[1.2.serp] — 4 4 3 1 — tmp+4 — str
perc: bd, cym, sd, td, tri
Cross-cued by Fritz Hoffmann for smaller instrumentations.
Breitkopf	Kalmus	Luck's	Schott

The Ring: An Orchestral Adventure, WWV 86 <1853–1874>   64'
4[1.2.3/pic2.pic1] 4[1.2.3.Eh] 4[1.2.3/Dcl.bcl] 3 — 8[hn5-8/Wag tb]
4[1.2.3.btp] 4[1.2.3.cb tbn] 1 — 2tmp+3 — 2hp — str[16.16.12.12.8]
perc: glock, field dr, tamtam, tri, cym, sus cym, 6anvils[in3 sizes]
Arr. Henk de Vlieger, 1991. Harps should be doubled or tripled if
possible. Trumpets 2 & 3 and timpanist 2 double on anvils. Movements
are played continuously.
1. Vorspiel	*4'*
2. Das Rheingold	*2'*
3. Nebelheim	*3'*
4. Walhall	*4'*
5. Die Walküren	*4'*
6. Feuerzauber	*4'*
7. Waldweben	*3'*
8. Siegfried's Heldentat	*7'*
9. Brünnhilde's Erwachen	*5'*
10. Siegfried und Brünnhilde	*5'*
11. Siegfried's Rheinfahrt	*6'*
12. Siegfried's Tod	*5'*
13. Trauermusik	*5'*
14. Brünnhilde's Opfertat	*7'*

Schott		

Der Ring ohne Worte für Orchester (The Ring Without Words) <1853–1874>   70'
4[1.2.3/pic.pic] 4[1.2.3.Eh] 4[1.2.3.bcl] 3 — 8[hn5-8/Wag tb]
4[1.2.3.btp] 4[1.2.3.4/cb tbn] 1 — tmp+3 — 2hp[ad lib 6] — str
perc: bd, cym, sd, tri, tamtam, glock, cowhorn, 3anvils
Compiled [zusammengestellt] by Lorin Maazel, 1996. Orchestration of
Wagner's *Der Ring des Nibelungen* with all vocal parts omitted and the
whole cleverly cut down from 4 full evenings to 70 minutes.
Schott		

Rule Britannia!, WWV 42 <1837>   10'
4[2fl, 2pic] 2 3[1.2.Ebcl] 3[1.2.cbn] — 4 4 3 1 — tmp+4 — str
perc: tri, field dr, cym, bd
Kalmus & Luck's (reprints of Breitkopf) ed. Felix Mottl; Schott ed., Egon
Voss.
Kalmus	Luck's	Schott

Siegfried, WWV 86c: Forest Murmurs (Waldweben) arr. Zumpe <1857–1871>   9'
2[1.2/pic] 2 2 2 — 4 2 3 0 — tmp+1 — str
perc: glock, tri
Arr. Herman Zumpe.
Kalmus	Luck's	Schott

Siegfried, WWV 86c: Forest Murmurs (Waldweben) arr. Hutschenruyter <1857–1871>   9'
3[1.2.3/pic] 3[1.2.Eh] 3 3 — 4 3 3 0 — tmp+1 — str
perc: glock, tri
Arr. Wouter Hutschenruyter.
   Said to be playable with: 2 2 2 2 — 2 2 3 0 — tmp — str
Breitkopf	Kalmus	Luck's

Siegfried Idyll, WWV 103 <1870>   18'
1 1 2 1 — 2 1 0 0 — str
In the first performance of this work Wagner used only one string player
to a part (including however 2 violas, the second player doubling on
trumpet). Thereafter he used orchestral strings.
Breitkopf	Kalmus	Luck's

Symphony, WWV 29, C major <1832>   38'

2 2 2 3[1.2.cbn] — 4 2 3 0 — tmp — str
Schott ed. Egon Voss.
   1. Sostenuto e maestoso; Allegro con brio   13'
   2. Andante ma non troppo, un poco maestoso   10'
   3. Allegro assai   6'
   4. Allegro molto e vivace   7'

Kalmus	Luck's	Schott

Symphony, WWV 35, E major <1834>   19'

2 2 2 2 — 4 2 3 0 — tmp — str
Completed and orchestrated by Felix Mottl (1887). Ed. Egon Voss.
   I. Allegro con spirito   14'
   II. Adagio cantabile   5'

Schott

Tannhäuser, WWV 70: Overture (Dresden version) <1843–1845>   14'

3[1.2.pic] 2 2 2 — 4 3 3 1 — tmp+3 — str
perc: tri, cym, tambn
There appears to be no structural difference between the advertised "original version" (Kalmus A5715, a reprint of Fürstner) and the "concert version ed. by F. Hoffmann" (Breikopf, reprinted Kalmus A2245). In the latter, however, the 2nd flute also doubles on piccolo; i.e., flute distribution for the Hoffmann version is as follows: 3[1.2/pic.pic].

Breitkopf	Kalmus	Luck's	Schott

Tannhäuser: Overture & Venusberg Music (Paris version) <1845–1861>   21'

3[1.2.3/pic] 2 2 2 — 4 3 3 1 — 2tmp+4 — hp — str
perc: tri, tambn, cast, cym

Kalmus	Luck's

Tannhäuser: Venusberg Music (Bacchanale) <1843–1847>   12'

3[1.2.3/pic] 2 2 2 — 4 3 3 1 — 2tmp+4 — hp — str
perc: tambn, tri, cast, cym, sus cym

Kalmus	Luck's

Tannhäuser: Arrival of the Guests at the Wartburg (Einzug der Gäste) <1843–1847>   8'

3[1.2/pic.3/pic] 2 2 2 — 4 3 3 1 — tmp+3 — str
perc: tri, cym, bd
Arr. for concert use by Fritz Hoffmann. Several of the instruments are optional. The amount of piccolo in the 2nd flute is minimal; all the piccolo music could easily be consolidated into the 3rd flute part.

Breitkopf	Kalmus	Luck's

Tannhäuser: Prelude, Act III <1843–1847>   4'

3[1.2.3/pic] 2 2 2 — 4 3 3 1 — tmp — str

Breitkopf	Kalmus	Luck's

Tristan und Isolde, WWV 90: Prelude & Liebestod <1857–1859>   17'

optional soprano solo
3[1.2.3/pic] 3[1.2.Eh] 3[1.2.bcl(A)] 3 — 4 3 3 1 — tmp — hp — str
A critical edition of the score with historical and analytical essays is available from Norton; it includes in addition Wagner's own concert ending of the *Prelude*.
   An early Breitkopf "concert edition" (no longer in print except for Kalmus and Luck's reprints) omits the voice part in the *Liebestod*, but has a few minor adjustments in instrumentation to accommodate that absence. Its provenance is unclear, though some copies bear the note, "Arranged for orchestra alone by the composer."
   Prelude   10'
   Liebestod   7'

Breitkopf	Kalmus	Luck's

Tristan und Isolde: Prelude (with concert ending) <1857–1859>   12'

3 3[1.2.Eh] 3[1.2.bcl] 3 — 4 2 3 1 — tmp — hp — str
Concert ending by the composer.

Breitkopf	Kalmus	Schott

Tristan und Isolde: Nachtgesang <1857–1859>   10'

2 3[1.2.opt Eh] 3[1.2.opt bcl] 3[bn3 opt] — 4 1 3 1 — tmp — hp — str
Arr. Arthur Seidel.

Breitkopf	Kalmus	Luck's

Tristan und Isolde: Prelude, Act III <1857–1859>   8'

0 2[1.Eh] 2 2 — 4 0 0 0 — tmp — str
Playable with 1 ob/Eh. Arr. Arthur Seidel.

Breitkopf	Kalmus	Luck's

Die Walküre, WWV 86b: Ride of the Valkyries (Walkürenritt) <1854–1856>   5'

4[1.2.pic1.pic2] 4[1.2.3.Eh] 4[1.2.3.bcl(A)] 3 — 8 3 4 1 — 2tmp+3 — str
perc: sd, tri, cym

Kalmus	Luck's	Schott

Die Walküre: Ride of the Valkyries (Walkürenritt) arr. Hutschenruyter <1854–1856>   5'

3[1.2.pic] 3[1.2.Eh] 4[1.2.3opt.bcl] 3[bn3 opt] — 6[hn5&6 opt] 3 3 1 — tmp+3 — str
perc: sd, tri, cym
Arr. Wouter Hutschenruyter; ending shortened in this arrangement.

Breitkopf	Kalmus	Luck's

Die Walküre: Ride of the Valkyries (Walkürenritt) arr. Sheffer <1854–1856>   5'

3[incl pic] 2 2 2 — 4 3 3 1 — tmp+2 — str
perc: sd, tri, cym
Reduced instrumentation by Jonathan Sheffer.

Fleisher	Sheffer

Die Walküre: Wotan's Farewell & Magic Fire Music (Wotans Abschied und Feuerzauber)   18'

2[1.2/pic] 2 2[1/Ebcl.2] 2 — 4 2 3 1 — tmp+2 — hp — str
perc: sus cym, tri, glock
Orchestral reduction by an unknown hand.

Kalmus	Luck's	Schott

Wesendonck Lieder, WWV 91 (Mottl/Wagner) <1857–1858>   21'

solo soprano
2 2 2 2 — 4 1 0 0 — tmp — str
Originally for soprano & piano. Orchestrated by Felix Mottl (nos.1-4) and by Wagner (no.5, for solo violin or soprano & orchestra).
   The 5 songs are published separately.
   Mapleson (via EMS) also offers No.5, *Träume*, a half-step higher in A major.
   1. Der Engel (G major)   3'
   2. Stehe still (C minor)   4'
   3. Im Treibhaus (D minor)   6'
   4. Schmerzen (C minor)   3'
   5. Träume (A-flat major)   5'

Kalmus	Luck's	Schott

Wesendonck Lieder, WWV 91 (Henze) <1857–1858>   21'

solo alto
2[1.afl] 2[1.Eh] 2 2 — 2 0 0 0 — hp — str[6.4.4.4.2]
Originally for soprano & piano. Orchestrated by Hans Werner Henze (1976).

1. *Der Engel (E major)*	3'
2. *Stehe still (A minor)*	4'
3. *Im Treibhaus (B minor)*	6'
4. *Schmerzen (A minor)*	3'
5. *Träume (F major)*	5'

Schott

Wesendonck Lieder, WWV 91 (Tarkmann) <1857–1858>   21'

solo voice (soprano, mezzo, or alto)
1 1 1 1 — 1 0 0 0 — str, or str 5t
Originally for soprano & piano. Orchestrated by Andreas N. Tarkmann.
    Available either in the original keys or transposed a minor 3rd lower.
    Another orchestration by Carl Stueber (also published by Bärenreiter) offers the same choices of key (*i.e.*, the original or a minor 3rd lower) in a slightly larger instrumentation: 1 1 2 2 — 2 3 0 0 — hp — str. Stueber employs the original Wagner orchestration of No.5.

1. *Der Engel (G major or E major)*	3'
2. *Stehe still (C minor or A minor)*	4'
3. *Im Treibhaus (D minor or B minor)*	6'
4. *Schmerzen (C minor or A minor)*	3'
5. *Träume (A-flat major or F major)*	5'

Bärenreiter

Waldteufel, Emile   1837-1915

(b Strasbourg, 9 Dec 1837; d Paris, 12 Feb 1915). French

Les Patineurs, op.183 (The Skaters' Waltz)   8'

2[1.pic] 2 2 2 — 4 2 3 1 — tmp+4 — str
perc: bd, cym, sd, tri, sleighbells
Kalmus ed. Clark McAlister.

Kalmus   Luck's

Walker, George   1922-

(b Washington, DC, 27 June 1922). American

Address for Orchestra <1959; rev 1991>   19'

3[1.2.pic] 3[1.2.Eh] 3[1.2.bcl] 3[1.2.cbn] — 4 2 2 1 — tmp+4 — hp — str

perc: sd, bd, cym, tri, tamtam, cast, glock, vib, chimes

MMB

Concerto, Violin <2007; rev 2009>   21'

3[1.2/afl.pic] 3[1.2.Eh] 3[1.2.bcl] 2 — 4 4 3 1 — tmp+4 — hp — cel/hpsd (ampd) — str

perc: bd, sus cym, sd, timbales, rototom, tri, tambn, tamtam, gong, glock, xyl, marim, vib, chimes, slgh-bells, whip, marac, claves, bass bow, glass windchimes

I. *quarter-note = 56*	10'
II. *eighth-note = 46*	5'
III. *quarter-note = 63*	6'

LKMP

Lyric for Strings <1947; rev 1990>   6'

str
Based on the 2nd movement of the composer's *String Quartet No.1*.

MMB

Overture in Praise of Folly <1981>   8'

3[1.2.pic] 3[1.2.Eh] 3[1.2.bcl] 3[1.2.cbn] — 4 4 3 1 — tmp+5 — hp — pf/cel — str

perc: tri, ratch, sus cym, tamtam, claves, woodblk, whip, templeblks, tambn, sd, bd, glock, chimes, vib, xyl, glass windchimes, anvil

MMB

Walker, Gwyneth   1947-

(b New York, 22 March 1947). American

About Leaves; Three Portraits for Chamber Orchestra Inspired by the Poetry of Robert Frost <1997>   12'

1 0 2 1 — str

I. *Treading on Leaves*	3'
II. *Light as Balloons*	3'
III. *The Last Color*	5'

MMB

Bicentennial Suite <1991>   13'

3[1.2.3/pic] 2 2 2 — 4 3 3 1 — tmp+3 — str
perc: bd, cym, sus cym, sd, td, tomtom, tri, glock, templeblks, bongos, marac; played by double bass section: ratchet, cowbell, whip
Orchestral transcription of the composer's *A Vermont Bicentenniale Suite* for band.

1. *The Governor's Salute*	1'
2. *Pastorale*	4'
3. *Ethan Allen Rides Again!*	2'
4. *The Floating Bridge*	3'
5. *Bicentennial March*	3'

MMB

Bicycle Waltz <1997>   4'

3[1.2.pic] 2 2 2 — 4 3[preferably crts] 3 1 — 3perc — str
perc: bd, cym, sus cym, sd, tri, tambn, cello bow; **sound effects:** bicycle bell, bicycle horn, card in wheel
Musicians vocalize special effects (pumping up bicycle tire, etc.).

MMB

A Concerto of Hymns and Spirituals <1997>   16'

solo trumpet
3[1.2.pic] 2 2 2 — 4 3 3 1 — tmp+2 — str
perc: bd, sus cym, td, tri, glock, chimes, 2tomtoms

I. *All Creatures (of Our God and King)*	5'
II. *Steal Away*	6'
III. *Go Tell It on the Mountain*	5'

MMB

Fanfare for the Family Farm <1989>   4'

2[1.pic] 2 2 — 4 2 3 1 — 3perc — str
perc: milkcan (played like conga), 4 pails (played with mallets), cowbell (with clapper)

MMB

Fanfare, Interlude and Finale <1978–1980>   11'

2 1 1 1 — 2 2 0 0 — tmp/perc — str
perc: sus cym, sd, td, congas

I. *Fanfare*	2'
II. *Interlude*	6'
III. *Finale*	3'

MMB

The Light of Three Mornings; Sketches of Braintree Hill <1987>   17'

1 1 1 0 — 1 1 1 0 — 1perc — str[min 4.2.1.1.1]
3rd movement, *Hints and Tappings*, may be performed separately.

1. When the Stars Begin to Fall	5'
2. First Light	7'
3. Hints and Tappings	5'

MMB

Match Point <1985>   6'

2 2 2 2 — 4 2 3 1 — tmp+2 — str
Musical dramatization of a tennis point; tennis props required.

1. Tuning Up	_'
2. Anticipation	_'
3. The Point	_'
4. March Triomphante	_'

MMB

Open the Door <1990>   4'

2 2 2 2 — 4 2 3 1 — tmp+2 — str

MMB

Overture of Diamonds <2002>   6'

3[1.2.pic] 2 2 2 — 4 3 3 1 — tmp+3 — str
perc: cym, sus cym, tri, glock, windchimes, woodblk, cowbell, claves, 4tomtoms

MMB

Suite for Strings <1996>   9'

str

I. First Run	3'
II. Bradenton Waltz	4'
III. Portable Rhythms	2'

MMB

Symphonic Dances <2004>   17'

3[1.2.pic] 2 2 2 — 4 3 3 1 — 3perc — pf — str
perc: bd, cym, sus cym, hi-hat, sd, td, set, tri, tambn, windchimes, templeblks, bongos, ratch, marac, cast, congas, 2tomtoms

1. Prance (A Two-Step)	3'
2. Petite Waltz/Grand Waltz (Dance of the Fireflies and Elephants)	4'
3. Dance of the Wild Ponies (A Trot and a Gallop)	2'
4. Tango	5'
5. Charleston	3'

MMB

Symphony of Grace <1999>   22'

2[1.2/pic] 2 2 2 — 3 2 1 0 — tmp+2 — pf — str
perc: bd, cym, sus cym, td, tri, tambn, glock, chimes, templeblks, whip, bongos, ratch, marac, congas, herdbell, 4tomtoms

I. For the Beauty of the Earth	7'
II. Companions for the Journey [strings]	5'
III. Many Creatures	4'
IV. The Spirit Within	6'

MMB

Up-Front Concerto <1993>   10'

solo percussion (hand drums)
1 1 1 1 — 1 1 1 0 — str
perc: (solo) marac, 2congas, large rainstick, grapes[rattle], cuíca

1. Rise and Shine	3'
2. About Rain	4'
3. Flying Tattoos!	3'

MMB

Walton, William   1902-1983

(b Oldham, 29 March 1902; d Ischia, nr Naples, 8 March 1983). English

As You Like It; a Poem for Orchestra after Shakespeare <1936>   13'

solo soprano
3[incl pic] 2[incl Eh] 2 2 — 4 2 2 0 — tmp+3 or 2 — 2hp[hp2 opt] — hpsd — str
Arr. by Christopher Palmer from the film score.

1. Prelude	3'
2. Moonlight	3'
3. Under the Greenwood Tree	2'
4. The Fountain	3'
5. Wedding Procession	2'

Oxford

Belshazzar's Feast <1931; rev 1948, 1957>   36'

chorus   baritone solo
3[1.2.pic] 2 3[1/Ebcl.2/bcl.3] 3[1.2.cbn] — 4 3 3 1 — asx[or Eh] — 2 opt brass ens, each 3tp, 3tbn, tuba — tmp+4 — 2hp — org, opt pf — str
perc: xyl, glock, tri, cast, tambn, gong, field dr, td, woodblk, cym, bd, whip, anvil
The parts for the 2 optional brass ensembles are cued into the orchestral brass.

1. Thus Spake Isaiah	5'
2. If I Forget Thee	6'
3. Babylon Was a Great City	2'
4. In Babylon Belshazzar the King	3'
5. Praise Ye the God of Gold	6'
6. Thus in Babylon, the Mighty City	3'
7. And in That Same Hour	2'
8. Then Sing Aloud to God Our Strength	4'
9. The Trumpeters and Pipers	1'
10. Then Sing Aloud to God Our Strength	4'

Oxford

Capriccio burlesco <1968>   7'

3[1.2.pic] 3[1.2.Eh] 4[1.2.Ebcl.bcl] 3[1.2.cbn] — 4 3 3 1 — tmp+3 — hp — str
perc: xyl, sd, field dr, td, bd, bongos, cast, whip, tambn

Oxford

CONCERTO, VIOLA   27'
Concerto, Viola [original version] <1928–1929; rev 1961>

3[1.2.pic] 3[1.2.Eh] 3[1.2.bcl] 3[1.2.cbn] — 4 3 3 1 — tmp — str
Original 1929 version. The 1930 piano reduction used a version of the solo part by Lionel Tertis, which diverged from Walton's original. A 1938 reduction, approved by Walton, used phrasings, articulations and bowings by Frederick Riddle, and corresponded to Riddle's 1937 recording.

I. Andante comodo	9'
II. Vivo; con molto preciso	5'
III. Allegro moderato	13'

Oxford

Concerto, Viola [1961 revision] <1928–1929; rev 1961>   27'

2[1.2/pic] 2[1.Eh] 2[1.2/bcl] 2 — 4 2 3 0 — tmp — hp — str
Revised in 1961. Through a mixup between the publisher and the composer, this edition is based on the Lionel Tertis version of the solo part with additional changes by Walton, rather than the Frederick Riddle solo part which Walton actually preferred. Scores and parts for this version have been withdrawn.

I. Andante comodo	9'
II. Vivo; con molto preciso	5'
III. Allegro moderato	13'

Concerto, Viola [definitive version] <1928–1929; rev 1961>   27'

2[1.2/pic] 2[1.Eh] 2[1.2/bcl] 2 — 4 2 3 0 — tmp — hp — str
The new Walton Edition of this work brings together for the first time the revised (1961) orchestration and the Frederick Riddle version of the solo part from 1937. This is believed to represent the composer's intention, though he also allowed for the possibility of performances of the original version.

I. Andante comodo	9'
II. Vivo; con molto preciso	5'
III. Allegro moderato	13'

Oxford

Concerto, Violin <1936–1939; rev 1943>   31'

2[1.2/pic] 2[1.2/Eh] 2 2 — 4 2 3 0 — tmp+2 — hp — str
perc: tambn, field dr, xyl, cym

I. Andante tranquillo	11'
II. Presto capriccioso all napolitana	7'
III. Vivace	13'

Oxford

Concerto, Violoncello <1955–1956>   30'

2[1.2/pic] 2[1.2/Eh] 2[1.2/bcl] 2[1.2/cbn] — 4 2 3 1 — tmp+3 — hp — cel — str
perc: vib, sd, sus cym, cym, xyl, field dr, tambn, bd, tamtam, cast

I. Moderato	9'
II. Allegro appassionato	7'
III. Lento; Allegro molto	14'

Oxford

Crown Imperial (Coronation March) <1937; rev 1963>   7'

3[1.2.3/pic] 3[1.2.Eh] 3[1.2.bcl] 3[1.2.cbn] — 4 3 3 1 — tmp+3 — hp — opt org — str
perc: sd, glock, tri, td, cym, bd, gong, chimes[F5,C6]
Playable with winds reduced to: 2 2 2 2 — 4 2 3 0
    Original 1937 uncut version, 9'; revised 1963 cut version, 7'.

Oxford

Façade <1922–1929; rev 1942, 1951, 1977>   39'

reciter
1[1/pic] 0 1[1/bcl] 0 — 0 1 0 0 — asx — 1perc — 1 or 2vc
perc: sd, sus cym, tri, templeblks, cast, tambn

Fanfare	1'
1. Hornpipe	1'
2. En Famille	3'
3. Mariner Man	1'
4. Long Steel Grass	2'
5. Through Gilded Trellises	3'
6. Tango-Pasodoble	2'
7. Lullaby for Jumbo	2'
8. Black Mrs. Behemoth	1'
9. Tarantella	1'
10. A Man from a Far Countree	2'
11. By the Lake	2'
12. Country Dance	2'
13. Polka	1'
14. Four in the Morning	2'
15. Something Lies Beyond the Scene	1'
16. Valse	4'
17. Jodelling Song	2'
18. Scotch Rhapsody	1'
19. Popular Song	2'
20. Fox-Trot "Old Sir Faulk"	2'
21. Sir Beelzebub	1'

Façade 2 <1929>   12'

reciter
1[1/pic] 0 1 0 — 0 1 0 0 — asx — 1perc — vc
perc: sd, sus cym, tri, templeblks, cast, tambn
8 more songs to go with the original Façade.

Flourish	1'
1. Came the Great Popinjay	1'
2. Aubade	4'
3. March	1'
4. Madam Mouse Trots	1'
5. The Octogenarian	1'
6. Gardener Janus Catches a Naiad	1'
7. Water Party	1'
8. Sad King Pompey	1'

Oxford

Façade: Four Additional Numbers <1923–1926; rev 1977>   6'

reciter
1 0 1 0 — 0 1 0 0 — asx — 1perc — 1vc
perc: sus cym, sd, tri
These 4 extra pieces were used in various early performances of Façade, but not selected for the 1951 publication, nor for the 1979 Façade 2.

1. Small Talk	1'
2. Daphne	2'
3. The White Owl	1'
4. The Last Galop	2'

Oxford

Façade: Suite No.1 <1926>   9'

2[1.2/pic] 2[1.2/Eh] 2 2 — 4[hn3&4 opt] 2 1 1 — tmp+3 — str
perc: xyl, field dr, tri, cast, glock, tambn, bd, cym, rattle

1. Polka	1'
2. Valse	3'
3. Swiss Jodelling Song	2'
4. Tango-Pasodoble	2'
5. Tarantella-Sevillana	1'

Oxford

Façade: Suite No.2 <1938>   10'

2[1.pic] 3[1.2.Eh(or asx)] 2 2 — 2 2 1 0 — 1perc — str
perc: sd, sus cym, cast, tri, templeblks, bd/ped

1. Fanfare	1'
2. Scotch Rhapsody	1'
3. Country Dance	2'
4. Noche espagnole	2'
5. Popular Song	2'
6. Old Sir Faulk	2'

Oxford

Hamlet; A Shakespeare Scenario: Concert Suite   35'

3[1.2.3/pic] 3[1.2.3/Eh] 3[1.2.3/Ebcl] 3[1.2.cbn] — 4 3 3 1 — tmp+4 — 1 or 2hp — hpsd/pf/cel — str
perc: bd, cym, sus cym, sd, td, field dr, tamtam, glock, xyl, chimes, woodblk, whip
Arr. Christopher Palmer from music for the film. A longer (43') version, intended for broadcast or recording, requires a speaker and extra brass & percussion.

Prelude	_'
Hamlet and Ophelia	_'
Fanfare	_'
The Mousetrap	_'
Ophelia's Death	_'
Retribution and Threnody	_'
Finale (Funeral March)	_'

Oxford

Hamlet and Ophelia; A Poem for Orchestra <1947>   14'

2[1.2/pic] 2[1.Eh] 2 2 — 4 2 3 0 — tmp+1 — hp — cel — str
perc: sd, glock; played by tmp: sus cym, gong, bd
Arr. Muir Mathieson from the film score.

Oxford

Hamlet: Funeral March <1947>   6'

2 2 2 2 — 4 2 3 1[opt] — tmp+4 — hp — str
perc: sd, td, sus cym, cym, 2bd, chimes[B4]
Arr. Muir Mathieson, from the film score.

Oxford

Henry V: Suite <1943–1944; rev 1963 (suite)>   15'

2[1/pic.2/pic] 2[1.2/Eh] 2 2 — 4 2 2 1[opt] — tmp+4 — hp — str
perc: bd, cym, sus cym, td, tambn, chimes, 2sd, tabor
Compiled and arranged in 1963 by Muir Mathieson, from the music for
the 1943 film. A similar suite, 21' in duration, and for larger orchestra
plus chorus, was prepared by the composer and is available from Oxford.

I. Overture: The Globe Playhouse	2'
II. Passacaglia: The Death of Falstaff	3'
III. Charge and Battle	6'
IV. "Touch her soft lips and part"	2'
V. Agincourt Song	3'

Oxford

Henry V; A Shakespeare Scenario <1943–1944>   53'

chorus   children's chorus   speaker
3[1.2/pic.3/pic] 3[1.2.3/Eh] 3[1.2.3/bcl] 2 — 4 3 3 1 — tmp+4 or 5 —
1 or 2hp — hpsd/pf/cel/opt org — str
perc: bd, cym, td, tri, tambn, tamtam, glock, xyl, chimes, crot, 2sd, tabor, rattle
Arranged in 1989 by Christopher Palmer, from the composer's music for
the 1943 film.
    Children's chorus is cued into the main chorus.

1. Prologue	9'
2. Interlude: At the Boar's Head	5'
3. Embarkation	3'
4. Interlude: "Touch her soft lips and part"	1'
5(i). Harfleur	4'
5(ii). The Night-watch	5'
6. Agincourt	15'
7. Interlude: At the French Court	5'
8. Epilogue	6'

Oxford

Improvisations on an Impromptu of Benjamin Britten   16'
<1969>

3[1.2.3/pic] 3[1.2.3/Eh] 3[1.2.3/bcl] 3[1.2.3/cbn] — 4 3 3 1 — tmp+3
— hp — str
perc: glock, xyl, bd, field dr, sd, cym, chimes, tambn, 3bongos

1. Lento	5'
2. Vivo	3'
3. Moderato	4'
4. Scherzando	4'

Oxford

Johannesburg Festival Overture <1956>   7'

3[1.2.3/pic] 3[1.2.Eh] 3 3[1.2.3/cbn] — 4 3 3 1 — tmp+3[or 4] — hp
— str
perc: xyl, glock, marac, tri, sd, td, cast, cym, sus cym, bd, tambn, claves
Reduced version by Vilem Tausky available, for:
    2 2[1.2/Eh] 2 2 — 4 2 3 1[opt] — tmp+1 (or 2) — hp — str

Oxford

Partita <1957>   16'

3[1.2.3/pic] 3[1.2.Eh] 3[1.2.3/bcl] 3[1.2.3/cbn] — 4 3 3 1 — tmp+4
— hp — cel — str
perc: bd, cym, sus cym, sd, fd, tri, tambn, glock, xyl, cast, tamtam, vib

Toccata	5'
Pastorale siciliana	6'
Giga burlesca	5'

Oxford

Portsmouth Point; An Overture <1924–1925>   6'

3[1.2/pic2.pic1] 3[1.2.Eh] 3[1.2.bcl] 3[1.2.cbn] — 4 3 3 1 —
tmp+3[or 4] — str
perc: sd, cast, xyl, tambn, cym, sus cym, bd, tri, tamtam
Reduced version by Constant Lambert available, for:
    2[incl pic] 1 2 1 — 2 2 1 0 — 1 or 2perc — str

Oxford

Prologo e fantasia <1951–1952>   6'

3[1.2.3/pic] 3[1.2.3/Eh] 3[1.2.3/bcl] 3[1.2.3/cbn] — 4 3 3 1 — tmp+4
— hp — pf — str
perc: xyl, field dr, tambn, cym, bd

Oxford

Scapino; A Comedy Overture <1940; rev 1949>   8'

3[1.2/pic.3/pic] 3[1.2.Eh] 3[1.2.bcl] 3[1.2.cbn] — 4 3 3 1 — tmp+3
— hp — str
perc: bd, cym, sus cym, sd, tri, tambn, glock, xyl, templeblks, cast

Oxford

Sinfonia concertante (original version) <1926–1927; rev   18'
1943>

piano obbligato
3[1.2.pic] 3[1.2.Eh] 3[1.2.bcl] 3[1.2.cbn] — 4 3 3 1 — tmp+3 — str
perc: bd, cym, sus cym, sd, tambn, glock, xyl, tri, cast
Ed. Lionel Friend.
    Percussion parts available that permit reduction from 3 to 2 players.

I. Maestoso; Allegro spiritoso	8'
II. Andante comodo	6'
III. Allegro molto	4'

Oxford

Sinfonia concertante (revised version) <1926–1927; rev   17'
1943>

piano obbligato
3[1.2.pic] 2[1.2/Eh] 2 2 — 4 2 3 1 — tmp+2 — str
perc: bd, cym, sus cym, sd, tambn, glock, xyl, field dr
Ed. Lionel Friend.

I. Maestoso; Allegro spiritoso	7'
II. Andante comodo	6'
III. Allegro vivo, sempre scherzando	4'

Oxford

Spitfire Prelude and Fugue <1942>   8'

2[1.pic] 2 2 — 4 2 3 1[opt] — tmp+1 — hp — str
perc: cym, sus cym, sd, chimes
From the film score The First of the Few.

| Prelude | 4' |
| Fugue | 4' |

Oxford

Symphony No.1, B-flat minor <1931–1935; rev 1968>   43'

2[1.2/pic] 2 2 2 — 4 3 3 1 — 2tmp+2 — str
perc: cym, field dr, tamtam
Percussion & 2nd tmp play only in 4th mvt.

I. Allegro assai	13'
II. Presto, con malizia	7'
III. Andante con malinconia	10'
IV. Maestoso - Brioso ed ardamente - Vivacissimo	13'

Oxford

Symphony No.2 <1957–1960>   28'

3[1.2.3/pic] 3[1.2.3/Eh] 3[1.2/Ebcl.3/bcl] 3[1.2.3/cbn] — 4 3 3 1 —
tmp+4 — 2hp — cel, pf — str
perc: vib, glock, xyl, tambn, sd, field dr, cym, bd, chimes[D5]

1. Allegro molto	9'
2. Lento assai	10'
3. Passacaglia: Rema - Risoluto	9'

Oxford

Variations on a Theme by Hindemith <1962–1963>   24'

3[1.2.3/pic] 3[1.2.Eh] 3[1.2.bcl] 3[1.2.3/cbn] — 4 3 3 1 — tmp+3 — hp — str

perc: glock, xyl, bd, field dr, sd, tri, tambn, sus cym, cym, bell

Tema (Andante con moto)	2'
Var. I, Vivace	2'
Var. II, Allegramente	2'
Var. III, Larghetto	2'
Var. IV, Moto perpetuo (con slancio)	1'
Var. V, Andante con moto	2'
Var. VI, Scherzando	1'
Var. VII, Lento molto	4'
Var. VII, Vivacissimo	1'
Var. IX, Maestoso	1'
Finale (Allegro molto)	6'

Oxford

The Wise Virgins: Suite <1940>   20'

2[1.pic] 2[1.Eh] 2 2 — 4 2 3 0 — tmp — hp — str

Arrangement of music of J.S. Bach.

1. What God Hath Done, Is Rightly Done	3'
2. Lord, Hear My Longing	2'
3. See What His Love Can Do	4'
4. Ah! How Ephemeral	2'
5. Sheep May Safely Graze	7'
6. Praise Be to God	2'

Wanhal, Johann Baptist   1739-1813

see: Vanhal, Johann Baptist (Jan Krt.), 1739-1813

Wański, Jan   ca.1762-ca.1830

(b Wielkopolska, ?1760–62; d ?1830). Polish

Symphony, D major (The Shepherd by the Vistula; Pasterz nad Wisłą)   22'

2 0 0 0 — 1 0 0 0 — str

On themes from the overture to the opera *Pasterz nad Wisla (The Shepherd by the Vistula)*.

1.	7'
2.	3'
3.	4'
4.	8'

PWM

Symphony, G major (The Peasant; Kmiotek) <1786–1788>   19'

2 0 0 0 — 1 0 0 0 — str

On themes from the overture to the opera *Kmiotek (The Peasant)*.

1.	5'
2.	5'
3.	4'
4.	5'

PWM

Ward, Robert   1917-2013

(b Cleveland, 13 Sept 1917; d Durham, NC, 3 Apr 2013). American

Adagio and Allegro <1944>   12'

2[1.2/pic] 2[1.2/Eh] 2 2 — 4 3 3 1 — tmp+1 — str

perc: cym

Peer

By the Way of Memories; A Nocturne for Orchestra <1991?>   8"

3[1.2.pic] 2[1.2/Eh] 2 2 — 4 3 2 0 — tmp+1 — hp — str

perc: cym, gong, glock, xyl

Vireo

Cherish Your Land <1999>   3'

bar solo   chorus

1 1 1 1 — dulcimer — tmp/perc — str

perc: xyl, marim

Banjo may substitute for xylophone in one brief passage (17 bars).

Vireo

City of Oaks <2008>   8'

3[1.2.pic] 3[1.2.Eh] 2 2 — 4 2 3 1 — tmp+3 — str

perc: cym, sd, td, xyl, bell

Vireo

Concert Music <1943>   8'

3[1.2.3/pic] 2 2 2 — 4 3 3 1 — tmp+4 — pf — str

perc: cym, sus cym, sd, tri, xyl

Galaxy

Concertino for Strings <1973>   14'

str

I. Introduction	1'
II. Scherzo	4'
III. Siciliano	4'
IV. Finale	5'

Highgate

Concerto, Piano <1968>   25'

3[1.2.3/pic] 3[1.2.Eh] 3[1.2.bcl] 2 — 4 3 3 1 — tmp+1 — str

perc: sus cym, sd

I. Adagio; Allegro	13'
II. Grave; Doppio movimento	12'

ECS

Concerto, Tenor Saxophone <1989>   14'

3[1.2.3/pic] 3[1.2.Eh] 3[1.2.bcl] 2 — 4 3 3 1 — tmp+2 — hp — str

perc: bd, cym, sus cym, sd, td, tri, glock

I. Lento	4'
II. Allegro	10'

Highgate

Concerto, Violin <1993; rev 1994>   21'

2[1.2/pic] 2[1.2/Eh] 2 2 — 4 3 3 0 — tmp+2 — cel[played by perc] — str

perc: sus cym, crot, sd, td, hi-hat, bd, xyl, gong, cel[played by perc]

I. Moderato	_'
II. Blues	_'
III. Allegro spiritoso	_'

Vireo

Dialogues, A Triple Concerto <1982–1987; rev 1998>   19'

solo violin, violoncello, & piano

2[1.2/pic] 2 2 2 — 2 2 0 0 — tmp+1 — str

perc: sd, glock, xyl, sus cym

The last movement may be performed separately, under the title "Dialogues for Solo Violin, Cello and Piano and Chamber Orchestra" (duration 9').

Dialogue I: On the Tides of Time	_'
Interlude	_'
Dialogue II: On the Joy of Living	_'

Highgate

Divertimento <1961> 14'

3[1.2.3/pic] 3[1.2.Eh] 3[1.2.bcl] 2 — 4 3 3 1 — tmp+2 — hp — str
perc: tri, cym, sus cym, woodblk, sd, td, bd, tamtam, glock
   I. Fanfare _'
   II. Intermezzo _'
   III. Finale _'

Highgate

Earth Shall Be Fair <1960> 26'

mixed chorus (or double chorus) and children's choir (or S solo)
2[1.2/pic] 2 2 2 — 4 2 2 0 — tmp+1 — str
perc: cym, sus cym, sd, tambn, chimes
Considerable discretion is possible with the choral forces; the score also
mentions a "junior choir" (treble only) and in another movement contrasts
a "youth choir" (SATBar) with the adult choir.
   I. Lord, Thou hast been our dwelling place _'
   II. Then the kings of the earth _'
   III. Thou changest man back to the dust _'
   IV. Earth might be fair _'
   V. Search me, O God, and know my heart _'

Highgate

Euphony for Orchestra <1954> 10'

2[1.2/pic] 2[1.2/Eh] 2 2 — 4 2 3 1 — tmp+1 — str
perc: cym

Highgate

Festival Triptych <1986> 21'

3[1.2.3/pic] 3[1.2.Eh] 3[1.2.3/bcl] 2 — 4 3 3 1 — tmp+2 — hp —
cel[played by perc] — str
perc: cym, sus cym, sd, td, tri, gong, glock, xyl, crot, 2woodblks, cel[played by
perc]
   I. Adagio; Allegro _'
   II. Lento _'
   III. Vivo _'

Highgate

Festive Ode for Orchestra <1966> 11'

3[1.2.3/pic] 3[1.2.Eh] 3[1.2.bcl] 2 — 4 3 3 1 — tmp+2 — str
perc: cym, sus cym, sd, td, xyl

Galaxy

First Symphonic Set (The New South) <1973; rev 1978> 18'

2[1.2/pic] 2[1.2/Eh] 2[1.2/bcl] 2 — 4 3 3 0 — tmp+2 — hp — str
perc: bd, cym, sus cym, sd, tri, xyl
Suite from the opera *Claudia Legare*.
   1. Aftermath of War _'
   2. Epitaph _'
   3. Industrialize and Rise _'
   4. From Trauma to Revival _'

Highgate

Five Times Five [5 x 5]; Four Variations on a Five-Part Theme <1989> 12'

2[1.2/pic] 2 2 2 — 4 3 3 1 — tmp+2 — str
perc: sd, tri, gong, glock, xyl

Highgate

Hymn and Celebration <1962; rev 1966> 10'

3[1.2.3/pic] 3[1.2.Eh] 3[1.2.bcl] 2 — 4 3 3 1 — tmp+1 — hp — str
perc: cym, sus cym, sd

Highgate

Hymn to the Night <1966> 7'

3[1.2.3/pic] 3[1.2.Eh] 2 2 — 4 3 3 1 — tmp+1 — hp — str
perc: bd, sd, tamtam, glock

Highgate

Invocation and Toccata <1963–1966> 9'

3[1.2.3/pic] 3[1.2.Eh] 3[1.2.bcl] 2 — 4 3 3 1 — tmp+2 — str
perc: cym, sus cym, sd, glock
A revision of his *Music for a Celebration*.
   I. Invocation: Adagio
   II. Toccata: Allegro _'

Highgate

Jonathon and the Gingery Snare <1949> 9'

narrator
2 2 2 2 — 4 3 3 0 — tmp+3 — hp — cel[played by perc] — str
perc: sd, ratch, glock, bd, cast, tambn, xyl, siren, woodblk, gong, sus cym, cym, tri,
whistle, cel[played by perc]
May be played with a reduced brass section: 3hn, 2tp, 1tbn, no tuba.

Vireo

Jubilation; An Overture <1945> 7'

3[1.2.3/pic] 3[1.2.Eh] 3[1.2.3/bcl] 3[1.2.cbn] — 4 3 3 1 — tmp — pf
— str

Highgate

Lady Kate: A Western Set <1964; rev 1994> 20'

2[1.2/pic] 3[1.2.Eh] 2 2 — 4 3 3 1 — tmp+2 — hp — str
perc: bd, cym, sus cym, sd, marac, claves
   I. Celebration Overture 4'
   II. Prairie Romance 6'
   III. Hootenanny 10'

Vireo

The Lamb <2007> 2'

children's chorus (SA)
str

Vireo

Let the Word Go Forth 10'

chorus SAATTBB
0 0 0 0 — 2 2 2 0 — hp — str

Highgate

Prairie Overture <1957; rev (orchd) 1963> 7'

3[1.2.3/pic] 2 2 2 — 4 3 3 1 — tmp+2 — str
perc: bd, cym, sd, td, tri, glock, cast
Originally for band; orchestrated by the composer.

Highgate

Processional March <1963; rev 1966> 5'

3[1.2.3/pic] 3[1.2.Eh] 3[1.2.bcl] 2 — 4 3 3 1 — tmp+3 — str
perc: bd, cym, sd, glock, xyl

Highgate

Sacred Songs for Pantheists <1951> 16'

solo soprano
2[1.2/pic] 1 3[1.2.bcl[or bn]] 0 — 2 2 2 0 — hp — str
   1. Pied Beauty 3'
   2. Little Things 3'
   3. Intoxication 2'
   4. Heaven-Haven 3'
   5. God's Grandeur 5'

Vireo

Sonic Structure <1980> 11'

3[1.2.3/pic] 3[1.2.Eh] 3[1.2.bcl] 3[1.2.cbn] — 4 3 3 1 — tmp+2 — hp
— str
perc: xyl, tri, sd, sus cym, cym, td, glock, crot

Highgate

Sweet Freedom's Song; A New England Chronicle <1965>   40'

narrator, solo S, Bar   chorus
2[1.2/pic] 2 2 2 — 2 2 2 0 — tmp+1 — hp — cel[played by perc] — str
perc: bd/cym, cym, sus cym, sd, glock, cel[played by perc]
Tmp doubles on bd/cym.

Largo e maestoso	_'
It was a great design	_'
O Lord God of my salvation	_'
Come ye thankful people, come	_'
Ballad of Boston Bay	_'
Damnation to the Stamp Act	_'
Here lies a soldier of the Revolution	_'
Sweet Freedom's Song	_'

> Highgate

Symphony No.1 <1941>   13'

3[1.2.3/pic] 3[1.2.Eh] 3[1.2.bcl] 3[1.2.cbn] — 4 3 3 1 — tmp — str

1. Allegro pesante	4'
2. Andante	4'
3. Allegro	5'

> ECS

Symphony No.2 <1947>   21'

3[1.2.3/pic] 3[1.2.Eh] 3[1.2.bcl] 3[1.2.cbn] — 4 3 3 1 — tmp+2 — pf/cel — str
perc: bd, cym, sus cym, sd, td, tri, xyl

1. Fast and energetic	8'
2. Slowly	8'
3. Fast	5'

> ECS

Symphony No.3 <1950>   21'

2[incl pic] 2[incl Eh] 2[incl bcl] 2 — 2 1 0 0 — pf — str

1. Adagio; Allegro	8'
2. Adagio	8'
3. Allegro	5'

> Highgate

Symphony No.4   23'

2 2[1.2/Eh] 2 2 — 2 2 0 0 — tmp — hp — str

1. Adagio; Allegro	8'
2. Grave	8'
3. Vivo	7'

> ECS

Symphony No. 5 (Canticles of America) <1976>   40'

soprano & baritone solos, narrator   chorus SATB
2[1.2/pic] 2[1.2/Eh] 2[1.2/bcl] 2 — 4 3 2 0 — tmp+2 — hp — str
perc: bd, cym, sus cym, td, tri, glock, xyl, windchimes, 2sd
4 soloists from chorus briefly in far corners of the auditorium.

Narration	_'
1. Behold, America	_'
2. A Psalm of Life	_'
3. Hymn to the Night	_'
4. All Peoples of the Globe Together Sail (Walt Whitman)	_'

> ECS

Symphony No.6 <1988>   18'

1[1/pic] 1 1 1 — pf — str

1. Maestoso	7'
2. Lento	5'
3. Allegro	6'

> ECS

Symphony No.7 (The Savannah) <2002–2003>   27'

3[1.2.pic] 2[1.2/Eh] 2 2 — 4 3 3 1 — tmp+2 — hp — str
perc: cym, sd, td, tri, glock, xyl, woodblk, ship's bell, bosun's whistle

I. Maestoso; Allegro	7'
II. Andante	9'
III. Vivace	5'
IV. Moderato; Allegro	6'

> ECS

Warlock, Peter   1894-1930

(b London, 30 Oct 1894; d London, 17 Dec 1930). English

Capriol Suite <1926; rev full orch: 1928>   11'

2[1.2/pic] 2 2 2 — 2 2 3 1 — 1perc — str
perc: sd w/o snares
Based on tunes from Thoinot Arbeau's *Orchésographie* (1588). Also available for purchase or rent in a version for string orchestra.

1. Basse-Danse	2'
2. Pavane	3'
3. Tordion	1'
4. Bransles	2'
5. Pieds-en-l'air	2'
6. Mattachins	1'

> Curwen

Warshauer, Meira Maxine   1949-

(b Wilmington, NC, 28 Feb 1949). American

Ahavah (Love) <1994>   19'

mezzo-soprano solo   chorus
3[incl 2pic] 3[incl Eh] 3[incl bcl] 3[incl cbn] — 4 3 3 1 — tmp+3 — hp — str

Sh'ma v'ahavta	9'
Hishamru	4'
V'samtem	6'

> Kol Meira

As the Waters Cover the Sea; A Tribute to Mozart <1991>   12'

3[all/pic] 2[incl Eh] 2 2 — 4 3 3 1 — tmp+2 — pf/cel — str

> MMB

Beyond the Horizon <2000>   5'

2[1/pic.2/pic] 2 2 2 — 4 2 2 1 — tmp+2 — str
perc: bd, sus cym, szl cym, tambn, glock, xyl, vib, slgh-bells, rainstick

> LKMP

Born on a River (The city of Wilmington, North Carolina)   20'

chorus SATB
2[1/pic.2/pic] 2 2[1.2/bcl] 2 — 2 2 0 0 — tmp+2 — pf — str
perc: bd, sd, tri, tamtam, glock, xyl, marim, slgh-bells, marktree, whip, guiro, claves, vibrslp, 3tomtom w/ snares, 2sus cym, 2tambn, 2woodblk
Brief S solo (member of chorus)

> Kol Meira

In memoriam September 11, 2001   6'

solo violoncello
str

> Kol Meira

Jerusalem, Open Your Gates <1998>   18'

2[1/pic.2/pic] 2 2 2 — 4 3 3 1 — tmp+3 — hp — pf — str
perc: bd, szl cym, tri, tambn, tamtam, glock, marim, vib, chimes, slgh-bells, cast, vibrslp, 2sus cym, 4tomtom, 3woodblk
I. Enter the Sacred Space   _'
II. Arise into Radiant Grace   _'
III. Open Your Gates and Receive God's Glory _'

LKMP

Like Streams in the Desert <1998>   8'

2[1/pic.2/pic] 2 2 2 — 4 2 3 1 — tmp+2 — 2hp — str
perc: szl cym, sd, tomtom, xyl, marim, vib, slgh-bells, bongos, 2sus cym, 2woodblk

LKMP

Revelation <1992>   8'

3[incl 2pic] 3[incl Eh] 3[incl bcl] 3[incl cbn] — 4 3 3 1 — tmp+3 — pf/cel — str

MMB

Shabbat with King David   12'

str

Oxford

Shacharit <1989>   35'

chorus   solo soprano, tenor/narrator
3[incl pic] 2 2 2 — 4 2 3 1 — tmp+4 — hp — str
An interpretation of the Sabbath Morning service.

Kol Meira

Symphony No.1 (Living, Breathing Earth) <2007>   25'

3[1/pic3.2/pic2.pic1/fl3] 3[1.2.Eh] 2[1.2/Ebcl] 2 — 4 3 3 1 — tmp+2 — hp — pf — str
perc: bd, sd, xyl, marim, vib, crot, guiro, cast, vibrslp, 2cabasa, rainstick, shaker, light metal chain, 4sus cym, 3szl cym, 4rototom, 3tambn, 2slgh-bells, 3woodblk, 2marac
I. Call of the Cicadas   _'
II. Tahuayo River at Night   _'
III. Wings in Flight   _'
IV. Living, Breathing Earth   _'

LKMP

Tekeeyah (a call); Concerto for Shofar/Trombone and   25'
Orchestra <2008–2009>

shofar/trombone solo
2[1/opt ocarina.2/pic] 2[1.2/Eh] 2 2[1.2/cbn] — 4 2 2 1 — tmp+2 — hp — str
perc: bd, sus cym, szl cym, glock, xyl, marim, vib, chimes, vibrslp, 2sd, 2tambn, 3tamtam, 4woodblk, tingsha (Tibetan bells), Tibetan bowl, rainstick, cabasa, chain
Trombone soloist, doubling on shofar. Shofar plays E4 & C5; if necessary, two separate shofars may be used.
   Woodwinds and shofar soloist use plastic megaphones for special effects. Contact publisher for advice on this and esoteric percussion.

Kol Meira

Yes! for Clarinet & Orchestra <1996>   8'

2 2 2 2 — 4 2 3 0 — tmp+2(or 3) — pf — str
perc: cym, hi-hat, set, tri, tambn, xyl, marim, slgh-bells, whip, guiro, marac, vibrslp, 3sus cym, 2szl cym, 2tomtom, 5woodblk, 2cowbell, cabasa

LKMP

Watkins, Huw   1976-

(b South Wales, UK, 13 July 1976). British

Concerto, Flute <2013>   20'

2[1.pic] 2 2[1.2/bcl] 2[1.2/cbn] — 4 2 0 0 — 1perc — hp — cel — str
perc: chimes, tri, cym, bd, woodblk
I. Allegro molto   _'
II. Andante   _'
III. Allegro molto   _'

Schott

Weber, Ben   1916-1979

(b St Louis, 23 July 1916; d New York, 16 June 1979). American

Dolmen, op.58 <1964>   9'

0 2 0 1 — 2 0 0 0 — str

Marks

Symphony on Poems of William Blake, op.33 <1952>   30'

baritone solo
1[incl pic] 1 2[incl bcl] 1 — 1 0 1 0 — 1perc — hp — cel — 1vc
To Autumn   11'
Never Seek to Tell Thy Love   6'
Mad Song   5'
To Spring   8'

CFE

Weber, Carl Maria von   1786-1826

(b Eutin, ?19 Nov 1786; d London, 5 June 1826). German

J = F.W. Jähns: *Carl Maria von Weber in seinen Werken: Chronologisch-thematisches Verzeichnis seiner sämmtlichen Compositionen* (Berlin, 1871; reprinted 1967)

Abu Hassan, J.106: Overture <1810–1811; rev 1812-13> 4'

2[1.pic] 2 2 — 2 2 1[btbn] 0 — tmp+3 — str
perc: bd, tri, cym

Breitkopf   Kalmus   Luck's

Andante & Rondo ongarese [original viola version], J.79 8'
<1809>

solo viola
2 2 0 2 — 2 2 0 0 — tmp — str
Ed. Georg Schünemann. This is the original 1809 version of the *Andante & Rondo ongarese*, although it was not published until 1938. Weber had revised it in 1813 for solo bassoon (J.158), in which form it became established in the repertoire.
   The orchestral materials for J.79 and J.158 are not interchangeable. However, the Kunzelmann edition by Hans-Hubert Schönzeler includes both the viola and the bassoon version.
   NB: A more elaborate version by William Primrose is well-known to violists in viola-piano score; however, the Primrose version will not work with the orchestra parts for either J.79 or J.158.

Kunzelmann   Luck's   Schott

Andante & Rondo ongarese [bassoon version], J.158, op.35 <1809; rev 1813>   9'

solo bassoon
2 2 0 2 — 2 2 0 0 — tmp — str
A revision by the composer of the original version for solo viola & orchestra (J.79, *q.v.*). The orchestral materials for J.79 and J.158 are not interchangeable.
   The Kunzelmann edition by Hans-Hubert Schönzeler includes both the viola and the bassoon version.

| C. Fischer | Kalmus | Kunzelmann | Peters | Universal |

Aufforderung zum Tanz, J. 260, op.65 (Invitation to the Dance) <1819>   9'

2[1.pic] 2 2 4 — 4 4 3 0 — tmp — 2hp — str
Originally for solo piano (in D-flat major); orchestrated by Berlioz, 1841 (transposed to D major).

| Breitkopf | Kalmus | Luck's |

Beherrscher der Geister, J.122, op.27 (Ruler of the Spirits) <1811>   7'

2[1.pic] 2 2 2 — 4 2 3 0 — tmp — str
A concert overture, being a revision, 1811, of the overture to the unfinished opera *Rübezahl* of 1805.

| Breitkopf | Kalmus | Luck's |

Concertino, Clarinet, J.109, op.26, E-flat major <1811>   10'

1 2 0 2 — 2 2 0 0 — tmp — str

| Breitkopf | Kalmus | Luck's |

Concertino, Horn, J.188, op.45, E major <1806; rev lost, and revised 1815>   12'

1 0 2 2 — 2 2 0 0 — tmp — str

| Kalmus | KaWe | Lienau | Luck's |

Concerto, Bassoon, J.127, op.75, F major <1811; rev 1822>   17'

2 2 0 2 — 2 2 0 0 — tmp — str
I. Allegro ma non troppo	8'
II. Adagio	5'
III. Rondo: Allegro	4'

| Breitkopf | Kalmus | Luck's |

Concerto, Clarinet, No.1, J.114, op.73, F minor <1811>   18'

2 2 0 2 — 3 2 0 0 — tmp — str
3rd hn in 2nd mvt only.
I. Allegro	7'
II. Adagio ma non troppo	4'
III. Rondo: Allegretto	7'

| Breitkopf | Kalmus | Luck's |

Concerto, Clarinet, No.2, J. 118, op.74, E-flat major <1811>   19'

2 2 0 2 — 2 2 0 0 — tmp — str
I. Allegro	8'
II. Romanza: Andante	7'
III. Alla polacca	4'

| Breitkopf | Kalmus | Luck's |

Concerto, Piano, No.1, J.98, op.11, C major <1810>   20'

2 2 0 2 — 2 2 0 0 — tmp — str
I. Allegro	9'
II. Adagio	4'
III. Presto	7'

| Kalmus | Lienau |

Concerto, Piano, No.2, J.155, op.32, E-flat major <1811–1812>   26'

2 0 2 2 — 2 2 0 0 — tmp — str
I. Allegro maestoso	12'
II. Adagio	7'
III. Rondo: Presto	7'

| Kalmus |

Die drei Pintos, J.Anh.5 (The Three Pintos): Entr'acte <1820–1821>   3'

2[1/pic.2/pic] 2 2 2 — 4 2 1 1 — tmp+1 — str
Completed by Gustav Mahler.

| Kahnt | Kalmus |

Euryanthe, J.291: Overture <1822–1823>   8'

2 2 2 2 — 4 2 3 0 — tmp — str

| Breitkopf | Kalmus | Luck's |

Der Freischütz, J.277: Overture <1817–1821>   10'

2 2 2 2 — 4 2 3 0 — tmp — str

| Breitkopf | Kalmus | Luck's |

Invitation to the Dance

see his: Aufforderung zum Tanz

Jubel Overture, J. 245, op.59 (Jubilation) <1818>   8'

4[2fl, 2pic] 2 2 2 — 4 2 3 0 — tmp+3 — str
perc: cym, bd, tri
The work ends with a full orchestral setting of *God Save the King*, known in German as *Heil Dir im Siegerkranz* (the German national anthem until 1922).

| Breitkopf | Kalmus | Luck's |

Konzertstück, Piano & Orchestra, J.282, op.79, F minor <1821>   17'

2 2 2 2 — 2 2 1[btbn] 0 — tmp — str

| Breitkopf | Kalmus | Luck's |

Mass, J.224, E-flat major (Missa sancta No.1; Freischützmesse) <1817–1818>   37'

chorus   solos SATB
2 2 2 2 — 2 2 0 0 — tmp — org — str
Faber ed. Christopher Brown. Faber and Schott editions do not include organ.
1. Kyrie	7'
2. Gloria	8'
3. Credo	8'
4. Sanctus	4'
5. Benedictus	6'
6. Agnus Dei	4'

| Faber | Kalmus | Luck's | Schott |

Oberon, J.306: Overture <1825–1826>   9'

2 2 2 2 — 4 2 3 0 — tmp — str

| Breitkopf | Kalmus | Luck's |

Peter Schmoll, J.8: Overture <1801–1802>   8'

2 2 2 2 — 2 2 1[btbn] 0 — tmp — str

| Breitkopf | Kalmus | Luck's |

Polonaise brillante, Piano & Orchestra, J.268, op.72 (arr. Liszt) <1819>   13'

2 2 2 2 — 2 2 3 0 — tmp+2 — str

perc: tri, cym

Orchestrated by Franz Liszt, from Weber's *Polacca brillante* for solo piano, 1819. (This Liszt orchestration, S.367, is not to be confused with his S.455, which is an embellished version of the same Weber work, but for solo piano without orchestra.) Liszt provides a lengthy introduction, partly adapted from Weber's *Grande polonaise* for solo piano (op.21, J.59), but mostly of his own invention.

C. Fischer	Kalmus	Lienau	Luck's

Preciosa, J.279: Overture <1820>   9'

2 2 2 2 — 2 2 0 0 — tmp+4 — str

perc: tri, tambn, sd, slgh-bells

Breitkopf	Kalmus	Luck's

Ruler of the Spirits

see his: Beherrscher der Geister

Silvana, J.87: Overture <1808–1810>   5'

2 2 2 2 — 2 2 1 0 — tmp — str

Kalmus	Luck's

Symphony No.1, J.50, op.19, C major <1806–1807; rev 1810>   25'

1 2 0 2 — 2 2 0 0 — tmp — str

I. Allegro con fuoco	7'
II. Andante	7'
III. Scherzo: Presto	4'
IV. Finale: Presto	7'

Alkor	Kalmus	Luck's

Symphony No.2, J.51, C major <1806–1807>   18'

1 2 0 2 — 2 2 0 0 — tmp — str

I. Allegro	10'
II. Adagio	5'
III. Menuetto	1'
IV. Scherzo	2'

Alkor	Kalmus	Luck's

Turandot, J.75: Overture & March <1809>   6'

2[1.pic] 2 2 2 — 2 2 1 0 — tmp+4 — str

perc: bd, cym, sd, tri

Breitkopf	Kalmus	Luck's

Webern, Anton   1883-1945

(b Vienna, 3 Dec 1883; d Mittersill,15 Sept 1945). Austrian

Das Augenlicht, op.26 (The Light of the Eye) <1935>   7'

chorus

1 1 1 0 — 1 1 1 0 — asx — mand — tmp+1 — hp — cel — str[4.4.4.4.0]

perc: glock, xyl, cym

Universal

Cantata No.1, op.29 <1938–1939>   8'

chorus   soprano solo

1 1 2[1.bcl] 0 — 1 1 1 0 — mand — tmp+3 — hp — cel — str[no db]

perc: cym, glock, bd, tamtam, tri

1. Zündender Lichtblitz	2'
2. Kleiner Flügel	2'
3. Tönen die seligen Saiten Apollos	4'

Universal

Cantata No.2, op.31   13'

chorus   solos SB

2[1.pic] 2[1.Eh] 2[1.2/bcl] 1 — 1 1 1 1 — asx — 1perc — hp — cel — str

perc: glock, chimes[C4,D#4]

1. Schweigt auch die Welt	2'
2. Sehr tiefverhalten	3'
3. Schöpfen aus Brunnen	2'
4. Leichteste Bürden	1'
5. Freundselig ist da Wort	3'
6. Gelockert aus dem Schosse	2'

Universal

Concerto, op.24 <1931–1934>   7'

1 1 1 0 — 1 1 1 0 — pf — vn, va

I. Etwas lebhaft	2'
II. Sehr langsam	3'
III. Sehr rasch	2'

Universal

Fünf Sätze, op.5 (Five Movements) <1909; rev 1928, 1929>   11'

str

Originally for string quartet, 1909; arr. by the composer for string orchestra, 1928; rev. 1929.

Universal

Fünf Stücke, op.10 (Five Pieces for Orchestra) <1911–1913>   6'

1[1/pic] 1 2[1/bcl.Ebcl] 0 — 1 1 1 0 — gtr, mand — 4perc — hp — cel, harm — vn, va, vc, db

perc: bd/cym, glock, cym, xyl, tri, sd, herdbells, bells

I. Sehr ruhig und zart	1'
II. Lebhaft und zart bewegt	1'
III. Sehr langsam und äusserst ruhig	2'
IV. Fliessend, äusserst ruhig	1'
V. Sehr fliessend	1'

Universal

Geistliche Lieder, op.15 (Sacred Songs) <1917–1922>   6'

high voice

1 0 1[cl/bcl] 0 — 0 1 0 0 — hp — vn/va

1. Das Kreuz, das musst' er tragen	1'
2. Morgenlied	1'
3. In Gottes Namen aufstehn	1'
4. Mein Weg geht jetzt vorüber	1'
5. Fahr hin, o Seel'	2'

Universal

Im Sommerwind <1904>   12'

3 3[1.2.Eh] 5[1.2.3.4.bcl] 2 — 6 2 0 0 — tmp+2 — 2hp — str

perc: cym, tri

C. Fischer

Langsamer Satz <1905>   9'

str

Transcribed by Gerard Schwarz, from an early work for string quartet.

C. Fischer

Lieder, op.8 <1910; rev 1925, 1926>   2'

medium voice

0 0 1[cl/bcl] 0 — 1 1 0 0 — hp — cel — vn, va, vc

1. Du, der ichs nicht sage	1'
2. Du machst mich allein	1'

Universal

Lieder, op.13 <1914–1918> 6'

solo soprano
1[1/pic] 0 2[1.bcl] 0 — 1 1 1 0 — 1perc — hp — cel — vn, va, vc, db
perc: glock

1. Wiese im Park	2'
2. Die Einsame	1'
3. In der Fremde	1'
4. Ein Winterabend	2'

Universal

Lieder, op.14 8'

high voice
0 0 2[1.bcl] 0 — vn, vc

1. Die Sonne: Täglich kommt die gelbe Sonne	2'
2. Abendland I: Mond, als träte ein Totes	1'
3. Abendland II: So leise sind die grünen Wälder	1'
4. Abendland III: Ihr grossen Städt steinern aufgebaut	2'
5. Nachts: Die Bläue meiner Augen	1'
6. Gesang einer gefangenen Amsel: Dunkler Odem im grünen Gezweig	1'

Universal

Lieder, op.19 2'

chorus
0 0 2[1.bcl] 0 — gtr — cel — vn

1. Weiss wie Lilien	1'
2. Ziehn die Schafe	1'

Universal

Passacaglia, op.1 <1908> 11'

3[1.2.pic] 3[1.2.Eh] 3[1.2.bcl] 3[1.2.cbn] — 4 3 3 1 — tmp+2 — hp — str
perc: tamtam, cym, tri, bd

Kalmus	Luck's	Universal

Sechs Stücke, op.6 [original version] (Six Pieces for Orchestra) <1909> 13'

4[1.2/afl.3/pic.4/pic] 4[2ob, 2Eh] 5[1.2.3/Ebcl.bcl1.bcl2] 2[1.2/cbn] — 6 6 6 1 — tmp+5 — 2hp — cel — str
perc: glock, cym, tamtam, tri, sd, bd, bells ["deep bell-sounds"], rute
Original version, 1909.

I. Langsam	1'
II. Bewegt	2'
III. Mässig	1'
IV. Sehr mässig	4'
V. Sehr langsam	3'
VI. Langsam	2'

Universal

Sechs Stücke, op.6 [1928 version] (Six Pieces for Orchestra) <1909; rev 1928> 13'

2[1.2/pic] 2 3[1.2.bcl] 2[1.2/cbn] — 4 4 4 1 — tmp+5 — hp — cel — str
perc: glock, cym, tamtam, tri, sd, bd, bells ["deep bell-sounds"]

I. Langsam	1'
II. Bewegt	2'
III. Mässig	1'
IV. Sehr mässig	4'
V. Sehr langsam	3'
VI. Langsam	2'

Universal

Symphony, op.21 <1927–1928> 10'

0 0 2[1.bcl] 0 — 2 0 0 0 — hp — str[no db]

I. Ruhig schreitend	7'
II. Variationen	3'

Universal

Variations for Orchestra, op.30 <1940> 8'

1 1 2[1.bcl] 0 — 1 1 1 1 — tmp — hp — cel — str

Universal

Weill, Kurt

1900-1950

(b Dessau, 2 March 1900; d New York, 3 April 1950). German composer, American citizen from 1943

Aufstieg und Fall der Stadt Mahagonny (Rise and Fall of the City of Mahagonny): Suite <1927–1929> 17'

2[1/pic.2/pic] 1 1 2 — 2 2 2 1[1/tbn3] — asx, tsx/ssx — banjo, bass gtr — tmp+1 — pf — str[no vn2]
perc: sd, tomtom, woodblk, sus cym, tamtam, chimes; played by tmp: bd, tri
Suite from the opera, arr. Wilhelm Brückner-Rüggeberg.
  Tbn3 is only 9 bars of quarternotes, all doubling the tuba; there is no separate tbn3 part.
  The movements lack titles; those given below were supplied by David Loebel.

I. Overture to Act I	1'
II. "Alabama Song"	2'
III. "Auf nach Mahagonny"	3'
IV. "Ich habe gelernt"	2'
V. Hurricane	2'
VI. Crane Duet	3'
VII. Finale	4'

Universal

Das Berliner Requiem <1928> 19'

solo tenor & baritone   male chorus
0 0 2 2 — 2 2 2 1[opt] — asx, asx/tsx — gtr, banjo — tmp+1 — org or harm — [no str]
perc: sd, sus cym
Ed. David Drew. If no chorus is available, the work may be done with solo voices T, Bar, B.

1. Grosser Dankchoral	3'
2. Vom ertrunkene Mädchen	2'
3. Hier ruht die Jungfrau	2'
4. Erster Bericht über den unbekannten Soldaten	4'
5. Zweiter Bericht über den unbekannten Soldaten	5'
6. Grosser Dankchoral	3'

Universal

Concerto, Violin & Wind Instruments, op.12 <1924> 33'

2[incl pic] 1 2 2 — 2 1 0 0 — tmp+1 — double basses
perc: sd[partially covered by tmp], bd, tri, cym, xyl

I. Andante con moto	10'
II. Notturno: Allegro un poco tenuto	3'
II. Cadenza: Moderato - Vivace	4'
II. Serenta: Allegretto	4'
III. Allegro molto, un poco agitato	4'

Universal

Dreigroschenoper (Threepenny Opera): Suite (arr. Max Schönherr) <1928> 17'

solo voice ad lib.
2[1.2/pic] 2 2 2 — 4 2 2 1 — gtr — tmp+2 — hp — cel/pf — str
perc: bd, sus cym, sd, toms, tri, tamtam, gong, glock, xyl, vib, woodblk
Arr. Max Schönherr for symphony orchestra. Not to be confused with Weill's own Kleine Dreigroschenmusik (see below).

1. Overture	3'
2. Die Moritat von Mackie Messer	2'
3. Liebeslied	3'
4. Die Ballade vom angenehmen Leben	3'
5. Polly's Lied	3'
6. Kanonen-Song	3'

Universal

Kleine Dreigroschenmusik (Suite from "Threepenny Opera") <1928>   20'

2[1/pic.2] 0 2 2 — 0 2 1 1 — asx, tsx[dbl opt ssx] — banjo/opt gtr, bandoneon — tmp/perc — hp[or gtr] — pf — [no str]
perc: sd, tomtom, bd, cym, woodblk, chimes[B3,C4]
Suite selected and arranged for wind orchestra by the composer.

1. Overture	*2'*
2. Die Moritat von Mackie Messer (The Moritat of Mack the Knife)	*2'*
3. Anstatt-dass Song (The Instead-of Song)	*2'*
4. Die Ballade von angenehmen Leben (The Ballad of the Easy Life)	*3'*
5. Pollys Lied (Polly's Song)	*2'*
6. Tango-Ballade (Tango Ballad)	*3'*
7. Kanonen-Song (Cannon Song)	*2'*
8. Dreigroschen-Finale (Threepenny Finale)	*4'*

Universal

Die sieben Todsünden (The Seven Deadly Sins) <1933>   39'

solo soprano   male quartet or possibly chorus
2[1/pic.2/pic] 1 2 1 — 2 2 1 1 — banjo/gtr — tmp+2 — hp — pf — str
perc: tri, cym, tamtam, bd, 3tomtoms (1 player if pedal bd used)
Ballet chanté in 8 parts.

Prologue	*5'*
No.1, Faulheit (Sloth)	*4'*
No.2, Stotz (Pride)	*5'*
No.3, Zorn (Anger)	*4'*
No.4, Völlerei (Gluttony)	*4'*
No.5, Unzucht (Lust)	*7'*
No.6, Habsucht (Covetousness)	*3'*
No.7, Neid (Envy)	*5'*
Epilogue	*2'*

Schott

Symphony No.1 (Berliner Sinfonie) <1921>   25'

2[1.2/pic] 1 2[1.2/bcl] 2 — 2[or 4] 1 1 0 — tmp+3 — str
perc: sd, glock, tri, tamtam, cym, bd, 4 deep bells [G2,A2,D3,E3]
In one movement.

Grave	*6'*
Allegro vivace; Sehr drängend	*4'*
Nicht schleppend (Sehr pathetisch)	*3'*
Andante religioso	*4'*
Larghetto; Wei ein Choral; Sehr ruhig, mystisch	*6'*
Langsam und feierlich	*1'*
Andante espressivo	*1'*

Schott

Symphony No.2 <1933–1934>   28'

2[1/pic.2/pic] 2 2 2 — 2 2 2 0 — tmp — str
Two additional percussion parts, not notated in the score, may be included in the set of parts; these were disavowed by the composer and should not be used.

1. Sostenuto - Allegro molto	*9'*
2. Largo	*11'*
3. Allegro vivace - Presto	*8'*

Heugel   Schott

Weinberger, Jaromir   1896-1967

(b Prague, 8 Jan 1896; d St Petersburg, FL, 8 Aug 1967). American composer of Czech birth

Schwanda, the Bagpiper (Svanda dudák): Polka & Fugue [original, B major] <1926>   8'

3[1.2.3/pic] 2 2 2 — 4 7[3onstage, 4backstage] 3 1 — tmp+4 — hp — opt org — str
perc: glock, tri, sd, cym, bd
Backstage trumpets play in unison.
  Two excerpts from different parts of the opera, joined together to form a concert piece. This version, in B major (plate number 9330), has been extracted from the opera with almost no change except the omission of the chorus. Not to be confused with the following entry, which has been transposed and reorchestrated.
  AMP handles this work for USA; Boosey outside of the USA.

Polka	2'
Fugue	6'

AMP	Boosey	Fleisher	Universal

Schwanda, the Bagpiper (Svanda dudák): Polka & Fugue [arrangement, G major] <1926>   8'

3[1.2.3/pic] 2 2 2 — 4 3 3 1 — tmp+3 — hp — opt org — str
perc: glock, tri, sd, cym, bd
Transposed to G major, and reorchestrated, possibly by the composer. Not to be confused with the B major original (see previous entry.) This G major version (which bears no plate number), while by no means easy, is less challenging than the B major version.
  NB: Despite a persistent rumor, there is no evidence that a version of this work in C major exists.
  AMP handles this work for USA; Luck's has a copy for rental.

Polka	2'
Fugue	6'

AMP	Luck's

Under the Spreading Chestnut Tree; Variations & Fugue on an Old English Tune <1939; rev 1941>   16'

3[1.2/pic.3/pic] 2 2 2 — 4 3 3 1 — tmp+3 — hp — pf, opt org — str
perc: tri, sd, cym, sus cym, bd

AMP

Weiner, Leó   1885-1960

(b Budapest, 16 April 1885; d Budapest, 13 Sept 1960). Hungarian

Divertimento No.5, op.39 (Impressioni ungheresi) <1951>   11'

2[1.2/pic] 2 2 2 — 4 2 3 0 — tmp — hp — str

1. Verbunk from Pereg	_'
2. Joking	_'
3. Tramp's Song	_'
4. Love Song	_'
5. Bagpiper from Nógrád	_'

EMB

Preludio, Notturno e Scherzo diabolico, op.31 <1950>   8'

2[1.2/pic] 2 2 2 — 4 2 3 0 — tmp — hp — str
Originally for piano, 1911; arranged by the composer, 1950.

Preludio	2'
Notturno	3'
Scherzo diabolico	3'

EMB

Weinzweig, John 1913-2006

(b Toronto, ON, 11 March 1913; d Toronto, ON, 24 August 2006). Canadian

Concerto, Harp <1967> 18'

1 1 1 1 — 1 0 0 0 — str 5t or str orch

Leeds Canada

Weiss, Adolph 1891-1971

(b Baltimore, MD, 12 Sept 1891; d Van Nuys, CA, 21 Feb 1971). American composer

American Life (Scherzo jazzoso) <1928> 6'

3[1.2.3/pic] 3[1.2.Eh] 3[1.2.bcl] 3[1.2.cbn] — 4 3 3 1 — ssx, asx, tsx — tmp+4 — str
Original publisher: New Music, San Francisco.

Fleisher

I segreti <1923> 12'

3[1.2.pic] 3[1.2.Eh] 3[1.2.bcl] 3[1.2.cbn] — 4 4 3 1 — tmp+3 — hp — cel — str

Fleisher

Welcher, Dan 1948-

(b Rochester, NY, 2 March 1948). American

Concerto da camera <1975> 24'

solo bassoon
1 1 1 0 — 1 1 0 0 — 1perc — pf — str
perc: sus cym, sd, tri, glock, xyl, vib, templeblks, tmp, 3tomtom
It is unclear whether the composer intends 5 individual string players, or small string sections. Probably it would work well either way.

I. Moderato	10'
II. Scherzo; Interlude	6'
III. Calmo	8'

Presser

Haleakala (How Maui Snared the Sun) <1991> 21'

narrator
3[incl 2pic] 3[incl Eh] 3[incl bcl] 3[incl cbn] — 4[incl 1 conch shell] 3 3 1 — tmp+4 — hp — pf/cel — str

Elkan-Vogel

Night Watchers (Symphony No.2) <1994> 29'

3[incl pic] 3[incl Eh] 3[incl Ebcl,bcl] 3[incl cbn] — 4 3 3 1 — tmp+4 — hp — pf/cel — str

1. Putting up the Stars (Fantasia)	_'
2. Music of the Spheres (Romanza)	_'
3. The Delight of God (Scherzo)	_'
4. Twilight of the Dawn (Finale)	_'

Elkan-Vogel

Prairie Light; Three Texas Water Colors of Georgia O'Keeffe <1985> 15'

3[1.2.pic] 2 2 2 — 4 3 3 1 — tmp+3 — hp — pf/cel — str[min 10.8.6.6.4]
perc: glock, xyl, vib, szl cym, templeblks, woodblk, tamtam, bd, cast, 2tri, 2sus cym, 4tomtom

I. Light Coming on the Plains	5'
II. Canyon with Crows	5'
III. Starlight Night	5'

Presser

Symphony No.5 <2009> 38'

3[1.2.pic] 3[1.2.Eh] 3[1.2.bcl/Ebcl] 3[1.2.cbn] — 4 3 3 1 — asx — tmp+4 — hp — pf/cel — str
perc: bd, szl cym, hi-hat, sd, brake dr, glock, xyl, marim, vib, crot, flexatone, templeblks, bongos, claves, glass windchimes, 4woodblk, 2sus cym, 5tomtom, 3tri, 5cowbell, 5stones

I. Broadly	_'
II. Scherzo	_'
III. Strong and passionate	_'
IV. Dancing	_'

Presser

Venti di mare (Sea Winds) <1998> 24'

solo oboe
2[incl pic] 0 1 1 — 2 0 0 0 — 1perc — hp — pf — str

1. Introduction (Calling the Winds)	_'
2. The Outbound Trades	_'
3. Scirocco (Scherzo/Rondo)	_'
4. Doldrums (Equatorial)	_'
5. Recalling the Winds	_'
6. The Homeward Trades	_'

Presser

Zion <1999> 10'

3[1.2.pic] 3[1.2.Eh] 3[1.2.bcl] 3[1.2.cbn] — 4 4 3 1 — tmp+4 — hp — pf — str
perc: bd, sus cym, sd, field dr, tambn, tamtam, gong, glock, xyl, marim, vib, chimes, templeblks, whip, bongos, claves, 4tomtom, 2tri, 2woodblk
Originally the second mvt of a work for wind ensemble.

Presser

Wellesz, Egon 1885-1974

(b Vienna, 21 Oct 1885; d Oxford, 9 Nov 1974). Austrian composer; lived in England from 1938

Prosperos Beschwörungen, op.53; Five Pieces after Shakespeare's "The Tempest" (Prospero's Incantation) <1934–1936> 30'

3[1.2.3/pic] 3[1.2.Eh] 2[1.2/bcl] 2[1.2/cbn] — 4 3 3 1 — tmp+4 — hp — str
perc: bd, cym, sd, tri, tambn, 2tamtam

I. Prosperos Beschwörung (Prospero's Incantation)	5'
II. Ariel und der Sturm (Ariel and the Storm)	5'
III. Ariels Gesang (Ariel's Song)	6'
IV. Caliban	5'
V. Ferdinand und Miranda — Epilog	9'

Doblinger

Suite, Violin & Chamber Orchestra, op.38 <1924> 18'

violin solo
1 1[Eh] 1 1 — 1va, 1vc

Universal

Wendel, Robert 1951-

(b Bridgeport, CT, 21 June 1951). American

Carol of the Bells <1998> 4'

3[1.2.pic] 2 2 2 — 4 3 3 1 — opt handbells — tmp+4 — hp — cel — str
perc: bd, sus cym, sd, tri, tamtam, glock, chimes, belltree, 3 Turandot gongs

Wendel

A Chanukah Overture <1996> 6'

3[1.2.pic] 2 2 2 — 4 3 3 1 — tmp+4 — str
perc: bd, cym, set, tri, tambn, glock
Composed jointly with Dana Friedman.

Wendel

Christmas a la Valse <1995>   6'

3[1.2.pic] 2 2 2 — 4 3 3 1 — tmp+4 — hp[opt] — str
perc: bd, cym, tri, tambn, tamtam, glock, chimes

> Wendel

Commemoration   4'

3[1.2.pic] 2[1.Eh] 2 2 — 4 4[or 2] 3 1 — tmp+3 — opt org — str
perc: sus cym, sd, tamtam, glock, chimes

> Wendel

Fanfare for Freedom <1994>   4'

3[1.2.pic] 2 2 2 — 4 3 3 1 — tmp+3 — opt pf — str
perc: cym, tri, glock, chimes

> Wendel

Fantasia on "Yerousalaim shel zahav" (Jerusalem of Gold)   5'

1 2[1.Eh] 1 1 — 1perc — hp — str
perc: non-pitched antique cym (or tri or windchime)

> Wendel

In the Manger <1998>   4'

2 2[1.Eh] 2 2 — 4 0 3[opt] 0 — opt handbell choir — 3perc — hp — cel — str
perc: tri, glock, chimes, belltree

> Wendel

Parade of the Percussionists <2000>   4'

3[1.2.pic] 2 2 2 — 4 3 3 1 — tmp+5 — opt pf — str
perc: bd, cym, sd, set, tri, tambn, tamtam, glock, xyl, chimes, woodblk, templeblk, whip, autohorn, starter's pistol

> Wendel

Ride of the Headless Horseman <2001>   5'

3[1.2.pic] 2[1.Eh] 2 2 — 4 3 3 1 — tmp+4 — hp — str
perc: bd, cym, set, tri, tamtam, glock, xyl, chimes, marktree

> Wendel

Take Flight <2003>   5'

3[1.2.pic] 2 3[1.2.opt bcl] 2 — 4 3 3 1 — tmp+3 — str
perc: bd, cym, sus cym, tri, tamtam, glock, marktree

> Wendel

Towers of Light; An Elegy for Orchestra <2006>   7'

2 2[1.2/Eh] 2 2 — 2[or 4] 0 0 0 — tmp+2 — hp — cel — str
perc: cym, sus cym, tri, tamtam, glock, chimes, marktrees [more than 1]

> Wendel

Virginia, 1861 <2011>   18'

SATB chorus   children's chorus   child or alto soloist
3[1.2.3/pic] 2 3[1.2.opt bcl] 2 — 4 3 3 1 — opt euph — tmp+3 — hp — pf/cel — str
perc: bd, cym, sus cym, sd, tri, tamtam, chimes
Child or alto soloist (3 bars only) in balcony. Chorus sings the phrase "Give us peace" in 21 different languages.

> Wendel

Wernick, Richard   1934-

(b Boston, 16 Jan 1934). American

Concerto, Violoncello, No.2   25'

3[incl pic] 3[incl Eh] 3[incl bcl] 3[incl cbn] — 4 3 3 1 — tmp+3 — hp — str

> Presser

The Name of the Game <2001>   20'

solo guitar
1[fl/afl] 0 1[cl/bcl] 1 — 1 0 0 0 — 2perc — hp — str 4t[vn, va, vc, db]
  I. The Name is the Game   _'
  II. The Game is the Name   _'

> Presser

Visions of Terror and Wonder <1976>   28'

solo mezzo-soprano
4[1/pic.2/pic.3/afl.4/afl] 4[1.2.3.4/Eh] 4[1.2.3/Ebcl.4/bcl/Ebcl] 4[1.2.3.4/cbn] — 4 3 3 1 — 2tmp+5 — hp — cel — str
Texts from the Bible (in Hebrew & Greek) and the Koran (Arabic), with transliterations and pronunciation guide.
  PART ONE
  1. The Vision from Judah (Isaiah 65:17-18)   _'
  2. The Vision from Mecca (Koran: Surahs XXI:104, XIV:48   _'
  PART TWO
  3. The Vision of the End (Revelations 20:1-2)   _'
  Coda-Recitative: The Vision of Paradise (Koran: Surah LVI:11, 12, 25, 26   _'

> Presser

Wharton, Philip   1969-

(b New Orleans, 9 Apr 1969). American

Symphony <2009–2010>   44'

2[1.2/pic] 2 2 2 — 4 2 2 1 — tmp+3 — pf — str
perc: bd, cym, sd, tri, tambn, tamtam, woodblk, whip, siren, anvil
The 4th mvt, *High Fooling*, may be performed separately.
Possible with 3perc if the timpanist doubles on percussion.
  1. Soundshapes   12'
  2. Laughing Corn   6'
  3. Verdant Twilight   14'
  4. High Fooling   5'
  5. Summer Tuning   7'

> Wharton

White, Paul   1895-1973

(b Bangor, ME, 22 Aug 1895; d Henrietta, NY, 31 May 1973). American

Five Miniatures for Orchestra   7'

1[1/pic] 1[1/Eh] 1 1 — 2 2 3 0 — 2perc — hp[or cel] — str
perc: cym, whip, tamtam, vib, woodblk, xyl, sandblks
  1. By the Lake   2'
  2. Caravan Song   2'
  3. Waltz for Teenie's Doll 1'
  4. Hippo Dance   1'
  5. Mosquito Dance   1'

> Elkan-Vogel

Whitehead, Gillian   1941-

(b Whangarei, 23 April 1941). New Zealander

Alice <2002>   35'

solo mezzo-soprano
3[1.2.3/pic] 3 4[1.2.3.bcl] 3[1.2.3/cbn] — 4 3 3 1 — tmp+3 — hp — str
perc: cym, tri, xyl, marim, vib, chimes, crot, woodblk, guiro, 2bd, 3sus cym, 7rototom, 2tamtam, 2windwhstle, 3pr stones, watergong, metalblks
Monodrama.
   1. On board the S.S. Fifeshire, travelling to New Zealand   _'
   2. Arrival in New Zealand   _'
   3. Exchange of letters between father and daughter   _'
   4. Alice discovers she has fallen pregnant   _'
   5. The death of her father   _'
   6. The death of her husband   _'
   7. Her return to the farm at Makarora   _'
   8. Alice looks forward to a new life in the North Island   _'

SOUNZ

the improbable ordered dance <2000>   18'

3[1.2.3/pic] 3[1.2.3/Eh] 3 3 — 4 3 3 1 — 3perc[incl tmp] — hp — pf — str
perc: xyl, vib, tamtam, bd, guiro, 2rainstick, 14rototom, metal chimes, stones, tmp, 5sus cym, flax bundle, 2claves, 5woodblk

SOUNZ

Resurgences <1989>   14'

3[1.2.3/pic] 3 3 3 — 4 3 3 1 — 3perc[incl tmp] — hp — str
perc: chimes, belltree, thunder, brake dr, marim, glock, bd, tamtam, guiro, 2gong, tmp, 5tomtom, 3sus cym, metal chimes , 2td

SOUNZ

Widor, Charles-Marie   1844-1937

(b Lyons, 21 Feb 1844; d Paris, 12 March 1937). French

Choral et variations <1900>   13'

solo harp
2[1.2/pic] 2 2 2 — 4 2 3 1 — tmp+3 — str
perc: bd, cym, tri

Heugel	Kalmus	Luck's

La korrigane (The Goblin): Suite <1880>   18'

2[1.2/pic] 2 2 2 — 4 4[2tp, 2crt] 3 1[oph] — tmp+4 — hp — str
perc: bd, cym, sd, tri, tambn
Harp only in the 5th movement; score lists "Harpes," but there is only a single part.
   1. Prélude; Alla marcia   _'
   2. Tempo di mazurka   _'
   3. Adagio   _'
   4. Scherzando   _'
   5. Valse lente   _'
   6. Finale   _'

Heugel

Symphony No.3, op.69, E minor   30'

solo organ
3[1.2.3/pic] 2 2 — 4 4[2tp, 2crt] 3 1 — tmp+2 — str
perc: bd, cym, sus cym
   I. Adagio; Andante sosteunto; Allegro   16'
   II. Vivace   14'

Kalmus	Luck's	Schott

Wieniawski, Henryk   1835-1880

(b Lublin, 10 July 1835; d Moscow, 31 March 1880). Polish

Concerto, Violin, No.1, op.14, F-sharp minor <1853>   25'

2 2 2 2 — 2 2 3 0 — tmp — str
   I. Allegro moderato   13'
   II. Prehiera [Prayer]: Larghetto   5'
   III. Rondo: Allegro giocoso   7'

Kalmus	Luck's	PWM

Concerto, Violin, No.2, op.22, D minor <1862>   22'

2 2 2 2 — 2 2 3 0 — tmp — str
   I. Allegro moderato   11'
   II. Romance   5'
   III. Allegro con fuoco - Allegro moderato (à la zingara)   6'

Kalmus	Luck's	PWM	Schott

Fantaisie brillante, on themes from Gounod's *Faust*, op.20 <1868>   18'

solo violin
3[1.2/pic.pic(opt)] 2 2 2 — 2 2 3 0 — tmp — str
Kalmus ed. Howard K. Wolf.

Kalmus	Kistner&Siegel

Légend, Violin & Orchestra, op.17 <1860>   9'

2 2 2 2 — 2 0 0 0 — tmp — str

Kalmus	Luck's	PWM

Polonaise brillante No.1, op.4, D major (Polonaise de concert) <1853>   6'

solo violin
2 2 2 2 — 2 2 1 0 — tmp — str
There appear to be multiple orchestrations of this work; the most commonly used one is listed above.
   PWM offers two versions:
   (1) by Jerzy Kornowicz: 1 2 1 1 — 2 0 0 0 — str
   (2) by Artur Malawski: 2 2 2 2 — 4 2 3 0 — 1perc — str

C. Fischer	Kalmus	Luck's	PWM

Polonaise brillante No.2, op.21, A major <1875>   7'

solo violin
2 2 2 2 — 2 2 3 0 — tmp — str
Some editions of the solo part (*e.g.*, Nathan Milstein's) require cuts and adjustments in the orchestral parts.

Kalmus	Luck's	PWM

Scherzo-tarantelle, op.16 <1856>   6'

solo violin
2 2 2 2 — 2 2[opt] 0 0 — tmp+2 — str
perc: tambn, tri
Orchestrated by Paul Gilson.

Kalmus	Luck's	Sikorski

Wigglesworth, Ryan   1979-

(b Yorkshire, UK, 31 Aug 1979). British

Locke's Theatre <2013>   12'

3[all/pic] 2[1.2/Eh] 3[1.2.3/bcl] 3[1.2.3/cbn] — 4 3 3 1 — tmp+4 — hp — cel — str[min 12.10.8.6.6]
perc: vib, xyl, templeblks, whip, claves, cym, Chinescym, szl cym, tamtam, tambn, crot, glock, bd, chimes, tri, 2sus cym, 2anvil, 4sd
   1. The First Music   _'
   2. Rustic Music   _'
   3. Curtain Music (with Storm)   _'

Schott

Wilder, Alec

1907-1980

(b Rochester, NY, 16 Feb 1907; d Gainesville, FL, 24 Dec 1980). American

Carl Sandburg Suite <1960>

16'

2[1.2/pic] 2[1.2/Eh] 2 2 — 2 2 2 0 — tmp+1 — hp — str
perc: xyl, vib, sd, bd, cym, sus cym, woodblk, gong
Based on folktunes from Carl Sandburg's *The American Songbag*.

AMP	Luck's

Concerto, Oboe

24'

tmp+2 — str
(Perhaps intended for tmp+1, using a drum set.)

AMP

Williams, John

1932-

(b New York, 8 Feb 1932). American

Concerto, Horn <2003>

24'

3[1.2.3/pic] 3[1.2.3/Eh] 3[1.2.3/bcl] 3[1.2.3/cbn] — 4 3 3 1 — tmp+5 — hp — pf/cel — str
perc: bd, sus cym, szl cym, rototom, tambn, glock, xyl, marim, vib, crot, belltree, templeblks, whip, ratch, guiro, 2chimes, 2tamtams, finger cym, 2tri, logdrum, metalpipe, puili, 2anvils

I. Angelus	_'
II. Battle of the Trees	_'
III. Pastorale	_'
IV. The Hunt	_'
V. Nocturne	_'

Kane

Concerto, Violin <1981; rev 1988>

30'

3[1.2.pic] 2[1.2/Eh] 2 2[1.2/cbn] — 4 3 3 1 — tmp+3 — hp — str
perc: bd, cym, sus cym, sd, glock, xyl, vib, chimes, 2tri

1. Moderato	11'
2. Slowly, in Peaceful Contemplation	10'
3. Broadly (Maestoso) — Quickly	9'

Kane

Star Wars: Suite <1977–?>

24'

3[1.2.3/pic] 2[1.2/Eh] 3[1.2.bcl] 2 — 4 3 3 1 — tmp+5 — hp — pf/cel — str
perc: bd, cym, sus cym, tri, tamtam, glock, vib, 2sd

I. Main Title	5'
II. Princess Leia's Theme	3'
III. The Imperial March (Darth Vader's Theme)	3'
IV. Yoda's Theme	5'
V. Throne Room & End Title	8'

Leonard

Wilson, Olly

1937-

(b St Louis, 7 Sept 1937). American

Expansions III <1993>

15'

3[1.2.pic] 3[1.2.Eh] 2 2 — 4 3 3 1 — tmp+2 — hp — pf — str
perc: xyl, marim, timbales, vib, gong, bd, chimes, tri, tamtam, 3sus cym, 2szl cym, 3Chinese gongs, wood drum, metal windchimes

Gunmar

Houston Fanfare <1986>

3'

2 2 2 2 — 4 3 3 1 — 3perc — hp — pf — str

Gunmar

Lumina <1981>

11'

3[incl pic] 2 2 2 — 4 3 3 1 — tmp+3 — hp — pf — str

Gunmar

Sinfonia <1984>

23'

3[1.2.pic/bfl] 3[incl Eh] 3[incl bcl] 3[incl cbn] — 4 3 3 1 — tmp+4 — hp — cel, pf — str

Gunmar

Voices <1970>

15'

2[1/pic.2] 3[1.2.Eh] 3[1.2.3/bcl] 3[1.2.cbn] — 4 3 3 1 — tmp+4 — pf — str

Gunmar

Wirén, Dag

1905-1986

(b Striberg, Narke, 15 Oct 1905; d Stockholm, 19 April 1986). Swedish

Serenade, op.11

15'

str

1. Preludium	3'
2. Andante expressivo	4'
3. Scherzo	3'
4. Marcia	5'

Gehrmans	Kalmus	Luck's

Witt, Friedrich

1770-1837

(b Niederstetten, Wurttemberg, 8 Nov 1770; d Wurzburg, 3 Jan 1836). German

Jena Symphony, C major

27'

1 2 0 2 — 2 2 0 0 — tmp — str
Ed. Fritz Stein. Formerly attributed to Beethoven.

I. Adagio - Allegro vivace	9'
II. Adagio cantabile	8'
III. Menuetto: Maestoso	4'
IV. Finale: Allegro	6'

Breitkopf	Kalmus	Luck's

Symphony in A

24'

1 2 0 2 — 2 0 0 0 — str

1. Adagio; Allegro vivace	8'
2. Menuetto: Allegro	4'
3. Andante	7'
4. Allegretto	5'

Breitkopf	Kalmus	Luck's

Wittry, Diane

1964-

(b Pasadena, CA, 11 Oct 1964). American

after the rain <2012>

8'

2[1.pic] 1 1 1 — 1 2 1 0 — 2perc — str 5t or small str section
perc: marim, templeblks, sus cym, woodblk, 3eggshakers, 2metal trashcan lids
Special seating required. Oboist and clarinetist each also play an egg shaker.

Peckham

Concerto for Homemade Instruments <2013>

5'

2[1.2/pic] 2 2 — 2 2 2 1 — 3perc — hp — str
perc: glock, xyl, chimes, ratch, marac, bd, tomtom, sd, sus cym, flowerpot chimes, tmp
Audience-participation piece; instruction sheets help young people construct homemade instruments representative of the families of the orchestra (strings, woodwinds, brass, percussion).

Peckham

Lamentoso <2010> 11'

3[1.2.3/pic] 2 2 2 — 4 3 3 1 — tmp+1 — str
perc: vib, tamtam, chimes, windchimes, 2sus cym
Timpanist covers one of the suspended cymbals.

Peckham

Mist <2008> 16'

2 2[1.2/Eh] 2 2 — 3 2 1 1 — tmp+1 — hp — str
perc: sus cym, glock, windchimes, 2nd tmp, water pan, 2rainsticks

Presser

Wolf, Hugo 1860-1903

(b Windischgraz, Styria [now Slovenjgradec, Slovenia], 13 March 1860; d Vienna, 22 Feb 1903). Austrian

Anakreons Grab (Anacreon's Grave) <1888; rev (orchd) 1890, 1893> 3'

medium voice
2 0 2 2 — 2 0 0 0 — str
Originally for voice & piano; orchestrated by the composer twice (1890 & 1893). No.29 from *Gedichte von J.W. v. Goethe* (1890). Key of D.

Kalmus	Luck's

Der Corregidor: Prelude & Interlude <1895> 8'

3[incl pic] 3[incl Eh] 2 2 — 4 3 3 1 — tmp+1 — str
Prelude 5'
Interlude 3'

Bote & Bock

Der Corregidor: Suite <1895> 16'

3[1.2.3/pic] 2[1.2/Eh] 2 2 — 4 2 3 1 — tmp+3 — str
perc: bd, cym, tri
Arr. Hans Gál.
1. Prelude _'
2. Fandango & March _'
3. Spanish Intermezzo _'
4. Notturno & Entr'acte _'

Boosey

Der Feuerreiter (The Fire Rider) <1888; rev 1892> 6'

chorus SATB
3[1.2.pic] 2 2 3 — 4 3 3 1 — tmp+1 — str
perc: tamtam
No.44 of the *Mörike Lieder*. Originally for voice & piano; arr. for chorus & orchestra by the composer (1892).

C. Fischer	Kalmus	MWV	Peters

Italian Serenade <1887> 8'

solo viola
2 2 2 2 — 2 0 0 0 — str
Originally for string quartet (1887). 1892 version for orchestra was to be the first movement of a larger work which was never finished. The fragment was edited by Max Reger and published posthumously. Wolf had at first alternated solo English horn with solo viola; later changed his mind and gave it all to the viola.

Bote & Bock	Breitkopf	Kalmus	Luck's	MWV

Penthesilea <1883–1885> 27'

3[1.2.pic] 3[1.2.Eh] 2 3 — 4 4 3 1 — tmp+4 — hp — str
perc: tri, sd, cym, sus cym, bd, tamtam
1. Aufbruch der Amazonen nach Troja 6'
2. Der Traum Penthesileas vom Rosenfest 5'
3. Kämpfe, Leidenschaften, Wahnsinn, Vernichtung 16'

Alkor	Breitkopf	Kalmus	MWV

Scherzo & Finale <1876> 15'

3[1.2.pic] 2 2 2 — 4 3 3 1 — 2tmp+1 — str
perc: Scherzo requires 2tmp; Finale requires tmp+2.
Originally for piano as *Rondo capriccioso*, op.15. Orchestrated by the composer as 2 mvts of a projected but unfinished symphony; scoring completed by H. Schultz.
Scherzo 8'
Finale 7'

Alkor	Breitkopf	Kalmus	Luck's

Spanisches Liederbuch: Two Sacred Songs <1891> 8'

mezzo-soprano solo
0 0 3 0 — 2 0 0 0 — str 5t
Instrumentation by Igor Stravinsky.
1. Herr, was trägt der Boden hier 5'
2. Wunden trägst du 3'

Boosey

Wolfe, Julia 1958-

(b Philadelphia, 18 Dec 1958). American

Cruel Sister <2004> 35'

str[min 6.5.4.3.1]

Red Poppy

Tell Me Everything <1994> 8'

1 1 1 1 — 1 1 1 0 — asx — 2perc — hp[ampd] — pf — str
perc: bd, glock, vib, 4sus cym, chain
May be performed with single strings, in which case the strings should be amplified for balance.

Red Poppy

The Vermeer Room <1989> 15'

1[fl/afl] 1 1[cl/bcl] 1 — 1 1 1 1[btbn] 0 — tmp+1 — hp — pf — str
perc: vib, crot, glock, brake dr, tamtam, tri, cym

Red Poppy

Window of Vulnerability 9'

3[1.2/pic.3/pic] 3 3[1.2.3/bcl] 3[1.2.cbn] — 4 3 3 1 — tmp+4 — hp — pf, Hammond org — str
perc: szl cym, hi-hat, sd, glock, xyl, vib, crot, 2bd, 2anvil, 3sus cym, 2tomtom, 2brake dr, 2tri, 3tamtam, 4cowbell
"Organ" = sampled Hammond B-3 organ performed on synthesizer with pitch wheel, amplified through Leslie speakers.

Red Poppy

Wolf-Ferrari, Ermanno 1876-1948

(b Venice, 12 Jan 1876; d Venice, 21 Jan 1948). Italian

Concertino, English Horn, op.34 <1947> 25'

0 0 0 0 — 2 0 0 0 — str
1. Preludio: Andante 7'
2. Capriccio: Allegro vivace 5'
3. Adagio 8'
4. Finale: Allegro moderato, pesante 5'

Leuckart

L'amore medico (Doctor Cupid): Intermezzo <1913> 3'

2 3[1.2.Eh] 3[1.2.bcl] 2 — 4 1 0 0 — tmp — hp — str

Kalmus

I gioielli della Madonna (The Jewels of the Madonna):   *4'*
Intermezzo No.1 (arr. Langey) <1911>

1 1 2 1 — 2 0 0 0 — pf — str

Arr. Langey. Additional parts for 2 cornets and one trombone consist of
nothing but cues; may be used if other instruments are missing.
    This is one of several versions of this work.

Luck's	Weinberger

I gioielli della Madonna (The Jewels of the Madonna):   *3'*
Intermezzo No.2 (arr. Langey) <1911>

1 1 2 1 — 2 2 1 0 — pf — str

Arr. Langey. This is one of several versions of this work.

Luck's	Weinberger

I gioielli della Madonna (The Jewels of the Madonna):   *3'*
Intermezzo No.2 (large orchestra) <1911>

3[1.2.pic] 3[1.2.Eh] 3[1.2.bcl] 3 — 4 3 3 1 — tmp+1 — hp — str
perc: tri

Kalmus	Luck's

Il segreto di Susanna (The Secret of Suzanne): Overture   *4'*
<1909>

3[1.2.pic] 2 2 2 — 4 2 3 0 — tmp — hp — str

Kalmus	Luck's	Weinberger

Sinfonia da camera, op.8, B-flat major   *37'*
(Kammersymphonie)

1 1 1 1 — 1 0 0 0 — pf — str[1.1.1.1.1]
1. Allegro moderato	*11'*
2. Adagio	*11'*
3. Vivace con spirito	*5'*
4. Adagio; Allegro moderato	*10'*

Kalmus

Wölfl, Joseph   **1773-1812**

(b Salzburg, 24 Dec 1773; d London, 21 May 1812). Austrian

Concerto, Piano, No.7, op.64, E major   *17'*

1 0 2 2 — 2 0 0 0 — tmp — str
I. Allegro moderato	*12'*
II. Andante	*2'*
III. Allegro	*3'*

Harmonic

Wolpe, Stefan   **1902-1972**

(b Berlin, 25 Aug 1902; d New York, 4 April 1972). American composer of German
birth and Russian parentage

C = Austin Clarkson, *Stefan Wolpe Chronological Catalog*, found on the
official website of the Stefan Wolpe Society, wolpe.org.

Chamber Piece No.1, C.161 <1964>   *9'*

1 2[1.Eh] 1 1 — 1 1 1 0 — pf — str 5t
Ed. Austin Clarkson.

Peer

Chamber Piece No.2, C.167 <1967>   *4'*

1 1 1 1 — 1 1 1 0 — 1perc — pf — str[1.0.1.1.1]
perc: bd, glock, vib, tmp
Ed. Austin Clarkson & Anthony Korf.

Southern

The Man from Midian, C.100: Part Two <1942>   *17'*

3[1.2/pic.3/pic] 3[1.2.Eh] 3[1/Ebcl.2/Ebcl.bcl] 3[1.2.cbn] — 4 3 2 1
— asx, tsx — tmp+4 — hp — pf — str[16.14.12.10.8]
perc: bd, cym, sd, tamtam, glock, xyl, guiro, cast
Originally a ballet for 2 pianos; orchestral version of Part Two by Antony
Beaumont, 2007.
8. Conversation with God	*3'*
9. Moses Meets Aaron	*1'*
10. March Through the Red Sea	*4'*
11. Restlessness	*1'*
12. Aaron's Desperation	*1'*
13. Joshua's Pleading	*1'*
14. Bacchanal	*1'*
15. Return of Moses	*1'*
16. Moses Walks Among the People	*1'*
17. Gathering of People	*3'*

McGinnis

The Man from Midian, C.100: Moses Meets Aaron, &   *4'*
March Through the Red Sea <1942>

3[1.2.pic] 2 2 2[1.cbn] — 3 0 0 0 — asx, tsx — str[12.10.8.6.4]
Mvts. 9 & 10 from the ballet, originally for 2 pianos; orchestral version
by Antony Beaumont, 2008.
Moses Meets Aaron	*1'*
March Through the Red Sea	*3'*

McGinnis

Passacaglia, op.23, C.66 <1936–1937>   *13'*

3[1.2.pic] 3[1.2.Eh] 3[1.2.bcl] 3[1.2.cbn] — 4 3 3 1 — tmp+2 — hp
— str
perc: bd, sd, xyl
Originally for piano (*On an All-Interval Row*, C.62: No.4 of *4 Studies on
Basic Rows*); arr. by the composer.

Presser

Piece for Two Instrumental Units, C.158 <1963>   *12'*

1 1 0 0 — 1perc — pf — str[1.0.0.1.1]
perc: tamtam, gong, glock, xyl, vib, bongos

Peer

Symphony No.1, C.138 <1955–1956>   *23'*

4[1/pic.2.3.pic] 4[1.2.3.Eh] 4[1.2.3.bcl] 4[1.2.3.cbn] — 4 3 3 1 —
tmp+4 — hp — pf/cel — str
perc: bd, cym, hi-hat, sd, tambn, gong, glock, xyl, 4tomtom, steelpan, 3bongos,
steelplate, 2sus cym, 2foghorns [or conch shells]
Ed. Robert Falck.
I. Not too slow	*5'*
II. Charged	*8'*
III. Alive	*10'*

Peer

Two Studies for Large Orchestra, C.52 (Zwei Studien für   *6'*
grosses Orchester) <1933>

2[1/pic.2/pic] 3[1.2.Eh] 4[1.2.3.bcl] 3[1.2.cbn] — 4 4 3 1 — tmp+1
— hp — cel — str
perc: bd, cym, sd, tamtam
First 4 bars of *Ouvertüre* have been lost.
   Ed. Martin Brody & Matthew Greenbaum.
I. Ouvertüre	*2'*
II. Pastorale in Form einer Passacaglia	*4'*

Peer

Wood, Hugh   1932-

(b Parbold, Lancashire, 27 June 1932). English

Beginnings: Three Early Songs, op.54   15'

solo mezzo-soprano
str
  1. *Tom O'Bedlam's Song (Anonymous)*   _'
  2. *Why East Wind Chills (Dylan Thomas)*   _'
  3. *O Unicorn Among the Cedars (W.H. Auden)* _'

  Chester

Concerto, Violin, No.2, op.50 <2009>   25'

3[1.2/pic.3/pic] 3[1.2.3/Eh] 3[1.2.3/bcl] 3[1.2.3/cbn] — 4 3 3 1 —
3perc — hp — pf/cel — str
perc: bd, sd, sus cym, cym, xyl, tri, tambn, whip, cast, 3bongos, 2tamtam, 2gong,
4woodblk
  I. Allegro appassionato e energico   _'
  II. Larghetto, calmo   _'
  III. Vivacissimo   _'

  Chester

Divertimento, op.51 <2007>   10'

str
  I. Maestoso   _'
  II. Adagietto   _'
  III. Allegro molto, feroce _'

  Chester

Woollen, Russell   1923-1994

(b Hartford, CT, 7 Jan 1923; d Charlottesville, VA, 16 March 1994). American

Elegy & Divertimento for Strings   11'

str
  Elegy   5'
  Divertimento 6'
  Calabrese

Wuorinen, Charles   1938-

(b New York, 9 June 1938). American

Chamber Concerto, Violoncello & 10 Players <1963>   17'

solo violoncello
1 1 1 1 — 2perc — pf — vn, va, db
  Peters

Concerto, Piano, No.3 <1983>   27'

3[1.2.3/pic] 2 3[1.2.bcl] 2 — 4 2 3 1 — tmp+3 — hp — str
perc: vib, bd, 2tri, 4herdbells, 4tomtoms or congas
  Peters

Contrafactum <1969>   20'

3[1.2.3/pic] 3[1.2.3/Eh] 3[1.2.3/bcl] 3[1.2.3/cbn] — 4 3 3 2 —
2tmp+5 — 2pf — str
  Peters

Crossfire <1984>   11'

3[1.2.pic] 2 3[1/Ebcl.2.bcl] 2 — 4 3 3 1 — tmp+2 — pf — str
perc: xyl, marim, glock, chimes, vib; played by tmp: bd
  Peters

Grand Bamboula <1971>   6'

str[min 6.5.4.4.2]
  Peters

Machault mon chou <1988>   11'

2 2[1.2/Eh] 3[1.2.bcl] 3[1.2.cbn] — 4 2 3 1 — tmp+1 — hp — str
perc: chimes, glock
Material is drawn from the *Messe de Nostre Dame* by Guillaume de
Machaut.

  Peters

The Magic Art <1979>   75'

1[1/pic] 2[1.2/Eh] 1[1/bcl] 2 — 2 2 1 0 — tmp — hp — pf — str[min
6.4.3.3.1]
An instrumental masque drawn from the works of Henry Purcell. Suites
of various lengths may be constructed from the individual movements.
  1.   6'
  2.   7'
  3.   6'
  4.   7'
  5.   6'
  6.   6'
  7. 17'
  8. 15'
  9.   5'

  Peters

Movers and Shakers <1984>   27'

3[1.2.3/pic] 3[1.2.3/Eh] 3[incl Ebcl,bcl] 3[1.2.3/cbn] — 4 3 3 1 —
tmp+5 — hp — pf — str
perc: xyl, glock, vib, chimes, marim, bd, 8bongos, 11tomtoms, 6herdbells, tmp2,
tmp3
  Peters

A Reliquary for Igor Stravinsky <1975>   17'

4[1.2.3.4/pic] 2 2[1.2/bcl] 3[incl cbn] — 4 2 3 1 — tmp+4 — hp — pf
— str
Incorporates fragments from an unfinished orchestra piece by Stravinsky.
  Peters

Two-Part Symphony <1978>   23'

3 2 2 2 — 4 2 2 1 — tmp+4 — hp — pf — str
  Part 1   12'
  Part 2   11'
  Peters

Wyner, Yehudi   1929-

(b Calgary, AB, 1 June 1929). Canadian-born American composer

Concerto, Piano (Chiavi in mano) <2004>   20'

2[1.2/pic] 2 2 2 — 4 2 3 1 — tmp+1 — str
perc: bd, bongos, sus cym (or brake dr), 2tomtom, washboard
A chamber orchestra version exists, with reduced brass: 3 2 1 0.
  AMP

Epilogue <1996>   9'

2[1.2/pic] 2[1.2/Eh] 2[1.2/bcl] 3[1.2.cbn] — 4 2 2 0 — tmp/crot — str
perc: crot[E5]
In memory of Jacob Druckman.
    Two reduced versions also available: one without trombones and
contrabassoon, the other without trumpets, trombones and contrabassoon.
  AMP

Fragments from Antiquity <1978>   25'

solo soprano
2[1.2/pic] 2 3[1.2.bcl] 2 — 4 2 2 0 — tmp+2 — str
perc: bd, Chinescym, hi-hat, set, tamtam, marim, crot, bongos, guiro, 2tomtom, 2 brake dr (pitched)
 I. A Night of Spring River and Flower Moon _'
 II. But it Breaks My Spirit _'
 III. …And the Time is Passing _'
 IV. The Time of Afterdeath _'
 V. Here I Lie Mournful with Desire _'

> AMP

Give Thanks for All Things <2010>   37'

chorus soloists: SABar
1[fl/pic] 1 1 — 1 1 1 0 — 2perc — hp — pf — str[min 6.6.4.4.2]
perc: bd, cym, sd, tamtam, bongos, bell, 4tomtom, 2woodblk
 I. Psalms 148 and 150 '
 II. Dear Lord, be good to me _'
 III. Psalm: Give thanks for all things _'
 IV. We well know that death shall come. Ay, but to die… _'
 V. Dear Lord, be good to me (II) _
 VI. Dirge for two veterans _'
 VII. Dear Lord, be good to me (III) _'
 VIII. Psalms 148 and 150 (reprise) _

> AMP

Intermedio <1974; rev 2004>   16'

solo soprano (textless)
str
 1. Torch Song _'
 2. Up Tempo _'
 3. Elegy _'

> AMP

Lyric Harmony <1995; rev 1996>   19'

2[1.2/pic] 2[1.2/Eh] 2[1.2/bcl] 3[1.2.cbn] — 4 2 3 1 — 2perc — hp — str
perc: bd, sus cym, sd, templeblks, tmp, 4tomtom, 4bongos

> AMP

Prologue and Narrative <1994>   28'

solo violoncello
3[1.2.pic] 3[1.2.Eh] 3[1.2.bcl] 2 — 4 3 3 1 — str

> AMP

Tuscan Triptych (Echoes of Hannibal) <1985; rev 2002>   25'

str
 I. Tense and incisive _'
 II. Interlude with Codetta _'
 III. Alla marcia _'
 IV. Postlude _'

> AMP

X

Xenakis, Yannis   1922 - 2001

(b Braïla, ?29 May 1922; d Paris, 4 Feb 2001). French composer of Greek parentage

Akrata <1964–1965>   12'

1[pic] 1 3[Ebcl.bcl.cbcl] 3[1bn, 2cbn] — 2 3 2 1 — [no str]

> Boosey

Anaktoria <1969>   11'

0 0 1 1[1/opt cbn] — 1 0 0 0 — str 5t
Contrabassoon is optional.

> Salabert

Analogique A <1958>   6'

3vn, 3vc, 3db

> Salabert

Atrees <1958–1962>   15'

1 0 2[1.bcl] 0 — 1 1 1 0 — 3perc — vn, vc

> Salabert

Eonta <1963–1964>   18'

0 0 0 0 — 0 2 3 0 — pf — [no str]
Brass sit, stand, move around.

> Boosey

Metastaseis <1953–1954>   8'

2[1.pic] 2 1[bcl] 0 — 3 2 2 0 — tmp+3 — str[12.12.8.8.6]
perc: xyl, woodblk, tri, sd, field dr, bd

> Boosey

Pithoprakta <1955–1956>   10'

0 0 0 0 — 0 0 2 0 — 2perc — str[12.12.8.8.6]
perc: xyl, woodblk

> Boosey

ST/48—1,240162 <1959–1962>   11'

2[1.pic] 2 2[1.bcl] 2[1.cbn] — 2 2 2 0 — tmp+3 — str[8.8.6.6.4]
perc: vib, marim, templeblks, woodblk, 4tomtoms

> Boosey

Syrmos <1959>   15'

str[12vn, 4vc, 2db]

> Boosey

Y

Yardumian, Richard   1917-1985

(b Philadelphia, 5 April 1917; d Bryn Athyn, PA, 15 Aug 1985). American composer of Armenian descent

Armenian Suite <1937>   18'

4[1.2.3.pic] 4[1.2.3.Eh] 4[1.2.Ebcl.bcl] 4[1.2.3.cbn] — 6 4 4 1 — tmp+5 — hp — str

1. Introduction: Harvest	1'
2. Song: Reminiscences of a Song from Childhood	3'
3. Lullaby	2'
4. Dance I: Love Song	1'
5. Interlude: The Bells Rang Out Good Morning	3'
6. Dance II: Allegro spiritoso	3'
7. Finale	5'

> Elkan-Vogel

Cantus animae et cordis (Song of the Soul and the Heart) <1955>   15'

str 4t or str orch
Originally for string quartet; arranged by the composer for string orchestra.

> Elkan-Vogel

Yasinitsky, Gregory   1953-

(b San Francisco, CA, 3 October 1953). American

As the Sun Descended   17'

solo trumpet
tmp — str

I. The Clouds Were Streaked with Coral	6'
II. And the Sky Was Cobalt Blue	5'
III. As the Sun Descended from the Heavens	6'

> Hoyt

Yi, Chen   1953-

see under: Chen Yi ["Chen" is surname]

Yoshimatsu, Takashi   1953-

(b Tokyo, 18 Mar 1953). Japanese

Threnody to Toki, op.12   12'

pf — str[12.12.8.8.6]
Double string orchestra, seated antiphonally. May be done with 6vn, 2va, 2vc, db, & piano.

> Ongaku

Youmans, Vincent   1898-1946

(b New York, 27 Sept 1898; d Denver, 5 April 1946). American

Tea for Two

see under: Shostakovich, Dmitry, 1906-1975
                 Tahiti Trot

Young, Kenneth   1955-

(b 11 Nov 1955). New Zealander

Concerto, Euphonium <2004>   24'

2[1.2/pic] 2[1.2/Eh] 2[1.2/bcl] 2[1.2/cbn] — 2 2 3 1 — tmp+2 — hp — cel — str
perc: bd, cym, sus cym, sd, td, tamtam, glock, 5rototom

I. Larghetto	5'
II. Allegro	4'
III. Adagio assai	9'
IV. Moderato	6'

> SOUNZ

Concerto, Piano <2004>   25'

2[1.2/pic] 2 2 2 — 2 2 0 0 — tmp — str

> SOUNZ

Dance <1997>   14'

3[1.2/pic.3/pic] 3[1.2.Eh] 3[1.2.3/Ebcl] 3[1.2.cbn] — 4 3 3 1 — tmp+3 — hp — cel — str
perc: sd, td, tri, tambn, glock, chimes, crot, cast, 2bd, 2sus cym, talking dr, 5rototom

> SOUNZ

Lux Aeterna <2009>   16'

2[1/pic.2/afl/pic] 2[1.2/Eh] 2[1.2/bcl] 2 — 4 2 3 1 — tmp+3 — hp — str
perc: bd, tri, tamtam, glock, marim, vib, talking dr

> SOUNZ

Remembering <2007>   13'

solo violin
2[1.2/pic] 2 2 2 — 2 2 0 0 — 1perc — hp — str
perc: sus cym, glock

> SOUNZ

Saffire Concerto (Concerto for 4 Guitars & Orchestra) <2007; rev 2008>   25'

2[1.2/pic] 2[1.2/Eh] 2 2 — 2 2 0 0 — 1perc — hp — cel — str
perc: cym, sus cym, szl cym, sd, glock, vib, crot, woodblk, cast
N.B.: One of the 4 solo guitars is an "octave-guitar."

> SOUNZ

Symphony [No.1]   41'

solo soprano
3[1.2.3/pic] 3[1.2.3Eh] 3[1.2.3/Ebcl/bcl] 3[1.2.3/cbn] — 4 3 3 1 — tmp+2 — hp — pf/cel — str
perc: bd, sus cym, szl cym, sd, td, tri, tamtam, glock, xyl, vib, chimes, crot, 3rototom, metal windchimes

I. Andante	13'
II. Presto	5'
III. Largo	10'
IV. Larghetto rubato; Andante moderato	13'

> SOUNZ

Symphony No.2 <2005>   25'

3[1/pic/afl.2/pic.3/pic] 3[1.2.3/Eh] 3[1.2.3/bcl] 3[1.2.3/cbn] —
4 3[1.2.3/flug] 3 1 — tmp+4 — hp — cel — str
perc: bd, cym, szl cym, hi-hat, td, tri, tamtam, glock, xyl, marim, woodblk,
templeblks, whip, cast, 3sus cym, 2sd, 4rototom, gamelan gong

> SOUNZ

Virgen de la Esperanza (The Virgin of Hope) <1997>   15'

3[1.2.3/pic] 3[1.2.3/Eh] 3[1.2.3/Ebcl] 3[1.2.cbn] — 4 3 3 1 — tmp+2
— hp — cel — str
perc: bd, cym, sus cym, tamtam, crot

> SOUNZ

Ysaÿe, Eugene   1858-1931

(b Liege, 16 July 1858; d Brussels, 12 May 1931). Belgian

Chant d'hiver, op.15 <1902>   12'

solo violin
2 2 2 2 — 2 0 0 0 — tmp — str

> Enoch   Kalmus

Exil!, op.25 (Exile!)   8'

str[no vc, no db]
Strings divided into eight parts:
    on the [conductor's] left: violin1 A&B, violin2 A&B
    on the right: violin3 A&B, viola1, viola2

> mph

Z

Zach, Jan   1699-1773

(b Celákovice, Bohemia, bap. 13 Nov 1699; d Ellwangen, 24 May 1773). Czech

Tantum ergo, B-flat major

see: Mozart, Wolfgang Amadeus (1756-1791)
    Tantum ergo, K.142

Zaimont, Judith Lang   1945-

(b Memphis, 8 Nov 1945). American

Chroma (Northern Lights) <1986>   11'

1 1 1 1 — 1 0 0 0 — 1perc — str
perc: sus cym, tri, tambn, tamtam, belltree, woodblk, templeblk, glass chimes,
finger cym
A reworking of the composer's *Borealis*, a movement of the mixed
quintet *Sky Curtains* (1984).

> Sounds Alive!

Elegy for Strings <1998>   9'

str
This work became the 2nd movement of *Remember Me* (Symphony
No.2).

> MMB

JoyDance in Spring <2012>   4'

str
Numerous solos scattered throughout.

> Subito

Monarchs <1988>   18'

3[1.2.pic] 3[1.2.Eh] 4[1.2.Ebcl.bcl] 2 — 4 3 3 1 — tmp+3 — pf/cel
— str
perc: bd, tri, tamtam, whip, sd, sus cym, vib, marim, glock, cym, 3tomtoms,
2woodblks

> Subito

Pure, Cool (Water) — Symphony No.4 <2011–2013>   48'

2 2 3[1.2.bcl] 2 — 4 1 3 1 — tmp+3 — str
perc: claves, tamtam, ratch, sd, field dr, bd, vib, marim, marac, finger cym, tri,
4tomtom, cym, sus cym, crystal bell [G]
Mvts 1, 2, 4, and 5 may be performed independently.
    Tmp also covers several perc insts. Brass in mvt 3 are asked at times to
blow through the instruments without producing a note.
    I. in a current (The River)   12'
    II. as a solid (Ice)   8'
    III. falling drops (Rainshower)   7'
    IV. still (The Tarn)   8'
    V. in waves and torrents (Ocean)   13'

> Subito

Remember Me (Symphony No.2) <1998–1999>   33'

str
2nd movement may be performed separately.
1. Ghosts   13'
2. Elegy   9'
3. Dancin' Over My Grave 11'

> MMB

Sacred Service for the Sabbath Evening <1975>   60'

baritone (or alto) solo   SATB chorus
2[1.2/pic] 2[1.2/Eh] 2 2 — 2 2 2 0 — tmp+ — pf — str
perc: cym, sus cym, tri, chimes, whip, glock
Brief passages for solo quartet (SATB drawn from the chorus).

> ECS

Stillness; Poem for Orchestra <2005>   20'

2[1.2/pic] 2[1.2/Eh] 2[1.2/bcl] 2 — 4 2 3 1 — tmp+3 — hp — cel[can
be played by perc] — str
perc: bd, cym, sus cym, sd, tamtam, vib, crot, woodblk, 3tri

> Subito

Symphony No.1 <1994>   28'

3[1.2.pic] 3[1.2.Eh] 3[1.2.bcl] 3[1.2.cbn] — 4 3 3 1 — tmp+4 — hp
— pf/cel — str
perc: bd, cym, sus cym, sd, td, toms, 2tri, tambn, tamtam, glock, vib, chimes, whip
One of the percussion parts may be covered by the timpanist.
1. Moderato   12'
2. Adagio molto - Molto più mosso 10'
3. Brisky, military   6'

> Subito

Tarantelle: Overture for Orchestra <1985>   7'

3[1.2.pic] 3[1.2.Eh] 2 2 — 4 2 3 1 — tmp+2(or 3) — str
perc: tri, cym, sus cym, woodblk, glock, tamtam, bd, sd, 2tomtom

> ECS

Zaninelli, Luigi   1932-

(b Raritan, NJ, 30 March 1932). American

Americana   8'

3[1.2.pic] 2 3[1.2.bcl] 2 — 4 4[tp4 opt] 3 1 — tmp+2 — hp or pf —
str
perc: sd, tamtam, glock, xyl, vib, chimes

> Shawnee

Aria festiva; for Trumpet, Trumpet Choir & Orchestra   5'

solo trumpet   trumpet choir (12 tp; 6 real parts)
2 2 2 2 — 3 0 3 1 — tmp+4 — str
perc: bd, cym, tamtam, glock, xyl, vib

> Zaninelli

Autumn Music   6'

solo trumpet or alto saxophone
str

> Shawnee

Battle Hymn of the Republic   7'

optional chorus or solo voice
3[1.2.pic] 2 3[1.2.bcl] 2 — 4 3 3 1 — tmp+7 — pf or hp — str
perc: bd, sus cym, sd, tamtam, glock, vib, chimes

> Zaninelli

Beginnings   22'

soprano (narrating & singing)
1 1 1 1 — 2 0 0 0 — 2perc — hp — pf — str
perc: bd, sus cym, sd, tri, tamtam, glock, xyl, vib
Father   _'
Mother   _'
Reading   _'
Alphabet   _'
Lightning Bugs _'
The Moon   _'
The Music Box   _'
On the Train   _'
The Memory   _'

> Zaninelli

Canto   8'

solo flute
tmp+1 — pf — str
perc: gong

> Elkan-Vogel

Capriccio spiritoso <1983>   6'

2[1.2/pic] 2 3[1.2.bcl] 2 — 4 3 3 1 — tmp+5 — hp — str
perc: bd, sus cym, sd, tri, gong, glock, xyl, vib

> Zaninelli

Concertino, Piano, 17 Winds & Percussion   14'

2 1 2[1.2/bcl] 1 — 4 3 3 1 — tmp+4 — [no str]
perc: bd, sus cym, tri, tamtam, glock, xyl

> Zaninelli

Five American Gospel Songs <1986>   11'

soprano solo
2[1.pic] 1 2[1.bcl] 1 — 4 3 3 1 — 6perc — hp — str
perc: bd, sus cym, tri, tambn, tamtam, glock, xyl, vib, chimes
1. His Eye is on the Sparrow   3'
2. The Sweet By and By   2'
3. Amazing Grace   2'
4. Old Time Religion   2'
5. Shall We Gather at the River 2'

> Zaninelli

Jubilate <1991>   7'

optional chorus SATB
2 2 2 2 — 4 3 3 1 — 5perc — hp — str
perc: bd, cym, tamtam, glock, chimes

> Zaninelli

A Lexicon of Beasties <1968>   26'

narrator   solo piano
1 1 1 1 — 1 1 1 1 — 2perc — opt str
perc: tmp, bd, sus cym, tri, tamtam, glock, xyl, vib, finger cym

> Zaninelli

Night Voices <1980>   14'

2[1.2/pic] 2 3[1.2.bcl] 2 — 4 3 3 1 — 2perc — pf, cel — str
perc: sus cym, tamtam, vib

> Zaninelli

The Steadfast Tin Soldier <1983>   23'

narrator
0 1 1 1 — 1 1 1 1 — 2perc — pf — str or str 5t
perc: bd, sus cym, sd, tamtam, glock, xyl, vib

> Zaninelli

The Tale of Peter Rabbit   19'

narrator
1[1/pic] 1 1[1/bcl] 1 — 1 1 0 1 — 1perc — hp — pf — str[no db]
perc: tmp, sus cym, tamtam, glock, xyl, vib

> Zaninelli

Through Eudora's Eyes <1997>   9'

narrator (optional)
3perc — str
perc: bd, sus cym, sd, tambn, glock, xyl, vib, chimes
Optional narration (from Eudora Welty) precedes each mvt; total duration
with narration: 12'.
To the Little Store	1'
Butterflies	3'
The Church	3'
Armistice Day	2'

> Zaninelli

Zappa, Frank   1940-1993

(b Baltimore, 21 Dec 1940; d Laurel Canyon, Los Angeles, 4 Dec 1993). American

Durpree's Paradise   8'

2 2[1/Eh.2/Eh] 3[1.2.bcl] 1[1/cbn] — 2 2 2 1 — 3perc — hp —
2pf[1/cel.2/cel] — str[3vn.2va.2vc.db]
perc: xyl, vib, cym, cast, Chinescym, 3chimes, 3bd, 3sd, 3tamtam, 2marim,
2glock, 2gong, 2marac, 2woodblk, 3whip, 2popgun

> Munchkin

The Perfect Stranger <1984>   13'

2[1/afl.2/afl] 2[1/Eh.2/Eh] 3[1.2.bcl] 1 — 2 2 2 1 — 3perc — hp —
2pf[1/cel.2/cel] — str[3vn.2va.2vc.db]
perc: tambn, vib, xyl, tamtam, Chinescym, 3chimes, 3bd, 3sd, 2marac, 2slgh-bells,
2cast, 2woodblk, 2tri, 2glock, 2marim, 2gong, 2belltree, 2whip, popgun

> Munchkin

Zemlinsky, Alexander   1871-1942

(b Vienna, 14 Oct 1871; d Larchmont, NY, 15 March 1942). Austrian

Lyrische Symphonie, op.18 (Lyric Symphony)   48'
<1922–1923>

solo soprano & baritone
4[incl 2pic] 3[incl Eh] 4[incl bcl] 3[incl cbn] — 4 3 3 1 — tmp+3 —
hp — cel, harm — str
perc: xyl, tamtam, tambn, tri, cym, bd, sd
1. Ich bin friedlos	11'
2. Mutter, der junge Prinz	7'
3. Du bist die Abendwolke	7'
4. Sprich zu mir, Geliebter	8'
5. Befrei' mich von den Banden	2'
6. Vollende denn das letzte Lied	5'
7. Friede, mein Herz	8'

> Universal

Psalm 23, op.14 <1910>   10'

chorus
4[1.2.3/pic.4/pic] 3[1.2.3/Eh] 3 3 — 4 3 3 1 — tmp+3 — 2hp — cel
— str
perc: glock, tambn, tri, bd, cym

> Universal

Die Seejungfrau (The Mermaid) <1902–1903>   40'

4[1.2.3/pic.4/pic] 3[1.2.Eh] 4[1.2.Ebcl.bcl] 3 — 6 3 4 1 — tmp+2 —
2hp — str
perc: cym, sus cym, tri, glock, chimes
Critical ed. (2013) by Antony Beaumont includes in the score both
versions of the 2nd mvt: the original and the revised.
I. Sehr mässig bewegt	15'
II. Sehr bewegt, rauschend	12'
III. Sehr gedehnt, mit schmerzvollem Ausdruck	13'

> Universal

Sinfonietta, op.23 <1934>   21'

2[1.2/pic] 2[1.2/Eh] 2[1.2/Ebcl] 2 — 4 3 3 0 — tmp+3 — hp — str
perc: cym, sd, tomtom, tri, tambn, glock, xyl
Ed. Antony Beaumont.
I. Sehr lebhaft	7'
II. Ballade: Sehr gemessen, doch nicht schleppend	8'
III. Rondo: Sehr lebhaft	6'

> Universal

Six Songs after Poems by Maeterlinck, op.13   16'
<1910–1913; rev orchd 1913, 1922>

solo voice (medium)
4[1/pic.2/pic.3.4] 3[1.2.Eh] 3[1.2.bcl] 2 — 2 3 3 0 — tmp+2 — hp —
cel/pf, harm — str
perc: cym, glock, bd, tri, tamtam
Universal also publishes an arrangement by Gösta Neuwirth for voice and
chamber orchestra, as well as arrangements of two of the songs (Nos.2 &
5) by Erwin Stein for chamber ensemble (fl, cl, pf, harm, str 5t).
1. Die drei Schwestern	3'
2. Die Mädchen mit den verbundenen Augen	2'
3. Lied der Jungfrau	2'
4. Als ihr Geliebter schied	2'
5. Und kehrt er einst Heim	3'
6. Sie kam zum Schloss gegangen	4'

> Universal

Symphony [No.1], D minor <1892–1893>   33'

2 2 2 2 — 4 2 3 0 — tmp — str
Ed. Antony Beaumont. Elsewhere listed as Symphony [No.2], counting a
fragment from 1891 (E minor) as No.1.
I. Allegro ma non troppo	11'
II. Scherzo	6'
III. Sehr innig und breit	8'
IV. Finale: Moderato	8'

> Ricordi

Symphony [No.2], B-flat major <1897>   43'

2 2 2 2 — 4 2 3 1 — tmp — str
Unnumbered by the publisher. Elsewhere listed as Symphony [No.3],
counting a fragment from 1891 (E minor) as No.1.
I. Allegro. Schnell, mit Feuer und Kraft	14'
II. Nicht zu schnell (Scherzo)	9'
III. Adagio	9'
IV. Moderato	11'

> Universal

Zwei Gedichte (Two Poems) <1896; rev 1903 [no.1] >   6'

chorus
str
Ed. Antony Beaumont. No.2 orchestrated by the editor from short-score.
1. Frühlingsglaube	4'
2. Geheimnis	2'

> Ricordi

Zhanhao, He   1933-

see: He Zhanhao ("He" is surname)

Zhou Long   1953-

(b Beijing, 8 July 1953). Chinese-American

Concerto, Taiko & Timpani <2005>   15'

timpani: 5 kettles with bowl chime
taiko: kotsuzumi, shime, sumo, chu, odaiko
3[1.2.pic] 3[1.2.Eh] 3[1.2.bcl] 3[1.2.cbn] — 4 3 3 1 — 3perc — hp —
pf/cel — str
perc: tamtam, templeblks, claves, 3chu, smallbells, 4Peking opera gongs on mat
Introduction   _'
Section I   _'
Cadenza I   _'
Section II   _'
Cadenza II   _'
Section III   _'
Coda   _'

> Oxford

Da Qu <1991>   22'

solo percussion
3[all/pic] 3 3 3[1.2.cbn] — 4 3 3 1 — tmp+3 — hp — str[min
14.14.10.10.8]
perc: (orchestra) cym, tomtom, tamtam, glock, xyl, chimes, 3bd, 2sus cym,
2Chinescym, 3tri, 3gong, crot[3sets], 2marktree, templeblks[2sets], buttongong, 6
flat gongs on mat
(soloist) 7 paigu or rototoms, 10 flat gongs, vib, marim, glock, bangzi &
namibangzi (or 2woodblks), templeblks[2sets], tamtam, piccolo drum, dagu or bd.
Another version of this work, for Chinese traditional orchestra, is also
published by Oxford.
I. San Xu   10'
II. Zhong Xu   6'
III. Po   6'

> Oxford

The Enlightened <2005>   15'

3[1.2.pic] 3[1.2.Eh] 3[1.2.bcl] 3[1.2.cbn] — 4 3 3 1 — tmp+4 — hp
— str
perc: bd, sd, tomtom, tri, tamtam, glock, xyl, marim, vib, marktree, bongos, crot[E,
on tmp head], 2sus cym, 5woodblk, 5Chinese opera gongs (6-12"), high plastic
block

> Oxford

The Future of Fire <2001>   6'

chorus SATB *or* children's chorus SA
3[1/pic.2/pic.3] 3[1.2.Eh] 3[1.2.bcl] 3[1.2.cbn] — 4 2 3 1 — tmp+4
— hp — cel — str[min 14.14.10.10.8]
perc: bd, Chinescym, tri, tamtam, glock, xyl, marim, vib, chimes, crot, marktree,
claves, buttongong, 2sus cym, 4rototom, templeblks[min 2 sets], handgong placed
on mat

> Oxford

The Immortal <2004>   13'

3[1.2.pic] 3[1.2.Eh] 3[1.2.bcl] 3[1.2.cbn] — 4 3 3 1 — tmp+4 — hp
— str
perc: bd, sd, tamtam, gong, glock, xyl, marim, vib, marktree, 3sus cym, 4Chinese
opera gong, crot on tmp head

> Oxford

King Chu Doffs His Armour; Concerto for Pipa &   15'
Orchestra <1991>

pipa
2[1.pic] 2[1.2/Eh] 2 2 — 2[or 4] 2 2[1.btbn] 0 — tmp+2 — str
perc: bd, tamtam, xyl, marktree, woodblk, 2sus cym, 4rototom, chime[G#3], small
bells

> Oxford

Out of Tang Court, for Tang Ensemble & Orchestra   10'
<2000>

Tang Ensemble: pipa, erhu, zheng, Chinese percussion
3[fl/afl.pic1.pic2] 2 2[1.2/bcl] 2 — 4 3 3 0 — tmp+2 — str[min
14.12.10.10.6]
perc: Chinese perc soloist: fangzian, 6 hand gongs, 3 gongs, chimestones,
templeblks, 3Chinescym, windgong, tamtam, 3Chinese tomtom, 3 Chinese bd,
clappers, 3temple chimes, high block.
Orchestral perc: bd, cym, tamtam, glock, xyl, marim, vib, windchimes, small bells,
nipplegong, 3sus cym, 3Chinescym, 3tri, templeblks[2sets], claves[2pr]; tmp
covers some perc.

> Oxford

Poems from Tang <1995>   30'

solo string quartet
3[1.2.pic] 3[1.2.3/Eh] 3[1.2.3/bcl] 3[1.2.cbn] — 4 3 3 1 — tmp+4 —
hp — str
perc: bd, cym, sus cym, timbales, tri, tamtam, glock, xyl, marim, vib, chimes, crot,
marktree, bongos, claves, congas, 2Chinescym, 2tomtom, 2gong, 2templeblks,
bamboo windchimes, 4bells, nipplegong, Chinese opera gong, sharp block,
windgong, 2sus cym w/ chain, handgong on mat
I. Hut Among the Bamboo   _'
II. The Old Fisherman (Song of the Ch'in)   _'
III. Hearing the Monk Xun Play the Qin   _'
IV. Song of Eight Unruly Tipsy Poets   _'

> Oxford

The Rhyme of Taigu <2003>   12'

3[1.2.pic] 3[1.2.Eh] 3[1.2.bcl] 3[1.2.cbn] — 4 3 3 1 — tmp+3 — hp
— pf/cel — str
perc: tamtam, templeblks, bongos, claves, conga, 3bd, bowl chime, 4gongs(4"–6"),
2bells (2")
Ethnic Chinese equivalents may be substituted for the bass drums, bongos
and conga.

> Oxford

Zimmermann, Bernd Alois   1918-1970

(b Bliesheim, nr Cologne, 20 March 1918; d Grosskönigsdorf [now Pulheim], nr
Cologne, 10 Aug 1970). German

Dialog; Concerto, 2 Pianos <1960; rev 1965>   18'

5[1-4/pic.5/pic/afl] 3[1.2.3/Eh] 5[1.2.3/Ebcl.4.5/bcl] 3[1.2/cbn1.3/cbn2]
— 5 4 4[1.2.3.cb tbn] 1 — asx1/tsx, asx2/bsx — gtr — 3tmp+9 — hp
— cel — str[14.12.10.8.7]
perc: xyl, tri, whip, chimes, vib, sd, bd, cym, glock, gong, td, hi-hat, 2tamtams,
2marim, 4sus cym, 3cowbells; all 3tmp participate in the percussion

> Schott

Heroische Prosodie <1948>   18'

3[1.2.3/pic] 3[1.2.Eh] 2 3[1.2.cbn] — 4 3 3 1 — tmp+3 — 2hp — org
— str
perc: tri, sus cym, tamtam, field dr, sd, bd

> Schott

Sinfonie in einem Satz (Symphony in One Movement)   17'
<1951; rev 1953>

3[1.2/pic.3/pic] 3[1.2.3/Eh] 3[1.2.3/bcl] 3[1.2.3/cbn] — 4 3 3 1 —
2tmp+4 — hp — pf/cel — str
perc: sd, bd, field dr, tamtam, xyl, marim, vib, cym, sus cym, 2tomtom, logdrum
String complement: 12 vn1, 10 vn2, 10 vn3, 6 va1, 6 va2, 10 vc, 8 db.
An earlier (1951) version is also available from the publisher.

> Schott

Stille und Umkehr (Stillness and Return) <1970>   9'

4 4[1.2.3.Eh] 4[1.2.3.4/bcl] 1[cbn] — 4 2 2[1.cb tbn] 0 — asx —
accordion — 3perc — hp — vn, va, 3vc, 3db
perc: sd, td, 2sus cym[bowed], 2db bows, crot[a, d; bowed]

> Schott

Zwilich, Ellen Taaffe   1939-

(b Miami, 30 April 1939). American

American Concerto <1994>   16'

solo trumpet
2[1.pic] 2[1.Eh] 2[1.bcl] 2[1.cbn] — 4 2 3 1 — tmp+ — str
perc: szl cym, hi-hat, set, tamtam, 3sus cym

> Presser

Celebration for Orchestra <1984>   10'

4[incl pic] 3[incl Eh] 3[incl bcl] 3[incl cbn] — 4 3 3 1 — tmp+3 —
hp — pf/cel — str
perc: marim, tri, sus cym, chimes, 3vib, 2gongs, 2handbells[C#4,D#4]

> Merion

Commedia dell'arte <2012>   17'

solo violin
str
Individual members of the string orchestra at certain times play simple
percussion parts: slapstick, tambourine, toy drum, 4 tube bells,
windchimes. (The slapstick and tube bells are provided with the rental of
parts.)

I. Arlechinno	_'
II. Columbina	_'
III. Capitano	_'
IV. Cadenza and Finale	_'

> Presser

Concerto Grosso <1985>   14'

1 2[incl Eh] 0 1 — 2 0 0 0 — hpsd — str
Based on Handel's *Sonata in D for Violin & Continuo*, HWV 371.

1. Maestoso	3'
2. Presto	2'
3. Largo	5'
4. Presto	1'
5. Maestoso	3'

> Mobart

Concerto, Bass Trombone <1989>   19'

tmp+1 — str[max 12.12.12.12.8]
perc: cym
This 1989 work is not to be confused with the composer's *Trombone
Concerto* of 1988, *q.v.*

1. Andante con moto	7'
2. Largo	5'
3. Vivace	7'

> Merion

Concerto, Clarinet <2002>   28'

1 1 0 1 — 2 1[crt] 0 0 — 1perc — str
perc: bd, szl cym, hi-hat, sd, set, tamtam, glock, 3sus cym, 5tomtom
May be done with string sections, or with 5 individual string players (2vn,
va, vc, db).

I. quarter-note = 132	5'
II. Elegy: September 11	9'
III. dotted quarter-note = 112	6'
IV. quarter-note = 66	8'

> Presser

Concerto, Horn <1993>   15'

str
In one mvt.

> Presser

Concerto, Oboe <1990>   20'

2[1.pic] 3[1.ob d'am.Eh] 2 2[1.cbn] — 4 2[2crt] 0 0 — tmp+2 —
perc: szl cym, glock, xyl, crot, 2sus cym, 4rototom
In one mvt.

> Presser

Concerto, Trombone <1988>   21'

3[1.2.pic] 3[1.2.Eh] 3[1.2.bcl] 3[1.2.cbn] — 6 3 3 1 — tmp+3 — pf
— str
perc: bd, sus cym, szl cym, sd, gong, glock, vib, 4tomtom
This 1988 work is not to be confused with the composer's *Concerto for
Bass Trombone* of 1989, *q.v.*

I. Allegro	7'
II. Lento	7'
III. Allegro moderato	7'

> Presser

Concerto, Violin <1997>   26'

2[1.pic] 2[1.Eh] 2[1.bcl] 2[1.cbn] — 2 2 0 0 — tmp — hp — str

I. quarter-note = 62	9'
II. quarter-note = 58	7'
III. quarter-note = 152	10'

> Presser

Concerto, Violin & Violoncello <1991>   17'

2 2[1.Eh] 2 2 — 2 2 0 0 — tmp — str

1. quarter note = c.72	8'
2. quarter note = c.132	9'

> Merion

Fantasy for Orchestra <1993>   17'

3[1.2.pic] 3[1.2.Eh] 3[1.2.bcl] 3[1.2.cbn] — 4 3 3 1 — tmp+3 — str
perc: glock, marim, sus cym, hi-hat, tamtam, bd, 2chimes (2sets, offstage), 3sus
cym

I. Fantasia	_'
II. Temporale	_'
III. Lento	_'
IV. Allegro vivo	_'

> Presser

Jubilation <1995>   6'

3[1.2.pic] 3[1.2.Eh] 3[1.2.bcl] 3[1.2.cbn] — 4 3 3 1 — tmp+4 — str
perc: glock, vib, cym, szl cym, 3sus cym

> Merion

Millennium Fantasy <2000>   20'

solo piano
2[1.2/pic] 2[1.Eh] 2[1.bcl] 2[1.cbn] — 2 2 0 0 — 1perc — str
perc: szl cym, hi-hat, set, 3sus cym

I. quarter-note = 60	8'
II. quarter-note = 180	12'

> Presser

One Nation; Reflections on the Pledge of Allegiance   5'
<1991>

chorus
0 0 0 0 — 2 4 3 1 — tmp — str
4 of the brass (2tp, 2tbn) deployed antiphonally right & left.

> Merion

Openings <2001; rev 2003>   4'

2[1.pic] 2[1.Eh] 2[1.bcl] 2[1.cbn] — 4 2 3 1 — tmp+2 — str
perc: glock, chimes, 3sus cym

> Merion

Partita <2000>   18'

solo violin
str
   I. Introduction and Allegro   _'
   II. Serenade   _'
   III. Tango   _'
   IV. Meditation   _'
   V. Finale   _'

   Presser

Peanuts Gallery <1997>   13'

solo piano
1 2 2 2 — 2 0 0 0 — 1perc — str
   1. Schroeder's Beethoven Fantasy   2'
   2. Lullaby for Linus   2'
   3. Snoopy Does the Samba   2'
   4. Charlie Brown's Lament   3'
   5. Lucy Freaks Out   2'
   6. Peppermint Patty & Marcie Lead the Parade   2'

   Merion

Prologue & Variations <1983>   14'

str

   Merion

Rituals <2003>   26'

5 solo percussionists
2 2[1.Eh] 2[1.bcl] 0[1.cbn] — 4 2 3 1 — str
The 5 solo percussionists use a vast array of instruments, many of them not commercially manufactured or readily availble, but rather from various world cultures. The composer provides a comprehensive legend, inviting players to use it as a guide, allowing for modifications for differences in taste as well as the availability of particular instruments.
   I. Invocation   6'
   II. Ambulation   6'
   III. Remembrances   6'
   IV. Contests   8'

   Presser

Romance; For Violin & Chamber Orchestra <1993>   7'

1 1 0 1 — 0 0 0 0 — str

   Merion

Shadows <2011>   20'

solo piano
1 2[1.Eh] 2[1.bcl] 1 — 2 0 0 0 — 1perc — pf —
perc: set, sd, td, tomtom, bd, szl cym, hi-hat, crot, djembe, 3sus cym
   I. Tranquillo
   II. quarter-note = 44

   Presser

Symphony No.1; Three Movements for Orchestra <1982>   17'

2[1.2/pic] 2[1.Eh] 2[1.2/bcl] 2[1.2/cbn] — 4 2 3 1 — tmp+3 — hp — pf — str
perc: glock, vib, crot, szl cym, cym, sd, tambn, guiro, chimes, bass bow, 2sus cym, 2bd
   I. half-note = 44   7'
   II. quarter-note = 52   6'
   III. quarter-note = 144   4'

   Margun

Symphony No.2 (Cello Symphony) <1985>   25'

3[incl pic] 3[incl Eh] 3[incl Ebcl,bcl] 3[incl cbn] — 4 3 3 1 — tmp+3 — pf — str
perc: sd, crot, szl cym, whip, gong, bd, 3sus cym
   1. Allegro   9'
   2. Lento   10'
   3. Presto   6'

   Merion

Symphony No.3 <1992>   19'

3[incl pic] 3[incl Eh] 3[incl bcl] 3[incl cbn] — 4 3 3 1 — tmp+3 — str
perc: xyl, tambn, vib, hi-hat, 4sus cym, 2szl cym, 2tamtams, 2bd, set (incl 2 ped bd)
   Movement 1   9'
   Movement 2   4'
   Movement 3   6'

   Merion

Symphony No.4 (The Gardens) <2000>   27'

chorus   children's chorus (also playing handbells)
3[1.2.pic] 3[1.2.Eh] 3[1.2.bcl] 3[1.2.cbn] — 4 3 3 1 — tmp+3 — str
perc: bd, 3 sus cym, szl cym, hi-hat, tamtam, gong, glock, vib, chimes
Children's chorus sings only in 4th mvt; plays several handbell notes (cued in percussion) at end of 3rd mvt.
   1. Litany of Endangered Plants   5'
   2. Meditation on Living Fossils   6'
   3. A Pastoral Journey   8'
   4. The Children's Promise   8'

   Merion

Symphony No.5 <2008>   24'

3[1.2.pic] 3[1.2.bclbcl] 3[1.2.bcl] 3[1.2.cbn] — 4 3 3 1 — tmp+4 — str
perc: bd, szl cym, hi-hat, sd, marim, vib, spiral cymbal, dumbek, 3sus cym, 4tomtom, 4buttongongs
   I. quarter-note = 60   _'
   II. quarter-note = 154   _'
   III. quarter-note = 44   _'
   IV. quarter-note = 120   _'

   Presser

Upbeat <1999>   4'

3[1.2.pic] 3[1.2.Eh] 3[1.2.bcl] 3[1.2.cbn] — 4 3 3 1 — tmp+2 — str
perc: sd, szl cym, hi-hat, 3sus cym, set, 3tomtoms
Based on the violin partita in E major of J.S. Bach (BWV 1006).

   Merion

APPENDICES

APPENDIX A
CHORUS

Double Chorus

Mixed Chorus
    Large Orchestra
    Medium Orchestra
    Small Orchestra
    String Orchestra
    Without Strings

Female Chorus

Male Chorus

Children's Chorus

Works within the larger categories are subdivided by duration. If solo voices are also required, these are given in parentheses. Works that fit in more than one category are repeated as appropriate. Initial articles in all languages are omitted from the titles in this appendix.

Within each category or subdivision, works are listed in *chronological order* according to the composer's birth date. This will make it possible for you to go immediately to the correct part of the list if you happen to be looking for something from a particular style-period (baroque, for example, or contemporary).

Once you have found works that suit your purpose, refer back to the main alphabetical listing by composer for full information.

DOUBLE CHORUS

Monteverdi—Vespro della beata vergine (SSTTTBB or SSATTBB)
Hofer—Te Deum
Vivaldi—Kyrie, RV 587 (opt SSAA); Lauda Jerusalem (SSSS)
Bach, J.S.—Cantatas Nos.50, 215 (STB); Matthäuspassion (SATBB); Motet No.2, BWV 226
Handel—Israel in Egypt (SSATBB); Occasional Oratorio (SSATB)
Mozart, W.A.—Mass, K.427 (SSTB); Venite populi, K.260
Berlioz—Te Deum (T)
Mendelssohn—Psalm 98
Schumann, R.—Scenen aus Goethes Faust (STBBB)
Verdi—Te Deum (S)

Wagner, Richard—Lohengrin: Elsa's Procession
Mahler—Symphony No.8 (SSSAATBB)
Delius—Mass of Life (SATBar)
Bartók—Cantata profana (TBar)
Miaskovsky—Symphony No.6 [4th mvt]
Howells—Hymnus Paradisi (ST)
Rosenberg—Symphony No.4
Thomson, V.—Four Saints in Three Acts (SSMsATBarBs)
Ward—Earth Shall Be Fair
Ligeti—Requiem (S, Ms)
Nørgård, Per—Symphony No.3
Jones—Symphony No.2
Hailstork—Earthrise
Rodríguez—Agnus Dei (SSTB); Forbidden Fire (Bs-Bar)
Golijov—Oceana (vocalist)
Trigos, Juan—Magnificat Guadalupano (STBar)

MIXED CHORUS

Large Orchestra

20' or less

Berlioz—Hymne des Marseillais
Verdi—Stabat Mater
Rimsky-Korsakov—Mlada: Suite
Roussel—Évocations (ATBar)
Zemlinsky—Psalm 23
Rachmaninoff—Three Russian Songs [chorus of altos & basses]
Schoenberg—Genesis Suite: Prelude [wordless]
Ravel—Daphnis et Chloé: Suite Nos.1, 2 [opt wordless chorus]
Ireland—These Things Shall Be (Bar or T)

Stravinsky—Star Spangled Banner
Kabalevsky—Symphony No.3
Barber—Prayers of Kierkegaard (S);
    Vanessa: Under the Willow Tree [opt
    chorus]
Britten—Ballad of Heroes (T or S)
Nono, Luigi—Victoire de Guernica
Van de Vate—Katyn
Colgrass—Theatre of the Universe
    (SMsTBarB)
Górecki—Ad matrem (S)
Jones—Seas of God
Pärt, Arvo—Credo
Hartway—Freedom Festival [opt chorus]
Mauldin—Prayer of Mesas
Warshauer—Ahavah (Ms)
Zhou—Future of Fire
Higdon—On the Death of the Righteous
Richman—Wake Me a Song
Boyer—Dream Lives On [opt chorus]

21'–30'

Dvořák—American Flag (ATB);
    Te Deum (SB)
Janáček—Amarus (TBar)
Mahler—Waldmärchen (SATBar)
Delius—Sea Drift (Bar)
Schmitt—Psalm 47 (S)
Scriabin—Prometheus
Ives—Symphony No.4
Carpenter—Skyscrapers
Stravinsky—Flood (TBB);
    Noces [orchd Stucky] (SMsTB);
    Symphony of Psalms
Szymanowski—Symphony no.3 (T)
Boulanger, L.—Psalm 130 (S or A)
Poulenc—Gloria (S)
Dallapiccola—Canti di liberazione
Holmboe—Symphony No.4
Kirchner—Of Things Exactly as They
    Are (SBar)
Husa—Apotheosis of This Earth
Nono—Canto sospeso (SAT)
Martino—Paradiso Choruses
    (3S, 4Mz, 3T, 2Bar)
Kilar—Angelus (S); Exodus
Zwilich—Symphony No.4
Adams, John—On the Transmigration of
    Souls
Saariaho—Oltra mar
Oliverio—Generations (2 females,
    2 males)
Boyer—On Music's Wings (SBar)

31'–45'

Berlioz—Lélio   (TTB); Symphonie
    funèbre et triomphale
Saint-Saëns—Requiem (SATB)
Janáček—Glagolitic Mass (SATB)

Elgar—Music Makers (A)
Mahler—Klagende Lied [2nd version]
    (SAT, opt boy alto)
Debussy—Enfant prodigue (STBar)
Delius—Appalachia (Bar);
    Song of the High Hills
Roussel—Aeneas
Rachmaninoff—Bells (STB)
Prokofiev—Alexander Nevsky (Ms)
Howells—English Mass
Milhaud—Choéphores (SSA);
    Symphony No.3
Orff—Trionfo di Afrodite (SSTTB)
Sessions—When Lilacs Last in the
    Dooryard Bloom'd (SABar)
Poulenc—Stabat Mater (S)
Duruflé—Requiem, op.9 (MsBar)
Walton—Belshazzar's Feast (Bar)
Moore, Undine—Scenes from the Life of
    a Martyr (SATB)
Shostakovich—Song of the Forests (TB)
Barber—Lovers (Bar)
Schuman, Wm.—Casey at the Bat (Bar,
    S); On Freedom's Ground (Bar)
Bernstein—Symphony No.3 (S)
Mechem—Songs of the Slave (Bs-Bar, S)
Górecki—Beatus vir, op.38 (Bar)
Glass—Symphony No.7
Adams, John—Harmonium
Psathas—Orpheus in Rarohenga (STBar)

46'–60'

Gounod—Messe solennelle (STB)
Saint-Saëns—Déluge (SATB)
Reznicek—Sieger (A)
Holst—First Choral Symphony (S)
Ravel—Daphnis et Chloé
Bloch, E.—Avodath Hakodesh (Bar)
Stravinsky—Perséphone (T)
Howells—Stabat Mater (T)
Walton—Henry V
Britten—Spring Symphony (SAT)
Reich—Desert Music
Kernis—Garden of Light (SMTBar, boy
    soprano)

Over 60'

Haydn, F.J.—Schöpfung [ed. Brown]
    (STB or SSTBB)
Rossini—Petite messe solennelle (SATB)
Berlioz—Damnation de Faust
    (MsTBarB); Requiem (T); Roméo et
    Juliette (ATB)
Liszt—Christus (SATB)
Verdi—Messa da requiem (SATB)
Dvořák—Requiem (SATB)
Elgar—Apostles (SATBBB); Dream of
    Gerontius (MsTB); Kingdom (SATB)

Mahler—Klagende Lied [orig] (SATBar,
    2boys[S&A]); Symphony No.2 (SA)
Debussy—Martyre de Saint Sébastien
    (SAA)
Vaughan Williams—Hodie (STB);
    Symphony No.1 (SBar)
Schmidt, F.—Buch mit sieben Siegeln
    (SATB, Heldentenor)
Schoenberg—Gurre-Lieder [2 ver-sions]
    (SATTB, Sprechstimme)
Prokofiev—Ivan the Terrible (ABar)
Honegger—Jeanne d'Arc au bûcher
    (SSSATB)
Hindemith—When Lilacs Last in the
    Door-Yard Bloom'd (MsBar)
Orff—Carmina burana (STBar)
Tippett—Mask of Time
Messiaen—Transfiguration de
    Jésus-Christ
Britten—War Requiem (STB)
Penderecki—Passio et mors domini
    nostri Iesu Christi secundum Lucam
    (SBarB)
Bolcom—Songs of Innocence and of
    Experience (SSSAATTBar, country
    singer, rock singer, folk singer, opt boy
    soprano)
Stucky—August 4, 1964 (SMsTBar)
Sierra—Missa latina (SBar)
Danielpour—American Requiem
    (MsTBar)
Heitzeg—Nobel Symphony (MsBar)

Medium Orchestra

10' or less

Mozart, W.A.—Kyrie, K.341
Beethoven—Meeresstille und glückliche
    Fahrt; Ruinen von Athen: March and
    Chorus
Schubert—Tantum ergo (SATB)
Berlioz—Sara la baigneuse; Tristia:
    Marche funèbre d'Hamlet [wordless
    chorus]
Mendelssohn—Kyrie; Tu es Petrus
Schumann, R.—Fest-Ouvertüre (SATB)
Franck—Psalm 150
Bruckner—Psalm 150 (S)
Bruch—Hebräische Gesänge
Buck—Festival Overture on the
    American National Air
Rimsky-Korsakov—Christmas Eve:
    Polonaise; Dubinushka
Wolf—Feuerreiter
Holst—Christmas Day (SATB)
Ives—Circus Band; Lincoln the Great
    Commoner; They Are There
Bacon—Hymn to the United Nations
Britten—Praise We Great Men (SATB);
    Welcome Ode

Hollingsworth—Death Be Not Proud; Song of David (T)
Boulez—Soleil des eaux (STB [1958] or S [1965]
Erb—Cummings Cycle
Zaninelli—Battle Hymn of the Republic
Rudow—Dark Waters of Elba; Spirit of America; Weeping Rocker III
Zwilich—One Nation
Chiarappa—Paean to the Scholar, the Athlete and the Artist
Ayers—Fanfare and Carol for Christmas; Veni Emmanuel
Rush, T.R.—Angels in the Snow (SATB)
Heitzeg—Together (Divided We Are Nothing)

11'–20'

Haydn, F.J.—Te Deum for the Empress Maria Therese
Beethoven—Fantasia, Piano, Chorus & Orch (SSATTB)
Schubert—Mirjams Siegesgesang (S)
Schubert—Offertorium (T)
Berlioz—Cinq mai (B); Tristia; Vox populi (TTBB)
Mendelssohn—Psalm 114
Schumann, R.—Adventlied (S); Neujahrslied (SAB); Requiem für Mignon (SSAAB)
Verdi—Inno delle nazioni (T)
Borodin—Prince Igor: Polovtsian Dances
Brahms—Gesang der Parzen; Nänie; Schicksalslied
Strauss, R.—Wanderers Sturmlied
Sibelius—Captive Queen
Vaughan Williams—Fantasia on Christmas Carols (Bar); Five Mystical Songs (Bar); Serenade to Music (4S, 4A, 4T, 4B); Toward the Unknown Region
Holst—Choral Fantasia (S)
Ives—New England Holidays: Thanksgiving and Forefathers' Day
Stravinsky—Canticum sacrum (TBar); Chorale-Variations; Requiem canticles (AB); Sermon, a Narrative, and a Prayer (AT)
Szymanowski—Stabat Mater (SABar)
Villa-Lobos—Chôros no.10
Howells—Sir Patrick Spens (Bar)
Castelnuovo-Tedesco—Genesis Suite: The Flood
Hanson—Cherubic Hymn; Lament for Beowulf; Song of Democracy
Poulenc—Sécheresses
Copland—Canticle of Freedom
Finzi—In terra pax (SBar)
Bonds, M.A.—Ballad of the Brown King (SATBar)
Britten—Ballad of Heroes (T or S)

Boulez—cummings ist der Dichter
Jones—Trumpet of the Swan
Corigliano—Fern Hill (Ms)
Stewart—Cindy, O Cindy
Rutter—Gloria
Rodríguez—Jargon; Scrooge (B)
Mauldin—Prayers of the Children
Locklair—Since Dawn
Wendel—Virginia, 1861 (treble or A)
Smith, Kile—Psalm 46 (Bar)
Heitzeg—Litanies for the Living
Boyer—Dreaming a World

21'–30'

Mendelssohn—Christus (STBB); Lauda Sion (SATB); Psalm 42 (STTBB); Psalm 95 (SST)
Schumann, R.—Königssohn (ATBarB)
Gade—Zion (Bar)
Bruckner—Te Deum (SATB)
Rimsky-Korsakov—Christmas Eve: Suite
Kodály—Psalmus hungaricus (T); Te Deum (SATB)
Honegger—Cantate de Noël (Bar)
Still—Lenox Avenue
Bacon—USania (B, opt S)
Tippett—Midsummer Marriage: Ritual Dances (opt SMsTB)
Shostakovich—Symphony No.2; Symphony No.3
Britten—Cantata academica, carmen basiliense (SATB)
Ward—Earth Shall Be Fair (S)
Maxwell Davies—Shepherds' Calendar (treble soloist)
Jones—Symphony No.2
Del Tredici—Pop-Pourri (S, opt T or Ms)
Svoboda—Journey (MsBar)
Kechley—Skylark Sings (S)
Rouse—Karolju
Danielpour—Symphony No.3 (S)

31'–45'

Schütz—Historia der Geburt Jesu Christi (STB)
Bach, J.S.—Cantata No.30 (SATB)
Haydn, F.J.—Mass, Hob.XXII:11 [3rd instrumentation] (SATB)
Mozart, W.A.—Litaniae de venerabili altaris sacramento, K.243 (SATB)
Beethoven—Cantata on the Death of Emperor Joseph II (SSATB); Mass, op.86 (SATB); Ruinen von Athen (SBarB)
Schubert—Mass No.1 (SSATTB); Mass No.5 (SATB); Stabat Mater (STB)
Berlioz—Huit scènes de Faust (SSSSATBarB)
Mendelssohn—Erste Walpurgisnacht (ATBB)

Schumann, R.—Manfred (SATBBBB); Mass (STB); Requiem (SATB); Des Sängers Fluch (SSATBarBarBs)
Bruckner—Missa solemnis (SATB)
Fauré—Requiem (SBar)
Parry—Ode on St. Cecilia's Day (SBar)
Coleridge-Taylor—Hiawatha's Wedding Feast (T); Death of Minnehaha (SB); Hiawatha's Departure (STB)
Kodály—Missa brevis (SATB)
Stravinsky—Threni (SATTBB)
Collins—Hymn to the Earth (SATB)
Bacon—Ecclesiastes (SB)
Walton—Belshazzar's Feast (Bar)
Tippett—Vision of Saint Augustine (Bar)
Ward—Sweet Freedom's Song (SBar); Symphony No. 5 (SBar)
Mechem—Songs of the Slave (Bs-Bar, S)
Glass—Passion of Ramakrishna (S Ms T Bs-Bar B)
Ptaszyńska—Holocaust Memorial Cantata (STBar)
Jenkins—Gloria (solo voice)
Tavener—Whale (MsBar)
Rutter—Magnificat (S or Ms)
Warshauer—Shacharit (ST)
Higdon—The Singing Rooms

46'–60'

Haydn, F.J.—Sieben letzten Worte [choral version] (SATB)
Mozart, W.A.—Davidde penitente (SST); Mass, K.427 (Robbins Landon) (SSTB); Mass, K.427 (Holl & Köhler) (SSATB)
Cherubini—Requiem, C minor; Messa solenne, G major
Beethoven—Christus am Ölberg (STB)
Schubert—Mass No.6 (SATTB); Rosamunde (A)
Berlioz—Messe solennelle (STB)
Bruckner—Mass No.1 (SATB); Mass No.3 (SATB)
Dubois, Th.—Sept paroles du Christ (STB)
Rheinberger—Stern von Bethlehem (STBarB)
Scriabin—Symphony No.1 (TMs)
Holst—First Choral Symphony (S)
Bliss—Beatitudes (ST)
Rosenberg—Symphony No.5 (A)
Bacon—By Blue Ontario (ABar); Last Invocation (S, B, opt A)
Harbison—Requiem (S A T Bs-Bar)
Zaimont—Sacred Service (Bar or A)
Horwood—Symphony No.2
Galbraith—Requiem
McClure—Caribbean Christmas Mass

Over 60'

Handel—Messiah [orchestrated by
  Mozart or Prout] (SATB)
Haydn, F.J.—Jahreszeiten (STB);
  Schöpfung (SSTBB or STB)
Mozart, W.A.—Betulia liberata, K.118
  (SSSATB); Mass, K.427 (Schmitt)
  (SMsTB); Mass, K.427 (Beyer)
  (SSATB)
Beethoven—Missa solemnis (SATB);
  Symphony No.9 (SATB)
Rossini—Stabat mater (SSTB)
Berlioz—Enfance du Christ
  (STTBarBBB)
Mendelssohn—Elijah (SSATB);
  Lobgesang (SST), St. Paul (SATBB)
Schumann, R.—Paradies und die Peri
  (SSMsATTBarB); Rose Pilgerfahrt
  (SSAATTBB)
Liszt—Legende von der heiligen
  Elisabeth (SMsB)
Franck—Rédemption (S)
Bristow—Oratorio of Daniel
  (SMzTTBarBBB)
Brahms—Deutsches Requiem (SBar)
Paine—Mass (SATB)
Dvořák—Spectre's Bride (STB); Stabat
  Mater (SATB)
Grieg—Peer Gynt (SSSBarB)
Parker—Hora novissima (SATB)
Beach—Grand Mass in E-flat (SATB)
Perosi—Risurrezione di Lazzaro
  (SSTBarB)
Vaughan Williams—Hodie (STB);
  Symphony No.1 (SBar)
Honegger—Roi David (SAT)
Hindemith—Unaufhörliche (STBarB)
Tippett—Child of Our Time (SATB)
Jones—Temptation of Jesus (B)
Adams, John—Niño (SMsBar)
Knehans—shoah requiem (SMsTBs-Bar)
Moravec, Paul—Blizzard Voices
  (SMaTBarB)
Golijov—Pasión según San Marcos
  (SABar)

Small Orchestra

10' or less

Monteverdi—Laudate dominum (SSTTB)
Vivaldi—Beatus vir, RV 598 (SSA)
Telemann—Laudate Jehovam
Bach, J.S.—Cantatas Nos.118 [2nd
  setting]; 141 (ATB); 145 (STB); Jesu,
  Joy of Man's Desiring (Cant. No.147)
Handel—Let Thy Hand be Strengthened;
  Zadok the Priest (SSAATBB)
Galuppi—Domine ad adjuvandum me
  (SA)
Haydn, F.J.—Mass, Hob.XXII:3

Gossec—Christmas Suite
Haydn, M—Veni Sancte Spiritus, MH 39;
  Salve Regina, MH 634
Mozart, W.A.—Alma dei creatoris,
  (SAT); Ave verum corpus; Benedictus
  sit deus, (S); Gloria from the Twelfth
  Mass; Inter natos mulierum; Litaniae
  lauretanae, K.109 (SATB);
  Misericordias domini; Regina coeli,
  K.276 (SATB); Sancta Maria; Scande
  coeli limina (S); Tantum ergo, K.142
  (S); Tantum ergo, K.197; Veni sancte
  spiritus (SATB)
Beethoven—Elegischer Gesang (SATB)
Donizetti—Ave Maria (S)
Schubert—Stabat Mater, D.175
Berlioz—Tristia: Méditation religieuse
Hensel—Hiob (SATB)
Mendelssohn—Hear My Prayer (S);
  Hymne (Ms or A); Jesu, meine Freude;
  Verleih' uns Frieden (Dona nobis
  pacem)
Fauré—Cantique de Jean Racine; Pavane
Elgar—Spanish Serenade
Zemlinsky—Zwei Gedichte
Ives—General William Booth Enters into
  Heaven; Three Harvest Home Chorales
Schoenberg—Friede auf Erden
Kodály—Kállai kettös
Webern—Augenlicht; Cantata No.1 (S);
  Lieder, op.19
Milhaud—Symphonie de chambre No.6
Thomson, V.—Dance in Praise
Britten—Te Deum (treble solo)
Ward—Cherish Your Land (Bar)
Husa—Festive Ode
Jones—Reunion Benediction
Rutter—Shepherd's Pipe Carol
Lang, David—statement to the court
Di Vittorio—San Michele Arcangelo
  (Bar)

11'-20'

Charpentier, M.-A.—Messe de minuit
  pour Noël (SSATTB)
Purcell—Te Deum & Jubilate (SSAATB)
Bach, J.S.—Cantatas Nos.2 (ATB); 6
  (SATB); 8 (SATB); 14 (STB); 15
  (SATB); 16 (ATB); 17 (SATB); 18
  (STB); 22 (ATB); 23 (SAT); 24
  (SATB); 25 (STB); 26 (SATB); 27
  (SATB); 28 (SATB); 31 (STB); 33
  (ATB); 34 (ATB); 37 (SATB); 38
  (SATB); 40 (ATB); 44 (SATB); 46
  (ATB); 48 (AT); 52 (S); 55 (T); 56 (B);
  59 (SB); 60 (ATB); 61 (STB); 65 (TB);
  67 (ATB); 68(SB); 71 (SATB); 72
  (SAB); 73 (STB); 77 (SATB); 79
  (SAB); 81 (ATB); 84 (S); 85 (SATB);
  86 (SATB); 87 (ATB); 89 (SAB); 90
  (ATB); 91 (SATB); 93 (SATB); 95

(STB); 96 (SATB); 98 (SATB); 99
  (SATB); 103 (AT); 104 (TB); 106
  (SATB); 107 (STB); 108 (ATB); 111
  (SATB); 112 (SATB); 116 (SATB); 121
  (SATB); 122 (SATB); 124 (SATB); 126
  (ATB); 127 (STB); 128 (ATB); 129
  (SAB); 130 (SATB); 132 (SATB); 133
  (SATB); 135 (ATB); 136 (ATB); 137
  (SATB); 138 (SATB); 139 (SATB); 142
  (ATB); 143 (STB); 144 (SAT); 147a
  (SATB); 148 (AT); 149 (SATB); 150
  (SATB); 151 (SATB); 154 (ATB); 155
  (SATB); 156 (ATB); 157 (TB); 158 (B);
  159 (ATB); 161 (AT); 162 (SATB); 163
  (SATB); 164 (SATB); 165 (SATB); 166
  (ATB); 167 (SATB); 168 (SATB); 171
  (SATB); 172 [both versions] (SATB);
  173 (SATB); 175 (ATB); 176 (SAB);
  179 (STB); 181 (SATB); 183 (SATB);
  185 (ATB); 186a (SATB); 190 (ATB);
  190a (ATB); 191 (ST); 192 (SB); 193
  (SA); 195 (SB); 197a (AB)
Handel—Jubilate for the Peace of Utrecht
  (AAB); Psalm 96: O Sing unto the Lord
  (ST)
Sammartini, Giov. Battista—Magnificat
  (SATB)
Bach, J.C.—Credo breve
Haydn, M—Masses MH 17 (SATB); MH
  182 (SATB)
Mozart, W.A.—Dixit et Magnificat
  (STB); Mass, K.258 (SATB); Missa
  brevis, K.65 (SATB); K.220 (SATB);
  K.259 (SATB); Regina coeli, K.108 (S);
  Regina coeli, K.127 (S); Te Deum
  laudamus
Schubert—Magnificat (SATB)
Hensel—Lobgesang (SA)
Mendelssohn—O Haupt voll Blut und
  Wunden (B); Psalm 115 (STBar)
Bruckner—Mass, WAB 25 (A)
Brahms—Liebeslieder Waltzes, from
  op.52 & 65
Vaughan Williams—Flos campi; Serenade
  to Music [reduced version]; Toward the
  Unknown Region
Schoenberg—Kol nidre
Webern—Cantata No.2 (SB)
Copland—Old American Songs, Sets 1-2
Lambert—Rio Grande (A)
Lockwood—Carol Fantasy
Britten—Cantata misericordium (TB)
Bernstein—Chichester Psalms (solo boy
  or countertenor)
Hollingsworth—Stabat Mater
Maxwell Davies—Veni sancte spiritus
  (SAB)
Harbison—Flight into Egypt (SBar)
Warshauer—Born on a River
Chen Yi—Tang Poems Cantata (T)
Amrhein—Missa humanis (SATB)

21'-30'

Dvořák—American Flag (ATB);
   Te Deum (SB)
Janáček—Amarus (TBar)
Mahler—Waldmärchen (SATBar)
Delius—Sea Drift (Bar)
Schmitt—Psalm 47 (S)
Scriabin—Prometheus (chor opt)
Ives—Symphony No.4
Carpenter—Skyscrapers (chorus opt)
Stravinsky—Flood (TBB); Noces (orchd
   Stucky) (SMsTB); Symphony of Psalms
Szymanowski—Symphony no.3 (T)
Boulanger, L.—Psalm 130 (S or A)
Poulenc—Gloria (S)
Dallapiccola—Canti di liberazione
Holmboe, Vagn—Symphony No.4
Kirchner—Of Things Exactly as They Are
   (SBar)
Husa—Apotheosis of This Earth
Nono, Luigi—Canto sospeso (SAT)
Martino—Paradiso Choruses   (3S, 4Mz,
   3T, 2Bar)
Kilar—Angelus (S); Exodus
Zwilich—Symphony No.4
Adams, John—On the Transmigration of
   Souls
Saariaho—Oltra mar
Oliverio—Generations (2 females, 2
   males)
Boyer—On Music's Wings (SBar)

31'-45'

Schütz—Historia der Geburt Jesu Christi
   (STB)
Haydn, F.J.—Mass, Hob.XXII:11 [3rd
   instr] (SATB)
Haydn, M—Masses MH 254; MH 796
   (SATB); MH 826 (SATB); Requiem
Mozart, W.A.—Litaniae de venerabili
   altaris sacramento, K.243 (SATB)
Beethoven—Cantata on the Death of
   Emperor Joseph II (SSATB); Mass,
   op.86 (SATB); Ruinen von Athen
   (SBarB)
Schubert—Mass No.1 (SSATTB); Mass
   No.5 (SATB); Stabat Mater (STB)
Berlioz—Huit scènes de Faust
   (SSSSATBarB)
Mendelssohn—Erste Walpurgisnacht
   (ATBB)
Schumann, R.—Manfred (SATBBBB);
   Mass (STB); Requiem (SATB); Des
   Sängers Fluch (SSATBarBarBs)
Bruckner—Missa solemnis (SATB)
Fauré—Requiem (SBar)
Parry—Ode on St. Cecilia's Day (SBar)
Coleridge-Taylor—Hiawatha's Wedding
   Feast (T); Death of Minnehaha (SB);
   Hiawatha's Departure (STB)

Kodály—Missa brevis (SATB)
Stravinsky—Threni (SATTBB)
Collins—Hymn to the Earth (SATB)
Bacon—Ecclesiastes (SB)
Walton—Belshazzar's Feast (Bar)
Tippett—Vision of Saint Augustine (Bar)
Ward—Sweet Freedom's Song (SBar),
   Symphony No. 5 (SBar)
Mechem—Songs of the Slave
   (Bs-Bar, S)
Glass—Passion of Ramakrishna (S Ms T
   Bs-Bar B)
Ptaszyńska—Holocaust Memorial Cantata
   (STBar)
Jenkins—Gloria (solo voice)
Tavener—Whale (MsBar)
Rutter—Magnificat (S or Ms)
Warshauer—Shacharit (ST)
Higdon—The Singing Rooms

46'-60'

Haydn, F.J.—Sieben letzten Worte
   [choral version]   (SATB)
Mozart, W.A.—Davidde penitente (SST);
   Mass, K.427 (Robbins Landon)
   (SSTB); Mass, K.427 (Holl & Köhler)
   (SSATB)
Cherubini—Requiem, C minor; Messa
   solenne, G major
Beethoven—Christus am Ölberg (STB)
Schubert—Mass No.6   (SATTB);
   Rosamunde (A)
Berlioz—Messe solennelle (STB)
Bruckner—Mass No.1 (SATB); Mass
   No.3 (SATB)
Dubois, Th.—Sept paroles du Christ
   (STB)
Rheinberger—Stern von Bethlehem
   (STBarB)
Scriabin—Symphony No.1 (TMs)
Holst—First Choral Symphony (S)
Bliss—Beatitudes (ST)
Rosenberg—Symphony No.5 (A)
Bacon—By Blue Ontario (ABar); Last
   Invocation (S, B, opt A)
Harbison—Requiem (SATBs-Bar)
Zaimont—Sacred Service (Bar or A)
Horwood—Symphony No.2
Galbraith—Requiem
McClure—Caribbean Christmas Mass

Over 60'

Handel—Messiah (orch Mozart or Prout)
   (SATB)
Haydn, F.J.—Jahreszeiten (STB);
   Schöpfung (SSTBB or STB)
Mozart, W.A.—Betulia liberata, K.118
   (SSSATB); Mass, K.427 (Schmitt)
   (SMsTB); Mass, K.427 (Beyer)
   (SSATB)

Beethoven—Missa solemnis (SATB);
   Symphony No.9 (SATB)
Rossini—Stabat mater (SSTB)
Berlioz—Enfance du Christ
   (STTBarBBB)
Mendelssohn—Elijah (SSATB);
   Lobgesang (SST); St. Paul (SATBB)
Schumann, R.—Paradies und die Peri
   (SSMsATTBarB); Rose Pilgerfahrt
   (SSAATTBB)
Liszt—Legende von der heiligen
   Elisabeth (SMsB)
Franck—Rédemption (S)
Bristow—Oratorio of Daniel
   (SMzTTBarBBB)
Brahms—Deutsches Requiem (SBar)
Paine—Mass (SATB)
Dvořák—Spectre's Bride (STB), Stabat
   Mater (SATB)
Grieg—Peer Gynt (SSSBarB)
Parker—Hora novissima (SATB)
Beach—Grand Mass in E-flat (SATB)
Perosi—Risurrezione di Lazzaro
   (SSTBarB)
Vaughan Williams—Hodie (STB);
   Symphony No.1 (SBar)
Honegger—Roi David (SAT)
Hindemith—Unaufhörliche (STBarB)
Tippett—Child of Our Time (SATB)
Jones—Temptation of Jesus (B)
Adams, John—Niño (SMsBar)
Knehans—shoah requiem (SMsTBs-Bar)
Moravec, Paul—Blizzard Voices
   (SMsTBarB)
Golijov—Pasión según San Marcos
   (SABar)

String Orchestra

15' or less

Monteverdi—Laudate dominum (SSTTB)
Buxtehude—Magnificat
Purcell—Ode for St. Cecilia's Day, Z.334
   (SB); Ode for St. Cecilia's Day, Z.339
   (SSATB)
Vivaldi—Beatus vir, RV 598 (SSA);
   Credo, RV 591; Magnificat, RV 610
   [Robbins Landon] (SSATB)
Telemann—Laudate Jehovam
Bach, J.S.—Cantata No.196 (STB)
Galuppi—Domine ad adjuvandum me
   (SA)
Pergolesi—Magnificat   (SATB)
Haydn, F.J.—Mass, Hob.XXII:1 (SS);
   Mass, Hob.XXII:3
Mozart, W.A.—Ave verum corpus; Inter
   natos mulierum; Litaniae lauretanae,
   K.109 (SATB); Misericordias domini;
   Missa brevis, K.140 (SATB); Sancta
   Maria, K.273

Beethoven—Elegischer Gesang (SATB)
Donizetti—Ave Maria (S)
Mendelssohn—Jesu, meine Freude
Zemlinsky—Zwei Gedichte
Vaughan Williams—Fantasia on
  Christmas Carols (Bar); Serenade to
  Music [strings & piano]
Finzi—In terra pax [orig] (SBar)
Britten—Te Deum (treble solo)
Jones—Reunion Benediction
Lang—statement to the court

16'–30'

Vivaldi—Magnificat, RV 610 or 611
  [Malipiero] (SSAT)
Durante—Vespro breve
Bach, Joh. Sebastian—Cantatas Nos.4;
  153 (ATB)
Galuppi—Laudate pueri (SAT)
Haydn, F.J.—Mass, Hob.XXII:7 (S);
  Salve regina (SATB)
Mozart, W.A.—Missa brevis, K.49
  (SATB); Missa brevis, K.192 (SATB);
  Missa brevis, K.194 (SATB); Missa
  brevis, K.275 (SATB)
Schubert—Mass No.2 (STB); Mass No.4
  (SATB)
Hollingsworth—Dumbarton Oaks Mass
Moravec, Paul—Songs of Love and War
  (Bar)

Over 30'

Schütz—Historia der Auferstehung
  (SSAATTBB)
Handel—Dixit Dominus (SSATB)
Saint-Saëns—Oratorio de Noël
  (SMsATBar)
MacMillan—Seven Last Words From the
  Cross

Without Strings

Bach, J.S.—Cantata No.118 [1st setting]
Schubert—Deutsche Messe
Bruckner—Mass No.2
Brahms—Begräbnisgesang
Respighi—Lauda per la natività (SSA or
  SAT)
Stravinsky—Mass (SATTB); Noces
  (SMsTB)
Boulanger, L.—Psalm 24
Dallapiccola—Canti di prigionia
Bernstein—Chichester Psalms (solo boy
  or countertenor)
Schnittke—Requiem (SSSAT)
Rutter—Gloria (original version)
Galbraith—Missa mysteriorum (SSATB)
Rival, Robert—Delights & Dischords

FEMALE CHORUS

Pergolesi—Stabat Mater (SA)
Berlioz—Sara la baigneuse; Tristia: La
  mort d'Ophélia
Mendelssohn—Midsummer Night's
  Dream (SS)
Liszt—Dante Symphony
Saint-Saëns—Nuit (S)
Chabrier—Ode à la musique (S)
Grieg—At the Cloistergate (SA)
Fauré—Caligula
Elgar—Apostles (SATBBB)
Mahler—Symphony No.3 (A)
Loeffler—Evocation
Debussy—Damoiselle élue (Ms);
  Nocturnes
Busoni—Turandot: Suite
Vaughan Williams—Magnificat (A);
  Symphony No.7 (S)
Holst—Planets
Bartók—Three Village Scenes
Shilkret—Genesis Suite: Creation
Bacon—From Emily's Diary (SA)
Messiaen—Trois petites liturgies
Van de Vate—Voices of Women (SA)
Maxwell Davies—Caroline Mathilde:
  Suite from Act II
Matthews, C.—Pluto, the Renewer
Ayers—and they gathered on Mount
  Carmel
Elfman—Serenada Schizophrana (S)
Chin—Troerinnen (SSMs)

MALE CHORUS

Charpentier, M.-A.—Magnificat
Mozart, W.A.—Laut verkünde unsre
  Freude (TTB); Maurerfreude (T)
Cherubini—Requiem, D minor
Schubert—Gesang der Geister über den
  Wassern; Rosamunde [mvt 4] (A)
Berlioz—Hymne des Marseillais; Sara la
  baigneuse
Liszt—Faust Symphony (T)
Wagner, Richard—Kaisermarsch;
  Lohengrin: Elsa's Procession
Bruckner—Helgoland
Strauss, Joh., Jr.—An der schönen blauen
  Donau
Borodin—Prince Igor: Polovtsian March
Brahms—Alto Rhapsody (A);
  Rinaldo (T)
Bruch—Seeräuberlied
Grieg—Landsighting (Bar)
Delius—Eventyr
Sibelius—Kullervo (SBar)
Busoni—Concerto, Piano
Ives—Johnny Poe

Schoenberg—Survivor from Warsaw
Stravinsky—Genesis Suite: Babel;
  Introitus; Oedipus rex (ATTBB);
  Roi des étoiles
Varèse—Ecuatorial; Nocturnal (S)
Boulanger, L.—Psalm 129
Weill—Berliner Requiem (TBar)
Weill—Sieben Todsünden (S)
Shostakovich—Symphony No.13 (B)
Bernstein—Chichester Psalms (solo boy
  or countertenor)
Crumb—Star-Child (S)
Chen Yi—Chinese Myths Cantata
Danielpour—Symphony No.3 (S)
Richman—Dachau Lied

CHILDREN'S CHORUS

Bach, J.S.—Matthäuspassion (SATBB)
Berlioz—Damnation de Faust
  (MsTBarB)
Berlioz—Hymne des Marseillais; Te
  Deum (T)
Liszt—Dante Symphony; Legende von
  der heiligen Elisabeth (SMsB)
Wagner, Richard—Lohengrin: Elsa's
  Procession
Tchaikovsky—Nutcracker
Fauré—Requiem [ed. Nectoux &
  DeLage] (solo treble & Bar)
Elgar—Apostles (SATBBB)
Mahler—Symphony No.3 (A);
  Symphony No.8 (SSSAATBB)
Ingelbrecht—Rapsodie de printemps
Kodály—Psalmus hungaricus   (T)
Stravinsky—Perséphone (T)
Stravinsky—Symphony of Psalms
Prokofiev—Ivan the Terrible (ABar)
Honegger—Cantate de Noël (Bar);
  Jeanne d'Arc au bûcher (SSSATB)
Hindemith—Unaufhörliche (STBarB
  solos)
Orff—Carmina burana (STBar)
Walton—Henry V [arr.]
Shostakovich—Song of the Forests (TB)
Britten—Children's Crusade; Spring
  Symphony (SAT); War Requiem
  (STB)
Ward—Earth Shall Be Fair; Lamb
Bernstein—Symphony No.3 (S)
Erb—New England's Prospect
Crumb—Star-Child (S)
Martino—Paradiso Choruses (3S, 4Mz,
  3T, 2Bar)
Penderecki—Passio et mors domini
  nostri Iesu Christi secundum Lucam
  (SBarB)
Jones—Eudora's Fable; Hear the Music;
  Temptation of Jesus (B)
Rudow—Spirit of America

Bolcom—Songs of Innocence and of
    Experience (SSSAATTBar, country
    singer, rock singer, folk singer, opt boy
    soprano)
Svoboda—Child's Dream
Zwilich—Symphony No.4
Pasatieri—In the Light of Angels (SMs)
Reuter—We Have a Dream
Adams, John—Niño (SMsBar); On the
    Transmigration of Souls
Mauldin—Prayers of the Children
Wendel—Virginia, 1861 (A or treble)
Zhou—Future of Fire
Amundson—Reindeer Rock
Rush, T.R.—Angels in the Snow (SATB)
Sheng—Two Chinese Folk Tunes (treble)
Heitzeg—Nobel Symphony (MsBar)
Kernis—Garden of Light (SMTBar, boy
    soprano)
Richman—I Remember a Lullaby (S)
Boyer—Dreaming a World;
    On Music's Wings (SBar)

APPENDIX B
SOLO VOICES
(INCLUDING SPEAKER OR NARRATOR)

Soprano
Alto or Mezzo-Soprano
Tenor
Baritone or Bass

Several Solo Voices
    2 Solo Voices
    3 Solo Voices
    4 Solo Voices (SATB)
    4 or more Solo Voices (not SATB)

Speaker (Narrator)

Works within the larger categories are subdivided by duration. Within each category or subdivision, works are listed in *chronological order* according to the composer's birth date. This will make it possible for you to go immediately to a particular part of the list if you happen to be looking for something from a certain style-period (baroque, for example, or contemporary). Initial articles in all languages are omitted from the titles in this appendix.

Refer back to the main alphabetical listing by composer for full information.

SOPRANO

10' or less

Mozart, W.A.—A questo seno/Or che il cielo; Ah se in ciel, benigne stelle; Al desio; Alcandro, lo confesso/Non so d'onde viene; Alma grande e nobil core; Basta, vincesti/Ah non lasciarmi; Bella mia fiamma/Resta, oh cara; Ch'io mi scordi di te/Non temer; Chi sà, chi sà, qual sia; Ergo interest; Kommet her, ihr frechen Sünder; Ma che vi fece; Mia speranza/Ah, non sai; Misera, dove son; Moto di gioia; Nehmt meinen Dank; No, no, che non sei capace; Vado, ma dove; Voi avete un cor fedele; Vorrei spiegarvi
Schubert—An die Musik; Salve Regina, D.223
Berlioz—Zaïde
Duparc, Henri—Chanson triste; Invitation au voyage; Manoir de Rosemonde

Mahler—Antonius von Padua Fischpredigt; Blicke mir nicht in die Lieder!; Ich atmet' einen Linden Duft; Ich bin der Welt abhanden gekommen; Irdische Leben; Liebst du um Schönheit?; Lob des hohen Verstandes; Revelge; Rheinlegendchen; Schildwache Nachtlied; Tamboursg'sell; Trost im Unglück; Um Mitternacht; Verlorne Müh'; Wer hat dies Liedlein erdacht?; Wo die schönen Trompeten blasen
Strauss, R.—Cäcilie; Morgen; Sechs Lieder [individual songs]; Vier letzte Lieder [individual songs]; Zueignung
Sibelius—Arioso; Luonnotar
Rachmaninoff—Vocalise
Varèse—Offrandes
Webern—Geistliche Lieder; Lieder, op.13; Lieder, op.14
Villa-Lobos—Bachianas brasileiras no.5
Rodrigo—Cuatro madrigales amatorios
Menotti—Nocturne

Ligeti—Mysteries of the Macabre
Boulez—Pli selon pli: Nos.1 & 2
Adler, S.—Those Were the Days
Previn—Vocalise
Górecki—Genesis: Monodram
Balassa—Cantata Y
Del Tredici—Acrostic Song
Tyzik—Twelve Gifts of Christmas
Smith, Kile—Poems of Gerard Manley Hopkins
Benjamin, G.—Mind of Winter
Richman—Sheva B'rachot

11'–20'

Scarlatti, A.—Christmas Cantata; Su le sponde del Tebro
Bach, J.S.—Cantata No.51
Mozart, W.A.—Ah, lo previdi/Ah, t'invola/Deh, non varcar; Exsultate jubilate; Popoli di Tessaglia
Beethoven—Ah, perfido
Schubert—Salve Regina, D.676

Wagner, Richard—Götterdämmerung: Brünnhilde's Immolation; Tristan und Isolde: Prelude & Liebestod
Mahler—Rückert Lieder
Loeffler—Canticum fratris solis
Schoenberg—Gurre-Lieder: Lied der Waldtaube
Glière—Concerto, Coloratura Soprano
Ravel—Shéhérazade [voice & orch]
Bloch, E.—Prelude and Two Psalms
Berg—Altenberg Lieder; Sieben frühe Lieder; Wein; Wozzeck: Three Excerpts
Hindemith—Drei Gesänge
Gerhard—Cancionero de Pedrell
Weill—Dreigroschenoper: Suite [arr. Schönherr]
Walton—As You Like It
Dallapiccola—Divertimento in quattro esercizi
Carter—Mirror on Which to Dwell
Barber—Andromache's Farewell; Antony and Cleopatra: Two Scenes; Knoxville: Summer of 1915
Britten—Quatre chansons françaises
Morawetz—From The Diary of Anne Frank
Ward—Sacred Songs for Pantheists
La Montaine—Songs of the Rose of Sharon
Boulez—Pli selon pli: Nos.1, 3, 4, 5
Previn—Magic Number
Wyner—Intermedio
Zaninelli—Five American Gospel Songs
Del Tredici—Alice Symphony: Illustrated Alice; Alice Sym: The Lobster Quadrille; Haddock's Eyes
Albert, Stephen—Flower of the Mountain
Harris, Ross—Floating Bride, the Crimson Village
Ran—Ensembles for 17
Knussen—Symphony No.2; Where the Wild Things Are: Songs and a Sea-Interlude
Brief—Cantares
Tan—On Taoism
O'Boyle—Conflict, Sadness, Victory, and Resolution
Boyer—perchance to dream...

21'–30'

Bach, J.S.—Cantatas Nos.82a; 199; 202; 204; 209
Berlioz—Cléopâtre
Wagner, Richard—Wesendonck Lieder
Chausson—Poème de l'amour et de la mer
Mahler—Sieben Lieder aus letzten Zeit
Loeffler—Five Irish Fantasies
Strauss, R.—Sechs Lieder, op.68; Three Hymns; Vier letzte Lieder

Schoenberg—Six Songs, op.8
Toch—Chinesische Flöte
Martin—Maria-Triptychon
Hindemith—Marienleben: Sechs Lieder
Finzi—Dies natalis
Tippett—Byzantium
Britten—Illuminations; Our Hunting Fathers
Lutoslawski—Chantefleurs et chantefables
Ohana—Tombeau de Claude Debussy
Foss—Time Cycle
Duffy—Time for Remembrance
Druckman—Lamia
Wyner—Fragments from Antiquity
Baker—Chat qui pêche
Zaninelli—Beginnings
Levy—Canto de los marranos
Rands—Canti lunatici
Del Tredici—Alice Symphony: In Wonderland; Quaint Events; Syzygy; Vintage Alice
Andriessen—Dances
Cresswell—Voice Inside
Harris, Ross—Symphony No.2
Pasatieri—Sieben Lehmannlieder
Saariaho—Quatre Instants
Sierra—Beyond the Silence of Sorrow
Sheng—Phoenix
Danielpour—Woman's Life
Golijov—Three Songs
Adamo—Late Victorians
McLoskey—Prex penitentialis

Over 30'

Bach, J.S.—Cantata No.210
Beethoven—Egmont
Mahler—Lieder aus "Des Knaben Wunderhorn"; Symphony No.4
Vaughan Williams—Symphony No.3
Turina—Canto a Sevilla
Berg—Lulu: Suite
Sessions—Idyll of Theocritus
Tippett—Symphony No.3
Britten—Fourteen Folk Songs
Foss—Song of Songs
Górecki—Symphony No.3
Amy—D'un espace déployé
Del Tredici—Alice Symphony; All in the Golden Afternoon; Child Alice; Final Alice; In Memory of a Summer Day
Corigliano—Mr. Tambourine Man
Harbison—Milosz Songs
Young—Symphony [No.1]

ALTO or MEZZO-SOPRANO

10' or less

Bach, J.S.—Cantatas Nos.53; 200
Mozart, W.A.—Ombra felice
Schubert—An die Musik
Berlioz—Captive; Jeune pâtre breton
Grieg—From Monte Pincio
Fauré—Pelléas et Mélisande: Melisande's Song
Duparc, Henri—Chanson triste
Mahler—Antonius von Padua Fischpredigt; Blicke mir nicht in die Lieder!; Ich atmet' einen Linden Duft; Ich bin der Welt abhanden gekommen; Irdische Leben; Liebst Du um Schönheit?; Lob des hohen Verstandes; Revelge; Rheinlegendchen; Schildwache Nachtlie; Tamboursg'sell; Trost im Unglück; Um Mitternacht; Verlorne Müh'; Wer hat dies Liedlein erdacht?; Wo die schönen Trompeten blasen
Wolf—Anakreons Grab; Spanisches Liederbuch: Two Sacred Songs
Strauss, R.—Morgen; Zueignung
Sibelius—Rapid-Rider's Brides
Ives—Charlie Rutlage; Evening
Ravel—Cinq mélodies populaires grecques
Canteloube—Chants d'Auvergne [each of 27 songs]
Respighi—Tre liriche
Stravinsky—Faun and the Shepherdess
Webern—Lieder, op.8
Collins—Daffodils; Piper; Prayer for C.H.S.; Song and Suds
Rodrigo—Cuatro madrigales amatorios
Dallapiccola—Liriche greche: Cinque frammenti
Rudow—Journey of Waters
Smith, Kile—Song of Sonia Sanchez
Richman—Homework Blues; Music Can Make Your Life Complete

11'–20'

Vivaldi—Stabat Mater, RV 621
Bach, J.S.—Cantata No.54
Mussorgsky—Songs and Dances of Death)
Mahler—Lieder eines fahrenden Gesellen; Rückert Lieder
Loeffler—Canticum fratris solis
Debussy—Trois Ballades de François Villon
Granados—Dante
Zemlinsky—Six Songs, op.13
Ravel—Trois poèmes de Stéphane Mallarmé

Falla—Siete canciones populares
Respighi—Tramonto
Berg—Sieben frühe Lieder
Prokofiev—Ugly Duckling
Rogers—Three Japanese Dances
Still—Here's One
Poulenc—Bal masqué
Weill—Dreigroschenoper: Suite [arr. Schönherr]
Britten—Phaedra
Argento—Casa Guidi
Adams, Leslie—Three Dunbar Songs
Schafer—Adieu Robert Schumann
Maxwell Davies—Stone Litany
Tan—On Taoism

21'–30'

Bach, J.S.—Cantatas Nos.35; 82, 170
Wagner, Richard—Wesendonck Lieder [Henze or Tarkmann]
Dvořák—Biblical Songs
Chausson—Poème de l'amour et de la mer
Elgar—Sea Pictures
Mahler—Kindertotenlieder; Sieben Lieder aus letzten Zeit
Falla—Amor brujo: Ballet Suite
Gruenberg—Creation
Copland—Eight Poems of Emily Dickinson
Fortner—Creation
Bernstein—Symphony No.1
Adler, S.—Symphony No.5
Druckman—Dark Upon the Harp
Schafer—Garden of the Heart
Wernick—Visions of Terror and Wonder
Larsen, L.—Mary Cassatt

Over 30'

Berlioz—Nuits d'été
Mahler—Lieder aus "Des Knaben Wunderhorn"
Falla—Sombrero de tres picos
Britten—Fourteen Folk Songs
Foss—Song of Songs
Boulez—Marteau sans maître

TENOR

10' or less

Mozart, W.A.—Clarice cara mia sposa; Con ossequio, con rispetto; Misero, o sogno; Per pietà, non ricercate; Se al labbro mio non credi; Si mostra la sorte
Schubert—An die Musik; Salve Regina, D.106
Berlioz—Jeune pâtre breton

Borodin—Mer
Leoncavallo—Mattinata
Mahler—Antonius von Padua Fischpredigt; Blicke mir nicht in die Lieder!; Ich atmet' einen Linden Duft; Ich bin der Welt abhanden gekommen; Irdische Leben; Liebst Du um Schönheit?; Lob des hohen Verstandes; Revelge; Rheinlegendchen; Schildwache Nachtlie; Tamboursg'sell; Trost im Unglück; Um Mitternacht; Verlorne Müh'; Wer hat dies Liedlein erdacht?; Wo die schönen Trompeten blasen
Strauss, R.—Cäcilie; Morgen; Sechs Lieder [each of 6 songs]; Zueignung
Rachmaninoff—Vocalise
Stravinsky—In memoriam Dylan Thomas
Webern—Geistliche Lieder; Lieder, op.14
Britten—Now Sleeps the Crimson Petal
Tyzik—Twelve Gifts of Christmas
Smith, Kile—Poems of Gerard Manley Hopkins
Richman—Sheva B'rachot

11'–20'

Bach, J.S.—Cantatas Nos.160, 189
Fauré—Shylock: Suite
Mahler—Rückert Lieder
Loeffler—Canticum fratris solis
Busoni—Rondò arlecchinesco
Berg—Sieben frühe Lieder
Gerhard—Cancionero de Pedrell
Weill—Dreigroschenoper: Suite (arr. Schönherr)
Barber—Knoxville: Summer of 1915
Britten—Quatre chansons françaises
Maderna—Venetian Journal
Del Tredici—Alice Symphony: The Lobster Quadrille
Tan—On Taoism

21'–30'

Verdi—Romanze
Sullivan—Merchant of Venice: Masquerade Suite
Chausson—Poème de l'amour et de la mer
Mahler—Sieben Lieder aus letzten Zeit
Loeffler—Five Irish Fantasies
Strauss, R.—Sechs Lieder, op.68; Three Hymns [high voice]
Casella—Giara: Symphonic Suite
Finzi—Dies natalis
Tippett—Songs for Dov
Carter—In Sleep, In Thunder
Britten—Gloriana: Symphonic Suite; Illuminations; Nocturne; Our Hunting Fathers; Serenade for Tenor, Horn &

Strings
London—Peter Quince at the Clavier
Rands—Canti del sole

Over 30'

Berlioz—Nuits d'été
Mahler—Lieder aus "Des Knaben Wunderhorn"
Vaughan Williams—Symphony No.3
Britten—Fourteen Folk Songs
Maxwell Davies—Eight Songs for a Mad King; Into the Labyrinth

BARITONE or BASS

10' or less

Mozart, W.A.—Alcandro, lo confesso/Non so d'onde viene, K.512; Bacio di mano; Così dunque; Ich möchte wohl der Kaiser sein; Io ti lascio; Mentre ti lascio, o figlia; Per questa bella mano; Rivolgete a lui lo sguardo
Schubert—An die Musik
Grieg—From Monte Pincio
Mahler—Antonius von Padua Fischpredigt; Blicke mir nicht in die Lieder!; Ich atmet' einen Linden Duft; Ich bin der Welt abhanden gekommen; Irdische Leben; Liebst Du um Schönheit?; Lob des hohen Verstandes; Revelge; Rheinlegendchen; Schildwache Nachtlied; Tamboursg'sell; Trost im Unglück; Um Mitternacht; Verlorne Müh'; Wer hat dies Liedlein erdacht?; Wo die schönen Trompeten blasen
Wolf—Anakreons Grab
Strauss, R.—Morgen; Zueignung
Sibelius—Rapid-Rider's Brides
Ives—Charlie Rutlage; Evening
Ravel—Cinq mélodies populaires grecques; Don Quichotte à Dulcinée
Canteloube—Chants d'Auvergne [each of 27 songs]
Respighi—Tre liriche
Stravinsky—Pribaoutki; Two Songs by Verlaine
Webern—Lieder, op.8
Collins—Daffodils; Piper; Prayer for C.H.S.; Song and Suds
Rudow—Journey of Waters
Richman—Homework Blues

11'–20'

Bach, J.S.—Cantata No.203
Mussorgsky—Songs and Dances of

Death
Mahler—Lieder eines fahrenden
  Gesellen; Rückert Lieder
Loeffler—Canticum fratris solis
Debussy—Trois Ballades de François
  Villon
Zemlinsky—Six Songs, op.1
Ravel—Trois poèmes de Stéphane
  Mallarmé
Falla—Siete canciones populares
Respighi—Tramonto
Stravinsky—Abraham and Isaac
Berg—Sieben frühe Lieder
Prokofiev—Lieutenant Kijé: Suite
Still—Here's One
Poulenc—Bal masqué
Weill—Dreigroschenoper: Suite (arr.
  Schönherr)
Foss—Song of Anguish
Adams, Leslie—Three Dunbar Songs
Adams, John—Wound-Dresser
Tan—On Taoism

21'–30'

Bach, J.S.—Cantata No.82
Cimarosa—Maestro di cappella
Dvořák—Biblical Songs
Chausson—Poème de l'amour et de la
  mer
Elgar—Sea Pictures
Mahler—Kindertotenlieder; Sieben
  Lieder aus letzten Zeit
Gruenberg—Creation
Copland—Eight Poems of Emily
  Dickinson
Fortner—Creation
Weber, Ben—Symphony on Poems of
  Wm Blake
Henze—Concerto, Violin, No.2
Nelson, Ron—Five Pieces
Schafer—Garden of the Heart
Gruber—Frankenstein!!
Tan—Orchestral Theatre II

Over 30'

Berlioz—Nuits d'été
Mahler—Lieder aus "Des Knaben
  Wunderhorn"
Schoenberg—Serenade
Britten—Fourteen Folk Songs
Maxwell Davies—Eight Songs for a Mad
  King

SEVERAL SOLO VOICES

2 Solo Voices

Bach, J.S.—Cantatas Nos.49 (SB); 58
  (SB); 152 (SB); 212 (SB); Tilge,
  Höchster, meine Sünden (SA)
Mozart, W.A.—Nun liebes Weibchen
  (SB)
Tchaikovsky—Romeo and Juliet [duet
  version] (ST)
Mahler—Lied von der Erde (AT or BarT)
Delius—Prelude and Idyll (SBar)
Nielsen, Carl—Symphony No.3 (SBar)
Sibelius—Autrefois (SA)
Roussel—Padmâvatî: Suite No.1 (TBar)
Zemlinsky—Lyrische Symphonie (SBar)
Copland—Tender Land: Suite [chamber
  ens] (ST)
Shostakovich—Symphony No.14 (SB)
Carter—Syringa (MsB)
Burgess—Symphony No.3 (TBar)
Bernstein—Arias and Barcarolles
  (MsBar)
Nono, Luigi—Canti di vita e d'amore
  (ST)
Maxwell Davies—Black Pentecost
  (MsBar)
Andriessen—Mausoleum (2Bar)
Tavener—Akhmatova: Requiem (SB)
Danielpour—Symphony No.2 (ST)

3 Solo Voices

Monteverdi—Combattimento di Tancredi
  e Clorinda (SAT)
Purcell—Ode for St. Cecilia's Day, Z.329
  (ATB)
Mozart, W.A.—Mandina amabile (STB)
Berlioz—Nuits d'été (MsTBar)
Stravinsky—Pulcinella (STB)
Reich—Music for Mallet Instruments,
  Voices & Organ (3 female voices)

4 Solo Vloices (SATB)

Bach, J.S.—Cantatas nos. 15, 42, 85, 86,
  88, 132, 151, 155, 162, 163, 164, 165,
  167, 168, 183, 185, 188
Beethoven— Elegischer Gesang
Milhaud—Symphonies de chambre: No.6
Schnittke—Symphony No.4

4 or more Solo Voices (not SATB)

Mozart, W.A.—Dite almeno in che
  mancai (STBB)
Vaiughan Williams—Serenade to Music
  (4S, 4A, 4T, 4B)
Stravinsky—Renard (TTBB)

Martin—Vin herbé (3S, 3A, 3T, 3B)
Bernstein—Songfest (SMsATBarB)
Berio—Sinfonia (SSAATTBB)
Boulez—cummings is der Dichter (4S,
  4A, 4T, 4B)
Moore, Carman—Gospel Fuse (SSAA)
Reich—Tehillim (SSSA)
Andriessen—Staat (4 female voices)

SPEAKER or NARRATOR

10' or less

Schoenberg—Moderne Psalm; Survivor
  from Warsaw; Genesis Suite: Babel
Toch—Genesis Suite: The Covenant
Milhaud—Genesis Suite: Cain and Abel
Copland—Preamble for a Solemn
  Occasion
Walton—Façade: Four Additional
  Numbers
Kubik—Gerald McBoing Boing
Foss—Elegy for Anne Frank
Kraft—Simple Introduction to the
  Orchestra
Zaninelli—Through Eudora's Eyes
Lankester—Pocket-Sized Guide to the
  Orchestra
Peck—Jack and Jill at Bunker Hill;
  Playing with Style
Beckel—Imagination
Ayers—Veni Emmanuel
Schaffner—Whirlwind Tour of the
  Orchestra
Rimelis—Cool Ghoul
Danielpour—Washington Speaks
Dorff—Blast Off!; Goldilocks and the
  Three Bears; Three Fun Fables: The
  Tortoise and the Hare
O'Boyle—Music That Goes with "The
  Tale of Peter Rabbit"
Richman—Be a Composer; Dachau Lied

11'–20'

Grieg—Bergliot
Loeffler—Evocation
Schoenberg—Kol nidre; Ode to Napoleon
Stravinsky—Sermon, a Narrative, and a
  Prayer
Shilkret—Genesis Suite: Creation
Castelnuovo-Tedesco—Genesis Suite:
  The Flood
Copland—Lincoln Portrait
Walton—Façade 2
Britten—Young Person's Guide to the
  Orchestra
Kleinsinger—Tubby the Tuba
Kirk—Orchestra Primer
Barab—G-A-G-E

Hollingsworth—Three Ladies Beside the Sea
Lees—Trumpet of the Swan
Schuller—Journey into Jazz
Lombardo—Drakestail
Biggs—Ballad of William Sycamore
Zaninelli—Tale of Peter Rabbit
Schickele—Zoo Called Earth
Del Tredici—Haddock's Eyes
Baksa—Variations from the Heart
Armer—Great Instrument of the Geggerets
Kolb—Chromatic Fantasy
Proto—Casey at the Bat
Bamert—Circus Parade
Bond, Victoria—Thinking Like a Mountain
Peck—Thrill of the Orchestra; Where's Red Robin?
Gilbert, J.—In the Beginning; Nine-in-One Grr! Grr!
Lieberson, Peter—Remembering JFK
Rodríguez—Colorful Symphony; Jargon; Trunks
Kechley—Alexander and the Wind-Up Mouse; Clocks and More Clocks
Mauldin—Enchanted Land
Tann—Adirondack Light
Beckel—Gardens of Stone; Liberty for All; Waltz of the Animals
Bryant—Dinosaurs
Locklair—Since Dawn
Mascari—Meet the Orchestra
Ayers—Passion of John Brown
Dorff—Billy and the Carnival; Three Fun Fables
Oliverio, James—Story of Snow White
Cotton—CityMusic
Itkin—Jonah
Smith, Gregory—Mr. Smith's Composition; Zoo Song
Tan—On Taoism
Heitzeg—On the Day You Were Born; Voice of the Everglades

Roter—TR: A "Bully" Portrait
Richman—I Remember a Lullaby
Boyer—Dreaming a World
Puts—John Brown's Body
Territo—John Henry vs. the Machine

21'–30'

Saint-Saëns—Carnaval des animaux
Vaughan Williams—Oxford Elegy
Prokofiev—Peter and the Wolf
Rogers—Musicians of Bremen
Bacon—Fables; USania; A Small Oratorio
Harsányi—Histoire du petite tailleur
Poulenc—Histoire de Babar
Gould—Jogger and the Dinosaur
Pinkham—Signs of the Zodiac
Laderman—Magic Prison
Duffy—Time for Remembrance
Erb—New England's Prospect
Nelson, Ron—This is the Orchestra
Shchedrin—Anna Karenina: Romantic Music
Zaninelli—Beginnings; Lexicon of Beasties; Steadfast Tin Soldier
Harmon—Earth Day Portrait
Schickele—Chenoo Who Stayed to Dinner
Corigliano—Creations
Monroe—Amazing Symphony Orchestra
Schwantner—New Morning for the World
Bond, Victoria—What's the Point of Counterpoint?
Gilbert, J.—Dream Carver; Khoj
Ott—First Trip to the Symphony
Welcher—Haleakala
Einhorn—My Many Colored Days
Davidson—Young Lutheran's Guide to the Orchestra
Adolphe—Carnival of the Creatures; Marita and Her Heart's Desire; Tyrannosaurus Sue

Smith, Gregory—Major-Minor Mystery; Melodic Life; Mr. Smith's Bowl of Notes; Orchestra Games
Allen—Nativity Scenes
Maltz—Aesop's Fables
Adamo—Late Victorians
Richman—Behold the Bold Umbrellaphant
Stookey—Composer is Dead

Over 30'

Beethoven—Ruinen von Athen
Berlioz—Lélio
Bruckner—Symphony No.9: Finale (Documentation)
Debussy—Martyre de Saint Sébastien
Schoenberg—Gurre-Lieder; Pierrot lunaire
Bloch, E.—Avodath Hakodesh
Stravinsky—Oedipus rex; Perséphone
Prokofiev—Ivan the Terrible
Honegger—Roi David
Bacon—Great River
Walton—Façade; Henry V [arr.]
Moore, Undine—Scenes from the Life of a Martyr
Ward—Sweet Freedom's Song
Bernstein—Symphony No.3
Duffy—Heritage: Symphonic Suite with Narration
Penderecki—Passio et mors domini nostri Iesu Christi secundum Lucam
Jones—Eudora's Fable: The Shoe Bird
Bach, Jan—Happy Prince
Bamert—Once Upon an Orchestra
Tavener—Whale
Paulus—Voices from the Gallery
Warshauer—Shacharit
Adolphe—Purple Palace
Corrin—How the Orchestra Grew
Abels—Frederick's Fables
Stephenson—Compose Yourself!
Boyer—Ellis Island
Dorman—Uzu and Muzu from Kakaruzu

APPENDIX C
SOLO INSTRUMENTS

Piano
Piano (left hand)
2 or more Pianists
Harpsichord
2 or more Harpsichords
Organ
Multiple Diverse Keyboards

Violin
2 or more Violins
Viola
Violoncello
Double Bass
Multiple Diverse Strings
    2 Solo Strings
    2 Violins & Violoncello
    Solo String Quartet
    Other Combinations of 3-13 Strings

Flute
2 or more Flutes
Recorder
Piccolo
Oboe
English Horn
Clarinet
Bassoon(s)

Saxophone(s)

Horn
2 or more Horns
Trumpet
2 Trumpets
Trombone
Tuba

Percussion
Harp(s)
Guitar
2 or more Guitars
Ethnic Instruments
Other Instruments
Multiple Diverse Soloists
    2 Soloists
    3 Soloists
    4 Soloists
    5 Soloists
    6 or more Soloists

Handbell Choir
Steelpan(s)
Jazz Soloists

Works within the larger categories are subdivided by duration. Within each category or subdivision, works are listed in *chronological order* according to the composer's birth date. This will make it possible for you to go immediately to a particular part of the list if you happen to be looking for something from a certain style-period (baroque, for example, or contemporary). Initial articles in all languages are omitted from the titles in this appendix.

Refer back to the main alphabetical listing by composer for full information.

PIANO

10' or less

Mozart, W.A.—Concertos, Piano, K.107 nos.2-3; Concert-Rondos, K.382, K.386
Beethoven—Rondo, Piano & Orch

Mendelssohn—Rondo brillant
Chopin—Grande polonaise brillante
Alkan—Andante romantique
Gottschalk—Grande Tarantelle
Saint-Saëns—Allegro appassionato, op.70; Rhapsodie d'Auvergne; Wedding Cake
Stravinsky—Movements
Turina—Rapsodia sinfónica

Honegger—Concertino, Piano & Orch
Gershwin—"I Got Rhythm" Variations
Ellington—New World A-Comin'
Addinsell—Warsaw Concerto
Françaix—Concertino, piano
Foss—Elegy for Anne Frank
Górecki—Concerto, Harpsichord (or Piano)
O'Boyle—Scottish Piano Rhapsody

11'–20'

Haydn, F.J.—Concerto, Harpsichord, Hob.XVIII:5
Mozart, W.A.—Concertos, Piano, Nos.1-4; K.107, no.1; No.6; No.8
Beethoven—Fantasia, Piano, Chorus & Orch, op.80
Wölfl—Concerto, Piano, No.7
Weber, C.M.—Concerto, Piano, No.1; Konzertstück, Piano & Orch; Polonaise brillante
Mendelssohn—Capriccio brillant
Chopin—Allegro de concert; Fantasy on Polish Airs; Krakowiak; Variations on "La ci darem la mano"
Schumann, R.—Concert-Allegro with Introduction; Introduction & Allegro appassionato
Liszt—Concerto, Piano, No.1; Concerto, Piano, op. posth.; Concerto pathétique; Fantasie über ungarische ; Fantasy on "Ruins of Athens"; Malédiction; Rhapsodie espagnole; Totentanz [2 versions]
Franck—Djinns; Symphonic Variations
Raff—Ode au printemps
Saint-Saëns—Africa
Tchaikovsky—Andante & Finale; Concerto, Piano, No.3
Rimsky-Korsakov—Concerto, Piano
Fauré—Ballade; Fantasy, Piano, op.111
Janáček—Capriccio for Piano (LH); Concertino
Albéniz—Rapsodia española
Strauss, R.—Burleske
Roussel—Concerto, Piano
Ravel—Concerto, Piano (LH)
Laparra—Dimanche basque
Respighi—Fantasia slava; Toccata
Bartók—Rhapsody, Piano & Orchestra
Stravinsky—Capriccio; Concerto for Piano & Winds
Becker—Concerto arabesque
Prokofiev—Concerto, Piano, No.1
Milhaud—Carnaval d'Aix; Concerto, Piano, No.1; Concerto, Piano, No.3; Suite concertante, Piano & Orchestra
Benjamin, A.—Concertino, Piano & Orchestra
Piston—Concertino
Hindemith—Kammermusik No.2
Still—Black Man Dances; Dismal Swamp
Cowell—Four Irish Tales
Tansman—Concertino, Piano
Gershwin—Rhapsody in Blue [3 versions; Second Rhapsody
Poulenc—Concerto, Piano
Tcherepnin, A.—Bagatelles, op.5
Antheil—Jazz Symphony [original 1925 version]

Copland—Concerto, Piano
Walton—Sinfonia concertante [2 versions]
Blacher—Variations on a Theme of Clementi
Kabalevsky—Concerto, Piano, No.3
Lambert—Rio Grande
Tippett—Fantasia on a Theme of Handel
Shostakovich—Concerto, Piano, No.2
Messiaen—Couleurs de la cité céleste; Oiseaux exotiques; Vitrail et des oiseaux
Szpilman—Concertino, Piano & Orch
Gould—Interplay
Perle—Concerto, Piano, No.2
Surinach—Concertino for Piano, Strings & Cymbals
Babbitt—Concerto, Piano
Kirchner—Concerto, Piano, No.2
Ustvolskaya, Galina—Concerto, Piano
La Montaine, John—Birds of Paradise
Chou—Pien
Hollingsworth—Concerto, Piano
Muczynski—Concerto, Piano, No.1
Wyner—Concerto, Piano
Takemitsu—Riverrun
Zaninelli—Concertino, Piano
Pärt, Arvo—Credo
Bolcom—Orphée-sérénade
Svoboda—Concerto, Piano, No.1
Zwilich—Millennium Fantasy; Peanuts Gallery; Shadows
Singleton—Blueskonzert
Schwantner—Distant Runes and Incantations
Cresswell—Concerto, Piano
Emerson—Concerto, Piano, No.1
Eötvös—CAP-KO
Bond, Victoria—Ancient Keys
Adams, John—Eros Piano
Horwood—Intravariations
Ran—Concert Piece
Rollin—Concerto romantique
Chen Yi—Concerto, Piano
Daugherty—Tombeau de Liberace
Picker—Keys to the City
Sheng—Red Silk Dance
Francesconi—Islands
Smith, Kile—Variations on a Theme of Schubert
Ince—Concerto, Piano
Martineau—Concertino, Piano
Amrhein—Concerto, Piano
Boyer—American Rhapsody

21'–30'

Mozart, W.A.—Concertos, Piano, Nos.5; 11; 12; 13; 14; 15; 17; 18; 19; 20; 21; 23; 25; 26
Beethoven—Concerto, Piano, No.2
Kuhlau—Concerto, Piano, op.7
Weber, C.M.—Concerto, Piano, No.2

Schubert—Wanderer Fantasy
Mendelssohn—Concertos, Piano, No.1-2
Liszt—Concerto, Piano, No.2
Schumann, Clara—Concerto, Piano
Rubinstein—Concerto, Piano, No.4
Saint-Saëns—Concertos, Piano, Nos.1-5
Tchaikovsky—Concerto, Piano, No.2 [Siloti version]; Fantasie de concert
Massenet—Concerto, Piano
Grieg—Concerto, Piano
Brüll—Concerto, Piano, No.1
Scharwenka—Concerto, Piano, No.1
Indy—Symphonie sur un chant montagnard français
Albéniz—Concerto, Piano, No.1
MacDowell—Concertos, Piano, Nos.1-2
Paderewski—Fantaisie polonaise
Arensky—Concerto, Piano, op.2
Debussy—Fantaisie, Piano & Orch [2 versions]
Delius—Concerto, Piano
Busoni—Indianische Fantasie
Beach—Concerto, Piano
Converse—Night & Day
Scriabin—Concerto, Piano; Prometheus
Vaughan Williams—Concerto, 1 Piano or 2 Pianos
Rachmaninoff—Concerto, Piano, No.1 [definitive final version]; Concerto, Piano, No.4 [1928 version or 1941 version]; Rhapsody on a Theme of Paganini
Ives—Emerson Overture (Concerto)
Schoenberg—Concerto, Piano
Hahn—Concerto, Piano
Ravel—Concerto, Piano, G major
Falla—Noches en los jardines de
Dohnányi—Variations on a Nursery Song
Bloch, E.—Concerto Grosso No.1
Bartók—Concertos, Piano, Nos.1, 2, 3; Scherzo
Szymanowski—Symphony No.4
Casella—Scarlattiana
Collins—Concerto, Piano, No.1; Concert Piece
Villa-Lobos—Bachianas brasileiras no.3; Mômoprecóce
Martin—Concerto, Piano, No.2
Martinů—Fantasia concertante, Piano & Orch
Prokofiev—Concerto, Piano, No.3; Concerto, Piano (LH), No.4; Concerto, Piano, No.5
Hindemith—Theme and Variations
Gerhard—Concerto, Piano
Poulenc—Aubade
Poulenc—Concerto champêtre
Antheil—Concerto, Piano, No.1
Krenek—Concertos, Piano, Nos.1-2
Serly—Concertino 3 x 3
Blacher—Concerto, Piano, No.1
Blitzstein—Concerto, Piano

Jolivet—Concerto, Piano
Badings—Concerto, Piano
Anderson, Leroy—Concerto, Piano
Carter—Concerto
Messiaen—Sept haïkaï
Barber—Concerto, Piano
Schuman, Wm.—Concerto, Piano
Lutoslawski—Concerto, Piano
Panufnik—Concerto, Piano
Perle—Concerto, Piano, No.1
Ginastera—Concerto, Piano, No.1
Ward—Concerto, Piano
Kirchner—Concerto, Piano, No.1
La Montaine—Concerto, Piano
Imbrie—Concerto, Piano, No.2
Ligeti—Concerto, Piano
Rorem—Concerto, Piano, No.3
Lees—Concerto, Piano, No.2
Schurmann—Concerto, Piano
Hoiby—Concerto, Piano, No.2,
Diemer—Concerto, Piano
Flagello—Concerto, Piano, No.2
Rautavaara—Concerto, Piano, No.3
Martino—Concerto, Piano
Biggs—Variations on a Theme of
  Shostakovich
Lazarof—Tableaux
Zaninelli—Lexicon of Beasties
Schnittke—Concerto, Piano
Wuorinen—Concerto, Piano, No.3
Kolb—Voyants
Stewart—Concerto, Piano
Schwantner—Concerto, Piano
Höller—Pensées
Pasatieri—Concerto, Piano
Adams, John—Century Rolls
Schoenfeld—Four Parables
Davis—Wayang No.5
Beaser—Concerto, Piano
Durand, Joël-François—Concerto, Piano
Young—Concerto, Piano
Danielpour—Metamorphosis
Moravec, Paul—Concerto, Piano
Lindberg—Concerto, Piano, [No.1]
Higdon—Concerto, Piano
Psathas—Three Psalms
Horne—Concerto, Piano
Dorman—Lost Souls

Over 30'

Viotti—Concerto, Piano, G minor
Mozart, W.A.—Concertos, Piano, Nos.9;
  22; 24; 27
Beethoven—Concertos, Piano, Nos.1, 3,
  4, 5, 6
Hummel—Concerto, Piano, op.113
Mendelssohn—Concerto, Piano &
  Strings, A minor
Chopin—Concerto, Piano, No.1 [3
  versions]; Concerto, Piano, No.2
Schumann, R.—Concerto, Piano

Alkan—Concerto, Piano
Litolff—Concerto symphonique, No.4
Rubinstein—Concerto, Piano, No.3
Brahms—Concertos, Piano, Nos.1-2
Goetz—Concerto, Piano, No.2
Tchaikovsky—Concertos, Piano, Nos.1-2
Dvořák—Concerto, Piano
Sinding—Concerto, Piano, op.6
Paderewski—Concerto, Piano
Busoni—Concerto, Piano
Pfitzner—Concerto, Piano, op.31
Stojowski—Concerto, Piano, No.1
Rachmaninoff—Concertos, Piano, Nos.2,
  3, 4 [1926 version]
Dohnányi—Concerto, Piano, No.1
Collins—Concerto, Piano, No.3
Atterberg—Concerto, Piano, op.37
Prokofiev—Concerto, Piano, No.2
Bacon—Concerto, Piano, No.2; Riolama
Gershwin—Concerto, Piano, F major [2
  versions]
Chávez—Concerto, Piano
Khachaturian—Concerto, Piano
Skalkottas—Concerto, Piano, No.3
Tippett—Concerto, Piano
Dorati—Concerto, Piano
Menotti—Concerto, Piano
Britten—Concerto, Piano, No.1
Burgess—Concerto, Piano, E-flat
Bernstein—Symphony No.2
Imbrie—Concerto, Piano, No.3
Henze—Concerto, Piano, No.2
Glass—Concerto, Piano, No.2
Corigliano—Concerto, Piano
Davies, Victor—Mennonite Piano
  Concerto
Svoboda—Concerto, Piano, No.2; Three
  Cadenzas
Danielpour—Concerto, Piano, No.2

PIANO (LEFT HAND)

Janáček—Capriccio for Piano (LH)
Strauss, R.—Parergon zur Sinfonia
  Domestica
Ravel—Concerto, Piano (LH)
Prokofiev—Concerto, Piano (LH), No.4
Britten—Diversions on a Theme
Rorem—Concerto, Piano (LH), No.4

2 OR MORE PIANISTS

Mozart, W.A.—Concerto, 3 Pianos, No.7;
  Concerto, 2 Pianos, No.10
Czerny—Concerto, Piano 4-hands
Mendelssohn—Concerto, 2 Pianos, A-flat
  major; Concerto, 2 Pianos, E major
Saint-Saëns—Carnaval des animaux
Bruch—Concerto, 2 Pianos, op.88a

Vaughan Williams—Concerto, 1 Piano or
  2 Pianos
Villa-Lobos—Chôros no.8
Piston—Concerto, 2 Pianos
Poulenc—Concerto, 2 Pianos
Bowles—Concerto, 2 Pianos, Percussion
  & Winds; Concerto, 2 pianos [full
  orchestra version]
Britten—Scottish Ballad
Zimmermann—Dialog
Imbrie—Little Concerto (4 hands)
Powell—Duplicates
Berio—Concerto, 2 Pianos
Pasatieri—Concerto, 2 Pianos & Strings
Adams, John—Grand Pianola Music [2
  solo pianos & 3 ampd female voices]

HARPSICHORD

15' or less

Bach, J.S.—Concertos, Harpsichord,
  Nos.4, 5, 6
Galuppi—Concerto, Harpsichord, F
  major
Haydn, F.J.—Concertino, Harpsichord,
  Hob.XIV:11; Concertos, Harpsichord,
  Hob.XVIII:5; Hob.XVIII:7;
  Hob.XVIII:F1
Bach, J.C.—Concerto, Harpsichord,
  op.13, no.2
Dittersdorf—Concerto, Harpsichord
Falla—Concerto, Harpsichord
Górecki—Concerto, Harpsichord

Over 15'

Bach, J.S.—Concertos, Harpsichord,
  Nos.1, 2, 3, 6
Bach, C.P.E.—Concerto, Harpsichord,
  H.427
Wagenseil—Concerto, Harpsichord
Haydn, F.J.—Concerto, Harpsichord,
  Hob.XVIII:4; Concerto, Harpsichord,
  Hob.XVIII:11
Bach, J.C.—Concerto, Harpsichord, op.7,
  no.5; Concerto, Harpsichord, op.13, no.4
Poulenc—Concerto champêtre
Bennett, Richard R.—Concerto,
  Harpsichord
Locklair—Concerto, Harpsichord, Str &
  Perc

2 or MORE HARPSICHORDS

Bach, J.S.—Concertos, 2 Harpsichords,
  Nos.1, 2, 3; Concertos, 3 Harpsichords,
  Nos.1-2; Concerto, 4 Harpsichords,
  BWV 1065

ORGAN

15' or less

Albinoni—Adagio, Organ & Strings
Handel—Concertos, Organ, op.4, nos.2, 5, 6; op.7, nos.1, 5, 6; Concerto, Organ, HWV 295; Concerto, Organ, HWV 304
Haydn, F.J.—Concerto, Organ, No.2, Hob.XVIII:8; Concerto, Organ, F major
Mozart, W.A.—Sonatas, Organ & Strings, Nos.1-17
Piston—Prelude & Allegro
Krenek—Concerto, Organ, op.230
Barber—Toccata festiva
Arnold—Concerto, Organ
Adler, S.—Lux perpetua
Jones—Mount Rainier Overture
Bolcom—Humoresk
Locklair—"Ere Long We Shall See ..."
Chen Yi—Dunhuang Fantasy
Theofanidis—Rex tremendae majestatis

Over 15'

Handel—Concertos, Organ, op.4, nos.1, 4; op.7, nos.2, 3, 4; Concerto, Organ, HWV 296a; Concerto, Organ, HWV 305a
Haydn, F.J.—Concerto, Organ, Hob.XVIII:1
Saint-Saëns—Symphony No.3
Guilmant—Symphony No.1, Organ & Orch
Rheinberger—Concertos, Organ, Nos.1-2
Widor—Symphony No.3
Jongen—Symphonie concertante
Respighi—Suite, P.58
Dupré—Symphony, op.25
Hindemith—Concerto, organ (1962); Kammermusik No.7
Sowerby—Medieval Poem
Poulenc—Concerto, Organ
Copland—Symphony for Organ & Orchestra
Khachaturian—Symphony No.3
Rorem—Concerto, Organ
Riley—At the Royal Majestic

MULTIPLE DIVERSE KEYBOARDS

Bach, C.P.E.—Concerto, Piano & Harpsichord, H.479
Carter—Double Concerto, Harpsichord & Piano
Messiaen—Trois petites liturgies; Turangalîla-symphonie [both with piano & ondes martenot]

VIOLIN

10' or less

Torelli—Concerto, Violin, op.8, no.8
Vivaldi—Concertos, Violin, op.3, nos.3, 6, 9, 12; op.4, nos.1, 2, 3, 4, 5, 8, 9, 10, 11; op.8, nos.5, 6, 7, 8, 10, 12; op.9, nos.1, 2, 5, 7, 8, 10, 11; Concerto, Violin, RV 270; Quattro stagioni: Estate, Autunno, Inverno
Telemann—Concerto, Violin, TWV 51:a2
Veracini—Concerto, Violin, D major
Mozart, W.A.—Adagio, Violin & Orch, K.261; Rondo, Violin, K.269; Rondo, Violin, K.373
Beethoven—Romance Nos.1-2
Paganini—Moto perpetuo, op.11
Schubert—Konzertstück
Chopin—Romanze
Vieuxtemps—Yankee Doodle (Souvenir d'Amerique)
Borodin—Nocturne [arr. N. Rimsky-Korsakov]
Saint-Saëns—Introduction & Rondo capriccioso; Romance, Flute (or Violin), op.37; Romance, Violin, op.48
Wieniawski—Légend; Polonaise brillante No.1; Polonaise brillante No.2; Scherzo-tarantelle
Bruch—Adagio appassionato
Svendsen—Romance
Tchaikovsky—Sérénade mélancolique; Souvenir d'un lieu cher: nos.1, 2, 3; Valse-scherzo
Massenet—Thaïs: Méditation
Sarasate—Introduction and Tarantella; Zigeunerweisen
Accolay—Concerto, Violin, No.1
Seitz—Concerto, Violin, op.13, no.2
Strauss, R.—Morgen
Sibelius—Humoresque I & II
Sinigaglia—Rapsodia piemontese
Brockway—Cavatina
Schmitt—Légende
Ravel—Tzigane
Bartók—Rhapsody No.1
Stravinsky—Pastorale
Atterberg—Adagio amoroso
Milhaud—Concertino de printemps
Hindemith—Trauermusik
Cowell—Fiddler's Jig
Finzi—Introit
Penderecki—Capriccio, Violin
Kancheli—V & V
Zwilich—Romance
Actor—Meditation
Daugherty—Metropolis Symphony: Lex
Dorff—Sunburst

O'Boyle—Snapshot Concertos: Tumbleweeds at Ten Paces
Frank, G.L.—Havana Jila

11'–20'

Torelli—Concerto, Violin, op.8, no.9
Vitali—Ciaccona [2 versions]
Albinoni—Concerto, Violin, op.9, no.10
Vivaldi—Concertos, Violin, op.4, nos.6, 12; op.8, no.11; op.9, nos.3, 4, 6, 12
Concerto, Violin, RV 179; RV 271; RV 582; RV 583; Quattro stagioni: Primavera
Bach, J.S.—Cantata No.147a; Concerto, Flute (or Violin), BWV 971; Concertos, Violin, Nos.1, 2
Veracini—Concerto grande da chiesa
Tartini—Concerto, Violin, No.57; Sinfonia pastorale
Leclair—Concertos, Violin, op.7, no.4-5
Sammartini, Giov. Battista—Concerto, Violin (or Violoncello Piccolo), C major
Pergolesi—Concerto, Violin, B-flat major
Benda, Joh.—Concerto, Violin, G major
Haydn, F.J.—Concerto, Violin, Hob.VIIa:1
Bach, J.C.—Sinfonia concertante, W. C34
Hofmann, Leopold—Concertos, Violin, Badley A2 & Badley Bb1
Saint-Georges—Concerto, Violin, No.1
Auber—Concerto, Violin, D major
Paganini—Concerto, Violin, No.1 [arr. Wilhelmj]
Spohr—Concerto, Violin, No.8
Schubert—Rondo, D.438
Berlioz—Rêverie et Caprice, op.8
Schumann, R.—Fantasia, op.131
Vieuxtemps—Concerto, Violin, No.5
Saint-Saëns—Concerto, Violin, No.1; Havanaise
Wieniawski—Fantaisie brillante
Goetz—Concerto, Violin, op.22
Tchaikovsky—Souvenir d'un lieu cher, op.42 [complete]
Dvořák—Romance, op.11
Rimsky-Korsakov—Fantasia on 2 Russian Themes
Sarasate—Carmen Fantasy
Chausson—Poème
Ysaÿe—Chant d'hiver
Conus—Concerto, Violin
Vaughan Williams—Concerto, Violin; Lark Ascending; Serenade to Music [orch version]
Carpenter—Concerto, Violin
Bloch, E.—Baal Shem; Suite hébraïque
Bartók—Rhapsody No.2; Two Portraits
Szymanowski—Concerto, Violin, No.2
Wellesz—Suite, Violin & Chamber Orch
Stephan—Musik für Geige und Orchester

Milhaud—Boeuf sur le toit
Rosenberg—Suite, Violin & Orchestra
Still—Suite, Violin & Orchestra
Rubbra—Improvisation
Dallapiccola—Tartiniana
Kabalevsky—Concerto, Violin
Hartmann—Concerto funèbre
Dahl—Elegy Concerto
Khrennikov—Concerto, Violin, op.14
Lutoslawski—Chain 2
Shulman—Pastorale and Dance; Poem
Ritchie, John—Pisces
Hollingsworth—Concerto, Violin
Perry—Concerto, Violin
Previn—Concerto, Violin & Viola
Takemitsu—Far Calls, Coming, Far
Van de Vate—Concerto, Violin, No.2
Maxwell Davies—Spell for Green Corn
Schnittke—Quasi una sonata
Riley—Zephir
Schwertsik—Concerto, Violin
Bolcom—Concerto-Serenade
Corigliano—Red Violin [Chaconne]
Harbison—Crane Sightings
Holliger—Meta arca
Svoboda—Concerto, Violin
Zwilich—Commedia dell'arte; Partita
Gruber—Nebelsteinmusik
Holloway—Romanza
Schwantner—Angelfire
Ran—Concerto, Violin
Tsontakis—Concerto, Violin, No.2
Chen Yi—Chinese Folk Dance Suite
Young—Remembering
Mackey—Beautiful Passing
Sleeper, Thomas—Concerto, Violin
Wagner, Melinda—Little Moonhead
Ince—In White
O'Boyle—Celtic Suite
Richman—I Remember a Lullaby
Stephenson—Violin Fantasie Concerto

21'–30'

Haydn, F.J.—Concertos, Violin,
 Hob.VIIa:4, Hob.VIIa:B2
Haydn, M.—Concerto, Violin, MH 207
Boccherini—Concerto, Violin, G.486
Viotti—Concerto, Violin, No.22
Mozart, W.A.—Concertos, Violin,
 Nos.1-4, 6-7
Spohr—Concerto, Violin, No.9
Mendelssohn—Concerto, Violin, op.64;
 Concerto, Violin (posth.), D minor
Schumann, R.—Concerto, Violin, A
 minor
Gade—Concerto, Violin, op.56
Vieuxtemps—Concerto, Violin, No.4
Lalo—Concerto, Violin
Saint-Saëns—Concertos, Violin, Nos.2-3
Wieniawski—Concertos, Violin, Nos.1-2

Bruch—Concertos, Violin, Nos.1-2;
 Scottish Fantasy
Delius—Concerto, Violin
Glazunov—Concerto, Violin
Karłowicz—Concerto, Violin
Respighi—Concerto, Violin
Bartók—Concerto, Violin, No.1
Stravinsky—Concerto, Violin
Szymanowski—Concerto, Violin, No.1
Berg—Concerto, Violin
Martin—Polyptyque
Martinů—Concerto, Violin, No.2, H.293
Prokofiev—Concertos, Violin, Nos.1-2
Milhaud—Concerto, Violin, No.2
Hindemith—Concerto, Violin;
 Kammermusik No.4
Sessions—Concerto, Violin
Korngold—Concerto, Violin
Antheil—Concerto, Violin
Rodrigo—Concierto de estío
Goldschmidt—Concerto, Violin
Khachaturian—Concerto-Rhapsody,
 Violin
Tubin—Concerto, Violin, No.2
Carter—Concerto, Violin
Barber—Concerto, Violin, op.14
Diamond—Concerto, Violin, No.3
Ginastera—Concerto, Violin
Ward—Concerto, Violin
Husa—Concerto, Violin
Walker, George—Concerto, Violin
Rorem—Concerto, Violin
Lees—Concerto, Violin
Henze—Concerto, Violin, No.2
Previn—Concerto, Violin, No.2
Van de Vate—Concerto, Violin, No.1
Biggs—Concerto, Violin
Williams—Concerto, Violin
He—Butterfly Lovers
Maxwell Davies—Concerto, Violin
 [No.1]; Concerto, Violin, No.2
Jones—Concerto, Violin
Bennett, Richard R.—Concerto, Violin
Finko—Concerto, Violin
Bolcom—Concerto, Violin
Corigliano—Red Violin
Zwilich—Concerto, Violin
Cresswell—Voice Inside
Eötvös—DoReMi [Violin Concerto No.2]
Harris, Ross—Concerto, Violin, No.1
Rouse—Concerto, Violin
Boelter—Concerto, Violin
Salonen—Concerto, Violin
Kernis—Lament and Prayer
Bacri—Prière
Stephenson—Tributes
Dorman—Concerto, Violin
Bates, Mason—Concerto, Violin
Greenberg—Concerto, Violin

Over 30'

Vivaldi—Quattro stagioni [complete]
Viotti—Concerto, Violin, No.19
Mozart, W.A.—Concerto, Violin, No.5;
 Serenade No.4
Beethoven—Concerto, Violin
Paganini—Concertos, Violin, No.1-3
Schumann, R.—Concerto, Violin, D
 minor
Lalo—Symphonie espagnole
Goldmark—Concerto, Violin
Joachim—Concerto, Violin, op.11
Brahms—Concerto, Violin
Bruch—Concerto, Violin, No.3; Serenade
Tchaikovsky—Concerto, Violin
Dvořák—Concerto, Violin
Elgar—Concerto, Violin
Strauss, R.—Concerto, Violin
Nielsen, Carl—Concerto, Violin
Sibelius—Concerto, Violin
Sinigaglia—Concerto, Violin
Schoenberg—Concerto, Violin
Dohnányi—Concerto, Violin, No.1
Bloch, E.—Concerto, Violin
Bartók—Concerto, Violin, No.2 (1938)
Gruenberg—Concerto, Violin
Atterberg—Concerto, Violin, op.7
Weill—Concerto, Violin
Walton—Concerto, Violin
Khachaturian—Concerto, Violin
Shostakovich—Concerto, Violin, No.1
Schuman, Wm.—Concerto, Violin
Menotti—Concerto, Violin
Britten—Concerto, Violin, No.1
Bernstein—Serenade
Rochberg—Concerto, Violin
Imbrie—Concerto, Violin
Feldman—Violin and Orchestra
Henze—Vitalino raddoppiata
Previn—Concerto, Violin
Gubaydulina—Offertorium
Penderecki—Concerto, Violin
Schnittke—Concerto, Violin, No.4
Riley—Palmian Chord Ryddle;
 SolTierraLuna
Glass—Concerto, Violin, No.2
Blake—Concerto, Violin
Corigliano—Concerto, Violin
Eötvös—Seven
Tavener—Lalishri
Adams, John—Concerto, Violin
Actor—Concerto, Violin
Dean—Lost Art of Letter Writing
O'Connor, Mark—Fiddle Concerto; Three
 Pieces for Violin & Orch
Higdon—Concerto, Violin; Singing
 Rooms

2 or MORE VIOLINS

Torelli—Concertos, 2 Violins, op.6, no.10; op.8, nos.1, 3, 7; Concerti grossi, 2 Violins, op.8, nos.2, 5, 6
Vivaldi—Concertos, 2 Violins, RV 512, RV 514, RV 519, RV 522, RV 530; Concerto, 3 Violins, RV 551; Concerto, 4 Violins, op.3, no.4, RV 550
Telemann—Concerto, 2 Violins, TWV 52:C2
Manfredini—Concerti grossi, op.3, nos.10, 12
Bach, J.S.—Concerto, 2 Violins
Locatelli—Concerto grosso, op.7, no.12 [4 violins]
Sammartini, Giuseppe—Concerto grosso, op.5, no.6
Saint-Georges—Symphonie concertante, op.13
Mozart, W.A.—Concertone, 2 Violins, K.190
Sarasate—Navarra
Holst—Concerto, 2 Violins
Arnold—Concerto, 2 Violins
Trimble—Duo concertante
Colgrass—Concertmasters [3 violins]
Schnittke—Concerto grosso No.3; Moz-Art à la Haydn
Hoover—Concerto, 2 Violins
Corigliano—Snapshot
Chen Yi—Romance and Dance; Romance of Hsiao and Ch'in
O'Boyle—Snapshot Concertos: Dueling Fiddles [2 versions]
Stookey—Double

VIOLA

Vivaldi—Concertos, Viola d'Amore, RV 392, RV 394
Telemann—Concerto, Viola, TWV 51:G9
Handel—Concerto, Viola
Stamitz, Joh.—Concerto, Viola, G major
Bach, J.C.—Concerto, Violoncello, C minor [spurious; also viola]
Hummel—Fantaisie, Viola
Weber, C.M.—Andante & Rondo ongarese, J.79
Bruch—Romance
Wolf—Italian Serenade
Schmitt—Légende
Holst—Lyric Movement
Bloch, E.—Suite hébraïque
Howells—Elegy
Hindemith—Trauermusik
Hanson—Lux aeterna, op.24

Partos—Yiskor
Hovhaness—Talin
Shulman—Homage to Erik Satie; Theme & Variations, Viola; Variations 1984
Kurtág—Movement, Viola
McCabe—Concerto funèbre
Chen Yi—Xian shi (Viola Concerto)
O'Boyle—Snapshot Concertos: The Songbird

VIOLONCELLO

15' or less

Vivaldi—Concertos, Violoncello, RV 401, R.404, RV 406, RV 418, RV 422
Veracini—Menuet et Gavotte
Boismortier—Concerto, Violoncello
Tartini—Concerto, violoncello, A major
Leo—Concerto, Violoncello, D major
Wagenseil—Concerto, Violoncello, A major
Bach, J.C.—Concerto, Violoncello, C minor
Hofmann, L.—Concertos, Violoncello, C major, Badley C1 & C3
Boccherini—Concerto, Violoncello, G.477
Mozart, W.A.—Concert-Rondo, K.371
Schumann, R.—Adagio & Allegro, op.70
Rubinstein—Melody in F
Saint-Saëns—Allegro appassionato, op.43; Carnaval des animaux: Le cygne; Romance, Horn (or Violoncello)
Bruch—Adagio nach keltischen Melodien; Ave Maria; Kol Nidrei
Tchaikovsky—Andante cantabile; Pezzo capriccioso
Dvořák—Rondo, op.94; Silent Woods
Popper—Hungarian Rhapsody; Tarantelle
Fauré—Elegy
Indy—Lied, op.19
Herbert—Yesterthoughts
Boëllmann—Symphonic Variations
Strauss, R.—Romanze
Glazunov—Chant du ménestrel
Bantock, Granville—Hamabdil
Holst—Invocation, op.19, no.2
Respighi—Adagio con variazioni
Malipiero—Concerto, Violoncello
Milhaud—Concerto, Violoncello, No.1
Hindemith—Trauermusik
Diamond—Kaddish
Shulman—Homage to Erik Satie; Kol nidre; Suite parisienne
Ligeti—Concerto, Violoncello
Previn—Vocalise
Van de Vate—Concertpiece, Violoncello
Balada—Concerto, Violoncello
Penderecki—Sonata, Violoncello & Orch

Tavener—Eternal Memory
Warshauer—In memoriam September 11, 2001
Chen Yi—Eleanor's Gift
Knehans—soar
Golijov—Mariel
Kernis—Air
Higdon—Soliloquy
O'Boyle—Snapshot Concertos: Changing Seasons
Richman—Prayer and Freylach

16'–30'

Bach, C.P.E.—Concerto, Violoncello, H.436
Wagenseil—Concerto, Violoncello, C major
Haydn, F.J.—Concertos, Violoncello, Hob.VIIb:1, Hob.VIIb:2, Hob.VIIb:2 [arr. Gevaert], Hob.VIIb:5
Hofmann, L.—Concerto, Violoncello, Badley D3
Boccherini—Concertos, Violoncello, G.474, G.482, G.482 [Grützmacher]
Stamitz, Carl—Concertos, Violoncello, Nos.1, 2, 3
Schumann, R.—Concerto, Violoncello
Offenbach—Concerto militaire
Lalo—Concerto, Violoncello
Rubinstein—Concerto, Violoncello, No.2
Saint-Saëns—Concertos, Violoncello, Nos.1-2
Tchaikovsky—Variations on a Rococo Theme [orig]; Variations on a Rococo Theme [Fitzenhagen]
Dvořák—Concerto, Violoncello [No.2]
Sullivan—Concerto, Violoncello
Elgar—Concerto, Violoncello
Herbert—Concertos, Violoncello, Nos.1-2
Delius—Concerto, Violoncello
Albert, Eugen d'—Concerto, Violoncello
Schoenberg—Concerto, Violoncello
Hahn—Concerto, Violoncello
Bridge—Oration
Bloch, E.—Schelomo; Voice in the Wilderness
Bartók—Concerto, Violoncello, op. posth. [Serly adaptation]
Enesco—Symphonie concertante
Toch—Concerto, Violoncello
Milhaud—Concerto, Violoncello, No.2
Hindemith—Concerto, Violoncello; Kammermusik No.3
Walton—Concerto, Violoncello
Blacher—Concerto, Violoncello
Goldschmidt—Concerto, Violoncello
Khachaturian—Concerto-Rhapsody, Violoncello; Concerto, Violoncello, No.2

Shostakovich—Concerto, Violoncello, No.1
Rózsa—Concerto, Violoncello
Bacewicz—Concerto, Violoncello, No.2
Holmboe, Vagn—Concerto, Violoncello
Barber—Concerto, Violoncello, op.22
Schuman, Wm.—Song of Orpheus
Menotti—Fantasia, Violoncello & Orch.
Lutoslawski—Concerto, Violoncello
Shulman—Concerto, Violoncello; Theme & Variations, Violoncello (1966)
Dutilleux—Tout un monde lointain ...
Bernstein—Mass: Three Meditations
Kirchner—Music for Cello and Orchestra
Babadjanyan—Concerto, Violoncello
Imbrie—Concerto, Violoncello
Foss—Cello Concert
Berio—Ritorno degli snovidenia
Henze—Ode an den Westwind
Previn—Concerto, Violoncello
Wyner—Prologue and Narrative
Takemitsu—Orion and Pleiades
Baker—Concerto, Violoncello
Martino—Concerto, Violoncello
Biggs—Concerto, Violoncello
Penderecki—Concerto, Viola [or vc]
Wernick—Concerto, Violoncello, No.2
Jones—Concerto, Violoncello
Rands—Hiraeth
Sallinen—Chamber Music III
Bennett, Richard R.—Reflections on a Scottish Folk Song; Sonnets to Orpheus
Hoover—Stitch-te Naku
Wuorinen—Chamber Concerto, Violoncello
McCabe—Concerto, Violoncello
Gruber—Concerto, Violoncello
Cresswell—Concerto, Violoncello
Harris, Ross—Concerto, Violoncello
Ran—Three Fantasy Movements
Rouse—Concerto, Violoncello
Sierra—Cuatro Versos
Danielpour—Through the Ancient Valley
Sleeper, Thomas—Concerto, Violoncello
Moravec, Paul—Montserrat
Tan—Crouching Tiger Concerto; Intercourse of Fire and Water
Lindberg—Zona
Amaya—Un Camino
Golijov—Azul solo
Bacri—Prière

Over 30'

Haydn, M.—Concerto, Violoncello, B-flat major
Dvořák—Concerto, Violoncello
Strauss, R.—Don Quixote
Prokofiev—Sinfonia concertante
Shostakovich—Concerto, Violoncello, No.2
Britten—Symphony for Cello & Orch

Maxwell Davies—Strathclyde Concerto No.2
Tavener—Protecting Veil
Danielpour—Concerto, Violoncello
Kernis—Colored Field (Violoncello)

DOUBLE BASS

Dittersdorf—Concerto, Double Bass, E major; Concerto, Double Bass, E-flat major
Vanhal—Concerto, Double Bass
Capuzzi—Concerto, Double Bass [2 editions: Ludwin or Schaffner]
Dragonetti—Concerto, Double Bass; Pezzo di concerto
Bottesini—Concerto, Double Bass, No.2 [2 versions]; Elegy; Grande allegro di concerto
Koussevitzky—Andante; Chanson triste; Concerto, Double Bass [3 versions]; Humoresque; Valse miniature
Tubin—Concerto, Double Bass
Menotti—Concerto, Double Bass
Miari—Concerto, Double Bass
Maxwell Davies—Strathclyde Concerto No.7
Harbison—Concerto, Bass Viol
Proto—Carmen Fantasy [db & orch]
Horwood—Concerto, Double Bass
O'Boyle—Snapshot Concertos: Quando, quando, basso
Eccles—Sonata in A minor

MULTIPLE DIVERSE STRINGS

2 Solo Strings

Vivaldi—Concerto, Violin & Violoncello, RV 547; Concerto, 2 Violoncellos, RV 531
Bach, J.S.—Concerto, Violin & Viola, G major
Graun—Concerto, Violin & Viola
Bach, J.C.—Sinfonia concertante, W. C34 [vn & vc]
Hofmann, Leopold—Concerto, Violin & Violoncello, Badley G1
Dittersdorf—Sinfonia concertante, Double Bass & Viola
Saint-Georges—Symphonie concertante, op.6, no.1 [2vn, or vn & vc]
Stamitz, Carl—Sinfonia concertante, D major [vn & va]
Mozart, W.A.—Sinfonia concertante, K.364 [vn & va]
Bottesini—Gran duo concertante [vn &

db—2 versions]
Brahms—Concerto, Violin & Violoncello
Delius—Concerto, Violin & Violoncello
Sessions—Concerto, Violin & Violoncello
Britten—Concerto, Violin & Viola
Kirchner—Concerto, Violin & Violoncello
Previn—Concerto, Violin & Double Bass; Concerto, Violin & Viola
Maxwell Davies—Strathclyde Concerto No.5 [vn & va]
Finko—Concerto, Viola & Double Bass
Harbison—Double Concerto, Violin & Violoncello
Holliger—Janus [vn & va]
Zwilich—Concerto, Violin & Violoncello
Beall—Concerto, Violin & Double Bass
Sierra—Concerto, Violin & Viola

2 Violins & Violoncello

Corelli—Concerti grossi, op.6, nos.1-12
Scarlatti, A.—Concerti grosso Nos.3, 6
Vivaldi—Concertos, 2 Violins & Violoncello, op.3, no.2, RV 578; op.3, no.11, RV 565; op.4, no.7, RV 185
Manfredini—Concerto grosso, op.3, no.9
Handel—Concerti grossi, op.3, no.2, HWV 313; No.7, HWV 318 op.6, nos.1-12
Marcello, B.—Concerti grossi, op.1, nos.1, 6, 7, 8, 9, 10
Geminiani—Concerto grosso, C major [after Corelli, op.5, no.3]
Locatelli—Concerto grosso, op.1, no.9
Boyce—Concerto grosso, B minor
Boccherini—Symphony No.2, G.491
Atterberg—Suite pastorale in modo antico [3 solo strings: 2vn & viola, or 2vn & vc, or 3 vn]
Tippett—Fantasia concertante

Solo String Quartet

Marcello, B.—Concert grossi, op.1, nos.2-5
Geminiani—Concerti grossi no.5; no.12; op.3, nos.1-6; op.7, no.1
Locatelli—Concerto grosso, op.7, no.6
Sammartini, Giov. Battista—Concerto, E-flat
Spohr—Concerto, String Quartet, op.131
Elgar—Introduction and Allegro, op.47
Vaughan Williams—Fantasia on a theme by Thomas Tallis
Bloch, E.—Concerto Grosso No.2
Piston—Concerto for String Quartet, Winds & Perc
Blacher—Orchesterfantasie, op.51
Holmboe—Concerto, String Quartet
Britten—Cantata misericordium

Lees—Concerto, String Quartet & Orch
Deussen—Peninsula Suite
Riley—Sands
Cresswell—Concerto, String Quartet
Zhou—Poems from Tang
Danielpour—Voices of Remembrance
Abels—Delights and Dances

Other Combinations of 3-13 Solo Strings

Vivaldi—Concertos, 4 Violins & Violoncello, op.3, nos.1, 7, 10
Bach, J.S.—Brandenburg Concerto No.3 3vn, 3va, 3vc]; Brandenburg Concerto No.6 [2va, 2va da gamba]
Locatelli—Concerto grosso, op.1, no.8 [2vn 2va, vc]
Saint-Georges—Symphonie concertante, op.10, no.2 [2 violins & viola]
Mozart, W.A.—Serenade No.6 [2vn, va, db]
Stravinsky—Pulcinella [2vn, va, vc, db] Pulcinella: Suite [2vn, va, vc, db]
Atterberg—Suite pastorale in modo antico [3 solo strings: 2vn & viola, or 2vn & vc, or 3 vn]
Howells—Elegy for Viola, String Quartet & String Orchestra
Rosenberg—Concerto No.3 [vn, va, vc]
Tippett—Concerto, Violin, Viola & Violoncello
Canning—Fantasy on a Hymn by Justin Morgan [2 solo string quartets]

FLUTE

15' or less

Vivaldi—Concertos, Flute, op.10, no.2, RV 439; op.10, no.3, RV 428; Concerto, Flute, RV 438
Telemann—Concerto, Flute, E minor
Bach, J.S.—Concerto, Flute (or Violin), BWV 971
Quantz—Concertos, Flute, C major & D major
Galuppi—Concerto, Flute, D major
Pergolesi—Concerto, Flute, G major
Frederick II—Concertos, Flute, Nos.3-4
Gluck—Concerto, Flute, G major
Stamitz, Joh.—Concerto, Flute, D major
Grétry—Concerto, Flute, C major
Mozart, W.A.—Andante, Flute & Orch, K.315; Rondo, Flute, K.373
Devienne—Concerto, Flute, No.7
Donizetti—Concertino, Flute
Gounod—Concertino, Flute
Doppler—Fantasie pastorale
Demersseman—Concerto italien

Saint-Saëns—Odelette; Romance, Flute (or Violin), op.37
Fauré—Fantasy, Flute
Foote—Night Piece
Chaminade—Concertino, Flute
Delius—Air and Dance
Busoni—Divertimento, Flute
Bloch, E.—Suite modale
Griffes—Poem
Atterberg—Adagio amoroso
Martin—Ballade, Flute & Orch [2 versions: orig & arr.]
Rogers—Soliloquy No.1
Hanson—Serenade, op.35
Moncayo—Amatzinac
Kennan—Night Soliloquy
Kirchner—Music for Flute and Orch
Arnold—Concerto, Flute
Boulez—Memoriale (…explosante-fixe…originel)
Gordeli—Concertino, Flute, op.8
Zaninelli—Canto
Sallinen—Chamber Music II [alto flute]
Rudow—Go Green!
Corigliano—Voyage (flute)
Tower—Concerto, Flute
Mauldin—Dreams of the Child of Light [Native American flute]
Larsen, L.—Atmosphere As a Fluid System
Beaser—Song of the Bells
Drattell—Fire Within
Higdon—Soliloquy [Eh, vc, cl or fl]
O'Boyle—Snapshot Concertos: Flipperdiperus
Frank, G.L.—Illapa

Over 15'

Telemann—Concerto, Flute, TWV 51:D2
Bach, J.S.—Suite (Overture) No.2, BWV 1067
Quantz—Concertos, Flute, C minor; D major (Pour Potsdam); G major
Bach, C.P.E.—Concerto, Flute, H.425
Stamitz, Joh.—Concerto, Flute, C major
Haydn, F.J.—Concerto, Flute, Hob.VIIf:D1
Boccherini—Concerto, Flute, G.489
Stamitz, Carl—Concerto, Flute, G major
Mozart, W.A.—Concertos, Flute, Nos.1-2
Mercadante—Concerto, Flute
Reinecke—Concerto, Flute
Nielsen, Carl—Concerto, Flute
Ibert—Concerto, Flute
Piston—Concerto, Flute
Rodrigo—Fantasía para un gentilhombre
Khachaturian—Concerto, Flute
Holmboe, Vagn—Concerto, Flute
Brant—Angels and Devils [solo flute, accompanied by a flute orchestra]
Gould—Concerto, Flute

Bernstein—Halil
Foss—Renaissance Concerto
Laderman—Concerto, Flute
Maxwell Davies—Strathclyde Concerto No.6
Hoover—Medieval Suite
Corigliano—Pied Piper Fantasy [solo flute doubling on tin whistle or piccolo]
Harbison—Concerto, Flute
Rutter—Suite antique
Aho—Concerto, Flute
Ran—Voices [flute soloist (dbl also on amplified alto flute & piccolo)]
Rouse—Concerto, Flute
Saariaho—Aile du songe
Chen Yi—Golden Flute
Wagner, Melinda—Concerto, Flute
Amaya—Indigo Concerto
Ritchie, Anthony—Concerto, Flute
Pann—Mercury Concerto
Watkins—Concerto, Flute

2 or MORE FLUTES

Vivaldi—Concerto, 2 Flutes, R.533
Telemann—Concerto, 2 Flutes, TWV 52:a2
Galuppi—Concerto, 2 Flutes, E minor
Haydn, F.J.—Concerto, 2 Flutes, Hob.VIIh:1
Cimarosa—Concerto, 2 Flutes, G major
Doppler—Concerto, 2 Flutes
Daugherty—Metropolis Symphony: MXYZPTLK [1.2/pic]

RECORDER

Vivaldi—Concerto, Recorder, op.44, no.19, RV 441
Telemann—Concert Suite, TWV 55:Es2; Concerto, Recorder. TWV 51:F1; Suite, TWV 55:a2
Sammartini, Giuseppe—Concerto, Recorder, F major

PICCOLO

Vivaldi—Concertos, Piccolo, RV 443; RV 445
Liebermann, Lowell—Concerto, Piccolo
O'Boyle—Snapshot Concertos: Mini Dance
Dorman—Concerto, Piccolo

OBOE

Marcello, A.—Concerto, Oboe, C minor
Albinoni—Concertos, Oboe, op.7, no.3;
  op.9, no.2; op.9, no.11
Vivaldi—Concertos, Oboe, RV 447;
  op.8, no.9, RV 454; RV 455; RV 456
Telemann—Concertos, Oboe,
  TWV 51:d1; TWV 51:e1; TWV 51:f1;
  Concerto, Oboe d'amore, TWV 51:A2
Graupner—Concerto, Oboe
Handel—Concertos, Oboe, Nos.1-3;
  Concerto, Oboe, E-flat major
Marcello, B.—Concerto, Oboe, C minor
  [now attributed to Alessandro Marcello]
Bach, C.P.E.—Concertos, Oboe, H.466;
  H.468
Stamitz, Joh.—Concerto, Oboe, C major
Haydn, F.J.—Concerto, Oboe,
  Hob.VIIg:C1
Cimarosa—Concerto, Oboe
Mozart, W.A.—Concerto, Oboe, K.314
Donizetti—Concertino, Oboe
Bellini—Concerto, Oboe
Strauss, R.—Concerto, Oboe
Vaughan Williams—Concerto, Oboe
Boughton—Concerto, Oboe, No.1
Martinů—Concerto, Oboe
Goossens—Concerto, Oboe
Bacon—Elegy
Skalkottas—Concertino, Oboe
Wilder—Concerto, Oboe
Carter—Concerto, Oboe
Barber—Canzonetta
Barlow—Winter's Past
Britten—Temporal Variations
Rochberg—Concerto, Oboe
Maderna—Concerto, Oboe, No.3
Arnold—Concerto, Oboe, op.39
Lees—Concerto, Oboe
Biggs—Concerto, Oboe
Maxwell Davies—Strathclyde Concerto
  No.1
Tull—Concertino, Oboe
Bennett, Richard R.—Concerto, Oboe
Bolcom—Serenata Notturna
Corigliano—Aria; Concerto, Oboe
Harbison—Concerto, Oboe
Svoboda—Meditation
Zwilich—Concerto, Oboe
Tavener—Kaleidoscopes
Avshalomov, D.—Concertino, Oboe
Welcher—Venti di mare
Lofstrom—Concertino, Oboe
Rouse—Concerto, Oboe
Francesconi—Plot in Fiction [ob/Eh]
Moravec, Paul—Concerto, Oboe
Higdon—Concerto, Oboe
O'Boyle—Snapshot Concertos: A Quiet
  Place
Hutter, Gregory—Still Life

ENGLISH HORN

Donizetti—Concertino, English Horn
Sibelius—Lemminkäinen Suite: Swan of
  Tuonela
Wolf-Ferrari—Concertino, English Horn
Alwyn—Autumn Legend
Persichetti—Concerto, English Horn
Francesconi—Plot in Fiction [ob/Eh]
Kernis—Colored Field (English horn)
Higdon—Soliloquy
O'Boyle—Snapshot Concertos: The
  Pretty Girl Milking Her Cow

CLARINET

15' or less

Molter—Concerto, Clarinet, No.1
Stamitz, Carl—Concerto, Clarinet, No.3
Baermann—Adagio, Clarinet & Strings
Weber, C.M.—Concertino, Clarinet
Rossini—Introduction, Theme &
  Variations; Variations, Clarinet [orig. &
  transposed versions]
Donizetti—Concertino, Clarinet
Schreiner—Immer kleiner
Rimsky-Korsakov—Concerto, Clarinet
Debussy—Rhapsody, clarinet & orchestra
Strauss, R.—Romanze, TrV 80
Busoni—Concertino, Clarinet
Stravinsky—Ebony Concerto
Milhaud—Scaramouche
Hindemith—Concertpiece
  (Konzertstück), Trautonium & Strings
  [often played on clarinet]
Gershwin—Promenade
Blacher—Concerto, Clarinet
Manevich—Concerto, Clarinet
Hovhaness—Talin
Lutoslawski—Dance Preludes
Shulman—Rendezvous
Bernstein—Prelude, Fugue and Riffs
Ritchie, John—Concertino, Clarinet
Hollingsworth—Dubious Piety
Adler, S.—Beyond the Pale
Albert, Stephen—Wind Canticle
Iannaccone—Concertante, Clarinet
Warshauer—Yes!
Ewazen—Ballade
Gross—Reaching
Drattell—Fire Dances [Eb cl & Bb cl]
McCarter—Landscape Scenes
Amaya—Wuaraira Repano
Higdon—Soliloquy [Eh, or vc, or cl, or
  fl]
O'Boyle—Snapshot Concertos: Liquorice
  Noodles [2 orchestrations]; Snapshot
  Concertos: Bassett Hound [bass clarinet]

Amrhein—Event Horizon [cl conc]
Pann—Rags to Richard

Over 15'

Stamitz, Carl—Concertos, Clarinet, E-flat
  major; F major
Mozart, W.A.—Concerto, Clarinet
Crusell—Concerto, Clarinet, No.2
Spohr—Concerto, Clarinet, No.1
Weber, C.M.—Concertos, Clarinet,
  Nos.1-2
Brahms—Concerto, Viola [or Clarinet],
  op.120, no.1
Nielsen, Carl—Concerto, Clarinet
Hindemith—Concerto, Clarinet
Copland—Concerto, Clarinet
Finzi—Concerto, Clarinet
Tomasi—Concerto, Clarinet
Swanson—Fantasy Piece
Britten—Movements for a Clarinet
  Concerto
Avshalomov, J.—Evocations
Arnold—Concerto, Clarinet, No.2
Skrowaczewski—Ricercari notturni
Laderman—Concerto, Clarinet
Denisov—Concerto, Clarinet
Deussen—Concerto, Clarinet
Maxwell Davies—Strathclyde Concerto
  No.4
Hoover—Concerto, Clarinet
Corigliano—Concerto, Clarinet
Tower—Concerto, Clarinet
Svoboda—Symphony No.6
Zwilich—Concerto, Clarinet
Tavener—Repentant Thief
Schiff—Canti di Davide
Adams, John—Gnarly Buttons
Saariaho—D'om le vrai sens
Dorff—Summer Solstice
Cotton—Concerto, Clarinet
Golijov—Dreams and Prayers of Isaac
  the Blind [klezmer clarinet, with
  numerous doublings]
Trigos, Juan—Concerto, Clarinet

BASSOON(S)

Vivaldi—Concertos, Bassoon, RV 477;
  RV 484; RV 485; RV 498; RV 501
Graupner—Concerto, Bassoon
Kozeluch—Concerto, Bassoon, C major
Stamitz, Carl—Concerto, Bassoon, F
  major
Mozart, W.A.—Concertos, Bassoon,
  K.191; No.2 [no.2 probably spurious]
Weber, C.M.—Andante & Rondo
  ongarese, J.158; Concerto, Bassoon,
  J.127
David—Concertino, Bassoon, op.12

Villa-Lobos—Ciranda das sete notas
Panufnik—Concerto, Bassoon
Maxwell Davies—Strathclyde Concerto No.8
Schickele—Concerto, Bassoon
Welcher—Concerto da camera
Buhr, Glenn—Concerto, Bassoon, No.2
Daugherty—Dead Elvis; Hell's Angels [3bn & cbn]
Amundson—Three's Company [3bn]
O'Boyle—Snapshot Concertos: A Bundle of Sticks
Stephenson—Dialogue of Self and Soul

SAXOPHONE(S)

Loeffler—Divertissement espagnole [asx]
Debussy—Rhapsody, Alto Saxophone
Glazunov—Concerto, Alto Saxophone
Schmitt—Légende [va or asx or vn]
Villa-Lobos—Fantasia [ssx or tsx]
Ibert—Concertino da camera [asx]
Martin—Ballade, Saxophone & Orch [asx]
Milhaud—Scaramouche [asx or cl]
Schulhoff—Hot-Sonate [asx]
Cowell—Air and Scherzo [asx]
Creston—Concerto, Alto Saxophone
Swanson—Fantasy Piece [ssx or cl]
Maurice—Tableaux de Provence [asx]
Dahl—Concerto, Alto Sax & Wind Orch
Ward—Concerto, Tenor Saxophone
Skrowaczewski—Ricercari notturni [ssx/asx/bsx]
Dubois, P.—Concerto, Alto Saxophone
Martino—Concerto, Alto Saxophone
Zaninelli—Autumn Music [tp or asx]
Bond, Victoria—Urban Bird [asx]
Peck—Upward Stream [tsx]
Horwood—Symphony No.3 [tsx]
Gellis—Corduroy [bsx]
Aho—Kellot [sax 4t: ssx, asx, tsx, bsx]
Actor—Concerto, Alto Saxophone
Chen Yi—Ba yin [sax 4t: ssx, asx, tsx, bsx]
Sierra—Concerto, Saxophone [tsx/ssx]
Drattell—Be Still My Spirit [asx]
Torke—Concerto, Soprano Saxophone
Higdon—Concerto, Soprano Saxophone
Thomas, Augusta Read—Hemke Concerto [asx]
Psathas—Zahara [ssx/tsx]
Dorman—Concerto, Soprano Saxophone

HORN

Telemann—Concerto, Horn, TWV 51:D8
Haydn, F.J.—Concertos, Horn, Nos.1-2
Haydn, M.—Concertino, Horn, MH 134

Mozart, W.A.—Concertos, Horn, Nos.1-4; Concert-Rondo, K.371
Weber, C.M.—Concertino, Horn, J.188
Rossini—Prelude, Theme, and Variations
Schumann, R.—Adagio & Allegro, op.70
Strauss, F.—Concerto, Horn, op.8
Saint-Saëns—Morceau de concert, Horn; Romance, Horn [or Violoncello]
Strauss, R.—Concertos, Horn, Nos.1-2
Dukas—Villanelle
Glazunov—Rêverie
Glière—Concerto, Horn
Hindemith—Concerto, Horn
Jacob—Concerto, Horn
Larsson, L-E.—Concertino, Horn, op.45, no.5
Schuman, Wm.—Three Colloquies
Hovhaness—Artik
Britten—Now Sleeps the Crimson Petal; Serenade for Tenor, Horn & Strings
Hamilton—Voyage
Ligeti—Hamburgisches Konzert
Lees—Concerto, Horn
Adler, S.—Concerto, Horn
Hoddinott—Concerto, Horn
Williams—Concerto, Horn
Jones—Concerto, Horn
Bennett, Richard R.—Actaeon
McCabe—Concerto, Horn
Zwilich—Concerto, Horn
Eötvös—Hommage à Domenico Scarlatti; Glass Bead Game
Actor—Concerto, Horn
Boelter—Images from Goldsmith
Smith, Kile—Exsultet
Stephenson—Sounds Awakened

2 or MORE HORNS

Vivaldi—Concertos, 2 Horns, RV 538; RV 539
Haydn, F.J.—Concerto, 2 Horns
Kuhlau—Concertino, 2 Horns
Schumann, R.—Concertstück, op.86 [4 solo horns]
Chávez—Concerto, 4 Horns
O'Boyle—Snapshot Concertos: Curly Bits [horn section soli]

TRUMPET

Torelli—Concertos, Trumpet, D major [2 separate concertos, though in the same key]; Sinfonia con tromba
Purcell—Sonata, Trumpet & Strings, Z.850
Scarlatti, A.—Su le sponde del Tebro [with soprano voice]

Albinoni—Concerto, Trumpet, A major
Clarke—Suite, D major
Bach, J.S.—Cantata No.51 [with soprano voice]
Fasch—Concerto, Trumpet, D major
Tartini—Concerto, Trumpet
Mozart, Leopold—Concerto, Trumpet, D major
Haydn, F.J.—Concerto, Trumpet, Hob.VIIe:1
Haydn, M.—Concertino, Trumpet, D major; Concerto, Trumpet, No.2, MH 60
Hummel—Concerto, Trumpet [available in E major (orig) or E-flat major]
Laparra—Suite italienne
Goedicke—Concert Etude
Bloch, E.—Proclamation
Tomasi—Concerto, Trumpet
Jolivet—Concertino, Trumpet
Larsson, L-E.—Concertino, Trumpet, op.45, no.6
Panufnik—Concerto in modo antico
Persichetti—Hollow Men
Arutiunian—Concerto, Trumpet
Arnold—Concerto, Trumpet, op.125
Husa—Concerto, Trumpet & Wind Orchestra
Chou—Soliloquy of a Bhiksuni
Ligeti—Mysteries of the Macabre
Zaninelli—Aria festiva [solo trumpet plus trumpet choir (12 tp; 6 real parts); Autumn Music
Maxwell Davies—Concerto, Trumpet
Tull—Concerto No.1, Trumpet; Rhapsody, Trumpet
Rudow—Dark Waters; Dark Waters of Elba
McCabe—Concerto, Trumpet
Zwilich—American Concerto
Cresswell—Alas! How Swift
Walker, Gwyneth—A Concerto of Hymns & Spirituals
Yasinitsky—As the Sun Descended
Curiale—Blue Windows
Moravec, Paul—Songs of Love and War [with baritone solo]
MacMillan—Epiclesis
Abels—American Variations on "Swing Low, Sweet Chariot" solo trumpet
O'Boyle—Snapshot Concertos: Lonesome Prairie [2 orchestrations]
Stephenson—Concertos, Trumpet, Nos.1-2

2 TRUMPETS

Vivaldi—Concerto, 2 Trumpets, RV 537
Prelleur—Concerto, 2 Trumpets
Stravinsky—Fanfare for a New Theatre [2 solo trumpets]

Hamilton—Circus
Adams, John—Tromba lontana

TROMBONE

Wagenseil—Concerto, Trombone
Albrechtsberger—Concerto, Trombone
David—Concertino No.4, Trombone
Rimsky-Korsakov—Concerto, Trombone
Bloch, E.—Symphony for Trombone &
  Orchestra
Milhaud—Concertino d'hiver
Jacob—Concerto, Trombone
Tomasi—Concerto, Trombone
Creston—Fantasy for Trombone
Larsson, L-E.—Concertino, Trombone,
  op.45, no.7
Hovhaness—Overture, op.76, no.1
Bassett—Concerto lirico
Erb—Concerto, Trombone
Jones—Concerto, Trombone
Zwilich—Concerto, Bass Trombone;
  Concerto, Trombone
Cresswell—Kaea
Rouse—Concerto, Trombone
Warshauer—Tekeeyah (a call)
  [shofar/trombone]
McTee—Solstice
Sleeper, Thomas—Translucence
Smith, Kile—Concerto, Trombone
Wagner, Melinda—Concerto, Trombone
O'Boyle—Snapshot Concertos: Buy,
  Swap or Sell!
Stephenson—Concerto, Trombone

TUBA

Vaughan Williams—Concerto, Tuba
Holmboe—Concerto, Tuba
Kleinsinger—Tubby the Tuba [solo tuba
  & narrator]
Jones—Concerto, Tuba
O'Boyle—Snapshot Concertos: Tuba
  Toothpaste
Petering—Concerto, Tuba
Territo—John Henry vs. the Machine
  [solo tuba & narrator]

PERCUSSION

Schreiner—Worried Drummer
Milhaud—Concerto, Marimba &
  Vibraphone, op.278 [1 soloist
  alternating marim & vib]; Concerto,
  Percussion & Small Orchestra, op.109
Jolivet—Concerto, Percussion
Creston—Concertino, Marimba

Liebermann, Rolf—Geigy Festival
  Concerto [solo Basle drum]
Kubik—Gerald McBoing Boing [with
  narrator]
Panufnik—Concertino, Timpani &
  Percussion [2 players]
Foss—Concerto, Percussion
Kraft—Configurations [4 perc]; Three
  Miniatures [4 perc]
Erb—Concerto for Solo Percussionist &
  Orchestra
Mayuzumi—Concertino, Xylophone
Van de Vate—Krakow Concerto [tmp+5]
Kagel—Konzertstück, Timpani & Orch
Colgrass—Rhapsodic Fantasy
Corigliano—Conjurer
Svoboda—Concerto, Marimba
Zwilich—Rituals [5 perc]
Schwantner—Concerto, Percussion [No.1
  (1 perc)]; Concerto, Percussion, No.2
  [tmp+3]
Peck—Glory and the Grandeur [3perc];
  Harmonic Rhythm [solo tmp]
Walker, Gwyneth—Up-Front Concerto
Gellis—Allegro sauvage [tmp]
Catán—Caribbean Airs [5 perc]
Stucky—Concerto, Percussion & Wind
  Orchestra; Spirit Voices
Tsontakis—Mirologhia
Actor—Concerto, Timpani
Chen Yi—Concerto, Percussion
Zhou—Concerto, Taiko & Timpani [2
  soloists]; Da Qu [1 perc]
Daugherty—Flamingo [2 tambourine
  soloists]; UFO [1 perc]
Dorff—Concerto, Percussion [1 perc];
  Concerto, Percussion: Allegro volante
  [xyl]
Oliverio—Concerto, Timpani, No.1;
  Dynasty [2 timpanists]; Messenger
Lang, David—loud love songs
MacMillan—Veni, veni, Emmanuel
O'Boyle—Concerto, Percussion [tmp+3];
  Snapshot Concertos: Galloping Goanna
Psathas—Djinn [marimba]; Planet
  Damnation [tmp]
Puts—Concerto, Marimba
Dorman—Uzu and Muzu from Kakaruzu
  [2 perc with narrator]

HARP(S)

Handel—Concerto, Harp, op.4, no.6,
  HWV 294
Dittersdorf—Concerto, Harp, A major
Boieldieu—Concerto, Harp
Reinecke—Concerto, Harp
Saint-Saëns—Morceau de concert, Harp
Widor—Choral et variations

Debussy—Danses sacrée et profane
Glière—Concerto, Harp
Ravel—Introduction & Allegro
Grandjany—Aria in Classic Style
Piston—Capriccio
Berezowsky—Concerto, Harp
Rodrigo—Concierto de Aranjuez [version
  for harp & orchestra]; Concierto
  serenata
Alwyn—Lyra angelica
Jolivet—Concerto, Harp
Badings—Concerto, Harp
Weinzweig—Concerto, Harp
Ginastera—Concerto, Harp
Previn—Concerto, Harp
Van de Vate—Concerto, Harp
Finko—Concerto, Harp
Hartway—Island Dances [2 solo harps]
Ott—Angel's Harp
Locklair—Concerto, Harp
Adamo—Four Angels
O'Boyle—Snapshot Concertos: Pale
  Moonlight

GUITAR

Vivaldi—Concerto, Guitar, RV 93
Giuliani—Concerto, Guitar
Ponce—Concierto del sur
Villa-Lobos—Concerto, Guitar
Castelnuovo-Tedesco—Concertos,
  Guitar, Nos.1-2
Rodrigo—Concierto de Aranjuez;
  Fantasía para un gentilhombre
Berkeley—Concerto, Guitar, op.88
Smith Brindle—Concerto, Guitar
Rochberg—EDEN: Out of Time and Out
  of Space
Arnold—Concerto, Guitar
Adler, S.—Concerto, Guitar
Takemitsu—To the Edge of Dream
Wernick—The Name of the Game
Bennett, Richard R.—Concerto, Guitar &
  Chmbr Ens
Corigliano—Troubadours
Brouwer—Concerto de Toronto;
  Concerto elegiaco; Retrats catalans
Schwantner—From Afar
Stucky—Concerto Mediterraneo
Márquez—Danzón No.3 [version for
  guitar & chamber orch]
Actor—Concerto, Guitar
Sierra—Folias
Daugherty—Bay of Pigs
Tan—Concerto, Guitar
Kernis—Concierto de "Dance Hits"
Trigos, Juan—Concertos, Guitar, Nos.1-2
Amrhein—Hamilton Street Concerto

2 or MORE GUITARS

Tailleferre—Concerto, 2 Guitars
Castelnuovo-Tedesco—Concerto, 2
  Guitars
Rodrigo—Concierto andaluz [4 guitars];
  Concierto madrigal [2 guitars]
Young—Saffire Concerto [4 guitars]

ETHNIC INSTRUMENTS

Tubin—Concerto, Balalaika
Davison—Arthur's Return [bagpipe]
Van de Vate—Peacock Southeast Flew
  [pipa]
Maxwell Davies—Cross Lane Fair
  [Northumbrian pipes & bodhran];
  Orkney Wedding With Sunrise
  [bagpiper]
Gilbert, J.—Suite for South Indian Veena
  [veena a.k.a. vina]
Warshauer—Tekeeyah (a call)
  [shofar/trombone]
Chen Yi—Fiddle Suite [huqin (= erhu,
  zhonghu, jinghu)]
Zhou—King Chu Doffs His Armour
  [pipa]; Out of Tang Court [Tang
  Ensemble: pipa, erhu, zheng, Chinese
  percussion (4 players)]
Sheng—Nanking! Nanking! [pipa]
Tan—Concerto for String Orchestra and
  Pipa or Zheng
Tan—Orchestral Theatre I [xun]
O'Boyle—Concerto, Didgerido

OTHER INSTRUMENTS

Vivaldi—Concerto, Mandolin, RV 425
Vaughan Williams—Romance
  [harmonica]
Arnold—Concerto, Harmonica
Piazzolla—Aconcagua [bandoneon]
O'Boyle—Concerto, Didgerido

MULTIPLE DIVERSE SOLOISTS

2 Soloists

Vivaldi—Concerto, Oboe & Bassoon,
  op.42, no.3, RV 545; Concertos, Oboe
  & Violin, RV 543 & RV 548; Concerto,
  Viola d'Amore & Lute, RV 540
Telemann—Concerto, Flute & Violin,
  TWV 53:A2; Concerto, Recorder &

Flute TWV 52:e1
Bach, J.S.—Concerto, Violin & Oboe,
  BWV 1060R
Handel—Concerto grosso, op.3, no.3,
  HWV 314, G major [vn & fl (or ob)]
Hertel—Double Concerto [tp & ob]
Haydn, F.J.—Concertos, Flute & Oboe,
  Hob.VIIh:2, Hob.VIIh:3, Hob.VIIh:4,
  Hob.VIIh:5; Concerto, Violin & Piano
  (or Harpsichord), Hob.XVIII:6
Stamitz, Carl—Concerto, Clarinet &
  Bassoon, B-flat major; Concerto,
  Clarinet & Violin (or 2 Clarinets)
Mozart, W.A.—Ch'io mi scordi di te—
  Non temer [soprano voice & piano];
  Concerto, Flute & Harp; Per questa bella
  mano, K.612 [bass voice & double bass]
Mendelssohn—Concerto, Violin & Piano
  [2 versions]
Saint-Saëns—Tarantelle [flute & clarinet]
Bruch—Concerto, Clarinet & Viola
Strauss, R.—Duet-concertino [cl & bn]
Holst—Fugal Concerto [fl & ob]
Bloch, E.—Concertino [fl & va (or cl)]
Berg—Chamber Concerto, op.8 [vn & pf]
Martin—Maria-Triptychon [soprano
  voice & violin]; Three Dances [ob & hp]
Martinů—Concerto, Flute & Violin
Honegger—Concerto da camera [fl & Eh]
Piston—Fantasy for English Horn, Harp
  & Strings
Hindemith—Concerto, Trumpet &
  Bassoon
Hanson—Concerto, Organ & Harp
Copland—Quiet City [tp & Eh (or ob)]
Shostakovich—Concerto, Piano, No.1
  [solo trumpet as well as solo piano]
Lutoslawski—Concerto, Oboe & Harp
Harrison—Suite, Violin, Piano & Chmbr
  Orch
Rorem—Water Music [clarinet & violin]
Berio—Concertino, Clarinet & Violin
Henze—Double Concerto, Oboe, Harp &
  Strings
Henze—Requiem [piano & trumpet]
Musgrave—Two's Company [ob & perc]
Russo—Street Music [harmonica & piano
  (may be played by one performer)]
Denisov—Concerto, Bassoon &
  Violoncello; Concerto, Flute & Harp
Maxwell Davies—Strathclyde Concerto
  No.3 [horn & trumpet]
Schnittke—Concerto, Oboe, Harp & Str
Finko—Concerto, Viola D'Amore &
  Harpsichord (or Guitar)
Hoover—Summer Night [flute & horn]
Bolcom—Fives [violin & piano]
Harbison—Concerto, Oboe, Clarinet
Eötvös—Shadows [flute & clarinet]
Larsen, L.—Mary Cassatt [mezzo-
  soprano voice & trombone]
Márquez—Danzón No.3 (fl & gtr]

Adolphe—Three Pieces for Kids &
  Chamber Orchestra: 1. Ta Woop! [flute
  & oboe]
Mackey—Deal [elec guitar & drum set]
Knehans—glow [violin & clarinet]
Psathas—Omnifenix [tenor saxophone &
  drumset]
Psathas—View from Olympus
  [percussion & piano]
Amrhein—Variants [flute & guitar]
Frank, G.L.—Compadrazgo [vc & pf]
Petering—Concerto, Clarinet [version for
  clarinet & violin soloists]

3 Soloists

Vivaldi—Concerto, Flute, Oboe &
  Bassoon, op.44, no.16, RV 570
Telemann—Concerto, Trumpet & 2
  Oboes, TWV 53:D2
Bach, J.S.—Brandenburg Concerto No.4
  [2 recorders & violin]; Brandenburg
  Concerto No.5 [harpsichord, flute,
  violin]; Concerto, Flute, Violin &
  Harpsichord, BWV 1044
Handel—Concerto, Organ, op.4, no.3
  [solo vn & solo vc, in addition to organ]
Beethoven—Concerto, Violin,
  Violoncello & Piano; Romance
  Cantabile [flute, bassoon, piano]
Martinů—Concertino, Piano Trio &
  String Orch [i.e., vn, vc, & pf]
Barber—Capricorn Concerto [fl, ob, tp]
Ohana—Tombeau de Claude Debussy
  [soprano, piano, one-third-tone zither]
Kubik—Symphony concertante [trumpet,
  viola, piano]
Ward—Dialogues, A Triple Concerto
  [violin, violoncello, & piano]
Argento—Bravo Mozart! [ob, hn, vn]
Previn—Triple Concerto [hn, tp, tuba]
Kagel—Das Konzert [fl/pic/afl, hp, perc]
Riley—SolTierraLuna [violin, 2 guitars]
Smith, Kile—Three Graces [ob, hn, vc]
Tan—On Taoism [voice, bcl, cbn]
Higdon—Concerto 4-3 [2 vn & db]
Greenberg—Concerto, Piano Trio &
  Orchestra [pf, vn, vc]

4 Soloists

Vivaldi—Concertos, 2 Oboes & 2
  Clarinets, RV 559; RV 560
Telemann—Concerto, 2 Horns & 2
  Violins, TWV 54:Es1
Bach, J.S.—Brandenburg Concerto No.2
  [recorder, oboe, trumpet, violin]
Haydn, F.J.—Sinfonia concertante, op.84,
  Hob.I:105 [ob, bn, vn, vc]

Mozart, W.A.—Sinfonia concertante, K.297b [oboe, clarinet, horn, bassoon]; Sinfonia concertante, K.297b [Levin] [flute, oboe, horn, bassoon]

Ponchielli—Gran quartetto concertante [flute, oboe, E-flat clar, clarinet (orig), *or* 3 flutes & alto flute]

Bartók—Concerto, 2 Pianos and Percussion [2pf, 2perc – orch accomp]; Sonata, 2 Pianos & Percussion [2pf, 2perc – no accompaniment]

Gál—Symphony No.4 [fl, cl, vn, vc]

Rosenberg—Sinfonie concertante [vn, va, ob, bn]

Crawford—Three Songs [oboe, percussion, piano, contralto voice]

Messiaen—Concert à quatre [flute, oboe, violoncello, piano]; Canyons aux étoiles [piano, horn, xylorimba, glockenspiel]

Berio—Tempi concertati [fl, vn, 2pf]

Adler, S.—Arcos Concerto [fl, ob, cl, bn]

Takemitsu—Quatrain [cl, vn, vc, pf]

Birtwistle—Nomos [fl, cl, hn, bn]

Del Tredici—Syzygy [soprano, horn, tubular bells (2 players)]

5 Soloists

Rossini—Variazioni a più strumenti [clarinet; solo string quartet]

Respighi—Concerto a cinque [oboe, trumpet, violin, double bass, piano]

Stravinsky—Capriccio, Piano & Orchestra [pf, vn, va, vc, db]

Hindemith—Concerto for Woodwinds, Harp & Orch [fl, ob, cl, bn, hp]

Britten—Young Apollo [piano, solo string quartet & orchestra]

Arnold—Grand, Grand Festival Overture [organ, 3 vacuum cleaners, floor polisher]

Foss—Night Music for John Lennon [2tp, hn, tbn, tuba (or 2nd tbn)]

Colgrass—Déjà vu [percussion quartet & jazz double bass]

Górecki—Concerto for Five Instruments and String Quartet [flute, clarinet, trumpet, xylophone, mandolin]

Maxwell Davies—Sinfonia concertante [fl, ob, cl, bn, hn]

Del Tredici—Alice Symphony: Lobster Quadrille [2ssx, accordion, mndolin, tenor banjo]

Perera—Chamber Concerto [brass 5t: 2tp, hn, tbn, tuba]

6 or more Soloists

Vivaldi—Concertos, 2 Oboes, Bassoon, 2 Horns, Violin, RV 569 & RV 574; Concerto, Violin & Woodwinds, RV 577 [violin, 2rec, 2ob, bn]; Concerto, 4 Violins, 4 Recorders, RV 585

Bach, J.S.—Brandenburg Concerto No.1 [3 oboes, 2 horns, violin]

Martin—Concerto, 7 winds [fl, ob, cl, bn, hn, tp, tbn]

Messiaen—Transfiguration de Jésus-Christ [fl, cl, xylorimba, vib, marimba, vc, pf]

Menotti—Triplo Concerto a Tre [pf, hp, perc, ob, cl, bn, vn, va, vc]

Raksin—Toy Concertino [8 toy insts]

Maxwell Davies—Strathclyde Concerto No.9 [pic, afl, Eh, Ebcl, bcl, cbn]

Svoboda—Symphony No.3 [organ; solo string quintet: 2vn, 2va, vc]

Rodríguez—Oktoechos [vn, cl, tp, perc, vc, bn, tbn, pf]

McCarthy—American Dance Music [2tp, hn, tbn, tuba, perc]

Smith, Kile—Alabanza [mezzo-soprano & Latin ens: vn, pf, bass gtr, 3perc]

Ince—F E S T [asx/siren, tsx/cl, perc, synth, elec gtr, elec bgtr, vn, vc]

Higdon—On a Wire [flute/piccolo/alto flute; clarinet/bass clarinet; violin/viola; violoncello; marimba; piano]

HANDBELL CHOIR

Rodriguez—Gathering of Angels

Amundson—Joyous Noel

STEELPAN(S)

Bach, Jan—Concerto, Steelpan

Teason—Trinity

McClure—Caribbean Christmas Mass

JAZZ SOLOISTS

Ellington—Grand Slam Jam [varied soloists, as many as possible]; New World A-Comin' [piano]; Trois rois noirs [soloist or combo]

Liebermann, Rolf—Concerto, Jazz Band [2asx, 2tsx, bsx, 4tp, 4tbn, pf, db, drums]

Brubeck, H.—Dialogues [combo]

Bernstein—Prelude, Fugue and Riffs [clarinet]

Lewis, J.—The Golden Striker [piano, bass, drums]; Jazz Ostinato [vibraphone, piano, bass, drums]

Kraft—Contextures [ssx, tp, bass, drums]

Rorem—Lions [asx, drum set, pf, db]

Schuller—Concertino, Jazz 4t [vib, pf, db, drums]; Journey into Jazz [asx, tsx, tp, db, drums, with narrator]

Russo—Street Music [harmonica & pf]; Symphony No.2

Amram—Triple Concerto [3 solo quintets: woodwind (fl, ob, cl, bn, hn), brass (2tp, hn, tbn, tuba), & jazz (asx, bsx, pf, db, drums)]

Baker—Chat qui pêche [textless soprano voice; jazz quartet (asx/tsx; pf/elec pf; db/elec db; drums)]

Proto—Casey at the Bat [tp, pf, db, drums, with narrator]; Fantasy on the Saints [tp, others opt]

Hartway—Cityscapes [asx, pf, db, drums]; Country Suite [fl, pf, db, drums]; Urban Pictures [2tenor sax (1 dbl soprano sax), piano, bass, drums]

Bond, Victoria—Urban Bird [asx]

Heath—Out of the Cool [sax (or fl or vn)]

Psathas—Omnifenix [tsx, drums]; Pounamu [vocals/gtr/bgtr]

Code	Strings	Woodwinds	Brass	Percussion	Other	Page
[1]		brass and/or percussion				627
[2]	works without strings	any	any	any	any	628
[3]	str orch					628
[4]	str orch				cnt	630
[5]	str orch			perc	hp, cel, pf, hpsd	631
[6]	Individual string players	any	any	any	any	631
[7]	str	single winds & percussion			hp, cel, pf	632
[8]	str	2fl or 2rec				633
[9]	str		2-8 hn			633
[10]	str	0202	2000		cnt	634
[11]	str	2202	2000		cnt	634
[12]	str	2202	2200	tmp	cnt	635
[13]	str	2222	2200	tmp		635
[14]	str	2222	2200	3	hp, cel, pf	636
[15]	str	2222	2231	1		637
[16]	str	2222	2331	4	hp, cel, pf	638
[17]	str	2222	4000	2	hp, kybd	639
[18]	str	2222	4200	3	2hp, 2kybd	639
[19]	str	2222	4330	tmp		640
[20]	str	2222	4230	4		640
[21]	str	2222	4331	5		641
[22]	str	2222	4431	5		642
[23]	str	2222	4431	5	hp, cel, pf	642
[24]	str	8 woodwinds	4300	tmp	cnt	644
[25]	str	3222	4331	4		644
[26]	str	3222	4431	5	hp, cel, pf	646
[27]	str	3322	4431	6	2hp, cel, pf	647
[28]	str	9/10 woodwinds	4331	4		648
[29]	str	9/10 woodwinds	4431	6	hp, cel, pf	648
[30]	str	3332	4331	5	hp, cel, pf	650
[31]	str	11 woodwinds	4431	5	hp, cel, pf	651
[32]	str	3333	4331	5		651
[33]	str	3333	4431	6	2hp, cel, pf	652
[34]	str	3333	larger than previous categories			655
[35]	str	13 woodwinds	4431	7	2hp, cel, pf	656
[36]	str	4454	6641	8	3hp, cel, pf	657
[37]		normal strings; otherwise larger than all previous categories				658
[38]		Indeterminate instrumentation				659
[39]		Multiple orchestras				659

Instrumentation Chart for Appendix D:
ORCHESTRAL WORKS LISTED BY INSTRUMENTATION

APPENDIX D
ORCHESTRAL WORKS
LISTED BY INSTRUMENTATION

This appendix is suitable for browsing. If you are looking for works that employ certain combinations of instruments—or perhaps works that do not exceed certain limits of instrumentation—this is the place. It includes orchestral works only— normally not accompaniments for solos or choral works.

Use the chart on the facing page (p.626). It progresses more or less from smaller to larger combinations. Find the category that best fits your needs. The right-most column will then send you to the appropriate pages.

Once there, the lists of pieces are *in a rough chronological order according to the composers' dates of birth.* The idea is that you can go to the part of each list that interests you: near the beginning of any list for the eighteenth century, near the end for twentieth or twenty-first, and so on.

If a category is large, it is subdivided by duration: 0'–10', 11'–20', and so on.

Once you get used to navigating the appendix, it should be easy to find a handful of works according to your specifications: short baroque pieces for strings and continuo, for example; or nineteenth-century works using double woodwinds, modest brass, and lasting less than 20 minutes.

The categories in the chart, of course, are far from exact. Many of the pieces call for somewhat fewer instruments than the category suggests. It will be necessary to turn back to the main portion of the book to establish the precise details for any work in which you are interested.

---

[1] BRASS and/or PERCUSSION

Brass only

Gabrieli—Canzona noni toni; Sonata pian' e forte [2 versions]
Dukas—Péri: Fanfare
Ruggles—Angels
Stravinsky—Fanfare for a New Theatre [2 solo tp]
Copland—Ceremonial Fanfare
Fuleihan—Fanfare for the Medical Corps
Perle—New Fanfares
Shulman—Top Brass
Jones—Festival Fanfare
Schickele—Fanfare for the Common Cold
Albert, Adrienne—Fanfare
Tower—Third Fanfare for the Uncommon Woman
Marshall—Fog Tropes
Larsen, L.—Northern Star Fanfare

Knussen—Fanfares for Tanglewood
Gross—Watchman, Tell Us of the Night
McCarter—Prelude and Excursion

Percussion only

Varèse—Ionisation

Brass and Percussion

Purcell—Funeral Music for Queen Mary
Janáček—Sokol Fanfare
Debussy—Martyre de Saint Sébastien: Two Fanfares
Strauss, R.—Feierlicher Einzug; Wiener Philharmoniker Fanfare
Roussel—Fanfare pour un sacre païen
Taylor—Fanfare for Russia
Goossens—Fanfare for the Merchant Marine
Piston—Fanfare for the Fighting French
Wagenaar—Fanfare for Airmen
Hanson—Fanfare for the Signal Corps

Thomson, V.—Fanfare for France
Cowell—Fanfare for the Forces of our Latin American Allies
Copland—Fanfare for the Common Man
Tomasi—Fanfares liturgiques
Creston—Fanfare for Paratroopers
Xenakis—Eonta
Duffy—Heritage Fanfare and Chorale
Druckman—Dark Upon the Harp [Ms solo]
Rautavaara—Requiem in Our Time
Jones—Aurum aurorae; Parliament of Owls
Corigliano—Salute; Utah Fanfare
Tower—Fanfare for the Uncommon Woman; Second Fanfare for the Uncommon Woman
Ran—Chicago Skyline
Knussen—Fanfares for Tanglewood
Daugherty—Asclepius
Sartor—Dies irae
Higdon—Spirit

[2]
WORKS WITHOUT STRINGS

15' or less

Purcell—Funeral Music for Queen Mary
Haydn, F.J.—Divertimento, Hob.II:46
Mozart, W.A.—Divertimentos, K.166, K.186, K.188; Entführung aus dem Serail: March
Cherubini—March, F major
Beethoven—Zapfenstreich March
Donizetti—Sinfonia for Winds
Schubert—Rosamunde [mvt 6]
Mendelssohn—Nocturno; Overture for Winds
Rimsky-Korsakov—Concerto, Trombone
Indy—Chanson et danses
Strauss, R.—Serenade, TrV 106
Joplin—Entertainer
Reger—Serenade, B-flat major
Ives—Over the Pavements
Grainger—Immovable Do
Stravinsky—Octet; Song of the Volga Boatmen; Symphonies of Wind Instruments [1920 & 1947]
Varèse—Hyperprism; Intégrales
Milhaud—Symphonie de chambre No.5
Poulenc—Suite française
Copland—Inaugural Fanfare
Brant—Galaxy 2; Verticals Ascending
Britten—Sword in the Stone
Persichetti—Serenade No.1
Bernstein—Prelude, Fugue and Riffs [solo cl]
Rochberg—Black Sounds
Delden—Piccolo concerto (Little Concerto)
Serocki—Segmenti
Xenakis—Akrata
Chou—Beijing in the Mist; Pien [solo pf]; Soliloquy of a Bhiksuni [solo tp]
Rorem—Sinfonia
Jones—Aurum aurorae; Parliament of Owls
Harbison—Music for 18 Winds
Kolb—Chromatic Fantasy [narrator]
Ferneyhough—Carceri d'invenzione III
Schwantner—From a Dark Millennium
Mauldin—Entrada
Stucky—Funeral Music for Queen Mary
Chen Yi—Dunhuang Fantasy [solo org]; KC Capriccio [chorus]
Higdon—Wind Shear
Petering—Swimming Pool

Over 15'

Handel—Royal Fireworks Music [2 versions]

Mozart, W.A.—Serenades Nos.10-12
Berlioz—Symphonie funèbre et triomphale
Gounod—Petite Symphonie
Raff—Sinfonietta
Strauss, R.—Suite, TrV 132; Symphony for Winds, TrV 291
Hahn—Bal de Beatrice d'Este: Suite
Varèse—Déserts
Berg—Chamber Concerto, op.8 [solo vn & pf]
Antheil—Ballet mécanique (1953 version)
Weill—Kleine Dreigroschenmusik
Brant—Angels and Devils [solo fl with flute orchestra]
Kurka—Good Soldier Schweik: Suite
Xenakis—Eonta
Zaninelli—Lexicon of Beasties [narrator & solo pf]
Birtwistle—Verses for Ensembles
Reich—Music for Mallet Instruments, Voices & Organ [3 female voices]
Boudreau—Versus
Ran—Double Vision

[3]
STRING ORCHESTRA

5' or less

Pachelbel—Canon
Purcell—Canon on a Ground Bass; Fantasias, Strings [13 individual works]
Veracini—Aria schiavona
Haydn, M.—Symphony, MH 181
Boccherini—Minuet in A, G.275
Reinagle—Madison's March & Mrs. Madison's Minuet
Chopin—Mazurka No.7
Schumann, R.—Träumerei
Bolzoni—Gavotte; Minuetto
Grieg—Erotik, op.43, no.5
Fauré—Shylock: Nocturne
Foote—Irish Folk Song
Elgar—Elegy, op.58
Delius—Air and Dance
Pierné—Serenade, op.7
Ropartz—Serenade
Sibelius—Andante festivo; Canzonetta; Romance
Kalinnikov—Chanson triste
Vaughan Williams—Prelude "49th Parallel"
Ives—Hymn (Largo cantabile)
Schreker—Intermezzo
Grainger—Immovable Do; Irish Tune from County Derry; Molly on the Shore
Cowell—Ballad
Riisager—Little Overture
Copland—Rodeo: Hoe-Down (str orch)

Crawford—Andante for Strings
Finzi—Prelude
Carter—Elegy
Dello Joio—Air; Arietta
Lutoslawski—Overture for Strings
Shulman—Bop Gavotte; Elizabethan Legend; Four Moods; Minuet; Minuet for Moderns; Nocturne; Portrait of Lisa; Viennese Lace
Starer—Elegy for Strings
Harmon—Prelude & Fugue for String Orchestra
Jones—Elegy
Pärt—Silouans Song
Bennett, Richard R.—Chelsea Reach
Skoryk—Melody
Peck—Don't Tread on Me
Zaimont—JoyDance in Spring
Kechley—Funky Chicken
Locklair—In Memory — H.H.L.
Buhr—Chant of Water and Sky; Chant of Wind and Thunder
Dorff—It Takes Four to Tango; Lamentations
Sartor—Black Ball Counts Double
Cotton—Elegy
Heitzeg—Wounded Fields
Higdon— Celebration Fanfare; String; To the Point
O'Boyle—She Moved Through the Fair [str orch]
Richman—Kol Nidre
Thomas, Augusta Read—Of Paradise and Light
Stephenson—Printemps
Dorman—Chorale
Rival—Elegy

6'–10'

Gabrieli—Canzona [arr. Napolitano]
Monteverdi—Orfeo: Sinfonie e ritornelli
Schein—Banchetto musicale: Suite No.1
Corelli—Sarabanda, Giga e Badinerie
Purcell—Chacony in G minor; Gordian Knot Untied: Suite No.2
Scarlatti, A.—Piccola Suite
Vivaldi—Sinfonia, RV 169
Durante—Concerto No.5
Marcello, B.—Introduction, Aria & Presto
Geminiani—Concerto grosso, op.2, no.2
Leclair—Sonata, D major (arr.)
Pergolesi—Concertino, E-flat major
Abel—Symphonies, op.1, nos.5–6
Beck, F.I.—Sinfonia, op.10, No.2
Boccherini—Sinfonia concertante, Strings, G.268; Symphony "A", G.500
Stamitz, Carl—Orchestral Quartet, op.1, no.3
Mozart, W.A.—Adagio & Fugue, K.546
Donizetti—Allegro in C major
Schubert—Overture, D.8 (arr. Hess)

Mendelssohn—Sinfonia Nos.1-5;
  Symphony Movement
Liszt—Angelus!
Borodin—Nocturne (arr. Malcolm
  Sargent)
Brahms—Es ist ein Ros' entsprungen
Saint-Saëns—Déluge: Prélude; Sarabande
Svendsen—Two Icelandic Melodies; Two
  Swedish Folk Melodies
Dvořák—Nocturne, op.40
Grieg—Two Elegiac Melodies, op.34;
  Two Melodies, op.53
Strong—Chorale on a Theme of Leo
  Hassler
Puccini—Crisantemi
Glazunov—Elegy
Nielsen, Carl—Bohemian-Danish Folk
  Tune
Kalinnikov—Serenade for Strings
Sinigaglia—Adagio tragico
Roussel—Sinfonietta
Reger—Weihnachten
Holst—Brook Green Suite
Suk—Meditation on an Old Bohemian
  Chorale
Ruggles—Portals
Respighi—Aria
Bartók—Romanian Folk Dances (str orch)
Cadman—American Suite
Webern—Langsamer Satz
Riegger—Study in Sonority
Villa-Lobos—Bachianas brasileiras no.5:
  Aria (strings); Bachianas brasileiras no.9
Prokofiev—Andante
Rosenberg—Overtura bianca-nera
Cowell—Hymn and Fuguing Tune No. 2;
  Hymn and Fuguing Tune No.5
Tansman—Tombeau de Chopin
Gershwin—Lullaby
Harris, Roy—Chorale
Finzi—Romance
Rodrigo—Zarabanda lejana y Villancico
Skalkottas—Five Greek Dances
Tippett—Little Music
Swanson—Music for Strings
Barber—Adagio for Strings; Serenade,
  op.1
Schuman, Wm.—Amaryllis
Hovhaness—Alleluia and Fugue;
  Armenian Rhapsody No.2; Celestial
  Fantasy
Fine, Irving—Serious Song
Panufnik—Jagiellonian Triptych
Shulman—Ben Franklin Suite; Ripe for
  Plucking; Suite; Threnody
Babbitt—Correspondences
Husa—Pastoral
Walker, George—Lyric for Strings
Ligeti—Ramifications
Rorem—Pilgrims
Adler, S.—Elegy for String Orchestra
Rautavaara—Fiddlers

Amram—Autobiography for Strings
Takemitsu—Requiem
Van de Vate—Gema Jawa
Deussen—Peninsula Suite
Kilar—Orawa
Wood, Hugh—Divertimento, op.51
Górecki—Three Pieces in Old Style
Penderecki—Emanations; Polymorphia;
  To the Victims of Hiroshima
Pärt—Festina lente
Riley—Half-Wolf Dances Mad in
  Moonlight
Schickele—Elegy
Albert, Adrienne—Interiors
Glass—Arioso no.2; Company
Corigliano—Fancy on a Bach Air;
  Snapshot [2 solo vn]; Voyage (strings)
Wuorinen—Grand Bamboula
Lauridsen—O magnum mysterium
Harris, Ross—Music for Jonny
Zaimont—Elegy for Strings
Avshalomov, D.—Elegy
Tann—Water's Edge
Walker, Gwyneth—Suite for Strings
Gellis—Hymn
Chen Yi—Shuo; Sprout
Adolphe—I'm Inclined to New Music
McCarter—Opening Ideas
Sartor—Reveries
Smith, Kile—Hymn and Fugue No.1
Knehans—lamentation
Amaya—Angelica
Wachsman—Fanfares for String Orchestra
McLoskey—Chanson pour cordes
Dorman—Prayer for the Innocents
Rival—Spring

11'–15'

Purcell—Fairy Queen: Suite No.2; Fairy
  Queen: Two Suites [Wm. Reed, ed.];
  Gordian Knot Untied: Suite No.1
Fux—Overture, C major
Telemann—Overture, TWV 55:C1
Rameau—Suite for String Orch
Durante—Concerto No.1
Scarlatti, D.—Five Sonatas
Tartini—Sinfonia, D major
Stamitz, Joh.—Symphony, op.3, no.3;
  Three Mannheim Symphonies [each]
Stamitz, Carl—Orchestral Quartets, op.1,
  nos.1, 2, 4-6
Mozart, W.A.—Divertimenti, K.136, 137,
  138 [individual works]
Rossini—Sonatas Nos.1-4
Mendelssohn—Sinfonia No.6; Sinfonia
  No.10
Grieg—Two Norwegian Airs
Parry—Suite in F
Foote—Suite, op.63, E major
Elgar—Serenade, op.20

Vaughan Williams—Fantasia on a theme
  by Thomas Tallis [solo str 4t]
Holst—St. Paul's Suite
Schoenberg—Waltzes
Stravinsky—Concerto in D
Webern—Fünf Sätze
Becker—Soundpiece No.2b
Martin—Passacaille (str orch)
Warlock—Capriol Suite
Hindemith—Five Pieces; Suite of French
  Dances
Tansman—Variations on a Theme by
  Frescobaldi
Copland—Two Pieces
Krenek—Sinfonietta; Symphonic Elegy
Wirén—Serenade, op.11
Thiriet, Maurice—Danseries françaises
Bacewicz—Concerto for String Orchestra
Hovhaness—Psalm and Fugue, op.40a
Dahl—Variations on a Theme by C.P.E.
  Bach
Françaix—Sei preludi
Montsalvatge—Tres reflejos sobre una
  pastoral de invierno
Coolidge—Pioneer Dances
Lutoslawski—Musique funèbre
Panufnik—Divertimento; Old Polish Suite
Diamond—Rounds
Hervig—In Summer Season
Kay, U.—Suite for Strings
Ward—Concertino for Strings
Yardumian—Cantus animae et cordis
Ritchie, John—Aquarius; Suite No.1
Xenakis—Syrmos
Woollen—Elegy & Divertimento
Rautavaara—Suite for Strings
Perkinson—Sinfonietta No.1
Górecki—Muzyczka 3
Sallinen—Chamber Music I
Schwertsik—Draculas Haus- und
  Hofmusik
Harbison—Merchant of Venice: Incidental
  music
Tower—In Memory
Holliger—Meta arca [solo vn]
Zwilich—Prologue & Variations
Antunes—Poetica II
Cresswell—Paesaggi dell'anima
Jenkins—Palladio
Peck—Signs of Life
Rutter—Suite for Strings
Sapieyevski—Surtsey
Mauldin—Petroglyph
Mozetich—Postcards from the Sky
Stucky—Colburn Variations
Warshauer—Shabbat with King David
McTee—Adagio for String Orchestra
Danielpour—Lacrimae beati
Drattell—Sorrow Is Not Melancholy
Smith, Kile—Four French Carols
Bartholomew—Suite for String Orchestra
Cotton—Lyra

Kats-Chernin—Zoom and Zip
Tüür—Action — Passion — Illusion
Golijov—Last Round
Kernis—Musica celestis
Torke—December
Abels—Delights and Dances [solo str 4t]
Miller—Scenes Unseen
Boyer—Three Olympians
Hutter—Deploration
Bates—Icarian Rhapsody
Tommasini—Tell Me …

16'–20'

Lully—Triomphe de l'amour: Ballet Suite
Purcell—Fairy Queen: Suite No.1
Veracini—Quatro pezzi
Stamitz, Joh.—Orchestral Trios, op.1,
 nos.1-3; op.4, no.3; op.5, no.3
Hofmann, Leopold—Sinfonia, Badley F1
Stamitz, Carl—Orchestral Quartets, op.14,
 nos.1 & 4
Mozart, W.A.—Eine kleine Nachtmusik
Beethoven—Grosse Fuge, op.133
Rossini—Sonatas Nos.5–6
Mendelssohn—Sinfonia No.12
Gade—Novelette No.2
Foote—Serenade
Arensky—Variations on a Theme by
 Tchaikovsky
Nielsen—Little Suite
Schmitt—Janiana
Vaughan Williams—Concerto grosso;
 Partita
Melartin—Serenade
Bridge—Suite
Ireland—Concertino pastorale
Respighi—Antiche danze ed arie: Suite III
Malipiero—Symphony No.6
Schoeck—Sommernacht, op.58, Pastoral
 Intermezzo
Villa-Lobos—Suite for Strings
Martin—Etudes for String Orch
Martinů—Sextet
Prokofiev—Visions fugitives
Rosenberg—Reflessioni no.2
Ben-Haim—Concerto for Strings
Tansman—Triptych
Bacon—Concerto Grosso
Tcherepnin, A.—Serenade, op.97
Antheil—Serenade [I]
Copland—Nonet for Strings
Skalkottas—Ten Sketches
Cushing—Divertimento
Scelsi—Chukrum
Tippett—Fantasia concertante
Tubin—Music for Strings
Gutche—Symphony No.5
Schuman, Wm.—Symphony No.5
Rota—Concerto, String Orchestra
Britten—Simple Symphony
Persichetti—Symphony No.5

Babbitt—Transfigured Notes
Kay, U.—Six Dances for String Orch
Delden—Concerto per due orchestre
 d'archi
Klein—Partita
Nørgård—Tributes
Perkinson—Sinfonietta No.2
Bennett, Richard R.—Reflections on a
 Sixteenth Century Tune
Maslanka—Music for String Orchestra
Bond, Victoria—Dreams of Flying
Peck—Signs of Life II
Coleman, L.R.—Hibernia Suite;
 Suite Antique
Tan—Symphony for Strings
Di Vittorio—Symphony No.1

21'–25'

Gossec—Symphony op.6, no.6
Beethoven—Quartet, Strings, op.95
Mendelssohn—Sinfonia No.7
Verdi—Symphony for Strings
Reinecke—Serenade, op.242
Grimm—Suite in Canonform
Brahms—Liebeslieder Waltzes, op.52
Grieg—Holberg Suite
Fuchs—Serenade, No.3
Parry—English Suite
Bossi—Intermezzi goldoniani
Karłowicz—Serenade
Respighi—Suite, P.41
Bartók—Divertimento (1939)
Miaskovsky—Sinfonietta, op.32, no.2
Gál—Musik für Streichorchester
Honegger—Symphony No.2
Rosenberg—Concerto No.1 for String
 Orchestra; Suite on Swedish Folktunes
Chávez—Symphony No.5
Jolivet—Symphonie pour cordes
Tippett—Concerto for Double String Orch
Shostakovich—Chamber Symphony,
 op.110a
Ginastera—Concerto for Strings, op.33
Overton—Symphony for Strings
Arnold—Symphony for Strings
Rorem—String Symphony
Wyner—Tuscan Triptych
Schnittke—Fragment-Suite
Glass—Symphony No.3
Larsen, Libby—String Symphony
Saariaho—Nymphea Reflection
Phillips, P.S.—Celestial Harmonies
Allen—Nativity Scenes
Frank, G.L.—Leyendas
Petering—Symphony No.2

26'–30'

Tchaikovsky—Serenade, op.48
Dvořák—Serenade, op.22
Chadwick—Serenade

Janáček—Idylla
Herbert—Serenade
Klengel—Serenade
Strauss, R.—Metamorphosen
Schoenberg—Suite for String Orch;
 Verklärte Nacht [1917 & 1943 versions]
Suk—Serenade, op.6
Stravinsky—Apollon Musagète [both]
Berg—Lyric Suite
Atterberg—Sinfonia per archi
Alwyn—Sinfonietta
Britten—Variations on a Theme of Frank
 Bridge
Gould—Stringmusic
Surinach—Concerto for String Orchestra
Adams, John—Shaker Loops

Over 30'

Purcell—Fantasias, Strings [complete]
Stamitz, Joh.—Three Mannheim
 Symphonies [all three together]
Mozart, W.A.—Divertimenti, K.136, 137,
 138 [all three]
Beethoven—Quartet, Strings, op.131, C-
 sharp minor (arr. Davis)
Schubert—Quartet (Tod und das
 Mädchen)
Mendelssohn—Octet, Strings, op.20;
 Sinfonia No.8 (string version);
 Sinfonia No.9 (Swiss)
Tchaikovsky—Souvenir de Florence
Korngold—Symphonic Serenade
Hartmann—Symphony No.4
Dello Joio—Meditations on Ecclesiastes
Corigliano—Symphony No.2
Zaimont—Remember Me
Avshalomov, D.—Pangs of Love
Cotton—Pyramus and Thisbe: Suite
Wolfe, Julia—Cruel Sister

+-----------------------------------+
| **[4]** |
| **STRING ORCHESTRA** |
| **WITH CONTINUO** |
+-----------------------------------+

10' or less

Biber—Battalia
Pachelbel—Canon
Torelli—Concerto, op.6, no.1; Sinfonia,
 op.6, no.6
Purcell—Dido and Aeneas: Suite; Double
 Dealer: Suite; Rival Sisters: Overture
Scarlatti, A.—Concerti grossi Nos.1–2
Albinoni—Concertos, op.5, nos.4 & 7
Vivaldi—Concertos for Orchestra, RV
 151, RV 152, RV 155, RV 158;
 Sinfonia No. 1, RV 719, No.2, RV 146,
 No.3, RV 149
Telemann—Overture, TWV Anh.55:G1

Manfredini—Sinfonia da chiesa, op.2, no.12
Handel—Alcina, HWV 34: Overture
Geminiani—Concerto grosso, op.2, no.3
Veracini—Aria schiavona
Sammartini, Giov. Battista—Concertino, G major; Sinfonia, J-C 39
Galuppi—Concerto a quattro, Nos.1-2
Frederick II—Symphonies Nos.1-2
Bach, C.P.E.—Symphonies, H.661 & H.662
Gluck—Overture, D major; Sinfonia, G major
Abel—Symphonies, op.1, nos.5-6
Menotti—Pastorale
Denisov—Crescendo e diminuendo
Jones—Organ Benediction

Over 10'

Monteverdi—Combattimento di Tancredi e Clorinda [solos SAT]
Purcell—Abdelazer: Suite; Fairy Queen: Suites Nos.1-2
Fux—Overture, C major
Vivaldi—Sinfonia Nos. 1 & 2, RV 719 & 146 [6' ea]
Telemann—Don Quichotte; Ouverture des nations anciens; Overture, TWV 55:fis1
Bach, J.S.—Chaconne (arr. Starr)
Locatelli—Concerto grosso, op.1, no.6; Trauer-Symphonie
Sammartini, Giov. Battista—Sinfonia, J-C 32
Bach, W.F.—Sinfonia, F major
Bach, C.P.E.—Symphonies, H.657, H.658, H.659, H.660
Avshalomov, D.—Concerto con timpani

---

[5]
STRING ORCHESTRA WITH HARP, PIANO, CELESTA, HARPSICHORD, and/or PERCUSSION

Purcell—Chacony in G minor
Mendelssohn—Sinfonia No.11
Reinecke—Kinder-Symphonie
Strauss, Joh., Jr.—Pizzicato Polka
Grieg—Erotik, op.43, no.5
Elgar—Sospiri, op.70
Mahler—Symphony No.5: Adagietto
Delius—Hassan: Intermezzo & Serenade
Sibelius—Andante festivo; Rakastava
Vaughan Williams—Fantasia on "Greensleeves"; Five Variants of "Dives and Lazarus"
Schoenberg—Ode to Napoleon
Coleridge-Taylor—Novelettes Nos.1-4

Ravel—Pavane pour une infante défunte
Bartók—Music for Strings, Percussion and Celesta
Becker—Soundpiece No.1b
Martin—Petite symphonie concertante
Martinů—Double Concerto
Still—Out of the Silence; Serenade
Copland—Rodeo: Hoe-Down (str orch)
Fine, Irving—Notturno
Panufnik—Lullaby
Diamond—Elegy in Memory of Ravel
Shulman—Ricky-Tick Serenade
Dutilleux—Mystère de l'instant
Perkinson—Grass
Shchedrin—Carmen Suite
Zaninelli—Through Eudora's Eyes
Górecki—Symphony No.1
Penderecki—Anaklasis
Pärt—Cantus; Festina lente; Fratres
Glass—Dracula; Phaedra
Avshalomov, D.—Trotzky's Train
McTee—Einstein's Dream
Yoshimatsu—Threnody to Toki
Curiale—Sea of Tranquility/Ocean of Storms
Danielpour—Apparitions
Smith, Kile—Three Dances
Cotton—Folia
Adamo—Alcott Music
Frank, G.L.—Escaramuza; Manchay tiempo

---

[6]
WORKS USING INDIVIDUAL STRING PLAYERS RATHER THAN SECTIONS

Small ensemble (10 insts or less)

Mozart, W.A.—Musikalischer Spass
Beethoven—Septet, op.20, E-flat major
Spohr—Nonet; Octet, op.32, E major
Rossini—Serenata per piccolo complesso; Sonatas Nos.1-6
Schubert—Octet, D.803
Mendelssohn—Octet, Strings, op.20
Bruckner—Symphony No.7 [chmbr orch]
Saint-Saëns—Carnaval des animaux; Septet, op.65
Ives—Evening; Unanswered Question
Schoenberg—Ode to Napoleon; Pierrot lunaire [Sprechstimme]
Ruggles—Angels
Grainger—Immovable Do
Stravinsky—Histoire du soldat [orig & Suite]; Septet
Varèse—Octandre
Webern—Concerto

Villa-Lobos—Bachianas brasileiras no.1
Milhaud—Création du monde; Symphonies de chambre Nos.1-4
Piston—Divertimento for Nine Insts
Thomson, V.—Parson Weems and the Cherry Tree
Harsányi—Histoire du petite tailleur
Revueltas—Ocho por radio
Walton—Façade; Façade 2; Façade: Four Additional Numbers
Wolpe—Piece for Two Instrumental Units
Dallapiccola—Piccola musica notturna [chmbr version]
Blitzstein—Surf and Seaweed: Suite
Swanson—Night Music
Barber—Serenade, op.1
Pentland—Symphony No.3
Britten—Sinfonietta
Ohana—Suite pour un mimodrame
Kubik—Gerald McBoing Boing [solo perc; narrator]
Babbitt—All Set
Rochberg—EDEN [solo gtr]
Xenakis—Anaktoria; Analogique A
Chou—Yü ko
Feldman—Atlantis
Musgrave—Chamber Concerto No.1
Stockhausen—Kontra-Punkte
Górecki—Muzyczka 3
Harbison—Merchant of Venice
Scherchen—Hsun
Schwantner—Distant Runes and Incantations [solo pf]
Adams, John—Christian Zeal and Activity; Shaker Loops
Beckel—Imagination
Chen Yi—Sparkle
Daugherty—Dead Elvis [solo bn]
Adolphe—Oceanophony
Dorff—It Takes Four to Tango
Francesconi—Da capo
Ince—Arches
Stephenson, James—Devil's Tale
Dorman—Prayer for the Innocents

Medium ens. (11–15 players)

Mozart, W.A.—Serenade No.10
Heinrich—Columbiad; Tower of Babel
Schubert—Fantasy, D.940 [arr. Davidson]
Wagner, Richard—Siegfried Idyll
Dvořák—Serenade, op.44
Mahler—Symphony No.4 [chmbr orch arr]
Debussy—Prélude à "L'après-midi d'un faune" [arr.]
Strauss, R.—Serenade, TrV 106
Joplin—Entertainer; Maple Leaf Rag; Ragtime Dance
Schoenberg—Chamber Symphony No.1; Five Pieces for Orchestra [chmbr orch]
Wolf-Ferrari—Sinfonia da camera

Stravinsky—Concertino for 12 Insts;
 Concerto in E-flat; Eight Instrumental
 Miniatures; Ragtime
Rogers, B—Musicians of Bremen
Hindemith—Kammermusik No.1; Suite of
 French Dances
Cowell—Sinfonietta
Revueltas—Homenaje a Lorca
Copland—Appalachian Spring [complete
 ballet *or* suite]; Tender Land: Suite
 [chmbr ens] [solo ST]
Wolpe—Chamber Piece No.1
Finney—Landscapes Remembered
Shostakovich—Suite for Jazz Orch, No.1
Carter—In Sleep, In Thunder [solo T]
Bacewicz—Contradizione
Schuman, Wm.—Newsreel
Lutosławski—Preludes & Fugue
Kubik—Divertimento I
Perle—Serenade No.2
Surinach—Apasionada
Babbitt—Composition for 12 Insts
Weber, Ben—Symphony on Poems of Wm
 Blake [Bar]
Rochberg—Music for the Magic Theater
Bentzon—Chamber Concert
Maderna—Serenata No.2
Xenakis—Atrees
Ligeti—Ramifications
Rorem—Eleven Studies for Eleven Players
Boulez—Éclat
Henze—Usignolo dell'imperatore
Musgrave—Largo, In Homage to
 B.A.C.H.
Denisov—Chamber Symphony No.2;
 Crescendo e diminuendo
Takemitsu—Rain Coming
Górecki—Muzyczka 3
Birtwistle—Carmen arcadiae mechanicae
 perpetuum
Davidovsky—Inflexions
Maxwell Davies—Carolísima Serenade;
 Mirror of Whitening Light; Welcome to
 Orkney
Reynolds—Quick Are the Mouths of
 Earth; Wedge
Sallinen—Chamber Music I
Schwartz—Texture
Bolcom—Orphée-sérénade [solo pf]
Harbison—Umbrian Landscape With Saint
Holliger—Meta arca [solo vn]
Kolb—Soundings
Antunes—Intervertige
Adams, John—Chamber Symphony
Horwood—Women of Trachis
Davis—Litany of Sins
McTee—Twittering Machine
Durand—Lichtung
Adolphe—Marita and Her Heart's Desire;
 Tyrannosaurus Sue
Francesconi—Inquieta limina
Maltz—Aesop's Fables

Torke—Adjustable Wrench
Seither—Kammersinfonie
Stephenson, James—Compose Yourself!
Amrhein—Event Horizon (alt.version)
Adès—Chamber Symphony; Living Toys
Territo—John Henry vs. the Machine

Large ens. *(over 15 players)*

Mussorgsky—Pictures at an Exhibition
 [arr. Yu]
Strauss, R.—Bourgeois Gentilhomme:
 Suite; Metamorphosen
Busoni—Berceuse élégiaque
Ives—Chromâtimelôdtune
Ruggles—Men and Mountains [1924]
Bartók—Three Village Scenes [female
 voices]
Webern—Fünf Stücke
Ibert—Divertissement
Prokofiev—Overture, op.42
Milhaud—Création du monde
Sessions—Concertino for Chamber
 Orchestra
Korngold—Much Ado About Nothing
Revueltas—Sensemayá [chmbr version]
Antheil—Jazz Symphony
Copland—Music for the Theatre
Krenek—Kleine Symphonie
Wolpe—Chamber Piece No.2
Carter—Penthode
Bacewicz—Pensieri notturni
Lutosławski—Venetian Games
Blomdahl—Game for Eight
Zimmermann—Stille und Umkehr
Arnold—Concerto for 28 Players
Powell—Modules
Brown—Available Forms 1
Feldman—Atlantis
Henze—Heure bleue
Takemitsu—Tree Line
Shchedrin—Geometry of Sound
Górecki—Muzyczka 3
Lachenmann—… zwei Gefühle…
Amy—Mouvements
Reich—Variations
Bach, Jan—Happy Prince [narrator]
Bolcom—Summer Divertimento
Eötvös—Chinese Opera
Adams, John—Son of Chamber
 Symphony
Murail—Pour adoucer le cours de temps…
Buhr—this is the murmur of yearning
Daugherty—Blue Like an Orange
Lindberg—Arena; Joy; Ritratto
Wolfe, Julia—Tell Me Everything
Turnage—Snapshots
Toovey—Black Light
Wittry, Diane—after the rain
Trigos, Juan—Symphony No.2

---

[7]
STRINGS
SINGLE WINDS & PERC
HARP, CELESTA, PIANO

10' or less

Purcell—Indian Queen: Trumpet Overture
Scarlatti, A.—Sinfonia No.2 & No.4
Handel—Agrippina: Overture
Mozart, Leopold—Kindersymphonie
Haydn, F.J.—Kindersymphonie
Mozart, W.A.—Contradances, K.609;
 March, K.544
Rossini—Serenata per piccolo complesso
Franck—Eight Short Pieces, Nos.1-4;
 Nos.5-8
Grieg—Lyric Pieces, op.68, nos.4 & 5
Debussy—Plus que lente
Debussy—Prélude à "L'après-midi d'un
 faune" (arr.)
Delius—Irmelin: Prelude
Pierné—Marche des petits soldats de
 plomb
Joplin—Entertainer; Maple Leaf Rag;
 Ragtime Dance
Vaughan Williams—Prelude "49th
 Parallel"; Two Hymn-Tune Preludes
Holst—Brook Green Suite
Ives—Charlie Rutlage;
 Chromâtimelôdtune; Evening; Fugue in
 Four Keys; New England Holidays:
 Washington's Birthday; Set of Pieces;
 Symphony No.4: Fugue; Tone Roads
 Nos.1 & 3
Respighi—Serenata, p.54
Stravinsky—Ragtime
Honegger—Pastorale d'été
Milhaud—Symphonies de chambre
 Nos.2-3
Cowell—Hymn and Fuguing Tune No.10;
 Polyphonica for Small Orchestra
Bacon—Elegy [solo ob]
Poulenc—Deux marches et un intermède
Revueltas—Ocho por radio
Copland—Symphony No.1: Prelude [arr.
 for chmbr orch]
Luening—Prelude to a Hymn Tune by
 William Billings
Finzi—Severn Rhapsody, op.3
Walton—Façade: Four Additional
 Numbers
Dallapiccola—Piccola musica notturna
 [chmbr version]
Swanson—Night Music
Françaix—Serenade for Small Orchestra
Glanville-Hicks—Gymnopédie No.1
Pentland—Symphony No.3
Britten—Sword in the Stone

Kubik—Gerald McBoing Boing [solo perc; narrator]
Babbitt—All Set; Composition for Twelve Instruments
La Montaine—Summer's Day
Piazzolla—Oblivion
Feldman—Atlantis
Musgrave—Chamber Concerto No.1
Van de Vate—Variations for Chambr Orch
Maxwell Davies—Welcome to Orkney
Pärt—Wenn Bach Bienen gezüchtet hätte…
Schwartz—Texture
Stock—Capriccio
Adams, John—Christian Zeal and Activity
Horwood—Do You Live for Weekends?
Davidson—Mexico-Bolivar Tango
Daugherty—Blue Like an Orange; Dead Elvis [solo bn]
Dorff—Goldilocks and the Three Bears
Bartholomew—Sunshine Music
Lentini—Dreamscape
Wolfe, Julia—Tell Me Everything
Golijov—ZZ's Dream
Turnage—Snapshots
Toovey—Black Light
Di Vittorio—Il tallone di Achille
Rival—Scherzo

11'–15'

Purcell—Fairy Queen: Suite No.2
Scarlatti, A.—Sinfonias Nos.6, 8, 10
Saint-Saëns—Septet
Vaughan Williams—Death of Tintagiles
Ives—Ragtime Dances
Malipiero—Oriente immaginario
Stravinsky—Septet
Becker—When the Willow Nods
Ibert—Divertissement; Symphonie marine
Piston—Divertimento for Nine Insts
Cowell—Sinfonietta
Bacon—Remembering Ansel Adams
Copland—Three Latin-American Sketches
Walton—Façade 2
Finney—Landscapes Remembered
Britten—Sinfonietta
Perle—Serenade No.2
Rochberg—Cheltenham Concerto
Xenakis—Anaktoria
Anderson, T. J.—Chamber Symphony
Shchedrin—Geometry of Sound
Birtwistle—Carmen arcadiae mechanicae perpetuum
Glass—Secret Agent: Three Pieces
Silvestrov—Symphony No.2
Baksa—Variations from the Heart
Kolb—Chromatic Fantasy
Schwantner—Distant Runes and Incantations [solo pf]
Zaimont—Chroma
Márquez—Danzón No.4 (chmbr orch)

Chen Yi—Sparkle
McTee—Twittering Machine
Sierra—Güell concert
Wolfe, Julia—Vermeer Room
Ince—Arches
Stephenson—Chamber Concerto
Amrhein—Event Horizon (alt.version)
Petering—Lake Summit

16'–20'

Roussel—Marchand de sable qui passe …
Schoenberg—Five Pieces for Orchestra, op.16 (chmbr orch)
Harty—John Field Suite
Respighi—Trittico Botticelliano
Hindemith—Kammermusik No.1; Tuttifäntchen: Suite
Tippett—Divertimento on "Sellinger's Round"
Bacewicz—Contradizione
Hovhaness—Symphony No.10
Kubik—Divertimento I
Surinach—Ritmo jondo
Kay, U.—Scherzi musicali
Ward—Symphony No.6
Imbrie—Chamber Symphony
Zaninelli—Tale of Peter Rabbit
Birtwistle—Endless Parade
Rands—Madrigali
Bolcom—Orphée-sérénade [solo pf]
Kolb—Soundings
Horwood—Women of Trachis
Walker, Gwyneth—Light of Three Mornings
Lindberg—Zona [solo vc]
Adès—Living Toys

Over 20'

Beethoven—Septet, op.20
Spohr—Nonet
Schubert—Octet
Adam—Giselle
Bruckner—Symphony No.7 [chmbr orch]
Saint-Saëns—Carnaval des animaux [2 solo pf]
Mussorgsky—Pictures at an Exhibition [arr. Yu]
Mahler—Symphony No.4 [chmbr version] [solo S]
Schreker—Kammersymphonie
Honegger—Symphony No.2
Milhaud—Carnaval de Londres
Rogers—Musicians of Bremen
Thomson, V.—Parson Weems and the Cherry Tree
Harsányi—Histoire du petite tailleur
Copland—Appalachian Spring [complete or suite]; Tender Land: Suite [chmbr ens] [solo ST]
Walton—Façade

Carter—In Sleep, In Thunder [solo T]
Barber—Medea [orig]
Britten—Plymouth Town
Surinach—Embattled Garden
Rorem—Eleven Studies for Eleven Players
Zaninelli—Lexicon of Beasties [solo pf]; Steadfast Tin Soldier
Maxwell Davies—Sinfonia for Chmbr Orch
Harbison—Umbrian Landscape With Saint
Svoboda—Concerto for Chmbr Orch
Adolphe—Marita and Her Heart's Desire; Tyrannosaurus Sue
Maltz—Aesop's Fables
Stephenson—Compose Yourself!

**[8]
STRINGS
2 FLUTES or 2 RECORDERS**

Charpentier, M.-A.—Noëls pour les instruments, H.531 & 534
Lalande—Symphonie de Noël
Scarlatti, A.—Sinfonia Nos.1 & 5
Bach, W.F.—Sinfonia, D minor
Abel—Symphonies, op.1, nos.5 & 6
Bach, Joh. Christian—Symphony, op.21, no.2, W. C18
Foote—Air and Gavotte
Vaughan Williams—Fantasia on "Greensleeves"
Tann—Water's Edge: Toward Dusk

**[9]
STRINGS
2 OR MORE HORNS**

Telemann—Suite, TWV 44:7
Sammartini, Giov. Battista—Sinfonia, J-C 4; Sinfonia, J-C 47
Galuppi—Sinfonia, D major; Sinfonia, F major
Gluck—Sinfonia, D major; Sinfonia, F major
Stamitz, Joh.—Symphony, op.3, no.3
Beck, F.I.—Sinfonia, op.13, no.1
Boccherini—Symphony "A", G.500
Mozart, W.A.—Divertimentos No.7, K.205; No.10, K.247; No.15, K.287; No.17, K.334; Marches, K.248, K.290, K.445; Musikalischer Spass; Serenade No.8
Grainger—Irish Tune from County Derry

[10]
STRINGS
WINDS 0202—2000
CONTINUO

10' or less

Lalande—Symphonie de Noël
Handel—Acis and Galatea: Overture; Alcina, HWV 34: Overture; Alessandro, HWV 21: Overture; Alexander's Feast, HWV 75: Overture; Belshazzar: Overture; Concerti grossi, op.3, nos.5-6; Judas Maccabaeus, HWV 63: Overture; Orlando: Overture; Rinaldo: Overture; Samson, HWV 57: Overture; Solomon, HWV 67: Overture; Solomon: Entrance of the Queen of Sheba; Xerxes: Overture
Leo—Santa Elena al Calvario: Sinfonia
Arne—Symphonies Nos.1-2
Boyce—Overture (Ode for His Majesty's Birthday [1769]); Overture (Ode for the New Year [1772]); Overture (Peleus and Thetis); Symphonies Nos.2, 3, 4, 6
Gluck—Orfeo ed Euridice: Dance of the Furies
Benda, Georg—Symphony No.4, F major
Abel—Symphonies, op.1, nos.5 & 6
Haydn, F.J.—Symphony No.2
Gossec—Christmas Suite
Bach, J.C.—Symphonies, op.3, no.2; op.6, no.1; op.21, no.3
Haydn, M.—Symphony, MH 473
Paisiello—Sinfonia, D major; Sinfonia in tre tempi
Boccherini—Overture, G.521; Symphony No.1, G.490; Symphony No.12, G.496
Cimarosa—Traci amanti: Overture
Salieri—Sinfonia (Veneziana)
Mozart, W.A.—Apollo et Hyacinthus: Prelude; Bastien und Bastienne: Overture; Contradances, K.462; Finta giardiniera: Overture; Idomeneo: March, F major [No.25]; Symphonies Nos.4, 5, 10, 11; Symphonies K.81 & K.196/121
Moncayo—Homenaje a Cervantes
Weber, Ben—Dolmen
Arnold—Sinfonietta No.1

11'-20'

Albinoni—Concerto, op.9, no.9
Bach, Joh. Ludwig—Suite, G major
Telemann—Overture, TWV 55:g4
Handel—Concerto grosso, op.3, no.4; Overtures to Rodrigo, Saul, Theodora
Tartini—Concerto No.58
Arne—Symphony No.3
Wagenseil—Sinfonia, G minor
Stamitz, Joh.—Sinfonia, op.4, nos.1, 2, 4, 6

Abel—Symphony, op.14, no.2, E-flat major
Haydn, F.J.—Symphony A, Hob.I:107; Symphony B Hob.I:108; Symphonies Nos.1, 3-5, 10-12, 14-19, 21-23, 25-29, 34-37, 40, 46, 58-59, 65, 67
Beck, F.I.—Sinfonia, Callen 30
Gossec—Sinfonia, op.12, nos.2 & 4
Bach, Joh.Christian—Symphonies, op.3, no.1; op.3, no.4; op.6, no.6; op.21, nos.1-2
Haydn, M.—Symphonies, MH 272 & MH 508
Hofmann, Leopold—Sinfonia, B-flat major, C major, D major; Sinfonia, B.F2, F major
Dittersdorf—Sinfonia, A major [G.A10]; Sinfonia, F major [G.F7]
Gołąbek—Symphony, D major [both]
Saint-Georges—Symphony No.1
Vanhal—Sinfonia, G minor
Boccherini—Symphonies Nos.13-20; No.26
Mozart, W.A.—Cassation No.2; Symphonies, K.Anh.214, K.Anh.216, K.Anh.220 (16a), K.Anh.221 (45a), K.Anh.223 (19a); Symphonies Nos.1-2, 6, 12-13, 15-17, 33; Symphonies, K.75 & K.76
Pleyel—Symphony, op.3, no.1
Moravec, Paul—Sempre diritto!

Over 20'

Telemann—Overture, TWV 55:D21
Bach, Joh Sebastian—Suite (Overture) No.1
Handel—Water Music: Suite No.1
Haydn, F.J.—Symphonies Nos.42-45, 47, 49, 51-52, 55, 64, 99, 68
Dittersdorf—Sinfonia, A minor [G.a2]; Sinfonia, D major [G.D16]; Sinfonia, D minor [G.d1]
Boccherini—Symphonies No.6, 11
Mozart, W.A.—Cassation No.1; Divertimento No.11, K.251; Symphony No.29
Amram—Shakespearian Concerto
Shchedrin—Music for Str, Ob, Hns & Cel

[11]
STRINGS
WINDS 2202-2000
CONTINUO

10' or less

Rameau—Platée: Suite des danses; Zaïs: Overture
Bach, Joh. Sebastian—Bist du bei mir
Handel—Concerto grosso, op.3, no.1
Sammartini, Giov. Battista—Sinfonia, J-C 47
Graun—Sinfonia, F major, M.95
Boyce—Symphonies Nos.1 & 7
Bach, C.P.E.—Symphonies, H.664, H.665, H.666
Gluck—Orfeo ed Euridice: Dance of the Blessed Spirits
Haydn, F.J.—Armida: Overture, Scherzandi, Hob.II:33-37
Bach, Joh. Christian—Clemenza di Scipione, W. G10: Overture
Haydn, M.—Symphony, MH 476
Boccherini—Overture, G.521
Cimarosa—Sinfonia, D major
Mozart, W.A.—Contradances, K.267; Contradance, K.610; Overtures to Finta semplice, Mitridate; Serenade No.2; Symphony No.24
Hindemith—Spielmusik, op.43, no.1

11'-20'

Rameau—Dardanus: Suite; Paladins Suite No.2
Bach, Joh. Sebastian—Suite (Overture) No.2, BWV 1067 [solo fl]
Handel—Water Music: Suite No.3, HWV 350
Arne—Symphony No.4
Boyce—Symphony No.8
Bach, C.P.E.—Symphony, H.663
Benda, Georg—Symphony No.5, G major
Haydn, F.J.—Notturno No.1; Scherzando, Hob.II:38; Symphonies Nos.9, 24, 30, 62, 63 [both versions], 77, 78, 85
Bach, Joh. Christian—Symphonies, op.18, nos.1, 3, 5-6
Haydn, M.—Symphonies, MH 334 & MH 399
Gołąbek—Symphony, C major
Boccherini—Symphonies Nos.7, 9-10, 18, 21, 23, 27
Mozart, W.A.—Symphonies Nos.14, 21, 27, 37
Berkeley—Windsor Variations
Badings—Symphonietta
Arnold—Concerto for 28 Players; Sinfonietta No.2
Schurmann—Variants

Musgrave—Night Music
Lazarof—Chamber Symphony
Zwilich—Concerto Grosso
Mozetich—Steps to Ecstasy
Heitzeg—Flower of the Earth
Wański—Symphony, G major

Over 20'

Telemann—Overture, TWV 55:C3
Haydn, F.J.—Symphonies Nos.6-8, 71, 74, 76, 79-81, 83-84, 87, 89, 91
Boccherini—Symphonies Nos.3, 5, 8, 25
Mozart, W.A.—Symphony No.40
Witt—Symphony in A
Schubert—Symphony No.5, D.485
Argento—Royal Invitation
Wański—Symphony, D major

---

[12]
STRINGS
WINDS 2202—2200
TIMPANI
CONTINUO

10' or less

Lully—Roland: Suite
Handel—Alceste, HWV 45: Inst Pieces; Occasional Oratorio, HWV 62: Overture
Boyce—Overture (Ode for the New Year [1758]); Symphony No.5
Gluck—Iphigénie en Aulide: Overture [orig & Wagner ending]; Orfeo ed Euridice: Overture
Piccinni—Iphigenie en Tauride: Overture
Haydn, F.J.—Isola disabitata: Overture; Ritorno di Tobia: Overture
Haydn, M.—Andromeda ed Perseo, MH 438: Overture
Paisiello—Scuffiara: Overture
Cimarosa—Maestro di cappella: Overture
Mozart, W.A.—Contradance, K.587 & K.603; German Dances, K.605; Idomeneo: March, D major [No.8]; Lucio Silla: Overture; Marches, K.62, K.189, K.214, K.215, K.237, K.249, K.335; Minuet, K.409; Re pastore: Overture; Symphonies, K.111/120 & K.141a; Symphonies Nos.22-23, 26
Nunés-Garcia—Sinfonia funebre
Schubert—Overture, D.470
Sibelius—Cassazione
Maxwell Davies—Threnody on a Plainsong

11'-20'

Rameau—Fêtes d'Hébé: Divertissement

Handel—Royal Fireworks Music (ed. Baines & Mackerras); Water Music: Suite No.2
Sammartini, Giov. Battista—Sinfonia, J-C 2
Bach, C.P.E.—Symphony, H.663
Haydn, F.J.—Symphonies Nos.20, 32-33, 37-38, 41, 50, 69-70, 75, 96
Bach, Joh. Christian—Symphony, op.18, no.4, W. C27
Dittersdorf—Sinfonia, C major
Salieri—Sinfonia
Mozart, W.A.—German Dances, K.536; Marches, K.408; Symphonies Nos.7-9, 20, 30; Symphonies, K.95, K.96, K.97, K.320; Thamos: Zwischenaktmusiken
Weber, C.M.—Symphony No.2
Hindemith—Suite of French Dances
Badings—Symphonietta

21'–30'

Gluck—Don Juan: Four Movements
Haydn, F.J.—Symphonies Nos.48, 53-54, 56-57, 60-61, 73, 82, 86, 88, 90, 92-95, 97-98, 102
Knecht—Portrait musical de la nature
Mozart, W.A.—Idomeneo: Ballet Music; Symphonies Nos.28, 34, 36, 38;
Witt—Jena Symphony
Weber, C.M.—Symphony No.1

Over 30'

Bach, J.S.—Musikalisches Opfer, BWV 1079 [Landshoff]
Handel—Water Music, HWV 348-350
Mozart, W.A.—Serenades No.3-5, 7, 9; Symphony, K.250; Symphony No.41

---

[13]
STRINGS
WINDS 2222—2200
TIMPANI

10' or less

Purcell—Gordian Knot Untied: Suite No.2; Virtuous Wife: Suite
Handel—Acis and Galatea: Overture (arr. Mozart)
Haydn, F.J.—March for the Royal Society of Musicians
Paisiello—Nina: Overture; Sinfonia funebre
Cimarosa—Giorno felice: Overture; Matrimonio segreto: Overture [2 versions]; Nemeci generosi: Overture

Salieri—Grotta di Trofonio: Overture
Mozart, W.A.—Contradance, K.535; Fantasia, K.608; German Dances, K.567 & K.602; Idomeneo: March; Maurerische Trauermusik; Overture, K.311a; Overtures to Clemenza di Tito, Così fan tutte, Don Giovanni. Idomeneo [both], Nozze di Figaro; Schauspieldirektor
Cherubini—March, F major
Méhul—Joseph: Overture
Beethoven—Coriolan Overture; Gratulations-Menuet; Prometheus: Overture
Weber, C.M.—Preziosa: Overture
Rossini—Guillaume Tell: Pas de six; Overtures to Cenerentola, Italiana in Algeri, Scala di seta, Signor Bruschino, Tancredi; Sinfonia di Bologna
Schubert—Deutsche Tänze; Overtures to Claudine von Villa Bella, Freunde von Salamanka, Häusliche Krieg, Spiegelritter, Teufel als Hydraulicus, Vierjährige Posten, Zwillingsbrüder; Overtures, D.8, D.556; D.590; D.591; Symphony, D.615
Arriaga—Esclavos felices: Overture
Mendelssohn—Hebrides; Heimkehr aus der Fremde: Overture; Märchen von der schönen Melusine; Midsummer Night's Dream extracts Intermezzo, Nocturne, Scherzo; Octet, Strings
Verdi—Traviata: Prelude to Act III
Brahms—Es ist ein Ros' entsprungen
Rimsky-Korsakov—Tale of the Tsar Saltan: Flight of the Bumblebee
Fauré—Pavane
Elgar—Salut d'amour
Delius—Two Pieces: On Hearing the First Cuckoo in Spring [7'], Summer Night on the River [5']
Glazunov—Serenade No.2
Sibelius—Autrefois [solo SA]; Kuolema: Valse triste & Scene with Cranes
Järnefelt—Berceuse
Vaughan Williams—Running Set
Ives—Unanswered Question
Kreisler—Liebesfreud
Dohnányi—Schleier der Pierrette: Walzer-Reigen & Menuett
Bartók—Romanian Folk Dances
Valen—Isla de las calmas
Martin—Ouverture en hommage à Mozart
Revueltas—Ocho por radio
Adaskin—Serenade Concertante
Montsalvatge—Cuatro variaciones sobre un tema de La flauta mágica
Etler—Elegy
Shulman—In Memoriam Sophie
London—Imaginary Invalid: Overture
Deussen—Ascent to Victory; Carmel by-the-Sea

Maxwell Davies—Ojai Festival Overture
Perera—Saints: Joyful Noise
Actor—Divertimento for Small Orchestra; Opening Remarks
Adolphe—Three Pieces: No.2 (Rainbow) & No.3 (T-D-T)
Fine, M.—Missouriana
Karidoyanes—Café Neon

11'–20'

Purcell—Gordian Knot Untied: Suite No.1; Married Beau: Suite
Handel—Saul: Overture (arr. Prout)
Abel—Symphony, op.7, no.6
Bach, Joh. Christian—Symphony, op.18, no.2
Mozart, W.A.—Divertimento No.1; German Dances, K.600; Symphonies Nos.3, 31, 35
Beethoven—Contradances, WoO 14; Musik zu einem Ritterballet
Heinrich—Tower of Babel
Schubert—Symphony, D.708a: Scherzo
Schumann, R.—Overture, Scherzo, & Finale
Wagner, Richard—Siegfried Idyll
Delibes—Roi s'amuse
Pachulski—Suite
Koechlin—Partita
Roussel—Concerto for Small Orch
Kodály—Summer Evening
Stravinsky—Concerto in E-flat
Prokofiev—Classical Symphony
Piston—Sinfonietta
Berkeley—Sinfonietta, op.34
Badings—Symphonietta
Britten—Sinfonietta
Effinger—Little Symphony No.1, op.31
Panufnik—Harmony
Shulman—Woodstock Waltzes
Surinach—Sinfonia chica
Ballard—Incident at Wounded Knee
Tower—Chamber Dance
Peck—Thrill of the Orchestra
Walker, Gwyneth—About Leaves; Fanfare, Interlude & Finale
Smith, Kile—Symphony (Lumen ad revelationem); Three Dances
Ritchie, A.—French Overture; Hanging Bulb
Torke—Lucent Variations
Goulet—Chocolats symphoniques

21'–30'

Haydn, F.J.—Symphonies Nos.99, 101, 103, 104
Mozart, W.A.—Petits Riens; Serenade No.1; Symphony No.39
Cherubini—Symphony, D major
Méhul—Symphony No.2

Beethoven—Symphonies Nos.1 & 8
Schubert—Symphonies Nos.1-3, 6
Arriaga—Symphony in D
Mendelssohn—Symphony No.4
Gounod—Symphony No.1
Saint-Saëns—Symphony, A major
Sibelius—Pelléas and Mélisande
Schoenberg—Chamber Symphony No.2
Valen—Symphony No.2
Cowell—Symphony No.10
Maxwell Davies—Strathclyde Concerto No.10
Sallinen—Concerto for Chamber Orch
Cresswell—Of Smoke and Bickering Flame
Davidson—Black & Blues

Over 30'

Mozart, W.A.—Symphony No.40
Beethoven—Prometheus, Symphonies Nos.2, 4, 7
Mendelssohn—Sinfonia No.8 (with winds); Symphony No.1
Maxwell Davies—Sinfonietta accademica; Symphony No.4
Bolcom—Symphony No.3

**[14]
STRINGS
WINDS 2222—2200
3 PERCUSSION
HARP, CELESTA, PIANO**

10' or less

Bach, J.C.—Symphony, W. G8
Mozart, W.A.—Entführung aus dem Serail: Overture [3 versions]; German Dances, K.571
Beethoven—Ruinen von Athen: Turkish March
Boieldieu—Calife de Bagdad: Overture
Rossini—Barbiere di Siviglia: Overture (critical ed); Italiana in Algeri: Overture (critical ed); Tancredi: Overture
Schumann, R.—Manfred: Suite
Chabrier—Habanera
Humperdinck—Hänsel und Gretel: Knusperwalzer
Elgar—Chanson de matin; Chanson de nuit
Debussy—Clair de lune (arr. Caplet); Danse; Sarabande
Delius—Hassan: Intermezzo & Serenade
Mascagni—Cavalleria rusticana: Intermezzo
Ropartz—Sérénade champêtre
Järnefelt—Praeludium

Pfitzner—Christ-Elflein: Overture
Vaughan Williams—Running Set; Wasps: Overture; Wasps: March Past of the Kitchen Utensils
Ives—Set of Pieces
Hahn—Mozart: Overture
Ravel—Ma Mère l'Oye: Prélude & Danse du rouet; Pavane pour une infante défunte
Falla—Amor brujo: Ritual Fire Dance
Wolf-Ferrari—Gioielli della Madonna: Intermezzo No.1 (arr.)
Kodály—Háry János: Song
Webern—Symphony, op.21
Butterworth—The Banks of Green Willow
Becker—Two Pieces: 1. Among the Reeds and Rushes
Ibert—Hommage à Mozart
Milhaud—Symphonie de chambre No.1
Benjamin, A.—Two Jamaican Pieces
Still—Lenox Avenue: Blues
Cowell—Carol for Orchestra
Dallapiccola—Piccola musica notturna
Bissell—Andante e Scherzo
Raksin—Toy Concertino
Duffy—American Fantasy Overture (chmbr orch)
Denisov—Little Suite
Nelson, Ron—Sarabande: For Katharine in April
Deussen—Tico; Transit of Venus
Martino—Divertisements for Youth Orchestra
Maxwell Davies—Chat Moss
Bennett, Richard R.—Sinfonietta
Rudow—Dark Waters of Elba; Dark Waters of the Chesapeake
Bolcom—Commedia for (Almost) 18th-Century Orchestra
McCartney—Spiral
Mauldin—Music for the Mountain Air; Three Dances from Chaco Canyon
Tann—With the Heather and Small Birds
Lofstrom—Irish Suite #1
Wendel—Fantasia on "Yerousalaim shel zahav"; Towers of Light
Chen Yi—Duo ye [No.1]
Kernis—Too Hot Toccata
Adamo—Lysistrata: Overture
O'Boyle—Scottish Piano Rhapsody
Richman—Jalopy and Blues
Di Vittorio—Il tallone di Achille
Amrhein—Serenade
Frank, G.L.—Concertino Cusqueño
Petering—Fanfare and Reflection
Dorman—Reflections

11'–20'

Rameau—Ballet Suite
Grétry—Zémire et Azor: Ballet Suite
Schumann, R.—Carnaval: 3 excerpts

Fauré—Masques et bergamasques
Debussy—Five Etudes; Petite suite
Sibelius—Belshazzar's Feast
Pfitzner—Kleine Sinfonie
Roussel—Festin de l'araignée
Vaughan Williams—Three Preludes on
    Welsh Hymn Tunes
Holst—St. Paul's Suite
Ravel—Tombeau de Couperin
Falla—Sombrero de tres picos: Suite No.1
Respighi—Uccelli
Malipiero—Dialogo no.1
Prokofiev—Summer Day
Cowell—Ongaku
Jolivet—Amants magnifiques
Talma—Full Circle
Liebermann, Rolf—Suite über sechs
    schweizerische Volkslieder
Britten—Suite on English Folk Tunes
Dello Joio—New York Profiles
Lutoslawski—Polish Dances
Maderna—Serenata No.2
Hollingsworth—Three Ladies Beside the
    Sea
Lees—Concerto for Chamber Orch
Henze—Aria de la Folía española;
    Symphony No.1
Druckman—Nor Spell Nor Charm
Flagello—Serenata
Schickele—Symphony No.2
Bennett, Richard R.—Country Dances,
    Bk 1; Diversions; Partita
Harbison—Most Often Used Chords
Tower—Duets
Boone—Second Landscape
León, Tania—Ácana
Horwood—Symphony No.1
Tann—Adirondack Light
Boelter—Dharma
Sierra—Serenata; Sinfonía No.1
Coleman, L.R.—For a Beautiful Land
Sheng—Postcards
Mackey—Square Holes, Round Pegs
Kernis—Concerto With Echoes
Boyer—Ghosts of Troy
Frank, G.L.—Elegia Andina; Raíces

Over 20'

Gluck—Airs de ballet, Suite No.2
Haydn, F.J.—Symphony No.100
Vorisek—Symphony
Falla—Amor brujo: Ballet Suite [solo Ms]
Martinů—Toccata e due canzoni, H.311
Honegger—Symphony No.4
Poulenc—Sinfonietta
Ward—Symphonies Nos.3-4
Husa—Symphony No.2
Previn—Diversions
Bennett, Richard R.—Symphony No.3
Bolcom—Summer Divertimento
Schwantner—New Morning for the World

Frank, G.L.—Peregrinos

```
        [15]
      STRINGS
  WINDS 2222—2231
   1 PERCUSSION
```

10' or less

Buxtehude—Chaconne, BuxWV 160
Bach, J.S.—Fugue, BWV 577 [arr. Holst]
Gluck—Alceste: Overture [2 versions]
Mozart, W.A.—Overtures to Don
    Giovanni (arr. Busoni), Zauberflöte
Cherubini— Overtures to Démophoon,
    Faniska, Hôtellerie portugaise
Nunés-Garcia—Zemira
Boieldieu—Dame blanche: Overture
Paganini—Moto perpetuo [arr. Molinari]
Weber, C.M.— Overtures to Peter
    Schmoll, Silvana
Schubert— Overtures to Alfonso und
    Estrella, Teufels Lustschloss; Overture,
    D.26; Symphony, D.2b; Symphony,
    D.759 (Newbould)
Bellini—Symphonies, C minor & D major
Adam—Si j'étais roi: Overture
Glinka—Kamarinskaya
Mendelssohn—Athalie: Kriegsmarsch der
    Priester; Trumpet Overture
Bruckner—March in D minor; Three
    Pieces for Orchestra
Saint-Saëns—Rigaudon
Balakirev—Overture on Three Russian
    Folk Songs
Mussorgsky—Scherzo, B-flat major
Dvořák—Humoresque
Sullivan—Overtures to Gondoliers,
    Iolanthe, Patience, Yeomen of the Guard
Janáček—Adagio
Vaughan Williams—Prelude on an Old
    Carol Tune
Ives—Circus Band
Stravinsky—Suite No.1
Collins—Lil' David Play on Yo' Harp
Valen—Cimetière marin
Cowell—Ancient Desert Drone
Copland—Down a Country Lane; Letter
    from Home
Crawford—Rissolty Rossolty
Walton—Façade: Suite No.2
Creston—A Rumor
Read—Prelude & Toccata
Benson—Five Brief Encounters
Adler, S.—Summer Stock
Van de Vate—Adagio for Orchestra
Maxwell Davies—Jimmack the Postie
Jones—Benediction
Rands—Fanfare for a Festival
Perera—Saints: Choirs

Lankester—Pocket-Sized Guide to the
    Orchestra
Peck—Playing with Style
Buhr—Akasha
Tommasini—Letter Home

11'–20'

Schubert—Rosamunde: Ballet Music
Mendelssohn—Midsummer Night's
    Dream: Overture
Schumann, R.—Overture, Scherzo, &
    Finale; Symphony, WoO 29
Bruckner—Overture, G minor
Holst—Egdon Heath; Hammersmith
Ives—Symphony No.3
Stravinsky—Danses concertantes
Honegger—Suite archaïque
Warlock—Capriol Suite
Finney—Landscapes Remembered
Swanson—Short Symphony
Rorem—Quaker Reader
Berio—Variazioni per orchestra da camera
Maxwell Davies—Carolísima Serenade;
    First Fantasia on Taverner's "In nomine"
Sallinen—Variations for Orchestra
Dorff—Billy and the Carnival
Caltabiano—Concertini
McLoskey—Moraine

Over 20'

Clementi—Symphonies Nos.1-4
Schubert—Rosamunde: Entr'actes;
    Symphonies, D.759, D.936a, D.944
Mendelssohn—Symphony No.5
Schumann, R.—Symphony No.2
Bennett, Wm. S.—Symphony, G minor
Grieg—Symphony, C minor
Vaughan Williams—Symphony No.5
Atterberg—Symphony No.8
Villa-Lobos—Sinfonietta No.1
Ibert—Histoires: Suite No.1
Milhaud—Saudades do Brazil, op.67
Weill—Symphony No.2
Carter—Symphony No.1
Britten—Plymouth Town
Gilbert, J.—Dream Carver
Aho—Symphony No.1
Adolphe—Purple Palace

**[16]
STRINGS
WINDS 2222—2331
4 PERCUSSION
HARP, CELESTA, PIANO**

10' or less

Monteverdi—Orfeo: Overture
Bach, J.S.—Musikalisches Opfer:
  Ricercare [arr. Webern]
Haydn, M.—Pastorello, MH 83
Weber, C.M.—Abu Hassan: Overture;
  Turandot: Overture & March
Rossini—Overtures to Barbiere di Siviglia,
  Cenerentola, Elisabetta, Italiana in
  Algeri, Turco in Italia, Viaggio a Reims
Lanner—Schönbrunner Walzer; Werber
  Walzer
Lortzing—Zar und Zimmermann:
  Overture
Glinka—Capriccio brillante; Valse
  fantaisie
Mendelssohn—Overtures to Athalie, St.
  Paul; Midsummer Night's Dream:
  Wedding March
Fry—Evangeline: Overture
Gounod—Marche funèbre d'une
  marionette
Strauss, Joh., Jr.—Accelerationen
Delibes—Coppélia: Entr'acte & Waltz
Balakirev—Overture on Three Russian
  Folk Songs
Chabrier—Roi malgré lui: Danse slav &
  Fête polonaise
Dvořák—Humoresque
Sullivan—Overtures to H.M.S. Pinafore,
  Mikado, Pirates of Penzance
Sousa—Glass-Blowers: Overture
Charpentier, G.—Louise: Prelude to Act
  III & "Air de Louise"
German—Henry VIII: Three Dances; Nell
  Gwyn: Three Dances
Pierné—Cydalise: Entrance of the Little
  Fauns
Glazunov—Seasons: Three Movements
Satie—Deux Préludes posthumes et une
  gnossienne; Jack in the Box; Trois
  petites pièces montées
Vaughan Williams—English Folk Song
  Suite; Poisoned Kiss: Overture
Holst—Capriccio
Ives—Central Park in the Dark; "Country
  Band" March; Gong on the Hook and
  Ladder; Overture and March "1776"; Set
  No.1
Coleridge-Taylor—Christmas Overture
Falla—La vida breve: Spanish Dance No.1
  [Chapelier]

Wolf-Ferrari—Gioielli della Madonna:
  Intermezzo No.2 [arr.]
Bartók—Dances of Transylvania;
  Hungarian Peasant Songs
Stravinsky—Pas de deux [Tchaikovsky];
  Suite No.2
Webern—Variations for Orchestra
Griffes—White Peacock
Riegger—Dance Rhythms
Atterberg—Varmlands Rhapsody
Villa-Lobos—Bachianas brasileiras no.5:
  Aria [full orch]
Martinů—Comedy on the Bridge: Little
  Suite
Milhaud—Genesis Suite: Cain and Abel
Hindemith—Cupid and Psyche: Overture
Jacob—Barber of Seville Goes to the
  Devil
White—Five Miniatures for Orchestra
Gerhard—Albada, interludi i dansa
Cowell—Hymn and Fuguing Tunes Nos.3
  & 16
Korngold—Theme and Variations
Revueltas—Alcancías; Homenaje a Lorca
Copland—Billy the Kid: Prairie Night &
  Celebration Dance; Billy the Kid: Waltz;
  John Henry; Rodeo: Corral Nocturne,
  Saturday Night Waltz; Variations on a
  Shaker Melody
Luening—Synthesis
Walton—Façade: Suite No.1; Portsmouth
  Point
Wolpe—Chamber Piece No.1
Dallapiccola—Piccola musica notturna
Kabalevsky—Comedians: Galop
Tubin—Toccata
Shostakovich—Tahiti Trot [small]
Barber—Die natali: Silent Night
Schuman, Wm.—Newsreel
Britten—Building of the House; Paul
  Bunyan: Overture; Soirées musicales
Gould—Notes of Remembrance
Lutoslawski—Prelude for GSMD
Arnold—Little Suite No.4
Foss—Salomon Rossi Suite
Xenakis—Pithoprakta
Chou—All in the Spring Wind;
  Landscapes
Benson—Chants and Graces
Frackenpohl—Short Overture
Lees—Spectrum
Cunningham—Lullabye for a Jazz Baby
Deussen—Trinity Alps
Martino—Divertisements for Youth
  Orchestra
Davidovsky—Inflexions
Tull—Capriccio
Jones—Hear the Music
Bennett, Richard R.—Lilliburlero
  Variations
Finko—Holocaust
Blake—Nursery Rhyme Overture

Corigliano—Elegy for Orchestra
León—Batá
Peck—Jack and Jill at Bunker Hill
Ayers—Fanfare and Carol for Christmas;
  Veni Emmanuel
Davis—Notes from the Underground
McTee—Circuits
Dorff—Pachelbel's Christmas; Three Fun
  Fables: The Tortoise and the Hare
Gordon—Romeo
Salonen—Giro
Janello—At the Sea of Clouds
McLoskey—post-
Richman—American Fanfare; Brentwood
  Rag; Christmas Wish: Reindeer
  Variations; Western Fanfare
Wittry, Diane—after the rain; Concerto for
  Homemade Instruments
Di Vittorio—Overtura Respighiana
Stephenson—Celebration Overture
Petering—Train & Tower

11'–20'

Bach, J.S.—Suites Nos.3-4
Gluck—Ballet Suite No.2 (arr. Mottl)
Sullivan—Tempest: Three Dances
Fauré—Four Pieces
Debussy—Children's Corner (arr.
  Abrahamsen)
Satie—Aventures de Mercure
Roussel—Petite suite
Vaughan Williams—England of Elizabeth:
  Three Portraits
Ives—Three Places in New England,
  versions 2-3
Ravel—Jardin magique; Ma Mère l'Oye:
  Suite
Bartók—Hungarian Sketches
Stravinsky—Scènes de ballet
Milhaud—Aubade, op.387; Boeuf sur le
  toit; Cortège funèbre; Création du
  monde; Suite française
Rosenberg—Bergslagsbilder
Rogers—Five Fairy Tales
Still—Darker America
Gerhard—Alegrías: Suite; Don Quixote:
  Dances
Sessions—Concertino for Chamber
  Orchestra
Thomson, V.—Louisiana Story: Acadian
  Songs and Dances; Plow That Broke the
  Plains: Suite
Cowell—Old American Country Set
Korngold—Much Ado About Nothing
Tansman—Sinfonietta
Auric—Chambre
Copland—Music for Movies
Weill—Aufstieg und Fall der Stadt
  Mahagonny: Suite
Goldschmidt—Ciaccona sinfonica
Jolivet—Symphonie de danses

Tubin—Estonian Dance Suite
Swanson—Concerto for Orchestra
Wilder—Carl Sandburg Suite
Holmboe—Symphony No.1
Hovhaness—Symphony No.10
Smith, Julia—Folkways Symphony
Montsalvatge—Manfred
Britten—Johnson over Jordan: Suite
Britten—Matinées musicales
Coolidge—Pioneer Dances
Diamond—Music for Shakespeare's
  Romeo and Juliet
Babbitt—Ars combinatoria
Avshalomov, J.—Cues from "The Little
  Clay Cart"
Kirchner—Toccata
Barab—G-A-G-E
Husa—Fantasies
Xenakis—ST/48–1,240162
Ligeti—Melodien
Powell—Modules
Rorem—Ideas for Easy Orchestra
Rautavaara—Cantus arcticus; Lintukoto
Stockhausen—Kontra-Punkte
Denisov—Postludio in memoriam Witold
  Lutoslawski
Colgrass—Letter from Mozart
Nørgård—Voyage into the Golden Screen
Maxwell Davies—Orkney Wedding With
  Sunrise [solo bagpiper]
Tull—Overture for a Legacy
Jones—Christmas Memory: Suite; Janus
Rands—Agenda
Bennett, Richard R.—Serenade
Hoover—Two Sketches
Tower—Made in America
Armer—Great Instrument of the Geggerets
McCabe—Lion the Witch and the
  Wardrobe: Suite
Svoboda—Nocturne
Plain—Clawhammer
Singleton—Yellow Rose Petal
Schwantner—Chasing Light
Peck—Thrill of the Orchestra
Rodríguez—Estampie
Kechley—Alexander and the Wind-Up
  Mouse
Mauldin—Desert Light; Enchanted Land
Bryant—Dinosaurs
Dorff—Three Fun Fables
Lindberg—Marea
Ince—Deep Flight; Domes
Liebermann, Lowell—Domain of Arnheim
Torke—Adjustable Wrench
McLoskey—Requiem, ver.2.001x
Amrhein—Bestiary; Little Nemo in
  Slumberland; Semi-Suite
Territo—John Henry vs. the Machine

Over 20'

Mozart, Leopold—Musikalische
  Schlittenfahrt
Chopin—Sylphides [various arrangements:
  Britten, Douglas reduction, Lanchbery]
Tchaikovsky—Nutcracker [reductions by
  Ceo or Itkin]
Chabrier—Suite pastorale
Strauss, R.—Bourgeois Gentilhomme:
  Suite
Vaughan Williams—Symphony No.8
Ravel—Ma Mère l'Oye
Casella—Serenata
Honegger—Dit des jeux du monde
Thomson, V.—River: Suite
Cowell—Symphonies Nos.7, 9, 16
Bacon—Fables
Poulenc—Histoire de Babar
Copland—Appalachian Spring [full orch
  versions: Suite or complete ballet];
  Dance Panels; Music for the Theatre
Weill—Symphony No.1
Blacher—Tanzszenen
Tippett—Concerto for Orchestra
Shostakovich—Hamlet: Incidental Music
Rózsa—Jungle Book [solo A]
Menotti—Sebastian: Suite
Gould—Jogger and the Dinosaur
Ginastera—Variaciones concertantes
Husa—Steadfast Tin Soldier
Rorem—Symphony No.2
Lees—Scarlatti Portfolio
Berio—Rendering
Schuller—Contours
London—In Heinrich's Shoes
Maxwell Davies—Caroline Mathilde:
  Suites from Act I or Act II
Bach, Jan—Happy Prince
Corigliano—Creations
Wuorinen—Magic Art
Tavener—Mystagogía
Adams, John—Chamber Symphony
Adolphe—Oceanophony
Abels—Frederick's Fables
Trigos, Juan—Symphony No.2
Wharton—Symphony
Greenberg—Neon Refracted

---

[17]
STRINGS
WINDS 2222—4000
2 PERCUSSION
HARP, KEYBOARD

Haydn, F.J.—Symphonies Nos.13, 31,
  39, 72
Vanhal—Sinfonia, G minor
Kraus—Symphony, C minor

Mozart, W.A.—Divertimento No.2;
  Symphonies Nos.18-19, 25
Cherubini—Médée (Medea): Overture
Méhul—Chasse du jeune Henri
Chopin—Nocturne, op.32, no.2 [arr.
  Stravinsky]
Verdi—Traviata: Prelude to Act I
Wagner, Richard—Tristan und Isolde:
  Prelude, Act III
Gounod—Colombe: Entr'acte
Bizet—Pecheurs de perles: Overture
Sibelius—Scènes historiques: Minnelied;
  Swanwhite: Suite
Satie—Gymnopédies
Dohnányi—Schleier der Pierrette: Pierrot's
  Complaint of Love
Oliverio, James—Go Gently my Friend

---

[18]
STRINGS
WINDS 2222—4200
3 PERCUSSION
2 HARPS, 2 KEYBOARDS

15' or less

Scarlatti, D.—Good-Humored Ladies:
  Suite
Mozart, W.A.—Betulia liberata: Overture;
  German Dances, K.605; Symphony
  No.32
Beethoven—Overtures: Egmont, Leonore
  No.1, Namensfeier, Ruinen von Athen
Hensel—Overture, C major
Wagner, Richard—Concert Overture No.1;
  König Enzio: Overture
Franck—Éolides
Bizet—Jeux d'enfants: Petite suite
Mussorgsky—Khovantchina: Introduction
  [both versions]
Goetz—Frühlings-Ouvertüre
Elgar—Dream Children
Mahler—Symphony No.1: Blumine
Debussy—Clair de lune [arr. Luck]
Glazunov—Serenade No.1
Satie—Gymnopédie No.2
Vaughan Williams—Wasps: Overture
Kodály—Háry János: Intermezzo
Malipiero—Symphony No.10
Martinů—Overture, H.345
Piston—Serenata
Thomson, V.—Pilgrims and Pioneers
Blacher—Two Inventions
Ginastera—Estancia: Four Dances
Biggs—Sousaphernalia
Horwood—Three Interludes
Beckel—Make a Joyful Noise
Rouse—Iscariot
Wendel—In the Manger
Torke—Ash

Rival, Robert—Lullaby

Over 15'

Lully—Ballet Suite
Handel—Pastor fido: Suite; Water Music Suite [arr. Harty]
Haydn, F.J.—Sieben letzten Worte [orch version]
Beethoven—Egmont [solo S]; Symphony No.3
Schubert—Symphony No.4
Mendelssohn—Symphonies No.2-3
Chopin—Sylphides [arr. McDermott]
Gade—Symphony No.4
Rubinstein—Symphonies No.3 & 5
Brahms—Serenade No.1
Bizet—Symphony No.1
Tchaikovsky—Suites Nos.1 & 4
Dvořák—Legends, op.59
Fauré—Pelléas et Mélisande: Suite; Shylock: Suite [solo T]
Parry—Symphony No.3
Debussy—Children's Corner [arr. Caplet]
Sibelius—Tempest: Suite No.2
Bartók—Suite No.2
Kodály—Dances of Galanta
Prokofiev—Sinfonietta
Bolcom—Symphony No.1
Kernis—Symphony in Waves

---

[19]
STRINGS
WINDS 2222—4330
TIMPANI

15' or less

Gluck—Iphigénie en Aulide: Overture [Wagner ending]
Cherubini—Overtures to Abencérages, Anacréon, Deux journées, Lodoïska
Beethoven—Overtures: Fidelio, Leonore No.2, Leonore No.3, Weihe des Hauses
Weber, C.M.—Overtures: Beherrscher der Geister, Euryanthe, Freischütz, Oberon
Rossini—Sinfonia di Odense
Marschner, Heinrich—Hans Heiling: Overture
Berwald—Estrella de Soria: Overture
Schubert—Overtures to Fierrabras, Rosamunde; Overture, D.648
Adam—Brasseur de Preston: Overture
Berlioz—Béatrice et Bénédict: Overture
Glinka—Life for the Tsar: Overture; Life for the Tsar: Krakoviak
Mendelssohn—Overtures to Hochzeit des Camacho, Ruy Blas

Schumann, R.—Fest-Ouvertüre [voices briefly]; Overtures to Genoveva, Manfred, Scenen aus Goethes "Faust"
Rietz—Concert Overture
Gade—Echoes of Ossian
Offenbach—'66': Overture
Goldmark—Scherzo, op.45
Borodin—In the Steppes of Central Asia
Brahms—Hungarian Dances Nos.5, 6 (arr. Parlow)
Paine—Oedipus tyrannus: Prelude
Svendsen—Norwegian Rhapsody No.3
Tchaikovsky—Eugene Onegin: Polonaise
Dvořák—Prague Waltzes
Massenet—Manon: Minuet & Gavotte
Rimsky-Korsakov—May Night: Overture
Indy—Fervaal: Introduction to Act I
Chadwick—Elegy
Strauss, R.—Intermezzo: Entr'acte after Act I
Nielsen, Carl—Symphonic Rhapsody
Sibelius—Scènes historiques: All' overtura
Stravinsky—Monumentum
Thomson, V.—Bugles and Birds
Hovhaness—Prelude and Quadruple Fugue
Tavener—Little Ceremonial
Lofstrom—Two Soldiers: Prelude & Wedding Scene
Wendel—In the Manger

16'–30'

Spohr—Symphony No.3
Berwald—Symphonies Nos.2-4
Schubert—Lebensstürme
Schumann, R.— Symphony No.1; Symphony No.4 [orig & rev]
Wagner, Richard—Symphony, WWV 35, E major
Gade— Symphonies Nos.2-3
Raff—Symphony No.6
Bruckner—Symphony No.3: Adagio 2 (1876)
Reinecke—Symphony No.1
Grimm—Symphony, op.19
Joachim—Hamlet
Borodin—Symphony No.3
Bruch—Symphony No.1
Dvořák—Symphonic Variations
Rimsky-Korsakov—Sinfonietta on Russian Themes; Symphony No.1
Stanford—Symphony No.7
Sibelius— Symphonies Nos.3, 5, 7
Valen— Symphonies Nos.2-3
Gould—Tap Dance Concerto [solo tap dancer]
Einem—Meditations

Over 30'

Berwald—Symphony No.1
Schubert—Rosamunde [solo A, chorus]; Symphony, D.729 [Weingartner or Newbould versions]
Schumann, R.—Symphony No.3
Gade—Symphony No.7
Raff—Symphonies Nos.1 & 8
Bruckner—Symphonies, Cahis 1 & 3; Symphonies Nos.2 [Cahis 4 or 8], 3 [Cahis 5, 9, 15], 4
Reinecke—Symphonies Nos.2-3
Borodin—Symphony No.1
Draeseke—Symphony No.1
Paine—Symphonies Nos.1-2
Goetz—Symphony, op.9, F major
Dvořák—Symphony No.7
Parry—Symphony No.3
Chadwick—Symphony No.2
Taneyev—Symphony No.1
Magnard—Symphony No.3
Zemlinsky—Symphony [No.1]

---

[20]
STRINGS
WINDS 2222—4230
4 PERCUSSION

10' or less

Auber—Overtures to Diamants de la couronne, Domino noir, Lestocq, Marco Spada, Part du diable, Zanetta
Donizetti— Overtures to Don Pasquale, Fille du régiment
Lortzing—Zar und Zimmermann: Overture
Glinka—Summer Night in Madrid
Nicolai—Merry Wives of Windsor: Overture
Flotow—Alessandro Stradella: Overture
Wagner, Richard—Concert Overture No.2; Siegfried: Forest Murmurs (Zumpe)
Litolff—Maximilian Robespierre
Offenbach— Overtures to Île de Tulipatan, Périchole, Vie parisienne
Suppé— Overtures to Banditenstreiche, Boccaccio, Fatinitza, Leichte Kavallerie, Morgen, Mittag und Abend in Wien, Schöne Galathée, Tantalusqualen
Strauss, Joh., Jr.—Fledermaus: Overture; Fledermaus: Du und du; Leichtes Blut; Märchen aus dem Orient; Seid umschlungen Millionen; Tausend und eine Nacht
Strauss, Joh., Jr.—Vergnügungszug; Wiener Blut; Wo die Citronen blüh'n; Zigeunerbaron: Einzugsmarsch
Strauss, Jos.—Delirien; Frauenherz

Brahms—Hungarian Dances Nos.2, 7 [arr. Hallén]; Nos.17-21 (arr. Dvořák)
Delibes—Roi l'a dit: Overture
Dvořák—My Homeland
Grieg—Wedding Day at Troldhaugen
Humperdinck—Hänsel und Gretel: Knusperwalzer
Janáček—Moravian Dances
Sibelius—Pan and Echo; Scènes historiques: Scena; Valse chevaleresque; Valse lyrique
Dohnányi—Schleier der Pierrette: Hochzeitswalzer
Milhaud—Kentuckiana; Ouverture méditerranéene
Moeran—Overture to a Masque
Tubin—Prélude solennel
Galbraith—Festive Violet Pulse
Chen Yi—Ge xu (Antiphony)
Dorff—Pachelbel's Christmas

Over 10'

Kuhlau—William Shakespeare: Overture
Rossini—Overtures to Guillaume Tell, Semiramide
Goldmark—Ländliche Hochzeit
Bruch—Swedish Dances, op.63, nos.1-7; Symphony No.2
Dvořák—Peasant a Rogue: Overture; Slavonic Dances, op.46 & op.72; Symphony No.5
Rimsky-Korsakov—Overture on Russian Themes [1880 version]
Sibelius—King Kristian II: Suite; Symphony No.4
Busoni—Rondò arlecchinesco [solo T backstage]
Stenhammar—Serenade, op.31, F major
Rabaud—Divertissement
Kodály—Dances of Marosszek
Casella—Giara: Symphonic Suite
Bliss—Checkmate
Prokofiev—Peter and the Wolf
Rosenberg—Symphony No.6
Luening—Rhapsodic Variations
Weill—Symphony No.1
Musgrave—Festival Overture
Harbison—Partita
Bond, Victoria—The Frog Prince

---

[21]
STRINGS
WINDS 2222—4331
5 PERCUSSION

10' or less

Gabrieli—Canzon XVI
Bach, J.S.—Jesu, Joy of Man's Desiring [arr.]
Auber—Fra Diavolo: Overture
Weber, C.M.—Drei Pintos: Entr'acte; Preziosa: Overture
Hérold—Zampa: Overture
Meyerbeer—Fackeltanz No.1
Rossini—Gazza ladra: Overture [both]
Schubert—Marche hongroise
Bellini—Overtures to Norma & Pirata
Schumann, R.—Julius Caesar: Overture
Thomas, Ambroise—Raymond: Overture
Flotow—Martha: Overture
Verdi—Aroldo: Overture; Ballo in maschera: Preludio; Nabucco: Overture
Gade—In the Highlands
Moniuszko—Halka: Mazur; Overtures to Halka & Hrabina
Suppé—Pique Dame: Overture
Strauss, Joh., Jr.—Egyptischer Marsch; Künstlerleben; Künstler Quadrille; Morgenblätter; Neu-Wien; Pizzicato Polka; Tritsch-Tratsch-Polka [crit. ed.]; Unter Donner und Blitz
Waldteufel—Patineurs
Mussorgsky—Intermezzo in the Classic Style
Svendsen—Andante funèbre
Dvořák—Festival March
Grieg—Wedding Day at Troldhaugen
Ivanovici—Donauwellen
Shelley—Santa Claus Overture
Delius—Marche caprice
Halvorsen—Entry of the Boyars
Nielsen, Carl—Pan and Syrinx
Sibelius—Finlandia; Lemminkäinen Suite: Lemminkäinen's Return; Scène de ballet
Holst—Somerset Rhapsody
Ives—Postlude in F
Stokowski, Leopold—Traditional Slavic Christmas Music
Stravinsky—Circus Polka; Four Norwegian Moods
Honegger—Prélude pour "La Tempête"
Milhaud—Murder of a Great Chief of State
Hindemith—Marsch über den alten Schweizerton
Jacob—Fantasia on the Alleluia Hymn
Rathaus—Praeludium and Gigue
Thomson, V.—Louisiana Story: Boy Fights Alligator

Cowell—Hymn and Fuguing Tunes Nos.3 & 16
Rubbra—Festival Overture
Walton—Façade: Suite No.1
Schuman, Wm.—Orchestra Song
McBride—Pumpkin-Eater's Little Fugue
Britten—Gloriana: Courtly Dances
Ward—Euphony
Arnold—Little Suites Nos.1, 2, 4; Symphonic Study
Bergsma—Music on a Quiet Theme
Bavicchi—Mont Blanc Overture
Xenakis—Metastaseis
Caviani—Ondee
Biggs—Passacaglia; Pastiche; Salutation
Bilik—American Civil War Fantasy
Birtwistle—Machaut à ma manière
Albert, Adrienne—Courage
Corigliano—To Music
Tower—For the Uncommon Woman [orch]
Zwilich—Openings
Peck—Playing with Style
Mauldin—Three Jemez Landscapes
Walker, Gwyneth—Fanfare for the Family Farm; Match Point; Open the Door
Locklair—Phoenix and Again
Warshauer—Beyond the Horizon
Ayers—Fanfare and Carol for Christmas
Rimelis—Cool Ghoul; Please Turn Your Cell Phones On!
Costa—Vignette
Rush, T.R.—Spirit of Freedom
Dorff—Fanfare Overture
Kallman—Holiday Hoedown
Bartholomew—Ah, My Children
Bremer—Early Light
Karidoyanes—Yerakína
Higdon—Machine; Peachtree Street
O'Boyle—Music That Goes with "The Tale of Peter Rabbit"
Goulet—Citius, altius, fortius!
Gilbertson—Reflections on Rushmore

11'–20'

Buxtehude—Four Chorale Preludes
Handel—Royal Fireworks Music [arr. Harty]
Berlioz—Roi Lear
Liszt—A la Chapelle Sixtine; Festklänge; Hungarian Rhapsody No.2 [arr. Müller-Berghaus]
Fry—Macbeth: Overture
Gade—Echoes of Ossian
Moniuszko—Fairy Tale
Franck—Rédemption: Morceau symphonique
Bruckner—Symphony No.4 (1878 version, Cahis 10): Finale 1878 (Volksfest)
Bizet—Ouverture
Bruch—Swedish Dances, op.63, nos.8-15

Svendsen—Romeo and Juliet
Sullivan—Overture di ballo; Overture in C
Foote—Francesca da Rimini
Elgar—Three Bavarian Dances
Ippolitov-Ivanov—Armenian Rhapsody
Sibelius—Lemminkäinen Suite:
  Lemminkäinen and the Maidens of the
  Island, & Lemminkäinen in Tuonela;
  Saga; Spring Song
Vaughan Williams—Variations for
  Orchestra
Rachmaninoff—Symphony, D minor
Holst—Suite for Orchestra [McPhee]
Ireland—London Overture
Ibert—Suite symphonique
Thomson, V.—Symphony on a Hymn
  Tune
Revueltas—Noche de los Mayas: Suite
  (Hindemith)
Tcherepnin, A.—Georgiana
Blacher—Concertante Musik; Studie im
  Pianissimo
Khachaturian—Masquerade: Suite
Tippett—Suite for the Birthday of Prince
  Charles
Glanville-Hicks—Sinfonia da Pacifica
Lutoslawski—Little Suite
Kay, U.—Fantasy Variations; Serenade for
  Orchestra
Ward—Adagio and Allegro; Five Times
  Five
Kirk—Orchestra Primer
Bergsma—Documentary One
Lees—Trumpet of the Swan
Rautavaara—Symphony No.1 (1988)
Sculthorpe—Mangrove
Adams, Leslie—Ode to Life
Biggs—Ballad of William Sycamore
Górecki—Three Dances
Maxwell Davies—Orkney Wedding With
  Sunrise [solo bagpiper]
Corigliano—Gazebo Dances
Tower—Tambor
Peck—Thrill of the Orchestra
Rodríguez—Jargon
Locklair—Hues
Picker—Keys to the City
Costa—Espranza; Providence
MacMillan—Confession of Isobel Gowdie
Tüür—Zeitraum
Burge, J.—The Canadian Shield;
  Snowdrift
Psathas—Seikilos
Rival—Northwest Passage Variations

Over 20'

Spohr—Symphony No.4
Liszt—Ideale
Bruckner—Symphony No.4 [Cahis 11,
  Suppl.1/14+]; Symphony No.5 (Cahis
  7); Symphony No.6 (Cahis 12)

Goldmark—Symphony No.2
Brahms—Symphony No.2
Bruch—Symphony No.3
Dvořák—Hero's Song; Symphonies
  Nos.6 & 8
Sullivan—Merchant of Venice:
  Masquerade Suite
Strauss, R.—Symphony, TrV 126
Nielsen, Carl—Aladdin: 7 pieces;
  Symphony No.6
Sibelius—Symphony No.2
Zemlinsky—Symphony No.2 (1897)
Vaughan Williams—Story of a Flemish
  Farm; Symphony No.4
Ives—Symphony No.1
Stravinsky—Jeu de cartes
Toch—Symphony No.6
Rosenberg—Symphony No.2
Hindemith—Mathis der Maler
  [Symphony]; Nobilissima visione: Suite;
  Symphonic Dances
Cowell—Symphony No.17
Antheil—Symphony No.3
Walton—Symphony No.1
Alwyn—Symphony No.4
Swanson—Symphony No.1
Markevitch—Rebus
Dello Joio—Triumph of Saint Joan
Bentzon—Symphony No.13
Schickele—Chenoo Who Stayed to Dinner
Davies, Victor—Short Symphony
Cresswell—Ylur
Rouse—Symphony No.1
Stephenson—Compose Yourself!

---

[22]
STRINGS
WINDS 2222—4431
5 PERCUSSION

Haydn, M.—Pastorello, MH 83
Mozart, W.A.—German Dances, K.605
Cherubini—Ali-Baba: Overture
Rossini—Robert Bruce: Overture
Berlioz—Carnaval romain; Corsaire;
  Roméo et Juliette: Introduction; Te
  Deum: Prelude; Troyens: Overture
Fry—Dying Soldier
Verdi—Vespri siciliani: Overture
Lalo—Roi d'Ys: Overture
Strauss, Joh., Jr.—Figaro-Polka
Strauss, E.—Bahn frei
Delibes—Coppélia: Valse de la poupée &
  Czardas
Massenet—Scènes alsaciennes; Scènes
  pittoresques
Sibelius—Overture, A minor
Hindemith—Konzertmusik, op.50
Curiale—Wind River

---

[23]
STRINGS
WINDS 2222—4431
5 PERCUSSION
HARP, CELESTA, PIANO

10'or less

Handel—Xerxes: Largo (arr.)
Adam—Si j'étais roi: Overture
Berlioz—Te Deum: Marche
Glinka—Capriccio brillante
Liszt—Hungarian Rhapsody No.5
Thomas, Ambroise—Mignon: Overture
Verdi—Forza del destino: Overture
Wagner, Richard—Götterdämmerung:
  Gesang der Rheintöchter & Siegfried's
  Rhine Journey; Rheingold: Entry of the
  Gods; Tristan und Isolde: Nachtgesang
Offenbach—Belle Hélène: Overture;
  Contes d'Hoffmann: Intermezzo &
  Barcarolle; Orphée aux enfers: Overture
Suppé—Dichter und Bauer: Overture
Strauss, Joh., Jr.—An der schönen blauen
  Donau; Frühlingsstimmen; Kaiser-
  Walzer; Perpetuum mobile; Rosen aus
  dem Süden; Tritsch-Tratsch-Polka [trad.
  version]; Wein, Weib, und Gesang;
  Zigeunerbaron: Overture;
  Zigeunerbaron: Schatz-Walzer
Minkus—Don Quixote: Pas de deux
Strauss, Jos.—Dorfschwalben aus
  Österreich; Mein Lebenslauf ist Lieb'
  und Lust; Sphärenklänge
Brahms—Hungarian Dance No.4 (arr.
  Juon)
Saint-Saëns—Princesse jaune: Overture
Delibes—Coppélia: Prelude & Mazurka;
  Lakmé: Airs de danse
Bruch—Loreley: Prelude
Dvořák—Festival March
Massenet—Hérodiade: Prelude, Act III
Grieg—Bell Ringing; Wedding Day at
  Troldhaugen
Humperdinck—Trauung in der Bastille
Elgar—Sursum corda
Mahler—Symphonic Prelude; What the
  Wild Flowers Tell Me
Delius—Walk to the Paradise Garden
Strauss, R.—Rosenkavalier: Waltzes (arr.
  Doebber)
Vaughan Williams—Prelude "49th
  Parallel"
Rachmaninoff—Prelude, op.3, no.2
Schoenberg—Begleitungsmusik
Bartók—Two Romanian Dances
Grainger—Shepherd's Hey
Stravinsky—Firebird: Berceuse & Finale
Weiner—Preludio, Notturno e Scherzo
  diabolico
Atterberg—Ballade & Passacaglia

Howells—Penguinski
Hindemith—When Lilacs Last in the
    Door-Yard Bloom'd: Prelude
Korngold—Military March; Schneemann:
    Overture
Bacon—Bearwalla; Muffin Man
Finzi—New Year Music
Walton—Crown Imperial; Hamlet:
    Funeral March; Johannesburg Festival
    Overture; Spitfire Prelude & Fugue
Alwyn—Moor of Venice
Siegmeister—Lonesome Hollow
Barber—Essay No.1
Liebermann, Rolf—Furioso
Britten—Soirées musicales
Gould—Symphonette No.2
Fine, I.—Diversions for Orchestra
Shulman—Hup-Two-Three-Four;
    Interstate 90; Prelude; Waltzes
Surinach—Feria magica
Ginastera—Oberatura para el "Fausto"
    Criollo
Ward—Jonathon and the Gingery Snare
Bernstein—Fancy Free: Three Dance
    Variations; West Side Story: Overture;
    West Side Story: Selections
Arnold—Four Scottish Dances; Roots of
    Heaven
Bergsma—Carol on Twelfth Night
Foss—American Fanfare
Smith, Hale—Contours
Duffy—Three Jewish Portraits [both]
Floyd—In Celebration
Flagello—Goldoni Overture
Musgrave—Scottish Dance Suite
Hoag—After-Intermission Overture
Zaninelli—Jubilate
Maxwell Davies—Five Klee Pictures
Rudow—Spirit of America
Wilson—Houston Fanfare
Mauldin—Dawn at San Juan Mesa
Beckel—Gospel Christmas
Márquez—Danzon No.2; Paisajes bajo el
    signo de cosmos
Ayers—Veni Emmanuel
Coleman, L. R.—In Good King Charles's
    Golden Days
Daugherty—Metropolis Symphony: Oh
    Lois!
Dorff—Blast Off!
Kallman—Holiday Hoedown
Heitzeg—Aqua; Mustang
Adamo—Prepositions and the Names of
    Fish
O'Boyle—Country Kazoo Overture; Silent
    Movie Music; Song Bird: Scissor Dance
Psathas—Tarantismo
Dorman—Astrolatry
Rival—Achilles & Scamander, Whirlwind
Tommasini—Sonic Dreams Made Real

11'–15'

Berlioz—Rob Roy
Wagner, Richard—Götterdämmerung:
    Siegfried's Death & Funeral Music
    (Stasny)
Strauss, Joh., Jr.—Geschichten aus dem
    Wienerwald
Minkus—Bayadère: Pas de deux
Bizet—Carmen: Suite No.1; Jolie fille de
    Perth: Scènes bohémiennes; Patrie;
    Variations chromatiques
Dvořák—Slavonic Rhapsodies, op.45,
    nos.2-3
Rimsky-Korsakov—Overture on Russian
    Themes (1880 version)
Debussy—Printemps; Symphony
Magnard—Chant funèbre
Vaughan Williams—Coastal Command:
    Suite; Serenade to Music [orch version]
Ives—New England Holidays:
    Thanksgiving and Forefathers' Day
Dohnányi—Symphonic Minutes
Schreker—Tanzspiel
Malipiero—Symphony No.11
Weiner—Divertimento No.5
Atterberg—Bäckahästen: Midsummer
    Dances
Ibert—Louisville Concerto
Martinů—Inventions
Bliss—Things to Come: Concert Suite
Rosenberg—Orpheus in Town: Dance
    Suite
Hanson—Elegy
Bacon—Erie Waters
Copland—Lincoln Portrait; Orchestral
    Variations; Prairie Journal
Walton—Hamlet and Ophelia; Henry V:
    Suite
Dallapiccola—Variazioni
Kabalevsky—Comedians
Hartmann—Miserae
Jolivet—Amants magnifiques
Creston—Invocation and Dance
Shostakovich—Ballet Suite No.1
Stevens—Sinfonia breve
Britten—Canadian Carnival; Prince of the
    Pagodas: Pas de six
Gould—Classical Variations
Kay, U.—Umbrian Scene
Thorne—Elegy for Orchestra
Benson—Delphic Serenade
Hollingsworth—Divertimento
Smith, Hale—Ritual and Incantations
Duffy—Heritage Dances
Musgrave—Peripeteia; Rainbow
Deussen—Reflections on the Hudson
Adams, Leslie—Ode to Life
Schickele—Zoo Called Earth
Albert, Adrienne—Western Suite
Del Tredici—Alice Symphony: The
    Lobster Quadrille

Tower—Sequoia
Bamert—Circus Parade
Schwantner—Aftertones of Infinity
Lankester—Make Your Own Orchestra
Bond, Victoria—Thinking Like a
    Mountain
Adams, John—Chairman Dances
Márquez—Danzón No.4 [full orch]
Tsontakis—Four Symphonic Quartets:
    2. Perpetual Angelus
Chen Yi—Linear
Coleman, L.R.—Elegy; Journeys; Lunatics
    and Lovers
Young—Lux Aeterna
Danielpour—First Light [both]
Kats-Chernin—Mythic
Higdon—blue cathedral
Wittry, Diane—Mist
Di Vittorio—Symphony No.2
Bates—Music from Underground Spaces;
    Sea-Blue Circuitry

16'–20'

Verdi—Birthday Variations [arr. McPhee]
Wagner, Richard—Walküre: Wotan's
    Farewell & Magic Fire Music
Offenbach—Kakadu: Ballet Suite
Delibes—Sylvia: Suite
Bizet—Carmen: Suite No.2
Tchaikovsky—Nutcracker and the Mouse
    King
Massenet—Cid: Ballet Music
Sullivan—Pineapple Poll: Suite
Grieg—Sigurd Jorsalfar: Three Orchestral
    Pieces
Widor—Korrigane
Fauré—Dolly
Foote—Four Character Pieces
Humperdinck—Dornröschen: Suite
Janáček—Lachian Dances
Schmitt—Musiques de plein air
Alfvén—Swedish Rhapsody No.3
Vaughan Williams—England of Elizabeth:
    Three Portraits
Ives—Three Places in New England
    [version 3]
Coleridge-Taylor—Hiawatha: Suite
Carpenter—Sea Drift
Bartók—Dance Suite
Villa-Lobos—Sinfonietta No.2
Martinů—Estampes
Hindemith—Sinfonietta
Still—Wood Notes
Thomson, V.—Louisiana Story: Suite
Krenek—Eleven Transparencies
McPhee—Symphony No.2
Weill—Dreigroschenoper: Suite (arr.
    Schönherr)
Walton—Wise Virgins: Suite
Khachaturian—The Valencian Widow:
    Suite

Alwyn—Elizabethan Dances
Ránki—Symphony No.1
Rózsa—Theme, Variations & Finale;
  Three Hungarian Sketches
Barber—Souvenirs: Suite
Hovhaness—Symphony No.1
Ward—First Symphonic Set
Foss—Exeunt
Rorem—Design
Smith, Hale—Ritual and Incantations
Duffy—Heritage Dances
Tower—Sequoia
Zwilich—Symphony No.1
Bond, Victoria—Thinking Like a
  Mountain
Zaimont—Stillness
Gilbert, J.—In the Beginning
Rodríguez—Trunks
Warshauer—Jerusalem, Open Your Gates
Coleman, L.R.—Celebration; Lunatics and
  Lovers
Curiale—Gates of Gold
Young—Lux Aeterna
Oliverio, James—Story of Snow White
Heitzeg—Mahkato Wakpa; On the Day
  You Were Born; Voice of the
  Everglades
Wittry, Diane—Mist
Di Vittorio—Symphony No.2

21'–30'

Minkus—Bayadère: Act II; Paquita: Suite
Delibes—Coppélia: Suite No.1
Mussorgsky—Pictures at an Exhibition
  [Goehr]
Janáček—Jenůfa-Rhapsodie
Ropartz—Symphony No.5
Zemlinsky—Sinfonietta
Vaughan Williams—Wasps: Suite
Stravinsky—Firebird: Suite (1919); Song
  of the Nightingale
Atterberg—Symphony No.7
Ibert—Tropismes pour des amours
  imaginaires
Bliss—Checkmate: Prologue & Five
  Dances
Still—Lenox Avenue
Bacon—Enchanted Isle; Symphony No.2
Ellington—River
Krenek—Symphony, op.137
Egk—Variations on a Caribbean Theme
Tippett—Midsummer Marriage: Ritual
  Dances
Badings—Symphony No.7
Rózsa—Jungle Book [solo A]
Carter—Minotaur: Ballet Suite; Variations
  for Orchestra
Barber—Medea [Ballet Suite]
Schuman, Wm.—Judith
Hovhaness—Symphony No.15
Britten—Death in Venice: Suite

Gould—Fall River Legend: Ballet Suite
Bernstein—Facsimile; Fancy Free
Rochberg—Music for the Magic Theater
Kay, H.—Cakewalk: Concert Suite
Suolahti—Sinfonia piccola
Bassett—Variations for Orchestra
Rorem—Symphony No.1
Lees—Symphony No.2
Duffy—Heritage: Suite; Symphony No.1;
  Time for Remembrance [solo S]
Henze—Symphony No.8
Deussen—Silver Shining Strand
Biggs—Concerto for Orchestra
McCabe—Symphony on a Pavane
Bond, Victoria—What's the Point of
  Counterpoint?
Gilbert, J.—Khoj
Walker, Gwyneth—Symphony of Grace
Davidson—Young Lutheran's Guide to the
  Orchestra
Sierra—Carnaval
Adolphe—Carnival of the Creatures
Sheng—H'un
Sleeper—Symphony No.4
Heitzeg—Symphony to the Prairie Farm
Higdon—All Things Majestic
Stookey—Composer is Dead
Frank, G.L.—Requiem for a Magical
  America
Rival—Symphony No.2

Over 30'

Adam—Corsaire; Giselle
Løvenskjold—Sylphide
Strauss, Joh., Jr.—Graduation Ball
Minkus—Don Quixote [McPhee red.];
  Paquita [McPhee red.]
Bizet—Roma
Tchaikovsky—Nutcracker [Golan red.]
Dvořák—Symphony No.4
Bendix—Symphony No.3
Stanford—Symphony No.3
Albéniz—Iberia [arr. Surinach]
Glazunov—Raymonda: Act III [McPhee
  red.]
Sibelius—Symphony No.1
Kalinnikov—Suite, D Major
Vaughan Williams—Job; Symphonies
  Nos.2-3
Melartin—Symphony No.3
Stravinsky—Firebird [McPhee red.];
  Firebird: Suite (1945)
Rosenberg—Symphony No.3
Gerhard—Symphony No.1
Bacon—Great River
Tippett—Symphony No.2
Burgess—Symphony No.3 [solo TBar]
Bentzon—Symphonies Nos.4 & 8
Duffy—Heritage: Symphonic Suite with
  Narration
Rautavaara—Symphony No.7

Maxwell Davies—Second Fantasia on
  Taverner's "In nomine"
Lofstrom—Woodcarver's Daughter: Suite
  [No.1]
Actor—Symphony No.1

```
[24]
STRINGS
8 WOODWINDS
BRASS 4300
TIMPANI
CONTINUO
```

Handel—Concerti a due cori, Nos.1-3;
  Royal Fireworks Music
Mozart, W.A.—Divertimento No.1
Szöllösy—Sonorità

```
[25]
STRINGS
WINDS 3222—4331
4 PERCUSSION
```

10' or less

Purcell—Trumpet Voluntary [arr.
  Westermann]
Bach, J.S.—Sheep May Safely Graze
Mozart, W.A.—Turkish March
Rossini—Siège de Corinthe: Overture
Donizetti—Linda di Chamounix: Prelude;
  Roberto Devereux: Overture
Schubert—Grande marche héroïque
Berlioz—Troyens: Chasse royale et Orage
Strauss, Joh., Sr.—Radetzky March
Chopin—Polonaise, op.40, no.1 [arr.]
Schumann, R.—Overtures to Braut von
  Messina, Hermann und Dorothea
Liszt—Hamlet; Huldigungs-Marsch;
  Rákóczi-Marsch; Ungarischer
  Sturmmarsch
Verdi—Aïda: Prelude; Luisa Miller:
  Overture
Wagner, Richard—Christoph Columbus:
  Overture; Tannhäuser: Arrival of the
  Guests; Tannhäuser: Prelude, Act III;
  Walküre: Ride of the Valkyries (Sheffer)
Gade—Michelangelo
Cornelius—Barbier von Bagdad: Overture
  (B minor)
Smetana—Bartered Bride: Overture; Ma
  vlast: 3. Sárka
Goldmark—Im Frühling
Borodin—Petite suite: Scherzo &
  Nocturne; Prince Igor: Overture

Brahms—Hungarian Dances Nos.1, 3, 10
(arr. Brahms); Nos.5, 6, 7 (arr.
Schmeling)
Saint-Saëns—Danse macabre
Buck—Festival Overture on the American
National Air
Mussorgsky—Fair at Sorochinski: Gopak;
Khovantchina: Prince Galitzin's Journey
Paine—As You Like It: Overture
Tchaikovsky—Eugene Onegin: Waltz;
Suite No.1: Marche miniature
Chabrier—Gwendoline: Prelude, Act II
Dvořák—Slavonic Rhapsody, op.45, no.1
Grieg—In Autumn
Rimsky-Korsakov—Tale of the Tsar
Saltan: Flight of the Bumblebee [arr.
Strimer]
Chadwick—Rip Van Winkle: Overture
Humperdinck—Hänsel und Gretel:
Prelude
MacDowell—Saracens
Reznicek—Donna Diana: Overture
Delius—Summer Evening
Mascagni—Cavalleria rusticana: Prelude
& Siciliana
Strauss, R.—Festmarsch
Nielsen, Carl—Fantasy Journey to the
Faroes; Maskarade: Overture;
Maskarade: Hanedans; Saga Dream;
Saul and David: Prelude to Act II
Sibelius—Karelia Overture
Busoni—Lustspiel Overture
Sinigaglia—Baruffe chiozzotte
Alfvén—Bergakungen
Ives—Variations on "America"
Coleridge-Taylor—Bamboula; Danse
nègre
Falla—La vida breve: Spanish Dance No.1
Becker—Two Pieces: 2. Mountains
Toch—Pinocchio
Prokofiev—March, op.99
Hanson—Before the Dawn
Revueltas—Janitzio
Anderson, Leroy—Goldilocks: Overture
Dahl—Quodlibet
Fine, I.—Blue Towers
Ward—Prairie Overture
Einem—Capriccio
Arnold—Tam O'Shanter Overture
Duffy—American Fantasy Overture;
Freedom Overture
Diemer—Homage to Tchaikovsky
Adler, S.—Drifting on Wind and Currents
Shchedrin—Symphonic Fanfares
Herman—Overtures to Hello Dolly &
Mame
Svoboda—Overture of the Season;
Serenade; Three Pieces
Rodríguez—Salutation Rag
Mauldin—Last Musician of Ur
Tann—Through the Echoing Timber

Walker, Gwyneth—Bicycle Waltz;
Overture of Diamonds
Chiarappa—Gettysburg Address
McTee—Finish Line
Sierra—Alegría; Joyous Overture
Rimelis—Phonefare
Oliverio, J.—UnStoppable
Sartor—Metamorphic Fanfare
Abels—Outburst
Stephenson—Ode to Peace [solo Ms]

11'–20'

Gluck—Ballet Suite No.1 [arr. Mottl]
Mozart, W.A.—German Dances, K.509 &
K.536
Beethoven—German Dances; Wellingtons
Sieg
Liszt—Hunnenschlacht; Triomphe funèbre
du Tasse; Von der Wiege bis zum Grabe
Wagner, Richard—Tannhäuser: Overture
(Dresden version)
Gade—Hamlet
Raff—Feste Burg ist unser Gott
Smetana—Bartered Bride: Three Dances;
Ma vlast: Nos.4. From Bohemia's
Forests and Meadows, 5. Tábor,
6. Blaník
Gottschalk—Symphony No.2
Brahms—Tragische Ouvertüre
Tchaikovsky—Tempest
Dvořák—Hussite Overture
Grieg—Peer Gynt: Suite No.1
Brüll—Serenade No.2
Chadwick—Melpomene
MacDowell—Hamlet & Ophelia; Lamia;
Lancelot and Elaine; Suite No.1
Reznicek—Lustspiel-Ouvertüre
Wolf—Corregidor: Suite; Scherzo &
Finale
Glazunov—Chopiniana; Overture
solennelle
Nielsen, Carl—Helios Overture
Sibelius—Karelia Suite
Pfitzner—Scherzo
Holst—Suites Nos.1 & 2
Coleridge-Taylor—Ballade; Petite suite de
concert; Toussaint L'Ouverture
Falla—Amor brujo: Suite (arr. Ryden)
Dohnányi—American Rhapsody
Stravinsky—Ode
Holmboe—Concerto for Orchestra
Read—Pennsylvania Suite
Fine, I.—Music for Orchestra
Einem—Ballade; Bruckner Dialog;
Philadelphia Symphony
Stock—Inner Space
Svoboda—Sinfoniette
Horwood—Amusement Park Suite
Tann—Open Field
Walker, Gwyneth—Bicentennial Suite

Gellis—Short Symphony on Eastern
Modes
Mascari—Meet the Orchestra
Actor—Premonition
Smith, Kile—Voice of One Who Spoke
Wittry, Diane—Lamentoso

21'–30'

Mozart, W.A.—German Dances, K.586
Beethoven—Minuets, WoO 7
Schumann, R.—Bilder aus Osten
Fry—Santa Claus
Gade—Symphonies Nos.6 & 8
Borodin—Petite suite
Brahms—Serenade No.2
Saint-Saëns—Symphony No.2
Rimsky-Korsakov—Maid of Pskov:
Overture & Entr'actes
MacDowell—Suite No.2
Reznicek—Symphonic Suite No.1
Nielsen, Carl—Symphony No.1
Kodály—Symphony
Stravinsky—Symphony in C
Hanson—Symphony No.4
Porter, Quincy—Symphony No.2
Blacher—Symphony
Giannini—Symphony No.2
Creston—Symphonies Nos.1 & 4
Shostakovich—Symphonies Nso.3 & 9
[chorus]
Bacewicz—Symphony No.3
Arnold—Symphony No.6
Finko—Symphony No.2
Svoboda—Dance Suite
Monroe—Amazing Symphony Orchestra

Over 30'

Beethoven—Symphony No.6
Schubert—Symphony, D.812
Gade—Symphony No.1
Raff—Symphonies Nos.3, 5, 9
Bruckner—Symphony No.1 (Cahis 2
or 17)
Rubinstein—Symphonies No.1,
No.2 [1851 version], No.4
Tchaikovsky—Suite No.1; Symphonies
Nos.1-6
Dvořák—Symphony No.2
Rimsky-Korsakov—Symphony No.3
Sinding—Symphony No.1
Arensky—Symphony No.1
Dukas—Symphony
Nielsen, Carl—Symphony No.2
Hadley—Symphony No.2
Suk—Symphony No.1
Glière—Symphony No.1
Einem—Wiener Symphonie
Arnold—Symphony No.3
Hailstork—Symphony No.3
Actor—Symphony No.3

> **[26]**
> **STRINGS**
> **WINDS 3222—4431**
> **5 PERCUSSION**
> **HARP, CELESTA, PIANO**

10' or less

Purcell—Trumpet Prelude
Auber—Masaniello: Overture
Berlioz—Damnation de Faust: Rákóczy
  March
Liszt—Hungarian Rhapsodies Nos.3 & 6;
  Polonaise No.2
Wagner, Richard—Götterdämmerung:
  Siegfried's Rhine Journey;
  Meistersinger: Prelude
Gounod—Mors et vita: Judex
Lalo—Rapsodie norvégienne
Cornelius—Barbier von Bagdad: Overture
  (D major)
Minkus—Don Quixote: Pas de deux (orig)
Borodin—Prince Igor: Polovtsian March
Saint-Saëns—Danse macabre; Marche
  héroïque; Rouet d'Omphale; Suite
  algérienne: Marche militaire française
Gomes—Guarany: Overture
Mussorgsky—Khovantchina: Dance of the
  Persian Maidens; Solemn March
Massenet—Phèdre: Overture
Grieg—Peer Gynt: Prelude
Rimsky-Korsakov—Fantasia on Serbian
  Themes; Snow Maiden: Dance of the
  Skomorokhi; Tsar's Bride: Overture
Chadwick—Euterpe
Humperdinck—Hänsel und Gretel:
  Hexenritt
Chausson—Tempête: 2 Excerpts
Delius—Sleigh Ride
Mascagni—Amico Fritz: Intermezzo;
  Cavalleria rusticana: Prelude & Siciliana
Glazunov—March des noces; Seasons: 1.
  Winter, 2. Spring; Valse de concert,
  No.2
Sibelius—Scènes historiques: An der
  Zugbrücke
Sinigaglia—Danze piemontesi Nos.1-2
Schmitt—Reflets d'Allemagne
Wolf-Ferrari—Segreto di Susanna:
  Overture
Cadman—Oriental Rhapsody
Grainger—Immovable Do; Molly on the
  Shore
Kodály—Háry János: Intermezzo
Stravinsky—Scherzo à la russe
Butterworth—Two English Idylls
Toch—Circus Overture
Moore, Douglas—Overture on an
  American Tune
Slonimsky—My Toy Balloon

Weinberger—Schwanda the Bagpiper:
  Polka & Fugue [both]
Korngold—Straussiana
Riisager, Knudåge—Qarrtsiluni
Copland—Outdoor Overture; Rodeo: Hoe-
  Down
Alwyn—Festival March
Anderson, Leroy—Goldilocks: Overture
Schuman, Wm.—Circus Overture
Menotti—Lewisohn Stadium Fanfare
Britten—Men of Goodwill
Gould—American Salute
Shulman—Popocatepetl
Ward—By the Way of Memories; Concert
  Music
Arnold—English Dances: Sets One &
  Two; Four Cornish Dances; Four Welsh
  Dances; Grand, Grand Festival Overture;
  Holly and the Ivy; Peterloo;
  Sound Barrier
Nelson, Ron—Savannah River Holiday
Deussen—American Hymn
Herman—Overtures to Cage aux folles,
  Hello Dolly, Mame, Milk and Honey
Bennett, Richard R.—Birthday Music
Corigliano—Promenade Overture
Earnest—Chasing the Sun
Zappa—Durpree's Paradise
Stewart—Overture in F
Rodríguez—Hot Buttered Rhumba; Piñata
Mauldin—High Places
Larsen, L.—Overture for the End of a
  Century
Galbraith—Fantasy
Wendel—Carol of the Bells; Chanukah
  Overture; Christmas a la Valse;
  Commemoration; Fanfare for Freedom;
  Ride of the Headless Horseman
Saariaho—Lumière et Pesanteur
Frazelle—From the Air
Kernis—New Era Dance
Abels—Dance for Martin's Dream; Global
  Warming
Richman—Be a Composer; Colonial
  Liberty Overture; Hanukkah Festival
  Overture
Stookey—Big Bang

11'–20'

Halévy—Juive: Overture
Berlioz—Troyens: Ballet
Liszt—Christus: Die heiligen drei Könige;
  Hungarian Rhapsody No.4; Mephisto
  Waltzes Nos.1 & 2; Nächtliche Zug;
  Préludes; Von der Wiege bis zum Grabe
Verdi—Aïda: Triumphal March & Ballet
Wagner, Richard—Fliegende Holländer:
  Overture; Meistersinger: Three Excerpts
  from Act III
Smetana—Ma vlast: 2. Vltava (Moldau);
  Richard III; Wallenstein's Camp

Brahms—Hungarian Dances Nos.11-16
  (arr. Parlow)
Saint-Saëns—Suite algérienne
Mussorgsky—Night on Bald Mountain
  [orig or Rimsky-Korsakov version]
Dvořák—Hussite Overture
Massenet—Scènes hongroises
Grieg—Bergliot; Lyric Suite; Norwegian
  Dances; Peer Gynt: Suite No.2
Rimsky-Korsakov—Russian Easter
  Overture; Sadko (1892 version); Skazka;
  Snow Maiden: Suite
Noskowski—Steppe
Chadwick—Sinfonietta
Humperdinck—Hänsel und Gretel: Three
  Excerpts
Elgar—Crown of India: Suite
Puccini—Capriccio sinfonico; Preludio
  sinfonico
Parker—Northern Ballad
Glazunov—Overture No.1; Seasons: 3.
  Summer; Stenka Razine
Bantock—Pierrot of the Minute
Pfitzner—Kätchen von Heilbronn:
  Overture
Rabaud—Procession nocturne
Rachmaninoff—Rock
Holst—Perfect Fool: Ballet Music
Coleridge-Taylor—Symphonic Variations
Respighi—Antiche danze ed arie: Suite I
Bartók—Mikrokosmos Suite
Kodály—Theater Overture
Gerhard—Pedrelliana
Hanson—Symphony No.5
Weinberger—Under the Spreading
  Chestnut Tree
Riisager, Knudåge—Fools' Paradise: Suite
  No.2; Twelve by the Mail: Six Dances
Szell—Variations on an Original Theme
Copland—Tender Land: Suite
Creston—Two Choric Dances
Phillips, B.—Selections from McGuffey's
  Reader
Anderson, Leroy—Irish Suite
Carter—Pocahontas: Suite
Coolidge—Pioneer Dances
Khrennikov—Symphony No.1
Ginastera—Pampeana No.3
Overton—Symphony No.2
Arnold—Four Irish Dances; Homage to
  the Queen: Suite
Flagello—Lautrec
Van de Vate—Dark Nebulae
Reynolds—Fiery Wind
Wilson—Lumina
Zappa—Perfect Stranger
Iannaccone—From Time to Time
Avshalomov, D.—Gems
Rodríguez—Colorful Symphony
Mauldin—Fajada Butte
Tann—Grey Tide and the Green
Walker, Gwyneth—Symphonic Dances

Welcher—Prairie Light
Warshauer—As the Waters Cover the Sea
Galbraith—De profundis ad lucem
Frazelle—Shivaree
Sleeper, Thomas—Symphony No.2
Cotton—CityMusic
Smith, Gregory—Mr. Smith's
   Composition; Zoo Song
Torke—Ecstatic Orange
Roter—With Courage and Compassion

21'–30'

Chopin—Sylphides (arr. Douglas)
Gade—Symphony No.5
Paine—Tempest
Grieg—Old Norwegian Melody with
   Variations; Symphonic Dances
Rimsky-Korsakov—Legend of the
   Invisible City of Kitezh: Suite
Arensky—Suite No.1
Kodály—Concerto for Orchestra;
   Variations on a Hungarian Folksong
Malipiero—Symphony No.2
Stravinsky—Orpheus
Rosenberg—Concerto No.2
Korngold—Märchenbilder
Copland—Billy the Kid: Suite
Shostakovich—Symphony No.1
Holmboe—Symphonies Nos.3 & 7
Ward—Symphony No.7
Arnold— Symphonies Nos.5 & 8
Reich—Four Sections
Wuorinen—Two-Part Symphony
Holloway—Scenes from Schumann
Horwood—National Park Suite
Mauldin—American West
Ott—First Trip to the Symphony
Sleeper, Thomas—Symphony No.1
Smith, Gregory—MAJOR-minor Mystery;
   Melodic Life; Mr. Smith's Bowl of
   Notes; Orchestra Games

Over 30'

Schumann, R.—Carnaval (orchd)
Liszt—Faust Symphony [solo T &
   male chor]
Wagner, Richard—Meistersinger:
   Orchestral Tribute
Minkus—Bayadère; Don Quixote [both]
Rubinstein—Symphony No.2 [1863 or
   1880 version]
Borodin—Symphony No.2
Tchaikovsky—Swan Lake [139'];
   Swan Lake: Suite [31']; Symphony No.7
Rimsky-Korsakov—Symphony No.2
Glazunov—Symphony No.7
Nielsen, Carl—Symphony No.5
Kalinnikov—Symphony No.2
Reger—Variations and Fugue on a Theme
   of Mozart

Shostakovich—Symphony No.15
Arnold—Symphony No.9

**[27]
STRINGS
WINDS 3322—4431
6 PERCUSSION
2 HARPS, CELESTA, PIANO**

10' or less

Weber, C.M.—Aufforderung zum Tanz
Meyerbeer—Huguenots: Overture
Schubert—Marche militaire
Berlioz—Damnation de Faust: Dance of
   the Sylphs; Troyens: Marche troyenne
Liszt—Hungarian Rhapsody, S.244, no.1;
   Légendes: Die Vogelpredigt
Ponchielli—Gioconda: Dance of the Hours
Mussorgsky—Fair at Sorochinski:
   Introduction
Paine—Poseidon and Amphitrite
Tchaikovsky—Fatum; Festival Coronation
   March; Marche solennelle; Mazeppa:
   Danse cosaque; Voyevoda, op.3
Dvořák—Carnival Overture
Chadwick—Pastoral Prelude
Wolf—Corregidor: Prelude & Interlude
Debussy—Enfant prodigue: Cortège et Air
   de danse; Marche écossaise; Prélude à
   "L'après-midi d'un faune"; Roi Lear
Delius—Dance Rhapsody No.2
Rachmaninoff—Vocalise (orch)
Schoenberg—Survivor from Warsaw
   [narrator & chor]
Laparra—Rythmes espagnols
Grainger—Children's March; Shepherd's
   Hey
Bax—Summer Music
Bacon—Nantucket Fling
Khachaturian—Gayane: Dance of the Rose
   Maidens, & Lullaby
Barber—Essay No.2
Muczynski—Dovetail Overture
Zaimont—Tarantelle
Warshauer—Like Streams in the Desert
Wendel—Parade of the Percussionists
Amundson—Angels' Dance; Joyous Noel
   [handbell choir]; Sola gratia
Amaya—Parasol
Koch—Adventures of Sinbad

11'–20'

Liszt—Christus: Hirtengesang; Légendes;
   Nächtliche Zug; Orpheus; Prometheus
Wagner, Richard—Tannhäuser:
   Venusberg Music
Smetana—Ma vlast: 1. Vysehrad

Goldmark—Sakuntala
Borodin—Prince Igor: Polovtsian Dances
Saint-Saëns—Jeunesse d'Hercule
Balakirev—Russia
Tchaikovsky—Capriccio italien; Hamlet;
   Overture 1812; Romeo and Juliet (final
   version); Storm: Overture
Dvořák—Othello Overture; Rhapsody;
   Watersprite
Massenet—Cigal: Suite
Rimsky-Korsakov—Capriccio espagnol
Luigini—Ballet égyptien
Chadwick—Tre pezzi
Liadov—Eight Russian Folk Songs
Ippolitov-Ivanov—Turkish Fragments
Glazunov—Seasons: 4. Autumn
Rachmaninoff—Caprice bohémien
Holst—Beni Mora
Ravel—Valses nobles et sentimentales
Falla—Sombrero de tres picos: Suite No.2
Respighi—Antiche danze ed arie: Suite II
Bloch, E.—Evocations; Hiver-Printemps
Bartók—Two Portraits
Enesco—Romanian Rhapsody, op.11,
   nos.1-2
Malipiero—Sinfonia per Antigenida;
   Symphonies Nos.8-9
Martinů—Sinfonia concertante
Milhaud—Suite provençale
Rosenberg—Symphony No.8
McPhee—Transitions
Rodrigo—A la busca del más allá
Walton—As You Like It
Dallapiccola—Due pezzi
Alwyn—Symphony No.5
Hovhaness—And God Created Great
   Whales; Floating World; Variations and
   Fugue
Moncayo—Tierra de temporal
Britten—Young Person's Guide to the
   Orchestra
Schuller—Five Etudes
Jones—Listen Now, My Children
Bennett, Richard R.—Gormenghast: Suite
Glass—Canyon
Wilson—Expansions III
Rodríguez—Sinfonía à la mariachi
Costa—Allure
Smith, Kile—Four French Carols
Ticheli—Radiant Voices
Thomas, Augusta Read—Terpsichore's
   Dream

21'–30'

Liszt—Héroïde funèbre; Hungaria
Wagner, Richard—Tannhäuser: Overture
   & Venusberg Music
Saint-Saëns—Foi: Trois tableaux
   symphoniques

Tchaikovsky—Francesca da Rimini;
    Romeo and Juliet (orig);
    Sleeping Beauty: Suite
Dvořák—Czech Suite
Massenet—Suite No.1
Ippolitov-Ivanov—Caucasian Sketches
Respighi—Boutique fantasque: Suite;
    Rossiniana
Malipiero—Symphony No.1
Villa-Lobos—Bachianas brasileiras no.2
Lajtha—Suite No.3
Alwyn—Symphony No.2
Nelson, Ron—This is the Orchestra
Reich—Variations
Einhorn—My Many Colored Days
Puts—Symphony No.1

Over 30'

Minkus—Paquita
Balakirev—Symphony No.1
Tchaikovsky—Sleeping Beauty;
    Suites Nos.2-3
Dvořák—Symphonies Nos.1, 3, 9
Rimsky-Korsakov—Sheherazade
Debussy—Boîte à joujoux
Kalinnikov—Symphony No.1
Rachmaninoff—Symphony No.1
Falla—Sombrero de tres picos [solo Ms]
Respighi—Boutique fantasque
Alwyn—Symphonies Nos.1, 3
Tubin—Symphony No.2
Shostakovich—Hamlet: Film Suite

```
┌─────────────────────────────┐
│             [28]            │
│           STRINGS           │
│       9/10 WOODWINDS        │
│         BRASS 4331          │
│         4 PERCUSSION        │
└─────────────────────────────┘
```

10' or less

Frescobaldi—Toccata
Handel—Overture, HWV 337
Gluck—Alceste: Overture
Beethoven—König Stephan: Overture
Weber, C.M.—Jubel Overture
Berlioz—Waverley
Glinka—Russlan and Ludmilla: Overture
Alkan—Ouverture de concert
Brahms—Akademische Festouvertüre
Fauré—Pénélope: Prelude
Humperdinck—Königskinder: Prelude,
    Introduction to Act II
Puccini—Manon Lescaut: Prelude, Act II
Strauss, R.—Feierlicher Einzug
Sibelius—Dryad; Tempest: Prelude
Ives—Yale-Princeton Football Game
    [Sinclair version]

Dohnányi—Schleier der Pierrette: Lustiger
    Trauermarsch
Moeran—Overture to a Masque
Hindemith—Rag Time
Still—Black Bottom
Thomson, V.—Fugue and Chorale on
    "Yankee Doodle"
Shostakovich—Age of Gold: Polka
Dahl—Quodlibet
Moncayo—Sinfonietta
Britten—Paul Bunyan: Overture
Dello Joio—Five Images for Orchestra
Panufnik—Tragic Overture
Ward—City of Oaks
Kraft—Simple Introduction to the
    Orchestra
Mechem—Jayhawk
Mamlok—Grasshoppers
Wyner—Epilogue for Orchestra
Schickele—Celebration with Bells
Svoboda—Swing Dance
Hailstork—Fanfare on "Amazing Grace"
Peck—Freedom Fanfare
Beckel—Musica Mobilis; Night Visions:
    The American Dream; Overture for a
    New Age
Gellis—Duplex
Wendel—Take Flight
Danielpour—Washington Speaks
Dorff—Fast Walk
Thomas, Augusta Read—Aureole
Stephenson—Ode to Peace [solo Ms]
Kuster—Iron Diamond

11'–20'

Berlioz—Franc-Juges; Roméo et Juliette:
    Love Scene
Mendelssohn—Meeresstille und
    glückliche Fahrt
Liszt—Hungarian Rhapsody No.2
Wagner, Richard—Faust-Ouvertüre
Brahms—Variations on a Theme of Joseph
    Haydn
Dvořák—In Nature's Realm; Midday
    Witch; Suite, op.98b
Duparc, Henri—Lénore
Elgar—Froissart
Schumann, G.—Liebesfrühling
Holst—Egdon Heath
Ives—Three Places in New England,
    version 1
Casella—Paganiniana
Honegger—Chant de Nigamon
Bennett, Robt. R.—Four Freedoms
Riisager—Fools Paradise: Suite No.1
Ellington—Nutcracker Suite (after
    Tchaikovsky)
Copland—Our Town
Adaskin—Saskatchewan Legend
Kay, Ulysses—Southern Harmony
Subotnick—Play No.2

Finko—Russia; Wailing Wall
Bond, Victoria—Variations on a Theme of
    Brahms
Actor—Celebration Overture;
    Dance Rhapsody
McLoskey—Symphoniae sacrae

Over 20'

Beethoven—Symphony No.5
Mendelssohn—Symphony No.5
Wagner, Richard—Symphony, WWV 29,
    C major
Brahms—Eleven Chorale Preludes;
    Symphonies Nos.1, 3, 4
Gernsheim—Symphony No.4
Elgar—Enigma Variations
Rott—Symphony No.1
Glazunov—Symphonies Nos.4, 6
Beach—Symphony No.2
Scriabin—Symphony No.2
Reger—Vier Tondichtungen
Ives—Symphony No.2
Stravinsky—Symphony No.1
Hindemith—Lustige Sinfonietta
Tippett—Symphony No.1
Rautavaara—Symphony No.2
Finko—Symphony No.1
Peck—Mozart Escapes the Museum
Zaimont—Pure, Cool (Water)
Hoyt—Symphony No.1

```
┌─────────────────────────────┐
│             [29]            │
│           STRINGS           │
│       9/10 WOODWINDS        │
│         BRASS 4431          │
│         6 PERCUSSION        │
│     HARP, CELESTA, PIANO    │
└─────────────────────────────┘
```

10' or less

Monteverdi—Orfeo: Toccata & ritornelli
Vivaldi—Concerto, op.3, no.11, RV 565
    (arr. Siloti)
Bach, J.C.—Symphony, W. G8
Weber, C.M.—Aufforderung zum Tanz
Wagner, Richard—Huldigungsmarsch
Smetana—Hakon Jarl, op.16
Borodin—Nocturne (arr. N. Tcherepnin)
Saint-Saëns—Marche du couronnement;
    Rouet d'Omphale
Delibes—Coppélia: Ballade & Thème
    slave varié
Tchaikovsky—Marche slave
Rimsky-Korsakov—Christmas Eve:
    Polonaise; Dubinushka
Chadwick—Elegy
Janáček—Jealousy

Liadov—Enchanted Lake
Puccini—Suor Angelica: Intermezzo
Delius—Irmelin: Prelude
Villanueva—Vals poético
Strauss, R.—Feierlicher Einzug
Glazunov—Carnaval Overture;
   Cortége solennel Nos.1-2
Sibelius—Bard
Busoni—Berceuse élégiaque
Granados—Goyescas: Intermezzo
Lehár—Gold und Silber Walzer
Schmitt—Rapsodie viennoise; Ronde
   burlesque
Vaughan Williams—Norfolk Rhapsody
   No.1; Prelude & Fugue
Holst—In the Bleak Midwinter
Ives—New England Holidays: The Fourth
   of July
Suk—Toward a New Life
Wolf-Ferrari—Amore medico: Intermezzo
Dohnányi—Schleier der Pierrette:
   Pierrettens Wahnsinnstanz
Stravinsky—Feu d'artifice; Greeting
   Prelude; Tango (1953 version)
Bax—Mediterranean
Collins—Cowboy's Breakdown; Valse
   elegante
Price—Dances in the Canebrakes
Milhaud—Ouverture philharmonique
Sowerby—Comes Autumn Time
Korngold—Captain Blood: Overture
Riisager—Mardi Gras
Tansman—Sonatine transatlantique
Gershwin—Promenade
Harris, Roy—Ode to Consonance
Chávez—Baile
Vladigerov—Improvisation and Toccata
Copland—Letter from Home;
   Rodeo: Saturday Night Waltz
Rodgers—Slaughter on Tenth Avenue;
   Sound of Music [symphonic picture]
Walton—Façade: Suite No.2
Styne—Gypsy: Overture
Siegmeister—American Holiday
Barber—Die natali: Silent Night
Dahl—Quodlibet
Gillis—Short Overture to an Unwritten
   Opera
Moncayo—Huapango
Brant—Verticals Ascending
Britten—Peter Grimes: Passacaglia
Gould—American Ballads: Nos.1. Star-
   Spangled Overture, 2. Amber Waves,
   3. Jubilo, 4. Memorials,
   5. Saratoga Quickstep, 6. Hymnal
Delden—In memoriam
Chou—And the Fallen Petals
Cunningham—Lullabye for a Jazz Baby
Previn—Overture to a Comedy
Zaninelli—Battle Hymn of the Republic;
   Capriccio spiritoso
Herman—Mack & Mabel: Overture

Fiser—Fifteen Prints after Dürer's
   Apocalypse
Svoboda—Festive Overture
Hailstork—American Port of Call
Perera—Saints: Marching In
Iannaccone—West End Express
León, Tania—Horizons
Avshalomov, D.—Siege
Adams, John—Tromba lontana
Mauldin—Kokopelli; Valley at Annacarla
Beckel—Christmas Fanfare (orch version);
   Night Visions: The American Dream;
   Toccata for Orchestra
Lofstrom—Irish Suite #1
Davis—Jacob's Ladder
Sheng—Black Swan
Amaya—Pájaros de tres alas
Ince—Hot, Red, Cold, Vibrant
Abels—Affectionate Objects
O'Boyle—Olympia Australis
Richman—Overture to Blanche
Di Vittorio—Overtura Palermo
Boyer—Celebration Overture
Puts—Network
Dorman—Azerbaijani Dance
Bates—Attack Decay Sustain Release

11'–20'

Berlioz—Benvenuto Cellini: Overture
Liszt—Hungarian Rhapsody No.1; Tasso
Wagner, Richard—Polonia;
   Rienzi: Overture
Gounod—Faust: Ballet Music
Lalo—Roi d'Ys: Overture
Bizet—Arlésienne: Suites Nos.1-2
Dvořák—Wood Dove
Stanford—Irish Rhapsody No.1
Janáček—Fiddler's Child; Lachian Dances
Elgar—Cockaigne
Herbert—Suite romantique
Glazunov—Valse de concert, No.1
Magnard—Hymne à la justice
Granados—Tres danzas españolas
Schmitt—Feuillets de voyage
Ives—New England Holidays:
   Thanksgiving and Forefathers' Day;
   Orchestral Set No.2; Three Places in
   New England, version 4
Grainger—In a Nutshell
Malipiero—Symphony No.3
Ponce—Chapultepec
Webern—Sechs Stücke, op.6 (1928)
Butterworth—Shropshire Lad
Coates—London Suite
Prokofiev—Lieutenant Kijé: Suite
Milhaud—Symphony No.12
Bennett, Robt. R.—Suite of Old American
   Dances
Hindemith—Concerto for Orchestra
Still—Suite, Violin & Orchestra
Copland—Prairie Journal; Salón México

Shostakovich—Age of Gold: Suite;
   Suite for Variety Orch, No.2
Siegmeister—Five Fantasies; Theater Set;
   Western Suite
Britten—Peter Grimes: Four Sea
   Interludes
Gould—Spirituals
Panufnik—Autumn Music
Shulman—Quilt
Ward—Lady Kate: A Western Set
Bernstein—On the Town: Three Dance
   Episodes
Delden—Symphony No.3
Kirchner—Forbidden
Arnold—Electra
Bergsma—Chameleon Variations
Foss—Quintets for Orchestra
Lees—Passacaglia
Berio—Requies
Henze—Antifone
Crumb—Echoes of Time and the River
Hoddinott—Sinfonietta No.3
Previn—Owls
Sculthorpe—Kakadu
Wyner—Lyric Harmony
Martino—Ritorno
Goehr, Alexander—When Adam Fell
Zaninelli—Night Voices
Schwartz—Island
Bach, Jan—Variations on a Theme of
   Brahms
Hoover—Two Sketches
Wuorinen—Crossfire; Machault mon chou
Iannaccone—Divertimento;
   Symphony No.3; Waiting for the Sunrise
   on the Sound
Maslanka—11:11 – A Dance at the Edge
   of the World
Lieberson, Peter—Remembering JFK
Adams, John—Common Tones in Simple
   Time
Mauldin—Santa Fe Magic
Beckel—Fantasy After Schubert; Waltz of
   the Animals
Dorff—Philly Rhapsody
Itkin—Jonah
Lindberg—Arena
Di Vittorio—Symphony No.3
Puts—Inspiring Beethoven
Lee—Beyond Rivers of Vision

21'–30'

Bizet—Carmen Symphony [Serebrier]
Dvořák—Golden Spinning Wheel
Rimsky-Korsakov—Christmas Eve: Suite
Chadwick—Symphonic Sketches
Glazunov—Scènes de ballet
Sibelius—Symphony No.6;
   Tempest: Suite No.1

Vaughan Williams—Story of a Flemish
   Farm; Symphony No.8
Enesco—Suite No.1
Wellesz—Prosperos Beschwörungen
Hanson—Symphony No.1
Gershwin—Catfish Row
Copland—City; Red Pony
Shostakovich—Suite for Variety Orch,
   No.1
Badings—Symphony No.7
Reed—Fiesta mexicana
Arnold—Symphony No.2
Laderman—Magic Prison
Williams—Star Wars: Suite
McCabe—Arthur: Three Portraits;
   Arthur Pendragon: Suite No.1
Svoboda—Symphony No.2
Eötvös—Chinese Opera
Adams, John—Fearful Symmetries
Mauldin—Mountain Light
Mozetich—Procession of Duos
Catán—Florencia en el Amazonas: Suite
Ran—Concerto for Orchestra
Larsen, L.—Solo Symphony
Tan—Death and Fire
Ince—Symphony No.2
Amrhein—Symphony of Seasons
Bates—B-Sides

Over 30'

Berlioz—Symphonie fantastique
Liszt—Ce qu'on entend sur la montagne
Franck—Symphony
Delibes—Coppélia; Sylvia
Balakirev—King Lear: Incidental Music;
   Symphony No.2
Stanford—Symphony No.4
Humperdinck—Hänsel und Gretel: Suite
Strauss, R.—Aus Italien
Glazunov—Raymonda: Suite;
   Symphony No.5
Scriabin—Symphony No.1 [chorus, solo T
   Ms]
Reger—Variations and Fugue on a Merry
   Theme of Hiller
Melartin—Symphony No.4 [solo S Ms A];
   Symphony No.5
Atterberg—Symphony No.2
Hindemith—Harmonie der Welt
Burgess—Mr W.S.
Bentzon—Symphony No.4
Arnold—Symphony No.4
Rautavaara—Symphony No.6
Glass—Symphony No.8
Svoboda—Symphony No.1
Ran—Symphony
Ritchie, Anthony—Symphony No.2

---

[30] STRINGS WINDS 3332—4331 5 PERCUSSION HARP, CELESTA, PIANO

10' or less

Couperin—Sultane: Overture and Allegro
Handel—Prelude & Fugue, HWV 316
Tchaikovsky—Voyevoda, op.78
Liadov—Kikimora
Puccini—Manon Lescaut: Intermezzo
Ravel—Barque sur l'ocean
Ireland—Forgotten Rite
Stravinsky—Tango (large orch);
   Variations
Still—American Scene: The East (Suite 1),
   The Old West (Suite 3), The Far West
   (Suite 4); Fanfare for American War
   Heroes; Festive Overture; In memoriam;
   Old California
Gershwin—Girl Crazy: Overture
Copland—Rodeo: Buckaroo Holiday;
   Rodeo: Hoe-Down
Khachaturian—Gayane: Sabre Dance;
   Gayane: Three Pieces
Barber—Fadograph of a Yestern Scene;
   Night Flight; School for Scandal:
   Overture; Vanessa: Intermezzo;
   Vanessa: Under the Willow Tree
Schuman, Wm.—American Festival
   Overture
Shulman—Laurentian Overture
Surinach—Drama jondo; Fandango
Ward—Hymn and Celebration; Hymn to
   the Night; Invocation and Toccata;
   Processional March
Rochberg—Time-Span II
Mennin—Canto
Feldman—Structures for Orchestra
Turok—Joplin Overture
Kilar—Pan Tadeusz: Polonaise
Tull—Final Covenant
Harmon—Fanfare for Our Common Earth;
   Suite of Migrations: Flight of the
   Monarch; Suite of Migrations: Geese
Hailstork—Celebration
Lavista—Clepsidra
Rodríguez—Gathering of Angels
Beckel—Celebrations
Saariaho—Asteroid 4179: Toutatis
Schaffner—Whirlwind Tour of the Orch
McTee—Unquestioned Answer
Amundson—Rejoicing
Mercurio—Mercurial Overture
Tan—Atonal Rock 'N Roll: Of Youth
Stephenson—American Fanfare; Stars and
   Stripes Fanfare

11'–20'

Dvořák—Scherzo capriccioso
Rimsky-Korsakov—Tale of the Tsar
   Saltan: Suite
Satie—Parade
Schmitt—Palais hanté
Hadley—San Francisco
Vaughan Williams—In the Fen Country
Karłowicz—Lithuanian Rhapsody
Respighi—Impressioni brasiliane
Grainger—Lincolnshire Posy
Malipiero—Armenia; Impressioni dal
   vero: Part I
Toch—Big Ben
Still—American Scene: The South (Suite
   2), A Mountain, a Memorial, and a Song
   (Suite 5); Poem; Symphony No.5
Gershwin—American in Paris
Harris, Roy—Symphony No.3
Copland—Inscape; Our Town
Barber—Andromache's Farewell [solo S];
   Die natali
Diamond—World of Paul Klee
Kay, U.—Theater Set for Orchestra
Ward—Divertimento; Festive Ode
Mennin—Concertato (Moby Dick)
Druckman—Aureole
Lombardo—Drakestail
Shchedrin—Seagull: Suite
Maxwell Davies—Prolation
Singleton—When Given a Choice
McGlaughlin—Solstice
Beckel—Gardens of Stone
Actor—Prelude to a Tragedy
Torke—Jasper
Stephenson—Celestial Suite

21'–30'

Tchaikovsky—Nutcracker: Suite No.1
Herbert—Hero and Leander
Suk—Fairy Tale
Carpenter—Adventures in a Perambulator
Stravinsky—Baiser de la fée: Divertimento
Martinů—Symphonies Nos.2-3
Still—Symphonies Nos.3-4
Sessions—Symphony No.2
Cowell—Symphony No.15
Khachaturian—Gayane: Suites Nos.2-3;
   Spartacus: Suite No.2
Adaskin—Algonquin Symphony
Swanson—Symphony No.3
Montsalvatge—Simfonia de Rèquiem
Persichetti—Night Dances;
   Symphony No.4
Ward—Festival Triptych
Bentzon—Symphony No.7
Mennin—Symphony No.6
Pinkham—Signs of the Zodiac
Druckman—Brangle; Prism
Harmon—Earth Day Portrait

Pasatieri—Symphony
Sierra—Sinfonía No.3
Tan—Orchestral Theatre II [solo B]
Puts—Symphony No.4

Over 30'

Spohr—Symphony No.7
Tchaikovsky—Nutcracker
Delius—Florida
Stojowski—Symphony, op.21
Vaughan Williams—Symphony No.3 [S]
Rachmaninoff—Symphony No.2
Stravinsky—Baiser de la fée
Atterberg—Symphony No.5
Prokofiev—Symphony No.7
Khachaturian—Gayane: Suite No.1
Tubin—Symphony No.4
Locklair—Symphony No.1

---

[31]
STRINGS
11 WOODWINDS
BRASS 4431
5 PERCUSSION
HARP, CELESTA, PIANO

10' or less

Bach, J.S.—Prelude & Fugue, BWV 558
Meyerbeer—Prophète: Coronation March
Wagner, Richard—Tristan und Isolde:
    Nachtgesang; Walküre: Ride of the
    Valkyries (Hutschenruyter)
Chabrier—Joyeuse marche
Sousa—Humoresque on "Swanee"
Elgar—Crown of India: March of the
    Mogul Emperors
Puccini—Edgar: Preludio
Busoni—Nocturne symphonique
Satie—Cinq grimaces
Alfvén—Bergakungen
Laparra—Habanera: Three Entr'actes
Stravinsky—Four Etudes
Riegger—Music for Orchestra
Martinů—Memorial to Lidice
Honegger—Mouvement symphonique
    no.3
Milhaud—Funérailles de Phocion
Hindemith—Neues vom Tage: Overture
Harris, Roy—Elegy for Orchestra
Finzi—Fall of the Leaf; New Year Music
Wolpe—Man from Midian: Moses Meets
    Aaron & March Through the Red Sea
Creston—Airborne Suite: Afternoon in
    Montreal
Shostakovich—Tahiti Trot [large]
Fine, Irving—Blue Towers
Panufnik—Heroic Overture

Nelhybel—Music for Orchestra
Berio—Nones
Adler, S.—Centennial
Deussen—Field in Pennsylvania
Chance—Elegy
Zaninelli—Americana
Maxwell Davies—Sir Charles His Pavan
Svoboda—Ex libris
Galbraith—Tormenta del sur
Picker—Old and Lost Rivers
Lang—how to pray
Ince—Before Infrared
Ritchie, Anthony—Bugle Will Do
O'Boyle—Ragtime Overture
Bates—Mothership

11'–20'

Handel—Royal Fireworks Music (ed.
    Baines & Mackerras)
Meyerbeer—Prophète: Ballet Music
Franck—Chasseur maudit
Ponchielli—Elegia
Duparc, Henri—Lénore
Sousa—Tales of a Traveler
Chaminade—Callirhoë Suite
Elgar—Crown of India: Suite
Strauss, R.—Don Juan
Dukas—Polyeucte: Overture
Sibelius—Night Ride and Sunrise
Gilbert, H.F.—Dance in the Place Congo
Roussel—Pour un fête de printemps
Schmitt—Musiques de plein air
Ives—Robert Browning Overture
Suk—Scherzo fantastique
Schreker—Ekkehard
Collins—Mardi Gras
Boulanger, L.—D'un soir triste
Korngold—Schauspiel-Ouvertüre
Ellington—Black, Brown and Beige:
    Suite; Night Creature
Copland—Lincoln Portrait
Berkeley—Symphony No.3
Siegmeister—Sunday in Brooklyn
Gould—Latin-American Symphonette
Panufnik—Nocturne
Zimmermann—Heroische Prosodie
Delden—Musica sinfonica
Husa—Two Sonnets by Michelangelo
Schuller—Five Bagatelles
Erb—Symphony of Overtures
Subotnick—Lamination
Wilson—Voices
Wuorinen—Reliquary for Igor Stravinsky
León—Desde …
Avshalomov, D.—Gems
Danielpour—Song of Remembrance
Dorff—Kiss
Tan—Orchestral Theatre I
Ince—Academica
Bates—Ode

Over 20'

Alkan—Symphony, op.39
Humperdinck—Maurische Rhapsodie
Janáček—Taras Bulba
Taneyev—Symphony no.4
Wolf—Penthesilea
Debussy—Pelléas et Mélisande symphonie
Melartin—Symphony No.6
Bloch, E.—Trois Poèmes juifs
Stravinsky—Symphony in Three
    Movements
Casella—Suite à Jean Huré
Hindemith—Pittsburgh Symphony
Hanson—Symphony No.2
Korngold—Sinfonietta
Chávez—Symphony No.4
Shostakovich—Symphony No.5
Hovhaness—Symphony No.22
Foss—Symphony No.1
Druckman—Mirage
Nelson, Ron—Five Pieces [solo Bar]
Maxwell Davies—Symphony No.2
Bennett, Richard R.—Concerto for
    Orchestra
Glass—Symphony No.2
Harris, Ross—Symphony No.4
Lieberson, Peter—Ashoka's Dream: Suite
Danielpour—Awakened Heart
Gordon—Dystopia; ReWriting
    Beethoven's Seventh Symphony
Ritchie, Anthony—Symphonies Nos.1, 3
Greenberg—Symphony No.5

---

[32]
STRINGS
WINDS 3333—4331
5 PERCUSSION

15' or less

Bach, J.S.—Passacaglia & Fugue, BWV
    582 (arr. Stokowski)
Wagner, Richard—Kaisermarsch;
    Lohengrin: Prelude, Act I; Lohengrin:
    Prelude, Act III; Lohengrin: Elsa's
    Procession; Siegfried: Forest Murmurs
    (Hutschenruyter)
Gottschalk—Souvenir de Porto Rico
Saint-Saëns—Orient et Occident
Rimsky-Korsakov—Legend of the
    Invisible City of Kitezh: Massacre at
    Kerzhentz; Maid of Pskov: Overture
Liadov—Baba-Yaga
Elgar—Pomp and Circumstance: No.5
Holst—Hammersmith
Schoenberg—Theme and Variations
Collins—Lament and Jig
Martin—Passacaille

Weiss—American Life
Honegger—Pacific 231; Rugby
Piston—Bicentennial Fanfare; Pine Tree Fantasy
Thomson, V.—Sea Piece with Birds; Solemn Music and a Joyful Fugue
Cowell—Chiaroscuro, HC 892; Synchrony
Tansman—Genesis Suite: Adam and Eve
Harris, Roy—When Johnny Comes Marching Home
Chávez—Resonancias
Walton—Portsmouth Point
Blacher—Orchester-Ornament
Farkas—Prelude & Fugue
Creston—Airborne Suite: Night in Mexico; Airborne Suite: Afternoon in Montreal
Shostakovich—Festive Overture
Gutche—Holofernes Overture
Messiaen—Hymne; Offrandes oubliées
Schuman, Wm.—American Festival Overture
Ward—Symphony No.1
Henze—Quattro poemi
Adler, S.—Art Creates Artists
Penderecki—Awakening of Jacob
Rudow—Force III
Hoover—Eleni
Corigliano—Jamestown Hymn
Zwilich—Jubilation; Upbeat
Singleton—After Fallen Crumbs
Peck—Thrill of the Orchestra
Actor—Circus Symphonicus
Chen Yi—Duo ye, No.2
McTee—Circuits; Finish Line; Tempus fugit
Sierra—Saludo
Higdon—SkyLine
Richman—United Symphony
Devore—Heartland

Over 15'

Liszt—Mazeppa
Wagner, Richard—Tristan und Isolde: Prelude & Liebestod
Bruckner—Symphony No.9: Finale [3 versions]
Borodin—Borodiniana Suite
Brahms—Eleven Chorale Preludes
Elgar—Severn Suite
Strauss, R.—Macbeth
Glazunov—Symphony No.8
Nielsen, Carl—Symphony No.3 [S & Bar]; Symphony No.4
Sibelius—Tapiola
Schoenberg—Chamber Symphony No.1 (orch version)
Karłowicz—Eternal Songs
Bloch, E.—Symphony in E-flat
Miaskovsky—Symphonies Nos.21-22

Stravinsky—Rite of Spring [McPhee or Rudolf]
Prokofiev—Symphony No.4 (1st version)
Honegger—Symphonies Nos.1, 5
Langgaard—Symphony No.7
Piston—Symphonies Nos.1-2
Hindemith—Philharmonic Concerto; Symphonic Metamorphosis; Symphony in E-flat
Hanson—Symphonies Nos.3, 6
Thomson, V.—Symphony No.2
Cowell—Symphony No.19
Chávez—Pasajes mexicanas
Thompson, R.—Symphony No.2
Copland—Statements
Blacher—Hamlet; Orchestra-Variations on a Theme of Paganini
Kabalevsky—Symphonies Nos.1-2
Tubin—Symphony No.5
Shostakovich—Symphony No.10
Messiaen—Ascension
Holmboe—Symphonies Nos.2, 8
Schuman, Wm.—Symphony No.6
Dello Joio—Variations, Chaconne & Finale
Brott, Alexander—Concordia
Diamond—Symphonies Nos.1-2
Kay, U.—Markings; Southern Harmony
Ward—Symphony No.2
Bentzon—Symphony No.9
Mennin—Symphony No.7
Laderman—Symphony No.7
Blackwood—Symphony No.5
Maxwell Davies—Symphonies Nos.3, 9
McCabe—Symphony No.7
Zwilich—Fantasy for Orchestra; Symphonies Nos.3, 5
Peck—Flying on Instruments
Actor—Symphony No.2
Chen Yi—Concerto, Piano
Durand—Athanor

```
[33]
STRINGS
WINDS 3333—4431
6 PERCUSSION
2 HARPS, CELESTA, PIANO
```

10' or less

Bach, J.S.—Fantasia & Fugue, BWV 537 [arr]; Fugue, BWV 578 [arr]; Sheep May Safely Graze [arr]
Berlioz—Roméo et Juliette: Queen Mab Scherzo
Alkan—Festin d'Esope
Wagner, Richard—Götterdämmerung: Siegfried's Rhine Journey

Saint-Saëns—Phaéton; Samson et Dalila: Bacchanale
Balakirev—Islamey [arr. Lyapunov]
Mussorgsky—Boris Godunov: Polonaise
Chabrier—España; Gwendoline: Overture
Lysenko—Taras Bulba: Overture
Rimsky-Korsakov—Coq d'or: Introduction & Wedding March
Drigo—Diane et Actéon Pas de deux
Humperdinck—Königskinder: Introduction to Act III
Liadov—From the Apocalypse
Martucci—Tarantella
Elgar—Pomp and Circumstance: Nos.1, 2, 4
Leoncavallo—Pagliacci: Intermezzo
Albéniz—Catalonia; Navarra
Loeffler—Villanelle du diable
Debussy—Berceuse héroïque; Triomphe de Bacchus
Strauss, R.—Salome: Salome's Dance [Boosey red]
Roussel—Rapsodie flamande
Lehár—Lustige Witwe: Overture
Schmitt—Mirages
Converse—Ormazd
Holst—Lure
Ives—New England Holidays: Decoration Day
Glière—Red Poppy: Russian Sailors' Dance
Ravel—Menuet antique
Brian—Symphony No.22
Falla—La vida breve: Interlude & Dance
Laparra—Habanera: Prélude
Ruggles—Men and Mountains [1936 version]
Wolf-Ferrari—Gioielli della Madonna: Intermezzo no.2 [large orch]
Bridge—Rebus
Bloch, E.—In the Night
Malipiero—Impressioni dal vero: Part III
Stravinsky—Canon
Turina—Procesion del rocio
Griffes—Clouds
Riegger—New Dance
Toch—Genesis Suite: The Covenant
Ibert—Bostoniana; Féerique; Rencontres: 3 pièces de ballet
Prokofiev—Love for Three Oranges: March & Scherzo; Overture, op.42
Grofé—Kentucky Derby
Honegger—Chant de joie; Nocturne
Boulanger, L.—D'un matin de printemps
Goossens—Tam O'Shanter
Piston—Symphonic Prelude; Toccata
Still—Bells
Thomson, V.—Seine at Night; Wheat Field at Noon
Cowell—Ancient Desert Drone
Tansman—Toccata

Gershwin—Overtures to: Let 'Em Eat Cake, Of Thee I Sing
Copland—Danzón cubano; Jubilee Variation; Preamble for a Solemn Occasion
Mosolov—Iron Foundry
Rodgers—Carousel: The Carousel Waltz
Walton—Crown Imperial; Johannesburg Festival Overture; Prologo e fantasia; Scapino
Blacher—Music for Cleveland
Kabalevsky—Colas Breugnon: Overture; Overture pathétique
Alwyn—Festival March
Finney—Hymn, Fuguing Tune & Holiday
Anderson, Leroy—Classical Jukebox
Carter—Holiday Overture
Barber—Music for a Scene from Shelley
Gould—Cheers
Lutoslawski—Postludium
Read—First Overture
Fine, I.—Toccata concertante
Perle—Six Bagatelles
Persichetti—Dance Overture
Kay, U.—Of New Horizons
Ward—Jubilation
Kirchner—Orchestra Piece
Husa—Celebration Fanfare; Overture
Foss—Ode
Walker, George—Overture in Praise of Folly
Berio—Ritirata notturna di Madrid
Martirano—Contrasto
Takemitsu—Green
Jones—Fanfare and Celebration [Version B]; Hear the Music; Overture for a City
Bennett, Richard R.—Troubadour Music
Rudow—Fanfare for My Hero
Bolcom—Ragomania!
Corigliano—Midsummer Fanfare
Harbison—Remembering Gatsby: Foxtrot
Earnest—Southern Exposure
Proto—Fantasy on the Saints
Iannaccone—Lysistrata
Schwantner—Freeflight
Hartway—Freedom Festival
Peck—Earth Pulse; Jack and Jill at Bunker Hill
McGlaughlin—Bela's Bounce
Kechley—Karasuma; Tuahku
Ott—Water Garden
Welcher—Zion
Rouse—Nevill Feast
Stucky—Jeu de timbres
Warshauer—Revelation
Asia—What About It
McTee—Timepiece; Unquestioned Answer
Sierra—Tropicalia: Celebration
Daugherty—Metropolis Symphony: Krypton; Route 66
Frazelle—Swans at Pungo Lake

Sheng—China Dreams: Fanfare; Shanghai Overture
Danielpour—Toward the Splendid City
Drattell—Syzygy
Phillips, P.S.—Brownian Motion
Lang—International Business Machine
Lentini—Sinfonia di festa
Wolfe, Julia—Window of Vulnerability
Heitzeg—Blue Liberty
Butler—Fixed Doubles
Lorenz—En tren vá changó
Higdon—Fanfare ritmico; Shine
O'Boyle—River Symphony: Suite; River Symphony: Fanfare
Richman—Playground Escapades
Thomas, Augusta Read—Helios Choros I
Guzzo—Fanfare for Mountains and Peace
Stephenson—Concertino and Fanfare
Boyer—Festivities; On Music's Wings: Silver Fanfare; Rolling River
Hutter—Skyscrapers; Urban Collision
Pann—Slalom
Puts—Hymn to the Sun; Millennium Canons; "… this noble company"
Devore—In Common Ragtime
Petering—Lamentations
Tommasini—Torn Threads Rewoven

11'–20'

Liszt—Hungarian Rhapsody No.1
Wagner, Richard—Tristan und Isolde: Prelude
Lalo—Namouna: Ballet Suite No.2
Balakirev—Tamara
Mussorgsky—Pictures at an Exhibition (Tushmalov)
Paine—Azara: Orchestral Scene & 3 Moorish Dances
Rimsky-Korsakov—Tale of the Tsar Saltan: Suite
Indy—Istar
Chadwick—Aphrodite
Chausson—Viviane
Elgar—In the South
Kelley—Pit and the Pendulum
Mahler—Totenfeier
Debussy—Six épigraphes antiques
Delius—In a Summer Garden
Strauss, R.—Josephslegende: Symphonic Fragment; Rosenkavalier: Waltzes, First Sequence
Dukas—Péri
Sibelius—Oceanides; Pohjola's Daughter
Roussel—Bacchus et Ariane: Suite No.1; Évocations, op.15, nos.1-2; Suite in F; Symphony No.4
Schmitt—Salammbô: Suite No.2
Converse—Endymion's Narrative; Festival of Pan; Flivver Ten Million; Mystic Trumpeter

Alfvén—Midsommarvaka; Swedish Rhapsody No.3
Mason—Chanticleer
Holst—Perfect Fool: Ballet Music
Schmidt, F.—Notre Dame: Entr'acte & Carnival Music
Glière—Zaporozhy Cossacks
Ravel—Shéhérazade [overture]
Falla—Homenajes
Bridge—Enter Spring
Respighi—Fontane di Roma
Bloch, E.—Poems of the Sea; Sinfonia breve
Bartók—Miraculous Mandarin: Suite; Two Pictures
Malipiero—Pause del silenzio I
Stravinsky—Agon
Turina—Danzas fantásticas
Bax—Tintagel
Webern—Passacaglia
Griffes—Pleasure Dome of Kubla Khan
Collins—Irish Rhapsody; Set of Four
Stephan—Musik für Orchester
Villa-Lobos—Danses africaines; Uirapurú
Martin—Quatre éléments
Bliss—Introduction and Allegro
Prokofiev—Love for Three Oranges: Symphonic Suite; Romeo and Juliet: Suite No.3; Russian Overture
Weiss—Segreti
Grofé—Mississippi Suite
Honegger—Impératrice aux rochers: Suite
Milhaud—Frenchman in New York; Symphony No.11
Moore, Douglas—Pageant of P.T. Barnum
Rogers—Three Japanese Dances
Piston—Concerto for Orchestra; Incredible Flutist: Suite; Lincoln Center Festival Overture; Symphony No.7; Three New England Sketches
Sowerby—Prairie
Auric—Phèdre: Suite symphonique
Chávez—Initium
Ellington—Trois rois noirs
Poulenc—Biches: Suite
Copland—Symphony No.2
Egk—French Suite
Walton—Improvisations on an Impromptu of Benjamin Britten; Partita
Wolpe—Man from Midian; Passacaglia
Khachaturian—Spartacus: Suite No.3
Kabalevsky—Colas Breugnon: Suite
Hartmann—Symphony No.2
Talma—Toccata
Gutche—Perseus and Andromeda XX
Carter—Adagio tenebroso; Concerto for Orchestra; Partita; Three Occasions for Orchestra
Stevens—Symphonic Dances
Holmboe—Symphony No.13
Barber—Antony and Cleopatra: Two Scenes

Hovhaness—Floating World; Fra
  Angelico; Meditation on Orpheus
Françaix—Ville mystérieuse
Britten—Prince of the Pagodas: Pas de six
Gould—Soundings
Lutoslawski—Livre; Mi-parti; Novelette;
  Three Postludes
Diamond—Symphony No.4 [reduced]
Babbitt—Relata I
Blomdahl—Sisyphos
Ginastera—Glosses sobre temes de Pau
  Casals [full orch]; Iubilum
Burgess—Manchester Overture
Kay, U.—Chariots; Suite
Ward—Sonic Structure
Rochberg—Night Music
Zimmermann—Sinfonie in einem Satz
Kirchner—Music for Orchestra
Arnold—Inn of the Sixth Happiness: Suite
Husa—Symphonic Suite
Imbrie—Legend; Symphony No.3
Bassett—Echoes from an Invisible World;
  From a Source Evolving
Ligeti—San Francisco Polyphony
Pinkham—Symphonies Nos.1–2
Starer—Samson agonistes
Schuller—American Triptych
Henze—Caprichos
Leeuw, T. de—Mouvements retrograde
Nelson, Marie—Ode to Antigone
Erb—Concerto, Brass; Seventh Trumpet
Peterson—Face of the Night
Musgrave—Concerto for Orchestra
Bloch, A.—Enfiando per orchestra
Hoddinott—Fioriture
Takemitsu—Dream/Window; Flock
  Descends into the Pentagonal Garden
Van de Vate—Chernobyl; Nemo: Suite;
  Pura Besakih; Western Front
Baker—Kosbro
Colgrass—As Quiet As …
Lazarof—Poema; Symphony No.7
Nørgård, Per—Twilight
Shchedrin—Self-Portrait
Maxwell Davies—Mavis in Las Vegas
Tull—Symphonic Treatise
Jones—Hymn to the Earth; Open Range;
  Reflections
Ketting—Symphony No.1
Sallinen—Shadows; Symphony No.1
Schwertsik—Fünf Naturstücke
Bennett, Richard R.—Anniversaries;
  Zodiac
Glass—Days and Nights in Rocinha
Bolcom—Seattle Slew
Corigliano—Fantasia on an Ostinato;
  Three Hallucinations; Tournaments
Skoryk—Hutsul Triptych
Singleton—Shadows
Albert, Stephen—Anthem and
  Processionals
Proto—Casey at the Bat

Whitehead—improbable ordered dance;
  Resurgences
Bamert—Snapshots
Matthews, D.—Symphony No.3
Schwantner—Sudden Rainbow
Cresswell—O!; Salm
Peck—Peace Overture
Kechley—Clocks and More Clocks;
  Transformations
Vivier—Orion
Catán—En un doblez del tiempo
Locklair—When Morning Stars Begin to
  Fall
Paulus—Concertante
Ran—Vessels of Courage and Hope
Stucky—Dreamwaltzes; Pinturas de
  Tamayo
Ayers—Jericho; Passion of John Brown
  [Bar]
Davis—Tales (Tails) of the Signifying
  Monkey
Tsontakis—Four Symphonic Quartets: 1.
  Other Echoes, 3. Dove Descending, 4.
  Winter Lightning
Chen Yi—Momentum; Symphony No.2
McTee—Double Play
Sierra—Bacchae; Borikén; Concerto for
  Orchestra; Fandangos; Sinfonía No.2
Zhou—Enlightened; Immortal
Beaser—Double Chorus for Orchestra
Daugherty—Metropolis Symphony: Red
  Cape Tango
Gross—You Must Remember This …
Young—Dance; Virgen de la Esperanza
Gordon—Beijing Harmony
Mackey—TILT
Sartor—Portent and Apotheosis
Knehans—ripple; winter steps
Lang—Grind to a Halt
Smith, Gregory—Mr. Smith's Composition
Tan—Symphonic Poem of 3 Notes
Wagner, Melinda—Falling Angels
Lindberg—Corrente II
Heitzeg—Nine Surrealist Studies
MacMillan—Britannia
Kernis—Newly Drawn Sky
Hagen—Gesture Drawings
Heggie—Dead Man Walking: Orchestral
  Excerpts
Higdon—river sings a song to trees
Roter—Camp David Overture; TR: A
  "Bully" Portrait
O'Boyle—An Australian in New York
Thomas, Augusta Read—Helios Choros II;
  Helios Choros III; Jubilee
Trigos—Sinfonia breve
Theofanidis—Rainbow Body
Boyer—Dream Lives On; New
  Beginnings; Titanic
Stookey—Mahl/er/werk
Frank, G.L.—Three Latin American
  Dances

Puts—Exalted Virelai; Falling Dream;
  John Brown's Body; Symphony No.2;
  Two Mountain Scenes
Wigglesworth, Ryan—Locke's Theatre
Greenberg—Skyline Dances

21'–30'

Lalo—Namouna: Ballet Suite No.1
Rimsky-Korsakov—Coq d'or: Suite;
  Legend of the Invisible City of Kitezh:
  Suite
Parry—Symphony No.5
Chausson—Symphony
Elgar—Falstaff
Foerster, J.B.—From Shakespeare
Mahler—Symphony No.10 [Krenek or
  Ratz]
Debussy—Nocturnes [orig or rev]
Strauss, R.—Rosenkavalier: Suite [1945];
  Tod und Verklärung
Glazunov—Kremlin
Roussel—Bacchus et Ariane: Suite No.2;
  Symphony No.3
Schmitt—Tragédie de Salomé: Suite
Hadley—Salome
Vaughan Williams—Symphony No.8
Rachmaninoff—Cinq Études-tableaux
Dohnányi—Ruralia hungarica
Bridge—Sea
Respighi—Vetrate di chiesa
Bartók—Miraculous Mandarin
Malipiero—Per una favola cavalleresca
Turina—Sinfonia sevillana
Collins—The Masque of the Red Death:
  Ballet Suite
Toch—Symphony No.3
Villa-Lobos—Bachianas brasileiras
  nos.4 & 8
Ibert—Ballade de la geôle de Reading
Prokofiev—Cinderella: Suites Nos.1-3
Honegger—Horace victorieux; Symphony
  No.3
Milhaud—Symphonies Nos.1-2, No.10
Piston—Symphonies Nos.4, 5, 6, 8
Hindemith—Symphonia serena
Gerhard—Concerto for Orchestra
Ben-Haim—Symphony No.1
Cowell—Symphonies Nos.5, 16
Bacon—From These States;
  Symphony No.1
Tcherepnin, A.—Symphony No.2
Antheil—Symphonies Nos.5–6
Copland—Music for a Great City
Walton—Symphony No.2; Variations on a
  Theme by Hindemith
Khachaturian—Spartacus: Suite No.1
Petrassi—Concerto for Orchestra No.1
Jolivet—Symphony No.1
Tubin—Symphony No.8
Badings—Symphony No.5
Gutche—Symphony No.6

Holmboe— Symphonies Nos.10-12
Barber—Symphony No.1
Reed—Fiesta mexicana
Schuman, Wm.—Judith; Symphonies
  Nos.7, 9; Undertow
Britten—Gloriana: Symphonic Suite;
  Sinfonia da requiem
Gould—Symphony of Spirituals
Lutoslawski— Symphonies Nos.1, 2, 4
Read—Symphony No.3
Fine, I.—Symphony
Panufnik—Symphony No.8
Blomdahl—Symphony No.3
Dutilleux—Symphony No.2
Ginastera—Popol vuh
Bernstein—Symphony No.1 [solo Ms]
Rochberg—Imago mundi; Symphony No.5
Arnold—Bridge on the River Kwai
Husa—Music for Prague; Symphony No.1
Foss—Symphony No.3
Bassett—Concerto for Orchestra
Rorem—Symphony No.3
Laderman—Concerto for Orchestra
Lees—Concerto for Orchestra; Symphony
  No.5
Schurmann—Six Studies of Francis Bacon
Schuller—Seven Studies on Themes of
  Paul Klee
Henze— Symphonies Nos.2-4
Argento—Fire Variations; In Praise of
  Music
Erb—Concerto for Orchestra; Evensong
Adler, S.—Symphony No.6
Druckman—Windows
Flagello—Theme, Variations & Fugue
Musgrave—Turbulent Landscapes
Rautavaara—Symphony No.8
Stockhausen—Punkte
Hoddinott— Symphonies Nos.3, 5
Goehr, Alexander—Symphony in One
  Movement
Shchedrin—Little Humpbacked Horse:
  Suite No.1
Blackwood—Symphony No.2
Maxwell Davies—Symphony No.5
Jones—Symphonic Requiem; Symphonies
  Nos.1, 3
Hoover—J. M. W. Turner: Impressions
Wilson—Sinfonia
Bolcom—Symphony No.5
Corigliano—Phantasmagoria
Harbison— Symphonies Nos.1, 3, 4, 6
Tower—Concerto for Orchestra; Silver
  Ladders
Wuorinen—Movers and Shakers
Davies, Victor—Dream Variations
Zwilich—Symphony No.2
Schwantner—Toward Light
Zaimont—Symphony No.1
Adams, John—Doctor Atomic Symphony
Welcher—Haleakala; Night Watchers
Paulus—Concerto for Orchestra

Rouse—Symphony No.2
Stucky—Concerto for Orchestra;
  Second Concerto for Orchestra
Asia— Symphonies Nos.1, 2
Buhr—winter poems
Daugherty—Motorcity Triptych
Picker—Symphony No.1
Sheng—China Dreams
Young—Symphony No.2
Danielpour—Concerto for Orchestra
Heitzeg—Sacred Stones;
  Symphony in Sculpture
Kernis—Symphony No.2
Higdon—City Scape
Richman—Behold the Bold
  Umbrellaphant
Trigos—Symphony No.1
Boyer—Symphony No.1
Stookey—Out of the Everywhere
Puts—Symphony No.3
Lee, James III—A Different Soldier's Tale
Bates—Alternative Energy; Liquid
  Interface

31'–40'

Saint-Saëns—Symphony No.3
Mussorgsky—Pictures at an Exhibition
  (Ravel)
Tchaikovsky—Nutcracker: Suite No.2
Indy—Jour d'été a la montagne
Rezniček—Symphony No.5
Busoni—Brautwahl: Suite; Turandot:
  Suite
Bantock—Hebridean Symphony
Converse—American Sketches
Vaughan Williams—Symphonies Nos.6, 9
Rachmaninoff—Symphony No.3
Bartók—Concerto for Orchestra
Stravinsky—Petrushka (1947)
Szymanowski—Symphony No.2
Taylor—Through the Looking Glass
Atterberg—Symphony No.3
Martinů— Symphonies Nos.1, 5
Bliss—Colour Symphony
Prokofiev—Chout: Symphonic Suite;
  Symphonies Nos.2-3
Grofé—Grand Canyon Suite
Piston—The Incredible Flutist; Symphony
  No.3
Bacon—Ford's Theatre
Thompson, R.—Symphony No.1
Antheil—Symphony No.4
Walton—Hamlet: Concert Suite
Shostakovich—Symphony No.12
Holmboe— Symphonies Nos.6, 9
Diamond—Symphony No.3
Bernstein—Symphony No.2
Rochberg—Symphony No.2
Husa—Concerto for Orchestra
Imbrie—Symphony No.1
Rorem—Air Music

Flagello—Symphony No.1
Maxwell Davies—Symphony No.8
Harbison—Symphony No.5 [solo Bar, Ms]
McCabe—Symphony "Edward II"
Holloway—Second Concerto for
  Orchestra
Vasks—Symphony No.2
McTee—Symphony No.1
Tan—Concerto for Orchestra
Higdon—Concerto for Orchestra

Over 40'

Liszt—Dante Symphony [chor: women or
  boys]
Brahms—Piano Quartet [arr. Schoenberg]
Tchaikovsky—Manfred
Indy—Symphony No.2
Elgar—Symphonies Nos.1, 3
Vaughan Williams—Job; Symphonies
  Nos.2, 7 [S & chorus]
Holst—Planets [female chorus]
Ives—A Concord Symphony
Schmidt, F.—Symphony No.4
Suk—Symphony No.2
Glière—Symphony No.2
Bloch, E.—America
Shilkret—Genesis Suite [complete;
  narrator, chorus]
Shostakovich—Gadfly: Suite;
  Symphony No.11
Rochberg— Symphonies Nos.1, 4
Hurwit—Symphony No.1
Nørgård—Symphony No.3 [2 chor]
Maxwell Davies— Symphonies
  Nos.1, 6, 7
Jones—Roundings
Bamert—Once Upon an Orchestra
Harris, Ross—Symphony No.3
Daugherty—Metropolis Symphony
Corrin—How the Orchestra Grew
Young—Symphony [No.1] [solo S]
Boyer—Ellis Island [actors]

```
        [34]
       STRINGS
    WOODWINDS 3333
 OTHERWISE LARGER THAN
   PREVIOUS CATEGORIES
```

20' or less

Bach, J.S.—Komm süsser Tod [arr.]
Fry—Niagara Symphony
Wagner, Richard—Christoph Columbus:
  Overture
Goldmark—Königin von Saba:
  Einzugsmarsch;
  Königin von Saba: Ballet Music

Paine—Azara: Orchestral Scene & 3
    Moorish Dances
Dvořák—Watersprite
Elgar—Cockaigne
Strauss, R.—Rosenkavalier: Concert Suite
    [Mandell]
Glazunov—Finnish Fantasy
Pfitzner—Palestrina: Prelude, Act III
Rachmaninoff—Isle of the Dead
Ravel—Alborada del gracioso; Bolero;
    Valse
Nielsen, Ludolf—Symphony No.3
Schreker—Geburtstag der Infantin: Suite
Grainger—In a Nutshell
Ibert—Escales
Langgaard—Sphinx
Hanson—Merry Mount: Suite
Weinberger—Schwanda the Bagpiper:
    Polka & Fugue [2 versions]
Gershwin—American in Paris
Harris, Roy—Horn of Plenty
Ellington—Trois rois noirs
Krenek—Kleine Symphonie
Halffter—Muerte de Carmen: Habanera
Shostakovich—Festive Overture;
    Suite for Jazz Orch, No.2
Gutche—Holofernes Overture
Carter—Symphony of Three Orchestras
Hovhaness—Symphony No.2
Ginastera—Ollantay
Foss—Folksong for Orchestra
Ligeti—Apparitions; Macabre Collage
Feldman—...Out of "Last Pieces"
Henze—Barcarola
Shchedrin—Concerto for Orchestra no.1
Miyoshi—Concerto for Orchestra
Penderecki—De natura sonoris No.2
Reynolds—Graffiti
Ishii—Sho-ko
Wuorinen—Contrafactum
Schwantner—From a Dark Millennium
Sapieyevski—Summer Overture
Lieberson, Peter—Drala
Locklair—Phoenix
Ran—Legends
Rouse—Rapture
Saariaho—Laterna Magica
Drattell—Lilith
Salonen—Insomnia
Turnage—Three Screaming Popes
Chin—santika Ekatala
O'Boyle—Ballycroy

21'–30'

Saint-Saëns—Symphony No.1
MacDowell—Suite No.2
Loeffler—Pagan Poem
Glière—Red Poppy: Suite
Carpenter—Skyscrapers
Respighi—Pini di Roma
Villa-Lobos—Bachianas brasileiras no.7

Harris, Roy—Symphony No.5
Copland—Symphony No.1
Hartmann—Symphony No.6
Jolivet—Symphony No.3
Scelsi—Uaxuctum [solos SSTB & chorus
    are textless]
Menotti—Apolcalypse
Britten—Sinfonia da requiem
Lutoslawski—Concerto for Orchestra
Foss—Baroque Variations
Górecki—Old Polish Music
Schnittke—In memoriam ...
Ishii—Kyō-Sō; Mono-Prism
Ferneyhough—Plötzlichkeit [3 female
    voices]
Rouse—Symphony No.3
Hartke—Symphony No.3 [Countertenor,
    2T, Bar]
Adès—Asyla

Over 30'

Bruckner—Symphonies Nos.7 (Cahis 13),
    8 (Cahis 14 *or* 16), 9 (Cahis 18)
Paderewski—Symphony, op.24
Reger—Symphonischer Prolog
Miaskovsky—Symphony No.6
Korngold—Symphony, op.40
Hartmann—Symphony No.7
Tippett—Symphony No.4
Messiaen—Turangalîla-symphonie [solo
    pf, ondes]
Pettersson, Allan—Symphony No.4
Shapey—Concerto fantastique
Rautavaara—Symphonies Nos.3, 5
Penderecki—Symphony No.2
Maw—Odyssey

**[35]
STRINGS
13 WOODWINDS
BRASS 4431
7 PERCUSSION
2 HARPS, CELESTA, PIANO**

10' or less

Bach, J.S.—Toccata & Fugue [arr]
Berlioz—Damnation de Faust:
    Will-o-the-Wisps (Menuet de follets)
Wagner, Richard—Rule Britannia
Franck—Psyché: Sommeil de Psyché,
    Psyché enlevée par les Zéphirs, Les
    Jardins d'Eros, Psyché et Eros
Chabrier—Bourée fantasque
Janáček—From the House of the Dead:
    Overture
Elgar—Pomp and Circumstance: No.3

Debussy—Images: Rondes de printemps;
    Isle joyeuse
Strauss, R.—Guntram: Prelude to Act I;
    Salome: Salome's Dance (Kalmus red)
Ruggles—Organum
Ingelbrecht—Rapsodie de printemps
Grainger—Immovable Do
Bax—Happy Forest; Overture to a
    Picaresque Comedy
Griffes—Bacchanale
Ibert—Bacchanale
Gershwin—Cuban Overture
Walton—Capriccio burlesco
Wolpe—Two Studies
Gutche—Epimetheus USA
Barber—Commando March; Night Flight
Galindo—Sones de mariachi
Schuman, Wm.—Circus Overture
Read—Night Flight
Bernstein—Candide: Overture; Slava!
Zimmermann—Stille und Umkehr
Schuller—Dramatic Overture
Flagello—Aria sinfonica
Holliger—Ardeur noire
Zwilich—Celebration for Orchestra
Adams, John—Lollapalooza; Short Ride in
    a Fast Machine
Rouse—Bump; Infernal Machine
Saariaho—Song for Betty
Torke—Javelin
Thomas, Augusta Read—Ceremonial

11'–20'

Bach, J.S.—Chaconne [arr. Casella]
Gottschalk—Symphony No.1
Chadwick—Tam O'Shanter
Janáček—Cunning Little Vixen: Suite
    [both versions]; From the House of the
    Dead: Suite [Jílek]
Dukas—Apprenti sorcier
Busoni—Sarabande & Cortège
Roussel—Padmâvatî: Suites Nos.1 [solo
    TBar] & 2
Converse—California
Tcherepnin, N.—Enchanted Kingdom
Malipiero—Impressioni dal vero: Part II
Bax—In the Faery Hills; Roscatha; Tale
    the Pine-Trees Knew
Becker—Symphony No.3
Ibert—Diane de Poitiers: Suite No.1
Martinů—Frescos of Piero della Francesca
Prokofiev—Steel Step: Suite
Honegger—Prelude, Fugue, Postlude
Sowerby—From the Northland
Still—Deserted Plantation
Sessions—Concerto for Orchestra;
    Montezuma: Suite;
    Symphonies Nos.1, 5, 6
Korngold—Symphonic Overture
Copland—Salón México
McPhee—Tabuh-Tabuhan

Blitzstein—Orchestra Variations
Creston—Dance Overture;
  Invocation and Dance
Barber—Essay No.3; Medea's Meditation
  and Dance of Vengeance
Schuman, Wm.—New England Triptych
Read—Pennsylvania Suite
Diamond—Symphony No.7
Perle—Three Movements
Bernstein—Divertimento
Rorem—Lions [combo]
Schuller—Capriccio stravagante
Aschaffenburg—Three Dances for
  Orchestra
Rautavaara—Symphony No.4
Previn—Night Thoughts
Felciano—Orchestra
Takemitsu—Music of Tree
Kelterborn—Changements
Jones—Let Us Now Praise Famous Men
Pärt—Nekrolog
Amy—Refrains
Glass—Music in Similar Motion
Höller—Aura
Zaimont—Monarchs
Adams, John—Slonimsky's Earbox
Rouse—Phantasmata
Stucky—Impromptus
Beaser—Chorale Variations for Orchestra
Lindberg—Era
Salonen—L.A. Variations
Amaya—Soledad y el Mar
Burge, John—The Canadian Shield
Dorman—Ellef Symphony; Variations
  Without a Theme

21'–30'

Albéniz—Iberia [arr. Arbós]
Strauss, R.—Rosenkavalier: Suite [1945]
Ravel—Gaspard de la nuit
Price—Symphony No.3
Ibert—Diane de Poitiers: Suite No.2
Martinů—Symphony No.6
Prokofiev—Romeo and Juliet: Suites
  Nos.1-2
Milhaud—Suite symphonique no.2
Still—Symphonies Nos.1-2
Sessions—Black Maskers: Suite;
  Symphonies Nos.3, 4, 7, 9
Chávez—Hija de Colquide: Symphonic
  Suite; Symphony No.3
Antheil—Symphony [No.5; withdrawn]
Creston— Symphonies Nos.2-3
Shostakovich—Symphony No.6
Barber—Symphony No.2
Reed—Fiesta mexicana
Diamond—Symphony No.5
Bernstein—On the Waterfront: Symphonic
  Suite; West Side Story: Symphonic
  Dances
Starer—Symphony No.3

Lewis, R.H.—Three Movements on
  Scenes of Hieronymous Bosch
Erb—Ritual Observances
Crumb—Variazioni
Gubaydulina—Light of the End
Kagel—Variationen ohne Fuge
Shchedrin—Anna Karenina: Romantic
  Music; Stikhira
Del Tredici—Happy Voices
Harbison—Symphony No.2
McCabe—Arthur: Three Portraits;
  Symphony No.4
Matthews, C.—Landscape
Rodríguez—Favola boccaccesca
Lloyd—Symphony No.2
Mackey—Eating Greens
Ince—Symphony No.3

**[36]
STRINGS
WINDS 4454—6641
8 PERCUSSION
3 HARPS, CELESTA, PIANO**

10' or less

Buxtehude—Chaconne, BuxWV 160
Bach, J.S.—Toccata & Fugue [arr]
Berlioz—Te Deum: Marche;
  Te Deum: Prelude
Wagner, Richard—Walküre: Ride of the
  Valkyries (Hutschenruyter)
Balakirev—Islamey [arr. Casella]
Rimsky-Korsakov—Mlada: Procession of
  the Nobles
Debussy—Images: Gigues; Martyre de
  Saint Sébastien: La Chambre magique
Pfitzner—Palestrina: Prelude, Act I,
  Prelude, Act II
Stenhammar—Sången: Mellanspel
Ives—Yale-Princeton Football Game
  [Schuller]
Varèse—Tuning Up
Pijper—Six Symphonic Epigrams
Harris, Roy—Epilogue to Profiles in
  Courage—J.F.K.
Revueltas—Sensemayá [full orch version]
Messiaen—Sourire
Cage—Suite for Toy Piano [orch]
Perle—Adagio for Orchestra
Kraft—Simple Introduction to the
  Orchestra
Ligeti—Atmosphères
Pinkham—Catacoustical Measures
Rorem—Eagles
Berio—Encore
Boulez—Notations I–IV
Baird—Variations Without a Theme
Shchedrin—Concerto for Orch No.2

Jones—Fanfare and Celebration [Version
  A]
Corigliano—Campane di Ravello
Matthews, C.—Pluto, the Renewer [female
  chor]
Knussen—Flourish with Fireworks
Asia—Gateways
Picker—Old and Lost Rivers
Gordon—Sunshine of Your Love
Boyer—Phoenix

11'–20'

Bach, J.S.—Passacaglia, BWV 582, C
  minor [orch. Respighi]
Berlioz—Roméo et Juliette: Romeo Alone,
  Festivities at Capulet's
Wagner, Richard—Grosser Festmarsch;
  Parsifal: Prelude;
  Parsifal: Good Friday Spell
Rimsky-Korsakov—Mlada: Suite
Debussy—Images: Ibéria; Jeux
Delius—Brigg Fair; Dance Rhapsody
  No.1; Eventyr
Strauss, R.—Frau ohne Schatten:
  Symphonic Fantasy; Till Eulenspiegel
Roussel—Padmâvatî: Suites Nos.1 [solo
  TBar], & 2
Schoenberg—Five Pieces for Orchestra
  [orig or rev]
Glière—Syrènes
Ravel—Daphnis et Chloé: Suite No.1;
  Rapsodie espagnole
Ruggles—Evocations
Respighi—Ballata delle gnomidi
Bloch, E.—Hiver-Printemps
Stravinsky—Scherzo fantastique
Szymanowski—Concert Overture
Bax—November Woods
Casella—Italia
Webern—Im Sommerwind; Sechs Stücke,
  op.6 [orig]
Berg—Three Pieces for Orchestra;
  Wozzeck: Three Excerpts [solo S]
Collins—Hibernia; Tragic Overture;
  Variations on an Irish Folksong
Gerhard—Epithalamion
Sessions—Symphony No.8
Harris, Roy—Symphony No.7
Chávez—Symphony No.2
Copland—Connotations; Dance
  Symphony; Emblems; Symphonic Ode
Bacewicz—Music for Strings, Trumpets &
  Percussion
Hovhaness—Floating World
Brant—Desert Forests
Diamond—Symphony No.4
Dutilleux—Métaboles;
  Timbres, espace, mouvement
Ginastera—Panambí: Suite
Yardumian—Armenian Suite
Walker, George—Address for Orchestra

Ligeti—Lontano
Samuel—Looking at Orpheus Looking;
  Requiem for Survivors
Schuller—Of Reminiscences and
  Reflections
Brown—Available Forms 2
Henze—Scorribanda sinfonica
Veerhoff—Sinfonia panta-rhei
Adler, S.—Concerto for Orchestra
Russo—Symphony No.2
Denisov—Bells in the Mist
London—Hero of our Time
Takemitsu—Twill by Twilight; Visions
Martino—Mosaic for Grand Orchestra
Kilar—Krzesany
Górecki—Refrain; Scontri
Rands—Agenda
Reich—Three Movements
Kolb—Grisaille
Eötvös—zeroPoints
Hartway—Star Dancer
Aho—Minea
Davis—ESU Variations
Chen Yi—Si Ji
Salonen—NYX
Ince—Ebullient Shadows
Thomas, Augusta Read—Tangle;
  Words of the Sea

21'–30'

Fry—Santa Claus
Debussy—Martyre de Saint Sébastien:
  Fragments symphoniques; Mer
Pierné—Cydalise et le chèvre-pied: Suite
  No.1
Schoenberg—Variations for Orchestra
Karłowicz—Stanisław and Anna
  Oświecimowie
Schreker—Vorspiel zu einem Drama
Respighi—Belkis, regina di Saba: Suite
Bartók—Four Orchestral Pieces
Kodály—Háry János: Suite
Stravinsky—Firebird: Suite (1911)
Stephan—Symphonischer Satz
Gerhard—Symphony No.4
Cowell—Symphony No.3
Harris, Roy—Symphonies Nos.5, 11
Poulenc—Animaux modèles: Suite
Wolpe—Symphony No.1
Skalkottas—Return of Ulysses
Hartmann—Symphony No.1 [solo A]
Messiaen—Chronochromie
Schuman, Wm.—Symphony No.4
Lutoslawski—Symphony No.3
Panufnik—Symphony No.10
Diamond—Symphony No.6
Perle—Transcendental Modulations
Persichetti—Symphony No.9
Lees—Symphony No.3
Orbón—Tres versiones sinfónicas

Schuller—Concerto for Orchestra, No.2;
  Spectra
Argento—Ring of Time
Gubaydulina—Feast During a Plague
Kagel—Broken Chords
Lazarof—Concerto for Orchestra
Maxwell Davies—St. Thomas Wake
Sallinen—Symphony No.3
Hoover—Night Skies
Svoboda—Symphonies No.3 [solo org;
  solo str 5t: 2vn, 2va, vc], & No.4
Schwantner—New Morning for the World
Aho—Symphony No.2
Saariaho—Orion
Lindberg—Sculpture
Salonen—Wing on Wing [2 solo S
  (textless)]

Over 30'

Berlioz—Symphonie funèbre et
  triomphale
Mussorgsky—Pictures at an Exhibition
  [arr. Funtek]
Mahler—Symphony No.5; Symphony
  No.10 [editions of Cooke, Wheeler,
  Gamzou]
Strauss, R.—Also sprach Zarathustra
Zemlinsky—Seejungfrau
Holst—Planets
Ives—Universe Symphony, S.6 [Austin
  realization]
Respighi—Sinfonia drammatica
Bartók—Suite No.1
Stravinsky—Petrushka [orig]
Bax—Symphonies Nos.1, 4
Collins—Symphony
Prokofiev—Romeo and Juliet
Gerhard—Metamorphoses
Shostakovich—Symphony No.8
Messiaen—Canyons aux étoiles [solo pf,
  hn, xylorimba, glock]
Schuman, Wm.— Symphonies Nos.3,
  8, 10
Ohana—Livre des prodiges
Rochberg—Symphony No.6
Nørgård—Symphony No.8
Blackwood—Symphony No.1
Górecki—Symphony No.3 [solo S]
Penderecki— Symphonies Nos.1, 4
Kancheli—Symphony No.7
Sallinen—Symphony No.5
Corigliano—Symphony No.1
Adams, John—City Noir; Harmonielehre
Greenberg—Intelligent Life

[37]
INSTRUMENTATION LARGER THAN ALL PREVIOUS CATEGORIES

20' or less

Bach, J.S. [orchd Schoenberg]—Komm,
  Gott, Schöpfer, heiliger Geist; Prelude &
  Fugue, BWV 552; Schmücke dich, o
  liebe Seele
Bach, J.S. [arr Stokowski]—Passacaglia &
  Fugue, BWV 582
Wagner, Richard—Götterdämmerung:
  Siegfried's Funeral Music;
  Walküre: Ride of the Valkyries
Rimsky-Korsakov—Concerto, Trombone
Pierné—Cydalise et le chèvre-pied: Suite
  No.2
Strauss, R.—Frau ohne Schatten:
  Symphonic Fantasy [arr. Ruzick];
  Salome: Salome's Dance
Busoni—Turandot: Verzweiflung und
  Ergebung
Granados—Dante [solo A]
Koechlin—Bandar-Log
Ravel—Daphnis et Chloé: Suite No.2
Ruggles—Sun-Treader
Stravinsky—Rite of Spring: Sacrificial
  Dance
Bax—Garden of Fand
Varèse—Arcana
Prokofiev—Scythian Suite
Chávez—Symphony No.1
Ellington—Harlem
Janssen—New Year's Eve in New York
Copland—Symphonic Ode
Schuman, Wm.—Credendum; Newsreel
Blomdahl—Forma ferritonans
Maderna—Aura
Shapey—Rituals
Kraft—Contextures [offstage jazz 4t]
Berio—Allelujah I; Still
Brown—Cross Sections and Color Fields
Henze—Symphony No.5
Felciano—Galactic Rounds
Penderecki—De natura sonoris No.1;
  Flourescences
Jones—Let Us Now Praise Famous Men
Rush, L.—Cloud Messenger
Leeuw, R. de—Abschied
Keuris—Sinfonia
Knussen—Choral

21'–40'

Balakirev—King Lear: Incidental Music
Mussorgsky—Pictures at an Exhibition
  [Stokowski]
Janáček—Sinfonietta

Pierné—Cydalise et le chèvre-pied:
  Suite No.1
Strauss, R.—Heldenleben
Glazunov—Kremlin
Koechlin—Course de printemps
Scriabin—Poem of Ecstasy;
  Prometheus [solo pf]
Ives—Symphony No.4 (Performance
  Edition) [chorus, solo pf]
Respighi—Feste romane
Bartók—Kossuth; Wooden Prince: Suite
Stravinsky—Rite of Spring
Varèse—Amériques [both]
Ibert—Chevalier errant: Symphonic Suite
Gershwin—Porgy and Bess: Symphonic
  Picture
Harris, Roy—Symphony No.9
Revueltas—Noche de los Mayas: Suite
  [Limantour]
Tippett—New Year: Suite
Schuman, Wm.—Symphony No.7
Stockhausen—Gruppen
Ayers—and they gathered on Mount
  Carmel
Elfman—Serenada Schizophrana [solo S,
  female chorus]

Over 40'

Wagner, Richard—Ring: An Orchestral
  Adventure; Ring ohne Worte
Mahler—Symphonies Nos.1, 2 [chor,
  solos SA], 3 [solo A, female chor],
  6, 7, 9; Symphony No.10 [Carpenter or
  Mazetti]
Strauss, R.—Alpensinfonie;
  Josephslegende; Symphonia domestica

Scriabin—Divine Poem
Ives—Universe Symphony [Porter or
  Reinhard]
Schmidt, F.—Symphony No.2
Schoenberg—Pelléas und Mélisande
Glière—Symphony No.3
Ravel—Daphnis et Chloé [wordless
  chorus]
Stravinsky—Firebird
Shostakovich—Symphonies Nos.4, 7
Adams, John—Naive and Sentimental
  Music

[38]
INSTRUMENTATION
INDETERMINATE

Ruggles—Angels
Cage—Atlas eclipticalis
Feldman—Intersection No.1;
  Marginal Intersection
Glass—Music in Similar Motion

[39]
MULTIPLE ORCHESTRAS

Gabrieli—Canzona
Vivaldi—Concerto, Violin & Double
  Orchestra, RV 582; Concerto, Violin &
  Double Str Orch, RV 583; Concerto, 4
  Violins, 4 Recorders, RV 585
Handel—Concerti a due cori, Nos.1-3
Bach, J.C.—Symphonies, op.18, nos.1 & 5
Mozart, W.A.—Serenade No.8

Spohr—Symphony No.7
Nielsen, Carl—Aladdin: 7 pieces
Vaughan Williams—Concerto grosso;
  Partita
Ives—Universe Symphony, S.6 [Austin
  realization]
Bartók—Music for Strings, Percussion and
  Celesta
Martin—Petite symphonie concertante
Martinů—Double Concerto; Sinfonia
  concertante
Hindemith—Symphonia serena
Tippett—Concerto for Double String
  Orch; Fantasia concertante [concertino:
  2vn, vc]
Carter—Symphony of Three Orchestras
Brant—Desert Forests; Verticals
  Ascending
Dutilleux—Symphony No.2
Delden—Concerto per due orchestre
  d'archi
Henze—Symphony No.6
Stockhausen—Gruppen
Shchedrin—Geometry of Sound
Penderecki—Emanations
Maxwell Davies—St. Thomas Wake
Schnittke—Moz-Art à la Haydn
  [2 solo vn]
Amy—D'un espace déployé
  [solo S & 2pf]
Bolcom—Fives [solo vn & pf]
Davies, Victor—Dream Variations
Kolb—Soundings
Tavener—Mystagogía
Rodríguez—Sinfonía à la mariachi
Chilcott—Tandem
Tan—Orchestral Theatre II [solo B]

APPENDIX E
ORCHESTRAL WORKS LISTED BY DURATION

This appendix is useful if you are looking for a particular sort of piece to fill out a program—a French baroque work, let us say, of about eight minutes in duration. Here is how it works.

Orchestral pieces (not accompaniments) are grouped here by duration. Within each group they are subdivided according the the composer's nationality; and within each subdivision they are listed *chronologically* by composer's birthdate. Thus the French baroque piece mentioned above would appear in the 6'-10' group, the "French & Belgian" subdivision, near the beginning of the list: Lully, Lalande, Couperin, Rameau and Leclair are possibilities.

The composer's nationality is normally taken to be the country of origin, though there are exceptions (Lully, though Italian by birth, is inextricably bound with the history of French music). See also Appendix H, in which composers are listed under more than one nationality, where appropriate.

For complete information on any work, refer to the main alphabetical listing by composer. Initial articles in all languages are omitted from the titles in this appendix.

5' OR LESS

American (United States)

Reinagle—Madison's March & Mrs. Madison's Minuet
Gottschalk—Souvenir de Porto Rico
Foote—Irish Folk Song
Sousa—Humoresque on "Swanee"
Albéniz—Navarra
Villanueva—Vals poético
Granados—Goyescas: Intermezzo
Joplin—Entertainer; Maple Leaf Rag; Ragtime Dance
Ives—Charlie Rutlage; Circus Band; "Country Band" March; Evening; Fugue in Four Keys; Gong on the Hook and Ladder; Hymn; Over the Pavements; Overture and March "1776"; Postlude in F; Tone Roads No.1, No.3; Yale-Princeton Football Game (2 versions)
Kreisler—Liebesfreud

Falla—Amor brujo: Ritual Fire Dance; Vida breve: Spanish Dance No.1
Ruggles—Angels
Stokowski,—Traditional Slavic Christmas Music
Griffes—Bacchanale; Clouds
Riegger—New Dance
Taylor—Fanfare for Russia
Becker—Two Pieces:
  1. Among the Reeds and Rushes, 2. Mountains
Collins—Cowboy's Breakdown; Lament and Jig; Lil' David Play on Yo' Harp; Valse elegante
Piston—Bicentennial Fanfare; Fanfare for the Fighting French
Wagenaar—Fanfare for Airmen
Sowerby—Comes Autumn Time
Still—Fanfare for American War Heroes; Lenox Avenue: Blues; Out of the Silence
Hanson—Before the Dawn; Fanfare for the Signal Corps
Thomson, V.—Bugles and Birds; Fanfare for France; Fugue and Chorale on

"Yankee Doodle"; Louisiana Story: Boy Fights Alligator; Sea Piece with Birds
Cowell—Ancient Desert Drone; Ballad; Fanfare for the Forces of our Latin American Allies; Polyphonica for Small Orchestra
Bacon—Bearwalla; Muffin Man
Gershwin—Of Thee I Sing: Overture; Promenade
Chávez—Baile
Copland—Billy the Kid: Prairie Night & Celebration Dance, Waltz (Billy and His Sweetheart); Ceremonial Fanfare; Down a Country Lane; Fanfare for the Common Man; Inaugural Fanfare; John Henry; Jubilee Variation; Rodeo: Corral Nocturne, Saturday Night Waltz; Rodeo: Hoe-Down; Symphony No.1: Prelude; Variations on a Shaker Melody
Fuleihan—Fanfare for the Medical Corps
Crawford—Andante for Strings; Rissolty Rossolty

[5' or less]

Wolpe—Chamber Piece No.2; Man from Midian: Moses Meets Aaron & March

Styne—Gypsy: Overture

Creston—Airborne Suite: Night in Mexico, Afternoon in Montreal; Fanfare for Paratroopers; Rumor

Anderson, Leroy—Classical Jukebox; Goldilocks: Overture

Carter—Elegy

Barber—Commando March; Die natali: Silent Night; Vanessa: Intermezzo, Under the Willow Tree

Schuman, Wm.—Orchestra Song

McBride—Pumpkin-Eater's Little Fugue

Dahl—Quodlibet

Gillis—Short Overture to an Unwritten Opera

Brant—Galaxy 2

Dello Joio—Air; Arietta

Etler—Elegy

Gould—American Ballads: 1. Star-Spangled Overture, 3. Jubilo, 5. Saratoga Quickstep; American Salute; Cheers

Fine, Irving—Blue Towers

Perle—New Fanfares

Shulman—Bop Gavotte; Elizabethan Legend; Four Moods; Hup-Two-Three-Four; In Memoriam Sophie; Interstate 90; Minuet; Minuet for Moderns; Nocturne; Popocatepetl; Portrait of Lisa; Ricky-Tick Serenade; Viennese Lace

Ward—Processional March

Bernstein—Overtures to: Candide, West Side Story; Slava!

La Montaine—Summer's Day

Piazzolla—Oblivion

Foss—American Fanfare

Chou—Soliloquy of a Bhiksuni; Yü ko

Kraft—Simple Introduction to the Orchestra

Pinkham—Catacoustical Measures

Frackenpohl—Short Overture

Starer—Elegy for Strings

Duffy—American Fantasy Overture; Freedom Overture; Heritage Fanfare and Chorale

Adler, S.—Art Creates Artists; Centennial; Summer Stock

Flagello—Aria sinfonica; Goldoni Overture

London—Imaginary Invalid: Overture

Muczynski—Dovetail Overture

Nelson, Ron—Sarabande: For Katharine in April

Deussen—American Hymn

Hoag—After-Intermission Overture

Herman—Overtures to: Cage aux folles, Hello Dolly!, Mack & Mabel, Mame, Milk and Honey

Harmon—Fanfare for Our Common Earth; Prelude & Fugue for String Orchestra

Jones—Elegy; Fanfare and Celebration (2 versions); Festival Fanfare; Hear the Music; Parliament of Owls

Rands—Fanfare for a Festival

Schickele—Fanfare for the Common Cold

Rudow—Fanfare for My Hero

Albert, Adrienne—Courage; Fanfare

Wilson—Houston Fanfare

Corigliano—Campane di Ravello; Jamestown Hymn; Midsummer Fanfare; Salute; To Music; Utah Fanfare

Tower—Fanfare for the Uncommon Woman [3]

Zwilich—Openings; Upbeat

Hailstork—Celebration; Fanfare on "Amazing Grace"

Perera—Saints: Choirs, Joyful Noise, Marching In

Peck—Don't Tread on Me; Freedom Fanfare

Zaimont—JoyDance in Spring

Rodríguez—Salutation Rag

Adams, John—Short Ride in a Fast Machine; Tromba lontana

Kechley—Funky Chicken

Mauldin—Dawn at San Juan Mesa; Entrada; Valley at Annacarla

Walker, Gwyneth—Bicycle Waltz; Fanfare for the Family Farm; Open the Door

Beckel—Celebrations; Christmas; Make a Joyful Noise; Musica Mobilis; Night Visions: The American Dream

Chiarappa—Gettysburg Address

Locklair—In Memory; Phoenix and Again

Rouse—Infernal Machine

Stucky—Jeu de timbres

Warshauer—Beyond the Horizon

Larsen, L.—Northern Star Fanfare

Ayers—Fanfare and Carol for Christmas

Galbraith—Festive Violet Pulse

Wendel—Carol of the Bells; Commemoration; Fanfare for Freedom; Fantasia on "Yerousalaim shel zahav"; In the Manger; Parade of the Percussionists; Ride of the Headless Horseman; Take Flight

Asia—Gateways

Davidson—Mexico-Bolivar Tango

Sierra—Joyous Overture; Saludo

Daugherty—Metropolis Symphony: Oh Lois!

Rimelis—Cool Ghoul; Phonefare

Adolphe—Three Pieces: 2. Rainbow, 3. T-D-T

Amundson—Angels' Dance; Joyous Noel

Curiale—Sea of Tranquility

Rush, T.R.—Spirit of Freedom

Dorff—Fanfare Overture; Fast Walk; It Takes Four to Tango; Lamentations; Pachelbel's Christmas

Fine, Marshall—Missouriana

Kallman—Holiday Hoedown

McCarter—Prelude and Excursion

Sartor—Black Ball Counts Double; Dies irae; Metamorphic Fanfare

Cotton—Elegy

Karidoyanes—Yerakína

Lang—International Business Machine

Tan—Atonal Rock 'N Roll: Of Youth

Amaya—Parasol

Heitzeg—Blue Liberty; Wounded Fields

Golijov—ZZ's Dream

Abels—Outburst

Adamo—Lysistrata: Overture; Prepositions and the Names of Fish

Higdon—Celebration Fanfare; Machine; Spirit; String; To the Point; Wind Shear

[5' or less]

Richman—American Fanfare; Brentwood Rag; Jalopy and Blues; Kol Nidre; Playground Escapades; Western Fanfare

Thomas, Augusta Read—Of Paradise and Light

Wittry, Diane—Concerto for Homemade Instruments

Stephenson—American Fanfare; Printemps; Stars and Stripes Fanfare

Amrhein—Serenade

Boyer—On Music's Wings: Silver Fanfare; Rolling River

Bates—Attack Decay Sustain Release

Eastern European

Gluck—Overtures to: Iphigénie en Aulide, Orfeo ed Euridice; Orfeo ed Euridice: Dance of the Furies; Overture, D major; Sinfonia, D major

Chopin—Mazurka No.7; Polonaise, op.40, no.1

Liszt—Ungarischer Sturmmarsch

Moniuszko—Halka: Mazur

Dvořák—Festival March; Humoresque

Lysenko—Taras Bulba: Overture

Janáček—Sokol Fanfare

Dohnányi—Schleier der Pierrette: Pierrot's Complaint of Love, Walzer-Reigen, Lustiger Trauermarsch, Menuett

Bartók—Dances of Transylvania

Kodály—Háry János: Intermezzo

Lutoslawski—Overture for Strings; Postludium; Prelude for GSMD

Husa—Celebration Fanfare; Overture

Kilar—Pan Tadeusz: Polonaise

Pärt—Silouans Song

Skoryk—Melody

French & Belgian

Rameau—Zaïs: Overture

Meyerbeer—Prophète: Coronation March

Berlioz—Damnation de Faust: Dance of the Sylphs, Rákóczy March, Will-o'-the-Wisp; Roméo et Juliette:

Introduction; Te Deum: Marche, Prelude; Troyens: Marche troyenne

Gounod—Colombe: Entr'acte; Mors et vita: Judex

Offenbach—Overtures to: Île de Tulipatan, Périchole, Vie parisienne; '66'

Franck—Psyché: Psyché enlevée par les Zéphirs, Les Jardins d'Eros

Saint-Saëns—Rigaudon; Suite algérienne: Marche militaire française

Delibes—Coppélia: Entr'acte & Waltz, Valse de la poupée & Czardas

Bizet—Pecheurs de perles: Overture

Chabrier—Bourée fantasque; Gwendoline: Prelude, Act II; Habanera; Joyeuse marche; Roi malgré lui: Danse slav

Massenet—Hérodiade: Prelude, Act III; Manon: Minuet & Gavotte

Fauré—Shylock: Nocturne

Debussy—Berceuse héroïque; Clair de lune; Martyre de Saint Sébastien: Chambre magique, Two Fanfares; Plus que lente; Roi Lear; Triomphe de Bacchus

Pierné—Cydalise: Entrance of the Little Fauns; Marche des petits soldats de plomb; Serenade, op.7

Ropartz—Serenade

Dukas—Péri: Fanfare

Satie—Cinq grimaces; Gymnopédie No.2; Trois petites pièces montées

Roussel—Fanfare pour un sacre païen

Hahn—Mozart: Overture

Laparra—Habanera: Prélude

Varèse—Hyperprism; Tuning Up

Ibert—Hommage à Mozart

Milhaud—Genesis Suite: Cain and Abel; Murder of a Great Chief of State; Ouverture méditerranéene; Symphonies de chambre Nos.1, 2, 3, .5

Boulanger, L.—D'un matin de printemps

German & Austrian

Pachelbel—Canon

Bach, J.S.—Bist du bei mir; Fugue, BWV 577; Fugue,

BWV 578; Jesu, Joy of Man's Desiring; Komm, Gott, Schöpfer, heiliger Geist; Komm süsser Tod; Prelude & Fugue, BWV 558; Schmücke dich, o liebe Seele; Sheep May Safely Graze

Handel—Overtures to: Acis and Galatea, Alcina, Alexander's Feast, Rinaldo, Solomon; Overture, HWV 337; Solomon: Entrance of the Queen of Sheba; Xerxes: Largo

Haydn, F.J.—March for the Royal Society of Musicians

Bach, J.C.—Clemenza di Scipione, W. G10: Overture

Haydn, M.—Andromeda ed Perseo, MH 438: Overture; Symphony, MH 181

Mozart, W.A.—Overtures to: Apollo et Hyacinthus, Bastien und Bastienne, Betulia liberata, Clemenza di Tito, Così fan tutte, Finta giardiniera, Idomeneo, Nozze di Figaro, Re pastore, Schauspieldirektor; Contradances, K.535, K.587, K.603, K.610; Entführung aus dem Serail: March; Idomeneo: Marches, D major [No.8], C major [No.14], F major [No.25]; Marches, K.62, K.189, K.214, K.215, K.237, K.248, K.249, K.290, K.445, K.544; Minuet, K.409; Turkish March

Beethoven—Gratulations-Menuet; Prometheus: Overture; Ruinen von Athen: Turkish March; Zapfenstreich March

Weber, C.M.—Abu Hassan: Overture; Drei Pintos: Entr'acte; Silvana: Overture

Schubert—Grande marche héroïque; Marche hongroise; Marche militaire; Symphony, D.2b; Overtures to: Teufel als Hydraulicus, Zwillingsbrüder

Strauss, Joh., Sr.—Radetzky March

Mendelssohn—Athalie: Kriegsmarsch der Priester; Midsummer Night's Dream: Intermezzo, Scherzo, Wedding March; Octet, Strings

Schumann, R.—Träumerei

[5' or less]

Wagner, Richard—Lohengrin: Prelude, Act III; Lohengrin: Elsa's Procession; Tannhäuser: Prelude, Act III; Walküre: Ride of the Valkyries [3 versions]

Bruckner—March in D minor

Strauss, Joh., Jr.—Egyptischer Marsch; Figaro-Polka; Fledermaus: Du und du; Leichtes Blut; Perpetuum mobile; Pizzicato Polka; Tritsch-Tratsch-Polka; Unter Donner und Blitz; Ver- gnügungszug; Zigeunerbaron: Einzugsmarsch

Strauss, Jos.—Frauenherz

Brahms—Hungarian Dances Nos.2, 7 (arr. Hallén)

Brahms—Hungarian Dance No.4 (arr. Juon)

Strauss, E.—Bahn frei

Humperdinck—Hänsel und Gretel: Hexenritt, Knusper- walzer; Königskinder: Introduction to Act II

Reznicek—Donna Diana: Overture

Strauss, R.—Wiener Philharmoniker Fanfare

Schreker—Intermezzo

Hindemith—Marsch über den alten Schweizerton; Rag Time; When Lilacs Last in the Door-Yard Bloom'd: Prelude

Korngold—Overtures to: Captain Blood, Schneemann

Italian

Gabrieli—Canzon XVI

Monteverdi—Orfeo: Overture; Orfeo: Toccata & ritornelli

Albinoni—Concerto, op.5, no.4, G major

Vivaldi—Concerto for Orchestra, RV 151

Veracini—Aria schiavona

Leo—Santa Elena al Calvario: Sinfonia

Galuppi—Concerto a quattro, No.2, G major

Paisiello—Nina: Overture

Boccherini—Minuet in A, G.275; Overture, G.521

Cimarosa—Overtures to: Giorno felice, Maestro di cappella, Nemeci generosi

Paganini—Moto perpetuo

Rossini—Signor Bruschino: Overture; Sinfonia di Bologna; Sinfonia di Odense

Donizetti—Sinfonia for Winds

Verdi—Ballo in maschera: Preludio; Traviata: Preludes to Act I & Act III

Bolzoni—Gavotte; Minuetto

Leoncavallo—Pagliacci: Intermezzo

Puccini—Manon Lescaut: Prelude, Act II; Manon Lescaut: Intermezzo, Act III; Suor Angelica: Intermezzo

Mascagni—Amico Fritz: Intermezzo; Cavalleria rusticana: Intermezzo

Busoni—Turandot: Verzweiflung und Ergebung

Wolf-Ferrari—Amore medico: Intermezzo; Gioielli della Madonna: Intermezzos Nos.1 & 2; Segreto di Susanna: Overture

Respighi—Serenata, p.54

Menotti—Lewisohn Stadium Fanfare

Berio—Encore

Russian

Glinka—Life for the Tsar: Krakoviak; Ruslan and Lyudmila: Overture

Borodin—Prince Igor: Polovtsian March

Mussorgsky—Fair at Sorochinski: Introduction, Gopak; Khovantchina: Introduction; Khovantchina: Prince Galitzin's Journey; Scherzo, B-flat major

Tchaikovsky—Eugene Onegin: Polonaise; Festival Coronation March; Marche solennelle; Mazeppa: Danse cosaque; Suite No.1: Marche miniature

Rimsky-Korsakov— Dubinushka; Legend of the Invisible City of Kitezh: Massacre at Kerzhentz; Mlada: Procession of the Nobles; Snow Maiden: Dance of the Skomorokhi; Tale of the Tsar Saltan: Flight of the Bumblebee

Liadov—Baba-Yaga

Glazunov—Cortège solennel No.2; Seasons: 2. Spring; Seasons Three Movements; Serenades Nos.1 & 2

Kalinnikov—Chanson triste

Rachmaninoff—Prelude, op.3 no.2

Glière—Red Poppy: Russian Sailors' Dance

Stravinsky—Canon; Circus Polka; Fanfare for a New Theatre; Feu d'artifice; Greeting Prelude; Ragtime; Scherzo à la russe; Song of the Volga Boatmen; Tango

Prokofiev—Love for Three Oranges: March & Scherzo; March, op.99

Mosolov—Iron Foundry

Khachaturian—Gayane: Dance of the Rose Maidens, Lullaby, Sabre Dance; Colas Breugnon: Overture; Comedians: Galop

Kabalevsky—Overture pathétique

Shostakovich—Age of Gold: Polka; Tahiti Trot

Shchedrin—Symphonic Fanfares

Spanish & Latin American

Albéniz—Navarra

Villanueva—Vals poético

Granados—Goyescas: Intermezzo

Falla—Amor brujo: Ritual Fire Dance; Vida breve: Spanish Dance No.1

Chávez—Baile

Piazzolla—Oblivion

Amaya—Parasol

Golijov—ZZ's Dream

United Kingdom

Purcell—Canon on a Ground Bass; Funeral Music for Queen Mary; Indian Queen: Trumpet Overture; Trumpet Prelude; Trumpet Voluntary

Boyce—Overture (Ode for the New Year [1758 & 1772]); Symphony No.2

Sullivan—Overtures to: H.M.S. Pinafore, Yeomen of the Guard

Elgar—Chanson de matin; Chanson de nuit; Crown of India: March of the Mogul Emperors; Elegy, op.58; Pomp and Circumstance: Nos.1-5; Salut d'amour

[5' or less]

Delius—Air and Dance;
  Hassan: Intermezzo &
  Serenade; Irmelin: Prelude;
  Marche caprice; Sleigh Ride;
  Two Pieces: Summer Night
  on the River
Vaughan Williams—Fantasia
  on "Greensleeves"; Prelude
  "49th Parallel"; Running Set;
  Wasps: March Past of the
  Kitchen Utensils
Holst—In the Bleak Midwinter
Coleridge-Taylor—Christmas
  Overture; Novelettes Nos.1,
  3, 4
Bax—Mediterranean
Howells—Penguinski
Benjamin, A.—Two Jamaican
  Pieces
Goossens—Fanfare for the
  Merchant Marine; Tam
  O'Shanter
Jacob—Barber of Seville Goes
  to the Devil
Finzi—Prelude
Britten—Building of the
  House; Paul Bunyan:
  Overture
Arnold—Roots of Heaven
Maxwell Davies—Sir Charles
  His Pavan; Threnody on a
  Plainsong; Welcome to
  Orkney
Bennett, Richard R.—Birthday
  Music; Chelsea Reach;
  Troubadour Music
Tann—Through the Echoing
  Timber; Water's Edge:
  Toward Dusk
Knussen—Fanfares for
  Tanglewood; Flourish with
  Fireworks
Turnage—Snapshots

Other Nationalities

Grieg—Bell Ringing; Erotik
Halvorsen—Entry of the
  Boyars
Nielsen, Carl—Maskarade:
  Overture, Hanedans
Sibelius—Andante festivo;
  Canzonetta; Kuolema: Scene
  with Cranes; Pan and Echo;
  Romance; Scènes historiques:
  All' overtura, Minnelied;
  Tempest: Prelude; Valse
  chevaleresque; Valse lyrique
Järnefelt—Berceuse;
  Praeludium

Stenhammar—Sången:
  Mellanspel
Alfvén—Bergakungen
Grainger—Children's March;
  Immovable Do; Irish Tune
  from County Derry; Molly on
  the Shore; Shepherd's Hey
Riisager—Little Overture
Glanville-Hicks—Gymnopédie
  No.1
Ran—Chicago Skyline
Saariaho—Asteroid 4179:
  Toutatis; Song for Betty
Chen Yi—KC Capriccio
Buhr—Akasha; Chant of Water
  and Sky; Chant of Wind and
  Thunder; this is the murmur
  of yearning
Sheng—China Dreams:
  Fanfare
O'Boyle—Country Kazoo
  Overture; Olympia Australis;
  Ragtime Overture; River
  Symphony: Fanfare; She
  Moved Through the Fair ;
  Silent Movie Music; Song
  Bird: Scissor Dance
Koch—Adventures of Sinbad
Dorman—Chorale
Rival—Elegy; Lullaby
Goulet—Citius, altius, fortius!

6'–10'

American (United States)

Fry—Dying Soldier;
  Evangeline: Overture
Buck—Festival Overture
Paine—As You Like It:
  Overture; Oedipus tyrannus:
  Prelude; Poseidon and
  Amphitrite
Chadwick—Elegy; Euterpe;
  Pastoral Prelude; Rip Van
  Winkle: Overture
Sousa—Glass-Blowers:
  Overture
Strong—Chorale on a Theme
  of Leo Hassler
Shelley—Santa Claus Overture
MacDowell—Saracens
Loeffler—Villanelle du diable
Converse—Ormazd
Ives—Central Park in the
  Dark; Chromâtimelôdtune;
  New England Holidays:
  Washington's Birthday,
  Decoration Day, Fourth of
  July; Set of Pieces; Set No.1;

Symphony No.4: Fugue;
  Unanswered Question;
  Variations on "America"
Ruggles—Men and Mountains
  (2 versions); Organum;
  Portals
Bloch, E.—In the Night
Cadman—American Suite;
  Oriental Rhapsody
Griffes—White Peacock
Riegger—Dance Rhythms;
  Music for Orchestra; Study in
  Sonority
Price—Dances in the
  Canebrakes
Weiss—American Life
Grofé—Kentucky Derby
Moore, Douglas—Overture on
  an American Tune
Piston—Pine Tree Fantasy;
  Symphonic Prelude; Toccata
Slonimsky—My Toy Balloon
Rathaus—Praeludium and
  Gigue
Still—American Scene: The
  East (Suite 1), The Old West
  (Suite 3), The Far West
  (Suite 4); Bells; Black
  Bottom; Festive Overture; In
  memoriam; Old California;
  Serenade
White—Five Miniatures for
  Orchestra
Thomson, V.—Pilgrims and
  Pioneers; Seine at Night;
  Wheat Field at Noon
Cowell—Carol for Orchestra;
  Hymn and Fuguing Tune No.
  2, No.3, No.5, No.10, No.16
Bacon—Elegy; Nantucket
  Fling
Gershwin—Cuban Overture;
  Girl Crazy: Overture; Let 'Em
  Eat Cake: Overture; Lullaby
Harris, Roy—Chorale; Elegy
  for Orchestra; Epilogue to
  Profiles in Courage—J.F.K.;
  Horn of Plenty; Ode to
  Consonance; When Johnny
  Comes Marching Home
Antheil—Jazz Symphony
Copland—Danzón cubano;
  Outdoor Overture; Preamble
  for a Solemn Occasion;
Luening—Prelude to a Hymn
  Tune by William Billings;
  Synthesis
Rodgers—Carousel: The
  Carousel Waltz; Slaughter on
  Tenth Avenue; Sound of
  Music [symphonic picture]

[6'–10']

Wolpe—Chamber Piece No.1;
Two Studies
Finney—Hymn, Fuguing Tune
& Holiday
Gutche—Epimetheus USA;
Holofernes Overture
Swanson—Music for Strings;
Night Music
Carter—Holiday Overture
Siegmeister—American
Holiday; Lonesome Hollow
Barber—Adagio for Strings;
Essay No.1, No.2; Fadograph
of a Yestern Scene; Music for
a Scene from Shelley; Night
Flight; School for Scandal:
Overture; Serenade, op.1
Schuman, Wm.—Amaryllis;
American Festival Overture;
Circus Overture; Newsreel
Hovhaness—Alleluia and
Fugue; Armenian Rhapsody
No.2; Celestial Fantasy;
Prelude and Quadruple Fugue
Cage—Suite for Toy Piano
(orch)
Raksin—Toy Concertino
Brant—Verticals Ascending
Dello Joio—Five Images for
Orchestra
Gould—American Ballads: 2.
Amber Waves, 4. Memorials,
6. Hymnal; Notes of
Remembrance; Symphonette
No.2
Read—First Overture; Night
Flight; Prelude & Toccata
Fine, Irving—Diversions for
Orchestra; Serious Song;
Toccata concertante
Kubik—Gerald McBoing
Boing
Diamond—Elegy in Memory
of Ravel
Perle—Adagio for Orchestra;
Six Bagatelles
Persichetti—Dance Overture;
Serenade No.1
Shulman—Ben Franklin Suite;
Laurentian Overture; Prelude;
Ripe for Plucking; Suite;
Suite Miniature; Threnody;
Top Brass; Waltzes
Surinach—Drama jondo;
Fandango; Feria magica
Babbitt—All Set; Composition
for Twelve Instruments;
Correspondences
Weber, Ben—Dolmen
Kay, U.—Of New Horizons

Ward—By the Way of
Memories; City of Oaks;
Concert Music; Euphony;
Hymn and Celebration; Hymn
to the Night; Invocation and
Toccata; Jonathon and the
Gingery Snare; Jubilation;
Prairie Overture
Bernstein—Fancy Free: Three
Dance Variations; Prelude,
Fugue and Riffs; West Side
Story: Selections
Rochberg—Time-Span II
Kirchner—Orchestra Piece
Bergsma—Carol on Twelfth
Night; Music on a Ouiet
Theme
Bavicchi—Mont Blanc
Overture
Foss—Ode; Salomon Rossi
Suite
Walker, George—Lyric for
Strings; Overture in Praise of
Folly
Chou—All in the Spring Wind;
And the Fallen Petals;
Landscapes
Mennin—Canto
Rorem—Eagles; Pilgrims;
Sinfonia
Benson—Chants and Graces;
Five Brief Encounters
Lees—Spectrum
Mechem—Jayhawk
Schuller—Dramatic Overture
Smith, Hale—Contours
Duffy—Three Jewish Portraits
Feldman—Atlantis; Marginal
Intersection; …Out of "Last
Pieces"; Structures for
Orchestra
Floyd—In Celebration
Diemer—Homage to
Tchaikovsky
Martirano—Contrasto
Kay—Drifting on Wind and
Currents; Elegy for String
Orchestra
Cunningham—Lullabye for a
Jazz Baby
Mamlok—Grasshoppers
Nelson, Ron—Savannah River
Holiday
Previn—Overture to a Comedy
Turok—Joplin Overture
Wyner—Epilogue for
Orchestra
Amram—Autobiography for
Strings
Felciano—Galactic Rounds
Van de Vate—Adagio for
Orchestra; Gema Jawa;

Variations for Chamber
Orchestra
Caviani—Ondee
Deussen—Ascent to Victory;
Carmel by-the-Sea; Field in
Pennsylvania; Peninsula
Suite; Tico; Transit of Venus;
Trinity Alps
Martino—Divertisements for
Youth Orchestra
Biggs—Passacaglia; Pastiche;
Salutation; Sousaphernalia
Chance—Elegy
Zaninelli—Americana; Battle
Hymn of the Republic;
Capriccio spiritoso; Jubilate;
Through Eudora's Eyes
Bilik—American Civil War
Fantasy
Reynolds—Graffiti; Wedge
Tull—Capriccio; Final
Covenant
Harmon—Suite of Migrations:
Flight of the Monarch,
Geese—Majestic Travelers
Jones—Aurum aurorae;
Benediction; Organ
Benediction; Overture for a
City
Riley—Half-Wolf Dances Mad
in Moonlight
Schickele—Celebration with
Bells; Elegy
Rudow—Dark Waters of Elba;
Dark Waters of the
Chesapeake; Spirit of
America
Schwartz—Texture
Albert, Adrienne—Interiors
Glass—Arioso no.2; Company
Bolcom—Commedia for
(Almost) 18th-Century
Orchestra; Ragomania!
Corigliano—Elegy for
Orchestra; Fancy on a Bach
Air; Promenade Overture;
Snapshot; Voyage (strings)
Harbison—Remembering
Gatsby: Foxtrot
Wuorinen—Grand Bamboula
Stock—Capriccio
Zwilich—Celebration for
Orchestra; Jubilation
Earnest—Chasing the Sun;
Southern Exposure
Singleton—After Fallen
Crumbs
Zappa—Durpree's Paradise
Hailstork—American Port of
Call
Proto—Fantasy on the Saints
Stewart—Overture in F

[6'–10']

Marshall—Fog Tropes

Iannaccone—Lysistrata; West End Express

Lauridsen—O magnum mysterium

León, Tania—Batá; Horizons

Schwantner—Freeflight

Hartway—Freedom Festival

Peck—Jack and Jill at Bunker Hill; Playing With Style

Zaimont—Elegy for Strings; Tarantelle

Avshalomov, D.—Elegy; Siege

McGlaughlin—Bela's Bounce

Rodríguez—Gathering of Angels; Hot Buttered Rhumba; Piñata

Adams, John—Christian Zeal and Activity; Lollapalooza

Horwood—Do You Live for Weekends?; Three Interludes

Kechley—Karasuma; Tuahku

Mauldin—High Places; Kokopelli; Last Musician of Ur; Music for the Mountain Air; Three Dances from Chaco Canyon; Three Jemez Landscapes

Ott—Water Garden

Walker, Gwyneth—Match Point; Overture of Diamonds; Suite for Strings

Beckel—Gospel Christmas; Imagination; Overture for a New Age; Toccata for Orchestra

Gellis—Duplex; Hymn

Welcher—Zion

Locklair—Phoenix; Irish Suite #1

Lofstrom—Two Soldiers: Prelude & Wedding Scene

Rouse—Bump; Nevill Feast

Stucky—Funeral Music for Queen Mary

Warshauer—Like Streams in the Desert; Revelation

Larsen, L.—Overture for the End of a Century

Ayers—Veni Emmanuel

Davis—Jacob's Ladder; Notes from the Underground

Galbraith—Fantasy; Tormenta del sur

Wendel—Chanukah Overture; Christmas a la Valse; Towers of Light

Actor—Circus Symphonicus; Divertimento for Small Orchestra; Opening Remarks

Schaffner—Whirlwind Tour of the Orchestra

Asia—What About It

McTee—Circuits; Finish Line; Tempus fugit; Timepiece; Unquestioned Answer

Sierra—Alegría; Tropicalia: Celebration

Coleman, L.R.—In Good King Charles's Golden Days

Daugherty—Asclepius; Blue Like an Orange; Dead Elvis; Metropolis Symphony: Krypton; Route 66

Picker—Old and Lost Rivers

Rimelis—Please Turn Your Cell Phones On!

Adolphe—I'm Inclined to New Music

Amundson—Rejoicing; Sola gratia

Costa—Vignette

Frazelle—From the Air; Swans at Pungo Lake

Gross—Watchman, Tell Us of the Night

Danielpour—Toward the Splendid City; Washington Speaks

Dorff—Blast Off!; Goldilocks and the Three Bears; Three Fun Fables: The Tortoise and the Hare

Drattell—Syzygy

Gordon—Romeo; Sunshine of Your Love

McCarter—Opening Ideas

Mercurio—Mercurial Overture

Oliverio, J.—Go Gently My Friend; UnStoppable

Phillips, P.S.—Brownian Motion

Sartor—Reveries

Smith, Kile—Hymn and Fugue No.1

Bartholomew—Ah, My Children; Sunshine Music

Bremer—Early Light

Karidoyanes—Café Neon

Knehans—lamentation

Lang, David—how to pray

Lentini—Dreamscape; Sinfonia di festa

Wolfe, Julia—Tell Me Everything; Window of Vulnerability

Heitzeg—Aqua; Mustang

Ince—Before Infrared; Hot, Red, Cold, Vibrant

Janello—At the Sea of Clouds

Kernis—New Era Dance; Too Hot Toccata

Wachsman—Fanfares for String Orchestra

Torke—Javelin

Abels—Affectionate Objects; Dance for Martin's Dream; Global Warming

Higdon—Fanfare ritmico; Peachtree Street; Shine; SkyLine

McLoskey—Chanson pour cordes; post- [sic]

Richman—Be a Composer; Christmas Wish: Reindeer Variations; Colonial Liberty Overture; Hanukkah Festival Overture; Overture to Blanche; United Symphony

Thomas, Augusta Read—Aureole; Ceremonial; Helios Choros I

Wittry—after the rain

Guzzo—Fanfare for Mountains and Peace

Stephenson—Celebration Overture; Concertino and Fanfare; Ode to Peace

Boyer—Celebration Overture; Festivities; Phoenix

Stookey—Big Bang

Hutter—Skyscrapers; Urban Collision

Frank, G.L.—Concertino Cusqueño; Escaramuza

Pann—Slalom

Puts—Hymn to the Sun; Millennium Canons; Network; "… this noble company"

Devore—Heartland; In Common Ragtime

Kuster—Iron Diamond

Petering—Fanfare and Reflection; Lamentations; Swimming Pool; Train & Tower

Bates—Mothership

Tommasini—Letter Home; Sonic Dreams Made Real; Torn Threads Rewoven

Gilbertson—Reflections on Rushmore

Eastern European

Gluck—Alceste: Overture; Iphigénie en Aulide: Overture; Orfeo ed Euridice: Dance of the Blessed Spirits; Sinfonia, G major

Benda, Georg—Symphony No.4, F major

[6'-10']

Stamitz, Carl—Orchestral Quartet, op.1, no.3

Chopin—Nocturne, op.32, no.2

Liszt—Angelus!; Hamlet; Huldigungs-Marsch; Hungarian Rhapsodies Nos.3, 5, 6, & S.244, no.1; Légendes: Die Vogelpredigt; Polonaise No.2; Rákóczi-Marsch

Moniuszko—Overtures to: Halka, Hrabina

Smetana—Bartered Bride: Overture; Hakon Jarl; Ma vlast: 3. Sárka

Minkus—Don Quixote: Pas de deux

Dvořák—Carnival Overture; My Homeland; Nocturne; Prague Waltzes; Slavonic Rhapsody, op.45, no.1

Ivanovici—Donauwellen

Janáček—Adagio; From the House of the Dead: Overture; Jealousy; Moravian Dances

Lehár—Gold und Silber Walzer; Lustige Witwe: Overture

Suk—Meditation on an Old Bohemian Chorale; Toward a New Life

Dohnányi—Schleier der Pierrette: Hochzeitswalzer, Pierrettens Wahnsinnstanz

Bartók—Hungarian Peasant Songs; Two Romanian Dances

Kodály—Háry János: Song

Weiner—Preludio, Notturno e Scherzo diabolico

Martinů—Comedy on the Bridge: Little Suite; Memorial to Lidice; Overture, H.345

Weinberger—Schwanda the Bagpiper: Polka & Fugue

Vladigerov—Improvisation and Toccata, op.36

Farkas—Prelude & Fugue

Tubin—Prélude solennel; Toccata

Bacewicz—Pensieri notturni

Lutoslawski—Chain 1

Panufnik—Heroic Overture; Jagiellonian Triptych; Lullaby; Tragic Overture

Nelhybel—Music for Orchestra

Husa—Pastoral

Serocki—Segmenti

Ligeti—Apparitions; Atmosphères; Ramifications

Baird—Variations Without a Theme

Kilar—Orawa

Górecki—Three Pieces in Old Style

Penderecki—Anaklasis; Awakening of Jacob; De natura sonoris No.1, No.2; Emanations; Polymorphia; To the Victims of Hiroshima

Fiser—Fifteen Prints after Dürer's Apocalypse

Pärt, Arvo—Cantus; Festina lente; Wenn Bach Bienen gezüchtet hätte …

Svoboda—Ex libris; Festive Overture; Overture of the Season; Serenade; Swing Dance; Three Pieces

Sapieyevski—Summer Overture

French & Belgian

Lully—Roland: Suite

Lalande—Symphonie de Noël

Couperin—Sultane: Overture and Allegro

Rameau—Platée: Suite des danses

Leclair—Sonata, D major

Gossec—Christmas Suite

Méhul—Joseph: Overture

Boieldieu—Overtures to: Calife de Bagdad, Dame blanche

Auber—Overtures to: Diamants de la couronne, Domino noir, Fra Diavolo, Lestocq, Marco Spada, Masaniello, Part du diable, Zanetta

Hérold—Zampa: Overture

Meyerbeer—Fackeltanz No.1; Huguenots: Overture

Adam—Overtures to: Brasseur de Preston, Si j'étais roi

Berlioz—Béatrice et Bénédict: Overture; Carnaval romain; Corsaire; Roméo et Juliette: Queen Mab Scherzo; Troyens: Overture, Chasse royale et Orage; Waverley

Thomas, Ambroise—Overtures to: Mignon, Raymond

Alkan—Festin d'Esope; Ouverture de concert

Gounod—Marche funèbre d'une marionette

Litolff—Maximilian Robespierre

Offenbach—Belle Hélène: Overture; Contes d'Hoffmann: Intermezzo & Barcarolle; Orphée aux enfers: Overture

Franck—Eight Short Pieces, Nos.1-4 [as a group], Nos.5-8 [as a group]; Psyché: Sommeil de Psyché, Psyché et Eros

Lalo—Rapsodie norvégienne

Saint-Saëns—Danse macabre; Déluge: Prélude; Marche du couronnement; Marche héroïque; Orient et Occident; Phaéton; Princesse jaune: Overture; Rouet d'Omphale; Samson et Dalila: Bacchanale; Sarabande

Delibes—Coppélia: Prelude & Mazurka, Ballade & Thème slave varié; Lakmé: Airs de danse; Roi l'a dit: Overture

Waldteufel—Patineurs

Chabrier—España; Gwendoline: Overture; Roi malgré lui: Fête polonaise

Massenet—Phèdre: Overture

Fauré—Pavane; Pénélope: Prelude

Indy—Fervaal: Introduction to Act I

Chausson—Tempête: 2 Excerpts

Charpentier, G.—Louise: Prelude to Act III & "Air de Louise"

Debussy—Danse; Enfant prodigue: Cortège et Air de danse; Images: Gigues, Rondes de printemps; Isle joyeuse; Marche écossaise; Prélude à "L'après-midi d'un faune"; Sarabande

Ropartz—Sérénade champêtre

Satie—Deux Préludes posthumes et une gnossienne; Gymnopédies; Jack in the Box

Roussel—Rapsodie flamande; Sinfonietta

Schmitt—Mirages; Rapsodie viennoise; Reflets d'Allemagne; Ronde burlesque

Ravel—Alborada del gracioso; Barque sur l'ocean; Ma Mère l'Oye: Prélude & Danse du rouet; Menuet antique; Pavane pour une infante défunte

Laparra—Habanera: Three Entr'actes; Rythmes espagnols

[6'–10']

Ingelbrecht—Rapsodie de printemps

Varèse—Ionisation; Octandre

Ibert—Bacchanale; Bostoniana; Féerique; Rencontres: 3 pièces de ballet

Honegger—Chant de joie; Mouvement symphonique no.3; Nocturne; Pacific 231; Pastorale d'été; Prélude pour "La Tempête"; Rugby

Milhaud—Funérailles de Phocion; Kentuckiana; Ouverture philharmonique; Symphonie de chambre No.4

Tansman—Toccata; Tombeau de Chopin

Poulenc—Deux marches et un intermède

Messiaen—Sourire

Françaix—Serenade for Small Orchestra

Boulez—Éclat; Notations I-IV

Amy—Mouvements

Scherchen—Hsun

German & Austrian

Schein—Banchetto musicale: Suite No.1

Buxtehude—Chaconne, BuxWV 160

Biber—Battalia

Telemann—Overture, TWV Anh.55:G1

Bach, J.S.—Fantasia & Fugue, BWV 537; Musikalisches Opfer: Ricercare (arr. Webern); Toccata & Fugue

Handel—Overtures to: Agrippina, Alessandro, Belshazzar, Judas Maccabaeus, Occasional Oratorio, Orlando, Samson, Xerxes; Alceste: Instrumental Pieces; Concerti grossi, op.3, nos.1, 5, 6; Prelude & Fugue, HWV 316

Graun—Sinfonia, F major, M.95

Bach, W.F.—Sinfonia, D minor

Frederick II—Symphonies Nos.1 & 2

Bach, C.P.E.—Symphonies, H.661, H.662, H.664, H.665, H.666

Mozart, Leopold—Kindersymphonie

Abel—Symphonies, op.1, nos.5 & 6

Haydn, F.J.—Overtures to: Armida, Isola disabitata, Ritorno di Tobia; Divertimento, Hob.II:46; Kindersymphonie; Scherzandi, Hob.II:33-37; Symphony No.2

Beck, F.I.—Sinfonia, op.10, No.2 & op.13, no.1

Bach, J.C.—Symphonies, op.3, no.; op.6, no.1; op.21, no.3; Symphony, W. G8

Haydn, M.—Pastorello, MH 83; Symphonies, MH 473 & MH 476

Mozart, W.A.—Adagio & Fugue, K.546; Contradances, K.267, K.462, K.609; Divertimento, K.188; Overtures to: Don Giovanni, Entführung aus dem Serail, Finta semplice, Lucio Silla, Mitridate, Zauberflöte; Fantasia, K.608; German Dances, K.567, K.571, K.602, K.605; Marches, K.335; Maurerische Trauermusik; Overture, K.311a; Serenade No.2; Symphonies Nos.4, 5, 10, 11, 22, 23, 24, 26, 32; Symphony, K.81; Symphony, K.111/120; Symphony, K.141a; Symphony, K.196/121

Beethoven—Overtures to: Coriolan, Egmont, Fidelio, König Stephan, Leonore No.1, Namensfeier, Ruinen von Athen

Weber, C.M.—Aufforderung zum Tanz; Beherrscher der Geister; Overtures to: Euryanthe, Freischütz, Jubel, Oberon, Peter Schmoll, Preziosa; Turandot: Overture & March

Marschner, Heinrich—Hans Heiling: Overture

Schubert—Overtures to: Alfonso und Estrella, Claudine von Villa Bella, Fierrabras, Freunde von Salamanka, Häusliche Krieg, Rosamunde, Spiegelritter, Teufels Lustschloss, Vierjährige Posten; also Overtures D.8, D.12, D.26, D.470, D.556, D.590, D.591, D.648; Deutsche Tänze; Symphony, D.615; Symphony, D.759

Lanner—Schönbrunner Walzer; Werber Walzer

Lortzing—Zar und Zimmermann: Overture

Mendelssohn—Overtures to: Athalie, Heimkehr aus der Fremde, Hochzeit des Camacho, Ruy Blas, St. Paul; Hebrides; Märchen von der schönen Melusine; Midsummer Night's Dream: Nocturne; Nocturno [for winds]; Overture for Winds; Sinfonias Nos.1-5; Symphony Movement; Trumpet Overture

Nicolai—Merry Wives of Windsor: Overture

Schumann, R.—Overtures to: Braut von Messina, Genoveva, Hermann und Dorothea, Julius Caesar, Scenen aus Goethes Faust; Fest-Ouvertüre; Manfred: Suite

Flotow—Alessandro Stradella: Overture; Martha: Overture

Wagner, Richard—Christoph Columbus: Overture; Concert Overtures Nos.1-2; Götterdämmerung: Gesang der Rheintöchter, Siegfried's Funeral Music, Siegfried's Rhine Journey; Huldigungs-marsch; Kaisermarsch; König Enzio: Overture; Lohengrin: Prelude, Act I; Meistersinger: Prelude; Rheingold: Entry of the Gods; Rule Britannia; Siegfried: Forest Murmurs (2 versions); Tannhäuser: Arrival of the Guests; Tristan und Isolde: Nachtgesang, Prelude, Act III

Suppé—Overtures to: Banditenstreiche, Boccaccio, Dichter und Bauer, Fatinitza, Leichte Kavallerie, Morgen Mittag und Abend in Wien, Pique Dame, Schöne Galathée, Tantalusqualen

Bruckner—Three Pieces for Orchestra

Cornelius—Barbier von Bagdad: Overture (2 versions)

Strauss, Joh., Jr.—Accelerationen; An der schönen blauen Donau; Fledermaus: Overture; Frühlingsstimmen; Kaiser-Walzer; Künstlerleben; Künstler Quadrille; Märchen aus dem Orient; Morgen-

[6'–10']

blätter; Neu-Wien; Rosen aus dem Süden; Seid um-schlungen Millionen; Tausend und eine Nacht; Wein, Weib, und Gesang; Wiener Blut; Wo die Citronen blüh'n; Zigeunerbaron: Overture, Schatz-Walzer

Strauss, Jos.—Delirien; Dorfschwalben aus Öster-reich; Mein Lebenslauf ist Lieb' und Lust; Sphärenklänge

Goldmark—Im Frühling; Königin von Saba: Einzugsmarsch

Brahms—Akademische Festouvertüre; Es ist ein Ros' entsprungen; Hungarian Dances Nos.1, 3, 10 (arr. Brahms); Hungarian Dances Nos.5, 6 (arr. Parlow); Hungarian Dances Nos.5, 6, 7 (arr. Schmeling); Hungarian Dances Nos.17-21 (arr. Dvořák)

Bruch—Loreley: Prelude

Humperdinck—Hänsel und Gretel: Prelude; Königs-kinder: Prelude, Introduction to Act III; Trauung in der Bastille

Mahler—Symphonic Prelude; Symphony No.1: Blumine; Symphony No.5: Adagietto; What the Wild Flowers Tell Me

Wolf—Corregidor: Prelude & Interlude

Strauss, R.—Feierlicher Einzug; Festmarsch; Guntram: Prelude to Act I; Intermezzo: Entr'acte after Act I; Rosenkavalier: Waltzes (arr. Doebber); Salome: Salome's Dance (several versions); Serenade, TrV 106

Pfitzner—Christ-Elflein: Overture; Palestrina: Preludes, Acts I, II, III

Reger—Serenade; Weihnachten

Schoenberg—Begleitungs-musik; Survivor from Warsaw

Webern—Concerto; Fünf Stücke; Langsamer Satz; Symphony, op.21; Variations for Orchestra

Toch—Circus Overture; Genesis Suite: The Covenant; Pinocchio

Hindemith—Overtures to: Cupid and Psyche, Neues vom Tage; Spielmusik, op.43, no.1

Korngold—Military March; Straussiana; Theme and Variations

Blacher—Music for Cleveland

Einem—Capriccio

Zimmermann—Stille und Umkehr

Henze—Heure bleue; Quattro poemi

Seither—Kammersinfonie

Italian

Gabrieli—Canzona; Canzona noni toni; Sonata pian' e forte

Monteverdi—Orfeo: Sinfonie e ritornelli

Frescobaldi—Toccata

Corelli—Sarabanda, Giga e Badinerie

Torelli—Concerto, op.6, no.1; Sinfonia, op.6, no.6

Scarlatti, A.—Concerti grossi Nos.1, 2; Piccola Suite; Sinfonias Nos.1, 2, 4, 5

Albinoni—Concerto, op.5, no.7

Vivaldi—Concerto, op.3, no.11, RV 565; Concertos for Orchestra, RV 152, RV 155, RV 158; Concerto, 4 Violins, 4 Recorders, RV 585; Sinfo-nias nos.3, RV 149, RV 169

Durante—Concerto No.5

Manfredini—Sinfonia da chiesa, op.2, no.12

Marcello, B.—Introduction, Aria & Presto

Geminiani—Concerti grossi, op.2, nos.2 & 3; Concertino, G major; Sinfonias, J-C 4, J-C 39, J-C 47

Galuppi—Concerto a quattro, No.1; Sinfonias, D major & F major (Della serenata)

Pergolesi—Concertino, E-flat major

Piccinni—Iphigenie en Tauride: Overture

Paisiello—Scuffiara: Overture; Sinfonia, D major; Sinfonia funebre; Sinfonia in tre tempi

Boccherini—Sinfonia concertante, G.268; Symphonies Nos.1, 12; Symphony "A", G.500

Cimarosa—Overtures to: Matrimonio segreto [2

versions], Traci amanti; Sinfonia, D major

Salieri—Grotta di Trofonio: Overture; Sinfonia (Veneziana)

Cherubini—Overtures to: Abencérages, Ali-Baba, Anacréon, Démophoon, Deux journées, Faniska, Hôtellerie portugaise, Lodoïska, Médée; March, F major

Rossini—Overtures to: Barbiere di Siviglia [2 versions], Cenerentola, Elisabetta, Gazza ladra [2 versions], Italiana in Algerii [2 versions], Robert Bruce, Scala di seta, Siège de Corinthe, Tancredi, Turco in Italia, Viaggio a Reims; Guillaume Tell: Pas de six; Serenata per piccolo complesso

Donizetti—Allegro in C major; Overtures to: Don Pasquale, Fille du régiment, Linda di Chamounix (Prelude), Roberto Devereux

Bellini—Overtures to: Norma, Pirata; Symphonies, C minor, D major

Verdi—Aïda: Prelude; Overtures to: Aroldo, Forza del destino, Luisa Miller, Nabucco, Vespri siciliani

Ponchielli—Gioconda: Dance of the Hours

Drigo, Riccardo—Diane et Actéon Pas de deux

Martucci—Tarantella

Puccini—Crisantemi; Edgar: Preludio

Mascagni—Cavalleria rusticana: Prelude & Siciliana

Busoni—Berceuse élégiaque; Lustspiel Overture; Nocturne symphonique

Sinigaglia—Adagio tragico; Baruffe chiozzotte; Danze piemontesi Nos.1 & 2

Respighi—Aria

Malipiero—Impressioni dal vero: Part III

Dallapiccola—Piccola musica notturna [2 versions]

Menotti—Pastorale

Berio—Allelujah I; Nones; Ritirata notturna di Madrid

Francesconi—Inquieta limina

[6'–10']
Di Vittorio—Overtura
Palermo; Overtura
Respighiana; Tallone di
Achille

Russian

Glinka—Capriccio brillante;
Kamarinskaya; Life for the
Tsar: Overture; Summer
Night in Madrid; Valse
fantaisie
Borodin—In the Steppes of
Central Asia; Nocturne [2
arrangements]; Petite suite:
Scherzo & Nocturne; Prince
Igor: Overture
Balakirev—Islamey [2
arrangements]; Overture on
Three Russian Folk Songs
Mussorgsky—Boris Godunov:
Polonaise; Intermezzo in the
Classic Style; Khovantchina:
Dance of the Persian
Maidens; Solemn March
Tchaikovsky—Eugene Onegin:
Waltz; Fatum; Marche slave;
Voyevoda, op.3 or Voyevoda,
op.78
Rimsky-Korsakov—Christmas
Eve: Polonaise; Coq d'or:
Introduction & Wedding
March; Fantasia on Serbian
Themes; Overtures to: Maid
of Pskov, May Night, Tsar's
Bride
Liadov—Enchanted Lake;
From the Apocalypse;
Kikimora
Glazunov—Carnaval Overture;
Cortége solennel No.1; Elegy;
March des noces; Seasons: 1.
Winter; Valse de concert,
No.2
Kalinnikov—Serenade for
Strings
Rachmaninoff—Vocalise
Stravinsky—Concertino for 12
Insts; Eight Instrumental
Miniatures; Firebird:
Berceuse & Finale; Four
Etudes; Four Norwegian
Moods; Monumentum; Pas de
deux (Tchaikovsky); Rite of
Spring: Sacrificial Dance;
Suites No.1 & No.2;
Variations
Prokofiev—Andante; Overture,
op.42
Khachaturian—Gayane: Three
Pieces

Shostakovich—Festive
Overture; Suites for Jazz
Orch, No.1 & No.2
Denisov—Crescendo e
diminuendo; Little Suite
Shchedrin—Concertos for
Orchestra No.1 & No.2
Finko—Holocaust

Spanish &
Latin American

Nunés-Garcia—Sinfonia
funebre; Zemira Overture
Arriaga—Esclavos felices:
Overture
Gomes—Guarany: Overture
Albéniz—Catalonia
Falla—Vida breve: Interlude &
Dance
Turina—Procesion del rocio
Villa-Lobos—Bachianas
brasileiras no.5: Aria (full
orch or strings); Bachianas
brasileiras no.9
Gerhard—Albada, interludi i
dansa
Revueltas—Alcancías;
Homenaje a Lorca; Janitzio;
Ocho por radio; Sensemayá [2
versions]
Rodrigo—Zarabanda lejana y
Villancico
Halffter, E.—Muerte de
Carmen: Habanera
Galindo—Sones de mariachi
Moncayo—Homenaje a
Cervantes; Huapango;
Sinfonietta
Montsalvatge—Cuatro
variaciones sobre un tema de
La flauta mágica
Ginastera—Oberatura para el
"Fausto" Criollo
Davidovsky—Inflexions
Lavista—Clepsidra
Márquez—Danzon No.2;
Paisajes bajo el signo de
cosmos
Amaya—Angelica; Pájaros de
tres alas
Lorenz—En tren vá changó

United Kingdom

Purcell—Chacony in G minor;
Suites from: Dido and
Aeneas, Double Dealer,
Virtuous Wife; Funeral Music
for Queen Mary; Gordian
Knot Untied: Suite No.2;
Rival Sisters: Overture

Arne—Symphonies Nos.1–2
Boyce—Overture (Ode for His
Majesty's Birthday [1769]);
Overture (Peleus and Thetis);
Symphonies Nos.1, 3–7
Sullivan—Overtures to:
Gondoliers, Iolanthe, Mikado,
Patience, Pirates of Penzance
Elgar—Dream Children;
Sospiri; Sursum corda
Delius—Dance Rhapsody
No.2; Summer Evening; Two
Pieces: On Hearing the First
Cuckoo; Walk to the Paradise
Garden
German—Henry VIII: Three
Dances; Nell Gwyn: Three
Dances
Vaughan Williams—English
Folk Song Suite; Norfolk
Rhapsody No.1; Poisoned
Kiss: Overture; Prelude &
Fugue; Prelude on an Old
Carol Tune; Two Hymn-Tune
Preludes; Wasps: Overture
Holst—Brook Green Suite;
Capriccio; Lure; Somerset
Rhapsody
Coleridge-Taylor—Bamboula;
Danse nègre; Novelette No.2
Brian—Symphony No.22
Bridge—Rebus
Ireland—Forgotten Rite
Bax—Happy Forest; Overture
to a Picaresque Comedy;
Summer Music
Butterworth—The Banks of
Green Willow; Two English
Idylls
Moeran, E. J.—Overture to a
Masque
Jacob—Fantasia on the
Alleluia Hymn
Finzi—Fall of the Leaf; New
Year Music; Romance;
Severn Rhapsody, op.3
Rubbra—Festival Overture
Walton—Capriccio burlesco;
Crown Imperial; Façade: Four
Additional Numbers; Façade:
Suites No.1 & 2; Hamlet:
Funeral March; Johannesburg
Festival Overture; Portsmouth
Point; Prologo e fantasia;
Scapino; Spitfire Prelude &
Fugue
Alwyn—Festival March; Moor
of Venice
Tippett—Little Music

[6'–10']

Britten—Gloriana: Courtly Dances; Men of Goodwill; Peter Grimes: Passacaglia; Soirées musicales; Sword in the Stone

Arnold—English Dances: Sets One & Two; Four Cornish Dances; Four Scottish Dances; Four Welsh Dances; Grand, Grand Festival Overture; Holly and the Ivy; Little Suites Nos.1, 2, 4; Peterloo; Sinfonietta No.1; Sound Barrier; Symphonic Study; Tam O'Shanter Overture

Musgrave—Chamber Concerto No.1; Largo, In Homage to B.A.C.H.; Scottish Dance Suite

Wood, Hugh—Divertimento, op.51

Birtwistle—Machaut à ma manière

Maxwell Davies—Chat Moss; Five Klee Pictures; Jimmack the Postie; Ojai Festival Overture

Bennett, Richard R.— Lilliburlero Variations; Sinfonietta

Blake—Nursery Rhyme Overture

McCartney—Spiral

Lankester—Pocket-Sized Guide to the Orchestra

Matthews, C.—Pluto, the Renewer

Tann—Water's Edge; With the Heather and Small Birds

Knussen—Choral

Butler—Fixed Doubles

Toovey—Black Light

Other Nationalities

Berwald—Estrella de Soria: Overture

Gade—In the Highlands; Michelangelo

Svendsen—Andante funèbre; Norwegian Rhapsody No.3; Two Icelandic Melodies; Two Swedish Folk Melodies

Grieg—In Autumn; Lyric Pieces, op.68, nos.4 & 5; Peer Gynt: Prelude; Two Elegiac Melodies, op.34; Two Melodies, op.53; Wedding Day at Troldhaugen

Nielsen, Carl—Bohemian-Danish Folk Tune; Fantasy Journey to the Faroes; Pan and Syrinx; Saga Dream; Saul and David: Prelude to Act II; Symphonic Rhapsody

Sibelius—Autrefois; Bard; Cassazione; Dryad; Finlandia; Karelia Overture; Kuolema: Valse triste; Lemminkäinen Suite: 4. Lemminkäinen's Return; Scène de ballet; Scènes historiques: Scena, An der Zugbrücke

Atterberg—Ballade & Passacaglia; Varmlands Rhapsody

Valen—Cimetière marin; Isla de las calmas

Martin—Ouverture en hommage à Mozart

Rosenberg—Overtura biancanera

Langgaard—Sphinx

Pijper—Six Symphonic Epigrams

Riisager—Mardi Gras; Qarrtsiluni

Skalkottas—Five Greek Dances

Adaskin—Serenade Concertante

Liebermann, Rolf—Furioso

Bissell—Andante e Scherzo

Pentland—Symphony No.3

Delden—In memoriam; Piccolo concerto (Little Concerto)

Xenakis—Analogique A; Metastaseis; Pithoprakta

Rautavaara—Fiddlers

Takemitsu—Green; Rain Coming; Requiem

Holliger—Ardeur noire

Harris, Ross—Music for Jonny

Saariaho—Lumière et Pesanteur

Chen Yi—Duo ye [No.1]; Duo ye, No.2; Ge; Shuo; Sprout

Sheng—Black Swan; Shanghai Overture

Salonen, E-P.—Giro

Ritchie, Anthony—Bugle Will Do

O'Boyle—Ballycroy; Music That Goes with "The Tale of Peter Rabbit"; River Symphony: Suite; Scottish Piano Rhapsody

Psathas—Tarantismo

Dorman—Astrolatry; Azerbaijani Dance; Prayer for the Innocents; Reflections

Rival – Achilles & Scamander; Scherzo; Spring; Whirlwind

11'–15'

American (United States)

Heinrich—Columbiad; Tower of Babel

Fry—Niagara Symphony; Macbeth: Overture; Suite, op.63, E major

Chadwick—Melpomene; Tre pezzi

Parker—Northern Ballad

Converse—California; Endymion's Narrative; Flivver Ten Million

Hadley—San Francisco

Mason—Chanticleer

Ives—New England Holidays: Thanksgiving and Forefathers' Day; Ragtime Dances

Ruggles—Evocations; Sun-Treader

Bloch, E.—Hiver-Printemps; Poems of the Sea

Griffes—Pleasure Dome of Kubla Khan

Becker—Soundpiece No.1b & No.2b; When the Willow Nods

Collins—Irish Rhapsody [1927]; Mardi Gras; Tragic Overture

Weiss—Segreti

Grofé—Mississippi Suite

Rogers—Five Fairy Tales; Three Japanese Dances

Piston—Concerto for Orchestra; Divertimento for Nine Insts; Lincoln Center Festival Overture; Serenata; Sinfonietta

Still—American Scene: The South (Suite 2), A Mountain, a Memorial, and a Song (Suite 5); Darker America; Poem; Suite, Violin & Orch

Hanson—Elegy; Merry Mount: Suite; Symphony No.5

Sessions—Concerto for Orchestra; Montezuma: Suite; Symphony No.8

[11'–15']

Thomson, V.—Louisiana Story: Acadian Songs and Dances; Plow That Broke the Plains: Suite; Solemn Music and a Joyful Fugue

Cowell—Chiaroscuro; Old American Country Set; Ongaku; Sinfonietta; Synchrony

Szell—Variations on an Original Theme

Bacon—Erie Waters; Remembering Ansel Adams

Ellington—Trois rois noirs

Copland—Emblems; Inscape; Lincoln Portrait; Orchestral Variations; Our Town; Prairie Journal; Salón México; Symphony No.2; Three Latin-American Sketches; Two Pieces

Krenek—Kleine Symphonie; Sinfonietta; Symphonic Elegy

McPhee—Transitions

Wolpe—Passacaglia; Piece for Two Instrumental Units

Blitzstein—Orchestra Variations

Creston—Dance Overture; Invocation and Dance; Two Choric Dances

Finney—Landscapes Remembered

Talma—Full Circle; Toccata

Swanson—Short Symphony

Stevens—Sinfonia breve; Symphonic Dances

Siegmeister—Five Fantasies; Theater Set

Barber—Andromache's Farewell; Essay No.3; Medea's Meditation and Dance of Vengeance

Hovhaness—And God Created Great Whales; Floating World; Meditation on Orpheus; Psalm and Fugue, op.40a; Symphony No.2; Variations and Fugue

Smith, Julia—Folkways Symphony

Dahl—Variations on a Theme by C.P.E. Bach

Brant—Desert Forests

Coolidge—Pioneer Dances

Gould—Classical Variations

Effinger—Little Symphony No.1, op.31

Fine, Irving—Notturno

Diamond—Rounds; World of Paul Klee

Perle—Serenade No.2

Shulman—Quilt; Woodstock Waltzes

Surinach—Sinfonia chica

Hervig—In Summer Season

Kay, U.—Chariots; Fantasy Variations; Suite for Strings; Theater Set for Orchestra; Umbrian Scene

Ward—Adagio and Allegro; Concertino for Strings; Divertimento; Festive Ode; Five Times Five; Sonic Structure; Symphony No.1

Yardumian—Cantus animae et cordis

Bernstein—Divertimento; On the Town: Three Dance Episodes

Rochberg—Black Sounds; Cheltenham Concerto

Rochberg—Night Music

Avshalomov, J.—Cues from "The Little Clay Cart"

Kirchner—Forbidden; Music for Orchestra; Toccata

Kirk—Orchestra Primer

Overton—Symphony No.2

Bergsma—Chameleon Variations

Imbrie—Legend

Shapey—Rituals

Foss—Folksong for Orchestra; Quintets for Orchestra

Thorne—Elegy for Orchestra

Bassett—From a Source Evolving

Chou—Beijing in the Mist; Pien

Mennin—Concertato

Powell—Modules

Rorem—Ideas for Easy Orchestra; Lions

Woollen—Elegy & Divertimento

Benson—Delphic Serenade

Hollingsworth—Divertimento; Three Ladies Beside the Sea

Lees—Passacaglia

Starer—Samson agonistes

Schuller—American Triptych; Five Bagatelles; Five Etudes; Of Reminiscences and Reflections

Brown—Available Forms 1

Feldman—Intersection No.1

Nelson, Marie—Ode to Antigone

Aschaffenburg—Three Dances for Orchestra

Anderson, T. J.—Chamber Symphony

Druckman—Aureole; Nor Spell Nor Charm

Previn—Owls

Van de Vate—Chernobyl; Dark Nebulae; Pura Besakih; Western Front

Baker—Kosbro

Deussen—Reflections on the Hudson

Martino—Ritorno

Adams, Leslie—Ode to Life

Colgrass—As Quiet As …

Perkinson—Sinfonietta No.1

Zaninelli—Night Voices

Subotnick—Lamination; Play No.2

Reynolds—Fiery Wind

Tull—Overture for a Legacy; Symphonic Treatise

Jones—Hymn to the Earth; Listen Now, My Children; Open Range

Rands—Agenda

Schickele—Zoo Called Earth

Reich—Three Movements

Rudow—Force III

Schwartz—Island

Albert, Adrienne—Western Suite

Del Tredici—Alice Symphony: The Lobster Quadrille

Glass—Music in Similar Motion; Phaedra; Secret Agent: Three Pieces

Hoover—Eleni; Two Sketches

Wilson—Expansions III; Lumina; Voices

Baksa—Variations from the Heart

Corigliano—Fantasia on an Ostinato; Gazebo Dances; Three Hallucinations; Tournaments

Harbison—Merchant of Venice: Incidental music; Music for 18 Winds

Tower—Chamber Dance; In Memory; Made in America; Tambor

Wuorinen—Crossfire; Machault mon chou

Boone—Second Landscape

Kolb—Chromatic Fantasy; Grisaille

Stock—Inner Space

Zwilich—Concerto Grosso; Prologue & Variations

Plain—Clawhammer

Zappa—Perfect Stranger

Proto—Casey at the Bat

[11'–15']

Iannaccone—Divertimento; From Time to Time; Waiting for the Sunrise on the Sound

León, Tania—Ácana

Schwantner—Aftertones of Infinity; Distant Runes and Incantations; From a Dark Millennium; Sudden Rainbow

Hartway—Star Dancer

Bond, Victoria—The Frog Prince

Peck—Peace Overture; Signs of Life; Thrill of the Orch

Zaimont—Chroma

Avshalomov, D.—Concerto con timpani; Gems

Lieberson, Peter—Remembering JFK

McGlaughlin—Solstice

Rodríguez—Jargon

Adams, John—Chairman Dances; Slonimsky's Earbox

Kechley—Clocks and More Clocks

Mauldin—Desert Light; Fajada Butte; Petroglyph; Santa Fe Magic

Walker, Gwyneth—About Leaves; Bicentennial Suite; Fanfare, Interlude & Finale

Beckel—Fantasy After Schubert; Gardens of Stone; Waltz of the Animals

Welcher—Prairie Light

Locklair—Hues; When Morning Stars Begin to Fall

Paulus—Concertante

Rouse—Iscariot; Rapture

Stucky—Colburn Variations; Dreamwaltzes

Warshauer—As the Waters Cover the Sea; Shabbat with King David

Davis—ESU Variations; Tales (Tails) of the Signifying Monkey

Tsontakis—Four Symphonic Quartets: Nos.1. Other Echoes, 2. Perpetual Angelus, 3. Dove Descending, 4. Winter Lightning

Actor—Celebration Overture; Prelude to a Tragedy; Premonition

Boelter—Dharma

McTee—Adagio for String Orchestra; Einstein's Dream; Twittering Machine

Sierra—Bacchae; Borikén; Fandangos; Güell concert; Sinfonía No.2

Beaser—Double Chorus for Orchestra

Coleman, L.R.—Elegy; For a Beautiful Land; Journeys

Daugherty—Metropolis Symphony: Red Cape Tango

Costa—Allure; Espranza; Providence

Curiale—Wind River

Frazelle—Shivaree

Gross—You Must Remember This …

Danielpour—First Light (2 versions); Lacrimae beati

Dorff—Billy and the Carnival; Kiss; Philly Rhapsody; Three Fun Fables

Drattell—Lilith; Sorrow Is Not Melancholy

Gordon—Beijing Harmony

Mackey—Square Holes, Round Pegs; TILT

Sartor—Portent and Apotheosis

Sleeper—Symphony No.2

Smith, Kile—Four French Carols; Three Dances

Bartholomew—Suite for String Orchestra

Cotton—CityMusic; Folia; Lyra

Knehans—ripple; winter steps

Lang—Grind to a Halt

Moravec, Paul—Sempre diritto!

Tan—Symphonic Poem of 3 Notes

Wagner, Melinda—Falling Angels

Wolfe, Julia—Vermeer Room

Heitzeg—Flower of the Earth

Ince—Academica; Arches; Deep Flight; Domes; Ebullient Shadows

Kernis—Musica celestis

Torke—Adjustable Wrench; Ash; December; Ecstatic Orange; Jasper; Lucent Variations

Abels—Delights and Dances

Higdon—blue cathedral

Miller—Scenes Unseen

Roter—Camp David Overture; With Courage and Compassion

McLoskey—Moraine; Requiem, ver.2.001x

Thomas, Augusta Read—Helios Choros III

Wittry—Lamentoso

Trigos—Sinfonia breve

Theofanidis—Rainbow Body

Stephenson—Chamber Concerto

Amrhein—Bestiary; Event; Little Nemo in Slumberland; Semi-Suite

Boyer—Dream Lives On; Ghosts of Troy; New Beginnings; Three Olympians; Titanic

Hutter, Gregory—Deploration

Frank, G.L.—Elegia Andina; Manchay tiempo; Raíces

Puts—Exalted Virelai; Inspiring Beethoven; John Brown's Body; Symphony No.2; Two Mountain Scenes

Petering—Lake Summit

Lee—Beyond Rivers of Vision

Bates—Icarian Rhapsody; Music from Underground Spaces; Ode; Sea-Blue Circuitry

Territo—John Henry vs. the Machine

Tommasini—Tell Me …

Greenberg—Skyline Dances

Eastern European

Gluck—Ballet Suite No.2; Sinfonia, F major

Stamitz, Joh.—Sinfonia pastorale, op.4, no.2; Symphony, op.3, no.3

Benda, Georg—Symphony No.5, G major

Gołąbek—Symphonies, C major & D major (I)

Vanhal—Sinfonia, G minor

Stamitz, Carl—Orchestral Quartets, op.1, nos.1, 2, 4–6

Liszt—Christus: Die heiligen drei Könige; Hungarian Rhapsodies Nos.1, 2 [2 versions], 4; Mephisto Waltz Nos.1–2; Nächtliche Zug; Orpheus; Prometheus; Triomphe funèbre du Tasse; Von der Wiege bis zum Grabe

Moniuszko—Fairy Tale

Smetana—Bartered Bride: Three Dances; Ma vlast: 1. Vysehrad, 2. Vltava, 4. From Bohemia's Forests and Meadows, 5. Tábor, 6. Blaník; Richard III; Wallenstein's Camp

Minkus—Bayadère: Pas de deux

Dvořák—Hussite Overture; In Nature's Realm; Midday Witch; Othello Overture;

[11'–15']

Peasant a Rogue: Overture; Scherzo capriccioso; Slavonic Rhapsodies, op.45, nos.2-3

Janáček—Cunning Little Vixen: Suite (Jílek); Fiddler's Child

Suk—Scherzo fantastique

Dohnányi—American Rhapsody; Symphonic Minutes

Bartók—Hungarian Sketches; Three Village Scenes; Two Portraits

Enesco—Romanian Rhapsodies, op.11, nos.1-2

Kodály—Dances of Marosszek; Theater Overture

Weiner—Divertimento No.5

Martinů—Inventions

Tubin—Estonian Dance Suite

Bacewicz—Concerto for String Orchestra

Lutosławski—Little Suite; Mi-parti; Musique funèbre; Polish Dances; Venetian Games

Panufnik—Divertimento; Old Polish Suite

Szöllösy—Sonorità

Ligeti—Lontano; Melodien; San Francisco Polyphony

Bloch, A.—Enfiando per orchestra

Lazarof—Poema

Górecki—Muzyczka 3; Three Dances

Penderecki—Flourescences

Pärt—Fratres; Nekrolog

Silvestrov—Symphony No.2

Skoryk—Hutsul Triptych

Eötvös—zeroPoints

Sapieyevski—Surtsey

Tüür—Action — Passion — Illusion; Zeitraum

French & Belgian

Charpentier, M.-A.—Noëls pour les instruments, H.531 & 534

Rameau—Ballet Suite; Dardanus: Suite; Suite for String Orch

Gossec—Sinfonias, op.12, nos.2, 4

Saint-Georges—Symphony No.1

Grétry—Zémire et Azor: Ballet Suite

Méhul—Chasse du jeune Henri

Halévy—Juive: Overture

Berlioz—Benvenuto Cellini: Overture; Franc-Juges; Rob Roy; Roméo et Juliette: Romeo Alone, Festivities at Capulet's; Troyens: Ballet

Gounod—Faust: Ballet Music

Franck—Chasseur maudit; Éolides; Rédemption: Morceau symphonique

Lalo—Namouna: Ballet Suite No.2; Roi d'Ys: Overture

Saint-Saëns—Septet

Delibes—Roi s'amuse

Bizet—Carmen: Suite No.1; Jeux d'enfants: Petite suite; Jolie fille de Perth: Scènes bohémiennes; Ouverture; Patrie; Variations chromatiques

Massenet—Cigal: Suite

Fauré—Four Pieces; Masques et bergamasques

Duparc—Lénore

Indy—Chanson et danses; Istar

Chausson—Viviane

Chaminade—Callirhoë Suite

Debussy—Petite suite; Printemps; Symphony

Pierné—Cydalise et le chèvre-pied: Suite No.2

Dukas—Apprenti sorcier; Polyeucte: Overture

Magnard—Chant funèbre; Hymne à la justice

Satie—Aventures de Mercure

Koechlin—Bandar-Log

Roussel—Concerto for Small Orch; Évocations, op.15, nos.1-2; Padmâvatî: Suite No.2; Petite suite; Pour un fête de printemps; Suite in F

Schmitt—Feuillets de voyage; Palais hanté; Salammbô: Suite No.2

Rabaud—Divertissement

Ravel—Bolero; Daphnis et Chloé: Suite No.1; Jardin magique; Shéhérazade [overture]; Valse

Varèse—Intégrales

Ibert—Divertissement; Escales; Louisville Concerto; Suite symphonique; Symphonie marine

Honegger—Chant de Nigamon; Prelude, Fugue, Postlude

Milhaud—Boeuf sur le toit; Cortège funèbre; Suite française

Boulanger, L.—D'un soir triste

Tansman—Genesis Suite: Adam and Eve; Sonatine transatlantique; Variations on a Theme by Frescobaldi

Poulenc—Suite française

Jolivet—Amants magnifiques

Thiriet—Danseries françaises

Messiaen—Hymne; Offrandes oubliées

Françaix—Sei preludi; Ville mystérieuse

Ohana—Suite pour un mimodrame

Dutilleux—Timbres, espace, mouvement

Amy—Refrains

Durand, Joël-François—Lichtung

German & Austrian

Fux—Overture, C major

Bach, J. L.—Suite, G major

Telemann—Overtures, TWV 55:C1, TWV 55:g4

Bach, J.S.—Chaconne (arr. Starr); Passacaglia, BWV 582 [2 versions]

Handel—Concerti a due cori, Nos.1 & 3; Concerto grosso, op.3, no.4; Royal Fireworks Music (arr. Harty); Saul: Overture [2 versions]; Theodora: Overture; Water Music: Suites Nos.2 & 3

Bach, W.F.—Sinfonia, F major

Bach, C.P.E.—Symphonies, H.657, H.658, H.659, H.660, H.663

Wagenseil—Sinfonia, G minor

Abel—Symphonies, op.7, no.6 & op.14, no.2

Haydn, F.J.—Notturno No.1; Scherzando, Hob.II:38; Symphonies A, B, Nos.1, 4, 9, 10, 14, 16, 17, 19, 20, 21, 24, 25, 27, 30, 34, 37, 38

Beck, F.I.—Sinfonia, Callen 30

Bach, J.C.—Symphonies, op.3, nos.1 & 4; op.6, no.6; op.18, nos.1, 2, 3, 4, 6; op.21, nos.1 & 2

Haydn, M.—Symphony, MH 508

Hofmann, Leopold—Sinfonias, B-flat major, D major, F major

Dittersdorf—Sinfonias, C major & F major

[11'–15']

Mozart, W.A.—Divertimentos, K.113, K.131, K.166, K.186; German Dances, K.536, K.600; Marches, K.408; Symphonies, K.Anh.214, 216, 220, 221, 223; Symphonies Nos.1, 2, 3, 7, 8, 9, 13, 16, 37; Symphonies, K.75, K.76, K.95, K.96, K.97
Beethoven—Contradances, WoO 14; Leonore Overtures Nos.2 & 3; Musik zu einem Ritterballet; Weihe des Hauses: Overture; Wellingtons Sieg
Kuhlau—William Shakespeare: Overture
Hensel—Overture, C major
Mendelssohn—Meeresstille und glückliche Fahrt; Midsummer Night's Dream: Overture; Sinfonias Nos.6 & 10
Schumann, R.—Carnaval: 3 excerpts; Manfred: Overture
Rietz—Concert Overture
Wagner, Richard—Faust-Ouvertüre; Fliegende Holländer: Overture; Götterdämmerung: Siegfried's Death & Funeral; Grosser Festmarsch; Meistersinger: Three Excerpts from Act III; Parsifal: Prelude, Good Friday Spell; Polonia; Rienzi: Overture; Tannhäuser: Overture (Dresden version), Venusberg Music; Tristan und Isolde: Prelude
Bruckner—Overture, G minor
Reinecke—Kinder-Symphonie
Strauss, Joh., Jr.—Geschichten aus dem Wienerwald
Goldmark—Königin von Saba: Ballet Music; Scherzo, op.45
Brahms—Hungarian Dances Nos.11-16 (arr. Parlow); Tragische Ouvertüre
Bruch—Swedish Dances, op.63, nos.1–7 & 8–15
Goetz—Frühlings-Ouvertüre
Brüll—Serenade No.2
Humperdinck—Hänsel und Gretel: Three Excerpts
Reznı̌ček—Lustspiel-Ouverture
Wolf—Scherzo & Finale
Strauss, R.—Frau ohne Schatten: Symphonic Fantasy; Rosenkavalier: Waltzes, First Sequence; Till Eulenspiegel

Schumann, G.—Liebesfrühling
Pfitzner—Kätchen von Heilbronn: Overture; Scherzo
Schoenberg—Theme and Variations; Waltzes
Schreker—Ekkehard; Tanzspiel
Webern—Fünf Sätze; Im Sommerwind; Passacaglia; Sechs Stücke, op.6 [2 versions]
Hindemith—Concerto for Orchestra; Five Pieces; Suite of French Dances
Korngold—Much Ado About Nothing
Blacher—Concertante Musik; Orchester-Ornament; Studie im Pianissimo; Two Inventions
Goldschmidt—Ciaccona sinfonica
Hartmann—Miserae
Einem—Ballade; Bruckner Dialog
Henze—Scorribanda sinfonica
Stockhausen—Kontra-Punkte
Schwertsik—Draculas Haus-und Hofmusik

Italian

Scarlatti, A.—Sinfonias Nos.6, 8, 10
Albinoni—Concerto, op.9, no.9, C major
Vivaldi—Sinfonias Nos. 1 & 2
Durante—Concerto No.1
Scarlatti, D.—Five Sonatas; Good-Humored Ladies: Suite
Tartini—Concerto No.58; Sinfonia, D major
Locatelli—Concerto grosso, op.1, no.6; Trauer-Symphonie
Sammartini, Giov. Battista—Sinfonias, J-C 2 & J-C 32
Boccherini—Symphonies Nos.9, 14–16, 18–19, 26
Rossini—Overtures to: Guillaume Tell, Semiramide; Sonatas Nos.1–4
Verdi—Aïda: Triumphal March & Ballet
Ponchielli—Elegia
Puccini—Preludio sinfonico
Busoni—Rondò arlecchinesco
Respighi—Fontane di Roma
Malipiero—Armenia; Dialogo no.1; Impressioni dal vero: Part I; Oriente immaginario; Pause del silenzio I; Symphonies Nos.10 & 11

Dallapiccola—Due pezzi; Variazioni
Berio—Requies; Still; Variazioni per orchestra da camera
Francesconi—Da capo
Di Vittorio—Symphony No.3

Russian

Borodin—Prince Igor: Polovtsian Dances
Balakirev—Russia
Mussorgsky—Night on Bald Mountain [2 versions]
Tchaikovsky—Capriccio italien; Storm: Overture
Rimsky-Korsakov—Capriccio espagnol; Mlada: Suite; Overture on Russian Themes; Russian Easter Overture; Sadko; Skazka; Snow Maiden: Suite
Liadov—Eight Russian Folk Songs
Ippolitov-Ivanov—Armenian Rhapsody; Turkish Fragments
Glazunov—Chopiniana; Overture No.1; Overture solennelle; Seasons: 3. Summer & 4. Autumn; Valse de concert, No.1
Rachmaninoff—Symphony, D minor
Tcherepnin, N.—Enchanted Kingdom
Stravinsky—Concerto in D; Concerto in E-flat; Octet; Ode; Scherzo fantastique; Septet; Symphonies of Wind Insts [2 versions]
Prokofiev—Classical Symphony; Love for Three Oranges: Symphonic Suite; Russian Overture; Steel Step: Suite; Summer Day
Kabalevsky—Comedians
Shostakovich—Ballet Suite No.1; Suite for Variety Orch, No.2
Denisov—Bells in the Mist; Postludio in memoriam Witold Lutoslawski
Shchedrin—Geometry of Sound; Moz-Art à la Haydn
Finko—Russia; Wailing Wall

Spanish & Latin American

Granados—Dante; Tres danzas españolas

[11'–15']

Falla—Amor brujo: Suite (Ryden); Sombrero de tres picos: Suites Nos.1–2
Ponce—Chapultepec
Gerhard—Alegrías: Suite; Pedrelliana; Resonancias; Symphonies Nos.1 & 2
Revueltas—Noche de los Mayas: Suite (Hindemith)
Moncayo—Tierra de temporal
Montsalvatge—Tres reflejos sobre una pastoral de invierno
Ginastera—Estancia: Four Dances; Iubilum; Ollantay; Panambí: Suite
Antunes—Intervertige; Poetica II
Catán—En un doblez del tiempo
Márquez—Danzón No.4 [2 versions]
Amaya—Soledad y el Mar
Golijov—Last Round

United Kingdom

Purcell—Abdelazer: Suite; Fairy Queen: Suite No.2; Fairy Queen: Two Suites; Gordian Knot Untied: Suite No.1; Married Beau: Suite
Arne—Symphonies Nos.3–4
Boyce—Symphony No.8
Sullivan—Overture di ballo; Overture in C; Tempest: Three Dances
Parry—Suite in F
Stanford—Irish Rhapsody No.1
Elgar—Cockaigne; Froissart; Serenade, op.20; Three Bavarian Dances
Delius—Dance Rhapsody No.1; In a Summer Garden
Bantock—Pierrot of the Minute
Vaughan Williams—Coastal Command: Suite; Death of Tintagiles; Fantasia on a theme by Thomas Tallis; Five Variants of "Dives and Lazarus"; In the Fen Country; Serenade to Music [orch version]; Three Preludes on Welsh Hymn Tunes; Variations for Orchestra
Holst—Beni Mora; Egdon Heath; Hammersmith; Perfect Fool: Ballet Music; St. Paul's

Suite; Suites Nos.1 & 2; Suite for Orchestra [McPhee]
Coleridge-Taylor—Ballade; Toussaint L'Ouverture
Ireland—London Overture
Bax—In the Faery Hills; November Woods; Roscatha; Tintagel
Butterworth—Shropshire Lad
Coates—London Suite
Bliss—Introduction and Allegro; Things to Come: Concert Suite
Warlock—Capriol Suite
Walton—As You Like It; Façade 2; Hamlet and Ophelia; Henry V: Suite
Berkeley—Sinfonietta, op.34; Symphony No.3; Windsor Variations
Britten—Canadian Carnival; Johnson over Jordan: Suite; Prince of the Pagodas: Pas de six; Sinfonietta; Suite on English Folk Tunes
Burgess—Manchester Overture
Arnold—Concerto for 28 Players; Electra; Four Irish Dances; Inn of the Sixth Happiness: Suite; Sinfonietta No.2
Musgrave—Festival Overture; Peripeteia; Rainbow
Hoddinott—Sinfonietta No.3
Goehr—When Adam Fell
Birtwistle—Carmen arcadiae mechanicae perpetuum
Maxwell Davies—First Fantasia on Taverner's "In nomine"; Mavis in Las Vegas; Orkney Wedding With Sunrise
Bennett, Richard R.—Country Dances, Bk 1; Serenade
McCabe—Lion the Witch and the Wardrobe: Suite
Ferneyhough—Carceri d'invenzione III
Jenkins—Palladio
Lankester—Make Your Own Orchestra
Tavener—Little Ceremonial
Rutter—Suite for Strings
Tann—Grey Tide and the Green; Open Field
MacMillan—Britannia
Turnage—Three Screaming Popes
Adès—Chamber Symphony
Wigglesworth, Ryan—Locke's Theatre

Other Nationalities

Gade—Echoes of Ossian; Hamlet
Svendsen—Romeo and Juliet
Grieg—Peer Gynt: Suites Nos.1 & 2; Two Norwegian Airs
Nielsen, Carl—Helios Overture
Sibelius—Belshazzar's Feast; Karelia Suite; Lemminkäinen Suite: Lemminkäinen in Tuonela; Oceanides; Rakastava; Spring Song
Alfvén—Midsommarvaka
Nielsen, Ludolf—Symphony No.3
Grainger—In a Nutshell
Atterberg—Bäckahästen: Midsummer Dances
Martin—Passacaille [2 versions]
Rosenberg—Orpheus in Town: Dance Suite
Riisager—Fools' Paradise: Suite No.2; Twelve by the Mail: Six Dances
Wirén—Serenade, op.11
Adaskin—Saskatchewan Legend
Badings—Symphonietta
Holmboe—Concerto for Orchestra; Symphony No.1
Liebermann, Rolf—Suite über sechs schweizerische Volkslieder
Glanville-Hicks—Sinfonia da Pacifica
Blomdahl—Forma ferritonans
Delden—Symphony No.3
Ritchie, John—Aquarius; Suite No.1
Xenakis—Akrata; Anaktoria; Atrees; ST/48–1,240162; Syrmos
Leeuw, T. de—Mouvements retrograde
Rautavaara—Lintukoto; Requiem in Our Time; Suite for Strings
Sculthorpe—Kakadu; Mangrove
Takemitsu—Dream/Window; Flock Descends into the Pentagonal Garden; Tree Line; Twill by Twilight; Visions
Kelterborn—Changements
Miyoshi—Concerto for Orchestra

[11'–15']

Sallinen, A.—Chamber Music
I; Shadows; Variations for
Orchestra
Holliger—Meta arca
Whitehead—Resurgences
Bamert—Circus Parade;
Snapshots
Cresswell—Paesaggi
dell'anima
Keuris—Sinfonia
Mozetich—Postcards from the
Sky; Steps to Ecstasy
Vivier—Orion
Ran—Vessels of Courage and
Hope
Chen Yi—Dunhuang Fantasy;
Linear; Momentum; Si Ji;
Sparkle
Yoshimatsu—Threnody to
Toki
Zhou—Enlightened; Immortal
Young—Dance; Virgen de la
Esperanza
Kats-Chernin—Mythic; Zoom
and Zip
Lindberg—Arena; Marea;
Ritratto
Ritchie, Anthony—French
Overture; Hanging Bulb
Burge—The Canadian Shield;
Snowdrift
Chin—santika Ekatala
Psathas—Seikilos
Dorman—Variations Without a
Theme
Rival—Northwest Passage
Variations
Goulet—Chocolats
symphoniques

16'–20'

American (United States)

Gottschalk—Symphonies
Nos.1 & 2
Paine—Azara: Orchestral
Scene & 3 Moorish Dances
Foote—Four Character Pieces;
Francesca da Rimini;
Serenade
Chadwick—Aphrodite;
Sinfonietta; Tam O'Shanter
Sousa—Tales of a Traveler
Kelley—Pit and the Pendulum
Herbert—Suite romantique
MacDowell—Hamlet &
Ophelia; Lamia; Lancelot and
Elaine; Suite No.1

Gilbert, H.F.—Dance in the
Place Congo
Converse—Festival of Pan;
Mystic Trumpeter
Ives—Orchestral Set No.2;
Robert Browning Overture;
Symphony No.3; Three
Places in New England [4
versions]
Carpenter—Sea Drift
Bloch, E.—Evocations;
Sinfonia breve
Becker—Symphony No.3
Collins—Hibernia; Set of Four;
Variations on an Irish
Folksong
Moore, Douglas—Pageant of
P.T. Barnum
Bennett, Robt. R.—Four
Freedoms; Suite of Old
American Dances
Piston—Incredible Flutist:
Suite; Symphony No.7; Three
New England Sketches
Sowerby—From the
Northland; Prairie
Still—Deserted Plantation;
Symphony No.5; Wood Notes
Sessions—Concertino for
Chamber Orchestra;
Symphonies Nos.1, 5, 6
Thomson, V.—Louisiana
Story: Suite; Symphony on a
Hymn Tune; Symphony No.2
Bacon—Concerto Grosso
Gershwin—American in Paris
Harris, Roy—Symphonies
Nos.3 & 7
Ellington—Black, Brown and
Beige: Suite; Harlem; Night
Creature; Nutcracker Suite
(after Tchaikovsky)
Janssen—New Year's Eve in
New York
Antheil—Ballet mécanique
(1953 version); Serenade [I]
Copland—Connotations;
Dance Symphony; Music for
Movies; Nonet for Strings;
Statements; Symphonic Ode;
Tender Land: Suite
Krenek—Eleven
Transparencies
Luening—Rhapsodic
Variations
McPhee—Symphony No.2;
Tabuh-Tabuhan
Weill—Aufstieg und Fall der
Stadt Mahagonny: Suite;
Dreigroschenoper: Suite (arr.
Schönherr); Kleine
Dreigroschenmusik

Wolpe—Man from Midian
Blitzstein—Surf and Seaweed:
Suite
Cushing—Divertimento
Gutche—Perseus and
Andromeda XX; Symphony
No.5
Phillips, B.—Selections from
McGuffey's Reader
Swanson—Concerto for
Orchestra
Wilder—Carl Sandburg Suite
Anderson, Leroy—Irish Suite
Carter—Adagio tenebroso;
Concerto for Orchestra;
Partita; Penthode;
Pocahontas: Suite; Symphony
of Three Orchestras; Three
Occasions for Orchestra
Siegmeister—Sunday in
Brooklyn; Western Suite
Barber—Antony and
Cleopatra: Two Scenes; Die
natali; Souvenirs: Suite
Schuman, Wm.—Credendum;
New England Triptych;
Symphony No.5
Hovhaness—Fra Angelico;
Symphonies Nos.1 & 10
Brant—Angels and Devils
Dello Joio—New York Profiles
Gould—Latin-American
Symphonette; Soundings;
Spirituals; Tap Dance
Concerto
Read—Pennsylvania Suite
Fine, Irving—Music for
Orchestra
Kubik—Divertimento I
Diamond—Music for
Shakespeare's Romeo and
Juliet; Symphonies Nos.4 & 7
Perle—Three Movements
Persichetti—Symphony No.5
Surinach—Ritmo jondo
Babbitt—Ars combinatoria;
Relata I; Transfigured Notes
Kay, U.—Markings; Scherzi
musicali; Serenade for
Orchestra; Six Dances for
String Orch; Southern
Harmony; Suite
Ward—First Symphonic Set;
Lady Kate: A Western Set;
Symphony No.6
Yardumian—Armenian Suite
Rochberg—EDEN: Out of
Time and Out of Space
Barab—G-A-G-E
Bergsma—Documentary One
Imbrie—Chamber Symphony;
Symphony No.3

[16'–20']

Kurka—Good Soldier Schweik: Suite

Foss—Exeunt

Walker, George—Address for Orchestra

Bassett—Echoes from an Invisible World

Kraft—Contextures

Pinkham—Symphony No.1; Symphony No.2

Rorem—Design; Quaker Reader

Lees—Concerto for Chamber Orch; Trumpet of the Swan

Samuel—Looking at Orpheus Looking; Requiem for Survivors

Schuller—Capriccio stravagante

Smith, Hale—Ritual and Incantations

Brown—Available Forms 2; Cross Sections and Color Fields

Duffy—Heritage Dances

Erb—Concerto, Brass; Seventh Trumpet; Symphony of Overtures

Peterson—Face of the Night

Adler, S.—Concerto for Orchestra

Flagello—Lautrec; Serenata

Russo—Symphony No.2

Crumb—Echoes of Time and the River

London—Hero of our Time

Previn—Night Thoughts

Wyner—Lyric Harmony

Felciano—Orchestra

Van de Vate—Nemo: Suite

Ballard—Incident at Wounded Knee

Lombardo—Drakestail

Martino—Mosaic for Grand Orchestra

Biggs—Ballad of William Sycamore

Colgrass—Letter from Mozart

Perkinson—Grass; Sinfonietta No.2

Zaninelli—Tale of Peter Rabbit

Reynolds—Quick Are the Mouths of Earth

Jones—Christmas Memory: Suite; Janus; Let Us Now Praise Famous Men; Reflections

Rands—Madrigali

Rush, L.—Cloud Messenger

Schickele—Symphony No.2

Reich—Music for Mallet Instruments, Voices & Organ

Bach, Jan—Variations on a Theme of Brahms

Glass—Canyon; Days and Nights in Rocinha

Bolcom—Fives; Orphée-sérénade; Seattle Slew; Symphony No.1

Harbison—Most Often Used Chords; Partita

Tower—Duets; Sequoia

Wuorinen—Contrafactum; Reliquary for Igor Stravinsky

Armer—Great Instrument of the Geggerets

Kolb—Soundings

Zwilich—Fantasy for Orchestra; Symphonies Nos.1 & 3

Singleton—Shadows; When Given a Choice; Yellow Rose Petal

Albert, Stephen—Anthem and Processionals

Iannaccone—Symphony No.3

León—Desde …

Maslanka—11:11 — A Dance at the Edge of the World; Music for String Orchestra

Schwantner—Chasing Light

Bond, Victoria—Dreams of Flying; Thinking Like a Mountain; Variations on a Theme of Brahms

Peck—Signs of Life II

Zaimont—Monarchs; Stillness

Gilbert, J.—In the Beginning

Lieberson, Peter—Drala

Rodríguez—Colorful Symphony; Estampie; Sinfonía à la mariachi; Trunks

Adams, John—Common Tones in Simple Time

Horwood—Amusement Park Suite; Symphony No.1; Women of Trachis

Kechley—Alexander and the Wind-Up Mouse; Transformations

Mauldin—Enchanted Land

Walker, Gwyneth—Light of Three Mornings; Symphonic Dances

Gellis—Short Symphony on Eastern Modes

Bryant—Dinosaurs

Mascari—Meet the Orchestra

Rouse—Phantasmata

Stucky—Impromptus; Pinturas de Tamayo

Warshauer—Jerusalem, Open Your Gates

Ayers—Jericho; Passion of John Brown

Galbraith—De profundis ad lucem

Actor—Dance Rhapsody

McTee—Double Play

Sierra—Concerto for Orchestra; Serenata; Sinfonía No.1

Beaser—Chorale Variations for Orchestra

Coleman, L.R.—Celebration; Hibernia Suite; Lunatics and Lovers; Suite Antique

Picker—Keys to the City

Curiale—Gates of Gold

Danielpour—Song of Remembrance

Oliverio, James—Story of Snow White

Smith, Kile—Symphony: Lumen ad revelationem; Voice of One Who Spoke

Itkin—Jonah

Smith, Gregory—Mr. Smith's Composition; Zoo Song

Tan—Orchestral Theatre I; Symphony for Strings

Ticheli—Radiant Voices

Caltabiano—Concertini

Heitzeg—Mahkato Wakpa; Nine Surrealist Studies; On the Day You Were Born; Voice of the Everglades

Kernis—Concerto With Echoes; Newly Drawn Sky

Hagen—Gesture Drawings

Heggie—Dead Man Walking: Orchestral Excerpts

Liebermann, Lowell—Domain of Arnheim

Adamo—Alcott Music

Higdon—river sings a song to trees

Roter—TR: A "Bully" Portrait

McLoskey—Symphoniae sacrae

Thomas, Augusta Read—Helios Choros II; Jubilee; Tangle; Terpsichore's Dream; Words of the Sea

Wittry—Mist

Stephenson—Celestial Suite

Stookey—Mahl/er/werk

Frank, G.L.—Three Latin American Dances

Puts—Falling Dream

[16'–20']

Eastern European

Gluck—Ballet Suite No.1 (arr. Mottl)
Stamitz, Joh.—Orchestral Trios, op.1, nos.1–3; Orchestral Trio, op.4, no.3; Orchestral Trio, op.5, no.3
Stamitz, Joh.—Sinfonias, op.4, nos.1, 4, 6
Gołąbek—Symphony, D major (II)
Stamitz, Carl—Orchestral Quartets, op.14, nos.1 & 4
Liszt—A la Chapelle Sixtine; Christus: Hirtengesang; Festklänge; Hunnenschlacht; Légendes; Mazeppa; Préludes; Tasso
Dvořák—Rhapsody; Slavonic Dances, op.46, nos.1–4; op.46, nos.5–8; op.72, nos.1–4 (9–12); op.72, nos.5–8 (13–16); Suite, op.98b; Water Goblin; Wood Dove
Noskowski—Steppe
Janáček—Cunning Little Vixen: Suite (Talich/Smetácek); From the House of the Dead: Suite (Jílek); Lachian Dances
Pachulski—Suite
Karłowicz—Lithuanian Rhapsody
Bartók—Dance Suite; Mikrokosmos Suite; Miraculous Mandarin: Suite; Two Pictures
Kodály—Dances of Galanta; Summer Evening
Szymanowski—Concert Overture
Martinů—Double Concerto; Estampes; Frescos of Piero della Francesca; Sextet; Sinfonia concertante
Weinberger—Under the Spreading Chestnut Tree
Tubin—Music for Strings
Ránki—Symphony No.1
Rózsa—Theme, Variations & Finale; Three Hungarian Sketches
Bacewicz—Contradizione; Music for Strings, Trumpets & Percussion
Lutoslawski—Livre; Novelette; Three Postludes
Panufnik—Autumn Music; Harmony; Nocturne

Klein—Partita
Husa—Fantasies; Symphonic Suite; Two Sonnets by Michelangelo
Ligeti—Macabre Collage
Kilar—Krzesany
Lazarof—Chamber Symphony; Symphony No.7
Górecki—Refrain; Scontri; Symphony No.1
Svoboda—Nocturne; Sinfoniette
Wański—Symphony, G major

French & Belgian

Lully—Ballet Suite; Triomphe de l'amour: Ballet Suite
Rameau—Fêtes d'Hébé: Divertissement; Paladins: Suite No.2
Meyerbeer—Prophète: Ballet Music
Berlioz—Roi Lear; Roméo et Juliette: Love Scene
Offenbach—Kakadu: Ballet Suite
Saint-Saëns—Jeunesse d'Hercule; Suite algérienne
Delibes—Sylvia: Suite
Bizet—Arlésienne: Suites Nos.1 & 2; Carmen: Suite No.2
Massenet—Cid: Ballet Music; Scènes hongroises; Scènes pittoresques
Widor—Korrigane
Fauré—Dolly; Pelléas et Mélisande: Suite; Shylock: Suite
Luigini—Ballet égyptien
Debussy—Children's Corner [2 versions]; Five Etudes; Images: Ibéria; Jeux; Six épigraphes antiques
Dukas—Péri
Satie—Parade
Koechlin—Partita
Roussel—Bacchus et Ariane: Suite No.1; Festin de l'araignée; Marchand de sable qui passe … ; Padmâvatî: Suite No.1; Symphony No.4
Schmitt—Janiana; Musiques de plein air
Rabaud—Procession nocturne
Hahn—Bal de Beatrice d'Este: Suite
Ravel—Daphnis et Chloé: Suite No.2; Ma Mère l'Oye: Suite; Rapsodie espagnole;

Tombeau de Couperin; Valses nobles et sentimentales
Varèse—Arcana
Ibert—Diane de Poitiers: Suite No.1
Honegger—Impératrice aux rochers: Suite; Suite archaïque
Milhaud—Aubade; Création du monde; Frenchman in New York; Suite provençale; Symphonies Nos.11 & 12
Tansman—Sinfonietta; Triptych
Auric—Chambre; Phèdre: Suite symphonique
Poulenc—Biches: Suite
Tomasi—Fanfares liturgiques
Jolivet—Symphonie de danses
Dutilleux—Métaboles; Mystère de l'instant
Murail—Pour adoucer le cours de temps …
Durand, Joël-François—Athanor

German & Austrian

Buxtehude—Four Chorale Preludes
Telemann—Don Quichotte; Ouverture des nations anciens; Overture, TWV 55:fis1; Suite, TWV 44:7
Bach, J.S.—Chaconne (arr. Casella); Prelude & Fugue, BWV 552; Suites (Overtures) Nos.2, 3, 4
Handel—Concerto a due cori, No.2; Rodrigo: Overture; Royal Fireworks Music [2 versions]; Water Music Suite (arr. Harty)
Haydn, F.J.—Symphonies Nos.3, 5, 11, 12, 15, 18, 22, 23, 26, 28, 29, 32, 33, 35, 36, 39, 40, 41, 46, 50, 58, 59, 62, 63 [2 versions], 65, 67, 69, 70, 75, 77, 78, 85, 96
Bach, J.C.—Symphony, op.18, no.5
Haydn, M.—Symphonies, MH 272, MH 334, MH 399
Hofmann, L.—Sinfonias, C major & F major
Dittersdorf—Sinfonia, A major [G.A10] (Nazionale nel gusto di cinque nazioni)
Mozart, W.A.—Cassation No.2; German Dances, K.509; Kleine Nachtmusik;

[16'–20']

Musikalischer Spass;
Serenade No.8; Symphonies
Nos.6, 12, 14, 15, 17, 18, 19,
20, 21, 27, 30, 31, 33, 35;
Symphony, K.320; Thamos:
Zwischenaktmusiken
Pleyel—Symphony, op.3, no.1
Beethoven—German Dances;
Grosse Fuge, op.133
Weber, C.M.—Symphony
No.2
Schubert—Fantasy, D.940, F
minor; Lebensstürme;
Rosamunde: Ballet Music;
Symphony, D.708a: Scherzo
Mendelssohn—Sinfonia No.12
Schumann, R.—Overture,
Scherzo, & Finale;
Symphony, WoO 29
Wagner, Richard—Siegfried
Idyll; Symphony, WWV 35,
E major; Tristan und Isolde:
Prelude & Liebestod;
Walküre: Wotan's Farewell &
Magic Fire Music
Raff—Feste Burg ist unser
Gott
Bruckner—Symphony No.3:
Adagio 2 (1876); Symphony
No.4 (1878 version, Cahis
10): Finale 1878 (Volksfest)
Goldmark—Sakuntala
Joachim—Hamlet
Brahms—Variations on a
Theme of Joseph Haydn
Humperdinck—Dornröschen:
Suite
Mahler—Totenfeier
Wolf—Corregidor: Suite
Strauss, R.—Don Juan; Frau
ohne Schatten: Symphonic
Fantasy (arr. Ruzick);
Josephslegende: Symphonic
Fragment; Macbeth;
Rosenkavalier: Concert Suite
[Mandell]
Pfitzner—Kleine Sinfonie
Schmidt, F.—Notre Dame:
Entr'acte & Carnival Music
Schoenberg—Five Pieces for
Orchestra [3 versions]; Ode to
Napoleon
Schreker—Geburtstag der
Infantin: Suite
Berg—Three Pieces for
Orchestra; Wozzeck: Three
Excerpts
Stephan—Musik für Orchester
Toch—Big Ben
Hindemith—Kammermusik
No.1; Konzertmusik, op.50;

Philharmonic Concerto;
Sinfonietta; Tuttifäntchen:
Suite
Korngold—Schauspiel-
Ouvertüre; Symphonic
Overture
Egk—French Suite
Blacher—Hamlet; Orchestra-
Variations on a Theme of
Paganini
Hartmann—Symphony No.2
Einem—Philadelphia
Symphony
Zimmermann—Heroische
Prosodie; Sinfonie in einem
Satz
Henze—Antifone; Aria de la
Folía española; Barcarola;
Caprichos; Symphonies
Nos.1 & 5; Usignolo
dell'imperatore
Veerhoff—Sinfonia panta-rhei
Schwertsik—Fünf Naturstücke
Höller—Aura

Italian

Veracini—Quatro pezzi
Boccherini—Symphonies
Nos.7, 10, 13, 17, 20, 21, 23,
27
Salieri—Sinfonia (Giorno
onomastico)
Rossini—Sonatas Nos.5 & 6
Verdi—Birthday Variations
[arr. J.McPhee]
Puccini—Capriccio sinfonico
Busoni—Sarabande & Cortège
Respighi—Antiche danze ed
arie: Suites I, II, III; Ballata
delle gnomidi; Impressioni
brasiliane; Trittico
Botticelliano; Uccelli
Malipiero—Impressioni dal
vero: Part II; Sinfonia per
Antigenida; Symphonies
Nos.3, 6, 8, 9
Casella—Italia; Paganiniana
Scelsi—Chukrum
Rota—Concerto, String
Orchestra
Maderna—Aura; Serenata
No.2
Di Vittorio—Symphonies
Nos.1 & 2

Russian

Borodin—Symphony No.3
Balakirev—Tamara
Mussorgsky—Pictures at an
Exhibition (Tushmalov)

Tchaikovsky—Hamlet;
Nutcracker and the Mouse
King; Overture 1812; Romeo
and Juliet (final version);
Tempest
Rimsky-Korsakov—Tale of the
Tsar Saltan: Suite
Arensky—Variations on a
Theme by Tchaikovsky,
op.35a
Glazunov—Finnish Fantasy;
Stenka Razin
Rachmaninoff—Caprice
bohémien; Isle of the Dead;
Rock
Glière—Syrènes; Zaporozhy
Cossacks
Miaskovsky—Symphony
No.21
Stravinsky—Agon; Danses
concertantes; Scènes de ballet
Prokofiev—Lieutenant Kijé:
Suite; Romeo and Juliet: Suite
No.3; Scythian Suite;
Sinfonietta; Visions fugitives
Tcherepnin, A.—Georgiana;
Serenade, op.97
Khachaturian—Masquerade:
Suite; Spartacus: Suite No.3;
Valencian Widow: Suite
Kabalevsky—Colas Breugnon:
Suite
Shostakovich—Age of Gold:
Suite
Khrennikov—Symphony No.1
Denisov—Chamber Symphony
No.2
Shchedrin—Seagull: Suite;
Self-Portrait

Spanish &
Latin American

Falla—Homenajes
Turina—Danzas fantásticas
Villa-Lobos—Bachianas
brasileiras no.1; Danses
africaines; Sinfonietta No.2;
Suite for Strings; Uirapurú
Gerhard—Don Quixote:
Dances; Epithalamion
Chávez—Initium; Pasajes
mexicanas
Rodrigo—A la busca del más
allá
Montsalvatge—Manfred
Ginastera—Glosses sobre
temes de Pau Casals;
Pampeana No.3

[16'–20']

United Kingdom

Purcell—Fairy Queen: Suite No.1
Sullivan—Pineapple Poll: Suite
Elgar—Crown of India: Suite; In the South; Severn Suite
Delius—Brigg Fair; Eventyr
Vaughan Williams—Concerto grosso; England of Elizabeth; Partita
Coleridge-Taylor—Hiawatha: Suite; Petite suite de concert; Symphonic Variations
Bridge—Enter Spring; Suite
Harty—John Field Suite
Ireland—Concertino pastorale
Bax—Garden of Fand; Tale the Pine-Trees Knew
Walton—Improvisations on an Impromptu of Benjamin Britten; Partita; Wise Virgins: Suite
Alwyn—Elizabethan Dances; Symphony No.5
Tippett—Divertimento on "Sellinger's Round"; Fantasia concertante; Suite for the Birthday of Prince Charles
Britten—Matinées musicales; Peter Grimes: Four Sea Interludes; Simple Symphony; Young Person's Guide to the Orchestra
Arnold—Homage to the Queen: Suite
Musgrave—Concerto for Orchestra; Night Music
Hoddinott—Fioriture
Birtwistle—Endless Parade
Maxwell Davies—Carolísima Serenade; Prolation
Bennett, Richard R.—Anniversaries; Diversions; Gormenghast: Suite; Partita; Reflections on a Sixteenth Century Tune; Zodiac
McCabe—Symphony No.7
Matthews, D.—Symphony No.3
Tann—Adirondack Light
MacMillan—Confession of Isobel Gowdie
Adès—Living Toys

Other Nationalities

Gade—Novelette No.2

Grieg—Bergliot; Lyric Suite; Norwegian Dances; Sigurd Jorsalfar: Three Orchestral Pieces
Nielsen, Carl—Little Suite
Sibelius—Lemminkäinen Suite: Lemminkäinen and the Maidens of the Island; Night Ride and Sunrise; Pohjola's Daughter; Saga; Tapiola; Tempest: Suite No.2
Alfvén—Swedish Rhapsody No.3
Melartin—Serenade
Grainger—Lincolnshire Posy
Schoeck—Sommernacht
Valen—Symphony No.3
Martin—Etudes for String Orch; Quatre éléments
Rosenberg—Bergslagsbilder; Reflessioni no.2; Symphony No.8
Langgaard—Symphony No.7
Ben-Haim—Concerto for Strings
Riisager—Fools' Paradise: Suite No.1
Skalkottas—Ten Sketches
Holmboe—Symphony No.13
Blomdahl—Sisyphos
Bentzon—Chamber Concert
Delden—Concerto per due orchestre d'archi; Musica sinfonica
Xenakis—Eonta
Schurmann—Variants
Rautavaara—Cantus arcticus; Symphonies Nos.1 & 4
Takemitsu—Music of Tree
Nørgård—Tributes; Twilight; Voyage into the Golden Screen
Ketting—Symphony No.1
Sallinen, A.—Symphony No.1
Ishii—Sho-ko
Leeuw, R. de—Abschied
Whitehead—improbable ordered dance
Cresswell—O!; Salm
Boudreau—Versus
Aho—Minea
Ran—Double Vision; Legends
Saariaho—Laterna Magica
Chen Yi—Concerto, Piano; Symphony No.2
Sheng—Postcards
Young—Lux Aeterna
Lindberg—Corrente II; Era; Zona
Salonen, E-P.—Insomnia; L.A. Variations; NYX

O'Boyle—Australian in New York
Dorman—Ellef Symphony

21'–25'

American (United States)

Fry—Santa Claus
Paine—Tempest
Loeffler—Pagan Poem
Hadley—Salome
Bloch, E.—Symphony in E-flat; Trois Poèmes juifs
Rogers—Musicians of Bremen
Piston—Symphonies Nos.2, 4, 5, 8
Still—Lenox Avenue; Symphonies Nos.1 & 3
Hanson—Symphony No.6
Sessions—Black Maskers: Suite; Symphonies Nos.4 & 7
Thomson, V.—Parson Weems and the Cherry Tree; River: Suite
Cowell—Symphonies Nos.3, 7, 9, 10, 15, 16, 17
Bacon—Enchanted Isle; From These States
Gershwin—Catfish Row; Porgy and Bess: Symphonic Picture
Harris, Roy—Symphonies Nos.5 & 11
Antheil—Symphonies Nos. 3 & 5
Copland—Appalachian Spring: Suite [2 versions]; Billy the Kid: Suite; City; Music for a Great City; Music for the Theatre; Red Pony; Symphony No.1
Krenek—Symphony, op.137
Weill—Symphony No.1
Wolpe—Symphony No.1
Giannini—Symphony No.2
Creston—Symphonies Nos.1-2
Swanson—Symphonies Nos.1 & 3
Carter—In Sleep, In Thunder; Minotaur: Ballet Suite; Variations for Orchestra
Barber—Symphony No.1
Reed—Fiesta mexicana
Schuman, Wm.—Judith; Undertow
Hovhaness—Symphony No.15
Dello Joio—Variations, Chaconne & Finale

[21'–25']

Gould—Fall River Legend: Ballet Suite; Jogger and the Dinosaur

Read—Symphony No.3

Fine, Irving—Symphony

Diamond—Symphonies Nos.1, 5, 6

Perle—Transcendental Modulations

Persichetti—Night Dances; Symphonies Nos.4 & 9

Surinach—Embattled Garden

Ward—Festival Triptych; Symphonies Nos.2, 3, 4

Bernstein—Facsimile; Fancy Free; On the Waterfront: Symphonic Suite; Symphony No.1; West Side Story: Symphonic Dances

Rochberg—Imago mundi; Symphony No.5

Kay, H.—Cakewalk: Concert Suite

Overton—Symphony for Strings

Foss—Baroque Variations

Bassett—Variations for Orchestra

Pinkham—Signs of the Zodiac

Rorem—String Symphony; Symphonies Nos.1, 2, 3

Laderman—Concerto for Orchestra; Magic Prison

Lees—Concerto for Orchestra; Scarlatti Portfolio

Starer—Symphony No.3

Schuller—Concerto for Orchestra, No.2; Contours; Seven Studies on Themes of Paul Klee; Spectra

Duffy—Heritage: Suite; Symphony No.1; Time for Remembrance

Lewis, R.H.—Three Movements on Scenes of Hieronymous Bosch

Argento—Fire Variations; Royal Invitation

Erb—Evensong

Adler, S.—Symphony No.6

Druckman—Brangle; Dark Upon the Harp; Mirage; Prism; Windows

Crumb—Variazioni

Nelson, Ron—Five Pieces; This is the Orchestra

Previn—Diversions

Wyner—Tuscan Triptych

Amram—Shakespearian Concerto

Deussen—Silver Shining Strand

Biggs—Concerto for Orchestra

Williams—Star Wars: Suite

Zaninelli—Steadfast Tin Soldier

Blackwood—Symphony No.2

Harmon—Earth Day Portrait

Jones—Symphonic Requiem; Symphony No.3

Schickele—Chenoo Who Stayed to Dinner

Reich—Four Sections; Variations

Del Tredici—Happy Voices

Glass—Symphony No.3

Hoover—J. M. W. Turner: Impressions; Night Skies

Wilson—Sinfonia

Bolcom—Summer Divertimento; Symphony No.5

Corigliano—Phantasmagoria

Harbison—Symphonies Nos.1, 2, 3, 4, 6; Umbrian Landscape With Saint

Tower—Silver Ladders

Wuorinen—Two-Part Symphony

Zwilich—Symphonies Nos.2 & 5

Monroe—Amazing Symphony Orchestra

Schwantner—Toward Light

Bond, Victoria—What's the Point of Counterpoint?

Pasatieri—Symphony

Peck—Mozart Escapes the Museum

Gilbert, J.—Dream Carver; Khoj

Rodríguez—Favola boccaccesca

Adams, John—Chamber Symphony; Doctor Atomic Symphony; Son of Chamber Symphony

Horwood—National Park Suite

Mauldin—American West; Mountain Light

Ott—First Trip to the Symphony

Walker, Gwyneth—Symphony of Grace

Welcher—Haleakala

Rouse—Symphonies Nos.1 & 3

Larsen, L.—String Symphony

Ayers—And they gathered on Mount Carmel

Actor—Symphony No.2

Einhorn—My Many Colored Days

Asia—Symphony No.1

Davidson—Black & Blues; Young Lutheran's Guide to the Orchestra

Sierra—Carnaval

Danielpour—Awakened Heart

Gordon—ReWriting Beethoven's Seventh Symphony

Mackey—Eating Greens

Phillips, P.S.—Celestial Harmonies

Sleeper—Symphony No.4

Smith, Gregory—MAJOR-minor Mystery; Melodic Life

Tan—Orchestral Theatre II

Allen—Nativity Scenes

Maltz—Aesop's Fables

Heitzeg—Sacred Stones; Symphony to the Prairie Farm

Ince—Symphonies Nos.2 & 3

Higdon—All Things Majestic

Trigos—Symphonies Nos.1-2

Amrhein—Symphony of Seasons

Boyer—Symphony No.1

Stookey—Out of the Everywhere

Frank, G.L.—Leyendas; Peregrinos; Requiem for a Magical America

Puts—Symphonies Nos.1 & 3

Petering—Symphony No.2

Lee, James III—A Different Soldier's Tale

Bates—B-Sides; Liquid Interface

Greenberg—Neon Refracted

Eastern European

Gluck—Airs de ballet, Suite No.2

Wański—Symphony, D major

Liszt—Hungaria

Minkus—Bayadère: Act II; Paquita: Suite

Dvořák—Czech Suite; Hero's Song; Legends, op.59: Nos.1-5; Legends, op.59: Nos.6-10; Serenade, op.44; Symphonic Variations

Janáček—Jenůfa-Rhapsodie; Sinfonietta; Taras Bulba

Karłowicz—Eternal Songs; Serenade; Stanisław and Anna Oświecimowie

Dohnányi—Ruralia hungarica

Bartók—Divertimento; Four Orchestral Pieces; Kossuth

Kodály—Concerto for Orchestra; Háry János: Suite;

[21'–25']
Variations on a Hungarian
Folksong
Martinů—Symphony No.2;
Toccata e due canzoni, H.311
Lutoslawski—Symphony No.4
Panufnik—Symphonies
Nos.8 & 10
Husa—Music for Prague;
Symphony No.2
Lazarof—Concerto for
Orchestra
Svoboda—Concerto for
Chamber Orch; Dance Suite

French & Belgian

Gossec—Symphony op.6, no.6
Gounod—Petite Symphonie
Lalo—Namouna: Ballet Suite
No.1
Saint-Saëns—Carnaval des
animaux; Symphony,
A major; Symphony No.2
Delibes—Coppélia: Suite No.1
Bizet—Carmen Symphony
Chabrier—Suite pastorale
Massenet—Scènes alsaciennes;
Suite No.1
Debussy—Martyre de Saint
Sébastien: Fragments
symphoniques; Mer;
Nocturnes (2 versions);
Pelléas et Mélisande
symphonie
Roussel—Bacchus et Ariane:
Suite No.2; Symphony No.3
Schmitt—Tragédie de Salomé:
Suite
Ravel—Gaspard de la nuit
Varèse—Amériques (1929
version); Déserts
Ibert—Histoires: Suite No.1;
Tropismes pour des amours
imaginaires
Honegger—Horace victorieux;
Symphonies Nos.1, 2, 5
Milhaud—Saudades do Brazil;
Suite symphonique no.2;
Symphony No.10
Poulenc—Animaux modèles:
Suite; Histoire de Babar
Jolivet—Symphonie pour
cordes; Symphonies Nos.1, 3
Messiaen—Chronochromie
Markevitch—Rebus

German & Austrian

Telemann—Overture, TWV
55:D21

Bach, J.S.—Suite (Overture)
No.1, BWV 1066, C major
Handel—Pastor fido: Suite
Mozart, Leopold—Musikal-
ische Schlittenfahrt
Haydn, F.J.—Symphonies
Nos.6–8, 13, 31, 43–45, 47,
49, 51–52, 55–57, 60–61, 64,
66, 68, 71–74, 76, 79–80, 83–
84, 87–91, 93–95, 97, 99–
100, 102
Dittersdorf—Sinfonias,
A minor [G.a2] & D minor
[G.d1]
Kraus—Symphony, C minor
Mozart, W.A.—Cassation
No.1; Divertimento No.7,
K.205; German Dances,
K.586; Idomeneo: Ballet
Music; Petits Riens;
Serenades Nos.11–12;
Symphonies Nos.25, 28, 34;
Symphony, K.204
Beethoven—Minuets, WoO 7;
Quartet, Strings, op.95
Witt—Symphony in A
Weber, C.M.—Symphony
No.1
Schubert—Rosamunde:
Entr'actes; Symphony, D.759
Mendelssohn—Sinfonia No.7
Schumann, R.—Bilder aus
Osten
Wagner, Richard—
Tannhäuser: Overture &
Venusberg Music
Raff—Sinfonietta
Bruckner—Symphony No.9:
Finale (Carragan or SPCM)
Reinecke—Serenade, op.242
Grimm—Suite in Canonform
Brahms—Eleven Chorale
Preludes; Liebeslieder
Waltzes, op.52
Fuchs—Serenade, No.3
Mahler—Symphony No.10
(Krenek): Movements I and
III only; Symphony No.10
(Ratz): 1st movement
(Adagio) only
Reznicek—Symphonic Suite
No.1
Strauss, R.—Rosenkavalier:
Suite [1945]; Suite, TrV 132;
Tod und Verklärung
Zemlinsky—Sinfonietta
Reger—Vier Tondichtungen
Schoenberg—Chamber
Symphony No.1 [2 versions];
Chamber Symphony No.2;
Variations for Orchestra

Schreker—Kammer-
symphonie; Vorspiel zu
einem Drama
Stephan—Symphonischer Satz
Toch—Symphony No.6
Gál—Musik für
Streichorchester
Hindemith—Mathis der Maler
(Symphony); Nobilissima
visione: Suite; Pittsburgh
Symphony; Symphonic
Metamorphosis
Korngold—Märchenbilder
Blacher—Symphony;
Tanzszenen
Einem—Meditations
Henze—Symphonies
Nos.2 & 3
Stockhausen—Gruppen;
Punkte
Kagel—Broken Chords;
Variationen ohne Fuge
Lachenmann—… zwei
Gefühle …

Italian

Monteverdi—Combattimento
di Tancredi e Clorinda
Boccherini—Symphonies
Nos.3, 5, 6, 11, 25
Clementi—Symphony No.2
Verdi—Symphony for Strings
Bossi—Intermezzi goldoniani
Respighi—Belkis, regina di
Saba: Suite; Boutique
fantasque: Suite; Feste
romane; Pini di Roma;
Rossiniana; Suite, P.41
Malipiero—Per una favola
cavalleresca; Symphonies
Nos.1 & 2
Casella—Giara: Symphonic
Suite; Serenata
Petrassi—Concerto for
Orchestra No.1
Scelsi—Uaxuctum
Menotti—Apolcalypse;
Sebastian: Suite
Berio—Rendering

Russian

Borodin—Borodiniana Suite;
Petite suite
Mussorgsky—Pictures at an
Exhibition (Goehr)
Tchaikovsky—Francesca da
Rimini; Nutcracker: Suite
No.1; Romeo and Juliet
(orig); Sleeping Beauty:
Suite; Suite No.4

[21'–25']

Rimsky-Korsakov—Christmas
 Eve: Suite; Coq d'or: Suite;
 Legend of the Invisible City
 of Kitezh: Suite; Maid of
 Pskov: Overture & Entr'actes;
 Sinfonietta on Russian
 Themes
Ippolitov-Ivanov—Caucasian
 Sketches
Scriabin—Poem of Ecstasy;
 Prometheus
Rachmaninoff—Cinq Études-
 tableaux
Miaskovsky—Sinfonietta,
 op.32, no.2
Stravinsky—Baiser de la fée:
 Divertimento; Firebird: Suite
 (1911 or 1919); Jeu de cartes;
 Song of the Nightingale;
 Symphony in Three
 Movements
Prokofiev—Peter and the Wolf
Khachaturian—Gayane: Suite
 No.3; Spartacus: Suite No.2
Kabalevsky—Symphony No.1
Shostakovich—Chamber
 Symphony, op.110a; Hamlet:
 Incidental Music; Suite for
 Variety Orch, No.1
Gubaydulina—Feast During a
 Plague; Light of the End
Shchedrin—Little Hump-
 backed Horse: Suite No.1;
 Music for Str, Ob, Hns & Cel;
 Stikhira; Fragment-Suite
Finko—Symphonies Nos.1 & 2

Spanish & Latin American

Falla—Amor brujo: Ballet
 Suite
Turina—Sinfonia sevillana
Villa-Lobos—Bachianas
 brasileiras nos.2 & 4;
 Sinfonietta No.1
Gerhard—Concerto for
 Orchestra
Chávez—Hija de Colquide:
 Symphonic Suite;
 Symphonies Nos.4 & 5
Montsalvatge—Simfonia de
 Rèquiem
Ginastera—Concerto for
 Strings; Popol vuh;
 Variaciones concertantes
Orbón—Tres versiones
 sinfónicas

United Kingdom

Bennett, Wm. S.—Symphony,
 G minor
Sullivan—Merchant of Venice:
 Masquerade Suite
Parry—English Suite
Vaughan Williams—Story of a
 Flemish Farm; Wasps: Suite
Bridge—Sea
Walton—Variations on a
 Theme by Hindemith
Tippett—Concerto for Double
 String Orch; Midsummer
 Marriage: Ritual Dances
Britten—Plymouth Town;
 Sinfonia da requiem
Arnold—Bridge on the River
 Kwai; Symphony for Strings;
 Symphony No.8
Musgrave—Turbulent
 Landscapes
Hoddinott—Symphonies
 Nos.3 & 5
Maxwell Davies—Mirror of
 Whitening Light; St. Thomas
 Wake; Sinfonia for Chamber
 Orchestra; Symphony No.9
Bennett, Richard R.—Concerto
 for Orchestra; Symphony
 No.3
McCabe—Arthur: Three
 Portraits; Symphony on a
 Pavane
Ferneyhough—Plötzlichkeit
Holloway—Scenes from
 Schumann
Lloyd—Symphony No.2
Chilcott—Tandem
Adès—Asyla

Other Nationalities

Berwald—Symphony No.2
Gade—Symphonies Nos.4 & 6
Grieg—Holberg Suite; Old
 Norwegian Melody with
 Variations
Nielsen, Carl—Aladdin:
 7 pieces
Sibelius—King Kristian II:
 Suite; Symphony No.7;
 Tempest: Suite No.1
Valen—Symphony No.2
Martin—Petite symphonie
 concertante
Rosenberg—Concerto No.1 for
 String Orchestra; Suite on
 Swedish Folktunes;
 Symphony No.6
Adaskin—Algonquin
 Symphony

Badings—Symphony No.7
Holmboe—Symphonies
 Nos.7, 11 & 12
Brott—Concordia
Blomdahl—Game for Eight;
 Symphony No.3
Suolahti—Sinfonia piccola
Rautavaara—Symphony No.2
Sallinen, A.—Concerto for
 Chamber Orch; Symphony
 No.3
Ishii—Kyō-Sō; Mono-Prism
Davies, Victor—Dream
 Variations; Short Symphony
Cresswell—Of Smoke and
 Bickering Flame
Harris, Ross—Symphony No.4
Mozetich—Procession of Duos
Aho—Symphony No.2
Saariaho—Nymphea
 Reflection; Orion
Buhr—winter poems
Sheng—China Dreams; H'un
Young—Symphony No.2
Lindberg—Sculpture
Rival—Symphony No. 2

26'–30'

American (United States)

Chadwick—Serenade;
 Symphonic Sketches
Herbert—Hero and Leander;
 Serenade
MacDowell—Suite No.2
Ives—Symphony No.4
Carpenter—Adventures in a
 Perambulator; Skyscrapers
Collins—The Masque of the
 Red Death: Ballet Suite
Price—Symphony No.3
Piston—Symphonies
 Nos.1 & 6
Still—Symphonies Nos.2 & 4
Hanson—Symphonies
 Nos.1, 2, 4
Sessions—Symphonies
 Nos.2, 3, 9
Cowell—Symphonies
 Nos.5 & 19
Porter, Q.—Symphony No.2
Bacon—Fables; Symphonies
 Nos.1 & 2
Harris, Roy—Symphony No.9
Ellington—River
Thompson, R.—Symphony
 No.2
Antheil—Symphony [No.5;
 withdrawn] Symphony No.6

[26'–30']
Copland—Dance Panels
Weill—Symphony No.2
Creston—Symphonies Nos.3, 4
Gutche—Symphony No.6
Carter—Symphony No.1
Barber—Medea [orig]; Medea (Ballet Suite); Symphony No.2
Schuman, Wm.—Symphonies Nos.4, 6, 7, 9
Hovhaness—Symphony No.22
Dello Joio—Triumph of Saint Joan
Gould—Stringmusic; Symphony of Spirituals
Surinach—Concerto for String Orchestra
Weber, Ben—Symphony on Poems of Wm Blake
Ward—Symphony No.7
Rochberg—Music for the Magic Theater
Foss—Symphony No.3
Bassett—Concerto for Orchestra
Mennin—Symphonies Nos.6-7
Rorem—Eleven Studies for Eleven Players
Lees—Symphonies Nos.2, 3, 5
Argento—In Praise of Music; Ring of Time
Erb—Concerto for Orchestra; Ritual Observances
Flagello—Theme, Variations & Fugue
London—In Heinrich's Shoes
Zaninelli—Lexicon of Beasties
Blackwood—Symphony No.5
Jones—Symphony No.1
Corigliano—Creations
Tower—Concerto for Orchestra
Wuorinen—Movers and Shakers
Schwantner—New Morning for the World
Zaimont—Symphony No.1
Lieberson, Peter—Ashoka's Dream: Suite
Adams, John—Fearful Symmetries; Shaker Loops
Welcher—Night Watchers
Paulus—Concerto for Orchestra
Rouse—Symphony No.2
Stucky—Concerto for Orchestra; Second Concerto for Orchestra
Larsen, L.—Solo Symphony
Davis—Litany of Sins
Hartke—Symphony No.3

Asia—Symphony No.2
Sierra—Sinfonía No.3
Daugherty—Motorcity Triptych
Picker—Symphony No.1
Adolphe—Carnival of the Creatures; Marita and Her Heart's Desire; Tyrannosaurus Sue
Danielpour—Apparitions; Concerto for Orchestra
Gordon—Dystopia
Sleeper—Symphony No.1
Smith, Gregory—Mr. Smith's Bowl of Notes; Orchestra Games
Tan—Death and Fire
Heitzeg—Symphony in Sculpture
Kernis—Symphony No.2
Higdon—City Scape
Richman—Behold the Bold Umbrellaphant
Stookey—Composer is Dead
Puts—Symphony No.4
Bates—Alternative Energy

Eastern European

Gluck—Don Juan: Four Movements
Vorisek—Symphony
Chopin—Sylphides (various)
Liszt—Héroïde funèbre; Ideale
Dvořák—Golden Spinning Wheel; Serenade, op.22
Janáček—Idylla
Foerster, J.B.—From Shakespeare
Suk—Fairy Tale; Serenade
Bartók—Miraculous Mandarin; Music for Strings, Percussion and Celesta; Wooden Prince: Suite
Enesco—Suite No.1
Kodály—Symphony
Martinů—Symphonies Nos.3 & 6
Lajtha—Suite No.3
Harsányi—Histoire du petite tailleur
Tubin—Symphony No.8
Rózsa—Jungle Book
Bacewicz—Symphony No.3
Lutoslawski—Concerto for Orchestra; Symphonies Nos.1-3
Husa—Steadfast Tin Soldier; Symphony No.1
Górecki—Old Polish Music
Svoboda—Symphonies Nos.2, 3, 4

Eötvös—Chinese Opera

French & Belgian

Méhul—Symphony No.2
Gounod—Symphony No.1
Saint-Saëns—Foi: Trois tableaux symphoniques; Symphony No.1
Bizet—Symphony No.1
Chausson—Symphony
Pierné—Cydalise et le chèvre-pied: Suite No.1
Ropartz—Symphony No.5
Koechlin—Course de printemps
Ravel—Ma Mère l'Oye
Varèse—Amériques (1922 version)
Ibert—Ballade de la geôle de Reading; Chevalier errant: Symphonic Suite; Diane de Poitiers: Suite No.2
Honegger—Symphonies Nos.3 & 4
Milhaud—Carnaval de Londres; Symphonies Nos.1 & 2
Poulenc—Sinfonietta
Messiaen—Ascension
Dutilleux—Symphony No.2

German & Austrian

Telemann—Overture, TWV 55:C3
Haydn, F.J.—Symphonies Nos.42, 48, 53, 54, 81, 82, 86, 92, 98, 101, 103
Dittersdorf—Sinfonia, D major
Knecht—Portrait musical de la nature
Mozart, W.A.—Divertimento No.11; Serenade No.1; Symphonies Nos.29, 36, 38, 39
Beethoven—Symphonies Nos.1 & 8
Witt—Jena Symphony
Spohr—Octet, op.32, E major; Symphony No.3
Schubert—Symphonies Nos.1, 2, 3, 5, 6, & D.936a
Mendelssohn—Symphonies Nos.2, 4, 5
Schumann, R.—Symphonies Nos.1 & 4 [both versions]
Raff—Symphony No.6
Reinecke—Symphony No.1
Grimm—Symphony, op.19
Brahms—Serenade No.2
Bruch—Symphony No.1
Klengel—Serenade

[26'–30']

Wolf—Penthesilea
Strauss, R.—Metamorphosen
Schoenberg—Suite for String
 Orch; Verklärte Nacht (both
 versions)
Berg—Lyric Suite
Wellesz—Prosperos
 Beschwörungen
Toch—Symphony No.3
Hindemith—Lustige
 Sinfonietta; Symphonia
 serena; Symphonic Dances
Egk—Variations on a
 Caribbean Theme
Hartmann—Symphonies
 Nos.1 & 6
Henze—Symphonies
 Nos.4 & 8

Italian

Boccherini—Symphony No.8,
 G.508
Clementi—Symphonies
 Nos.1, 3, 4
Cherubini—Symphony, D
 major
Respighi—Vetrate di chiesa
Casella—Suite à Jean Huré

Russian

Mussorgsky—Pictures at an
 Exhibition (Stokowski)
Tchaikovsky—Serenade, op.48
Rimsky-Korsakov—Symphony
 No.1
Arensky—Suite No.1
Glazunov—Kremlin; Scènes
 de ballet
Glière—Red Poppy: Suite
Stravinsky—Apollon Musagète
 (both versions); Histoire du
 soldat: Suite; Orpheus;
 Symphony in C
Prokofiev—Cinderella: Suites
 Nos.1, 2, 3; Romeo and Juliet:
 Suites No.1, 2; Symphony
 No.4 (1st version)
Tcherepnin, A.—Symphony
 No.2
Khachaturian—Gayane: Suite
 No.2; Spartacus: Suite No.1
Kabalevsky—Symphony No.2
Shostakovich—Symphonies
 Nos.1, 3, 6, 9
Shchedrin—Anna Karenina:
 Romantic Music
Schnittke—In memoriam …

Spanish & Latin American

Arriaga—Symphony in D
Albéniz—Iberia (arr. Arbós)
Villa-Lobos—Bachianas
 brasileiras no.7 & no.8
Gerhard—Symphony No.4
Chávez—Symphony No.3
Catán—Florencia en el
 Amazonas: Suite

United Kingdom

Parry—Symphony No.5
Stanford—Symphony No.7
Elgar—Falstaff
Vaughan Williams—
 Symphonies Nos.4 & 8
Bliss—Checkmate: Prologue &
 Five Dances
Walton—Symphony No.2
Alwyn—Sinfonietta;
 Symphony No.2
Tippett—New Year: Suite
Britten—Death in Venice:
 Suite; Gloriana: Symphonic
 Suite; Variations on a Theme
 of Frank Bridge
Arnold—Symphonies
 Nos.2, 5, 6
Goehr, Alexander—Symphony
 in One Movement
Birtwistle—Verses for
 Ensembles
Maxwell Davies—Caroline
 Mathilde: Suite from Act I;
 Strathclyde Concerto No.10;
 Symphony No.5
McCabe—Arthur Pendragon:
 Suite No.1; Symphony No.4
Matthews, C.—Landscape

Other Nationalities

Berwald—Symphonies
 Nos.3 & 4
Gade—Symphonies
 Nos.2, 3, 5, 8
Grieg—Symphonic Dances
Nielsen, Carl—Symphony
 No.1
Sibelius—Pelléas and
 Mélisande; Swanwhite: Suite
Sibelius—Symphonies
 Nos.3, 5, 6
Atterberg—Sinfonia per archi;
 Symphony No.7
Rosenberg—Concerto No.2
Ben-Haim—Symphony No.1
Skalkottas—Return of Ulysses

Badings—Symphony No.5
Holmboe—Symphonies
 Nos.2, 3, 10
Bentzon—Symphony No.7
Schurmann—Six Studies of
 Francis Bacon
Rautavaara—Symphony No.8
Cresswell—Ylur
Aho—Symphony No.1
Ran—Concerto for Orchestra
Lindberg—Joy
Salonen, E.-P.—Wing on Wing
Ritchie, Anthony—Symphony
 No. 3

31'–40'

American (United States)

Paine—Symphony No.1
Chadwick—Symphony No.2
Converse—American Sketches
Hadley—Symphony No.2
Ives—Symphonies Nos.1 &.2;
 Universe Symphony (Austin
 realization)
Taylor—Through the Looking
 Glass
Collins—Symphony
Grofé—Grand Canyon Suite
Piston—The Incredible Flutist;
 Symphony No.3
Hanson—Symphony No.3
Bacon—Ford's Theatre
Dawson—Negro Folk
 Symphony
Thompson, R.—Symphony
 No.1
Antheil—Symphony No.4
Copland—Appalachian Spring
 (complete ballet; 2 versions)
Schuman, Wm.—Symphonies
 Nos.3, 8, 10
Dello Joio—Meditations on
 Ecclesiastes
Diamond—Symphonies
 Nos.3, 8
Surinach—Apasionada
Bernstein—Symphony No.2
Rochberg—Symphonies
 Nos.2, 6
Imbrie—Symphony No.1
Foss—Symphony No.1
Rorem—Air Music
Laderman—Symphony No.7
Flagello—Symphony No.1
Blackwood—Symphony No.1

[31'–40']

Bach, Jan—Happy Prince
Glass—Dracula; Symphony No.8
Bolcom—Symphony No.3
Corigliano—Symphony No.2
Harbison—Symphony No.5
Albert, Stephen—RiverRun; Symphony No.2
Maslanka—Symphony No.6
Zaimont—Remember Me
Avshalomov, D.—Pangs of Love; Trotzky's Train
Adams, John—City Noir; Harmonielehre
Welcher—Symphony No.5
Locklair—Symphony No.1
Lofstrom—Woodcarver's Daughter: Suite [No.1]
Actor—Symphonies Nos.1, 3
Elfman—Serenada Schizophrana
McTee—Symphony No.1
Adolphe—Oceanophony; Purple Palace
Cotton—Pyramus and Thisbe: Suite
Tan—Concerto for Orchestra
Wolfe, Julia—Cruel Sister
Kernis—Symphony in Waves
Abels—Frederick's Fables
Higdon—Concerto for Orchestra
Trigos—Symphony No.3
Greenberg—Intelligent Life; Symphony No.5

Eastern European

Stamitz, Joh.—Three Mannheim Symphonies
Liszt—Ce qu'on entend sur la montagne
Minkus—Paquita (2 versions)
Dvořák—Symphonies Nos.1, 3, 4, 5, 7, 8, 9
Stojowski—Symphony, op.21
Bartók—Concerto for Orchestra; Suites Nos.1 & 2
Enesco—Symphony No.1
Szymanowski—Symphony No.2
Martinů—Symphonies Nos.1, 4, 5
Tubin—Symphonies Nos.2, 4, 5, 6
Lutoslawski—Preludes & Fugue for 13 Solo Strings
Husa—Concerto for Orchestra
Penderecki—Symphonies Nos.1, 2, 4

Svoboda—Symphonies Nos.1, 5
Vasks—Symphony No.2

French & Belgian

Berlioz—Symphonie funèbre et triomphale
Alkan—Symphony, op.39
Franck—Symphony
Saint-Saëns—Symphony No.3
Bizet—Roma
Indy—Jour d'été a la montagne; Symphony No.3
Charpentier, G.—Impressions d'Italie
Debussy—Boîte à joujoux
Dukas—Symphony
Magnard—Symphony No.3
Roussel—Symphony No.2
Ohana—Livre des prodiges
Amy—D'un espace déployé

German & Austrian

Handel—Water Music: Suite No.1, HWV 348, F major
Mozart, W.A.— Divertimenti, K.136, 137, 138 (as a group); Divertimenti Nos.2, 10, 15; Serenades Nos.3, 5, 9; Symphony, K.250; Symphonies Nos.40, 41
Beethoven—Quartet, Strings, op.131; Septet, op.20; Symphonies Nos.2, 4, 5, 6, 7
Spohr—Nonet; Symphonies Nos.4 & 7
Schubert—Quartet (Tod und das Mädchen); Symphony No.4; Symphony, D.729 [2 versions]
Mendelssohn—Octet, Strings, op.20; Sinfonias No.8 [2 versions], No.9, No.11; Symphonies Nos.1, 3
Schumann, R.—Carnaval; Symphonies Nos.2 & 3
Wagner, Richard—Symphony, WWV 29, C major
Raff—Symphonies Nos.3, 5, 9
Bruckner—Symphony No.9: Finale (Documentation)
Reinecke—Symphonies Nos.2 & 3
Goldmark—Symphony No.2
Brahms—Symphonies Nos.3, 4
Draeseke—Symphony No.1
Bruch—Symphonies Nos.2, 3
Gernsheim—Symphony No.4
Goetz—Symphony, op.9, F major

Humperdinck—Hänsel und Gretel: Suite
Reznicek—Symphony No.5
Strauss, R.—Also sprach Zarathustra; Bourgeois Gentilhomme: Suite; Heldenleben; Symphony for Winds, TrV 291
Zemlinsky—Seejungfrau; Symphony [No.1], D minor
Reger—Symphonischer Prolog; Variations and Fugue on a Merry Theme of Hiller; Variations and Fugue on a Theme of Mozart
Schoenberg—Pierrot lunaire
Berg—Chamber Concerto, op.8; Lulu: Suite
Hindemith—Harmonie der Welt; Symphony in E-flat
Korngold—Symphonic Serenade
Hartmann—Symphonies Nos.4, 7
Einem—Wiener Symphonie
Henze—Symphony No.6

Italian

Busoni—Brautwahl: Suite; Turandot: Suite
Wolf-Ferrari—Sinfonia da camera
Respighi—Boutique fantasque

Russian

Rubinstein—Symphonies Nos.1, 2 [1851 version], 3, 5
Borodin— Symphonies Nos.1 & 2
Balakirev—King Lear: Incidental Music; Symphony No.2
Mussorgsky—Pictures at an Exhibition [many versions]
Tchaikovsky—Nutcracker: Suite No.2; Souvenir de Florence; Suite No.2; Swan Lake: Suite; Symphonies Nos.2, 7
Rimsky-Korsakov— Symphonies Nos.2, 3
Taneyev—Symphony No.1
Arensky—Symphony No.1
Glazunov—Raymonda: Act III; Raymonda: Suite; Symphonies Nos.4, 5, 6, 7
Kalinnikov—Suite, D Major; Symphonies Nos.1, 2
Rachmaninoff—Symphonic Dances; Symphony No.3

[31'–40']

Glière—Symphony No.1
Miaskovsky—Symphony
  No.22
Stravinsky—Firebird: Suite
  (1945); Petrushka [2
  versions]; Rite of Spring
  [multiple versions];
  Symphony No.1
Prokofiev—Chout: Symphonic
  Suite; Steel Step; Symphonies
  Nos.2, 3, 4 [rev. version]
Khachaturian—Gayane:
  Suite No.1
Shostakovich—Hamlet: Film
  Suite; Symphony No.12
Kancheli—Symphony No.7

Spanish &
Latin American

Falla—Sombrero de tres picos
Gerhard—Metamorphoses;
  Symphony No.1
Revueltas—Noche de los
  Mayas: Suite (Limantour)

United Kingdom

Purcell—Fantasias, Strings
Parry—Symphony No.3
Stanford—Symphony No.3
Elgar—Enigma Variations
Delius—Florida
Bantock—Hebridean
  Symphony
Vaughan Williams—
  Symphonies Nos.3, 5, 6, 9
Bax— Symphonies Nos.1, 6
Bliss—Colour Symphony
Walton—Façade; Hamlet:
  Concert Suite
Alwyn—Symphony No.4
Tippett—Concerto for
  Orchestra; Symphonies
  Nos.1, 2, 4
Burgess—Mr W.S.; Symphony
  No.3
Arnold—Symphony No.3
Maxwell Davies—Caroline
  Mathilde: Suite from Act II;
  Second Fantasia on
  Taverner's "In nomine";
  Sinfonietta accademica;
  Symphony No.8; Worldes
  Blis
McCabe—Symphony "Edward
  II"
Holloway—Second Concerto
  for Orchestra

Other Nationalities

Berwald—Symphony No.1
Gade—Symphonies Nos.1, 7
Grieg—Symphony, C minor
Bendix, Victor—Symphony
  No.3
Sinding—Symphony No.1
Nielsen, Carl—Symphonies
  Nos.2, 3, 4, 5, 6
Sibelius— Symphonies
  Nos.1, 4
Stenhammar—Serenade,
  op.31, F major
Melartin— Symphonies
  Nos.3, 4, 5, 6
Atterberg— Symphonies
  Nos.3, 5, 8
Rosenberg— Symphonies
  Nos.2, 3
Holmboe— Symphonies
  Nos.6, 8, 9
Pettersson, A.—Symphony
  No.4
Bentzon— Symphonies
  Nos.4, 9, 13
Rautavaara— Symphonies
  Nos.3, 5, 6, 7
Nørgård, Per—Symphony
  No.8
Sallinen, A.—Symphony No.5
Ran—Symphony
Lindberg—Aura
Ritchie, Anthony—
  Symphonies Nos. 1.2

```
┌─────────────────┐
│     41'–60'     │
└─────────────────┘
```

American (United States)

Paine—Symphony No.2
Beach—Symphony No.2
Ives—Concord Symphony
Bloch, E.—America
Shilkret—Genesis Suite
Bacon—Great River
Copland—Symphony No.3
Diamond—Symphony No.2
Rochberg—Symphony No.4
Shapey—Concerto fantastique
Duffy—Heritage: Symphonic
  Suite with Narration
Hurwit—Symphony No.1
Jones—Roundings
Glass—Symphony No.2
Corigliano—Symphony No.1
Hailstork—Symphony No.3
Melby—Symphony No.1
Zaimont—Pure, Cool (Water)

Adams, John—Naive and
  Sentimental Music
Hoyt—Symphony No.1
Daugherty—Metropolis
  Symphony
Corrin—How the Orchestra
  Grew
Stephenson—Compose
  Yourself!; Devil's Tale
Wharton—Symphony
Boyer—Ellis Island

Eastern European

Liszt—Dante Symphony
Dvořák—Symphonies
  Nos.2, 6
Paderewski—Symphony, op.24
Suk—Symphonies Nos.1, 2
Górecki—Symphony No.3

French & Belgian

Berlioz—Symphonie
  fantastique
Indy—Symphony No.2
Ravel—Daphnis et Chloé
Honegger—Dit des jeux du
  monde

German & Austrian

Bach, J.S.—Musikalisches
  Opfer (Landshoff)
Handel—Water Music,
  HWV 348-350
Mozart, W.A.—Divertimento
  No.17, K.334; Serenades
  Nos.4, 10
Beethoven—Egmont;
  Symphony No.3
Schubert—Rosamunde;
  Symphonies, D.812 & D.944
Wagner, Richard—
  Meistersinger: Orchestral
  Tribute
Raff—Symphony No.8
Bruckner—Symphony, F
  minor (Cahis 1); Symphony
  (Cahis 3), D minor (Nullte);
  Symphony No.1 (Cahis 2 &
  17); Symphony No.2 (1877,
  Cahis 8); Symphony No.3
  (1889, Cahis 15); Symphony
  No.6 (Cahis 12)
Strauss, Joh., Jr.—Graduation
  Ball
Goldmark—Ländliche
  Hochzeit
Brahms—Piano Quartet (arr.
  Schoenberg); Serenade No.1;
  Symphonies Nos.1 & 2

[41'–60']

Humperdinck—Maurische
  Rhapsodie
Rott—Symphony No.1
Mahler—Symphonies
  Nos.1 & 4
Strauss, R.—Alpensinfonie;
  Aus Italien; Josephslegende;
  Symphonia domestica;
  Symphony, TrV 126
Zemlinsky—Symphony No.2
  (1897)
Schmidt, F.—Symphonies
  Nos.2 & 4
Schoenberg—Pelléas und
  Mélisande
Korngold—Sinfonietta;
  Symphony, op.40

Italian

Respighi—Sinfonia
  drammatica

Russian

Rubinstein—Symphony No.2
  [1863 version]
Balakirev—Symphony No.1
Tchaikovsky—Manfred; Suites
  Nos.1 & 3; Symphonies
  Nos.1, 3, 4, 5, 6
Rimsky-Korsakov—
  Sheherazade
Taneyev—Symphony no.4
Glazunov—Symphony No.8
Scriabin—Divine Poem;
  Symphonies Nos.1 & 2
Rachmaninoff—Symphonies
  Nos.1 & 2
Glière—Symphony No.2
Stravinsky—Baiser de la fée;
  Firebird [2 versions]
Prokofiev—Chout;
  Symphonies Nos.5 & 6
Khachaturian—Symphony
  No.2
Shostakovich—Gadfly: Suite;
  Symphonies Nos.4, 5, 10, 11,
  15
Shchedrin—Carmen Suite

Spanish &
Latin American

Albéniz— Iberia (arr.
  Surinach)

United Kingdom

Stanford—Symphony No.4

Elgar—Symphonies Nos.1-3
Vaughan Williams—Job;
  Symphonies Nos.2 & 7
Holst—Planets
Bax— Symphonies Nos.3–5, 7
Bliss—Checkmate
Walton—Symphony No.1
Alwyn— Symphonies Nos.1, 3
Arnold— Symphonies Nos.4, 9
Maxwell Davies—Symphonies
  Nos.1, 2, 3, 4, 6, 7
Tavener—Mystagogía

Other Nationalities

Sibelius—Symphony No.2
Atterberg—Symphony No.2
Bentzon—Symphony No.8
Nørgård, Per—Symphony
  No.3
Bamert—Once Upon an
  Orchestra
Harris, Ross—Symphony No.3
Young—Symphony [No.1]

OVER 60'

American (United States)

Ives—Universe Symphony
  (Porter or Reinhard)
Rochberg—Symphony No.1
Wuorinen—Magic Art

Eastern European

Liszt—Faust Symphony
Minkus—Bayadère; Don
  Quixote (multiple versions)

French & Belgian

Adam—Corsaire; Giselle
Delibes—Coppélia; Sylvia
Messiaen—Des canyons aux
  étoiles; Turangalîla-
  symphonie

German & Austrian

Haydn, F.J.—Sieben letzten
  Worte [orch version]
Beethoven—Prometheus
Schubert—Octet
Wagner, Richard—Ring: An
  Orchestral Adventure; Ring
  ohne Worte
Raff—Symphony No.1

Bruckner—Symphonies Nos.2
  (1872, Cahis 4), No.3 (1873,
  Cahis 5), No.3 (1877, Cahis
  9, No.4 (1874, Cahis 6), No.4
  (1878/80 version, Cahis 11),
  No.4 (1888 version, Cahis
  Suppl.1/14+), No.5 (Cahis 7),
  No.7 (Cahis 13), No.7
  (chamber orch), No.8 (1887
  version, Cahis 14), No.8
  (1890 version, Cahis 16),
  No.9 (Cahis 18)
Mahler—Symphonies Nos.2, 3,
  5, 6, 7, 9, 10 [multiple
  versions]

Russian

Rubinstein—Symphony No.2
  [1880 version]; Symphony
  No.4
Tchaikovsky—Nutcracker
  [multiple versions]; Sleeping
  Beauty; Swan Lake
Glière—Symphony No.3
Miaskovsky—Symphony No.6
Stravinsky—Histoire du soldat
Prokofiev—Romeo and Juliet
Shostakovich—Symphonies
  Nos.7 & 8

United Kingdom

Maw—Odyssey

Other Nationalities

Løvenskjold—Sylphide

APPENDIX F
WORKS INTENDED
FOR YOUTH CONCERTS

In the vast repertoire for orchestra, there is no dearth of music that is suitable and appropriate for youth concerts. Almost any composition or excerpt can be made to work, if put in the right context.

This appendix, however, is concerned with works intended *primarily* for young audiences. These tend to be works using narrations and composed after 1925 or so. The conspicuous exception is Saint-Saëns' well-loved *Carnival of the Animals*, which was intended neither for children nor spoken commentary, but rather for family entertainment. It is included here because, with the addition of humorous narrative—usually verse—it has often come to be used to entertain youngsters.

The works listed here are divided into several categories:

      A. Stories Told with Music
      B. Descriptive Music
      C. Introduction to the Orchestra and/or its Instruments
      D. Explanations of Various Aspects of Music
      E. Other—that is, music for youth that does not fall
            into one of the previous categories.

A. Stories Told with Music

Abels, Michael

Frederick's Fables   37'
Contents—Frederick; The Greentail Mouse; Theodore & the Talking Mushroom; Alexander & the Wind-Up Mouse.
Based on stories by Leo Lionni. Movements are available separately.

Adolphe, Bruce

Marita and Her Heart's Desire   27'
Libretto and story by Louise Gikow. An actress with multiple voices is needed.

The Purple Palace   34'
The inhabitants of the land of Chromatica are personifications of colors (Queen Red, King Blue, their daughter Purple, etc.). When the spoiled daughter Purple ascends to the throne, she decrees that all colors save purple be banished from Chromatica. She soon learns the error of her ways, and invites the colors all to return. Everyone lives happily ever after. Text by Louise Gikow.

Tyrannosaurus Sue: A Cretaceous Concerto   28'
Contents—I. Birth of Sue; II. Youth — Sue Explores Her World; III. Competing for Food with the Troodon; IV. Chasing the Parasaurolophus; V. Battle with the Triceratops; VI. Old Age and the Death of Sue; VII. Dawning of a New World (After the Dinosaurs)
The birth, life, and death of a T. Rex, personified by the trombone.

Bach, Jan

The Happy Prince 38'

A rather dark though heartwarming fairy tale by Oscar Wilde. Perhaps best used in a family concert in which the children in the audience are accompanied by supportive adults.

Barab, Seymour

G-A-G-E, A Christmas Story 20'

A fanciful version of the creation of the Christmas hymn "Silent Night" (Stille Nacht) by Franz Gruber.

Beckel, James A., Jr.

Imagination; A Children's Narrative Work for Chamber Ensemble 8'

In this case, the audience creates its own story, by filling in such blanks as "This is a story about _____"; "Normally all was well, but one day something happened _____." Then the narrator reads this spontaneous creation, while the ensemble accompanies.

Waltz of the Animals 14'

A girl visits her forest friends, such as "Strawinsky the Squirrel" and "Ludwig von Blackbird." The music reflects the styles of composers thus alluded to.

Bond, Victoria

The Frog Prince 15'

A princess befriends a frog in order to recover her favorite bauble from a deep well, but once it is recovered she breaks her promise to include him in her royal life. The king explains to her that promises must be honored, especially by princesses! Finally stricken with remorse, she kisses the frog, who turns into a handsome prince. They marry and live happily ever after. Story from the Grimm brothers.

Dorff, Daniel

Blast Off! 10'

Narrative about space travel. Audience participates in the countdown to launch.

Goldilocks and the Three Bears 8'

The well-known story, from the Grimm brothers.

Three Fun Fables 11'

Contents—The Fox and the Crow (tp & db); The Dog and His Reflection (tbn & vn/hp/perc); The Tortoise and the Hare (cbn & cl)
The characters of each fable are represented by particular instruments. Stories from Aesop.

Three Fun Fables: The Tortoise and the Hare 6'

The contrabassoon and clarinet represent the protagonists. Story from Aesop.

Dukas, Paul

L'apprenti sorcier (The Sorcerer's Apprentice) 12'

The well-known story of the hapless apprentice who knows enough to initiate a magical action, but doesn't know how to stop it. The story's origin is a poem by Goethe.

Gilbert, Jan

Dream Carver; A Story from Oaxaca 22'
Contents—(A) Village Fiesta Music I / Zapotec Ruins; (B) Carving Music I;
(C) Parade of the Dream Animals I; (D) Freely/Mateo and his Father; (E)
Mateo's longing; (F) Dream Music I; (G) Carving Music II; (H) Carving Music
III; (J) Parade of the Dream Animals II; (K) Andante / Mateo's love for his
father / Dream Music II; (FIESTA-INSERT) *El Toro Relajo* (*The Disturbed
Bull*); (L) Village Fiesta Music II
*Mateo and his father carve wooden animals to sell at fiesta. Mateo dreams of
carving larger animals painted in bizarre untraditional colors; despite
parental resistance, he follows his dream, learns to carve what his imagination
sees, and wins his father's approval. Based on a book by Diana Cohn,
illustrated by Amy Cordova.*

In the Beginning 20'
Contents—(A) The Soft Darkness; (B) Raven Arrives; (C) The Ghosts; (D) The
Fish; (E) Calypso I; (F) The Magic Spring; (G) Raven's Waltz; (H) Storytelling
by the Fire; (I) Bossa Nova; (J) Storytelling; (K) Calypso II; (L) Raven's
Escape; (M) The Wobbly Flight; (N) The Creation of the Crooked Rivers; (O)
The Endless Night
*Out of the Alaskan coastal wilderness, Raven creates the earth and then tricks
Ganook to help him form all the rivers of the world. This is also the story of
how the raven came to be black. A creation myth from the Tlingit people of the
Pacific Northwest Coast.*

Khoj; The Search for Light 23'
Contents—(A) The Earth is Dark; (B) The Koel Bird; (C) The Flight of the
Flamingos; (D) The Camels; (E) March of the Elephants; (F) The Wonder of
the Child Elephants; (G) The River; (H) The Sea Turtles; (I) The Cheetal Deer;
(J) The Western Wind; (K) The Search for Light; (L) Dance of the Peacocks;
(M) The Enchanted Night
*Thirteen miniatures for orchestra with interspersed narration. The animals of
Northern India (the koel bird, flamingoes, elephants, camels, sea turtles, deer,
and peacocks) search for the light of the moon. Based on a story by Gita Kar.
The Hindi word* khoj *means "the wonder of discovery."*

Nine-in-One Grr! Grr! 17'
*A mother tiger wants to learn how large her family will be. She travels to the
kingdom of the great god Shao, who tells her she will have nine baby tigers
every year, as long as she remembers his words. She happily travels through
the forest singing "Nine-in-One Grr! Grr!" But the clever Eu Bird is worried
about an overpopulation of tigers, and sets out to trick Tiger into forgetting her
all-important song. A Hmong folk tale, told by Blia Ziong and adapted by
Cathy Spagnoli.*

Gould, Morton

The Jogger and the Dinosaur; For Rapper (Narrator) & Orchestra 22'
in 7 Scenes
*An amiable dinosaur escapes from the museum and makes friends with a
passing jogger.*

Harsányi, Tibor

L'histoire du petite tailleur (The Story of the Little Tailor) 30'
Composed for marionettes, after a tale of the Grimm brothers.

Heitzeg, Steve

The Tin Forest 10'
*A parable with an ecological message. Based on the book by Helen Ward,
illustrated by Wayne Anderson.*

Jones, Samuel

Eudora's Fable: The Shoe Bird   51'

A fable about animals learning not to shortchange their native gifts to follow fashion. Children's chorus has a substantial role, somewhat in the manner of a Greek chorus. Narrator must be a skilled actor to portray a dozen different characters. Text from Eudora Welty's children's book. A teachers' guide is available.

Kechley, David

Alexander and the Wind-Up Mouse   17'

Alexander the mouse makes friends with Willy, a toy mouse, and wants to be just like him until he discovers that Willy is to be thrown away. Based on a children's book by Leo Lionni.

Clocks and More Clocks   13'

Mr. Higgins can't understand why his four clocks never agree, until the Clockmaker assures him they are all correct. Based on a book by Pat Hutchins.

Kleinsinger, George

Tubby the Tuba   13'

The neglected tuba finally gets to play the tune. Narrator must be an actor with different voices.

Kubik, Gail

Gerald McBoing Boing   9'

Young Gerald doesn't speak words—he makes sound effects instead. Dejected and feeling outcast at one point, he finds fame and fortune providing sound effects for a radio station. From a children's book by Dr. Seuss.

Lees, Benjamin

The Trumpet of the Swan   17'

Knowing how to read and write is not enough for Louis, a voiceless trumpeter swan; his determination to learn to play a stolen trumpet takes him far from his wilderness home. From the children's book by E. B. White.

Lombardo, Mario

Drakestail; A Symphonic Fairy Tale for Children   18'

An undersized duck sets off to the palace to confront an evil king; he survives various trials, and ultimately becomes king himself. Adaptation of a French fairy tale.

Maltz, Richard

Aesop's Fables   22'

Contents—Overture; The Hare and the Tortoise; The Fox and the Grapes; The Ants and the Grasshopper; The Oak and the Reeds; The Milkmaid and Her Pail; Finale
Classic fables.

O'Boyle, Sean

Music That Goes with "The Tale of Peter Rabbit"   7'

Beatrix Potter's classic tale.

Oliverio, James

The Story of Snow White; A Child's Introduction to the Symphony Orchestra   17'

The familiar tale, from the Grimm brothers, with various instruments representing the characters.

Peck, Russell

Jack and Jill at Bunker Hill 9'
An action-packed story of American history and idealism.

Where's Red Robin? (Song of the Little Robin) 17'
A nature story of joy, sadness, humor, mystery, and dramatic danger, with a happy ending of springtime return.

Poulenc, Francis

L'histoire de Babar, le petit éléphant (The Story of Babar, the Little Elephant) 22'
Jean de Brunhoff's classic children's story.

Prokofiev, Serge

Peter and the Wolf, op.67 (Petya i volk) 25'
Boy captures wolf with aid of animal friends, despite his grandfather's strict prohibitions. Text by the composer in Russian; English version by Thomas Dunhill; Spanish text by Juan Serrallonga, and doubtless narrations in many other languages exist.

Richman, Lucas

I Remember a Lullaby 12'
The stories of five children who were each influenced by a lullaby to choose a path in the arts.

Rodríguez, Robert Xavier

A Colorful Symphony 20'
A boy named Milo enters a strange world in which all color is the product of music played by a celestial orchestra. Text from Norman Juster's children's book The Phantom Tollbooth.

Trunks; A Circus Story for Narrator & Orchestra 18'
Xenobia, the circus elephant, befriends David, the veterinarian's son. When the circus leaves town, Xenobia refuses to be parted from her new friend. A stubborn elephant is a serious problem, but David cleverly saves the day! Based on a story by H.C. Bunner.

Rogers, Bernard

Five Fairy Tales (Once Upon a Time) 13'
Contents—1. The Tinder-Box Soldier; 2. The Song of Rapunzel; 3. The Story of a Darning Needle; 4. Dance of the Twelve Princesses; 5. The Ride of Koschei the Deathless
Classic tales from Hans Christian Andersen (nos.1 & 3), the Grimm brothers (nos.2 & 4), and Slavic folklore (no.5).

The Musicians of Bremen 22'
A donkey runs away from his evil master to go to Bremen; on the journey he accumulates friends: a dog, a cat, and a rooster. The four subdue a band of robbers and live happily ever after. Based on a folk tale by the brothers Grimm.

Schickele, Peter

The Chenoo Who Stayed to Dinner 22'
Based on a Native American Micmac legend. For narrator & orchestra; may be performed without narrator under the title Legend.

Schuller, Gunther

Journey into Jazz 16'
Boy learns to play jazz on the trumpet.

Smith, Gregory

A MAJOR-minor Mystery 22'
Inspector Beckensteiner tries to discover which member of the orchestra keeps changing major into minor.

The Melodic Life 23'
Prop: small noise-making device, preferably electronic (other non-electronic possibilities: gong, whistle, handbell, sopranino recorder, duck call, balloon, etc.)
The life and times of a melody named "Bob," from childhood through middle age.

Zoo Song 17'
Sara McCullough McCartney goes to the zoo and is enchanted by an elusive sound made by some animal. She searches through all the animals in the zoo and their distinctive cries, until she finally identifies it as a peacock.

Stookey, Nathaniel

The Composer is Dead 30'
A "whodunit" with text by Lemony Snicket. The composer is dead. An Inspector comes to investigate. He questions all the instruments of the orchestra, as well as the conductor, but all have alibis. "Besides," they say, "all of us have murdered a composer at one time or another... If you want to hear the work of the world's greatest composers, you're going to have to allow for a little murder here and there."

Tchaikovsky, Piotr Ilyich

The Nutcracker and the Mouse King 17'
Contents—1. Overture; 2. Drosselmeyer; 3. Sleep; 4. Night; 5. Midnight; 6. Mice; 7. Everything Gets Bigger; 8. Battle; 9. Clara and the Nutcracker Prince; 10. Chinese Dance; 11. Russian Dance; 12. Waltz of the Flowers; 13. Sugarplum Fairy and Her Prince; 14. Farewell
The familiar music and story of the "Nutcracker," much condensed. The tale was originally by E.T.A. Hoffmann.

Territo, James

John Henry vs. the Machine 12'
John Henry, personified by the tuba, proves a man can beat a machine and becomes a legend. The familiar folk tune does not appear. The real John Henry, if he actually existed, was believed to have been born a slave in the American South in the 1840s.

Welcher, Dan

Haleakala (How Maui Snared the Sun) 21'
Maui the trickster, in order to assuage his mother's weeping, captures the sun and creates the seasons of winter and summer. Retelling of a myth about the Polynesian demigod Maui.

Zaninelli, Luigi

The Steadfast Tin Soldier 23'
The tin soldier remains steadfast in his love for a ballerina through many misfortunes. Based on a fairytale of Hans Christian Andersen.

The Tale of Peter Rabbit 19'
Story by Beatrix Potter.

B. Descriptive Music

Bamert, Matthias

Circus Parade   12'

Contents—Ringmaster; Horses; Tightrope Walkers; Bears; Jugglers; Lions; Magician; Little Monkeys; Clowns.
Meet the denizens of the circus!

Bryant, Curtis

Dinosaurs; A Primeval Symphony   17'

Contents—1. Ultimate Tangle; 2. Plated March; 3. Pterrible Flight; 4. Duckbilled Ragtime; 5. Tyrannical Tarantelle
Five scenes of dinosaur doings, each preceded by a humorous verse.

Cotton, Jeffery

CityMusic   12'

Will be most effective with urban youngsters who are familiar with such things as subways.

Dello Joio, Norman

Five Images for Orchestra   8'

Contents—Cortège; Promenade; Day Dreams; The Ballerina; The Dancing Sergeant
Intended primarily for youth audiences; the composer suggests using as few or as many of the movements as desired.

Einhorn, Richard

My Many Colored Days By Dr. Seuss   25'

Contents—I. Some Days; II. Bright Red Days; III. Bright Blue Days; IV. Sort of Brown Days; V. A Yellow Day; VI. Gray Day; VII. My Orange Days; VIII. Green Days; IX. On Purple Days; X. Happy Pink Days; XI. My Black Days; XII. Mixed Up Days / Finale
Brief characterizations of different colored days in Dr. Seuss' inimitable style, followed in each case by longer descriptive music.

Heitzeg, Steve

On the Day You Were Born   18'

The animals, the planet, the stars, the sun and moon, the sea, and the plants and trees welcome the birth of a new baby. Based on the book by Debra Frasier; accompanying slides are available from publisher.

Horwood, Michael

Amusement Park Suite   17'

Contents—The Sky Ride; The Log Flume; The Carousel; The Dark Ride; The Roller-Coaster
Hang on for a series of exciting rides!

Monroe, Ervin

The Amazing Symphony Orchestra   24'

Contents—I. Moods; II. Pictures; III. Dances
Thirty excerpts from familiar orchestral works tied together with a narration describing the expressive powers of the orchestra. Movements may be performed independently.

Richman, Lucas

Behold the Bold Umbrellaphant 29'

Contents—Behold the Bold Umbrellaphant; The Bizarre Alarmadillos; The Ballpoint Penguins; The Lynx of Chain; The Pop-up Toadsters; Shoehornets; Here Comes a Panthermometer; The Circular Sawtoise; The Limber Bulboa; The Clocktopus; The Eggbeaturkey; Hatchickens; The Trumpetoos and Tubaboons; The Tweasels of the Forest; The Tearful Zipperpotamuses; The Ocelock; The Solitary Spatuloon; Finale

Amusing poems by Jack Prelutsky about outlandish animals.

Playground Escapades 3'

Musical depiction of children during recess featuring the games they play, the brass section as the bullies, and the English horn as the teacher who intervenes.

Rimelis, David

The Cool Ghoul 3'

Creepy music with ghoulish laughter; musicians shriek and howl at various points. Not just for Halloween.

Saint-Saëns, Camille

Le carnaval des animaux (Carnival of the Animals) 21'

Contents—1. Introduction et Marche royale du lion (Introduction and Royal March of the Lion); 2. Poules et coqs (Hens and Roosters); 3. Hémiones—Animaux véloces (Wild Donkeys—Fleet Animals); 4. Tortues (Tortoises); 5. L'éléphant; 6. Kangourous (Kangaroos); 7. Aquarium; 8. Personnages à longues oreilles (People with Long Ears); 9. Le coucou au fond des bois (Cuckoo in the Depths of the Woods); 10. Volière (Aviary); 11. Pianistes (Pianists); 12. Fossiles (Fossils); 13. Le cygne (The Swan); 14. Final (Finale)

Humorous narratives may precede each movement; see main entry. A children's picture book by John Lithgow is available.

Schickele, Peter

A Zoo Called Earth 15'

Visitors from another galaxy, who live for millions of earth years, visit their "zoo" (= Planet Earth) from time to time to see what has changed since their last visit. An exhortation to preserve our world.

Smith, Gregory

The Orchestra Games 27'

Explores the various instruments' personalities and acquaints the listener with basic musical elements, as it sprints through an Olympic array of events.

Zaninelli, Luigi

A Lexicon of Beasties 26'

Each "beastie" represented by a humorous verse (adapted from Edward Lear) and music; 26 beasties, one for each letter of the alphabet. Fewer beasties may be used, in which case the title should be rendered as A Bevy of Beasties.

C. Introduction to the Orchestra and/or its Instruments

Britten, Benjamin

Young Person's Guide to the Orchestra, op.34 (Variations and Fugue on a Theme of Purcell) 18'

Instruments introduced via the variations; a climactic fugue ensues.

Corrin, Gary

How the Orchestra Grew   55'

Featured composers—Vivaldi, Handel, Gluck, Boyce, Haydn, Mozart, Beethoven, Berlioz, Tchaikovsky, Dvorak, Stravinsky.

Using a number of props, the narrator traces the development of the orchestra from a small group of strings to the full modern ensemble. Each instrument is introduced individually, then added to the orchestra in music that features that instrument and illustrates a new stage in the development of the orchestra.

Dorff, Daniel

Billy and the Carnival; A Children's Guide to the Instruments   14'

Intended as a guide to the instruments for children in grades kindergarten through 4. A companion coloring book is available.

Kirk, Theron

An Orchestra Primer   13'

The various instruments are introduced, and then a composition is built from scratch.

Kraft, William

A Simple Introduction to the Orchestra   4'

Instruments are demonstrated.

Lankester, Michael

Make Your Own Orchestra; A Piece for Home-Made Instruments & Orchestra   15'

Instruments are constructed on the spot from junk; then the 6-person "junk band" is pitted against the full orchestra, in the manner of a concerto grosso.

A Pocket-Sized Guide to the Orchestra (The Time-Machine, Part 1)   8'

Instruments enter the stage one by one, introduced by rap-style poetry.

Mascari, Edward Paul

Meet the Orchestra   17'

Charming and clever introduction to the instruments.

Nelson, Ron

This Is the Orchestra   22'

An introduction to the orchestra.

O'Boyle, Sean

SNAPSHOT CONCERTOS

Pick and choose from this series of 1-minute character pieces with delightfully fanciful titles, each featuring a specific instrument.

Mini Dance   1'

Piccolo

Flipperdiperus   1'

Flute

A Quiet Place   1'

Oboe

The Pretty Girl Milking Her Cow   1'

English horn

Liquorice Noodles   1'

Clarinet

Liquorice Noodles (small orchestra)   1'
Clarinet

Bassett Hound   1'
Bass clarinet

A Bundle of Sticks   1'
Bassoon

The Big Broomstick   1'
Contrabassoon

Curly Bits   1'
The horn section

Lonesome Prairie   1'
Trumpet

Lonesome Prairie (small orchestra)   1'
Trumpet

Buy, Swap or Sell!   1'
Trombone

Tuba Toothpaste   1'
Tuba

Galloping Goanna   1'
Xylophone

The Big Bang   1'
Percussion

Pale Moonlight   1'
Harp

Dueling Fiddles   1'
2 violins

Dueling Fiddles (small orchestra)   1'
2 violins

Tumbleweeds at Ten Paces   1'
Violin

The Songbird   1'
Viola

Changing Seasons   1'
Cello

Quando, quando, basso   1'
Double Bass

Oliverio, James

Voyage Through the Musical Universe; A Child's Introduction to the Symphony Orchestra   17'
Visiting the String Sector, the Woodwind Zone, the Brass Belt, and Planet Percussion, ably led by Captain Conductor. Finally we visit the most dangerous of all: the Synthesizer System! We are being pulled into an Electronic Black Hole, until Captain Conductor heroically marshalls all the United Forces of the Galactic Orchestra to save us, and return us safely home to re-entry and landing. Mission accomplished!
A coloring book handout is also available from the publisher.

Ott, David

First Trip to the Symphony 23'

First the instrument families, and then the individual instruments are introduced; all join in a grand finale.

Proto, Frank

Doodles; An Introduction to the Orchestra var

Variations on Yankee Doodle, *each variation featuring a different instrument. Alternative variations for certain instruments; the composer has added new variations from time to time. (It is not intended that all variations be performed, hence the variable duration from 8'-30')*
Interactive possibilities: *a variation in which the audience responds with clapped rhythm to musical cues; also an audience sing-along.*

Richman, Lucas

The United Symphony 8'

Contents—Toccata for Percussion; Hornpipe for Brass; Arabesque for Winds; Scherzo for Strings; The United Symphony
Each movement preceded by a demonstration of the instruments to be used therein. The sections are finally united for a big finish.

Schaffner, Steven

A Whirlwind Tour of the Orchestra 6'

A very quick demonstration of the instruments, with rhyming text.

Schuman, William

The Orchestra Song 4'

An orchestration of the familiar children's song.

Stephenson, James

Compose Yourself! 45'

A complete 45' program in which, among other things, kids from the audience choose options that result in a complete piece of music. A charismatic narrator is required. Humorous and engaging.

Walker, Gwyneth

Up-Front Concerto 10'

Contents—1. Rise and Shine; 2. About Rain; 3. Flying Tattoos!
Percussion soloist is front and center with an unusual array of hand drums, including congas, cuica, rain stick, and grapes.

Wittry, Diane

Concerto for Homemade Instruments 5'

Audience members have made their instruments in advance according to instruction sheets. Each instrumental group (strings, woodwinds, brass, percussion) rehearses a particular rhythm assigned to the group. Then: the performance!

D. Explanations of Various Aspects of Music

Bond, Victoria

What's the Point of Counterpoint? 25'

A tune, guided by a little bird, travels through the musical cities of Rhythm, Harmony, and Counterpoint and meets their denizens.

Peck, Russell

Playing With Style   10'
Demonstrates the conductor's responsibilities with respect to tempo, dynamics, and articulation.

The Thrill of the Orchestra   13'
Introduces the sections of the orchestra and how they are combined to achieve thrilling music.

Richman, Lucas

Be a Composer   8'
Children participate by choosing 3 notes at random, which are then combined into a brief orchestral piece. Instrumentation may be flexible.

Music Can Make Your Life Complete   5'
A catchy song, celebrating the wonders of music, and how musical works are put together.

A Western Fanfare (Be a Conductor)   3'
Young people will learn the basics of conducting in 2/4 and 3/4 time.

Smith, Gregory

Mr. Smith's Bowl of Notes   30'
Costume & props: judge's wig, handkerchief, backpack, feathers, sealed bowl, rose branches, water bottle, folded paper, shirt with painted stripes, tennis shoe (painted).
Mr. Smith interrupts a concert to explain that 12 notes are all there are, using quotations from a dozen composers, as well as his own music. He also describes his own goofy adventures of the morning: being chased by dogs and ducks, sitting on a freshly-painted bench, and losing a shoe in wet concrete. The conductor also interacts with Mr. Smith.

Mr. Smith's Composition   19'
Mr. Smith, a composer, sits down to write a piece; he tries things out, erases them, makes changes, and gradually constructs the piece. Oops! He forgot to write the ending—but it is delivered to the stage by messenger just in time.

E. Other

Adolphe, Bruce

THREE PIECES for Kids & Chamber Orchestra   3'
1. Ta Woop!
Audience participation, introducing the principle of refrain and episode — like a baroque concerto.

2. Rainbow   4'
Audience participation.

3. T-D-T (Texture-Dynamics-Timbre)   5'
Audience participation, demonstrating several basic elements of music.

Baksa, Robert

Variations from the Heart   13'
Contents—Theme; Var.I: Being Frightened; Var.II: Getting Angry; Var.III: Feeling Sad; Var.IV: Feeling Happy.
Explores the feelings that all human beings—including children—share.

Bamert, Matthias

Once Upon an Orchestra   50'
May be danced or mimed. Excerpts suitable for concert performance without narrator.

Jones, Samuel

Hear the Music   2'
Commissioned by the Seattle Symphony for use as a signature song for their youth concerts. May be customized to serve the same purpose for your own orchestra.

O'Boyle, Sean

Country Kazoo Overture   2'
Orchestra members play kazoos and make animal sounds in the middle section.

Oliverio, James

Generations   25'
An oratorio-like work that acknowledges and honors the bond between parent and child, between brother and sister, and between those who came before and those who are yet to come. Suitable for family concerts.

Perera, Ronald

THE SAINTS; Three Pieces for Orchestra with Audience Participation   3'
1. Choirs
Audience participation: singing in unison.

2. Joyful Noise   3'
Audience participation: sound effects!

3. Marching In   3'
Audience participation, singing "When the Saints Come Marching In."

Richman, Lucas

Homework Blues   3'
Can be used interactively with youth audiences. Teaches them about the "blue note" in jazz.

APPENDIX G
SIGNIFICANT ANNIVERSARIES
OF COMPOSERS

Taking the composers represented in this book, this appendix lists the significant anniversaries (multiples of 50 years from their birth and death dates) for the years 2016–2026.

2016

Milton Babbitt	1916-2011
William Sterndale Bennett	1816-1875
Karl-Birger Blomdahl	1916-1968
Howard Brubeck	1916-1993
Ferruccio Busoni	1866-1924
George Butterworth	1885-1916
Gaspar Cassadó	1897-1966
Francesco Cilea	1866-1950
Jules Demersseman	1833-1866
Henri Dutilleux	1916-2013
Julius Fucik	1872-1916
Friedrich Gernsheim	1839-1916
Vittorio Giannini	1903-1966
Alberto Ginastera	1916-1983
Enrique Granados	1867-1916
Vassili Kalinnikov	1866-1901
Eduard Nápravník	1839-1916
Giovanni Paisiello	1740-1816
Quincy Porter	1897-1966
John Psathas	b.1966
Max Reger	1873-1916
Erik Satie	1866-1925
Georg Schumann	1866-1952
Anton Simon	1850-1916
Eduard Strauss	1835-1916
Deems Taylor	1885-1966
Ben Weber	1916-1979

2017

Amy Marcy Cheney Beach	1867-1944
Anthony Burgess	1917-1993
Salvatore Di Vittorio	b.1967
Friedrich Johann Eck	1767-1838
Niels Gade	1817-1890
Umberto Giordano	1867-1948
Enrique Granados	1867-1916
Lou Harrison	1917-2003
Richard Hervig	1917-2010
Scott Joplin	1868-1917
Ulysses Kay	1917-1995
Justin Heinrich Knecht	1752-1817

Zoltán Kodály	1882-1967
Charles Koechlin	1867-1950
Paule Maurice	1910-1967
Etienne-Nicolas Méhul	1763-1817
Ludwig Minkus	1826-1917
Georg Matthias Monn	1717-1750
Claudio Monteverdi	1567-1643
Oskar Morawetz	1917-2007
José Mauricio Nunés-Garcia	1767-1830
Johann Schobert	c1735-1767
Reginald Smith Brindle	1917-2003
Joh. Wenzel Anton Stamitz	1717-1757
Billy Strayhorn	1915-1967
Georg Philipp Telemann	1681-1767
Christopher Theofanidis	b.1967
Robert Ward	1917-2013
Jaromir Weinberger	1896-1967
Richard Yardumian	1917-1985

2018

Granville Bantock	1868-1946
Leonard Bernstein	1918-1990
Franz Berwald	1796-1868
Karl-Birger Blomdahl	1916-1968
Arrigo Boito	1842-1918
Lili Boulanger	1893-1918
Giuseppe Antonio Capuzzi	1755-1818
Mario Castelnuovo-Tedesco	1895-1968
François Couperin	1668-1733
Claude Debussy	1862-1918
Gottfried von Einem	1918-1996
Henry F. Gilbert	1868-1928
Charles Gounod	1818-1893
Anne Guzzo	b.1968
Scott Joplin	1868-1917
Henry Charles Litolff	1818-1891
Hubert Parry	1848-1918
George Rochberg	1918-2005
Bernard Rogers	1893-1968
Gioachino Rossini	1792-1868
Friedrich Seitz	1848-1918
Leone Sinigaglia	1868-1944
Leo Sowerby	1895-1968
Bernd Alois Zimmermann	1918-1970

2019

Jacob Avshalomov	1919-2013
Grażyna Bacewicz	1909-1969
Niels Viggo Bentzon	1919-2000
Hector Berlioz	1803-1869
Giovanni Bolzoni	1841-1919
Julius Conus	1869-1942
Lex van Delden	1919-1988
Georg Druschetzky	1745-1819
Louis Moreau Gottschalk	1829-1869
Armas Järnefelt	1869-1958
Hershy Kay	1919-1981
Leon Kirchner	1919-2009
Theron Kirk	1919-1999
Gideon Klein	1919-1945
Ruggero Leoncavallo	1857-1919
Frank Loesser	1910-1969
Alessandro Marcello	1669-1747
Jason Martineau	b.1969
Stanislaw Moniuszko	1819-1872
Douglas Moore	1893-1969
Leopold Mozart	1719-1787
Vaclav Nelhybel	1919-1996
Jacques Offenbach	1819-1880
Horatio Parker	1863-1919
Hans Pfitzner	1869-1949
Albert Roussel	1869-1937
Clara Wieck Schumann	1819-1896
James Stephenson	b.1969
Zygmunt Stojowski	1869-1946
Franz von Suppé	1819-1895
Galina Ustvolskaya	1919-2006
Philip Wharton	b.1969

2020

Karen Amanda Amrhein	b.1970
Aleksandr Grigori Arutiunian	1920-2012
John Barbirolli	1899-1970
Ludwig van Beethoven	1770-1827
Peter Boyer	b.1970
Howard Brockway	1870-1951
Max Bruch	1838-1920
Ingolf Dahl	1912-1970
Anis Fuleihan	1900-1970
Roberto Gerhard	1896-1970
Charles Tomlinson Griffes	1884-1920
David Horne	b.1970
Jiri Jaroch	1920-1986
Hall Johnson	1887-1970
John La Montaine	1920-2013
Franz Lehár	1870-1948
John Lewis	1920-2001
Herman Løvenskjold	1815-1870
Bruno Maderna	1920-1973
George Frederick McKay	1899-1970
Saverio Mercadante	1795-1870
Hall Overton	1920-1972
Cesare Pugni	1802-1870
Florent Schmitt	1870-1958
Nathaniel Stookey	b.1970
Josef Strauss	1827-1870
Heikki Suolahti	1920-1936
George Szell	1897-1970
Giuseppe Tartini	1692-1770
Bartolomeo Tromboncino	1470-1534
Henri Vieuxtemps	1820-1881
Friedrich Witt	1770-1837
Bernd Alois Zimmermann	1918-1970

2021

Thomas Adès	b.1971
Richard Adler	1921-2012
Tomaso Albinoni	1671-1750
Malcolm Arnold	1921-2006
Daniel-François-Esprit Auber	1782-1871
Arno Babadjanyan	1921-1983
Seymour Barab	1921-2014
William Bergsma	1921-1994
Giovanni Bottesini	1821-1889
Frederick Shepherd Converse	1871-1940
Franz Doppler	1821-1883
Marcel Dupré	1886-1971
Johann Gottlieb Graun	1703-1771
Henry Hadley	1871-1937
Engelbert Humperdinck	1854-1921
Karel Husa	b.1921
Gregory Hutter	b.1971
Andrew Imbrie	1921-2007

Jiang Kui	1155-1221
Robert Kurka	1921-1957
Henryk Pachulski	1859-1921
Astor Piazzolla	1921-1992
John Ritchie	b.1921
Carl Ruggles	1876-1971
Camille Saint-Saëns	1835-1921
Ralph Shapey	1921-2002
Wilhelm Stenhammar	1871-1927
Igor Stravinsky	1882-1971
András Szöllösy	1921-2007
Henri Frédien Tomasi	1901-1971
Bernard Wagenaar	1894-1971
Adolph Weiss	1891-1971
Alexander Zemlinsky	1871-1942

2022

Hugo Alfvén	1872-1960
John Bavicchi	b.1922
Georg Anton Benda	1722-1795
Margaret Allison Bonds	1913-1972
Havergal Brian	1876-1972
John Barnes Chance	1932-1972
Lukas Foss	1922-2009
César Franck	1822-1890
Gabriela Lena Frank	b.1972
Julius Fucik	1872-1916
Ferde Grofé	1892-1972
Iain Hamilton	1922-2000
Anton Peter Koch	b.1972
Johann Kuhnau	1660-1722
Stanislaw Moniuszko	1819-1872
Hall Overton	1920-1972
Carter Pann	b.1972
Lorenzo Perosi	1872-1956
Kevin Puts	b.1972
Joachim Raff	1822-1882
Heinrich Schütz	1585-1672
Alexander Scriabin	1872-1915
Kazimierz Serocki	1922-1981
Franz Strauss	1822-1905
Maurice Thiriet	1906-1972
Francis Thorne	b.1922
Ralph Vaughan Williams	1872-1958
George Walker	b.1922
Stefan Wolpe	1902-1972
Yannis Xenakis	1922-2001

2023

Karl Friedrich Abel	1723-1787
Leslie Bassett	b.1923
Chou Wen-chung	b.1923
Ferdinand David	1810-1873
Derek Devore	b.1973
Alvin Etler	1913-1973

Joseph Jongen	1873-1953
William Kraft	b.1923
Kristin Kuster	b.1973
Édouard Lalo	1823-1892
György Ligeti	1923-2006
Bruno Maderna	1920-1973
Gian Francesco Malipiero	1882-1973
Daniel Gregory Mason	1873-1953
Peter Mennin	1923-1983
Aleksandr Vasil'yevich Mosolov	1900-1973
Mark Petering	b.1973
Daniel Pinkham	1923-2006
Mel Powell	1923-1998
Johann Joachim Quantz	1697-1773
Henri Rabaud	1873-1949
Sergei Rachmaninoff	1873-1943
Max Reger	1873-1916
Ned Rorem	b.1923
Stanisław Skrowaczewski	b.1923
Nikolay Tcherepnin	1873-1945
Lester Trimble	1923-1986
Paul White	1895-1973
Joseph Wölfl	1773-1812
Russell Woollen	1923-1994
Jan Zach	1699-1773

2024

Kurt Atterberg	1887-1974
Warren Benson	1924-2005
Anton Bruckner	1824-1896
Ferruccio Busoni	1866-1924
Jeremiah Clarke	ca.1674-1707
Peter Cornelius	1824-1874
Théodore Dubois	1837-1924
Edw. Kennedy "Duke" Ellington	1899-1974
Gabriel Fauré	1845-1924
Arthur Frackenpohl	b.1924
Victor Herbert	1859-1924
Stanley Hollingsworth	1924-2003
Gustav Holst	1874-1934
Charles Ives	1874-1954
André Jolivet	1905-1974
Serge Koussevitzky	1874-1951
Ezra Laderman	b.1924
Benjamin Lees	1924-2010
Frank Martin	1890-1974
Darius Milhaud	1892-1974
Luigi Nono	1924-1990
Julia Perry	1924-1979
Giacomo Puccini	1858-1924
Carl Reinecke	1824-1910
Knudåge Riisager	1897-1974
Gerhard Samuel	1924-2008
Xaver Scharwenka	1850-1924
Franz Schmidt	1874-1939
Arnold Schoenberg	1874-1951

Gerard Schurmann	b.1924
Bedrich Smetana	1824-1884
Gaspare Spontini	1774-1851
Charles Villiers Stanford	1852-1924
Robert Starer	1924-2001
Josef Suk	1874-1935
Giovanni Battista Viotti	1755-1824
Egon Wellesz	1885-1974

2025

Franco Alfano	1875-1954
Leroy Anderson	1908-1975
William Sterndale Bennett	1816-1875
Luciano Berio	1925-2003
Georges Bizet	1838-1875
Boris Blacher	1903-1975
Arthur Bliss	1891-1975
François Boieldieu	1775-1834
Marco Enrico Bossi	1861-1925
Pierre Boulez	b.1925
George Frederick Bristow	1825-1898
André Caplet	1878-1925
Samuel Coleridge-Taylor	1875-1912
Marius Constant	1925-2004
Bernhard Henrik Crusell	1775-1838
Luigi Dallapiccola	1904-1975
Avner Dorman	b.1975

Andre Esphai	b.1925
Reinhold Glière	1875-1956
Marcel Grandjany	1891-1975
Reynaldo Hahn	1875-1947
Bernard Herrmann	1911-1975
Fritz Kreisler	1875-1962
James Lee III	b.1975
Kirke Mechem	b.1925
Erkki Melartin	1875-1937
Julián Orbón	1925-1991
Maurice Ravel	1875-1937
Robert Carl Rival	b.1975
Antonio Salieri	1750-1825
Giovanni Battista Sammartini	1701-1775
Erik Satie	1866-1925
Alessandro Scarlatti	1660-1725
Gunther Schuller	b.1925
Dmitry Shostakovich	1906-1975
Hale Smith	1925-2009
Johann, Jr. Strauss	1825-1899
Jan Václav Vorísek	1791-1825

2026

Juan Crisóstomo Arriaga	1806-1826
Victor Bendix	1851-1926

Havergal Brian	1876-1972
Benjamin Britten	1913-1976
Earle Brown	1926-2002
John Alden Carpenter	1876-1951
John Dowland	1563-1626
John Duffy	1926-
Manuel de Falla	1876-1946
Morton Feldman	1926-1987
Carlisle Floyd	1926-
Hermann Goetz	1840-1876
Hans Werner Henze	1926- 2011
Lee Hoiby	1926- 2011
Mieczyslaw Karłowicz	1876-1909
György Kurtág	1926-
Michel-Richard de Lalande	1657-1726
Raoul Laparra	1876-1943
Ton de Leeuw	1926-1996
Robert Hall Lewis	1926-1996
Alexander Manevich	1908-1976
Ludwig Minkus	1826-1917
Marie Barker Nelson	1926-
Ludolf Nielsen	1876-1939
Walter Piston	1894-1976
Jerry Ross	1926-1955
Carl Ruggles	1876-1971
Carlos Veerhoff	1926-
Huw Watkins	1976-
Carl Maria von Weber	1786-1826
Ermanno Wolf-Ferrari	1876-1948

APPENDIX H
COMPOSER GROUPS
FOR THEMATIC PROGRAMMING

Occasionally it is necessary to find one or more works from a particular group of composers, such as Polish composers, black composers, women composers. This appendix is intended to help in that process.

Obviously, many composers belong to more than one of these groups. Meyerbeer, for example, was Jewish, born in Germany, and did much of his important work in France. Tania León is black, female, born in Cuba, and has lived in the United States for many years. Any such multi-group composer appears in all relevant lists.

The list of Jewish composers here has been researched and updated by Helen Rowin, music librarian, Detroit Public Library (retired) ever since it first appeared in the 2nd edition of this book.

American (United States)	Czech	Mexican
American Indian	Danish	Moravian
(Native American)	Dutch	New Zealander
Argentinian	Estonian	Norwegian
Armenian	Finnish	Polish
Australian	French	Puerto Rican
Basque	Georgian	Rumanian
Belgian	German & Austrian	Russian
Black Composers	Greek	Scottish
Brazilian	Hungarian	Spanish
British	Irish	Swedish
Bulgarian	Israeli	Swiss
Canadian	Italian	Turkish
Catalan	Japanese	Ukrainian
Chinese	Jewish	Venezuelan
Cuban	Korean	Welsh
Cypriot	Latvian	Women Composers
	Macanese	

AMERICAN (UNITED STATES)

Michael Abels, 1962-
Lee Actor, 1952-
Mark Adamo, 1962-
John Adams, 1947-
John Luther Adams, 1953-
Leslie Adams, 1932-
Samuel Adler, 1928-
Bruce Adolphe, 1955-
Adrienne Albert, 1937-
Stephen Albert, 1941-1992
Brett Lensley Allen, 1958-
Efraín Amaya, 1959-

David Amram, 1930-
Karen Amanda Amrhein, 1970-
Steven Amundson, 1955-
Leroy Anderson, 1908-1975
T.J. Anderson, 1928-
George Antheil, 1900-1959
Dominick Argento, 1927-
Harold Arlen, 1905-1986
Elinor Armer, 1939-
Walter Aschaffenburg, 1927-
Daniel Asia, 1953-
David Avshalomov, 1946-
Jacob Avshalomov, 1919-2013
Jesse Ayers, 1951-
Milton Babbitt, 1916-2011
Jan Bach, 1937-

Ernst Bacon, 1898-1990
David Baker, 1931-
Robert Baksa, 1938-
Leonardo Balada, 1933-
Louis Ballard, 1931-2007
Seymour Barab, 1921-2014
Samuel Barber, 1910-1981
Wayne Barlow, 1912-1996
Greg Bartholomew, 1957-
Leslie Bassett, 1923-
Mason Bates, 1977-
John Bavicchi, 1922-
Amy Marcy Cheney Beach, 1867-1944
John Beall, 1942-
Robert Beaser, 1954-

[AMERICAN (UNITED STATES)]
James A. Beckel, Jr., 1948-
John J. Becker, 1886-1961
Robert Russell Bennett, 1894-1981
Warren Benson, 1924-2005
Nicolai Berezowsky, 1900-1953
William Bergsma, 1921-1994
Irving Berlin, 1888-1989
Leonard Bernstein, 1918-1990
John Biggs, 1932-
Jerry H. Bilik, 1933-
William Billings, 1746-1800
Easley Blackwood, 1933-
Arthur Bliss, 1891-1975
Marc Blitzstein, 1905-1964
Ernest Bloch, 1880-1959
Jerry Bock, 1928-2010
Karl Boelter, 1952-
William Bolcom, 1938-
Victoria Bond, 1945-
Margaret Allison Bonds, 1913-1972
Charles Boone, 1939-
Paul Bowles, 1910-1999
Peter Boyer, 1970-
Henry Brant, 1913-2008
Carolyn Bremer, 1957-
Todd Brief, 1953-
George Frederick Bristow, 1825-1898
Howard Brockway, 1870-1951
Earle Brown, 1926-2002
Howard Brubeck, 1916-1993
Curtis Bryant, 1949-
Dudley Buck, 1839-1909
Charles Wakefield Cadman,
  1881-1946
John Cage, 1912-1992
Ronald Caltabiano, 1959-
Thomas Canning, 1911-1989
David Carlson, 1952-
John Alden Carpenter, 1876-1951
Elliott Carter, 1908-2012
Ronald Joseph Caviani, 1931-2004
George Whitefield Chadwick,
  1854-1931
John Barnes Chance, 1932-1972
Richard Chiarappa, 1948-
Chou Wen-chung, 1923-
Anthony J. Cirone, 1941-
Cy Coleman, 1929-2004
Linda Robbins Coleman, 1954-
Michael Colgrass, 1932-
Edward Collins, 1886-1951
Frederick Shepherd Converse,
  1871-1940
Peggy Stuart Coolidge, 1913-1982
Aaron Copland, 1900-1990

John Corigliano, 1938-
Gary Corrin, 1955-
John Vasconcelos Costa, 1955-
Jeffery Cotton, 1957-2013
Henry Cowell, 1897-1965
Ruth Crawford (Seeger), 1901-1953
Paul Creston, 1906-1985
George Crumb, 1929-
Arthur Cunningham, 1928-1997
Joseph Curiale, 1955-
Charles Cushing, 1905-1982
Ingolf Dahl, 1912-1970
Richard Danielpour, 1956-
Michael Daugherty, 1954-
Randall Davidson, 1953-
Anthony Davis, 1951-
John Davison, 1930-1999
William Dawson, 1899-1990
Norman Dello Joio, 1913-2008
David Del Tredici, 1937-
Nancy Bloomer Deussen, 1931-
Derek Devore, 1973-
David Diamond, 1915-2005
Emma Lou Diemer, 1927-
Antal Dorati, 1906-1988
Daniel Dorff, 1956-
Deborah Drattell, 1956-
Jacob Druckman, 1928-1996
John Duffy, 1926-
Joël-François Durand, 1954-
John David Earnest, 1940-
Cecil Effinger, 1914-1990
Richard Einhorn, 1952-
Danny Elfman, 1953-
Edw. Kennedy "Duke" Ellington,
  1899-1974
Donald Erb, 1927-2008
Alvin Etler, 1913-1973
Eric Ewazen, 1954-
Richard Felciano, 1930-
Morton Feldman, 1926-1987
Irving Fine, 1914-1962
Marshall Fine, 1956-
Vivian Fine, 1913-2000
David Finko, 1936-
Ross Lee Finney, 1906-1997
Nicolas Flagello, 1928-1994
Carlisle Floyd, 1926-
Arthur Foote, 1853-1937
George Forrest, 1915-1999
Lukas Foss, 1922-2009
Primous Fountain III, 1949-
Arthur Frackenpohl, 1924-
Gabriela Lena Frank, 1972-
Benjamin Franklin, 1706-1790
Kenneth Frazelle, 1955-

William Henry Fry, 1813-1864
Anis Fuleihan, 1900-1970
Nancy Galbraith, 1951-
Herbert Sidney Gellis, 1948-
George Gershwin, 1898-1937
Vittorio Giannini, 1903-1966
Henry F. Gilbert, 1868-1928
Jan Gilbert, 1946-
Michael Gilbertson, 1987-
Don Gillis, 1912-1978
Philip Glass, 1937-
Osvaldo Golijov, 1960-
Michael Gordon, 1956-
Louis Moreau Gottschalk, 1829-1869
Morton Gould, 1913-1996
Percy Grainger, 1882-1961
Jay Greenberg, 1991-
Charles Tomlinson Griffes, 1884-1920
Ferde Grofé, 1892-1972
Murray Gross, 1955-
Louis Gruenberg, 1884-1964
Gene Gutche, 1907-2000
Anne Guzzo, 1968-
Henry Hadley, 1871-1937
Daron Aric Hagen, 1961-
Adolphus Hailstork, 1941-
Marvin Hamlisch, 1944- 2012
Howard Hanson, 1896-1981
John Harbison, 1938-
John Harmon, 1935-
Roy Harris, 1898-1979
Lou Harrison, 1917-2003
Stephen Hartke, 1952-
James Hartway, 1944-
Jake Heggie, 1961-
Anthony Philip Heinrich, 1781-1861
Steve Heitzeg, 1959-
Victor Herbert, 1859-1924
Jerry Herman, 1933-
Bernard Herrmann, 1911-1975
Richard Hervig, 1917-2010
Jennifer Higdon, 1962-
Paul Hindemith, 1895-1963
Charles Kelso Hoag, 1931-
Lee Hoiby, 1926- 2011
Stanley Hollingsworth, 1924-2003
Katherine Hoover, 1937-
Michael Horwood, 1947-
Alan Hovhaness, 1911-2000
George Hoyt, 1947-2014
Albert Hurwit, 1931-
Karel Husa, 1921-
Gregory Hutter, 1971-
Anthony Iannaccone, 1943-
Andrew Imbrie, 1921-2007
Kamran Ince, 1960-

[AMERICAN (UNITED STATES)]
David Itkin, 1957-
Charles Ives, 1874-1954
David A. Janello, 1960-
Werner Janssen, 1899-1990
Samuel Jones, 1935-
Scott Joplin, 1868-1917
Daniel Kallman, 1956-
John Kander, 1927-
Steven Karidoyanes, 1957-
Hershy Kay, 1919-1981
Ulysses Kay, 1917-1995
David Kechley, 1947-
Edgar Stillman Kelley, 1857-1944
Kent Kennan, 1913-2003
Jerome Kern, 1885-1945
Aaron Jay Kernis, 1960-
Leon Kirchner, 1919-2009
Theron Kirk, 1919-1999
George Kleinsinger, 1914-1982
Douglas Knehans, 1957-
Barbara Kolb, 1939-
William Kraft, 1923-
Fritz Kreisler, 1875-1962
Ernst Krenek, 1900-1991
Gail Kubik, 1914-1984
Robert Kurka, 1921-1957
Kristin Kuster, 1973-
Ezra Laderman, 1924-
Bun-Ching Lam, 1954-
John La Montaine, 1920-2013
Burton Lane, 1912-1997
David Lang, 1957-
Libby Larsen, 1950-
Jonathan Larson, 1960-1996
Morten Lauridsen, 1943-
Henri Lazarof, 1932-
James Lee III, 1975-
Benjamin Lees, 1924-2010
Mitch Leigh, 1928-2014
James Lentini, 1958-
Tania León, 1943-
Marvin David Levy, 1935-
John Lewis, 1920-2001
Robert Hall Lewis, 1926-1996
Lowell Liebermann, 1961-
Peter Lieberson, 1946-2011
Andrew Lippa, 1964-
Dan Locklair, 1949-
Normand Lockwood, 1906-2002
Charles Martin Loeffler, 1861-1935
Frank Loesser, 1910-1969
Frederick Loewe, 1901-1988
Doug Lofstrom, 1949-
Mario Lombardo, 1931-
Edwin London, 1929-

Otto Luening, 1900-1996
Peter Christian Lutkin, 1858-1931
Edward MacDowell, 1860-1908
Steven Mackey, 1956-
Richard Maltz, 1958-
Ursula Mamlok, 1928-
Ingram Marshall, 1942-
Jason Martineau, 1969-
Donald Martino, 1931-2005
Salvatore Martirano, 1927-1995
Edward Paul Mascari, 1949-
David Maslanka, 1943-
Daniel Gregory Mason, 1873-1953
Michael Mauldin, 1947-
Clark McAlister, 1946-
Robert McBride, 1911-
Kevin McCarter, 1956-
Daniel McCarthy, 1955-
Glenn McClure, 1964-
William McGlaughlin, 1946-
George Frederick McKay, 1899-1970
Lansing McLoskey, 1964-
Colin McPhee, 1900-1964
Cindy McTee, 1953-
Kirke Mechem, 1925-
John Melby, 1941-
Peter Mennin, 1923-1983
Gian Carlo Menotti, 1911-2007
Steven Mercurio, 1956-
Scott Aaron Miller, 1962-
Ervin Monroe, 1942-
Carman Moore, 1936-
Douglas Moore, 1893-1969
Undine Smith Moore, 1904-1989
Paul Moravec, 1957-
Robert Muczynski, 1929-2010
Marie Barker Nelson, 1926-
Ron Nelson, 1929-
Mark O'Connor, 1961-
James Oliverio, 1956-
David Ott, 1947-
Hall Overton, 1920-1972
John Knowles Paine, 1839-1906
Carter Pann, 1972-
Horatio Parker, 1863-1919
Thomas Pasatieri, 1945-
Stephen Paulus, 1949-2014
Russell Peck, 1945-2009
Terry Pennington, 1943-
Ronald Perera, 1941-
Coleridge Taylor Perkinson,
  1932-2004
George Perle, 1915-2009
Julia Perry, 1924-1979
Vincent Persichetti, 1915-1987
Mark Petering, 1973-

Wayne Peterson, 1927-
Burrill Phillips, 1907-1988
Paul Schuyler Phillips, 1956-
Tobias Picker, 1954-
Daniel Pinkham, 1923-2006
Walter Piston, 1894-1976
Gerald Plain, 1940-
Cole Porter, 1891-1964
Quincy Porter, 1897-1966
Mel Powell, 1923-1998
André Previn, 1929-
Florence Price, 1887-1953
Frank Proto, 1941-
Kevin Puts, 1972-
David Raksin, 1912-2004
Bernard Rands, 1935-
Karol Rathaus, 1895-1954
Gardner Read, 1913-2005
H. Owen Reed, 1910-2014
Steve Reich, 1936-
Alexander Reinagle, 1756-1809
Paul Reuter, 1945-
Roger Reynolds, 1934-
Lucas Richman, 1964-
Wallingford Riegger, 1885-1961
Terry Riley, 1935-
David Rimelis, 1954-
George Rochberg, 1918-2005
Richard Rodgers, 1902-1979
Robert Xavier Rodríguez, 1946-
Bernard Rogers, 1893-1968
Catherine Rollin, 1952-
Sigmund Romberg, 1887-1951
Harold Rome, 1908-1993
Ned Rorem, 1923-
Jerry Ross, 1926-1955
Bruce Craig Roter, 1962-
Christopher Rouse, 1949-
Miklós Rózsa, 1907-1995
Vivian Adelberg Rudow, 1936-
Carl Ruggles, 1876-1971
Loren Rush, 1935-
Tracey Ryan Rush, 1955-
William Russo, 1928-2003
Gerhard Samuel, 1924-2008
David P. Sartor, 1956-
Steven Schaffner, 1952-
Peter Schickele, 1935-
David Schiff, 1945-
Harvey Schmidt, 1929-
Paul Schoenfeld, 1947-
Gunther Schuller, 1925-
William Schuman, 1910-1992
Joseph Schwantner, 1943-
Elliott Schwartz, 1936-
Tibor Serly, 1901-1978

[AMERICAN (UNITED STATES)]

Roger Sessions, 1896-1985
Ralph Shapey, 1921-2002
Harry Rowe Shelley, 1858-1947
Bright Sheng, 1955-
Nathaniel Shilkret, 1889-1982
Alan Shulman, 1915-2002
Elie Siegmeister, 1909-1991
Roberto Sierra, 1953-
Alvin Singleton, 1940-
Thomas Sleeper, 1956-
Nicolas Slonimsky, 1894-1995
Gregory Smith, 1957-
Hale Smith, 1925-2009
Julia Smith, 1911-1989
Kile Smith, 1956-
Stephen Sondheim, 1930-
John Philip Sousa, 1854-1932
Leo Sowerby, 1895-1968
Robert Starer, 1924-2001
James Stephenson, 1969-
Halsey Stevens, 1908-1989
David Nisbet Stewart, 1941-
William Grant Still, 1895-1978
David Stock, 1939-
Eric Stokes, 1930-
Leopold Stokowski, 1882-1977
Nathaniel Stookey, 1970-
Billy Strayhorn, 1915-1967
George Templeton Strong, 1856-1948
Charles Strouse, 1928-
Steven Stucky, 1949-
Jule Styne, 1905-1994
Morton Subotnick, 1933-
Carlos Surinach, 1915-1997
Tomás Svoboda, 1939-2007
Howard Swanson, 1907-1978
George Szell, 1897-1970
Louise Talma, 1906-1996
Tan Dun, 1957-
Deems Taylor, 1885-1966
Deborah Fischer Teason, 1951-
James Territo, 1978-
Christopher Theofanidis, 1967-
Augusta Read Thomas, 1964-
Randall Thompson, 1899-1984
Virgil Thomson, 1896-1989
Francis Thorne, 1922-
Frank Ticheli, 1958-
Frederick Tillis, 1930-
Ernst Toch, 1887-1964
Matthew Tommasini, 1978-
Michael Torke, 1961-
Joan Tower, 1938-
Juan Trigos, 1965-
Lester Trimble, 1923-1986

George Tsontakis, 1951-
Fisher Tull, 1934-1994
Paul Turok, 1929-
Jeff Tyzik, 1952-
Vladimir Ussachevsky, 1911-1990
Nancy Van de Vate, 1930-
Edgard Varèse, 1883-1965
Dianne Wachsman, 1960-
Bernard Wagenaar, 1894-1971
Melinda Wagner, 1957-
George Walker, 1922-
Gwyneth Walker, 1947-
Robert Ward, 1917-2013
Meira Maxine Warshauer, 1949-
Ben Weber, 1916-1979
Kurt Weill, 1900-1950
Jaromir Weinberger, 1896-1967
Hugo Weisgall, 1912-1997
Adolph Weiss, 1891-1971
Dan Welcher, 1948-
Robert Wendel, 1951-
Richard Wernick, 1934-
Philip Wharton, 1969-
Paul White, 1895-1973
Alec Wilder, 1907-1980
Frank Wildhorn, 1959-
John Williams, 1932-
Meredith Willson, 1902-1984
Olly Wilson, 1937-
Diane Wittry, 1964-
Christian Wolff, 1934-
Julia Wolfe, 1958-
Stefan Wolpe, 1902-1972
Russell Woollen, 1923-1994
Robert Wright, 1914-2005
Charles Wuorinen, 1938-
Yehudi Wyner, 1929-
Richard Yardumian, 1917-1985
Gregory Yasinitsky, 1953-
Vincent Youmans, 1898-1946
Judith Lang Zaimont, 1945-
Luigi Zaninelli, 1932-
Frank Zappa, 1940-1993
Zhou Long, 1953-
Ellen Taaffe Zwilich, 1939-

AMERICAN INDIAN (NATIVE AMERICAN)

Louis Ballard, 1931-2007

ARGENTINIAN

Mario Davidovsky, 1934-
Alberto Ginastera, 1916-1983
Osvaldo Golijov, 1960-
Mauricio Kagel, 1931-2008
Astor Piazzolla, 1921-1992
Carlos Veerhoff, 1926-

ARMENIAN

Aleksandr Grigori Arutiunian, 1920-2012
Arno Babadjanyan, 1921-1983
Alan Hovhaness, 1911-2000
Aram Khachaturian, 1903-1978

AUSTRALIAN

Richard Yardumian, 1917-1985
Arthur Benjamin, 1893-1960
Brett Dean, 1961-
Peggy Glanville-Hicks, 1912-1990
Percy Grainger, 1882-1961
Elena Kats-Chernin, 1957-
Douglas Knehans, 1957-
Anton Peter Koch, 1972-
Sean O'Boyle, 1963-
Peter Sculthorpe, 1929-2014

BASQUE

Juan Crisóstomo Arriaga, 1806-1826
Maurice Ravel, 1875-1937

BELGIAN

Jean-Baptiste Accolay, 1833-1900
Jules Demersseman, 1833-1866
César Franck, 1822-1890
François Joseph Gossec, 1734-1829
André Grétry, 1741-1813
Joseph Jongen, 1873-1953
Eugene Ysaÿe, 1858-1931

BLACK COMPOSERS

Michael Abels, 1962-
Leslie Adams, 1932-
T.J. Anderson, 1928-
Margaret Allison Bonds, 1913-1972
Samuel Coleridge-Taylor, 1875-1912
Arthur Cunningham, 1928-1997
Anthony Davis, 1951-
William Dawson, 1899-1990
Edw. Kennedy "Duke" Ellington,
  1899-1974
Antônio Carlos Gomes, 1836-1896
Adolphus Hailstork, 1941-
Scott Joplin, 1868-1917
Ulysses Kay, 1917-1995
James Lee III, 1975-
Tania León, 1943-
John Lewis, 1920-2001
Carman Moore, 1936-
José Mauricio Nunés-Garcia,
  1767-1830
Coleridge Taylor Perkinson,
  1932-2004
Florence Price, 1887-1953
Joseph Boulogne Saint-Georges,
  1739-1799
Alvin Singleton, 1940-
Hale Smith, 1925-2009
William Grant Still, 1895-1978
Billy Strayhorn, 1915-1967
Howard Swanson, 1907-1978
Frederick Tillis, 1930-
George Walker, 1922-
Olly Wilson, 1937-

BRAZILIAN

Jorge Antunes, 1942-
Antônio Carlos Gomes, 1836-1896
José Mauricio Nunés-Garcia,
  1767-1830
Heitor Villa-Lobos, 1887-1959

BRITISH

Richard Addinsell, 1904-1977
Thomas Adès, 1971-
William Alwyn, 1905-1985
Thomas Arne, 1710-1778
Malcolm Arnold, 1921-2006
Granville Bantock, 1868-1946
John Barbirolli, 1899-1970

Lionel Bart, 1930-1999
Arnold Bax, 1883-1953
Arthur Benjamin, 1893-1960
George Benjamin, 1960-
Richard Rodney Bennett, 1936-2012
William Sterndale Bennett,
  1816-1875
Lennox Berkeley, 1903-1989
Harrison Birtwistle, 1934-
Howard Blake, 1938-
Arthur Bliss, 1891-1975
Rutland Boughton, 1878-1960
William Boyce, 1711-1779
Havergal Brian, 1876-1972
Frank Bridge, 1879-1941
Benjamin Britten, 1913-1976
John Bull, ca.1562-1628
Anthony Burgess, 1917-1993
Martin Butler, 1960-
George Butterworth, 1885-1916
Bob Chilcott, 1955-
Jeremiah Clarke, ca.1674-1707
Muzio Clementi, 1752-1832
Eric Coates, 1886-1957
Samuel Coleridge-Taylor, 1875-1912
Frederick Delius, 1862-1934
John Dowland, 1563-1626
George Dyson, 1883-1964
Henry Eccles, ca.1680-ca.1740
Edward Elgar, 1857-1934
Keith Emerson, 1944-
Brian Ferneyhough, 1943-
Gerald Finzi, 1901-1956
Roberto Gerhard, 1896-1970
Edward German, 1862-1936
Alexander Goehr, 1932-
Berthold Goldschmidt, 1903-1996
Eugene Goossens, 1893-1962
Iain Hamilton, 1922-2000
George Frideric Handel, 1685-1759
Dave Heath, 1956-
Alun Hoddinott, 1929-2008
Robin Holloway, 1943-
Gustav Holst, 1874-1934
Herbert Howells, 1892-1983
John Ireland, 1879-1962
Gordon Jacob, 1895-1984
Oliver Knussen, 1952-
Constant Lambert, 1905-1951
Michael Lankester, 1944-
Henry Charles Litolff, 1818-1891
Jonathan Lloyd, 1948-
Andrew Lloyd Webber, 1948-
Colin Matthews, 1946-
David Matthews, 1943-
Nicholas Maw, 1935-2009

Peter Maxwell Davies, 1934-
John McCabe, 1939-
Paul McCartney, 1942-
E. J. Moeran, 1894-1950
Sean O'Boyle, 1963-
Maurice Ohana, 1913-1992
Andrzej Panufnik, 1914-1991
Hubert Parry, 1848-1918
Peter Prelleur, 1705-1741
Henry Purcell, 1659-1695
Bernard Rands, 1935-
Edmund Rubbra, 1901-1986
John Rutter, 1945-
Gerard Schurmann, 1924-
John Stafford Smith, 1750-1836
Reginald Smith Brindle, 1917-2003
Jule Styne, 1905-1994
Arthur Sullivan, 1842-1900
Thomas Tallis, c1505-1585
John Tavener, 1944-2013
John Taverner, ca.1490-1545
Michael Tippett, 1905-1998
Andrew Toovey, 1962-
Mark-Anthony Turnage, 1960-
Ralph Vaughan Williams, 1872-1958
William Walton, 1902-1983
Peter Warlock, 1894-1930
Huw Watkins, 1976-
Andrew Lloyd Webber, 1948-
Ryan Wigglesworth, 1979-
Hugh Wood, 1932-

BULGARIAN

Henri Lazarof, 1932-
Pancho Vladigerov, 1899-1978

CANADIAN

Murray Adaskin, 1906-2002
Keith Bissell, 1912-1992
Walter Boudreau, 1947-
Henry Brant, 1913-2008
Alexander Brott, 1915-2005
Glenn Buhr, 1954-
John Burge, 1961-
Michael Colgrass, 1932-
Victor Davies, 1939-
Maxime Goulet, 1980-
Stewart Grant, 1948-
Michael Horwood, 1947-
Galt MacDermot, 1928-
Colin McPhee, 1900-1964
Oskar Morawetz, 1917-2007

[CANADIAN]

Marjan Mozetich, 1948-
Barbara Pentland, 1912-2000
Robert Carl Rival, 1975-
R. Murray Schafer, 1933-
Claude Vivier, 1948-1983
John Weinzweig, 1913-2006
Yehudi Wyner, 1929-

CATALAN

Roberto Gerhard, 1896-1970
Xavier Montsalvatge, 1912-2002

CHINESE

Chen Gang, 1935-
Chen Yi, 1953-
Chou Wen-chung, 1923-
He Zhanhao, 1933-
Jiang Kui, 1155-1221
Bun-Ching Lam, 1954-
Bright Sheng, 1955-
Tan Dun, 1957-
Zhou Long, 1953-

CUBAN

Leo Brouwer, 1939-
Ernesto Lecuona, 1896-1963
Tania León, 1943-
Julián Orbón, 1925-1991

CYPRIOT

Anis Fuleihan, 1900-1970

CZECH or BOHEMIAN

Georg Anton Benda, 1722-1795
Johann (Georg) [Jan Jiří] Benda, 1713-1752
Heinrich von Biber, 1644-1704
Karl Ditters von Dittersdorf, 1739-1799
Georg Druschetzky, 1745-1819
Antonín Dvořák, 1841-1904
Lubos Fiser, 1935-1999
Josef Bohuslav Foerster, 1859-1951
Julius Fučik, 1872-1916

Christoph Willibald Gluck, 1714-1787
Anthony Philip Heinrich, 1781-1861
Karel Husa, 1921-
Leoš Janáček, 1854-1928
Jiří Jaroch, 1920-1986
Johann Antonin Kozeluch, 1738-1814
Johann Kuhnau, 1660-1722
Robert Kurka, 1921-1957
Bohuslav Martinů, 1890-1959
Ludwig Minkus, 1826-1917
Oskar Morawetz, 1917-2007
Josef Mysliveček, 1737-1781
Eduard Nápravník, 1839-1916
Vaclav Nelhybel, 1919-1996
Franz Xaver Pokorny, 1729-1794
David Popper, 1843-1913
Erwin Schulhoff, 1894-1942
Bedřich Smetana, 1824-1884
Anton Stamitz, 1750-ca.1809
Carl Stamitz, 1745-1801
Johann Wenzel Anton Stamitz, 1717-1757
Josef Suk, 1874-1935
Tomás Svoboda, 1939-2007
Johann Baptist (Jan Krt.) Vanhal, 1739-1813
Jan Václav Vorísek, 1791-1825
Jaromir Weinberger, 1896-1967
Hugo Weisgall, 1912-1997
Jan Zach, 1699-1773

DANISH

Victor Bendix, 1851-1926
Niels Viggo Bentzon, 1919-2000
Niels Gade, 1817-1890
Vagn Holmboe, 1909-1996
Friedrich Kuhlau, 1786-1832
Rued Immanuel Langgaard, 1893-1952
Herman Løvenskjold , 1815-1870
Carl Nielsen, 1865-1931
Ludolf Nielsen, 1876-1939
Per Nørgård, 1932-
Knudåge Riisager, 1897-1974

DUTCH

Louis Andriessen, 1939-
Henk Badings, 1907-1987
Lex van Delden, 1919-1988
Otto Ketting, 1935-

Tristan Keuris, 1946-1996
Reinbert de Leeuw, 1938-
Ton de Leeuw, 1926-1996
Willem Pijper, 1894-1947
Gerard Schurmann, 1924-
Bernard Wagenaar, 1894-1971

ESTONIAN

Arvo Pärt, 1935-
Eduard Tubin, 1905-1982
Erkki -Sven Tüür, 1959-

FINNISH

Kalevi Aho, 1949-
Bernhard Henrik Crusell, 1775-1838
Armas Järnefelt, 1869-1958
Magnus Lindberg, 1958-
Erkki Melartin, 1875-1937
Einojuhani Rautavaara, 1928-
Kaija Saariaho, 1952-
Aulis Sallinen, 1935-
Esa-Pekka Salonen, 1958-
Jean Sibelius, 1865-1957
Heikki Suolahti, 1920-1936

FRENCH

Adolph-Charles Adam, 1803-1856
Charles-Valentin Alkan, 1813-1888
Gilbert Amy, 1936-
Daniel-François-Esprit Auber, 1782-1871
Georges Auric, 1899-1983
Nicolas Bacri, 1961-
Hector Berlioz, 1803-1869
Georges Bizet, 1838-1875
Léon Boëllmann, 1862-1897
François Boieldieu, 1775-1834
Joseph Bodin de Boismortier, 1691-1755
Lili Boulanger, 1893-1918
Pierre Boulez, 1925-
Joseph Canteloube, 1879-1957
André Caplet, 1878-1925
Henri Casadesus, 1879-1947
Emmanuel Chabrier, 1841-1894
Cécile Chaminade, 1857-1944
Gustave Charpentier, 1860-1956
Marc-Antoine Charpentier, 1643-1704
Ernest Chausson, 1855-1899

[FRENCH]

Marius Constant, 1925-2004
François Couperin, 1668-1733
Claude Debussy, 1862-1918
Léo Delibes, 1836-1891
François Devienne, 1759-1803
Pierre Max Dubois, 1930-1995
Théodore Dubois, 1837-1924
Paul Dukas, 1865-1935
Henri Duparc, 1848-1933
Marcel Dupré, 1886-1971
Joël-François Durand, 1954-
Maurice Duruflé, 1902-1986
Estienne Du Tertre, fl. mid-16th c.
Henri Dutilleux, 1916-2013
Gabriel Fauré, 1845-1924
Jean Françaix, 1912-1997
César Franck, 1822-1890
Jacques Gallot, d.ca.1690
Claude Gervaise, fl.-1540-1560
Charles Gounod, 1818-1893
Marcel Grandjany, 1891-1975
Alexandre Guilmant, 1837-1911
Ernest Guiraud, 1837-1892
Reynaldo Hahn, 1875-1947
Fromental Halévy, 1799-1862
Louis Joseph F. Hérold, 1791-1833
Leontzi Honauer, 1737-1790
Arthur Honegger, 1892-1955
Jacques Ibert, 1890-1962
Vincent d'Indy, 1851-1931
Désiré-Émile Ingelbrecht, 1880-1965
André Jolivet, 1905-1974
Charles Koechlin, 1867-1950
Michel-Richard de Lalande,
  1657-1726
Édouard Lalo, 1823-1892
Raoul Laparra, 1876-1943
Jean-Marie Leclair, 1697-1764
Henry Charles Litolff, 1818-1891
Alexandre Luigini, 1850-1906
Jean-Baptiste Lully, 1632-1687
Guillaume de Machaut, ca.1300-1377
Albéric Magnard, 1865-1914
Igor Markevitch, 1912-1983
Jules Massenet, 1842-1912
Paule Maurice, 1910-1967
Etienne-Nicolas Méhul, 1763-1817
Marin Mersenne, 1588-1648
Olivier Messiaen, 1908-1992
Giacomo Meyerbeer, 1791-1864
Darius Milhaud, 1892-1974
Tristan Murail, 1947-
Jacques Offenbach, 1819-1880
Maurice Ohana, 1913-1992
Gabriel Pierné, 1863-1937

Francis Poulenc, 1899-1963
Henri Rabaud, 1873-1949
Jean-Philippe Rameau, 1683-1764
Maurice Ravel, 1875-1937
Joseph Guy Ropartz, 1864-1955
Albert Roussel, 1869-1937
Joseph Boulogne Saint-Georges,
  1739-1799
Camille Saint-Saëns, 1835-1921
Erik Satie, 1866-1925
Tona Scherchen, 1938-
Florent Schmitt, 1870-1958
Claude-Michel Schönberg, 1944-
Anton Simon, 1850-1916
Germaine Tailleferre, 1892-1983
Alexandre Tansman, 1897-1986
Maurice Thiriet, 1906-1972
Ambroise Thomas, 1811-1896
Henri Frédien Tomasi, 1901-1971
Edgard Varèse, 1883-1965
Henri Vieuxtemps, 1820-1881
Emile Waldteufel, 1837-1915
Charles-Marie Widor, 1844-1937

GEORGIAN

Otar Gordeli, 1928-1994
Giya Kancheli, 1935-

GERMAN & AUSTRIAN

Karl Friedrich Abel, 1723-1787
Samuel Adler, 1928-
Eugen d'Albert, 1864-1932
Johann Georg Albrechtsberger,
  1736-1809
Carl Philipp Emanuel Bach,
  1714-1788
Johann Christian Bach, 1735-1782
Johann Ludwig Bach, 1677-1731
Johann Sebastian Bach, 1685-1750
Wilhelm Friedemann Bach,
  1710-1784
Heinrich Joseph Baermann,
  1784-1847
Franz Ignaz Beck, 1734-1809
Ludwig van Beethoven, 1770-1827
Paul Ben-Haim, 1897-1984
Alban Berg, 1885-1935
Heinrich von Biber, 1644-1704
Boris Blacher, 1903-1975
Johannes Brahms, 1833-1897
Max Bruch, 1838-1920

Anton Bruckner, 1824-1896
Ignaz Brüll, 1846-1907
Dietrich Buxtehude, ca.1637-1707
Christian Cannabich, 1731-1798
Peter Cornelius, 1824-1874
Carl Czerny, 1791-1857
Ferdinand David, 1810-1873
Karl Ditters von Dittersdorf,
  1739-1799
Felix Draeseke, 1835-1913
Friedrich Johann Eck, 1767-1838
Johann Gottfried Eckard, 1735-1809
Werner Egk, 1901-1983
Gottfried von Einem, 1918-1996
Johann Friedrich Fasch, 1688-1758
Friedrich von Flotow, 1812-1883
Wolfgang Fortner, 1907-1987
Frederick II ("The Great"), 1712-1786
Robert Fuchs, 1847-1927
Johann Joseph Fux, 1660-1741
Hans Gál, 1890-1987
Friedrich Gernsheim, 1839-1916
Alexander Goehr, 1932-
Hermann Goetz, 1840-1876
Karl Goldmark, 1830-1915
Berthold Goldschmidt, 1903-1996
Johann Gottlieb Graun, 1703-1771
Christoph Graupner, 1683-1760
Julius Otto Grimm, 1827-1903
H.K. Gruber, 1943-
George Frideric Handel, 1685-1759
Karl Amadeus Hartmann, 1905-1963
Josef Matthias Hauer, 1883-1959
Franz Joseph Haydn, 1732-1809
Michael Haydn, 1737-1806
Anthony Philip Heinrich, 1781-1861
Fanny Mendelssohn Hensel,
  1805-1847
Hans Werner Henze, 1926- 2011
Johann Wilhelm Hertel, 1727-1789
Johann Adam Hiller, 1728-1804
Paul Hindemith, 1895-1963
Andreas Hofer, 1629-1684
Georg Melchior Hoffmann,
  ca.1685-1715
Leopold Hofmann, 1738-1793
York Höller, 1944-
Johann Nepomuk Hummel,
  1778-1837
Engelbert Humperdinck, 1854-1921
Joseph Joachim, 1831-1907
Mauricio Kagel, 1931-2008
Daniel Kallman, 1956-
Julius Klengel, 1859-1933
Justin Heinrich Knecht, 1752-1817
Erich Wolfgang Korngold, 1897-1957

[GERMAN & AUSTRIAN]

Joseph Martin Kraus, 1756-1792
Johann Ludwig Krebs, 1713-1780
Fritz Kreisler, 1875-1962
Ernst Krenek, 1900-1991
Friedrich Kuhlau, 1786-1832
Helmut Lachenmann, 1935-
Joseph Lanner, 1801-1843
Franz Lehár, 1870-1948
György Ligeti, 1923-2006
(Gustav) Albert Lortzing, 1801-1851
Gustav Mahler, 1860-1911
Heinrich Marschner, 1795-1861
Felix Mendelssohn, 1809-1847
Giacomo Meyerbeer, 1791-1864
Ludwig Minkus, 1826-1917
Johann Melchior Molter, 1696-1765
Leopold Mozart, 1719-1787
Wolfgang Amadeus Mozart,
  1756-1791
Georg Muffat, 1653-1704
Wenzel Müller, 1759-1835
Otto Nicolai, 1810-1849
Carl Orff, 1895-1982
Johann Pachelbel, 1653-1706
Hans Pfitzner, 1869-1949
Ignaz Pleyel, 1757-1831
Johann Joachim Quantz, 1697-1773
Joachim Raff, 1822-1882
Hermann Friedrich Raupach,
  1728-1778
Max Reger, 1873-1916
Carl Reinecke, 1824-1910
Emil Nikolaus von Reznicek, 1860-
  1945
Joseph Rheinberger, 1839-1901
Julius Rietz, 1812-1877
Hans Rott, 1858-1884
Gerhard Samuel, 1924-2008
Emil Sauer, 1862-1942
Xaver Scharwenka, 1850-1924
Johann Hermann Schein, 1586-1630
Franz Schmidt, 1874-1939
Johann Schobert, c1735-1767
Arnold Schoenberg, 1874-1951
Adolf Schreiner, 1841-1894
Franz Schreker, 1878-1934
Franz Schubert, 1797-1828
Erwin Schulhoff, 1894-1942
Clara Wieck Schumann, 1819-1896
Georg Schumann, 1866-1952
Robert Schumann, 1810-1856
Heinrich Schütz, 1585-1672
Kurt Schwertsik, 1935-
Charlotte Seither, 1965-
Friedrich Seitz, 1848-1918

Ludwig (Louis) Spohr, 1784-1859
Rudi Stephan, 1887-1915
Karlheinz Stockhausen, 1928-2007
Gottfried Heinrich Stölzel,
  1690-1749
Eduard Strauss, 1835-1916
Franz Strauss, 1822-1905
Johann Strauss Jr., 1825-1899
Johann Strauss Sr., 1804-1849
Josef Strauss, 1827-1870
Richard Strauss, 1864-1949
Franz von Suppé, 1819-1895
Georg Philipp Telemann, 1681-1767
Ernst Toch, 1887-1964
Nancy Van de Vate, 1930-
Carlos Veerhoff, 1926-
Georg Joseph Vogler, 1749-1814
Georg Christoph Wagenseil,
  1715-1777
Richard Wagner, 1813-1883
Carl Maria von Weber, 1786-1826
Anton Webern, 1883-1945
Kurt Weill, 1900-1950
Egon Wellesz, 1885-1974
Friedrich Witt, 1770-1837
Hugo Wolf, 1860-1903
Joseph Wölfl, 1773-1812
Stefan Wolpe, 1902-1972
Albert Zabel, 1834-1910
Alexander Zemlinsky, 1871-1942
Bernd Alois Zimmermann,
  1918-1970

GREEK

Steven Karidoyanes, 1957-
John Psathas, 1966-
Nikos Skalkottas, 1904-1949
Christopher Theofanidis, 1967-
Yannis Xenakis, 1922-2001

HUNGARIAN

Sándor Balassa, 1935-
Béla Bartók, 1881-1945
Ernö [Ernst von] Dohnányi,
  1877-1960
Franz Doppler, 1821-1883
Antal Dorati, 1906-1988
Zsolt Durkó, 1934-1997
Peter Eötvös, 1944-
Ferenc Farkas, 1905-2000
Tibor Harsányi, 1898-1954
Emmerich Kálmán, 1882-1953

Zoltán Kodály, 1882-1967
György Kurtág, 1926-
László Lajtha, 1892-1963
Franz Lehár, 1870-1948
György Ligeti, 1923-2006
Franz Liszt, 1811-1886
Ödön Partos, 1907-1977
György Ránki, 1907-1992
Sigmund Romberg, 1887-1951
Miklós Rózsa, 1907-1995
Tibor Serly, 1901-1978
Eduard Strauss, 1835-1916
Johann Strauss Jr., 1825-1899
Johann Strauss Sr., 1804-1849
Josef Strauss, 1827-1870
George Szell, 1897-1970
András Szöllösy, 1921-2007
Sándor Veress, 1907-1992
Leó Weiner, 1885-1960

IRISH

John Field, 1782-1837
Hamilton Harty, 1879-1941
Victor Herbert, 1859-1924
E. J. Moeran, 1894-1950
Sean O'Boyle, 1963-
Charles Villiers Stanford, 1852-1924

ISRAELI

Paul Ben-Haim, 1897-1984
Avner Dorman, 1975-
Ödön Partos, 1907-1977
Shulamit Ran, 1949-

ITALIAN

Mark Adamo, 1962-
Tomaso Albinoni, 1671-1750
Franco Alfano, 1875-1954
Vincenzo Bellini, 1801-1835
Luciano Berio, 1925-2003
Giovanni Battista Besardo, c1567-
  c1625
Luigi Boccherini, 1743-1805
Arrigo Boito, 1842-1918
Giovanni Bolzoni, 1841-1919
Marco Enrico Bossi, 1861-1925
Giovanni Bottesini, 1821-1889
Ferruccio Busoni, 1866-1924
Giuseppe Antonio Capuzzi,
  1755-1818

[ITALIAN]

Fabritio Caroso, c1527/35-after 1605
Alfredo Casella, 1883-1947
Mario Castelnuovo-Tedesco,
  1895-1968
Alfredo Catalani, 1854-1893
Luigi Cherubini, 1760-1842
Francesco Cilea, 1866-1950
Domenico Cimarosa, 1749-1801
Muzio Clementi, 1752-1832
Arcangelo Corelli, 1653-1713
Luigi Dallapiccola, 1904-1975
Salvatore Di Vittorio, 1967-
Gaetano Donizetti, 1797-1848
Domenico Dragonetti, 1763-1846
Riccardo Drigo, 1846-1930
Francesco Durante, 1684-1755
Luca Francesconi, 1956-
Girolamo Alessandro Frescobaldi,
  1583-1643
Giovanni Gabrieli, 1554/7-1612
Vincenzo Galilei, 1520s-1591
Baldassare Galuppi, 1706-1785
Francesco Geminiani, 1687-1762
Carlo Gesualdo, c1561-1613
Bernardo Gianoncelli, fl 1650
Remo Giazotto, 1910-1998
Umberto Giordano, 1867-1948
Mauro Giuliani, 1781-1829
Leonardo Leo, 1694-1744
Ruggero Leoncavallo, 1857-1919
Pietro Locatelli, 1695-1764
Jean-Baptiste Lully, 1632-1687
Bruno Maderna, 1920-1973
Gian Francesco Malipiero, 1882-1973
Francesco Manfredini, 1684-1762
Alessandro Marcello, 1669-1747
Benedetto Marcello, 1686-1739
Giuseppe Martucci, 1856-1909
Pietro Mascagni, 1863-1945
Gian Carlo Menotti, 1911-2007
Saverio Mercadante, 1795-1870
Giangiacomo Miari, 1929-
Simone Molinaro, c1570-after 1633
Claudio Monteverdi, 1567-1643
Marjan Mozetich, 1948-
Luigi Nono, 1924-1990
Nicolò Paganini, 1782-1840
Giovanni Paisiello, 1740-1816
Bernardo Pasquini, 1637-1710
Giovanni Battista Pergolesi,
  1710-1736
Lorenzo Perosi, 1872-1956
Goffredo Petrassi, 1904-2003
Niccolò Piccinni, 1728-1800
Amilcare Ponchielli, 1834-1886

Giacomo Puccini, 1858-1924
Cesare Pugni, 1802-1870
Ottorino Respighi, 1879-1936
Ludovico Roncalli, late 17th century
Gioachino Rossini, 1792-1868
Nino Rota, 1911-1979
Antonio Salieri, 1750-1825
Giovanni Battista Sammartini,
  1701-1775
Giuseppe Sammartini, 1695-1750
Alessandro Scarlatti, 1660-1725
Domenico Scarlatti, 1685-1757
Giacinto Scelsi, 1905-1988
Leone Sinigaglia, 1868-1944
Alessandro Stradella, 1644-1682
Giuseppe Tartini, 1692-1770
Matthew Tommasini, 1978-
Giuseppe Torelli, 1658-1709
Bartolomeo Tromboncino,
  1470-1534
Francesco Maria Veracini,
  1690-ca.1750
Giuseppe Verdi, 1813-1901
Giovanni Battista Viotti, 1755-1824
Tomaso Antonio Vitali, 1663-1745
Antonio Vivaldi, 1678-1741
Ermanno Wolf-Ferrari, 1876-1948
Riccardo Zandonai, 1883-1944

JAPANESE

Maki Ishii, 1936-2003
Toshirō Mayuzumi, 1929-1997
Akira Miyoshi, 1933-
Toru Takemitsu, 1930-1996
Takashi Yoshimatsu, 1953-

JEWISH

Lee Actor, 1952-
Murray Adaskin, 1906-2002
Samuel Adler, 1928-
Charles-Valentin Alkan, 1813-1888
David Amram, 1930-
George Antheil, 1900-1959
Harold Arlen, 1905-1986
David Avshalomov, 1946-
Jacob Avshalomov, 1919-2013
Nicolas Bacri, 1961-
Lionel Bart, 1930-1999
Victor Bendix, 1851-1926
Paul Ben-Haim, 1897-1984
Arthur Benjamin, 1893-1960
Irving Berlin, 1888-1989

Leonard Bernstein, 1918-1990
Jerry H. Bilik, 1933-
Marc Blitzstein, 1905-1964
Ernest Bloch, 1880-1959
Jerry Bock, 1928-2010
Henry Brant, 1913-2008
Ignaz Brüll, 1846-1907
Ferruccio Busoni, 1866-1924
Mario Castelnuovo-Tedesco,
  1895-1968
Daniel Catán, 1949-
Cy Coleman, 1929-2004
Aaron Copland, 1900-1990
Richard Danielpour, 1956-
Ferdinand David, 1810-1873
Mario Davidovsky, 1934-
Lex van Delden, 1919-1988
David Diamond, 1915-2005
Antal Dorati, 1906-1988
Avner Dorman, 1975-
Jacob Druckman, 1928-1996
Paul Dukas, 1865-1935
Danny Elfman, 1953-
Morton Feldman, 1926-1987
Irving Fine, 1914-1962
Marshall Fine, 1956-
David Finko, 1936-
Gerald Finzi, 1901-1956
Lukas Foss, 1922-2009
Friedrich Gernsheim, 1839-1916
George Gershwin, 1898-1937
Philip Glass, 1937-
Reinhold Glière, 1875-1956
Karl Goldmark, 1830-1915
Osvaldo Golijov, 1960-
Louis Moreau Gottschalk, 1829-1869
Morton Gould, 1913-1996
Jay Greenberg, 1991-
Murray Gross, 1955-
Louis Gruenberg, 1884-1964
Reynaldo Hahn, 1875-1947
Fromental Halévy, 1799-1862
Marvin Hamlisch, 1944- 2012
Lou Harrison, 1917-2003
Fanny Mendelssohn Hensel,
  1805-1847
Jerry Herman, 1933-
Bernard Herrmann, 1911-1975
Albert Hurwit, 1931-
David Itkin, 1957-
Joseph Joachim, 1831-1907
Mauricio Kagel, 1931-2008
Emmerich Kálmán, 1882-1953
John Kander, 1927-
Hershy Kay, 1919-1981
Jerome Kern, 1885-1945

[JEWISH]

Aaron Jay Kernis, 1960-
Leon Kirchner, 1919-2009
Gideon Klein, 1919-1945
Erich Wolfgang Korngold,
  1897-1957
Serge Koussevitzky, 1874-1951
Fritz Kreisler, 1875-1962
György Kurtág, 1926-
Ezra Laderman, 1924-
Burton Lane, 1912-1997
Jonathan Larson, 1960-1996
Henri Lazarof, 1932-
Mitch Leigh, 1928-2014
Marvin David Levy, 1935-
Rolf Liebermann, 1910-1999
György Ligeti, 1923-2006
Andrew Lippa, 1964-
Frank Loesser, 1910-1969
Gustav Mahler, 1860-1911
Ursula Mamlok, 1928-
Alexander Manevich, 1908-1976
Felix Mendelssohn, 1809-1847
Giacomo Meyerbeer, 1791-1864
Darius Milhaud, 1892-1974
Oskar Morawetz, 1917-2007
Jacques Offenbach, 1819-1880
Maurice Ohana, 1913-1992
Ödön Partos, 1907-1977
Paul Schuyler Phillips, 1956-
Mel Powell, 1923-1998
André Previn, 1929-
Shulamit Ran, 1949-
Karol Rathaus, 1895-1954
Steve Reich, 1936-
Lucas Richman, 1964-
Richard Rodgers, 1902-1979
Bernard Rogers, 1893-1968
Sigmund Romberg, 1887-1951
Harold Rome, 1908-1993
Jerry Ross, 1926-1955
Bruce Craig Roter, 1962-
Anton Rubinstein, 1829-1894
Vivian Adelberg Rudow, 1936-
Camille Saint-Saëns, 1835-1921
Gerhard Samuel, 1924-2008
Tona Scherchen, 1938-
David Schiff, 1945-
Arnold Schoenberg, 1874-1951
Paul Schoenfeld, 1947-
Claude-Michel Schönberg, 1944-
Franz Schreker, 1878-1934
Erwin Schulhoff, 1894-1942
William Schuman, 1910-1992
Nathaniel Shilkret, 1889-1982
Alan Shulman, 1915-2002

Elie Siegmeister, 1909-1991
Leone Sinigaglia, 1868-1944
Nicolas Slonimsky, 1894-1995
Stephen Sondheim, 1930-
Robert Starer, 1924-2001
Charles Strouse, 1928-
Jule Styne, 1905-1994
Morton Subotnick, 1933-
Wladyslaw Szpilman, 1911-2000
Alexandre Tansman, 1897-1986
Ernst Toch, 1887-1964
Pancho Vladigerov, 1899-1978
Emile Waldteufel, 1837-1915
Ben Weber, 1916-1979
Kurt Weill, 1900-1950
Jaromir Weinberger, 1896-1967
John Weinzweig, 1913-2006
Hugo Weisgall, 1912-1997
Egon Wellesz, 1885-1974
Richard Wernick, 1934-
Henryk Wieniawski, 1835-1880
Frank Wildhorn, 1959-
Stefan Wolpe, 1902-1972
Yehudi Wyner, 1929-
Alexander Zemlinsky, 1871-1942

KOREAN

Unsuk Chin, 1961-

LATVIAN

Peteris Vasks, 1946-

MACANESE

Bun-Ching Lam, 1954-

MEXICAN

Daniel Catán, 1949-
Carlos Chávez, 1899-1978
Blas Galindo, 1910-1993
Mario Lavista, 1943-
Arturo Márquez, 1950-
José Pablo Moncayo (García),
  1912-1958
Manuel Ponce, 1882-1948
Silvestre Revueltas, 1899-1940
Juan Trigos, 1965-
Felipe Villanueva, 1862-1893

MORAVIAN

Gideon Klein, 1919-1945

NEW ZEALANDER

Lyell Cresswell, 1944-
Ross Harris, 1945-
John Psathas, 1966-
Anthony Ritchie, 1960-
John Ritchie, 1921-
Gillian Whitehead, 1941-
Kenneth Young, 1955-

NORWEGIAN

Edvard Grieg, 1843-1907
Johan Halvorsen, 1864-1935
Herman Løvenskjold, 1815-1870
Christian Sinding, 1856-1941
Johan Svendsen, 1840-1911
Fartein Valen, 1887-1952

POLISH

Grażyna Bacewicz, 1909-1969
Tadeusz Baird, 1928-1981
Augustyn Bloch, 1929-
Fryderyk Franciszek Chopin,
  1810-1849
Franz Doppler, 1821-1883
Jakub Gołąbek, 1739-1789
Henryk Mikołaj Górecki, 1933-2010
Feliks Janiewicz, 1762-1848
Mieczyslaw Karłowicz, 1876-1909
Wojciech Kilar, 1932-2013
Witold Lutosławski, 1913-1994
Stanislaw Moniuszko, 1819-1872
Zygmunt Noskowski, 1846-1909
Henryk Pachulski, 1859-1921
Ignacy Jan Paderewski, 1860-1941
Andrzej Panufnik, 1914-1991
Krzysztof Penderecki, 1933-
Marta Ptaszyńska, 1943-
Karol Rathaus, 1895-1954
Jerzy Sapieyevski, 1945-
Xaver Scharwenka, 1850-1924
Kazimierz Serocki, 1922-1981
Stanisław Skrowaczewski, 1923-
Zygmunt Stojowski, 1869-1946
Wladyslaw Szpilman, 1911-2000

[POLISH]

Karol Szymanowski, 1882-1937
Alexandre Tansman, 1897-1986
Jan Wański, ca.1762-ca.1830
Henryk Wieniawski, 1835-1880

PUERTO RICAN

Roberto Sierra, 1953-

RUMANIAN

Marius Constant, 1925-2004
Georges Enesco, 1881-1955
Iosif Ivanovici, 1845-1902

RUSSIAN

Anton Arensky, 1861-1906
Boris Vladimirovich Asaf'yev,
 1884-1949
Mily Balakirev, 1837-1910
Nicolai Berezowsky, 1900-1953
Irving Berlin, 1888-1989
Alexander Borodin, 1833-1887
Julius Conus, 1869-1942
Edison Denisov, 1929-1996
David Finko, 1936-
Boris Fitingof-Shel, 1829-1901
Yuli Gerber, 1831-1883
Alexander Glazunov, 1865-1936
Reinhold Glière, 1875-1956
Mikhail Glinka, 1804-1857
Alexander Goedicke, 1877-1957
Sofiya Asgatovna Gubaydulina,
 1931-
Mikhail Ippolitov-Ivanov, 1859-1935
Dmitri Kabalevsky, 1904-1987
Vassili Kalinnikov, 1866-1901
Giya Kancheli, 1935-
Aram Khachaturian, 1903-1978
Tikhon Khrennikov, 1913-2007
Serge Koussevitzky, 1874-1951
Anatol Liadov, 1855-1914
Alexander Manevich, 1908-1976
Nikolai Miaskovsky, 1881-1950
Aleksandr Vasil'yevich Mosolov,
 1900-1973
Modest Mussorgsky, 1839-1881
Eduard Nápravník, 1839-1916
Peter Oldenburg, 1812-1881
Serge Prokofiev, 1891-1953
Sergei Rachmaninoff, 1873-1943

Nikolai Rimsky-Korsakov,
 1844-1908
Anton Rubinstein, 1829-1894
Alfred Schnittke, 1934-1998
Alexander Scriabin, 1872-1915
Rodion Shchedrin, 1932-
Dmitry Shostakovich, 1906-1975
Anton Simon, 1850-1916
Nicolas Slonimsky, 1894-1995
Vasily Pavlovich Solov'yov-Sedoy,
 1907-1979
Igor Stravinsky, 1882-1971
Sergey Ivanovich Taneyev, 1856-1915
Piotr Ilyich Tchaikovsky, 1840-1893
Alexander Tcherepnin, 1899-1977
Nikolay Tcherepnin, 1873-1945
Vladimir Ussachevsky, 1911-1990
Galina Ustvolskaya, 1919-2006
Stefan Wolpe, 1902-1972
Albert Zabel, 1834-1910
Valery Viktorovich Zhelobinsky,
 1913-1946

SCOTTISH

Lyell Cresswell, 1944-
David Horne, 1970-
James MacMillan, 1959-
Georg Muffat, 1653-1704
Thea Musgrave, 1928-

SPANISH

Isaac Albéniz, 1860-1909
Juan Crisóstomo Arriaga, 1806-1826
Leonardo Balada, 1933-
Gaspar Cassadó, 1897-1966
Manuel de Falla, 1876-1946
Roberto Gerhard, 1896-1970
Enrique Granados, 1867-1916
Ernesto Halffter, 1905-1989
Xavier Montsalvatge, 1912-2002
Maurice Ohana, 1913-1992
Julián Orbón, 1925-1991
Joaquín Rodrigo, 1901-1999
Gaspar Sanz, mid-17th c-early 18th c
Pablo de Sarasate, 1844-1908
Antonio Soler, 1729-1783
Carlos Surinach, 1915-1997
Joaquín Turina, 1882-1949

SWEDISH

Hugo Alfvén, 1872-1960
Kurt Atterberg, 1887-1974
Franz Berwald, 1796-1868
Karl-Birger Blomdahl, 1916-1968
Bernhard Henrik Crusell, 1775-1838
Joseph Martin Kraus, 1756-1792
Lars-Erik Larsson, 1908-1987
Allan Pettersson, 1911-1980
Hilding Rosenberg, 1892-1985
Wilhelm Stenhammar, 1871-1927
Eduard Tubin, 1905-1982
Dag Wirén, 1905-1986

SWISS

Matthias Bamert, 1942-
Ernest Bloch, 1880-1959
Roberto Gerhard, 1896-1970
Heinz Holliger, 1939-
Arthur Honegger, 1892-1955
Rudolf Kelterborn, 1931-
Rolf Liebermann, 1910-1999
Frank Martin, 1890-1974
Maurice Ravel, 1875-1937
Othmar Schoeck, 1886-1957
Sándor Veress, 1907-1992

TURKISH

Kamran Ince, 1960-

UKRAINIAN

Reinhold Glière, 1875-1956
Mykola Lysenko, 1842-1912
Igor Markevitch, 1912-1983
Aleksandr Vasil'yevich Mosolov,
 1900-1973
Valentin Silvestrov, 1937-
Myroslav Skoryk, 1938-

VENEZUELAN

Efraín Amaya, 1959-
Reynaldo Hahn, 1875-1947
Ricardo Lorenz, 1961-

WELSH

Alun Hoddinott, 1929-2008
Karl Jenkins, 1944-
Hilary Tann, 1947-
Huw Watkins, 1976-

WOMEN COMPOSERS

Adrienne Albert, 1937-
Karen Amanda Amrhein, 1970-
Elinor Armer, 1939-
Grażyna Bacewicz, 1909-1969
Amy Marcy Cheney Beach,
 1867-1944
Victoria Bond, 1945-
Margaret Allison Bonds, 1913-1972
Lili Boulanger, 1893-1918
Carolyn Bremer, 1957-
Cécile Chaminade, 1857-1944
Chen Yi , 1953-
Unsuk Chin, 1961-
Linda Robbins Coleman, 1954-
Peggy Stuart Coolidge, 1913-1982
Ruth Crawford (Seeger), 1901-1953
Nancy Bloomer Deussen, 1931-

Emma Lou Diemer, 1927-
Deborah Drattell, 1956-
Vivian Fine, 1913-2000
Gabriela Lena Frank, 1972-
Nancy Galbraith, 1951-
Jan Gilbert, 1946-
Peggy Glanville-Hicks, 1912-1990
Sofiya Asgatovna Gubaydulina,
 1931-
Anne Guzzo, 1968-
Fanny Mendelssohn Hensel,
 1805-1847
Jennifer Higdon, 1962-
Katherine Hoover, 1937-
Elena Kats-Chernin, 1957-
Barbara Kolb, 1939-
Kristin Kuster, 1973-
Bun-Ching Lam, 1954-
Libby Larsen, 1950-
Tania León, 1943-
Ursula Mamlok, 1928-
Paule Maurice, 1910-1967
Cindy McTee, 1953-
Undine Smith Moore, 1904-1989
Thea Musgrave, 1928-
Marie Barker Nelson, 1926-
Barbara Pentland, 1912-2000
Julia Perry, 1924-1979

Florence Price, 1887-1953
Marta Ptaszyńska, 1943-
Shulamit Ran, 1949-
Catherine Rollin, 1952-
Vivian Adelberg Rudow, 1936-
Tracey Ryan Rush, 1955-
Kaija Saariaho, 1952-
Tona Scherchen, 1938-
Clara Wieck Schumann, 1819-1896
Charlotte Seither, 1965-
Julia Smith, 1911-1989
Germaine Tailleferre, 1892-1983
Louise Talma, 1906-1996
Hilary Tann, 1947-
Deborah Fischer Teason, 1951-
Augusta Read Thomas, 1964-
Joan Tower, 1938-
Galina Ustvolskaya, 1919-2006
Nancy Van de Vate, 1930-
Dianne Wachsman, 1960-
Melinda Wagner, 1957-
Gwyneth Walker, 1947-
Meira Maxine Warshauer, 1949-
Gillian Whitehead, 1941-
Diane Wittry, 1964-
Julia Wolfe, 1958-
Judith Lang Zaimont, 1945-
Ellen Taaffe Zwilich, 1939-

APPENDIX I
ORCHESTRALOGY

This appendix would be called "Bibliography," were it not that it includes institutions, organizations, and websites, as well as books. Hence my contrived title "Orchestralogy."

This includes the resources that I personally find most useful, in hopes that others may find the same. It is divided into three sections:

      A. Books
      B. Institutions and Organizations
      C. Websites

A. BOOKS

General

Jerzy Chwialkowski. *The Da Capo Catalog of Classical Music Compositions*. Da Capo Press, 1996.

    A ponderous paperback, listing the complete works of 132 major composers, from Monteverdi to Stockhausen. Useful in surprising and unpredictable ways. Includes thematic index numbers not just for Mozart and Bach, but for composers you never thought had them (Albéniz, W.F. Bach, and Martinu, for example). Includes lists of opera excerpts: Do you need to check the name of an aria from Rossini's *Elisabetta*, Act II? More than a dozen of them are there, on page 1040, in the order in which they occur in the opera, though, alas, without identification as to which character sings them.

Theodor Müller-Reuter. *Lexikon der deutschen Konzertliteratur: ein Ratgeber für Dirigenten, Konzertveranstalter, Musikschriftsteller und Musikfreunde*. 2 vols. Leipzig: G.F. Kahnt, 1909-1921. (Reprints: Da Capo Press, 1972 [may be out of print]; Ulan Press, 2012 [v.2 only?]).

    About a century old, but I still often turn to it. Gives full and detailed information on individual works, including instrumentation, duration, movement titles, and rich background information. An oddly idiosyncratic selection of 15 composers. Although the title proclaims it a lexicon of German concert literature, it includes Berlioz and Liszt amongst the Germans and Austrians—but Beethoven, Brahms, and Haydn were not included until the 1921 supplement, and Mozart never made it at all! Includes some now-obscure composers (Draeseke and Gernsheim), and others presently enjoying a revival of interest (Raff, Reinecke).

Wilhelm Buschkötter & Hansjürgen Schaefer. *Handbuch der internationalen Konzertliteratur (Manual of International Concert Literature)*. 2nd ed., revised and expanded. Berlin: Walter de Gruyter, 1996.

    Analogous to the present book. In German, and reflective of German repertoire; the foreword and the list of abbreviations are in English as well as German.

Jennifer Goodenberger. *Subject Guide to Classical Instrumental Music*. Lanham, MD: Scarecrow Press, 2001 (paperback reprint of original 1989 edition).

Originally intended for producers of film, television, and radio, but useful to musicians as well. Lists of instrumental compositions (not just orchestral) organized by subject matter or topic, such as *Arabia, Autumn, Bears, Bells,* and the like. May be helpful in planning thematic programs.

Robert A. Fradkin. *The Well-Tempered Announcer: A Pronunciation Guide to Classical Music*. Bloomington & Indianapolis: Indiana University Press, 1996.

Intended for radio announcers at classical music stations, but useful to all of us who are required by our jobs to mangle names and titles in a variety of languages.

Ballet

Matthew Naughtin. *Ballet Music: A Handbook*. Lanham, MD: Rowman & Littlefield, 2014.

The book I wish I had owned 40 years ago. Explains how ballet companies work, the supremacy of the choreographer (as opposed to the composer) in determining the shape and order of a production, the necessity of a good relationship with the rehearsal pianist, and many other factors that may seen topsy-turvy to someone from the orchestra world. The author is Music Librarian of the San Francisco Ballet. Detailed information on over 120 ballets in the standard repertoire. In addition to the usual duration, instrumentation, and publisher for each ballet, it includes synopses, alternative versions, and the various interpolations that have been made over time to classic ballets. Helpful appendices deal with Grand Rights, commissioning agreements, Master Use licenses, and the like.

Chamber Orchestra

Dirk Meyer. *Chamber Orchestra & Ensemble Repertoire: A Catalog of Modern Music*. Lanham, MD: Scarecrow Press, 2011.

Includes nearly 4000 works by 1100 composers of the 20th and 21st centuries. A clever system of appendices will be particularly useful in designing programs. An especially welcome feature is the list of the 22 arrangements for large chamber ensemble created for the **Verein für Musikalische Privataufführungen** (Society for Private Musical Performances)—the legendary group formed by Arnold Schoenberg and Alban Berg in 1918.

Choral

Jonathan Green. *A Conductor's Guide to Choral-Orchestral Works*. Lanham, MD & London: Scarecrow Press, 1994-   .

An ongoing series, of which six volumes have appeared: 20th-century works with English texts (1994); Rachmaninof through Penderecki (1998); J.S. Bach (2000); Haydn and Mozart (2001); Nineteenth Century (2008); and Selected Baroque Works (2013). An omnibus edition, combining all these, is in preparation. Rich detail on each work, including background,

performing forces, duration, contents and performance issues.

Translations and Annotations of Choral Repertoire. Corvallis, OR: Earthsongs, 1988-2009.

> Vol.1: Sacred Latin Texts (Ron Jeffers)
> Vol.2: German Texts (Ron Jeffers & Gordon Paine)
> Vol.3: French & Italian Texts (Gordon Paine)
> Vol.4: Hebrew Texts (Ethan Nash & Joshua Jacobson)

Translations are given at the micro-level (word-by-word) and the macro-level (line-by-line). Excellent background information on each text and its source. An International Phonetic Alphabet (IPA) pronunciation guide is also available for vol.2 (German Texts).

Opera

Nicholas Ivor Martin. *The Opera Manual*. Lanham, MD: Scarecrow Press, 2014.

Just about everything you need to know to produce one of the almost 900 operas in this book. Each entry includes the number of acts, scenes, and sets; durations; hazards; roles (categorized as major, minor, or bit); chorus; dance or movement; orchestration; stageband if any; publisher; and the copyright owner (if not in the public domain).

Nico Castel. *Operatic Libretti Series*. Mt. Morris, NY: Leyerle Publications, 197?- .

A monumental series of opera librettos, in a 3-line format: the original opera text in boldface, a phonetic version directly above (in the International Phonetic Alphabet), and a word-for-word English translation directly below. Where needed, a fourth (lowest) line gives an idiomatic English version. 23 volumes are currently available in the series, with more in preparation. Each volume contains several operas, so consult castelopera.com to determine which volume you need.

John Yaffé & David Daniels. *Arias, Ensembles, & Choruses: An Excerpt Finder for Orhestras*. Lanham, MD: Scarecrow Press, 2012.

Lists vocal excerpts suitable for concert performance from operas, oratorios, cantatas, musicals, and the like, with instrumentation, duration, publisher, and often helpful commentary.

Percussion[1]

Russ Girsberger. *A Practical Guide to Percussion Terminology*. Ft. Lauderdale, FL: Meredith Music Publications, 1998.

A handy dictionary of percussion instruments, terms and technique. Includes a compendium of lengthy explanatory phrases used in standard orchestral repertoire from Berlioz to Bartók.

Raynor Carroll. *Symphonic Repertoire Guide for Timpani and Percussion*. Pasadena, CA: Batterie Music, 2005.

One of the best of several books that give percussion assignments for orchestral works. 3000

---

[1] See also **Percussion Orchestrations Ltd. (percorch.com)**, under Websites, below.

orchestral works are covered: each entry lists (a) how many timpanists and percussionists are required, (b) what instruments are needed, and (c) a schema for who plays what. A polyglot glossary in the back of the book defines over 600 percussion instruments and gives in each case an example of a composition that makes characteristic use of the instrument in question.

Pops

Lucy Manning. *Orchestral "Pops" Music: A Handbook*. 2nd edition. Lanham, MD: Scarecrow Press, 2013.

 Analogous to the present book, but emphasizing music for pops concerts.

B. INSTITUTIONS AND ORGANIZATIONS

MOLA (Major Orchestra Librarians' Association) www.mola-inc.org

 MOLA is open to orchestras, opera and ballet companies, concert bands, music schools, and music festivals worldwide. Membership is by institution; individuals become members only by being voted Honorary or Emeritus status. There is an annual conference, a quarterly newsletter (*Marcato*—to which non-members may subscribe), and an online forum. Especially helpful features of the website are the errata lists, and the section of "Publishers, Agencies & Dealers" (PAD), constantly updated.

Conductors Guild guild@conductorsguild.net
719 Twinridge Lane publications@conductorsguild.net
Richmond, VA 23235 www.conductorsguild.org
USA

 Membership is open to any conductor, student, institution, library or individual interested in supporting the art and profession of conducting. There is an annual conference, a semi-annual *Journal* for scholarly articles, an online newsletter (*Podium Notes*), a monthly *Conductor Opportunities Bulletin* (conducting vacancies, study opportunities, competitions, workshops), an *Annual Membership Directory*, an internet mailing list (*GuildList*). The Guild's *Mentoring & Consulting Program* allows members to receive guidance from experienced colleagues. The Guild store offers various books and other materials at discounted prices.

CODA (College Orchestra Directors Association) www.codaweb.org

 An international organization for college and university orchestra directors, as well as conductors of youth and community orchestras and student conductors. Founded 2003, with more than 200 members in 41 U.S. states and around the globe. It offers a library of bowings, program notes, and errata lists, and provides support in promotion and tenure efforts. Peer-reviewed journal and newsletter. Repertoire ideas on such things as music for less experienced orchestras. Information on technology in the classroom, fund-raising, touring and pedagogical materials. A biennial international composition competition, and an annual conference, which includes masterclasses with prominent conductors.

OPAS (Orchestra Planning and Administration System)

Fine Arts Software
112 Covington Square Drive
Cary, NC 27513

Tel/Fax: 919-380-0172
www.fineartssoftware.com

A comprehensive software program specifically designed to manage virtually every facet of orchestra administration. Its most powerful version integrates the repertoire, artistic, scheduling, personnel, finance, library, and tour operations of any performing ensemble. In use by over 200 organizations worldwide. Available in three configurations: OPAS Lite, Basic, and Extended. Price structure is based on the organization's total annual expenses.

Center for Black Music Research (CBMR)

Street address:
618 S. Michigan Avenue, 6th floor
Chicago, IL

Mailing address:
600 South Michigan Ave.
Chicago, IL 60605-1996
Tel: 312-369-7559

A unit of Columbia College Chicago, devoted to the research, preservation and dissemination of information about the history of black music on a global scale. Orchestral music of black composers constitutes just one part of the Center's activities, but the staff responds very promptly to research inquiries about concert music and can provide repertoire suggestions as well as background information. For direct access to reference services, e-mail: cbmrref@colum.edu.

National Anthem Protocols

U.S. Army Band, Fort Myer, VA

Tel: 703-696-3648

The United States government has assigned to the U.S. Army Band at Fort Myer, Virginia, the responsibility for keeping track of correct, current national anthems for all nations. Band arrangements, which can easily be adapted for orchestral use, may usually be obtained from this source. Governments of other nations are likely to maintain similar arrangements through either their military or foreign affairs departments.

If more than one anthem is to be played for a particular occasion, protocol dictates that the anthem of the home country (e.g., U.S.A. when on U.S. soil) be played last. If there is to be more than one preceding anthem, these should be played in alphabetical order.

National anthem sites exist on the Internet, but there is no guarantee that their information is either current or correct. Rather than risk embarrassment—or even an international incident—one might prefer to consult an official government source such as the Department of State, an embassy or consulate, or the Army Band. Nevertheless, the following sites might be useful in certain circumstances:

(1) www.nationalanthems.info has extensive information on each of more than 400 anthems, with music as well as lyrics in the original language and in English translation.

(2) www.colin-kirkpatrick.com/national-anthems/links.html ("Colin Kirkpatrick's National Anthems Online") makes parts available for 65 anthems, freely downloadable. The arrangements consist of six independent parts in different transpositions and various octaves, making them usable for almost any sort of ensemble.

Edwin A. Fleisher Collection of Orchestral Music
Please see **Fleisher** in Appendix L: Publishers & Sources.

IAMIC (International Association of Music Information Centres)

Rue Saint Michel 38
BE-1000 Brussels
Belgium

Tel: +32 2 504 90 99
iamic@iamic.net
www.iamic.net

A worldwide network of organizations promoting new music. Member-organizations exist in some 40 countries. Complete contact information for all members may be found on the IAMIC website. Each is an excellent source of information on new music in its particular region.

Opera America
330 Seventh Avenue
New York, NY 10001
Tel: 212-796-8620
Fax: 212-796-8621
info@operaamerica.org
www.operaamerica.org

Opera.ca
6286-2100 Bloor St. W.
Toronto, Ontario M6S 5A5
Canada
416-591-7222
www.opera.ca

Opera Europa
23 rue Léopold
B-1000 Brussels
Belgium
Tel & Fax: +32 2 217 6705
info@opera-europa.org
www.opera-europa.org

Service organizations for opera, with memberships of about 150 professional companies (U.S.), 13 companies (Canada), and 148 companies from 39 different countries (Europe).

Pocket Publications
25 Plymouth Road
Penarth
South Glamorgan UK
CF64 3DA

Tel & Fax: +44 (0) 2920 703447
tony@pocket-publications.com
www.pocket-publications.com

A specialist publisher of orchestral reductions of opera scores, under the direction of Tony Burke, formerly librarian of the Welsh National Opera Orchestra. Reductions as well as sets of full orchestrations are for hire; a great many individual arias and ensembles (reduced or full) are also available, as are choral and purely orchestral works. Often there are several different reductions of the same work for varying size ensembles.

C. WEBSITES

Almost everything these days—be it a publisher, an organization, a business—has a website. The list that follows, however, consists of useful websites and listserves at least some of which have no independent existence in the "real" world.

Gaylord Music Library Necrology   **http://library.wustl.edu/units/music/necro**
Founded by the late Nathan Eakin, at Washington University in St. Louis. This is one of the best of the various online music necrologies.

Gigfix.com   **admin@gigfix.com**

An intriguing website apparently designed for freelance musicians in the UK. There are many links useful for musicians all over the world, however. One of the best features is a searchable repertoire database where, for example, flutists can check the repertoire being played to see whether they should bring their piccolos.

Music-In-Print   **www.emusicquest.com**

Successor to the Music-In-Print series of books from Musicdata, Inc., which began in 1973. Donald Reese started emusicquest in 2000 to provide an Internet-based searchable sheet music index for piano, band, and popular guitar—areas not covered by Music-In-Print. He later acquired the assets of Musicdata, Inc., and expanded his index to include 15 specific music areas, the most relevant for users of this book being "Orchestral."

Access to the site is available via annual subscription. Pricing information may be found on the site. Trial subscriptions are available.

Searches in the Orchestral area of the emusicquest site will yield publication information, instrumentation, and duration. There is a very complete Publisher Directory. The databases are frequently updated, and Mr. Reese is eager to make corrections as needed.

Orchestra Library Information Yahoo! Group   **OrchLibInfo@yahoogroups.com**
                                            http://launch.groups.yahoo.com/group/OrchLibInfo

This group serves primarily as a way to pick the brains of Clinton F. Nieweg, Principal Librarian, the Philadelphia Orchestra (ret.), who has been a pedagogue and mentor to students of orchestral librarianship for many years. The listserve owner is Thomas Pease of the Library of Congress. It is possible to peruse past messages, post new ones, and subscribe for either the daily digest or individual e-mails.

Orchestral Music   **www.orchestralmusic.com**

The complete database of this book, updated monthly with new additions and corrections. In existence since 2008, it is to receive a general makeover to coincide with the publication of this 5th edition. Annual subscriptions are available, as is a 30-day free trial period.

Orchestralist   **http://launch.groups.yahoo.com/group/orchestralist**

An international listserve for the orchestra world, created by conductor/composer Andrew Levine. Regular participants include many conductors, composers, players, publishers, and the like. Ask a question and receive prompt answers from others in the field. Very long threads tend to develop on certain subjects. No-cost subscriptions may be set to receive either a daily digest or individual messages as they are posted. Archives may be searched.

Oxford Music Online   www.grovemusic.com

All musicians know *The New Grove Dictionary of Music and Musicians* (2nd edition, 2000, ed. Stanley Sadie and John Tyrrell) as a peerless English-language reference source. It is the cornerstone of the ever-growing Oxford Music Online, which now includes in addition the following:

> *The Oxford Companion to Music*
> *The Oxford Dictionary of Music*
> *Encyclopedia of Popular Music*
> *The Grove Dictionary of American Music*
> *The Grove Dictionary of Musical Instruments*
> *The New Grove Dictionary of Jazz*
> *The New Grove Dictionary of Opera*

One annual subscription—not inexpensive, but worth it—gives the subsciber access to all of these via one easy search mechanism: just type what you want to find in the search box and you are rewarded with a whole list of articles from these works to which you can link. All the components are updated frequently.

Percussion Orchestrations Ltd.   www.percorch.com

Founded in 2004 by Ed Cervenka, a British percussionist (and, one might add, cimbalom player). The site gives the percussion requirements for over 8000 works, including orchestral, operatic, and contemporary repertoire. Each work displays, in a clever and clear grid system, the number of players and the list of instruments required, movement by movement.

Special features include a dictionary of percussion instrument names in five languages, the ability to search for works which require a specific number of percussionists, a "scheduler" for linking works to a season calendar, and even lists of works that require no percussion at all. The site itself may be read in five languages.

The site is constantly being upgraded with new features. It is available by subscription, with prices varying depending on the status of the user. Free trial subscriptions are possible.

Symphony Orchestra Library Center   www.orchestralibrary.com

This one should be called "The Mother of All Websites," at least for orchestral information. Created and maintained by Steven Sherrill, Principal Librarian of the Atlanta Symphony (ret.). The home page consists almost entirely of links—several hundred of them—invitingly arranged for browsing or for searching. You'll find just about anything here, including transposed parts for those nasty bass clarinets in A or in bass clef, and D clarinet parts transposed for E-flat instruments.

APPENDIX J
EXTENDED CONTENTS

A few of the entries in this book are simply too long to fit into the format of the main body of the book. These are given here, with durations of individual movements, which are often helpful in planning rehearsals.

Handel, George Frideric   1685-1759

(b Halle, 23 Feb 1685; d London, 14 April 1759). German; naturalized English from 1726

Messiah, HWV 56 <1741>   159'

chorus   solos SATB

0 2 0 2 — 0 2 0 0 — tmp — cnt,m org — str

N.B.: Numbering varies from one edition to another.

PART I

1. *Sinfony*	4'
2/3. *Comfort ye my people / Every valley shall be exalted*	7'
4. *And the glory of the Lord*	3'
5. *Thus saith the Lord of Hosts*	2'
6. *But who may abide the day of His coming*	5'
7. *And He shall purify the sons of Levi*	3'
8/9. *Behold a virgin shall conceive / O Thou that tellest*	7'
10/11. *For behold / The people that walked in darkness*	6'
12. *For unto us a Child is born*	5'
13. *Pifa (Sinphonia pastorale)*	3'
14/15/16. *There were shepherds abiding in the fields*	2'
17. *Glory to God in the highest*	2'
18. *Rejoice greatly, o daughter of Zion*	5'
19/20. *Then shall the eyes of the blind / He shall feed His flock*	6'
21. *His yoke is easy, His burthen is light*	3'

PART II

22. *Behold the Lamb of God*	3'
23. *He was despised and rejected*	11'
24. *Surely, He hath borne our griefs*	3'
25. *And with His stripes we are healed*	2'
26. *All we like sheep have gone astray*	4'
27. *All they that see Him, laugh Him to scorn*	1'
28. *He trusted in God that He would deliver Him*	3'
29/30. *Thy rebuke / Behold and see if there be any sorrow*	3'
31/32. *He was cut off / But Thou didst not leave His soul*	3'
33. *Lift up your heads, O ye gates*	4'
34/35. *Unto which of the angels / Let all the angels of God*	2'
36. *Thou art gone up on high*	4'
37. *The Lord gave the word*	1'
38. *How beautiful are the feet of them*	4'
39. *Their sound is gone out into all lands*	1'
40. *Why do the nations so furiously rage*	3'
41. *Let us break their bonds asunder*	2'
42/43. *He that dwelleth in heaven / Thou shalt break them*	3'
44. *Hallelujah*	4'

PART III

45. *I know that my Redeemer liveth*	7'
46. *Since by man came death*	2'
47/48. *Behold I tell you a mystery / The trumpet shall sound*	10'
49/50. *Then shall be brought / O death, where is thy sting?*	2'
51. *But thanks be to God*	2'
52. *If God is for us, who can be against us*	5'
53. *Worthy is the Lamb that was slain / Amen*	7'

Honegger, Arthur   1892-1955

(b Le Havre, 10 March 1892; d Paris, 27 Nov 1955). Swiss-French

Le roi David [large orchestra version, 1923]   74'
(King David) <1921; reorchestrated 1923>

chorus   solos SAT   speaker

2[1.2/pic] 2[1.2/Eh] 2[1.2/bcl] 2[1.2/cbn] — 4 2 3 1 — tmp+3 — hp — cel, org — str

perc: cym, sd, bd, gong, tambn, tambn prov

Originally for small orchestra; rescored by the composer.

PART I:

1. *Introduction*	2'
2. *Song of the Shepherd David*	2'
3. *Psalm: All Praise to Him*	2'
3a. *Fanfare and Entry of Goliath*	1'
4. *Song of Victory*	1'
5. *March & Reprise of No.4*	2'
6. *Psalm: In the Lord I Put My Faith*	2'
7. *Psalm: Oh, Had I Wings Like a Dove*	3'
8. *Song of the Prophets*	2'
9. *Psalm: Pity Me, Lord!*	2'
10. *The Camp of Saul*	2'
11. *Psalm: God, the Lord Shall Be My Light*	2'
12. *Incantation of the Witch of Endor*	3'
13. *March of the Philistines*	1'
14. *Lament of Gilboa*	5'

PART II:

15. *Song of the Daughters of Israel*	2'
16. *The Dance Before the Ark*	12'

PART III:

17. *Song: Now My Voice in Song Up-Soaring*	2'
18. *Song of the Handmaid*	2'
19. *Psalm of Penitence*	2'
20. *Psalm: Behold in Evil I was Born*	4'
21. *Psalm: O Shall I Raise Mine Eyes unto the Mountains?*	2'
22. *The Song of Ephraim*	1'
23. *March of the Hebrews*	3'
24. *Psalm: Thee Will I Love O Lord*	3'
25. *Psalm: In My Distress*	1'
26. *The Crowning of Solomon*	2'
27. *The Death of David*	6'

Mendelssohn, Felix   1809-1847
(b Hamburg, 3 Feb 1809; d Leipzig, 4 Nov 1847). German

Elijah, op.70 (Elias) <1846; rev 1847>   *133'*
chorus   solos SSATB (or more)
2 2 2 2 — 4 2 3 1 — tmp — org — str
Breitkopf ed. Christian Martin Schmidt.
PART I

Introduction: As God the Lord of Israel liveth	*1'*
Overture	*4'*
1. Chorus: Help, Lord!	*4'*
2. Duet with Chorus: Lord, bow thine ear to our pray'r	*2'*
3. Tenor Recit.: Ye people, rend your hearts	*1'*
4. Tenor Aria: If with all your hearts ye truly seek me	*3'*
5. Chorus: Yet doth the Lord see it not	*4'*
6. Alto Recit.: Elijah, get thee hence Elijah	*1'*
7. Double Quartet: For He shall give His angels charge	*4'*
8. Aria & Duet: What have I to do with thee	*6'*
9. Chorus: Blessed are the men who fear Him	*3'*
10. Recit. with Chorus: As God the Lord of Sabaoth liveth	*4'*
11. Chorus: Baal, we cry to thee	*3'*
12. Recit. & Chorus: Call him louder! For he is a God	*1'*
13. Recit. & Chorus: Call him louder! He heareth not	*2'*
14. Bass Aria: Lord God of Abraham, Isaac, and Israel	*3'*
15. Quartet: Cast thy burden upon the Lord	*2'*
16. Bass Solo with Chorus: O Thou, who makest thine Angels	*3'*
17. Bass Aria: Is not His word like a fire!	*2'*
18. Alto Arioso: Woe, woe unto them who forsake Him	*3'*
19. Recit. with Chorus: O man of God, help thy people	*6'*
20. Chorus: Thanks be to God	*4'*
PART II	
21. Soprano Aria: Hear ye, Israel!	*5'*
22. Chorus: Be not afraid, said God the Lord	*4'*
23. Recit. with Chorus: The Lord hath exalted thee	*3'*
24. Chorus: Woe to him! He shall perish	*2'*
25. Recit.: Man of God, now let my words	*3'*
26. Bass Aria: It is enough, O Lord	*5'*
27. Tenor Recit.: See, now he sleepeth	*1'*
28. Terzetto: Lift thine eyes to the mountains	*2'*
29. Chorus: He, watching over Israel	*4'*
30. Recit.: Arise, Elijah	*2'*
31. Alto Aria: O rest in the Lord	*3'*
32. Chorus: He that shall endure to the end	*2'*
33. Recit: Night falleth round me, O Lord	*2'*
34. Chorus: Behold, God the Lord passed by	*5'*
35. Recit. & Quartet: Holy is God the Lord	*4'*
36. Chorus–recit. & Bass Solo: Go, return upon thy way	*1'*
37. Bass Arioso: For the mountains shall depart	*3'*
38. Chorus: Then did Elijah the prophet break forth	*2'*
39. Tenor Aria: Then, then shall the righteous shine forth	*3'*
40. Soprano Solo: Behold, God hath sent Elijah the prophet	*1'*
41. Chorus & Quartet: But the Lord, from the north hath raised	*6'*
42. Chorus: And then, then shall your light break forth	*4'*

Mendelssohn, Felix   1809-1847
(b Hamburg, 3 Feb 1809; d Leipzig, 4 Nov 1847). German

St. Paul, op.36 (Paulus) <1836>   *125'*
chorus   solos SATBB
2 2 2 3[1.2.cbn] — 4 2 3 1[serp] — tmp — org — str
The composer's indication "contrafagotto e serpente"
suggests the doubling of the cbn part with a tuba.
However, no separate tuba part is provided in published
materials.
   Bärenreiter ed. Michael Cooper; Breitkopf edition by
Michael Märker, 1997.

Overture	*7'*
PART ONE	
1. Chorus: Herr, der du bist der Gott	*4'*
2. Chorale: Allein Gott in der Höh' sei Ehr'	*2'*
3. Recit.: Die Menge der Gläubigen	*2'*
4. Chorus: Dieser Mensch hört nicht auf zu reden	*3'*
5. Recit. & Chorus: Und sie sahen auf ihn Alle	*5'*
6. Aria: Jerusalem, die du tödtest die Propheten	*3'*
7. Recit. & Chorus: Sie aber stürmten auf ihn ein	*2'*
8. Recit. & Chorale: Und sie steinigten ihn	*3'*
9. Recit.: Und die Zeugen legten ab	*1'*
10. Chorus: Siehe, wir preisen selig	*4'*
11. Recit. & Aria: Saulus aber zerstörte die Gemeinde	*2'*
12. Recit. & Arioso: Und zog mit einer Schaar gen Damaskus	*3'*
13. Recit. & Chorus: Und als er auf dem Wege war	*2'*
14. Chorus: Mache dich auf, werde Licht	*5'*
15. Choral: Wachet auf! Ruft uns die Stimme	*2'*
16. Recit.: Die Männer aber die seine Gefährten waren	*1'*
17. Aria: Gott sei mir gnädig	*5'*
18. Recit.: Es war aber ein Jünger zu Damaskus	*2'*
19. Aria with Chorus: Ich danke dir, Herr mein Gott	*4'*
20. Recit.: Und Ananias ging hin	*2'*
21. Chorus: O welch' eine Tiefe des Reichtums	*5'*
PART TWO	
22. Chorus: Der Erdkreis ist nun des Herrn	*4'*
23. Recit.: Und Paulus kam zu der Gemeinde	*1'*
24. Duettino: So sind wir nun Botschafter	*2'*
25. Chorus: Wie lieblich sind die Boten	*3'*
26. Recit. & Arioso: Und wie sie ausgesandt	*3'*
27. Recit. & Chorus: Da aber die Juden das Volk sah'n	*1'*
28. Chorus: Ist das nicht der zu Jerusalem	*5'*
29. Recit.: Paulus aber und Barnabas sprachen	*1'*
30. Duet: Denn also hat uns der Herr geboten	*2'*
31. Recit.: Und es war ein Mann zu Lystra	*1'*
32. Chorus: Die Götter sind den Menschen gleich geworden	*1'*
33. Recit.: Und nannten Barnabas Jupiter	*1'*
34. Chorus: Seid uns gnädig, hohe Götter	*3'*
35. Recit. & Aria with Chorus: Da das die Apostel hörten	*8'*
36. Recit.: Da ward das Volk erreget wider sie	*1'*
37. Chorus: Hier ist des Herren Tempel	*2'*
38. Recit.: Und sie alle verfolgten Paulus	*1'*
39. Cavatina: Sei getreu bis in den Tod	*3'*
40. Recit.: Paulus sandte hin und liess fordern	*2'*
41. Chorus & Recit.: Schone doch deiner selbst	*3'*
42. Chorus: Sehet, welch' eine Liebe	*3'*
43. Recit.: Und wenn er gleich geopfert wird	*1'*
44. Chorus: Nicht aber ihm allein	*4'*

Minkus, Ludwig   **1826-1917**

(b Vienna, 23 March 1826; d Vienna, 7 Dec 1917). Czech composer
of Austrian birth, active in Russia

Don Quixote <1869>   137'

3[1.2.3/pic] 2 2 2 — 4 4[2tp, 2crt] 3 1 — tmp+4 — hp —
pf/cel — str

perc: bd, cym, tri, tambn, sd, glock, xyl, cast

The uncut Bolshoi material, which includes traditional added
music by Vasily Solov'yev-Sedoy, Reinhold Glière, Anton
Simon, Valery Zhelobinsky, Riccardo Drigo, Yuly Gerber,
Cesare Pugni, & Eduard Napravnik.

Piano, celesta, harp 2, and xylophone only required for
certain of these added movements.

No.00. Introduction	*4'*
PROLOGUE	
No. 00a. Tableau	*1'*
1. Entrée de Don Quichotte	*3'*
1a. Allegro assai	*1'*
2. Scène de Don Quichotte et Sancho Panza	*4'*
ACTE I	
3. Place en Barcelone	*1'*
4. Entrée de Kitri	*1'*
5. Entrée de Basilio	*1'*
6. Kitri et Basilio (Pas de deux)	*2'*
7. Moreño	*1'*
8. Scène (Lorenzo, Kitri et Basilio)	*2'*
9. Entrée de Gamache	*2'*
10. Seguidilla	*2'*
11. Scène des Toréadors	*2'*
12. La Danseuse de la Rue	*1'*
12a. Course de Taureaux	*1'*
13. Scène des Toréadors	*1'*
14. Pas des couteaux	*2'*
15. Coda (Toréadors)	*1'*
15a. Presto assai	*1'*
16. Entrée de Don Quichotte et Sancho Panza	*3'*
17. Sancho Panza et les filles (Polka)	*3'*
18. Les amies de Kitri	*4'*
19. Scène (Basilio et Kitri)	*5'*
20. Variation I (Basilio)	*1'*
21. Variation II (Kitri)	*1'*
22. Coda	*3'*

ACTE II	
23. Introduction	*2'*
24. Entrée de Kitri et Basilio	*5'*
25. Carmencita—Vasily Solov'yev-Sedoy (1907–1979)	*5'*
26. Variation d'Espada–Sola a gitana—R. Glière (1875–1956)	*1'*
27. Danse espagnole de Mercedes—Anton Simon (1850–1916)	*4'*
28. Danse des matelots— Vasily Solov'yev-Sedoy	*2'*
29. Scène	*2'*
30. Scène (Le suicide burlesque de Basilio)	*3'*
31. Coda	*2'*
32. Campement des Tziganes	*1'*
33. Entrée de Don Quichotte, Kitri et Basilio	*2'*
34. Danse des Tziganes I	*2'*
35. Danse des Tziganes II—Valery Zhelobinsky (1913–1946)	*4'*
36. Théâtre des Marionettes	*1'*
37. Scène	*1'*
38. Bataille avec les moulins à vent	*1'*
39. Scène (Forêt)	*2'*
40. Le Rêve de Don Quichotte	*3'*
40a. Les Dryades	*2'*
40b. Souvenir du bal (Valse)—Anton Simon, orchd Drigo	*2'*
40c. L'Amour (variation from "Paquita")	*1'*
40d. Variation de Dulcinée—Riccardo Drigo (1846–1930)	*2'*
40e. Coda	*4'*
41. Le Réveille de Don Quichotte (Scène de la chasse)	*1'*
ACTE III	
42. Marche—Yuly Gerber (1831–1883)	*3'*
43. Bolero—Cesare Pugni (1802–1870)	*2'*
44. Scène	*2'*
45. L'Amour	*3'*
46. Fandango—Eduard Napravnik (1839–1916)	*2'*
47. Pas de deux (Kitri et Basilio)	*1'*
a) Valse	*1'*
b) Adage	*4'*
Variation I (L'Amour)	*1'*
Variation II (Basilio)	*1'*
Variation III (Kitri)	*1'*
Variation IV—Riccardo Drigo (1846–1930)	*1'*
Coda	*1'*
48. Finale	*4'*
Addendum: Variation (alternative var. from "La Bayadère")	*1'*

APPENDIX K
TITLE INDEX

Distinctive titles of compositions—as well as subtitles, nicknames, title translations and distinctive titles of excerpts—are followed here by the composer and title of the work as it appears in the main list. If you are not sure under which title, for example, *Vesna svyashchennaya* or *Sacre du printemps* may be entered in the main list, you may look up either one right here, and be referred to Stravinsky's *Rite of Spring*. The Title Index is also useful should you momentarily forget who composed, say, *La bayadère*—but ignore the "La" and look under "B"! That's because *initial articles in all languages are omitted* in this title index.

Punctuation has occasionally been omitted from titles in order to make the alphabetization more user-friendly (the computer has its own way of alphabetizing punctuation, sometimes rendering things more difficult for the casual user).

Generic titles (symphony, suite) are not listed unless they are modified so as to become distinctive titles themselves (e.g., *Symphony of Psalms; Suite provençale*).

11:11
Maslanka—11:11 — A Dance at the Edge of the World
1812 god
Tchaikovsky—Overture 1812
1905 god
Shostakovich—Symphony No.11
1917 god
Shostakovich—Symphony No.12
66
Offenbach—'66': Overture

A

A la busca del más allá
Rodrigo—A la busca del más allá
A la Chapelle Sixtine
Liszt—A la Chapelle Sixtine
A memória de Mozart
Villa-Lobos—Sinfonietta No.1
A mrtvého domu
Janáček—From the House of the Dead
A Pastoral Prelude
Chadwick—Pastoral Prelude
A questo seno
Mozart, W.A.—A questo seno / Or che il cielo
Aallottaret
Sibelius—Oceanides
Abdelazer
Purcell—Abdelazer
Abduction from the Seraglio
Mozart, W.A.—Entführung aus dem Serail
Abencérages
Cherubini—Abencérages
About Leaves
Walker, Gwyneth—About Leaves

Abraham and Isaac
Stravinsky—Abraham and Isaac
Abschied
Leeuw, R. de—Abschied
Abschieds-Symphonie
Haydn, F.J.—Symphony No.45
Abu Hassan
Weber, C.M.—Abu Hassan
Academic Festival Overture
Brahms—Akademische Festouvertüre
Academica
Ince—Academica
Acadian Songs and Dances
Thomson, V.—Louisiana Story: Acadian Songs and Dances
Ácana
León—Ácana
Accelerationen (Accelerations)
Strauss, Joh., Jr.—Accelerationen
Accompaniment to a Cinematographic Scene
Schoenberg—Begleitungsmusik
Accordi più usati
Harbison—Most Often Used Chords
Accursed Huntsman
Franck—Chasseur maudit
Ach Gott, vom Himmel sieh darein
Bach, J.S.—Cantata No.2
Ach Gott, wie manches Herzeleid
Bach, J.S.—Cantatas Nos.3 & 58
Ach Herr, mich armen Sünder
Bach, J.S.—Cantata No.135
Ach wie flüchtig, ach wie nichtig
Bach, J.S.—Cantata No.26

Ach, ich sehe, jetzt
Bach, J.S.—Cantata No.162
Ach, lieben Christen, seid getrost
Bach, J.S.—Cantata No.114
Achilles & Scamander
Rival—Achilles & Scamander
Achilles' Heel
Di Vittorio—Tallone di Achille
Acis and Galatea
Handel—Acis and Galatea
Aconcagua
Piazzolla—Aconcagua
Across the Sea
Saariaho—Oltra mar
Acrostic Song
Del Tredici—Acrostic Song
Actaeon
Bennett, Richard R.—Actaeon
Action — Passion — Illusion
Tüür—Action — Passion — Illusion
Actus tragicus
Bach, J.S.—Cantata No.106
Ad matrem
Górecki—Ad matrem
Adagio
Hartmann—Symphony No.2
Adagio
Penderecki—Symphony No.4
Adagio amoroso
Atterberg—Adagio amoroso
Adagio for Orchestra
Van de Vate—Adagio for Orchestra
Adagio for String Orchestra
McTee—Adagio for String Orchestra

Adagio for Strings
Barber—Adagio for Strings
Adagio nach keltischen Melodien (Adagio on Keltish Melodies)
Bruch—Adagio nach keltischen Melodien
Adagio tenebroso
Carter—Adagio tenebroso
Adagio tragico
Sinigaglia—Adagio tragico
Adam and Eve
Tansman—Genesis Suite: Adam and Eve
Address for Orchestra
Walker, George—Address for Orchestra
Adieu Robert Schumann
Schafer—Adieu Robert Schumann
Adirondack Light
Tann—Adirondack Light
Adjustable Wrench
Torke—Adjustable Wrench
Adventlied
Schumann, R.—Adventlied
Adventures in a Perambulator
Carpenter—Adventures in a Perambulator
Adventures of Sinbad
Koch—Adventures of Sinbad
Adventures of Vixen Bystroušky
Janáček—Cunning Little Vixen
Aeneas
Roussel—Aeneas
Aerøsymfonien
Bentzon—Symphony No.9
Aesop's Fables
Maltz—Aesop's Fables

Chansons plaisantes
Stravinsky—Pribaoutki

Chant d'hiver
Ysaÿe—Chant d'hiver

Chant de joie
Honegger—Chant de joie

Chant de la nuit
Szymanowski—Symphony no.3

Chant de Nigamon
Honegger—Chant de Nigamon

Chant du ménestrel
Glazunov—Chant du ménestrel

Chant du rossignol
Stravinsky—Song of the
Nightingale

Chant éternel
Karłowicz—Eternal Songs

Chant funèbre
Magnard—Chant funèbre

Chant of Water and Sky
Buhr—Chant of Water and Sky

Chant of Wind and Thunder
Buhr—Chant of Wind and
Thunder

**Chant sur la mort de
l'Empereur Napoléon**
Berlioz—Cinq mai

**Chante de berger de Haute-
Auvergne**
Canteloube—Chants d'Auvergne,
1st series

Chantefleurs et chantefables
Lutoslawski—Chantefleurs et
chantefables

Chanticleer
Mason—Chanticleer

Chants and Graces
Benson—Chants and Graces

Chants bibliques
Dvořák—Biblical Songs

Chants d'Auvergne
Canteloube—Chants d'Auvergne

Chanukah Overture
Wendel—Chanukah Overture

Chapultepec
Ponce—Chapultepec

Chariots
Kay, Ulysses—Chariots

Charlie Rutlage
Ives—Charlie Rutlage

Chasing Light
Schwantner—Chasing Light

Chasing the Sun
Earnest—Chasing the Sun

Chasse
Haydn, F.J.—Symphony No.73

Chasse du jeune Henri
Méhul—Chasse du jeune Henri

Chasse royale et Orage
Berlioz—Troyens: Chasse royale
et Orage

Chasseur danois
Berlioz—Chasseur danois

Chasseur maudit
Franck—Chasseur maudit

Chat Moss
Maxwell Davies—Chat Moss

Chat qui pêche
Baker—Chat qui pêche

Chayka
Shchedrin—Seagull

Checkmate
Bliss—Checkmate

Cheers!
Gould—Cheers

Chelsea Reach
Bennett, Richard R.—Chelsea
Reach

Cheltenham Concerto
Rochberg—Cheltenham Concerto

Chemises des noces
Dvořák—Spectre's Bride

Chenoo Who Stayed to Dinner
Schickele—Chenoo Who Stayed
to Dinner

Cherish Your Land
Ward—Cherish Your Land

Chernobyl
Van de Vate—Chernobyl

Cherubic Hymn
Hanson—Cherubic Hymn

Cheval de bronze
Auber—Cheval de bronze

Chevalier errant
Ibert—Chevalier errant

Chi sà, chi sà, qual sia
Mozart, W.A.—Chi sà, chi sà, qual
sia

Chiaroscuro
Cowell—Chiaroscuro

Chiavi in mano
Wyner—Concerto, Piano

Chicago Skyline
Ran—Chicago Skyline

Chichester Psalms
Bernstein—Chichester Psalms

Child Alice
Del Tredici—Child Alice

Child of Our Time
Tippett—Child of Our Time

Child's Dream
Svoboda—Child's Dream

Childhood of Christ
Berlioz—Enfance du Christ

Children's Corner
Debussy—Children's Corner (arr.
Caplet)

Children's Crusade
Britten—Children's Crusade

Children's March
Grainger—Children's March

Chimes
Shchedrin—Concerto for
Orchestra No.2

China Dreams
Sheng—China Dreams

Chinese Flute
Toch—Chinesische Flöte

Chinese Folk Dance Suite
Chen Yi—Chinese Folk Dance
Suite

Chinese Myths Cantata
Chen Yi—Chinese Myths Cantata

Chinese Opera
Eötvös—Chinese Opera

Chinesische Flöte
Toch—Chinesische Flöte

Chio mi scordi di te
Mozart, W.A.—Ch'io mi scordi di
te / Non temer

Chocolats symphoniques
Goulet—Chocolats symphoniques

Choéphores
Milhaud—Choéphores

Choice of Hercules
Handel—Choice of Hercules

Choirs
Perera—Saints: Choirs

Chopiniana
Glazunov—Chopiniana

Choral
Knussen—Choral

Choral et variations
Tailleferre—Choral et variations
Widor—Choral et variations

Choral Fantasia
Holst—Choral Fantasia
Beethoven—Fantasia, Piano,
Chorus & Orch

Choral Symphony
Beethoven—Symphony No.9

Chorale
Harris, Roy—Chorale

Chorale for String Orchestra
Dorman—Chorale

**Chorale on a Theme of Leo
Hassler**
Strong—Chorale on a Theme of
Leo Hassler

**Chorale Variations for
Orchestra**
Beaser—Chorale Variations for
Orchestra

**Chorale-Variations on "Vom
Himmel hoch da komm' ich
her"**
Stravinsky—Chorale-Variations

Chôros
Villa-Lobos—Chôros

Chout
Prokofiev—Chout

Christ lag in Todesbanden
Bach, J.S.—Cantata No.4

Christ on the Mount of Olives
Beethoven—Christus am Ölberg

**Christ unser Herr zum Jordan
kam**
Bach, J.S.—Cantata No.7

Christ-Elflein
Pfitzner—Christ-Elflein

Christen, äzet diesen Tag
Bach, J.S.—Cantata No.63

Christian Zeal and Activity
Adams, John—Christian Zeal and
Activity

Christmas
Reger—Weihnachten

Christmas a la Valse
Wendel—Christmas a la Valse

Christmas Cantata
Bonds, M.A.—Ballad of the
Brown King
Honegger—Cantate de Noël
Scarlatti, A.—Christmas Cantata

Christmas Concerto
Corelli—Concerto grosso, op.6,
no.8
Manfredini—Concerto grosso,
op.3, no.12
Sammartini, Giuseppe—Concerto
grosso, op.5, no.6
Torelli—Concerto grosso, 2
Violins, op.8, no.6

Christmas Day
Holst—Christmas Day

Christmas Elf
Pfitzner—Christ-Elflein

Christmas Eve
Rimsky-Korsakov—Christmas
Eve

Christmas Fanfare
Beckel—Christmas Fanfare

Christmas Memory
Jones—Christmas Memory

Christmas Music
Haydn, M.—Pastorello

Christmas Oratorio
Bach, J.S.—Weihnachtsoratorium
Saint-Saëns—Oratorio de Noël
Schütz—Historia der Geburt Jesu
Christi

Christmas Overture
Coleridge-Taylor—Christmas
Overture

Christmas Story
Mennin—Christmas Story

Christmas Suite
Gossec—Christmas Suite

Christmas Symphony
Fry—Santa Claus
Lalande—Symphonie de Noël
Manfredini—Sinfonia da chiesa,
op.2, no.12
Penderecki—Symphony No.2

Christmas Wish
Richman—Christmas Wish

Christoph Columbus
Wagner, Richard—Christoph
Columbus: Overture

Christum wir sollen loben schon
Bach, J.S.—Cantata No.121

Christus
Liszt—Christus
Mendelssohn—Christus

Christus am Ölberg
Beethoven—Christus am Ölberg

Lyric Symphony (Lyrische Symphonie)
Zemlinsky—Lyrische Symphonie

Lyrischen Suite
Berg—Lyric Suite

Lyrisk suite
Grieg—Lyric Suite

Lysistrata
Adamo—Lysistrata: Overture
Iannaccone—Lysistrata

Lyubov' k tryom apel'sinam
Prokofiev—Love for Three
Oranges

M

Ma che vi fece
Mozart, W.A.—Ma che vi fece /
Sperai vicino il lido

Ma Mère l'Oye
Ravel—Ma Mère l'Oye

Má vlast
Smetana—Má vlast

Macabre Collage
Ligeti—Macabre Collage

Macbeth
Fry—Macbeth
Strauss, R.—Macbeth

MacDonald Dances
Maxwell Davies—Spell for Green
Corn

Machault mon chou
Wuorinen—Machault mon chou

**Machaut à ma manière
(Machaut in My Manner)**
Birtwistle—Machaut à ma manière

Mache dich, mein Geist, bereit
Bach, J.S.—Cantata No.115

Machine
Higdon—Machine

Machines
Jones—Machines

Mack & Mabel
Herman—Mack & Mabel

Made in America
Tower—Made in America

**Madison's March & Mrs.
Madison's Minuet**
Reinagle—Madison's March &
Mrs. Madison's Minuet

Madrigali
Rands—Madrigali

Maestro di cappella
Cimarosa—Maestro di cappella

Magic Art
Wuorinen—Magic Art

Magic Bird
Villa-Lobos—Uirapurú

Magic Fire Music
Wagner, Richard—Walküre:
Wotan's Farewell & Magic Fire
Music

Magic Flute
Mozart, W.A.—Zauberflöte

Magic Garden
Ravel—Jardin magique

Magic Number
Previn—Magic Number

Magic Prison
Laderman—Magic Prison

Magnificat Guadalupano
Trigos—Magnificat Guadalupano

Magnificent Lovers
Jolivet—Amants magnifiques

Magyar induló
Liszt—Ungarischer Sturmmarsch,
S.119

Magyar képek
Bartók—Hungarian Sketches

Magyar parasztdalok
Bartók—Hungarian Peasant Songs

Mahkato Wakpa
Heitzeg—Mahkato Wakpa

Mahl/er/werk
Stookey—Mahl/er/werk

Mährische Volkstänze
Janáček—Moravian Dances

Maid of Blue
Amaya—Soledad y el Mar

Maid of Pskov
Rimsky-Korsakov—Maid of
Pskov

Majnun
Hovhaness—Symphony No.24

MAJOR-minor Mystery
Smith, Gregory—MAJOR-minor
Mystery

Make a Joyful Noise
Beckel—Make a Joyful Noise

Make Your Own Orchestra
Lankester—Make Your Own
Orchestra

Mala suita (Mała suita)
Lutoslawski—Little Suite

Malédiction
Liszt—Malédiction

Malen'kaya suita
Denisov—Little Suite

Malheureux qui à une femme
Canteloube—Chants d'Auvergne,
3rd series

Malorossiskaia
Tchaikovsky—Symphony No.2

Malurous qu'o uno fenno
Canteloube—Chants d'Auvergne,
3rd series

Mame
Herman—Mame

Man from Midian
Wolpe—Man from Midian

Man singet mit Freuden
Bach, J.S.—Cantata No.149

Manchay tiempo
Frank, G.L.—Manchay tiempo

Manchester Overture
Burgess—Manchester Overture

Mandina amabile
Mozart, W.A.—Mandina amabile

Manfred
Montsalvatge—Manfred

Manfred
Schumann, R.—Manfred

Manfred
Tchaikovsky—Manfred

Mangrove
Sculthorpe—Mangrove

Manoir de Rosemonde
Duparc, Henri—Manoir de
Rosemonde

Manon
Massenet—Manon

Manon Lescaut
Puccini—Manon Lescaut

Manzoni requiem
Verdi—Messa da requiem

Maple Leaf Rag
Joplin—Maple Leaf Rag

March des noces
Glazunov—March des noces

**March for the Royal Society of
Musicians**
Haydn, F.J.—March for the Royal
Society of Musicians

**March of the Little Lead
Soldiers**
Pierné—Marche des petits soldats
de plomb

March of the Mogul Emperors
Elgar—Crown of India: March of
the Mogul Emperors

**March Past of the Kitchen
Utensils**
Vaughan Williams—Wasps:
March Past of the Kitchen
Utensils

March with Trio alla turca
Mussorgsky—Solemn March

Marchand de sable qui passe…
Roussel—Marchand de sable qui
passe…

Marche caprice
Delius—Marche caprice

**Marche des petits soldats de
plomb**
Pierné—Marche des petits soldats
de plomb

Marche du couronnement
Saint-Saëns—Marche du
couronnement

Marche écossaise
Debussy—Marche écossaise

Marche funèbre d'Hamlet
Berlioz—Tristia: Marche funèbre
d'Hamlet

**Marche funèbre d'une
marionette**
Gounod—Marche funèbre d'une
marionette

Marche héroïque
Saint-Saëns—Marche héroïque

Marche hongroise
Schubert—Marche hongroise

Marche militaire
Schubert—Marche militaire

Marche militaire française
Saint-Saëns—Suite algérienne:
Marche militaire française

Marche militaire hongroise
Liszt—Ungarischer Sturmmarsch,
S.119

Marche slave
Tchaikovsky—Marche slave

Marche solennelle
Mussorgsky—Solemn March
Tchaikovsky—Marche solennelle

**Marche solennelle du
couronnement**
Tchaikovsky—Festival Coronation
March

Marche troyenne
Berlioz—Troyens: Marche
troyenne

Märchen
Suk—Fairy Tale

Märchen aus dem Orient
Strauss, Joh., Jr.—Märchen aus
dem Orient

**Märchen von der schönen
Melusine**
Mendelssohn—Märchen von der
schönen Melusine

Märchenbilder
Korngold—Märchenbilder

Marching In
Perera—Saints: Marching In

Marco Spada
Auber—Marco Spada: Overture

Mardi Gras
Collins—Mardi Gras
Riisager—Mardi Gras

Marea
Lindberg—Marea

Marginal Intersection
Feldman—Marginal Intersection

Maria Theresia
Haydn, F.J.—Symphony No.48

Maria-Triptychon
Martin—Maria-Triptychon

Mariazeller Messe
Haydn, F.J.—Mass, Hob.XXII:8

Mariel
Golijov—Mariel

Marienleben
Hindemith—Marienleben

Marionetten Trauer Marsch
Gounod—Marche funèbre d'une
marionette

Marita and Her Heart's Desire
Adolphe—Marita and Her Heart's
Desire

Markings
Kay, Ulysses—Markings

Markus-Passion
Golijov—Pasión según San
Marcos

Maroon Dreams
Amaya—Maroon Dreams

Marosszéki táncok
Kodály—Dances of Marosszek

APPENDIX L
PUBLISHERS & SOURCES

The worldwide network of music publishers and agents is complex and changeable from week to week—even from day to day. No list will remain correct for very long. This one reflects the best of my knowledge at press time. As always, I will be grateful to be informed of any corrections or changes.

ACA American Composers Alliance
802 W. 109th St., 1st Floor
New York, NY 10040
USA
Tel: 212-362-8900 or 212-925-0458
Fax: 212-925-6798
info@composers.com
bd55@umail.umd.edu (University of Maryland)
www.composers.com
   All ACA scores are housed at the Performing Arts Library of the University of Maryland.

University of Maryland
Performing Arts Library
College Park, MD 20742
Tel: 301-405-9256
Fax: 301-314-7170

Accessibility Accessibility Music Publishing
433 Sylvan Avenue #44
Mountain View, CA 94041
USA
Tel: 650-625-8572
ndeussen@sbcglobal.net
www.nancybloomerdeussen.com
   *Music of **Nancy Bloomer Deussen**.*

Adjustable Adjustable Music
rental-sales@michaeltorke.com
US agent: Holab
   *Music of **Michael Torke** composed after 1991. Earlier works are from **Boosey**.*

Aeolus Aeolus Music Publications, Inc.
P.O. Box 5581
Winter Park, FL 32793
USA
Fax: 407-425-1981
joe@kreines.com
www.kreines.com
*Music of **Joseph Kreines**, including band and orchestra transcriptions.*

Alfred Alfred Publishing
P.O. Box 10003
Van Nuys, CA 91410-0003
USA
Tel: 818-891-5999; rentals, x157
Fax: 818-891-2369; rentals, 818-895-1846
customerservice@alfred.com
rental@alfred.com
www.alfred.com
US agent: Luck's

[rental return shipping
16320 Roscoe Blvd, Ste. 100
Van Nuys, CA 91406

Alkor Alkor-Edition
Heinrich-Schütz-Allee 35
D - 34131 Kassel
Germany
Tel: +49 (0)561 3105-282
Fax: +49 (0)561 37755
order.alkor@baerenreiter.com
perusal scores: ny@baerenreiter.com
www.alkor-edition.com
US agent: EAM
Subsidiary of Bärenreiter
*Founded 1934 in Leipzig as a subsidiary of the firm **Oscar Brandstetter**. Renamed **Bruckner-Verlag Leipzig** in 1944 for the publication of the Critical Bruckner Gesamtausgabe. Since 1955, Alkor-Edition has been a subsidiary of **Bärenreiter**.*

Alliance Alliance Publications, Inc.
9171 Spring Road
Fish Creek, WI 54212-9619
USA
Tel: 920-868-3100
Fax: 608-748-4491
apimusic@dcwis.com
www.APImusic.org
*Also known as **Czech Music Alliance**. Specializing in Czech and Slovak composers (living and dead); Wisconsin composers; and women composers.*

Amadeus Amadeus Verlag
Hermannstrasse 7
8400 Winterthur
Switzerland
Tel: +41 052 233 28 66
Fax: +41 052 233 54 01
order@amadeusmusic.ch
info@amadeusmusic.ch
verlag@amadeusmusic.ch
www.amadeusmusic.ch
Founded 1973 by Bernhard Päuler.

AME American Music Edition
US agent: Presser

AMP Associated Music Publishers
US agent: G. Schirmer, rentals; Hal Leonard, sales
*Founded 1927 in New York City. Acquired by **G. Schirmer** in 1964, for which it became the **BMI** affiliate, complementing Schirmer's ASCAP affiliation.*

Amphion Éditions Amphion
didier.langlois@bmg.com (sales)
location.rental.durand-salabert-eschig@bmg.com (rental)
www.durand-salabert-eschig.com
*French firm founded 1943. Purchased by **Durand** in 1986.*

Aperto Aperto Press
rental-sales@kevinputs.com
www.kevinputs.com
US agent: Holab
*Music of **Kevin Puts**.*

Apollo Apollo-Verlag Paul Lincke
Weihergarten 5
6500 Mainz
Germany
Tel: +49 (06131) 246300
Fax: +49 (06131) 236211
International agent: Schott

A-R Editions A-R Editions, Inc.
8551 Research Way, Suite 180
Middleton, WI 53562
USA
Tel: 608-836-9000; US orders 800-736-0070
Fax: 608-831-8200
orders@areditions.com
www.areditions.com
    Scholarly editions of music and books dealing with music.

Arcana Arcana Editions
227 Douro First Line
Douro-Dummer
RR2 Indian River, Ontario K0L 2B0
Canada
Tel: 705-652-0446
Fax: 705-652-0683
www.patria.org/arcana
International agent (excluding USA and Canada): Schott
    *Music of **R. Murray Schafer**.*

Argon Argon Press Publishers
3646 W. Wrightwood Ave., Ste.1000
Chicago, IL 60647
USA
Tel: 312-520-0110
djanello@argon-tech.com

Armadillo Armadillo Edition
PO Box 42535
Cincinnati, OH 45242-0535
USA
Tel: 513-237-8281
info@armadilloedition.com
www.armadilloedition.com
    *Music of **Douglas Knehans**.*

Ars Viva Ars Viva Verlag
Weihergarten
D - 6500 Mainz 1
Germany
US agent: EAM
 Founded 1950 by Hermann Scherchen to promote avant-garde composers.
Acquired by **Schott** *1955.*

Art of Sound Art of Sound Music
47 Ettl Circle
Princeton, NJ 08540
USA
Tel: 609-759-0278
Fax: 928-447-4131
www.artofsoundmusic.com
 Founded 2007 by Ed Hirschman and Craig Levesque. Offers web-printable music
as well as printed scores and parts.

Artaria Artaria Editions
Level 11, Cyberport 1
100 Cyberport Road
Hong Kong
SAR
Tel: (+852) 2760-7818
Fax: (+852) 2989-9181
customer.service@artaria.com
www.artaria.com
Rental agent for Europe: Schott
 Founded 1995 "to bring the music of the Viennese eighteenth century back to life."

ASCAP American Society of Composers, Authors & Publishers
1 Lincoln Plaza
New York, NY 10023
USA
Tel: 212-621-6000
Fax: 212-724-9064
www.ascap.com
 One of the three major US performing rights organizations, the others being **BMI**
and **SESAC**.

Augener Augener, Ltd.
US agent: ECS
 Founded in 1853 in London. Owned at various times by **Schott** *(briefly),* **Galaxy**,
and ultimately **Stainer and Bell**.

Ayers   Jesse Ayers Music
228 17th Street NW
Canton, OH 44703
USA
info@jesseayers.com
http://jesseayers.com
     *Music of **Jesse Ayers**.*

Babel   BabelScores
39, quai de l'horloge
75001 Paris
France
www.babelscores.com
     Specializing in contemporary music of the last 40 years. Scores available online by subscription. Parts may be rented for public performance.

Bacon   Ernst Bacon Society, Inc.
8 Drovers Lane
Syracuse, NY 13214
USA
Tel: 315-446-6447
ellenbacon@baldcom.net
mail@ernstbacon.org
www.ernstbacon.org

8 Johnson Road
Sharon, MA 02067

     *Founded 1996 to promote awareness and appreciation of the music and other works of **Ernst Bacon**.*

Bärenreiter   Bärenreiter-Verlag
Heinrich-Schütz-Allee 35
D - 34131 Kassel
Germany
Tel: +49 (0)561 3105-0
Fax: +49 (0)561 3105-176
info@baerenreiter.com; perusal scores: ny@baerenreiter.com
https://www.baerenreiter.com
US agent: EAM
     *Founded in 1924 in Augsburg; soon moved to Kassel. Associated early on with German musicology, and became publisher of scholarly editions of various composers of the 17th and 18th centuries, and, during and after the 1950s, 19th and 20th centuries. Took over the **Nagels Musik-Archiv** series in 1952, and founded the subsidiary **Alkor-Edition** in 1955.*

Barnard Barnard Street Music
79 Wheeler Avenue
Cranston, RI 02905-2707
USA
Tel: 401-338-1383
orchestra@brown.edu
*Music of **Paul Phillips**.*

Barnhouse C.L. Barnhouse Company
Box 680
205 Cowan Avenue West
Oskaloosa, IA 52577
USA
Tel: 515-673-8397; 877-673-8397
Fax: 515-673-4718; 888-673-4718
bhouse@se-iowa.net
bbarnhouse@barnhouse.com
www.barnhouse.com
*Distributes Keith Brion's Sousa editions for **Willow Blossom Music**.*

Willow Blossom Music

Barry Barry Editorial, Com., Ind., S.r.l.
Talcahuano 638
Planta Baja H
C1013AAN Buenos Aires
Argentina
Tel: +54 (0)11 4371 1313
Fax: +54 (0)11 4383 0745
contacto@barryeditorial.com.ar
www.barryeditorial.com.ar
US agent: Boosey
Founded 1945.

BBC BBC Music Library
Unit 7 Ariel Way
London W12 7SL
United Kingdom
Tel: 020 8576 0208
Fax: 020 8225 9984
peter.linnitt@bbc.co.uk
www.cecilia-uk.org [then navigate to BBC]

Beall Dr. John Beall
Creative Arts Center
West Virginia University
P.O. Box 6111
Morgantown, WV 26506
USA
john.beall@mac.com; jobeall@mail.wvu.edu
*Music of **John Beall**.*

Beckel James A. Beckel, Jr.
6039 Harlescott Rd.
Indianapolis, IN 46220
USA
Tel: 317-842-3662
musbeck@msn.com
www.jimbeckelmusic.com
*Music of **James Beckel**.*

Belaieff M. P. Belaieff
www.belaieff-music.com/en_UK
US agent: EAM
Schott handles worldwide distribution
*Russian publishing house established in 1885 in Leipzig. Music publishing was taken over by the state after the Russian Revolution, but later the firm was acquired by **Peters**; in 2006 taken over by **Schott**.*

Bellbird Bellbird Publications
229 Helensburgh Road
Dunedin
New Zealand
Tel: (03) 476-2541
www.anthonyritchie.co.nz/bellbird
*Music of **Anthony Ritchie**.*

Belmont Belmont Music Publishers
P.O. Box 231
1221 Bienveneda Avenue
Pacific Palisades, CA 90272
USA
Tel: 310-454-1867
Fax: 310-573-1925
belmontmusic90272@yahoo.com
www.schoenbergmusic.com
Music of **Schoenberg** *in the US (name is a play on words:* schön-berg = bel-mont*). Owned and operated by Schoenberg's three surviving children. Cooperates with the* **Arnold Schönberg Center** *in Vienna (www.schoenberg.at). If Belmont doesn't have the work being sought, they will help find it.*

Belwin CPP/Belwin
15800 NW 48th Ave
Miami, FL 33014
USA
Tel: 305-620-1500
Fax: 305-621-4869; (305) 621-1094
US agent: Luck's
Founded 1918. In 1969, merged with Mills Music Publishers to form **Belwin-Mills,** *which also purchased the catalog of* **Franco Colombo, Inc.** *In 1985 the firm was sold from hand to hand, emerging in 1988 as CPP/Belwin. Mills split off in 1993. CPP/Belwin was purchased (and that name retained) by* **Warner-Chappell** *Music in 1994; its publications are now handled by* **Luck's**.

Benjamin Anton J. Benjamin Musikverlag GmbH
Werderstraße 44 — Postfach 2561
D-2000 Hamburg 13
Germany
US agent: Boosey (rentals); Leonard (sales)
Founded 1818 in Altona and soon moved to Hamburg. Acquired **Rahter** *(1917),* **A. E. Fischer** *(1925), and* **Simrock** *(1929). Sold under duress to* **Sikorski** *in 1938 but restored in 1951. Also known as* **Benjamin-Rahter-Simrock** *and as* **Richard Schauer Music Publisher**s. *Sold to* **Boosey & Hawkes** *in 2002.*

Bent Pen Bent Pen Music
BentPen@jakeheggie.com
US agent: Holab
Music of **Jake Heggie**.

Berandol   Berandol Music, Ltd.
1266 Minaki Rd.
Mississauga Ontario L5G 2X4
Canada
Tel: 905-278-6338
Fax: 905-278-9409
grahamcoles@on.aibn.com
www.berandolmusic.com
    Formed in 1969 to handle the music-publishing division of **BMI Canada**.

Bèrben   Bèrben Edizioni musicali
Via Redipublia 65
60122 Ancona
Italy
Tel: ++39 071 204428
Fax: ++39 071 57414
info@berben.it
www.berben.it
US agent: Presser
    Special interest in guitar music.

Billaudot   Gérard Billaudot, Éditeur
14 rue de l'Échiquier
75010 Paris
France
Tel: (33 1) 47 70 14 46
Fax: (33 1) 45 23 22 54
info@billaudot.com
www.billaudot.com
US agent: Presser
    Founded 1896 as **Éditions Billaudot***; purchased the firm* **Costallat** *in 1958 (but sold it to* **Jobert** *in 1995) and* **Éditions Françaises de Musique** *in 1988. In 1958 changed the name to Gérard Billaudot, Éditeur.*

Birchard   C.C. Birchard
Boston, MA
USA
US agent: Alfred
    Founded 1901. Taken over by Summy in 1957 to become **Summy-Birchard**. *Later acquired the* **Arthur P. Schmidt Co.** *of Boston. Bought by* **Warner/Chappell** *in 1988.*

BKJ BKJ Publications
Attn. John Bavicchi
Box 610377
Newton Highlands, MA 02161
USA
Tel: 617-965-9788
www.gasilvis.net/jb.htm
  *Music of **John Bavicchi**.*

Blackwood Blackwood Enterprises
5300 South Shore Drive
Chicago, IL 60615
USA
Tel: 312-324-0219
  *Music of **Easley Blackwood**.*

BMG BMG Editions
Chemin de la Moraine 42
1162 Sr. Prex, Vaud
Switzerland
Tel: +41-21-806-3757
Fax: +41-21-806-3757
bmgeditions.classicgeneral@bmg.com (general)
bmgeditions.classiclicence@bmg.com (rentals)
bmgeditions.classiclicence@bmg.com (print)
bmgeditions.classicpromo@bmg.com (promotion)
www.bmgmusicsearch.com
US agent: Boosey
European agent: Ricordi
  *Subsidiary of the German media group **Bertelsmann**. BMG Edition companies are **Amphion**, **Durand**, **Eschig**, **Editio Musica Budapest**, **Ricordi**, **Rideau Rouge**, **Salabert**. Acquired both **Forberg** and **Mannheimer** in 2006. BMG itself was acquired in 2006 by **Universal Music Publishing Group**.*

BMI Broadcast Music, Inc.
7 World Trade Center
250 Greenwich Street
New York, NY 10007-0030
USA
Tel: 212-220-3176
Fax: 212-220-4450
bpetersen@bmi.com
www.bmi.com
  *One of the three major US performing rights organizations, the others being **ASCAP** and **SESAC**.*

Boccaccini Boccaccini & Spada Editori
Via Arezzo, 17
00040 Pavona di Albano Laziale
Rome
Italy
Tel: +39 (0) 6 - 931 0217; 931 0561
Fax: +39 (0) 6 - 9311903
info@boccacciniespada.com
sales@boccacciniespada.com
www.boccacciniespada.it
US agent: Presser
  Founded 1996.

Boelke Boelke-Bomart / Mobart Music Publishers
US agent: EAM
  *Publications from Boelke-Bomart and Mobart Music (its BMI affiliate) are
  available worldwide from **Schott**.*

Boelter Karl Boelter
School of Music   4888 E. Shorewood Dr.
SUNY Fredonia   Dunkirk, NY 14048
Fredonia, NY 14163   Tel: 716-432-7708
USA
Tel: 716-673-3151
Fax: (716) 673-3154
boelter@fredonia.edu
US agent: Fleisher
  *Music of **Karl Boelter**.*

Mario Bois Editions Mario Bois
19 rue de Rocroy
75010 Paris
France
Tel: +33 1 42 82 10 46
Fax: +33 1 42 82 10 19
editions@mariobois.com
www.mariobois.pagesperso-orange.fr
US agent: Presser

Bongiovanni Casa Musicale Francesco Bongiovanni
via Ugo Bassi 31/f
40121 Bologna
Italy
Tel: 39 051 22 57 22
Fax: 39 051 22 61 28
giancarlo@bongiovanni70.com
andrea@bongiovanni70.com
www.bongiovanni70.com

Boonin Joseph Boonin, Inc.
Hackensack, NJ
USA
US agent: EAM
  *Purchased in 1977 by **Schott** and **Universal** to form **EAM**.*

Boosey Boosey & Hawkes, Inc.
35 E. 21st St.
New York, NY 10010-6212
USA
Tel: 212-358-5300; rentals 212-358-5370
Fax: rentals 212-358-5301; perusals 212-358-5306
info.ny@boosey.com
usrental@boosey.com
www.boosey.com

Boosey & Hawkes Rental
601 West 26th Street, Suite 312
New York, NY 10001
  Tel: 212-358-5300

  *Boosey & Co. founded in London about 1792. From 1851, also manufactured wind instruments. In 1930 joined with Hawkes & Son (founded 1865) to become Boosey & Hawkes. Acquired **Ed. Russe de Musique** in 1947 and **Bote & Bock** in 1996.*
  Many full scores may be examined online at the Boosey website.

Bote Bote & Bock GmbH & Co.
Lützowufer 26
10787 Berlin
Germany
Tel: (030) 250013-00
Fax: (030) 250013-99
musikverlag@boosey.com
US agent: Boosey (rentals); Leonard (sales)
  *Founded in Berlin in 1838 by the purchase of the preexisting firm **C.W. Froehlich & Co.** Later acquisitions: **Moritz Westphal** (1840), **Thomas Brandenburg** (1845) and **Lauterbach & Kuhn** (1908). Acquired by **Boosey & Hawkes** in 1996.*

Boys Art Boys Art Music
721 SE 6th Street
Minneapolis, MN 55414
USA
Tel: 612-331-3168
Fax: 612-378-9389
davidson@boyhsartmusic.com
www.boysartmusic.com
Music of **Randall Davidson**.

Brass Press The Brass Press
136 8th Avenue North
Nashville, TN 37203
USA
www.editions-bim.com
US agent: King

Editions BIM
P.O. Box 300
CH-1674 Vuarmarens
Switzerland
Tel: +41-(0)21-909 1000
Fax: +41-(0)21-909 1009

Founded 1970. Later acquired by **Editions BIM**.

Breitkopf Breitkopf & Härtel
Walkmühlstrasse 52
D-65195 Wiesbaden
Germany
Tel: +49 611 45008 0
Fax: +49 611 45008 59-61
info@breitkopf.com [contact form is on website]
sales@breitkopf.com; hir@breitkopf.de
www.breitkopf.com
US agent: Schirmer (rentals)

Established by Bernhard Christoph Breitkopf in 1719 in Leipzig; Gottfried Christoph Härtel joined the firm in 1795. From 1945, the firm was divided into two independent sections, in Leipzig (East Germany) and Wiesbaden (West Germany) respectively; it was reintegrated in 1991. Took over **Deutscher Verlag für Musik** *in 1992;* **Musica Rara** *in 2000. Cooperates with* **Henle** *since 2003 to provide orchestral materials based on the new complete editions of Beethoven and Brahms, among others. In 2005 initiated "Breitkopf Urtext," a series of critical/practical editions.*

Broude Bros. Broude Brothers, Ltd.
141 White Oaks Rd.
Williamstown, MA 01267
USA
Tel: 800-225-3197; 800-525-8559; 413-458-8131
Fax: 413-458-5242
broudebrothers@verizon.net; broudeeuropa@gmail.com
www.broude.us; www.broudeeuropa.com

Broude Europa
Rosmarinstrasse 15
D-55232 Alzey Germany
Fax: +49 (0)6731 549

    Publisher of orchestra scores and parts, including new compositions, transcriptions, and offprints from its scholarly editions as well as reprints of standard repertory works. Broude Brothers is also a retailer, selling both its own publications and those of all other publishers of orchestral music. Not to be confused with Alexander Broude Inc., q.v.

Brown Curtis Brown Ltd.
10 Astor Place
New York, NY 10003
USA
Tel: 212-473-5400
cb@curtisbrown.co.uk
www.curtisbrown.co;m www.curtisbrown.co.uk

Haymarket House
28-29 Haymarket
London SW1Y 4SP UK
Tel: +44 (0) 207 393
Fax: +44 (0) 207 393

    Not a music publisher; this firm holds the rights for the Ogden Nash verses for Camille Saint-Saëns' Carnival of the Animals.

Bryant Curtis Bryant Music
5485 Lakeside Dr.
Union City, GA 30291
USA
Tel: 770-964-3063
cbmusic@bellsouth.net
www.curtisbryantmusic.com
    *Music of **Curtis Bryant**.*

Burke&Bagley Burke & Bagley
1824 North 53rd St.
Seattle, WA 98103-6116
USA
Tel: 206-632-4487
office@burkeandbagley.com
www.burkeandbagley.com
    *Music of **Greg Bartholomew**, **Douglas DaSilva**, **Dale Dykins**, and **Georgia Lockwood**.*

Calabrese Rosalie Calabrese Management
Box 20580 Park West Station
New York, NY 10025-1512
USA
Tel: 212-663-6620
Fax: 212-663-5941
rcmgt@yahoo.com
www.musicalworld.com/managers/rosalie-calabrese-

Campanile Campanile Press
cf-info@carlfischer.com; sj@samueljones.net
www.samueljones.net
US agent: C. Fischer
*Music of **Samuel Jones**.*

Canticle Canticle Distributing
1727 Larkin Williams Road
Fenton, MO 63026-2024
USA
Tel: 800-647-2117 (USA only); 636-305-0100 (outside USA
                              and within metro St. Louis)
Fax: 636-305-0121
www.morningstar@morningstarmusic.com
*Handles sales for **ECS**, **Randol Bass Music**, **MorningStar Music**, **Aureole
Editions**, **Prime Music**, and **Laurendale Associates**.*

Carisch Carisch S.p.A.
via Campania, 12
20098 San Giuliano Milanese
Italy
Tel: +39 02 98 222 1212
info@carisch.it
www.carisch.com
US agent: Boosey
Founded 1887.

Carlanita Carlanita Music Co.
US agent: Schirmer (rentals); Leonard, sales
*Music of **Carlos Chávez**.*

Carus Carus-Verlag GmbH
Sielminger Str. 51
D-70771 Lf.-Echterdingen
Germany
Tel: +49 711-797 330-0
Fax: +49 711-797 330-29
info@carus-verlag.com
www.carus-verlag.com
Founded in 1972 to publish sacred choral music in editions with high scholarly standards.

CeBeDeM Centre Belge de Documentation Musicale
Belgian Documentation Centre for Contemporary Music
Tour & Taxis
Avenue du Port 86C, Box 214
Be-1000 Brussels
Belgium
Tel: +32 02 230.94.30
Fax: +32 02 230.94.37
info@cebedem.be
www.cebedem.be

CFE Composers Facsimile Edition
US agent: ACA

Chant Le Chant du Monde
31 / 33 Rie Vandrezanne
75013 Paris
France
Tel: +33 (0)1 53 80 12 30
Fax: +33 (0)1 53 80 12 18
cdm@harmoniamundi.com
www.chantdumonde.com
US agent: Schirmer
*Founded 1938; in 1993 Chant du Monde joined the group **Harmonia Mundi**.*

Chappell Chappell & Co., Inc.
www.warnerchappell.com
US agent: Alfred
*Founded in 1810. Sold in 1980s to an American group, which was in turn taken over in 1987 by Warner Communications. Is now **Warner/Chappell Music, Inc.***

Chester J. & W. Chester, Ltd.
Chester Music and Novello & Co.
14-15 Berners St.
London W1V 3LJ
United Kingdom
Tel: +44 (0) 20 7612 7400
Fax: +44 (0) 20 7612 7545
www.musicsalesclassical.com
US agent: Schirmer
Founded in 1874 when John Chester and his son took over the branch office of **Augener***. Merged with* **Hansen** *in 1950s. In 1989 Chester was taken over by* **Music Sales***. Rental library is now combined with that of* **Novello***.*
Many scores may be perused online; click on **OnDemand***.*

Chiltern Chiltern Music
Maudlin House
Westhampnett, Chichester West Sussex PO18 0PB
United Kingdom
Tel: 01243 776325
Fax: 01243 539604

Choudens Choudens Editions   Import Diffusion Music SA
38, rue Jean Mermoz   29 R De Bitche
F-75008 Paris   92400 Courbevoie, France
France   Tel: +33 141 88 98 98
Tel: (33) 01 42 66 62 97   Fax: +33 147 68 74 28
Fax: (33) 01 42 66 62 79
editions.choudens@wanadoo.fr
US agent: Schirmer
Founded in Paris in 1844. Acquired by **Music Sales** *in 2007.*

Clear Mud Clear Mud Publications
www.cmpub.com
Music of **Richard Chiarappa***.*

Clyde R. Clyde Music Publisher
6 Whitelands Avenue
Chorleywood, Rickmansworth, Herts WD3 5RD
England
Tel: +44 (0)1923 283600
Fax: +44 (0)1923 283600
r.clyde@dial.pipex.com
Specializing in the music of **Arthur Sullivan***.*

CMC   Centre de Musique Canadienne
National Office
Chalmers House
20 St. Joseph Street
Toronto, Ontario M4Y 1J9
Canada
Tel: 416-961-6601
Fax: 416-961-7198
info@musiccentre.ca
www.musiccentre.ca
   *Music of **Canada**. Regional offices in Vancouver, Calgary, Toronto, Montréal, and Sackville NB.*

Coho   Coho Music Publications
12 Halsdorf St.
Albany, NY 12208
USA
Tel: 518-438-4651
broter@ix.netcom.com
   *Music of **Bruce Roter**.*

Coleman   Coleman Creative Services
1137 - 37th Street
Des Moines, IA 50311-3616
USA
Tel: 515-277-8893
LindaRobbinsColeman@att.net
www.lindarobbinscoleman.com
   *Music and poetry of **Linda Robbins Coleman**, and writings of **William S.E. Coleman**.*

Colombo   Franco Colombo Publications
US agent: Alfred
   *Originally the New York branch of **Ricordi**; purchased after World War II by Franco Colombo, who had been its managing director since 1949. In 1962 the firm's name became Franco Colombo, Inc. The Colombo catalog was purchased by **Belwin-Mills** in 1969.*

Compusic   Edition Compusic
Amsterdam
Netherlands
www.woodbrass.com/en/edition+compusic+-+amsterdam

Concordia Concordia Publishing House
3558 S. Jefferson Ave.
St. Louis, MO 63118
USA
Tel: 800-325-3040; 314-268-1000
Fax: 314-268-1329
www.cph.org
The official publisher of the Lutheran Church—Missouri Synod. Music publishing is only one part of its mission.

Consort Consort Press
1225 S. Rice Road #41
Ojai, CA 93023
USA
Tel: 805-646-4779
office@consortpress.com
www.consortpress.com
*Principally music of **John Biggs**. Scores and parts for orchestral works are available from **Fleisher**.*

Coppenrath Musikverlag Alfred Coppenrath
Martin-Moser-Strasse 23
Postfach 11 58
D-84495 Altötting
Germany
Tel: +49 0 86 71/50 65-20
Fax: +49 0 86 71/50 65.25
mail@coppenrath.com
www.coppenrath.com
Agent: Carus

Corrin Gary Corrin
176 Indian Road
Toronto, Ontario M6R 2W3
Canada
Tel: 416-539-8745
gcorrin@tso.ca

Costa John Vasconcelos Costa
6165 Rodeo Lane
Salt Lake City, UT 84121
USA
Tel: 801-274-3721
jvascsta@aol.com
*Music of **John Vasconcelos Costa**.*

Costallat Éditions Costallat
US agent: King
*Founded in 1895 in Paris; acquired **Richault** in 1898. In 1958 Costallat was purchased by **Billaudot** and in 1995 sold to **Jobert**.*

Cotton Jeffery Cotton
Wired Musician, Inc.
1329 Tasker St.
Philadelphia, PA 19148
USA
Tel: 215-589-3191
jcotton@wiredmusician.net
library@jefferycotton.net
www.wiredmusician.net
*Music of **Jeffery Cotton**.*

Counterpoint Counterpoint Music Library Services Inc.
42 Frater Avenue
Toronto, ON M4C 2H6
Canada
Tel: 416-696-5377
Fax: 416-996-8625
library@cpmusiclibrary.ca
cpmusiclibrary.ca
Canadian composers.

556112 Mulmur-Melancthon
TLine
Melancthon, ON L9V 1W5
Tel: 519-925-3360

Curci Edizioni Curci
Galleria del Corso 4
1-20122 Milano
Italy
Tel: +39 02 79 47 46
Fax: +39 02 76 014 504
info@edizionicurci.it
laura.moro@edizionicurci.it
www.edizionicurci.it
US agent: Curci USA Corp
International agent: Pagani
Founded in Naples in 1912; moved later to Rome and in 1936 to Milan.

Curwen J. Curwen & Sons
US agent: Schirmer
Music Sales
Established in mid-19th century to publish educational music. Orchestral music added in the early 20th century.

Czech Czech Music Fund (Cesky Hudebni Fond)
Note Music Hire Service [Rental Dept]
Radická 99
150 00 Prague 5
Czech Republic
Tel: 420 251 554 940
Fax: 420 251 554 940
chf-phm@cbox.cz
www.hudebnifond.cz
US agent: Boosey
Established by the Czech Music Fund Foundation in 1998.

Dako Dako Publishers
2751 Quaint St.
Secane, PA 19018-3426
USA
Tel: 610-543-6280
david@davidfinko.org
http://davidfinko.org
US agent: Presser
*Music of **David Finko**.*

Dantalian Dantalian, Inc.
11 Pembroke St.
Newton, MA 02458-2122
USA
Tel: 617-244-7230
Fax: 617-244-7230
dantinfo@dantalian.com
www.dantalian.com
*Music of **Donald Martino**.*

DCI Music DCI Music
8370 Fullerton Street
Lantana, TX 76226
USA
Tel: 940-725-0494
DCIMusic@yahoo.com
www.dcimusic.com
*Compositions and arrangements of **David Itkin**.*

Deutscher Deutscher Verlag für Musik
US agent: Schirmer
*Founded in Leipzig in 1954; purchased by **Breitkopf** in 1992.*

DNS DNSMusic
Box 1516
Royal Oak, MI 48068-1516
USA
dns.assoc@pobox.com
www.dnsmusic.com
   *Music of **David Nisbet Stewart**.*

Doblinger Musikverlag Doblinger
Dorotheergasse 10
A-1010 Wien
Austria
Tel: ++43/1 515 03-0
Fax: ++43/1 515 03-51
music@doblinger.at; rent@doblinger.at
www.doblinger-musikverlag.at
   Ludwig Doblinger purchased an existing Viennese publishing business in 1857.
*Began the distinguished series **Diletto musicale** in 1958.*

Donemus Donemus
Music Center The Netherlands
Rokin 111
1012 KN Amsterdam
Netherlands
Tel: +31 020 344 6000
Fax: +31 020 673 3588
info@mcn.nl
rental.sales@donemus.nl
www.donemus.nl
US agent: Presser
   Begun in 1947 with foundation assistance to preserve and publish modern Dutch
music. Name is an abbreviation of Documentatie in Nederland voor Muziek.

Dover Dover Publications, Inc.
31 E. Second St.
Mineola, NY 11501
USA
Tel: 516-294-7000
Fax: 516-742-6953
http://store.doverpublications.com/by-subject-music.html
   Excellent and inexpensive reprints of orchestral scores and other music, largely in
the public domain. Dover does not publish orchestral sets of parts.

Dragon Carmen Dragon Music Library
28908 Grayfox Street
Malibu, CA 90265
USA
Tel: 310-457-9902
Fax: 310-457-8470
dragon.music@verizon.net
www.carmendragon.com
*Rental of pops and light classic scores orchestrated by conductor **Carmen Dragon**.*

Duma Duma Music, Inc.
557 Barron Avenue
Woodbridge, NJ 07095
USA
Tel: 732-636-5406
Fax: 732-636-5220
dumamuse@aol.com
www.dumamusic.com
Emphasizing Ukrainian music especially, along with composers of other nationalities.

Dunvagen Dunvagen Music Publishers, Inc.
40 Exchange Place, Suite 1906
New York, NY 10005
USA
Tel: 212-979-2080
Fax: 212-473-2842
info@dunvagen.com
www.dunvagen.com
US agent: Schirmer
Outside the US: Chester
*Music of **Philip Glass**.*

Durand   Durand SA Editions Musicales, France
Durand-Salabert-Eschig
16 rue des Fossés Saint-Jacques
F-75005 Paris
France
Tel: +33-1 44 41 50 90
Fax: +33-1 44 41 50 91
durand-salabert-eschig@bmg.com
rentals: location.rental.durant-salabert-eschig@bmg.com
www.durand-salabert-eschig.com
US agent: Boosey (rentals); Leonard (sales)
   *Founded 1869 in Paris. Went through several name changes (**Durand-Schoenewerk & Cie; A. Durand & Fils; Durand & Cie**). Purchased **Amphion** in 1986, and **Éditions Max Eschig** in 1987. Now a member of **BMG**.*

EAM   European American Music Distributors Company
254 West 31st Street, 15th Floor
New York, NY 10001-2813
USA
Tel: 212-461-6940
Fax: 212-810-4565
rental@Eamdc.com
perusals: cory.bracken@eamdc.com
www.eamdc.com
US agent: EAM (rentals); Hal Leonard (sales)

EAM rentals c/o Subito
60 Depot St.
Verona, NJ 07044
   Tel: 973-857-3440

   *Established in 1977 by **Schott** and **Universal** as a joint agency for the USA. In 2005 it became a fully-owned subsidiary of Schott, and acts as the rental and licensing agent in North America for various other firms. EAM's Rental Service Center now shares space with **Subito** in Verona, NJ, though rental orders are still placed via EAM in New York.*

EAMH   Editions Anna-Marie Holmes
Kevin Galiè
19 Fort Avenue
Boston, MA 02119
USA
Tel: 617-427-2342
kevinjngalie@gmail.com
kevingalie.com
   ***Kevin Galiè** orchestrations of Russian ballets, including divertissements.*

EBP Editio Bärenreiter Praha
Bechovická 26
100 00 Praha 10
Czech Republic
Tel: ++420/ 274 781 006
Fax: ++420/ 274 001 927
musicpbl@editio-baerenreiter.cz
www.ebp.cz
> *Emphasis on works by Czech and Slovak composers.*

ECFAM Edward Collins Fund for American Music
c/o Jon Becker
Arts & Education Consultant
Post Office Box 3292
Madison, WI 53704
USA
Tel: 877-223-8068; 608-242-8525
jonbecker@aol.com
Consultant@ecfam.org
www.ecfam.org
> *Music of **Edward Collins**.*

ECS ECS Publishing Corporation
1727 Larkin Williams Road
Fenton, MO 63026
USA
Tel: 800-647-2117; 636-305-0100
Fax: 636-305-0121
office@ecspublishing.com
www.ecspublishing.com
> *Founded as **E.C. Schirmer** in 1921 in Boston; name changed 1993 to ECS. Parent company to **Galaxy**, **Highgate** and **Ione Press**.*
> *Sales for USA and Canada are handled by **Canticle**; rentals remain with ECS.*

Ed. Russe Édition Russe de Musique
US agent: Boosey
> *Founded 1909 as **Russkoye Muzïkal'noye Izdatel'stvo** by Sergey and Nataliya Koussevitzky in Moscow and St. Petersburg to promote new Russian music. Bought the firm **Gutheil** in 1914; moved to Paris, 1920. Éd. Russe purchased by **Boosey**, 1947.*

EDY Les Éditions Doberman-Yppan
C.P. 2021
Saint-Nicolas, Québec G7A 4X5
Canada
Tel: 418-831-1304
Fax: 418-836-3645
www.dobermaneditions.com
Emphasis on music for guitar.

EFdM Éditions Françaises de Musique
US agent: Presser
International agent: Billaudot
*Originally the publications section of Radio France. Acquired by **Billaudot**, 1988.*

Einhorn Richard Einhorn Music
320 Riverside Drive #15C
New York, NY 10025
USA
Tel: 212-932-1972
Richardein@mac.com
www.richardeinhorn.com
*Music of **Richard Einhorn**.*

EJR Ediciones Joaquín Rodrigo
General Yagüe 11, 4 J
28020 Madrid
Spain
Tel: +34 91 5552728
Fax: +34 91 5564335
ediciones@joaquin-rodrigo.com
www.joaquin-rodrigo.com
*Music of **Joaquin Rodrigo**; founded 1989 by his only child, Cecilia Rodrigo.*

Elkan-Vogel Elkan-Vogel, Inc.
US agent: Presser
*Founded 1928 in Philadelphia. Represented French agencies **Durand**, **Jobert** et al.
Also acquired **Lemoine**, **Éditions Rideau Rouge**, **Hamelle** and others. In 1970
became a subsidiary of **Presser**.*

Elkin Elkin Music International, Inc.
94 Merrills Chase
Asheville, NC 28803
USA
Tel: 800-367-3554; 828-951-9828
Fax: 800-291-5590; 828-651-9655
timsloan@elkinmusic.com
www.elkinmusic.com
    Founded 1903 in London.

Elkus J.B. Elkus & Sons
US agent: MMB

EMB Editio Musica Budapest
Vörösmarty tér 1, POB 322
H-1370 Budapest
Hungary
Tel: +36-1-2361-100
Fax: +36-1-2361-101
emb@emb.hu
www.emb.hu
US agent: Boosey
    Founded by the state of Hungary in 1950; privatized in 1993. Is now a part of
BMG *Editions.*

Editio Musica Budapest
Victor Hugo Street 11-15
H-1132 Budapest Hungary

EMF Editions Musica Ferrum
Kranias 2
15344 Gerakas
Greece
Tel: +30 210 6019675
www.musica-ferrum.com
    Focuses on contemporary concert music.

EMI EMI Music Publishing
550 Madison Ave., 5th Floor
New York, NY 10022
USA
Tel: 212-833-7730
mediauk@emimusicpub.com
www.emimusicpub.com
US agent: Schirmer
    Founded 1931 as Electric and Musical Industries Ltd; later adding publishing to
its main business of recording.

27 Wrights Lane
London W8 5SW United
Tel: +44 203 059 3059
Fax: +44 203 059 2059

EMM Ediciones Mexicanas de Musica S.A.
Avenida Juarez 18
Despacho 206 06050 Mexico, D.F.
Mexico
Tel: (52) - (5) - 5215855
US agent: Peer
Founded 1947 by a group of preeminent Mexican composers.

EMS Educational Music Service   EMS—Music of All
(for North America & East Asia)   Fünter Weg 35
33 Elkay Dr.   D-45472 Mülheim Germany
Chester, NY 10918   Tel: +49-(0)208-941 366
USA   Fax: +49-(0)208-941 366
Tel: 845-469-5790
Fax: 845-469-5817
sales@emsmusic.com (for North America & East Asia)
sales@ems-musicworldwide.com (for Europe & South
www.emsmusic.com
Founded in 1979. More active as a retailer than a publisher. Celebrated for up-to-the-minute knowledge of changes in the music publishing industry. EMS acquired **Mapleson** *in 1996.*
A number of works that are now available only on rental were purchased by EMS when it was possible to do so and are now available as rentals either from EMS or from the copyright holder.
Bowing masters are also available for a large number of works; search for "bowing masters" on the website.

EMT Éditions Musicales Transatlantiques
151-153 avenue Jean - James
75019 Paris
France
www.editions-transatlantiques.com
US agent: Schirmer
Purchased by **Music Sales** *in 2010.*

Enoch Enoch & Cie.
193 Blvd. Pereire
F-75017 Paris
France
Tel: +33 (0) 1 45 74 01 72
Fax: +33 (0) 1 45 72 57 53
contact@editions-enoch.com
www.editions-enoch.com/editions-enoch
US agent: Schirmer
Founded in Paris, 1880. Taken over in 1927 by the English firm **Edwin Ashdown**, *which was subsequently absorbed by* **Music Sales** *in 1982.*

Eschig Éditions Max Eschig
Durand-Salabert-Éschig
16 rue des Fossés Saint-Jacques
F-75005 Paris
France
Tel: +33-1 44 41 50 90
Fax: +33-1 44 41 50 91
www.durand-salabert-eschig.com
US agent: Boosey (rentals); Leonard (sales)
   Founded 1907 in Paris; purchased by **Durand** *in 1987. Is now, along with Durand and others, a part of* **BMG** *Editions.*

Escobar Edition Escobar
Tel: +358-400-298227
Fax: +358-420-298227
edition@escobar.com
www.edition.escobar.com
US agent: EMS (Europe and America)
   Founded 1999 to specialize in interesting rarities.

Eufonia Edizioni Musicali Eufonia
Via Trento, 5
25055 Pisogne (BS)
Italy
Tel: 0364 97069
Fax: 0364 97069
info@edizionieufonia
www.edizionieufonia.it

Eulenburg Edition Eulenburg
www.schott-music.com/shop/1/Eulenburg_Pocket_Scores
US agent: EAM
   Founded 1874 in Leipzig. Moved to London 1939. Taken over by **Schott** *in 1957; in 2012 the Eulenburg performance materials were transferred to* **Breitkopf**, *which plans to supplement further Eulenburg study scores with complete performing materials.*

Faber   Faber Music Ltd.
74-77 Great Russell Street
London WC1B 3DA
United Kingdom
Tel: +44 (0)20 7908 5310
Fax: +44 (0)20 7908 5339
information@fabermusic.com
hire@fabermusic.com
www.fabermusic.com
US agent: EAM (rental); Alfred (sales)
   Established 1965, London, as an offshoot of the book publishers Faber and Faber, from which it separated in 1988.

Falla   Manuel de Falla Ediciones
C / Bretón de los Herreros 55
28003 Madrid
Spain
Tel: (+34) 91 441 77 43
Fax: (+34) 91 399 45 08
info@manueldefallaediciones.es
   *Music of **Manuel de Falla**.*

Fazer   Fazer Music, Inc.
Finland
US agent: Boosey (rentals); Leonard (sales)
International agent: Fennica.
   *Founded in Helsinki, 1897. In 1993 acquired by **Warner**. In 1998 the name "Fazer" ceased to exist. In 2002, Warner leased the rights to the classical catalog to **Gehrmans** Musikförlag Ab of Stockholm. Gehrmans in turn created a subsidiary, **Fennica Gehrman**, q.v., to handle this catalog. As of 2007, Fennica Gehrman owns the serious catalog of **Warner/Chappell Music Finland**, including the former Fazer catalog.*

Fennica   Fennica Gehrman
P.O. Box 158
Fin-00121 Helsinki
Finland
Tel: +358-10-3871220
Fax: +358-10-3871221
info@fennicagehrman.fi; hire@fennicagehrman.fi (rentals)
www.Fennicagehrman.fi
US agent: Boosey (rentals); Leonard (sales)
   *Finnish music publisher. Fennica Gehrman owns the Finnish music originally published by **Fazer** or by its successor firm, **Warner Chappell Music Finland**.*

FIMIC   Music Finland [Finnish Music Information Centre]
Urho Kekkosen kau 2 C, 6th floor
00100 Helsinki
Finland
Tel: +358 (0)20 730 2230
info@musicfinland.fi
www.musicfinland.fi
   The product of a 2012 merger of **Music Export Finland** *and the* **Finnish Music Information Centre** *(FIMIC). Promotes Finnish music, sells commercially unpublished music of Finnish composers, and handles rentals of parts for these works.*

C. Fischer   Carl Fischer, Inc.
65 Bleecker St., 8th Floor
New York, NY 10012
USA
Tel: 212-777-0900; 800-762-2328 (ask for rentals)
Fax: 212-477-6996; 610-644-7110
cf-info@carlfischer.com
www.carlfischer.com
US agent: Presser
   Established in the late 19th century. Purchased by **Boosey** *in 1998 but sold a year later back to the great-grandson of the firm's founder. Since 2005 operating jointly with* **Presser**.

Fleisher   Edwin A. Fleisher Collection of Orchestral Music
Free Library of Philadelphia
1901 Vine Street
Philadelphia, PA 19103-1116
USA
Tel: 215-686-5313
fleisher@freelibrary.org
www.freelibrary.org
   The largest lending library of orchestral music in the world. Originally the library of a youth training orchestra. Given to the Free Library of Philadelphia in 1929.
   Finding sets of orchestral works through the online catalog used to be tricky, but has now been simplified: just be sure to type Fleisher Collection *in the search box along with the composer, title, and/or keyword for the work you seek.*

Foetisch Foetisch Frères
Grand Pont 4
CH - 1002 Lausanne
Switzerland
Tel: 00 41 21 310 4810
Fax: 00 41 21 320 2430
fredy.henry@hugmusique.ch
US agent: Boosey (for US & Canada)
Agent for all other nations (except Switzerland): Ricordi
  Swiss firm founded 1865. Became Foetisch Frères around 1905 under founder's four sons. Two grandsons left in 1947 to start **M.P. Foetisch** *(a different firm). Foetisch Frères bought by* **Hug** *& Co. 1978.*

Forberg Robert Forberg — P. Jurgenson Musikverlag
Mirbachstraße 9
D - 5300 Bonn - Bad Godesberg
Germany
US agent: Boosey
  Founded 1862 in Leipzig; in the late 19th century helped spread works of Russian composers and others. Moved to Bonn 1949 and Bad Godesberg in 1951. Acquired by **BMG** *in 2006.*

Fountain Park Fountain Park Music Publishing
2728 Asbury Road, Suite 200
Dubuque, IA 52001
USA
Tel: 563-690-0151
Fax: 563-690-0152
fpmusicpub@aol.com
www.fountainparkmusic.com
  Formerly **Castle Enterprises** *and* **Stoskopf Music Publishing.**

Four Hands Four Hands Music
15 Birchmead Close
St. Albans Hertfordshire AL3 6BS
United Kingdom
Tel: 01727 858485
Fax: 01727 858485
  Specializing in music for piano 4-hands, including, for example, the Czerny Concerto for Piano 4-Hands, op.153.

Fox Sam Fox Publishing Co. Inc.
US agent: Alfred
  Long out of business. The works of **Alan Shulman** *originally published by Fox now have a home with* **LudwigMasters**.

Fujihara Fujihara Music Co. Inc.
18206 51st Avenue So.
Seattle, WA 98188-4640
USA
Tel: 206-246-9880
hovanessfuji@aol.com; contact@hovhaness.com
www.hovhaness.com
*Works of **Alan Hovhaness**.*

PO Box 88381
Seattle, WA 98188-2381

Furore Furore Verlag
Naumburger Str. 40
D-34127 Kassel
Germany
Tel: ++49-(0)561-89 73 52
Fax: ++49-(0)561-8 34 72
info@furore-verlag.de
www.furore-verlag.de
Music by women composers.

Fürstner Adolf Fürstner Ltd.
US agent: Schott (EAM) or Boosey (see below)
*Founded 1868 in Berlin. Moved to England in 1933 and formed Fürstner Ltd. Rights to some works sold to **Boosey** 1943. In 1986, **Schott** took over the remainder of the catalog.*

Galaxy Galaxy Music Corporation
US agent: ECS
*Founded NYC 1931. Purchased **Augener** in 1962. In 1989, Galaxy became an imprint of **ECS**.*

Garland Garland Publishing, Inc.
19 Union Square W., 8th floor
New York, NY 10003
USA
Tel: 212-414-0650
Fax: 212-414-0659
info@garland.com

Orders & inquiries: 47G
Runway Rd.
Levittown, PA 19057
Tel: 800-821-8312; 215
Fax: 215-269-0343

Gehrmans　Carl Gehrmans Musikförlag
Box 42026
S-126 12 Stockholm
Sweden
Tel: +46 8 610 06 10 (sales); +46 8 610 06 20 (rentals)
Fax: +46 8 610 06 27 (sales); +46 8 610 06 27 (rentals)
sales@gehrmans.se
hire@gehrmans.se (rentals)
info@gehrmans.se
www.gehrmans.se
US agent: Boosey
　　*Founded 1893. Acquired **Hirsch's Förlag** in 1943. Later acquired the catalog of*
Körlings Förlag *AB. In 2007 acquired the catalog of **Warner/Chappell Music***
***Scandinavia**.*

Gems　Gems Music Publications
P.O. Box 6253
Fort Lauderdale, FL 33310
USA
Tel: 352-682-6297
gemsmusicpublications@yahoo.com
www.gemsmusicpublications.com
　　Specializing in viola music.

Geocoso　Geocoso Music
15716 Condor Ridge Road
Canyon County, CA 91387
USA
Tel: 661-250-1263
Fax: 661-250-0256
info@gregorysmithmusic.com
www.gregorysmithmusic.com
US agent: Stanton
　　*Music of **Gregory Smith**.*

Gershwin Music　George Gershwin Music
US agent: EAM

Glocken　Glocken Verlag
glockenverlag@jwmail.co.uk
US agent: EAM
　　Franz Lehar founded Glocken Verlag in Vienna in 1935 to publish his own music.
*Glocken Verlag's business is administered by **Weinberger**.*

Goodmusic Goodmusic Publishing
P.O. Box 100
Tewkesburg GL20 7YQ
United Kingdom
Tel: +44 01684 773883
Fax: +44 01684 773884
sales@goodmusic-uk.com
US agent: Presser
*Began as retail business 1974; added music publishing 1995. Acquired **Roberton Publications** in 2003. Mail order only.*

Gray H. W. Gray Co., Inc.
US agent: Alfred
*Founded 1906; was sole agent for **Novello** until 1937. In 1971 became a division of **Belwin-Mills**; ultimately acquired by **Warner/Chappell** in 1994. However, publications continue under the Gray imprint.*

Griggs-Janower David Griggs-Janower
Department of Music
University at Albany
1400 Washington Avenue
Albany, NY 12222
USA
Tel: 518-438-6548
Fax: 518-442-4182
janower@albany.edu

Gross Murray Gross
614 W. Superior St.
Alma, MI 48801-1599
USA
Tel: 989-463-7119
murraygross@gmail.com
www.murraygross.com
*Music of **Murray Gross**.*

GunMar *See* Margun
US agent: Schirmer
*The ASCAP sister company of **Margun**, which is BMI.*

Gutheil Gutheil [Gutkheyl']
Moscow
Russia
> *Founded 1859. Published Rachmaninoff's works from 1892 to 1914. Purchased by Koussevitzky's firm **Édition Russe de Musique** in 1914.*

Guzzo Anne M. Guzzo
Music Department 3039
1000 E. University Avenue
University of Wyoming
Laramie, WY 82071
USA
guzzo@uwyo.edu
> *Music of **Anne Guzzo**.*

Hamelle Hamelle & Cie, France
175 Rue St. Honore
F-75040 Paris
France
Tel: (1) 42.96.89.11
US agent: King
> *Founded in 1877 in Paris; taken over by **Leduc** in 1993.*

Handlo Handlo Music
Bath
England
khudson@handlo.com
www.handlo.com
> *Specializing in choral music.*

Hansen Edition Wilhelm Hansen
Bornholmsgade 1
DK-1266 Copenhagen K
Denmark
Tel: +45 33 11 78 88
Fax: +45 33 14 81 78
ewh@ewh.dk
www.ewh.dk
US agent: Schirmer
> *Founded 1853 in Copenhagen. Purchased by **Music Sales** in 1988.*

Hänssler Hänssler Verlag
Max-Eyth-Str. 41
Industriegebiet Buch/Sol
D-71088 Holzgerlingen
Germany
Tel: +49 (70 31) 74 14 - 130 or - 131
Fax: +49 (70 31) 74 14 - 109
kundenservice@haenssler.de
Agent: Carus
Founded 1919 in Stuttgart. Produces scholarly yet practical editions, largely of Lutheran church music.

Happy Lemon Happy Lemon Music Publishing
6808 Old Harford Road
Baltimore, MD 21234
USA
info@karenamrhein.com
www.happylemonmusicpublishing.com
*Music of **Karen Amrhein**.*

Hard Wall Hard Wall Publishing
536 Jacob Way #103
Rochester, MI 48307
USA
ac2554@wayne.edu
*Music of **James Hartway**.*

Harmonia Harmonia BV
P.O. Box 744
NL-8440 AS Heerenveen
Netherlands
Tel: +31 (0)513 653053
Fax: +31 (0)513 618016
sales@dehaske.com; music@dehaske.com
*Specializing in choral music since 1922. Part of **De Haske Publications** since 2003.*

Harmonic Harmonic Services Group
436 River Rock Court
San Jose, CA 95136
USA
Tel: 408-269-2301
hsginfo@harmonicservicesgroup.com .
http://Harmonicservicesgroup.com

Harth   Harth Musikverlag/Pro musica Verlag GmbH
Bergisch-Gladbach
D - 04004 Leipzig
Germany
Tel: (02204)2003-0
Fax: (02204) 200333
musikverlag.hans.gerig@harth-musikverlag.de

Heinrichshofen   Heinrichshofens Verlag
Liebigstrasse 16
D-26389 Wilhelmshaven
Germany
Tel: 0 44 21/92 67.0
Fax: 0 44 21/20 20 07
heinrichshofen@t-online.de
www.heinrichshofen.de
US agent: Peters
Founded 1806 in Magdeburg.

Helicon   Schott Helicon Music Corp. (BMI)
US agent: EAM (rentals); Leonard (sales)
*A member of the **Schott** Music Group.*

Hendon   Hendon Music, Inc.
US agent: Boosey

Henle   G. Henle Verlag   G. Henle USA, Inc.
Forstenrieder Allee 122   P.O. Box 460127
81476 München   St. Louis, MO 63146
Germany   Tel: 314-514-1791
Tel: ++49 (89) 759 82 - 0   Fax: 314-514-1269
Fax: ++49 (89) 759 82 - 40
info@henle.de (Germany)
info@henleusa.com (USA)
www.henle.com
Founded 1948 in Munich.

Heugel Heugel & Cie
175 Rue St. Honoré
F-75040 Paris
France
Tel: (1) 42.96.89.11
US agent: King
Founded 1839 in Paris. Acquired by **Leduc** *in 1980.*

Highgate Highgate Press
US agent: ECS

Hildegard Hildegard Publishing Company
P.O. Box 18860
Mount Airy, PA 19119
USA
Tel: 610-667-8634
Fax: 215-359-0654
mail@hildegard.com
www.hildegard.com
US agent: Presser
Founded 1988; music of women composers.

Hinrichsen Hinrichsen Edition Ltd. / Edition Peters Ltd.
Hinrichsen House
10-12 Baches Street
GB - London N1 6DN
United Kingdom
Tel: +44 / (0)20 / 7553-4000
Fax: +44 / (0)20 / 7490-4921
sales@editionpeters.com
www.edition-peters.com
US agent: Peters
Founded 1938 in London by Max Hinrichsen, who had family connections with the
C.F. Peters firm. Hinrichsen Edition was renamed **Peters Edition Ltd.** *in 1975.*

Hinshaw Hinshaw Music Inc.
Box 470
Chapel Hill, NC 27514-0470
USA
Tel: 919-933-1691; 800-568-7805
Fax: 919-967-3399
www.hinshawmusic.com
Established 1975, specializing in choral music.

HNH   HNH International Ltd.
Level 11, Cyberport 1
100 Cyberport Road
Hong Kong
SAR
Tel: 852-2760-7818; 852-2993-5649
Fax: 852-2760-1962; 852-2989-9181
Klaus.Heymann@Naxos.com
Edith.Lei@Naxos.com

Hofmeister   Friedrich Hofmeister Verlag
Büttnerstrasse 10
D-04103 Leipzig
Germany
Tel: +49-341 / 9 60 07 50
Fax: +49-341 / 9 60 30 55
sales: info@hofmeister-musikverlag.com
rentals: orchester@hofmeister-musikverlag.com
http://hofmeister-musikverlag.com
   Founded 1807. Sales may be handled through any dealer; rentals are direct from Hofmeister.

Holab   Bill Holab Music
377 Sterling Place, No.4
Brooklyn, NY 11238
USA
Tel: 718-499-3946
Fax: 719-228-8085
bill@holabmusic.com
www.billholabmusic.com
   Publishing/rental agent for **Mason Bates, Alla Borzova, Peter Boyer, Paul Brantley, Kenji Bunch, Richard Danielpour** *[all works since 2009],* **Michael Daugherty** *[all works since 2011],* **Scott Eyerly, Mark Grey, Jake Heggie, Pierre Jalbert, Gabriel Kahane, Anthony Korf, Cindy McTee, Joel Puckett, Kevin Puts, Neil Rolnick, D.J. Sparr, Michael Torke** *[all works since 1992].*

Hollins   Hollins and Park Music Company
211 Goodwood Gardens
Baltimore, MD 21210-2531
USA
www.VivianAdelbergRudow.com
   Music of **Vivian Adelberg Rudow.**

Hoyt   Hoyt Editions
13463 Peekaboo Ave. NW
Poulsbo, WA 98370-7051
USA
info@hoyteditions.com
tbaplr@aol.com

Hug   Hug & Co. Musikverlage
Limmatquai 28-30
Postfach
CH-8022 Zürich
Switzerland
Tel: 00 41 21 310 4810
Fax: 00 41 21 320 2430
info.zuerich@musikhug.ch
www.hug-musikverlage.ch
US agent: Boosey (US & Canada)
Agent for all other nations (except Switzerland): Ricordi
Founded 1817 as Gebrüder Hug. Emphasis on Swiss composers, educational materials and musicological works; also dealt in musical instruments. Took over **Foetisch Frères** *in 1978. Publisher of the series* **Musica Instrumentalis***.*

Ibu Music   Ibu Music
c/o Ingram Marshall
17 Rolfe Rd.
Hamden, CT 06517
USA
IngramMar@aol.com
Music of **Ingram Marshall***.*

IMSLP   International Music Score Library Project
imslp.org

An online public domain library of music scores and parts. Also known as the **Petrucci Music Library***, the site is based in Canada, and thus subject to Canadian copyright laws, which differ from those of other countries.*

International   International Music Company
5 West 37 Street
New York, NY 10018
USA
Tel: 212-391-4200
Fax: 212-391-4306
info@internationalmusicco.com
www.internationalmusicco.com

Inter-Note   Inter-Note GmbH
Siebenbürgerhof 6
69493 Hirschberg
Germany
Tel: 0049 [0] 6201 24 987 0
Fax: 0049 [0] 6201 24 987 99
info@inter-note.com
www.inter-note.com
Founded 2006. An Internet print-on-demand service. Copies are printed, bound, and delivered in three working days. Individual parts may be ordered.

Ione   Ione Press
US agent: ECS

Ipsilon   Ipsilon Music Services
604 Riverside Dr., Suite 3-C
New York, NY 10031
USA
Tel: 646-265-5666
E-mail: info@ipsilonmusic.com
www.ipsilonmusic.com
Ipsilon provides many services, including state-of-the-art music notation, editing, score and part preparation, arranging, orchestration, transcriptions, proofreading, musical theater workshop production, and recording production.
Extractions from opera, oratorio, and the like, are provided on demand (only for works in the public domain); allow preparation time by ordering early. Ipsilon can also provide photocopies (or PDFs) of the piano-vocal versions of extracts (public domain only).
Ipsilon is under the supervision of John Yaffé, coauthor of Arias, Ensembles, & Choruses, *Scarecrow, 2012.*

Israeli   Israeli Music Institute
Israel Music Information Centre
55 Menachem Begin Road
P.O.Box 51197
IL-67138 Tel Aviv
Israel
Tel: 972-(0)3-624 70 95
Fax: 972-(0)3-561 28 26
musicinst@bezeqint.net
www.imi.org.il
US agent: Presser

P.O. Box 51197
IL-6713813 Tel Aviv

Established in 1961 as a publicly owned publishing house supported by the Israel Ministry of Education and Culture. IMI also serves as the **Israel Music Information Center***, a member of the IAMIC.*

Israeli MP Israeli Music Publications, Ltd.
25 Keren Hayesod
Jerusalem 94188
Israel
US agent: Presser

Jobert Societé des Éditions Jobert
info@jobert.fr
www.jobert.fr
Agent: Lemoine
*Established 1922 in Paris as the successor firm to **Eugène Fromont**. As of January 2008, complete distribution and rights representation for Éditions Jobert reside with **Lemoine**.*

Jurgenson P. Jurgenson
US agent: Peters
*Founded 1861 by Pyotr Ivanovich Jürgenson, specializing in Russian music. Nationalized in 1918 to become the music section of the Soviet State Publishing House under various names (see **Muzyka**). Current arrangements with foreign agents are listed under the rubric **Russian**, q.v. The firm P. Jurgenson was revived in 2004 by the great-grandson of the founder.*

Kahnt C. F. Kahnt Musikverlag
US agent: Peters
Founded 1851 in Leipzig.

Kallisti Kallisti Music Press
810 South Saint Bernard St.
Philadelphia, PA 19143-3309
USA
Tel: 215-724-6511; 800-260-2881
kallisti@ix.netcom.com
www.kallistimusic.com
Founded 1991.

Kalmus   Edwin F. Kalmus & Co., Inc.   (Rentals)
P.O. Box 5011   6403 W. Rodgers Circle
Boca Raton, FL 33431-0811   Boca Raton, FL 33487
USA
Tel: 800-434-6340; 561-241-6340
Fax: 561-241-6347
efkalmus@aol.com
www.efkalmus.com
   Founded 1926 in New York. Mainly publishes reprints of public domain works. Not
*to be confused with **Kalmus.com**, an online retailer with offices in South Carolina*
and in Barcelona.

Kane   JoAnn Kane Music Service
3526 Hayden Avenue
Culver City, CA 90232
USA
Tel: 310-231-9733
Fax: 310-733-4126
library@joannkanemusic.com
rentals@joannkanemusic.com
www.joannkanemusic.com
   Specializing in film music as well as music preparation services.

KaWe   Edition KaWe
Brederodestraat 90
NL-1054 VC Amsterdam 13
Netherlands
US agent: King
   No longer in business. Some of the horn solos and concertos published by KaWe
are still available at www.pizka.de/KaWe.htm.

Keiser Classical
US agent: LKMP
   *The BMI subsidiary of **LKMP** (Lauren Keiser Music Publishing), q.v.*

Kenter Canyon   Kenter Canyon Music
1019 Grant Street, Unit B
Santa Monica, CA 90405
USA
Tel: 310-450-5650
Fax: 640-450-5694
adrienne@adriennealbert.com
www.adriennealbert.com
   *Music of **Adrienne Albert**.*

King   Robert King Music Co.
140 Main St.
North Easton, MA 02356
USA
Fax: 508-238-2571
commerce@RKingMusic.com
rental@RKingMusic.com
www.rkingmusic.com
US agent: Schirmer
   *Founded 1940 in Wakefield, MA, as a specialist in brass music. Sold in two transactions (1987, 1990) to **Leduc**. Currently handles all rentals for Leduc, **Bornemann**, **Costallat**, **Heugel**, and **Hamelle**. The official corporate name became "Alphonse Leduc — Robert King, Inc." The whole was acquired by **Music Sales** in 2014.*

Kistner&Siegel   Fr. Kistner & C.F.W. Siegel & Co.
Uhlstraße 82–84
D-50321 Brühl
Germany
Tel: +49 (0) 2232-9494-240
Fax: +49 (0) 2232-9494-219
info@kistner-siegel.de
www.kistnerundsiegel.de

Musikverlag Kistner und
Wippinger Weg 26
53859 Niederkassel
   Tel: +49 02208 / 768094
   Fax: +49 02208 / 768095

   Formed in 1923 by a merger of Kistner (founded 1823, originally under the name Probst) and Siegel (1846).

Kjos   Neil A. Kjos Music Company
4382 Jutland Dr.
San Diego, CA 92117
USA
Tel: 858-270-9800
email@kjos.com
www.kjos.com
   Founded 1936; specializing in educational music.

Kneusslin   Editions Kneusslin
Amselstrasse 43
CH-4059 Basel 24
Switzerland
US agent: Peters

Kol Meira Kol Meira Publications
3526 Broundbrook Lane
Columbia, SC 29206
USA
Tel: 803-787-4332
meira@musician.org
meirawarshauer.com
  *Music of **Meira Warshauer**.*

Kunzelmann Edition Kunzelmann
Grütstrasse 28
CH-8134 Adliswil
Switzerland
Tel: +41 44 710 36 81
Fax: +41 44 710 38 17
edition@kunzelmann.com
www.kunzelmann.ch
US agent: Peters
  Founded 1979.

Edition Kunzelmann
Grütstrasse 28
CH-8134 Adliswil/ZH
Tel: 0041/(1) 710 3681
Fax: 0041/(1) 710 3817

Kuster Kristin Kuster
School of Music, Theatre & Dance
Earl V. Moore Building
1100 Baits Drive
Ann Arbor, MI 48109-2085
USA
kkuster@kristinkuster.com
www.kristinkuster.com
  *Music of **Kristin Kuster**.*

LaFi Latin American Frontiers International Publishers, Ltd.
P.O. Box 345
Plymouth Meeting, PA 19462-0345
USA
Tel: 610-825-3262
lafi@lafipublishers.com
www.lafipublishers.com
  Latin American contemporary music, visual arts and literature.

LarkFrost LarkFrost Publishing
1761 N. 130th St.
Seattle, WA 98133
USA
Tel: 877-600-2219

Lawdon Lawdon Press
1008 Spruce St. #3F
Philadelphia, PA 19107
USA
Tel: 215-592-1847
Fax: 215-592-1095
LawdonPress@aol.com
www.jenniferhigdon.com
  *Music of **Jennifer Higdon**.*

LeDor LeDor Music
118 N. Peters Road, #330
Knoxville, TN 37923
USA
Tel: 865-691-0428; 888-624-9094
Fax: 568-691-0448
info@ledorgroup.com
www.ledorgroup.com
  *Mostly music of **Lucas Richman**.*

Leduc Alphonse Leduc Éditions
85 rue Gabriel Péri
92120 Montrouge
France
Tel: +33 (0)1 42 96 89 11
Fax: +33 (0)1 42 86 02 83
AlphonseLeduc@wanadoo.fr
www.alphonseleduc.com
US agent: Schirmer
  *Founded in Paris 1842. Acquired **Heugel** in 1980 and **Hamelle** in 1993. **Robert King** has been a subsidiary of Leduc since 1990. Acquired by **Music Sales** in 2014.*

Leeds Canada Leeds Canada
MCA Building
2450 Victoria Park Avenue
Willowdale, Ontario M2J 4A2
Canada
US agent: EAM (rentals); Alfred (sales)

Lemoine   Henry Lemoine et Cie.
27 boulevard Beaumarchais
F-75004 Paris
France

Tel: +33 01 56 68 86 65
Fax: +33 01 56 68 90 66
orchestre@editions-lemoine.fr
www.henry-lemoine.com
Founded in Paris in 1772. No US agent since 2009; send rental requests direct to the Paris address.

Rental library:
c/o Hexamusic
246, avenue de la Couronne
de Prés
CS 10604 Epône
F-78417 Aubergenville
Tel: 33 (0) 1 30 90 56 36
Fax: 33 (0) 1 30 90 10 23

Lengnick   Alfred Lengnick & Co.
27 Grove Road
Beaconsfield Bucks HP9 1UR
United Kingdom
Tel: +44 (0) 1494 681 216
Fax: +44 (0) 1494 670 443
sally@alfredlengnick.co.uk
www.ricordi.co.uk/lengnick_catalogue/
US agent: Schirmer (rentals); Leonard (sales)
Music Sales (rentals); Faber (sales)
*Founded 1893 in London. Was the British agent for the firm **Simrock**, which it ultimately purchased. Lengnick was purchased by **Complete Music Ltd.** in 1991. The Lengnick catalog is now handled by **Ricordi, London**.*

Leonard   Hal Leonard Publishing Corp.
Box 13819; 7777 W. Bluemound Rd.
Milwaukee, WI 53213
USA
Tel: 646-562-5880, (414) 774-3630
Fax: 212-575-9270, (414) 774-3259
halinfo@halleonard.com
rental inquiries: www.laurenkeisermusic.com
www.halleonard.com

Hal Leonard Corporation
960 East Mark St.
Winona, MN 55987

*Sales arm of **Music Sales** and many other publishers. Purchased **Shawnee** in 2009. Leonard does not sell directly, however, but through music retailers or through its ever-evolving subsidiaries such as **Music Dispatch**, **SheetMusicDirect**, **OrchestraMusicDirect**, and the like. Leonard also administers rentals for the **MJQ** catalog.*

Leuckart F.E.C. Leuckart
Rheingoldstrasse 4
D-80639 Munich
Germany
Tel: +49 (0)8917 3928
Fax: +49 (0)8917 6054
US agent: Peters (for North America)
Sole selling agent: Thomi-Berg
Founded 1782 in Breslau.

Liben Liben Music Publishers
1191 Eversole Rd.
Cincinnati, OH 45230
USA
Tel: 513-232-6920
Fax: 513-232-1866
info@liben.com
sales@liben.com
www.liben.com
*Music of **Frank Proto**.*

Lienau Robert Lienau Musikverlag
Strubbergstrasse 80
D-60489 Frankfurt am Main
Germany
Tel: +49-69-978-286-6
Fax: +49-69-978-286-79
info@lienau-frankfurt.de
www.zimmermann-frankfurt.de
US agent: Peters
Subsidiary of Allegra Musikverlag.
*A successor firm to **Schlesinger** of Berlin in 1864. Acquired the firms Haslinger (1875), Rättig (1910), Krentzlin (1919), Wernthal (1925), and Köster (1928). Taken over in 1991 by **Musikverlag Zimmermann**. Now owned by **Allegra Musikverlag**, together with Zimmermann and others.*

Little Miracles Little Miracles Music
735 Grant Street
Downers Grove, IL 60515
USA
Tel: 630-901-9828
Lmiracles@aol.com
www.douglofstrom.com
*Music of **Doug Lofstrom**.*

Little Piper Little Piper
915 South Main Street
Royal Oak, MI 48065
USA
Tel: 248-850-8123
Fax: 248-336-2320
piper@little-piper.com
www.little-piper.com
Specializing in flute music.

LKMP Lauren Keiser Music Publishing
10750 Indian Head Industrial Blvd
St. Louis, MO 63132
USA
Tel: 203-560-9436
Fax: 314-270-5305
info@laurenkeisermusic.com; rental@laurenkeisermusic.com
www.laurenkeisermusic.com/

Rentals
1210 Innovation Drive
Winona, MN 55987
Tel: 855-259-6495
Fax: 507-454-8334

Founded 2009 as a music publisher and rental library, with the acquisition of
MMB *Music. Acquired* **Southern Music Company** *(San Antonio, TX) in 2012.*
Full scores may be examined online at the LKMP website.

Luck's Luck's Music Library
32300 Edward
P.O. Box 71397
Madison Heights, MI 48071
USA
Tel: 800-348-8749; 248-583-1820
Fax: 248-583-1114
sales@lucksmusic.net
helpdesk@lucksmusic.net
www.lucksmusic.com

Founded in Detroit in the 1940s. Publishes under its own imprint and retails
orchestral music of all publishers. A number of works that are now available only on
rental were purchased by Luck's when it was possible to do so and are now available
as rentals either from Luck's or from the copyright holder.

LudwigMasters LudwigMasters Publications
6403 West Rogers Circle
Boca Raton, FL 33487
USA
Tel: 800-434-6340; 561-241-6169
Fax: 561-241-6343
www.ludwigmasters.com
Ludwig Music Publishing Company founded 1921 emphasizing educational music. In 2008 consolidated with **Great Works Publishing** *and* **Masters Publications** *to form LudwigMasters.*

Ludwin Ludwin Music
3618 Cazador St.
Los Angeles, CA 90065
USA
Tel: 323-257-5735
Fax: 323-255-5946
norman@ludwinmusic.com; ludwinmusic@yahoo.com
www.ludwinmusic.com
US agent: Luck's
Specializing in double bass music. All solo bass works from Ludwin are available in two keys to accommodate the tuning used by the soloist: solo tuning (low to high: F#, B, E, A) or a whole step lower for standard orchestral tuning (E, A, D, G). A useful way to think of it: in solo tuning, the double bass is effectively in a D transposition.

Lyche Harald Lyche & Co.
Postboks 2171 Stromso
N-3001 Drammen
Norway
Tel: 33-83-39-70
US agent: Walton

Madigan Madigan New Music
Brooklyn, NY 11215
USA
Tel: 347-987-4145
mary@madigannewmusic.com
www.madigannewmusic.com
Advances commissioning and performance projects with various project partners: composers, performers, commissioners, presenters. Also offers professional guidance, contract negotiation, and advising on grant proposals.

Malcolm Malcolm Music Ltd.
US agent: Shawnee

Maltz Richard Maltz Music
Etherredge Center
471 University Parkway
Aiken, SC 29801
USA
Tel: 803-641-3625
richardmaltz@richardmaltz.com
www.richardmaltz.com
> *Music of **Richard Maltz**.*

Mapleson Mapleson Music Rental Library
US agent: EMS
> *Lionel Mapleson was the first librarian of the Metropolitan Opera of New York. The firm bearing his name remained in the family for many years. The Mapleson Rental Library was purchased by **EMS** in 1996.*

Margun Margun Music Inc. / GunMar Music Inc.
US agent: Leonard
> *Founded 1975 by composer Gunther Schuller. Acquired by **Shawnee** in 1999. Shawnee in turn was acquired by **Leonard** in 2009. Margun is a BMI affiliate; GunMar is ASCAP.*

Marks Edward B. Marks Music Corp.
126 East 38th Street
New York, NY 10016
USA
Tel: 212-779-7977
Fax: 212-779-7920
bkalban@carlinamerica.com
www.ebmarks.com
US agent: Presser (rentals); Leonard (sales)

Massey Massey University Music Department
Private Bag 11222
Palmerston North
New Zealand

Masters Music Masters Music Publications, Inc.

> *See: LudwigMasters*

Matalex Matalex Press
244 Ocean View Dr.
Vista, CA 92084
USA
Tel: 760-758-5856
matthew@matthewtommasini.com
Music of Matthew Tommasini.

Matzi Werner Matzi
Postfach 106, Badhausgasse 7 /7
Wien A-1071
Tel: +43 1 786 36 63; +43 664 481 21 18
werner.matzi@gmx.at
www.wernermatzi.at

Mauldin Michael Mauldin
12713 Summer Avenue NE
Albuquerque, NM 87112
USA
Tel: 505-293-5666
Michael@mmauldin.com
www.mmauldin.com
Music of Michael Mauldin.

MCA MCA Music
1755 Broadway, 8th Floor
New York, NY 10019
USA
Tel: 212-841-8000
Fax: 212-582-7340
US agent: EAM (rentals); Leonard (sales)
*Formed in 1924 as Music Corporation of America, a talent agency. Purchased **Leeds Music** in 1964 and began publishing. Acquired by Matsushita Electric Industrial Company in 1991 and by the Canadian firm Seagram Company Ltd. to be part of its **Universal Music Group**.*

McCarter Kevin McCarter
389 Glastonbury Lane
Somerset, NJ 08873
USA
Tel: 732-568-9008

kevin.mccarter@usa.net
Music of Kevin McCarter.

McClure   McClure Productions, Inc.
PO Box 293
Geneseo, NY 14454
USA
Tel: 585-243-0324
info@artforbrains.com
www.artforbrains.com
    *Music of **Glenn McClure**.*

McGinnis   McGinnis & Marx Music Publishers
APNM/Music Publishing Service
236 West 26th St., #11S
New York, NY 10001-6736
USA
Tel: 212-243-5233
Fax: 212-675-1630
pabloski1@earthlink.net
US agent: Peer

McTier   McTier Music
106 Hounslow Road
Twickenham Middlesex TW2 7HB
United Kingdom
Tel: 020 8894 5381
Fax: 020 8898 4591
music@mctier.globalnet.co.uk
    Specializing in double bass music.

Meadow   Meadow Music
P.O. Box 403
Wasco, IL 60183
USA
janbach@comcast.net
http://www.janbach.com
    *Music of **Jan Bach**.*

Medici   Medici Music Press
5017 Veach Road
Owensboro, KY 42303
USA
Tel: 270-684-9233
ronalddishinger@yahoo.com
www.medicimusic.com

Melartin Erkki Melartin Society (Erkki Melartin — Seura)
www2.siba.fi/Melartinseura/?page=toiminta
Fennica
Website is in Finnish.

Mercury Mercury Music Corp.
US agent: Presser
*Owned by **Presser**.*

Merion Merion Music Inc.
US agent: Presser
*Owned by **Presser**.*

Metamorphic Metamorphic Music
2010 Lakeview Ct.
Hermitage, TN 37076
USA
Tel: 888-421-6881
mail@metamorphicmusic.com
http://metamorphicmusic.com
*Music of **David Sartor**.*

Migdal Migdal Publishing
4352 Churchill Blvd.
Cleveland, OH 44118
USA
Tel: 216-691-3158
pschoenfield@gmail.com; psps@umich.edu
http://www.paulschoenfield.org
*Music of **Paul Schoenfeld**. Although a number of his works are published under the name Paul Schoenfield, and that is the spelling that appears on his website, the composer has more recently dropped the "i" from the spelling of his name.*

Milken The Milken Archive of American Jewish Music
1250 Fourth Street
Santa Monica, CA 90401
USA
Tel: 310-570-4800
Fax: 310-570-4801
info@milkenarchive.org
www.milkenarchive.org
American Jewish Music from the past 350 years.

777 West End Avenue, Ste. 10-E
New York, NY 10025

Mills Mills Music, Inc.
US agent: Schirmer (rentals); Alfred (sales)
  *Founded 1919 in New York, originally as Jack Mills, Inc., later as Mills Music. At first published popular music but moved into the classical field by mid-century. In 1969 merged with Belwin to become **Belwin-Mills**, which also purchased the catalog of **Franco Colombo, Inc.** Belwin-Mills became **CCP/Belwin** in 1988, but Mills split off again in 1993.*

MJQ MJQ Music, Inc.
US agent: Leonard (sales & licensing); LKMP (rentals)
  *Named after the Modern Jazz Quartet; publisher of jazz-influenced music. Now administered by **Hal Leonard Corporation**; rentals from **LKMP**.*

MMB MMB Music Inc.
US agent: LKMP
  *Founded 1964 as **Magnamusic-Baton**. Special interest in Orff-Schulwerk, plus a strong catalog of contemporary music, principally American. Music publishing business acquired in 2009 by Lauren Keiser Music Publishing (**LKMP**). [MMB remains active as a dealer in Orff instruments for the music education field.]*

Mobart Mobart Music Publishers
www.musicassociatesofamerica.com
US agent: EAM
  *Publications from Boelke-Bomart and Mobart Music (its BMI affiliate) are available worldwide from **Schott**.*

Modern Works Modern Works Music Publishing
Tel: NYC: 646-494-7131; Nashville 615-280-0088
Fax: 212-656-1767
info@ModernWorksMusicPublishing.com
www.modernworksmusicpublishing.com
  Founded 2004. Offices in New York, Nashville, and Tucson. All genres, including jazz, classical, and world music.

Moeck   Moeck Verlag
Lückenweg 4
D-29227 Celle   Postfach 3131
Germany   D-29231 Celle, Germany
Tel: +49-5141-8853-0; 0 800 6 63 25 46
Fax: +49-5141-8853-42
info@moeck-music.de
www.moeck-music.de
US agent: Boosey

    Founded 1930 and very influential in the promotion of recorder music. Also an instrument maker, specializing in copies of renaissance and baroque woodwinds. After 1958 Moeck began publishing avant-garde music of Polish composers and others.

Möseler   Karl Heinrich Möseler Verlag
Hoffmann-von-Fallersleben-Strasse 8-10
Postfach 1661
D-38304 Wolfenbüttel
Germany
Tel: +49-5331-95970
Fax: +49-5331-959720
info@moeseler-verlag.de
www.moeseler-verlag.de/

    *Founded in 1821 in Wolfenbüttel as C.H. Hartmann. Purchased in 1947 and name changed to Möseler. Since 2000, **Schott** has handled some of the rentals for Möseler.*

mph   Musikproduktion Höflich
Enhuberstrasse 6-8 Rgb.
D-80333 München
Germany
Tel: +49 089-52 20 81
Fax: +49 089-52 54 11
hoeflich@musikmph.de
www.musikmph.de

    *Creator of **Repertoire Explorer** and **Opera Explorer**, two series dedicated to the publication of unjustly neglected works otherwise unavailable. These are largely in full score or study score format; parts are available only for selected items.*

MTI   Music Theatre International
421 West 54th Street
New York, NY 10019
USA
Tel: 212-541-4684
Fax: 212-397-4684
Licensing@MTIshows.com
www.MTIshows.com

       Library & Shipping Dept.
31A Industrial Park Road
New Hartford, CT 06057

Founded in 1952. Specializing in theatrical licensing of Broadway, Off-Broadway, and West End musicals. Supplies scripts, scores, and parts. For international licensing, representatives for other countries and regions are listed on the website.

Munchkin   Munchkin Music
munchkinmusic@zappa.com
http://www.zappa.com/munchkinmusic/
*Music of **Frank Zappa**.*

Music Assoc   Music Associates of America
224 King Street
Englewood, NJ 07631
USA
Tel: 201-569-2898
Fax: 201-569-7023
maasturm@sprynet.com
www.musicassociatesofamerica.com

Music Sales   Music Sales Group
14-15 Berners St.
London W1T 3LJ
United Kingdom
Tel: +44 (0) 20 7612 7400
Fax: +44 (0) 20 7612 7547
[contact form on website]
www.musicsales.com
US agent: Leonard (sales).

       257 Park Avenue South,
20th Floor
New York, NY 10010
Tel: 212-254-2100
Fax: 212-254-2013

*An international organization with headquarters in London and offices all over the world. Owns numerous catalogs, including **Chester**, **Novello**, **Curwen**, **Schirmer**, **Hansen**, and **UME**.*

A very large number of scores are available for online perusal; click on "OnDemand."

MusicaNeo   MusicaNeo
Load.CD GmbH
Rothausstrasse 1
8280 Kreuzlingen
Switzerland
www.musicaneo.com
A web-based platform for distribution and promotion of the music of contemporary composers. Formerly known as Load.CD. Scores and parts may be downloaded.

Musica Rara   Musica Rara
US agent: Schirmer (rental)
Subsidiary of Breitkopf
*Taken over by **Breitkopf** in 2000.*

Musica Viva   Musica Viva
262 King's Drive
Eastbourne - Sussex BN21 2XD
United Kingdom

MusikFabrik   Musik Fabrik Music Publishing (La Fabrique Musique)
18 rue Marthe Aureau
77400 Lagny sur Marne
France
Tel: 00.33.1.64.30.1384

Muzyka   Muzyka [Muzïka]

    *The firm **P. Jurgenson** (founded 1861) was nationalized in 1918 and went through a series of name changes:*
    *1918-1922 **Gosmuzizdat** (State Music Publishing House)*
    *1922-1930 **Gosizdat Muzsektor** (State Publisher, Music Sector)*
    *1930-1964 **Muzgiz** (Gosudarstvennoye Muzïkal'noye Izdatel'stvo, State Music Publishing House)*
    *1964-2006 **Muzyka** [Muzïka]*
    *Muzyka was the new joint name taken when Muzgiz combined with **Sovetskiy Kompozitor** ("Soviet Composer," founded 1956). The imprint Muzyka was no longer used after 2006. In 2004, the firm P. Jurgenson was revived by the great-grandson of the founder.*
    *Current agreements with foreign agents for the above imprints are listed under the rubric **Russian**, q.v.*

MWV Musikwissenschaftlicher Verlag
Dorotheergasse 10
A-1010 Wien
Austria
Tel: 43-1-515-0343
Fax: 43-1-515-0351
office@mwv.at
www.mwv.at
US agent: Peters
International Bruckner Society and International Hugo Wolf Society.

Nagel Nagels Verlag
Subsidiary of Bärenreiter.

*In 1835, became the successor firm to George Christian Bachmann in Hannover. In the 20th century specialized in practical editions of baroque and classic works in the series Nagels Musik-Archiv. Taken over by **Bärenreiter** in 1952.*

Newbould Brian Newbould
Department of Music
University of Hull
Hull HU6 7RX
United Kingdom
Tel: 00 44 1482 465998
B.R.Newbould@hull.ac.uk
*Various completions and reconstructions of **Schubert**.*

Nordiska Nordiska Musikförlaget
St. Eriksgatan 58   Vendevägen 85 B
S-112 34 Stockholm   Box 533
Sweden   S-18215 Danderyd, Sweden
Tel: +46 8 650 13 13   Tel: (46) 8-755 12 10
Fax: +46 8 650 19 19   Fax: (46) 8-753 48 88
US agent: Schirmer
*Founded in Stockholm in 1915 as a subsidiary of **Hansen**. Taken over by **Music Sales** in 1988, then sold to **Fazer**, and in 1993 to **Warner/Chappell**.*

Norton W. W. Norton
500 5th Avenue
New York, NY 10110
USA
Tel: 212-354-5500
Fax: 212-869-0856
www.wwnorton.com
*Publisher of the **Norton Critical Edition** scores; no orchestral parts.*

Norwegian MIC   Norwegian Music Information Centre
Norsk Musikkinformasjonssenteret
Tollbugata 28
N-0157 Oslo
Norway
Tel: +47 22 42 90 90
Fax: +47 22 42 90 91
info@mic.no
www.mic.no

Notevole   Notevole Publishing
US agent: Subito
*The BMI division of **Subito**.*

Noteworthy   Noteworthy Music
132 Loucks Avenue
Los Altos, CA 94022-1045
USA
Tel: 650-948-2060
markstarr@sbcglobal.net
*Orchestrations and reconstructions by **Mark Starr** of rare and unusual works.*

Novello   Novello & Co.
www.chesternovello.com
US agent: Schirmer
*Established in 1811 in London. Acquired the firms **Ewer** (1867), **Elkin** (1960), **Goodwin & Tabb** (1971), and **Paxton** (1971). Subject to various takeovers; purchased by **Music Sales** in 1993.*

Nuove Cons   Nuove Consonanze S.r.l.
Edizione Musicali
Via Bellini 20
20040 Busnago (MI)
Italy

Obrasso   Obrasso-Verlag AG
Baselstrasse 23c
CH-4537 Wiedlisbach
Switzerland
Tel: ++41 (0)32 636 37 27
Fax: ++41 (0)32 636 37 27
info@obrasso.ch
www.obrasso.ch

O'Connor   Mark O'Connor Musik International
P.O. Box 398
Bonsall, CA 92003
USA
www.markoconnor.com
   *Music of **Mark O'Connor**.*

Odhecaton   Ochecaton Z Music
14532 142nd Court Circle South
Miami, FL 33186-7262
USA
Tel: 305-562-8211
Fax: 305-284-4448
lmcloskey@miami.edu
www.lansingmcloskey.com
   *Music of **Lansing McLoskey**.*

Oiseau Lyre   Éditions de L'Oiseau-Lyre

*Founded in Paris in 1932; moved to Monaco in 1947. Special emphasis on French music of the 17th and 18th centuries—both scholarly and performing editions. For a time, became a record label in conjunction with Decca. In 2013, Éditions de L'Oiseau-Lyre ended its presence in Europe, reverting to **Lyrebird Press** at the University of Melbourne, Australia.*

OMI Music   OMI Music Group
c/o James Oliverio
University of Florida
PO Box 115800
102 Fine Arts Building A
Gainesville, FL 32611-5800
USA
Tel: 352-222-1144
james@jamesoliverio.com
www.jamesoliverio.com
   *Music of **James Oliverio**. [Not to be confused with **Old Manuscripts & Incunabula** (also abbreviated OMI).]*

Ongaku   Ongaku-No-Tomo-Sha Co Ltd.
Kagurazaka 6-30, Shinjuku-ku
Tokyo 162-8716
Japan
home@ongakunotomo.co.jp
www.ongakunotomo.co.jp
US agent: Presser

Opus Opus Ceskoslavenske Hudobne Vydaratelstro
Mlynski nivy 73
827 99 Bratislava
Slovakia
US agent: Boosey
  *Split off from **Supraphon** in 1971, to handle Slovak composers at the time of the gradual separation of Czechoslovakia into the Czech Republic and the Slovak Republic.*

Opus 125 Opus 125 Publishing
opus125publishing@gmail.com
www.theofanidismusic.com
US agent: Holab
  *Music of **Christopher Theofanidis**.*

Orchard Road Orchard Road Music
c/o Christopher Owens
22858 Cass Ave.
Woodland Hills, CA 91364
USA
Tel: 818-427-6298
josephcuriale@gmail.com
www.josephcuriale.net
  *Music of **Joseph Curiale**.*

Oxford Oxford University Press
Music Department
Great Clarendon Street
Oxford OX2 6DP
United Kingdom
Tel: +44 1865 355067; rent: +44 (0)1865 353323
Fax: +44 1865 355060; rent: +44 (0)1865 353767
rentals@cfpeters-ny.com (for USA and Latin America)
counterpoint_musical@compuserve.com (for Canada)
music.hire.uk@oup.com (for rest of world)
music.enquiry.uk@oup.com
www.oup.co.uk/music; www.oup.com/us/music
US agent: Peters
Agent for rentals in USA, Mexico, Central & South America: Peters.
For rentals in Canada: Counterpoint Musical Services
  A venerable publisher whose important music offerings, however, began only with the 20th century.

198 Madison Ave.
New York, NY 10016-4314
  Tel: 212-726-6109;
  Fax: 212-726-6441;

Packard   Packard Humanities Institute
Editorial Office
11A Mt. Auburn Street
Cambridge, MA 02138
USA
Tel: 617-876-1317
Fax: 617-876-0074

Main Office
300 Second Street
Los Altos, CA 94022
Tel: 650-948-0150
Fax: 650-948-4135

> *Parts will be provided in PDF form, to be printed out by the user.*

Pagani   Edizioni Musicali A. Pagani SRL
Via N. Sauro, 5
22073 Fino Mornasco (CO)
Italy
Tel: +39 031.92 76 42
Fax: +39 031.88 13 35
info@apagani.it
www.apagani.it

> *Founded 1990. A catalog of **Astor Piazzolla** may be downloaded at the website.*

Panastudio   Edizioni Panastudio
Corso Via La Mantia, 72
90138 Palermo
Italy
Tel: 011.39.091.325.284
info@panastudio.it; panasci@panastudio.it
www.panastudio.it
Ricordi

> *Music of **Salvatore Di Vittorio** and of **Ottorino Respighi**.*

Papagena   Papagena Press
Box 20484 Park West Station
New York, NY 10025-1514
USA
Tel: 212-749-3012
Fax: 212-316-2235
contactus@papagenapress.com
www.papagenapress.com
US agent: Presser

> *Music of **Katherine Hoover**.*

Park Press   Park Press
107 Mark Street
Destin, FL 32541
USA
Tel: 888-562-3077
*Music of **David Ott**.*

Paterson   Paterson's Publications Ltd.
8-10 Lower James Street
London W1R 3PL
United Kingdom
US agent: Schirmer
*Founded in Edinburgh ca. 1819. Bought by **Novello** in 1989.*

Payne   Lars Payne
40 Durand Gardens
London SW9 0PP
United Kingdom
Tel: +44 (0)20 7735 7948
larspayne@btinternet.com
Newly computer-engraved editions of ballet repertoire. Authentic original orchestrations, as well as the traditional insertions, supplements, and transpositions as used by professional ballet companies. Lars Payne can provide material for particular productions, with cuts and reordering of movements as desired.

Peckham   Peckham Publications
5 Syme Ave
West Orange, NJ 07052
USA
Tel: 973-731-3031
Fax: 973-731-3031
info@PackhamPublications.com
www.PeckhamPublications.com

Pecktackular   Pecktackular Music
3605 Brandywine Dr.
Greensboro, NC 27410
USA
Tel: 336-288-7034
Fax: 336-286-2940
PeckMusic@RussellPeck.com
www.russellpeck.com
*Music of **Russell Peck**.*

Peer Peermusic Classical
810 Seventh Ave.
New York, NY 10019
USA
Tel: 212-265-3910
Fax: 212-489-2465
peerclassical@peermusic.com
info@peermusic-classical.de
www.peermusicclassical.com; www.peermusic-classical.de
US agent: Rentals: Subito; sales: Leonard
Founded 1928 in New York as **Southern Music Publishing Co.** *by Ralph Peer.*
Subsequent names: **Peer International Corporation, Peer-Southern,** *and* **Peermusic**
Classical. *(NB: Southern Music Publishing, Peer's progenitor, is not to be confused*
with **Southern Music Company** *of San Antonio, abbreviated* **SMC** *in this book.)*

Peermusic Classical GmbH
Muehlenkamp 45
D22303 Hamburg Germany
Tel: ++49-40 278-379-18
Fax: ++49-40 278-379

Pegasus Pegasus Press
91 Maple Street
Boston, MA 02132
USA
Tel: 617-325-0645
Fax: 617-325-0645
http://orchestraconductor.com
Music of **Steven Karidoyanes***.*

Pembroke Pembroke Music Co., Inc.
US agent: C. Fischer
A division of **Carl Fischer***.*

Petering Mark Petering
431 44th St. #2
Kenosha, WI 53140
USA
markpetering@hotmail.com
www.markpetering.com
Music of **Mark Petering***.*

Peters C. F. Peters Corp.
70-30 80th Street
Glendale, NY 11385
USA
Tel: 718-416-7800; rentals 718-416-7826
Fax: 718-416-7805
sales@cfpeters-ny.com
rentals@cfpeters-ny.com
rentals.us@editionpeters.com
info@edition-peters.de
www.edition-peters.com; www.edition-peters.de

*C.F. Peters purchased a preexisting firm in Leipzig in 1814. During and after World War II, the Leipzig firm was taken over by the state. Now Peters has become an international group of independent companies in Frankfurt, London, and New York. Important acquisitions included **M.P. Belaieff** (1971), **Schwann** (1974), and **Kahnt** (1989).*

C.F. Peters Musikverlag
Kennedyallee 101
D - 60596 Frankfurt/Main,
Tel: +49 / (0)69 / 630099
Fax: +49 / (0)69 / 630099

Picker Tobias Picker Music
US agent: Subito
*Music of **Tobias Picker**.*

Piedmont Piedmont Music Co.
US agent: Alfred
*Music of **Alan Shulman**.*

Pine Valley Pine Valley Press
P.O. Box 582
Williamstown, MA 01267
USA
Fax: 413-458-3202
info@pinevalleypress.com
www.pinevalleypress.com
*Music of **David Kechley**.*

Polygames Polygames
15374 Tamson Court
Monte Sereno, CA 95030
USA
Tel: 408-395-2911
Fax: 408-395-2911
info@leeactor.com
www.leeactor.com
*Music of **Lee Actor**.*

Presser Theodore Presser Co.
588 North Gulph Road
King of Prussia, PA 19406
USA
Tel: 610-592-1222
Fax: 610-592-1229; 888-525-3636
presser@presser.com
rental@presser.com
sales@presser.com
www.presser.com
  *Founded in 1883 in Philadelphia. Significant acquisitions include **Church** (1930), **Ditson** (1931), **Mercury** (1969), **Elkan-Vogel** (1970), and most of the titles of **AME** (1981). Since 2005 Presser is operating jointly with **Fischer**.*
  *Full scores may be examined online at the Presser website. Under **Rental**, click on **Scores for Online Perusal** for a list of about 100 composers whose works may be perused.*

Promethean Promethean Editions Ltd.   United Music Publishers
P.O. Box 10143   42 Rivington Street
Wellington   London EC2A 3BN UK
New Zealand   Tel: +44 (0)20 7729 4700
Tel: +64 4 473 5033   Fax: +44 (0)20 7739
Fax: +64 4 473 5066
info@promethean-editions.com
info@ump.co.uk
www.promethean-editions.com

PromoMusica PromoMusica International Ed.
info@promusint.com
www.promusint.com
  *Music of **Juan Trigos**.*

Propulsive Propulsive Music
3736 N. Hollingsworth Road
Altadena, CA 91001
USA
Tel: 626-398-3377
Fax: 626-398-3373
Info@PropulsiveMusic.com
www.PropulsiveMusic.com
US agent: Holab
  *Music of **Peter Boyer**.*

PWM   Polskie Wydawnictwo Muzyczne
Al. Krasinskiego 11A
PL31-111 Kraków
Poland
Tel: +48 12 422 70 44 ext. 153
internet@pwm.com.pl
www.pwm.com.pl
US agent: EAM
*Successor firm (1945) to the **Towarzystwo Wydawnicze Muzyki Polskiej** (Polish Music Publishing Society), which was founded in 1928. Early and avant-garde Polish music, as well as critical editions of foremost Polish 19th- and 20th-century composers.*

Queensland   Queensland Orchestra
53 Ferry Road West End Q 4101
GPO Box 9994
Brisbane Q 4001
Australia
Tel: 7 3377 5000
Fax: 7 3377 5001
info@thequeenslandorchestra.com.au
enquiries@seanoboyle.com.au
*Music of **Sean O'Boyle**.*

Raven   Raven Music
2402 4th Street No.5
Santa Monica, CA 90405
USA
Tel: 310-392-2641
davshalomov@earthlink.net
www.davshalomov.com
*Music of **David Avshalomov**.*

RBP   RBP Music Publishers
2615 Waugh Dr. #198
Houston, TX 77006
USA
rbpviola@aol.com
*Specializing in viola arrangements by **Robert Bridges**.*

Real Real Musical Publicaciones y Ediciones, S.A.
Carlos III.1
28013 Madrid
Spain
Tel: 902 101 666
informacion@realmusical.com

Red Poppy Red Poppy Music
80 Hanson Pl #701
Brooklyn, NY 11217
USA
www.redpoppymusic.com
US agent: Schirmer
*Founded 1993; music of **Michael Gordon**, **David Lang**, and **Julia Wolfe**. Scores may be examined online at musicsales.com; click on **OnDemand**.*

Reichert Dr. Ludwig Reichert Verlag
Tauernstrasse 11
D - 65199 Wiesbaden
Germany
Tel: ++49 611 461851 or 9465911
Fax: ++49 611 468613
reichert.verlag@t-online.de
www.reichert-verlag.de
Not principally a music publisher, but a specialist in art, culture, and the like.

Reift Editions Marc Reift
Case Postale 303 — Route du Golf
CH-3963 Crans-Montana
Switzerland
Tel: 027-483 12 00
Fax: 027-483 42 43
reift@tvs2net.ch
www.reift.ch
US agent: Solid Brass
Specializing in wind music.

RepEx Repertoire and Opera Explorer
Musikproduktion Jürgen Höflich
Enhuberstrasse 6-8 Rgb.
D-80333 München
Germany
Tel: +49.89.52 20 81
Fax: +49.89.52 54 11
hoeflich@musikmph.de
www.musikmph.de
 Miniature scores (though not always parts) of unjustly neglected works.

Richault Verlag S. Richault
Paris
France
 *Founded in Paris in 1816. Bought in 1898 by **Costallat**, which itself was purchased by **Billaudot** (1958) and later **Jobert** (1995).*

Ricordi G. Ricordi & Co.
Via Liguria 4, fr. Sesto Ulteriano   Via Berchet 2
20098 S. Giuliano Milanese (MI)   20121 Milano Italy
Italy
Tel: (02) 98813.4220/4302
Fax: (02) 98813.4258
rental.ricordi@bmg.com
promozione.ricordi@bmg.com
www.ricordi.com; www.ricordi.it
US agent: Boosey (rentals); Leonard (sales)
 *Founded in Milan in 1808. The New York branch split off from the parent company after World War II, and in 1962 changed its name to **Franco Colombo, Inc.**, q.v. In 1995, Ricordi merged with BMG Ariola to form BMG Ricordi S.p.a. In 2006 **BMG** was acquired by **Universal Music Publishing Group**.*

Ries Ries & Erler
Wandalenallee 8
D-14052 Berlin
Germany
Tel: +49 030-825 10 49
Fax: +49 030-825 97 21
verlag@rieserler.de
www.rieserler.de
US agent: C.Fischer
 Founded in Berlin in 1881.

Ritchie Anthony Ritchie
9 Delta Street
Dunedin
New Zealand
contact@anthonyritchie.co.nz
www.anthonyritchie.co.nz
*Music of **Anthony Ritchie**.*

Rival Robert Carl Rival
info@robertrival.com
www.robertrival.com
*Music of **Robert Rival**.*

Robbins Robbins Music Corp.
US agent: Alfred
*An imprint of **CPP/Belwin**.*

R&H Rodgers & Hammerstein Concert Library
229 W. 28th St., 11th floor
New York, NY 10001
USA

Tel: 212-268-9300
Fax: 212-268-1245
concert@rnh.com
www.rnh.com
Not just Rodgers & Hammerstein, but also many other composers of the US musical theatre.

Rodgers & Hammerstein
For rental of musical shows:
1065 Avenue of the
Americas, Ste. 2400
New York, NY 10018
Tel: 212-541-6600
Fax: 212-586-6155

Rondure Rondure Music Publishing
Tel: 214-559-2549
mctee@unt.edu
http://cindymctee.com
US agent: Holab
*Music of **Cindy McTee**.*

Rongwen Rongwen Music, Inc.
US agent: Broude Bros.

Rouart Rouart-Lerolle et Cie.
US agent: Boosey (rentals); Leonard (sales)
*Founded in Paris in 1905; purchased by **Salabert**, 1941.*

Rudow Vivian Adelberg Rudow
211 Goodwood Gardens
Baltimore, MD 21210-2531
USA
Tel: 410-889-3939
Fax: 410-889-0610
VivianAR@aol.com; VivianAR@jhu.edu
www.VivianAdelbergRudow.com
*Music of **Vivian Adelberg Rudow**.*

Russian Russian Authors' Society (RAO)
bld. 73/1, Novoslobodskaya
Moscow 127055
Russia
Tel: +7 (495) 418-00-22
Fax: +7 (495) 685-48-18
office@rp-union.ru
www.rp-union.ru/en
US agent: Schirmer

The Russian Authors' Society (RAO; Российское Авторское Общество) was created in 1993 to administer property rights of authors and composers. It has reciprocal representation contracts with 117 societies in 68 countries.

In the Soviet era, the official state publisher entered into agreements with various foreign firms, by which each of the latter would act as publisher in its own national or regional sphere. After the dissolution of the USSR, these agreements were largely renegotiated along similar lines. Here are listings as of June 2005:

> ***Schirmer**—US, Canada, and Mexico*
> ***Boosey**—UK and British Commonwealth (except Canada) and Ireland*
> ***Sikorski**—Germany, Greece, Denmark, Sweden, Norway, Holland, Portugal, Spain (but see below), Iceland, Switzerland, Turkey, and Israel*
> ***Real**—Spain (for works written after Jan.1, 1985)*
> ***Chant du Monde**—France*
> ***Ricordi**—Italy*
> ***Universal**—Austria*
> ***Fennica Gehrman**—Finland*
> ***Zen-On**—Japan*

Saga Saga Music Publishing Ltd.
Thames Publishing, c/o William Elkin Music Services
Station Road Industrial Estate, Salhouse
Norwich NR13 6NS
United Kingdom
Tel: 01603 721302
Fax: 01603 721801
info@elkinmusic.co.uk
www.elkinmusic.co.uk

Salabert Éditions Salabert
Durand-Salabert-Eschig
16 rue des Fossés Saint-Jacques
F-75005 Paris
France
Tel: +33-1 44 41 50 90
Fax: +33-1 44 41 50 91
www.durand-salabert-eschig.com; www.salabert.fr [same
US agent: Boosey (rentals); Leonard (sales)
*Founded in Paris in 1894. Significant acquisitions include **Dufresne** (1923), **Gaudet** (1927), **Mathot** (1930), **Christiné** (1937), **Rouart-Lerolle** (1941), **Senart** (1941), and **Deiss** (1946). Now a member of **BMG** Editions.*

Samfundet Samfundet Til Udgivelse af Dansk Musik
(Society for the Publication of Danish Music)
Gråbrødrestraede 18, 1.sal
DK-1156 Copenhagen K
Denmark
Tel: +45 33 13 54 45
sales@samfundet.dk
www.edition-s.dk
US agent: Peters
*Founded in 1871 as a private non-commercial enterprise. Now functions like any private publisher, though supported by the Danish Arts Council. Publishes a fine musicological series under the imprint **Dania**. Restructured in 2007 with a name change to **Edition-S**. Many published works may still bear the Samfundet imprint, however.*

Schaffner Schaffner Publishing Company
224 Penn Avenue
Westmont, NJ 08180-1839
USA
Tel: 856-854-3760
Fax: 856-854-5584
SchaffnerPublishing@gmail.com
www.schaffnerpublishing.com
*Music of **Steven Schaffner**.*

P.O. Box 1162
Merchantville, NJ 08109

Schirmer G. Schirmer, Inc.
180 Madison Avenue
New York, NY 10016
USA
Tel: 212-254-2100; rental 845-469-4699
Fax: 212-254-2013; for quotes, 845-469-7544; rental 845
schirmer@schirmer.com
perusals@schirmer.com
rental@schirmer.com
quotes@schirmer.com
www.musicsalesclassical.com

G. Schirmer Rental &
2 Old Route 17
Chester, NY 10918
Tel: 845-469-2271
Fax: 845-469-7544

Established 1866, having bought out a previous firm. **Associated Music Publishers** *became Schirmer's BMI subsidiary in 1964. Schirmer was purchased by US book publisher Macmillan in 1968. In 1986, music publishing was taken over by* **Music Sales***; sales of music given to* **Hal Leonard***; book publishing (Schirmer Books) remained with Macmillan, and rentals remained with Schirmer. In 1989, Schirmer acquired* **Shawnee Press***.*

When requesting **perusal scores***, email schirmer@schirmer.com and use this precise phrase in the subject line: Schirmer Promotion Department.*

Full scores of many works may be examined online at the indicated website; click on **OnDemand***.*

Schirmer, E.C. E.C. Schirmer Music Co.
see: ECS

Schmidt Arthur P. Schmidt

Established in Boston, 1876. **Schott** *bought the European rights to the Schmidt catalog in 1910. After 1916, focus turned to educational music. Purchased by* **Summy-Birchard** *in 1959.*

Schott   Schott Music GmbH
Weihergarten 5, Postfach 3640
D-55116 Mainz
Germany
Tel: +49 6131 246-0
Fax: +49 6131 246-211
info@schott-music.com
www.Schott-Music.com
US agent: EAM (rentals); Leonard (sales)

*Founded 1770 in Mainz. A Brussels branch of Schott became independent in 1889 under the name Schott Frères. Took over **Augener** (briefly) in 1910; **Ars Viva**, 1955; **Eulenburg**, 1957. In 1977 Schott and **Universal** established **EAM** in the USA as a joint agency; in 2005 EAM became a fully-owned subsidiary of Schott Music. Schott purchased **Fürstner** in 1981, **Cranz** in 1992, **Panton International** in 1998, and **Hohner** in 1998. Alternative names: **B.Schott's Söhne; Schott & Co. Ltd.; Schott Music Corporation**.*

Many scores may be perused on the Schott website: search the site for the work desired; if a blue box appears labeled "View Score," click on it.

***PSNY** (Project Schott New York) is the digital publishing edition of Schott Music.*

Schuberth   Schuberth Musikverlag
Gwinnerstrasse 39
60388 Frankfurt/M
Germany
Tel: 69 94 76 00 45
Fax: 69 94 76 00 46
juergen.grahl@t-online.de

*In existence 1888. Offices destroyed during World War II; firm reconstituted after the war. Also known as **Musikverlag Schuberth**. The firm requests that communications be made by fax.*

Scores Ref   Scores Reformed
More House
13 Warwicks Bench
Guildford Surrey GU1 3SZ
United Kingdom
Tel: 01483 456646
admin@scoresreformed.co.uk
www.ScoresReformed.co.uk

Founded 2009. Newly computer-engraved editions of arias and orchestral works, some of which are still under copyright protection in the USA. US orchestras could purchase these copyrighted materials, but would still need to pay a fee to the US agent whenever they are performed.

Scottish   Scottish Music Centre
City Halls
Candleriggs
Glasgow Scotland G1 1NQ
United Kingdom
Tel: + 44 (0) 141 552 5222
Fax: + 44 (0) 141 553 2789
info@scottishmusiccentre.com
www.scottishmusiccentre.com

Serenissima   Serenissima Music, Inc.
205 S. Charles St.
Edwardsville, IL 62025
USA
Tel: 618-656-5143
serenissima18@att.net
www.serenissimamusic.com
Digitally-enhanced reprints of standard works, selected titles of lesser-known composers, and new editions. Available through Sheet Music Plus, Amazon.com, and online.

SESAC   SESAC
55 Music Square East
Nashville, TN 37203
USA
Tel: 615-320-9627
Fax: 615-329-9627
www.sesac.com

SESAC International
67 Upper Berkeley Street
London W1H 7QX, England
Tel: 0207 616 9284
Fax: 0207 563 7029

*One of the three major US performing rights organizations, the others being **BMI** and **ASCAP**.*

Shawnee   Shawnee Press, Inc.
421 E. Iris, Ste. 202
Nashville, TN 37204
USA
Tel: 800-962-8584; 615-320-5300
Fax: 800-971-4310; 615-320-7306
shawnee-info@shawneepress.com
shawnee-sales@shawneepress.com
www.shawneepress.com
US agent: Leonard
*Founded 1939 as "Words and Music, Inc." and renamed Shawnee Press in 1947. Purchased by **Music Sales** in 1989 as an independent subsidiary. Acquired both **Margun Music** and **Mark Foster Music** in 1999. Shawnee was sold to **Hal Leonard** in 2009.*

Sheffer   Jonathan Sheffer
39 West 10th St.
New York, NY 10011
USA
Tel: 212-420-0005
  jsheffer@nyc.rr.com

Shulman   Shulman
P.O. Box 602
Claverack, NY 12513
USA
Tel: 518-851-9791
shulmuse@capital.net
www.capital.net/com/ggjj/shulman
   *Music of **Alan Shulman**.*

Sikorski   Internationale Musikverlage Hans Sikorski
Johnsallee 23, Postfach 13-2001
D-20148 Hamburg
Germany
Tel: +49 (0)40 41 41 00 - 0
Fax: +49 (0)40 41 41 00 - 41
contact@sikorski.de
www.sikorski.de
US agent: Schirmer (rentals); Leonard (sales)
   Founded 1935 in Berlin; moved 1948 to Hamburg. Handled a number of Jewish firms temporarily during World War II.

Simrock   Nicholas Simrock Musikverlag (a division of Anton J.
    Benjamin)
Werderstraße 44
20144 Hamburg
Germany
Tel: +49 040 451225
US agent: Boosey (rentals); Leonard (sales)
   *Founded in Bonn in 1793. After acquiring the firms **Bartolf Senff** (1907) and **Eos** (1925), Simrock was sold to the **Anton J. Benjamin-Verlag** in 1929 but the name was retained as an imprint. Benjamin was held by **Sikorski** 1938-1951 but then restored to the previous owners, known variously as **Anton J. Benjamin Musikverlag**, **Benjamin-Rahter-Simrock**, and **Richard Schauer Music Publishers**.*

SMC Southern Music Company
info@southernmusic.com
www.smcpublications.com
US agent: LKMP (rentals); Leonard (sales)
*Founded 1937 in San Antonio, Texas. Purchased by **LKMP** in 2012.*
*SMC is not to be confused with **Southern Music Publishing Co., Inc.**, which was the predecessor of **Peermusic Classical**.*

Sonzogno Casa Musicale Sonzogno
Via Bigli, 11
20121 Milano
Italy
Tel: +39 02 76 00 00 65
Fax: +39 02 76 01 45 12
sonzogno@sonzogno.it
www.sonzogno.it
US agent: Presser
Founded 1874, though the Sonzogno family had been active as book publishers since 1804. Gained the rights to numerous French operas and operettas, and subsequently championed young Italian composers, especially of the verismo school.

Sounds Alive! Sounds Alive!
Brazinmusikanta
73 Ireland Place, Ste.108
Amityville, NY 11701
USA
Musinskus@aol.com

SOUNZ SOUNZ, the Centre for New Zealand Music
Level 3, Toi Poneke Arts Centre
61 Abel Smith Street
Te Aro
Wellington 6011
New Zealand
Tel: +64 4 801 8602
Fax: +64 4 801 8604
info@sounz.org.nz
sounz.org.nz

postal address:
PO Box 27347
Marion Square
Wellington 6141

A music information center for New Zealand composers. It can supply scores and parts for many works.

Southern Southern Music Publishing Co., Inc.
www.peermusic.com
US agent: Rentals: Subito; sales: Leonard
  Original name of the company now known as **Peermusic**, q.v. *Founded 1928 in New York by Ralph Peer. Subsequent names:* **Peer International Corporation**, **Peer-Southern**, *and* **Peermusic Classical**.
  N.B. *Southern Music Publishing Co. is not to be confused with* **Southern Music Company** *of San Antonio, Texas (under the abbreviation* **SMC** *in this book).*

Spurwink Spurwink River Publishing
96 Wells Road
Cape Elizabeth, ME 04107
USA
Tel: 207-767-3483
info@spurwinkriverpublishing.com
spurwinkriverpublishing.com
  Nutcracker *reduction by* **Lawrence Golan**. *Also ensemble music for strings.*

Stainer Stainer & Bell Ltd.
PO Box 110, Victoria House
23 Gruneisen Rd.
London N3 1DZ
United Kingdom
Tel: +44 20 8343 3303 (sales); +44 20 8343 2535 (rentals)
Fax: +44 20 8343 3024
post@stainer.co.uk
www.stainer.co.uk
US agent: ECS
  Founded in London in 1907 to promote British music. Acquired **Augener** *in 1972.*

Stangland Thomas C. Stangland Co.
P.O.Box 19263
7804 S.W. 45th Ave., Suite 47
Portland, OR 97280-0263
USA
Tel: 503-244-0634
Fax: 208-485-4393
Info@TomasSvoboda.com
www.tomassvoboda.com
  Music of **Tomás Svoboda**.

Stanton   Stanton Management
45-05 Newtown Road
Astoria, NY 11103-1622
USA
Tel: 718-956-6092
Fax: 718-956-5385
TDStanton@StantonMgt.com
www.stantonmgt.com

Stephenson   Stephenson Music, Inc.
264 Park Ave.
Lake Forest, IL 60045
USA
Tel: 847-830-5882
ComposerJim@gmail.com
www.stephensonmusic.com
   *Music of **James Stephenson**.*

Stone Circle   Stone Circle Music
1693 Ashland Ave.
St. Paul, MN 55104
USA
Tel: 651-644-4700; 612-226-6489
steve@steveheitzeg.com
www.steveheitzeg.com
   *Music of **Steve Heitzeg**.*

Strauss Ed.   Strauss Edition Wien
Verlagsgruppe Hermann
Goldschmiedgasse 10
A-1010 Wien
Austria
Tel: +43-1-534 62 40
Fax: +43-1-534 62 67
office@strauss.at
sales@strauss.at
www.strauss.at
Worldwide rentals: Schott
   *Founded 1989 as **Edition Contemp Art**; took the name Strauss Edition Wien in
1992. Under the patronage of the Vienna Philharmonic since 1994.*

Subito Subito Music Corporation
60 Depot Street
Verona, NJ 07044
USA
Tel: 973-857-3440
Fax: 973-857-3442
mail@subitomusic.com
rental@subitomusic.com
www.subitomusic.com
  *Founded in 1980. Acquired **Seesaw Music** in 2006.*

Suecia Edition Suecia
http://svenskmusik.org/om/edition-suecia/
US agent: Fleisher
Germany, Austria, Switzerland, Netherlands & Belgium:
Breitkopf
Spain: SEEMSA.
  *Edition Suecia was founded in 1930 by the Society of Swedish Composers (FST), and was taken over by **Svensk Musik** in 1965. Promotes contemporary Swedish music. Suecia is now enabling free downloading of certain scores from its website—a very limited trial at the moment.*

Supraphon Editio Supraphon
Palckého 1 / 740
CS - 112 99 Praha 1
Czech Republic
Tel: +420 221 966 600
Fax: +420 221 966 630
info@supraphon.com
www.supraphon.com
US agent: EAM
  *Originally (1930s) a Czech record company, **Gramofonové Závody-Supraphon**. Czech music publishing, after nationalization in 1949, had been under two imprints: **Orbis** and **Hudební Matice**. In 1953 these were brought together to become the state publisher under various names, most notably **Státní Hudebni Vydavatelství** and, in 1967, **Editio Supraphon**. (In 1971 the Slovak composers were taken over by **Opus**.) Taken over 1994-1997 by Bärenreiter (as **Bärenreiter Editio Supraphon**) but then became independent again.*

Suvini Edizioni Suvini Zerboni
see: Zerboni

Swedish MIC Swedish Music Information Centre (Svensk Musik)
P.O. Box 27327
Stockholm SE-102 54   Sandhamnsgatan 79
Sweden   Stockholm
Tel: +46 8 783 8800   Sweden
Fax: +46 8 783 9510
info@svenskmusik.org
www.svenskmusik.org
   The Swedish Music Information Centre, a member of the International Association of Music Information Centres. Owned since 2008 by STIM (the Swedish Performing Rights Society). Sales and rentals of performing material and recordings, along with information on Swedish composers.

Symphonia Symphonia Verlag
US agent: Warner

Tams Tams-Witmark Music Library, Inc.
560 Lexington Ave.
New York, NY 10022
USA
Tel: 212-688-9191; 800-221-7196
Fax: 212-688-5656; 800-826-7121
www.tams-witmark.com

Teason Deborah Fischer Teason
61 Woodstock Rd.
Hamden, CT 06517
USA
Tel: 203-248-0475
dteason@aol.com
   *Music of **Deborah Fischer Teason**.*

Templeton Templeton Publishing Inc.
US agent: Shawnee

Tempo Tempo Music Resource
312 El Capitan Loop
Stevensville, MT 59870
USA
tmr.mus@gmail.com
www.tempomusicresource.org
   *Music of **Steven Amundson** and **Matthew Peterson**.*

Territo   James Territo
8851 Allen Rd.
Clarkston, MI 48348
USA
jterrito1978@gmail.com
www.jimterrito.com
*Music of **James Territo**.*

Tetra   Tetra
US agent: LudwigMasters

Thomi-Berg   Thomi-Berg Musikverlag
Postfach 1736
Pasingerstrasse 38 a
D - 82152 Planegg bei München
Germany
Tel: +49 (0)89 / 859 99 44
Fax: +49 (0)89 / 859 33 23
info@Thomi-Berg
www.thomi-berg.de
US agent: Peters (North America)
*Founded in 1926 in Leipzig as Philipp Grosch; transferred to Munich, 1957. Acquired by Thomi-Berg, 1977. Took over **C.L. Schultheiss**, 1980. Sole selling agency for **Leuckart**, **Vieweg**, and many other firms.*

Tonos   Tonos Music oHG
Hinterbildstraße 8a
78234 Engen
Germany
Tel: +49 7733 99640-0
Fax: +49 7733 99640-25
mail@tonosmusic.com
www.tonosmusic.com
US agent: Alfred
*Specializing in tango music, including the works of **Astor Piazzolla**.*

Tritó Tritó Edicions, S.L.
Enamorats, 35-37, baixos
08013 Barcelona
Spain
Tel: (34) 93 342 61 75
Fax: (34) 93 302 26 70
info@trito.es
www.trito.es
   A Catalan music publisher specializing in the Catalan, Spanish, and Ibero-American repertoire.

Tritó, S.L.
Apartat de Correus 2254
08080 Barcelona Spain

Tropp Tropp Music Editions, LLC
PO Box 807
Lake Forest, IL 60045
USA
Tel: 224-649-6000
info@galantmusic.com
www.galantmusic.com
   Specializing in liturgical music of the galant style: critical performing editions of previously unpublished 18th-century works, under the aegis of "The Galant Masters Project."

Tuba-Euph Tuba-Euphonium Press
3811 Ridge Road
Annandale, VA 2203-1832
USA
Fax: 703-916-0711
dymiles@verizon.net

UME Unión Musical Ediciones
Marques de la Ensenada 4, 3
Madrid, 28004
Spain
Tel: 34.91.308.4040
Fax: 34.91.310.4429
US agent: AMP
   *Founded in Bilbao in 1900 as **Casa Dotesio**, a successor firm to Casa Romero (founded 1856). Soon acquired Zozaya, Fuentes y Asenjo, and Eslava. In 1914 name changed to **Unión Musical Española**. In 1942 acquired Editorial Orfeo Tracio (which itself had acquired Vidal Llimona y Boceta, Luis Tena, and Salvat). Purchased in 1990 by **Music Sales**, whereupon the name was changed to Unión Musical Ediciones.*

UMP   United Music Publishers Ltd.
33 Lea Road, Waltham Abbey
Essex EN9 1ES
United Kingdom
Tel: +44 01992 703110
Fax: +44 01992 703189
info@ump.co.uk
www.ump.co.uk
US agent: Presser

UMPC   Universal Music Publishing Classical
c/o Universal Music Publishing
20 Fulham Broadway
London SW6 1AH
United Kingdom
umpg.classical@umusic.com
www.universalmusicpublishingclassical.com
Formed in 1996 under the ownership of Seagram Company Ltd of Canada.
*Acquired music publishers **MCA**, **Ricordi**, **Durand-Salabert-Eschig**, and **EMB**.*
*Not to be confused with **Universal-Edition**, Vienna.*

Universal   Universal-Edition
Karlsplatz 6   254 West 31st St., Floor 15
A-1010 Vienna   New York, NY 10010-2813
Austria   Tel: 212-461-6953
Tel: * 43 / 1 / 337 23 - 0   Fax: 212-810-4565
Fax: * 43 / 1 / 337 23 - 400
office@universaledition.com
www.universaledition.com
US agent: EAM (rentals); Presser (sales)
*Founded in Vienna in 1901. Purchased **Aibl**, 1904. Universal, jointly with **Schott**,*
*established **European American Music** (**EAM**) in 1977. Not to be confused with*
***Universal Music Publishing Group**, based in the USA.*

UnivPacific   University of the Pacific Library
3601 Pacific Avenue
Stockton, CA 95211
USA
Tel: 209-946-2431
http://library.pacific.edu *or* http://library.uop.edu

Uroboros Uroboros Music
10310 SW 89 St.
Miami, FL 33176
USA
Tel: 305-972-5651
mercurious@sleepermusic.com
www.sleepermusic.com
*Music of **Thomas Sleeper**.*

VHSource VHSource
302 West 105th Street, #3C
New York, NY 10025
USA
Tel: 917-815-8899
VHSource@vherbert.com
www.vherbert.com
*Music of **Victor Herbert**. The creation of Alyce Mott. The only source of computerized scores and parts of original Herbert material. Available as pdf downloads from the website, or as hard copies direct from VHSource. Alyce Mott is also very helpful providing information about Victor Herbert music from other publishers and sources.*

Vieweg Chr. Friedrich Vieweg, Musikverlag
Nibelungenstrasse 48
D - 8000 München 19
Germany
US agent: Peters (North America)
International agent: Thomi-Berg
*Founded in Berlin 1786; moved to Braunschweig 1799. After a takeover by Pergamon-Verlag in 1966, became part of the Bertelsmann group (**BMG**) in 1974.*

Vireo Vireo Press
US agent: ECS

Waiteata Waiteata Music Press
New Zealand School of Music
Victoria University of Wellington
PO Box 600
Wellington
New Zealand
Tel: +64-4-4635853
waiteata-music@vuw.ac.nz
Established by Douglas Lilburn, 1967. A non-profit organization specializing in music and recordings of New Zealand composers.

Walton   Walton Music Corp.
1028 Highlandwoods Road
Chapel Hill, NC 27517
USA
Tel: 919-929-1330
Fax: 919-929-2232
writeus@waltonmusic.com
www.waltonmusic.com
US agent: Boosey
Founded by conductor Norman Luboff; specializing in choral music.

Warner   Warner/Chappell Music, Inc.   Warner Bros. Publications
10585 Santa Monica Blvd.   15800 N.W. 48th Avenue
Los Angeles, CA 90025-4950   Miami, FL 33014
USA   Tel: 305-521-1685
Tel: 310-441-8600   Fax: 305-521-1680
Fax: 310-441-1448
rentals: eamdllc@eamdllc.com
http://warnerchappell.com; www.warnerbrospub.com
US agent: EAM
*Formed by Warner Bros. in Los Angeles in 1929. Originally the **Music Publishers Holding Corporation**, which included the popular music publishers **Harms**, **Remick**, **Witmark**, and **New World Music**. In 1968 became known as **Warner Bros. Music**. In 1987 the parent company (Warner Communications) acquired **Chappell**, becoming **Warner/Chappell Music Group**. In 1989 it merged with Time, Inc., to create **Time Warner**. In 1994 it acquired **CPP/Belwin**, which it merged with its print division, Warner Bros. Publications.*

Weinberger   Josef Weinberger Wien GmbH   Josef Weinberger Ltd.
Neulerchenfelderstrasse 3-7   12-14 Mortimer St.
A-1160 Vienna   London W1T 3JJ England
Austria   Tel: 44 + (0)20 7580
Tel: +43 (0)1 403 59 91-0   Fax: 44 + (0)20 7436
Fax: +43 (0)1 403 59 91-13
musik@weinberger.co.at
general.info@jwmail.co.uk
www.weinberger.co.at; www.josef-weinberger.com
*Founded 1885 in Vienna. In 1938 taken over by **Sikorski** for the duration of World War II but restored after the war. Administers the business affairs of **Glocken Verlag** (music of Franz Lehar) since the end of World War II.*

Weintraub   Weintraub Music Co.
US agent: Schirmer (rentals)
*Founded in 1950 in New York. The firm was acquired by **Music Sales** in 1987.*

Wendel Robert Wendel Music
467 West 163rd Street, 3rd Floor
New York, NY 10032-4302
USA
Tel: 212-928-9094
Fax: 212-928-9094
bobwen@pipeline.com
www.wendelmusic.com
Downloadable perusal scores for many works may be examined on the Robert Wendel Music website. In addition, sound files for various special effects (e.g., Pines of Rome nightingale; 1812 Overture *cannon) or rare instruments (e.g., low E bell for* Also sprach Zarathustra*) may be found there.*

WGS William Grant Still Music
809 W. Riordan Road, Suite 100, Box 109
Flagstaff, AZ 86001-0810
USA
Tel: 928-526-9355
Fax: 928-526-0321
discovermusic@williamgrantstill.com
www.williamgrantstill.com
Music of **William Grant Still** *and other minority composers.*

Wharton Philip Wharton
23 W. 73rd St. No.514
New York, NY 10023
USA
pdwharton@aol.com
pdwharton@gmail.com
www.philipwharton.com
Music of **Philip Wharton**.

Willow Blossom Willow Blossom Music
Box H9, Erector Square
319 Peck Street
New Haven, CT 06513
USA
Tel: 203-562-5663
WillowBlos@aol.com
http://newsousaband.com
US agent: Barnhouse
Keith Brion arrangements & editions, principally of the music of **John Philip Sousa**.

Wimbledon   Wimbledon Music Inc./Trigram Music Inc.
1801 Century Park E. Ste.2400
Los Angeles, CA 90067-2326
USA
Tel: 310-556-9683
Fax: 310-277-1278

Wollenweber   Verlag Walter Wollenweber
Schiffmannstrasse 4 - Postfach 1165
D - 8032 Gräfelfing von München
Germany
US agent: Peters

Woodbury   Woodbury Music Company
P.O. Box 447
33 Grassy Hill Road
Woodbury, CT 06798
USA
Tel: 203-263-0696
Fax: 203-263-5102
info@woodburymusic.com
www.LeroyAnderson.com
US agent: Presser (rental partial); Wendel (rental partial);
*Music of **Leroy Anderson**.*

Ximart   Ximart Ediciones Musicales S.L.
c/ Rodríguez San Pedro, no. 13 - 1°
28015 Madrid
España
Tel: 34 91 593 26 43
Fax: 34 91 445 17 15
ximart@asesores-musicales.com
www.asesores-musicales.com/ximart

Ytalianna   Ytalianna Music Publishing
www.osvaldogolijov.com
US agent: Boosey
*Music of **Osvaldo Golijov**.*

Zaimont   Judith Lang Zaimont
20928 North John Wayne Parkway
C-13 #145
Maricopa, AZ 85239
USA
jzaimont@worldnet.att.net
www.jzaimont.com
  *Music of **Judith Lang Zaimont**.*

Zanibon   Edizioni G. Zanibon
US agent: Boosey
  *Founded in Padua, 1908. In 1992, moved to Milan as part of **Ricordi** but retained its own imprint.*

Zaninelli   Luigi Zaninelli
Box 5318
University of Southern Mississippi
Hattiesburg, MS 39406
USA
luigiz132@comcast.net
  *Music of **Luigi Zaninelli**.*

Zen-On   Zen-On Music, Ltd.
2-13-3 Kami-ochiai, Shinjuku-ku
Tokyo 161-0034
Japan
Tel: +81-3-3227-6283
Fax: +81-3-3227-6288
hirelibrary@zen-on.co.jp
www.zen-on.co.jp/cms/docs/rental/about2.html
US agent: EAM (rentals); Leonard (sales)
Canada, Mexico: EAM
France, Monaco, Luxemburg: Leduc
Other European countries: Boosey (German office)
  Founded 1931.

Zerboni   Edizioni Suvini Zerboni
Galleria del Corso 4
20122 Milan
Italy
Tel: +39.02.77070701
Fax: +39.02.77070261
suvini.zerboni@sugarmusic.com
www.esz.it
US agent: EAM
   Founded in Milan in 1907.

Zimmermann   Musikverlag Zimmermann
Strubbergstrasse 80
D-60459 Frankfurt am Main
Germany
Tel: +49-69-978-286-6
Fax: +49-69-978-286-79
info@zimmermann-frankfurt.de
lektorat@zimmermann-frankfurt.de
www.zimmermann-frankfurt.de
US agent: Peters
   Founded 1876 in St. Petersburg. Moved to Leipzig in 1886. Acquired the firm
Robert Lienau *in 1991.*
   (Not to be confused with **Zimmerman Press** *in Bennington, Vermont—a small publisher specializing in double bass music.)*

Zinfonia   Zinfonia: Music Publisher Portal
info@zinfonia.com
www.zinfonia.com
   Zinfonia is neither a publisher nor a dealer, but rather a free online service for classical music rentals and sales. Zinfonia describes itself as a "Music Publisher Portal."
   Created in 2011 by Peter Grimshaw of BTM Innovation Pty Ltd, Zinfonia provides a one-stop web location where the user can search for particular classical works that are available for rental or sale from a vast number of publishers; orders may be placed with these publishers directly through the Zinfonia website. User-interfaces are available in English, French, German, Italian, and Polish. Registered users may create individualized repertoire lists using the "My Catalog" option. Use of the website is free; certain ancillary services are available by subscription.

ABOUT THE AUTHOR

This was supposed to be a little summer project back in 1968—a modest handbook of orchestral repertoire. After nearly five decades of work on it, the subject still hasn't lost its fascination for David Daniels.

When not doing the housekeeping chores for this database, he taught at Oakland University in Michigan for 28 years and directed several orchestras. He hasn't lifted a baton now since the Spring of 2014—or was it the Spring of 2013? It doesn't seem to matter so much.

He received an A.B. degree from Oberlin College, an M.A. in musicology from Boston University, and both an M.F.A. in organ and a Ph.D. in orchestral literature and conducting from the University of Iowa.